CONCISE
ETYMOLOGICAL DICTIONARY
OF THE
ENGLISH LANGUAGE

A CONCISE
ETYMOLOGICAL
DICTIONARY
OF THE
English Language

BY THE REV.

WALTER W. SKEAT

Litt.D., LL.D., D.C.L., Ph.D.

A PERIGEE BOOK

Perigee Books
are published by
G.P. Putnam's Sons
200 Madison Avenue
New York, New York, 10016

First Perigee Printing, 1980

SBN: 399-50049-9

Tenth Impression

Manufactured in the United States of America

CONTENTS

PAGE

INTRODUCTION   vii
    KEY TO THE GENERAL PLAN OF THE DICTIONARY   xi

    LIST OF ABBREVIATIONS   xii

CONCISE ETYMOLOGICAL DICTIONARY
    OF THE ENGLISH LANGUAGE   I

APPENDIX:

    I. LIST OF PREFIXES   624

    II. SUFFIXES   630

    III. SELECT LIST OF LATIN WORDS   632

         SELECT LIST OF GREEK WORDS   644

    IV. DISTRIBUTION OF WORDS ACCORDING TO THE
         LANGUAGES FROM WHICH THEY ARE DERIVED   647

INTRODUCTION

THE first edition of my 'Concise Etymological Dictionary of the English Language' was published in 1882, and it has since passed through several editions.

Each successive edition contained several corrections and additions, in order that the work might be, to some extent, brought up to date.

Meanwhile, numerous and important contributions have been made, by many writers, to the study of Indo-germanic philology; more exact methods of analysing phonetic changes have been adopted, and important advances have been made at many points. Such works as Kluge's Etymological Dictionary of German, Franck's Etymological Dictionary of Dutch, Godefroy's Dictionary of Old French, the Modern French Dictionary by Hatzfeld and Darmesteter, in addition to other highly important books such as the Comparative Grammar of the Indo-germanic languages by Brugmann, have all contributed to a much clearer and more exact view of the science of comparative philology. Hence the time has come when partial emendations of my Concise Dictionary, however diligently made, have (as I fear) failed to keep pace with the requirements of the present day; and I have accordingly rewritten the book from beginning to end, making improvements in nearly every article, whilst at the same time introducing into the body of the work words which have hitherto necessarily been relegated to a continually increasing Supplement. The result is less a new edition than a new book.

Since the year 1882 above-mentioned, a great advance has been made in English lexicography. An entirely new edition of Webster appeared in 1890, and The Century Dictionary, of which the publication was begun in 1889, was completed in 1891. In both of these works my name appears in the 'List of Authorities cited'; though it is seldom expressly mentioned except in cases of considerable difficulty, where the writer preferred not to risk an opinion of his own. But the chief event during this period has been the publication of The New English Dictionary on Historical Principles, the unique value of which is even now too little understood and respected by the general public. The first part of this great national work appeared in 1884.

The chief difference between the second and later editions of my Concise Etymological Dictionary and the present one can now be readily explained. The former editions were mainly reproduced from the first edition, at a time when, from the nature of the case, little help could be had from the works above-mentioned, owing to the fact that they either did not exist or could not be much utilised. But in the present work, I have endeavoured to glean from them all their most important results. The work has been collated with the Century Dictionary throughout, and with the New English Dictionary from A to H (excepting a small portion of G). I have endeavoured to make good use of Kluge, Franck, Brugmann, and other authorities; and have gladly adopted a large number of corrections. In particular, I have now marked the quantities of all the vowels in Latin words, as this often throws much light upon Romance phonology. And in many cases where the result is tolerably certain I have given the primitive types of Teutonic and even of Indo-germanic words.

In all former editions, I endeavoured, by help of cross-references, to arrange derivative words under a more primitive form. Thus *ex-cite*, *in-cite*, *re-cite* and *resus-cit-ate* were all given under *Cite*. But experience has shewn that this endeavour was more ambitious than practical, often causing needless delay and trouble. Hence the only truly practical order, viz. an alphabetical one, has been here adopted, so that the required word can now be found at once. But in order to retain the chief advantages of the old plan, I have prepared two lists, one of Latin and one of Greek words, which account for a large number of derivatives. These will be found in the Appendix, § III, at pp. 632 and 644.

I have much pleasure in mentioning two more circumstances by which I have been greatly assisted and encouraged. Some few years ago, my friend the Rev. A. L. Mayhew was so good as to go patiently through every word of the Concise Etymological Dictionary, making hundreds of suggestions for improvement; and finally sent me the copy in which all these suggestions were entered. They have all been carefully considered, and in a very large number of instances have been fully adopted. Again, while the revises were passing through the press, they were read over by Mr. H. M. Chadwick, M.A., Fellow of Clare College, Cambridge, author of 'Studies in Old English' published by the Cambridge Philological Society in 1899; and his exact knowledge of Indo-germanic phonology has been suggestive of many improvements. I have only to add, in justice to these scholars, that they are not responsible for all the results here given. In some few cases I have held to my own preconceived opinion; perhaps not always wisely. Still it was best that the final form of each article should be left to the author's decision; for the reader is then sure as to where he must lay any blame.

Many articles which, in former editions, appeared only in the Supplement have now been incorporated with the rest, so that the number of words now explained (in alphabetical order) amounts to more than 12,750.

Considerable pains have been taken to ensure accuracy in the printing of the forms cited; and I have received much help from the care exercised by the press-reader. At the same time, I shall be thankful to any reader who will kindly send me a note of any error which he may detect. I have myself discovered, for example, that under the word *Cemetery* the 'Skt. çi' is an error for the 'Skt. çī.' A few belated corrections appear at pp. 662–3.

As I frequently allude to the ordinary vowel-changes in the course of the work, I may note here those which are the most elementary and common. They deserve to be learnt by heart at once.

ANGLO-SAXON. The most usual vowel-change is that produced by the occurrence of an *i* or *j* (which often disappears by a subsequent contraction of the word) in the following syllable. Owing to this, we frequently find that the vowels, as arranged in row (1) below, are changed into the corresponding vowels in row (2).

(1) *a, u* (*o*), *ea,*   *eo,*   *ā, ō, ū,*   *ēa,*   *ēo.*
(2) *e, y, ie*(*y*), *ie*(*y*), *ǣ, ē, ȳ, ie*(*ȳ*), O. Merc. *ē*), *ie*(*ȳ*).

Example :—*fyllan,* to fill, for *fulljan ; from *full,* full.

Moreover, substantives and secondary verbs are often formed from bases seen in the past tense singular, past tense plural, or past participle of a strong verb, rather than from the infinitive mood. Thus *band* and *bend* are from the base seen in the A. S. *band,* pt. t. of *bindan,* to bind ; whilst *bundle* is derived from that which appears in the pp. *bund-en.* By way of distinction, I refer to *bind-* as the 'prime grade,' to *band-* as the 'second grade,' and to *bund-* as the 'weak grade.'

Lastly, our modern words of native origin belong rather to the Midland (or Old Mercian) dialect than to the 'Anglo-Saxon' or Wessex ; and Old Mercian employs *a* (mutated to *e*) where the A. S. has *ea,* and sometimes *e* for A. S. *eo.*

ICELANDIC. This language abounds in somewhat similar vowel-changes, but very few of these appear *in English.* But we must not pass over the frequent formation of derivatives from the past tenses (singular or plural) and the past participles of strong verbs. Thus *bait,* Icel. *beita,* lit. 'to cause to bite,' is the causal of *bīta,* to bite ; its form may be explained by the fact that the pt. t. of *bīta* is *beit.*

Again, as regards the Romance languages, especially French, it must be borne in mind that they are also subject to phonetic laws. These laws are sufficiently illustrated in Mr. Paget Toynbee's translation of Brachet's Historical French Grammar. In particular, I may note that most French substantives are derived from Latin *accusatives* ; and that to derive *bounty* from *bonitās* (nom.), or *honour* from Lat. *honor* (nom.), is simply impossible.

For fuller information, the reader is referred to my Principles of English Etymology, First and Second Series ; the former deals chiefly with the native, and the latter with the foreign elements of the language. My Primer of English Etymology contains some of the more important facts.

I subjoin a key to the plan of the work, and a list of abbreviations.

KEY TO THE GENERAL PLAN OF
THE DICTIONARY.

§ 1. **Order of Words.** Words are given in their alphabetical order; but a few secondary derivatives are explained under some more important form. Thus *campaign* is given under *Camp*, and *cannon* under *Cane*.

§ 2. **The Words selected.** The word-list contains nearly all primary words of most frequent occurrence, with a few others that are remarkably prominent in literature, such as *unaneled*. Homonymous forms, such as *bay* (used in *five* senses), are numbered.

§ 3. **Definitions.** Definitions are omitted in the case of common words; but explanations of original forms are added wherever they seemed to me to be necessary.

§ 4. **Language.** The language to which each word belongs is distinctly marked, in every case, by means of letters within marks of parenthesis. Here the symbol — or − is to be read as 'derived from.' Thus *Abbey* is (F.—L.—Gk.—Syriac); i. e. a French word derived from Latin; the Latin word being, in its turn, from Greek, whilst the Greek word is of Syriac origin.

The order of derivation is always upward or backward, from late to early, and from early to earlier forms.

The symbol **+** is employed to distinguish forms which are merely *cognate*, and are adduced merely by way of illustrating and confirming the etymology. Thus, *bite* is a purely *English* word, derived from the Anglo-Saxon *bītan*. The other Teutonic forms, viz. the Du. *bijten*, Icel. *bīta*, Swed. *bita*, Dan. *bide*, G. *beissen*, and the other Indo-germanic forms, viz. Lat. *findere* (base *fid-*) and Skt. *bhid*, to cleave, are merely cognate and illustrative. On this point, there commonly exists the most singular confusion of ideas; and there are many Englishmen who are accustomed to derive English, of all things, from *Modern High German!* I therefore introduce this symbol **+** by way of warning. It has its usual algebraical value of *plus* or *additional*; and indicates 'additional information to be obtained from the comparison of cognate forms.'

The symbol > means ' older than,' or ' more primitive than '; the symbol < means ' younger than,' or ' derived from.'

§ 5. **Symbols of Languages.** The symbols, such as F.=French, are not used in their usual vague sense, so as to baffle the enquirer who wishes to find the words referred to. Every symbol has a *special sense*, and has reference to certain books, in one at least of which the word cited may be found, as I have ascertained for myself by looking them all out. I have purposely used, as far as was practicable, the most easily accessible authorities. The exact sense of each symbol is given in the list below.

§ 6. **Roots.** In some cases, a word is traced back to its original Indo-germanic root. The root is denoted by the symbol √, to be read as ' root.' Thus *bear*, to carry, is from √BHER. Some of these roots are illustrated by the lists in § III of the Appendix.

§ 7. **Derivatives.** The symbol **Der.**, i. e. Derivatives, is used to introduce forms related to the primary word. Thus, under *Act*, I note such derivatives as *act-ion*, *act-ive*, &c., which cause no difficulty.

LIST OF ABBREVIATIONS.

Arab.—Arabic; as in Richardson's Persian and Arabic Dict., ed. F. Johnson; 1829. See also Devic's Supplement to Littré's F. Dict.

A. S.—Anglo-Saxon; as in the dictionaries by Bosworth and Toller, Ettmüller, and Grein; in the Vocabularies edited by T. Wright and Prof. Wülker; and in Sweet's Oldest English Texts.

Bavar. — Bavarian; as in Schmeller's Bayerisches Wörterbuch; 1827–1837.

Bret.—Breton; as in Legonidec's Bret. Dict., ed. 1821.

Brugm.—Brugmann, Grundriss der vergleichenden Grammatik, &c.; vol. i. (2nd ed.), 1897; vol. ii. 1889–90.

C.—Celtic; used as a general term for Irish, Gaelic, Welsh, Breton, Cornish, &c.

Corn.—Cornish; as in Williams' Dict.; 1865.

Dan.—Danish; as in Ferrall and Repp; 1861.

Dan. dial.—Danish dialects; as in Molbech, 1841.

Du.—Dutch; as in Calisch and in the Tauchnitz Dutch Dict. Middle Dutch words are from Oudemans, Hexham (1658), or Sewel (1754).

E.—Modern English; as in N. E. D. (New English Dictionary); and in the Century Dictionary.

M.E.—Middle English (English from the thirteenth to the fifteenth centuries inclusive); as in Stratmann's Old English Dict., new edition, 1891.

F.—French. Most of the forms cited are not precisely *modern* French, but from Cot. = Cotgrave's Dictionary, ed. 1660. This accounts for citation of forms, such as F. *recreation*, without accents; the F. accents being mostly modern. Such words are usually marked M. F. (Middle French). See also the dictionaries by Hatzfeld and Littré.

O. F.—Old French; as in the dictionaries by Godefroy, Burguy, or Roquefort.

Fries.—Friesic; as in Richthofen, 1840.

Gael. — Gaelic; as in Macleod and Dewar, 1839; or Macbain, 1896.

G.—German; as in Flügel, 1883.

Low G.—Low German; as in the Bremen Wörterbuch, 1767.

M. H. G.—Middle High German; as in Schade, Altdeutsches Wörterbuch, 1882.

O. H. G.—Old High German; as in the śame volume.

Gk.—Greek; as in Liddell and Scott's Lexicon.

Goth. — Mœso‑Gothic; as in Balg's Glossary, 1887‑9.

Heb.—Hebrew; as in Gesenius' Dict., 1893.

Hind.—Hindustani; as in Forbes, Bate, or Wilson's Glossary of Indian Terms.

Icel.—Icelandic; as in Cleasby and Vigfusson, 1874.

Idg. — Indo‑germanic; the family of languages which includes Sanskrit, Greek, Latin, English, &c.

Irish.—Irish; as in O'Reilly, 1864.

Ital.—Italian; as in Meadows, 1857; Torriano, 1688; and Florio, 1598.

L.—Latin; as in Lewis and Short, 1880.

Late L.—Late Latin; as in the latest edition of Ducange; by L. Favre, 1884‑7. (Low L. = Late L. words of non‑Latin origin.)

Lith.—Lithuanian; as in Nesselmann's Dict., 1851.

Low G.—Low German; see under G. above.

Malay.—As in Marsden's Dict., 1812; cf. Notes by C. P. G. Scott.

Mex. — Mexican; as in the Dict. by Siméon, Paris, 1885.

M. E.—Middle English; see under E. above.

M. H. G.—Middle High German; see under G. above.

Norw.—Norwegian; as in Aasen's Norsk Ordbog, 1873.

O. F.—Old French; see under F. above.

O. H. G.—Old High German; see under G. above.

O. Sax.—Old Saxon; as in the Heliand, &c., ed. Heyne.

O. Slav — Old Slavonic; as in Miklosich, Etym. Dict., Vienna, 1886.

Pers.—Persian; as in Richardson's Arab. and Pers. Dict.; or in Palmer's Pers. Dict., 1876; cf. Horn, Neupersische Etymologie, 1893.

Peruv.—Peruvian; as in the Dict. by Gonçales, Lima, 1608.

Port.—Portuguese; as in Vieyra, 1857.

Prov.—Provençal; as in Raynouard's Lexique Roman, and Bartsch's Chrestomathie Provençale.

Russ.—Russian; as in Reiff's Dict., 1876.

Scand.—Scandinavian; used as a general term for Icelandic, Swedish, Danish, and Norwegian.

Skt.—Sanskrit; as in Benfey's Dict., 1866.

Span.—Spanish; as in Neumann, ed. Seaone, 1862; Pineda, 1740; or Minsheu, 1623.

Swed.—Swedish; as in the Tauchnitz Dict., or in Widegren, or in Öman.

Swed. dial. — Swedish dialects; as in Rietz (1867).

Teut. — Teutonic; a general term for English, Dutch, German, Gothic, and Scandinavian.

Turk.—Turkish; as in Zenker's Dict., 1866‑1876.

W.—Welsh; as in Spurrell, 1861.

OTHER ABBREVIATIONS.

acc.—accusative case.
adj.—adjective.
adv.—adverb.
A.V.—Authorised Version of the Bible, 1611.
cf.—confer, i. e. compare.
Ch.—Chaucer.
comp.—comparative.
conj.—conjunction.
dat.—dative case.
decl.—declensional.
Der.—Derivative.
dimin.—diminutive.
f. or fem.—feminine.
frequent.—frequentative.
gen.—genitive case.
i. e.—id est, that is.
inf.—infinitive mood.
interj.—interjection.
lit.—literally.
m. or masc.—masculine.
n. or neut.—neuter.

nom.—nominative case.
obs.—obsolete.
orig.—original or originally.
pl.—plural.
pp.—past participle.
prep.—preposition.
pres. part.—present participle.
pres. t.—present tense.
prob.—probably.
pron.—pronoun.
prov.—provincial.
pt. t.—past tense.
q. v.—quod vide = which see.
s. v.—sub verbo = under the word.
sb.—substantive.
Shak.—Shakespeare.
sing.—singular.
str. vb.—strong verb.
superl.—superlative.
tr.—translated, or translation.
trans.—transitive.
vb.—verb.

Some of the longer articles are marked off into sections by the use of the Greek letters β, γ. This is merely intended to make matters clearer, by separating the various statements from each other.

Notes at the end of an article are marked off by beginning with the symbol ¶. XIV, XV, XVI, mean that the word was introduced in the 14th, 15th, or 16th century, respectively. Hyphens are freely introduced to shew the *etymological* division of a word. Thus the word *concede* is derived from Lat. *con-cēdere*; meaning that *concēdere* can be resolved into *con-* and *cedere*. This etymological division is often very different from that usually adopted in printed books when words have to be divided; thus *capacious* can only be divided, etymologically, as *cap-ac-i-ous*, because *cap-* is the root-syllable; whereas, when divided according to the pronunciation, it becomes *ca-pa-ci-ous*.

Theoretical forms are marked by an asterisk preceding them. Thus, under *Barrow* (1), the Teutonic type **bergoz*, a hill, is the primitive Teutonic form whence the A. S. *beorg* and the G. *berg* are alike descended; and under *Beetle* (2), the A. S. form *bȳtel* must have been **bētel* in Old Mercian.

The symbols ð and þ are both written for *th*.   In Icelandic, þ has the sound of *th* in *thin*, and ð that of *th* in *that*; but the M.E. and A.S. symbols are confused.   The M.E. symbol ȝ commonly represents *y* at the beginning of a word, and *gh* in the middle.   A.S. short and long vowels, such as *a* and *ā*, are as distinct from each other as ε and η, or ο and ω in Greek.

The distinction between the two values of A.S. long *æ* (as made by Dr. Sweet in his A.S. Dict.) has been carefully observed. Thus the A.S. *ǣ* invariably represents the mutation of A.S. *ā* (as usual), and corresponds to Goth. *ai*; but A.S. *ǽ* represents the Wessex sound corresponding to the Anglian and Kentish *ē*, and to Goth. *ē*.   For example, *heal* is from A.S. *hǣlan*, cognate with Goth. *hailjan*, G. *heilen*; but *deed* is from O. Merc. *dēd* (Wessex *dǽd*), cognate with Goth. *dēds*, G. *that*.

A

CONCISE ETYMOLOGICAL DICTIONARY

OF THE

ENGLISH LANGUAGE

A, indef. art. (E.) See **An.**

A- (1), as in *a-down* = A.S. *ofdūne.* (E.) Here *a-* = A.S. *of*; see **Of, Off.**

A- (2), as in *a-foot.* (E.) For *on foot*; see **On.** ¶ This is the commonest value of the prefix *a-.*

A- (3), as in *a-long.* (E.) Here *a-* = A.S. *and-*; see **Along.**

A- (4), as in *a-rise.* (E.) Here *a-* = A.S. *ā-*; see **Arise.**

A- (5), as in *a-chieve, a-stringent.* (F. –L.; or L.) Here *a* = F. prefix *a* = L. *ad*, to; see **Ad-.**

A- (6), as in *a-vert.* (L.) Here *a-* = L. *ā*; see **Ab-** (1).

A- (7), as in *a-mend.* (L.) Here *a-mend* is for *e-mend*; and *e-* = L. *ē* or *ex*; see **Ex-.**

A- (8), as in *a-las.* (F.) See **Alas.**

A- (9), as in *a-byss.* (Gk.) Here *a-* = Gk. *ἀ-* or *ἀν-*; see **Un-, Abyss.**

A- (10). as in *a-do.* (E.) For *at do*; see **At, Ado.**

A- (11), as in *a-ware.* (E.) Here *a-* is for M.E. *y-, i-,* A.S. *ge-*; see **Aware.**

A- (12), as in *a-vast.* (Du.) For Du. *houd vast*; see **Avast.**

Ab- (1), *prefix.* (L.) L. *ab*, from; cognate with E. *of*; see **Of.** In F., it becomes *a-* or *av-*; see **Advantage.**

Ab- (2), *prefix.* (L.) For L. *ad*, to, by assimilation; see **Abbreviate.**

Aback. (E.) For *on back.* A.S. *onbæc*; see **A-** (2) and **Back.**

Abaft. (E.) From the prefix *a-* (2), and *b-aft*, short for *bi-aft*, by aft. Thus *a-b-aft* = on by aft, i.e. at the part which lies to the aft. Cf. M.E. *biaften*, Gen. and Exod. 3377; A.S. *beæftan.* See **A-** (2), **By,** and **Aft.**

Abandon. (F. – Low L. – O.H.G.) M.E. *abandounen*, vb. – F. *abandonner.* – F. *à bandon*, at liberty; orig. in the power (of). – L. *ad*, at; Low L. *bandum, bannum*, an order, decree; from O.H.G. *ban*, summons, ban; see **Ban.**

Abase. (F. – L.) M.E. *abasen*, from **A-** (5) and **Base**; imitating O.F. *abaissier*, to lower.

Abash. (F.) M.E. *abaschen, abaischen, abasen.* – O.F. *esbaïss-*, stem of pres. part. of *esbair* (F. *ébahir*), to astonish. – O.F. *es-* (= L. *ex*, out, very much); and *bair, bahir*, to cause astonishment, a word of imitative origin from the interj. *bah!* of astonishment. ¶ Sometimes confused with *abase* in M.E. See **Bashful.**

Abate. (F. – L.) M.E. *abaten.* – O.F. *abatre.* – Late L. **abbattere*, to beat down (as in Ital.). – L. *ad*, to; and *batere*, for *batuere*, to beat. ¶ Hence *bate*, for *a-bate.* Cf. **Ab-** (2).

Abbot. (L. – Gk. – Syriac.) M.E. *abbot, abbod*, A.S. *abbod.* – L. *abbāt-* (nom. *abbas*), an abbot, lit. a father – Gk. ἀββᾶς. – Syriac *abbā*, a father; Rom. viii. 15.

abbess. (F. – L. – Gk. – Syriac.) M.E. *abbesse.* – O.F. *abesse, abaesse.* – Late L. *abbāt-issa.* – L. *abbāt-* (as above); and *-issa* = Gk. *-ισσα*, fem. suffix.

abbey. (F. – L. – Gk. – Syriac.) M.E. *abbeye.* – O.F. *abeie.* – Late L. *abbāt-ia.* – L. *abbāt-* (above).

Abbreviate. (L.) From pp. of L. *abbreuiāre*, to shorten.—L. *ab-*, for *ad*, to, by assimilation; and *breuis*, short. See Ab- (2) and Brief.

Abdicate. (L.) From pp. of L. *abdicāre*, to renounce.—L. *ab*, from; *dicāre*, to proclaim. Allied to Diction.

Abdomen. (L.) L. *abdōmen* (stem *abdōmin-*), lower part of the belly.

Abduction. (L.) L. *abductiōnem*, acc. of *abductio*, a leading away.—L. *abdūcere*, to lead away.—L. *ab*, from; *dūcere*, to lead. Cf. Duke.

Abed. (E.) For *on bed*; see A- (2) and Bed.

Aberration. (L.) From acc. of L. *aberrātio*, a wandering from; from pp. of L. *ab-errāre*.—L. *ab*, from; *errāre*, to wander, err. See Err.

Abet, to incite. (F.—Scand.) O.F. *abeter*, to excite, set on (Godefroy).—F. *a-* (Lat. *ad-*); and O.F. *beter*, to bait (a bear), to set on, from Icel. *beita*, to make to bite, causal of *bīta*, to bite. See Bait, Bite. Der. *bet*, short for *abet*, sb.

Abeyance, expectation, suspension. (F.—L.) A.F. *abeiance*, suspension, waiting (Roq.).—F. *a*; and *beant*, pres. pt. of O.F. *beer* (F. *bayer*), to gape, expect anxiously.—L. *ad*, at; and *badāre*, to gape.

Abhor. (L.) L. *ab-horrēre*, to shrink from in terror.—L. *ab*, from; *horrēre*, to dread. Cf. Horrid.

Abide (1), to wait for. (E.) A.S. *ā-bīdan*; from *ā-*, prefix, and *bīdan*, to bide. See A- (4) and Bide.

Abide (2), to suffer for, pay for. (E.) In Sh.; corrupted from M. E. *abyen*, to pay for, lit. to buy up, redeem.—A.S. *ābycgan*, to pay for. See A- (4) and Buy.

Abject, mean, lit. cast away. (L.) L. *ab-iectus*, cast away, pp. of *ab-icere*, to cast away.—L. *ab*, away; *iacere*, to cast. Cf. Jet (1).

Abjure. (L.) L. *ab-iūrāre*, to deny; lit. to swear away from.—L. *ab*, from; *iūrāre*, to swear.—L. *iūr-*, from nom. *iūs*, law, right. Cf. Jury.

Ablative. (L.) L. *ablātīuus*, lit. taking away.—L. *ab*, from; and *lātum* (= *tlātum*), to bear, take; allied to *tollere*, to take. See Tolerate.

Ablaze. (E.) For *on blaze*; see A- (2) and Blaze.

Able, powerful, skilful. (F. — L.) M. E. *able*, *hable*.—O. F. *habile*, able, able. —L. *habilis*, easy to handle, active.—L.

habēre, to have. Cf. Habit. Der. *ability* from L. acc. *habilitātem*.

Ablution. (F.—L.) F.; from L. acc. *ab-lūtiōnem*, a washing away.—L. *ablūtus*, pp. of *ab-luere*, to wash away.—L. *ab*, from; *luere*, to wash.

Abnegate. (L.) From pp. of L. *ab-negāre*, to deny.—L. *ab*, from; *negāre*, to say no. Cf. Negation.

Aboard. (E.) For *on board*; see A- (2) and Board.

Abode, sb. (E.) M.E. *abood*, delay, abiding. Formed as if from A.S. *ābād*, 2nd stem of *ābīdan*, to abide. See Abide.

Abolish. (F.—L.) F. *aboliss-*, stem of pres. pt. of *abolir*.—L. *abolēre*, to abolish.

Abominate. (L.) From pp. of L. *ab-ōminārī*, to turn away from that which is of ill omen.—L. *ab*, away; *ōmin-*, for *ōmen*, an omen.

Aborigines, original inhabitants. (L.) L. *aborīgines*, the nations which, previous to historical record, drove out the Siculi (Lewis and Short). Formed from L. *ab orīgine*, from the beginning; where *orīgine* is the abl. of *orīgo* (Vergil, Æn. i. 642).

Abortion. (L.) From acc. of L. *abortio*, an untimely birth.—L. *abortus*, pp. of *ab-orīrī*, to fail.—L. *ab*, away; *orīrī*, to arise, begin. Cf. Orient.

Abound. (F.—L.) A.F. *abunder*, O.F. *abonder*.—L. *ab-undāre*, to overflow. —L. *ab*, away; *unda*, a wave.

About. (E.) M. E. *abuten*, *abouten*. A.S. *ābūtan*, *onbūtan*; short for *on-be-ūtan*; where *be* answers to E. *by*, and *ūtan* outward, is related to E. *ūt*, out. See A- (2), By and Out.

Above. (E.) M. E. *aboven*, *abufen*. A.S. *ābufan*, for *on-be-ufan*; where *be* answers to E. *by*, and *ufan*, upward, is extended from Goth. *uf*, up. See A- (2), By, Up. (A.S. *ufan* = G. *oben*. A.S. *be-ufan* = Du. *boven*.)

Abrade, to scrape off. (L.) L. *ab-rādere*, to scrape off.—L. *ab*, off; *rādere*, to scrape. Der. *abrasion* (from L. pp. *abrāsus*).

Abreast. (E.) Put for *on breast*; see A- (2) and Breast.

Abridge. (F.—L.) M. E. *abreggen*. A. F. *abregger*, O. F. *abreger*, *abregier*, to shorten.—L. *abbreuiāre*, to shorten.—L. *ab-*, put for *ad-*, to; and *breuis*, short. Cf. Brief. Doublet, *abbreviate*.

Abroach, to set. (E. *and* F.) Put for *to set on broach*; see **A-** (2) and **Broach.**

Abroad. (E.) M. E. *abrood*; put for *on brood*; lit. on broad; see **A-** (2) and **Broad.**

Abrogate. (L.) From pp. of L. *ab-rogāre*, to repeal a law.—L. *ab*, away; *rogāre*, to ask, propose a law.

Abrupt. (L.) L. *abruptus*, pp. of *ab-rumpere*, to break off.—L. *ab*, off; *rumpere*, to break.

Abscess. (L.) A gathering of humours into one place; lit. a going away.—L. *abscessus*, a going away; abscess (Celsus). — L. *abscessus*, pp. of *abs-cēdere*, to go away.—L. *abs*, away; *cēdere*, to go, cede.

Abscind. (L.) From L. *ab-scindere*, to cut off.—L. *ab*, off; *scindere*, to cut. Der. *abscissa*, from fem. of L. *abscissus*, pp. of *abscindere*.

Abscond, to go into hiding. (L.) L. *abscondere*, to hide. — L. *abs*, away; *condere*, to hide. *Condere* is from *con-* (*cum*), together, and *-dere*, to put, allied to Skt. *dhā*, to put. (√DHĒ, to place; Brugm. i. § 589.) See **Do.**

Absent, adj. (F.—L.) XIV cent. O. F. *absent*, adj.—L. *absent-*, stem of *absens*, being away.—L. *ab-*, away; *-sens*, being, occurring also in *præ-sens*. Cf. Skt. *sant*, pres. pt. of *as*, to be; from √ES, to be. Cf. **Present, Sooth.** Der. *absence*, F. *absence*, L. *absentia*.

Absolute, unrestrained, complete. (L.) L. *absolūtus*, pp. of *ab-soluere*, to set free. — L. *ab*, from; *soluere*, to loosen.

absolve. (L.) L. *ab-soluere*, to set free (above). Der. *absolut-ion*, from the pp. above.

Absorb. (L.) L. *absorbēre*, to swallow.—L. *ab*, away; *sorbēre*, to sup up.+ Gk. ῥοφέειν, to sup up. (Brugm. ii. § 801.) Der. *absorpt-ion*, from pp. *absorptus*.

Abstain. (F.—L.) F. *abstenir* (O.F. *astenir*).—L. *abs-tinēre*, to refrain from.—L. *abs*, from; *tenēre*, to hold. Der. *abstinence*, F. *abstinence*, from L. *abstinentia*, sb.: *abstent-ion*, from the pp.

Abstemious. (L.) L. *abstēmius*, refraining from strong drink. — L. *abs*, from; *tēmētum*, strong drink, whence *tēmu-lentus*, drunken.

Abstract. (L.) L. *abstractus*, pp. of *abs-trahere*, to draw away.—L. *abs*, away; *trahere*, to draw.

Abstruse. (L.) L. *abstrūsus*, diffi-cult, concealed; pp. of *abs-trūdere*, to thrust away.—L. *abs*, away; *trūdere*, to thrust. See **Intrude.**

Absurd. (L.) L. *absurdus*, inharmonious, foolish.—L. *ab*, from; *surdus*, deaf, inaudible, harsh. Cf. **Surd.**

Abundance. (F.—L.) F. *abondance*. —L. *abundantia*. See **Abound.**

Abuse, vb. (F.—L.) F. *abuser*, to use amiss.—L. *abūsus*, pp. of *ab-ūtī*, to use amiss.—L. *ab*, away (amiss); *ūtī*, to use.

Abut, to project towards. (F.—L. *and* G.) O. F. *abouter*, to thrust towards.— L. *ad*, to; O.F. *bouter*, *boter*, to thrust. See **A-** (5) and **Butt** (1).

Abyss, a bottomless gulf. (L.—Gk.) Milton. L. *abyssus*.—Gk. ἄβυσσος, bottomless.—Gk. ἀ-, short for ἀν-, neg. prefix; and βυσσός, depth. See **A-** (9), **Un-** (1).

Acacia, a tree. (L.—Gk.) L. *acacia*. —Gk. ἀκακία, the thorny Egyptian acacia. —Gk. ἀκίς, a point, thorn. (√AK.) See Brugm. ii. § 52 (4).

Academy. (F. — L. — Gk.) F. *académie*.—L. *academīa*.—Gk. ἀκαδήμεια, a grove where Plato taught, named from the hero *Akademus*.

Accede. (L.) L. *ac-cēdere*, to come towards, assent to.—L. *ac-* (for *ad*), to; *cēdere*, to come, cede.

Accelerate. (L.) From pp. of L. *accelerāre*, to quicken.—L. *ac-* (for *ad*), to; *celer*, quick. Cf. **Celerity.**

Accent. (F.—L.) F. *accent*, sb.—L. acc. *accentum*, a tone.—L. *ac-* (for *ad*); *cantus*, a singing, from *canere*, to sing.

Accept. (F.—L.) F. *accepter*.—L. *acceptāre*, frequentative of *ac-cipere*, to receive.—L. *ac-* (for *ad*), to; *capere*, to take.

Access. (L.) L. *accessus*, a coming unto.—L. *accessus*, pp. of *ac-cēdere*, to accede.—L. *ac-* (for *ad*), to; *cēdere*, to come, cede.

Accident. (F.—L.) F. *accident*, a chance event (Cot.).—L. *accident-*, base of pres. pt. of *ac-cidere*, to happen.—L. *ac-* (for *ad*), to; *cadere*, to fall. Der. *accidence*, F. *accidence*, L. *accidentia*.

Acclaim. (L.) Formed from L. *ac-clāmāre*, to cry out at.—L. *ac-* (for *ad*), at; *clāmāre*, to cry out. For the spelling, cf. **Claim.**

Acclivity. (L.) XVII cent. From L. *acclīuitātem*, acc. of *acclīuitas*.—L. *ac-* (for *ad*); and *clīu-us*, sloping, a slope; see **Lean** (1). (√KLEI; Brugm. i. § 463.)

Accolade, the dubbing of a knight. (F. – Ital. – L.) F. *accollade*, in Cotgrave, ed. 1660; lit. an embrace round the neck, then a salutation, light tap with a sword in dubbing a knight. – Ital. *accollata*, fem. of pp. of *accollare*, to embrace about the neck (Florio). – L. *ac-* (for *ad*), to, about; *collum*, the neck.

Accommodate. (L.) From pp. of L. *accommodāre*, to fit, adapt. – L. *ac-* (for *ad*), to; and *commodus*, fit. – L. *com-* (= *cum*), with; and *modus*, measure, mode.

Accompany. (F. – L.) F. *accompagner*, to accompany. – F. *a* (L. *ad*), to; and O. F. *compaing*, companion; see Company.

Accomplice. (F. – L.) Put for *a complice*; *a* is the indef. art. – F. *complice*, 'a complice, confederate;' Cot. – L. acc. *complicem*, from *complex*, confederate, lit. 'interwoven.' – L. *com-* (*cum*), together; and stem *plic-*, allied to *plicāre*, to weave. Cf. **Ply.**

Accomplish. (F. – L.) M. E. *acomplisen*. – O. F. *acomplis-*, stem of pres. part. of *acomplir*, to complete. – L. *ad*, to; *complēre*, to fulfil. – L. *com-* (*cum*), together; *plēre*, to fill.

Accord. (F. – L.) A. F. *acorder*, to agree. – Late L. *accordāre*. – L. *ac-* (for *ad*), to; and *cord-*, stem of *cor*, heart. Cf. **Concord.**

Accordion, a musical instrument. (Ital. – L.) From Ital. *accord-are*, to accord, to tune an instrument; with suffix *-ion* (as in *clar-ion*). – Late L. *accordāre*, to agree. See above.

Accost, to address. (F. – L.) F. *accoster*, lit. 'to go to the side of.' – Late L. *accostāre* (same). – L. *ac-* (for *ad*), to; *costa*, rib, side. See **Coast.**

Account, vb. (F. – L.) A. F. *acounter*, *acunter*. – O. F. *a*, to; *conter*, *compter*, to count. – L. *ad*; and *com-putāre*, to compute, from *com-* (*cum*), and *putāre*, to think.

Accoutre. (F. – L.?) F. *accoutrer*, formerly also *accoustrer*, to dress, array. Etym. quite uncertain; perhaps from O. F. *coustre*, *coutre*, a sacristan who had charge of sacred vestments, from Late L. *custor* = L. *custos*, a custodian, keeper.

Accretion, increase. (L.) From acc. of L. *accrētio*, increase. – L. *accrētus*, pp. of *ac-crescere*, to increase. – L. *ac-* (for *ad*); *crescere*, to grow, inchoative form from *cre-are*, to make. Cf. **Create.**

Accrue, to come to by way of increase. (F. – L.) From A. F. *acru*, O. F. *acreu*, pp. of *acroistre* (F. *accroître*), to increase. – L. *accrescere*; see above.

Accumulate. (L.) From pp. of L. *ac-cumulāre*, to amass. – L. *ac-* (*ad*), to; *cumulāre*, to heap up, from *cumulus*, a heap.

Accurate. (L.) From pp. of L. *accūrāre*, to take pains with. – L. *ac-* (*ad*), to; *cūrāre*, to care for, from *cūra*, care. See **Cure.**

Accursed, cursed. (E.) Pp. of M. E. *acursien*. A. S. *ā-*, prefix; and *cursian*, to curse; see A- (4) and **Curse.**

Accuse. (F. – L.) A. F. *acuser*. – L. *accūsāre*, to lay to one's charge. – L. *ac-* (*ad*), to; and *causa*, *caussa*, a suit at law, a cause.

Accustom. (F. – L.) A. F. *acustumer* (F. *accoutumer*), to make usual. – F. *a* (from L. *ad*, to); and A. F. *custume*, custom. See **Custom.**

Ace, the ' one ' on dice. (F. – L. – Gk. ?) M. E. *as*. – O. F. *as*. – L. *as*. [Said to be the Tarentine *ăs*, for Gk. *εἶς*, one.]

Acephalous, headless. (Gk.) Gk. ἀκέφαλ-ος, headless; with suffix *-ous*. – Gk. ά-, un- ; and κεφαλή, head. See A- (9).

Acerbity. (F. – L.) XVI cent. F. *acerbité*. – L. acc. *acerbitātem* (nom. *acerbitas*), bitterness. – L. *acer-b-us*, bitter; cf. *ăc-er*, sharp, lit. piercing. – L. *acēre*, to be sour.

Ache, verb. (E.) M. E. *aken*, vb.; pt. t. *ook*. A. S. *acan*. (√AG, to drive.) ¶ Spelt *ache* by confusion with M. E. *ache*, sb., from A. S. *æce*, a pain. The verb survives, spelt as the obs. sb.

Achieve. (F. – L.) M. E. *acheven*. – A. F. *achever*, to achieve; lit. to come to a head. – O. F. *a chef*, to a head. – L. *ad*, to; *caput*, a head. Cf. **Chief.**

Achromatic, colourless. (Gk.) See A- (9) and **Chromatic.**

Acid, sour, sharp. (F. – L.; *or* L.) F. *acide*. – L. *ac-idus*, lit. piercing. (√AK, to pierce.) Der. *acid-i-ty*; *acid-ul-at-ed* (from L. *acid-ul-us*, dimin. of *acid-us*).

Acknowledge. (E.) XVI cent. M. E. *knowlechen*; from the sb. *knowleche*, mod. E. *knowledge*; see **Knowledge.** The prefix is due to M. E. *aknowen* (= A. S. *oncnāwan*), with the same sense; hence the prefix is A- (2).

Acme, top. (Gk.) Gk. ἀκ-μή, top, sharp edge. (√AK, to pierce.)

Acolyte, a servitor. (F.—Low L.—Gk.) F. *acolyte,* Cot.—Late L. *acolŷthus.*—Gk. ἀκόλουθος, a follower.—Gk. ἀ-, with (akin to Skt. *sa-,* with); κέλευθος, a path; so that ἀκόλουθος = a travelling-companion.

Aconite, monk's-hood. (F.—L.—Gk.) F. *aconit.*—L. *aconītum.*—Gk. ἀκόνῑτον, a plant; perhaps so called from growing ἐν ἀκόναις, on steep sharp rocks.—Gk. ἀκ-όνη, a whetstone, sharp stone.

Acorn. (E.) M. E. *acorn.* A. S. *æcern,* fruit; properly 'fruit of the field,' from A. S. *æcer,* a field; see **Acre.**+Icel. *akarn,* Dan. *agern* Goth. *akran,* fruit; from Icel. *akr,* Dan. *ager,* Goth. *akrs,* a field. ¶ Not from *oak.*

Acoustic. (Gk.) Gk. ἀκουστικός, relating to hearing (or sound).—Gk. ἀκούειν, to hear.

Acquaint. (F.—L.) M. E. *acqueynten,* earlier *acointen.*—O. F. *acointer, acointier,* to acquaint with.—Late L. *adcognitāre,* to make known (Brachet).—L. *ad,* to; and **cognitāre,* formed from *cognitus,* pp. of *cognoscere,* to know. See **Quaint.**

Acquiesce. (L.) L. *acquiescere,* to rest in.—L. *ac-* (for *ad*), to; *quiescere,* to rest. See **Quiet.**

Acquire. (L.) L. *acquīrere,* to get, obtain.—L. *ac-* (for *ad*), to; *quærere,* to seek. **Der.** *acquisit-ion;* from pp. *acquīsītus.*

Acquit. (F.—L.) M. E. *aquiten.*—O. F. *aquiter,* to settle a claim; Late L. *acquiētāre.*—L. *ac-* (for *ad*), to; *quiētāre,* vb., formed from *quiētus,* discharged, free, orig. at rest. See **Quiet.**

Acre. (E.) M. E. *aker.* A. S. *æcer.*+Du. *akker,* Icel. *akr,* Swed. *åker,* Dan. *ager,* Goth. *akrs,* G. *acker;* L. *ager,* Gk. ἀγρός, Skt. *ajra.* Teut. type **akroz;* Idg. type, **agros.* The orig. sense was 'pasture.' (√AG.) **Der.** *acor-n,* q. v.

Acrid, tart. (L.) Coined by adding *-d* to L. *ācri-,* stem of *ācer,* sharp; on the analogy of *ac-id.*

Acrimony. (F.—L.) F. *acrimoine.*—L. *ācri-mōn-ia.*—L. *ācri-,* stem of *ācer* (above).

Acrobat, a tumbler. (F.—Gk.) F. *acrobate.*—Gk. ἀκρόβατος, lit. walking on tiptoe.—Gk. ἄκρο-ν, a point, neut. of ἄκ-ρος, pointed; and βατός, verbal adj. of βαίνειν, to walk; see **Come.**

Acropolis, a citadel. (Gk.) Lit.

'upper city.'—Gk. ἄκρο-s, pointed, upper; and πόλις, a city.

Across. (E. *and* Scand.) For *on cross;* see **A-** (2) and **Cross.**

Acrostic, a short poem in which the initial letters spell a word. (Gk.) Gk. ἀκροστιχίς.—Gk. ἄκρο-s, pointed, also first; and στίχος, a row, line, from weak grade of στείχειν, to go. (√STEIGH.)

Act, sb. (F.—L.) F. *acte.*—L. *actus,* m., and *actum,* n.—L. *actus* done; pp. of *agere,* to do, drive. See **Agent.** **Der.** *act-ion;* *act-ive* (F. *actif*); *act-or;* *act-u-al* (L. *actuālis*); *act-uary* (L. *actuārius;* *act-u-ate* (from pp. of Late L. *actuāre,* to perform, put in action).

Acumen. (L.) L. *ac-ū-men,* sharpness, acuteness. Cf. *acuere,* to sharpen.

Acute. (L.) L. *acūtus,* sharp; pp. of *ac-u-ere,* to sharpen. (√AK, to pierce.)

Ad-, *prefix.* (L.) L. *ad,* to, cognate with E. **At.** ¶ L. *ad* becomes *ac-* before *c; af-* bef. *f; ag-* bef. *g; al-* bef. *l; an-* bef. *n; ap-* bef. *p; ar-* bef. *r; as-* bef. *s; at-* bef. *t.*

Adage, a saying. (F.—L.) F. *adage.*—L. *adāgium.*—L. *ad;* and *āgium,* a saying; cf. *āiō,* I say.

Adamant. (F.—L.—Gk.) M. E. *adamaunt,* a diamond, a magnet.—O. F. *adamant.*—L. *adamanta,* acc. of *adamas.*—Gk. ἀδάμας, a very hard metal or stone; lit. 'unconquerable.'—Gk. ἀ- (= E. *un-*); and δαμάω, I conquer, tame. See **Tame.**

Adapt. (F.—L.) Early XVII cent.—F. *adapter.*—L. *ad-aptāre,* to fit to.—L. *ad,* to; *aptāre,* to fit, from *aptus,* fit, apt.

Add. (L.) M. E. *adden.*—L. *addere,* lit. to put to.—L. *ad;* and *-dere,* to put. See **Abscond.**

Adder, a viper. (E.) M. E. *addere;* also *naddere, neddere.* [*An* adder resulted from *a nadder,* by mistake.] A. S. *nǽdre, nǽddre,* a snake.+G. *natter,* a snake; also cf. Icel. *naðr,* Goth. *nadrs* (with short *a*).

Addict. (L.) From L. *addict-us,* pp. of *ad-dīcere,* to adjudge, assign.—L. *ad,* to; *dīcere,* to say, appoint. Cf. **Diction.**

Addled, corrupt, unproductive. (E.) Due to an attributive use of the M. E. sb. *adel,* filth, used in the compound *adel-ey,* lit. 'filth-egg' = Late L. *ōvum ūrīnæ,* urine-egg; mistaken form of L. *ōuum ūrīnum,* wind-egg, due to Gk. οὔριον ᾠόν, wind-egg. Orig. 'mud,' from A.S. *adela,* mud (Grein). Cf. Low G. *adel,* a puddle.

Address, vb. (F.—L.) F. *adresser.*

5

—F. *a*, to; *dresser*, to direct, dress; see Dress.

Adduce. (L.) L. *ad-dūcere*, to lead to, bring forward.—L. *ad*, to; *dūcere*, to lead, bring.

Adept, a proficient. (L.) L. *adeptus*, one who has obtained proficiency; pp. of *adipisci*, to obtain.—L. *ad*, to; *apisci*, to obtain, perhaps related to *aptus*, fit. Cf. **Apt.**

Adequate. (L.) L. *adæquātus*, pp. of *adæquāre*, to make equal to.—L. *ad*, to; *æquāre*, to make equal, from *æquus*, equal.

Adhere. (L.) L. *ad-hærēre*, to stick to.—L. *ad*, to; *hærēre*, to stick.

Adieu, farewell. (F.) M. E. *a dieu*. —F. *à dieu*, (I commit you) to God.—L. *ad Deum*, to God. See **Deity.**

Adipose, fatty. (L.) Late L. *adipōsus*, fatty.—L. *adip-*, stem of *adeps*, sb., fat. Connection with Gk. ἄλειφα, fat, is doubtful.

Adit, access to a mine. (L.) L. *adit-us*, approach, entrance.—L. *adit-um*, supine of *ad-īre*, to go to.—L. *ad*, to; *īre*, to go.

Adjacent, near to. (L.) From base of pres. pt. of L. *ad-iacēre*, to lie near.— L. *ad*, near; *iacēre*, to lie.

Adjective. (F.—L.) F. *adjectif* (fem. *-ive*).—L. *ad-iectīuus*, lit. put near to.— L. *ad-iectus*, pp. of *ad-icere*, to put near.— L. *ad*, to; *iacere*, to cast, throw.

Adjoin, to lie next to. (F.—L.) O. F. *adjoindre*.—L. *ad-iungere* (pp. *adiunctus*), to join to.—L. *ad*, to; *iungere*, to join.

Adjourn, to put off till another day. (F.—L.) O. F. *ajorner*, properly to draw near to day, to dawn; also, to appoint a day for one.—Late L. *adjurnāre*, 'diem dicere alicui;' Ducange.—L. *ad*, to; and Late L. *jurnus* (Ital. *giorno*), a day, from L. adj. *diurnus*, daily.—L. *diēs*, a day.

Adjudge. (F.—L.) M. E. *adiugen*; also *aiugen* (=*ajugen*).—O. F. *ajuger*, to decide.—L. *adiūdicāre*, to award.—L. *ad*, to; *iūdicāre*, to judge, from *iūdic-*, base of *iūdex*, a judge. See **Judge.**

Adjudicate. (L.) From pp. of L. *adiūdicāre* (above).

Adjure. (L.) L. *ad-iūrāre*, to swear to; in late L., to put to an oath.—L. *ad*, to; *iūrāre*, to swear. See **Jury.**

Adjust, to fit exactly. (F.—L.) From F. *adjuster*,' to adjust, place justly;' Cot. L. *ad*, to; *iustus*, just, exact; see **Just.**
¶ A new F. formation, due to misunder-

standing the sense of O. F. *ajoster*, to put side by side, arrange.—L. *ad*, to; and *iuxtā*, near; see **Joust.**

Adjutant, lit. assistant. (L.) From L. *adiūtant-em*, acc. of pres. part. of *adiūtāre*, to assist, frequent. of *ad-iuuāre*, to aid.—L. *ad*, to; *iuuāre*, to help. Cf. **Aid.**

Administer. (F.—L.) M. E. *aministren*.—O. F. *aministrer*.—L. *ad-ministrāre*, to minister (to).—L. *ad*, to; *ministrāre*, to serve, from *minister*, a servant. See **Minister.**

Admiral. (F.—Arab.) M. E. *admiral*, more often *amiral*.—O. F. *amiral*, *amirail*, also *amire*; cf. Low L. *admiraldus*, a prince, chief.—Arab. *amīr*, a prince; see **Emir.** The suffix is due to Arab. *al* in *amīr-al-bahr*, prince of the sea.

Admire. (F.—L.) F. *admirer* (O. F. *amirer*).—L. *admīrāri*, to wonder at.— L. *ad*, at; *mīrāri*, to wonder.

Admit. (L.) L. *ad-mittere*, to let to, send to.—L. *ad*, to; *mittere*, to send. Der. *admiss-ion*; from pp. *admiss-us*.

Admonish. (F.—L.) M. E. *amonesten*; so that *admonish* has taken the place of *amonest*, with changed suffix due to verbs in *-ish*. 'I *amoneste* or warne'; Wyclif, 1 Cor. iv. 14.—O. F. *amonester*.— Late L. *admonestāre*, new formation from L. *admonēre*, to advise.—L. *ad*, to; *monēre*, to advise. Cf. **Monition.**

A-do, to-do, trouble. (E.) M. E. *at do*, to do; a Northern idiom, whereby *at* was used as the sign of the infin. mood, as in Icel., Swedish, &c. See **Do** (1).

Adolescent, growing up. (L.) L. *adolescent-em*, acc. of pres. pt. of *ad-olescere*, to grow up. See **Adult.**

Adopt. (L.) L. *ad-optāre*, to adopt, choose.—L. *ad*, to; *optāre*, to wish.

Adore. (L.) L. *ad-ōrāre*, to pray to. —L. *ad*, to; *ōrāre*, to pray, from *ōs* (gen. *ōr-is*), the mouth. Cf. **Oral.**

Adorn. (L.) L. *ad-ornāre*, to deck. —L. *ad*, to; *ornāre*, to adorn.

Adown, downwards. (E.) M. E. *adune*. A.S. *of-dūne*, lit. from a down or hill.—A.S. *of*, off, from; and *dūne*, dat. of *dūn*, a hill; see **A-** (1) and **Down** (2).

Adrift. (E.) For *on drift*; see **A-** (2) and **Drift.**

Adroit. (F.—L.) F. *adroit*, dexterous. —F. *à droit*, rightfully.—F. *à* (L. *ad*), to; Late L. *dīrectum*, right, justice, neut. of L. *dīrectus*, pp. of *dī-rigere*, to direct, from L. *dī-* (for *dis-*), apart, and *regere*, to rule.

Adulation, flattery. (F.−L.) F. *adulation.*−L. acc. *adulātiōnem,* from *adulātio,* flattery.−L. *adulātus,* pp. of *adulārī,* to flatter.

Adult. (L.) L. *adultus,* grown up; pp. of *ad-olescere,* to grow up.−L. *ad,* to; **olescere,* inceptive form related to *alere,* to nourish; see **Aliment.**

Adulterate, to corrupt. (L.) XVI cent.−L. *adulterātus,* pp. of *adulterāre,* to corrupt.−L. *adulter,* an adulterer, a debaser of money.

Adultery. (F.−L.) M. E. *avoutrie*; but a later form was *adulterie,* in imitation of Latin. Cf. O. F. *avoutrie, avouterie,* adultery; from *avoutre,* an adulterer, which represented L. *adulter* (see above); so that *avoutrie* was equivalent in sense to L. *adultērium,* adultery.

Adumbrate. (L.) From pp. of L. *ad-umbrāre,* to shadow forth.−L. *ad,* to; *umbra,* a shadow.

Advance, to go forward. (F. − L.) XVI cent. A mistaken form; for M. E. *auancen, avancen.*−F. *avancer,* to go forward or before.−F. *avant,* before.−L. *ab,* from; *ante,* before. See **Ante-, Van.**

Advantage, profit. (F.−L.) A mistaken form for M. E. *avantage.*−F. *avantage*; formed with suffix *-age* from *avant,* before; see above.

Advent, approach. (L.) L. *aduentus,* approach.−L. *aduentus,* pp. of *ad-uenīre,* to approach.−L. *ad,* to; *uenīre,* to come. Cf. **Venture.**

Adventure. (F.−L.) M.E. *aventure*; with F. *a-* replaced by L. *ad-.*−F. *aventure,* a chance, occurrence.−L. *aduentūra,* fem. of *aduentūrus,* about to happen, fut. part. of *aduenīre,* to approach; see above.

Adverb. (F.−L.) Used to qualify a verb. F. *adverbe.*−L. *aduerbium.*−L. *ad,* to; *uerbum,* a word, a verb.

Adverse. (F.−L.) M.F. *advers* (O.F. *avers*).−L. *aduersus,* turned towards, also opposed to; pp. of L. *aduertere,* to turn to (see below). **Der.** *advers-ary, adversity.*

Advert. (L.) L. *ad-uertere,* to turn to, regard, heed.−L. *ad,* to; *uertere,* to turn; see **Verse. Der.** *in-advert-ent,* not regarding.

Advertise. (F.−L.) M.E. *avertisen,* later *advertise.* From the base of *avertiss-ant,* pres. pt. of *avertir,* to inform,

---

warn.−Late L. *aduertēre,* put for L. *aduertere,* to turn to, heed; see above.

Advice. (F.−L.) M.E. *auis (avis),* without *d.*−O. F. *avis,* an opinion; orig. a compound word, put for *a vis,* i. e. according to my opinion.−L. *ad,* according to; *uīsum,* that which has seemed good to one, orig. neut. of *uīsus,* pp. of *uidēre,* to see.

Advise. (F.−L.) M.E. *aduisen,* also *auisen (avisen),* without *d.*−O.F. *aviser,* to be of opinion.−O. F. *avis* (above).

Advocate, sb. (F.−L.) M.F. *advocat,* 'an advocate;' Cot.−L. *aduocātus,* an advocate, one 'called upon' to plead.− L. *aduocātus,* pp. of *ad-uocāre,* to call to, call upon.−L. *ad,* to; *uocāre,* to call.

Advowson. (F. − L.) A.F. *avoeson,* also *advouson,* patronage; hence the right of presentation to a benefice (Roquefort).− Late L. *aduocātiōnem,* acc. of *aduocātio,* patronage.−Late L. *aduocātus,* a patron; the same as L. *aduocātus,* an advocate.

Adze, a cooper's axe. (E.) M.E. *adse, adese.* A. S. *adesa,* an adze.

Aerial. (L.−Gk.) Formed with suffix *-al* from L. *aëri-us,* dwelling in the air.− L. *aër,* air.−Gk. ἀήρ, air; see **Air.**

Aerolite, a meteoric stone. (Gk.) Also *aerolith,* which is a better form.− Gk. ἀερο-, from ἀήρ, air; λίθ-ος, a stone.

Aeronaut, a balloonist. (F.−Gk.) F. *aéronaute.*−Gk. ἀερο-, from ἀήρ, air; ναύτ-ης, a sailor, from ναῦς, a ship.

Aery, an eagle's nest, brood of eagles or hawks. (F.−Late L.)−F. *aire,* 'an airie or nest of hawkes;' Cot.−Late L. *ārea,* a nest of a bird of prey; of uncertain origin. ¶ Sometimes misspelt *eyry,* by confusion with M. E. *ey,* an egg; see **Egg.**

Æsthetic, refined. (Gk.) Gk. αἰσθητικός, perceptive.−Gk. αἰσθέσθαι, to perceive. (√AW; see Brugm. ii. § 841.)

anæsthetic, relieving pain, dulling sensation.−Gk. ἀν-, not; and αἰσθητικός.

Afar. (E.) For *on far.*

Affable. (F.−L.) F. *affable.*−L. *affābilis,* easy to be spoken to.−L. *af- = ad,* to; *fārī,* to speak.

Affair. (F.−L.) M.E. *affere.*−O. F. *afeire, afaire,* a business; orig. *a faire,* i. e. (something) to do.−L. *ad,* to; *facere,* to do.

Affect. (L.) L. *affectāre,* to apply oneself to (hence, to act upon); frequent. of *afficere,* to aim at, treat.−L. *af- = ad,* to; *facere,* to do, act. **Der.** *dis-affect.*

Affeer, to assess, confirm. (F.–L.) O. F. *afeurer,* to fix the price of a thing (officially). – Late L. *afforāre,* to fix a price. – L. *af-* (for *ad*); and *forum,* market, price.

Affiance. (F.–L.) O. F. *afiance,* trust; cf. *affier, afier,* to trust (whence E. *affy*). – O. F. *a* (L. *ad*), to; and *fīdant-,* stem of pres.. pt. of Late L. *fīdāre,* to trust, from L. *fīdere* to trust. Cf. Late L. *fīdantia,* a pledge.

Affidavit, an oath. (L.) Late L. *affī-dāuit,* 3 p. s. pt. t. of *affīdāre,* to pledge. – L. *af-* = *ad,* to ; Late L. *fīdāre,* for L. *fīdere,* to trust.

Affiliation. (F.–L.) F. *affiliation,* an adoption as a son. – Late L. acc. *affiliā-tiōnem.* – L. *af-* = *ad,* to ; *filius,* a son.

Affinity. (F.–L.) F. *affinité.* – L. *affinitātem,* acc. of *affinitas,* nearness. – L. *affinis,* near, bordering on. – L. *af-* (for *ad*), to, near; *finis,* boundary, end.

Affirm. (F.–L.) M. E. *affermen.* – O. F. *afermer,* to fix. – L. *affirmāre.* – L. *af-* (for *ad*), to ; *firmāre,* to make firm, from *firmus,* strong ; see **Firm.**

Affix. (L.) Late L. *affixāre* (Ducange), frequent. of L. *affigere* (pp. *affix-us*), to fasten to. – L. *af-* (for *ad*), to; *figere,* to fix.

Afflict, to harass. (L.) XVI cent. – L. *afflictus,* pp. of *affligere,* to strike to the ground. – L. *af-* (for *ad*), to; and *fligere,* to dash. So also *conflict,* from pp. *con flictus; inflict;* and cf. *pro-flig-ate.*

Affluence. (F.–L.) F. *affluence.* – L. *affluentia,* abundance. – L. *affluent-em* (acc.), flowing towards, pres. part. of *affluere,* to flow to, abound. – L. *af-* (for *ad*), to ; *fluere,* to flow.

Afford. (E.) Altered from *aforth,* M.E. *aforthen,* to provide, P. Pl. B. vi. 201. – A. S. *geforðian, forðian,* to further, promote, provide. – A. S. *ge-,* prefix ; and *forð,* forth, forward ; see **Forth.**

Affray, to frighten. (F.–L. *and* Teut.) XIV cent. M. E. *affrayen.* – O. F. *effraier, esfreër,* to frighten. – Low L *exfridāre,* to break the king's peace, cause an affray or fray ; hence, to disturb, frighten. – L. *ex* ; and O. H. G. *fridu* (G. *friede*), peace. (See *Romania,* 1878, vii. 121.) Der. *affray,* sb., also spelt *fray* ; and *afraid,* q. v.

Affreightment, the hiring of a vessel to convey cargo. (F.–L. *and* G.) An E. spelling of F. *affretement,* now written *affrétement,* the hiring of a ship. – F. *affreter* (now *affréter*), to hire a ship. – F.

af-, for L. *ad-,* prefix ; and F. *fret,* the freight of a ship. See **Fraught, Freight.**

Affright, to frighten. (E.) The double *f* is late. From M. E. *afright,* used as a pp., affrighted. – A. S. *āfyrht, āfyrhted,* pp. affrighted ; from infin. *āfyrhtan* (not used). – A. S. *ā-,* intensive ; and *fyrhtan,* to terrify, from *fyrhto,* fright ; see **Fright.**

Affront. (F.–L.) M. E. *afronten.* – O. F. *afronter,* to confront, oppose face to face. – Late L. *affrontāre.* – L. *af-* (for *ad*), to; *front-em,* acc. of *frons,* forehead, brow.

Afloat. (E.) For *on float.*

Afoot. (E.) For *on foot.*

Afore. (E.) For *on fore* ; A. S. *on-foran,* afore.

Afraid. (F.–L. *and* Teut.) Orig. *affrayed,* i. e. 'frightened.' Pp. of **Affray,** q. v.

Afresh. (E.) For *on fresh* or *of fresh* ; see **Anew.**

Aft, After. (E.) A. S. *æftan,* behind ; *æfter,* after, both prep. and adv. + Icel. *aptan,* behind, *aptr, aftr,* backwards; Dan. and Swed. *efter,* Du. *achter,* O. H. G. *aftar,* prep. and adv. behind. β. *Aftan* is extended from Goth. *af,* off ; see **Of.** *Af-ter* is a comp. form, like Gk. ἀπω-τέρ-ω, further off; it means more off, further off, hence behind. Der. *ab-aft,* q v. ; *after-ward* (see **Toward**).

Aftermath, a second crop of mown grass. (E.) Here *after* is an adj. ; and *math* means 'a mowing,' unaccented form of A. S. *mǣþ.* Allied to **Mead, Mow.** Cf. G. *mahd,* a mowing ; *nachmahd,* aftermath.

Aftermost, hindmost. (E.) A. S. *æftemest,* Goth. *aftumists* ; but affected by *after* and *most.* The Goth. *af-tu-m-ists* is a treble superl. form. See **Aft.**

Aga, Agha, a chief officer. (Turk.) Turk. *aghā,* master.

Again. (North E.) Cf. M. E. *ayein,* A. S. *ongegn* (*ongēan* . – A. S. *on*; and *gegn,* of which the primary meaning seems to have been ' direct,' or ' straight.' (N. E. D.) + Dan. *igien,* Swed. *igen,* again.

against. (North E.) The *t* is added. Cf. M. E. *ayeines,* against ; extended from M. E. *ayein,* against, with adv. suffix -*es.* – A. S. *ongēan,* against ; the same as A. S. *ongēan, ongegn,* again ; see above. + Icel. *í gegn,* G. *entgegen,* against.

Agate. (F.–It. – L. – Gk.) O.F. *agate, agathe.* – Ital. *agata, agatha,* an agate (Florio). – L. *achātem,* acc. of *achātes.* –

Gk. ἀχάτης, an agate; so named from being found near the river *Achates* (Sicily).

Age. (F. – L.) O. F. *aage*, *edage*. – Late L. *ætāticum*. – L. *ætāti-*, stem of *ætās* (from **æui-tās*), age. – L. *æuum*, life, period.+ Gk. αἰών; Goth. *aiws*; Skt. *āyus*, life. Brugm. ii. § 112.

Agent. (L.) XVI cent. L. *agent-*, stem of pres. pt. of *agere* (pp. *actus*), to do, drive, conduct.+Gk. ἄγειν; Icel. *aka*; Skt. *aj*, to drive. (√ AG.)

Agglomerate, to mass together. (L.) From pp. of L. *agglomerāre*, to form into a mass. – L. *ag-* (= *ad*); and *glomer-*, stem of *glomus*, a mass, ball, clue of thread, allied to *globus*, a globe; see **Globe**.

Agglutinate. (L.) From pp. of *agglūtināre*, to glue together. – L. *ag-* (= *ad*), to; *glūtin-*, for *glūten*, glue.

Aggrandise. (F. – L.) M. F. *aggrandis-*, stem of pres. pt. of *aggrandir*, to enlarge. Also *agrandir* (with one *g*). – F. *a* (for L. *ad*); and *grandir*, to increase, from L. *grandīre*, to enlarge, which is from L. *grandis*, great.

Aggravate. (L.) From pp. of L. *aggrauāre*, to add to a load. – L. *ag-* (= *ad*), to; *grauāre*, to load, from *grauis*, heavy.

Aggregate. (L.) From pp. of L. *aggregāre*, to collect into a flock. – L. *ag-* (for *ad*), to; *greg-*, stem of *grex*, a flock.

Aggress, to attack. (F. – L.) M.F. *aggresser.* – L. *aggressus*, pp. of *aggredī*, to assail. – L. *ag-* (for *ad*), to; *gradī*, to advance.

Aggrieve. (F. – L.) M. E. *agreven.* – O. F. *agrever*, to overwhelm. – O. F. *a*, to; *grever*, to burden. – L. *ad*, to; *grauāre*, to weigh down, from *grauis*, heavy, grave. See **Grave** (2).

Aghast, horror-struck. (E.) Misspelt for *agast*, which is short for *agasted*, pp. of M. E. *agasten*, to terrify; Ch. C. T. 2341; Leg. of Good Women, Dido, 248. – A. S. *ā-*, prefix; and *gæstan*, to terrify, torment. β. A. S. *gæstan* is from the base *gās-* = Goth. *gais-* in *us-gais-jan*, to terrify. (√ GHwAIS.) Brugm. ii. § 802.

Agile. (F. – L.) XVI cent. F. *agile*. – L. *agilis*, nimble; lit. easily driven about. – L. *agere*, to drive.

Agistment, the pasturage of cattle by agreement. (F. – L.) From the F. vb. *agister*, to assign a resting-place. – F. *a* (= L.*ad*),to; and O.F.*giste*, a couch,lodging, verbal sb. from O. F. *gesir* (F. *gésir*), to lie, from L. *iacēre*, to lie.

Agitate. (L.) L. *agitātus*, pp. of *agitāre*, to keep driving about, frequent. of *agere*, to drive; see **Agent.** (√AG.)

Aglet, a tag of a lace. (F. – L.) Also *aygulet*, Spenser, F. Q. ii. 3. 26. – F. *aiguillette*, dimin. of *aiguille*, a needle. – Late L. *acūcula*, dimin. of *ac-us*, a needle, pointed thing. Cf. **Acme.** (√AK.)

Agnail, (1) a corn on the foot, (2) a sore beside the nail. (E.) The sense has been confused or perverted. From A. S. *angnægl*, a corn on the foot (see A. S. Leechdoms, ii. 81, § 34); with which cf. O. Friesic *ogneil*, *ongneil*, apparently used in a similar sense. From a prefix *ang-*, signifying afflicting, paining, and A. S. *nægl*, a nail (as of iron), hence a hard round-headed excrescence or wart fixed in the flesh; see **Anger and Nail.** β Soon misunderstood as referring to the *nails* of the toes or fingers, and so made to mean 'a sore beside the nail'; prob. by comparing (wrongly) the Gk. παρονυχία, a whitlow (lit. beside the nail), or by confusion with F. *angonaille*, a sore (Cot.). See N. E. D.

Agnate, allied. (L.) L. *agnātus*, allied; pp. of *agnascī* = *ad-gnascī*. – L. *ad*, to; *nascī*, earlier form *gnascī*, to be born.

Ago, Agone, gone away, past. (E.) M. E. *ago*, *agon*, *agoon*, pp. of the verb *agon*, to pass by, pass away. A. S. *āgān*, pp. of *āgān*, to pass away. See **A-** (4) and **Go.**

Agog, in eagerness. (F.) For *a-gog*, in activity, in eagerness, where *a-* is the prefix **A-** (2). Adapted from O. F. *en gogues* (Littré), or *a gogue* (Godefroy), in mirth. Cot. has *estre en ses gogues*, 'to be frolicke, . . . in a veine of mirth.' The origin of O. F. *gogue*, fun, diversion, is unknown.

Agony. (F. – L. – Gk.) M. E. *agonie*. – F. *agonie*. – L. *agōnia*. – Gk. ἀγωνία, orig. a contest. – Gk. ἀγών, contest. – Gk. ἄγειν, to drive. (√ AG.)

Agouti, a rodent animal, of the guinea-pig family. (F. – Sp. – Brazil.) F. *agouti*. – Sp. *aguti*. – Brazil. *aguti*, *acuti*.

Agraffe, a kind of clasp. (F. – O.H.G.) F. *agrafe*; also *agraphe* (in Cotgrave), a hook, clasp; *agrafer*, to clasp. The verb is from F. *a* (= L. *ad*), to; and M. H. G. *krapfe*, O. H. G. *crapo*, *chrapfo*, a hook, which is allied to E. *cramp*.

Agree, to accord. (F. – L.) O. F. *agreer*, to receive favourably. – O. F. *a gre*, favourably.—O. F. *a* (=L. *ad*), according to ; *gre, gret*, pleasure, from L. *grātum*, neut. of *grātus*, dear, pleasing. Cf. **Grace**. Der. *dis-agree*.

Agriculture. (L.) L. *agrī cultūra*, culture of a field.—L. *agrī*, gen. of *ager*, a field ; and *cultūra*. See **Acre** and **Culture**.

Agrimony, a plant. (F.—L.—Gk.) M. E. *agremoine, egremoine*.—M. F. *aigrimoine*. — L. *argemōnia, argemōnē*.—Gk. ἀργεμώνη. (Lewis and Short, L. Dict.)

Aground. (E.) For *on ground*.

Ague, a fever-fit. (F.—L.) Lit. 'acute' attack.—O. F. *ague*, fem of *agu* (F. *aigu*), acute.—L. *acūta* (*febris*), acute (fever) ; fem. of *acūtus* ; see **Acute**.

Ah! (F.—L.) M. E. *a*!—O. F. *a*!— L. *ah*!

Ahead. (E.) For *on head*, i.e. in a forward direction. See A- (2).

Ai, a sloth. (Brazil.) From Brazil. *ai*.

Aid. (F.—L.) M. E. *aiden*. — O. F. *aider*. — L. *adiūtāre*, frequent. of *adiuuāre*, to assist. —L. *ad* ; and *iuuāré*, to help, pp. *iūtus*. Cf. Brugm. ii. § 583.

Ail, v. (E.) M. E. *eilen*. A. S. *eglan*, to pain ; cognate with Goth. *agljan*.— A.S. *egle*, troublesome (allied to Goth. *aglus*, hard). Cf. A. S. *ege*, terror, orig. pain ; see **Awe**.

Aim, to endeavour after. (F.—L.) M. E. *eimen*. From confusion of (1) A. F. *esmer*, from L. *æstimāre*, to estimate, aim at, intend ; and (2) O. F. *aesmer*, from L. *ad-æstimāre*, comp. with prefix *ad-*, to. See **Esteem**.

Air (1). (F.—L.—Gk.) M. E. *air, eir*. —F. *air*.—L. *āer*.—Gk. ἀήρ, air.

air (2), mien, affected manner ; tune. (F.—It.—L.—Gk.) F. *air*, look, tune.— Ital. *aria*, 'a looke,. . a tune ;' Florio.— Folk-L. neut. pl. *āëra*, treated as a fem. sing. (Diez).—L. *āër*.—Gk. ἀήρ (above).

Airt, a point of the compass. (Gael.) Gael. *aird*, a quarter or point of the compass. Cf. O. Irish *aird*, a point, limit.

Aisle, the wing of a church. (F.—L.) Better spelt *aile* —F. *aile*.—L. *āla*, a wing. Prob. for *axla*, dimin. of **Axis**.

Ait. (E.) See **Eyot**.

Aitch-bone, the rump-bone. (Hyb.; F.—L. *and* E.) Orig. spelt *nache bone*.— O. F. *nache*, sing. of *naches*, the buttocks ; and E. *bone*. *Naches* = Late L. *naticās*, acc. of *naticæ*, dimin. of L. *natēs*, the buttocks.

Ajar. (E.) From *a char, on char*, on the turn (G. Douglas, tr. of Virgil, b. vii, prol.). —A.S. *on cierre*, on the turn ; cf. A.S. *cyrran, cierran*, to turn. See **Char** (2).

Akimbo, in a bent position. (Scand.) M. E. *in kenebowe*, Beryn, 1838. Perhaps from Icel. *ī keng*, into a crook ; with E. *bow*, i. e. bend, superfluously added. Here *keng* is the acc. of *kengr*, a crook, twist, kink. Cf. also Icel. *kengboginn*, bent into a crook, from *kengr*, a crook, twist, kink, and *boginn*, bowed, pp. of lost verb *bjūga*, to bow. See **Kink** and **Bow** (1). (Very doubtful ; a guess.)

Akin, of kin. (E.) For *of kin*.

Alabaster. (F.—L.—Gk.) M.E. *alabastre*.—O. F. *alabastre* (F. *albâtre*).—L. *alabaster, alabastrum*.—Gk. ἀλάβαστρον, ἀλάβαστος. Said to be derived from *Alabastron*, a town in Egypt. (Pliny.)

Alack. (E.) Prob. a corruption of M.E. *a ! lack !* alas ! a shame ! lit. 'lack.' (It cannot be the same as *alas*.)

Alacrity. (L.) Formed by analogy with *celerity*, from L. *alacritātem*, acc. of *alacritās*, briskness.—L. *alacer*, brisk.

Alarm, a call to arms. (F.—Ital.—L.) M. E. *alarme*.—F. *alarme*.—Ital. *all'arme*, to arms ! for *alle arme*. — Late L. *ad illas armas*, for L. *ad illa arma*, to those arms ! to your arms !

alarum. (F.—Ital.—L.) The same word, with an old pronunciation, in which the *r* was strongly trilled.

Alas! (F.—L.) M. E. *alas*.—O. F. *alas* (cf. F. *hélas*).—O. F. *a*, ah ! and *las*, wretched that I am!—L. *ah*! and *lassus*, tired, wretched. (Allied to **Late**.)

Alb, a white vestment. (F.—L.) M. E. *albe* —O. F. *albe*.—Late L *alba*, sb. ; orig. fem. of L. *albus*, white.

Albacore, a kind of tunny. (Port.— Arab.) Port. *albacor, albacora*. Said to be of Arab. origin.

Albatross, a large sea-bird. (Port.— Span.—Arab.—Gk.) Formerly also *algatross*.—Port. *alcatraz*, a cormorant, albatross ; Span. *alcatraz*, a pelican —Port. *alcatruz*, a bucket, Span. *arcaduz*, M. Span. *alcaduz* (Minsheu), a bucket on a waterwheel. —Arab *al-qādūs*, the same (Dozy). Similarly Arab. *saqqā*, a water-carrier, a pelican, because it carries water in its pouch. (Devic ; supp. to Littré.)

Album, lit. that which is white. (L.) L. *album*, a tablet, orig. neut. of *albus*, white.

albumen, white of egg. (L.) L. *albūmen oui* (also *album oui*), white of egg.— L. *albus*, white.

Alcayde, a judge ; see **Cadi**.

Alchemy. (F.—Arab –Gk.) O. F. *alchemie.*—Arab. *al*, the ; and *kīmīā*, alchemy.—Late Gk. χημεία, chemistry ; probably confused with χὔμεία, a mingling, from Gk. χέειν, to pour out, mix.

Alcohol. (Med. L.—Arab.) Med. L. *alcohol*, applied to pure spirit, though the orig. sense was a fine impalpable powder. —Arab. *al*, the ; and *kohl* or *kuḥl*, a collyrium, very fine powder of antimony, used to paint the eyelids with.

Alcoran ; see **Koran**.

Alcove, a vaulted recess. (F.—Span.— Arab.) F. *alcôve.*—Span. *alcoba*, a recess in a room.—Arab. *al*, the ; and *qobbah*, a vault, dome, cupola ; hence a vaulted space.

Alder, a tree. (E.) M. E. *alder, aller* (*d* being excrescent).—A. S. *alor* (*aler, alr*).✛Du. *els* ; Icel. *ölr* (for *ŏlr*) ; Swed. *al* ; Dan. *elle, el* ; G. *erle* ; O. H. G. *erila*, earlier *elira* ; Span. *aliso* (from Gothic). Teut. stems *alur-*, *aliz-*, *alis-*. Allied to Lith. *alksnis*, L. *alnus* (for *alsnos*) ; Russ. *olĕkha* ; and perhaps to **Elm**.

Alder-, prefix, of all. In *alder-liefest* (Sh.) ; here *alder* is for *aller*, O. Merc. *alra*,·A.S. *ealra*, gen. pl. of *al, eal*, all. See **All**.

Alderman. (E.) Merc. *aldorman*, A. S. *ealdorman.*—Merc. *aldor* (*ealdor*), a chief ; and *man*, man. Allied to O. Fries. *alder*, a parent ; G. *eltern*, pl. parents ; and to L. *al-tor*, a bringer up, from *alere*, to nourish. Cf. **Old**.

Ale. (E.) M. E. *ale.*—A. S *ealu*, gen. *aloþ* (stem *alut*).✛Icel., Swed., and Dan. *öl* ; Lithuan. *alus* ; Russ. *olovina*.

Alembic, a vessel for distilling. (F.— Span.—Arab.—Gk.) M. E. *alembyk.*—F. *alambique* (Cot.).—Span. *alambique.* — Arab. *al*, the ; and *anbiq* (pronounced *ambiq*), a still.—Gk. ἄμβιξ, a cup, goblet ; cap of a still. Cf. **Limbeck**.

Alert. (F.—Ital.—L.) F. *alerte* ; formerly *allerte*, and (in Rabelais) *a l'herte*, i. e. on the watch.—Ital. *all'erta*, on the watch ; from the phr. *stare all'erta*, to stand erect, be on one's guard.—Ital. *alla* (for *a la*), at the, on the ; *erta*, fem. of *erto*, erect.—L. *ad*, to, at ; *illam*, fem. acc. of *ille*, he ; *ērectam*, fem. acc. of *ērectus*, erect ; see **Erect**.

Algebra. (Late L.—Arab.) Late L.

algebra, computation. — Arab. *al*, the ; and *jabr*, setting, repairing ; also, the reduction of fractions to integers in arithmetic ; hence, algebra.—Arab. root *jabara*, to set, con· solidate.

Alguazil, a police-officer. (Span.— Arab.) Span. *alguazil.*—Arab. *al*, the ; *wazīr*, a vizier, officer ; see **Vizier**.

Algum, sandal-wood. (Heb. — Skt.) In 2 Chron. ii. 8, ix. 10 ; spelt *almug*, 1 Kings x. 11.—Heb. *algŭmmīm*, or (transposed) *almugīm* ; a borrowed word. Supposed by Max Müller (*Sci. Lang.* i. 232) to be from Skt. *valgu-ka*, sandal-wood ; where *-ka* is a suffix.

Alias. (L.) L. *aliās*, otherwise.—L. *alius*, another ; see **Alien**.

alibi. (L.) L. *alibi*, in another place. —L. *ali-*, as in *alius* ; and suffix *-bi* as in *i-bi*, there, *u-bi*, where. See below.

alien. (F.—L.) M. E. *aliene.*—O. F. *alien.*—L. *aliēnus*, strange ; a stranger.—L. *alius*, another. ✛ Gk. ἄλλος, another ; O. Irish *aile*, W. *aill*, all ; Goth. *aljis* (stem *aljo-*), other ; see **Else**.

Alight (1), to descend from. (E.) M. E. *alihten*, to alight from horseback ; A. S. *ālīhtan*, the prefix *a-* being = A. S. *ā-*. The simple form *līhtan* also occurs in A. S., meaning to make light, relieve of weight, alight (from a horse) ; from *līht*, light, adj. See **Light** (3).

alight (2), to light upon. (E.) M. E. *alihten*, with reference to the *completion* of the action of alighting. See above.

Align ; see **Aline**.

Alike, similar. (E.) M. E. *alike, olike.* A. S. *onlīc*, like ; from *līc*, like, with prefix *on-* = **on**, prep.

Aliment, food. (F.—L.) F. *aliment.* —L. *alimentum*, food ; formed with suffix *-mentum* from *alere*, to nourish. (✓AL.)

alimony, money allowed for a wife's support upon her separation from her husband. (L.) L. *alimōnia*, nourishment. —L. *alere*, to nourish ; see above.

Aline, Align, to range in a line. (F. —L.) Adapted from mod. F. *aligner*, to range in a line. From the phr. *à ligne*, into line.—L. *ad*, to ; *līnea*, a line. See **Line**. (*Aline* is the better spelling for the E. word.)

Aliquot. (L.) L. *aliquot*, some, several (hence, ˈproportionate).—L. *ali-us*, other ; and *quot*, how many.

Alive, in life. (E.) From A.S. *on līfe*,

in life; where *life* is dat. of *līf*, life; see **Life.**

Alkali, a salt. (Arab.) Arab. *al,* the; and *qalī,* ashes of salt-wort, which abounds in soda.

All. (E.) M. E. *al,* sing.; *alle,* pl. – O. Merc. *al, all*; A. S. *eal,* pl. *ealle.*+Icel. *allr*; Swed. *all*; Dan. *al*; Du. *al*; O. H. G. *al*; Goth. *alls,* pl. *allai.* Teut. type **alnoz*; allied to Irish *uile,* all, from Idg. type **oljos.*

all, adv., utterly. In the phr. *all-to brake* (correctly *all to-brake*), Judges ix. 53. Here the incorrect *all-to,* for 'utterly,' came up about A.D. 1500, in place of the old idiom which linked *to* to the verb; cf. '*Al is tobrosten* thilke regioun,' Chaucer, C. T. 2757. See **To-,** *prefix.*

almost. (E.) A. S. *eal-mǣst,* i. e. quite the greatest part, nearly all; affected by mod. E. *most.* See **Most.**

alway, always. (E.) (1) A. S. *ealne weg,* every way, an accus. case. (2) M. E. *alles weis,* in every way, a gen. case.

Allay. (E.) M. E. *aleyen, alaien,* the stem of which is due to A. S. *āleg-es, ālegeð,* 2 and 3 pres. t. sing. of A.S. *ālecgan,* to lay down, put down, which produced also M. E. *aleggen,* to lay or set aside. – A. S. *ā-,* prefix; and *lecgan,* to lay, place; see **A-** (4) and **Lay** (1). β. But much confused with other forms, especially with M. E. *aleggen,* to alleviate, from O. F. *aleger, alegier,* L. *alleuiāre*; and with old forms of *alloy.* See N. E. D.

Allege. (F.–L.) M.E. *alegen, aleggen.* In form, the word answers to A. F. *alegier, aligier* = O. F. *esligier* (see Godefroy); from A. F. *a-* = O. F. *es-,* and *ligier.* – L. *ex-*; and *lītigāre,* to contend (Ducange), from L. *lis* (gen. *līt-is*), strife. Latinised as *adlēgiāre* (Ducange), and treated as if allied to L. *allēgāre* (F. *alléguer*); hence the sense usually answers to that of L. *allēgāre,* to adduce. – L. *al-* (for *ad*), to ; *lēgāre,* to dispatch, to tell, from *lēg-,* base of *lex,* law.

Allegiance, the duty of a subject to his lord. (F.–O. H. G.) M. E. *alegeaunce.* Formed from F. *a* (=L. *ad*), to ; O. F. *ligance, ligeance,* homage, from O. F. *lige, liege,* liege. See **Liege.** ¶ The form *ligance* (Godefroy) was due to a supposed connexion with L. *ligāre,* to bind.

Allegory. (L.–Gk.) XVI cent. L. *allēgoria.* – Gk. ἀλληγορία, a description of one thing under the image of another. –

Gk. ἀλληγορεῖν, to speak so as to imply something else ; Galat. iv. 24. – Gk. ἄλλο-, stem of ἄλλος, other ; and ἀγορεύειν, to speak, from ἀγορά, a place of assembly ; cf. ἀγείρειν, to assemble. Gk. ἄλλος = L. *alius*; see **Alien.**

Allegro, lively. (Ital.–L.) Ital. *allegro.* – L. *alacrem,* acc. of *alacer,* brisk.

Alleluia. (Heb.) See **Hallelujah.**

Alleviate. (L.) From pp. of Late L. *alleuiāre,* used for L. *alleuāre,* to lighten. L. *al-* (for *ad*), to ; *leuāre,* to lift, lighten, from *leuis,* light.

Alley, a walk. (F.–L.?) M. E. *aley.* – O. F. *alee,* a gallery ; a participial sb. – O. F. *aler,* to go ; F. *aller.* β. The etymology of *aller,* much and long discussed, is not yet settled ; the Prov. equivalent is *anar,* allied to Ital. *andare,* to go.

Alliance ; see **Ally.**

Alligator. (Span. – L.) Lit. 'the lizard.' – Span. *el lagarto,* the lizard, i. e. the great lizard. – L. *ille,* he, that; *lacerta,* a lizard. See **Lizard.**

Alliteration, repetition of initial letters. (L.) Coined from L. *al-* (for *ad*,, to ; and *lītera,* a letter ; see **Letter.** .

Allocate, to set aside. (L.) From pp. of Late L. *allocāre,* to allot. – L. *al-* (=*ad*), to ; *locāre,* to place, from *locus,* a place. Cf. **Allow** (1).

Allocution, an address. (L.) From L. *allocūtiō,* an address. – L. *al-* (for *ad*), to ; *locūtiō,* a speaking, from *locūtus,* pp. of *loquī,* to speak.

Allodial. (Late L. – O. Frankish.) Late L. *allōdiālis,* from *allōdium, alōdium,* a derivative of *alōdis,* a free inheritance (Lex Salica). It means 'entirely '(one's) property,' from O. Frank. *alōd* ; where *al-* is related to E. *all,* and *ōd* signifies 'property' or 'wealth.' This O. Frank. *ōd* is cognate with O. H. G. *ōt,* A. S. *ēad,* Icel. *auðr,* wealth. Cf. Goth. *audags,* blessed.

Allopathy, a treatment by medicines which produce an opposite effect to that of disease. (Gk.) Opposed to *homœopathy,* q. v. – Gk. ἄλλος, for ἄλλος, other; and παθ-εῖν, to suffer ; see **Alien** and **Pathos.**

Allot, to assign a portion to. (F. – L. and E.) A. F. *aloter.* – A. F. *a,* from L. *ad,* to ; and M. E. *lot,* A. S. *hlot*; see **Lot.**

Allow (1), to assign, grant. (F.–L.) F. *allouer,* to let out for hire, assign for an expense. – Late L. *allocāre,* to allot. – L. *al-* (for *ad*), to ; and *locāre,* to place, from *locus,* a place.

Allow (2), to approve of. (F. – L.) M. E. *alouen.* – O. F. *alouer*, later *allouer*, to approve of. – L. *allaudāre.* – L. *al-* (for *ad*), to; *laudāre*, to praise, from *laud-*, stem of *laus*, praise.

Alloy, a due proportion in mixing metals. (F. – L.) Formerly *allay*; M. E. *alay.* – O. F. *alay, aley, alloy.* – O.F. *aleier, aleyer*, to combine. – L. *alligāre*, to bind together; see **Ally**. The O. F. *alei*, sb., became *aloi*, which was misunderstood as being *à loi* = L. *ad lēgem*, according to rule or law (Littré).

Allude. (L.) L. *allūdere*, to laugh at, allude to (pp. *allūsus*). – L. *al-* (= *ad*), at; *lūdere*, to sport. Der. *allus-ion.*

Allure, to tempt by a bait. (F. – L. *and* G.) A. F. *alurer*; from F. *a leurre* = to the bait or lure. – I.. *ad*, to; M. H. G. *luoder* (G. *luder*), a bait. See **Lure**.

Alluvial, washed down, applied to soil. (L.) L. *alluui-us*, alluvial. – L. *al-* (= *ad*), to, in addition; *luere*, to wash.

Ally, to bind together. (F. – L.) M. E. *alien.* – O. F. *alier*, to bind up. – L. *ad*, to; *ligāre*, to bind. Der. *alli-ance*, M. E. *aliaunce.*

Almanac, Almanack. (Late L.) Late L. *almanach.* ¶ Origin unknown; *not* of Arab. origin (Dozy).

Almighty. (E.) O. Merc. *almæhtig*, A. S. *ælmihtig.* The prefix is O. Merc. *al-*, O. Sax. *alo-*, O. H. G. *ala-*, related to **All**. And see **Might**.

Almond. (F. – L. – Gk.) M. E. *almaund.* – O. F. *almandre*, more correctly, *amandre* ; the *al* being due to Span. and Arab. influence; mod. F. *amande.* – L. *amygdala, amygdalum*, an almond; whence the forms *amygd'la, amyd'la, amynd'la, amyndra* (see Brachet). – Gk. ἀμυγδάλη, ἀμύγδαλον, an almond.

Almoner; see **Alms**.

Almost. (E.) A. S. *ealmǣst*; see **All**.

Alms. (L. – Gk.) M. E. *almesse*, later *almes.* A. S. *ælmæsse.* – Folk-L. **alimosina* (whence O. F. *almosne*, F. *aumône*, Ital. *limosina*) ; Late L. *eleëmosyna.* – Gk. ἐλεημοσύνη, pity; hence alms. – Gk. ἐλεήμων, pitiful. – Gk. ἐλεεῖν, to pity. – Gk. ἔλεος, pity. ¶ Thus *alms* is a *singular* form.

almoner. (F. – L. – Gk.) O.F. *almosnier*, a distributor of alms. – O. F. *almosne*, alms; F. *aumône.* – Folk-L. **alimosina* (above).

Almug, the same as **Algum**, q. v.

Aloe, a plant. (L. – Gk.) I.. *aloë* (Pliny). – Gk. ἀλόη ; John xix. 39.

Aloft. (Scand.) Icel. *ā lopt* (pron. *loft*), aloft, in the air. – Icel. *ā* (= A. S. *on*), in ; *lopt*, air. See **Loft**.

Alone. (E.) M. E. *al one, al oon*, written apart ; here *al*, adv., means 'entirely,' and *oon* is the M. E. form of *one*. Cf. Du. *alleen*, G. *allein*. See **All** and **One**.

Along (1), lengthwise of. (E.) M. E. *along.* A. S. *andlang*, along, prep. with gen.; orig. (like O. Sax. *antlang*) an adj., meaning complete (from end to end). – A.S. *and-*, prefix (allied to Gk. ἀντί, Skt. *anti*, over against); *lang*, long. The sense is 'over against in length,' or 'long from end to end.' + G. *entlang*, along. See **A-** (3) and **Long** (1) ; and see **Anti-**.

Along (2) ; in phr. *all along of you*, &c. (E.) Equivalent to M. E. *ilong*, Layamon, 15502. – A. S. *gelang*, 'depending on,' as in *on ðām gelang*, along of that. – A. S. *ge-*, prefix ; *lang*, long.

Aloof, away. (E. *and* Du.) For *on loof* ; answering to Du. *te loef*, to windward. Cf. Du. *loef houden*, to keep the luff or weather-gage, Dan. *holde luven*, to keep to the windward; which suggested our phrase 'to hold aloof,' i. e. to keep away (from the leeward shore or rock). See **Luff**.

Aloud, loudly. (E.) From *a-*, prefix, due to A. S. *on*, prep. ; and A.S. *hlūd*, loud. See **A-** (2) and **Loud**.

Alp. (L.) L. *Alpes*, the Alps ; of Celtic origin. Connected with L. *albus*, white (Stokes). Der. *trans-alp-ine*, i. e. beyond the Alps.

Alpaca. (Span. – Peruvian.) Span. *alpaca*; from *paco*, the Peruvian name, with the Arab. def. art. *al* prefixed.

Alphabet. (Late L. – Gk. – Phœnician.) Late L. *alphabētum.* – Gk. ἄλφα, βῆτα, the names of α and β, the first two letters of the alphabet ; Heb. *āleph*, an ox, the name of the first letter ; and *bēth*, a house, the name of the second letter.

Already. (E.) M. E. *al redy*, quite ready; from *al*, quite, representing the neut. of O. Merc. *al*, all, used adverbially, and **Ready**.

Also. (E.) M. E. *al so*, quite so; A. S. *ealswā* ; see above.

Altar. (L.) A.S. *altāre*, Matt. v. 24. – L. *altāre*, an altar, high place. – I.. *altus*, high.

Alter. (L.) Late L. *alterāre*, to alter.

– L. *alter*, other. **–** L. *al-* (as in *al-ius*); with comparative suffix *-tero-*.

altercation, a dispute. (F. – L.) M. E. *altercation.* – O. F. *altercation.* – L. *altercātiōnem*, acc. of *altercātiō.* – L. *altercātus*, pp. of *altercārī*, to dispute, speak in turns. **–** L. *alter*, other, another.

alternate. (L.) L. *alternātus*, pp. of *alternāre*, to do by turns. **–** L. *alternus*, reciprocal. **–** L. *alter* (with suffix *-no-*).

Although. (E.) M. E. *al thogh*; see **Already** and **Though.**

Altitude. (F. – L.) XIV cent. **–** F. *altitude.* **–** L. *altitūdo*, height. **–** L. *altus*, high.

alto, high voice. (Ital. – L.) Ital. *alto.* **–** L. *altus*, high.

Altogether. (E.) M. E. *al together*, quite together. See **Already.**

Altruism, regard for others. (Ital. – L.; *with* Gk. *suffix*.) Coined from Ital. *altrui*, another, others, a form of *altro*, another, when preceded by a preposition. Orig. a dat. case. **–** L. *alteri huic*, to this other; datives of *alter*, other, and *hīc*, this.

Alum. (F. – L.) M. E. *alum.* **–** O. F. *alum*; F. *alun.* **–** L. *alūmen*, alum.

Alway, Always. (E.) See **All.**

Am. (E.) See **Are.**

Amain. (E.) For *on main*, in strength, with strength; see **A-** (2) and **Main,** sb.

Amalgam. (F. *or* Late L. – Gk. ?) F. *amalgame*, Late L. *amalgama*, a mixture, esp. of quicksilver with other metals. Origin unknown; said by some to be a corruption or an alchemist's anagram of *malagma*, a mollifying application; perhaps with Arab. *al* (= the) prefixed. – Gk. μάλαγμα, an emollient. – Gk. μαλάσσειν (for *μαλάκ-γειν), to soften. – Gk. μαλακός, soft.

Amanuensis, one who writes to dictation. (L.) L. *āmanuensis.* – L. *ā manū*, by hand; with suffix *-ensis.*

Amaranth, an unfading flower. (L. – Gk.) Properly *amarant*, as in Milton; but *-anth* is due to confusion with Greek ἄνθος, a flower. **–** L. *amarantus.* **–** Gk. ἀμάραντος, unfading, or as sb. unfading flower. **–** Gk. ἀ-, not; and μαραίνειν, to fade. (√MER.)

Amass, to heap up. (F. – L. – Gk.) F. *amasser*, to heap up. **–** F. *à masse*, into a mass. **–** L. *ad*, to; *massa*, a mass. **–** Gk. μᾶζα, a barley-cake. See **Mass** (1).

Amatory. (L.) L. *amatōrius*, loving. **–** L. *amātor*, a lover. **–** L. *amāre*, to love; with suffix *-tōr-, -tor*, of agent.

Amaze, to astound. (E.) M. E. *amasen.* A. S. *āmasian*, pp. *āmasod*; Wulfstan's Hom. p. 137, l. 23. From A. S. *ā-* (prefix); and ***masian*, to perplex. See **Maze.**

Amazon, a female warrior. (Gk.) Gk. ἀμαζών, one of a warlike nation of women in Scythia. ¶ To account for the name, the Greeks said that these women cut off the right breast to shoot better; from Gk. ἀ-, not; and μαζός, the breast. Obviously an invention.

Ambassador, Embassador. (F. – Late L. – C.) F. *ambassadeur.* **–** F. *ambassade*, an embassy; prob. borrowed from Ital. *ambasciata.* **–** Late L. *ambascia* (Lex Salica); more correctly **ambactia*; a mission, service. **–** L. *ambactus*, a servant, emissary; Cæsar, de Bell. Gall. vi. 15. The L. word is borrowed from an O. Gaulish (Celtic) word (*ambactos?*) a slave, lit. one driven about, a pp. form from *ambi-*, prefix, about, and the verb *ag-*, cognate with L. *agere*; cf. O. Irish *imm-agim*, I drive about, send about. (Fick, 1894, ii. 34; Brugm. ii. § 79.) Cf. W. *amaeth*, a husbandman.

Amber. (F. – Span. – Arab.) M. E. *aumbre.* **–** F. *ambre.* **–** Span. *ambar.* **–** Arab. *'anbar* (pronounced *'ambar*), ambergris, a rich perfume. ¶ The resinous amber was so called from a resemblance to ambergris, which is really quite a different substance.

ambergris, i. e. gray amber. Called *gris amber* in Milton, P. R. ii. 344. The F. *gris*, gray, is from O. H. G. *grīs*, gray; cf. G. *greis*, hoary.

Ambi-, Amb-, prefix. (L.) L. *ambi-*, about; cf. Gk. ἀμφί, on both sides, whence E. prefix *amphi-*. Related to L. *ambo*, Gk. ἄμφω, both. Cf. A. S. *ymb*, Irish *im*, about.

Ambient, going about. (L.) L. *ambient-*, stem of pres. part. of *amb-īre*, to go about, from *īre*, to go.

Ambiguous, doubtful. (L.) L. *ambiguus*, doubtful, lit. driving about (with *-ous* (= L. *-ōsus*) in place of L. *-us*). **–** L. *amb-*, about; and *agere*, to drive.

Ambition. (F. – L.) F. *ambition.* **–** L. *ambitiōnem*, acc. of *ambitiō*, a going round, esp. used of going round to solicit votes; hence, a seeking for preferment. **–** L. *amb-*

ītum, supine of *amb-īre*, to go about (but note that *ambĭtio* retains the short *i* of *ĭtum*, the supine of *īre*-, the simple verb).

Amble. (F.–L.) M. E. *amblen*.–O.F. *ambler*, to go at an easy pace.–L. *ambulāre*, to walk.

ambulance, a moveable hospital. (F. –L.) F. *ambulance*. – L. *ambulant*-, stem of pres. part. of *ambulāre*, to walk.

ambulation, a walking about. (L.) From L. *ambulātio*, a walking about.–L. *ambulātus*, pp. of *ambulāre*.

Ambrosia, food of the gods. (Gk.) Gk. ἀμβροσία; fem. of ἀμβρόσιος, lengthened form of ἄμβροτος, immortal. – Gk. ἀ-, not (E. *un*-); and *μβροτός, for *μροτός (Gk. βροτός), mortal; see **Mortal**. Cf. Skt. *a-mṛta*, immortal. See **Amaranth**.

Ambry, Aumbry, a cupboard. (F.–L.) M. E. *awmebry*, *awmery*, Prompt. Parv.; the *b* is excrescent.– O. F. *aumaire*, *almaire*, *armarie*, a repository; properly, for arms; but also a cupboard. – Late L. *armāria*, a cupboard; *armārium*, a repository for arms.–L. *arma*, arms.

Ambulance, -ation; see Amble.

Ambuscade. (Span.–Late L.) From Span. *emboscada*, an ambush. Orig. pp. of *emboscar*, to set in ambush.–Late Lat. *imboscāre*, lit. to set in a bush or thicket.–L. *im*- (for *in*), in; and Late L. *boscum*, a bush. See **Bush**.

ambush. (F.–Late L.) Formerly *embush*.–O.F. *embuscher*, *embuissier*, to set in ambush. – Late L. *imboscāre*; as above.

Ameer, the same as **Emir**, q. v.

Ameliorate. (F.–L.; *with* L. *suffix*.) Formed with suffix -*ate* (= L. -*ātus*) from F. *améliorer*, to better, improve.– F. *à* (= L. *ad*), in addition; -*meliorer* (= Late L. *meliōrāre*), to make better.– L. *meliōr*-, from *melior*, better.

Amen. (L.–Gk.–Heb.) L. *āmēn*.– Gk. ἀμήν, verily.– Heb. *āmēn*, verily, so be it.– Heb. *āmēn*, firm, true.– Heb. *āman*, to confirm; orig. ' to be firm.'

Amenable, easy to lead. (F.–L.) From F. *amener*, to lead to, bring to.– F. *à*, to; *mener*, to conduct, drive.–L. *ad*, to; Late L. *mināre*, to conduct, lead about, also to drive out, chase away; L. *minārī*, to threaten.–L. *minæ*, threats.

Amend. (F.–L.) M. E. *amenden*.– F. *amender*.–L. *ēmendāre*, to free from fault.–L. *ē*, from; *mendum*, a fault.

amends. (F. – L.) M. E. *amendes*.

sb. pl.–O. F. *amende*, reparation.–O.F. *amender* (above).

Amenity, pleasantness. (F.–L.) M F. and F. *amenité*.–L. *amænitātem*, acc. of *amænitās*.–L. *amænus*, pleasant. Cf. L. *amāre*, to love.

Amerce, to fine. (F.–L.) A. F. (not O. F.) *amercier*, to fine.–O.F. *a* (=L. *ad*), to; *mercier*, to pay, acquit, but usually to thank; cf. Late L. *merciāre*, to fix a fine. Cf. O. F. *mercit* (F. *merci*), thanks, pardon. –L. *mercēdem*, acc. of *mercēs*, reward, wages, also pity, indulgence, thanks (passing into the sense of ' fine ').–L. *merc*-, stem of *merx*, merchandise, traffic.

Amethyst, a gem. (L.–Gk.) L. *amethystus*.–Gk. ἀμέθυστος, an amethyst; so called because supposed to prevent drunkenness. – Gk. ἀμέθυστος,not drunken. – Gk. ἀ-, not; and μεθύειν, to be drunken, from μέθυ, strong drink; see **Mead**.

Amiable. (F.–L.) O. F. *amiable*, friendly; also loveable, by confusion with *aimable* (from L. *amābilis*).–L.*amīcābilis*, friendly.–L. *amīcus*, a friend.–L. *amāre*, to love.

amicable.(L.) L.*amīcābilis*, friendly; as above.

Amice (1), an oblong piece of linen, variously worn by priests. (F.–L.) M. E. *amyse*, and (earlier) *amit*.–O. F. *amis*, *amit* (Burguy).–L. *amict-us*, a covering. –L. *amictus*, pp. of *amicīre*, to throw round.–L. *am*- (*amb*-), around; *iacere*, to cast.

Amice (2), a pilgrim's robe. (O. F.– Span.?–Teut.?) ' In *amice* gray;' Milton, P.R. iv. 427.–O. F. *aumuce* (F. *aumusse*); Late L. *almucia*.–Span. *almucio* (Pineda); where *al* seems to be the Arab. def. art. (cf. Port. *murça*).–G. *mütze*, a cap (cf. Lowl. Sc. *mutch*). But G. *mütze* may be from Late L.

Amid, Amidst, in the middle of. (E.) *Amids-t* is lengthened from M. E. *amiddes*. Again, *amidde-s* was due to adding the adv. suffix -*s* to *amidde* = A. S. *on middan*, in the middle; where *middan* is the dat. of *midde*, sb., the middle.–A. S. *mid*, *midd*, adj., middle. *Amid* = A. S. *on middan* (as before). See **Mid**.

Amiss, adv. wrongly. (E. *or* Scand.) M. E. *on misse*, i. e. in error.–Icel. *ā mis*, amiss.–Icel. *ā* (= A. S. *on*), in; *mis*, adv., wrongly (due to an older lost pp.). See **Miss** (1).

Amity. (F.–L.) O. F. *amiste*, *amisted*,

amistet. — Late L.**amīcitātem,* acc. of **amī-citās,* friendship. — L. *amīcus,* friendly. — L. *amāre,* to love.

Ammonia, an alkali. (L. — Gk. — Egyptian.) Suggested by L. *sal ammōniacum,* rock-salt. — Gk. *ἀμμωνιακόν,* sal ammoniac, rock-salt. — Gk. *ἀμμωνιάς,* Libyan. — Gk. *ἄμμων,* the Libyan Zeus-Ammon ; a word of Egyptian origin ; Herod. ii. 42. ¶ It is said that *sal ammoniac* was first obtained near the temple of Ammon.

ammonite, a fossil shell. (Gk.) Coined with suffix *-ite* (Gk. *-ιτης*) from the name Ammon ; because the shell resembles the twisted ram's horn on the head of the image of Jupiter Ammon.

Ammunition, store for defence. (F. — L.) From Mid. F. *amunition,* a soldier's corruption of *munition,* due to substituting *l'amunition* for *la munition* (Littré). — L. acc. *mūnītiōnem,* a defending. — L. *mūnītus,* pp. of *mūnīre,* to defend.

Amnesty, lit. a forgetting of offences. (F. — L. — Gk.) F. *amnestie.* — L. *amnēstia.* — Gk. *ἀμνηστία,* forgetfulness, esp. of wrong. — Gk. *ἄμνηστος,* forgotten. — Gk. *ἀ-,* not ; and *μνάομαι,* I remember. (√MEN.)

Among, Amongst. (E.) The earliest M. E. form is *amonge,* whence *amonges* with added *s* (a common adverbial suffix) ; and hence *amongs-t* with excrescent *t.* — A. S. *onmang,* prep., among. — A. S. *on,* in ; *mang,* a mixture, crowd. Cf. **Mingle.**

Amorous. (F. — L.) O. F. *amoros;* F. *amoureux.* — L. *amorōsus.* — L. *amor,* love.

Amorphous, formless. (Gk.) From Gk. *ἀ-,* not ; and *μορφ-ή,* shape, form.

Amount, to mount up to. (F. — L.) O. F. *amonter,* to amount to. — O. F. *a mont,* towards a mountain or large heap. — L. *ad,* to ; *montem,* acc. of *mons,* a mountain.

Amour. (F. — L.) F. *amour.* — L. *amōrem,* acc. of *amor,* love.

Amphi-, *prefix.* (Gk.) Gk. *ἀμφί,* on both sides, around ; see **Ambi-.**

Amphibious. (Gk.) Gk. *ἀμφίβιος,* living a double life, on land and water. — Gk. *ἀμφί,* on both sides ; *βίος,* life.

Amphibrach, a foot in prosody. (Gk.) The foot composed of a short syllable on each side of a long one (◡–◡). Gk. *ἀμφίβραχυς.* — Gk. *ἀμφί,* on both sides ; and *βραχύς,* short ; see **Amphi-** and **Brief.**

Amphitheatre. (Gk.) Gk. *ἀμφιθέā-*

τρον, a theatre with seats all round the arena. — Gk. *ἀμφί,* around ; *θέατρον,* a theatre.

Ample, full. (F. — L.) F. *ample.* — L. *amplus,* spacious.

Amputate. (L.) From pp. of L. *amputāre,* to cut off round about. — L. *am-,* short for *amb-, ambi-,* round about ; *putāre,* to cleanse, also to lop or prune trees. — L. *putus,* clean.

Amulet. (F. — L.) F. *amulette.* — L. *amulētum,* a talisman hung round the neck. [Once thought to be of Arabic origin ; but now given up.]

Amuse, to divert. (F. — L.) F. *amuser,* ' to amuse, make to muse or think of, to gaze at ;' Cot. — F. *à* (= L. *ad*), to, at ; O. F. *muser,* to gaze at, stare at, muse ; see **Muse** (1).

An, A, *indefinite article.* (E.) *A* is short for *an ;* and *an* is an unaccented form of A. S. *ān,* one ; see **One.**

An-, A-, *neg. prefix.* (Gk.) Gk. *ἀν-, ἀ-,* cognate with L. *in-,* and E. *un-* ; see **Un-, In-, A-** (9).

An, if. See **And.**

Ana-, An-, *prefix.* (Gk.) Gk. *ἀνα-, ἀν-;* from Gk. *ἀνά,* upon, on, up, back, again; cognate with E. *on;* see **On.**

Ana, Anna, a sixteenth of a rupee. (Hind.) Hind. *āna,* a sixteenth part, esp. of a rupee. (H. H. Wilson.)

Anabaptist. (Gk.) One who baptizes again. Coined from Gk. *ἀνά,* again ; and *baptist.* See **Baptize.**

Anachronism, error in chronology. (Gk.) Gk. *ἀναχρονισμός.* — Gk. *ἀναχρονίζειν,* to refer to a wrong time. — Gk. *ἀνά,* up, back (wrong) ; *χρόνος,* time.

Anaconda, a large serpent. (Ceylon.) Now used of a S. American boa ; but at first applied to a large snake in Ceylon. The Tamil *ānai-kondra* means ' which killed an elephant ' (Yule).

Anæmia, bloodlessness. (L. — Gk.) A Latinised form of Gk. *ἀναιμία,* want of blood. — Gk. *ἀν-,* not ; *αἷμα,* blood.

Anæsthetic, rendering insensible to pain. (Gk.) Coined from Gk. *ἀν-,* not ; and *αἰσθητικός,* full of perception ; see **An-** and **Æsthetic.**

Anagram, a change in a word due to transposition of letters. (F. — L. — Gk.) F. *anagramme.* — L. *anagramma.* — Gk. *ἀνά-γραμμα.* — Gk. *ἀνά,* up, here used distributively ; *γράμμα,* a letter of the alphabet. — Gk. *γράφειν,* to write.

Analogy, proportion. (F.—L.—Gk.)
F. *analogie.*—L. *analogia.*—Gk. ἀναλογία,
equality of ratios.—Gk. ἀνά, upon,
throughout; -λογία, from λόγ-ος, a word,
statement, from λέγειν, to speak.

Analysis. (Gk.) Gk.ἀνάλυσις,a resolv-
ing into parts, loosening.—Gk. ἀναλύειν,to
undo, resolve.—Gk. ἀνά, back; and λύειν,
to loosen. (√LEU.) **Der.** *analyse,* verb, a
coined word.

Ananas, the pine-apple plant. (Span.
—Braz.) Span. *ananas* (Pineda); mod.
Span. *anana.* — Brazil. *nanas* or *nana.*
¶ The Peruv. name is *achupalla.*

Anapæst, Anapest, a foot in prosody. (Gk.) L. *anapæstus.*—Gk. ἀνά-
παιστος, struck back, rebounding ; because
it is the *reverse* of a dactyl.—Gk. ἀναπαίειν,
to strike back.—Gk. ἀνά, back ; and παίειν,
to strike.

Anarchy. (F.—L.—Gk.) XVI cent.
F. *anarchie.*—L. *anarchia.*—Gk. ἀναρχία,
lack of government.—Gk. ἄναρχος, without
a ruler.—Gk. ἀν-, neg. prefix ; ἄρχος, a
ruler, from ἄρχειν, to rule, to be first.

Anathema, a curse. (L.—Gk.) L.
anathema.—Gk. ἀνάθεμα, a thing devoted
or accursed.—Gk. ἀνατίθημι, I devote.—
Gk. ἀνά, up ; τίθημι, I place, set. Cf.
Theme.

Anatomy. (F.—L.—Gk.) F. *ana-
tomie.*—L. *anatomia.*—Gk. ἀνατομία, the
same as ἀνατομή, dissection.—Gk. ἀνατέμ-
νειν, to cut up.—Gk. ἀνά, up ; τέμνειν, to
cut. Cf. **Tome.**

Ancestor. (F.—L.) M.E. (1) *ancestre,*
O. F. *ancestre,* from L. *antecessor,* nom.,
a predecessor, foregoer ; and M. E. (2) *ancessour,* O. F. *ancessour,* from L. *ante-
cessōrem,* acc.—L. *ante,* before ; *cess-us,*
pp. of *cēdere,* to go.

Anchor. (L.—Gk.) The current spelling imitates the false L. form, *anchora.*
A. S. *ancor.*—L. *ancora* (wrongly *anchora*).
—Gk. ἄγκυρα, an anchor, lit. a bent hook ;
cf. Gk. ἀγκών, a bend. (√ANQ.)

Anchoret, Anchorite, a recluse.
(F.—Late L.—Gk) F. *anachorete* (Cot.).
—Late L. *anachōrēta.*—Gk. ἀναχωρητής,
one who retires from the world.—Gk. ἀνα-
χωρεῖν, to retire.—Gk. ἀνά, back ; and
χωρεῖν, to withdraw, from χῶρος, space,
room. (√GHĒ, GHŌ.)

Anchovy, a fish. (Span.—Basque ?)
Span. *anchova* ; cf. Basque *anchoa, anchua,*
an anchovy. Perhaps ' dried fish ' ; from
Basque *antzua,* dry.

Ancient (1), old. (F.—L.) With
excrescent *t.* M. E. *auncien.*—F. *ancien.*
—Late L. *antiānus,* old, belonging to
former time. Formed with suffix -*ānus*
from *ante,* before.

Ancient (2), a banner, standard-bearer.
(F.—L.) Confused with *ancient* (1) ; but
from O. F. *enseigne,* m. ' ensigne, auncient,
standard-bearer ; ' Cot. ; also for O. F. *enseigne,* f., ' a banner; ' Cot. See **Ensign.**

And. (E.) A. S. *and, end.* ✚ O. Fries.
anda, ende ; O. H. G. *anti, unta,* G. *und.*
Prob. related to L. *ante,* before, Gk. ἀντί,
over against.

an, if. (E.) Formerly also *and* ;
Havelok, 2861,&c ; the same word as the
above. *An if* = if if, a reduplication. *But
and if* = but if if ; Matt. xxiv. 48.

Andante, slowly. (Ital.) Ital.*andante,*
moving slowly, pres. pt. of *andare,* to
go.

Andiron, a fire-dog. (F.—L.) Not
connected with *iron,* but corrupted from
M. E. *anderne, aunderne, aundire.*—O. F.
andier ; mod. F. *landier,* put for *l'andier,*
where *l'* is the def. art. Cf. Late L. *ande-
rius, andena,* a fire-dog.

Anecdote. (F.—L.—Gk.) F. *anecdote.*—Late L. *anecdota,* orig. a neut. pl.—
Gk. ἀνέκδοτα, neut. pl. of ἀνέκδοτος,
unpublished ; hence an unpublished story,
story in private life.—Gk. ἀν-, not ; ἐκ,
out ; and δοτός, given, allied to δίδωμι, I
give.

Anemone, a flower. (Gk.) Gk. ἀνε-
μώνη, lit. wind-flower.—Gk. ἄνεμος, wind.

Anent, regarding, with reference to.
(E.) M. E. *anent, anentis* ; older form
onefent, where the *t* is excrescent. A. S.
anefen, onefen, near ; later form *onemn.*
—A. S. *on,* on ; *efen,* even. Hence *onefn* =
even with, on an equality with. Cf. G.
neben, near (for *in eben*). See **Even.**

Aneroid, dry, applied to a barometer
having no liquid mercury in it. (Gk.)
Coined from Gk. ἀ-, not ; νηρό-s, wet ;
εἶδ-os, form, kind.

Aneurysm, a tumour due to dilatation. (Gk.) Gk. ἀνεύρυσμα, a widening.
—Gk. ἀν-, for ἀνά, up ; and εὐρύνειν, to
widen, from εὐρύς, wide. Also *aneurism.*

Anew. (E.) M. E. *of-newe.* A. S. *of-
niowe,* John iii. 7 (Rushworth). From **Of**
and **New.**

Angel. (F.—L.—Gk.) O. F. *angele.*
—L. *angelus.*—Gk. ἄγγελος, a messenger.
Cf. Gk. ἄγγαρος, a mounted courier, from

O. Persian. **Der.** *arch-angel*, q. v., *ev-angel-ist*, q. v. ¶ The A. S. form was *engel*, directly from L. *angelus*.

Anger. (Scand.) M. E. *anger*, often with the sense of vexation, trouble. — Icel. *angr*, grief; Dan. *anger*, Swed. *ånger*, regret. **+** L. *angor*, a strangling, anguish. (√ANGH.) See below.

Angina, acute pain. (L.) L. *angina*, quinsy, lit. choking. — L. *angere*, to choke.

Angle (1), a corner. (F. — L.) M. E. *angle*. — F. *angle*. — L. *angulus*, an angle. Cf. Gk. ἀγκύλος, bent.

Angle (2), a hook, fish-hook. (E.) A. S. *angel*, a fish-hook; dimin. of *anga*, *onga*, a sting, prickle; cf. Icel. *angi*, a prickle, Gk. ἄγκυρα, a bent hook, Skt. *aṅka(s)*, a hook. **+** Dan. *angel*; G. *angel*, dimin. of O. H. G. *ango*, a prickle, fish-hook. Allied to **Anchor. Der.** *angle*, verb, to fish.

Anguish. (F. — L.) M. E. *anguise*, *angoise*. — O. F. *anguisse*; F. *angoisse*. — L. *angustia*, narrowness, poverty, perplexity. — L. *angustus*, narrow. — L. *angere*, to choke. (√ANGH.)

Aniline, a substance which furnishes a number of dyes. (F. — Span. — Arab. — Pers. — Skt.) Formed, with suffix *-ine*, from *anil*, a dye-stuff. — F. *anil*. — Span. *añil*, azure. — Arab. *an-nīl*; for *al-nīl*, where *al* is the def. art., and *nīl* is borrowed from Pers. *nil*, blue, or the indigo-plant. — Skt. *nīla*, blue; *nīlī*, the indigo-plant.

Animal. (L.) L. *animal*, a living creature. — L. *anima*, breath, life. (√AN.)

animadvert, to censure. (L.) L. *animaduertere*, to turn the mind to, hence, to criticise. — L. *anim-*, for *animus*, the mind (allied to *anima*, breath); *ad*, to; and *uertere*, to turn (see **Verse**).

animate. (L.) L. *animātus*, pp. of *animāre*, to endue with life. — L. *anima*, life. **Der.** *in-animate*, *re-animate*.

animosity. (F. — L.) F. *animosité*. — L. *animōsitātem*, acc. of *animōsitās*, vehemence. — L. *animōsus*, vehement, full of mind or courage. — L. *animus*, mind, courage, passion.

Anise, a herb. (F. — L. — Gk.) M. E. *anese*, *anys*. — F. *anis* (Cot.). — L. *anīsum*; also *anēthum*. — Gk. ἄνισον, ἄνησον, orig. ἄνηθον, anise.

Anker, a liquid measure. (Du. — Late L.) Du. *anker*, the same. — Late L. *anceria*, the same. **+** Swed. *ankare*; G. *anker*; from the same.

Ankle. (E.) M. E. *ancle*; also *an-*

clowe. — O. Fries. *ankel*; also A.S. *ancléow*, with a longer suffix (cf. O. Fries. *onklef*).**+** Dan. and Swed. *ankel*; Icel. *ökkla* (for *önkla = *ankula*); Du. and G. *enkel*. Perhaps allied to Skt. *aṅguli*, a finger, *aṅga*, a limb.

Anna, a small coin; see **Ana.**

Annals. (F. — L.) F. *annales*, pl. sb. — L. *annālēs*, pl. adj., for *librī annālēs*, yearly books, chronicles; from *annālis*, yearly. — L. *annus*, a year.

Anneal, to temper by heat. ((1) E.; (2) F. — L.) Two distinct words have been confused. **1.** M. E. *anelen*, to inflame, kindle, heat, melt, burn. A. S. *onǣlan*, to burn, kindle; from *on*, prefix, and *ǣlan* to burn. Cf. A. S. *ǣled*, fire. **2.** M. E. *anelen*, to enamel glass. — Prefix *a-* (perhaps = F. *à*, L. *ad*); and O. F. *neeler*, *nieler*, to enamel, orig. to paint in black on gold or silver. — Late L. *nigellare*, to blacken. — L. *nigellus*, blackish; from *niger*, black.

Annex. (F. — L.) F. *annexer*. — L. *annexus*, pp. of *annectere*, to knit or bind to. — L. *an-* (for *ad*), to; and *nectere*, to bind.

Annihilate. (L.) L. *annihilātus*, pp. of *annihilāre*, to reduce to nothing. — L. *an-* (for *ad*), to; and *nihil*, nothing.

Anniversary. (L.) For 'anniversary memorial.' — L. *anniuersārius*, returning yearly. — L. *anni-* (from *anno-*), from *annus*, a year; and *uersus*, pp. of *uertere*, to turn (see **Verse**).

Annotate, to make notes on. (L.) From pp. of L. *annotāre*, to make notes on. — L. *an-* (for *ad*), to, on; *notāre*, to mark, from *nota*, a mark. See **Note.**

Announce. (F. — L.) F. *annoncer*. — L. *annuntiāre*, to announce. — L. *an-* (= *ad*), to; *nuntiāre*, to bring tidings, from *nuntius*, a messenger. See **Nuncio.**

Annoy, to vex. (F. — L.) M. E. *anoien*, *anuien*. — O. F. *anoier*, *anuier*, to annoy. — O. F. *anoi*, *anui* (F. *ennui*), vexation. Cf. Span. *enojo*, O. Venetian *inodio*, vexation. — L. *in odiō*, lit. in hatred, common in the Late L. phr. *in odiō habui*, lit. I had in hatred, I was annoyed with; cf. L. *in odiō esse*, to be hated by (Cicero). — L. *in*, in; *odiō*, abl. of *odium*, hatred.

Annual, yearly. (F. — L.) M. E. *annuel*. — F. *annuel*. — L. *annuālis*, yearly. — L. *annus*, a year.

annuity. (A. F. — L.) A F. *annuité*; A. D. 1304. — Late L. *annuitātem*, acc. of *annuitās*. — L. *annus*, a year.

Annul. (L.) L. *annullāre*, to bring to

nothing. —L. *an-* (for *ad*), to; *nullus*, no one; see **Null.**

Annular, like a ring. (L.) L. *annulāris,* adj.; from *annulus,* a ring, earlier spelling *ānulus*; dimin. of L. *ānus,* a rounding, a circular form (Lewis).

Anodyne, a drug to allay pain. (L.—Gk.) XVI cent. Late L. *anōdynus,* a drug relieving pain. —Gk. ἀνώδυνος, free from pain. — Gk. ἀν-, not; and ὀδύνη, pain.

Anoint. (F.—L.) M. E. *anoint,* used as a pp.=anointed.—O. F. *enoint,* pp. of *enoindre,* to anoint.—O. F. *en,* upon; *oindre,* to smear.—L. *in,* upon; *ungere,* to anoint. See **Unguent.**

Anomaly. (Gk.) Gk. ἀνωμαλία, deviation from rule. — Gk. ἀνώμαλος, uneven. — Gk. ἀν-, not; and ὁμαλός, even, related to ὁμός, one and the same.

Anon, immediately. (E.) M. E. *anon, anoon*; also *onan.* A.S. *on ān,* lit. 'in one moment.' — A. S. *on,* on, in; *ān,* one.

Anonymous, nameless. (Gk.) Gk. ἀνώνυμ-ος, nameless; with *-ous* added. — Gk. ἀν-, neg. prefix; and ὄνομα, name.

Another. (E.) For *an other,* one other.

Answer, to reply. (E.) A. S. *andswerian, andswarian,* to answer, speak in reply; a weak verb. — A. S. *andswaru,* a reply. — A. S. *and-,* against, in reply; *swerian,* to speak, to swear. The A. S. *and-*=G. *ant-* (in *ant-worten*)=Gk. ἀντί; see **Anti-** and **Swear.**

Ant. (E.) M. E. *amte,* short for *amete.* A. S. *ǣmette,* an emmet, ant. **Doublet,** *emmet,* q. v.

Antagonist, an opponent. (L.—Gk.) Late L. *antagōnista.* — Gk. ἀνταγωνιστής, an opponent. — Gk. ἀντ-, for ἀντί, against; and ἀγωνίζομαι, I struggle, from ἀγών, a contest. (√AG.)

Antarctic. (L.—Gk.) L. *antarcticus.* — Gk. ἀνταρκτικός, southern, opposite to arctic. — Gk. ἀντ-, for ἀντί, opposite to; and ἀρκτικός, arctic. See **Arctic.**

Ante-, prefix, before. (L.) L. *ante,* before. Allied to **Anti-,** q. v.

Antecedent. (L.) L. *antecēdent-,* stem of pres. part. of *antecēdere,* to go before. — L. *ante,* before; *cēdere,* to go.

Antediluvian, before the flood. (L.) L. *ante,* before; *dīluuium,* deluge, a washing away. — L. *dīluere,* to wash away. — L. *dī-,* apart; *luere,* to wash.

Antelope. (F. — L. — Gk.) In Spenser,

F. Q. i. 6. 26. — O. F. *antelop.* — Late L. *antalopus.* — Late Gk. ἀνθόλοπ-, the stem of ἀνθόλοψ, used by Eustathius of Antioch to signify some uncertain quadruped. Of unknown origin.

Antennae, feelers of insects. (L.) L. *antennæ,* pl. of *antenna,* properly the yard of a sail.

Antepenultima, the last syllable but two in a word. (L.) L. *ante,* before; *pænultima,* fem. adj., last but one, from *pæn-e,* almost, *ultima,* last.

Anterior. (L.) L. *anterior,* former, more in front, compar. adj. from *ante,* before.

Anthem. (L.—Gk.) Formerly *antem.* A. S. *antefn.* — Late L. *antiphōna,* an anthem. — Gk. ἀντίφωνα, considered as fem. sing., but really neut. pl. of ἀντίφωνος, sounding in response to; from the alternate singing of the half-choirs. — Gk. ἀντί, over against; φωνή, voice, sound.

Anther, the summit of the stamen of a flower. (Gk.) From Gk. ἀνθηρός, blooming. — Gk. ἀνθεῖν, to bloom; ἄνθος, a young bud or sprout.

anthology, a collection of choice poems. (Gk.) Lit. a collection of flowers. — Gk. ἀνθολογία, a gathering of flowers. — Gk. ἀνθολόγος, flower-gathering. — Gk. ἀνθο-, for ἄνθος, a flower; and λέγειν, to cull.

Anthracite, a kind of hard coal. (Gk.) Gk. ἀνθρακίτης, resembling coals. — Gk. ἀνθρακ-, stem of ἄνθραξ, coal.

Anthropophagi, cannibals. (Gk.) Lit. 'men-eaters.' — Gk. ἀνθρωποφάγος, man-eating. — Gk. ἄνθρωπος, a man; and φαγεῖν, to eat. (√BHAGw; Brugm. i. § 641.)

Anti-, Ant-, *prefix,* against. (Gk.) Gk. ἀντί, against; allied to L. *ante,* before. Cf. Skt. *anti,* over against, allied to *anta,* end; see **End.** ¶ In *anti-cipate,* the prefix is for L. *ante.*

Antic, fanciful, odd; as sb. a trick. (Ital.—L.) Orig. an adj. Adopted in the XVI cent. from Ital. *antico,* with the sense of 'grotesque'; lit. antique, old.— L. *antiquus,* old. See **Antique.**

Antichrist. (F. — L. — Gk.) O. F. *Antecrist.* — L. *Antichristus* (Vulgate). — Gk. ἀντιχρίστος (1 John ii. 18). — Gk. ἀντί, against; χρίστος, Christ.

Anticipate. (L.) From the pp. of L. *anticipāre,* to take beforehand. — L. *anti-,* before; and *capere,* to take.

Anticlimax. (Gk.) From **Anti-** and **Climax.**

Antidote. (F. – L. – Gk.) F. *antidote.* – L. *antidotum,* a remedy. – Gk. ἀντίδοτον, a remedy; a thing given as a remedy. – Gk. ἀντί, against; δοτόν, neut. of δοτός, given, from δίδωμι, I give.

Antimony, a metal. (Late L.) Late L. *antimōnium.* (XI cent.) Origin unknown.

Antipathy. (Gk.) From Gk. ἀντιπάθεια, antipathy, lit. ' a suffering (feeling strongly) against.' – Gk. ἀντί, against ; παθεῖν, to suffer. See **Pathos.**

Antiphon. (L. – Gk.) Late L. *antiphōna,* an anthem ; see **Anthem.**

Antiphrasis. (Gk.) See **Anti-** and **Phrase.**

Antipodes. (Gk.) Gk. ἀντίποδες, pl., men with feet opposite to ours, from nom. sing. ἀντίπους. – Gk. ἀντί, opposite to; and πούς, foot, cognate with **Foot.**

Antique, old. (F. – L.) F. *antique.* – L. *antīquus,* also *antīcus,* formed with suffix *-īcus* from *ante,* before ; as *postīcus* is from *post,* behind. **Doublet,** *antic.*

Antiseptic, counteracting putrefaction. (Gk.) Gk. ἀντί, against ; and σηπτικός, putrefying, σηπτ-ός, rotten, from σήπειν, to rot.

Antistrophe. (Gk.) From **Anti-** and **Strophe.**

Antithesis. (Gk.) From **Anti-** and **Thesis.**

Antitype. (Gk.) From **Anti-** and **Type.**

Antler. (F.) M. E. *auntelere,* for *auntolier* (?). – O. F. *antoillier,* said to have been once in use (Littré). In this case the O. F. word is supposed to be equivalent to a Late L. **antoculārem,* acc., i. e. the branch (of the horn) in front of the eyes ; cf. G. *augen-sprosse,* a brow-antler (lit. eye-sprout). See *Romania,* iv. 349. From *ante,* before, and *oculus,* the eye.

Anus, the lower orifice of the bowels. (L.) L. *ānus.*

Anvil. (E.) M. E. *anvelt, anfeld, anfelt.* A.S. *anfilte, onfilti.* – A. S. *an, on,* on, upon; and a verb **fieltan* (see below), causal of **fealtan,* to infix, redupl. verb cognate with O. H. G. **falzan,* M. H. G. *valzen,* whence G. *falz,* a groove. ¶ Some derive it from *on* and *fealdan,* to fold; however, the O. H. G. *anafalz,* an anvil, is not derived from *ana,* on, and *faldan,*

to fold up, but from M. H. G. *valzen,* as above. Cf. L. *incūs,* an anvil, from *in,* on, and *cūdere,* to strike ; and note the A.S. gloss : ' *Cudo, percutio,* anfilte ;' Voc. 217. 5.

Anxious. (L.) L. *anxi-us,* distressed ; with suffix *-ous.* – L. *angere,* to choke, distress.

Any. (E.) A. S. *ǣnig,* any ; from *ān,* one, with suffix *-ig* (E. *-y*). + Du. *eenig,* from *een,* one; G. *einiger,* from *ein,* one. See **One.**

Aorta. (L. – Gk.) Late L. *aorta.* – Gk. ἀορτή, the great artery ' rising ' from the heart. – Gk. ἀείρεσθαι, to rise up ; ἀείρειν, to raise.

Apace. (E. and F.) For *a pace,* i. e. at a (good) pace ; where *a* is put for *on* (cf. *a-foot*) ; see **A-** (2). *Pace,* M. E. *pas,* is from F. *pas* (L. *passus*). See **Pace.**

Apart, aside. (F. – L.) F. *à part,* apart, alone, singly ; Cot. – L. *ad partem,* lit. to the one part or side, apart. – L. *ad,* to ; *partem,* acc. of *pars,* a part.

apartment, a separate room. (F. – Ital. – L.) F. *appartement.* – Ital. *appartamento,* an apartment, a partition, lit. separation. – Ital. *appartare,* to separate. – Ital. *a parte,* apart. – L. *ad partem* ; see above.

Apathy. (Gk.) From Gk. ἀπάθεια, want of feeling. – Gk. ἀ-, not ; παθεῖν, to suffer. See **Pathos.**

Ape. (E.) M. E. *ape* ; A. S. *apa.* + Du. *aap* ; Icel. *api* ; Swed. *apa* ; G. *affe* ; Irish *apa* (from E.) ; O. Bohem. *op.*

Aperient. (L.) XVII cent. Lit. ' opening.' – L. *aperient-,* stem of pres. pt. of *aperīre,* to open. Perhaps from *ap-,* old form of *ab,* from, away, and *-uer-* = Lith. *wer-* in *werti,* to move (to and fro), whence Lith. *at-werti,* to open. Brugm. i. § 361.

Apex. (L.) L. *apex,* summit.

Aph-, *prefix.* (Gk.) See **Apo-.**

Aphæresis, the taking away of a letter or syllable from the beginning of a word. (L. – Gk.) Late L. *aphæresis.* – Gk. ἀφαίρεσις, a taking away. – Gk. ἀφ-, for ἀπό, away ; αἵρεσις, a taking, from αἱρεῖν, to take. See **Heresy.**

Aphelion, the point in a planet's orbit farthest from the sun. (Gk.) Coined from Gk. ἀφ-, for ἀπό, from ; ἥλιος, the sun.

Aphorism, a definition. (Gk.) Gk. ἀφορισμός, a definition. – Gk. ἀφορίζειν, to define, limit. – Gk. ἀφ-, for ἀπό, off; ὁρίζειν, to limit, from ὅρος, a boundary.

Apiary, a place for bees. (L.) L. *apiārium*, neut. of *apiārius*, belonging to bees. – L. *api-*, stem of *apis*, a bee.

Apiece. (E. *and* F.) Orig. (at so much) *a piece*, where *a* is the indef. article.

Apo-, *prefix*, off. (Gk.) Gk. ἀπό, off, from; cognate with E. *of, off*; see **Of.** It becomes *aph-* before an aspirate.

Apocalypse. (L.–Gk.) M. E. *apocalips* (Wyclif). – L. *apocalypsis*. – Gk. ἀποκάλυψις, a revelation. – Gk. ἀποκαλύπτειν, to uncover, reveal. – Gk. ἀπό, off; and καλύπτειν, to cover. Cf. καλιά, a cot.

Apocope. (L.–Gk.) L. *apocopē.* – Gk. ἀποκοπή, a cutting off (of a letter). – Gk. ἀπό, off; and κόπτειν, to hew, cut.

Apocrypha. (Gk.) Lit. 'hidden things;' hence, uncanonical books of the Old Testament. – Gk. ἀπόκρυφα, neut. pl. of ἀπόκρυφος, hidden. – Gk. ἀποκρύπτειν, to hide away. – Gk. ἀπό, from, away; κρύπτειν, to hide.

Apogee, the point of the moon's orbit furthest from the earth. (F.–L.–Gk`F. *apogée* (Cot.). – L. *apogæum.* – Gk. ἀπόγαιον, neut. of ἀπόγαιος, away from earth. – Gk. ἀπό, away from; γῆ, earth.

Apologue, a fable, story. (F.–L.– Gk.) F. *apologue.* – L. *apologus.* – Gk. ἀπόλογος, a fable. – Gk. ἀπό, off; λόγος, speech, from λέγειν, to say.

apology, a defence. (L.–Gk.) L. *apologia.* – Gk. ἀπολογία, a speech made in defence. – Gk. ἀπό, off; λόγος, a speech (above).

Apophthegm, Apothegm. (Gk.) Gk. ἀπόφθεγμα, a thing uttered, a terse saying. – Gk. ἀπό, off, out; and φθέγγομαι, I cry aloud, utter.

Apoplexy. (F.–Late L.–Gk.) F. *apoplexie.* – Late L. *apoplēxia.* – Gk. ἀποπληξία, stupor, apoplexy. – Gk. ἀποπλήσσειν, to cripple by a stroke. – Gk. ἀπό, off; πλήσσειν, to strike.

Apostasy. (F.–Late L.–Gk.) F. *apostasie.* – Late L. *apostasia.* – Gk. ἀποστασία, late form for ἀπόστασις, revolt, lit. 'a standing away from.' – Gk. ἀπό, off, away; στάσις, a standing, from στα-, base allied to ἵστημι, I place. Cf. **Statics.**

apostate. (Late L. – Gk.) M. E. *apostata.* – Late L. *apostata.* – Gk. ἀποστάτης, a deserter, apostate. – Gk. ἀπό, off; στάτης, standing, from στα- (see above).

Apostle. (L.–Gk.) A. S. *apostol.* –

L. *apostolus.* – Gk. ἀπόστολος, one who is sent off. – Gk. ἀπό, off; στέλλειν, to send.

Apostrophe. (L. – Gk.) L. *apostrophē.* – Gk. ἀποστροφή, a turning away; in rhetoric, a turning away to address some one else. – Gk. ἀπό, away; στρέφειν, to turn. ¶ In the sense of a mark used to denote an omission, it should be *apostroph* (L. *apostrophus*, Gk. ἀπόστροφος).

Apothecary. (F. – Late L. – Gk.) M. E. *apotecary,* *potecary.*–O. F. *apotecaire.* – Late L. *apothēcārius*, lit. a store-keeper. – Late L. *apothēca*, a store-house (esp. for drugs). – Gk. ἀποθήκη, a store-house. – Gk. ἀπό, away; τί-θη-μι, I put.

Apotheosis, deification. (L. – Gk.) L. *apotheōsis.* – Gk. ἀποθέωσις, deification. – Gk. ἀποθεόω, I deify, set aside as a god. – Gk. ἀπό, away, fully; θεός, a god.

Appal, to terrify. (F.–L.) The present sense is late; the M. E. *apalled* meant 'rendered pale'; cf. Chaucer, C. T., 10679 (F 365). – O. F. *apallir, apalir, appalir,* to wax pale, also to make pale (Cot.). – O. F. *a-*, prefix; O. F. *pale, palle,* pale. – L. *ad*, to; *pallidus,* pale. Cf. **Pale.**

Appanage, Apanage, provision for a dependent, &c. (F.–L.) O. F. *apanage* (also *appanage*), properly, a provision for maintenance. – O. F. *apaner,* lit. to supply with bread (Late L. *appānāre*). – L. *ap-* (for *ad*), to, for; *pān-is,* bread.

Apparatus, gear. (L.) L. *apparātus,* preparation. – L. *apparātus,* pp. of *apparāre,* to prepare for. – L. *ad,* for; *parāre,* to get ready.

Apparel, to clothe. (F.–L.) M. E. *aparailen.* – O. F. *apareiller,* to dress, apparel. – O. F. *a,* to; *pareiller, parailler,* to assort, put like things with like, to arrange, from *pareil,* like, similar. – L. *ad,* to; Med. L. *pariculus* (Ducange has *paricla, paricula*), similar, from L. *pari-,* stem of *par,* equal. Cf. **Par. Der.** *apparel, s.*

Apparition. (F.–L.) F. *apparition.* –L. acc. *appāritiōnem.* – L. *appārēre,* to appear. See **Appear.**

apparitor, an officer who attends magistrates to execute their orders; an officer who serves the process of a spiritual court. (L.) L. *appāritor,* an attendant, lictor. – L. *appārēre,* to appear as attendant, wait on. See **Appear.**

Appeal, v. (F.–L.) M. E. *apelen.* – O. F. *apeler,* to call. – L. *appellāre,* to address, call upon; a secondary form, from *appellere*, to drive to, incline towards; from L. *ap-* (for *ad*), to ; *pellere*, to drive.

Appear, to become visible. (F.–L.) M. E. *aperen*. – O. F. *aper-*, tonic stem (as in pres. subj. *apere*) of O. F. *apareir*, *aparoir*, to appear. – L. *appārēre*. – L. *ap-* (for *ad*), to, forth ; *pārēre*, to come in sight, also spelt *parrēre*. Cf. **Apparition**.

Appease. (F. – L.) , M. E. *apesen*, *apaisen*. – A. F. *apeser*, *apeiser*, O. F. *apeser* (F. *apaiser*), to bring to a peace. – O. F. *a peis*, *a pais*, to a peace. – L. *ad pācem*, to a peace. See **Peace**.

Appellant. (F.–L.) F. *appellant*, pres. pt. of *appeller*, O. F. *apeler*, to appeal ; see **Appeal**.

Append, to attach. (F.–L.) Formerly also M. E. *apenden*, to pertain to. – O. F. *apendre*, to depend on. – L. *appendĕre*, for L. *appendēre*, to hang to or upon. – L. *ap-* (for *ad*), to ; *pendēre*, to hang.

appendix, an addition. (L.) L. *appendix*. – L. *appendĕre*, to suspend upon. – L. *ap-* (for *ad*), to ; *pendĕre*, to weigh.

Appertain. (F.–L.) M. E. *apertenen*. – O F. *apartenir* (F. *appartenir*), to belong to. – L. *ap-* (for *ad*), to ; *pertinēre*, to belong. See **Pertain**.

Appetite. (F.–L.) O. F. *appetit*. – L. *appetītus*, an appetite ; lit. 'assault upon.' – L. *appetere*, to attack. – L. *ap-* (for *ad*), to ; *petere*, to seek, attack.

Applaud. (L.) L. *applaudere*, to applaud. – L. *ap-*.(for *ad*), at ; *plaudere*, to applaud, clap (hands). Der. *applause*, from pp. *applausus*.

Apple. (E.) M. E. *appel*. A. S. *æppel*, *æpl*. + Du. *appel* ; Icel. *epli* ; Swed. *äple* ; Dan. *æble* ; G. *apfel* ; Irish *abhal* ; Gael. *ubhal* ; W. *afal* ; Russ. *iabloko* ; Lithuan. *obolys*. Origin unknown. Some connect it with Abella in Campania ; cf. Verg. Æn. vii. 740.

Apply. (F.–L.) M. E. *aplyen*. – O. F. *aplier*. – L. *applicāre*, to join to, turn or apply to. – L. *ap-* (for *ad*), to ; *plicāre*, to fold, twine. Der. *appli-ance* ; also *appli-cation* (F. *application*).

Appoggiatura, a grace-note or passing tone prefixed, as a support, to an essential note of a melody. (Ital.–L. *and* Gk.) Ital. *appoggiatura*, lit. a support. – Ital. *appoggiare*, to lean upon. – Ital. *ap-* (for *ad*), to, upon ; *poggio*, a place to stand or lean on, &c. – L. *ad*, to ; *podium*, an elevated place, a balcony, from Gk. πόδιον. See **Pew**.

Appoint. (F.–L.) M. E. *apointen*. – O. F. *apointer*, to prepare, arrange, settle. – Late L. *appunctāre*, to repair, appoint, settle a dispute ; Ducange. – L. *ap-* (for *ad*); Late L. *punctāre*, to mark by a point, from Late L. *puncta*, a prick, fem. of *punctus*, pp. ; see **Point**. Der. *disappoint*.

Apportion. (F.–L.) F. *apportioner*, to portion out to. – F. *ap-* (put for *a* before *p*, in imitation of L. *ap-=ad*), to ; *portion*, a portion ; see **Portion**.

Appose. (F.–L.) F. *apposer*; formed to represent L. *appōnere*, on the analogy of *composer*, *exposer*, and other presumed representatives of compounds of L. *pōnere* ; but really formed on F. *poser* (from L. *pausāre*). See **Pose**.

Apposite. (L.) L. *appositus*, suitable ; pp. of *appōnere*, to put near. – L. *ap-* (for *ad*), to ; *pōnere*, to put. See **Position**.

Appraise. (F.–L.) M. E. *apraisen*, to value. – O. F. **apreiser* (cf. O. F. *apre-tier* in Roquefort). – O. F. *a-*, prefix ; *preiser*, to value, from *preis*, value, price. – L. *ad*, at ; *pretium*, a price.

appreciate. (L.) From pp. of L. *appretiāre*, to value at a price. – L. *ap-* (for *ad*), at ; *pretium*, a price.

Apprehend. (F.–L.) F. *apprehendre* (Cot.). – L. *apprehendere*, orig. to lay hold of. – L. *ap-* (for *ad*), to, at ; *prehendere*, to grasp. See **Prehensile**.

apprentice. (F.–L.) O. F. *aprentis*, nom. of *aprentif* (see Godefroy, s. v. *aprentic*). The O. F. *aprentis*, *aprentif*, represent Late L. **apprenditīvus*, nom., and **apprenditīvum*, acc., from a Late L. **apprenditus*, used as a pp. of L. *apprendere*, to learn, short for L. *apprehendere*, to lay hold of (above).

apprise, to inform. (F.–L.) From the M. E. sb. *aprise*, information, teaching. – O. F. *aprise*, instruction. – O. F. *appris*, *apris*, pp. of *aprendre*, to learn. – L. *apprendere* (above).

Approach. (F.–L.) M. E. *approchen*, *aprochen*. – O. F. *aprochier*, to approach. – L. *appropiāre*, to draw near to (Exod. iii. 5). – L. *ap-* (for *ad*), to ; *prope*, near.

Approbation. (F.–L.) F. *approba-tion*. – L. acc. *approbātiōnem*, approval. – L. *approbātus*, pp. of *approbāre*, to approve. See **Approve**.

Appropriate. (L.) From pp. of L. *appropriāre*, to make one's own. – L. *ap-* (for *ad*), to ; *proprius*, one's own. See **Proper**.

Approve. (F.—L.) O. F. *approver.*—
L. *approbāre,* to approve.—L. *ap-* (for *ad*),
to; *probāre,* to test, try, esteem as good.
Der. *appro-val*; *dis-approve.*

Approximate. (L.) From pp. of L.
approximāre, to draw near to.—L. *ap-*
(for *ad*), to; *proximus,* very near, superl.
adj. from *prope,* near.

Appurtenance. (F.—L.) A.F. *apur-
tenaunce* (O. F. *apartenance*), that which
belongs to.—O. F. *apartenir,* to belong to.
See **Appertain.**

Apricot. (F.—Port. — Arab. — Gk.—
L.) Formerly also *apricock,* from Port.
albricoque directly. Also *abricot.* — F.
abricot, ‘the abricot, or apricock plum;’
Cot.—Port. *albricoque.*—Arab. *al barqūq,*
where *al* is the def. art.—Mid. Gk. πραικό-
κιον (Dioscorides); pl. πραικόκια. The
pl. πραικόκια was borrowed from L. *prœ-
coqua,* apricots, neut. pl. of *prœcoquus,*
another form of *prœcox,* precocious, early
ripe (Pliny; Martial, 13. 46).—L. *prœ,*
beforehand; and *coquere,* to cook, ripen.
See **Precocious** and **Cook.** ¶ Thus the
word reached us in a very indirect manner.

April. (L.) L. *Aprīlis*; said to be so
named because the earth then opens to
produce new fruit.—L. *aperīre,* to open;
see **Aperient.**

Apron. (F.—L.) Formerly *napron.*—
O. F. *naperon,* a large cloth; augmentative
form of O. F. *nape,* a cloth (F. *nappe*).—
L. *mappa,* a napkin, cloth (with change of
m to *n,* as in F. *natte,* a mat). See
Map.

Apse. (L.—Gk.) Now used of a recess
at the end of a church; formerly *apse,*
apsis, a turning-point of a planet’s orbit.—
L. *apsis,* pl. *apsides,* a bow, turn.—Gk.
ἁψίς, a tying, fastening, felloe of a wheel,
curve, bow, arch.—Gk. ἅπτειν, to tie, bind.

Apt, fit. (L.) XIV cent. L. *aptus,*
used as pp. of *apiscī,* to reach, get, but
really pp. of O. Lat. *apere,* to fit or join
together.

Aquatic. (L.) L. *aquāticus,* pertaining to water.—L. *aqua,* water.

aqua-fortis.—L. *aqua fortis,* strong
water.

aquarium.—L. *aquārium,* a water-
vessel.—L. *aqua,* water.

aquarius.—L. *aquārius,* a water-
bearer.—L. *aqua,* water.

aqueduct.—L. *aquæductus,* a conduit; from *aquæ,* gen. of *aqua,* water, and
ductus, a duct; see **Duct.**

aqueous. As if from L. **aqueus,* adj.,
a form not used.—L. *aqua,* water.

Aquiline, like an eagle. (F.—L.) F.
aquilin; hence *nez aquilin,* ‘a nose like
an eagle;’ Cot.—L. *aquilīnus,* adj. from
aquila, an eagle. Cf. **Eagle.**

Arabesque. (F.—Ital.—Arab.) XVII
cent. F. *Arabesque,* Arabian-like; also
full of flourishes, like fine Arabian work.
—Ital. *Arabesco*; where *-esco* = E. *-ish.*—
Arab. ‘*arab,* Arabia.

Arable. (F. — L.) F. *arable.* — L.
arābilis, that can be ploughed.—L. *arāre,*
to plough. (√AR.) See **Ear** (3).

Arbiter. (L.) In Milton.—L. *arbiter,*
a witness, judge, umpire.

arbitrary. (L.) In Milton. — L.
arbitrārius, orig. like the decision of an
umpire.—L. *arbitrāre,* to act as umpire.
—L. *arbiter* (above).

arbitrate. (L.) From pp. of L.
arbitrāre, to act as umpire (above).

Arboreous, belonging to trees. (L.)
L. *arbore-us,* adj. from *arbor,* a tree; with
suffix *-ous.*

Arbour, a bower. (F.—L.) The word
seems to be really due to M. E. *herbere,*
also *erbere,* from O. F. *herbier,* L. *her-
bārium,* a herb-garden, also an orchard.—
L. *herba,* grass, herb. The special sense
was due to confusion with L. *arbor,* a
tree.

Arc. (F.—L.) XIV cent. F. *arc.*—
L. *arcum,* acc. of *arcus,* a bow, arch, arc.

arcade. (F.—Ital.—L.) F. *arcade.*
—Ital. *arcata,* an arched place; fem. of
pp. of *arcare,* to arch.—Ital. *arco,* a bow,
—L. acc. *arcum* (above).

Arcana. (L.) L. *arcāna,* things kept
secret, secrets.—L. *arcēre,* to keep.

Arch (1), a vault, &c. (F.—L.) O. F.
arche, a chest, box (L. *arca,* see **Ark**);
also, by confusion, an arch, owing to the
use of Med. Lat. *arca* with the sense of
L. *arcus,* a bow, arch. See **Arc.**

Arch (2), roguish, waggish. (L.—Gk.)
‘So *arch* a leer;’ Tatler, no. 193. The
examples in the New E. Dictionary prove
that it is nothing but the prefix Arch-,
chief (for which see below), used separately
and peculiarly. Cf. ‘The most *arch* act’
in Shak. Rich. III. iv. 3. 2; ‘An heretic,
an *arch* one;’ Hen. VIII. iii. 2. 102.
Also ‘Byends . . . a very *arch* fellow, a
downright hypocrite’; Bunyan’s Pilgrim’s
Progress. A. S. *arce-,* O. F. *arche-,* L.
archi-, Gk. ἀρχι- (prefix). See below.

Arch-, *prefix,* chief. (L. – Gk.) The form *arch-* is due to A. S. *arce-,* as in *arcebisceop,* an archbishop, and to O. F. *arche-,* as in *arche-diacre,* an archdeacon. This form was borrowed from L. *archi-* = Gk. ἀρχι-, as in ἀρχι-επίσκοπος, an archbishop. – Gk. ἄρχειν, to be first, to rule; cf. Gk. ἀρχή, beginning. Der. *arch-bishop, archdeacon,* &c. ; but, in *arch-angel,* the *ch* remained hard (as *k*) in the Romance languages, on account of the following *a.* Cf. Ital. *arcangelo,* Span. *arcangel.*

archæology. (Gk.) Gk. ἀρχαιολογία. – Gk. ἀρχαῖος, ancient, which is from ἀρχή, the beginning; and the suffix *-logy,* Gk. *-λογία,* due to λόγος, discourse, from λέγειν, to speak.

archaic. (Gk.) Gk. ἀρχαϊκός, antique, primitive. – Gk. ἀρχαῖος, old. – Gk. ἀρχή, beginning.

archaism. (Gk.) Gk. ἀρχαϊσμός, an antiquated phrase. – Gk. ἀρχαίζειν, to speak antiquatedly. – Gk. ἀρχαῖος, old (above).

Archer. (F. – L.) M. E. *archer.* – A. F. *archer;* O. F. *archier,* a bow-man. – Late L. *arcārius,* a bow-man; from *arcus,* a bow.

Archetype, the original type. (F. – L. – Gk.) F. *archetype,* 'a principall ype;' Cot. – L. *archetypum,* the original pattern. – Gk. ἀρχέτυπον, a model; neut. of ἀρχέτυπος, stamped as a model. – Gk. ἀρχε- = ἀρχι-, prefix (see Archi-); τύπος, a type.

Archi-, *prefix,* chief. (L. – Gk.) L. *archi-,* for Gk. ἀρχι- ; see Arch-.

archimandrite. (L. – Gk.) L. *archimandrīta,* a chief or principal of monks, an abbot. – Late Gk. ἀρχιμανδρίτης, the same. – Gk. ἀρχι-; chief; μάνδρα, an enclosure, fold, afterwards a monastery. See Arch- and Madrigal.

archipelago, chief sea, i. e. Aegean sea. (Ital. – Gk.) Ital. *arcipelago,* modified to *archipelago.* – Gk. ἀρχι-, chief; and πέλαγος, sea.

architect. (F. – L. – Gk.) F. *architecte.* – L. *architectus,* the same as *architectōn.* – Gk. ἀρχιτέκτων, a chief builder or artificer. – Gk. ἀρχι-, chief (see Archi-); τέκτων, a carpenter, builder.

architrave. (F. – Ital. – L. *and* Gk.) In Milton. – F. *architrave.* – Ital. *architrave,* the part of an entablature resting immediately on the column. A barbarous compound; from Gk. ἀρχι-, prefix, chief,

principal, and Lat. *trabem,* acc. of *trabs,* a beam. See **Trave.**

Archives, s. pl., public records ; but properly an *archive* is a place where records are kept. (F. – L. – Gk.) F. *archif,* pl. *archives;* Cot. – L. *archīuum, archīum.* – Gk. ἀρχεῖον, a public building, residence of magistrates. – Gk. ἀρχή, a beginning, a magistracy.

Arctic. (F. – L. – Gk.) M. E. *artik.* – O. F. *artique;* F. *arctique.* – L. *arcticus.* – Gk. ἀρκτικός, near the constellation of the Bear, northern. – Gk. ἄρκτος, a bear. Cognate with L. *ursus;* see **Ursine.** Der. *ant-arctic.*

Ardent. (F. – L.) XIV cent. M. E. *ardaunt.* – O. F. *ardant,* pres. part. of *ardre,* to burn. – L. *ardent-em,* acc. of pres. pt. of *ardēre,* to burn.

ardour. (F. – L.) O.F. *ardour, ardor,* heat. – L. *ardōrem,* acc. of *ardor,* a burning, fervour. – L. *ardēre,* to burn.

Arduous. (L.) L. *ardu-us,* steep, difficult, high; with suffix *-ous.*+Irish *ard,* high ; Gk. ὀρθός, upright.

Are, pres. pl. of the verb substantive. (E.) O. Northumbrian *aron,* O. Merc. *earun,* as distinguished from A.S. (Wessex) *sint, sind, sindon.* Cf. Icel. *er-u,* they are. From the Idg. √ES, to be ; from whence also are Skt. *s-anti,* Gk. εἰσ-ίν, L. *s-unt,* G. *s-ind,* Icel. *er-u* (for **es-u),* they are.

am, O. Northumb. *am,* O. Merc. *eam,* A. S. *eom.*+Skt. *as-mi,* Gk. εἰ-μί, Goth. *i-m,* Icel. *e-m* ; &c.

art. O. Northumb. *arð,* O. Merc. *earð* ; A.S. *eart* (with *t* due to *-t* in *sceal-t,* shalt, &c.). Icel. *est, ert.*

is. A. S. *is.*+Icel. *es,* later *er.* Cf. also Goth. and G. *is-t,* Skt. *as-ti,* Gk. ἐσ-τί, L. *es-t.* See also **Be, Was.**

Area. (L.) XVI cent. L. *ārea,* an open space.

Areca, a genus of palms. (Port. – Canarese.) Port. *areca.* – Canarese *adiki, adike,* areca-nut ; *r* being substituted for the cerebral *d* (H. H. Wilson). Accented on the first syllable.

Arefaction; see **Arid** (below).

Arena. (L.) L. *arēna,* sand ; the sanded space in which gladiators fought. Orig. *harēna;* cf. Sabine *fasēna,* sand.

Argent. (F. – L.) White; in heraldry. – F. *argent.* – L. *argentum,* silver ; from its brightness. Cf. Gk. ἄργυρος, silver, Skt. *arjuna(s),* white. (√ARG, to shine.) Brugm. i. §§ 529, 604. See below.

Argillaceous, clayey. (L.) L. *argillāceus,* adj. from *argilla,* clay, esp. white clay. Cf. Gk. ἀργός, white.

Argonaut. (L.–Gk.) L. *argonauta.* –Gk. ἀργοναύτης, one who sailed in the ship Argo. –Gk. ἀργώ, the name of Jason's ship (lit. swift, from ἀργός, swift); and ναύτης, a sailor; see **Nautical.**

Argosy, a merchant-vessel. (Dalmatian.) Formerly spelt *arguze* and *ragusy* (see N. and Q. 6 S. iv. 490; Arber's Eng. Garner, ii. 67). The orig. sense was 'a ship of Ragusa,' which is the name of a port in Dalmatia. Ragusa appears in XVI cent. E. as *Aragouse.*

Argue. (F.–L.) M. E. *arguen.* – O. F. *arguer.* –Late L. *argūtāre* (L. *argūtarī*), frequent. of *arguere,* to prove by argument, lit. to make clear; cf. *argūtus,* clear.

Arid, dry. (L.) XVII cent. L. *āridus,* dry. –L. *ārēre,* to be dry.

arefaction. (L.) XVI cent. Coined from L. *ārefacere,* to make dry. –L. *ārē-re,* to be dry; and *facere,* to make.

Aright. (E.) For *on right,* in the right way.

Arise. (E.) M. E. *arisen.* A. S. *ārīsan.* – A. S. *ā-,* prefix; *rīsan,* to rise. See **Rise.**

Aristocracy. (Gk.) Modified from Gk. ἀριστοκρατία, government by the nobles or ' best' men. –Gk. ἄριστο-, for ἄριστος, best; and κρατεῖν, to be strong, govern, from κρατύς, strong. The form ἄρ-ιστος is a superlative from the base ἀρ- seen in ἀρ-ετή, excellence. Der. *aristocratic;* whence *aristocrat,* for ' aristocratic person.'

Arithmetic. (F.–L.–Gk.) In Sh. –F. *arithmétique;* Cot. –L. *arithmētica.* –Gk. ἀριθμητική, the science of numbers; fem. of ἀριθμητικός, adj., from ἀριθμέ-ειν, to number. –Gk. ἀριθμός, number, reckoning.

Ark, a chest, box; hence a large floating vessel. (L.) A. S. *arc.* –L. *arca,* a chest, box; cf. L. *arcēre,* to keep.

Arm (1), part of the body. (E.) M. E. *arm.* A. S. *earm.*+Du. *arm;* Icel. *armr;* Dan., Swed., and G. *arm;* Goth. *arms;* L. *armus,* the shoulder; Russ. *ramo,* shoulder. See Brugm. i. § 524.

Arm (2), to furnish with weapons. (F. –L.) F. *armer.* – L. *armāre,* to furnish with arms. –L. *arma,* arms.

armada, a fleet. (Span.–L.) Span

armada, an armed fleet; fem. of *armado,* pp. of *armar,* to arm. –L. *armāre,* to arm (above). **Doublet,** *army.*

armadillo, an animal. (Span. –L.) Span. *armadillo,* lit ' the little armed one,' because of its hard shell. Dimin. of *armado,* pp. of *armar,* to arm; as above.

armament. (L.) L. *armāmentum,* an equipment. –L. *armāre,* to arm, equip. –L. *arma,* arms.

armature, doublet of **armour.**

armistice. (F.–L.) F. *armistice.* – Mod. L. **armistitium,* coined on the analogy of *sōl-stitium,* i. e. solstice. –L. *armi-,* for *arma,* arms; and *-stitium,* for *-statium* (through atonic position), from *statum,* supine of *stāre,* to stand. (Cf. **Solstice.**)

armour. (F.–L.) M. E. *armour, armure.* –O. F. *armure, armeüre.* –L. *armātūra,* armour. – L. *armātus,* pp. of *armāre,* to arm. –L. *arma,* arms. **Doublet,** *armature.*

arms, s. pl. weapons. (F.–L.) M. E. *armes.* –O. F. *armes,* pl. –L. *arma,* neut. pl., arms, lit. ' fittings.' (√AR, to fit.)

army. (F.–L.) O. F. *armee,* fem. of pp. of *armer,* to arm. –L. *armāta,* fem. of pp. of *armāre,* to arm. –L. *arma,* arms.

Aroint thee! begone! Origin unknown. The usual reference to *ryntye* in Ray does not help us.

Aroma, a sweet smell. (L.–Gk.) Late L. *arōma.* –Gk. ἄρωμα, a spice, sweet herb. Der. *aromat-ic,* from the Gk. stem ἀρωματ-.

Around, prep. and adv. (E. *and* F.– L.) M. E. *around;* for *on round;* see **A-** (2) and **Round.**

Arouse. (E. *and* Scand.) From **A-** (4) and **Rouse.**

Arquebus, a kind of gun. (F.–Du.) F. *arquebuse,* 'an harquebuse, or handgun,' Cot.; Walloon *harkibuse,* dialectal variation of Mid. Du. *haeckbusse,* Du. *haakbus,* lit. ' a gun with a hook.' This refers to the hook whereby it was attached to a point of support. –Mid. Du. *haeck,* Du. *haak,* a hook; and Mid. Du. *busse,* Du. *bus,* a hand barrel, a gun. See **Hackbut.**

Arrack, an ardent spirit. (Arab.) Arab. *'araq,* sweat, juice, essence, distilled spirit. – Arab. root *'araqa,* to sweat. ¶ Sometimes shortened to *Rack;* cf. Span. *raque,* arrack.

Arraign. (F.−L.) M. E. *arainen.*−
O. F. *areisnier,* to speak to, discourse
with, cite, arraign.−O. F. *a* (L. *ad*), to ;
reisner, reisoner, to reason, from O. F.
reson, raison, reason, advice, from L. acc.
ratiōnem ; see **Reason.**

Arrange. (F. − L. *and* O. H. G.)
M. E. *arayngen, arengen.*−O. F. *arengier,*
to put into a rank.−O. F. *a* (L. *ad*), to ;
rangier, rengier, to range, from O. F.
rang, reng, a rank. See **Rank.**

Arrant, knavish, notoriously bad. (F.
−L.) This word is now ascertained to
be a mere variant of *errant* (cf. *parson* for
person). Chaucer has *theef erraunt,* arrant
thief, C. T. 17173 ; and see Piers Plowman, C. vii. 307. See **Errant.**

Arras, tapestry. (F.) So named from
Arras, in Artois, north of France.

Array, verb. (F.−L. *and* O. Low G.)
O. F. *arraier,* to array.−O. F. *arrai,
arroi,* preparation.−L. *ad* (becoming *ar-*
before *r*), to, for ; O. Low G. and O. Fries.
rēde (cf. Goth. *garaid-s*), ready, A. S.
rēde, ready ; so that to *array* is 'to get
ready.' See **Ready.**

Arrears, sb. pl. (F.−L.) From M. E.
arere, adv., in the rear.−O. F. *arere* (F.
arrière), behind.−Late L. *ad retro,* backward.−L. *ad,* to ; *retro,* behind. ¶ What
we now call *arrears* answers to M. E.
arerages, s. pl. formed from M. E. *arere*
with F. suffix *-age.*

Arrest, to stop. (F.−L.) O. F. *ares-
ter* (F. *arrêter*), to stay.−O. F. *a* (= L.
ad), to ; L. *restāre,* to stay, remain, from
re-, back, and *stāre,* to stand ; see **Rest**
(2).

Arrive. (F.−L.) F. *arriver.*−Late
L. *arrīpāre, adrīpāre,* to come to shore,
land.−L. *ad,* to ; *rīpa,* shore, bank. **Der.**
arriv-al.

Arrogate. (L.) From pp. of L. *arro-
gāre,* to ask, adopt, attribute to, add to.−
L. *ar-* (for *ad*), to ; *rogāre,* to ask. **Der.**
arrogant, from the pres. pt.

Arrow. (E.) M. E. *arewe, arwe.* A.S.
arwe, and *earh* (rare).+Icel. *ör,* an arrow
(gen. *örvar*) ; allied to Goth. *arhwazna,*
an arrow. From Teut. base *arhw-* ; cognate with L. *arc-us,* a bow.

arrow-root. (E.) So called, it is said,
because the tubers of the *Maranta* were
used as an antidote against poisoned
arrows.

Arse. (E.) M. E. *ars, ers.* A. S. *ærs.*
+Gk. ὄρρος, the rump. Idg. type **orsos.*

Arsenal. (Span.−Arab.) Span. *arsenal,* a magazine, dock-yard, arsenal ;
longer forms, *atarazanal, atarazana,* where
the *a-* answers to Arab. *al,* def. article.
Cf. Ital. *darsena,* a wet dock.−Arab. *dār
aç-çinā'ah,* a house of construction, place
for making things, dock-yard. − Arab. *dār,*
a house ; *al,* the ; and *çinā'ah,* art, trade,
construction.

Arsenic. (L. − Gk. − Arab. − Pers.)
Late L. *arsenicum.*−Gk. ἀρσενικόν, arsenic ;
seeming to mean a male principle (the alchemists had a strange fancy that metals were of
different sexes). But really borrowed from
Arab. *az-zernīkh* ; where *az* is for *al,* the,
def. art., and *zernīkh,* orpiment, is from
Pers. *zernī,* orpiment, yellow arsenic (from
zar, gold). See Devic, p. 4.

Arson, incendiarism. (F.−L.) O. F.
arson, incendiarism.−Late L. acc. *ar-
siōnem,* a burning.−L. *ars-us,* pp. of
ardēre, to burn. See **Ardent.**

Art (1), ᵖ p. s. pres. of verb. (E.) See
Are.

Art (2), skill. (F.−L.) M. E. *art.*−
O. F. *art.*−L. *artem,* acc. of *ars,* skill.

Artery. (L.−Gk.) L. *artēria,* properly
the wind-pipe ; also, an artery.−Gk. ἀρτη-
ρία, wind-pipe, artery.

Artesian, adj. (F.) *Artesian wells* are
named from F. *Artésien,* adj. formed from
Artois, a province in the north of France,
where these wells were early in use.

Artichoke. (Ital.−Arab.) Ital. *arti-
ciocco,* a corrupt form ; Florio also gives
the spellings *archiciocco, archicioffo* ; also
(without the *ar,* which answers to the
Arab. def. art. *al,* the) the forms *carciocco,
carcioffo.* Cf. Span. *alcachofa,* an artichoke.−Arab. *al kharshūf,* or *harshaf,* an
artichoke. ¶ Not Arab. *ar'dī shaukī*
(Diez), which is a modern corrupt form
borrowed from Italian.

Article, a small item, part of speech.
(F.−L.) F. *article.*−L. *articulus,* a joint,
knuckle, article in grammar ; lit. ' a small
joint.' Dimin. of *artus,* a joint, limb.

articulate. (L.) L. *articulātus,* distinct ; pp. of *articulāre,* to supply with
joints, divide by joints.−L. *articulus,* a
joint (above).

Artifice. (F.−L.) In Milton.−F.
artifice.−L. *artificium,* a trade, handi-
craft ; hence skill.−L. *arti-,* stem of *ars,*
art ; and *-fic-,* for *facere,* to make. **Der.**
artific-er, a skilled workman.

artillery. (F.−L.) O. F. *artillerie,*

equipment of war, machines of war, including cross-bows, &c., in early times. — O. F. *artiller*, to equip. — Late L. *artillāre, to make machines; a verb inferred from the sb. *artillātor*, a maker of machines. Extended from *arti*-, stem of *ars*, art. We also find *artilliātor*, answering to an older *articulātor; also Late L. *articulum*, artifice; *articula*, art.

artisan, a workman. (F. — Ital. — L.) F. *artisan*. — Ital. *artigiano*, a workman. — Late L. *artītiānus, not found, but formed from L. *artītus*, cunning, artful. — L. *arti*·, stem of *ars*, art.

As, conj. (E.) M. E. *as, als, alse, also, al so. As* is a contraction of *also*. (Proved by Sir F. Madden.) See **Also.**

Asafœtida, Assafœtida, a gum. (Med. L. — Pers. *and* L.) From Pers. *āzā*, mastic; the L. *fœtida*, fetid, refers to its offensive smell. See **Fetid.**

Asbestos, a mineral. (Gk.) Gk. ἄσβεστος, unquenchable; because it is incombustible. — Gk. ἀ-, neg. prefix; and -σβεστος, quenchable, from σβέννυμι, I quench, extinguish. See Brugm. i. § 653.

Ascend. (L.) L. *ascendere*, to climb up. — L. *ad*, to ; *scandere*, to climb. See Scan. Der. *ascens-ion*, from pp. *ascensus*.

Ascertain. (F. — L.) From O. F. *acertainer, acertener*, to make certain (with *s* inserted). — F. *a* (= L. *ad*, to); and *certain*, certain. See **Certain.**

Ascetic. (Gk.) Gk. ἀσκητικός, given to exercise, industrious; applied to hermits, who strictly exercised themselves in religious devotion. — Gk. ἀσκητής, one who practises an art, an athlete. — Gk. ἀσκεῖν, to work, exercise ; also, to mortify the body, as an ascetic.

Ascititious, incidental. (L.) Coined, as if from L. *ascītīcius, from *ascītus*, pp. of *asciscere*, or *adsciscere*, to receive, learn. — L. *ad*, to; *sciscere*, to learn, inceptive form of *scīre*, to know.

Ascribe. (L.) L. *ascrībere*, to write down to one's account. — L. *a*- (for *ad*), to ; *scrībere*, to write.

Ash, a tree. (E.) M. E. *asch*. A. S. *æsc*. + Du. *esch* ; Icel. *askr* ; Dan. and Swed. *ask* ; G. *esche*. Teut. type *askiz. Cf. Russ. *iasene*, Lith. *ŭsis*, ash.

Ashamed. (E.) A. S. *āscamod*, pp. of *āscamian*, to put to shame. — A. S. *ā*-, extremely ; *scamian*, to shame, from *scamu*, shame. β. Or for A. S. *ofscamod*, with the same sense (with prefix *of*-, off, very).

Ashes. (E.) The pl. of *ash*, which is little used. M. E. *asche, axe*, sing. ; the pl. is commonly *aschen, axen*, but in Northern E. it is *asches, askes*. A. S. *æsce*, pl. *æscan, æxan, ascan.* + Du. *asch* ; Icel. and Swed. *aska* ; Dan. *aske* ; Goth. *azgo*, pl. *azgon* ; G. *asche*. Teut. stems *askōn-, *azgōn-.

Ashlar, Ashler, a facing made of squared stones. (F. — L.) It consists of thin slabs of stone for facing a building ; formerly applied to a square hewn stone ; and, probably, so called because it took the place of the *wooden* beams used for the same purpose. — O. F. *aiseler* (Livre des Rois), extended from O. F. *aiselle, aisiele*, a little board, dimin. of *ais*, a plank. — L. *axilla*, dimin. of L. *axis* an axis, also, a board, a plank.

Ashore. (E.) For *on shore*.

Aside. (E.) For *on side*.

Ask. (E.) M. E. *asken, axien*. A. S. *āscian, āhsian, ācsian* ; the last answers to prov. E. *ax*. + Du. *eischen* ; Swed. *äska* ; Dan. *æske* ; G. *heischen*, O. H. G. *eiscōn*. Teut. types *aiskōn, *aiskōjan. Cf. Russ. *iskate*, Lith. *jëskóti*, to seek ; Skt. *ichchhā*, a wish, desire, *esh*, to search.

Askance, obliquely. (Ital. — L.) Spelt *a-scance* by Sir T. Wyat ; *ascanche* by Palsgrave, who gives *de trauers, en lorgnant*, as the F. equivalent. Etym. doubtful ; but prob. due to Ital. *scansare*, ' to go a-slope or *a-sconce*, or a-skew, to go sidelin ;' Florio. — Ital. *s*- (= Lat. *ex*, out of the way) ; and *cansare*, ' to go a-slope, give place ;' Florio. This is derived, according to Diez, from L. *campsāre*, to turn round a place, bend round it ; cf. Gk. κάμπτειν, to bend.

Askew, awry. (O. Low G.) For *on skew* ; Hexham gives M. Du. *scheef*, ' askew, awry ;' see **Skew.**

Aslant. (Scand.) For *on slant*.

Asleep. (E.) For *on sleep* ; Acts xiii. 36.

Aslope. (E.) For *on slope*.

Asp, Aspic, a serpent. (F. — L. — Gk.) F. *aspe, aspic*. — L. *aspidem*, acc. of *aspis*. — Gk. ἀσπίς (gen. ἀσπίδος), an asp.

Asparagus, a vegetable. (L. — Gk. — Pers. ?) L. *asparagus*. — Gk. ἀσπάραγος. Supposed to be of Pers. origin ; cf. Zend *çparegha*, a shoot, a prong; Lithuan. *spurgas*, a shoot (Fick, Prellwitz).

Aspect. (L.) L. *aspectus*, look. — L. *aspectus*, pp. of *aspicere*, to look. — L. *a*- (for *ad*), to, at ; *specere*, to look.

27

Aspen, Asp, a tree. (E.) M. E. *asp,* Chaucer, C. T. 2923; *aspen* is an adj. (like *golden*), and is used for *aspen-tree*; cf. Ch. C. T. 7249. A. S. *æspe, æps.* + Du. *esp*; Icel. *ösp,* Dan. and Swed. *asp*; G. *espe, äspe.* Cf. Lithuan. *apuszis*; Russ. *osina.*

Asperity. (F. — L.) F. *aspérité.* — L. *asperitātem,* acc. of *asperitās,* roughness — L. *asper,* rough.

Asperse, to cast calumny upon. (L.) From L. *aspersus,* pp. of *aspergere,* to besprinkle. — L. *as-* (for *ad*); *spargere,* to scatter.

Asphalt. (Gk.) Gk. ἄσφαλτος, ἄσφαλ-τον, asphalt, bitumen. A foreign word.

Asphodel. (Gk) Gk. ἀσφόδελος. a plant of the lily kind. **Der.** *daffodil,* q. v.

Asphyxia, suffocation. (Gk.) Gk. ἀ-σφυξία, a stopping of the pulse; cf. ἄ-σφυκτος, without pulsation. — Gk. ἀ-, not; and σφύξις, the pulse, from σφύζειν, to pulsate; cf. σφυγμός, pulsation.

Aspire. (F. — L.) F. *aspirer,* to breathe, covet, aspire to. — L. *aspīrāre,* lit. to breathe towards. — L. *a-* (for *ad*), to; *spīrāre,* to breathe. **Der.** *aspir-ate,* v. to pronounce with a full breathing.

Ass. (C. — L.) M. E. *asse.* A. S. *assa.* — Irish *assan.* — L. *asinus*; whence also W. *asyn,* Swed. *åsna,* Icel. *asni.* Hence also (or from L. dimin. *asellus*) came Irish *asal,* Du. *ezel,* Dan. and G. *esel,* Goth. *asilus.* Prob. of Semitic origin; cf. Arab. *atān,* Heb. *āthōn,* a she-ass.

Assail. (F. — L.) M. E. *asailen.* — O. F. *asaillir,* to attack. — Late L. *assalīre*; L. *assilīre.* — L. *ad,* to; *salīre,* to leap, rush forth. See **Salient.**

Assart, the offence of grubbing up trees and destroying the coverts of a forest. (F. — L.) From A. F. *assarter* F. *essarter,* to grub up, clear ground of shrubs. — L. *ex,* out, thoroughly; Late L. *sartāre,* frequent. of L. *sarrīre, sarīre,* to grub up weeds.

Assassin, a secret murderer. (F. — Arab.) F. *assassin.* From Arab. *ḥashāshīn,* pl., eaters of 'hashish,' the name of a sect in the 13th century; the 'Old Man of the Mountain' roused his followers' spirits by help of this preparation, and sent them to stab his enemies, esp. the leading crusaders. — Arab. *ḥashīsh,* an intoxicating preparation from the *dried* leaves of *Cannabis indica,* a kind of hemp. Cf. Arab. *ḥashīy,* dry.

Assault. (F. — L.) O. F. *assalt.* — L.

ad, to; *saltus,* a leap, attack, from *saltus,* pp. of *salīre,* to leap. See **Assail.**

Assay, s.; the same as **Essay,** q. v.

Assemble. (F. — L.) O. F. *assembler.* — Late L. *assimulāre,* to collect (different from L. *assimulāre,* to feign). — L. *as-* (for *ad*), to; *simul,* together.

Assent. (F. — L.) O. F. *assentir* — L. *assentīre,* to assent, agree to. — L. *as-* (for *ad*), to; *sentīre,* to feel, perceive.

Assert. (L.) From L. *assertus,* pp. of *asserere,* to add to, claim, assert. — L. *as-* (for *ad*), to; *serere,* to join, connect.

Assess, to fix a tax. (F. — L.) O. F. *assesser.* — Late L. *assessāre,* to sit as assessor, to assess; cf. L. sb. *assessor,* one who adjusted taxes; orig. a judge's assistant, one who sat by him. — L. *assessus,* pp. of *assidēre,* to sit near. See **Assize** (1).

Assets, sufficient effects of a deceased debtor. (F. — L.) O. F. *assez* (pron. *assets*), sufficient (to pay with); properly an adv., but, in E., mistaken to be a pl. sb. — L. *ad satis,* up to what is enough.

Asseverate. (L.) L. *asseuērātus,* pp. of *asseuērāre,* to speak in earnest. — L. *as-* (for *ad*), to; *seuērus,* earnest.

Assiduous. (L.) L. *assidu-us,* sitting down to, applying closely to; with suffix *-ous.* — L. *assidēre,* to sit near. — L. *as-* (for *ad*), at, near; *sedēre,* to sit. See **Sit.**

Assign. (F. — L.) O. F. *assigner.* — L. *assignāre,* to assign, mark out to. — L. *as-* (for *ad*), to; *signāre,* to mark, from *signum,* a mark, sign.

Assimilate. (L.) From pp. of L. *assimilāre,* to make like to. — L. *as-* (for *ad*), to; *similis,* like. See **Similar.**

Assist. (F. — L.) F. *assister.* — L. *assistere,* to step to, approach, assist. — L. *as-* (for *ad*), to; *sistere,* to place, stand, from *stāre,* to stand.

Assize (1), a session of a court of justice. (F. — L.) M. E. *assise.* — O. F. *assise,* an assembly of judges; also a tax, an impost. Probably fem. pp. of O. F. *asseoir,* to sit near, assist a judge. — L. *assidēre,* to sit near; see **Assiduous, Assess.**

assize (2), a fixed quantity or dimension. (F. — L.) O. F. *assise,* a tax, impost; the Late L. *assīsa* was also used in the sense of a fixed allowance of provisions. The same word as the above. Another form is **Size,** q. v.

Associate. (L.) From pp. of L. *associāre,* to join to. — L. *as-* (for *ad-*), to; *sociāre,* to join, associate. — L. *socius,* a companion, lit. follower.—L. *sequī,* to follow. See **Sequence.**

Assoil, to absolve, acquit. (F.—L.) M. E. *assoilen.*—O. F. *as(s)oille,* pres. subj. of *assoudre, asoldre,* to absolve.—L. *absoluere,* to absolve. — L. *ab,* from ; *soluere,* to loosen. See **Solve.** Doublet, *absolve.*

Assonant. (L.) L. *assonant-,* stem of *assonans,* sounding like ; pres. pt. of *assonāre,* to respond to.—L. *as-* (for *ad-*), to ; *sonāre,* to sound, from *sonus,* sound.

Assort. (F.—L.) O. F. *assortir,* to sort, assort, match (15th century).—O. F. *as-* (=L. *as-,* for L. *ad*), to ; *sort-,* stem of L. *sors,* lot. See **Sort.**

Assuage. (F.—L.) O. F. *asouagier, asoagier,* to soften, appease ; (Prov. *asuaviar*).—F. *a* (=L. *ad*), to ; and L. *suāuis,* sweet. See **Suave.**

Assume. (L.) L. *assūmere* (pp. *assumptus*), to take to oneself.—L. *as-* (for *ad*), to ; *sūmere,* to take, which is from *emere,* to take, with a prefix of doubtful origin. Der. *assumpt-ion* (from the pp.).

Assure. (F.—L.) M. E. *assuren.*— O. F. *aseürer,* to make secure.—O. F. *a* (= L. *aa*), to ; *seür,* sure, from L. *sēcūrus,* secure, sure. See **Sure.**

Aster, a flower. (Gk.) Gk. ἀστήρ, a star. See **Star.**

asterisk. (Gk.) Gk. ἀστερίσκος, a little star, also an asterisk *, used for distinguishing fine passages in MSS.—Gk. ἀστερ-, stem of ἀστήρ, a star.

asteroid, a minor planet. (Gk.) Properly an adj., signifying ' star-like.'—Gk. ἀστερο-ειδής, star-like.—Gk. ἀστερο-, for ἀστήρ, a star ; and εἶδ-ος, form, figure.

Asthma, difficulty in breathing. (Gk.) Gk. ἄσθμα, panting.—Gk. ἀά(ειν, to breathe hard. Cf. Gk. ἄημι, I blow. See **Air.**

Astir. (E.) For *on stir* ; Barbour's Bruce, xix. 577.

Astonish, Astound. (F.—L.) The addition of *ish,* as in *extingu-ish,* is due to analogy with other verbs in *-ish.* M. E. *astonien, astunien, astonen* ; whence later *astony,* afterwards lengthened to *astonish* ; also *astound,* by the addition of excrescent *d* after *n,* as in *sound,* from F. *son.* All from O. F. *estoner* (mod. F. *étonner*), to amaze.—Late L. **extonāre,* to thunder out, from *ex,* out, and *tonāre,* to thunder. Cf. L. *attonāre,* to thunder at, astound (with prefix *at-* for L. *ad,* at).

Astray. For *on stray* ; Barbour's Bruce, xiii. 195. See **Stray.**

Astriction. (L.) From L. acc. *astrictiōnem,* a drawing together.—L. *astrictus,* pp. of *astringere* ; see **Astringent.**

Astride. (E.) For *on (the) stride.*

Astringent. (L.) From stem of pres. pt. of *astringere,* to bind or draw closely together.—L. *a-* (for *ad*), to ; *stringere,* to draw tight.

Astrology. (F.—L.—Gk.) F. *astrologie.*—L. *astrologia,* (1) astronomy ; (2) astrology, or science of the stars.—Gk. ἀστρολογία, astronomy.—Gk. ἀστρο-, for ἄστρον, a star ; and -λογία, allied to λόγος, a discourse, from λέγειν, to speak.

Astronomy. (F.—L.—Gk.) F. *astronomie.*—L. *astronomia.*—Gk. ἀστρονομία.—Gk. ἄστρο-ν, a star ; and -νομία, allied to νόμος, law, from νέμειν, to distribute.

Astute. (L.) L. *astūtus,* crafty, cunning.—L. *astus,* craft.

Asunder. (E.) For *on sunder.* A. S. *on-sundran,* apart. See **Sunder.**

Asylum. (L.—Gk.) L. *asȳlum.*—Gk. ἄσυλον, an asylum ; neut. of ἄσυλος, adj. unharmed, safe from violence.—Gk. ἀ-, not ; and σύλη, a right of seizure ; cf. συλάω, I despoil an enemy.

Asymptote, a line which, indefinitely produced, does not meet the curve which it continually approaches. (Gk.) Gk. ἀσύμπτωτος, not falling together, not coincident. — Gk. ἀ-, not ; σύμ, for σύν, together ; and πτωτός, falling, from πίπτειν (pt. t. πέπτωκα), to fall. (√PET.)

At. (E.) M. E. *at,* A. S. *æt.* + Icel. *at* ; Goth. *at* ; Dan. *ad* ; Swed. *åt* ; L. *ad.*

Atabal, a kettle-drum. (Span.—Arab.) Span. *atabal.*—Arab. *at* (for *al,* def. article); *tabl,* a drum.

Ataghan ; see **Yataghan.**

Atheism. (Gk.) Coined from Gk. ἄθε-ος, denying the gods, without a god ; with suffix *-ism.*—Gk. ἀ-, negative prefix ; θεός, a god.

Athirst. (E.) M. E. *ofthurst, athurst,* very thirsty ; orig. pp. of a verb. A. S. *ofþyrsted,* very thirsty ; pp. of *ofþyrstan,* to be very thirsty. — A. S. *of,* very (prefix) ; and *þyrstan,* to thirst ; see **Thirst.**

Athlete. (L.—Gk.) L. *athlēta.*—Gk. ἀθλητής, a combatant, contender in games. — Gk. ἀθλέ-ειν, to contend for a prize.—Gk. ἆθλος (for ἀϝεθλος), a contest ; ἆθλον (for ἀϝεθλον), a prize. See **Wed.**

Athwart, across. For *on thwart,* on the transverse, across ; see **Thwart.**

Atlas. (Gk.) Named after Atlas, the demi-god who was said to bear the world on his shoulders; his figure used often to appear on the title-page of atlases. − Gk. Ἄτλας (gen. Ἄτλαντος), prob. 'the sustainer' or bearer, from √TEL, to bear.

atlantic, an ocean, named after Mt. Atlas, in the N.W. of Africa. (Gk.) From Ἀτλαντι-, stem of Ἄτλας; with suffix -κος.

Atmosphere. (Gk.) Lit. 'a sphere of air round the earth.' Coined from ἀτμό-, stem of ἀτμός, vapour, air; and **Sphere.**

Atoll, a group of coral islands forming a ring. (Maldive Islands.) 'We derive the expression from the Maldive islands . . . where the form of the word is *atolu*. It is prob. connected with the Singhalese prep. *ätul*, inside.' (Yule.)

Atom. (F. − L. − Gk.) F. *atome* (Cot.). − L. *atomus.* − Gk. ἄτομος, sb., an indivisible particle; allied to ἄτομος, adj., indivisible. − Gk. ἀ-, not; τομ-, o-grade of τεμ-, as seen in τέμ-νειν, to cut, divide.

Atone, to set at one, to reconcile. (E.) Made up from the words *at* and *one*, and due to the frequent use of the phrase *at oon*, at one (i. e. reconciled) in Middle English. *Al at on* = all agreed; Rob. of Glouc. p. 113. Tyndall has *atonemaker*, i. e. reconciler, Works, p. 158. **Der.** *atonement*, i. e. *at-one-ment*; we actually find the word *onement*, reconciliation, in old authors; see Hall, Satires, iii. 7. 69.

Atrocity. (F. − L.) F. *atrocité*, Cot. − L. *atrōcitātem*, acc. of *atrōcitās*, cruelty. − L. *atrōci-*, from *atrox*, cruel.

Atrophy. (Gk.) Gk. ἀτροφία, want of nourishment or food, hunger, wasting away of the body, atrophy. − Gk. ἀ-, not; and τρέφειν (pt. t. τέ-τροφ-α), to nourish.

Attach. (F. − Teut.?) O. F. *attacher*, to attach, fasten. − O. F. *a*, for L. *ad*, to; and (perhaps) a Low G. word with the sense of E. *tack*, a nail. See **Tack.** Cf. Picard *ataker*, to attach; Bret. *tacha*, to fasten, from *tach*, a tack, nail; and see **Detach, Attack.** **Der.** *attach-ment.*

    attack. (F. − Ital. − Teut.?) F. *attaquer.* − Ital. *attaccare*, to fasten, attach; *attaccare battaglia*, 'to ioyne battell,' Florio. Cognate with F. *attacher*; so that *attack* is a doublet of *attach.*

Attain. (F. − L.) M. E. *ateinen.* − O. F. *ateign-*, pres. stem of *ateindre*, *ataindre*, to reach to. − L. *attingere*, to

attain. − L. *at-* (for *ad*), to; *tangere*, to touch.

attainder. (F. − L.) From the O. F. *ateindre*, verb, to convict; used substantively; see above.

attaint, to convict. (F. − L.) From M. E. *atteynt*, *ateynt*, convicted, whence the verb has been evolved; orig. pp. of O. F. *ateindre* (above). ¶ In no way allied to *taint.*

Attar of Roses. (Arab.) Also, less correctly, *otto of roses*, i.e. perfume. − Arab. ʿiṭr, perfume. − Arab. root ʿaṭara, to smell sweetly.

Attemper. (F. − L.) O. F. *atemprer*, to modify. − O.F. *a* (= L. *ad*), to; *temprer*, *temperer*, to temper. − L. *temperāre*, to apportion, regulate, qualify. See **Temper.**

Attempt. (F. − L.) O. F. *atempter*, to undertake. − L. *attentāre*, to attempt. − L. *at-* (for *ad*), to; *tentāre*, to try; see **Tempt.**

Attend. (F. − L.) O. F. *atendre*, to wait. − L. *attendere* (pp. *attentus*), to stretch towards, give heed to. − L. *at-* (for *ad*), to; *tendere*, to stretch. **Der.** *attention* (from the pp.); *attent*, adj., 2 Chron. vi. 40, vii. 15.

Attenuate. (L.) From pp. of L. *attenuāre*, to make thin. − L. *at-* (for *ad*), to; *tenu-is*, thin. See **Thin.**

Attest. (L.) L. *attestārī*, to be witness to. − L. *at-* (= *ad*), to; *testārī*, to be witness, from L. *testis*, a witness.

Attic, a small upper room. (L. − Gk.) It orig. meant the whole of a parapet wall, terminating the upper façade of an edifice. Named from the *Attic* order of architecture; see Phillips, ed. 1706. − L. *Atticus.* − Gk. Ἀττικός, Attic, Athenian. Cf. F. *attique*, an attic; *Attique*, Attic.

Attire. (F. − Teut.?) M. E. *atir*, *atyr*, sb.; *atiren*, *atyren*, verb. − O. F. *atirier*, to adorn (Roquefort). − O. F. *a* (= L. *ad*, prefix); and O. F. *tire*, *tiere*, a row, file; so that *atirier* is properly 'to arrange.' Cf. O. Prov. *tiera*, a row (Bartsch). See **Tier.**

Attitude. (Ital. − L.) Orig. a painter's term, from Italy. − Ital. *attitudine*, aptness, skill, attitude. − L. *aptitūdinem*, acc. of *aptitūdo*, aptitude. − L. *aptus*, apt.

Attorney. (F. − L.) M. E. *attourne.* − O. F. *atorne* [i. e. *atorné*], lit. 'one appointed or constituted;' pp. of *atorner*, to direct, prepare, constitute. − F. *a* (= L. *ad*), to; O. F. *torner*, to turn, from L. *tornāre*. See **Turn.**

Attract. (L.) From L. *attractus*, pp. of *attrahere*, to attract. – L. *at-* (=*ad*), to ; *trahere*, to draw.

Attribute. (L.) From *attribūtus*, pp. of L. *attribuere*, to assign. – L. *at-* (=*ad*), to ; *tribuere*, to assign ; see **Tribute**.

Attrition. (L.) From L. acc. *attrītiōnem*, a rubbing or wearing away. – L. *attrītus*, pp. of *atterere*, to rub away. – L. *at-* (=*ad*), at ; *terere*, to rub. See **Trite**.

Attune, to bring to a like tune. (L. and L. – Gk.) From L. *at-* (=*ad*), to ; and E. **Tune**, q. v.

Auburn. (F. – L.) M. E. *aborne*, *auburne*, orig. citron-coloured or light yellow. – O. F. *alborne*, *auborne*, blond (Godefroy). – Late L. *alburnus*, whitish, light-coloured. Torriano explains Ital. *alburno* by ' that whitish colour of women's hair called an *aburn* colour.' Cf. L. *alburnum*, the sap-wood or inner bark of trees (Pliny). – L *albus*, white.

Auction. (L.) L. *auctiōnem*, acc. of *auctio*, a sale by auction, lit. ' an increase,' because the sale is to the highest bidder. – L. *auctus*, pp. of *augēre*, to increase. See **Eke**.

Audacious. (F. – L.) F. *audacieux*, bold, audacious. – L. **audāciōsus*, not found ; extended from L. *audāci-*, from *audax*, bold. – L. *audēre*, to dare.

Audience. (F. – L.) F. *audience*, ' an audience or hearing ; ' Cot. – L. *audientia*, a hearing. – L. *audient-*, stem of pres. pt. of *audīre*, to hear. For **auisdīre* ; cf. Gk. αἰσθέσθαι, to perceive, for ἀϝισθεσθαι. Brugm. i. § 240.

audible. (L.) Late L. *audībilis*, that can be heard. – L. *audīre*, to hear.

audit. (L.) From L. *audītus*, a hearing. – L. *audīre*, to hear ; whence also *audi-tor*.

Auger. (E.) For *nauger*. M.E. *nauegar* (=*navegar*), *nauger*, a tool for boring holes. – A. S. *nafogār*, an auger, lit. nave-piercer, for boring holes in the nave of a wheel. – A. S. *nafu*, a nave ; *gār*, a piercer, that which gores ; see **Nave** (1) and **Gore** (3). + Du. *avegaar* (for *navegaar*) ; Icel. *nafarr* ; Dan. *naver* ; Swed. *nafvare* ; O. H. G. *nabagēr*.

Aught. (E.) M. E. *aht*, *aght*, *aught*. A. S. *āht*, earlier *āwiht* ; from *ā*, ever, and *wiht*, a creature, wight, whit ; lit. ' e'er a whit.' See **Whit**.

Augment. (F. – L.) F. *augmenter*. – L. *augmentāre*, to enlarge. – L. *augmentum*,

an increase. – L. *augēre*, to increase. See **Auction**.

Augur. (L.) M. E. *augur*. – L. *augur*, a sooth-sayer ; said to mean a diviner by the flight and cries of birds. Hence a supposed etymology (not certain) from *auis*, a bird, and -*gur*, telling, allied to *garrīre*, to shout. Cf. L. *au-ceps*, a bird-catcher.

August. (L.) L. *augustus*, venerable ; whence E. *august*, venerable, and *August*, the month named after Augustus Caesar. Cf. Skt. *ōjas*, strength. Brugm. i. § 213.

Auk, a sea-bird. (Scand.) Swed. *alka* ; Dan. *alke* ; Icel. *alka*, *ālka*, an auk.

Aunt. (F. – L.) M. E. *aunte*. – A. F. *aunte* ; O. F. *ante* (mod. F. *t-ante*). – L. *amita*, a father's sister. Cf. G. *amme*, nurse.

Aureate. (L.) Late L. *aureātus*, gilt, from *aureus*, golden ; in place of L. *aurātus*, gilded, pp. of *aurāre*, to gild. – L. *aurum*, gold ; O. L. *ausum*. Der. *aurelia*, a gold-coloured chrysalis ; *aur-e-ol-a*, *aur-e-ole*, the halo of golden glory in paintings ; *auriferous*, gold-producing, from *ferre*, to bear.

Auricula, a plant. (L.) L. *auricula*, the lobe of the ear ; used to mean the ' bear's ear,' a kind of primrose ; see below.

auricular, told in the ear, secret. (L.) Late L. *auriculāris*, in the phr. *auriculāris confessio*, auricular confession. – L. *auricula*, the lobe of the ear ; double dimin. from *auri-s*, the ear. See **Ear**.

Aurora, the dawn. (L.) L. *aurōra*, the dawn ; from prehistoric **ausōsa*. + Gk. Æolic αὔως, Ion, ἠώς, dawn, from prehistoric **αὔσως*. See **East**.

Auscultation, a listening. (L.) L. *auscultātiōnem*, acc. of *auscultātio*, a listening ; from the pp. of *auscultāre*, to listen. – L. **aus-*, base of *auris*, the ear. See **Ear**.

Auspice, favour, patronage. (F. – L.) F. *auspice*, a token of things by the flight of birds, an omen, good fortune. – L. *auspicium*, a watching of birds for the purpose of augury. Short for **auispicium*. – L. *aui-*, for *auis*, a bird ; and *spicere*, *specere*, to spy, look into.

Austere. (F. – L. – Gk.) M. E. *austere*. – O. F. *austere*. – L. *austērus*, harsh, severe. – Gk. αὐστηρός, making the tongue dry, harsh. – Gk. αὔειν, to dry. See **Sere**.

Austral. (F. – L. ; *or* L.) We find F. *australe*, ' southerly ; ' Cot. – L. *Austrālis*, southerly. – L. *Auster*, the South wind.

Authentic. (F. – L. –Gk.) M. E. *autentike, autentik.* –O. F. *autentique,* later *authentique* (Cot.). – L. *authenticus,* original, written with the author's own hand. –Gk. αὐθεντικός, vouched for, warranted. –Gk. αὐθέντης, also αὐτο-έντης, one who does things with his own hand, a 'self-worker'; see Auto-. β. Gk. ἕντης (for *σέντης) is prob. allied to L. *sons* (gen. *sontis*), guilty, responsible.

Author. (F. – L.) M. E. *autour, autor;* later *author* (with *th* once sounded as *t,* but now as *th* in thin). –O. F. *autor* (Bartsch). –L. *auctōrem,* acc. of *auctor,* an originator, lit. 'increaser, grower.' –L. *augēre,* to increase. Cf. Auction.

Auto-, prefix. (Gk.) Gk. αὐτο-, stem of αὐτός, self. Der. *auto-biography,* a biography written by oneself (see Biography); *autograph,* something in one's own handwriting, from Gk. γράφειν, to write (see Graphic).

autocracy. (Gk.) Adapted (with suffix *-cy* for Gk. -τεια) from Gk. αὐτοκράτεια, absolute power. –Gk. αὐτο-, self; -κράτεια (in compounds), power; from κρατέειν, to rule. – Gk. κρατύς, strong; cognate with E. Hard.

automaton, a self-moving machine. (G.) Gk. αὐτόματον, neut. of αὐτόματος, self-moving. –Gk. αὐτό-, for αὐτός, self; and -ματος, cognate with Skt. *matás,* thought, considered, known, pp. of *man,* to think. (√MEN.)

autonomy, self-government. (Gk.) Gk. αὐτονομία, independence. –Gk. αὐτόνομος, free, living by one's own laws. –Gk. αὐτό-, self; and νόμος, law, from νέμομαι, I sway, νέμειν, to distribute.

autopsy, personal inspection. (Gk.) Gk. αὐτοψία, a seeing with one's own eyes. –Gk. αὐτο-, self; ὄψις, sight (see Optic).

Auto-da-fe. (Port. –L.) Lit. 'decree of faith;' a judgment of the Inquisition, also, the execution of such judgment, when the decree or sentence is read to the victims. –Port. *auto,* action, decree; *da,* short for *de a,* of the; *fé,* faith. [The Span. form is *auto de fé,* without the article *la* = Port. *a.*] –L. *actum,* acc. of *actus,* act, deed; *dē,* prep.; *illa,* fem. of *ille,* he; *fidem,* acc. of *fidēs,* faith.

Autumn. (F. –L.) M. E. *autumpne.* –O.F. *autompne.* –L. *autumnus, auctumnus,* autumn. (Perhaps allied to *augēre,* to increase.)

Auxiliary. (L.) L. *auxiliārius,*

helping, assisting. –L. *auxilium,* help. – L. *augēre,* to increase.

Avadavat, a finch-like E. Indian bird. (Arab. *and* Pers.) Formerly *amadavat* (N. E. D.); or *amudavad,* N. and Q. 6 S. ii. 198. Named from the city of *Ahmedābād,* whence they were imported. –Arab. *Ahmed,* a proper name; Pers. *ābād,* a city.

Avail. (F. –L.) M. E. *auailen* (= *availen*). Compounded of O. F. *a,* to; and *vail-,* tonic stem of O. F. *valoir* (*valer*), to be of use. –L. *ad,* to; *ualēre,* to be strong.

Avalanche. (F. –L.) F. *avalanche,* the descent of snow into a valley. –F. *avaler,* to swallow; but the old sense was 'to let fall down.' –F. *aval,* downward, lit. 'to the valley.' –F. *a* (=L. *ad*), to; *val,* vale, from L. *uallem,* acc. of *uallis,* a valley.

Avarice. (F. – L.) M. E. *auarice* (with *u* for *v*). –F. *avarice.* –L. *auāritia,* greediness. – L. *auārus,* greedy; cf. L. *auidus,* greedy. –L. *auēre,* to wish, desire.

Avast, stop, hold fast. (Du.) Du. *hou vast, houd vast,* hold fast. –Du. *hou,* short form of *houd,* imper. of *houden,* to hold (see Hold); and *vast,* fast (see Fast).

Avatar. (Skt.) Skt. *avatāra,* descent; hence, the descent of a Hindu deity in incarnate form. –Skt. *ava,* down; and *tr̥ī,* to pass over, pass.

Avaunt, begone! (F. – L.) A.F. *avaunt;* O.F. *avant,* forward! See Advance.

Ave, hail. (L.) Short for *Auē Maria,* hail, Mary (Luke i. 28). –L. *auē,* hail! imper. sing. of *auēre,* to fare well.

Avenge. (F. –L.) O. F. *avengier,* to avenge. – F. *a* (L. *ad*), to; *vengier,* to avenge, from L. *uindicāre,* to lay claim to, also, to avenge. See Vindicate.

Aventail, the mouth-piece of a visor. (F. –L.) A.F. *aventaille;* O.F. *esventail,* air-hole. –O.F. *esventer,* to expose to air. – L. *ex,* out; *uentus,* wind. See Ventail.

Avenue. (F. –L.) F. *avenue, advenue,* access; hence an approach to a house (esp. one shaded by trees); fem. of *avenu,* pp. of F. *avenir,* to come to. –L. *ad,* to; *uenīre,* to come.

Aver. (F. –L.) A.F. and O. F. *averer.* –Late L. *auērāre, aduērāre,* to affirm to be true. –L. *ad,* to; *uērus,* true.

Average, an equalised estimate. (F.) Formerly a duty, tax, impost; then, an extra charge on goods, the incidence of such a charge, the general estimate or apportionment of loss of goods, &c. Formed, with suffix *-age*, from F. *avar-ie*, now usually ' damage ' (cf. Span. *averia*, *haberia*, ' the custom paid for goods that are exported ' (Pineda), Port. and Ital. *avaria*, Late L. *avaria*, *averia*). A Mediterranean maritime term, orig. signifying ' duty charged on goods ' (G. P. Marsh, in N. E. D.). Origin unknown ; perhaps from Ital. *avere*, *havere*, goods, chattels (F. *avoir*), a sb. use of *havere*, *haver* (L. *habēre*), to possess. ¶ Not from Arab. *'avār*, damage, which is borrowed from Ital. *avaria*, in a late sense.

Avert. (L.) L. *ā-uertere*, to turn away. ─ L. *ā* (= *ab*), off, away ; *uertere*, to turn. Der. *averse*, from L. pp. *āuersus*.

Aviary. (L.) L. *auiārium*, a place for birds ; neut. of adj. *auiārius*, belonging to birds.─ L. *aui-*, stem of *auis*, a bird.

Avidity. (F.─ L.) F. *avidité*, greediness, eagerness.─ L. *auiditātem*, acc. of *auiditās*, eagerness.─ L. *auidus*, greedy, desirous.─ L. *auēre*, to crave.

Avocation. (L.) From L. *āuocātiōnem*, acc. of *āuocātio*, a calling away of the attention, hence a diversion, amusement ; afterwards used in the sense of employment.─ L. *āuocātus*, pp. of *ā-uocāre*, to call away.─ L. *ā* (= *ab*), from, away ; *uocāre*, to call. See Vocation.

Avoid, to shun. (F.─ L.) M. E. *auoiden* (= *avoiden*), to empty, empty out, get rid of ; later, to keep away from, shun. ─ O. F. *esvuidier*, to empty out, get quit of.─ O. F. *es-*, prefix (L. *ex*, out) ; and O. F. *vuit*, *vuide* (F. *vide*), empty, void. See Void.

Avoirdupois. (F. ─ L.) Formerly *avoir de pois* (Anglo-F. *aveir de peis*), goods of weight, i. e. heavy articles.─ F. *avoir*, goods, orig. ' to have ;' *de*, of ; O. F. *pois*, A. F. *peis*, weight.─ L. *habēre*, to have ; *dē*, of ; *pensum*, that which is weighed out, neut. of *pensus*, pp. of *pendere*, to weigh. ¶ The F. *pois* is now misspelt *poids*. See Poise.

Avouch. (F.─ L.) M. E. *avouchen*. ─ O. F. *avochier*, to call upon as guarantor (Godefroy).─ L. *aduocāre*, to call to or summon (a witness).─ L. *ad*, to ; *uocāre*, to call. Cf. Vouch.

avow, to confess, to declare openly. (F. ─ L.) M. E. *avowen*.─ O. F. *avouer*, *avoer*. ─ L. *aduocāre*, to call upon ; Med. L. to call on as patron or client, to acknow-

ledge, recognise. ─ L. *ad*, to ; *uocāre*, to call. ¶ Another M. E. *avowen*, to bind with a vow, to vow, is obsolete ; see Vow. Doublet, *avouch* (above).

Await. (F.─ L. *and* O. H. G.) O. F. *awaitier*, *agaitier*, to wait for.─ O. F. *a* (= L. *ad*), for ; *waitier*, to wait, from O. H. G. *wahtēn*, to watch, from the sb. *wahta* (G. *wacht*), a watching. See Wait.

Awake, Awaken. (E.) M. E. *awakien*, *awaken* ; and *awaknen*, *awakenen* ; both orig. intransitive. Two A. S. verbs are confused ; *āwacian*, wk. vb. ; and *onwæcnan*, with wk. pres. t., but strong pt. t. *onwōc*, pp. *onwacen*. The prefix is either A- (2) or A- (4). See Wake, Waken.

Award, vb. (F.─ L. *and* O. Low G.) M. E. *awarden*.─ A. F. *awarder* ; O. F. *eswarder*, *esgarder*, to examine, adjudge. ─ O. F. *es-* (= L. *ex*), out ; O. F. *warder*, to ward, guard, from O. Low G., as in O. Sax. *wardōn* (cf. G. *warten*), to watch, guard. See Ward, Guard.

Aware. (E.) A corruption of M. E. *iwar*, *ywar*, aware (common) ; from A. S. *gewær*, aware. ─ A. S. *ge-*, a common prefix, not altering the sense ; *wær*, ware, wary ; see Wary.

Away. (E.) For *on way*, i. e. on one's way, so as to depart. A. S. *onweg*, away. See Way.

Awe. (Scand.) M. E. *aȝe*, *aghe*, *awe*. [Also *eȝe*, *eghe*, *eye* ; all orig. dissyllabic. The latter set are from A. S. *ege*, awe.]─ Icel. *agi*, awe, fear ; Dan. *ave*.+A. S. *ege*) Goth. *agis*, fear, anguish ; Irish *eagal*, fear, terror ; Gk. ἄχος, anguish, affliction. (√AGH.) Der. *aw-ful*.

Awkward, clumsy. (Scand. *and* E.) Orig. an adv., signifying ' transversely,' or ' in a backhanded manner.' M. E. *awkward*, *awkwart* ; ' *aukwart* he couth him ta ' = he gave him a backhanded stroke, Wallace, iii. 175. β. The suffix *-ward* is E., as in *for-ward*, *on-ward*, &c. The prefix is M. E. *auk*, *awk*, contrary, perverse, wrong ; this is a contraction of Icel. *öfug-* [Swed. *afvug*, in Widegren], like *hawk* from A. S. *hafoc*.─ Icel. *öfugr*, often contracted to *öfgu*, adj., turning the wrong way, back foremost, contrary. γ. Here *öf-* is for *af-*, off, from, away ; and *-ug-* is a suffix. Cf. O. H. G. *ap-uh*, M. H. G. *eb-ich*, turned away, perverse ; from *apa* = G. *ab*, off, away, and the suffix *-h*. δ. Thus the sense of *awk* is ' turned away ' ;

from Icel. *af-*, cognate with E. *of*, *off*, Gk. ἄπο.

Awl. (E.) M. E. *awel*, *aul* [we also find *al*, *el*]. A.S. *awel*, *awul*; perhaps cognate with L. *acūleus*, a sting, spine, allied to L. *acus*, a needle. ¶ The A. S. *æl* or *ǽl*, an awl, seems to be a distinct word, and allied to Icel. *alr*; G. *ahle*; Skt. *ārā* (Kluge).

Awn. (E.) M. E. *agune* (13th cent.), *awene*, *awne*. A.S. pl. *ægnan*, Corp. Gl. ✚ Icel. *ögn*, chaff, a husk; Dan. *avne*, chaff; Swed. *agn*, only in pl. *agnar*, husks; Goth. *ahana*; O. H. G. *agana*, chaff. Cf. Gk. pl. ἄχναι, chaff; O. L. *agna*, a straw.

Awning. (O. F. ?) In Sir T. Herbert's Travels, ed. 1665, p. 8 ; the proper sense seems to be 'a sail or tarpauling spread above a ship's deck, to keep off the sun's heat.' Perhaps from O. F. *auvan*, *auvant*, mod. F. *auvent*, 'a pent-house of cloth before a shop-window ;' Cot. Cf. Prov. *anvan*, Late L. *antevanna*, *auvanna*, *avanna*. Perhaps from L. *ante*, before ; *uannus*, a fan (fem. sb.).

Awry. (E.) For *on wry*, on the twist; Barbour, Bruce, iv. 705. See **Wry**.

Axe, Ax. (E.) M. E. *ax*, *ex*. A. S. *æx*, older forms *acus*, *æcus*.✚Du. *aaks*; Icel. *öx*, *öxi*; Swed. *yxa*; Dan. *öxe*; Goth. *akwizi* ; O. H. G. *acchus*; G. *axt*; L. *ascia* (if for **acscia*) ; Gk. ἀξίνη.

Axiom. (Gk.) XV cent.—Gk. ἀξίωμα (gen. ἀξιώματος), worth, quality.; in science, an assumption.—Gk. ἀξιόω, I deem worthy.—Gk. ἄξιος, worthy, worth, lit. 'weighing as much as.'—Gk. ἄγειν, to drive ; also, to weigh. (√AG.)

Axis, axle. (L.) L. *axis*, an axis, axle-tree. ✚ Gk. ἄξων; Skt. *aksha*, an axle, wheel, cart. Cf. also A. S. *eax*, an axle; Du. *as*; G. *achse*; Russ. *os*'; Lith. *aszis*. (√AG, to drive.) See below.

axle. (Scand.) M. E. *axel*. [A.S. has *eaxl*, but only with the sense of shoulder.] —Icel. *öxull*, axis; whence *öxul-trē*, an axle-tree; Swed. and Dan. *axel*, axle. β. It is a dimin. of the form appearing in L. *axis*; see **Axis**. Cf. W. *echel*, axle. Der. *axle-tree*, where *tree* is a block of wood.

Ay! interj. (E.) M. E. *ey!* A natural interjection. ¶ The phr. *ay me* is French ; O. F. *aymi*, alas for me ! Cf. Ital. *ahimè*, Span. *ay di me*, Gk. οἴμοι. See **Ah**.

Ay, Aye, yea, yes. (E.?) Spelt *I* in old edd. of Shak., &c. Origin uncertain; perhaps a variant of **Yea**.

Ayah, a native waiting-maid, in India. (Port.—L.) Port. *aia*, a nurse, governess (fem. of *aio*, a tutor). Prob. from L. *auia*, a grandmother.—L. *auus*, a grandfather.

Aye, adv., ever. (Scand.) M. E. *ay*.— Icel. *ei*, ever.✚A. S. *ā*, ever, also *āwa* ; Goth. *aiw*, ever, case-forms from Teut. **aiwoz* (Goth. *aiws*), an age, which is allied to L. *æuum*, Gk. αἰών, an age. Cf. Gk. αἰεί, ἀεί, ever.

Aye-Aye, a kind of lemur. (F.—Madagascar.) F. *aye-aye*, supp. to Littré. From the native name *ai-ay* in Madagascar ; said to be named from its cry.

Azimuth. (Arab.) *Azimuthal* circles are great circles on the sphere that pass through the *zenith*. Properly, *azimuth* is a pl. form, answering to Arab. *as-samūt*, ways, or points (or quarters) of the horizon ; from *al samt*, sing., the way, or point (or quarter) of the horizon.—Arab. *al*, the ; and *samt*, a way, quarter, direction; whence also E. *zenith*. See **Zenith**.

Azote, nitrogen. (F.—Gk.) So called because destructive to animal life.—F. *azote*.—Gk. ἀ-, negative prefix ; ζωτικός, preserving life, from ζω-ή, life, ζάειν, to live.

Azure, blue. (F.—Arab.—Pers.) M. E. *asur*, *azure*.—O. F. *azur*, azure ; a corrupted form, standing for *lazur*, which was mistaken for *l'azur*, as if the initial *l* indicated the def. article ; Low L. *lazur*, an azure-coloured stone, also called *lapis lazuli*.—Arab. *lāzward* (see Devic).—Pers. *lājuward*, lapis lazuli, a blue colour. So called from the mines of Lajwurd, where the lapis lazuli was found (Marco Polo, ed. Yule).

B

Baa, to bleat. (E.) In Shak.; an imitative word.

Babble. (E.) M. E. *babelen*, to prate, mumble, chatter. The suffix *-le* is frequentative ; the word means 'to keep on saying *ba*, *ba*,'syllables imitative of a child's attempts to speak.✚Du. *babbelen*; Dan. *bable* ; Icel. *babbla*; G. *bappeln*; and cf. F. *babiller*.

Babe. (E.) M. E. *bab*, earliest form *baban*. Probably due to infantile utterance; cf. **Babble**.

Babirusa, Babiroussa, a kind of wild hog. (Malay.) Malay *bābī rūsa*, lit. ' deer-hog,' or ' hog like a deer '; from *rūsa*, deer, and *bābī*, hog.

Baboon. (F. or Low L.) O. F. *babuin*, F. *babouin* ; we also find M. E. *babion*, *babian*, *babewine* ; Low L. *babewynus*, a baboon (A. D. 1295). Origin uncertain. Cf. O. F. *babou*, a grimace (Godefroy). Prob. from the motion of the lips. Cf. **Babble.**

Bacchanal. (L. – Gk.) L. *Bacchānālis*, a worshipper of *Bacchus*, god of wine. – Gk. Βάκχος, god of wine.

Bachelor. (F. – L.) M. E. *bacheler*. – O. F. *bacheler*. – Late L. **baccalāris*, but only found as *baccalārius*, a holder of a small farm or estate, called in Late L. *baccalāria*. Remoter origin unknown, and much disputed. Hardly from Late L. *bacca*, for L. *uacca*, a cow.

Back. (E.) M. E. *bak*. A. S. *bæc*.✛ Icel. *bak*; O. Sax. *bak*; O. Fries. *bek*. Der. *a-back*, q. v.; *back-bite*, M. E. *bak-biten* (P. Pl. B. ii. 80); *back-ward*, M. E. *bacward* (Cursor Mundi, 2042).

backgammon, a game. (E.) In Butler's Hudibras, pt. iii. c. 2. The sense is ' back-game,' because the pieces, when taken, are put back. See **gammon** (2).

Bacon. (F. – Teut.) M. E. *bacon*. – O. F. *bacon*; Low L. *baco*. – O. H. G. *bacho*, M. H. G. *bache*, buttock, ham, a flitch of bacon. Cf. G. *bache*, a wild sow; M. Du. *bak*, a pig; M. Dan. *bakke*, a pig.

Bad. (E.) M. E. *badde*. Formed from A. S. *bæddel*, s., a hermaphrodite; and allied to A. S. *bædling*, an effeminate man.

Badge. (Unknown.) M. E. *bage*; Prompt. Parv. Low L. *bagia*, *bagea*, ' signum, in-signe quoddam ;' Ducange ; apparently, a Latin version of the E. word. Origin unknown.

badger. (Unknown.) Spelt *bageard* in Sir T. More ; a nickname for the *brock*. Dr. Murray shews that *badger* = animal with a *badge* or stripe. See above.

Badinage, jesting talk. (F. – Prov. – L.) F. *badinage*. – F. *badiner*, to jest. – F. *badin*, adj., jesting. – Prov. *bader* (= F. *bayer*), lit. to gape ; hence, to be silly. – Late L. *badāre*, to gape ; prob. of imitative origin, from *ba*, expressive of opening the mouth. Cf. **Babble.**

Baffle, to foil, disgrace. (F. ? – G. ?) A Scotch word, as explained in Hall's Chron.

Hen. VIII, an. 5. *To baffull* is ' a great reproach among the Scottes '; it means to disgrace, vilify. Cf. Lowland Sc. *bauchle* (XV cent. *bachle*), to vilify. Origin doubtful ; but cf. F. *beffler*, to deceive, mock (Cot.), *bafouer* (Cot. *baffouer*, to baffle, revile, disgrace) ; allied to Ital. *beffare*, to flout, scoffe (Florio), from *beffa*, a scoff ; Norman F. *baffer*, to slap in the face ; Prov. *bafa*, a scoff. Prob. from M. H. G. *beffen*, to scold ; cf. G. *bäffen*, Du. *baffen*, to bark, yelp ; of imitative origin, like Du. *paf*, a pop, a box on the ear.

Bag. (Scand.) M. E. *bagge*. – Icel. *baggi*, O. Swed. *bagge*, a bag, pack, bundle. Not found elsewhere in Teutonic. (Gael. *bag* is from E.)

bagatelle, a trifle, a game. (F. – Ital. – Teut.) F. *bagatelle*, a trifle. – Ital. *bagat-tella*, a trifle, dimin. of Parmesan *bagata*, a little property ; from Lombard *baga*, a wine-skin, of Teut. origin ; see **Bag**, **baggage** (1).

baggage (1), luggage. (F. – Scand.) M. E. *baggage*, *bagage*. – O. F. *bagage*, a collection of bundles. – O. F. *bague*, a bundle.

baggage (2), a worthless woman. (F. – Scand.) The same as **Baggage** (1), in a depraved sense. Perhaps influenced by F. *bagasse*, ' a baggage, quean,' Cot. ; Ital. *bagascia*, ' a baggage-wench ;' Florio.

Bail (1), security : as verb, to secure. (F. – L.) O. F. *bail*, s. custody; from *bailler*, a law term, to secure, to keep in custody. – L. *bāiulāre*, to carry a child about, to take charge of a child. – L. *bāiulus*, a porter, carrier.

bailiff. (F. – L.) M. E. *bailif*. – O. F. *baillif*, Cot. – Late L. *bājulīvum*, acc. of *bājulīvus*, a custodian, &c. – L. *bāiulāre* (above).

bailiwick. (F. – L. ; *and* E.) From M. E. *baili*, short for *bailif* (above) ; and M. E. *wik*, A. S. *wīc*, a district ; hence, ' district of a bailiff ;' later, ' office ' of the same.

Bail (2), a bucket. See **Bale** (3).

Bail (3), at cricket. (F. – L.?) O. F. *bail*, an iron-pointed stake ; Godefroy adds that ' in the arrondissements of Vervins and Avesnes, *bail* is the name of a horizontal piece of wood fixed upon two stakes.' Perhaps from L. *baculum*, a stick. (Doubtful.)

Bairn, a child. (E.) M. E. *barn*. A. S. *bearn*. ✛ Icel., Swed., Dan., and Goth. *barn*. Lit. ' that which is born ;' Teut.

type *barnom, neut. sb., from bar, 2nd grade of ber-an, to bear ; with suffix -no-. See **Bear** (1).

Bait, to feed. (Scand.) Lit. ' to make to bite ;' a bait is ' an enticement to bite.' M. E. baiten, beiten. — Icel. beita, to make to bite, causal of bīta, to bite ; Swed. beta, to pasture ; Swed. bete, Dan. bed, a bait. See **Bite**.

Baize, coarse woollen stuff. (F. – L.) An error for bayes, pl. of F. baye, ' the cloth called bayes ;' Cot. – O. F. bai, bay-coloured. – L. badius, bay. From the orig. colour. Cf. Span. bayo, bay, bayeta, baize ; &c. See **Bay** (1).

Bake. (E.) M. E. baken. A. S. bacan, pt. t. bōc, pp. bacen. + Icel. and Swed. baka ; Dan. bage ; Du. bakken ; G. backen ; cf. Gk. φώγειν, to roast. (√ BHOG.)

Bakshish, Backsheesh, a present, small gratuity. (Pers.) Pers. bakhshīsh, a gratuity ; from bakhshīdan, to give ; baksh, a share, portion. Cf. Zend. baksh, to distribute ; Skt. bhaj, to divide.

Balance. (F. – L.) M. E. balance. – F. balance, ' a ballance, pair of weights or ballances ;' Cot. Cf. Ital. bilancia. – L. bilancem, acc. of bilanx, having two scales. – L. bi-, for bis, double, twice ; and lanx, a dish, platter, scale of a balance.

Balas-ruby, a variety of ruby, of a pale rose-red or orange colour. (F. – Low L. – Arab. – Pers.) Formerly balais. – F. balais ; Med. L. balascus, balascius. – Arab. balakhsh, a ruby (Devic). – Pers. badakhshī, a ruby ; named from Badakh-shān, N. of the river Amoo (Oxus).

Balcony. (Ital. – Teut.) Ital. balcone, palcone, orig. a stage. – O. H. G. balcho, a beam. + O. Sax. balko, a beam. See **Balk** (1).

Bald. (C.) M. E. balled ; the orig. sense was ' shining, white,' as in ' bald-faced stag,' a stag with a white streak on its face ; cf. prov. E. ball, a white-faced horse. – Gael. and Irish bal, ball, a spot, mark, speckle (properly a white spot or streak) ; Bret. bal, a white streak on an animal's face ; W. bali, whiteness in a horse's forehead. Cf. Gk. φάλιος, white, φαλακρός, bald-headed ; Lith. baltas, white.

Baldachin (pronounced baoldakin or bældakin), a canopy over an altar, throne, &c. (F. or Ital. – Arab.) F. baldaquin ; Ital. baldacchino, a canopy, tester, orig hangings or tapestry made at Bagdad. – Ital. Baldacco, Bagdad. – Arab. Baghdād, Bagdad.

Balderdash, poor stuff. (Scand. ?) It formerly meant a jumbled mixture of liquors. Cf. Dan. balder, noise, clatter ; and daske, to slap, flap. Hence it appears (like slap-dash) to have meant a confused noise ; secondarily a hodge-podge (Halliwell) ; and generally, any mixture. (Uncertain.)

Baldric, a girdle. (F. – M. H. G. – L.) O. F. *baldric (not recorded), older form of O. F. baldret, baldrei ; Low L. baldringus. – M. H. G. balderich, a girdle ; extended from O. H. G. balz, a belt. – L. balteus, a belt. See **Belt**.

Bale (1), a package ; see **Ball** (2).

Bale (2), evil. (E.) M. E. bale. A.S. bealu, balu, evil. + O. Fries. and O. S. balu ; Icel. böl, misfortune ; O. H. G. balo, destruction. Teut. *balwom, neut. of *balwoz, adj. evil ; cf. Goth. balwawesei, wickedness. Der. bale-ful.

Bale (3), to empty water out of a ship. (F. – Teut.) XVII cent. It means to empty a ship by means of bails, i. e. buckets. – F. baille, a bucket. Cf. Du. balie, a tub ; Swed. balja, Dan. ballie, G. balje, a tub. – Late Lat. *bacula (Diez), dimin. from Du. bak, M. Du. back, a trough.

Balk (1), a beam, ridge of land. (E.) M. E. balke. A. S. balca, a ridge, heap ; which explains balked = laid in heaps, 1 Hen. IV, i. 1. 69. + O. Sax. balko, a beam ; Du. balk, a beam, bar ; Swed. balk, a beam, partition ; G. balken. Teut. stem *balkon-, a bar. Cf. **Phalanx**.

balk (2), **baulk,** to hinder. (E.) M. E. balken. To put a balk or bar in a man's way.

Ball (1), a spherical body. (F. – O. H. G.) M. E. bal, balle. – F. balle. – M. H. G. balle, O. H. G. ballo (G. ball), a ball, sphere. + Icel. böllr.

bale (1), a package. (F. – O. H. G.) M. E. bale. – F. bale, a ball, also a pack, as of merchandise ; Cot. The same as F. balle, a ball ; hence, a round package.

Ball (2), a dance. (F. – Late L.) F. bal. – F. baller, to dance. – Late L. ballāre, to dance. + Gk. βαλλίζειν, to dance.

ballad. (F. – Prov. – Late L.) M. E. balade. – O. F. balade ; F. ballade. – Prov. balada, a song for dancing to. – Late L. ballāre, to dance.

Ballast, a load to steady a ship. (Scand. or O. Low G.) Three forms are found : (1) O. Dan. barlast, i. e. bare load, mere weight, Swed. barlast ; (2) O. Low G.

ballast, i.e. ' bale last,' useless load, Du., Dan., E. Fries. *ballast* ; (3) Dan. *bag-last,* i.e. back load. Of these, (3) seems due to popular etymology ; and (2) arose out of (1). See **Last** (4) ; also **Bare, Bale** (2), **Back.** Cf. M. Du. *bal-daedt,* evil deed (Hexham).

Ballet. (F. – Late L.) F. *ballet,* dimin. of *bal,* a dance. See **Ball** (2).

Balloon, a large ball. (F.–O. H. G.) Formerly *baloon,* a ball used in a game like football ; (also *ballone,* from Ital. *ballone,* in Florio). – O. F. *balon,* 'a little ball, or pack ; a football or baloon ;' Cot. Mod. F. *ballon* ; Span. *balon* ; Ital. *pallone* ; augmentative form of F. *balle,* &c., a ball. See **Ball** (1).

ballot. (Ital. – O. H. G.) Ital. *ballot-tare,* 'to cast lots with bullets, as they vse in Venice ;' Florio. – Ital. *ballotta,* a little ball used for voting ; dimin. of Ital. *balla,* a ball. See **Ball** (1).

Balm. (F. – L. – Gk.) A modified spelling ; M. E. *basme, bame, baume.* – O. F. *basme.* – L. *balsamum.* – Gk. βάλσα-μον, fragrant resin of the βάλσαμος, or balsam-tree. Prob. Semitic ; cf. Heb. *bāsām,* balsam.

balsam. (L. – Gk.) L. *balsamum* ; as above.

Baluster, a rail of a staircase, small column. (F. – Ital. – L. – Gk.) F. *balustre* ; *balustres,* ' ballisters, little, round, and short pillars, ranked on the outsides of cloisters, terraces,' &c. ; Cot. – Ital. *balaustro,* a baluster ; so called from a fancied resemblance to the flower of the wild pomegranate. – Ital. *balausto, balaustra,* the flower of the pomegranate. – L. *balaus-tium.* – Gk. βαλαύστιον, the flower of the wild pomegranate. **Der.** *balustr-ade,* F. *balustrade,* from Ital. *balaustrata,* furnished with balusters.

Bamboo. (Malay – Canarese.) XVI cent. Malay *bambū.* – Canarese *banbu,* or *banwu,* bamboo.

Bamboozle, to hoax. (Unknown.)

Ban, a proclamation. (E.) Chiefly in the pl. *banns* (of marriage). M. E. *ban.* A.S. *gebann,* a proclamation (the prefix *ge-* making no difference). Cf. A.S. *ābannan,* to summon, order out. Influenced by O. F. *ban,* of G. origin (as below).+ Du. *ban,* excommunication ; Icel. and Swed. *bann,* Dan. *band,* O. H. G. *ban,* a ban. All from Teut. strong vb. **bannan-,* to proclaim ; as in O. H. G. *bannan.* Cf.

L. *fāma,* a rumour. (√BHA.) Brugm. i. § 559.

Banana, the plantain-tree. (Span.) Span. *banana,* fruit of the *banano* ; said to be of African origin (from Guinea).

Band (1), **Bond.** (Scand.) M. E. *band* ; variant, *bond.* – Icel. *band* ; Swed. *band* ; Dan. *baand* ; cf. Du. and G. *band.* Teut. **bandom,* n. ; from *band-,* 2nd grade of *bind-an,* to bind ; see **Bind.** Allied to A. S. *bend,* Goth. *bandi,* a band. Cf. Skt. *bandha,* a binding. **Der.** *band-age* (F. *bandage*) ; *band-box* ; *bandog,* q. v.

band (2), a company of men. (F. – Teut.) F. *bande* ; whence G. *bande,* a gang, set. – Low Lat. *banda,* a gang ; allied to Low L. *bandum,* a banner. See **Banner** and **Bind.**

Bandanna, a silk handkerchief with white spots. (Hind.) Hind. *bāndhnū,* 'a mode of dyeing in which the cloth is tied in different places, to prevent the parts tied from receiving the dye . . . a kind of silk cloth ;' Shakespear's Hind. Dict.

Bandicoot, a large Indian rat.(Telugu.) Telugu *pandi-kokku,* lit. pig-rat (Yule). – Tel. *pandi,* a pig, *kokku,* a rat.

Bandit. (Ital. – O. H. G.) In Sh. – Ital. *bandito,* outlawed, pp. of *bandire,* to proscribe. – Low L. *bannire,* to proclaim. – O. H. G. *bannan,* to summon ; whence O. H. G. *ban,* cognate with E. *ban.*

Bandog, a large dog. (E.) Orig. *banddog,* a dog that is tied up. See Prompt. Parv. p. 43. See **Band** (1).

Bandy, to beat to and fro, contend. (F. – Teut.) Orig. to *band* (Turbervile). – F. *bander,* ' to bind ; also, to bandie, at tennis ;' Cot. *Se bander,* to league against. – F. *bande,* a band ; see **Band** (2).

bandy-legged, bow-legged. (F. – Teut. *and* Scand.) Prob. from *bandy,* formerly the name of a bent stick for playing a game called *bandy,* in which a ball was *bandied* about. See above.

Bane, harm. (E.) A.S. *bana,* a murderer, bane.+O. Sax. and O. H. G. *bano* ; Icel. *bani,* Dan. and Swed. *bane,* death, murder. Teut. stem **banon-,* m. Cf. Goth. *banja,* a wound. **Der.** *bane-ful.*

Bang (1), to beat. (Scand.) In Sh. – Icel. *banga,* Dan. *banke,* to beat ; O. Swed. *bång,* Icel. *bang,* a hammering. Cf. G. *bengel,* a cudgel.

Bang (2), a narcotic drug. (Pers. – Skt.) Pers. *bang.* – Skt. *bhangā,* hemp ; the drug being made from the wild hemp.

Bangle, a kind of bracelet. (Hind.) Hind. *bangrī*, a bracelet, bangle. (H. H. Wilson.)

Banian; see Banyan.

Banish. (F.—O. H. G.) M. E. *banis-shen.* —O. F. *banis-*, stem of pres. part. of *banir, bannir*, to proscribe. — Low L. *ban-nīre*, to proclaim ; see Bandit.

Banisters; a corruption of Balusters.

Banjo, a six-stringed musical instrument. (Ital. — Gk.) A negro corruption of *bandore, bandora,* or *pandore.* — Ital. *pandora,* a musical instrument, usually with three strings. — Gk. πανδοῦρα, the same. Perhaps of Egypt. orig.

Bank (1), a mound of earth. (Scand.) M. E. *banke.* — O. Scand. **banke*, orig. form of Icel. *bakki*, ridge, eminence, bank of a river; cf. Dan. *bakke,* Swed. *backe,* bank ; whence also Norman F. *banque,* a bank. Teut. stem **bankon-*. Cf. O. Sax. and Du. *bank,* O. H. G. *banch,* A. S. *benc,* a bench (see Bench).

bank (2), for money. (F. — Teut.) F. *banque,* a money-changer's table or bench. —M. Du. *banck,* M. H. G. *banc,* a bench, table. See above.

bankrupt. (F. — Ital. — Teut. *and* L.) Modified from F. *banqueroute,* bankruptcy, by a knowledge of the relation of the word to L. *ruptus*, broken. — Ital. *banca rotta,* a broken bank, due to the money-changer's failure. — M. H. G. *banc,* a bench (see above) ; and L. *rupta,* fem. of *ruptus,* pp. of *rumpere,* to break.

Banner. (F. — Teut.) M. E. *banere.* — O. F. *banere* (supp. to Godefroy, s. v. *baniere*), also *baniere.* — Low L. **bandāria* (Ducange gives *bandēria*), a banner. — Low L. *bandum, bannum,* a standard. From a Teut. (Langobardic) source ; cf. Goth. *bandwa,* a sign, token. ' Uexillum, quod *bandum* appellant ;' Paulus, *de Gestis Langob.* i. 20. Prob. allied to Band (1) and Band (2).

banneret, orig. a knight who had men under his own banner. (F. — Teut.) M. E. *baneret.* — O. F. *baneret* (F. *banneret*) ; lit. ' bannered.' — O. F. *banere* (above) ; with suffix *-et* = L. pp. *-ātus.*

Bannock, a cake. (C. — L. ?) Gael. *bannach,* a cake. Perhaps from L. *pāni-cium,* a thing baked ; from *pāni-s,* bread.

Banns, pl. of Ban, q. v.

Banquet. (F. — Ital. — Teut.) F. *banquet.* — Ital. *banchetto* (Torriano), a feast ; also a bench ; dimin. of *banco,* a bench. —

M. H. G. *banc,* a bench, table ; see bank (2).

Banshee, a female spirit supposed to warn families of a death. (C.) Gael. *beanshith,* a banshee, from Gael. *bean,* a woman ; *sith,* a fairy ; O. Irish *ban-side,* fairies (Windisch, s. v. *side*), from O. Ir. *ben* (= E. *quean*), a woman, *side,* fairies.

Bantam. (Java.) A fowl from *Bantam,* in Java.

Banter, raillery. (Unknown.)

Bantling, an infant. (G. ?) Prob. considered as *band-ling,* one wrapped in swaddling bands ; with double dimin. suffix *-l-ing;* but really an adaptation of G. *bänkling* (with the same sense as *bank-art*), an illegitimate child ; from *bank,* a bench ; i. e. ' a child begotten on a bench,' not in the marriage-bed (Mahn). Cf. bank (2).

Banyan, a tree. (Port. — Skt.) An English, not a native name for the tree. So called because used as a market-place for merchants or ' bannyans,' as we termed them ; see Sir T. Herbert, Travels, ed. 1665, pp. 51, 123. — Port. *banian,* an Indian merchant. — Skt. *banij,* a merchant.

Baobab, a tree. (African.) The native name in Senegal (Adanson).

Baptise, Baptize. (F.—L. — Gk.) Formerly *baptise* ; M. E. *baptisen.* — O. F. *baptiser.* — L. *baptizāre.* — Gk. βαπτίζειν ; from βάπτειν, to dip. Der. *baptist,* Gk. βαπτιστής, a dipper ; *baptism,* Gk. βάπτισμα, βάπτισμος, a dipping.

Bar, a rail. (F. — Late L.) M. E. *barre.* — O. F. *barre.* — Late L. *barra,* a bar.

Barb (1), hook on an arrow. (F. — L.) F. *barbe.* — L. *barba,* a beard. Hence O. F. *flesche barbelée,* ' a bearded or barbed arrow ;' Cot. See Beard.

barbel, a fish. (F. — L.) M. E. *bar-belle.* — O. F. *barbel.* — F. *barbeau.* — L. *barbellus,* dimin. of *barbus,* a barbel. — L. *barba,* a beard. ¶ Named from four beard-like appendages near the mouth.

barber. (F. — L.) M. E. *barbour.* — A. F. *barbour,* with suffix *-our* = Lat. acc. *-ātorem ;* cf. O. F. *barbier,* a barber. — F. *barbe,* a beard ; from L. *barba,* beard.

Barb (2), a horse. (F. — Barbary.) F. *barbe,* a Barbary horse ; named from the country.

Barbarous. (L. — Gk.) L. *barbar-us* ; with suffix *-ous.* — Gk. βάρβαρος, foreign, lit. stammering ; a name given by Greeks to express the strange sound of foreign languages. Cf. L. *balbus*, stammering.

Barbed, accoutred, armed; said of horses. (F. – Scand.?) Also (more correctly), *barded*. – F. *bardé*, 'barbed as a horse,' Cot. – F. *barde*, horse-armour. – Icel. *barð*, a brim, edge; also, a beak or armed prow of a warship (cf. *barði*, a shield); whence it may have been applied to horses (Diez).

Barbel, Barber; see Barb (1).

Barberry, Berberry, a shrub. (Med. L.) From Med. L. *barbaris*, a barberry-tree; of unknown origin. Hence also M. F. *berberis*, Sp. *berberis*, and even mod. Arab. *barbārīs*. ¶ The spelling should be *berbery* or *barbary*; no connexion with *berry*.

Barbican. (F.) M. E. *barbican*. – F. *barbacane*, a barbican or outwork of a castle; also, a loop-hole; also, an outlet for water. Hardly from Arab. *barbakh*, an aqueduct, a sewer (Devic).

Bard. (C.) W. *bardd*, Irish and Gael. *bard*, a poet. Cf. Gk. φράζειν, to speak.

Bare. (E.) M. E. *bar*. A. S. *bær*. **+** Icel. *berr*; G. *bar, baar*. Teut. type *bazoz*; cf. Lith. *basas*, O. Slav. *bosŭ*, barefooted.

Bargain. (F. – Late L.) M. E. *bargayn*, sb. – O. F. *bargaignier, bargenir*, to chaffer. – Late L. *barcāniāre*, to change about. Remoter origin unknown.

Barge. (F. – Late L. – C.?) M. E. *barge*. – F. *barge*. – Late L. *barga*, variant of *barca*; see Bark (1).

bark (1), **barque.** (F. – Late L. – C.?) *Bark* is an E. spelling of F. *barque*, a little ship. – Late L. *barca*, a sort of ship or large boat, a lighter. Perhaps of Celtic origin (Thurneysen). – O. Irish *barc* (fem. *a*-stem), a bark.

Bark (2), the rind of a tree. (Scand.) M. E. *bark*. – Swed. *bark*; Dan. *bark*; Icel. *börkr*. Teut. type *barkuz*.

Bark (3), to yelp as a dog. (E.) M. E. *berken*. – A. S. *beorcan*, to bark. Cf. Icel. *berkja*, A. S. *borcian*, to bark. Perhaps of imitative origin.

Barley. (E.) M. E. *barli*. – A. S. *bærlic*. Cf. A. S. *bere*, barley (Lowl. Sc. *bear*); and *-lic*, for *līc*, like. Cf. also Goth. *barizeins*, made of barley; L. *far*, corn.

barn. (E.) M. E. *berne*. A. S. *bern*, contr. form of *ber-ern* (Luke iii. 17). – A. S. *bere*, barley; and *ern, ærn*, a place

for storing. A. S. *ærn* is for *ran(n)*, cognate with Icel. *rann*; see Ransack.

Barm (1), yeast. (E.) M. E. *berme*. A. S. *beorma*. **+** Low G. *barm*; Swed. *bärma*; G. *bärme*. Teut. stem *bermon-*; perhaps allied to Ferment.

Barm (2), the lap. (E.) M. E. *barm*. A. S. *bearm*, lap, bosom. **+** O. Sax., Swed., Dan. *barm*; Icel. *barmr*; Goth. *barms*. Teut. type *barmoz*; from *bar-*, 2nd grade of *ber-an*, to bear; see Bear (1).

Barn. (E.) See Barley.

Barnacle (1), a kind of goose. (F. – Med. L.) Dimin. from F. *bernaque* (Cot.); Med. L. *bernaca*. 'Bernacæ, aues aucis palustribus similes;' Ducange. Used by Giraldus Cambrensis. Cf. Port. *bernaca, bernacha*; Span. *bernicla* (Neuman). (See Max Müller, Lectures, 2nd Series.)

barnacle (2), a sort of shell-fish. (F. – Med. L.) The same as Barnacle (1). See N. E. D.; and Max Müller, Lect. on Science of Language, ed. 7, ii. 583.

Barnacles, spectacles, orig. irons put on the noses of horses to keep them quiet. (F.) The sense of 'spectacles' is late, and due to a humorous allusion. M. E. *bernak*, dimin. *bernakill*. 'Bernak for hors, *bernakill*, Chamus' (i. e. L. *camus*); Prompt. Parv. We find *bernac* in A. F. (in an Eng. MS.); Wright's Vocab. i. 100, l. 3. Origin unknown.

Barometer, an instrument for measuring the weight of the air. (Gk.) Gk. βαρο-, for βάρος, weight; and μέτρον, a measure; see Metre.

Baron, a title. (F. – Late L.) M. E. *baron*. – F. *baron*; older form *ber*, nom. (Prov. *bar*), the suffix *-on* marking the acc. case (Diez). Cf. Ital. *barone*, Sp. *varon*, Port. *varão*. – Late L. *baro*, acc. *-ōnem*, a man, a male. Origin unknown.

Barouche, a carriage. (G. – Ital. – L.) G. *barutsche*. – Ital. *baroccio, biroccio*, a chariot, orig. a two-wheeled car. – L. *birotus*, two-wheeled; with suffix *-occio* assimilated to that of *carr-occio*, a chariot (Diez). – L. *bi-*, double; and *rota*, a wheel.

Barracks. (F. – Ital.) F. *baraque*. – Ital. *baracca*, a tent for soldiers; cf. Sp. *barraca*. Prob. connected with Late L. *barra*, a bar, pale.

Barrator, one who incites to quarrels and lawsuits. (F.) Formerly *barratour, baratour*; from M. E. *barat*, deceit, strife. – F. *barat*, 'cheating, deceit, guile, also a barter,' Cotgrave. Allied to Barter.

¶ Influenced by Icel. *barátta*, a fight, a turmoil.

Barrel. (F.) M. E. *barel.* – O. F. (and F.) *baril.* Perhaps from Late L. *barra*, a bar, pale ; from the staves of it.

Barren. (F.) M. E. *barain.* – A. F. *barain, -e*; O. F. *brehaing*, fem. *brehaingne, baraigne*; F. *bréhaigne*, sterile. Of unknown origin.

Barricade. (F. – Span.) F. *barricade.* – Span. *barricada*, a barricade, lit. one made with barrels full of earth. – Span. *barrica*, a barrel. Perhaps from Span. *barra*, a bar ; see **Barrel**.

Barrier. (F.) M. E. *barrere.* – O. F. *barrere* (Godefroy, s. v. *bassein*) ; F. *barrière.* – F. *barrer*, to bar up. – F. *barre*, a bar. See **Bar**.

barrister. (Low L.) A barbarous word ; formed with suffix *-ister* (= Low L. *-istārius*) from the sb. *bar.* Spelman gives the Low L. form as *barrastērius*.

Barrow (1), a burial-mound. (E.) For *berrow* (like *parson* for *person*, &c.). M. E. *bergh, berw*, a hill, mound. O. Merc. *berg*; A. S. *beorg, beorh*, a mountain, hill, mound. **+** O. Sax., Du., G. *berg.* Teut. type ******bergoz*, a hill. Cf. O. Irish *bri*, a mountain ; Skt. *bṛhant*, large.

Barrow (2), a wheel-barrow. (E.) M.E. *barewe.* – A. S. *bar-*, 2nd grade of *ber-an*, to bear, carry. Cf. M. H. G. *rade-ber*, wheel-barrow, from *rad*, wheel.

Barter, to traffic. (F.) M. E. *bartryn.* – O. F. *bareter, barater*, ' to cheat, beguile, also to barter ; ' Cot. O. F. *barat*, ' cheating, also a barter ; ' Cot. β. Of doubtful origin ; perhaps Celtic (Littré). Cf. Bret. *barad*, treachery, Irish *brath*, W. *brad*, treachery, Gael. *brath*, advantage by unfair means ; Irish *bradach*, Gael. *bradach*, thievish, roguish ; W. *bradu*, to plot.

Barton, a court-yard, manor. (E.) O. Northumb. *bere-tūn* (Matt. iii. 12). – A. S. *bere*, barley ; and *tūn*, an enclosure ; see **Barley** and **Town**.

Barytes, in chemistry. (Gk.) Named from its weight. – Gk. βαρύτης, weight. – Gk. βαρύς, heavy. See **Grave** (2).

barytone. (Ital. – Gk.) Better *baritone* ; a musical term for a deep voice. – Ital. *baritono*, a baritone. – Gk. βαρύ-s, heavy, deep ; and τόνος, a tone ; see **Tone**.

Basalt. (L.) Also *basaltes.* L. *basaltes*, a hard kind of marble in Æthiopia. An African word (Pliny).

Base (1), low. (F. – L.) M. E. *bass*.

base. – F. *bas*, m., *basse*, fem. – Late L. *bassus*, low ; the same word as L. *Bassus*, proper name, which seems to have meant ' stout, fat,' rather than merely ' low.'

Base (2), a foundation. (F. – L. – Gk.) M. E. *bas.* – F. *base.* – L. *basis.* – Gk. βάσις, a step, a pedestal, base. – Gk. base βα-, to go (as in βαίνειν, to go) ; with suffix *-σι-* (for *-τι-*) ; cf. Skt. *ga-ti*(*s*), a going, from *gam*, to go. See **Come**.

Basement, lowest floor of a building. (F. – Ital. – L.) Appears in F. as *soubassement*, the basement of a building ; formed from *sous*, under, and *-bassement*, borrowed from Ital. *bassamento*, lit. an abasement. – Ital. *bassare*, to lower. – Ital. *basso*, low. – Late L. *bassus* ; see **Base** (1).

Basenet, Basnet ; see **Basinet**.

Bashaw ; the old form of Pasha.

Bashful. (F. *and* E.) For *abash-ful*; see **Abash**. Prob. by confusion with *abase* and *base*.

Basil (1), a plant. (F. – L. – Gk.) O.F. *basile* (Supp. to Godefroy) ; short for *basilic* ; cf. F. *basilic*, ' herb basill ; ' Cot. – L. *basilicum*, neut. of *basilicus*, royal. – Gr. βασιλικόν, basil ; neut. of βασιλικός, royal. – Gk. βασιλεύς, a king.

basilica, a large hall. (L. – Gk.) L. *basilica*, fem. of *basilicus*, royal.

basilisk, a fabled serpent. (L. – Gk.) L. *basiliscus.* – Gk. βασιλίσκος, lit. royal ; also a lizard or serpent, named from a spot on the head like a crown (Pliny, viii. 21). – Gk. βασιλεύς, a king.

Basil (2), the hide of a sheep tanned. (F. – Span. – Arab.) A. F. *baseyne* (Liber Albus, 225). – F. *basane*, M. F. *bassane.* – Span. *badana*, a dressed sheep-skin. – Arab. *biṭānah*, the [inner] lining of a garment, for which basil-leather was used. Cf. Arab. *baṭn*, the inside.

Basin. (F. – Late L.) M. E. *bacin, basin.* – O. F. *bacin, bachin* ; F. *bassin.* – Late L. *bachīnus, bacchīnus*, a basin (Duc.). Supposed to be from Late L. *bacca*, water-vessel (Isidore). Cf. Du. *bak*, a bowl, trough.

basinet, basenet, basnet, a light helmet. (F. – Late L.) In Spenser ; F. Q. vi. I. 31. – O. F. *bacinet*, dimin. of *bacin*, a basin ; from its shape.

Basis. (L. – Gk.) L. *basis.* – Gk. βάσις ; see **Base** (2).

Bask. (Scand.) M. E. *baske*, to bathe oneself, Palsgrave ; and cf. *bathe hire*, to bask herself, Ch. C. T. Nonnes Prestes

40

Tale, 447. – Icel. *baðask* (later *baðast*), for *baða sik*, to bathe oneself. Cf. also Swed. dial. *at basa sig i solen*, to bask in the sun, *badfisk*, fishes basking in the sun (Wedgwood). See **Bathe.** ¶ Formed like Busk.

Basket. (F. ?) M. E. *basket*. Mod. Norman F. *basquette* (Moisy). Origin unknown.

Basnet; see Basinet.

Bass (1), the lowest part, in music. (F. – L.) The same word as **Base** (1); but so spelt in imitation of Ital. *basso*, base.

Bass (2), **Barse**, a fish. (E.) - M. E. *barse*; also *base*, *bace* (with loss of *r*). A.S. *bærs*, a perch.+Du. *baars*; G. *bars*, *barsch*, a perch. Named from its prickles. From *bars-*, 2nd grade of Teut. root *bers*, whence also **Bristle**, q. v. Cf. Skt. *bhṛshti*, pointed.

Bassoon, a base instrument. (F. – L.) F. *basson*, augmentative from F. *basse*, base (in music), fem. of *bas*, base. See Base (1).

Bast. (E.) M. E. *bast*; *bast-tre*, a lime-tree. A.S. *bæst*, inner bark of a lime-tree; whence bast is made.+Icel., Swed., Dan., G. *bast*. Often spelt *bass*.

Bastard, an illegitimate child. (F.) M. E. *bastard*, applied to Will. I. – O. F. *bastard*, the same as *fils de bast*, lit. 'the son of a pack-saddle,' not of a bed. [The expression *a bast ibore*, illegitimate, occurs in Rob. of Glouc. p. 516.] – O. F. *bast*, a pack-saddle (F. *bât*); with suffix *-ard*, from O. H. G. *hart*, hard, first used as a suffix in proper names and then generally.

Baste (1), to beat. (Scand. ?) The form *bas-it* occurs as a pp. in 1553. Cf. Swed. *basa*, to strike, beat, whip.

Baste (2), to pour fat over meat. (Unknown.) In Sh. ' *To baste*, linire;' Levins, ed. 1570.

Baste (3), to sew slightly. (F. – M. H.G.) M. E. *basten.* – O. F. *bastir*, F. *bâtir*, to sew slightly; a tailor's term. – M. H. G. *besten* (for *bastjan*), to bind; orig. to tie with bast. – G. *bast*, bast. See Bast.

Bastile, a fortress. (F.) O.F. *bastille*, a building. – O. F. *bastir* (F. *bâtir*), to build. Origin uncertain; perhaps allied to Baton.

Bastinado. (Span.) From Span. *bastonada*, a beating. – Span. *baston*, a stick. – Late L. *bastōnem*, acc.; see Baton.

Bastion. (F. – Ital.) F. *bastion*. – Ital. *bastione*, part of a fortification. – Ital. *bastire*, to build; allied to O. F. *bastir*, to build. See **Bastile.**

Bat (1), a cudgel. (E.) M. E. *batte*. – A. S. *batt* (Eng. Studien, xi. 65). Cf. Irish *bata*, *bat*, a staff. **Der.** *bat-let*, with double dimin. suffix *-l-et*.

Bat (2), a winged mammal. (Scand.) *Bat* has taken the place of M. E. *bakke*. – Dan. *bakke*, now only in comp. *aften-bakke*, evening-bat. Cf. O. Swed. *natt-backa*, 'night-bat' (Ihre); for which we find Swed. dial. *natt-batta* (Rietz).

Batch. (E.) A *batch* is as much as is baked at once; hence, a quantity. M. E. *bacche*, a baking; from A. S. *bacan*, to bake. See **Bake.**

Bate (1), to beat down, diminish. (F. – L.) Short for **Abate**, by loss of *a*.

Bate (2), strife. (F. – L.) M. E. *bate*; a clipt form of **Debate**, in the sense of strife. ¶ So also *fence* for *de-fence*.

Bath. (E.) M. E. *bap*. A. S. *bæð*.+ Icel. *bað*; O. H. G. *bad*; Swed., Dan., Du., G. *bad*. Teut. *ba-þom*, neuter. The orig. sense was a place of warmth; cf. O. H. G. *bâjan* (G. *bähen*), to foment.

bathe. (E.) A. S. *baðian*, to bathe. – A. S. *bæð*, a bath. And see Bask.

Bathos. (Gk.) Lit. depth, sinking. – Gk. βάθος, depth; cf. βαθύς, deep.

Baton, Batoon, a cudgel. (F.) F. *bâton*, O. F. *baston*. – Late L. *bastōnem*, acc. of *basto*, a cudgel. Origin doubtful; connected by Diez with Gk. βαστάζειν, to support.

Battalion. (F. – Ital. – L.) F. *bataillon*. – Ital. *battaglione*, a battalion. – Ital. *battaglia*, a battle; see Battle below.

Batten (1), to grow fat; to fatten. (Scand.) Orig. intransitive. – Icel. *batna*, to grow better, improve, recover. Cf. Goth. *ga-batnan*, to. be bettered; Icel. *bat-i*, s., improvement, E. **Better**, q. v., and **Boot** (2). Cf. also Du. *baten*, to yield profit; *baat*, profit.

Batten (2), a wooden rod. (F.) To *batten* down is to fasten with *battens*. *Batten* is merely another spelling of Baton.

Batter (1), to beat. (F. – L.) M. E. *bat-er-en*; with frequentative suffix *-er-*. – F. *battre*. – L. *battere*, popular form of *battuere*, to beat.

batter (2), a compound of eggs, flour, and milk. (F. – L.) M. E. *batour*, *bature*. – O. F. *bature*, a beating. – F. *battre*, to beat (above). So called because beaten up.

battery. (F.–L.) F. *baterie, batterie,* 'beatir battery;' Cot.–F. *battre,* to beat.

bat le. (F.–L.) M. E. *bataille, bataile.* –O. . *bataille,* (1) a fight, (2) a battalion. – Folk-L. *battālia,* neut. pl. (turned into a fem. sing.), fights; Late L. *battuālia,* neut. pl. of adj. *battuālis,* fighting.–Late L. *battuere,* to beat.

battledoor. (Prov.–L.) M. E. *batyldoure,* Prompt. Parv.–Prov. *batedor,* Span. *batidor,* a washing-beetle, which was also at first the sense of the E. word. [The corruption to *battledoor* was due to confusion with *battle,* vb. to fight.]–Prov. *batre,* Span. *batir,* the same as F. *battre,* to beat; with suffix *-dor,* which in Prov. and Span.=L. suffix *-tōrem,* acc. form from nom. *-tor,* expressing the agent.

Battlement. (F.) M. E. *batelment, batilment,***bateillement,* from O. F. *bateillier,* to fortify; formed from *bataille,* battle, fight, but confused with O. F. *bastiller,* to fortify, derivative of O. F. *bastir,* to build. See Battle and Bastile.

Bauble (1), a fool's mace; (2) a plaything. (F.) (1) M. E. *babyll, bable, babel,* Gower, C. A. i. 224; (2) M. E. *babel,* Tudor E. *bauble.* From O. F. *baubel, babel,* a child's plaything (Godefroy). Perhaps connected with M. Ital. *babbola,* a toy (Florio); and with L. *babulus,* a fool. Cf. E. Babble.

Bavin, a faggot. (F.) Prov. E. (Wilts.) *bavin,* a faggot; hence, as adj., soon kindled and burnt out, 1 Hen. IV. iii. 2. 61.– O. F. *baffe,* a faggot, bundle (Godefroy, Roquefort). Remoter origin unknown.

Bawd, a procurer or procuress, go-between. (F.–O. H. G.) The full M. E. form is *bawdstrot,* P. Plowm. A. iii. 40 (another MS. has *bawde*).–O. F. *baldestrot (found only in the later form *baudetrot*), equivalent to Lat. *pronuba,* a bride-woman.–O. H. G. *bald,* bold, gay, lively (cognate with E. *bold*); and M. H. G. *strotzen,* vb. (E. *strut*).

Bawl. (Scand.) Icel. *baula,* to low as a cow; Swed. *böla,* to bellow: see Bull, Bellow.

Bay (1), reddish brown. (F.–L.) M. E. *bay.*–O. F. *bai.*–L. *badius,* bay-coloured.

bayard. (F.–L.) A bay horse; from the colour; also, any horse. The suffix *-ard* is Teutonic; see Bastard.

Bay (2), a kind of laurel; properly, a berry-tree. (F.–L.) M. E. *bay,* a berry –F. *baie,* a berry.–L. *bāca,* a berry.

Bay (3), inlet of the sea. (F.–L.) F. *baie,* an inlet.–Late L. *baia,* a harbour (Isidore). β. Confused with *bay,* a recess in a wall.–O. F. *baee,* a gap.–Late L. *badāta,* fem. of pp. of *badāre,* to gape.

Bay (4), to bark as a dog. (F.–L.) M. E. *bayen.*–O. F. *baier,* to yelp (Godefroy). Cf. Ital. *baiare,* 'to barke,' Florio. From the sound.

Bay (5), in phr. *at bay.* (F.–L.) For *at abay.*–F. *abois, abbois; être aux abois,* to be at bay, lit. 'to be at the baying of the dogs.' Pl. of F. *aboi,* the bark of a dog; verbal sb. from F. *aboyer,* O. F. *abaier,* to yelp, bay.–O. F. *a* (for L. *ad*); and *baier* (above).

Bay-window; from Bay (3, sect. β) and Window.

Bayonet. (F.) XVII cent. F. *baïonnette; bayonette,* a knife; Cot. Probably named from *Bayonne* (France), where first made or used.

Bazaar. (Pers.) Pers. *bāzār,* a market.

Bdellium. (L.–Gk.–Heb.) A precious substance.–L. *bdellium.*–Gk. βδέλλιον.–Heb. *bedōlakh* (Gen. ii. 12).

Be-, prefix. (E.) A.S. *be-,* prefix; often causative, as in *be-numb,* to make numb. Note also *be-head,* to deprive of the head; *be-set,* to set upon, set round; *be-mire,* to cover with mire; &c.

Be, to exist. (E.) M. E. *been.* A.S. *bēon,* to be.+W. *bod,* to be; Russ. *buite;* L. *fore* (pt. t. *fui*); Gk. φύειν; Skt. *bhū.* (√BHEU.)

Beach. (E.?) XVI cent. Orig. 'shingle.' Prob. E., and the same as prov. E. *bache,* a valley; also, a sandbank near a river. A.S. *bæc,* a valley; Kemble, Cod. Dipl. iii. 386.

Beacon. (E.) M. E. *beken.* A.S. *bēacn, bēcn.*+O. Sax. *bōkan;* O. H. G. *bouhhan.* Teut. type **bauknom,* neut.

Bead. (E.) Orig. 'a prayer;' hence a perforated ball, for counting prayers. M. E. *bede,* a prayer, a bead. A.S. *bed, gebed,* a prayer.–A. S. *biddan* (=*bidjan), to pray.+Du. *bede;* G. *bitte;* Goth. *bida,* a prayer. See Bid (1).

Beadle. (F.–Teut.) M. E. *bedel.*– O. F. *bedel,* F. *bedeau,* a beadle; lit. 'proclaimer,' or 'messenger.'–M. H. G. *bütel,* O. H. G. *butil.*–O. H. G. *but-,* weak

grade of *biotan*, G. *bieten* ; cognate with
A. S. *bēodan*, to bid. Cf. A. S. *bydel*, a
beadle, from *bēodan*. See **Bid** (2).

Beagle, a dog. (Unknown.) M. E.
begle, Squire of Low Degree, l. 771.

Beak. (F.−C.) M. E. *bec.*−F. *bec.*−
Late L. *beccus*, of Gaulish origin. Cf.
Irish *bacc*, W. *bach*, a crook, a hook.

Beaker. (Scand.−L.−Gk.) M. E.
biker, *byker.*−Icel. *bikarr*, a cup. + O.
Sax. *bikeri* ; Du. *beker* ; G. *becher* ; Ital.
bicchiere. β. Perhaps from Late L. *bicā-
rium*, a wine-cup.−Gk. *βῖκos*, an earthen
wine-vessel ; a word of Eastern origin.

Beam (1), a piece of timber. (E.)
M. E. *beem*. A. S. *bēam*, a tree. + Du.
boom ; G. *baum*. Cf. also Icel. *baðmr*, a
tree ; Goth. *bagms*.

Beam (2), a ray. (E.) [Usually identified with **Beam** (1), specially used to
signify a column of light; cf. A. S. *byr-
nende bēam*, ' the pillar of fire.'] But A. S.
bēam, a beam (as in *sunne-bēam*, a sun-
beam) answers to a Teut. type *bau-moz*,
prob. cognate with Gk. φαῦ-σιs, light, φάos
(for φάƒos), also φῶs, light. See **Phosphorus.**

Bean. (E.) M. E. *bene*. A. S. *bēan*.
+ Du. *boon* ; Icel. *baun* ; O. H. G. *pōna*,
bōna (G. *bohne*). Teut. type *baunā*, f.

Bear (1), to carry. (E.) M. E. *beren*.
A. S. *beran*. + Icel. *bera* ; O. H. G. *beran* ;
Goth. *bairan* ; also L. *ferre* ; Gk. φέρειν ;
Skt. *bhṛ* ; O. Ir. *berim*, I bear ; Russ. *brate*,
to take, carry ; Pers. *burdan*, to bear.
(√BHER.) Der. *upbear.*

Bear (2), an animal. (E.) M. E. *bere*.
A. S. *bera*.+Icel. *bera* (*björn*) ; O. H. G.
bero, *pero*, G. *bär* ; Du. *beer*. Cf. Lith.
bēras, brown (Kluge). Teut. type *beron-*.

Beard. (E.) M. E. *berd*. A. S. *beard*.
+Du.*baard* ; G. *bart*. Teut. type *bardoz*.
Allied to Russ. *boroda* ; Lith. *barzda* ; L.
barba, beard ; from Idg. type *bhardhā*.

Beast. (F.−L.) M. E. *beste*.−O. F.
beste (F. *bête*).−L. *bestia*, a beast.

Beat. (E.) M. E. *beten*. A. S. *bēatan*.
+Icel. *bauta* ; O. H. G. *pōzan*, M. H. G.
bōzen. Teut. type *bautan-*.

Beatify. (F.−L.) F. *béatifier.*−L.
beātificāre, to make happy.−L. *beāti-*, for
beātus, pp. of *beāre*, to bless, make happy;
and *-fic-*, for *facere*, to make.

beatitude. (F.−L.) F. *béatitude*.
−L. *beātitūdinem*, acc. from nom. *beāti-
tūdo*, blessedness.−L. *beāti-*, for *beatus*,
blessed ; with suffix *-tūdo*.

Beau, a dressy man. (F.−L.) F. *beau* ;
O. F. *bel.*−L. *bellus*, fair.   For *ben-lus* ;
from *ben-* (as in *ben-e*), variant of *bon-*, as
in *bon-us*, good. Brugm. ii. § 67.

beauty. (F.−L.) M. E. *beute.*−A.F.
beute, O. F. *beaute*, *beltet.*−L. *bellitātem*,
acc. of *bellitās*, fairness.−L. *bellus*, fair
(above). Der. *beauti-ful*, *beaute-ous*.

Beaver (1), an animal. (E.) M. E.
bever. A. S. *befer*, *beofor*. + Du. *bever* ;
Icel. *bjórr* ; Dan. *bæver* ; Swed. *bäfver* ;
G. *biber* ; Russ. *bobr'* ; Lith. *bebrus* ; L.
fiber. Skt. *babhrus* (1) brown ; (2) a large
ichneumon. Teut. type *bebruz* ; Idg. type
bhebhrus, reduplicated deriv. of *bhru-*,
brown, tawny. Brugm. i. § 566. See
Brown.

Beaver (2), **Bever,** lower part of a
helmet. (F.)   Altered by confusion with
beaver-hat.−M. E. *baviere.*−O. F. *bavière*,
a child's bib ; also, the bever (beaver) of
a helmet.−F. *baver*, to slaver.−F. *bave*,
foam, slaver.   Perhaps from the movement of the lips ; cf. Bret. *babouz*, slaver.

Beaver (3), **Bever,** a short immediate repast. (F.−L.) M. E. *beuer* (=
bever).−A. F. *beivre*, a drink ; substantival
use of O. F. *bevre*, *beivre*, to drink.−L.
bibere, to drink.

Becalm, to make calm. See **Be-** and
Calm.

Because. (E. *and* F.−L.) See **Cause.**

Bechance. (E. *and* F.−L.) See
Chance.

Beck (1), to nod, give a sign. (E.)
M. E. *bek-yn*, the same as *bek-nyn*, to
beckon (Prompt. Parv.). See **Beckon.**

Beck (2), a stream. (Scand.)   M. E.
bek.−Icel. *bekkr* ; Swed. *bäck* ; Dan. *bæk* ;
a stream. Teut. type *bakkiz*. Also
Teut. type *bakiz* ; whence Du. *beek*, a
beck ; G. *bach*.

Beckon. (E.)   M. E. *beknen*. A. S.
bēcnan, *bēacnian* (also *biecnan*), to make
signs.−A. S. *bēacn*, a sign. See **Beacon.**

Become. (E.)   A. S. *becuman*, to
arrive, happen, turn out, befall. + Goth.
bi-kwiman ; cf. G. *be-quem*, suitable, becoming.   From **Be-** and **Come.**

Bed. (E.) M. E. *bed*. A. S. *bed*, *bedd*.
+Du. *bed* ; Goth. *badi* ; G. *bett*.   Teut.
type *badjom*, n.

bedrid, bedridden. (E.)   M. E.
bedrede (Ch. C. T. 7351) ; *bedreden* (P.
Pl. B. viii. 85). A. S. *bedrida*, *bedreda*, lit.
' a bedrider ; ' one who can only ride on a
bed, not on a horse.−A. S. *bed*, a bed ; and

43

*,*ḥid-a,* one who rides, from the weak grade of *rīdan,* to ride.

bedstead. (E.) M. E. *bcdstcde.* — A. S. *bed,* a bed; and *stede,* a stand, station; see Stead.

Bedabble, Bedaub, Bedazzle, Bedew, Bedim, Bedizen. See Dabble, Daub, &c.

Bedell. (Low L. — Teut.) From the Latinised form (*bedellus*), of O. F. and M. E. *bedel;* see Beadle.

Bedlam. (Palestine.) M. E. *bedlem,* corruption of Bethlehem, in Palestine. Now applied to the hospital of St. Mary of Bethlehem, for lunatics.

Bedouin. (F. — Arab.) O. F. *bedouin,* a wandering Arab; orig. pl. — Arab. *badawīn,* pl. of Arab. *badawīy,* wandering in the desert. — Arab. *badw,* a desert.

Bedridden, Bedstead; see Bed.

Bee. (E.) M. E. *bee.* A. S. *bēo,* earlier *bīo.*+Du. *bij;* O. H. G. *bīa.* Cf. G. *bie-ne;* Lith. *bi-tte;* Ir. *bea-ch.* Perhaps 'flutterer'; cf. Skt. *bhī,* to fear; O. H. G. *bi-bēn,* to tremble.

Beech. (E.) A. S. *bōēce, bēce,* a beech; *bēcen,* adj., beechen; both derivatives (by mutation) from the older form *bōc.* See Book.

Beef. (F. — L.) M. E. *beef.* — A. F. *bēf;* O. F. *boef* (F. *bœuf*). — L. *bouem,* acc. of *bōs,* an ox.+Gk. βοῦς, ox; Ir. *bó,* Gael. *bò,* W. *buw,* Skt. *go,* A. S. *cū,* a cow; see Cow.

beef-eater, a yeoman of the guard. (Hyb.) Lit. 'an eater of beef;' hence, an attendant. Cf. A. S. *hlāf-ǣta,* a loaf-eater, a servant. ¶ The usual derivation (from Mr. Steevens' imaginary *beaufetier,* later spelt *buffetier*) is historically baseless.

Beer. (E.) M. E. *bere.* A. S. *bēor.* + Du. and G. *bier;* Icel. *bjórr.*

Beestings; see Biestings.

Beet. (L.) M. E. *bete.* A. S. *bēte.* — L. *bēta,* beet (Pliny).

Beetle (1), an insect. (E.) Prov. E. *bittle.* A. S. *bitela,* lit. 'biting one.' — A. S. *bit-,* weak grade of *bītan,* to bite; with adj. suffix *-ol;* cf. *wac-ol,* wakeful. See Bite.

Beetle (2), a large mallet. (E.) M. E. *betel.* A. S. *bȳtel* (= O. Wes. **bīetel,* O. Merc. *bētel); cf. Low G. *bötel.* Teut. type**baut-iloz,* 'a beater;' from**baut-an-,* to beat; see Beat.

Beetle (3), to overhang. (E.) From the M. E. adj. *bitel-brouwed,* 'beetle-browed;' P. Plowm. A. v. 109. Orig. sense doubtful; either from M. E. *bitel,*

sharp, or from M. E. *bitil,* a beetle. In either case from *bit-,* weak grade of *bītan,* to bite.

Befall, Befool, Before; see Fall, &c.

Beg. (F.) M. E. *beggen.* A. F. *begger,* Langtoft, i. 248; used as equiv. to *be-guigner,* Britton, I. 22. § 15. Formed from the sb. *beggar;* see below.

Beget, Begin; see Get, Gin (1).

Beggar. (F.) M. E. *beggare;* cf. *Begger* = a Beguin or Beghard, Rom. Rose, 7256 (F. text, *Beguin*). — O. F. *begard, begart,* Flemish *beggaert,* Late L. *Beghardus.* Formed, with suffix *-ard* (G. *-hart*), from Bègue, a man's name. See Beguine.

Begone, Beguile; see Go, Guile.

Beguine, one of a class of religious devotees. (F.) Chiefly used in the fem.; F. *béguine,* Low L. *beghīna,* one of a religious order, first established at Liège, about A. D. 1207. Named af'er Lambert Le Bègue, priest of Liège (12th c.); whence also Beguin, Beghard, masc. Le Bègue means 'stammerer,' from the verb *bègui,* to stammer, in the dialect of Namur; allied to Picard *béguer,* F. *bégayer.*

Begum, in the E. Indies, a lady of the highest rank. (Pers. — Turk.) Pers. *begum,* a queen, lady of rank. — Turk. *beg,* *bey,* a bey, governor. See Bey.

Behalf, interest. (E.) Formerly in the M. E. phrase *on my behalue* = on my behalf, on my side; substituted for the A. S. phr. *on (mīn) healfe,* on the side of (me), by confusion with *be healfe (mē),* used in the same sense. From A. S. *be,* by; and *healf,* sb., side. See Half.

Behave. (E.) I. e. to *be-have* oneself, or control oneself; from *have* with prefix *be-,* the same as prep. *by.*

behaviour. (E.; *with* F. *suffix.*) Formed abnormally from the verb to *behave;* confused with F. sb. *avoir,* (1) wealth, (2) ability. Cf. Lowl. Sc. *havings,* (1) wealth, (2) behaviour.

Behead. (E.) From Be- and Head.

Behemoth. (Heb. — Egypt.) Heb. *behēmōth,* said to be pl. of *behēmāh,* a beast; but probably of Egypt. origin.

Behest, Behind, Behold. (E.) See Hest, Hind, Hold (1).

Behoof, advantage. (E.) M. E. *to bihoue,* for the advantage of. A. S. *behōf,* advantage.+O. Fries. *bihōf,* Du. *behoef,* advantage; G. *behuf;* Swed. *behof;* Dan. *behov,* need. β. The prefix *be* is A. S. *be,*

44

E. *by.* The simple sb. appears in Icel. *hóf,* moderation, measure; cf. Goth. *gahobains,* temperance, self-restraint. From A. S. *hóf,* 2nd stem of the vb. **Heave.**

behove, to befit. (E.) A. S. *behófian,* verb formed from the sb. *behóf* above. + Du. *behoeven,* from sb. *behoef*; Swed. *behöfva*; Dan. *behöve.*

Belabour, Belay; see **Labour, Lay.**

Belch. (E.) M. E. *belken.* A. S. *bealcian, bælcan,* to utter; translating L. *ēructāre,* used figuratively. Cf. *bælc,* sb. + Du. *balken,* to bray. See **Bellow** and **Bell.**

Beldam. (F. – L.) Ironically for *beldame,* i. e. fine lady. – F. *belle dame.* – L. *bella,* fem. of *bellus,* fair; and *domina,* lady, fem. of *dominus,* lord. See **Beau.**

Beleaguer. (Du.) See **Leaguer.**

Belemnite, a fossil. (Gk.) Gk. βελεμνίτης, a stone shaped like the head of a dart. – Gk. βέλεμνον, a dart. – Gk. βάλλειν, to cast. (√GwEL.)

Belfry. (F. – G.) Orig. 'a watchtower.' Corrupted (partly by influence of *bell*) from M. E. *berfray, berfrey,* a watchtower. – O. F. *berfrei, berfroi, belfroi* (F. *beffroi*). – M. H. G. *bercfrit,* a watch-tower. – M. H. G. *berc-,* for *berg-,* base of *bergen,* to protect; and M. H. G. *frit, fride,* a place of security, a tower, the same word as G. *friede,* peace; hence the lit. sense is ' a protecting shelter,' watch-tower. Allied to **Borough** and **Free.**

Belie. (E.) A. S. *belēogan,* to tell lies about. From *be-,* by, prefix; and *lēogan,* to lie. See **Lie** (2).

Believe. (E.) M. E. *beleuen (beleven).* The prefix *be-* was substituted for older *ge-.* – O. Merc. *gelēfan,* A.S. *gelīefan, gelȳfan,* to believe; lit. to hold dear. + Du. *gelooven*; O. H. G. *gilouban,* G. *g-lauben*; Goth. *ga-laubjan.* Teut. type **laubjan,* with A.S. *ge-,* prefix; from *laub,* 2nd stem of Teut. root **leub* = Idg. √LEUBH, to like. See **Lief.**

Bell. (E.) M. E. *belle.* A. S. *belle,* a bell. + Du. *bel.* Perhaps named from its loud sound; cf. A.S. *bellan,* to roar, bellow. See **Bellow.**

Belle, a fair lady. (F. – L.) F. *belle,* fem. of F. *beau,* O. F. *bel,* fair. – L. *bellus,* fair, fine. See **Beau.**

belladonna. (Ital. – L.) Ital. *bella donna,* fair lady. – L. *bella domina*; see **Beldam.** A name given to the nightshade, from the use of it by ladies to give ex-

pression to the eyes, the pupils of which it expands.

Belligerent. (L.) More correctly, *belligerant.* – L. *belligerant-,* stem of pres. pt. of *belligerāre,* to carry on war. – L. *belli-,* for *bello-,* stem of *bellum,* war; *gerere,* to carry on (war). *Bellum* is for O. Lat. *duellum*; see **Duel.**

Bellow. (E.) M. E. *belwen* (c. 1300). Not fully explained. It may have resulted from confusion of A.S. *bellan,* to roar, bellow, with the str. verb *belgan,* to be angry, or with the rare verb *bylgian,* to bellow (which would have given *billow*). See **Bell.** Cf. **Bull.**

Bellows. (Scand.) M.E. *beli, bely, below,* a bag, but also used in the special sense of ' bellows.' *Bellows* is the pl. of M. E. *below,* a bag, from Icel. *belgr*; and M. E. *beli* (from A.S.) also means *belly.* Cf. G. *blase-balg,* a ' blow-bag,' a pair of bellows; A.S. *blǣst-belg,* bellows, lit. ' blast-bag.' See below.

belly. (E.) M. E. *bely.* A.S. *bælg, belg,* a bag, skin (for holding things); hence (later), belly. + Icel. *belgr,* bag; Du. *balg,* skin, belly; Swed. *bälg,* belly, bellows; Dan. *bælg,* husk, belly; G. *balg*; Goth. *balgs,* bag. Teut. type **balgiz.* From *balg-,* 2nd stem of Teut. root *balg* (= Idg. √BHELGH), to swell. Cf. Irish *bolg,* bag, belly; *bolgaim,* I swell; W. *bol,* belly. Der. *bellows,* q. v.

Belong, Beloved, Below; see **Long, Love, Low.**

Belt, a girdle. (L.) M. E. *belt.* A.S. *belt.* + Icel. *belti*; Irish and Gael. *balt,* a belt, border; O. H. G. *balz*; Swed. *bälte*; Dan. *bælte.* All borrowed from L. *balteus,* a belt.

Beltane, Old May-day. (C.) O. Irish *bel-tene* (Windisch); lit. ' fire-kindling,' from an old custom. Celtic type **belo-te(p)niā*; where *belo-* is cognate with A.S. *bǣl,* a blaze, and *tepniā* is from **tepnos,* type of O. Irish *ten,* fire; cf. L. *tep-ēre,* to be warm (Fick. ii. 125, 164).

Bemoan. (E.) From **Be-** and **Moan.**

Bench. (E.) M. E. *benche.* – A.S. *benc.* + Du. *bank,* a bench, table, bank for money; Swed. *bänk*; Dan. *bænk*; Icel. *bekkr*; G. *bank.* Teut. type **bankiz.* Doublet, *bank.*

Bend (1), to bow, curve. (E.) M. E. *benden.* A. S. *bendan,* orig. to string a bow, fasten a band or string to it; cf. A. S.

bend, a band (= Teut.*bandiz); from *band,* 2nd stem of *bind-an,* to bind. See **Bind.** So also Icel. *benda,* to bend a bow ; allied to *band,* a cord.

bend (2), an oblique band, in heraldry. (F. − G.) O. F. *bende,* also *bande,* a band ; see Cotgrave. The same word as F. *bande,* a band of men ; see **Band** (2).

Beneath. (E.) M. E. *benethe.* A. S. *beneoðan,* prep. below.− A. S. *be-,* by ; *neoðan,* adv. below, from the base *neoð-* in *neoð-era,* nether ; with adv. suffix *-an.* Cf. G. *nied-en, nied-er* ; see **Nether.**

Benediction. (F.−L.) F. *bénédic-tion.* − L. *benedictiōnem,* acc. of *benedictio,* a blessing.− L. *benedictus,* pp. of *bene-dīcere,* to speak well, bless.− L. *bene,* well ; and *dicere,* to speak (see **Diction**).

benison. (F.−L.) M. E. *beneysun.* −O. F. *beneison.*− L. acc. *benedictiōnem.*

Benefactor. (L.) L. *benefactor,* a doer of good.− L. *bene,* well ; and *factor,* a doer, from *facere,* to do.

benefice. (F.−L.) M. E. *benefice.* −F. *bénéfice* (Cot.).−Late L. *beneficium,* a grant of an estate ; L. *beneficium,* a well-doing, a kindness.− L. *bene,* well ; and *facere,* to do.

benefit. (F.−L.) Modified (badly) from M. E. *benfet.* − O. F. *bienfet* (F. *bienfait*).− L. *benefactum,* a kindness conferred ; neut. of pp. of *benefacere,* to do well, be kind.

Benevolence. (F.−L.) F. *bénévolence* (Cot.).− L. *beneuolentia,* kindness.− L. acc. *bene uolentem,* kind, lit. well-wishing.− L. *bene,* well ; and *uolentem,* acc. of *uolens,* wishing, from *uolo,* I wish (see **Voluntary**).

Benighted. (E.) See **Night.**

Benign. (F. − L.) O. F. *benigne* (F. *bénin*).− L. *benignus,* kind ; short for **benigenus.*− L. *beni-,* for **benus,* variant of *bonus,* good ; and *-genus,* born (as in *indigenus*), from *genere,* old form of *gignere,* to beget.

Benison, blessing ; see **Benediction.**

Bent-grass. (E.) M. E. *bent.* A. S. *beonet,* for earlier **binut,* bent-grass (in place-names).+O. H. G. *binuz,* G. *binse,* bent-grass.

Benumb. From **Be-** and **Numb.**

Benzoin, a resinous substance. (F. − Ital. − Arab.) F. *benjoin,* 'gum benzoin or gum benjamin ;' Cot. − Ital. *ben-zoino, bengivi* (Torriano). The Ital. *lo*

bengivi seems to have been substituted for the Arab. name, *lubān jāwī,* lit. frankincense of Java. (Further corrupted to *gum benjamin.*)

Bequeath. (E.) A. S. *becweðan* to assert, bequeath. − A. S. *be-,* prefix ; and *cweðan,* to say, assert. See **Quoth.**

bequest. (E.) M. E. *biqueste, biquiste.* Formed, with added *-te* (cf. M. E. *requeste*), from A. S. **bicwiss,* *becwiss (not found), sb. due to *becweðan,* to bequeath, assert, say. The components of this form occur ; viz. *be-, bi-,* prefix, and *cwiss* (in *ge-cwis*), a saying. *Cwiss* is from Teut. **kwessiz,* Idg.**g(w)ettis,* formed (with suffix *-ti-*) from Idg. base **g(w)et-,* whence *cweðan,* to say (Sievers, A. S. Gr. § 232) ; and *becwiss* is thus a regular deriv. of *becweðan,* to bequeath.

Bereave. (E.) A.S. *berēafian,* to dispossess ; see **Reave.**

Bergamot (1), an essence. (Ital.) Ital. *bergamotta,* the essence called bergamot. − Ital. *Bergamo,* a town in Lombardy.

Bergamot (2), a kind of pear. (F.− Ital. − Turk.) F. *bergamotte* (Cot.).− Ital. *bergamott-a* (pl. *-e*), 'a kind of excellent pears, come out of Turky ;' Torriano. −Turk. *beg armūdi,* 'prince's pear.' − Turk. *beg,* prince ; *armūd,* pear.

Berry. (E.) M. E. *berie.* A. S. *berie.* +Du. *bes, bezie* ; Icel. *ber* ; Swed. *bär* ; Dan. *bær* ; G. *beere* ; Goth. *basi.* All from a base *bas-.* Lit. 'edible fruit ;' cf. Skt. *bhas,* to eat. **Der.** *goose-berry,* &c.

Berth. (E.) Formerly 'convenient sea-room' ; prob. from the M. E. *ber-en,* to bear ; as if 'bearing-off room.' Cf. prov. E. *berth,* a foothold, grasp, position. See **Bear** (1) ; and cf. **Birth.**

Beryl. (L.− Gk.− Skt.) M. E. *beril.* −O. F. *beril.*−L. *bēryllus.*−Gk. βήρυλλος ; cf. Arab. *billaur,* crystal, beryl.− Skt. *vaidūrya* (Prakrit *velūriya*), orig. beryl, brought from Vidûra in S. India (Yule ; Böhtlingk).

Besant, Bezant, a gold circle, in heraldry. (F.−L.−Gk.) Intended to represent a gold coin of Byzantium.− O. F. *besant,* 'an ancient gold coin ;' Cot.−L. *Byzantium.*−Gk. Βυζάντιον, the name of Constantinople.

Beseech. (E.) M. E. *besechen.* From *be-,* prefix ; and *sechen,* Southern form corresponding to Northern *seken,* to seek. See **Seek.**

Beseem, Beset, Beshrew, Beside, Besiege; see Seem, Sit, Shrew, &c.

Besom, a broom. (E.) M. E. *besum, besme.* A. S. *besma.*+Du. *bezem;* G. *besen.* Teut. type **besmon-,* m.

Besot, Bespeak; see Sot, Speak.

Best; see Better.

Bestead; from Be- and Stead.

Bestial. (F. – L.) F. *bestial.* – L. *bestiālis,* beast-like. – L. *bestia,* a beast. See Beast.

Bestow, Bestrew, Bestride; see Stow, &c.

Bet, to wager. (F. – Scand.) Short for *abet,* in the sense to maintain, or 'back,' as *abet* is explained in Phillips, ed. 1706. See Abet. Der. *bet,* sb.

Betake. (E. *and* Scand.) See Take.

Betel, a species of pepper. (Port. – Malayalim.) Port. *betel, betele.* – Malayalim *vettila,* i. e. *veru ila,* mere leaf (Yule).

Bethink, Betide, Betimes, Betoken; see Think, &c.

Betray. (F. – L.; *with* E. *prefix.*) From *be-,* prefix; and O. F. *traïr* (F. *trahir*), to deliver up, from L. *trādere.* ¶ The prefix *be-* was due to confusion with *bewray.* See Tradition.

Betroth. (E.) See Troth.

Better, Best. (E.) 1. From the Teut. base **bat,* good, was formed the Teut. comp. stem **batizon-,* as in Goth. *batiza,* better, A. S. *betera* (with mutation from *a* to *e*), M. E. *better.* The A. S. *bet,* M. E. *bet,* is adverbial and comparative. 2. From the same base was formed Goth. *batista,* best, A. S. *betst* (for *bet-ist*), M. E. *best.* Similarly Du. *beter, best;* Icel. *betri, beztr;* Dan. *bedre, bedst;* Swed. *bättre, bäst;* G. *besser, best.* **Der.** (from the same base) *batten, boot* (2).

Between. (E.) A. S. *betweonan,* between; earlier *betweonum.* – A. S. *be,* by; *twēonum,* dat. pl. of *twēone,* double, allied to *twā,* two; see Two. Here *twēonum* (also *twīnum*) answers to Goth.*tweihnaim,* dat. pl. of *tweihnai,* 'two each.' Cf. L. *bīnī.*

betwixt. (E.) (M. E. *betwix;* to which *t* was afterwards added. – A. S. *betwix, betwux, betweox, betweohs,* apparently extended from A. S.*betwīh,* between. From A. S. *be,* by; and **twīh,* answering to *tweih-* in Goth. *tweih-nai,* two each. See above.

Bevel, sloping; to slope, slant. (F.)

In Sh. Sonn. 121. – O. F. **bivel,* **buvel,* only found in mod. F. *biveau,* and in F. *buveau,* 'a kind of squire [carpenter's rule], having moveable and compasse branches, or the one branch compasse and the other straight; some call it a *bevell;*' Cot. Cf. Span. *baivel.* Origin unknown.

Bever, a potation; see Beaver (3).

beverage. (F. – L.) O. F. *bevrage* (Supp. to Godefroy), drink. – O. F. *bevre, boivre,* to drink. – L. *bibere,* to drink.

bevy. (F. – L.) It answers to O. F. *bevee,* a drink; from O. F. *bevre,* to drink (above). Cf. Ital. *beva,* a bevy (Florio); also, a drink (Torriano).

Bewail, Beware, Bewilder, Bewitch; see Wail, Ware, Wild, Witch.

Bewray, to disclose. (E.) Properly to accuse. M. E. *bewraien, biwreyen,* to disclose. A. S. *be-,* prefix (see Be-); and *wrēgan,* to accuse (for older **wrōgian,* with mutation from *ō* to *ē*). Cf. Icel. *rægja* (for *vrægja*), to slander, Swed. *röja,* to discover; O. Fries. *biwrōgia,* to accuse; Goth. *wrōhjan,* to accuse; G. *rügen,* to censure. β. These are causal verbs, from the base *wrōh-* seen in Goth. *wrōhs,* accusation, Icel. *rōg,* a slander.

Bey, a governor. (Turk.) Turk. *beg* (pron. nearly as *bay*), a lord, prince.

Beyond. (E.) M. E. *beyonde.* A. S. *begeondan,* beyond. – A. S. *be-,* for *be* or *bi,* by; and *geond,* prep. across, beyond, from *geon,* yon. Cf. Goth. *jaindrē,* thither, *jaind,* there; from *jains,* that, yon. See Yon.

Bezel, the part of a ring in which the stone is set. (F.) Also spelt *basil;* it also means a sloping edge. – O. F. *bisel* (Roquefort); mod. F. *biseau,* a bezel, basil, slant, sloped edge. Cf. Span. *bisel,* the slanting edge of a looking-glass. Perhaps from L. *bis,* double.

Bezique, a game at cards. (F. – Pers.) F. *besigue* (with *g*); also *bésy* (Littré). β. The first form = Pers. *bāzīchah,* sport, a game; the second = Pers. *bāzī,* play. – Pers. *bāzīdan,* to play. [A guess.]

Bezoar, a stone. (F. – Span. – Arab. – Pers.) O. F. *bezoar,* F. *bézoard.* – Span. *bezoar.* – Arab. *bādizahr.* – Pers. *pād-zahr,* bezoar; lit. 'counter-poison,' from its supposed virtue. – Pers. *pād,* expelling; and *zahr,* poison.

Bezonian, a beggarly fellow. (F.) In 2 Hen. IV. v. 3. 118. Formerly *bisonian*; made by adding E. *-ian* to F. *bisogne*, spelt *bisongne*, in Cotgrave, 'a filthe knave ... bisonian.' Or from Ital. *bisogno*, need, want; whence *bisogni*, pl. 'new-levied souldiers, such as come ... needy to the wars'; Torriano (not in Florio). Origin unknown.

Bi-, prefix. (L.) L. *bi-*, for **dui-*, twice. – L. *duo*, two. So also Gk. δι-, Skt. *dvi*. See **Two.**

Bias. (F. – L.) F. *biais*, a slant, slope; hence, inclination to one side. Cf. Ital. *s-biesco, s-biescio*, oblique. Origin unknown.

Bib. (L.) A cloth under a child's chin; from M. E. *bibben*, to drink. – L. *bibere*, to drink. Hence *wine-bibber* (Luke vii. 34) ; L. *bibens uīnum* (Vulg.).

Bible. (F. – L. – Gk.) M. E. *bible*. – F. *bible*. – Late L. *biblia*, fem. sing.; for L. *biblia*, neut. pl. – Gk. βιβλία, collection of writings, pl. of βιβλίον, little book, dimin. of βίβλος, a book. – Gk. βύβλος, Egyptian papyrus; hence, a book.

bibliography. (Gk.) Gk. βιβλίο-, for βιβλίον; and γράφειν, to write.

bibliomania. (Gk.) Gk. βιβλίο-, for βιβλίον; and **Mania.**

Bice. (F.) Properly 'grayish'; hence *blew byce*, grayish blue. – F. *bis*, dusky. Cf. Ital. *bigio*, gray. Origin unknown.

Bicker, to skirmish. (Uncertain.) M. E. *biker*, a fight; *bikeren*, to skirmish. Cf. M. E. *beken*, to peck; *biken*, to thrust with a pointed weapon. Apparently from O. F. *bequer*, to strike with the beak (see **Beak**); or from A. S. *becca*, a pick-axe. Cf. Du. *bikken*, to notch a mill-stone; also E. Fries. *bikkern*, to hack, gnaw, from *bikken*, to hack, *bikke*, a pickaxe (G. *bicke*).

Bicycle. (Hybrid.) In use since 1868. Coined from **Bi-** and **Cycle.**

Bid (1), to pray. (E.) Nearly obsolete; preserved in *bidding-prayer*, and in to *bid beads* (pray prayers). M. E. *bidden.* A. S. *biddan.* + Du. *bidden*; G. *bitten*; Icel. *biðja*; Goth. *bidjan.* Teut. type **bidjan-*, allied to L. *fīdo*, I trust; Gk. πείθω, I prevail upon; from √BHEIDH. See Brugm. i. § 589; ii. § 890.

Bid (2), to command. (E.) M. E. *beden*. – A. S. *bēodan*, to command.+Du. *bieden*, to offer; Icel. *bjōða*; G. *bieten*; Goth. *ana-biudan*; Gk. πεύθομαι, I enquire; Skt. *budh*, to understand. Teut. type **beudan-*. (√BHEUDH.) Confused with **Bid** (1),

the forms of which have taken the place of those of **Bid** (2).

Bide, to await, wait. (E.) M. E. *biden*. A. S. *bīdan.* + Du. *beiden*; Icel. *bīða*; Swed. *bida*; Dan. *bie*; Goth. *beidan*; O. H. G. *bītan.* Teut. type **bīdan-*.

Biennial, lasting two years. (L.) Formed as if from *bienni-um*, a space of two years; the true L. word is *biennālis*. – L. *bi-* two; and *annālis*, lasting a year, yearly. – L. *annus.* So also *tri-ennial*, from *tri-* (for *tres*), three; *quadr-ennial*, more correctly *quadri-ennial*, from *quadri-* (for *quadrus*), belonging to four; *quinqui-ennial*, from *quinqui-* (for *quinque*), five; *dec-ennial*, from *dec-em*, ten; *cent-ennial*, from *centum*, a hundred; *mill-ennial*, from *mille*, a thousand, &c.

Bier, a frame on which a corpse is borne. (E.) M. E. *beere, bære.* A. S. *bǣr, bēr.* – A. S. *bēr-*, 3rd stem of *beran*, to carry. + Du. *baar*; O. H. G. *bāra* (G. *bahre*); allied to Icel. *barar*, fem. pl.; L. *feretrum*; Gk. φέρετρον.

Biestings, Beestings, the first milk given by a cow after calving. (E.) A. S. *bȳsting, bȳst* (for **bīest*), thick milk. From A. S. *bēost*, first milk after calving. +Du. *biest*; G. *biest-milch*.

Bifurcated, two-pronged. (L.) Late L. *bifurcātus*, pp. of *bifurcāri*, to part in two directions. – L. *bi-furcus*, two-pronged; from *bi-(s)*, double; *furca*, a fork.

Big. (Scand. ?) M. E. *big*; also *bigg*, rich (Hampole). Not A. S. Cf. prov. E. *bug*, big, *bog*, boastful. Prob. of Scand. origin. Cf. Norw. *bugge*, a strong man.

Bigamy, a double marriage. (F. – L. *and* Gk.) F. *bigamie*. – Late L. *bigamia*; a clumsy compound from L. *bi-*, double (see **Bi-**), and Gk. -γαμία, from γάμος, marriage. It should rather have been *digamy* (Gk. διγαμία).

Biggen, a night-cap. (F.) M. F. *beguin*, 'a biggin for a child;' Cot. Named from the caps worn by beguines; see **Beguine.**

Bight, a coil of rope, a bay. (E.) M. E. *bight.* A. S. *byht*, as in *wæteres byht*, a bight (bay) of water (see Grein). – A. S. *bug-*, weak grade of *būgan*, to bow, bend; with mutation of *u* to *y*.+G. *bucht.* Teut. type **buhtiz.* See **Bow** (1).

Bigot, an obstinate devotee to a creed. (F.) F. *bigot*, 'an hypocrite, superstitious fellow;' Cot. Applied by the

French to the Normans as a term of reproach (Wace). Of unknown origin. It is an older word than *beguine*, with which it seems to have been somewhat confused at a later period.

Bijou, a trinket. (F.—C.?) F. *bijou*. Perhaps from Bret. *bizou*, a ring with a stone, a finger-ring, from *biz*, a finger. Cf. Corn. *bisou* (the same), from *bis*, *bes*, a finger; W. *byson*, ring, from *bys*, finger.

Bilberry, a whortle-berry. (Scand.) Dan. *böllebær*, a bilberry; where *bær* is E. *berry*. In M. Dan., *bölle* had the sense of Dan. *bugle*, i. e. boss (Kalkar). Cf. Norw. *bola*, a swelling, tumour. ¶ North Eng. *blea-berry = blue-berry*; see **Blaeberry.** In both cases, *-berry* takes the E. form; see **Berry.**

Bilbo, a sword; **Bilboes,** fetters. (Span.) Both named from Bilboa or Bilbao in Spain, famous for iron and steel.

Bile (1), secretion from the liver. (F.—L.) F. *bile*.—L. *bīlis*. L. *bīlis* is for **bislis*, Brugm. i. § 877; cf. W. *bustl*, Bret. *bestl*, bile (Fick, ed. 4. ii. 175). Der. *bili-ous*.

Bile (2), a boil. (E.) See **Boil** (2).

Bilge. (F.—C.) A variant of *bulge*, which orig. meant the bottom of a ship's hull; whence *bilge-water* (N. E. D.). See **Bulge.**

Bill (1), a chopper, sword. (E.) M. E. *bil*, sword, axe. A. S. *bill*, sword, axe. + O. Sax. *bil*, O. H. G. *bill*, n.; (cf. G. *bille*, axe, f.). Teut. type **biljom*, n.

bill (2), a bird's beak. (E.) M. E. *bile*. A. S. *bile* (Teut. type **biliz*?). Allied to **Bill** (1).

Bill (3), a writing, account. (F.—L.) A. F. *bille*.—Late L. *billa*, a writing; the dimin. is *billēta*, *bullēta*, shewing that *billa* is a corruption of L. *bulla*, a papal bull, &c.; see **Bull** (2).

billet (1), a note. (F.—L.) A. F. *billette*.—Late L. *billetta*, *billēta*, dimin. of *billa*, a writing; see **Bill** (3) above.

Billet (2), a log of wood. (F.) F. *billette*, *billot*, a billet of wood. Dimin. of *bille*, a log, stump. Origin unknown.

billiards. (F.) F. *billard*, 'a billard, or the stick wherewith we touch the ball at billyards;' Cot. Formed with suffix *-ard* (G. *-hart*) from *bille*, a log, stick, as above.

Billion; see **Million.**

Billow, a wave. (Scand.) Icel. *bylgja*, a billow; Swed. *bölja*; Dan. *bölge*.+M. H. G. *bulge*, a billow, a bag. Lit. 'a swell' or surge; cf. Icel. *belgja*, to inflate, puff out. The Icel. *bylgja* has mutation of *u* to *y*, and, like M. H. G. *bulg-e*, is from *bulg-*, 3rd stem of *belgan*, to swell with anger.

Bin. (E.) M. E. *binne*. A. S. *binn*, a manger; Lu. ii. 7.+Du. *ben*, G. *benne*, a sort of basket. Perhaps of Celtic origin; cf. Gaulish Lat. *benna*, body of a cart; W. *ben*, a cart.

Binary, twofold. (L.) L. *bīnārius*, consisting of two things.—L. *bīnus*, two-fold.—L. *bī-*, double; see **Bi-.**

Bind. (E.) M. E. *binden*. A. S. *bindan*. + Du. and G. *binden*; Icel. and Swed. *binda*; Dan. *binde*; Goth. *bindan*; Skt. *bandh*, to bind. (√BHENDH.)

Bing, a heap of corn; *obs.* (Scand.) In Surrey's Poems.—Icel. *bingr*, Swed. *binge*, a heap.+M. H. G. *bīge*, a heap of corn; whence Ital. *bica*. ¶ Distinct from *bin*, though perhaps confused with it.

Binnacle, a box for a ship's compass. (Port.—L.) A singular corruption of the older word *bittacle*, by confusion with *bin*, a chest.—Port. *bitacola*, a bittacle (i. e. binnacle); Vieyra. Cf. Span. *bitacora*, F. *habitacle*, the same. The Port. *bitacola* stands for **habitacola*, the first syllable being lost.—L. *habitāculum*, a little dwelling, i. e. the 'frame of timber in the steerage of a ship where the compass stands' (Bailey).—L. *habitāre*, to dwell; frequent. of *habēre*, to have.

Binocular, having two eyes. (L.) From Lat. *bīn-ī*, two each; *ocul-us*, eye; with suffix *-āris*.

Binomial, having two terms. (L.) From Late L. *binōmi-us*, equiv. to L. *binōminis*, adj. having two names; with suffix *-ālis*. From L. *bi-*, two; *nōmin-*, for *nōmen*, a name.

Biography. (Gk.) A written account of a life; from βίο-, for βίος, life; and γράφειν, to write. The sb. βίος is allied to **Quick.**

biology. (Gk.) Science of life; from Gk. βίο-, for βίος, life; and -λογία, a discoursing, from λόγος, a discourse.

Biped. (L.) L. *biped-*, stem of *bipes*, two-footed; from *bi-*, two; *pēs*, foot.

Birch, a tree. (E.) M. E. *birche*. A. S. *birce*, f.+G. *birke*, f.<Teut. **birk-jōn-*. β. Also A. S. *berc*, *beorc*. + Du.

berk ; Icel. *björk*, Swed. *björk*, Dan. *birk* (cf. North E. *birk*).<Teut. **berkā*, f. Cf. also O. Slav. *brĕza*, Russ. *berĕza* ; Lith. *beržas*. Also Skt. *bhūrja*, a kind of birch.

Bird. (E.) M. E. *brid* (the *r* being shifted) ; A. S. *bridd*, a bird, esp. the young of birds.

Biretta, a clerical cap. (Ital.–L.– Gk.) Ital. *beretta* (Torriano) ; cf. Late L. *birrētum*, orig. a scarlet cap.–Late L. *birrus, burrus*, reddish. See **Bureau.**

Birth. (Scand.) M. E. *burthe, birthe.* Cf. Icel. *burðr*, m. ; Swed. *börd*, Dan. *byrd*, f. (= O. Icel. *byrð*, f.). + A. S. *gebyrd*, f. ; O. H. G. *giburt* (G. *geburt*) ; Goth. *gabaurths*, f.<Teut. **burðiz* = Idg. **bhrtis* (Skt. *bhr̥tis*, f. nourishment). All from the weak grade of √BHER, to bear. See **Bear** (1).

Biscuit, a kind of cake. (F.–L.) F. *biscuit*, lit. twice cooked.–F. *bis* (L. *bis*), twice ; and *cuit*, cooked, from L. *coctum*, acc. of *coctus*, pp. of *coquere*, to cook.

Bisect. (L.) From L. *bī-*, short for *bis*, twice ; and *sect-um*, supine of *secāre*, to cut.

Bishop. (L.–Gk.) A. S. *biscop.*–L. *episcopus.*–Gk. ἐπίσκοπος, a bishop ; lit. ' overseer.'–Gk. ἐπί, upon ; σκοπός, one that observes, from σκοπ-, *o*-grade of σκεπ-, as in σκέπ-τομαι, I spy, overlook. See **Species.**

Bismuth, a metal. (G.) G. *bismuth*; also spelt *wismut, wissmut, wissmuth.* Origin unknown.

Bison, a quadruped. (L.–Teut.) L. *bison* (Pliny) ; Late Gk. βίσων. Not a L. word, but borrowed from Teutonic ; O. H. G. *wisunt*, G. *wisent*, a bison ; A. S. *weosend*, a wild ox ; Icel. *vīsundr.* See O. H. G. *wisunt* in Schade.

Bissextile, a name for leap-year. (L.) Late L. *bissextīlis annus*, bissextile year.–L. *bissextus*, an intercalary day; so called because the intercalated day (formerly Feb. 24) was called the *sixth* of the calends of March; there being thus two days with the same name.–L. *bis*, twice ; *sextus*, sixth, from *sex*, six.

Bisson, purblind. (E.) In Sh. M. E. *bisen.* O. Northumb. *bisen*, blind (Matt. ix. 28). Origin unknown.

Bistre, a dark brown. (F.–G. ?) F. *bistre*, a dark brown. Perhaps from prov. G. *biester*, dark, gloomy, also bistre (Flügel).

Bit (1), a mouthful, small piece. (E.)

M. E. *bite* (2 syll.). A. S. *bita*, a morsel. From A. S. *bit-*, weak grade of *bītan*, to bite.+Du. *beet*; Icel. *biti*; Swed. *bit*; Dan. *bid.*<Teut. type **biton-*, m.

bit (2), a curb for a horse. (E.) M. E. *bitt.* A. S. *bite*, m. a bite, a biting.<Teut. type **bitiz*, a bite ; cf. *bitol*, a curb.+Du. *gebit*; Icel. *bitill* (dimin.) ; Swed. *bett*; Dan. *bid*; G. *gebiss.*

Bitch. (E.) M. E. *biche, bicche.* A. S. *bicce.*+Icel. *bikkja* ; also *grey-baka.*

Bite. (E.) M. E. *biten.* A. S. *bītan.* +Du. *bijten*; Icel. *bīta* ; Swed. *bita* ; Dan. *bide*; G. *beissen.* Teut. type **bītan-.* Allied to L. *findere* (pt. t. *fīdi*), to cleave ; Skt. *bhid*, to cleave. (√BHEID.)

bitter. (E.) M. E. *biter.* A. S. *biter, bitor*, lit. ' biting.'–A. S. *bit-*, weak grade of *bītan*, to bite.+Du. *bitter*; Icel. *bitr* ; Swed., Dan., G. *bitter.*

Bittern, a bird. (F.–Late L.) The *n* is added. M. E. *botor, bitoure.*–F. *butor*, ' a bittor [bittern] ;' Cot. Prob. named from its cry ; cf. L. *būtire, bubire*, to cry like a bittern ; whence also L. *būtio*, said to mean ' bittern,' though the same word as *būteo*, i. e. buzzard.

Bitts, naval term. (Scand. ?) The *bitts* are two strong posts on deck to which cables are fastened. Prob. from Icel. *biti*, a bit, mouthful (see **Bit** (1)); also, a cross-beam in a house ; a thwart (L. *transtrum*) in a ship. [F. *bites*, bitts (see Cot.), Span. *bitas*, may have been borrowed from E.] Cf. also A. S. *bǣting*, a cable for holding a ship, from *bǣtan*, to restrain, curb, equivalent (in form) to Icel. *beita* ; see **Bait.** Also Swed. *beting*, a bitt, whence *betingbult*, a bitt-bolt, bitt-pin ; Dan. *beding* : used also on land for tethering horses, as in Swed. *betingbult*, a peg for tethering, from *beta*, to pasture, bait.

Bitumen. (L.) L. *bitūmen*, mineral pitch. Cf. Brugm. i. § 663.

Bivalve. (F.–L.) From **Bi-** and **Valve.**

Bivouac. (F.–G.) F. *bivouac*, orig. *bivac.*–Swiss G. *beiwacht*, an additional watch at night (Stalder) ; cf. *bei-geben*, to add.–G. *bei*, in addition ; *wacht*, a watch, from *wachen*, to wake. See **Wake** (1). Cf. G. *beiwache.*

Bizarre, odd. (F.–Span.) F. *bizarre*, strange, capricious ; orig. ' valiant.' –Span. *bizarro*, valiant, gallant. Perhaps of Basque origin ; cf. Basque *bizarra*, a beard. Cf. Span. *hombre de bigote*, a man of spirit; where *bigote* means 'moustache.'

Blab, to tell tales. (E.)   M. E. *blabbe*, a tell-tale; *blaberen*, to babble. Cf. Dan. *blabbre*, to babble; Dan. dial. *blaffre*, G. *plappern*, to babble, prate. Of imitative origin; cf. Gael. *plab*, a soft noise; *plabair*, a babbler; *blabaran*, a stammerer, *blabh-dach*, babbling, garrulous.

Black. (E.)   M. E. *blak*. A. S. *blac*, *blæc* [which editors have often confused with *blǣc*, bright, shining]. Cf. Icel. *blakkr*, dark; also A. S. *blæc*, Low G. *blak*, O. H. G. *blach*, Icel. *blak*, Swed. *bleck*, Dan. *blæk*, all meaning 'ink.' Connexion with Du. *blaken*, to scorch, is doubtful.

blackguard, a term of reproach. (E. and F.)   From *black* and *guard*. A name given to scullions, turnspits, and kitchen menials, from the dirty work done by them. See Trench, Select Glossary.

Bladder. (E.)   M. E. *bladdre*. A. S. *blǣddre*, *blǣdre*, a blister, bladder (lit. blowing out).+Du. *blaar* [Icel. *blaðra*?]; O. H. G. *blātara* (G. *blatter*).   Teut. type *blǣdrōn-*, wk. fem. From Teut. stem *blǣ-*, to blow (see **Blow** (1)); with suffix *-drōn* similar to Gk. *-τρᾰ* (cf. χύτρα, a pot).

Blade, a leaf, flat of a sword. (E.)   M. E. *blade*. A. S. *blæd*, a leaf.+Icel. *blað*, Swed., Dan., Du. *blad*, a leaf, blade; G. *blatt*. Teut. type *bla-dom*, neut., with sense of 'blown,' i. e. 'flourishing;' pp. form (with suffix *-do-* = Idg. *-tó-*) from √BHLŌ. See **Blow** (2).

Blaeberry, Bleaberry, a bilberry. (Scand. and E.)   From North E. *blae*, livid, dark; and *berry*. The form *blae* is from Icel. *blā-r*, livid; see under **Blue**.

Blain, a pustule. (E.)   M. E. *blein*. A. S. *blegen*, a boil.+Du. *blein*; Dan. *blegn*. Cf. O. H. G. *plehen-ougi*, weak-eyed.

Blame, vb. (F. – L. – Gk.)   M. E. *blamen*.–O. F. *blasmer*, to blame.–L. *blasphēmāre*, to speak ill, also to blame. – Gk. βλασφημεῖν; see **Blaspheme**.

Blanch (1), to whiten. (F. – O. H. G.)   From F. *blanchir*, to whiten.–F. *blanc*, white; see **Blank** below.

Blanch (2), the same as **Blench**.

Bland. (L.)   L. *blandus*, mild.

blandish, to flatter. (F. – L.)   M. E. *blandisen*.–O. F. *blandis-*, stem of pres. part of *blandir*, to flatter.–L. *blandīrī*, to caress.–L. *blandus*, bland.

Blank, white. (F. – O. H. G.)   In Milton, P. L. x. 656.–F. *blanc*.–O. H. G.

blanch, white. Nasalised form from O. H. G. *blah*, shining; cf. Gk. φλόγ-εος, flaming, shining, from φλέγ-ειν, to shine.

blanket. (F.– O. H. G.)   Orig. of a white colour. M. E. *blanket*.–A. F. *blanket* (F. *blanchet*), dimin. from *blanc*, white; see above.

Blare, to make a loud noise. (E.)   M. E. *blaren*. Cf. Du. *blaren*, Low G. *blarren*, to bleat; M. H. G. *blēren*, *blerren* (G. *plärren*), to bleat, blubber. Prob. imitative, like *bleat*; but cf. **Blaze** (2).

Blason; see **Blazon.**

Blaspheme, to speak injuriously. (L. – Gk.)   L. *blasphēmāre*.–Gk. βλασφη-μεῖν, to speak ill of.– Gk. βλάσφημος, adj., speaking evil.– Gk. βλασ-, for *βλαβεσ-, i. e. hurtful (cf. βλάβ-η, hurt); and φημί, I say: see **Fame**. Brugm. i. § 744.

Blast, a blowing. (E.)   M. E. *blast*. A. S. *blǣst*, a blowing; cf. Icel. *blāstr*, a breath, blast of a trumpet; O. H. G. *blāst*. Formed with Idg. suffix *to-* from the old base of **Blaze** (2).

Blatant, noisy, roaring. (E.)   Spenser has 'blatant beast'; F. Q. vi. 12 (heading); also *blattant*, id. vi. 1. 7. Prob. imitative. Cf. Lowl. Sc. *blad*, to abuse; *blatter*, a rattling noise; G. *platz*, a crash.

Blay, a bleak (fish). (E.)   A. S. *blǣge*. +Du. *blei*; G. *bleihe*.

Blaze (1), a flame. (E.)   M. E. *blase*. A. S. *blæse*, a flame, in comp. *bǣl·blæse*, a bright light; *blæse*, f. a torch; < Teut. type *blasōn*. Cf. M. H. G. *blas*, a torch; also G. *blässe*, Icel. *blesi*, a 'blaze' or white mark on a horse, Swed. *bläs*, same.

Blaze (2), to proclaim, noise abroad. (Scand.)   Mark i. 45.   M. E. *blasen*. – Icel. *blāsa*, to blow, blow a trumpet, sound an alarm; Swed. *blāsa*, to sound; Dan. *blæse*, Du. *blazen*, to blow a trumpet; G. *blasen*. Also Goth. *uf-blēsan*, to puff up. < Teut. type *blēs-an-*, to blow; whence A. S. *blǣst*, E. *blast*. Much confused with *blazon*.

Blazon (1), **Blason,** a proclamation. Hamlet, i. 5. 21; Shak. Son. 106. A corruption from **Blaze** (2), M. E. *blasen*, to proclaim; due to confusion with **Blazon** (2) below.

Blazon (2), to pourtray armorial bearings. (F.)   M. E. *blason, blasoun*, a shield; whence *blazon*, verb, to describe a shield. –F. *blason*, a coat of arms, orig. a shield (Brachet). Cf. Span. *blason*, heraldry, blazonry, glory, *hacer blason*, to blazon, *blasonar*, to blazon, brag, boast; suggesting a (very doubtful) connexion with G. *blasen*, to blow the trumpet, as done by heralds, to proclaim a victor's fame; see **Blaze** (2) above. (See Scheler.) Or if the orig. sense was a bright mark on a shield, it is allied to **Blaze** (1).

Bleaberry; see **Blaeberry.**

Bleach. (E.) Orig.'to whiten;' M. E. *blechen*, Ancren Riwle, p. 324, l. 1. A. S. *blǣcan*.—A. S. *blāc*, shining, bright, pale. See **bleak** below.＋Icel. *bleikja* ; Du. *bleeken* ; G. *bleichen* ; ＜Teut. *＊blaikjan-*.

bleak (1), orig. pale. (Scand.) M. E. *bleik*.—Icel. *bleikr*, pale ; Swed. *blek* ; Dan. *bleg*.＋A. S. *blāc* ; Du. *bleek* ; G. *bleich*. Teut. type ＊*blaikoz*. From ＊*blaik-*, strong grade of Teut. ＊*bleikan-* (A. S. *blican*), to shine.

bleak (2), a fish. (Scand.) From its pale colour.

Blear-eyed, having watery, inflamed, or dim eyes. (E.) M. E. *bleer-eyed*. Cognate with Low G. *blarr-oged*, bleareyed ; cf. *blarr-oge*, an eye wet with tears, from *blarren*, to howl, weep ; which seems to be allied to E. *blare*.

Bleat. (E.) M. E. *bleten*. A. S. *blǣtan*, *blētan*, to bleat as a sheep.＋Du. *blaten* ; O. H. G. *plāzan*. Cf. Russ. *blejate*, to bleat ; L. *flēre*, to weep.

Bleb, Blob, a small bubble or blister. (E.) Cf. M. E. *blober*, a bubble on water ; *blubber*, a bubble. By comparing *blobber*, *blubber*, with *bubble*, having much the same meaning, we see the probability that they are imitative, from the action of forming a bubble with the lips.

Bleed. (E.) M. E. *bleden*. A. S. *blēdan*, formed (by mutation of *ō* to *ē*) from A. S. *blōd*, blood.＜Teut. type ＊*blōdjan-*, to lose blood＞Icel. *blæða*.

Blemish, to stain. (F.) M. E. *blemisshen*.—O. F. *blemis-*, stem of pres. part. of *blemir*, *blesmir*, to wound, stain, make pale.—O. F. *bleme*, *blesme*, wan, pale. Of unknown origin.

Blench, to shrink from. (E.) M. E. *blenchen*, to avoid, elude. A.S. *blencan*, to deceive ; as if from a Teut. type ＊*blankjan-*, causal of ＊*blinkan-*, to blink. But proof is wanting.

Blend, to mix together. (Scand.) M. E. *blenden*. Due to *blend-*, base of the pres. indic. of Icel. *blanda* (Swed. *blanda*, Dan. *blande*), to blend ; cognate with

A. S. and Goth. *blandan*, str. redupl. vb., O. H. G. *blantan*, to mix.

Bless, to consecrate, &c. (E.) The orig. sense may have been 'to consecrate by blood,' i. e. either by sacrifice or by the sprinkling of blood, as the word can be clearly traced back to *blood*. M. E. *blessen*, A. S. *blētsian*, O. Northumb. *blēdsia*, *bloedsia* (Matt. xxv. 34, xxvi. 26), which can be explained from *blōd*, blood, with the usual vowel-change from *o* to *oe* or *ē*. Teut. type ＊*blōdisōn*. Cf. *bleed*. (Suggested by Sweet ; Anglia, iii. 156.)

Blight. (E.) XVII cent. Of unknown origin ; perhaps allied to M. E. *blichening*, mildew. And cf. M. H. G. *blicze*, G. *blitz*, lightning.

Blind. (E.) A. S. *blind*.＋Du. *blind*; Icel. *blindr* ; Sw., Dan., G. *blind* ;＜Teut. type ＊*blindoz* (Idg. base ＊*bhlendh-*). Cf. Lith. *blęsti-s* (3 pr. s. *blendzia-s*), to become dim (of the sun).

blindfold, vb. (E.) M. E. *blindfolden*, verb (Tyndale) ; corruption of *blindfelden* (Palsgrave), where the *d* is excrescent. The true word is *blindfellen*, to 'fell' or strike blind, Ancren Riwle, p. 106.—A.S. *blind*, blind ; and *fellan*, to strike ; see **Fell.**

Blindman's buff; see **Buff.**

Blink, to wink, to glance. (E.) M. E. *blenken*, to shine, to glance ; whence mod. E. *blink*, by change of *en* to *in*, as in many words. Allied to A. S. *blanc*, white (as in *blanc-a*, a white horse), cognate with O. H. G. *blanch*, M. H. G. *blanc* ; see **Blank.** Cf. Du., G. *blinken*, Swed. *blinka*, Dan. *blinke*, all late forms ; and A. S. *blīcan*, to shine.

Bliss. (E.) see **Blithe.**

Blister. (F.—Teut.) M. E. *blester*, *blister*. (Not found before 1300.)—O. F. *blestre*, 'tumeur,' Godefroy. Of Teut. origin ; cf. Icel. *blāstr* (dat. *blǣstri*), a blast, also a swelling, allied to E. **Blast.** From the notion of blowing out.

Blithe. (E.) M. E. *blithe*. A. S. *blīðe*, sweet, happy.＋O. Sax. *blīði*, bright, glad ; Du. *blijde*, *blij* ; Icel. *blīðr* ; Swed., Dan. *blid* ; O. H. G. *blīdi*, glad ; Goth. *bleiths*, merciful, kind.

bliss. (E.) M. E. *blis*. A. S. *blis*, *bliss* ; contr. from A. S. *blīðs*, happiness, lit. blitheness. — A. S. *blīðe* (above). ＋ O. Sax. *blīzza*, *blīdsea*, happiness. Teut. stem ＊*blissiā* ; with *ss* ＜*tt*, the suffix being -*tiā*, as in L. *laeti-tia*.

Bloat, to swell. (Scand.) We now generally use *bloated* to mean 'puffed out' or 'swollen,' as if allied to *blow*. But the M. E. form was *blout*, soft ; connected with Icel. *blautr*, soft, effeminate, imbecile, *blotna*, to become soft, lose courage. Cf. Swed. *blöt*, Dan. *blöd*, soft, pulpy, mellow. Allied to Icel. *blauðr*, soft ; A. S *blēaþ*, G. *blöde*, weak.

bloater, a prepared herring. (Scand.) A *bloater* is a cured fish, cured by smoke ; but formerly a 'soaked' fish. — Icel. *blautr*, soft. Cf. Swed. *blötfisk*, soaked fish ; from *blöta*, to soak, steep ; from *blöt*, soft (above).

Blob, a bubble. (E.) See **Bleb.**

Block, a large piece of wood. (F. — M. H. G.) M. E. *blok*. — O. F. *bloc*. — M. H. G. *bloch*, a block ; cf. Du. *blok*, Dan. *blok*, Swed. *block*. **Der.** *block-ade*.

Blond. (F.) XV cent. F. *blond*, m. *blonde*, fem. 'light yellow ;' Cot. Referred by Diez to Icel. *blandinn*, mixed ; cf. A. S. *blonden-feax*, having hair of mingled colour, gray-haired. See **Blend.** ¶ But the Low L. form is *blundus*, pointing to a Teut. type *blundo-*, answering to Skt. *bradhna-s*, reddish, pale yellow (Kluge). Cf. O. Slav. *bron'*, white ; Brugm. i. § 814.

Blood. (E.) M. E. *blod*, *blood*. A. S. *blöd*.+Du. *bloed*, Icel. *blöð*, Swed. *blod*, Goth. *blōth* ; G. *blut* ; < Teut. type *blōdom*, n. Hence *bleed*.

Bloom, a flower. (Scand.) M. E. *blome* ; not in A. S. — Icel. *blōm*, *blōmi*, a flower ; Swed. *blomma* ; Dan. *blomme*.+ Du. *bloem* ; Goth. *blōma* ; allied to O. Ir. *blāth*, L. *flōs* ; see **Flower.** And see below.

blossom. (E.) M. E. *blosme*, also *blostme*. A. S. *blōstma*, a blossom ; from base *blō-* of A. S. *blō-wan*, with suffixes *-st* and *-ma* (Teut. *-mon*).+Du. *bloesem* ; M. H. G. *bluost* (with suffix *-st*). See above.

Blot (1), a spot. (Scand. ?) M. E. *blot*, *blotte*. Origin unknown. It has some resemblance to Icel. *blettr*, a blot, stain ; Dan. dial. *blat*, a spot, a blot.

Blot (2), at backgammon. (Scand.) A *blot* is an 'exposed' piece. — Dan. *blot*, bare, naked ; whence *give sig blot*, to lay oneself open, expose oneself ; Swed. *blott*, naked ; *blotta*, to lay oneself open.+Du. *bloot*, naked, *blootstellen*, to expose ; G. *bloss*, naked. Allied to Icel. *blautr*, soft ; see **Bloat.**

Blotch, a large blot. (E.) A mod. variant of *blot*, perhaps suggested by *botch*.

Blouse, a loose outer frock. (F.) From F. *blouse*, a frock much used by workmen (XVIII cent.). Origin unknown.

Blow (1), to puff. (E.) M. E. *blowen*. A. S. *blāwan*.+G. *blähen*, O. H. G. *blā-han* ; allied to L. *flāre*.

Blow (2), to bloom, flourish as a flower. (E.) M. E. *blowen*. A. S. *blōwan*.+Du. *bloeijen* ; G. *blühen*, O. H. G. *bluojan*. Allied to L. *flōrēre* ; see **Flourish.**

Blow (3), a stroke, hit. (E.) M. E. *blowe*. Not in A. S. ; but we find M. Du. strong verb *blouwen* (pt. t. *blau*), to strike, dress flax by beating ; O. H. G. *bliuwan*, whence G. *bläuen*, to beat ; Goth. *bliggwan*, to strike ; all from Teut. *bliwwan-*, to strike. (History obscure.)

Blubber. (E.) M. E. *blober*, a bubble ; *bloberen*, to bubble up, to weep copiously. Of imitative origin ; cf. **Blob.** The *blubber* of the whale consists of bladder-like cells filled with oil. *Blubber-lipped*, with swollen lips. Cf. E. Fries. *blubber*, a bubble, a blob of fat ; *blubbern*, to bubble.

Bludgeon. (E. or F.) XVIII cent. Of unknown origin.

Blue, a colour. (F. — O. H. G.) M. E. *blew*, *bleu*. — A. F. *blu*, *blew*, O. F. *bleu*, blue. — O. H. G. *blāo*, blue, livid, G. *blau*. +Icel. *blār*, livid ; Swed. *blå*, Dan. *blaa* ; A. S. *blǣw* (O. E. Texts, p. 588) ; < Teut. type *blēwoz*. Cognate with Lat. *flāuus*, yellow.

Bluff, downright, rude. (Du. ?) A *bluff* is a steep headland. It appears to be Dutch. M. Du. *blaf*, flat, broad ; *blaffaert*, one having a broad flat face, also, a boaster (Oudemans) ; *blaf van het voor-hooft*, 'the flat of a forehead' (Hexham) ; *blaffen*, *bleffen*, to mock (id.). Cf. E. Fries. *bluffen*, to make a noise, bluster, impose on.

Blunder, to flounder about, err. (Scand.) M. E. *blondren*, to confuse, to move blindly or stupidly. Formed (as a frequentative) from Icel. *blunda*, to doze, slumber ; Swed. *blunda*, to shut the eyes ; Dan. *blunde*, to nap. Cf. Icel. *blundr*, Dan. and Swed. *blund*, a doze, a nap. From the sense of 'confusion.' Allied to **Blend** and **Blind.**

Blunderbuss, a short gun. (Hyb.) In Pope. Formerly spelt *blanterbusse*, *plantierbusse* (Palmer, Folk-Etymology) ;

i. e. 'a gun on a rest.' Apparently from
L. *plantāre*, to plant (see **Plant**); and
Du. *bus*, a gun, orig. a box, barrel; see
Box (1). But the corresponding Du. word
is *donderbus*, i. e. thunder-gun.

Blunt, dull. (Scand. ?) M. E. *blunt*,
blont, dull, dulled. Origin unknown;
perhaps allied to Icel. *blunda*, Dan.
blunde, to sleep, doze; see **Blunder.**

Blur, to stain; a stain. (Scand. ?)
Properly 'to dim'; metaphorically, 'to
deceive.' We find: '*A blirre*, deceptio;
to blirre, fallere;' Levins (1570). Of
uncertain origin. Cf. Swed. dial. *blura*,
to blink, partially close the eyes; Swed.
plira, Swed. dial. *blira*, to blink; *blirra*
fojr augu, to quiver (be dim) before the
eyes, said of a haze caused by heat;
Bavarian *plerr*, a mist before the eyes.

Blurt, to utter impulsively. (E.)
Lowl. Sc. *blirt*, to make a noise in weep-
ing; cf. M. E. *bleren*, to make a loud
noise, to *blare*. Of imitative origin.

Blush. (E.) M. E. *bluschen*, *blusshen*,
to glow. A. S. *blyscan*, used to translate
L. *rutilāre*, to shine (Mone, Quellen, 355);
cf. *āblysian*, *āblisian*, to blush; from A. S.
blys in *bǣl-blys*, lit. 'a fire-blaze.' + Du.
blozen, to blush, from *blos*, a blush; Dan.
blusse, to flame, glow, from *blus*, a torch;
Swed. *blossa*, to blaze, from *bloss*, a torch.
From Teut. root *bleus*, to glow.

Bluster, to be boisterous. (E.) Doubtless associated in idea with *blast* (Icel.
blāstr, Swed. *blåst*). Cf. E. Fries. *blüs-
tern*, to be tempestuous (esp. of wind);
blüster, *blüser*, a breeze; *blüsen*, to blow
strongly; *blüse*, wind.

Boa, a large snake. (L.) L. *boa*
(Pliny); perhaps allied to *bos*, an ox; from
its size.

Boar, an animal. (E.) M.E. *bore*, *boor*.
A.S. *bār*. + Du. *beer*; M. H. G. *bēr*.
Teut. type *bairoz*, m.

Board (1). (E.) M. E. *bord*. A. S.
bord, board, side of a ship, shield. + Du.
boord; Icel. *borð*, plank, side of a ship; G.
bord; Goth. -*baurd* in *fotu-baurd*, a foot-
stool. Cf. Irish, Gael., W., and Corn.
bord, a board (from E.). Teut. type
bordom, n. ¶ The sense 'side of a ship'
explains *star-board*, *lar-board*, *on board*,
over-board. Der. *board*, to have meals as
a lodger; from *board*, a table.

  board (2), to go on board a ship, to
accost. (F. – Teut.) The sb. *board* is E.,
but the verb, formerly spelt *borde*, *bord*, is

short for *aborde*, used by Palsgrave. – F.
aborder, 'to approach, accost, abboord,
or lay aboord;' Cot. – F. *a*, to (L. *ad*);
bord, edge, brim, side of a ship, from
Icel. *borð*, Du. *boord*, side of a ship. See
Board (1).

Boast. (E.) M. E. *bost*. [W. *bost*,
Corn. *bost*, Irish and Gael. *bosd*, are all
borrowed from E.] Origin unknown, but
perhaps a late formation (with suffix -*st*)
from A. S. *bogan*, *bōn*, to boast; cf. prov.
E. *bog*, to boast.

Boat. (E.) M. E. *boot*. A. S. *bāt*.
Cf. Icel. *bātr*; Swed. *båt*; Du. *boot*; Russ.
bot'; W. *bad*; Gael. *bāta*, a boat. β. The
Icel. word is borrowed from A. S.; and
the other forms either from E. or Icel.
Teut type *baitoz*, m.

  boat-swain. (E.) Lit. 'boat-lad;'
Icel. *sveinn*, a lad (= A. S. *swān*).

Bob, to jerk. (E.) Perhaps imitative.

Bobbin, a wooden pin on which thread
is wound; round tape. (F.) Formerly
bobin. – F. *bobine*, 'a quil for a spinning
wheele, a skane;' Cot. Orig. unknown.

Bode, to foreshew. (E.) M. E. *boden*,
bodian. – A. S. *bodian*, to announce. – A. S.
boda, a messenger; *bod*, a message. From
bod-, weak grade of *bēodan*, to command,
announce. See **Bid** (2).

Bodice, stays. (E.) A corruption of
bodies (pl. of *body*), which was the old
spelling. (Cf. F. *corset*, from *corps*.)

Bodkin, orig. a small dagger. (?)
M. E. *boydekin*, Ch. Origin unknown.

Body, the frame of an animal. (E.)
M. E. *bodi*; A. S. *bodig*. + O. H. G. *potach*.

Boer; the same as **Boor.**

Bog. (C.) Irish *bogach*, a bog, from
bog, soft; cf. Irish *bogaim*, I shake; a *bog*
being a soft quagmire. So also Gael.
bogan, a quagmire; *bog*, soft, moist; *bog*,
to soften, also to agitate. Cf. O. Irish
bocc, soft.

Boggard, Boggart, a spectre. (C.;
with F. *suffix.*) From *bog*, variant of
Bug (1); with suffix -*ard*, -*art* (F. -*ard*
as in *bast-ard*). See below.

Boggle, to start aside, swerve for fear.
(C.?) Prob. coined from prov. E. *boggle*,
bogle, a spectre. Cf. W. *bwg*, a goblin;
bygel, a scarecrow; *bwgwl*, a threat,
bygylu, to threaten; *bwgwth*, to scare.
See **Bug** (1).

Bohea, a kind of tea. (Chinese.) So
named from the *Bohea* hills; the mountain called *Bou-y* (or *Wu-i*) is situated in

the province of *Fokien* or *Fukian*, on the
S. E. coast of China.

Boil (1), to bubble up. (F.—L.) O. F.
boillir, to boil (F. *bouillir*).—L. *bullīre*, to
bubble up, boil.—L. *bulla*, a bubble; see
Bull (2). Cf. Norman F. *boillir*, to
boil.

Boil (2), a small tumour. (E.) Prov.
E. *bile*; prob. affected by *boil* (1). M. E.
byle. A. S. *bȳl*, a boil, swelling.+Du.
buil; G. *beule*. Cf. Goth. *ufbauljan*, to
puff up; Icel. *beyla*, a hump (with mutation). See Bowl (2).

Boisterous. (F.) Lengthened from
M. E. *boistous*, Ch.; lit. 'noisy.' *Boistous*
answers to O. F. *boistous*, lame, but the
difference in sense is remarkable. The
O. F. *boistous* also meant 'rough,' as
applied to a bad road; hence perhaps
M. E. *boistous*, rough, coarse, noisy.

Bold. (E.) M. E. *bold*, *bald*; A.S.
beald, *bald*, *balþ*.+Icel. *ballr*; Du. *boud*;
O. H. G. *bald*; cf. Goth. *balthaba*, adv.,
boldly. Teut. type *balþoz*.

Bole, stem of a tree. (Scand.) M. E.
bole.—Icel. *bolr*, *bulr*, the trunk of a tree,
stem; Swed. *bål*; Dan. *bul*. Cf. Gk.
φάλ-αγξ, a log, trunk. Cf. Balk (1).

Bolled, swollen. (Scand.) Earlier
forms are M. E. *bollen*, pp., and *bolned*,
pp. The latter is the pp. of M. E. *bolnen*,
to swell.—Dan. *bulne*, Swed. *bulna*, Icel.
bólgna, to swell, inchoative forms from
wk. grade of *belg*- (cf. Icel. *belgja*, to inflate). Cf. A. S. *belgan* (pp. *bolgen*), to
swell with anger. See Bellows, Billow.

Bolster. (E.) A. S. *bolster*, with suffix
ster as in *hol-ster*. From its round shape.
+Du. *bolster*, *bulster*; Icel. *bolstr*; O.
H. G. *bolstar* (G. *polster*). Teut. type
bul-stroz; from Teut. *bul*, weak grade
of *beul*, to puff up. See Boil (2). (See
Franck.)

Bolt (1), a stout pin of iron, an arrow.
(E.) A. S. *bolt*.+Du. *bout*, formerly *bolt*;
Dan. *bolt*; G. *bolz*, *bolzen*. Root unknown.

Bolt (2), **Boult,** to sift meal. (F.—
L.—Gk.) Spelt *boulte* in Palsgrave.—
O. F. *bulter*; mod. F. *bluter*; oldest form
buleter, a corruption of *bureter*, to sift
through coarse cloth; cf. M. Ital. *burat-
tare*, to boult (Florio). — O. F. and F.
bure, coarse woollen cloth. — Late Lat.
bura, *burra*, coarse red cloth. — Lat.
burrus, reddish. — Gk. πυρρός, reddish.—
Gk. πῦρ, fire. See Bureau and Fire.

Bolus, a large pill. (L.—Gk.) Late

L. *bŏlus* (not L. *bŏlus*), a Latinised form
of Gk. βῶλος, a clod, lump.

Bomb, a shell for cannon. (F *or* Span.
—L.—Gk.) F. *bombe*; Span. *bomba*.—L.
bombus, a humming noise.—Gk. βόμβος,
the same. See Boom (1).

bombard. (F.—L.—Gk.) The verb
is from E. *bombard*, a great gun; Sh.—F.
bombarde, a cannon; extended from F.
bombe; see Bomb. Der. *bombard-ier*, F.
bombardier (Cot.).

Bombast, orig. cotton wadding; hence
padding, affected language. (F.—L.—
Gk.) From O. F. *bombace* (with added *t*),
cotton wadding. — Late L. *bombācem*, acc.
of *bombax*, cotton; for L. *bombyx*. — Gk.
βόμβυξ, silk, cotton; orig. a silkworm.
Cf. 'to talk *fustian*.'

bombazine, bombasine, a fabric
of silk and worsted. (F.—L.—Gk.) F.
bombasin.—Late L. *bombācinum*.—L. *bom-
bȳcinus*, adj. silken; from *bombyx*, silk;
see above.

Bond. (E.) See Band (1).

Bondage, servitude. (F. — Scand.)
M. E. and A. F. *bondage*, servitude; the
sense being due to confusion with the verb
to bind. But it orig. meant the condition
of a *bondman*, called in A. S. *bōnda*, a
word borrowed from Icel. *bóndi*, a husbandman. And *bóndi* = *búandi*, a tiller;
from Icel. *búa*, to till, prepare, cognate
with A. S. *búan*, to dwell, and G. *bauen*.
Thus A. S. *bōnda* is allied in sense and
origin to E. *boor*, q. v.

Bone. (E.) M. E. *boon*; A.S. *bān*.
+Du. *been*; Icel. *bein*; Swed. *ben*; Dan.
been; O. H. G. *bein*. Teut. type *bainom*.

bonfire. (E.) Orig. a bone-fire.
'*Bane-fire*, ignis ossium;' Catholicon
Anglicanum, A. D. 1483; where *bane* is
the Northern form of *bone*. Cf. Picard *fu
d'os*, a bonfire.

Bonito, a kind of tunny. (Span.—
Arab.) Span. *bonito.* — Arab. *baynīth*,
a bonito.

Bonnet. (F.) F. *bonnet*; O. F. *bonet*
(A. D. 1047), the name of a stuff of which
bonnets or caps were made. Origin
unknown.

Bonny, fair. (F.—L.) From F. *bonne*,
fair, fem. of *bon*, good.—L. *bonus*, good;
O. L. *duonus*.

Bonze, a priest. (Port.—Japanese.)
Port. *bonzo.*—Jap. *bonzo*, a religious man.

Booby. (Span.—L.) Span. *bobo*, a
blockhead, booby (related to F. *baube*,

stammering). **–** L. *balbus*, stammering; hence, stupid.

Book. (E.) M. E. *book*; A. S. *bōc*, a book; also, a beech-tree. The orig. 'books' were pieces of writing scratched on a beechen board.**+**Du. *boek*; Icel. *bōk*; Swed. *bok*; Dan. *bog*; G. *buch*; all in the sense of 'book'; Goth. *bōka*, a letter, pl. *bōkōs*, writings. **β**. With A. S. *bōc*, beech, cf. L. *fāgus*, a beech, Gk. *φηγός*, a tree with edible fruit.

Boom (1), to hum. (E.) M. E. *bommen*; not found in A. S.**+**Du. *bommen*, to boom, to give out a hollow sound like an empty barrel. An imitative word; like L. *bombus*, Gk. *βόμβος*, a humming.

Boom (2), a pole. (Du.) Du. *boom*; the Du. form of **Beam** (1).

Boomerang, a wooden missile weapon. (Australian.) From the native Australian name.

Boon (1), a petition. (Scand.) M. E. *bone*, Ch. **–** Icel. *bōn*; Dan. and Swed. *bön*, a petition.**+**A. S. *bōen*, *bēn* (whence *bene* in Wordsworth). The sense of 'favour' arose from confusion with **Boon** (2).

Boon (2), good. (F.**–**L.) In the phr. '*boon* companion.' **–** F. *bon*, good. **–** L. *bonus*. See **Bonny.**

Boor, a peasant. (Du.) Du. *boer*, a peasant, lit. 'tiller of the soil.' **–** Du. *bouwen*, to till. **+** A. S. *būan*, to dwell in, whence *gebūr*, s., a peasant (only preserved in *neigh-bour*). So also G. *bauen*, to till, whence *bauer*, a peasant; Icel. *būa*, Goth. *bauan*, to dwell. Teut. stem **bū-*, related to Bə. (Streitberg, § 90.)

Boot (1), advantage, profit. (E.) M. E. *bote*, *boot*. A. S. *bōt*, profit.**+**Du. *boete*; Icel. *bōt* (cf. *bati*), advantage, cure; Dan. *bod*, Swed. *bot*, remedy; G. *busse*, atonement; Goth. *bōta*. Teut. type **bōtā*, f. From *bōt-*, strong grade of *bat-*; see **Better.** Der. *boot-less*, profitless.

Boot (2), a covering for the foot. (F.) M. E. *bote*. **–** O. F. *bote* (F. *botte*); cf. Span., Port., Late L. *bota*. Origin unknown.

Booth. (Scand.) M. E. *bothe*. **–** M. Dan. *bōth* (Kalkar), Dan. *bod*; Swed. *bod* (cf. Icel. *būð*, a dwelling, booth). **–** Dan. *boe*, Swed. *bo*, Icel. *būa*, to dwell; see **Boor.** **+** G. *bude*, a stall. Teut. type **būþā*, f. Cf. also Irish *both*, a hut, W. *bôd*, a residence; Lith. *buta*, *buttas*, a house. See **Build.**

Booty. (F.**–**Low G.) Formerly spelt *butin.* **–** F. *butin*, 'a booty, prey;' Cot.

– M. Du. *büte*, Du. *buit*; cf. Icel. *bȳti*, Dan. *bytte*, Swed. *byte*, exchange, barter, also booty, spoil; G. *beute*, spoil.

Borage. (F. **–** Span. **–** Arab.) Formerly *bourage.* **–** F. *bourrache.* **–** Span. *borraja.* **–** Arab. *abū rashh*, lit. 'father of sweat;' because it is a sudorific.

Borax. (Low L. **–** Arab. **–** Pers.) Low L. *borax*; also *boracum.* **–** Arab. *būrāq.* **–** Pers. *būrah*, borax (Vullers).

Border, an edge. (F. **–** Low L. **–** Teut.) M. E. *bordure*, *bordeure.* **–** O. F. *bordeüre* (Span. *bordadura*), an edging. **–** Low L. *bordātūra*, edging. **–** Low L. *bordāre* (Ital. *bordare*, Span. *bordar*, F. *border*), to edge. **–** Low L. *bordus* (F. *bord*). **–** Teut. (O. Low G.) *bord*, side; see **Board.**

Bore (1), to perforate. (E.) M. E. *borien*, A. S. *borian.* **+** Du. *boren*; Icel. *bora*; Swed. *borra*; Dan. *bore*; G. *bohren*. Also L. *forāre*, to bore; Gk. *φαρειν*, to plough. Brugm. i. § 510. (√BHER, to cut.)

bore (2), to worry. (E.) Possibly a metaph. use of the verb above; Hen. VIII, i. 1. 128.

Bore (3), a tidal surge in a river. (Scand.?) Perhaps from Icel. *bāra*, a billow caused by wind; Norw. *baara*, a billow, swell in the sea.

Boreas, the north wind. (L.**–**Gk.) L. *Boreas.* **–** Gk. *Βορέας*, *Βορρᾶς*, the N. wind.

Borough. (E.) M. E. *burgh*, *borgh*; also *borwe*. A. S. *burh*, *burg* (gen. and dat. *byrig*), a fort. Perhaps from Teut. *burg-*, weak grade of **bergan-*, to protect; whence Goth. *bairgan*, to hide, keep; see **Barrow. +** Du. *burg*; Icel. *borg*; Swed. and Dan. *borg*; G. *burg*; Goth. *baurgs*. See below. Brugm. i. § 566; ii. § 160.

borrow. (E.) M. E. *borwen*; A. S. *borgian*, lit. to give a pledge.**–**A. S. *borg*, *borh*, a pledge.**–**A. S. *borg-*, weak grade of *beorgan*, to keep, protect; see **Barrow** and **Borough.**

Bosom. (E.) M. E. *bosom*. A. S. *bōsm*.**+**Du. *boezem*; G. *busen*.

Boss, a knob. (F.**–**O. H. G.) M. E. *boce*, *bos*.**–**O. F. *boce* (F. *bosse*); cf. Ital. *bozza*, a swelling; M. Ital. *bozzare*, to rough-hew, to bungle. Prob. from O. H. G. *bōzan*, to beat; a bump being the effect of a blow. Cf. *botch*, *beat*.

Botany. (F. **–** Gk.) F. *botanique*,

orig. an adj. — Gk. βοτανικός, belonging to plants. — Gk. βοτάνη, grass. — Gk. βόσκειν, to pasture; cf. βοτόν, a grazing animal.

Botargo, a cake made of the roe of the sea-mullet. (Ital. — Arab.) M. Ital. *botargo*, pl. *botarghe*; see Florio and Torriano. — Arab. *butarkha*, botargo; given by Devic. Supposed to be composed of *bu*, Coptic def. article, and Gk. τάριχος, dried fish (Journ. des Savants, Jan. 1848, p. 45).

Botch (1), to patch. (E.) Origin unknown. Similar is M. Du. *butsen*, to strike, beat, also to patch up; cf. Du. *botsen*, to beat.

Botch (2), a swelling. (F. — G.) M. E. *boche*. — O. North F. *boche*; Picard *boche*; O. F. *boce* (F. *bosse*), a swelling; see Boss.

Both. (Scand.) M. E. *bāþe*, Scot. *baith*. — Icel. *bāðir*, both, dual adj.; Dan. *baade*; Swed. *båda*.+G. *beide*. And cf. A. S. *bā*, both; Lat. -*bo* in *ambo*; Gk. -φω in ἄμ-φω; Skt. -*bha* in *u-bha*, both. Icel. -*ðir* is for *ðeir*, they, the; so that *bo-th* was orig. *two* words; cf. Goth. *ba þō skipa*, both the ships (Luke v. 7).

Bother, vb. and sb. (E.) In Swift. Cf. *pother*; prov. E. *pudder*, confusion; M. E. *putheren*, to bestir oneself. Origin unknown.

Bots, small worms. (E.) Lowl. Sc. *bats*. Of unknown origin.

Bottle (1), a hollow vessel. (F. — Late L. — Gk.) M. E. *botel*. — F. *bouteille*. — Late Lat. *buticula*, double dimin. of Late L. *butis*, *buttis*, a cask, a butt; see Butt (2).

Bottle (2), a bundle of hay. (F. — O. H. G.) M. E. *botel*. — O. F. *botel*, *botelle*, a small bundle, dimin. of *botte*, a bundle, as of hay. — O. H. G. *bōzo*, a bundle of straw or flax; allied to O. H. G. *bōzan*, to beat (see Beat); perhaps from the beating of flax.

Bottom. (E.) M. E. *botum*, *bothom*. A. S. *botm*.+Du. *bodem*; Icel. *botn*; Swed. *botten*; Dan. *bund*; G. *boden*; Lat. *fundus*; Gk. πυθμήν; Vedic Skt. *budhnā*, depth, ground. Allied to Irish *bonn*, sole of the foot; Gael. *bonn*, sole, bottom; W. *bon*, base, stock. See Fundament. Brugm. i. §§ 103, 704.

Boudoir. (F.) F. *boudoir*, a private room for a lady; lit. a place to sulk in. — F. *bouder*, to sulk. Cf. E. *pout*.

Bough. (E.) M. E. *bough*. A. S. *bōg*,

bōh; of which the orig. sense was 'an arm.'+Icel. *bógr*, Swed. *bog*, Dan. *bov*, the shoulder of an animal, hence the bow (shoulder) of a ship; G. *bug*; Gk. πῆχυς, the fore-arm; Skt. *bāhus*, the arm. Teut. type **bōguz*; Idg. type **bhāghus*. See Bow (4). Brugm. i. § 184.

Bought, a bend, turn, fold. (Low G.) In Spenser, F. Q. i. 1. 15. Low G. *bugt*, a bend; Du. *bogt*, *bocht*; Dan. *bugt*. Cf. G. *bucht*. The E. form is Bight. And see Bout.

Boulder, a large stone. (E.?) Etym. obscure; cf. Swed. dial. *bullersteen*, a large rolling stone; so called from its rolling down stream with a crash. — Swed. *bullra*, to thunder, roar; and *steen*, a stone. Danish has *buldre*, to roar, *bulder*, a crash.

Boult, to sift meal; see Bolt (2).

Bounce, to jump up quickly. (E.) M. E. *bunsen*, to beat. Cf. Low G. *bunsen*, to beat, knock at a door; Du. *bonzen*, to bounce, throw, from Du. *bons*, a bounce, thump; G. *bumps*, bounce; Icel. *bops*, bump! Prob. imitative.

Bound (1), to leap. (F. — L. — Gk.) F. *bondir*, to bound; but orig. to resound. — L. *bombitāre*, to resound. — L. *bombus*, a humming sound. — Gk. βόμβος, the same. Der. *re-bound* (F. *rebondir*).

Bound (2), a boundary. (F. — C.?) M. E. *bounde*, Ch.; with excrescent *d*, as in *soun-d*. A. F. *bounde*, *bunde*; O. F. *bonne*, a boundary; also spelt *bodne* (Burguy); Late Lat. *bodina* (contr. form *bonna*), a bound, limit. Perhaps of Celtic origin; Thurneysen, 91. Der. *bound-ary*.

Bound (3), ready to go. (Scand.) In 'the ship is *bound* for Spain,' &c. Formed, with excrescent *d*, from M. E. *boun*, ready, Ch. C. T. 11807. — Icel. *buinn*, prepared; pp. of *būa*, to till, prepare.+A. S. *būan*; see Boor.

Bounden, the old pp. of Bind. (E.) As in '*bounden* duty.'

Bounty, orig. goodness. (F. — L.) M. E. *bountee*. — O. F. *bontet*. — L. acc. *bonitātem*, from *bonitās*, goodness. — L. *bonus*, good. See Bonny.

Bouquet. (F. — Late L.) F. *bouquet*; O. F. *bosquet*, orig. 'a little wood,' dimin. of O. F. *bos* (F. *bois*), a wood. — Late L. *boscum*, *buscum*, acc. of *boscus*, *buscus*, a wood; of unknown origin. Cf. Bush.

Bourd, a jest; to jest. (F.) M. E. *bourde*, sb.; *bourden*, v. — F. *bourde*, a game; *bourder*, to play. Of unknown origin. (Not as in Diez.)

Bourn (1), a boundary. (F.) In Sh. — F. *borne*, a bound; for O. F. *bodne*, variant of O. F. *bonne*, a boundary; see Bound (2).

Bourn (2), **Burn**, a stream. (E.) M. E. *bourne*. A. S. *burna*, a fountain, stream, well. + Icel. *brunnr*; Swed. *brunn*; Dan. *brönd*; G. *brunnen*; Goth. *brunna*, a spring, well.

Bouse, Bouze, Boose, to drink deeply. (Du.) M. E. *bousen* (ab. 1300). —M. Du. **büsen*, later *buyzen*, to drink deeply.—M. Du. *büse* (Latinised as *büsa* by Erasmus), *buyse*, a large cup, also a tap, a conduit (Kilian); Du. *buis*, a conduit, pipe. Cf. O. F. *buse*, a conduit; G. *bausen*, to bouse.

Bout, a turn, a round, occasion. (Low G.) The same as **Bought** (above); prob. influenced by *bout*.

Bow (1), to bend. (E.) M. E. *bowen, bogen, bugen*. A. S. *būgan.* + Du. *buigen*; O. H. G. *biogan*; Goth. *biugan*; Teut. type **beugan-* or **būgan-*. Cf. Skt. *bhuj*, to bend; Lat. *fugere*, to take to flight, give way; Gk. φεύγειν, to flee. Brugm. i. §§ 658, 701.

bow (2), a bend. (E.) From the verb.

bow (3), a weapon to shoot with. (E.) M. E. *bowe*. A. S. *boga*, a bow; because it is bent or *bowed.* + Du. *boog*; Icel. *bogi*; Swed. *båge*; Dan. *bue*; O. H. G. *bogo*; G. *bogen*. From A. S. *bog-*; cf. *bog-en*, pp. of *būgan*, to bend.

bow-window. (E.) A window of semi-circular form; not the same as *bay-window*.

Bow (4), the 'shoulder' of a ship. (Scand.) From Icel. *bōgr*, shoulder; see Bough. + Du. *boeg*, bow of a ship.

Bowel. (F.—L.) M. E. *bouel.*—O. F. *boël*; (mod. F. *boyau*).—Lat. acc. *botellum*, a sausage; in Late L., an intestine; dimin. of *botulus*, a sausage.

Bower, an abode, chamber, arbour. (E.) M. E. *bour*. A. S. *būr*, a chamber. —A. S. *būan*, to dwell. + Icel. *būr*, a chamber; Dan. *buur*, Swed. *bur*; O. Sax. *būr*; O. H. G. *būr*. Teut. types **būrom*, n., **būroz*, m. ; see Boor. Cf. Booth.

Bowl (1), a round wooden ball. (F.— L.) M. E. *boule.*—F. *boule.*—L. *bulla*, a bubble; hence, a round thing, a ball.

Bowl (2), a drinking-vessel. (E.)

M. E. *bolle*. A. S. *bolla*; from its round form. + Du. *bol*, ball; Icel. *bolli*, O. H. G. *bolla*, bowl (G. *bolle*). From Teut. **bul-*, weak grade of **beul-*, to swell; cf. Goth. *uf-bauljan*, to puff up. See Boil (2).

Bow-line. (Scand.) *Not* so called because it keeps a sail *bowed* (for it rather keeps it straight), but because fastened to the ship's *bow*. — Norw. and Swed. *boglina*, bow-line, from *bog*, bow of a ship; Du. *boeglijn*, from *boeg*, bow. For the pronunciation, cf. *bow-sprit*. See Bow (4) and Line.

Bow-window; see Bow (1).

Box (1), the name of a tree. (L.—Gk.) M. E. *box*; A. S. *box.*—Lat. *buxus*, the box-tree.—Gk. πύξος, the box-tree.

box (2), a chest or case to put things in. (L.—Gk.) M. E. *box*; A. S. *box.*—L. *buxum*, anything made of box-wood; hence, a box.—Lat. *buxus*, the box-tree. (Hence a *box* at a theatre; a shooting-*box*; a Christmas *box* or present; &c.) Cf. Pyx.

Box (3), to fight with fists; a blow. (E.) The verb is from M. E. *box*, sb., a blow. Cf. N. Fries. *bakke*, Silt *bokke*, a blow (Outsen); M. H. G. *buc*, a blow; Du. *beuken*, G. *pochen*, to beat.

Box (4), in phr. 'to box the compass.' Apparently one of the numerous uses of the vb. formed from **box** (2). See N. E. D.

Boy. (E.) M. E. *boi, boy.* Preserved in E. Friesic *boi, boy*, a boy (Koolman); allied to M. Du. *boeve*, a boy, Du. *boef*, a knave. + Icel. *bófi*, a knave; G. *bube*, Bavarian *bueb, bua, bui*, a boy. Cf. A. S. *Bōfa*, personal name.

Boycott, to combine with others in refusing to have dealings with any one. (E.) From the treatment accorded to Capt. *Boycott*, of Lough Mask House, co. Mayo, Ireland, in Dec. 1880.

Brabble, to quarrel. (E.) Cf. Du. *brabbelen*, to stammer, confound; whence *brabbeltaal*, foolish talk. See Blab, Babble.

Brace, orig. a firm hold. (F.—L.) From the notion of embracing.—O. F. *brace*, the two arms (Bartsch); hence a measure of 5 feet, formed with extended arms (Cot.); and hence, a grasp.—Lat. *brāchia*, pl. of *brāchium*, the arm. + Irish *brac*, W. *braich*, the arm; Gk. βραχίων.

bracelet. (F. — L.) F. *bracelet*; dimin. of O. F. *bracel*, an armlet (Bartsch).

—L. *brāchiāle*, an armlet. —L. *brāchium*, an arm.

Brach, a kind of hunting-dog. (F.—G.) M. E. *brache*, pl. *braches*. — A. F. *brachez*, pl. of *brachet*, dimin. of O. F. *brac* (F. *braque*). —O. H. G. *bracco* (G. *brack*), a dog that hunts by the scent.

Bracken, fern. (Scand.) M. E. *braken*. From O. Icel. **brakni*, not found; represented by Swed. *bräken*, Dan. *bregne*, fern; cf. Icel. *burkni*, fern.

Bracket, a corbel, &c. (F.—C.?) Formerly spelt *bragget*, as in Minsheu, ed. 1627. So named from the resemblance to the front part of a pair of breeches, as formerly made. — F. *braguette*, 'a codpiece,' Cot. (the front part of a pair of breeches); the allied Span. *bragueta* also meant a projecting mould in architecture, a bracket or corbel. Dimin. of O. F. *brague*, 'a kind of mortaise,' Cot.; from *bragues*, breeches; so also Span. *bragueta* is the dimin. of Span *bragas*, breeches.— L. *brācæ*, breeches; said to be of Celtic (or Teutonic?) origin. See **Breeches.**

Brackish. (Du.) Du. *brak*, briny, nauseous; older form *wrack*, brackish (Hexham); allied to M. Du. *wracke*, a wreck, Du. *wraken*, to reject, blame, disapprove. — Du. *wrak*, orig. 2nd grade of *wreken*, to wreak; orig. to drive. See **Wreck.** [So also *wrang*, sour, is allied to *wringen*, to wring. See Franck.]

Bract. (L.) Lat. *bractea*, a thin plate or leaf of metal.

Brad. (Scand.) M. E. *brod*.—Icel. *broddr*, a spike; Swed. *brodd*, Dan. *brodde*, a frost-nail.+A. S. *brord*, a spike. Teut. type **brozdoz*. Cf. O. Irish *brot*, Ir. *brod*, W. *brath*, a sting.

Brae, brow of a hill, steep bank, slope. (Scand.) M. E. *brā*, *brō* (North).—Icel. *brā*, brow; hence, brow of a hill; see **Brow.**

Brag, to boast. (Uncertain.) M. E. *braggen*, to sound loudly, to vaunt. Etym. unknown; cf. Gael. *bragh*, an explosion, crack; A.S. *gebræc*, a breaking, crash, noise; Icel. *brak*, a creaking, *braka*, to creak; cognate with L. *fragor*, noise. Also (late) M. F. *braguer*, 'to flaunt, brag,' Cot.; M. F. *bragard*, 'gay, gallant, braggard,' whence E. *braggart*. We find also W. *bragal*, to vociferate (from E.); Bret. *fraga*, to brag (from F.). Cf. **Bray.**

Bragget. (W.) M. E. *bragot*.—W. *bragot*, a kind of mead; allied to Irish

bracat, malt liquor. — W. *brag*, malt; Irish and Gael. *braich*, malt, fermented grain. Cf. Gael. *brach*, to ferment.

Brahman, Brahmin. (Skt.) Skt. *brāhma*na, a brahman, holy man. — Skt. *brahman*, prayer; also devotion, lit. 'a greatness' of the soul; cf. *brhant*, great. (✓BHERGH, to be great.)

Braid (1), to weave. (E.) M.E. *breiden*. A.S. *bregdan*, *brēdan*, to brandish, weave, braid. + Icel. *bregða*, to brandish, turn about, change, start, braid, &c.; whence *bragð*, a sudden movement.

braid (2), full of deceit. (E.) In All's Well, iv. 2. 73, *braid* is short for *braided*, i. e. full of *braids* or tricks. M.E. *braid*, trick, deceit. — A.S. *brægd*, deceit; from A. S. *brægd*, 2nd grade of *bregdan*, to draw out, weave, knit, braid.

Brail, a kind of ligature or fastening. (F.—C.?) O.F. *braiel*, a cincture; orig. for fastening up breeches. — F. *braie*, breeches. —L. *brācæ*, breeches.

Brain. (E.) M.E. *brayne*. A.S. *brægn*, *brægen*, the brain. + Du. *brein*. Cf. Gk. βρεχμός, the top of the head.

Brake (1), a machine for breaking hemp, a name for various mechanical contrivances. (O. Low G.) M. E. *brake*. —Low G. *brake*, a flax-brake; M. Du. *braecke*, 'a brake to beat flax;' Hexham; Du. *braak*. — Du. *brak*, 2nd grade of *breken*, to break; see **Break.**

Brake (2), bush. (E.) M. E. *brake*. +Low G. *brake*, willow-bush (Bremen); also stumps of broken trees, rough growth. From A.S. *brecan*, (pt. t. *bræc*), to break. ¶ In the sense of 'fern,' modified from **Bracken.**

Bramble. (E.) M. E. *brembil*. A.S. *brēmel*, *brembel*. Allied to Du. *braam*, a blackberry; Swed. *brom-bär*, Dan. *brom-bær*, G. *brombeere*, a blackberry. Here Du. *braam*, G. *brōm* (O.H.G. *brāma*) answer to A. S. *brōm* (see **Broom**); of which A.S. *brēm-el* (for Teut.**brǣmiloz*) is the diminutive).

Bran. (F.) M.E. *bran*. —O. F. *bran*, *bren*. Cf. Gael. Irish *bran*, husks, chaff(from E.); Bret. *brenn*, bran (from F.).

Branch. (F.—L.) F. *branche*. —Late L. *branca*, the paw of an animal.

Brand, a burning piece of wood, scar of fire, a sword. (E.) M. E. *brond*, A.S. *brand*, a burning, a sword : from *brann*, 2nd stem of Teut. **brennan-*, to burn ; see **Burn.** + Icel. *brandr*, a fire-brand, sword-blade (from its flashing) ; Swed. and Dan. *brand*, fire-brand, fire ; M. H. G. *brant*, a brand, sword.

brandish. (F.—Scand.) M.E.*braundisen.* — F.*brandiss-ant*, pres. pt. of *brandir*, to brandish a sword. — A.F. *brand*, a sword. — Icel. *brandr* ; see Brand above.

brandy. (Du.) Formerly *brand-wine*, *brandy-wine* ; whence *brandy*. — Du. *brande-wijn*, M. Du. *brandwijn*, brandy ; lit. 'burnt' (i. e. distilled) wine (or, acc. to Kilian, because it easily burns). — Du. *branden*, to burn ; and *wijn*, wine ; see Burn.

Branks, a punishment for scolds. (E.) See Jamieson. Hence were borrowed Gael. *brangas* (O. Gael. *brancas*), a sort of pillory ; Gael. *brang*, Irish *brancas*, a halter. ┿ Du. *pranger*, pincers, barnacle, collar ; G. *pranger*, a pillory ; Du. *prangen*, to pinch. Cf. Goth. *ana-praggan*, to harass.

Bran-new. (E.) Short for *brand-new*, i. e. new from the fire. See Brand.

Brant-fox, Brant-goose or **brent-goose.** The prefix is Scand., as in Swed. *brandräf*, a brant-fox, *brandgås*, a brent-goose. The orig. sense is 'burnt,' with the notion of redness or blackness.

Brasier, Brazier, a pan to hold coals. (F.—Scand.) F. *brasier*. — F. *braise*, live coals. — Swed. *brasa*, fire (below).

Brass. (E.) M.E. *bras*. A.S. *bræs*. Perhaps allied to the verb seen in Icel. *brasa*, to harden by fire ; Dan. *brase*, to fry ; cf. Swed. *brasa*, fire. Der. *braz-en*, A.S. *bræsen*.

braze (1), to harden. (E.) K. Lear, i. 1. 11. It means to harden like *brass*; see below.

braze (2), to ornament with brass. (E.) In Chapman, tr. of Homer, Od. xv. 113 ; from *brass*, sb. 'Aero, *ic brasige*;' Ælfric, Gram. p. 215.

Brassart, the piece of armour which protected the upper part of the arm. (F.—L.) F. *brassart* (Cot.), *brassard* (Littré); also *brassal*. Formed with suffix *-ard* from F. *bras*, arm. — L. *brāchium*, arm.

Brat (1), a cloak, rough mantle. (C.) It also meant a rag, clout, or pinafore. — Gael. and Irish *brat*, a cloak, rag ; O. Irish *brat*, a rough cloak ; W. *brethyn*, woollen cloth. (W. *brat* is from E.)

Brat (2), a child ; esp. 'a beggar's *brat*.' Perhaps 'a rag,' the same as Brat (1).

Brattice, a fence of boards in a mine.

(F. — Teut. ?) M. E. *bretasche*, *bretasce*, *brutaske*, a parapet, battlement. — O. F. *bretesche*, a small wooden outwork, battlement; cf. Prov. *bertresca*, Ital. *bertesca*, the same. A difficult word ; prob. formed from G. *brett*, a plank.

Bravado. (Span.) See Brave.

Brave. (F.—Ital.) F. *brave*, 'brave, gay, fine, proud, braggard, valiant;' Cot. — Ital. *bravo*; the same as Span. and Port. *bravo*; Prov. *brau*. Etym. unknown; none of the explanations are satisfactory; the Bret. *brav*, O. Swed. *braf*, appear to be borrowed from F.

bravado. (Span.) Altered from Span. *bravada*, 'a bravado;' Minsheu's Span. Dict. — Span. *bravo*, brave.

bravo, a daring villain. (Ital.) Ital. *bravo*, brave ; as a sb., a cut-throat, villain.

bravo! well done! (Ital.) Ital. *bravo*, brave ; used in the voc. case masc.

Brawl (1), to quarrel. (E. ?) M. E. *brawlen*. Perhaps E. Cf. Du. *brallen*, to brag, boast ; Dan. *bralle*, to prate, chatter; G. *prahlen*, to brag.

Brawl (2), a sort of dance. (F.—Scand. or O. H. G.) 'A French *brawl*,' L. L. L. iii. 9. — F. *bransle*, 'a totter, swing, ... *brawl* or dance;' Cot. — F. *bransler*, to reel ; mod. F. *branler*. Allied to O. F. *brandeler* (Littré), *brandiller*, to shake (Cot.), frequent. forms of F. *brandir*, to brandish. See Brandish.

Brawn, muscle. (F.—O. H. G.) M. E. *braun*, muscle, boar's flesh. — O. F. *braon*, a slice of flesh; cf. Prov. *bradon*, the same. — O. H. G. *brāton*, acc. of *brāto*, a slice of flesh for roasting. — O. H. G. *brātan* (G. *braten*), to roast. ┿ A. S. *brǣdan*.

Bray (1), to bruise, pound. (F.—G.) M. E. *brayen*. — O. F. *breier* (F. *broyer*). — O. Sax. *brekan* (G. *brechen*), to break ; see Break.

Bray (2), to make a roaring noise. (F.—C.) A. F. *braier*; F. *braire* (Med. Lat. *bragīre*). Of Celtic origin; cf. Gael. *bragh*, a burst, explosion, *braigh*, to crackle (Thurneysen) ; and cf. L. *frag-or*, noise.

Braze ; see Brass.

Brazier ; see Brasier.

Breach. (E.) M. E. *breche*, a fracture. — A. S. *brece*, as in *hlāf-gebrece*, a piece of bread (more commonly *brice*, a breaking); O. Fries. *breke*. — A. S. *brecan*, to break. ¶ M. E. *breche* is also partly from O. F. *breche* (F. *brèche*), a fracture. — G. *brechen*, to break.

Bread. (E.) M. E. *breed.* A. S. *brēad.*
+Du. *brood*; Icel. *brauð*; Swed. and Dan.
bröd; G. *brot.* Teut. type **braudom*, n. ;
or **braudoz*, neut. form in *-oz.* It sometimes means 'bit' or 'piece'; cf. A. S.
'*brēadru*, frusta *pānis*,' Blickling Glosses ;
O. Northumb. *brēad*, a bit, morsel ; John
xiii. 27.

Breadth. (E.) The final *-th* is late ;
from M. E. *brede*, breadth ; Ch. – A. S.
brǣdu.+Icel. *breidd*; O. H. G. *breitī* (G.
breite); Goth. *braidei*, f. From Teut.
*braidoz, broad ; see **Broad.**

Break. (E.) M. E. *breken*; pt. t. *brak*;
pp. *broken.* A. S. *brecan*, pt. t. *brǣc*, pp.
brocen.+Du. *breken*; Goth. *brikan*; G.
brechen. Cf. Icel. *braka*, to creak; Swed.
braka, to crack ; Dan. *brække* ; Lat. *frangere*, to break ; Gael. *bragh*, an explosion.
(√BHREG.) The orig. sense is to break
with a noise, to crack.

Bream, a fish. (F. – Teut.) M. E. *breem.*
– O. F. *bresme* (F. *brème*). – M. H. G.
brahsem (G. *brassen*); O. H. G. *brahsina*
(Kluge). Cf. Du. *brasem.*

Breast. (E.) M. E. *brest, breest.* A. S.
brēost. + Icel. *brjōst* (Swed. *bröst*, Dan.
bryst) : Teut. type **breustom*, n. Also G.
brust, Du. *borst*, Goth. *brusts* : Teut. stem
*brust- (with weak grade).

Breath. (E.) M. E.*breeth,breth.* A. S.
brǣð.+O. H. G. *brādam*, G. *brodem,broden*,
brodel, steam, vapour, exhalation.

Breech. (E.) See **Breeches.**

Breeches. (E.) Really a double
plural, the form *breech* being, in itself, a pl.
form. A. S. *brēc*, breeches; pl. of *brōc*, with
the same sense.+Du. *broek*, a pair of
breeches; Icel. *brōk* (pl. *brækr*); M. H. G.
bruoch. Cf. L. *brācæ*, said to be a word
of Celtic (but rather of Teutonic) origin.
See **Brogues.**

breech. (E.) M. E. *breech*; A. S.
brēc, the breech; A. S. Leechdoms, ii.
146. Cf. A. S. *brēc*, breeches, pl. of *brōc*;
see above.

Breed. (E.) A. S. *brēdan*, to produce
or cherish a brood. – A. S. *brōd*, a brood
(with mutation from *ō* to *ē*).+G. *brüten*;
from *brut.* See **Brood.**

Breeks, breeches. (Scand.) Northern
E. From Icel. *brækr*, pl. of *brōk*; see
Breeches.

Breeze (1), a gadfly. (E.) M. E. *brese.*
A. S. *brīosa.*

Breeze (2),a strong wind. (F.) Formerly
brize. – O. F. *brise*, used by Rabelais in the

same sense as F. *bise*, the N. wind ; cf.
Span. *brisa*, Port. *briza*, the N.E. wind;
Ital. *brezza*, a cold wind. Orig. unknown.

Breeze (3), cinders. (F. – Scand.)
O. F. *brese* (*breze* in Cot.), F. *braise*, live
coals. See **Brasier.**

Breve. (Ital. – L.) Orig. a *short* note ;
now the longest in use. – Ital. *breve*, brief.
– L. *breuis*, short. Der. *semi-breve.*

brevet. (F. – L.) F. *brevet*, ' a brief,
breviate, little writing;' Cot. Dimin. from
F. *bref*, brief. – L. *breuis*, short.

breviary. (F. – L.) F. *bréviaire.* –
L. *breuiārium*, a summary. – L. *breuis.*

brevity. (F. – L.) F. *brièveté.* – L.
acc. *breuitātem*, shortness. – L. *breuis*,
short.

Brew. (E.) M. E. *brewen.* A. S.
brēowan, pt. t. *brēaw*, pp. *gebrowen.*+Du.
brouwen; G. *brauen*; Icel. *brugga*; Swed.
brygga; Dan. *brygge.* Cf. L. *dē-fru-tum*,
new wine boiled down ; Thracian βρῦτον,
beer. (√ BHREU, to decoct.)

Brewis, Browis, pottage. (F. –
O. H. G.) M. E. *brewes, browes*. – O. F.
brouez, broez, nom. of *brouet, broet*, soup
made with broth of meat ; dimin. of *breu*,
pottage (Roquefort). – O. H. G. *brod, brot*,
broth; see **Broth.** Also spelt *brose.*

Briar, Brier. (E.) M. E. *brere.*
A. S. *brēr*, O. Merc. *brēr.*

Bribe. (F.) M. E. *bribe.* – O. F. *bribe*,
a piece of bread given to a beggar.
Cf. *briber*, to beg; Span. *briba*, idleness ;
bribar, to loiter about; Ital. *birba*, fraud;
birbante, an idle beggar. Origin unknown ; not Celtic.

Brick. (F. – M. Du.) F. *brique*, a
brick; also a fragment, bit. – M. Du. *bricke*,
a brick ; cf. Walloon *briquet*, a large slice
of bread. – Du. *breken*, to break. Der.
brick-bat (see **Bat**).

Bride. (E.) M. E. *bride*; also *birde*,
brude, burde. A. S. *brȳd*, a bride. + Du.
bruid; Icel. *brūðr*; Swed. and Dan. *brud*;
O. H. G. *brūt*; G. *braut*; Goth. *brūths.*
Teut. type **brūdiz*, f.

bridal. (E.) Formerly *bride-ale*, a
bride-feast. A. S. *brȳd-ealo*, a bride-ale,
bride-feast. – A. S. *brȳd*, bride; and *ealo*,
ale, also a feast; see **Ale.**

bridegroom. (E.) For *bridegoom*;
the second *r* is intrusive; by confusion
with *groom.* A. S. *brȳd-guma*, lit. bride-
man; where *guma* is cognate with L.
homo, a man ; see **Homage.**+Du. *bruide-
gom*; Icel. *brūðgumi*; Swed. *brudgum* ;

61

Dan. *brudgom*; G. *bräutigam*, O. H. G. *brūtigomo*.

Bridge. (E.) M. E. *brigge*, *brugge*. A. S. *brycg*.+Icel. *bryggja*; Swed. *brygga*; Dan. *brygge*, a pier ; Du. *brug*; G. *brücke*. Teut. type **brugjā*, f. Allied to Icel. *brū*, Dan. *bro*, a bridge, pavement; O. Swed. *bro*, a paved way.

Bridle. (E.) M. E. *bridel*. A. S. *brīdel*.+ Du. *breidel*; O. H. G. *brīdel*, *brittil* (whence F. *bride*). A. S. *brīdel* represents an earlier **brigdel* (cf. *brigdils*, a bridle, O. E. Texts, p. 44, l. 127).—A. S. *bregd-an*, to pull, twitch (with change of *e* to *i*). See **Braid.**

Brief (1), short. (F.—L.) M. E. *bref*. —F. *bref.*—L. *breuis*, short.+Gk. βραχύς, short.

brief (2), a writ, &c. (F.—L.) F. *brief*, a brief; Cot. The same as F. *bref* above; from its being in a short form.

Brig, Brigade; see **Brigand.**

Brigand. (F.—Ital.) F. *brigand*, a robber.—Ital. *brigante*, an intriguer, robber; orig. pres. part. of *brigare*, to strive after.—Ital. *briga*, strife, quarrel, trouble. Orig. uncertain.

brig; short for **brigantine.**

brigade. (F.—Ital.) F. *brigade*, a crew, troop.—Ital. *brigata*, a troop; orig. fem. of pp. of *brigare*, to strive, fight, as above.

brigandine, a kind of armour. (F. —Ital.) F. *brigandine*, a kind of armour, worn by brigands.—F. *brigand*, a robber; see above.

brigantine, brig, a ship. (F.— Ital.) *Brig* is merely short for *brigantine*. —F. *brigantin*, a kind of ship. — Ital. *brigantino*, a pirate-ship.—Ital. *brigante*, a robber. See **Brigand.**

Bright. (E.) M. E. *bright*. A. S. *beorht*, *berht*. + Icel. *bjartr*; M. H. G. *berht*; Goth. *bairhts*, shining. Teut. type **berhtoz*, shining. Cf. Gk. φορκός, white.

Brill, a fish. (E.) Origin unknown.

Brilliant, shining. (F.—L.—Gk.— Skt.) F. *brillant*, pres. part. of *briller*, to glitter; cf. Ital. *brillare*, to sparkle. The orig. sense was to sparkle as a beryl. —L. *beryllus*, a beryl; see **Beryl.**

Brim. (E.) M. E. *brim*. (Not in A. S.) Cf. Icel. *barmr*, brim; Swed. *bräm*, border, edge; Dan. *bræmme*; M. Du. *breme*; G. *gebräme*, border.

Brimstone, sulphur. (E.) M. E. *brimston*, *bremstoon*, also *brenstoon* (Wy-

clif).—M. E. *brenn-en*, to burn, and *stoon*, stone. So also Icel. *brennisteinn*, brimstone. See **Burn.**

Brindled, Brinded, streaked. (Scand.) Icel. *brönd-*, as in *bröndöttr*, brinded, said of a cow.—Icel. *brandr*, a brand, flame, sword. Thus *brinded* = *branded.*

Brine. (E.) M. E. *brine*. A. S. *brȳne* (for *brīne*), brine, salt liquor.+M. Du. *brijne*; Du. *brijn*, pickle.

Bring. (E.) A. S. *bringan*, also *brengan*, pt. t. *bröhte*.+Du. *brengen*; G. *bringen*; Goth. *briggan* (written for *bringan*), pt. t. *brāhta.*

Brink. (Scand.) M. E. *brink.*—Dan. *brink*, verge; Swed. *brink*, descent or slope of a hill; Icel. *brekka* (for *brinka*), a slope, crest of a hill; allied to Icel. *bringa*, a grassy slope, orig. the breast.

Brisk. (F.—Ital.) Spelt *bruisk* in Lowl. Sc. (1560).—F. *brusque*, 'brisk, lively, quicke, rash, harsh;' Cot.—Ital. *brusco*, tart, harsh; see **Brusque.**

Brisket. (F.) O. F. *brischet* (Brachet), s. v. *brechet*), also *bruschet* (Ducange); *brichet*, 'the brisket, or breast-piece,' *bruchet*, 'the craw-bone of a bird;' Cot. Mod. F. *brechet*. Cf. Bret. *bruched*, the breast; spelt *brusk* in the dialect of Vannes.

Bristle. (E.) M. E. *bristle*, *berstle*, *birstle*; dimin. of A. S. *byrst*, a bristle.+ Du. *borstel*; Icel. *burst*; Swed. *borst*; G. *borste*. From Teut. **burs-*, weak grade of **bers* = Idg. **bhers*, to bristle; cf. Skt. *sahasra-bhṛshti*, having a thousand points. See **Burr.**

Brittle. (E.) M. E. *britel*, *brotel*, *brutel*. For A. S. **brytel* = Teut. **brutiloz*, from *brut-*, weak grade of A. S. *brēotan*, to break. It means 'fragile.' Cf. Icel. *brjóta*, Swed. *bryta*, Dan. *bryde*, to break.

Broach. (F.—L.) M. E. *setten on broche* = to set a-broach, tap liquor.—F. *mettre en broche*, to tap, by piercing a barrel. — F. *brocher*, to pierce; *broche*, 'a broach, spit,' Cot.; see **Brooch.**

Broad. (E.) M. E. *brood*. A. S. *brād*. + Du. *breed*; Icel. *breiðr*; Swed. and Dan. *bred*; Goth. *braids*; G. *breit.*

Brocade. (Span.—L.) Span. *brocado*, brocade; orig. embroidered, the pp. of a verb **brocar* (not used) answering to F. *brocher*, 'to broach, also, to stitch . . . with great stitches;' Cot. — F. *broche.*—Late L. *brocca*, L. *broccus*; see **Brooch.**

broccoli. (Ital.–L.) Ital. *broccoli*, sprouts; pl. of *broccolo*, a sprout. Dimin. of *brocco*, a skewer, a shoot, stalk.–L. *broccus*, projecting, like teeth.

brochure, a pamphlet. (F.–L.) F. *brochure*, a few leaves stitched together.– F. *brocher*, to stitch; see Brocade.

Brock, a badger. (C.) A.S. *broc.*– W., Corn., and Bret. *broch*; Irish, Gael., and Manx *broc*, a badger. Named from his white-streaked face; cf. Gael. *brocach*, speckled, grayish, as a badger; Gk. φορκός, white, gray. (Cf. E. *gray*, a badger.)

Brocket, a red deer two years old. (F.–L.) F. *brocart*, the same; so called because he has but one tine to his horn.– F. *broche*, a spit, also, a tine of a stag's horn; see Brooch.

Brogues, coarse shoes, leggings. (C. –E.) Gael. and Irish *brōg*, shoe; M. Irish *brōcc*, shoe.–A.S. *brōc*, breeches; *or* Icel. *brōk*. See Breeches.

Broided, braided. (E.) The wk. pp. *broided* took the place of the str. pp. *broiden*, woven, itself due to confusion of *browden* with *broider* (below). *Browden* represents A.S. *brogden*, pp. of *bregdan*, to braid. See Braid.

Broider, to adorn with needlework. (F.) [In 1 Tim. ii. 9, *broidered* (as in some edd.) is an error for *broided*; see above.] Used as the equivalent of F. *broder*, 'to imbroyder,' Cot. The *oi* is due to confusion with *broided.* – O.F. *brouder*, also *brosder* (Supp. to Godefroy); cf. Late L. *brusdus, brosdus*, embroidered work (Ducange). Of unknown origin; perhaps from Teut. **brozd-*, whence A.S. *brord*, Icel. *broddr*, a spike; see Brad.

Broil (1), to fry, grill. (F.) M.E. *broilen.* – A. F. *broiller* (Bozon), O. F. *bruiller*, to boil, roast (Roquefort). Origin unknown; cf. O.F. *bruir*, to roast; perhaps from M.H.G. *brüejen*, to scald; see Brood.

Broil (2), a tumult. (F.) F. *brouiller*, to jumble, confuse, confound. Cf. Ital. *brogliare*, to disturb, *broglio*, confusion (whence E. *im-broglio*). Origin unknown.

Broker. (F. – L.) M. E. *brocour*, an agent, witness of a transaction.–A.F. *brocour*, an agent; orig. a ' broacher' or seller of wine.– Late L. *broccātor*, one who broaches.– Late L. *brocca*, i. e. spike; see Brooch.

Bromine, a chemical element. (Gk.)

Named from its ill odour. Formed, with suffix *-ine*, from Gk. βρῶμ-ος, a stink.

Bronchial. (Gk.) Gk. βρόγχια, neut. pl., the ramifications of the windpipe.– Gk. βρόγχος, the windpipe; cf. βράγχος, a gill. Der. *bronch-itis*; from βρόγχος.

Bronze. (F. – Ital.–L.) F. *bronze.* –Ital. *bronzo*; *bronzino*, made of bronze (*z = ds*).–L. *æs Brundusīnum.*–L. *Brundusium*, Brindisi (in Italy); where bronze mirrors were made (Pliny, xxxiii. 9).

Brooch. (F.–L.) Named from the pin which fastens it. M. E. *broche*, a pin, peg, brooch.–F. *broche*, a spit, point.– Late L. *brocca*, a pointed stick; *broca*, a spike; L. *broccus*, projecting, like teeth.

Brood. (E.) M.E. *brod.* A.S. *brōd* (rare); 'hi *brēdað* heora *brōd*' = they nourish their brood; Ælfric's Hom. ii. 10. +Du. *broed*; G. *brut.* Teut. stem **brō-ð-*, from a verbal base **brō-*, preserved in G. *brü-hen*, to scald (orig. to heat), Du. *broe-ien*, to brood, hatch; from the idea of ' heat' or ' warmth.' Der. *breed.*

Brook (1), to endure, put up with. (E.) M. E. *broken, brouken.* A.S. *brū-can*, to use, enjoy; which was the orig. sense. +Du. *gebruiken*, Icel. *brūka*, G. *brauchen*, Goth. *brukjan*, to use; cf. L. *frui*, to enjoy. See Fruit. (√BHREUG.) Brugm. i. § 111.

Brook (2), a small stream. (E.) M. E. *brook.* A.S. *brōc.*+Du. *broek*, G. *bruch*, a marsh.

brook-lime, a plant. (E.) M. E. *brok-lemke, brok-lemok.* From A.S. *brōc*, a brook, and *hleomoc*, brook-lime.

Broom. (E.) M. E. *brome, broom.* A.S. *brōm*, the plant broom; hence, a besom made from twigs of it.+Du. *brem*; Low G. *braam*, broom. Teut. type **brǣ-moz.* Allied to Bramble, q. v.

Brose, a later form of *browis* or *brewis*; see Brewis.

Broth. (E.) A.S. *broþ.*+Icel. *broð*; O. H. G. *brod.* Teut. type **broþom*, n.; from *bro-, bru-*, weak grade of *breu-*, as in A.S. *brēowan*, to brew. Lit. ' brewed.'

Brothel. (E.; *confused with* F.– Teut.) 1. M. E. *brothel*, a lewd person, base wretch. – A.S. *broð-en*, pp. of *brēoðan*, to perish, become vile; whence also *ābroðen*, degenerate, base. Hence was made *brothel-house*, a house for vile people (Much Ado, i. 1. 256), afterwards contracted to *brothel.* 2. Orig. distinct from M. E. *bordel*, which was used, however, in much the same sense. **—** O. F. *bordel*, a hut, orig. of boards. **—** Du. *bord*, a plank, board; see **Board**.

Brother. (E.) M. E. *brother*. A. S. *brōðor*.**+**Du. *broeder*; Icel. *brōðir*; Goth. *brothar*; Swed. and Dan. *broder*; G. *bruder*; Gael. and Ir. *brathair*; W. *brawd*; Russ. *brat'*; Lat. *frāter*; Gk. φρατήρ; Skt. *bhrātṛ*. Teut. stem **brōther-*; Idg. stem **bhrāter-*.

Brougham, a kind of carriage. (Personal name.) Date 1839. Named after the first Lord Brougham.

Brow. (E.) M. E. *browe*. A.S. *brū*. **+**Icel. *brún*, eyebrow; Lith. *bruwis*; Russ. *brove*; Gk. ὀφρύς; Pers. *abrū*; Skt. *bhrū*. Brugm. i. § 554.

Brown. (E.) M. E. *broun*. A.S. *brūn*.**+**Du. *bruin*; Icel. *brūnn*; Swed. *brun*; Dan. *bruun*; G. *braun*; Lith. *brunas*. Cf. Gk. φρῦνος, a toad; Skt. *ba-bhru(s)*, tawny.

Browse. (F. **—** M. H. G.) For *broust*; lit. 'to feed on young shoots.' **—** M. F. *brouster* (F. *brouter*), to nibble off young shoots. **—** M. F. *broust* (F. *brout*), a sprig, shoot, bud. **—** M. H. G. *broz*, a bud; Bavar. *brosst*, *bross*, a bud. From the weak grade of O. H. G. *briozan*, to break, also, to break into bud; which is cognate with A. S. *brēotan*. See **Brittle**.

Bruin. (Du.) In Reynard the Fox, the bear is called *bruin*, i. e. brown. **—** Du. *bruin*, brown. See **Brown**.

Bruise. (E.; *partly* F.) A. S. *(tō)-brȳsan*, to bruise. Influenced by O. F. *bruiser*, *briser*, to break, perhaps of Celtic origin; cf. Gael. *bris*, to break, Irish *brisim*, I break. (The spelling *ui*, from A. S. *ȳ*, occurs in S. Eng. Legendary, 295. 58.)

Bruit, a rumour. (F. **—** L.?) F. *bruit*, a noise. **—** F. *bruire*, to make a noise. Scheler derives F. *bruire* from L. *rugīre*, to roar, with prefixed *b*. **—** F. *bruit* **=** Late L. *brugītus*, a clamour (Ducange); cf. L. *rugītus*, a roaring. Partly imitative; cf. G. *brüllen*, to roar.

Brunette. (F. **—** G.) F. *brunette*, fem. of *brunet*, brownish. **—** M. H. G. *brūn*, brown; see **Brown**.

Brunt. (E.) Prob. imitative; cf. *dint* (*dunt*), a blow; influenced by North E. *brunt*, i. e. 'burnt,' as if the 'hot' part of the fight.

Brush. (F. **—** Teut. ?) M. E. *brusche*, a brush; also brush-wood, which is the older sense, the orig. brush being made of twigs. **—** O. F. *broce*, F. *brosse*, brushwood; also, later, a brush. **—** Low L. *bruscia*, a thicket. Derived by Diez from O. H. G. *burstā*, G. *borste*, a bristle; but perhaps Celtic (Thurneysen).

Brusque, rough in manner. (F. **—** Ital.) F. *brusque*. **—** Ital. *brusco*, sharp, tart, sour, applied to fruits and wine. Origin uncertain.

Brute. (F. **—** L.) F. *brut*, fem. *brute*. **—** L. *brūtus*, stupid.

Bryony. (L. **—** Gk.) L. *bryōnia*. **—** Gk. βρυωνία, βρυώνη, bryony. **—** Gk. βρύειν, to teem, grow luxuriantly.

Bubble. (E.) Cf. Swed. *bubbla*, Dan. *boble*, a bubble; also Du. *bobbel*, a bubble, *bobbelen*, to bubble. Of imitative origin.

Buccanier. (F. **—** West Indian.) F. *boucanier*, a pirate. **—** F. *boucaner*, to broil on a sort of wooden frame. **—** F. *boucan*, a wooden frame, used by hunters for smoking and drying flesh. The word *boucan* is said to be a F. spelling of a Tupi (Brazilian) word, and to mean 'a frame on which meat is smoke-dried.'

Buck (1), a male deer, goat. (E.) M. E. *bukke*. A. S. *buc*, male deer, *bucca*, a he-goat.**+**Du. *bok*, Icel. *bukkr*, Swed. *bock*, a he-goat; Dan. *buk*, a he-goat, ram, buck; G. *bock*; also W. *bwch*, Gael. *boc*, Irish *boc*. Brugm. i. § 800.

Buck (2), to steep clothes in lye. (E.) M. E. *bouken*. As if from A. S. **būcian*, not found. Prob. from A. S. *būc*, a pitcher (prov. E. *bouk*, a pail, tub); but M. E. *bouken* has the specific sense of 'steep in lye,' like M. H. G. *büchen*, Swed. *byka*, Dan. *byge*, Low G. *būken*, *büken* (whence Ital. *bucare*, F. *buer*).

bucket. (E.) A. F. *boket* (Bozon). Formed with A. F. dimin. suffix -*et* from A. S. *būc*, a pitcher. Cf. Gael. *bucaid*, Irish *buicead*, a bucket (from E.).

Buckle. (F. **—** L.) M. E. *bokel*. **—** O. F. *bucle* (F. *boucle*), the boss of a shield, a ring, a buckle. **—** Late L. *bucula*, the boss of a shield; *buccula*, beaver of a helm, boss of a shield, buckle. **—** Lat. *buccula*, the cheek, dimin. of *bucca*, the cheek.

buckler. (F. **—** L.) M. E. *bokeler*. **—** O. F. *bucler* (F. *bouclier*), a shield; so named from the boss on it; see above.

Buckram, a coarse cloth. (F. **—** Ital.) M. E. *bokeram*. **—** O. F. *boquerant* (F. *bougran*), a coarse kind of cloth; Low L. *boquerannus* or (in Italy) *būchirānus* (for Ital. *buchirano*), late Ital. *bucherame*.

Origin uncertain; perhaps from Bokhara (Tartary).

Buckwheat. (E.) Lit. beech-wheat; from the resemblance of its seeds to the mast of the beech-tree. The form *buck* is from A. S. *bōc*, as in *buck-mast*, beech-mast. So also Du. *boekweit*, buckwheat; G. *buchweizen*. See Beech.

Bucolic, pastoral. (L. – Gk.) L. *būcolicus.* – Gk. βουκολικός, pastoral. – Gk. βουκόλος, a cowherd. – Gk. βοῦ-s, an ox; and κέλλειν, to drive.

Bud. (E.?) M. E. *bodde, budde,* a bud; *budden,* to bud. Not found in A.S. Cf. Du. *bot,* a bud; *botten,* to bud, sprout.

Budge (1), to stir. (F. – L.) F. *bouger,* to stir; answering to Ital. *bulicare,* to bubble up (Diez). – L. *bullīre*; see Boil (1) above. Cf. Span. *bullir,* (1) to boil, (2) to stir.

Budge (2), a kind of fur. (F.?) Perhaps related to O. F. *bochet, bouchet,* a young kid.

Budget, a leathern bag. (F. – C.) F. *bougette,* dimin. of *bouge,* a bag. – L. *bulga,* a leathern bag (Gaulish). – O. Irish *bolg, bolc,* a sack.

Buff (1), the colour of dressed buffalo-skin. (F. – L. – Gk.) F. *buffle,* a buffalo. – L. *būfalus*; see Buffalo.

Buff (2), in Blindman's buff. (F.) Formerly *blindman-buff,* a game; in which game boys used to *buffet* one (who was blinded) on the back, without being caught, if possible. From O. F. *bufe,* F. *buffe,* a buffet, blow; cf. Low G. *buff, puf,* a blow (Lübben). See Buffet (1).

Buffalo. (Port. *or* Ital. – L. – Gk.) Port. *bufalo,* Ital. *buffalo,* orig. a kind of wild ox. – L. *būfalus,* also *būbalus.* – Gk. βούβαλος, a buffalo; a kind of deer or antelope. (Not a true Gk. word.)

Buffer (1), and (2); see Buffet (1).

Buffet (1), a blow; to strike. (F.) M. E. *boffet, buffet,* a blow, esp. on the cheek. – O. F. *bufet,* a blow, dimin. of *bufe,* a blow, esp. on the cheek; cf. *bufer, buffer,* to puff out the cheeks, also to buffet; mod. F. *bouffer.* Prob. of imitative origin, allied to *pouffer,* to puff; see Buff (2), Puff.

buffer (1), a foolish fellow. (F.) Orig. a stammerer; hence, a foolish fellow. M.E. *buffen,* to stammer. – O. F. *bufer,* to puff out the cheeks (hence, to puff or blow in talking).

buffer (2), a cushion, to deaden concussion. (F.) Lit. 'a striker;' from M. E.

buffen, to strike, orig. to buffet on the cheek; see Buffet (1).

buffoon. (F.) F. *bouffon,* a buffoon, jester, one who makes grimaces. – F. *bouffer,* to puff.

Buffet (2), a side-board. (F.) F. *buffet,* a side-board. Origin unknown.

Bug (1), a spectre. (C.) In Sh. – W. *bwg,* a hobgoblin, spectre; Gael. and Ir. *bocan,* a spectre. + Lithuan. *baugus,* terrific, from *bugti,* to terrify, allied to Skt. *bhuj,* to turn aside; see Bow (1). Brugm. i. § 701.

Bug (2), an insect. (C.?) Said to be so named because an object of terror, exciting disgust; see Bug (1). But cf. A.S. *scearn-budda,* dung-beetle (Voc.), prov. E. *shorn-bug* (Kent).

Bug-bear. (C. *and* E.) A supposed spectre in the shape of a bear; see Bug (1).

Bugle (1), a wild ox; a horn. (F. – L.) *Bugle,* a horn, is short for *bugle-horn*; a *bugle* is a wild ox. – O. F. *bugle,* a wild ox. – L. acc. *būculum,* a young ox; double dimin. of *bōs,* an ox.

Bugle (2), a kind of ornament. [Low L. *bugoli,* pl., the name of a kind of pad for the hair (A.D. 1388), throws no light on the word.] Etym. unknown.

Bugle (3), a plant. (F.) F. *bugle*; Cot.; cf. Span. and Late L. *bugula.* Cf. L. *bugillo,* (perhaps) bugle.

Bugloss, a plant. (F. – L. – Gk.) Lit. 'ox-tongue.' – F. *buglosse.* – L. *būglōssa*; also *būglōssus.* – Gk. βούγλωσσος, ox-tongue; from the shape of the leaves. – Gk. βοῦ-s, ox; γλῶσσα, tongue.

Build. (E.) M.E. *bulden.* Late A. S. *byldan,* to build. – A. S. *bold,* a house, variant of *botl,* a dwelling, n. = Teut. **bu-þlom,* from *bu-,* related to *bū-an,* to dwell; see Bower. Cf. A. S. *bytlian,* to build, from *botl* (above). [Cf. O. Swed. *bylja,* to build (Ihre). – O. Swed. *bol,* a house, dwelling; Icel. *ból,* a house, Dan. *bol,* a small farm.]

Bulb. (F. – L. – Gk.) F. *bulbe.* – L. *bulbus,* a bulb. – Gk. βολβός, a bulbous root, onion.

Bulbul, a nightingale. (Pers.) Pers. *bulbul,* a bird with a melodious voice, resembling the nightingale. Of imitative origin.

Bulge, to swell out. (F. – C.) Formed from M. E. *bulge,* a wallet, pouch. – O. F. *boulge (bouge),* a bag. – L. *bulga,* a bag (Gaulish). See **Budget**. **Doublet,** *bilge*.

Bulk (1), size. (Scand.) M. E. *bolke*, a heap. – Icel. *būlki*, a heap; O. Swed. *bolk*; Dan. *bulk*, a lump. Cf. Swed. *bulna*, to swell.

Bulk (2), the trunk of the body. (Du.) In Sh. – M. Du. *bulcke*, thorax (Kilian). (Prob. confused with Du. *buik*, Icel. *būkr*, the trunk; Swed. *buk*, Dan. *bug*, G. *bauch*, the belly.)

Bulk (3), a stall of a shop. (Scand.) Perhaps related to **Balk**. Cf. Dan. dial. *bulk*, a half-wall; Icel. *bālkr*, a beam, also, a partition; Linc. *bulker*, a beam, a wooden hutch in a workshop. **Der.** *bulk-head*, a partition.

Bull (1), male of the cow. (E.) M. E. *bole, bule*. Not found in A. S., but the dimin. *bulluc*, a bullock, occurs. Prob. ' the bellower;' cf. M. H. G. *bullen*, to roar; and see **Bellow**. + Du. *bul*; Icel. *boli*; G. *bulle*; Lithuan. *bullus*. **Der.** *bull-ock*, A. S. *bulluc*, as above.

Bull (2), a papal edict. (L.) M. E. *bulle*. – Lat. *bulla*, a bubble, boss, knob, leaden seal on an edict; a bull (in late Latin).

bullet. (F. – L.) M. F. *boulet*, dimin. of F. *boule*, a ball. – L. *bulla*, a boss, knob, &c.

bulletin. (F. – Ital. – L.) F. *bulletin*, a ticket. – Ital. *bullettino*, a safe-conduct, pass, ticket. Dimin. of *bulletta*, a passport, lottery ticket, dimin. of *bulla*, a seal, bull. – L. *bulla*, a boss, &c.

Bullace, wild plum. (F. ?) M. E. *bolas*. Apparently related to O. F. *beloce*, a bullace; cf. Bret. *bolos, polos*, bullace; Low L. *bolluca*; Walloon. *biloc* (Remacle).

Bullet, Bulletin; see Bull (2).

Bullion. (F. – L.) The A. F. *bullion* meant a mint, and Late L. *bulliōna, bullio* meant a mass of. metal, apparently, from its being melted; cf. F. *bouillon*, a boiling. – Late L. *bulliōnem*, acc. of *bullio*, a boiling. – L. *bullīre*, to bubble up, boil. – L. *bulla*, a bubble.

Bully, a noisy rough fellow. (O. Low G.) In Sh. The oldest sense, in E., is ' dear one, lover.' – M. Du. *boel*, a lover (of either sex); borrowed from M. H. G. *buole* (G. *buhle*), lover.

Bulrush. (E.) M.E. *bulrysche*, Prompt. Parv., p. 244, col. 2. Perhaps ' stem-rush '; from its stout stem; cf. Shetl. *bulwand*, a bulrush. – Dan. *bul*, stem, trunk; see

Bole. Or *bull* may mean ' large,' with ref. to a *bull*. Cf. *bull-daisy*, &c. (Britten).

Bulwark. (Scand.) Dan. *bulværk*, Swed. *bolverk* (Ihre); cf. Du. *bolwerk*, G. *boll-werk* (whence F. *boulevard*). Compounded of Dan. *bul*, Swed. *bol*, trunk of a tree, log, Icel. *bulr, bolr*, the stem of a tree; and Dan. *værk*, Swed. *verk*, a work. Lit. ' log - work,' or ' bole-work '; see **Bole**.

Bum-bailiff, under-bailiff. (E. *and* F.) A slang term. Todd quotes passages to shew that it arose from the pursuer catching at a man by the hinder part of his garment.

Bumble-bee, a bee that booms or hums. See **Boom** (1).

Bumboat. (E.) From *bum* and *boat*. Orig. a scavenger's boat on the Thames (A. D. 1685); afterwards used to supply vegetables to ships.

Bump (1), to thump; a blow. (E.) Of imitative origin; cf. M. Dan. *bumpe*, to strike with the fist; W. *pwmpio*, to thump; *pwmp*, a lump; Corn. *bom, bum*, a blow. The senses are: (1) to strike, (2) a blow, (3) its effect. See **Bunch**.

Bump (2), to boom. (E.) Imitative; cf. **Boom** (1), and **Bumble-bee**.

Bumper, a full glass. (E.) From *bump*; with the notion of a *bumping* or full glass; cf. *thumping*, i. e. great.

Bumpkin, a thick-headed fellow. (Du.) M. Du. *boomken*, a little tree (Hexham); dimin. of *boom*, a tree, a beam, bar; see **Beam** (1). The E. *bumkin* also meant a luff-block, a thick piece of wood (Cotgrave, s. v. *Chicambault*, and see *bumkin* in the E. index); hence, readily applied to a block-head, thick-skulled fellow.

Bun. (F.) Cf. prov. F. *bugne*, a kind of fritters; perhaps the same as O. F. *bugne*, a swelling or bump due to a blow (Burguy), also spelt *bigne*, ' a bump, knob;' Cot. O. F. *bugnete*, a fritter (Godefroy); also *bugnet* (id., Supp. p. 393). ' *Bignets*, little round loaves, buns,' &c.; Cot. Minsheu has Span. *buñuelos*, ' pancakes, cobloaves, buns.' See **Bunion**. (Doubtful.)

Bunch. (E. ?) M. E. *bunche*. Cf. M. E. *bunchen*, to beat. Prob. imitative, like *bump, bounce*. And see **Bunk**.

Bundle. (E.) M. E. *bundel*. Dimin. of O. Northumb. *bund*, a bundle (Matt. xiii. 30). – A. S. *bund-*, weak grade of *bindan*, to bind. + Du. *bondel*; G. *bündel*.

Bung, a stopple. (Du.–L.) M. Du. *bonge* (Du. *bom*), a bung; dialectal form of **bonde*, as preserved in F. *bonde*, a bung. Cognate with Swiss *punt* (Weigand, s. v. *Spund*).–L. *puncta*, an orifice; orig. fem. pp. of *pungere*, to prick. Cf. W. *bwng*, an orifice, also, a bung.

Bungalow, a Bengal thatched house. (Hind.) Hind. *bangalah*, of or belonging to Bengal, a bungalow; Rich. Dict. p. 293. From the name *Bengal*.

Bungle. (Scand.?) Of imitative origin. Cf. Swed. dial. *bangla*, to work ineffectually; O. Swed. *bunga*, to strike (Rietz, Ihre.) And cf. **Bang.**

Bunion. (F.–G.) O. F. *buignon*, only in the sense of a fritter (Godefroy); but really an augmentative of O. F. *buigne* (F. *bigne*, 'a bump, swelling,' Cot.).– O. H. G. *bungo*, a lump (Graff, in Schmeller); cf. Icel. *bunga*, convexity. So also Ital. *bugnone*, augment. of *bugno*, a boil, a swelling. See **Bun.**

Bunk, a wooden case or box, berth. (Scand.) Cf. O. Swed. *bunke*, the planking of a ship forming a shelter for merchandise, &c. (Ihre); the usual sense of Swed. *bunke* is a heap, pile, something prominent; M. Dan. *bunke*, room for cargo.

Bunt, the belly of a sail. (Scand.) It answers in form to Dan. *bundt*, Swed. *bunt*, a bundle, a bunch; from the weak stem of the verb to **Bind.** ¶ But the right words for 'bunt' are Dan. *bug*, Swed. *buk*, Du. *buik*, G. *bauch*; see **Bulk** (2).

Bunting (1), a bird. (E.?) M. E. *bunting*; also *buntyle* (= *buntel*), Lowl. Sc. *buntlin*. Origin unknown.

Bunting (2), a thin woollen stuff for flags. (E.) Perhaps 'sifting-cloth'; from M. E. *bonten*, prov. E. *bunt*, to sift. Cf. F. *étamine*, in the same senses.

Buoy. (Du.–F.–L.) Du. *boei*, a buoy; also a shackle, a fetter.–O. F. *buie*, a fetter, F. *bouée*, a buoy.–Late L. *boia*, a fetter, clog.–L. *boiæ*, pl. a collar for the neck, orig. of leather.

Bur, Burdock; see **Burr.**

Burbot, a fish. (F.) F. *bourbotte* (also *barbote*).–F. *bourbetter*, 'to wallow in mud,' Cot.–F. *bourbe*, mud; of unknown origin.

Burden (1), **Burthen,** a load carried. (E.) A. S. *byrðen*, a load. From Teut. **bur-*, weak grade of **beran-*, to bear; see **Bear** (1). **✢** Icel. *byrðr*, *byrði*; Swed.

börda; Dan. *byrde*; Goth. *baurthei*; G. *bürde*; from the same root, with varying suffixes. For the form *burden*, see below.

Burden (2), the refrain of a song. (F.–Late L.) F. *bourdon*, a drone-bee, humming of bees, drone of a bagpipe; see Cot.–Late L. *burdōnem*, acc. of *burdo*, a drone. Prob. of imitative origin; cf. Lowland Sc. *birr*, to make a whizzing noise, E. *buzz*. ¶ Confused with **Burden** (1).

Bureau. (F.–L.) F. *bureau*, a desk, writing-table; so called because covered with brown baize.–F. *bureau*, O. F. *burel*, coarse woollen stuff, russet-coloured. – O. F. *buire*, M. F. *bure*, dark brown; F. *bure*, coarse cloth.–L. *burrus*, reddish. – Gk. πυρρός, reddish.–Gk. πῦρ, fire.

Burgeon, a bud. (F.–Teut.) F. *bourgeon*, a young bud. Lengthened from Languedoc *boure*, a bud, eye of a shoot (Diez).–M. H. G. *buren*, O. H. G. *purjan*, to raise, push up, push out.–M. H. G. *bor*, *por*, an elevation; whence G. *empor* (= *in por*), upwards.

Burgess. (F.–M. H. G.) M. E. *burgeys*.–O. F. *burgeis*.–Low Lat. *burgensis*, belonging to a fort or city.–Low Lat. *burgus*, a fort.–M. H. G. *burc* (G. *burg*); cognate with A. S. *burg*; see **Borough.**

burgher. (Du.) Formerly *burger*.– Du. *burger*, a citizen.–Du. *burg*, a city; cognate with E. **Borough.**

burglar. (A. F.–E.) A. F. *burgler*, *burglour*; Law L. *burgulātor*.–Law L. *burgulāre*, to break into a house.–A. S. *burh*, *burg*; see **Borough.**

burgomaster. (Du. *and* F.) Du. *burge-meester*, a town-master.–Du. *burg*, cognate with E. **Borough**; and *meester*, a master, from O. F. *meistre*; see **Master.**

Burgonet, a helmet. (F.) F. *bourguignote*, 'a burganet,' Cot. So called because first used by the Burgundians.– F. *Bourgogne*, Burgundy.

Burial. (E.) M. E. *buriel*, *biriel*, a tomb; also spelt *beriels*, *biriels*.–A. S. *byrgels*, a tomb. – A. S. *byrgan*, to bury; see **Bury.** The spelling with *-al* is due to association with *funer-al*, &c.

Burin, an engraver's tool. (F.–G.) F. *burin*; Ital. *borino*. Prob. from M. H. G. *boren* (G. *bohren*), to bore; see **Bore** (1).

Burke, to murder by suffocation; to murder, stifle. (Personal name.) From the name of *Burke*, an Irishman who committed murders by suffocation; executed at Edinburgh, Jan. 28, 1829.

Burl, to pick knots and loose threads from cloth. (F. – L.) To *burl* is to pick off *burls*. M. E. *burle*, a knot in cloth. – O. F. *bourle*; dimin. of F. *bourre*, a flock or lock of wool or hair. – Late L. *burra*, a woollen pad; allied to L. *burræ*, trifles, trash, Late L. *reburrus*, rough.

burlesque, comic. (F. – Ital. – L.) F. *burlesque*. – Ital. *burlesco*, ludicrous. – Ital. *burla*, waggery, a trick. A dimin. from L. *burræ*, trifles, nonsense (Ausonius). See **Burl**.

Burly. (E.) M. E. *burli*, *burliche*, *borli*; prov. E. *bowerly*; Shetland *boorly*. Formed by adding the suffix -*ly* (A. S. -*lic*) to A. S. *būr*, a bower, a lady's chamber; hence, the old senses of 'fit for a bower,' stately, excellent, large, great; and, finally, stout, big. E. g. 'a *burly* bed.'

Burn (1), verb. (E.) M.E. *bernen*; also *brennen*. There are two forms. α. intrans. A.S. *beornan*, *byrnan*, strong verb, pt. t. *bearn*, *bran*, pp. *bornen*.+O. Icel. *brinna*; Goth. *brinnan*; Teut. type **brennan-*; cf. A. S. *bryne*, flame. β. trans. A. S. *bærnan*, wk. vb.+Icel. *brenna*, Dan. *brænde*, Swed. *bränna*; G. *brennen*; Goth. *brannjan*; Teut. type **brannjan-*, causal to the former.

Burn (2), a brook; see **Bourn** (2).

Burnet, a plant. (F. – O. H. G.) Low L. *burneta*. – O. F. *brunete*, the name of a flower: *burnette*, *brunette*, a kind of dark brown cloth, also a brunette. See **Brunette**: Named from the dark brown colour of the flowers.

burnish, to polish. (F. – O. H. G.) M. E. *burnishen*; also *burnen*. – O. F. *burnir*, *brunir* (pres. part. *burnis-ant*), to embrown, to polish. – O. H. G. *brünen* (<**brünjan*). – O.H.G. *brün*, brown; see **Brown**.

Burnouse, Burnoose, an upper cloak worn by the Arabs. (F. – Arab.) F. *burnous*, *bournous*. – Arab. *burnus*, a kind of high-crowned cap, worn formerly in Barbary and Spain; whence Span. *al-bornoz*, a kind of cloak with a hood.

Burr, Bur. (E.) M. E. *burre*, knob on a burdock; *borre*, roughness in the throat. Not in A. S. N. Fries. *burre*, *borre*, a burr, burdock.+Swed. *borre*, a sea-urchin; *kardborre*, a burdock; Dan. *borre*, burdock. From Teut. base **burz-*<**burs-*, weak grade of Teut. root **bers*, to bristle. See **Bristle**. Der. *bur-dock*.

Burrow, a shelter for rabbits. (E.) M. E. *borwgh*, a cave, shelter; merely a varied spelling of *borough*. Der. *burrow*, verb.

Bursar. (Med. L. – Gk.) Med. L. *bursārius*, a purse-bearer. – Med. L. *bursa*, a purse. – Gk. βύρσα, a hide, wine-skin.

Burst. (E.) M. E. *bersten*, *bresten*, pt. t. *brast*. A. S. *berstan*, to burst asunder; break; str. vb.+Du. *bersten*; G. *bersten*; Icel. *bresta*; Swed. *brista*; Dan. *briste*; also O. Irish *briss-im* (for **brest-im*), I break.

Bury (1), vb. (E.) M. E. *burien*, A.S. *byrigan*, *byrgan*, to hide in the ground, bury. From *burg-*, weak grade of *beorg-an*, to hide; see **Borough**.

Bury (2), a town. (E.) As in Canterbury. – A. S. *byrig*, dat. of *burh*, a borough. See **Borough**.

Bus, a shortened form of *omnibus*. (L.) See **Omnibus**.

Bush (1), a thicket. (Scand. – L.) M. E. *busch*, *busk*. – Dan. *busk*, Swed. *buske*, a bush, shrub.+Du. *bosch*; O. H. G. *busc*; G. *busch*. All from Late L. *boscus*, a bush; a word of unknown origin.

Bush (2), the metal box in which an axle works. (Du. – L. – Gk.) M. E. *busse*. – Du. *bus*, a box, barrel (of a gun); G. *büchse*. – Late L. *buxis*, a box. – Gk. πύξις, a box. – Gk. πύξος, box-wood, box-tree. See **Pyx**.

bushel, a measure. (F. – L. – Gk.) M.E. *bushel*. – A.F. *bousselle*, Q. F. *boissel*; Late L. *bustellus*, a small box; for **boistel*, dimin. of O. F. *boiste*, a box. – Late L. *buxida*, acc. of *buxis*, a box (above).

Busk (1), to get oneself ready. (Scand.) Icel. *būask*, to get oneself ready. – Icel. *būa*, to prepare; and -*sk*, for *sik*, oneself. See **Bound** (3); and cf. **Bask**.

Busk (2), a support for a woman's stays. (F.) M. F. *busque*, 'a buske, or buste;' Cot. Mod. F. *busc*. Of uncertain origin. Cf. M. F. *buc*, 'a busque;' Cot.

Buskin. (Du.) Du. *broosken*, buskin (Sewel); mod. Du. *broos*, with dimin. suffix -*ken*. Or from M.F. *brousequin*, now *brodequin*; or from Span. *borcegui*. Origin unknown.

Buss, to kiss. (E.) [The old word was *bass*. – F. *baiser*, to kiss. – Lat. *basium*, a kiss.] The modern *buss*, of imitative origin, may have been partly suggested by it. Cf. prov. G. (Bavarian) *bussen*, to kiss; Lith. *buczoti*, to kiss; also Gael. and W. *bus*, mouth, lip.

Bust. (F. – Ital.) F. *buste*. – Ital. *busto*, the bust, trunk of human body, stays; Late L. *bustum*, the trunk of the body. Etym. uncertain.

Bustard, a bird. (F. – L.) Formerly also *bistard* (Sherwood). – O. F. *bistarde*, ' a bustard; ' Cot. (Mod. F. *outarde*.) – L. *auis tarda*, a slow bird (Pliny, N. H. x. 22). Cf. Port. *abetarda*, also *betarda*, a bustard. ¶ Both O. F. *bistarde* and F. *outarde* are from *auis tarda*; in the former case, initial *a* is dropped; in the latter, *outarde* stands for an older *oustarde*, where *ous* = L. *auis*. See Diez. *Auis tarda*, lit. 'slow bird,' is far from being truly descriptive; so that it is prob. a substitution for some form foreign to Latin.

Bustle. (Scand.) A variant of (obsolete) *buskle*, to prepare; also, to hurry about. Frequent. of *busk*, to prepare oneself; see Busk (1). Cf. Icel. *bustla*, to splash about as a fish.

Busy. (E.) M. E. *bisy*. A. S. *bisig* (*bysig*), active; whence *bisgu*, exertion. + Du. *bezig*, busy.

But (1), prep. and conj., except. (E.) A. S. *be-ūtan*, *būtan*, *būta*, lit. 'without.' – A. S. *be*, by; *ūtan*, adv. without, from *ūt*, out. + Du. *buiten*.

But (2); see Butt (1), Butt (2).

Butcher. (F. – G.) M. E. *bocher*. – O. F. *bochier*, orig. one who kills goats. – O. F. *boc* (F. *bouc*), a goat. – G. *bock*, a goat. See Buck.

Butler. (F. – Late L. – Gk.) M. E. *boteler*, one who attends to bottles; from M. E. *botel*, a bottle; see Bottle.

Butt (1), a push, thrust; to thrust. (F. – O. Low G.) [The senses of the sb. may be referred to the verb; just as F. *botte*, a thrust, depends on *bouter*, to strike.] M. E. *butten*, to push, strike. – O. F. *boter*, to push, butt, strike. – O. Frank. *bōtan, corresponding to M. Du. *booten*, to beat, M. H. G. *bōzen*, O. H. G. *bōzan*, to beat. **Der.** *butt* (mound to shoot at), from M. F. *butte*, the same, allied to F. *but*, a mark, from *buter*, O.F. *boter*, to hit. **Der.** *a-but*. See Beat.

Butt (2), a large barrel. (F. – L.) We find A. S. *bytt*; but our mod. word is really F. – O. F. *boute*, F. *botte*, ' the vessel which we call a *butt*;' Cot. – Late Lat. *butta, buttis*, a cask.

Butt (3), a thick end. (E.) M. E. *but*,

butte. Cognate with Icel. *buttr*, short; see Buttock. **Der.** *butt-end*.

Butt (4), a kind of flat fish. (E.) Allied to Swed. *butta*, a turbot, M. Dan. *butte*, Low G. *but*, Du. *bot*, a butt. Prob. from *but*, stumpy; see Buttock.

Butter. (L. – Gk.) M. E. *botere*; A. S. *butere*. – L. *būtyrum*. – Gk. βούτυρον, butter. Probably of Scythian origin.

butterfly. (E.) A. S. *buttor-flēoge*, lit. butter-fly. So called from its excrement resembling butter, as shewn by the M. Du. *boter-schijte*, a butter-fly, lit. butter-voider (Kilian). + Du. *botervlieg*; G. *butter-fliege*.

Buttery, a place for provisions, esp. liquids. (F. – Late L.) A corruption of M. E. *botelerie*, properly a place for a butler; from M. E. *boteler*, a butler; see Butler. (Thus *buttery* = *bottlery*.) Confused with the word *butter*.

Buttock. (E.) M. E. *buttok*. Formed, with dimin. suffix *-ok* (A. S. *-uc*), from *butt*, a thick end, a stump. Cf. Icel. *buttr*, short, *būtr*, a log; Dan. *but*, Swed. *butt*, stumpy, surly; Du. *bot*, blunt, dull. See Butt (3).

Button. (F. – O. Low G.) M. E. *boton*, also, a bud. – O. F. *boton* (F. *bouton*), a bud, a button; properly a round knob pushed out. – O. F. *boter*, to push, push out; see Butt (1).

buttress, a support, in architecture. (F. – O. Low G.) M. E. *boteras*; Palsgrave has *bottras, butteras*. Orig. a plural form, as if for *butterets. – O. F. *bouterez*, pl. of *bouteret*, a prop. – F. *bouter*, to thrust, prop. Cotgrave also has *boutant*, a buttress, from the same verb; see Butt (1).

Butty, a companion or partner in a work. (F. – Low G.) Shortened from *boty-felowe* or *booty-fellow*, one who shares booty with others. From *boty*, old spelling of *booty* = F. *butin*, booty. Of Low G. origin; see Booty.

Buxom. (E.) M. E. *boxom, buhsum*; the old sense was obedient, obliging, good-humoured. Lit. 'bow-some.' – A.S. *būg-an*, to bow, bend, obey; and *-sum*, suffix, as in *win-some*. + Du. *buigzaam*; G. *bieg-sam*. See Bow (1).

Buy. (E.) From A. S. *byg-*, as in *byg-est, byg-eð*, 2 and 3 p. sing. pres. of A. S. *bycgan*, to purchase, whence M. E. *buggen, biggen*. + Goth. *bugjan*. **Der.** *abide* (2), q. v. See Sweet, N. E. G. § 1293.

Buzz. (E.) An imitative word; cf.

Lowl. Sc. *bizz*, to hiss ; Ital. *buzzicare*, to hum, whisper.

Buzzard. (F. – L.) M. E. *bosard*, *busard*, an inferior kind of falcon. – F. *busard*. – F. *buse*, a buzzard ; with suffix -*ard* (from O.H.G. *hart*). – Late L. *busio* = L. *buteo*, a sparrow-hawk.

By, prep. (E.) M. E. *bi*. A. S. *bī*, *big*. + Du. *bij* ; G. *bei* ; Goth. *bi*. Cf. Skt. *a-bhi*, Gk. ἀμ-φί.

By-law, a law affecting a township. (Scand.) Formerly also *birlaw*. – Icel. *bœ̄-r*, *bȳ-r*, a village (gen. *bæjar*, whence *bir-*) ; *lög*, a law. So also Dan. *by-lov*, a town-law. Icel. *bēr* is allied to *būa*, to dwell. See Boor.

Byre, a cow-house. (E.) A Northern E. deriv. of *bower*. A. S. *bȳre*, a shed, hut. – A. S. *būr*, a bower ; cf. Icel. *būr*, a pantry. See Bower.

C.

Cab (1) ; see Cabriolet.

Cab (2), a Heb. measure. (Heb.) Heb. *qab*, the 18th part of an ephah. The literal sense is 'hollow' ; cf. Heb *qābab*, to form in the shape of a vault ; see Alcove.

Cabal. (F. – Heb.) Orig. ' a secret.' F. *cabale*, ' the Jewes Caball, a hidden science ;' Cot. – Heb. *qabbālāh*, reception, mysterious doctrine. – Heb. *qābal*, to receive ; *qibbēl*, to adopt a doctrine.

Cabbage (1), a vegetable. (F. – L.) M. E. *cabache*, *caboche*. – F. (Picard) *caboche*, lit. ' great head ;' cf. Picard *cabus*, F. *choux cabus*, large-headed cabbage. – L. *cap-ut*, head ; with augmentative suffix ; cf. Ital. *capocchia*, head of a nail.

Cabbage (2), to steal. (F.) From F. *cabasser*, to put into a basket ; Norman *cabasser*, to cabbage (and see Supp. to Godefroy). – F. *cabas*, a basket ; Norman *cabas*, tailor's cabbage ; of unknown origin.

Caber, a pole. (C. – L.) Gael. *cabar*, a rafter. – L. type **caprio*, a rafter ; see Chevron.

Cabin. (F.) M.E *cabane*. – F. *cabane*. – Prov. *cabana*. – Late L. *capanna*, a hut (Isidore).

cabinet. (F.) F. *cabinet*, dimin. of F. *cabane*, a cabin (above).

Cable. (F. – L.) M. E. *cable*. – O. F. *cable*. – Late L. *capulum*, *caplum*, a strong (holding) rope. – L. *capere*, to hold.

Caboose, the cook's cabin on board ship. (Du.) Formerly *camboose*. – Du. *kombuis*, a cook's cabin ; also ' the chimney in a ship,' Sewel. (Hence also Dan. *kabys*, Swed. *kabysa*, caboose.)

Cabriolet. (F. – Ital. – L.) *Cab* is short for *cabriolet*. – F. *cabriolet*, a cab ; from its supposed lightness. – F. *cabriole*, a caper, leap of a goat ; formerly *capriole*. – Ital. *capriola*, a caper, a kid. – Ital. *caprio*, wild goat ; *capra*, a she-goat. – L. *caper*, goat ; fem. *capra*.

Cacao, a tree. (Span. – Mexican.) Span. *cacao* ; from the Mexican name (*cacauatl*) of the tree whence chocolate is made. ¶ Not the same as *cocoa*.

Cachinnation. (L.) L. acc. *cachinnātiōnem*, loud laughter. – L. *cachinnāre*, to laugh. Cf. Cackle.

Cachucha, a dance. (Span.) Span. *cachucha*.

Cacique, a W. Indian chief. (Span. – W. Indian.) Span. *cacique*, an Indian prince. From the old language of Hayti.

Cack, to go to stool. (L.) M. E. *cakken*. – L. *cacāre*.

Cackle. (E.) M.E. *kakelen*, a frequentative form. Not in A. S. + Du. *kakelen* ; Swed. *kackla* ; Dan. *kagle* ; G. *gackeln*. The sense is ' to keep on saying *kak* ;' cf. *gabb-le*, *gobb-le*, *gagg-le*.

Cacophony, a harsh sound. (Gk.) Gk. κακοφωνία, a harsh sound. – Gk. κακό-φωνος, harsh. – Gk. κακό-s, bad ; and φων-ή, sound. Der. *cacophonous* (Gk. κακό-φωνος).

Cad, a low fellow. (F. – L.) Short for Lowl. Sc. *cadie*, an errand-boy ; see Jamieson. – F. *cadet* ; see Cadet.

Cadaverous, corpse-like. (L.) L. *cadāuerōsus*. – L. *cadāuer*, a corpse. – Lat. *cad-ere*, to fall, fall dead.

Caddis, a kind of worsted lace or tape. (F.) In Wint. Tale, iv. 4. 208. M. E. *cadas*, explained by *bombicinium* in Prompt. Parv. ; (hence Irish *cadas*, caddis). Though also used to denote ' worsted,' it was orig. coarse silk. – F. *cadarce*, ' the coursest part of silke, whereof sleave is made ;' Cot. Cf. Span. *cadarzo*, coarse, entangled silk, that cannot be spun on a reel ; Port. *cadarço*, a coarse silk. Origin unknown ; probably Eastern. Der. *caddis-worm*, from the caddis-like shape of the case of the larva.

Caddy, a small box for tea. (Malay.) Better spelt *catty*. A small package of tea, less than a half-chest, is called in the tea-trade a *caddy* or *catty*. – Malay *kātī*, a

70

weight equal to 1⅛ lb. avoirdupois. This weight is also used in China and Japan, and tea is often made up in packages containing one catty.

Cade, a barrel, cask. (F. – L. – Gk. – Heb.) F. *cade.* – L. *cadus,* a barrel, cask. – Gk. κάδος, a cask, jar. – Heb. *kad,* a pail.

Cadence, a fall of the voice. (F. – Ital. – L.) M. E. *cadence.* – F. *cadence,* ' a cadence, just falling of words ; ' Cot. – Ital. *cadenza.* – Late L. *cadentia,* a falling. – L. *cadent-,* stem of pres. pt. of *cadere,* to fall. +Skt. *çad,* to fall.

Cadet, orig. a younger son. (F. – L.) F. *cadet,* a younger brother; Prov. *capdel. Capdel* is a Gascon form = Late L. *capitellum* (the substitution of *t* for *ll* being regular in Gascon ; P. Meyer) ; lit. a little (younger) head, dimin. from L. *caput,* a head.

Cadi, a judge. (Arab.) Arab. *qādī, qāzī,* a cadi or cazi, a judge. Hence Span. *alcalde,* the judge (E. *alcayde*) ; where *al* is the Arab. def. article.

Caducous, falling. (L.) L. *cadūc-us,* falling ; with suffix *-ous.* – L. *cadere,* to fall. See Cadence.

Cæsura. (L.) L. *cæsūra,* a cutting ; a pause in a verse. – L. *cæs-us,* pp. of *cædere,* to cut.

Caftan, a Turkish garment. (Turk.) Turk. *qaftān,* a dress.

Cage. (F. – L.) F. *cage.* – Late L. *cavea,* L. *cauea,* a cave, den, cage. – L. *cauus,* hollow. See **Cave.**

Caïque, a boat. (F. – Turk.) F. *caïque.* – Turk *kaik,* a boat.

Cairn, a pile of stones. (C.) Gael., Irish, W., Bret. *carn,* a crag, rock ; also a pile of stones.

Caitiff. (F. – L.) M. E. *caitif.* – A. F. *caitif,* a captive, a wretch (F. *chétif*). – L. *captiuum,* acc. of *captiuus;* see Captive.

Cajole. (F.) F. *cajoler,* to cajole ; formerly, to chatter like a jay. Perhaps of imitative origin ; cf. *cackle.*

Cajuput, Cajeput (with *j* as *y*), a tree yielding an oil. (Malay.) Malay *kāyu pūtih,* lit. ' white wood.' – Malay *kāyu,* wood ; *pūtih,* white.

Cake. (E. *or* Scand.) M. E. *cake.* N. Fries. *kāk, kāg,* late Icel. and Swed. *kaka;* Dan. *kage.* Teut. stem **kakōn-,* fem. ; from Teut. root **kak-,* of which the strong grade is **kōk-* (whence prov. E. *cookie,* Du. *kock,* G. *kuchen,* a cake).

Calabash, the shell of a gourd. (F. – Span. – Arab. – Pers.) F. *calebasse.* – Span. *calabaza* (Port. *calabaça*). – Arab. – Pers. *kharbuz,* a melon ; lit. ' ass-gourd,' i. e. large gourd. – Pers. *khar,* ass (hence, coarse) ; *buzah,* odoriferous fruit. Cf. Skt. *khara,* an ass.

Calamint, a herb. (F. – L. – Gk.) M. F. *calament,* Cot. – Late L. *calamintha.* – Gk. καλαμίνθη.

Calamity. (F. – L.) F. *calamité.* – L. acc. *calamitātem,* a misfortune.

Calash, a sort of carriage. (F. – G. – Slavonic.) F. *calèche.* – G. *kalesche.* – Pol. *kolaska,* a small carriage, dimin. of *kolasa,* a carriage ; Russ. *koliaska,* a carriage. – Pol. *koło,* a wheel ; O. Slav. *kolo.* (√QEL.)

Calcareous. (L.) Should be *calcarious.* – L. *calcārius,* pertaining to lime. – L. *calc-,* stem of *calx,* lime.

calcine. (F. – L.) F. *calciner.* – Mod. L. *calcināre,* to reduce to a calx. – L. *calc-,* stem of *calx,* lime.

calculate. (L.) L. *calculāt-us,* pp. of *calculāre,* to reckon by help of small pebbles. – L. *calculus,* pebble ; dimin. of *calx,* a stone.

Caldron, Cauldron. (F. – L.) M. E. *cauderon,* A. F. *caudrun.* – O. North F. (Picard) *cauderon,* for O. F. *chauderon,* mod. F. *chaudron* (Ital. *calderone,* Span. *calderon*), a vessel for hot water. Extended from L. *caldār-ia,* a hot bath. – L. *caldus,* contr. form of *calidus,* hot. – L. *calēre,* to be hot.

Calendar. (L.) L. *calendārium,* an account-book kept by money-changers ; so called because interest was due on the *calends* (1st day) of each month ; also, a calendar. – L. *calendæ,* calends.

Calender (1), a machine for pressing cloth. (F. – L. – Gk.) F. *calandre.* – Med. L. **calendra, celendra,* a calender ; an adaptation of L. *cylindrus,* a cylinder ; see Cylinder. Der. *calender,* a smoother of linen, a mistaken form for *calendrer.*

Calender (2), a kind of wandering monk. (F. – Pers.) F. *calender.* – Pers. *qalandar,* a kind of wandering Muhammadan monk, who abandons everything and retires from the world.

Calends. (L.) L. *calendæ,* s. pl., the first day of the (Roman) month. Orig. obscure; but certainly from the base *cal-,* as in O. Lat. *calāre,* to proclaim. + Gk. καλεῖν, to summon. Allied to **Hale** (2).

Calenture, a feverous madness. (F.

—Span. –L.) F. *calenture.* – Span. *calentura.* – L. *calent-,* stem of pres. pt. of *calēre,* to be hot.

Calf (1). (E.) M.E. *kalf.* O. Merc. *calf;* A.S. *cealf.*+Du. *kalf;* Icel. *kálfr;* Swed. *kalf;* Dan. *kalv;* Goth. *kalbō;* G. *kalb.* **Der.** *calve,* vb., A.S. *cealfian.* Perhaps allied to Skt. *garbha,* womb, a fœtus. Brugm. i. § 656.

Calf (2), the thick hind part of the shank. (E.) Perhaps the same as the above; cf. Gaulish L. *galba,* great-bellied; Icel. *kálfi,* calf of the leg. See **Cave in.**

Caliber, Calibre, bore of a gun. (F.) F. *calibre,* size of a bore; Span. *calibre* (1623). Etym. unknown. Perhaps from Arab. *qālib,* a form, mould, model, Rich. Dict. p. 1111 (Diez). Mahn suggests L. *quā lībrā,* with what measure.

Calico, cotton - cloth. (E. Indian.) Named from *Calicut,* on the Malabar coast, whence it was first imported.

Calif, Caliph. (F. – Arab.) F. *calife,* a successor of the prophet. – Arab. *khalīfah,* successor. – Arab. *khalafa,* to succeed. **Doublet,** *khalifa.*

Caligraphy, Calligraphy, good writing. (Gk.) Gk. καλλιγραφία. – Gk. καλλι-, prefix (for κάλλος, beauty, from καλός, good, fair); and γράφειν, to write.

calisthenics, callisthenics, graceful exercises. (Gk.) From Gk. καλλισθεν-ής, adorned with strength. – Gk. καλλι- (for κάλλος, beauty, from καλός, fair); and σθέν-ος, strength.

Calipers, compasses. (F.) For *caliber-compasses,* i. e. compasses for measuring diameters; see **Caliber.**

Calisthenics; see **Caligraphy.**

Caliver, a sort of musket. (F.) Named from its *caliber* or bore; see Kersey's Dict. See **Caliber.**

Calk; usually **Caulk,** q. v.

Call. (E.) M. E. *callen.* A.S. *ceallian;* cf. *hildecalla,* a herald. E. Fries. *kallen.*+ Icel. and Swed. *kalla;* Dan. *kalde;* Du. *kallen;* O. H. G. *challōn.* Teut. type **kallōn-* or **kallōjan-,* weak verb; cf. W. *galw,* to call, Russ. *golos',* voice, sound.

Callet, Callat, a worthless woman. (F. – Low L. – Low G.) In Oth. iv. 2. 121. – F. *caillette,* a gossip, chatterer; lit. a little quail; dimin. of *caille,* a quail, also a woman. Littré gives *caille coiffée,* femme galante. See **Quail.** (Doubtful.)

Callous, hard. (F. – L.) F. *calleux.* –

L. *callōsus,* thick-skinned. – L. *callus, callum,* hard skin.

Callow, unfledged, bald. (L.) M. E. *calu, calewe.* A. S. *calu,* bald.+Du. *kaal,* bald; Swed. *kal;* G. *kahl.* Teut. **kalwoz,* early borrowed from L. *caluus,* bald.

Calm. (F. – L. – Gk.) F. *calme,* adj. Allied to Prov. *chaume,* the time when the flocks rest; F. *chômer* (formerly *chaumer*), to rest from work; Ital. *calma,* rest. – Late L. *cauma,* the heat of the sun (whence, time for rest); Job xxx. 30. [It is suggested that the change from *au* to *al* was due to association with L. *cal-ēre,* to be hot.] – Gk. καῦμα, heat. – Gk. καίειν, to burn. **Der.** *be-calm.*

Calomel, a preparation of mercury. (Gk.) Coined to express a *white* product from a *black* substance. – Gk. καλό-ς, fair; and μέλ-ας, black.

Caloric. (F. – L.) F. *calorique.* – L. *calor,* heat. – L. *calēre,* to be hot.

calorific, making hot. (L.) L. *calōrificus,* making hot. – L. *calōri-,* stem of *calor,* heat; and *-fic-,* for *facere,* to make.

Calthrop, Caltrap, a star-thistle, a ball with spikes for annoying cavalry. (L. *and* Teut.) M. E. *kalketrappe,* A. S. *calcetreppe,* a star-thistle. Coined from L. *calci-,* stem of *calx,* the heel; and the Teutonic word *trap.* Lit. 'heel-trap'; see **Trap.** So also F. *chaussetrappe,* the same.

Calumet, a kind of pipe for tobacco. (F. – L. – Gk.) Norman F. *calumet,* a pipe; parallel form to O. F. *chalemel,* F. *chalumeau,* a pipe. – L. *calamus,* a reed. – Gk. κάλαμος, a reed. See **Shawm.**

Calumny. (F. – L.) F. *calomnie.* – L. *calumnia,* false accusation. – L. *calui,* *caluere,* to deceive.

Calve; see **Calf.**

Calx. (L.) L. *calx,* stone, lime (stem *calc-*); in Late L., a calx.

Calyx. (L. – Gk.) L. *calyx.* – Gk. κάλυξ, a covering, calyx (or cup) of a flower. Allied to **Helm** (2).

Cam, a projection on a wheel. (Du.) Du. *kamm,* a comb (see Kilian); Low G. *kamm;* cf. Dan. *kam,* comb, also a ridge on a wheel, cam, or cog. See **Comb.**

Cambric. (Flanders.) Named from *Kamerijk,* also called *Cambray,* a town in Flanders, where it was first made.

Camel. (F. – L. – Gk. – Heb.) M. E. *camel, camail, chamel.* – O. North F. *camel;* O. F. *chamel.* – L. *camēlus.* – Gk. κάμηλος. – Heb. *gāmāl.* Cf. Arab. *jamal.*

camelopard, a giraffe. (L.—Heb. *and* Gk.) Formerly *camelopardalis.*—L. *ca-mēlopardālis.* — Gk. καμηλοπάρδαλις, giraffe; partly like a camel, partly like a pard. — Gk. κάμηλο-s, a camel (Heb. *gāmāl*); and πάρδαλις, a pard ; see **Pard.**

Camellia. (Personal name.) A plant named (by Linnæus) after Geo. Jos. Kamel, a Moravian Jesuit (17th cent.), who described the plants in the island of Luzon.

Camelopard ; see **Camel.**

Cameo. (Ital.) Ital. *cammeo*, a cameo, precious stone carved in relief. Origin unknown.

Camera. (L. L. *camera*, a chamber ; hence *camera obscūra*, a dark chamber, box for photography ; see **Chamber.**

Camlet, a stuff. (F.—Arab.) Formerly *camelot.*—M. F. *camelot*, Cot.; supposed to be named from containing *camel's* hair. Really from Arab. *khamlat, khamalat*, camlet ; Rich. Dict. p. 628.

Camomile ; see **Chamomile.**

Camp. (F.—Ital.—L.) F. *camp* (Cot.). — Ital. *campo*, a field, camp. — L. *campum*, acc. of *campus*, a field, ground held by an army. Brugm. i. § 563.

campaign, orig. a large field. (F.— Ital.—L.) F. *campaigne, campagne*, an open field. — Ital. *campagna*, a field ; also a campaign. — L. *campānia*, open field. — L. *campus*, a field. (Also spelt *champaign*, and even *champion* in old authors.)

campestral, growing in fields. (L.) From L. *campestr-is*, growing in fields; with suffix -*al.*— L. *campus*, a field.

Campanula. (L.) Lit. 'a little bell ;' dimin. of L. *campāna*, a bell. Hence also *campani-form.*

Camphor. (F.—Arab.—Malay.) Formerly spelt *camphire* with an inserted *i*). —F. *camphre*, ' camphire ;' Cot. — Low L. *camphora* (whence the form *camphor*). — Arab. *kāfūr*, camphor; cf. Skt. *karpūra*, camphor. — Malay *kāpūr*, lit. chalk; *kāpūr Bārūs*, chalk of Barous, a name for camphor. *Barous* is in Sumatra.

Can (1), I am able. (E.) A.S. *can, cann*, 1st and 3rd persons sing. pres. of *cunnan*, to know. The pres. t. *can* is really an old perf. t. ; the same peculiarity occurs in Du. *kunnen*, Icel. and Swed. *kunna*, Dan. *kunde*, to know, to be able ; G. *können*, to know. β. The pt. t. is *could*, with intrusive *l*; M.E. *coude*, A.S. *cūðe* ; cf. Goth. *kuntha*, Du. *konde*, G. *könnte* ; shewing that A.S. *cūðe* (for

cunðe) has lost an *n*. γ. The pp. *couth*, A.S. *cūð*, known, only survives in *un-couth*, which see. Allied to **Ken** and **Know.** (✓ GEN.)

Can (2), a drinking-vessel. (E.) A.S. *canne*, a can. + Du. *kan* ; Icel. *kanna* ; Swed. *kanna* ; Dan. *kande* ; G. *kanne*, a tankard, mug. (Apparently a true Teut. word.)

Canal. (F.—L.) F. *canal* (whence also Du. *kanaal*). — L. *canālis*, a channel, trench.

Canary, a bird, a wine, a dance. (Canary Islands.) All named from the *Canary* Islands.

Cancel. (F.—L.) F. *canceller.*—Law L. *cancellāre*, to cancel a deed by drawing lines across it. — L. *cancellus*, a grating, pl. *cancellī*, lattice-work, crossed lines ; dimin. of pl. *cancrī*, lattice-work.

Cancer. (L.) L. *cancer*, a crab ; also an ' eating ' tumour. Cf. Gk. καρκίνος, Skt. *karkata*, a crab ; cf. Skt. *karkara*, hard. Named from its hard shell. Brugm. i. § 464.

Candelabrum. (L.) L. *candēlābrum*, a candle-holder ; from *candēla*, a candle.

Candid. (F.—L.) F. *candide*, white, fair, sincere.—L. *candidus*, white, shining. —L. *candēre*, to shine.—L. *candēre*, to set on fire (in comp. *in-cendere*).+Skt. *chand* (for *çchand*), to shine. (✓SQEND.) Brugm. i. §§ 456, 818 (2).

candidate. (L.) L. *candidātus*, white-robed ; because candidates for office wore white. — L. *candidus*, white.

candle. (L.) A.S. *candel.*—L. *candēla*, a candle. — L. *candēre*, to glow.

candour. (F.—L.) F. *candeur.*—L. acc. *candōrem*, brightness (hence, sincerity).

Candy, crystallised sugar. (F.—Ital.— Skt.) F. *sucre candi*, sugar-candy; whence F. *se candir*, ' to candie ;' Cot.—Ital. *candire*, to candy ; *candi*, candy ; *zucchero candi*, sugar-candy.— Arab. *qand*, sugar ; whence Arab. *qandī*, made of sugar. The word is Aryan; cf. Skt. *khāndava*, sweetmeats, *khanda*, a broken piece, from *khand*, to break. **Der.** *sugar-candy*, Ital. *zucchero candi.*

Candytuft, a plant. (Hyb.) From *Candy*, i. e. Candia (Crete) ; and *tuft.*

Cane. (F.—L.—Gk.) M.E. *cane, canne.*—F. *canne.*—L. *canna.*—Gk. κάννα, a reed. Cf. Heb. *qāneh*, reed; Arab. *qanāh*, cane.

canister. (L.—Gk.) L. *canistrum*, a light basket.—Gk. κάναστρον, the same. —Gk. κάνη—κάννα, a reed.

cannon. (F. – Ital. – L. – Gk.) F. *canon.* – Ital. *cannone,* a cannon, orig. a great tube, a gun-barrel. – L. *canna,* a reed; see **Cane.** ¶ The Span. *cañon,* a tube, a deep gorge, is cognate.

canon (1), a rule. (L. – Gk.) A. S. *canon.* – L. *canon,* a rule. – Gk. κανών, a rod, rule. – Gk. κάνη = κάννα, a (straight) cane.

canon (2), a dignitary of the church. (F. – L. – Gk.) M. E. *canun, canoun.* – O. F. *canogne,* now *chanoine.* – Lat. *canonicum,* acc. of *canonicus,* adj., one on the church-roll or list. – L. *canon,* the church-roll; also, a rule. See **canon** (1).

Canine. (L.) L. *caninus,* belonging to a dog. – L. *canis,* a dog; see **Hound.**

Canister; see **Cane.**

Canker. (F. – L.) North F. *cancre.* (F. *chancre*). – L. *cancrum,* acc. of *cancer,* a crab, a canker. See **Cancer.** ¶ The G. *kanker* may be Teutonic (Kluge); so perhaps E. *canker* in the sense of 'disease of trees'; cf. Gk. γόγγρος, an excrescence on trees.

Cannel-coal. (L. *and* E.) Lit. a 'candle-coal,' because it burns brightly. Prov. E. *cannel,* a candle. See **Candle.**

Cannibal. (Span. – W. Indian.) Formerly *canibal.* – Span. *canibal;* for *Caribal,* a Carib, native of the Caribbean Islands. The W. Indian (Hayti) word *carib* means 'brave.' Hence also *Caliban.*

Cannon (1); see **Cane.**

Cannon (2), at billiards. (F. – Span.) A corruption of *carrom,* shortened form of F. *caramboler,* v., to make a cannon at billiards, to touch two other balls with one's own; see Hoyle's Games. Orig. sense, to touch the red ball; whence *caramboler,* to cannon (as above) and *carambolage,* sb, a cannon. – Span. *carambola,* a manner of playing at billiards, a device, trick, cheat. Origin unknown.

Canoe. (Span. – W. Ind.) Span. *canoa;* orig. a Haytian word for 'boat.'

Canon (1) and (2); see **Cane.**

Canopy. (F. – Ital. – L. – Gk.) Should be *conopy;* but we find F. *canopé,* borrowed from Ital. *canopè.* (Also F. *conopée.*) – L. *conōpēum,* Judith xiii. 9. – Gk. κωνωπεῖον, an Egyptian bed with mosquito curtains (hence, any sort of hangings). – Gk. κωνωπ-, stem of κώνωψ, a mosquito, gnat; lit. 'cone-faced' or 'cone-headed,' from the shape of its head. – Gk. κῶνο-ς, a cone; and ὤψ, face, appearance, from Gk. base ΟΠ, to see (see **Optics**).

Canorous, tuneful. (L.) L. *canōr-us;* with suffix -*ous.* – L. *canere,* to sing. Brugm. i. § 181.

cant (1), to sing in a whining way, whine. (L.) L. *cantāre* (whence Picard and Walloon *canter,* to sing); frequent. of *canere,* to sing. *Cant* was at first a beggar's whine; hence, hypocrisy; see **Recant.**

canticle. (L.) L. *canticulum,* a little song; dimin. of *canticum,* a song; dimin. of *cantus,* a song; cf. *cantus,* pp. of *canere,* to sing.

canto. (Ital. – L.) Ital. *canto,* a singing, section of a poem. – L. acc. *cantum,* a singing, song (above).

canzonet. (Ital. – L.) Ital. *canzonetta,* dimin. of *canzone,* a hymn, song. – L. *cantiōnem,* acc. of *cantio,* a song. – L. *cantus,* pp. of *canere,* to sing.

Cant (2), an edge; as verb, to tilt. (Du. – L.) Du. *kant,* an edge, corner. +Dan. and Swed. *kant,* edge; G. *kante,* a corner. β. All from Late L. *cantus,* a corner; which is prob. from L. *canthus* = Gk. κάνθος, the corner of the eye felloe of a wheel.

Canteen. (F. – Ital.) F. *cantine.* – Ital. *cantina,* a cellar, cool cave (hence the sense of vessel for liquids). Origin doubtful. Perhaps from Late L. *cantus,* a corner.

Canter, an easy gallop. (Proper name.) Short for *Canterbury* gallop, the pace at which pilgrims rode thither.

Canticle, Canto; see **Cant** (1).

Cantle, a small piece. (F. – L. ?) O.F. *cantel,* a small piece (F. *chanteau*), dimin. of Picard *cant* (F. *chant*), a corner; Late L. *cantus.* Prob. from L. *canthus,* corner of the eye; see **Cant** (2).

Canton, a region. (F. – Ital.) F. *canton.* – Ital. *cantone,* a nook, angle; also, a corporation, township (Torriano); Late L. *cantōnum, canto,* a region, province. Origin doubtful. ¶ *Canton* (in heraldry), a corner of a shield, is from F. *canton,* a corner, Ital. *cantone,* from Ital. *canto,* an edge; see **Cant** (2).

Canvas. (F. – L. – Gk.) M. E. *canevas.* North F. *canevas.* – Late L. *canabācius,* hempen cloth. – L. *cannabis,* hemp. – Gk. κάνναβις, hemp. Cf. Skt. *çana,* hemp; see **Hemp.**

canvass. (F. – L. – Gk.) Orig. to toss in a *canvas* sheet, to criticize or discuss thoroughly. From *canvas,* sb.

Canzonet; see **Cant** (1).

Caoutchouc. (F.—Carib.) F. *caout-chouc*; orig. a Caribbean word, *cahuchu*.

Cap, a head-covering. (Late L.) A. S. *cæppe.*—Late L. *cappa*, a cap (Isidore).

Capable. (F.—L.) F. *capable.*—Late L. *capābilis*, comprehensible; afterwards, able to hold.—L. *capere*, to hold (below).

capacious, able to contain. (L.) Coined from L. *capāci-*, stem of *capax*, able to hold.—L. *capere*, to hold, contain; see **Heave.** Brugm. i. § 635. (√QAP.)

Caparison, trappings of a horse. (F. —Span.—Late L.) O. F. *caparasson.*— Span. *caparazon*, cover for a saddle; augmentative from Med. L. *caparo*, a cowl; from Span. *capa*, a cloak, cover.—Late L. *cāpa*, a cape; as below.

Cape (1), a covering for the shoulders. (F.—Late L.) O. North F. *cape.*—Late L. *cāpa*, a cape (Isidore of Seville); whence also Prov., Span., Port. *capa*, Icel. *kāpa*, &c. Allied to *cap*. Doublet, *cope*.

Cape (2), a headland. (F.—Ital.—L.) F. *cap.*—Ital. *capo*, head, headland.—L. *caput*, head.

Caper (1), to dance about. (Ital.—L.) Abbreviated from *capreole* (Sir P. Sidney). —Ital. *capriolare*, to skip as a goat.—Ital. *capriola*, 'a caper in dancing,' Florio; also, a kid; dimin. of *capra*, a she-goat. —L. *capra*, a she-goat; cf. *caper*, he-goat. +Gk. κάπρος, a goat; A.S. *hæfer*, Icel. *hafr*.

Caper (2), the flower-bud of a certain plant. (F.—L.—Gk.) M. F. *capre* (F. *câpre*).—L. *capparis*.—Gk. κάππαρις, caper-plant; its fruit; cf. Pers. *kabar*, capers.

Capercailzie. (Gael.) Here *z* represents M. E. *ȝ*, pron. as *y*.—Gael. *capull-coille*, great cock of the wood; lit. horse of the wood.—Gael. *capull*, a horse (see **Cavalier**); *coille*, gen. of *coill*, a wood, cognate with E. **Holt**.

Capillary, like hair. (L.) L. *capil-lāris*, adj.; from *capillus*, hair. Perhaps allied to *cap-ut*, the head.

Capital (1), chief. (F.—L.) F. *capital.* —L. *capitālis*, belonging to the head.—L. *capit-*, stem of *caput*, the head.+Skt. *kapā-la(m)*, skull; A. S. *hafela*, head. Brugm. i. § 641.

capital (2), stock of money. (F.— L.) F. *capital.*—Late L. *capitāle*, wealth; neut. of *capitālis*, chief; see **Capital** (1).

capital (3), head of a pillar. (L.; *or* F.—L.) L. *capitellum*, head of a pillar; dimin. from L. *caput*, head. Or from O.

North F. *capitel* (F. *chapiteau*); from L. *capitellum* (above).

capitation, poll-tax. (F.—L.) F. *capitation.*—Late L. acc. *capitātiōnem*, poll-tax.—L. *capit-*, stem of *caput*, poll, head.

capitol. (L.) The temple of Jupiter, at Rome, called *Capitōlium.*—L. *capit-*, stem of *caput*, a head; but the reason for the name is obscure; see Smith, Class. Dict.

capitular, relating to a chapter. (L.) Med. L. *capitulāris*, adj. of *capitulum*, a chapter of a cathedral, or a chapter of a book; see **Chapter**.

capitulate. (L.) Late L. *capitulātus*, pp. of *capitulāre*, to divide into chapters, also to propose terms (for surrender).— Late L. *capitulum*, a chapter; see **Chapter**. Der. *re-capitulate*.

Capon. (L.—Gk.) A. S. *capun.*—L. acc. *capōnem*, from nom. *capo.*—Gk. κάπων, a capon.

Caprice. (F.—Ital.—L.?) F. *caprice.* —Ital. *capriccio*, a whim. Perhaps from Ital. *capro*, a he-goat; so that *capriccio* might mean a frisk like a goat's; see **Caper** (1).

capricorn. (L.) L. *capricornus*, horned like a goat.—L. *capri-*, for *capro-*, stem of *caper*, goat; and *corn-u*, horn.

capriole, a peculiar frisk of a horse. (F.—Ital.—L.) F. *capriole* (see Cot.).— Ital. *capriola*, the leap of a kid; see **Caper** (1).

Capsize, to upset. (Span.?—L.) Perhaps from Span. *capuzar*, to sink (a ship) by the head; apparently a derivative of L. *caput*, the head. (A guess.)

Capstan. (F.—Span.—L.?) F. *cabe-stan*; Prov. *cabestan.*—Span. *cabestrante*, *cabrestante*, a capstan. Of these forms, *cabestrante* is the better, and is allied to Span. *cabestrage*, a halter, or a haltering, and to *cabestrar*, to halter.—L. *capistrant-*, stem of pres. pt. of *capistrāre*, to halter. —L. *capistrum* (Span. *cabestro*), a halter. —L. *cap-ere*, to hold; with double suffix *-is-tro*.

Capsule, seed-vessel. (F.—L.) F. *capsule*, a small case.—L. *capsula*, dimin. of *capsa*, a case; see **Case** (2).

Captain. (F.—L.) M. E. *capitain.*— O. F. *capitain.*—Late L. *capitāneus*, *capit-ānus*, a leader of soldiers.—L. *capit-*, stem of *caput*, head.

Captious. (F.—L.) F. *captieux*, cavilling. – L. *captiōsus.* – L. *captio*, a taking, a sophistical argument. – L. *captus*, pp. of *capere*, to hold.   See **Capacious.**

captive. (F. – L.)   F. *captif* (fem. *captive*). – L. *captīuus*, a captive. – L. *captus*, pp. of *capere*, to take. + W. *caeth*, a captive; O. Irish *cacht*, a female captive.

captor. (L.)   L. *captor*, a taker. – L. *cap-*, as in *capere*, to take; with suffix *-tor.*

capture. (F. – L.)   F. *capture.* – L. *captūra*, a taking. – L. *cap-*, as in *capere*, to take; with fem. suffix *-tūra.*

Capuchin, hooded friar, hood. (F. – Ital. – Late L.)   M. F. *capuchin*; F. *capucin.* – Ital. *cappucino*, a small hood, hence a hooded friar; dimin. of *cappuccio*, a cowl. – Ital. *cappa*, a cape; see **Cap** and **Cape** (1).

Car. (F. – C.)   M. E. *carre.* – O. North F. *carre*, a car (Ducange, s. v. *Marcellum*). – Late L. *carra*, f.; allied to L. *carrus*, a car; of Gaulish origin. – Bret. *karr*, a chariot; W. *car*, O. Gael. *cár*, Irish *carr.* Allied to L. *currus*, a chariot; Brugm. i. § 516.

Caracole. (F. – Span.)   F. *caracol*, *caracole*, a snail; whence *faire le caracole*, applied to a manœuvre by soldiers, and to turns made by a horse. – Span. *caracol*, a snail, winding staircase, turning about (from the snail-shell's spiral form). Perhaps of Celtic origin; cf. Gael. *carach*, circling, winding; *car*, a turn, twist.

Carafe, a glass water-bottle. (F. – Span. – Arab.)   F. *carafe.* – Span. *garrafa*, a cooler, vessel to cool wines in. – Arab. *ghiráf*, draughts of water; Arab. root *gharafa*, to draw water. (Dozy, Devic.) ¶ Or from Pers. *qarābah*, a large flagon; but see **Carboy.**

Carat. (F. – Ital. – Arab. – Gk.)   F. *carat*, a very light weight. – Ital. *carato.* – Arab. *qirrāt*, a pod, husk, carat, 24th part of an ounce. – Gk. κεράτιον, fruit of the locust-tree; also, a carat; lit. 'a small horn.' – Gk. κερατ-, stem of κέρας, a horn; see **Horn.**

Caravan. (F. – Pers.)   F. *caravane.* – Pers. *kārwān*, a caravan, convoy.

caravansary. (Pers.)   Pers. *kārwānsarāy*, an inn for caravans. – Pers. *kārwān*, caravan; *sarāy*, public building, inn.

Caraway, Carraway. (Span. – Arab.)   Span. *al-carahueya*, a caraway; where *al* is merely the Arab. def. art.; also written *carvi.* – Arab. *karwiyā-a*,

karawiyā-a, caraway-seeds or plant. Cf. Gk. κάρος, κάρον, cumin.

Carbine. (F. – Gk.)   Formerly *carabine*, a musket, the weapon of a *carabin*, or musketeer. – F. *carabin*, ' an arquebuzier;' Cot. Perhaps from O. F. *calabrin*, a light-armed soldier; of uncertain origin.

Carbon. (F. – L.)   F. *carbone.* – L. acc. *carbōnem*, a coal.

carbonado, broiled meat. (Span. – L.)   Span. *carbonada*, meat broiled over coals. – Span. *carbon*, coal; see above.

carbuncle. L. *carbunculus*, (1) a small coal, (2) a carbuncle, gem, from its glowing, (3) a red tumour. Double dimin. of L. *carbo*, coal.

Carboy, a large glass bottle, protected by wicker-work. (Pers.)   Pers. *qarābah*, a large flagon; which is prob. of Arab. origin. Cf. Arab. *qirbah*, a water-skin, water-bottle.

Carcanet. (F. – Teut.)   Dimin. of F. *carcan*, a collar of jewels, or of gold. – O. H. G. *querca*, the throat; cf. Icel. *kverkr*, pl. the throat; Lith. *gerkle*, throat, *gerti*, to drink.   Brugm. i. § 653.

Carcase, Carcass. (F. – Ital.)   From M. F. *carquasse*, a dead body. – Ital. *carcassa*, a kind of bomb-shell, a shell; also, a skeleton, frame; cf. Port. *carcassa*, a carcase, a very old woman. Of unknown origin.

Card (1), piece of pasteboard. (F. – Ital. – Gk.)   Corruption of F. *carte*, 'a card,' Cot. – Ital. *carta*; L. *charta.* – Gk. χάρτη, χάρτης, a leaf of papyrus. **Der.** *cardboard.*   **Doublet**, *chart.*

Card (2), an instrument for combing wool. (F. – L.)   F. *carde.* – Med.L. *cardus*, L. *carduus*, a thistle; for wool-combing.

Cardinal. (L.)   L. *cardinālis*, principal, chief; orig. relating to the hinge of a door. – L. *cardin-*, stem of *cardo*, a hinge.

Cardoon, a plant. (F. – Prov. – L.)   F. *cardon*, Cot. – Prov. *cardon*; with augment. suffix from Med. L. *card-us*, a thistle.   See **Card** (2).

Care. (E.)   M. E. *care.* A. S. *caru*, *cearu*, anxiety. + O. Sax. *kara*, sorrow; O. H. G. *chara*, a lament; Goth. *kara*; Teut. type **karā*, f. Hence, *care*, vb.; A.S. *carian.*   ¶ Not allied to L. *cūra.*

Careen. (F. – L.)   Lit. 'to clean the keel;' hence to lay a ship on its side. – F. *carine*, *carène*, keel. – L. *carīna*, keel.

Career. (F. – C.)   F. *carrière*, a racecourse. **-** Late L. *carrāria uia*), a road for cars. **-** Late L. *carra*, L. *carrus*, a car; of Celtic origin; see **Car.**

Caress. (F. **-** Ital. **-** L.) F. *caresse*, a fondling. **-** Ital.*carezza*, a caress, fondling. **-** Late L. *cāritia*, dearness. **-** L. *cārus*, dear. Brugm. i. § 637.

Carfax. (F. **-** L.) M. E. *carfoukes*, a place where four roads meet. **-** O. F. pl. *carrefourgs*, the same: from sing. *carrefourg.* **-** Late L. *quadrifurcus*, four-forked. **-** L. *quadri-* (from *quatuor*), four; and *furca*, a fork. See **Fork.**

Cargo. (Span. **-** C.) Span.*cargo*,freight, load; cf. *cargar*, to load. **-** Late L. *carricāre*, to load a car; see **Charge.**

caricature. (Ital. **-** C.) Ital. *caricatura*, a satirical picture; so called because exaggerated or ' overloaded.' **-** Ital. *caricare*, to load, burden. **-** Late L. *carricāre*, to load a car; see **Charge.**

Caries. (L.) L. *cariēs*, rottenness.

Cark, burden, anxiety. (F. **-** C.) A. F. *karke*, North. F. form of F. *charge*, i. e. load; see **Charge.** Cf. M. E. *karke*, a load; as in ' a *karke of pepper*.'

Carkanet; see Carcanet.

Carminative, expelling wind from the body. (F. **-** L.) F. *carminatif*, 'wind-voiding;' Cot. **-** L. *carmināt-us*, pp. of *carmināre*, to card wool (hence, in old medicine, to cleanse from gross humours); with suffix *-īuus.* **-** L. *carmin-*, from *carmen*, a card for wool. **-** L. *cārere*, to card.

Carmine. (Span. **-** Arab. **-** Skt.) Span. *carmin*, short form of *carmesin*, adj.; from *carmesi*,crimson. **-** Arab.*qirmizī*, crimson; from *qirmiz*,cochineal. **-** Skt. *kṛmi*,a worm, the cochineal insect.

Carnage; see below.

Carnal. (L.) L. *carnālis*, fleshly. **-** L. *carn-*, stem of *caro*, flesh. Brugm. i. § 515.

carnage. (F. **-** L.) F. *carnage*, flesh-time, slaughter of animals. **-** Late L. *carnāticum*, a tribute of flesh-meat; cf. *carnātum*, time for eating flesh. **-** L. *carn-*, stem of *caro*, flesh.

carnation. (F. **-** L.) F. *carnation*, flesh colour (Littré). **-** L. acc. *carnātiōnem*, fleshiness. **-** L. *carn-*, stem of *caro*, flesh.

carnival. (F. **-** Ital. **-** L.) F. *carnaval*,Shrovetide. **-** Ital.*carnevale, carnovale*, the last three days before Lent. **-** Med. L. *carnelevāle,carnelevāmen*,removal of flesh, Shrovetide. **-** L. *carne-m*,acc.of *caro*, flesh;

and *leuāre*, to lift, remove, take away, from *leuis*, light.

carnivorous. (L.) L. *carniuorus*, flesh-eating. **-** L. *carni-*,decl. stem of *caro*, flesh; and *uor-āre*, to devour.

Carob-tree, the locust-tree. (F. **-** Arab.) M. F. *carobe, caroube.* **-** Arab. *kharrūb*, bean-pods.

Caroche, Carroche, a kind of coach. (F. **-** Ital. **-** C.) Nearly obsolete; but the present sense of *carriage* is due to it. **-** F. *carroche*, variant of *carrosse*, ' a carosse or caroach;' Cot. **-** Ital. *carroccia, carrozza*, a chariot. Extended from Ital. *carro*, a car. See **Car.**

Carol, a song. (F. **-** L. **-** Gk.?) Formerly, a kind of dance. **-** O. F. *carole*, a (singing) dance. Godefroy (s. v. *carole*) cites Swiss Rom. *coraula*, a round-dance, also a dance-song. Prob. from L. *choraulēs*, a flute-player to a chorus. **-** Gk. χοραύλης, the same. **-** Gk. χορ-ός, a chorus, round-dance; and αὐλός, a flute.

Carotid, adj. (Gk.) Gk. καρωτίδες, s. pl., the two great arteries of the neck; it was thought that an alteration in the flow of blood through them caused stupor. **-** Gk. καρόω, I stupefy; κάρος, stupor.

Carousal, (1) a drinking-bout; (2), a pageant. (1. F. **-** G.; 2. F. **-** Ital) **1.** Sometimes used as if from the verb *carouse* below. **2.** But, in old authors, *cárousél* (also *carousal*) means a sort of pageant, of which some kind of chariot-race formed a principal part; Dryden, Virgil, Æn. v. 777. **-** F. *carrousel*, a tilting-match. **-** Ital. *carosello*, also spelt *garosello*, a tournament; of uncertain origin.

Carouse. (F. **-** G.) F. *carous*, ' a carousse of drinke,' Cot. **-** G. *garaus*, right out; used of emptying a bumper. **-** G. *gar*, quite; and *aus*, out. (Raleigh even writes *garouse*; directly from G. *garaus*.) **Der.** *carous-al*, but only in one sense of that word; see above.

Carp (1), a fish. (F.) M. E. *carpe*. XV cent. **-** O. F. *carpe* (Span. Port. *carpa*, Ital. *carpa*, Florio); also Du. *karper*; Icel. *karfi*; Dan. *karpe*; Swed. *karp*; G. *karpfen*; O. H. G. *charpho*; Russ. *karp*'; Lith. *karpa*.

Carp (2), to cavil at. (Scand.) M. E. *carpen*, which often merely means to talk, say. **-** Icel. *karpa*, to boast; Swed. dial. *karpa*, to boast, talk much. ¶ The present sinister sense is due to confusion with L. *carpere*, to pluck.

Carpenter. (F.—C.) A. F. *carpenter*; O. North F. *carpentier* (F. *charpentier*).— Late L. *carpentārius*, sb.; *carpentāre*, to work in timber.—L. *carpentum*, a carriage; a word of Celtic origin.—O. Irish *carpat*, Gael. and Irish *carbad*, W. *cerbyd*, a carriage, chariot, litter.

Carpet. (F.—L.) O.F. *carpite*.—Late L. *carpīta*, *carpeta*, a kind of thick cloth; also *carpia* (F. *charpie*), lint.—L. *carpere*, to pluck, pull to pieces (lint being made of rags pulled to pieces, and carpet, probably, from shreds).

Carrack. (F.) O.F. *carraque*, a ship of burden; Late Lat. *carraca*, the same. Of unknown origin.

Carriage. (F.—C.) M.E. *cariage*, that which is carried about (as in Bible, A. V.). —O. F. *cariage*; from *carier*, to carry; see **Carry**. ¶ Its modern use is due to confusion with *caroch*, a vehicle (Massinger, Renegado, i. 2); see **Caroche**.

Carrion. (F.—L.) M. E. *caroigne*, a carcase.—O. North F. *caroigne*; Late L. *carōnia*, a carcase.—L. *caro*, flesh.

Carronade, a sort of cannon. (Scotland.) So named because made at *Carron*, in Stirlingshire.

Carrot. (F.—L.—Gk.) F. *carote*, *carotte*.—L. *carōta*.—Gk. καρωτόν, a carrot.

Carry. (F.—C.) O. F. *carier*.—Late L. *carricāre*.—L. *carrus*, a car; see **Car**.

Cart. (E.) A. S. *cræt*, *crat*; cf. Du. *krat*. Or from Icel. *kartr*, a cart; whence, probably, Picard *carti*, a cart.

Carte, a bill of fare. (F.—Gk.) Chiefly in the F. phr. *carte blanche*, lit. white paper.—Late L. *carta*; see **Card** (1).

cartel. (F.—Ital.—Gk.) F. *cartel.*— Ital. *cartello*, lit. a small paper; dimin. of *carta*, paper, bill; see **Card** (1).

Cartilage. (F.—L) F. *cartilage*, gristle.—L. *cartilāginem*, acc. of *cartilāgo*. Der. *cartilagin-ous*.

Cartoon. (F.—Ital.—Gk.) F. *carton*.— Ital. *cartone*, lit. a large paper; from *carta*, a card; see **Card** (1).

cartouche, cartridge. (F.—Ital. —Gk.) *Cartridge* (with intrusive *r*) is for *cartridge*, corrupt form of *cartouche*.—F. *cartouche*, a roll of paper.—Ital. *cartoccio*, a roll of paper, cartridge.—Ital. *carta*, paper; Late L. *carta*; see **Card** (1). ¶ The *cartridge* took its name from the paper in which it was rolled up.

cartulary, a register. (Late L.—Gk.) Late L. *cartulārium*, *chartulārium*, a

register.—Late L. *chartula*, a document; dimin. of *charta*, a paper; see **Card** (1).

Carve. (E.) M. E. *keruen*. A.S. *ceorfan*; pt. t. *cearf*, pl. *curfon*, pp. *corfen*. [The A. S. *ceorfan* would have given **charve*; *c* was retained from the pt. pl. and pp.] **+** Du. *kerven*; G. *kerben*, to notch, cut; also Dan. *karve*, Swed. *karfva*, to notch, from the 2nd stem. Gk. γράφειν. Brugm. i. § 791.

Cascade. (F.—Ital.—L.) F. *cascade*.— Ital. *cascata*, a waterfall; orig. fem. pp. of *cascare*, to fall. For **casicare*.—L. *cāsāre*, to totter.—L. *cāsum*, sup. of *cadere*, to fall.

Case (1), an event. (F.—L.) M. E. *cas.*—F. *cas.*—L. acc. *cāsum*, a fall, a case.—L. *cāsus*, pp. of *cadere*, to fall.

Case (2), a receptacle. (F.—L.) O. F. *casse.*—L. *capsa*, a box, cover.—L. *capere*, to hold.

Casemate. (F.—Ital.) F. *casemate*, a loop-hole in a fortified wall.—Ital. *casamatta*, a chamber built under a wall or bulwark, to hinder those who enter the ditch to scale the wall of a fort. It seems to mean 'dark chamber.'—Ital. and L. *casa*, house, cottage, room; and Ital. *matta*, fem. of *matto*, orig. mad, but the Sicilian *mattu* means 'dim.'

Casement, frame of a window. (F.—L.) Coined with the sense of *encasement*, that which encases or encloses. From *case*, verb; with suffix *-ment*.

Cash, coin. (F.—L.) Orig. a till or box to keep money in.—F. *casse*, a case; see **Case** (2) above. Der. *cash-ier*, sb., one who keeps a money-box or cash.

Cashew-nut, the nut of a W. and E. Indian tree. (F.—Brazilian?) *Cashew* is a corruption of F. *acajou*, which is said to be from the native Brazilian name *acajaba* or *acajaiba*. (Mahn, Littré.)

Cashier, to dismiss from service. (Du.—F.—L.) Du. *casseren*, to cashier; merely borrowed from F. *casser*, 'to breake, burst, . . also to casseere, discharge;' Cot. [Du. words, borrowed from F., end in *-eren*.]—L. *quassāre*, to shatter, frequent. of *quatere*, to shake; which annexed the senses of L. *cassāre*, to annul, discharge, from L. *cassus*, void, null.

Cashmere, a soft wool. (India.) So called from the vale of *Cashmere*, in India. Also spelt *cassimere*, *kerseymere*.

Casino, a room for dancing. (Ital.—L.) Ital. *casino*, dimin. of *casa*, a cottage, house.—L. *casa*, a cottage.

Cask. (Span.—L.) Span. *casco*, a skull, sherd, coat of an onion ; also a cask of wine, a casque or helmet. The orig. sense is 'husk' ; cf. Span. *cascara*, peel, rind, shell, Port. *casca*, rind. — Span. *cascar*, to burst open ; formed (as if from Lat. **quassicāre*) from an extension of L. *quassāre*, to break, burst ; see **Quash.**

  casque, a helmet. (F.—Span.—L.) F. *casque.* — Span. *casco*, a helmet, headpiece ; see above.

Casket, a small box. (Span.—L.) Apparently confused with F. *cassette*, 'a small casket ;' Cot. Formally, it is a dimin. of **Cask.**

Casque ; see **Cask.**

Cassava, a plant. (Span. — Hayti.) Span. *cazabe*; also *cazavi*, 'the bread made in the W. Indies of the fruit called the *yuca* ;' Pineda. It properly means the plant, which is also called manioc ; said to be from the Hayti *casabbi*, with the same sense. See R. Eden's works, ed. Arber, p. 175. See **Tapioca.**

Cassia, a species of laurel. (L. — Gk. — Heb.) L. *casia, cassia.* — Gk. κασία, a spice like cinnamon. — Heb. *qetsī'ōth*, in Ps. xlv. 8, a pl. form from *qetsī'ōh*, cassia-bark. — Heb. root *qātsa'*, to cut away ; because the bark is cut off.

Cassimere ; see **Cashmere.**

Cassock, a vestment. (F.—Ital.) F. *casaque.* — Ital. *casacca*, an outer coat. Of uncertain origin.

Cassowary, a bird. (Malay.) First brought from Java. Malay *kasuwāri*.

Cast. (Scand.) Icel. *kasta*, to throw ; Swed. *kasta* ; Dan. *kaste.* **Der.** *re-cast.*

Castanets, instruments used for making a snapping noise. (F.—Span.— L.—Gk.) F. *castagnettes*, 'finger-knackers, wherewith players make a pretty noise in some dances ;' Cot. — Span. *castañetas*, castanets ; pl. of *castañeta*, a snapping noise resembling the cracking of roasted chestnuts. — Span. *castaña*, a chestnut. — Lat. *castanea*, the chestnut-tree. — Gk. κάστανον ; see **Chestnut.**

Caste, a breed, race. (Port.—L.) Port. *casta*, a race, orig. a 'pure' breed ; a name given by the Port. to classes of men in India. — Port. *casta*, fem. of *casto*, pure. — L. *castus*, pure, chaste.

  castigate. (L.) L. *castīgātus*, pp. of *castīgāre*, to chasten ; lit. 'to keep pure.' — L. *castus*, chaste. **Doublet,** *chastise.*

Castle. (L.) A. S. *castel.* — L. *cas-*

tellum, dimin. of *castrum*, a fortified place. **Der.** *castell-an*, O. North F. *castelain*, O. F. *chastelain*, the keeper of a *chastel*, or castle ; also *châtelaine* (fem. of F. *châtelain* = O. F. *chastelain*), now applied to a lady's chain or 'keeper' of keys, &c.

Castor. (L. — Gk.) L. *castor.* — Gk. κάστωρ, a beaver. But of Eastern origin ; cf. Malay *kastūri*, Skt. *kastūrī*, musk ; Pers. *khaz*, beaver.

  castor-oil. Named from some confusion with *castoreum*, 'a medicine made of the liquor contained in the little bags that are next the beaver's groin ;' Kersey. But it is really a vegetable production.

Castrate. (L.) L. *castrātus*, pp. of *castrāre*, to cut.

Casual. (F.—L.) F. *casuel.* — L. *cāsuālis*, happening by chance. — L. *cāsu-*, stem of *cāsus*, chance. See **Case** (1).

Cat. (E.) A. S. *cat.* + Du., Dan. *kat*, Icel. *köttr*, Sw. *katt*, G. *kater, katze* ; L. *cātus*, W. *cath*, Ir. Gael. *cat*, Russ. *kot'*, *koshka*, Arab. *qitt*, Turk. *kedī*. (Prob. Eastern.)

Cata-, prefix. (Gk.) Gk. κατά, down, thoroughly.

Cataclysm, deluge. (Gk.) Gk. κατακλυσμός, a dashing over, flood. — Gk. κατά, down ; κλύζειν, to dash, wash, as waves.

Catacomb. (Ital. — L.) Ital. *catacomba*, a sepulchral vault. — Late L. *catacumbas* ; of which the sense and origin are unknown.

Catafalque, a stage or platform, chiefly used at funerals. (F.—Ital.) F. *catafalque.* — Ital. *catafalco* ; of unknown origin. See **Scaffold.**

Catalepsy, a sudden seizure. (Gk.) Formerly *catalepsis.* — Gk. κατάληψις, a grasping, seizing. — Gk. κατά, down ; λαμβάνειν, to seize.

Catalogue. (F.—Gk.) F. *catalogue.* — Late Lat. acc. *catalogum.* — Gk. κατάλογος, a counting up, enrolment. — Gk. κατά, fully ; λέγειν, to say, tell ; see **Logic.**

Catamaran, a sort of raft. (Tamil.) In Forbes, Hindustani Dict., ed. 1859, p. 289, we have '*katmaran*, a raft . . ; the word is orig. Tamil, and means *tied logs*.' — Tamil *kattu*, binding ; *maram*, wood (Yule).

Cataplasm, a poultice. (F.—L.— Gk.) F. *cataplasme.* — L. *cataplasma.* — Gk. κατάπλασμα, a plaster, poultice. — Gk. καταπλάσσειν, to spread over. — Gk. κατά,

fully; and πλάσσειν, to mould; see
Plaster.

Catapult. (Late L.—Gk.) Late L.
catapulta, an engine for throwing stones.—
Gk. καταπέλτης, the same.—Gk. κατά,
down; πάλλειν, to swing, hurl.

Cataract. (L.—Gk.) L. *cataracta*,
Gen. vii. 11.—Gk. καταρράκτης, as sb., a
waterfall; as adj., broken, rushing down.
Prob. allied to καταρρήγνυμι, I break
down; the 2 aor. κατερράγην was used
of the rushing down of waterfalls and
storms.—Gk. κατά, down; ῥήγνυμι, I
break.

Catarrh. (F.—Late L.—Gk.) F.
catarrhe.—Late L. *catarrhus*.—Gk.
κατάρροος, a flowing down (of rheum),
a cold in the head.—Gk. κατά, down; and
ῥέειν, to flow.

Catastrophe. (Gk.) Gk. καταστροφή,
an overturning, sudden turn.—Gk. κατά,
down; στρέφειν, to turn.

Catch. (F.—L.) O. Picard *cachier*,
variant of O. F. *chacier*, to hunt, chase;
hence, to catch. It answers to Ital. *cac-
ciare*, Late L. **captiāre*, extended form of
L. *captāre*, to catch.—L. *captus*, pp. of
capere, to seize. ¶ We even find M. Du.
kaetsen, to catch, borrowed from Picard
cachier. The M. E. pt. t. *cauȝte* imitated
lauȝte, pt. t. of M. E. *lacchen*, to catch.
Doublet, *chase* (1).

Catechise. (L.—Gk.) Late L. *cate-
chizāre*.—Gk. κατηχίζειν, to catechise,
instruct; lengthened form of κατηχέειν, to
din into one's ears, lit. 'to din down.'—
Gk. κατ-ά, down; ἠχεῖν, to sound; cf.
ἦχος, a ringing in the ears; see **Echo.**

Category, a class. (Gk.) Gk. κατη-
γορία, an accusation; but in logic, a predicament or class.—Gk. κατηγορεῖν, to
accuse.—Gk. κατ-ά, down, against; *ἀγο-
ρεῖν*, with the sense of ἀγορεύειν, to declaim,
address an assembly, from ἀγορά, an
assembly.

Catenary, belonging to a chain; used
of the curve in which a chain hangs. (L.)
From L. *catēna*, a chain; see **Chain.**

Cater, to buy provisions. (F.—L.)
Formed as a verb from M. E. *catour*, a
buyer of provisions (whom we should now
call a *cater-er*). *Catour* is short for
acatour, formed from *acat*, a buying, purchase, Ch. prol. 571.—O. F. *acat* (mod.
F. *achat*), a buying.—Folk-L. *acaptum*, a
purchase; for *accaptum*.—Folk-L. *accap-
tāre*, to purchase (A. D. 1060), frequent. of

accipere, to receive, also to buy; see
Accept and **Cates.**

Cateran, a Highland robber. (Gael.)
Low L. *cateranus*, answering to Gael.
ceathairne, lit. 'common people;' cf.
ceathairne-choille, s. pl., freebooters, out-
laws. From Irish *cethern, ceithern*, a
troop, band; cf. L. *caterua*, a band of
men. See **Kern.**

Catercousin. (F.—L.) Nares (ed.
1876) has: '*Cater-cousins*, friends so
familiar that they eat together.' If so,
the word is from *cater*, vb., and
cousin.

Caterpillar. (F.—L.) Adapted from
O. F. *chatepelose*, a caterpillar (Godefroy);
the latter half of the word was assimilated
to *piller*, one who *pills*, or robs or spoils.
O. F. *chatepelose* is lit. 'hairy she-cat.'—
O. F. *chate*, fem. of *chat*, cat; *pelose*,
hairy.—L. *cātus*, cat; *pilōsus*, hairy, from
pilus, a hair.

Caterwaul. (E.) M. E. *caterwawen*;
coined from *cat*, and *wawen*, to make a
wailing noise.

Cates, provisions. (F.—L.) So called
because provided by the *catour*, mod. E.
cater-er; see **Cater.** '*Cater*, a steward, a
provider of *cates*;' Baret (1580).

Cathartic, purging. (Gk.) Gk. καθαρ-
τικός, purgative.—Gk. καθαίρειν, to cleanse,
purge.—Gk. καθαρός, pure.

Cathedral. (L.—Gk.) L. *cathe-
drālis ecclesia* = a cathedral church, or one
which has a bishop's throne.—Late L.
cathedra, a throne.—Gk. καθέδρα, a seat.
—Gk. καθ-, for κατά, down; and ἕδρα, a
seat, chair, from ἕζομαι (=ἑδ-γομαι), I sit;
see **Sit.**

Catholic. (L.—Gk.) L. *catholicus*
(Tertullian.)—Gk. καθολικός, universal.
—Gk. καθόλ-ου, adv., on the whole, in
general.—Gk. καθ-, for κατά, according
to; and ὅλου, gen. of ὅλος, whole.

Catkin. (Du.) A loose spike of
flowers, named from its soft downy appearance.—M. Du. *katteken*, 'a kitling,'
Hexham. (It also meant 'catkin'; cf.
F. *chattons* in Cot.) Dimin. of Du. *kat*, a
cat (M. Du. *katte*).

Catoptric, relating to optical reflec-
tion. (Gk.) Gk. κατοπτρικός, reflexive.—
Gk. κάτοπτρον, a mirror.—Gk. κατ-ά,
down, inward; ὄπ-τομαι, I see, with suffix
-τρον, of the instrument.

Cattle. (F.—L.) M.E. *catel*, property;
hence, live stock, cattle.—O. North F.

catel. – Late L. *capitāle*, capital, property ; see **Capital** (2) and **Chattels**.

Caucus, a name applied to certain political meetings. (American Indian?) Said to be from an Algonkin word meaning to speak, to counsel, whence *kaw-kaw-asu,* a counsellor. 'Their elders, called *cawcawwassoughes;*' Capt. Smith's Works, ed. Arber, p. 347. '*Caucorouse,* which is captaine;' id. p. 377. ¶ This is more likely than the entirely unsupported story about *caulkers'* meetings.

Caudal, belonging to the tail. (L.) L. *cauda,* the tail.

Caudle, a warm drink. (F. – L.) O. North F. *caudel,* O. F. *chaudel,* a sort of warm drink. – O. F. *chaud, chald,* hot. – L. *caldus,* for *calidus,* hot.

Caul, a net, covering, esp. for the head. (F.) O. F. *cale,* 'a kind of little cap ;' Cot. Origin unknown.

Cauldron; see **Caldron**.

Cauliflower. (F. – L.) Formerly *colyflory.* From M. E. *col* (O. F. *col*), a cabbage ; and *flory,* from O. F. *flori, fleuri,* pp. of *fleurir,* to flourish. The O. F. *col* is from L. acc. *caulem,* from *caulis,* a cabbage ; and *fleurir* is from L. *flōrēre,* to flourish. See **Cole** and **Flourish**.

Caulk, Calk. (F. – L.) M. E. *cauken,* to tread; hence, to squeeze in (as oakum into a ship's seams). – O. F. *cauquer,* to tread; to tent a wound with lint. – L. *calcāre,* to tread, force down by pressure. – L. *calc-,* stem of *calx,* the heel.

Cause. (F. – L.) F. *cause.* – L. *causa, caussa,* a cause. Der. *cause,* vb.

Causeway, a paved way, raised way. (F. – L.; *and* E.) Formerly *caus-ey-way ;* by adding *way* to M. E. *causè, causie, causey.* – O. North F. *caucie* (mod. F. *chaussée,* Prov. *causada,* Span. *calzada*). – Late L. *calciāta,* for *calciāta uia,* a paved way. – Late L. *calciātus,* pp. of *calciāre,* to make a roadway by treading it down ; from L. *calcāre,* to tread. – L. *calc-,* stem of *calx,* heel ; see **Caulk**.

Caustic. (L. – Gk.) L. *causticus.* – Gk. καυστικός, burning. – Gk. καυστύς, burnt. – Gk. καίειν (fut. καύσω), to burn.

cauterise. (F. – Late L. – Gk.) F. *cauteriser.* – Late L. *cautērizāre,* to sear. – Gk. καυτηριάζειν, to sear. – Gk. καυτή-ριον, a branding-iron. – Gk. καίειν, to burn (above).

Caution. (F. – L.) F. *caution.* – L. acc. *cautiōnem,* heed. – L. *cautus,* pp. of

cauēre, to beware. Cf. Skt. *kavi(s),* wise. Brugm. i. § 635. Der. *pre-caution.*

Cavalier. (F. – Ital. – L.) F. *cavalier,* a horseman. – Ital. *cavaliere,* the same. – L. *caballārium,* acc. of *caballārius,* the same. – L. *caballus,* a horse. See **Chevalier**.

cavalcade. (F. – Ital. – L.) F. *cavalcade.* – Ital. *cavalcata,* a troop of horsemen; orig. fem. of pp. of *cavalcare,* to ride. – Ital. *cavallo,* a horse. – L. *caballum,* acc. of *caballus,* a horse.

cavalry. (F. – Ital. – L.) O. F. *cavallerie.* – Ital. *cavalleria,* cavalry. – Ital. *cavaliere,* a knight ; see **Cavalier**.

Cave. (F. – L.) M. E. *caue.* – O. F. *cave,* a ·cave. – Folk-L. *cava,* a cave. – L. *cauus,* hollow. (√KEU.) Der. *cav-ity*; *cav-ern* (F. *caverne,* L. *cauerna*).

Cave in. (M. Du.) Properly to *calve in,* a phrase introduced by Du. navvies. Cf. W. Flanders *inkalven,* to cave in ; E. Friesic *kalfen,* to calve as a cow, whence *kalfen in,* to cave in. The falling portion of earth is compared to a calf dropped by a cow. Confused with *cave,* a hollow.

Caveat, a caution. (L.) L. *caueat,* lit. let him beware. – L. *cauēre,* to beware.

Caviare, roe of the sturgeon. (F. – Ital.) F. *caviar.* – Ital. *caviaro;* whence also Turk. *khāvyār,* caviare.

Cavil. (F. – L.) O. F. *caviller.* – L. *cauillārī,* to banter; hence, to wrangle, object to. – L. *cauilla,* a jeering, caviling.

Caw. (E.) An imitation of the cry of the crow or daw. Cf. Du. *kaauw,* Dan. *kaa,* a jackdaw : which are imitative.

Cayman, an American alligator. (Caribbean.) Also *caiman.* The spelling *cayman* is Spanish. – Caribbean *acayūman* (Littré).

Cease. (F. – L.) F. *cesser.* – L. *cessāre,* to loiter, go slowly, cease ; frequent. of *cēdere* (pp. *cessus*), to yield, go away, go.

Cedar, a tree. (F. – L. – Gk.) O. F. *cedre.* – L. *cedrus.* – Gk. κέδρος.

Cede. (L.) A late word (A. D. 1633). – L. *cēdere,* to go, to come, to yield.

Ceil, Ciel, to line the inner roof or walls of a room. (F. – L.) Hence the sb. *ceil-ing* or *ciel-ing.* M. E. *celen,* to ceil ; from the sb. *syle* or *cyll,* a canopy. – F. *ciel,* a canopy ; the same word as *ciel,* heaven. [Cf. Ital. *cielo,* heaven, a canopy, a cieling.]—L. *cælum*, heaven. ¶ Not to be confused with E. *sill*, nor with *seal*; nor with *seel* (F. *siller*); nor with L. *cēlāre*, to hide. The L. *cælāre*, to emboss, seems to have had some influence on the word, but did not originate it; cf. M. E. *celure*, a canopy, Late L. *cælātūra*.

Celandine, a plant. (F.–Gk.) O. F. *celidoine*.—Late L. *celidonia*. — L. *chelidonia*.—Gk. χελιδόνιον, swallow-wort.— Gk. χελιδον-, stem of χελιδών, a swallow. (The *n* is intrusive.)

Celebrate. (L.) L. *celebrātus*, pp. of *celebrāre*, to frequent, to solemnise, honour.—L. *celeber*, frequented, populous.

Celerity. (F.–L.) F. *célérité.* — L. acc. *celeritātem*, speed.—L. *celer*, quick. Cf. Gk. κέλης, a runner; Brugm. i. § 633.

Celery. (F.–L.–Gk.) F. *céleri*, introduced from the Piedmontese Ital. *selleri*; for Ital. *selini*, pl. of *selino*, parsley. — L. *selinon*, parsley.— Gk. σέλινον, a kind of parsley.

Celestial. (F.–L.) O. F. *celestiel.* — L. *cælesti-s*, heavenly. — L. *cælum*, heaven.

Celibate. (L.) The orig. sense was 'a single life'; it was afterwards an adj., and again a sb., meaning 'one who is single.'—L. *cælibātus*, sb. celibacy, single life.—L. *cælib-*, stem of *cælebs*, single, unmarried. Der. *celibacy* (for **cælibātia*).

Cell. (L.) M. E. *celle.* — L. *cella*, small room, hut. Cf. *cēlare*, to hide. See **Helm** (2). (✔KEL.)

cellar. (F.–L.) M. F. *celer.* A. F. *celer*; O. F. *celier.*—L. *cellārium*, a cellar. —L. *cella* (above).

Celt (1), a name originally given to the Gauls. (C.) From L. pl. *Celtæ*, the Celts; the word probably meant 'warriors'; cf. A.S. *hild*, Icel. *hildr*, war; Lith. *kalti*, to strike; L. *per-cellere*, to strike through, beat down (Rhys).

Celt (2), a primitive chisel or axe. (Late L.) Late L. *celtis*, assumed nom. of the abl. *celte* (=with a chisel), in the Vulgate Version of Job xix. 24. But this reading is due to some error, and there seems to be no such word in Latin.

Cement. (F.–L.) O. F. *ciment.*— L. *cæmentum*, rubble, chippings of stone; hence, cement. Perhaps for **cædmentum*, from *cædere*, to cut (Brugm. i. § 587).

Cemetery. (L.–Gk.) Late L. *cæmētērium.* — Gk. κοιμητήριον, a sleeping-place, cemetery. — Gk. κοιμάω, I lull to sleep; in

pass., to fall asleep. Allied to κεῖμαι, I lie down ; Skt. *çi*, to lie down.

Cenobite. (L. – Gk.) L. *cænobīta*, a member of a (social) fraternity (Jerome). —L. *cænobium*, a convent.—Gk. κοινόβιον, a convent.—Gk. κοινόβιος, living socially. —Gk. κοινό-s, common ; βίος, life.

Cenotaph. (F. – L. – Gk.) O. F. *cenotaphe.* — L. *cenotaphium.*—Gk. κενοτάφιον, an empty tomb. — Gk. κενό-s, empty ; τάφ-ος, a tomb.

Censer. (F.–L.) M. E. *censer.* — O. F. *censier, senser* (Godefroy); shortened from O. F. *encensier.*—Late L. *incensārium*, also *incensōrium* (whence mod. F. *encensoir*). — L. *incensum*, incense; from pp. of *incendere*, to kindle. See **Incense**.

Censor. (L.) L. *censor*, a taxer, valuer, assessor, critic. — L. *censēre*, to give an opinion, appraise.+Skt. *çaṁs*, to praise.

censure. (F.–L.) F. *censure.*—L. *censūra*, orig. opinion. — L. *censēre* (above).

census. (L.) L. *census*, a registering.—L. *censēre* (above).

Cent, a hundred, as in *per cent*. (L.) In America, the hundredth part of a dollar. — L. *centum*, a hundred ; see **Hundred**.

centenary. (L.) L. *centēnārius*, relating to a hundred. — L. *centēnus*, a hundred (usu. distributively).—L. *centum*.

centennial. (L.) Coined to mean relating to a century.—L. *cent-um*, hundred ; *ann-us*, a year.

centesimal. (L.) L. *centēsim-us*, hundredth.—L. *cent-um*, hundred.

centigrade. (L.) Divided into a hundred degrees.—L. *centi-*, for *centum*, hundred ; *grad-us*, a degree ; see **Grade**.

centipede, centiped. (F.–L.) F. *centipède.* — L. *centipeda*, a many-footed (lit. hundred-footed) insect.—L. *centi-*, for *centum*, hundred ; and *ped-*, stem of *pēs*, foot.

centuple. (L.) L. *centuplex* (stem *centuplic-*), a hundredfold.—L. *centu-m*, hundred ; *plic-āre*, to fold.

centurion. (L.) L. acc. *centuriōnem*, a captain of a hundred. — L. *centuria* (below).

century. (F.–L.) F. *centurie.*— L. *centuria*, a body of a hundred men ; number of one hundred. — L. *centu-m*, hundred.

Centaur. (L. – Gk.) L. *Centaurus.*

－Gk. κένταυρος, a centaur, a creature half man and half horse; which some have compared with Skt. *gandharvas*, a demi-god.

centaury, a plant. (L.－Gk.) L. *centaurēa.*－Gk. κεντάυρειον, centaury; a plant named from the *Centaur* Chiron.

Centenary, Centennial, Centuple, Centurion, &c.; see Cent.

Centre, Center. (F.－L.－Gk.) F. *centre.* － L. *centrum.* － Gk. κέντρον, a spike, goad, prick, centre. － Gk. κεντέω, I goad on. Cf. W. *cethr*, a spike.

centrifugal, flying from a centre. (L.) L. *centri-,* for *centro-,* stem of *centrum*; and *fug-ere*, to fly.

centripetal, tending towards a centre. (L.) L. *centri-* (above); *pet-ere,* to seek.

Ceramic, relating to pottery. (Gk.) Gk. κεραμικ-ός, adj. － Gk. κέραμ-ος, potter's earth. Cf. κεράννυμι (fut. κεράσω), I mix.

Cere, to coat with wax. (L.) L. *cērāre,* to wax.－L. *cēra*, wax.+Gk. κηρός, wax.

cerecloth. (L. *and* E.) Lit. a waxed cloth.

cerement. (L.) From *cere*; with suffix *-ment* (L. *-mentum*).

ceruse, white lead. (F.－L.) O. F. *ceruse.*－L. *cērussa,* white lead.－L. *cēra,* wax.

Cereal, relating to corn. (L.) L. *cereālis.*－L. *ceres,* corn.

Cerebral, relating to the brain. (L.) From L. *cerebr-um,* the brain. Cf. Gk. κάρα, the head. Brugm. i. § 619.

Cerecloth, Cerement; see Cere.

Ceremony. (F. － L.) M. E. *ceremonie.*－ F. *cérémonie.*－L. *cærimōnia,* a ceremony, rite.

Certain. (F. － L.) O. F. *certein, certain.* － L. *cert-us,* sure; with suffix *-ānus.* Allied to L. *cernere,* to discriminate; Gk. κρίνειν, to separate, decide.

certify. (F.－L.). M. E. *certifien.*－ F. *certifier.*－Late L. *certificāre,* to make sure.－L. *certi-,* for *certo-,* stem of *certus* (above); and *-fic-,* for *fac-ere,* to make.

Cerulean, azure. (L.) L. *cæruleus, cærulus,* blue; for **cæluleus, *cælulus,* from *cælum,* sky. Brugm. i. § 483.

Ceruse, white-lead; see Cere.

Cervical, belonging to the neck. (L.) From L. *ceruīc-,* stem of *ceruix,* neck.

Cervine, relating to a hart. (L.) L. *ceruīn-us.*－L. *ceru-us,* a hart; see **Hart.**

Cess, limit, measure. (F.－L.) In

1 Hen. IV. ii. 1. 8. Orig. a tax, rate, rating, assessment; see Spenser, State of Ireland, Globe ed., p. 643, col. 2. For *sess*; from *sess,* verb, to rate; which is short for **Assess.**

Cessation. (F.－L.) F. *cessation.*－ L. acc. *cessātiōnem,* a ceasing.－L. *cessā-tus,* pp. of *cessāre,* to cease.－L. *cessus* (below).

cession. (F. － L.) F. *cession.* － L. acc. *cessiōnem,* a yielding.－L. *cessus,* pp. of *cēdere,* to yield, to cede.

Cess-pool. (Hybrid.) Most probably equiv. to *(se)cess-pool*; see N. E. D. Cf. Ital. *cesso,* a privy (Torriano); which is a shortened form of *secesso,* a retreat.－ L. *sēcessus,* 'the draught;' Matt. xv. 17 (Vulgate).

Cetaceous, of the whale kind. (L.－ Gk.) L. *cētus.*－Gk. κῆτος, a sea-monster.

Ch.

Chablis, a white wine. (F.) From *Chablis,* 12 mi. E. of Auxerre, in the department of Yonne, France.

Chafe, to warm by friction, vex. (F.－ L.) M. E. *chaufen,* to warm. － O. F. *chaufer* (F. *chauffer*), to warm; cf. Prov. *calfar,* to warm.－Late L. **calefāre,* to warm; for L. *calefacere,* to warm, make to glow.－ L. *calē-re,* to glow; *facere,* to make.

Chafer, Cockchafer. (E.) A.S. *cefer* (also *ceafor*), a kind of beetle.+Du. *kever*; G. *käfer.*

Chaff. (E.) A.S. *ceaf,* later *chæf,* husk of grain.+Du. *kaf*; Low G. *kaff.* ¶ The verb *to chaff* = *to chafe,* i. e. vex. So also *chaff-wax,* for *chafe-wax.*

chaffinch, a bird. (E.) I. e. *chaff-finch*; it frequents barn-doors.

Chaffer. (E.) The verb is from the M. E. sb. *chapfare,* also *chaffare,* a bargaining.－A. S. *cēap,* a bargain, and *faru,* a journey, also business; see **Cheap** and **Fare.**

Chaffinch; see **Chaff.**

Chagrin. (F.) F. *chagrin,* melancholy. [Diez identifies it with F. *chagrin,* shagreen; but wrongly.]

Chain. (F.－L.) O. F. *chaine, chaëne.* －L. *catēna,* a chain.

Chair. (F.－L.－Gk.) M. E. *chaire, chaere.*－O. F. *chaiere, chaere.*－L. *cathe-dra,* a throne, raised seat, chair.－Gk. καθέδρα, a seat.－Gk. καθ-, for κατά, down;

ἔδρα, a seat, from ἔζομαι (= ἐδ-γομαι), I sit; see **Cathedral, Sit.**

chaise, a light carriage. (F.–L.–Gk.) F. *chaise*, a chair, also, a chaise; a Parisian modification of F. *chaire*, a pulpit, orig. a seat.

Chalcedony, a kind of quartz. (L.–Gk.) L. *chalcēdōnius*, Rev. xxi. 19.–Gk. χαλκηδών, Rev. xxi. 19.

Chaldron, a coal-measure. (F.–L.) O. F. *chaldron*, orig. a caldron; see **Caldron.**

Chalice, a cup. (F.–L.) A.F.*chalice*; O. F. *calice.*–L. *calicem*, acc. of *calix*, a cup. Allied to *calyx*, but not the same word.

Chalk. (L.) M. E. *chalk.*–A.S. *cealc* (Southern).–L. *calc-*, stem of *calx*, lime.

Challenge. (F.–L.) M. E. *chalenge*, *calenge*, often in the sense 'a claim.'–A.F. *chalenge*, O. F. *chalonge*, *calenge*, a dispute, claim; an accusation.–L. *calumnia*, false accusation; see **Calumny.**

Chalybeate. (L.–Gk.) Used of water containing iron. Coined from L. *chalyb-s*, steel.–Gk. χάλυψ (stem χαλυβ-), steel; named from the *Chalybes*, a people of Pontus, who made it.

Chamber. (F.–L.–Gk.) F. *chambre*; Prov. *cambra.*–L. *camera*, *camara*, a vault, vaulted room, room.–Gk. καμάρα, a vaulted place.

chamberlain. (F.–O.H.G.–L.–Gk.) F.*chamberlain*, O.F.*chambrelenc.*–O. H. G. *chamerlinc*, M. H. G. *kamerlinc*, one who has the care of rooms; formed with suffix -*l-inc* (the same as E. -*l-ing*), from L. *camera* (above).

Chameleon. (L.–Gk.) L. *chamæleōn.*–Gk. χαμαι-λέων, lit. a ground-lion, dwarf-lion; a kind of lizard.–Gk. χαμαί, on the ground (also dwarf, in comp.); and λέων, lion. Cf. L. *humī*, on the ground.

chamomile. (Late L.–Gk.) Late L. *camomilla* (*chamomilla*).–Gk. χαμαί-μηλον, lit. ground-apple, from the apple-like smell of the flower.–Gk. χαμαί-, on the ground (see above); μῆλον, apple.

Chamois. (F.–G.) F. *chamois*; borrowed from some Swiss dialectal form; cf. Piedmontese *camossa.*–M. H. G. *gamz* (for **gamuz*), a chamois (G. *gemse*).

Champ, to eat noisily. (E.) Formerly *cham* or *chamm*; of imitative origin, like *jam*, to crush. Cf. Swed. dial. *kämsa*, to chew with difficulty.

Champagne. (F.–L.) A wine named from *Champagne* in France, which means 'a plain'; see below.

champaign, open country. (F.–L.) In Sh. F.*champaigne*, of which the Picard form was *campaigne*; see **Campaign.**

Champak, a tree. (Skt.) Skt. *champaka*, the champak.

Champion. (F.–L.) O. F. *champion.*–L. *campiōnem*, acc. of *campio*, a combatant (Isidore).–L. *campus*, a place for military exercise; a peculiar use of *campus*, a field. See **Camp.**

Chance, hap. (F.–L.) M. E. *cheaunce.*–O. F. *cheance*, *chaance.*–Late L. *cadentia*, a falling, a chance.–L. *cadere*, to fall, happen; see **Cadence.**

Chancel. (F.–L.) So called because orig. fenced off by a latticed screen.–O. F. *chancel*, an enclosure fenced off with an open screen.–Late L. *cancellus*, a chancel, screen; L. *cancellī*, pl., a grating; see **Cancel.**

chancellor. (F.–L.) O. F. *chancelier.*–Late L. acc. *cancellārium*, a chancellor; orig. an officer who stood near the screen before the judgment-seat.–L. *cancellī*, a grating; see **Chancel, Cancel.**

chancery. (F.–L.) For *chancelry.* M. E. *chancelerie.*–O. F. *chancellerie.*–Late L. *cancellāria*, the record-room of a *cancellārius*; see **Chancellor.**

Chandelier. (F.–L.) O. F. *chandelier*, a candle-holder.–Late L. *candēlārius*, m.; cf. *candēlāria*, a candle-stick.–L. *candēla*; see **Candle.**

chandler. (F.–L.) O.F.*chandelier*, a chandler.–Late L. *candēlārius*, a candle-seller.–L. *candēla*; see **Candle.** Der. *corn-chandler*, where *chandler* merely means seller, dealer.

Change, vb. (F.–L.) O. F. *changer*, *changier.*–Late L. *cambiāre*, to change (Lex Salica).–L. *cambīre*, to exchange. Cf. Late L. *cambium*, exchange; whence F. *change*, E. *change*, sb.

Channel. (F.–L.) M. E. *chanel*, *canel.*–O. F. *chanel*, *canel*, a canal.–L. acc. *canālem*; see **Canal.**

Chant. (F.–L.) F. *chanter*, vb.–L. *cantāre*, to sing; frequent. of *canere*, to sing. Der. *chant-ry*, M. E. *chaunterie*, Late L. *cantāria*; *chanti-cleer*, M. E. *chaunte-cleer*, clear-singing.

Chaos. (Gk.) L. *chaos*, Lat. spelling of Gk. χάος, chaos, abyss, lit. a cleft. Cf. Gk. χάσκειν, to gape. See **Chasm.**

Chap (1), to cleave, crack. (E.) M. E.

chappen, to cut; hence, to gape open like a wound made by a cut. E. Fries. *kappen*, to cut; not found in A. S.+M. Du. *kappen*, to cut; Swed. *kappa*, Dan. *kappe*, to cut; G. *kappen*, to cut, lop. See **Chop** (1).

Chap (2); see **Chapman**.

Chapel. (F.—L.) O. F. *chapele*.— Late L. *cappella*, orig. a shrine in which was preserved the *cāpa* or cope of St. Martin (Brachet).—Late L. *cāpa, cappa*, cape, hooded cloak; see **Cape** (1).

chaperon. (F.—L.) F. *chaperon*, a protector; orig. a kind of hood.—F. *chape*, a cope.—Late L. *cāpa*; as above.

Chapiter, the capital of a column. (F.—L.) O. F. *chapitre*, usually a chapter of a book, but representing L. *capitulum*, which meant 'chapiter' as well as 'chapter.' See **Chapter.**

Chaplet. (F.—L.) M. E. *chapelet*.— O. F. *chapelet*, a head-dress, wreath.— O. F. *chapel*, head-dress. — O. F. *chape*, a cope; see **Chaperon.**

Chapman, a merchant. (E.) The familiar *chap* is merely short for *chapman*. — A. S. *cēapman*, a merchant.—A. S. *cēap*, price, barter (see **Cheap**); and *man*, man.

Chaps, Chops, the jaws. (E.) A late word, of unknown origin; possibly from **Chap** (1). ¶ Perhaps suggested by North E. *chafts* or *chaffs*, jaws (Cleveland Gloss.).—Icel. *kjaptr* (*pt* pron. as *ft*), the jaw; Swed. *käft*, Dan. *kiæft*, jaw.

Chapter, a division of a book, synod of clergy. (F.—L.) M.E. *chapitre*, in both senses.—F. *chapitre*, variant of an older form *chapitle*. — L. *capitulum*, a chapter of a book (little head); also, in Late L., a synod; dimin. of *caput*, a head.

Char (1), a turn of work. (E.) Also *chare, chore, chewre*; M. E. *cher, char*, orig. a turn, hence, a space of time, turn of work, &c.—A. S. *cerr* (below). Hence, *char-woman*, a woman who does a turn of work. See **Ajar.**

char (2), usually **chare,** to do a turn of work. (E.) M. E. *cherren, charren*, to turn; A.S. *cerran*, to turn.—A.S. *cerr* (*cierr, cyrr*), a turn. ¶ The sense 'burn' is later than the appearance of the sb. *char-coal.*

Char (3), a fish. (C.?) Of unknown origin; perhaps named from its red belly [the W. name is *torgoch*, red-bellied, from *tor*, belly, and *coch*, red].—O. Gael. *ceara*, red, from *cear*, blood; Irish *cear*, red, also blood.

Character. (L.—Gk.) L. *charactēr*. — Gk. χαρακτήρ, an engraved or stamped mark.—Gk. χαράσσειν, to furrow, scratch, engrave.

Charade. (F.—Prov.) F. *charade*, introduced from Provençal *charrada*, a long talk, from *charrà*, to chatter (Supp. to Littré); cf. Languedoc *charrade*, idle talk. Cf. also Span. *charrada*, speech or action of a clown, from Span. *charro*, a clown, peasant.

Charcoal. (E.) From *char* and *coal*; but the sense of *char* remains unknown; some refer it to M. E. *cherren*, to turn (as if to turn to coal), but there is no proof of this. See *char* (2).

Charge. (F.—C.) F. *charger*, to load.—Late L. *carricāre*, to load a car.— L. *carrus*, a car, a Gaulish word; see **Cark, Car.** Der. *charg-er*, a dish or horse, because carrying a burden.

chariot. (F.—C.) F. *chariot*, augmentative of F. *char*, a car.—L. *carrus*, a car; see **Car.**

Charity. (F.—L.) O. F. *charitet*.— L. acc. *cāritātem*, love.—L. *cārus*, dear. Brugm. i. § 637. ¶ Not allied to Gk. χάρις.

Charlatan. (F.—Ital.) F. *charlatan*. — Ital. *ciarlatano*, a mountebank, great talker, prattler.—Ital. *ciarlare*, to prattle; *ciarla*, prattle; prob. of imitative origin.

Charlock, a kind of wild mustard. (E.) Prov. E. *carlock*. — A.S. *cerlic*; origin unknown.

Charm. (F.—L.) M. E. *charme*, sb. — O. F. *charme*, an enchantment.—L. *carmen*, a song, enchantment.

Charnel. (F.—L.) Properly an adj.; containing carcases, as in *charnel-house*.— O. F. *charnel*, adj. carnal; as sb. a cemetery.—Late L. *carnāle*, glossed by *flǣschūs* (flesh-house); Wright-Wülker, Voc. 184. 37.—L. *carnālis*; see **Carnal.**

Chart. (F.—L.—Gk.) O. F. *charte*. —L. *charta*, a paper.—Gk. χάρτη, a leaf of paper. **Doublet,** *card* (1).

charter. (F. — L. — Gk.) M. E. *chartre.*—O. F. *chartre.*—Late L. *cartula*, a small paper or document.—L. *charta*, a paper; see above.

Chary, careful, cautious. (E.) M. E. *chari.* A.S. *cearig*, full of care, sad.— A. S. *cearu, caru*, care.+Du. *karig*, G. *karg*, sparing. *Chary* meant (1) sorrowful, (2) heedful. See **Care.**

Chase (1), to hunt after. (F.—L.)

O. F. *chacier, chacer,* to pursue; see **Catch**.

Chase (2), to enchase; short for *enchase,* which see.

Chase (3), a printer's frame. (F.—L.) F. *châsse,* a shrine. — L. *capsa,* a box; see **Case** (2).

Chasm. (L. — Gk.) L. *chasma,* a gulf. — Gk. χάσμα, a yawning cleft. Allied to χάσκειν, to gape; see **Chaos**.

Chaste. (F.—L.) O. F. *chaste.* — L. *castus,* chaste; see **Caste**.

chasten. (F.—L.) Used in place of M. E. *chasty* or *chastien;* see below.

chastise. (F.—L.) M. E. *chastisen;* shorter form *chastien.* — O. F. *chastier.* — L. *castīgāre,* lit. ' to make pure.' — L. *castus,* chaste; see **Castigate**.

Chasuble, a vestment. (F.—L.) F. *chasuble.* — Late L. *casubula,* with the same sense as Late L. *casula,* a little house; hence, a mantle. — L. *casa,* a cottage.

Chat, Chatter. (E.) M. E. *chateren,* also *chiteren,* to chatter, twitter; frequentative form of *chat.* An imitative word; cf. Du. *kwetteren,* to warble, chatter, Swed. *kvittra,* to chirp.

Chateau. (F.—L.) F. *château,* O. F. *chastel.* — L. *castellum,* dimin. of *castrum,* a fortified place. **Der.** *castell-an;* also *châtelaine;* for which see **Castle**.

Chattels. (F.—L.) Pl. of M. E. *chatel,* property, also cattle. — O. F. *chatel,* O. North F. *catel,* property; see **Cattle**.

Chatter; see **Chat**.

Chaudron, entrails. (F.) Macb. iv. I. 33. The *r* is inserted by confusion with F. *chaudron,* a caldron. — O. F. *chaudun,* older forms *caudun, caldun,* entrails (Godefroy). [Cf. G. *kaldaunen,* entrails; from Mid. Low G. *kaldūne,* the same.] Thought to be from Late L. *caldūna,* a dish containing entrails (Ducange). Perhaps from L. *calidus,* warm (F. *chaud*).

Chaw; see **Chew**.

Chaws, by-form of **Jaws;** see **Jaw**.

Cheap, at a low price; orig. a sb. (E.) M.E. *chep, cheep,* barter, price; always a sb. Hence, *good cheap,* in a good market (F. *bon marché*); whence E. *cheap,* used as an adj. A.S. *cēap,* price; whence the verb *cēapian,* to cheapen, buy. So also Du. *koop,* a bargain, *koopen,* to buy; G. *kauf,* purchase, *kaufen,* to buy; Icel. *kaup,* Swed. *köp,* Dan. *kiöb,* a purchase; Goth. *kaupon* (weak vb.), to traffic. ¶ Some say that these words are borrowed from

L.; in particular, that O. H. G. *choufo,* a huckster, is from L. *caupo,* a huckster. But this is now held to be unlikely (Kluge, Franck).

Cheat, to defraud. (F.—L.) *Cheat* is merely short for *escheat;* cf. M. E. *chete,* an escheat (Prompt. Parv.). The *escheaters* were often *cheaters;* hence the verb. See **Escheat**.

Check, a sudden stop, repulse. (F. — Pers.) M. E. *chek,* a stop; also check! in playing chess. The word is due to the game, which is very old. The orig. sense of *check* was ' king!' i. e. mind the king, the king is in danger. — O. F. *eschec,* ' a check at chess-play,' Cot. — Pers. *shāh,* a king, king at chess; whence *shāh-māt,* check-mate, lit. ' the king is dead,' from Arab. *māt,* he is dead. Similarly we have F. *échec,* a check, repulse, defeat, pl. *échecs,* chess; Ital. *scacco,* a square of a chess-board, also a check, defeat. See **chess** below. ¶ Devic shews that O. F. *eschec* represents Arab. *esh-shāg;* where *esh* is for *al,* the def. art., and *shāg* is the Arab. pron. of Pers. *shāh.*

checker, chequer, to mark with squares. (F. — Pers.) To mark with squares like those on a chess-board. M. E. *chekker, chekere,* a chess-board. (Hence *The Checkers,* an inn-sign.) — O. F. *eschequier,* a chess-board, also, an exchequer. — Low L. *scaccārium,* a chess-board. — Low L. *scaccī,* chess, pl. of *scaccus,* from the Arab. form of Pers. *shāh,* king.

checkers, chequers, an old name for the game at draughts; from the *checker* or chess-board; see above.

check-mate. (F. — Pers. *and* Arab.) From Arab. **shāg-māt,* for *shāh-māt,* the king is dead; see **Check**.

cheque. (F. — Pers.) A pedantic spelling of *check,* from confusion with *exchequer;* it is really a name given to a draft for money, of which one keeps a memorandum or *counter-check.*

chess, the game of the kings. (F. — Pers.) Equivalent to *checks,* i. e. kings; see **Check** above. — O. F. *esches,* chess; really the pl. of *eschec,* check, orig. ' king.' ¶ From Pers. *shāh,* a king, were formed O. F. *eschec,* F. *échec,* E. *check,* Ital. *scacco,* Span. *xaque, jaque,* Port. *xaque,* G. *schach,* Du. *schaak,* Dan. *skak,* Swed. *schack,* Low Lat. *lūdus scaccōrum* — game of checks, or of kings.

Cheek. (E.) M. E. *cheke, cheoke.* O.

CHEER

CHICORY

Merc. *cēce*, A. S. *ceāce*, cheek. + Du.
kaak, jaw, cheek; Swed. *käk*, jaw.

Cheer. (F.–L.) M. E. *chere*, orig.
the mien; hence, 'to be of good *cheer*.'
–O. F. *chere*, the face.–Late L. *cara*,
face. (Relationship to Gk. *κάρα*, the head,
is doubtful.) Der. *cheer-ful*.

Cheese. (L.) M. E. *chese*. O. Merc.
cēse (A. S. *cȳse*, for earlier **cīese<*cēasi*),
with *i*-mutation; prehistoric A. S. **cāsi*
< **cāsioz*. – L. *cāseus*, cheese; whence
other forms (G. *käse*, Du. *kaas*) are borrowed. Sievers, 2nd ed. § 75. 2.

Cheeta, Cheetah, the hunting leopard, a leopard used for the chase. (Hind.
–Skt.) Hind. *chītā*. – Skt. *chitraka*, a
cheeta; from *chitra*, spotted, also visible, clear.–Skt. *chit*, to perceive. See
Chintz.

Chemise. (F.–L.) F. *chemise*.–
Late L. *camisia*, a shirt, thin dress;
whence O. Irish *caimmse*, shirt (Stokes).

Chemist, Chymist; short for *alchemist*; see Alchemy.

Cheque, Chequer; see Check.

Cherish. (F. – L.) O. F. *cheris-*,
stem of pres. pt. of *cherir*, to hold dear.–
F. *cher*, dear. – L. *cārus*, dear.

Cheroot, a cigar. (Tamil.) Tamil
shuruttu, a roll; hence, a roll of tobacco
(Yule).

Cherry. (F.–L.–Gk.) M. E. *cheri*, a
mistake for *cheris*, the final *s* being mistaken for the pl. inflexion.–O. North F.
cherise, O. F. *cerise*; representing Folk-
L. **ceresia*, **ceresea*.–L. *cerasus*, a cherry-
tree. – Gk. *κέρασος*, a cherry-tree; usually
said to come from *Cerasos*, in Pontus;
a story which Curtius doubts.

Chert, a kind of quartz. (?) Unknown.
Cf. Irish *ceart*, a pebble.

Cherub. (Heb.) The true pl. is *cherub-
im*. – Heb. *k'rūv* (pl. *k'rūvīm*), a mystic
figure.

Chervil, a plant. (L.–Gk.) A.S. *cer-
fille*. – L *chærephylla*, pl. of *chærephyllum*.
–Gk. *χαιρέφυλλον*, chervil, lit. pleasant
leaf.–Gk. *χαίρ-ειν*, to rejoice; *φύλλον*,
leaf.

Chess; see Check.

Chest. (L.–Gk.) M. E. *cheste, chiste.*
A.S. *cist*.–L. *cista*.–Gk. *κίστη*, a chest,
box (whence G. *kiste*, &c.).

Chestnut, Chesnut. (F.–L.–Gk.)
Chesnut is short for *chestnut*, which is
short for *chesten-nut*, nut of the *chesten*,
which is the old name of the tree, called

in M. E. *chestein*.–O.F. *chastaigne* (F.
châtaigne).–L. *castanea*, chestnut-tree.–
Gk. *κάστανον*, a chestnut. Chestnuts are
said to have been called *κάστανα*, or *κάρυα*
Κασταναῖα, from Κάστανα, Castana, the
name of a city in Pontus where they
abounded; but more probably from Armen.
kaskeni, a chestnut-tree, from *kask*, a chestnut (Kluge).

Cheval-de-frise, an obstruction with
spikes. (F.) Lit. 'horse of Friesland,' a
jocular name; the pl. *chevaux-de-Frise* is
commoner. See below.

chevalier. (F.–L.) F. *chevalier*, a
horseman.–F. *cheval*, a horse.–L. *caballum*, acc. of *caballus*, a horse.

Cheveril, kid leather. (F.–L.) O. F.
chevrele, fem., a little kid. Dimin. of
O.F. *chevre*, F. *chèvre*, a goat, kid.–L.
capram, acc. of *capra*, a she-goat.

chevron, an ordinary, in heraldry, re
sembling two rafters of a house. (F.–L.)
(Most likely meant to represent the saddle-
peak.)–F. *chevron*, 'a kid, a chevron in
building, a rafter;' Cot. Augmentative
form of *chevre*, a she-goat.–L. *capra*, a
she-goat; see Caper (1). Cf. L. *capre-
olus*, which likewise means a prop.

Chew, Chaw. (E.) M.E. *chewen.*
A. S. *cēowan*, to chew. eat.+Du. *kaauwen*;
G. *kauen*; O. H. G. *kiuwan*; Russ. *jevate*.
Cf. also Icel. *tyggja, tyggva*, to chew
(Streitberg).

Chibouk, a Turkish pipe. (Turk.)
Turk. *chibūk, chybūk*, a stick, tube, pipe
(Zenker, p. 349).

Chicanery. (F.–Pers.?) F. *chica-
nerie*, wrangling, pettifogging; Cot.–F.
chicaner, to wrangle; orig. to dispute in
the game of the mall or *chicane* (Brachet).
Perhaps from the medieval Gk. *τζυκάνιον*,
a word of Byzantine origin (id.); from
Pers. *chaugān*, a club, bat.

Chicken. (E.) Sometimes shortened
to *chick*; but the M. E. word is *chiken*.
A.S. *cīcen*, earlier **ciucin*. + Du. *kieken,
kuiken*, a chicken, Low G. *küken*; cf. G.
küchlein, a chicken, Icel. *kjūkling*, Swed.
kyckling; related to Cock, which shews the
weak grade **cuc-*; see Cock (1). Sievers,
2nd ed. § 165.

Chicory, a plant, succory. (F.–L.–
Gk.) F. *chicorée*.–L. *cichorium*.–Gk.
κιχόρια, neut. pl.; also *κιχώριον, κιχώρη*,
succory. β. *Succory* is a corrupter form
of the word, apparently for *siccory* or
cichory, from L. *cichorium*.

87

Chide. (E.) M.E. *chiden*. A.S. *cīdan*, to chide, brawl; pt. t. *cīdde*.

Chief. (F. – L.) M.E. *chef, chief.* – O.F. *chef, chief,* the head. – L. type **capum* (Ital. *capo*). – L. *caput*, head. Der. *ker-chief*, q. v.

Chieftain. (F. – L.) O.F. *chevetaine.* – Late L. *capitāneus, capitānus*, a captain. – L. *capit-*, from *caput*, a head.

Chiffonier, a cupboard. (F.) Lit. a place to put rags in. – F. *chiffonier*, a rag-picker, also a cupboard. – F. *chiffon*, augment. of *chiffe*, a rag. Orig. unknown.

Chignon. (F. – L.) Hair twisted; another spelling of F. *chaînon*, a link. – F. *chaîne*, O.F. *chaine*, a chain. – L. *catēna*, a chain.

Chilblain. (E.) A *blain* caused by a *chill.*

Child. (E.) M. E. *child*. A.S. *cild*. Teut. type **kiljom*, neut.; cf. Goth. *kilthei*, the womb.

Chill, cold. (E.) Orig. a sb. A.S. *cele, ciele,* chilliness. Teut. type **kaliz*, sb.; from **kal-an*, to be cold, as in A.S. *calan*, to be cold, Icel. *kala*, to freeze. + Du. *kil*, a chill; cf. L. *gelu*, frost.

Chime, sb. (F. – L. – Gk.) M. E. *chimbe*, of which the orig. sense was cymbal; hence the chime or ringing of a cymbal. Shortened from O. F. *chimbale*, dialectal form of O. F. *cimbale*, a cymbal. – L. *cymbalum*. – Gk. κύμβαλον; see Cymbal. N.B. We find M. E. *chyme-belle*, which looks like a popular form for *cymbal*. Der. *chime*, verb.

Chimera, Chimæra. (L. – Gk.) L. *chimæra.* – Gk. χίμαιρα, a she-goat; also, a fabulous monster, with a goat's body. – Gk. χίμαρος, he-goat.

Chimney. (F. – L. – Gk.) F. *cheminée*, 'a chimney;' Cot. – Late L. *camīnāta*, provided with a chimney; hence, a chimney. – L. *camīnus*, an oven, a fire-place. – Gk. κάμινος, oven, furnace.

Chimpanzee, an ape. (African.) I am informed that the name is *tsimpanzee* in the neighbourhood of the gulf of Guinea.

Chin. (E.) M.E. *chin*. A.S. *cin*. + Du. *kin*, Icel. *kinn*, Dan. *kind*, Swed. *kind*; Goth. *kinnus*, the cheek; G. *kinn*, chin; L. *gena*, cheek; Gk. γένυς, chin; cf. Skt. *hanus*, jaw.

China. (China.) Short for *china-ware*, or ware from *China*. The name of the people was formerly *Chineses*; we have dropped the final *s*, and use *Chinese* as a pl.; hence *Chinee* in the singular, by a second dropping of *se*.

Chinchilla, a small rodent animal. (Span. – L.) Span. *chinchilla*, lit. 'a little bug,' as if from its smell; but undeservedly so named. – Span. *chinche*, a bug. – L. *cimicem*, acc. of *cimex*, a bug.

Chinchona; the same as Cinchona.

Chincough, whooping-cough. (E.) For *chink-cough*; cf. Scotch *kink-cough, kink-host* (*host* means *cough*). A *kink* is a catch in the breath, nasalised form of a base **kik*, to gasp. + Du. *kinkhoest*; M. Du. *kieckhoest*; Swed. *kikhosta*, chincough, *kikna*, to gasp; G. *keichen*, to gasp.

Chine. (F. – O.H.G.) O.F. *eschine* (F. *échine*), the back-bone. – O.H.G. *skina*, a needle, prickle (G. *schiene*, a splint). For the sense, cf. L. *spīna*, a thorn, spine, backbone.

Chink (1), a cleft. (E.) Formed with suffixed *k*, from the base of M. E. *chine*, a cleft, rift. – A.S. *cinu*, a chink. – A.S. *cin-*, weak grade of *cīnan*, to split (strong vb.). + Du. *keen*, a chink, also a germ, *kenen*, to bud; cf. G. *keimen*, Goth. *keinan*, to bud. (Germinating seeds make a crack in the ground.)

Chink (2), to jingle. (E.) An imitative word; cf. *clink, clank;* and see Chincough. E. Fries. *kinken* (a strong vb.); M. Dan. *kinke*.

Chintz. (Hindustani – Skt.) For *chints*, pl. of *chint*. Hind. *chhīnt*, spotted cotton cloth, named from the variegated patterns on it; *chhīt*, chintz, also a spot. – Skt. *chitra*, variegated, spotted. See Cheeta.

Chip, vb. (E.) Related (with a lighter vowel) to *chap* (1) or *chop*; as if to cut a little at a time. Cf. A.S. *for-cyppod*, gloss to *praecisus* (Lye); E. Fries. *kippen*, to cut.

Chirography, handwriting. (Gk.) From Gk. χειρογραφεῖν, to write with the hand. – Gk. χειρο-, from χείρ, the hand; γράφειν, to write. Cf. *chiro-mancy*, fortune-telling by the hand; *chiro-pod-ist*, one who handles (and cures) the feet.

Chirp. (E.) Also *chirrup*. M. E. *chirpen*. Also M. E. *chirken, chirmen*, to chirp. The forms *chir-p, chir-k, chir-m* are from an imitative base; cf. Du. *kirren*, to coo.

Chirurgeon, the old spelling of *surgeon*. (F. – L. – Gk.) F. *chirurgien*, 'a surgeon;' Cot. – F. *chirurgie*, surgery. – L. *chīrurgia*. – Gk. χειρουργία, a

working with the hands, skill with the
hands, art, surgery. — Gk. χειρο-, from
χείρ, the hand ; and ἔργειν, to work.

Chisel. (F.—L.) M. E. chisel.—A. F.
chisel, O. F. cisel (F. ciseau). Cf. Late L.
cīsellus, scissors (A. D. 1352). O. F. cisel
answers to Late L. *cīsellum, with the
sense of L. cīsōrium, a cutting instrument
(Vegetius) ; see Scheler's note to Diez.—
L. *cīsum, for cæs-um, supine of cædere,
to cut ; whence also Late L. incīsor, a
carver, cutter ; see Cæsura.

Chit (1), a pert child. (E.) M. E. chit,
a whelp, cub, kitten. Allied to kit-ling
(Icel. ketlingr), and to kit-ten; cf. G. kitze,
a female cat.

Chit (2), a shoot, sprout. (E.) In Holland's Pliny, xiii. 4. Perhaps allied to
M. E. chithe, a sprout (N. E. D.).—A. S.
cīð, a germ, sprout. Cf. Goth. keinan, to
produce a shoot ; G. keim, a germ.

Chivalry. (F.—L.) M. E. chivalrie.—
O.F.chevalerie, horsemanship, knighthood.
—F. cheval, a horse.—Late L. caballum,
acc. of caballus, a horse.

Chlorine, a pale green gas. (Gk.)
Named from its colour. — Gk. χλωρ-ός, pale
green.

chloroform. (Gk. and L.) The latter
element relates to formyl and formic acid,
an acid formerly obtained from red ants. —
L. formīca, an ant.

Chocolate, a paste made from cacao.
(Span. — Mex.) Span. chocolate. — Mex.
chocolatl, chocolate ; Clavigero, Hist.
Mex. i. 433. ¶ Not allied to cacao.

Choice. (F. — Teut.) Not E. M. E.
chois. — O. F. chois (F. choix). — O. F.
choisir, O. North F. coisir, to choose. Of
Teut. origin. — Goth. kausjan, to try,
test; causal of kiusan, to choose. See
Choose.

Choir. (F.—L.—Gk.) The choir of a
church is the part where the choir sit.
Also spelt quire ; M. E. queir, quer.—
O. F. cuer, later choeur, 'the quire of a
church, a troop of singers ;' Cot. — L.
chorum, acc. of chorus, a choir. — Gk.
χορός, a dance, a band of dancers or
singers. See Chorus.

Choke. (E.) M. E. choken, cheken,
cheoken. A. S. cēocian ; only in the derivative ācēocung, to translate L. ruminatio,
which the glossator hardly seems to have
understood, and in the pp. ācēocod, Ælfric,
Hom. i. 216 : with change from ēo to eō,
shortening of ō to o in M. E., and subse-

quent lengthening. Cf. Icel. koka, to
gulp ; kok, the gullet.

Choler, the bile, anger. (F. — L. — Gk.)
Anger was supposed to be due to excess of
bile. M.E. coler. — O.F. colere. — L. cholera,
bile ; also cholera, bilious complaint. — Gk.
χολέρα, cholera ; χολή, bile ; χόλος, bile,
wrath. See Gall.

cholera. (L. — Gk.) L. cholera, as
above. And see Melancholy.

Choose. (E.) M. E. chesen, chusen.
A. S. cēosan (also ceósan), to choose
(pt. t. cēas, ceós). + Du. and G. kiesen,
Icel. kjōsa, Goth. kiusan; Teut. type
*keus-an-. Allied to L. gus-tare, to taste,
Gk. γεύομαι, I taste, Skt. jush, to relish.
(√GEUS.) See Gust. Brugm. i. § 602.

Chop (1), to cut ; a later form of
Chap (1).

Chop (2), to barter. (E.) Probably a
variant of chap, a verb which seems to
have been evolved from the sb. chapman.

Chopine, a high-heeled shoe. (F.—
Span.) In Hamlet, ii. 2. 447 ; for chapine.
—O.F. chapin ; later chappin (Cotgrave).
—Span. chapin, a clog with a cork sole,
woman's shoe, high cork shoe. Perhaps
from Span. chapa, a thin plate (of metal),
used to strengthen the work it covers.

Chops ; see Chaps.

Chord. (L. — Gk.) L. chorda. — Gk.
χορδή, the string of a musical instrument,
orig. a string of gut. Brugm. i. § 605.
¶ The same word as Cord.

Chorus. (L. — Gk.) L. chorus, a band
of singers. — Gk. χορός, a dance, a band of
dancers or singers. See Choir. Der.
chor-al, chor-i-ster.

Chough, a bird. (E.) M. E. choȝe,
chough. Not found in A. S., which has
(however) the forms cēo, cīo, and the early
forms ciae, chyae. Somewhat similar forms
are seen in Du. kaauw, Dan. kaa, Swed.
kaja, a jackdaw.

Chouse, to cheat. (Turk. ?) To act as a
chouse or cheat. Ben Jonson has chiaus in
the sense of 'a Turk,' with the implied
sense of 'cheat'; Alchemist, i. 1. The
allusion is alleged to be to a Turkish
chiaus or interpreter, who committed a
notorious fraud in 1609. — Turk. chā'ush,
a sergeant, mace-bearer, Palmer's Pers.
Dict. ; châwush, a sergeant, herald, messenger, Rich. Dict. p. 534. Or (medi-
ately) from M. Ital. ciaus.

Chrism ; see below.

Christ, the anointed one. (L. — Gk.)

A. S. *Crist.* – L. *Chrīstus.* – Gk. χριστός, anointed. – Gk. χρίω, I rub, anoint. **Der.** *Christ-ian, Christ-en-dom,* &c. ; *Christ-mas* (see **Mass**) ; *anti-christ,* opponent of Christ (from Gk. ἀντί, against; see 1 John ii. 18).

chrism, holy unction. (L. – Gk.) Also spelt *chrisome,* whence *chrisome-child,* a child wearing a *chrisome-cloth,* or cloth which a child wore after holy unction; cf. O. F. *cresme,* ' the crisome, or oyle ; ' Cot. – Late L. *chrisma,* holy oil. – Gk. χρῖσμα, an unguent. – Gk. χρίω (as above).

Chromatic, relating to colours. (Gk.) Gk. χρωματικός, adj. – Gk. χρωματ-, stem of χρῶμα, colour; allied to χρώς, skin.

chrome, chromium. (Gk.) A metal ; its compounds exhibit beautiful colours. – Gk. χρῶμ-α, colour.

Chronicle. (F. – Late L. – Gk.) M. E. *cronicle,* with inserted *l* ; also *cronike, cronique.* – A. F. *cronicle* ; O. F. *cronique,* pl. *croniques,* chronicles, annals. – Late L. *chronica,* fem. sing. ; for neut. pl. – Gk. χρονικά, pl., annals. – Gk. χρονικός, adj. from χρόνος, time. **Der.** *chron-ic* (= χρονικός).

chronology, science of dates. (Gk.) From χρόνο-s, time ; -λογία, from λόγ-os, discourse ; see **Logic**.

chronometer, time-measurer. (Gk.) From χρόνο-s, time ; μέτρον, measure ; see **Metre**.

Chrysalis, the form taken by some insects. (Gk.) Gk. χρυσαλλίς, the gold-coloured sheath of butterflies, chrysalis. – Gk. χρυσ-ός, gold.

chrysanthemum, a flower. (L. – Gk.) L. *chrȳsanthemum.* – Gk. χρυσάν-θεμον, a marigold. – Gk. χρυσ-ός, gold ; ἄνθεμον, a bloom, from ἀνθεῖν, to bloom, related to ἄνθος, a flower, a bud.

chrysolite, a yellow stone. (F. – L. – Gk.) O. F. *crisolite.* – L. *chrȳsolithus,* Rev. xxi. 20. – Gk. χρυσόλιθος. – Gk. χρυσό-s, gold ; λίθος, stone.

chrysoprase. (L. – Gk.) L. *chrȳsoprasus,* Rev. xxi. 20. – Gk. χρυσόπρασος, a yellow-green stone. – Gk. χρυσό-s, gold ; πράσον, a (green) leek.

Chub, a fish. (E.) Etym. unknown. Cf. Dan. *kobbe,* a seal, prov. Swed. *kubbug,* chubby, fat; Norw. *kubben,* stumpy; Swed. *kubb,* a block, log. This does not explain the *ch* ; but see **Chump**.

chubby, fat. (E.) Lit. ' like a chub;' cf. prov. Swed. *kubbug* (above).

Chuck (1), to strike gently, toss. (F. – Teut.) Formerly written *chock* (Turberville). – F. *choquer,* to give a shock, jolt. – Du. *schokken,* to jolt, shake; allied to E. *shock* and *shake.*

Chuck (2), to chuck as a hen. (E.) An imitative word ; Ch. has *chuk* to express the noise made by a cock; C. T. 15180 (B. 3464). Cf. *cluck.* **Der.** *chuck-le,* in the sense ' to cluck '

Chuck (3), a chicken. A variety of *chick,* for *chicken.* See above.

Chuckle. (E.) To *chuckle* is to laugh in a suppressed way; cf. **Chuck** (2).

Chump, a log. (E.) Cf. Swed. dial. *kumpa,* to chop into logs; *kumping,* a log, round stick; also Icel. *kumbr, trō-kumbr,* a log of wood, from Icel. *kumbr,* nasalised form of *kubbr,* a chopping; Icel. *kubba,* to chop. **Der.** *chump-end,* i. e. thick end.

Church. (Gk.) M. E. *chirche, chireche.* A. S. *cirice,* later *circe* ; (cf. Icel. *kirkja* ; G. *kirche,* Du. *kerk*). – Gk. κυριακόν, a church, neut. of κυριακός, belonging to the Lord ; or (possibly) from Gk. κυριακά, pl., treated as a fem. sing. – Gk. κύριος, a lord, orig. mighty. – Gk. κῦρος, strength. Cf. Skt. *çūra,* a hero.

Churl. (E.) M. E. *cherl, cheorl.* A. S. *ceorl,* a man. + Du. *kerel,* G. *kerl* ; Dan. Sw. Icel. *karl.* Teut. types, **kerloz, *karloz.*

Churn, sb. (E.) A. S. *cyrin* ; older form *cirin* (printed *cirm*), Corp. gloss. 1866. + Icel. *kirna,* Swed. *kärna,* Dan. *kierne,* a churn; cf. O. Swed. *kerna.* Swed. *kärna,* Dan. *kierne,* to churn, Du. *kernen,* to churn.

Chutney, Chutny, a kind of hot relish. (Hind.) Hind. *chaṭnī* (Yule).

Chyle, milky fluid. (F. – L. – Gk.) F. *chyle.* – L. *chȳlus.* – Gk. χυλός, juice. – Gk. χέω (= χέϝ-ω), I pour. (√GHEU.)

chyme, liquid pulp. (L. – Gk.) Formerly *chymus.* – L. *chȳmus.* – Gk. χυμός, juice. – Gk. χέ-ω; as above.

Chymist ; see **Alchemist.**

Ci—Cz.

Cicatrice, scar. (F. – L.) F. *cicatrice.* – L. *cicātrīcem,* acc. of *cicātrix,* a scar.

Cicerone. (Ital. – L.) Ital. *cicerone,* a guide; orig. a Cicero. – L. acc. *Cicerōnem,* proper name.

Cid, lit. a chief or commander. (Span.

—Arab.) Usually a title of Ruy Diaz, the national hero of Spain.—Arab. *sayyid*, a lord; Richardson's Dict. p. 864.

Cider. (F. – L. – Gk. – Heb.) It merely means strong drink. M. E. *sicer, cyder.*—F. *cidre*; O. F. *cisdre* (for **cisre*).—L. *sicera.*—Gk. σίκερα, strong drink.—Heb. *shĕkār*, strong drink.—Heb. *shākar*, to be intoxicated.

Cieling; see **Ceil.**

Cigar, Segar. (Span.) Span. *cigarro*; whence also F. *cigare.*

Cinchona, Peruvian bark. (Span.) Named after the Countess of *Chinchon*, wife of the governor of Peru, cured by it A.D. 1638. Chinchon is S.E. of Madrid. (Should be *chinchona*.)

Cincture. (L.) L. *cinctūra*, a girdle. —L. *cinctus*, pp. of *cingere*, to gird.

Cinder. (E.) Misspelt for *sinder* (by confusion with F. *cendre* = L. *cinerem*; see **Cinerary**). A.S. *sinder*, 'scoria,' slag. +Icel. *sindr*; Swed. *sinder*; G. *sinter*, dross, whence Du. *sintels*, cinders. ¶ The A.S. *sinder* occurs in the 8th century.

Cinerary, relating to the ashes of the dead. (L.) L. *cinerārius.* – L. *ciner-*, stem of *cinis*, dust, ashes of the dead.+ Gk. κόνις, dust. **Der.** *cineraria*, a flower; named from the ash-coloured down on the leaves. Brugm. i. § 84.

Cinnabar, Cinoper. (L.–Gk.– Pers.) L. *cinnabaris.* – Gk. κιννάβαρι, vermilion. From Pers. *zinjifrah, zinjarf,* red lead, vermilion, cinnabar.

Cinnamon, a spice. (L.–Gk.–Heb.) L. *cinnamōmum.*—Gk. κιννάμωμον.—Heb. *qinnāmōn*; said to be of Malay origin (Genesius). Cf. Malay *kayu manis*, cinnamon; from *kayu*, wood, *manis*, sweet.

Cipher. (F. – Span. – Arab.) O. F. *cifre* (F. *chiffre*), a cipher, zero.—Span. *cifra.*—Arab. *sifr*, a cipher; lit. 'empty thing;' from *sifr*, adj. empty; Rich. Dict. p. 937. (A translation of Skt. *çūnya*, (1) empty; (2) a cipher.) **Der.** *de-cipher*, from L. *dē*, in the verbal sense of *un-*, and *cipher*; cf. M. F. *dechiffrer*, 'to decypher;' Cot.

Circle. (F.–L.) A.S. *circul*; but M.E. *cercle.*—F. *cercle.*—L. *circulus*, dimin. of *circus*, a ring, circle; see **Ring** (1). **Der.** *encircle, semi-circle*; and see *circum-*.

circus, a ring. (L.) L. *circus* (above).

Circuit. (F.–L.) F. *circuit.* – L. acc. *circuitum*, a going round.—L. *circuitus*, also *circumitus*, pp. of *circumīre*

(also *circuīre*), to go round.—L. *circum*, round; *īre*, to go.

Circum-, *prefix*, round. (L.) L. *circum*, around, round; orig. acc. of *circus*, a circle; see **Circle.** **Der.** *circumambient* (see **Ambient**); *circum-ambulate* (see **Amble**); and see below.

circumcise. (L.) L. *circumcīs-us*, pp. of *circumcīdere*, to cut round. – L. *circum*, round; and *cædere*, to cut.

circumference. (L.) L. *circumferentia*, boundary of a circle. – L. *circumferent-*, stem of pres. pt. of *circum-ferre*, to carry round; from *ferre*, to bear.

circumflex. (L.) L. *syllaba circumflexa*, a syllable marked with a circumflex (∧) or 'bent' mark.—L. *circumflexus*, pp. of *circum-flectere*, to bend round; from *flectere*, to bend.

circumjacent, lying near. (L.) From stem of pres. part. of *circum-iacēre*, to lie around; from *iacēre*, to lie.

circumlocution. (L.) L. *circumlocūtio*, a periphrasis.—L. *circumlocūtus*, pp. of *circum-loquī*, to speak in a roundabout way; from *loquī*, to speak.

circumscribe. (L.) L. *circumscrībere*, to write or draw around, to limit; from *scrībere*, to write.

circumspect, prudent. (L.) L. *circumspectus*, prudent; orig. pp. of *circum-spicere*, to look around; from *specere*, to look.

circumstance. (F.–L.) Adapted from O. F. *circonstance.*—L. *circumstantia*, lit. a standing around, also an attribute, circumstance (influenced by F. *circonstance*).—L. *circumstant-*, stem of pres. pt. of *circum-stāre*, to stand round; from *stāre*, to stand.

Circus; see **Circle.**

Cirrus, a fleecy cloud, tendril. (L.) L. *cirrus*, a curl, curled hair.

Cist, a sort of tomb. (L.–Gk.) L. *cista*, a chest.—Gk. κίστη, a box, chest.

cistern. (F.–L.–Gk.) F. *cisterne.* —L. *cisterna*, a reservoir for water.—L. *cista*, as above.

cistvaen, a British monument. (L. and W.) W. *cistfaen*, a stone chest, monument made with four upright stones, and a fifth on the top.—W. *cist*, a chest (from L. *cista*); and *maen*, a stone.

Cit, Citadel; see **Civil** (below).

Cite, to summon, quote. (F.–L.) F. *citer.*— L. *citāre*, frequent. of *ciēre*, to rouse, excite, call. + Gk. κίω, I go.

(√KI.) See **Hie. Der.** *ex-cite, in-cite, re-cite.*

Cithern, Cittern, a kind of guitar. (L. – Gk.) [Also M. E. *giterne*; from O. F. *guiterne*, a guitar.] The *n* is excrescent, as in *bitter-n*, in imitation of M. E. *giterne.* – L. *cithara.* – Gk. κιθάρα, a kind of lyre or lute.

Citizen; see Civil (below).

Citron. (F. – L. – Gk.) F. *citron.* – Late L. acc. *citrōnem.* – L. *citrus,* orange-tree. – Gk. κίτρον, a citron; κιτρία, citrontree.

City; see Civil (below).

Civet. (F. – Arab.) F. *civette,* civet; also the civet-cat; Ital. *zibetto;* borrowed from medieval Gk. ζαπέτιον (Brachet). – Arab. *zabād,* civet; Rich. Dict. p. 767.

Civil. (F. – L.) F. *civil.* – L. *cīuīlis,* belonging to citizens. – L. *cīuis,* a citizen. Allied to A. S. *hīwan,* members of a household. **Der.** *civil-ise, civil-i-an.*

cit; short for **citizen** (below).

citadel. (F. – Ital. – L.) F. *citadelle.* – Ital. *cittadella,* a small town, fort; dimin. of *cittade = cittate (città),* a city. – L. *cīuitātem,* acc. of *cīuitās,* a city. – L. *cīuis,* a citizen (above).

citizen. (F. – L.) M. E. *citesein,* from A. F. *citisein,* in which *s* was an insertion. – O. F. *citeain* (F. *citoyen*); formed from O. F. *cite (cité)* city, by help of the suffix *-ain* – L. *-ānus;* see below.

city. (F. – L.) M. E. *cite, citee.* – O.F. *cite* (F. *cité*). – Late L. type*civ'tātem,* for *cīuitātem,* acc. of *cīuitās;* see citadel.

Clachan, a small village with a church. (Gael.) Gael. *clachan,*(1) a circle of stones, (2) a small rude church, (3) a small village with a church. – Gael. *clach,* a stone. So also Irish *clachán,* a hamlet; *clach,* O. Ir. *cloch,* a stone.

Clack. (E.) M. E. *clacken.* Imitative; allied to **Crack.** E. Fries. *klakken.*+ Icel. *klaka,* to chatter; Du. *klakken,* to clack, crack; Irish *clag,* the clapper of a mill.

Claim, to demand, call out for. (F. – L.) O. F. *claimer, clamer.* – L. *clāmāre,* to call out; cf. O. L. *calāre,* to proclaim; Gk. καλεῖν, to summon. **Der.** *ac-claim, de-claim, ex-claim, pro-claim, re-claim;* also (from pp. *clamātus*) *ac-clamat-ion, de-clamat-ion, ex-clamat-ion, pro-clamat-ion, re-clamat-ion.*

clamour. (F. – L.) M. E. *clamour.* – O. F. *clamour.* – L. acc. *clāmōrem,* an

outcry. – L. *clāmāre* (above). **Der.** *clamorous.*

Clamber, to climb by grasping tightly. (E.; *perhaps* Scand.) XV. cent. M. E. *clameren, clambren.* Cf. Icel. *klambra,* to pinch closely together; Dan. *klamre,* to grip firmly; see **Clamp.** Affected by **Climb,** of which the M. E. pt. t. was *clamb, clam.*

Clammy, viscous. (E.) Earliest form *claymy,* perhaps-from A. S. *clǣm,* clay (see Clay); but confused with an adj. *clam,* sticky; with which cf. E. Fries. and Du. *klam,* Dan. *klam,* clammy, moist. See **Clamp.**

Clamour; see **Claim.**

Clamp. (Du.) XV. cent. Du. *klampe,* a holdfast; whence *klampen,* to clamp, grapple, also to board a ship. + Dan. *klamme,* a cramp-iron; Swed. *klamp,* the same; Icel. *klömbr,* a smith's vice; Teut. base **klamp,* answering to the 2nd grade of M. H. G. *klimpfen,* to press tightly together. Cf. **Clump.**

Clan. (Gael.) Gael. *clann,* offspring, children; Irish *cland, clann,* descendants, a tribe; W. *plant,* pl. offspring, children. Cf. Skt. *kula(m),* a herd, family. Brugm. i. § 669.

Clandestine. (L.) L. *clandestīnus,* secret, close. Allied to *clam,* secretly.

Clang, to resound. (L.) L. *clangere,* to resound; whence *clangor,* a loud noise. +Gk. κλαγγή, a clang; allied to κλάζειν, to clash (fut. κλάγξω). **Der.** *clang-or.* See below.

Clank, a heavy ringing sound. (Du.) XVII cent. – Du. *klank,* 'a ringing;' Hexham. Cf. Du. *klonk,* pt. t. of *klinken,* to clink. See **Clink. Der.** *clank,* vb.

Clap. (E.) M. E. *clappen.* [We only find A.S. *clæppetan,* to palpitate; Voc. 473.] E. Fries. *klappen,* to clap hands. The orig. sense is to make a noise by striking. + Icel. *klappa,* Swed. *klappa,* Dan. *klappe,* Du. *klappen,* M. H. G. *klaffen,* to pat, clap, prate, make a noise. Allied to **Clack, Clatter.**

Claret. (F. – L.) Orig. a light red wine. M. E. *claret.* – O. F. *claret, clairet* (F. *clairet*), adj.; dimin. of *clair,* clear. – L. *clārus,* clear. See **Clear.**

clarify. (F. – L.) O. F. *clarifier.* – L. *clārificāre,* to make clear. – L. *clāri-,* from *clārus,* clear; and *-fic-,* for *facere,* to make.

clarion. (F. – L.) M. E. *clarioun.* –

O. F. *clarion, claron (F. clairon), a clear-sounding horn. — Late L. acc. clāriōnem. — L. clāri- (as above).

Clash. (E.) An imitative word; suggested by clack and crash, dash, &c. Cf. E. Fries. klatsen, to crack a whip.

Clasp. (E.) M. E. claspe, clapse, sb.; claspen, clapsen, vb. The base seems to be klap-s-, extended from klap- (see Clap), and influenced by M. E. clippen, to embrace. Cf. G. klafter, a fathom; Lith. glēbys, an armful; and cf. Grasp.

Class. (F. — L.) F. classe, a rank. — L. acc. classem, a class, assembly, fleet.

Clatter. (E.) A frequentative of clat, which is a by-form of Clack. A. S. clatrung, a clattering; E. Fries. klattern, to clatter. + Du. klateren, to clatter. Of imitative origin.

Clause. (F. — L.) F. clause. — Late L. clausa, a passage from a book, a clause. — L. clausus, pp. of claudere, to shut. + O. Fries. slūta, to shut. See Slot (1). (√SKLEU.) Brugm. i. § 795.

Clavicle, the collar-bone. (F. — L.) F. clavicule, the collar-bone. — L. clāuicula, lit. a small key; dimin. of clāuis, a key. Allied to claudere; see Clause.

Claw. (E.) M. E. clau, clee. A. S. clawu (also clēa), a claw. + Du. klaauw; G. klaue; Icel. klō, Dan. Swed. klo. Allied to Clew; from a Teut. base *klau-, 2nd grade of *kleu-, to draw together; cf. O. H. G. kluwi, forceps.

Clay. (E.) M. E. clai, cley. A. S. clǣg. + Du. and Low G. klei, Dan. klæg. Teut. type *klai-jā, fem.; from *klai-, 2nd grade of Teut. root *klei-; cf. A. S. clām (for *klai-moz), earthenware; Gk. γλοι-ός, sticky matter. See Cleave (2) and Glue.

Claymore, a Scottish broadsword. (Gael.) Gael. claidheamh mor, a great sword. Here claidheamh is cognate with W. cleddyf, O. Ir. claideb, sword; and Gael. mor, great, is allied to W. mawr, great. Cf. W. cledd, a sword.

Clean. (E.) M. E. clene. A. S. clǣne, clear, pure. + O. Sax. clēni, cleini; O. Fries. klēn; Du. klein, small; G. klein, O. H. G. chleini, pure, bright, fine, small. All from Teut. *klaini-, orig. ' clear, pure.'

cleanse. (E.) A. S. clǣnsian, to make clean. — A. S. clǣne, clean.

Clear. (F. — L.) M. E. cleer, cler. — O. F. cler, clair. — L. clārus, bright, clear, loud.

Cleat, a piece of iron for strengthening the soles of shoes; a piece of wood or

iron to fasten ropes to. (E.) M. E. clete, a wedge (as if from A. S. *clēat), also clite, clote, a lump; cognate with Du. kloot, a ball, G. kloss, a clot, lump. Allied to Clot; and see Clout.

Cleave (1), to split. (E.) Strong verb. A. S. clēofan, pt. t. clēaf, pp. clofen (= E. cloven). + Du. klieven, Icel. kljūfa (pt. t. klauf), Swed. klyfva, Dan. klöve, G. klieben. Teut. base *kleub; cf. Gk. γλύφειν, to hollow out.

cleft, clift. (Scand.) The old spelling is clift. — Icel. kluft, Swed. klyft, Dan. klöft, a cleft, chink, cave. — Icel. kluf-, weak grade of kljūfa (above); cf. Swed. klyfva, to cleave.

Cleave (2), to stick. (E.) Weak verb. The correct pt. t. is cleaved, not clave, which belongs to the verb above. A. S. clifian, cleofian, pt. t. clifode. + Du. kleven, Swed. klibba sig, G. kleben, to adhere, cleave to. All from Teut. base *klib-, weak grade of Teut. root *kleib-, found in A. S. clīfan (pt. t. clāf), Du. be-klijven, to cleave to. Allied to Clay, Climb.

Clef, a key in music. (F. — L.) F. clef. — L. clāuem, acc. of clāuis, a key.

Cleft; see Cleave (1).

Clematis, a plant. (Gk.) Gk. κληματίς, a creeping plant. — Gk. κληματ-, stem of κλῆμα, a shoot, twig. — Gk. κλάειν, to break off, prune (Brugm. ii. § 661).

Clement. (F. — L.) F. clement. — L. clēmentem, acc. of clēmens, mild.

Clench; see Clinch.

Clerestory, an upper story in a church, furnished with windows. (F. — L.) Old spelling of clear-story. The triforium below is sometimes called the blind-story. See Story (2).

Clerk. (F. — L. — Gk.) A. S. and O. F. clerc. — L. clēricus. — Gk. κληρικός, one of the clergy. — Gk. κλῆρος, a lot; in late Gk., the clergy, whose portion is the Lord, Deut. xviii. 2, 1 Pet. v. 3; cf. Acts i. 17. (St. Jerome.)

clergy. (F. — L.) M. E. clergie, often also (2) ' learning.' — (1) O. F. clergie, as if from L. *clēricia; (2) mod. F. clergé, from Late L. clēricātus, clerkship. — Late L. clēricus, a clerk (above).

Clever. (E.) Cleverly is in Butler's Hudibras, i. 1. 398 (1663). For M. E. cliver, adj., meaning ready to seize, allied to M. E. cliver, a claw, and to Cleave (2). So also E. Fries. klüfer, clever, Dan. dial. klöver, klever (Molbech). ¶ It took the place of M. E. *deliver*, quick, nimble, Ch. prol. 84.—O. F. *dclivre*, free, prompt, alert ; compounded of L. *dē*, prefix, and *līber*, free ; see **Deliver**.

Clew, Clue, a ball of thread. (E.) M. E. *clewe*. A. S. *clīwen*, a clew ; also *clēowe* (Epinal gl. *cleouuae*).+Du. *kluwen*, whence *kluwenen*, to wind on clews (E. *clew* up a sail) ; M. Low G. *kluwen* ; and cf. G. *knäuel* (for **kläuel*), a clew. Perhaps allied to L. *gluere*, to draw together. Cf. **Claw**.

Click. (E.) An imitative word, expressing a lighter and thinner sound than **Clack**. E. Fries. *klikken*. Cf. Du. *klik-klakken*, to clash.

Client. (F.—L.) F. *client*, a suitor.— L. *clientem*, acc. of *cliens = cluens*, orig. a hearer, one who listens to advice ; pres. pt. of *cluere*, to hear. (✓KLEU.)

Cliff, a steep rock, headland. (E.) A. S. *clif*, a rock, cliff.+Du. and Icel. *klif*; O. H. G. *klep*. Cf. G. and Dan. *klippe*, Swed. *klippa*, a crag ; and Icel. *kleif*, a ridge of cliffs.

Climate. (F.—L.—Gk.) M.E. *climat*. —F. *climat*.—Late L. *climat-*, stem of *clima*.—Gk. κλιματ-, stem of κλίμα, a slope, zone, region of the earth, climate.— Gk. κλίνειν, to lean, slope ; see **Lean**.

climacter, a critical time of life. (F. —Gk.) M.F. *climactere*, adj. ; whence *l'an climactere*, ' the climaticall (*sic*) year ; every 7th, or 9th, or the 63 yeare of a man's life, all very dangerous, but the last, most ;' Cot.—Gk. κλιμακτήρ, a step of a ladder, a dangerous period of life.—Gk. κλῖμαк-, stem of κλῖμαξ, a ladder, climax, with suffix -τηρ of the agent ; see below.

climax, the highest degree. (Gk.) Gk. κλῖμαξ, a ladder, staircase, highest pitch of expression (in rhetoric).—Gk. κλίνειν, to slope. Der. *anti-climax*.

clime. (L.—Gk.) L. *clima*, a climate. —Gk. κλίμα ; see **Climate**.

Climb. (E.) M. E. *climben*, pt. t. *clomb*. A. S. *climban*, pt. t. *clamb*, pl. *clumbon*.+ Du. *klimmen*, M.H.G. *klimmen*. Teut. type **klimban-*. The *m* was orig. inserted in the present stem, and did not belong to the root ; as is shewn by Icel. *klifa*, to climb. Hence it is allied to **Cleave** (2).

Clime ; see **Climate**.

Clinch, Clench, to rivet. (E.) M.E. *clenchen*, *klenken*, to strike smartly, to make to clink ; causal of *klinken*, to clink.

Cf. Du. *klink*, a latch, rivet ; also, a blow ; and O. H. G. *klenkan*, to knot or bind together.

Cling. (E.) M. E. *clingen*, to become stiff, be matted together. A.S. *clingan* (pt. t. *clang*, pp. *clungen*), to dry up, shrivel up.+Dan. *klynge*, to cluster. Allied to Swed. *klänga*, to climb ; O. H. G. *clunga*, a clew.

Clinical. (F.—L.—Gk.) F. *clinique*, ' one that is bedrid ;' Cot.—L. *clīnicus*, the same.—Gk. κλινικός, belonging to a bed, a physician ; ἡ κλινική, his art.—Gk. κλίνη, a bed.—Gk. κλίνειν, to lean ; see **Lean** (1).

Clink. (E.) E. Fries. *klinken*. Nasalised form of **Click**.+Du. *klinken*, to sound, pt. t. *klonk*, pp. *geklonken* ; Swed. *klinka*, to jingle. Cf. **Clank**.

clinker, a hard cinder. (Du.) Du. *klinker*, a clinker, named from the tinkling sound which they make when they strike each other.—Du. *klinken*, to clink ; cognate with E. *clink*.

clinquant, glittering. (F.—Du.) In Shak. Lit. ' tinkling.'—F. *clinquant*, pres. pt. of O.F. *clinquer*, to clink.—Du. *klinken* (above).

Clip, to cut. (Scand.) M. E. *klippen*.— Icel. *klippa*, Swed. *klippa*, Dan. *klippe*, to clip, shear hair. Cf. **Snip**. Der. *clipper*, a ' cutter,' a fast vessel.

Clique, a gang. (F.—Du.) F. *clique*, a gang, noisy set.—O. F. *cliquer*, to click, make a noise.—Du. *klikken*, to click, clash ; also to inform, tell ; cf. Du. *klikker*, a tell-tale. See **Click**.

Cloak, Cloke. (F.—C.) M. E. *cloke*.— O. North F. *cloque*, O. F. *cloche*.—Late I.. *cloca*, a bell ; also a horseman's cape, which resembled a bell in shape : see below.

clock. (C.) The orig. sense was ' bell '; bells preceded clocks for notifying times. Either from M. Du. *clocke* (Du. *klok*), a bell ; or from O. North F. *cloque*, a bell.— Late L. *cloc(c)a*, a bell ; of Celtic origin.— Irish *clog*, a bell, clock ; *clogaim*, I ring or sound as a bell ; O. Irish *cloc*, a bell. Cf. W. *cloch*, a bell, &c. The G. *glocke* is a borrowed word ; so also Du. *klok*, &c.

Clod. (E.) M. E. *clod*, *clodde*. A. S. *clod* (in compounds), a lump of earth. Teut. type **klu-do-*, from the weak grade of Teut. root **kleu-*, to stick together. See **Clew, Cloud**. Cf. **Clot**.

Clog, a hindrance ; a wooden sole of a shoe ; wooden shoe. (E.) M. E. *clog*, a log, clump. Not found in A. S. A late word; cf. Dan. *klagge*, mud (Molbech).

Cloister. (F.−L.) M. E. *cloister.*− O. F. *cloistre* (F. *cloître*).−L. *claustrum*, lit. enclosure.−L. *claus·us*, pp. of *claudere*, to shut. See **Clause.**

close (1), to shut in. (F.−L.) M. E. *closen.*−O. F. *clos*, 1 pr. s. of O. F. *clore*, to shut in.−L. *claudere* (above). Der. *close*, a field; *dis-close, en-close, in-close.*

close (2), shut up. (F.−L.) M. E. *clos, cloos.*−O. F. *clos*, pp. of *clore* (above).

closet. (F.−L.) O. F. *closet*, dimin. of *clos*, an enclosed space.−O. F. *clos*, pp. ; see **close** (2).

Clot. (E.) M. E. *clot, clotte*, a ball, esp. of earth. A. S. *clott, clot*, a lump.+ G. *klotz*, a lump. Teut. type **klut-to-*, from the weak grade of Teut. base **kleut* ; see **Cleat, Clout, Cluster.**

Cloth. (E.) M. E. *cloth, clath.* A. S. *clāð.*+Du. *kleed*, G. *kleid*, a dress. Der. *clothes*, A. S. *clāðas*, pl. of *clāð.*

clothe, to cover with a cloth. (E.) M. E. *clothen, clathen*, pt. t. *clothede* (or *cladde*), pp *clothed* (or *clad*). Formed from A. S. *clāð.*+Du. *kleeden*, from *kleed* ; so also G. *kleiden*, from *kleid.* ¶ But the pt. t. and pp. *clad* are of Scand. origin : cf. Icel. *klædd-r*, pp. of *klæða*, to clothe ; Swed. *klädd*, pp. of *kläda.*

Cloud. (E.) M. E. *cloud*, orig. a mass of vapours ; the same word as M. E. *clūd*, a mass of rock. A. S. *clūd*, a round mass, mass of rock, hill. From Teut. root **kleu*, to stick together ; see **Clew, Clod.**

Clough, a hollow in a hill-side. (E.) M. E. *clough, cloȝe.* Answering to A. S. **clōh*, not found ; cognate with O. H. G. *klāh.* The A. S. **clōh* (= O.H. G. *klāh*, as in *Klah-uelde*, Förstemann) represents a Teut. type **klanχo-*, from **klanχ*, 2nd grade of **klinχ*; cf. G. *klinge*, O. H. G. *chlinga*, a clough (Acad., Aug. and Sept. 1889).

Clout, a patch. (E.) M. E. *clout.* A.S. *clūt*, a patch ; whence W. *clwt*, Corn. *clut*, a patch, clout ; Ir. and Gael. *clud*, the same. Orig. sense 'mass, piece of stuff'; orig. type **klūt-oz*, from Teut. root **klūt-*, **kleut-*, as seen in **Clot.** Closely allied to **Cleat** (which is from the 2nd grade of the same root).

Clove (1), a kind of spice. (F.−L.) M. E. *clow* ; the change to *clove*, in the XVIth cent., was due to the influence of Ital. *chiovo.* − F. *clou*, a nail ; *clou de girofle*, 'a clove,' Cot. ; from the semblance to a nail. Cf. Span. *clavo*, a nail, also a clove.−L. *clāuum*, acc. of *clāuus*, a nail.+O. Irish *clo*, a nail.

Clove (2), a bulb, or spherical shell of a bulb of garlic, &c. (E.) A.S. *clufu*, f. ; cf. *cluf-wyrt*, a buttercup (lit. clove-wort). Named from its cleavage into shells.− A. S. *cluf-*, weak grade of *clēofan*, to split; see **Cleave** (1). Cf. Icel. *klofi*, a cleft.

Clove (3), a weight. (F.−L.) A. F. *clou* ; the same word as **Clove** (1).−Late L. *clāvus*, a weight (for wool).

Clover. (E.) M. E. *claver.* A. S. *clāfre, clǣfre*, trefoil.+Du. *klaver*, whence Swed. *klöfver*, Dan. *klöver*; Low G. *klever* ; cf. G. *klee.* ¶ The supposed connexion with *cleave* (1) is impossible.

Clown. (Scand.) Icel. *klunni*, a clumsy, boorish fellow : Swed. dial. *klunn*, a log, *kluns*, a clownish fellow ; Dan. *klunt*, a log; cf. Dan. *kluntet*, clumsy. Allied to **Clump.** Orig. sense 'log' or 'clod.'

Cloy. (F.−L.) Orig. to stop up, hence, to sate. M.F. *cloyer*, 'to cloy, stop up,' Cot.; a by-form of F. *clouer* (O. F. *cloer*), to nail, fasten up. [A horse pricked with a nail, in shoeing, was said to be *cloyed.*]−O. F. *clo*, F. *clou*, a nail; see **Clove** (1). ¶ *Cloy* (in E.) is usually short for *ac-cloy* or *a-cloy*, where the prefix *a-* represents F. *en-* ; see F. *enclouer, enclouer* in Cotgrave.

Club (1), a heavy stick. (Scand.) M.E. *clubbe.* − Icel. *klubba, klumba*, a club; Swed. *klubb*, a club, log, lump; Dan. *klub*, club, *klump*, lump. A mere variant of *Clump* below. See **Golf.**

club (2), an association. (Scand.) XVII cent. Lit. 'a clump of people.' Cf. Swed. dial. *klubb*, a clump, lump, also a knot of people (Rietz). See above.

Cluck. (E.) M. E. *clokken*, to cluck as a hen ; a mere variant of **Clack.**+ Du. *klokken*, Dan. *klukke*, G. *glucken*; L. *glocīre.* An imitative word.

Clue ; see **Clew.**

Clump, a mass, block. (E.) XVI cent. Not in A.S., except as in *clymp-re*, a clump. Cf. Dan. *klump*, Swed. *klump*; Du. *klomp*, Low G. *klump*, a clump, lump, log ; (Icel. *klumba*, a club, with *b* for *p*). From *klump-*, weak grade of Teut. **klemp-*, as in M.H.G. *klimpfen*, to press tightly together. Cf. **Clamp.**

Clumsy. (Scand.) Cf. M. E. *clumsed, clomsed*, benumbed ; benumbed fingers are clumsy. This is the pp. of *clomsen*, to benumb, or to feel benumbed. Cf. Swed. dial. *klummsen*, benumbed (Rietz) ; Icel. *klumsa*, lock-jawed. Cf. Du. *klemmen*, to pinch; *kleumen*, to be benumbed, *kleumsch*, numb with cold ; also A. S. *clom, clam*, a bond, clasp. See **Clammy**.

Cluster, a bunch. (E.) A. S. *cluster*, *clyster*, a bunch. ╋ Low G. *kluster*. Suggests a Teut. type **klut-tro-*, a cluster ; formed with suffix *-tro* from **klut-*, weak grade of Teut. root **kleut-*, to mass together ; for which see **Clot, Cleat, Clout**.

Clutch, to seize. (E.) M. E. *clucchen, clicchen*. A. S. *clyccan* (whence pp. *ge-cliht*, Somner). We find also M. E. *cloke*, a claw; which was superseded by the verbal form.

Clutter, a clotted mass ; also *clutter*, vb., to clot. (E.) *Clutter*, vb., is a variant of *clotter*, to run into clots; see **Clot**, and cf. E. Fries. *klutern*, to become clotted. *Clutter* also meant confusion, a confused heap, turmoil, din ; by association with **Clatter**. Cf. E. Fries. *klöter*, a rattle.

Clyster. (L. – Gk.) L. *clyster*, an injection into the bowels. ━ Gk. *κλυστήρ*, a clyster, syringe. ━ Gk. *κλύζειν*, to wash. ╋ L. *cluere*, to wash. (√KLEU.)

Co-, prefix. (L.) L. *co-*, together ; used for *con-* (=*cum*), together, before a vowel. Hence, *co-efficient, co-equal, co-operate, co-ordinate*. See others below ; and see **Con-**.

Coach. (F. – Hung.) F. *coche*, ' a coach ;' Cot. Etym. disputed. Said, as early as A. D. 1553, to be a Hungarian word ; from Hung. *kocsi*, a coach, so called because first made at a Hung. village called *Kocsi* or *Kocs*, near Raab ; see Littré, and Beckmann, Hist. of Inventions.

Coadjutor. (F. – L.) XV cent. A. F. *coadjutour*. ━ L. *co-*, for *con-* = *cum*, together; and *adiūtor*, an assistant, from vb. *adiu-uāre*, to assist. ━ L. *ad-*, to ; *iuuāre*, to help.

Coagulate, to curdle. (L.) L. *coāgu-lātus*, pp. of *coāgulāre*, to curdle. ━ L. *coāgulum*, rennet, which causes milk to run together. ━ L. *co-* (*cum*), together ; *ag-ere*, to drive.

Coal. (E.) M. E. *col*. A. S. *col*. ╋ Du. *kool*, Icel. Swed. *kol*, Dan. *kul*, G. *kohle*. Cf. Skt. *jval*, to blaze.

Coalesce, to grow together. (L.) L. *coalescere*. ━ L. *co-*, for *con-* = *cum*, together ; and *alescere*, to grow, inceptive of *alere*, to nourish.

Coarse, rough. (F. – L.) Formerly *course*, an adj. which arose from the phrase *in course* to denote anything of an ordinary character; cf. mod. E. *of course*. See **Course**.

Coast. (F. – L.) M. E. *coste*. ━ O. F. *coste* (F. *côte*), a rib, slope of a hill, shore. ━ L. *costa*, a rib.

Coat. (F. – G.) M. E. *cote*. ━ O. F. *cote* (F. *cotte*) ; Low L. *cota, cotta*, a coat. ━ M. H. G. *kotte, kutte*, a coarse mantle; O. Sax. *cot*, the same.

Coax. (E. ?) Formerly *cokes*, vb., from *cokes*, sb., a simpleton, dupe. Perhaps allied to **Cocker** or to **Cockney**.

Cob (1), a round lump, knob. (E.) As applied to a pony, it means short and stout. M. E. *cob*, a great person (Hoccleve). In some senses, it seems to be allied to A. S. *copp*, a top, summit.

cobble (1), a small round lump. (E.) M. E. *cobylstone*, a cobble-stone. Dimin. of *cob* (above).

Cob (2), to beat. (E.) Cf. W. *cobio*, to thump ; *cob*, a bunch ; prov. E. *cop*, to strike, esp. on the *cop* or head. See **Cob** (1).

Cobalt, a mineral. (G.) G. *kobalt*, cobalt ; a nickname given by the miners, because considered poisonous ; better spelt *kobold*, meaning (1) a demon, (2) cobalt. Of G. origin (Kluge).

Cobble (1) ; see **Cob** (1).

Cobble (2), to patch up. (E.) Origin unknown ; cf. **Cob** (2), of which it seems to be the frequentative.

Cobra, a hooded snake. (Port. – L.) Port. *cobra*, also *cobra de capello*, i. e. snake with a hood. ━ L. *colubra*, snake ; *de*, of; *capellum*, acc. of *capellus*, hat, hood, dimin. of *cāpa*, a cape. See Notes and Queries, 7 S. ii. 205.

Cobweb. (E.) M. E. *copweb, coppe-web* ; from M. E. *coppe*, a spider, and *web*. Cf. M. Du. *kop, koppe*, ' a spider, or a cob,' Hexham. From A. S. *coppa*, as in *āttor-coppa*, a spider ; lit. poison-bunch ; from A. S. *āttor, ātor*, poison, and *cop*, a head.

Coca, a Peruvian plant. (Span. – Peruv.) Span. *coca*. ━ Peruv. *cuca*; Garcilasso, Peru, bk. 8. c. 15. Distinct both from *cocoa* (or *coco*) and *cacao*. **Der.** *coca-ine*.

Cochineal. (F. – Span. – L. – Gk.) F. *cochenille*. ━ Span. *cochinilla*, cochineal (made from insects which look like berries). ━ L. *coccinus*, of a scarlet colour ; see Isaiah i. 18 (Vulgate). ━ L. *coccum*, a berry;

also kermes, supposed to be a berry. — Gk. *κόκκος*, a berry, cochineal.

Cock (1), a male bird. (E.) M. E. *cok*. A. S. *cocc* ; from the bird's cry. ' Cryde anon *cok! cok!* ' Ch. C. T. Nun's Priest's Tale, 457. Cf. Skt. *kukkuṭa*, a cock; Malay *kukuk*, crowing of cocks. And cf. **Cuckoo.**

cock, the stop-cock of a barrel, is the same word. So also G. *hahn*, (1) a cock, (2) a stop-cock.

cock, part of the lock of a gun. From its original shape; cf. G. *den Hahn spannen*, to cock a gun.

cockade, a knot of ribbon on a hat. (F.) F. *coquarde*, fem. of *coquard*, saucy ; also *coquarde, bonnet à la coquarde*, ' any bonnet or cap worn proudly;' Cot. Formed with suffix -*ard* from F. *coq*, a cock (from the bird's cry).

cockerel, a young cock. (E.) Double dimin. of **Cock** (1). Cf. *pik-erel*.

cockloft, upper loft. (E. *and* Scand.) From *cock* and *loft*. So also G. *hahnbalken*, a roost, cockloft; Dan. *loftkammer*, a loft-chamber, room up in the rafters.

Cock (2), a pile of hay. (Scand.) Dan. *kok*, a heap; prov. Dan. *kok*, a hay-cock, *at kokke höet*, to cock hay; Icel. *kökkr*, lump, ball; Swed. *koka*, clod of earth.

Cock (3), to stick up abruptly. (E.) Apparently with reference to the posture of a *cock's* head when crowing; or to that of his crest or tail. Cf. Gael. *coc*, to cock; as in *coc do bhoineid*, cock your bonnet ; *coc-shronach*, cock-nosed. And see **Cockade.**

Cock (4), **Cockboat,** a small boat. (F. — L. — Gk.) O. F. *coque*, a kind of boat, orig. a shell. Cf. Span. *coca*, Ital. *cocca*, a small ship. Derived (by Diez) from L. *concha*, a shell; from Gk. *κόγκη*, a cockle ; see **Cockle** (1).

Cockade; see **Cock** (1).

Cockatoo, a kind of parrot. (Malay.) Malay *kakatūa*; from the bird's cry. Cf. Malay *kukuk*, crowing of cocks. Skt. *kukkuṭa*, a cock. See **Cock** (1).

Cockatrice. (F. — Late L. — L.) By confusion with *cock*, it was said to be a monster hatched from a cock's egg. — O.F. *cocatrice*. — Late L. *cōcātrīcem*, acc. of *cōcātrix, caucātrix*, answering to a Latin type **calcātrix*, i. e. ' the treader or tracker,' used to render the Gk. *ἰχνεύμων*, and afterwards transferred to mean ' crocodile' (see account in N. E. D.). — L. *calcā-re*, to

tread; with fem. suffix -*trix*, of the agent.

Cocker, to pamper. (E. ?) M. E. *cokeren* (whence W. *cocri*, to fondle, indulge). Cf. M. Du. *kokelen, keukelen,* ' to cocker, to foster,' Hexham ; M. F. *coqueliner*, ' to dandle, cocker, pamper (a child) ;' Cot. Perhaps from *cock*, as if to make a nestle-cock or chick of.

Cockerel; see **Cock** (1).

Cockle (1), a sort of bivalve. (F. — L. — Gk.) M. E. *cokel*. [Cf. *cock*, a cockle (P. Plowman, C. x. 95) ; A. S. *sǣ-cocca* ; (where *sǣ* = sea).] — F. *coquille*, a cockle-shell ; cf. Ital. *cochiglia*. — Lat. type **cochylium*, for *conchylium*, a cockle, shell-fish. — Gk. *κογχύλιον*, a cockle, dimin. of *κογκύλη*, from *κόγκη*, a cockle or mussel.

Cockle (2), a weed among corn. (E.) A. S. *coccel*, tares; whence Gael. *cogall*, tares, husks, cockle; *cogull*, corn-cockle; Irish *cogall*, corn-cockle.

Cockle (3), to be uneven, pucker up. (Scand.) Of Scand. origin; cf. Norw. *koklutt*, lumpy, uneven, ' cockled up ;' from Norw. *kokle*, a little lump, dimin. of *kok*, a lump; see **Cock** (2). Cf. Swed. *kokkel*, dimin. of *koka*, a clod.

Cockloft; see **Cock** (1).

Cockney, orig. an effeminate person. (E.) Florio has: ' *Caccherelli*, cacklings of hens ; also egs, as we say *cockanegs*.' From M. E. *cokenay*, a foolish person, Ch. C. T. 4208. Lit. ' cocks' egg ;' i.e. yolk-less egg. From M. E. *coken*, gen. pl. of *cok*, a cock ; and *ay, ey*, A. S. *æg*, egg. See C. S. Burne, Shropshire Folk-lore, p. 229.

Cockroach. (Span.) From Span. *cucaracha*, a wood-louse, cockroach ; from *cuca* (also *cuco*), a kind of caterpillar. Origin uncertain.

Cocoa (1), **Coco,** the cocoa-nut palm. (Port.) Port. and Span. *coco*, a bugbear, an ugly mask to frighten children ; hence applied to the cocoa-nut on account of the monkey-like face at the base of the nut. Cf. Span. *cocar*, to make grimaces.

Cocoa (2), a corrupt form of **Cacao.**

Cocoon, case of a chrysalis. (F. — L. — Gk.) F. *cocon*, a cocoon ; from *coque*, a shell. See **Cock** (4).

Cod (1), a fish. (E. ?) Spelt *codde* in Palsgrave. Perhaps named from its rounded shape; cf. M. Du. *kodde*, a club (Hexham) ; and see below. Der. *cod-ling*, a young cod ; M. E. *codlyng*.

Cod (2), a husk, bag, bolster. (E.) Hence, *peas-cod*, husk of a pea. A. S. *codd*, a bag.+Icel. *koddi*, pillow, *koðri*, scrotum; Swed. *kudde*, a cushion.

Coddle, to pamper, render effeminate. (F. – L.?) Perhaps for *caudle*, vb. (in Shak.), to treat with *caudle*; see **Caudle.** Cf. prov. E. *coddle*, to parboil, stew.

Code, a digest of laws. (F.–L.) F. *code.*–L. *cōdicem*, acc. of *cōdex*, a tablet, book; older form *caudex*, a trunk of a tree.

codicil. (L.) L. *cōdicillus*, a codicil to a will; dimin. of *cōdex* (stem *cōdic-*).

Codling (1), **Codlin,** a kind of apple. (C.?) Earlier spellings *querdling, quadling, quodling*. Apparently formed, with E. suffix *-ling*, from Irish *cueirt*, an apple-tree.

Codling (2); see **Cod** (1).

Coerce. (L.) L. *coercēre*, to compel. –L. *co-*(*cum*), together; *arcēre*, to enclose, confine, allied to *arca*, a chest; see **Ark.**

Coffee. (Turk.–Arab.) Turk. *qahveh.*–Arab. *qahwah*, coffee.

Coffer. (F.–L.–Gk.) M. E. *cofre.* –O. F. *cofre*, also *cofin*, a chest.–L. acc. *cophinum.*–Gk. κόφινος, a basket.

coffin. (F.–L.–Gk.) Orig. a case, chest.–O. F. *cofin*, as above. (Doublet of *coffer.*)

Cog (1), a tooth on a wheel-rim. (Scand.) M. E. *cogge* [whence Gael. and Irish *cog*, a mill-cog; W. *cocos, cocs*, cogs of a wheel]. Not in A. S. –M. Dan. *kogge*, a cog, *kogge-hjul*, a cog-wheel (Kalkar); Swed. *kugge*, a cog; M. Swed. *kugg* (Ihre).

Cog (2), to trick. (Scand.) Prob. to catch as with a *cog*; to *cog* a die, to check it so as to make it fall as desired. Cf. Swed. dial. *kugg*, Norw. *kogga*, to dupe; Swed. *kugga*, 'to cheat, to cog;' Öman.

Cogent. (L.) L. *cōgent-*, stem of pres. part. of *cōgere*, to compel; for *co-agere* (=*con-agere*), lit. to drive together. Brugm. i. § 968.

Cogitate. (L.) L. *cōgitātus*, pp. of *cōgitāre*, to think; for *co-agitāre*, from *co-, con-*, together, and *agitāre*, to agitate, frequent. of *agere*, to drive.

Cognate. (L.) L. *co-gnātus*, allied by birth.–L. *co-* (for *cum*), together; *gnātus*, born, old form of *nātus*, pp. of *nasci*, to be born; see **Natal.**

Cognisance, knowledge, a badge. (F. –L.) Formerly *conisaunce.*–O. F. *connoissance*, knowledge; M. F. *cognoissance.* – O. F. *conoissant*, pres. pt. of O. F. *conoistre*, to know. – L. *cognoscere*, to know. – L. *co-* (*cum*), together, fully; *gnoscere*, to know; see **Know.**

cognition, perception. (L.) From acc. of L. *cognitio.*–L. *cognitus*, pp. of *cognoscere* (above).

cognomen, a surname. (L.) L. *cognōmen*, a surname.–L. *co-* (*cum*), with; *nōmen*, a name, altered to *gnōmen* by confusion with *gnoscere, noscere*, to know. See **Noun, Name.**

Cohabit. (L.) L. *co-habitāre*, to dwell together with.–L. *co-* (*cum-*), together; *habitāre*, to dwell. See **Habitation.**

Cohere. (L.) L. *co-hærēre*, to stick together (pp. *cohæsus*).–L. *co-*, together; *hærēre*, to stick. Der. *cohes-ion, cohes-ive*, from the pp.

Cohort, a band of soldiers. (F.–L.) F. *cohorte.*–L. acc. *cohortem*, from *cohors*, a court, also a band of soldiers. See **Court**, of which it is a doublet.

Coif, Quoif, a cap. (F.–G.–L.) O. F. *coife, coiffe*; Low L. *cofea*, a cap.– M. H. G. *kuffe, kupfe*, a cap worn under the helmet; O. H. G. *chuppha*; stem **kupp-jōn-.*–O. H. G. *chuph* (G. *kopf*), a cup; also, the head.–L. *cuppa*; see **Cup.**

Coign; see **Coin.**

Coil (1), to gather together. (F.–L.) 'Coiled up in a cable;' Beaumont and Fletcher. – O. F. *coillir*, to collect. – L. *colligere*; see **Collect.**

Coil (2), a noise, bustle. (F. – L.?) Orig. a colloquial or slang expression; prob. from **Coil** (1). We find 'a *coil* of hay,' a heap; and *coil*, to twist.

Coin. (F.–L.) M. E. *coin.* – O. F. *coin*, a wedge, stamp on a coin, a coin (stamped by means of a wedge). – L. *cuneum*, acc. of *cuneus*, a wedge. Perhaps allied to **Cone.**

coign. (F.–L.) F. *coing, coin*, a corner; lit. a wedge (as above).

Coincide, to agree with. (L.) L. *co-* (for *con-*=*cum*, with); and *incidere*, to fall upon, from *in*, upon, and *cadere*, to fall.

Coistrel, a mean fellow. (F. – L.) For *coustrel*, the older form (Palsgrave). An E. adaptation of M. F. *coustillier*, an armour-bearer, lackey; lit. 'one who carries a poinard.' – M. F. *coustille*, a poniard; variant of O. F. *coustel*, better *coutel*, a knife. – L. *cultellum*, acc. of *cultellus*, a knife; dimin. of *culter*. See Coulter.

Coit; see Quoit.

Coke, charred coal. (E. ?) ' *Coke*, pit-coal or sea-coal charred;' Ray, 1674. Etym. unknown; cf. M. E. *colk*, the core (of an apple).

Colander, Cullender, a strainer. (L.) Equivalent to Med. L. *cōlātōrium*, a strainer; apparently coined from L. *cōlant-*, stem of pres. part. of *cōlāre*, to strain. – L. *cōlum*, a sieve. Or the M. E. *colindore* may have been taken from Span. *colador*, a strainer (from L. *cōlāre*).

Cold. (E.) M. E. *cold, kald*, adj.; O. Merc. *cald*, A. S. *ceald*, adj. + Icel. *kaldr*, Swed. *kall*, Dan. *kold*, Du. *koud*, Goth. *kalds*, G. *kalt*. Teut. **kal-doz*, cold; from Teut. **kal*, to be cold (as in Icel. *kala*, to freeze), with suffix *-doz* = Gk. *-tós*. Cf. Lat. *gel-idus*, cold; see Congeal, Chill, Cool.

Cole, Colewort, cabbage. (L.) For *-wort*, see Wort. M. E. *col, caul*. A. S. *cāul, cāwel* (or Icel. *kāl*). – L. *caulis*, a stalk, cabbage.+Gk. *κανλός*, a stalk.

Coleoptera, sheath - winged insects. (Gk.) Gk. *κολεό-s*, a sheath; *πτερ-όν*, a wing.

Colic. (F. – L. – Gk.) Short for *colic pain.* – F. *colique*, adj. – L. *cōlicus.* – Gk. *κωλικός*, for *κολικός*, suffering in the colon. – Gk. *κόλον*. See Colon (2).

Coliseum. (Med. L. – Gk.) The same as *colossēum*, a large amphitheatre at Rome, so named from its magnitude (Gibbon). The Ital. word is *coliseo*. See Colossus.

Collapse, to shrink together, fall in. (L.) First used in the pp. *collapsed*. Englished from L. *collapsus*, pp. of *collābī*, to fall together. – L. *col-* (for *con-*, i. e. *cum*), together; *lābī*, to slip. See Lapse.

Collar. (F. – L.) M. E. and A. F. *coler.* – O. F. *colier*, a collar. – L. *collāre*, a band for the neck. – L. *collum*, the neck.+ A. S. *heals*, G. *hals*, the neck.

collet, the part of the ring in which the stone is set. (F. – L.) F. *collet*, a collar. – F. *col*, neck. – L. *collum*, neck.

Collateral. (L.) Late L. *collaterālis*, side by side. – L. *col-* (for *com- = cum*), with; *laterālis*, lateral, from *later-*, for **lates-*, stem of *latus*, side.

Collation, a comparison; formerly, a

conference. (F. – L.) O. F. *collation*, a conference. – L. acc. *collātiōnem*, a bringing together, a conferring. – L. *collātum*, supine in use with the verb *conferre*, to bring together (but from a different root). – L. *col-* (for *con- = cum*), together; *lātum*, supine of *tollere*, to take, bear. See Tolerate.

Colleague (1), a partner. (F. – L.) M. F. *collegue.* – L. *collēga*, a partner in office. – F. *col-* (for *con-, cum*), with; *legere*, to choose; see Legend.

Colleague (2), to join in an alliance. (F. – L.) O. F. *colliguer, colleguer*, to colleague with. – L. *colligāre*, to bind together. – L. *col-* (for *con-, cum*), to-gether; *ligāre*, to bind. See League (1).

Collect, vb. (F. – L.) O. F. *collecter*, to collect money (Roquefort). – Late L. *collectāre* (the same), from *collecta*, a collection, orig. fem. of pp. of *colligere*, to collect. – L. *col-* (for *con-, cum*), with; *legere*, to gather; see Legend.

collect, sb. (L.) Late L. *collecta*, a collection in money, an assembly for prayer, hence a short prayer; see above.

Colleen, a girl. (Irish.) Irish *cailin*, a girl; dimin. of *caile*, a country-woman. Gael. *cailin*, dimin. of *caile*.

College, an assembly, seminary. (F. – L.) O.F. *college.* – L. *collēgium*, society of colleagues or companions. – L. *collēga*, a colleague; see Colleague (1).

Collet; see Collar.

Collide. (L.) L. *collīdere*, to dash to-gether. – L. *col-* (for *con-, cum*), together; *lædere*, to strike, hurt. Der. *collis-ion* (from pp. *collīs-us*).

Collie, Colly, a kind of shepherd's dog. (E.) Formerly, *coally, coley*; prob. the same as *coal-y*, coal-coloured, black. Cf. obs. *colly*, adj., coal-black; *collied* in Shak. M. N. D. i. 1. 145.

Collier. (E.) M. E. *colier*; from M.E. *col*, coal. Cf. *bow-yer, saw-yer*.

Collocate, to place together. (L.) From pp. of L. *col-locāre*, to place together. – L. *col-* (for *con-, cum*), together; *locāre*, to place, from *locus*, a place.

Collodion, a solution of gun-cotton. (Gk.) From Gk. *κολλώδ-ης*, glue-like. – Gk. *κόλλ-α*, glue; *-είδης*, like, *είδος*, appearance.

Collop, a slice of meat. (E. ?) M. E. *coloppe, col-hoppe*; pl. *col-hoppes* (P. Plow-man), whence M. Swed. *kollops*, Swed. *kalops*. Here *col-* = coal (see Coal); cf.

Swed. dial. *glö(d)hoppa*, a cake baked over gledes or hot coals. (E. Björkman).

Colloquy. (L.) From L. *colloquium*, conversation. **–** L. *col-loquī*, to converse with, lit. to speak together. **–** L. *col-* (for *con-, cum*), together; *loquī*, to speak.

Collude, to act with others in a fraud. (L.) L. *collūdere* (pp. *collūsus*), to play with, act in collusion with. **–** L. *col-* (for *con-, cum*), with; *lūdere*, to play. Der. *collus-ion*, from the pp.

Colocynth, Coloquintida, pith of the fruit of a kind of cucumber. (Gk.) From the nom. and acc. cases of Gk. κολοκυνθίς (acc. κολοκυνθίδα), a kind of round gourd or pumpkin.

Colon (1), a mark (:) in writing and printing. (Gk.) Gk. κῶλον, a limb, clause; hence, a stop marking off a clause.

Colon (2), part of the intestines. (Gk.) Gk. κόλον, the same.

Colonel. (F. – Ital. – L.) Sometimes *coronel*, which is the Span. spelling; whence the pronunciation as *kurnel*. **–** F. *colonel, colonnel*. **–** Ital. *colonello*, a colonel; lit. a little column, as being ' the upholder of the regiment;' Torriano. The colonel was he who led the company at the head of the regiment. Dimin. of Ital. *colonna*, a column. **–** L. *columna*, a column. See Column.

colonnade. (F. – Ital. – L.) F. *colonnade*. **–** Ital. *colonnata*, a range of columns. **–** Ital. *colonna*, a column (above).

Colony. (F. – L.) F. *colonie*. **–** L. *colōnia*, a colony, band of husbandmen. **–** L. *colōnus*, a husbandman. **–** L. *colere*, to till. *Colere* is for **quelere*; cf. L. *inquilīnus*, a sojourner. Brugm. i. § 121.

Colophon, an inscription at the end of a book, with title, and (sometimes) name and date. (Gk.) Late L. *colophōn*. **–** Gk. κολοφών, a summit; hence, a finishing-stroke. Allied to Column.

Coloquintida; see Colocynth.

Colossus. (L. – Gk.) L. *colossus*. **–** Gk. κολοσσός, a large statue. Der. *coloss-al*, i. e. large; *coliseum*, q.v.

Colour. (F. – L.) M. E. *colour*. **–** O. F. *colour* (F. *couleur*). **–** L. acc. *colōrem*, from *color*, a tint.

Colporteur, a hawker of wares. (F. – L.) Lit. ' one who carries wares on his neck;' F. *colporteur*. **–** F. *colporter*, to carry on the neck. **–** F. *col*, neck; *porter*, to carry. **–** L. *collum*, neck; *portāre*, to carry.

Colt. (E.) A. S. *colt*, a young camel, young ass, &c.+Swed. dial. *kullt*, a boy; Swed. *kull*, Dan. *kuld*, a brood; cf. Dan. dial. *koltring*, a lad.

Columbine, a plant. (F. – L.) M. F. *colombin*. **–** Late L. *columbīna*, a columbine; L. *columbīnus*, dove-like; from a supposed resemblance. **–** L. *columba*, a dove. See Culver.

Column, a pillar, body of troops. (F. – L.) L. *columna*, a pillar; cf. *columen, culmen*, a summit, *collis*, a hill, Gk. κολωνός, a hill. See Hill. (√QEL.)

Colure, one of two great circles on the celestial sphere, at right angles to the equator. (L. – Gk.) So called because a part of them is always beneath the horizon. The word means docked, clipped. **–** L. *colūrus*, curtailed; a colure. **–** Gk. κόλουρος, dock-tailed, truncated; a colure. **–** Gk. κόλ-ος, docked, clipped; and οὐρά, a tail.

Colza oil, a lamp-oil made from the seeds of a variety of cabbage. (F. – L. *and* Du.) F. *colza*, better *colzat*. **–** Du. *koolzaad*, rape-seed, cabbage-seed. **–** Du. *kool* (borrowed from L. *caulis*), cole, cabbage; and Du. *zaad* = E. *seed*.

Com-, prefix. (L.) For L. *cum*, with, together; when followed by *b, f, m, p*. See Con-.

Coma. (Gk.) Gk. κῶμα, a deep sleep.

Comb. (E.) A. S. *camb*, a comb, crest, ridge.+Du. *kam*, Icel. *kambr*, Dan. Swed. *kam*; G. *kamm*. Teut. type **kamboz*; Idg. type **gombhos*; cf. Gk. γόμφος, a pin, peg; Skt. *jambha-s*, a tooth.

Comb, Coomb, a dry measure. (E.) A.S. *cumb*, a cup.+Du. *kom*, a bowl; G. *kumpf, kumme*, a bowl.

Combat. (F. – L.) Orig. a verb. **–** F. *combattre*, O. F. *combatre*, to fight with. **–** F. *com-* (for L. *cum*), with; and F. *battre*, O. F. *batre*, to fight, from **battere*, for L. *battuere*, to beat. Der. *combat-ant*, from the F. pres. pt.

Combe, a hollow in a hill-side. (C.) W. *cwm*, Corn. *cwm*, a hollow, dale; Celtic type **kumbā*, a valley; cf. Irish *cumar*, a valley.

Combine. (L.) L. *combīnāre*, to unite, join two things together. **–** L. *com-* (*cum*). together; and *bīnus*, twofold. See Binary.

Combustion. (F. – L.) F. *combustion*. **–** L. acc. *combustiōnem*, a burning up. **–** L. *combust-us*, pp. of *com-būrere*, to burn up. **–** L. *com-* (for *cum*), together; and (perhaps) *ūrere*, to burn, with *b* inserted by association with *amb-ūrere*.

Come. (E.) A.S. *cuman*, pt. t. *c(w)ōm*, pp. *cumen.*+Du. *komen*, Icel. *koma*, Dan. *komme*, Sw. *komma*, Goth. *kwiman*, G. *kommen*; L. *uen-īre*, (**guen-īre*), Gk. βαίνειν, Skt. *gam*, to go. (✓GwEM.)

Comedy. (F.–L.–Gk.) O.F. *comedie*, 'a play;' Cot.–L. *cōmædia.*–Gk. κωμῳ-δία, a comedy. – Gk. κωμῳδός, a comic actor. – Gk. κῶμο-s, a banquet, revel, festal procession; ἀοιδός, a singer, from ἀείδειν, to sing. A comedy was a festive spectacle, with singing, &c. See **Ode**.

comic. (L.–Gk.) L. *cōmicus.*–Gk. κωμικός, belonging to a κῶμος, as above.

Comely. (E.) M.E. *comli*, *kumli*. A.S. *cymlic*, earlier form *cȳmlic*, beautiful, fair. The A.S. *cȳme*, exquisite, is closely allied to O.H.G. *cūmig*, weak, tender, and to O.H.G. *kūm*, with difficulty (G. *kaum*). The A.S. *ȳ* was shortened before *ml*, and the M.E. *comli* was associated with M.E. *comen*, to come, and so gained the sense of 'becoming,' pleasing, decorous. Cf. M.E. *kime*, a weak person.

Comet. (L.–Gk.) Late A.S. *cometa*. –L. *comēta.*–Gk. κομήτης, long-haired; a tailed star, comet.–Gk. κόμη, hair.+L. *coma*, hair. ¶ Also O.F. *comete*.

Comfit, sb., a sweatmeat. (F.–L.) Formerly *confit*, *confite.*–O.F. *confit*, lit. confected, prepared; pp. of *confire.*–L. *confectum*, pp. of *conficere*, to prepare, put together.–L. *con-* (*cum*), together; *facere*, to make. See **Confect**.

Comfort, vb. (F.–L.) M.E. *con-forten*, later *comforten.*–O.F. *conforter*, to comfort. – Late L. *con-fortāre*, to strengthen. – L. *con-* (*cum*), together; and *fort-is*, strong; see **Force** (1).

Comfrey, a plant. (F.–L.) O.F. *confire*, *cumfirie;* Late L. *cumfiria;* probably for Lat. *conferua* (Pliny), comfrey, a name given to the plant from its supposed healing powers.–L. *conferuēre*, to grow together, heal up (Celsus). – L. *con-* (*cum*), together; *feruēre*, (orig.) to boil. ¶ It was also called *confirma* (from L. *firmāre*, to make firm), and *consolida* (from L. *solidāre*, to make solid).

Comic; see **Comedy**.

Comity, urbanity. (L.) L. *cōmitātem*, acc. of *cōmitās*, urbanity. – L. *cōmis*, friendly, courteous.

Comma. (L.–Gk.) L. *comma.*–Gk. κόμμα, that which is struck, a stamp, a

clause of a sentence, a comma (that marks the clause). – Gk. κόπ-τειν, to hew, strike.

Command. (F. – L.) O.F. *commander*, *comander*. – L. *commendāre*, to entrust to; confused with Late L. *commandāre*, as if an intensive form of *mandāre*, to command. Both forms are from L. *com-* (*cum*), together; and *mandāre*, to put into the hands of, entrust to, command. See **Mandate**.

Commemorate. (L.) From the pp. of L. *commemorāre*, to call to mind.–L. *com-* (for *cum*), together; *memorāre*, to mention, from *memor*, mindful.

Commence. (F.–L.) F.*commencer;* O.F. *comencer* (with one *m*; cf. Ital. *cominciare*). – L. *com-* (*cum*), together; *initiāre*, to begin; see **Initiate**.

Commend. (L.) L. *commendāre*, to entrust or commit to; see **Command**.

Commensurate. (L.) From L. *commensūrātus*, as if from **commensurāre*, to measure in comparison with; a coined word.–L. *com-* (*cum*), with; *mensūra*, a measure; see **Measure**.

Comment, vb. (F.–L.) F.*commenter*. –Late L. *commentāre*, for L. *commentārī*, to consider, make a note on.–L. *com-mentus*, pp. of *comminiscī*, to devise.–L. *com-* (*cum*), with; *-min-* for **men*, to think, as in *me-min-ī* (= **me-men-ī*), I remember, and *men-s*, mind. See **Mental**.

Commerce, traffic. (F.–L.) F. *commerce.*–L. *commercium*, trade.–L. *com-* (=*cum*), with; *merc-*, stem of *merx*, merchandise, with suffix *-i-um*.

Commination, a threatening, denouncing. (F.–L.) F. *commination.*–L. acc. *comminātiōnem*, a threatening.–L. *comminātus*, pp. of *com-minārī*, to threaten. – L. *com-* (*cum*), intensive prefix; and *minārī*, to threaten. See **Menace**.

Commingle. (L. and E.) From Com- and **Mingle**.

Comminution, a reduction to small fragments. (L.) Formed from L. *com-minūt-us*, pp. of *com-minuere*, to break into small pieces; see **Minute**.

Commiseration. (F.–L.) M.F. *commiseration.*–L. acc. *commiserātiōnem*, part of an oration intended to excite pity. –L. *commiserārī*, to excite pity (pp. *-āt-us*). – L. *com-* (*cum*), with; *miserārī*, to pity, from L. *miser*, wretched, pitiable.

Commissary, an officer to whom something is entrusted. (L.) Med. L. *commissārius*, a commissary. – L. *com-*

missus, pp. of *committere*, to commit; see below.

commit, to entrust to. (L.) L. *committere*, to send out, begin, entrust, consign; pp. *commissus.*—L. *com-* (*cum*), with; *mittere*, to send, put forth. **Der.** *commiss-ion*, F. *commission*, from L. acc. *commissiōnem*, perpetration.

Commodious. (F.—L.) O. F. *commodieux*; Med. L. *commodiōsus*, useful.— L. *commodus*, fit, suitable. — L. *com-* (*cum*), with; *modus*, measure.

Commodore, the commander of a squadron. (Du. — F. — L.) Formerly spelt *commandore* (1695); also *commandeur*, as in Dutch; Hexham has: 'den *Commandeur van een Stadt*, The Commandeur of a Towne.'—F. *commandeur*, a commander. — L. acc. type *commandātōrem*, from Late L. *commandāre*; see Command.

Common. (F.—L.) M. E. *commun*, *comoun.* — O. F. *comun.* — L. *commūnis*, common, general. — L. *com-* (*cum*), together with; and *mūnis*, ready to serve (Plautus); cf. *mūnus*, service. (As if 'helping each other.') Cf. Lith. *mainas*, Russ. *miena*, barter. Brugm. i. § 208. **Der.** *commun-ion*, *commun-ity*.

commune, verb. (F. — L.) M. E. *comunen.*—O. F. *communer*, to commune with; Late L. *commūnāre.* — L. *commūnis*, common (above).

communicate. (L.) L. *commūnicātus*, pp. of *commūnicāre.* — L. *commūnis*, common. **Der.** *excommunicate*.

Commotion. (F.—L.) F. *commotion.* —L. *commōtiōnem*, acc. of *commōtio.*—L. *commōt-us*, pp. of *commouēre*, to disturb. —L. *com-* (*cum*), intensive; and *mouēre*, to move. See Move.

Commute, to exchange. (L.) L. *commūtāre*, to exchange with.—L. *com-* (*cum*), with; *mūtāre*, to change.

Compact (1), adj., fastened together, fitted, close, firm. (F.—L.) M. F. *compacte.*—L. *compactus*, fitted together, pp. of *compingere.*—L. *com-* (*cum*), together; *pangere*, to fasten. See Pact.

Compact (2), sb., a bargain, agreement. (L.) L. *compactum*, sb.—L. *compactus*, pp. of *compacisci*, to agree with.— L. *com-* (*cum*), with; *pacisci*, to make a bargain, inceptive form of O. Lat. *pacere*, to agree. See Pact.

Company. (F.—L.) M. E. *companye.* —O. F. *companie.* [Cf. also O. F. *compain*,

a companion, O. F. *companion* (F. *compagnon*), a companion.] — Med. L. *compāniem*, acc. of *compāniēs*, a taking of meals together.—L. *com-* (*cum*), together; and *pānis*, bread; see Pantry. **Der.** *companion*, from O. F. *companion*. Also *accompany*, O. F. *accompaignier*, from F. *a* (for L. *ad*) and O. F. *compaignier*, to associate with, from *compaignie*, company.

Compare, to set together, so as to examine likeness or difference. (F.—L.) F. *comparer.*—L. *comparāre*, to adjust, set together.—L. *compar*, co-equal.—L. *com-* (*cum*), together; *par*, equal.

Compartment. (F.—Ital.—L.) F. *compartiment*, 'a partition;' Cot. — Ital. *compartimento.*—Ital. *compartire*; Late L. *compartīre*, to share. — L. *com-* (*cum*), together; *partīre*, to share, to part, from *parti-*, decl. stem of *pars*, a part.

Compass. (F. — L.) F. *compas*, a circuit, circle, limit; also, a pair of compasses.—Late L. *compassus*, a circuit.—L. *com-* (*cum*), with; *passus*, a pace, step, passage, track; so that *compassus* = a track that joins together, circuit. See Pace. **Der.** *compass*, verb; *compasses*, s. pl., an instrument for drawing circles.

Compassion. (F. — L.) F. *compassion.* — L. *compassiōnem*, acc. of *compassio*, sympathy.—L. *com-* (*cum*), with; *passio*, suffering, from *patī*, to endure.

compatible. (F.—L.) F. *compatible*, 'compatible, concurrable;' Cot. — Late L. *compatibilis*, adj., used of a benefice which could be held together with another.—L. *compatī*, to endure together with. — L. *com-* (*cum*), with; *patī*, to endure.

Compeer, an associate. (F. — L.) M. E. *comper.*—F. *com-*, together; O. F. *per*, a peer, equal. — L. *com-* (*cum*), together; *parem*, acc. of *par*, equal; see Peer.

Compel. (L.) L. *com-pellere*, to compel, lit. to drive together.—L. *com-* (*cum*), together; *pellere*, to drive. **Der.** *compulsion*, from pp. *compuls-us*.

Compendious, brief. (F. — L.) F. *compendieux.*—L. *compendiōsus*, adj., from *compendium*, an abridgment, lit. a saving, sparing of expense. — L. *compendere*, to weigh together. — L. *com-* (*cum*), with; *pendere*, to weigh.

compensate. (L.) From pp. of L. *compensāre*, to weigh one thing against another.—L. *com-* (*cum*), together; *pen-*

sāre, to weigh, frequent. of *pendere*, to weigh (pp. *pensus*).

Compete. (L.) L. *competere*. ‒ L. *com-* (*cum*), together; *petere*, to strive after.

competent. (F.‒L.) M. F. *competent*; orig. pres. part. of *competer*, to be sufficient for. ‒ L. *competere*, to be sufficient for. ‒ L. *com-* (*cum*), with; *petere*, to seek.

competitor. (L.) L. *competītor*, a rival candidate. ‒ L. *com-* (*cum*), with; *petītor*, a seeker, from *petītus*, pp. of *petere*, to seek.

Compile. (F.‒L.) O. F. *compiler*. ‒ L. *compīlāre*, to plunder, pillage, rob; so that the word had, at first, a sinister meaning. ‒ L. *com-* (*cum*), with; *pīlāre*, to rob. See Pill (2).

Complacent. (L.) From stem of pres. pt. of *complacēre*, to please. ‒ L. *com-* (*cum*), intensive; *placēre*, to please.

complaisant. (F. ‒ L.) F. *complaisant*, obsequious, pres. part. of *complaire*, to please. ‒ L. *complacēre*, to please (above).

Complain. (F. ‒ L.) O. F. *complaign-*, a stem of *complaindre*. ‒ Late L. *complangere*, to bewail. ‒ L. *com-* (*cum*), with; *plangere*, to bewail, lit. to strike, beat the breast.

Complement. (L.) L. *complēmentum*, that which completes. ‒ L. *complēre* (below). Doublet, *compliment*.

complete, perfect. (L.) L. *complētus*, pp. of *complēre*, to fulfil. ‒ L. *com-* (*cum*), together; *plēre*, to fill. Allied to *plē-nus*, full. See Plenary.

Complex. (L.) L. *complexus*, entwined round; hence, intricate; pp. of *complectī*, to embrace. ‒ L. *com-* (*cum*), together; and *plectere*, to plait, allied to *plic-āre*, to twine. See Pleach.

complexion. (F. ‒ L.) F. *complexion*, appearance. ‒ L. *complexiōnem*, acc. of *complexio*, a comprehending, compass, habit of body, complexion. ‒ L. *complexus*, pp. of *complectī*, to surround, entwine. ‒ L. *com-* (*cum*), together; *plectere*, to plait.

complicate. (L.) From pp. of L. *complicāre*, to fold together. ‒ L. *com-* (*cum*), together; *plicāre*, to fold.

complicity. (F.‒L.) F. *complicité*, 'a bad confederacy;' Cot. ‒ F. *complice*, a confederate. ‒ L. *complicem*, acc. of *complex*, interwoven, confederate with; see Complex.

Compliance, Compliant; formed with F. suffixes *-ance, -ant*, from the verb to *comply*, which, however, is not of F. origin; see Comply.

Compliment. (F. ‒ Ital. ‒ L.) F. *compliment*. ‒ Ital. *complimento*, compliment, civility. ‒ Ital. *complire*, to fill up, to suit. ‒ L. *complēre*, to fill up; see Complete. Doublet, *complement*.

compline. (F.‒L.) M. E. *complin*, the last church-service of the day; it was orig. an adj. (like *gold-en* from *gold*), and stands for *complin song*; the sb. is *complie* (Ancren Riwle). ‒ O. F. *complie* (mod. F. *complies*, which is pl.), compline. ‒ Late L. *complēta* (sc. *hōra*), fem. of *complētus*, complete; because it completed the 'hours' of the day's service; see Complete.

comply, to yield, accord with. (Ital. ‒ L.) It has no doubt been supposed to be allied to *ply* (whence *compliant*, by analogy with *pliant*), but is quite distinct, and of Ital. origin. ‒ Ital. *complire*, to fill up, fulfil, to suit, 'also to use compliments, ceremonies, or kind offices and offers;' Torriano. Cf. Span. *complir*, to fulfil, satisfy. ‒ L. *complēre*, to fill up; see Complete. Cf. *supply*.

Complot, a conspiracy; see Plot (1).

Component, composing. (L.) L. *compōnent-*, stem of pres. pt. of *compōnere*, to compose. ‒ L. *com-* (*cum*), together; *pōnere*, to put. See Compound.

Comport, to behave, suit. (F.‒L.) F. *se comporter*, to behave. ‒ L. *comportāre*, to carry together. ‒ L. *com-* (*cum*), together; *portāre*, to carry.

Compose. (F. ‒ L. and Gk.) F. *composer*, to compound, make; Cot. ‒ F. *com-* (L. *cum*), together; and F. *poser*, to put, of Gk. origin, as shewn under Pose, q.v. ¶ Distinct from *compound*.

Composition. (F.‒L.) F. *composition*. ‒ L. acc. *compositiōnem*, acc. of *compositio*, a putting together. ‒ L. *compositus*, pp. of L. *compōnere*; see compound.

compost, a mixture. (F.‒L.) O. F. *compost*, a mixture. ‒ L. *compositum*, neut. of *compositus*, pp. of *compōnere* (below).

compound. (F.‒L.) The *d* is excrescent; M. E. *compounen*. ‒ O. F. *ponre* (Bartsch). ‒ L. *compōnere*, to compound, put together. ‒ L. *com-* (*cum*), together; *pōnere*, to put. See Component.

Comprehend. (L.) L. *com-prehendere*, to grasp. ‒ L. *com-* (*cum*), together, and *prehendere*, to seize; see Prehensile.

Compress. (L.) L. *compressāre*, to oppress. — L. *com-* (*cum*), together ; *pressāre*, frequent. of *premere*, to press.

Comprise. (F. — L.) From O. F. *compris*, comprised, comprehended ; pp. of *comprendre*, to comprehend. — L. *comprehendere* ; see **Comprehend**.

Compromise, a settlement by concessions. (F. — L.) F. *compromis*, 'a compromise, mutual promise;' Cot. Orig. pp. of F. *compromettre*, 'to put unto compromise;' Cot. — L. *comprōmittere*, to make a mutual promise. — L. *com-* (*cum*), mutually ; *prōmittere*, to promise ; see **Promise**.

Comptroller, another spelling of *controller* ; see **Control**.

Compulsion. (F. — L.) See **Compel**.

Compunction, remorse. (F. — L.) O. F. *compunction*. — Late L. acc. *compunctiōnem*. — L. *compunctus*, pp. of *compungī*, to feel remorse, pass. of *compungere*, to prick. — L. *com-* (*cum*) ; *pungere*, to prick.

Compute. (L.) L. *computāre*, to reckon. — L. *com-* (*cum*), together ; *putāre*, to clear up, reckon. Doublet, *count* (2).

Comrade. (F. — Span. — L.) F. *camarade*. — Span. *camarada*, a company ; also an associate, comrade. — Span. *camara*, a chamber, cabin. — L. *camera*, a chamber.

Con (1), to study, peruse, scan. (E.) M. E. *cunnen* ; A. S. *cunnian*, to test. Allied to A. S. *cunnan*, to know ; see **Can** (1). Der. *ale-conner*, i. e. ale-tester.

Con (2), short for *contra*, against. (L.) In the phrase ' pro and *con*.'

Con-, *prefix*. (L.) For *com-* (*cum*), with, when the following letter is *c, d, g, j, n, q, s, t,* or *v*. Before *b, m, p,* it is *com-* ; before *l, col-* ; before *r, cor-* ; before *f, m* or *n*.

Concatenate. (L.) L. *concatēnātus*, pp. of *concatēnāre*, to link together. — L. *con-* (*cum*), together ; *catēna*, a chain.

Concave. (F. — L.) F. *concave*. — L. *concauus*, hollow. — L. *con-* (*cum*), with, together ; *cauus*, hollow.

Conceal. (F. — L.) O. F. *conceler*. — L. *concēlāre*, to hide. — L. *con-* (*cum*), completely ; *cēlāre*, to hide. See **Helm** (2).

Concede. (L.) L. *concēdere*, to retire, yield. — L. *con-* (*cum*), together ; *cēdere*, to yield. Der. *concess-ion* (from pp. *concessus*).

Conceit. (F. — L.) M. E. *conceit, conceite*. Formed as if from the pp. of O. F.

concevoir, to conceive, though the real pp. was *conceu* (F. *conçu*) ; by analogy with *deceit*, q.v. See below.

conceive. (F. — L.) M. E. *conceven, conceiven*. — A. F. *conceiv-*, a stem of O. F. *concever, concevoir*, to conceive. — L. *concipere*, to conceive. — L. *con-* (*cum*), altogether ; *capere*, to take.

conception. (F. — L.) F. *conception*. — L. *conceptiōnem*. — L. *concept-us*, pp. of *concipere*, to conceive (above).

Concentre, to draw to a centre. (F. — L. *and* Gk.) F. *concentrer*. — L. *con-* (*cum*), together ; and *centr-um*, a centre, from Gk. κέντρον ; see **Centre**. Der. *concentr-ic, concentr-ate* (modern).

Concern, vb. (F. — L.) F. *concerner*. — L. *concernere*, to mix ; in Late Lat., to refer to, regard. — L. *con-* (*cum*), with ; and *cernere*, to separate, decree, observe. + Gk. κρίνειν, to separate, decide ; Lith. *skir-ti*, to separate, distinguish. Brugm. ii. § 612. (√SKER.)

concert. (F. — Ital. — L.) Often confused with *consort* in old writers. — F. *concerter*, ' to consort, or agree together ;' Cot. — Ital. *concertare*, ' to agree or tune together, sing in consort,' Florio ; cf. *concerto*, sb., agreement. The Ital. forms shew that it was derived from L. *concertāre*, to contend, struggle together ; indeed, we find also Span. *concertar*, to settle or adjust, covenant, bargain ; which also points to the same origin. [It would seem that the L. vb. took up the sense of to settle by debate, and so, to agree.] — L. *con-* (*cum*), together ; *certāre*, to contend, vie with ; orig. ' to decide by contest ;' frequent. of *cernere*, to decide. See **Concern**. Der. *concert*, sb., *concert-ina*.

Concession. (F. — L.) F. *concession*. — L. acc. *concessiōnem*. — L. *concessus*, pp. of *concēdere*, to concede ; see **Concede**.

Conch, a marine shell. (L. — Gk.) L. *concha*. — Gk. κόγχη (also κόγκος), a cockleshell. + Skt. *çaṅkha*, a conch. Der. *conchology* (from κόγκο-s).

Conciliate. (L.) From the pp. of L. *conciliāre*, to bring together, conciliate. — L. *concilium*, a council ; see **Council**.

Concise. (F. — L. ; *or* L.) F. *concis*. — L. *concīsus*, brief, cut short ; pp. of *concīdere*. — L. *con-* (*cum*), intensive ; *cædere*, to cut. Der. *concis-ion*.

Conclave. (F. — L.) F. *conclave*, a small room (to meet in). — L. *conclāue*, a room ; later, a place of assembly of cardinals, assembly. Orig. a locked up place. — L. *con-* (*cum*), together ; *clāuis*, a key.

Conclude. (L.) L. *conclūdere*, to shut up, close, end. — L. *con-* (*cum*), together ; and *-clūdere* = *claudere*, to shut. Der. *conclus-ion*. Similarly *ex-clude*, *in-clude*, *pre-clude*, *se-clude* ; whence *in-clus-ive*, *pre-clus-ion*, *se-clus-ion* (from pp. *-clūsus* = *clausus*).

Concoct. (L.) From L. *concoctus*, pp. of *concoquere*, to cook together, digest. — L. *con-* (*cum*) ; *coquere*, to cook.

Concomitant, accompanying. (L.) From L. *con-* (*cum*), together ; and *comitant-em*, acc. of pres. pt. of *comitāri*, to accompany, from *comit-*, stem of *comes*, a companion ; see Count (1).

Concord. (F. — L.) F. *concorde.* — L. *concordia*, agreement. — L. *concord-*, stem of *con-cors*, agreeing. — L. *con-* (*cum*) ; *cor* (stem *cord-*), the heart.

concordant. (F. — L.) F. *concord-ant*, pres. pt. of *concorder*, to agree. — L. *concordāre*, to agree. — L. *concord-* (above).

concordat. (F. — L.) F. *concordat*, an agreement. — Late L. *concordātum*, a convention, thing agreed on, esp. between the pope and F. kings ; pp. of *concordāre*, to agree (above).

Concourse. (F. — L.) F. *concours.* — L. acc. *concursum*, a running together. — L. *concursus*, pp. of *con-currere*, to run together. — L. *con-* (*cum*), together ; and *currere*, to run. See Concur.

Concrete, formed into one mass. (L.) L. *concrēt-us*, pp. of *concrescere*, to grow together. — L. *con-* (*cum*), together ; *crescere*, to grow.

Concubine. (F. — L.) O. F. *concubine.* — L. *concubīna.* — L. *con-* (*cum*), together ; *cubāre*, to lie.

Concupiscence. (F. — L.) F. *concupiscence.* — L. *concupiscentia*, desire. — L. *concupiscere*, to desire ; inceptive form of *concupere.* — L. *con-* (*cum*), intensive ; and *cupere*, to long for.

Concur. (L.) L. *concurrere*, to run together, agree. — L. *con-* (*cum*), together ; *currere*, to run. Der. *concourse*.

Concussion. (F. — L.) F. *concussion.* — L. *concussiōnem*, acc. of *concussio*, a violent shaking. — L. *concussus*, pp. of *concutere*, to shake together. — L. *con-* (*cum*), together ; *quatere*, to shake.

Condemn. (F. — L.) O. F. *condemner.* — L. *condemnāre*, to condemn wholly, pro-

nounce to be guilty. — L. *con-* (*cum*), wholly ; *damnāre*, to condemn.

Condense. (F. — L.) F. *condenser.* — L. *condensāre.* — L. *condensus*, very thick. — L. *con-* (*cum*), very ; *densus*, thick, dense.

Condescend. (F. — L.) F. *condescendre.* — Late L. *condēscendere*, to grant (lit. to descend with). — L. *con-* (*cum*), with ; *dēscendere*, to descend ; see Descend. Der. *condescens-ion*, from the pp.

Condign, well merited. (F. — L.) O. F. *condigne.* — L. *condignus*, very worthy. — L. *con-* (*cum*), very ; *dignus*, worthy.

Condiment. (L.) L. *condīmentum*, seasoning, sauce. — L. *condīre*, to season, spice, preserve (as fruit).

Condition. (F. — L.) F. *condition.* — L. *conditiōnem*, acc. of *conditio*, a late spelling of *condicio*, a covenant, condition. — L. *condīcere*, to talk over together, agree upon. — L. *con-* (*cum*), together ; *dīcere*, to speak.

Condole. (L.) L. *condolēre*, to grieve with. — L. *con-* (*cum*), with ; *dolēre*, to grieve.

Condone. (L.) L. *condōnāre*, to remit, pardon. — L. *con-* (*cum*), wholly ; *dōnāre*, to give ; see Donation.

Condor, a large bird. (Span. — Peruvian.) Span. *condor.* — Peruv. *cuntur*, a condor.

Conduce. (L.) L. *condūcere*, to draw together towards, lead to. — L. *con-* (*cum*), together ; *dūcere*, to lead.

conduct, sb. (L.) Late L. *conductus*, defence, protection, guard, escort. — L. *conductus*, pp. of *con-dūcere* (above).

conduit. (F. — L.) M. E. *conduit.* — O. F. *conduit*, a conduit. — Late L. *conductus*, a defence, escort ; also, a canal, tube ; see above.

Cone. (F. — L. — Gk.) M. F. *cone.* — L. *cōnus.* — Gk. κῶνος, a cone, peak, peg. + Skt. *çāna-s*, a whetstone ; cf. L. *cōs*, the same. See Hone. Brugm. i. § 401.

Coney ; see Cony.

Confabulate. (L.) From pp. of L. *confābulāri*, to talk together. — L. *con-* (*cum*), with ; *fābulāri*, to converse, from *fābula*, a discourse ; see Fable.

Confect, to make up into sweetmeats. (L.) L. *confectus*, pp. of *conficere*, to put together, make up. — L. *con-* (*cum*), together ; *facere*, to put. Der. *confect-ion*, *confection-er*. See Comfit.

Confederate. (L.) L. *confœderātus*, united by a covenant, pp. of *confœderāre*.

— L. *con-* (*cum*), together; *fœder-*, for *fœdes-*, stem of *fœdus*, a treaty. See Federal.

Confer. (L.) From L. *conferre*, to bring together, collect, bestow. — L. *con-* (*cum*), together; *ferre*, to bring, bear. ¶ Not from F.

Confess. (F.—L.) O. F. *confesser.* — Late L. *confessāre.* — L. *confessus*, pp. of *confitēri*, to confess. — L. *con-* (*cum*), fully; *fatēri*, to acknowledge, allied to *fārī*, to speak. Cf. Gk. φάτις, a speech. Brugm. i. § 195.

Confide. (L.) L. *confīdere*, to trust fully. — L. *con-* (*cum*), fully; *fīdere*, to trust, allied to *fides*, faith; see Faith.

Configuration. (F. — L.) F. *configuration.* — L. *configūrātiōnem*, a conformation. — L. *configūrātus*, pp. of *configūrāre*, to put together. — L. *con-* (*cum*); *figūrāre*, to fashion, from *figūra*, a figure. See Figure.

Confine, to limit. (F.—L.) F. *confiner*, to keep within limits. — M. F. *confin*, near; Cot. — L. *confinis*, bordering on. — L. *con-* (*cum*), with; *fīnis*, boundary. See Final. ¶ Mod. F. has only *confins*, sb. pl., confines; representing O. F. *confines*, L. *confinia*, pl.; whence E. *confines*, pl.

Confirm. (F.—L.) M. E. *confermen.* — O. F. *confermer.* — L. *confirmāre*, to make firm, strengthen. — L. *con-* (*cum*), fully; *firmāre*, to strengthen, from *firmus*, firm.

Confiscate, to adjudge to be forfeit. (L.) L. *confiscātus*, pp. of *confiscāre*, to lay by in a coffer, to confiscate, transfer to the treasury. — L. *con-* (*cum*); *fiscus*, a purse.

Conflagration. (F. — L.) F. *conflagration.* — L. acc. *conflāgrātiōnem*, a great burning. — L. *con-* (*cum*), together; *flāgrāre*, to burn. See Flagrant.

Conflict, an encounter. (L.) L. *conflictus*, a striking together; from the pp. of *conflīgere*, to strike together. — L. *con-* (*cum*), together; *flīgere*, to strike.

Confluent. (L.) From stem. of pres. pt. of *con-fluere*, to flow together; see Flueht. So also *conflux*, sb., from the pp. *confluxus*.

Conform. (F.—L.) F. *conformer.* — L. *conformāre*, to fashion like. — L. *con-*, together; *formāre*, to form, from *forma*, form.

Confound. (F.—L.) F. *confondre.* —

L. *confundere*, to pour together, confound. — L. *con-* (*cum*), together; *fundere*, to pour. See Fuse (1).

Confraternity. (F.—L.) From L. *con-* (*cum*), with; and Fraternity, q v.

Confront. (F.—L.) F. *confronter*, to bring face to face. — Med. L. *confrontārī*, to be near to. — L. *con-* (*cum*), together; *front-*, stem of *frons*, forehead, front.

Confuse. (L.) M. E. *confus*, used as a pp. in Chaucer. — L. *confūsus*, pp. of *confundere*, to confound; see Confound.

Confute. (F.—L.) F. *confuter.* — L. *confūtāre*, to cool by mixing cold water with hot, to allay, also to confute. — L *con-* (*cum*), together; **fūtāre*, to pour out (?); cf. *fūtis*, a water-vessel to pour from, from the L. base *fū-*, to pour. Brugm. i. § 605. See Futile, Refute and Fuse (1).

Congeal. (F.—L.) F. *congeler.* — L. *congelāre*, to cause to freeze together. — L. *con-*, together; *gelāre*, to freeze, from *gelu*, frost. See Gelid.

Congee, Congé, leave to depart. (F. —L.) F. *congé*, ' leave, dismission ; ' Cot. O. F. *congie*, *cunge*, *congiet* (Burguy); the same as Prov. *comjat.* — Late L. *comiātus*, leave, permission (VIII cent.); the same as L. *commeātus*, a travelling together, also leave of absence. — L. *com-* (*cum*), together; *meātus*, a course, from pp. of *meāre*, to go.

Congenial, kindred. (L.) Coined from L. *con-* (*cum*), with; and *genial*, adj. from L. *genius*; see Genial.

Congenital. (L.) Coined by adding *al* to the obs. word *congenite* (XVII cent.). — L. *congenitus*, born with. — L. *con-* (*cum*), with; *genitus*, born, pp. of *gignere*, to produce. See Genital.

Conger, a sea-eel. (F. — L. — Gk.) M. E. *congre.* — O. F. *congre.* — L. *congrum*, acc. of *congrus*, by-form of *conger*, a sea-eel. — Gk. γόγγρος, the same.

Congeries, a mass of particles. (L.) L. *congeriēs*, a heap. — L. *congerere*, to bring together. — L. *con-* (*cum*), together; *gerere*, to carry.

congestion, accumulation. (L.) From L. acc. *congestiōnem.* — L. *congestus*, pp. of *congerere* (above).

Conglobe, to form into a globe. (L.) L. *con-globāre.* — L. *con-* (*cum*), together; *globus*, a globe.

Conglomerate. (L.) From pp. of *conglomerāre*, to wind into a ball, heap together. — L. *con-* (*cum*), together; and *glomer*-, for *glomes-, stem of *glomus*, a ball, clew of yarn.

Conglutinate. (L.) From pp. of L. *conglūtināre*, to glue together. — L. *con*- (*cum*), together; *glūtināre*, to glue, from *glūtin*-, stem of *glūten*, glue.

Congou, a kind of tea. (Chinese.) In the Amoy dialect, called *kang-hu tê*, where *kang-hu* is lit. 'work, labour;' i. e. tea on which labour has been expended (Douglas). The true Chinese is *kung-fu ch'a*, with the same sense.

Congratulate. (L.) From pp. of L. *congrātulārī*, to wish much joy. — L. *con*- (*cum*), fully; *grātulārī*, to wish joy, from adj. *grātus*, pleasing. See **Grace.**

Congregate. (L.) From pp. of L. *congregāre*, to collect into a flock. — L. *con*- (*cum*), together; *gregāre*, to assemble a flock, from *greg*-, stem of *grex*, a flock.

Congress, a meeting together. (L.) L. *congressus*. — L. *congressus*, pp. of *congredī*, to meet together. — L. *con*-, together; *gradī*, to advance, walk.

Congrue, to agree, suit. (L.) L. *congruere*, to suit. (Root uncertain.) Der. *congru-ous*, from L. *congruus*, suitable; *congru-ity*.

Conjecture. (F. — L.) F. *conjecture*. — L. *coniectūra*, a casting together, a guess. — L. *coniectus*, pp. of *conicere*, to throw or put together. — L. *con*- (*cum*), together; *iacere*, to throw.

Conjoin. (F. — L.) O. F. *conjoindre*. L. *coniungere* (pp. *coniunctus*), to join together. — L. *con*- (*cum*), together; *iungere*, to join. See **Join.** Der. *conjunction*, *conjunct-ive*, from the pp.

conjugal, relating to marriage. (F. — L.) F. *conjugal*. — L. *coniugālis*, adj. — L. *coniugem*, acc. of *coniux*, a spouse. — L. *con*-, together; *iug*-, allied to *iungere*, to join, *iugum*, a yoke; see **Join.**

conjugation. (L.) From L. *coniugātio*, a conjugation (Priscian); lit. a yoking together. — L. *coniugātus*, pp. of *coniugāre*, to yoke together. — L. *con*- (*cum*), together; *iug-um*, a yoke.

Conjure. (F. — L.) M. E. *coniuren*. — F. *conjurer*. — L. *coniūrāre*, to swear together, combine by oath. — L. *con*-, together; *iūrāre*, to swear; see **Jury.**

Connect. (L.) L. *connectere*, to tie together. — L. *con*- (*cum*), together; and *nectere*, to bind (pp. *nexus*). Der. *con-nex-ion* [not *connection*], from the pp.

Connive. (F. — L.) F. *conniver*. — L. *connīuēre*, to close the eyes at, overlook. — L. *con*- (*cum*), together; and *nīguere, to wink; cf. *nic-tāre*, to wink. + Goth. *hneiwan*, to bow; Brugm. i. § 664.

Connoisseur, a critical judge. (F. — L.) F. *connaisseur*, formerly *connoisseur*, a knowing one. — O. F. *connoiss-ant*, pres. pt. of O. F. *conoistre*; see **Cognisance.**

Connubial. (L.) L. *connūbiālis*, relating to marriage. — L. *co*(*n*)*nūbium*, marriage. — L. *con*- (*cum*), with; *nūbere*, to marry. See **Nuptial.**

Conquer. (F. — L.) M. E. *conqueren*. — O. F. *conquerre*. — L. *conquīrere*, to seek after, go in quest of; in Late L., to conquer. — L. *con*- (*cum*), with; *quærere*, to seek. Der. *conquest*, M. E. *conqueste*, from Late L. *conquesta*, L. *conquīsīta*, fem. of *conquīsītus*, pp. of *conquīrere*.

Consanguineous. (L.) From L. *consanguine-us*, related by blood, with suffix *-ous*. — L. *con*- (*cum*), together; *sanguin*-, stem of *sanguis*, blood.

Conscience. (F. — L.) F. *conscience*. L. *conscientia*, consciousness. — L. *conscient*-, stem of pres. pt. of *conscīre*, to know along with. — L. *con*- (*cum*), with; *scīre*, to know. See **Science.** Der. *conscionable*, an ill-contrived word, used as a contraction of *conscien*(*ce*)-*able*.

conscious. (L.) From L. *consci-us*, aware, with suffix *-ous*. — L. *conscīre*, to be aware of (above).

Conscript. (L.) L. *conscriptus*, enrolled, pp. of *conscrībere*, to write down together. — L. *con*- (*cum*), together; *scrībere*, to write.

Consecrate. (L.) From pp. of L. *consecrāre*, to render sacred. — L. *con*- (*cum*), with, wholly; *sacrāre*, to consecrate; see **Sacred.**

Consecutive. (F. — L.) M. F. *consecutif*, Cot. Formed with suffix *-if* (L. *-īuus*) from L. *consecūt-us*, pp. of *consequī*, to follow together. — L. *con*- (*cum*), together; *sequī*, to follow. See **Sequence.**

consequent. (L.) L. *consequent*-, stem of pres. pt. of *consequī* (above).

Consent, vb. (F. — L.) F. *consentir*. — L. *consentīre*, to agree to. — L. *con*- (*cum*), with; *sentīre*, to feel. See **Sense.**

Conserve, vb. (F. — L.) F. *conserver*. — L. *conseruāre*, to preserve. — L. *con*- (*cum*), fully; *seruāre*, to keep. Der. *conserve*, vb; *conserv-atory*. See **Serve.**

Consider. (F. — L.) O. F. *considerer*.

—L. *consīderāre*, to consider, orig. to contemplate the stars (Festus). **—** L. *con-* (*cum*), together; *sīder-*, for **sīdes-*, stem of *sīdus*, a star.

Consign. (F.—L.) F. *consigner.* **—** L. *consignāre*, to attest, register, record. **—** L. *con-* (*cum*), together; *signāre*, to mark; see **Sign.**

Consist. (F.—L.) F. *consister*, to consist, rest, abide, &c. **—** L. *consistere*, to stand together, consist. **—** L. *con-* (*cum*), together; *sistere*, causal form from *stāre*, to stand; see **State.** Der. *consistory.*

Console. (F.—L.) F. *consoler.* **—** L. *consōlārī*, to comfort. **—** L. *con-* (*cum*), with; *sōlārī*, to comfort; see **Solace.**

Consolidate. (L.) From pp. of L. *consolidāre*, to render solid. **—** L. *con-* (*cum*), together; *solidāre*, to make solid, from *solidus*, solid. Der. *consols*, a familiar abbreviation for *consolidated annuities.*

Consonant, agreeing with. (F.—L.) F. *consonant*, accordant; Cot. **—** L. *consonant-*, stem of pres. pt. of *consonāre*, to sound together. **—** L. *con-* (*cum*), together; *sonāre*, to sound; see **Sound** (3).

Consort, sb. (F.—L.) F. *consort.* **—** L. *consort-*, stem of *consors*, one who shares property with another, a partner. **—** L. *con-* (*cum*), together; *sort-*, stem of *sors*, a lot, share. See **Sort.**

Conspicuous. (L.) L. *conspicu-us*, visible, with suffix *-ous*. **—** L. *conspicere*, to see thoroughly. **—** L. *con-*, fully; *specere*, to see. See **Species.**

Conspire. (F.—L.) F. *conspirer.* **—** L. *conspīrāre*, to breathe together, combine, plot. **—** L. *con-* (*cum*), together; *spīrāre*, to breathe.

Constable, a peace-officer. (F.—L.) O. F. *conestable* (F. *connétable*). **—** L. *comes stabulī*, lit. ' count of the stable,' the title of a dignitary of the Roman empire and afterwards in use among the Franks. See **Count** (1) and **Stable.**

Constant, firm. (F.—L.) F. *constant.* **—** L. *constant-*, stem of *constans*, firm; orig. pres. pt. of *constāre*, to stand together. **—** L. *con-* (*cum*), together; *stāre*, to stand; see **State.**

Constellation. (F.—L.) F. *constellation.* **—** L. acc. *constellātiōnem*, cluster of stars. **—** L. *con-* (*cum*), together; *stellāt-us*, pp. of *stellāre*, to set with stars, from *stella*, a star. See **Star.**

Consternation. (F.—L.) F. *con-*

sternation. **—** L. acc. *consternationem*, fright. **—** L. *consternātus*, · pp. of *consternāre*, to frighten; intensive form of *consternere*, to bestrew, throw down. **—** L. *con-* (*cum*), together; *sternere*, to strew; see **Stratum.**

Constipate. (L.) From pp. of L. *constīpāre*, to join closely, press together. **—** L. *con-* (*cum*), together; *stīpāre*, to press, cram.

Constitute. (L.) L. *constitūtus*, pp. of *constituere*, to cause to stand together, establish. **—** L. *con-* (*cum*), together; *statuere*, to set up, denom. vb. from *status*, a position; see **Statute.**

Constrain, to compel. (F.—L.) O. F. *constraign-*, a stem of *constraindre*, later *contraindre*. **—** L. *constringere*, to bind together, fetter. **—** L. *con-* (*cum*), together; *stringere*, to draw tight.

Construct. (L.) From L. *constructus*, pp. of *construere* (below).

construe. (L.) L. *construere*, to heap together, build, construct; in Late L., to construe a passage. **—** L. *con-* (*cum*), together; *struere*, to pile, build. Der. *mis-construe.*

Consul. (L.) L. *consul*, a consul. Etym. doubtful; but allied to *consulere*, to consult: see below.

consult. (F.—L.) F. *consulter.* **—** L. *consultāre*, to consult; frequent. form of *con-sulere*, to consult. Root uncertain; prob. allied to *sedēre*, to sit; cf. *solium*, a seat.

Consume. (L.) L. *consūmere*, lit. to take up wholly. **—** L. *con-* (*cum*), together, wholly; *sūmere*, to take up, from **sups-*, allied to *sub*, under, up, and *emere*, to take, buy. Brugm. i. § 240. Der. *consumption*, from the pp.

Consummate. (L.) From pp. of L. *consummāre*, to bring into one sum, to perfect. **—** L. *con-* (*cum*), together; *summāre*, to sum, from *summa*, a sum; see **Sum.**

Consumption; see **Consume.**

Contact, sb. (L.) L. *contactus*, a touching. **—** L. *contactus*, pp. of *contingere*, to touch closely; see **Contingent.**

contagion. (F.—L.) F. *contagion.* **—** L. *contāgiōnem*, acc. of *contāgio*, a touching, hence contagion. **—** L. *con-* (*cum*), with; *tāg-*, 2nd grade of *tag-*, as in **tagtus* (>*tac-tus*), pp. of *tangere*, to touch.

Contain. (F.—L.) From a tonic stem of O. F. *contenir.* **—** L. *continēre*, to hold together, contain; pp. *contentus.* − L. *con-* (*cum*), together; *tenēre*, to hold.

Contaminate. (L.) From pp. of L. *contăminăre*, to defile. − L. *contămin-*, stem of *contămen*, contagion; which stands for **contagmen*. − L. *con-* (*cum*); *tag-*, as in *tactus*, for **tag-tus*, pp. of *tangere*, to touch. Brugm. i. § 768.

Contemn. (F. − L.) M. F. *contemner.* − L. *contemnere*, to despise. − L. *con-* (*cum*), with, wholly; *temnere*, to despise.

contempt. (F. − L.) M. F. *contempt*; Cot. − L. *contemptus*, scorn. − L. *contemptus*, pp. of *contemnere* (above).

Contemplate. (L.) From pp. of *contemplāri*, to observe, consider; used at first of augurs. − L. *con-* (*cum*); *templum*, an open space for observation (by augurs); see **Temple.**

Contemporaneous. (L.) L. *contemporāne-us*, adj., at the same time; with suffix *-ous*. − L. *con-* (*cum*), with; *tempor-*, for **tempos-*, stem of *tempus*, time.

contemporary. (L.) L. *con-*, with; and L. *temporārius*, temporary, adj., from *tempor-* (above).

Contend. (F. − L.) O. F. *contendre.* − L. *contendere*, to stretch out, exert, fight. − L. *con-* (*cum*), fully; *tendere*, to strive. Der. *content-ion* (from the pp. *contentus*).

Content, adj. (F. − L.) F. *content*, satisfied. − L. *contentus*, content; pp. of *continēre*; see **Contain.** Der. *dis-content.*

Contest, vb. (F. − L.) F. *contester.* − L. *contestāri*, to call to witness, to bring an action. − L. *con-* (*cum*), together; *tes-tāri*, to witness, from *testis*, a witness. Der. *contest*, sb.

Context. (L.) L. *contextus*, a joining together, order (hence, context of a book). − L. *contextus*, pp. of *contexere*, to weave together. − L. *con-* (*cum*), together; *texere*, to weave.

Contiguous. (L.) L. *contigu-us*, that may be touched, near; with suffix *-ous*. − L. *con-* (*cum*), with; and *tag-*, as in *tac-tus* (for **tag-tus*), pp. of *tangere*, to touch; see **Contingent.**

Continent. (F. − L.) F. *continent*, adj., moderate. − L. *continent-*, stem of pres. pt. of *continēre*; see **Contain.**

Contingent, dependent on. (L.) From stem of pres. pt. of *contingere*, to touch, relate to. − L. *con-* (*cum*); *tangere*, to touch. See **Tangent.**

Continue. (F. − L.) F. *continuer.* − L. *continuāre*, to continue. − L. *continuus* (below). Der. *dis-continue.*

continuous. (L.) L. *continu-us*, lit. holding together; with suffix *-ous*. − L. *continēre*, to hold together, contain. See **Contain.**

Contort. (L.) L. *contortus*, pp. of *contorquēre*, to twist together. − L. *con-* (*cum*), together; *torquēre*, to twist.

Contour, an outline. (F. − Ital. − L.) F. *contour*, esp. in an artistic sense. − Ital. *contorno*, a circuit; *contornare*, 'to encircle;' Florio. − L. *con-* (*cum*), together; *tornāre*, to round off, to turn; see **Turn.**

Contra-, prefix. (L.) L. *contrā*, against; orig. the abl. fem. of an obs. adj. **con-t(e)r-us*, a comparative form from *con-*, prep. together; cf. *extrā* from *exterus*.

Contraband. (Span. − Ital. − L. and Teut.) Span. *contrabando*, prohibited goods. − Ital. *contrabbando*, prohibited goods. − Ital. *contra* (= L. *contrā*), against; *bando*, a ban, from Late L. *bannum*, a word of Teut. origin, viz. from O. H. G. *ban*, a command. See **Ban.**

Contract (1), to draw together. (L.) L. *contractus*, pp. of *contrahere*, to draw together. − L. *con-* (*cum*), together; *trahere*, to draw.

contract (2), a bargain. (F. − L.) M. F. *contract*; Cot. − L. *contractum*, acc. of *contractus*, sb., a drawing together, a bargain. − L. *contractus*, pp. (above).

Contradict. (L.) L. *contrādictus*, pp. of *contrādicere*, to speak against. − L. *contrā*, against; *dicere*, to speak.

Contralto. (Ital. − L.) Ital. *contr-alto*, counter-tenor. − Ital. *contra*, opposite to, and *alto*, high. − L. *contrā*, against; *altus*, high.

Contrary. (F. − L.) A. F. *contrarie*; F. *contraire*. − L. *contrārius*, contrary; from *contrā*, against; see **Contra-.**

Contrast, vb. (F. − L.) F. *contraster*, to strive, contend against (hence to be in opposition to, &c.). − Late L. *contrāstāre*, to stand against. − L. *contrā*, against; *stāre*, to stand.

Contravene, to hinder. (F. − L.) F. *contrevenir*, 'to thwart;' Cot. − Late L. *contrāuenīre*, to oppose; to break a law. − L. *contrā*, against; *uenīre*, to come.

Contribute. (L.) From pp. of L. *contribuere*, to contribute, lit. pay together. − L. *con-* (*cum*), together; *tribuere*, to bestow; see **Tribute.**

Contrite. (F.–L.) F. *contrit.*–L. *contrītus*, thoroughly bruised, hence, penitent; pp. of L. *conterere*, to rub together, bruise.–L. *con-* (*cum*), together; *terere*, to rub. See **Trite.**

Contrive. (F. – L. *and* Gk.) An altered spelling; M. E. *controuen, controuen* (= *controven, contreven*). – O. F. *controver*, to find, find out (Bartsch).– O. F. *con-* (L. *con-*, for *cum*) ; O. F. *trover*, to find; see **Trover.** ¶ *Contrive* (cf. *retrieve*) is from M. E. *contreve*, answering to O. F. *contréuv-*, stressed stem of *cóntrovér.*

Control, sb. (F.–L.) *Control* is short for *contre-roll*, old form of *counter-roll.* – O. F. *contre-rol(l)e*, a duplicate register, used to verify the official or first-made roll.– O. F. *contre*, over against; *rol(l)e*, a roll.– L. *contrā*, against; *rotulum*, acc. of *rotulus*, a roll; see **Roll.**

Controversy. (F.–L.) A. F. *controversie* (1 327).–L. *contrōuersia*, a quarrel. – L. *contrōuersus*, opposed. – L. *contrō-*, masc. or neut. form corresponding to fem. *contrā*, against; *uersus*, pp. of *uertere*, to turn. See **Contra-.**

Contumacy. (F.–L.) A. F. *contumacie* (1303). – L. *contumācia*, obstinacy.– L. *contumāci-*, stem of *contumax*, stubborn.– L. *con-* (*cum*), very; and **tum-ax*, prob. from *tum-ēre*, to swell with pride; see **Tumid.**

Contumely. (F.–L.) M. F. *contumelie.* – L. *contumēlia*, insult, reproach; prob. allied to *contumācia*; see **Contumacy.**

Contuse, to bruise severely. (L.) L. *contūsus*, pp. of *contundere*, to bruise severely.– L. *con-* (*cum*), with, much ; and *tundere*, to strike.+Skt. *tud*, to strike; Goth. *stautan*, to strike. (√STEUD.) Brugm. i. § 818.

Conundrum. (Unknown.) Formerly used in the sense of whim, crotchet, or hoax. Also *quonundrum*; orig. in univ. slang; prob. of L. origin.

Convalesce. (L.) L. *conualescere*, to begin to grow well; an inceptive form. –L. *con-* (=*cum*), fully; *ualēre*, to be strong.

Convene, to assemble. (F.–L.) F. *convenir*, to assemble.–L. *conuenīre*, to come together.–L. *con-* (*cum*), together; *uenīre*, to come.

convenient, suitable. (F. – L.) From stem of L. *conueniens*, suitable;

orig. pres. pt. of *conuenīre*, to come together, suit (above).

convent. (L.) L. *conuentus*, an assembly.–L. *conuentus*, pp. of *con-uenīre*.

convention. (F.–L.) F. *convention*, 'a compact;' Cot.–L. acc. *conuentiōnem*, a meeting, compact.–L. *conuentus*, pp. of *con-uenīre*, to meet.

Converge. (L.) Late L. *conuergere*, to incline together (Isidore). – L. *con-* (*cum*), together; *uergere*, to bend, incline.

Converse, vb. (F.–L.) F. *converser*, to associate with; Cot.–L. *conuersārī*, to live with.–L. *con-* (*cum*), with; *uersārī*, to dwell (lit. turn oneself about), orig. pass. of the frequent. of *uertere*, to turn.

convert, vb. (F.–L.) O. F. *convertir.*–Folk-L. **convertīre*, for L. *con-uertere*, to turn wholly, change.–L. *con-* (*cum*), wholly; *uertere*, to turn.

Convex. (L.) L. *conuexus*, arched, vaulted ; related to *conuehere*, to bring together (hence, to unite by an arch).–L. *con-* (for *cum*), together; *uehere*, to carry, bring. See **Vehicle.**

Convey, Convoy, vb. (F. – L.) M. E. *conueien, conuoien* (*conveien, convoien*), to convey, also to convoy.–A. F. *conveier*, O. F. *convoier*, to convey, convoy, accompany on the way.–Late L. *conuiāre*, to accompany.–L. *con-* (*cum*), with; *uia*, way. ¶ *Convey* is the A. F. or Norman form ; *convoy* is Parisian.

Convince. (L.) L. *conuincere*, to overcome by proof. – L. *con-* (*cum*), wholly ; *uincere*, to conquer. Der. *convict*, verb and sb., from A. F. *convict*<L. *conuictus*, pp. of *conuincere*.

Convivial. (L.) Coined as adj. from L. *conuīui-um*, a feast.–L. *con-* (*cum*), together ; *uīuere*, to live (hence, eat).

Convoke. (F.–L.) F. *convoquer.*– L. *conuocāre*, to call together.–L. *con-*, together; *uocāre*, to call.

Convolve. (L.) L. *conuoluere*, to roll together, writhe about.–L. *con-* (*cum* , together; *uoluere*, to roll. Der. *convolution*, from pp. *conuolūtus* ; *convolv-ul-us*, L. *conuoluulus*, a twining plant.

Convoy; see **Convey.**

Convulse, to agitate violently. (L.) L. *conuulsus*, pp. of *conuellere*, to pluck up, convulse. – L. *con-* (*cum*), with, severely ; *uellere*, to pluck.

Cony, Coney, a rabbit. (F. – L.) M. E. *coni* ; also *conyng.* Anglo-F. *conil*, *conin*; O. F. *connil.* – L. *cunīculus*, a rabbit; a word of uncertain origin.

Coo. (E.) A purely imitative word; also spelt *croo.* Cf. *cuckoo, cock.*

Cook. (L.) M. E. *coken*, to cook; A. S. *cōc*, a cook. – L. *coquus*, a cook; *co-quere*, to cook.+Gk. πέσσειν; Skt. *pach*, to cook; Russ. *pech(e)*, to bake. (√PEQ; whence Lat. **pequere*, becoming **quequere* by assimilation, and then *coquere*; Gk. **πέq-ειν*, whence πέσσειν.) Brugm. i. § 661. A. S. *cōc*＝Late L. *cōcus*, for *coquus.*

Cookie, a cake; see **Cake.**

Cool. (E.) A. S. *cōl*, cool.+Du. *koel*; Teut. type **kōl-uz*; also, with mutation, Dan. *köl*, G. *kühl*; from *kōl-*, 2nd grade of *kal-*, as in A. S. *calan*, Icel. *kala*, to freeze (pt. t. *kōl*); see **Cold.**

Coolie, Cooly, an East Indian porter. (Hind. *or* Tamil.) Hind. *kūlī*, a labourer, porter, cooley (Forbes); prob. from *Kōlī*, a tribal name (Yule). Or from Tamil *kūli*, daily hire or wages; hence, a day-labourer (Wilson).

Coomb; see **Comb.**

Coop. (L.) M. E. *cupe*, a basket; answering to A. S. **cūpe*, not found, though *cȳpe* (with *i*-mutation) occurs as a gloss to *dolium.* – L. *cūpa*, a tub, whence also Du. *kuip*, Icel. *kūpa*, a bowl; also Late L. *cōpa*, whence G. *kufe*, tub, vat, coop; O. Sax. *cōpa*, a tub. Cf. Skt. *kūpa*, a pit, hollow. Der. *coop-er*, tub-maker.

Co-operate. (L.) From pp. of L. *co-operārī*, to work with; from *co-* (*cum*), with; and *operārī*, to work; see **Operate.**

Co-ordinate. (L.) From L. *co-* (*cum*), with; and the pp. of *ordināre*, to order. See **Ordinate.**

Coot. (E.) M. E. *cote, coote*, a water-fowl.+Du. *koet*, a coot. Origin unknown.

Copal. (Span. – Mexican.) Span. *copal.* – Mex. *copalli*, resin.

Co-parcener, a co-partner. (F. – L.) *Parcener* is the true old spelling of *partner*; see **Partner.**

Cope (1), orig. a cape. (Late L.) M. E. *cope*, earlier *cape*; A. S. **cāpa*, not found; but Icel. *kāpa* occurs. – Late L. *cāpa*, a cape; see **Cape.** [Cf. *pope*, from A. S. *pāpa.*] Der. *coping-stone.*

Cope (2), to vie with. (F. – L. – Gk.) M. E. *copen, coupen*, to fight. – O. F. *coper, couper, colper*, to strike (F. *couper*, to cut). – O. F. *cop, coup, colp*, a blow. – Late L. *colpus*, L. *colaphus*, a blow. – Gk. κόλαφος, a blow on the ear. See **Coupon.**

Copeck, a small Russian coin, worth less than ½*d.*; a hundredth part of a rouble. (Russ.) Russ. *kopieïka*, a copeck; dimin. of Russ. *kopeï*, a lance. So called from the figure of Ivan IV, holding a *lance* (1535). See **Rouble.**

Copious, ample. (F. – L.) O. F. *co-pieux.* – L. *cōpiōsus*, plentiful. – L. *cōpia*, plenty; for **co-opia.* – L. *co-* (for *cum*), together; *op-*, base of *op-ēs*, wealth. Cf. *in-opia*, want.

Copper, a metal. (Cyprus.) M.E. *coper.* A. S. *copor.* – Late L. *cuper*, L. *cuprum*, a contraction for *Cuprium æs*, Cyprian brass. – Gk. Κύπριος, Cyprian; Κύπρος, Cyprus; whence the Romans got copper.

copperas, sulphate of iron. (F. – L.) M. E. *coperose.* – O. F. *coperose (couperose)*; cf. Ital. *copparosa.* According to Diez, from L. *cuprī rosa*, rose of copper, a translation of Gk. χάλκ-ανθος, brass-flower, copperas. But this is prob. only a popular etymology; and the Late L. *cuprōsa* seems to be merely an adj. form from *cuprum.* See N. E. D.

Coppice, Coppy, Copse, a small wood. (F. – L. – Gk.) *Coppy* is short for *coppice*, and *copse* is contracted. – O. F. *copeiz* [Low L. *copecia*], underwood frequently cut, brushwood. – O. F. *coper* (F. *couper*), to cut. – O. F. *cop* (F. *coup*), a stroke. – Low L. *colpus*, L. *colaphus*, stroke, blow. – Gk. κόλαφος, a blow. ¶ O. F. *copeiz* answers to a Late L. type **colpātīcium*, from *colpāre*, to strike. *Coppy* arose from *coppice* being taken as *coppies*, pl.; and *copse* (*cops*) from reducing a supposed pl. **coppis* to *cops.*

Coprolite. (Gk.) Lit. ‘dung-stone.’ Made from Gk. κόπρο-s, dung; and λίθ-os, a stone. For *-lite*, cf. **Aerolite.**

Copulate. (L.) From pp. of L. *cōpulāre*, to join. – L. *cōpula*, a band; see **Couple.**

Copy. (F. – L.) M. E. *copy*, abundance; the mod. sense is due to the multiplication of an original by means of *copies.* – O. F. *copie*, abundance; also a copy. – L. *cōpia*, plenty; see **Copious.**

Coquette. (F.) F. *coquette*, ‘a pratling or proud gossip,’ Cot.; fem. of *coquet*, a little cock, dimin. of *coq*, a cock. Cf. prov. E. *cocky*, i. e. strutting as a cock.

Coracle, a light wicker boat. (W.) W. *corwgl, cwrwgl*, coracle; dimin. of *corwg, cwrwg*, a boat, frame. So Gael. *curachan*, coracle, from *curach*, boat of wicker-work ; cf. Ir. *corrach*, O. Ir. *curach*, a boat.

Coral. (F.–L.–Gk.) O. F. *coral.* – L. *corallum*, *corālium*. – Gk. κοράλλιον, coral. See Schade, p. 1374.

Corban, a gift. (Heb.) Heb. *qorbān*, an offering to God, in fulfilment of a vow ; from *qārab*, to draw near. Cf. Arab. *qurbān*, a sacrifice.

Corbel. (F.–L.) O. F. *corbel*, a raven, a corbel (in architecture), from the notion of a projecting beak. – Folk-L. *corbellum*, for *corvellum*, acc. of *corvellus*, dimin. of L. *coruus*, a raven. ¶ Distinct from *corbeil*, a basket full of earth (F. *corbeille*, L. *corbicula*, dimin. of *corbis*, a basket).

Cord. (F.–L.–Gk.) M. E. *corde.* – F. *corde*. – Late L. *corda*, a thin rope ; the same as L. *chorda*. – Gk. χορδή, the string of a musical instrument. **Der.** *cord-age* (F. *cordage*) ; *cord-on* (F. *cordon*) ; *cord-elier* (F. *cordelier*, a twist of rope, also a Gray Friar, who used such a twist ; from *cordeler*, to twist ropes). See **Chord.**

Cordial. (F.–L.) F. *cordial*, hearty. – L. *cordi-*, decl. stem of *cor*, heart ; with suffix *-ālis* ; see **Heart.**

Corduroy, a thick-ribbed or corded stuff. (F.–L.) F. *corde du roi*, a trade-name, invented in England ; lit. 'king's cord.' See **Cord** and **Royal.**

Cordwainer, shoemaker. (F.–Span.) M. E. *cordewaner*, a worker in *cordewane*, i.e. leather of Cordova. – O. F. *cordouan*, Cordovan leather. – Late L. *Cordoa*, Cordova in Spain (L. *Corduba*).

Core, hard centre in fruit, &c. (F.–L.?) Etym. doubtful. Perhaps from F. *cor*, a horn, also, a corn on the foot, callosity. – L. *cornu*, a horn, a horny excrescence.

Coriander. (F.–L.–Gk.) F. *coriandre.* – L. *coriandrum* (whence A. S. *cellendre*). – Gk. κορίαννον, κόριον, coriander.

Cork. (Span. – L.) Apparently from O. Span. *alcorque*, a cork shoe, which seems to be an Arab. form allied to Span. *al-cornoque*, the cork-tree, where *al* is the Arab. def. art., and *corn-oque* is formed from L. *quern-us* (for **quercnus*), oaken, adj. from L. *quercus*, an oak. ¶ But the *bark* of the tree was called, in Span., *corche*, *corcho.* – L. *corticem*, acc. of *cortex*, bark. Hence *cork* is often derived from Span. *corcho*, though *k* for *ch* seems improbable.

Cormorant, a bird. (F.–L.) The *t* is excrescent. – F. *cormoran* ; O. F. *corma-*

rant, *cormaran* (Littré). – O. F. *corp*, a crow ; and O. F. **marenc*, belonging to the sea, deriv. of L. *mare*, sea, with G. suffix *-ing* ; cf. F. *flamant*, flamingo. – L. *coruum*, acc. of *coruus*, a crow ; &c. Cf. Port. *corvomarinho*, a cormorant ; lit. ' marine crow ;' from L. *coruus marīnus*. But probably *-moran* was due to, or confused with, Bret. *morvran*, a cormorant (from *mor*, sea, and *bran*, a crow).

Corn (1), grain. (E.) A. S. *corn.*+Du. *koren*, Icel. Dan. Swed. G. *korn*, Goth. *kaurn*. Teut. type **kurnom*, Idg. type **gr̥nom*, corn ; whence O. Slav. *zrŭno*, Russ. *zerno*, corn. Cf. Lat. *grānum*, grain ; Skt. *jīrṇa-*, worn down, pp. of *jr̄i*. Doublet, *grain.* See **Churn.** Brugm. i. § 628. (√GER.)

Corn (2), a hard excrescence on the foot. (F.–L.) O. F. *corn* (F. *cor*), a horn, horny swelling. – L. *cornū*, a horn ; see **Horn.**

cornea, horny membrane in the eye. (L.) L. *cornea*, fem. of *corneus*, horny. – L. *cornū*, a horn.

cornel, a shrub. (Du. – L.) M. Du. *kornelle*, 'the fruit of the cornelle-tree,' Hexham ; cf. M. H. G. *cornelbaum*, cornel-tree ; Weigand. [Cf. M. F. *cornille*, a cornel-berry ; *cornillier*, cornel-tree.] – Late L. *cornolium*, cornel-tree. – L. *cornus*, a cornel-tree ; from the hard, horny nature of the wood. – L. *cornū*, a horn.

cornelian, a kind of chalcedony. (F.–L.) Formerly *cornaline.* – F. *cornaline*, 'the cornix or cornaline, a flesh-coloured stone ;' Cot. Cf. Port. *cornelina* ; also Ital. *corniola*, (1) a cornel-tree, (2) a cornelian, prob. so named because its colour resembles that of the fruit of the cornel-tree (Schade). – Late L. *corniola*, cornel-berry ; *cornolium*, cornel. – L. *corneus*, adj. of *cornus*, a cornel. ¶ Altered to *carneolus* in Late L. (Schade, p. 1379), *carnelian* in E., and *carneol* in G., from a popular etymology which connected it with L. *carn-*, stem of *caro*, flesh. Cf. *onyx* = Gk. ὄνυξ, finger-nail.

corner. (F.–L.) A. F. *cornere* ; O. F. *corniere.* – Med. L. *cornēria*, corner, angle. – Med. L. *corna*, angle. – L. *cornua*, pl. of *cornū*, horn, projection ; taken as a fem. sing.

cornet. (F.–L.) M. E. *cornet*, a horn ; later, a troop of horse (who carried a *cornette* or standard) ; also an officer of such a troop. – F. *cornet*, *cornette*, dimin. of F.

corne, a horn.—Med. L. *corna*, a horn (above).

Cornice. (F.—Ital.) M. F. and Picard *cornice*; F. *corniche*. — Ital. *cornice*, a ledge for hanging tapestry (Florio); usually, a crow (from L. acc. *cornīcem*, a crow). Origin uncertain; by some identified with *corōnix*, a square frame. — Gk. κορωνίς, curved; as sb., a wreath.

Corolla. (L.) L. *corolla*, dimin. of *corōna*, a crown. See **Crown**.

corollary. (L.) L. *corollārium*, a present of a garland, a gratuity; also, an additional inference. — L. *corolla* (above).

coronal, a crown. (F. — L.) Properly an adj. — F. *coronal*, adj. — L. *corōnālis*, belonging to a crown. — L. *corōna*, a crown.

coronation. (L.) Late L. acc. *corōnātiōnem*, from pp. of *corōnāre*, to crown. — L. *corōna*, a crown.

coroner. (F. — L.) Also *crowner*; both forms represent A. F. *coruner*, *coroner*, Latinised as *corōnārius*, a crown-officer, a coroner (afterwards Latinised as *corōnātor*). — O. F. *corone*, a crown. — L. *corōna*, a crown.

coronet. (F. — L.) Dimin. of O. F. *corone*, a crown. — L. *corōna*, a crown.

Coronach, a dirge. (Gael.) Gael. *corranach*, a dirge, lit. ' a howling together.' — Gael. *comh-* (= L. *cum*), together; *rànaich*, a howling, from the verb *ràn*, to howl, cry, roar, which is from *ràn*, sb., an outcry. So also Irish *coranach*, a dirge.

Corporal (1), a subordinate officer. (F. — L.) O. F. *corporal*. — Late L. *corporālis*, a captain; a leader of a body of troops. — L. *corpor-*, for **corpos-*, stem of *corpus*, body. ¶ F. has now the form *caporal*, from Ital. *caporale*, a chief of a band; as if from Ital. *capo*, head (L. *caput*); but this does not explain the *-or-*.

corporal (2), belonging to the body. (F. — L.) O. F. *corporal*, *corporel*. — L. *corporālis*, bodily. — L. *corpor-*, for **corpos-*, stem of *corpus*, the body. Der. (from L. *corpor-*) *corpor-ate*, *corpor-e-al* (L. *corpore-us*), &c. Brugm. i. § 555.

corps, corpse, a body. (F. — L.) [Here *corps* is F.; *corse* is from the O. F. *cors*.] M. E. *cors*, *corps*. — O. F. *cors*, M. F. *corps*, the body. — L. *corpus*, body.

corpulent. (F. — L.) F. *corpulent*. — L. *corpulentus*, fat. — L. *corpus*, body.

corpuscle. (L.) L. *corpus-cu-lum*, double dimin. of *corpus*, body.

Corral, an enclosure for animals, pen.

(Span. — L.) Span. *corral*, a court, yard, enclosure. — Span. *corro*, a circle, a ring of people met to see a show. From the phrase *correr toros*, to hold a bull-fight, lit. to run bulls. — L. *currere*, to run (Diez). See **Kraal**.

Correct, adj. (L.) L. *correctus*, pp. of *corrigere*, to correct. — L. *cor-* (for *con-* = *cum*), together; *regere*, to rule.

corregidor, a Spanish magistrate. (Span. — L.) Span. *corregidor*, lit. ' corrector.' — Span. *corregir*, to correct. — L. *corrigere* (above).

Correlate, to relate or refer mutually. (L.) Coined from L. *cor-* (= *cum*), together; and **Relate**, q. v.

Correspond. (F. — L.) F. *correspondre*. — L. *cor-* (for *con-*, *cum*), together; and **Respond**, q. v.

Corridor. (F. — Ital. — L.) F. *corridor*. — Ital. *corridore*, a swift horse; also, a long (running along) gallery. — Ital. *correre*, to run. — L. *currere*, to run.

Corrie. (Gael.) Gael. *coire*, a circular hollow surrounded with hills, a mountain dell; also, a cauldron. [Cf. G. *kessel*, a kettle, a ravine.] + O. Irish *coire*, *core*, a kettle; W. *pair*, A. S. *hwer*, a cauldron. Brugm. i. § 123.

Corroborate. (L.) From pp. of L. *corrōborāre*, to strengthen. — L. *cor-* (for *con-* = *cum*), wholly; *rōbor-*, stem of *rōbur*, strength.

Corrode. (F. — L.) F. *corroder*. — L. *corrōdere*, to gnaw to pieces. — L. *cor-* (for *con-* = *cum*), wholly; *rōdere*, to gnaw. Der. *corrosive*, from pp. *corrōs-us*.

Corrody, Corody, allowance, pension. (Low Lat. — Teut.) A. F. *corodie*. — Low Lat. *corrōdium*, earlier *corrēdium*, L. form of A. F. *conrei*, preparation, provision, allowance. See **Curry** (1).

Corrugate. (L.) From pp. of L. *corrūgāre*, to wrinkle. — L. *cor-* (*cum*), wholly; and *rūgāre*, to wrinkle, from *rūga*, a wrinkle.

Corrupt, adj. (F. — L.) A. F. *corupt*. — L. *corruptus*, pp. of *corrumpere*, to break wholly, corrupt. — L. *cor-* (for *con-* = *cum*), wholly; *rumpere*, to break.

Corsair. (F. — Ital. — L.) F. *corsaire* (Prov. *corsari*, one who makes the course, *corsa*). — Ital. *corsare*, earlier *corsaro*, a pirate. — Med. L. *cursārius*, a pirate. — L. *cursus*, a course. See **Course**.

Corse, a body. (F. — L.) M. E. *cors*. — O. F. *cors*. — L. *corpus*, a body.

corset. (F. – L.) F. *corset*, a pair of stays; dimin. of O. F. *cors*, body.

corslet. (F. – L.) F. *corselet*, 'a little body,' Cot.; hence, body-armour. Double dimin. of O. F. *cors*, body (above).

Cortège. (F. – Ital. – L.) F. *cortège*, a train, retinue. – Ital. *corteggio*, a retinue. – Ital. *corte*, a court. – L. *cŏrtem*, *cohortem*, acc. of *cohors*, a court; see Court (1).

cortes, the Span. national assembly. (Span. – L.) Span. *cortes*, pl. of *corte*, a court. – L. *cŏrtem* (above).

Cortex, bark. (L.) L. *cortex* (gen. *corticis*), bark. Der. *cortical.*

Coruscate. (L.) From pp. of L. *coruscāre*, to glitter.

Corvette, a small frigate. (F. – Port. – L.) F. *corvette*. – Port. *corveta*; Span. *corbeta*, a corvette. – L. *corbīta*, a slow-sailing ship of burden; – L. *corbis*, a basket.

Cosmic, relating to the world. (Gk.) Gk. κοσμικός, adj., from κόσμος, order, also the world, universe. Der. *cosmo-gony*, *cosmo-graphy*, *cosmo-logy*, *cosmo-polite* (citizen of the world, Gk. πολίτης, a citizen).

cosmetic, that which beautifies. (Gk.) Gk. κοσμητικός, skilled in adorning; whence also F. *cosmétique*. – Gk. κοσμέω, I adorn. – Gk. κόσμος, order, ornament.

Cossack, a light-armed S. Russian soldier. (Russ. – Tatar.) Russ. *kozak'*, *kazak'*; of Tatar (Tartar) origin. – Turki *quzzāq*, a vagabond; a predatory horse-man (Yule).

Cosset, to pet. (E.) From 16th cent. *cosset*, a pet-lamb, a pet. Prob. the same as A. F. *coscet*, *cozet*, a cottar; A. S. *cot-sǣta*, a dweller in a cot, 'cot-sitter.' From A. S. *cot*, cot; *sǣta*, dweller, from *sittan*, to sit. Cf. prov. G. *kossat*, a cottager. [So Ital. *casiccio*, pet lamb (Florio); from *casa*, a cottage.]

Cost, vb. (F. – L.) M. E. *costen*. – O. F. *coster* (F. *coûter*), to cost. – L. *constāre*, to stand together, last; also to cost. – L. *con-* (*cum*), together; and *stāre*, to stand.

Costal, relating to the ribs. (L.) From L. *costa*, a rib. See Coast.

Costermonger. (F. *and* E.) Formerly *costard-monger*, or *costard-monger*, a seller of *costards* or apples. [The suffix *-monger* is E.; see **Monger.**] M. E. *costard*, an apple, where the suffix *-ard* is F.; prob. from O. F. *coste*, F. *côte*, a rib; cf. F. *fruit côtelé*, ribbed fruit (Hamilton).

Costive. (F. – L.) From O. F. *costevé*. – L. *constipātus*, constipated. See *constiper* in Littré; and **Constipate.**

Costume. (F. – Ital. – L.) O. F. *costume*, a costume. – Ital. *costume*; Low L. *costūma*; see **Custom.** Doublet of *custom.*

Cosy, Cozy, comfortable, snugly sheltered. (C.?) Lowland Scotch *cosie*, *cozie* (Burns). Etym. unknown; perhaps cf. Gael. *còsach*, *còsagach*, abounding in recesses, also snug, sheltered; Gael. *còs*, a hollow, recess, cave; Irish *cuas*, a cave.

Cot, a small dwelling; **Cote,** an enclosure. (E.) M. E. *cote*. A. S. *cot*, *cote*, a cot, den; Northumbrian *cot*. + Du. *kot*, Icel. *kot*, cot, hut; prov. G. *koth*, cot. Der. *cott-age* (with F. suffix); *cott-ar* or *cott-er*; *sheep-cote.*

coterie, a set of people. (F. – Teut.) F. *coterie*, a set of people, company; allied to O. F. *coterie*, servile tenure (Littré); Low L. *coteria*, a tenure by cottars who clubbed together. – Low L. *cota*, a cot. – Du. *kot* (above).

Cotillon, Cotillion, a dance for 4 or 8 persons. (F. – M. H. G.) F. *cotillon*, lit. a petticoat; see Cotgrave. Formed, with suffix *-ill-on*, from O. F. *cote*, a coat, frock; see **Coat.**

Cotton (1), a downy substance. (F. – Span. – Arab.) M. E. and A. F. *cotoun*. – F. *coton*. – Span. *coton*, *algodon*, cotton (where *al* is the Arab. art.). – Arab. *qutn*, *qutun*, cotton.

cotton (2), to agree. From a technical use of *cotton*, to form a down upon; from Cotton (1); see Nares.

Cotyledon, seed-lobe. (Gk.) Gk. κοτυληδών, a cup-shaped hollow. – Gk. κοτύλη, a hollow vessel, cup.

Couch, to lay down, place, set. (F. – L.) M. E. *couchen*, to set, arrange. – O. F. *coucher*, *colcher*, to place. – L. *collocāre*, to put together. – L. *col-* (*cum*), together; and *locāre*, to place, from *locus*, a place. Der. *couch*, sb., a place on which one is *couched* or laid.

Couch-grass, a grass which is troublesome as a weed. (E.) Here *couch* is a variant of *quitch*, palatalised form of *quick*, i. e. tenacious of life; see **Quick.**

Cough. (E.) M. E. *coughen*, *cowhen*. A. S. *cohhian, only found in the deriv. *cohhetan*, to make a noise. [The usual A. S. word is *hwōstan*.] Cf. Du. *kuchen*, to cough; M. H. G. *kūchen*, G. *keuchen*,

to gasp. From an imitative base *keuh,
*kuh, to gasp ; see **Chincough.**

Could ; see **Can (1).**

Coulter, part of a plough. (L.) M. E.
colter. A. S. *culter.* — L. *culter,* a coulter,
knife. Cf. *per-cellere,* to strike.

Council. (F. — L.) F. *concile.* — L. *concilium,* an assembly called together. — L.
con- (*cum*), together ; and *calāre,* to
summon. ¶ Often confused with *counsel.*

Counsel. (F. — L.) M. E. *conseil.* —
O. F. *conseil.* — L. *consilium,* deliberation.
— L. *consulere,* to consult ; see **Consult.**
¶ Often confused with *council.*

Count (1), a title of rank. (F. — L.)
The orig. sense was 'companion.' A. F.
counte (not in M. E.). — O. F. *conte* ; also
comte. — L. *comitem,* acc. of *comes,* a companion (stem *com-it-*). — L. *com-* (for *cum-*),
together ; and *it-um,* supine of *īre,* to go.
Der. *count-ess* ; also *count-y* (below).

Count (2), to reckon. (F. — L.) F.
conter, formerly also *compter.* — L. *computāre,* to compute ; see **Compute.**

Countenance. (F. — L.) O. F. *con-
tenance,* gesture, demeanour ; also look,
visage. — L. *continentia,* continence, which
in Late L. meant 'gesture, demeanour.' —
L. *continent-,* stem of pres. pt. of *continēre* ;
see **Continent.** Der. *dis-countenance,* vb.

Counter, a piece to count with, a
bureau. (F. — L.) M. E. *countour.* — O. F.
conteour, countour. From O. F. *conter* ;
see **Count (2).**

Counter-, *prefix.* (F. — L.) F. *contre,*
against. — L. *contrā,* against.

Counteract. (F. — L.) See **Counter-,**
prefix, and **Act.**

Counterfeit, imitated. (F. — L.)
M. E. *counterfeit.* — O. F. *contrefait,* pp.
of *contrefaire,* to imitate. — F. *contre,* over
against, like ; *faire,* to make. — L. *contrā,*
against ; *facere,* to make.

Countermand, to revoke an order.
(F. — L.) F. *contremander,* to recall a
command. — F. *contre* (L. *contrā*), against ;
mander (L. *mandāre*), to command.

Counterpane (1), a coverlet for a bed.
(F. — L.) An altered form, in place of
counterpoint, as in Shak. — M. F. *contre-
poinct,* the back-stitch or quilting-stitch,
also a quilt ; Cot. β. Thus named, by a
popular etymology, from a fancied connection with M. F. *contrepoincter,* to work the
back-stitch (from *contre* = L. *contrā*). But
really connected with M. F. *contrepointer,*
to quilt (also in Cotgrave). In fact, *contre-*

poinct is a corruption of O. F. *coutepointe,*
a counterpane (see *courtepointe* in Littré).
— L. *culcita puncta,* a counterpane, a
stitched quilt (see Ducange). — L. *culcita,*
a quilt ; *puncta,* fem. of *punctus,* pp. of
pungere, to prick. See **Quilt.**

Counterpane (2), counterpart of a
deed. (F. — L.) M. F. *contrepan, contre-
pant* ; Cot. — F. *contre* (L. *contrā*), over
against ; *pan,* a piece, part ; see **Pane.**

Counterpoint, the composing of
music in parts. (F. — L.) M. F. *contre-
poinct,* 'a ground or plain song, in music ; '
Cot. The lit. sense is *point against point,*
from the *points* or dots which represented
musical notes, and were placed on staves
over or against each other in compositions
in two or more parts. — F. *contre* (L. *contrā*), against ; *point,* a point ; see **Point.**

Counterpoise. (F. — L.) From *counter* and *poise* ; see **Poise.**

Counterscarp, exterior slope of a
ditch. (F. — Ital. — L. *and* Teut.) F. *con-
trescarpe* ; Cot. — Ital. *contrascarpa.* —
Ital. *contra,* over against ; *scarpa,* a scarp.
See **Counter-** and **Scarp.**

Countersign, to attest by signing in
addition. (F. — L.) F. *contresigner,* 'to
subsigne ; ' Cot. — F. *contre,* over against ;
signer, to sign ; see **Counter-** and **Sign.**

Countertenor. (F. — Ital. — L.) M. F.
contreteneur ; Cot. — Ital. *contratenore,* a
countertenor, the highest adult male voice.
— Ital. *contra,* against, over against ; *tenore,*
a tenor ; see **Tenor.**

Countervail. (F. — L.) M. E. *con-
trevailen.* — O. F. *contrevail-,* a stem of
contrevaloir, to avail against. — O. F. *contre,* against ; *valoir,* to avail. — L. *contrā,*
against ; *ualēre,* to be strong.

Country. (F. — L.) M. E. *contree.* —
O. F. *contree* (= Ital. *contrada*). — Late L.
contrāda, contrāta, a region, lit. that which
lies opposite ; cf. G. *gegend,* country, lit.
opposite, from *gegen,* opposite. — L. *contrā,*
opposite ; see **Contra-.**

Country-dance. (F.) From *country*
and *dance.* (The F. *contredanse* was borrowed from this E. form.)

County, orig. a province governed by a
count. (F. — L.) M. E. *countee.* — O. F.
counte (i. e. *coun-té*), F. *comté,* a province.
— Late L. *comitātum,* acc. of *comitātus,* a
county (though the old meaning was a company or suite). — L. *comit-,* stem of *comes,*
a count ; see **Count (1).**

Couple. (F. — L.) O. F. *cople,* later

couple. — L. *cōpula*, a bond, band, that which joins ; short for *co-ap-ula.* — L. *co-(cum)*, together ; and O. L. *apere*, to join, preserved in the pp. *aptus* ; see **Apt.**

Coupon, one of a series of conjoined tickets or certificates. (F. — L. — Gk.) F. *coupon*, a piece cut off, a coupon. — F. *couper*, to cut, slash. — F. *coup*, a blow. — Late L. *colpus*, short for *colaphus*, a blow. — Gk. κόλαφος, a blow on the ear.

Courage. (F. — L.) F. *courage*, O. F. *corage* ; formed with suffix -*age* (L.-*āticum*) from O. F. *cor*, heart. — L. *cor*, heart. **Der.** *encourage.*

Courier. (F. — Ital. — L.) M.F. *courier*, a runner ; F. *courrier.* — Ital. *corriere*, lit. ' runner.' — Ital. *correre*, to run. — L. *currere*, to run.

course. (F. — L.) F. *course.* — L. *cursum*, acc. of *cursus*, a course ; from pp. of *currere.* **Der.** *cours-er*, a swift horse.

Court (1), a yard ; royal retinue, judicial assembly. (F. — L.) M. E. *cort*, *curt.* — O. F. *cort*, *curt* (F. *court*), a court, a yard, also a tribunal. — L. acc. *cōrtem*, *cohortem* (nom. *cohors*), a pen, enclosure, cattle-yard, court, also a cohort, or band of soldiers. — L. *co-* (*cum*), together ; and *hort-*, as in *hort-us*, a garden, yard, cognate with *yard.* (√GHER.)

court (2), to seek favour. (F. — L.) From the sb. *court* ; hence, to practise arts in vogue at court.

courteous, of courtly manners. (F. — L.) M. E. *corteis*, later *corteous.* — O. F. *corteis*, courteous. — O. F. *cort*, a court ; with suffix -*eis* (L. -*ensis*).

courtesan. (F. — Ital. — L.) Fem. of F. *courtisan*, a courtier. — Ital. *cortigiano* (in Florio *cortegiano*), a courtier. For **cortesiano*, an extension of *cortese*, courteous ; from Ital. *corte*, court. — L. acc. *cōrtem* ; see **Court** (1).

courtesy. (F. — L.) M. E. *cortesie.* — O. F. *cortesie*, courtesy. — O. F. *corteis*, courteous ; see **courteous.**

courtier. (F. — L.) M. E. *courteour.* From A. F. **cortei-er* (O. F. *cortoi-er*), to live at court ; with suffix -*our* (L. -*ātōrem*). — O. F. *cort*, a court.

Court cards ; a corruption of *coat cards*, pictured cards, the old name.

Courteous, &c. ; see **Court.**

Cousin. (F. — L.) M. E. *cosin.* — O. F. *cosin* (F. *cousin* ; Late L. *cosīnus*, Ital. *cugino*, Romaunsch *cusrin*, *cusdrin*). — L. *consobrīnus*, the child of a mother's sister,

a cousin. — L. *con- (cum)*, together ; *sobrīnus*, for **swesr-īnus*, belonging to a sister ; from L. *soror* (for **swesōr*), a sister ; cf. Skt. *svasṛ*, a sister. See **Sister.** (Cf. Brugm. i. § 319.)

Cove, a nook. (E.) A. S. *cofa*, a chamber, a cave. + Icel. *kofi*, a hut ; Swed. *kofva* ; G. *koben*, a cabin. ¶ Distinct from *cave*, *coop*, *alcove.* Brugm. i. § 658.

Covenant, agreement. (F. — L.) O.F. *covenant*, also *convenant*, agreement. — O. F. *co*(*n*)*venant*, pres. pt. of *co*(*n*)*venir*, to assemble, agree. — L. *conuenīre*, to assemble, come together ; see **Convene.**

Cover, to hide. (F. — L.) O. F. *covrir* (*couvrir*). — L. *coöperīre*, to cover. — L. *co-(cum)*, wholly ; *operīre*, to shut, hide. For **op-uerīre* ; cf. Lith. *aż-weriu*, I shut, *wartai*, doors, Oscan acc. *veru*, a door. Brugm. i. § 350.

coverlet. (F. — L.) M. E. *coverlite.* — A. F. *coverlet*, *coverlit* (not in O. F.), a bed-cover. — O. F. *covrir*, to cover ; *lit*, a bed, from L. *lectum*, acc. of *lectus*, a bed.

covert. (F. — L.) O. F. *covert*, pp. of *covrir*, to cover (above).

Covet. (F. — L.) M. E. *coueiten* (*coveiten*). — A. F. *coveiter* (F. *convoiter*). Cf. Ital. *cubitare* (for *cupitare*), to covet. Formed, as if from L. **cupiditāre*, from *cupiditā-tem*, acc., eager desire, which is from *cupidus*, desirous of. — L. *cupere*, to desire. See **Cupid.**

Covey. (F. — L.) O. F. *covee* (F. *couvée*), a brood of partridges ; fem. of pp. of *cover* (F. *couver*), to hatch, sit. — L. *cubāre*, to lie down, sit. Cf. Gk. κυφός, bent.

Covin, secret agreement, fraud ; a law-term. (F. — L.) M. E. *covine.* — O. F. *covine*, agreement. — O. F. *covenir*, to assemble, agree. — L. *conuenīre*, to come together. See **Convene, Covenant.** (The O. F. *covine* answers to Late L. *convenia*, pl. of *convenium*, an agreement.)

Cow (1), female of the bull. (E.) A.S. *cū* ; pl. *cȳ*, whence M. E. *ky*, and the double pl. *ky-en* = *kine.* Teut. stem **kū-*, whence also Icel. *kȳr.* + Du. *koe*, Swed. Dan. *ko*, G. *kuh* ; Teut. stem **kō-.* Also Irish and Gael. *bō*, W. *buw*, L. *bōs* (gen. *bou-is*), Gk. βοῦς, Pers. *gāw*, Skt. *go-* (nom. *gāus*) ; cf. Russ. *goviado*, oxen. Idg. stems **g(w)ōu-*, **g(w)ow-.* See **Beef.**

kine, cows. (E.) A *double* pl., made by adding -*n*, short for -*en* (A. S. -*an*), to M. E. *ky*, A. S. *cȳ*, cows. The A. S. *cȳ*, pl. of *cū*, a cow, is formed by vowel-change from *ū* to *ȳ*.

Cow (2), to dishearten. (Scand.) Icel. *kūga*, to tyrannise over; Dan. *kue*, to coerce, subdue; Swed. *kufva*, to suppress.

Coward. (F.–L.) A.F. *couard*, a hare, a coward, F. *couard*, a coward; cf. Ital. *codardo*, a coward. Probably named from the 'bob-tailed' hare.–O. F. *coe* (Ital. *coda*), a tail; with F. suffix *-ard*, from Teut. *-hart*, orig. hard. – L. *cauda*, a tail.

Cower. (Scand.) M. E. *couren.*–Icel. *kūra*, Dan. *kure*, to doze, lie quiet; Swed. *kura*, to cower, lie quiet; Swed. dial. *kura*, to sit hunched up. Cf. G. *kauern*, to cower.

Cowl (1), a monk's hood. (L.) M. E. *cūle, coule.* A.S. *cugele, cugle.*–L. *cuculla*, a cowl; cf. also *cucullus.*

Cowl (2), a vessel carried on a pole. (F.–L.) M.E. *couel.*–O.F. *cuvel* (*cuveau*), a little tub; dimin. of *cuve*, a vat, tub.– L. *cūpa*, a tub. **Der.** *cowl-staff.*

Cowry, a small shell used for money. (Hind.–Skt.) Hind. *kaurī*, a small shell (*Cypræa moneta*) used as coin in the lower provinces of India.–Skt. *kaparda.*

Cowslip, a flower. (E.) M. E. *cou-sloppe.* A.S. *cū-sloppe, cū-slyppe,* lit. cowslop, i. e. a piece of dung. (Other A.S. names of plants are of a very homely character.) Cf. *oxlip,* q. v.; and prov. E. *bull-slop,* a large kind of oxlip (Britten).

Coxcomb. (E.) A fool, named from his *cock's comb,* or fool's cap, cap with a cock's crest.

Coxswain. (F. *and* Scand.) For *cock-swain;* from *cock* (4), a boat, and *swain.*

Coy. (F.–L.) O. F. *coi,* older form *quei,* quiet, still; spelt *coy, quoy,* in Cotgrave. – Folk-L. **quētum,* acc. of **quētus,* for L. *quiētus,* still. See **Quiet.**

Coyote, a prairie-wolf. (Mexican.) From *coyote,* Span. pron. of Mex. *coyotl.*

Cozen. (F.–L.) To *cozen* is to act as *cousin* or kinsman, to sponge upon, beguile. – F. *cousiner,* to call cousin, to sponge, live on other people; see Hamilton and Cotgrave.–F. *cousin,* a cousin; see **Cousin.**

Crab (1), a shell-fish. (E.) A S. *crabba.*+Icel. *krabbi,* Swed. *krabba,* Dan. *krabbe,* Du. *krab,* G. *krabbe.* Allied to E. Fries. and Du. *krabben,* to scratch.

claw; G. *krebs* (O. H. G. *crebiz*), a crab, Du. *kreeft,* a crab. See **Crayfish.**

crabbed, peevish, cramped. (E.) From *crab,* sb.; i. e. crab-like, snappish or awkward. Cf. Du. *krabben,* to scratch, *kribben,* to be peevish.

Crab (2), a kind of apple. (E.) Cf. Swed. *krabbäple,* crab-apple. Perhaps allied to **crabbed** (above).

Crabbed; see **Crab** (1).

Crack. (E.) A. S. *cracian,* to crack. +Du. *kraken,* to crack, creak; G. *krachen.* Cf. Gael. *crac,* a fissure, *cnac,* a crack, to crack (from E.). Imitative, like *crake, creak, croak, crash, gnash, knock.*

cracknel. (F.–Du.) Formerly *crakenel,* corruption of F. *craquelin,* a cracknel. –Du. *krakeling,* a cracknel. Named from its crispness.–Du. *kraken,* to crack.

crake, corncrake, a bird. (E.) From its cry; M. E. *craken,* to cry out. Allied to *crack, croak.*

Cradle. (E.) A.S. *cradol.* Cf. O.H.G. *cratto,* a basket; also O. H. G. *crezzo,* prov. G. *krätze,* a basket.

Craft, skill. (E.) A. S. *cræft.*+Du. *kracht,* Icel. *kraptr, kraftr,* Swed. Dan. G. *kraft,* force. Cf. A. S. *crafian,* to crave, demand. **Der.** *handi-craft.*

Crag. (C.) W. *craig,* Gael. *creag,* crag, rock; Irish *creag,* a rock; cf. W. *careg,* Gael. *carraig,* rock, cliff, Bret. *karrek,* O. Irish *carric,* a rock.

Crake; see **Crack.**

Cram. (E.) A.S. *crammian,* to stuff. + Icel. *kremja,* Swed. *krama,* Dan. *kramme,* to squeeze. From *cramm-,* 2nd grade of the str. vb. *crimm-an,* to crumble. And cf. **Cramp.**

Cramp. (F.–Teut.) F. *crampe,* 'the crampe,' Cot.; cf. *crampon,* 'a crampiron.'–Du. *kramp,* a cramp, spasm. From the 2nd grade of Teut. **krempan-, *krim-pan-,* to draw together, as in O.H.G. *krimphan,* to draw together, str. vb. Cf. E. *crimp, cramp, crumple;* Icel. *krappr,* cramped; *kreppa,* to pinch. And compare **Crank.**

Crane, a bird. (E.) A. S. *cran.*+Du. *kraan,* Icel. *trani* (for *krani*), Swed. *trana,* Dan. *trane,* G. *kran-ich;* W. and Bret. *garan,* Gk. γέρανος, a crane, also a crane for raising weights. Cf. L. *grus,* a crane, Lith. *garnys,* a stork. From √GER, to cry out; cf. Gk. γῆρυς, voice (Prellwitz).

cranberry. (Low G.) Modern; from

Low G. *kraanbere* (Berghaus), G. *kran-beere*, lit. craneberry; cf. Dan. *tranebær* (from *trane* = krane, as above); Swed. *tranbär*.

Cranium. (L.–Gk.) Med. L. *cränium*.–Gk. *κρανίον*, skull; allied to *κάρα*, head.

Crank (1), a bend. (E.) M. E. *cranke*. Allied to E. Fries. *krunken*, pp., bent. Cf. Du. *kronkel*, a wrinkle, *kronkelen*, to wrinkle, turn, wind. Teut. base **krenk-*, variant of **kreng-*. Cf. Cringe, Crinkle.

crank (2), easily upset, as a boat. (E.) I. e. easily bent or twisted aside. Cf. Du. *krank*, ill, poor; also *krengen*, to careen a boat; Swed. *kränga*, Dan. *krænge*, to heel over; see Cringe.

crank (3), lively. (E.) The same word, from the idea of turning quickly. Cf. Norw. *kring*, active, brisk; Dan. dial. *kræng*, dexterous.

Cranny. (F. – L.?) M. E. *crany*. –F. *cran*, a notch; with E. suffix -*y*. Allied to Ital. *crena*, a notch (Florio). Cf. Late L. *crēna*, a notch (a word of doubtful authority). See Crenellate.

Crants, a garland. (M. Du.–G.) M. Du. *krants*, Du. *krans*, a garland, wreath (whence Dan. *krands*, Sw. *krans*). All from G. *kranz*, a wreath.

Crape. (F.–L.) F. *crêpe*, formerly *crespe*, 'frizzled, crisped, crisp;' Cot. From its wrinkled surface.–L. *crispus*, curled. See Crisp.

Crare, a small ship. (F.) In Cymb. iv. 2. 205. M. E. *crayer*.–O. F. *craier*, *creer*, a war-vessel. Of unknown origin.

Crash, vb. (E.) Of imitative origin; closely allied to *crack*. Cf. *clash*, *dash*; and see Craze.

Crasis. (Gk.) Gk. *κρᾶσις*, a mixing; hence, contraction. – Gk. *κεράννυμι*, I mix.

Crass. (L.) L. *crassus*, thick, dense.

Cratch, a crib, manger. (F. –O.H.G.) M. E. *crecche*. – O. F. *creche* (*crèche*); Prov. *crepcha*.–O. H. G. *crippea* (whence G *krippe*), a crib. See Crib.

Crate. (L.) L. *crātes*, a hurdle; hence, a wicker-case, &c.

Crater. (L.–Gk.) L. *crātēr*, a bowl, a crater.–Gk. *κρᾱτήρ*, a large bowl in which things were mixed. – Gk. *κεράννυμι*, I mix.

Cravat. (F.–Slavonic.) F. *cravate*, (1) a Croatian, (2) a cravat. *Cravats* were introduced into France in 1636, as

worn by the *Croatians*, who were called in F. *Croates* or *Crovates* or *Cravates*. *Croat* is a name of Slavonic origin; cf. Russ. *Kroat'*, a Croatian.

Crave. (E.) A. S. *crafian*, to crave, ask. Cf. Icel. *krefja*, Swed. *kräfva*, Dan. *kræve*, to demand; Icel. *krafa*, a demand.

Craven. (F.–L.?) The oldest form is M. E. *cravant*, with the sense of beaten, foiled, or overcome. 1. Mr. Nicol suggested that it is a clipped form of O. F. *cravanté*, pp. explained by Cotgrave by 'oppressed, foiled'; this is the pp. of O. F. *cravanter*, to break, oppress = Late L. **crepantāre*, formed from *crepant-*, stem of pres. pt. of *crepāre*, to crack, break. Cf. Span. *quebrantar*, to crack, break. 2. But it seems rather to be due to a confusion of the E. vb. to *crave* with M. E. *creaunt*, used in the precise sense of recreant, craven, beaten; this answers to O. F. *creant*, trusting, from Lat. acc. *crēdentem*, believing; from *crēdere*, to believe, in Late L., to yield, to fear (cf. *re-creant*). Cf. prov. E. *cradden*, *cradant*, a coward; prob. from an A.F. form of L. *crēdentem*.

Craw, crop of fowls. (E.?) M. E. *crawe*. As if from A. S. **craga*, the neck; not found; N. Fries. *krage*, neck, craw. Allied to Du. *kraag*, G. *kragen*, neck, collar (whence Late Icel. *kragi*, Swed. *krage*, Dan. *krave*, a collar). Note also Dan. *kro*, the craw of a bird; Swed. *kräfva*.

Crawfish, the same as Crayfish.

Crawl. (Scand.) Prov. E. *craffle*, *croffle*, to crawl.–Icel. *krafla*, to paw, crawl; Swed. *krafla*, to grope; Dan. *kravle*, to crawl. Cf. N. Fries. *krabli*, *krawli*, to crawl; Low G. *kraueln*. Frequentative from Teut. base **krab-*, to scratch, claw; see Crab.

Crayfish. (F. – O. H. G.) Altered from M. E. *crevise*. – O. F. *crevisse*, *escrevisse* (*écrevisse*). – O. H. G. *crebiz*, G. *krebs*, a crab; allied to G. *krabbe*, a crab; see Crab (1).

Crayon. (F.–L.) F. *crayon*; extended from F. *craie*, chalk.–L. *crēta*, chalk.

Craze. (Scand.) M. E. *crased*, i.e. cracked. – Swed. *krasa*, Dan. *krase*, to crackle; whence also F. *écraser*, to break in pieces. Cf. Swed. *slå in kras*, Dan. *slaae i kras*, to break in shivers.

Creak. (E.) M. E. *kreken*. Allied to *crake*, *crack*. Cf. Du. *kriek*, a cricket,

M. F. *criquer*, to creak, allied to *craquer*, to crack. Of imitative origin.

Cream. (F.—L.—Gk.) O. F. *cresme* (F. *crème*) ; really the same word as O. F. *cresme* (F. *chrême*), chrism (though confused with L. *cremor*, thick juice).—Late L. *chrisma*, consecrated oil.—Gk. χρῖσμα, an unguent; see **Chrism**.

Crease (1), a wrinkle, as in folding paper, &c. (F.—L.) Earliest spelling *creast*, a ridge (later, a furrow). Variant of *crest*, ridge (as of a roof). Cf. Walloon *cress*, a crest, ridge of a roof, *kretlé*, wrinkled (Remacle) ; Prov. *crest*, *creis*, a ridge; and prov. E. *crease*, a ridge-tile of a roof. (*Athen.* Sept. 18, 1897.)

Crease (2), **Creese**, a dagger. (Malay.) Malay *krīs*, 'a dagger, kris, or creese;' Marsden.

Create. (L.) From pp. of L. *creāre*, to make.+Skt. *kṛ*, to make. **Der.** *creature*, O. F. *creature*, L. *creātūra*. And see **Crescent.** Brugm. i. § 641.

Creed. (L.) M. E. *crede*; A. S. *crēda*. —L. *crēdo*, I believe : the first word of the creed. + O. Irish *cretim*, I believe ; Skt. *çrad-dadhāmi*, I believe. **Der.** *credence* (O. F. *credence*, L. *crēdentia*); *credible* ; *credit* (L. pp. *crēditus*) ; *cred-ulous* (L. *crēdulus*), &c. Brugm. i. § 539.

Creek. (E. ?) M. E. *creke*, a creek.+ Du. *kreek*, M. Du. *krēke*; cf. Icel. *kriki*, a crack, nook (whence F. *crique*). The orig. sense is 'a bend,' as in Swed. dial. *armkrik*, bend of the arm ; *krik*, an angle, nook.

Creel, an angler's osier basket. (F.—L.) O. F. *creil*, wicker-work (Ducange), s.v. *cleia*).—L. type *crāticulum*, for *crāticula*, wicker-work, double dimin. of *crātes*, a hurdle. See **Crate** and **Grill**.

Creep. (E.) M. E. *crepen*; A. S. *crēopan*.+Du. *kruipen*, Icel. *krjūpa*, Swed. *krypa*, Dan. *krybe*, to crawl. Teut. type *kreupan-*, str. vb.

Creese ; see **Crease** (2).

Cremation, burning. (L.) L. *cremā-tiōnem*, acc. of *cremātio* ; from pp. of *cre-māre*, to burn.

Crenate, notched. (L.) From Late L. *crēna*, M. Ital. *crena*, a notch.

crenellate. (Late L.—F.—L.) From pp. of Late L. *crēnellāre*, to furnish with battlements.—O. F. *crenel*, a battlement ; dimin. of O. F. *cren*, F. *cran*, a notch, from Late L. *crēna* (above).

Creole, one born in the W. Indies, but of European blood. (F.—Span.—L.) F. *créole*.—Span. *criollo*, a negro corruption of **criadillo*, dimin. of *criado*, one educated, instructed, or brought up ; hence, a child of European blood. *Criado* is pp. of *criare*, to create, also, to educate.—L. *creāre*, to create, make. ¶ Cf. Span. *criadilla*, dimin. of *criada*, a servant-maid.

Creosote, a liquid distilled from tar. (Gk.) Lit. 'flesh-preserver.'—Gk. κρεο-, for κρέας, flesh ; and σωτ-, short for σωτ-ήρ, preserver, from σώζειν, to preserve. (Ill-formed.)

Crescent. (L.) The 'increasing' moon.—L. *crescent-*, stem of pres. pt. of *crescere*, to grow, increase (pp. *crē-tus*), inchoative form allied to *cre-āre*, to make ; see **Create**.

Cress. (E.) M. E. *cres*, also *kerse* (by shifting of *r*). A. S. *cærse*, *cerse*, *cressa*. +Du. *kers*, M. Du. and Low G. *kerse*, G. *kresse*, O. H. G. *cressa*.

Cresset. (F. — L.) M. E. *cresset*, a light in a cup at the top of a pole.— O. F. *cresset*, *craisset*, a cresset (with grease in an iron cup).—O. F. *craisse* (F. *graisse*), grease; Littré.—Folk-L. **crassia*, grease, from L. *crassus*, thick, dense. So also Walloon *craché*, a cresset, from *crache*, grease.

Crest. (F.—L.) O. F. *creste* (F. *crête*.) — L. *crista*, a comb or tuft on a bird's head, crest.

Cretaceous, chalky. (L.) L. *crē-tāce-us*, adj. from *crēta*, chalk ; with suffix *-ous*.

Crevice, Crevasse. (F.—L.) M. E. *crevice*, *crevase*, *crevasse*.—O. F. *crevasse*, a rift (Late L. *crepātia*).—O. F. *crever*, to burst asunder.— L. *crepāre*, to crackle, burst.

Crew. (F.—L.) Formerly *crue*, short for *accrue*, a re-inforcement.—O. F. *ac-creue*, increase ; orig. fem. of pp. of *ac-croistre*, to increase.—L. *accrescere*, to grow to.—L. *ac-* (for *ad*), to ; *crescere*, to grow.

Crewel, a thin worsted yarn. Origin unknown.

Crib, a manger. (E.) A. S. *crib*.+ O. Sax. *kribbia*, Du. *krib*, G. *krippe*; allied to Icel. Swed. *krubba*, Dan. *krybbe*. Allied perhaps to M. H. G. *krebe*, a basket; but not to Du. *korf*, G. *korb*, if these are from L. *corbis*. **Der.** *crib*, verb, to put by in a crib, purloin ; *cribb-age*, where *crib* is the secret store of cards

Crick, a spasm or twist in the neck, (E.) M. E. *crykke*; also used in the sense of wrench. Prob. allied to **Crack**.

Cricket (1), an insect. (F. – Teut.) M. E. *criket*. – O. F. *crequet, criquet,* cricket. – O. F. *criquer,* to creak, rattle, chirp. – Du. *kriek,* a cricket; *krikkrakken,* to rattle. From the imitative base *krik*; cf. prov. E. *cracket, creaker,* a cricket. Hexham has M. Du. *kricken,* ' to creake.'

Cricket (2), a game. (F. – Du.) The game was once played with a hooked stick (Cot., s. v. *crosse*). – O. F. *criquet,* ' bâton servant de but au jeu de boule ; ' Godefroy. – M. Du. *krick, kricke,* a crutch; Hexham. Cf. A. S. *cricc, crycc,* a crutch, staff.

Crime. (F. – L.) F. *crime.* – L. *crīmen,* an accusation, fault (stem *crīmin*-) ; allied to *cernere,* to decide. + Gk. κρῖμα, κρῖμα, a decision ; κρίνειν, to judge. Der. *crimin-al, crimin-ate* ; hence, *recriminate*

Crimp, to wrinkle. (E.) In late use ; answering to an A.S. **crempan,* E. Fries. *krempen,* causal deriv. of **Cramp**. The orig. str. vb. occurs as E. Fries. and Du. *krimpen,* O. H. G. *krimfan*; Teut. type **krempan- (krimpan-),* to draw oneself together, shrink up ; pt. t. **kramp,* pp. **krumpano-.* See **Cramp** and **Crumple**.

Crimson. (F. – Arab. – Skt.) M. E. *cremosin.* – O.F. *cramoisin, cramoisyne* (see *cramoisi* in Littré) ; Low L. *cramesīnus,* also *carmesīnus,* crimson (Span. *carmesi,* Ital. *chermisi*). – Arab. *qirmizī,* crimson ; from *qirmiz,* the cochineal insect. – Skt. *kṛmi(s̒),* a worm. Brugm. i. § 418.

Cringe. (E.) M. E. *crengen* ; causal derivative of A. S. *cringan, crincan,* to sink in battle, fall beneath the foe. *Crincan* is a strong verb; see **Crank, Crinkle**.

Cringle, an iron ring. (Low G.) Low G. *kringel,* a ring (Lübben); E. Fries. *kringel* ; allied to Icel. *kringla,* a circle (cf. *kringar,* pl., the pullies of a drag-net). Dimin. of E. Fries. *kring,* a ring, Du. *kring,* a circle; allied to **Crinkle, Crank** (1), and **Cringe**.

Crinkle. (E.) M. E. *crinkled, crencled,* twisted. A frequent form of the causal deriv. of *crink,* which occurs in the A. S. str. vb. *crincan,* to sink in a heap; see **Cringe**.

Crinoline, a lady's stiff skirt. (F. – L.) F. *crinoline,* (1) hair-cloth, (2) crino-

line. – F. *crin* (L. acc. *crīnem*), hair ; and *lin,* flax, hence thread, from L. *līnum,* flax, also, a thread.

Cripple. (E.) M. E. *crepel, crupel* ; O. Northumb. *crypel,* Luke v. 24. Lit. ' a creeper.' – A. S. *crup*-, weak grade of *crēopan* (pt. t. *crēap*), to creep ; with suffix *-el* (for *-ilo*-) of the agent. + Du. *kreupel,* Icel. *kryppill,* G. *krüppel.* Cf. Dan. *kröbling* (from *krybe,* to creep). See **Creep**.

Crisis ; see **Critic**.

Crisp, wrinkled, curled. (L.) A. S. *crisp.* – L. *crispus,* curled. Brugm. i. § 565.

Critic. (L. – Gk.) L. *criticus.* – Gk. κριτικός, able to discern ; cf. κριτής, a judge. – Gk. κρί-νειν, to judge. Der. *criterion,* Gk. κριτήριον, a test ; *dia-critic,* from Gk. διακριτικός, fit for distinguishing between.

crisis. (Gk.) Gk. κρίσις, a discerning, a crisis. – Gk. κρί-νειν, to judge.

Croak. (E.) Cf. A. S. *crǣcetung,* a croaking. Of imitative origin. Allied to *crake, creak.*

Crochet. (F. – Late L.) F. *crochet,* a little hook ; dimin. of *croc,* a crook. – Late L. *croccum,* acc. of *croccus,* a hook.

Crock, a pitcher. (C.) A.S. *crocca.* Of Celtic origin. Cf. E. Irish *crocan,* Gael. *crog,* Irish *crogan,* W. *crochan,* a pitcher, pot. + Gk. κρωσσός (for κρωκγός), a pitcher. So also Du. *kruik,* Icel. *krukka,* Swed. *kruka,* Dan. *krukke,* G. *krug.*

Crocodile. (F. – L. – Gk.) F. *crocodile.* – L. *crocodīlus.* – Gk. κροκόδειλος, a lizard, a crocodile.

Crocus. (L. – Gk.) L. *crocus.* – Gk. κρόκος, crocus, saffron. Perhaps Semitic ; cf. Arab. *karkam,* Heb. *karkōm,* saffron.

Croft. (E.) A. S. *croft,* a field. + Du. *krocht, kroft,* a field on the downs.

Cromlech. (W.) W. *cromlech,* a flagstone laid across others. – W. *crom,* fem. of *crwm,* crooked, bent ; *llech,* flat stone.

Crone, an old woman. (F. – L.) Tusser has *crone,* an old ewe. Prob. from Picard *carone,* carrion ; whence M. Du. *karonie, kronie,* an old sheep. See **Carrion**.

Crony, an old chum. (Gk. ?) Pepys has *chrony* (N. E. D.). Perhaps for Gk. χρόνιος, a 'long-lasting' friend ; as it arose in college slang (Skinner). Butler rimes *cronies* with *monies.*

Crook, a hook, bend. (Scand.) M. E. *crok* (Ancren Riwle). – Icel. *krókr,* Swed. *krok,* Dan. *krog,* hook, bend, angle.

Crop. (E.) A. S. *cropp,* the top of a

plant, the craw of a bird; orig. a bunch. [Hence the verb to *crop*, to cut off the tops; and hence *crop*, a harvest.]+Du. *krop*, G. *kropf*, bird's crop; Icel. *kroppr*, a hunch; Swed. *kropp*, Dan. *krop*, trunk of the body. Cf. W. *cropa*, Gael. and Ir. *sgroban*, bird's crop. [To *crop out* is to bunch out.]

croup (2), hinder part of a horse. (F. —Teut.) F. *croupe*, crupper; orig. protuberance.—Icel. *kroppr*, a hunch (above).

crupper. (F.—Teut.) F. *croupière* (O. F. *cropiere*).—F. *croupe* (O. F. *crope*, above).

Croquet, a game. (F.—Late L.) From N. French *croquet*, a little hook, bent stick; the same as F. *crochet*. See **Crochet.**

Crosier. (F.—Late L.) M. E. *crocer*, *croser*, &c. Formed, with suffix -*er*, from M. E. *croce*, in the same sense of 'bishop's staff.'—O. F. *croce*, 'a crosier,' Cot.; mod. F. *crosse*; Late L. *crocia*.—O. F. *croc*, a hook; see Crochet. ¶ Not from *cross*, though early confused with M. E. *croisier*, a coinage from O. F. *crois*, a cross.

Cross. (L.) M. E. *cros*; from Icel. *kross*, adopted from O. Irish *cros*.—L. *cruc-em*, acc. of *crux*, a cross. Der. *a-cross*.

cross, adj. (L.) Orig. transverse, from the shape of a cross; hence, peevish.

Crotchet, in music. (F.—Late L.) F. *crochet*, 'a small hook, a quaver in music;' Cot. (The *hooked* mark now called a quaver was called *crochet* in French.) See Crochet.

Croton, plant. (Gk.) Gk. κρότων, a tick, which the castor-berry resembles.

Crouch. (F.—Late L.) M. E. *crouchen*, to stoop, bend. — O. F. *crochir*, to grow crooked (Godefroy). — O. F. *crôche*, a crook; also *croc*.—Late L. *croccum*, acc. of *croccus*, a hook.

Croup (1), a disease. (E.) From Lowland Sc. *croupe*, *crope*, to croak, make a harsh noise. Of imitative origin; associated with *crow*, *croak*, and with North E. *roup*, *rope*, to call, shout hoarsely, from Icel. *hrópa*, weak vb., to cry out. Cf. A.S. *hrópan* (pt. t. *hréop*), to cry out; G. *rufen* (pt. t. *rief*).

Croup (2), of a horse; see Crop.

Crow (1), vb. (E.) A.S. *cráwan* (pt. t. *créow*), to crow.+Du. *kraaijen*, G. *krähen*, weak verbs; and cf. O. Slav. *grajati*, Lith. *groti*, to crow. Of imitative origin

crow (2), a bird. (E.) A.S. *cráwe* (see above).+O. S. *kráia*, Du. *kraai*, G. *krähe*. Der. *crow-bar*, bar with a crow-like beak.

Crowd (1), to push, throng. (E.) A.S. *crúdan* (pr. s. *crýdeþ*, pt. t. *créad*), to push; whence *croda*, *gecrod*, a crowd, throng. + M. Du. *kruyden*, *kruyen*, Du. *kruien*, to push along; E. Fries. *kröden*, *krüden*. Teut. type **krúdan*-, str. vb.

Crowd (2), a fiddle. (W.) M. E. *croude*.—W. *crwth*, a trunk, belly, crowd, violin, fiddle; Gael. *cruit*, harp; O. Irish *crot*, harp.

Crown. (F.—L.—Gk.) M. E. *corone*, *coroune* (whence *croune*).— O. F. *corone* (F. *couronne*). —L. *corōna*, a wreath. —Gk. κορώνη, end, tip; κορώνις, a wreath, garland.—Gk. κορωνός, bent, curved. Cf. Gk. κυρτός, L. *curuus*, bent.

Crucial. (F.—L.) F. *crucial*, 'cross-like;' Cot.—L. *cruci*-, decl. stem of *crux*, a cross; with suffix -*ālis*.

crucify. (F.—L.) O. F. *crucifier*.—Late L. **crucificāre*, for L. *crucifigere* (pp. *crucifixus*), to fix on a cross.—L. *cruci*, dative of *crux*; *figere*, to fix; see Fix. Der. *crucifix*, -*ion*.

Crucible. (L.) From Late L. *crucibolum*, (1) a night-lamp, (2) a vessel for melting metals. The lamp may have been so named from having four nozzles with wicks, forming a cross (still a common Ital. pattern); as if from *cruci*-, decl. stem of *crux*, a cross; with suffix -*bolum* =-*bulum*, as in *tūribulum*, a censer.

Crude. (L.) L. *crūdus*, raw. Allied to Raw.

cruel. (F.—L.) O. F. *cruel*. — L. *crūdēlis*, cruel; allied to *crūdus*, raw (above).

Cruet. (F.—Teut.) A. F. *cruet*, a small vessel (Godefroy); dimin. of O. F. *cruie*, *crue*, pot.—Low L. *crūga*, a pitcher. —O. H. G. *kruog*, G. *krug*, a pitcher; allied to Crock.

Cruise. (Du.—L.) Du. *kruisen*, to cruise, cross the sea.—Du. *kruis*, a cross. —L. acc. *crūc-em*, from *crux*, a cross; with lengthening of *ū*.

Crumb. (E.) Prov. E. *croom*. A. S. *crūma*. (The final *b* is excrescent.)+Du. *kruim*, Dan. *krumme*, G. *krume*, a crumb. Cf. Ital. *grumo*, a clot. Der. *crumb-le*, verb; cf. Du. *kruimelen*, G. *krümeln*, to crumble.

Crumpet, a kind of cake. (E.) Wyclif

has *crompid cake* to render Lat. *laga-num* (Ex. xxix. 23); cf. prov. E. *crumpy cake*, crisp cake. For *crump-ed*, pp. of M. E. *crumpen*, to curl up (whence E. *crumple*). Cf. G. *krümpen*, *krumpen*, to crumple, curl up; *krumm*, curved; Du. *krommen*, to crook, curve. See below.

Crumple, vb. (E.) Frequentative of obs. *crump*, to curl up. From *crump-*, weak grade of A. S. **crimpan*, str. vb.; see Cramp and Crimp.

Crunch. (E.) An imitative word. Cf. prov. E. *crinch*, *cranch*, to crunch.

Crupper; see Crop.

Crural. (L.) L. *crūrālis*, belonging to the leg. ─ L. *crūr-*, stem of *crūs*, the leg.

Crusade. (F. *and* Span. ─ L.) The form is due to confusion of F. *croisade* with Span. *cruzada.* ─ Late L. *cruciāta*, sb. fem., a marking with the cross, pp. f. of *cruciāre*, to cross. ─ L. *cruci-*, decl. stem of *crux*, a cross.

Cruse, a small pot. (E.) M. E. *cruse.* W. Fries. *kröss*, E. Fries. *krös.* + Icel. *krūs*, a pot; Swed. *krus*, Dan. *kruus*, a mug; Du. *kroes*, cup, pot, crucible; M. H. G. *krūse*, G. *krause*, mug.

Crush. (F. ─ Teut.) O. F. *crusir*, *cruisir*, *croissir*, to crack, break ; (Span. *cruxir*, Ital. *crosciare*). From a Teut. type **kraustjan-* (see Diez), causal form from Goth. *kriustan*, to gnash with the teeth.

Crust. (F. ─ L.) O. F. *crouste* (F. *croûte*). ─ L. *crusta*, crust of bread. Cf. Gk. κρύος, frost; see Crystal. Der. *crust-y*, hard like a crust, stubborn, harshly curt (of people).

Crutch. (E.) M. E. *crucche* ; from A. S. *crycc*, a crutch, staff. + Du. *kruk*, Swed. *krycka*, Dan. *krykke*, G. *krücke.*

Cry. (F. ─ L.) M. E. *crien.* ─ F. *crier.* (Fuller forms occur in Ital. *gridare*, Span. *gritar*, Port. *gritar.*) ─ L. *quirītāre*, to shriek, cry, lament (Brachet) ; lit. 'to implore the aid of the *Quirītes*' or Roman citizens (Varro).

Crypt. (L. ─ Gk.) L. *crypta.* ─ Gk. κρυπτή, a vault, hidden cave ; orig. fem. of κρυπτός, hidden. ─ Gk. κρύπτειν, to hide.

Crystal. (F. ─ L. ─ Gk.) Formerly *cristal.* ─ O. F. *cristal.* ─ L. *crystallum*, crystal. ─ Gk. κρύσταλλος, ice, crystal. ─ Gk. κρυσταίνειν, to freeze. ─ Gk. κρύος, frost.

Cub. (E.?) Etym. unknown. Cf.

Shetl. *coob*, to bring forth young, applied only to a seal ; Icel. *kobbi*, *kōpr*, a young seal.

Cube. (F. ─ L. ─ Gk.) F. *cube.* ─ L. acc. *cubum.* ─ Gk. κύβος, a cube, die.

Cubeb, a spicy berry. (F. ─ Span. ─ Arab.) F. *cubebe*, in Cotgrave. ─ Span. *cubeba.* ─ Arab. *kabāba(t)*, pl. *kabābah*, cubeb, an aromatic.

Cubit. (L.) L. *cubitus*, an elbow, bend ; the length from the elbow to the middle finger's end. Allied to L. *cubāre*, to lie down, recline ; see Covey.

Cuckold. (F. ; *with* G. *suffix*.) M. E. *kokewold*, *kokeweld*, *cokold.* ─ O. F. *cucuault*, *coucual* (Godefroy), a cuckold. ─ O. F. *cucu* (F. *coucou*), a cuckoo ; with depreciatory suffix *-ault*, *-al*, from G. *-wald* (Diez, *Gram.* ii. 346). Cf. O. F. *cucu* (F. *coucou*), a cuckoo ; secondly, a man whose wife is unfaithful. (There are endless allusions to the comparison between a cuckoo and a cuckold ; see Shak. L. L. L. v. 2. 920, &c.)

Cuckoo. (F.) F. *coucou* ; from the bird's cry. Cf. L. *cuculus*, a cuckoo ; Gk. κόκκυξ, a cuckoo ; κόκκυ, its cry ; Skt. *kokila-*, a cuckoo ; Irish *cuach*, W. *côg.* Cf. *cock*, *cockatoo.* And see Coo.

Cucumber. (L.) The *b* is excrescent ; M. E. *cucumer.* ─ L. *cucumerem*, acc. of *cucumis*, a cucumber.

Cud. (E.) M. E. *cude*, *code*, *quide.* A. S. *cwidu*, *cweodu*, *cudu.* Teut. type **kwedwom*, neut. Cf. Skt. *jatu-*, resin ; also Icel. *kwāða*, resin. Orig. sense, 'glutinous substance.'

Cuddle. (E.) Perhaps for **couthle*, to be familiar, to fondle ; from *couth*, adj. familiar, well known ; A. S. *cūð*, known, pp. of *cunnan*, to know. See Can (1). Cf. prov. E. *couth*, loving ; *cootle*, to fondle.

Cudgel. (E.) M. E. *kuggel.* A. S. *cycgel* ; in Gregory's Pastoral Care, ed. Sweet, p. 297. Cf. Cog.

Cudweed. (E.) From *cud* and *weed*; 'the plant being administered to cattle that had lost their cud.' So also *cud-wort.*

Cue, for an actor. (L.?) Sometimes written *q* or *qu* in the 16th cent., and supposed to be for L. *quando*, when.

Cuff (1), to strike. (Scand. ?) Cf. Swed. *kuffa*, to thrust, push, M. Swed. *kuffa*, to strike, to cuff (Ihre).

Cuff (2), part of the sleeve. (L. ?) M. F. *cuffe*, *coffe.* Cf. Late A. S. *cuffie*, a

kind of cap (Leo); M. H. G. *kupfe,*
kuppe, kuffe, a coif; see Coif. [Very
doubtful.]

Cuirass. (F.–Ital.–L.) Formerly
curace.–O. F. *cuirace* (F. *cuirasse*).–Ital.
corazza, a cuirass. Formed from L.
coriāceus, leathern.– L. *corium,* leather
(whence F. *cuir,* leather).

Cuisses, pl. (F.–L.) O. F. *cuissaux,*
armour for the thighs. – F. *cuisse,* thigh. –
L. *coxa,* hip. Brugm. i. § 609.

Culdee. (C.) Irish *ceilede,* a Culdee, a
servant of God.– Ir. *ceile* (O. Irish *cēle*),
servant; and *dē,* gen. of *dīa,* God.

Culinary. (L.) L. *culīnārius,* belonging to the kitchen. – L. *culīna,*
kitchen.

Cull, to collect, select. (F.–L.) M. E.
cullen.–O. F. *coillir, cuillir,* to collect.–
L. *colligere,* to collect. See Coil (1) and
Collect.

Cullender; see Colander.

Cullion, a wretch. (F.–L.) A coarse
word. F. *couillon* (Ital. *coglione*).–L.
cōleus.

Cullis, a strong broth, boiled and
strained. (F.–L.) Formerly *colys, coleys.*
– O. F. *coleïs, couleïs,* later *coulis,* 'a
cullis,' Cot.; substantival use of *coleïs,*
later *coulis,* 'gliding,' Cot.– L. type **cōlā-*
tīcius ; from *cōlāre,* to strain. Cf. Portcullis.

Culm, a stem. (L.) L. *culmus,* a
stalk; allied to *calamus,* a stalk. See
Haulm.

Culminate. (L.) From pp. of L.
culmināre, to come to a top.–L. *culmin-,*
stem of *culmen* (= *columen*), a top. See
Column.

Culpable. (F.–L.) M. E. *coupable.*
O. F. *culpable, colpable, coupable* (F. *coup-*
able). – L. *culpābilis,* blameworthy.– L.
culpāre, to blame.–L. *culpa,* a fault.

culprit. (F.–L.) In Dryden. Not
orig. a single word, but due to a fusion of
A. F. *cul-* (for *culpable,* i. e. guilty) and
prist or *prest* (i. e. ready to prove it);
signifying that the clerk of the crown was
ready to prove the indictment (N. E. D.).

Culter; see Coulter.

Cultivate. (L.) Late L. *cultīvātus,*
pp. of *cultīvāre,* to till.–Late L. *cultīvus,*
fit for tilling.–L. *cultus,* pp. of *colere,* to
till. Brugm. i. § 121.

culture. (F.–L.) F. *culture.*–L.
cultūra· allied to *cult-us,* pp. of *colere,*
to till.

Culver. (E.) A.S. *culfre,* a dove.

Culverin. (F.–L.) Corrupt form,
for **culevrin.*–F. *coulevrine,* a culverin;
a piece of ordnance named from its long
shape, like a snake.–O. F. *couleuvrin,*
adder-like; from *couleuvre,* an adder.–L.
colubra, coluber, an adder.

Culvert, an arched drain. (F.–L.)
Of doubtful origin; perhaps formed, with
added *t,* from O. F. *coulouёre,* 'a channel,
gutter,' Cot.–F. *couler,* to trickle.–L.
cōlāre, to strain, drain. Compare Portcullis and Cullis.

Cumber. (F.–Late L.) M. E. *com-*
bren.–O. F. *combrer,* to hinder (rare) ;
usual form *en-combrer.*–Late L. *cumbrus,*
a heap, a barrier; of doubtful origin.
[Cf. L. *cumulus,* a heap; but also G.
kummer, grief, oppression, prov. G. *kum-*
mer, rubbish. Thus *cumber* = to put a
heap in the way.] Der. *en-cumber,* from
O. F. *encombrer,* to encumber, load.

Cumin, Cummin, a plant. (L.–
Gk.–Heb.) M. E. *comin.* A. S. *cumin,*
cymen.–L. *cumīnum,* Matt. xxiii. 23.–
Gk. κύμῑνον.–Heb. *kammōn,* cumin.

Cumulate. (L.) From pp. of L.
cumulāre, to heap up.–L. *cumulus,* a
heap.

Cuneate, wedge-shaped. (L.) Formed,
with suffix -*ate,* from L. *cune-us,* a wedge.
Allied to Cone. Der. *cunei-form* ; i. e.
wedge-shaped. See Coin.

Cunning, adj. (E.) Orig. pres. pt. of
M. E. *cunnen,* to know; hence, 'knowing.'
From A. S. *cunnan,* to know ; see Can (1).

cunning, sb. (E.) M. E. *cunninge.*
From A. S. *cunnan,* to know. Perhaps
suggested by Icel. *kunnandi,* knowledge ;
from Icel. *kunna,* to know.

Cup. (L.) A. S. *cuppe,* a cup.–Late L.
cuppa, variant of L. *cūpa,* a tub, in Late
L., a drinking-vessel ; whence also Du.
Dan. *kop,* F. *coupe,* &c. See Coop.

cupboard. (L. *and* E.) M. E. *cup-*
borde, orig. a side-board for holding cups ;
Allit. Poems, B. **1440**; Morte Arth.
206.

Cupid, god of love. (L.) L. *cupīdo,*
desire.–L. *cupere,* to desire. **+** Skt. *kup,*
to become excited. Der. *cupid-i-ty,* F.
cupidité, from L. acc. *cupiditātem.*

Cupola. (Ital.–L.) Ital. *cupola,* a
dome; from its shape.–L. *cūpula,* a small
cask, a little vault; dimin. of L. *cūpa,* a
cask.

Cupreous, coppery. (L.) L. *cupre-us,*

of copper; with suffix -ous.—L. cuprum, copper.

Cur. (E.) M. E. kur-dogge (ab. 1225). +M. Du. korre, a house-dog; cf. Swed. dial. kurre, a dog. Named from growling. Cf. prov. E. curr, to purr; Low G. kurren, to snarl (Lübben); Icel. kurra, to murmur, grumble; Swed. kurra, to rumble.

Curate; see Cure.

Curb. (F. — L.) M. E. courben, to bend. — F. courber, to bend, bow. — L. curuāre, to bend; from curuus, bent.

Curd. (E.) M. E. curd, crud. Prob. from A. S. crud-, related to crūdan, to crowd, press together. Cf. Ir. gruth, Gael. gruth, curds. (Fick, ii. 119.)

Cure. (F.—L.) O. F. cure.—L. cūra, attention (prim. Ital. *koizā). Brugm. i. § 874. ¶ Not allied to care.

curate. (L.) Med. L. cūrātus, a priest, curate; cf. cūrātum beneficium, a benefice with cure of souls. — L. cūra, cure.

curious. (F.—L.) O. F. curios.—L. cūriōsus, attentive.—L. cūra, attention.

Curfew. (F.—L.) A. F. coeverfu, covrefeu, curfeu; O. F. covrefeu (F. couvre-feu), a fire-cover, covering of fires, time for putting out fires.—O. F. covrir, to cover; feu, fire (<L. focum, acc. of focus, hearth, fire); see Cover and Focus.

Curious; see Cure.

Curl, sb. (E.) M. E. crul (with shifting of r); from M. E. crul, adj., curly (A. D. 1300). Not in A. S. E. Fries. krulla, krull, krul, a curl.+Du. krul, a curl, krullen, to curl; Dan. krölle, a curl, Swed. krullig, curly; G. krolle, a curl, M. H. G. krülle. Cf. Norw. krull, a curl, something rolled together; krulla, to curl, bend or bow together. Allied to E. Fries. krillen, to bend, turn, wind; Low G. krellen, to turn; N. Fries. krall, close-twisted; suggesting Teut. base *krellan-, to wind, str. vb. (Franck, Koolman).

Curlew, a bird. (F.) M. F. corlieu, 'a curlue;' Cot. Cf. Ital. chiurlo, a curlew, chiurlare, to howl, Swed. kurla, to coo; so that it is named from its cry.

Curmudgeon. (E.?) Origin unknown. In one instance spelt corn-mudgin (Phil. Holland), as if a hoarder of corn, hence, a stingy fellow; where mudgin is for mudging, pres. pt. of mudge, to hoard, also spelt mooch (M. E. muchen), to skulk; from O. F. mucer, to hide. But this is a

forced spelling, giving a wrong clue. In 1596, we find cormullion, with the same sense. The first syllable seems to be cur, a whelp; and we find Lowl. Sc. murgeon, to mock, to grumble; mudgeon, a grimace.

Currant. (F.—L.—Gk.) Formerly raysyns of coraunt.—F. raisins de Corinthe, 'currants;' Cot. Hence, currant is a corruption of Corinth (L. Corinthus, Gk. Κόρινθος).

Current, running, flowing. (F.—L.) M. E. currant, O. F. curant, pres. pt. of curre, corre (F. courir), to run.—L. currere, to run. Prob. for *cursere. Brugm. i. §§ 499, 516. Perhaps allied to Horse.

curricle. (L.) L. curriculum, a running; also, a light car.—L. currere, to run.

Curry (1), to dress leather. (F.—L. and Teut.) O. F. correier (Godefroy), earlier forms conreder, conreër, later conroyer, courroier, to curry, dress leather, orig. to prepare.—O. F. conrei, older form cunreid, gear, preparation. A hybrid word; made by prefixing con- (=L. con, cum) to O. F. rei, order (Ital. -redo in arredo, array). β. This O. F. rei is of Scand. origin; from Dan. rede, order (also to set in order), Icel. reiði, tackle. Precisely the same O. F. rei helps to form E. ar-ray; see Array. ¶ To curry favour is a corruption of M. E. to curry favel, to rub down a horse; Favel was a common old name for a horse.

Curry (2), a seasoned dish. (Tamil) From Tamil kari, sauce, relish for rice (Yule).

Curse. (E.) A. S. cursian, verb; curs, sb., an imprecation. Cf. O. Ir. cūrsaigim, 'I reprehend' (Windisch). Der. ac-cursed, from M. E. acorsien, to curse extremely, where the prefix a-=A. S. ā-, very; see A- (4).

Cursive. (L.) Med. L. cursīvus, flowing; said of handwriting.—L. curs-us, pp. of currere, to run. See Current.

cursory. (L.) Late L. cursōrius, hasty.—L. cursōri-, decl. stem of cursor, a runner.—L. curs-us (above).

Curt. (L.) L. curtus, short, cut short.

curtail. (F.—L.) It has nothing to do with tail, but is an alteration of the older form curtal, verb, to dock; from the adj. curtal, having a docked tail (All's Well, ii. 3. 65).—O. F. courtault, later courtaut, 'curtall, being curtalled;' Cot. The same as Ital. cortaldo, 'a curtall, a orse without a taile,' Florio. Formed, with suffix -*ault* (=Ital. -*aldo*, Low L. -*aldus*, < G. *wald*, power), from O. F. *court*, short.—L. *curtus*, short.

Curtain. (F.—L.) M. E. *cortin.*— O. F. *cortine.*—Late L. *cortīna*, a curtain (Exod. xxvi. 1, Vulgate), a screen, plain wall of a fort, orig. a small yard.—L. *cōrt-em*, acc. of *cōrs*, a court. See **Court**.

Curtleaxe. (F.—L.) A perversion of *cuttleaxe*, which was a perversion of *cuttelas*, an old spelling of *cutlass*. See **Cutlass**.

Curtsey. (F.—L.) The same word as *courtesy*, i. e. a courtly act.

Curve, a bent line. (L.) Late L. *curvus*, L. *curuus*, bent. + Gk. κύρτος, bent. **Der.** *curv-ature*, L. *curuātūra*, from pp. of *curuāre*, to bend; from *curuus*.

curvet. (Ital.—L.) Ital. *corvetta*, a curvet, leap, bound; dimin. from M. Ital. *corv-o* (Ital. *curvo*), bent.—L. *curuus* (above).

Cushat, the ring-dove. (E.) A.S. *cū-sceote*, a wild pigeon; also *cūscote*. Here *sceote* probably means 'shooter, darter,' from *scēotan*, to shoot (cf. A. S. *scēota*, a kind of trout); and perhaps *cū* refers to the ' coo' of the bird. Cf. Lowl. Sc. *cow-shot*, a cushat.

Cushion. (F.—L.) M. E. *quisshin*, *cusshin.*—O. F. *coissin, coussin*, a cushion. [It is supposed that O. F. *coissin* was the true form, altered to *coussin* (perhaps) by the influence of O. F. *coute*, a quilt.]—L. type *coxīnum*, a support for the hip, from *coxa*, hip, thigh (like L. *cubital*, elbow-cushion, from *cubitus*, elbow). Cf. Ital. *cuscino*, cushion, *coscia*, hip; Span. *cojin*, cushion, *cuja*, hip. (*Romania*, 1892, p. 87.)

Cusp. (L.) L. *cuspis*, a point.

Custard. (F.—Ital.—L.) For M. E. *crustade*, by shifting of *r*. Formerly *cus-tade, crustade*, and orig. used with the sense of 'pasty.'—F. *croustade*, a pasty. —Ital. *crostata*, ' a kinde of daintie pye;' Florio.—L. *crustāta*, fem. pp. of *crustāre*, to encrust.—L. *crusta*, a crust.

Custody. (L.) L. *custōdia*, a keeping guard.—L. *custōd(i)*-, stem of *custos*, a guardian; lit. 'hider.' Cf. Gk. κεύθειν, to hide. See **Hide**. (√KEUDH.) Brugm. i. § 699.

Custom. (F.—L.) M. E. *custume.*— O. F. *custume, costume* (F. *coutume*).

From a L. type **costumne*, for **cos-tudne*, shortened form of *consuētudinem*, acc. of *consuētudo*, custom.—L. *consuētus*, pp. of *consuescere*, to accustom, inchoative form of **consuēre*, to be accustomed.—L. *con-* (*cum*), together, very; *suescere* (pp. *suētus*), to be accustomed; possibly from *suus*, own; so that *suescere*=to have it one's own way.

Cut. (Scand.) M. E. *cutten*, a weak verb. Of Scand. origin, but the traces of it are not many. Cf. Mid. Swed. *kotta*, to cut (Ihre); Swed. dial. *kuta, kåta*, to cut small with a knife, also spelt *kvòta, kòta, käta*; *kuta*, or *kytti*, a knife (Rietz); Icel. *kuti*, a little knife; Norw. *kyttel, kytel, kjutul*, a knife for barking trees.

Cuticle. (L.) L. *cutīcula*, double dimin. of *cutis*, hide, skin. See **Hide**. **Der.** *cut-an-e-ous*, from *cut-is*.

Cutlass. (F.—L.) F. *coutelas*, ' a cut-telas, or courtelas, or short sword;' Cot. (Cf. Ital. *coltellaccio*, ' a curtleax,' Florio; which is the same word.)—O. F. *coutel, cultel* (F. *couteau*), a knife; cf. Ital. *col-tello*, knife; with acc. suffix -*āceum.*—L. acc. *cultellum*, a knife; dimin. of *culter*, a coulter. ¶ The F. -*as*, Ital. -*accio*=L. -*āceum*; but F. *coutelas* was actually turned into E. *curtleaxe*. Yet a *curtle-axe* was a sort of sword!

cutler. (F.—L.) M. E. *coteler.*— O. F. *cotelier.*—Late L. *cultellārius*, knife-maker.—L. *cultellus*, a knife (above).

Cutlet. (F.—L.) F. *côtelette*, a cutlet; formerly *costelette*, a little rib; dimin. of O. F. *coste*, rib.—L. *costa*, a rib; see **Coast**.

Cuttle, a fish. (E.) Formerly *cudele*. A.S. *cudele*, a cuttle-fish. Cf. G. *kuttel-fisch* (perhaps from E.).

Cycle. (F.—L.—Gk.) F. *cycle.*—L. *cyclum*, acc. of *cyclus*.—Gk. κύκλος, a circle, cycle. + Skt. *chakra-*, a wheel, circle. Allied to **Wheel**. **Der.** *cyclone* = Gk. κυκλῶν, whirling round, pres. pt. of κυκλόω, I whirl round; *epi-cycle*; *bi-cycle*.

Cygnet, a young swan. (F.—L.—Gk.) Dimin. of O. F. *cigne*, a swan. Strangely enough, this O. F. word is *not* immediately from L. *cycnus*, a swan; but the oldest O. F. spelling was *cisne* (as in Spanish), from Late L. *cicinus*, a swan, variant of *cycnus.*—Gk. κύκνος, a swan. Cf L. *ciconia*, a stork. See Diez; 4th ed. p. 714.

Cylinder. (F.—L.—Gk.) O. F. *cil-indre*, later *cylindre*. — L. *cylindrus*. — Gk. κύλινδρος, a roller, cylinder. — Gk. κυλίνδειν, to roll; from κυλίειν, to roll. Cf. O. Slav. *kolo*, a wheel. (√QEL.)

Cymbal. (F.—L.—Gk.) M.E. *cimbale*. — O. F. *cimbale*. — L. *cymbalum*. — Gk. κύμβαλον, a cymbal; named from its cup-like shape. — Gk. κύμβη, a cup. + Skt. *kumbha-*, a jar. Allied to **Cup**; and see **Comb** (2). (√KEUBH.)

Cynic, lit. dog-like. (L.—Gk.) L. *cynicus*. — Gk. κυνικός, dog-like, a Cynic. — Gk. κυν-, as in κυνός, gen. of κύων, a dog (E. *hound*).

cynosure. (L.—Gk.) L. *cynosūra*, the stars in the tail of the constellation of the Lesser Bear; one of these is the Pole-star (hence, a centre of attraction). — Gk. κυνόσουρα, the Cynosure, tail of the Lesser Bear; lit. ' dog's tail.' — Gk. κύνος, gen. of κύων, a dog; οὐρά, a tail.

Cypress (1), a tree. (F.—L.—Gk.) M. E. *cipres*. — O. F. *cypres*, later *cyprès*. — L. *cupressus, cyparissus*. — Gk. κυπάρισσος, cypress-tree. Cf. Heb. *gōpher*.

Cypress (2), a cloth of gold, a kind of satin, a kind of crape. (F.—L.) Pals-grave explains F. *crespe* by ' a cypres for a womans neck'; Cotgrave has ' *crespe, cipres*, cobweb lawn'; which suggests some confusion of *cypress* with *crape*. The origin of *cypress* is doubtful; but it occurs as *cipres, cypirs* in Piers Plow-man, and as *cyprus* in Sir Degrevant. It seems to have been imported from the isle of *Cyprus*.

Cyst, a pouch (in animals) containing morbid matter. (L. — Gk.) Formerly written *cystis*. — Late L. *cystis*. — Gk. κύστις, a bag, pouch.

Czar, the emperor of Russia. (Russ. — Teut. — L.) Russ. *tsare* (with *e* mute), a king. O. Slav. *cěsař*. — Goth. *kaisar*. — L. *Cæsar*. ¶ This has been disputed; but see Matt. xiii. 24 in Schleicher, Indogermanische Chrestomathie, p. 275, where O.Slav. *cesarstvo* occurs for Russ. *tsarstvo*, kingdom; &c. Der. *czarowitz*, from Russ. *tsarevich'*, czar's son; *czaritsa*, from Russ. *tsaritsa*, empress; *czar-ina*, with Ital. suffix *-ina*, from G. fem. suffix *-in*.

D.

Dab (1), to strike gently. (E.) M. E. *dabben*; also *dabbe*, a blow. Not in A. S.

Cf. M. Du. *dabben*, to pinch, fumble, dabble; G. *tappen*, to grope, prov. G. *tappe*, fist, blow. See **Dub, Tap.**

dabble. (E.) To keep on dabbing; frequent. of *dab*. + M. Du. *dabbelen*, to fumble, dabble; frequent. of M.Du. *dabben* (above).

Dab (2), expert. (E.?) Prob. from *dab* (1); perhaps influenced by *dapper* or by *adept*.

Dab (3), a fish. (E.) M. E. *dabbe*. Prob. allied to *dab*, a light blow, a soft mass dabbed down. See **Dab** (1), **dabble**.

Dabble; see **Dab** (1).

Dab-chick. (E.) Formerly *dap-chick, dop-chick*. Cf. A.S. *dop-enid*, a moorhen, lit. ' dipping duck;' *doppettan*, to dip often, immerse; Du. *dobber*, a float. See **Dip.**

Dace. (F. — O. Low G.) Formerly *darce*. — O. F. *dars*, nom. case of the word also spelt *dart*, meaning (1) a dart, (2) a dace. The fish is also called a *dart* or a *dare*, from its swift motion. See **Dare** (2), **Dart.**

Dacoit, a robber. (Hind.) Hind. *ḍākāit*, a robber belonging to an armed gang; from *ḍākā*, robbery by a gang (Wilson). Der. *dacoit-y*, robbery.

Dactyl. (L.—Gk.) L. *dactylus*, the metrical foot marked −∪∪. — Gk. δάκτυλος, a finger, a dactyl.

Dad. (E.) A child's word for ' father.' So also W. *tad*, Irish *daid*, Bret. *tat, tad*, father; Gk. τάτα, Skt. *tata*, dad.

Dado. (Ital.—L.) Formerly used of the die, or square part in the middle of the pedestal of a column; afterwards applied to the part of an apartment between the plinth and the impost moulding. — Ital. *dado*, a die, cube, pedestal. (Cf. Prov. *dat-z*, a die.) — Folk-L. *datum*, assumed to mean ' a die'; lit. ' a thing given, a lot.' — L. *datum*, neut. of pp. of *dare*, to give. See **Die** (2).

Daffodil. (F.—L.—Gk.) The *d* is a later addition; perhaps from M. F. *fleur d'affrodille*, translated ' daffodil-flower.' M. E. *affodile*; Prompt. Parv. — M. F. *asphodile*, also *affrodille*, ' th'affodill, or asphodill flower;' Cot.—L. *asphodelus*.— Gk. ἀσφόδελος, a kind of lily. See **Asphodel.**

Daft, foolish; the same as **Deft.**

Dagger. (F.) M. E. *daggere*; allied to *daggen*, to pierce. — F. *dague*, a dagger; of unknown origin (not Celtic). Cf. Ital. Span. *daga*, Port. *adaga*, dagger. The

Port. form suggests an Eastern origin;
cf. Heb. *dākhāh*, to strike.

Daggle, to moisten, wet with dew or
spray. (Scand.) Frequentative verb from
Swed. *dagg*, Icel. *dögg* (gen. *daggar*), dew.
Cf. Icel. *döggva*, to bedew. See **Dew.**

Daguerreotype. (F. *and* Gk.)
Formed by adding *-o-type* to F. *Daguerre*,
a personal name, the inventor (A. D. 1838).

Dahlia. (Swed.) Named after *Dahl*,
a Swedish botanist (A. D. 1791).

Dainty, a delicacy. (F. – L.) M. E.
deintee, orig. a sb., a pleasant thing; cf.
A. F. *deyntee*, greediness (Bozon). –
O. F. *daintie* (i. e. *daintié*), agreeableness.
– L. acc. *dignitātem*; see **Dignity.**
¶ The O. F. *daintie* is the true popular
O. F. form; *digniteit* is a pedantic form;
cf. O. F. *dain*, old spelling of *digne*,
worthy.

Dairy. (Scand.) M. E. *deyerye*, a
room for a *deye*, i. e. a milk-woman, farm-
servant. – O. Norw. *deigja*, Swed. *deja*, a
maid, dairy-maid, who was also the bread-
maker; the orig. sense is 'kneader of dough.'
– Teut. type *daig-jōn-*, sb. f., as if from
(Goth.) *deigan* (pt. t. *daig*), to mould;
whence also Goth. *daigs*, Icel. *deig*, Swed.
deg, dough; see **Dough.** ¶ The cognate
or borrowed A. S. *dǣge* occurs once only;
see Thorpe, *Dipl.* p. 641.

Dais, a raised floor in a hall. (F. – L.
– Gk.) Now used of the raised platform
on which the high table in a hall stands.
Properly, it was the table *itself*; but was
also used of a canopy over a seat of state,
or of the seat of state. M. E. *deis, deys.* –
A. F. *deis,* O. F. *dois,* a high table (Supp.
to Godefroy). – L. *discum,* acc. of *discus,*
a quoit, platter; in Late L. a table. – Gk.
δίσκος, a quoit, disc. See **Disc.**

Daisy. (E.) M. E. *dayĕsyĕ* (4 syllables). A. S. *dæges ēage*, eye of day, i. e.
the sun, which it resembles.

Dale, a valley. (E.) M. E. *dale.* –
A. S. *dæl* (pl. *dal-u*). + Icel. *dalr,* Dan.
Swed. *dal,* a dale; Du. *dal*; Goth. *dals*;
G. *thal*; also O. Slav. *dolŭ* (Russ. *dol'*) ;
cf. Gk. θόλος, a vault. Der. *dell.*

Dally, to trifle. (F. – Teut.) M. E.
dalien, to play, trifle. – A. F. *and* O. F.
dalier, to converse, chat, pass the time in
light converse (Bozon). Of Teut. origin;
cf. Bavarian *dalen,* to speak and act as
children (Schmeller); mod. G. (vulgar)
dahlen, to trifle.

Dalmatic, a vestment. (F. – Dal-

matia.) F. *dalmatique.* – L. *dalmatica*
(*uestis*); fem. of *Dalmaticus,* belonging to
Dalmatia.

Dam (1), a mound, bank against water.
(E.) A. S. *damm,* only in the derived
verb *for-demman,* to dam up; O. Fries.
dam; North. Fries. *dām.* + Du. *dam,*
Icel. *dammr,* Dan. *dam,* Swed. *damm,*
M. H. G. *tam,* G. *damm,* a dam, dike.
Cf. Goth. *faurdammjan,* to dam up.

Dam (2), a mother, applied to animals.
(F – L.) The same word as **Dame.**

Damage. (F. – L.) M. E. *damage.* –
A. F. *damage* (F. *dommage*); cf. Prov.
damnatje, answering to Late L. **damnāti-
cum,* harm; we find Late L. *damnāticus,*
condemned to the mines. – L. *damnātus,*
pp. of *damnāre*; see **Damn.**

Damask. (Ital. – Syria.) M. E. *da-
maske,* cloth of Damascus. – Ital. *damasco.*
– Heb. *dmeseq,* damask, *Dammeseq,* Damascus (Gen. xiv. 15). Der. *damask-
rose*; *damask-ine,* to inlay with gold (F.
damasquiner, from *damasqu-in,* adj.).

Dame. (F. – L.) M. E. *dame.* – O. F.
dame, a lady. – L. *domina*; fem. of *dominus,* a lord. See **Don** (2).

Damn, to condemn. (F. – L.) M. E.
damnen, dampnen. – F. *damner.* – L. *damnāre,* to condemn, fine. – L. *damnum,* loss,
fine, penalty. Brug. i. § 762.

Damp. (E.) Cf. M. E. *dampen,* to
suffocate; E. Fries. *damp,* vapour.+Du.
damp, vapour, steam; Dan. *damp,* G.
dampf, vapour; Swed. *damb,* dust. From
the 2nd grade of Teut. **dempan-,* pt. t.
*damp, pp. **dumpano-,* as in M. H. G.
dimpfen, timpfen, str. vb., to reek; cf.
Swed. dial. *dimba,* str. vb., to reek. See
Dumps.

Damsel. (F. – L.) M. E. *damosel.* –
O. F. *dameisele,* a girl, fem. of *dameisel,* a
young man, squire, page. – Late L. *domi-
cellus,* a page, short for **dominicellus,*
double dimin. of *dominus,* a lord. (Pages
were often of high birth.)

Damson. (L. – Syria.) M. E. *dama-
scene.* – L. *Damascēnum* (*prūnum*), plum
of Damascus. See **Damask.**

Dance. (F. – O. H. G.) M. E. *daun-
cen.* – F. *danser.* – O. H. G. *dansōn,* to
drag along (as in a round dance). –
O. H. G. *dans,* 2nd grade of *dinsen,* to
pull, draw; allied to E. **Thin.** Cf. Goth.
at-thinsan, to draw towards one.

Dandelion, a flower. (F. – L.) F.
dent de lion, tooth of a lion; named from

the jagged leaves.—L. *dent-em*, acc. of *dens*, tooth; *dē*, prep.; *leōnem*, acc. of *leo*, lion.

Dandle. (E.) Prob. of imitative origin; cf. M. F. *dodiner, dodeliner*, 'to rock, dandle, lull,' Cot.; M. Ital. *dandolare, dondolare*, 'to dandle or play the baby,' Florio; *dandola, dondola*, a toy. Godefroy gives M. F. *dandiner*, to balance or sway the body. Cf. E. Fries. *dindannen*, to walk unsteadily, sway from side to side.

Dandriff, scurf on the head. (E.) Formerly also *dandruffe*. Of unknown origin; but cf. prov. E. *dan*, scurf, *dander*, a slight scurf on the skin; and (perhaps) *drib*, a driblet, or *drift*, a fine shower. ¶ The W. *marw-don*, dandriff, is from *marw*, dead, and *ton*, skin.

Dandy, a beau (E.?). Origin unknown. Prov. E. *dandy*, gay, fine. Note M. Dan. *dande*, brave, excellent. *Dandy* is also a form of *Andrew*. [F. *dandin*, 'a meacock, noddy, ninny,' Cot., is unsuitable.]

Danger. (F.—L.) M. E. *daungere*, power, esp. power to harm.—O. F. *dangier* (F. *danger*), also *dongier* (XIII cent.), absolute power, irresponsible authority. This answers to a Late L. type *domniārium, *dominiārium*, not found, but regularly formed from Late L. *dom(i)nium*, power, authority.—Late L. *domnus*, L. *dominus*, a lord.

Dangle, to swing about. (Scand.) Dan. *dangle*, Swed. dial. *dangla*, to swing about; cf. Swed. and Icel. *dingla*, Dan. *dingle*, to swing about; frequentative forms from *ding* (pt. t. *dang*), to throw about. See **Ding**.

Dank, moist. (Scand.) M. E. *dank*, wet (esp. with ref. to dew).—Swed. dial. *dank*, marshy ground; Icel. *dökk* (stem *dankwō-*), a pool. Cf. Swed. dial. *dänka*, to moisten, Dan. dial. *dönke, dynke*, Norw. *dynka*, to wet; also Dan. dial. *dunkel*, moist, Swed. dial. *dunkelhet*, moisture; North. E. *danker*, a dark cloud; Swed. dial. and M. Dan. *dunken*, musty; G. *dunkel*, dark.

Dapper. (Du.) Orig. good, valiant; hence brave, fine, spruce. XV cent.—Du. *dapper*, brave.+O. H. G. *taphar*, weighty, valiant, G. *tapfer*, brave; Russ. *dobrui*, good. Brugm. i. § 563.

Dapple, a spot on an animal. (Scand.) Icel. *depill*, a spot, dot; a dog with spots over the eyes is also called *depill*. The orig. sense is 'a little pool,' from Norweg.

dape, a pool, a wet splotch; whence the idea of 'splash' or 'blot.'

Dare (1), to venture. (E.) M. E. *dar*, I dare; pt. t. *dorste, durste*. A. S. *ic dearr*, I dare; *he dearr*, he dare; pt. t. *dorste*; infin. **durran*. + Goth. *ga-dars*, I dare, *-daursta*, I durst, infin. *-daursan*; O. H. G. *tar*, I dare, infin. *turran*. Also Gk. θαρσεῖν, to be bold, θρασύς, bold; Skt. *dṛsh*, to dare. (√DHERS.) Brugm. i. § 502.

Dare (2), a dace. (F.—O. Low G.) A new form, made by taking *darce* (old form of *dace*) as a pl. form (= *dars*), and thence making a singular *dar*, now *dare*. See **Dace**.

Dark. (E.) M. E. *derk*. A. S. *deorc*, with a broken vowel; for older **derc*. The O. H. G. *tarchanjan*, to hide (answering to W. Germ. **dark-n-jan*) is from the 2nd grade **dark* of the same base. Cf. also O. Sax. *der-ni*, A. S. *derne*, O. H. G. *tar-ni*, secret, dark; see **Tarnish**.

darkling, in the dark. (E.) Formed with adv. suffix *-ling*, as in *flat-ling*, M. E. *hedling* (headlong), A. S. *bæc-ling*, backwards.

Darling. (E.) M. E. *derling*. A. S. *dēorling*, a favourite. — A. S. *dēor-e* (in comp. *dēor-*), dear; with double dimin. suffix *-l-ing*. See **Dear**.

Darn. (E.) XVII cent. Prob. from M. E. *dernen*, to conceal, from *derne*, adj., secret, hidden; cf. prov. E. *dern, darn*, to hide, to stop up a hole.—A. S. *derne, dyrne*, secret, hidden. + O. Sax. *derni*, O. H. G. *tarni*, secret. See **Dark**.

Darnel. (F.) M. E. *darnel, dernel*. From an O. F. word, now only preserved in Walloon (Rouchi), *darnelle*, darnel (Hécart). Hitherto unexplained; but cf. Swed. *dår-*, as in *dår-repe*, or *repe*, darnel (Lowl. Sc. *dornel*); and O. F. *nielle, nelle* (Late L. *nigella*), darnel (Godefroy). The Swed. *dåra* means to stupefy (as with *lolium temulentum*); cf. Dan. *daare*, a fool; Walloon *darnise, daurnise*, drunken (Grandgagnage).

Dart. (F.—O. Low G.) M. E. *dart*.—O. F. *dart* (F. *dard*). Of Teut. origin; cf. A. S. *daroð*, a dart, Swed. *dart*, a dagger, Icel. *darraðr*, a dart, O. H. G. *tart*, a dart.

Dash. (E.) M. E. *daschen*. Cf. Low G. *daschen*, to thrash (Berghaus); Dan. *daske*, to slap, Swed. *daska*, to beat; we speak of water *dashing* against rocks.

Dastard. (Scand.; *with* F. *suffix*.)

M. E. *dastard*; where *-ard* is a F. suffix, as in *dull-ard, slugg-ard.* *Dast* appears to be for *dazed*; cf. Icel. *dæstr*, exhausted, pp. of *dæsa*, to be out of breath ; *dasaðr*, exhausted, weary, pp. of *dasask*, to be weary; see **Daze**. Cf. Icel. *dasi*, a lazy fellow, M. Du. *dasaert*, a fool (whence M. E. *das-art* (i. e. *daz(e)ard*), a dullard, in N. E. D.) ; Low G. *däskopp*, a block-head (Berghaus). The orig. sense is 'slug-gard.'

Date (1), a given point of time. (F.— L.) M. E. *date.*—F. *date*, date.—Late L. *data*, a date; L. *data*, neut. pl. of *datus*, given, dated.—L. *dare*, to give.+Gk. δί-δωμι, I give ; δοτός, given ; Skt. *dadāmi*, I give ; Russ. *date*, to give. (√DŌ.) Brugm. i. §§ 167, 168.

Date (2), fruit of the palm. (F.— L.— Gk.) M. E. *date.*—O. F. *date* (F. *datte*), also *datele*, a date.—L. *dactylum*, acc. of *dactylus.*—Gk. δάκτυλος, a finger ; also a date (somewhat like a finger). But it is probable that δάκτυλος, a date, was a word of Semitic origin, assimilated to the word for 'finger.' Cf. Aramaic *diqlā*, a palm-tree (see Gen. x. 27); Arab. *daqal.*

Daub. (F.—L.) M. E. *dauben.*—O. F. *dauber*, to plaster; answering to an older form **dalber.*—L. *dealbāre*, to whiten, plaster.—L. *dē*, down, very ; *albāre*, to whiten, from *albus*, white; see **Alb.** Cf. Span. *jalbegar* (= **dealbicāre*), to plaster. Der. *be-daub.*

Daughter. (E.) M. E. *doghter, doh-ter.* A. S. *dohtor.*+Du. *dochter*, Dan. *dat-ter, dotter*, Swed. *dotter*, Icel. *dōttir*, Goth. *dauhtar*, G. *tochter* ; Russ. *doche*, Lith. *dukte*, Gk. θυγάτηρ, Pers. *dukhtar*, Skt. *duhitṛ.* Orig. sense doubtful.

Daunt. (F.—L.) M. E. *daunten.*— O. F. *danter*; also *donter.*—L. *domitāre*, to tame, subdue; frequent. of *domāre*, to tame ; see **Tame.**

Dauphin. (F.—L.—Gk.) F. *dauphin*, a dolphin ; see **Dolphin.** A title of the eldest son of the king of France, who took it from the province of *Dauphiny* (A. D. 1349); and the province had formerly had several lords named *Dauphin.*

Davit, a support for ship's boats. (Heb. ?) Formerly spelt *David*, as if from a proper name (A. D. 1626). Also called *daviot* in A. F., a dimin. of O. F. *Davi*, David.

Daw. (E.) From the noise made by the bird ; cf. *caw.*+O. H. G. *tāha*, a daw ;

dimin. *tāhele* (now G. *dohle*), a daw ; whence Ital. *taccola*, a daw (Florio). **Der.** *jack-daw.*

Dawk, transport by relays of men and horses. (Hindi.) Hindi *ḍāk*, post, trans-port, &c. (Yule).

Dawn ; see **Day.**

Day. (E.) M. E. *day, dai, dæi.* A. S. *dæg*, pl. *dagas.*+Du. Dan. Swed. *dag*, Icel. *dagr*, G. *tag*, Goth. *dags.* Allied to Lith. *dagas*, hot time, autumn ; *dègti*, to burn. Teut. type **dagoz* ; Idg. type **dhoghos* ; from √DHEGH, to burn ; Skt. *dah*, to burn, *ni-dāgha-*, hot season. *Day* is the hot, bright time; as opposed to *night.* ¶ In no way allied to L. *diēs.*

dawn, vb. (Scand.) M. E. *dawnen*; from the older sb. *dawning.*—Swed. Dan. *dagning*, a dawning, dawn ; as if from a verb **dag-na*, to become day, from Swed. Dan. *dag*, day. 2. We also find M. E. *dawen*, to dawn ; from A. S. *dagian*, to become day, dawn.—A. S. *dag-*, base of *dæg*, day. (Cf. *fawn*, vb.)

Daywoman, dairy-woman. (Scand. and E.) In Shak. L. L. L. i. 2. 137. The addition of *woman* is needless. *Day* = M. E. *deye.*=O. Norw. *deigja*, a maid ; esp. a dairymaid ; see **Dairy.**

Daze. (Scand.) M. E. *dasen*, to stupefy. —Swed. *dasa*, to lie idle ; Icel. *dasask*, to be wearied, lit. to daze oneself, where *-sk* is the reflexive suffix; *dasi*, a lazy man; *dasinn*, lazy ; Dan. dial. *dase*, to be idle ; Low G. *däsen, dösen*, to be listless; *in 'n däs' sein*, to be in a 'daze' (Berghaus).

dazzle, to confuse. (Scand.) From *daze* ; with frequent. suffix *-le.* **Der.** *be-dazzle.*

De- (1), *prefix.* (L. ; *or* F.—L.) L. *dē*, down, away, from, very; hence sometimes F. *dé-, de-*, O. F. *de-.*

De- (2), *prefix.* (F.—L.) F. *dé-*, O. F. *des-* ; from L. *dis-* ; see **Dis-.**

Deacon. (L. — Gk.) M. E. *deken.* A. S. *diacon.*—L. *diaconus.*—Gk. διάκονος, a servant, a deacon. Cf. ἐγ-κονέω, I am quick, ἐγ-κονίς, a maid-servant.

Dead. (E.) M. E. *deed.* A. S. *dēad*, dead.+Du. *dood*, Dan. *död*, Swed. *död*, Icel. *dauðr*, Goth. *dauths.* Teut. type **dau-ðoz*, orig. a pp. with Idg. suffix *-to-* (Teut. *-ðo-*) from the vb. **dau-jan-* (Icel. *deyja*), to die. See **Die** (1).

Deaf. (E.) M. E. *deef.* A. S. *dēaf.*+ Du. *doof*, Dan. *döv*, Swed. *döf*, Icel. *daufr*, Goth. *daubs*, G. *taub.* Orig. 'obfuscated ;'

allied to Gk. τῦφος, smoke, darkness, stupor, τύφ-λος, blind. (√DHEUBH.)

Deal (1), a share. (E.) M. E. *deel.* A. S. *dǽl,* a share. + Du. *deel,* Dan. *deel,* Swed. *del,* Goth. *dails,* G. *theil.* Cf. O. Slav. *dĕlŭ,* a part. Brugm. i. § 279 (2).

deal (2), to divide, distribute. (E.) M. E. *delen.* A. S. *dǽlan.* — A. S. *dǽl,* a share (above). + Du. *deelen,* Dan. *dele,* Swed. *dela,* Icel. *deila,* Goth. *dailjan,* G. *theilen* ; cf. the respective sbs. (above).

Deal (3), a thin board. (Du.) Du. *deel,* a plank. + G. *diele* ; see **Thill.**

Dean. (F. — L.) M. E. *dene.* — O. F. *deien* (F. *doyen*). — L. *decānum,* acc. of *decānus,* one set over ten soldiers, or over ten monks, a dean. — L. *decem,* ten.

Dear. (E.) M. E. *dere.* A. S. *dēore, dȳre,* dear, precious. + Dan. and Swed. *dyr,* dear, costly, Icel. *dȳrr,* dear, precious ; O. Sax. *diuri* ; G. *theuer.*

dearth, scarcity. (E.) M. E. *derthe,* dearness ; hence, dearth. Not in A. S. ; but formed as *heal-th, warm-th,* &c. + Icel. *dȳrð,* value, from *dȳrr* (above) ; O. Sax. *diuritha,* value, from *diuri,* dear, precious ; O. H. G. *tiurida,* from *tiuri* (G. *theuer*).

Death. (E.) M. E. *deeth.* A. S. *dēað.* + Du. *dood,* Dan. Swed. *död,* Goth. *dauthus,* G. *tod* ; cf. Icel. *dauði.* Teut. type **dau-ðuz,* formed with Idg. suffix *-tu-,* Teut. *-ðu-,* from the base **dau-* ; see **Dead.**

Debar (F.) F. *débarrer* ; O. F. *des-barrer.* From **De-** (2) and **Bar.**

Debase. (L., *and* F. — L.) Formed from *base* by prefixing L. *dē,* down.

Debate. (F. — L.) M. E. *debaten.* — O. F. *debatre,* to debate, argue. — L. *dē,* down ; *battere,* to beat. See **Batter** (1).

Debauch. (F. — L. *and* Teut.) O. F. *desbaucher,* (F. *débaucher*), ' to debosh, mar, seduce, mislead ; ' Cot.' Diez supposes that the orig. sense was ' to entice away from a workshop ' ; it is certainly derived from the O. F. prefix *des-* (L. *dis-*), away, and O. F. *bauche,* explained by Roquefort as ' a little house,' and by Cotgrave as ' a course of stones or bricks in building.' Cf. M. F. *embaucher,* to use in business, employ, *esbaucher,* to rough-hew, frame. Godefroy gives *desbaucher* only in the sense of ' rough-hew,' but his Supp. adds—' detach from one's service, turn aside, distract.' The orig. sense of *bauche* was prob. ' balk,' i. e. beam, hence frame of a building, course in building,

small building, &c. ; of Teut. origin ; see **Balk.**

Debenture, acknowledgment of a debt. (L.) Formerly *debentur* (Bacon). — L. *dēbentur,* lit. ' they are due,' because such receipts began with the words *dēbentur mihi* (Webster) ; pr. pl. pass. of *dēbeo,* I owe ; see **Debt.**

Debilitate. (L.) From pp. of L. *dēbilitāre,* to weaken. — L. *dēbilis,* weak. — L. *dē,* away, not ; *-bilis,* prob. allied to Skt. *bala-,* strength ; cf. *dur-bala-* (for *dus-bala-*), feeble. Brugm. i. § 553.

Debonair. (F.) M. E. *debonere, debonaire* ; A. F. *debonaire,* for *de bon aire,* lit. of a good stock. — L. *dē,* of ; *bon-us,* good ; and O. F. *aire,* place, stock, race, a word of uncertain origin. Diez suggests that it represents Lat. acc. *agrum,* field.

Debouch. (F. — L.) F. *déboucher,* to uncork, to emerge from ; hence, to march out of a narrow pass. — F. *dé* (= O. F. *des-* < L. *dis-*), away ; and *bouche,* mouth, opening, from L. *bucca,* mouth.

Debris, broken pieces. (F. — L. *and* Teut.) F. *débris,* fragments. — O. F. *de-brisier,* to break to pieces. — O. F. *de-,* from L. *dē,* down ; and *brisier* (F. *briser*), to break ; see **Bruise.**

Debt. (F. — L.) A bad spelling of *dett,* M. E. *dette.* — O. F. *dette* (but in M. F. misspelt *debte*). — L. *dēbita,* a sum due ; fem. of *dēbitus,* owed, pp. of *dēbēre,* to owe. *Dēbēre = dē-hibēre* (Plautus), i. e. to have away, have on loan. — L. *dē-,* down, away ; *habēre,* to have. Der. *debt-or,* M. E. *det-tur,* from O. F. *deteur,* L. acc. *dēbitōrem.*

Debut. (F. — L. *and* O. H. G.) A first appearance in a play. — F. *début,* a first stroke, first cast or throw at dice, first play in the game of bowls ; verbal sb. of *débuter,* M. F. *desbuter,* ' to put from the mark he aimed at ' (at bowls), Cot. ; hence, to come in first, be entitled to lead. From L. *dis-,* from, and F. *but,* mark. See **Butt** (1).

Decade. (F. — L. — Gk.) F. *decade,* 'a decade,' Cot. ; i. e. an aggregate of ten. — L. *decadem,* acc. of *decas.* — Gk. δεκάδα, acc. of δεκάς, a company of ten. — Gk. δέκα, ten ; see **Ten.**

decagon. (Gk.) Named from its ten angles. — Gk. δέκα, ten ; γων-ία, a corner, angle, allied to γόνυ, knee ; see **Knee.** Der. *hendeca-gon* (ἕνδεκα, eleven) ; *dodeca-gon* (δώδεκα, twelve).

decahedron. (Gk.) Named from its ten sides or bases. – Gk. δέκα, ten: ἕδ-ρα, a base, lit. 'seat,' from ἕζομαι (for ἕδγομαι), I sit; see Sit. Der. *do-deca-hedron* (Gk. δώδεκα, twelve).

decalogue. (F. – L. – Gk.) F. *décalogue.* – L. *decalogum*, acc. of *decalogus*. – Gk. δεκάλογος, the ten commandments. – Gk. δέκα, ten; λόγος, a speech, saying; see Logic.

decasyllabic, having ten syllables. (Gk.) Gk. δέκα, ten; συλλαβή, a syllable. Der. *hendecasyllabic* (Gk. ἕνδεκα, eleven).

Decadence, decay. (F. – L.) F. *décadence.* – Med. L. *dēcadentia,* – L. *dē*, down; *cadentia*, a falling; see Cadence.

Decamp, to depart. (F. – L.) L. *dé-camper*; O. F. *descamper*, orig. to remove a camp. – L. *dis-*, away; and *campus*, a field, later, a camp. See De- (2) and Camp.

Decanal. (L.) Belonging to a dean. – L. *decān-us*, a dean; with suffix *-al* (L. *-ālis*); see Dean.

Decant. (F. – L. and Gk.) F. *décanter* (Span. *decantar*). – Med. L. *dēcanthāre* (a word of the alchemists), to pour out. – L. *dē*, from; *canthus*, the 'lip' of a cup, a peculiar use of Gk. κάνθος, corner of the eye (Hatzfeld). Der. *decant-er*, a wine-vessel.

Decapitate. (L.) From pp. of Late L. *dēcapitāre*, to behead. – L. *dē*, off; and *capit-*, stem of *caput*, head.

Decay, to fall into ruin. (F. – L.) O. North F. *decair* (Span. *decaer*); variant of O. F. *dechair*, *decheoir*. – O. F. *de-*; and *cheoir* (F. *choir*), to fall. – L. *dē*, down; and Folk-L. *cadīre*, *cadēre*, to fall, variants of L. *cadere*, to fall.

Decease. (F. – L.) M. E. *deces.* – O. F. *deces* (F. *décès*), death. – L. acc. *dēcessum*, departure, death. – L. *dēcessus*, pp. of *dēcēdere*, to depart. – L. *dē*, from; *cēdere*, to go away.

Deceive. (F. – L.) A. F. *deceivre*; O. F. *deceveir*, *decevoir*, pres. subj. *deceive*. – L. *dēcipere* to take away, deceive. – L. *dē*, away; and *capere*, to take. Der. *deceit*, from O. F. *deceit*, pp. of *deceveir*.

December. (L.; *or* F. – L.) O. F. *Decembre.* – L. *December.* – L. *decem*, ten; as it was the tenth month of the Roman year.

Decemvir, one of ten magistrates. (L.) L. *decemuir*, one of the *decemuirī*, or ten men joined in a commission. – L.

decem, ten (see **Ten**); and *uir*, a man (see **Virile**).

Decennial, belonging to ten years. (L.) For L. *decenn-ālis*, of ten years; cf. *bi-ennial.* – L. *dec-em*, ten; *annus*, a year.

Decent. (F. – L.) O. F. *decent.* – L. *decentem*, acc. of pres. pt. of *decēre*, to become, befit; cf. *decus*, honour.

Deception. (F. – L.) O. F. *deception.* – L. acc. *deceptiōnem.* – L. *deceptus*, pp. of *decipere*, to deceive; see **Deceive.**

Decide. (F. – L.) F. *décider.* – L. *dēcīdere*, pp. *dēcīsus*, to cut off, decide. – L. *dē*, down; and *cædere*, to cut. Der. *decis-ion* (from pp. *dēcīsus*).

Deciduous, falling off. (L.) L. *dēcidu-us*, that falls down; with suffix *-ous*. – L. *dēcidere*, to fall down. – L. *dē*, down; and *cadere*, to fall. See **Decay.**

Decimal. (F. – L.) O. F. *decimal.* – Late L. *decimālis*, belonging to tithes. – L. *decima*, a tithe; fem. of *decimus*, tenth. Cf. L. *decem*, ten.

decimate. (L.) From pp. of L. *decimāre*, to select every tenth man, for punishment. – L. *decem*, ten.

Decipher. (F. *and* Arab.) Formed after F. *déchiffrer*, to decipher. – F. *dé-*, O. F. *des-*, L. *dis-*, apart; **Cipher,** q. v.

Deck, to cover. (Du.) Du. *dekken*, to cover; *dek*, a cover, a ship's deck. Cognate with E. **Thatch**, q. v.

Declaim. (L.) Formerly *declame.* – L. *dēclāmāre*, to cry aloud. – L. *dē*, down, fully; *clāmāre*, to cry; see **Claim.**

Declare. (F. – L.) O. F. *declarer.* – L. *dēclārāre*, to make clear, declare. – L. *dē*, fully; *clārus*, clear.

Declension. (F. – L.) O. F. *declinaison*, used for the 'declension' of a noun. – L. *dēclīnātiōnem*, acc. of *dēclīnātio*, declination, declension. – L. *dēclīnātus*, pp. of *dēclīnāre* (below).

decline. (F. – L.) O. F. *decliner.* – L. *dēclīnare*, to lean or bend aside from. – L. *dē-*, from; *-clīnāre* (only in comp.), to lean; see **Incline, Lean** (1).

Declivity. (F. – L.) F. *déclivité.* – L. *dēcliuitātem*, acc. of *dēcliuitās*, a downward slope. – L. *dēclīuis*, sloping downward. – L. *dē*, down; *clīuus*, a slope, hill. See **Lean** (1).

Decoct. (L.) L. *dēcoctus*, pp. of *dēcoquere*, to boil down. – L. *dē*, down, away; *coquere*, to cook.

Decollation, a beheading. (F. – L.)

O. F. *decollation.*—Late L. acc. *dĕcollā-tiōnem.* From pp. of *dĕcollāre,* to behead. —L. *dē,* off; *collum,* the neck.

Decompose. (F.—L. *and* Gk.) F. *décomposer* (XVI c.); from *de-,* prefix, and *composer,* to compose. See Compose.

Decorate. (L.) From pp. of *decorāre,* to adorn.—L. *decŏr-* (for **decos-*), stem of *decus,* honour, ornament; cf. L. *decēre,* to be fit.

decorum. (L.) L. *decōrum,* seemliness; neut. of *decōrus,* seemly.—L. *decŏr-,* stem of *decor,* seemliness, allied to *decus* (above). **Der.** *in-decōrum.*

Decoy, a contrivance for catching wild-ducks. (F. *and* Du.) Coined from prov. E. *coy,* a decoy, by prefixing the E. *de-* (F. *dé-,* L. *dē*). E. *coy* is from Du. *kooi,* a cage, decoy, M. Du. *koye,* older form *kouwe* (Hexham); from L. *cauea,* whence also F. and E. *cage*; see Cage. ¶ The prefixing of *de-* was probably due to confusion with M. E. *coyen,* to quiet; so that *de-coy* seemed to mean a 'quieting down.'

Decrease. (F.—L.) A. F. *descrees, descreis,* O. F. *descrois,* sb., a decrease; from *descroistre,* vb., to decrease.—Late L. *discrescere,* used for L. *dēcrescere,* to diminish (pp. *dēcrētus*). — L. *dē,* down, away; *crescere,* to grow.

decrement. (L.) L. *dēcrēmentum,* a decrease. — L. *dēcrē-tus,* pp. of *dēcrescere.*

Decree. (F.—L.) M. E. *decree.* — O. F. *decret.*—L. *dēcrētum.*—L. *dēcrētus,* pp. of *dēcernere,* to decree, lit. to separate. —L. *dē,* away; *cernere,* to distinguish.

decretal. (F.—L.) O. F. *decretal.* —Late L. *dēcrētāle,* a decree.—L. *dēcrētus.*

Decrepit. (L.) L. *dēcrepitus,* noise-less, creeping about like an old man, aged. —L. *dē,* away; *crepitus,* noise, allied to *crepitus,* pp. of *crepāre,* to crackle, make a noise.

Decry, to condemn. (F.—L.) O. F. *descrier,* to cry down, disparage.—O. F. *des-* (L. *dis-*), implying the reversal of an act, and here opposed to 'cry up'; *crier,* to cry. See Cry.

Decussate, to cross at an acute angle. (L.) From pp. of L. *decussāre,* to cross, to put into the form of an X.—L. *decussis,* a coin worth ten asses (as-es), and therefore marked with X, i. e. ten.—L. *decem,* ten; *assi-,* stem of *as,* an ace; see Ace.

Dedicate, to devote. (L.) L. *dēdicā-tus,* pp. of *dēdicāre,* to devote.—L. *dē,*

down; *dicāre,* to proclaim; from *dic-,* weak grade of *dīc-,* as in *dīcere,* to say.

Deduce. (L.) L. *dēdūcere,* to bring down (hence, to infer).—L. *dē,* down; *dūcere,* to bring. See Duke.

deduct. (L.) Orig. to derive from. —L. *dēduct-us,* pp. of *dēdūcere,* to bring down (above).

Deed. (E.) M. E. *deed.* O. Merc. *dēd,* A. S. *dēd.*+Du. *daad,* Icel. *dáð,* Swed. *dåd,* Dan. *daad,* Goth. *dēds,* G. *that,* O. H. G. *tāt.* Teut. type **dædiz*; Idg. type **dhētis*; from √DHĒ, to place, put, do. See Do.

Deem. (E.) M. E. *demen.* A. S. *dē-man,* to judge, give a doom.—A. S. *dōm,* a doom; see Doom. Cf. Du. *doemen,* Icel. *dæma* (for *dœma*), Swed. *döma,* Dan. *dömme,* Goth. *dōmjan,* O. H. G. *tuomian.* Teut. type **dōmjan-,* from **dōmoz,* doom.

Deep, profound. (E.) M. E. *deep.* A. S. *dēop.*+Du. *diep,* Dan. *dyb,* Swed. *djup,* Icel. *djúpr,* G. *tief,* Goth. *diups.* Teut. type **deupoz*; see Dip.

depth, deepness. (E.) From *deep*; cf. Icel. *dýpð,* depth, from *djúpr,* deep.+Du. *diepte*; Goth. *daupitha.*

Deer. (E.) M. E. *deer,* an animal. A. S. *dēor,* a wild animal.+Du. *dier,* Dan. *dyr,* Swed. *djur,* Icel. *dýr,* Goth. *diuŝ,* G. *thier.* Teut. type **deuzom*; Idg. type **dheusom,* prob. 'animal'; from **dheus-,* to breathe (Kluge). Brugm. i. § 539 (2). Der. *wilder-ness,* q. v.

Deface. (F.—L.) M. E. *defacen.*— O. F. *desfacier,* to deface, disfigure. — O. F. *des-* (<L. *dis-*), apart; *face,* face; see Face.

Defalcate, to abate, deduct. (L.) From pp. of Late L. *diffalcāre* or *dēfalcāre,* to abate, deduct, take away.—L. *dif-* (=*dis-*), apart, or else *dē,* away; Late L. *falcāre,* to cut with a sickle, from L. *falx* (stem *falc-*), a sickle.

Defame. (F.—L.) M. E. *defamen,* *diffamen.*—O. F. *diffamer,* to take away a man's character.—L. *diffāmāre,* to spread a bad report.—L. *dif-* (for *dis-*), apart; *fāma,* a report. See Fame.

Default. (F.—L.) M. E. *defaute.*— O. F. *defaute,* a default, from *defaillir,* to fail; imitating *faute* from *faillir.* See De-(1) and Fault.

Defeasance, a rendering null. (F.— L.) A. F. law-term *defesance,* a rendering void.—O. F. *defesant, defeisant,* pres. part. of *defaire, desfaire,* to render void.—O. F.

des- (L. *dis-*), apart; *faire* (L. *facere*), to make.

defeat. (F.–L.) M. E. *defaiten*, to defeat.–A. F. *defeter*, formed from O. F. *defait*, *desfait*, pp. of *defaire*, *desfaire*, to render void (above).

Defecate. (L.) From pp. of *dēfaecāre*, to free from dregs.–L. *dē*, out; *faec-*, stem of *faex*, pl. *faecēs*, dregs.

Defect. (L.) L. *dēfectus*, a want.–L. *dēfectus*, pp. of *dēficere*, to fail, orig. to undo.–L. *dē*, away; *facere*, to make. Der. *defect-ion*, *-ive*.

Defend. (F.–L.) M. E. *defenden.* – O. F. *defendre.*–L. *dēfendere*, to defend, lit. strike down or away.–L. *dē*, down; **fendere*, to strike, only in comp. *dē-fendere*, *of-fendere*. Cf. G. θείνειν, to strike; Skt. *han.* (√GHwEN.) Brugm. i. § 664.

defence. (F.–L.) M. E. *defence.* – O. F. *defense.*–L. *dēfensa*, a defending (Tertullian). – L. *dēfens-us*, pp. of *dēfendere* (above). Also M. E. *defens*, O. F. *defens*, from L. *dēfensum*, neut.

Defer (1), to delay. (F.–L.) M. E. *differren.*–O. F. *differer*, to delay.–L. *differre*, to bear different ways, delay.–L. *dif-* (for *dis-*), apart; *ferre*, to bear.

defer (2), to lay before, submit oneself. (F.–L.) O. F. *deferer*, to admit or give way to an appeal.–L. *dēferre*, to bring down, bring before one.–L. *dē*, down; *ferre*, to bear, carry.

Deficient. (L.) From stem of pres. pt. of *dēficere*, to fail; see Defect.

deficit, lack. (L.) L. *dēficit*, it fails; 3 p. s. pres. of *dēficere* (above).

Defile (1), to pollute. (F.–L.; *confused with* L. *and* E.) M. E. *defoulen*, to trample under foot; later spelling *defoyle*; see Foil (1). This word is obsolete, but it suggested a hybrid compound made by prefixing L. *dē*, down, to the old word *file*, to defile (Macb. iii. 1. 65) = A. S. *fȳlan* (for **fūljan*), to defile, make foul, formed (by vowel-change of *ū* to *ȳ*) from A. S. *fūl*, foul; see Foul.

Defile (2), to march in a file. (F.–L.) F. *défiler*, to defile. – F. *dé-* = O. F. *des-* (L. *dis-*), apart; *filer*, to spin threads, from L. *filum*, thread. Der. *defile*, sb., F. *défilé*, a narrow passage; orig. pp. of *défiler.*

Define. (F.–L.) O. F. *definer*, to define, conclude.–L. *dēfinīre*, to limit. –L. *dē* down; *finīre*, to end, from *finis*, end.

Deflect. (L.) L. *dēflectere*, to bend

down or aside.–L. *dē*, down; *flectere*, to bend. Der. *deflex-ion*, from *deflex-us*, pp.

Deflour, Deflower. (F.–L.) M. E. *deflouren.*–O. F. *defleurer*, Cotg.–Late L. *dēflōrāre*, to gather flowers.–L. *dē*, away; *flōr-*, for *flōs*, a flower.

Defluxion. (L.) From acc. of L. *dēfluxio*, a flowing down.–L. *dē*, down; *flux-us*, pp. of *fluere*, to flow.

Deforce, to dispossess. (F. – L.) Legal.–A. F. *deforcer*, to dispossess (Med. L. *difforciāre*).–O. F. *de-* = *des-* (L. *dis-*), away; and F. *force*. See Force.

Deform. (F.–L.) M. E. *deformen*, chiefly in pp. *deformed.*–O. F. *difformer*, to deform; Godefroy. – O. F. *difforme*, adj., deformed, ugly; Cot.–L. *dēformis*, ugly.–L. *dē*, away; *forma*, shape, beauty.

Defraud. (F.–L.) O. F. *defrauder.* –L. *dēfraudāre*, to deprive by fraud.–L. *dē*, away; *fraud-*, stem of *fraus*, fraud.

Defray. (F.–L. *and* O. H. G.) O. F. *desfrayer*, to pay expenses; Littré.–O. F. *des-* (L. *dis-*); *fraier*, to spend. *Fraier* is from O. F. **frai*, **fre*, later *frait*, mostly used in the pl. *frais*, *fres* (F. *frais*), expenses; cf. Low L. *fredum*, a fine, composition. – O. H. G. *fridu* (G. *friede*), peace; also, a fine for a breach of the peace. See Affray.

Deft, neat, dexterous. (E.) M. E. *deft*, *daft.* A. S. *dæfte*, as seen in *ge-dæfte*, mild, gentle, meek; *ge-dæftlīce*, fitly, seasonably; *dæftan*, to prepare. Cf. A. S. *ge-daf-en*, fit, pp. of a lost strong vb. **dafan*; Goth. *gadaban*, to befit, *gadōbs*, fitting.

Defunct, dead. (L.) L. *dēfunctus*, i. e. having fully performed the course of life, pp. of *dēfungī*, to perform fully.–L. *dē*, fully; and *fungī*, to perform; see Function.

Defy. (F.–L.) M. E. *defyen.*–O. F. *defier*, *deffier*, *desfier*, orig. to renounce one's faith.–Late L. *diffidāre*, to renounce faith.–L. *dif-* (for *dis-*), apart; *-fidāre* (from *fidus*, faithful), to trust; cf. L. *fidere*, to trust. See Faith.

Degenerate. (L.) From pp. of L. *dēgenerāre*, to become base.–L. *dēgener*, adj., base. – L. *dē*, down; *gener-* (for **genes-*), stem of *genus*, race. See Genus.

Deglutition, swallowing. (F. – L.) F. *déglutition.*–L. *dē*, down; *glūtītus*, pp. of *glūtīre*, to swallow.

Degrade. (F.–L.) O. F. *degrader*, to deprive of rank or office.–Late L. *dē-*

gradāre, the same. – L. *dē*, from ; *gradus*, rank. See **Grade**.

degree. (F. – L.) O. F. *degre, degret*, a step, rank ; orig. a step *down* (used of stairs). – L. *dē*, down ; *gradus*, a step.

Dehiscent, gaping. (L.) L. *dēhiscent-*, stem of pres. pt. of *dēhiscere*, to gape open. – L. *dē*, down ; *hiscere*, to gape, inceptive of *hiāre*, to yawn ; see **Hiatus.**

Deify, Deist ; see **Deity.**

Deign. (F. – L.) M. E. *deignen.* – A. F. *deign-*, a stem of O. F. *dign(i)er*, to deign. – L. *dignāre*, by-form of *dignārī*, to deem worthy. – L. *dignus*, worthy. Brugm. ii. § 66.

Deity. (F. – L.) M. E. *deite.* – O. F. *deite.* – L. *deitātem*, acc. of *deitās*, deity, Godhead. – L. *dei-*, for *deus*, God ; cf. *dīuus*, godlike. Cf. W. *duw*, Gael. and Ir. *dia*, Skt. *dēva-*, a god ; Gk. δῖος, Skt. *daiva-*, divine. See **Tuesday.**

deify. (F. – L.) M. E. *deifyen.* – O. F. *deifier*, 'to deifie;' Cot. – Late L. *deificāre*, accounting as gods. – L. *dei-*, for *deus*, a god ; and *-fic-*, for *facere*, to make. **Der.** *deificat-ion*, due to pp. of *deificāre.*

deist. (F. – L.) F. *déiste.* From L. *de-us* ; with suffix *-ist*.

Deject, to cast down. (L.) From L. *dēiectus*, pp. of *dēicere* (*dēiicere*), to cast down. – L. *dē*, down ; *iacere*, to throw.

Delay, vb. (F. – L.) O. F. *delayer, dilaier*; also *deleer* (Godefroy). It answers in sense to L. *dīlātāre*, to defer, delay, put off ; which would properly give O. F. *dileer*. *Dīlātāre* is from *dīlātus*, deferred, put off ; from L. *dī-* (*dis-*), apart ; *lātus*, borne, pp. of *tollere*, to lift, sustain, bear. ¶ The O. F. spelling with *ai* causes a difficulty. **Der.** *delay*, sb. ; O. F. *delai*.

Delectable. (F. – L.) Late M. E. *delectable.* – F. *délectable.* – L. *dēlectābilis*, delightful. – L. *dēlectāre*, to delight ; frequent. of *dēlicere*, to allure. See **Delicious.**

Delegate, a chosen deputy. (L.) L. *dēlēgātus*, pp. of *dēlēgāre*, to depute, appoint. – L. *dē*, away ; *lēgāre*, to depute. See **Legate.**

Delete, to erase. (L.) L. *dēlētus*, pp. of *dēlēre*, to destroy. See below.

Deleterious. (Gk.) Late L. *dēlē-tēri-us*, with suffix *-ous*. For Gk. δηλη-τήριος, noxious. – Gk. δηλητήρ, a destroyer. – Gk. δηλέομαι, I harm, injure.

Delf. (Du.) Earthenware first made at *Delft*, formerly *Delf*, a town in S. Holland, about A. D. 1310 (Haydn). The town was named from its *delf* or canal ; cf. **Delve.**

Deliberate, carefully weighed and considered. (L.) L. *dēlīberātus*, pp. of *dē-līberāre*, to consult. – L. *dē*, thoroughly ; *lībrāre*, to weigh, from *lībra*, a balance.

Delicate, dainty, refined. (L.) L. *dēlicātus*, luxurious ; probably allied to *dēlicia* (or *dēliciæ*, pl.), pleasure, delight, and to L. *dēlicere*, to amuse (below).

delicious. (F. – L.) M. E. *delicious.* – O. F. *delicious.* – Late L. *dēliciōsus*, pleasant. – L. *dēlicia*, pleasure. – L. *dē-licere*, to amuse, allure. – L. *dē*, away ; *lacere*, to entice.

delight. (F. – L.) Misspelt for *delite.* M. E. *deliten*, verb. – O. F. *deliter, delei-ter.* – L. *dēlectāre* ; see **Delectable.**

Delineate. (L.) From pp. of L. *dēlineāre*, to sketch in outline. – L. *dē*, down ; *lineāre*, to mark out, from *līnea*, a line. See **Line.**

Delinquent, failing in duty. (L.) L. *dēlinquent-*, stem of pres. pt. of *dēlinquere*, to fail, to omit one's duty. – L. *dē*, away, from ; *linquere*, to leave.

Deliquesce, to become liquid. (L.) L. *dēlīquescere*, to become liquid. – L. *dē*, away; *līquescere*, inceptive form of *līquēre*, to be wet. See **Liquid.**

Delirious. (L.) A coined word (with suffix *-ous*), from L. *dēlīri-um*, madness, which is also adopted into English. – L. *dēlīrus*, mad ; lit. 'going out of the furrow.' – L. *dē*, from ; and *līra*, a furrow. Cf. O. H. G. *leisa*, G. *g-leise*, a track.

Deliver. (F. – L.) O. F. *delivrer*, to set free. – Late L. *dēlīberāre*, to set free. – L. *dē*, from ; *līberāre*, to free, from *līber*, free.

Dell, a dale. (E.) M. E. *delle.* A. S. *dell*, neut. ; Cart. Sax. i. 547 ; ii. 71. Teut. type **daljom*; see **Dale.**

Delta. (Gk.) Gk. δέλτα, the letter Δ ; answering to Heb. *daleth*, the name of the 4th letter of the alphabet ; orig. ' a door of a tent.' (Orig. Phœnician.) **Der.** *deltoid.*

Delude. (L.) L. *dēlūdere* (pp. *dēlūsus*), to mock at, cajole. – L. *dē*, down ; *lūdere*, to play. **Der.** *delus-ion*, from the pp.

Deluge. (F. – L.) O. F. *deluge.* – L. *dīluuium*, a washing away. – L. *diluere*, to wash away. – L. *dī-* (*dis-*), apart ; *luere*, to wash, allied to **Lave.**

Delve, to dig. (E.) M. E. *deluen.*

A. S. *delfan*, pt. t. *dealf*, pp. *dolfen*.+Du. *delven* ; M. H. G. *telben*. Cf. Russ. *dolbite*, to hollow out. Brugm. i. § 521 (2).

Demagogue. (F. – Gk.) F. *démagogue*. – Gk. δημαγωγός, a popular leader. – Gk. δῆμ-ος, people ; ἀγωγός, leading, from ἄγ-ειν, to lead.

Demand. (F. – L.) F. *demander*, to demand, require. – L. *dēmandāre*, to entrust ; in late L., to demand. – L. *dē*, away ; *mandāre*, to commission, order.

Demarcation. (Span. – L. and M. H. G.) From Span. *demarcacion* (see N. E. D.) ; whence also F. *démarcation*. – L. *dē*, down ; and Span. *marcar*, to mark, a word of German origin ; see **Marque.**

Demean (1), to conduct ; *reflex.*, to behave. (F. – L.) M. E. *demenen*. – O. F. *demener*, to conduct, guide, manage. – O. F. *de* (= L. *dē*), down, fully ; *mener*, to conduct, from Late L. *mināre*, to drive cattle, conduct, from L. *minārī*, to threaten. See **Menace.**

demeanour. (F. – L.) M. E. *demenure* (XV cent.) ; a coined word, from M. E. *demenen*, to demean, behave ; see **Demean** (1).

Demean (2), to debase, lower. (Hybrid ; L. *and* E.) Made, like *debase*, from the prefix **De-** (1), and the adj. *mean*. See **Mean** (2).

Demented, mad. (L.) Pp. of the old verb to *dement*. – L. *dēmentāre*, to drive out of one's mind. – L. *dē*, from ; *ment-*, stem of *mens*, mind.

Demerit, ill desert. (F. – L.) Also merit, in a *good* sense ; Cor. i. 1. 276. – O. F. *demerite*, desert ; also a fault, demerit. – Late L. *dēmeritum*, a fault ; from pp. of L. *dēmerēre*, *dēmererī*, to deserve (in a *good* sense). – L. *dē*, fully ; *merēre*, *mererī*, to deserve. See **Merit.**

Demesne. (F. – L.) A. F. *demeine*, *demene*, also *demesne* (with silent *s*) ; other spellings of **Domain**, q. v.

Demi-, half. (F. – L.) O. F. *demi*, half. – L. acc. *dīmidium*, half. – L. *dī-* = *dis-*, apart ; *medius*, middle ; see **Medium.**

Demijohn, a kind of large bottle. (F.) From F. *dame-jeanne* ; cf. Span. *damajuana*. Much disputed, but *not* of Eastern origin. The F. form is right as it stands, though often much perverted. From F. *dame* (Sp. *dama*), lady ; and *Jeanne* (Sp. *Juana*), Jane, Joan. See N. E. D.

Demise, transference, decease. (F. – L. O. F. *demise*, *desmise*, fem. of pp. of *desmettre*, to displace, dismiss. – L. *dīmittere* ; see **Dismiss.**

Democracy. (F. – Gk.) Formerly *democraty* (Milton). – M. F. *democratie* ; Cot. – Gk. δημοκρατία, popular government, rule by the people. – Gk. δημο-, for δῆμος, a country-district, also the people ; and κρατεῖν, to rule. Cf. O. Ir. *dām*, a retinue.

Demolish. (F. – L.) O. F. *demoliss-*, inchoative stem of *demolir*, to demolish. – L. *dēmōlīrī*, *dēmōlīre*, to pull down. – L. *dē*, from ; *mōles*, heap, mass.

Demon. (L. – Gk.) Formerly *dæmon*. – L. *dæmon*. – Gk. δαίμων, a god, genius, spirit. Cf. δαίομαι, I impart.

Demonstrate. (L.) From pp. of L. *dēmonstrāre*, to show fully. – L. *dē*, down, fully ; *monstrāre*, to show, from *monstrum*, a portent. See **Monster.**

Demoralise, to corrupt in morals. (F. – L.) Mod. F. *démoraliser*. – F. *dé-*, O. F. *des* (L. *dis-*), apart ; *moral*, moral ; with suffix *-ise* (= F. *-iser*, for Gk. *-ιζειν*). See **Moral.**

Demur, vb. (F. – L.) O. F. *demourer*, *demeurer*, to tarry ; hence, to hesitate. – L. *dēmorārī*, to delay fully. – L. *dē*, fully ; *morārī*, to delay, from *mora*, delay.

Demure. (F. – L.) XIV cent. Coined by prefixing *de-* (see **De-** (1)), to M. E. *mure*, mature, calm, demure. – O. F. *meur* (F. *mûr*), mature. – L. *mātūrus* ; see **Mature.**

Demy ; a spelling of *demi-*.

Den. (E.) M. E. *den* ; A. S. *denn*, a cave, allied to *denu*, a valley.+ M. Du. *denne*, a cave (Kilian).

Denary, relating to tens. (L.) L. *dēnārius*, containing ten. – L. *dēnī* (= *decni*), pl. ten by ten. – L. *dec-em*, ten. Hence *denier*, L. *dēnārius*, piece of ten (as-es).

Dendroid. (Gk.) Gk. δένδρο-ν, a tree ; *-ειδης*, like, from εἶδος, form, shape.

Denizen, a naturalised citizen, inhabitant. (F. – L.) Formerly *deynsein*. – A. F. *and* O. F. *deinzein* (also *denzein*), used in the Liber Albus to denote a trader *within* the privilege of the city franchise, as opposed to *forein*. Formed by adding the suffix *-ein* (= L. *-āneus*) to O. F. *deinz*, now spelt *dans*, within. – L. *dē intus*, from within. – L. *dē*, from ; *intus*, within, allied to **Interior.**

Denominate. (L.) From pp. of L. *dēnōmināre*, to name. – L. *dē*, down, fully ;

135

nŏmināre, to name, from *nŏmin-*, stem of *nōmen*, a name; see **Noun**.

Denote. (F. – L.) F. *dénoter*. – L. *dēnotāre*, to mark out. – L. *dē*, down; *notāre*, to mark, from *nota*, a mark. See **Note**.

Denouement, the undoing of a knot. (F. – L.) F. *dénouement*, sb., from *dénouer*, to undo a knot. – L. *dis-*, apart; *nōdāre*, to knot, from *nōdus*, a knot. See **Node**.

Denounce. (F. – L.) O. F. *denoncer*. – L. *dēnuntiāre*, to declare. – L. *dē*, down, fully; *nuntiāre*, to tell, from *nuntius*, a messenger. See **Nuncio**. Der. *denunciation*, from L. pp. *dēnunciātus*.

Dense. (L.) L. *densus*, thick. +Gk. δασύς, thick. Brugm. i. § 851. Der. *condense*.

Dent; see **Dint**.

Dental. (L.) Formed with suffix *-al* (F. *-al*, L. *-ālis*) from L. *dent-*, stem of *dens*, a tooth, cognate with E. **Tooth**.

dentated, furnished with teeth. (L) L. *dentātus*, toothed. – L. *dent-*, stem of *dens*, a tooth.

denticle, a little tooth. (L.) L. *denticulus*, double dimin. of *dens*, a tooth.

dentifrice, tooth-powder. (F. – L.) F. *dentifrice*. – L. *dentifricium* (Pliny). – L. *denti-*, decl. stem of *dens*, a tooth; *fric-āre*, to rub.

dentist. (F. – L.) F. *dentiste*. Coined from L. *dent-*, stem of *dens*, a tooth.

dentition. (L.) L. *dentītiōnem*, acc. of *dentitio*, cutting of teeth. – L. *dentītus*, pp. of *dentīre*, to cut teeth. – L. *denti-*, decl. stem of *dens*, a tooth.

Denude, to lay bare. (L.) L. *dēnūdāre*, to make fully bare. – L. *dē*, fully; *nūdāre*, to lay bare, from *nūdus*, bare. See **Nude**.

Denunciation; see **Denounce**.

Deny. (F. – L.) M. E. *denien*. – M. F. *denier*, earlier form *deneier*. – L. *dēnegāre*, to deny fully. – L. *dē*, fully; *negāre*, to deny. See **Negation**.

Deodand, lit. a thing to be given to God. (L.) From L. *deō*, dat. of *deus*, God; *dandum*, neut. of *dandus*, to be given, from *dare*, to give.

Depart. (F. – L.) O. F. *departir*, *despartir*, to divide, to part from. – L. *dis-*, away from; *partīre*, to part; see **Part**. Cf. L. *dispertīre*.

Depend. (F. – L.) O. F. *dependre*, to depend, hang on; Cot. – L. *dēpendēre*, to

hang down or from. – L. *dē*, down, from; *pendēre*, to hang. See **Pendant**.

Depict. (L.) Formerly used as a pp. – L. *dēpictus*, pp. of *dēpingere*, to depict, lit. paint fully. – L. *dē*, fully; *pingere*, to paint. Cf. **Picture**.

Depilatory, removing hair. (L.) Formed, in imitation of M. F. *depilatoire* (Cot.), from a L. adj. **dēpilātōrius*, not found. – L. *dēpilā-re*, to pluck out hair. – L. *dē*, away; *pilāre*, to pluck away hair, from *pilus*, hair.

Depletion. (L.) '*Depletion*, an emptying;' Blount. Formed, in imitation of *repletion*, from L. *dēplētus*, pp. of *dēplēre*, to empty. – L. *dē*, away; *plēre*, to fill. See **Plenary**.

Deplore. (F. – L.; *or* L.) O. F. *deplorer*. – L. *dēplōrāre*, to lament over. – L. *dē*, fully; *plōrāre*, to cry out, wail, weep. Brugm. i. § 154.

Deploy, to open out, extend. (F. – L.) F. *déployer*, to unroll, unfold; O. F. *desploier*, to unfold. – L. *dis-*, apart; *plicāre*, to fold. A doublet of **Display**.

Deponent, one who testifies. (L.) L. *dēpōnent-*, stem of the pres. pt. of *dēpōnere*, to lay down, also (in late L.) to testify. – L. *dē*, down; *pōnere*, to lay. See **Position**.

Depopulate. (L.) From pp. of L. *dēpopulāre*, to lay waste; in Late L. to deprive of people or inhabitants. Orig. to ravage by means of multitudes. – L. *dē*, fully; *populāre*, to populate, fill with people, from *populus*, people; see **People**.

Deport. (F. – L.) M. F. *deporter*, to bear, endure; se *deporter*, to forbear, quiet oneself. – L. *dēportāre*, to carry down, remove; with extended senses in Late Latin. Der. *deportment*, O. F. *deportement*, behaviour. ¶ For the varying senses, see F. *déporter*.

Depose. (F. – L. *and* Gk.) O. F. *deposer*, to displace. – O. F. *de-* (L. *dē*), from; and F. *poser*, to place, of Gk. origin, as shown under **Pose**. ¶ Much confused with derivatives from L. *pōnere*, to place. See below.

Deposit, vb. (F. – L.) Obs. F. *depositer*, to entrust. – L. *dēpositāre*, to lay down. – L. *dēpositum*, a thing laid down, neut. of pp. of *dēpōnere*; see **Deponent**.

deposition. (F. – L.) O. F. *deposition*. – L. acc. *dēpositiōnem*, a depositing. – L. *dēpositus*, pp. of *dēpōnere*, to lay down (above).

depot, a store. (F.–L.) F. *dépôt*; O. F. *depost.* – L. *depositum*, a thing laid down (hence, stored); neut. of *depositus*, pp. of *deponere*; see Deponent.

Deprave. (F.–L.) M.E. *deprauen.* – O. F. *depraver.* – L. *deprauare*, to make crooked, distort, vitiate. – L. *de*, fully; *prauus*, crooked, depraved.

Deprecate. (L.) From pp. of L. *deprecari*, to pray against, pray to remove. – L. *de*, away; *precari*, to pray. See Precarious.

Depreciate. (L.) From pp. of L. *depretiare*, to lower the price of. – L. *de*, down; *pretium*, price. See Precious.

Depredate. (L.) From pp. of L. *deprædari*, to plunder. – L. *de*, fully; *prædari*, to rob, from *præda*, prey; see Prey.

Depress. (F.–L.) O. F. *depresser* (Godefroy). – L. type **depressare*; from L. *depressus*, pp. of *deprimere*, to press down. – L. *de*, down; *premere*, to press.

Deprive. (F.–L.) O. F. *depriver* (Godefroy). – Late L. *deprivare*, to deprive of office, degrade. – L. *de*, fully; *priuare*, to deprive. See Private.

Depth; see Deep.

Depute. (F.–L.) M. F. *deputer*; Cot. – L. *deputare*, to cut off, also to impute, destine. – L. *de*, down; *putare*, to cut off, orig. to cleanse. **Der.** *deput-y*, M. F. *deputé*, one deputed, pp. of *deputer*.

Derange. (F.–L. and O. H. G.) F. *déranger*, to disarrange; formerly *des-rangier.* – L. *dis-*, apart; O. F. *rangier*, *rengier*, to range; see Range.

Dereliction, complete abandonment. (L.) L. acc. *derelictionem*, complete neglect. – L. *derelictus*, pp. of *derelinquere*, to forsake. – L. *de*, from; *relinquere*, to leave behind, from *re-*, back, and *linquere*, to leave. See Relinquish.

Deride. (L.) L. *deridere*, to laugh down, laugh at; from *de*, down, and *ridere*, to laugh. **Der.** *deris-ive*, from pp. *derisus*.

Derive. (F.–L.) O. F. *deriver*, to derive, also to drain. – L. *deriuare*, to drain off water. – L. *de*, from; *riuus*, a stream. See Rivulet.

Derm, skin. (Gk.) Gk. δέρμα, skin. – Gk. δέρειν, to flay; cognate with E. **Tear,** vb., to rend.

Derogate. (L.) From pp. of L. *derogare*, to repeal a law, detract from. – L. *de*, away; *rogare*, to ask, propose a law. See Rogation.

Derrick, a kind of crane. (Du.) Orig. the gallows; and named from a Dutch hangman; see T. Dekker, Seven Deadly Sins of London, ed. Arber, p. 17. – Du. *Dierryk, Dirk, Diederik*; answering to G. *Dietrich*, A. S. *Þeodric*, 'ruler of the people.'

Dervis, Dervish, a Persian monk, ascetic. (Pers.) Pers. *darvish*, poor; a dervish, who professed poverty. Cf. Zend *driγu-*, poor (Horn).

Descant. (F.–L.) Orig. a variation in a song. – O. North F. *descant* (O. F. *deschant*), a kind of song. – Late L. *discantus*, a refrain, kind of singing. – L. *dis-*, apart; and *cantus*, a song. See Cant (1).

Descend. (F.–L.) M. F. *descendre*. Cot. – L. *descendere*, lit. to climb down. – L. *de*, down; *scandere*, to climb; see Scan.

Describe. (L.) L. *describere*, to write down, describe fully; pp. *descriptus* (whence *description*). – L. *de*, down; *scribere*, to write. See Scribe.

descry. (F.–L.) M. E. *descryen*, to discern. – O. F. *descrire*, short form of O. F. *descrivre*, to describe. – L. *describere*. ¶ Sense affected by O. F. *descrier*, to proclaim, publish; from O. F. *des-* (L. *dis-*), and *crier*, to cry.

Desecrate. (L.) From pp. of L. *desecrare* or *desacrare*, to consecrate; (with change of sense due to O. F. *dessacrer*, to profane, from L. *dis-*, apart). – L. *de*, fully; *sacrare*, to account as sacred; see Sacred.

Desert (1), a waste. (F.–L.) O. F. *desert*, a wilderness. – L. *desertum*, neut. of *desertus*, waste; pp. of *deserere* to desert, abandon. – L. *de*, away (negative); *serere*, to join.

Desert (2), merit. (F.–L.) O. F. *desert*, fem. *deserte*, lit. a thing deserved, pp. of *deservir*, to deserve; see below.

deserve. (F.–L.) O. F. *deservir.* – L. *deseruire*, to serve fully; in Late L., to deserve. – L. *de*, fully; *seruire*, to serve. See Serve.

Deshabille, careless dress. (F.–L.) F. *déshabille*, undress. – F. *déshabiller*, to undress. – F. *dés* (L. *dis-*), apart, away, un-; *habiller*, to dress; see Habiliment.

Desiccate, to dry up. (L.) From pp. of L. *desiccare*, to drain dry. – L. *de*, away; *siccare*, to dry, from *siccus*, dry.

Desiderate; see Desire.

Design, vb. (F.–L.) O. F. *designer*, to denote, to design. – L. *designare*, to denote, mark down.—L. *dē*, down; *signāre*, to mark, from *signum*, sign. **Der.** *design-ate.*

Desire, to long for. (F.—L.) O. F. *desirer, desirrer.*—L. *dēsīderāre*, to long for, regret, miss. Perhaps (like *consīderāre*) allied to *sīdus*, a star, as if to turn the eyes from the stars, to regret, miss. **desiderate.** (L.) L. *dēsīderātus*, pp. of *dēsīderāre* (above).

Desist. (F.—L.) O. F. *desister*, to cease.—L. *dēsistere*, to put away, also to desist.—L. *dē*, away; *sistere*, to put, also to stand still, from *stāre*, to stand.

Desk, a sloping table. (L.—Gk.) M. E. *deske, desk*; in Chaucer, C. T., F. 1128.—Med. L. *desca*, a desk; cf. Ital. *desco*, 'a desk;' Florio.—L. *discum*, acc. of *discus*, a disc, table. See **Disc, Dish.**

Desolate, solitary. (L.) L. *dēsōlātus*, forsaken; pp. of *dēsōlāre*, to forsake.—L. *dē*, fully; *sōlāre*, to make lonely, from *sōlus*, alone.

Despair; see **Desperate.**

Despatch; see **Dispatch.**

Desperate, hopeless. (L.) L. *dēspērātus*, pp. of *dēspērāre*, to lose all hope.—L. *dē*, from; *spērāre*, to hope; from *spēr-*, as in *spēr-es*, O. Lat. pl. of *spēs*, hope. **despair**, vb. (F.—L.) M. E. *despeiren, desperen.*—O. F. *despeir-*, tonic stem of *desperer*, to despair.—L. *dēspērāre* (above).

desperado, a desperate man. (Span.—L.) M. Span. *desperado.*—L. *dēspērātus*, pp. of *dēspērāre* (above).

Despise, to contemn. (F.—L.) M. E. *despisen.*—O. F. *despis-*, stem of the pres. part., &c., of *despire*, to despise.—L. *dēspicere*, to look down, look down on (below). **Der.** *despic-able*, from L. *dēspicārī*, to look down on, allied to *dēspicere.*

despite, spite, hatred. (F.—L.) M.E. *despit.*—O. F. *despit*, 'despight, spight :' Cot. ⸗ L. *dēspectum*, acc. of *dēspectus*, contempt.—L. *dēspectus*, pp. of *dēspicere*, to despise.—L. *dē*, down; *specere*, to look; see **Species.**

Despoil. (F.—L.) O. F. *despoiller* (F. *dépouiller*), to despoil.—L. *dēspoliare*, to plunder.—L. *dē*, fully; *spoliāre*, to strip of clothing, from *spolium*, spoil; see **Spoil.**

Despond. (L.) L. *dēspondēre*, (1) to promise fully, (2) to give up, yield (hence,

to despair).—L. *dē*, (1) fully, (2) away; *spondēre*, to promise.

Despot, a tyrant. (F.—L.—Gk.) O.F. *despot.*—Med. L. *despotus.* ⸗ Gk. δεσπότης, a master; lit. ' master of the house.' The syllable δεσ-= Idg. **dems*, ' of a house ;' cf. Skt. *dam-pati-*, master of the house. The syllable πoτ- is allied to Gk. πόσις, husband, Skt. *pati-*, lord, and to **Potent.** Brugm. i. § 408.

Desquamation, a scaling off. (L.) From pp. of L. *dēsquāmāre*, to remove scales.—L. *dē*, off; *squāma*, a scale.

Dessert. (F.—L.) O. F. *dessert*, the last course at dinner.—O. F. *desservir*, to do ill service to; also, to take away the courses at dinner.—O. F. *des-*, from L. *dis-*, away; *servir*, from *seruīre*, to serve.

Destine. (F.—L.) O. F. *destiner*, to ordain.—L. *dēstināre*, to destine, ordain; allied to L. *dēstina*, a prop, support.—L. *dē*, down; and **stanāre*, to cause to stand, derivative of *stāre*, to stand. Cf. Cretic στανύω, I set. Brugm. ii. § 603.

Destitute. (L.) L. *dēstitūtus*, left alone; pp. of *dēstituere*, to place alone.— L. *dē*, away; *statuere*, to place, causal of *stāre*, to stand.

Destroy. (F.—L.) M. E. *destroien, destruien.*—O. F. *destruire* (F. *détruire* ; Ital. *distruggere*).—L. type **dēstrugere*, for L. *dēstruere*, to pull down, unbuild, overthrow (pp. *dēstructus*).—L. *dē*, down; *struere*, to pile up. **destruction.** (F.—L.) O. F. *destruction.*—L. acc. *dēstructiōnem*; from *dēstruct-us*, pp. of *dēstruere* (above).

Desuetude, disuse. (L.) L. *dēsuētūdo*, disuse.—L. *dēsuētus*, pp. of *dēsuescere*, to grow out of use, opposed to *con-suescere*; see **Custom.**

Desultory, jumping from one thing to another. (L.) L. *dēsultōrius*, orig. belonging to a *dēsultor*; hence, inconstant.— L. *dēsultor*, one who leaps down, or from horse to horse.—L. *dēsultus*, pp. of *dēsilīre*, to leap down.—L. *de*, down; *salīre*, to leap.

Detach. (F.—L. *and* G.) F. *détacher*, to unfasten.—F. *dé-*=O. F. *des-* (L. *dis-*), apart ; F. *tache*, a nail, tack; see **Tack.** **Der.** *detachment.* Cf. **Attach.**

Detail, a small part. (F.—L.) O. F. *detail*, 'a peece-mealing, also retaile, or a selling by parcels :' Cot.—O. F. *detailler*, to cut into pieces. ⸗ O. F. *de-* (L. *dē-*), down fully ; *tailler*, to cut ; see **Tailor.**

Der. *detail,* verb (which is from the sb. in E., though in F. it is the other way).

Detain. (F.—L.) From a tonic stem of O. F. *detenir.*—L. *dētinēre,* to hold back; pp. *dētentus.*—L. *dē,* down; *tenēre,* to hold. Der. *detention* (from the pp.).

Detect. (L.) From L. *dētectus,* pp. of *dētegere,* to uncover, expose.—L. *dē,* away; *tegere,* to cover. See Tegufrom.

Detention; see Detain.

Deter. (L.) L. *dēterrēre,* to frighten from.—L. *dē,* from; *terrēre,* to frighten. See Terror.

Deterge, to wipe off. (L.) L. *dētergēre,* to wipe off.—L. *dē,* off; *tergēre,* to wipe. Der. *deterg-ent,* from the pres. pt.

Deteriorate. (L.) L. *dēteriōrātus,* pp. of *dēteriōrāre,* to make worse.—L. *dēterior,* worse. Formed from *dē,* away, from; with comp. suffixes *-ter-ior.* (So also *in-ter-ior* from *in.*)

Determine. (F.—L.) O. F. *determiner.*—L. *dētermināre,* to bound, end.—L. *dē,* down, fully; *termināre,* to bound, from *terminus,* a boundary; see Term. Der. *pre-determine.*

Detest. (F.—L.) M. F. *detester,* to loathe.—L. *dētestārī,* to execrate, imprecate evil by calling down the gods to witness.—L. *dē,* down; *testārī,* to witness, from *testis,* a witness.

Dethrone. (F.—L. *and* Gk.) M. F. *desthroner,* 'to unthrone;' Cot. — O. F. *des-* (L. *dis-*), apart; L. *thronus,* from Gk. θρόνος, a throne. See Throne.

Detonate, to explode. (L.) L. *dētonātus,* pp. of *dētonāre,* to explode.—L. *dē,* fully; *tonāre,* to thunder.

Detour, a winding way. (F.—L.) F. *détour,* a circuit; verbal sb. from F. *détourner,* to turn aside.—F. *dé-* (L. *dis-*), aside, apart; *tourner,* to turn. See Turn.

Detraction. (F.—L.) O. F. *detraction.*—L. *dētractiōnem,* acc. of *dētractio,* a withdrawal; hence a taking away of one's credit.—L. *dētractus,* pp. of *dētrahere,* to take away, also to disparage. — L. *dē,* away; *trahere,* to draw. See Trace (1).

Detriment. (F.—L.) O. F. *detriment.* —L. *dētrīmentum,* loss; lit. 'a rubbing away.'—L. *dētrī-tus,* pp. of *dēterere,* to rub down; with suffix *-mentum.*—L. *dē,* down; *terere,* to rub. See Trite.

Detrude. (L.) L. *dētrūdere,* to thrust down.—L. *dē,* down; *trūdere,* to thrust.

Deuce (1), a two, at cards. (F.—L.)

O. F. *deus* (F. *deux*), also *dous,* two.—L. *duōs,* acc. of *duō,* two.

deuce (2), the devil. (Low G.—F.—L.) Low G. *de duus!* the deuce! (Bremen Wörterbuch); G. *der daus!* Orig. an exclamation on throwing the *deuce* or two at dice, as it was a losing throw.— O. F. *dous,* two (above).

Deuteronomy. (L.—Gk.) Late L. *deuteronomium.* — Gk. δευτερονόμιον, a second giving of the law.—Gk. δεύτερο-ς, second; νόμ-ος, law.

Devastate. (L.) From pp. of L. *dēuastāre,* to lay waste. — L. *dē,* down; *uastāre,* to lay waste, from adj. *uastus,* waste.

Develop, to unfold, open out. (F.— L. *and* Teut.) F. *développer,* O. F. *desveloper, desvoluper.* — O. F. *des-* (L. *dis-*), apart; and the base *velop-* or *volup-,* which appears also in *envelope.* This base represents Teut. *wlap-,* as in M. E. *wlappen,* to wrap up; see Lap (3), Wrap.

Devest, to unclothe. (F.—L.) From M. F. *desvestir,* to devest.—L. *dis-,* off; and *uestīre,* to clothe. Doublet, *divest.*

Deviate. (L.) From pp. of L. *dēuiāre,* to go out of the way.—L. *dē,* from; *uia,* way.

devious. (L.) L. *dēui-us,* going out of the way; with suffix *-ous.*—L. *dē,* from; *uia,* way.

Device, a plan. (F. — L.) M. E. *deuys, deuise* (*devys, devise*).—O. F. *devis, devise,* a device, also a division.—Late L. *dīuīsum, dīuīsa,* a division; also a judgment, device; orig. neut. and fem. of pp of *dīuīdere,* to divide; see Divide.

devise, to plan. (F.—L.) M. E. *deuisen* (*devisen*). — O. F. *deviser.* — O. F. *devis* or *devise,* sb. (above).

Devil. (L.—Gk.) A.S. *dēoful, dēofol.* —L. *diabolus.*—Gk. διάβολος, the slanderer, the devil.—Gk. διαβάλλειν, to throw across, traduce, slander.—Gk. διά, through, across; βάλλειν, to throw; see Belemnite.

Devious; see Deviate.

Devise; see Device.

Devoid, quite void. (F. — L.) M. E. *deuoid;* due to *deuoided,* pp. of *deuoiden* (*devoiden*), to empty.—O. F. *desvuidier, desvoidier,* to empty out. — O. F. *des-* (L. *dis-*); *voidier,* to empty, from *voide, vuide,* adj. empty; see Void.

Devoir, duty. (F.—L.) M.E. *deuoir.* — M. F. *devoir,* O. F. *deveir,* to owe; used as a sb.—L. *dēbēre,* to owe; see Debt.

Devolve. (L.) L. *dēuoluere*, to roll down, bring or transfer to. – L. *dē*, down ; *uoluere*, to roll. ¶ A frequent old sense of *devolve* was ' to transfer.' **Der.** *devolution*, from the pp. *dēvolūtus*.

Devote, vb. (L.) L. *dēuōtus*, pp. of *dēuouēre*, to devote, vow fully. – L. *dē*, fully ; *uouēre*, to vow. See **Vote**.

Devour. (F. – L.) O. F. *devorer* (1 p. s. pr. *devoure*). – L. *dēuorāre*, to consume, eat up. – L. *dē*, fully ; *uorāre*, to gulp down. See **Voracity**.

Devout. (F. – L.) M. E. *deuot* (*devot*), also spelt *devoute*. – O. F. *devot*, devoted. – L. *dēuōtus*, pp. of *dēuouēre* ; see **Devote**.

Dew. (E.) M. E. *deu*, *dew*. A. S. *dēaw*, dew. ✛ Du. *dauw*, Icel. *dögg* (gen. *döggvar*), Dan. *dug*, Swed. *dagg*, G. *thau*. Teut. type **dauwo-*. Perhaps allied to Skt. *dhāv*, to run, flow ; Gk. θέειν, to run.

Dexter. (L.) L. *dexter*, on the right hand side, right. ✛ Gk. δεξιός, right, Skt. *dakshiṇa-*, on the right or south, Goth. *taihswa*, right hand, W. *deheu*, right, southern, Gael. and Irish *deas* (the same). The Skt. *dakshiṇa-* is orig. ' clever ' ; cf. Skt. *daksha-*, able, *daksh*, to be strong.

Dey, a governor of Algiers. (F. – Turk.) F. *dey*. – Turk. *dāi*, a maternal uncle ; afterwards, in Algiers, an officer, chieftain.

Dhow, a slave ship (?). Mod. Arab. *dāo*, but not an Arab. word (Yule). Orig. language unknown.

Di- (1), prefix ; apart. (L.) L. *dī-*, shorter form of *dis-* ; see **Dis-**.

Di- (2), prefix ; twice, double. (Gk.) Gk. δι- (for δίς), twice. ✛ L. *bis*, *bi-* ; Skt. *dvis*, *dvi-*. Allied to **Two**.

Dia-, prefix. (Gk.) Gk. διά, through, between, apart ; allied to **Di-** (2), and to **Two**. ¶ In nearly all words beginning with *dia-*, except *dial*, *diamond*, *diary*.

Diabetes, a disease accompanied with excessive discharge of urine. (Gk.) Gk. διαβήτης, a pair of compasses, a siphon, diabetes. – Gk. διαβαίνειν, to stand with the legs apart (like compasses or a siphon). – Gk. διά, apart ; βαίνειν, to go ; see **Come**.

Diabolical. (L. – Gk.) L. *diabolic-us*, devilish. – Gk. διαβολικός, devilish. – Gk. διάβολος, the devil ; see **Devil**.

Diaconal, belonging to a deacon. (F. – L. – Gk.) F. *diaconal*. – Late L. *diāconālis*, from L. *diāconus*, a deacon ; see **Deacon**.

Diacritic. (Gk.) Gk. διακριτικός, dis-tinctive. – Gk. διακρίνειν, to separate. – Gk. διά, apart ; κρίνειν, to judge.

Diadem, a fillet, crown. (F. – L. – Gk.) M. E. and O. F. *diademe*. – L. *diadēma*. – Gk. διάδημα, a fillet. – Gk. διά, apart, across ; δέ-ω, I bind, allied to Skt. *dā*, to bind (whence *dāman*, a garland). (✓DĒ.) Brugm. ii. § 707.

Diæresis, a mark (¨) of separation. (L. – Gk.) L. *diæresis*. – Gk. διαίρεσις, a dividing. – Gk. δι-ά, apart ; αἵρεσις, a taking, from αἱρεῖν, to take.

Diagnosis, scientific determination of a disease. (Gk.) Gk. διάγνωσις, a dis-tinguishing. – Gk. διά, between ; γνῶσις, enquiry, from γνῶναι, to know.

Diagonal. (F. – L. – Gk.) F. *diagonal*. – L. *diagōnālis*, running from corner to corner. – Gk. διαγώνιος (the same). – Gk. διά, through, between ; γωνία, an angle, bend, allied to γόνυ, knee ; see **Knee**.

Diagram. (L. – Gk.) L. *diagramma*, a scale, gamut (hence, sketch, plan). – Gk. διάγραμμα, a figure, plan, gamut. – Gk. διαγράφειν, to mark out by lines, describe. – Gk. διά, through ; γράφειν, to write.

Dial. (L.) M. E. *dial*. – Med. L. *diālis*, relating to a day ; hence a plate for shew-ing the time of day. – L. *diēs*, day. Brugm. i. § 223.

Dialect, a variety of a language. (F. – L. – Gk.) F. *dialecte*. – L. *dialectus*, f. – Gk. διάλεκτος, f., discourse, language, dialect. – Gk. διαλέγομαι, I discourse. – Gk. διά, between ; λέγειν, to speak.

dialogue, a discourse. (F. – L. – Gk.) F. *dialogue*. – L. *dialogum*, acc. of *dialogus*. – Gk. διάλογος, a conversation. – Gk. δια-λέγομαι, I discourse (above).

Diameter, the line measuring the breadth across or thickness through. (F. – L. – Gk.) Mid. F. *diametre*, ' a dia-meter ; ' Cot. – L. *diametros*. – Gk. διά-μετρος, f. – Gk. διά, through ; μέτρον, a measure ; cf. μετρεῖν, to measure.

Diamond. (F. – L. – Gk.) M. E. *dia-mant*. – O. F. *diamant*, altered form of *adamant* ; so also Ital. Span. *diamante*, G. *diamant*, *demant*. See **Adamant**.

Diapason, a whole octave, harmony. (L. – Gk.) L. *diapāsōn*, an octave, con-cord of a note with its octave. – Gk. δια-πᾱσῶν, concord of first and last notes of an octave, lit. ' through all ' the notes. – Gk. διά, through ; πᾱσῶν, gen. pl. fem. of πᾶς, all (χορδῶν being understood) ; see **Pan-**, prefix.

Diaper, figured linen cloth. (F.–L.–Gk.) Cf. O. F. *diapré*, diapered; from the verb *diaprer*, to diaper, or 'diversifie with flourishings;' Cot. The verb is formed from O. F. *diaspre*, later *diapre*, a fine cloth, often described as *blanc* (white). – Late L. *diasprus*, adj., also used as a sb. (tunica de *diaspra alba*). – Late Byzantine Gk. διασπρος, adj., pure white; from δι-ά, wholly, ἄσπρος, white (see N. E. D.). ¶ Not the same as Ital. *diaspro*, a jasper; but cf. Prov. *diaspes*, *diaspres*, diaper, costly cloth (Bartsch); also Late L. *asperī*, white money (Ducange).

Diaphanous, transparent. (Gk.) Gk. διαφαν-ής, transparent; with suffix *-ous*. – Gk. διά, through; allied to φαίνειν, to shew. Brugm. i. § 195.

Diaphoretic, causing perspiration. (L.–Gk.) L. *diaphorēticus*, sudorific. – Gk. διαφορητικός (the same). – Gk. διαφόρησις, perspiration. – Gk. διαφορεῖν, to carry off (by perspiration). – Gk. διά, through; φορεῖν, to carry, allied to φέρειν, to bear; see Bear.

Diaphragm, a dividing membrane. (F.–L.–Gk.) F. *diaphragme.* – L. *diaphragma.* – Gk. διάφραγμα, partition, midriff. – Gk. διά, between; φράσσω (fut. φράξω), I fence in, enclose.

Diarrhœa. (L.–Gk.) L. *diarrhœa.* – Gk. διάρροια, lit. 'a flowing through.' – Gk. διαρρέειν, to flow through. – Gk. διά, through; ῥέειν, to flow.

Diary. (L.) L. *diārium*, a daily allowance, also a diary. – L. *diēs*, a day. See **Dial.**

Diastole, dilatation of the heart. (Gk.) Gk. διαστολή, a drawing asunder, dilatation. – Gk. διαστέλλειν, to put aside or apart. – Gk. διά, apart; στέλλειν, to put.

Diatonic, proceeding by tones. (Gk.) Gk. διατονικός, from διάτονος (lit. stretched out), diatonic. – Gk. διατείνειν, to stretch out. – Gk. διά, fully; τείνειν, to stretch.

Diatribe. (F.–L.–Gk.) F. *diatribe.* – L. *diatriba*, a learned disputation. – Gk. διατριβή, a wearing away of time, waste of time, discussion. – Gk. διατρίβειν, to waste time, to discuss. – Gk. διά, thoroughly; τρίβειν, to rub, waste away (with long ι).

Dib, to dab lightly. (E.) A lighter form of *dab.* Hence *dibber*, a dibble; see below.

dibble, an instrument for setting plants, by making holes. (E.) M. E. *debil, de-*

bylle; apparently formed from **Dab**; see above.

Dice, pl. of **Die** (2), q. v.

Dicker, half a score. (L.) M. E. *diker* (cf. Icel. *dekr*). – L. *decuria*, a set of ten. – L. *dec-em*, ten.

Dicotyledon, a plant with two seedlobes. (Gk.) From Gk. δι-, double; κοτυληδών, a cup-shaped hollow, from κοτύλη, a cup.

Dictate. (L.) L. *dictātus*, pp. of *dictāre*, to dictate, frequentative of *dīcere*, to say (below). Der. *dictat-or*.

diction, talk. (F.–L.) F. *diction.* – L. *dictiōnem*, acc. of *dictio*, a saying. – L. *dictus*, pp. of *dīcere*, to say, appoint; allied to *dicāre*, to tell, publish. ╋Gk. δείκνυμι, I shew; Skt. *diç*, to shew; Goth. *gateihan*, to announce, G. *zeigen*, to accuse, point out. Brugm. i. § 207. (√DEIK.)

dictionary. (L.) Late L. *dictiōnārium*, formed from *dictiōn-*, stem of *dictio*, a saying, word (above).

Didactic, instructive. (Gk.) Gk. διδακτικός, instructive. – Gk. διδάσκειν, to teach (= *διδακ-σκειν); allied to δοκεῖν, to think, δέκομαι, Ionic for δέχομαι, I accept; cf. L. *discere*, to learn, *docēre*, to teach. Brugm. i. § 707. (√DEK.)

Didapper, Divedapper, a bird; see **Dive.**

Die (1), to lose life. (Scand.) M. E. *dyen, deyen*; Late A. S. *dēȝan.* – Icel. *deyja*; Swed. *dö*, Dan. *döe*, to die.╋ M. H. G. *touwen*; cf. Russ. *davit(e)*, to strangle. The Teut. base is *dau*, whence *dau-jan* (Icel. *dey-ja*). Cf. **Dead, Death.**

Die (2), a small cube for gaming. (F.–L.) Used as sing. of M. E. *dys*, more usually *dees*, dice. – O. F. *dez*, dice, pl. of *det*, a die (F. *dé*). Cf. Prov. *dat*, Ital. Span. *dado*, a die. – Late L. *datum*, lit. a thing given or decreed; hence applied to a die for casting lots. – L. *datus*, pp. of *dare*, to give. See **Date** (1).

Diet (1), regimen. (F.–L.–Gk.) M. E. *diete.* – O. F. *diete*, daily fare. – L. *dicta, diæta*, a ration of food. – Gk. δίαιτα, mode of life, diet. Brugm. i. § 650.

Diet (2), an assembly. (F.–L.–Gk.) M. F. *diete*, 'a diete, parliament;' Cot. – Med. L. *diæta*, a public assembly; also a ration of food, diet. – Gk. δίαιτα, a mode of life, diet; see **Diet** (1). ¶ The peculiar use of the word was due to a popular etymology which connected *diæta* (often spelt *diēta*) with *diēs*, a day; we even

find *diæta* used to mean ' a day's journey ';
and *diēta* for ' a day's work ' and ' a daily
office or duty '; Ducange.

Differ. (F.—L.) M. F. *differer*.—L.
differre, to carry apart, to differ. —L. *dif-*
(for *dis-*), apart; *ferre*, to bear. Cf. **Defer.**

Difficulty. (F.—L.) M.E. *difficultee.*
—O. F. *difficulte*.—L. *difficultātem*, acc.
of *difficultas* (for *difficilitas, like *facultas*
for *facilitas*), difficulty.—L. *difficilis*, hard.
—L. *dif-* (for *dis-*), apart; *facilis*, easy ;
see **Facile.**

Diffident. (L.) L. *diffīdent-*, stem of
diffidens, pres. pt. of *diffīdere*, to distrust.
—L. *dif-*(=*dis-*), apart; *fīdere*, to trust,
allied to *fidēs*, faith. See **Faith.**

Diffuse. (L.) L. *diffūsus*, pp. of *dif-
fundere*, to shed abroad.—L. *dif-* (=*dis-*),
apart; *fundere*, to pour; see **Fuse** (1).

Dig. (F.—Du.) F. *diguer*, to make a
dike.—F. *digue*, a dike.—Flem. *and* Du.
dijk, a dike; see **Dike.**

Digest, to assimilate food. (L.) M.E.
digest, used as a pp.=digested.—L. *dīges-
tus*, pp. of *dīgerere*, to carry apart, separate, dissolve, digest.— L. *dī-* (for *dis-*),
apart; *gerere*, to carry.

Dight, adorned. (L.) *Dight* as a pp. is
short for *dighted*, from the obs. verb *dight*,
to arrange, prepare, M. E. *dihten*, to prepare. A.S. *dihtan*, to set in order, arrange ;
borrowed from L. *dictāre*, to dictate, prescribe ; see **Dictate.**

Digit, a finger, figure. (L.) L. *digitus*,
a finger ; hence a figure, from counting on
the fingers.

Dignity. (F.—L.) M.E. *dignitee.*—
O. F. *digneté*.—L. *dignitātem*, acc. of
dignitās, worthiness.—L. *dignus*, worthy.
Brugm. i. § 762 (3).

dignify. (F.—L.) O. F. *dignifier*.—
Med. L. *dignificāre*, to make worthy.—L.
digni-, for *dignus*, worthy ; *-ficāre*, for
facere, to make.

Digress, lit. to step aside. (L.) L.
digressus, pp. of *dīgredī*, to go aside.—L.
dī- (for *dis-*), apart; *gradī*, to go. See
Grade.

Dike, a trench, trench and embankment,
bank. (E.) M. E. *dik*. A.S. *dīc*, masc.
+Du. *dijk*, Icel. *dīki*, Dan. *dige*, Swed.
dike, G. *teich*, pond, tank. Der. *dig*, q. v.
See **Ditch.**

Dilacerate. (L.) From pp. of L.
dīlacerāre, to tear apart.—L. *dī-* (for *dis-*),
apart; *lacerāre*, to tear. See **Lacerate.**

Dilapidate, to pull down stone build-

ings, to ruin. (L.) From pp. of L. *dīla-
pidāre*, to scatter like stones.—L. *dī-* (for
dis-), apart ; *lapid-*, stem of *lapis*, a stone.

Dilate. (F.—L.) O. F. *dilater*, to
widen.—L. *dīlātāre*, to widen.—L. *dī-*
(for *dis-*), apart; *lātus*, broad. See **Latitude.** Der. *dilat-ory*, A. F. *dilatorie.*

Dilemma, a perplexity. (L.—Gk.) L.
dilemma.—Gk. δίλημμα, a double proposition, or argument in which one is caught
between two difficulties.—Gk. δι-, twice,
double ; λῆμμα, an assumption, premiss.
See **Lemma.**

Dilettante, a lover of the fine arts.
(Ital.—L.) Ital. *dilettante*, lit. ' delight-
ing in.'—Ital. *dilettare*, to delight.—L.
dēlectāre, to delight ; see **Delectable.**

Diligent, industrious. (F.—L.) O.F.
diligent.—L. *dīligent-*, stem of *dīligens*,
careful, diligent, lit. loving (fond) ; pres.
pt. of *dīligere*, to love, select, lit. choose
between.—L. *dī-* (=*dis-*), apart ; *legere*, to
choose. See **Legend.**

Dill, a plant. (E.) . M. E. *dille*. A.S.
dile.+Du. *dille*, Dan. *dild*, Swed. *dill*, G.
dill, dille, O. H. G. *tilli.*

Dilute. (L.) L. *dīlūtus*, pp. of *dīluere*,
to wash away, also to mix with water.—L.
dī- (for *dis-*), apart ; *luere*, to wash.

Dim. (E.) M.E. *dim*. A.S. *dim*, dark.
+Icel. *dimmr*, dim ; M. Dan. *dim*. Cf.
M. H. G. *timmer*, dim ; Swed. *dimma*, a
fog, haze ; O. Irish *deim*, dark.

Dime, the tenth part of a dollar. (F.—
L.) F. *dîme*, O. F. *disme*, tenth. —L.
decima, a tithe ; fem. of L. *decimus*, tenth,
allied to *decem*, ten. See **Ten.**

Dimension. (F.—L.) O. F. *dimension.*—L. acc. *dimensiōnem*, a measuring.
—L. *dīmensus*, pp. of *dīmetīrī*, to measure
off.—L. *dī-* (for *dis-*), apart ; *metīrī*, to
measure. See **Measure.**

Diminish, to lessen. (F.—L.) Coined
from L. *dī-* (=*dis-*), apart, and E. *minish* ;
in imitation of L. *dīminuere*, to diminish
(below). See **Minish.**

diminution. (F.—L.) F. *diminution.*—L. acc. *dīminūtiōnem*, diminution.
—L. *dīminūtus*, pp. of *dīminuere*, to
lessen.—L. *dī-* (=*dis-*), apart ; *minuere*,
to lessen. See **Minute.**

Dimissory, giving leave to depart.
(L.) L. *dīmissōrius*, giving leave to go
before another judge.—L. *dīmissus*, pp. of
dīmittere. to send away.—L. *dī-* (for *dis-*),
away ; *mittere*, to send.

Dimity, a white stuff. (Ital.—L.—Gk.)

Ital. *dimito* (pl. *dimiti*), 'a kind of course cotton or flanell;' Florio. — Late L. *dimitum* (pl. *dimita*), silk woven with two threads. — Gk. δίμιτος, made with a double thread. — Gk. δι-, double; μίτος, a thread of the woof.

Dimple, a small hollow. (E.?) M. E. *dympull.* Perhaps from a base **dump-*, allied to *dip.* Cf. Dan. dial. *dump*, a hollow in a field; *dybbel*, a pool, a hollow in the upper lip (Molbech); Du. *dompelen*, to dive; G. *dumpfel*, M. H. G. *tümpfel*, O. H. G. *tumphilo*, a deep pool. Also Lith. *dùbus*, hollow; *dùbti*, to be hollow (pres. t. *dumb-u*).

Din, clamour. (E.) M. E. *dine, dune.* A. S. *dyne, dyn*; *dynnan*, to resound. **+** Icel. *dynr*, Swed. *dån*, Dan. *dön*, noise; Skt. *dhuni-*, roaring, *dhvani-*, a din, *dhvan*, to resound.

Dine. (F. — L.) M. E. *dinen.* — O. F. *disner*, F. *dîner*, to dine. — Late L. **disiūnāre*, short for **disiēiūnāre*, to break one's fast. — L. *dis-*; *iēiūnāre*, to fast, from *iēiūnus*, fasting. (Romania, viii. 95.)

dinner. (F. — L.) M. E. *diner*; from O. F. *disner*, to dine; the infinitive mood being used as a sb.

Ding, to throw violently, beat. (E.?) M. E. *dingen*, pt. t. *dang*, pp. *dungen*; as a strong verb; though not found in A. S. Cf. Icel. *dengja*, Dan. *dænge*, Swed. *dänga*, to bang; all weak verbs. Cf. M. Dan. *dinge*, to blunt an edge by beating on it; O. H. G. *tangol*, a hammer. From a Teut. type **dengan-*.

Dingle, a deep dell. (E. *or* Scand.) M. E. *dingle.* Cf. *dimble*, in a similar sense. Of uncertain origin. Cf. Dimple.

Dingo, the native dog of Australia. (New S. Wales.) New S. Wales *dingo*, written *teingo* in 1798 (Morris).

Dingy, dirty. (E.) Orig. soiled with dung. Cf. A. S. *dingiung* (for **dyng(i)ung*, with *g* as *j*), a dunging; from *dung*, dung; so also Swed. *dyngig*, dungy, from *dyng*, dung; see Dung. For the pronunciation, cf. *stingy* (allied to *sting*).

Dingy (with hard *g*), **Dingey,** a small boat. (Bengali.) Beng. *dingy*, a small boat; 'it has become legitimately incorporated in the vocabulary of the British Navy, as the name of the smallest ship's boat' (Yule).

Dinner; see Dine.

Dint, a blow, force. (E.) M. E. *dint, dunt*; also *dent.* A. S. *dynt*, a blow.**+**

Icel. *dyntr*, a dint, *dynta*, to dint; Swed. dial. *dunt*, a stroke, *dunta*, to strike.

Diocese. (F. — L. — Gk.) M. E. *diocise.* — O. F. *diocise* (F. *diocèse*). — L. *diœcēsis.* — Gk. διοίκησις, administration, a province, diocese. — Gk. διοικέω, I keep house, govern. — Gk. δι- (for διά), throughout; οἰκέω, I dwell, occupy, from οἶκος, a house; see Wick, a town.

Dioptrics, the science of the refraction of light. (Gk.) Gk. τὰ διοπτρικά, dioptrics. — Gk. διοπτρικός, relating to the δίοπτρα, an optical instrument for taking heights, &c. — Gk. δι-ά, through; base **οπ-* (fut. ὄψομαι), to see; -τρα, fem. instrumental suffix. See Optics.

Diorama, a scene seen through a small opening. (Gk.) Gk. δι- (for διά), through; ὅραμα, a sight, from ὁράω, I see.

Dip, to plunge, immerge. (E.) M. E. *dippen.* A. S. *dyppan*, later *dippan*; for **dup-jan*, causal form from the base *dup-*, weak grade of *deup-*, as seen in A. S. *dēop*, deep; see Deep. Cf. Dan. *dyppe*, to dip.

Diphtheria. (Gk.) From Gk. διφθέρα, leather; from the leathery nature of the false membrane formed in the disease. Cf. Gk. δεψεῖν, to make supple.

Diphthong, a union of two vowel-sounds in one syllable. (F. — L. — Gk.) Formerly *dipthong* (Ben Jonson). — M. F. *dipthongue.* — L. acc. *diphthongum*, f. — G. δίφθογγος, with two sounds. — Gk. δι- (for δίς), double; φθόγγος, sound, from φθέγγομαι, I cry out.

Diploma. (L. — Gk.) L. *diplōma*, a document conferring a privilege. — Gk. δίπλωμα, a thing folded double; also, a licence, diploma (prob. orig. folded double). — Gk. διπλόος, double. — Gk. δι- (δίς), double; -πλόος, folded. **Der.** *diplomat-ic*, from διπλωματ-, stem of δίπλωμα.

Diptera, two-winged insects. (Gk.) From Gk. δι- (δίς), double; πτερόν, a wing, from the weak grade of πέτομαι, I fly.

Diptych, a double-folding tablet. (L. — Gk.) Late L. pl. *diptycha.* — Gk. δίπτυχα, a pair of tablets; neut. pl. of δίπτυχος, folded in two. — Gk. δι- (δίς), double; πτυχή, a fold, πτύσσειν, to fold.

Dire. (L.) L. *dīrus*, fearful.

Direct, adj. (L.) L. *directus*, pp. of *dīrigere*, to direct. — L. *dī-* (for *dis-*), apart; *regere*, to rule.

dirge. (L.) Formerly *dīrige*; from the first word of the anthem '*dīrige*, Dominus meus,' in the office for the dead. — L.

dīrige, direct thou (cf. Ps. v. 8); 2 p. imper. sing. of *dīrigere* (above).

Dirk, a dagger. (Du. ?) Spelt *dork* (A. D. 1602); also *durk*. Perhaps from Du. *dolk*, a dagger; a word of Slavonic origin. Cf. Polish *tulich*, a dagger. ¶ Irish *duirc*, a poniard, is borrowed from E.

Dirt. (Scand.) From M. E. *drit* (with shifted *r*). — Icel. *drit*, dirt, excrement of birds. Cf. Icel. *drīta*, to void excrement.+ M. Du. *drete*, Du. *dreet*, sb., *drijten*, vb.

Dis-, *prefix*. (L.) L. *dis-*, apart ; cf. Gk. δι-, apart ; see **Di-**. Hence O. F. *des-*, which sometimes becomes *dis-* in E., and sometimes *de-*, as in *de-feat*. The prefix *dis-* commonly expresses the reversal of an act, somewhat like the E. verbal prefix *un-*. For most words beginning with this prefix, see the simpler forms. For example, for *dis-abuse*, see *abuse* ; and so on.

Disaster. (F. — L.) M. F. *desastre*, ' a disaster, misfortune ; ' Cot. Lit. ' ill-fortune.' — O. F. *des-*, for L. *dis-*, with a sinister or bad sense ; and M. F. *astre*, a star, planet, also destiny, fortune, from L. *astrum*, a star.

Disburse. (F. — L. *and* Gk.) O. F. *desbourser*, to take out of a purse. — O. F. *des-* (L. *dis-*), away ; F. *bourse*, a purse, from Late L. *bursa*, Gk. βύρσα, a skin (hence, a bag). See **Bursar**.

Disc, Disk, a round plate. (L. — Gk.) L. *discus*, a quoit, a plate. — Gk. δίσκος, a quoit. — Gk. δικεῖν, to cast, throw. Brugm. i. § 744. See **Dish, Desk, Dais**.

Discern. (F. — L.) F. *discerner*. — L. *discernere*, to separate, determine. — L. *dis-*, apart ; *cernere*, to separate. Cf. **Concern**.

Disciple. (F. — L.) F. *disciple*. — L. *discipulum*, acc. of *discipulus*, a learner. — L. *discere*, to learn ; allied to *docēre*, to teach ; see **Docile**. Der. *discipl-ine*, O. F. *discipline*, L. *disciplīna*, learning.

Disclose. (F. — L.) M. E. *disclosen*. — O. F. *desclos-*, pres. stem of *desclorre*, to unclose, open. — L. *disclaudere*, to unclose. — L. *dis-*, apart ; *claudere*, to close. See **Clause**.

Discomfit. (F. — L.) M. E. *discomfit* (Bruce). — O. F. *disconfit*, discomfited, pp. of *desconfire*, ' to discomfit, vanquish,' Cot. — O. F. *des-* ; and *confire*, to preserve, make ready. — L. *dis-*, apart ; and *conficere*, to preserve, complete, from L. *con-* (*cum*), together, *facere*, to put, make. See **Fact**.

Disconsolate. (L.) Late L. *disconsōlātus*, comfortless. — L. *dis-*, apart ; *consōlātus*, pp. of *consōlārī*, to console ; from *con-* (*cum*), with, *sōlārī*, to comfort. See **Solace**.

Discord, sb. (F. — L.) O. F. *descord*, discord, variance ; formed from O. F. *descorder*, vb., to be at variance. — L. *discordāre* (the same). — L. *discord-*, stem of *discors*, adj. discordant. — L. *dis-*, apart ; *cord-*, stem of *cor*, heart.

Discount, verb. (F. — L.) Formerly *discompt*. — O. F. *descompter*, to reckon back or off. — O. F. *des-* (L. *dis-*), away ; *compter*, to count ; see **Count** (2).

Discourse. (F. — L.) O. F. *discours*, sb. — L. *discursum*, acc. of *discursus*, a running about ; also, conversation. — L. *discursus*, pp. of *discurrere*, to run about. — L. *dis-*, apart ; *currere*, to run.

Discover. (F. — L.) M. E. *discoueren* (*discoveren*). — O. F. *descouvrir*, to uncover, disclose. — O. F. *des-* (L. *dis-*), apart ; *couvrir*, to cover. See **Cover**.

Discreet, prudent. (F. — L.) O. F. *discret*. — L. *discrētus*, pp. of *dis-cernere*, to discern ; see **Discern**. Der. *discret-ion*.

Discrepant, differing. (F. — L.) M. F. *discrepant*. — L. *discrepant-*, stem of pres. part. of *discrepāre*, to differ (in sound). — L. *dis-*, apart ; *crepāre*, to crackle, sound.

Discriminate. (L.) L. *discrīminātus*, pp. of *discrīmināre*, to separate. — L. *discrīmin-*, stem of *discrīmen*, a separation. — L. *discernere* (pt. t. *discrē-uī*), to distinguish. — L. *dis-*, apart ; *cernere*, to separate.

Discursive. (L.) From L. *discursus*, pp. of *discurrere*, to run about ; with suffix *-ive*. See **Discourse**.

Discuss. (L.) M. E. *discussed*, pp. driven away. — L. *discussus*, pp. of *discutere*, to shake asunder ; in Late L., to discuss. — L. *dis-*, apart ; *quatere*, to shake.

Disdain, sb. (F. — L.) M. E. *disdeyn*. — O. F. *desdein*, sb. — O. F. *desdegnier*, to disdain. — O. F. *des-* (L. *dis-*), apart ; *degnier* (L. *dignārī*), to think worthy, from *dignus*, worthy. ¶ O. F. *desdegnier* seems to have been substituted for L. *dēdignārī*, to disdain (with prefix *dē-*, down).

Disease. (F.) O. F. *desaise*, want of ease. — O. F. *des-* (L. *dis-*) ; *aise*, ease.

Disembark. (F.) M. F. *desembarquer*. — O. F. *des-* (L. *dis-*), away ; *embarquer*, to embark ; see **Embark**.

Disembogue, to flow into the sea, as a river. (Span.—L.) Span. *desembocar*, to disembogue. — Span. *des-* (L. *dis-*), apart ; *embocar*, to enter the mouth, from *em-* (L. *in*), into, and *boca* (L. *bucca*), mouth.

Disgorge. (F.—L.) O. F. *desgorger*. —O. F. *des-* (L. *dis-*), away ; *gorge*, the throat ; see **Gorge**.

Disgrace. (F.—Ital.—L.) M.F. *disgrace.*—Ital. *disgrazia.*—L. *dis-*, apart ; *grātia*, grace. See **Grace**.

Disguise, vb. (F.—L. *and* O. H. G.) O. F. *desguiser*, to disguise. — O. F. *des-* (L. *dis-*), apart ; and *guise*, guise ; see **Guise**. Lit. ' to change the guise of.'

Disgust, vb. (F.—L.) M. F. *desgouster*, ' to distaste, loath ; ' Cot. —O. F. *des-* (L. *dis-*), apart ; *gouster*, to taste, from L. *gustāre*, to taste ; see **Gust** (2).

Dish, a platter. (L.—Gk.) M. E. *disch.* A. S. *disc*, a dish.—L. *discus*, a quoit, platter ; see **Disc**.

Dishabille ; see **Deshabille**.

Dishevil. (F.—L.) M. F. *discheveler* (Cot.), ' to dischevell,' i. e. to disorder the hair. — O. F. *des-* (L. *dis-*), apart ; *chevel* (F. *cheveu*), a hair, from L. *capillum*, acc. of *capillus*, hair.

Disinterested. (F. — L.) From Dis- (2) and *interested* ; see **Interest** (2).

Disk ; see **Disc**.

Dislocate, to put out of joint. (L.) From pp. of Late L. *dislocāre*, to put out of place.—L. *dis-*, apart ; *locāre*, to place, from *locus*, place.

Dismal. (F.—L.) Orig. A. F. *dis mal*, unlucky days (A. D. 1256). [The phrase was misunderstood, and *dismal* was treated as an adj., with the addition of *days* ; and later, of other sbs.]—L. *diēs malī*, evil days. Cf. F. *Lun-di* = Mon-day.

Dismantle. (F.—L.) M. F. *desmanteller*, ' to take a mans cloake off his backe; also, to raze walls ; ' Cot. — O. F. *des-* (L. *dis-*), apart ; *manteler*, to cloak, from *mantel*, sb. ; see **Mantle**.

Dismay, to discourage. (F.—L. *and* O. H. G.) O. F. **desmayer*, not found (except *dismayé*, pp., in Palsgrave, p. 519). but exactly the same as Span. *desmayar* (Port. *desmaier*, Ital. *smagare*), to dismay, terrify. The O. F. **desmayer* was early supplanted by *esmayer* in the same sense, which only differed in substituting the prefix *es-* (L. *ex-*) for *des-* (L. *dis-*). The latter part (*-mayer*) of these words is from

O. H. G. *magan* (G. *mögen*), to have power, be able. Hence **desmayer* and *esmayer*, at first used in the intrans. sense, to lack power, faint, be discouraged, but afterwards, actively, to discourage. Cf. Ital. *smagare* (for **dis-magare*), orig. to lose courage, also to dismay (Florio). See **May** (1).

Dismiss, to send away. (F.—L.) A coined word ; suggested by F. *desmettre*, pp. *desmis*, ' to displace, dismiss ; ' Cot. The true L. form is *dīmittere*, to send away.—L. *dī-* (for *dis-*), apart, away ; *mittere*, to send.

Disparage, to offer indignity, to lower in rank or esteem. (F.—L.) M. E. *desparagen.*—O. F. *desparager.*—O. F. *des-*, apart ; *parage*, rank. — L. *dis-*, apart ; Late L. *parāticum*, society, rank, equality of rank, from L. *par*, equal (Diez). See **Par**.

disparity. (F. — L.) F. *disparité* (Montaigne). From L. *dis-*, apart ; and F. *parité*, equality ; see **Parity**. Suggested by L. *dispar*, unequal.

Dispatch, Despatch. (Span.—L.) Formerly spelt *dis-*, not *des-*.—Span. *despachar*, to dispatch, expedite.—L. *dis-*, away ; and L. type **pactāre*, to fasten, fix, from *pactus*, pp. of *pangere*, to fasten. (See N. E. D.) Cf. Ital. *spacciare*, to dispatch (Florio), answering to a L. type **dispactiāre*.

Dispel. (L.) L. *dispellere*, to drive asunder, — L. *dis-*, apart ; *pellere*, to drive.

Dispense. (F.—L.) O. F. *dispenser*, to dispense with.—L. *dispensāre*, to weigh out, frequent. form of *dispendere*, to weigh out.—L. *dis-*, apart ; *pendere*, to weigh.

Disperse, to scatter abroad. (F.—L.) M. F. *disperser*. From L. pp. *dispersus*, pp. of *dispergere*, to scatter abroad.—L. *dī-* (for *dis-*), apart ; *spargere*, to scatter.

Display. (F.—L.) A. F. *desplayer*, O. F. *desploier*, to unfold, shew.—L. *dis-*, apart ; *plicāre*, to fold. **Doublet,** *deploy*.

Disport. (F.—L.) M. E. *disporten*, to amuse.—O. F. *se desporter*, to amuse oneself, orig. to cease from labour ; later *deporter*, and confused with **Deport**.—L. *dis-*, away, *portāre*, to carry (hence, to remove oneself from or cease from labour). Hence *sport*, q. v.

Dispose. (F.—L *and* Gk.) O. F. *disposer*, to arrange.—O. F. *dis-* (L. *dis-*), apart ; F. *poser*, to place ; see **Pose**.

Disposition. (F.—L.) F. *disposi-*

tion. − L. acc. *dispositiōnem*, a setting in order. − L. *dispositus*, pp. of *dispōnere*, to set in various places, to arrange. − L. *dis-*, apart; *pōnere*, to place, put.

Dispute. (F. − L.) F. *disputer.* − L. *disputāre*, to argue. − L. *dis-*, apart; *putāre*, to think. See **Putative.**

Disquisition, an investigation. (L.) From L. *disquīsītiō*, a search into. − L. *disquīsītus*, pp. of *disquīrere*, to examine. L. *dis-*, apart; *quærere*, to seek.

Disruption. (L.) From L. *disruptio*, *dīruptio*, a breaking asunder. − L. *disruptus*, *dīruptus*, pp. of *disrumpere*, *dīrumpere*, to break apart. − L. *dis-*, *dī-*, apart; *rumpere*, to burst.

Dissect. (L.) From L. *dissect-us*, pp. of *dissecāre*, to cut apart. − L. *dis-*, apart; *secāre*, to cut.

Dissemble. (F. − L.) O. F. *dis-* (L. *dis-*), apart; *sembler*, to seem, appear; cf. O. F. *dissimuler*, to dissemble. − L. *dis-*, apart, away; *simulare*, to pretend; cf. L. *dissimulāre*, to pretend that a thing is not. See **Simulate.**

Disseminate. (L.) From pp. of L. *dissēmināre*, to scatter seed. − L. *dis-*, apart; *sēmināre*, to sow, from *sēmin-*, for *sēmen*, seed.

Dissent, vb. (L.) L. *dissentīre* (pp. *dissensus*), to differ in opinion. − L. *dis-*, apart; *sentīre*, to feel, think. **Der.** *dissens-ion*, from the pp. *dissensus.*

Dissertation, a treatise. (L.) From L. *dissertātio*, a debate. − L. *dissertātus*, pp. of *dissertāre*, to debate; frequent. of *disserere*, to disjoin, discuss. − L. *dis-*, apart; *serere*, to join.

Dissever. (F. − L.) O. F. *dessevrer.* − Late L. *dissēparāre.* − L. *dis-*, apart; *sēparāre*, to separate.

Dissident. (L.) L. *dissident-*, stem of pres. pt. of *dissidēre*, to sit apart, to disagree. − L. *dis-*, apart; *sedēre*, to sit.

Dissimilar, unlike. (F. − L.) M. F. *dissimilaire.* − O. F. *dis-* (L. *dis-*), apart; and *similaire*, like; see **Similar.**

dissimilitude, dissimulation; from L. *dis-*, apart, and similitude, simulation.

Dissipate. (L.) From pp. of L. *dissipāre*, to disperse. − L. *dis-*, apart; and O. L. *supāre*, to throw; we find also *insipāre*, to throw into. Cf. Skt. *kship*, to throw. Brugm. i. § 761.

Dissociate. (L.) From the pp. of L. *dissociāre*, to separate from. − L. *dis-*,

apart; *sociāre*, to associate, from *socius*, a companion. See **Sociable.**

Dissolute. (L.) L. *dissolūtus*, licentious; pp. of L. *dissoluere* (below).

dissolve. (L.) L. *dissoluere*, to dissolve, loosen, relax. − L. *dis-*, apart; *soluere*, to loosen. See **Solve. Der.** *dissolut-ion* (from pp. *dissolūtus*).

Dissonant. (F. − L.) M. F. *dissonant*; Cot. − L. *dissonant-*, stem of pres. pt. of *dissonāre*, to be unlike in sound. − L. *dis-*, apart; *sonāre*, to sound, from *sonus*, sound.

Dissuade. (F. − L.) F. *dissuader*; Cot. − L. *dissuādēre*, to persuade from. − L. *dis-*, apart; *suādēre*, to persuade; see **Suasion.**

Distaff. (E.) A distaff is a *staff* *bedizened* with flax, ready to be spun off. ' I *dysyn* a *dystaffe*, I put the flaxe upon it to spynne; ' Palsgrave. M. E. *distaf*, *dysestaf.* A. S. *dīstæf.* The A. S. *dīstæf* stands for **dīse-stæf*, where *stæf =* E. *staff*, and **dīse =* Low G. *diesse*, the bunch of flax on a distaff (Bremen); also spelt *dise*, *disene* (Lübben); E. Fries. *dīssen.* See **Dizen.**

Distain. (F. − L.) M. E. *disteinen.* − O. F. *desteign-*, a stem of *desteindre*, to distain, take away colour. − O. F. *des-* (L. *dis-*), away; and *teindre*, from L. *tingere*, to dye.

Distant. (F. − L.) O. F. *distant.* − L. *distantem*, acc. of *distans*, pres. pt. of *distāre*, to stand apart. − L. *dī-*, apart; *stāre*, to stand.

Distemper (1), to derange the temperament of body or mind. (F. − L.) M.E. *distemperen.* − O. F. *destemprer*, to mix; whence pp. *destempré*, immoderate, excessive. − O. F. *des-* (L. *dis-*), apart; *temprer* (mod. F. *tremper*), from L. *temperāre*, to regulate. See **Temper.**

distemper (2), a kind of painting. (F. − L.) O. F. *destemprer*, later *destremper*, ' to soake, steepe, moisten, make fluid, liquid, or thin,' Cot.; the same verb as above.

Distend. (L.) L. *distendere*, to stretch apart. − L. *dis-*, apart; *tendere*, to stretch; see **Tend. Der.** *distent-ion* (from the pp. *distent-us*).

Distich, a couplet. (L. − Gk.) L. *distichus*, *distichon.* − Gk. δίστιχον, a couplet (in verse); neut. of δίστιχος, having two rows. − Gk. δι- (δίς), double; στίχος, a row, allied to στείχειν, to go. (√STEIGH.)

146

Distil. (F.–L.) O.F. *distiller.*–L. *distillāre, dēstillāre,* to drop or trickle down.–L. *dē,* down; *stillāre,* to drop, from *stilla,* a drop. See Still (2).

Distinguish, to mark off. (F.–L.) O.F. *distinguer,* to distinguish; the suffix *-ish* has been added by analogy, and cannot be accounted for in the usual way.–L. *distinguere,* to mark with a prick, distinguish (pp. *distinctus*).–L. *dī-* (for *dis-*), apart; **stinguere* (not in use), to prick, allied to Gk. στίζειν, to prick, and E. *stick,* vb. See Instigate. Brugm. i. § 666.

distinct. (F.–L.) O.F. *distinct.*– L. *distinctus,* distinguished; pp. of *distinguere.*

Distort. (L.) L. *distortus,* pp. of *distorquēre,* to twist aside.–L. *dis-,* apart; *torquēre,* to twist; see Torture.

Distract, vb. (L.) From L.*distractus,* pp. of *distrahere,* to draw apart.–L. *dis-,* apart; *trahere,* to draw; see Trace (1).

Distrain. (F.–L.) O.F. *destreign-,* a stem of *destraindre,* to strain, press, vex extremely, constrain (hence to seize goods for debt).–L. *distringere,* to pull asunder (see below).–L.*dī-* (*dis-*), apart; *stringere,* to draw tight; see Stringent.

distress, calamity. (F.–L.) O.F. *destresse,* oldest form *destrece*; from a Folk-L. **districtia* (not used), regularly formed from L. *districtus,* pp. of *distringere,* to pull asunder (in Late L. to punish, afflict); see Distrain.

Distraught. (L.) A modification of *distract* (=distracted); from L.*distract-us*; see Distract.

Distribute, to allot, deal out. (L.) From *distribūt-us,* pp. of L. *distribuere,* to deal out, allot separately.–L. *dis-,* apart; *tribuere,* to assign; see Tribute.

District, a region. (F.–L.) M.F. *district.* – Late L. *districtus,* territory wherein a lord has power to enforce justice. –L. *districtus,* pp. of *distringere*; see Distrain.

Disturb. (F.–L.) M.E. *destorben, distourben.*–O.F. *destorber,* to vex.–L. *disturbāre,* to disturb.–L. *dis-,* apart; *turbāre,* to disorder, from *turba,* a tumult, crowd. See Turbid.

Ditch. (E.) M.E. *diche*; cf. A.S. *dīce,* dat. of *dīc,* fem. [also masc.], a dike; see Dike.

Dithyramb, a kind of hymn. (L.–Gk.) L. *dīthyrambus.*–Gk. διθύραμβος, a hymn in honour of Bacchus.

Dittany, a plant. (F.–L.–Gk.) M.E. *dytane.*–O.F. *ditan, dictam.*–L. *dictamnum,* acc. of *dictamnus.*–Gk. δίκταμνος, δίκταμνον, dittany; named from Mount *Dictè* in Crete, where it grew.

Ditto. (Ital.–L.) Ital. *ditto, detto,* that which has been said.–L. *dictum,* neut. of pp. of *dīcere,* to say.

Ditty. (F.–L.) M. E. *ditee.*–O. F. *dité,* a kind of poem.–L. *dictātum,* a thing dictated; neut. of *dictātus,* pp. of *dictāre,* frequent. of *dīcere*; see Dictate.

Diuretic, provoking discharge of urine. (F.–L.–Gk.) M.F. *diuretique*; Cot.–L. *diūrēticus.*–Gk. διουρητικός. – Gk. διουρέειν, to pass urine.–Gk. δι-ά, through; οὖρον, urine; see Urine.

Diurnal. (L.) L. *diurnālis,* daily.– L. *diurnus,* daily.–L. *diēs,* a day.

Divan, a council-chamber, sofa. (Pers.) Pers. *dīvān,* a tribunal; Arab. *daywān,* a royal court, tribunal, council of state.

Divaricate, to fork, diverge. (L.) From pp. of L. *dīuāricāre,* to spread apart. –L. *dī-* (for *dis-*), apart; *uāricus,* straddling, from *uārus,* crooked.

Dive. (E.) M.E. *diuen, duuen* (*u* = *v*). A. S. *dȳfan,* to immerse, weak verb; confused with *dūfan,* strong verb (pt. t. *dēaf,* pp. *dofen*), to dive. + Icel. *dȳfa,* to dip. Allied to Dove, Deep, Dip.

didapper, a bird. (E.) Short for *divedapper.* Cf. A.S. *dūfedoppa,* a pelican.*Here *dapper* (= A.S. *doppa*) means a dipper or diver; and *dive-dapper* = dive-dipper, a reduplicated word.

Diverge. (L.) Coined from L. *dī-* (for *dis-*), apart; and *verge,* vb. See Verge (2).

Divers, Diverse, various. (F.–L.) O. F. *divers,* masc., *diverse,* fem., 'divers, differing;' Cot.–L. *dīuersus,* various; orig. pp. of *dīuertere,* to turn asunder, separate, divert (below).

divert. (F.–L.) M.F. *divertir,* 'to divert, alter;' Cot.–L. *dīuertere,* to turn aside.–L. *dī-* (*dis-*), apart; *uertere,* to turn. Der. *divers-ion,* from pp. *dīuersus.*

Divest. (L.) Late L. *dīuestīre,* in place of L. *dēuestīre,* to strip off clothes. –L. *dī-* (for *dis-*), apart, substituted for L. *dē-,* down, away; *uestīre,* to clothe, from *uestis,* clothing. See Vest.

Divide. (L.) L. *dīuidere,* to divide, separate (pp. *dīuīsus*).–L. *dī-* (*dis-*), apart; and **uidere,* a lost verb, prob.

meaning 'to separate'; see **Widow.**
(√WIDH.) Brugm. i. § 589, ii. 528.
Der. *divis-ion* (from the pp.).

Divine. (F.−L.) M.E. *devin.* −O.F.
devin. − L. *dīuīnus*, divine, god-like;
allied to *dīuus*, godlike, *deus*, god; see
Deity.

Divorce, sb. (F.−L.) O.F. *divorce.* −
L. *dīuortium*, a separation.−L. *dīuortere*,
the same as *dīuertere*, to turn aside, separate; see **Divert.**

Divulge. (F.−L.) F. *divulguer*, 'to
divulge, reveal;' Cot.−L. *dīuulgāre*, to
publish abroad. −L. *dī-*, for *dis-*, apart;
uulgāre, to publish, from *uulgus*, the
people, a crowd; see **Vulgar.**

Dizen, to deck out. (E.) To *dizen* was
orig. to furnish a distaff with flax, hence
to deck out. See **Distaff.** Der. *be-dizen*.

Dizzy. (E.) M.E. *dysy, dusi.* A.S.
dysig, foolish, stupid. **+** E. Fries. *dusig*,
dizzy, foolish; O.H.G. *tusīc*. From
Teut. **dus-*, as in Low G. *dusen*, to loiter
(Lübben); allied to Teut. **dūs-*, as in Du.
duizelen, to be dizzy. Perhaps further
allied to A.S. *dwǽs*, Du. *dwaas*, foolish
(Franck), from Teut. stem **dwǽs-*.

Do, to perform. (E.) M.E. *doon.* A.S.
dōn, pt. t. *dyde*, pp. *gedōn*; the orig. sense
is 'put' or 'place.' **+** Du. *doen*, O.H.G.
tuon, G. *thun*. Teut. stem **dō-*. Allied
to Gk. τί-θη-μι, I put, Skt. *dhā*, to place.
(√DHĒ.) Brugm. i. § 129.

Docile. (F.−L.) F. *docile.* −L. *docilis*,
teachable. −L. *docēre*, to teach. Allied to
Disciple and **Didactic.**

doctor. (F.−L.) M.E. *doctour.* −
O.F. *doctour.* −L. *doctōrem*, acc. of *doctor*,
a teacher. −L. *docēre*, to teach.

doctrine. (F.−L.) F. *doctrine.* −L.
doctrīna, lore, learning. − L. *doctor*, a
teacher. −L. *docēre*, to teach.

document. (F.−L.) F. *document.*
−L. *documentum*, a proof. −L. *docēre*, to
teach, shew.

Dock (1), to curtail. (E.?) From
dock, sb., the stump of a tail, stump, cut
end. Cf. E. Fries. *dokke, dok*, a bundle,
bunch (as of straw); Du. *dok*, a little
bunch (of straw); Dan. *dukke*, a skein,
short column, baluster; G. *docke*, a skein,
rail, plug, peg; Low G. *dokke*, a bunch,
stump, peg (Berghaus).

Dock (2), a plant. (E.) A.S. *docce.* **+**
M.Du. *docke* (as in *docken bladeren*, dock-
leaves, Hexham); M.Dan. *å-dokka*, water-
dock (Kalkar). So also Gael. *dogha*, a

burdock; Irish *meacan-dogha*, a great burdock, where *meacan* means a tap-rooted
plant, as a carrot. Der. *bur-dock*.

Dock (3), a basin for ships. (Du.?)
M. Du. *docke*, a harbour (whence Dan.
dokke, Swed. *docka*, G. *docke*); Du. *dok*.
¶ History obscure.

Docket, a label, ticket. (E.?) Orig. an
abstract; apparently allied to **Dock** (1).
¶ History obscure.

Doctor, Doctrine, Document;
see **Docile.**

Dodecagon. (Gk.) Named from its
12 angles. Formed like *decagon*, with
Gk. δώδεκα, twelve, instead of δέκα, ten.
See **Decagon.**

Dodecahedron. (Gk.) Formed with
Gk. δώδεκα, twelve, in place of δέκα, ten;
see **Decahedron.**

Dodge, to go hither and thither, to
quibble. (E.) XVI cent. Orig. to walk
unsteadily, hence to go from side to side
as if to escape; perhaps allied to prov. E.
dade, to walk unsteadily, Scotch *daddle*,
doddle, to waddle, *dod*, to jog, *dodge*, to
jog along, *dodgel*, to hobble, North E.
dodder, to shake, totter, *dadge*, *dodge*, to
walk clumsily. (Very doubtful.)

Dodo, an extinct bird. (Port.) Port.
doudo, silly, foolish; the bird being of a
clumsy make. Said to be borrowed from
Devonsh. *dold*, stupid, the same as E. *dolt*
(Diez). See **Dolt.**

Doe. (E.) M.E. *doo.* A.S. *dā.*+Dan.
daa. Swed. *dof-*, in *dofhjort*, a buck, may
be allied to G. *damhirsch*, a buck, wherein
the syllable *dam-* is thought to be borrowed
from L. *dāma*, a deer. But A.S. *dā* may
be Teutonic.

Doff, to put off clothes. (E.) Short for
do off, i.e. put off. Cf. *don, dup.*

Dog. (E.) M.E. *dogge.* A.S. *docga.*
(Du. *dog*, Swed. *dogg*, a mastiff; Dan.
dogge, a bull-dog; Low G. *dogge*, F. *dogue*;
all borrowed from E.) Der. *dog*, verb, to
track, follow as a dog; *dogg-ed*, sullen;
dog-cheap, very cheap (see N.E.D.);
dog-wood.

Doge, a duke of Venice. (Ital.−L.)
Ital. *doge*, prov. form of **doce*, a duke.−L.
duc-em, acc. of *dux*, a leader. See **Duke.**

Doggerel, wretched poetry. (E.?)
M.E. *dogerel*, Ch. C.T. 13853. Origin
uncertain; but prob. formed from *dog.*
Cf. *dog-rime*, poor verses (N.E.D.).

Dogma, a definite tenet. (Gk.) Gk.
δόγμα, an opinion stem δογματ-). −Gk.

δοκέω, I am of opinion. Allied to **Do-cile**. Der. *dogmat-ic, dogmat-ise.*

Doily, a small napkin. (Personal name.) Formerly we read of '*doily* stuff,' and '*doily* petticoats.' Said to be named after 'the famous *Doily*'; Spectator, no. 283, Jan. 24, 1712. Mentioned in Dryden's Kind Keeper, iv. 1 (1679).

Doit, a small coin. (Du.—Scand.) Du. *duit,* a doit. — Icel. *þveit,* a piece, bit, small coin, doit. — Icel. *þvíta (pt. t. *þveit), to cut, a lost verb, but the same as A.S. *þwítan* ; see **Thwite**.

Dole, a portion. (E.) M.E. *dol, dale.* A.S. *dāl,* a division (Exod. viii. 23). A variant of **Deal** (1), q.v.

Doleful, sad. (Hybrid ; F.—L. *and* E.) The suffix *-ful* is E. M.E. *doel, duel, dol* (Scotch *dool*), sorrow, grief. —O.F. *doel, dol* (F. *deuil*), grief; verbal sb. of O.F. *doloir,* to grieve. —L.*dolium,*in *cor-dolium,* grief of heart. —L. *dolēre,* to grieve.

dolour. (F. — L.) M.E. *dolour.* — O.F. *dolour.* —L. *dolōrem,* acc. of *dolor,* grief. —L. *dolēre,* to grieve.

Doll. (Gk.) From *Doll,* for *Dorothy* ; a familiar name, of Gk. origin (see N.E.D.). Cf. Lowl. Sc. *doroty,* a doll.

Dollar. (Low G.—G.) Low G. *daler* ; Du. *daalder,* a dollar. Adapted and borrowed from G. *thaler,* a dollar. The G. *thaler* is short for *Joachimsthaler,* a coin made from silver found in *Joachims-thal* (Joachim's dale) in Bohemia, ab. A.D. 1519.

Dolman, a kind of loose jacket. (F.— G.—Hung.—Turk.) F. *dolman.* —G. *dol-man, dollman.* — Hung. *dolmany.* — Turk. *dōlāmān, dōlāmah,* a kind of long robe.

Dolmen, a monument of two upright stones, with a third across them. (F.—C.) F. *dolmen.* — Bret. *dolmen,* lit. 'stone-table;' Legonidec. — Bret. *tōl, taol,* a table (from L. *tābula*) ; and *men,* a stone ; according to Legonidec. But (see N.E.D.) this is due to some mistake; the F. *dolmen* seems to represent the Cornish *tolmēn,* stone with a hole beneath; from Corn. *toll,* a hole (W. *twll*), and *mēn* (W. *maen*), a stone.

Dolomite, a kind of rock. (F.) Named in 1794 from M. *Dolomieu,* a French geologist (1750–1801).

Dolour; see **Doleful**.

Dolphin, a fish. (F.—L.—Gk.) M.E. *dolphine.* —O.F. *daulphin* (now *dauphin*). —Folk-L. *dalfinum,* for L. *delphīnum,*

acc. of *delphīnus,* a dolphin. —Gk. δελφίν-, stem of δελφίς, a dolphin.

Dolt. (E.) Cf. Devonsh. *dold,* a dolt. M.E. *dult* (=*dulled*) ; from M.E. *dul,* dull ; see **Dull**.

Domain. (F.—L.) F. *domaine,* sb. ; from O.F. *demaine,* adj., belonging to as one's own. —L. *dominicus,* adj., belonging to a lord (the neut. *dominicum* was used for L. *dominium,* lordship). —L. *dominus,* a lord ; allied to L. *domāre,* to tame, subdue ; see **Tame**. Doublet, *demesne.*

Dome. (F. — Ital. — L.) F. *dôme.* — Ital. *duomo, domo,* a cathedral church (house of God). — L. *domum,* acc. of *domus,* a house, a building. (√DEM.) See **Timber**. Brugm. i. § 138.

domestic. (F.—L.) F. *domestique.* —L. *domesticus,* belonging to a household. —L. *dom-us,* a house (above).

domicile. (F.—L.) O.F. *domicile,* a mansion. —L. *domicilium,* a habitation. —L. *domi-,* for *domus,* a house; and *-cilium,* possibly allied to **Cell**.

Domesday; see **Doom**.

Dominate. (L.) From pp. of *domi-nārī,* to be lord over. —L. *dominus,* a lord.

domineer. (Du.—F.—L.) M. Du. *domineren,* to feast luxuriously (Oude-mans); borrowed from O.F. *dominer,* to govern, rule. —L. *dominārī,* to be lord over (above).

dominical. (F.—L.) O.F. *domini-cal.* —Late L. *dominicālis,* belonging to the Lord's day, or to the Lord. —L. *dominic-us,* belonging to a lord. —L. *dominus,* a lord.

dominion. (F. — Late L.) O.F. *dominion.* —Late L. *dominiōnem,* acc. of *dominio,* lordship ; allied to L. *domin-ium,* lordship. —L. *dominus* (above).

domino. (F. — L.) F. *domino,* a masquerade-dress ; orig. a master's hood. —L. *dominus,* a master (above). Der. *dominoes,* sb. pl., a game.

Don (1), to put on clothes. (E.) Short for *do on,* i.e. put on. Cf. *doff, dout, dup.*

Don (2), a Spanish title. (Span.—L.) Span. *don,* sir. — L. *dominum,* acc. of *dominus,* a lord.

Donation. (F.—L.) F. *donation.* — L. acc. *dōnātiōnem,* a gift, from the stem of the pp. of *dōnāre,* to give. —L. *dōnum,* a gift. Cf. Gk. δῶρον, a gift.

Donjon; see **Dungeon**.

Donkey. (C. *and* E.) Double dimin. with suffix *-k-ey* (= Lowl. Sc. *-ick-ie*, as in *hors-ickie*, a little-little horse, Banffsh.), from *dun*, familiar name for a horse, from its colour (Romeo. i. 4. 41); see Dun (1). ¶ So also M.E. *don-ek*, prov. E. *dunnock*, a hedge-sparrow, from its colour. *Donkey* (first found in 1785) was a prov. E. word, which seems to have rimed with *monkey* (whence the spelling). Cf. Somersets. *duung-kee*, pron. of *donkey*.

Donna. (Ital.—L.) Ital. *donna*.—L. *domina*, mistress, fem. of *dominus*, a master. **Doublet,** *duenna*.

Doom, a judgment, decision. (E.) M. E. *dōm*. A. S. *dōm*, lit. a thing set or decided on ; from *dōn*, to set, do ; see Do. ╋ Swed. Dan. *dom*, Icel. *dōmr*, Goth. *dōms*, O. H. G. *tuom*. Teut. type **dōmoz*, a statute. Cf. Gk. θέμις, law (from τίθημι, I set). Der. *deem*.

doomsday, domesday. (E.) A.S. *dōmes dæg*, day of doom or judgment.

Door, a gate. (E) M.E. *dore*, *dure*. A.S. *dor*, n. ; *duru*, f. ╋ O. Sax. *dor*, Goth. *daur*, G. *thor*, n. ; and Icel. *dyrr*, f. pl. ; Dan. *dör*, Swed. *dörr*, Du. *deur*, G. *thür*, f. sing. Teut. types **durom*, n. ; **dures*, f. pl. Cf. L. *fores*, Lith. *dùrys*, f. pl. ; O. Irish *dorus*, n., W. *drws*, m. ; Russ. *dver(e)*, Gk. θύρα. Skt. *dvār*, f. Brugm. i. § 462.

Dormant, sleeping. (F.—L.) F. *dormant*, pres. pt. of *dormir*, to sleep.—L. *dormīre*, to sleep. ╋Skt. *drā*, to sleep ; Gk. δαρθάνειν.

dormer-window. (F. *and* Scand.) A *dormer* was a sleeping-room. — O. F. *dormeor*.—L. *dormītōrium* (below).

dormitory. (L.) L. *dormītōrium*, a sleeping-chamber ; neut. of *dormītōrius*, adj., belonging to sleeping.—L. *dormītor*, a sleeper.—L. *dormīre*, to sleep.

Dormouse. (F. *and* E.) M. E. *dormous*. The prefix is perhaps short for North E. *dorm*, to doze (whence *dorm-mouse*). Cf. Icel., Norw., and Swed. dial. *dorma*, to doze ; all apparently from F. *dormir*, to sleep ; see **Dormant.** We find also prov. E. *dorrer*, a sleeper, as if from *dor*, to sleep.

Dornick, a kind of cloth ; *obsolete.* (Flemish.) Named from Flem. *Dornick*, better known by the F. name of *Tournay* (Lat. *Tornacus*).

Dorsal. (F.—L.) F. *dorsal*, belonging to the back.—Late L. *dorsālis*.—L. *dorsum*, the back.

Dory, a fish ; see John Dory.

Dose. (F.—L.—Gk.) O. F. *dose*, a quantity of medicine given at once. — Med. L. *dosis*.—Gk. δόσις, a giving.—Gk. δίδωμι (stems δω-, δο-), I give. Brugm. i. § 167.

Dot. (E.) A. S. *dott*, only in the sense 'head of a boil.' Cf. Du. *dot*, a little bundle of spoilt wool, &c., good for nothing (Sewel); Swed. dial. *dott*, a little heap, small lump; M. Dan. *dot*, a bunch ; E. Fries. *dot*, *dotte*, a heap, bunch, lump. Cf. Norw. *dotten*, pp. of *detta*, to fall, to fall to pieces.

Dote. (E.) M. E. *dotien*, *doten*, to be foolish (Layamon). ╋ M. Du. *doten*, to dote, mope ; Du. *dutten*, to doze ; Icel. *dotta*, to nod with sleep, M. H. G. *getotzen*, to doze, *tūzen*, to mope.

dotage. (E. ; *with* F. *suffix.*) M. E. *dotage* ; from M. E. *dot-en* ; with F. suffix *-age* (L. *-āticum*). Cf. F. *radotage*, from *radoter*, to dote.

dotard. (E. *with* F. *suffix.*) From *dote*, with F. suffix *-ard* (O. H. G. *hart*).

dotterel, a kind of plover. (E.) A bird easily caught ; from *dote*, vb., with suffix as in *cock-erel*.

Double. (F.—L.) O. F. *doble*, later *double*. — L. *duplus*, lit. twice-full. — L. *du-o*, two ; *-plus*, allied to *plēnus*, full.

doublet. (F.—L.) M. E. *dobbelet*.— O. F. *doublet*, an inner (double) garment. — F. *double*, double ; with suffix *-et*.

doubloon. (F.—Span.—L.) F. *doublon*.—Span. *doblon*, a coin, the *double* of a pistole.—Span. *doblo*, double.—L. *duplus* (above).

doubt. (F. — L.) M. E. *douten*.— O. F. *douter*.—L. *dubitāre*, to be of two minds ; allied to *dubius*, doubtful ; see Dubious.

Douceur. (F.—L.) F. *douceur*, lit. sweetness (hence, pleasant gift).—L. *dulcōrem*, acc. of *dulcor*, sweetness.—L. *dulcis*, sweet. See Dulcet.

Douche, a shower-bath. (F.—Ital.—L.) F. *douche*, a shower-bath. — Ital. *doccia*, a conduit, water-pipe. — Ital. *docciare*, to pour ; equivalent to Late Lat. **ductiāre*, derivative of L. *ductus*, a duct ; see Duct.

Dough. (E.) M. E. *dah*, *dogh*. A.S. *dāh* (stem *dāg-*).╋Du. *deeg*, Dan. *deig*, Swed. *deg*, Icel. *deig*, Goth. *daigs*, a kneaded lump, G. *teig*. The Goth. *daigs* is from *daig*, 2nd stem of *deigan*, to knead ; see Dike. (√DHEIGH.) Brugm. i. § 604.

Doughty. (E.) M. E. *dohti, duhti,*
valiant. A. S. *dohtig,* earlier form *dyhtig,*
valiant. ─ A. S. *dugan,* to be worth, be
strong. + Dan. *dygtig,* Swed. *dugtig,* Icel.
dygðugr, G. *tüchtig;* variously formed from
the Teut. verb **dugan-.*

Douse, to immerse. (E.?) Allied to
M. Du. *doesen,* 'to smite with violence'
(Hexham). See **Dowse** (1).

Dout, to extinguish. (E.) Short for *do
out,* i. e. put out.

Dove, a bird. (E.) A. S. *dūfe,* only
in comp. *dūfe-doppa,* lit. a diver. ─ A. S.
dūfan, to plunge into. + O. Sax. *dūva,*
Goth. *dubo,* G. *taube,* a dove, lit. diver.
[So also L. *columba,* a dove, is allied to
Gk. κολυμβίς, a diver, sea-bird. First
applied to sea-gulls, &c.]

dovetail, to fasten boards together.
(E.) From *dove* and *tail;* from the shape
of the fitted ends of the board (◁).

Dowager, a widow with a jointure.
(F. ─ L.) O. F. *douagere;* from *douage,*
an endowment. Again *douage* is coined
(with suffix *-age*) from F. *dou-er,* to endow.
─ L. *dōtāre,* to endow. ─ L. *dōt-,* stem of
dōs, a gift, dowry. Allied to *dō-num,* a
gift, *dare,* to give. **Der.** *en-dow,* from
F. *en* and *douer.* Brugm. i. § 167.

dower, an endowment. (F. ─ L.)
M. E. *dowere.* ─ O. F. *doaire,* later *douaire.*
─ Late L. *dōtārium.* ─ L. *dōtāre,* to endow
(above). **Der.** *dowr-y,* short for *dower-y.*

Dowdy; see **Duds.**

Dowlas, a coarse linen. (Bret.) From
Daoulas, S. E. of Brest, in Brittany.

Down (1), soft plumage. (Scand.)
M. E. *down.* ─ Icel. *dūnn,* Swed. *dun,*
Dan. *duun,* down; whence Du. *dons.*

Down (2), a hill. (C.) A. S. *dūn,* a
hill. ─ Irish *dūn,* a fortified hill, fort;
Gael. *dun,* W. *din,* a hill-fort. + A. S.
tūn; see **Town.**

down (3), prep. and adv. (E. *and* C.)
A corruption of *adown* = A. S. *ofdūne* = off
the hill, downwards. ─ A. S. *of,* off; *dūne,*
dat. of *dūn,* a hill; see **Down** (2).

dune, a low sand-hill. (C.) XVIII
cent. ─ F. *dune.* ─ M. Du. *dune* (Du.
duin); of Celt. origin. See **Down** (2).

Dowse (1), to strike in the face.
(E.?) Apparently the same as **Douse**
(above). Cf. Norw. *dūs,* a push, blow;
M. Du. *doesen,* to strike, E. Fries. *dössen,*
to strike.

Dowse (2), to immerse; see **Douse.**
Prob. the same as **Dowse** (1).

Dowse (3), to extinguish. The same
as **Dowse** (1); sense perhaps suggested
by *dout,* q. v.

Doxology. (L. ─ Gk.) L. *doxologia.*
─ Gk. δοξολογία, an ascription of praise.
─ Gk. δοξο-, for δόξα, glory, orig. a
notion; -λογια, from λέγειν, to speak.

Doxy. (M. Du.) A cant term. Cf.
E. Fries. *doktje,* dimin. of *dokke,* a doll.
Prob. introduced from the Netherlands. ─
M. Du. *docke,* a doll. Cf. O. H. G. *tocchā,*
a doll, also a term of endearment (G.
docke).

Doze. (Scand.) Swed. dial. *dusa,* Dan.
döse, to doze, mope; Icel. *dūsa,* to doze;
M. Dan. *dåse,* to be torpid. Allied to
Dizzy.

Dozen, twelve. (F. ─ L.) O. F. *do-
saine* (F. *douzaine*), a dozen. ─ O. F. *doze* (F.
douze), twelve; with suffix *-aine* (L. *-ēna,*
as in *cent-ēna*). ─ L. *duodecim,* twelve. ─ L.
duo, two; *decem,* ten. See **Two** and **Ten.**

Drab (1), a slut. (E.) Cf. Irish *drabog,*
Gael. *drabag,* a slut; Gael. *drabach,* dirty;
Irish *drab,* a spot, stain (all from E.). E.
Fries. *drabbe,* puddle-water. Also Du.
drabbe, f. dregs, draff; allied to **Draff.**

Drab (2), dull light brown. (F. ─ L.)
The colour of undyed cloth. ─ F. *drap,*
cloth. See **Drape.**

Drachm; see **Dram.**

Draff, dregs. (E.) M. E. *draf* (Layamon). + Du. *draf,* hogswash, *drabbe,* draff;
Icel. *draf,* Swed. *draf,* Dan. *drav,* dregs;
G. *träber,* pl. [Cf. Gael. and Irish *drabh,*
draff, from E.]

Draft; see **Draught.**

Drag, vb. (Scand.) M. E. *draggen;* a
Northern form allied to Icel. *draga,* to
draw. Cf. Swed. *dragg,* a drag, grapnel;
dragga, to drag. See **Draw.**

Dragoman, an interpreter. (Span. ─
Arab.) Span. *dragoman;* [Late Gk. δρα-
γούμανος], an interpreter. ─ Arab. *tarjumān,* an interpreter, translator; see
Targum.

Dragon. (F. ─ L. ─ Gk.) F. *dragon.*
─ L. acc. *dracōnem,* from nom. *draco.* ─
Gk. δράκων, a dragon, lit. 'seeing;' from
his supposed sharp sight. ─ Gk. δρακ-,
weak grade of δέρκομαι, I see. ¶ Such is
the usual account.

dragoon. (F. ─ L. ─ Gk.) F. *dragon,*
a dragoon; so called because the dragoons
orig. had a *dragon* on their standard; or
rather, because they were armed with a
short carbine called (in F.) *dragon.*

Drain. (E.) A. S. *drēhnigean, drēh-nian*, to drain away, strain off, Matt. xxiii. 24, also spelt *drēahnian*; orig. ' to become dry.' — A. S. **drēag-* = Teut. **draug-*, second grade of Teut. **dreug-an-*, to be dry. Cf. Icel. *draugr*, a dry log. See **Dry**.

Drake, male of the duck. (L. — Gk.?) M. E. *drake.* Not found in A. S.; cf. *drake*, a drake, in Low G. (Bremen); M. Swed. *drake*, (1) a dragon, (2) a drake, (3) a boy's kite. Supposed to correspond to the latter part of Swed. *and-drake*, a drake (a form thought to be borrowed from Low G.). Cf. Swed. *and*, duck, *anddrake*, drake; Low G. *anderik*, drake (Lübben); G. *ente*, duck; *enterich*, drake; O. H. G. *antrahho*, a drake. β. The Swed. *and*, A.S. *ened*, a duck, is cognate with L. *anas* (stem *anat-*), a duck. The M. E. *drake* may be the same as A. S. *draca*, a dragon, borrowed from L. *draco*; see **Dragon**.

Dram, Drachm. (F. — L. — Gk.) M. F. *drame, drachme*, ' a dram, eighth part of an ounce;' Cot. — L. *drachma.* — Gk. δραχμή, a handful, a drachma, used both as weight and coin; cf. δράγμα, as much as one can grasp. — Gk. δράσσομαι, I grasp. Brugm. i. § 509.

Drama. (L. — Gk.) L. *drāma.* — Gk. δρᾶμα (stem δράματ-), an act, a drama. — Gk. δράω, I perform; cf. Lith. *darau*, I make. (√DAR.) Der. *dramat-ic* (from δραματ-); &c.

drastic, effective. (Gk.) Gk. δραστικός, effective; allied to δραστέος, verbal adj. of δράω, I perform.

Drape, to cover with cloth. (F. — L.) F. *draper*, to make cloth. — F. *drap*, cloth; Late L. *drappus.* Of unknown origin. Der. *drap-er, drap-er-y*; and see *drab* (2).

Drastic; see **Drama**.

Draw. (E.) M. E. *drawen.* A. S. *dragan* (A. S. *-aga-* becoming M.E. *-awe-*). + Du. *dragen*, Icel. Swed. *draga*, Dan. *drage*, Goth. *dragan*, G. *tragen*, to pull along, carry. Teut. type **dragan-*, pt. t. **drōg.*

draught, draft. (E.) *Draft* is a phonetic spelling. M. E. *draught, draht.* From A. S. *drag-an*; with suffixed *t*. + Du. *dragt*, a load, from *dragen*, to carry; Dan. *dret*; Icel. *dráttr*, a draught of fishes; G. *tracht*, a load, from *tragen*.

drawl. (Du.) Frequentative of *draw*; parallel to *draggle* from *drag*. Introduced from Du. *drālen*, to be slow; from *dragen*,

to draw. + E. Fries. *draulen*; Low G. *draueln.*

dray. (E.) A.S. *dræge*, that which is drawn; as in *dræge, dræg-net*, a draw-net. + Swed. *drög*, a sledge, dray.

Dread, vb. (E.) A. S. **drēdan*, in comp. *on-drēdan*, to dread, fear. + O. Sax. *ant-drādan*; O. H. G. *in-trātan.* Teut. type **drēdan-*.

Dream, a vision. (E.) M. E. *dreem.* A. S. **drēam*, a dream; not found. [Quite distinct from A.S. *drēam*, a sweet sound, harmony, also joy, glee, happiness.] + O. Sax. *drōm*, dream; Du. *droom*, Icel. *draumr*, Dan. Swed. *dröm*, G. *traum.* Kluge suggests comparison with G. *trug-bild*, a phantom; if correct, the Teut. sb. was **draugmoz*, m.; from Teut. **draug*, strong grade of Teut. **dreugan-* (O. H. G. *triogan*, G. *trügen*), to deceive. From the Idg. root **dhreugh*, whence also Skt. *drōgha(s)*, a crafty wounding; O. Pers. *drauga* (Pers. *durūgh*), a deceit, lie; Icel. *draugr*, a ghost. Brugm. i. §§ 681, 689.

Dreary, Drear. (E.) *Drear* is short for *dreary.* M. E. *drery.* A. S. *drēorig*, sad; orig. ' gory ;' formed with suffix *-ig* from A. S. *drēor*, gore. — A. S. *drēosan*, to drip. + Icel. *dreyrigr*, gory, from *dreyri*, gore ; G. *traurig*, sad, orig. gory, from O. H. G. *trōr*, gore. From Teut. **dreusan-*, vb.

Dredge (1), a drag-net. (E.) North E. *dreg.* Answering to A. S. **drecg, *drecge* (not found), for **drag-jo-*; from A. S. *dragan*; see **Draw**. And see **Dregs**.

Dredge (2), to sprinkle flour on meat. (F. — Late L. — Gk.) To *dredge* is to sprinkle, as in sowing *dredge* (M. E. *drage*) or mixed corn. — O. F. *dragée*, mixed corn; also a sweetmeat, sugar-plum. [Prov. *dragea*; Ital. *treggea*, a sugar-plum.] — Late L. *dragāta, drageia*, a sugar-plum; altered form of *tragēmata*, pl. of *tragēma.* — Gk. τράγημα, something nice to eat. — Gk. τρώγειν (2 aor. ἔτραγον), to gnaw.

Dregs, lees. (Scand.) Pl. of M. E. *dreg*, mire; we also find M. E. *dregges*, dregs. — Icel. *dregg*, pl. *dreggjar*, dregs; Swed. *drägg*, pl. dregs, lees. Perhaps from Icel. *drag-a*, to draw. Distinct from L. *fracēs*, dregs of oil; Brugm. i. § 417.

Drench, vb. (E.) M. E. *drenchen.* A. S. *drencan*, causal of *drincan*; hence ' to make drink.' + Du. *drenken*, Icel. *drekkja*, Swed. *dränka*, Goth. *dragkjan*, G. *tränken.* See **Drink**.

Dress. (F. — L.) O. F. *dresser, dresser*,

to erect, set up, dress; answering to a Late L. form *dīrectiāre. — L. dīrectus, pp. of dīrigere, to direct; see **Direct**.

Dribble. (E.) Frequentative of obs. E. *drib*, to drip slightly; which is a weakened form of *drip*. Cf. *drib-let*. See **Drip**. So also Dan. dial. *drible*.

Drift; see **Drive**.

Drill (1), to pierce, to train soldiers. (Du.) Borrowed from Du. *drillen*, to drill, to bore, to turn round, shake, brandish, drill soldiers, form to arms. Allied to M. H. G. *drellen*, to turn round (pp. *ge-drollen*), Low G. *drall*, twisted tight. Teut. type **threllan-* (pt. t. **thrall*), to twist; cf. A.S. *pearl*, strict. ¶ Perhaps allied to **Thrill**.

Drill (2), to sow corn in rows. (E.) The same as *drill*, to trickle, which seems to be a variant of *trill*, to trickle.

Drilling, a coarse cloth used for trousers. (G. — L.) Corrupted from G. *drillich*, ticking, huckaback. — L. *trilīc-*, stem of *trilix*, having three threads. — L. *tri-*, from *tres*, three; *licium*, a thread. See **Three**.

Drink. (E.) A.S. *drincan*, pt. t. *dranc*, pp. *druncen*. + Du. *drinken*, Icel. *drekka*, Swed. *dricka*, Dan. *drikke*, Goth. *drigkan* (= *drinkan*), G. *trinken*. Teut. **drenkan-*.

Drip. (Scand.) M. E. *dryppen*. — Dan. *dryppe*, to drip (= Teut. **drup-jan-*). From Teut. **drup-*, weak grade of **dreupan-*, as seen in Icel. *drjúpa*, to drip, A.S. *dréopan* (obs. E. *dreep*), G. *triefen*. Cf. O. Ir. *trucht*, a dew-drop. See **Drop**.

Drive. (E.) M. E. *driuen*. A.S. *drífan* (pt. t. *dráf*, pp. *drifen*). + Du. *drijven*; Icel. *drífa*, Swed. *drifva*, Dan. *drive*, Goth. *dreiban*, G. *treiben*. Teut. **dreiban-*.

drift. (E.) M. E. *drift*. Formed from *drif-*, weak grade of *drífan*; with suffix *-t*. + Du. *drift*, Icel. *drift*, Swed. Dan. *drift*, G. *trift*. Der. *a-drift* = on the drift; see **A-** (2).

drove. (E.) M. E. *drof*. A.S. *dráf*, a drove. From *dráf*, 2nd grade of *drífan*.

Drivel, vb. (E.) M.E. *drevelen*. A.S. *dreflian*, to dribble or run at the nose. Cf. M. E. *dravelen*, to drivel. From the base *draf-*, as in M. E. *draf*, draff. See **Draff**.

Drizzle, to rain slightly. (E.) Formerly *drisel* or *drisle*, to keep on dripping. Frequent. form of M. E. *dresen*, A.S. *dréosan*, to drip; see **Dreary**. Cf. Dan. *drysse*, to fall in drops; Swed. dial. *drösla*.

Droll. (F. — Du.) M. F. *drole*, 'a pleasant wag;' Cot. — Du. *drollig*, odd, strange; M. Du. *drol*, 'a juglar;' Hexham. Perhaps from Du. *droll-*, pp. stem of *drillen*, to turn, wheel, whirl about; see **Drill** (1).

Dromedary. (F. — L. — Gk.) M. E. *dromedarie*. — O. F. *dromedaire* (older form **dromedarie*). — Late L. *dromadārius*. — L. *dromad-*, stem of *dromas*, a dromedary. — Gk. δρομαδ-, stem of δρομάς, fast running. — Gk. δραμεῖν, to run. + Skt. *dram*, to run.

Drone (1), to hum. (E.) M.E. *dronen* (also *drounen*). Not in A.S. Cf. Icel. *drynja*, Swed. *dröna*, Dan. *dröne*, to drone, roar, rumble, &c. Cf. Goth. *drunjus*, a sound, Gk. θρῆνος, a dirge; Skt. *dhran*, to sound.

Drone (2), a non-working bee. (Low G.) M. E. *dran*. A. S. *drān*; which (like E. Fries. *drāne*) was prob. borrowed from O. Sax. *drān*. Cf. M.H.G. *treno* (G. *drohne* being borrowed from Low G.). Teut. stems **drēn-*, **dren-*; cf. Gk. ἀν-θρήνη, a wild-bee, θρῶναξ (Hesychius). ¶ With the parallel stems **drēn-*, **dren-*, cf. the stems of **Queen** and **Quean**.

Droop; see below.

Drop, sb. (E.) M.E. *drope*, sb.; hence *dropien*, *droppen*, vb. — A.S. *dropa*, sb.; *dropian*, vb. These are from the weak grade **drup-* (A.S. *drop-*) of the Teut. vb. **dreupan-* (A.S. *dréopan*), to drop, drip. + Du. *drop*, sb., Icel. *dropi*, Swed. *droppe*, Dan. *draabe*, G. *tropfen*. See also **Drip**.

droop, to sink, fail. (Scand.) M. E. *droupen*. — Icel. *drúpa*, to droop; weak vb., allied to *drjúpa*, strong vb., to drip = Teut. **dreupan-* (whence also G. *triefen*); see above. Cf. 'I am ready to *drop*,' i. e. I *droop*.

Dropsy; see **Hydropsy**.

Droshky, Drosky, a kind of carriage. (Russ.) Russ. *drozhki, drojki,* a low four-wheeled carriage (the *j* sounded as in French). Dimin. of *drogi,* a waggon; which was orig. pl. of *droga,* a perch (of a carriage).

Dross. (E.) M.E. *dros*. A.S. *drōs*, dross, dregs; cf. also obs. E. *drosen*, A.S. *drōsna*, pl., lees, dregs. + M. Du. *droes*, lees (Kilian); Du. *droesem*, dregs, lees, G. *drusen*, pl. dregs; O. H. G. *trusana*, *truosana*, husks of pressed grapes.

Drought, Drouth; see **Dry**.

Drove; see **Drive**.

Drown. (Scand.) M. E. *drounen*, dru-

nen. – M. Dan. *drukne, drougne, drovne, drone,* to sink, be drowned (Kalkar); Icel. *drukna.* The *-nkn-* was preserved in Swed. *drunkna,* A. S. *druncnian,* to be drunk, also to sink, to be drowned. See **Drunken.** (E. Björkman.)

Drowse, Drowze, to be sluggish. (E.) Formerly *drouse.* A.S. *drūsian,* to be sluggish; allied to A. S. *drēosan,* to fail; also to drip, to fall. See **Dreary.** Der. *drowz-y.*

Drub, to beat. (Arab.?) ' *Drub,* to beat the soles of the feet with a stick, a punishment used in Turkey;' (Phillips). Apparently a travellers' word. Perhaps from Arab. *ḍarb (zarb),* a beating with a stick; from Arab. root *ḍaraba (zaraba),* he beat; Rich. Dict. p. 952. (N. E. D.)

Drudge, vb. (E.) M. E. *druggen.* A. S. **drycgean,* not found; but regularly formed from *drug-,* weak grade of *drēogan,* to work, perform, endure (= Teut. **dreugan-,* Goth. *driugan,* Lowl. Sc. *dree*). Cf. Icel. *drjūg-virkr,* one who works slowly but surely. The Gael. *drugair,* a drudge, is from E.

Drug. (F.) M. E. *drogge. drugge.* – O. F. *drogue,* a drug. Also Ital. and Span. *droga.* Origin unknown; perhaps Oriental. Der. *drugg-ist.*

Drugget. (F.) M.F. *droguet,* 'a kind of stuff that's half silk, half wool;' Cot. Dimin. of *drogue,* used in the sense of rubbish, poor stuff; from the coarseness of the material; cf. E. 'a *drug* in the market.' ¶ Probably not the same word as F. *drogue,* a drug.

Druid, a priest of the ancient Britons. (F. – L. – C.) F. *Druide.* – L. (Gaulish) pl. *Druides, Druidae* (Lewis and Short). Cf. O. Irish *druid,* dat. and acc. of *drui,* a magician, sorcerer; Ir. *draoi, druidh,* Gael. *druidh* (whence also A. S. *drȳ,* a magician).

Drum. (Du.) XVI cent. Imperfectly adapted from M. Du. *tromme, trommel,* a drum; Low G. *trumme;* Du. *trom.* + O. H. G. *trumbā, trumpā,* M. H. G. *trumme,* a pipe, trumpet; Icel. *trumba,* a pipe, trumpet; *So* also Ital. *tromba,* Span. *trompa.*] Of imitative origin.

Drunkard. (E.; *with* F. *suffix.*) From A. S. *drunc-,* base of pp. of *drincan,* to drink; with F. suffix *-ard* (G. *hart*).

drunken, drunk. (E.) A. S. *druncen,* pp. of *drincan,* to drink.

Drupe, a fleshy fruit containing a stone.

(F. – L. – Gk.) F. *drupe.* – L. *drūpa,* an over-ripe olive. – Gk. δρύππᾱ, the same.

Dry. (E.) M. E. *druȝe.* A. S. *drȳge.* Cf. Du. *droog,* dry; G. *trocken,* dry; Icel. *draugr,* a dry log.

drought. (E.) M. E. *droȝte, drouȝte;* also *drouthe* (P. Plowman). A.S. *drūgaþ,* drought. – A. S. *drūgian,* to be dry; *drȳge,* dry. + Du. *droogte,* drought; from *droog,* dry. Doublet, *drouth* (Milton).

Dryad, a nymph of the woods. (L. – Gk.) L. *Dryad-,* stem of *Dryas,* a wood-nymph. – Gk. δρυαδ-, stem of δρυάς, the same. – Gk. δρῦς, a tree; see **Tree.**

Dual, consisting of two. (L.) L. *duālis,* dual. – L. *duo,* two; see **Two.**

Dub, to confer knighthood by a stroke. (F.) M. E. *dubben.* A. S. *dubban;* A. S. Chron. an. 1086. [So also Swed. *dubba.*] Usually derived from O. F. *aduber, adouber, adober,* to dub a knight; a Romanic word of unknown origin (Ital. *addobbare,* O. Span. and Prov. *adobar,* O. Port. *adubar*). ¶ Diez derives *adouber,* conversely, from *dubban;* which is hardly tenable; see N. E. D.

Dubious. (L.) From L. *dubiōsus,* doubtful. – L. *dubium,* doubt; neuter of L. *dubius,* doubtful, moving in two directions. – L. *du-o,* two. See **Two.**

Ducal. (F. – L.) F. *ducal,* adj.; from *duc,* a duke; see **Duke.**

ducat, a coin. (F. – Ital. – L.) O. F. *ducat.* – Ital. *ducato,* a ducat, also a duchy; named from L. *ducātus* (duchy of Apulia) alluded to in the legend upon it; see **duchy** below.

duchess. (F. – L.) O. F. *duchesse* (Late L. *ducissa*), fem. of *duc,* duke; see **Duke.**

duchy. (F. – L.) F. *duché.* – Late L. *ducātum,* acc. of *ducātus,* a dukedom. – L. *duc-,* stem of *dux,* a duke. ¶ Also O. F. *duchée,* fem., as if from Late L. **ducitātem.*

Duck (1), to dive, bob the head. (E.) M. E. *duken, douken.* Not in A. S. + Du. *duiken,* to stoop, dive; G. *tauchen,* to plunge, dive. Teut. type **deukan-,* pt. t. **dauk* (whence G. *tauch-en*), pp. **duk-ano-.* From the weak grade *duk-* we have Dan. *dukke,* Swed. *dyka;* to which the shortening of the vowel in mod. E. *duck* may have been partly due.

duck (2), bird. (E.) M. E. *doke, duke.* Lit. 'diver;' the suffix *-e* represents the A. S. f. suffix of the agent. A. S.

dūce, a duck. From the verb above. Cf. Dan *dukand*, lit. 'diving duck;' Swed. *dykfågel*, 'diving fowl.' **Der.** *duck-l-ing*, with double dimin. suffix.

Duck (3), a pet, darling. (E.) Apparently the same as **Duck** (2).

Duck (4), light canvas. (Du.) A nautical word. − Du. *doek*, linen cloth, canvas. +Dan. *dug*, Swed. *duk*, Icel. *dūkr*, G. *tuch*, O. H. G. *tuoh*.

Duct, a conduit-pipe. (L.) L. *ductus*, a leading (hence, a duct). − L. *ductus*, pp. of *dūcere*, to lead. See **Duke**.

ductile. (F.−L.) F. *ductile*, malleable. − L. *ductilis*, easily led. − L. *duct-us*, pp. of *dūcere* (above).

Dude, an exquisite, a dandy. Of unknown origin. (Ab. 1883.)

Dudgeon (1), resentment. Of unknown origin.

Dudgeon (2), haft of a dagger. (Unknown.) M. E. *dogeon*, a kind of wood used for the handles of daggers. Etym. unknown.

Duds, clothes. (Scand.) Jamieson has *dudis* as well as *duds*; the *u* was prob. once long. − Icel. *dūði*, swaddling clothes; *dūða*, to wrap up. Cf. E. *dowd*, a woman's cap, a slut; *dowd-y*, ill-dressed.

Due. (F.−L.) M. E. *dew*, *dewe*. − O. F. *deu*, masc., *deue*, fem.; pp. of *devoir*, to owe. − L. *debēre*. See **Devoir**.

Duel. (Ital.−L.) Ital. *duello*, a duel. − L. *duellum*, a fight between two men (archaic form of L. *bellum*, war). − L. *du-o*, two.

duet. (Ital.−L.) Ital. *duetto*, music for two. − Ital. *due*, two. − L. *duo*, two.

Duenna. (Span.−L.) Span. *dueña*, a married lady, duenna. − L. *domina*, fem. of *dominus*, a lord. See **Donna**.

Duet; see **Duel**.

Duffel, coarse woollen cloth. (Du.) Du. *duffel*; so called from *Duffel*, a place near Antwerp.

Duffer, a stupid person. (Scand.) Lowl Sc. *dowfart*, formed with suffix *-art* from the adj. *dowf*, stupid, dull; lit. 'deaf.' − Icel. *dauf-r*, deaf; see **Deaf**.

Dug, a teat. (Scand.) Perhaps allied to Swed. *dägga*, Dan *dægge*, to suckle. Cf. Goth. *daddjan*, O. H. G. *tāan*, to suckle. ¶ But cf. Skt. *duh*, to milk.

Dugong, a sea-cow. (Malay.) Malay *dūyong*, *dūyōng*, a sea-cow.

Duke, a leader. (F.−L.) M. E. *duk*. − O. F. *duc*, acc. formed from O. F. nom.

dux. − L. *dux*, a leader. − L. *dūcere*, to lead. (√DEUK.) ¶ The L. acc. *ducem* would have given O. F. *dois*, F. *doix*; like F. *noix* from *nucem*, *croix* from *crucem*. (N. E. D.) Brugm. i. § 592.

Dulcet, sweet. (F.−L.) M. F. *doucet* (Cot.), refashioned after L. *dulcis* (cf. Ital. *dolcetto*). − O. F. *dols* (F. *doux*), sweet. − L. *dulcis*, sweet.

dulcimer. (F. − Span. − L.) Roquefort has F. *doulcemer* (undated); cf. O. F. *doulcemele* (Godefroy). − Span. *dulcemele*, a dulcimer; named from its sweet sound. − L. *dulce melos*, sweet sound; see **Melody**.

Dull, stupid. (E.) M. E. *dul*; cognate with Low G. *dull*; answering to Teut. **dul-joz*. Closely allied to A. S. *dol*, foolish, cognate with Du. *dol*, mad, G. *toll*, mad, answering to Teut. **dul-oz*. Both are from Teut. **dul-* (<**dwul*), weak grade of **dwel-an*, as seen in A. S. *dwelan*, to err, to be stupid; see **Dwell**. Cf. A. S. *gedwol-god*, a false god, idol; Irish and W. *dall*, blind. Brugm. i. § 375 (6).

Dulse, an edible seaweed. (C.) Irish *duileasg*, Gael. *duileasg*, dulse. According to Macleod, it means 'water-leaf,' from Ir. and Gael. *duille*, leaf, and *uisg(e)*, water.

Dumb. (E.) M. E. *domb*. A. S. *dumb*, mute. + Du. *dom*, Icel. *dumbr*, Swed. *dumb*, Dan. *dum*, Goth. *dumbs*, G. *dumm*, O. H. G. *tumb*, *tump*, stupid. The orig. sense seems to have been 'stupid,' and perhaps Goth. *dumbs* is allied to Goth. *daubs*, deaf; see **Deaf**. **Der.** *dumm-y* (=*dumb-y*).

Dump (1), an ill-shapen piece. (E.?) Prov. E. *dump*, a clumsy lump, a bit; *dumpy*, short and thick. Probably 'a thing thrown down in a mass'; see **Dump** (2).

dumpling, a kind of pudding. (E.?) A small solid ball of pudding; *dump-l-ing* is a double dimin. of *dump* (1).

Dump (2), to strike, fling down. (Scand.?) Cf. Lowl. Sc. *dump*, to beat. Dan. *dumpe*, to plump, plunge; Norw. *dumpa*; Swed. dial. *dompa*. − Swed. dial. *dump-*, as in *dump-id*, supine of str. vb. *dimpa*, to fall down plump.

Dumps, melancholy. (Scand.) Swed. dial. *dumpin*, melancholy, orig. pp. of *dimba*, to steam, reek; Dan. *dump*, dull, low. + Du. *domp*, damp, hazy, G. *dumpf*, damp, dull. Allied to **Damp**; cf. 'to *damp* one's spirits.'

Dun (1), brown. (C.) A. S. *dunn*, dark. — Irish and Gael. *donn*, brown; W. *dwn*, dun, dusky. Celtic type **donnos*.

Dun (2), to urge for payment. (Scand.) Said (in 1708) to be derived from the name of *Joe Dun*, a famous bailiff in the time of Henry VII. But perhaps from the notion of noisiness. Cf. M. E. *dunning*, a loud noise. — Icel. *duna*, to thunder; *koma einum dyn fyrir dyrr*, to make a din before one's door; Swed. *dåna*, to make a noise. Allied to Din.

Dunce, a stupid person. (Scotland.) From the phr. ' a *Duns* man,' i. e. a native of *Dunse*, in Berwickshire. In ridicule of the disciples of John *Duns* Scotus, schoolman, died A. D. 1308. ¶ Not to be confused with John Scotus Erigena, died A. D. 875.

Dune, a low sand-hill. (F. — Du. — C.) F. *dune*. — M. Du. *düne* (Du. *duin*); cognate with A. S. *dün*, a down; see Down (2). Brugm. i. § 112.

Dung. (E.) A. S. *dung.*+Swed. *dynga*, dung; Dan. *dynge*, a heap, mass; G. *dung*. Root uncertain; it answers, in form, to the pp. of Ding; as if it were ' what is thrown down or away.' Cf. Swed. dial. *dong*, (1) heap, (2) dung.

Dungeon, Donjon. (F. — L.) M. E. *dongeon*. — O. F. *donjon*, the chief tower of a castle. — Late L. *domniōnem*, acc. of *domnio*, a dungeon-tower, chief-tower; shortened from *dominio*, properly dominion, feudal power; see Dominion.

Duniwassal, a Highland gentleman, yeoman. (C.) In Sir W. Scott's *Bonny Dundee*. — Gael. *duine uasal*, gentleman. — Gael. *duine*, a man (W. *dyn*); *uasal*, noble, gently born (W. *uchel*), orig. ' exalted;' see Brugm. i. § 219 (4).

Duodecimo. (L.) *In duodecimo* = with 12 leaves to the sheet. — L. *duodecimō*, abl. of *duodecimus*, twelfth; cf. L. *duodecim*, twelve; see Dozen.

Duodenum, the first of the small intestines. (L.) Late L. *duodēnum*, so called because about 12 finger-breadths long. — L. *duodēnī*, twelve apiece, distributive form of *duodecim*, twelve; see Dozen.

Dup. (E.) Short for *do up*, i. e. lift up (a latch); to open a door.

Dupe, a person easily deceived. (F.) F. *dupe*, a dupe. The M. F. *dupe* meant a hoopoe; whence *dupe*, a dupe, because the bird was easily caught. (So also Bret. *houperik*, a hoopoe, a dupe.) Perhaps of imitative origin.

Duplicate, two-fold. (L.) L. *duplicātus*, pp. of *duplicāre*, to double. — L. *duplic-*, stem of *duplex*, two-fold (below).

duplicity. (F. — L.) Lit. doubleness. — F. *duplicité*. — L. acc. *duplicitātem*. — L. *duplici-*, decl. stem of *duplex*, two-fold. — L. *du-o*, two; *plic-āre*, to fold.

Durance, Duration; see Dure.

Durbar, a hall of audience, levee. (Pers.) Pers. *darbār*, a prince's court, levee; lit. ' door of admittance.' — Pers. *dar*, door (= E. *door*); and *bār*, admittance, court.

Dure, to last. (F. — L.) F. *durer*. — L. *dūrāre*, to last. — L. *dūrus*, hard, lasting. +Irish and Gael. *dur*, firm; W. *dur*, steel. Cf. Gk. δύναμις, force. Der. *during*, orig. pres. pt. of *dure*; *dur-able*, &c.

durance, captivity. (F. — L.) The orig. sense was long endurance of hardship. O. F. *durance*, duration. — F. *durer*, to last; with suffix *-ance*; see above.

duration. (F. — L.) O. F. *duration*. — Late L. *dūrātiōnem*, acc. of *dūrātio*. A coined word; from the pp. of L. *dūrāre*, to last.

duress, hardship. (F. — L.) M. E. *duresse*. — O. F. *duresce*. — L. *dūritia*, harshness. — L. *dūrus*, hard, severe.

Durian, a fruit. (Malay.) Malay *dūrīan*, a fruit with a prickly rind. — Malay *dūrī*, a thorn, prickle.

Dusk, dim. (Scand.) Properly an adj. M. E. *dosk*, dark, dim; *deosc*, the same. Prob. a Northern form (as the *sk* did not become *sh*). Cf. A. S. *dox* (for **dosc*), translating L. *flāuus*; Vocab. 239. 36. — Swed. dial. *duska*, to drizzle; *duskug*, misty, dim; Norw. *dusk*, mist, *duskregn*, fine rain. Der. *dusk*, sb.; whence *dusk-y*, adj.

Dust. (E.) A. S. *dūst.*+Du. *duist*, Icel. *dust*, dust, Dan. *dyst*, meal; G. *dunst*, vapour, fine dust. All from a Teut. base **dunst-* (for **dwuns-t-*), the *n* being lost except in G. Cf. Skt. *dhvaṁs*, to fall to pieces (pp. *dhvas-ta-*).

Dutch, belonging to Holland. (G.) Formerly applied to the Germans. — G. *Deutsch*, German; lit. belonging to the people; M. H. G. *diut-isk*, where the suffix *-isk* = E. *-ish*, and *diut* is cognate with A. S. *þéod*, Goth. *thiuda*, a people, nation; Ir. *tuath*, a people; cf. Oscan *touto*, a city. Brugm. i. § 218.

Duty. (A. F. — L.) M. E. *duete(e)*. — A. F. *ducté*, duty (O. F. has only *devoir*).

A coined word; from A. F. *deu, du*, due, and the suffix *-té* (L. *-tātem*). See **Due.**

Dwale; see **Dwell.**

Dwarf. (E.) M.E. *dwerȝ, dwergh*; the *f* represents the guttural. O. Merc. *dwerg*, A.S. *dweorg*, a dwarf.+Du. *dwerg*, Icel. *dvergr*, Swed. Dan. *dverg*, G. *zwerg*. Teut. type *dwerg-oz.*

Dwell. (E.) M.E. *dwellen*, to linger. A.S. *dwellan*, in the active sense to retard, also to seduce; also *dwelian*, to go astray, err, tarry, dwell. Causal of A.S. *dwelan* (pt. t. *dwæl*, pp. *dwolen*), to be torpid or dull, to err.+Icel. *dvelja*, to dwell, delay, orig. to hinder; Swed. *dväljas*, to dwell (reflexive); Dan. *dvæle*, to linger; M.H.G. *twellen*, to hinder, delay. Teut. type *dwaljan*, causal of the str. vb. *dwelan*- (pt. t. *dwal*, pp. *dwulano*-), to be torpid, to cease, to err (A.S. *dwelan*, O. H. G. *gi-twelan*). Cf. Skt. *dhvr*, to bend aside, *dhūr-ta*-, fraudulent. (√DHWEL.) And see **Dull.**

dwale, deadly nightshade. (Scand.) Named from its soporific effects. Dan. *dvale*, stupor, *dvaledrik*, a soporific, ' dwale-drink;' Swed. *dvala*, a trance. Cf. A.S. *dwala*, an error, stupefaction, from the 2nd grade of A.S. *dwelan* (above).

Dwindle. (E.) The frequent. form of M.E. *dwinen*, to dwindle, A.S. *dwinan* (pt. t. *dwān*), to dwindle, languish.+ Icel. *dvína*; Swed. *tvina*, to dwindle, pine away; Du. *ver-dwijnen*, to vanish.

Dye, to colour; a colour. (E.) M.E. *deyen*, vb.; *deh*, sb. A.S. *dēagian*, vb., to dye; from *dēah*, sb., dye, colour. A.S. *dēah* (gen. *dēag-e*), sb. f., answers to Teut. type *daug-ā.* ¶ Not allied to L. *fūcus*, which is from Gk. φῦκος.

Dyke; see **Dike.**

Dynamic, relating to force. (Gk.) Gk. δυναμικός, powerful. – Gk. δύναμις, power. – Gk. δύναμαι, I am strong; see **Dure.** (√DEU.)

dynasty, lordship. (F. – L. – Gk.) F. *dynastie*. – Late L. *dynastīa*. – Gk. δυναστεία, lordship. – Gk. δυνάστης, a lord. – Gk. δύναμαι, I am strong.

Dysentery, disease of the entrails. (L. – Gk.) L. *dysenteria.* – Gk. δυσεντερία. – Gk. δυσ-, prefix, with a bad sense; ἔντερα, pl., the inwards, bowels, from ἔντος, within, ἐν, in; see **Interior.**

Dyspepsy, indigestion. (L. – Gk.) L. *dyspepsia.* – Gk. δυσπεψία. – Gk. δύσπεπτος,

hard to digest. – Gk. δυσ-, prefix, with a bad sense; πέπτειν, to cook, digest; see **Cook.** Der. *dyspeptic* (from δύσπεπτ-ος).

E.

E-, prefix; see **Ex-.**

Each, every one. (E.) M.E. *eche, elch.* A.S. *ǣlc*, each, short for *ā-gi-līc*, i.e. aye-like (ever-like or ever alike).+Du. *elk*, each; O. H. G. *eogalīh*, M. H. G. *iegelīch*, G. *jeglicher*. See **Aye.**

Eager. (F. – L.) M.E. *egre*. – A.F. *egre* (F. *aigre*). – L. *acrem*, acc. of *ac-er*, sharp. See **Acid.** Der. *vin-egar.*

Eagle. (F. – L.) M.E. *egle*. – A.F. *egle*, O.F. *aigle* (F. *aigle*). – L. *aquila.* See **Aquiline.**

Eagre, tidal wave in a river. (F. – L.) O. F. *aiguere*, a flood (Godefroy). – Late L. *aquāria*, a conduit; cf. *aquāre*, to irrigate. – L. *aqua*, water. See **Ewer.**

Eanling, a lamb. (E.) *Eanling* is from the verb *ean*, which is *y-ean* without the prefix *y-* (=A.S. *ge-*). See **Yean.**

Ear (1), organ of hearing. (E.) M.E. *ere.* A.S. *ēare.*+Du. *oor*, Icel. *eyra*, Swed. *öra*, Dan. *öre*, G. *ohr*, Goth. *auso.* Teut. type *auzon-.* Cf. also Russ. *ucho*, L. *auris*, Lith. *ausis*, Gk. οὖς, O. Irish *ō.*

earwig, an insect. (E.) A.S. *ēar-wicga*, from its being supposed to creep into the ear. Cf. A.S. *wicga*, a kind of insect; prov. E. *wiggle*, to wriggle.

Ear (2), spike of corn. (E.) M.E. *er.* A.S. *ēar* (pl.); Northumb. *eher.*+Du. *aar*, Icel. Dan. Swed. *ax* (for *ahs*), Goth. *ahs*, G. *ähre.* Teut. type *ahoz*, *ahiz*-, cognate with L. *acus* (gen. *aceris*). Brugm. i. § 182. Allied to **Awn.** (√AK.)

Ear (3), to plough. (E.) M.E. *eren.* A.S. *erian*, to plough.+Icel. *erja*, Goth. *arjan*, L. *arāre*, Lith. *arti*, Russ. *orat(e)*; also Irish *araim*, I plough, Gk. ἀρόω, I plough. (√AR.)

Earl. (E.) M.E. *erl.* A.S. *eorl.*+ Icel. *jarl*, O. Sax. *erl*, a man. O. Norse (runic) type *erila R.*

Early, soon. (E.) M.E. *erly.* A.S. *ǣrlīce*, adv.; from *ǣrlīc*, adj., not used. – A.S. *ǣr*, soon; *līc*, like. See **Ere.**

Earn. (E.) M.E. *ernien.* A.S. *earnian.* +O. H. G. *arnōn* (cf. also G. *ernten*, to reap, from *ernte*, harvest). Teut. type *az(a)nōjan*, to get the profit of labour; from the sb. *az(a)nā* (Icel. *önn*), labour;

cf. O. H. G. *aran*, Goth. *asans*, a harvest. (√AS.) ¶ Others connect it with Gk. *ἀρνυμαι*, I earn.

Earnest (1), seriousness. (E.) Properly a ª sb., as in ' in earnest.' M. E. *ernest*, sb. A. S. *eornost*, sb.+Du. *ernst*, sb.; G. *ernst*, O. H. G. *ernust*. Teut. type *ernustiz*.

Earnest (2), a pledge. (F.–L.–Gk.–Heb.) The *t* is added. M. E. *ernes*; also spelt *erles, arles*. Dimin. of O. F. *erres, arres* (F. *arrhes*), f. pl.–L. *arrha, arrhabo*.–Gk. *ἀρραβών*, a pledge.–Heb. *'erāvōn*, security; from *'ārav*, to give security.

Earth. (E.) M. E. *erthe*. A. S. *eorðe*. +Du. *aarde*, Icel. *jörð*, Dan. Swed. *jord*, Goth. *airtha*, G. *erde*. Teut. types *erthā*, *erthōn-*, f. Cf. Gk. *ἔρα*, earth.

Earwig; see Ear (1).

Ease. (F.) M. E. *ese*.–O. F. *aise*, ease. Cf. Ital. *agio*, ease, Port. *azo*, occasion. Orig. unknown. Der. *dis-ease*.

Easel. (Du.–L.) Du. *ezel*, an ass; also a support, a painter's easel. [G. *esel*; Goth. *asilus*.]–L. *asellus*, dimin. of L. *asinus*, ass.

East, the quarter of sun-rise. (E.) M.E. *est*. A. S. *ēast*, adv., in the east; *ēastan*, from the east.+Du. *oost*, G. *ost*, Dan. *öst*; Swed. *östan*, G. *osten*; Du. *ooster-*, G. *oster-*, Dan. Swed. *öster*, Icel. *austr* (gen. *austr-s*). Teut. types *aus-to-*, *aus-to-no-*; also *aust-ro-*, for Idg. *aus-ro-* (see easter). Cf. L. *aur-ōra*, dawn, Gk. *ἠώς, ἕως, αὔως*, dawn, Skt. *ushās*, dawn. Brugm. i. § 218 (4).

easter. (E.) M. E. *ester*. A.S. *ēastor-*, in comp.; *ēastre*, Lu. xxii. 1, Easter.–A.S. *ēastre*, a goddess whose festivities were at the vernal equinox; see Beda, De Temporum Ratione, c. 15. Cf. Lith. *auszra*, f. dawn; Skt. *usra-*, m. a ray.

Eat. (E.) M. E. *eten*. A.S. *etan*.+Du. *eten*, Icel. *eta*, Swed. *äta*, Dan. *æde*, Goth. *itan*, G. *essen*. Teut. type *etan-*. Cf. L. *edere*, Gk. *ἔδειν*, Skt. *ad*, to eat. (√ED.)

Eaves, the clipped edge of a thatched roof. (E.) Also E. dial. (Essex) *oavis*. M. E. *euese*; pl. *eueses* (= *eaveses*); also *ouese*. A.S. *efes*, a (clipped) edge of thatch, whence *efesian* to shear, also *oefes*, whence *oefsung*, Corp. gl. 474.+Icel. *ups*, Swed. dial. *uffs*; Goth. *ubizwa*, a porch, from the projection of the eaves; O. H. G. *opasa*. Teut. type *obeswā*. Prob. allied to **Over.** Der. *eavesdropper*,

one who stands under droppings from the eaves, a secret listener.

Ebb. (E.) M. E. *ebbe*. A. S. *ebba*, ebb of the tide.+Du. *eb, ebbe*, sb. [whence Dan. *ebbe*, sb. and vb., Swed. *ebb*, sb.]. Perhaps the Teut. type is *affon-*, with the sense of going off; see **Off.**

Ebony, a hard wood. (F.–L.–Gk.–Heb.) Formerly *ebene*.–M.F. *ebene*, ebony. –L. *hebenus, ebenus*.–Gk. *ἔβενος, ἐβένη*. –Heb. *hovnīm*, pl. ebony wood; prob. a non-Semitic word.

Ebriety, drunkenness. (F.–L.) F. *ébriété*.–L. acc. *ēbrietātem*.–L. *ēbrius*, drunken. Der. *in-ebriate*, to make drunken.

Ebullition, a boiling over. (F.–L.) O. F. *ebullition*.–L. acc. *ēbullītiōnem*; a rare word, from *ēbullītus*, pp. of *ēbullīre*, to bubble up.–L. *ē*, out; *bullīre*, to bubble; see **Boil** (1).

Écarté, a game at cards. (F.–L. *and* Gk.) In this game, cards may be *discarded* and exchanged; hence the name.–F. *écarté*, discarded, pp. of *écarter*, to discard.–L. *ex*, out, away; F. *carte*, from Late L. *carta*, from Gk. *χάρτη*, a leaf of paper, hence a card.

Eccentric, departing from a centre, odd. (F.–L.–Gk.) F. *excentrique*.–Late L. *eccentricus*.–Gk. *ἔκκεντρ-os*, out of the centre; with suffix *-icus*.–Gk. *ἐκ*, out; *κέντρον*, centre. See **Centre.**

Ecclesiastic. (L.–Gk.) Late L. *ecclēsiasticus*.–Gk. *ἐκκλησιαστικός*, belonging to the *ἐκκλησία*, i. e. assembly, church.–Gk. *ἔκκλητος*, summoned.–Gk. *ἐκκαλέω*, I call forth.–Gk. *ἐκ*, out; *καλέω*, I call.

Echelon. (F.–L.) F. *échelon*, an arrangement of troops in parallel divisions; orig. a round of a ladder.–F. *échelle*, a ladder (O. F. *eschiele*).–L. *scāla*, a ladder; see **Scale** (3).

Echo. (L.–Gk.) M. E. *ecco*.–L. *ēchō*.–Gk. *ἠχώ*, a sound, echo; cf. *ἦχος, ἠχή*, a ringing noise. Der. *cat-ech-ise*, q. v.

Eclat. (F.–Teut.) F. *éclat*, splendour; lit. 'a bursting forth.'–F. *éclater*, to burst forth; O. F. *s'esclater*, to burst. Origin doubtful; perhaps from L. type *exclappitare*, formed from Low G. *klappen*, to clap, make a noise; see **Clap.**

Eclectic, choosing out; hence, a philosopher who selected doctrines from various sects. (Gk.) Gk. *ἐκλεκτικός*, selecting; as sb. an Eclectic.–Gk. *ἐκλέγειν*, to select.–Gk. *ἐκ*, out; *λέγειν*, to choose.

Eclipse. (F.—L.—Gk.) M. E. *eclips, clips.*—O. F. *eclipse.*—L. *eclīpsis.*—Gk. ἔκλειψις, a failure, esp. of light of the sun.—Gk. ἐκλείπειν, to leave out, fail, suffer eclipse.—Gk. ἐκ, out; λείπειν, to leave.

Eclogue, a pastoral poem. (L.—Gk.) L. *ecloga* (the F. word was *églogue*).—Gk. ἐκλογή, a selection, esp. of poems.—Gk. ἐκλέγειν, to choose out; see **Eclectic.**

Economy. (F.—L.—Gk.) Formerly *œconomy.*—M. F. *œconomie.*—L. *œconomia.*—Gk. οἰκονομία, management of a household.—Gk. οἰκονόμος, a steward.—Gk. οἰκο-, for οἶκος, a house; and νέμειν, to deal out.

Ecstasy. (F.—L.—Gk.) O. F. *extasie* (H.).—Late L. *ecstasis*, a trance.—Gk. ἔκστασις, displacement; also, a trance.—Gk. ἐκ, out; στάσις, a standing, allied to ἵσταμαι, I stand.

Ecumenical, general. (L. — Gk.) Late L. *œcūmenicus*; with suffix *-al.*—Gk. οἰκουμενικός, universal. — Gk. οἰκουμένη (sc. γῆ), the inhabited world, fem. of οἰκούμενος, pres. pt. pass. of οἰκέω, I inhabit.—Gk. οἶκος, a house. Brugm. i. § 611.

Eczema, a breaking-out of pustules on the skin. (Gk.) Gk. ἔκζεμα, a pustule.—Gk. ἐκζεῖν, to boil over.—Gk. ἐκ, out; ζέειν, to boil. See **Yeast.**

Eddy. (Scand.) M. E. *ydy* (= *idy*). Icel. *iða*, an eddy, whirlpool; cf. *iða*, to whirl about; Swed. dial. *iða, idǎ,* Dan. dial. *ide,* an eddy. Perhaps formed from Icel. *ið-,* A. S. *ed-,* Goth. *id-* (prefix), backwards. Cf. Brugm. i. § 574.

Edge. (E.) M. E. *egge.* A. S. *ecg,* an edge, border.+Du. *egge,* Icel. Swed. *egg,* Dan. *eg,* G. *ecke.* Teut. type **agja.* Cf. L. *acies,* Gk. ἀκίς, a point, Skt. *açri-,* edge, corner. (√AK.)

Edible, eatable. (L.) Late L. *edibilis.*—L. *edere,* to eat; see **Eat.**

Edict. (L.) L. *ēdictum,* neut. of pp. of *ēdīcere,* to proclaim.—L. *ē,* out; *dīcere,* to speak.

Edify. (F.—L.) O. F. *edifier.*—L. *ædificāre,* to build (hence, instruct).—L. *ædi-,* stem of *ædēs,* a building, orig. a hearth; *-fic-,* for *facere,* to make. **Der.** *edifice,* F. *édifice,* L. *ædificium,* a building; *edile,* L. *ædilis,* a magistrate who had the care of public buildings. Brugm. i. § 202.

Edition. (F.—L.) O. F. *edicion* (H.).—L. *ēditiōnem,* acc. of *ēditio,* a publishing.—L. *ēditus,* pp. of *ēdere,* to give out, publish.—L. *ē,* out; *dare,* to give. **Der.** *edit,* a

coined word, from the sb. *editor* (L. *ēditor*).

Educate. (L.) From L. *ēducātus,* pp. of *ēducāre,* to educate; allied to L. *ēdūcere,* to bring out.—L. *ē,* out; *dūcere,* to bring.

educe. (L.) L. *ēdūcere,* to bring out. **Der.** *eduction* (from pp. *ēduct-us*).

Eel. (E.) M. E. *ēl.* A. S. *ǣl.* + Du. *aal,* Icel. *āll,* Dan. *aal,* Swed. *ål,* G. *aal.* Teut. type **ǣloz.*

Eery, timid, affected by fears, melancholy, strange. (E.) See Jamieson. M. E. *arʒ, arh, areʒ, arʒe, erʒe,* timid; spelt *eri* in Cursor Mundi, 17685.—A. S. *earg, earh,* timid, cowardly. Cf. Icel. *argr, ragr*; G. *arg*; Du. *erg,* bad.

Efface. (F.—L.) F. *effacer.*—F. *ef-* (L. *ef-,* for *ex,* out); and *face,* from Folk-L. **facia* (for L. *faciem,* acc. of *faciēs*). face. See **Face.**

Effect. (F.—L.) A. F. *effect* (F. *effet*).—L. *effectum,* acc. of *effectus,* an effect.—L. *effectus,* pp. of *efficere,* to work out.—L. *ef-,* for *ex,* thoroughly; *facere,* to do.

Effeminate. (L.) From pp. of L. *effēmināre,* to make womanish.—L. *ef-,* for *ex,* thoroughly; *fēmina,* a woman. See **Feminine.**

Effendi, sir, master. (Turkish—Gk.) Turk. *ēfendi,* sir.—Mod. Gk. ἀφέντης, for Gk. αὐθέντης, a despotic master, ruler; see **Authentic.**

Effervesce. (L.) L. *efferuescere.*—L. *ef-,* for *ex,* out; *feruescere,* to begin to boil, inceptive of *feruēre,* to boil.

Effete, exhausted. (L.) L. *effētus,* weakened by having brought forth young.—L. *ef-,* for *ex,* out; *fētus,* that has brought forth; allied to L. *fuī,* I was (Brugm. i. § 361; ii. § 587).

Efficacy, force, virtue. (L.) L. *efficācia,* effective power.—L. *efficāc-,* stem of *efficax,* efficacious.—L. *efficere*; to effect (below).

efficient. (L.) From stem of pres. pt. of *efficere,* to effect; see **Effect.**

Effigy. (F.—L.) F. *effigie.*—L. *effigiem,* acc. of *effigiēs,* an image.—L. *effig-,* base of *effingere,* to form.—L. *ef-,* for *ex,* out; *fingere,* to form. See **Figure.**

Efflorescence. (F.—L.) F. *efflorescence,* lit. 'a flowering.' From L. *efflōrescere,* inceptive form of *efflōrēre,* to blossom out.—L. *ef-* = *ex,* out; *flōrēre,* to blossom. See **Floral.**

Effluence, a flowing. (L.) From the

pres. pt. of *effluere*, to flow out. – L. *ef-*, for *ex*, out ; *fluere*, to flow. See **Fluent**.

Effort. (F. – L.) F. *effort*, an effort ; verbal sb. from F. *s'efforcer*, to endeavour. – Med. L. *exfortiāre*, to use force. – L. *ex*, out ; *forti-s*, strong. See **Force**.

Effrontery. (F. – L.) XVIII cent. – F. *effronterie*, 'impudency ;' Cot. – O. F. *effronté*, shameless. – O. F. *ef-* (L. *ef-*, for *ex*), out ; *front*, face, forehead (as if putting forward the forehead). Cf. F. *af-fronter*, to oppose face to face. See **Front**.

Effulgent, bright. (L.) From stem of pres. pt. of L. *effulgēre*, to shine forth. – L. *ef-*, for *ex*, out ; *fulgēre*, to shine.

Effuse. (L.) L. *effūsus*, pp. of *effundere*, to pour out. – L. *ef-*, for *ex*, out ; *fundere*, to pour.

Egg (1), the oval body whence chickens, &c. are hatched. (Scand.) M. E. *eg*, pl. *egges*. – Icel. *egg*, Dan. *æg*, Swed. *ägg* + A.S. *ǣg* (= M. E. *ey*) ; Du. *ei*, G. *ei*. Prob. allied to Irish *ugh*, Gael. *ubh*, W. *wy*, L. *ōuum*, Gk. *ᾠόν*, egg. Brugm. i. § 309 (2).

Egg (2), to instigate. (Scand.) M. E. *eggen*. – Icel. *eggja*, to goad on – Icel. *egg*, an edge (point). See **Edge**.

Eglantine. (F. – L.) F. *églantine*, M. F. *aiglantine*, *aiglantier*, sweet-briar. – O. F. *aiglant*, the same. – L. type *aculent-us*, prickly (not found). – L. *acu-s*, a needle ; *-lentus* (as in *uiru-lentus*). Cf. L. *aculeus*, a prickle, dimin. of *acus*. See **Aglet**. (√AK.)

Egotist, Egoist, a self-opinionated person. (L.) Coined from L. *ego*, I ; see I. Cf. F. *égoïste* (A.D. 1755).

Egregious, excellent. (L.) L. *ēgregi-us*, chosen out of a flock, excellent ; with suffix *-ous*. – L. *ē*, out ; *greg-*, stem of *grex*, a flock.

Egress, a going out. (L.) L. *ēgressus*. – L. *ēgressus*, pp. of *ēgredi*, to go out. – L. *ē*, out ; *gradi*, to go.

Egret, the lesser white heron. (F. – O. H. G.) M. F. *egrette*, *aigrette*, dimin. of a form *aigre* (whence also Prov. *aigron*, O. F. *hair-on*, E. *her-on*). – O. H. G. *heigir*, *heiger*, a heron. See **Heron**.

Eh ! interj. (E.) M. E. *ey*. Cf. A. S. *ēa* ; Du. *he !* G. *ei !* F. *eh !*

Eider-duck. (Swed. *and* E.) The E. *duck* is here added to the Swed. spelling of Icel. *æðr*, an eider-duck (*æ* pronounced like *i* in *time*) ; whence Dan. *ederfugl*

(eider-fowl), Swed. *ejder* ; and cf. Swed. dial. *åd*. Der. *eider down*, Icel. *æðardūn*.

Eight. (E.) M. E. *eightė*. A. S. *eahta*. + Du. *acht*, Icel. *ātta*, Dan. *otte*, Swed. *åtta*, Goth. *ahtau*, G. *acht* ; Irish *ocht*, Gael. *ochd*, W. *wyth*, L. *octo*, Gk. *ὀκτώ*, Pers. *hasht*, Zend *ashta*, Skt. *ashṭau*. Idg. type *oktō(u)*. Der. *eigh-teen*, A.S. *eahtatēne*, *eahtatȳne* ; *eigh-ty*, A. S. (*hund*)-*eahtatig* ; *eigh-th*, A. S. *eahtoða*.

Eisel, vinegar. (F. – L.) In Shak. M. E. *eisel*, *eisil*, *aisil*. – O. F. *aisil*, *eisil*, also *aisi*, vinegar (Godefroy). *Aisil* appears to be a dimin. form of *aisi*. – Late L. *acītus*, bitter ; closely related to L. *acētum*, vinegar. The Goth. *akeit*, vinegar, A. S. *ecid*, G. *essig*, is due to Late L. *acītum* or L. *acētum*.

Eisteddfod, a congress of (Welsh) bards. (W.) W. *eisteddfod*, a sitting, congress. – W. *eistedd*, to sit.

Either. (E.) M. E. *either*, *aither*. A. S. *ǣgþer*, contracted form of *ǣghwæþer*. Comp. of *ā-gi-hwæþer* ; where *ā* = aye, *gi* (for *ge-*) is a prefix, and *hwæþer* = whether. + Du. *ieder*, G. *jeder*, O. H. G. *ēohwedar*.

Ejaculate, to jerk out an utterance. (L.) From pp. of L. *ēiaculārī*, to cast out. – L. *ē*, out ; *iaculum*, a missile, from *iacere*, to cast.

eject. (L.) L. *ēiectāre*, frequentative of L. *ēicere*, to cast out. – L. *ē*, out ; *iacere*, to cast.

Eke (1), to augment. (E.) M. E. *eken*. O. Merc. *ēcan*, A. S. *īecan*, weak vb. Teut. type *aukjan-*, weak vb. ; allied to Icel. *auka*, Goth. *aukan* (neuter), str. vb. ; cf. L. *augēre*. (√AUGw.) Brugm. i. §635.

eke (2), also. (E.) M. E. *eek*, *eke*. A. S. *ēac*. + Du. *ook*, Icel. *auk*, Swed. *och* (and), Dan. *og* (and), G. *auch*. All from the Teut. base *auk-* above.

Elaborate. (L.) L. *ēlabōrātus*, pp. of *ēlabōrāre*, to labour greatly. – L. *ē*, out, greatly ; *labōrāre*, to work, from *labōr-*, stem of *labor*, labour.

Eland, a S. African antelope. (Du. – G. – Lith.) Du. *eland*, an elk. – G. *elend*. – Lithuan. *élnis*, an elk. Cf. W. *elain*, a hind, Russ. *olene*, a stag. See **Elk**.

Elapse, to glide away. (L.) From L. *ēlapsūs*, pp. of *ēlābī*, to glide away. – L. *ē*, away ; *lābī*, to glide.

Elastic. (Gk.) Formerly *elastick*. Gk. *ἐλαστικός*, propulsive, coined from Gk. *ἐλάω* = *ἐλαύνω*, I drive (fut. *ἐλάσ-ω*). Cf. Gk. *ἐλαστής*, also *ἐλατήρ*, a driver.

Elate, lifted up, proud. (L.) L. *ēlātus,* lifted up.—L. *ē,* out ; *lātus,* used as pp. of *ferre,* but allied to *tollere,* to lift.

Elbow, the bend of the arm. (E.) M. E. *elbowe.* A. S. *elboga,* also *eln-boga,* —A. S. *eln,* signifying ' ell,' orig. ' arm ; ' and *boga,* a bow, a bending (see **Bow**). A. S. *eln* is allied to Goth. *aleina,* a cubit, W. *elin,* Irish *uile,* L. *ulna,* Gk. *ὠλένη,* Skt. *aratni-,* the elbow. See **Ell.**+Du. *elle-boog,* Icel. *öln-bogi,* Dan. *al-bue,* G. *ellen-bogen.*

Eld, old age. (E.) M. E. *elde,* old age ; O. Merc. *œldo,* old age ; from *ald,* old. Cf. A. S. *ieldu, yldu* ; from *eald,* old. +Icel. *elli* ; Dan. *ælde.* See **Old.**

elder (1), older. (E.) Both as adj. and sb. O. Merc. *œldra* (A. S. *yldra*), elder, adj. ; comparative of *œld* (A. S. *eald*), old.

eldest. (E.) O. Merc. *œldesta* (A. S. *yldesta*), superl. of *ald* (A. S. *eald*), old.

Elder (2), a tree. (E.) The *d* is excrescent. M. E. *eller.* A. S. *ellen, ellœrn.*+ Low G. *elloorn.* ¶ Distinct from *alder.*

Elecampane, a plant. (L.) A. S. *eolone, elene,* perverted from L. *inula* ; and M.F.*enule-campane* (Cot.).—L. *inula cam-pāna,* elecampane. Here *campāna* prob. means wild, growing in the fields ; from L. *campus,* a field.

Elect, chosen. (L.) L. *ēlectus,* pp. of *ēligere,* to choose out.—L. *ē,* out ; *legere,* to choose.

Electric. (L.—Gk.) Coined from L. *electrum,* amber, which has electric properties.—Gk. *ἤλεκτρον,* amber, also shining metal ; allied to *ἠλέκτωρ,* gleaming.

Electuary, a kind of confection. (F. —L.—Gk.) M. E. *letuarie.* ◻ O. F. *lectuaire,* M. F. *electuaire.* ◻ Late L. *ēlectuā-rium, ēlectārium,* a medicine that dissolves in the mouth. Perhaps for **e(c)lict-ārium,* from Gk. *ἐκλεικτόν,* an electuary, from *ἐκλείχειν,* to lick out.— Gk. *ἐκ,* out ; *λείχειν,* to lick.

Eleemosynary, relating to alms. (Late L.—Gk.) Late L. *eleēmosynārius,* an almoner ; from *eleēmosyna,* alms.—Gk. *ἐλεημοσύνη,* pity, alms. See **Alms.**

Elegant, choice, neat. (F.—L.) M. F. *elegant.* ◻ L. *ēlegant-,* stem of *ēlegans,* tasteful, neat.—L. *ē,* out ; *leg-,* base of *legere,* to choose.

Elegy, a funeral ode. (F.—L.—Gk.) M. F. *elegie.* ◻ L. *elegīa.* ◻ Gk. *ἐλεγεία,* fem. sing., an elegy ; orig. neut. pl. of

ἐλεγεῖον, a distich (of lament). ◻ Gk. *ἔλεγος,* a lament. **Der.** *elegi-ac.*

Element. (F.—L.) O. F. *element.* ◻ L. *elementum,* a first principle.

Elephant. (F. — L. — Gk.) M. E. *elyphaunt, olifaunt.*◻O. F. *olifant, ele-fant.* ◻ L. *elephantem,* acc. of *elephas.* ◻ Gk. *ἐλέφας,* an elephant. Origin unknown ; some compare Heb. *eleph,* an ox.

Elevate. (L.) From pp. of L. *ēleuāre,* to lift up.—L. *ē,* out ; *leuāre,* to lighten, lift, from *leuis,* light. See **Levity.**

Eleven. (E.) M. E. *enleuen.* A. S. *en(d)leofan, endlufon* ; O. Northumb. *œllefne.*+Du. *elf,* Icel. *ellifu,* Dan. *elleve,* Swed. *elfva,* Goth. *ainlif,* G. *elf,* O. H. G. *einlif.* β. A compound of Teut. **ain-,* one ; and *-lif-* = Lithuan. *-lika* (in *vēno-lika,* eleven). Lith. *-lika* perhaps means 'remaining' ; cf. L. *linquere,* to leave. Brugm. ii. § 175.

Elf. (E.) M. E. *elf.* O. Merc. *œlf.*+ Icel. *álfr,* Dan. *alf* ; also G. *alp,* a nightmare. **Der.** *elf-in,* adj., for **elf-en* ; but prob. suggested by the M. E. gen. pl. *elvene,* of elves (in the Southern dialect).

Elicit, to coax out. (L.) From pp. of L. *ēlicere,* to draw out by coaxing.— L. *ē,* out ; *lacere,* to entice. And see **Lace.**

Elide. (L.) L. *ēlīdere,* to strike out.— L. *ē,* out ; *lædere,* to dash. **Der.** *elis-ion* (from pp. *ēlīs-us*).

Eligible. (F.—L.) F. *éligible.*—Med. L. *ēligibilis,* fit to be chosen.—L. *ēligere,* to choose out ; see **Elect.**

Eliminate. (L.) From pp. of L. *ēlīmināre,* to thrust out of.—L. *ē,* forth ; *limin-,* stem of *līmen,* a threshold. See **Limit.**

Elision ; see **Elide.**

Elixir. (Ar.—Gk.) Med. L. *elixir* ; for Arab. *el iksīr,* the philosopher's stone, esp. a sort of powder (Devic) ; where *el* is the definite article.—Gk. *ξήριον,* dry powder, or *ξηρόν,* dry (residuum).

Elk, a kind of deer. (G.) Prob. adapted from M. H. G. *elch,* an elk ; O.H.G. *elaho.* Cf. Icel. *elgr,* Swed. *elg,* an elk ; Russ. *olene,* a stag ; L. *alces,* Gk. *ἄλκη.* (History obscure.) Found in A. S. as *elch, elh.*

Ell. (E.) M. E. *elle, elne.* A. S. *el(i)n,* a cubit.+Du. *elle, el* ; Icel. *alin,* the arm from the elbow to the tip of the middle finger ; Swed. *aln,* Dan. *alen,* Goth. *aleina,* G. *elle,* ell ; L. *ulna,* elbow, cubit ; Gk. *ὠλένη,* elbow. *Ell* = *el-* in *el-bow.*

Ellipse. (L. – Gk.) Formerly *ellipsis*. – L. *ellīpsis*. – Gk. ἔλλειψις, a defect, an ellipse of a word; also, an oval figure, because its plane forms with the base of the cone a less angle than that of a parabola. – Gk. ἐλλείπειν, to leave in, leave behind. – Gk. ἐλ-, for ἐν, in; λείπειν, to leave, cognate with L. *linquere*. **Der.** *elliptic*, adj., Gk. ἐλλειπτικός.

Elm, a tree. (E.) A.S. *elm.*+O. H. G. *elm* ; cf. Icel. *ālmr*, Dan. *alm*, Swed. *alm* ; also L. *ulmus* (whence G. *ulme*, Du. *olm*).

Elocution. (L.) From L. *ēlocūtiōnem*, acc. of *ēlocūtio*, clear utterance. – L. *ēlocūtus*, pp. of *ēloquī*, to speak out. – L. *ē*, out; *loquī*, to speak. Cf. **Eloquent.**

Eloign, Eloin, to remove and keep at a distance, to withdraw. (F. – L.) O. F. *esloigner*, to remove, keep away (Law L. *exlongāre*). – O. F. *es*, away; *loing* (F. *loin*), far off. – L. *ex*, away; *longē*, adv. far off. See **Long.**

Elope. (A. F. – Scand.) A. F. *aloper*, to run away (from a husband; see N. E. D.). – A. F. *a-* prefix (perhaps for O. F. *es-*, away, as in E. *a-bash*); and M. E. *lopen*, to run (Cath. Anglicum), from Icel. *hlaupa*, cognate with E. **Leap.** β. Or from A. S. *ōphlop-en*, pp. of *ōphlēopan*, to escape; from A. S. *ōþ-*, away, and *hlēopan*, to run, to leap.

Eloquent. (F. – L.) M. E. *eloquent*. – O. F. *eloquent*. – L. *ēloquent-*, stem of pres. pt. of *ēloquī*, to speak out or clearly. – L. *ē*, out; *loquī*, to speak.

Else, otherwise. (E.) A.S. *elles*, adv.; stem **aljo-*, signifying ' other,' as in Goth. *aljis*, other.+Swed. *eljest*; allied to L. *alias*, and to **Alien.** The suffix *-es* marks the gen. case, neuter.

Elucidate. (L.) From pp. of Late L. *ēlūcidāre*, to make clear. – L. *ē*, out, very; *lūcid-us*, lucid, clear. See **Lucid.**

Elude, to avoid slily. (L.) L. *ēlūdere* (pp. *ēlūsus*), to mock, deceive. – L. *ē*, out; *lūdere*, to play. **Der.** *elus-ory*, from the pp.

Elysium, a heaven. (L. – Gk.) L. *ēlysium*. – Gk. ἠλύσιον, short for ἠλύσιον πεδίον, the Elysian field (Od. 4. 563).

Em-, *prefix*. (F. – L.) F. *em-*<L. *im-* (for *in*), in, before *b* and *p*. Hence *embalm*, to anoint with balm; *em-bank*, to enclose with a bank, cast up a bank; *embody*, to invest with a body, &c.

Emaciate. (L.) From pp. of L. *ēmaciāre*, to make thin. – L. *ē*, very;

maci-, base of *maciēs*, leanness; cf. *macer*, lean.

Emanate. (L.) From L. *ēmānātus*, pp. of *ēmānāre*, to flow out. – L. *ē*, out; *mānāre*, to flow.

Emancipate. (L.) From pp. of L. *ēmancipāre*, to set free. – L. *ē*, out; *mancipāre*, to transfer property. – L. *mancip-*, stem of *man-ceps*, lit. one who takes property in hand or receives it. – L. *man-us*, hand; *capere*, to take.

Emasculate, to deprive of virility. (L.) From pp. of L. *ēmasculāre*. – L. *ē*, away from; *masculus*, male. See **Masculine.**

Embargo. (Span.) Span. *embargo*, an arrest, a stoppage of ships; lit. a putting a bar in the way. – Late L. type **imbarricāre*, to bar in. Formed with prefix *em-* (=Lat. *in*) from Span. *barra*, a bar. See **Bar, Barricade.**

Embark. (F. – Late L.) F. *embarquer*. – Late L. *imbarcāre*, to put in a bark. – L. *im-* (for *in*), in; *barca*, a bark; see **Bark** (1).

Embarrass. (F. – Span.) F. *embarrasser*, to perplex; lit. to hinder, put a bar in one's way. – Span. *embarazar*, the same. – Span. *em-* (L. *im-*, for *in*), in; *barra*, a bar. Cf. **Embargo**; and **Bar.**

Embassy, a mission. (F. – Late L. – C.) A modification of O. F. *ambassee*; cf. M. F. *embassade*, Ital. *imbasciata*, weakened form of *ambasciata*. All from Late L. *ambasciāta*, sb., orig. fem. of pp. of *ambasciāre*, to send on a mission, from *ambascia*, a mission. See **Ambassador.**

Embattle, to furnish with battlements. (F.) M. E. *embattelen*. – O. F. *em-* (L. *im-*, for *in-*, prefix); and O. F. *bastiller*, to fortify. See **Battlement.**

Embellish. (F. – L.) M. E. *embelissen*. – O. F. *embeliss-*, stem of pres. pt. of *embellir*, to beautify. – O. F. *em-* (L. *in*) ; and *bel*, fair. See **Belle.**

Ember-days. (E.) M. E. *ymber*, as in *ymber-weke*. A. S. *ymbren-*, prob. from *ymbryne*, a circuit, or period; the ember-days are days that *recur* at each of the four seasons of the year. The A. S. *ymb-ryne* is lit. ' a running round.' – A. S. *ymb*, round (= G. *um*, Gk. ἀμφί) ; and *ryne*, a run, course; see **Run.** Prob. confused with L. *quatuor tempora*, four seasons; whence G. *quatember*.

Embers, ashes. (E.) M. E. *emeres*. A. S. *ǣmyrgean*, embers; A. S. Leechdoms, iii. 30 (rare). **+** Icel. *eimyrja,* Dan. *emmer,* Swed. *mörja,* O. H. G. *eimurja,* sb. ember. Cf. Icel. *eim-r,* vapour; prov. E. *ome* (= A.S. *ām), vapour.

Embezzle, to filch. (F.) A. F. *enbesiler,* to make away with (A. D. 1404). – O. F. *en-* (for L. *in-,* prefix) ; and O. F. *besillier,* to maltreat, destroy, apparently from O. F. *bes-* (Late L. *bis-,* used as a pejorative prefix). Cf. O. F. *besil,* illtreatment, torture ; and see Bezzle in the N. E. D. ¶ Certainly influenced, in the 16th cent., by a supposed etymology from *imbécill,* to weaken, an obsolete verb formed from the adj. *imbecile,* q.v.

Emblem. (F.–L.–Gk.) M. F. *embleme.*– L. *emblēma.* – Gk. ἔμβλημα, a thing put on, an ornament.–Gk. ἐμ-, for ἐν, in, on ; βάλλειν, to throw, to put. See Belemnite.

Emblements, the produce of sown lands, crops which a tenant may cut after the determination of his tenancy. (F.–L.) O. F. *emblaement,* harvest. – O. F. *emblaër, emblader* (F. *emblaver*), to sow with corn.– Late Lat. *imbladāre,* to sow. –L. *im-* (for *in*), in ; Late L. *blādum* =L. *ablātum,* a crop, corn, lit. 'what is carried away' (F. *blé*).

Embolism. (F.–L.–Gk.) O. F. *embolisme.*– L. *embolismus.* – Gk. ἐμβολισμός, an intercalation or insertion of days, to complete a period. – Gk. ἐμ, for ἐν, in ; βάλλειν, to cast ; cf. ἐμβολή, an insertion.

Embonpoint, plumpness of person. (F. – L.) F. *embonpoint,* plumpness. For *en bon point,* in good case.–L. *in,* in ; *bonum,* neut. of *bonus,* good ; *punctum,* point.

Emboss (1), to adorn with bosses or raised work. (F.–L. *and* G.) From Em-, prefix ; and Boss.

Emboss (2), to take shelter, or drive to shelter in a wood, &c. (F.–Late L.) O F. *embosquer,* to shroud in a wood.– O.F. *em-* (L. *in*), in ; O. F. *bosc,* a wood ; see Bouquet.

Embouchure. (F.–L.) F. *embouchure,* the mouth or opening (of a river). –F. *emboucher,* to put in or to the mouth. –L. *in,* in, F. *bouche,* from *bucca,* the mouth.

Embrace. (F.–L.) O.F. *embracer,* to grasp in the arms.– O.F. *em-,* for *en* (L. *in*) ; and *brace,* the grasp of the arms; see Brace.

Embrasure. (F.) F. *embrasure,* an aperture with slant sides.–M. F. *embraser,* to slope the sides of a window. –O.F. *em-* (L. *in*), in ; M. F. *braser,* 'to skue, or chamfret ;' Cot. (Of unknown origin.)

Embrocation, a fomenting. (F.– Late L.–Gk.) O. F. *embrocation.*– Med. L. *embrocātus,* pp. of *embrocāre,* to foment. – Gk. ἐμβροχή, a fomentation.– Gk. ἐμβρέχειν, to soak in. – Gk. ἐμ-=ἐν, in ; βρέχειν, to wet, soak.

Embroider. (F.) From Em- and Broider. Cf. O. F. *embroder,* to embroider.

Embroil. (F.) From F. *embrouiller,* to confuse. – F. *em-* (L. *im-,* for *in*) ; *brouiller,* to confuse. See Broil (2) ; and cf. Imbroglio.

Embryo. (F.–Gk.) Formerly *embryon.* – M. F. *embryon.* – Gk. ἔμβρυον, the embryo, fœtus. –Gk. ἐμ-=ἐν, within ; βρύον, neut. of pres. pt. of βρύειν, to be full of, swell out.

Emendation. (L.) Coined from the pp. of L. *ēmendāre,* to free from fault.– L. *ē,* free from ; *mendum, menda,* a fault.

Emerald, a green gem. (F.–L.–Gk.) M. E. *emeraude.*–O.F. *esmeraude* (Span. *esmeralda*) ; also *esmeragde.* – L. *smaragdum,* acc. of *smaragdus.* – Gk. σμάραγδος, an emerald. Cf. Skt. *marakata-,* an emerald.

Emerge, to rise from the sea, appear. (L.) L. *ēmergere,* to rise out of water. – L. *ē,* out ; *mergere,* to dip ; see Merge.

Emerods; see Hemorrhoids.

Emery, a hard mineral. (F.–Ital.– Gk.) Formerly *emeril;* XVII cent.– F. *émeri;* M. F. *emeril, esmeril.*–Ital. *smeriglio.*– Gk. σμῆρις, σμύρις, emery.

Emetic. (L.–Gk.) L. *emeticus.*– Gk. ἐμετικός, causing sickness. – Gk. ἐμέω, I vomit ; see Vomit.

Emigrate. (L.) From pp. of L. *ēmigrāre,* to wander forth. – L. *ē,* out ; *migrāre,* to wander ; see Migrate.

Eminent, excellent. (L.) L. *ēminent ,* stem of pres. pt. of *ēminēre,* to project, excel.–L. *ē,* out ; **minēre,* to project ; for which cf. *im-minent, pro-minent.*

Emir, a commander. (Arab.) Arab. *amīr,* a nobleman, prince.–Arab. root *amara,* he commanded. Der. *admir-al.*

Emit, to send forth. (L.) L. *ēmittere,* to send forth ; pp. *ēmissus.*–L. *ē,* out ; *mittere,* to send. Der. *emiss-ion, emissary,* from the pp.

Emmet, an ant. (E.) M. E. *emete, amote.* A. S. *ǣmette,* or *ǣmette,* an ant.+ G. *ameise,* O. H. G. *āmeiza,* or *ameiza,* an ant. Doublet, *ant.*

Emmew; see **Enew.**

Emollient, softening. (F. – L.) M.F. *emollient.* – L. *ēmollient-,* stem of pres. pt. of *ēmollīre,* to soften. – L. *ē,* out, very; *mollīre,* to soften, from *molli-s,* soft.

Emolument, gain. (F. – L.) O. F. *emolument.* – L. *ēmolumentum,* what is gained by labour. – L.*ēmōlīrī,*to work out, accomplish. – L. *ē,* out, greatly; *mōlīrī,*to work, from *mōles,* heap, also effort. ¶ So usually explained; but the short vowels in -*mŏlŭ*- suggest a derivation from *ēmŏlere,* to grind thoroughly.

Emotion. (L.) Coined from L. *ēmōtus,* pp. of *ēmouēre,* to move away or much. – L. *ē,* out, much; *mouēre,* to move.

Emperor, a ruler. (F. – L.) O. F. *empereor.* – L. *imperātōrem,* acc. of *imperātor,* a ruler. – L. *imperāre,* to rule. – L. *im-* (for *in-*), upon, over; *parāre,* to make ready, order. Der. *empr-ess.*

Emphasis, stress of voice. (L. – Gk.) L. *emphasis.* – Gk. ἔμφασις, a declaration, emphasis; orig. appearance. – Gk. ἐμφαίνομαι, I appear. – Gk. ἐμ- (ἐν), in; φαίνομαι, I appear, whence φάσις, an appearance; see **Phase.** Der. *emphatic,* from Gk. ἐμφατικός, significant.

Empire. (F. – L.) F. *empire.* – L. *imperium,* command. – L. *im-* (*in-*), upon, over; *parāre,* to make ready, order.

Empiric, a quack doctor. (F. – L. – Gk.) M. F. *empirique.* – L. *empīricus.* – Gk. ἐμπειρικός, experienced; also one of a certain set of physicians. – Gk. ἐμ- = ἐν, in; πεῖρα (=*περια), a trial, experience, allied to πόρος, a way, and to E. **Fare.** Brugm. i. § 293.

Employ. (F. – L.) M. F. *employer,* to employ. – L. *implicāre,* to implicate (in Late L., to use for, employ). – L. *im-* (for *in-*), in; *plicāre,* to fold; see **Implicate, Imply.**

Emporium, a mart. (L. – Gk.) L. *emporium.* – Gk. ἐμπόριον, a mart; neut. of ἐμπόριος, commercial. – Gk. ἐμπορία, commerce, ἔμπορος, a traveller, merchant. – Gk. ἐμ- = ἐν, in; πόρος, a way; see **Fare.**

Emprise, enterprise. (F. – L.) M. E. *emprise.* – O. F. *emprise;* orig. fem. of *empris,* pp. of O. F. *emprendre,* to take in hand. – L. *im-* (*in-*), in; *prehendere,* to take. See **Comprehend.**

Empty, void. (E.) M. E. *empti.* A.S. *ǣmtig, ǣnetig,* lit. full of leisure. – A. S. *ǣmta, ǣmetta,* leisure, older form *ǣmota* (Epin. Glos. 680). Perhaps *ǣmetta* is for **ǣmōtjon ,* from *ǣ-,* prefix, privative, and *mōt,* a meeting for business.

Empyrean, Empyreal, pertaining to elemental fire. (L. – Gk.) Adjectives coined from L. *empȳræ-us,* Gk. **ἐμπύραιος,* extended from ἔμ-πυρος, exposed to fire. – Gk. ἐμ- = ἐν, in; πῦρ, fire; see **Fire.**

Emu, Emeu, a bird. (Port.) Port. *ema,* an ostrich.

Emulate. (L.) From pp. of L. *æmulārī,* to try to equal. – L. *æmulus,* striving to equal.

Emulsion, a milk-like mixture. (F. – L.) M. F. *emulsion;* formed from L. *ēmuls-us,* pp. of *ēmulgēre,* to milk out. – L. *ē,* out; *mulgēre,* to milk; see **Milk.**

En-, *prefix.* (F. – L.) F. *en-.* – L. *in-,* in; sometimes used with a causal force, as *en-case, en-chain,* &c. See **Em-.**

Enact. (F. – L.) In Shak. – F. *en,* in (L. *in*); and **Act.** Lit. 'to put in act.'

Enamel, vb. (F. – O. H. G.) M. E. *enamaile,* sb., *enamelen,* vb. – A. F. *enameller, enamailler,* vb. – F. *en* (L. *in*), on; *amaile,* for O. F. *esmail,* enamel (= Ital. *smalto*), from O. Low G. *smalt* (Lübben). See **Smalt.**

Enamour. (F. – L.) O. F. *enamorer,* to inflame with love. – F. *en amour,* in love; where F. *en* is from L. *in,* in, and *amour* from L. acc. *amōrem,* love.

Encamp. (F. – L.) Coined from *en-* (F. *en,* L. *in*) and *camp;* hence 'to form into a camp.' See **Camp.**

Encase. (F. – L.) Cf. F. *encaisser,* 'to put into a case;' Cot. – F. *en,* in (L. *in*); and M. F. *caisse, casse,* a case; see **Case** (2).

Encaustic, relating to designs burnt in. (F. – L. – Gk.) F. *encaustique.* – L. *encausticus.* – Gk. ἐγκαυστικός, relating to burning in. – Gk. ἐν, in; καίω, I burn. See **Calm.**

Enceinte, pregnant. (F. – L.) F. *enceinte.* – Late L. *incincta,* ungirt, said of a pregnant woman, fem. of pp. of *cingere,* to gird, with neg. prefix *in-.* ¶ Isidore explains Late L. *incincta* as meaning 'ungirt;' so also Ital. *incinta* (Florio).

Enchant. (F. – L.) F. *enchanter,* to charm. – L. *incantāre,* to repeat a chant. – L. *in-,* upon; and *cantāre,* to sing; see **Cant** (1).

Enchase. (F.−L.) M. F. *enchasser*, ' to enchace or set in gold ; ' Cot. Hence to emboss. − F. *en*, in (L. *in*) ; and *chasse* (F. *châsse*), the same as *casse*, a case ; see Case (2).

Encircle. (F.−L.) From En- and Circle.

Encline. (F.−L.) M. E. *enclinen.* − O.F. *encliner.* − L. *inclīnāre*; see Incline.

Enclitic. (Gk.) Gk. ἐγκλιτικός, en-clining, dependent ; used of a word which ' leans ' its accent upon another. − Gk. ἐγκλίνειν, to lean upon, encline. − Gk. ἐν, on ; κλίνειν, to lean ; see Lean (1).

Enclose. (F.−L.) From En- and Close (1). Cf. A.F. *enclos*, pp. of *enclorre*, to shut in.

Encomium, commendation. (L.−Gk.) Latinised from Gk. ἐγκώμιον, neut. of ἐγκώμιος, laudatory, full of revelry. − Gk. ἐν, in ; κῶμος, revelry.

Encore, again. (F.−L.) F. *encore* (= Ital. *ancora*), still, again. − L. *hanc hōram*, for *in hanc hōram*, to this hour ; see 'Hour. ¶ Somewhat disputed.

Encounter, vb. (F.−L.) O.F. *en-contrer*, to meet in combat. − F. *en*, in ; *contre*, against. − L. *in*, in ; *contrā*, against.

Encourage. (F.−L.) F. *encourager*; from F. *en* (L. *in*) and *courage* ; see Courage.

Encrinite, the ' stone lily ' ; a fossil. (Gk.) Coined from Gk. ἐν, in ; κρίνον, a lily ; with suffix -ιτης.

Encroach. (F.−L. *and* Teut.) Lit. to hook away, catch in a hook. − O.F. *encrochier*, to seize upon. − F. *en*, in ; *croc*, a hook ; cf. F. *accrocher*, to hook up. − L. *in*, in ; and M. Du. *kroke*, Icel. *krōkr*, &c.; see Crook.

Encumber. (F.−L. ?) O.F. *encom-brer*, to block up (a way). − Late L. *in-combrāre*, to obstruct. − L. *in-*, in ; and Late L. *combrus*, an obstacle. See Cumber.

Encyclical, circular, said of a letter sent round (ecclesiastical). From Gk. ἐγκύκλι-ος, circular (said of a letter) ; with suffix -*c-al.* − Gk. ἐν, in ; κύκλο-ς, a circle.

encyclopædia. (L.−Gk.) Latinised from (a coined) Gk. *ἐγκυκλοπαιδεία, for ἐγκύκλιος παιδεία, circular (or complete) instruction ; from ἐγκύκλιος (above), and παιδεία, instruction.

End, sb. (E.) M.E. *ende*. A.S. *ende*, sb. +Du. *einde*, Icel. *endir*, Sw. *ände*, Dan. *ende*, Goth. *andeis*, G. *ende*. Teut. type

and-joz. Cf. O. Irish *ind*, Skt. *anta-*, end, limit. ¶ Hence the prefixes *ante-*, *anti-*, *an-* in *an-swer*.

Endeavour, to attempt. (F. − L.) Coined from the M. E. sb. *dever*, *devoir*, duty, with F. prefix *en-* (= L. *in*). Compare the old phrase ' to do his *dever* ' = to do his duty (Ch. C. T. 2598) ; see Devoir.

Endemic, peculiar to a district. (Gk.) Gk. ἔνδημ-ος, belonging to a people. − Gk. ἐν, in ; δῆμος, a people ; see Demo-cracy.

Endive, a plant. (F.−L.) F. *endive* (Ital. *endivia*). − Lat. type *intibea*, adj.; from L. *intibus*, *intubus*, endive.

Endogen, a plant that grows from within. (F.−Gk.) F. *endogène* (1813). From Gk. ἔνδο-ν, within ; γεν-, base of γίγνομαι, I am born, allied to γένος, race.

Endorse. (F.−L.) Formerly *endosse*. O. F. *endosser*, to put on the back of. − F. *en*, on ; *dos*, the back, from L. *dorsum*, the back (whence the spelling with *rs*).

Endow. (F.−L.) A.F. *endower*. From F. *en-* and *douer.* − L. *in-*, in, and *dōtāre*, to give a dowry, from *dōt-*, stem of *dōs*, a dowry; cf. *dare*, to give.

Endue (1), to endow. (F.−L.) An-other spelling of *endow*; XV cent. − O. F. *endoer* (later *endouer*), to endow (Burguy). − L. *in*, in ; and *dōtāre*, to endow ; see above. ¶ Confused both with O.F. *en-duire*, to introduce (from L. *indūcere*), and with Endue (2) below.

Endue (2), to clothe. (L.) A corrup-tion of *indue*; as in ' *endue* thy ministers with righteousness.' − L. *induere*, to clothe. See Indue (2) ; and see above.

Endure. (F.−L.) M. E. *enduren.* − F. *endurer.* − F. *en* (L. *in*) ; and *durer* (L. *dūrāre*), to last. See Dure.

Enemy. (F. − L.) M. E. *enemi.* − O. F. *enemi.* − L. *inimīcus*, unfriendly. − L. *in*, not ; *amīcus*, friendly, from L. *amāre*, to love.

Energy. (F.−L.−Gk.) O.F. *energie.* − Late L. *energīa.* − Gk. ἐνέργεια, vigour, action. − Gk. ἐνεργός, at work. − Gk. ἐν, in ; ἔργον, work ; see Work.

Enervate. (L.) From pp. of L. *ēneruāre*, to deprive of nerve or strength. − L. *ē*, out of ; *neruus*, a nerve ; see Nerve.

Enew. (F.−L.) Misspelt *emmew* in Shak.; read *enew*, to drive into the water. − F. *en*, in ; A.F. *ewe* (F. *eau*), water, from L. *aqua.* Cf. O. F. *enewer,* to soak in water (Godefroy).

Enfeoff, to endue with a fief. (F. – L. *and* O. H. G.) The spelling is Norman F.; formed from F. *en* (L. *in*), in; and *fief,* a fief. See **Fief.**

Enfilade, a straight line or passage. (F. – L.) F. *enfilade,* a long string (of things). – F. *enfiler,* to thread. – F. *en-* (L. *in*), in; *fil,* a thread, from L. *filum,* a thread. See **File** (1).

Engage. (F. – L.) O. F. *engager,* to bind by a pledge. – F. *en* (L. *in*), in; *gage,* a pledge; see **Gage.** Der. *disengage.*

Engender, to breed. (F. – L.) M. E. *engendren.* – O. F. *engendrer.* – L. *ingenerāre,* to produce. – L. *in,* in; *generāre,* to breed, from *gener-* (for **genes-*), stem of *genus,* a race, See **Genus.**

Engine. (F. – L.) O. F. *engin,* a tool. – L. *ingenium,* natural capacity, also, an invention. – L. *in,* in; *geni-,* as in *genius;* see **Genius.**

English, belonging to the Angles. (E.) A. S. *Englisc, Ænglisc.* – A. S. *Engl-e, Ængl-e,* pl., the Angles; with suffix *-isc,* -ish. Cf. A. S. *Angel-cynn,* Angle kin (*gens Anglōrum*).

Engrailed, indented with curved lines; in heraldry. (F. – L. *and* Teut.) O. F. *engresle,* pp. of *engresler,* to engrail (indent as with hailstones). – O. F. *en,* in; *gresle* (F. *grêle*), hail. – L. *in,* in; and (perhaps) G. *gries,* grit. See **Grail** (3).

Engrain, Ingrain, to dye of a fast colour. (F. – L.) M. E. *engreynen,* to dye *in grain,* i.e. of a fast colour. Coined from F. *en* (L. *in*); and O. F. *graine,* 'the seed of herbs, also grain, wherewith cloth is died *in grain,* scarlet die, scarlet in graine;' Cot. From Late L. *grāna,* the cochineal 'berry' or insect; a fem. sb. formed from the pl. (*grāna*) of *grānum,* a grain.

Engrave. (F. *and* E.) From En- and Grave (1); imitating O. F. *engraver* (from L. *in* and O. H. G. *graban,* Low G. *graven,* cognate with E. *grave*).

Engross, to write in large letters, to occupy wholly. (F. – L.) The former (legal) sense is the older. A. F. *engrosser.* From F. *en grosse,* i. e. in large characters. – L. *in,* in; Late L. *grossa,* large writing, from L. *grossus,* thick.

Enhance, to raise, exalt, increase. (F. – I.) A. F. *enhauncer,* a form of O. F.

enhaucer, enhaucier, to lift (Ital. *innalzai e*). – L. *in;* and Late L. *altiāre,* to lift, from *altus,* high.

Enigma. (L. – Gk.) L. *ænigma.* – Gk. αἴνιγμα (stem αἰνίγματ-), a riddle, dark saying. – Gk. αἰνίσσομαι, I speak in riddles. – Gk. αἶνος, a tale, story. Der. *enigmat-ic* (from the stem).

Enjoin, to bid. (F. – L.) O. F. *enjoindre* (1 p. pres. *enjoin-s*). – L. *iniungere,* to bid, ordain, orig. to join into. – L. *in,* in; *iungere,* to join. See **Join.**

Enjoy, to joy in. (F. – L.) M. E. *enioien* (=*enjoyen*); A. F. *enioier.* – F. *en* (L. *in*); O. F. *ioie,* F. *joie;* see **Joy.**

Enlighten, vb. (E.; *with* F. *prefix.*) Coined with F. prefix *en-* (L. *in*), from *lighten,* vb.; see **Lighten.**

Enlist, to enter on a list. (F. – G.; *with* F. – L. *prefix.*) Coined by prefixing F. *en* (L. *in*) to List (2).

Enmity. (F. – L.) M. E. *enmite.* – A. F. *enemite;* O. F. *enamistie(t).* – O. F. *en-* (L. *in-*), neg. prefix; and *amistie(t),* amity; see **Amity.**

Ennui. (F. – L.) Mod. F. *ennui,* annoyance; O. F. *anoi.* See **Annoy.**

Enormous, great beyond measure. (F. – L.) Formed from *enorm* (obsolete) with suffix *-ous.* – M. F. *enorme,* huge. – L. *ēnormis,* out of rule, huge. – L. *ē,* out of; *norma,* rule. See **Normal.**

Enough. (E.) M. E. *inoh, enogh;* pl. *inohe, enoghe.* A.S. *genōh, genōg,* pl. *genōge,* sufficient; allied to A.S. *geneah,* it suffices.+Icel. *gnōgr,* Dan. *nok,* Swed. *nog,* Du. *genoeg,* G. *genug,* Goth. *ganōhs.* The *ge-* is a prefix. Cf. L. *nanciscī,* to obtain (pp. *nac-tus*); Skt. *naç,* to attain.

Enquire. (F. – L.) M. E. *enqueren;* altered from *enquere* to *enquire,* and later to *inquire,* under the influence of the L. form. – O. F. *enquerre, enquerir.* – L. *inquīrere,* to search into. – L. *in,* in; *quærere,* to seek. Der. *enquir-y,* often turned into *inquiry; enquest* (now *inquest*), from O. F. *enqueste,* L. *inquīsīta* (*rēs*), a thing enquired into.

Ensample. (F. – L.) M. E. *ensample.* – A. F. *ensample,* corrupt form of *essample, exemple.* – L. *exemplum,* a sample, pattern. – L. *eximere,* to select a sample. – L. *ex,* out; *emere,* to take. Der. *sample.*

Ensign. (F. – L.) O. F. *ensigne,* more correctly *enseigne,* 'a sign, ensigne, standard;' Cot. – Late L. *insignia,* pl. of L. *insigne,* a standard. – L. *insignis,* remarkable. **—** L. *in*, upon; *signum*, a mark; i. e. 'with a mark on it.' See **Sign.**

Ensilage, the storing of grain, &c., underground. (F. — Span. — L. *and* Gk.) F. *ensilage*. **—** Span. *ensilar*, to store up underground. **—** Span. *en*, in; *silo*, a pit for storing grain. **—** L. *in*, in; *sirus*, borrowed from Gk. σιρός, a pit for storing grain.

Ensue. (F. — L.) O. F. *ensu-*, a stem of *ensivre*, to follow after. **—** Late L. *insequere*, for L. *insequi*, to follow upon. **—** L. *in*, on; *sequi*, to follow.

Ensure, to make sure. (F. — L.) A. F. *enseurer*. **—** F. *en* (L. *in*), in; and O. F. *seür*, sure; see **Sure.**

Entablature. (F. — L.) Obs. F. *entablature*, 'an intablature;' Cot. [Cf. Ital. *intavolatura*, 'a planking,' Torriano; from *intavolare*, 'to board,' Florio.] Properly 'something laid flat,' and, though now applied to the part of a building surmounting the columns, orig. applied to a panel or flooring. **—** L. *in*, upon; **tabulāre*, a verb formed from the sb. *tabulātum*, boardwork, a flooring, from *tabula*, a plank; see **Table.**

Entail, to bestow as a heritage. (F. — L.) Orig. to convert an estate into *fee-tail* (*feodum talliātum*, where *talliātum* means 'limited' in a certain way). From F. *en-* (L. *in*) and *tailler* (*talliāre*). In another sense we find M. E. *entailen*, to cut, carve. **—** O. F. *entailler*, to carve, grave. **—** F. *en-* (L. *in*), in; and *tailler*, to cut; see **Tailor, Tail** (2), **Tally.**

Entangle; from **En-** and **Tangle,** q. v.

Enter. (F. — L.) M. E. *entren*. **—** O. F. *entrer*. **—** L. *intrāre*, to go into. **—** L. *in*, in; and **trāre*, to go through (cf. *pene-trāre* and *trans*); allied to Skt. *tara-*, a passage. See Brugm. ii. § 579. **Der.** *entr-ance*.

Enterprise. (F. — L.) O. F. *entreprise*, *enterprinse*, an enterprise. **—** O. F. *enterpris*, pp. of *enterprendre*, to undertake. **—** Late L. *interprendere*. **—** L. *inter*, among; *prendere*, short for *prehendere*, to lay hold of. See **Prehensile.**

Entertain. (F. — L.) O. F. *entretenir*. **—** Late L. *intertenēre*, to entertain, lit. 'to hold or keep among.' **—** L. *inter*, among; *tenēre*, to hold.

Enthusiasm, inspiration. (L. — Gk.) Late L. *enthūsiasmus*. **—** Gk. ἐνθουσιασμός, inspiration. **—** Gk. ἐνθουσιάζω, I am inspired.

— Gk. ἔνθεος, full of the god, having a god within, inspired. **—** Gk. ἐν, in; θεός, a god.

Entice. (F. — L.) M. E. *enticen*. **—** O. F. *enticier*, *enticher*, to excite. **—** Lat. type **intitiāre*, to kindle, set on fire. **—** L. *in*; and **titius*, for *titio*, a firebrand. Cf. F. *attiser*, Ital. *attizzare*, to set on fire.

Entire. (F. — L.) O. F. *entier*, whole. **—** L. *integrum*, acc. of *integer*, whole. See **Integer.**

Entity, being. (L.) A coined word, with suffix *-ty*, from L. *enti-*, decl. stem of **ens*, a thing, a being; see **Essence.**

Entomology. (F. — Gk.) F. *entomologie* (A. D. 1764). From Gk. ἔντομο-ν, an insect; neut. of ἔντομο-s, cut into, so called from the very thin middle part (see **Insect).** **—** Gk. ἐν, in; τέμνειν, to cut; with suffix -λογια, discourse, from λέγειν, to speak.

Entrails, the inward parts. (F. — L.) O. F. *entraille*, intestines. **—** Late L. *intrālia*, also (more correctly) *intrānea*, entrails. **—** L. *interānea*, entrails, neut. pl. of *interāneus*, inward, adj., from *inter*, within. ¶ The O. F. *entraille* was a fem. sing. made from a neut. pl.

Entreat. (F. — L.) Orig. to treat; then to treat with, beseech. O. F. *entraiter*, to treat of. **—** F. *en* (< L. *in*), in, concerning; F. *traiter* < L. *tractāre*, to handle, treat; see **Treat.**

Enumerate. (L.) From pp. of L. *ēnumerāre*, to reckon up. **—** L. *ē*, out, fully; *numerāre*, vb., from *numerus*, number.

Enunciate. (L.) From pp. of L. *ēnunciāre*, better spelt *ēnuntiāre*, to utter, declare fully. **—** L. *ē*, fully; *nuntiāre*, to tell, from *nuntius*, a messenger.

Envelop. (F. — Teut.) M. E. *envolupen*. O. F. *envoluper*, later *enveloper*, to wrap in, wrap round, enfold. **—** F. *en* (L. *in*), in; and O. F. *voluper*, *voloper*, *vloper*, to wrap, from a base *vlop-*, to wrap. This base resembles M. E. *wlappen*, to wrap; which, however, is not known outside English. See **Lap** (3). Note Walloon *ewalpé*, to envelop (Remacle); M. Ital. *goluppare*, to wrap (Florio). Cf. **Develop.**

Environ, to surround. (F. — L.) O. F. *environner*, to surround. **—** F. *environ*, round about. **—** F. *en* (L. *in*), in; O. F. *viron*, a circuit, from *virer*, to turn, veer; see **Veer.**

Envoy. (F. — L.) O. F. *envoy*, a sending. **—** O. F. *envoier*, to send. **—** F. *en voie*, on the way.—L. *in uiam*, on the way. Cf. Ital. *inviare*, to send.

Envy, sb. (F.—L.) M. E. *enuie* (*envie*).—O. F. *envie.*—L. *inuidia*, envy; see Invidious.

Epact. (F. — Late L. — Gk.) O. F. (and F.) *epacte*, an addition, the epact (a term in astronomy).—Late L. *epacta.*—Gk. ἐπακτή (for ἐπακτός ἡμέρα), late fem. of ἐπακτός, added.—Gk. ἐπάγειν, to bring in, add.—Gk. ἐπ-, for ἐπί, to; and ἄγειν, to lead, bring. (√AG.)

Epaulet, a shoulder-knot. (F.—L.—Gk.) F. *épaulette*; dimin. from *épaule* (O. F. *espaule*), a shoulder. — Late L. *spatula*, shoulder-blade; L. *spatula*, a broad blade; see Spatula.

Epergne, an ornamental stand for the centre of a table. (F.—L. *and* G.) F. *épergne*, commonly spelt *épargne*, lit. thriftiness, sparingness. So called from the method of ornamentation; the F. *taille d'épargne* is applied to a sort of ornamentation in which certain parts are cut away and filled in with enamel, leaving the design *in relief*, i. e. *spared* or left uncut. See Littré, and Cotgrave (s. v. *espargne*).—F. *épargner*; O. F. *espargner, espergner*, to spare.—O. H. G. *sparōn*, G. *sparen*, to spare; see Spare.

Ephah, a Hebrew measure. (Heb.—Egypt.) Heb. *ēphāh*, a measure; of Egyptian origin; cf. Coptic *ōpi*, measure.

Ephemera, sing. (Gk.) orig. pl., flies that live for a day. (Gk.) XVII cent.—Gk. ἐφήμερα, neut. pl. of ἐφήμερος, lasting for a day.—Gk. ἐφ-=ἐπί, for; ἡμέρα, a day. Der. *ephemer-al*, adj.; *ephemer-is* (Gk. ἐφημερίς, a diary).

Ephod, part of the priest's habit. (Heb.) Heb. *ēphōd*, a vestment.—Heb. *āphad*, to put on.

Epi-, *prefix.* (Gk.) Gk. ἐπί, upon, to, besides; spelt *eph-* in *eph-emeral*, *ep-* in *ep-isode, ep-och, ep-ode*.

Epic, narrative. (L.—Gk.) L. *epicus.*—Gk. ἐπικός, narrative.—Gk. ἔπος, word, narrative, song; see Voice.

Epicene, of common gender. (L.—Gk.) L. *epicænus.*—Gk. ἐπίκοινος, common.—Gk. ἐπί, among; κοινός, common.

Epicure, a follower of Epicurus. (L.—Gk.) L. *Epicūrus.*—Gk. Ἐπίκουρος, a proper name; lit. 'assistant.'

Epicycle, a small circle, with its centre on the circumference of a larger one. (L.—Gk.) L. *epicyclus.*—Gk. ἐπίκυκλος.

—Gk. ἐπί, upon; κύκλος, a circle; see Cycle.

Epidemic, affecting a people. (L.—Gk.) Formed from L. *epidēmus*, epidemic.—Gk. ἐπίδημος, among the people, general.—Gk. ἐπί, among; δῆμος, people. See Endemic.

Epidermis, cuticle. (L.—Gk.) L. *epidermis.*—Gk. ἐπιδερμίς, upper skin.—Gk. ἐπί, upon; δέρμ-α, skin. See Derm.

Epiglottis, the cartilage forming a lid over the glottis. (Gk.) Gk. ἐπιγλωττίς.—Gk. ἐπί, upon; γλωττίς, glottis; see Glottis.

Epigram, a short and pithy poem or saying. (F.—L.—Gk.) F. *épigramme.*—L. *epigramma.*—Gk. ἐπίγραμμα, an inscription, epigram.—Gk. ἐπιγράφειν, to inscribe. — Gk. ἐπί, upon; γράφειν, to write. See Grammar.

Epilepsy. (F.—L.—Gk.) M. F. *epilepsie*, 'the falling sickness;' Cot.—L. *epilēpsia.*—Gk. ἐπιληψία, ἐπίληψις, a seizure.—Gk. ἐπιλαμβάνειν, to seize upon.—Gk. ἐπί, on; λαμβάνειν, to seize. Der. *epileptic* (Gk. ἐπιληπτικός).

Epilogue. (F.—L.—Gk.) F. *épilogue.*—L. *epilogus.*—Gk. ἐπίλογος, a concluding speech.—Gk. ἐπί, upon; λόγος, a speech.

Epiphany, Twelfth Day. (F.—L.—Gk.) O. F. *epiphanie.*—L. *epiphania.*—Gk. ἐπιφάνια, manifestation; orig. neut. pl. of ἐπιφάνιος, manifest, but used as equivalent to ἐπιφάνεια, sb.—Gk. ἐπιφαίνειν, to shew forth.—Gk. ἐπί, to, forth; φαίνειν, to shew. See Phantom.

Episcopal. (F. — L. — Gk.) O. F. *episcopal.*—L. *episcopālis*, belonging to a bishop.—L. *episcopus*, a bishop.—Gk. ἐπίσκοπος, an over-seer, bishop.—Gk. ἐπί, upon; σκοπός, one that watches. See Scope.

Episode, a story introduced into another. (Gk.) Gk. ἐπεισόδιον, orig. neut. of ἐπεισόδιος, coming in besides.—Gk. ἐπ-(ἐπί), besides; εἰσόδιος, coming in, from εἰς, in, ὁδός, a way.

Epistle, a letter. (F. — L. — Gk.) O. F. *epistle*, also *epistre.*—L. *epistola.*—Gk. ἐπιστολή, message, letter.—Gk. ἐπιστέλλειν, to send to.—Gk. ἐπί, to; στέλλειν, to send. See Apostle.

Epitaph. (F.—L.—Gk.) F. *épitaphe.*—L. *epitaphium.*—Gk. ἐπιτάφιος, upon a tomb.—Gk. ἐπί, on; τάφος, a tomb.

Epithalamium, a marriage-song. (L.—Gk.) L. *epithalamium.*—Gk. ἐπιθαλάμιον, bridal song. – Gk. ἐπί, upon, for ; θάλαμος, bride-chamber.

Epithet. (L. – Gk.) L. *epitheton*. – Gk. ἐπίθετον, an epithet; neut. of ἐπίθετος, attributed. – Gk. ἐπί, besides; θε-τός, placed, from θε-, weak grade of τίθημι, I place.

Epitome. (L. – Gk.) L. *epitomē*. – Gk. ἐπιτομή, a surface-incision, also an abridgment. – Gk. ἐπί, upon ; τέμνειν, to cut.

Epoch. (L. – Gk.) Late L. *epocha*. – Gk. ἐποχή, a stop, pause, fixed date. – Gk. ἐπ- (ἐπί), upon ; ἔχειν, to hold, check. (√SEGH.) Brugm. i. § 602.

Epode. (F. – L. – Gk.) O. F. *epode*. – L. *epōdos*. – Gk. ἐπῳδός, an epode, something sung after. – Gk. ἐπ-ί, upon, after ; ἀείδειν, to sing.

Equal. (L.) L. *æquālis*, equal. – L. *æquus*, just, exact.

  equanimity, evenness of mind. (L.) From L. *æquanimitas*, the same. – L. *æquanimis*, of even temper, kind. – L. *æqu-us*, equal ; *animus*, mind.

  equation, a statement of equality. (L.) L. acc. *æquātionem*, an equalising ; from pp. of *æquāre*, to make equal. – L. *æquus*, equal. So also *equator* < L. *æquātor*.

  equilibrium, even balancing. (L.) L. *æquilībrium*. – L. *æquilībris*, evenly balanced. – L. *æqui-*, for *æquus*, even ; *lībra*, a balance ; see Librate.

  equinox. (F. – L.) F. *équinoxe*. – L. *æquinoctium*, time of equal day and night. – L. *æqui-*, for *æquus* ; *nocti-*, decl. stem of *nox*, a night ; see Night.

  equipollent, equally potent. (F. – L.) O. F. *equipolent*. – L. *æquipollent-*, stem of *æquipollens*, of equal power. – L. *æqui-*, for *æquus* : *pollens*, pres. pt. of *pollēre*, to be strong.

  equity. (F. – L.) O. F. *equité*. – L. *æquitātem*, acc. of *æquitas*, equity. – L. *æquus*, equal.

  equivalent. (F. – L.) M. F. *equivalent*. – L. *æquiualent-*, stem of pres. pt. of *æquiualēre*, to be of equal force. – L. *æqui-*, for *æquus* : *ualēre*, to be worth ; see Value.

  equivocal. (L.) Formed from L. *æquiuoc-us*, of doubtful sense. – L. *æqui-*, *æquus* ; *uoc-*, stem of *uocāre*, to call ; see Voice. Der. *equivoc-ate*, to speak doubtfully. ¶ So also *equi-angular*, *equi-multiple*, &c.

Equerry, an officer who has charge of horses and stables. (F. – O. H. G.) Properly *equerry* means a stable, and mod. E. *equerry* stands for *squire of the equerry*. – F. *écurie*, O. F. *escurie*, a stable ; Low L. *scūria*, a stable. – O. H. G. *skūra*, *skiura* (G. *scheuer*), a shelter, stable ; allied to O. H. G. *skūr*, a shelter. Brugm. i. § 109. (√SKEU.) ¶ Altered to *equerry* by confusion with *equus*, a horse.

Equestrian ; see Equine.

Equilibrium ; see Equal.

Equine. (L.) L. *equīnus*, relating to horses. – L. *equus*, a horse. + Gk. ἵππος, (ἵκκος) ; Skt. *açva* ; Pers. *asp* ; O. Irish *ech* ; A.S. *eoh*. Brugm. i. § 116.

  equestrian. (L.) Formed from L. *equestri-*, stem of *equester*, belonging to horsemen. – L. *eques*, a horseman. – L. *equus*, a horse.

Equinox ; see Equal.

Equip, to furnish, fit out. (F. – Scand.) M. F. *equiper*, O. North F. *esquiper*, to fit out ; A. F. *eskipper*. – Icel. *skipa*, to set in order, perhaps allied to *skip*, a ship. Der. *equip-age*, *-ment*.

Equipollent, Equity ; see Equal.

Equivalent, Equivocal ; see Equal.

Era. (L.) L. *æra*, an era, fixed date. From a particular sense of *æra*, counters (for calculation), pl. of *æs*, brass, money.

Eradicate. (L.) From pp. of L. *ērādīcāre*, to root out. – L. *ē*, out ; *rādīcāre*, to root, from *rādīc-*, stem of *rādix*, root. See Radix.

Erase. (L.) L. *ērāsus*, pp. of *ērādere*, to scratch out. – L. *ē*, out ; *rādere*, to scrape.

Ere, before. (E.) M. E. *er*. A. S. *ǣr*, soon, before ; adv. prep. and conj. + Du. *eer*, O. H. G. *ēr*, G. *eher* ; Goth. *airis*, sooner, comp. of *air*, Icel. *ār*, adv., early, soon. ¶ The two last are positive, not comparative, forms. Cf. Gk. ἦρι, early.

  early, soon. (E.) M. E. *erly*. A. S. *ǣrlīce*, adv. ; from **ǣrlīc*, adj., not used. – A. S. *ǣr*, soon ; *līc*, like.

  erst, soonest. (E.) M. E. *erst*. A. S. *ǣrest*, superlative of *ǣr*, soon.

Erect, adj. (L.) L. *ērectus*, upright ; pp. of *ērigere*, to set up straight. – L. *ē*, out, up ; *regere*, to make straight, rule.

Ermine, a beast. (F. – O. H. G.) M. E. *ermine*. – O. F. *ermine* (F. *hermine*). – O. H. G. *harmīn*, ermine-fur (G.

hermelin). **–** O. H. G. *harmo*, an ermine. **+**A.S.*hearma*; Lithuan. *szarmŭ*, a weasel. ¶But Hatzfeld supports the derivation from *Armenius mūs*, an Armenian mouse; cf. *Ponticus mūs*, supposed to be an ermine.

Erode. (F.–L.) F. *éroder.* **–** L. *ērō-dere*, to eat away. **–** L. *ē*, out; *rōdere*, to gnaw. Der. *eros-ion* (from pp. *ērōs-us*).

Erotic. (Gk.) Gk. ἐρωτικός, relating to love. **–**Gk. ἐρωτι-, crude form of ἔρως, love; allied to ἔραμαι, I love.

Err, to stray. (F.–L.) M. E. *erren.* **–** O. F. *errer.* **–**L. *errāre*, to wander (for **ers-āre*).**+**G. *irren*, to stray, Goth. *airz-jan*, to make to stray. Brugm. i. § 878.

erratum, an error. (L.) L. *errā-tum*, neut. of pp. of *errāre*, to make a mistake.

erroneous, faulty. (L.) Put for L. *errōne-us*, wandering; with suffix *-ous.* **–** L. *errāre* (above).

error. (F. – L.) M. E. *errour.* **–** O. F. *errour.* **–**L. *errōrem*, acc. of *error*, a mistake. **–**L. *errāre* (above).

Errand. (E.) M. E. *erende.* A. S. *ǽrende*, a message, business.**+**O. Sax. *ārundi*, O. H. G. *ārunti*, a message; cf. Icel. *eyrendi*, *örendi*, Swed. *ärende*, Dan. *ærende*. Usually connected with A. S. *ār*, Icel. *ārr*, Goth. *airus*, a messenger; which is hardly possible.

Errant, wandering. (F.–L.) F. *er-rant*, pres. pt. of O. F. *errer*, *eirer*, to wander. **–**Late L. *iterāre*, to travel. **–**L. *iter*, a journey. ¶ It sometimes represents the pres. pt. of *errāre*, to wander. Doublet, *arrant*.

Erratum, Erroneous, Error; see Err.

Erst; see Ere.

Erubescent. (L.) L. *ērubescent-*, stem of pres. pt. of *ērubescere*, to grow red. **–**L. *ē*, out, much; *rubescere*, to grow red, inceptive form of *rubēre*, to be red. See Red.

Eructate. (L.) From pp. of L. *ēruc-tāre*, to belch out. **–**L. *ē*, out; *ructāre*, to belch; allied to *ē-rūgere*, to belch; cf. Gk. ἐρεύγεσθαι. Brugm. i. § 221.

Erudite, learned. (L.) L. *ērudītus*, pp. of *ērudīre*, to free from rudeness, to teach. **–**L. *ē*, from; *rudis*, rude.

Eruption. (L.) From L. *ēruptiōnem*, acc. of *ēruptio*, a breaking out. **–**L.*ēruptus*, pp. of *ērumpere*, to break out. **–**L. *ē*, out; *rumpere*, to break. See Rupture.

Erysipelas, a redness on the skin.

(L.–Gk.) L. *erysipelas.* **–**Gk. ἐρυσίπελας, redness on the skin. **–**Gk. ἐρυσι-, allied to ἐρυθ-ρός, red; πέλλα, skin. Cf. ἐρυσίβη, red blight on corn.

Escalade, a scaling of walls. (F.– Span.–L.) F. *escalade.* **–**Span. *escalado*, *escalada*, a scaling; from *escalar*, to scale. **–** Span. *escala*, a ladder. **–** L. *scāla*, a ladder; see Scale (3). Cf. Ital. *scalata*, an escalade; Florio also has ' *Scalada*, an escalade,' from Spanish.

Escape. (F.–L.) M. E. *escapen.* **–** O. North F.*escaper* (F. *échapper*),to escape, lit. to slip out of one's cape; Picard *écaper.* **–**L. *ex cappā*, out of one's cape; see Cape (1).

Escarpment. (F. – Ital.–Teut.) F. *escarpement*. Formed from F. *escarpe*, a scarp; with suffix *-ment* (L. *-mentum*); see Scarp.

Escheat. (F. – L.) M. E. *eschete* (also *chete*), a forfeit to the lord of the fee. **–**O. F. *eschete*, rent, that which falls to one, orig. fem. pp. of *escheoir* (F. *échoir*). **–**Late L. *excadere*, to fall to one's share. **–**L. *ex*, out; and *cadere*, to fall. Hence *cheat.*

Eschew, to shun. (F. – O. H. G.) M. E. *eschewen.* **–**O. F. *eschiver*, *eschever*, to shun. **–**O. H. G. *sciuhan*, to frighten, also to fear. **–**O. H. G. **scioh*, M. H. G. *schiech*, shy, timid. See Shy.

Escort, a guide, guard. (F.–Ital.–L.) O. F. *escorte.* **–**Ital. *scorta*, a guide; fem. of pp. of *scorgere*, to see, perceive, guide (orig. to set right). **–** L. *ex*, entirely; *corrigere*, to correct; see Correct.

Escrow, a deed delivered on condition. (F.–Teut.) A. F. *escrouwe*, M. E. *scroue*, *scrowe*; the orig. word of which *scro-ll* is the diminutive. **–**O. F. *escroe*, a slip of parchment. **–**M. Du. *schroode*, a shred, slip of paper (Kilian); cf. O. H. G. *scrōt*, a shred. See Shred and Scroll.

Escuage, a pecuniary satisfaction in lieu of feudal service. (F.–L.) O. F. *escuage* < Late L. *scūtāgium*. Formed with suffix *-age* from O. F. *escu*, a shield; because *escuage* was first paid in lieu of service in the field. **–**L. *scūtum*, a shield.

Esculent, eatable. (L.) L. *esculentus*, fit for eating. **–**L. *ēsca*, food. For **ed-sca.* **–**L. *edere*, to eat. Brugm. i. § 753.

Escutcheon, Scutcheon, a painted shield. (F. – L.) Formerly *escochon*; XV cent.; A.F. *escuchon.* **–**O. North F. *escuchon*, O. F. *escusson*, the same; answering to a Late L. acc. *scūtiōnem*, extended from L. *scūtum*, a shield.

Esophagus, gullet. (L.–Gk.) Late L. *æsophagus.* –Gk. οἰσοφάγος, the gullet, lit. conveyer of food. –Gk. οἰσο- (of doubtful origin) ; φαγ-, base of φαγεῖν, to eat.

Esoteric. (Gk.) Gk. ἐσωτερικός, inner ; hence, secret. –Gk. ἐσώτερος, inner, comp. of ἔσω, adv., within ; from ἐς = εἰς, into, prep. Opposed to *exoteric.*

Espalier, frame-work for training trees. (F.–Ital.–L.–Gk.) M.F. *espallier* ; Cot.–Ital. *spalliera*, back of a chair, support, espalier. –Ital. *spalla*, shoulder. –L. *spatula* ; see **Epaulet.**

Especial. (F.–L.) O.F. *especial.* –L. *speciālis*, belong to a special kind. –L. *speciēs*, a kind. Doublet, *special.*

Espionage; see **Espy.**

Esplanade, a level space. (F.–Ital.–L.) M.F. *esplanade*, 'a planing, levelling, evenning of ways ;' Cot. Formed from O.F. *esplaner*, to level ; the suffix being due to an imitation of Ital. *spianata*, an esplanade, a levelled way ; from *spia-nare*, to level. –L. *explānāre*, to level. –L. *ex*, out ; *plānāre*, to level, from *plānus*, flat. See **Plain.**

Espouse. (F.–L.) O.F. *espouser*, to espouse, wed. –L. *sponsāre*, to betroth. –L. *sponsus*, pp. of *spondēre*, to promise. See **Spouse, Sponsor.**

Espy, to spy, see. (F.–O.H.G.) M.E. *espyen.* –O.F. *espier.* –O.H.G. *spehōn* (G. *spähen*), to spy ; see **Species.** Der. *espi-on-age*, F. *espionnage*, from M.F. *espion*, a spy, borrowed from Ital. *spione*, a spy, from O.H.G. *spehōn*, to spy.

Esquire, a shield-bearer. (F.–L.) M.E. *squyer.* –O.F. *escuyer*, *escuier*, a squire. –Late L. *scūtārius*, a shield-bearer. –L. *scūt-um*, a shield, cover (F. *écu*). (√SKEU.) Brugm. i. § 109. Doublet, *squire.*

Essay, Assay, an attempt, trial. (F.–L.) O.F. *essai*, a trial. –L. *exagium*, a trial of weight ; cf. *exāmen*, a weighing, a swarm. –L. *ex*, out ; *ag-ere*, to drive, impel, move. (√AG.)

Essence, a quality, being. (F.–L.) F. *essence* –L. *essentia*, a being. –L. **es-sent-*, fictitious stem of pres. pt. of *esse*, to be. Der. *essenti-al* ; and see *entity.*

Essoin, an excuse for not appearing in court. (F.–L. *and* Teut.) O.F. *essoine*, M.F. *exoine*, 'an essoine, or excuse ;' Cot. –O.F. *essonier*, to excuse (Godefroy). –

O.F. *es-* (L. *ex*), away ; and Low L. *sunnia*, O.H.G. *sunne* (for **sundjā*, Braune, xiv. 9), lawful excuse. Cf. Goth. *sunjōn sik*, to excuse oneself, *ga-sunjōn*, to justify, from *sunja*, truth ; Skt. *satja-*, true. Brugm. i. § 287.

Establish. (F.–L.) M.E. *establis-sen.* –O.F. *establiss-*, base of pres. pt. of *establir*, to establish. – L. *stabilīre*, to establish. –L. *stabilis*, firm ; see **Stable** (2).

Estate. (F.–L.) O.F. *estat.* – L. *statum*, acc. of *status*, state ; see **State.**

Esteem, to value. (F.–L.) O.F. *estimer.* –L. *æstimāre*, O.L. *æstumāre*, to value. Allied to Goth. *aistan*, to regard. Brugm. ii. § 692.

estimate. (L.) From pp. of L. *æsti-māre*, to value (above).

Estop, to bar. (F.–L.) The same as **Stop.**

Estovers, supplies of various necessaries. (F.–L.) A.F. *estovers*, M.E. *stovers*, pl. of *stover* ; see **Stover.**

Estrange, to make strange. (F.–L.) O.F. *estranger*, to make strange. –O.F. *estrange*, strange. –L. *extrāneum*, acc. of *extrāneus*, foreign, on the outside. – L. *extrā*, without ; see **Extra.**

Estreat, a true copy, in law. (F.–L.) Lit. 'extract.' A.F. *estrete*, fem. of pp. of *estraire*, to extract. –L. *extracta*, fem. of pp. of *extrahere* ; see **Extract.**

Estuary, mouth of a tidal river. (L.) L. *æstuārium*, the same. –L. *æstuāre*, to surge, foam as the tide. –L. *æstus*, heat, surge, tide. Allied to **Ether.**

Etch, to engrave with acids. (Du.–G.) Du. *etsen*, to etch. –G. *ätzen*, to corrode, etch ; orig. 'to make to eat ;' causal of G. *essen*, to eat. See **Eat.**

Eternal. (F.–L.) M.E. *eternel.* – O.F *eternel.* –L. *æternālis*, eternal. –L. *æternus*, lit. lasting for an age ; for *æui-ternus.* –L. *æui-*, for *æuum*, an age. See **Age.**

Ether, pure upper air. (L.–Gk.) L. *æther.* –Gk. αἰθήρ, upper air ; from its brightness. –Gk. αἴθειν, to glow. (√AIDH.) Brugm. i. § 202.

Ethic, relating to morals. (L.–Gk.) L. *ēthicus*, moral. –Gk. ἠθικός, moral. – Gk. ἦθος, custom, moral nature ; cf. ἔθος, manner, custom. + Skt. *svadhā-*, self-will, strength, from *sva*, self, *dhā*, to place ; cf. Goth. *sidus*, G. *sitte*, custom.

Ethnic, relating to a nation. (L.–Gk.)

L. *ethnicus.* — Gk. ἐθνικός, national. — Gk. ἔθνος, a nation.

Etiolate, to blanch plants. (F. — L.) F. *étioler*; with suffix *-ate*. From a dialectal form answering to *s'éteuler*, to grow into haulm or stalk, like etiolated plants. — F. *éteule*, O. F. *esteule*, a stalk. — Late L. *stupula*, for L. *stipula*, straw. See **Stubble.**

Etiquette, ceremony. (F. — G.) F. *étiquette*, a label, ticket, also a form of introduction; cf. M. F. *etiquet* (O. F. *estiquet*), 'a little note, such as is *stuck up* on the gate of a court,' &c.; Cot. — G. *stecken,* to stick, put, set, fix; causal of G. *stechen,* to stick, pierce. See **Stick** (I). Doublet, *ticket.*

Etymon, the true source of a word. (L. — Gk.) L. *etymon.* — Gk. ἔτυμον; neut. of ἔτυμος, real, true.

etymology. (F. — L. — Gk.) F. *étymologie.* — L. *etymologia.* — Gk. ἐτυμολογία, etymology. — Gk. ἔτυμο-s, true; -λογία, account, from λέγειν, to speak.

Eu-, prefix, well. (Gk.) Gk. εὖ, well; neut. of ἐύς, good. Cf. Skt. *vasu,* wealth.

Eucalyptus, a genus of trees, including the blue gum-tree. (Gk.) Latinised from Gk. εὖ, well; καλυπτός, covered, surrounded. The reference is to the hood protecting the stamens.

Eucharist, the Lord's Supper, lit. thanksgiving. (L. — Gk.) L. *eucharistia.* — Gk. εὐχαριστία, a giving of thanks. — Gk. εὖ, well; χαρίζομαι, I show favour, from χάρις, favour. Cf. **Yearn.**

Eulogy, praise. (L. — Gk.) From L. *eulogium.* — Gk. εὐλογία, praise, lit. good speaking; with suffix suggested by L. *elogium,* an inscription. — Gk. εὖ, well; λέγειν, to speak.

Eunuch, one who is castrated. (L. — Gk.) L. *eunūchus.* — Gk. εὐνοῦχος, a chamberlain; one who had charge of sleeping apartments. — Gk. εὐνή, a couch; ἔχειν, to keep, have in charge.

Euphemism, a softened expression. (Gk.) Gk. εὐφημισμός, the same as εὐφημία, the use of words of good omen. — Gk. εὖ, well; φημί, I speak. (√BHĀ.)

Euphony. (Gk.) Gk. εὐφωνία, a pleasing sound. — Gk. εὔφωνος, sweet-voiced. — Gk. εὖ, well; φωνή, voice. (√BHĀ.)

Euphrasy, the plant eye-bright. (Gk.) Supposed to be beneficial to the eyes; lit. 'delight.' — Gk. εὐφρασία, delight. — Gk. εὐφραίνειν, to delight, cheer; cf. εὔφρων, cheerful. Allied to Gk. εὖ, well; φρεν-, stem of φρήν, midriff, heart, mind.

Euphuism, affectation in speaking. (Gk.) So named from a book *Euphues,* by J. Lyly (1579). — Gk. εὐφυής, well-grown, excellent. — Gk. εὖ, well; φυή, growth, from φύομαι, I grow. (√BHEU.)

Euroclydon, a tempestuous wind. (Gk.) Gk. εὐροκλύδων, supposed to mean 'a storm from the east.' — Gk. εὖρο-s, S.E. wind; κλύδων, surge, from κλύζειν, to surge, dash as waves. ¶ Only in Acts xxvii. 14; where some read εὐρακύλων, i. e. *Eur-aquilo*; from L. *Eur-us,* E. wind, and *Aquilo,* N. wind.

Euthanasia, easy death. (Gk.) Gk. εὐθανασία, easy death; cf. εὐθάνατος, dying well. — Gk. εὖ, well; θανεῖν, to die.

Evacuate. (L.) From pp. of L. *ēuacuāre,* to empty. — L. *ē,* out; *uacuus,* empty.

Evade, to shun. (F. — L.) F. *évader.* — L. *ēuādere* (pp. *ēuāsus*), to escape. — L. *ē,* away; *uādere,* to go. Der. *evas-ion* (from the pp.).

Evanescent. (L.) From stem of pres. pt. of L. *ēuānescere,* to vanish away. — L. *ē,* away; *uānescere,* to vanish, from *uānus,* empty, vain.

Evangelist, writer of a gospel. (F. — L. — Gk.) O. F. *evangeliste.* — L. *euangelista.* — Gk. εὐαγγελιστής. — Gk. εὐαγγελίζομαι, I bring good news. — Gk. εὖ, well; ἀγγελία, tidings, from ἄγγελος, a messenger; see **Angel.**

Evaporate. (L.) From pp. of L. *ēuaporāre,* to pass off in vapour. — L. *ē,* out; *uapor,* vapour.

Evasion; see **Evade.**

Eve, Even, the latter part of the day. (E.) *Eve* is short for *even.* (For *evening,* see below.) M. E. *eue, euen.* A. S. *ǽfen, ēfen.* + O. Sax. *āband,* Du. *avond,* G. *abend.* Of doubtful origin. Der. *even-tide,* A. S. *ǽfentíd.* Brugm. i. § 980.

evening, even. (E.) M. E. *euening.* A. S. *ǽfnung*; formed from *ǽfnian,* to grow towards evening, with suffix *-ung*; from *ǽfen,* even (above).

Even, level. (E.) M. E *euen* (*even*). A. S. *efen, efn.* + Du. *even,* Icel. *jafn,* Dan. *jævn,* Swed. *jämn,* Goth. *ibns,* G. *eben.*

Event, result. (L.) L. *ēuentus, ēuentum,* sb. — L. *ēuentus,* pp. of *ēuenīre,* to come out, result. — L. *ē,* out; *uenīre,* to come, allied to **Come.**

Ever. (E.) M. E. *euer* (*ever*). A. S. *æfre*, ever. Related to A.S. *ā*, Goth. *aiw*, ever. Der. *ever-lasting, ever-more.*

every, each one. (E.) M. E. *eueri, euerich.*—A. S. *æfre,* ever; and *ælc,* each. *Ever-y* = *ever-each* ; see **Each.**

everywhere. (E.) M. E. *euerihwar.*—A. S. *æfre,* ever; *gehwǣr,* where. The word really stands for *ever-ywhere,* i. e. ever-where; *y-* is a prefix (=*ge-*).

Evict. (L.) From L. *ēuict-us,* pp. of *ēuincere,* to evince; also, to expel. See **Evince.**

Evident. (F.—L.) O. F. *evident.*— L. *ēuident-,* stem of *ēuidens,* visible, pres. pt. of *ēuidēre,* to see clearly. —L. *ē,* out, clearly; *uidēre,* to see.

Evil. (E.) M. E. *euel.* A. S. *yfel,* adj. and sb.+Du. *euvel,* G. *übel,* Goth. *ubils.* Teut. type *ubiloz.* Prob. allied to *over* (G. *über*), as meaning ' excessive.'

Evince. (L.) L. *ēuincere,* to conquer, to prove beyond doubt.—L. *ē,* out, extremely; *uincere,* to conquer.

Eviscerate, to gut. (L.) From pp. of L. *ēuiscerāre,* to gut. — L. *ē,* out; *uiscera,* entrails.

Evoke. (F.—L.) F. *évoquer.*—L. *ēuocāre,* to call forth.—L. *ē,* forth; *uocāre,* to call. See **Vocal.**

Evolve. (L.) L. *ēuoluere,* to unroll, disclose.—L. *ē,* out; *uoluere,* to roll. Der. *evolut-ion,* from pp. *ēuolūtus.*

Ewe. (E.) M. E. *ewe.* A.S. *ewe,* Laws of Ine, 55 ; *eowu,* a female sheep.+ Du. *ooi,* Icel. *ær,* M. H. G. *ouwe* ; Lithuan. *avis,* a sheep, Russ. *ovtsa,* L. *ouis,* Gk. *öïs,* O. Irish *oi* ; Skt. *avi-,* a sheep. Cf. Goth. *awi-str,* a sheep-fold.

Ewer. (F.—L.) M. E. *ewer.*—A. F. *ewer, *eweire* ; spelt *ewer,* Royal Wills, pp. 24, 27.—L. *aquārium,* a vessel for water; cf. A. F. *ewe,* water; mod. F. *eau.* —L. *aqua,* water.

Ex-, E-, *prefix.* (L.) L. *ex, ē,* out. + Gk. *ἐκ, ἐξ,* out; Russ. *iz',* Lith. *isz.*

Exacerbate, to embitter. (L.) From pp. of *exacerbāre,* to irritate.—L. *ex,* very; *acerbus,* bitter; see **Acerbity.**

Exact (1), precise. (L.) From L. *ex-actus,* pp. of *exigere,* to drive out, weigh out.—L. *ex,* out; and *agere,* to drive.

exact (2), to demand. (F.—L.) From M. F. *exacter;* Cot. (obsolete).—Late L. *exactāre.*—L. *ex,* out; and *actus,* pp. of *agere* (above).

Exaggerate. (L.) From pp. of L.

exaggerāre, to heap up, amplify.—L. *ex,* very; *agger,* a heap, from *ag-*=*ad,* to; *gerere,* to bring.

Exalt. (F.—L.) F. *exalter.*—L. *exaltāre,* to lift out, exalt.—L. *ex,* out; *altus,* high.

Examine, to test. (F.—L.) F. *examiner.*—L. *exāmināre,* to weigh carefully. — L. *exāmin-,* stem of *exāmen,* the tongue of a balance, for *exāgmen;* cf. *exigere,* to weigh out.—L. *ex,* out; *agere,* to drive, move. Brugm. i. § 768.

Example. (F.—L.) O. F. *example;* F. *exemple.*—L. *exemplum,* a sample.—L. *exim-ere,* to take out; with suffix *-lum;* for the inserted *p* cf. the pp. *exem-p-tus.*— L. *ex,* out; *emere,* to take, procure.

Exasperate, to provoke. (L.) From the pp. of *exasperāre,* to roughen, provoke. —L. *ex,* very; *asper,* rough.

Excavation. (F.—L.) F. *excavation.*—L. acc. *excauātiōnem,* a hollowing out.—L. *excauātus,* pp. of *excauāre,* to hollow out.—L. *ex,* out; *cauāre,* to hollow, from *cauus,* hollow.

Exceed. (F.—L.) O. F. *exceder.*—L. *excēdere,* lit. to go out. — L. *ex,* out; *cēdere,* to go.

Excel, to surpass. (F.—L.) O. F. *exceller.* — L. *excellere,* to rise up, surpass. — L. *ex,* out; *cellere,* to rise, only in comp. *ante-, ex-, præ-cellere,* and in *cel-sus,* high, orig. ' raised.' Cf. Lithuan. *kélti,* to raise ; see **Hill.** Brugm. i. § 633.

Except, to exclude. (F.—L.) F. *excepter,* to except; Cot. — L. *exceptāre,* frequent. of *excipere,* to take out.—L. *ex,* out; *capere,* to take. Der. *except,* prep.; *except-ion.*

Excerpt, a selected passage. (L.) L. *excerptum,* an extract; neut. of pp. of *excerpere,* to select.—L. *ex,* out; *carpere,* to cull. See **Harvest.**

Excess. (F.—L.) O. F. *exces.*—L. acc. *excessum,* lit. a going out or beyond. —L. *excess-,* as in *excessus,* pp. of *excēdere;* see **Exceed.**

Exchange. (F.—L.) O. F. *eschange,* sb. ; *eschangier,* vb., to exchange.—O. F. *es-* (< L. *ex*) ; and O. F. *change,* sb., *changier,* to change. See **Change.**

Exchequer, a court of revenue. (F.—Pers.) M. E. *eschekere.*—O. F. *eschequier,* a chess-board; hence, a checkered cloth on which accounts were reckoned by means of counters (Low L. *scaccārium*).—O. F. *eschec,* check; see **Check.**

Excise, a duty, tax. (Du.—F.—L.) A misspelling of M. Du. *aksiis* or *aksys*, excise. (Cf. G. *accise*, excise.) — O. F. *acceis*, a tax, given in the N. E. D. ; allied to Low L. *accisia* (Ducange) ; also spelt *exsisa* (id.). — Late L. *accensus*, a payment, rent ; cf. *accensāre*, to tax.—L. *ac-* (for *ad*), to ; and *census*, a tax. ¶ For the sound-change, cf. Du. *spijs*, food, from Late L. *spensa* (for *dispensa*), a larder, a spence.

Excision. (F.—L.) F. *excision*, 'a destroying ;' Cot.—L. acc. *excisiōnem*, a cutting out, a destroying. —L. *excisus*, pp. of *excīdere*, to cut out.—L. *ex*, out ; and *cædere*, to cut.

Exclaim. (F.—L.) F. *exclamer*.—L. *exclāmāre*, to call out.—L. *ex*, out ; *clā-māre*, to call. See **Claim.**

Exclude. (L.) L. *exclūdere*, to shut out.—L. *ex*, out ; *claudere*, to shut. See **Clause.**

Excommunicate. (L.) From pp. of L. *excommūnicāre*, to put out of the community.—L. *ex*, out of ; *commūnis*, common. See **Communicate.**

Excoriate. (L.) From pp. of L. *ex-coriāre*, to strip off skin. — L. *ex*, off ; *corium*, hide, skin. See **Cuirass.**

Excrement (1). (L.) L. *excrēmen-tum*, refuse, ordure.—L. *excrētus*, pp. of *excernere*, to separate, sift out.—L. *ex*, out ; *cernere*, to sift.

Excrement (2), out-growth. (L.) In Shak. From L. *excrēmentum*.—L. *excrē-tus*, pp. of *excrescere*, to grow out (below).

excrescence. (F.—L.) O. F. *ex-crescence*.—L. *excrescentia*, an outgrowth. —L. *excrescent-*, stem of pres. pt. of *ex-crescere*, to grow out.—L. *ex*, out ; *crescere*, to grow. See **Crescent.**

Excretion. (F.—L.) M. F. *excretion* ; formed (with suffix *-ion*) from L. *excrētus*, pp. of *excernere* ; see **Excrement** (1).

Excruciate, to torture. (L.) From pp. of L. *excruciāre*, to torment greatly. — L. *ex*, very ; *cruciāre*, to torture on a gibbet, from *cruci-*, decl. stem of *crux*, a cross.

Exculpate. (L.) From pp. of Late L. *exculpāre*, to clear of blame.—L. *ex*, out of ; *culpa*, blame.

Excursion. (L.) L. *excursiōnem*, acc. of *excursio*, a running out.—L. *ex-cursus*, pp. of *excurrere*, to run out.—L. *ex*, out ; *currere*, to run.

Excuse. (F. — L.) F. *excuser*.—L. *excūsāre*, to release from a charge. —L. *ex*, out ; and *causa*, a charge, a cause.

Execrate. (L.) From pp. of L. *exe-crārī*, for *exsecrārī*, to curse greatly. —L. *ex*, greatly ; *sacrāre*, to consecrate, also to declare accursed. — L. *sacr-um*, neut. of *sacer*, sacred ; also, accursed.

Execute. (F.—L.) O. F. *executer*.— L. *execūtus*, *exsecūtus*, pp. of *exsequī*, to follow out, pursue, perform.—L. *ex*, out ; *sequī*, to follow.

Exegesis, exposition. (Gk.) Gk. ἐξή-γησις, interpretation. —Gk. ἐξηγεῖσθαι, to explain.—Gk. ἐξ, out ; ἡγεῖσθαι, to guide, perhaps allied to **Seek.** Brugm. i. § 187.

Exemplar. (F.—L.) M.E. *exem-plaire*.—O. F. *exemplaire*.—L. *exemplā-rium*, late form of *exemplar*, a copy (to which the mod. E. word is now conformed). —L. *exemplāris*, adj., serving as a copy. —L. *exemplum* ; see **Example.** Der. *ex-emplar-y*, from L. *exemplāris*.

exemplify, to shew by example. (F. —L.) A coined word ; as if from F. **ex-emplifier*. — Late L. *exemplificāre*, pro-perly 'to copy out.'—L. *exempli-*, for *ex-emplum*, a copy ; *fic-*, for *facere*, to make.

Exempt, freed. (F.—L.) O. F. *ex-empt* ; whence *exempter*, to exempt, free. —L. *exemptus*, pp. of *eximere*, to take out, deliver, free.—L. *ex*, out ; *emere*, to take. Cf. Lith. *im-ti*, to take.

Exequies. (F.—L.) O. F. *exeques*, *exequies*, 'funerals ;' Cot. —L. *exsequiās*, acc. pl. of *exsequiæ*, funeral obsequies, lit. 'followings.'—L. *exsequī*, to follow out. —L. *ex*, out ; *sequī*, to follow.

Exercise, sb. (F.—L.) M.E. *exer-cise*.—O. F. *exercice*.—L. *exercitium*, exer-cise.—L. *exercitus*, pp. of *exercēre*, to drive out of an enclosure, drive on, set at work.—L. *ex*, out ; *arcēre*, to enclose ; see **Ark.** Der. *exercise*, vb.

Exergue, the small space left beneath the base-line of a subject engraved on a coin. (F.—Gk.) The final *-ue* is not pronounced ; cf. *prologue*, &c.—F. *exergue*, so called because lying 'out of the work.' —Gk. ἐξ, out of ; ἔργον, work.

Exert. (L.) Lit. to 'put forth.' L. *exertus*, better spelt *exsertus*, thrust forth ; pp. of *exserere*, to thrust out.—L. *ex*, out ; *serere*, to join, to put.

Exfoliate. (L.) From pp. of L. *ex-foliāre*, to strip off leaves ; from *ex*, off, and *folium*, a leaf.

Exhale. (F.—L.) F. *exhaler*.—L. *ex-*

hălăre, to breathe out. – L. *ex*, out; *hălăre*, to breathe.

Exhaust. (L.) From L. *exhaustus*, pp. of *exhaurīre*, to draw out, drink up. – L. *ex*, out; *haurīre*, to draw water.

Exhibit, to show. (L.) From L. *exhibit-us*, pp. of *exhibēre*, to hold forth. – L. *ex*, out; *habēre*, to have.

Exhilarate, to cheer. (L. – Gk.; *with* L. *prefix*.) From pp. of L. *exhilarāre*, to gladden greatly. – L. *ex*, very; *hilaris*, *hilarus*, glad, cheerful, from Gk. *ἱλαρός*, cheerful. See Hilarity.

Exhort. (F. – L.) O. F. *ex(h)orter*. – L. *exhortārī*, to encourage greatly. – L. *ex*, out, very; *hortārī*, to encourage; see Hortatory.

Exhume, to disinter. (F. – L.) F. *exhumer*. – Late L. *exhumāre*. – L. *ex*, out of; *humus*, the ground.

Exigent, exacting. (L.) From the stem of pres. pt. of *exigere*, to exact. – L. *ex*; and *agere*, to drive.

Exile, banishment. (F. – L.) O. F. *essil*; later *exil*, 'an exile, banishment;' Cot. – L. *exilium*, better *exsilium*, banishment; cf. *exsul*, a banished man. – L. *ex*, out of; and (perhaps) *sed-ēre*, to sit, abide. Cf. Consul. Der. *exile*, verb; hence, *exile*, sb. (= one who is *exiled*).

Exist, to continue to be. (L.) L. *existere*, better *exsistere*, to stand forth, arise, be. – L. *ex*, out; *sistere*, to set, stand, from *stāre*, to stand.

Exit. (L.) L. *exit*, i. e. 'he goes out,' used as a stage direction; 3rd pers. s. pres. of *exīre*, to go out. – L. *ex*, out; *īre*, to go. ¶ *Exit*, departure, is from L. *exitus*, sb.

Exodus, departure. (L. – Gk.) L. *exodus*. – Gk. *ἔξοδος*, a going out. – Gk. *ἐξ*, out; *ὁδός*, a way, a march. (√SED.)

Exogen, a plant that increases outwardly. (F. – Gk.) F. *exogène* (1813). From Gk. *ἐξ-ω*, outside, from *ἐξ*, out; and *γεν-*, base of *γίγνεσθαι*, to be born.

Exonerate. (L.) From pp. of L. *exonerāre*, to free from a burden. – L. *ex*, away; *onerāre*, to burden, from *oner-* (for *ones-*), stem of *onus*, a burden.

Exorbitant, extravagant. (F. – L.) F. *exorbitant*. – L. *exorbitant-*, stem of pres. pt. of *exorbitāre*, to fly out of a track. – L. *ex*, out; *orbita*, a track of a wheel, from *orbi-*, stem of *orbis*, a wheel, with suffix *-ta*.

Exorcise. (L. – Gk.) Late L. *exor-*

cizāre. – Gk. *ἐξορκίζειν*, to drive away by adjuration. – Gk. *ἐξ*, away; *ὁρκίζειν*, to adjure, from *ὅρκος*, an oath.

Exordium. (L.) L. *exordium*, a beginning. – L. *exordīrī*, to begin, to weave. – L. *ex*; and *ordīrī*, to begin, weave.

Exoteric, external. (Gk.) Gk. *ἐξωτερικός*, external. – Gk. *ἐξωτέρω*, more outward, comp. of adv. *ἐξω*, outward, from *ἐξ*, out.

exotic, foreign. (L. – Gk.) L. *exōticus*. – Gk. *ἐξωτικός*, outward, foreign. – Gk. *ἐξω*, adv., outward, from *ἐξ*, out.

Expand. (L.) L. *expandere* (pp. *expansus*), to spread out. – L. *ex*, out; *pandere*, to spread out; causal from *patēre*, to lie open. Cf. Gk. *πίτνημι*, I spread out. Der. *expanse*, from the pp.

Expatiate. (L.) From pp. of L. *expatiārī*, better *exspatiārī*, to wander. – L. *ex*, out; *spatiārī*, to roam, from *spatium*, space.

Expatriate. (L.) From pp. of Late L. *expatriāre*, to banish. – L. *ex*, out of; *patria*, native country, from *pater*, father.

Expect. (L.) L. *expectāre*, better *exspectāre*, to look for anxiously. – L. *ex*, thoroughly; *spectāre*, to look, frequentative of *specere*, to see.

Expectorate. (L.) From pp. of L. *expectorāre*, to expel from the breast. – L. *ex*, out of; *pector-* (for **pectos*), stem of *pectus*, the breast.

Expedite. (L.) From pp. of L. *expedīre*, to extricate the foot, release, get ready. – L. *ex*, out; *ped-*, stem of *pēs*, foot. Der. *expedient*, from the stem of the pres. pt.

Expel. (L.) L. *expellere*, to drive out. – L. *ex*, out; *pellere*, to drive. Der. *expulsion*, O. F. *expulsion*, L. acc. *expulsiōnem*, from pp. *expuls-us*.

Expend, to spend. (L.) L. *expendere*, to weigh out, lay out. – L. *ex*, out; *pendere*, to weigh. Der. *expense*, from A. F. *expense*, L. *expensa*, money spent, fem. of pp. *expensus*; *expendit-ure*, from Late L. *expenditus*, a mistaken form of the pp. *expensus*.

Experience, knowledge due to trial. (F. – L.) O. F. *experience*. – L. *experientia*, a proof, trial. – L. *experient-*, stem of pres. pt. of *experīrī*, to make a thorough trial of (below). Der. *experi-ment*, M. F. *experiment*, L. *experīmentum*, a trial.

expert, experienced. (F. – L.) O. F. *expert*. – L. *expertus*, pp. of *experīrī*, to make full trial of. –L. *ex*, thoroughly; and **perīrī*, an obs. vb. of which the pp. *perītus* is common. See **Peril**.

Expiate. (L.) From pp. of L. *expiāre*, to atone for fully. –L. *ex*, fully; *piāre*, to propitiate, from *pius*, devout.

Expire. (F.–L.) O.F. *expirer*. –L. *expīrāre*, *exspīrāre*, to breathe out, die. – L. *ex*, out; *spīrāre*, to breathe.

Explain. (F.–L.) M.F. *explaner*, Cot. – L. *explānāre*, to make plain. – L. *ex*, thoroughly; *plānāre*, to make plain, lit. to flatten, from *plānus*, flat. See **Plain**.

Expletive. (L.) L. *explētīuus*, filling up. –L. *explētus*, pp. of *explēre*, to fill up. – L. *ex*, fully; *plēre*, to fill. See **Plenary**.

Explicate, to explain. (L.) From pp. of L. *explicāre*, to unfold, explain. – L. *ex*, out; *plicāre*, to fold.

explicit. (L.) L. *explicitus*, old pp. of *explicāre*, to unfold, make plain (above). Cf. F. *explicite*.

Explode, to drive away noisily, burst. (F.–L.) M.F. *exploder*, 'to explode, publicly to disgrace or drive out;' Cot. – L. *explōdere* (pp. *explōsus*), to drive off the stage by noise (the old sense in E.). –L. *ex*, away; *plōdere*, *plaudere*, to clap hands. Der. *explos-ive*, *-ion*, from the pp.

Exploit. (F.–L.) M.E. *esploit*, success, Gower, C. A. ii. 258. –O.F. *esploit*, revenue, profit; later, an exploit, act. – L. *explicitum*, a thing settled, ended, or displayed; neut. of *explicitus*; see **explicit**. Cf. Late L. *explicta*, revenue.

Explore. (F.–L.) F. *explorer*. –L. *explōrāre*, to search out, lit. to make to flow out. – L. *ex*, out; *plōrāre*, to make to flow. Cf. *de-plore*, *im-plore*. Brugm. i. § 154.

Exponent. (L.) L. *exponent-*, stem of pres. pt. of *expōnere*, to expound, indicate. – L. *ex*, out; *pōnere*, to put.

Export. (L.) L. *exportāre*, to carry away. – L. *ex*, away; *portāre*, to carry.

Expose. (F.–L. *and* Gk.) O.F. *exposer*, to lay out. –O.F. *ex*- (L. *ex*), out; F. *poser*, to place, lay. See **Pose** (1).

Exposition. (F.–L.) F. *exposition*. –L. acc. *expositiōnem*. –L. *expositus*, pp. of *expōnere*, to set forth, expound. See **Expound**.

Expostulate. (L.) From pp. of L. *expostulāre*, to demand earnestly. – L. *ex*, fully; *postulāre*, to ask.

Expound. (L.) The *d* is excrescent,

but was suggested by the form of the O.F. infinitive. M.E. *expounen*. – O.F. *espondre*, to explain. –L. *expōnere*, to set forth, explain. –L. *ex*, out; *pōnere*, to put. See **Exposition**.

Express, adj., exactly stated. (F.–L.) O.F. *expres*. –L. *expressus*, distinct; pp. of *exprimere*, to press out. –L. *ex*, out; *premere*, to press; see **Press**.

Expulsion; see **Expel**.

Expunge. (L.) L. *expungere*, to prick out, blot out. [In MSS., *expunction* of a word is denoted by *dots under it*.] –L. *ex*, out; *pungere*, to prick. Der. *expunct-ion*, from the pp. *expunctus*.

Expurgate. (L.) From pp. of L. *expurgāre*, to purify thoroughly. –L. *ex*, thoroughly; *purgāre*, to purge, purify; see **Purge**.

Exquisite, sought out, excellent. (L.) L. *exquīsītus*, pp. of *exquīrere*, to seek out. – L. *ex*, out; *quærere*, to seek.

Exsequies; see **Exequies**.

Extant, existing. (L.) Late L. *extant-*, stem of *extans*, for *exstans*, pres. pt. of *exstāre*, to stand forth, exist. – L. *ex*, out; *stāre*, to stand.

Extasy; see **Ecstasy**.

Extempore. (L.) From L. *ex tempore*, at the moment. – L. *ex*, from, out of; *tempore*, abl. of *tempus*, time.

Extend. (L.) M. E. *extenden*. –L. *extendere*, to stretch out; pp. *extentus*, *extensus*. – L. *ex*, out; *tendere*, to stretch. Der. *extens-ion*, *-ive* (from the pp.).

extent. (F.–L.) O.F. *extente*, commonly *estente*, extent. –Late L. *extenta*, fem. of *extentus*, pp. of *extendere* (above).

Extenuate. (L.) From pp. of L. *extenuāre*, to thin, reduce, palliate. –L. *ex*, out, very; *tenu-is*, thin. See **Thin**.

Exterior, outward. (F.–L.) Formerly *exteriour*. – M.F. *exterieur*. –L. *exteriōrem*, acc. of *exterior*, outward, comparative of *exterus* or *exter*, outward. –L. *ex*, out; with compar. suffix *-tero-*.

Exterminate. (L.) From pp. of L. *extermināre*, to put or drive beyond bounds. –L. *ex*, out; *terminus*, boundary.

External, outward. (L.) From L. *extern-us*, outward, extended form from *exterus*, outward. See **Exterior**.

Extinguish. (L.) Coined, with suffix *-ish*, from L. *extinguere*, better *exstinguere* (pp. *extinctus*, *exstinctus*), to quench. – L. *ex*, out; **stinguere*, to prick, also to quench. **Der.** *extinct* (from pp. *extinctus*). Cf. **Distinguish.**

Extirpate. (L.) From pp. of L. *extirpāre*, to root out, better spelt *exstirpāre*, to pluck up by the stem. ─ L. *ex*, out; *stirp-s, stirp-es*, the stem of a tree.

Extol. (L.) L. *extollere*, to lift or raise up. ─ L. *ex*, out, up; *tollere*, to lift.

Extort. (L.) L. *extort-us*, pp. of *extorquēre*, to twist out, wring out. ─ L. *ex*, out; *torquēre*, to twist.

Extra. (L.) L. *extrā*, beyond, beyond what is necessary; O. L. *extrād*, allied to L. *exter*; see **Exterior.**

extraneous. (L.) L. *extrāne-us*, external, with suffix *-ous*; extended from *extrā* (above). Cf. **Strange.**

Extract, vb. (L.) L. *extract-us*, pp. of *extrahere*, to draw out. ─ L. *ex*, out; *trahere*, to draw.

Extraordinary. (L.) L. *extrā-ordinārius*, beyond what is ordinary, rare. ─ L. *extrā*, beyond; *ordinārius*, ordinary. See **Ordinary.**

Extravagant. (F. ─ L.) F. *extravagant*. ─ Late L. *extrāvagant-*, stem of *extrāvagans*, extravagant, lit. wandering beyond. ─ L. *extrā*, beyond; *uagans*, pres. pt. of *uagārī*, to wander.

Extravasate, to force (blood) out of its (proper) vessel. (L.) Coined from *extrā*, beyond; *uās*, a vessel; with suffix *-ate.*

Extreme. (F. ─ L.) O. F. *extreme*. ─ L. *extrēmus*, superl. of *exterus*, outward; see **Exterior.**

Extricate. (L.) From pp. of L. *extrīcāre*, to disentangle. ─ L. *ex*, out of; *trīcæ*, impediments, perplexities.

Extrinsic, external. (F. ─ L.) It should rather be *extrinsec*. ─ O. F. *extrinseque*, outward. ─ Late L. acc. *extrinsecum*, auj.; allied to L. *extrinsecus*, adv., from without. ─ L. *extrin* (= *extrim*), adverbial form from *exter*, outward; and *secus*, beside; so that *extrin-secus* = on the outside; cf. *interim*. *Secus* is allied to *secundum*, according to, from *sequī*, to follow; see **Sequence.**

Extrude. (L.) L. *extrūdere*, to thrust out. ─ L. *ex*, out; *trūdere*, to thrust. Cf. **Intrude.**

Exuberant. (L.) From stem of pres. pt. of L. *exūberāre*, to be fruitful or luxuriant. ─ L. *ex*, very; and *ūberāre*, to be fruitful, from *ūber*, fertile, allied to *ūber*, an udder, fertility; see **Udder.**

Exude. (L.) From L. *exūdāre*, better *exsūdāre*, to sweat out, distil. ─ L. *ex*, out; *sūdāre*, to sweat. See **Sweat.**

Exult, to leap for joy. (F. ─ L.) F. *exulter*. ─ L. *exultāre*, better spelt *exsultāre*, to leap up, exult. ─ L. *exsultus*, pp. of *exsilere*, to leap out. ─ L. *ex*, out; *salīre*, to leap. See **Salient.**

Exuviæ, cast skins of animals. (L.) L. *exuuiæ*, things stripped off. ─ L. *exuere*, to strip off. Cf. *induuiæ*, clothes.

Eyas, a nestling. (F. ─ L.) For *nias*; by substituting *an eyas* for *a nias*. ─ F. *niais*, a nestling; Cot. He also gives *niard*, whence *faulcon niard*, 'a nias faulcon.' Cp. Ital. *nidiace*, or *nidaso falcone*, 'an eyase-hawk, a young hawk taken out of her nest;' Torriano. Formed as if from Late L. **nīdācem*, acc. of **nīdax*, adj. from L. *nīdus*, a nest. See **Nest.**

Eye. (E.) M. E. *eye, eighe*; pl. *eyes, eyen* (whence *eyne*). O. Merc. *ēge*; A. S. *ēage*, pl. *ēagan.*+Du. *oog*, Icel. *auga*, Dan. *oie*, Swed. *öga*, Goth. *augō*, G. *auge*. Perhaps allied to Russ. *oko*, L. *oculus* (dimin. of **ocus*); Gk. ὄσσε (dual); Lith. *akis*, Skt. *akshi*. Brugm. i. § 681. **Der.** *dais-y*, q. v.; *window*, q. v.

Eyelet-hole. (F. ─ L.; *and* E.) *Eyelet* is for M. E. *oilet*, from M. F. *oeillet*, 'a little eye, an oilet hole,' Cot.; dimin. of O. F. *oeil*, from L. *oculum*, acc. of *oculus*, eye.

Eyot, a little island. (E.) Also spelt *ait, eyet, eyght*. Late A. S. *ȳget* (Kemble, Cod. Dipl. v. 17, l. 30); for A. S. *īgoð, īgeoð*, a dimin. from *īg, īeg*, an island; see **Island.**

Eyre, a circuit. (F. ─ L.) M. E. *eire*, circuit, esp. of a judge. ─ O. F. *eire*, journey, way. ─ O. F. *eirer*, to journey, wander about. ─ Late L. *iterāre*, to journey (for L. *itinerāre*); from L. *iter*, a journey. See **Errant.**

Eyry, a nest; see **Aery.**

F.

Fable, a story. (F. ─ L.) F. *fable*. ─ L. *fābula*, a narrative. ─ L. *fā-ri*, to speak, tell. See **Fate.**

Fabric. (F. ─ L.) F. *fabrique*. ─ L. *fabrica*, workshop, fabric. ─ L. *fabri-*, for *faber*, a workman. From L. base **fab-*, to be skilful; cf. Lith. *dab-inù*, I adorn, clean; Goth. *ga-dab-ith*, it is fit; Russ. *dob-ruii*, good. See **Deft**. **Der**. *fabricate*, from pp. of L. *fabricārī*, to construct; from *fabrica* (above). Brugm. i. § 563.

Façade, face of a building. (F. − Ital. − L.) M. F. *facade* (Cot.). − Ital. *facciata*, face of a building. − Ital. *faccia*, face. − Folk-L. *facia*, for L. *faciēs* (below).

face. (F. − L.) F. *face*. − Folk-L. *facia*, for L. *faciēs*, the face, appearance.

Facetious. (F. − L.) F. *facétieux* (Cot.). − M. F. *facetie*, 'witty mirth,' id. − L. *facētia*, wit; common in pl. − L. *facētus*, witty, courteous; orig. 'fine.'

Facile, easy to do. (F. − L.) F. *facile*. − L. *facilis*, i. e. do-able. − L. *facere*, to do. **Der**. *facility*; *faculty*.

fac-simile. (L.) For *fac simile*, make thou like. − L. *fac*, imp. s. of *facere*, to make; *simile*, neut. of *similis*, like; see **Similar**. ¶ We also find *factum simile*, i. e. made like.

fact, a deed, reality. (L.) L. *factum*, a deed; orig. neut. of *factus*, pp. of *facere*, to make, do.

faction. (F. − L.) F. *faction*, a sect. − L. *factiōnem*, acc. of *factio*, a doing, taking part, faction. − L. *factus*, pp. of *facere*, to do.

factitious. (L.) L. *factiti-us*, artificial; with suffix *-ous*. − L. *factus*, pp. of *facere*, to make.

factotum. (L.) A general agent. − L. *fac(ere) tōtum*, to do everything.

faculty, facility to act. (F. − L.) M. E. *facultee*. − F. *faculté*. − L. *facultātem*, acc. of *facultas* (=*facilitas*), facility. − L. *facilis*, easy; see **Facile**.

Fad, a folly. (F. − Prov. − L.) Apparently shortened from F. *fadaise*, fiddle-faddle; cf. '*fadeses*, follies, toyes, fooleries;' Cot. − Prov. *fadeza*, folly (Hatzfeld). − Prov. *fat* (Gascon *fad*), foolish. − L. *fatuus*, foolish.

Fade, vb. (F. − L.) O. F. *fader*; from F. *fade*, adj., tasteless, weak, faint. − L. *uapidum*, acc. of *uapidus*, vapid. See **Vapid**. ¶ *Vade*, for *fade*, is from M. Du. *vadden*; from O. F. *fader*.

Fadge, to fit, suit, be content with, succeed. (E.) Formed, in some unexplained way, from the Teut. base *fag-*, to suit, whence also O. Sax. *fōgian*, A. S. *fēgan*, to join, suit, M. E. *fēʒen*, to adapt, fit, G. *fügen*, Du. *voegen* (see Kluge and Franck). Cf. Goth. *fulla-fah-jan*, to satisfy, O. H. G. *gifag*, content, Du. *vage-*

fuur, cleansing fire, purgatory. See **Fair**.

Fæces. (L.) L. *fæcēs*, dregs; pl. of *fæx*, the same. **Der**. *fec-ulent*, L. *fæc-ulentus*, adj. from *fæx*.

Fag, to drudge. (E.?) 'To *fag*, deficere;' Levins (1570). The orig. sense was 'to droop.' Perhaps a corruption of *flag*; see **Flag** (1); and see below.

Fag-end, remnant. (E.?) In Massinger, Virg. Mart. ii. 3. Perhaps for *flag-end* = loose end; see above. Cf. 'the *flagg* or the *fagg federis*' (feathers); Book of St. Albans, fol. B 1 *a*.

Faggot, **Fagot**. (F. − Ital. − L.?) F. *fagot*, 'a fagot, a bundle of sticks;' Cot. Of doubtful origin; perhaps borrowed from Ital. *fagotto*, 'a faggot,' Florio; a dimin. from L. *fāg-us*, a beech-tree (Körting).

Fail. (F. − L.) F. *faillir*; cf. Ital. *fallire*. − Folk-L. **fallīre*, for L. *fallere*, to beguile, also, to be defective; *fallī*, to err. Brugm. i. § 757.

Fain. (E.) M. E. *fayn*. A. S. *fægen*, glad. +O. Sax. *fagan*, Icel. *feginn*, glad. Cf. A. S. *gefēon* (pt. t. *gefeah*), to rejoice. Teut. root **feh-*, as in A. S. *ge-fēon* (for **-feh-an*); cf. Goth. *fah-ēths*, joy.

Faint. (F. − L.) M. E. *feint*. − O. F. *feint*, weak, pretended; orig. pp. of *feindre*, to feign. − L. *fingere*, to form, feign. See **Figure**.

Fair (1), pleasing, beautiful. (E.) M. E. *fayr*, A. S. *fæger*, fair.+Icel. *fagr*; Dan. Swed. *fager*, Goth. *fagrs*, fit, O.H.G. *fagar*. Teut. type **fagroz*. Cf. Gk. πήγ-νυμι, I fasten. Brugm. i. §§ 200, 701.

Fair (2), a holiday. (F. − L.) M. E. *feire*. − A. F. *feire* (F. *foire*). − L. *fēria*, a holiday, later, a fair; commoner as pl. *fēriæ*, for **fēs-iæ*, feast-days; allied to **Feast**. Brugm. ii. § 66.

Fairy. (F. − L.) M. E. *faerie*, *fayrye*, enchantment. [The mod. use of the word is new; *fairy* = enchantment, the old word for 'elf' being *fay*.] − O. F. *faerie*, enchantment. − O. F. *fae*, a fay; see **Fay**.

Faith. (F. − L.) M. E. *feith*; also *fey*. Slightly altered from O. F. *feid*, *fei*, faith. − L. *fidem*, acc. of *fides*, faith; allied to *fidere*, to trust. Cf. Gk. πίστις, faith. (√BHEIDH.) Allied to **Bide**. Brugm. i. § 202.

Falchion, a sword. (F. − Ital. − L.) M. E. *fauchon*. − O. F. *fauchon*. − Ital. *falcione* (*ci* pron. as *ch*). − Late L. *falciō-*

nem, acc. of *falcio*, a bent sword.—L. *falci-*, decl. stem of *falx*, a sickle. Allied to *flectere*, to bend.

falcon. (F.—L.) M. E. *faucon.*— O. F. *faucon, faulcon.* — Late L. *falcōnem,* acc. of *falco*, a falcon, so named from its hooked claws.—L. *falc-*, stem of *falx*, a sickle.

Faldstool, a folding-stool. (Low L.— O. H. G.) Low L. *faldistolium.*—O.H.G. *fald-an*, to fold; *stuol* (G. *stuhl*), a stool. Cf. F. *fauteuil.* See **Fold.**

Fall, to drop down. (E.) M. E. *fallen.* O. Merc. *fallan*; A. S. *feallan.*+Du. *vallen*, Icel. *falla*, Dan. *falde* (for *falle*), Swed. *falla*, G. *fallen.* Teut. **fallan-.* Cf. Lith. *pùlti*, to fall; and perhaps L. *fallere*, to deceive, *fallī*, to err. Brugm. i. § 757. **Der.** *be-fall*, from A. S. *be-feallan*, to fall out, happen; *fell* (1).

Fallacy. (F.—L.) Formed by adding -*y* to M. E. *fallace*, a fallacy, deceit.—F. *fallace.*—L. *fallācia*, deceit.—L. *fallāc-*, stem of *fallax*, deceitful.—L. *fallere*, to deceive. See above.

fallible. (L.) L. *fallibilis*, liable to err.—L. *fallī*, to err; *fallere*, to deceive.

Fallow (1), orig. 'harrowed;' of land. (E.) A. S. *fælging*, fallow-land.—A. S. *fealh*, a harrow. Cf. E. Fries. *falgen*, to fallow land; O. H. G. *felgā*, a harrow.

Fallow (2), used with reference to colour. (E.) O. Merc. *falu*; A. S. *fealu*, *fealo*, pale red, yellowish.+Du. *vaal*, Icel. *fölr*, pale, G. *fahl*, pale, also *falb*; Lith. *palvas*; cf. also L. *pallidus*, Gk. πολιός, gray, Skt. *palita-*, gray. See **Pale.**

False. (F.—L.) M. E. *fals.* — O. F. *fals* (F. *faux*).—L. *falsus*, false; pp. of *fallere*, to deceive.

Falter, to totter, stammer. (E.?) M. E. *faltren*, to totter; frequentative from a base *falt-.* Of obscure origin. Perhaps connected with Icel. refl. vb. *faltra-sk*, to be cumbered, to be puzzled.

Fame, report. (F.—L.) F. *fame.*—L. *fāma*, report. — L. *fārī*, to speak; see **Fate.**

Family. (F.—L.) F. *famille.*—L. *familia*, a household. — L. *famulus*, a servant, Oscan *famel*; cf. Oscan *faamat*, he dwells. **Der.** *famili-ar* (L. *familiāris*).

Famine. (F.—L.) F. *famine.*—Late L. **famīna*, unrecorded, but plainly an extension from L. *famēs*, hunger. **Der.** *fam-ish*, formed (by analogy with *lan-*

guish, &c.) from L. *fam-ēs*, hunger; cf. O. F. *afamer*, to die of hunger.

Fan, an instrument for blowing. (L.) A. S. *fann.*—Late L. *vannus*, L. *uannus*, a fan (whence also F. *van*); see **Van** (2). Brugm. i. § 357.

Fanatic, religiously insane. (F.—L.) F. *fanatique.*—L. *fānāticus*, (1) belonging to a temple, (2) inspired by a divinity, enthusiastic.—L. *fānum*, a temple; see **Fane.**

Fancy. (F.—L.—Gk.) Short for M.E. *fantasie.*—O. F. *fantasie.*—Late L. *phantasia.*—Gk. φαντασία, a making visible (hence, imagination).—Gk. φαντάζειν, to display; see **Phantom.**

Fandango, a Spanish dance. (Span.) Span. *fandango*, 'a dance used in the W. Indies;' Pineda (1740).

Fane, a temple. (L.) L. *fānum*, a temple; shortened from an earlier form **fasnom*; cf. Oscan *fīsnam*, a temple; allied to L. *fēstus, fēria.* Brugm. ii. § 66.

Fanfare, a flourish of trumpets. (F.— Span.?) F. *fanfare.* Prob. of imitative origin, or borrowed from Span. *fanfarria*, bluster, vaunting, which is of similar formation. **Der.** *fanfarr-on-ade*, bluster.

Fang, a talon, claw. (E.) A. S. *fang*; lit. a seizing.—A. S. **fōhan*, to seize, only used in the contracted form *fōn*, pt. t. *fēng*, pp. *gefangen*; the pp. form having alone survived, evolving an infin. mood in dialects.+Du. *vangen*, to catch; Icel. *fā* (cf. *fang*, sb., a catch of fish), Dan. *faae*, Swed. *få*, Goth. *fāhan*, G. *fangen*, to catch, *fang*, sb., a catch, also a fang. Allied to L. *pangere*; Brugm. i. § 421.

Fantastic. (Gk.) Gk. φανταστικός, able to represent or shew.—Gk. φαντάζειν, to display. See **Fancy.**

Fantasy, older form of **Fancy**, q. v.

Faquir, Fakir, an Oriental religious mendicant. (F.—Arab.) F. *faquir, fakir.* —Arab. *faqīr*, one of a religious order of mendicants; lit. 'poor, indigent;' Richardson's Dict. p. 1096.

Far. (E.) M. E. *fer.* A. S. *feor.*+Du. *ver*, Icel. *fjarri*, Swed. *fjerran*, adv., Dan. *fjern*, G. *fern*; Goth. *fairra*, adv. Allied to Gk. πέραν, beyond; Skt. *paras*, beyond, *para-*, far. (√PER.) The comp. *farther* [for M. E. *ferrer* (i. e. *far-er*)] is due to confusion with *further*, comp. of **Forth.**

Farce. (F.—L.) The orig. sense is 'stuffing'; hence, a jest inserted into a comedy.—F. *farce*, stuffing, a farce.—F.

farcir, to stuff. – L. *farcīre*, to stuff. +Gk. φράσσειν (for *φράκ-γειν), to shut in.

Fardel, a pack, bundle. (F. – Arab.) M. E. *fardel.* – O. F. *fardel* (F. *fardeau*). Dimin. of O. F. *farde*, a burden. Prob. from Arab. *fardah*, a package (Devic). Perhaps borrowed through Spanish ; cf. Span. *fardel, fardo*, a bundle.

Fare, to travel, speed. (E.) A. S. *faran*, to go, travel. + Du. *varen*, Icel. Swed. *fara*, Dan. *fare*, G. *fahren*, Goth. *faran*, to go ; Teut. **faran-* (pt. t. **fōr*). Cf. Gk. πορεύομαι, I travel ; L. *experior*, I pass through, Skt. *pr*, to bring over. (√PER.) Der. *fare-well*, i. e. may you speed well ; *thorough-fare*, a passage through ; *wel-fare*, successful practice or journey.

Farina, ground corn. (L.) L. *farīna*, meal. – L. *far*, a kind of grain ; allied to Barley. Der. *farinaceous*, from L. *farīnāceus*. Brugm. i. § 180.

farrago. (L.) L. *farrāgo*, mixed food for cattle, a medley. – L. *far* (gen. *farr-is*), grain (above).

Farm. (L.) M. E. *ferme*. [Cf. A. S. *feorm*, a feast, food, property, use.] – Late L. *firma*, a feast, farm, tribute ; fem. of L. *firmus*, durable. (From the *fixed* rent ; also food, from its *support*.) See Firm.

Farrier. (F. – L.) Formerly *ferrier*, a worker in iron. – O. F. *ferrier* (the same). – L. *ferrārius*, a blacksmith. – L. *ferrum*, iron.

Farrow, to litter pigs. (E.) From the sb. *farrow*, a litter of pigs. – A. S. *fearh*, a pig ; pl. *fearas.* + M. H. G. *varch*, a pig ; G. *ferk-el* ; L. *porcus* ; see Pork.

Farther ; see Far.

Farthing, fourth part of a penny. (E.) M. E. *ferthing.* A. S. *fērþing, fēorðing*, older form *fēorþling.* – A. S. *fēorð-a*, fourth ; with dimin. suffix *-ing* or *-l-ing*. Allied to A. S. *fēower*, four.

Farthingale, Fardingale, a hooped petticoat. (F. – Span. – L.) M.F. *verdugalle*, ' a vardingall ; ' Cot. – Span. *verdugado*, a farthingale, lit. ' provided with hoops.' – Span. *verdugo*, young shoot of a tree, rod, hoop. – Span. *verde*, green. – L. *uiridis*, green. See Verdant.

Fascinate. (L.) From pp. of L. *fascināre*, to enchant. – L. *fascinum*, a spell.

Fascine, a bundle of rods. (F. – L.) F. *fascine.* – L. *fascīna*, a bundle of twigs. – L. *fascis*, a bundle.

Fashion. (F. – L.) O. F. *faceon, fachon*, make, shape. – L. *factiōnem*, acc. of *factio*, a making ; see Faction.

Fast (1), firm. (E.) A. S. *fæst.* + Du. *vast*, Dan. Swed. *fast*, Icel. *fastr*, G. *fest* ; Armen. *hast.* Der. *fast* (2), *fast* (3). Brugm. ii. § 79.

fast (2), to abstain from food. (E.) A. S. *fæstan*, orig. to make fast, observe, be strict ; from *fæst* (above). +Du. *vasten*, Dan. *faste*, Swed. and Icel. *fasta*, G. *fasten* ; Goth. *fastan*, to observe, fast.

fast (3), quick. (Scand.) A peculiar use of *fast* (1) above ; this use is Scand. Cf. Icel. *drekka fast*, to drink hard, *sofa fast*, to be fast asleep, *fastr ī verkum*, hard at work, *fylgja fast*, to follow fast, &c. It means firm, close, urgent, quick.

fasten. (E.) A. S. *fæstnian*, to make fast or firm. – A. S. *fæst*, firm.

fastness. (E.) M. E. *festnes, fastness*, orig. ' strength.' – A. S. *fæstness*, the firmament, a fastness ; orig. that which is firm. – A. S. *fæst*, firm.

Fastidious. (L.) L. *fastīdiōsus*, disdainful. – L. *fastīdium*, loathing ; perhaps for **fastutīdium* (Vaniček). – L. *fastu-s*, arrogance ; *tædium*, disgust ; so that *fastīdium* = arrogant disgust.

Fastness ; see Fast.

Fat (1), gross. (E.) M. E. *fatt, fet, fat.* A. S. *fætt*, orig. a pp., contr. from **fǣted*, fattened, enriched. +O. H. G. *feizit* (G. *feist*), pp. of a Teut. vb. **faitjan-*, formed from Teut. adj. **faitoz*, which is represented by Icel. *feitr* (Swed. *fet*, Dan. *fed*), fat. Cf. Gk. πίων, Skt. *pīvan*, fat.

Fat (2), a vat ; see Vat.

Fate, destiny. (F. – L.) M. E. *fate.* – O. F. *fat, fate* (not common). – L. *fātum*, what is spoken ; neut. of pp. of *fārī*, to speak. +Gk. φημί, I say. Perhaps allied to Boon (1). Brugm. i. § 187. (√BHĀ.)

Father. (E.) M. E. *fader.* A. S. *fæder.* The pron. with *th* is due to dialectal influences. +Icel. *faðir*, Du. *vader*, Dan. Swed. *fader*, Goth. *fadar*, G. *vater*, L. *pater*, Gk. πατήρ, O. Irish *athir*, Pers. *pidar*, Skt. *pitṛ.* Idg. type **pater-*.

Fathom. (E.) M. E. *fadme.* A. S. *fæðm*, the space reached by the extended arms, a grasp, embrace. +Du. *vadem*, Icel. *faðmr*, a fathom, Dan. *favn*, Swed. *famn*, an embrace, G. *faden.* Allied to Patent.

Fatigue, sb. (F. – L.) O. F. *fatigue* ; from *fatiguer*, to weary. – L. *fatīgāre*, to weary.

Fatuous. (L.) L. *fatu-us*, silly, feeble; with suffix *-ous*. Der. *in-fatuate*, from pp. of L. *infatuāre*, to make a fool of.

Fauces. (L.) L. *faucēs*, pl., the upper part of the throat.

Faucet, a spigot, vent. (F. − L.?) F. *fausset*, a faucet; *faulset*, Cot. Origin unknown; but cf. M. F. *faulser*, to falsify, forge; also *faulser un escu*, to pierce a shield; hence, to pierce. − L. *falsāre*, to falsify. − L. *falsus*, false.

Fault. (F. − L.) Formerly *faut*. M. E. *faute*. − O. F. *faute*, a fault. (Span. and Ital. *falta*, a defect.) − Folk-L. **fallita*, a defect, fem. of **fallitus*, new pp. of *fallere*, to deceive; cf. F. *faillir*. See **Fail, Fallible, False.** Hence also O. F. *fauter*, Span. *faltar*, Ital. *faltare*, to be lacking.

Faun, a rural (Roman) deity. (L.) L. *faunus*. − L. *fauēre*, to be propitious (?)

Fauteuil, an arm-chair. (F. − Low L. − O. H. G.) F. *fauteuil*, O. F. *fauldetueil* (Cot.). − Low L. *faldistolium*, a faldstool; see **Faldstool.**

Favour, sb. (F. − L.) O. F. *favour*. − L. *fauōrem*, acc. of *fauor*, favour. − L. *fauēre*, to befriend, orig. ' to venerate.'

favourite. (F. − Ital. − L.) M. F. *favorit*; cf. F. *favori*, pp. of O. F. *favorir*, to favour. But the final *t* is really due to borrowing from Ital. *favorito*, pp. and sb.; orig. pp. of *favorire*, to favour. − Ital. *favore*, favour. − L. *fauōrem* (above).

Fawn (1), to cringe to, rejoice servilely over. (E.) A. S. *fahnian, fagnian*, to rejoice; variants of *fægenian*, to fawn, from *fægen*, fain, glad. + Icel. *fagna*, to rejoice, welcome one; allied to *feginn*, fain. See **Fain.**

Fawn (2), a young deer. (F. − L.) O. F. *fan, faon*, earlier *feön*, a fawn; answering to a Late L. form **fētōnem* (not found), acc. of **fētō*, a young one. − L. *fētus, fœtus*, offspring. See **Fetus.**

Fay, a fairy. (F. − L.) F. *fée*, O. F. *fae*, a fay. Cf. Port. *fada*, Ital. *fata*, a fay. − Late L. *fāta*, a fate, goddess of destiny, a fay. − L. *fāta*, pl. of L. *fātum*, fate. See **Fate.** Der. *fai-ry*.

Fealty, true service. (F. − L.) O. F. *fealte, feelteit*, fidelity. − L. *fidēlitātem*, acc. of *fidēlitās*, fidelity. − L. *fidēlis*, faithful; from *fidēs*, faith.

Fear. (E.) M. E. *feer*. A. S. *fǣr*, a sudden peril, danger, fear. Orig. used of

the peril of travelling. − A. S. *fǣr-*, 3rd stem of *faran*, to go, travel. + Icel. *fār*, harm, G. *gefahr*, Du. *gevaar*, danger. Cf. L. *perīculum*, danger.

Feasible, easy to be done. (F. − L.) [Also *feisable*.] − M. F. *faisible, faisable*, ' feasible, doable;' Cot. − O. F. *fais-*, as in *fais-ant*, pres. pt. of *faire*, to do. − L. *facere*, to do. See **Fact.**

Feast. (F. − L.) M. E. *feste*. − O. F. *feste* (F. *fête*). − Late L. *festa*, fem. sb. − L. *festa*, lit. festivals, pl. of *festum*. See **Festal.**

Feat, a deed well done. (F. − L.) M.E. *feet, fete*. − A. F. *fet*; O. F. *fait*. − L. *factum*, a deed; see **Fact.**

Feather. (E.) M. E. *fether*. A. S. *feðer*. + Du. *veder*, Dan. *fjæder*, Swed. *fjäder*, Icel. *fjöðr*, G. *feder*; L. *penna* (for **pet-sna*), Skt. *patra-*, Gk. πτερόν, a wing. See **Pen.** (√PET.)

Feature, make, form. (F. − L.) M. E. *feture*. − A. F. *feture*; O. F. *faiture*, fashion. − L. *factūra*, work, formation. − L. *factus*, pp. of *facere*, to make.

Febrile, relating to fever. (F. − L.) F. *fébrile*. − L. *febrīlis*. − L. *febri-s*, fever.

February. (L.) L. *februārius*, the month of expiation. − L. *februa*, neut. pl., a festival of expiation on Feb. 15. − L. *februum*, purification; *februāre*, to expiate. Of Sabine origin.

Feckless, ineffective. Also *fectless*; short for *effect-less*; see **Effect.**

Feculent, foul. (F. − L.) F. *féculent*. − L. *fæculentus*, full of dregs. − L. *fæcēs*, dregs. See **Fæces.**

Fecundity. (F. − L.) M. F. *fecondité* (Cot.). − L. acc. *fēcunditātem*, fruitfulness. − L. *fēcundus*, fruitful; allied to *fētus*, offspring. See **Fetus.**

Federal. (F. − L.) F. *fédéral*. Formed, with suffix *-al*, from L. *fœder-* (for **fœdes-*), stem of *fœdus*, a treaty. Akin to *fides*, faith.

Fee, a lordship, a payment. (F. − O. H. G.?) A. F. *fee*, O. F. *fiu* (F. *fief*), a fee, fief. − Late L. *fevum*, a fief (Ducange). Prob. from O. H. G. *fehu*, property. + Du. *vee*, Icel. *fē*, Dan. *fæ*, Swed. *fä*, Goth. *faihu*, L. *pecus*; Skt. *paçu-*, cattle. (√PEK.) So also A. S. *feoh*, cattle, whence M. E. *fee*, cattle, property. now obsolete. ¶ We also find Late L. *feudum*; see **Feudal.**

Feeble. (F. − L.) M. E. *feble*. − A. F. *feble*, M. F. *foible*, O. F. *fleble* (Godefroy);

cf. Ital. *fievole* (<*flevole*), feeble [since Ital. *fi*<*fl*].—L. *flēbilis*, doleful; hence, weak.—L. *flēre*, to weep. Brugm. ii. § 590.

Feed, to take food, give food. (E.) M.E. *feden*. A.S. *fēdan*; for **fōdian*; with vowel-change from *ō* to *ē*.—A.S. *fōda*, food.+Du *voeden*, Icel. *fœða*, Swed. *föda*, Dan. *föde*, O. H. G. *fuotan*, Goth. *fōdjan*; Teut. type **fōdjan*-. See **Food**.

Feel. (E.) M.E. *felen*. A.S. *fēlan*.+Du. *voelen*, G. *fühlen*. Teut. **fōljan*-; from Teut. base *fal*- (2nd grade, *fōl*-), whence also Icel. *falma*, to grope, A.S. *folm*, palm of the hand (L. *palma*). Allied to **Palm** (1).

Feeze, Feaze, Pheeze. (E.) Properly 'to put to flight, drive away, chase away, harass, worry'; often misexplained by 'whip.' M.E. *fesen*; O. Merc. *fēsian*, A.S. *fȳsian*, to drive away quickly, chase. Cf. Norw. *föysa* (=Icel. **feysa*), Swed. *fösa*, to drive. From Teut. base **faus*- (sense unknown). ¶ Distinct from A.S. *fȳsan*, to hurry, from *fūs*, prompt.

Feign. (F.—L.) M.E. *feinen*.—O.F. *feign*-, as in *feign ant*, pres. pt. of *feindre*. —L. *fingere*, to form, feign. See **Figure**. Der. *feint* (from F. pp. *feint*).

Feldspar, a kind of mineral. (G.) Corrupted from G. *feldspath*, lit. field-spar.

Felicity. (F.—L.) O.F. *felicité*.—L. acc. *fēlicitātem*.—L. *fēlīci*-, decl. stem of *fēlix*, happy, fruitful; allied to **Feline**.

Feline. (L.) L. *fēlīnus*, belonging to cats.—L. *fēles*, a cat; perhaps allied to Gk. θῆλυς, female.

Fell (1), to cause to fall. (E.) O. Merc. *fællan*, A.S. *fyllan*, causal of O. Merc. *fallan*, A.S. *feallan*, to fall. So also Du. *vellen*, Dan. *fælde*, Swed. *fälla*, Icel. *fella*, G. *fällen*; all causal forms. Teut. type **falljan*-, causal of *fallan*-, to fall. See **Fall**.

Fell (2), a skin. (E.) M.E. *fel*. A.S. *fel*, *fell* +Du. *vel*, Icel. *fell*, Goth. *-fill*, M. H. G. *vel*; L. *pellis*, Gk. πέλλα, skin. Doublet, *pell*; cf. *fil-m*.

Fell (3), cruel, dire. (F.—Late L.—L.?) M.E. *fel*.—O.F. *fel*, cruel (cf. Ital. *fello*, cruel).—Late L. *fello*, *felo*, a malefactor, felon, traitor. Perhaps from L. *fel*, gall (N. E. D.); cf. Du. dial. *fel*, sharp, biting. acrid (Molema). See **Felon**.

Fell (4), a hill. (Scand.) M. E. *fel*.—Icel. *fjall*, *fell*, a hill; Dan. *field*, Swed.

fjäll, a fell. Allied to G. *fels*, a rock (Kluge).

Fellah, a peasant. (Arab.) Pl. *fellahīn*. —Arab. *fellāḥ*, *fallāḥ*, a farmer, peasant. —Arab. root *falaḥa*, to plough, till.

Felloe; see **Felly**.

Fellow, a partner. (Scand.) M. E. *felawe*.—Icel. *fēlagi*, a partner in a 'félag.' —Icel. *fēlag*, companionship; lit. a laying together of property.—Icel. *fē*, property; *lag*, a laying together, a law; see **Law**. The Icel. *fē* is cognate with A.S. *feoh*, cattle, property, L. *pecus*, cattle.

Felly, Felloe, part of a wheel-rim. (E.) M. E. *felwe*. A.S. *felg*, *felga*, a felly.+Du. *velg*, Dan. *fælge*, G. *felge*.

Felon, a wicked person. (F.—Late L. —L.?) M. E. *felun*.—O. F. *felon*, a traitor.—Late L. *felōnem*, acc. of *felo*, *fello*, a traitor, rebel. See **Fell** (3).

Felt. (E.) M. E. *felt*. A.S. *felt*.+Du. *vilt*, Low G., Swed., Dan. *filt*, G. *filz*. Teut. type **feltoz*, n.; allied to G. *falzen*, to groove, join together. Der. *filter*, *feuter*.

Felucca, a ship. (Ital.—Arab.) Ital. *feluca*.—Arab. *fulk*, a ship. (See Devic.)

Female. (F.—L.) For *femell*, by confusion with *male*. M. E. *femelle*.—O.F. *femelle*.—L. *fēmella*, a young woman; dimin. of *fēmina*, a woman (below).

feminine. (F.—L.) O.F. *feminin*. —L. *fēminīnus*, womanly.—L. *fēmina*, a woman. Cf. *fēlare*, to suckle; Gk. θῆλυς, female, θηλή, the breast; Skt. *dhātrī*, a nurse.

Femoral, belonging to the thigh. (L.) L. *femorālis*; adj. from *femor*-, stem of *femur*, thigh.

Fen, a bog. (E.) M. E. *fen*. A.S. *fenn*.+Du. *veen*, Icel. *fen*, Goth. *fani*, mud. Teut. type **fanjom*, n.

Fence; short for *defence*; see **Defend**.

Fend; short for **Defend**, q. v.

Fender; short for *defender*.

Fennel, a plant. (L.) M. E. *fenel*. A.S. *finol*, *finugle*.—L *faeniculum*, fennel; double dimin. of *faenum*, hay.

Fenugreek, a plant. (F.—L.) F. *fenugrec*.—L. *faenum Graecum*, lit. Greek hay.

Feoff; see **Fief**.

Ferment. (L.) L. *fermentum* (short for **ferui-mentum*), leaven.—L. *feruēre*, to boil. See **Fervent**.

Fern. (E.) A.S. *fearn*.+Du. *varen*; G. *farn(kraut)*; Skt. *parṇa*-, a wing,

feather, leaf, plant, the orig. sense being
'feather.' Brugm. i. § 973. Cf. also
Lith. *papartis*, Russ. *paporot(e)*, Irish
raith, W. *rhedyn*, fern; Gk. πτέρις, fern,
πτερόν, a wing, feather.

Ferocity. (F.–L.) M.F. *ferocité.*–
L. acc. *ferōcitātem*, fierceness.–L. *ferōci-*,
decl. stem of *ferox*, fierce.–L. *ferus*,
fierce, wild. Brugm. i. § 319.

Ferreous. (L.) L. *ferreus*, made of
iron; with suffix *-ous.*–L. *ferrum*, iron.

ferruginous. (L.) L. *ferrūgin-us*,
same as *ferrūgineus*, rusty; with suffix
-ous.–L. *ferrūgin-*, stem of *ferrūgo*, rust
of iron.–L. *ferrum*, iron.

Ferret (1), an animal. (F.–Low L.–
L.?) O. F. *furet*, a ferret.–Late L. *fūrē-
tus*, *fūrectus*, a ferret. Also *fūrō*; said to
be the same as Late L. *fūrō*, a thief, from
L. *fūr*, a thief. Cf. Gk. φώρ, a thief;
from the strong ō-grade of φέρειν, to bear,
carry off.

Ferret (2), a kind of silk tape. (Ital.
–L.) From Ital. *fioretti*, 'little flowers,
flourishings'; also foret or ferret silke,'
Florio. Pl. of *fioretto*, dimin. of *fiore*, a
flower.–L. *flōrem*, acc. of *flōs*, a flower;
see **Flower.** Cf. F. *fleuret*, ferret; from
fleur, flower.

Ferruginous; see **Ferreous.**

Ferrule, a metal ring at the end of a
stick. (F.–L.) Corrupted spelling (due
to confusion with *ferrum*, iron) of the
older form *virrol*; XVI cent.–O.F. *virol*
(F. *virole*), a ferrule; Late L. *virola*, the
same. From L. *uiriola*, a little bracelet;
dimin. of **uiria*, an armlet, only found in
pl. *uiriæ*. (Diez.) Doubtful.

Ferry, vb. (E.) M.E. *ferien*. A.S.
ferian, to convey across; causal of A.S.
faran, to go. **+** Icel. *ferja*, to carry;
causal of *fara*, to go; Goth. *farjan*, to
travel by ship. See **Fare.** (N.E.D.)

Fertile. (F.–L.) F. *fertile.*–L. *fer-
tilis*, fertile.–L. *ferre*, to bear. See
Bear (1).

Ferule, a rod or bat for punishing
children. (L.) Formerly *ferula.*–L.
ferula, a rod; orig. the plant 'giant-
fennel.'

Fervent, hot, zealous. (F.–L.) O.F.
fervent.–L. *feruent-*, stem of pres. pt. of
feruēre, to boil. Allied to O. Irish *berb-
aim*, I boil. Der. *fervour*, from O. F.
fervour<L. acc. *feruōrem*, heat; *feruid*,
from L. *feruidus*.

Fess, a horizontal band in heraldry.

(F.–L.) O. F. *fesse* (Roquefort); mod.
F. *fasce*, a fess.–L. *fascia*, a girth; allied
to *fascis*, a bundle; see **Fascine.**

Festal. F.–L.) O.F. *festal.* Formed
(with F. suffix *-al*<L. *-ālis*) from L. *festum*, a feast, orig. neut. of *festus*, festive,
joyful. Allied to **Fair** (2) and **Fane.**

festival. (F.–Late L.–L.) Properly an adj.–O. F. *festival*, festive.–
Late L. *festīvālis.*–L. *festīuus* (below).

festive. (L.) L. *festīuus*, belonging
to a feast.–L. *festum*, a feast.

Fester, a sore. (F.–L.) O. F. *festre*,
also spelt *fistle*, an ulcer; whence *festrir*,
to fester (Godefroy).–L. *fistula*, a running
sore. See **Fistula.**

Festival, Festive; see **Festal.**

Festoon. (F.–Ital.–L.) F. *feston*, a
garland, festoon.–Ital. *festone*, a garland.
Usually derived from L. *festum*, a feast.

Fetch. (E.) M. E. *fecchen*, pt. t.
fehte, *fæhte*. A. S. *feccan*, to fetch, Gen.
xviii. 4; Luke xii. 20. Prob. *fecc(e)an* is
a later form of *fetian*, to fetch (Anglia, vi.
177). Allied to A. S. *fæt*, a pace, step,
journey; Icel. *fet*, a step, foot-measure;
and to L. *pēs* (gen. *ped-is*), a foot. ¶ Cf.
A.S. *gefeccan*, O. E. T., p. 178. **Der.**
fetch, sb., a stratagem.

Fête. (F.–L.) Mod. F. *fête*, the same
as O. F. *feste*; see **Feast.**

Fetich, Fetish, an object of superstitious dread. (F.–Port.–L.) F.
fétiche.–Port. *feitiço*, sorcery, lit. artificial;
also, a name given by the Port. to the
roughly made idols of Africa.–L. *factītius*,
artificial.–L. *fact-us*, pp. of *facere*, to
make.

Fetid. (F.–L.) O. F. *fetide.*–L.
fētidus, *fœtidus*, stinking.–L. *fētēre*, to
stink.

Fetlock. (Scand.) As if the 'lock'
or tuft of hair behind a horse's pas-
tern-joint. Cf. Low G. *fitlock* (Lübben);
M. H. G. *vizzeloch* (Kluge). The syllable
-l-ock is due to a double suffix, but was
thought to refer to Icel. *lokkr*, A. S. *locc*,
a lock of hair. *Fet-* is prob. allied to
Icel. *fet*, a pace, step, *feti*, a pacer (used
of horses); and to Icel. *fōtr*, a foot; cf.
G. *fessel*, pastern; and see **Fetch, Foot.**
(Kluge, s. v. *Fuss*.)

Fetter, a shackle. (E.) M. E. *feter*.
A. S. *fetor*, a shackle for the foot; from
*fet-, č-grade of *fōt*, foot.+Du. *veter*, Icel.
fjöturr; cf. L. *ped-ica* and *com-pēs*, Gk.
πέδη, a fetter. **Der.** *fetter*, vb.

Fetus, offspring. (L.) L. *fētus*, a bringing forth, offspring. – L. **fuēre*, an obsolete verb, to generate, produce; allied to *fu-i*, I was; see **Future, Be.** Brugm. i. § 361, ii. § 587.

Feu, a fief; a variant of **Fee.**

Feud (1), hatred, perpetual hostility. (F. – O. H. G.) M. E. *fede, feid.* Modified in spelling in some unexplained way, perhaps by the influence of *foe.* – O. F. *feide, faide, fede,* perpetual hostility. – O. H. G. *fēhida* (G. *fehde*), enmity; cognate with A. S. *fǣhð,* enmity, from A. S. *fāh,* hostile. See **Foe.**

Feud (2), a fief. (Low L. – F. – O. H. G.) Low L. *feudum,* a Latinised form allied to O. F. *fiu,* also spelt *fief*; see **Fee, Fief.** (The intrusive *d* is unexplained.) Der. *feud-al,* adj.

Feuter, to lay spear in rest. (F. – Teut.) From M. E. *feuter,* a rest for a spear. – O. F. *feutre,* older *feltre,* a piece of felt, also a rest (prob. at first felted) for the lance. Cp. Ital. *feltro,* felt. Of Teut. origin; from Low G. *filt,* felt. See **Felt.**

Feuterer, a dog-keeper. (F. – Low L. – C.) In Ben Jonson, Every Man out of his Humour, ii. 1; see Nares. Older spelling *vewter,* for *veutr-er.* – O. F. *veutre,* mod. F. *vautre,* a mongrel between a hound and a mastiff. – Low Lat. acc. *veltrum*; for L. *vertagus, vertagra, vertraga,* a greyhound. Said to be Celtic. Perhaps from Celtic *ver-,* intensive prefix, and *trag-,* to run; see Fick, ii. 136, 283.

Fever, a kind of disease. (L.) M. E. *feuer* (*fever*). A. S. *fēfer, fēfor*; see Matt. viii. 15; A. F. *fevre.* – L. *febris,* fever.

feverfew, a plant. (L.) A. S. *fēferfuge*; A. F. *feverfue.* – Late L. *febrifuga,* for L. *febrifugia,* 'fever-dispelling.' – L. *febri-s,* fever; *fugāre,* to put to flight.

Few. (E.) M. E. *fewe.* A. S. pl. *fēawe.* +Icel. *fār,* Dan. *faa,* Swed. *få*; Goth. *fawai,* pl.; cf. L. *paucus,* Gk. παῦρος, small.

Fey, doomed to die. (E.) A. S. *fǣge,* doomed to die.+Icel. *feigr,* Du. *veeg*; G. *feige,* cowardly; Swed. *feg,* Dan. *feig,* cowardly.

Fez, a red Turkish cap, without a brim. (F. – Morocco.) F. and Turk. *fez,* a cap; so called because made at Fez, in Morocco.

Fiasco, lit. 'a bottle.' (Ital.) Ital. *far fiasco,* to make a bottle, also, to fail,

break down. See **Flask.** (Origin of phrase unknown.)

Fiat, a decree. (L.) L. *fīat,* let it be done. – L. *fio,* I become; used as pass. of *facere,* to do, but really allied to *fui,* I was. Cf. A. S. *bēo,* I am. Brugm. i. § 282.

Fib. (Low G.) Allied to *fob, fub off,* to delude (Shak.); cf. G. *foppen,* to banter (formerly, to lie); Westphal. *fip-ken,* a small lie, fib (Woeste).

Fibre. (F. – L.) F. *fibre.* – L. *fibra,* a thread.

Fickle. (E.) M. E. *fikel.* A. S. *ficol*; from **fician,* to deceive, in comp. *be-fician,* to deceive; cf. *fic,* sb., fraud, *fǣcne,* deceitful; *fācen,* fraud.

Fiction. (F. – L.) F. *fiction.* – L. *fictiōnem,* acc. of *fictio,* a feigning. – L. *fictus,* pp. of *fingere,* to feign. See **Figure.**

Fiddle, a violin. (L.) M. E. *fithel*; A. S. *fiðele:* cf. Icel. *fiðla,* Dan. *fiddel,* Du. *vedel,* G. *fiedel.* Apparently borrowed from Late L. *uitula, uidula,* a viol; see **Viol.**

Fidelity. (F. – L.) M. F. *fidelité.* – L. *fidēlitātem,* acc. of *fidēlitās,* faithfulness. – L. *fidēli-,* stem of *fidēlis,* faithful. – L. *fidēs,* faith. See **Faith.**

Fidget. (Scand.) A dimin. form of *fidge,* to be continually moving up and down, like *fike* in North of England, M. E. *fiken,* to fidget, to hasten. Cf. Icel. *fika,* to climb up nimbly, as a spider; Swed. *fika,* to hunt after, Norw. *fika,* to take trouble, *fika etter,* to hasten after, pursue.

Fiducial, shewing trust. (L.) From Late L. *fidūciālis,* adj. – L. *fidūcia,* trust. – L. *fidere,* to trust.

Fie. (F. – L.) M. E. *fy.* – F. *fi.* – L. *fī.* Cf. Icel. *fy,* Dan. *fy,* Swed. *fy,* G. *pfui,* Lat. *phu, phy,* Skt. *phut,* expressions of disgust.

Fief, land held of a superior. (F. – O. H. G.) O. F. *fief,* formerly spelt *fiu* (Roland). See **Fee.** Der. *feoff,* vb., to put in legal possession; from A. F. *feoffer,* to endow with a *feof* or *fief.* Also *feoffee,* A. F. *feoffé,* pp. of *feoffer.*

Field. (E.) M. E. *feld.* A. S. *feld.*+ Du. *veld.* G. *feld* (whence Dan. *felt,* Swed. *fält*). Allied to A. S. *folde,* earth, land. Teut. type **felthuz.* Cf. Russ. *polé,* a field; Skt. *prthivī,* earth. Brugm. i. § 502.

fieldfare, a bird. (E.) A. S. *feldefare* [miswritten *feldeware*], lit. 'field-traveller:' see **Fare.**

Fiend. (E.) M. E. *fend.* A. S. *fiond,*
feond, lit. ' a hating one,' an enemy, the
enemy; orig. pres. pt. of *feog(e)an,* to
hate. + Du. *vijand,* Dan. Swed. *fiende;*
Icel. *fjāndi,* pres. pt. of *fjā,* to hate ; Goth.
fijands, from *fijan,* to hate ; G. *feind.* Cf.
Skt. *pīy,* to hate (Fick). See **Foe.**

Fierce. (F. – L.) M. E. *fers.* – O. F.
fers, fiers, old nom. of O. F. *fer, fier,*
fierce (F. *fier,* proud). – L. *ferus,* wild.

Fife. (F. – O. H. G. – L.) F. *fifre.* –
O. H. G. *pfīfa,* G. *pfeife,* a pipe. – O. H. G.
pfīfen, to blow, whistle. – Late L. *pīpāre,*
to pipe ; L. *pīpāre,* to chirp (as a bird).
See **Pipe.**

Fig. (F. – Prov. – L.) F. *figue.* – Prov.
figa. – Folk-L. **fīca,* used for L. *fīcus,* a
fig. (Cf. O. F. *fie,* a fig; immediately
from *fīca.*)

Fight. (E.) M. E. *fihten, fehten,* vb.
O. Merc. *fehtan,* to fight ; *fehte,* a fight. +
Du. *vechten,* G. *fechten,* to fight (whence
Dan. *fegte,* Swed. *fäkta*). Teut. **fehtan-.*

Figment. (L.) L. *figmentum,* an invention. – L. *fig-,* base of *fingere,* to feign
(pp. *fic-tus,* for **fig-tus*).

figure. (F. – L.) F. *figure.* – L.
figūra, a thing made. – L. *fingere* (base
fig-), to make, fashion, feign. + Skt.
deigan, to knead, Skt. *dih,* to smear.
(√DHEIGH.) Brugm. i. § 589. **Der.**
dis-figure, pre-figure, trans-figure.

Filament. (F. – L.) F. *filament.* –
Late L. *filāmentum,* thin thread. – Late
L. *filāre,* to wind thread. – L. *filum,*
thread ; see **File** (1).

Filbert, fruit of hazel. (F. – O. H. G.)
Formerly *philiberd* (Gower) ; short for
Philiberd or *Philibert nut,* from the
proper name *Philibert;* (S. Philibert's
day is Aug. 22) ; North F. *noix de filbert*
(Moisy). – O. H. G. *filu-berht,* very bright ;
from *filu* (G. *viel*), greatly, *berht,* bright.
¶ Called in Germany *Lambertsnuss,* i. e.
nut from Lombardy (Weigand).

Filch. (E.) Etym. unknown ; possibly
related to M. E. *felen,* to conceal. Cf. Icel.
fela, to hide, bury ; Goth. *filhan,* to hide.

File (1), string, line, order. (F. – L.)
Partly from O. F. *file,* a file, from *filer,* to
thread ; from · Late L. *filāre* (see **Filament**) ; partly from F. *fil,* thread, from
L. *filum,* a thread.

File (2), a steel rasp. (E.) O. Merc.
fil ; A. S. *fēol.* + Du. *vijl,* O. H. G. *fīhala,*
G. *feile* ; as if from a base **fenh-.* The
Icel. form is *þél,* as if from a base **thenh-.*

File (3), to defile. (E.) A. S. *fȳlan,*
to make foul; for **fūlian.* – A. S. *fūl,*
foul. See **Defile** (1) and **Foul.**

Filial. (L.) From L. *fīli-us,* a son,
fīlia, daughter; orig. infant : cf. L. *fēlāre,*
to suck. Cf. **Feminine.** (√DHE.)

Filibuster, a freebooter. (Span. – Du.)
Span. *filibuster,* a mere corruption of Du.
vrijbuiter, a freebooter. – Du. *vrijbuiten,*
to rob, plunder. – Du. *vrij,* free ; *buit,*
booty, plunder. See **Booty.**

Filigree. (F. – Ital. – L.) Formerly
filigrane; XVII cent. – F. *filigrane.* – Ital.
filigrana, filigree-work, fine wrought work.
– Ital. *filo,* a thread or row, *filare,* to
spin ; *grano,* grain or texture ; so called
because the chief texture of it was wrought
in silver wire. From L. *filum,* thread ;
grānum, grain. ¶ The Span. *filigrana* is
merely borrowed from Italian (Monlau).

Fill, vb. (E.) A. S. *fyllan;* formed
from *ful,* i. e. full, by vowel-change from *u*
to *y.* + Du. *vullen,* Icel. *fylla,* Dan. *fylde,*
Swed. *fylla,* Goth. *fulljan,* G. *füllen.*

Fillet. (F. – L.) M. E. *filet.* – O. F.
filet, dimin. of *fil,* a thread. – L. *filum,* a
thread. See **File** (1).

Fillibeg, Philibeg, a kilt. (Gaelic.)
Gael. *feileadh-beag,* the modern kilt. –
Gael. *feileadh, feile,* a kilt, prob. from L.
uēlum, a veil (Macbain) ; and *beag,* little,
small. Cf. W. *bach,* little.

Fillip, to strike with the finger-nail,
when jerked from the thumb. (E.) Another
form of *flip;* see **Flippant.**

Fills, used for *thills.* (E.) See **Thill.**

Filly, a female foal. (Scand.) Icel.
fylja, a filly, allied to *foli,* a foal, cf.
Dan. Swed. *föl,* G. *füllen.* See **Foal.**

Film, a thin skin. (E.) A. S. *filmen*
(*fylmen*), neut., membrane (O. Fries. *fil-
mene,* f., skin). For W. Teut. **filmin-jo-,*
from **felmen, -mon-,* as in A. S. *ǣgerfelma,*
skin of an egg. Extended from the base
fel- in A. S. *fel,* skin, Goth. *fill,* skin. See
Fell (2).

Filter, to strain. (F. – O. Low G.) F.
filtrer, orig. to strain through felt. – F.
filtre, a strainer, orig. felt (Littré). – Low
G. *filt,* felt ; see **Felt.**

Filth, foul matter. (E.) A. S. *fȳlð.* –
A. S. *fūl,* foul (by vowel-change of *ū* to
ȳ). So also O. Sax. *fūlithā,* filth, from
fūl, foul. See **Foul.**

Fin. (E.) A. S. *finn,* a fin. + Du. *vin,*
Swed. *fena,* Dan. *finne* ; L. *pinna.* See
Pin.

Final. (F. – L.) O. F. *final.* – L. *finālis,* final. – L. *finis,* end.

Finance, revenue. (F. – L.) O.F. *finance.* – Late L. *finantia,* payment. – Late L. *fināre,* to pay a fine. – Late L. *finis,* a settled payment, a *finish* or end, i. e. final arrangement ; L. *finis,* end.

Finch, a bird. (E.) M. E. *finch.* A. S. *finc.*+Du. *vink,* Dan. *finke,* Swed. and G. *fink.* Cf. W. *pinc,* a chaffinch ; Gk. σπίγγος, σπίζα, a finch ; prov. E. *spink.* **Der.** *chaf-finch,* q. v., *bull-finch,* &c.

Find. (E.) A. S. *findan.*+Du. *vinden,* Dan. *finde,* Swed. and Icel. *finna* (= *finþa*), Goth. *finthan,* G. *finden.* Teut. **fenth-an-*; Idg. base **pent-*, whence O. Irish *ēt-aim,* I find. Perhaps allied to L. *petere,* to seek after ; see **Petition.** Brugm. ii. § 634.

Fine (1), exquisite, thin. (F. – L.) O. F. *fin,* witty, perfect. – Late L. *finus,* fine ; used in place of L. *finitus,* well rounded or ended, said of a sentence (Brachet), orig. pp. of *finire,* to end. – L. *finis,* end. ¶ *Finus* is a back-formation from *finire.*

fine (2), a tax. (Law L.) Law L. *finis,* a fine, a final arrangement ; L. *finis,* end. See **Finance** (above).

Finger. (E.) A. S. *finger.*+Du. *vinger,* Icel. *fingr,* Dan. Swed. G. *finger,* Goth. *figgrs* (= *fingrs*). Teut. type **fin-groz* ; orig. sense unknown.

Finial. (L.) A coined word ; from L. *finis,* end. Cf. *final.*

finical. (F. – L.) A coined word ; extended from **Fine** (1) above.

finish, vb. (F. – L.) M. E. *finischen.* – O. F. *finiss-*, base of pres. pt. of *finir,* to finish. – L. *finire,* to end. – L. *finis,* end.

finite, limited. (L.) L. *finitus,* pp. of *finire* (above).

Fiord, a sea-loch, deep inlet of the sea. (Scand.) Norw. *fjord,* Dan. *fiord, fjord* ; Icel. *fjörðr.* See **Frith.**

Fir, a tree. (Scand.) M. E. *fir* ; answering to a mutated form due to A. S. *furh,* which occurs in *furhwudu,* a pine-tree ; but prob. of Scand. origin. Cf. Icel. *fyri-skōgr,* a fir-wood (written *fyriskōgr*) ; from Icel. *fura,* a fir ; cf. Dan. *fyr,* Swed. *fura* +G. *föhre,* W. *pyr.* Cognate with L. *quercus,* an oak ; and O. Lombardic *fereha,* 'æsculus.'

Fire. (E.) A. S. *fȳr.*+Du. *vuur,* Icel. *fȳri,* Dan. and Swed. *fyr,* G. *feuer,* M.H.G.
viur, O. H. G. *fuir.* Teut. type **fū-ir.* Cognate with Gk. πῦρ. Cf. Skt. *pāvaka-* (from *pū*), purifying, also fire. (√PŪ.)

Firk, to conduct, drive, beat. (E.) A. S. *fercian,* to conduct, support. Prob. from A. S. *fær,* a journey ; allied to **Fare.**

Firkin, the fourth part of a barrel. (M. Du.) M. E. *ferdekin.* From Du. *vierde,* fourth ; with suffix *-kin* (as in *kil-der-kin*) answering to the M. Du. double dimin. suffix *-k-in* (G. *-ch-en* in *mädchen*). *Vierde* is from Du. *vier,* four ; see **Four.**

Firm (1), adj. (F. – L.) M. E. *ferme.* – O. F. and F. *ferme.* – L. *firmus,* steadfast. **Der.** *farm.*

firm (2), a partnership. (Span. – L.) The older sense was 'signature' of the house or (as we call it) the firm. – Span. *firma,* a signature. – Span. *firmar,* to confirm, sign. – L. *firmāre,* to make firm. – L. *firmus,* firm (above).

firmament, celestial sphere. (F. – L.) O. F. *firmament.* – L. *firmāmentum,* a support ; also, expanse of the sky (Vulgate). – L. *firmāre,* to strengthen ; from *firmus,* firm.

Firman, a mandate. (Pers.) Pers. *fermān,* a mandate, order ; O. Pers. *framāna* (Horn) ; cf. Skt. *pramāna-*, a decision, from *pra,* before (Gk. πρό) and *mā,* to measure.

First. (E.) A. S. *fyrst,* the superl. of *fore,* with vowel-change of *u* (A. S. *o*) to *y.*+Icel. *fyrstr* ; Dan. *förste* ; Swed. *första.* Teut. type **furistoz,* superl. from the base **fur-* ; see **Fore.**

Firth ; see **Frith.**

Fiscal, pertaining to the revenue. (F. – L.) O. F. *fiscal.* – Late L. *fiscālis.* – L. *fiscus,* a basket of rushes, also a purse.

Fish. (E.) A. S. *fisc.*+Du. *visch,* Icel. *fiskr,* Dan. and Swed. *fisk,* G. *fisch* ; Goth. *fisks.* Teut. type **fiskoz.* Cognate with L. *piscis,* Irish and Gael. *iasg,* O. Ir. *iasc* (with loss of initial *p*).

Fissure. (F. – L.) O. F. *fissure.* – L. *fissūra.* – L. *fissus,* pp. of *findere,* to cleave. +Skt. *bhid,* to cleave ; A. S. *bītan,* to bite. (√BHEID.) And see **Vent** (1). Brugm. i. § 567.

Fist. (E.) M. E. *fist, fest, fust.* A. S. *fyst.*+Du. *vuist,* G. *faust,* O. H. G. *fūst.* Teut. **fūstiz.* ¶ If the orig. Teut. form was **funhstiz,* it may be identified with Russ. *piaste,* fist, O. Slav. *pęsti* ; from an Idg. base **pǝnksti-*, which is allied to **Five.**

Fistula, a deep, narrow abscess. (L.) From the shape; L. *fistula,* a pipe.

Fit (1), to suit; as adj., apt. (Scand.) M. E. *fitten,* to arrange. — Icel. and Norw. *fitja,* to knit together; Swed. dial. *fittja,* to bind together; cf. G. *fitzen,* to bind into skeins, from *fitze,* a skein. From Icel. *fit,* a hem, also 'web' of a bird's foot; cf. M. Dan. *fidde,* to knit; Dan. *fid,* a skein. Perhaps allied to **Fit** (2). ¶ Influenced as to sense by M. E. *fete,* well done; from O. F. *fait,* Lat. *factus*; see **Feat.**

Fit (2), a part of a poem, attack of illness. (E.) M. E. *fit.* A. S. *fitt,* (1) a song, (2) a struggle; which perhaps are the same word. Cf. **Fit** (1).

Fitch, the same as **Vetch,** q. v.

Fitchet, Fitchew, a pole-cat. (F. — M. Du.) *Fitchew* is from Picard *ficheux,* M. F. *fissau,* a polecat; older form, *fissel.* — M. Du. *fisse,* a polecat; from the smell. Cf. Icel. *fisa,* to make a smell.

Fitz, son. (A. F. — L.) Formerly *fiz* (with *z* as *ts*). — A. F. *fiz* (with *z* as *ts*); also O. F. *filz, fils.* — L. *filius,* a son.

Five. (E.) M. E. *fif*; sometimes *fiue,* as a plural. A. S. *fif* (for **fimf*). **+** Du. *vijf,* Dan. Swed. *fem,* Icel. *fimm,* Goth. *fimf,* G. *fünf*; W. *pump,* O. Ir. *coic,* L. *quinque,* Lith. *penki,* Gk. πέντε (Æol. πέμπε), Skt. *pancha.* Idg. type **penqe.* Der. *fif-th,* A. S. *fifta*; *fifteen,* A. S. *fiftene*; *fif-ty,* A. S. *fiftig.*

Fix. (F. — L.) O. F. *fix,* fixed. — L. *fixus,* fixed; pp. of *figere,* to fix.

Fizz. (Scand.) Imitative; cf. Icel. *fisa,* Dan. *fise,* with the sense of L. *pedere.*

Flabby; weakened form of *flappy*; see **Flap.** Cf. Low G. *flabbe,* a hanging lip; *flabbsig,* flabby (Danneil).

Flaccid. (F. — L.) F. *flaccide.* — L. *flaccidus,* limp. — L. *flaccus,* flabby.

Flag (1), to droop, grow weary. (E.) Weakened form of *flack,* to hang loosely; M. E. *flakken,* to flap about. From the base *flac-* of A. S. *flac-or,* flying, roving. **+** Icel. *flakka,* to rove; *flaka,* to flap; *flökra, flögra,* Dan. *flagre,* to flutter; G. *flackern,* to flutter. All from the imitative base *flak-,* allied to *flap, flicker.* And partly from O. F. *flaquir,* to be limp; from O. F. *flaque,* limp, L. *flaccus.*

flag (2), an ensign. (Scand.?) Dan. *flag,* Swed. *flagg,* a flag; from base of Icel. *flögra,* to flutter (above).

flag (3), a reed; the same word as *flag* (2); from its waving in the wind.

Flag (4), **Flagstone,** a paving-stone. (Scand.) Icel. *flaga,* a flag or slab of stone. This might give E. dial. *flaw* (see **Flaw**), but cf. Icel. *flagna,* to flake off, Dan. dial. *flag-törv,* Sc. *flag,* a cut turf. A weakened form of **Flake.**

Flagellate. (L.) From pp. of L. *flagellāre,* to scourge. — L. *flagellum,* dimin. of *flagrum,* a scourge. See **Flail.**

Flageolet, a sort of flute. (F. — Prov.) M. F. *flageolet,* dimin. of *flageol,* with the same sense. — Prov. *flajols, flaujols,* a flageolet; which cannot represent a Late L. **flautiolus,* a little flute, as suggested by Diez.

Flagitious. (L.) L. *flāgitiōs-us,* shameful; with suffix *-ous-.* — L. *flāgitium,* a disgraceful act; cf. L. *flāgitāre,* to act with violence. Perhaps allied to **Flagrant.**

Flagon. (F. — Late L.) O. F. *flacon,* another form of *flascon.* — Late L. *flascōnem,* acc. of *flasco,* a flask. — Late L. *flasca,* a flask. See **Flask.**

Flagrant, glaring, as a fault. (F. — L.) O. F. *flagrant,* properly burning. — L. *flagrant-,* stem of pres. pt. of *flagrāre,* to burn. **+** Gk. φλέγειν, to burn; Sk. *bhrāj.* (√BHLEG.) Brugm. i. § 539 (2).

Flail. (L.) M. E. *fliƺel, fleƺl, fleil.* [Later, *flayel* (from O. F. *flaël* > F. *fléau*).] From L. *flagellum,* a whip, in Late L., a flail; dimin. of *flagrum,* a scourge. See **Flagellate.**

Flake, a thin slice. (Scand.) Norw. *flak,* a slice, an ice-floe; cf. Icel. *flakna,* *flagna,* to flake off, Swed. *flaga,* a flake. Perhaps allied to **Flay.**

Flambeau. (F. — L.) F. *flambeau,* a torch; dimin. of O. F. *flambe* (below).

flame, sb. (F. — L.) O. F. *flame,* *flamme*; also *flambe.* — L. *flamma* (**flagma*?), a flame; perhaps from the base *flag-,* to burn. See **Flagrant.**

Flamen. (L.) L. *flāmen,* a priest of Rome. Prob. for **flag-men,* he who burns the sacrifice; cf. *flagrare,* to burn. Or else allied to Goth. *blōtan,* to sacrifice.

Flamingo. (Span. — Prov. — L.) Span. *flamenco,* a flamingo; but said to be a Provençal word; the Prov. form is *flamenc,* where the suffix *-enc* is supposed to be an adaptation of the Teut. suffix *-ing.* The F. form is *flamant,* lit. 'flaming,' but it seems to have been confused with F. *Flamand,* a *Fleming,* whence the peculiar form of the Prov. form may have arisen; Palsgrave has 'Flemmyng, *flammant.*'

Still, the etymology is certainly from L. *flamma*, a flame; from the flame-like colour of the bird.

Flange, a projecting rim. (F. – Teut.) The same as prov. E. *flanch*, a projection; cf. *flanch* in heraldry, an ordinary on each side (or *flank*) of the shield. – O. F. *flanche* (A. F. *flanke*), fem. sb. allied to F. *flanc*, side. See below.

flank, the side. (F. – Teut.) M. E. *flanc.* – F. *flanc*, side. – O. H. G. *hlancha*, *lanka*, hip, bend, loin; cf. Mid. Du. '*de Lancke*, the flancks;' Hexham. Allied to A. S. *hlanc*, slender; see **Lank**. (Disputed; but probable; see Kluge, s. v. *Gelenk*.)

Flannel. (W.) Prov. E. *flannen*, a better form. – W. *gwlanen*, flannel, from *gwlan*, wool. Allied to **Wool**.

Flap, to beat with the wings. (E.) M. E. *flappen*, to beat; not in A. S. E. Fries. *flappen*. Imitative; like *flack*, to beat; see **Flag** (1). + Du. *flappen*, to flap. Der. *flabby* (flappy); *flap*, sb.

Flare; see below.

Flash, to blaze. (E.) M. E. *flaschen*, to dash; cf. Swed. dial. *flasa*, to burn violently; Icel. *flasa*, to rush, *flas*, a swift rushing.

flare. (Scand.) Norweg. *flara*, to blaze; apparently a variant of Swed. dial. *flasa* (above).

Flask. (Late L.?) A. S. *flasce*, *flaxe*; we also find Icel. *flaska*, Dan. *flaske*, Swed. *flaska*, G. *flasche*; but it is hardly a Teut. word. – Late L. *flasca*, a flask; cf. also W. *fflasg*, Gael. *flasg* (from E.). Remoter origin uncertain. See **Flagon**.

Flat. (Scand.) M. E. *flat.* – Icel. *flatr*, Swed. *flat*, Dan. *flad.*

Flatter. (F. – Teut.; *or* E.) M. E. *flateren*, a frequentative form. Either, with suffix *-er-*, from O. F. *flat-er*, mod. F. *flatter*, to flatter; or formed from an E. base *flat-*, of imitative origin; cf. M. Du. *flattéren*, to flatter (Hexham) from O. F. *flater*, which is from Icel. *flat-r*, flat; from the notion of making smooth. Cf. the base *flak-*, seen in M. Swed. *fleckra*, to flatter, Swed. dial. *fleka*, to caress; also M. E. *flakken*, to move to and fro, and G. *flach*, flat; see **Flag** (1). The sb. *flattery* is plainly adapted from O. F. *flaterie*, F. *flatterie*.

Flatulent, windy. (F. – L.) M. F. *flatulent.* – Late L. *flātulentus.* – L. *flātus*, breath. – L. *flāre*, to blow; see **Blow** (1).

Flaunt, to display ostentatiously. (Unknown.) It seems to have been particularly used of the display of fluttering plumes, &c. Of unknown origin; most words in *-aunt* are French. Somewhat similar is Swed. dial. *flankt*, flutteringly, loosely, from *flanka*, to waver; perhaps allied to *flakka*, to waver, answering to M. E. *flakken*; see **Flag** (1).

Flavour. (F. – L.) The form seems to have been influenced by that of the word *savour*. O. Lowl. Sc. *flewoure*, *flewer.* – O. F. *fleur*, *fleiur*, *flaur*, smell. Cf. Ital. *fiatore*, a bad odour; answering to Late L. acc. **flātorem.* – L. *flātus*, pp. of *flāre*, to blow. (Körting, § 3316.)

Flaw, a crack. (Scand.) M. E. *flawe.* – Swed. *flaga*, a crack, flaw, also a flake; see **Flake**. Cf. prov. E. *flaw*, a flake (as of snow); also, a gust of wind, like Du. *vlaag*.

Flawn, a kind of custard. (F. – O.H G.) M. E. *flaun.* – F. *flan*, O. F. *flaon*, a flawn; (cf. Span. *flaon*, Ital. *fiadone*). – O. H. G. *flado*, a broad flat cake; G. *fladen*. Allied to Gr. πλατύς, broad.

Flax, a plant. (E.) A. S. *fleax.* + Du. *vlas*, G. *flachs*. Perhaps allied to Goth. *flah-ta*, a plaiting, Gk. πλέκ-ειν, to weave.

Flay, to strip off skin. (E.) M. E. *flean.* A. S. *flēan*, to flay. + Icel. *flā*, pt. t. *flō*, pp. *fleginn*. Teut. type **flahan-* (pt. t. *flōh), to strike. Cognate with Lith. *plakù*, I strike; cf. Lat. *plāga*, a stroke. See **Plague**. Brugm. i. § 569.

Flea. (E.) M. E. *flee*, pl. *fleen.* A. S. *flēah*, a flea. + Du. *vloo*, Icel. *flō*, G. *floh*. Teut. base **flauh-*, or perhaps **þlauh-*, allied to the verb *to flee*. See **Flee**.

Fleam, a kind of lancet. (F. – L. – Gk.) O. F. *flieme*, F. *flamme*, a fleam; Hamilton. – Late L. *flētoma*, a lancet (Vocab. 400. 11); shortened from Late L. *flevotomum*, *phlebotomum*, a lancet. – Gk. φλεβοτόμον, a lancet. – Gk. φλεβο-, decl. stem of φλέψ, a vein; τομ-, o-grade of τέμνειν, to cut. Hence also M. H. G. *fliedeme*, G. *fliete*, Du. *vlijm*, a fleam.

Fleck, a spot. (Scand.) M. E. *flek.* – Icel. *flekkr*, a spot; *flekka*, to stain; Swed. *fläck*, a spot. + Du. *vlek*, G. *fleck*.

Flection; see **Flexible**.

Fledge, to be furnished with feathers. (E.) The pp. *fledged* is now used in the place of M. E. *flegge*, adj., ready to fly. *Flegge* is a Kentish form of M. E. *flygge*, ready to fly. From A. S. *flycge; found

in the compound *unflycge*, as in '*inplumes*,
unfligge,' Academy, 2 June, 1894 (Napier).
E. Fries. *flügge.* **+** Du. *vlug* (M. Du.
vlugge) ; O. H. G. *flucchi.* Teut. type
*flugjoz, adj. ; from **flug-*, weak grade of
*fleugan-, to fly. See Fly.

Flee, to escape. (E.) M. E. *fleen*, pt. t.
fleh, fleih. [The M. E. pt. t. also appears
as *fledde*, whence mod. E. *fled*, of Scand.
origin.] A. S. *fléon* (pt. t. *fléah*).**+**O. Sax.
fliohan, G. *fliehen* ; also Icel. *flýja* (pt. t.
flö, also *flýða*) ; Swed. *fly* (pt. t. *flydde*) ;
Goth. *thliuhan.* Teut. type **thleuhan-*
(pt. t. *thlauh*) ; so that *fl* was orig. *thl*, and
there was *no* orig. connexion with the
verb *to fly*, which has from an early date
been confused with it.

Fleece. (E.) M. E. *flees.* A. S. *fléos*,
earlier *flíus* ; also *flýs.***+**Du. *vlies*, M.H.G.
vlius ; cf. G. *fliess* ; also G. *flaus*, a woollen
coat, M. H. G. *vlús*, a sheep-skin. Teut.
stems **fleusi-*, **fleuso-*, **flúso-* ; possibly
allied to L. *plú-ma.* See Plume.

Fleer, to mock. (Scand.) M. E.
flerien. ━ Norw. *flira*, to titter, giggle ;
also spelt *flisa* ; Dan. dial. *flire*, to jeer ;
Swed *flissa*, to titter.

Fleet (1), a number of ships. (E.)
M. E. *flete, fleote.* A S. *fléot*, a ship ; or
(collectively) a number of ships. ━ A. S.
fléotan, to float. **+** O. Sax. *fliotan*, Du.
vlieten, to flow ; O. H. G. *fliozzan* to
float, flow, G. *fliessen*, to flow ; Icel.
fljóta, Swed. *flyta*, Dan. *flyde.* Teut.
*fleutan- (pt. t. *flaut*, pp. *flutanoz*) ; Idg.
base **pleud*, as in Lith. *plúdis*, a float of
a fishing-net. (√PLEU.) Cf. Gk. πλέειν,
to sail, Skt. *plu, pru*, to swim, float,
flow.

fleet (2), a creek. (E.) A.S. *fléot*, a
creek, a place where water flows ; *fléote*,
a stream. ━ A.S. *fléotan*, to float, swim ;
see Fleet (1). Cf. O. Fries. *flét*, stream.

fleet (3), swift. (E.) Cf. A. S. *fléotig*,
swift ; Icel. *fljótr*, swift. From the verb ;
see Fleet (1).

fleet (4), vb., to move swiftly. (E.)
From A. S. *fléotan* ; see Fleet (1).

Flesh. (E.) M. E. *flesch.* A.S. *flǽsc*,
flesh. **+** Icel. *flesk*, bacon ; Dan. *flesk*,
Swed. *fläsk*, bacon : Du. *vleesch* ; G.
fleisch. Teut. type **flaiskoz*, n.

Fleur-de-lis, flower of the lily.
(F. ─ L.) O. F. *fleur de lis.* Here *lis* =
Late L. *lílius*, corrupt form of L. *lílium*,
a lily ; see Flower and Lily.

Flexible. (F. ─ L.) M. F. *flexible.* ─ L.

flexibilis, easily bent. ━ L. *flexus*, pp. of
flectere, to bend. **Der.** *in-flexible.*

flection, a bending. (L.) Better
flexion ; from L. acc. *flexiōnem*, a bending. ─ L. *flexus*, pp. of *flectere.* So also
flex-or, flex-ure. (Cf. F. *flexion.*)

Flick, a light blow. (E.) Imitative ;
cf. *flip.* E. Fries. *flik*, a flick ; *flik-flakken*,
to strike lightly.

Flicker, to flutter. (E.) M. E. *flikeren.*
━ A. S. *flicorian*, to flutter. Imitative ; a
weakened form of *flacker*, frequent. of M. E.
flakken, to flap about. Cf. A. S. *flacor*,
adj., flying ; G. *flackern*, to flutter. See
Flag (1).

Flight, act of flying. (E.) A.S. *flyht*,
allied to *flyge*, flight.**+**Swed. *flykt*, G.
flucht, Du. *vlucht.* Teut. **fluhti-* ; from
flug-, weak grade of **fleugan-*, to fly. See
Fly.

Flimsy, weak, slight. (E.) Modern ;
first recorded in 1702 (Kersey). Prob.
imitative, and suggested by *film* ; note E.
Fries. *flém, flím*, a film ; Dan. dial. *flems*,
flims, a skim on milk. 'For the ending,
cf. *tipsy, bumpsy* ; also *limpsy*, given by
Webster as a U. S. synonym of *flimsy* ';
N. E. D.

Flinch. (F. ─ Teut. ?) XVI cent. ━
O. F. *flenchir, flainchir, flechir*, to turn
aside, bend. Of unknown origin ; perhaps
from O. H. G. **hlencan*, answering to G.
lenken, to turn, bend. The G. *lenken* is
from O. H. G. *hlanca*, the side (Kluge) ;
see Flank, Flange. ¶ The initial *fl*
would then be accounted for precisely as
in the case of *flank*, viz. from O. H. G. *hl.*
Cf. Link (1).

Fling. (Scand.) Cf. Swed. *flänga*, to
use violent action, romp, race about ; *i
fläng*, at full speed (taking one's fling) ;
M. Swed. *flenga*, to strike ; Icel. *flengja*,
to whip ; Dan. *flenge*, to slash ; *i fleng*,
indiscriminately. These forms presuppose
a strong verb **flinga*, which the E. form
perhaps represents.

Flint. (E.) A.S. *flint.***+**Dan. *flint* ;
Swed. *flinta.* Perhaps cognate with Gk.
πλίνθος, a brick. Brugm. i. §§ 575, 704.

Flip (1), vb., to fillip, jerk lightly. (E.)
Of imitative origin, like *flick.* Cf. **Flap.**

Flip (2), a mixture of beer and spirit
with sugar, heated. (E.) Prob. from *flip*,
to beat up. Moisy (Dict. of Norman
patois) spells it *phlippe*, as if from F.
Philippe ; but wrongly.

Flippant. (Scand.) *Flippant* is for

flippand, the North. M. E. pres. pt. ; *flip-pand* = prattling, saucy. Or else, the suffix *-ant* imitates the French (heraldic) suffix in *ramp-ant*, &c. Cf. prov. E. *flip*, nimble, flippant ; from the base *flip-*, as in Icel. *fleipa*, to prattle ; Swed. dial. *flepa*, to talk nonsense ; cf. Swed. dial. *flip*, the lip.

Flirt. (E.) Often written *flurt*, meaning to mock, gibe, scorn ; the oldest sense of *flirt* was to jerk lightly away. Of imitative origin ; cf. *flip*, *flick*. So also E. Fries. *flirr*, *flirt*, a light blow ; *flirtje*, a giddy girl.

Flit, to remove from place to place. (Scand.) M. E. *flitten*. — Icel. *flytja*, to cause to flit ; Swed. *flytta*, to flit, remove ; Dan. *flytte* ; causal of Icel. *fljóta*, Swed. *flyta*, Dan. *flyde*, to float. See **Fleet** (1), **Float**.

Flitch, side of bacon. (E.) M. E. *flicche*. A. S. *flicce*.+Icel. *flikki*, a flitch ; *flík*, a flap, tatter. Perhaps allied to G. *flick-*, a patch ; and to E. **Fleck**.

Float, to swim on a liquid surface. (E.) M. E. *floten*, *flotien*. A. S. *flotian*. +Icel. *flota*, Du. *vlotten*. Teut. **flutōjan-*, wk. vb. ; from **flut-*, weak grade of **fleu-tan-*, to float, whence mod. E. *fleet*. See **Fleet** (1). ¶ Confused with F. *flotter* (O. F. *floter*), to float, from the same Teut. base **flut-*.

Flock (1). a company of sheep, &c. (E.) M. E. *flok*. A. S. *flocc*.+Icel. *flokkr*, Dan. *flok*, Swed. *flock*.

Flock (2), a lock of wool. (F.—L.) O. F. *floc*. — L. *floccus*, a lock of wool.

Floe, a flake of ice. (Dan.) Dan. *flage* ; as in *iis-flage*, an ice-floe, lit. 'ice-flake.' Cf. Norw. *isflak*, *isflōk*, the same. See **Flake**.

Flog, to beat. (L. ?) A late word ; and (in 1676) a cant term. Cf. *flack* ; or probably suggested by *flagellate*, q. v. Cf. Low G. *flogger*, a flail, variant of G. *flegel*, a flail, from Late L. *flagellum*, a flail ; see **Flail**.

Flood. (E.) A. S. *flōd*, a flood ; from *flōwan*, to flow.+Du. *vloed*, Icel. *flōð*, Swed. Dan. *flod*, Goth. *flōdus*, a river, G. *fluth*. Teut. **flō-ðuz*, act of flowing, also a flood ; from Teut. base **flō-* ; see **Flow**.

Floor. (E.) A. S. *flōr*.+Du. *vloer*, G. *flur*. Teut. **flōruz*; cognate with W. *llawr*, Bret. *leur*, Irish *lār*. Idg. **plārus*, a floor ; from **plā-*, to spread out, whence also L. *plā-nus*, plain. See **Plain**.

Floral, pertaining to flowers. (L.) L.

flōrālis, belonging to *Flōra*, goddess of flowers. — L. *flōr-*, as the stem of *flōs*, a flower ; cf. *flōrēre*, to flourish, allied to **Blow** (2) and **Bloom**.

florid. (L.) L. *flōridus*, lit. abounding with flowers ; hence, rosy. — L. *flōri-*, decl. stem of *flōs*, a flower (above).

florin, a coin. (F.—Ital.—L.) M. E. *floren* (about A. D. 1303).—O. F. *florin*, a florin.—Ital. *fiorino* (=*florino*), a coin of Florence, so called because it bore a lily, the symbol of that town.—Ital. *fiore*, a flower.—L. *flōrem*, acc. of *flōs*, a flower.

floscule. (L.) L. *flōsculus*, a little flower ; double dimin. of *flōs*.

Floss, rough silk ; as in *floss-silk*. (F.—L.) From M. F. *flosche*; Cot. has : '*soye flosche*, sleave silke.' [So also Ital. *floscio*, Venetian *flosso*, soft, weak ; *floscia seta*, floss-silk.] An adj. formation from O. F. *flocher*, to form into 'flocks' or tufts. — F. *floc* ; see **Flock** (2).

Flotilla. (Span.—Teut.) Span. *flotilla*, a little fleet ; dimin. of *flota*, a fleet, cognate with O. F. *flote*, a fleet of ships, a crowd of people. This O. F. *flote* (fem.), F. *flotte* (whence G. *flotte*) is from a Teut. source ; cf. Du. *vloot*, Icel. *floti*, a fleet, A. S. *flota*, a ship. From the base **flut-* ; see **Float**. Cf. M. E. *flote*, a fleet. (Körting, § 3349.)

flotsam, goods lost in shipwreck, and floating on the waves. (Law F.—E.) An A. F. law-term, formerly *flotson* (Blount). A. F. *floteson* ; O. F. *flotaison*, a flooding of fields (Godefroy).—Low L. type **flot-tātiōnem*, from **flottāre*, to float, to flood (F. *flotter*). From the Teut. base **flut-* (above). Cf. **Jetsam**.

Flounce (1), to plunge about. (E.) Cf. Swed. dial. and M. Swed. *flunsa*, to plunge. Of imitative origin.

Flounce (2), a plaited border on a dress. (F.—L.?) Changed from M. E. *frounce*, a plait. —O. F. *fronser*, *froncer*, to gather, plait, wrinkle ; *fronser le front*, to knit or wrinkle the forehead. Prob. from Late L. **frontiāre*, not found, but regularly formed from *fronti-*, decl. stem of *frons*, forehead ; see **Front**. (Körting, § 3477.)

Flounder (1), to flounce about. (E.) XVI cent. An imitative word ; perhaps suggested by *flounce* (1) and *flood*. Cf. Du. *flodderen*, to dangle, flap, splash through mire ; Swed. *fladdra*, to flutter.

Flounder (2), a fish. (F.—Scand.)

A. F. *floundre.* – O. F. *flondre* (in Normandy). – Swed. *flundra,* Dan. *flynder,* Icel. *flyðra* ; E. Fries. *flunder.*

Flour, finer part of meal. (F. – L.) Short for 'flower of wheat.' – F. *fleur,* short for *fleur de farine,* flour; see **Flower** below (which is a doublet).

flourish, vb. (F. – L.) M. E. *florisshen* – O. F. *floriss-,* stem of pres. pt. of *florir,* to flourish. – Folk-L. *flōrīre,* for L. *flōrēre,* to blossom ; cf. L. *flōrescere,* inceptive form of *flōrēre.* See **Floral.**

Flout, to mock. (F.) Prob. from M. E. *flouten,* to play the flute. Similarly, M. Du. *fluyten* (Du. *fluiten*), to play the flute, also had once the meaning 'to mock, jeer'; Oudemans. See **Flute.**

Flow, to stream. (E.) M. E. *flowen* ; A. S. *flōwan,* pt. t. *flēow*; cf. Du. *vloeijen,* to flow; Icel. *flōa,* to flood. Teut. base **flō-* ; cognate with Gk. πλώειν, to float. See **Flood.**

Flower, sb. (F. – L.) M. E. *flour.* – O. F. *flour* (F. *fleur*). – L. *flōrem,* acc. of *flōs,* a flower. See **Floral.**

Fluctuate, to waver. (L.) From pp. of *fluctuāre,* to float about. – L. *fluctus,* a wave. – L. *fluctus,* old pp. of *fluere,* to flow.

Flue (1), a chimney-pipe. (F. – L. ?) Of doubtful origin. [*Flue,* in Phaer's Virgil, x. 209, is prob. a misprint for *flute.*] Prob. from M. E. *fluen,* to flow, as the pipe conducts the flow of the smoke; 'To flue, *fluere,*' Cath. Angl. – F. *fluer,* 'to flow, glide ;' Cot. – L. *fluere,* to flow.

Flue (2), light, floating down. (E. ?) Cf. prov. E. *fluff,* flue. Perhaps a derivative of the verb **Fly** (cf. A. S. pt. t. pl. *flug-on*). We find Low G. *flog,* E. Fries. *flüg, flog,* flue ; cf. G. *flug,* flight.

Fluent. (L.) From stem of pres. pt. of L. *fluere,* to flow.

fluid. (F. – L.) O. F. *fluide.* – L. *fluidus,* flowing. – L. *fluere,* to flow.

Fluke (1), a fish. (E.) M. E. *floke, fluke.* A. S. *flōc,* a kind of plaice + Icel. *flōki,* a kind of halibut. Lit. 'flat' fish. The base **flōc-* is the strong grade of Teut. **flac-,* as seen in G. *flach,* flat.

Fluke (2), part of an anchor. (E. ?) Also spelt *flook.* Perhaps 'the flat' end ; and the same word as *fluke* (1). Apparently distinct from G. *flunke,* the hook of an anchor.

Flummery, a light food. (W.) W. *llymru, llymruwd,* flummery, sour oat-meal boiled and jellied. Cf. W. *llymus,* sharp, tart.

Flunkey, a footman. (F. – O. H. G.) Modern. Lowl. Sc. *flunkie,* a servant in livery. Apparently from F. *flanqueur,* a scout (see *Flanker* in N. E. D.). – F. *flanquer,* ' to flank, to be at one's elbow for a help at need ;' Cot. – F. *flanc,* side ; see **Flank.**

Fluor, Fluor-spar, a mineral. (L.) The L. *fluor* (lit. a flowing) was formerly in use as a term in alchemy and chemistry. – L. *fluere,* to flow.

Flurry, hurry. (E.) Swift has *flurry,* a gust of wind. From *flurr,* to whirr (N. E. D.). Imitative ; cf. Swed. dial. *flurig,* disordered (as hair) ; *flur,* disordered hair, whim ; Norweg. *flurutt,* shaggy, disordered. And cf. E. *flutter.*

Flush (1), to inundate. (E.) Apparently of imitative origin ; cf. *flush,* to fly up quickly (N. E. D.). Perhaps influenced by F. *flux,* 'a flowing, a flux ; also, a *flush* at cards ;' Cot. See **Flux.** Cf. *flusch,* a pool of water (G. Douglas) ; M. Du. *fluysen,* to gush or break out violently (Hexham) ; Dan. dial. *fluse,* to gush out.

Flush (2), to blush, to redden. (E.) XVIII cent. Perhaps the same as **Flush** (1), but much influenced by **Flash.** Cf. Swed. dial. *flossa,* to burn, flare ; Norweg. *flosa,* passion, vehemence. And see **Fluster.**

Flush (3), level. (E. ?) This is a derived sense ; it meant in full flow, abundantly full ; hence, level. From **Flush** (1).

Fluster, to heat with drinking, confuse. (Scand.) Icel. *flaustra,* to be flustered ; *flaustr,* fluster, hurry; cf. E. Fries. *flöstern, flustern,* to rustle (as wind). Cf. **Flush** (2) and **Flash.**

Flute, a musical pipe. (F.) M. E. *flowte, floite.* – O. F. *flaute, fleute, flahute, flehute,* a flute (mod. F. *flûte*). Prov. *flauta.* Of uncertain origin. The *fl* may have been suggested by L. *flāre,* to blow.

Flutter, to flap the wings. (E.) M. E. *floteren,* to fluctuate. A. S. *flotorian,* to float about; cf. A. S. *flot,* the sea; *flota,* a ship. – A. S. *flot-,* stem of *flot-en,* pp. of *flēotan,* to float. Cf. E. Fries. *fluttern.*

Flux. (F. – L.) O. F. *flux,* a flux. – L. *flūxum,* acc. of *flūxus,* a flowing ; from the pp. of *fluere,* to flow.

Fly (1), to float in air. (E.) M. E. *flēꝫen, flēꝫen.* A. S. *flēogan* ; pt. t. *flēah* ; pp. *flogen.* + Du. *vliegen,* Icel. *fljūga,* Dan.

flyve, Swed. *flyga*, G. *fliegen*. Teut. type
*fleugan-. Cf. L. *plūma*, a feather.
(√PLEUGH.) Not allied to **Flee**. **Der.**
fly, an insect, A. S. *fléoge*, *flȳge* ; G. *fliege*.

Fly (2), a vehicle. (E.) A name given
to a kind of four-wheeled vehicle drawn
by men at Brighton, in 1816. Called *fly-
coach* in 1818 (Scott, Heart Midl. ch. 1).
From *fly*, vb. See above.

Foal. (E.) M. E. *fole*, A. S. *fola*.+Du.
veulen, Icel. *foli*, Dan. *fole*, Swed. *fåle*,
Goth. *fula*, G. *fohlen*. Teut. *fulon-.
Cognate with L. *pullus*, young of an
animal ; Gk. πῶλος.

Foam. (E.) M. E. *fome*. A. S. *fām*.
+Prov. G. *faim* ; O. H. G. *feim*. Teut.
*faimo-. Cognate with Russ. *piena*, foam ;
Skt. *phēna*, foam ; and prob. with Lat.
spūma (for *spoima), foam, and Lat. *pūmex*, pumice. Allied to **Spume**.

Fob, watch-pocket. (O. Low G.) An
O. Low G. word, only preserved in the
cognate H. G. (Prussian) *fuppe*, a pocket ;
for which see Bremen Wört. i. 437.

Focus, a point where light-rays meet.
(L.) L. *focus*, a hearth ; hence, a centre
of fire.

Fodder, food for cattle. (E.) M. E.
fodder. A. S. *fōdor*, *fōddor* ; extended
form of *fōda*, food.+Du. *voeder*, Icel. *fōðr*,
Dan. Swed. *foder*, G. *futter*. Teut. type
*fōdrom, neut. Allied to **Food**, q. v.

Foe. (E.) M. E. *foo*. A. S. *fāh*, adj.
hostile. Teut. type *faihoz ; Idg. *poiqos
(whence Irish *oech*, a foe, with loss of
p). From the weak grade *piq- we have
Gk. πικρός, bitter, Lith. *piktas*, unkind.
Brugm. i. § 646.

Fœtus ; see **Fetus**.

Fog. (E.) In several senses ; M. E.
fogge is 'coarse grass' ; hence *foggy*,
mossy, boggy, murky (whence perhaps
the sb. *fog*, a mist). Origin unknown ; cf.
Dan. *fog*, as in *snee-fog*, a blinding fall
of snow, *fyge*, to drift (as snow) ; but
there is no clear connexion.

Foible, a weak point in character.
(F.—L.) O. F. *foible*, F. *faible*, weak,
feeble ; see **Feeble**.

Foil (1), to defeat. (F.—L.) M. E.
foylen, to trample under foot. — O. F.
fouler, to trample on, also to oppress,
foil, over-charge extremely (Cot.). — Late
L. *fullāre*, *folāre*, to full cloth ; see **Full**
(3). **Der.** *foil*, a blunt sword, for practice
in *foiling*, i. e. parrying ; *foil*, a defeat.

Foil (2), a set-off, as in setting a gem.

(F.—L.) M. F. *feuille*, a leaf, 'also the
foyle of precious stones,' Cot. ; Norman
foille, fem. ; cf. Ital. *foglia*, Span. *hoja*,
a leaf.—L. *folia*, pl. of *folium*, a leaf ;
afterwards used as a fem. sing. See
Foliage. Also O. F. *fueil*, *foil*, m. ; from
L. *folium*.

Foin, to thrust with a sword. (F.—L.)
Obsolete. Lit. 'to thrust with an eel-
spear or trident.'—O. F. *foine*, *foisne*, an
eel-spear. — L. *fuscina*, a trident, the
weapon used by a *retiārius*, or gladiator
with a net.

Foison, plenty. (F.—L.) O. F. *foison*,
abundance. — Folk-L. *fūsiōnem*, for L.
fūsiōnem, acc. of *fūsio*, a pouring out,
hence profusion.—L. *fūsus*, pp. of *fundere*,
to pour. See **Fuse**.

Foist, to palm or put off, to intrude
surreptitiously. (Du.) XVI cent. — Du.
vuisten, to take in the fist or hand ; see
N. E. D. (Low G. *vūsten*, to take in the
hand) ; hence, to 'palm' a die, to cheat.
—Du. *vuist*, fist ; see **Fist**.

Fold (1), to double together. (E.) M. E.
folden, O. Merc. *faldan*, A. S. *fealdan* (pt.
t. *fēold*), to fold.+Dan. *folde*, Swed. *fålla*
(=*falda*), Icel. *falda*, Goth. *falthan*, G.
falten. Teut. type *falthan-. Allied to Gk.
δι-πλάσιος, doubled ; πλάσσειν, to form,
mould. See **Plaster**. **Der.** *fold*, sb.,
a plait ; *-fold*, suffix, as in *two-fold*, &c.

Fold (2), a pen for sheep. (E.) A. S.
fald, also *falod*, *falud*. Not connected
with *fold* (1), but with Dan. *fold*, a sheep-
pen ; Du. *vaalt*, a dung-pit ; Low G. *faal*.

Foliage, a cluster of leaves. (F.—L.)
Modified from M. F. *fueillage*, from M. F.
fueille, a leaf.—L. *folia*, pl. of *folium*, a
leaf ; used as fem. sing. + Gk. φύλλον,
leaf. Cf. **Foil** (2).

folio. (L.) From the L. phr. *in foliō*,
where *foliō* is the abl. of *folium*, a leaf,
sheet.

Folk, a crowd of people. (E.) A. S.
folc.+Icel. *folk*, Dan. Swed. *folk* ; Du. G.
volk. Teut. type *folkom, neut. ¶ Lithuan.
pulkas, a crowd, Russ. *polk'*, an army,
were probably borrowed (at an early date)
from Teutonic.

Follicle, seed-vessel. (F. — L.) F.
follicule, little bag.—L. *folliculus*, double
dimin. of *follis*, a bag.

Follow. (E.) M. E. *folwen*. A. S.
folgian, also *fylgan*, weak verb, to follow.
+O. Fries. *folgia*, *fulia*, O. Sax. *folgōn*,
Du. *volgen* ; Icel. *fylgja*, Dan. *følge*, Swed.

fŏlja; G. *folgen*. We also find A. S. *ful-gangan*, (pt. t. *ful-ēode*), with the same sense, but derived from A. S. *ful*, full, and *gangan*, to go; and, in like manner, O. H. G. *follegān*. Hence the orig. sense was, perhaps, 'to go in full numbers,' to go in a crowd, to accompany; and it is a derivative of Teut. **fulloz*, full. See **Full**. Cf. A.S. *fylstan*, to assist, *fultum*, assistance; also from A. S. *full*.

Folly. (F.–L.) M. E. *folye*.–O. F. *folie*, folly.–O.F. *fol*, foolish. See **Fool** (1).

Foment. (F.–L.) M. F. *fomenter*.–L. *fōmentāre*.–L. *fōmentum*, short for **fouimentum*, a warm application, lotion. –L. *fouēre*, to warm.

Fond, foolish. (E.) M. E. *fond*, more commonly *fonn-ed*, pp. of *fonnen*, to be weak, to act as a fool; from the M. E. sb. *fon, fonne*, a fool. The sb. answers to O. Fries. *famne, fomne*, Fries. *fone* (see Hettema), E. Fries. *fone, fōn*, a maid, girl, weakling, simpleton (see Koolman). All allied to A. S. *fǣmne*, a virgin. **Der.** *fond-le*, vb.

Font (1), basin of water. (L.) A. S. *font*.–L. *fontem*, acc. of *fons*, a fount. See **Fount.**

Font (2), **Fount,** an assortment of types. (F.–L.) F. *fonte*, a casting of metals.–F. *fondre*, to melt. See **Found** (2).

Food. (E.) M. E. *fode*. A. S. *fōda*, what one eats. The A. S. *fōd-* is the strong grade of the base **fad*, corresponding to Gk. πατ- in πατ-έεσθαι, to feed. From the Idg. root *pā-*, to feed, whence L. *pā-nis*, bread, *pā-bulum*, food, and *pā-scere*, to feed. See **Pasture. Der.** *fodder*; *feed*.

Fool (1), a jester. (F.–L.) M. E. *fōl*, sb. and adj. O. F. *fol* (F. *fou*), a fool.–L. *follem*, acc. of *follis*, a wind-bag; pl. *follēs*, puffed cheeks, whence the term was easily transferred to a vain or foolish person; as in Late L. *follis*, a fool. **Der.** *be-fool*.

fool (2), a dish of crushed fruit, &c. (F.–L.) From **Fool** (1); named like *trifle*. Florio has: '*Mantiglia*, a kind of clouted creame, called a *foole* or a *trifle* in English.'

fools-cap, paper so called from the water-mark on it.

Foot. (E.) M. E. *fot, foot*, pl. *fet, feet*. A.S. *fōt*, pl. *fēt*. + Du. *voet*, Icel. *fōtr*, Dan. *fod*, Swed. *fot*, Goth. *fōtus*, G. *fuss*. Teut. type **fōt* (consonant-stem), corresponding to Idg. type **pōd*, with the variants **ped, *pod*. Cf. L. *pēs*, foot (gen.

ped-is); Gk. πούς (Æolic πώς), foot (gen. ποδ-ός), πεζός (=πεδγός), on foot; Skt. *pād*, a foot (gen. *pad-as*). Cf. **Fetter, Fetlock, Fetch.** Brugm. i. § 578.

Footy, paltry, mean. (E.) A variant of *foughty*, musty (N. E. D.). Orig. 'damp;' from A. S. *fūht*, damp, with suffix *-y*.+Du. *vochtig*, damp; Swed. *fuktig*, Dan. *fugtig*. Cf. G. *feucht*, O. H. G. *fūhti, fūht*. From a Teut. type **fūhtuz*, damp; from Teut. base **feuk*, as in Icel. *fjūka*, to drift as snow or dust, whence also Norw. *fuk*, vapour (Franck).

Fop, a coxcomb. (E.) M. E. *fop*, a fool. Cf. Du. *foppen*, to prate, cheat; *fopper*, a wag; *fopperij*, cheating (= E. *foppery*). Cf. *fob off*, to delude (Johnson).

For (1), prep. and conj. (E.) Orig. a prep. A.S. *for, fore*, before, for; see **Fore.**+Du. *voor*, Icel. *fyrir*, Dan. *for*, Swed. *för*, G. *für*. Cf. L. *prō*, for; Gk. πρό, before, παρά, near.

For- (2), *prefix*. (E.) *For-* has usually an intensive force, or preserves something of the sense of *from*, to which it is related. (Quite distinct from *fore-*, though ultimately allied to it.) A.S. *for-*; Icel. *for-*, Dan. *for-*, Swed. *för-*, Du. *ver-*, G. *ver-*, Goth. *fra-*, *fair-*, Skt. *parā-*. The Skt. *parā* is an old instrumental sing. of *para-*, far; perhaps the orig. sense was 'away' or 'forth.' **Der.** *for-bear, for-bid, for-fend, for-go* (misspelt *fore-go*), *for-get, for-give, for-lorn, for-sake, for-swear*; see **Bear, Bid,** &c.

For- (3), *prefix*. (F.–L.) Only in *for-close* (misspelt *foreclose*), *for-feit*, which see.

Forage, fodder, chiefly obtained by pillage. (F.–Low L.–Teut.) M. E. *forage, fourage*.–O. F. *fourage*.–O. F. *forrer*, to forage.–O. F. *forre* (F. *feurre*), fodder.–Low L. *fōdrum*, fodder.–Teut. type **fōdrom*, fodder; see **Fodder.**

Foraminated, perforated. (L.) From L. *forāmin-*, stem of *forāmen*, a small hole.–L. *forāre*, to bore; see **Bore.**

Foray, Forray, a raid for foraging. (F.–Low L.–Teut.) *Foray, forray* are old Lowl. Scotch spellings, with the sense of 'foraging expedition.' Apparently coined from the M. E. *forrier, forreyer*, a forager. – O. F. *forrier*, a forager; from O. F. *forrer*, to forage; see **Forage.**

Forbear (1), vb. (E.) From **For-** (2) and **Bear.** A. S. *forberan*.

Forbear (2), sb., an ancestor. (E.)

M. E. *forbear* (Wallace). For *fore-be-er*, one who is before. See Fore and Be.

Forbid. (E.) From For- (2) and Bid (2). A. S. *forbēodan.*+Du. *verbieden*, Goth. *faurbiudan*, G. *verbieten*.

Force (1), strength. (F.–L.) M. E. *force, fors.*–O. F. *force.*–Late L. *fortia*, strength.–L. *forti-*, decl. stem of *fortis*, strong; O. L. *forctis*. Allied to Borough. Brugm. i. §§ 566, 756. Cf. **Fort.**

Force (2), to stuff fowls ; see **Farce.**

Force (3), **Foss,** waterfall. (Scand.) Dan. *fos*, Swed. *fors*, Icel. *fors, foss*, a waterfall.

Forceps, pincers. (L.) L. *forceps*, orig. used for holding hot iron ; for **for-miceps* (Vaniček). – L. *formus*, hot ; *capere*, to hold.

Ford. (E.) M. E. *ford*; also *forth*. A. S. *ford*, a ford, passage.+G. *furt*. Teut. type **furduz*. From Idg. **por*, weak grade of √PER, to go; see **Fare.** Allied to L. *portus*, a harbour, O. Welsh (*p*)*rit*, Welsh *rhyd*, a ford, and to *frith*; see **Frith** and **Pore.** Brugm. ii. § 108.

Fore, in front, coming first. (E.) A. S. *fore*, for, before, prep. ; *fore, foran*, before, adv.+Du. *voor*, G. *vor*, Goth. *faura* ; cf. Icel. *fyrir*, Dan. *for*, Swed. *för*. Allied to Gk. πάρος, before; Skt. *puras*, before, in front, Skt. *purā*, formerly. Also to For- (1), prefix, q. v. Der. *fore-arm, -bode, -cast, -castle, -date, -father, -finger, -foot, -front, -go* (in the sense 'to go before' only), *-ground, -hand, -head, -judge, -know, -land, -lock, -man, -noon, -ordain, -part, -rank, -run, -see, -ship, -shorten, -show, -sight, -stall* (A. S. *fore-steall*, sb. lit. 'a position in front'), *-taste, -tell, -thought, -token, -tooth, -top, -warn* ; all easily understood.

Foreclose, to preclude, exclude. (F.– L.) Formerly spelt *forclose.*–O. F. *forclos*, pp. of *forclorre*, to exclude, shut out. – O. F. *for-*, from L. *forīs*, outside ; and *clorre*, to shut, from L. *claudere*. See **Forfeit** and **Close.**

Forego, to relinquish ; see **Forgo.**

Foreign. (F.–L.) The *g* is wrongly inserted. M. E. *foraine, foreyne.*–O. F. *forain*, alien, strange. – Folk-L. **forānus* ; for Late L. *forāneus*, adj., from L. *forās*, out of doors, adv. with acc. pl. form, allied to L. *forēs*, doors ; cf. L. *forum*, a market-place, and E. *door*.

Forejudge (1), to prejudge. From **Fore** and **Judge.**

Forejudge (2) ; see **Forjudge.**

Foremost, most in front. (E.) A double superl., the old superl. form being misunderstood. For M.E. *formest*, through secondary influence of *most.*–A.S. *formest*, by-form of the regular *fyrmest* (<*furmistoz*), through the influence of A. S. *forma*, which is cognate with Goth. *fruma*, first, Gk. πρᾶμος, πρόμος, first. Further allied to Gk. πρό, before. Brugm. i. § 518.

Forensic, belonging to law-courts. (L.) Coined from L. *forens-is*, belonging to the forum.–L. *forum*, market-place, meeting-place ; orig. a vestibule or door-way. Allied to L. *forēs*, doors, and E. *door*.

forest. (F.–L.) O. F. *forest.*– Late L. *forestis*, free space of hunting-ground ; *foresta*, a wood (medieval writers oppose the *forestis*, open hunting-ground, to the *parcus*, enclosed park).–L. *forīs*, out of doors; adv. allied to L. *forēs*, doors. Der. *forest-er*, also *forster, foster*.

Forfeit, a thing forfeited or lost by misdeed. (F.–L.) M. E. *forfete*; whence *forfeten*, vb.–A. F. *forfait*, O.F. *forfait*, a crime punishable by fine, a fine ; also a pp. of O. F. *forfaire, forsfaire*, to trespass. – Late L. *forisfactum*, a trespass, fine ; orig. pp. (neut.) of *forisfacere*, to trespass, lit. 'to do beyond.'–L. *forīs facere*, to do or act beyond or abroad ; from *foris*, out of doors ; and *facere*, to do. See **Fore-close.**

Forfend, Forefend, to avert. (Hybrid ; E. *and* F.) M. E. *forfenden*. An extraordinary compound of E. *for-*, prefix, with *fend*, a familiar abbreviation of *defend*. See **For-** (2) and **Defend**; also **Fend, Fence.**

Forge. (F.–L.) O. F. *forge*, a work-shop. – Folk-L. **faurga*, for **favrega* (Schwan) ; for L. *fabrica*, a workshop. See **Fabric.** Der. *forge*, vb.

Forget. (E.) From **For-** (2) and **Get.** A.S. *forgetan* (E. E. T.), *forgitan*. +Du. *vergeten*, G. *vergessen*.

Forgive. (E.) From **For** (2) and **Give.** A.S. *forgefan.*+Du. *vergeven*, G. *vergeben* ; Goth. *fragiban*, to grant.

Forgo, Forego, to give up. (E.) Better *forgo*. A.S. *forgān*, to pass over. From **For-** (2) and **Go.**

Forjudge, to deprive of by a judgement. (F.–L.) O. F. *forjugier.*–Low L. *forisjudicāre.*–L. *forīs*, outside : and *iūdi-*

cāre, to judge. See **Forfeit** and **Judge**.

Fork. (L.) A.S. *forca.* – L. *furca*, a fork. Der. *bi-furcated.*

Forlorn, quite lost. (E.) M. E. *forlorn.* A.S. *forloren*, pp. of *forlēosan*, to lose utterly; from *for-*, prefix, and *lēosan*, to lose; see **For-** (2) and **Lose.** So also Dan. *forloren*, Du. and G. *verloren*, similarly derived.

Form. (F. – L.) O. F. *forme.* – L. *forma*, shape. Brugm. ii. § 72. (√DHER.) ¶ O. F. *forme* also means ' a bench,' like E. *form.* Der *form-ula.*

Former, more in front. (E.) Not early; XII cent.; a false formation, to suit M. E. *formest*, i. e. foremost; see **Foremost.** Formed by adding -*er* to the base *form-* of A. S. *form-a*, first, really a superl. form, where -*m*- is an Idg. superl. suffix. Cf. L. *prī-mus*, first.

Formic, pertaining to ants. (L.) For *formic-ic*; from L. *formīca*, an ant.

Formidable, causing fear. (F. – L.) F. *formidable.* – L. *formīdābilis*, terrible. – L. *formīdāre*, to dread; *formīdo*, fear.

Formula, a prescribed form. (L.) L. *formula*, dimin. of *forma*, a form. See **Form.**

Fornicate. (L.) From pp. of L. *for-nicārī*, to commit lewdness, seek a brothel. – L. *fornic-*, base of *fornix*, a vault, arch, brothel. Perhaps allied to **Furnace**; cf. O. L. *fornus*, L. *furnus*, an oven (of vaulted shape).

Forsake. (E.) M. E. *forsaken.* A.S. *forsacan*, to neglect, orig. to contend against, or oppose; from *for-*, prefix, and *sacan*, to contend, whence the E. sb. *sake.* See **For-** (2) and **Sake.** So also Swed. *försaka*, Dan. *forsage*, Du. *verzaken.*

Forsooth. (E.) M. E. *for sothe*, for a truth. A.S. *for sōðe*; where *for* = for, and *sōðe* is dat. of *sōð*, truth; see **Sooth.**

Forswear. (E.) From **For-** (2) and **Swear.** A.S. *forswerian.*

Fort. (F. – L.) O. F. *fort*, sb., a fort; a peculiar use of F. *fort*, adj., strong. – L. acc. *fort-em*, from nom. *fortis*, strong. See **Force.**

fortalice, small fort. (F. – L.) O. F. *fortelesce*; Late L. *fortalitia*; see **Fortress** (below).

forte, loud. (Ital. – L.) Ital. *forte.* – L. acc. *fort-em*, strong (above).

fortify. (F. – L.) O. F. *fortifier*, to make strong. – L. *fortificāre.* – L. *forti-*,

decl. stem of *fortis*, strong; -*ficāre*, for *facere*, to make.

fortitude. (F. – L.) F. *fortitude.* – L. *fortitūdo*, strength. – L. *forti-s*, strong; with suffix -*tūdo.*

Forth, forward. (E.) M. E. *forth.* A.S. *forþ*, adv.; related to *fore*, before; see **Fore.** + Du. *voort*, from *voor*; G. *fort*, M. H. G. *vort*, from *vor*; cf. Goth. *faurthis*, further, from *faur-a*, before. Teut. type **fur-þo-*; Idg. type **pr̥-to-.* See **Further.**

Fortify, Fortitude; see **Fort.**

Fortnight, two weeks. (E.) M. E. *fourtenight*; also *fourten night.* – M. E. *fourten*, i. e. fourteen; *night*, old pl., i. e. nights. A. S. *fēowertȳne niht.* So also *sennight* = seven night.

Fortress. (F. – L.) M. E. *fortresse.* – O. F. *forteresce, fortelesce.* – Late L. *fortalitia*, a small fort. – Late L. *fortis* (*domus*), a fort; L. *fortis*, strong. See **Fort, Fortalice.**

Fortune. (F. – L.) O. F. *fortune.* – L. *fortūna*, chance. – L. *fortū-*, allied to *forti-*, decl. stem of *fors*, chance; orig. ' that which is brought,' or ' an event'; from *ferre*, to bring; see **Fertile.**

fortuitous. (L.) L. *fortuit-us*, casual; with suffix -*ous.* – L. *fortū-* (as above).

Forty; see **Four.**

Forward. (E.) M. E. *forward.* A.S. *foreweard*, adj. – A.S. *fore*, before; ·*weard*, suffix; see **Toward.** Der. *forward-s*, M. E. *forwardes*, where -*es* is the suffix of gen. case, used adverbially. And see **Further.**

Fosse. (F. – L.) F. *fosse.* – L. *fossa*, a ditch. – L. *fossa*, fem. of *fossus*, pp. of *fodere*, to dig. Brugm. i. § 166.

fossil, petrified remains obtained by digging. (F. – L.) M. F. *fossile*, ' that may be digged;' Cot. – L. *fossilis*, dug up. – L. *foss-us*, pp. of *fodere* (above).

Fosset, a spigot; see **Faucet.**

Foster, to nourish. (E.) A.S. *fōstrian*, vb. – A.S. *fōstor*, nourishment; Teut. type *fōstrom, for *fōd-trom, neut.; allied to *fōda*, food. + Icel. *fōstr*, nursing, whence *fōstra*, to nurse; Swed. *fostra*, Dan. *fostre*, to rear, bring up.

Fother, a load, heavy mass. (E.) A.S. *fōðer.* + M. Du. *voeder*, Du. *voer*; O. H. G. *fuodar*, G. *fuder.* Teut. type *fōþ-rom, n. From **fōþ-*, strong grade of **faþ-*; see **Fathom.**

Foul. (E.) M. E. *foul*. A. S. *fūl.* +
Du. *vuil*, Icel. *fūll*, Dan. *fuul*, Swed. *ful*,
Goth. *fuls*, G. *faul*. Teut. type **fū-loz*;
cf. Icel. *fū-inn*, rotten. Akin to Putrid.
(√PŪ.) Brugm. i. § 113.

foumart, a polecat. (E.) M. E. *ful-
mart*, *fulmard*; comp. of M. E. *ful*, foul
(as above), and A. S. *mearð*, a marten.
See Marten.

Found (1), to lay the foundation of.
(F.−L.) M. E. *founden.* − O. F. *fonder.*
− L. *fundāre*, to found. − L. *fundus*, a
bottom, foundation. See Fund. Der.
found-ation.

Found (2), to cast metals. (F.−L.)
O. F. *fondre.* − L. *fundere*, to pour, cast
metals. (√GHEU.) See Fuse (1).
Der. *found-ry*, F. *fond-erie.*

Founder, to go to the bottom. (F.−
L.) M. E. *foundren*, said of a horse falling. − O. F. *fondrer*, chiefly in comp.
afondrer (obsolete), *effondrer*, to fall in
(still in use); orig. to sink in.− F. *fond*,
bottom. − L. *fundus*, bottom. See Found
(1).

Foundling, a deserted child. (E.)
M. E. *fundling*; formed with suffix *-l-ing*
from A. S. *fund-*, weak grade of *findan*,
to find. + Du. *vondeling.* See Find.

Fount (1), a spring. (F.−L.) Formed,
by analogy with *mount*, from F. *font.* − L.
fontem, acc. of *fons*, a fountain. Der.
fount-ain, O. F. *fontaine*, Late L. *fon-
tāna.*

Fount (2), **Font,** an assortment of
types. (F.−L.) O. F. *fonte*, a casting of
metals. − O. F. *fondre*, to cast. − L. *fundere*, to pour, cast metals. See Found (2).

Four. (E.) M. E. *feowur*, *fower*, *four.*
A. S. *fēower.* + Icel. *fjōrir*, Dan. *fire*,
Swed. *fyra*, Du. *vier*, Goth. *fidwor*, G.
vier; also W. *pedwar*, Gael. *ceithir*, O.
Irish *cethir*, L. *quatuor*, Gk. τέτταρες,
τέσσαρες, πίσυρες, Russ. *chetvero*, Lith.
peturi, Pers. *chehār*, Skt. *chatvāras.* Idg.
type, **qetwer-.* Der. *four-th*, A. S. *fēorþa*;
four-teen, A. S. *fēowertēne*; *for-ty*, A. S.
fēowertig.

Fowl. (E.) M. E. *foul*, A. S. *fugol*, a
bird. + Du. *vogel*, Icel. *fugl*, Dan. *fugl*,
Swed. *fogel*, Goth. *fugls*, G. *vogel*. Teut.
type **fugloz*, masc.; prob. for **flugloz*, by
dissimilation; the form *fluglas*, pl. occurs
in Matt. xiii. 32 (Rushworth gloss), and
cf. the adj. *flugol*, flying. From **flug-*,
weak grade of Teut. **fleug-an-*, to fly.
See Fugleman and Fly. Brugm. i. § 491.

Fox. (E.) A. S. *fox.* + Du. *vos*, G.
fuchs. Teut. type **fuh-s-*, masc. We also
find Icel. *fōa*, Goth. *fauhō*, fem. a vixen;
Teut. type **fuhā.* A connexion with Skt.
puchchha-, 'tail,' is doubtful. Der. *vix-en.*
q. v.

foxglove. (E.) A. S. *foxes glōfa*, i. e.
fox's glove; a fanciful name. Cf. Norw.
revbjölla, a foxglove; lit. 'fox-bell.'

Foy, a parting entertainment, by or to
a wayfarer. (Du.−F.) From Du. *fooi*
(in Hexham, *foy*, 'a banquet given by one
at parting from his friends'). − F. *foi*, lit.
faith, from L. acc. *fidem*; cf. Late L.
fidēs, in the sense of 'payment.' (So
Franck.) But rather from F. *voie*, a way;
L. *uia.* Cf. Voyage.

Fracas. (F.−Ital.−L.) F. *fracas*, a
crash. − F. *fracasser*, to shatter. − Ital.
fracassare, to break in pieces. − Ital. *fra*,
prep., among, and *cassāre*, to break: (imitated from L. *interrumpere*). Ital. *fra* is
from L. *infrā*, below. *Cassāre* = L. *quassāre*, to shatter; see Quash.

Fraction. (F.−L.) F. *fraction.* − L.
acc. *fractiōnem*, a breaking. − L. *fractus*,
pp. of *frangere*, to break. Cognate with
break; see Break.

fracture. (F.−L.) O. F. *fracture.*
− L. *fractūra*, a breach. − L. *fractus*, pp.
of *frangere*, to break.

Fractious, peevish. (E.; *and* F.−L.)
A prov. E. word, as if from North. E. *fratch*,
to squabble, chide; the same as M. E.
fracchen, to creak as a cart. But it also
occurs (in 1705) in the sense of *refractory*,
being formed from *fraction*, in the sense
of 'dissension,' a sense now obsolete; see
N. E. D. See Fraction.

Fragile. (F.−L.) F. *fragile.* − L.
fragilis, easily broken. − L. *frag-*, base of
frangere, to break. See Fraction.
Doublet, *frail.*

fragment. (F.−L.) F. *fragment.* −
L. *fragmentum*, a broken piece. − L. *frag-*,
base of *frangere*; with suffix *-mentum.*

Fragrant. (F.−L.) F. *fragrant.* −
L. *frāgrantem*, acc. of *frāgrans*, pres. pt.
of *frāgrāre*, to emit an odour.

Frail. (F.−L.) M. E. *freel*, *freyl.* −
O. F. *fraile*, brittle. − L. *fragilem*, acc. of
fragilis; see Fragile.

Frame, to construct. (E.) M. E. *fra-
mien*; also *fremien*. A. S. *framian*, to
be profitable, avail; cf. also *fremien*,
fremman, to promote, effect, do, lit. to
further. − A. S. *fram*, strong, good, lit.

forward; cf. *fram*, prep., from, away; see **From**. + Icel. *frama*, *fremja*, to further, from *framr*, adj., forward, *fram*, adv., forward, allied to *frā*, from. Cf. G. *fromm*, good. Der. *frame*, sb.

Frampold, quarrelsome. (Low G.) Obsolete. Also *frampald*, *frompall*. Allied to prov. E. *rantipole*, a romping child. Cf. E. Fries. *frante-pot*, *wrante-pot*, a peevish man; M. Du. *wranten*, to chide, Dan. *vrante*, to be peevish, *vranten*, peevish. Cf. also Dan. *vrampet*, warped; Low G. *wrampachtigh*, morose (Lübben); E. Fries. *franten*, *wranten*, to be cross. Note also Sc. *frample*, to disorder, and E. *frump*. The second element is prob. from E. *poll*, head.

Franc, a French coin. (F. – G.) M. E. *frank*. – O. F. *franc*; said to be short for *Francorum Rex* (on a coin of 1360). See **Frank**.

franchise. (F. – G.) M. E. *franchise*. – O. F. *franchise*, privileged liberty. – O. F. *franchis-*, stem of pres. pt. of *franchir*, to free. – O. F. *franc*, free; see **Frank**. Der. *dis-franchise*, *en-franchise*.

Frangible. (L.) Late L. *frangibilis*, breakable; a coined word. – L. *frangere*, to break. See **Fraction**.

Franion, a dissolute person. (F. – L.) O. F. *fraignant*, one who infringes (law); pres. pt. of *fraindre*, to break, hence to infringe. – L. *frangere*, to break. See **Fragile**.

Frank, free. (F. – Low L. – O. H. G.) O. F. *franc*. – Low L. *francus*, free; orig. a Frank. – O. H. G. *franko*, a Frank; perhaps named from a weapon; cf. A. S. *franca*, a javelin. The *Franks* were a Germanic people.

frankalmoign, the name of the tenure by which most church-lands are held. (F. – O. H. G. *and* L. – Gk.) Lit. 'free alms.' – F. *franc*, free; Anglo-F. *almoine* = O. F. *almosne*, alms. See **Frank** and **Almoner**.

frankincense. (F. – G. *and* L.) O. F. *franc encens*, pure incense; see **Frank** (above) and **Incense**.

franklin, a freeholder. (F. – G.) M. E. *frankelein*. – A. F. *fraunkelayn*, Langtoft, ii. 212; Low L. *francalānus*, *franchilānus*. – Low L. *francus*, free; see **Frank** (above). The suffix is possibly from O. H. G. *-linc* (= E. *-l-ing* as in *dar-ling*); precisely as in *chamberlain*.

Frantic. (F. – L. – Gk.) M. E. *frene-*

tik, shorter form *frentik*. – O. F. *frenatique*. – L. *phrenēticus*, *phrenīticus*, mad. – Gk. φρενιτικός, mad, suffering from φρενῖτις, frenzy. See **Frenzy**.

Fraternal. (F. – L.) O. F. *fraternel*. – Late L. *frāternālis*, the same as L. *frāternus*, brotherly. – L. *frāter*, cognate with E. **Brother**.

fraternity. (F. – L.) O. F. *fraternitee*. – L. acc. *frāternitātem*, brotherhood. – L. *frāternus*, brotherly. – L. *frāter*, brother. Der. *con-fraternity*.

fratricide (1), murderer of a brother. (F. – L.) O. F. *fratricide*. – L. *frātricīda*, a brother-slayer. – L. *frātri-*, stem of *frāter*, brother; *-cīda*, a slayer, from *cædere*, to kill; see **Cæsura**.

fratricide (2), murder of a brother. (F. – L.) O. F. *fratrecide* (Littré). – L. *frātricīdium*, the killing of a brother. – L. *frātri-*, stem of *frāter*, brother; *-cīdium*, a slaying, from *cædere*, to kill.

Fraud. (F. – L.) O. F. *fraude*. – L. *fraudem*, acc. of *fraus*, deceit, guile.

Fraught, to lade a ship. (Low G. *or* Friesic.) We now use *fraught* only as a pp. M. E. *frahten*, *fragten*, only in the pp. *fraught*. Cf. Swed. *frakta*, to fraught or freight, from *frakt*, a cargo; Dan. *fragte*, from *fragt*, a cargo; E. Fries. *fracht*, *fragt*, (1) a cargo, (2) charge for transport; also Du. *bevrachten*, from *vracht*; G. *frachten*, from *fracht*. See further under **Freight**.

Fray (1), an affray. (F. – L.) Short for *affray*, or *effray*, orig. 'terror,' as shewn by the use of *fray* in the sense of terror, Bruce, xv. 255. See **Affray**.

fray (2), to terrify. (F. – L.) Short for *affray*; see **Affray**.

Fray (3), to wear away by rubbing. (F. – L.) O. F. *freier* (also *froier*), to rub (Godefroy). – L. *fricāre*, to rub.

Freak (1), a whim, caprice. (E.) A quick movement; from M. E. *frek*, quick, vigorous. – A. S. *frec*, bold, rash; whence *frician*, to move briskly. + Icel. *frekr*, voracious; Swed. *fräck*, impudent, Dan. *fræk*, audacious; G. *frech*, saucy, O. H. G. *freh*, greedy; Goth. *faihu-friks*, covetous.

Freak (2), to streak. (E.) A coined word; to streak capriciously (Milton); from **Freak** (1).

Freckle, a small spot. (Scand.) We find both *frekell* and *freken* or *frakin*. – Icel. *freknur*, pl., freckles; Swed. *fräkne*, Dan. *fregne*, a freckle. Cf. **Fleck**.

Free. (E.) M. E. *frē.* A. S. *frēo.*+
Du. *vrij*; Goth. *freis*; G. *frei.* Teut.
type **frijoz*; allied to Skt. *priya-*, beloved,
agreeable; also to E. **Friend.** Orig. sense
'dear, beloved'; hence applied to those
of the household who were children, not
slaves; cf. L. *līberī*, free, also 'children.'
Der. *freedom*, A. S. *frēodōm*; *free-stone*,
transl. of F. *pierre franche.*

Free-booter, a rover, pirate. (Du.)
Borrowed from Du. *vrijbuiter*, a free-
booter, robber. – Du. *vrijbuiten*, to rob;
vrijbuit, plunder, lit. 'free booty.' Du.
vrij = E. *free.* And see Booty, p. 56.

Freeze. (E.) M. E. *fresen.* A. S.
frēosan; pp. *froren.*+Icel. *frjōsa*, Swed.
frysa, Dan. *fryse*, Du. *vriezen*, G. *frieren.*
Teut. type **freusan-.* L. *prūrīre*, to itch,
originally to burn (cf. *pruīna*, hoarfrost),
Skt. *plōsha-*, a burning. Brugm. i. § 562;
ii. § 657. (√PREU.)

Freight, a cargo. (F.–O.H.G.) M.E.
freyte; later *freyght*; an altered spelling
of F. *fret*, the freight of a ship, the *gh*
being inserted by (a true) connexion with
fraught, q. v. – F. *fret*, 'the fraught or
freight of a ship, also, the hire that's paid
for a ship;' Cot.–O. H. G. *frēht*, 'earn-
ings,' hire. This O. H. G. *frēht* is thought
to be the same as G. *fracht*, a cargo; and
frēht has been supposed to represent a
Teut. type **fra-aihtiz*; from *fra-*, prefix
(see **Fret**), and **aihtiz*>A. S. *ǣht*, ac-
quisition (from *āgan*, to own). See **Own.**

Frenzy. (F.–L.–Gk.) M.E.*frenesye.*
–O. F. *frenisie.*–L. *phrenēsis.* – Late
Gk.φρένησις,for Gk. φρενῖτις, inflammation
of the brain.–Gk. φρεν-, base of φρήν,
midriff, heart, senses. See **Frantic.**

Frequent. (F.–L.) M. F. *frequent.*
–L.*frequentem*, acc. of *frequens*, crowded,
frequent; pres. part. of a lost verb **frequēre*,
to cram, allied to *farcīre*, to cram; see
Farce. Brugm. ii. § 713.

Fresco. (Ital.–O. H. G.) A painting
on *fresh* plaster.–Ital. *fresco*, cool, fresh.
–O. H. G. *frisc* (G. *frisch*). See below.

fresh. (E.; *and* F.–Teut.) M. E.
fresh; also *fersh*, representing A. S. *fersc.*
The form *fresh* is from O. F. *fres*, *freis*
(fem. *fresche*); cf. mod. F. *frais*, fresh. –
O. H. G. *frisc* (G. *frisch*), fresh. Teut.
type **friskoz.* Allied to Lith. *prēskas*,
sweet, unsoured, i. e. unleavened (applied
to bread); Russ. *priesnuii*, fresh.

Fret (1), to eat away. (E.) A.S.
fretan, for Teut. **fra-etan*, to devour

entirely. + Goth. *fra-itan*, to devour
entirely, from *fra-*, entirely, and *itan*, to
eat; Du. *vreten*, G. *fressen* (=*ver-essen*).
See **For-** (2) and **Eat.**

Fret (2), to ornament, variegate.
(F.–L.; *and* E.) M. E. *fretten*, to adorn
with interlaced work. – O. F. *freter*, to
strengthen (as with iron), also to adorn;
also spelt *ferter.* – O. F. *frete*, a ferrule
(Cot.), also a *fret* (in heraldry); see **Fret**
(3). Probably influenced by M. E. *fretien*,
A. S. *frætwan*, to adorn; from *frætwe*,
ornament.

Fret (3), a kind of grating. (F.–L.)
Common in heraldry.–O. F. *frete*, a
ferrule; *frettes*, pl., an iron grating (Diez);
fretter, to hoop; *fretté*, fretty (in heraldry).
[Cf. Span. *fretes*, frets (in heraldry); allied
to Ital. *ferriata*, an iron grating.] – F. *fer*,
iron. – L. *ferrum*, iron.

fret (4), a stop on a musical instrument. (F.–L.) *Frets* are bars across the
neck of the instrument; probably the same
word as *fret* (3). See N. E. D.

Friable, easily crumbled. (F.–L.)
M. F. *friable.*–L. *friābilis.*–L. *friāre*, to
rub, crumble.

Friar. (F.–L.) M. E. *frere.*–O. F.
frere, *freire*, lit. a brother.–L. *frātrem*,
acc. of *frāter*, a brother. See **Brother.**

Fribble, to trifle. (F.–L.) Of imitative origin; but prob. suggested by obsolete *frivol*, adj. frivolous, M. E. *frevol.*–
F. *frivole.* – L. *frīuolus*; see **Frivolous.**

Fricassee, a dish of fowls cut up.
(F.) F. *fricassée*, a fricassee; fem. of pp.
of *fricasser*, to fricassee, also, to squander
money. A fricassee is made of chickens,
&c. cut up into small pieces. Of unknown
origin. Some have suggested L. *frīgere*,
to roast, or L. *fricāre*, to rub (Körting).

Friction. (F.–L.) F. *friction.*–L.
acc. *frictiōnem*, a rubbing.–L. *frictus*,
contr. pp. of *fricāre*, to rub; allied to
friāre, to rub; see **Friable.**

Friday. (E.) A.S. *frīge-dæg*, translating L. *diēs Veneris*; where *frīge* is gen.
of *Frīg*, the wife of Woden. Teut. type
*frijā, fem. of **frijoz*, dear, beloved, also
'free'; Skt. *priyā*, wife, loved one. See
Free, Friend.

Friend. (E.) M. E. *frend.* A. S.
frēond, orig. 'loving,' pres. pt. of *frēogan*,
to love.+Icel. *frændi*, Dan. *frænde*, Swed.
frände, only in the sense of 'kinsman';
also Du. *vriend*, G.*freund*; Goth. *frijōnds*,
a friend, pres. pt. of *frijōn*, to love. Cf.

Skt. *prī*, to love. Allied to **Free.**
Brugm. i. § 567. **Der.** *friend-ship*, A. S.
frĕond-scipe.

Frieze (1), a coarse woollen cloth. (F.
—Du.?) M. F. *frize, frise*, ' frise;' Cot.
Perhaps due to *drap de frise*, i. e. cloth of
Friesland; with which Cotgrave identifies
it.—Du. *Vriesland*, Friesland, *Vries*, a
Frieslander, belonging to Friesland. So
also *cheval de Frise*, a horse of Friesland;
whence *chevaux de Frise*, spikes to resist
cavalry, a jesting term. ¶ Hence O. F.
friser, to cover with a nap, to curl hair,
to *frizz*. See Körting.

Frieze (2), part of the entablature of a
column. (F.) M. F. *frize*, ' the broad and
flat band that's next below the cornish
[cornice], or between it and the architrave;'
Cot. Span. *friso*, a frieze; allied to Ital.
fregio, a fringe, lace, border, ornament.
The Ital. *fregio* represents L. *Phrygium*
(*opus*), Phrygian work.

Frigate. (F.—Ital.) M. F. *fregate*,
' a frigate;' Cot.—Ital. *fregata*, a frigate.
Origin uncertain.

Fright. (E.) M. E. *fryght*. O. Northumb. *fryhto*, A. S. *fyrhto, fyrhtu*, fright,
allied to *forht*, timid.+O. Sax. *forhta*, Dan.
frygt, Swed. *fruktan*, G. *furcht*, Goth.
faurhtei, fright; allied to O. Sax. *forht*,
O. H. G. *foracht*, Goth. *faurhts*, fearful.

Frigid. (L.) L. *frīgidus*, cold, adj.—
L. *frīgēre*, to be cold.—L. *frigus*, cold, sb.
+Gk. ῥῖγος, cold. Brugm. i. § 875.

Frill, a ruffle on a shirt. (F. ?)
[*Frill*, vb., was a term in hawking; a hawk
that shivered, from feeling *chilly*, was said
to *frill*.—O. F. *friller*, to shiver with
cold. Hence some have deduced the
sense of a hawk ruffling his feathers; but
for this there is no authority. The sb.
answers, in sense, to O. F. *fresel, freisel*,
a ruffle, frill; cf. mod. F. *fraise*, a frill.
It is remarkable that both F. *fraise* and
E. *frill* mean ' the mesentery of a calf.']
Perhaps from M. F. *vrille*; Cot. has:
' *vrilles*, hook-like edges, or ends of leaves,
. . . scrols.' F. *vrille* also means a gimlet,
a tendril; prob. from Dan. *vrilde*, to twist,
from *vride*, to writhe; see **Writhe.**

Fringe, a border of loose threads. (F.
—L.) M. E. *fringe*.—O. F. *frenge* (Palsgrave), oldest form of F. *frange*, fringe;
the Wallachian form is *frimbie*, for *fim-
brie* (by metathesis).—L. *fimbria*, fringe;
allied to *fibra*, a fibre; see **Fibre.**

Frippery, worn-out clothes, trash.

(F.—L.) Stuff sold by a *fripier*.—M. F.
fripier, ' a fripier, or broker, trimmer up
of old garments, and a seller of them so
mended;' Cot.—O. F. *frepe* (also *ferpe*,
felpe), frayed out fringe, old clothes.
Prob. from L. *fibra*, fibre (Körting).

Frisk, to skip about. (F.—Teut.)
From the adj. *frisk*, brisk.—M. F. *frisque*,
' friske, blithe, briske;' Cot.; O. F. *frique*.
—O. H. G. *frech*, greedy, M. H. G. *vrech*,
bold, lively. Cf. A. S. *frec*, bold. See
Freak (1).

Frith (1), an enclosure, forest, wood.
(E.) Obsolescent; M. E. *frith*, peace, also
enclosure, park. Cf. W. *ffridd*, park, forest,
which is borrowed from M. E.—A. S. *frið*,
peace; *friðu*, peace, security, asylum.
Cf. Icel. *friðr*, Dan. Swed. *fred*, Du.
vrede, G. *friede*, peace. Teut. type
*frithuz; from **fri-*, base of **fri-joz*, free.
See **Free.** ¶ The M. E. *frith* is also
' wooded country.' This is prob. a different
word; A. S. *gefyrhðe* (Birch, iii. 120).

Frith (2), **Firth**, an estuary. (Scand.)
M. E. *frith*.—Icel. *fjörðr*, a firth, bay;
Dan. *fiord*, Swed. *fjärd*, the same. Allied
to **Ford.** Brugm. ii. 108.

Fritillary, a plant. (L.) So named
because the chequered markings on the
corolla were in some way associated with
a *fritillus*.—L. *fritillus*, a dice-box.

Fritter (1), a kind of pancake. (F.—
L.) M. E. *frytowre, fritoure*. [Cf. F.
friteau, ' a fritter,' Cot.]—O. F. *friture*,
a frying, dish of fried fish.—O. F. *frit*,
fried.—L. *frictus*, pp. of *frigere*, to fry.

Fritter (2), a fragment; Shak. (F.—L.)
O. F. *freture*.—L. *fractūra*, a fracture.
See **Fracture.**

fritter away, to diminish, waste.
(F.—L.) A derivative from *fritter* (2),
a fragment; whence *fritter*, vb., to cut
up into fragments. See above.

Frivolous, trifling. (L.) From L.
friuol-us, silly; with suffix *-ous*. The orig.
sense seems to have been ' rubbed away ';
hence *friuola* meant broken potsherds,
&c. — L. *friāre, fricāre*, to rub; see
Friable.

Friz, Frizz, to curl, render rough.
(F.—Du.?) M. F. *frizer*, ' to frizle, crispe,
curle;' Cot. [Cf. Span. *frisar*, to frizzle,
raise the nap on frieze, from *frisa*, frieze.]
Similarly the F. *friser* is from *frise, frize*,
frieze; see **Frieze** (1). **Der.** *frizz-le*, frequent. form, in commoner use; cf. O. Fries.
frisle, fresle, a lock of hair.

Fro. (Scand.) The Scand. form of *from.* — Icel. *frā,* Dan, *fra,* from. See **From.**

Frock. (F.—Low L.) M. E. *frok.* — O. F. *froc* ; Low L. *froccus,* a monk's frock, also spelt *floccus* (Ducange). Prob. so called because woollen ; see **Flock** (2). Cf. Port. *froco,* a snow-flake, from L. *floccus.* ¶ So Diez ; but Brachet derives it from O. H. G. *hroch* (G. *rock*), a coat, in which the initial *h* is unoriginal.

Frog (1), an animal. (E.) M. E. *frogge.* A. S. *frogga, frocga.* Also A. S. *frox,* a frog. + Icel. *froskr,* Du. *vorsch,* G. *frosch.*

Frog (2), a substance in a horse's foot. (L. ?) It is shaped like a fork ; perhaps a corruption of *fork,* q. v. ; the F. name is *fourchette.* In any case, it has been conformed to **Frog** (1).

Frolic, adj., sportive. (Du.) XVI cent. Orig. an adj. — Du. *vrolijk,* frolic, merry. +G. *fröhlich,* merry. Formed with suffix *-lijk* (= E. *like, -ly*) from the O. Sax. *frō-* (as in *frō-līko,* adv.), O. Fries. *frō* (= G. *froh*), merry. Der. *frolic,* sb. and verb.

From, away, forth. (E.) A.S. *from, fram.* + Icel. *frā,* from ; O.H.G. *fram,* forth ; Goth. *fram,* from. Cf. also Icel. *fram,* adv. forward (Swed. *fram,* Dan. *frem*) ; Goth. *framis,* adv., further. Allied to **Frame.**

Frond, a branch. (L.) L. *frond-,* stem of *frōns,* a leafy branch.

Front. (F.—L.) M. E. *front,* forehead. — O. F. *front,* forehead, brow. — L. *frontem,* acc. of *frōns,* forehead, brow.

frontal, a band worn on the forehead. (F. — L.) O. F. *frontel.* — L. *frontāle,* an ornament for a horse's forehead. — L. *front-,* stem of *frōns,* forehead.

frontier. (F.—L.) O. F. *frontiere,* fem. — Late L. *frontēria, frontāria,* borderland. — L. *front-,* stem of *frōns,* front (hence, border).

frontispiece. (F.—L.) For *frontispice* ; through the influence of *piece.* — F. *frontispice,* ' the frontispiece or fore-front of a house ; ' Cot. — Late L. *frontispicium,* a front view. — L. *fronti-,* decl. stem of *frōns ; specere,* to see ; see **Species.**

frontlet. (F.—L.) O. F. *frontel-et,* dimin. of O. F. *frontel* ; see **frontal** (above).

Frore, frozen. (E.) A. S. *froren,* pp. of *frēosan,* to freeze. See **Freeze.**

frost. (E.) M. E. *frost, forst* ; A. S. *forst* (for *frost*).+Du. *vorst,* Icel. Dan. Swed. G. *frost.* Teut. types **frustoz,* m. ; **frustom,* n. From **frus-,* weak grade of **freusan-,* to freeze. See **Freeze.**

Froth. (Scand.) M. E. *frothe.* — Icel. *froða, frauð,* Dan. *fraade* [Swed. *fradga*], froth, foam on liquids. From the Teut. verb **freuthan-,* to froth up ; as in A.S. *ā-frēoðan.*

Frounce, to wrinkle, curl, plait. (F.—L.) The older form of *flounce* ; see **Flounce** (2).

Froward, perverse. (Scand. *and* E.) M. E. *froward,* commonly *fraward* (Northern). From Icel. *frā,* fro ; and *ward.* Cf. A.S. *fromweard,* only in the sense ' about to depart ' ; but we still keep the orig. sense of from-ward, i. e. averse, perverse. (Cf. *wayward,* i. e. away-ward.) And see **Toward.**

Frown. (F. — Teut.) M.E. *frounen.* — O. F. *frongnier,* whence F. *refrogner,* to frown, look sullen. Cf. Ital. *infrigno,* frowning, Ital. dial. (Lombardic) *frignare,* to whimper, make a wry face. Of Teut. origin. From Teut. **frunjan-,* as in Swed. dial. *fryna,* Norw. *fröyna,* to make a wry face. (Körting, § 3324.)

Fructify. (F.—L.) F. *fructifier.* — L. *frūctificāre,* to make fruitful. — L. *frūcti-,* for *frūctus,* fruit ; *-ficāre,* for *facere,* to make. See **fruit.**

frugal, thrifty. (F.—L.) F. *frugal.* — L. *frūgālis,* economical ; lit. belonging to fruits. — L. *frūg-ī,* frugal ; orig. dat. of *frux* (pl. *frūgēs*), fruit of the earth. Allied to **fruit.**

fruit. (F.—L.) M. E. *fruit.* — O. F. *fruit.* — L. *frūctum,* acc. of *frūctus,* fruit. — L. *frūctus,* pp. of *fruī,* to enjoy ; allied to **Brook** (1). (√BHREUG.) Brugm. i. § 111 ; ii. § 532.

fruition. (F. — L.) O. F. *fruition,* enjoyment. — Late L. *fruitiōnem,* acc. of *fruitio,* enjoyment. — L. *fruit-us,* the same as *frūctus,* pp. of *fruī,* to enjoy.

frumenty, furmety, wheat boiled in milk. (F.—L.) O. F. *fromentee,* f. ; ' furmenty, sodden wheat ; ' Cot. Lit. made with wheat ; the suffix *-ee* = L. *-āta,* made with. — O. F. *froment,* wheat. — Late L. *frūmentum* ; L. *frūmentum,* corn ; allied to L. *frūgēs,* fruit.

Frump, an ill-tempered person. (E.) Of doubtful origin ; but cf. *frampold.* A *frump* formerly meant a ' sneer,' or expression of contempt. Cf. Low. Sc. *framble*, to disorder; *frumple*, to crease; *frump*, an unseemly fold : Dan. *vrampet*, warped.

Frustrate, to render vain. (L.) From pp. of L. *frustrārī*, to render vain. — L. *frustrā*, in vain ; orig. abl. fem. of obsolete adj. *frūstros* (= **frūd-tros*), deceitful. Allied to **Fraud**.

Frustum, a piece of a cone or cylinder. (L.) L. *frūstum*, a piece cut off. Cf. Gk. θραῦσμα, a fragment, from θραύειν, to break in pieces. Prellwitz; Brugm. i. § 853.

Fry (1), to dress food. (F.—L.) M. E. *frien.* — O. F. *frire* — L. *frīgere*, to roast. Cf. Gk. φρύγειν, to parch; Skt. *bhrajj*, to fry.

Fry (2), spawn of fishes. (Scand.) A. F. *fry* ; M. E. *fri*, also used (like the Goth. word) in the sense of 'offspring.' — Icel. *fræ*, *frjō*, spawn, fry; Dan. Swed. *frö.* +Goth. *fraiw*, seed, offspring. Teut. type **fraiwom*, neut. Brugm. i. § 1029.

Fuchsia, a flower. (G.) Named after L. *Fuchs*, German botanist, ab. 1542.

Fudge. (F.) Picard *fuche! feuche!* an interjection of contempt (Corblet).

Fuel. (F.—L.) M. E. *fewell* (Barbour). A. F. *fewaile*, O. F. *fouaille* (Low L. *foallia*), fuel. — Late L. *focālia*, pl. of *focāle*, fuel. — L. *focus*, a hearth. See **Focus.**

Fugitive. (F.—L.) O. F. *fugitif.* — L. *fugitīuus*, fleeing away. — L. *fugit-um*, supine of *fugere*, to flee. +Gk. φεύγειν, to flee; Skt. *bhuj*, to bend, turn aside. Allied to **Bow** (1). Der. *centri-fugal*, q. v. ; *febri-fuge*, *fever-few.*

Fugleman, the leader of a file. (G.) For *flugleman.* — G. *flügelmann*, the leader of a wing or file of men. — G. *flügel*, a wing, from *flug*, flight, from *fliegen*, to fly; *mann*, a man. See **Fly.**

Fugue, a musical composition. (F.— Ital.—L.) F. *fugue.* — Ital. *fuga*, a fugue, lit. a flight.—L. *fuga*, flight. See **Fugitive.**

Fulcrum, a point of support. (L.) L. *fulcrum*, a support.—L. *fulcīre*, to prop.

Fulfil. (E.) M. E. *fulfillen.* A. S. *fulfyllan*, to fill full, fulfil. — A. S. *ful*, full ; *fyllan*, to fill. See **Full, Fill.**

Fulgent, shining. (L.) From stem of pres. pt. of L. *fulgēre*, to shine. +Gk. φλέγειν, to burn ; Skt. *bhrāj*, to shine. Der. *ef-fulgent* (*ef-* = L *ex*) ; *re-fulgent.*

Fuliginous, sooty. (L.) L. *fūliginō-*

sus, sooty. — L. *fūligin-*, stem of *fūlīgo*, soot. Cf. Skt. *dhū-li-*, dust. Allied to **Fume.** Brugm. i. § 481.

Full (1), complete. (E.) A. S. *ful.* + Du. *vol*, Icel. *fullr*, Dan. *fuld* (for *full*), Swed. *full*, Goth. *fulls*, G. *voll.* Teut. type **fulloz* ; Idg. type **polnos.* Cf. Lith. *pilnas*, full, filled ; Russ. *polnuii*, full ; O. Irish *lān* (<**plān*), full ; W. *llawn* ; Skt. *pūrna-*, Pers. *pur* ; cf. Gk. πλήρης, L. *plēnus.* Idg. root **pol*, **plē*, to fill. Brugm. i. §§ 393, 461. Der. *fill, fulfil, fulsome.*

Full (2), to full cloth, felt. (F.—L.) O. F. *fuler*, F. *fouler*, 'to full, or thicken cloath in a mill;' Cot. Also 'to trample on.' — Late L. *fullāre*, (1) to cleanse clothes, (2) to full.—L. *fullo*, a fuller.

fuller, a bleacher of cloth. (L.) A. S. *fullere*, a bleacher. — L. *fullo*, a fuller, bleacher. (See above.)

Fulminate, to thunder, hurl lightning. (L.) From pp. of L. *fulmināre*, to thunder. — L. *fulmin-*, for *fulmen*, a thunderbolt (= **fulg-men*). — L. *fulgēre*, to shine.

Fulsome, cloying. (E.) M. E *fulsum*, from M. E. *ful*, full ; with suffix *-sum* (= E. *-some* as in *winsome*). See **Full** (1).

Fulvous, Fulvid, tawny. (L.) From L. *fuluus*, tawny ; Late L. *fuluidus*, somewhat tawny. Cf. **Yellow** ; Brugm. i. § 363.

Fumble, to grope about. (Du.) XVI cent. — Du. *fommelen*, to fumble. +Swed. *fumla* (also *famla*) ; Dan. *famle.* Apparently *ml* is for *lm* ; cf. Icel. *fálma*, to grope about, from the sb. appearing as A. S. *folm*, the palm of the hand, allied to L. *palma* ; see **Palm.**

Fume. (F. — L.) O. F. *fum.* — L. *fūmum*, acc. of *fūmus*, smoke. +Skt. *dhūma-*, smoke ; Gk. θυμός, spirit, anger. (√DHEU.) Allied to **Fuliginous.**

fumigate. (L.) From pp. of L. *fūmigāre*, to fumigate. — L. *fūm-*, for *fūmus*, vapour ; *-igāre*, for *agere*, to drive about.

fumitory, a plant. (F.—L.) Formerly *fumiter.* — F. *fumeterre*, fumitory (for *fume de terre*). — Late L. *fūmus terræ*, smoke of the earth ; so named from its abundance (and perhaps its curly appearance). Cf. G. *erdrauch*, fumitory, lit. 'earth-smoke'; W. *cwd y mwg*, lit. 'bag of smoke.'

Fun, merriment. (E.) XVIII cent. It orig. meant 'a trick'; from an obs. vb. *fun*, to cheat, hoax ; prob. from M. E.

fon, fonne, a foolish person. See **Fond.**
Cf. Irish *fonn,* delight, pleasure, song;
Gael. *fonn*; prob. borrowed from E.

Funambulist, a rope-dancer. (Span.
– L.) Formerly *funambulo.* – Span. *funambulo,* a funambulist. – L. *fūn-is,* a rope;
ambul·āre, to walk; see **Amble.**

Function, performance, office. (F. –
L.) M. F. *function* (F. *fonction*). – L. acc.
functiōnem, performance. – L. *functus,* pp.
of *fungi,* to perform, orig. to use. + Skt.
bhuṅj, to enjoy. Brugm. ii. § 628.

Fund, a store. (F. – L.) M. F. *fond,*
'a bottom, a merchant's stock;' Cot. –
L. *fundus,* bottom; cognate with E.
Bottom.

fundament, base. (F. – L.) M. E.
fundement. – O. F. *fondement,* foundation.
– L. *fundāmentum,* foundation. – L. *fundāre*; see **Found** (1).

Funeral, relating to a burial. (F. – L.)
O. F. *funeral.* – Late L. *fūnerālis,* adj.,
from L. *fūner-* (for **fūnes-*), stem of *fūnus,*
a burial. Der. *funere-al,* from L. *fūnere-us,*
funereal.

Fungus, a spongy plant. (L.) L.
fungus. + Gk. σπόγγος, a sponge; see
Sponge.

Funnel. (F. – L.) M. E. *fonel.* Prob.
from an O. F. **fonil,* preserved in Bret.
founil, a funnel; cf. Span. *fonil,* Port.
funil, Prov. *founil, enfounilh.* – Late L.
fundibulum (Lewis and Short); L. *in-
fundibulum,* a funnel. – L. *infundere,* to
pour in. – L. *in,* in; *fundere,* to pour.

Fur. (F. – O. Low G.) M. E. *forre.* –
O. F. *forre, fuerre,* a sheath, case, whence
the vb. *forrer,* to line with fur; Chaucer
translates *forree* by 'furred,' R. R. 408.
[Cf. Span. *forro,* lining for clothes, Ital.
fodero, lining, fur, scabbard.] – Goth. *fodr,*
scabbard, orig. 'protection;' Icel. *fōðr,*
lining; allied to G. *futter,* a case, lining,
fur. + Skt. *pātra(m),* a receptacle; cf. Gk.
πῶμα, a cover. Brugm. i. § 174.

Furbelow, a flounce. (F.) Prov. F.
farbala, a flounce, in the dialect of
Hainault (Diez); the usual form is F.
Span. Ital. Port. *falbala,* a flounce. Origin
unknown.

Furbish, to polish, trim. (F. – O.H.G.)
O. F. *forbiss-,* inceptive stem of *forbir,*
to furbish, polish. – O. H. G. **furbjan,*
M. H. G. *fürban,* to purify, clean, rub
bright.

Furl, to roll up a sail. (F. – Arab.)
Formerly spelt *furdle, farthel,* to roll up

in a bundle. From *fardel,* a bundle; see
Fardel. Cf. F. *fardeler,* 'to truss, to
make into fardles;' Cot. [F. *ferler,* to
furl, is from E.]

Furlong, ⅛th of a mile. (E.) A. S.
furlang, orig. a furrow-long, or the length
of a furrow. – A. S. *furh,* a furrow; *lang,*
long.

Furlough, leave of absence. (Du. –
Scand.) Orig. *vorloffe.* – Du. *verlof,*
leave, furlough; the same as Dan. *forlov,*
Swed. *förlof,* leave. Cf. G. *urlaub,* furlough; Dan. *orlov.* β. As to the prefix,
Du. *ver-,* Dan. *for-,* Swed. *för-,* are the
same as E. *for-*; whilst Dan. *or-,* G. *ur-* =
Goth. *us,* out. The syllable *lof,* leave, is
shortened from *-lōf-,* the equivalent of G.
-laub-, as seen in G. *er-laub-en,* to permit,
and in A. S. *lēaf,* permission. See **Leave**
(2); also **Believe, Lief.**

Furmety; see **Frumenty.**

Furnace, an oven. (F. – L.) M. E.
forneis. – O. F. *fornaise.* – L. *fornācem,*
acc. of *fornax,* an oven. – L. *fornus,* an
oven; allied to *formus,* warm. Cf. Skt.
gharma-, warmth, glow. See **Warm.**
Brugm. i. § 146.

Furnish, to fit up, equip. (F. – O.H.G.)
O. F. *fourniss-,* inceptive stem of *fournir,*
to furnish, of which an older spelling is
fornir, the same word as Prov. *formir,*
fromir. – O. H. G. *frumjan,* to provide,
furnish; cf. O. H. G. *fruma,* utility, profit,
gain; G. *fromm,* good. Allied to **Former,
Frame.** And see **Veneer.**

Furrow. (E.) M. E. *forwe.* A. S.
furh, a furrow. + Du. *voor,* Icel. *for,* Dan.
fure, Swed. *fåre*; G. *furche,* a furrow.
Teut. type **furh-,* f. Cf. W. *rhych,* a
furrow; L. *porca,* a ridge between two
furrows. Der. *fur-long.*

Further. (E.) Probably the comp.
of *fore,* but also explained as comp. of
forth. M. E. *furðer.* A. S. *furðra,* adj.
m.; *furðor,* further, adv. + Du. *vorders,*
adv., further; O. Fries. *fordera,* adj.;
O. Sax. *forthora,* adj.; O. H. G. *fordar,*
G. *vorder,* adj. Teut. type **furthero-* (i. e.
*fur-ther-o-) answering to Gk. πρό-τερ-ος,
comp. of πρό. ¶ In this view the comp.
suffix is *-ther* (Gk. -τερ-). Der. *further,*
vb., A. S. *fyrðran,* formed from *furðor*
by vowel-change of *u* to *y.*

furthest, a late form, made as the
superl. of *forth,* and due to regarding
further as the comp. of the same. The
true superl. of *fore* is *first.*

Furtive. (F.–L.) M. F. *furtif,* fem. *furtive.*–L. *furtīuus,* stolen, secret.–L. *furtum,* theft. – L. *fūrāri,* to steal.–L. *fūr,* a thief.+Gk. φώρ, a thief, allied to φέρειν, to bear, carry (away). (√BHER.) Brugm. ii. § 160 (3).

Fury. (F.–L.) F. *furie.*–L. *furia,* rage.–L. *furere,* to rage.

Furze. (E.) M. E. *firse.* A. S. *fyrs*; older form *fyres.*

Fuscous, brown. (L.) L. *fusc-us,* brown; with suffix *-ous.*

Fuse (1), to melt by heat. (L.) A late word. Due to *fus-ible* (in Chaucer), *fus-ion,* in Sir T. Browne.–L. *fūsus,* pp. of *fundere,* to pour, melt. Allied to Gk. χέειν (for *χεϝ-ειν), Goth. *giutan,* to pour. (√GHEU.) Der: *fus-ible* (from O. F. *fusible*); *fus-ion.* See **Gush.**

Fuse (2); see Fusee (1).

Fusee (1) **Fuse.** (F.–L.; *or* Ital.–L.) ' *Fuse, fusee,* a pipe filled with wild-fire, and put into the touch-hole of a bomb;' Kersey (1715). 1. *Fuse* is from Ital. *fuso,* a spindle, a shaft (of a column); also, a fuse.–L. *fūsus,* a spindle. 2. *Fusee* is from F. *fusée,* a fusee, i. e. a spindle-shaped pipe; see below.

fusee (2), a spindle in a watch. (F.–L.) O. F. *fusée,* orig. a spindleful of thread.–Late L. *fūsāta,* the same; fem. of pp. of *fūsāre,* to use a spindle.–L. *fūsus,* a spindle.

Fusil (1), a light musket. (F.–L.) Orig. not the musket itself, but the steel against which the flint struck. From F. *fusil,* ' a fire-steele for a tinder-box;' Cot. Also in mod. F., a fusil. [Cf. Span. *fusil,* a fusil.]–L. *focile,* a steel for kindling fire. –L. *focus,* a hearth; see **Focus.** Der. *fusil-eer, fusillade.*

Fusil (2), a spindle, in heraldry. (L.) A. F. *fusel* (see O. F. *fuisel* in Godefroy). Dimin. of L. *fūsus,* a spindle.

Fusil (3), easily molten. (L.) L. *fūsilis,* easily molten.–L. *fūsus,* pp. of *fundere,* to pour. See **Fuse** (1).

Fuss, haste, flurry. (E.) Probably of imitative origin, descriptive of spluttering and puffing. Cf. *fuff,* i. e. to puff, and *hiss.* ¶ It cannot be connected with M. E. *fūs,* adj., eager; A. S. *fūs,* eager, prompt.

Fust (1), to become mouldy. (F.–L.) In Hamlet, iv. 4. 39. Coined from *fusty* (A. D. 1398), answering to O. F. *fusté,* ' fusty, tasting of the cask,' Cot.–O. F.

fust, a cask; orig. a stock, trunk, log.– L. *fustem,* acc. of *fustis,* a cudgel.

fust (2), the shaft of a column. (F.– L.) In Kersey (1715).–O. F. *fust,* a trunk.–L. *fustem,* acc. of *fustis,* a cudgel, thick stick.

Fustian, a kind of coarse cloth. (F.– Ital.–Low L.–Egypt.) M. E. *fustane*; also *fustian*; A. F. *fustiane, fustain*; O. F. *fustaine.*–Ital. *fustagno*; Low L. *fustāneum.* – Arab. *fustāt,* a suburb of Cairo, in Egypt, whence the stuff first came. ¶ Introduced through Genoese commerce.

Fustigate, to cudgel. (L.) From pp. of L. *fustigāre,* to cudgel.–L. *fust-,* stem of *fustis,* a cudgel; *-igāre,* for *agere,* to drive, wield.

Fusty; see Fust (1).

Futile, vain. (F.–L.) F. *futile.*–L. *fūtilis, futtilis,* that which easily pours forth, also vain, empty, futile. From L. *fū-,* allied to *fundere,* to pour; cf. Gk. χέειν. See Fuse (1).

Futtocks, certain timbers in a ship. (E.) ' *Futtocks,* the compassing timbers in a ship, that make the breadth of it;' Kersey (1715). Called *foot-stocks* in Florio, s. v. *stamine.* The first syllable is for *foot*; *futtocks* is thought to be for *foot-hooks,* and was so explained in 1644; *hook* referring to the bent shape of the timbers. Bailey gives the form *foot-hooks.*

Future, about to be. (F.–L.) O. F. *futur,* fem. *future.*–L. *futūrus,* about to be; fut. part. from *fu-ī,* I was; allied to Be. (√BHEU.)

Fuzzball, a spongy fungus. (E.) Cf. prov. E. *fuzzy, fozy,* light and spongy; Low G. *fussig,* loose, weak; Du. *voos,* spongy.

Fylfot, a peculiarly formed cross. (E.) Modern; and due to a mistake. MS. Lansd. 874, leaf 190, has *fylfot,* meaning a space in a painted window at the bottom, that *fills* the *foot.* Erroneously connected with the ' gammadion.'

G.

Gabardine, Gaberdine. (Span.– Teut.) Span. *gabardina,* a coarse frock. We also find M. E. *gawbardyne*; which is from O. F. *galvardine, gualvardine,* a loose frock. Perhaps a ' pilgrim's ' frock; from M. H. G. *walfart* (G. *wallfahrt*), pilgrimage. — M. H. G. *wallen*, to wander ; *fart*, travel, from *faran*, to go (E. *fare*).

Gabble, to prattle. (E.) Frequent. of *gab*, to prattle. Of imitative origin ; cf. *jabber*. ¶ The M. E. *gabben*, to mock, is from O. F. *gaber*, to mock, which is also perhaps of imitative origin, or is allied to *gape*.

Gabion. (F. — Ital. — L.) F. *gabion*, a gabion, large basket filled with earth. — Ital. *gabbione*, a gabion ; augment. of *gabbia*, a cage, also spelt *gaggia*, and allied to Span. *gavia*, a cage (for madmen). — L. *cauea*, a hollow place, cage, den, coop ; see **Cage**.

Gable, a peak of a house-top. (F. — Scand.) M. E. *gable*. — O. F. *gable*. — Icel. *gafl*, Dan. *gavl*, Swed. *gafvel*, a gable. + A. S. *geafol*, a fork ; Du. *gaffel*, a fork ; G. *gabel*, a fork. Further allied to O. Irish *gabul*, a fork, gallows ; W. *gafl*, the fork of the thighs. With a different gradation, we find Goth. *gibla*, pinnacle, G. *giebel*, Du. *gevel*, gable ; O. H. G. *gebal*, head, Gk. κεφαλή, head (root-form **ghebh-*). See **Gaff**.

Gaby, a simpleton. (Scand.) M. Dan. *gabe*, a fool ; Dan. dial. *gabenar*, a simpleton, allied to Dan. *gabe*, to gape (Dan. *nar* means 'fool'). Cf. Icel. *gapi*, a heedless man ; *gapamuðr* (lit. gape-mouthed), the same ; Icel. *gapa*, to gape ; Norw. *gapa*, stupid.

Gad (1), a wedge of steel, goad. (Scand.) M. E. *gad*, a goad. — Icel. *gaddr*, a goad, spike, sting ; cognate with Goth. *gazds*, a rod, Irish *gath*, L. *hasta*, a spear.

gad (2), to ramble idly. (Scand.) In Levins. The orig. sense was to run about. — Icel. *gadda*, to goad. — Icel. *gaddr* (above). Cf. *on the gad*, 'on the move.

Gaff, a light fishing-spear, a sort of boom. (F. — Teut.) A ship's *gaff* is named from the *forked* end against the mast ; the fishing-spear is hooked. — O. F. *gaffe*, a gaff, iron hook. — Low G. *gaffel*, a two-pronged hay-fork ; E. Fries. *gaffel*, a fork, a ship's gaff ; Du. *gaffel*, a pitchfork, ship's gaff. Allied to G. *gabel*, a fork. See **Gable**.

Gaffer, an old man, grandfather. (F. — L. ; *and* E.) From *gramfer*, West E. form of *grand-father*. See **Gammer**.

Gag. (E.) M. E. *gaggen*, to suffocate. Apparently of imitative origin ; cf. *gaggle*, *guggle*. Also, W. *cegio*, to choke ; *ceg*, the mouth.

Gage (1), a pledge. (F. — Teut.) M. E. *gage*. — F. *gage*, a pledge (Low L. *uadium*). — Teut. **wadjom*, n., a pledge ; as in Goth. *wadi*, A. S. *wed*, a pledge. See **Wed** ; and see **Wage**. From the same source are Ital. *gaggio*, Span. and Port. *gage*, a pledge.

Gage (2), to gauge ; see **Gauge**.

Gaggle, to cackle as geese. (E.) A frequent. form from the imitative base *gag*. Cf. *cackle*, *gabble* ; also Icel. *gagl*, a wild goose ; *gagg*, the cry of a fox ; Lith. *gagéti*, to gaggle.

Gaiety. (F. — Teut.) F. *gaieté*. — F. *gai*, gay. See **Gay**.

Gain (1), profit. (F. — Teut.) O. F. *gain*, F. *gagne*, from the verb below. [It partly displaced the M. E. *gain*, advantage, which was of Scand. origin ; from Icel. *gagn*, gain, advantage ; Swed. *gagn*, profit, Dan. *gavn*.]

gain (2), to win. (F. — Teut.) 'Yea, though he *gaine* and cram his purse with crunes ;' and again, 'To get a *gaine* by any trade or kinde ;' Gascoigne, Fruits of War, st. 69 and st. 66. — O. F. *gaigner*, F. *gagner*, to gain. This F. *gagner*, O. F. *gaagnier* (Ital. *guadagnare*), is from O. H. G. *weidenôn* > *weidenen*, to pasture, which was the orig. sense of the F. word ; from O. H. G. *weida* (G. *weide*), pasture-ground. Cognate with G. *weide* are A. S. *wâð*, Icel. *veiðr*, hunting, the chase. Cf. L. *uē-nāri*, to hunt. **Der.** *regain*.

Gainly ; see **Ungainly**.

Gainsay, to speak against. (Scand. *and* E.) The prefix is Icel. *gegn*, against ; cf. A. S. *gegn*, *gēan* ; see **Against**.

Gait, manner of walking. (Scand.) A particular use of M. E. *gate*, a way ; see **Gate** (2). See also **Gantlet** (2).

Gaiter, a covering for the ankle. (F. — Teut.) F. *guêtre*, formerly *guestre* (Cot.). The spelling with *gu* shews the word to be Teutonic (*gu* < G. *w*). Origin doubtful ; possibly allied to M. H. G. *wester*, a child's chrisom-cloth, lit. a covering ; Goth. *wasti*, clothing ; see **Vest**.

Gala. (F. — Ital. — M. H. G.) F. *gala*, borrowed from Ital. *gala*, festive attire ; whence *di gala*, merrily ; cf. *galante*, gay, lively. See **Gallant**.

Galaxy, the milky way. (F. — L. — Gk.) M. E. *galaxie*. — O. F. *galaxie*. — L. *galaxiam*, acc. of *galaxias*. — Gk. γαλαξίας, milky way. — Gk. γαλακς-, for γαλακτ-, stem of γάλα, milk. See **Lacteal**.

Gale (1), a strong wind. (Scand.) XVI cent. Of doubtful origin; but cf. Dan. *gal*, furious; Norweg. *ein galen storm*, a furious storm, *eit galet veer*, stormy weather. Cf. Icel. *galinn*, furious, from *gala*, to cry out. See **Yell**. Note F. *galerne*, a north-west wind.

Gale (2), the bog-myrtle. (E.) A. S. *gagel*.+Du. *gagel*.

Galeated, helmeted. (L.) L. *galeātus*. ─L. *galea*, a helmet.

Galingale, the pungent root of a plant. (F.─Span.─Arab.─Pers.) M. E. *galingale*. ─ O. F. *galingal*, *garingal*. ─ Span. *galanga*, galingale. ─ Arab. *khalanjān*, galingale. ─ Pers. *khūlanjān*, galingale; said to be of Chinese origin.

Galiot; see **Galliot**.

Gall (1), bile. (E.) M. E. *galle*. O. Merc. *galla*. + Du. *gal*, Icel. *gall*, Swed. *galla*, Dan. *galde* (for *galle*), G. *galle*; L. *fel*, Gk. χολή. Allied to **Yellow**. Cf. Russ. *jelch(e)*, gall (*j = zh*); *jeltuii*, yellow.

Gall (2), to rub a sore place. (F.─L.) M. F. *galler*; M. F. *galle*, a galling, itching. Cf. Ital. *galla*, *gala*, 'a disease called a windgalle;' Florio. Also Late L. *galla*, a soft tumour; app. the same word as L. *galla*, a gall-nut; see below. ¶ But also partly E.; cf. A. S. *gealla*, (1) gall, bile, (2) a gall on a horse. So also Du. *gal*. See above.

Gall (3), a gall-nut. (F.─L.) O. F. *galle*. ─L. *galla*, a gall-nut, oak-apple.

Gallant, gay, splendid, brave. (F.─ M. H. G.) O. F. *gallant*, better *galant*, with one *l*. Orig. pres. part. of O. F. *galer*, to rejoice. ─ O. F. *gale*, shows, mirth, festivity. (Cf. Ital. Span. Port. *gala*, festive attire.) Perhaps from M. H. G. *wallen*, O. H. G. *wallōn*, to go on pilgrimage.

Galleon, a large galley. (Span.) Span. *galeon*, a galleon. ─ Late L. *galea*, a galley. See **Galley**.

Gallery. (F.) M. F. *gallerie*, *galerie*, a gallery to walk in. ─ Late L. *galeria*, a long portico, gallery. Of unknown origin; possibly from Gk. κᾶλον, wood, timber (Körting). See below.

Galley, a low-built ship. (F.─Late L. ─Gk.?) M. E. *galeie*. ─O. F. *galie*; Late L. *galea*, a galley; Late Gk. γαλέα, γαλαῖα. Orig. unknown. Körting suggests Gk. κᾶλον, wood, also sometimes a ship.

Galliard, a lively dance. (Span.─C.?) Span. *gallarda* (with *ll* as *ly*), a kind of

lively Spanish dance; perhaps through F.; cf. *galop gaillard*, 'the galliard;' Cot.─Span. *gallardo*, gay, lively. M. F. *gaillard* meant valiant or bold; perhaps of Celtic origin; cf. Bret. *galloud*, power, W. *gallad*, able, *gallu*, to be able; O. Irish *gal*, boldness (Thurneysen).

Gallias, a sort of galley. (F.─Ital.─ Late L.) O. F. *galeace*.─Ital. *galeazza*, a heavy galley. ─ Ital. and Late L. *galea*; see **Galley**.

Galligaskins, large hose or trousers. (F. ─ Ital. ─ L.) Corruption of F. *garguesques*, *greguesques*, 'slops, gregs, gallogascoins, Venitians;' Cot.─Ital. *Grechesco*, Greekish. ─ Ital. *Greco*, a Greek. ─ L. *Græcus*, Greek. The name was given to a particular kind of hose worn at Venice.

Gallinaceous. (L.) L. *gallīnāce-us*, belonging to poultry; with suffix *-ous*.─ L. *gallīna*, a hen.─L. *gallus*, a cock.

Galliot, small galley. (F.─Late L.) O. F. *galiote*; Late L. *galeota*, small galley; dimin. of *galea*; see **Galley**.

Gallipot, a small glazed earthen pot. (F.) From *galley* and *pot*, as being brought over in *galleys*. So also *galley-tile*; cf. *galy-halfpeny*, a galley-halfpenny, coin brought over by *galley-men*, who landed wines at a place called *Galley-key* (Thames Street).

Gallon. (F.) M. E. *galon*, *galun*. ─ O. F. *gallon*, *jalon*, a gallon; orig. 'a large bowl;' augmentative form of the wor[ ] which appears as mod. F. *jale*, a bo[ ] Orig. unknown.

Galloon. (F.─M. H. G.) F. [ ] 'galoon-lace,' Cot.; cf. O. F. *galo[ ]* adorn the head (with ribbons, &c.[ ] Span. *galon*, galloon.]─O. F. [ ] *gala*, festivity; see **Gallant**.

Gallop. (F.─Scand.) M[ ] also spelt *walopen*.─O. F. [ ] *galop*, *walop* (Bartsch), sb[ ] borrowed O. H. G. *walopi[ ]* so that it is not of [ ] ─O. Norweg. **wall-ho[ ]* a gallop (Aasen); li[ ] a field, 'field-hop.'─[ ] *vall-*, Icel. *völlr*, [ ] with E. **Wold**); [ ] jump, skip, fr[ ] **Hop** (1).

Gallow, t[ ] iii. 2. 44. [ ] to terrify; [ ]

Galloway, a nag, pony. (Scotland.) Named from *Galloway*, Scotland.

Gallowglas, Galloglas, a heavy-armed foot-soldier. (Irish.) Irish *galloglach*, a servant, a galloglas. – Irish *gall*, a foreigner, an Englishman; *oglach*, a youth, servant, soldier (from *ōg*, young, O. Ir. *ōac*, *ōc*, cognate with E. **Young**). It meant 'an English servitor,' as explained by Spenser, View of the State of Ireland, Globe ed. p. 640. (See N. and Q. 6 S. x. 145.)

Gallows. (E.) M. E. *galwes*, pl. A.S. *galga*, *gealga*, cross, gibbet; whence mod. E. *gallow*, the *s* being the pl. termination. + Icel. *gālgi*, Dan. Swed. *galge*, Du. *galg*, Goth. *galga*, a cross, G. *galgen*. Teut. type **galgon-*; cf. Lith. *żalga*, a pole (*ż = zh*).

Galoche, a kind of shoe. (F. – Late L. – Gk.) F. *galoche*, answering to a Romance type **galopia*, **calopia*; formed from **calopūs*, sing. of Late L. *calopodes*, wooden shoes; we also find Late L. *calopedia* (see Brachet), a clog, wooden shoe, and *calopodium*. – Gk. καλοπόδιον, dimin. of καλόπους, καλάπους, a shoemaker's last. – Gk. κᾶλο-ν, wood; πούς, a foot.

Galore, in plenty. (C.) Irish *goleor*, *gu leor*, *gu leoir*, sufficiently. Formed ~~i~~sh and Gael. *leor*, sufficient, by ~~~~ *or gu*, lit. 'to,' but used to ~~~~ an adverb.

~~~~**t,** clay and marl. ~~~~ hard ground, ~~~~dden hard;

~~~~ M.E. ~~~~ *lt*, ~~~~ m ~~~~ o.

[Also ~~~~ to ~~~~ Span. ~~~~ E. *galopen*; ~~~~ *galoper*, vb.; [Hence was ~~~~ o gallop ~~~~igin.] ~~~~

~~~~ of. G ~~~~ *Cambo*~~~~ whence it w~~~~ e h o t f ,

Gambol, a frisk, caper. (F. – Ital. – L.) Formerly *gambold*, *gambauld*, *gambaud*. – M. F. *gambade*, 'a gamboll;' Cot. – Ital. *gambata*, a kick. – Ital. *gamba*, the leg; the same as F. *jambe*, O. F. *gambe*, Late L. *gamba*, a joint of the leg. Cf. Gael. and W. *cam*, crooked, answering to O. Celt. **kambos* (fem. **kambā*), crooked; Stokes-Fick, 78.

Game. (E.) M. E. *game*, also *gamen*. A. S. *gamen*, sport. + Icel. *gaman*, Dan. *gammen*, M. Swed. *gamman*, O. H. G. *gaman*, joy, mirth. See **Gammon** (2).

Gammer, an old lady, grandmother. (F. – L.; *and* E.) For *grammer*, West. E. form of *grand-mother*.

Gammon (1), the preserved thigh of a hog. (F. – L.) M. E. *gambon*. A. F. *gambon* (F. *jambon*), a gammon; from O. F. *gambe*, leg. See **Gambol**.

Gammon (2), nonsense; orig. a jest. (E.) M. E. *gamen*, a game; see **Game**. And see **Backgammon**.

Gamut. (F. – Gk.; *and* L.) Comp. of O. F. *game*, *gamme*, and *ut*. Here *gamme* represents the Gk. γάμμα (γ), because the musical scale was represented by *a*, *b*, *c*, *d*, *e*, *f*, *g*, the last being *g* = γ. *Ut* is the old name for *do*, the 1st note in singing, because it began an old hymn to St. John, '*Ut* queant laxis,' &c., used in learning singing. *Gamut* is the scale, from γ (*g*) to *ut* (*a*).

Gander. (E.) M. E. *gandre*. A. S. *gandra*, also spelt *ganra* (the *d* being, in fact, excrescent). + Du. *gander*. Cf. also Low G. *gante*, a gander (see *ganta* in Pliny). Teut. type **ganron-*, m. Allied to **Gannet** and **Goose**.

Gang (1), a crew of persons. (E.) A. S. *gang*, a going, progression; but the sense was affected by the related word *genge*, a gang.

gang (2), to go. (Scand.) Icel. *ganga*, to go; cf. A. S. *gang*, a going, path, course (whence E. *gang-way*); see **Go.**

Ganglion, a tumour on a tendon. (L. – Gk.) L. *ganglion*. – Gk. γάγγλιον.

Gangrene, a mortification of the flesh. (F. – L. – Gk.) M. F. *gangrene*. – L. *gangræna*. – Gk. γάγγραινα, an eating sore. Allied to γέρ-ων, an old man, from √γέρ, to grow old; cf. Skt. *jaras*, old age, *jaraya*, to consume (see Prellwitz).

Gannet, solan goose, a sea-fowl. (E.) A. S. *ganot*. + Low G. *gante*, Du. *gent*, a gander; M. H. G. *ganze*, O. H. G. *ganazo*, a gander. From a base *gan-*; see Gander.

Gantlet (1); see Gauntlet.

Gantlet (2), **Gantlope,** a military punishment. (Swed.) Formerly *gantlope*; corrupted by confusion with *gauntlet*. Again, *gantlope* is a corruption of Swed. *gatlopp*, lit. ' a running down a lane;' to ' run the gantlope' is to run between two files of soldiers, who strike the offender as he passes. — Swed. *gata*, a lane, street (see Gate (2)); and *lopp*, a running, from *löpa*, to run, cognate with E. Leap.

Gaol, Jail, a cage, prison. (F. – L.) A. F. *gaole*, *geiole* (F. *geôle*), a prison, birdcage. – Late L. *gabiola*, *caveola*, a cage, dimin. of L. *cauea*, a den, cave, cage. – L. *cauus*, hollow; see Cage.

Gap. (Scand.) M. E. *gappe.* – Icel. and Swed. *gap*, a gap, abyss. – Icel. and Swed. *gapa*, to gape (below).

gape. (Scand.) M. E. *gapen.* – Icel. and Swed. *gapa*, Dan. *gabe.*+E. Fries. and Du. *gapen*, G. *gaffen.* Cf. Skt. *jabh*, *jambh*, to gape.

Gar (1), **Garfish,** a fish. (E.) A fish with slender body and pointed head. From A. S. *gār*, a spear; cf. Garlic. So also *pike*, *ged*.

Gar (2), to cause. (Scand.) Icel. *gǫrua* (Noreen), Swed. *göra*, Dan. *gjöre*, to make, cause; lit. to make ready. – Icel. *gǫrr*, *görr*, ready; see Yare.

garb (1), dress. (F. – O. H. G.) Shak. – O. F. *garbe*, a garb, good fashion. – O. H. G. *garawī*, *garwī*, dress, preparation; cf. O. H. G. *garawen*, M. H. G. *garwen*, to get ready. – O. H. G. *garo*, ready; cognate with E. *yare*; see Gear.

Garb (2), a wheatsheaf, in heraldry. (F.—O. H. G.) A. F. and Picard *garbe.* F. *gerbe*, a sheaf. – O. H. G. *garba* (G. *garbe*), a sheaf. Lit. ' what is grabbed' or caught up into a bundle by grasping. Cf. E. *grab*, Swed. *grabba*, to grasp; Skt. *grah*, Vedic *grabh*, to seize. Brugm. i. § 531.

garbage, refuse. (F. – O. H. G.) M. E. *garbage*, entrails of fowls. This agrees in form with O. F. *garbage*, *gerbage*, a tax paid in garbs or sheaves. Prob. similarly formed from O. F. *garbe*, in the sense of ' handful,' small bundle, a sense which occurs for Low L. *garba*.

Garble, to select for a purpose; hence, to corrupt an account. (F. – Span. – Arab.) Orig. to pick out, sort, sift out. – O. F. *gar-*

beller (see N. E. D.), the same as *grabeller*, to garble or sort out spices, orig. to sift. The same as Span. *garbillar*, Ital. *garbel-lare*, to garble or sift wares. – Span. *gar-billo*, a coarse sieve. – Pers. *gharbīl*, Arab. *ghirbāl*, a sieve; Arab. *gharbalat*, sifting, searching. Rich. Dict. p. 1046.

Garboil, a commotion. (F.) M. F. *garbouil*, ' a garboil, hurliburly;' Cot. Cf. Span. *garbullo*, a crowd; Ital. *gar-buglio*, a garboil, disorder. Of unknown origin. Prob. imitative. Florio has Ital. *garabullare*, to rave.

Garden. (F. – O. Frankish.) M. E. *gardin.* – A. F., O. North F. *and* Picard *gardin*, F. *jardin.* – O. Frank. *gardin* (O. H. G. *gartin*), gen. and dat. of *gardo*, a yard, cognate with E. Yard, q. v. Cf. O. H. G. *gartin-āri*, a gardener.

Garfish; see Gar (1).

Gargle. (F. – Late L. – Gk.) Modified from F. *gargouiller*, ' to gargle;' Cot. — F. *gargouille*, the weasand of the throat, also a gargoyle, or mouth of a spout. So also Span. *gargola*, a gargoyle; Ital. *gar-gozza*, the gullet. From an imitative base *garg-*, as seen in L. *garg-arizāre*, to gargle, from Gk. γαργαρίζειν, to gargle; cf. Gk. γαργαρεών, the uvula. Hence also Ital. *gargagliare*, to murmur, *gargatta*, the throat. The parallel L. base is *gurg-*; see Gorge, Gurgle.

gargoyle, a spout. (F. – L.) F. *gar-gouille* (above).

Garish, staring, showy. (E.) Also formerly spelt *gaurish*. Allied to M. E. *gauren*, to stare (Chaucer). Cf. M. E. *gawen*, to stare; Icel. *gā*, to heed, mark.

Garland. (F.—Teut.?) M. E. *gerlond.* – O. F. *garlonde.* Cf. Span. *guirnalda*, Ital. *ghirlanda* (whence Mod. F. *guir-lande*), a garland. Prob. formed, with suffix *-ande*, from M. H. G. **wierelen*, frequentative of *wieren*, to adorn, from O. H. G. *wiara*, M. H. G. *wiere*, refined gold, fine ornament, crown. Cf. Wire.

Garlic, a plant. (E.) A. S. *gārlēac*, lit. ' spear-leek.' – A. S. *gār*, a spear; *lēac*, a leek, plant. See Gore (3) and Leek.

Garment. (F. – O. Low G.) M. E. *garnement.* – O. F. *garnement*, *garniment*, a robe (defence). – O. F. *garnir*, to protect; see Garnish.

Garner. (F. – L.) M. E. *garner.* – O. F. *gernier*, variant of *grenier*, a granary. – L. *grānārium*, a granary. – L. *grānum*, corn; see Grain.

garnet. (F.–L.) M. E. *garnet*, also spelt *granat;* – O. F. *granate* ; M. F. *grenat,* ' a precious stone called a granat or garnet,' Cot.; Late L. *grānātus.* So called from its resemblance to the seeds of the pomegranate, or *mālum grānātum*, lit. seeded apple. – L. *grānum*, a grain, seed.

Garnish. (F.–O. Low G.) Also *warnish.* – O. F. *garnis-, warnis-,* stem of pres. pt. of *garnir, warnir,* to defend oneself, fortify, garnish. – O. Frank. **warnjan* ; cf. O. H. G. *warnōn*, M. H. G. *warnen,* to guard against, provide oneself with ; cf. O. H. G. *warna,* foresight, care. See **Warn.**

garniture. (F.–O. Low G.) F. *garniture,* garnishment. – Low L. *garnītūra.* – Low L. *garnītus,* orig. pp. of *garnīre,* to adorn, which is merely a Latinised form of O. F. *garnir* (above).

Garret. (F.–G.) M. E. *garite.* – O. F. *garite* (F. *guérite*), place of refuge, watch-tower. – O. F. *garir, warir,* to preserve. – O. H. G. *warjan,* to defend. Allied to **Wary.**

Garrison. (F.–O. Low G.) Confused with M. E. *garisoun, warisoun,* a reward ; but the true form is M. E. *garnison, warnison,* defence, stores, supply. – O. F. *garnison,* store, supply. – O. F. *garnis-ant,* pres. pt. of *garnir,* to supply, garnish ; see **Garnish.** And see **Warison.**

Garrote, Garrotte. (Span. – C.) Span. *garrote,* a cudgel, tying a rope tight, strangling by means of an iron collar. Formed, with dimin. suffix -*ote,* from Span. *garra,* a claw, talon, clutch, grasp. – Bret., W., and Corn. *gar,* the shank of the leg (Diez). See **Garter.**

Garrulous. (L.) L. *garrulus,* talkative. – L. *garrīre,* to chatter. Brugm. i. § 638.

Garter. (F.–C.) A. F. *garter* ; O.F. *gartier* (North of France, Hécart), spelt *jartier* in Cotgrave (F. *jarretière*). – O. F. and Norm. *garet* (F. *jarret*), the ham of the leg ; a dimin. form. – Bret. *gar,* W. *gar,* shank of the leg ; Celt. type **garris.*

Gas. (Du.) The Belgian chemist Van Helmont (died A. D. 1644) invented two terms, *gas* and *blas* ; the latter did not come into use. He tells us that *gas* was suggested by the Gk. χάος. See N. E. D.

Gasconade, boasting. (Gascony.) F. *gasconnade,* boasting ; said to be a vice of Gascons ; at any rate named from them.

Gash, to hack, cut deeply. (F.–Late L. –Gk.) Formerly *garsh, garse.* – O. F. *garser,* to scarify, pierce with a lancet. – Late L. *caraxāre,* short for *incaraxāre, incharaxāre,* to pierce, incise. Cf. Late L. *garsa,* scarification, by making incisions in the skin, called in Gk. ἐγχάραξις ; whence the Late L. vb. was formed. See **Character.**

Gasp. (E.) M. E. *gaspen, gaispen.* The latter answers to Icel. *geispa,* Swed. *gäspa,* to yawn (cf. Dan. *gispe*). The former represents the cognate A. S. **gāspan* (not found). Icel. *geispa* is for **geipsa* ; cf. Du. *gijpen,* to gasp ; A. S. *gipung,* a gaping.

Gastric, belonging to the belly. (Gk.) Coined from Gk. γαστρό-, from γαστήρ, the belly.

Gate (1), a door, hole, opening. (E.) M. E. *gate, yate.* A. S. *gæt, geat,* a gate, opening (whence M. E. *yate*) ; pl. *gatu* (whence M. E. *gate*). **+** Du. *gat,* a hole, opening, gap ; O. Fries., O. Sax., Icel. *gat,* an opening.

Gate (2), a street. (Scand.) Common in the North ; it also means ' a way.' – Icel. *gata,* Swed. *gata,* a way, path, street, lane ; Dan. *gade* ; cf. Goth. *gatwō,* G. *gasse.* Perhaps allied to **Gate** (1), and also to the vb. **Go.** β. *Gate* (1) answers to Teut. type **gatom,* n., but *gate* (2) to Teut. type **gatwōn-,* f. See **Gait** and **Gantlet** (2).

Gather. (E.) M. E. *gaderen.* A. S. *gaderian, gædrian,* to collect, get together. – A. S. *gader-,* together; also *gador-, geador.* **+** Du. *gaderen,* to collect, from (*te*)*gader,* together. Cf. A. S. *gæd,* a company, society (whence also A. S. *gædeling,* a comrade ; *ge-gada,* a companion) ; Du. *gade,* a spouse, G. *gatte* a husband ; Goth. *gadiliggs,* a cousin. Perhaps allied to **Good.**

Gaud, a show, ornament. (L.) M. E. *gaude.* – L. *gaudium,* gladness, joy ; hence, an ornament. – L. *gaudēre,* to rejoice (base *gāuid-,* as in *gāuīsus sum,* used as pt. t.). **+** Gk. γηθέειν, to rejoice ; allied to γαίειν (= γαϝ-ίειν), to rejoice ; γαῦρος, proud. Brugm. i. § 589 ; ii. § 694. Der. *gaud-y,* adj.

Gauge, Gage, to measure the content of a vessel. (F.–Low L.) Spelt *gage* in Shak. – O. North F. *gauger,* F. *jauger,* ' to gage,' Cot. – O. North F. *gauge,* F. *jauge,* ' a gage, instrument wherewith a

cask is measured,' Cot.; Low L. *gaugia*
(A. D. 1446). Of unknown origin.

Gaunt, thin, lean. (Scand. ?) An East-
Anglian word; perhaps Scand. Also spelt
gant (1691). Cf. Norweg. *gand*, a thin
stick, a tall and thin man, an overgrown
stripling (Aasen); Swed. dial. *gank*, a lean,
half-starved horse (Rietz). Doubtful.

Gauntlet. (F.—Scand.) O. F. *gante-
let*, a double dimin. of *gant*, a glove.—O.
Swed. *wante*, a glove; Dan. *vante*, a
mitten, Icel. *vöttr* (stem *vantu-*), a glove.
Cf. Du. *want*, a mitten (prob. borrowed
from Scand.). Prob. from **Wind**, verb
(Noreen); cf. G. *gewand*, a garment; Low
G. *want*, cloth (Lübben).

Gauntlet; see **Gantlet** (2).

Gauze, a thin silken fabric. (F.—
Palestine.) M. F. *gaze*; Span. *gasa*. Cf.
Low L. *gazzātum*, gauze; *gazētum*, wine
from Gaza. Said to be from *Gaza*, in
Palestine, whence it was first brought.

Gavelkind, a sort of tenure. (E.)
M. E. *gauelkynde*; answering to an A.S.
form **gafol-cynd*. — A. S. *gafol*, tribute,
payment; and *cynd*, kind, sort, condition.
The A. S. *gaf-ol* (whence Low L. *gabulum*)
is from Teut. **gab*, 2nd grade of **Give**, q. v.

Gavial, the crocodile of the Ganges.
(F.—Hind.) F. *gavial* (a corrupt form).
— Hind. *ghaṛiyāl*, a crocodile.

Gavotte, a dance. (F.) M. F. *gavote*,
orig. a dance of the *Gavots*. *Gavot* is a
sobriquet, in Provence, of the moun-
taineers of the Alps (see Hatzfeld).

Gawk, Gawky, awkward. (F.—
Scand.) From E. dial. *gawk-handed*,
gaulick-handed, left-handed; *gawk*, clumsy.
Here *gawk* is short for *gaul-ick*, where
-ick is a suffix. Of F. origin; cf. Burgund.
gôle, numb with cold, said of the fingers.
—Swed. Dan. *val-händt*, Norw. *val-hendt*,
having numb⸗d hands. ¶ Prob. not from
F. *gauche* (N. E. D.).

Gay. (F. — O. H. G.) O. F. *gai*. —
O. H. G. *wāhi*, fine, beautiful.

Gaze. (Scand.) M. E. *gasen*.—Swed.
dial. *gasa*, to gaze, stare at.

Gazelle, an animal. (F. — Span.—
Arab.) Formerly *gazel*. — O. F. *gazel*,
gazelle.—Span. *gacela*.—Arab. *ghazāl*, a
wild goat, gazelle.

Gazette. (F.—Ital.) O. F. *gazette*, an
abstract of news, issued at Venice.—Ital.
gazzetta, a gazette; the orig. sense is
either (1) a magpie, from Ital. *gazzetta*,

a magpie, dimin. of *gazza*, a magpie,
whence it may have meant 'tittle-tattle';
or (2) a *very* small coin (perhaps paid for
the privilege of reading the news), from
Ital. *gazzetta*, a coin less than a farthing,
probably from Gk. γάζα, a treasury.

Gear, dress, harness, tackle. (Scand.)
M. E. *gere*. — Icel. *gervi*, *görvi*, gear,
apparel. Cf. *görr*, *geyrr*, skilled, dressed,
pp. of *göra*, to make. ╋A. S. *gearwe*, fem.
pl., preparation, dress, ornament; A. S.
gearo, ready; see **Yare**. And see **Gar**
(2), **Garth** (1).

Geck, a dupe. (Du.) In Tw. Nt. v.
351.—Du. *gek*, formerly *geck*, a fool, sot;
cf. G. *geck*, the same; Dan. *gjek*, fool;
Icel. *gikkr*, a pert, rude person. ¶ Not
to be confused with A. S. *gēac*, cuckoo;
nor with *gowk*; nor with *gawky*.

Gecko, a nocturnal lizard. (Malay.)
Also F. *gecko*. — Malay *gēkoq*, a gecko;
so named from an imitation of its cry.

Ged, the fish called a pike. (Scand.)
Icel. *gedda*, Swed. *gädde*, Dan. *giedde*, a
ged; allied to *gaddr*, a goad; see **Gad** (1).
Named from the sharp, thin head; hence
also called *pike*.

Gelatine. (F.—Ital.—L.) F. *gélatine*,
kind of jelly.—Ital. *gelatina*.—L. *gelātus*,
pp. of *gelāre*, to freeze.—L. *gelu*, frost;
see **Gelid**.

Geld, to emasculate. (Scand.) M. E.
gelden. — Icel. *gelda*, Dan. *gilde*, Swed.
gälla (for *gälda*); cf. Icel. *geldr*, Swed.
gall, barren. Perhaps related to Goth.
giltha, a sickle. Cf. **Galt** (2). **Der.**
geld-ing, from Icel. *gelding*, the same.

Gelid, cool. (L.) L. *gelidus*.—L. *gelu*,
frost. Allied to **Cool**. Brugm. i. § 481.

Gem. (F. — L.) M. E. *gemme*. — F.
gemme. — L. *gemma*, a bud; also a gem,
jewel. Brugm. i. § 413 (4).

Gemini. (L.) L. *geminī*, twins; pl.
of *geminus*, double.

Gender (1), kind. (F.—L.) M. E.
gendre (with excrescent *d*).—O. F. *genre*,
kind.—L. *genere*, abl. case of *genus*, kind,
kin. ¶ The unusual deriv. from the abl.
case is due to the common phrases *genere
nātus*, *hoc genere*, *omni genere*; so also
Ital. *genere*.

gender (2), to produce. (F. — L.)
M. E. *gendren*. — O. F. *gendrer* (Godefroy).—L. *generāre*, to beget.—L. *gener-*,
for **genes*, stem of *genus* (above). And
see **Engender**.

Genealogy. (F. — L. — Gk.) M. E.

genealogie. – O. F. *genealogie.* – L. *genea-
logia.* – Gk. γενεαλογία, an account of a
family, pedigree (1 Tim. i. 4). – Gk. γενεά,
birth (allied to γένος, see **genus**); and
λογία, an account, allied to λόγος (see
Logic).

General, relating to a genus, common.
(F. – L.) O. F. *general.* – L. *generālis,*
belonging to a *genus* (stem *gener-,* for
*genes); see **genus.** Hence *general,* sb.,
a leader; *general-issimo,* from Ital. *general-
issimo,* a supreme commander, with superl.
suffix *-issimo.*

generate. (L.) From pp. of L.
generāre, to produce. – L. *gener-,* decl.
stem of *genus.*

generic, pertaining to a genus. (L.)
Coined from L. *gener-,* decl. stem of
genus.

generous. (F. – L.) O. F. *genereus,*
later *généreux.* – L. *generōsus,* (properly)
of noble birth. – L. *gener-,* as above.

Genesis, creation. (L. – Gk.) L.
genesis. – Gk. γένεσις, origin, source;
related to γένος, race; see **genus.**

Genet, an animal. (F. – Span. – Arab.)
F. *genette,* 'a kind of weessel;' Cot. –
Span. *gineta.* – Arab. *jarneit* (Dozy).

Genial. (F. – L.) O. F. *genial.* – L.
geniālis, pleasant; adj. from *genius;* see
genius.

Geniculate, jointed. (L.) In botany.
From L. *geniculum,* a little knee, joint in
a plant; double dimin. of *genū,* a knee.
Allied to **Knee.**

Genie, a demon; see **Jinn.**

Genital. (F. – L.) O. F. *genital.* – L.
genitālis, generative. – L. *genit-um,* supine
of *gignere,* to beget.

genitive. (F. – L.) O. F. *genitif.* –
L. *genetīuus,* belonging to birth, applied
in grammar to a certain case of nouns. –
L. *genitum* (above).

genius, inborn faculty. (L.) L.
genius, the tutelar spirit of any one; also
wit, lit. 'inborn nature.' Allied to **genus.**

Gennet; see **Jennet.**

Genteel. (F. – L.) XVI cent.; F.
gentil. – L. *gentīlis,* belonging to the same
clan, a gentile (afterwards applied to mean
well-bred, &c.). – L. *genti-,* decl. stem of
gens, a clan, tribe. Allied to **genus.**

Gentian, a plant. (F. – L.) O. F. *gen-
tiane.* – L. *gentiāna;* named after *Gentius,*
an Illyrian king, abt. B.C. 180.

Gentile. (F. – L.) O. F. *gentil.* – L.
gentīlis, gentile; see **Genteel.**

gentle. (F. – L.) O. F. *gentil* (above).

gentry. (F. – L.) M. E. *gentrie,* high
birth; shortened from M. E. *gentrise,* the
same. – O. F. *genterise,* another form of
gentilise, rank (= Late L. **gentīlitia*). –
L. *gentīlis;* see **Genteel.**

Genuflection, Genuflexion, a
bending of the knee. (F. – L.) M.F. *genuflexion.* – Late L. acc. *genūflexiōnem.* – L.
genū, knee; *flex-us,* pp. of *flectere,* to
bend.

Genuine. (L.) L. *genuīnus,* of the
true *genus* or stock; allied to L. *genus*
(below).

genus, kin. (L.) L. *genus* (gen.
generis, for **geneses*), kin, race. + Gk.
γένος, race; A.S. *cyn,* kin. See **Kin.**
(√GEN.) Brugm. i. § 604.

Geography. (F. – L. – Gk.) M. F.
geographie. – L. *geōgraphia.* – Gk. γεω-
γραφία, lit. earth-description. – Gk. γεω- =
γηο-, a combining form of γῆ, earth;
-γραφία, description, from γράφειν, to
write.

geometry. (F. – L. – Gk.) O. F.
geometrie. – L. *geōmetria.* – Gk. γεωμετρία,
land-measurement. – Gk. γεω- (as above);
-μετρία, measurement, from μετρέω, I
measure, μέτρον, a measure; see **Metre.**

georgic. (L. – Gk.) L. *geōrgicus,*
relating to husbandry. – Gk. γεωργικός,
the same. – Gk. γεωργία, tillage. – Gk. γεω-
(as above); ***ἔργειν > ἔρδειν, to work. See
Work.

Geranium, a plant. (L. – Gk.) L.
geranium, Latinised from Gk. γεράνιον, a
geranium or crane's bill (from the shape
of the seed-pod). – Gk. γέρανος, a crane;
allied to **Crane.**

Gerfalcon; see **Gyrfalcon.**

Germ, a seed. (F. – L.) F. *germe.* –
L. *germen* (stem *germin-*), a sprout, germ.
Der. *germin-ate* (from the stem).

german, germane, akin. (F. – L.)
Cousins-german are cousins having the
same grandfather. Formerly spelt *germain.*
– M. F. *germain.* – L. *germānum,* acc. of
germānus, closely akin. Allied to **Germ.**

Germander. (F. – L. – Gk.) F. *ger-
mandrée,* germander; O. F. *germandree,
gemandree* (Godefroy, Supp.); cf. G. *ga-
mander.* – Late L. *gamandria,* a popular
alteration of Late Gk. χαμανδρυά, germander. – Gk. χαμαίδρυς, germander; lit.
'ground-tree,' i.e. low tree. – Gk. χαμαί,
on the ground; δρῦς, tree.

Gerund, a part of a Latin verb. (L.)

L. *gerundium*, a gerund. — L. *gerundus*, that which is to be done or carried on; a verbal adj. from *gerere* (pp. *ges-tus*), to carry on, perform, bring. (√GES.)

gestation, the carrying of the young in the womb. (F.—L.) M. F. *gestation*.— L. acc. *gestātiōnem*, a carrying. — L. *gestātus*, pp. of *gestāre*, to carry, frequent. form of *gerere* (pp. *gest-us*), to bring.

gesticulate, to make gestures. (L.) From pp. of *gesticulārī*, to make mimic gestures. — L. *gesticulus*, a gesture, double dimin. of *gestus*, a gesture.— L. *gestus*, pp. of *gerere*.

gesture. (L.) Late L. *gestūra*, a mode of action.— L. *gestus*, pp. of *gerere*.

Get. (Scand.) M. E. *geten*, pt. t. *gat*, pp. *geten*. — Icel. *geta*, pt. t. *gat*, pp. *getinn*. +A. S. *-getan*, pt. t. *-gæt*, pp. *-geten*, to get, obtain; Goth. *-gitan*; cognate with L. *-hendere* (base *hed*), in *prehendere*, to seize; Gk. χανδάνειν (base χαδ), to seize; Russ. *gadate*, to conjecture. (√GHwED.) Der. *be-get, for-get*. Brugm. i. § 632.

Gewgaw, a plaything, specious trifle. (F.) Formerly *gugaw*, (perhaps) answering to M. E. *giuegoue*, Ancren Riwle, p. 196. The pron. of M. E. *giuegoue* is uncertain. Origin unknown; prob. F. One sense of E. *gewgaw* is a Jew's harp; cf. Burgundian *gawe*, a Jew's harp (Mignard). Cf. Swed. dial. *guva*, to blow; Norw. *guva*, *gyva* (pt. t. *gauv*).

Geysir. (Icel.) Icel. *geysir*, lit. 'gusher.' — Icel. *geysa*, to gush; allied to *gjósa* (pt. t. *gaus*), to gush. See **Gush.**

Ghastly, terrible. (E.) M. E. *gastly*. Formed from M. E. *gasten*, A. S. *gǣstan*, to terrify; allied to Goth. *usgaisjan*, to terrify. See **Aghast.** Allied words are *gasted*, terrified, K. Lear, ii. 1. 57; *gastness*, Oth. v. 1. 106. See **Ghost.**

Ghaut, a landing-place, quay, way down to a river; mountain-pass. (Hind.) Hind. *ghāt*, Bengāli *ghāt*. See Wilson.

Ghee, boiled or clarified butter. (Hind. —Skt.) Hind. *ghī*. — Skt. *ghṛta*, clarified butter; orig. pp. of *ghṛ*, to sprinkle.

Gherkin, small cucumber. (Du. — Slav. — Low L. — Gk. — Pers.) Short for *agherkin*. — Du. *agurkje*, a gherkin (of which an older form was doubtless *agurken* (= *agurk-ken*), because M. Du. used the dimin. suffix *-ken* where mod. Du. uses *-je*; in fact, the form *augurken* is preserved in E. Friesic.). Without the final *n*, we have Du. *agorke* (Sewel). —

Pol. *ogurek, ogorek, ogorka*, a cucumber; Bohem. *okurka*. — M. Ital. *anguria*, a cucumber (Florio); Low L. *angūrius*, a water-melon. — Byzantine Gk. ἀγγούριον, a water-melon. — Pers. *angārah*, a melon, a cucumber; Rich. Dict., p. 194.

Ghost, a spirit. (E.) M. E. *gost, goost*. A. S. *gāst*. +Du. *geest*, G. *geist*. Teut. type *gaistoz*. Of uncertain origin; perhaps allied to Icel. *geisa*, to rage (like fire), and to Goth. *us-gais-jan*, to terrify. Brugm. i. § 816 (2).

Ghoul, a kind of demon. (Arab.) Pers. *ghōl*, an imaginary sylvan demon; Arab. *ghuwal*, a demon of the woods; from Arab. *ghawl*, attacking suddenly.

Giant. (F.—L.—Gk.) M. E. *giant, geant, geaunt*.—A. F. and O. F. *giant, geant*. — L. *gigantem*, acc. of *gigas*. — Gk. γίγας (stem γιγαντ-), a giant. Der. *gigant-ic*, from L. *gigant-*, stem of *gigas*.

Giaour, an infidel. (Pers.) *Giaour* is an Ital. spelling usual among the Franks of the Levant (Byron). Pers. *gawr*, an infidel, a fire-worshipper; variant of Pers. *gabr*, a Gueber; see **Gueber.**

Gibberish, idle talk. (Arab.?) The hard *g* separates it from the verb *gibber*, to gabble, which is the frequentative of *jibe*, and allied to *jabber*. Fuller has *Geberish*, and Camden *Gebrish*; apparently in allusion to *Gebir*, an Arabian alchemist of the 8th century, and to the jargon of alchemy. Or it may be merely imitative.

Gibbet. (F.) M. E. *gibbet, gibet*. — O. F. *gibbet* (F. *gibet*), a gibbet. Prob. allied to O. F. *gibet*, a large stick, perhaps a dimin. of O. F. *gibe*, *gibbe*, a sort of stick shod with iron, an implement for stirring up earth. Or is *gib-et* a dimin. from M. Du. *wippe*, 'a gibbet,' in Hexham?

Gibbon, a kind of ape. (F.) F. *gibbon*, in Buffon; of unknown origin.

Gibbous, humped, swelling. (L.) From L. *gibbōsus*, humped (whence also *gibbose*). — L. *gibbus, gibba*, a hump, hunch; cf. *gibbus*, bent.

Gibe, Jibe, to mock. (E.) Of imitative origin; cf. E. Fries. *gībeln*, to mock, Du. *gijbelen*, to sneer. Note also Icel. *geipa*, to talk nonsense, Icel. *geip*, idle talk; Norw. *geipa*, to make grimaces.

Giblets, the internal eatable parts of a fowl, removed before cooking. (F.) M. E. *gibelet*. — O. F. *gibelet*, which, according to Littré, answers to mod. F *gibelotte*, stewed rabbit. Of unknown origin; perhaps related to F. *gibier*, game.

Giddy. (E.) M. E. *gidi, gedy*, adj.; late A. S. *gidig*, insane, answering to earlier **gydig*, which would mean 'possessed by a god'; cf. A. S. *gyden*, a goddess. From A. S. *god*.

Gier-eagle, a kind of eagle. (Du. *and* F.) The first syllable is from Du. *gier*, a vulture; cf. G. *geier*, M. H. G. *gīr*, a vulture. Allied to G. *gier-ig*, greedy, and to E. **Yearn**.

Gift. (E.) M. E. *gift, yift*. = A. S. *gift*, a gift (rare); common in the pl. *gifta*, nuptials; E. Fries. *gift*. = A. S. *gifan*, to give. + Icel. *gipt*, Du. *gift*, G. *-gift* (in *mitgift*, a dowry). ¶ The hard *g* is due to Scand. influence. See **Give**. Der. *gift-ed*.

Gig, a light carriage, light boat. (Scand.) In Shak., a *gig* is a boy's top. M. E. *gigge*, apparently a whirling thing, Ch. Ho. Fame, iii. 852 (whence E. *whirligig*). Prob. of Scand. origin; cf. Icel. *geiga*, to take a wrong direction, to rove at random. Cf. **Jig**. Prob. of imitative origin.

Gigantic; see **Giant**.

Giggle, to titter. (E.) Of imitative origin; cf. *gaggle*. Cf. E. Fries. *gicheln*, Low G. *giggeln* (Danneil), G. *kichern*, to giggle.

Giglet, Giglot, a wanton woman. (E.?) Dimin. of *gigle*, a flirt, used by Cotgrave (s. v. *gadrouillette*); from M. E. *gigge*, the same, Plowm. Tale, 759. Perhaps allied to **Gig** or **Giggle**.

Gild, to overlay with gold. (E.) M. E. *gilden*. A. S. *gyldan*, to gild; cf. A. S. *gylden*, golden. Formed (with vowelmutation from Teut. *u* (>A. S. *o*) to *y*) from *gold*, gold. See **Gold**.

Gill (1), organ of respiration in fishes. (Scand.) M. E. *gille*. = Dan. *giælle*, Swed. *gäl*, a gill; M. Dan. *gælle*, M. Swed. *gel*.

Gill (2), a ravine, chasm. (Scand.) Also *ghyll*. = Icel. *gil*, ravine; Norw. *gil*.

Gill (3), with *g* soft, a quarter of a pint. (F. = Late L.) M. E. *gille*. = O. F. *gelle*, a sort of wine-measure, Late L. *gella*; cf. Late L. *gillo*, a wine-vessel.

Gill (4), with *g* soft, a woman's name, a pitcher, ground-ivy. (L.) Short for *Gilliān*, from L. *Iuliāna*, a fem. name due to L. *Iulius*; see **July**. Der. *flirtgill* or *gill-flirt, jilt*.

Gillie, a boy, page. (C.) Gael. *gille, giolla*, Irish *giolla*, boy, lad; O. Irish *gilla*, a servant.

Gillyflower, a flower. (F. = L. = Gk.) Formerly *gilofer, geraflour*. Formed (by confusion with *flower*) from M. F. *giroflée*, 'a gilloflower;' Cot. From F. *clou de girofle*, the same. = Late L. *caryophyllum*, Latinised from Gk. καρυόφυλλον, a clove tree, lit. 'nut-leaf.' = Gk. κάρυο-ν, a nut; φύλλον, leaf.

Gimbals, a contrivance for suspending a ship's compass, to keep it horizontal. (F. = L.) Formerly *gimmals*; also called *gemmow* or *gemmow-ring*, a double ring, with two or more links. The forms *gemmow* and *gimmal* correspond to M. F. *gemeau*, and O. F. *gemel*, a twin. = L. *gemellus*, a twin, a dimin. form of L. *geminus*, double.

Gimlet, Gimblet. (F. = Teut.) M.F. *gimbelet*, 'a gimlet or piercer;' Cot.; *guimbelet*, Godefroy (F. *gibelet*); Norman dial. *guinblet*. Of M. H. G. origin; formed from a base *wind-*, to turn or wind; cf. mod. G. *wendel-bohrer*, a wimble. Note also Icel. *vindla*, to wind up, *vindill*, a wisp. See **Wimble**, of which *gimlet* is the dimin.

Gimmal-ring; see **Gimbals**.

Gimp, a kind of trimming, made of twisted silk, cotton, or wool. (F. = O.H.G.) See Bailey's Dict. vol. ii., ed. 1731. Named from a resemblance to some kind of wimple. = M. F. *guimpe*, a nun's wimple; also *guimple* (see index to Cotgrave, s. v. *wimple*). = O. H. G. *wimpal*, a light robe, a fillet for the head; G. *wimpel*, a streamer; see **Wimple**. ¶ Prob. confused with F. *guipure*, a thread or silk lace. See **Guipure**.

Gin (1), to begin. (E.) Obsolete; often needlessly written *'gin*, as though *be-* were omitted. M. E. *ginnen*. A. S. *ginnan*, to begin, commonly *on-ginnan* (pt. t. *ongann*, pp. *ongunnen*). + Goth. *ginnan*, in the comp. *du-ginnan*, to begin. Brugm. i. § 376.

Gin (2), a trap, snare. (F. = L.) M. E. *gin*, short for M. E. *engin*, a contrivance. See **Engine**.

Gin (3), a kind of spirit. (F. = L.) Short for *geneva*, corruption of M. F. *genevre*, juniper. = L. acc. *iūniperum*; see **Juniper**.

Ginger, the root of a certain plant. (F. = Gk. = Skt.) M. E. *ginger, gingeuere* (=*gingevere*). = O. F. *gengibre* (F. *gingembre*). = Late L. *gingiber*; L. *zingiber*. = Gk. ζιγγίβερις. = Skt. *çṛñgavera*, ginger;

lit. ' horn-shaped,' from the horns on it. —
Skt. *çṛṅga*, a horn; *vera*, a body.

Gingerly, with soft steps. (F. — L.)
From the adj. **ginger*, soft, delicate (with
soft *g*). Apparently adapted from O. F.
genzor, gensor, more delicate, comp. of
gent, fine, delicate, noble; orig. ' well-
born.' — Folk-L. **gentum*, L. *genitum*,
acc. of *genitus*, born (well-born), pp. of
gignere, to beget. (N.E.D.)

Gingham, a kind of cotton cloth.
(F. — Malay.) F. *guingan*. — Malay *ging-
gang*, striped cloth, gingham. — Malay and
Javanese *ginggang*, striped (C. P. G. Scott).

Gingle; the same as **Jingle.**

Gipsy; the same as **Gypsy.**

Giraffe, a long-legged animal. (F. —
Span. — Arab.) M. F. *giraffe* (F.
girafe). — Span. *girafa.* — Arab. *zaráf,
zaráfa(t)*.

Gird (1), to enclose, bind round. (E.)
M. E. *gurden, girden.* A. S. *gyrdan*, to
gird. + O. Sax. *gurdian*, Du. *gorden*, Icel.
gyrða, to gird, Dan. *giorde*, G. *gürten*.
Teut. type **gurdjan-*; from **gurd-*, weak
grade of Teut. **gerdan-* (pt. t. **gard*), to
enclose; cf. Goth. *bigairdan*, to begird.
Allied to **Garth, Garden,** and **Yard.**

Gird (2), to jest at, jibe. (E.) A peculiar
use of M. E. *girden, gurden*, to strike, cut.
To *gird at* = to strike at, jest at; a *gird*
is a cut, sarcasm; Tam. Shrew, v. 2. 58.

Girdle. (E.) A. S. *gyrdel*, that which
girds. — A. S. *gyrdan*, to gird; see **Gird** (1).
+ Du. *gordel*, Icel. *gyrðill*, Swed. *gördel*,
G. *gürtel*.

Girl. (E.) M. E. *girle, gerle, gurle*,
often used to mean ' a boy'; a child.
Answering to an A.S. form **gyrel-*, Teut.
*guril-, a dimin. form from Teut. base
*gur-. Allied to N. Fries. *gör*, a girl;
Low G. *gör, göre*, a child. Cf. Swiss
gurre, gurrli, a depreciatory term for a
girl (Sanders, Ger. Dict.).

Giron, Gyron, in heraldry, the eighth
part of a shield, made by drawing a diagonal line from the top corner to the centre,
.and from the centre horizontally towards
the same side; a right-angled triangle.
(F. — O. H. G.) F. *giron*, a giron (Littré).
— O. H. G. *gêrun*, acc. of *gêro*, a lance,
spear; M. H. G. *gêre*, a gore or gusset in
a garment, a triangular piece. — O. H. G.
gêr, a spear, cognate with A. S. *gár*, a
spear. See **Gore** (2). (Diez, Schade.)

Girth. (Scand.) M. E. *gerth.* — Icel.
gjörð, a girdle, girth; *gerð*, girth round

the waist; Dan. *giord.* + Goth. *gairda*, a
girdle. Teut. type **gerdâ.* See **Gird** (1).

Gist, the pith of a matter. (F. — L.)
The *gist* is the point wherein the matter
lies. — O. F. *gist* (mod. F. *gît*), it lies;
whence the proverb ' c'est là que *gît* le
lièvre,' that is where the difficulty is, lit.
' that's where the hare lies.' From the F.
verb *gesir* (now *gésir*), to lie. — L. *iacēre*,
to lie. (O. F. *gist* = L. *iacet*.) See **Jet** (1).

Gittern; see **Cithern.**

Give. (Scand.) M. E. *giff* (Northern),
geuen, yeuen (Southern); pt. t. *gaf* (N.),
yaf (S.), pp. *gifen* (N.), *yiuen, youen* (S.).
— Icel. *gefa*, Dan. *give*, Swed. *gifva.* +
A. S. *gifan*, pt. t. *geaf*, pp. *gifen*; Du.
geven; Goth. *giban*, G. *geben.* Teut. type
*geban-, pt. t. **gab*. Cf. O. Irish *gab-im*,
I give, I take.

Gizzard. (F. — L.) M. E. *giser* (the
d being added). — O. F. *gezier, jugier*,
juisier (F. *gésier*). — L. *gigērium*, only in
pl. *gigēria* (Late L. *gizēria*), cooked
entrails of poultry.

Glabrous, smooth. (L.) From L.
glaber, smooth. Idg. stem **gladh-ro-*;
see **Glad.** Brugm. i. § 589.

Glacial, icy. (F. — L.) F. *glacial.* — L.
glaciālis, icy. — L. *glaciēs*, ice.

glacier, a mountain ice-field. (F. — L.)
F. *glacier* (a Savoy word). — F. *glace*, ice. —
Folk-L. *glacia*, for L. *glaciēs*, ice.

glacis, smooth slope. (F. — L.) F.
glacis. — M. F. *glacer*, to cover with ice. —
F. *glace* (above).

Glad. (E.) A. S. *glæd*, shining, bright,
cheerful, glad. + Du. *glad*, smooth, bright,
Icel. *glaðr*, bright, glad, Dan. Swed. *glad*,
G. *glatt*, smooth, polished. Cf. Russ.
gladkii, even, smooth; L. *glaber*, smooth;
see **Glabrous.**

Gladden, Gladen, a plant; *Iris
pseudacorus.* (L.) A. S. *glædene*; altered
from L. *gladiolus*, a sword-lily. Dimin.
of L. *gladius*, a sword; see **Gladiator.**

Glade, an open space in a wood. (E.)
The orig. sense was prob. an opening for
light, passage through a wood; from A.S.
glæd, bright, shining. Cf. Swed. dial.
glad-yppen, completely open, said of a
lake whence the ice has all melted away.

Gladiator, a swordsman. (L.) L. *gla-
diátor.* — L. *gladius*, a sword.

Glair, the white of an egg. (F. — L.)
M. E. *gleyre.* — O. F. *glaire.* — L. *clāra*,
fem. of *clārus*, bright; Late L. *clāra ōuī*,
the white of an egg.

Glaive, a sword. (F. – L.) A. F. *glaive,* a sword ; O. F. *glaive,* a sword, lance. – L. *gladium,* acc. of *gladius,* a sword.

Glamour ; see Gramarye.

Glance, a swift dart of light, quick look ; as a verb, to glide off or from, to graze, to flash. (F. – L.) The sb. is from the verb. A nasalised form (influenced by M. E. *glenten,* to glance) of O. F. *glacer, glacier,* to glide, slip, glance. – F. *glace,* ice ; see Glacial. 2. M. E. *glenten* answers to the causal form of the strong verb *glinta,* to shine, still found in Swed. dialects (Rietz). See Glint.

Gland, a fleshy organ in the body, secreting fluid. (F. – L.) M. F. and F. *glande,* a gland ; O. F. *glandre.* – L. *glandula,* a gland ; dimin. of *glans* (stem *gland-*), an acorn. + Gk. βάλανος, an acorn. Brugm. i. § 665.

glanders, glandular swellings. (F. – L.) M. F. *glandres,* pl. – Lat. pl. acc. *glandulās,* swollen glands ; from L. *glans* (above).

Glare, to shine brightly. (E.) M. E. *glaren ;* cf. A. S. *glǣr,* amber. + Low G. *glaren,* to glow. Perhaps allied to Glass. Cf. Dan. *glar,* Icel. *gler,* glass (below).

Glass. (E.) A. S. *glæs.* + Du. *glas,* G. *glas ;* cf. Dan. *glar,* M. Swed. *gler,* Icel. *gler,* glass. Orig. sense prob. ' shining.' See above.

Glaucous, grayish blue. (L. – Gk.) L. *glauc-us ;* with suffix *-ous.* – Gk. γλαυκός, gleaming, bluish.

Glaze, to furnish with glass. (E.) M. E. *glasen.* – M. E. *glas,* glass ; see Glass.

Gleam, a beam of light. (E.) A. S. *glǣm ;* Teut. type *glaimiz.* + O. Sax. *glīmo,* brightness ; O. H.G. *glīmo, gleimo,* a glow-worm (from base *gleim-*). Allied to Gk. χλι-αρός, warm. See Glimmer.

Glean. (F.) M. E. *glenen.* – O. F. *glener, glaner* (F. *glaner*), to glean ; Low L. *glenāre* (A.D. 561) ; cf. Low L. *glena, gelina, gelima,* a handful. Of unknown origin. The A. S. *gilm,* a handful, whence prov. E. *yelm,* to provide handfuls of straw ready for a thatcher, will not account for the O. F. form. ¶ We also find the form to *gleame* (Levins), also spelt *gleme.*

Glebe, soil. (F. – L.) M. F. *glebe,* ' glebe, land belonging to a parsonage ; ' Cot. – L. *glēba,* soil, a clod of earth.

Glede (1), a kite, a bird so called. (E.)

M. E. *glede.* A. S. *glida,* a kite, lit. ' glider,' from its smooth flight. – A. S. *glīd-,* weak grade of *glīdan,* to glide ; see Glide. Cf. Icel. *gleða* (the same).

Glede (2), **Gleed,** a glowing coal. (E.) A. S. *glēd* (where *ē* is from *ō,* by vowel-change). – A. S. *glōwan,* to glow ; see Glow. Cf. Dan. Swed. *glöd,* the same.

Glee, joy, singing. (E.) A. S. *glēo,* earlier *gliu,* joy, mirth, music. + Icel. *glȳ,* glee, gladness ; Swed. dial. *gly,* mockery. Cf. Gk. χλεύη, a jest. Brugm. i. § 633.

Gleek (1), a scoff, jest. See Nares. Prob. a particular use of Gleek (2).

Gleek (2), a game at cards ; in which a *gleek* meant three cards *alike* (as three kings). (F. – Du.) See Nares. – O. F. *glic,* a game at cards ; also spelt *ghelicque* (Godefroy). – M. Du. *gelijck,* alike. – M. Du. *ge-, ghe-,* Du. *ge-,* prefix (= A. S. *ge-,* Goth. *ga-*) ; M. Du. *-lijck,* Du. *-lijk,* cognate with E. *like ;* see Like. ¶ Hexham has *gelijk ofte ongelijk spelen,* to play at even or odds.

Glen, a narrow valley. (C.) Gael. and Irish *gleann,* O. Irish *glenn ;* W. *glyn,* a valley, glen. Celtic type *glennos.*

Glib (1), smooth, voluble. (E.) Cf. E. Fries. *glibberig, glibberig,* slippery ; *glippen,* to slip. + Du. *glibberig,* slippery, *glibberen,* to slide ; Du. and Low G. *glippen,* to slip away.

Glib (2), a lock of hair. (C.) Irish and Gael. *glib,* also Ir. *clib,* a lock of hair.

Glib (3), to castrate. (E.) The same as *lib,* with prefixed *g-* = A. S. *ge-,* a common prefix. Cognate with Du. *lubben,* to castrate, M. Du. *lubben.* See Left.

Glide. (E.) M. E. *gliden,* pt. t. *glood.* A. S. *glīdan.* + Du. *glijden,* Dan. *glide,* Swed. *glida,* G. *gleiten.* Teut. type *gleidan-,* pt. t. *glaid,* pp. *glidanoz.*

Glimmer, verb. (E.) M. E. *glimeren.* + Low G. *glimmern,* frequent. of *glimmen,* to shine ; Dan. *glimre,* vb., cf. *glimmer,* sb., glitter ; Swed. dial. *glimmer,* vb., *glimmer,* sb., glitter. Frequent. of Dan. *glimme,* Swed. *glimma,* to shine. Cf. Swed. dial. *glim,* a glance, A. S. *gleomu* (for *glimu*), splendour ; from *glim-,* weak grade of *gleim-* ; see Gleam.

glimpse, a slight gleam. (E.) Formerly *glimse ;* M. E. *glimsen,* to glimpse ; formed with suffix *-s-* from *glim* (above).

Glint, to shine, glance. (Scand.) M. E. *glenten.* – Swed. dial. *glänta, glinta,* to shine ; nasalised from Icel. *glita,* to shine.

+M.H.G. *glinzen*, to glint, Swed. *glindra*. See Glitter.

Glisten, Glister, to glitter. (E.) Extended from base *glis-* of M. E. *glisien*, to shine. A. S. *glisian*; whence also *glisnian*, to shine. We also find M. E. *glisteren, glistren*, to glitter. Cf. Du. *glinsteren*, to glitter; Swed. dial. *glisa*.

Glitter. (E.) M. E. *gliteren*, to shine. A. S. *glitinian*, to shine; extended from A. S. *glitian*, to shine.**+**Icel. *glitra*, to glitter, frequent. of *glita*, to shine; Swed. *glittra*, to glitter; *glitter*, sb., a sparkle. Cf. Goth. *glit-munjan*, to glitter. From **glit-*, weak grade of **gleit-*, as in O. Sax. *glītan*, G. *gleissen*, to shine.

Gloaming, twilight. (E.) A Scot. form of *glooming*, i. e. the time of becoming dusk; A. S. *æfen-glommung*, gloom of eve, Hymn. Surtees, 16. 16. See Gloom.

Gloat, to stare, gaze with admiration. (E.) Formerly *glote* (XVI cent.). **+** Icel. *glotta*, to grin, smile scornfully; Swed. dial. *glotta, glutta*, to peep; G. *glotzen*, to stare. Cf. Russ. *gliadiet(e)*, to look at.

Globe. (F.–L.) O. F. *globe.* –L. *globum*, acc. of *globus*, a ball; cf. *glomus*, a ball, clue.

Glomerate. (L.) From pp. of *glomerāre*, to collect into a ball. –L. *glomer-*, for **glomes*, stem of *glomus*, a ball or clew of yarn. See Globe.

Gloom. (E.) A. S. *glōm*, gloom, twilight; cf. A. S. *-glommung*, twilight (see Gloaming), and prov. E. *glum*, overcast. **+**Norw. *glyma*, an overcast sky; Low G. *glum*, turbid. See Glum.

Glory. (F.–L.) M. E. *glorie.* –A. F. and O. F. *glorie* (F. *gloire*). – L. *glōria.*

Gloss (1), lustre. (Scand.) Icel. *glossi*, a blaze, *glys*, finery; Swed. dial. *glossa*, to glow; Norw. *glosa*, to glow.**+**M. H. G. *glosen*, to glow, *glos*, lustre; Du. *gloren* (Franck), E. Fries. *gloren*.

Gloss (2), a commentary, explanation. (F.–L.–Gk.) M. E. *glose.*–O. F. *glose*, 'a glosse;' Cot.–L. *glōssa*, a difficult word requiring explanation.–Gk. γλῶσσα, the tongue, a language, word needing explanation. **Der.** *gloss*, vb., *gloze.*

glossary. (L.–Gk.) L. *glōssārium*, a glossary; formed with suffix *-ārium* from L. *glōss-a* (above).

glossographer. (Gk.) Coined from *glōsso-*, from Gk. γλῶσσα, a hard word; γράφειν, to write.

glottis. (Gk.) Gk. γλωττίς, the

---

mouth of the windpipe. – Gk. γλῶττα, Attic form of γλῶσσα, the tongue. **Der.** *epi-glottis*.

Glove. (E.) A. S. *glōf*, a glove; cf. Icel. *glōfi*, prob. borrowed from A. S. *glōf*. Possibly from *g-* (for *ge-*), prefix; and Icel. *lōfi*, Goth. *lōfa*, the palm of the hand. **Der.** *fox-glove*.

Glow. (E.) M. E. *glowen.* A. S. *glōwan*, to be ardent, to shine brightly.**+** Icel. *glōa*, Dan. *gloe*, to glow, stare, Swed. *glo*, to stare, Du. *gloeijen*, G. *glühen*. Brugm. i. § 156. **Der.** *glede* (2).

Glower, to look frowningly. (E.) E. Fries. *glüren*. Cf. Low G. *gluren*, M. Du. *gloeren*, 'to look awry, to leare,' Hexham; Du. *gluren*. ¶ M. E. *gloren*, to stare, is allied to *glare*.

Gloze, to interpret, flatter. (F.–L.– Gk.) M. E. *glosen*, to make glosses.– M. E. *glose*, a gloss; see Gloss (2).

Glue. (F.–L.) O. F. *glu.*–Late L. *glūtem*, acc. of *glūs* (gen. *glūtis*), glue; allied to L. *glūten*, glue, *glūtus*, tenacious. **+**Gk. γλοιός, mud, gum. Allied to Clay. Brugm. i. § 639.

Glum, sullen. (E.) M. E. *glommen, glomben, gloumen*, to look gloomy. E. Fries. *glumen, glümen*, to look sullen.**+** Low G. *gluum*, a sullen look, *glummen*, to make turbid; Norw. *glyme*, a sullen look, *glyma, gloma*, to look sullen. See Gloom.

Glume, a bracteal covering, in grasses. (L.) L. *glūma*, a husk, hull. –L. *glūbere*, to peel, take off the husk. See Cleave (1).

Glut, to swallow greedily. (F.–L.) M. E. *glotien.*–O. F. *glo.ir*, *gloutir.*–L. *glūtīre, glūttīre*, to swallow; cf. *gula*, the throat. **Der.** *glutton*.

Glutinous, gluey. (L.) L. *glūtinōsus*, sticky.–L. *glūtin-*, for *glūten*, glue.

Glutton. (F.–L.) M. E. *gloton.*– O. F. *gloton.*–L. *gluttōnem, glūtōnem*, acc., a glutton. –L. *glūtīre*, to devour.

Glycerine, a viscid fluid, of sweet taste. (F.–Gk.) F. *glycérine*; from Gk. γλυκερός, sweet; from Gk. γλυκύς, sweet.

Glyptic, relating to carving in stone. (Gk.) Gk. γλυπτικός, carving. – Gk. γλυπτός, carved.–Gk. γλύφειν, to hollow out, engrave. See Cleave (1).

Gnarl, to snarl, growl. (E.) Frequentative of *gnar*, to snarl, an imitative word. Cf. A. S. *gnyrran*, to creak; E. Fries. *gnarren*, to creak, snarl.**+**Du. *knorren*, Dan. *knurre*, to growl, Dan. *knarre*, to creak; Swed. *knorra*, G. *knurren*, to growl, G. *knarren*, to creak.

Gnarled, knotty, twisted. (E.) *Gnarled* is full of gnarls, where *gnar-l* is a dimin. of *gnar* or *knar*, M. E. *knarre*, a knot in wood. See **Knurr.**

Gnash. (E.) M. E. *gnasten*, to gnash the teeth. E. Fries. *gnastern*, *gnästern*, to gnash.+Swed. *knastra*, to crash (between the teeth); Dan. *knaske*, to gnash; Icel. *gnastan*, sb., a gnashing, *gnesta* (pt. t. *gnast*), to crack; G. *knastern*, to crackle. Imitative; so also Dan. *knase*, to crackle; Icel. *gnísta*, to gnash, E. Fries. *gnísen*.

Gnat. (E.) A.S. *gnætt*. Said to be named from the whirring of the wings; cf. Icel. *gnata*, to clash, *gnat*, clash of weapons.

Gnaw. (E.) M. E. *gnawen*, pt. t. *gnew*, *gnow*. A.S. *gnagan*, to gnaw, pt. t. *gnóh*, pp. *gnagen.*+Du. *knagen*, Low G. *gnauen*, O. Icel. *knaga*, mod. Icel. *naga*, Dan. *gnave*, Swed. *gnaga*. Without the *g*, we have G. *nagen*; also Dan. *nage*, to gnaw, Swed. *nagga*, whence prov. E. *nag*, to worry.

Gneiss, a rock. (G.) G. *gneiss*; from its sparkling. — O. H. G. *gneistan*, to sparkle; *gneista*, a spark. + A.S. *gnást*, Icel. *gneisti*, a spark.

Gnome, a kind of sprite. (F. – Gk.) F. *gnome*, a gnome; a word due to Paracelsus; from the notion that gnomes could reveal secret treasures. — Gk. γνώμη, intelligence. — Gk. γνῶναι, to know. (√GEN.)

gnomon, index of a dial. (L. – Gk.) L. *gnōmōn.* — Gk. γνώμων, an interpreter (one who knows); the index of a dial. — Gk. γνῶναι, to know.

gnostic, one of a certain sect. (Gk.) Gk. γνωστικός, wise, good at knowing. — Gk. γνωστός, from γνωτός, known. — Gk. γνῶναι, to know.

Gnu, a kind of antelope. (Hottentot.) Found in S. Africa. Said to belong to the Hottentot language.

Go, to move about, proceed, advance. (E.) M. E. *gon, goon.* A.S. *gán.*+Du. *gaan*, Dan. *gaae*, Swed. *gå*; G. *gehen*; O. H. G. *gán, gén.* ¶ 'The Teut. *gai-* (= A.S. *gā-*, O. H. G. *gē-*) supplanted the Idg. √I, to go, in Lat. *íre*, Gk. *ίέναι*, Skt. *i.* Since Teut. *gai-* has no old primitive noun-derivatives in Teut., and takes the place of Idg. √I (the Goth. aorist *iddja* = A. S. *éode* still remains), and as it is inflected after the -*mi*- conjugation, the

supposition arises that Teut. *gaim, *gais, *gaith are contracted from the verbal particle *ga-* and the inherited *īm, īz, īth* = Skt. *ēmi, ēshi,·ēti*; cf. Gk. εἶμι.' – Kluge. But this is mere conjecture.

Goad. (E.) M. E. *gode.* A.S. *gád.* Teut. type *gaidā, f.+Lombardic *gaida*, a gore (Duc.); from the base **gai-*, Idg. **ghai-*, whence also A.S. *gā-r*, Icel. *gei-rr*, O. Irish *gai*, a spear; see **Gore** (2).

Goal, the winning-post in a race. (E.) M. E. *gōl*, Shoreham, p. 145. Answering to A.S. *gāl, prob. 'an impediment;' whence A. S. *gǽlan*, to impede. *Goal* may have meant 'stopping-place.'

Goat. (E.) M. E. *goot.* A.S. *gát.*+ Du. *geit*, Dan. *ged*, Swed. *get*, Icel. *geit*, G. *geiss, geisse*; Goth. *gaits.* Teut. base **gait-*; allied to L. *hædus.*

Gobbet, a mouthful, a small piece. (F. – C.) M. E. *gobet*, a small piece. – O. F. *gobet*, a morsel of food (see Littré); allied to M.F. *gob*, a gulp (in swallowing). – O. F. *gober*, to devour. – Gael. *gob*, beak, bill, mouth; Irish *gob*, mouth, beak.

gobble (1), to devour. (F. – C.) Frequentative, with suffix -*le*, from O. F. *gob-er*, to devour; see **Gobbet.**

Gobble (2), to make a gabbling noise. (E.) Imitative; a variant of *gabble.*

Gobelin, a French tapestry. (F.) Named from Giles *Gobelin*, wool-dyer of Paris, in the 15th cent.

Goblet. (F. – L.) F. *gobelet*, 'a goblet;' Cot. Dimin. of O. F. *gobel*, a cup. — Late L. *cūpellum*, acc. of *cūpellus*, a cup; dimin. of L. *cūpa*, a vat; see **Coop.** Cf. Picard *gobe*, a great cup.

Goblin. (F. – L. – G.) O.F. *gobelin.* — Low L. *gobelīnus*, a goblin; properly 'a household-god'; cf. A. S. *cof-godas*, 'penates.' — M. H. G. *kobel*, a hut; dimin. of M. H. G. *kobe*, a stall, cognate with Icel. *kofi*, a hut, A. S. *cofa*, a chamber (Kluge). See **Cove.**

Goby, a fish. (L. – Gk.) For L. *gōbius*, orig. applied to the gudgeon. — Gk. κωβιός, a kind of fish, gudgeon, tench. **Der.** *gudgeon.*

God. (E.) A.S. *god.*+Du. *god*, Icel. *goð, guð*, Dan. *gud*, Swed. *gud*, Goth. *guth*, G. *gott.* Teut. type *guthom; Idg. type *ghutom, perhaps 'the being worshipped,' a pp. form; from Idg. root *ghu, to worship, as in Skt. *hu*, to sacrifice (to), whence *huta-*, one to whom sacrifice is offered. ¶ *Not* allied to *good*, adj.

goddess. (E.; *with* F. *suffix*.) M. E. *goddesse* (*godesse*). Made from *god* by adding the O. F. suffix *-esse* (= L. *-issa* = Gk. *-ισσα*).

godfather. (E.) M. E. *godfader*, father in baptism ; from *god* and *fader*.

godhead. (E.) M. E. *godhed*, also *godhod* ; the suffix answers to A. S. *hád*, office, state, dignity; see **-hood** (suffix).

Godwit, a bird. (E.) Origin unknown. Can it mean 'good creature'? A. S. *gód wiht*, a good wight, good creature (*wiht* being often applied to animals and birds). See **Wight**.

Goffer, Gauffer, to plait or crimp lace, &c. (F.—O. Low G.) M. F. *gauffrer*, to goffer ; orig. to mark like the edges of wafers.—M. F. *gauffre, goffre*, a wafer ; see **Wafer**.

Goggle-eyed, having rolling and staring eyes. (E.) M. E. *gogil-eyid*. 'They *gogle* with their eyes hither and thither ;' Holinshed, Descr. of Ireland, c. 1. Cf. Irish and Gael. *gogshuileach*, goggle-eyed, having wandering eyes, from *gog*, to move slightly, and *suil*, eye. But *gog* seems to be from E., and of imitative origin. Cf. prov. E. *coggle*, Bavar. *gageln*, to be unsteady.

Goitre. (F.—L.) F. *goître*, a swelled throat ; from O. F. *goitron*, the same, esp. in Savoy.—Late L. acc. type **guttriōnem*, from L. *guttur*, throat.

Gold. (E.) A. S. *gold*.+Du. *goud* (for *gold*), Icel. *gull*, Swed. Dan. *guld*, G. *gold*, Goth. *gulth*. Teut. type **gul-thom*, n. ; Idg. type **ghal-tom* ; cf. Russ. *zoloto*, Skt. *hātaka-*, gold ; also Pers. *zar*, gold, Zend *zaranya-*, Skt. *hiranya-*. Named from its colour. Allied to **Yellow**. (√GHEL.) Der. *mari-gold, gild*.

Golf, a game. (Du.) Mentioned A. D. 1457 (Jam.). The name is from that of a Du. game played with club and ball.—Du. *kolf*, a club used to strike balls with.+Low G. *kulf*, hockey-stick ; Icel. *kólfr*, clapper of a bell, *kylfa*, a club ; Dan. *kolbe*, butt-end of a weapon, *kolv*, bolt, shaft, arrow, Swed. *kolf*, butt-end, G. *kolbe*, club, mace, knob.

Golosh ; the same as **Galoche**.

Gondola. (Ital.—Gk.—Pers. ?) Ital. *gondola*, dimin. of *gonda*, a boat.—Gk. *κόνδυ*, a drinking-vessel ; from the shape (Diez). Said to be of Pers. origin; cf. Pers. *kandū*, an earthen vessel.

Gonfanon, Gonfalon, a kind of

banner. (F.—M. H. G.) M. E. *gonfanon*. —O. F. *gonfanon*.—M. H. G. *gundfano*, lit. 'battle-flag.'—M. H. G. *gund, gunt*, battle ; *fano* (G. *fahne*), a banner, flag. Here *gunt* is cognate with A. S. *gūð* (for **gunth*), battle, war ; cf. Skt. *han*, to kill. *Fano* is allied to **Vane**.

Gong. (Malay.) Malay *agóng* or *góng*, the gong, a sonorous instrument.

Good. (E.) M. E. *good*. A. S. *gód*.+Du. *goed*, Icel. *góðr*, Dan. Swed. *god*, Goth. *góds*, G. *gut*. Teut. type **gōdoz* ; from **gōd-*, strong grade of **gad-*, 'fit ;' see **Gather**. Allied to Russ. *godnuii*, suitable, O. Slav. *godŭ*, fit season. Der. *good-s*, sb. pl., i. e. good things, property ; *good-will*, &c. Also *good-man*, i. e. master of the house, *good-wife*, mistress of the house.

Goodbye, farewell. (E.) A familiar, but meaningless, contraction of *God be with you*, the old form of farewell ; very common; often written *God b'w'y*. ¶ *Not* for *God be by you* ; the form *God buy you* = *God be-with-you you* (*you* repeated).

Goodman ; see **Good**.

Goose, a bird. (E.) A. S. *gós*, pl. *gés* (lengthened *o* caused loss of *n*, and *gōs* = **gons* < **gans*).+Du. *gans*, Dan. *gaas*, Swed. *gas*, Icel. *gás*, G. *gans*. Teut. type **gans* ; Idg. type **ghans-* ; cf. L. *anser*, Gk. χήν ; Skt. *haṃsa*, a swan ; O. Irish *geis*, a swan ; Lith. *ż̨sis*, a goose.

Gooseberry. (E.; cf. F.—M. H. G.) In Levins. From *goose* and *berry* ; cf. *goose-grass*, &c. **a**. We also find North. E. *grosers*, gooseberries ; Burns has *grozet*, a gooseberry. Apparently from O. F. **grose, *groise*, a gooseberry, not recorded, but occurring not only in the O. F. dimin. form *groisele, grosele*, a gooseberry, but also in Irish *grois-aid*, Gael. *grois-eid*, W. *grwys*, a gooseberry, all borrowed from M.E. The spelling *groisele* is as old as the 13th century (Bartsch) ; and answers to the form *crosela* in the dialect of Como (Monti). **β**. The orig. O. F. **groise* or **grose* was borrowed from M. H. G. *krūs*, curling, crisped, whence G. *krausbeere*, a cranberry, a rough gooseberry. Cf. Swed. *krusbär*, a gooseberry, from *krus*, crisp, curled, frizzled. The name was first given to the rougher kinds of the fruit, from the curling hairs on it ; similarly, Levins gives the Lat. name as *uua crispa* (frizzled grape).

Gopher, a kind of wood. (Heb.) Heb. *gōpher*, a wood.

Gorbellied, having a fat belly. (E.) Compounded of E. *gore*, lit. filth, dirt (also the intestines) ; and *belly.* So also Swed. dial. *gårbälg*, a fat paunch, from *går*, dirt, contents of the intestines, and *bälg*, belly. See Gore (1).

  gorcrow, carrion-crow. (E.) I. e. *gore-crow* ; see above.

Gordian. (L. – Gk.) Only in the phr. '*Gordian* knot,' i. e. intricate knot. Named from the Phrygian king *Gordius* (Γόρδιος), who tied it. An oracle declared that whoever undid it should reign over Asia. Alexander cut the knot, and applied the oracle to himself.

Gore (1), clotted blood. (E.) It formerly meant filth. A. S. *gor*, filth, dirt.+ Icel *gor*, gore; Swed. *gor*, dirt; M. Du. *goor*; O. H. G. *gor*, filth. Origin uncertain.

Gore (2), a triangular piece let into a garment, a triangular slip of land. (E.) M. E. *gore*. A. S. *gāra*, a gore, projecting piece of land ; from *gār*, a dart, a spear-point. Named from the shape. [So also Icel. *geiri*, a triangular slip of land, from *geirr*, a spear ; G. *gehre*, a wedge, gusset, gore ; Du. *geer*, a gusset, gore.] β. The A. S. *gār* (Icel. *geirr*, O. H. G. *gēr*) is from Teut. type **gaizoz*, m. ; allied to Gaulish L. *gaesum*, a javelin, O. Irish *gai*, a spear.

Gore (3), to pierce. (E.) From A. S. *gār*, a spear-point (with the usual change from *ā* to long *o*).

Gorge, the throat, a narrow pass. (F. –L.) O. F. *gorge*, throat. – Late L. *gorga*, variant of L. *gurgēs*, a whirlpool, hence (in Late L.) the gullet, from its voracity. Cf. L. *gurgulio*, gullet.+Skt. *gargara-*, a whirlpool.

gorgeous, showy, splendid. (F.–L.) O. F. and M. F. *gorgias*, 'gorgeous;' Cot. The O. F. *gorgias* also meant a gorget ; the sense of 'gorgeous' was orig. proud, from the swelling of the throat in pride. Cotgrave gives F. *se rengorger*, ' to hold down the head, or thrust the chin into the neck, as some do in pride, or to make their faces look the fuller ; we say, to bridle it.' Hence the derivation is from F. *gorge*, throat (above).

  gorget, armour for the throat. (F. – L.) From *gorge*, i. e. throat.

Gorgon, a monster. (L. – Gk.) L. *Gorgon, Gorgō*. – Gk. Γοργώ, the Gorgon.

– Gk. γοργός, fearful. + O. Ir. *garg*, fierce.

Gorilla, a kind of large ape. (O. African.) An old word revived. In the Periplus of Hanno, near the end, some creatures are described 'which the interpreters called *Gorillas*'—in Greek, γορίλλας.

Gormandise; see Gourmand.

Gorse. (E.) Formerly *gorst*. – A. S. *gorst*, gorse. Cf. Skt. *hṛsh*, to bristle.

Goshawk. (E.) Lit. 'goose-hawk.' A. S. *gōshafuc*. – A. S. *gōs*, goose ; *hafuc*, hawk.

gosling. (E.) Formed from A. S. *gōs*, goose (M. E. *gos*), with double dimin. suffix *-l-ing*.

Gospel, the life of Christ. (E.) M. E. *gospel.* A. S. *godspell.* – A. S. *god*, God, i. e. Christ ; *spell*, a story. Lit. ' narrative of God,' i. e. life of Christ. ¶ Orig. *gōd spell*, i. e. *good spell*, a translation of Gk. εὐαγγέλιον ; but soon altered to *godspell*; for the E. word was early introduced into Iceland in the form *guðspjall* (where *guð-* = god, as distinguished from *gōð-* = good), and into Germany as O. H. G. *gotspell* (where *got* = god, as distinguished from *guot*, good).

Gossamer. (E.) M. E. *gossomer, gosesomer*, lit. '*goose-summer*.' The prov. E. name (in Craven) is *summer-goose*. Named from the time of year when it is most seen, viz. during St. Martin's summer (early November) ; geese were eaten on Nov. 11 formerly. Cf. Lowl. Sc. *go-summer* (popular variant), Martinmas. ¶ Also called *summer-colt* (Whitby) ; also *summer-gauze.* Cf. G. *sommerfäden* (lit. summer-threads), gossamer ; Du. *zomer-draden*, Swed. *sommertråd*, the same. [But in G. it is also called *mädchensommer*, lit. Maiden-summer, *der altweibersommer*, the old women's summer ; which also means St. Martin's summer.] It would appear that *summer* is here used in the sense of 'summer-film,' so that *gossamer* = goose-summer-film. (Better spelt *gossomer* or *gossummer*.)

Gossip. (E.) Now a crony ; formerly a sponsor in baptism. M. E. *gossib*, also *godsib*, lit. 'related in god.' – M. E. *god*, god ; *sib*, related, from O. Northumb. *sibbo*, pl. relatives, allied to Goth. *sibja*, relationship, G. *sippe*, affinity, *sippen*, kinsmen. Cf. Skt. *sabhya-*, fit for an assembly, trusty, from *sabhā*, an assembly. Brugm. i. §§ 124 (4), 567.

Gouge, a hollow-bladed chisel. (F. — Low L.) F. *gouge.* — Low L. **gobia, *gubia,* only recorded in the form *guvia* (Span. *gubia*). Cf. Ital. *sgorbia,* gouge; Gascon *goujo.*

Gourd. (F.—L.) F. *gourde,* formerly *gouhourde* and *cougourde* (Cot.).—L. *cucurbita,* a gourd.

Gourmand, a glutton. (F.) F. *gourmand,* 'a glutton, gormand, belly-god;' Cot. Etym. unknown. Der. *gormandise* (for *gourmand-ise*).

Gout (1), a drop, disease. (F.—L.) M. E. *goute,* a disease supposed to be due to defluxion of humours.—O. F. *goute, goutte,* a drop.—L. *gutta,* a drop.

Gout (2), taste. (F.—L.) F. *goût,* taste.—L. *gustus,* taste; see **Gust** (2).

Govern. (F.—L.—Gk.) M. E. *gouernen.*—O. F. *governer.*—L. *gubernāre,* to steer a ship, rule.—Gk. κυβερνᾶν, to steer. Cf. Lith. *kumbriti,* to steer.

Gowan, a daisy. (Scand.) North. E. *gowlan,* Sc. *yellow gowan,* corn marigold. Named from the colour.—Icel. *gulr,* Swed. *gul,* Dan. *guul,* Norw. *gul, gaul,* yellow. See **Yellow.**

Gowk, a simpleton. (Scand.) Icel. *gaukr,* a cuckoo, Swed. *gök.*+G. *gauch,* a cuckoo, simpleton.

Gown, a loose robe. (C.) M. E. *goune.* — W. *gwn,* a loose robe. [Irish *gunn,* Gael. and Corn. *gun,* Manx *goon,* are from E. O. F. *goune* is Gaulish.] Stokes-Fick, p. 281.

Grab, to seize. (E.) Cf. E. Fries. *grabbig,* greedy; *grabbelen,* to grab at; Du. *grabbel,* a scramble, *grabbelen,* to scramble for; Low G. *grabbeln,* to grab at; Swed. *grabba,* to grasp.+Skt. *grah,* O. Skt. *grabh,* O. Pers. and Zend *grab,* to seize. See **Garb** (2). Cf. **Grasp.**

Grace. (F.—L.) O. F. *grace.* — L. *grātia,* favour.—L. *grātus,* dear, pleasing. Brugm. i. §§ 524, 632.

Grade, a degree. (F.—L.) F. *grade,* a degree.—L. *gradum,* acc. of *gradus,* a degree, step.—L. *gradī* (pp. *gressus*), to step, walk, go. (√GHREDH.) Brugm. i. § 635; ii. § 707.

gradient, a gradually rising slope. (L.) L. *gradient-,* stem of pres. pt. of *gradī,* to walk, advance.

gradual, advancing by steps. (L.) Orig. *gradual,* sb., a service-book called in Lat. *graduāle,* and in E. *gradual* or *grayl.*—Late L. *graduālis,* only in neut.

graduāle, a service-book of portions sung *in gradibus,* i. e. on the steps (of the choir).—L. *gradu-s,* a step.

graduate. (L.) Late L. *graduātus,* one who has taken a degree; pp. of Late L. *graduāre.*—L. *gradu-s,* degree.

Graft, Graff, to insert buds on a stem. (F.—L.—Gk.) *Graft* is a later form of *graff,* and due to confusion with *graffed,* pp. Shak. has pp. *graft,* Rich. III, iii. 7. 127. M. E. *graffen,* to graff, from *graffe,* sb.—O. F. *graffe,* a sort of pencil, also a slip for grafting, because it resembled a pointed pencil in shape.—L. *graphium,* a style to write with.—Gk. γραφίον, γραφεῖον, the same.—Gk. γράφειν, to write.

Grail (1), a gradual, a service-book. (F.—L.) M. E. *graile, grayle.* — O. F. *graël.*—Late L. *gradāle,* also called *graduāle;* see **gradual.**

Grail (2), the Holy Dish at the Last Supper. (F.—L.—Gk.) The etymology was very early falsified by an easy change from *San Greal* (Holy Dish) to *Sang Real* (Royal Blood, strangely taken to mean Real Blood).—O. F. *graal, greal, grasal,* a flat dish; with numerous other forms, both in O. F. and Late L. It would appear that the word was corrupted in various ways from Late L. type **crātālis* (cf. Late L. *grādāle,* a bowl); from Late L. *crāt-us,* a bowl, equivalent to L. *crāter,* a bowl; see **Crater.** (Diez.)

Grail (3), fine sand. (F. — L.) In Spenser, F. Q. i. 7. 6; Vis. Bellay, st. 12. —O. F. *graisle, graile* (F. *grêle*), thin, small. — L. *gracilem,* acc. of *gracilis,* slender.

Grain. (F.—L.) M. E. *grein.*—O. F. *grain.*—L. *grānum,* a grain, corn.+Irish *grān,* W. *gronyn.* Cognate with E. **Corn.**

Grallatory. (L.) A term applied to wading birds.—L. *grallātor,* a walker on stilts.—L. *gralla* (for **gradla*), stilts.—L. *gradus,* a step; *gradī,* to walk.

Gramarye, magic. (F.—L.—Gk.) M. E. *gramery,* skill in grammar, and hence skill in magic.—O. F. *gramaire,* grammar; see **Grammar.** Cf. O. F. *gramaire,* (1) a grammarian, (2) a magician. ¶ The word *glamour* is a mere corruption of *gramarye* or *grammar,* meaning (1) grammar, (2) magic.

Gramercy, thanks. (F. — L.) Formerly *graund mercy,* Chaucer, C. T. 8964.— F. *grand merci,* great thanks; see **Grand** and **Mercy.**

Gramineous. (L.) From L. *grāmin-*, for *grāmen*, grass; with suffix *-e-ous*.

Grammar. (F. – L. – Gk.) M. E. *grammere.* – O. F. *gramaire* (XIII cent.). – Late L. *grammatica*, grammar (Schwan). – Gk. γραμματική, grammar. – Gk. γραμματικός, knowing one's letters; see below.

grammatical. (F. – L. – Gk.) M. F. *grammatical*; from L. *grammaticus*, grammatical. – Gk. γραμματικός, versed in one's letters. – Gk. γραμματ-, stem of γράμμα, a letter. – Gk. γράφειν, to write. See Graphic.

Grampus, a large fish. (F. – L.) Spelt *grampasse*, A. D. 1655. – A. F. *grampais*; Blk. Bk. Adm. i. 152. – L. *grandem piscem*, acc. of *grandis piscis*, great fish.

Granary, store-house for grain. (L.) L. *grānāria*, pl. – L. *grānum*, corn. See Garner.

Grand, great. (F. – L.) O. F. *grand.* – L. *grandem*, acc. of *grandis*, great.

grandee, a Spanish nobleman. (Span. – L.) Span. *grande*, great; also, a nobleman. – L. *grandem*, acc. of *grandis*, great.

grandeur, greatness. (F. – L.) F. *grandeur*; formed with suffix *-eur* (L. *-ōrem*), from *grand*, great.

grandiloquent, pompous in speech. (L.) Coined from L. *grandi-*, decl. stem of *grandis*, great; and *loquent-*, stem of pres. pt. of *loquī*, to speak; see Loquacious. The true L. form is *grandiloquus.*

Grange, a farm-house. (F. – L.) O. F. *grange*, a barn, a farm-house. – Late L. *grānea*, a barn. – L. *grānum*, corn.

granite, a hard stone. (Ital. – L.) Ital. *granito*, granite, speckled stone. – Ital. *granito*, pp. of *granire*, to reduce to grains (hence, to speckle). – Ital. *grano*, a grain. – L. *grānum*, a grain; see Grain.

Grant. (F. – L.) M. E. *graunten.* – O. F. *graanter*, *graunter*, later spelling of *crēanter*, *crēanter*, to caution, assure, guarantee; whence the later senses, to promise, yield; Late L. *crēantāre*, for *crēdentāre.* – L. *crēdent-*, stem of pres. pt. of *crēdere*, to trust. See Creed.

Granule, a little grain. (L.) L. *grānulum*, dimin. of *grānum*, a grain.

Grape. (F. – M. H. G.) A. F. *grape*, M. F. *grappe*, 'bunch, or cluster of grapes;' Cot. [In E., the sense has changed, from cluster to single berry.] The orig. sense of *grappe* was 'a hook,' then clustered

fruit. – M. H. G. *krapfe*, O. H. G. *krapfo*, a hook. Allied to Cramp. The senses of 'hook' and 'cluster' result from that of 'clutching.'

Graphic, descriptive, pertaining to writing. (L. – Gk.) L. *graphicus*, belonging to painting or drawing. – Gk. γραφικός, the same. – Gk. γράφειν, to write. Allied to Carve.

Grapnel, a grappling-iron. (F. – M. H. G.) M. E. *grapenel.* Dimin. of M. F. *grappin*, a grapnel. – O. F. *grappe*, a hook. – O. H. G. *krapfo*, a hook; see Grape.

grapple, to clutch. (F. – M. H. G.) Properly to seize with a grapnel. – M. F. *grappil*, sb., 'the *grapple* of a ship;' Cot. – O. F. *grappe*, a hook (above).

Grasp. (E.) M. E. *graspen*, used in the sense 'to grope.' Also *grapsen*, in Hoccleve. Prob. for **grab-sen*, closely allied to Grab, q. v. Cf. E. Fries. *grapsen*, to clutch; Low G. *grapsen*; E. Fries. *graps*, a handful; also Lith. *gróp-ti*, to grab (Kluge).

Grass. (E.) M.E. *gras*, *gres*, also *gers*. A.S. *gærs*, *græs*.✛Du. Icel. Goth. G. *gras*; Swed. *gräs*, Dan. *græs*. Teut. type **gra-som*, n.; from **gra-*, the sense of which is doubtful; cf. *grow*.

Grate (1), a framework of iron bars. (Late L. – L.) M. E. *grate.* – Late L. *grāta*, *crāta*, a grating. – L. *crātēs*, hurdles. See Crate.

Grate (2), to rub, scrape. (F. – Teut.) O. F. *grater* (F. *gratter*). – Swed. *kratta*, Dan. **kratte*, to scrape; O. H. G. *chrazzōn* (< **krattōn*), to scrape.

Grateful, pleasant. (Hybrid; F. – L. *and* E.) The first syllable is from O. F. *grat*, pleasing, from L. *grātus*; with E. suffix *-ful.*

gratify. (F. – L.) M. F. *gratifier.* – L. *grātificāre*, *grātificārī*, to please. – L. *grāti-*, for *grātus*, pleasing; and *-ficāre*, for *facere*, to make. **Der.** *gratific-at-ion.*

gratis, freely. (L.) L. *grātīs*, adv., freely; for *grātiis*, abl. pl. of *grātia*, grace; see Grace.

gratitude. (F. – L.) F. *gratitude.* – Late L. *grātitūdinem*, acc. of *grātitūdo*, thankfulness. – L. *grātus*, pleasing.

gratuitous, freely given. (L.) L. *grātuīt-us*, freely given; with suffix *-ous.* From *grātus.*

gratuity, a present. (F. – L.) O. F. *gratuité*, 'a free gift;' Cot. – Late L.

grātuītātem, acc. of *grātuītās.*—L. *grā-tuītus* (above).

gratulate, to congratulate. (L.) From pp. of L. *grātulārī*, to wish a person joy. As if for **grāti-tulārī*; from L. *grātus*, pleasing. Brugm. i. § 986.

Grave (1), to cut, engrave. (E.) M. E. *grauen.* A. S. *grafan*, pt. t. *grōf.*+Du. *graven*, Dan. *grave*, Icel. *grafa*, M. Swed. *grafva*, Goth. *graban*, G. *graben.* Teut. type **graban-*, pt. t. **grōb.* Cf. Russ. *grob'*, a tomb, grave. **Der.** *grave*, sb., a thing cut or dug out ; A. S. *græf.*

Grave (2), sad. (F. – L.) F. *grave.*—L. *grauem*, acc. of *grauis*, heavy.+Goth. *kaurus*; Gk. βαρύς, Skt. *guru-*, heavy. Brugm. i. § 665.

Gravel. (F. – C.) M. E. *grauel.*—O. F. *gravele*, dimin. of O. F. *grave*, gravel. Of Celtic origin ; from Celt. base **gravo-*, as in Bret. *grouan*, gravel, Corn. *grow*, gravel, W. *gro*, pebbles.

Gravy. (E.) Formerly *greavy*, orig. an adj. formed from *greave* (for *greaves*, q.v.), refuse of tallow. Hence *gravy* is (1) tallowy, (2) fat, gravy.

Gray. (E.) M. E. *gray, grey.* O. Merc. *grēg*, A. S. *grǣg.*+Du. *graauw*, Icel. *grār*, Dan. *graa*, Swed. *grå*, G. *grau*, O. H. G. *grā* (gen. *grāw-es*). Teut. stems **grǣg-*, **grǣw-*, <**grǣgwoz.*

Graze (1), to scrape slightly. (E. ?) Formerly *grase.* Apparently a peculiar use of *graze*, to crop grass ; perhaps confused with *rase*, i. e. to scrape. See **Rase**; and see **Glance.** (Doubtful.)

Graze (2), to feed as cattle. (E.) M. E. *grasen*, vb. A. S. *grasian.*—A. S. *grǣs*, grass ; see **Grass.** Der. *graz-i-er* (cf. *bow-y-er, law-y-er*).

Grease. (F. – L.) M. E. *grese, grece.*—A. F. *greisse, craisse*, fatness, Ps. xvi. 10.—Late L. type **crassia.*—L. *crassus*, thick, fat. See **Crass.**

Great. (E.) M. E. *gret, greet.* A. S. *grēat.*+Du. *groot*, G. *gross.* Teut. type **grautoz.*

Greaves (1), **Graves,** sediment of melted tallow. (E.) E. Fries. *gräfe*; pl. *gräfen*, greaves.+M. Swed. *grefwar*, dirt ; *ljus-grefwar*, lit. ' light-dirt,' refuse of tallow in candle-making ; Swed. dial. *grevar*, pl., graves ; Low G. *greven*, greaves; G. *griebe*, O. H. G. *griubo, griupo.*

Greaves (2), leg-armour. (F.) O. F. *greves*, ' boots, also greaves;' Cot. Cf. Span. *grebas*, greaves, pl. of *greba.*—O. F.

greve, Picard *greve*, the shank, shin. Origin unknown.

Grebe, a bird. (F.) F. *grèbe.* Cot. gives *griaibe*, ' a sea-mew,' as a Savoyard word. Of unknown origin.

Greedy. (E.) A. S. *grǣdig, grēdig.*+Du. *gretig*, Icel. *grāðugr*, Dan. *graadig*, Goth. *grēdags*; cf. Skt. *gṛdhra-*, greedy, from *gṛdh*, to be greedy. The sb. *greed*, hunger, answers to Icel. *grāðr*, Goth. *grēdus*, hunger ; Teut. type **grǣduz.*

Green. (E.) M. E. *green.* A. S. *grēne.*+Du. *groen*, Icel. *grænn*, Dan. Swed. *grön*, G. *grün.* Teut. type **grōnjoz*, earlier type **grō-niz* (Sievers). Cf. A. S. *grō-wan*, to grow. Allied to **Grow.** *Green* is the colour of *growing* herbs. Der. *greens*, pl. sb. See **Sward.**

Greengage, a green plum. Named from Sir W. *Gage*, of Hengrave Hall, near Bury, before A. D. 1725. There is also a *blue Gage, a yellow Gage*, and a *purple Gage.*

Greet (1), to salute. (E.) M. E. *greten.* A.S. *grētan*, to visit, address.+Du. *groeten*, G. *grüssen*; O. Sax. *grōtian.* Teut. type **grōt-jan-*; from the sb. **grōt-*, as in Du. *groet*, G. *gruss*, a salutation.

Greet (2), to cry, weep. (E.) M. E. *greten.* A. S. *grǣtan, grētan.*+Icel. *grāta*, Dan. *græde*, Swed. *gråta*, Goth. *grētan.*

Gregarious. (L.) L. *gregārius*, belonging to a flock. – L. *greg-*, stem of *grex*, a flock.+O. Irish *graig*, a herd of horses.

Grenade, a war-missile. (F. – Span. – L.) Formerly also *granado*, which is like the Span. form. Named from its likeness to a pomegranate, being filled with combustibles as that is with seeds. – F. *grenade*, ' a pomegranet, a ball of wild-fire ; ' Cot. – Span. *granada*, the same ; *granado*, full of seeds. – L. *grānātus*, full of seeds. – L. *grānum*, a grain ; see **Grain.** Der. *grenad-ier.*

Grey; the same as **Gray.**

Greyhound. (E.) M. E. *greihound, grehound.* A. S. *grīghund*; where *grīg-* = *grīeg-* (Icel. *grey-*), for Teut. **graujo-.* Cf. Icel. *greyhundr*, a greyhound, from Icel. *grey*, a dog, *hundr*, a hound ; *grey-baka*, a bitch. ¶ Not allied to *gray*, which is represented in Icelandic by *grār.*

Griddle, a pan for baking cakes. (F. – L.) Also *girdle.* M. E. *gredil.*—O. F. *gredil* (Moisy, Dict. of Norman patois), *grëil* (Godefroy) ; cf. *grediller*, vb., to grill (same).—Late L. **crātīculum*, for L. *crātīcula*, a gridiron, dimin. of *crātis*, a hurdle. **Der.** Hence M. E. *gredire*, a griddle, afterwards turned into *gridiron*, by confusion with M. E. *ire* = E. *iron*. See **Grill** and **Creel**.

Gride, to pierce, cut through. (E.) See Spenser, F. Q. ii. 8. 36. A metathesis of *gird*, M. E. *girden*, to strike, pierce ; see **Gird** (2).

Gridiron; see **Griddle**.

Grief. (F.−L.) M. E. *grief, gref.* − O. F. *grief, gref,* burdensome, sad, heavy. −L. *grauis,* heavy ; see **Grave** (2). **Der.** *grieve,* vb., O. F. *grever,* L. *grauāre,* to burden ; from *grauis.*

Griffin, Griffon. (F. − L. − Gk.) Better *griffon.* M. E. *griffon.* − F. *griffon* ; formed from Late L. *griffus,* a griffon. − L. *gryphus,* extended form of *gryps,* a griffon. − Gk. γρύψ (stem γρυπ-), a griffon, a fabulous animal supposed to have a hooked beak. − Gk. γρυπός, curved, hook-beaked. ¶ Confused with Gk. γύψ, a vulture.

Grig, a small eel, a cricket. (E.) App. of imitative origin. Cf. *crick,* still preserved in *crick-et* ; Lowl. Sc. *crick,* a tick, louse ; Du. *kriek,* a cricket. ¶ In phr. 'as merry as a *grig,*' *grig* is for *Greek* (Troil. i. 2. 118) ; *Merygreek* is a character in Udall's Roister Doister ; from L. *græcārī,* to live like Greeks, i. e. luxuriously.

Grill, to boil on a gridiron. (F.−L.) F. *griller,* to broil. − F. *gril,* 'a gridiron,' Cot. ; O. F. *greil, grail.* − Late L. **crātīculum,* for *crātīcula,* a small gridiron (whence F. *grille,* a grating). − L. *crātis,* a hurdle. See **Crate**, **Creel**, and **Griddle**.

Grilse, the young salmon on its first return from the sea to fresh water. (C. ?) Said to represent Irish *grealsach,* the name of a fish.

Grim, fierce. (E.) A. S. *grim* ; allied to *gram,* fierce, angry, furious. + Icel. *grimmr,* grim, gramr, angry ; Dan. *grim,* grim, *gram,* angry ; G. *grimm,* fury, *gram,* hostile. From Teut. root **grem-* (2nd grade, **gram-*). Allied to Gk. χρεμετίζειν, to neigh, χρόμη, χρόμος, noise. Brugm. i. § 572.

Grimace. (F.−Teut.) F. *grimace,* 'a crabd looke;' Cot. Of uncertain origin. Perhaps from Icel. *grimmr,* Dan. *grim,* grim, angry (above) ; cf. E. Fries. and Low G. *grimlachen,* to laugh maliciously. Derived by Diez from Icel. *grima,* a mask.

Grimalkin, a cat. (E.; *partly* O.H.G.) Prob. for *gray Malkin,* the latter being a cat's name. *Malkin* = *Mald-kin,* dimin. of A. F. *Mald* = *Maud,* i. e. Matilda ; from O. H. G. *Mahthilt.* Here *maht* = might; *hilt* means battle. Cf. Macb. i. 1. 8.

Grime. (Scand.) Swed. dial. *grima,* a smut on the face; Dan. *grim, griim,* lamp-black, soot, grime. Cf. Low G. *grimmeln,* to become smutty; E. Fries. *gremen,* to begrime.

Grin, to snarl, grimace. (E.) M. E. *grennen.* A. S. *grennian,* to grin. + Icel. *grenja,* to howl. Perhaps cf. Du. *grijnen,* to weep, fret; Dan. *grine,* to grin, simper, Swed. *grina,* G. *greinen* (Noreen, § 149). See **Groan**.

Grind. (E.) A. S. *grindan,* pt. t. *grand,* pp. *grunden.* Allied to L. *frendere,* to gnash.

Grip, sb. (E.) M. E. *gripe.* A. S. *gripe,* a grip ; from the weak grade of *gripan* (below).

gripe. (E.) A. S. *grīpan,* pt. t. *grāp,* pp. *gripen,* to seize. + Du. *grijpen,* Icel. *grīpa,* Swed. *gripa,* Dan. *gribe,* Goth. *greipan,* G. *greifen.* Teut. type **greipan-,* pt. t. **graip,* pp. **gripanoz.* Cf. Lith. *graibyti,* to grasp at.

Grise, Grize, a step. (F.−L.) Also spelt *greece, greese,* &c. The proper spelling is *grees,* and the proper sense is 'a flight of steps,' though often used as meaning a single step. *Grees* is the pl. of M. E. *gree, gre,* a step. − O. F. *gre,* a step (Roquefort) ; cf. F. *de-gré,* E. *de-gree.* − L. *gradus,* a step. **Der.** Prov. E. (Norf.) *grissens,* steps = *gree-s-en-s,* a treble plural.

Grisette, a gay young Frenchwoman of the lower class. (F. − M. H. G.) F. *grisette* ; named from the cheap gray dress which they used to wear. − F. *gris,* gray ; see **Grizzly**.

Griskin. (Scand.) The lit. sense is 'little pig,' now spine of a hog. Dimin. from M. E. *gris,* a pig. − Icel. *gríss,* a young pig ; Dan. *griis,* Swed. *gris,* pig. ¶ Or is it for **gris-skin,* where *skin* represents Dan. *skinne,* a splint? Cf. **Grizzly**.

Grisled; see **Grizzly**.

Grisly, terrible. (E.) A. S. *grīslīc,* terrible. Formed with suffix *-līc* (like) from *grīs-an* (pt. t. *grās*), to shudder. E. Fries. *grīselīk,* terrible, from *grīsen,* to shudder. + Du. *af-grijsselijk,* horrible ; *af-grijzen,* horror.

Grist, a supply of corn to be ground. (E.) A. S. *grīst.* From the base of Grind.

gristle. (E.) A. S. *gristel,* cartilage; allied to *grist,* and A. S. *grīstbitian,* to gnash the teeth. From the base of *grind,* with reference to the necessity of crunching it if eaten. So also Du. *knarsbeen,* gristle, from *knarsen,* to crunch.

Grit, coarse sand. (E.) Formerly *greet,* A. S. *grēot,* grit. **+** O. Fries. *grēt,* Icel. *grjōt,* G. *gries.* Allied to **Grout, Groat** (1).

Grizzly, Grizzled, grayish. (F. – M. H. G.) From M. E. *grisel,* a gray-haired man. **–** F. *gris,* gray. **–** M. H. G. *grīs,* gray; cf. G. *greis,* a gray-haired man. **+** Du. *grijs,* O. Sax. *grīs,* gray.

Groan. (E.) M. E. *gronen.* A. S. *grānian,* to groan. Teut. type **grainōjan-,* from **grain,* 2nd grade of **greinan-,* as in O. H. G. *grīnan,* G. *greinen,* to weep, grin; Du. *grijnen,* to weep. Perhaps allied to **Grin.**

Groat (1), a particle, atom. (E.) M. E. *grot.* A. S. *grot.* From **grut-,* weak grade of **greut-* (as in A. S. *grēot*). See **Grit, Grout.**

Groat (2), a coin worth 4*d.* (Du. – Low G.) M. E. *grote.* **–** M. Du. *groote.* **–** O. Low G. *grote,* a coin of Bremen; meaning 'great,' because large in comparison with the copper coins (*Schwaren*) formerly in use there; cf. Du. *groot,* great, cognate with E. *great.*

Groats, grain of oats. (E.) M. E. *grotes.* A. S. *grātan,* pl. groats; A. S. Leechdoms, iii. 292.

Grocer. (F. – L.) Formerly *grosser* or *engrosser,* a wholesale dealer. **–** O. F. *grossier,* a wholesale dealer. **–** O. F. *gros,* great; see **Gross.** Der. *grocer-y,* formerly *grossery.*

grog, spirits and water. (F. – L.) Short for *grogram*; it had its name from Admiral Vernon, nicknamed *Old Grog,* from his *grogram* breeches (ab. A. D. 1745); he ordered the sailors to dilute their rum with water.

grogram, a stuff. (F. – L.) Formerly *grogran,* so called from its coarse grain. **–** M. F. *grosgrain,* grogram. **–** O. F. *gros,* coarse; *grain,* grain.

Groin, the depression of the human body in front, at the junction of the thigh with the trunk. (Scand.) [Confused with F. Cot. gives '*groin de porc,* the head or

upper part of the shoulder-blade,' and *groin,* 'snowt of a hog.' The O. F. *groin* also means 'extremity, headland.' – Late L. type **grunnium,* from L. *grunnīre,* to grunt.] It answers to prov. E. *grain,* the place where the branch of a tree forks, the groin (Drayton, Pol. i. 495). **–** Icel. *grein,* a branch, arm; Dan. *green,* Swed. *gren,* branch, arm, fork. Der. *groin-ed,* having angular curves that fork off.

Gromwell, a plant. (F. – L.) Formerly *gromelle, grumelle, gromel, grumel.* **–** O. F. *gremil, grenil,* 'the herb gromil, or graymil;' Cot. Prob. from L. *grānum,* a grain; from its hard seeds.

Groom. (Low G. *or* F. – Low G.) M. E. *grome.* Either from M. Du. *grom,* Icel. *gromr,* a boy, lad (Egilsson); or from O. F. **grome,* in the dimin. *gromet,* a lad, boy, servant, valet (whence F. *gourmet*), which is prob. from the same M. Du. *grom.* And see **Bridegroom.** Der. *grummet.*

Groove. (Du.) Du. *groef, groeve,* a trench, a channel, a groove. **–** Du. *graven* (pt. t. *groef*), to dig; see **Grave** (1). **+** M. E. *grōfe,* a cave.

Grope. (E.) A. S. *grāpian,* to seize, handle; hence, to feel one's way. **–** A. S. *grāp,* 2nd grade of *grīpan,* to seize. See **Gripe.**

Gross. (F. – L.) O. F. *gros* (fem. *grosse*), gross, great. **–** L. *grossus,* fat, thick.

Grot. (F. – Ital. – L. – Gk.) F. *grotte,* a cave. **–** Ital. *grotta.* **–** L. *crypta.* **–** Gk. κρυπτή, a vault; see **Crypt.**

grotesque. (F. – Ital. – L. – Gk.) F. *grotesque,* ludicrous. **–** Ital. *grotesca,* curious painted work, such as was employed on the walls of grottoes. **–** Ital. *grotta* (above).

grotto. (Ital. – L. – Gk.) Better *grotta.* **–** Ital. *grotta* (above).

Ground. (E.) A. S. *grund.* **+** Du. *grond,* G. *grund*; Goth. *grundu-.* Teut. type **grunduz*; also **grunthuz,* whence Icel. *grunnr,* Dan. Swed. *grund.*

groundling, a spectator in the pit of a theatre. (E.) From *ground,* with double dimin. suffix *-l-ing,* with a contemptuous force.

grounds, dregs. (E.) So called from being at the bottom. Cf. Gael. *grunndas,* lees, from *grunnd,* bottom, ground; Irish *gruntas,* dregs, from *grunnt,* the bottom.

groundsel, a small plant. (E.) Also *groundswell* (Holland's tr. of Pliny). A. S. *grundeswelge*, as if ' ground-swallower,' but really from the older form *gundeswelge*, lit. ' swallower of pus,' from its supposed healing qualities ; from A. S. *gund*, pus.

groundsill, threshold. (E.) From *ground* and *sill*, q. v. Also spelt *grunsel* (Milton).

Group. (F. — Ital. — G.) F. *groupe.* — Ital. *groppo*, a knot, heap, group. ▬ O.H.G. *kropf*, a crop, wen on the throat, orig. a bunch ; Low G. *kropp* ; see **Crop.**

Grouse, a bird. (F. — L. — Gk.) *Grouse* appears to be a false form, evolved from the old word *grice*, which seems to have been taken as a pl. form (cf. *mouse, mice*). ▬ M. F. *griesche*, gray, speckled ; *perdrix griesche*, the gray partridge, *poule griesche*, ' a moorhen, the hen of the *grice* or moorgame ;' Cot. The oldest form is *greoches* (13th cent., in Littré, s. v. *grièche*), variant of *Griesche*, fem. adj., Greek. ▬ Late L. *Graecisca*, f. of *Graeciscus*, Greekish. ▬ L. *Graecus*, Greek. ▬ Gk. Γραικός, Greek. ¶ The meaning was changed to ' gray ' by the influence of F. *gris*, gray.

Grout, coarse meal ; **Grouts,** dregs. (E.) M. E. *grut.* ▬ A. S. *grūt*, coarse meal. Cf. Du. *grut* ; Icel. *grautr*, porridge, Dan. *gröd*, Swed. *gröt*, boiled groats ; G. *grütze*, groats ; allied to Lithuan. *grudas*, corn ; L. *rūdus*, rubble. Cf. **Grit.**

Grove, a collection of trees. (E.) M. E. *groue* (with *u* = *v*). ▬ A. S. *grāf*, a grove.

Grovel, to fall flat on the ground. (Scand.) Due to M. E. *groveling*, properly an adv., signifying flat on the ground; also spelt *grofling*, *groflinges*, where the suffixes -*ling*, -*linges* are adverbial ; cf. *head-long*, *dark-ling.* ▬ Icel. *grūfa*, in phr. *liggja ā grūfu*, to lie grovelling, *symja ā grūfu*, to swim on the belly ; cf. also *grūfa*, *grufla*, to grovel ; Swed. dial. *gruva*, flat on one's face, *ligga å gruve*, to lie on one's face.

Grow. (E.) A. S. *grōwan*, pt. t. *grēow*, pp. *grōwen*. ▬ Du. *groeijen*, Icel. *grōa*, Dan. *groe*, Swed. *gro*. Esp. to produce shoots, as herbs ; allied to **Green. Der.** *grow-th* ; from Icel. *grōðr*, growth.

Growl, to grumble. (F. — Low G.) Picard *grouler.* ▬ E. Fries. *grullen* ; cf. Du. *grollen*, to grumble ; G. *grollen*, to rumble ; Norw. *gryla*, to growl. (See *grol* in Franck.)

Grub, to grope in dirt. (E.) M. E.

grobben. Cf. E. Fries. *grubbeln*, to grope about. ✛ Low G. *grubbeln*, the same ; G. *grübeln*, O. H. G. *grubilōn*, to rake, dig, grub. Allied to **Grave** (1).

Grudge, to grumble. (F.) M. E. *grochen*, *grucchen*, to murmur. ▬ O. F. *groucier*, *groucher*, to murmur ; Low L. *groussāre*, A. D. 1358. Probably *gru-dge*, *gru-nt*, *grow-l* are all from the same imitative base ; cf. Gk. γρῦ, a grunt.

Gruel. (F. ▬ O. Low G.) O. F. *gruel* (F. *gruau*). ▬ Low L. *grūtellum*, dimin. of *grūtum*, meal. ▬ O. Low G. *grūt*, Du. *gruit*, grout, coarse meal ; see **Grout.**

Gruesome, horrible. (Scand.) Dan. *grusom*, cruel. ▬ Dan. *gru*, horror ; with suffix -*som*, as in *virk-som*, active. Cf. Dan. *grue*, to dread, *gruelig*, horrid. ✛ Du. *gruwzaam*, G. *grausam* ; M. H. G. *grūsam*, *grūwesam*, from M. H. G. *grūwe*, horror. Allied to O. Sax. *gruri*, A. S. *gryre*, horror, A. S. *be-grēosan*, to overwhelm with terror.

Gruff, rough, surly. (Du.) Du. *grof*, big, coarse, loud, blunt. ✛ G. *grob*, coarse (whence Swed. *grof*, Dan. *grov*) ; O. H. G. *gerob* ; E. Fries. *gruffig*.

Grumble, to murmur. (F. — G.) F. *grommeler* (Cot.). ▬ Low and prov. G. *grummelen*, to grumble, frequent. of *grummen*, *grommen*, to grumble ; M. Du. *grommelen*, frequent. of *grommen*. From *grumm-*, weak grade of Teut. *gremman-*, to rage, as in M. H. G. and A. S. *grimman*, to rage. Cf. G. *gram*, anger, and E. **Grim.**

Grume, a clot of blood. (F. — L.) Rare. M. F. *grume*, a cluster. ▬ L. *grūmus*, a little heap.

Grummet, Gromet, a ship-boy, a ring of rope. (F. — Teut.) O. F. *gromet*, a serving-boy ; cf. Span. *grumete*, a shipboy. ▬ M. Du. *grom*, a boy ; see **Groom.**

Grunsel ; see **Groundsill.**

Grunt. (E.) M. E. *grunten*. A. S. *grunnettan*, extension of A. S. *grunian*, to grunt. ✛ Dan. *grynte*, Swed. *grymta*, G. *grunzen* ; so also L. *grunnīre*, Gk. γρύζειν. All imitative ; cf. Gk. γρῦ, the noise made by a pig.

Guaiacum, a kind of resin, from lignum vitae. (Span. — Hayti.) Span. *guayaco*, *guayacan*, lignum vitae. From the language of Hayti.

Guanaco, a kind of Peruvian sheep. (Span. — Peruv.) Span. *guanaco* (Pineda). ▬ Peruv. *huanacu*, a wild sheep.

Guano. (Span. — Peruv.) Span. *guano*, *huano.* ▬ Peruv. *huanu*, dung.

Guarantee, sb. (F.–O. H. G.) Formerly *guaranty* or *garanty*, which are better spellings.–O. F. *garantie, garrantie,* a warranty ; fem. of pp. of *garantir,* to warrant. – O. F. *garant, warant,* a warrant ; see **Warrant.** Der. *guarantee,* vb.; cf. F. *garantir.*

Guard, vb. (F.–O. Low G.) O. F. *garder,* earliest form *warder,* to guard.– O. Sax. *wardon,* to watch ; cognate with A. S. *weardian,* to watch, from *weard,* sb.; see **Ward.** Der. *guard-ian* ; see **Warden.**

Guava. (Span.–W. Ind.) Span. *guayaba* ; borrowed from the native name in Guiana.

Gudgeon. (F.–L.–Gk.) M. E. *goione.–*F. *goujon.–*L. *gobionem,* acc. of *gobio,* a by-form of *gobius.–*Gk. κωβιός, a gudgeon, tench.

Gueber, Gheber, a fire-worshipper. (F.–Pers.) F. *Guèbre.–*Pers. *gabr,* a priest of fire-worshippers ; Rich., Dict., p. 1228.

Guelder-rose. (Du.) Here *guelder* stands for *Gueldre,* the F. spelling of the province of *Gelderland* in Holland.

Guerdon, recompense. (F.–O. H. G. and L.) O.F. *guerdon* (Ital. *guidardone*).–Low L. *widerdonum,* a singular compound of O. H. G. *widar,* back, again, and L. *donum,* a gift. The word is really a half-translation of the true form O. H. G. *widarlon =* a recompense. Here *widar =* G. *wieder,* back again ; and *lon* (G. *lohn*) is cognate with A. S. *lean,* Du. *loon,* a reward, allied to L. *lu-crum,* gain ; Brugm. i. § 490. So also A. S. *wiðer-lean,* a recompense.

Guerilla, Guerrilla, irregular warfare. (Span.–O. H. G.) Span. *guerrilla,* a skirmish, lit. 'little war;' dimin. of *guerra,* war.–O. H. G. *werra,* war; see **War.**

Guess. (Scand.) M. E. *gessen.–*Dan. *gisse,* Swed. *gissa,* to guess.+E. Fries. and Du. *gissen,* Icel. *giska* ; N. Fries. *gezze, gedse.* Allied to Dan. *gjette,* to guess; the Icel. *giska* may be for **git-ska,* a denominative vb. from a base **git-isko-,* ingenious, acute, from *geta,* to get, also, to guess. See **Get.**

Guest. (Scand.) M. E. *gest.* – Icel. *gestr,* Dan. *giest,* Swed. *gäst.+*A. S. *gæst, giest* ; Du. *gast,* Goth. *gasts,* G. *gast.* Teut. type **gastiz* ; Idg. type **ghostis* ; cf. Russ. *gost(e),* a guest, alien ; L. *hostis,*

a stranger, also an enemy. Allied to **Hostile.**

Guide. (F. – Ital. – Teut.) M. E. *gyden* (also *gyen*).–F. *guider,* to guide.– Ital. *guidare* ; cf. O. F. *guier,* Span. *guiar.* The *gu* (for *w*) shows the word to be of Teut. origin.–O. Sax. *witan* (A. S. *witan*), to pay heed to; O. H. G. *wizan.* Allied to **Wit.** Cf. **Guy-rope.**

Guild, Gild. (Scand.) The spelling *guild* indicates the hard *g.* M. E. *gilde.* –Icel. *gildi,* a payment, a guild; Dan. *gilde.* –Icel. *gjalda* (pres. t. *geld*), to pay; cognate with A. S. *geldan,* to pay, yield ; see **Yield.+**Du. *gild* ; whence G. *gilde.*

Guilder, a Du. coin. (Du. – G.) Adaptation of M. Du. *gulden,* 'a gilder,' Hexham. From Teut. adj. type **gulthinoz,* golden, from Teut. **gulth-om,* gold. See **Gold.**

Guile, a wile. (F.–O. Low G.) O. F. *guile.* From a Low G. **wil*; cf. A. S. *wil,* a wile (A. S. Chron. 1128). Der. *beguile,* vb., with E. prefix *be-* (= *by*).

Guillotine. (F.) Named after a French physician, *J. I. Guillotin,* died A. D. 1814. First used, 1792.

Guilt, crime. (E.) M. E. *gilt.* A. S. *gylt,* a trespass; also, a fine for a trespass. Teut. ·type **gultiz,* m. ; perhaps related to A. S. *geldan,* to pay, yield; see **Yield.**

Guinea. (African.) First coined of African gold from the *Guinea* coast, A. D. 1663. Der. *guinea-fowl* (from *Guinea*). ¶ The *guinea-pig* is from S. America; so that it may mean *Guiana pig.*

Guipure, a lace of cords, kind of gimp. (F.–Teut.) F. *guipure.–*Teut. **wip-an,* to wind, weave ; as in Goth. *weipan,* to crown (whence *waips,* a wreath) ; G. *weifen,* to reel, wind.

Guise, way, wise. (F. – O. H. G.) M. E. *gise, guise.–*O. F. *guise,* way, wise, manner. – O. H. G. *wisa* (G. *weise*), a wise ; cognate with **Wise** (2).

Guitar. (F.–L.–Gk.) F. *guitare.–*L. *cithara.* – Gk. κιθάρα, a lyre ; see **Cithern.**

Gules, red. (F.–L.) M. E. *goules.–*F. *gueules,* gules, red ; answering to Late L. *gulæ·*(pl. of *gula*), meaning (1) mouth, (2) reddened skin, (3) gules. (See *Gula* in Ducange.)–L. *gula,* the throat.

Gulf. (F. – Ital. – Gk.) Formerly *goulfe.–*F. *golfe.*– Ital. *golfo.*– Late Gk. κόλφος, a variant of Gk. κόλπος, the bosom, also, a deep hollow, bay, creek. **Der.** *en-gulf.*

Gull (1), a bird. (C.) Corn. *gullan*, a gull; W. *gwylan*; Bret. *gwelan*; O. Irish *foilenn*, 'alcedo.'

Gull (2), a dupe. (C.) The same; from the notion that a *gull* was a stupid bird. ¶ But cf. Du. *gul*, soft, good-natured; M. Du. *gulle*, 'a great wench without wit,' Hexham.

Gullet, the throat. (F.–L.) M. E. *golet.* – M. F. *goulet* (Cot.); dimin. of O. F. *gole*, *goule* (F. *gueule*), the throat. – L. *gula*, the throat. Brugm. i. § 499.

gully, a channel worn by water. (F.– L.) Formerly *gullet.* – M. F. *goulet*, 'a gullet, a deep gutter of water ;' Cot. The same word as **Gullet** (above).

Gulp. (E.) M. E. *gulpen*, *gloppen*, *glubben.* Cf. E. Fries. and Du. *gulpen*, to swallow eagerly; Du. *gulp*, a great billow, draught, gulp. Prob. of imitative origin. Cf. Swed. *glupa*, to devour.

Gum (1), flesh of the jaws. (E.) M. E. *gōme.* A. S. *gōma*, jaws, palate. **+** Icel. *gōmr*, Swed. *gom*; cf. G. *gaumen*, Lith. *gomurys*, the palate. Brugm. i. § 196.

Gum (2), resin of certain trees. (F.– L. – Gk.) M. E. *gomme.* – F. *gomme.* – L. *gummi.* – Gk. κόμμι, gum. (Prob. of Egyptian origin; Coptic *komē*, gum.)

Gun. (E. ?) M. E. *gonne*; whence W. *gwn*, a gun (as early as the fourteenth cent.). Of obscure origin.

Gunny, a coarse kind of sacking. (Hind. – Skt.) Hind. and Mahratti *gon*, *gonī*, a sack, sacking. – Skt. *goṇi*, a sack (Yule).

Gunwale, upper edge of a ship's side. (E.) See *gunwale* or *gunnel* in Kersey (1715). A *wale* is an outer timber on a ship's side; and the *gun-wale* is a *wale* from which *guns* were pointed. A *wale* is a 'beam'; see **Wale.**

Gurgle, to purl. (Ital. – L.) In Spenser, Thestylis, 3. Imitated from Ital. *gorgogliare*, to purl, bubble, boil; *gorgoglio*, gurgling of a stream. – Ital. *gorgo*, a whirlpool. – L. *gurges*, whirlpool; cf. *gurgulio*, gullet. See **Gorge.** So also Du. *gorgel*, G. *gurgel*, throat; from L. *gurgulio.* Brugm. i. § 499.

Gurnard, Gurnet, a fish. (F.–L. ; *with* Teut. *suffix*.) *Gurnard* is the better and fuller form. The word means 'a grunter,' from the sound which the fish makes when taken out of the water.–

M. F. *grongnard* (F. *grognard*), grunting, grunter, whence M. F. *gournauld*, *grougnaut*, gurnard (Cot.). – M. F. *grogner*, to grunt ; with suffix *-ard* (= G. *hart*). – L. *grunnire*, to grunt ; see **Grunt.**

Gush. (E.) M. E. *guschen.* E. Fries. *gûsen*, to gush out.**+**M. Du. *guysen*, to gush out (Kilian); Icel. *gusa*, allied to *gjōsa* (pt. t. *gauss*), Norw. *gjosa*, to gush. Allied to Icel. *gjōta*, to pour, Goth. *giutan*, L. *fundere.* Cf. Du. *gudsen*, to gush. (√GHEU.) See **Gut, Geysir.**

Gusset. (F.) F. *gousset*, 'a gusset,' Cot. Also 'the piece of armour by which the arm-hole is covered,' id. Named from its supposed resemblance to a husk of a bean or pea; dimin. of F. *gousse*, husk of bean or pea; cf. Ital. *guscio*, a shell, husk ; of unknown origin.

Gust (1), a sudden blast, gush of wind. (Scand.) Icel. *gustr*, a gust. – Icel. *gus-*, weak grade of *gjōsa*, to gush; see **Gush.** So also Swed. dial. *gust*, stream of air from an oven, Norw. *gust*, a gust.

Gust (2), relish, taste. (L.) L. *gustus*, a tasting; cf. *gustāre*, to taste. (√GEUS.) Allied to **Choose.** **Der.** *dis-gust.*

Gut, the intestinal canal. (E.) (The word is allied to M. E. *gote*, prov. E. *gut*, a channel.) M. E. *gutte.* A. S. *gut*; pl. *guttas*; orig. 'a channel.' Mone, Quellen, p. 333, l. 198.–A. S. *gut-*, weak grade of Teut. **geutan-*, A.S. *gēotan*, to pour. (√GHEU.) **+** Dan. *gyde*, a lane, M. Du. *gote*, a channel, G. *gosse*, a drain. See **Gush.**

Gutta-percha. (Malay.) The spelling *gutta* is due to confusion with L. *gutta*, a drop, with which it has nothing to do. – Malay *gatah*, *gutah*, gum, balsam ; *percha*, the name of the tree producing it.

Gutter. (F.–L.) M. E. *gotere.* – A. F. *guttere*; O. F. *gutiere*, *goutiere* (Littré, s. v. *gouttière*, a gutter). Esp. used for catching drops from the eaves of a roof. – F. *goutte.* – L. *gutta*, a drop.

Guttural. (F.–L.) F. *guttural.* – L. *gutturālis*, belonging to the throat. – L. *guttur*, the throat.

Guy, a hideous creature, fright. (F.– Ital. – Teut.) Orig. used of an effigy of *Guy* Fawkes. – F. *Guy.* – Ital. *Guido* ; of Teut. origin. Cf. **Guide.**

Guy-rope, Guy, a guide-rope, used to steady a weight in heaving. (F. – Teut.) O. F. *guie*, a guide. – O. F. *guier*, to guide; see **Guide.** Cf. Span. *guia*, a guy-rope.

Guzzle. (F.) Apparently suggested by O. F. *goziller, gosillier*, to vomit (Godefroy), understood to mean 'to swallow greedily.' The O.F. *desgosiller* had both senses (Godefroy). Cf. O. F. *gosillier*, the throat, allied to F. *gosier*, the throat. Remoter source unknown.

Gymnasium. (L. – Gk.) L. *gymnasium.* – Gk. γυμνάσιον, an athletic school, where men practised naked. – Gk. γυμνά-ζειν, to train naked, exercise. – Gk. γυμνός, naked. **Der.** *gymnast* = γυμναστής, a trainer of athletes; *gymnast-ic.*

Gypsum. (L. – Gk. – Arab.) L. *gypsum*, chalk. – Gk. γύψος, chalk. Prob. from Pers. *jabsīn*, lime, Arab. *jibs*, plaster, mortar; Rich. Dict., p. 494.

Gypsy. (F. – L. – Gk. – Egypt.) Spelt *gipsen*, Spenser, M. Hubbard, 86. Short for M. E. *Egypcien.* – O. F. *Egyptien.* – Late L. *Ægyptiānus*; from L. *Ægyptius*, an Egyptian. – Gk. Αἰγύπτιος. – Gk. Αἴγυπτος, Egypt. ¶ The supposition that they came from *Egypt* was false; their original home was India.

Gyre, circular course. (L. – Gk.) L. *gȳrus.* – Gk. γῦρος, ring, circle. **Der.** *gyr-ate*, from pp. of L. *gȳrāre.*

Gyrfalcon, Gerfalcon, bird of prey. (F. – Teut. *and* L.) Formerly *gerfaulcon*; also *girefaucon* (used by Trevisa to translate L. *gȳrofalco*). – O. F. *gerfaucon.* – M. H. G. *gīrvalke.* – O. H. G. *gīr-*, for *giri*, greedy (whence also G. *geier*, a vulture); and L. *falco*, a falcon. ¶ L. *gȳrofalco* is a mistaken form.

Gyron; see Giron.

Gyves, fetters. (F.) M. E. *giues, gyues.* – A. F. *gives*, fetters (Godefroy). Cf. O. H. G. *be-wīfen*, to fetter.

H.

Ha, interj. (E.) An exclamatory sound. Cf. O. Fries. *haha*, to denote laughter; G. *he*; O. F. *ha!*

Haberdasher, a seller of small wares. (F.) So named from his selling a stuff called *hapertas* in A.F.; see Liber Albus, ed. Riley, pp. 225, 231. The name of this stuff is of unknown origin.

Habergeon, armour for neck and breast. (F. – O. H. G.) M. E. *habergeon, haubergeoun.* – O. F. *haubergeon, hauberjon*, a hauberk; deriv. (treated as dimin.) of O. F. *hauberc*; see Hauberk.

Habiliment, dress. (F. – L.) F. *habillement*, clothing. – F. *habiller*, to clothe, orig. 'to get ready.' – F. *habile*, ready, fit. – L. *habilis*, easy to handle, active. – L. *habēre*, to have; see Able.

Habit, practice, custom, dress. (F. – L.) O. F. *habit*, a dress, a custom. – L. *habitum*, acc. of *habitus*, a condition, dress. – L. *habitus*, pp. of *habēre*, to have, keep. See Brugm. i. § 638.

habitable. (F. – L.) F. *habitable.* – L. *habitābilis*, that can be dwelt in. – L. *habitāre*, to dwell, frequent. of *habēre*, to have.

habitant. (F. – L.) F. *habitant*, pres. pt. of *habiter*, to dwell. – L. *habitāre*, frequent. of *habēre* (above).

habitat, the natural abode of a plant. (L.) L. *habitat*, it dwells (there); 3 pres. s. of *habitāre*, to dwell (above).

habitation, abode. (F. – L.) F. *habitation.* – L. acc. *habitātiōnem.* – L. *habitātus*, pp. of *habitāre*, to dwell, frequent. of *habēre*, to have.

habitude. (F. – L.) F. *habitude*, custom. – L. *habitūdo*, condition. – L. *habit-*, as in *habitus*, pp. of *habēre*, to have.

Hacienda, a farm, estate, farm-house. (Span. – L.) Span. *hacienda*, an estate, orig. employment. [The *c* is pronounced as *th* in *thin*.] O. Span. *facienda.* – L. *facienda*, things to be done; gerundive neut. pl. of *facere*, to do.

Hack (1), to cut, mangle. (E.) M. E. *hakken.* A. S. *haccian*, to cut, in the comp.*tō-haccian*.+Du.*hakken*, Dan. *hakke*, Swed. *hacka*, G. *hacken*, to chop, hack. Teut. types **hakkōn-, *hakkōjan-.*

Hack (2); see Hackney.

Hackbut. (F. – Low G.) Also *hagbut.* – M. F. *haquebute*, 'a haquebut, a caliver' (i. e. a sort of musket); Cot. A corruption of Low G. *hakebusse* (Du. *haakbus*), an arquebus; due, apparently, to some confusion with O.F. *buter*, to thrust. Lit. 'hook-gun;' so called from the hook on the gun, by which it was hung on to a support. – Low G. *hake*, (Du. *haak*), hook; *busse* (Du. *bus*), a gun. See Arquebus; and see Hook.

Hackle (1), **Hatchel,** an instrument for dressing flax; see Heckle.

Hackle (2), long shining feathers on the neck of a cock. (E.) Probably allied to Hackle (1).

Hackney, Hack, a horse let out for hire. (F.) M. E. *hakeney.* – O. F. *haquenee*, 'an ambling horse;' Cot. (Cf. O. Span. *facanea*, Span. *hacanea*, Ital. *chinea*, short for *acchinea*, the same.) Extended from O. F. *haque*, O. Span. *faca*, Span. *haca*, a nag, gelding; a word of unknown origin. ¶ *Hack* is short for *hackney*, and quite a late form; hence *hack*, verb, i. e. to use as a hack or hackney.

Haddock, a fish. (E.) M. E. *haddok* (XIV cent.). Orig. doubtful; the Irish for 'haddock' is *codog*.

Hades, the abode of the dead. (Gk.) Gk. ᾅδης, αἴδης (Attic), ἀΐδης (Homeric), the nether world; in Homer, the god of the nether world. Of unknown origin.

Hadji, Hajji, one who has performed the pilgrimage to Mecca. (Arab.) Arab. *ḥājī*, 'a Christian who has performed the pilgrimage to Jerusalem, or a Muhammedan [who has performed] that to Mecca;' Rich. Dict., p. 549. Orig. the latter.

Hæmatite, Hæmorrhage; see Hematite, Hemorrhage.

Haft, handle. (E.) A. S. *hæft*, a handle. — A. S. *haf-*, base of *hebban*, to lift; see **Heave.** + Du. *heft*, Icel. *hepti* (pron. *hefti*), G. *heft*, a handle. Lit. 'that which is caught up.'

Hag. (E.) M. E. *hagge*; with same sense as A.S. *hægtis*, a fury, a witch, a hag. + G. *hexe*, M. H. G. *hecse*, a witch, O. H. G. *hazissa*, also *hagazussa*, a fury. Perhaps connected with A. S. *haga*, a hedge, enclosure; but this is uncertain.

Haggard (1), wild, said of a hawk. (F. – G.) M. F. *hagard*, wild; esp. used of a wild falcon; see Cotgrave. Perhaps the orig. sense was hedge-falcon; formed, with suffix -*ard* (< O. H. G. *hart*), from M. H. G. *hag* (G. *hag*), a hedge; see Haw.

Haggard (2), lean, meagre. (F. – G.) Really the same as the word above (Cot.). We also find *hagg-ed*, i. e. hag-like, from *hag*. 'The ghostly prudes with *hagged* face,' Gray, A Long Story, near end. ¶ Mod. G. *hager* may be from M. F. *hagard*; for G. *hagerfalk* means a haggard hawk.

Haggis, a dish of sheep's entrails, chopped up, seasoned, and boiled in the sheep's maw. (E.) M. E. *hagas, hageis*. Of unknown origin. Perhaps from *hag*, to cut; see Haggle (1). (The Gael. *taigeis* is from E.)

Haggle (1), to hack awkwardly, mangle.

(Scand.) Frequent. of North E. *hag*, to cut; as *hackle* is of *hack*, to cut. The form *hag* is from Icel. *höggva*, to hew, cognate with E. *hew*; see **Hew.** Cf. Norman dial. *haguer*, to hack.

Haggle (2), to be slow in making a bargain. (E.) In Cotgrave, s. v. *harceler*. Cf. Du. *hakkelen*, 'to hackle, mangle, faulter,' i. e. stammer (Sewel); *hakketeren*, to wrangle, cavil. It is probably the same word as Haggle (1). Cf. also *higgle*, to bargain.

Hagiographa, holy writings. (Gk.) Gk. ἁγιόγραφα (βιβλία), books written by inspiration. — Gk. ἅγιο-ς, holy; γράφ-ειν, to write.

Ha-ha, Haw-haw, a sunk fence. (F.) From F. *haha*, an interjection of laughter; hence a surprise in the form of an unexpected obstacle (that laughs at one). The F. word also means an old woman of surprising ugliness, a 'caution.'

Hail (1), frozen rain. (E.) M. E. *haghel, hayl*. A.S. *hægl, hagol*. + Icel. *hagl*, Du. Dan. Swed. G. *hagel*. Teut. types *hag(a)loz*, m., *hag(a)lom*, n. Cf. Gk. κάχληξ, a round pebble.

Hail (2), to salute, greet. (Scand.) M. E. *heilen*; a verb coined from M. E. *heil, hail*, sb.; which is an adaptation of Icel. *heill*, prosperity, good luck, a sb. formed from the adj. *heill*, hale, sound, fortunate. Cf. A.S. *hæl*, safety, luck. See Hale (1).

hail (3), an exclamation. (Scand.) Icel. *heill*, hale, sound; used in greeting. This word is common in greeting persons, as *far heill* = farewell, *kom heill*, welcome, hail! The Scand. verb is Icel. *heilsa*, Swed. *helsa*, Dan. *hilse*, to greet. See Hale (1).

Hair. (E.; *influenced by* F.) The true E. form was M. E. *heer*. From A.S. *hǽr, hér*. + Du. *haar*, Icel. *hár*, Dan. *haar*, Swed. *hår*; G. *haar*, O. H. G. *hár*. Teut. type *hǽrom*, neut. Further related to Icel. *haddr*, hair, Teut. type *hazdoz*; and to Lith. *kassa*, plaited hair; also to Russ. *chesat(e)*, to comb out, L. *carere*, to card wool. β. But the mod. E. form is due to confusion with A. S. *hǽre*, hair-cloth, which was replaced by M. E. *haire*, borrowed from O. F. *haire*, with the same sense; and this O. F. *haire* was from O. H. G. *hárra* (for *hárjá*), haircloth, a derivative of O. H. G. *hár*, hair.

Hake, a fish. (Scand.) Cf. Norw.

hakefisk, lit. 'hook-fish;' from the hooked underjaw. (See Hatch (1).)

Hakim, a physician, doctor. (Arab.) Arab. *ḥakīm*, wise; also, a doctor, physician. ─ Arab. root *ḥakama*, he exercised authority.

Halberd, Halbert, a kind of pole-axe. (F.─M. H. G.) O. F. *halebarde*. ─ M. H. G. *helmbarte*, mod. G. *hellebarte*; sometimes explained as an axe with a long handle; cf. M. H. G. *halm* (?), a helve (helm), or handle. But it has been better interpreted as an axe for splitting a *helm*, i. e. helmet. β. The O. H. G. *barta*, G. *barte*, a broad axe, or axe with a broad blade, is from G. *bart*, a beard. [Similarly the Icel. *skeggja*, an axe, is from *skegg*, a beard; and see Barb (1).] Cf. Icel. *barða*, halberd.

Halcyon, a kingfisher; as adj. serene. (L. ─ Gk.) *Halcyon* days = calm days; it was supposed that the weather was calm when kingfishers were breeding. ─ L. *halcyon, alcyon*, a kingfisher. ─ Gk. ἀλκυών, ἀλκυών, a kingfisher. Allied to L. *alcēdo*, the true L. name. ¶ The incorrect aspirate in Gk. was due to a fanciful etymology from ἅλ-ς, sea, and κύων, conceiving.

Hale (1), whole. (E.) M. E. *hale, hal*. O. Northumb. *hāl*, which became *hale*, while the A. S. (Wessex) *hāl* became M. E. *hool*, now spelt *whole*. Cognate with Goth. *hails*. See Whole.

Hale (2), **Haul**, to drag, draw violently. (F.─O. H. G.) M. E. *halien, halen*. ─ F. *haler*, to haul a boat, &c. (Littré). ─ O. H. G. *halōn, holōn* (whence G. *holen*). + O. Sax. *halōn*, Du. *halen*, O. Fries. *halia*, E. Fries. *halen*, Low G. *halen*, to pull, haul; cf. also A. S. *geholian*, to acquire, get; L. *calāre*, to summon; Gk. καλεῖν, to summon. (√KAL.) ¶ *Hale* dates from the XIV cent.; *haul* is later, appearing as *hall* in 1581.

Half, adj. (E.) M. E. *half*. O. Merc. *half*, O. Fries. *half*; A. S. *healf*. + Du. *half*, Icel. *hālfr*, Swed. *half*, Dan. *halv*, Goth. *halbs*, G. *halb*. 2. Allied to *half*, sb., from O. Merc. *half*, A. S. *healf*, sb.+Icel. *hālfa*, Goth. *halba*, G. *halb*; in all these languages the oldest sense of the sb. is 'side.' Der. *halve*, vb.; *be-half*.

Halibut, Holibut, a fish. (E.) So called because excellent eating for holidays; the lit. sense is 'holy (i. e. holiday) plaice.' From M. E. *hali*, holy (see Holy), and *butte*, a plaice (Havelok, l.

759). So also Du. *heilbot*, halibut, from *heilig*, holy, *bot*, a plaice; Swed. *helgeflundra*, a halibut, from *helig*, holy, *flyndra*, a flounder; Dan. *helleflynder*, a halibut, from *hellig*, holy, *flynder*, flounder. See Butt (4).

Halidom, a holy relic. (E.) M. E. *halidom, halidam*. A. S. *hāligdōm*, holiness, a sanctuary, a holy relic. ─ A. S. *hālig*, holy; *-dōm*, suffix, orig. the same as *dōm*, doom. See Holy and Doom.+Du. *heiligdom*; Icel. *helgidōmr*, Dan. *helligdom*, G. *heiligthum*. ¶ By my halidam (with *-dam* for *-dom*) was imagined to refer to Our Lady (*dame*).

Hall. (E.) M. E. *halle*. O. Merc. *hall*; A. S. *heall, heal*, a hall, orig. a shelter. + Du. *hal*, Icel. *hall, höll*, Swed. *hall*, Dan. *hal*. Teut. type **hallā*, for **halnā*, fem.; from **hal*, 2nd grade of **helan-*, to cover (A. S. *helan*). Allied to Helm (2), Hell.

Hallelujah, Alleluia, an expression of praise. (Heb.) Heb. *halelū jāh*, praise ye Jehovah. ─ Heb. *halelū*, praise ye (from *hālal*, to shine, praise); *jāh*, Jah, Jehovah.

Halliard; see Halyard.

Halloo, Hallow, to shout. (F.) M. E. *halowen*. ─ O. F. *halloer*, to pursue with shouts. Of imitative origin.

Hallow, to sanctify. (E.) M. E. *halwen, halewen, halowen*. A. S. *hālgian*, to make holy, from *hālig*, holy; see Holy. So also Icel. *helga*, G. *heiligen*.

hallowmass, feast of All Hallows, i. e. All Saints. (Hybrid; E. *and* L.) Short for *All Hallows' Mass*, mass (or feast) of All Saints. Here *hallows'* is the gen. of *hallows*, pl. due to M. E. *halowe* or *halwe*, a saint=A. S. *hālga*, a saint, def. form of the adj. *hālig*, holy; see Holy and Mass.

Hallucination, wandering of mind. (L.) From L. *hallūcinātio*, a wandering of the mind. ─ L. *hallūcinārī*, better *allūcinārī, alūcinārī*, to wander in mind, dream, rave. + Gk. ἀλύειν, ἀλύειν, to wander in mind; cf. ἠλεός, distraught.

Halm; see Haulm.

Halo, a luminous ring. (F. ─ L. ─ Gk.) F. *halo*. ─ L. acc. *halō*, from nom. *halōs*. ─ Gk. ἅλως, a round threshing-floor, in which the oxen trod out a circular path.

Halser; see Hawser.

Halt, lame. (E.) M. E. *halt*. O. Merc. *halt*; A. S. *healt*.+Icel. *haltr*, Dan. Swed. *halt*, Goth. *halts*, O. H. G. *halz*. Teut.

type *_haltoz_. Cf. L. _claudus_, lame. Der. _halt_, vb., A. S. _healtian_.

Halt! (F. – G.) F. _halte_. – G. _halt_, hold! See **Hold** (1).

Halter. (E.) M. E. _halter_ (an _f_ has been lost). A. S. _hælftre_, a halter.+M. Du. and G. _halfter_, O. H. G. _halftra_; O. Low G. _haliftra_ (Schade). Teut. types *_halftr-_, *_haliftr-_ (Franck). From the base *_halb-_, app. signifying 'to hold'; see **Helve.** I. e. 'something to hold by;' cf. L. _capistrum_, a halter.

Halyard, Halliard, a rope for hoisting sails. (F. – O. H. G.) As if for _hale-_ or _haul-yard_, because it _hales_ or _hauls_ the _yards_ into their places; but really a perversion of M. E. _halier_, meaning simply 'that which _hales_.' See **Hale** (2).

Ham. (E.) M. E. _hamme_. A. S. _hamm_. +Du. _ham_, M. Du. _hame_, Icel. _höm_ (gen. _hamar_); prov. G. _hamme_; O. H. G. _hamma_. Brugmann (i. § 421) connects these with Gk. κνήμη, the lower part of the leg.

Hamadryad, a wood-nymph. (L. – Gk.) L. _hamadryad-_, stem of _hamadryas_. – Gk. ἁμαδρυάς, a wood-nymph; the life of each nymph depended on that of the tree to which she was attached. – Gk. ἅμα, together with; δρῦ-s, tree.

Hame; Hames, pl., the bent sticks round a horse-collar. (E.) M. E. _hame_. +Du. _haam_. Cf. Mid. Du. _hamme_, 'a cratch of wood to tie beasts to, or a yoke;' Hexham. See **Hem** (1).

Hamlet. (F. – Teut.) M. E. _hamelet_, dimin. of O. F. _hamel_ (F. _hameau_), a hamlet. Formed, with dimin. suffix -_el_, from O. Fries. _hām_, _hēm_, O. Sax. _hēm_, a home, dwelling; see **Home.**

Hammer. (E.) A. S. _hamor_. + Icel. _hamarr_, Dan. _hammer_, Swed. _hammare_, Du. _hamer_, G. _hammer_. Thought to be allied to Russ. _kamen(e)_, a stone; as if orig. 'a stone implement;' Icel. _hamarr_ also means 'a rock.'

Hammercloth. (Du. _and_ E.?) Formerly _hamer-cloth_ (1465). The cloth which covers a coach-box. Origin unknown. Perhaps orig. a cover-cloth; adapted from Du. _hemel_, heaven, also a cover, tester, canopy. 'Den _hemel_ van een koetse, the seeling of a coach;' Hexham. Cf. M. Du. _hemelen_, 'to hide, cover, adorne;' Hexham.

Hammock, a slung net for a bed. (W. Ind.) Formerly _hamaca_; Span.

hamaca. A West Indian (Caribbean) word.

Hamper (1), to impede. (E.) M. E. _hampren_; from the same root as Icel. _hamla_, to stop, hinder, Norw. _hamla_, to strive against; cf. Swed. dial. _hamla_, to be awkward, to grope about. Perhaps further allied to Icel. _hemja_, to restrain, G. _hemmen_, to check. See **Hem** (1). 2. Or a nasalised form allied to Low G. _hapern_, E. Fries. _haperen_, to stop short; cf. Swed. dial. _happla_, to stammer, _happa_, to back a horse; Dan. _happe_, to stutter. See **Hopple.**

Hamper (2), a kind of basket. (F. – G.) Formerly spelt _hanaper_. – O. F. _hanapier_, Low L. _hanapērium_, orig. a vessel to keep cups in. – O. F. _hanap_ (Low L. _hanapus_), a drinking-cup. – O. Frankish *_hnapp-_, Du. _nap_, O. H. G. _hnapf_, M. H. G. _napf_, a cup.+A. S. _hnæp_, a cup, bowl.

hanaper, old form of **Hamper** (above). Hence _Hanaper office_, named from the basket in which writs were deposited.

Hand. (E.) A. S. _hand_, _hond_.+ Du. _hand_, Icel. _hönd_, Dan. _haand_, Swed. _hand_, Goth. _handus_, G. _hand_. Teut. type *_handuz_, fem. Root unknown.

handcuff. (E.) A _cuff_ for the _hand_. ¶ XVIII cent.; too late for connexion with A. S. _handcops_, a handcuff.

handicap, a race for horses of all ages. (E.) From _hand i' cap_, hand in the cap, a method of drawing lots; hence, a mode of settlement by arbitration, &c.

handicraft. (E.) A. S. _handcræft_, a trade; the _i_ being inserted in imitation of _handiwork_ (below).

handiwork. (E.) M. E. _handiwerc_. A. S. _handgeweorc_. – A. S. _hand_, hand; _geweorc_, from _weorc_, O. Merc. _werc_, work. The _i_ is due to A. S. _ge_.

handle, vb. (E.) A. S. _handlian_; formed from _handle_, a handle (below). Cf. Du. _handelen_, Icel. _höndla_, Dan. _handle_, Sw. _handla_, G. _handeln_, to handle, or to trade.

handle, sb. (E.) A. S. _handle_; Cp. Glos. 1904.–A. S. _hand_, hand.

handsel, hansel, first instalment of a bargain. (Scand.) Icel. _handsal_, the conclusion of a bargain by shaking hands; lit. 'handgiving,' expressed by 'hand-sale'; so also Dan. _handsel_, Swed. _handsöl_, a handsel. See **Sale.** ¶ The late A. S.

handselen, glossed 'mancipatio,' occurs but once; but cf. O. E. Texts, Charter 44, l. 8.

handsome. (E.) M. E. *handsum*, orig. tractable, or dexterous. — A. S. *hand*, hand; *-sum*, suffix, as in *wyn-sum*, winsome. + Du. *handzaam*, E. Fries. *handsām*, tractable, serviceable.

handy (1), dexterous. (E.) From *hand*, with suffix *-y*. ¶ The M. E. form was *hendi* (never *handi*); A. S. *hendig*, skilful; formed from *hand*, hand, with suffix *-ig* and vowel-change. + Du. *handig*, Dan. *hændig*, *behændig*, Swed. *händig*, dexterous.

handy (2), near. (E.) From *hand*, with suffix *-y*. ¶ The M. E. form was *hende*; A. S. *gehende*, near, at hand. — A. S. *hand*, hand.

Hang, to suspend, to be suspended. (E.) The history of this vb. involves that of two A. S. and one O. Norse vb.; viz. (1) the A. S. *hōn* (for **hanhan-*), pt. t. *hēng*, pp. *hangen*; (2) the A. S. weak vb., *hangian*, pt. t. *hangode*; and (3) the Icel. causal vb. *hengja*, from *hanga* (pt. t. *hēkk*, for **hēnk*, pp. *hanginn*). Cf. G. *hängen*, weak vb., from G. *hangen* (pt. t. *hing*, pp. *gehangen*). Allied to L. *cunctārī*, to delay, Skt. *çank*, to hesitate. Brugm. i. § 420.

Hanger, a short sword. (E.) So called because *hung* from the belt.

Hangnail; for *ang-nail*, a form of *Agnail*, q. v.

Hank, a parcel of skeins of yarn. (Scand.) Icel. *hönk*, a hank, coil; *hanki*, a hasp, clasp; Swed. *hank*, a string, Dan. *hank*, a handle, ear of a vessel. Cf. also Low G. *hank*, a handle (Lübben), G. *henkel*, a handle, ear of a vessel. Prob. allied to **Hang**; cf. O. H. G. *henkan* (<**hangian*), to hang up.

Hanker, to long after. (E.) Cf. prov. E. *hank*, to hanker after, of which it is a frequent form; cf. the phr. 'to *hang* about.' From the verb *to hang*. Verified by M. Du. *hengelen*, to hanker after (from *hangen*), *honkeren* (Du. *hunkeren*), to hanker after (Sewel); also Dan. *hang*, bias, inclination, E. Fries. *hang*, *hank*, bias.

Hanseatic, pertaining to the Hanse towns in Germany. (F. – O. H. G.) O. F. *hanse*, the hanse, i. e. society of merchants; with L. suffix *-āticus*. — O. H. G. *hansa* (G. *hanse*), an association; cf. Goth. *hansa*, A. S. *hōs*, a band of men. (From about A. D. 1140.)

Hansel; see **Handsel**.

Hansom, a kind of cab. (E.) From the name of the inventor (no doubt the same word as *handsome*). A. D. 1834.

Hap. (Scand.) M. E. *hap*. — Icel. *happ*, hap, chance, good luck; cf. A. S. *gehæp*, fit. [The W. *hap* must be borrowed from E.] Der. *happ-y*, i. e. lucky; *hap-less*, i. e. luckless; *hap-ly*, by luck (*happily* is used in the same sense); *mis-hap*; *per-haps*.

happen. (Scand.) M. E. *happenen*, *hapnen*, extended from *happen*, i. e. to hap. From the sb. above.

Hara-kiri, suicide by disembowelment. (Japanese.) From Japan. *hara*, belly; *kiri*, to cut (Yule).

Harangue. (F. – O. H. G.) O. F. *harangue*, an oration; Low L. *harenga*. The same as Span. *arenga*, Ital. *aringa*. Orig. a speech made in the midst of a *ring* of people; as shown by Ital. *aringo*, an arena, lists, also a pulpit. — O. H. G. *hrinc* (G. *ring*), a ring, ring of people, an arena, circus, lists. Cognate with A. S. *hring*, a ring. See **Ring**.

Harass. (F.) F. *harasser*, to tire out, vex, disquiet; Cot. Perhaps from O. F. *harer*, to set a dog at a beast. — O. H. G. *haren*, to call out, cry out (hence cry to a dog).

Harbinger, a forerunner. (F. – O. H. G.) M. E. *herbergeour*, one who provided lodgings for a man of rank. — O. F. *herberg-er*, to lodge, to harbour; with suffix *-our* (L. *-ātōrem*). — O. F. *herberge*, a lodging, harbour. — O. H. G. *heriberga* (below).

harbour (1), shelter. (Scand.) M. E. *hereberȝe*, *herberwe*. — Icel. *herbergi*, a harbour, lit. 'army-shelter.' — Icel. *herr*, an army; *barg*, 2nd grade of *bjarga*, to shelter. So likewise O. H. G. *heriberga*, a camp, lodging, from O. H. G. *heri* (G. *heer*), an army, *bergan*, to shelter (whence F. *auberge*, Ital. *albergo*). Cf. **Harry** and **Borough**. Der. *harbour*, vb.

Harbour (2), see **Arbour**.

Hard. (E.) A. S. *heard*; O. Fries. *herd*. + Du. *hard*; Icel. *harðr*, Dan. *haard*, Swed. *hård*, Goth. *hardus*, G. *hart*. Teut. type **harduz*, Idg. type **kartús*; cf. Gk. κρατύς, strong. Brugm. i. § 792.

Hardock, Hordock, the corn-bluebottle; *Centaurea cyanus*. (E.) *Hardokes*, pl., is the reading in K. Lear, iv. 4. 4, ed.

1623; the quartos have *hordocks*. The same as *haudod*, used in Fitzherbert's Husbandry to mean the corn-bluebottle; see Glossary, and pref. p. xxx. Mr. Wright (note to K. Lear) shows that *hardhake* meant the *Centaurea nigra*. Both plants were called, indifferently, *knobweed, knotweed*, and *loggerheads*. Named from the *hardness* of the head of the *Centaurea nigra*; for which reason it was also called *iron-weed, iron-heads*, &c. See Plant-names, by Britten and Holland.

Hards, fibres of flax. (E.) M. E. *herdes*. A. S. *heordan*, pl.+M. Du. *heerde, herde*, hards (Kilian), later *hēde* (Hexham); E. Fries. *hēde*. Teut. type **hizdōn-* or **hezdōn-*; cf. **Meed.** ¶ Distinct from *hard*.

Hardy, stout, brave. (F. — Teut.) M. E. *hardi*.—O. F. *hardi*, brave; orig. pp. of *hardir*, lit. to harden. — Teut. **hartjan*, as in O. H. G. *hertan*, to harden, make strong.—O. H. G. *harti* (G. *hart*), hard; see **Hard.**

Hare. (E.) A. S. *hara*. + Dan. Swed. *hare*, Icel. *hēri* (formerly *here*); Du. *haas*, G. *hase*. Teut. types **hazon-, *hason-*, Idg. type **kason-*; cf. O. Pruss. *sasins* (for **kasins*), W. *cein-ach*, fem. (Rhys), Skt. *çaça*, for *çasa*, a hare. The Skt. word means 'jumper,' from *çaç* (Idg. *kas-*), to jump, leap along.

harebell. (E.) From *hare* and *bell*.

Harem, set of apartments for females. (Arab.) Also *haram*. — Arab. *ḥaram*, women's apartments, lit. 'sacred,' or 'prohibited.'—Arab. root *ḥarama*, he prohibited (because men were prohibited from entering). The initial is the 6th letter of the Arab. alphabet. Rich. Dict., p. 563.

Haricot (1), a stew of mutton, (2) kidney bean. (F.) F. *haricot*, 'mutton sod with little turneps,' &c.; Cot. The sense of 'bean' is late; that of 'minced mutton with herbs,' O. F. *hericot*, is old. Origin unknown.

Hark, Hearken. (E.) M. E. *herken*, also *herknen*. *Herknen* is from A. S. *hercnian, heorcnian*, to listen to. *Herken* corresponds to a shorter type, A.S. **heorcian* (not found), O. Fries. *herkia*; also O. Fries. *harkia* (from the 2nd grade), E. Fries. *harken*. Teut. type **herkan-*, pt. t. **hark*, pp. **hurkanoz*. The O. H. G. *hōrechen*, M. H. G. *hōrchen*, with long *ō*, must have been associated with O. H. G. *hōrjan*, G. *hören*, to hear; cf. G. *horchen*. But the

Teut. type **herkan-* can hardly be related to **Hear.**

Harlequin. (F.—Ital.) F. *arlequin, harlequin*, a harlequin.—Ital. *arlecchino*, a buffoon, jester. The Ital. word seems to correspond to the O. F. *Hellequin, Herlekin, Hierlekin*; the usual O. F. phrase was *la maisnie hierlekin* (Low L. *harlequīnī familias*), a troop of demons that haunted lonely places at night. A popular etymology connected the word with *Charles Quint*; Max Müller, Lect. ii. 581. Prob. of Teut. origin; cf. O. H. G. *hella cunni*, the kindred of hell; which may have been confused with O. F. *herle, hierle*, tumult.

Harlot. (F.) Orig. used of either sex, and not always in a very bad sense; equiv. to mod. E. 'fellow;' Ch. C. T. 649.— O. F. *herlot, arlot*, a vagabond; Prov. *arlot*, a vagabond; Ital. *arlotto* (Baretti), Low L. *arlotus*, a glutton. Of disputed origin. ¶ W. *herlod* is from E.

Harm, sb. (E.) M. E. *harm*. A. S. *hearm*, grief, also harm. + Icel. *harmr*, grief, Dan. *harme*, wrath, Swed. *harm*, anger, grief, G. *harm*, grief; Teut. type **harmoz*. Cf. Russ. *srame*, shame. Brug. ii. § 72. **Der.** *harm*, vb.

Harmony, concord. (F.—L.—Gk.) M. E. *harmonie*.—F. *harmonie*.—L. *harmonia*.—Gk. ἁρμονία, a joint, proportion, harmony. — Gk. ἁρμός, a joining. — Gk. **ἄρειν* (ἀραρίσκειν), to fit. (√AR.)

Harness. (F.) The old sense was 'armour.' O. F. *harneis, harnois*, armour; whence Bret. *harnez*, old iron, armour (Thurneysen). Of unknown origin; the G. *harnisch* is from F.

Harp. (E.) M. E. *harpe*. A. S. *hearpe*. + Du. *harp*, Icel. *harpa*, Swed. *harpa*, Dan. *harpe*, G. *harfe*. Teut. type **harpōn-*, fem.; whence F. *harpe*.

Harpoon. (F.—L.—Gk.) Formerly also *harpon*, which is the F. spelling.—F. *harpon*, a cramp-iron, a grappling-iron; whence also Du. *harpoen*.—O. F. *harpe*, a dog's claw or paw, a clamp, cramp-iron; cf. *se harper*, to grapple.—Late L. *harpē*, a sickle-shaped sword. — Gk. ἅρπη, a sickle. Cf. also Span. *arpon*, a harpoon, *arpar*, to claw, rend.

Harpsichord. (F.—Teut. *and* Gk.) Also *harpsechord*; with intrusive *s*. — F. *harpechorde*, 'a harpsichord;' Cot. From Teutonic and Greek; see **Harp** and **Chord.** Cf. Ital. *arpicordo* (Florio).

Harpy. (F.—L.—Gk.) O. F. *harpie*.

- L. *harpȳia*, usually in pl. *harpȳiæ*. **-** Gk. pl. ἅρπυιαι, lit. ' spoilers ' or ' snatchers.' **-** Gk. ἁρπ-, base of ἁρπάζειν, to seize ; allied to L. *rapere*. See **Rapacious.**

Harquebus ; see **Arquebus.**

Harridan, a jade, a worn-out woman. (F.) A variant of M. F. *haridelle*, ' a poor tit, leane ill-favored jade,' Cot. ; i. e. a worn-out horse ; also used in the sense of a gaunt, ugly woman (Littré). The form remains unexplained.

Harrier (1), a hare-hound. (E.) Formerly *harier*; from *hare*. Cf. *bow-yer* from *bow*.

Harrier (2), a kind of buzzard. (E.) I. e. *harry-er*, because it destroys small birds ; see **Harry.**

Harrow, sb. (E.) M. E. *harwe*. North Fries. *harwe*. Not found in A. S. +Icel. *herfi*, Dan. *harv*, a harrow ; Swed. *harf*, a harrow. Apparently allied to M. Dan. *harge*, Du. *hark*, Swed. *harka*, G. *harke*, a rake. Base *har-*? Cf. L. *car-ere*, to card wool.

Harry, to ravage. (E.) M. E. *harwen*, *herien*, *herȝien*. A. S. *hergian*, to lay waste, as is done by an army.+Icel. *herja*, to ravage, Dan. *hærge*, O. H. G. *harjōn*. Teut. type *harjōn-*, to harry ; from *har-joz*, an army (A. S. *here*, Icel. *herr*, Dan. *hær*, O. H. G. *hari*, G. *heer*, Goth. *harjis*). Allied to O. Pruss. *karjis*, an army ; Lith. *karas*, war.

Harsh. (Scand.) M. E. *harsk*. **-** Dan. *harsk*, rancid ; Swed. *härsk*, rank, rancid, rusty. **+** G. *harsch*, harsh, rough. Cf. Lithuan. *kartùs*, harsh, bitter (of taste) ; see **Hard.**

Hart. (E.) M. E. *hert*. A. S. *heort*, *heorot*, *herut*.+Du. *hert*, Icel. *hjörtr*, Dan. *hiort*, Swed. *hjort*, G. *hirsch*, O.H.G. *hiruz* ; Teut. stem *herut-*. Allied to L. *ceruus*, W. *carw*, a hart, horned animal ; Russ. *serna*, a chamois; cf. Gk. κέρας, a horn. See **Horn**.

Harvest. (E.) A. S. *hærfest*, autumn ; orig. ' crop.' **+** Du. *herfst*, G. *herbst*, autumn ; Icel. *haust*, Dan. Swed. *höst* (contracted forms). Allied to Gk. καρπός, fruit ; L. *carpere*, to gather, Lith. *kerpu*, I shear. Brugm. i. § 631. And cf. Gk. κείρειν, to shear.

Hash, a dish of meat cut into slices, &c. (F.-G.) [O. F. *hachis*, hash.] **-** F. *hacher*, to hack. **-** F. *hache*, an ax. **-** O. H. G. *happja*, whence O. H. G. *heppa*, M. H. G. *hepe*, a bill, a sickle.

Hashish, Hasheesh, an intoxicating drink. (Arab.) See **Assassin.**

Haslets, Hastelets, Harslets, the inwards of a pig, &c., for roasting. (F.-L.) From O. F. *hastelet*, meat roasted on a spit. **-** O. F. *haste*, a spit. **-** L. *hasta*, a spit ; see **Hastate.**

Hasp. (E.) A. S. *hæpse*, a fastening, clasp, catch of a door.+Icel. *hespa*, a hasp, a skein (of wool), Dan. Swed. G. *haspe*, hasp ; cf. M. Du. *hasp*, *haps*, a skein of wool. Cf. Low G. *happen*, *hapsen*, to snatch, clutch ; F. *happer*, to lay hold of.

Hassock. (E.) M. E. *hassok*, orig. coarse grass or sedge ; of which the old hassocks were made. A. S. *hassuc*, a tuft of coarse grass. ¶ Not from W. *hesg*, sb. pl., sedges.

Hastate, spear-shaped. (L.) L. *hastā-tus*, spear-like. **-** L. *hasta*, a spear. Allied to **Yard** (2).

Haste, sb. (F.-Teut.) M. E. *hast*, *haste*. **-** O. F. *haste*, haste (F. *hâte*). **-** W. Germanic *hai(f)sti-*, violence ; as in O. Fries. *haest* (Richtofen, s. v. *hast*),O. H. G. *heisti*, adj., violent ; A. S. *hǣst*, violence. Cf. Goth. *haifsts*, fem., strife. ¶ Du. *haast*, G. Dan. Swed. *hast*, haste, are all borrowed from F. **Der.** *haste*, vb. ; *hast-en*, XVI cent.

Hat. (E.) A. S. *hæt.* **+** Icel. *hött*, a hood, later *hattr*, Swed. *hatt*, Dan. *hat*. Teut. type *hattuz*, m. If it is related to *hood*, it stands for an earlier form *hadnuz*. See **Hood.**

Hatch (1), a half-door. (E.) M. E. *hacche* ; a *hatch* also corresponds to North E. *heck*. A. S. *hæc* (gen. *hæcce*), a hurdle (?). **+** Du. *hek*, fence, rail, gate, Swed. *häck*, coop, rack. Teut. *hakjā*, f. Prob. so named as being lightly fastened with a hook. Cf. A. S. *hac-a*, a fastening of a door ; see **Hake, Hook. Der.** *hatch-es*, pl. sb., a frame of cross-bars over an opening in a ship's deck ; *hatch-way.*

Hatch (2), to produce a brood by incubation. (E.) M. E. *hacchen*. **+** Swed. *häcka*, to hatch ; Dan. *hækkebuur*, a breeding-cage. Origin unknown.

Hatch (3), to shade by minute lines, crossing each other. (F. **-** G.) F. *hacher*, to hack, also to hatch or engrave ; see **Hash.**

Hatches ; see **Hatch** (1).

Hatchet, a small ax. (F.-G.) F. *hachette*, dimin. of *hache*, an ax. See **Hash.**

Hatchment, escutcheon. (F. – L.)
Shortened from *achievement*, an escutcheon; which was contracted to *átcheament* (Ferne, 1586), *hachement* (Hall, 1548); &c.

Hate, sb. (E.) M. E. *hate.* A. S. *hete,* hate; the mod. E. sb. takes the vowel from the verb *hatian*, to hate.+Du. *haat*, Icel. *hatr*, Swed. *hat*, Dan. *had*, Goth. *hatis*, G. *hass*, hate. Cf. Gk. κήδειν, to vex; W. *cawdd*, displeasure. Der. *hate*, vb.

hatred. (E.) M. E. *hatred, hatreden.* The suffix is A. S. *rǣden*, law, mode, condition, state, as in *hīw-rǣden*, a household; and see *kindred*.

Hauberk, a coat of ringed mail. (F. – O. H. G.) M. E. *hauberk.* – O. F. *hauberc.* – O. H. G. *halsberc*, lit. neck-defence. – O. H. G. *hals*, neck; *bergan*, to protect. See **Collar** and **Bury.**

Haughty. (F. – L.) For M. E. *hautein*, arrogant; ' Hawty, *haultain* ;' Palsgrave. Cf. *booty*, from *butin*. – O. F. *hautain*, ' hauty ;' Cot. – O. F. *haut*; oldest form *halt*, high. – L. *altus*, high; see **Altitude.**

Haul; see **Hale** (2).

Haulm, Halm, stalk. (E.) A. S. *healm.* + Du. *halm*, Icel. *hálmr*, Dan. Swed. *halm;* Russ. *soloma*, straw; L. *culmus*, stalk, Gk. κάλαμος, reed; W. *calaf*, stalk. Brugm. ii. § 72.

Haunch, hip, bend of the thigh. (F. – O. H. G.) F. *hanche;* O. F. *hanche, hanke;* Low L. *hancha* (1275). Of Teut. origin ; from Frankish **hankā*, represented by M. Du. *hancke*, ' haunch or hip ;' Hexham. See Körting, § 3872.

Haunt, to frequent. (F.) M. E. *hanten, haunten.* – O. F. *hanter*, to haunt, frequent. Origin disputed.

Hautboy, a musical instrument. (F. – L.) F. *hautbois.* – F. *haut*, high ; *bois*, wood. – L. *altus*, high ; Late L. *boscus, buscus*, L. *buxus*, box-tree ; see **Box** (1). It is a wooden instrument with a high tone. Hence Ital. *oboè*, E. *oboe*, borrowed from F. *hautbois.*

Have. (E.) M. E. *hauen*, pt. t. *hadde*, pp. *had.* A. S. *habban*, pt. t. *hæfde*, pp. *gehæfd.* + Du. *hebben*, Icel. *hafa*, Swed. *hafva*, Dan. *have*, Goth. *haban*, G. *haben.* Teut. stem **habē-.* If cognate, as usually supposed, with L. *habēre*, to have, the Idg. base must be **khabh-*.

Haven, harbour. (Scand.) A. S. *hæfen, hæfene.* – Icel. *höfn*, Dan. *havn*,

Swed. *hamn.* + Du. *haven*, G. *hafen*, a harbour. Cf. also M. H. G. *habe*, haven ; which seems to be allied to M. H. G. *hab*, Icel. Swed. *haf*, Dan. *hav*, A. S. *heaf*, sea.

Haversack, soldier's provision-bag. (F. – G.) F. *havresac.* – G. *habersack, hafersack*, lit. ' oat-bag.' – G. *haber, hafer*, oats ; *sack*, a sack.

Havoc, destruction. (F.) Cf. A. F. *crier havok;* where *havok* is for O. F. *havot.* – O. F. *havot*, plunder ; whence *crier havot*, E. ' cry havoc ' (Godefroy). Cf. O. F. *haver*, to grapple with a hook (Cot.); and G. *haft*, seizure. Prob. from G. *heben*, to lift. ¶ The W. *hafoc*, destruction, is borrowed from E.

Haw, a hedge; also, berry of hawthorn. (E.) M. E. *hawe*, a yard. A. S. *haga*, an enclosure, yard.+Icel. *hagi*, Swed. *hage*, enclosure ; Dan. *have*, garden ; Du. *haag*, G. *hag*, hedge. Teut. base **hag-*; Idg. base **kagh-*, as in W. *cae*, an enclosure ; see **Quay.** Der. *haw-thorn.* See **Hedge.**

Hawk (1), a bird of prey. (E.) M. E. *hauk, hauek* (= *havek*). A. S. *hafoc, heafoc,* a hawk.+Du. *havik*, Icel. *haukr*, Swed. *hök*, Dan. *høg*, G. *habicht*, O. H. G. *hapuh.* Prob. ' a seizer ;' allied to E. *heave*, L. *capere* ; see **Heave.** So also Low L. *capus*, a falcon, from *capere* ; and L. *accipiter*, a hawk.

Hawk (2), to carry about for sale. (O. Low G.) A verb formed from the sb. *hawker* ; see **Hawker.**

Hawk (3), to clear the throat. (E.) Imitative. Cf. Dan. *harke*, Swed. *harska*, to hawk; W. *hochi*, to hawk, *hoch*, the throwing up of phlegm.

Hawker, pedlar. (O. Low G.) Introduced from abroad ; Du. *heuker*, a hawker, M. Du. *hoecker, hucker;* cf. *heukeren*, to hawk, sell by retail. So also Dan. *höker*, a chandler, huckster, *hökre*, to hawk; Swed. *hökare*, a chandler, huckster. See further under **Huckster.**

Hawse, Hawse-hole. (Scand.) *Hawse* is a round hole through which a ship's cable passes, so called because made in the ' neck ' of the ship. – Icel. *háls, hals*, the neck ; also, part of a ship's bows.+ O. Merc. *hals*, A. S. *heals;* Du. G. *hals;* allied to L. *collum*, neck.

Hawser, a tow-rope. (F. – L.) Cf. F. *haussière*, a hawser. But *hawse-r* is from M. E. *hawse*, to lift. – O. F. *halcier*, F. *hausser*, to lift, raise. – Late L. *altiāre*, to elevate. – L. *altus*, high. See **Altitude.**

Cf. M.Ital. *alzaniere*, 'a halsier [hawser] in a ship' (Florio) ; from *alzare*, to raise. ¶ Not allied to Hoist.

Hawthorn; see Haw.

Hay (1). (E.) M. E. *hey*. O. Merc. *hēg*; A. S. *hīg*. + Du. *hooi*, Icel. *hey*, Dan. Swed. *hö*, Goth. *hawi*, grass; G. *heu*. Teut. type **hau-jom*, n. Properly 'cut grass' ; from the verb *to hew*; see **Hew.**

Hay (2), a hedge. (E.) A. S. *hege*, m. Teut. type **hagiz*. Allied to **Haw** and **Hedge. Der.** *hay-ward*, i. e. hedge-warden.

Hazard. (F. — Span. — Arab.?) F. *hasard.* — Span. *azar*, a hazard; orig. an unlucky throw (at dice) ; cf. M. Ital. *zara*, a game at dice. — Arab. *al zahr*, lit. the die (Devic) ; *al* being the Arab. def. art. But Arab. *zahr* is of doubtful authority.

Haze, a mist. (E.?) Ray has: 'it *hazes*, it misles.' Etym. unknown. We may perhaps compare the Lowl. Sc. *haar*, a sea-fog, a mist.

Hazel. (E.) M. E. *hasel.* A. S. *hæsel.* + Du. *hazelaar*, Icel. *hasl*, *hesli*, Dan. Swed. *hassel*, G. *hasel*; Teut. type **haselo-*; from the Idg. type **koselo-* we have L. *corulus* (for **cosulus*), W. and O. Irish *coll* (for **cosl*), a hazel.

He. (E.) A. S. *hē*; gen. *his*, dat. *him*, acc. *hine.* Fem. sing. nom. *hēo*, gen. dat. *hire*, acc. *hie*, *hī*; neut. sing. nom. *hit*, gen. *his*, dat. *him*, acc. *hit.* Pl. (all genders), nom. acc. *hie*, *hī*, gen. *hira*, *heora*, dat. *him*, *heom.* + Du. *hij*, O. Sax. *he*, *hi* ; Goth. neut. *hita.* Allied to Lith. *szis*, this, L. *ci-trā*, on this side, Gk. *ἐ-κεῖ*, there, *κεῖνος*, that one. Brugm. i. §§ 83, 604. **Der.** *hence*, *her*, *here*, *hither.*

Head. (E.) M. E. *hed*, *heed*, *heued* (= *heved*). A. S. *hēafod.* + Du. *hoofd*, Goth. *haubith*, G. *haupt*, O. H. G. *houbit* ; also O. Icel. *haufoð*, later *höfuð*, Dan. *hoved*, Swed. *hufvud*, M. Swed. *havud.* Teut. types **haubud-*, **haubid-*, neut. ; answering to Idg. types **koupot-*, **koupet-*, which are not exactly represented. The L. *caput* (with short *a*) does not correspond in the vowel-sound, but is allied to A. S. *hafela*, *heafola*, head. (The difficulties as to this word are not yet cleared up.)

headlong, rashly, rash. (E.) M. E. *hedling*, *heuedling*, *hedlinges.* Thus the suffix is adverbial, answering to A. S. suffix *-l-ing*, really a double suffix. Cf. A. S. *bæc-ling*, backwards, *fær-inga*, suddenly.

Heal. (E.) M. E. *helen.* A. S. *hǣlan*, to make whole; formed from *hāl*, whole, with *i*-mutation of *ā* to *ǣ* ; see **Whole.** So also G. *heilen*, from *heil*; Goth. *hailjan*, from *hails.*

health. (E.) A. S. *hǣlð*, health (Teut. type **hailithā*, f.), from *hāl*, whole ; see **Heal** (above).

Heap, sb. (E.) M. E. *heep.* A. S. *hēap*, a heap, crowd. + Du. *hoop* (whence Icel. *hōpr*, Dan. *hob*, Swed. *hop*, O. H. G. *houf*) ; cf. also G. *haufe*, O. H. G. *hūfo.* + Lith. *kaupas*, O. Slav. *kupŭ*, a heap. Brugm. i. § 421 (7). **Der.** *heap*, vb.

Hear. (E.) M. E. *hēren*, pt. t. *herde*, pp. *herd.* O. Merc. *hēran* ; A. S. *hȳran*, pt. t. *hȳrde*, pp. *gehȳred.* + Du. *hooren*, Icel. *heyra*, Dan. *höre*, Swed. *höra*, Goth. *hausjan*, G. *hören.* Cf. Gk. *ἀ-κούειν*, to hear. (Not allied to **Ear.**)

Hearken; see Harken.

Hearsay. (E.) From *hear* and *say*, the latter being in the infin. mood. Cf. A. S. *ic secgan hȳrde* = I heard say (Beowulf, 1346).

Hearse. (F. — L.) M. E. *herse*, hearse. The orig. sense was a triangular harrow, then a triangular frame for supporting lights at a church service, esp. at a funeral, then a bier, a carriage for a dead body. All these senses are found. — M. F. *herce*, a harrow, a frame with pins on it. (Mod. F. *herse*, Ital. *erpice*, a harrow.) — L. *hirpicem*, acc. of *hirpex*, a harrow. **Der.** *rehearse.*

Heart. (E.) M. E. *herte.* A. S. *heorte.* + Du. *hart*, Icel. *hjarta*, Swed. *hjerta*, Dan. *hierte*, Goth. *hairtō*, G. *herz*; Teut. type **herton-*. Further allied to Lith. *szirdis*, Irish *cridhe*, W. *craidd*, Russ. *serdtse*, L. *cor* (gen. *cordis*), Gk. *καρδία*, *κῆρ.*

Hearth. (E.) M. E. *herth*, *herthe.* A. S. *heorð.* + Du. *haard*; Swed. *härd*, a hearth, a forge, G. *herd*; Teut. type **herthoz*, m. Cf. Goth. *haurja*, pl., Icel. *hyrr*, embers, burning coals. Idg. base **ker-*; cf. L. *cremāre*, to burn.

Heart's-ease, a pansy. (E.) Lit. *ease of heart*, i. e. giving pleasure.

hearty. (E.) M. E. *herty*; also *hertly* ; from M. E. *herte* ; see **Heart.**

Heat. (E.) M. E. *hete.* A. S. *hǣtu*, *hǣto*, from **haitiu*, for **haitjō-*, f. ; formed from *hāt*, hot, with the usual vowel-change. + Du. *hitte*, Dan. *hede*, Swed. *hetta*, Icel. *hiti*, G. *hitze* ; all from the weak grade *hit-*; see **Hot.** We also find A. S. *hǣtan*, verb, to heat.

Heath. (E.) M. E. *heth.* A. S. *hǣð.* +Du. G. *heide,* Icel. *heiðr,* Dan. *hede,* Swed. *hed,* Goth. *haithi,* a waste; Teut. type **haithī,* fem. Cf. W. *coed,* O. W. *coit,* a wood.

heathen, a pagan. (E.) A. S. *hǣðen,* adj. So also Icel. *heiðenn,* G. *heiden,* a heathen; Goth. *haithnō,* a heathen woman. Lit. a dweller on a heath, orig. 'wild'; cf. Goth. *haithiwisks,* wild (Mk. i. 6); A. S. *hǣðen,* a wild creature (Beow. 986). From A. S. *hǣð,* a heath (above). [Similarly L. *pagānus* meant (1) a villager, (2) a pagan.]

Heather. (E.) Usually associated with *heath* ; but the Nhumb. form *hadder* points to some different origin.

Heave. (E.) M. E. *hēuen* (= *hēven*). From A. S. *hef-,* a pres. stem of A. S. *hebban,* pt. t. *hōf,* pp. *hafen.* + Du. *heffen,* Icel. *hefja,* Swed. *häfva,* Dan. *hæve,* Goth. *hafjan,* G. *heben.* Teut. type **hafjan-,* pt. t. **hōf;* corresponding to L. *capio,* I seize; cf. Gk. κώπη, handle. (Distinct from *have.*)

Heaven. (E.) M. E. *heuen* (= *heven*). A.S. *heofon, hefon.* +O. Sax. *heban.* [Icel. *himinn,* Goth. *himins,* G. *himmel,*O.H.G. *himil,* O. Sax. *himil,* Du. *hemel,* heaven, may be from a different source.] Cf. A. S. *hūs-heofon,* a ceiling, so that the sense may have been 'canopy.'

Heavy. (E.) Hard to heave, weighty. M. E. *heui* (= *hevi*). A. S. *hefig,* heavy, hard to heave.—A. S. *haf-,* stem of *hebban* (pt. t. *hōf*), to heave; with *i*-mutation of *a.*+Icel. *höfugr, höfigr,* heavy, from *hefja,* to heave; Low G. *hevig;* O. H. G. *hebīg.* See Heave.

Hebdomadal, weekly. (L. – Gk.) L. *hebdomadālis.* – Gk. ἑβδομαδ-, stem of ἑβδομάς, a week.—Gk. ἑπτά, seven; see Seven.

Hebrew. (F. – L.–Gk.– Heb.) F. *hébreu* (*hébrieu* in Cotgr.).—L. *Hebræus.* Gk. Ἑβραῖος.—Heb. *'ivrī,* a Hebrew (Gen. xiv. 13), a name given to Israelites as coming from E. of the Euphrates—Heb. *'āvar,* he crossed over.

Hecatomb. (F.–L.–Gk.) M. F. *hecatombe.*—L. *hecatombē.*—Gk. ἑκατόμβη, a sacrifice of a hundred oxen.—Gk. ἑκατόν, a hundred; βοῦς, ox. See Hundred and Cow.

Heckle, Hackle, Hatchel, an instrument for dressing flax or hemp. (E.) M. E. *hechele, hekele,* E. Fries. *häkel, hekel.*

+Du. *hekel,* a heckle; Dan. *hegle;* Swed. *häckla* ; G. *hechel,* a heckle. Teut. type **hakilā;* from a base *hak-,* to pierce, bite, as in O. H. G. *hecchen,* M. H. G. *hecken* (for **hakjan*), to pierce, bite as a snake; cf. A.S. *hacod,* a pike (fish), from its sharp teeth. Cf. Hack (1).

Hectic, continual, as a fever. (F.– Gk.) F. *hectique* (as if from Late L. **hecticus*).—Gk. ἑκτικός, hectic, consumptive. — Gk. ἕξις, a possession; also, a habit of body.—Gk. ἕξ-ω, fut. of ἔχειν, to have, hold. (√SEGH.)

Hector, a bully. (L. –Gk.) From L. *Hector.*—Gk. Ἕκτωρ, the celebrated hero of Troy. Lit. 'holding fast;' from ἔχειν, to hold (above).

Hedge. (E.) A. S. *hecg,* f. (dat. *hecge*); Teut. type **hag-jā,* allied to *haga,* a haw.+Du. *hegge, heg,* allied to *haag,* a haw; G. *hecke,* f., a hedge. See Haw.

Heed, vb. (E.) M. E. *heden.* A. S. *hēdan,* pt. t. *hēdde.* Formed as if from sb. **hōd,* care (not found); though we find the corresponding O. Fries. sb. *hōde, hūde,* and the G. sb. *hut,* O. H. G. *huota,* care. +Du. *hoeden,* from *hoede,* care; G. *hüten,* from *hut* (O. H. G. *huota*), care, guard. Brugm. i. § 754. Prob. allied to Hood.

Heel (1), part of the foot. (E.) A. S. and O. Fries. *hēla,* heel (whence Du. *hiel*). + Icel. *hæll,* Dan. *hæl,* Swed. *häl.* The A. S. *hēla* is prob. contracted from **hōh-ila,* dimin. of A. S. *hōh,* heel. See Hough.

Heel (2), to lean over, incline. (E.) Modified from M. E. *helden, hilden,* to incline on one side. A. S. *hieldan, hyldan,* to tilt, incline; cf. *niðer-heald,* bent downwards.+Du. *hellen* (for **heldan,* O. Sax. *af-heldian*), to heel over; Icel. *halla* (for **halða*), to heel over (as a ship), from *hallr* (<**halth-*), sloping; Dan. *helde,* to tilt, cf. *held,* a slope; Swed. *hälla,* to tilt. The adj. is A.S. *-heald,* O. Fries. *hald,* Icel. *hallr,* O. H. G. *hald,* inclined, bent forward; Teut. type **halthoz.* Allied to A.S. *hold,* G. *hold,* faithful, true (to a master), Goth. *hulths,* gracious.

Heft, a heaving. (E.) In Wint. Tale, ii. 1.45. Formed from *heave,* just as *haft* is from *have.*

Hegira. (Arab.) Arab. *hijrah,* separation; esp. used of the flight of Mohammed from Mecca; the era of the Hegira begins on July 16, A.D. 622. Cf. Arab. *hajr,* separation.

Heifer. (E.) M. E. *hayfare, hekfere.*

A. S. *heahfore*, a heifer ; also spelt *heahfre*, *heahfru*. The form is still unexplained.

Heigh-ho. (E.) An exclamation ; *heigh*, a cry to call attention ; *ho*, an exclamation.

Height. (E.) A variant of *highth* (Milton) ; we find M. E. *highte* as well as *heȝþe* (*heghthe*). A.S. *híehðu*, *héahðu*, height. − A. S. *héah*, *héh*, high. + Du. *hoogte*, Icel. *hǽð*, Swed. *höjd*, Dan. *höide*, Goth. *hauhitha*. See High.

Heinous. (F.−O. Low G.) M. E. *heinous*, *hainous*.−O. F. *haïnos*, odious ; formed with suffix *-os* (L. *-ōsus*) from O. F. *haïne* (F. *haine*), hatred.−F. *haïr*, to hate. From an O. Teut. form, such as Goth. *hatjan*, O. Fries. *hatia*, to hate ; see Hate.

Heir. (F.−L.) M. E. *heire*, *heir*, also *eyr*.− O. F. *heir*, *eir*.−Late L. *hērem*, for L. *hērēdem*, acc. of *hērēs*, an heir. Cf. Gk. χήρα, a widow (relict). Der. *heir-loom*, where *loom* signifies ' a piece of property,' but is the same word as E. *loom*. See Loom (1).

Heliacal, relating to the sun. (L.− Gk.) From Late L. *hēliacus*.−Gk. ἡλιακός, belonging to the sun.−Gk. ἥλιος, sun ; see Solar.

heliotrope, a flower. (F.−L.−Gk.) F. *héliotrope*.− L. *hēliotropium*.−Gk. ἡλιοτρόπιον, a heliotrope, lit. ' sun-turner ;' from its turning to the sun.−Gk. ἥλιο-s, sun ; τροπ-, 2nd grade of τρέπειν, to turn ; see Trope.

Helix, a spiral figure. (L.−Gk.) L. *helix*, a spiral. − Gk. ἕλιξ, a spiral, a twist. −Gk. ἑλίσσειν, to turn round. Allied to Volute.

Hell. (E.) M. E. *helle*. A.S. *hel*, gen. *helle* ; orig. ' that which hides,' from Teut. **helan-*, A.S. *helan*, (pt. t. *hæl*), to hide. + Du. *hel*, Icel. *hel*, G. *hölle*, Goth. *halja*. Teut. type *haljā, fem. Allied to Cell, Conceal.

Hellebore. (F.−L.−Gk.) Also *ellebore*.−O. F. *ellebore*.−L. *helleborus*.−Gk. ἑλλέβορος, the name of the plant.

Helm (1), an implement for steering a ship. (E.) Orig. the tiller or handle. A. S. *helma*.+Icel. *hjálm* (for **helm-*), a rudder ; E. Fries. *helm*. The prov. E. *helm* means ' handle' ; so also M. E. *halm* (Gawain, 330). Prob. allied to Helve.

Helm (2), armour for the head. (E.) M. E. *helm*. A.S. *helm*.+Du. *helm* ; Icel. *hjálmr*, Dan. *hielm*, Swed. *hjelm*, G. *helm*,

Goth. *hilms*. Teut. type *hel-moz, m. ; lit. ' a covering ;' from **helan-*, to cover. Allied to Skt. *çarman-*, shelter, protection. Lith. *szalmas*, a helmet, O. Slav. *shlēmŭ*, are prob. borrowed from Teut. Brugm. i. § 420. Der. *helm-et*, dimin. form. Allied to Hell.

Helminthology, history of worms. (Gk.) Coined from Gk. ἕλμινθο-, decl. stem of ἕλμινς, a worm ; -λογία, a discourse, from λέγειν, to speak. The sb. ἕλμινς, also ἕλμις, means ' that which curls about' ; allied to Helix.

Helot, a (Spartan) slave. (L.−Gk.) L. pl. *Hēlōtes*, from Gk. εἵλωτες, pl. of εἵλως, a helot, bondsman ; fabled to have meant an inhabitant of *Helos* (a town of Laconia), enslaved by the Spartans.

Help, vb. (E.) M. E. *helpen*, pt. t. *halp*, pp. *holpen*. A. S. *helpan*, pt. t. *healp*, pp. *holpen*. + Du. *helpen*, Icel. *hjálpa*, Dan. *hielpe*, Swed. *hjelpa*, Goth. *hilpan*, G. *helfen*. Teut. type **helpan-*. Allied to Lithuan. *szelpti*, to help. Der. *help*, sb., A. S. *help*, *helpe* ; *help-mate*, suggested by *help meet* (Gen. ii. 18).

Helve, a handle. (E.) M. E. *helue* (= *helve*). A.S. *hielf*, also *helfe*, a handle. + M. Du. *helve*, handle, Low G. *helft*, M. H. G. *halp*, handle ; allied to Halter and Helm (1).

Hem (1), border. (E.) A. S. *hem*. Orig. ' an enclosure ;' cf. O. Fries. *ham*, *hem* (dat. *hemme*), North Fries. *ham*, an enclosure (Outzen) ; prov. G. *hamme*, a fence, hedge (Flügel, 1861). Der. *hem*, vb., to enclose within a border, hem in ; cf. G. *hemmen*, Swed. *hämma*.

Hem (2), a slight cough to call attention. (E.) An imitative word ; allied to Hum. + M. Du. *himmen*, *hemmen*, ' to call one with a hem,' Hexham.

Hematite, an ore of iron. (L.−Gk.) Named from the red colour of the powder. −L. *hæmatītes*.−Gk. αἱματίτης, bloodlike.−Gk. αἱματ-, stem of αἷμα, blood.

Hemi-, half. (Gk.) From a Lat. transcription of Gk. ἡμι-, half, cognate with L. *sēmi-*, half ; see Semi-. Der. *hemisphere*, &c.

hemistich, a half-line, in poetry. (L.−Gk.) L. *hēmistichium*. − Gk. ἡμιστίχιον, a half-verse. − Gk. ἡμι-, half ; στίχος, a row, verse.

Hemlock. (E.) M. E. *hemlok*, *humlok*. A.S. *hemlic*, *hymlice* ; also *hymblice* (Ep. Gl.). The origin of *hym-* is unknown ;

the second syllable is perhaps an unstressed form of A. S. *līc*, like.

Hemorrhage, a great flow of blood. (F.—L.—Gk.) M. F. *hemorrhagie.*—L. *hæmorrhagia.*—Gk. αἱμορραγία, a violent bleeding. — Gk. αἷμο-, for αἷμα, blood; ραγ-, a stem of ῥήγνυμι, I burst, break; the lit. sense being a bursting out of blood.

Hemorrhoids, Emerods, painful bleeding tubercles on the anus. (F.—L.—Gk.) M. F. *hemorrhoïde*, sing., a flowing of blood.—L. *hæmorrhoidæ*, pl. of *hæmorrhoida.*—Gk. αἱμορροΐδες, pl. of αἱμορροΐς, adj., liable to a flow of blood.—Gk. αἷμο-, for αἷμα, blood; *ρο-* (as in *ρο-os*, a stream), allied to ῥέειν, to flow, cognate with Skt. *sru*, to flow; see **Stream.**

Hemp, a plant. (L. — Gk.) M. E. *hemp* (short for *henep*). A. S. *henep, hænep.* Borrowed at a very early period from some Eastern language, whence also L. *cannabis*, Gk. κάνναβις, Pers. *kanab*, hemp, so that the word suffered consonantal letter-change. Cf. Skt. *çana*, hemp (prob. not an Idg. word). So also Du. *hennep*, Icel. *hampr*, Dan. *hamp*, Swed. *hampa*, G. *hanf*; all of foreign origin.

Hen. (E.) A. S. *henn, hen, hæn*; a fem. form (Teut. type **han-jā*) from A. S. *hana*, a cock, lit. 'a singer,' from his crowing; cf. L. *canere*, to sing.+Du. *hen*, fem. of *haan*, a cock; G. *henne*, f. of *hahn*; Icel. *hæna*, f. of *hani*; Dan. *höne*, f. of *hane*; Swed. *höna*, f. of *hane*. (√KAN.) See **Chant.**

Hence. (E.) M. E. *hennes*, older form *henne* (whence *henne-s* by adding adv. suffix -*s*). A. S. *heonan*, for **hinan*, adv., closely allied to A. S. *hine*, masc. acc. of *hē*, he. See **He.**

Henchman, a page, servant. (E.) Formerly *hengestman, henseman, henshman*; cf. *Hinxman* as a proper name. For *hengest-man*, i. e. groom; from M. E. *hengest*, A. S. *hengest*, a horse. Cf. Du. and G. *hengst*, Dan. *hingst*, a horse, Icel. *hestr*, a horse.

Hendecagon, a plane figure having eleven sides. (Gk.) Named from its eleven angles.—Gk. ἕνδεκα, eleven; γωνία, an angle; see **Decagon.**

Henna, a paste used for dyeing the nails, &c., of an orange hue. (Arab.) Arab. *ḥinnā-a, ḥinā*, or *ḥinna-at*, the dyeing or colouring shrub (*Lawsonia inermis*); Rich. Dict., p. 582.

Hent, a seizure; see **Hint.**

Hep, hip; see **Hip** (2).

Hepatic, relating to the liver. (F.—L.—Gk.) M. F. *hepatique.*—L. *hēpaticus.*—Gk. ἡπατικός, belonging to the liver.—Gk. ἡπατ-, stem of ἧπαρ, the liver.+L. *iecur*, Skt. *yakṛt*, the liver. See **Liver.** Der. *hepatica*, liver-wort, a flower.

Heptagon, a plane seven-sided figure. (Gk.) Lit. 'seven-angled.' — Gk. ἑπτά, seven; γωνία, an angle, allied to γόνυ, knee. See **Seven** and **Knee.**

heptahedron, a solid seven-sided figure. (Gk.) From Gk. ἑπτά, seven; ἕδρα, a base, seat (allied to E. **Sit**).

heptarchy, a government by seven persons. (Gk.) XVII cent.—Gk. ἑπτ-, for ἑπτά, seven; and -αρχία, from ἄρχ-ειν, to rule.

Her. (E.) M. E. *hire*; from A. S. *hire*, gen. and dat. of *hēo*, she, fem. of *hē*, he; see **He.** Der. *her-s*, M. E. *hirs, hires* (XIV cent.); *her-self.*

Herald. (F.—O. H. G.) M. E. *heraud.* —O. F. *heralt* (Low L. *heraldus*); O.H.G. *herolt* (G. *herold*), a herald; note also O. H. G. *Heriold, Hariold*, as a proper name, Harold. β. The proper name is for **hari-wald*, i. e. army-rule.—O. H. G. *hari*, an army (G. *heer*); *wald, walt*, rule, power (G. *gewalt*). ¶ The precise history of the word is very uncertain.

Herb. (F. — L.) M. E. *herbe.* — F. *herbe.* — L. *herba*, grass, fodder, herb; prob. allied to O. L. *forbea*, Gk. φορβή, pasture.

Herd (1), a flock. (E.) M. E. *herde.* A. S. *heord, hiord*, a flock. + Icel. *hjörð*, Dan. *hiord*, Swed. *hjord*, G. *heerde*, Goth. *hairda.* Teut. type *herdā*, f. Cf. Skt. *çardha(s)*, a herd, troop. Brugm. i. § 797.

herd (2), one who tends a herd. (E.) Usually in comp. *shep-herd, cow-herd*, &c. M. E. *herde.* A. S. *hierde, hirde*, keeper of a herd; from A.S. *heord,* a flock. + Icel. *hirðir*, Dan. *hyrde*, Swed. *herde*, G. *hirte*, Goth. *hairdeis*; all similarly derived. Cf. Lith. *kerdzus*, shepherd.

Here. (E.) M. E. *her, heer.* A. S. *hēr*, adv.; related to *hē*, he. + Du. *hier*, Icel. *hēr*, Dan. *her*, Swed. *här*, G. *hier*, Goth. *hēr.* Cf. L. *cis*, on this side.

Hereditary, adj. (L.) L. *hērēditārius.* —L. *hērēditāre*, to inherit. — L. *hērēdi-*, decl. stem of *hērēs*, an heir. See **Heir.**

Heresy. (F.—L.—Gk.) M. E. *here-sye.* — O. F. *heresie.* — L. type **hæresia*; for L. *hæresis.* — Gk. αἵρεσις, a taking,

choice, sect, heresy.—Gk. αἱρεῖν, to take.
Der. *heretic*, L. *hæreticus*, Gk. αἱρετικός,
able to choose, heretical (from the same
verb).

Heriot, a tribute paid to the lord of a
manor on the decease of a tenant. (E.)
A. S. *heregeatu*, lit. military apparel;
hence, equipments which, after the death
of a vassal, escheated to his lord; afterwards extended to include horses, &c.—
A. S. *here*, an army; *geatu*, *geatwe*,
apparel, adornment. See **Harry.**

Heritage. (F.—L.) O. F. *heritage*.
Formed, with suffix -*age* (=L. -*āticum*),
from O. F. *heriter*, to inherit.—L. *hērēditāre*, to inherit. See **Heir.**

Hermaphrodite, an animal or plant
of both sexes. (L.—Gk.) L. *hermaphro-
dītus*. — Gk. ἑρμαφρόδιτος; coined from
Ἑρμῆς, Mercury (representing the male)
and Ἀφροδίτη, Venus (representing the
female principle).

Hermeneutic, explanatory. (Gk.)
Gk. ἑρμηνευτικός, skilled in interpreting.—
Gk. ἑρμηνευτής, an interpreter; also ἑρμη-
νεύς, the same. Allied to L. *sermo* (stem
sermōn-); see **Sermon.**

Hermetic. (Gk.) Low L. *hermēticus*,
relating to alchemy; coined from *Hermēs*,
from the notion that the great secrets of
alchemy were discovered by *Hermēs Tris-
megistus.*—Gk. Ἑρμῆς, Mercury. ¶ *Hermetically* was a term in alchemy; a glass
bottle was *hermetically* sealed when the
orifice was fused and then closed against
any admission of air.

Hermit. (F.—L.—Gk.) [M. E. *here-
mite*, directly from L. *herēmīta*.] = F.
hermite.—Late L. *herēmīta*, more commonly *erēmīta.*—Gk. ἐρημίτης, a dweller
in a desert.—Gk. ἐρημία, a desert.—Gk.
ἐρῆμος, deserted, desolate. **Der.** *hermit-
age.*

Hern; see **Heron.**

Hernia. (L.) L. *hernia*, a kind of
rupture.

Hero. (F.—L.—Gk.) M. F. *heroë.*—
L. *hērōem*, acc. of *hērōs*, a hero.—Gk.
ἥρως, a hero, demi-god. **Der.** *hero-ic*,
M. F. *heroïque*, L. *hērōïcus*.

heroine. (F.—L.—Gk.) M.F. *heroïne.*
L. *hērōïnē.*—Gk. ἡρωίνη, fem. of ἥρως, a
hero.

Heron, Hern, a bird. (F.—O.H.G.)
M. E. *heroun*, *heiron*, *hern.*—O. F. *hairon*
(F. *héron*, Span. *airon*, Ital. *aghirone*).—
O. H. G. *heigir*, M. H. G. *heiger*, a heron;

with suffixed -*on* (Ital. -*one*). + Swed.
häger, Icel. *hegri*, Dan. *heire*, a heron.
¶ Distinct from G. *häher*, a jackdaw.

heronshaw, hernshaw, a young
heron; also (by confusion) a heronry.
(F.—O. H. G.) 1. Spenser has *herneshaw*,
a heron; M. E. *heronsewe*, a young heron
(still called *heronsew* in the North). From
O. F. *herounçeau*, later form of *herounçel*,
a young heron (Liber Custumarum, p.
304), dim. of *hairon* (above); cf. *lionceau*,
lioncel, a young lion. The usual form is
F. *héronneau*, O. F. *haironneau*. 2. But
heronshaw, a heronry, is due to a (false)
popular etymology from *heron*, a heron,
and *shaw*, a wood; Cotgrave has ' *hairon
niere*, a heron's neast, a herneshaw, or
shaw of wood wherein herons breed.'

Herring, a fish. (E.) M. E. *heering.*
A. S. *hǣring*. [Sometimes said to be
connected with A. S. *here*, a host, army;
which seems impossible.]+Du. *haring*;
G. *häring*; O. H. G. *hâring* (Kluge).

Hesitate. (L.) From pp. of L.
hæsitāre, to stick fast; intensive form of
hærēre, to stick. + Lithuan. *gaiszti*, to
tarry. (√GHAIS.) Brugm. i. § 627.

Hest, a command. (E.) M. E. *hest*,
the final *t* being excrescent, as in *whils-t*,
amongs-t, &c. A. S. *hǣs*, a command;
Teut. type **haittiz*, f. (>**haissiz*, with *ss*
for *tt*).—A. S. *hātan*, to command; Teut.
type **haitan-*. Cf. Icel. *heit*, a vow, from
heita, to call, promise; O. H. G. *heiz* (G.
geheiss), a command, from *heizan* (G.
heiẞen), to call, bid, command. Cf.
Goth. *haitan*, to call, name. **Der.** *be-hest.*
See **Hight.**

Heteroclite, irregularly inflected. (L.
—Gk.) L. *heteroclitus.*—Gk. ἑτερόκλιτος,
otherwise (i. e. irregularly) inflected.—Gk.
ἕτερο-s, another; -κλιτος, formed from
κλίνειν, to lean (hence, to vary as a case
does); see **Lean** (1).

heterodox, of strange opinion, heretical. (Gk.) Gk. ἑτερο-s, another; δόξ-α,
opinion, from δοκεῖν, to think.

heterogeneous, dissimilar in kind.
(Gk.) Gk. ἑτερο-s, another; γέν-os, kind,
kin, sort; see **Kin.**

Hetman, a captain. (Pol.—G.)
Polish *hetman* (Russ. *ataman'*), a captain (of Cossacks). — G. *hauptmann*, a
captain.—G. *haupt*, head; *mann*, man.

Hew. (E.) M. E. *hewen*. A. S. *hēa-
wan*, to cut.+Du. *houwen*, Icel. *höggva*,
Swed. *hugga*, Dan. *hugge*, G. *hauen*;

Russ. *kovate*, to hammer, forge ; Lith. *kauti*, to fight ; cf. Lith. *kowà*, battle. Brugm. i. § 639. Allied to L. *cūdere*, to beat. Der. *hay*, q. v.

Hexagon, a plane six-sided figure. (L. – Gk.) L. *hexagōnum.* – Gk. ἐξάγωνος, six-cornered. – Gk. ἕξ, six ; γωνία, an angle, from γόνυ, a knee ; see Knee.

hexameter. (L. – Gk.) L. *hexameter.* – Gk. ἐξάμετρος, orig. an adj., i. e. having six measures or feet. – Gk. ἕξ, six ; μέτρον, a measure, metre.

Hey, interj. (E.) M. E. *hei, hay* ; a natural exclamation.+G. and Du. *hei.*

heyday (1), interj. (G. *or* Du.) Also *heyda* (Ben Jonson). Borrowed either from G. *heida,* hey there ! hallo ! or from Du. *hei daar,* hey there ! The G. *da* and Du. *daar* both mean ' there.'

Heyday (2), frolicsome wildness. (E.) The ' *heyday* of youth ' means the ' *high day* of youth.' The spelling *hey* is a preservation of M. E. *hey,* the usual spelling of *high* in the 14th century.

Hiatus, a gap. (L.) L. *hiātus,* a gap ; from pp. of *hiāre,* to gape. Allied to Yawn and Chasm.

Hibernal, wintry. (F. – L.) F. *hibernal.* – L. *hibernālis,* wintry (Vulg.). – L. *hibernus,* wintry ; allied to *hiems,* winter. Also to Gk. χειμερινός, wintry, Gk. χι-ών, snow, Skt. *hi-ma-,* frost. Der. *hibern-ate.*

Hiccough, Hiccup, Hicket, a spasmodic inspiration, with closing of the glottis, causing a slight sound. (E.) The spelling *hiccough* seems to be due to a popular etymology from *cough,* certainly wrong ; no one ever so pronounces the word. Properly *hiccup,* or, in old books *hicket* and *hickock,* which are still better forms. *Hick-et, hick-ock,* are diminutives of *hick* or *hik,* a catch in the voice, imitative of the sound. Cf. ' a *hacking* cough ;' and see Hitch. + M. Du. *huck-up,* ' the hick, or hock,' Hexham ; M. Du. *hick,* ' the hick-hock,' Hexham ; Du. *hik,* the hiccup, *hikken,* to hiccup ; Dan. *hikke,* sb. and vb. ; Swed. *hicka,* sb. and vb. ; Bret. *hîk, hak,* a hiccough ; W. *ig,* a sob, *igio,* to sob. And cf. Chincough.

Hickory, a N. American tree. (Americ. Indian.) Formerly *pohickery* ; from the American-Indian (Virginian) name.

Hidalgo, a Span. nobleman of the lowest class. (Span. – L.) Span. *hidalgo* ; O. Span. *fidalgo,* Port. *fidalgo,* a nobleman ; sometimes written *hijodalgo* (Min-

sheu). Lit. ' son of something,' a son to whom a father has left an estate. – Span. *hijo,* son ; *de,* of ; *algo,* something. – L. *filium,* acc. of *filius,* son (whence O. Span. *figo,* later *hijo*) ; *dē,* of ; *aliquō,* something. (So Körting. The explanation from *filius Italicus* is baseless.)

Hide (1), to cover. (E.) M. E. *hīden, hūden.* A. S. *hȳdan.* + Gk. κεύθειν, to hide ; cf. W. *cuddio* (base **koud*-), to hide. (√KEUDH.)

Hide (2), a skin. (E.) M. E. *hide, hude.* A. S. *hȳd,* the skin. + Du. *huid,* Icel. *hūð,* Dan. Swed. *hud,* O. H. G. *hūt,* G. *haut* ; L. *cutis,* Gk. κύτος, σκῦτος, skin, hide. (√SKEU.) ¶ The roots of *hide* (1) and *hide* (2) are prob. connected.

hide (3), to flog. (E.) Colloquial ; to ' skin ' by flogging. So also Icel. *hȳða,* to flog, from *hūð,* skin.

Hide (4), a measure of land. (E.) Estimated at 120 to 100 acres, and less. (Low L. *hida.*) A. S. *hīd,* a contracted form ; the full form is *hīgid. Hīgid* and *hīwisc* were used in the same sense, to mean enough land for one family or household. They are probably closely allied words, and therefore allied to *hind* (2) ; for *hīwisc* is merely the adj. formed from *hīw-a,* a domestic, one of a household ; see Hind (2). ¶ Not connected with Hide (1).

Hideous, ugly. (F. – L. ?) M. E. *hidous.* – O. F. *hidos, hidus,* later *hideux,* hideous ; the earliest form is *hisdos.* Supposed by some to be from L. *hispidōsus,* roughish ; from *hispidus,* rough, shaggy. (See Körting, § 3363.)

Hie, to hasten. (E.) M. E. *hien, hyen, hizen.* A. S. *hīgian (higian* ?), to strive after, be intent on. Cf. Du. *hijgen,* to pant ; and (perhaps) Skt. *çīgh-ra-,* quick.

Hierarchy. (F. – L. – Gk.) M. F. *hierarchie* ; Cot. – Late L. *hierarchia.* – Gk. ἱεραρχία, power of a ἱεράρχης, a steward or president of sacred rites. – Gk. ἱερ-, for ἱερός, sacred ; and ἄρχειν, to rule. ¶ Milton has *hierarch* = Gk. ἱεράρχης.

hieroglyphic. (L. – Gk.) L. *hieroglyphicus,* symbolical. – Gk. ἱερογλυφικός, relating to sacred writings. – Gk. ἱερό-ς, sacred ; γλύφ-ειν, to hollow out, engrave, incise. See Glyptic.

hierophant, a priest. (Gk.) Gk. ἱεροφάντης, teaching the rites of worship. – Gk. ἱερό-ς, sacred ; φαίνειν, to shew, explain. See Phase.

Higgle, to bargain. (E.) Merely a weakened form of **Haggle.**

High. (E.) M. E. *heigh, hey, hy.* A. S. *hēah, hēh.* **+** Du. *hoog,* Icel. *hār,* Swed. *hög,* Dan. *höi,* Goth. *hauhs,* G. *hoch.* Teut. type **hauhoz.* See **How** (2); and cf. G. *hügel,* a bunch, knob, hillock; also Lith. *kaukaras,* a hill; *kaukas,* a boil, swelling; Skt. *kucha-,* the female breast. (√KEUK.)

highland. (E.) From *high* and *land*; cf. *up-land, low-land.*

Hight, was or is called. (E.) The only passive vb. found in E.; *he hight =* he was named. M. E. *highte;* also *hatte, hette.* A. S. *hātte,* I am called, I was called; pr. and pt. t. passive of A. S. *hātan,* to call. So also Icel. *heiti,* I am named, from *heita,* to call; G. *ich heisse,* I am named, from *heissen,* to call, bid. β. Best illustrated by Goth. *haitan,* to call, 3 p. pres. tense (passive) *haitada;* as in ' Thomas, saei *haitada* Didymus ' = Thomas, who is called Didymus, John xi. 6.

Hilarity, mirth. (F. – L. – Gk.) F. *hilarité.* – L. acc. *hilaritātem;* from *hilaris,* adj., cheerful; also *hilarus.* – Gk. ἱλαρός, cheerful. ¶ *Hilary* Term is so called from the festival of St. Hilary (L. *Hilarius*), who died Jan. 13, 367.

Hilding, a base wretch. (E.) Also *helding;* XVI cent. Prob. from M. E. *helden,* to incline, bend down. Cf. M. E. *heldinge,* a bending aside; Dan. *helding,* bias; A. S. *hylding,* a bending; see **Heel** (2).

Hill. (E.) M. E. *hil, hul.* A. S. *hyll.* **+** M. Du. *hil;* L. *collis,* a hill; Lithuan. *kalnas,* a hill, *kelti,* to raise; Gk. κολωνός, a hill. Brugm. i. § 633. Allied to **Holm** and **Culminate. Der.** *down-hill, up-hill.*

Hilt, sword-handle. (E.) A. S. *helt, hilt.* **+** Icel. *hjalt,* Dan. *hialte,* N. Fries. *heelt,* O. H. G. *helza.* Cf. O. F. *helt,* from Teut. ¶ *Not* allied to *hold;* rather, to *helve.* Cf. Low G. *helft,* ax-handle.

Him; see **He.**

Hin, a liquid measure. (Heb.) Heb. *hīn,* a hin; said to be of Egyptian origin.

Hind (1), female of the stag. (E.) A. S. *hind.* **+** Du. *hinde;* Icel. Dan. and Swed. *hind,* M. H. G. *hinde,* O. H. G. *hinta,* a doe. Perhaps allied to Gk. κεμ-άς, young deer.

Hind (2), a peasant. (E.) The final *d* is excrescent. M. E. *hine,* a domestic.

A. S. **hīna,* a domestic, unauthenticated as a nominative, and really a gen. pl., so that *hīna* stands for *hīna man =* a man of the domestics; cf. *hīna ealdor =* chief of the domestics, a master of a household. *Hīna = hīgna,* gen. pl. of *hīwan,* domestics; cf. *hīwen,* a family, *hīwrēden,* a household; also G. *heirath,* marriage, Goth. *heiwa-frauja,* master of a household. Cf. L. *cīuis,* a citizen. Brugm. i. § 609.

Hind (3), adj., in the rear. (E.) We now say ' *hind* feet '; but the older form is ' *hinder* feet.' We even find M. E. *hynderere* (as if hinder-er). – A. S. *hindan,* adv., at the back of, *hinder,* adv., backwards. **+** Goth. *hindar,* prep., behind; *hindana,* beyond; G. *hinter,* prep., behind, *hinten,* adv., behind; O. H. G. *hintaro,* comp. adj., hinder. We also find Goth. *hindumists,* hindmost. In O. H. G. *hintaro,* the comp. suffix is like the Gk. -τερο-; and in Goth. *hin-dum-ists,* the superl. suffix is like the L. -*tim-*(*us*) in *op-timus,* followed by -*ists =* E. -*est.* Extended from A. S. *hin-,* as in *hin-,* *heon-an,* hence; from *hi-,* base of *he;* see **Hence.**

hinder, vb. (E.) M. E. *hindren.* A. S. *hindrian,* to put behind, keep back. – A. S. *hinder* (above). **+** Icel. *hindra,* G. *hindern;* similarly formed. **Der.** *hindr-ance* (for *hinder-ance*).

hindmost. (E.) From *hind* and *most;* a late formation. The M. E. form was *hinderest;* cf. A. S. *hin-dema,* hindmost, a superl. form with suffix -*dema* (cf. L. *op-timus*). **+** Goth. *hindumists,* hindmost (= *hin-dum-ists,* with double superl. suffix).

Hinge. (E.) M. E. *heng,* that on which the door hangs; from M. E. *hengen,* to hang, a later variant of M. E. *hangien* (A. S. *hangian*), to hang; suggested by A. S. *hengen,* a hanging, or by Icel. *hengja,* to hang. Cf. A. S. *henge-clif,* a steep cliff; and *Stone-henge;* Dan. dial. *hinge, hænge,* a hinge (Dan. *hængsel*). For the sound, cf. *singe, swinge.* See **Hang.+** M. Du. *henge, hengene,* a hinge.

Hint, a slight allusion. (E.) *Hint* is apparently ' a thing taken ' or caught up; cf. Lowl. Sc. *hint,* an opportunity; *in a hint,* in a moment; *hint,* to lay hold of. From M. E. *henten,* to seize. – A. S. *hentan,* to seize. Allied to **Hunt,** and to Goth. *fra-hinthan,* to seize.

Hip (1), the haunch. (E.) M. E. *hipe, hupe.* A. S. *hype.* **+** Du. *heup,* Icel. *huppr,*

Dan. *hofte,* Swed. *höft,* Goth. *hups,* G. *hüfte,* O. H. G. *huf.* Perhaps allied to Gk. *κύβος,* the hollow near the hips of cattle.

Hip (2), **Hep,** fruit of the dog-rose. (E.) M. E. *hepe.* A. S. *hēope,* a hip; *hēopbrēmel,* a hip-bramble.╋O. Sax. *hiopo,* M. H. G. *hiefe,* O. H. G. *hiufo,* a bramble-bush.

Hippish. (Gk.) Equivalent to *hypochondriacal,* adj. of Hypochondria, q. v. Hence *hippish* = *hyp-ish.* The contraction *hipped* (= *hyp'd*) was prob. suggested by *hipped,* lamed in the hip (an older word).

Hippopotamus. (L.—Gk.) L. *hippopotamus.* — Gk. ἱπποπόταμος, the river-horse of Egypt. — Gk. ἵππο-s, horse; ποταμό-s, river. Gk. ἵππος is cognate with L. *equus;* see Equine.

Hire, sb. (E.) M. E. *hire.* A. S. *hȳr,* hire, wages.╋Du. *huur,* Swed. *hyra,* Dan. *hyre,* prov. G. *heuer,* hire, rent; Low G. *hüren,* to hire. Teut. type *hūr-jā,* f.

Hirsute. (L.) L. *hirsūtus,* bristly, rough. Cf. L. *horrēre,* to bristle; see Horrid.

His ; see He.

Hiss. (E.) M. E. *hissen, hisshen.* ╋ M. Du. *hisschen;* Low G. *hissen,* to say *hiss !* in setting on dogs; Gascon *hissa,* to hiss (Moncaut). An imitative word; like G. *zischen,* to hiss.

hist, an interjection enjoining silence. (E.) Also *ist, 'st.* Cf. Dan. *hys,* silence ! *hysse,* to hush. Milton has *hist* = summon silently, Il Pens. 55.

Histology, the science treating of the minute structure of tissues of plants, &c. (Gk.) Gk. ἱστό-s, a web (hence, tissue); -λογια, discourse, from λέγειν, to speak. Gk. ἱστό-s (also a mast) is allied to ἵστημι, to set, place. (√STA.)

History. (L.—Gk.) M. E. *historie.* — L. *historia.* — Gk. ἱστορία, a learning by enquiry, information. — Gk. ἱστορ-, stem of ἵστωρ, ἴστωρ, knowing; for *ἴδ-τωρ.* — Gk. Ϝιδ-, base of εἰδέναι, to know. (√WEID.) Allied to Wit. Doublet, *story,* q. v.

Histrionical, relating to the stage. (L.) From L. *histriōnicus,* relating to an actor. — L. *histriōn-,* stem of *histrio,* an actor.

Hit, to light upon, strike, attain to. (Scand.) M. E. *hitten.* — Icel. *hitta,* to hit upon; Dan. *hitte;* Swed. *hitta,* to find.

Hitch, to move by jerks, catch slightly. (E.) M. E. *hicchen,* to move, remove. Cf. Lowl. Sc. *hatch, hotch,* to move by jerks; *hitch,* a motion by a jerk; prov. E. *hike,* to toss, *hikey,* a swing. It describes a jerky movement; cf. Low G. and E. Fries. *hikken,* to peck. ¶ Not allied to *hook.*

Hithe, Hythe, a small haven. (E.) M. E. *hithe.* A. S. *hȳð,* a haven.

Hither. (E.) M. E. *hider, hither.* A. S. *hider.* From the base of *he,* with Idg. suffix -*t*(*e*)*r.* — So also Icel. *hēðra,* O. Icel. *hiðra,* Goth. *hidrē,* L. *citrā.*

Hive, a house for bees. (E.) A. S. *hȳf,* fem.; Teut. type *hūfiz.*╋Du. *huif,* a hive (see Franck); Dan. dial. *hyve;* cf. L. *cūpa,* a tub, cup. Allied to Cupola.

Ho, Hoa, a call to excite attention. (E.) A natural exclamation. Cf. Icel. *hō!* ho! *hōa,* to shout out ho !

Hoar, white. (E.) M. E. *hoor.* A. S. *hār.*╋Icel. *hārr,* hoar; G. *hehr,* exalted, O. H. G. *hēr,* proud, lofty, orig. ' reverend.' Teut. type **hairoz;* lit. ' shining,' hence, white := **hai-roz.* The base **hai-* occurs in Goth. *hai-s,* a torch; G. *hei-ter,* orig. ' bright,' Icel. *hei-ð,* brightness; cf. Skt. *kētu*(*s*), a sign, a meteor (Kluge).

Hoard, a store. (E.) A. S. *hord.*╋ Icel. *hodd,* G. *hort,* Goth. *huzd.* Teut. type **huzdo-,* due to Idg. **kudh-dho-,* ' a thing hidden ;' from the weak grade of √KEUDH, as in Gk. κεύθ-ειν, A. S. *hȳdan;* see Hide (1). Brugm. i. § 699.

Hoarding, a kind of fence. (F.—Du.; or Du.) Not old. Either from Du. *horde,* a hurdle, or from M. F. *hourd,* a scaffold (Cot., index), which is the same word (borrowed). See Hurdle.

Hoarhound, Horehound, a plant. (E.) The true *hoarhound* is the white, *Marrubium vulgare.* The final *d* is excrescent. M. E. *hor*(*e*)*houne.* A. S. *hārhūne,* also called simply *hūne.* — A. S. *hār,* hoar; *hūne,* hoarhound, the origin of which is unknown.

Hoarse, having a rough, harsh voice. (E.) The *r* is intrusive, but sometimes occurs in M. E. *hors,* also spelt *hoos,* hoarse. A. S. *hās,* hoarse. ╋ Dan. *hæs,* Swed. *hes,* Du. *heesch,* G. *heiser.* ¶ Icel. *hāss* seems distinct (Noreen).

Hoary ; see Hoar.

Hoax. (Low L.) Short for *hocus,* i. e. to juggle, cheat. See Hocus-pocus.

Hob (1), **Hub,** the nave of a wheel,

part of a grate. (E.) **The true sense is** 'projection'; the *hob* of a fire-place was orig. 'a boss or mass of clay behind the fire-place'; N. E. D.   E. Fries. *hobbe*, a rough tump of grassy land rising out of water; *hubbel*, a projection. **+** Du. *hobbel*, a knob; G. *hübel*, O. H. G. *hubel*, a hillock. Cf. Lith. *kup-stas*, a tump of grass; Du. *heuvel*, a hill; A.S. *hofer*, a hump. **Der.** *hob-nail*, a nail with a projecting head.

Hob (2), a clown, rustic, a fairy. (F. —O. H. G.) 'Elves, *hobs*, and fairies;' Beaumont and Fletcher, Mons. Thomas, iv. 6. *Hob* was a common personal name, a corruption of *Robin* (like *Hodge* from *Roger*). The name *Robin* is F., and is a form of *Robert*, a name of O. H. G. origin. **Der.** *hob-goblin*; see **Goblin.**

Hobble, to limp. (E.) M. E. *hobelen*. Equivalent to *hopp-le*; frequentative of *hop*.**+**Du. *hobbelen*; prov. G. *hoppeln*.

Hobbledehoy, a lad approaching manhood. (E.) Of unknown origin. Prob. an invention, perhaps for *hobbledy*, founded on *hobble* (above), with the addition of *hoy*, an unmeaning suffix. The Scottish *hoy* means 'shout,' both as sb. and vb.

Hobby (1), **Hobby-horse,** a toy like a horse, ambling nag, a favourite pursuit. (F.—O. H. G.) Corruption of M. E. *hobin*, a nag [whence F. *hobin*, 'a hobby;' Cot.]. *Hobin* is a variant of *Robin*; see Hob (2). Cf. *Dobbin*, a name for a horse.

Hobby (2), a small falcon. (F. — O. Low G.) M. E. *hobi*, *hoby*. From O. F. *hobet*, a hobby; allied to F. *hobreau* (=*hob-er-el*), 'the hawke tearmed a hobby;' Cot. — F. *hober*, to stir, move about.—M. Du. *hobben*, to toss, move up and down. Cf. Hop (1).

Hobgoblin; see Hob (2).

Hobnail; see Hob (1).

Hobnob, Habnab, with free leave, at random. (E.) Compounded of *hab* and *nab*, to have or not to have, hence applied to taking a thing or leaving it, implying free choice, and hence a familiar invitation to drink, as in 'to *hob-nob* together.' *Hab* is from A. S. *habban*, to have; *nab* is from A. S. *nabban*, for *ne hæbban*, not to have; see Have. Cf. *willy-nilly*.

Hock (1); see Hough.

Hock (2), a wine. (G.) From *Hochheim*, the name of a place in Germany, on the

river Main, whence the wine comes. It means 'high home.'

Hockey, a game. (E.)   Also called *hawkey*; because played with a *hooked* stick so called. See N. E. D.

Hocus-pocus, a juggler's trick, a juggler. (Low L.) As far as it can be said to belong to any language, it is a sort of Latin, having the L. termination *-us*. But it is merely an invented term, used by a juggler (temp. James I) in performing tricks; see Todd's Johnson and N. E. D. Cf. L. *iocus*, a game. **Der.** *hocus*, a juggler, a trick; *hocus*, vb., to trick, to *hoax*.

Hod a kind of trough for carrying bricks. (F.) Modified from M. E. *hotte*, F. *hotte*, a basket, dosser; influenced by *hod*, a prov. E. form of *hold*; see Hold. In Linc. and York. *hod* means 'hold' or 'receptacle'; as in (Whitby) *powder-hod*, powder-flask; *cannle-hod*, candlestick.

Hodge-podge; see Hotchpot.

Hoe. (F. — G.) Formerly *howe*. — F. *houe*, a hoe; Norman dial. *hoe*. — O. H. G. *houwa* (G. *haue*), a hoe, lit. a hewer. — O. H. G. *houwan*, to hew; see Hew.

Hog. (E.) M. E. *hogge*, 'maialis, est enim porcus carens testiculis;' Cathol. Anglic. p. 187. Cf. *hog-sheep*, one clipped the first year. Origin uncertain; prob. from an A. S. **hocg*; perhaps seen in *Hocges-tūn*, Cod. Dipl. Moisy gives Norman dial. *hogge*, a six-months' lamb, a pig; and *hogastre*, a two-year-old sheep; but these are prob. from E. ¶ Not borrowed from Corn. *hoch*, W. *hwch*, a sow; for which see Sow.

Hogshead. (E.) Of E. origin; for *hog's head*; but the reason for the name is uncertain. Hence M. Du. *hockshoot*, *okshoofd*, *oxhoofd*, a hogshead; M. Dan. *hogshoved*; also Dan. *oxhoved*, Swed. *ox-hufvud*, a hogshead, but made to seem to mean 'ox-head.'

Hoiden, Hoyden, a romping girl. (M. Du.) Formerly applied to males, and meaning a rustic.—M. Du. *heyden* (Du. *heiden*), a heathen; also, a gipsy. See Heathen. ¶ The W. *hoeden* is borrowed from English.

Hoist, to heave. (M. Du.) The final *t* is due to the pp. *hoist*, used for *hoised*. The verb is really *hoise*; spelt *hyce* in Palsgrave. (Cf. *graft* for *graff*.) — M. Du. *hyssen*, Du. *hijsschen*, to hoise (*y* sounded as E. long *i*); cf. Dan. *heise*, *hisse*; Swed.

hissa, to hoist (cf. F. *hisser*, from Teut.).
¶ *Not* allied to F. *hausser*, to elevate.

Hold (1), to keep. (E.) O. Merc.
haldan; A. S. *healdan*.+Du. *houden*, Icel.
halda, Swed. *hålla*, Dan. *holde*, Goth.
haldan, G. *halten*. Teut. type **haldan-* ;
pt. t. **he-hald*. **Der.** *hold*, sb. ; also *behold*, with prefix *be-* (E. *by*) ; *up-hold*.

Hold (2), the cavity of a ship. (Du.)
For *hole*, with excrescent *d*, due to
confusion with the verb to *hold*. — Du.
hol, a hole, cave, esp. used of the hold of
a ship (Sewel). See below.

Hole. (E.) M. E. *hole*, *hol*. A. S. *hol*,
a cave. + Du. *hol*, Icel. *hol*, Dan. *hul*,
Swed. *hål*. Teut. type **hulom*, n.; orig.
neut. of **huloz*, adj., hollow, as in A. S.
hol, Du. *hol*, Icel. *holr*, Dan. *huul*, G.
hohl. Cf. Goth. *us-hulōn*, to hollow out,
hul-undi, a cave. β. Prob. A. S. *hol* is
from *hol-*, weak grade of str. vb. *helan*, to
cover; see **Hell**. Not allied to Gk.
κοῖλος, hollow.

Holibut; see Halibut.

Holiday, a festival. (E.) For *holy day*.
See **Holy**.

Holla, Hallo, stop! wait! (F.) Not
the same word as *halloo*, to shout; but
differently used in old authors. See Oth.
i. 2. 56; As You Like It, iii. 2. 257. — F.
holà, ' an interjection, hoe there ;' Cot. —
F. *ho*, interj. ; and *là*, there (= L. *illāc*).
¶ The form *hallo* is due to a confusion
with *halloo*.

Holland, Dutch linen. (Du.) From
Holland, the name of the province. So
also *hollands*, spirits from Holland.

Hollow. (E.) M. E. *holwe*, adj. A. S.
holh, sb., a hollow place, also spelt *holg*.
Cf. O. H. G. *huliwa*, a pool, puddle.
Perhaps extended from A. S. *hol*, hollow ;
see **Hole**.

Holly. (E.) M. E. *holin* ; so that an
n has been dropped. A. S. *holen*, *holegn*,
holly.+W. *celyn*, Corn. *celin*, Bret. *kelen*,
Gael. *cuilionn*, Irish *cuileann*, holly ; Idg.
type **kolenno-*. Cf. also Du. *hulst*, G.
hülst, holly, O. H. G. *hulis* (whence F.
houx).

Hollyhock, a kind of mallow. (E.)
M. E. *holihoc*, i. e. holy hock. Compounded of *holy*, and A. S. *hoc*, ' mallow.'
[We also find W. *hocys*, mallows, *hocys
bendigaid*, hollyhock, lit. ' blessed mallow,'
where *bendigaid* = L. *benedictus*. W. *hocys*
is from A. S. *hoccas*, pl. of *hoc*.] In A. S.
the mallow is also called *hoclēaf*.

Holm, an islet in a river, flat land by a
river. (Scand.) M. E. *holm*. — Icel. *hōlmr*,
hōlmi, *holmr*, an islet, flat meadow ; Dan.
holm, Swed. *holme* ; whence G. *holm*,
island. Cf. A. S. *holm*, billow, sea ; L.
culmen, hill-top. Allied to **Hill** and
Culminate.

Holm-oak, the evergreen oak. (E.)
Here *holm* is a corruption of M. E. *holin*,
a holly. ' *Holme*, or holy [holly];'
Prompt. Parv. ; and see Way's note. The
Quercus ilex, an evergreen plant ; the
leaves of which resemble those of holly.

Holocaust. (L. – Gk.) L. *holocaus-
tum*, Gen. xxii. 8. — Gk. ὁλόκαυστον, a
sacrifice burnt whole ; neut. of ὁλόκαυστος,
burnt whole. — Gk. ὅλο-ς, whole ; and
καίειν, to burn. See **Caustic**.

Holster, a leathern case for a pistol.
(Du. – O. H. G.) Du. *holster* ; Low G.
holster, a pistol-case. – G. *holfter*, a pistol-
case (with change of *ft* to *st*) ; M. H. G.
hulfter, a quiver ; from O. H. G. *hulft*, a
cover, case (Kluge). Cf. M. Dan. *holfte*,
a gun-case. ¶ So Franck ; who rejects
the connection with Icel. *hulstr*, A. S.
heolster.

Holt, a wood. (E.) M. E. and A. S.
holt. + Du. *hout*, M. Du. *holt* ; Icel. *holt*,
G. *holz*. Teut. stem **hulto-*, Idg. stem
*kl̥do-. Allied to O. Irish *caill*, *coill*
(for **caild*), a wood ; W. *celli*, a grove,
Russ. *kolóda*, a log, Gk. κλάδος, a twig.

Holy, sacred. (E.) [This word is equivalent to the M. E. *hool*, whole, with suffix
-y; and therefore closely allied to *whole*.]
M. E. *holi*, *holy*. A. S. *hālig*, holy.+Du.
heilig, holy, Icel. *heilagr*, *helgr*, Dan.
hellig, Swed. *helig*, G. *heilig*; Goth.
hailag, neut. (in an inscription). Teut.
type **hailagoz*, a deriv. of **hailoz* (A. S.
hāl), whole, or of **hailoz-* or **hailiz-*, sb.,
good omen. Cf. Irish *cēl*, W. *coel*, an
omen. See **Whole**.

Homage. (F. – L.) M. E. *homage*. –
O. F. *homage*, the service of a vassal to his
lord. – Late L. *homāticum*, *homināticum*,
the service of a vassal or man. – L. *hom-o*
(stem *homin-*), a man. See **Human**.

Home. (E.) M. E. *hoom*. A. S. *hām*.
+Du. *heim*, *heem* ; Icel. *heimr*, an abode;
Dan. *hiem*, Swed. *hem*, G. *heim* ; Goth.
haims, a village. Teut. base **haimo-*,
*haimi- ; cf. Lithuan. *kēmas*, a village ;
and perhaps Skt. *kshēma-*, safety, from
kshi, to dwell.

Homer, a large measure. (Heb.) Heb.

khōmer, a homer, also a heap (with initial *cheth*). — Heb. root *khāmar*, to surge up.

Homicide, man-slaughter, also a man-slayer. (F. — L.) F. *homicide*, meaning (1) manslaughter, from L. *homicīdium*; (2) a man-killer, from L. *homicīda.* — L. *hom-o*, a man; *-cīdium*, a killing, or *-cīda*, a slayer, from *cædere*, to kill.

Homily. (L. — Gk.) L. *homīlia.* — Gk. ὁμιλία, a living together; also converse, instruction, homily. — Gk. ὅμιλος, a throng, concourse. — Gk. ὁμ-ός, like, same, together, cognate with E. **Same**; and (possibly) ἴλη, εἴλη, a crowd, from εἴλειν, to compress, shut in.

Hominy, maize prepared for food. (W. Indian.) W. Indian *auhúminea*, parched corn (Webster); Trumbull gives *appumineónash*, with the same sense.

Hommock; see Hummock.

Homœopathy. (Gk.) Englished from Gk. ὁμοιοπάθεια, likeness in feeling or condition. — Gk. ὅμοιο-s, like; παθ-εῖν, aorist infin. of πάσχειν, to suffer. See **Same** and **Pathos.**

Homogeneous, of the same kind throughout. (Gk.) Englished from Gk. ὁμογεν-ής, of the same race. — Gk. ὁμό-s, same (cognate with E. **Same**), and γέν-os, a race (cognate with E. **Kin**). So also *homo-logous*, corresponding, from λόγος, a saying, λέγειν, to say.

Homonymous, like in sound, but differing in sense. (L. — Gk.) L. *homōnymus*; with suffix *-ous.* — Gk. ὁμώνυμος, having the same name. — Gk. ὁμό-s, same; ὄνυμα, ὄνομα, name. See **Same** and **Name.** Der. *homonym*, F. *homonyme*.

Hone. (E.) A. S. *hān*, a stone (with change from *ā* to long *o*, as in *bān*, bone); Birch, ii. 458. **+** Icel. *hein*, Swed. *hen*. Teut. stem *hainā*, f. Cf. Skt. *çi*, to sharpen. Brugm. i. § 200.

Honest. (F. — L.) O. F. *honeste* (F. *honnête*). — L. *honestus*, honourable ; for *hones-tus*, related to *honos*, honour See Honour.

Honey. (E.) M. E. *huni*. A. S. *hunig.* **+**Du. *honig*, Icel. *hunang*, Dan. *honning*, Swed. *honing*, G. *honig*.

honeycomb. (E.) A. S. *hunigcamb*, a honey-comb ; where *comb* is the usual E. word, though the likeness to a *comb* is rather fanciful.

honeymoon. (E.) Wedded love was compared to the full moon, that soon wanes ; Huloet, 1522. See N. E. D.

honeysuckle. (E.) Lye gives A. S. *hunigsucle*, unauthorised ; but we find A. S. *hunigsūce*, *hunigsūge*, privet, similarly named. From A. S. *sūcan*, to suck.

Honour. (F. — L.) A. F. *honur.* — L. *honōrem*, acc. of *honor*, *honos*, honour.

Hood, covering. (E.) A. S. *hōd.* **+**Du. *hoed*, G. *hut*, O. H. G. *huot*, *hōt*, a hat. Allied to **Heed** and **Hat.**

-hood, -head, suffix. (E.) A. S. *hād*, state, quality ; cognate with Goth. *haidus*, manner, way. Cf. Skt. *kētu(s)*, a sign by which a thing may be recognised ; from *kit*, to perceive. Brugm. ii. § 104.

Hoodwink. (E.) To make one *wink* or close his eyes, by covering him with a *hood.*

Hoof. (E.) M. E. *hoof*, *huf*; pl. *hoves.* A. S. *hōf.* **+**Du. *hoef*, Icel. *hōfr*, Dan. *hov*, Swed. *hof*, G. *huf.* Teut. type *hōfoz*, m. Allied to Russ. *kopuito*, Skt. *capha*, hoof.

Hook. (E.) M. E. *hok*. A. S. *hōc.*+ Du. *hoek* ; also (with *a*-grade) Du. *haak*, Icel. *haki*, Dan. *hage*, Swed. *hake*, A. S. *haca*, a hook. Allied to **Hake.**

Hookah, Hooka. (Arab.) Arab. *huqqa(t)*, a vase, water-pipe for smoking.

Hoop (1), a pliant strip of wood or other material bent into a band. (E.) M. E. *hoop*, *hope*. A. S. *hōp.* **+**Du. *hoep*; E. and N. Fries. and O. Fries. *hōp*.

Hoop (2), **Whoop,** to call out, shout. (F.) M. E. *houpen*, to shout. — O. F. *houper*, 'to hoop unto ;' Cot. Of imitative origin ; from *houp!* interj. ; cf. Goth. *hwōpan*, to boast.

hooping-cough, a cough accompanied by a *hoop* or convulsive noisy catch in the breath. (Formerly called *chin-cough*.)

Hoopoe, the name of a bird. (F. — L.) Formerly *houpe*, *hoope.* — F. *huppe*, apparently confused with O. F. *pupu*, another form of the same word. — L. *upupa*, a hoopoe ; the E. initial *h* is due to the F. *huppe.* **+** Gk. ἔποψ, a hoopoe. Of imitative origin. ¶ The F. *huppe*, a tuft of feathers, is from *huppe*, a hoopoe (from its tufted head) ; not vice versâ.

Hoot. (Scand.) M. E. *houten.* — O. Swed. *huta*, to hoot. — Swed. *hut!* interj. begone ! of onomatopoetic origin. So also Norm. dial. *houter*, to hoot; W. *hwt!* Irish *ut!* expressions of dislike. See Hue (2).

Hop (1), to leap on one leg. (E.) M. E. *hoppen*, *huppen.* A. S. *hoppian*, to leap,

245

dance. **+** Du. *hoppen*, Icel. *hoppa*, Swed. *hoppa*, Dan. *hoppe*, G. *hüpfen*. Brugm. i. § 421 (7). **Der.** *hopp-er* (of a mill); *hopp-le*, a fetter for horses ; *hop-scotch*, a game in which children *hop* over *scotches*, i. e. lines scored on the ground. Cf. **Hobble.**

Hop (2), a plant. (Du.) Introduced from the Netherlands ; XV cent. **–** M. Du. *hoppe* (Du. *hop*), hop. **+** G. *hopfen*, hop. We also find A. S. *hymele*, Icel. *humall*, Swed. Dan. *humle*, M. Du. *hommel* (whence Late L. *humulus*) ; also F. *houblon*, which can hardly be allied words.

Hope (1), expectation. (E.) M. E. *hope*. A. S. *hopa*, hope; whence *hopian*, to hope. **+** Du. *hoop*, Dan. *haab*, Swed. *hopp*, M. H. G. *hoffe*, sb.; whence Du. *hopen*, Dan. *haabe*, Swed. *hoppas*, G. *hoffen*, to hope.

Hope (2), a troop. (Du.) Only in the phr. ' a forlorn hope,' i. e. troop. **–** Du. *verloren hoop* = lost band, where *hoop* = E. *heap*; see **Heap.** ' Een *hoop krijgs-volck*, a troupe or band of souldiers,' Hexham ; *verloren hoop* (Kilian). (Now obsolete in Dutch.)

Horde, a wandering tribe. (F. **–** Turk. **–** Tatar.) F. *horde*. **–** Turk. *ordū*, a camp. **–** Tatar *ūrdū*, a royal camp, horde of Tatars (Tartars) ; see Pavet de Courteille, p. 54.

Hordock; see Hardock.

Horehound; see Hoarhound.

Horizon. (F. **–** L. **–** Gk.) F. *horizon*. **–** L. *horīzōn* (stem *horīzont-*). **–** Gk. ὁρίζων, the bounding or limiting circle ; orig. pres. pt. of ὁρίζειν, to limit. **–** Gk. ὅρος, a boundary. **Der.** *horizont-al*.

Horn. (E.) A. S. *horn*. **+** Icel. Dan. Swed. G. *horn* ; Du. *horen*, Goth. *haurn* ; W. Gael. Irish *corn*, L. *cornu*. Allied to Gk. κέρ-ας, a horn, and to **Hart.**

Hornblende, a mineral. (G.) A *blende* named from its horn-like cleavage. G. *hornblende*. **–** G. *horn*, horn ; *blende*, a ' deceitful ' mineral, yielding little ore ; from *blenden*, to deceive, blind, dazzle ; from *blind*, blind.

Hornet, a kind of large wasp. (E.) So called from its resounding hum. A. S. *hyrnet*, a hornet. **–** A. S. *horn*, a horn, to which the word was later conformed. Cf. O. Sax. *horno-bero*, a hornet, lit. ' horn-bearer ;' A. S. *horn-bora*, a trumpeter. Hexham has M. Du. *horener*, *hornte*, a hornet, *horentoren*, a wasp, from *horen*, a

horn. ¶ It is strange that G. *hornisse*, O. H. G. *hornaz* (without vowel-change) is referred to a Teut. type **hurz-natoz* (cf. Du. *horz-elen*, to buzz), allied to L. *crābro* (for **cras-ro*), a hornet, Lith. *szirszū* (gen. *szirsz-ens*), a hornet; see Brugm. i. § 626.

Horologe, a clock. (F. **–** L. **–** Gk.) O. F. *horologe* (later *horloge*). **–** L. *hōrologium*. **–** Gk. ὡρολόγιον, a sun-dial, water-clock. **–** Gk. ὡρο-, for ὥρα, hour ; -λογιον, teller, from λέγειν, to tell.

horoscope. (F. **–** L. **–** Gk.) F. *horoscope*. **–** L. *hōroscopus*, a horoscope, from *hōroscopus*, adj., observing the hour. **–** Gk. ὡροσκόπος, observing the hour (also as sb.). **–** Gk. ὡρο-, for ὥρα, hour ; σκοπεῖν, to consider, allied to σκέπτομαι, I consider ; see **Sceptic.**

Horrible. (F. **–** L.) O. F. *horrible*. **–** L. *horribilis*, dreadful. **–** L. *horrēre*, to dread (below).

horrid. (L.) Spenser has it in the sense of ' rough'; F. Q. i. 7. 31. **–** L. *horridus*, rough, bristly. **–** L. *horrēre* (for **hors-ēre*), to bristle ; also to dread, with reference to the bristling of the hair through terror. Cf. Skt. *hṛsh*, to bristle, esp. as a token of fear or of pleasure.

horrify. (L.) Coined, by analogy with F. words in *-fy*, from L. *horrificāre*, to cause terror. **–** L. *horri-*, for *horrēre*, to dread ; *-ficāre*, for *facere*, to make.

horror, dread. (L.) L. *horror*. **–** L. *horrēre*, to dread (above).

Horse. (E.) M. E. *hors*. **–** A. S. *hors*, pl. *hors*, it being a neut. sb. **+** Icel. *hross*, *hors*, Du. *ros*, G. *ross*, O. H. G. *hros*. Prob. ' a runner ;' cf. L. *currere* (sup. *curs-um*), to run. Brugm. i. § 516, ii. § 662.

Hortatory, full of encouragement. (L.) As if from L. **hortātōrius*, coined from *hortātor*, an encourager. **–** L. *hortārī*, to encourage ; prob. allied to L. *horior*, I urge, and to E. **Yearn.**

Horticulture, gardening. (L.) Coined from L. *hortī*, gen. case of *hortus*, a garden ; *cultūra*, cultivation ; see **Culture** L. *hortus* is allied to E. *yard* (1).

Hosanna, an expression of praise. (Gk. **–** Heb.) Gk. ὡσαννά. **–** Heb. *hōshī'-āh nnā*, save, we pray. **–** Heb. *hōshī'a*, save (from *yāsha'*) ; and *nā*, a particle signifying entreaty.

Hose. (E.) M. E. *hose*, pl. *hosen*. A.S. *hosa*, pl. *hosan*, hose, stockings. **+** Du. *hoos*, Icel. *hosa*, Dan. *hose*, G. *hose* (whence

O. F. *hose*). **Der.** *hos-i-er* (cf. *bow-yer*, *law-yer*).

Hospice. (F. – L.) F. *hospice.* – L. *hospitium*, a house for guests. – L. *hospiti-*, decl. stem of *hospes*, a host; see **host** (1).

hospitable. (F. – L.) M. F. *hospitable.* From Late L. *hospitāre*, to receive as a guest. – L. *hospit-*, stem of *hospes*, a host.

hospital. (F. – L.) M. E. *hospital.* – O. F. *hospital.* – Late L. *hospitāle*, a large house, a sing. formed from L. pl. *hospitālia*, apartments for strangers. – L. *hospit-*, stem of *hospes* (below).

host (1), one who entertains guests. (F. – L.) M. E. *host, hoste.* – O. F. *hoste.* Cf. Port. *hospede*, a host, guest. – L. *hospitem*, acc. of *hospes*, (1) a host, (2) a guest. ¶ Some make L. *hospit-* short for **hostipot-*, where *hosti-* is the decl. stem of *hostis*, a stranger, enemy, see **Host** (2); and *-pot-* means 'lord,' being allied to L. *potens*, powerful; cf. Skt. *pati-*, a master, governor, lord; see **Possible.** Thus *hospes = *hostipotis*, guest-master, a master of a house who receives guests. Cf. Russ. *gospode*, the Lord, *gospodare*, a governor, master, from *goste*, a guest, and *-pode* (= Skt. *pati-*), lord. Brugm. i. §§ 158, 240. **Der.** *host-ess*, from M. F. *hostesse*, 'an hostesse,' Cot.; F. *hôtesse*.

Host (2), an army. (F. – L.) The orig. sense is 'enemy' or 'foreigner.' M. E. *host, ost.* – O. F. *host*, a host, army. – L. *hostem*, acc. of *hostis*, an enemy (orig. a stranger, a guest); hence, a hostile army, a host. **+** Russ. *goste*, a guest, stranger; A. S. *gæst*; see **Guest.** **Doublet,** *guest.*

Host (3), the consecrated bread of the eucharist. (L.) L. *hostia*, a victim in a sacrifice; O. Lat. *fostia*, lit. 'that which is slain.' – L. *hostīre*, O. Lat. **fostīre*, to strike.

Hostage. (F. – L.) O. F. *hostage*, a hostage (F. *otage*, Ital. *ostaggio*, O. Prov. *ostatje*). We also find Ital. *statico*, a hostage; and (according to Diez), both *ostaggio* and *statico* answer to a Late L. form **obsidāticus*, from Late L. *obsidātus*, the condition of a hostage. – L. *obsid-*, stem of *obses*, a hostage, one who remains behind with the enemy. – L. *obsidēre*, to stay. – L. *ob*, at, on, near; *sedēre*, to sit. ¶ Another explanation is from Late L. **hospitāticum*, a receiving as a guest; from L. *hospit-*, for *hospes*, a host; see

host (1). So Körting. The words may have been confused.

Hostel, an inn. (F. – L.) O. F. *hostel.* – Late L. *hospitāle*; see **hospital.**

hostler, ostler. (F. – L.) Orig. the innkeeper himself, and so named from his *hostel* (above).

Hot. (E.) M. E. *hoot* (with long *o*). A. S. *hāt*, hot. **+** Du. *heet*, Icel. *heitr*, Swed. *het*, Dan. *hed*, G. *heiss.* Teut. type **haitoz.* Allied to Icel. *hiti*, G. *hitze*, heat, Goth. *heito*, fever; and cf. Goth. *hais*, a torch, Lithuan. *kaitra*, heat. **Der.** *heat.*

Hotch-pot, Hodgepodge. (F. – Du.) *Hodgepodge* is a corruption of *hotchpot*, a confused medley. – F. *hochepot*, a medley. – F. *hocher*, to shake; and *pot*, pot (see Cot.). Imitated or borrowed from M. Du. *hutspot* (lit. shake-pot), hodgepodge, beef or mutton cut into small pieces. – M. Du. *hutsen, hotsen*, to shake; *pot*, a pot. Cf. E. Fries. *hotjen*, to shake. See **Hustle** and **Pot.**

Hotel, an inn. (F. – L.) Mod. F. *hôtel*, the same as O. F. *hostel*; see **Hostel.**

Hottentot, a native of the Cape of Good Hope. (Du.) A name given them by the Dutch, in derision of their speech, which sounded like stammering, or a repetition of the syllables *hot* and *tot.* *En* is Dutch for 'and'; hence Du. *hot en tot* = 'hot' and 'tot.' Cf. M. Du. *hateren*, to stammer, Du. *tateren*, to stammer.

Houdah, Howdah, a seat fixed on an elephant's back. (Hind. – Arab.) Hind. *haudah.* – Arab. *hawdaj*, a litter carried by a camel, a seat placed on an elephant's back.

Hough, Hock, the joint in the hindleg of an animal, between knee and fetlock; in man, the back part of the knee-joint. (E.) Now usually *hock*; formerly *hough.* M. E. *hough.* A. S. *hōh*, the heel; Teut. type **hanhoz.* **+** Icel. *hā-*, the hock, in *hā-sin*, hock-sinew. See **Heel.** *Hock* is a later form; and prob. arose from the comp. 'hough-sinew,' spelt *hōhsinu* in A. S., and *hōxene, hōxne* in O. Fries. (A. S. *hs* > *x*). See G. *hechse* (in Kluge); and see **Hox. Der.** *hough*, vb.; *hox*, q. v.

Hound, a dog. (E.) A. S. *hund.* **+** Du. *hond*, Icel. *hundr*, Dan. Swed. G. *hund*, Goth. *hunds.* Teut. type **hun-doz*, m. Allied to L. *canis*, Gk. κύων (gen. κυνός), Skt. *çvan-*, a dog; also to Irish *cu*,

W. *ci*, a dog, Russ. *suka*, a bitch, Lith. *szŭ* (stem *szun-*), a dog. Brugm. i. § 609. The final *-d* may have been suggested by confusion with Teut. **henthan-*, to catch. See Hunt.

Hour. (F.–L.–Gk.) O. F. *hore* (F. *heure*).–L. *hōra*. – Gk. ὥρα, a season, hour. Allied to **Year**.

Houri, a nymph of Paradise. (Pers.–Arab.) Pers. *ḥūrī*, one virgin of Paradise, *ḥūrā*, *ḥūr*, a virgin of Paradise, black-eyed nymph. From Arab. *ḥawrā*, fem. of *aḥwar*, having fine black eyes.

House. (E.) M. E. *hous*. A. S. *hūs*. +Du. *huis*, Icel. *hūs*, Dan. *huus*, Swed. *hus*, Goth. *hūs*, G. *haus*. Teut. type **hūsom*, n. Possibly allied to **Hut**, **Hoard**; from √KEUDH, to hide. See Hoard, Hide (1). Brugm. i. § 796.

Housel, the eucharist. (E.) The orig. sense is 'sacrifice.' M. E. *housel*. A. S. *hūsel*.+Goth. *hunsl*, sacrifice. Allied to Lith. *szwentas*, holy, consecrated; Zend *spənta-*, holy. Brugm. i. § 377.

Housings, trappings of a horse. (F.–Teut.) The old form was *hous*; *-ings* has been added.–F. *housse*, a coverlet, 'a foot-cloth for a horse;' Cot. (Low L. *hucia*, *husia*, *hussia*, the same). Low L. type **hulstia*.–O. H. G. *hulst*, a cover. +Icel. *hulstr*, a case, sheath; A. S. *heolstor*, Goth. *hulistr*, a covering. From **hul-*, weak grade of Teut. **helan-* (A. S. *helan*), to cover, hide; cf. O. H. G. and Du. *hullen*, to cover.

Hovel, a small hut. (F.–Teut.?) M. E. *hovel*, *hovil*, a shed. Perhaps from O. F. **huvel-*, as in *huvelet*, a penthouse. – O. H. G. *hūba* (G. *haube*), a hood; M. Du. *huyve*, a tilt of a cart.

Hover. (E.) A frequentative of M. E. *hōuen* (=*hōven*), to be poised, to stay, tarry, wait. Origin uncertain; cf. *heave*. ¶ The W. *hofio*, to hover, is borrowed from M. E. *houen*.

How (1). (E.) M. E. *hou*, *hu*; A. S. *hū*. Closely related to A. S. *hwā*, who; see Who. +O. Fries. *hū*, O. Sax. *hwō*, Du. *hoe*. Cf. Goth. *hwaiwa*, how; Gk. πῶς.

How (2), a hill. (Scand.) M. E. *hogh*. Icel. *haugr*, a hill; Swed. *hög*, a mound; Dan. *höi*, a hill. Allied to Icel. *hār*, Swed. *hög*, Dan. *höi*, high; see High.

Howdah; see Houdah.

Howitzer, a short cannon. (G.–Bohemian.) Borrowed from G. *haubitze*, a howitzer; formerly spelt *hauffnitz*. –

Bohemian *haufnice*, orig. a sling for casting a stone; Jungmann, Bohem. Dict. i. 662. Cf. F. *obus*, from the same.

Howl. (E.) M. E. *houlen*. + M. Du. *huylen*; Dan. *hyle*; G. *heulen*, to howl. Of imitative origin; cf. L. *ululāre*, to howl, whence O. F. *huller*.

Hox, to hamstring. (E.) For *hocks*, which is from *hock-sinew*, sb., O. Fries. *hôxene*, *hôxne*, A. S. *hôh-sinu*, hough-sinew. – A.S. *hôh*, hough; *sinu*, sinew; see Hough. Cf. E. Fries. *haksene*, lit. 'heel-sinew,' but also the hamstring (of a horse).

Hoy (1), a kind of sloop. (Du.) Du. *heu*, *heude*, a flat-bottomed merchant-ship; M. Du. *hode*, *heude*; Flemish *hui*, a hoy.

Hoy (2), stop! (E.) M. E. *hoy*. Cf. Du. *hui!* hoy! come! well! Allied to Ho.

Hoyden; see Hoiden.

Hub, a projection; the same as Hob (1).

Hubbub. (E.) Imitative. Cf. Gael. *ub*, interj. of aversion. Formerly also *whoobub*, a confused noise. *Hubbub* was confused with *hoop-hoop*, reduplication of *hoop*; and *whoobub* with *whoop-hoop*. See Hoop (2), Whoop.

Huckaback, a sort of linen cloth. (Low G. ?) The orig. sense was prob. 'pedlar's ware;' cf. Low G. *hukkebak*, G. *huckebak*, pick-a-back. See Huckster.

Huckle-berry. (E.) The same as *hurtle-*, *whortle-*, *hurt-*, *hart-berry*. A.S. *heorot-berge*, i. e. hart-berry.

Huckle-bone, the hip-bone. (E.) A. *huckle* is a 'small joint.' Cf. E. Fries. *hukken*, to bend, stoop, crouch; see below.

Huckster. (O. Low G.) M. E. *hukstere*, *hucster*. Formed with the fem. suffix *-ster* (for which see Spinster), from M. Du. *hucker*, Low G. *höker*, a hawker, also a stooper, bender, one who stoops. β. The *hawker* or *huckster* was so named from his bowed back, bent under his burden; from M. Du. *hucken*, to stoop under a burden. Cf. Icel. *hokinn*, bent, pp. of a lost strong verb (Teut. **heukan-*); also Icel. *hūka*, to sit on one's hams, Low G. *hūken*, to crouch. See Du. *heuker*, *huiken* in Franck.

Huddle. (E.) M. E. *hoderen*, *hodren*, which is an equivalent form, meaning to huddle together, as under a covert or shelter. Frequentative related to M. E. *hūden*, to hide; see Hide (1). ¶ But the mod. E. sense of *huddle* seems to be due to Du. *hoetelen*, 'to doe a thing unskilly,' Hexham; cf. G. *hudeln*, to bungle.

Hue (1), show, appearance, colour. (E.) M. E. *hewe*. A. S. *hiw, heow, heó,* appearance.＋Swed. *hy,* skin, complexion; Goth. *hiwi,* form, show.

Hue (2), clamour, outcry. (F.－Teut.) In the phr. *'hue* and cry;' A. F. *hu et cri.* M. E. *hue,* a loud cry.－O. F. *hu,* a cry; *huer,* to hoot.－M.H.G. *hû,* interj.; *hûzen,* to hoot; M. Swed. *huta,* to hoot; see **Hoot**.

Huff, to puff, bluster, bully. (E.) The old sense is to puff, blow hard; hence to bluster, vapour. An imitative word, like *puff.* Cf. Lowl. Sc. *hauch,* a forcible puff, *hech,* to breathe hard; G. *hauchen,* to breathe. ¶ To *huff,* at draughts, simply means 'to blow'; it was customary to *blow upon* the piece removed; cf. Lowl. Sc. *blaw,* to blow, also to huff at draughts; Dan. *blæse en brikke,* to huff (lit. blow) a man at draughts.

Hug, to embrace closely. (Scand. ?) XVI cent. Uncertain. Perhaps of Scand. origin; cf. Icel. *hugga,* to soothe, comfort; *hugga barnið,* to soothe a child, *huga,* to mind; *hugna,* to please; M. Du. *heuge,* joy.

Huge, vast. (F.－Teut. ?) M. E. *huge, houge.* An initial *a* has dropped.－A. F. *ahoge;* O. F. *ahuge, ahugue,* huge, vast (12th cent.). Of unknown origin; perhaps allied to Icel. *haugr,* a hill, whence O. F. *hoge, hogue,* a hill; see **How** (1).

Huguenot, a French protestant. (F. －G.) F. *huguenot;* as if from the personal name *Huguenot.* This name was in use two centuries at least before the Reformation, and is a dimin. of F. *Hugon,* acc. case from the nom. *Hugues,* Hugh. －M. H. G. *Hûg,* Hugh. 2. But this form was due to popular etymology. The orig. form was G. *eidgenoss,* a confederate, appearing as Swiss Romance *eingenot, higueno,* a protestant (Wedgwood). From G. *eid,* an oath (see **Oath**), and *genoss* = A. S. *genéat,* a companion. ¶ 15 false etymologies of this word are noted by Scheler.

Hulk, a heavy ship. (Late L.－Gk.) M. E. *hulke.* A. S. *hulc.*－Late L. *hulka,* also *hulcum, holcas,* a kind of ship.－Gk. ὁλκάς, a ship which is towed, also a heavy ship, merchantman.－Gk. ἕλκειν, to draw, drag. Cf. L. *sulcus,* a furrow. Der. *hulking,* i. e. bulky, unwieldy. ¶ Distinct from M. E. *hulke,* A. S. *hulc,* a hovel.

Hull (1), husk. (E.) M. E. *hule.* A. S.

hulu, a husk, lit. 'covering;' from the same root as G. *hülse,* a husk, viz. Teut. **hul-,* weak grade of Teut. **helan-* (A. S. *helan*), to cover See **Hell**.

Hull (2), body of a ship. (Du.) From Du. *hol,* hold. '*Het* hol *van een schip,* the ship's hold or hull;' Sewel. See **Hold** (2). Or the same as *hull* (1).

Hum (1), to buzz. (E.) M. E. *hummen;* an imitative word. ＋ G. *hummen,* Du. *hommelen,* to hum. Cf. **Hem** (2).

hum (2), to trick, cajole. (E.) A particular use of *hum,* to buzz; it also meant to utter a sound expressive of contempt (Cor. v. 1. 49); also to applaud; see Richardson, and Todd's Johnson. Hence it meant to flatter, cajole, trick. So also Port. *zumbir,* to buzz, *zombar,* to jest; Span. *zumbar,* to hum, also to jest. **Der.** *hum,* sb., a hoax.

Human. (F.－L.) Formerly *humaine.* －F. *.humain,* 'humane, manly;' Cot.－ L. acc. *humānum,* human.－L. *homo,* a man; lit. 'a creature of earth,' from *humus,* ground; see **humble.** ＋ A. S. *guma,* a man.

humane. (L.) Directly from L. *humānus,* (1) human, (2) kind (above).

humble. (F.－L.) F. *humble.*－L. *humilem,* acc. of *humilis,* humble, lowly, near the ground.－L. *humus,* the ground. Cf. Gk. χαμαί, on the ground, Russ. *zemlia,* earth, land. Brugm. i. § 604.

Humble-bee, a humming-bee. (E.) From the verb *humble,* for *hummle,* frequentative of *hum.* Cf. Du. *hommel,* a humble-bee, from *hommelen,* to hum; G. *hummel,* a humble-bee, from *hummen,* to hum; Swed. *humla,* a humble-bee.

Humbug, a hoax, piece of trickery. (E.) '*Humbug,* a false alarm, a bugbear,' Dean Milles MS. (cited in Halliwell). 'Drolleries, bonmots, and *humbugs*;' about A. D. 1740. Compounded of *hum,* hoax, and *bug,* a spectre, ghost, bugbear; the orig. sense being 'sham bugbear'; see **hum** (2) and **Bug**. Der. *humbug,* vb.

humdrum, dull, droning. (E.) Compounded of *hum,* a buzzing noise, and *drum,* a droning sound; see **Drum.**

Humeral, belonging to the shoulder. (L.) Late L. *humerālis,* belonging to the shoulder.－L. *humerus,* the shoulder; better *umerus.*＋Gk. ὦμος, Goth. *amsa,* Skt. *aṁsa-,* the shoulder. Brugm. i. § 163.

Humid, moist. (F.－L.) F. *humide.* －L. *hūmidus,* better *ūmidus,* moist.－L.

hūmēre, ūmēre, to be moist; cf. *ūuens, ūuidus, ūdus,* moist; Gk. ὑγρός, moist.

Humiliate. (L.) From pp. of L. *humiliāre,*to humble. – L. *humilis,*humble; see Humble.

humility. (F. – L.) M. E. *humilitee.* – O. F. *humiliteit,* humility. – L. *humili-tātem,* acc. of *humilitās,* humility. – L. *humilis,* humble.

Hummock, Hommock, a mound, hillock, rounded mass. (E.) It appears to be a variant of *hump* or *hunch.*

Humour, orig. moisture. (F. – L.) See Trench, Select Glossary, and Study of Words. The four *humours,* according to Galen, caused the four temperaments of mind, viz. choleric, melancholy, phlegmatic, and sanguine. – O. F. *humor* (F. *humeur*). – L. *ūmōrem,* acc. of *ūmor,* moisture. – L. *ūmēre,* to be moist; see Humid.

Hump, a lump, bunch, esp. on the back. (E.) ' *Hump,* a hunch, or lump,' *West-moreland*;' Halliwell. Not found in M. E. Cf. E. Fries. *humpe, hump,* a bit, lump.+Du. *homp,* a lump, bunch; Low G. *hümpel,* a heap. Cf. Lithuan. *kumpas,* hunched. Parallel to *hunch,* q. v.

Hunch, a hump, round mass. (E.) A palatalised form of prov. E. *hunk,* a lump. Apparently a parallel form of *hump*; with *nk* for *mp.* Cf. W. Flem. *hunke brood,* a hunk of bread (De Bo); and perhaps Du. *honk,* a starting-post, orig. ' a stump;' see Franck.

Hundred. (E.) M. E. *hundred.* A. S. *hundred*; a compound word. – A. S. *hund,* a hundred; and *-red,* with the sense of ' reckoning ' or rate, to denote the rate of counting. Cf. Icel. *hund-rað,* orig. 120; G. *hund-ert.* This suffix is allied to Goth. *raþjo,* number, L. *ratio*; see **Rate** (1). β. The A. S. *hund* is cognate with L. *centum,* answering to an Idg. form *ꝁəm-tóm,* perhaps for *dekmtóm,* a decad, allied to Goth. *taihunte-hund,* a hundred, which Brugmann explains as δεκάδων δεκάς. Cf. also Gk. ἑκατόν, Skt. *çatam,* Pers. *sad,* Lith. *szimtas,* Russ. *sto,* Irish *cead,* W. *cant,* a hundred. Brugm. i. § 431, ii. § 179. See **Ten.**

Hunger. (E.) A. S. *hungor.* + Icel. *hungr,* Swed. Dan. *hunger,* Du. *honger,* G. *hunger*; Goth. *hūhrus,* hunger. Teut. types **hungruz, *hunhruz,* m. Allied to Lith. *kanka,* suffering. Brugm. i. § 639.

Hunt, to chase wild animals. (E.) M. E. *hunten.* A. S. *huntian,* to capture;

cf. *hunt,* sb., a hunting. Related to Teut. **hunth-,* weak grade of **henthan-,* to seize; see Hent. Cf. Brugm. i. § 701.

Hurdle. (E.) M. E. *hurdel.* A. S. *hyrdel*; a dimin. from a Teut. base **hurd-*; see the cognate words. + Du. *horde,* Icel. *hurð,* G. *hürde,* M. H. G. *hurt,* a hurdle; Goth. *haurds,* a door. Allied to L. *crātēs,* a hurdle, Gk. κάρ-ταλος, a (woven) basket. Cf. Skt. *kṛt,* to spin. The sense is a ' plaited ' thing. Brugm. i. §§ 529, 633. (√QERT.)

Hurdygurdy, a kind of violin, played by turning a handle. (E.) From Lowl. Sc. *hirdygirdy,* a confused noise; also *hirdum-dirdum,* the same. Cf. Lowl. Sc. *hurr,* to snarl, *gurr,* to growl. ' Som vseþ strange wlaffyng, chytering, *harryng and garryng'* = some people use a strange babbling, chattering, snarling and growling ; Spec. of English, ed. Morris and Skeat, p. 241, l. 163. Formed on the model of *hurlyburly.* See Hurry.

Hurl. (E.) M. E. *hurlen, horlen.* Not in A. S.; perhaps of Scand. origin. Cf. E. *hurleblast,* a hurricane, *hurlepool,* whirlpool, *hurlewind,* whirlwind. Also E. Fries. *hurrel,* a gust of wind ; *hurreln,* to blow in gusts ;. *hurrel-wind,* a whirl-wind. Explained by Swed. dial. *hurra,* to whir, whirl round ; whence *hurrel,* a whirl, *hurrel-wind,* a whirlwind. Of imitative origin; cf. Dan. *hurre,* to buzz, Icel. *hurr,* a noise. So also M. H. G. *hurren,* to move quickly ; from the sound. Cf. Hurly-burly, Hurry.

Hurlyburly, a tumult. (F. – L.) A reduplicated word, the second syllable being an echo of the first. [Cf. M. F. *hurluberlu,* tumult, in Rabelais (v. prol.).] The short form *hurly* also occurs ; see K. John, iii. 4. 169. – O. F. *hurlee,* a howling, outcry, great noise ; orig. fem. pp. of *hurler,* to howl. – L. *ululāre,* to howl. Prob. confused with Hurl.

Hurrah. (G.) From G. *hurra,* M. H. G. *hurrā.* Of imitative origin ; see Hurl.

Hurricane, whirlwind. (Span. – Caribbean.) Span. *huracan.* – Carib. *huracan* (Oviedo).

Hurry. (E.) Not allied to *harry.* Formed from an older base *hurr-*; like *scurr-y* from *skir.* M. E. *horien,* to hurry (Allit. Poems, ed. Morris, B. 883). + M. Swed. *hurra,* to swing, whirl round; Swed. dial. *hurra,* to whirl, *hurr,* sb., hurry, haste. Cf. Dan. *hurre*, to hum, whir; Icel. *hurr*, a noise; M. H. G. *hurren*, to move swiftly. See **Hurl**; and cf. *whir*, *whiz*, of similar imitative origin; whence *whurry*, to hurry (Nares).

Hurst, a wood. (E.) M. E. *hurst*; A. S. *hyrst*. **+** M. H. G. *hurst*, a shrub, thicket; G. *horst*; E. Fries. *hörst*.

Hurt, to dash against, to harm. (F.) M. E. *hurten*, *hirten*, (1) to push, dash against; (2) to injure.—O. F. *hurter* (F. *heurter*), to strike or dash against. Of unknown origin. Hardly from Celtic (Thurneysen, p. 81). The Ital. form is *urtare*, possibly from L. **urtum*, unused supine of *urgēre*, to press on (Körting).

hurtle, to dash. (F.) M. E. *hurtlen*, frequent. of *hurten* (above).

Husband. (Scand.) Icel. *húsbóndi*, the master of a house, the goodman; short for *húsbúandi*.—Icel. *hús*, house; *búandi*, dwelling in, pres. pt. of *búa*, to dwell; see **Boor**. So also Swed. *husbonde*, Dan. *husbond*. Der. *husband-man*, *husband-ry*.

Hush. (E.) M. E. *husht*, whist, silent; prob. taken to be a pp. Cf. Swed. *hyssja*, Dan. *hysse*, to hush; Dan. *hys*, hush! A purely imitative word, allied to *hiss*.

Husk, shell. (E.) M. E. *huske*. The *-k* is a dimin. suffix; from A. S. *hús*, a house. Cf. Low G. *húske*, a little house; E. Fries. *húske*, a little house, core of an apple, small case; M. Du. *huysken*, a little house, a case, a husk of fruit (Kilian). See **House**.

Husky, hoarse. (E.) Apparently allied to prov. E. *husk*, dry, parched; with reference to the dryness of *husks*.

Hussar. (G.—Hungarian.—Servian.—Gk.—L.) 'Hussars, Husares,' Coles (1684).—G. *Husar*.—Hung. *Huszar*.—Serv. χusar, hussar, robber, sea-robber (Popovic').—Late Gk. κουρσάριος, a corsair, pirate (Ducange).—Late L. *cursārius*, a corsair.—L. *cursus*, a course; see **Corsair**. ¶ The word is older than the story about Mathius Corvinus (1458); see N. and Q. 8 S. ii. 156; Miklosich, p. 148.

Hussif, Hussy. (E.) Short for *huswife*, i. e. *house-wife*; cf. *hus-* in *husband*; see **Husband** and **House**. ¶ In the sense of ' case for needles, thread, &c.,' it must mean ' house-wife's companion'; it is, however, remarkable that Icel. *húsi* means ' a case.'

Hustings. (Scand.) The mod. use is incorrect; it is properly *husting*, sing., and means a council, an assembly for the choice of a candidate. M. E. *husting*. A. S. *hústing*.—Icel. *húsþing*, a council, meeting.—Icel. *hús*, a house; *þing*, a thing, also an assembly; see **House** and **Thing**. Cf. Swed. Norw. and Dan. *ting*, the same as Icel. *þing*.

Hustle, to jostle. (Du.) For *hutsle*. —Du. *hutselen*, to shake up and down, huddle together; frequent. of M. Du. *hutsen*, Du. *hotsen*, to shake. See **Hotchpot**. Cf. Du. *hotten*, to curdle; *hot*, curds; prov. G. *hotze*, a cradle, a swing; Lowl. Sc. *hott*, to move by jerks, *hotter*, to jolt.

Hut. (F.—O. H. G.) M. E. *hotte*.—F. *hutte*, a cottage; Cotgrave. — O. H. G. *hutta* (G. *hütte*), a hut. **+** Swed. *hydda*, a hut. Perhaps related to **Hide** (1).

Hutch, a box. (F.—Low L.) M. E. *huche*, *hucche*.—F. *huche*, a hutch, bin.— Late L. *hūtica*, a hutch, box; of unknown origin. Perhaps Teutonic; cf. O. H. G. *huotan* (G. *hüten*), to take care of. See **Heed.**

Huzzah, Hurrah. (E.) *Huzzah* is also written *huzza*. Cf. G. *hussa*, huzzah! M. H. G. *hurrā*, hurrah! So also Swed. and Dan. *hurra*, hurrah! Cf. M. H. G. *hurren*, to move quickly; Dan. *hurre*, to hum, buzz. See **Hurry.**

Hyacinth, a flower. (F.—L.—Gk.) F. *hyacinthe*.—L. *hyacinthus*.—Gk. ὑάκινθος, an iris, larkspur (not our hyacinth). Doublet, *jacinth*.

Hyæna; see **Hyena.**

Hybrid, mongrel. (L.) L. *hibrida*, *hybrida*, a mongrel, a hybrid. Some connect it with Gk. ὕβριδ-, stem of ὕβρις, insult, wantonness, violation; but it may be Latin.

Hydra, a water-snake. (L.—Gk.) L. *hydra*. — Gk. ὕδρα, water-snake. — Gk. ὕδ-ωρ, water. Cf. Skt. *udra-s*, a water-animal, otter, A. S. *oter*. Doublet, *otter*. And see **Water**. Brugm. i. § 572.

hydrangea, a flower. (Gk.) A coined name, referring to the cup-form of the capsule, or seed-vessel. From Gk. ὕδρ-, for ὕδωρ, water; ἀγγεῖον, a vessel.

hydraulic, relating to water in motion. (F.—L.—Gk.) F. *hydraulique*. —L. *hydraulicus*.—Gk. ὑδραυλικός, belonging to a water-organ.—Gk. ὕδραυλις, an organ worked by water.—Gk. ὕδρ-, for ὕδωρ, water; αὐλός, a pipe, tube (allied to ἄημι, I blow; see Air).

hydrodynamics, the science relating to the force of water in motion. (Gk.) Gk. ὕδρο-, for ὕδωρ, water; and E. *dynamics,* a word of Gk. origin; see Dynamics.

hydrogen, a very light gas. (Gk.) The name means 'generator of water.' — Gk. ὕδρο-, for ὕδωρ, water; and the base γέν-, to produce; see Genesis.

hydropathy, the water-cure. (Gk.) Gk. ὕδρο-, for ὕδωρ, water; πάθ-ος, suffering, endurance of treatment; see Pathos.

hydrophobia, fear of water. (L.— Gk.) Late L. *hydrophobia.* Coined from Gk. ὕδρο-, for ὕδωρ, water; φόβος, fear, fright, allied to φέβομαι, I flee. (√BHEG.)

hydropsy, dropsy. (F.—L.—Gk.) Formerly *dropsie* or *ydropsie;* the form *dropsie* being due to loss of *y*-.—M. F. *hydropisie.*—L. *hydropisis, hydropisïa.*— Late L. *ὑδρώπισις,* not found, from Gk. ὕδρωψ, dropsy, extended from ὕδρο-, for ὕδωρ, water. Der. *dropsi-c-al.*

hydrostatics, the science which treats of fluids at rest. (Gk.) Gk. ὕδρο-, for ὕδωρ, water; and Statics, q. v.

Hyena, Hyæna, a hog-like quadruped. (L.—Gk.) [M. E. *hyene;* from O. F. *hyene.*] L. *hyæna.*—Gk. ὕαινα, a hyena; lit. 'sow-like.'—Gk. ὕ-s, a sow, cognate with E. Sow; with fem. adj. suffix -αινα.

Hymen. (L.—Gk.) L. *hymen.*—Gk. ὑμήν, the god of marriage. Cf. Skt. *siv,* to connect, lit. to sew; see Sew.

Hymn. (F.—L.—Gk.) M. E. *ympne* (with excrescent *p*).—O. F. *ymne* (later *hymne*).—L. *hymnum,* acc. of L. *hymnus.* —Gk. ὕμνος, a song, festive song, hymn.

Hypallage, an interchange. (L.—Gk.) L. *hypallagē.* — Gk. ὑπαλλαγή, an interchange, exchange. — Gk. ὑπ-ό, under; ἀλλαγή, change, from ἀλλάσσειν, to change; from ἄλλος, another. See Alien.

Hyper-, prefix, denoting excess. (L.— Gk.) L. *hyper-,* for Gk. ὑπέρ, above, beyond, allied to L. *super.* Hence *hyperbaton,* a transposition of words (from natural order, lit. 'a going beyond' (from βαίνειν, to go); *hyper-bole,* exaggeration, Gk. ὑπερβολή (from βάλλειν, to throw, cast) ; *hyper-borean,* extreme northern (from βορέας, north wind).

Hyphen, a short stroke (-) joining two parts of a compound word. (L.—Gk.)

L. *hyphen,* for Gk. ὑφέν, lit. 'under one.' — Gk. ὑφ-, for ὑπό, under; ἕν, neut. of εἷς, one (allied to L. *sim-* in *simplex;* see Simple).

Hypo-, prefix. (Gk.) Gk. ὑπό, under; cognate with L. *sub.*

Hypochondria, a mental disorder inducing melancholy. (L.—Gk.) Named from the spleen (which was supposed to cause it), situate under the cartilage of the breast-bone.—Late L. *hypochondria,* fem. sb.; for L. *hypochondria,* s. pl.—Gk. ὑποχόνδρια, sb. pl., the parts beneath the breast-bone.—Gk. ὑπό, under; χόνδρος, a corn, grain, gristle, cartilage of the breast-bone (cognate with G. *grand,* gravel, and allied to E. *grind*). Der. *hipp-ish,* q. v.

Hypocrisy, pretence to virtue. (F. — L.—Gk.) M. F. *hypocrisie.*—L. *hypocrisis,* 1 Tim. iv. 2. — Gk. ὑπόκρισις, a reply, answer, playing a part on a stage, acting of a part.—Gk. ὑποκρίνομαι, I reply, play a part.—Gk. ὑπό, under; κρίνομαι, I contend, middle voice of κρίνω, I judge. See Critic. Der. *hypocrite,* F. *hypocrite,* L. *hypocrita,* Gk. ὑποκριτής, a dissembler, Matt. vi. 2.

Hypogastric, belonging to the lower part of the abdomen. (F. — L. — Gk.) M. F. *hypogastrique.* — Late L. *hypogastricus,* belonging to the lower part of the belly.—Gk. ὑπογάστριον, lower part of the belly; see Hypo- and Gastric.

Hypostasis. (L.—Gk.) L. *hypostasis.*—Gk. ὑπόστασις, a standing under, groundwork, subsistence, substance, a Person of the Trinity.—Gk. ὑπό, under; στάσις, a standing, from √STA, to stand. See Statics.

Hypotenuse. (F.—L.—Gk.) Also *hypothenuse* (badly).—F. *hypoténuse.*—L. *hypotēnūsa.*—Gk. ὑποτείνουσα, the subtending (line); fem. of pres. part. of ὑποτείνειν, to subtend, lit. to stretch under. (√TEN.)

Hypothec, a legal lien on property. (F. — L. — Gk.) Englished from M. F. *hypotheque,* a mortgage.—L. *hypothēca* (the same).—Gk. ὑποθήκη, lit. 'support;' a pledge, mortgage.—Gk. ὑπό, under; θη-, as in τί-θη-μι, I place. (√DHE.)

hypothesis, a supposition. (L. — Gk.) L. *hypothesis.*—Gk. ὑπόθεσις, a placing under, supposition.—Gk. ὑπό, under; θέσις, a placing; from the same root as the above. See Thesis.

Hyson, a kind of tea. (Chinese.) In

the Amoy dialect called *chhun-tê*, lit. 'spring tea,' from *chhun*, spring, and *tê*, tea. Said to have been orig. from *hi chhun*, lit. 'blooming spring,' i. e. early crop. From Chin. *hi*, blooming ; *chhun*, spring.

Hyssop, a plant. (F. – L. – Gk. – Heb.) M. E. *ysope.* – O. F. *hyssope.* – L. *hyssōpus.* – Gk. ὕσσωπος, an aromatic plant (not our hyssop). – Heb. *ēzōbh*, a plant (it is not exactly known what plant).

Hysteric, convulsive, said of fits. (F. – L. – Gk.) M. F. *hysterique.* – L. *hystericus.* – Gk. ὑστερικός, suffering in the womb ; hysterical. – Gk. ὑστέρα, the womb. Prob. from Gk. ὕστερος, latter, lower, comparative from the Idg. base *ud-*, out ; see **Uterine** and **Out.**

I.

I, nom. case of first pers. pronoun. (E.) M. E. (Northern) *ik, i* ; (Southern) *ich, uch, i.* A. S. *ic.*+Du. *ik*, Icel. *ek*, Dan. *jeg*, Swed. *jag*, Goth. *ik*, G. *ich*, Lith. *asz*, Russ. *ia*, L. *ego*, Gk. ἐγώ, ἐγών, Skt. *aham*. Idg. base, EGH- and EG- ; Brugm. ii. § 434. ¶ *Me* is from a different base.

I-, neg. prefix ; see **In-** (3).

Iambic, a certain m̄etre, a short and a long syllable (◡ –). (L. – Gk.) L. *iambicus.* – Gk. ἰαμβικός. – Gk. ἴαμβος, an iambic foot, iambic verse, lampoon. (Origin doubtful.)

Ibex, a genus of goats. (L.) L. *ibex.*

Ibis, a bird. (L. – Gk. – Egypt.) L. *ibis.* – Gk. ἶβις, an Egyptian bird. Of Egypt. origin ; cf. Coptic *hippen* (Peyron).

Ice. (E.) M. E. *ys, iis.* A. S. *īs.*+Du. *ijs*, Icel. *īss*, Dan. *iis*, Swed. *is*, G. *eis*. Teut. type **īsom*, neut. **Der.** *ice-berg*, quite a modern word ; the latter element is the Du., Norw., Swed., and G. *berg*, a mountain ; cf. Du. *ijsberg*, Norw. and Swed. *isbjerg*, Dan. *iisbjerg*, G. *eisberg*, an iceberg ; (prob. a Norw. word). Also *ice-blink*, Dan. *iis-blink*, a field of ice, from Dan. *blinke*, to gleam.

icicle. (E.) M. E. *isikel, iseyokel* ; from M. E. *ys*, ice, and *ikel*, a point of ice. – A. S. *īs-gicel*, an icicle ; also written *īses gicel*, where *īses* is the gen. case. *Gicel*, O. Merc. *gecile* (Sweet, O. E. T.), means 'a small piece of ice.'+Icel. *īss-jökull* ; though *jökull* is gen. used by itself in the sense of icicle ; Low G. *is-*

hekel, isjäkel. 2. Icel. *jökull* is the dimin. of Icel. *jaki*, a piece of ice, cognate with Irish *aig*, W. *ia*, ice. Brugm. i. § 305.

Ichneumon. (L. – Gk.) L. *ichneumon.* – Gk. ἰχνεύμων, an ichneumon (lizard) ; lit. 'a tracker,' because it tracks out (and devours) crocodiles' eggs. – Gk. ἰχνεύειν, to track. – Gk. ἴχνος, a footstep.

Ichor, the juice in the veins of gods. (Gk.) Gk. ἰχώρ, juice.

Ichthyography, description of fishes. (Gk.) Gk. ἰχθυο-, from ἰχθύς, a fish ; -γραφία, from γράφειν, to describe. So also *ichthyology*, from λόγος, a discourse, λέγειν, to speak.

Icicle ; see **Ice.**

Iconoclast, a breaker of images. (Gk.) Coined from Gk. εἰκόνο-, from εἰκών, an image ; κλάστης, a vine-pruner (but lit. a breaker), from κλάειν, to break.

Icosahedron, a solid figure with twenty equal faces. (Gk.) From Gk. εἴκοσι, twenty ; ἕδρα, a base, lit. a seat, from the base ἑδ-, to sit ; see **Sit.**

Idea. (L. – Gk.) L. *idea.* – Gk. ἰδέα, the look or semblance of a thing, species (hence, notion). – Gk. ἰδεῖν, to see. (√ WEID.) See **Wit.**

Identical, the very same. (L.) Formerly *identic, identick.* Formed as if from Med. (scholastic) L. *identicus*, adj. suggested by *identi-tās* ; see below.

identity, sameness. (F. – Late L. – L.) F. *identité.* – Late L. acc. *identitātem*, sameness. – L. *identi-*, occurring in *identidem*, repeatedly ; with suffix *-tas.* – L. *idem*, the same. – L. *i-*, and *-dem* ; from Idg. pronominal bases I and DE.

Ides, the 15th day of March, May, July, October ; 13th of other months. (F. – L.) F. *ides.* – L. *īdūs*, ides.

Idiom, peculiar mode of expression. (F. – L. – Gk.) F. *idiome.* – L. *idiōma.* – Gk. ἰδίωμα, an idiom, peculiarity of language. – Gk. ἰδιόω, I m̄ake my own. – Gk. ἴδιος, own.

idiosyncrasy, peculiarity of temperament. (Gk.) Cf. F. *idiosyncrasie.* From Gk. ἴδιο-ς, own ; σύγ-κρασις, a blending together, from σύγ- (= σύν), together, κρᾶσις, a mingling. See **Crasis.**

idiot. (F. – L. – Gk.) F. *idiot.* – L. *idiōta*, an ignorant, uneducated person. – Gk. ἰδιώτης, a private person ; hence, one who is inexperienced (1 Cor. xiv. 16). – Gk. ἰδιόω, I make my own. – Gk. ἴδιος, own.

Idle. (E.) M. E. *idel*. A. S. *īdel*, vain, empty, useless. + Du. *ijdel*, vain ; Dan. *idel*, Swed. *idel*, mere ; G. *eitel*, vain, trifling. Origin doubtful.

Idol. (F.–L.–Gk.) O. F. *idole*.–L. *īdōlum*. – Gk. εἴδωλον, an image, likeness. – Gk. εἴδομαι, I appear, seem ; ἰδεῖν, to see. (√WEID.) Der. *idolatry*, O. F. *idolatrie*, Late L. *īdōlatrīa*, shortened form of *īdōlōlatrīa*, from Gk. εἰδωλο-λατρεία, service to idols (where λατρεία, service, is from λατρίς, a hired servant, λάτρον, hire). Hence *idolater*, &c.

idyl, idyll, a pastoral poem. (L.– Gk.) L. *īdyllium*. – Gk. εἰδύλλιον, a short descriptive poem. – Gk. εἶδος, form, shape, figure. – Gk. εἴδομαι, I appear (see above).

If, conj. (E.) M. E. *if*, A. S. *gif*.+Icel. *ef*, *if*, O. Fries. *ief*, *gef*, *ef*, O. Sax. *ef*; Goth. *ibai*, interrog. particle, *jabai*, if ; with which cf. Du. *of*, if, whether, G. *ob*, whether; also O. H. G. *ibu*, if, lit. ' on the condition,' dat. of *iba*, condition, doubt. Cf. also Icel. *if*, *ef*, sb., doubt. See Kluge, s. v. *ob*.

Ignition, a setting on fire. (L.) F. *ignition*. As if from L. *ignītio.–L. *ig-nītus*, pp. of *ignīre*, to set on fire.–L. *ignis*, fire. + Skt. *agni-*, fire, base **egni-* ; cf. Russ. *ogone*, Lith. *ugnìs*, fire, base **ogni-*. Brugm. i. § 148. Hence also *ignis fatuus*, a vain fire ; *igne-ous*, adj.

Ignoble. (F.–L.) F. *ignoble*, not noble.–L. *i-gnōbilis*, where *i-* = *in*, not ; see Noble.

Ignominy, disgrace. (F.–L.) F. *ignominie*.–L. *ignōminia*.–L. *i-* (for *in*), not ; *gnōmin-*, for *gnōmen*, old form of *nōmen*, name, fame ; see Noun.

Ignore, to disregard. (F.–L.) F. *ignorer*.–L. *ignōrāre*, not to know.–L. *i-* (for *in*), not ; and base *gnō-*, as in *gnō-scere* = *nōscere*, to know; see Know. Der. *ignor-ant*, *-ance* ; also *ignōrāmus*, lit. ' we ignore' that, an old law-term.

Iguana, a kind of American lizard. (Span.–W. Indian.) Span. *iguana*. Of West Indian origin. – Hayti *iuanna*, *yuana* (Eden.).

iguanodon, a fossil dinosaur, with teeth like an iguana. From *iguan-a*, and Gk. ὀδον-τ-, stem of ὀδούς, tooth.

Il- (1), for *in-*, prefix, when *l* follows, prep., when *l* follows. Exx. : *il-lapse*, *il-lusion*, &c.

Il- (2), for *in-*, negative prefix when *l* follows. Exx. *il-legal*, *il-legible*, *il-legiti-mate*, *il-liberal*, *il-limitable*, *il-literate*, *il-*

logical ; for which see *legal*, *legible*, &c. And see *illicit*.

Iliac, pertaining to the smaller intestines. (F.–L.) F. *iliaque*, belonging to the flanks. Formed from L. *īlia*, sb. pl., flanks, groin. See also Jade (2).

Iliad, an epic poem. (L.–Gk.) L. *Iliad-*, stem of *Ilias*, the Iliad. – Gk. Ἰλιάδ-, stem of Ἰλιάς, the Iliad. – Gk. Ἴλιος, Ilios, commonly known as Troy ; said to have had its name from (a mythical) *Ilus*, grandfather of Priam, and son of *Tros* (whence *Troy*).

Ill, bad. (Scand.) M. E. *ille*. – Icel. *illr* (later *illr*), ill, adj. ; Swed. *illa*, Dan. *ilde*, ill, adv. ¶ Not allied to Evil.

Illapse, a gliding in, a sudden entrance. (L.) L. *illapsus*, sb., a gliding in.–L. *il-* (for *in*), in ; *lapsus*, a gliding, from pp. of *lābī*, to glide. See Lapse.

Illation, an inference. (F.–L.) F. *illation*.–L. acc. *illātiōnem*, a bringing in, inference.–L. *il-* (for *in*), in ; *lātus* (= *tlātus*), borne, brought (= Gk. τλητός). See Tolerate.

Illicit, unlawful. (F.–L.) F. *illicite*, 'illicitous,' Cot.–L. *illicitus*, not allowed. –L. *il-* (for *in-*), not ; *licitus*, pp. of *licēre*, to be allowed. See Licence.

Illision, a striking against. (L.) From L. *illīsio*, a striking against.–L. *illīsus*, pp. of *illīdere*, to strike against.–L. *il-* (for *in*), upon ; *lædere*, to strike. See Lesion.

Illude, to deceive. (F.–L.) F. *illuder*, 'to illude ;' Cot.–L. *illūdere*, to mock at.–L. *il-* (for *in*), upon, at ; *lūdere*, to jest, play. See Ludicrous.

Illuminate, to enlighten. (L.) From pp. of L. *illūmināre*, to throw light upon. –L. *il-* (for *in*), upon ; *lūmin-*, for *lumen*, light ; see Luminary. ¶ We also use *illumine*, *illume*, from F. *illuminer*<L. *illūmināre*.

Illusion. (F.–L.) F. *illusion*.–L. acc. *illūsiōnem*.–L. *illūsus*, pp. of *illūdere*; see Illude (above).

Illustrate. (L.) From the pp. of *illustrāre*, to throw light upon.–L. *il-* (for *in*), upon ; *lustrāre*, to shine (below).

illustrious. (F.–L.; *or* L.) A badly coined word ; from F. *illustre*, or from the L. *illustri-s*, bright, renowned. (Imitation of *industrious*.) β. In L. *illūstris*, the prefix *il-* (= *in*), upon ; *-lustris* stands for *lou-c-stris, from the base *lūc-*, as in Lucid, q. v. See Brugm. i. § 760.

Im- (1), prefix. (F.−L.) In some words, *im-* stands for *em-*, the O. F. form of L. *im-*, prefix. Or for L. *in*, in, before *b*, *m*, or *p*.

Im- (2), prefix. (E.) For E. *in*; as in *im-bed*, for *in-bed*.

Im- (3), prefix. (L.) L. *im-* (for *in*), in, when *b*, *m*, or *p* follows.

Im- (4), prefix. (F.−L.; *or* L.) Negative prefix; for L. *in-*, not. Exx.: *immaterial, im-mature, im-measurable, immemorial, im-moderate, im-modest, immoral, im-mortal, im-movable,im-mutable, im-palpable,im-parity,im-partial,im-passable, im-passive, im-patient, im-peccable, im-penetrable, im-penitent, im-perceptible, im-perfect, im-perishable, im-personal, impertinent, im-perturbable, im-piety, impious, im-placable, im-polite, im-politic, im-ponderable, im-possible, im-potent, impracticable, im-probable, im-proper, improvident, im-prudent, im-pure*; for which see *material, mature,* &c.

Image, a likeness, statue. (F.−L.) F. *image.*−L. *imāginem,* acc. of *imāgo,* a likeness. Formed, with suffix *-āgo,* from the base *im-* in *im-itārī,* to imitate; see Imitate.

imagine. (F.−L.) F. *imaginer,* to think.−L. *imāginārī,* to picture to oneself, imagine.−L. *imāgin-,* stem of *imāgo,* an image, picture; see above. Der. *imaginary, imagin-ation.*

Imam, Imaum, a Muhammedan priest. (Arab.) Arab. *imām,* a leader, chief, prelate, priest.−Arab. root *amma,* 'he tended towards.' Rich. Dict., p. 163.

Imbecile, feeble. (F.−L.) Formerly rare as an adj.; but the verb *imbécil,* to enfeeble, is found, and was confused with *embezzle.* − F. *imbécile*; M. F. *imbecille,* ' feeble;' Cotgrave.−L. *imbēcillum,* acc. of *imbēcillus* (also *imbēcillis*), feeble. (Root unknown.)

Imbibe, to drink in. (F.−L.; *or* L.) F. *imbiber* (16th cent.).−L. *imbibere,* to drink in.−L. *im-* (for *in-*), in; *bibere,* to drink.

Imbricated, bent and hollowed like a gutter-tile. (L.) Botanical. From pp. of L. *imbricāre,* to cover with gutter-tiles. − L. *imbric-,* stem of *imbrex,* a gutter-tile. − L. *imbri-,* decl. stem of *imber,* a shower of rain.+Gk. ἀφρός, foam; Skt. *abhra-,* a rain-cloud; Brugm. i. § 466.

Imbroglio, intrigue, perplexity. (Ital.)

Ital. *imbroglio,* perplexity. − Ital. *imbrogliare,* to entangle. − Ital. *im-* (for *in*), in ; *broglio,* a broil, confusion; see Broil (2).

Imbrue,Embrue, to moisten, drench. (F.−L.) M. F. *embruer*; *s'embruer,* ' to imbrue or bedable himself with;' Cot. Variant of O. F. *embevrer, embreuver,* to moisten.−F. *em-* (L. *in,* in) ; and a causal verb *-bevrer,* to give to drink, turned into *-brever* in the 16th cent., and then into *-bruer*; see F. *abreuver* in Hatzfeld. O.F. *bevrer* answers to a L. type *biberāre,* to give to drink; from L. *bibere,* to drink. See Beverage.

Imbue, to cause to drink in, tinge deeply. (F.−L.) O. F. *imbuer.*−L. *imbuere,* to cause to drink in ; where *-buere* is a causal form, apparently allied to *bibere,* to drink.

Imitate. (L.) From pp. of L. *imitārī,* to imitate; frequentative of *imāre,* not found ; cf. L. *imā-go.* See Image.

Immaculate. (L.) L. *im-maculātus,* unspotted.−L. *im-* (for *in-*), not ; *maculātus,* spotted. See Maculate.

Immediate, without intervention or means. (F. − L.) M. F. *immediat.* − L. *im-* (for *in-*), not ; *mediātus,* pp. of L. *mediāre,* to be in the middle.−L. *medius,* middle. See Medium.

Immense. (F.−L.) F. *immense.* − L. *immensus,* immeasurable.−L. *im-* (for *in-*), not ; *mensus,* pp. of *metīrī,* to measure. See Measure.

Immerge, to plunge into. (L.) L. *immergere* (pp. *im-mersus*), to plunge into.−L. *im-* (for *in*), in ; *mergere,* to plunge. See Merge. Der. *immers-ion.*

Immigrate. (L.) From pp. of L. *immigrāre,* to migrate to. (*Im- = in,* in.) See Migrate.

Imminent, near at hand. (L.) L. *imminent-,* stem of pres. pt. of *im-minēre,* to project over.−L. *im-* (for *in*), upon ; *-minēre,* to project, as in *ē-minēre.*

Immit, to inject. (L.) In Kersey (1715). L. *im-mittere,* to send into (pp. *immissus*).−L. *im-* (= in), in ; *mittere,* to send. See Missile. Der. *immiss-ion.*

Immolate, to offer in sacrifice. (L.) From pp. of L. *immolāre,* to sacrifice, lit. to throw meal upon a victim.−L. *im-* (for *in*), upon ; *mola,* meal, cognate with E. Meal (1).

Immunity, freedom from obligation. (F.−L.) F. *immunité,* immunity. − L. *immūnitātem,* acc. of *immūnitās,* exemption.—L. *immūnis*, exempt from public services.—L. *im-* (for *in*), not; *mūnis*, serving, obliging (whence also *commūnis*, common). See **Common**.

Immure. (F.—L.) For *emmure*. — M. F. *emmurer*, to shut up in prison, lit. to enclose with a wall.—L. *im-* (=*in*), in; *mūrus*, a wall.

Imp, a graft, offspring, demon. (Late L.—Gk.) Formerly in a good sense, meaning a scion, offspring. M. E. *imp*, a graft on a tree (A. S. *impe*); *impen*, to graft.—Late L. *impotus*, a graft (Lex Salica); [whence also Dan. *ympe*, Swed. *ympa*, G. *impfen*, O. H. G. *impitōn*, to graft].—Gk. ἔμφυτος, engrafted; James i. 21.—Gk. ἐμφύειν, to implant. — Gk. ἐμ- (for ἐν), in; φύειν, to produce, from √BHEU, to be; see **Be**.

Impact, a striking against. (L.) L. *impact-us*, pp. of *impingere*, to impinge. See **Impinge**.

Impair, to make worse, injure, weaken. (F.—L.) M. E. *empeiren*.—O. F. *empeirer*, later *empirer*, 'to impaire;' Cot.—Late L. *impēiōrāre*, to make worse.—L. *im-* (for *in*), prep., with intensive force; and *pēior*, worse, a comparative form from a lost positive. Cf. **Pessimist**.

Impale, to fix on a stake. (L.) Late L. *impālāre* (whence F. *empaler*).—L. *im-* (for *in*), on; *pālus*, a stake. See **Pale** (1).

Impart. (F.—L.) M. F. *impartir*.—L. *impartīre*, *impertīre*, to give a share to. —L. *im-* (=*in*), to, upon; *partīre*, to part, from *parti-*, decl. stem of *pars*, a part. See **Part**.

Impassive. From Im- (4) and Passive.

Impawn. From Im- (3) and Pawn (1).

Impeach, to charge with a crime. (F. —L.) The original sense was 'to hinder'; as, 'to *impeach* and stop their breath,' Holland, tr. of Pliny, b. xi. c. 3.—O. F. *empescher*, 'to hinder, stop, bar, impeach;' Cot. Older spelling *empeëscher*, where the *s* is adventitious. [Littré and Scheler connect the mod. F. *empêcher* with Prov. *empedegar*, from Late L. *impedicāre*, to fetter. —L. *im-* (for *in*), on, upon; *pedica*, a fetter, from *ped-*, stem of *pes*, a foot.] β. At the same time the usual sense of E. *impeach* and some (at least) of the senses of O. F. *empescher* above are due to O. F. *empacher*, Span. *empachar*, Ital. *impacciare*, to delay; from a Late L. frequent. form (**impacticāre*, in Körting, § 4110) of L.

impingere (pp. *impactus*), to bind, fasten; see **Pact**. See **Dispatch**.

Impede, to obstruct. (L.) From L. *impedīre*, to entangle the feet, obstruct.— L. *im-* (=*in*), in; *ped-*, stem of *pes*, foot. Der. *impedi-ment*.

Impel. (L.) L. *im-pellere*, to urge on. —L. *im-* (for *in*), on; *pellere*, to drive; see **Pulsate**. Der. *impulse*, L. *impulsus*, sb., from the pp. *impulsus*.

Impend, to hang over. (L.) L. *im-pendēre*, to hang over.—L. *im-* (for *in*), on, over; *pendēre*, to hang. See **Pendant**.

Imperative. (F.—L.) F. *impératif*, imperious.—L. *imperātīuus*, due to a command.—L. *imperātum*, a command; neut. of *imperātus*, pp. of *imperāre*, to command. See **Emperor**.

imperial. (F.—L.) O. F. *emperial*, later *impérial*.—L. *imperiālis*, belonging to an empire.—L. *imperium*, an empire. See **Empire**.

Impertinent. From Im- (4) and Pertinent.

Impervious. From Im- (4) and Pervious.

Impetus. (L.) L. *impetus*, lit. 'a falling on;' a rush, attack.—L. *im-* (*in*), on; *petere*, to fall, fly, seek. See **Petition**.

Impinge, to strike against. (L.) L. *impingere*, to strike against.—L. *im-* (*in*), on, upon; *pangere*, to fasten, also to strike. See **Pact**.

Implement, a tool. (Late L.—L.) Late L. *implēmentum*, an accomplishing; hence, means for accomplishing.—L. *implēre*, to fill in, execute.—L. *im-* (for *in*), in; *plēre*, to fill. See **Plenary**.

Implicate. (L.) From pp. of L. *implicāre*, to involve. — L. *im-* (*in*), in; *plicāre*, to fold. See **Ply**.

implicit. (F.—L.) F. *implicite*.— L. *implicitus*, old pp. of *implicāre* (above).

Implore. (F.—L.) F. *implorer*.—L. *implōrāre*, to implore.—L. *im-* (=*in*), on, upon; *plōrāre*, to wail. Cf. *de-plore*.

Imply. (F.—L.) Coined from L. *im-* (*in*), and *ply*; as if from a F. **implier*; but the F. form was *impliquer*, still earlier *emploier* (whence E. *employ*). See **Ply**.

Import. (F.—L.; or L.) In two senses: (1) to signify. — M. F. *importer*, to signify.—L. *importāre*, to import, bring in, introduce, cause: (2) to bring in from abroad; directly from the same L. *im-*

portāre.—L. *im-* (*in*), in; *portāre,* to bring. Der. *import-ant,* i. e. importing much. See Port (1).

importable, intolerable; *obsolete.* (F. —L.) M. F. *importable.*—L. *importābilis,* that cannot be borne.—L. *im-* (*in*-), not; *portāre,* to bear.

Importune, to molest. (F.—L.) From M. E. *importune,* adj., troublesome.—F. *importun,* 'importunate;' Cot.—L. *importūnus,* unfit, unsuitable, troublesome. Orig. 'hard of access;' from L. *im-* (*in*-), not; *portus,* access, a harbour. See Port (2). Der. *importun-ate,* from pp. of Late L. *importūnāri,* to vex, dep. vb.

Impose. (F.—L. and Gk.) F. *im-poser,* to lay upon.—F. *im-* (L. *in*), upon; F. *poser,* to lay. See Pose (1).

Imposition. (F.—L.) F. *imposition.* —L. acc. *impositiōnem,* a laying on.—L. *impositus,* pp. of *impōnere,* to lay on.—L. *im-* (*in*), on; *pōnere,* to lay.

impost. (F.—L.) O. F. *impost,* a tax.—L. pp. neut. *impositum* (above), a thing imposed.

Imposthume, an abscess. (F.—L.— Gk.) Better *apostume,* as in Cotgrave.— M. F. *apostume,* 'an apostume, an inward swelling full of corrupt matter.' A still better spelling is M. F. *aposteme,* also in Cotgrave.—L. *apostēma.*—Gk. ἀπόστημα, a standing away from; hence, a separation of corrupt matter.—Gk. ἀπό, away; στη-, base of ἵστημι, I set, place, stand. (√STA.)

Impostor. (L.) L. *impostor,* a de-ceiver; from L. *impōnere,* to impose, also, to impose upon, cheat. See Imposition.

Impotence. (F.—L.) F. (and O. F.) *impotence.*—L. *impotentia,* inability.—L. *impotent-,* stem of *impotens,* powerless. See Im- (4) and Potent.

Impoverish. (F.—L.) From O. F. *empovris-,* stem of pres. pt. of *empovrir,* to impoverish.—F. *em-* (= L. *in*), ex-tremely; O. F. *povre,* poor, from Lat. *pauperem,* acc. of *pauper,* poor. See Poverty and Poor.

Imprecate. (L.) From pp. of L. *im-precāri,* to call down upon by prayer.—L. *im-* (*in*), upon; *precāri,* to pray. See Pre-carious and Pray.

Impregnable. (F.—L.) The *gn* orig. represented the sound of *n* followed by a slight glide; cf. M. E. *regne,* pron. (ren'yə), whence E. *reign.*—F. *imprenable,* 'impregnable;' Cot.—F. *im-* (= L. *in*-),

not; F. *prendre,* from L. *prehendere,* to take, seize. See Prehensile.

Impregnate, to render pregnant. (L.) From pp. of L. *imprægnāre,* to impreg-nate.—L. *im-* (for *in*), in; **prægnāre,* only used in the pres. pt. *prægnans* ; see Pregnant.

Imprese, an heraldic device, with a motto. (F.—Ital.—L.) In Rich. II. iii. 1. 25. Also spelt *impresa* (Nares).—O. F. *imprese.*—Ital. *impresa,* an imprese, an embleme; also, an enterprise;' Florio. Fem. of *impreso,* undertaken (hence, adopted), pp. of *imprendere,* to undertake. —L. *in,* in; *prehendere,* to lay hold of. Doublet, *emprise,* an enterprise, Spenser, F. Q. ii. 4. 12 ; from F. *emprise,* fem. pp. of *emprendre,* to undertake (Cotgrave) = Ital. *imprendere.* Der. *impresario,* an undertaker, stage-manager ; from *impresa* an undertaking.

Impress. (L.) L. *impressāre,* fre-quent. of *imprimere,* to press upon.—L. *im-* (*in*), on; *premere,* to press. See Press.

imprint. (F.—L.) The verb, in Sir T. More, is formed as if from *im-* and *print*; but *print* itself is short for *emprint.* —O. F. *empreinte,* 'a stamp, print;' Cot. Orig. fem. of pp. of *empreindre,* 'to print, stamp;' id.—L. *imprimere,* to impress, press upon (above). See Print.

Imprison. (F.—L.) For *emprison.*— O. F. *emprisonner,* to imprison.—O. F. *em-* (for L. *in*), in; *prison,* a prison. See Prison.

Impromptu, a thing said off hand. (F.—L.) F. *impromptu.*—L. *in promptū,* in readiness ; where *promptū* is abl. of *promptus,* a sb. formed from *prōmere,* to bring forward ; see Prompt.

Impropriate, to appropriate to private use. (L.) Coined from L. *im-* (*in*), in ; *propriāre,* to appropriate, from *proprius,* one's own. See Proper.

Improve. (F.—L.) Formerly *emprove,* for late M. E. *enprowen* (Skelton), which was itself an alteration of M. E. *approwen,* to benefit.—O. F. *aproer, apprower,* to benefit.—O. F. *a* (for L. *ad,* to), and *prou,* sb., profit, answering to Ital. *prode,* sb., benefit. Cf. Ital. *prode,* adj., good, valiant; see Prowess. ¶ The O. F. sb. *emprovement,* improvement, occurs in Godefroy.

Improvise. (F.—Ital.—L.) F. *im-proviser.*—Ital. *improvvisare,* to sing extemporaneous verses.—Ital. *improvviso*, sudden, unprovided for.—L. *improuīsus*, unforeseen.—L. *im-* (for *in-*), not; *prō*, before; *uīsus*, pp. of *uidēre*, to see. See Vision.

Impudent, shameless. (F.—L.) F. *impudent*. —L. *impudent-*, stem of *impudens*, shameless.—L. *im-* (for *in*), not; *pudens*, modest, pres. pt. of *pudēre*, to feel shame.

Impugn. (F.—L.) F. *impugner*.—L. *impugnāre*, to fight against.—L. *im-* (for *in*), against; *pugnāre*, to fight, from *pugna*, a battle; cf. *pugnus*, a fist.

Impulse; see Impel.

Impunity. (F.—L.) F. *impunité*.—L. acc. *impūnitātem*, acc. of *impūnitās*, impunity.—L. *impūni-s*, without punishment.—L. *im-* (=*in-*), not; *pœna*, punishment. See Pain.

Impute. (F.—L.) F. *imputer*.—L. *imputāre*, to ascribe.—L. *im-* (*in*), towards; *putāre*, to reckon. See Putative.

In, prep. (E.) A.S. *in.*+Du. *in*, Icel. *i*, Swed. Dan. *i*, Goth. *in*, G. *in*, W. *yn*, O. Irish *in*, L. *in*, Gk. ἐν, ἐνί. L. *in* is for O. L. *en* (as in *en-do*)=Gk. ἐν. Der. *inn-er*, A. S. *innera*; *in-most*, A.S. *inne-mest* (i. e. *inne-m-est*, a double superl. form). The form *innermost* is also a corruption of A. S. *innemest*. Also *in-ward*, *there-in*, *where-in*, *with-in*, *in-as-much*, *in-so-much*, *in-ter-*, *in-tro-*. And see Inn.

In- (1), prefix. (E.) In some words, it is only the prep. *in* in composition. Exx.: *in-born*, *in-breathe*, *in-bred*, *in-land*, &c. And see Im- (1).

In- (2), prefix. (L.) In some words, it is the L. prep. *in* in composition. Exx.: *in-augurate*, *in-carcerate*, &c. Sometimes, it has passed through French; as *in-dication*, &c. ¶ It becomes *il-* before *l*, *im-* before *b*, *m*, and *p*, *ir-* before *r*.

In- (3), negative prefix. (L.; or F.—L.) From L. neg. prefix *in-*, cognate with E. neg. prefix *un-*; see Un- (1), An-, A- (9). ¶ It becomes *i-* before *gn*, as in *i-gnoble*; *il-* before *l*; *im-* before *b*, *m*, and *p*; *ir-* before *r*. Der. *in-ability*, *in-accessible*, &c., &c.; for which see *able*, *access*, &c.

Inane, empty, silly, useless. (L.) L. *inānis*, void, empty. Root unknown. Der. *inan-i-ty*.

inanition, exhaustion from lack of food. (F.—L.) F. *inanition*, 'an emptying;' Cot. From the pp. of *inānīre*, to empty; from *inānis* (above).

Inaugurate. (L.) From pp. of L. *in-augurāre*, to practise augury, to consecrate, begin formally.—L. *in*, in, upon; *augur*, an augur; see Augur.

Inca, a royal title. (Peruv.) Peruv. *inca*, a title. Cf. Peruv. *ç̧apay kapac Inca*, king of Peru (*ç̧apay* = only; *kapac* = lord). *Inca* was orig. the chief of a tribe (Oviedo).

Incandescent, glowing hot. (L.) From stem of pres. pt. of *in-candescere*, to glow; where *candescere* is the inceptive form of *candēre*, to glow. See Candid.

Incantation. (F.—L.) F. *incantation*.—L. *incantātiōnem*, acc. of *incantātio*, an enchanting.—L. *incantāre*, to enchant. — L. *in*, on, upon; *cantāre*, to sing, frequent. of *canere*, to sing. See Enchant and Cant (1).

Incarcerate, to imprison. (L.) L. *in*, in; and *carcerātus*, pp. of *carcerāre*, to imprison, from *carcer*, a prison.

Incarnadine, to dye of a red colour. (F.—Ital.—L.) F. *incarnadin*, carnation colour (Cot.).—Ital. *incarnadino*, carnation colour (Florio); also spelt *incarnatino*.—Ital. *incarnato*, incarnate; also, of flesh colour.—L. *incarnātus*, pp. of *incarnāre*, to clothe with flesh (below).

incarnation. (F.—L.) F. *incarnation*.—L. acc. *incarnātiōnem*, embodiment in flesh.—L. *incarnātus*, pp. of *incarnāre*, to clothe with flesh.—L. *in*, on; and *carn-*, decl. base of *caro*, flesh. See Carnal.

Incendiary. (L.) L. *incendiārius*, setting on fire.—L. *incendium*, a burning.—L. *incendere*, to set on fire.—L. *in*, upon; and **candēre*, to burn (not found), allied to Skt. *chand*, to shine.

incense (1), to inflame. (L.) From L. *incensus*, pp. of *incendere*, to set on fire; see above.

incense (2), smell of burnt spices. (F.—L.) F. *encens*, incense, burnt spices. —L. *incensum*, that which is burnt; neut. of pp. of *incendere*, to set on fire (above).

Incentive. (L.) L. *incentīuus*, striking up a tune, inciting.—L. **incentus*, unused pp. of *incinere*, to sound an instrument.—L. *in*, into; and *canere*, to sound, sing. See Chant.

Inceptive. (F.—L.) O. F. *inceptif*, adj., beginning (Godefroy).—Late L. **inceptīvus* (not found).—L. *incept-us*, pp. of *incipere*, to begin; see Incipient.

Incessant, ceaseless. (F.—L.) F. *incessant*.—L. *incessant-* stem of *incessans*, unceasing. — L. *in-*, not; *cessans*, ceasing, pres. pt. of *cessāre*, to cease, frequent. of *cēdere*, to yield. See **Cease** and **Cede**.

Incest, impurity. (F.—L.) M. E. *incest.* — F. *inceste*, sb. m. — L. *incestus* (gen. *-ūs*), incest. — L. *incestus*, unchaste. — L. *in-*, not; *castus*, chaste. See **Chaste**.

Inch (1), the twelfth part of a foot. (L. — Gk.) M. E. *inche.* A. S. *ynce.* — L. *uncia*, an inch; also an ounce, one-twelfth of a pound. — Sicilian οὐγκία, the same. — Gk. ὄγκος, bulk, weight. **Doublet,** *ounce* (1). And see **Uncial**.

Inch (2), an island. (Gael.) Gael. *innis*, an island.+Irish *inis*; W. *ynys*; Bret. *enez*; Corn. *enys*.

Incident. (F. — L.) F. *incident*, ' an incident;' Cot. — L. *incident-*, stem of pres. pt. of *incidere*, to fall upon. — L. *in*, on; and *cadere*, to fall. See **Cadence**.

Incipient. (L.) L. *incipient-*, stem of pres. pt. of *incipere*, to begin. — L. *in*, upon; *capere*, to lay hold of. See **Capacious**.

Incise, to cut into. (F.—L.) F. *inciser.* — L. *incīsus*, pp. of *in-cīdere*, to cut into. — L. *in*, in; *cædere*, to cut. See **Cæsura**.

Incite. (F. – L.) F. *inciter.* – L. *incitāre*, to urge on. — L. *in*, on; *citāre*, to urge. See **Cite**.

Incline, to lean towards. (F.—L.) F. *incliner.* — L. *inclīnāre.* — L. *in*, towards; **clīnāre*, to lean, cognate with E. **Lean** (1), q. v. **Doublet,** *encline*.

Inclose. (F. – L.) For *enclose.* — O. F. *enclos*, pp. of *enclore*, to include. — L. *inclūdere*, to shut in. — L. *in*, in; *claudere*, to shut. See **Clause**.

include. (L.) From L. *inclūdere* (above).

Incognito, lit. unknown. (Ital.—L.) Ital. *incognito*, unknown. — L. *in-cognitus*, not known. — L. *in-*, not; *cognitus*, known. See **Cognition**.

Income, gain, revenue. (E.) Properly that which *comes in*; from *in* and *come*. So also *out-come*, i. e. result.

Incommode. (F.—L.) F. *incommoder*, to inconvenience. — L. *incommodāre*, to inconvenience. — L. *in*, not; *commodus*, fit; see **Commodious**.

Incony, fine, delicate, very dear. (E.) In Shak. For *in-conny*; where *in-* is intensive, as in M. E. *in-ly*, very; and *conny* (also *canny*) is North E., meaning skilful, gentle, pleasant, &c. From E.

can, I know (how); cf. Icel. *kunnigr*, knowing, wise.

Incorporate. (L.) L. *incorporātus*, pp. of *incorporāre*, to furnish with a body; hence to form into a body. — L. *in*, in; *corpor-*, stem of *corpus*, a body. See **Corporal** (2).

Increase. (F.—L.) M. E. *incresen*, *encresen.* — F. *en* (L. *in*); and A. F. *creiss-*, stem of pres. pt. of A. F. *creistre*, O. F. *croistre* (F. *croître*), to grow, from L. *crescere*, to grow. See **Crescent**. **Der.** *increase*, sb.; A. F. *encrees*.

increment. (L.) L. *incrēmentum*, an increase. L. *in*, in, used intensively; *crē-*, as in *crē-tum*, supine of *crescere*, to grow, with suffix *-mentum*. Cf. *de-cre-ment*.

Incubate. (L.) From pp. of Lat. *incubāre*, to sit on eggs to hatch them. — L. *in*, upon; *cubāre*, to lie down, to sit.

incubus. (L.) L. *incubus*, a nightmare. — L. *in-cubāre*, to lie upon (above).

Inculcate. (L.) From pp. of L. *inculcāre*, lit. to tread in, hence, to enforce by admonition. — L. *in*, in; *calcāre*, to tread. See **Calk**.

Inculpate. (L.) From pp. of Late L. *inculpāre*, to bring blame upon. — L. *in*, upon; *culpāre*, to blame. See **Culpable**.

Incumbent. (L.) L. *incumbent-*, stem of pres. pt. of *incumbere*, to recline on, rest on or in (remain in); where **cumbere* is a nasalised form allied to *cubāre*, to lie down. So also *pro-cumbent*, prostrate; *re-cumbent*, lying back upon; *suc-cumb*, to lie under, yield to.

Incur. (L.) L. *incurrere*, to run into, run upon. — L. *in*, upon; *currere*, to run. See **Current**.

incursion. (F.—L.) M. F. *incursion.* — L. *incursiōnem*, acc. of *incursio*, an inroad. — L. *incursus*, pp. of *incurrere*, to run into, attack (above).

Incurvate, to crook. (L.) From pp. of L. *incuruāre*, to bend into a curve. — L. *in*, in; *curuāre*, to bend. See **Curve**.

Indeed, truly. (E.) For *in deed*, i. e. in fact; see **Deed**.

Indelible. (F.—L.) For *indeleble.* — M. F. *indelebile*, 'indelible;' Cot. — L. *indēlēbilis*, indelible. — L. *in-*, not; *dēlēbilis*, destructible, from *dēlēre*, to destroy. See **Delete**.

Indemnify, to make damage good. (L.) Ill coined; from L. *indemni-s*, unharmed, free from loss; and F. *-fier*, for L. *-fic-āre*, for *facere*, to make (as in *magni-fy*). L. *indemnis* is from L. *in-*, not; and *damnum*, loss. See **Damn**.

indemnity. (F.–L.) F. *indemnité*. –L. acc. *indemnitātem*.–L. *in-demni-s*, unharmed, free from loss (*damnum*).

Indent (1), to cut into points like teeth. (Law L.) A law term.–Law L. *indentāre*, to notch.–L. *in*, in; *dent-*, stem of *dens*, a tooth. Der. *indenture* (F. *endenture*); so called because duplicate deeds were cut with notched edges to fit one another.

Indent (2), to make a dint in. (E.) From E. *in*, prep.; and *dent*, a dint. See **Dint**. Suggested by *indent* (1), but quite a distinct word.

Index. (L.) L. *index* (stem *indic-*), a discloser, something that indicates.–L. *indicāre*, to point out.–L. *in*, in, to; *dicāre*, to appoint, declare, allied to *dīcere*, to say; see **Diction**.

indicate. (L.) From pp. of L. *in-dicāre*, to point at, point out (above).

indict. (F.–L.) For *indite* (which is the French spelling), and so pronounced. See **Indite**.

indiction, a cycle of fifteen years. (L.) O. F. *indiction*, an appointment of tributes arranged for fifteen years; the lit. sense is merely 'appointment.'–L. *in-dictiōnem*, acc. of *indictio*, an appointment, esp. of a tax.–L. *indictus*, pp. of *indīcere*, to appoint, impose a tax.–L. *in*, upon; *dicere*, to say. See **Diction**.

Indigenous, native. (L.) Late L. *indigen-us*, native; with suffix *-ous*.–L. *indi-* = O. Lat. *indu*, within (cf. Gk. ἔνδον); and *gen-*, as in *gen-i-tus*, born, pp. of *gignere*, to beget; see **Genus**.

Indigent, destitute. (F.–L.) M. F. *indigent*.–L. *indigent-*, stem of pres. part. of *indigēre*, to be in want.–L. *ind-*, for *indu*, an O. Lat. extension from *in*, in (cf. Gk. ἔνδον, within); *egēre*, to want, be in need; cf. L. *indigus*, needy. Cf. Gk. ἀχήν, poor, needy (Theocritus).

Indigo, a blue dye. (F.–Span.–L. –Gk.–Pers.–Skt.) F. *indigo*.–Span. *indico*.–L. *indicum*, indigo; neut. of *Indicus*, Indian (hence Indian dye).–Gk. ἰνδικόν, indigo; neut. of Ἰνδικός, Indian.– Pers. *Hind*, India; a name due to the river Indus.–Skt. *sindhu-*, the river Indus; a large river.–Skt. *syand*, to flow. ¶ The Persian changes initial *s* into *h*.

Indite. (F.–L.) For *endite*. M. F. *endicter*, O. F. *enditer*, to indict, accuse; also spelt *inditer*.–Late L. *indictāre*, to point out, frequent. of *indīcere*, to appoint. See **Indicate**. Doubtless confused with the closely related L. *indicāre*, to point out.

Indolence. (F.–L.) F. *indolence*.– L. *indolentia*, freedom from pain; hence, ease, idleness.–L. *in-*, not; *dolent-* stem of pres. pt. of *dolēre*, to grieve. See **Doleful**.

Indomitable. (L.) Coined from *in-*, not; *domitāre*, to subdue, frequent. of *domāre*, to tame. See **Daunt**.

Indubitable. (F.–L.) M.F. *indubitable*.–L. *indubitābilis*, not to be doubted. –L. *in-*, not; *dubitābilis*, doubtful, from *dubitāre*, to doubt; see **Doubt**.

Induce. (L.) L. *indūcere*, to lead to. –L. *in*, in, to; *dūcere*, to lead; see **Duke**.

induct. (L.) From L. *induct-us*, pp. of *indūcere*, to bring in (above).

Indue (1), to invest or clothe with, supply with. (L.) In Spenser, F. Q. iii. 6. 35.–L. *induere*, to put into, put on, clothe with. The prefix is *ind-*, not *in-* (for this prefix see **Indigent**); cf. *ex-uuiæ*, spoils, *ind-uuiæ*, clothes. See **Exuviæ**.

Indue (2), a corruption of **Endue**, q.v.

Indulgence. (F.–L.) F. *indulgence*. –L. *indulgentia*.–L. *indulgent-*, stem of pres. pt. of *indulgēre*, to be courteous to, indulge. (Of unknown origin.)

Indurate, to harden. (L.) From pp. of L. *indūrāre*, to harden.–L. *in*, intensive; *dūrāre*, to harden, from *dūrus*, hard. See **Dure**.

Industry. (F.–L.) F. *industrie*.– L. *industria*. – L. *industrius*, diligent. Origin uncertain.

Inebriate. (L.) From L. *inēbriātus*, pp. of *inēbriāre*, to make drunk.–L. *in*, in, very; *ēbriāre*, to make drunk, from *ēbrius*, drunk. See **Ebriety**.

Ineffable. (F.–L.) F. *ineffable*.– L. *ineffābilis*, unspeakable.–L. *in-*, not; *ef-* (for *ex*), out; *fā-rī*, to speak; with suffix *-bilis*. See **Fate**.

Inept, foolish. (F.–L.) XVII cent. –M. F. *inepte*.–L. *ineptus*, improper, foolish.–L. *in-*, not; and *aptus*, fit. (Also *inapt*, from *in-*, not, and *apt*.) See **Apt**.

Inert. (L.) L. *inert-*, stem of *iners*, unskilful, inactive.–L. *in-*, not; *ars*, skill. See **Art** (2).

Inexorable. (F. – L.) F. *inexorable.*
– L. *inexōrābilis,* that cannot be moved
by intreaty. – L. *in-,* not; *exōrāre,* to
gain by intreaty, from L. *ex,* out, greatly,
and *ōrāre,* to pray. See **Oration.**

Infamy. (F. – L.) F. *infamie.* – L.
infāmia, ill fame. – L. *infāmi-s,* adj., of
ill fame. – L. *in-,* not, bad; *fāma,* fame.
See **Fame.**

Infant. (L.) L. *infant-,* stem of *in-*
fans, not speaking, hence, a very young
babe. – L. *in-,* not; *fans,* pres. pt. of
fārī, to speak.

infantry. (F. – Ital. – L.) F. *infan-*
terie. – Ital. *infanteria,* foot-soldiers; orig.
a band of 'infants,' as young men were
called. – Ital. *infante,* an infant. – L.
infantem, acc. of *infans* (above).

Infatuate. (L.) From pp. of L.
infatuāre, to make a fool of. – L. *in,* in,
greatly; *fatuus,* foolish. See **Fatuous.**

Infect, to taint. (F. – L.) M. E.
infect, as pp.; also *infecten,* vb. – O. F.
infect, infected. – L. *infectus,* pp. of *in-*
ficere, to put in, dye, stain. – L. *in,* in;
facere, to put. See **Fact.**

Infer, to imply. (F. – L.) M. F. *in-*
ferer; F. *inférer.* – L. *inferre,* to bring in,
introduce. – L. *in,* in; *ferre,* to bring.
See **Fertile.**

Inferior. (F. – L.) M. F. *inferieur.* –
L. *inferiōrem,* acc. of *inferior,* lower,
comp. of *inferus,* low, nether. Strictly,
inferus is itself a compar. form, which
some connect with Skt. *adhara,* lower;
which is doubtful. See Brugm. i. § 589
(note).

infernal. (F. – L.) F. *infernal.* – L.
infernālis, belonging to the lower regions.
– L. *infernus,* lower; extended from *in-*
ferus (above).

Infest, to harass. (F. – L.) F. *infester.*
– L. *infestāre,* to attack. – L. *infestus,*
attacking, hostile; orig. unsafe. Origin
doubtful.

Infidel. (F. – L.) M. F. *infidele,* 'in-
fidell;' Cot. – L. *infidēlis,* faithless. – L.
in-, not; *fidēlis,* faithful, from *fidē-s,* faith.
See **Faith.**

Infinite. (F. – L.) O. F. *infinit* (F.
infini). – L. *infinītus,* unended. – L. *in-,*
not; *fīnītus,* pp. of *fīnīre,* to end, from
fīnis, end. See **Final.**

Infirm. (L.) L. *infirmus,* not strong,
weak. – L. *in-,* not; *firmus,* firm. See
Firm. Der. *infirm-ar-y, infirm-i-ty.*

Inflate. (L.) From pp. of L. *inflāre,*

to blow into, puff up. – L. *in,* in; *flāre,* to
blow. See **Flatulent.**

Inflect, to modulate the voice, &c.
(L.) L. *inflectere,* lit. to bend in. – L.
in, in; *flectere,* to bend. See **Flexible.**

Inflict. (L.) From L. *inflictus,* pp. of
inflīgere, to inflict, lit. to strike upon. – L.
in, upon; and *flīgere,* to strike. See
Afflict.

Inflorescence, mode of flowering.
(F. – L.) F. *inflorescence.* From the
pres. pt. of L. *inflōrescere,* to burst into
blossom. – L. *in,* into; and *flōrescere,*
inceptive form of *flōrēre,* to bloom. See
Flourish.

Influence. (F. – L.) O. F. *influence,*
a flowing in, esp. used of the influence of
planets. – Late L. *influentia.* – L. *influent-,*
stem of pres. pt. of *influere,* to flow into.
– L. *in,* into; *fluere,* to flow. See
Fluent.

influenza. (Ital. – L.) Ital. *influenza,*
influence, also used of a severe catarrh. A
doublet of **Influence** (above).

influx. (F. – L.) O. F. *influx.* – L. *in-*
fluxus, a flowing in. – L. *in,* in; *fluxus,*
pp. of *fluere,* to flow.

Inform, to impart knowledge to. (F.
– L.) F. *informer.* – L. *informāre,* to
put into form, mould; also, to tell, inform.
– L. *in,* into; *forma,* form. See **Form.**

Infraction, violation of law. (F. –
L.) F. *infraction.* – L. acc. *infractiōnem,*
a weakening, breaking into. – L. *infractus,*
pp. of *in-fringere* (below).

infringe. (L.) L. *infringere,* to
break into, violate law. – L. *in,* into;
frangere, to break. See **Fragile.**

Infuriate. (Ital. – L.) Ital. *infuriato,*
pp. of *infuriare,* to fly into a rage. – Ital.
in furia, 'in a fury, ragingly;' Florio. –
L. *in,* in; *furia,* rage. See **Fury.** ¶ Or
from Late L. pp. *infuriātus* (Ducange).

Infuse. (F. – L.) F. *infuser.* – L. *in-*
fūsus, pp. of *infundere,* to pour in. – L.
in, in; *fundere,* to pour. See **Fuse** (1).

Ingenious. (F. – L.) M. F. *ingenieux*
(Cot.). – L. *ingeniōsus,* clever. – L. *ingen-*
ium, natural capacity; see **Engine.**

ingenuous. (L.) L. *ingenu-us,* in-
born, free-born, frank; with suffix *-ous.* –
L. *in,* in; *gen-,* as in *gen-i-tus,* born, pp.
of *gignere,* to beget. See **Genus.**

Ingle (1), fire. (C.) Lowl. Sc. *ingle,*
fire. Perhaps from Gael and Irish *aingeal,*
fire. Allied to Irish *ong,* Russ. *ogone,* fire.
See **Ignition.**

Ingle (2), a darling, paramour. (Du. or Fries. – L. – Gk.) Also *engle* (Nares). M. Du. *ingel, engel,* an angel (hence, a term of endearment). Koolman notes E. Fries. *engel,* an angel, as being commonly used as a term of endearment and as a female name. – L. *angelus.* – Gk. ἄγγελος. See **Angel.**

Ingot, a mass of unwrought metal. (E.) M. E. *ingot,* Chaucer, C. T. 16677, &c., where it means a mould for molten metal. But the true sense is 'that which is poured in,' a mass of metal. – A.S. *in,* in; and *got-en,* poured, pp. of *gēotan,* to pour, fuse metals. Cf. Du. *ingieten,* Swed. *ingjuta,* to pour in. Also Du. *gieten,* G. *giessen,* Icel. *gjóta* (pp. *gotinn*), Dan. *gyde,* Swed. *gjuta,* Goth. *giutan,* to pour, shed, fuse; cognate with L. *fundere.* (✓GHEU.) Hence F. *lingot,* for *l'ingot.* + G. *einguss,* a pouring in, also an ingot; Swed. *ingöte,* the neck of a mould for metals.

Ingrain, to dye of a fast colour. (F. – L.) M. E. *engreynen.* – M. F. *engrainer* (Palsg.). – F. *en graine,* in grain, with a fast colour. – F. *en,* in (L. *in*); Late L. *grāna,* cochineal dye, from *grānum,* a grain. See **Grain** and **Cochineal.**

Ingrate, ungrateful. (F. – L.) F. *ingrat.* – L. *ingrātus,* not pleasing. – L. *in-,* not; *grātus,* pleasing. See **Grateful.**

Ingratiate, to commend to the favour of. (L.) Coined from L. *in,* in; *grātia,* favour, grace. See **Grace.**

Ingredient, that which enters into a compound. (F. – L.) F. *ingrédient* (the same). – L. *ingredient-,* stem of pres. pt. of *ingredī,* to enter upon, begin (hence to enter into). – L. *in,* in; *gradī,* to go. See **Grade.**

ingress. (L.) L. *ingressus,* an entering. – L. *ingressus,* pp. of *ingredī* (above).

Inguinal, relating to the groin. (L.) L. *inguinālis* (the same). – L. *inguin-,* stem of *inguen,* the groin.

Inhabit. (F. – L.) M. F. *inhabiter.* – L. *inhabitāre,* to dwell in. – L. *in,* in; *habitāre,* to dwell. See **Habitation.**

Inhale. (L.) L. *inhālāre,* to breathe in, draw in breath. – L. *in,* in; *hālāre,* to breathe. Cf. **Exhale.**

Inherent. (L.) L. *inhærent-,* stem of pres. pt. of *in-hærēre,* to stick in. Hence *inhere,* as a verb. See **Hesitate.**

Inherit. (F. – L.) O. F. *enheriter.* – Late L. *inhērēditāre.* – L. *in,* in; *hērēd-em,* acc. of *hērēs,* an heir. See **Heir.**

Inhibit, to check. (L.) From L. *inhibitus,* pp. of *inhibēre,* to keep in, hold in. – L. *in,* in; *habēre,* to have, keep. See **Habit.**

Inimical. (L.) L. *inimīcālis,* extended from *inimīcus,* hostile. – L. *in-,* not; and *amīcus,* friendly. See **Enemy** and **Amiable.**

Iniquity, vice. (F. – L.) M. E. *iniquitee.* – F. *iniquité.* – L. *inīquitātem,* acc. of *inīquitās,* injustice. – L. *in-,* not; *æquitas,* equity. See **Equity.**

Initial, pertaining to the beginning. (F. – L.) F. *initial.* – L. *initiālis,* adj. from *initium,* a beginning. – L. *initum,* supine of *in-īre,* to go in, to enter into or upon. – L. *in,* in; *īre,* to go.

initiate, to begin. (L.) From pp. of L. *initiāre,* to begin. – L. *initium* (above).

Inject. (L.) From *iniectus,* pp. of L. *inicere,* to cast in, throw into. – L. *in,* in; *iacere,* to throw. See **Jet** (1).

Injunction, command. (L.) From L. *iniunctio,* an order. – L. *iniunctus,* pp. of *iniungere,* to bid. See **Enjoin.**

Injure. (F. – L.) F. *injurier.* – Late L. *iniūriāre;* for L. *iniūriārī,* to harm. – L. *iniūria,* harm. – L. *iniūrius,* wrong. – L. *in-,* not; *iūr-,* for *iūs,* law, right. See **Just.**

Ink. (F. – L. – Gk.) M. E. *enke.* – O. F. *enque* (F. *encre*). – Late L. *incaustum;* L. *encaustum,* the purple-red ink used by the later Roman emperors; neut. of *encaustus,* burnt in. – Gk. ἔγκαυστος, burnt in. – Gk. ἐν, in; καίω, I burn. (Cf. Ital. *inchiostro,* ink.) See **Encaustic.**

Inkle, a kind of tape. (Origin unknown.) Perhaps from M. Du. *enckel,* Du. *enkel,* single, as opposed to double; but there is no obvious connexion.

Inkling, a hint, intimation. (Scand.?) M. E. *inkling,* a whisper, murmur, low speaking. Alexander, when in disguise, feared he was discovered, because he 'herd *a nyngkiling* of his name'; Allit. romance of Alexander, 2968; where *a nyngkiling* stands for *an yngkiling.* 'To *incle* the truthe' = to hint at the truth, Alisaunder (in app. to Wm. of Palerne), 616. Origin unknown; perhaps allied to Swed. *enkel,* single; cf. *et enkelt ord,* a single word; M. Du. *enckelinge,* 'a falling or a diminishing of notes;' Hexham.

Inn, sb. (E.) M. E. *in, inn.* – A. S. *inn, in,* sb., room, dwelling. – A. S. *in,* *inn*, adv., within, indoors. – A.S. *in*, prep., in. +Icel. *inni*, an inn ; *inni*, adv., indoors. See In.

inning. (E.) Properly the securing or housing of grain, from *inn*, vb., due to *inn*, sb. (above). Also *innings*, at cricket, invariably used in the plural, because the side which is *in* consists of several players.

Innate, in-born. (L.) L. *innātus*, in-born. – L. *in*, in ; *nātus*, born ; see Natal.

Innocent. (F. – L.) F. *innocent*. – L. *innocent-*, stem of *innocens*, harmless. – L. *in-*, not ; *nocens*, pres. pt. of *nocēre*, to hurt. See Noxious.

innocuous. (L.) L. *innocu-us*, harmless ; with suffix *-ous*. – L. *in-*, not ; *nocēre*, to hurt.

Innovate, to introduce something new. (L.) From pp. of L. *innouāre*, to renew, make new. – L. *in*, in ; *nouus*, new. See Novel.

Innuendo, an indirect hint. (L.) Not to be spelt *inuendo*. From L. *innuendo*, by intimating ; gerund of *innuere*, to nod towards, intimate. – L. *in*, in, at ; *nuere*, to nod. See Nutation.

Inoculate. (L.) In old authors it means 'to engraft.' – L. *inoculātus*, pp. of *inoculāre*, to engraft, insert a graft. – L. *in*, in ; *oculus*, an eye, also a bud of a plant. See Ocular.

Inordinate. (L.) L. *inordinātus*. – L. *in-*, not ; *ordinātus*, ordered, controlled, pp. of *ordināre* ; see Ordain. And see Order.

Inquest. (F. – L.) Later spelling of M. E. *enqueste*. – O. F. *enqueste*. – Late L. *inquesta*, sb., from *inquesta*, fem. of Late L. *inquestus*. – L. *inquīsītus*, pp. of *inquīrere*, to search into. – L. *in*, into ; *quaerere*, to search. See Query.

inquire, late spelling of Enquire, q. v.

inquisition. (F. – L.) F. *inquisition*. – L. acc. *inquīsītiōnem*, a search into. – L. *inquīsītus*, pp. of *inquīrere* ; see Inquest (above).

Inscribe. (L.) L. *inscrībere*, to write in or upon ; pp. *inscriptus* (whence *inscription*). – L. *in*, upon ; *scrībere*, to write. See Scribe.

Inscrutable, that cannot be scrutinised. (F. – L.) F. *inscrutable*. – L. *in-scrūtābilis*. – L. *in-*, not ; *scrūtāri*, to scrutinise. See Scrutiny.

Insect. (F. – L.) F. *insecte*. – L. *in-sectum*, lit. 'a thing cut into,' i. e. nearly divided, from the shape. – L. *insectus*, pp. of *insecāre*, to cut into. – L. *in*, into ; *secāre*, to cut. See Secant.

Insert. (L.) From L. *insertus*, pp. of *inserere*, to introduce, put in. – L. *in*, in ; *serere*, to join, put. See Series.

Insidious. (F. – L.) F. *insidieux*, deceitful. – L. *insidiōsus*, treacherous. – L. *insidiæ*, pl. troops of men who lie in wait, also cunning wiles. – L. *insidēre*, to lie in wait, lit. 'to sit in.' – L. *in*, in ; *sedēre*, to sit. See Sedentary.

Insignia. (L.) L. *insignia*, marks of office ; pl. of *insigne*, which is the neuter of *insignis*, remarkable. – L. *in*, upon ; *signum*, a mark. See Sign.

Insinuate. (L.) From pp. of L. *in-sinuāre*, to introduce by winding or bending. – L. *in*, into ; *sinus* (gen. *sinūs*), a bend. See Sinus.

Insipid. (L.) L. *insipidus*. – L. *in-*, not ; *sapidus*, savoury. See Sapid.

Insist. (F. – L.) F. *insister*. – L. *in-sistere*, to set foot on, persist. – L. *in*, in ; *sistere*, to set, stand, from *stāre*, to stand. See State.

Insolent. (F. – L.) M. E. *insolent*. – F. *insolent*, saucy. – L. *insolent-*, stem of *insolens*, not customary, unusual, insolent. – L. *in-*, not ; *solens*, pres. pt. of *solēre*, to be accustomed, be wont.

Inspect. (L.) L. *inspectāre*, to observe ; frequent. of *inspicere*, to look into. – L. *in*, into ; *specere*, to look. See Species.

Inspire. (F. – L.) O. F. *enspirer*, M. F. *inspirer* (Cot.). – L. *inspīrāre*, to breathe into. – L. *in*, into ; *spīrāre*, to breathe. See Spirit.

Inspissate, to make thick. (L.) From pp. of L. *inspissāre*, to thicken. – L. *in*, in ; *spissus*, thick, dense.

Instance. (F. – L.) F. *instance*, 'instance, urgency ;' Cot. – L. *instantia*, a being near, urgency. – L. *instant-*, stem of pres. pt. of *instāre*, to be at hand, to urge. – L. *in*, upon, near ; *stāre*, to stand. See State.

Instead. (E.) For *in stead*, i. e. in the place. See Stead.

Instep, the upper part of the foot, where it rises to the front of the leg. (E.) Formerly *instup* and *instop* (Minsheu). These forms may be related to A. S. *stōp-*, as seen in *stōp-el*, a footprint, O. Sax. *stōp-o*, a step (cf. Du. *stoep*, a set of steps,

G. *stufe,* a step, stair); from *stôp,* strong grade of *stapan,* to advance (whence the secondary verb *steppan,* to step). The reference seems to be to the movement of the foot in walking. See **Step.**

Instigate, to urge on. (L.) From pp. of *instīgāre,* to goad on.—L. *in,* on; and base **stīg-,* to prick, allied to L. *stinguere,* to prick; see **Distinguish.** See Brugm. i. § 633.

Instil. (F.—L.) F. *instiller.* — L. *instillāre,* to pour in by drops.—L. *in,* in; *stillāre,* to drop, from *stilla,* a drop. See **Still** (2).

Instinct. (F.—L.; *or* L.) F. *instinct,* sb.—L. *instinctum,* acc. of *instinctus,* an impulse.—L. *instinctus,* pp. of *instinguere,* to goad on.—L. *in,* on; *stinguere,* to prick. See **Distinguish.**

Institute. (L.) From L. *institūtus,* pp. of *instituere,* to set, establish.—L. *in,* in; *statuere,* to place, from *statu-s,* verbal sb. from *stāre,* to stand. See **State.**

Instruct. (L.) From L. *instructus,* pp. of *instruere,* to build into, instruct. — L. *in,* in; *struere,* to pile up, build. See **Structure.**

instrument. (F.—L.) F. *instrument.*—L. *instrūmentum,* an implement, tool.—L. *instruere* (above); with suffix *-mentum.*

Insular. (L.) L. *insulāris,* insular. — L. *insula,* an island. Cf. **Isle.**

Insult, vb. (F.—L.) F. *insulter.*—L. *insultāre,* to leap upon, scoff at, insult; frequent. of *insilere,* to leap upon.—L. *in,* on; *salīre,* to leap. See **Salient.**

Insurgent. (L.) L. *insurgent-,* stem of pres. pt. of *insurgere,* to rise up or on, to rebel.—L. *in,* on; *surgere,* to rise. See **Surge.**

insurrection. (F.—L.) F. *insurrection.*—L. acc. *insurrectiōnem,* from nom. *insurrectio.*—L. *insurrectus,* pp. of *insurgere,* to rebel (above).

Intaglio, a kind of carved work. (Ital. —L.) Ital. *intaglio,* a sculpture, carving. —Ital. *intagliare,* to cut into.—Ital. *in* (= L. *in*), in; *tagliare* = Late L. *taliāre,* *taleāre,* to cut twigs, to cut, allied to *tālia, tālea,* a slip, twig.

Integer, a whole number. (L.) L. *integer,* whole, entire; lit. untouched, i. e. unharmed.—L. *in-,* not; **tag-,* base of *tangere,* to touch. See **Tangent.** Brugm. i. 244 (3); ii. § 632.

Integument. (L.) L. *integumentum,*

a covering, skin.—L. *in,* upon; *tegere,* to cover; see **Teguement.**

Intellect. (F.—L.) M.F. *intellect.*—L. *intellectus,* perception, discernment.—L. *intellectus,* pp. of *intelligere,* to discern.—L. *intel-,* for *inter,* between; *legere,* to choose. See **Legend.**

intelligence. (F.—L.) F. *intelligence.*—L. *intelligentia,* perception.—L. *intelligent-,* stem of pres. pt. of *intelligere,* to discern, understand (above).

intelligible. (F.—L.) F. *intelligible.*—L. *intelligibilis,* perceptible to the senses.—L. *intelligere,* to discern (above); with suffix *-bilis.*

Intend. (F.—L.) M. E. *entenden.*—F. *entendre.*—L. *intendere,* to stretch to, bend or apply the mind to, design.—L. *in,* to; *tendere,* to stretch. See **Tend** (1).

intense. (F.—L.) O. F. *intense.*—L. *intens-us,* stretched out, pp. of *intendere* (above).

intent, design. (F.—L.) M. E. *entente.*—F. *entente,* intention; participial sb. from F. *entendre,* to intend; see **Intend.** And see below.

intent, adj. (L.) L. *intentus,* bent on; pp. of *intendere;* see **Intend.**

Inter. (F.—L.) M. E. *enterren.*—F. *enterrer,* to bury.—Late L. *interrāre,* to put into the ground.—L. *in,* in; *terra,* ground. See **Terrace.** Der. *inter-ment,* F. *enterrement.*

Inter-, *prefix,* amongst. (L.) L. *inter,* among; a comparative form, answering to Skt. *antar,* within; closely allied to **Interior,** q. v. Also **Intel-** (before *l*).

Intercalate, to insert. (L.) From pp. of L. *intercalāre,* to proclaim that a day has been inserted in the calendar, to insert.—L. *inter,* amongst; *calāre,* to proclaim. See **Calends.**

Intercede. (F.—L.) F. *intercéder.*—L. *intercēdere,* lit. to go between; hence, to mediate.—L. *inter,* between; *cēdere,* to go. See **Cede.** Der. *intercession,* from the pp. *intercess-us.*

Intercept. (F.—L.) F. *intercepter.*—L. *intercept-us,* pp. of *intercipere,* lit. to catch between.—L. *inter,* between; *capere,* to take. See **Capacious.**

Intercourse. (F.—L.) Formerly *entercourse.* — F. *entrecours,* intercourse, commerce. — Late L. *intercursus,* commerce; lit. a running amongst.—L. *inter,* amongst; *cursus,* a running, course, from the pp. of *currere,* to run. See **Course.**

Interdict, sb. (L.) Law L. *inter-dictum,* a kind of excommunication; in Latin, a decree.—L. *interdictus,* pp. of *interdīcere,* to pronounce a judgment between two parties.—L. *inter,* between; *dīcere,* to say. See **Diction.**

Interest (1), profit, advantage. (F.—L.) M. F. *interest* (F. *intérêt*), an interest in a thing, interest for money (Cot.).—L. *interest,* it is profitable; 3 pers. sing. of *interesse,* to concern, lit. 'be among.'—L. *inter,* among; *esse,* to be. See **Inter-** and **Essence.**

interest (2), to engage the attention of another. (F.—L.) A curious word; formed (by partial confusion with the verb above) from the pp. *interess'd* of the obsolete verb *to interess,* used by Massinger and Ben Jonson.—M. F. *interessé,* 'interessed, or touched in;' Cot.—L. *interesse,* to concern (as above). **Der.** Hence *dis-interested,* from the verb *dis-interest,* orig. a pp. and spelt *disinteress'd.*

Interfere. (F.—L.) Formerly *enterfeir,* to dash one heel against the other (Blount). O. F. *s'entreferir,* to exchange blows.—F. *entre,* between; *ferir,* to strike.—L. *inter,* between; *ferīre,* to strike. See **Ferule.**

Interior. (F.—L.) O. F. *interior.*—L. *interiōrem,* acc. of *interior,* comp. of *interus,* within. *In-terus* itself was orig. a comparative form, answering to Skt. *antara-,* interior. The positive is the L. *in*; in; see **In.** Brugm. i. § 466.

Interjacent. (L.) From pres. pt. of L. *interiacēre,* to lie between.—L. *inter,* between; *iacēre,* to lie. See **Jet** (1).

interjection. (F.—L.) F. *interjection,* an interjection, a word *thrown in* to express emotion.—L. acc. *interiectiōnem,* a throwing between, insertion, interjection. — L. *interiectus,* pp. of L. *intericere,* to cast between; (*-icere = iacere,* to cast).

Interloper, an intruder. (Du.—F.—L. and Du.) Low G. and Du. *enterloper* (Brem. Wört.). Lit. 'a runner between;' coined from F. *entre* (< L. *inter*), between; and Du. *looper,* a runner, from *loopen,* to run, cognate with E. *leap*; see **Leap.**

Intermit, to interrupt, cease awhile. (L.) L. *intermittere,* to send apart, interrupt; pp. *intermissus.*—L. *inter,* between; *mittere,* to send. See **Missile. Der.** *intermiss-ion,* F. *intermission,* L. acc. *intermissiōnem*; from the pp.

Intern, to confine within limits. (F.—

L.) F. *interner.*—F. *interne,* internal, kept within.—L. *internus,* inward; from *inter,* within, and suffix *-nus.* See **Inter-.**

internal. (L.) Cf. O. F. *internel.* From L. *intern-us* (above); with suffix *-al* (L.-*ālis*).

Internecine, thoroughly destructive. (L.) L. *internecīnus,* thoroughly destructive.—L. *internecio,* utter slaughter.—L. *inter,* thoroughly (see Lewis); and *necāre,* to kill, from *nec-,* stem of *nex,* death. Cf. Gk. *νέκυς,* a corpse. Brugm. i. § 375.

Interpellation. (F.—L.) F. *interpellation.*—L. acc. *interpellātiōnem.*—L. *interpellātus,* pp. of *interpellāre,* to drive between, to hinder, interrupt.—L. *inter,* between; *pellere,* to drive. See **Pulsate.**

Interpolate. (L.) From pp. of L. *interpolāre,* to furbish up, patch, interpolate.—L. *interpolus, interpolis,* polished up. — L. *inter,* in, between; *polīre,* to polish. See **Polish.**

Interpose. (F.—L. *and* Gk.) F. *interposer,* to put between.—L. *inter,* between; F. *poser,* to put; see **Pose** (1).

Interposition. (F.—L.) F. *interposition.* — L. acc. *interpositiōnem,* a putting between. — L. *interpositus,* pp. of *interpōnere,* to put between. — L. *inter,* between; *pōnere,* to put. See **Position.**

Interpret, to explain. (F.—L.) M. E. *interpreten.*—M. F. *interpreter.*—L. *interpretārī,* to expound.—L. *interpret-,* stem of *interprēs,* an interpreter, properly an agent, broker. The latter part of the word is perhaps allied to L. *pret-ium,* price; see **Price.**

Interregnum. (L.) From L. *inter,* between; *regnum,* a reign, rule, from *regere,* to rule. See **Regent.**

Interrogate. (L.) From pp. of L. *interrogāre,* to question. — L. *inter,* thoroughly; *rogāre,* to ask. See **Rogation.**

Interruption. (F.—L.) F. *interruption.*—L. acc. *interruptiōnem,* a breaking into. — L. *interruptus,* pp. of *interrumpere,* to break into. — L. *inter,* amongst; *rumpere,* to break. See **Rupture.**

Intersect. (L.) From L. *intersectus,* pp. of *intersecāre,* to cut between or apart. — L. *inter,* between; *secāre,* to cut. See **Secant.**

Intersperse. (L.) From L. *interspersus,* pp. of *interspergere,* to sprinkle amongst. — L. *inter,* among; *spargere,* to scatter. See **Sparse.**

Interstice. (F.—L.) F. *interstice.*— L. *interstitium*, an interval of space.—L. *inter*, between ; *stătus*, pp. of *sistere*, to place, from *stāre*, to stand. See **State.**

Interval. (F.—L.) M.F. *intervalle*, interval.—L. *interuallum*, lit. the space between the rampart of a camp and the soldiers' tents.—L.*inter*, between ; *uallum*, rampart. See **Wall.**

Intervene, to come between. (F.—L.) F. *intervenir*; Cot. — L. *interuenīre*, to come between.—L. *inter*, between; *uenīre*, to come. See **Venture.**

Intestate, without a will. (F.—L.) M. F. *intestat.* — L. *intestātus*, that has made no will.—L. *in-*, not ; *testātus*, pp. of *testārī*, to make a will. See **Testament.**

Intestine. (F.—L.) F. *intestin*, adj., 'intestine, inward ; ' Cot.—L. *intestīnus*, inward. Formed from L. *intus*, within, cognate with Gk. ἐντός, within ; extended from L. *in*, in. Cf. **Entrails.**

Intimate (1), to announce, hint. (L.) From pp. of L. *intimāre*, to bring within, to announce. — L. *intimus*, inmost, superl. corresponding to comp. *interior*; see **Interior.**

intimate (2), familiar. (L.) This form is due to confusion with the word above. It is really founded on M. F. *intime*, inward, ' secret, deer, entirely affected;' Cot.; from L. *intimus* (above).

Intimidate. (L.) From pp. of Late L. *intimidāre*, to frighten. — L. *in*, intensive prefix ; *timidus*, timid. See **Timid.**

Into, prep. (E.) M. E. *into*; orig. two words. A. S. *in tō*, in to, where *in* is used adverbially, and *tō* is a preposition ; see **In** and **To.**

Intone, to chant. (Late L.—L. *and* Gk.) Late L. *intonāre*, to sing according to tone.—L *in tonum*, according to tone ; where *tonum* is acc. of *tonus*, borrowed from Gk. τόνος ; see **Tone.**

Intoxicate. (Late L.—L. *and* Gk.) From pp. of Late L. *intoxicāre*, to make drunk.—L. *in*, into; *toxicum*, poison, borrowed from Gk. τοξικόν, poison for arrows. Gk. τοξικόν is der. from τόξον, a bow, of which the pl. τόξα is used to mean arrows. With Gk. τόξον cf Gk. τέχ-νη, art, or perhaps L. *taxus*, a yew-tree. See **Technical.**

Intrepid. (L) L. *intrepidus*, fearless, not alarmed.—L. *in-*, not ; *trepidus*, alarmed. See **Trepidation.**

Intricate, perplexed, obscure. (L.) From the pp. of L. *intrīcāre*, to perplex.— L. *in*, in ; *trīcæ*, pl. sb., hindrances, vexations, wiles. See **Extricate.**

intrigue, to form secret plots. (F.— Ital.—L.) F. *intriguer*, (also M. F. *intriquer*, ' to intricate, perplex, insnare ; ' Cot.).—Ital. *intrigare* (also *intricare*), ' to intricate, entrap ; ' Florio.—L. *intrīcāre* (above).

Intrinsic, inherent. (F.—L.) For **intrinsec.* M. F. *intrinseque*, 'inward ;' Cot.—L. *intrinsecus*, lit. ' following inwards.' — L. **intrim*, allied to *intrā*, within (cf. *interim*) ; *sec-us*, lit. following, from *sequī*, to follow. See **Sequence.**

Intro-, *prefix*, within. (L.) L. *intrō*; an adv. closely allied to L. *intrā*; from *interus*, inner. See **Interior.**

Introduce. (L.) L. *intrōdūcere*, to bring in.—L. *intrō*, within ; *dūcere*, to bring. See **Duke.** Der. *introduct-ion* (from the pp. *introduct-us*).

Introit, an antiphon sung as the priest approaches the altar. (F.—L.) F. *introït.* —L. acc. *introitum*, from *introitus*, lit. 'entrance.'—L. *introitus*, pp. of *introīre*, to enter.—L. *intrō*, within ; *īre*, to go.

Introspection. (L.) Coined from L. *introspect-us*, pp. of *introspicere*, to look into (with suffix *-ion*).—L. *intrō-*, within ; *specere*, to look. See **Species.**

Intrude, to thrust oneself into. (L.) L. *intrūdere*, to thrust into.—L. *in*, in, into ; *trūdere* (pp. *trūsus*), to thrust. Allied to **Threaten.** Der. *intrus-ion*, from the pp.

Intuition. (F.—L.) F. *intuition.* Formed, by analogy with *tuition*, from L. *intuitus*, pp. of *intuērī*, to look upon. —L. *in*, upon ; *tuērī*, to watch. See **Tuition.**

Intumescence, a swelling. (F.—L.) F. *intumescence.* From stem of pres. pt. of L. *intumescere*, to begin to swell.— L. *in*, very ; *tumescere*, inceptive form of *tumēre*, to swell. See **Tumid.**

Inundation. (F.—L.) Imitated from F. *inondation.*—L. *inundātiōnem*, acc. of *inundātio*, an overflowing.—L. *inundāre*, to overflow.—L. *in*, upon, over ; *unda*, a wave. See **Undulate.**

Inure, to habituate. (F.—L.) Also spelt *enure*, i. e. *en ure* ; the word arose from the phrase *in* (F. *en*) *ure*, i. e. in operation, in work, in employment, for-

merly common. Here *in* is the E. prep.
in; *ure* is from O. F. *eure*, also spelt *uevre*,
ovre, work, action; from L. *opera*, work.
(Cf. *man-ure* = *man-œuvre*.) See also
manure, *manœuvre*. See Operate.

Invade. (F.−L.) M. F. *invader.*−
L. *inuādere* (pp. *inuāsus*), to enter, invade.−L. *in*, in; *uādere*, to go. Der.
invas-ion, from the pp.

Invecked, Invected, in heraldry,
indented with successive cusps, with the
points projecting inwards. (L.) Lit.
'carried in.'−L. *inuectus*, pp. of *inuehere*,
to carry inwards.−L. *in*, in; *uehere*, to
carry. See Vehicle.

Inveigh, to attack with words, rail.
(F.−L.) From F. *envahir*, O. F. *envaïr*,
enveïr, to invade, from L. *inuādere* (see
Invade); but popularly connected with L.
inuehere, to carry into or to, to introduce,
attack, inveigh against.−L. *in*, against;
uehere, to bring. β. The latter etymology
was suggested by the use of E. *invective*,
borrowed from F. *invective*, 'an invective;'
Cot.; from L. *inuectīuus*, adj., scolding,
due to *inuectus*, pp. of *inuehere*. Hence
Cot. has '*invectiver*, to inveigh.'

Inveigle. (F.−L.) In Spenser, F. Q.
i. 12. 32. [Indirectly from F. *aveugler*,
to blind; cf. E. *aveugle*, to cajole, seduce,
A. D. 1547, in Froude's Hist. v. 132; and
A. D. 1543, State Papers, ix. 247.] It
precisely answers to Anglo-F. *enveoglir*,
to blind, in Will. of Wadington's Manuel
des Peches, l. 10639; spelt also *enveogler*
in N. Bozon. These are mere (ignorant)
variants of F. *aveugler*, to blind (like *imposthume* for *apostume*), from F. *aveugle*
(A. F. *enveogles* in Bozon), blind.−Late
L. **aboculum*, acc. of **aboculus*, blind
(Ducange has *avoculus*, also *aboculis*, adj.).
−L. *ab*, without; *oculus*, eye. ¶ Baret
(1580) has: '*inveigle* ones minde, *occæcare
animum*.'

Invent. (F.−L.) F. *inventer*, to devise. Formed, with suffix *-er* (L. *-āre*),
from L. *inuent-us*, pp. of *inuenīre*, to
come upon, find out.−L. *in*, upon; *uenīre*,
to come. See Venture. Der. *invention*, &c.

Inverse, opposite. (F.−L.) M. E.
invers.−M. F. *invers.*−L. *inuersus*, pp.
of *inuertere* (below).

invert. (L.) L. *inuertere*, to turn
towards or up, to invert.−L. *in*, towards;
uertere, to turn. See Verse.

Invest. (F.−L.) F. *investir.* − L.

inuestīre, to clothe in or with. − L. *in*,
in; *uestīre*, to clothe. See Vest.

Investigate. (L.) From pp. of L.
inuestīgāre, to track out.−L. *in*, in, upon;
uestīgāre, to trace, allied to *uestīgium*,
a foot-track. See Vestige.

Inveterate. (L.) L. *inueterātus*, pp.
of *inueterāre*, to retain for a long time. −
L. *in*, in; *ueter-*, for **uetes-*, stem of
uetus, old. See Veteran.

Invidious. (L.) From L. *inuidiōsus*,
causing odium or envy.−L. *inuidia*, envy.
−L. *inuidēre*, to envy, lit. to look upon
(in a bad sense).−L. *in*, upon; *uidēre*, to
look. See Vision.

Invigorate, to give vigour to. (L.)
As if from pp. of Late L. **inuigorāre*, to
give vigour to.−L. *in*, towards; *uigor*,
vigour; see Vigour. Cf. Ital. *invigorire*.

Invincible. (F.−L.) F. *invincible.*
−L. *inuincibilis.*−L. *in-*, not; *uinci-
bilis*, easily overcome, from *uincere*, to
conquer; see Vanquish.

Invite. (F. − L.) F. *inviter.* − L.
inuītāre, to ask, request, invite. Allied
to **uītus*, willing, in *in-uītus*, unwilling.
Brugm. i. § 343. Doublet, *vie*, q. v.

Invocation. (F.−L.) F. *invocation.*
−L. *inuocātiōnem*, acc. of *inuocātio*, a
calling upon.−L. *inuocātus*, pp. of *inuocāre*, to call upon.−L. *in*, upon; *uocāre*,
to call. See Vocation.

invoke. (F.−L.) F. *invoquer.*−L.
inuocāre, to call upon (above).

Invoice, a particular account of goods
sent out. (F.−L.) A corruption of *envois*,
pl. of F. *envoi*, O. F. *envoy*, a sending;
see Envoy. Cf. E. *voice*, from O. F. *vois*.

Involve. (F.−L.) F. *involver*, 'to
involve;' Cot.−L. *inuoluere*, to roll in,
roll up.−L. *in*, in; *uoluere*, to roll. See
Voluble. Der. *involut-ion*, *involute*,
from the pp. *inuolūtus*; also *involucre*,
from L. *inuolūcrum*, an envelope.

Iodine, an elementary body. (Gk.)
Named from the violet colour of its
vapour. [Cf. F. *iode*, iodine.]−Gk. ἰώδ-
ης, contr. form of ἰοειδής, violet-like; with
suffix *-ine.* − Gk. ἰο-ν, a violet; εἶδ-ος,
appearance. See Violet.

Iota. (Gk.−Heb.) Gk. ἰῶτα, a letter
of the Gk. alphabet. − Heb. *yōd*, the
smallest letter of the Heb. alphabet,
with the power of *y*. (Of Phœnician
origin.) See Jot.

Ipecacuanha, a medical root. (Port.
− Brazilian.) Port. *ipecacuanha* (Span.

ipecacuana). From the Brazilian name of the plant; Guarani *ipé-kaa-guaña*. *Ipé=peb*, small; *kaa*, plant; *guaña*, causing sickness.

Ir- (1), *prefix.* (L.; *or* F.−L.) For L. *in*, in, prep., when *r* follows.

Ir- (2), *prefix.* (L.; *or* F.−L.) For L. neg. prefix *in*-, when *r* follows.

Ire. (F.−L.) F. *ire.*−L. *īra*, anger.

irascible. (F.−L.) F. *irascible.*− L. *īrascibilis*, choleric; from *īrascī*, to become angry; with suffix *-bilis.*−L. *īra*, anger.

Iris, a rainbow. (L.−Gk.) L. *īris.*− Gk. ἶρις, a rainbow. Der. *irid-esc-ent*; *irid-ium*; from *īrid-*, stem of *īris*. And see **Orris.**

Irk, to weary. (E.) M. E. *irken, erken*, to tire; also *irk, erk*, adj. weary. Not in A.S.+M. H. G. *erken*, to loathe; *erklich*, loathsome; Bavarian *erkel*, sb., nausea (Schmeller).

Iron, a metal. (E.) M. E. *iren*, also *ire*. A. S. *īren*, older forms *īsern*, *īsaern*, adj. and sb. + Du. *ijzer*; O. Icel. *īsarn*; O. H. G. *īsarn*, G. *eisen*; Goth. *eisarn*, sb. (whence *eisarneins*, adj.). And cf. W. *haiarn*, Corn. *hoern*, Irish *iarann*, O. Ir. *iarn*, Bret. *houarn*, iron. β. The Celtic forms answer to an O. Celt. form **īsarno-* (**eisarno-*, Stokes, in Fick, ii. 25); from which the Germanic forms may have been borrowed. At any rate, Icel. *jārn* and Dan. Swed. *jern* are from O. Ir. *iarn*. Remoter origin unknown.

ironmonger, a dealer in iron goods. (E.) From *iron* and *monger*; see **Monger.**

iron-mould. (E.) See **Mould** (3).

Irony. (F. − L. − Gk.) F. *ironie* (Minsheu). − L. *īronīa*. − Gk. εἰρωνεία, dissimulation, irony. − Gk. εἴρων, a dissembler, one who says less then he thinks or means. Allied to Ionic εἴρομαι, Attic ἔρομαι, I ask, enquire, seek out (cf. εἰρωτέω, Ion. for ἐρωτάω, I ask), ἔρευνα, enquiry, search (base **reu*; Prellwitz).

Irradiate. (L.) From pp. of L. *irradiāre*, to shine upon.−L. *ir-*, for *in*, on; *radiāre*, to shine, from *radius*, a ray. See **Radius.**

Irrefragable, not to be refuted. (F. −L.) F. *irréfragable.*−L. *irrefrāgābilis*, not to be withstood.−L. *ir-* (= *in*-, not); *refrāgārī*, to oppose, thwart, from *re-*, back, and (probably) L. *frag-*, base of *frangere*, to break. (For the long *a*, cf. L. *suffrāgium*, prob. from the same root.)

Irrigate, to water. (L.) From pp. of L. *irrigāre*, to flood.−L. *in*, upon; *rigāre*, to wet, moisten.

Irritate. (L.) From pp. of L. *irritāre*, to incite, excite, provoke, tease. App. related to *irrīre*, *hirrīre*, to snarl as a dog; which is prob. an imitative word.

Irruption. (F.−L.) F. *irruption*, 'a forcible entry;' Cot.−L. acc. *irruptiōnem*, a breaking into.−L. *ir-* (for *in*), into; *rupt-us*, pp. of *rumpere*, to break. See **Rupture.**

Is. A. S. *is*; from √ES, to be. The general Idg. form is ES-TI, as in Skt. *as-ti*, Gk. ἐσ-τί, L. *es-t*, G. *is-t*; also O. Icel. *es*, E. *is*. See also **Be, Was.**

Isinglass, a glutinous substance made from a fish. (Du.) A corruption of M. Du. *huyzenblas* (mod. Du. *huisblad*), isinglass, lit. 'sturgeon-bladder,' whence isinglass is obtained; see Sewel.−M. Du. *huys*, sturgeon; *blaese*, bladder (Kilian). Cf. G. *hausenblase*, sturgeon-bladder, isinglass; from G. *hausen*, a sturgeon, *blase*, a bladder, from *blasen*, to blow. Cf. O. H. G. *hūso*, a sturgeon.

Islam, the religious system of Muhammed. (Arab.) Arab. *islām*, lit. 'submission.'−Arab. root *salama*, he was resigned. See **Moslem.**

Island. (E.) The *s* is inserted by confusion with F. *isle*. M. E. *iland*. A. S. *īgland.*−A. S. *īg*, an island; *land*, land; perhaps by confusion of A.S. *īg*, island, with A.S. *ēa-land*, island, lit. 'water-land.' The A. S. *īg* is also *īeg*, O. Merc. *ēg* (cf. *Angles-ey*); cognate with Icel. *ey*, Dan. Swed. *ö*, island; G. *aue*, meadow near water. The orig. Teut. form was **agwiā*, fem. of **agwioz*, belonging to water, an adj. formed from **ahwa*, water, represented by A. S. *ēa*, O. H. G. *aha*, Goth. *ahwa*, a stream, cognate with L. *aqua*, water.

Isle, an island. (F. -L.) O. F. *isle* (F. *île*). − L. *insula*, an island. See **Insular.**

Isochronous, performed in equal times. (Gk.) Gk. ἴσο-s, equal; χρόνος, time (see **Chronicle**). Brugm. i. § 345 c.

isosceles, having two equal legs or sides as a triangle. (L.−Gk.) L. *isosceles.* −Gk. ἰσοσκελής, isosceles. − Gk. ἴσο-s, equal; σκέλ-ος, a leg, side of a triangle.

Isolate, to insulate. (Ital.−L.) Suggested by Ital. *isolato*, detached, used as a term in architecture (whence also F.

isolé). — Ital. *isola*, an island. — L. *insula*, an island. See **Insular**.

Issue, progeny, result. (F. — L.) M. E. *issue*, sb. — F. *issue*, O. F. *issuë (eissuë)*, ' the issue, end, event ; ' Cot. Fem. of *issu*, pp. of *issir*, to depart, go out. — L. *exīre*, to go out. — L. *ex*, out ; *īre*, to go.

Isthmus, a neck of land connecting a peninsula with the mainland. (L. — Gk.) L. *isthmus*. — Gk. *ἰσθμός*, a narrow passage; allied to *ἴθμα*, a step. (✓EI, to go.)

It. (E.) M. E. *hit*. A. S. *hit*, neut. of *hē*, he. +Icel. *hit*, neut. of *hinn* ; Du. *het*, neut. of *hij* ; Goth. *hita*. The old gen. case was *his*, afterwards *it*, and finally *its* (XVII cent.). See **He**.

Italics, a name for letters printed thus— *in sloping type*. (L.) Named from Aldo Manuzio, an *Italian*, about A. D. 1501. — L. *Italicus*. — L. *Italia*, Italy.

Itch. (E.) North E. *yuke*. M. E. *iken, icchen*, fuller form *ʒiken, ʒichen*. A. S. *giccan*, to itch, for **gyccan* ; cf. A. S. *gyhða*, an itching. + E. Fries. *jöken*, Du. *jeuken*, G. *jucken*, to itch ; O. H. G. *jucchan*. Teut. type **jukjan-*.

Item, a separate article or particular. (L.) L. *item*, likewise; in common use for enumerating particulars; closely allied to *ita*, so. Cf. Skt. *ittham*, thus, *iti*, thus.

iterate, to repeat. (L.) From pp. of L. *iterāre*, to repeat. — L. *iterum*, again; a compar. form (with suffix *-ter*) from the pronominal base I, as in *i-tem, i-ta*. Cf. Skt. *i-tara(s)*, another.

Itinerant, travelling. (L.) From pres. part. of O. Lat. *itinerāre*, to travel. — L. *itiner-*, stem of *iter*, a journey. — L. *it-um*, supine of *īre*, to go. (✓EI, to go.)

Ivory. (F. — L.) M. E. *iuorie* (= *ivorie*). — O. F. *ivurie*, later *ivoire*. — L. *eboreus*, adj., made of ivory. — L. *ebor-*, stem of *ebur*, ivory. Perhaps allied to Skt. *ibha-*, an elephant.

Ivy, an evergreen. (E.) A. S. *ifig*; also *ifegn*. + O. H. G. *ebahewi* (G. *epheu*) ; Kluge. The A. S. *if-ig* seems to be a compound word. The syllable *if-* is equivalent to Du. *ei-* in *ei-loof*, ivy (where *loof* = E. *leaf*) ; and to *eba(h)-* in O. H. G. *ebah-* ; but the sense is unknown.

Iwis, certainly. (E.) M. E. *ywis, iwis*. A. S. *gewis*, adj., certain (whence *gewislīce*, adv., certainly). +Du. *gewis*, adj. and adv.; G. *gewiss*, adv. Cf. Icel. *viss*, certain, sure. From Teut. type **wissoz* (for **wittoz*, Idg. **wid-tos*), pp. from the base *wit-*

in *wit-an*, to know ; see **Wit**. (✓WEID.) ¶ The M. E. prefix *i-* (A. S. *ge-*) is sometimes written apart from the rest of the word, and with a capital letter. Hence, by the mistake of editors, it has been printed *I wis*, and explained as 'I know.' This is the origin of the fictitious word *wis*, to know, given in some dictionaries.

J.

Jabber, to chatter. (F. ?) Formerly *jaber* and *jable*, of imitative origin; similar to *gabber* and *gabble*. Godefroy gives O. F. *jaber* as a variant of *gaber*, to mock. Cf. Du. *gabberen*, to jabber ; Sewel. See **Gabble**.

Jacinth, a precious stone. (F. — L. — Gk.) F. *jacinthe*. — L. *hyacinthus*, a jacinth. — Gk. *ὑάκινθος*, a jacinth ; Rev. xxi. 20. See **Hyacinth**.

Jack (1), a saucy fellow, sailor. (F. — L. — Gk. — Heb.) M. E. *Jacke, Jakke*, often used as a term of reproach, as in '*Jakke* fool,' Chaucer, C. T. 3708. Generally used formerly (as now) as a pet substitute for *John*, and perhaps due to the dimin. form *Jankin*. *John* is from A. F. *Johan*. — L. *Iohannes*. — Gk. Ἰωάννης. — Heb. *Yehōkhanān, Yōkhānān*, lit. ' God is gracious.' β. Apparently confused with F. *Jacques*, a common name in France. *Jaques* is from L. *Iacōbus*. — Gk. Ἰάκωβος. — Heb. *Ya'aqōb*, Jacob; lit. one who seizes by the heel. — Heb. root *'āqab*, to seize by the heel, supplant. ¶ The name was extended to denote various implements, such as a *smoke-jack*, a *boot-jack* ; so also *Jack-o'-lent, Jack-o'-lantern, Jack-pudding, Jack-an-apes* (= *Jack on apes*, with *on* = *of*).

jack (2), a coat of mail. (F. — L. — Gk. — Heb.) O. F. *Jaque*, ' James, also a Jack, or coat of maile ; ' Cot. Cf. Ital. *giaco*, a coat of mail, Span. *jaco*, a soldier's jacket, G. *jacke*, a jacket. Of obscure origin ; but prob. due to the *Jacquerie*, or revolt of the peasantry nicknamed *Jacques Bonhommes*, A. D. 1358 ; and hence due to F. *Jaques*, James ; see above.

Jackal, a kind of wild animal. (Turk. — Pers.) Turk. *chakāl*. — Pers. *shaghāl*. Cf. Skt. *çrgāla-*, a jackal, a fox.

Jackanapes. For *Jack on apes*, i. e. Jack of apes. See **Jack** (1).

Jacket, a short coat. (F. — L. — Gk. — Heb.) O. F. *jaquette*, a jacket ; dimin. of O. F. *jaque*, a jack of mail ; see **jack** (2).

jacobin. (F.—L.—Gk.—Heb.) M.E. *jacobin.*—F.*jacobin.*—Late Lat. *Jacōbīnus*, adj., formed from *Iacōbus*, and applied to a friar of the order of St. Dominick. See **Jack** (1). β. Hence one of the *Jacobin* club in the French Revolution, which first met in the hall of the *Jacobin* friars in Paris, Oct. 1789. Also the name of a hooded (friar-like) pigeon.

jacobite, an adherent of James II. (L.—Gk.—Heb.) From L. *Iacōb-us*, James (above).

Jade (1), a sorry nag, an old woman. (Scand.?) M.E. *iade* (Ch.) The initial *j* is perhaps from *y*. Cf. Lowland Sc. *yaud, yawd*, a jade; Dunbar has *yald*. Of unknown origin; perhaps from Icel. *jalda*, a mare; prov. Swed. *jäldä*, a mare (Rietz).

Jade (2), a hard dark-green stone. F.—Span.—L.) F. *jade*. The jade brought from America by the Spaniards was called *piedra de ijada*, because it was believed to cure pain in the side; for a similar reason it was called *nephritis* (from Gk. νεφρός, kidneys).—Span. *ijada*, also *ijar*, the flank; cf. Port. *ilhal, ilharga*, the flank, side.—L. *īlia*, pl., the flanks.

Jag, a notch, tooth. (Unknown.) Perhaps a variant of *dag*. 'I *agge*, or dagge of a garment;' Palsg. 'I *iagge*, or cut a garment;' ib. Cf. **Tag.** ¶ Or perhaps cf. Icel. *jaki*, a piece of ice.

Jaggery, a coarse brown sugar. (Canarese — Skt.) A corruption of Canarese *sharkare*, unrefined sugar; H. H. Wilson.—Skt. *çarkarā*; see **Sugar.**

Jaguar, a beast of prey. (F.—Brazil.) '*Jagua* in the Guarani [Brazilian] language is the common name for tygers and dogs; the generic name for tygers is *jaquarete*;' Clavigero, Hist. of Mexico, tr. by Cullen, ii. 318. But there is no *j* in Tupi-Guarani (Cavalcanti). The spelling *jaguar* is F. (in Buffon). The Dict. of Trévoux has *janouare* (error for *jauouare*); for Brazil. *yāuāra*, a dog. Spelt *jaguara*, Hist. Nat. Brasiliæ, p. 235.

Jail; see **Gaol.**

Jalap, the root of a plant. (Mexican.) Named from *Jalapa* or *Xalapa*, in Mexico. Orig. *Xalapan*, 'sand by the water.'—Mex. *xal(li*, sand ; *a(tl)*, water ; *pan*, on, near ; where *-li, -tl* are suppressed.

Jam (1), to press, squeeze. (E.) Prob. a variant of *cham*, to chew, to champ;

prov. E. *champ*, to mash, crush, also to chew ; so also *champ*, hard, firm, i. e. *chammed* or pressed down. See **Champ.** ¶ But Ashe (1775) has : '*Jamb*, to confine as between two posts;' as if from **Jamb,** q. v.

jam (2), a conserve of fruit. (E.) A soft substance, like that which is chewed. 'And if we have anye stronger meate, it must be *chammed* afore by the nurse, and so put into the babes mouthe;' Sir T. More, Works, p. 241 *h.* See above.

Jamb, side-post of a door. (F.—L.) F. *jambe*, a leg, also a jamb (see Cotgrave).—Folk-L. *gamba*, a leg. See **Gambol.** Der. (perhaps) *jamb*, vb.; see **Jam** (1).

Jane, Jean, a twilled cloth. (F.—Ital.) Also '*gene* fustian,' 1580; cf. M.E. *Gene*, Genoa.—M.F. *Genes.*—Ital. *Genova*, Genoa.

Jangle, to sound discordantly. (F.—Scand.) M.E. *janglen.*—O.F. *jangler*, to jangle, prattle. Of Scand. origin.—Swed. dial. and Norw. *jangla*, to quarrel ; cf. Du. *jangelen*, to importune, frequent. of *janken*, to howl, yelp. An imitative word ; cf. L. *gannīre*, to yelp.

Janizary. (F.—Ital.—Turk.) F. *Janissaires*, 'the Janizaries;' Cot.—M. Ital. *ianizzeri*, 'the Turkes gard,' Florio. Of Turk. origin ; it means 'new soldiery'; from Turk. *yeñi*, new ; and *cheri*, soldiery (Devic). And *cheri* is from Pers. *charīk*, auxiliary forces (Zenker).

January. (L.) Englished from L. *Iānuārius*, a month named from the god *Iānus*, who was supposed to have doors under his protection ; cf. L. *iānua*, a door.

Japan, a name given to certain kinds of lacquered work. (Japan.) Named from the country. Der. *japan*, vb., to polish.

Jape, to mock, jest, befool. (F.) Obsolete. M.E. *japen.* Apparently from O.F. *japer* (F. *japper*), to yap (as a dog). Imitative ; cf. E. *yap.*

Jar (1), to make a harsh noise. (E.) Imitative; cf. M.E. *garren*, to chide, M.E. *ȝirren*, A.S. *georran*, to creak ; Du. *gieren*, to cry ; Bavar. *garren*, to jar. Parallel to prov. E. *char*, to chide, M.E. *charken*, to creak (Prompt. Parv.) ; cf. A.S. *ceorian*, *cerian*, to murmur ; M. Du. *karren, kerren*, 'to crake [creak] like a cart,' Hexham ; O. H. G. *kerran*, to give a loud harsh sound. Cf. **Jargon** and **Garrulous.**

Jar (2), an earthen pot. (F.—Arab.)

M. F. *jare*, ' a jarre,' Cot.; F. *jarre*. [Cf. Span. *jarra, jarro*, Ital. *giara*.] ▬ Arab. *jarra*, a jar (Devic).

Jargon, a confused talk. (F. – L. ?) F. *jargon*, orig. the chattering of birds, jargon; O. F. *gargon, gergon*. Cf. Span. *gerigonza*, jargon; Ital. *gergone*. Prob. from an imitative base *garg* (cf. *garg-le, gurg-le*); cf. L. *garrīre*, to prate, croak. Cf. M. E. *charken*, to creak. See **Jar** (1).

Jargonelle, a kind of pear. (F. – Ital. – Pers. ?) F. *jargonelle*, a kind of pear, very stony (Littré) ; formed (acc. to Littré) from F. *jargon*, a yellow diamond, small stone. ▬ Ital. *giargone*, a sort of yellow diamond. Perhaps from Pers. *zargūn*, gold-coloured (Zend *zairi-gaona-*) ; from *zar*, gold, and *gūn*, colour (Devic).

Jasmine, Jessamine, a plant. (F. – Arab. – Pers.) F. *jasmin*. (So also Span. *jazmin*.) ▬ Arab. *yāsemīn* (Devic). ▬ Pers. *yāsmīn*, jasmine ; *yāsamīn*, jessamine.

Jasper, a precious stone. (F. – L. – Gk. – Arab.) O. F. *jaspre* (Littré), an occasional spelling of *jaspe*, a jasper. ▬ L. *iaspidem*, acc. of *iaspis*. ▬ Gk. ἴασπις. ▬ Arab. *yasb, yasf, yashb*, jasper; whence Pers. *yashp, yashf*, jasper. Cf. Heb. *yāshpheh*, a jasper.

Jaundice. (F. – L.) M. E. *iaunis*; the *d* being excrescent. ▬ F. *jaunisse*, yellowness; hence, the jaundice. ▬ F. *jaune* (oldest spelling *jalne*), yellow. ▬ L. *galbinus*, greenish yellow. ▬ L. *galbus*, yellow ; (perhaps of Teut. origin ; cf. G. *gelb*, yellow).

Jaunt, to ramble. (F. ?) Of doubtful origin. Cf. M. F. *jancer un cheval*, ' to stirre a horse in the stable till he swart [sweat] withall; or (as our) to jaunt (an old word); ' Cot. Der. *jaunt*, sb., an excursion.

Jaunty, Janty, fantastical. (F. – L.) Also *janty, jantee*, variants of *jantyl*, old spelling of *gentle* or *genteel*. Cf. Burgundy *jantais*, ' gentil ; ' Mignard.

Javelin. (F. – C. ?) M. F. *javelin*, ' a javeling,' Cot.; allied to *javelot*, ' a gleave, dart,' id. Perhaps Celtic. Cf. O. Irish *gabul*, a fork ; *gablach*, pointed, Irish *gabhla*, a spear, *gabhlan*, a fork of a tree ; Gael. *gobhlan*, a prong; W. *gafl*, a fork, *gaflach*, a dart. See **Gaff.**

Jaw. (F. – L.) M. E. *iowe* (*jowe*). – O. F. (and F.) *joue*, ' the cheek, the jowle;' Cot. (Cf. Prov. *gauta*, Ital. *gota*, cheek, jaw.) ▬ Late L. *gabata, gavata*, a bowl; from the rounding of the cheek. (Diez,

Körting.) ¶ Perhaps influenced by *chaw*, *chew*; Palsgrave has *chawe-bone* for *jaw-bone*.

Jay, a bird. (F.) O. F. *jay*, a jay (F. *geai*). Cf. Span. *gayo*, a jay. Of doubtful origin ; perhaps from O. H. G. *gāhi* (G. *jähe*), quick, lively (Diez).

Jealous. (F. – L. – Gk.) M. E. *jalous, gelus.* – O. F. *jalous* (later *jaloux*). ▬ Late L. *zēlōsus*, full of zeal. ▬ L. *zēlus*, zeal. ▬ Gk. ζῆλος, zeal. See **Zeal.** Der. *jealous-y*, F. *jalousie*.

Jeer. (Du.) Doubtful; perhaps from M. Du. phrase *den gek scheeren*, lit. to shear the fool, hence to jeer at one ; whence the word *gekscheeren*, or simply *scheeren*, to jeer. Now spelt *scheren*. Cf. G. *scheren*, ' to shear, fleece, cheat, plague, tease ; ' Flügel ; E. Fries. *scheren*, the same.

Jehovah. (Heb.) Heb. *yahōvāh*, or, more correctly, *yahweh*, a proper name, rendered in the A.V. by ' the Lord.'

Jejune, hungry, meagre. (L.) L. *iēiūnus*, fasting, hungry, dry.

Jelly. (F. – L.) Formerly *gelly*. ▬ F. *gelée*, ' gelly ; ' Cot. Orig. fem. of pp. of *geler*, to freeze. ▬ L. *gelāre*, to freeze. See **Gelid.**

Jennet, Gennet, a small Spanish horse. (F. – Span. – Arab.) M. F. *genette*, ' a genet, or Spanish horse ; ' Cot. ▬ Span. *ginete*, a nag; but orig. ' a horse-soldier.' Of Moorish origin ; traced by Dozy to Arab. *zenāta*, a tribe of Barbary celebrated for its cavalry.

Jenneting, a kind of early apple. (F. – L. – Gk. – Heb.) Prob. for *jeanneton* ; a dimin. from F. *pomme de S. Jean*, an early apple, called in Italian *melo de San Giovanni*, i. e. St. John's apple. So called because, in France and Italy, it ripened about June 24, St. John's day. So also, there is an early pear, called *Amirè Joannet* or *Jeanette*, or *petit St. Jean* ; G. *Johannisbirne*. F. *Jean*<Lat. acc. *Iohannem* ; from Gk. Ἰωάννης, John. ▬ Heb. *Yōkhānān*, the Lord is gracious.

Jeopardy, hazard. (F. – L.) M. E. *jupartie*, later *jopardye, jeopardie.* ▬ O. F. *jeu parti*, lit. a divided game ; a game in which the chances were equal, hence, a risk, hazard. ▬ Late L. *iocus partītus*, the same ; also an alternative. ▬ L. *iocus*, a game ; *partītus*, pp. of *partīrī*, to part, divide, from *parti-*, decl. stem of *pars*, a part. ¶ The diphthong *eo* = F. *eu* ; cf. *people* (= F. *peuple*). See **Joke.**

Jerboa, a rodent quadruped. (Arab.) Arab. *yarbū*, (1) the flesh of the back or loins, an oblique descending muscle; (2) the jerboa, from the use it makes of the strong muscles in its hind legs, in taking long leaps.

Jereed, a wooden javelin used in mock fights. (Arab.) Arab. *jarīd*, a palm-branch stripped of its leaves, a lance.

Jerk. (E.) We find *jerk, jert,* and *yerk* all used in much the same sense, orig. to strike with a lash, whip or rod. Of these, *jert* was regarded as equivalent to *gird* (Index to Cot.); see **Gird** (2).

Jerked beef. (Peruvian.) A singular corruption of *ccharqui,* the S. American name for 'jerked' beef, or beef dried in a particular way; see Prescott, Conquest of Peru, ch. v. From Peruv. *ccharqui,* a slice of dried beef. Also called *jerkin beef;* from Peruv. *ccharquini,* vb., to make dried beef.

Jerkin, a jacket, short coat. (Du.) Dimin. of Du. *jurk,* a frock (Sewel), by help of the once common Du. dimin. suffix *-ken,* now supplanted by *-je* or *-tje.* Cf. Westphal. *jürken,* a sort of overcoat; E. Fries. *jurken,* a child's frock. Cf. *fir-kin, kilder-kin.*

Jersey, fine wool, a woollen jacket. (Jersey.) From *Jersey,* one of the Channel Islands.

Jessamine; see Jasmine.

Jesses, straps round a hawk's legs. (F.–L.) Double pl.; from M. E. *ges, jesses.* – O. F. *ges, gies,* pl. of *get, giet,* a short thong, for throwing off the hawk; orig. 'a cast.' Cf. M. F. *ject,* a cast; *les jects d'un oyseau,* 'a hawkes Iesses,' Cot. – O. F. *geter,* to cast. – L. *iactāre,* to cast; see **Jet** (1).

Jest, a joke. (F.–L.) Orig. a story, merry tale. M. E. *geste,* a story. – O. F. *geste,* an exploit, romance, tale of exploits. –L. *gesta,* for *rēs gesta,* a thing done, an exploit. – L. *gestus,* pp. of *gerere,* to carry, carry on. See **Gesture, Gerund.**

Jesuit; see below.

Jesus, the Saviour. (L.–Gk.–Heb.) L. *Iēsus.* –Gk. Ἰησοῦς. – Heb. *Yēshū'a,* Jeshua (Nehem. viii. 17); contr. form of *Yehōshu'a,* Jehoshua (Numb. xiii. 16) signifying saviour, lit. 'help of Jehovah.' –Heb. root *yāsha',* to be large, to save. Der. *jesu-it,* one of the society of Jesus.

Jet (1), to throw out, fling about, spout. (F.–L.) Formerly, to *jet* was to strut

about. M. E. *ietten,* to strut. – O. F. *jetter, geter, getter,* to throw, fling, push forth. – L. *iactāre,* to fling; frequent. of *iacere,* to throw. Der. *jet,* sb., formerly in the sense of guise or fashion, &c.

Jet (2), a black mineral. (F.–L.–Gk.) O. F. *jet, jaet,* also *jayet, gaiete,* jet (F. *jais*).–L. *gagātem,* acc. of *gagātēs,* jet.– Gk. γαγάτης, jet; so called from Γάγαι, a town in Lycia, in the S. of Asia Minor.

Jetsam. (F.–L.) Also *jettison.* An old term in Law F. for things thrown overboard from a wrecked vessel. – A. F. *getteson,* a casting; O. F. *getaison.* – L. acc. *iactātiōnem.* – L. *iactāre,* to cast; see **Jet** (1).

jetty, a kind of pier. (F.–L.) M. F. *jettée* (F. *jetée*), a cast, throw, 'also a jetty or jutty;' Cot. Orig. fem. of pp. of M. F. *jetter* (F. *jeter*), to throw; see **Jet** (1).

Jew. (F.–L.–Gk.–Heb.) M. E. *Iewe,* a Jew.–A. F. *Ieu, Geu* (F. *juif*). – L. *Iūdæus,* a Jew. – Gk. Ἰουδαῖος, an inhabitant of Ἰουδαία, Judæa. – Heb. *Yehūdāh,* Judah, son of Jacob, lit. 'illustrious.' – Heb. root *yādāh,* to throw, praise, celebrate. Der. *Jew-ry,* M. E. *Iewerie,* O. F. *Iuerie,* lit. a Jews' district; also *Jews'-harp,* a name given in derision; cf. 'the harp of David.'

Jewel, a valuable ornament. (F.–L.) M. E. *iowel, iuel.* – O. F. *joel, joiel, jouel, juel* (later *joyau*). – Late L. *iocāle,* usually in pl. *iocālia,* jewels (lit. trinkets). – L. *iocārī,* to play (O. F. *joer, jouer*). – L. *iocus,* play. See **Joke.** (Toynbee, §§ 76, 143.)

Jib (1), the foremost sail in a ship. (Dan.) So called because easily shifted from side to side; see 3 b (2) below.

jib (2), to shift a sail from side to side. (Dan.) '*Jib,* to shift the boom-sail from one side of the mast to another;' Ash (1775). Also spelt *jibe, gybe.* – Dan. *gibbe,* to jibe, jib; Swed. dial. *gippa,* to jerk up. Allied to Swed. *guppa,* to rock; see **Jump.** ¶ The form *gibe* answers to Du. *gijpen,* E. Fries. *gīpen,* to turn suddenly, said of a sail.

jib (3), to move restively, as a horse. (F.–L.) O. F. *giber,* to struggle with the hands and feet (Roquefort); whence O. F. *regiber* (F. *regimber*), to kick as a horse. Cf. also O. F. *giper,* to jib, as a horse (Godefroy). – Swed. dial. *gippa,* to jerk up (above).

Jibe, the same as Gibe, q. v.

Jig, a lively tune or dance. (F.– M. H. G.) O. F. *gige, gigue,* a fiddle, dance.– M. H. G. *gîge* (G. *geige*), a fiddle.

Jilt, a flirt. (L.) Formerly *jillet,* dimin. of *jill,* a flirt, orig. *Jill* or *Gillian,* a personal name.– L. *Jūliāna.* See Gill (4).

Jingle, to clink. (E.) M. E. *ginglen*; a frequentative verb from the base *jink,* allied to *chink*; see Chink (2). Also allied to Jangle.

Jinn, a demon. (Arab.) Formed from Arab. *jinna(t),* demons, pl.; the sing. form being *jinnīy,* Englished as *jinnee* or *genie.*

Job (1), to peck with the beak. (E. ?) Perhaps imitative. M. E. *iobben.* Cf. Gael. and Irish *gob,* mouth, beak.

Job (2), a small piece of work. (F. ?) M. E. *iob,* a piece, lump. ' *Gob,* a lump; also, to work by the *gob*;' Halliwell.– O. F. *gob,* a mouthful; *gobet,* a morsel. Perhaps of Celtic origin. See Job (1).

Jockey. (F. – L. – Gk. – Heb.) A North E. pron. of *Jackey,* dimin. of *Jack* as a personal name. See Jack (1).

Jocose, merry. (L.) L. *iocōsus,* sportive. – L. *iocus,* sport. See Joke.

jocular. (L.) L. *ioculāris.* – L. *ioculus,* a little jest, dimin. of *iocus,* a jest.

Jocund. (F. – L.) M. E. *joconde.* – O. F. *jocond,* pleasant, agreeable (Godefroy).– L. *iōcundus, iūcundus,* pleasant; orig. helpful.– L. *iuuare* (supine *iū-tum*), to help; see Adjutant.

Jog, to push slightly, jolt. (F. – Teut. ?) M. E. *ioggen.* Cf. W. *ysgogi,* to wag, stir, shake, E. *shog,* M. E. *schoggen,* to shake up and down; Kentish *jock,* to jolt. All apparently from M. E. *schokken*; see Shock. ¶ We also find Norw. and Swed. dial. *jukka,* to jump up and down, as in riding.

John Dory, the name of a fish. (F. – L.) *John dory* is the vulgar name of the fish called the *dory. John* appears to be a mere sailor's prefix, like the *jack* in *jackass*; it can hardly be from an alleged F. *jaune dorée,* which would be tautological nonsense. *Dory* is borrowed from F. *dorée,* a dory; lit. ' gilded,' *dorée* being the fem. of the pp. of *dorer,* to gild.– L. *dēaurāre,* to gild. – L. *dē aurō,* of gold; see Aureate.

Join. (F. – L.) O. F. and F. *joign-,* a stem of *joindre.*– L. *iungere* (pp. *iunctus*), to join. **+** Gk. ζευγνύναι; Skt. *yuj,* to join. Allied to Yoke.

joint. (F. – L.) O. F. *joinct, joint,* a

joint, sb. – O. F. *joinct, joint,* pp. of *joindre,* to join; see Join (above).

Joist, one of a set of timbers to support the boards of a floor. (F. – L.) Sometimes pronounced *jist* (with *i* as in *mice*). M. E. *giste.* – O. F. *giste,* a bed, couch, place to lie on, a joist; because these timbers support the floor. – O. F. *gesir* (F. *gésir*), to lie, lie on. – L. *iacēre,* to lie. Cf. Gist.

Joke, a jest. (L.) From L. *iocus,* a jest, game. Brugm. i. § 302.

Jole; see Jowl.

Jolly. (F. – Scand.) M. E. *ioly,* earliest form *iolif.* – O. F. *jolif,* later *joli,* ' jolly, gay, trim, fine;' Cot. Orig. sense ' festive.' – Icel. *jōl,* a great feast in the heathen time; cognate with A. S. *geōla,* yule. See Yule.

Jolly-boat. (Port. *and* E.) We find ' grete bote and *jolywat*' in 1495; but it was also spelt *gallevat* and *galleywat* (Yule). – Port. *galeota,* a galliot; see Galliot. Perhaps the form of the word has been influenced by F. *joli.* See Jolly.

Jolt, to jerk. (E.) From *joll,* vb., to knock the *jole* or head; cf. All's Well, i. 3. 59. Cf. *jolt-head,* a stupid fellow; one whose head has been *joll'd* or knocked about. See Jowl.

Jonquil, a flower. (F. – Span. – L.) F. *jonquille.* – Span. *junquillo*; named from its rush-like leaves. – Span. *junco,* a rush. – L. *iuncus,* a rush. See Junk (2).

Jordan, a pot. (Unknown.) M. E. *iordan, iurdan, iordeyne*; Late L. *iurdānus* (Prompt. Parv. and Vocab.). It was orig. an alchemist's bottle (Halliwell, Way); perhaps once used for keeping water from the Jordan.

Joss, a Chinese idol. (Port. – L.) Not Chinese, but corrupted from Port. *Deos,* God. Cognate with Span. *Dios,* God; O. F. *deus.* – L. *Deus,* nom., God.

Jostle, Justle, to push against. (F. – L.; *with* E. *suffix.*) A frequent. form, with suffix -*le,* from M. E. *jousten,* to tilt, push against. See Joust.

Jot. (L. – Gk. – Heb.) Englished from L. *iota,* Matt. v. 18 (Vulgate). – Gk. ἰῶτα, a letter of the Gk. alphabet. – Heb. *yōd,* the smallest letter of th: Heb. alphabet, with the power of *y.* See Iota.

Journal. (F. – L.) Properly an adj., signifying ' daily.' – F. *journal,* daily. – L. *diurnālis,* daily; see Diurnal.

journey. (F. – L.) M. E. *iournee.* a

day's travel. — F. *journée*, a day, orig. a day's work. — Late L. *diurnāta, orig. the fem. pp. of Late L. *diurnāre*, to sojourn. — L. *diurnus*, daily. — L. *diēs*, a day.

Joust, Just, to tilt. (F. — L.) O. F. *jouster* (F. *jouter*), to tilt. — Late L. *iuxtāre*, to approach (hence, to approach with hostile intent, as in tilting). — L. *iuxtā*, close to, hard by (whence O. F. *jouste*, close to). β. The form *iuxtā* is short for *iug-is-tā, fem. abl. of the superlative form of L. *iūg-is*, continual. From the base *iūg-* of *iungere*, to join. (√YEUG.) Brugm. i § 760. Der. *jostle*.

Jovial. (F. — L.) O. F. *jovial*, sanguine, lit. born under the lucky planet Jupiter. — L. *Iouiālis*, pertaining to Jupiter. — L. *Ioui-*, decl. stem of O. Lat. *Iouis*, Jove, whence L *Iū-piter* (= Jove-father). *Iouis* represents *Diouis* (cf. Oscan dat. *Diuv-ei*), allied to *diēs*, day, and to *deus*, god; cf. Gk. Διός, gen. case of Ζεύς. See **Deity, Tuesday.** Brugm. i. §§ 120, 223.

Jowl, Jole, the jaw or cheek. (E.) M. E. *jolle*; all the forms are corruptions of M. E. *chol*, *chaul*, which is a contraction of M. E. *chaule* (*chavel*), the jowl. — A. S. *ceafl*, the jaw; pl. *ceaflas*, the jaws, chaps. Cf. O. Sax. *kaflōs*, pl., the jaws; Du. *kevels*, pl. the gums; G. *kiefer*, jaw, jawbone; also Icel. *kjaptr*, Swed. *käft*, Dan. *kiæft*, jaw. ¶ The successive spellings are A.S. *ceafl*, *chæfle* (Layamon), *chauel*, *chaul*, *chol*, *jole*, *jowl* (all found).

Joy. (F. — L.) M. E. *ioye*. — O. F. *ioye*, *joye*; oldest form *goye* (F. *joie*); cf. Ital. *gioia*, joy, also a gaud, jewel, Span. *joya*, a gaud. — L. *gaudia*, pl. of *gaudium*, joy; afterwards turned into a fem. sing. — L. *gaudēre*, to rejoice. See **Gaud.**

Jubilation, a shouting for joy. (L.) From L. *iūbilātio*, sb. — L. *iūbilātus*, pp. of *iūbilāre*, to shout for joy. — L. *iūbilum*, a shout of joy. ¶ Quite distinct from *jubilee*.

Jubilee, a season of great joy. (F. — L. — Heb.) M. E. *jubilee*. — M. F. *jubilé*, 'a jubilee;' Cot. — L. *iūbilæus*, the jubilee (Levit. xxv. 11); masc. of adj. *iūbilæus*, belonging to the jubilee (Levit. xxv. 28). — Heb. *yōbel*, a blast of a trumpet, shout of joy. ¶ Distinct from the word above.

Judge. (F. — L.) F. *juge*. — L. *iūdicem*, acc. of *iūdex*, a judge, lit. ' one who points out law.' — L. *iū-s*, law; *dic-āre*, to point out. See **Jury** and **Diction.**

judicature. (F. — L.) F. *judicature*. — Late L. *iūdicātūra*, office of a judge, judgment. — L. *iūdicātus*, pp. of *iūdicāre*, to judge. — L. *iūdic-*, stem of *iūdex*, a judge.

judicial. (F. — L.) M. F. *judiciel*. — L. *iūdiciālis*, pertaining to courts of law. — L. *iūdicium*, a trial. — L. *iūdic-*, stem of *iūdex*, a judge (above).

judicious. (F. — L.) F. *judicieux*; as if from a L. form *iūdiciōsus. — L. *iūdic-*, stem of *iūdex*, a judge.

Jug, a kind of pitcher. (Heb.) Drinking-vessels were formerly called *jacks*, *jills*, and *jugs*, all of which represent Christian names. *Jug* and *Judge* were usual as pet female names, and equivalent to *Jenny* or *Joan*; see *Jannette*, *Jehannette* in Cotgrave. Cf. *Jock* for *John*; fem. form *Jacquetta*. Of Heb. origin; see **Jenniting.**

Juggernaut, the name of an Indian idol. (Skt.) Skt. *jagannātha-*, lord of the universe, monarch of the world (Benfey, p. 465). — Skt. *jagat*, world; *nātha-*, protector, lord.

Juggler. (F. — L.) M. E. *iogelour*. — O. F. *jogleor*, *jougleor*; later *jongleur*. — L. *ioculātōrem*, acc. of *ioculātor*, a jester. — L. *ioculāri*, to jest. — L. *ioculus*, a little jest, dimin. of *iocus*, joke. See **Joke.**

Jugular, pertaining to the side of the neck. (L.) From L. *iugul-um*, or *iugul-us*, the collar-bone, which joins the neck and shoulders; dimin. of *iugum*, a yoke. See **Yoke.**

Juice. (F. — L.) M. E. *iuce*, *iusc*. — O. F. *jus*, juice, broth. — L. *iūs*, broth; lit. ' mixture.' + Skt. *yūsha-*, soup. (√YU.) Brugm. i. §§ 911, 922.

Jujube, a fruit. (F. — L. — Gk. — Pers.) M. F. *jujubes*, pl. (Cot.). — L. *zizyphum*, a jujube; fruit of the tree called *zizyphus*. — Gk. ζίζυφον, fruit of the tree ζίζυφος. — Pers. *zayzafūn*, *zīzfūn*, *zīzafūn*, the jujube-tree.

Julep, a drink. (F. — Span. — Pers.) F. *julep*. — Span. *julepe*. — Pers. *julāb*, julep, a sweet drink; also *gulāb*, rose-water, also julep. — Pers. *gul*, a rose; *āb*, water. For Pers. *gul*, see **Rose.** Pers. *āb* is cognate with Skt. *ap-*, water.

July. (F. — L.) O. F. *Julie*. — L. *Iūlius*, a month (formerly called *Quinctīlis*) named after Julius Cæsar, who was born in July.

Jump (1), to leap, spring, skip. (Scand.) Swed. dial. *gumpa*, to spring, jump; *gimpa*, to wag about; allied to Swed. *guppa*, to move up and down; Dan. *gumpe*, to jolt; Icel. *goppa*, to skip.+M. H. G. *gumpen*, *gampen*, to jump, *gumpeln*, to play the buffoon; prov. G. *gampen*, to jump, hop, sport (Schmeller); M. Du. *gumpen*, to dance, leap. From a Teut. str. vb. **gim-pan-* (for **gempan-*); whence Dan. dial. *gimpe*, to swing, wag, Lowl. Sc. *jimp*, to jump.

jumble, to mix together confusedly. (Scand.) We also find M. E. *jombren*, Ch. Troil. ii. 1037; and *jumper*, to mix harmoniously (More). In fact, *jumb-le, jomb-ren, jump-er* are all frequentative forms of the verb to *jump*, used transitively. Thus *jumb-le* = to make to jump, jolt together, make a discord; or, otherwise, to shake together, make to agree. See **Jump** (1).

jump (2), exactly, pat; also, as a verb. (Scand.) From the verb above; cf. Hamlet, i. 1. 65. Also used in the sense to agree or tally, esp. in the phr. *to jump with.* 'They *jump* not;' Oth. i. 3. 5; cf. Tam. Shrew, i. 1. 195.

Junction, a joining. (L.) From L. *iunctio*, a joining. — L. *iunctus*, pp. of *iungere*, to join. See **Join.**

juncture, a union, a critical moment. (L.) The sense 'critical moment' is astrological, from the 'union' of planets. — L. *iunctūra*, a joining. — L. *iunctus* (above).

June. (F. — L.) O. F. and F. *Juin.* — L. *Iūnius*, the name of the month and of a Roman *gens* or clan.

Jungle. (Hind. — Skt.) Hind. *jangal*, waste land. — Skt. *jañgala-*, adj., dry, desert; hence *jungle* = waste land. ¶ The Hind. short *a* sounds like *u* in *mud*.

Junior, younger. (L.) L. *iūnior*, comp. of *iuuenis*, young; short for **iuuenior.* See **Juvenile.**

Juniper, an evergreen shrub. (L.) L. *iūniperus, iūnipirus*, a juniper. Of doubtful origin.

Junk (1), a Chinese vessel. (Port. — Malay. — Chin.?) Port. (and Span.) *junco*, a junk. — Malay *jōng*; also *ajōng*. Said to be borrowed from Chinese *chw'an*, a ship, boat, bark, junk; Williams, Chinese Dict. p. 120.

Junk (2), pieces of old cordage. (Port. — L.) Port. *junco*, a rush; also junk, as a nautical term; i. e. rush-made ropes. — L. *iuncum*, acc. of *iuncus*, a rush. ¶ *Junk* also means salt meat, tough as old ropes. But *junk*, a·lump, is for *chunk*.)

junket, a kind of sweetmeat. (F. — Ital.

— L.) F. *joncade* (Cot.). Orig. a kind of cream-cheese, served up on rushes, whence its name. — Ital. *giuncata*, a kind of cream-cheese on rushes, also a junket (Florio). — Ital. *giunco*, a rush. — L. *iuncum*, acc. of *iuncus*, a rush.

Junta, a council. (Span. — L.) Span. *junta*, a congress; a fem. form of *junto* (below).

junto, a knot of men, a faction. (Span. — L.) Span. *junto*, united, conjoined. — L. *iunctus*, pp. of *iungere*, to join. See **Join.**

Juridical, Jurisdiction, Jurist, Juror; see **Jury.**

Jury, a body of sworn men. (F. — L.) O. F. *jurée*, a jury, a company of sworn men; orig. the fem. pp. of *jurer*, to swear. — L. *iūrāre*, to swear, bind by an oath. — L. *iūr-*, for *iūs*, law.+Skt. *yu*, to bind.

juridical, pertaining to courts of law or to a judge. (L.) From L. *iuridic-us*, relating to the administration of justice; with suffix *-ālis*. — L. *iūri-*, decl. stem of *iūs*, law; *dicāre*, to proclaim. See **Just** (1) below.

jurisdiction. (F. — L.) M. F. *juris-diction* (F. *juridiction*). — L. *iūrisdic-tiōnem*, acc. of *iūrisdictio*, administration of justice. — L. *iūris*, gen. of *iūs*, law (see **Just** (1) below); and see **Diction.** ¶ So also *juris-prudence*.

jurist, a lawyer. (F. — L.) F. *juriste* (Cot.). — Late L. *iūrista*, a lawyer. — L. *iūr-*, for *iūs*, law; with suffix *-ista* (= Gk. -ιστης).

juror, one of a jury. (F. — L.) Imitated from F. *jureur*, a swearer, a juror. — L. *iūrātōrem*, acc. of *iūrātor*, one who swears. — L. *iūrāre*, to swear; see **Jury** (above).

Jury-mast, a temporary mast. (F. — L.) Short for *ajury-mast*; where *ajury* = O. F. *ajuirie*, aid, succour (Godefroy). From L. *adiūtāre*, to aid; see **Aid.** Cf. M. E. *iuwere*, assistance; Prompt. Parv.

Just (1), upright. (F. — L.) M. E. *iust.* — F. *juste*. — L. *iustum*, acc. of *iustus*, just, according to right; with suffix *-tus*. — L. *iūs*, right, that which is fitting; cf. Skt. *yu*, to join.

justice. (F. — L.) F. *justice.* — L. *iūstitia*, justice; Late L. *iūstitia*, a tribunal, a judge. — L. *iūsti-*, for *iūstus*, just; see **Just** (1) above.

justify. (F. — L.) F. *justifier.* — L. *iūstificāre* to shew to be just. — L. *iusti-*

for *iustus*, just; *-ficāre*, for *facere*, to make.

Just (2), to joust; see **Joust**.

Justle; see **Jostle**.

Jut, to project. (F.—L.) Merely a corruption of *jet*; in the same way a *jetty* or pier was formerly called a *jutty*; see **Jetty**.

jutty, a projection. (F.—L.) For *jetty*; see above. Der. *jutty*, vb., to project beyond.

Jute, a substance resembling hemp. (Bengali.) Bengali *jūt*, the fibres of the bark of the *Corchorus olitorius* (Wilson). From *jhōto*, vulgarly *jhuto*, the native name in Orissa (Yule).

Juvenile, young. (F.—L.) M. F. *juvenile*; F. *juvenil*.—L. *iuuenīlis*, youthful.—L. *iuuenis*, young. See **Young**.

Juxtaposition. (L. *and* F.—L.) Coined from L. *iuxtā*, near; and *position*. See **Joust** and **Position**.

K.

Kail, Kale, cabbage. (L.) Northern E. form of *cole*; see **Cole**.

Kails, ninepins. (Du.) Formerly also *keyles*; see *quille* in Cotgrave. These *kails* were cone-shaped.—Du. *kegel*, a pin, kail; *met kegels spelen*, to play at ninepins. ╋ Dan. *kegle*, a cone, *kegler*, nine-pins; Swed. *kägla*, a pin, cone; G. *kegel* (whence F. *quille*). Apparently a dimin. of Du. *keg*, a wedge.

Kaleidoscope, an optical toy. (Gk.) From Gk. καλ-ός, beautiful; εἶδο-s, form; σκοπ-εῖν, to behold; because it enables one to behold beautiful forms.

Kalendar; see **Calends**.

Kangaroo, a quadruped. (Australian.) Said to be *not* the native Australian name, but to have arisen from some mistake; but even this is doubtful (see Morris).

Kayles; see **Kails**.

Kecksies, hemlocks. (C.) For *keckses*; and *kecks* is also written *kex*. See **Kex**.

Kedge (1), to warp a ship. (F.—L.?) To *kedge* is to drag a ship slowly forward, by help of a kedge-anchor, against tide. A *kedge-anchor* was formerly called a *catch-anchor* or *catch* (N. E. D.). Hence *kedge* may represent *ketch*; for *catch*.

Kedge (2), **Kidge**, brisk, lively. (E.) An East-Anglian word. M. E. *kygge*,

kydge. Cf. prov. E. *cadgy*, cheerful; and perhaps Dan. *kaad*, frolicsome; M. Dan. *kæde*, joy; Swed. *kätja*, to be wanton.

Keel (1), the bottom of a ship. (Scand.) Icel. *kjölr*, Dan. *kiöl*, Swed. *köl*, the keel of a ship (whence G. Du. *kiel*, a keel). Teut. type **kiluz*. Cf. A. S. *celae*, the beak of a ship (O. E. T.). Distinct from A. S. *cēol*, O. H. G. *kiol*, M. H. G. *kiel*, a ship.

keelhaul. (Scand. *and* E.) Also *keel-hale*, 'to punish in the seaman's way, by dragging the criminal under water on one side of the ship and up again on the other;' Johnson. From *keel* and *haul* or *hale*. Cf. Du. *kiel-halen*, G. *kielholen*.

keelson, kelson, a set of timbers next a ship's keel. (Scand.) Formerly *kelsine* (Chapman).—Swed. *kölsvin*, Dan. *kiölsviin* (Norweg. *kjölsvill*), a keelson; E. Fries. *kolswīn*.╋G. *kielschwein*. Lit. 'keel-swine;' but this can hardly have been the orig. sense. A better sense is given by Norw. *kjölsvill*, where *svill* answers to G. *schwelle*, E. *sill*; see **Sill**. This suffix, not being understood, may easily have been corrupted to *swine*, and afterwards, in English, to *-son*.

Keel (2), to cool. (E.) To *keel* a pot is to keep it from boiling over, lit. to cool it.—A. S. *cēlan*, to cool; for **cōljan*.—A. S. *cōl*, cool. See **Cool**.

Keelson; see **Keel** (1).

Keen, sharp. (E.) M. E. *kene*. A. S. *cēne*, where *ē* is due to an older *ō*; O. Merc. *cōene*. The orig. sense is 'skilful, experienced.'╋Du. *koen*, bold, daring; Icel. *kænn* (for *kœnn*), wise, also able; G. *kühn*, bold, O. H. G. *chuoni*. Teut. type **kōnjoz*, able; from Teut. root **ken* (√GEN), to know; see **Can** (1).

Keep. (E.) M. E. *kepen*. A. S. *cēpan*, to observe, notice, attend to, keep.╋M.Du. *kepen*, to keep, retain (Hexham). Teut. type **kōpjan-*; cf. A. S. *ge-cōp*, fit, suitable.

Keg, a small cask. (Scand.) Formerly also *cag*.—Icel. *kaggi*, a keg; Swed. *kagge*, Norweg. *kagge*, a keg, a round mass or heap. Der. *kails*.

Kelp, calcined ashes of sea-weed. Origin unknown. Also spelt *kilp*.

Ken, to know. (Scand.) M. E. *kennen*.—Icel. *kenna*, Swed. *känna*, Dan. *kiende*, to know; so also G. *kennen*; A. S. *cennan* (to declare), Goth. *kannjan*. Teut. type **kannjan-*. Causal form of *cunnan*, to know, derived from Teut. base *kann* (cf. *can*) by vowel-change of *a* to *e*. See Can (1).

Kennel (1), a house for dogs. (F.–L.) M. E. *kenel*. A Norman form of O. F. *chenil*, a kennel.–Late L. 'canīle, domus canis' in Wrt. Vocab. 198. 29.–L. *can-is*, a dog, with suffix -*īle*, as in *ou-īle*, a sheepfold. Cf. Norman F. *ken*, O. F. *chen* (F. *chien*), a dog, from L. acc. *canem*, a dog.

Kennel (2), a gutter. (F.–L.) A corruption of M. E. *canel*, a channel.–A. F. *canel*, Charlemagne, ed. Michel, l. 556; O. F. *chanel*; see Channel.

Kerbstone. (F.–L.; and E.) Here *kerb* is for *curb*; so called because the stone was sometimes placed, as round a well, on a *curved* edge. See Curb.

Kerchief. (F.–L.) M. E. *curchief*, *couerchef* (*coverchef*). – O. F. *covrechef*, lit. a head-covering.–O. F. *covrir*, to cover; *chef*, the head; see Cover and Chief.

Kermes, the dried bodies of insects used in dyeing crimson. (Arab.–Skt.) See Crimson.

Kern (1), **Kerne,** an Irish soldier. (Irish.) Irish *ceatharnach*, a soldier.–O. Irish *cethern*, a troop. See Cateran.

Kern (2); see Quern.

Kernel. (E.) A. S. *cyrnel*, a grain: dimin. of A. S. *corn*, a grain (with the usual change from Teut. *u* (A. S. *o*) to *y*). Teut. stem *kurnilo-*. See Corn.

Kersey, coarse woollen cloth. (E.) Named from *Kersey* (of A. S. origin), a village three miles from Hadleigh, in Suffolk, where a woollen trade was once carried on. ¶ Not from *Jersey*, which is also used as the name of a material.

Kerseymere, a twilled cloth of fine wool. (Cashmere.) A corruption of *Cashmere* or *Cassimere*, by confusion with *kersey* above.

Kestrel, a base kind of hawk. (F.–L.) For *kesrel*; the *t* is excrescent, as in *whils-t*, &c.–M.F.*quercerelle*,'a kastrell;' Cotgrave; F. *crécerelle*. Extended from O. F. *crecele*, *cercelle*, M. F. *quercelle*, a kestrel. Of imitative origin; cf. O. F. *cercelle*, F. *sarcelle*, a teal, from L. *querquēdula*, a kind of teal.

Ketch, a small yacht or hoy. (B.) M. E. *cache*. Prob. from the verb *to catch*; see N. E. D.; s. v. Catch. ¶ The Du. *kits*, F. *quaiche*, a ketch, are borrowed from E. ¶ Distinct from *caïque*, q. v.

Ketchup, a sauce. (Malay.) Malay *kēchap*, *kīchap*, a sauce; soy. (In Dutch spelling, *ketjap*.)–C. P. G. Scott.

Kettle. (Scand.–L.) M. E. *ketel*. Icel. *ketill*; borrowed from L.' *catillus*, a small bowl (whence also Goth. *katils*, A. S. *cetel*, Du. *ketel*, G. *kessel*, &c.). Dimin. of *catīnus*, a bowl, deep vessel for cooking food. Perhaps allied to Gk. κότυλος, a cup (Prellwitz); see Cotyledon.

Kex, hemlock, a hollow stem. (W.–L.) M. E. *kex*.–W. *cecys*, pl., hollow stalks, hemlock, allied to *cegid*, hemlock; Corn. *cegas*, hemlock; prob. borrowed from L. *cicūta*, hemlock. ¶ *Kex*=*kecks*, and is properly a plural form.

Key. (E.) M. E. *keye*. A.S. *cāg*, a key; O. Fries. *kāi*, *kēi*, a key.

Khan, a prince. (Pers.–Tatar.) Pers. *khān*, lord, prince; of Tatar origin. Cf. *Chingis Khan*, i. e. great lord, a Tatar title (Chaucer's *Cambuscan*).

Khedive, a prince. (F.–Pers.) F. *khédive*.–Pers. *khadīw*, *khidīw*, a great prince, sovereign; *khidēwī*, the khedive, viceroy of Egypt (Palmer). Cf. Pers. *khodā*, God.

Kibe, a chilblain. (C.?) W. *cibwst*, chilblains; explained by Pugh as standing for *cib-gwst*.–W. *cib*, a cup; *gwst*, a humour, malady, disease; hence 'a cup-like malady,' from the rounded form. The E. word has preserved only the syllable *cib*, rejecting the latter syllable. (Doubtful.)

Kick. (Perhaps Celtic.) M. E. *kiken*. Cf. W. *cicio*, to kick (colloquial); O. W. *cic*, a foot; as in W. *cic-wr*, footman. (Doubtful.)

Kickshaws, a dainty dish. (F.–L.) A sing. sb.; the pl. is *kickshawses* (Shak.). A curious corruption of F. *quelque chose*, something, hence, a trifle, a delicacy. Spelt *quelquechose* by Dryden. – F. *quelque chose*. –L. *quāl-is*, of what sort, with suffix -*quam*; *caussa*, a cause, a thing. ¶ Moisy gives Norman F. *quiquechose*.

Kid, a young goat. (Scand.) M. E. *kid*. –Dan. *kid*, Swed. *kid*, Icel. *kið*, a kid.+ G. *kitze*.

kidnap, to steal young children. (Scand.) *Kid*, in Tudor E. slang, means a child; *nap* is our *nab*.–Dan. *kid*, a kid; *nappe*, to nab; see Nab.

Kiddle, a kind of weir formed of basketwork placed in a river to catch fish. (A.F.) Anglo-F. *kidel*, pl. *kideux*; O. F. *cuidel*

(Godefroy); later form *quideau*, ' a wicker engine whereby fish is caught ; ' Cotgrave. Late L. *kidellus* ; Breton *kidel*.

Kidney. (E. ? *and* Scand.) Corruption of M. E. *kidnere, kidneer* ; *nere* is also used alone. 1. Here *kid* answers to A. S. **cyd-*, perhaps related to A. S. *codd*, a bag, pod, husk, M. E. *cod*, belly. 2. M. E. *nere* is a Scand. word. ▬ Icel. *nȳra*, Dan. *nyre*, Swed. *njure*, a kidney ; cognate with Du. *nier*, G. *niere*, and allied to Gk. νεφρός, kidney. ¶ The former element is doubtful.

Kilderkin. (Du.) A corruption of M. Du. *kindeken*, also *kinneken*, the eighth part of a vat. The lit. sense is ' little child,' because the measure is a small one as compared with a tun, vat, or barrel. Formed, with dimin. suffix *-ken* (now nearly obsolete), from Du. *kind*, a child ; allied to Icel. *kundr*, a son, and to E. **Kin.** The mod. Du. name is *kinnetje*, by substitution of *-tje* for *-ken*.

Kill. (E.) M. E. *killen*, more commonly *cullen*. The M. E. *cullen* prob. answers to an A. S. type **cyllan*, from the weak grade *c(w)ul-* of *cwel-an*, to die. Cf. E. Fries. *küllen*, to vex, strike, beat, a parallel form ; O. H. G *chollen*, by-form of *quellan*, to vex, kill, martyr. Thus *kill* is closely related to **Quell**, q. v. For the loss of *w*, cf. *dull*, which is related to *dwell*.

Kiln. (L.) A. S. *cyln*, also *cylen* ; merely borrowed from L. *culina*, a kitchen (hence, a drying-house) ; whence also W. *cylyn*, a kiln, a furnace. See **Culinary**.

Kilt. (Scand.) The sb. is derived from the verb *kilt*, to tuck up. ▬ Dan. *kilte*, to truss, tuck up ; Swed. dial. *kilta*, to swaddle. Cf. Icel. *kilting*, a skirt. Perhaps related to Swed. dial. *kilta*, the lap, Icel. *kjalta*, lap.

Kimbo ; see Akimbo.

Kin, genus, race. (E.) M. E. *kin, kun.* A. S. *cynn*, orig. a tribe.+Icel. *kyn*, kin ; O. Sax. *kunni*, O. H. G. *chunni* ; Goth. *kuni*, tribe. Teut. type **kunjom*, neut. From the weak grade of Teut. root **ken-*, Idg. *gen-*. Allied to **Genus**. (√GEN.)

kind (1), sb., nature, sort. (E.) M. E. *kund, kind.* A. S. *cynd, ge-cynd*, nature ; whence the adj. below. Der. *kind-ly*, natural.

kind (2), adj., natural, loving. (E.) M. E. *kunde, kinde.* A. S. *cynde, ge-cynde.*

natural, in-born ; allied to Goth. *-kunds*, of such a nature. Allied to **Kin**.

kindle (1), to bring forth young. (E.) M. E. *kindlen, kundlen* ; from M. E. *kindel, kundel*, sb., a progeny ; from the A. S. *cynd*, nature, or from the adj. *cynde*, natural.

Kindle (2), to inflame. (Scand.) It appears to be the same word as **Kindle** (1); see Anc. Riwle. But it can hardly be separated from Icel. *kynda*, to inflame, kindle, Swed. dial. *kynda, kinda*, a sense which seems to have been suggested by Icel. *kyndill*, a torch. And Icel. *kyndill* is a mere borrowing from A. S. *candel* ; from L. *candēla*, a candle. See **Candle**.

Kindred. (E.) The former *d* is excrescent. M. E. *kinrede.* ▬ A. S. *cyn*, kin ; *-rēden*, signifying law, state, condition (so also *hat-red* from *hate*). *Rēden* is allied to the adj. *ready* ; cf. Goth. *ga-raideins*, an ordinance.

Kine, cows ; see **Cow**.

King, a chief ruler. (E.) A. S. *cyning*, a king ; lit. ' a man of good birth ;' (cf. A. S. *cyne-*, royal, Icel. *konr*, one of gentle birth) ;▬ A. S. *cyn*, a tribe, kin, race ; with suffix *-ing*, as in *Ælfred Æpelwulfing =* Ælfred the son of Æthelwulf. ✛ O. Sax. *kuning*, from *kuni*, tribe ; O. Fries. *kining* ; Icel. *konungr* ; Swed. *konung* ; Dan. *konge* ; Du. *koning* ; G. *könig*, O. H. G. *chuning* (from O. H. G. *chunni*, a kin, race). Teut. type **kuningoz*, m.

kingdom. (E.) Late M. E. *kingdom* ; not really a compound of *king* and suffix *-dom*, but a substitution for early M. E. *kinedom*, A. S. *cynedōm*, a kingdom. The A. S. *cyne-* signifies ' royal,' very common in composition, and is allied to A. S. *cyn*, a tribe.

Kink, a twist in a rope. (Scand.) A Northern word. ▬ Swed. *kink*, Norweg. *kink*, a twist in a rope. (So also Du. *kink.*) Allied to Norweg. *kika, kinka*, to writhe, Icel. *kikna*, to sink at the knees under a burden, Icel. *keikr*, bent back ; Norw. *keika*, to bend aside, to twist. (Teut. base **keik-*, to bend.)

Kiosk, a small pavilion. (Turk. ▬ Pers.) F. *kiosque.* ▬ Turk. *kushk, köshk* (pronounced with *k* as *ki*), a kiosk. ▬ Pers. *kūshk*, a palace, villa, portico.

Kipper, to cure salmon. (E.) This meaning is an accidental one, arising from a habit of curing *kipper-salmon*, i. e. salmon during the spawning season, which were cured because of inferior quality. A salmon, after spawning, was called a *kipper* (Pennant). A. S. *cypera*, a kipper-salmon.

Kirk, a church. (Scand. − E. − Gk.) M. E. *kirke*. − Icel. *kirkja*; borrowed from A. S. *cirice, circe*, a church. See **Church.**

Kirtle, a sort of gown or petticoat. (L. ; *with* E. *suffix*.) M. E. *kirtel*. A. S. *cyrtel*, a tunic ; Icel. *kyrtill*, Dan. *kiortel*, Swed. *kjortel* ; evidently dimin. forms. All from L. *curtus*, short, which appears also in Du. *kort*, G. *kurz*, short. See **Curt.**

Kiss, a salute with the lips. (E.) The vowel *i* is due to the *verb*, which is formed from the *sb.* by vowel-change. M. E. *coss*, sb., a kiss; whence *kissen*, verb. A. S. *coss*, sb.; whence *cyssan*, verb.+Du. *kus*, Icel. *koss*, Dan. *kys*, Swed. *kyss*, G. *kuss*, a kiss. Teut. type **hussuz*, sb. Cf. Goth. *kukjan*, to kiss; E. Fries. *kük*, a kiss.

Kit (1), a milk-pail, tub; also, an outfit. (O. Low G.) M. E. *kit*. − M. Du. *kitte*, a wooden bowl, a tub; Du. *kit*. Cf. Norweg. *kitte*, a corn-bin.

Kit (2), a small violin. (F. − L. − Gk.) Shortened from Norman F. *quiterne* (Moisy); answering to O. F. *guiterne* (Godefroy). From L. *cithara*. − Gk. κιθάρα, a kind of lyre. See **Cithern.**

Kit (3), a brood, family, quantity. (E.) A variant of *kith*. ' The whole *kit* ' = the whole kith. See **Kith.**

Kit-cat, Kit-kat, the name given to portraits of a particular size. (Personal name.) The size adopted by Sir G. Kneller for painting members of the *Kit-Kat* club, which used to meet at a house kept by *Christopher Kat* (Haydn). *Kit* is for *Christopher* (Gk. Χριστο-φόρος, lit. 'Christbearing').

Kitchen. (L.) M. E. *kichene*. A. S. *cycene*, f. − L. *coquina*, a kitchen. − L. *coquere*, to cook ; see **Cook.**

Kite, a bird, a toy for flying. (E.) M.E. *kite*. A. S. *cȳta*, a kite.

Kith, kindred, acquaintance. (E.) M.E. *cuȝȝe*, kith. A. S. *cȳȝ*, native land, relationship. − A. S. *cūȝ*, known, pp. of *kunnan*, to know. See **Can** (1).

Kitten. (Scand.; *with* F. *suffix*.) M.E. *kitoun*, where the suffix *-oun* is F., suggested by O. F. *chatton*, a kitten. *Kit* is a mutated form of *cat*, appearing in the E. form *kit-ling*, from Icel. *ketlingr*, a kitten ; and in (obs.) *kittle*, to produce kittens.

Knack, a snap, dexterity, trick. (E.)

Imitative, like **Knap.** Cf. Du. *knakken*, G. *knacken*, to crack. [The Gael. *cnac*, Irish *cnag*, a crack, W. *cnec*, a snap, are borrowed from E. *crack*.] It meant (1) a snap, (2) a snap with the finger or nail, (3) a jester's trick, piece of dexterity, (4) a joke, trifle, toy, &c. Cf. **Knock.**

Knacker, a dealer in old horses. (Scand.) It formerly meant a saddler and harness-maker (Ray). − Icel. *hnakkr*, a saddle.

Knag, a knot in wood, peg. (E.) M.E. *knagge*, a peg, a knot in wood. Not in A.S. Low G. *knagge*, a kind of peg ; Swed. *knagg*, a knag, knot ; Dan. *knag*, a peg, cog. We find also Irish *cnag*, a knob, peg, *cnaig*, a knot in wood, Gael. *cnag*, knob, pin, peg (all from E.).

Knap, to snap. (Du.) Du. *knappen*, to snap, crack, crush, eat (whence *knapper*, hard gingerbread, a lie) ; Cf. Dan. *kneppe*, to snap ; Swed. *knäpp*, a snap, *knep*, a trick. A parallel word to *knack*, and of imitative origin. Cf. Gael. *cnap*, to strike, beat, thump, Irish *cnapaim*, I strike ; from E. See **Knop.**

knapsack. (Du.) Du. *knapzak*, a knapsack, lit. a provision-bag. − Du. *knap*, eating, *knappen* to crush, eat ; *zak*, a sack (a word of Hebrew origin) ; see **Sack.**

Knapweed, Knopweed, a weed with a hard head or *knop* ; see **Knop.**

Knar ; see **Gnarled.**

Knave, a boy, servant, sly fellow. (E.) M. E. *knaue* (*knave*), a boy, servant. A.S. *cnafa*, older form *cnapa*, a boy. + So also Du. *knaap*, a lad, servant ; Icel. *knapi*, servant-boy ; G. *knabe*, a boy. It is probable that the initial *kn-* represents the weak grade of Teut. **ken-* (Idg. **gen-*), to produce ; cf. **Knight.** But the rest of the word remains unexplained.

Knead, to mould by pressure. (E.) M. E. *kneden*. A. S. *cnedan* (pt. t. **cnæd*, pp. *cneden*), a strong verb, to knead.+ Du. *kneden*, Icel. *knoȝa*, Swed. *knåda*, G. *kneten*; (all from Teut. base**kneȝ-*). Allied to Russ. *gnetate, gnesti*, to press, squeeze ; from the corresponding Idg. root **gnet*.

Knee. (E.) M. E. *kne*, pl. *knees* ; also *cneo*, pl. *cneon*. A. S. *cnēo*.+Du. *knie*, Icel. *knē*, Dan. *knæ*, Swed. *knä*, G. *knie*, O. H. G. *chniu*, Goth. *kniu*. Teut. type **knewom*, n. Cf. L. *genu*; Gk. γόνυ ; Skt. *jānu*. The Idg. related bases are **genu-* (as in L.), **gonu-* (as in Gk), **gneu-* (whence Teut. **kneu-*). Cf. Gk.

γνυ-πετεῖν, to fall on the knees. See **Genuflection, Pentagon,** &c.

kneel, to fall on the knees. (E.) M. E. *cneolien, knēlen*; A. S. *cneowlian.+* Du. *knielen*; Low G. *knelen* (Lübben); Dan. *knæle* (formed from *knæ*, knee).

Knell, Knoll, to sound as a bell, toll. (E.) M. E. *knillen, knollen.* A. S. *cnyllan*, to knock, beat noisily. Cf. Du. *knallen*, to give a loud report, Dan. *knalde*, to explode; Swed. *knalla*, to resound, G. *knallen*, to make a loud noise; Icel. *gnella*, to scream; M. H. G. *knüllen*, to beat. Perhaps of imitative origin, to denote a loud noise; cf. Du. *knal*, Dan. *knald*, Swed. *knall*, G. *knall*, a loud noise. From Teut. base **knel-* (**knal-, *knul-*).

Knickerbockers, loose knee-breeches. (Du.) Named from Diedrich *Knickerbocker*, the pretended author of W. Irving's Hist. of New York; taken as the type of a New York Dutchman.

Knick-knack, a trick, trifle, toy. (E.) A reduplication of *knack*, in the sense of trifle, toy. Cf. Du. *knikken*, to snap, weakened form of *knakken*, to crack. See **Knack.**

Knife. (E.) M. E. *knif*, pl. *kniues* (with *u=v*). A. S. *cnīf*, a knife.+ Du. *knijf*, Icel. *knīfr*, Dan. *kniv*, Swed. *knif*, prov. G. *kneif*; Low G. *knīf, knīp*, a knife (Lübben). (Cf. F. *canif*, from G.) Possibly related to **Nip** and **Nibble.**

Knight, a youth, servant, man-at-arms. (E.) M. E. *knight.* A. S. *cniht*, O. Merc. *cneht*, a boy, servant.+ Du. *knecht*, a servant; Dan. *knegt*, man-servant, knave (at cards); Swed. *knekt*, soldier, knave (at cards); G. *knecht.* β. Perhaps *cneht=* **cn-eht*, belonging to the kin or tribe; cf. Gk. γν-ήσιος, legitimate, from γέν-ος, kin (where γν- is the weak grade of γεν-); see **Kin.** The suffix *-eht, -iht* is adjectival; as in *þorn-iht*, thorny, from *þorn*, a thorn.

Knit. (E.) A. S. *cnyttan*, to form into a knot, to knot; formed (by vowel-change) from Teut. **knut-*, the base of *cnotta*, a knot (Teut. type **knut-ton-*). Allied to Icel. *knýta*, Dan. *knytte*, Swed. *knyta*, to knit; and to Icel. *knūtr*, Dan. *knude*, Swed. *knut*, a knot. See **Knot.**

Knob, a form of *knop.* M. E. *knobbe.* Cf. Low G. *knobbe*, Du. *knobbel*, a knob. See **Knop.**

Knock, to strike, rap. (E.) M. E. *knocken.* A. S. *cnucian*; Icel. *knoka.* Cf. Irish *cnagaim*, I knock; W. *cnocio*, to

knock; Corn. *cnoucye*, to knock. An imitative word, from Teut. **knuk-*, weak grade of **Knack.**

Knoll (1), a hillock. (E.) M. E. *knol.* A. S. *cnol.+*Du. *knol*, a turnip, from its roundness, Dan. *knold*, a knoll, Swed. *knöl*, a bump, G. *knollen*, a knoll, clod, lump. Cf. W. *cnol*, a knoll, hillock; Swed. dial. *knall*, a knoll.

Knoll (2); see **Knell.**

Knop, Knob, a bump, protuberance, boss. (E.) M. E. *knop*, a rose-bud. O. Fries. *ersknop*, the rump-bone.+Du. and Dan. *knop*, a knob, bud; Swed. *knopp*, a bud, *knop*, a knot, G. *knopf*, knob, button, knot. Apparently allied to M. E. *knap*, a knob; A. S. *cnæp*, a knob-top, Icel. *knappr*, a knob; whence Gael. *cnap*, a knob, button, boss, stud, hillock, also a slight blow; also the verb *cnap*, to thump, beat (hence, to raise a bump); W. *cnap*, a knob; Irish *cnap*, knob, bunch, hillock, *cnapaim*, I strike. See **Knap.**

Knot. (E.) M. E. *knotte.* A. S. *cnotta*, a knot. + Du. *knot.* Cf. also O. H. G. *chnodo*, G. *knoten*, a knot (with a different dental sound). Also (with a long vowel) Icel. *knūtr*, a knot, Dan. *knude*, Swed. *knut.* And (with orig. *a*) Icel. *knöttr* (Teut. **knattuʒ*), a ball.

knout, a scourge. (Russ. — Scand.) Russ. *knute*, a whip, scourge. ◼ Swed. *knut*, Icel. *knūtr*, a knot.

Know, to be assured of. (E.) M. E. *knowen.* A. S. *cnāwan* (pt. t. *cnēow*, pp. *cnāwen*). + Icel. *knā*, O. H. G. *chnāan.* Further allied to Russ. *znate*, to know; L. *noscere* (for *gnoscere*); Gk. γι-γνώσκειν; Pers. *far-zān*, knowledge; O. Irish *gnāth*, known, accustomed, W. *gnawd*, a custom; Skt. *jnā*, to know. All from a base **gnō*, a secondary form of √GEN, to know.

knowledge. (E.) M. E. *knowlege*, *knauleche*; from *knowlechen*, vb., to acknowledge. Here *-lēchen* = A. S. *-lǣcan* (as in M. E. *nēhlēchen*, A. S. *nēahlǣcan*, to approach). And *-lǣcan* is from the A. S. *-lāc*, the same word as A. S. *lāc*, a game, sport, play. See **Wedlock.**

Knuckle, the projecting joint of the fingers. (E.) M. E. *knokil*; O. Fries. *knokele.+* M. Du. *knokel*, Du. *kneukel*, Dan. *knokkel*, G. *knöchel*, a knuckle. A dimin. form; the shorter form appears in M. Du. *knoke*, a bone, knuckle, G. *knochen*, a bone, Swed. *knoge*, a knuckle.

Knurr, Knur, a knot in wood,

wooden ball. (O. Low G.) M. E. *knor.*
Not in A. S.—M. Du. *knorre,* a hard
swelling, knot in wood. **+** Dan. *knort,*
a knot; G. *knorren,* a lump. Allied to
M. E. *knarre,* a knot. See **Gnarled.**

Koran, sacred book of the Mohamme-
dans. (Arab.) Arab. *qurān,* reading aloud,
recitation; also, the Koran.—Arab. root
qara-a, he read. (The *a* is long.)
    alcoran; the same word, with the
Arab. def. art. *al* (the) prefixed.

Kraal, an enclosure, a collection of huts,
an African village. (Du.—Port.—L.) Du.
kraal, an African village.—Port. *curral,*
an enclosure; the same word as Span.
corral. See **Corral.**

Kythe, to make known. (E.) A.S.
cӯðan, to make known.—A. S. *cūð,* known,
pp. of *cunnan,* to know. See **Can** (1),
and **Uncouth.**

L.

Label, a small slip of paper, &c. (F.)
M. E. *label.* — O. F. *label, lambel,* a label
(in heraldry), a shred; mod. F. *lambeau.*
Of uncertain origin; cf. O. Lat. *lamberāre,*
to tear in pieces (Ascoli).

Labial. (L.) Late L. *labiālis,* pertaining to the lips.—L. *labium,* the lip. See
Lip.

labellum, a pendulous petal. (L.)
L. *labellum,* dimin. of *labium,* a lip.

labiate. (L.) A botanical term.—L.
labi-um, a lip; with suffix *-ate* (L. *-ātus*).

Laboratory. (L.) Formerly *elabora-
tory* (Blount).—M. F. *elaboratoire* (Cot.).
Formed from L. *ēlaborātus,* pp. of *ēlabo-
rāre,* to elaborate, work out.—L. *ē,* out;
laborāre, to work, from *labor,* labour.

laborious. (F.—L.) M. E. *laborious.*—F. *laborieux.*—L. *labōriōsus,* toil-
some. **—** L. *labōr-,* for *labor,* labour; with
suffix *-ōsus.*

labour, toil. (F.—L.) M. E. *labour.*
— O. F. *labour* (later *labeur*).—L. *labōrem,*
acc. of *labor, labōs,* toil.

Laburnum, a tree. (L.) L. *laburnum,*
in Pliny, xvi. 18.

Labyrinth, a maze. (F.—L.—Gk.—
Egypt.) F. *labyrinthe.*—L. *labyrinthus.*
—Gk. λαβύρινθος, a maze, a place full of
lanes or alleys. Of Egyptian origin
(Maspero).

Lac (1), a resinous substance. (Pers.—

Skt.) Pers. *lak,* gum-lac, whence crimson
lake is obtained for dyeing.—Skt. *lākshā,*
lac; also *laktaka, raktaka,* lac; *rañj,* to
dye. Der. *gum-lac, shel-lac.*

Lac (2), a hundred thousand. (Hind.—
Skt.) A *lac* of rupees = 100,000 rupees. —
Hindustani *lak* (also *lākh*), a lac.—Skt.
laksha, a hundred thousand; originally,
'a mark.'

Lace, a cord, tie. (F.—L.) M. E. *las,
laas.*—O. F. *las, laqs* (F. *lacs*), a snare,
noose.—L. *laqueus,* a noose, snare, knot.
Allied to L. *lacĕre,* to allure; cf. E. *elicit,
delight.* See **Lasso, Latchet.**

Lacerate, to tear. (L.) From pp. of
L. *lacerāre,* to tear.—L. *lacer,* mangled,
torn.**+**Gk. λακερός, torn; λακίς, a rent.

Lachrymal, Lacrimal, pertaining
to tears. (L.) The spelling *lachrymal* is
bad.—L. *lacryma,* better *lacruma, lacrima,*
a tear; O. L. *dacrima,* a tear. Cognate
with Gk. δάκρυ, a tear, and E. *tear;* see
Tear (1). Der. (from L. *lacrima*) *lachry-
mose,* tearful; *lachrymatory,* a tear-bottle.

Lack (1), want. (E.) The old sense is
often 'failure' or 'fault.' M. E. *lak, lac.*
Not in A. S., but cf. O. Fries. *lek,* damage,
harm, *lakia,* to attack.**+**Du. *lak,* blemish,
stain, *laken,* to blame; Low G. *lạk,* defect,
blame, Icel. *lakr,* defective, lacking.

lack (2), to be destitute of. (E.) M. E.
lakken; weak verb; from *lak,* sb. See
above.

Lacker; see **Lacquer.**

Lackey, Lacquey, a footman, menial
attendant. (F.—Span.?—Arab.?) From
M. F. *laquay,* 'a lackey, footboy;' Cot.
(F. *laquais*). There was also an O. F.
form *alacay;* Littré shews that, in the
15th cent., a certain class of soldiers (esp.
crossbow-men), were called *alagues, ala-
cays,* or *lacays.* (The prefix *a-* is prob.
due to Arab. *al,* the def. article.) Prob.
from Span. *lacayo,* Port. *lacaio,* a lackey;
Port. *lacaia,* a woman-servant in dramatic
performances. — Arab. *luka',* worthless,
servile; as a sb., a slave; *lak'ā,* fem., mean,
servile. Cf. *lakā', lakī',* servile, *laka'i,*
slovenly. ¶ This is a guess; it is much
disputed; Diez connects it with Ital.
leccare, G. *lecken,* to lick.

Laconic, brief and pithy. (L.—Gk.)
L. *Lacōnicus,* Laconian.—Gk. Λακωνικός,
Laconian.—Gk. Λάκων, a Laconian, Spartan. These men were celebrated for their
brief and pithy locution.

Lacquer, Lacker, a sort of varnish.

(F. – Port. – Pers. – Skt.) M. F. *lacre* (Cot.). – Port. *lacre*, sealing-wax. – Port. *laca*, gum-lac. – Pers. *lak*, gum-lac; see **Lac** (1).

Lacteal, relating to milk. (L.) From L. *lacte-us*, milky. – L. *lact-*, stem of *lac*, milk. + Gk. γαλακτ-, stem of γάλα, milk. Allied to *lettuce*.

Lad, a youth. (E.) M. E. *ladde*. Prob. the sense was 'one led,' i. e. a follower, dependant. From M. E. *lad*, led, pp. of *lēden*, to lead. See **Lead** (1). (H. Bradley, in *Athenæum*, June 1, 1894.)

Ladanum; see **Laudanum.**

Ladder. (E.) M. E. *laddre*. A. S. *hlǣder*, *hlǣdder*, a ladder. + Du. *ladder*, ladder, rails of a cart; O. H. G. *hleitra*, G. *leiter*, a ladder. Cognate with Gk. κλῖ-μαξ, a ladder; see **Climax.** Named from sloping; see **Lean** (1). (√KLEI.)

Lade (1), to load. (E.) Formerly a strong verb; we still use the pp. *laden*. M. E. *laden*. A. S. *hladan* (pt. t. *hlōd*, pp. *hladen*), meaning (1) to load, heap up, heap together, (2) to draw out water, lade out, drain. + Du. *laden*, Icel. *hlaða*, Dan. *lade*, Swed. *ladda*, Goth. *-hlathan* (in *afhlathan*), G. *laden*, to lade. Teut. base *hlad* (not *hlath*), to lade (Kluge). Allied to Russ. *klade*, a lading.

lade (2), to draw out water, drain. (E.) The same word as **Lade** (1).

ladle, a large spoon. (E.) M. E. *ladel*; A. S. *hlædel*; so named from being used for dipping out or *lading* water from a vessel; from M. E. *laden*, A. S. *hladan*, to lade out; see above.

Lady. (E.) Perhaps 'loaf-kneader.' A. S. *hlǣfdīge*, a lady. – A. S. *hlāf*, a loaf; and (perhaps) A. S. *dīge*, a kneader, from the root seen in Goth. *deigan*, to knead; see **Dike,** and see **Dairy.** ¶ *Lady* was specially used to mean the Virgin Mary; hence *lady-bird*, *lady's-slipper*, &c.

Lag, late, sluggish. (C.) W. *llag*, slack, loose, sluggish; Corn. *lac*, loose, remiss; Gael. and Ir. *lag*, weak, feeble, faint; O. Irish *lac*, weak. + L. *laxus*, lax; see **Lax, Languid, Slack.**

Lagan, goods cast out in a shipwreck. (F.) A law-term; usually explained so as to force a false connexion with L. *ligāre*, to tie. – O. F. *lagan*, *lagand*, wreckage cast ashore (Godefroy). Low L. *laganum*. Origin unknown. Perhaps from O. Icel. *laginn*, 'positus,' old pp. pass. of *leggja*, to lay, place (Egilsson),

also, to be driven (Vigf.). Cf. also O. F. *alagane* (Godefroy).

Lagoon. (Ital. – L.) Ital. *lagone*, a pool; also *laguna*. [Or from Span. *laguna*.] The former is an augmentative of L. *lacus*; the latter is from L. *lacūna*, extended from *lacus*. See **Lake** (1).

Laic. (L. – Gk.) L. *laicus*, belonging to the laity. – Gk. λαικός (the same). See **Lay** (3).

Lair, den or retreat of a wild beast. (E.) M. E. *leir*. A. S. *leger*, a lair, couch, bed. – A. S. stem *leg-*, as in A. S. *leg-*, base of *licgan*, to lie down, rest. See **Lie** (1). + Du. *leger*, a bed, lair, from *liggen*; G. *lager*, O. H. G. *legar*, a couch, from O. H. G. *liggan*, to lie; Goth. *ligrs*, a couch. Doublet, *leaguer.*

Laity, the lay people. (F. – L. – Gk.; with F. suffix.) A coined word; from *lay*, adj.; cf. *gaie-ty* from *gay*, &c. See **Lay** (3).

Lake (1), a pool. (L.) A. F. *lac*. – L. *lacus*, a lake. + Gk. λάκκος, a hollow, hole, pit, pond; O. Irish *loch*, A. S. *lagu.*

Lake (2), a crimson colour. (F. – Pers. – Skt.) F. *laque* (Cot.). – Pers. *lāk*, lake. – Pers. *lak*, gum-lac; see **Lac** (1).

Lakh; the same as **Lac** (2).

Lama (1), a high priest. (Thibetan.) We speak of the *grand lama* of Thibet, i. e. chief or high priest (Webster).

Lama (2); see **Llama.**

Lamb. (E.) M. E. *lamb*, *lomb*. A. S. *lamb*, pl. *lambru*. + Du. *lam*, Icel. *lamb*, Dan. *lam*, Swed. and G. *lamm*, Goth. *lamb*, a young sheep. Teut. type *lamboz*, neut.

Lambent, flickering. (L.) 'A *lambent* flame.' – L. *lambent-*, stem of pres. pt. of *lambere*, to lick, sometimes applied to flames. Allied to **Lap** (1).

Lame, disabled, esp. in the legs. (E.) M. E. *lame*. A. S. *lama.* + Du. *lam*, Icel. *lami*, Dan. *lam*, Swed. *lam*, G. *lahm.* The orig. sense is bruised, maimed; from a base *lam-*, to break. Cf. Russ. *lomate*, to break; Icel. *lama*, to bruise; prov. E. *lam*, to bruise.

Lament, vb. (F. – L.) F. *lamenter.* – L. *lāmentārī*, to wail. – L. *lāmentum*, a mournful cry; from the base *lā-*, to utter a cry; cf. *lā-trāre*, to bark. Cf. also Russ. *laiate*, to bark, scold.

Lamina. (L.) L. *lāmina*, a thin plate of metal. Cf. **Omelette.**

Lammas, a name for Aug. 1. (E.)

A.S. *hlāf-mæsse*, lit. 'loaf-mass;' later spellings *hlammæsse, lammasse.* A loaf was on this day offered as a first-fruits of harvest. See **Mass** (2).

Lamp. (F.–L.–Gk.) O. F. *lampe.*– L. *lampas.*–Gk. λαμπάς, a torch, light.– Gk. λάμπειν, to shine. Cf. **Lantern.**

Lampoon. (F.–Teut.) F. *lampon*, orig. a drinking-song; from the exclamation *lampons!* = let us drink (Littré).–F. *lamper*, nasalised form of O. F. *lapper*, to lap up; of Teut. origin.–M. Du. *lappen*, 'to lap or licke like a dogge;' Hexham. See **Lap** (1).

Lamprey, an eel-like fish. (F.–L.) A. F. *lampreie*, O. F. *lamproie* (Ital. *lampreda*). – Late L. *lamprēda*; once spelt *lampetra*, as if 'licker of rocks,' because the fish cleaves to them, from L. *lambere*, to lick, *petra*, a rock; but this is doubtful. Cf. **Limpet.**

Lance. (F.–L.) F. *lance.*–L. *lancea.* + Gk. λόγχη, a lance. Der. *lance*, vb., to pierce; *lanc-er.*

lancegay, a kind of spear. (F.–L.; *and* F.–Span.–Moorish.) Obsolete. A corruption of *lance-zagaye*, compounded of *lance* (as above), and F. *zagaye*, a kind of Moorish pike. The latter word answers to Span. *azagaya* (= *al zagaya*), where *al* is the Arab. def. article, and *zagaya* is an O. Span. word for 'dart,' of Moorish origin. So Port. *azagaia*, whence E. *assegai.*

lanceolate, lance-shaped. (L.) L. *lanceolātus*, furnished with a spike.–L. *lanceola*, a spike; dimin. of *lancea* (above).

lancet. (F.–L.) M. E. *launcet.*– F. *lancette*, dimin. of *lance*, a lance (above).

lanch, another spelling of *lance*, vb., to pierce; also of *launch* (below).

launch, lanch, to hurl a spear, send (a ship) into the water. (F.–L.) M. E. *launchen, launcen*, to hurl.–O.F.*lanchier, lancier*, Picard *lancher*, F. *lancer*, to hurl, fling, dart, also to prick, pierce.–L. *lanceāre*, to wield a lance.–L. *lancea*, a lance.

Land. (E.) M. E. *land, lond.* A.S. *land.* + Du. Icel. Dan. Swed. Goth. G. *land.* Teut. type **landom*, neut. Allied to Celtic type **landā*, fem., whence Ir. *lann*, land, W. *llan*, a yard, churchyard, Corn. *lan*, Bret. *lann* (whence F. *lande*, a plain). See **Lawn.** Der. *up-land, outland-ish.*

landau, a kind of coach. (G.) Said to be named from *Landau*, a town in Bavaria. *Land* is cognate with E. *land*; G. *au* is allied to *i-* in M. E. *i-land*; see **Island.**

landgrave, a count of a province. (Du.) Du. *landgraaf.*–Du. *land*, land; *graaf*, a count. Der. *landgrav-ine*, from Du. *landgravin*, fem. of *landgraaf*; see **Margrave.**

landrail, a bird; see **Rail** (3).

landscape. (Du.) Formerly *landskip*; borrowed from Dutch painters.– Du. *landschap*, a landscape, a province.– Du. *land*, land; and *-schap*, a suffix corresponding to E. *-ship* in *friend-ship*, allied to the E. verb *shape*. ¶ The Du. *sch* sounds to us more like *sk* than *sh*; hence our spelling with *sc*.

Lane. (E.) M. E. *lane, lone.* A.S. *lane, lone*, a lane; O. Fries. *lana, lona.* + Du. *laan*, a lane, narrow passage.

Language. (F.–L.) M. E. *langage.* –M. F. *language* (Cot.), now *langage.*–F. *langue*, the tongue.–L. *lingua*, tongue. See **Lingual.**

Languish. (F.–L.) M.E. *languishen.* –F. *languiss-*, stem of pres. part. of *languir*, to languish.–L. *languēre*, to be weak. Allied to Gk. λαγαρός, slack; Icel. *lakra*, to lag; and to **Lag.** See Brugm. ii. § 632. (√SLAG.)

languid. (L.) L. *languidus*, feeble. –L. *languēre*, to be languid or weak.

languor, dullness. (F.–L.) M. E. *languor.*–F. *langueur.*–L. *languōrem*, acc. of *languor.*–L. *languēre* (above).

Laniard; see **Lanyard.**

Laniferous, wool-bearing. (L.) From L. *lāna*, wool; *ferre*, to bear. L. *lāna* is allied to **Wool.**

Lank, slender, thin. (E.) M. E. *lank.* A.S. *hlanc*, slender.

Lanner, Lanneret, a kind of falcon. (F.–L.) F. *lanier*, 'a lanner;' Cotg.– L. *laniārius*, a butcher, one that tears and rends.–L. *laniāre*, to rend. (So Diez.) Der. Hence perhaps *lanyard.*

Lansquenet, a German foot-soldier, a game at cards. (F.–G.) F. *lansquenet*, 'a lance-knight [a mistaken form] or German footman;' Cot.–G. *landsknecht*, a foot-soldier.–G.*lands*, for *landes*, gen. of *land*, country; *knecht*, a soldier (E. *knight*). Thus *lansquenet* = *land's-knight*; orig. a soldier from Germany.

Lantern. (F.–L.–Gk.) M. E. *lan-*

terne. – F. *lanterne.* – L. *lanterna, lāterna,*
a lantern (not a true L. word). *Lanterna*
<*lamterna*<*lampterna,* borrowed from
Gk. λαμπτήρ, a light, torch. – Gk. λάμπειν,
to shine. ¶ Sometimes spelt *lanthorn,*
because *horn* was used for the sides of
lanterns.

Lanyard, Laniard, a certain small
rope in a ship. (F. – L.) Formerly spelt
lannier, M. E. *lainere;* the final *d* being
excrescent, or due to *yard.* – M. F. *laniere,*
'a long and narrow band or thong of
leather;' also *lanieres,* pl. 'hawks' lunes;'
Cot. Perhaps from F. *lanier,* a kind of
hawk. See **Lanner.**

Lap (1), to lick up with the tongue.
(E.) M. E. *lappen.* A. S. *lapian,* to lap.
+ M. Du. *lappen* (Hexham); Icel. *lepja,*
Dan. *labe;* O. H. G. *laffan,* to lap up.+
L. *lambere,* to lap with the tongue.
(√LAB; Brug. ii. § 632.) Allied to
lambent.

Lap (2), the loose part of a coat, an
apron, part of the body covered by an
apron, a fold. (E.) M. E. *lappe.* A.S.
læppa, a loosely hanging portion. + Du.
lap, Dan. *lap,* Swed. *lapp,* G. *lappen,* a
patch, shred, rag. Cf. Icel. *lapa,* to hang
down; Lith. *lópas,* a patch, rag. ¶ Hence
lap-el, a flap of a coat, dimin. of E. *lap;*
lapp-et, also dimin. of E. *lap;* also the
verb *to lap over.* Cf. **Limp** (1).

Lap (3), to wrap. (E.) M. E. *lappen,*
also *wlappen,* another form of *wrappen;*
see **Wrap.** Quite distinct from *lap* (2).

Lapidary, one who sets precious
stones. (L.) Englished from L. *lapidā-
rius,* a stonemason. – L. *lapid-,* stem of
lapis, a stone. Allied to Gk. λέπας, a
bare rock, λεπίς, a flake, λέπειν, to peel
(Prellwitz). See **Leper.**

Lapse, vb. (L.) From L. *lapsāre,* to
slip, frequent. of *lābī* (pp. *lapsus*), to glide,
slip, trip. Der. *col-, e-, il-, re-lapse.*

Lapwing, a bird. (E.) M. E. *lappe-
winke.* A.S. *hlēapewince,* as if 'one who
turns about in running'; from A.S. *hlēapan,* to run; **wince,* one who turns; see
Winch. ¶ But the older form is *laepae-
uincæ* (O. E. T., p. 504); the sense of
which is unknown.

Larboard. (E.?) Cotgrave has:
'*Babort,* the larboard side of a ship.'
Hakluyt (Voyages, i. 4) has the spelling
leereboord; where *leere* answers to prov. E.
leer, empty, A.S. **lǣre* (cognate with G.
leer, O. H. G. *lāri*); whence A.S. *lǣrnes,*

emptiness. The steersman formerly stood
on the *starboard* (steer-board) side; the
other side was free.

Larceny, robbery. (F. – L.) The *-y*
is an E. addition. – O. F. *larrecin* (F.
larcin), larceny. – L. *latrocinium,* robbery;
formed with suffix *-cinium* (as in *tīrō-
cinium*) from *latro,* a robber. Allied to
Gk. λάτρις, a hireling, used in a bad
sense; and to λάτρον, hire.

Larch, a tree. (F. – L. – Gk.) O. F.
larice (Godefroy), also *larege,* 'the larch;'
Cot. – L. *laricem,* acc. of *larix,* a larch. –
Gk. λάριξ, a larch.

Lard. (F. – L.) O. F. *lard.* – L. *lardum,*
also *lārida,* lard, fat of bacon. Cf. Gk.
λᾱρός, nice, λᾱρῑνός, fat. **Der.** *lard-er,*
from O. F. *lardier,* a tub to keep bacon in
(Cot.), hence a room in which to keep
bacon and meat. Also *inter-lard.*

Large. (F. – L.) F. *large.* – L. *larga,*
fem. of *largus,* great. Cf. O. F. *larc,* m.

largess, a liberal gift. (F. – L.) F.
largesse, bounty. – Late L. **largītia,* not
found, for L. *largītio,* a bestowing. – L.
largītus, pp. of *largīrī,* to bestow. – L.
largus, large, liberal.

Lark (1), a bird. (E.) Another form
is *lavrock* (Burns). M. E. *larke,* also
laverock. – A. S. *lāwerce,* later *lāuerce,*
lāferce. + Icel. *lævirki,* a lark; Low G.
lewerke, O. H. G. *lērehha,* G. *lerche,* Du.
leeuwrik, E. Fries. *lēverke,* Swed. *lärka,*
Dan. *lærke.* A compound word, of unknown origin.

Lark (2), a game, fun. (E.) The same
word as the above; from the cheerful note
of the bird. The fuller form *lavrock*
(whence *larrick*) produced the form *lar-
rikin'* for *larking,* now used as a slang
adj., in the sense of rollicking or rowdy.
See N. and Q. 7 S. vii. 345.

Larum; short for **Alarum.**

Larva. (E.) L. *larua,* a ghost, a
mask; used as a scientific name for a caterpillar or grub.

Larynx. (L. – Gk.) L. *larynx.* – Gk.
λάρυγξ (gen. λάρυγγ-ος), throat, gullet,
larynx. **Der.** *laryng-itis.*

Lascar, a native E. Indian soldier.
(Pers.) Pers. *lashkarī,* a soldier; from
lashkar, an army.

Lascivious. (L.) Corruptly formed
from L. *lascīuus,* lustful. Cf. Skt. *lash,*
to desire.

Lash (1), a thong, stripe. (E.) M. E.
lasshe, the flexible part of a whip; cf. E.

Fries. *laske*, a bit of wood fastened on, Low G. *laske*, a flap, G. *lasche*, a flap, groove for scarfing timber; M. Du. *lassche*, 'a peece of cloath sowne into a garment,' M. H. G. *lasche*, a shred, strip; Norw. *laske*, a strip, shred, bit of wood. *Lash* in the sense of thong is from its use in lashing or binding things together; Swed. *laska*, to stitch; Norw. *lask*, a seam. The verb *lash*, to scourge, is to use a *lash*.

Lash (2), to bind firmly together. (E.) Cf. Du. *lasschen*, to join, scarf together; *lasch*, a piece, joint, seam. So also Swed. *laska*, Dan. *laske*, to scarf; Swed. Dan. *lask*, a scarf, joint. The verb is from the sb.; see above.

Lass, a girl. (Scand. ?) M. E. *lasse*, *lasce* (Mätzner). Cf. Icel. *löskr*, weak; M. Swed. *lösk*, a person having no fixed abode. Vigfusson cites O. Swed. *loska kona*, a spinster. (H. Bradley; in *Ath.* June 16, 1894.) Cf. Bavarian *lasch*, a woman (a term of contempt); Schmeller.

Lassitude, weariness. (F.–L.) F. *lassitude*. – L. *lassitūdo*, weariness. – L. *lassus*, wearied; for *lad-tus, and allied to E. **Late**.

Lasso, a rope with a noose. (Span.– L.) From Mexican Span. *laso*; O. Span. *laso*, Minsheu. – L. *laqueus* (Folk L. *laceus*), a noose, snare, knot. See **Lace**. ¶ The mod. Span. has *lazo* (with *z* sounded as E. voiceless *th*).

Last (1), latest; see **Late**.

Last (2), a wooden mould of the foot for a shoemaker. (E.) M. E. *last*, *lest*. A. S. *lāst*, *lǣst*, a foot-track, path, trace of feet (whence the mod. sense follows).+ Du. *leest*, a last, form; Icel. *leistr*, the foot below the ankle; Swed. *läst*, Dan. *lǽst*, G. *leisten*, a shoemaker's last; Goth. *laists*, a foot-track. The Teut. base appears in Goth. *laist-*, with orig. sense 'foot-track'; from *lais-*, 2nd grade of Teut. **leisan-*; cf. Goth. *lais*, I know (find or trace out). Cf. L. *līra*, a track; see **Delirious**. Akin to **Learn**.

last (3), to endure. (E.) M. E. *lasten*, *lesten*; A. S. *lǣstan*, to observe, perform, last; orig. 'to follow in the track of;' from *lāst*, a foot-track (above). + Goth. *laistjan*, to follow after; G. *leisten*, to follow out. Cf. Goth. *laists*, G. *leisten*, sb.

Last (4), a load, large weight, ship's cargo. (E.) M. E. *last*. A. S. *hlǽst*, a burden. Formed from A. S. *hladan*, to lade, load.+Dan. *last*, cargo; Swed. Du.

and G. *last*, a burden. See **Lade**. ¶ A. S. *hlǽst* is for **hlad-sto-* (> **hlasto-*); from *hlad-*, with suffix *-sto-*. Cf. Icel. *hlass* (< **hlad-to-*), a cart-load.

Latch (1), a catch, fastening. (E.) M. E. *lacche*, a latch, from *lacchen*, to catch.– A. S. *lǽccan*, to seize, catch hold of.

Latch (2), vb., to moisten. (E.) In Shak. M. N. D. iii. 2. 36. Cf. M. Du. *laken*, to flow (Oudemans); Swed. *laka*, to distil, fall by drops, *laka pâ*, to pour on to; from *lak*, 2nd grade of Icel. *leka*, to drip; see **Leak**. Also prov. E. *letch*, a vessel for making lye; A. S. *leccan*, to moisten: Low G. *lake*, brine.

Latchet, a little lace, thong. (F.–L.) M. E. *lachet*.– O. F. *lachet*, Norman and Picard form of O. F. *lacet*, a lace; dimin. of O. F. *laqs*, F. *lacs*; see **Lace**.

Late. (E.) M. E. *lat*; comp. *later*, *latter*, superl. *latest*, *latst* (Ormulum, 4168), *last*. A. S. *lǣt*, slow, late.+ Du. *laat*, Icel. *latr*, Dan. *lad*, Swed. *lat*; Goth. *lats*, slothful, G. *lass*, weary. Allied to L. *lassus* (for *lad-tus), weary. From the weak grade of the verb *to let*, i. e. let go; *late* orig. meant slothful, slow. See **Let** (1). Brugm. i. § 197.

latter, another form of *later* (above).

last (1), latest; contracted form of *latest*.

Lateen; see **Latin**.

Latent, hidden. (L.) L. *latent-*, stem of pres. pt. of *latēre*, to lie hid.

Lateral. (L.) L. *laterālis*, belonging to the side.– L. *later-*, for **lates-*, stem of *latus*, side.

Lath. (E.) North E. *lat*. M. E. *latte*. A. S. *lætt*, a lath; pl. *lætta*.+ Du. *lat*; G. *latte* (whence F. *latte*); allied to G. *laden*, a board, plank, shutter. The mod. form *lath* seems to have been influenced by W. *llath*, a rod, staff, Ir. *slat*, a rod; which is cognate.

Lathe (1), a machine for turning wood, &c. (Scand.) Icel. *löð* (gen. *löð-ar*), a smith's lathe; Dan. *dreie-lad*, a turning-lathe.

Lathe (2), a division of a county. (E.) A. S. *lǣð*, M. E. *leð*, a lathe, province; Thorpe, Ancient Laws, i. 184, 455. Perhaps allied to Icel. *leið*, *leiðangr*, a levy.

Lather. (E.) M. E. *lather*. A. S. *léaðor*, lather; whence *lýðran*, to anoint. + Icel. *lauðr*, froth, foam, soap; Swed. *löder*, lather. For the form, cf. Gk.

λουτρόν, a bath. Allied to **Lye** and **Lave**.

Latin. (F. – L.) F. *Latin.* – L. *Latīnus,* belonging to *Latium.* Der. *latim-er,* an interpreter ; for *Latiner.*

lateen, triangular, applied to sails. (F. – L.) F. *latine,* as in *voile latine,* a lateen sail ; *latine* is the fem. of *Latin,* Latin (i. e. Roman).

Latitude, breadth. (F. – L.) M. E. *latitude.* – F. *latitude.* – L. *lātitūdo* (stem *lātitūdin-*), breadth. – L. *lātus,* broad ; short for O. L. *stlātus.* Brugm. i. § 529.

Latten, a mixed metal, like pinchbeck. (F.) M. E. *latoun.* – O. F. *laton* (F. *laiton*), latten. Origin unknown. Cf. Low L. *lato, latōnus ;* Span. *laton ;* Port. *latão ;* Ital. *ottone,* latten.

Latter ; see **Late.**

Lattice. (F. – G.) Formerly *lattis.* M. E. *latis.* – F. *lattis,* lath-work, latticework. – F. *latte,* a lath. – G. *latte,* a lath ; see **Lath.**

Laud, to praise. (L.) M. E. *lauden.* – L. *laudāre,* to praise. – L. *laud-,* stem of *laus,* praise.

Laudanum. (L. – Gk. – Pers.) Now a preparation of opium, but formerly applied to a different drug. Thus Minsheu's Span. Dict. (1623) has : ' *Laudano,* the gum labdanum vsed in pomanders.' ' *Laudanum, Ladanum, Labdanum,* a sweet-smelling transparent gum gathered from the leaves of *Cistus Ledon,* a shrub, of which they make pomander, it smells like wine mingled with spices ; ' Blount, 1674. (Laudanum has a like strong smell.) – L. *lādanum, lēdanum,* resin from the shrub *lada* (Pliny). – Gk. λήδανον, λάδανον (same). – Gk. λῆδον, a certain shrub. – Pers. *lādan,* the gum-herb lada (Richardson).

Laugh. (E.) M. E. *laughen, lehghen.* O. Merc. *hlæhhan,* A.S. *hlihan* (pt. t. *hlōh*), to laugh. +Du. *lagchen,* Icel. *hlæja,* Dan. *lee,* Swed. *le,* G. *lachen,* Goth. *hlahjan* (pt. t. *hloh*). (Base **hlah* = Idg. **klak ;* cf. Lith. *kleg-èti,* to laugh, Gk. κλώσσειν, to cluck.) Of imitative origin. Der. *laughter,* A. S. *hleahtor.*

Launch (1) ; see **Lanch.**

Launch (2), a large ship's boat. (Span.) Span. *lancha,* ' the pinnace of a ship ;' Pineda (1740). Port. *lancha,* the same. Cf. Port. *lanchara,* a kind of ship ; perhaps of Malay origin (Yule).

Laundress, a washerwoman. (F. –

L.) Formed by adding F. suffix *-ess* to M. E. *launder* or *lavander,* a washerwoman. – O. F. *lavandiere,* ' a launderesse or washing-woman ;' Cot. – Late L. *lauandāria,- dēria,* (same). – L. *lauand-,* gerundial stem of *lauāre,* to wash. See **Lave.** Der. *laundr-y = launder-y.*

Laurel. (F. – L.) M. E. *lorel, lorer, laurer.* – O. F. *lorier* (F. *laurier*), a laureltree. – O. F. *lor* (the same) ; with suffix *-ier* (L. *-ārius*). – L. *laurum,* acc. of *laurus,* a laurel-tree.

laureate. (L.) L. *laureātus,* crowned with laurel. – L. *laurea,* a laurel ; orig. fem. of *laureus,* adj. from *laurus* (above).

Lava. (Ital. – L.) Ital. *lava,* a stream (esp. of molten rock). – L. *lauāre,* to wash, lave. See **Lave.**

Lave, to wash. (F. – L.) F. *laver.* – L. *lauāre.* + Gk. λούειν, to wash. Der. *lav-er,* M.F. *lavoir,* a washing-pool (Cot.); *lav-at-or-y,* F. *lavatoire,* L. *lauātōrium,* neut. of *lauātōrius,* adj., belonging to a washer. And cf. **Lather.**

Laveer, to tack. (Du. – F. – Du.) In Dryden. – Du. *laveeren ;* M.Du. *laveren, loeveren,* ' to saile up and downe,' Hexham. – M. F. *loveër* (Littré) ; F. *louvoyer.* – F. *lof,* luff, weather-side. – Du. *loef.* See **Luff.**

Lavender, a plant. (F. – Ital. – L.) M. E. *lavendre,* the *r* being an E. addition. – F. *lavande,* lavender ; Cot. – Ital. *lavanda,* lavender ; used for being laid in freshly washed linen. – Ital. *lavanda,* a washing. – L. *lauāre,* to wash. See **Lave.**

Lavish, profuse, prodigal. (E.) Formerly spelt *lavish, laves ;* also *lavy.* Formed with suffix *-ish* (A. S. *-isc*) from the obsolete verb *lave,* to pour out, lade out water ; M. E. *lauen,* to bale out water, whence the *metaphorical* use of *lauen,* to give bountifully. ' He *lauez* hys gyftez ' = God *lavishes* His gifts ; Allit. Poems, A. 607. It answers to A. S. *lafian,* to lave, wash, pour. Cf. Du. *laven,* G. *laben,* to refresh. ¶ The Teut. verb was perhaps early borrowed from L. *lauāre ;* see **Lave.** Cf. Norman dial. *laver,* to spend lavishly. Der. *lavish,* vb.

Law, a rule of action, edict. (Scand.) M. E. *lawe.* A. S. *lagu* (not common ; the usual A. S. word is *ǣ*) ; borrowed from Scand. Cf. O. Sax. *lag,* law. – Icel. *lög,* pl., but in sing. sense, a law, from *lag,* a stratum, order ; Swed. *lag ;* Dan. *lov.*

From Teut. *lag*, 2nd stem of *ligjan, to lie; see **Lie** (1). The sense is 'that which lies,' or is fixed (cf. Gk. κεῖται νόμος, the law is fixed, from κεῖμαι, I lie). **Der.** *law-y-er* (cf. *saw-y-er*). See **Lie** (1).

Lawn (1), a space of grass-covered ground, a glade. (F. — C.) M. E. *laund* (the *d* has been dropped). — O. F. *lande*, 'a land or laund, a wild, untilled, shrubby, or grassy plain;' Cot. Cf. Ital. and Span. *landa*, a heath. β. Of disputed origin; referred by Littré to G. *land* (= E. *land*), open country; but by Diez (rightly) to Bret. *lann*, a bushy shrub, of which the pl. *lannou*, like F. *landes*, means 'waste lands.' It comes to the same thing; for E. and G. *land* are cognate with Irish *lann*, a piece of land. Cf. W. *llan*, Gael. *lann*, an enclosure, piece of land. See **Land**.

Lawn (2), fine linen. (F. place-name.) Palsgrave has *Laune lynen*, prob. for *Lan lynen*, where *Lan* is the 16th cent. spelling of *Laon*, to the N. W. of Rheims. *Lawn* was also called 'cloth of Remes,' i. e. Rheims; see Baret's Alvearie.

Lax, slack. (L.) L. *laxus*, slack, loose. Allied to **Slack**. Brugm. i. § 193.

laxative, loosening. (F. — L.) F. *lax-atif.* — L. *laxātīuus*, loosening. — L. *laxā-tus*, pp. of *laxāre*, to loosen. — L. *laxus*, lax.

Lay (1), to cause to lie down, set. (E.) M. E. *leien*, *leggen*, pt. t. *leide*, pp. *leid*. A. S. *lecgan*, pt. t. *legde*, pp. *geleg'd*; causal of *licgan*, to lie. + Du. *leggen*, Icel. *leggja*, Dan. *lægge*, Swed. *lägga*, G. *legen*, Goth. *lagjan*. Teut. type **lag-jan-*, causal verb; from *lag, 2nd grade of **ligjan-*, to lie; see **Lie** (1). For the modern forms, see Sweet, E. Gr. § 1293.

layer, a stratum, tier, bed. (E.) Different from *lay-er*, he who lays; a graphic variant of M. E. *leir*, a lair, couch, place for lying down in; hence a bed, stratum, &c. See **Lair**.

Lay (2), a song, poem. (F. — C.) M. E. *lai.* — O. F. *lai*, said to be a Breton word. Not preserved in Breton, but it answers to Irish *laoi*, *laoidh*, O. Ir. *lded*, a song, poem, Gael. *laoidh*, a verse, hymn, sacred poem.

Lay (3), pertaining to the laity. (F. — L. — Gk.) M. E. *lay.* — O. F. *lai*, secular. — L. *laicus*. — Gk. λαικός, belonging to the people. — Gk. λαός (Attic λεώς), the people. See **Laic, Laity**.

Lay (4), as in **Lay-figure**. (Du.) The old word was *lay-man* (Richardson). Lit. 'joint-man,' i. e. man made with joints. — Du. *leeman*, a lay-man. Here *lee-* is for *lede-*, in compounds (Sewel); and Du. *leden* is the pl. of *lid*, a joint, cognate with A. S. *liθ*, Goth. *lithus*, G. *g-lied*, a joint. Prob. allied to **Limb** (Kluge).

Layer; see **Lay** (1).

Lazar, a leper. (F. — L. — Gk. — Heb.) M. E. *lazar.* — F. *lazare.* — L. *Lazarus.* — Gk. Λάζαρος, the name of the beggar in Luke, xvi. 20; contracted from Heb. name *Eleazar.* — Heb. *El' āzār*, he whom God helps. **Der.** *lazar-etto*, a plague-hospital, Ital. *lazzaretto*.

Lazy. (Low G.) *Laezie* (Spenser). — Low G. *lasich*, variant of *losich*, languid, idle (Lübben); *läösig*, lazy (Danneil); Pomeran. *läsig*, cf. *laassam*, lazy (Bremen); Du. *leuzig*, lazy. Allied to **Loose**.

Lea, Lay, Ley, a meadow. (E.) M. E. *lay*, *ley*, untilled land. A. S. *lēah*, *lēa* (gen. *lēage*), a lea; cf. *Hæd-lēah*, i. e. Hadleigh. Cognate with prov. G. *loh*, a morass, low plain, Low G. *loge*, Flem. *loo* as in *Water-loo*; also with Lithuan. *lau-kas*, an open field, L. *lūcus*, a glade, open space in a wood. Orig. 'a clearing.' Allied to **Lucid**. Brugm. i. § 221.

Lead (1), to conduct. (E.) M. E. *leden*, pt. t. *ladde*, pp. *lad.* — A. S. *lēdan*, to lead. + Icel. *leiða*; Swed. *leda*; G. *leiten*; Du. *leiden*. Teut. type **laidjan-*; from *laith (by Verner's Law), 2nd grade of **leithan-* (A. S. *līðan*), to travel. See **Lode**.

Lead (2), a metal. (E.) M. E. *leed*. A. S. *lēad.*+Du. *lood*, Swed. *lod*, Dan. *lod*, G. *loth*, M. H. G. *lōt*. Teut. type *laudom, neut. Cf. O. Irish *luaidhe*, lead.

Leaf. (E.) M. E. *leef*, pl. *leues* (= *leves*). A. S. *lēaf*, neut., pl. *lēaf.*+Du. *loof*, foliage; Icel. *lauf*, Swed. *löf*, Dan. *löv*, Goth. *laufs*, G. *laub*. Teut. stem **laubo-*.

League (1), a bond, alliance. (Ital. — L.) Ital. *lega*, 'a league;' Florio. — Late L. *liga*, a league. — L. *ligāre*, to bind. See **Ligament**.

League (2), about three miles. (F. — L. — C.) O. F. *legue* (Roquefort); F. *lieue* (Gascon *lega*). — Late L. *lēga*, *leuca*; L. *leuga*, *leuca*, a Gallic mile; a word of Celtic origin. Cf. Bret. *leō lev* a league; also *leu* (in Vannes).

Leaguer, a camp. (Du.) In All's Well, iii. 6. 27. — Du. *leger,* a lair, a camp. See **Lair, Lie** (1). **Der.** *be-leaguer.*

Leak. (Scand.) M. E. *leken.* — Icel. *leka,* to drip, dribble, leak as a ship, str. vb. (pt. t. *lak*); cf. the causal forms seen in Swed. *läcka,* Dan. *lække,* Du. *lekken,* G. *lecken,* to leak, drop; A. S. *leccan,* to wet. ¶ The mod. E. word is Scand.; not from A. S. *leccan.* [We also find A. S. *hlec,* leaky.] **Der.** *leak,* sb., from Icel. *leki,* a leak. Prob. allied to **Lack** (Franck).

Leal, loyal, true. (F. — L.) M. E. *lēl.* — A. F. *leal,* O. F. *leial,* legal, hence just, loyal. — L. *lēgālis,* legal. **Doublets,** *legal, loyal.* See **Legal.**

Lean (1), to incline, stoop. (E.) M. E. *lenen.* A. S. *hlǣnan,* to make to lean, weak verb; (cf. A. S. *hlinian,* to lean, weak verb). + Du. *læne,* Swed. *läna,* causal forms; G. *lehnen,* intrans. Allied to L. *-clīnāre,* in *inclīnāre,* to incline; Gk. κλίνειν, to cause to lean, make to bend. (√KLEI.)

lean (2), slender, frail. (E.) M. E. *lene.* A. S. *hlǣne,* lean; orig. bending, stooping, hence thin; cf. L. *dēclīuis,* declining. Teut. type **hlainjoz.* Cf. O. Irish *clōen,* sloping, bad. Allied to A. S. *hlǣnan,* to lean (above).

Leap. (E.) M. E. *lepen,* pt. t. *leep,* pp. *lopen.* A. S. *hlēapan,* pt. t. *hlēop,* to run, jump. + Du. *loopen,* Icel. *hlaupa,* Dan. *löbe,* Swed. *löpa,* Goth. *hlaupan,* G. *laufen,* chiefly in the sense 'to run.' Teut. type **hlaupan-.*

Learn. (E.) M. E. *lernen.* A. S. *leornian.* + G. *lernen,* to learn. Teut. type **liznōn;* from **liz(a)noz,* pp. of **leisan-,* to trace out, of which the pt. t. *lais* occurs in Goth. with the sense 'I know,' i. e. have found out. Hence also Teut. **laizjan-,* to teach, as in A. S. *lǣran* (G. *lehren*), to teach. Brugm. i. § 903 (c). And see **Last** (2), **Lore.**

Lease (1), to let a tenement. (F. — L.) F. *laisser,* to let go. — L. *laxāre,* to slacken, let go. — L. *laxus,* loose. See **Lax.**

Lease (2), to glean. (E.) M. E. *lesen.* A. S. *lesan,* to gather. + Du. *lezen,* to gather, to read; G. *lesen;* Goth. *lisan,* pt. t. *las,* to gather; Lith. *lèsti,* to snap up.

Leash, a thong to hold in a dog. (F. — L.) M. E. *lees.* — O. F. *lesse* (F. *laisse*), a leash. — Late L. *laxa,* a thong, a loose rope. — L. *laxus,* slack. See **Lax.** ¶ The number usually leashed together was three.

Leasing, falsehood. (E.) M. E. *lesing.* A. S. *lēasung,* falsehood; from *lēas,* false. Cf. Icel. *lausung,* falsehood; Du. *loos,* false. See **Loose.**

Least; see **Less.**

Leat, a conduit for water. (E.) A. S. *ge-lǣte,* a course, direction. From *lǣtan,* to let, permit. Cf. *in-let, out-let.* See **Let** (1).

Leather. (E.) M. E. *lether.* A. S. *leðer.* + Du. *leder,* Icel. *leðr,* Dan. *læder,* Swed. *läder,* G. *leder,* leather. Teut. type **lethrom,* neut.; Idg. type **letrom,* as in O. Irish *lethar,* W. *lledr.* **Der.** *leather-n.*

Leave (1), to forsake, quit. (E.) M. E. *leuen* (*leven*). A. S. *lǣfan,* to leave a heritage, leave behind one. + Icel. *leifa,* to leave. Teut. type **laibjan-,* to leave; from**laib-,* as seen in A. S. *lāf,* a remainder, Icel. *leif,* a heritage. And **laib* is the 2nd stem of Teut. **leiban-,* to remain, as in A. S. *be-līfan,* O. H. G. *bi-līban* (whence G. *bleiben*). Idg. root **leip,* as in Gk. λῑπαρής, persistent; the weak grade **lip* appears in Skt. *lip,* to smear, Gk. λίπος, grease, Russ. *lipkii,* sticky, Lith. *lipti,* to adhere to. See **Live.** Brugm. i. § 87.

Leave (2), permission, farewell. (E.) 'To take *leave*' = to take permission to go. 'By your *leave*' = by your permission. M. E. *leue* (*leve*). A. S. *lēaf,* permission. From the same root as A. S. *lēof,* dear, pleasing. The orig. sense was pleasure; hence a grant, permission. + Du. *-lof,* as in *oor-lof,* permission, *ver-lof,* leave; Icel. *leyfi,* leave, *lofan,* permission, *lob* (1) praise, (2) permission; Dan. *lov,* Swed. *lof,* praise, leave; G. *ur-laub, ver-laub,* leave, *er-lauben,* to permit, *lob,* praise. From Teut. base **leub-* (whence A. S. *lēof*), 2nd grade **laub-* (>A. S. *lēaf*), weak grade **lub-* (>A. S. *luf-u,* love) See **Lief, Love, Furlough.** (√LEUBH.)

Leaven, ferment. (F. — L.) M. E. *leuain* (*levain*). — F. *levain.* — L. *leuāmen,* an alleviation; here used in the orig. sense of 'that which raises.' — L. *leuāre,* to raise. — L. *leuis,* light. See **Levity.**

Lecher. (F. — G.) M. E. *lechur, lechour.* — O. F. *lecheor, lecheur,* lit. one who licks up, a man addicted to gluttony and lewdness. — O. F. *lecher* (F. *lécher*), to lick. — O. H. G. *lecchōn* (G. *lecken*), to lick. See **Lick.**

Lectern, Lecturn, a reading-desk. (F. — Late L.) M. E. *leterone, lectorne, lectrone, lectrun* (Prompt. Parv.).

– O. F. *letrun* (Godefroy) ; *lectrun, letrin* (Littré, s. v. *lutrin*).– Late L. *lectrīnum*, a reading-desk, pulpit. – Late L. *lectrum*, a pulpit. Prob. from Gk. λέκτρον, a couch, support ; akin to Gk. λέχος, a couch, bed ; cf. L. *lectus*, a couch. But other forms, like Late L. *lectōrīnum, lectōrium*, shew that it was popularly connected with L. *lectio* (below).

Lection, a reading, portion to be read. (L.) From L. *lectio*, a reading.– L. *lectus*, pp. of *legere*, to read. See **Legend**.

lecture, a discourse. (F. – L.) F. *lecture*, a reading.– Late L. *lectūra*, a commentary.– L. *lectus*, pp. of *legere*, to read.

Ledge, a slight shelf, ridge. (E.) Palsgrave has *ledge* (i. e. support) of a shelf. Cf. Norfolk *ledge*, a bar of a gate, rail of a chair ; M. E. *legge*. Allied to Swed. *lagg*, the rim of a cask, Icel. *lögg*, the ledge or rim at the bottom of a cask ; Norweg. *logg* (pl. *legger*), the lowest part of a vessel ; M. H. G. *lekke*. Cf. also Norw. *lega*, a couch, lair, bed, support on which anything rests ; *lege*, a ledge, as of rock. All from Teut. *lag, 2nd stem of **ligjan-*, to lie. Cf. A. S. *licgan*, Icel. *liggja*, Swed. *ligga*, Dan. *ligge*, to lie. The sense is 'support.' See **Lie** (1).

Ledger, a flat slab ; also, a book in which a summary of accounts is preserved. (E.) (We also find *leger ambassadors*, i. e. such as *remained* for some time at a foreign court.) A *ledger-book* is one that lies always ready. Similarly, in Middle-English, a large book was called a *liggar* (that which lies), because not portable. From M. E. *liggen*, A. S. *licgan*, to lie ; see **Lie** (1). Cf. Du. *legger*, one that lies down (the nether mill-stone is also so called) ; from Du. *leggen*, to lie, a common corruption of *liggen*, to lie (like *lay* for *lie* in English). ¶ Howell uses *leger-book* for 'portable book,' which is from O. F. *legier*, light. See *ledger* in Richardson.

Lee, a sheltered place ; part of a ship away from the wind. (Scand.) M. E. *lee*, shelter.– Icel. *hlé*, lee (of a ship) ; Dan. *læ*, Swed. *lä*.+Du. *lij* ; A. S. *hléo, hleow*, a covering, a shelter (distinct from prov. E. *lew*, warm ; see **Lew**). ¶ The peculiar use is Scand.; the pronunciation *lew-ard* is due to the *w*; cf. *steward* for *sty-ward*. The Teut. type is **hlewo-* (Franck).

Leech (1), a physician. (E.) M. E. *leche*. A. S. *láce*, one who heals. + Goth. *lēkeis*, a leech ; cf. Icel. *læknir*, Dan. *læge*,

Swed. *läkare*. Also A. S. *lácnian*, to heal, Icel. *lækna*, Dan. *læge*, Swed. *läka*, Goth. *lēkinon*, to heal. Also O. Irish *liaig*, a leech.

leech (2), a blood-sucking worm. (E.) A. S. *láce*, lit. 'the healer;' the same word as the above.

Leech (3), **Leach**, the border or edge of a sail at the sides. (E.) Cf. Icel. *lík*, a leech-line ; Swed. *lik*, Dan. *lig*, a bolt-rope.+M. Du. *lyken*, a bolt-rope (Sewel) ; Du. *lijk* (see Franck).

Leek. (E.) M. E. *leek*. O. Merc. *léc*; A. S. *léac*.+ Du. *look*, Icel. *laukr*, Dan. *lög*, Swed. *lök*, G. *lauch*. Teut. type **lauko-*; cf. A. S. *lúcan*, str. vb. (pt. t. *léac* = Teut. *lauk), to weed. Der. *gar-lic*, *char-lock, hem-lock* (latter syllable).

Leer, a sly look. (E.) The verb is a development from the sb., which is an old word. M. E. *lere*, the cheek, face, complexion, mien ; usually in a good sense, but Skelton has it in a bad sense. A. S. *hléor*, the cheek ; hence, the face, look, mien.+Icel. *hlýr*, pl., the cheeks.

Lees, dregs of wine. (F.) Pl. of a sing. form *lee*, not used.– F. *lie*, 'the lees;' Cot. (Gascon *lio*, 'lie de vin.')– Late L. *lia*, pl. *liæ*, lees (10th cent.). Origin unknown.

Leet, an assembly of a township. (E.) M. E. *lete*. Prob. from A. S. *látan*, to let, permit, cause. See **Let** (1).

Left, the weaker hand. (E.) M. E. *left, lift, luft*. A. S. *left*; Dr. Sweet points out that 'inanis, *left*,' occurs in a gloss (Mone, Quellen, i. 443), and that the same MS. has *senne* for *synne* (sin) ; so that *left* is for *lyft*, with the sense 'worthless' or 'weak'; cf. A. S. *lyft-ádl*, palsy. + North Fries. *leeft, leefter hond*, left hand ; M. Du. *luft, lucht*, left ; E. Fries. *lüchter*, left, *luf*, weak. β. The form of the base is *lub; cf. Du. *lubben* (Franck). See **Lib**.

Leg. (Scand.) M. E. *leg* (pl. *legges*).– Icel. *leggr*, a leg ; Dan. *læg*, the calf of the leg ; Swed. *lägg* (the same). Brugm. i. § 647(5).

Legacy. (L.) M. E. *legacie* ; a coined word (as if = L. *lēgātia, not found) from L. *lēgātum*, a bequest, neut. of pp. of *lēgāre*, to appoint, bequeath ; allied to *lex* (stem *lēg-*), the law (below).

legal, pertaining to the law. (F.– L.) M.F. *legal*.– L. *lēgālis*, legal.– L. *lēg-*, stem of *lex*, law. Allied to L. *legere* ; Gk.

λέγειν, to collect. Brugm. i. § 134. (√LEG.)

legate, a commissioner. (F. — L.) M. E. *legate.* — O. F. *legat* (F. *légat*), a pope's ambassador. — L. *lēgātus,* a deputy; pp. of *lēgāre,* to appoint. — L. *lēg-,* stem of *lex,* law. See **legal.**

legatee. (L.; *with* F. *suffix.*) A law term; coined from L. *lēgāt-us,* appointed, with F. suffix *-é* (= L. *-ātus*). See above.

legend, a marvellous story. (F. — L.) M. E. *legende.* — O. F. *legende* (F. *légende*), a legend, story. — Late L. *legenda,* a legend; fem. sing. from L. *legenda,* neut. pl., things to be read. — L. *legendus,* fut. pass. part. of *legere,* to read, orig. to gather, collect. + Gk. λέγειν, to tell, speak. (√LEG.)

Legerdemain, sleight of hand. (F. — L.) O. F. *legier de main,* lit. light of hand. (Cf. Ital. *leggiere, leggiero,* light.) The O. F. *legier* answers to a Late L. type *leuiārius,* made by adding *-ārius* to L. *leui-s,* light. F. *de* = L. *dē,* of. F. *main* = L. *manum,* acc. of *manus,* a hand. See **Levity.**

leger-line, ledger-line, in music, a short line added above or below the staff. (F. — L.) Properly *leger-line*; where *leger* = F. *léger* (formerly *legier*), light; because these lines are small and short. See the word above. ¶ So usually explained; but mod. F. employs the phrase *lignes additionnelles.*

Legible, readable. (F. — L.) O. F. *legible.* — L. *legibilis,* legible. — L. *legere,* to read. See **legend.**

legion, a large body of soldiers. (F. — L.) M. E. *legioun.* — O. F. *legion.* — L. *legiōnem,* acc. of *legio,* a Roman legion, body of from 4200 to 6000 men. — L. *legere,* to gather, select a band.

Legislator. (L.) L. *lēgislātor,* a proposer of a law. — L. *lēgis,* gen. of *lex,* a law; *lātor,* a proposer, lit. bringer, from *lātum* (for *tlātum*), to bear, bring, from √TEL; see **Tolerate.** Brugm. i. § 585 (2). **Der.** *legislate,* &c. See **legal.**

legist. (F. — L.) O. F. *legiste* (F. *légiste*). — Late L. *legista,* one skilled in the laws. — L. *lēg-,* stem of *lex,* law (with Gk. suffix *-ista* = -ιστης).

legitimate. (L.) Late L. *lēgitimātus,* pp. of *lēgitimāre,* to declare to be lawful. — L. *lēgitimus,* according to law. — L. *lēgi-,* for *lex,* law; with suffix *-ti-mus.*

Legume, a pod. (F. — L.) F. *légume,*

pulse, a pod. — L. *legūmen* (stem *legūmin-*), pulse, bean-plant. Brugm. i. § 667. **Der.** *legumin-ous.*

Leisure, freedom from employment. (F. — L.) M. E. *leyser.* — A. F. *leisir* (F. *loisir*), leisure; orig. an infin. mood, meaning 'to be permitted.' — L. *licēre,* to be permitted. ¶ The form is bad; it should be *leiser* or *leisir*; *pleasure* is in the same case. The suffix has been changed from *-er* or *-ir* to *-ure* (as in *measure*).

Leman, Lemman, a sweetheart. (E.) I. e. *lief man.* M. E. *lemman,* also *leofman.* — A. S. *lēof,* dear; *mann,* a man or woman. See **Lief.**

Lemma, an assumption. (L. — Gk.) L. *lēmma.* — Gk. λῆμμα, a thing taken; in logic, a premiss taken for granted; allied to Gk. εἴ-λημμαι, perf. pass. of λαμβάνειν, to take (base λαβ-). Brugm. i. § 852.

Lemming, Leming, a kind of Norwegian rat. (Norweg.) Norweg. *lemende*; also occurring as *lemming, limende, lomeldre, lomund, lomhund.* Cf. Swed. *lemel,* a lemming; Icel. *lōmundr.* Origin obscure; Aasen derives it from Norweg. *lemja,* to strike, beat, maim, lit. 'lame,' and explains it to mean 'destroying'; from the destruction committed by them; see **Lame.** But this is 'popular etymology.' The word may be Lapp; the Lapp name is *loumek.*

Lemniscate, a curve like the figure 8. (L. — Gk.) From L. *lēmniscāt-us,* adorned with a ribbon. — L. *lēmniscus,* a pendent ribbon. — Gk. λημνίσκος, a fillet. Said to be from Gk. λῆνος, wool; which is allied to **Wool.**

Lemon. (F. — Pers.) Formerly *limon.* — F. *limon.* — Pers. *līmūn, līmūnā,* a lemon, citron.

Lemur, a nocturnal animal. (L.) L. *lemur,* a ghost; so nicknamed by naturalists from its nocturnal habits.

Lend. (E.) The final *d* is excrescent. M. E. *lenen.* A. S. *lǣnan,* to lend. — A. S. *lǣn,* a loan. + Icel. *lāna,* Dan. *laane,* Swed. *lāna,* G. *lehnen,* derivatives from the sb. See **Loan.**

Length. (E.) M. E. *lengthe.* A. S. *lengð,* fem.; for **langiðā,* with mutation of *a* to *e.* — A. S. *lang,* long. + Du. *lengte*; Dan. *længde*; Swed. *längd*; Icel. *lengd.* See **Long. Der.** *length-en.*

Lenient, mild. (L.) From pres. part. of L. *lēnīre,* to soothe. — L. *lēnis,* soft, mild.

lenity. (F. – L.) O. F. *lenité*, mildness (obsolete). – L. *lēnitātem*, acc. of *lēnitas*, mildness. – L. *lēnis* (above).

Lens, a piece of glass used in optics. (L.) So called from the resemblance of a double-convex lens to the shape of the seed of a lentil. – L. *lens*, a lentil.

Lent, a fast of 40 days, beginning with Ash-Wednesday. (E.) The fast is in spring-time; the old sense is simply spring. M. E. *lent*, *lenten*. A.S. *lencten*, the spring; supposed to be derived from *lang*, long, because in spring the days lengthen; Kluge suggests that it represents a Teut. form *langi-tīno-*, 'long day,' where *-tīno-* is allied to Skt. *dina-*, Lith. *dĕna*, a day. + Du. *lente*, spring; G. *lenz*, O. H. G. *lenzo*, *lenzin*, *lengizen*. Der. *lenten*, adj., from A. S. *lencten*, sb.

Lentil, a plant. (F. – L.) M. E. *lentil*. – O. F. (and F.) *lentille*. – L. *lenticula*, a little lentil; double dimin. of *lent-*, stem of *lens*, a lentil. See **Lens.**

Lentisk, the mastic-tree. (F. – L.) F. *lentisque.* – L. *lentiscum*, *lentiscus*, named from the clamminess of its resin. – L. *lentus*, sticky, pliant.

Leo, a lion. (L. – Gk. – Egypt. ?) L. *leo.* – Gk. λέων, a lion. We also find Du. *leeuw*, G. *löwe*, Russ. *lev'*, Lithuan. *lavas*, a lion; all borrowed forms. Cf. Heb. *lāvī'*, a lion. Probably of Egyptian origin; see Lion.

leopard. (F. – L. – Gk.) O.F. *leopard.* – L. *leopardus.* – Gk. λεόπαρδος, a leopard; supposed to be a mongrel between a pard (panther) and a lioness. – Gk. λεο-, for λέων, a lion; πάρδος, a pard.

Leper. (F. – L. – Gk.) The sense has changed; *lepre* formerly meant the disease itself; and what we now call a *leper* was called *a leprous man.* 'The *lepre* of him was clensid;' Wyclif, Matt. viii. 3. – M. F. *lepre*, 'a leprosie;' Cot. – L. *lepra.* – Gk. λέπρα, leprosy; so called because the skin scales off. – Gk. λέπρος, scaly, scabby. – Gk. λέπος, a scale; λέπειν, to peel. Cf. Russ. *lupite*, Lithuan. *lùpti*, to peel.

lepidoptera, a term applied to insects whose wings are covered with scales. (Gk.) Gk. λεπίδο-, for λεπίς, a scale; πτερά, pl. of πτερόν, a wing (allied to E *feather*).

Leporine, belonging to a hare. (L.) L. *leporinus*, adj., from *lepor-*, for *lepos*, stem of *lepus*, a hare.

Leprosy. (F. – L. – Gk.) A coined

word, from the adj. *leprous*; which is from M. F. *lepreux* = L. *leprōsus*, afflicted with *lepra*, i.e. leprosy. See **Leper.**

Lesion, an injury. (F. – L.) M. F. *lesion*, hurt; Cot. – L. *læsiōnem*, acc. of *læsio*, an injury. – L. *læsus*, pp. of *lædere*, to hurt. Der. (from *lædere*) *col-lide*, *e-lision.*

Less, smaller. (E.) Used as comp. of *little*, but from a different root. M. E. *lessè*, *lassè*, adj., *les*, adv. A. S. *lǣssa*, less, adj.; *lǣs*, adv. + O. Fries. *lēssa*, less. β. The form *lǣs-sa* is for **lǣs-ra*, by assimilation. The Teut. type is **lais-izon*, from a base **lais-*; cf. Lith. *lēsas*, thin, small. The Teut. type of the adv. is **laisiz*. Der. *less-er*, a double comp.; *less-en*, vb.

least. (E.) M. E. *lestè*, adj., *lest*, adv. A. S. *lǣsest*, whence *lǣst* by contraction; a superlative form from the same base **lais-*.

lest, for fear that, that not. (E.) Not for *least*, but due to A. S. phrase *ðy̆ lǣs ðe* = for the reason less that; wherein *ðy̆* (for the reason) was soon dropped, and *lǣs ðe* coalesced into *lest*. Here *lǣs* = less, adv.; and *ðe* is the indeclinable relative.

-less, suffix; see **Loose.**

Lessee. (F. – L.) O. F. *lesse* (*lessé*), pp. of *lesser*, later *laisser*, to let go (lease). See **Lease** (1).

Lesson. (F. – L.) M. E. *lesson.* – F. *leçon.* – L. *lectiōnem*, acc. of *lectio*, a reading; see **Lection.** Doublet, *lection.*

Lest; see **Less.**

Let (1), to permit. (E.) M. E. *leten*, strong verb, pt. t. *lat*, *leet*, pp. *laten*, *leten.* A. S. *lǣtan*, *lētan*, pt. t. *lēt*, *leort*, pp. *lǣten.* + Du. *laten* (*liet*, *gelaten*) ; Icel. *lāta* (*lēt*, *lātinn*) ; Dan. *lade*, Swed. *låta*, Goth. *lētan* (*lailōt*, *lētans*) ; G. *lassen* (*liess*, *gelassen*). Teut. type **lǣtan*, pt. t. **lelōt*, pp. **lǣtanoz.* Idg. √LĒD; weak grade LAD, whence E. **Late.** Brugm. i. § 478.

Let (2), to hinder. (E.) M. E. *letten* ; A. S. *lettan*, to hinder, make late. – A.S. *lǣt*, late, slow. + Du. *letten*, Icel. *letja*, Goth. *latjan*, to tarry ; from the adj. **Late.** Teut. type **lat-jan-* ; from **lat-*, slow. See **Late.**

Lethal, deadly. (F. – L.; *or* L.) M.F. *lethal*, 'deadly;' Cot. – L. *lēthālis*, for *lētālis*, mortal. – L. *lētum*, death.

Lethe, oblivion. (L. – Gk.) L. *lēthē*. – Gk. λήθη, a forgetting; the river of oblivion; allied to λαθ-, base of λανθάνειν, to lie hid.

lethargy, a heavy sleep. (F.–L.–Gk.) M. F. *lethargie*, a lethargy; Cot.– L. *lēthargia*.–Gk. ληθαργία, drowsiness. – Gk. λήθαργος, forgetful. – Gk. λήθη, oblivion (above).

Letter, a character. (F.–L.) M. E. *lettre*. – F. *lettre*. – L. *littera*, for older *lītera* (also *leitera*), a letter. See Brugm. i. § 930.

Lettuce, a succulent plant. (F.–L.) M. E. *letuce*.–O. F. **letuce*, only found in the form *lectus* (Palsgrave, s. v. *Lettes*); and in the Latinised form *lētūsa*, Wrt. Vocab. 787. 15.–L. **lactūcea*, fem. adj. from L. *lactūca*, a lettuce (whence F. *laitue*, Ital. *lattuga*).–L. *lact-*, stem of *lac*, milk, succulent juice. See **Lacteal.**

Levant, the E. of the Mediterranean Sea. (Ital.–L.) Ital. *levante*, E. wind, eastern country or part (where the sun rises).–L. *leuant-*, stem of pres. part. of *leuāre*, to raise; whence *sē leuāre*, to rise. –L. *leuis*, light.

levee, a morning assembly. (F.–L.) For F. *le lever* (Littré). – F. *lever*, to raise. –L. *leuāre* (above).

Level, an instrument for determining that a thing is horizontal. (F.–L.) M. E. *liuel*, *leuel* (*livel*, *level*).–O. F. *livel*, later spelling *liveau*; mod. F. *niveau*, a level. –L. *lībella*, a level; dimin. of *lībra*, a balance. See **Librate.** ¶ Hence the adj. *level*.

Lever. (F.–L.) M. E. *levour*.–F. *leveur*, a raiser, lifter.–L. *leuātōrem*, acc. of *leuātor*, a lifter.–L. *leuāre*, to lift.–L. *leuis*, light.

Leveret. (F.–L.) A. F. *leveret* (pl. *leveres*, Gaimar, Chron. l. 6239); O. F. *levrault*, ' a leveret, or young hare;' Cot.; with change of suffix. [The suffix *-ault* = Late L. *-aldus*, from O. H. G. *wald*, power, common as a suffix.] The base *lever-* is from L. *lepor-* for **lepos*, stem of *lepus*, a hare.

Leviathan. (L.–Heb.) Late L. *leviathan*, Job xl. 20 (Vulgate). – Heb. *livyāthān*, an aquatic animal, dragon, serpent; named from its twisting itself in curves. – Heb. root *lāvāh*; Arab. root *lawa'*, to bend, whence *lawā*, the twisting or coiling of a serpent.

Levigate, to make smooth. (L.) Out of use. – L. *lēuigātus*, pp. of *lēuigāre*, to make smooth. – L. *lēu-is*, smooth;

-igāre, for *agere*, to make. Cf. Gk. λεῖος, smooth.

Levin, lightning. (Scand.) M. E. *leyfnyng*, lightning; Wrt. Voc. 735.42. Prob. Scand.; not found in A. S. Cf. Icel. *leiptr* (pronounced *leiftr*), lightning.

Levite, one of the tribe of Levi. (L.– Gk. – Heb.) L. *Leuita*. – Gk. Λευίτης, Lu. x. 32.–Heb. *Levī*, one of the sons of Jacob.

Levity, lightness, frivolity. (L.) From L. *leuitas*, lightness.–L. *leuis*, light.

levy, the act of raising men for an army; the force raised. (F.–L.) F. *levée*, ' a levy, or levying of an army;' Cot. Fem. of pp. of *lever*, to raise.–L. *leuāre*, to raise.–L. *leuis* (above).

Lew, Lew-warm, tepid. (E.) M. E. *lew*, Wyclif, Rev. iii. 16. A.S. *hlēowe*, warm (found once).+Du. *lauw*, warm; Icel. *hlār*, *hlȳr*; G. *lau*, O. H. G. *lāo* (*lāw-*). Teut. base (perhaps) **hlēw-*, *hlǣw-*.

Lewd, ignorant, base. (L. – Gk.?) M. E. *lewed*, ignorant. A.S. *lǣwede*, adj., ignorant, also lay, belonging to the laity. [It may have been confused with the pp. of *lǣwan*, to betray; cf. Goth. *lēwjan*, to betray, from *lēw*, occasion, opportunity.] But it is supposed to be of Latin origin; answering to L. type **lāicātus*, belonging to the laity, parallel to Late L. *clēricātus* (whence E. *clergy*). If so, it is formed from L. *lāicus*, a word of Gk. origin. See **Laic.** (Sievers, § 173; Pogatscher, § 340.)

Lexicon. (Gk.) Gk. λεξικόν, a dictionary; neut. of λεξικός, adj., belonging to words. – Gk. λέξι-s, a saying. – Gk. λέγειν, to speak; see **legend.**

Ley, a meadow; see **Lea.**

Liable, responsible. (F.–L.) Formed, with suffix *-able*, from F. *li-er*, to tie.–L. *ligāre*, to tie. See **Ligament.**

Liane, Liana, a climbing tropical plant. (F.–L.) F. *liane* (the same); from Norman and Guernsey *lian*, a band.–L. *ligāmen*; see **Lien, Limehound.**

Lias, a formation of limestone. (F.) F. *lias*, *liais*, O. F. *liois*, a hard freestone.

Lib, to castrate. (E.) Answers to an A.S. type **lybban*; only found in the cognate Du. *lubben*, with the same sense; E. Fries. and Westphal. *lübben*. Der. *g-lib*, vb., the same (obsolete); cf. O. Du. *gelubt*, ' gelt,' Hexham. Also *lef-t*, q.v.

Libation, the pouring forth of wine in honour of a deity. (F.–L.) F. *libation*.

—L. acc. *lībātiōnem.*—L. *lībātus*, pp. of *lībāre*, to taste, sip, pour out.+Gk. λείβειν, to pour out, shed, offer a libation. Brugm. i. § 553.

Libel, a written accusation. (F.—L.) M.E. *libel*, a brief piece of writing ; A. F. *libel.*—L. *libellum*, acc. of *libellus*, a little book, a notice (Matt. v. 31) ; dimin. of *liber*, a book. See **Library.**

Liberal. (F.—L.) M. E. *liberal.*—O. F. *liberal.*—L. *līberālis*, befitting a free man, generous.—L. *līber*, free.

liberate. (L.) From pp. of L. *līberāre*, to set free.—L. *līber*, free ; Brugm. i. § 102.

libertine. (L.) Cf. Acts vi. 9.—L. *lībertīnus*, adj., belonging to a freed man, also sb., a freed man ; later applied to denote the licentious liberty of a certain sect (Acts vi. 9).—L. *lībertus*, a freed man.—L. *līber*, free.

liberty. (F.—L.) M.E. *libertee.*—F. *liberté.*—L. *lībertātem*, acc. of *lībertās*, freedom.—L. *līber*, free.

Libidinous, lustful. (F. — L.) *libidineux.* — L. *libīdinōsus*, lustful. — L. *libīdin-*, stem of *libīdo*, *lubīdo*, lust, pleasure.—L. *libet*, *lubet*, it pleases. Cf. Skt. *lubh*, to desire. Allied to **Love.**

Library. (F.—L.) F. *librairie.*—L. *librāria*, a book-shop ; fem. of *librārius*, belonging to books. — L. *libr-*, stem of *liber*, a book, orig. the bark of a tree (one of the earliest writing materials). Allied to Gk. λέπειν, to peel ; Brugm. i. § 499.

Librate, to balance, be poised, move slightly when balanced. (L.) The verb is rare, and due to the sb. *libration* (Kersey). —L. acc. *lībrātiōnem*, a poising.—L. *lībrātus*, pp. of *lībrāre*, to balance.—L. *lībra*, a balance, a level ; also a pound of 12 oz.+ Gk. λίτρα, a pound of 12 oz. Brugm. i. § 589.

Licence, License, leave, abuse of freedom. (F.—L.) M. E. *lycence.* — F. *licence.*—L. *licentia*, freedom to act.—L. *licent-*, from *licēre*, to be allowable. See Brugm. ii. § 587. **Der.** *licence*, more usually *license*, vb.

licentiate, one who has a grant to exercise a profession. (L.) Englished from Late L. *licentiātus*, pp. of *licentiāre*, to licence.—L. *licentia*, licence (above).

licentious. (F.—L.) F. *licencieux.* — L. *licentiōsus*, full of licence. — L. *licentia*, licence (above).

Lichen, a moss. (L.—Gk.) L. *līchēn.*

—Gk. λειχήν, lichen, tree-moss ; also, an eruption on the skin. Generally connected with Gk. λείχειν, to lick up ; from its encroachment. Cf. Russ. *lishai*, a lichen, a tetter.

Lichgate, a churchyard gate. (E.) So called because a corpse (in a bier) may be rested under it. The former syllable is M. E. *lich*, a corpse, but orig. the living body ; from A. S. *līc*, a body ; see **Like** (1).

Lick, to lap. (E.) M. E. *likken.* A.S. *liccian.* + Du. *likken*, G. *lecken.* A secondary verb allied to the primary forms seen in Goth. *bilaigon* (be-lick) ; Russ. *lizate*, O. Irish *ligim*, I lick, L. *lingere*, Gk. λείχειν, Pers. *lishtan*, Skt. *lih*, *rih*, to lick. (√LEIGH.) Brugm. i. § 604.

Licorice, Liquorice. (F.—L.—Gk.) M. E. *licoris.*—A. F. *lycorys*, Liber Albus, p. 224 ; M. F. *liquerice*, 'lickorice ;' Cot. —L. *liquirītia*, liquorice ; a corrupted form of *glycyrrhīza* (Pliny, Nat. Hist. xxii. 9. 11).—Gk. γλυκύρριζα, liquorice, lit. 'sweet root.'—Gk. γλυκύ-s, sweet ; ρίζα, root. See **Wort.**

Lictor, an officer in Rome. (L.) L. *lictor*, perhaps ' binder ' ; from the fasces or ' bound ' rods which he bore, or from binding culprits. Allied to *ligāre*, to bind. See **Ligament.** (Doubtful.)

Lid, a cover. (E.) M. E. *lid.* A.S. *hlid*, a lid.—A.S. *hlid-*, weak grade of *hlīdan*, to cover.+Du. *lid*, a lid ; Icel. *hlið*, a gate, gateway, gap, breach ; M. H. G. *lit*, *lid*, a cover (obsolete).

Lie (1), to rest, abide. (E.) A strong verb. M. E. *lyen*, also *liggen*, pt. t. *lay*, *ley*, pp. *lein*, *lein.* A.S. *licgan*, pt. t. *læg*, pp. *legen.*+Du. *liggen*, Icel. *liggja*, Dan. *ligge*, Swed. *ligga*, G. *liegen*, Goth. *ligan.* Related to Russ. *lejate* ; Lat. base *leg-* (in *lectus*, bed) ; Gk. base λεχ- (in λέχος, bed). (√LEGH.) ¶ On the mod. E. form see Sweet, E. Gr. § 1293.

Lie (2), to tell a falsehood. (E.) M.E. *līʒen*, *lēʒen*, pt. t. *leh*, pp. *lowen.* O. Merc. *lēgan* ; A.S. *lēogan*, pt. t. *lēag*, pp. *logen.* +Du. *liegen*, Icel. *ljúga*, Dan. *lyve*, Swed. *ljuga*, Goth. *liugan*, G. *lügen.* Teut. type *leugan-*, pt. t. *laug*, pp. *luganoz.* Cf. Russ. *lgate*, *luigate*, to lie ; *loje*, a lie. (√LEUGH.)

Lief, dear. (E.) M. E. *leef.* A. S. *lēof.* +Du. *lief*, Icel. *ljúfr*, Swed. *ljuf*, Goth. *liubs*, G. *lieb.* Teut. type *leuboz.* Cf.

Russ. *lioboi*, agreeable, *liobite*, to love; L. *lubet*, *libet*, it pleases; Skt. *lubh*, to desire. (√LEUBH.) Allied to Love.

Liege, faithful, subject. (F.—O. H. G.) [The sense has been altered by confusion with L. *ligātus*, bound. In old use, we could speak of ' a *liege* lord ' as meaning a *free* lord, in exact opposition to the imported notion.] M. E. *lige*, *lege*; *lege poustee* = free sovereignty, Bruce, v. 165.— O. F. *lige*, *liege*, liege, leal; also, free; a *liege* lord was a lord of a free band, and his *lieges* were privileged free men, faithful to him, but free from other service.— M. H. G. *ledic*, *lidic* (G. *ledig*), free, esp. from all obligations of service. Cf. Icel. *liðugr*, free, M. Du. *ledig*, free. (Disputed; see Körting, § 4736.)

Lieger, Leiger, an ambassador; see Ledger.

Lien, a legal claim, charge on property. (F.—L.) F. *lien*, a band, or tie, anything that fastens or fetters.—L. *ligāmen*, a tie.— L. *ligāre*, to tie. See **Ligament.**

Lieu, place, stead. (F.—L.) F. *lieu.* —L. *locum*, acc. of *locus*, a place. See **Locus.**

lieutenant, a 'locum tenens,' deputy, &c. (F.—L.) F. *lieu tenant.*—L. *locum-tenent-*, stem of *locum tenens*, one who holds another's place. — L. *locum*, acc. of *locus*, a place ; *tenens*, pres. pt. of *tenēre*, to hold. See **Tenable.**

Life. (E.) M. E. *lif*, *lyf*; gen. *lyues* (*lives*), dat. *lyue* (*live*). A.S. *lîf*, gen. *lîfes*, dat. *lîfe*. From the base of Teut. **leiban-* (pt. t. **laib*, pp. **libanoz*), to remain; as seen in Goth. *bi-leiban*, A.S. *be-lîfan*, G. *bleiben*, Du. *blijven*, to remain. +Icel. *lîf, lîfi*, Dan. *liv*, Swed. *lif*, O.H.G. *lîp*, life (whence G. *leib*, the body). The weak grade appears in Live, q. v. And see Leave (1). (√LEIP ?)

lifeguard. (E.) From *life* and *guard.* ¶ Cf. G. *leibgarde*, a body-guard, which is a cognate word, with the orig. sense of ' life-guard,' from O. H. G. *lîp*, life.

lifelong ; better livelong, q. v.

Lift (1), to elevate. (Scand.) M. E. *liften.*—Icel. *lypta* (pron. *lyfta*), to lift, exalt in air, from *lopt*, air ; Dan. *löfte*, Swed. *lyfta*, from *luft*, air. The Icel. *y* results, by mutation, from Teut. *u*; see Loft. Der. *up-lift.*

Lift (2), to steal. (E.) We speak of a *shop-lifter*, a thief; see Shak. Troil. i. 2. 129. To take up; hence, to take

away. The same as **Lift** (1). ¶ Not allied to Goth. *hliftus*, a thief.

Ligament, a band, band of tissue connecting the moveable bones. (F.—L.) F. *ligament.*—L. *ligāmentum*, a tie, band. —L. *ligā-re*, to tie ; with suffix *-mentum.*

ligature, a bandage. (F.—L.) F. *ligature*, a tie, bandage.—L. *ligātūra*, a binding.—L. *ligātus*, pp. of *ligāre*, to tie.

Light (1), illumination. (E.) M. E. *light.*—O. Merc. *lēht*; A. S. *lēoht*, light.+ Du. and G. *licht*; cf. Goth. *liuh-ath*, light, shewing that the *t* is a suffix. Teut. type **leuhtom*, neut. sb. ; related to the adj. **leuhtos*, as seen in E. *light*, i. e. bright, adj., G. and Du. *licht*. Co-radicate with L. *lux* (stem *lūc-*), light, Gk. λευκ-ός, white, Skt. *ruch*, to shine. (√LEUQ.) See Lucid.

lighten (1), to illuminate, flash. (E.) 1. INTRANS., to shine as lightning; ' it *lightens*.' M. E. *lightenen*, more correctly *light-n-en*, where the *-n-* is formative, and gives the sense ' to become light.' 2. TRANS. This is only the intrans. form incorrectly used with a trans. sense. The correct trans. form is simply *to light* = O. Merc. *līhtan*, from *lēoht*, sb.

lightning, an illuminating flash. (E.) Formed with suffix *-ing* from M. E. *lightnen*, to lighten (above).

Light (2), not heavy. (E.) M. E. *light.* A. S. *lēoht* (for **līht*). + Du. *licht*, *ligt*; Icel. *lēttr*, Dan. *let*, Swed. *lätt*, Goth. *leihts*, G. *leicht*, O. H. G. *līht*, *līhti.* Teut. type **līhtoz*, for **linχtoz*, **lenχtoz.* Allied to Lith. *lengwas*, light; and to Lung. See Brugm. i. § 684; Sievers, § 84.

light (3), to alight, settle, descend. (E.) M. E. *lihten.* A.S. *līhtan*, vb., to alight from, lit. to make light, relieve a horse of his burden.—A.S. *lēoht* (*līht*) (above). The sense ' to descend upon ' (the earth) is secondary, due to the completed action of descending from a horse.

lighten (2), to alleviate. (E.) The *-en* is merely formative, as in *strength-en.*— A.S. *līhtan*, to make light (above).

lighten (3), to alight on. (E.) Extended from **light** (3) above.

lighter, a boat for unlading ships. (Du.) Borrowed from Du. *ligter*, a lighter, i. e. unloader.—Du. *ligt*, light.

lights, lungs. (E.) So named from their lightness. So also Russ. *legkiia*, lights ; from *legkii*, light.

Lighten (1), to flash, **Lightning;** see Light (1).

Ligneous, woody. (L.) L. *ligne-us*, wooden; with suffix *-ous.* - L. *lignum*, wood.

lign-aloes, a kind of tree. (F.-L. *and* Gk.) O. F. *lignaloes* (Godef.).-L. *lignum aloës*, lit. 'wood of aloes.' *Aloës* is gen. of *aloë*, from Gk. ἀλόη, aloe. See Aloe.

Ligule, a strap-shaped petal. (L.) In botany.-L. *ligula*, a little tongue, also spelt *lingula*, dimin. of *lingua*, tongue. See Lingual.

Ligure, a precious stone. (L. - Gk.) L. *ligurius.* - Gk. λιγύριον, a sort of gem (amber or jacinth); Exod. xxviii. 19.

Like (1), similar. (E.) M. E. *lyk, lik.* A.S. *ge-līc*; as suffix, *-līc.* + Du. *ge-lijk*, Icel. *līkr*, *g-līkr*, Dan. *lig*, Swed. *lik*, Goth. *ga-leiks*, G. *g-leich*, O. H. G. *ka-līh.* β. Lit. 'having the same form,' and derived from the sb. meaning 'form, shape,' viz. A. S. *līc*, form, body, Icel. *līk*, Goth. *leik*, the body, Du. *lijk*, a corpse, Dan. *lig*, Swed. *lik*, a corpse, G. *leiche*, O. H. G. *līh.* See Lichgate. Cf. Lith. *lygus*, like.

like (2), to be pleased with. (E.) The construction has altered; M. E. *liketh*, it pleases, is impersonal, as in mod. E. *if you like* = if it may please you.-A. S. *līcian*, to please, orig. to be like or suitable for.- A. S. *-līc, ge-līc*, like; see Like (1).+Du. *lijken*, to suit; Icel. *līka*, to like; Goth. *leikan*, to please (similarly derived).

liken, to compare. (E.) M. E. *liknen*, to liken; but the true sense is intransitive, viz. to be like. Cf. Swed. *likna*, (1) to resemble, (2) to liken, from *lik*, like; Dan. *ligne*, the same, from *lig*, like.

Lilac, a shrub. (Span. - Arab. - Pers.) Span. *lilac.* - Arab. *līlak*, a lilac. - Pers. *līlaj, lilanj, līlang*, of which the proper sense is indigo-plant. The initial *l* stands for *n*, and the above forms are from *nīl*, blue, whence *nīlak* (>Arab. *līlak*), bluish. The plant is named from the 'bluish' tinge on the flowers in some varieties. (Devic). Cf. Skt. *nīla-*, dark blue.

Lilt, to sing, dance. (Scand.) M. E. *lilting-horn*, horn to dance to; cf. M. E. *lulten*, to resound. Formed (with added *-t*) from Norweg. *lilla*, to sing in a high tone. Cf. O. Swed. *lylla*, to lull to sleep (Rietz). Allied to Lull.

Lily, a plant. (L.-Gk.) A.S. *lilie.* - L. *līlium.* - Gk. λείριον, a lily.

Limb (1), a member, branch of a tree. (E.) M. E. *lim.* A.S. *lim.* +Icel. *limr*, Dan. Swed. *lem.* Allied to A.S. *li-ð*, Goth. *li-thus*, G. *g-lie-d*, a joint. Cf. Lith. *lēmů*, stature, growth. See Lay (4).

Limb (2), the edge or border of a sextant, &c. (L.) L. *limbus*, a border, edging, edge.

limbo, limbus, the borders of hell. (L.) The orig. phrase is *in limbo*, where *limbo* is the abl. case of *limbus*, a border; the *limbus patrum* was a supposed place on the border of hell, where the patriarchs abode till Christ's descent into hell.

Limbeck, the same as Alembic.

Limber (1), active, flexible. (E.) In Baret(1580). Apparently allied to Limp(1).

Limber (2), part of a gun-carriage, a frame with two wheels and a pole. (F. ?) Cf. prov. E. *limmers*, thills, shafts (the *b* being excrescent). G. Douglas has *lymnaris*, shafts. Probably from O. F. *limonier*, adj., belonging to the shafts; from *limon*, a shaft. Cf. F. *limonière*, part of a carriage including the two shafts. Etym. unknown; perhaps allied to Icel. *lim* (pl. *limar*), branches of a tree.

Limbo, Limbus; see Limb (2).

Lime (1), bird-lime, mortar. (E.) M. E. *lym, liim*, viscous substance. A. S. *līm*, bitumen, cement.+Du. *lijm*, Icel. *līm*, Dan. *liim*, Swed. *lim*, glue; G. *leim*, glue; L. *līmus*, slime. Idg. type *leimo-*. See Loam.

Lime (2), the linden-tree. (E.) *Lime* is a corruption of *line*, as in Shak. Temp. v. 10; and *line* is a corruption of *lind*, the lengthening of *i* having occasioned the loss of *d*. (Sweet, E. Gr. § 1607.) See Lind.

Lime (3), a kind of citron. (F. - Pers.) F. *lime.* - Pers. *līmū*, (also *līmūn*), a lemon, citron. See Lemon.

Limehound, a dog in a leash. (Hybrid; F. - L., *and* E.) Short for *liam-hound*, used by Turberville. The M. E. *liam* or *lyam* means 'a leash.'-O. F. *liem*, now spelt *lien*, a band; Guernsey *liam, lian.* - L. *ligāmen*, a tie. See Lien, Liane.

Limit. (F.-L.) F. *limite*, a limit.- L. *limitem*, acc. of *līmes*, a boundary; akin to *līmen*, a threshold. Cf. L. *līmus*, transverse.

Limn, to illuminate, paint. (F.-L.) M. E. *limnen*, contracted form of *luminen*, to illuminate (Prompt. Parv.). Again, *luminen* is for *enluminen.*-O. F. *enlu-*

miner, to illuminate, burnish, limn. **–** L. *illumināre*; see Illuminate.

Limp (1), flaccid, pliant. (E.) Not in early use. Apparently related, by gradation, to Bavarian *lampecht*, flaccid, downhanging, from the verb *lampen*, to hang loosely down; cf. Skt. *lamba*, depending, *lamb*, to hang down.

Limp (2), to walk lamely. (E.) In Shak. Mer. Ven. iii. 2. 130. We find A. S. *lemp-healt*, earlier *laempi-halt* (Ep. Gl.), adj., halting; and a cognate form in M. H. G. *limphin*, to limp. Cf. Low G. *lumpen*, to limp.

Limpet, a small shell-fish. (L.) Formerly *lempet* (Phillips, 1706). A. S. *lempedu*, orig. a lamprey, which also sticks to rocks. **–** Late L. *lemprida*, for L. *lampedra*, a lamprey. See Lamprey. Cf. '*Lemprida*, lempedu;' Wright's Vocab. 438. 17.

Limpid, pure, bright. (F. **–** L.) F. *limpide*. **–** L. *limpidus*, clear. Allied to Lymph. Brugm. i. § 102.

Linch-pin, a pin to fasten a wheel on an axle. (E.) Formerly *lins-pin*, lit. 'axle-pin.' **–** A. S. *lynis*, an axle-tree.**+** Du. *luns*, a linch-pin, O. Low G. *lunisa*, Low G. *lunse*, G. *lünse*, a linch-pin. Teut. base **lunis-* (cf. Goth. *akw-izi*, an ax); from **lun-*, as in O. H. G. *lun*, a bolt, peg, pin. Perhaps from Idg. root. **leu*, (cf. Gk. λύ-ειν), to loosen.

Lind, Linden, the lime-tree. (E.) The true form of the sb. is *lind*, and *lind-en* is the adj. from it. Hence *lind-en tree* = *lind*; the same thing. M. E. *lind*. A. S. *lind*, the tree; also a shield, commonly of this wood.**+**Du. *linde*, Icel. Dan. Swed. *lind*, G. *linde*. Cf. Lith. *lenta*, a board. Doublet, *lime* (2).

Line, a thread, thin cord; also a stroke, row, rank, verse (L.; *or* F. **–** L.). In the sense 'cord,' we find A. S. *līne*, directly from L. *līnea*. In the other senses, it is from F. *ligne*, also from L. *līnea*. β. The L. *līnea* meant orig. a string made of flax, being fem. of adj. *līneus*, made of flax. **–** L. *līnum*, flax. Cf. Gk. λίνον, flax; whence perhaps the L. word. Der. *out-line*.

lineage. (F. **–** L.) F. *lignage*, a lineage.**–**F. *ligne*, a line, rank.**–**L. *līnea*, a line (above).

lineal. (L.) L. *līneālis*, belonging to a line. **–** L. *līnea*, a line (above).

lineament, a feature. (F. **–** L.) M. F. *lineament*, Cot. **–** L. *līneāmentum*, a draw-ing, delineation. **–** L. *līneāre*, to draw a line. **–** L. *līnea*, a line (above).

linear. (L.) L. *līneāris*, belonging to a line. **–** L. *līnea*, a line (above).

linen, cloth made of flax. (L.) Used as a sb., but really an old adj., A. S. *līn-en*; the old sb. being M. E. *lin*, A. S. *līn*, flax. **–** L. *līnum*, flax. (Cf. *gold-en* from *gold*.) See linseed.

Ling (1), a fish. (E.) M. E. *lenge* (Havelok). Named from its long slender shape. Cf. A. S. *lengu*, length. **+** Du. *leng*, a ling, from *lang*, long; Icel. *langa*, Norw. *langa*, *longa*, a ling; Swed. *långa*; G. *länge*, a ling, also called *läng-fisch*, long fish. See Long.

Ling (2), heath. (Scand.) M. E. *lyng..* **–** Icel. *lyng*, ling, heather; Dan. *ling*, Swed. *ljung*.

Linger, to tarry. (E.) Frequent. form of M. E. *lengen*, to tarry. **–** A. S. *lengan*, to prolong, put off. **–** A. S. *lang*, long. Cf. Icel. *lengja*, to lengthen, Du. *lengen*, to lengthen, G. *verlängern*, to prolong. See Long.

Lingo, a language. (Port. **–** L.) Port. *lingoa* (also *lingua*), a language. **–** L. *lingua*, a tongue, language (below).

lingual, pertaining to the tongue. (L.) Coined from L. *lingua*, the tongue, O. Lat. *dingua*, cognate with E. tongue.

linguist, one skilled in languages. (L.) From L. *lingua*, a tongue, language; with suffix *-ista* (= Gk. -ιστης).

Liniment, salve, ointment. (F. **–** L.) F. *liniment*. **–** L. *linimentum*, ointment. **–** L. *linere*, to smear; cf. Skt. *lī*, to melt. Brugm. i. § 476 (5); ii. § 608.

Lining. (L.) Formed, with suffix -*ing*, from the verb *to line*, i. e. to cover the inside of a garment with *line*, i. e. linen; see linen.

Link (1), a ring of a chain. (Scand.) O. Icel. **hlenkr*, whence Icel. *hlekkr* (by assimilation); Dan. *lænke*, Swed. *länk*; G. *gelenk*, a joint, link, ring. Cf. A. S. *hlence*, or *hlenca* (which would have given *linch*). Also M. H. G. *lenken*, to bend, O. H. G. *hlanca*, hip, loin (whence perhaps Flank).

Link (2), a torch; see Linstock.

Linnet, a bird. (F. **–** L.) M. E. *linet*. [A. S. *linece*.] O.F. *linette*; cf. F. *linotte*, 'a linnet,' Cot. Named from feeding on flax-seed and hemp-seed (cf. G. *hänfling*, a linnet, from *hanf*, hemp).**–**L. *līnum*, flax. We also find A. S. *līnetwige*, a linnet (whence Lowl. Sc. *lintwhite*).

linseed, flax-seed. (L. *and* E.) From M. E. *lin* = A. S. *līn,* flax, borrowed from L. *līnum,* flax ; and E. *seed.*

linsey-woolsey, made of linen and woollen mixed. (L. *and* E.) Made up from M. E. *lin,* linen, and E. *wool.* See linen, under **Line.**

Linstock, Lintstock, a stick to hold a lighted match. (Du.) Formerly *lintstock* (Coles, 1684) ; but properly *luntstock,* from *lunt,* ' a match to fire guns with,' Phillips. — Du. *lontstok,* ' a lintstock,' Sewel. — Du. *lont,* a match ; *stok,* a stick (see **Stock**) ; cf. Dan. *lunte-stok* ; from *lunte,* a match, *stok,* a stick. Du. *lont* seems to have been formed from M. Du. *lompe,* ' a bundle of linnen,' Hexham ; lit. a lump. See **Lump.**

link (2), a torch. (Du.) A corruption of *lint,* as it appears in *lint-stock* (above). Cf. Lowl. Sc. *lunt,* a torch, Du. *lont,* a match (whence Dan. *lunte,* Swed. *lunta*).

Lint, scraped linen. (L.) Cf. Late L. *linta,* from L. *linteum,* a linen cloth ; neut. of *lin-teus,* linen. — L. *līnum,* flax.

Lintel, the headpiece of a door. (F. – L.) M. E. *lintel.* – O. F. *lintel* (F. *linteau*). – Late L. *lintellus,* a lintel, for **līmitellus,* dimin. of L. *līmes* (stem *līmit-*), a boundary, border ; see **Limit.**

Lion. (F. – L. – Gk. – Egypt.) F. *lion.* – L. *leōnem,* acc. of *leo,* a lion. – Gk. λέων. Cf. Heb. *lāvī',* a lion. Prob. of Egypt. origin ; from Egypt. *labai, lawai,* a lioness (whence Gk. λέαινα) ; see **Leo.**

Lip. (E.) M. E. *lippe.* A. S. *lippa, lippe,* the lip. + Du. *lip,* Dan. *læbe,* Swed. *läpp,* G. *lippe, lefze.* Also L. *lab-rum, labium,* lip ; Pers. *lab,* lip. But the relations are not clear. Brugm. i. § 563.

Liquefy, Liquescent; see **Liquid.**
Liquid, moist. (F. – L.) F. *liquide.* – L. *liquidus,* liquid. – L. *liquēre,* to be clear.

liquefy, to become liquid. (F. – L.) M. F. *liquefier* (see Cot.). As if from Late L. **liquefīcāre,* to make liquid ; but we only find L. *liquefierī,* to become liquid.

liquescent, melting. (L.) L. *liquescent-,* stem of pres. part. of *liquescere,* inceptive form of *liquēre,* to be wet.

liquidate, to make clear ; hence, to clear off an account. (L.) From pp. of Late L. *liquidāre,* to clarify, make clear. – L. *liquidus,* liquid, clear.

liquor, moisture, strong drink. (F. – L.) M. E. *licour, licur.* – A. F. *licur* ; F.

liqueur, moisture. – L. *liquōrem,* acc. of *liquor,* moisture. – L. *liquēre,* to be moist. ¶ Now accommodated to L. spelling ; we also use mod. F. *liqueur.*

Liquorice ; see **Licorice.**
Lisp. (E.) M. E. *lispen, lipsen.* A. S. **wlispian,* to lisp, not found ; regularly formed from A. S. *wlisp,* also *wlips,* adj., lisping, imperfect in utterance. + Du. *lispen,* Dan. *læspe,* Swed. *läspa,* G. *lispeln.* (Imitative.)

Lissom ; see **Lithe.**
List (1), a border of cloth, selvage. (E.) M. E. *list.* A. S. *līst.* + Du. *lijst,* Icel. *lista,* Dan. *liste,* Swed. *list,* G. *leiste,* O. H. G. *līsta.* (The *i* was orig. long.)

list (2), a catalogue. (F. – G.) F. *liste,* a list, roll ; also, a list or selvage. It meant (1) a border, strip, (2) a roll or list of names. – O. H. G. *līsta,* G. *leiste,* a border ; see **List** (1).

List (3) ; see **Lists.**
List (4), to please. (E.) M. E. *lusten, listen* ; ' if thee *list* ' = if it please thee, Ch. C. T. 1183. – A. S. *lystan,* to desire, used impersonally. – A. S. *lust,* pleasure. + Du. *lusten,* Icel. *lysta,* Dan. *lyste,* Swed. *lysta,* Goth. *luston,* G. *gelüsten* ; all from the sb. See **Lust.**

List (5), to listen ; see below.
Listen. (E.) We also find *list* ; also M. E. *lust-n-en* and *lust-en,* the former being deduced from the latter by a formative *n,* as in Goth. *full-n-an,* to become full. A. S. *hlystan,* to listen to. – A. S. *hlyst,* hearing ; Teut. type **hlus-ti-,* from a base **hlus,* weak grade of Teut. base **hleu-s.* Cf. A. S. *hlos-nian,* to hearken ; Icel. *hlusta,* to listen, from *hlust,* the ear ; W. *clust,* the ear ; also L. *clu-ere,* Gk. κλύ-ειν, to hear, Skt. *çru,* to hear. (√KLEU.) See **Loud.**

Listless, careless. (E.) The same as *lust-less* ; Gower has *lustles,* C. A. ii. 111. From *lust,* q.v. And see **List** (4).

Lists, ground enclosed for a tournament. (F.) M. E. *listes,* sb. pl., the lists. The *t* is excrescent ; and *liste* stands for **lisse.* – M. F. *lisse* (F. *lice*), ' a list or tiltyard ;' Cot. Cf. Ital. *lizza;* Span. *liza,* Port. *liça,* a list for tilting ; Late L. *liciæ,* sb. pl., barriers ; *liciæ duelli,* the lists. Origin disputed. Cf. Late L. *licia,* a stake ; perhaps from Late L. *licius,* oaken < L. *īliceus* (from * īlex,* holm-oak).

Litany, a form of prayer. (F. – L. – Gk.) M. E. *letanie,* afterwards altered to *litanie.* – O. F. *letanie.* – L. *litanīa.* – Gk. λιτανεία, a prayer. – Gk. λιταίνειν, to pray. – Gk. λίτομαι, I beg, pray, λιτή, prayer, entreaty.

Literal. (F. – L.) O. F. *literal.* – L. *līterālis,* according to the letter. – L. *lītera;* see Letter.

literature. (F. – L.) M.F. *literature.* – L. *līterātūra,* scholarship. – L. *līterātus,* learned, skilled in letters. – L. *lītera,* a letter; see Letter.

Litharge, protoxide of lead. (F. – L. Gk.) M. E. *litarge.* – F. *litharge,* 'litargie, white lead;' Cot. – L. *lithargyrus.* – Gk. λιθάργυρος, lit. 'stone-silver.' – Gk. λίθ-ος, a stone; ἄργυρος, silver; see Argent.

Lithe, pliant, flexible, active. (E.) M. E. *lithe.* A.S. *līðe, līð,* gentle, soft (for **linðe,* the lengthened *i* causing loss of *n*). + G. *gelinde,* O. H. G. *lindi,* soft, tender. Allied to Icel. *linr,* L. *lēnis,* soft; L. *lentus,* pliant. Der. *lissom,* i. e. *lithe-some.*

Lither, pestilent, stagnant, dull. (E.) In 1 Hen. VI. iv. 7. 21, '*lither* sky' means pestilent or dull lower air; cf. '*luther* eir,' pestilent air, P. Pl., C. xvi. 220. M. E. *luther, lither.* – A.S. *lȳðre,* evil, base, poor (hence, sickly, dull). Not to be confused with *lithe,* pliant.

Lithography, writing on stone. (Gk.) Coined from Gk. λίθο-ς, a stone; γράφειν, to write.

lithotomy, cutting for stone. (L. – Gk.) L. *lithotomia.* – Gk. λιθοτομία. – Gk. λίθο-ς, stone; τομ-, 2nd grade of τεμ-, as in τέμνειν, to cut; see Tome.

Litigation, a contest in law. (L.) From L. *lītigātio,* a disputing. – L. *lītigātus,* pp. of *lītigāre,* to dispute. – L. *līt-,* stem of *līs,* strife; *-igāre,* for *agere,* to carry on. L. *līs* = O. Lat. *stlīs,* strife.

litigious, contentious. (F. – L.) It also once meant debateable. – F. *litigieux,* 'debatefull;' Cot. – L. *lītigiōsus,* adj.; from *lītigium,* contention. – L. *lītigāre,* to dispute (above).

Litmus, a kind of dye. (Du.) Corrupted from Du. *lakmoes,* a blue dye-stuff. – Du. *lak,* lac; *moes,* pulp; (whence G. *lackmus,* litmus). See Lac (1).

Litter, a portable bed. (F. – L.) M.E. *litere.* – O. F. *litiere.* – Late L. **lectīcāria,* formed from *lectīca,* a litter. – L. *lectus,* a bed; see Lectern. Allied to Gk. λέχ-ος, a bed; and to Lie (1).

litter, materials for a bed, heap of straw to lie on, confused mass of things scattered. (F. – L.) The same word applied to a straw bed for animals, &c.

litter, a brood. (F. – L.) The same word; see the various senses of M. E. *lytere* in the Prompt. Parv.; and cf. F. *accoucher,* E. ' :o be in the straw.'

Little. (I) M. E. *litel, lutel.* A. S. *lȳtel* (or *lytel*), little; we also find *lȳt* (or *lyt*). + Du. *luttel,* little, *lutje,* a little; O. Sax. *luttil;* O. H. G. *luzil, luzzil, liuzil.* Compare also A. S. *lytig,* deceitful, *lot,* deceit; Goth. *liuts,* deceitful, *luton,* to betray. All from Teut. base **leut,* orig. to stoop; see Lout. ¶ Not allied to *less.* The Icel. *lītill,* Swed. *liten,* Goth. *leitils,* little, seem to be from a different Teut. base **leit.* It is difficult to see how they can be related.

Littoral, belonging to the sea-shore. (L.) L. *littorālis,* adj., from *littor-* (for **littos-*), stem of *littus* or *lītus,* sea-shore.

Liturgy, public prayer. (F. – L. – Gk.) O. F. *liturgie, lyturgie.* – Late L. *līturgia.* – Gk. λειτουργία, public service. – Gk. λεῖτο-ς, public; ἔργον, work, cognate with E. *work.*

Live (1), to exist. (E.) M. E. *liuien* (*livien*). O. Merc. *lifgan,* A. S. *libban,* to live, dwell; orig. to remain, be left behind. + Du. *leven,* to live; Icel. *lifa,* to be left, to live; Dan. *leve,* Swed. *lefva,* Goth. *liban,* to live; G. *leben,* to live, O. H. G. *lëbēn.* From Teut. **lib-,* weak grade of **leiban-,* to remain. See Life.

live (2), adj., alive. (E.) Short for *alive,* which is not a true orig. adj., but due to the phrase *a liue* (*a live*) = A. S. *on life,* in life, hence, alive. *Life* is the dat. case of *līf,* life; hence the *i* in *live* is long.

livelihood. (E.) Corruption of M.E. *liuelode* (*livelode*), i.e. life-leading, means of living; older spelling *liflode, liflade.* From A.S. *līf,* life; *lād,* a leading, way, provisions to live by, a course, a lode; see Life and Lode.

livelong, long-lasting. (E.) The same as *life-long,* i.e. long as life is; but *livelong* is the older spelling.

lively. (E.) M. E. *lifly,* i.e. life-like.

Liver. (E.) M. E. *liuer* (= *liver*). A.S. *lifer.* + Du. *lever,* Icel. *lifr,* Dan. *lever,* Swed. *lefver,* G. *leber.* Cf. Russ. *liver',* the pluck of animals (from Teut.). Allied to Armen. *leard,* liver; but not to L. *iecur.* Brugm. i. §§ 280, 557 (2).

Livery, a delivery, a thing delivered, uniform allowed to servants. (F. − L.) M. E. *liuere* (= *liverè*, three syllables). − A. F. *liveree*; F. *livrée*, 'a delivery of a thing that is given, the thing so given, a livery;' Cot. Orig. fem. of pp. of *livrer*, to deliver, give freely. − L. *līberāre*, to set free, give freely; see **Liberate.**

Livid, discoloured. (F.−L.) F. *livide*. − L. *līuidus*, bluish. − L. *līuēre*, to be bluish. Cf. W. *lliw*, O. Irish *lī*, colour, hue. Þrugm. i. § 94.

Lizard, a four-footed reptile. (F.−L.) M. E. *lesarde*. − O. F. *lesarde*. − L. *lacerta*, a lizard. Cf. **Alligator.**

Llama, a quadruped. (Peruvian.) *Llama* is a Peruvian word, meaning 'flock'; Prescott. But the Peruv. Dict. gives '*llama*, carnero de la tierra,' sheep of the country.

Llano, a level steppe or plain. (Span. −L.) Commoner in the pl. *llanos.* − Span. *llano*, pl. *llanos*, a plain; from *llano*, adj., plain, flat. − L. *plānus*, flat. See **Plain.**

Lo, behold! (E.) M. E. *lo.* A. S. *lā*, an interjection.

Loach, Loche, a small fish. (F.) F. *loche*, 'the loach,' Cot.; whence also Span. *loja, locha.* Cf. Norman *loque*, a loach, a slug (Le Hérichèr). Origin unknown.

Load, a burden. (E.) The sense of 'burden' seems to be due to confusion with the verb **Lade** (1); but cf. prov. E. *lead*, in the sense 'to carry.' M. E. *lāde*, a course, way, lode; also, a load. A. S. *lād*, a lode; also, carriage. See **Lode.**

Load-star, Load-stone; see **Lode.**

Loaf. (E.) M. E. *lof*, *loof*. A. S. *hlāf*. +Icel. *hleifr*, Goth. *hlaifs*, *hlaibs*, G. *laib*. Cf. Lithuan. *klēpas*, bread (from Teut.).

Loam, clay. (E.) M. E. *lam*. A. S. *lām*.+Du. *leem*, G. *lehm*, O. H. G. *leim*, *leimo.* Teut. type *laimoz.* Cf. Icel. *lęir* (Teut. type *laizom*), loam. Akin to **Lime** (1).

Loan, a lending, money lent. (Scand.) M. E. *lone* (= *lāne*). This corresponds to the rare A. S. *lān*, borrowed from Norse. [The true A. S. form is *lǣn*, a loan.] − Icel. *lān*, a loan; Dan. *laan*, Swed. *lån.* + A.S. *lǣn*, a loan; Du. *leen*, a grant, a fief; G. *lehn*, *lehen*, a fief. β. All from the verb seen in A. S. *lēon* (pt. t. *lāh*), to grant, Icel. *ljā*, G. *leihen*, to lend, Goth. *leihwan*; akin to L. *linquere* (pt. t. *līqui*),

Gk. λείπειν, Skt. *rich*, to leave, O. Irish *lecim*, I leave. (√LEIQ; Brugm. i. § 463.) Hence the Teut. verb **leihwan-* (as in Gothic); and the sb. **laihwniz*, **laihwnoz*, a loan, from the second grade **laihw* with suffix *-niz* or *-noz.*

Loath. (E.) M. E. *loth.* A.S. *lāð*, hateful, hostile.+Icel. *leiðr*, Dan. Swed. *led*, odious; O. H. G. *leit*, odious, orig. mournful. Teut. type **laithoz*, where *-thoz* is prob. a suffix. Allied to G. *leiden*, to suffer; but prob. *not* allied to A. S. *līðan* (pt. t. *lāð*), to travel, sail; as usually said (Kluge). Der. *loath-ly*; *-some*, suggested by M. E. *wlatsom*, detestable; also *loathe*, vb.

Lobby, a small hall, passage. (Ital. − G.) Probably from N. Ital. (Piedmontese) *lobia* (see Diez); the Ital. form is *loggia* (see **Lodge**). Cf. Late L. *lobia, laubia, lobium*, a portico, gallery, covered way; as if from a Germ. form **laubjā.* − M. H. G. *loube*, an arbour, bower, open way along the upper story of a house (as in a Swiss *chalet*); mod. G. *laube*, a bower. Orig. made with foliage. − M.H.G. *loub* (G. *laub*), a leaf; see **Leaf.**

Lobe, flap of the ear, &c. (F. − Low L. −Gk.) F. *lobe.* − Late L. *lobus.* − Gk. λοβός, a lobe of the ear or liver. Brugm. i. § 667.

Lobster, a kind of shell-fish. (L.) A. S. *loppestre*, a corrupter form of A. S. *lopust*, a corruption of L. *locusta*, a lobster, (2) a locust. It was perhaps confused with A. S. *loppe*, a flea.

Local, Locate; see **Locus.**

Loch, a lake. (Gaelic.) Gael. *loch*, a lake. + O. Irish *loch*, Corn. and Bret. *lagen*; L. *lacus*; Stokes, p. 237. See **Lake** (1).

Lock (1), a fastening. (E.) M. E. *loke.* A. S. *loc*, a fastening. + Icel. *loka*, a lock; Swed. *lock*, a lid; G. *loch*, a dungeon. From Teut. base **luk*, weak grade of Teut. root **leuk*, to fasten, whence also A. S. *lūcan*, Du. *luiken*, Icel. *lūka*, to shut, Goth. *galūkan*, to shut up.

locket, a little hinged case worn as an ornament. (F. − Scand.) Orig. a fastening (Hudibras, pt. ii. c. i. 808). − F. *loquet*, the latch of a door, dimin. of O. F. *loc*, a lock, borrowed from Icel. *loka*, a lock.

Lock (2), a tuft of hair or wool. (E.) M. E. *lok.* A. S. *locc.* + Du. *lok*, Icel. *lokkr*, Dan. *lok*, Swed. *lock*, G. *locke.* Orig. 'a curl;' cf. Icel. *lykkr*, a loop, bend, crook; also Lith. *lugnas*, pliable.

Locket; see Lock (1).

Lockram, a kind of cheap linen. (F. — Bret.) F. *locrenan,* a sort of unbleached linen; named from the place where it was made, viz. *Loc-Renan,* or *S. Renan,* near Quimper, in Brittany. — Bret. *Lok-Ronan,* cell of St. Ronan; from Bret. *lok* (L. *locus*), a cell.

Locomotion; see Locus.

Locus, a place. (L.) L. *locus,* a place. O. Lat. *stlocus,* a place.

local. (F.—L.) F. *local.* — L. *locālis,* belonging to a place. — L. *locus,* a place.

locate, to place. (L.) From pp. of L. *locāre,* to place. — L. *locus,* a place.

locomotion, motion from place to place. (L.) Coined from *loco-,* for *locus,* a place; and *motion.*

Locust, a winged insect. (L.) M. E. *locuste.* — L. *locusta,* a shell-fish, also a locust.

Lode, a vein of ore, a water-course. (E.) The true sense is 'course.' A. S. *lād,* a way, course, journey; cf. A. S. *lǣdan,* to lead, conduct.+Icel. *leið,* lode, way, course; Swed. *led,* a course. Teut. type **laidā,* fem. From the 2nd grade of Teut. **leithan-* (A. S. *līðan*), to travel. See Lead (1). Der. *lode-star.* ¶ And see Load.

lodestar, loadstar, the polar star. (E.) Lit. 'way-star,' star that leads or guides; see Lode above.

lodestone, loadstone, a magnet. (E.) Compounded of *lode* and *stone,* in imitation of *lodestar;* it means a stone that leads or draws.

Lodge, a small house, cot, resting-place. (F.—G.) M. E. *loge, logge.* — O. F. *loge;* cf. Ital. *loggia,* Late L. *lobia,* a gallery. — O. H. G. **laubjā,* allied to *loubā,* M. H. G. *loube,* an arbour, mod. G. *laube,* a bower. — O. H. G. *loub,* G. *laub,* a leaf; see Leaf. Doublet, *lobby.*

Loft, an upper room. (Scand.) M. E. *loft,* properly 'air'; the peculiar sense is Scand. — Icel. *lopt* (pron. *loft*), (1) air, sky, (2) an upper room; Dan. Swed. *loft,* a garret. Allied to A. S. *lyft,* air, sky, Goth. *luftus,* Du. *lucht* (for *luft*), G. *luft,* the air. Der. *a-loft;* also *lofty,* i. e. 'in the air;' *lift,* vb.

Log (1), a block, piece of wood. (Scand.) The vowel has been shortened. Cf. Norw. *laag,* a fallen trunk; Icel. *lāg,* a felled tree, log; Swed. dial. *låga,* a felled tree, a tree that has been blown

down. So called from its *lying* on the ground, as distinguished from the living tree. From the 3rd (pt. pl.) grade, viz. *lāg-,* of Icel. *liggia,* to lie; see Lie (1) and Low. Der. *logg-ats, logg-ets,* a game with bits of wood; *log-wood,* so called because imported in *logs,* and also called *blockwood* (Kersey).

log (2), a piece of wood with a line, for measuring the rate of a ship. (Scand.) The same word. The Swed. *logg,* as a sea-term, whence *log-lina,* a log-line, *log-bok,* a log-book, *logga,* to heave the log, Dan. *log, log-line, log-bog, logge,* vb., seem to have been all borrowed back from E.

logger-head, a dunce, a piece of timber (in a whale-boat) over which a line is passed to make it run more slowly. (Scand. *and* E.) A similar formation to *blockhead.* Cf. Icel. *lāgar,* gen. of *lāg.*

Log (3), a liquid measure. (Heb.) In Lev. xiv. 10. — Heb. *lōg,* a liquid measure, 12th part of a *hin;* orig. ' a basin.'

Logarithm. (Gk.) Coined from Gk. λογ-, stem of λόγος, a word, a proportion, ratio; and ἀριθμός, a number; the sense being ' ratio-number.' See Arithmetic.

Loggerhead; see Log (1).

Logic, the science of reasoning correctly. (F. — L. — Gk.) O. F. *logique.* — L. *logica,* for *ars logica,* logic art. — Gk. λογική, for λογικὴ τέχνη, logic art; where λογική is fem. of λογικός, reasonable. — Gk. λόγος, a speech. — Gk. λέγειν, to say.+L. *legere,* to speak; see Legend. Hence all words in *-logy,* the chief being *astro-logy, bio-, chrono-, concho-, doxo-, entomo-, etymo-, genea-, geo-, meteoro-, minera-, mytho-, necro-, noso-, ornitho-, osteo-, patho-, philo-, phraseo-, phreno-, physio-, psycho-, tauto-, theo-, zoo-logy;* see these in their due places.

Loin. (F.—L.) M. E. *loine.* — O. F. *logne,* also *longe.* — Late L. **lumbea,* fem. of an adj. **lumbeus* (not found), from L. *lumbus,* loin. See Lumbar.

Loiter, to delay. (Du.) M. E. *loitren,* Pr. Parv. — M. Du. and Du. *leuteren,* to linger, loiter, trifle, M. Du. *loteren,* to delay, deceive, vacillate; cf. E. Fries. *lötern, lötern,* to loiter. Allied to M. Du. *lutsen,* with the same sense (Hexham). Perhaps allied to Lout.

Loll, to lounge about. (E.) M. E. *lollen, lullen.* Cf. Icel. *lolla,* 'segniter agere,' Halldórsson; M. Du. *lollen,* to sit over the fire; the orig. sense was prob. to doze; M. Du. *lolle-banck*, 'a sleeping seate,' Hexham. Allied to **Lull**.

Lollard, a name given to the followers of Wyclif. (M. Du.) It was confused with M. E. *loller*, i. e. one who lolls, a lounger, lazy fellow; see **Loll** above; but the words are prob. related. Latinised as *Lollardus* from M. Du. *lollaerd*, (1) a mumbler of prayers and hymns, (2) a Lollard, lit. 'God-praiser' or 'singer'; first applied to a sect in Brabant. Formed with suffix *-aerd* (same as E. *-ard* in *drunk-ard*) from M. Du. *lollen*, *lullen*, to sing; see **Lull**.

Lone, short for *alone*; see **Alone**.

Long (1), to desire, yearn. (E.) M. E. *longen*. A. S. *langian*, impers. vb. with acc., to long after, crave, desire; (distinct from *langian*, to grow long).**+** O. Sax. *langôn*, impers.; Icel. *langa*, impers. and pers.; O. H. G. *langôn*, impers. Perhaps allied to G. *gelingen*, to succeed. Cf. G. *ver-langen*, to wish for. Der. *be-long*.

Long (2), extended. (E.) M. E. *long*. A. S. *lang*, *long* +Du. *lang*, Icel. *langr*, Dan. *lang*, Swed. *lång*, Goth. *laggrs* (=*langrs*), G. *lang*; L. *longus*. Brugm. i. § 642.

longevity, length of life. (L.) From L. *longæuitas*, long life. **–** L. *long-us*, long; *æuitas*, usually *ætas*, age; from *æui-*, a stem formed from *æuum*, life. See **Age**.

longitude. (F. –L.) F. *longitude.* **–** L. *longitūdō*, length; in late Lat., the longitude of a place. **–** L. *longi-*, stem formed from *longus*, long; with suffix *-tū-dō*. Der. *longitudin-al*, from stem *longitudin-*.

Loo, a game at cards. (F.) Formerly called *lanterloo*. **–** F. *lanturelu*, *lanturlu*, interj., nonsense! fudge! also a game at cards. The expression was orig. the refrain of a famous vaudeville (ab. 1630), afterwards used to give an evasive answer. Being purposely nonsensical, it admits of no further etymology.

Loof; see **Luff**.

Look, to see. (E.) M. E. *loken*. A. S. *lōcian*, to look. **+** O. Sax. *lōkōn*, to look; cf. M. H. G. *luogen*, to mark, behold, G. *lugen*, to look out. Brugm. i. § 421(7).

Loom (1), a machine for weaving cloth. (E.) M. E. *lome*, a tool, implement. A. S. *ge-lōma*, a tool, implement, instrument. Der. *heir-loom*, where *loom* meant any implement, hence a piece of furniture.

Loom (2), to appear faintly or at a distance. (E. ?) Orig. sense doubtful. (Not = M. E. *lumen*, to shine, as that has a different vowel.) If it meant orig. 'to come slowly towards,' it answers exactly to E. Fries. *lōmen*, Swed. dial. *loma*, to move slowly; cf. M. H. G. *luomen*, to be weary, from the adj. *luomi*, slack. Kilian has M. Du. *lome*, slow, inactive. The Teut. base of the adj. is **lōm-*, connected by gradation with E. **Lame**. See **Loon** (2). Cf. Lowl. Sc. *loamy*, dull, slow; E. Fries. *lōmig*.

Loon (1), **Lown**, a base fellow. (O. Low G.) M. E. *lown* (spelt *lowen*, but rhyming on *-oun*), St. Cuthbert, 7957. Cf. M. Du. *loen*, 'homo stupidus,' Kilian.

Loon (2), a water-bird, diver. (Scand.) A corruption of the Shetland name *loom*. **–** Icel. *lōmr*, Swed. Dan. *lom*, a loon. Prob. from the *lame* or awkward motion of diving-birds on land; cf. Swed. dial. *loma*, E. Fries. *lōmen*, to move slowly; see **Loom** (2) above.

Loop, a noose. (Scand.) G. Douglas has *lowp-knot* (Æn. xii. 603). **–** Icel. *hlaup*, lit. 'a leap'; cf. Swed. *löp-knut*, a running-knot; Dan. *löb*, a course, *löb-knude*, or *lob-öie*, a running-knot. **–** Icel. *hlaupa*, to leap, run. See **Leap**. Thus the orig. sense was 'running knot'; hence, loop of a string, &c.

Loop-hole, a small aperture in a wall. (F. –Low G.) M. E. *loupe*, P. Pl. **–** O. F. **loupe* (not found); Languedoc *loup*, a small window in a roof (Wedgwood). **–** M. Du. *lūpen*, Du. *luipen*, to lurk (see Franck); Low G. *lupen*, in the same sense as Low G. *glupen*, to peep (Lübben). Hence, the sense was 'peep-hole.' Cf. Low L. *loupus* (unexplained).

Loose, slack. (Scand.) M. E. *lous*, *los*; Prof. Zupitza shews (in Anglia, vii. 152) that it is due to the Scand. form. [The true M. E. form is *lees*, answering to A. S. *lēas*, (1) loose, (2) false.] **–** Icel. *lauss*, Swed. Dan. *lös*, loose; O. Sax. *lōs*, M. Du. *loos*, (1) loose, (2) false (where mod. Du. has *los*, loose, *loos*, false); G. *los*, loose; Goth. *laus*, empty, vain. Teut. type **lausoz*; from **laus-*, 2nd grade of Teut. **leusan-*, to lose. See **Lose**.

-less, suffix. (E.) M. E. *-lees*, *-les*; A. S. *-lēas*, the same as *lēas*, loose, free from (above).

loose, loosen, vb. (E.) The true form is *loose*, later *loosen* by analogy with *strengthen*, &c. A late derivative from the adj. above. Other languages derive the verb directly from the adj.; thus Du. *lossen*, Icel. *leysa*, Swed. *lösa*, Dan. *löse*, G. *lösen*, Goth. *lausjan*, to loosen, are derived (respectively) from Du. *los*, Icel. *lauss*, Swed. and Dan. *lös*, G. *los*, Goth. *laus*, loose, vain.

Loot, plunder. (Hindi.—Skt.) Hindi *lūṭ* (with cerebral *t*), loot, plunder. The cerebral *t* shews that *r* is elided.—Skt. *lotra*, shorter form of *loptra*, booty, spoil. —Skt. *lup*, to break, spoil; allied to L. *rumpere*, to break. See Rupture, Rob. *Loot* = that which is *robbed*. (Cf. Horn, Pers. Dict. § 608.)

Loover; see Louver.

Lop. (M. Du.) M. Du. *luppen*, to maim, castrate, mod. Du. *lubben*. Cf. Lithuan. *lùpti*, to peel. See Lib.

Loquacious, talkative. (L.) Coined from L. *loquāci-*, decl. stem of *loquax*, talkative. — L. *loquī*, to speak.

Lord, a master. (E.) Lit. ' loaf-keeper.' A.S. *hláford*, a lord; early form *hláfard*, for **hláfweard*, a loaf-ward; see Loaf and Ward. ¶ For the loss of *w*, cf. A.S. *fulluht*, from *fulwiht*, baptism.

Lore, learning. (E.) M.E. *lore*; A.S. *lāre*, gen., dat., and acc. of *lār*, lore.+Du. *leer*, G. *lehre*, O.H.G. *lēra*, doctrine. Teut. type **laizā*, fem.; cf. Teut. **laizjan* (A.S. *lēran*, G. *lehren*), to teach; from **lais-*, 2nd grade of **leisan-*, to trace out; see Learn, Last (2).

Lorel; see losel.

Lorimer, a maker of horses' bits, spurs, &c. (F.—L.) Also *loriner*.—O.F. *lorinier*, *loreinier*, M.F. *lorimier*, later *lormier*, ' a spurrier;' Cotgrave.—O.F. *lorein*, *lorain*, rein, bridle, bit. —Late L. *lōrēnum*, *lōrānum*, a rein, bit.—L. *lōrum*, a thong.

Loriot, the golden oriole. (F.—L.) F. *loriot*, corruptly written for *l'oriot*, where *oriot* is another form of *oriol*; see Oriole.

Lorn, lost. (E.) M.E. *loren*, pp. of *lēsen*, to lose; see Lose.

Lory, a bird of the parrot kind. (Malay.) Also called *lury*; and (formerly) *nory*, *nury*.—Malay *lūrī*, *nūrī*, a lury or lory.

Lose. (E.) The form formerly in use was *lese*; M.E. *lesen*. [The mod. form *lose* has got its sound of (uu) from the influence of M.E. *lōsen*, to loose, con-

fused with M.E. *losien*, to be lost.] The M.E. *lesen* is from A.S. *-lēosan*, strong verb, to lose (pt. t. *-lēas*, pp. *-loren*). This is cognate with Du. *-liezen* (only in comp. *ver-liezen*), G. *-lieren* (only in comp. *ver-lieren*), Goth. *-liusan* (only in *fra-liusan*, to loose). Teut. type **leusan-*. Cf. L. *lu-ere*, Gk. λύ-ειν, to set free. Der. *lorn*, lost, A.S. pp. *-loren*; also *forlorn*, q. v.

loss, sb. (E.) M.E. *los*. A.S. *los*, destruction. Allied to Lose; being derived from Teut. **lus*, weak grade of **leusan-*, to lose (above).

losel, lorel, a worthless fellow, reprobate. (E.) One devoted to perdition; cf. A.S. *los*, destruction, *los-ian*, to be lost, to perish. From *lus-* (A.S. *los-*), weak grade of the strong verb *lēosan*, to lose, pp. *lor-en* (for older **los-en*). *Lor-el* is formed from the base *lor-* of the pp. in use, and *los-el* from the older form of the same. For the suffix, cf. A.S. *wac-ol*, watchful.

Lot, a portion, share. (E.) M.E. *lot*. A.S. *hlot* (<**hlutom*), lot, share.—A.S. *hlut-*, weak grade of *hlēotan* (pt. t. *hlēat*). to obtain by lot. + Du. *lot*; Icel. *hluti*, allied to str. vb. *hljóta*, to obtain by lot; Dan. *lod*, Swed. *lott*. All from the weak grade of Teut. **hleutan-*, to obtain by lot; cf. A.S. *hlīet*, *hlȳt*, G. *loos*, Goth. *hlauts*, a lot, from **hlaut*, 2nd grade of the same verb.

Loth; see Loath.

Lotion, a washing, external medicinal application. (L.) L. *lōtiōn-em*, acc. of *lōtio*, a washing.—L. *lōtus*, pp. of *lauāre*, to wash. See Lave. Brugm. i. § 352(3).

Loto, Lotto, a game. (Ital.—Teut.) F. *loto*; a F. form of the Ital. *lotto*, a lottery, a word of Teut. origin; see Lot.

lottery. (E.; *with F. suffix.*) In Levins, ed. 1570. Formed by adding *-ery* to E. *lot*; cf. *brew-ery*, *fish-ery*. The F. *loterie* is borrowed from English or from Ital. *lotteria* (Torriano).

Lotus, the Egyptian water-lily. (L.— Gk.) L. *lōtus*, *lōtos*.—Gk. λωτός, (1) the Gk. lotus, (2) the Cyrenean lotus, the eaters of which were called *lōtophagī*, (3) the lily of the Nile.

Loud. (E.) M.E. *loud*. A.S. *hlūd*. +Du. *luid*, G. *laut*. Teut. type **hlūdoz*, for earlier *hlūthós* (with the accent on *o*); allied to the Idg. type **klutós* (with weak grade **klu*) as seen in L. *-clutus*, in *inclutus*, renowned, Gk. κλυτός, renowned,

Skt. *çruta-*, heard, from *çru*, to hear. (√KLEU.) Brugm. i. §§ 100, 113.

Lough, a lake. (Irish.) Ir. *loch*; see **Loch.**

Lounge, to loll about. (F.–L.) From *lungis*, an idle fellow or lounger, not an uncommon word in the 16th and 17th centuries.–F. *longis*, an idle, drowsy, and stupid fellow (Cot.). Littré supposes that this sense of *longis* was due to a pun, having reference to L. *longus*, long, hence a long and lazy man; for, strictly speaking, *Longis* is a proper name, being the O. F. form of L. *Longius* or *Longinus*, the name (in the old mysteries) of the centurion who pierced the body of Christ. This name first appears in the apocryphal gospel of Nicodemus, and was doubtless suggested by Gk. λόγχη, a lance, in John xix. 34.

Louse, an insect. (E.) M. E. *lous*, pl. *lys*. A. S. *lūs*, pl. *lȳs* (lice).+Du. *luis*, Dan. *luus*, Swed. *lus*, Icel. *lūs*, G. *laus*. Teut. type **lūs*, fem.

Lout, a clown. (E.) The lit. sense is 'stooping,' from M. E. *louten*, to stoop, bow.–A. S. *lūtan*, to stoop.+Icel. *lūtr*, stooping, bent (which prob. suggested our use of the word), from *lūta*, to stoop; cf. Swed. *luta*, Dan. *lude*, to stoop, lean.

Louver, Loover, an opening in the roofs of ancient houses. (F.) M. E. *lover* (used to translate O. F. *louvert* in the Romance of Partenay, 1175), but really from O. F. *lovier*, *lover*, used as a gloss to Late L. *lōdium*, a word also explained by M. E. *lover*.–Romanic type **lōdārium*, adj. form due to Late L. *lōdium*, a loover. (For the intercalated *v*, cf. F. *pouvoir*, from O. F. *pooir* = Span. *poder*.) Prob. an opening over a fireplace; from Icel. *hlōð*, n. pl., a hearth. (Academy, Dec. '94.)

Lovage, an umbelliferous plant. (F.–L.) M. E. *louache* (Alphita).–O. F. *levesche*, *luvesche* (Wright's Voc. i. 139). Cf. Ital. *levistico*, lovage.–L. *ligusticum*. lovage, a plant of *Liguria*.–L. *Ligusticus*, belonging to *Liguria*, a country of Cisalpine Gaul.

Love, affection. (E.) M. E. *loue* (*love*). A. S. *lufu*, love. From the weak grade (*lub*) of Teut. base **leub*. + Goth. *lubo*; O. H. G. *luba*; cf. also G. *liebe*; Russ. *liobov'*; Skt. *lobha*, covetousness, *lubh*, to desire. Closely allied to Lief. (√LEUBH.) Der. *love*, vb.; *belove*, first appearing in M. E. *bilufien*, to love greatly.

Low (1), humble, inferior. (Scand.) M. E. *louh*, also *lah*.–Icel. *lāgr*, low; N. Fries. *leeg*; Swed. *låg*, Dan. *lav*. The orig. sense is that which lies down, or lies low (as we say); from Icel. *lāg-*, stem of pt. pl. of *liggja*, to lie. See Lie (1). Der. *be-low* (= by low); also *lower*, vb., i. e. to let down, from *low-er*, comparative of *low*, adj.

Low (2), to bellow. (E.) M. E. *lowen*. A. S. *hlōwan*, to bellow, resound. + Du. *loeijen*, O. H. G. *hlōjan*. Cf. L. *clā-māre*.

Low (3), a hill. (E.) In place-names. A. S. *hlāw*, *hlǣw*, a hill; properly a slope. + Goth. *hlaiw*, a grave; *hlains*, a hill; Lat. *clīuus*, a hill. From a Teut. base **hlai-*, 2nd grade of the Teut. root **hlei-* (Idg. √KLEI), to lean, incline. Allied to **Lean** (1).

Low (4), flame. (Scand.) Icel. *logi*, flame; cf. L. *lūx*. Allied to **Lucid.**

Lower (1), to let down. (E.) From *low-er*, comparative of adj. *low*.

Lower (2), to frown. (E.) M. E. *louren*, *luren*, to lower, frown. Cf. M. Du. *loeren*, ' to leere, to frowne,' Hexham; Low G. and E. Fries. *lūren*, to lower, frown, peer; M. H. G. *lūren*, G. *lauern*. Cf. Icel. *lūra*, to doze.

Lown; see **Loon** (1).

Loyal, faithful. (F.–L.) F. *loyal* (Cot.).–L. *lēgālis*, legal (hence, just, loyal); see **Legal.**

Lozenge, a rhombus; a small cake of flavoured sugar, &c., orig. of a diamond shape. (F.) Formerly *losenge*, esp. a shield of a diamond shape (in heraldry).–O. F. *losenge*, *lozenge* (F. *losange*), a lozenge. Origin disputed; prob. from O. F. *lauze*, a flat stone. Cf. Span. *losanje*, a lozenge, rhombus; prob. from *losa*, a square stone for paving (whence *losar*, to pave). See *lausa*, *lauza*, a flat stone for buildings (Ducange).

Lubber, a dolt. (E.) M. E. *lobre*, *lobur*. Cf. M. Du. *lobben*, ' a lubbard, a clowne,' Hexham; Low G. *lobbes* (the same); Norw. *lubb*, *lubba*, one of round thick figure; *lubben*, short and thick. Also W. *llob*, a dolt, lubber, *llabi*, a stripling, looby. Cf. *lob* in Shakespeare, M. N. D. ii. 1. 16. Allied to **Lump**; cf. E. Fries. *lobbe*, *lob*, a flabby lump.

Lubricate, to make slippery. (L.) From pp. of L. *lūbricāre*, to make slippery. –L. *lūbricus*, slippery. Allied to Goth. *sliupan*, to slip. See **Slip.**

Luce, the pike; a fish. (F. — Late L. — Gk.) Lit. 'wolf-fish.' — M. F. *lucs*, *lus*, a pike; Cot. — Late L. *lucius*, a pike. — Gk. λύκος, a wolf; also a (ravenous) fish. Cf. 'Pyke, fysche, *dentrix, lucius, lupus*;' Prompt. Parv. ' Luce, fysche, *lucius*;' id.

Lucid, bright. (L.) L. *lūcidus*, bright. — L. *lūcēre*, to shine; cf. *lūx*, light.+Gk. λευκός, bright; Skt. *ruch*, to shine. Allied to **Light** (1). (√LEUK.) Der. *luci-fer*, i. e. light-bringer, morning-star, from *ferre*, to bring.

Luck, fortune. (Du. — M. H. G.) M. E. *lukke* (15th c.). Not found in A.S.; and Fries. *luk* is late. — Du. *luk*. From M.H.G. *ge-lücke*, good fortune; G. *glück* (for *ge-lück*). The Fries. *luk*, Swed. *lycka*, Dan. *lykke* (like Du. *luk*) are borrowed from G. (Kluge). Perhaps akin to G. *locken*, to entice, allure.

Lucre, gain, profit. (F. — L.) F. *lucre*. — L. *lucrum*, gain. Allied to Irish *luach*, price, wages, G. *lohn*, reward, Gk. λεία (for *λαϝία), booty, Russ. *lovite*, to take as booty. Der. *lucr-at-ive*, F. *lucratif*, L. *lucrātīuus*, from pp. of *lucrārī*, to gain, from *lucrum*, gain. Brugm. i. § 490.

Lucubration, a production composed in retirement. (L.) Properly, a working by lamp-light; from L. *lūcubrātio*, the same. — L. *lūcubrātus*, pp. of *lūcubrāre*, to bring in lamps, to work by lamp-light. — L. *lūcubrum*, prob. a faint light; at any rate, obviously formed from *lūc-*, stem of *lūx*, light; cf. *lūcēre*, to shine. See **Light** (1), **Lucid.**

Ludicrous, laughable. (L.) L. *lūdicr-us*, done in sport; with suffix *-ous*. — L. *lūdi-*, for *lūdus*, sport. — L. *lūdere*, to play.

Luff, Loof, to turn a ship towards the wind. (E.) From M. E. *lōf*, a contrivance for altering a ship's course; see Layamon, iii. 476. It seems to have been a sort of large paddle, used to assist the helm in keeping the ship right. Prob. named from the resemblance of a paddle to the palm of the hand; cf. Lowl. Sc. *loof*, Icel. *lófi*, Goth. *lōfa*, palm of the hand. Cf. also Du. *loef*, Dan. *luv*, Swed. *lof*, weather-gage; Dan. *luve*, to luff; and perhaps Bavarian *laffen*, blade of an oar, flat part of a rudder. See E. Fries. *lōf*, *lūf* in Koolman. Der. *laveer*.

Lug, to drag. (Scand.) Swed. *lugga*, to pull by the hair; cf. *lugg*, the forelock; Norw. *lugga*, to pull by the hair; cf. *lugg*, hair of the head. Also cf. Low G. *luken*, to pull, pull by the hair; A.S. *lūcan*, to pull up weeds; Dan. *luge*, to weed. β. The A.S. *lūcan* is a strong verb, allied to a Teut. type *leuk-an-*, to pull (pt. t. *lauk*, pp. *lukanoz*). *Lug* is from the weak grade *luk*. Der. *lugg-age*, with F. suffix as in *bagg-age*.

Lugsail, a sort of square sail. (Scand. and E.) Prob. from the verb *to lug*; the sail is easily hoisted by a pull at the rope attached to the yard. Or named from *lugger*, its apparent derivative, as if a ship furnished with lugsails; but cf. Du. *logger*, which seems to mean 'slow ship,' from Du. *log*, slow, E. Fries. *lug*. (Doubtful.)

Lugubrious, mournful. (L.) From L. *lūgubri-s*, mournful; with suffix *-ous*. — L. *lūgēre*, to mourn. Cf. Gk. λυγρός, sad.

Lukewarm, partially warm. (E.) M. E. *luke*, *leuk*, tepid. (*Luke-warm* = tepidly warm.) Cf. Du. *leuk*, luke-warm; E. Fries. *lūk*, *luke*, tepid, weak, slack. ¶ Distinct from *lew-warm*.

Lull, to sing to rest. (E.?) M. E. *lullen*. Not in A.S.+Swed. *lulla*, Dan. *lulle*, to hum, lull; M. Du. *lullen*, to sing in a humming voice; E. Fries. *lollen*, to sing badly, howl, cry. From the repetition of *lu lu*, in lulling children to sleep. This is a drowsier form of *la!* *la!* used in cheerful singing; cf. *lilt*; and see **Lollard.** Cf. Gk. λαλεῖν, to speak.

Lumbar, relating to the loins. (L.) L. *lumbāris.* adj.; whence *lumbāre*, an apron (Jerem. xiii. 1). — L. *lumbus*, the loin.+A.S. *lendenu*, pl., the loins, Du. *lendenen*, pl.; Swed. *länd*, Dan. *lend*, loin; G. *lende*, haunch. Brugm. i. § 360.

lumbago, pain in the loins. (L.) L. *lumbāgo*, pain in the loins. — L. *lumbus*, loin.

Lumber (1), useless furniture. (F. — G.) Formerly *lombor* (1487); *lumbar* (Blount). Perhaps the *lumber-room* was orig. *Lombard-room*, where the Lombard broker bestowed his pledges. Cf. *Lombardeer*, a broker, *Lombard*, a bank for usury or pawns; Blount. — F. *Lombard*, a Lombard (who acted as pawnbroker in the 14th century). — L. *Longobardus*, also *Langobardus.* — G. *Langbart*, a name given to the men of this tribe. Cf. A. S. *Langbeardas*, the Lombards. See Ducange. (Etym. disputed.)

Lumber (2), to make a great noise. (Scand.) In Palsgrave. A frequent. verb of Scand. origin. — Swed. dial. *lomra*, to resound; cf. Swed. *ljumm*, a great noise, Icel. *hljōmr*, a sound, a tune. From Teut. base **hleu-*, to hear, whence also Goth. *hliuma*, hearing. See **Loud**.

Luminary, a bright light. (F. – L.) O. F. *luminarie*, later *luminaire*, a light, lamp. – L. *lūmināre*, a light; neut. of *lūmināris*, light-giving. – L. *lūmin-*, for *lūmen*, light. *Lūmen* = **lūc-men*; from *lūcēre*, to shine. See **Lucid**.

luminous, bright. (F. – L.) F. *lumineux*. – L. *lūminōsus*, bright; from *lūmin-*, for *lūmen*, light (above).

Lump. (Scand.) M. E. *lompe*, *lumpe*. – Swed. dial. and Norw. *lump*, a block, stump, piece hewn off a log; Swed. *lumpor*, pl., rags; Swed. Dan. *lumpen*, paltry. Cf. Du. *lomp* (whence G. *lumpen*), a rag, lump, *lomp*, clumsy; E. Fries. *lump*, clumsy, thick, vile, lumpy.

Lunar. (L.) L. *lūnāris*, adj.; from *lūna*, moon. L. *lūna* = **loucsnā*, giver of light. – L. *lūcēre*, to shine. Brugm. i. § 218. Der. *lun-ette*, *inter-lunar*; and see below.

lunatic. (F. – L.) F. *lunatique*. – L. *lūnāticus*, mad; lit. affected by the moon. – L. *lūna*, moon.

Lunch, a large piece of bread, &c. (E. ?) *Lunch*, 'a gobbet, or peece;' Minsheu. Connected with *lump*, like *hunch* with *hump*, *bunch* with *bump*. See **Lump**.

luncheon, lunch, a slight meal. (E. ?) *Lunch* is now used as short for *luncheon*, though *luncheon* itself is an extension from *lunch*, a lump. Cot. gives M.F. *caribot*, ' a *lunchion*, or big piece of bread,' &c.; also ' *horion*, a cuff, thump, also a *luncheon* or big piece.' *Lunchion* appears to be for *lunshin*, as in ' a huge *lunshin* of bread,' Thoresby to Ray (1703), which is prob. merely short for *lunchin(g)*. At any rate, *luncheon* is clearly from *lunch*, a large piece (above). ¶ Quite distinct from *nuncheon*.

Lung. (E.) M. E. *lunge*, pl. *lunges*, *longes*, A.S. *lungen*, pl. *lungena*.+Du. *long*, Icel. *lunga*, pl., Dan. *lunge*, Swed. *lunga*, G. *lungen*, pl. Allied to A. S. *lungre*, quickly (orig. lightly), also to Gk. ἐλαχύς, Skt. *laghu-*, light. The *lungs* are named from their lightness; cf. E. *lights*, i.e. *lungs*; Russ. *legkoe*, lung, as compared with Russ. *legkii*, light; Port. *leves*, lungs, from Port. *leve*, light; see **Light** (2). Brugm. i. § 691.

Lunge, a thrust, in fencing. (F. – L.) Formerly *longe*. The E. *a longe* is a mistaken substitute for F. *allonge* (formerly *alonge*), a lengthening; i.e. an extension of the body in delivering the thrust. – F. *allonger*, to lengthen (formerly *alonger*). – F. *a* (from L. *ad*), to; and L. **longāre*, only used in comp. *ē-longāre*, to lengthen, from *longus*, long. See **Long**.

Lupine, a kind of pulse. (F. – L.) F. *lupin*. – L. *lupīnum*, a kind of pulse; orig. neut. of *lupīnus*, wolfish, though the reason is not clear. – L. *lupus*, a wolf; see **Wolf**.

Lurch (1), to lurk, dodge, pilfer. (E.) Allied to **Lurk**. Cf. *birch*, *birk*. The senses are (1) to lie in wait, lurk, (2) to pilfer, steal. Der. *lurch-er*, ' one that lies upon the lurch, or upon the catch, also a kind of hunting-dog;' Phillips.

Lurch (2), the name of a game. (F.) ' To leave in the *lurch*' is due to an old game. – M. F. *lourche*, ' the game called lurche, or lurch in a game; *il demoura lourche*, he was left in the lurch;' Cot. Cot. also gives *ourche*, ' the game at tables called lurch.' Perhaps from L. *orca*, a dice-box. Cf. Ital. *lurcio*, ' the game lurch,' Torriano. Cf. Low L. *lurculus*, ' parvus lusus;' Ducange.

Lurch (3), to devour; *obsolete*. (F. ? – L.) ' To *lurch*, devour, or eate greedily;' Baret. – O. F. **lurcher* (?); cf. Ital. *lurcare*, ' to lurch or devour greedily,' Torriano. – Late L. *lurcārī*, *lurcāre*, to devour greedily.

Lurch (4), a sudden roll sideways. (E. ?) ' *A lee lurch*, a sudden roll (of a ship) to the leeward;' Webster. Obscure; perhaps merely *lurch* (1) in the sense to stoop or dodge; see **Lurch** (1).

Lure, a bait. (F. – G.) M. E. *lure*. – O. F. *loerre*, *loirre*, later *leurre*, ' a faulconer's lure;' Cot. – Teut. **lōthrom*, neut.; as seen in M. H. G. *luoder* (G. *luder*), a bait, decoy, lure. Perhaps from Teut. **lōth*, 2nd grade of **lath-*, to invite? Cf. A. S. *laðian*, Icel. *laða*, Goth. *lathōn*, G. *laden*, to invite, weak verbs.

Lurid, wan, gloomy. (L.) L. *lūridus*, pale yellow, wan.

Lurk, to lie in wait. (Scand. ?) M. E. *lurken*, *lorken*. – Norw. *lurka*, to sneak away, go slowly; Swed. dial. *lurka*, to do anything slowly; E. Fries. *lurken*, to shuffle along. Perhaps extended from *lūr-*, as in Norw. *lura*, Dan. *lure*, to lie in wait, Dan. *lure*, (also) to listen, Swed. *lura*, to lie in wait; G. *lauern*, to lurk. See **Lower** (2).

Lury; see Lory.

Luscious, delicious. (F.–L.) Of doubtful origin. Still, we find in The Anturs of Arthur, ed. Morton, st. 36, 'with *lucius* drinkes;' and in Sir Amadace, st. 27, 'with *licius* drinke.' The latter form is short for *delicious*; so that *luscious* may be the same, but confused with *lusty*. Also *lushious* (Spenser); *lussyouse* (Palsgrave).

Lust. (E.) The usual old meaning is pleasure. A.S. *lust*, pleasure.+Du. *lust*, Icel. *lyst*, Dan. *lyst*, Swed. and G. *lust*, Goth. *lustus*, pleasure. Allied to Skt. *lash*, to desire; Gk. λιλαίομαι. Brugm. i. § 518 (2). **Der.** *lust-y*, formerly 'pleasant.'

Lustration; see Lustre (2).

Lustre (1), splendour. (F.–Ital.–L.) F. *lustre.*–Ital. *lustro*, 'a lustre, a glasse, a shining,' Florio; cf. Late L. *lustrum*, a window.–L. *lustrāre*, to shine. Prob. from a lost adj. **lustrus* (for **lucstrus*), shining; from *lūcēre*, to shine.

Lustre (2), **Lustrum**, a period of five years. (L.) L. *lustrum*, an expiatory sacrifice; also a period of five years, because every five years a lustrum was performed. The orig. sense is 'a purification'; from *luere*, to wash, purify.

lustration, a purification by sacrifice. (L.) From L. *lustrātio*, an expiation. – L. *lustrātus*, pp. of *lustrāre*, to purify.–L. *lustrum*, an expiatory sacrifice (above).

Lute (1), a musical instrument. (F.–Arab.) M. E. *lute.*–M. F. *lut* (Cotgrave), mod. F. *luth*. We also find Prov. *laut*, Span. *laud*, Port. *alaude*, Ital. *liuto*, Du. *luit*, Dan. *lut*, G. *laute*. The Port. form shews the Arab. origin; since *al-* in *alaude* is for *al*, the Arab. def. art.–Arab. *al*, the; *'ūd*, wood, timber, a staff, stick, wood of aloes, lute, or harp.

Lute (2), a kind of loam. (F.–L.) O. F. *lut*, clay, loam.–L. *lutum*, mud, that which is washed down.–L. *luere*, to wash. Allied to **Lave**.

Lutestring, a lustrous silk. (F.–Ital.–L.) A curious corruption of *lustring*, a sort of shining silk (Kersey).–F. *lustrine*, lutestring,lustring. –Ital. *lustrino*, lustring, tinsel; from its gloss.–L. *lustrāre*, to shine; see Lustre (1).

Luxury. (F.–L.) M. E. *luxurie.*–O. F. *luxurie* (Hatzfeld), F. *luxure.*–L. *luxūria*, luxury.–L. *luxus*, pomp, excess, luxury.

-ly, a common suffix. (E.) A.S. *-līc*, adj. suffix; *-līce*, adv. suffix; from *līc*, like; see Like (1).

Lye, a mixture of ashes and water, for washing. (E.) M. E. *ley.* A.S. *lēah.*+ Du. *loog*, G. *lauge*, O. H. G. *louga*, lye. Perhaps allied to Icel. *laug*, a bath; and to L. *lauāre*, to wash. Cf. **Lather.**

Lym, a lime-hound: K. Lear, iii. 6. 72. Short for **Limehound.**

Lymph, a colourless fluid. (L.) L. *lympha*, O. L. *lumpa* (Brugm. i. § 102), water, lymph, also a water-nymph. The spelling with *y* is prob. due to a supposed connexion with Gk. νύμφη, a nymph (prob. false). It is rather allied to Limpid.

Lynch, to punish by mob-law. (E.) From *Charles Lynch*, a Virginian planter (1736–96); Cent. Dict. The name is from A.S. *hlinc*, a ridge of land. See **Link** (1).

Lynx, a keen-sighted quadruped. L.–Gk.) M. E. *lynx.*–L. *lynx.*–Gk. λύγξ, a lynx; allied to λευκός, bright, and named from its bright eyes. Cf. Skt. *ruch*, to shine, *loch*, to see. Cognate forms are A.S. *lox*, Swed. *lo*, G. *luchs*, Lith. *luszis*, a lynx; and (probably) Russ. *ruise*, Pers. *rūs*, Zend *raozha* ; Student's Pastime, p. 393.

Lyre. (F.–L.–Gk.) F. *lyre.* – L. *lyra.* – Gk. λύρα, a lyre, lute. **Der.** *lyr-ic.*

M.

Macadamise, to pave a road with small broken stones. (Gael. *and* Heb.; with F. *suffix.*) Named after Mr. John *Macadam*, A.D. 1819. *Macadam* = son of Adam.–Gael. *mac*, son; Heb. *ādām*, a man, from root *ādam*, to be red.

Macaroni, Maccaroni. (Ital.–L.) Ital. *maccaroni*, 'a kinde of paste meate;' Florio. Prob. from Ital. *maccare*, 'to bruise, batter, to pester,' Florio; i.e. to reduce to pulp. – L. *mac-*, base of *mācerāre*, to macerate. See **Macerate.** **Der.** *macaronic*, i. e. in a confused or mixed state (applied to a jumble of languages).

macaroon. (F. – Ital. – L.) F. *maca-ron*, pl. *macarons*, 'macarons, little fritter-like buns, . . also the same as macaroni;' Cot. – Ital. *maccaroni* (above). ¶ Now applied to a kind of biscuit.

Macaw, a kind of parrot. (Caribbean.) Said to be the native name in the Antilles (Webster). Brazilian *macao* (Cent. Dict.).

Mace (1), a kind of club. (F. – L.) O. F. *mace* (F. *masse*). – Folk-L. **mattea*, a beetle, only preserved in dimin. *mateola*, a little beetle. See Körting. ¶ But see Franck (s. v. *metselen*).

Mace (2), a kind of spice. (F. – L. – Gk. – Skt.?) F. *macis*, mace (O. F. *maceis, macis*, Godefroy). It seems to have been confused with M. F. *macer*, which 'is not mace, as many imagine, but a reddish, aromaticall, and astringent rind of a certain Indian root'; Cot. Both prob. from L. *macer, macir*, i. e. the 'rind of a great root, which beareth the name of the tree itself,' Holland, tr. of Pliny, xii. 8. – Gk. μάκερ; doubtless of Eastern origin.

Macerate, to soften by steeping. (L.) From pp. of L. *mācerāre*, to steep; frequent. from a base *māc-*.

Machine. (F. – L. – Gk.) F. *machine*. – L. *māchina*. – Gk. μηχανή, a device, machine; cf. μῆχος, means. (√MAGH.) Allied to **May** (1).

Mackerel, a fish. (F. – L.) O. F. *makerel* (F. *maquereau*). From Late L. *maquerellus*. Of unknown origin.

Mackintosh, a waterproof overcoat. (Gael.) Gael. *Mack-intosh*, the name of the inventor.

Macrocosm, the whole universe. (Gk.) Gk. μακρό-s, long, great; κόσμος, the world. Cf. *microcosm*.

Maculate, to defile. (L.) From pp. of L. *maculāre*, to spot. – L. *macula*, a spot, dimin. of a form **maca*, not used. **Der.** *immaculate*, orig. a pp.

Mad. (E.) The vowel was formerly sometimes long. M. E. *maad, mad*. The M. E. *măd* is from A. S. *(ge)-mǣded*, maddened, shortened to *(ge-)mēdd* (cf. *fat*); pp. of *ge-mǣdan*, to drive mad. The M. E. *maad* answers to A.S. *mǣd*; cf. A.S. *ge-maad*, Corp. Gloss. 2105; hence *mād-mōd*, madness (Grein). + O. Sax. *ge-mēd*, foolish; O. H. G. *gimeit*, vain; Icel. *meiddr*, pp. of *meiða*, to maim, hurt; Goth. *ga-maids*, maimed. The orig. sense seems to be ' severely injured '; the prefix *ge-, gi-, ga-* is unessential.

Madam, my lady. (F. – L.) F. *madame*, i. e. *ma dame*, my lady. – L. *mea domina*, my lady; see **Dame.**

Madder, a plant. (E.) M. E. *mader, madir*. A. S. *mǣddre*; also *mǣdere*. + Icel. *maðra*, Du. *mede, mee*.

Madeira, a sort of wine. (Port. – L.) Named from the isle of *Madeira*, i.e. ' the well-wooded.' – Port. *madeira*, wood, timber. – L. *māteria*, stuff, wood, timber. See **Matter** (1).

Mademoiselle, miss. (F. – L.) F. *ma*, my ; *demoiselle*, damsel ; see **Damsel.**

madonna, my lady. (Ital. – L.) Ital. *ma*, my ; *donna*, lady, from L. *domina* ; see **Dame.**

Madrepore, coral. (F. – Ital. – L. and Gk.) F. *madrépore*. – Ital. *madrepora*. The lit. sense is ' mother-stone,' a fanciful name, due to the existence of such terms as *madre-selva*, honeysuckle (lit. mother-wood), *madre-bosco*, woodbine (lit. mother-bush), *madre-perla*, mother-of-pearl. Here *madre* is from L. *mātrem*, acc. of *māter*, mother; see **Mother.** *Pora* is from Gk. πῶρος, a light friable stone, also a stalactite. ¶ But the word has certainly been *understood* (prob. *mis-understood*) as connected with *pore*, whence numerous scientific terms such as *cateni-pora, tubi-pora, denti-pora, gemmi-pora.* ' Scientific ' etymology is usually clumsy, and frequently wrong. We may conclude that F. and E. *pore* have been understood in the place of Gk. πῶρος, by confusion of ideas. See **Pore.**

Madrigal, a pastoral song. (Ital. – L. – Gk.) Ital. *madrigale*, a short song, pastoral ditty; for **mandrigale*. Florio also gives *mandriale, mandriano*, a herdsman, also a madrigal. – Ital. *mandra*, a herd, flock. – L. *mandra*, a stall, stable. – Gk. μάνδρα, a fold. + Skt. *mandurā*, stable. (The suffix *-ig-ale* = L. suffix *-ic-ālis*.)

Magazine. (F. – Ital. – Arab.) O.F. *magazin* (F. *magasin*). – Ital. *magazzino*, a storehouse. – Arab. *makhāzin*, pl. of *makhzan*, a storehouse. – Arab. *khasn*, a laying up in store.

Maggot, a grub. (C.) M. E. *magot, magat*. Cf. W. *maceiad, macai*, a maggot; *magiaid*, grubs. Allied to W. *magiad*, breeding, *magad*, a brood; from *magu*, to breed. Cf. Bret. and Corn. *maga*, to feed; O. Celtic **makō*, I feed. See **Maid.** ¶ But if the W. word is from E., *maggot* must be referred to Norw. *makk*, Icel. *maðkr*; see **Mawkish**.

Magi, priests of the Persians. (L. – Gk. – Pers.) L. *magi*, pl. ‒ Gk. μάγοι, pl. of μάγος, a Magian, one of a Median tribe; also an enchanter, properly a wise man who interpreted dreams. ‒ O. Pers. *magu-*, Pers. *mugh*, *mūgh*, one of the Magi, a fire-worshipper (Horn, § 984). Der. *mag-ic*, short for *magic art; mag-ic-i-an*.

Magistrate. (F. – L.) F. *magistrat*, a magistrate, ruler. ‒ L. *magistrātus*, (1) a magistracy, (2) a magistrate. ‒ L. *magister*, a master. L. *mag-is-ter* is a double compar. form; cf. *mag-nus*, great.

Magnanimity, Magnate; see under **Magnificent**.

Magnesia; see **Magnet**.

Magnet, the lodestone. (F. – L. – Gk.) M. E. *magnete*. ‒ O. F. *magnete*, also *manete* (13th cent.). ‒ L. *magnētem*, acc. of *magnēs*, for *Magnēs lapis* = Magnesian stone, the lodestone. ‒ Gk. Μάγνης (stem Μαγνητ-), also Μαγνήτης, Μαγνήσιος, belonging to Magnesia, in Thessaly; whence λίθος Μαγνήσιος (or Μαγνήτης), Magnesian stone, lodestone, or a metal like silver. Der. *magnesia*, an old name (in Chaucer, C. T. 16923, *or* G. 1455), for a mineral brought from Magnesia; now differently applied. See Schade, p. 1395.

Magnificent. (L.) L. *magnificent-*, stem of *magnificens*, lit. doing great things, hence, grand. ‒ L. *magni-*, for *magnus*, great; *-ficens*, for *faciens*, doing, from *facere*, to do. See **magnitude**.

magnify. (F. – L.) M. E. *magnifien*. ‒ F. *magnifier*. ‒ L. *magnificāre*, lit. to make large. ‒ L. *magni-*, for *magnus*, great; *-ficāre*, for *facere*, to do.

magniloquence. (L.) L. *magniloquentia*, elevated language. ‒ L. *magni-*, for *magnus*, great; *loquent-*, stem of pres. pt. of *loquī*, to speak; see **Loquacious**.

magnitude, greatness. (L.) L. *magnitūdo*, size. ‒ L. *magnus*, great. **+** Gk. μέγας, great; Skt. *mahant-*, great; A. S. *micel*. See **Mickle**.

magnanimity, greatness of mind. (F. – L.) F. *magnanimité*. ‒ L. acc. *magnanimitātem*. ‒ L. *magnus*, great; *animus*, mind.

magnanimous, high-minded. (L.) L. *magnanim-us*; with suffix *-ous* (L. *-ōsus*). ‒ L. *magnus*, great; *animus*, mind.

magnate, a great man, noble. (F. – L.) F. *magnat*. ‒ L. *magnātem*, acc. of *magnās*, a prince (Judith v. 26). ‒ L. *magnus*, great. ¶ *Magnate* is due to the use of L. *magnās* in Hungary and Poland.

Magnolia. (F.) A genus of plants named after Pierre *Magnol*, of Montpellier, in France; died A. D. 1715.

Magpie, a bird. (F. – L. – Gk.; *and* F. – L.) Also called *magot-pie, maggoty-pie*. *Mag* is short for *Magot* = F. *Margot*, a familiar form of F. *Marguerite*, also used to denote a magpie. This is from L. *Margarīta*, Gk. μαργαρίτης, a pearl; cf. Pers. *murwārīd*, a pearl, from Skt. *manjarī*, a pearl. *Pie* = F. *pie*, from L. *pīca*, a magpie; see **Pie** (1).

Maguey, the American aloe. (Cuba.) Of Cuban origin (Oviedo). Not Mexican, which has no *g*; the Mex. name is *metl*.

Maharajah, great king. (Hind. – Skt.) From Skt. *mahā-rāja-*, great king. Cf. L. *magnus rex*. So also *mahā-rānī*, great queen; from Hind. *rānī*, Skt. *rājñī*, queen.

Mahdi, a spiritual director. (Arab.) Arab. *mahdī*, the guided one; from *ma*, prefix, and *hady*, to guide. Cf. *hādī*, a guide. (Rich. Dict. pp. 1661, 1670.)

Mahogany, a tree. (Hayti.) From *mahagoni*, in the old Carib dialect of Hayti. (Garden and Forest, no. 438, July 15, 1896.)

Mahometan; see **Mohammedan**.

Mahout, an elephant-driver. (Hind.) Hind. *mahāwat*.

Maid, Maiden. (E.) M. E. *mayde*, merely short for earlier *maiden, meiden*. A. S. *mægden*, a maiden, cognate with O. H. G. *magatīn*, a maiden (with fem. suffix *-īn*). The form without this suffix is A. S. *mægeð*, a maiden, cognate with Goth. *magaths*, a virgin, G. *magd*. Related to A. S. *magu*, a son or kinsman, cognate with Goth. *magus*, Icel. *mögr*, and perhaps with Corn. *maw*, a boy. See Stokes (in Fick, ii. 198). Kluge compares O. Irish *macc*, W. *mab*, son. Der. *maiden-hood*, also spelt *maiden-head*.

Mail (1), steel network for armour. (F. – L.) O. F. *maille*, mail, also a mesh of a net. ‒ L. *macula*, a spot, speck, hole, mesh of a net; see **Maculate**.

Mail (2), a letter-bag. (F. – O. H. G.) M. E. *male*. ‒ O. F. *male* (F. *malle*), a bag, wallet. ‒ O. H. G. *malaha*, a leathern wallet. Cf. Gael. and Irish *mala*, a bag (from F.); Gk. μολγός, hide, skin.

Mail (Black), a forced tribute. (F. –

L.) *Mail* is a Scottish term for rent.
Blackmail or *black rent* is the rent paid in
cattle, as distinct from *white money* or
silver. — F. *maille*, 'a French halfpenny;'
Cotgrave. O. F. *meaille, maaille.* — Folk-
L. **metallea*, Late L. *medālia*, lit. 'medal.'
See **Medal**.

Maim, a bruise, hurt. (F. — G.?) Also
spelt *mahim* in Law-books (Blount). M.E.
maim. — A. F. *mahaym*, Liber Albus, p.
281; M. F. *mehaing*, 'a maime, or abate-
ment of strength by hurts received;' Cot.
Cf. Ital. *magagna*, a defect, blemish. Orig.
uncertain; cf. Bret. *machañ*, mutilation,
machaña, to mutilate. Some derive Ital.
magagnare, to maim, from G. *man*, man,
and O. H. G. **hamjan*, to mutilate,
from the O. H. G. adj. *ham*, maimed
(Körting).

Main (1), sb., strength. (E.) M. E.
main. A. S. *mægen*, strength. + Icel.
megin, O. Sax. *megin*, strength. Allied
to **May** (1) and **Might** (1).

Main (2), adj., chief, principal. (F. —
L.) O. F. *maine, magne*, chief. — L. *magnus*, great. ¶ Distinct from *main*, sb.,
which is of A. S. origin; see above.

Mainour. (F. — L.) In the phr. 'taken
with the mainour' or 'taken in the manner'; i. e. caught in the act. Anglo-F.
meinoure, mainoure, O. F. *maineuvre*, lit.
manœuvre; hence, act. See **Manœuvre**.
We find also 'to be taken *with* the
manner,' i. e. with the stolen chattel in
hand; A. F. *ove mainoure*.

Maintain, to keep in a fixed state,
support. (F. — L.) M. E. *maintenen.* — F.
maintenir. — L. *manū tenēre*, to hold in
the hand; or more likely (in late L.) to
hold by the hand, to abet. — L. *manū*,
abl. of *manus*, hand; *tenēre*, to hold; see
Manual and **Tenable**.

Maize, Indian corn. (Span. — W.
Indian.) Span. *maiz.* — W. Indian *mahiz*,
mahis, in the old Carib dialect of the isle
of Hayti.

Majesty. (F. — L.) M. E. *magestee.*
— O. F. *majestet* (F. *majesté*). — L. *maies-
tātem*, acc. of *maiestās*, dignity, honour.
Here *mā-ies-* is related by gradation to
mā-ior, comparative of *mag-nus*, great.
See **Magnitude**. Brugm. ii. § 135.

major, a title of rank. (L.) L. *māior*,
greater; comparative of *magnus*, great.
Der. *major-domo*, imitated from Span.
mayor-domo, a house-steward.

Make. (E.) M. E. *maken.* A. S. *ma-*

cian, pt. t. *macode*, to make. + Du. *maken*;
G. *machen*. Allied to **Match** (1), q. v.

Mal-, *prefix*, bad. (F. — L.) F. *mal.* —
L. *malus*, bad; see **Malice**.

Malachite, a green stone. (Gk.)
Named from its colour, which resembles
that of mallow-leaves. Formed with
suffix *-ītēs* (Gk. *-ιτης*) from μαλάχ-η, a
mallow. See **Mallow**.

Malady. (F. — L.) F. *maladie.* — F.
malade, sick; oldest spelling *malabde.*
Cf. O. Prov. *malaptes, malaudes*, sick. — L.
male habitus, out of condition (hence sick,
ill); cf. *male habens*, sick, Matt. iv. 24
(Vulgate). — L. *male*, badly, from *malus*,
bad; *habitus*, pp. of *habēre*, to have;
see **Habit**. ¶ So Schwan. Not from
male aptus (Diez); this would mean
'foolish.'

malapert, saucy. (F. — L.) O. F.
mal apert. — O. F. *mal*, ill; *apert, aspert*,
open, also expert. ready, skilful. The sense
is 'badly expert,' i. e. mischievous. — L.
male, badly; *expertus*, skilful, confused
with *apertus*, pp. of *aperire*, to open;
see **Expert** and **Aperient**.

malaria, noisome exhalation. (Ital. —
L. *and* Gk.) Ital. *mal'aria*, for *mala aria*,
bad air. — L. *mala*, fem. of *malus*, bad;
and Ital. *aria*, air, which represents Late
L. **āria*, for *āeria*, fem. of *āerius*, adj.
from *āēr*, air. See **Air**.

Male. (F. — L.) O. F. *masle* (later
mâle); F. *mâle.* — L. *masculus*, male.
See **Masculine**.

Malediction, a curse. (F. — L.) M. F.
malediction. — L. acc. *maledictiōnem*, a
curse. — L. *maledictus*, pp. of *maledīcere*,
to speak evil of. — L. *male*, adv., evilly;
dīcere, to speak. So also *male-factor*, an
ill-doer, from *factor*, a doer; from *facere*,
to do. So also *malevolent*, lit. wishing
ill; from *uolent-*, stem of *uolens*, pres. pt.
of *uelle*, to will, to wish.

Malice, ill will. (F. — L.) M.E. *malice.*
F. *malice.* — L. *malitia*, badness. — L. *malus*, bad.

malign, unfavourable. (F. — L.) O.F.
maling, fem. *maligne* (F. *malin*). — L. *ma-
lignus*, ill-disposed, for **mali-genus*, ill-
born (like *benignus* for **beni-genus*). —
L. *mali-*, for *malus*, bad; *gen-*, base of
gignere, to produce; see **Genus**.

malinger, to feign sickness. (F. — L.
and G.) From F. *malingre*, adj., diseased,
formerly ugly, loathsome (Cot.). — F. *mal*,
badly; O. F. *haingre, heingre*, thin, ema-

ciated. – L. *male*, adv., badly; G. *hager*, thin, lean (Körting).

malison, a curse. (F. – L.) A. F. *maleison*; O. F. *malison*, popular form of *malediction*; see **Malediction** above. (So also *benison* for *benediction*.)

Malkin, a kitchen-wench. (F. – O.H.G.) *Malkin* is for *Mald-kin*, the dimin. of *Mald*, *Mold*, or *Maud*, i. e. *Matilda*. See **Grimalkin**. ¶ Not the dimin. of *Mary*; cf. 'Malkyne, or Mawt, Molt, Mawde, *Matildis*, *Matilda*;' Prompt. Parv.

Mall (1), a large wooden hammer. (F. – L.) M. E. *malle*. – O. F. *mal*, *mail*, F. *mail*, 'a mall'; Cot. – L. *malleum*, acc. of *malleus*, a hammer.

mall (2), the name of a public walk. (F. – Ital. – G. *and* L.) In *Pall Mall*, and the *Mall* in St. James's Park. Named from E. *pall-mall*; M. F. *pale-maille*, because the game so called was played there; this game of *pall-mall* was like the modern *croquet*, which is imitated from it. – M. Ital. *palamaglio*, 'a stick with a mallet at one end,' for playing the game of pall-mall; Florio. Also spelt *pallamaglio*; lit. 'mallet-ball.' – Ital. *palla*, a ball; *maglio*, a mall. A hybrid word. – O. H. G. *palla*, M. H. G. *balle*, G. *ball*, a ball; L. *malleum*, acc. of *malleus*, a hammer. See **Ball**.

malleable. (F. – L.) M. F. *malleable*, 'malleable, hammerable, pliant to the hammer;' Cot. From obs. L. **malleāre*, to hammer, of which the pp. *malleātus* occurs. – L. *malleus*, a hammer.

mallet, a small mall. (F. – L.) M. E. *maillet*. – F. *maillet*, 'a mallet'; Cot. Dimin. of F. *mail*; see **Mall** (1) above.

Mallard, a wild drake. (F. – L.) M. E. *malard*. – O. F. *malard*; formed, with suffix *-ard* (of G. origin, from G. *hart*), from O. F. *male*, male. See **Male**. The suffix *-ard* was particularly applied to males, so that the idea of 'male' appears twice.

Malleable, Mallet; see Mall.

Mallecho, malefaction, mischief. (Span. – L.) Hamlet, iii. 2. 147. – Span. *malhecho*, 'misdone; an euill deed;' Minsheu. – Span. *mal*, ill; *hecho*, done, pp. of *hacer*, to do. – L. *male*, ill; *factus*, pp. of *facere*, to do. See **Fact**.

Mallow, a plant. (L.) M. E. *malwe*. – A. S. *malwe*; borrowed from L. *malua*,

a mallow. **+** Gk. μαλάχη (=*μαλϜάχη), a mallow; named from its emollient properties; cf. Gk. μαλάσσειν, to make soft, μαλακός, soft, mild. Cf. **Malachite**.

Malmsey, a strong sweet wine. (F. – Gk.) A corruption of M. E. *malvesie*, malmsey. – A. F. *malvesy* (Ducange); F. *malvoisie*, 'malmesie'; Cot. From *Malvasia*, now called *Napoli di Malvasia* or *Monemvasia* (μον-εμβασία), a town on the E. coast of Lacedæmonia in Greece.

Malt, grain steeped in water. (E.) M. E. and O. Merc. *malt*. A.S. *mealt*, malt. – Teut. **malt-*, 2nd grade of **meltan-*, to melt, hence to steep, soften. **+** Du. *mout*; Icel. Dan. Swed. *malt*; O.H.G. *malz*, malt, also soft, allied to Skt. *mṛdu-*, L. *mollis*, soft. See **Melt**.

Maltreat. (F. – L.) F. *maltraiter*, to treat ill. – L. *male*, ill; *tractāre*, to handle, treat; see **Treat**.

malversation. (F. – L.) F. *malversation*, 'misdemeanor;' Cot. (Hence fraudulent behaviour.) – F. *malverser*, to behave ill. – L. *male*, ill; *uersārī*, to be engaged in, from *uersāre*, frequent. form of *uertere*, to turn; see **Verse**.

Mamaluke, Mameluke, an Egyptian light horse-soldier. (F. – Arab.) M. F. *Mamaluc*; Cot. – Arab. *mamlūk*, a purchased slave or captive, lit. 'possessed.' – Arab. root *malaka*, he possessed.

Mamma. (E.) Also *mama*; for *ma ma*, a mere repetition of *ma*, an infantine syllable. Many other languages have something like it; cf. F. *maman*, Span. Du. and G. *mama*, Ital. and L. *mamma*, a child's word for mother.

Mammalia, the class of animals that suckle their young. (L.) From L. *mammālis* (neut. pl. *mammālia*), belonging to the breasts. – L. *mamma*, the breast. Brugm. i. § 587 (3).

mammillary, pertaining to the breasts. (L.) From L. *mammillāris*, adj.; formed from L. *mamma*, the breast.

Mammon. – Gk. – Syriac.) L. *mammōna*. – Gk. μαμωνâς, Matt. vi. 24. – Syr. *mamōnā*, which occurs in Chaldee Targums, and in the Syriac version of St. Matthew, and means 'riches.' Cf. Heb. *matmōn*, a hidden treasure, from *tāman*, to hide.

Mammoth. (Russ. – Tatar.) Russ. *mamant'*, a mammoth, species of elephant. – Siberian *mammont*. From Tatar *mamma*, the earth; because the Siberian peasants thought the animal burrowed in the earth like the mole, as they could not otherwise account for the finding of the remains of these animals.

Man. (E.) M. E. *man.* A. S. *mann.* +Du. *man,* Icel. *mann-, maðr,* Swed. *man,* Dan. *mand,* Goth. *manna,* G. *mann* ; allied to Skt. *manu-,* a man.

manikin, manakin, a dwarf, small man. (F. – Du.) M. F. *manequin,* 'a puppet.' – M. Du. *manneken* (Hexham) ; double dimin. of Du. *man,* a man.

mankind, the race of men. (E.) A. S. *mancynn,* mankind. – A. S. *man,* man ; *cynn,* kind, race ; see **Kin.**

Manacle, a handcuff. (F. – L.) M. E. *manacle,* also *manycle.* – F. *manicle.* – L. *manicula,* dimin. of *manica,* a long sleeve, gauntlet, handcuff. – L. *manus,* the hand. See **Manual.**

manage, government of a horse, control, administration. (F. – Ital. – L.) Orig. a sb., but now superseded by *management.* See Rich. II. iii. 3. 179. – M.F. *manege,* 'the manage, or managing of a horse ;' Cot. – Ital. *maneggio,* 'a managing, a handling ;' Florio. – Ital. *mano,* the hand. – L. *manus,* the hand. Der. *manage,* vb.

Manatee, a sea-cow. (Span. – W. Indian.) Span. *manati,* a sea-cow. From its name in the language of Hayti.

Manchineel, a tree. (F. – Span. – L.) So called from its apple-like fruit. – F. *mancenille,* the fruit of the manchineel tree. – Span. *manzanilla,* the same ; also *manzanillo,* a little apple-tree, the manchineel tree ; dimin. of Span. *manzana,* an apple ; O. Span. *mazana* (Diez). – L. *Matiāna,* fem. of *Matiānus,* adj., the epithet of a kind of apple ; lit. ' Matian.' – L. *Matius,* the name of a Roman gens.

Manciple, a purveyor, esp. for a college. (F. – L.) M. E. *manciple.* – O. F. *mancipe, manciple,* a slave, servant ; cf. M. Ital. *mancipio,* a slave, farmer, mancipale. – L. *mancipium,* a slave ; orig. ' possession.' – L. *mancip-,* for *manceps,* a taker in hand. – L. *man-us,* hand ; *cap-ere,* to take.

Mandarin, a Chinese governor of a province. (Port. – Malay. – Skt.) Not a Chinese, but Skt. word (through the Portuguese). – Port. *mandarim,* a mandarin. – Malay (and Hindu) *mantrī,* a counsellor, minister of state. – Skt. *mantrin-,* a counsellor ; *mahāmantrin-,* the prime minister. – Skt. *mantra-,* advice, counsel. – Skt. *man,* to think.

Mandate, a command. (F. – L.) M.F. *mandat.* – L. *mandātum,* a charge. – L. *mandātus,* pp. of *mandāre,* to enjoin ; lit. to put into one's hand. – L. *man-us,* hand ; *dare,* to give ; see **Manual** and **Date.** Brugm. i. § 589 (2, b).

Mandible, a jaw. (L.) L. *mandibula,* jaw. – L. *mandere,* to chew.

Mandilion, a soldier's cloak. (Ital. – Span. – Arab. – L.) See Nares. Ital. *mandiglione,* 'a mandillion, souldier's iacket ;' Florio. – Span. *mandil,* a coarse apron. – Arab. *mandīl,* a table-cloth, towel, mantle. – L. *mantīle,* a napkin.

Mandolin, a guitar. (F. – Ital. – Gk.) F. *mandoline.* – Ital. *mandolino,* dimin. of *mandola, mandora,* a kind of guitar. Variants of Ital. *pandora.* See further under **Banjo.**

Mandrake, a narcotic plant. (F. – L. – Gk.) M. E. *mandrake, mandrage ;* fuller form *mandragores ;* cf. *mandragora,* Othello, iii. 3. – O. F. *mandragore* (Ital. and Span. *mandragora*). – L. *mandragoras.* – Gk. μανδραγόρας, the mandrake.

Mandrel, the revolving axis to which turners fix their work in a lathe. (F. – Gk. ?) From F. *mandrin,* a punch, a mandrel. Perhaps from Gk. μάνδρα, an enclosed space, sheepfold, also used to mean ' the bed in which the stone of a ring is set,' much like E. *mandrel.* See **Madrigal.** But cf. Oscan *mamphur,* part of a lathe ; Brugm. i. §§ 571, 757.

Mane. (E.) A. S. *manu* ; cf. Icel. *mön* (gen. *man-ar*), a mane ; Swed. and Dan. *man.* +Du. *maan,* M. Du. *mane ;* G. *mähne,* O. H. G. *mana.* Cf. W. *myngen,* mane, from *mwn,* neck ; Irish *muince,* collar, from *muin,* neck ; Skt. *manyā,* the tendon forming the nape of the neck ; L. *monīle,* neck-lace. Orig. sense ' neck ' ; hence ' hair on the neck.'

Manege, the same as **Manage.**

Manganese, a metal. (F. – Ital. – Gk.) An old term, newly applied. ' Manganese, so called from its likeness in colour and weight to the *magnes* or loadstone, is the most universal material used in making glass ;' Blount, ed. 1674. – M.F. *manganese* (Cot.). – Ital. *manganese,* ' a stuffe or stone to make glasses with ; also, a kind of minerall stone ;' Florio. A perverted form of *magnesia,* as shewn in the Cent. Dict. ; cf. *mangnet* for *magnet* in Palsgrave ; see **Magnet.**

Mange, scab or itch in dogs. (F. – L.)

Made out of adj. *mangy*, an older word. —
F. *mangé*, eaten, fed on; pp. of *manger*,
to eat. — L. *mandūcāre*, to eat. — L. *man-
dūcus*, a glutton. — L. *mandere*, to chew.
Cf. M. F. *mangeson*, an itch.

manger, a feeding-trough. (F. — L.)
M. E. *maungeur*, Cath. Angl. — O. F.
mangeure; F. *mangeoire.* — F. *manger*, to
eat (above).

Mangel-wurzel, (properly) a kind
of beet. (G.) Corrupted from G. *man-
gold-wurzel*, lit. ' beet-root.' — G. *mangold*
(M. H. G. *mangolt*), beet, derived by
Schade from the personal name *Manegold*;
wurzel, root, allied to E. **Wort** (1).

Mangle (1), to mutilate. (Perhaps
F. — G.) In Sir T. More. Works, p. 538.
We find Anglo-F. *mangler*, to mangle
(Godefroy); and *mahangler*, to maim, in
Langtoft's Chron. i. 254. Frequent. form
of O. F. *mahaigner*, to maim. — O. F.
mahaing, a maim, hurt. See **Maim.**

Mangle (2), a roller for smoothing
linen; to smooth linen. (Du. — Late L. —
Gk.) Borrowed from Du. *mangelen*, to
mangle, roll with a rolling-pin; *mangel-
stok*, a rolling-pin, cylinder for smoothing
linen. The corresponding Ital. word is
mangano, 'a kind of presse to presse
buckrom;' Florio. Both Du. and Ital.
words are from Late L. *manganum, mangona*, a military instrument for throwing
stones, worked with an axis and winch.
Indeed, the Ital. *mangano* also means a
mangonel. — Gk. μάγγανον, a machine for
defending forts, also the axis of a pulley.

mangonel, a war-engine. (F. — Late
L. — Gk.) O. F. *mangonel* (later *man-
gonneau*), a mangonel. — Late L. *man-
gonellus*, dimin. of *mangona* (above).

Mango, a fruit. (Port. — Malay. —
Tamil.) Port. *manga.* — Malay *manggā*,
formerly *mangkā*, the mango-fruit. The
Malay word is of Tamil origin. — Tamil
mānkāy, i. e. ' *mān*-fruit,' the tree being
māmarum, i. e. *mān*-tree' (Yule).

Mangonel; see **Mangle** (2).

Mangosteen, a fruit. (Malay.) Formerly *mangostan.* — Malay *manggustan*
(Scott); *manggīsta* (Marsden).

Mangrove. (Hybrid; Malay *and* E.)
' A sort of trees called *mangroves*;' Eng.
Garner, vii. 371; A. D. 1689. Meant, as I
suppose, for *mang-groves*, from the peculiar growth in groves or thickets. — Malay
manggi-manggi, the name for the tree
(Crawfurd).

Mania, frenzy. (L. — Gk.) L. *mania*.
— Gk. μανία, frenzy, orig. mental excite-
ment; cf. μένος, mind. **Der.** *mania-c*,
F. *maniaque*.

Manifest, apparent. (F. — L.) F.
manifeste. — L. *manifestus*, evident. The
lit. sense is doubtful. — L. *mani-*, for
manus, hand; *-festus*, apparently the same
as in *in-festus*, hostile. It has been doubtfully connected with *-fendere*, to strike, as
in *of-fendere*.

manifesto, a written declaration.
(Ital. — L.) Ital. *manifesto*, sb. — Ital.
manifesto, adj., manifest: — L. *manifestus*
(above).

Manifold; see **Many.**

Manikin; see **Man.**

Manioc, the cassava-plant. (Brazil.)
Brazil. *manioc*; whence Port. *mandioca*.

Maniple, a handful, small band of
men, priest's scarf. (L.) L. *manipulus*, a
handful, a wisp of straw used as an ensign,
a band of men round such an ensign. —
L. *mani-*, for *manus*, hand; *-pulus*, lit.
filling, from the weak grade (*pul*) of the
root **plē*, to fill; cf. L. *plē-nus*, full. Cf.
L. *disci-pulus*, a disciple.

manipulate, to handle. (L.) A
coined word, and ill coined. Cf. L.
manipulātim, adv., by troops; but it was
rather made directly out of the sb. *manipulus* (above).

Manito, a spirit, fetish. (Algonkin.)
Algonkin *manito, manitu*, a spirit, demon.
(Cuoq.)

Mankind; see **Man.**

Manna. (L. — Gk. — Heb.) L. *manna*.
— Gk. μάννα. — Heb. *mān*, manna. β.
Hardly from Heb. *mān hu*, what is this?
Exod. xvi. 15; but from *mān*, (it is) a
gift; cf. Arab. *mann*, favour, also manna.

Manner, way. (F. — L.) M.E. *manere*.
— A. F. *manere*, M. F. *maniere*, manner,
habit (Cot.); Late L. *manēria.* — L.
manus, the hand.

manœuvre. (F. — L.) F. *manœuvre*,
properly, handiwork. — Late L. *manuopera*,
also *manopera*, a working with the hand.
— L. *manū*, abl. of *manus*, hand; *opera*,
work; see **Operate.**

Manor, (formerly) a residence for a
nobleman. (F. — L.) O. F. *manoir*, a
mansion. — O. F. *manoir, maneir*, to dwell.
— L. *manēre*; see **Mansion.**

manse, a clergyman's house, in Scotland. (L.) Late L. *mansa*, a farm, dwelling. — L. *mansus*, pp. of *manēre* (below).

mansion. (F.—L.) O. F. *mansion*, a dwelling-place.—L. *mansiōnem*, acc. of *mansio*, an abiding, abode.—L. *mansus*, pp. of *manēre*, to remain, dwell. + Gk. μένειν, to stay, remain. (√MEN.)

Mantel, a shelf over a fire-place. (F.—L.) The same word as *mantle* below; in old fire-places, it projects like a hood, to catch the smoke. Der. *mantel-shelf*, *mantel-piece*.

mantilla, a long head-dress. (Span. —L.) Span. *mantilla*; dimin. of *manto*, a cloak, veil (below).

mantle, a cloak, covering. (F.—L.) M. E. *mantel*.—O. F. *mantel*, later *manteau*, 'a cloke, also the mantle-tree of a chimney;' Cot.—L. *mantellum*, a napkin, also a cloak; cf. L. *mantīle*, a towel. We also find Late L. *mantum*, a short cloak, whence Ital. and Span. *manto*, F. *mante*, a mantle. Der. *mantle*, vb., to form a covering upon, to gather a scum on a surface. Brugm. i. §§ 134 (1), 483 (7).

Mantua, a lady's gown. (Ital.) '*Mantoe* or *Mantua gown*', a loose upper garment,' &c.; Phillips (1706). *Manto* is from Ital. *manto*, a mantle (see **mantle**); but *Mantua gown* must refer to *Mantua* in Italy, though this connexion arose from mere confusion. Der. *mantua-maker*.

Manual, done by the hand. (F.—L.) Formerly *manuel*. — L. *manuālis*, adj., from *manus*, the hand; (√ME, to measure; Brugm. ii. § 106.)

manufacture. (F.—L.) F. *manufacture*, M. F. *manifacture*, lit. a making by the hand.—L. *manū*, abl. of *manus*, hand; *factūra*, a making, from *facere*, to make.

manumit, to release a slave. (L.) L. *manumittere* (pp. *manumissus*), to release, lit. to send away from one's hand.—L. *manū*, abl. of *manus*, hand; *mittere*, to send; see **Mission.** Der. *manumission*, from the pp.

manure, vb. (F. — L.) Formerly simply ' to till,' or to work with the hand; Othello, i. 3. 328. A contracted form of *manœuvre*; which see.

manuscript, written by the hand. (L.) Properly an adj., but also as a sb.— Late L. *manuscriptum*, a thing written by the hand.—L. *manū*, abl. of *manus*, hand; *scriptum*, neut. of pp. of *scrībere*, to write; see **Scribe.**

Many. (E.) M. E. *many*, *moni*. A.S. *manig*, *monig*, many; see Sweet, N. E. Gr.

§ 1608. + Du. *menig*; Dan. *mange*, Swed. *månge*, (perhaps) Icel. *margr* (Noreen, 359), Goth. *manags*, G. *manch*, O. H. G. *manac*. Teut. type **managoz*. Allied to Irish *minic*, Gael. *minig*, W. *mynych*, frequent, Russ. *mnogie*, pl. many. Der. *mani-fold*; see **Fold.**

Map. (F.—L.) The oldest maps represented the world, and were called *mappemounde*. This is an O. F. form of L. *mappa mundī*, map of the world. L. *mappa* meant a napkin, hence a painted cloth. See **Mop.** Der. *apron*, *napery*, *napkin*.

Maple, a tree. (E.) M. E. *maple*, *mapul*. A.S. *mæpel-*, *mapul-*; whence *mapul-trēo*, *mapulder*, a maple-tree.

Mar, to injure. (E.) M. E. *merren*. O. Merc. *-merran*, in comp. *āmerran*, to hinder; A.S. *āmyrran*, to obstruct, waste, hinder; cf. *gemearr*, an impediment. + M. Du. *merren*, Du. *marren*, to retard; O. H. G. *marrjan*, to hinder, vex; Goth. *marzjan*, to cause to stumble. Teut. base **marz-*. Brugm. i. § 903 b.

marline, a small cord used for binding ropes. (Du.) Du. *marlijn*, also *marling*, a marline.—Du. *marren*, to bind, tie; and *lijn*, *-ling*, from F. *ligne*, a line. See **Moor** (2); and **Line.** Der. *marline-spike*.

Marabou, Marabout, a kind of African stork; also, its downy feathers. (F.—Port.—Span.—Arab.) F. *marabout*. — Port. *marabuto*. — Span. *morabito*, a Mahommedan sage. — Arab. *murābit*, quiet, still; a hermit, sage; a religious sage among the Berbers (whence the bird's name came). Cf. **Maravedi.**

Maranatha, our Lord cometh. (Syriac.) Syriac *māran athā*, our Lord cometh; cf. Arab. *mār*, lord (from Syriac).

Maraschino, a cordial. (Ital.—L.) Ital. *maraschino*.— Ital. *marasca,amarasca*, a black and sour cherry.—L. *amārus*, bitter.

Maraud, to wander in quest of plunder. (F.) M. F. *marauder*, 'to play the rogue, beg;' Cot.—F. *maraud*, a rogue, vagabond. Etym. disputed. Bugge connects it with F. *mal*, evil; as if for **malaud* (Late L. **malaldus*).

Maravedi, a very small coin. (Span. —Arab.) Span. *maravedi*, the smallest Spanish coin; orig. a gold coin first struck during the dynasty of the *Almoravides* at Cordova, A. D. 1094–1144. Cf. Port. *maravedim*, *marabitino*, a maravedi.

— Arab. *Murābitīn*, the Arab. name of the above-mentioned dynasty; pl. of *murābit*; see **Marabou**.

Marble. (F. – L.) M. E. *marbel*; also *marbre*. – O. F. *marbre*. – L. *marmorem*, acc. of *marmor*, marble, considered as a masc. sb.; but it is commonly neuter. + Gk. μάρμαρος, explained as a glistening white stone, as if from μαρμαίρειν, to sparkle; cf. μαῖρα, dog-star, lit. ʿsparkler.ʾ See **Marmoset**.

Marcasite, a kind of iron pyrites. (F. – Span. – Pers.) F. *marcassite*. – Span. *marquesita*. – Pers. *marqashīshā* (Devic, Vüllers).

Marcescent, withering. (L.) L. *marcescent*-, stem. of pres. pt. of *marcescere*, inceptive form of *marcēre*, to wither, lit. to grow soft. Brugm. i. § 413 (8).

March (1), a border, frontier. (E.) M. E. *marche*. A. S. *mearc* (gen. dat. acc. *mearce*), a mark, boundary. Cf. A. F. *marche*. See **Mark** (2).

March (2), to walk with regular steps. (F. – L.? or G.?) F. *marcher*, to march. Of disputed origin; perhaps from a Late L. **marcare*, to beat (hence to tramp), from *marcus*, a hammer (Scheler).

March (3), the name of a month. (F. – L.) A. F. *Marz* (pron. marts). – L. *Martius*, the month dedicated to *Mars*.

Marchioness. (Low L. – G.) The proper F. form is *marquise*; the E. *marchioness* answers to Low L. *marchiōnissa*, formed with fem. suffix *-issa* (Gk. -ισσα) from Low L. *marchiōnem*, acc. of *marchio*, a prefect of the marches. – Low L. *marcha*, a boundary. – O.H.G. *marcha*, a boundary. See **Mark** (2).

Marchpane, a sweet cake, made with almonds and sugar. (F. – Ital.) O. F. *marcepain*; now *massepain*. – Ital. *marciapane, marzapane*, a marchpane; Florio. Origin of *marcia* unexplained, but prob. from a proper name (such as L. *Martia*): *pane* is from Lat. acc. *pānem*, bread.

Mare. (E.) M. E. *mere*. A. S. *mere*, fem. form of *mearh*, a horse.+Icel. *merr*, fem. of *marr*, a steed; Dan. *mær*, Swed. *märr*, E. Fries. *märe*, Du. *merrie*; G. *mähre*, O. H. G. *meriha*, fem. of O. H. G. *marah*, a battle-horse. Cf. Irish and Gael. *marc*, W. and Corn. *march*, a horse, a stallion. Idg. masc. type **markos*, a horse. Cf. **Marshal.**

Margin. (L.) L. *margin*-, stem of

margo, a border, brink; cognate with **Mark** (2).

Margrave, a lord of the marches. (Du.) Du. *markgraaf*, a margrave. – Du. *mark*, a boundary, march; *graaf*, a count. So also G. *markgraf*. (That the word is Du. appears from the fem. form *margravine*, which answers to Du. *markgravin*, not to G. *markgräfin*.)

Marigold, a plant. (Heb. *and* E.) Compounded of *Mary* (from the Virgin Mary) and *gold* (from its colour).

Marine. (F. – L.) F. *marin*. – L. *marīnus*, belonging to the sea. – L. *mare*, sea; cognate with **Mere** (1). **Der.** *marin-er*.

Marish, a marsh. (F. – L.) M. E. *maris, marais*. – A. F. *mareis*. – Late L. **marensis*, adj. from L. *mare*, lake, sea. Prob. confused with Late L. *mariscus*, from Low G. *marsch*, a marsh. See **Marsh.**

Marital, belonging to a husband. (F. – L.) F. *marital*. – L. *marītālīs*, adj. formed from *marītus*, a husband. This is a masc. sb. made to accompany L. *marīta*, a woman provided with a husband. – L. *mari*-, for *mās*, a man, husband; see **Masculine.**

Maritime, pertaining to the sea. (F. – L.) F. *maritime*. – L. *maritimus*, formed with suffix *-timus* from *mari*-, for *mare*, sea.

Marjoram, a plant. (F. – L. – Gk.) M. E. *majoran* (without *r*). – O. F. *majorane* (Godefroy); F. *marjolaine*. Cf. Ital. *majorana*, Span. *mayorana*, Port. *maiorana*, marjoram, Late L. *majorāna, majoraca*; variously corrupted from L. *amāracus*. – Gk. ἀμάρακος, marjoram.

Mark (1), a stroke, sign. (E.) M. E. *merke*. A. S. *mearc*, fem., mark, sign.+ Du. *merk*, Icel. *mark*, Swed. *märke*, Dan. *mærke*, G. *marke*, M. H. G. *marc*, a mark. Cf. also Lith. *margas*, marked, variegated. Perhaps related to **Mark** (2), which seems to be an older word.

Mark (2), a march, limit, boundary. (E.) A. S. *mearc*, fem.+O. Sax. *marka*; Du.*mark*; G. *mark*, fem., O.H.G.*marcha*; Goth. *marka*, confine, coast. So also Icel. *mörk*, f., a forest (orig. a boundary). Teut. type, **markā*, fem. Allied to L. *margo*, a margin, Zend *merezu*, Pers. *marz*, a border; O. Irish *mruig*.

Mark (3), a coin. (E.) M. E. *mark*, A.S. *mearc, marc*, a coin; a weight equal to half a pound; O. Fries. *merk.*+Du. *mark*; G. *mark*, a weight of silver, a coin; Icel. *mörk*. **β**. Orig. a particular weight. There is nothing to connect it with Mark (1).

Market. (F.—L.) Late A. S. *market*, from Picard F. *market*. [Cf. Du. G. *markt*; F. *marché*, O. Prov. *mercatz*, Ital. *mercato*, a market.]—L. *mercātus*, traffic, also a market (whence G. *markt*, &c.).—L. *mercātus*, pp. of *mercārī*, to trade; see Mercantile. (Pogatscher.)

Marl, a rich earth.   (F.—L.—C.) O. F. *marle* (F. *marne*); Picard *marle.* —Late L. *margila*, dimin. of Late L. *marga*, marl; of Celtic origin (Pliny).

Marline; see Mar.

Marmalade.   (F.—Port.—L.—Gk.) F. *marmelade*, Cot. — Port. *marmelada*, orig. a conserve of quinces.—Port. *marmelo*, a quince.—L. *melimēlum*, lit. honey-apple; also a quince.—Gk. μελίμηλον, a sweet apple, apple grafted on a quince.— Gk. μέλι, honey; μῆλον, an apple; see Melon.

Marmoset, a small American monkey. (F.—L.) Much older than the discovery of America; M. E. *marmosette*, a kind of ape (Maundeville, p. 210).—M. F. *marmoset*, F. *marmouset*, 'the cock of a cistern or fountain, any antick image from whose teats water trilleth, any puppet or antick;' Cot. Thus it meant a grotesque creature, orig. a grotesque ornament on a fountain. Formed, by a Parisian change of *r* to *s*, as in *chaise* for *chaire* (a chair), from Late L. *marmorētum*, a thing made in marble, applied to fountains. [Thus the *rue des marmousets* in Paris was called in Late Latin *vīcus marmorētōrum*; Littré.]—L. *marmor*, marble; see Marble. ¶ This seems to be correct; at the same time, the transference in sense from 'image' to 'ape' was certainly helped on by confusion with F. *marmot*, 'a marmoset, or little monkey;' which is a different word from E. *marmot* (see below).

Marmot, a mountain-rat. (F.—Ital. —L.) F. *marmotte.*—Ital. *marmotta*, an ape, substituted for *marmotana*, 'the mountain-rat, a marmotan' (Torriano), a marmot. From the Romansch (Grisons) name *murmont*; O. H. G. *murmuntī*, *muremunto*, a marmot.—L. *mūr-*, stem of *mūs*, mouse; and *mont-*, stem of *mons*, mountain. Thus the sense is 'mountain-mouse.' (See Diez.)

Maroon (1), brownish crimson. (F.) F. *marron*, a chestnut (hence, chestnut-colour. Cf. Ital. *marrone*, M. Ital. *marone*, a chestnut (of unknown origin).

Maroon (2), to put ashore on a desolate island. (F.—Span.) From F. *marron*, adj., fugitive, applied to a fugitive slave who takes refuge in woods. [Hence E. *maroon*, to treat as a fugitive, cause to be fugitive.] A clipped form of Span. *cimarron*, wild, unruly; hence, savage. Of unknown origin. ¶ *Negro cimarron* or *cimarron* was an everyday phrase for a fugitive slave hidden in the mountains, in Cuba, about A. D. 1846.

Marque, letters of. (F.—G.) A *letter of marque* was a permission by a ruler to make reprisals on the country of another ruler; it had particular reference to passing beyond the *march* or limit of one's own country. — O. F. *marque*, a boundary.—M. H. G. *marke*, a boundary; see Mark (2) above. See *marcha* (1) in Ducange.

marquee, a large tent. (F.—Low L.—G.) For *marquees*; the *s* being dropped because it was thought to be a plural form. An E. spelling of F. *marquise*, a large tent; orig. a tent for a marchioness or lady of rank. — F. *marquise*, a marchioness, fem. of *marquis*, a marquis; see marquis below.

marquess.   (Span.—Low L.—G.) Span. *marques*, a marquis; see marquis.

marquis. (F.—Low L.—G.) M. E. *markis.*—O. F. *markis*, later *marquis*, 'a marquesse, governour of a frontiere town;' Cot.—Low L. *marchensis*, a prefect of the marches.—O. H. G. *marcha*, a march or boundary. See Mark (2). ¶ The true O. F. form was *marchis*; altered to *markis* by the influence of Ital. *marchese*.

Marquetry, inlaid work. (F. — M. H. G.) F. *marqueterie*, inlaid work. —F. *marqueter*, to inlay, diversify, orig. to mark slightly with spots; iterative form of *marquer*, to mark.—F. *marque*, a mark. — M. H. G. *mark*, G. *marke*, a mark. See Mark (1).

Marrow, pith. (E.) M. E. *marow*, *mary*. O. Merc. *merg*, A. S. *mearh* (dat. *mearge*). + Du. *merg*, Icel. *mergr*, Swed. *merg*, Dan. *marv*, G. *mark*, O. H. G. *marag*; also W. *mer*, Corn. *maru*. Further allied to Russ. *mozg'*, Zend *mazga*, marrow; Skt. *majjan*, marrow of bones, pith of trees. Idg. type *mazgho·*; Brugm. i. § 642.

Marry. (F.—L.) M. E. *marien.*—
F. *marier.*—L. *marītāre*, to marry.—L.
marītus, a husband; see **Marital.**

Marsh, a swamp. (E.) M. E. *mersch.*
A. S. *mersc*, a marsh; early form *merisc<*
*mar-isc, lit. mere-ish, i. e. full of meres or
pools.—A. S. *mere* (for *mari), a mere,
lake. See **Mere** (1).

Marshal, master of the horse. (F.—
O. H. G.) Lit. 'horse-servant,' a groom;
it rose to be a title of honour. — M. F.
mareschal (F. *maréchal*), 'a marshall, a
farrier,' Cot. — O. H. G. *marascalh*, lit.
horse-servant, a groom.—O. H. G. *marah*,
a horse; *scalh*, a servant; cf. Goth. *skalks*,
a servant. See **Mare.**

Marsupial. (L. — Gk.) Applied to
animals that carry their young in a sort
of pouch.—L. *marsūpium*, a pouch.—Gk.
μαρσύπιον, a little pouch, dimin. of
μάρσυπος, a bag.

Mart, a shortened form of *market.*
(F.—L.) In Hamlet, i. 1. 74. Prob. influenced by Du. *markt*, market (of Latin
origin). See **Market.**

Martello tower, a watch-tower.
(Ital.—L.; *and* F.—L.) So called because the watchmen gave the alarm by
striking a bell with a hammer; see
Ariosto, *Orlando*, x. 51; xiv. 100. From
Ital. *martello*, a hammer; Late L. *mar-
tellus.* Dimin. of Late L. *martus* = L.
marcus, a hammer. See *martus* in Ducange.

Marten, a kind of weasel. (F.—Low
L.—Teut.) Short for *martern* (16th cent.);
M. E. *martrin* (Lydg.), adj. made of marten's fur; from O. F. *martrin*, the same.
The M. E. sb. was *marter, martre.*—F.
martre—Low L. pl. *martures.* Of Teut.
origin; cf. Du. *marter*, G. *marder*, a
marten; A.S. *mearð*, Icel. *mörðr*, Swed.
mård, Dan. *maar* (for *maard), a marten.

Martial, brave. (F.—L.) F. *martial.*
—L. *Martiālis*, dedicated to *Mars*, god of
war.

Martin, a bird. (F.—L.) F. *martin*, (1)
a proper name, Martin, (2) the same name
applied to various birds and animals. Thus
martin-pêcheur is a kingfisher; *oiseau de
S. Martin* is the ring-tail, and *martinet*
is a martin (Cot.). A nickname, like our
robin, jenny-wren, &c.; so that the bird
is named after *Martin* as a proper name.
From L. *Mart-*, stem of *Mars.*

martinet, a strict disciplinarian. (F.)
So called from a F. officer named *Martinet*

(temp. Louis XIV); dimin. form of
F. *Martin.*

martinmas, martlemas, the feast
of St. Martin; Nov. 11. (F. *and* L.)
Martlemass is a corrupt form of *Martin-
mass*, suggested by *Bartle* for *Bartholomew.*
See **Mass** (2).

martlet (1), a kind of bird, martin.
(F.—L.) Variant of M. E. *martnet*, short
for *martinet.*—F. *martinet*, 'a martlet or
martin,' Cot.; dimin. of F. *Martin.* Cf.
Picard *martinet*, called *martelot* in the
dep. of the Meuse (Corblet).

Martingale, a strap fastened to a
horse's girth to hold his head down. (F.—
Span.—Arab.?) Also applied to a short
spar, in ships, under the bowsprit; but
this is only due to a supposed resemblance
to a horse's martingale.—F. *martingale*,
'a martingale for a horse;' Cot. [Re-
ferred by Littré to the wearing of breeches,
called *chausses à la martingale* (Rabelais); but this is quite another word.]
—Span. *al-martaga*, 'a kinde of headstall
for a horse, trimmed, gilt, and embroidered;'
Minsheu (1623); where *al* is merely the
Arab. def. article. The sb. may be derived
from Arab. *rataka*, in the sense 'to cause
to go with a short step'; see Yule. I find
Arab. *rataka* given by Richardson as a
verbal root, whence *ratak*, going with a
short quick step.

Martinmas, Martlet (1); see
Martin.

Martlet (2), the bird called the swift,
as depicted in heraldry. (F.—L.) An E.
substitution for F. *merlette*, 'a martlet, in
blazon,' Cot. Lit. 'a little blackbird';
dimin. of *merle*, a blackbird.—L. *merula*;
see **Merle.** We find O. F. *merlos*, mart-
lets; Roll of Caerlaverock, p. 7.

Martyr. (L.—Gk.) A. S. *martyr.*—L.
martyr.—Gk. μάρτυρ, μάρτυς, a witness, lit.
one who remembers, records, or declares.
Cf. Skt. *smṛ*, to remember.

Marvel. (F.—L.) M. E. *mervaile.*—
F. *merveille.*—L. *mīrābilia*, neut. pl.,
wonderful things.—L. *mīrābilis*, wonderful.
—L. *mīrārī*, to wonder. See **Miracle.**

Mascle, in heraldry, a perforated
lozenge. (F.—L.) M. E. *mascule, mascle.*
— O. F. *mascle*, erroneous spelling of
macle, a mesh of a net (hence, a lozenge
perforated).—L. *macula*, a mesh; perhaps
confused with O. H. G. *masca*, a mesh.
Doublet, *mail* (1), q. v.

Masculine. (F.—L.) F. *masculin.*—

L. *masculīnus*, extended from *masculus*, male. ━ L. *mas-*, stem of *mās*, a male; with double dimin. suffix *-cu-lus*.

Mash, to beat into a mixed mass. (E.) A *mash* is properly a mixture; and to *mash* was, formerly, to mix, the M. E. form of the verb being *mēshen*, as if from A. S. **mǣscan*, from a sb. **mǣsc.* (The vowel has been shortened.) We find A. S. *mǣx-wyrt* (for **mǣsc-wyrt*), mash-wort, new beer; so that the word is English; but it is commoner in Scandinavian, whence Lowl. Sc. *mask.* Cf. Swed. dial. *mask,* Swed. *mäsk,* brewer's grains, whence *mäska,* to mash; Dan. and North Fries. *mǣsk,* grains, mash, Dan. *mǣske,* to mash, fatten pigs with grains; Norw. *meisk,* sb., *meiska,* vb. ✛ G. *meisch,* a mash, *meischen,* to mash. The sb. form appears to be the original. Cf. also Lithuan. *maisz-yti,* to stir things in a pot, from *misz-ti,* to mix. The form of the Teut. base is **maisk-*, so that it may be connected by gradation with *mix.* See **Mix.**

Mask, Masque, a disguise for the face; masked entertainment. (F. ─ Span. ─ Arab.) The sense of 'entertainment' is the true one; the sense of 'disguise' is secondary. 'A jolly company in maner of a *maske*;' F. Q. iii. 12. 5. 'Some haue I sene daunce in a *maske*;' Sir T. More, Works, p. 1039. More uses *maskers* in the sense of 'visors' (correctly, according to the Spanish use).━F. *masque,* a mask, visor; a clipped form, due to F. vb. *masquer,* really short for **masquerer*; the fuller form comes out in M. F. *masquarizé,* masked, *masquerie, masquerade,* 'a mask or mummery;' Cot.━Span. *mascara,* a masker, a masquerader; also a mask.━Arab. *mask-harat,* a buffoon, jester, man in masquerade, a pleasantry, anything ridiculous.━Arab. root *sakhira,* he ridiculed (Dozy). **Der.** *masquerade,* M. F. *masquerade,* F. *masca-rade,* Span. *mascarada.*

Mason. (F.─G.?) O. F. *masson*; F. *maçon*; Low L. *macio,* a mason; we also find the forms *machio, macho, maco, mactio, mattio, matio.* From Teut. stem **mat-jon-*, i. e. cutter; from a base **mat-*, to cut or hack, whence also E. *mattock.* Cf. O.H.G. *mezzo,* a mason, whence G. *steinmetz,* a stonemason.

Masque; see Mask.
Mass (1), a lump. (F.─L.─Gk.) F. *masse.*━L. *massa.*━Gk. μᾶζα, a barley cake; allied to μάγμα, any kneaded mass.

━Gk. μάσσειν, to knead. **Der.** *mass-ive, mass-y*; also *a-mass.*

Mass (2), the celebration of the Eucharist. (L.) M. E. *messe.* O. Merc. *messe* (Matt. viii. 4); A.S. *mæsse,* (1) the mass, (2) a church-festival. ━ Folk-L. *messa* (Ital. *messa*); Late L. *missa,* (1) dismissal, (2) the mass. Usually said to be from the phr. *ite, missa est* (go, the congregation is dismissed) used at the end of the service; in any case, the derivation is from L. *missus,* pp. of *mittere,* to send away. Cf. Du. *mis,* mass. ¶ For the change of vowel from *i* to *e,* cf. Icel. *messa,* Swed. *messa,* Dan. *messe,* O.H.G. *messa* (as well as *missa*), all in the sense of 'mass'; also O. F. *messe,* Ital. *messa.* And see **Missal.** **Der.** *Candle-mas, Christ-, Hallow-, Lam-, Martin-, Michael-mas,* which see.

Massacre. (F.─O. Low G.?) F. *massacre,* a massacre; *massacrer,* to massacre. Of disputed origin; it may perhaps be referred to Low G. *matsken,* to cut, hew, Du. *matsen,* to maul, kill. Cf. G. *metzelei,* a massacre; from *metzeln,* frequent. of *metzen,* to cut, kill. And see **Mason.**

Mast (1), a pole, to hold the sails of a ship. (E.) M. E. *mast.* A. S. *mæst,* stem of a tree, bough, mast. ✛ Du. *mast,* Swed. and Dan. *mast,* G. *mast.* Probably cognate with L. *mālus* (<**mazdos*), a mast; Brugm. i. § 587.

Mast (2), fruit of beech-trees. (E.) The orig. sense is 'edible fruit,' used for feeding swine. A. S. *mæst,* mast.✛G. *mast,* mast; *mästen,* to fatten. Prob. allied to Skt. *mēda(s),* fat; Brugm. i. § 698.

Master. (F.─L.) M.E. *maister.*━O. F. *maistre.* ━ L. *magistrum,* acc. of *magister,* a master; see **Magistrate.** **Der.** *master-y,* O. F. *maistrie.*

Mastic, Mastich, a kind of gum resin. (F.─L.─Gk.) F. *mastic,* 'mastich, a sweet gum'; Cot.━L. *mastichē.*━Gk. μαστίχη, the gum of the tree σχῖνος, called in Latin *lentiscus.* So called because used for chewing in the East. ━ Gk. μαστ-, base of μάσταξ, mouth, μαστάζειν, to chew; cf. Gk. μασάομαι, I chew.

masticate. (L.─Gk.) From pp. of L. *masticāre,* to chew, quite a late word; properly, to chew mastic. ━ L. *mastichē,* mastic (above). ¶ The true L. word for to chew is *mandere.*

Mastiff. (F.─L.) The A. F. form was *mastin,* as in O. F.; hence F. *mâtin,* a mastiff. The O. F. *mastin* also meant 'a domestic'; see Godefroy. Hence the Late L. *mastīnus*, a mastiff, has been conjectured to stand for *masnātinus, house-dog; as if from Late L. *masnāta*, a household (see Menagerie). The Late L. *mastīnus* seems to have been mistaken for *mastīuus* (Ducange); and confusion set in both with M. E. *masty*, fat, large (adj. formed from *mast* (2)), and with O. F. *mestif*, mongrel, Late L. *mixtivus, from L. *miscēre* (pp. *mixt-us*), to mix. See Mix.

Mastodon, an extinct elephant. (Gk.) Named from the nipple-like projections on its molar teeth. ─ Gk. μαστ-ός, the female breast; ὀδον-, short for ὀδοντ-, stem of ὀδούς, a tooth; see Tooth.

Mat. (L.) M. E. *matte*. A. S. *meatte*. ─ L. *matta* (Late L. *natta*), a mat; whence Du. *mat*, G. *matte*, F. *natte*, &c.

Matador, the slayer of the bull in a bull-fight. (Span. ─ L.) Span. *matador*, lit. slayer. ─ Span. *matar*, to kill. ─ L. *mactāre*, to kill.

Match (1), an equal, a contest, marriage. (E.) M. E. *macche*, *mache*, orig. a comrade. ─ A. S. -*mæcca*, whence *gemæcca*, a comrade, companion, spouse; from the more original form -*maca*, Durh. Rit. 165 (whence M. E. *make*, Ch.), *gemaca*. ✛ Icel. *maki*, Swed. *make*, Dan. *mage*, O. Sax. *gimako*, a mate, comrade. β. All closely related to the adj. seen in Icel. *makr*, suitable, M. H. G. *gemach*, suitable; and further to A. S. *macian*, to make, or 'fit together.' ¶ *Mate*, as used by sailors, is prob. Dutch; see Mate (1).

Match (2), a prepared rope for firing a cannon. (F. ─ L. ─ Gk.) M. E. *macche*. ─ O. F. *mesche*, *meiche* (F. *mèche*), wick of a candle, match to fire a gun, 'match of a lamp;' Cot. ─ Late L. *myxa* (= Gk. μύξα); Late L. *myxus*, the nozzle of a lamp, through which the wick protrudes; also, a wick. ─ Gk. μύξα, the nozzle of a lamp; older senses being (1) mucus (2) nostril. Allied to Mucus. Der. *match-lock*, the lock of a gun holding a match; hence, the gun itself.

Mate (1), a companion. (O. Low G.) M. E. *mate*, a fellow (Prompt. Parv.); Low G. *mate*, mate (Lübben); *maat* (Bremen); M. Du. *maet*, 'a mate,' Hexham; Du. *maat*. ✛ O. H. G. *gi-mazzo*, a meat-companion, mess-mate. Cf. Goth. *matjan*, to eat, *mats*, food. See Meat.

Mate (2), to check-mate, confound. (F.

─ Pers. & Arab.) From the game of chess. *Check-mate* means 'the king is dead'; cf. M. F. *eschec et mat*, 'check-mate'; Cot. [Here *et* is not wanted.] Godefroy has '*mat* du roi,' i. e. death of the king. ─ Pers. *shāh māt*, the king is dead, check-mate. ─ Pers. *shāh*, king (see Check); *māt*, he is dead, from Arab. root *māta*, he died. Cf. Heb. *mūth*, to die. ¶ Hence Turk. and Pers. *māt*, astonished, confounded, amazed, receiving check-mate; F. *mat*, 'mated, quelled, subdued,' Cot.; M. E. *mate*, confounded.

Material, substantial. (F. ─ L.) O. F. *materiel*. ─ L. *māteriālis*, adj., formed from *māteria*, matter. See Matter.

Maternal. (F. ─ L.) F. *maternel*. ─ Late L. *māternālis*. ─ L. *māternus*, belonging to a mother. ─ L. *māter*, mother; cognate with Mother.

Mathematic, pertaining to the science of number. (F. ─ L. ─ Gk.) O. F. *mathematique*. ─ L. *mathēmaticus*. ─ Gk. μαθηματικός, disposed to learn, belonging to the sciences, esp. to mathematics. ─ Gk. μαθηματ-, stem of μάθημα, a lesson. ─ Gk. μαθή-σομαι, future of μανθάνειν, to learn.

Matins, Mattins, morning prayers. (F. ─ L.) F. *matins*, a pl. sb. from F. *matin*, morning, orig. an adj. ─ L. *mātūtīnum*, acc. of *mātūtīnus*, adj., belonging to the morning. Cf. Ital. *mattino*, morning. ─ L. *Mātūta*, the goddess of dawn, as if from a masc. *mātūtus, with the sense of 'early,' or 'timely.'

Matrass, a long-necked glass bottle; in chemistry. (F.) F. *matras*; also (in Cot.) *matrac*, *matraz*, *matelas*; Span. *matraz*. Perhaps Arabic; see Devic.

Matricide, murderer of a mother. (F. ─ L.) F. *matricide*, adj., 'mother-killing'; Cot. ─ L. *mātrīcīda*, a matricide. ─ L. *mātri-*, decl. stem of *māter*, mother; *cædere*, to slay; see Mother, Cæsura. ¶ We also use *matricide* to represent L. *mātrīcīdium*, the slaying of a mother.

matriculate, to enrol in a college. (L.) From pp. of Late L. *mātriculāre*, to enrol; a coined word. ─ L. *mātricula*, a register; dimin. of *mātrix* (stem *mātrīc-*), meaning (1) a breeding animal, (2) womb, matrix, (3) a public register, roll, list, lit. parent-stock. See matrix (below).

matrimony. (F. ─ L.) O. F. *matri-monie*. ─ L. *mātrimōnium*, marriage, lit. motherhood. ─ L. *mātri-*, decl. stem of *māter*, mother; with suffix -*mōn-io-*.

matrix, the womb, cavity or mould. (L.) L. *mātrix*, a breeding animal, the womb. – L. *mātri-*, for *māter*, mother.

matron, a married woman. (F. – L.) F. *matrone*. – L *mātrōna*; extended from *mātr-*, stem of *mater*, a mother.

Matter (1), substance. (F. – L.) M. E. *matere, materie*. – O. F. *matere, matiere*, (F. *matière*). – L. *māteria*, stuff, materials, useful for building, &c. Brugm. i. § 407.

matter (2), pus, a fluid in abscesses. (F. – L.) The same word as **matter** (1); see Littré, s. v. *matière*, § 8.

Mattins; see Matins.

Mattock. (E.) A. S. *mattuc*. Cf. W. *matog*, a mattock, hoe; Gael. *madag*, a pickaxe; Russ. *motuika*, Lithuan. *matikkas*, mattock (from Teutonic); see **Mason**.

Mattress. (F. – Arab.) O. F. *mate-ras*; Picard and Walloon *matras*; F. *matelas*. Cf. Span. *al-madraque*, a mattress; where *al* is the Arab. def. art. – Arab. *matrah*, a situation, place, a place where anything is thrown; this word came to mean also anything hastily thrown down, hence, something to lie upon, a bed (Devic). – Arab. root *taraha*, he threw prostrate.

Mature, ripe. (L.) L. *mātūrus*, ripe.

Matutinal, pertaining to the morning. (L.) L. *mātūtīnus*, adj., belonging to the morning. See Matins.

Maudlin, sickly sentimental. (F. – L. – Gk. – Heb.) Orig. 'shedding tears of penitence,' like Mary Magdalen. From M.E. *Maudelein*, the same as *Magdelaine*. – O. F. *Maudeleine, Magdeleine*. – L. *Magdalēnē*. – Gk. Μαγδαληνή, i. e. belonging to Magdala; Luke viii. 2. – Heb. *migdol*, a tower; whence *Magdala* as a proper name.

Maugre, in spite of. (F. – L.) The proper sense is 'ill will,' as in P. Plowman, B. vi. 242. – O. F. *malgre, maugre*, lit. ill will; but also with sense 'in spite of.' – O. F. *mal*, ill; *gre, gret*, a pleasant thing. – L. *malus*, bad; *grātum*, neut. of *grātus*, pleasing.

Maul, to beat grievously. (F. – L.) M. E. *mallen*, to strike with a mall, or mace; from M. E. *malle*, sb., a mall, mace; see **Mall** (1).

Maulstick, a stick used by painters to steady the hand. (G.) G. *malerstock*, lit. 'painter's stick.' – G. *maler*, a painter, from *malen*, to paint; *stock*, a stick. *Malen* was orig. to mark, from G. *mahl*, O. H. G. *māl*, a mark, point of time; see **Meal** (2) and **Stock**.

Maund (1), a basket. (E.) A. S. *mand*, a basket; in MSS. of the 8th century. + Du. *mand*; prov. G. *mand, mande, manne* (whence F. *manne*); E. Fries. *mande*.

Maund (2), a (very variable) weight. (Arab.) Arab. *mann*; Pers. *man*. Cf. Heb. *māneh*, Gk. μνᾶ. See Yule.

Maundy Thursday, the day before Good Friday. (F. – L.; *and* E.) *Maundy* is M. E. *maundee*, a command, used with esp. reference to the text '*Mandatum nouum*,' John xiii. 34. The 'new commandment' is 'that ye love one another'; but in old times it was applied to the particular form of devotion to others exemplified by Christ, when washing His disciples' feet (on the first *Maundy Thursday*). See my note to P. Plowman, B. xvi. 140. This M. E. *maundee* = O. F. *mandé*, that which is commanded; from L. *mandātum*, a mandate, command. ¶ Not connected with *maund*. Cf. O. H. G. *mandāt*, the washing of feet (Otfrid); from L. *mandātum*.

Mausoleum, a magnificent tomb. (L. – Gk.) L. *mausōlēum*, a splendid tomb, orig. the tomb of Mausolus. – Gk. Μαυσω-λεῖον; from Μαύσωλος, Mausōlus, a king of Caria.

Mauve, mallow colour. (F. – L.) F. *mauve*, a mallow. – L. *malua*, mallow. See **Mallow**.

Mavis, the song-thrush. (F. – C. ?) M. E. *mavis*. – F. *mauvis*, a throstle; cf. Span. *malvis*, a thrush. Perhaps Celtic; cf. Bret. *milfid, milvid*, a mavis, also *milchouid* (at Vannes); Corn. *melhues*, O. Corn. *melhuet*, a lark.

Mavourneen, my darling. (Irish.) From Irish *mo*, my; and *mhuirnin*, mutated form of *muirnin*, darling, from *muirn*, affection. (*Mh = v*.)

Maw, stomach. (E.) M. E. *mawe*. A. S. *maga*. + Du. *maag*, Icel. *magi*, Swed. *mage*, Dan. *mave*, G. *magen*.

Mawkish, squeamish. (Scand.; *with* E. suffix.) The older sense is loathsome, lit. 'maggoty.' Formed, with E. suffix *-ish*, from M. E. *mawk, mauk*, a maggot, a contracted form of M. E. *maðek*, a maggot. – Icel. *maðkr*, Dan. *maddik*, a maggot (whence Norw. *makk = E. mawk*). Derived from the form which appears as A. S. *maða*, Du. G. *made*, maggot. See **Moth**.

Maxillar, Maxillary, belonging to the jawbone. (L.) L. *maxillāris*, adj.; from *maxilla*, jaw-bone.

Maxim, a proverb. (F. – L.) F. *maxime.* – L. *maxima,* for *maxima sententiārum,* an opinion of the greatest importance, chief of opinions, hence a maxim (Duc.). Orig. fem. of *maximus,* greatest, superlative of *magnus,* great. **maximum.** (L.) Neut. of *maximus,* greatest (above).

May (1), I am able, I am free to do. (E.) Pres. t. *may,* pt. t. *might*; the infin. (not in use) should take the form *mow.* M. E. *mowen,* infin.; pres. t. *may*; pt. t. *mighte.* A. S. *mugan,* to be able; pres. t. *mæg*; pt. t. *mihte.* (Here *mæg* is the old perfect of a strong verb.)+O. Sax. *mugan,* pres. *mag,* pt. *mahta*; Icel. *mega,* pres. *må,* pt. *måtti*; Du. *mogen,* pres. *mag,* pt. *mogt*; Dan. pres. *maa,* pt. *maatte*; Swed. pres. *må,* pt. *måtte*; G. *mögen,* pres. *mag,* pt. *mochte*; Goth. *magan,* pres. *mag,* pt. *mahta*; Russ. *moche,* to be able, pres. *mogu*; cf. Gk. μηχανή, means.

May (2), the fifth month. (F. – L.) O. F. *Mai.* – L. *Māius,* May.

Mayor. (F. – L.) M. E. *maire.* – F. *maire.* – L. *māior,* nom. greater; see **Major** (above). ¶ *Mayor* is a late spelling, introduced in the middle of the 16th century; it answers to O. F. *maior,* from L. *māiōrem,* acc.; cf. Span. *mayor.*

Mayweed, Anthemis cotula. (E.) Formerly *mathe-weed*; from A. S. *mægþa.*

Maze. (E.) M. E. *mase*; we also find M. E. *masen,* to confuse. The A. S. *masian appears in the comp. pp. *ā-masod.* Cf. Norweg. *masa-st* (where -*st* is reflexive), to lose one's senses and begin to dream, *masa,* to pore over a thing, also to prate, chatter; Icel. *masa,* to prate, chatter; Swed. dial. *masa,* to bask in the sun, to be lazy, lounge about. Cf. E. *in a maze* = in a dreamy perplexity. The orig. sense seems to have been ' to be lost in thought,' dream or pore over a thing, whence the idea of ' perplexity ' for the sb.

Mazer, a large drinking-bowl. (F. – O. H. G.) M. E. *maser.* – A. F. *mazer* (Bozon); O. F. *masere,* a bowl of maplewood, also of metal. – O. H. G. *masar,* mark in wood, also maple.+Icel. *mösurr,* a maple-tree, spotted wood; whence *mösur-bolli,* a mazer-bowl, so called because made of maple-wood; the maplewood was called *mösurr* or ' spot-wood' from its being covered with spots. But the word for spot is only preserved in

other languages, as in M. H. G. *mase,* a spot, and in E. **Measles,** q. v.

Mazurka, a dance. (Pol.) From Pol. *Mazurka,* lit. a woman of Massovia or Mazovia, a province of Poland containing Warsaw. Similarly, *polka* means ' a Polish woman '; and secondly, a dance.

Mazzard, the head. (F. – O. H. G.) From *mazer,* a bowl; see **Mazer.**

Me. (E.) A. S. *mē* (also *mec,* in the accusative only).+Du. *mij*; Icel. *mēr,* dat., *mik,* acc.; Swed. Dan. *mig*; Goth. *mis,* dat., *mik,* acc.; G. *mir,* dat., *mich,* acc. For the stem, cf. Corn. and Bret. *me*; Irish, Gael. W. *mi*; L. *mihi,* dat., *mē,* acc.; Gk. μοί, ἐμοί, dat., μέ, ἐμέ, acc.; Skt. *mah-yam, me,* dat., *mām, mā,* acc.

Mead (1), a drink made from honey. (E.) M. E. *mede.* A. S. *medu, meodu.*+Du. *mede,* Icel. *mjöðr,* Dan. *miöd,* Swed. *mjöd,* G. *meth*; also Irish *mid,* W. *medd,* Lith. *middus,* Russ. *med',* Gk. μέθυ; Skt. *madhu,* sweet, also as sb., honey, sugar. Idg. type **medhu,* Brugm. ii. § 104. Cf. Lith. *medùs,* honey.

Mead (2), a meadow. (E.) So called because ' mown.' M. E. *mede.* A. S. *mǣd,* a mead. [Allied to prov. E. *math,* a mowing, as in *aftermath,* and A. S. *māwan,* to mow; G. *mahd,* a mowing, M. H. G. *māt,* a mowing, a mead.] Cf. M. H. G. *mate,* a meadow, Swiss *matt,* a meadow (as in Zermatt, Andermatt). Also Gk. ἄ-μητος, a harvest, ἀμάειν, to mow. See **Mow** (1).

meadow. (E.) This fuller form is due to the inflected form (dat. *mǣdwe*) of A. S. *mǣd,* a mead.

Meagre, thin. (F. – L.) M. E. *megre.* – F. *maigre.* – L. *macrum,* acc. of *macer,* thin, lean; whence A. S. *mæger,* Icel. *magr,* Dan. Swed. G. *mager,* thin, were perhaps borrowed at an early period (unless cognate). Cf. Gk. μακρός, long.

Meal (1), ground grain. (E.) M. E. *mele.* A. S. *melu, meolo.*+Du. *meel,* Icel. *mjöl,* Dan. *meel,* Swed. *mjöl,* G. *mehl.* Teut. type **melwom,* neut. All from Idg. root MEL, to grind, as in O. Irish *mel-im,* Ch. Slav. *mel-jǫ,* I grind; the 2nd grade is Teut. **mal,* to grind, as in Icel. *mala,* Goth. *malan,* O. H. G. *malan,* to grind, cognate with Lith. *malti,* L. *molere.*

Meal (2), a repast. (E.) M. E. *mele.* A. S. *mǣl,* (1) a time, portion of time, stated time; (hence a common meal at a stated time, not a hastily snatched repast). +Du. *maal,* (1) time, (2) meal; Icel. *māl,* measure, time, meal; Dan. *maal*, Swed. *mål*, measure, meal; Goth. *mēl*, a time; G. *mahl*, a meal, *māl*, time. From Idg. √ME(MĒ); cf. **Mete** and **Moon**. See Prellwitz, s.v. μέδομαι.

Mean (1), to have in the mind, intend. (E.) M. E. *menen*. A. S. *mǣnan*, to intend. + Du. *meenen*, Dan. *mene*, Swed. *mena*, G. *meinen*. Cf. the sb. seen in O. H. G. *meina*, thought, allied to *minni*, memory. See **Mind**.

Mean (2), common. (E.) M. E. *mene*. A. S. *mǣne*, usually *ge-mǣne*, common; O. Fries. *mēne*, common. See **Common**. ¶ The peculiar sense of base, vile, may be due to A. S. *mǣne*, wicked, false, evil; from A. S. *mān*, wickedness. Cf. Icel. *meinn*, mean, hurtful, from *mein*, a hurt; M. H. G. *mein*, false (cf. G. *mein-eid*, perjury).

Mean (3), intermediate. (F.–L.) A.F. *meien* (F. *moyen*).–L. *mediānus*, extended form from *medius*, middle; see **Mid**. **Der.** *mean*, sb., common in pl. *means*.

Mean (4), to lament. (E.) In M. N. D. v. 1. 330 (ed. 1623). A. S. *mǣnan*, to bemoan; see **Moan**. So also, probably, in Merch. Ven. iii. 5. 82.

Meander, a winding course. (L.–Gk.) L. *Mæander*.–Gk. Μαίανδρος, a winding stream; Pliny, v. 29.

Measles, a contagious fever accompanied by small red spots on the skin. (E.) 'Rougeolle, the *meazles*;' Cot. M. E. *maseles* (14th cent.). From A. S. *mǣsle-*, a spot (Toller). Cf. Du. *mazelen*, measles; also called *masel-sucht*, ' measell-sicknesse,' Hexham. The lit. sense is 'small spots'; cf. M. Du. *maesche, masche, maschel*, 'a spot, blot,' Hexham. The orig. word occurs in M. H. G. *mase*, O. H. G. *māsa*, a spot. See **Mazer**. ¶ Wholly unconnected with M. E. *mesel*, a leper, which merely meant orig. ' a wretch,' from O. F. *mesel*, L. *misellus*, from L. *miser*, wretched.

Measure. (F.–L.) M. E. *mesure*.– O. F. *mesure*.–L. *mensūra*, measure.–L. *mensus*, pp. of *mētīrī*, to measure. See Brugm. ii. § 771.

Meat. (E.) M. E. *mete*. A.S. *mete* (for **matiz*).+Icel. *matr*, Dan. *mad*, Swed. *mat*, Goth. *mats*, O. H. G. *maz*, food. Cf. L. *mandere*, to chew.

Mechanic, pertaining to machines. (F.–L.–Gk.) M. E. *mechanike*, in the sense ' mechanic art.'–O. F. *mechanique*,

mechanical.–L. *mēchanica*.–Gk. μηχανική, science of machines.–Gk. μηχανή, a device, machine. See **Machine**.

Medal. (F.–Ital.–L.–Gk.) O. F. *medaille*.–Ital. *medaglia* (Low L. *medālia*, *medalla*, a small coin).–Late L. **metāllea*, adj. fem. – L. *metallum*, metal. See **Metal**.

Meddle. (F.–L.) M. E. *medlen*, simply in the sense ' to mix.' – A. F. *medler*; O. F. *meller, mesler*, to mix (F. *mêler*).–Late L. *misculāre*, to mix; cf. L. *miscellus*, mixed.–L. *miscēre*, to mix. See **Miscellaneous**.

Mediate, adj., acting by or as a means. (L.) From L. *mediātus*, pp. of *mediāre*, to be in the middle (Palladius). – L. *medius*, middle. See **Medium**. **Der.** *mediat-ion, mediat-or*.

Medic, a kind of clover. (L.–Gk.) L. *mēdica*.–Gk. Μηδική, Median grass; fem. of Μηδικός, belonging to *Media*.

Medicine, a remedy. (F.–L.) O. F. *medecine*.–L. *medicīna*.–L. *medicus*, a physician. – L. *medērī*, to heal. Cf. Zend *madh*, to treat medically. **Der.** *medical*, Late L. *medicālis*, from *medicus* (above); *medicate*.

Medieval, relating to the Middle Ages. (L.) Also written *mediæval*. Coined from L. *medi-us*, middle; *æu-um*, age; see **Medium** and **Age**.

Mediocre, middling. (F. – L.) F. *médiocre*.–L. *mediocrem*, acc. of *mediocris*, middling; formed from *medi-us*, middle. See **Medium**.

Meditate. (L.) From pp. of L. *meditārī*, to ponder. Cf. Gk. μέδομαι, I attend. Brugm. i. § 591.

Mediterranean, inland, said of a sea. (L.) L. *mediterrāne-us*, situate in the middle of the land.–L. *medi-us*, middle; *terra*, land; see **Medium** and **Terrace**.

Medium. (L.) L. *medium*, the midst, also a means; neut. of *medius*, middle. Allied to **Mid**.

Medlar. (F.–L.–Gk.) The name of a tree, bearing fruit formerly called *medles*. M. E. *medler*, the tree, also called *medle-tree* (A. F. *medle* = O. F. *mesle*). – O. F. *mesle*, a medlar (whence *meslier*, the tree); Gascon *mesplo*. – L. *mespilum*. – Gk. μέσπιλον, a medlar (whence also F. *nèfle*).

Medley, confusion, mixture. (F.–L.) M. E. *medlee*.–A. F. *medlee*; O. F. *medle*,

melle, mesle (fem. *medlee, mellee, meslee*),
pp. of the verb *medler*, to mix, confuse.
See **Meddle**. The fem. form *medlee* = F.
mêlée.

Medullar, belonging to the marrow.
(L.) L. *medullāris,* adj. — L. *medulla,*
marrow.

Meed. (E.) M. E. *mede, meed.* — A. S.
mēd, beside *meord* (with *r* for older *z*).
+ G. *miethe,* hire; Goth. *mizdō;* Russ.
mz ta, Gk. μισθός, pay, Pers. *muzd,* wages.
Idg. types *meizdhā, *mizdhā, *misdhos.*
Brugm. i. § 226.

Meek. (Scand.) M. E. *meke, meek;*
spelt *meoc,* Ormulum, 667. — Icel. *mjūkr,*
soft, agile, meek, mild ; N. Fries. *mjöck,*
Swed. *mjuk,* Dan. *myg,* soft. Cf. Du.
muik; Goth. *mūks,* in comp. *mūka-*
mōdei, gentleness. Teut. types *meukoz,*
mūkoz.

Meerschaum, a substance used for
making pipes. (G.) G. *meerschaum,* lit.
sea-foam (because it is white and light).
— G. *meer,* lake, sea; *schaum,* foam, lit.
scum ; see **Mere** (1) and **Scum**.

Meet (1), fit. M. E. *mete.* A. S. *gemet,*
meet, fit (the prefix *ge-* making no difference). — A.S. *metan,* to mete. Cf. G. *mässig,*
frugal, from *messen,* to mete. See **Mete**.

Meet (2), to encounter, find, assemble.
(E.) M. E. *meten* O. Merc. *mōetan;* A.S.
mētan, to find, meet (for *mōtian*). Formed
by mutation from A.S. *mōt,* a meeting,
assembly.**+**Icel. *mæta, mæta,* from *mōt ;*
Goth. *gamōt-jan,* Swed. *möta,* Dan. *möde,*
to meet. See **Moot**.

Megatherium, a fossil quadruped,
(Gk.) Lit. ' great wild beast.' — Gk. *μέγα-s.*
great ; θηρίον, dimin. of θήρ, a wild beast.

megalosaurus. (Gk.) Lit. ' great
lizard.' — Gk. μεγάλο-, decl. stem allied to
μέγα-s, great ; σαῦρος, a lizard.

Megrim, a pain affecting one side of
the head. (F. — L. — Gk.) F. *migraine,*
' the megrim;' Cot. — Late L. *hēmigrānea,*
megrim. — Gk. ἡμικράνιον, half of the
skull. — Gk. ἡμι-, half ; κρανίον, cranium.

Melancholy, sadness. (F. — L. — Gk.)
Supposed to be due to an excess of ' black
bile.' M. E. *melancolie.* — O. F. *melan-*
colie. — L. *melancholia.* — Gk. μελαγχολία,
melancholy. — Gk. μελάγχολος, jaundiced.
— Gk. μέλαν-, stem of μέλας, black ; χολή,
bile, gall, cognate with E. *gall.*

Melilot, a plant. (F. — L. — Gk.) M.F.
melilot (Cot.). — L. *melilōtos.* — Gk. μελί-
λωτος, μελίλωτον, a kind of clover, named

from the honey in it. — Gk. μέλι, honey ;
λωτός, lotus, clover.

Meliorate, to make better. (L.)
From pp. of Late L. *meliōrāre,* to make
better. — L. *melior,* better. **+** Gk. μᾶλλον,
rather, comp. of μάλα, adv., very much.

Mellifluous, sweet. (L.) Lit. ' flowing sweetly,' ' flowing like honey.' — L.
melli-, decl. stem of *mel,* honey; *-fluus,*
flowing, from *fluere,* to flow ; see **Fluent**.
Cf. Gk. μέλι, Goth. *milith,* Irish *mil,*
W. *mêl,* honey.

Mellow, fully ripe. (E.) M. E. *melwe,*
orig. soft, pulpy. Pegge notes that, in
Derbyshire, a *mellow* apple or pear is
called a *mealy* one; and *mellow* may be
an adjectival use of *meal.* The M. E.
melwe may represent A. S. *melw-,* as in
melwe, dat. of *melu,* meal. Cf. Du.
malsch, Low G. *mals,* soft, mellow ; from
Teut. *malan-,* to grind ; see **Meal** (1).
Note also Du. *molnen,* to moulder, *mul,*
soft; Goth. *gamalwiths,* crushed ; Du.
mollig, soft. See Franck, s. v. *mollig.*
¶ Perhaps confused with O. Merc. *merwe,*
tender (Mat. xxiv. 32) ; A. S. *mearu,* G.
mürbe, mellow.

Melocotone, a quince, a pear grafted
on a quince. (Span. — L. — Gk.) In Nares.
Span. *melocoton* (Pineda). — Late L. *mēlum*
cotōneum (Ducange). — Gk. μῆλον Κυδώνιον, a quince. See **Quince**.

Melodrama. (F. — Gk.) Formerly
melodrame. — F. *mélodrame,* acting, with
songs. — Gk. μέλο-s, a song ; δρᾶμα, an
action, drama ; see **Drama**.

melody. (F. — L. — Gk.) M.F. *melodie.*
— L. *melōdia.* — Gk. μελῳδία, a singing. —
Gk. μελῳδός, adj , musical — Gk. μέλ-ος, a
song; ᾠδή, a song, ode; see **Ode**.

Melon, a fruit. (F. — L. — Gk.) O. F.
melon. — L. *mēlōnem,* acc. of *mēlō,* an
apple-shaped melon. — Gk. μῆλον, an
apple, also applied to other fruits. Cf. L.
mālum, apple, prob. borrowed from Gk.

Melt. (E.) M. E. *melten,* pt. t. *malt,*
pp. *molten.* — A.S. *meltan,* pt. t. *mealt.***+**
Gk. μέλδειν, to melt. Allied to Skt.
mṛdu, O. Slavonic *mladu,* soft; Brugm.
i. § 580, ii. § 690. (√MEL.) See **Mild**.

Member. (F. — L.) F. *membre.* — L.
membrum, a member. Brugm. i. § 875.

membrane. (F. — L.) F. *membrane.*
— L. *membrāna,* a skin covering a member
of the body, a membrane. — L. *membrum.*

Memento, a memorial. (L.) L. *me-*
mentō (Luke xxiii. 42), remember me ;

imperative of *meminī*, I remember; Brugm. ii. § 846. (✓MEN.)

Memory. (F.–L.) M. E. *memorie*. – A.F. *memorie*; F. *mémoire*. – L. *memoria*, memory. – L. *memor*, mindful, remembering. This L. *memor* appears to be a reduplicated form; cf. Gk. μέρ-μερ-ος, anxious, μέρ-ιμνα, care, thought. Allied to Skt. *smṛ*, to remember. (✓SMER.)

memoir, a record. (F.–L.) Commoner in the pl. *memoirs*. – O. F. *memoires*, notes for remembrance, records; pl. of *mémoire*, memory (above).

Menace. (F.–L.) O. F. *menace*. – L. pl. *mināciæ*, threats. – L. *mināc-*, stem of *minax*, full of threatenings, also, projecting forward. – L. *minæ*, things projecting forward, hanging over and ready to fall, hence threats. – L. *-minēre*, as in *ē-minēre*, to project, jut out.

Menagerie, a place for keeping wild animals. (F.–L.) F. *ménagerie*, orig. a place for keeping *household* animals (Brachet). – F. *ménager*, to keep house. – F. *ménage*, O. F. *mesnage*, a household. – O. F. *mesnee*, *meisnee*, *maisnee*, a family; the same word as Late L. *mansnada*, *maisnada*, *masnata*, Ital. *masnada*, a family (answering to a Lat. type *mansiōnāta*). – L. *mansiōn-*, stem of *mansio*, an abiding, abode; see **Mansion**.

Mend. (F.–L.) M. E. *menden*, short for M. E. *amenden*, to amend, by loss of *a*; see **Amend**.

Mendacity. (L.) From L. *mendācitās*, falsehood. – L. *mendāc-*, stem of *mendax*, false.

Mendicant, a beggar. (L.) L. *mendīcant-*, stem of pres. pt. of *mendīcāre*, to beg. – L *mendīcus*, beggarly, poor.

Menial, one of a household, servile. (F.–L.) Properly an adj.; M. E. *meyneal*, as 'her *meyneal* chirche' = the church of their household, Wyclif, Rom. xvi. 5. – O. F. *mesnee*, *meisnee*, a household; whence M. E. *meinee*, *mainee*, a household, troop, retinue, once a common word; with suffix *-al*. See **Menagerie**.

Meniver, Miniver, a kind of fur. (F.–L.) M. E. *meniuer* (*meniver*). – O. F. *menu ver*, *menu vair*, miniver; lit. 'little vair.' – O. F. *menu*, small, from L. *minūtus*, small; *vair*, a fur, from L. *uarius*, variegated. See **Minute** and **Vair**.

Menses. (L.) L. *mensēs*, monthly discharges; pl. of *mensis*, a month. Allied to **Month**.

menstruous. (L.) From L. *menstru-us*, monthly. – L. *mensis*, a month.

menstruum. (L.) Late L. *menstruum*, a solvent; a word in alchemy; from the notion of some connexion of its action with the phases of the moon.

Mensuration, measuring. (L.) From L. *mensūrātio*, a measuring. – L. *mensūrātus*, pp. of *mensūrāre*, to measure. – L. *mensūra*, measure; see **Measure**.

Mental. (F.–L.) F. *mental*. – Late L. *mentālis*, mental. – L. *ment-*, stem of *mens*, mind. Brugm. i. § 431 (2).

mention, a notice. (F.–L.) F. *mention*. – L. acc. *mentiōnem*. – L. *menti-*, decl. stem of *mens*, mind (above).

Mentor, an adviser. (Gk.) Gk. Μέντωρ, Mentor (Homer, Od. ii); explained as 'adviser'; cf. L. *monitor* (Vaniček). See **Monition**.

Mephitis, a pestilential exhalation. (L.) L. *mephitis* (Vergil).

Mercantile, commercial. (F.–L.) M. F. *mercantil*, 'merchantly;' Cot. – Late L. *mercantilis*. – L. *mercant-*, stem of pres. pt. of *mercārī*, to trade. – L. *merc-*, stem of *merx*, merchandise. Cf. Gk. μάρπτειν, to seize (Prellwitz).

mercenary. (F.–L.) F. *mercenaire*. – L. *mercēnārius*, older form *mercennārius*, a hireling. For *merced-nārius*; from *mercēd-*, stem of *mercēs*, pay. – L. *merc-*, stem of *merx*, merchandise.

mercer. (F.–L.) F. *mercier*, lit. 'a trader.' – Late L. *mercērius*, a trader. – L. *merc-*, stem of *merx*, merchandise.

merchandise. (F.–L.) M. E. *marchandise*. – F. *marchandise*, merchant's wares. – F. *marchand*, a merchant (below).

merchant. (F.–L.) M. E. *marchant*. – M. F. *marchant* (F. *marchand*). – L. *mercant-*, stem of pres. pt. of *mercārī*, to trade; see **Mercantile**.

mercury, quicksilver. (F.–L.) M.E. *mercurie*, quicksilver, named after the planet Mercury. – A. F. *Mercurie*; F. *mercure* – L. *Mercurium*, acc. of *Mercurius*, Mercury, god of traffic. – L. *merc-*, stem of *merx*, merchandise.

mercy. (F.–L.) F. *merci*; O. F. *mercit*. – L. *mercēdem*, acc. of *mercēs*; see **mercenary**.

Mere (1), a lake. (E.) M. E. *mere*. A.S. *mere*, sea, lake, m.; orig. type *mari*. n. + Du. *meer*; Icel. *marr*, sea; G. *meer*, sea; Goth. *marei*, Russ. *more*, Lithuan.

mãrès, pl., W. *môr*, Gael. Irish *muir*, L. *mare*, sea.

Mere (2), pure, simple. (L.) L. *merus*, pure, unmixed (as wine).

Merelles, a game. (F.) From F. *mérelle*, a counter ; Low L. *merellus*. Of unknown origin.

Meretricious, alluring by false show. (L.) L. *meretrīci·us*, pertaining to a courtesan; with suffix *-ous*. — L. *meretrīc-*, stem of *meretrix*, a courtesan. — L. *merēre*, to gain, receive hire.

Merge, to sink, plunge under water. (L.) L. *mergere*, to dip. **+** Skt. *majj*, to dip, bathe. Brugm. i. § 816.

Meridian, pertaining to mid-day. (F. — L.) O. F. *meridien*. — L. *merīdiānus*. — L. *merīdiēs*, mid-day ; formed from the old locative *merī-diē*, as if meaning ' in the clear day,' from L. *merus*, clear, *diēs*, day ; but really for **medī-diē*, from *medius*, mid. Brugm. i. 587 (7).

Merino, a variety of sheep. (Span. — L.) Span. *merino*, roving from pasture to pasture. — Span. *merino*, an inspector of sheep-walks. — Late L. *mājorīnus*, a major-domo, steward of a household ; cf. Late L. *mājorālis*, a head-shepherd. From L. *māior*, greater ; see **Major**.

Merit, excellence, worth. (F. — L.) M. E. *merite*. — O. F. *merite*. — L. *meritum*, a thing deserved ; orig. neut. of *meritus*, pp. of *merēre*, to deserve ; orig. ' to receive as a share,' if it is allied to Gk. μέρος, a share, μείρομαι, I receive a share.

Merle, a blackbird. (F. — L.) O. F. *merle*. — L. *merula*, a blackbird. Cf. W. *mwyalch*, a blackbird. See **Titmouse**.

merlin, a kind of hawk. (F. — L. ?) M. E. *merlion*. — M. F. *esmerillon*, *emerillon*, ' the hawk termed a marlin ;' Cot. Cf. Ital. *smerlo*, a kind of hawk. Prob. from L. *merula*, a blackbird ; the initial *s* being unoriginal (Diez).

Mermaid. (E.) M. E. *mermaid*. — A. S. *mere*, sea, lake ; *mægden*, maiden.

Merry. (E.) M. E. *merie*, *mirie*. A. S. *myrge*, *myrige* (*mirige*), merry. Cf. O. H. G. *murg-fâri*, fragile, transitory ; Gk. βραχύς, short ; so that A. S. *myrg-e* (for **murgjoz*) means 'lasting a short time,' and so ' making the time short.' Cf. Goth. *gamaurgjan*, to shorten. Brugm. ii. § 104. Der. *mirth*.

Mesentery. (L. — Gk.) L. *mesenterium*. — Gk. μεσεντέριον, a membrane in the midst of the intestines. — Gk. μέσ-ος,

middle, cognate with L. *medius* ; ἔντερον, entrail. See **Mid** and **Entrail**.

Mesh, the opening between the threads of a net. (E.) M. E. *maske*. A. S. *max* (= **masc*, by the common interchange of *sc* and *cs = x*) ; cf. A. S. *mascre*, a mesh, dimin. form. **+** Du. *maas*, Icel. *möskvi*, Dan. *maske*, Swed. *maska*, G. *masche*, W *masg*. Orig. sense ' a knot,' from knots in a net ; cf. Lithuan. *mazgas*, a knot, *magstas*, a knitting-needle, allied to *megsti*, verb (pres. t. *mezg-u*), to knot, weave nets. From an Idg. root **mezg*, to weave. Brugm. i. § 816 (2).

Mesmerise, to operate on the nervous system of a patient. (G.) Named from *Mesmer*, a German physician (about 1766).

Mess (1), a dish of meat, portion of food. (F. — L.) M. E. *messe*. — O. F. *mes*, a dish, course at table (now spelt *mets*, badly). Cf. Ital. *messo*, a course at table. — O. F. *mes*, that which is sent, pp. of *mettre*, to send. — L. *missum*, acc. (or neut.) of *missus*, pp. of *mittere*, to send ; in late Lat., to place. See **Missile**.

Mess (2), a mixture, disorder. (E.) A corruption of the older form *mesh*, which again stands for *mash*, sb. ' *Mescolare*, to mixe, to *mash*, to mesh ;' Florio. ' *Mescolanza*, a medlie, a *mesh*, a mixture ;' id. See **Mash**.

Message. (F. — L.) F. *message*. — Late L. *missāticum*, a message. — L. *missus*, pp. of *mittere*, to send. Der. *messenger*, with inserted *n*, for M. E. *messager*, formed from *message* with suffix *-er*.

Messiah, the anointed one. (Heb.) Heb. *māshīakh*, anointed. — Heb. *māshakh*, to anoint.

Messuage, a dwelling-house with offices. (F. — L.) M. E. *mesuage*. — A. F. *mesuage*, a manor-house ; Low L. *messuā-gium*, *mansuāgium*. — Late L. *mansionā-ticum*, a mansion ; prob. shortened by confusion with *mansāticum*, acc. of *mans-āticus*, a mansion. — L. *mansiōnem*, acc. of *mansio*, a mansion ; confused with Late L. *mansa*, with a like sense and origin. See **Mansion** and **Manse**.

Meta-, prefix. (Gk.) Gk. μετά, prep., among, with, after ; as a prefix, it commonly signifies ' change.' **+** Goth. *mith* A. S. *mid*, G. *mit*, with ; Icel. *með*.

Metal. (F. — L. — Gk.) M. E. *metal*. — O. F. *metal*. — L. *metallum*, a mine, metal. — Gk. μέταλλον, a cave, mine, mineral, metal. Allied to μεταλλαω, I search after, explore.

metallurgy, a working in metals. (F. – L. – Gk.) O. F. *metallurgie.* – Late L. **metallurgia.* – Gk. *μεταλλουργός,* adj., working in metals. – Gk. *μέταλλο-ν,* metal; ἔργον, work; see **Work.** ¶ L. *ū* = Gk. *ου* < *οε.*

Metamorphosis, transformation. (L. – Gk.) L. *metamorphōsis.* – Gk. *μεταμόρφωσις,* a change of form. – Gk. *μετά,* here denoting 'change'; and *μορφόω,* I form, from *μορφή,* sb., shape.

Metaphor. (F. – L. – Gk.) M.F. *metaphore,* 'metaphor;' Cot. – L. *metaphora.* – Gk. *μεταφορά,* a transferring of a word from its literal signification. – Gk. *μεταφέρειν,* to transfer. – Gk. *μετά,* signifying 'change'; *φέρειν,* to bear; see **Bear** (1).

Metaphrase. (Gk.) From Gk. *μετάφρασις,* a paraphrasing; lit. change of phrase. – Gk. *μετά,* signifying 'change'; and *φράσις,* a phrase; see **Phrase.**

Metaphysics, the science of mind. (L. – Gk.) Formerly also *metaphysic.* – L. *metaphysica,* neut. pl. metaphysics. – Gk. *μετὰ τὰ φυσικά,* after physics; because the study was supposed to follow that of physics or natural science.

Metathesis. (L. – Gk.) L. *metathesis.* – Gk. *μετάθεσις,* transposition. – Gk. *μετά,* implying 'change'; *θέσις,* a placing; see **Thesis.**

Mete, to measure. (E.) M. E. *meten.* A. S. *metan,* to measure. + Du. *meten,* Icel. *meta* (to value), Swed. *mäta,* Goth. *mitan,* G. *messen.* Cf. L. *modus,* measure, Gk. *μέδ-ομαι,* I provide for. (√MED.)

Metempsychosis, transmigration of souls. (Gk.) Gk. *μετεμψύχωσις.* – Gk. *μετεμψυχόω,* I make the soul pass from one body to another. – Gk. *μετ-ά,* denoting 'change'; *ἐμ-* (for *ἐν*), in, into; *ψυχ-ή,* the soul. See **Psychical.**

Meteor. (F. – Gk.) M.F. *meteore,* 'a meteor;' Cot. – Gk. *μετέωρον,* a meteor; neut. of adj. *μετέωρος,* raised above the earth, soaring in air. – Gk. *μετά,* among; **ἄϝορος,* prob. from *ἀείρειν,* to lift (see Prellwitz).

Metheglin, mead. (W.) W. *meddyglyn,* mead, lit. mead-liquor. – W. *medd,* mead; *llyn,* liquor. See **Mead** (1).

Methinks. (E.) Lit. 'it seems to me;' here *me* is the dat. case, and *thinks* is an impers. verb, from M. E. *þinken,* to seem. A. S. *mē þynceð,* it seems to me; from

þyncan, to seem; +O. Sax. *thunkian,* Icel. *þykkja,* Goth. *thugkjan,* i. e. **thunkjan,* G. *dünken,* to seem. Allied (by gradation) to A. S. *þanc,* a thought, and *þencan,* to think. See **Thank, Think.**

Method. (F. – L. – Gk.) M.F. *methode,* 'a method;' Cot. – L. *methodus.* – Gk. *μέθοδος,* an enquiry into, method, system. – Gk. *μεθ-,* for *μετ-ά,* among, after; *ὁδός,* a way; the lit. sense is 'a way after,' a following after. (√SED.)

Methylated, used of spirits of wine when mixed with methyl to make it undrinkable. (L. – Gk.) Formed with suffix *-ated* from *methyl,* meaning a gas procured by the destructive distillation of wood. *Methyl* was a Latinised spelling coined from Gk. *μεθ'* (= *μετά,* by means of), and *ὕλη,* wood.

Metonymy, the putting of one word for another. (L. – Gk.) L. *metōnymia.* – Gk. *μετωνυμία,* change of name. – Gk. *μετά,* implying 'change'; *ὄνομα,* name.

Metre, Meter, rhythm, verse. (F. – L. – Gk.) M. E. *metre.* – M. F. *metre,* 'meeter;' Cot. – L. *metrum.* – Gk. *μέτρον,* that by which anything is measured, a rule, metre. Lit. 'measure;' cf. Skt. *mā,* to measure. See Brugm. ii. § 62. Der. *baro-meter, chrono-meter, geo-metry, hexa-meter, hydro-meter, hygro-meter, penta-meter, thermo-meter, trigono-metry, tri-meter,* &c.

Metropolis, a mother-city. (L. – Gk.) L. *mētropolis.* – Gk. *μητρόπολις,* a mother-state; the city of a primate. – Gk. *μήτρο-,* for *μήτηρ,* a mother; *πόλις,* a city. See **Mother** and **Police.**

Mettle, spirit, ardour. (F. – L. – Gk.) Another spelling of *metal;* in Shakespeare, no distinction is made between the two words in old editions, either in spelling or in use (Schmidt). With special allusion to the *metal* (or *mettle*) of a sword-blade.

Mew (1), to cry as a cat; a word of imitative origin. (E.) M. E. *mawen.* + Pers. *maw,* Arab. *mua,* mewing of a cat. Der. *mewl,* from F. *miauler,* to mew.

Mew (2), a sea-gull. (E.) M. E. *mawe.* A. S. *mǣw, mēaw, mēu,* a mew. + N. Fries. *mēwe,* E. Fries. *mēve,* Du. *meeuw,* Icel. *mār,* Dan. *maage,* Swed. *måke,* G. *möwe.* Cf. O. H. G. *mēh,* a mew.

Mew (3), a cage for hawks, &c. (F. – L.) The pl. *mews* now means a range of stabling, because the royal stables were rebuilt (A. D. 1534) in a place where the royal falcons had been kept (Stow). M. E. *mewe, mue,* a cage where hawks were kept when moulting. – O. F. *mue,* a moulting, also a mew for hawks; Guernsey *mue,* a mew. – F. *muer,* to change, moult. – L. *mūtāre,* to change. Der. *mew-s,* as above. See **Mutable.**

Mewl; see Mew (1).

Mews; see Mew (3).

Mezzotinto, a mode of engraving. (Ital. – L.) Ital. *mezzo tinto,* half tinted. – Ital. *mezzo,* mid; *tinto,* pp. of *tingere,* to tint. – L. *medius,* mid; *tingere,* to dip, dye.

Miasma, pollution, infectious matter. (Gk.) Gk. μίασμα, a stain. – Gk. μιαίνειν, to stain.

Mica, a glittering mineral. (L.) ' *Mica,* a crum, little quantity of anything that breaks off; also, a glimmer, or cat-silver, a metallick body like silver, which shines in marble,' &c.; Phillips (1706). – L. *mīca,* a crumb; cf. F. and Span. *mica,* mica. But it seems to have been applied to the mineral from the notion that this sb. is related to L. *micāre,* to shine, which is probably not the case.

Mich, to skulk, play truant. (E.) M.E. *muchen,* to pilfer. A. S. **myccan*; not found, but allied to G. *meuchlings,* insidiously. Der. *mich-er, mich-ing* (Shak.).

Michaelmas, the feast of St. Michael. (F. – Heb. *; and* L.) M. E. *michelmesse*; where *Michel* = F. *Michel,* from Heb. *Mīkhāel,* lit. ' who is like unto God?' The suffix *-mas* = M. E. *messe* = A.S. *mæsse*; from L. *missa*; see **Mass** (2).

Mickle, great. (E.) M. E. *mikel, mukel, michel, muchel.* – A.S. *micel* (*mycel*). + Icel. *mikill* (*mykill*), Goth. *mikils*; Gk. μεγάλη, great. Cf. also Gk. μέγας, great, L. *magnus.* See **Much.**

Microcosm, a little world. (F. – L. – Gk.) F. *microcosme.* – L. *microcosmus.* – Gk. μικρόκοσμος, a little world. – Gk. μικρό-s, little, for σμικρός, little; κόσμος, world; see **Cosmetic.**

microscope, an instrument for viewing small objects. (Gk.) Gk. μικρό-s, little; σκοπ-εῖν, to see; see **Scope.**

Mid, middle. (E.) M. E. *mid.* A. S. *mid, midd,* adj. + Du. Dan. Swed. *mid-* (in compounds); Icel. *miðr,* Goth. *midjis,* O. H. G. *mitti,* L. *medius,* Gk. μέσος, Æolic μέσσος, Skt. *madhya-,* adj., middle. Cf. Ir. *mid-,* as in *mid-nogt,* midnight. See **Medium, Middle.**

Midden, a dunghill. (Scand.) M. E.

midding. – Dan. *mödding* (for **mögdynge*). – Dan. *mög* (Icel. *myki*), muck; Dan. *dynge,* a heap; lit. ' muck-heap '). Dan. *dynge* = Swed. *dynga,* dung; allied to E. *dung.* And see **Muck.**

Middle, adj., intervening; also as sb. (E.) M. E. *middel,* adj.; *middel,* sb. A.S. *middel,* adj. and sb. – A. S. *midd,* adj., middle. + Du. *middel,* adj. adv. and sb. ; G. *mittel,* sb., means; O. H. G. *mittil,* adj. Cf. Icel. *meðal,* prep., among. Der. *middl-ing*; *middle-most,* an ill-coined superlative, on the model of *after-most, foremost.*

midriff, the diaphragm separating the heart from the stomach, &c. (E.) M. E. *midrif.* A. S. *midrif,* also *midhrif.* – A. S. *mid,* middle; *hrif,* the belly. + O. Fries. *midref,* from *mid,* middle, *ref, rif,* the belly; Du. *middel-rif.* With A.S. *hrif* cf. L. *corp-us,* body.

midship, short for *amid-ship*; hence *midship-man.*

midst, the middle. (E.) *In middest,* Spenser, F. Q. vi. 3. 25; formed, with added *t,* from M. E. *in middes,* equivalent to *amiddes*; see **Amid.**

midwife. (E.) M. E. *midwif*; rarely *medewif* (Wyclif), from a false etymology which connected it with M. E. *mede* or *meed,* reward. – A. S. *mid,* prep., together with; *wif,* a woman. Thus the lit. sense is ' a woman who is with another,' a helper. Cf. A.S. *mid-wyrcan,* to work with. So also Span. *co-madre,* lit. ' co-mother,' a midwife. Cf. Du. *medehelpen,* to assist (from *mede,* with, *helpen,* to help); G. *mit-helfer,* a helper with, assistant.

Midge. (E.) M. E. *migge, mygge.* A. S. *micg,* better *mycg,* a midge, gnat. + Du. *mug,* Low G. *mugge,* Swed. *mygg,* Dan. *myg,* G. *mücke.* Teut. type **mugjā,* f., or **mugjoz,* m.; prob. ' buzzer;' cf. Gk. μύζειν, to mutter, μυῖα, a fly (Prellwitz); also Icel. *mȳ,* a midge.

Midriff, Midship, Midst, Midwife; see **Mid.**

Mien, look. (F. – C.) F. *mine.* ' the look;' Cot. (Whence Ital. *mina*; Hatzfeld.) Prob. from Bret. *min,* muzzle, beak (also used of men). Cf. W. *min,* lip; Ir. *men,* mouth; Corn. *mein, men,* lip, mouth (Thurneysen). Celtic type **maknā* (**mekno-*), open mouth (Stokes).

Might (1), strength. (E.) M. E. *mi ʒt.* A. S. *miht.* O. Merc. *mæht.* + Du. *magt,* Icel. *māttr,* Dan. Swed. *magt,* Goth.

mahts, G. *macht*. Teut. type **mah-tiz*, f. ; from the verb **mag-an-*. See **May** (1).

Might (2), pt. t. of *may*. (E.) See **May** (1).

Mignonette, a plant. (F.) F. *mignonette*, dimin. of *mignon*, darling ; see **Minion**.

Migrate. (L.) From pp. of L. *migrāre*, to wander. Cf. Gk. ἀμείβειν, to change.

Milch ; see **Milk**.

Mild. (E.) M. E. *mild, milde*. A. S. *milde*.+Du. *mild*, Icel. *mildr*, Dan. Swed. G. *mild* ; O. Sax. *mildi*, O. H. G. *milti*. Goth. *-milds*, in *un-milds*, without natural affection. Perhaps allied to Gk. μαλθακός, soft, mild, O. Irish *meld*, pleasant. Brugm. i. § 591.

Mildew. (E.) M. E. *meldew*. A. S. *meledēaw, mildēaw*, lit. honey-dew. – A. S. *mele, mil*, allied to L. *mel*, honey ; *dēaw*, dew. So also Irish *milceog*, mildew ; from *mil*, honey. And cf. Gk. μέλι, honey.

Mile. (L.) M. E. *mile*. A. S. *mil*. – L. pl. *mīlia*, commonly *millia*, a Roman mile. – L. *mille*, sing., a thousand ; whence *mille* (pl. *millia*) *passuum*, a thousand paces, a Roman mile. Cf. Du. *mijl*, G. *meile*, Swed. *mil*, Dan. *miil* ; all from L.

milfoil, yarrow. (F.–L.) Lit. ' thousand-leaf.' – F. *mille*, thousand ; A. F. *foille*, F. *feuille*, leaf. – Late L. *millefolium*, milfoil. – L. *mille*, thousand ; *folium*, leaf ; see **Foil** (1).

Militate, to contend. (L.) From pp. of L. *mīlitāre*, to serve as a soldier. – L. *mīlit-*, stem of *mīles*, a soldier.

militia, troops. (L.) L. *mīlitia*, (1) warfare, (2) troops. – L. *mīlit-*, stem of *mīles*, a soldier.

Milk. (E.) M. E. *milk*. O. Merc. *milc* (Sweet, O. E. T.) ; A. S. *meolc, meoluc*.+ Du. *melk*, O. Sax. *miluk* ; Icel. *mjólk*, Dan. *melk*, Swed. *mjölk* ; Goth. *miluks*, G. *milch*. Teut. stem **meluk-*, fem. Allied to the old strong Teut. vb. **melk-an-*, as seen in A. S. *melcan*, Du. and G. *melken*, to stroke a cow, milk ; allied to Gk. ἀμέλγειν, L. *mulgēre*, to milk, Lith. *milszti*, to stroke, to milk ; O. Irish *blig-im*, I milk. (√MELG.)

milch, milk-giving. (E.) M. E *milche, melche*, adj. ; cf. A. S. *milc-en*, adj., milky. + Icel. *milkr, mjólkr*, adj., milk-giving, from *mjólk*, milk. So also G. *melk*, adj., milch.

milksop, an effeminate man. (E.) M. E. *milksoppe*, Ch. C. T. 13916 (B 3100).

Lit. ' bread sopped in milk ;' hence, a soft fellow. – M. E. *milk*, milk ; *soppe*, a sop ; see **Sop**.

Mill. (L.) M. E. *miln, myln, mulne* ; whence *mille, mulle*, by assimilation of *n*. A. S. *myln, mylen*. – Late L. *mulīna*, for *molīna*, a mill ; extended from *mola*, a mill. See **Molar**.

Millennium, a thousand years. (L.) L. *millennium*. – L. *mille*, thousand ; *annus*, year ; see **Annual**.

Millet, a plant. (F.–L.) F. *millet* ; dimin. of *mil*, millet. – L. *milium*, millet (whence A. S. *mil*, millet).+Gk. μελίνη, millet.

Milliner. (Ital.) Formerly also *millaner* (Ben Jonson). Disputed ; but certainly for *Milaner*, a dealer in goods brought from *Milan*, in Italy.

Million, a thousand thousand. (F.–L.) F. *million* ; Late L. *millio*, lit. ' great thousand,' an augmentative form. – L. *mille*, thousand. Der. Hence *b-illion, tr-illion, quadr-illion* are formed, by a sort of analogy, in order to express shortly the ideas of *bi-million, tri-million*, &c. ; where *bi-* means ' to the second power,' not ' twice.'

Milt (1), the spleen. (E.) M. E. *milte*. A. S. *milte*. + Du. *milt*, Icel. *milti*, Dan. *milt*, Swed. *mjälte*, the spleen ; G. *milz*, O. H. G. *milzi*, milt. From the verb *to melt* in the sense to digest ; cf. Icel. *melta*, (1) to malt, (2) to digest. See **Melt**.

Milt (2), soft roe. (Scand.) A corruption of *milk*, due to confusion with *milt* (1). M. E. *mylke* of fyshe ; Vocab. 591. 16. – Swed. *mjölke*, milt, from *mjölk*, milk ; Dan. *fiskemelk*, soft roe of fishes, lit. ' fish-milk ;' G. *fischmilch*, milt. Cf. M. Du. *melcker van een visch*, ' the milt of a fish,' Hexham.

Mimic. (L.–Gk.) L. *mīmicus*, farcical. – Gk. μιμικός, imitative. – Gk. μῖμος, an imitator, actor, mime.

Minaret, a turret on a mosque. (Span. – Arab.) Span. *minarete*, a high slender turret. – Arab. *manārat*, a lamp, light-house, minaret. – Arab. *manār*, candle-stick, lamp, lighthouse. Allied to Arab. *nār*, fire.+Heb. *manōrāh*, a candlestick ; from *nūr*, to shine.

Mince, to cut up small. (F.–L.) M.E. *mincen*. – M.F. *mincer*, O.F. *mincier*, to mince ; cf. *mince*, adj., small. – Late L. **minūtiāre*, to mince (Schwan, § 199) ; from Late L. *minūtia*, a small piece. – L.

minūtus, small. Cf. A.S. *minsian*, to diminish. See **Minish**. Der. *mince-pie*, formerly *minced-pie*, i.e. pie of minced meat.

Mind. (E.) M.E. *mind*. A.S. *gemynd*, memory. — A.S. *munan*, to think ; *gemunan*, to remember (whence *gemynd* for **ga-mundi-*, by mutation).+Goth. *ga-munds*, f., remembrance. Teut. type **mundi-*, for **munthi-*, by Verner's law ; Idg. type *manti-* (cf. L. *ment-is*, gen. of *mens*, mind ; Skt. *mati-*, mind). From the weak grade of √MEN, to think. Brugm. i. § 431.

Mine (1), belonging to me. (E.) M.E. *min*, pl. *mine* ; often shortened to *my*. A.S. *mīn*, poss. pron. (declinable), from *min*, gen. of 1st pers. pronoun. + Goth. *meins*, poss. pron. ; allied to *meina*, gen. case of 1st pers. pronoun ; so in other Teut. tongues. Cf. L. *meus*. See **Me**.

my. (E.) M.E. *mi*, *my* ; short for *min* (above), by loss of final *n*. Der. *my-self*, M.E. *mi-self*, formerly *me-self*.

Mine (2), to excavate. (F.—C.) F. *miner*. Of Celtic origin. Cf. Bret. *mengleuz*, a mine (cf. *cleuz*, hollow) ; W. *mwn*, ore, a mine, *mwn-glawdd*, a mine (cf. *clawdd*, a pit), O. W. *mwyn*, ore (Davies) ; Irish *mein*, ore ; Gael. *mein*, *meinn*, ore, a mine (Thurneysen). Celtic type *meini, ore (Stokes).

mineral. (F.—C.) M.F. *mineral*, 'a minerall ;' Cot. — F. *miner*, to mine (above). Cf. Span. *minera*, a mine.

Minever ; see Meniver.

Mingle, to mix. (E.) A frequentative form of *ming*, to mix (Surrey) ; M.E. *mengen*, *mingen*, to mix. A.S. *mengan*, to mix, to become mixed ; a causal verb. — A.S. *mang*, a mixture, usually *gemang*, *gemong*, a mixture, crowd, assembly.+Du. *mengelen*, to mingle, from *mengen*, to mix ; Icel. *menga*, G. *mengen*, to mingle. See **Among, Monger**.

Miniature, a small painting. (Ital.—L.) Ital. *miniatura*, a miniature. — Ital. *miniato*, pp. of *miniare*, to dye, paint, 'to colour or limne with vermilion or red lead ;' Florio.—L. *minium*, cinnabar, red lead ; said to be of Iberian origin.

Minikin, a little darling. (Du.) Used by Florio, to translate Ital. *mignone*. — Du. *minnekyn*, a cupid, (Sewel) ; M. Du. *minneken*, my darling, dimin. of *minne*, love (Hexham). Cf. O. H. G. *minna*, love ; allied to **Mind**. (√MEN.)

Minim, a note in music ; ₆¹₀th of a drachm. (F.—L.) O. F. *minime*, lit. very

small. — L. *min-ima*, very small ; superl. fem. allied to *min-or*, less. See **Minor**.

Minion, a favourite. (F.) F. *mignon*, sb., a favourite. — F. *mignon*, adj., minion, dainty, also pleasing, kind. Of doubtful origin. Cf. G. *minne*, love ; see **Minikin**. Or from Celt. *min-*, small (Körting).

Minish, to lessen. (F.—L.) M. E. *menusen*. — F. *menuiser*, to minish (answering to Late L. *minūtiāre). — L. *minūtus*, small ; see **Minute**. Doublet, *mince*.

minister. (F.—L.) M. E. *ministre*. — F. *ministre*. — L. acc. *ministrum* ; nom. *minister*, a servant. L. *min-is-ter* is formed with suffix *-ter* from *min-es, allied to *min-or*, smaller ; from the base *min-*, small ; see **Minor**.

Miniver ; see Meniver.

Minnow, a small fish. (E.) M. E. *menow*. A.S. *myne*, a minnow ; cf. O.H.G. *muniwa*, a minnow (Kluge). ¶ We find another word, viz. M.E. *menuse*, a small fish ; from O. F. *menuise*, a small fish. — Late L. type *minūtia. — L. *minūtus*, minute, small ; see **Minute**.

Minor, less. (L.) L. *min-or*, less ; the positive form occurs in A. S. *min* (?), Irish *min*, small.+Icel. *minnr*, adv., less ; Goth. *minniza*, less. Brugm. i. § 84.

Minster. (L.—Gk.) A. S. *mynster* ; cf. O. H. G. *munistri*. From L. *monastērium* ; see **Monastery**.

Minstrel. (F.—L.) M. E. *ministral*, or *menestrel*. — O. F. *menestrel*, *menestral*. — Late L. *ministrālis*, a servant, retainer, hence one who played instruments or acted as jester. — L. *minister*, a servant ; see **Minister**. Der. *minstrel-cy*, M. E. *minstralcie*.

Mint (1), a place where money is coined. (L.) M. E. *mint*, *mynt*. A.S. *mynet* ; cf. O.H.G. *munizza* (G. *münze*). From L. *monēta*, (1) a mint, (2) money (Pogatscher). *Monēta* was a surname of Juno, in whose temple at Rome money was coined. — L. *monēre*, to warn ; Brugm. ii. § 79. See **Money**.

Mint (2), a plant. (L.—Gk.) A. S. *minte*. — L. *menta*, *mentha*. — Gk. μίνθα, mint.

Minuet, a dance. (F.—L.) So called from the small steps taken in it. — M. F. *menuët*, 'smallish, little, pretty ;' Cot. Dimin. of M.F. *menu*, small. — L. *minūtus*, small ; see **Minute**.

minus, less. (L.) Neut. of *minor*, less ; see **Minor**.

minute, sb. (L.) M. E. *minute*, sb. — L. *minūta*, a small part; orig. fem. of *minūtus*, small, pp. of *minuere*, to make small. — L. *min-*, small; base of *min-or*, less. See **Minor.**

Minx, a pert wanton woman. (Low G.) Low G. *minsk*, (1) masc. a man, (2) neut. a pert female. Cf. G. *mensch*, neut., a wench. The G. *mensch* was orig. an adj., from *mann*, a man. Cf. A. S. *mennisc*, human; from *mann*, a man. See **Man.**

Miocene, less recent. (Gk.) Gk. μείο-, for μείων, less; καιν-ός, new, recent.

Miracle. (F. — L.) F. *miracle*. — L. *mīrāculum*, a wonder. — L. *mīrārī*, to wonder at. — L. *mīrus*, wonderful. Cf. Skt. *smaya-*, wonder, from *smi*, to smile. Allied to **Smile.** Brugm. i. § 389.

mirage. (F. — L.) F. *mirage*, an optical illusion. — F. *mirer*, to look at. — L. *mīrārī* (above).

Mire, deep mud. (Scand.) M. E. *mire*, *myre*. — Icel. *mȳrr*, mod. *mȳri*, a bog; Swed. *myra*, Dan. *myre*, *myr*, a bog. + O. H. G. *mios*, M. H. G. *mies*, moss, swamp. Teut. base **meus- > *meuz-*. Allied to **Moss.**

Mirror. (F. — L.) M. E. *mirour*. — O. F. *mireör*, later *miroir*, a looking-glass, mirror (answering to Late L *mīrātōrium*). — Late L. *mīrāre*, to behold; L. *mīrārī*. See **Miracle.**

Mirth. (E.) M. E. *mirthe*. A. S. *myrgð*, *mirhð*, *mirigð*, mirth. — A. S. *myrge*, merry. See **Merry.**

Mis- (1), prefix. (E.) The A. S. *mis-* occurs in *mis-dêd*, a misdeed, and in other compounds. It answers to Du. Dan. Icel. *mis-*, Swed. G. *miss-*, Goth. *missa-*, with the sense of 'wrong.' Teut. type **misso-*; Idg. type **mit-to-*; allied to O. H. G. *mīdan* (G. *meiden*), to avoid; Lat. *mittere*, to send away, pp. *missus*. Brugm. i. § 794. Der. *mis-become, -behave, -believe, -deed, -deem, -do, -give, -lay, -lead, -like, -name, -shape, -time, -understand.* Also prefixed to words of F. and L. origin, as in *mis-apply, -calculate, -carry, -conceive, -conduct, -construe, -date, -demeanour, -employ, -fortune, -govern, -guide, -inform, -interpret, -judge, -place, -print, -pronounce, -quote, -represent, -rule, -spend, -term, -use,* &c. Also to Scand. words, as in *mis-call, -hap, -take.* See **Miss** (1).

Mis- (2), prefix. (F. — L.) The proper spelling is M. E. *mes-*, as in *mes-chief*, mischief. The same as O. F. *mes-*, Span.

menos-, from L. *minus*, less; with the sense of 'bad.' Frequently confused with the prefix above. Der. *mis-adventure* (q. v.), *-alliance, -chance* (q. v.), *-chief* (q. v.), *-count* (q. v.), *-creant* (q. v.), *-nomer* (q. v.), *-prise* (q. v.).

Misadventure. (F. — L.) O. F. *mesaventure*; see **Mis-** (2) and **Adventure.**

Misanthrope. (Gk.) Gk. μισάνθρωπος, adj., hating mankind. — Gk. μισ-εῖν, to hate, from μῖσ-ος, hatred; ἄνθρωπος, a man. Der. *misanthrop-ic, -ist, -y* (Gk. μισανθρωπία).

Miscellaneous, various. (L.) L. *miscellāne-us*; with suffix *-ous*. — L. *miscellus*, mixed. — L. *miscēre*, to mix; see **Mix.**

Mischance. (F. — L.) M. E. and O. F. *meschance*; see **Mis-** (2) and **Chance.**

Mischief. (F. — L.) M. E. *meschief*. — O. F. *meschief*, a bad result. Cf. Span. *menos-cabo*, diminution, loss. See **Mis-** (2) and **Chief.**

Miscount. (F. — L.) O. F. *mesconter*; see **Mis-** (2) and **Count.**

Miscreant, a wretch. (F. — L.) Orig. an unbeliever, infidel. — M. F. *mescreant*, 'misbelieving;' Cot. Here *mes- < L. minus*; see **Mis-** (2). *Creant* is from L. *crēdent-*, stem of pres. pt. of *crēdere*, to believe. Cf. Ital. *miscredente*, misbelieving; and E. *re-creant*. See **Creed.**

Miser, a niggard. (L.) Also 'a wretch': Spenser, F. Q. ii. 1. 8. — L. *miser*, wretched. Cf. Ital. and Span. *misero* (1) wretched, (2) avaricious.

miserable. (F. — L.) M. F. *miserable*. — L. *miserābilis*, pitiable. — L. *miserārī*, to pity. — L. *miser*, wretched.

Mishap. (Scand.) M. E. *mishappen*, verb, to fall out ill; see **Mis-** (1) and **Hap.**

Mishna, a digest of Jewish traditions. (Heb.) Heb. *mishnah*, a repetition, a second part. — Heb. root *shānāh*, to repeat.

Misnomer, a misnaming. (F. — L.) It answers to an O. French *mesnommer*, to misname; used as a sb. with the sense 'a misnaming.' — O. F. *mes-*, badly; *nommer*, to name. See **Mis-** (2) and **Nominal.**

Misprise, Misprize, to slight. (F. — L.) In As You Like It, i. 1. 177. — M. F. *mespriser*, 'to disesteem, contemn;' Cot. — O. F. *mes-*, badly; Late L. *pretiāre*,

to prize, esteem, from L. *pretium*, price.
See **Mis-** (2) and **Price.**

Misprision, a mistake, neglect. (F. –
L.) M. F. *mesprison*, 'misprision, error,
offence;' Cot. Cf. F. *méprise,* a mistake.
–O. F. *mes-*, badly, ill; Late L. *prensiōnem,* acc. of *prensio* (short for L. *prehensio*),
a seizing, taking, apprehending, from L.
prehendere; to take. ¶ Quite distinct
from *misprise.*

Miss (1), to fail to hit. (E.) M. E.
missen. A. S. *missan,* to miss; also, to
escape one's notice (rare). From a base
*mith-, weak grade of **meith-*, as in A. S.
and O. S. *mīðan,* to conceal, avoid, escape
notice (as well as in G. *meiden,* O. H. G.
mīdan, to avoid). See **Mis-** (1).**+**Du.
missen, Icel. *missa,* Dan. *miste* (with excrescent *t*), Swed. *missa,* O.H.G. *missan,* to
miss; also Du. *mis,* Icel. *mis,* adv., amiss;
also Du. *mis-,* Icel. *mis-,* Dan. *mis-,* Swed.
G. *miss-,* wrongly. Allied to L. *mittere,*
to send; see **Missile.** (√MEIT.) **Der.**
miss, sb., a fault, M. E. *misse,* Will. of
Palerne, 532; *miss-ing.*

Miss (2), an unmarried woman. (F. –
L.) A contraction of *mistress*; Evelyn's
Diary, Jan. 9, 1662. See **Mistress.**

Missal, a mass-book. (L.) Late L.
missāle, a mass-book. – Late L. *missa,*
mass; see **Mass** (2).

Missel-thrush; see Mistle-thrush.

Missile, a weapon that may be thrown.
(L.) Properly an adj., 'that may be
thrown.' – L. *missilis,* that may be thrown.
– L. *missus,* pp. of *mittere,* (perhaps for
*mītere), to throw, send; pt. t. *mīsi.***+**
O. H. G. *mīdan,* to avoid; see **Miss** (1).
Brugm. i. § 930.

mission. (L.) O. F. and F. *mission.*
– L. *missiōnem,* acc. of *missio,* a sending. – L. *miss-us,* pp. of *mittere,* to send.

missive. (F. – L.) F. *missive,* 'a
letter sent;' Cot. Coined from L. *miss-us,*
pp. of *mittere,* to send.

Mist. (E.) A S. *mist,* gloom, darkness.
+Icel. *mistr,* Du. Swed. *mist,* mist. Teut.
type **mih-stoz.* Apparently formed from
the base **mig-* (>*mih-* before *st*), Idg.
*migh- (weak grade of root **meigh*); as
seen in Lithuan. *migla,* Russ. *mgla,* Gk.
·ὀμίχλη, mist, Skt. *mih-ira-,* a cloud; also
Skt. *mēgh-a-,* a cloud, from the stronger
grade. (√MEIGH, to darken; perhaps
distinct from √MEIGH, as appearing in
L. *mingere.*)

Mistake, to err. (Scand.) Icel. *mis-*

taka, to take by error, make a slip. – Icel.
mis-, wrongly; *taka,* to take. See **Mis-**
(1) and **Take.**

Mister, Mr., a title of address. (F. –
L.) A corruption of *master,* due to the
influence of *mistress,* which is an older
word than *mister*; see below.

mistress, a lady of a household. (F.
– L.) O. F. *maistresse,* 'a mistress, dame;'
Cot. (F. *maîtresse.*) Fem. of O. F. *maistre,*
a master; see **Master.**

Mistery, Mystery, a trade, handi-
craft. (F. – L.) The *mystery plays* (better
spelt *mistery plays*) were so called because
acted by craftsmen; from M. E. *mistere,* a
trade, craft, Ch. C. T. 615. – O. F. *mestier,*
a trade, occupation (F. *métier*). – Late L.
misterium (also written *mysterium* by confusion with that word in the sense of
'mystery'), short form of L. *ministerium,*
employment. – L. *minister,* a servant; see
Minister.

Mistle-thrush. (E.) So called from
feeding on the berries of the mistletoe;
from A. S. *mistel,* mistletoe (below). **+** G.
misteldrossel, mistle-thrush.

mistletoe. (E.) A final *n* has been
lost. A. S. *misteltān.* – A. S. *mistel,* also
(like G. *mistel*) with the sense of mistletoe;
tān, a twig, cognate with Icel. *teinn,* Du.
teen, Goth. *tains,* Dan. *teen,* Swed. *ten,*
twig, spindle.**+**Icel. *mistelteinn,* mistletoe.
Perhaps *mistel* is related to G. *mist,* dung.
Cf. M. Du. *mistel,* bird-lime (Kilian),
'glew' (Hexham).

Mistress; see Mister.

Misty (1), adj. formed from Mist.

Misty (2), doubtful, ambiguous, as applied to language. (F. – L. – Gk.) In the
phrases 'misty language' and '*mistiness*
of language,' *misty* is not from E. *mist,*
but is short for *mystic*; see Palmer, Folk-
Etymology. See **Mystic.**

Mite (1), an insect. (E.) M. E. *mite,*
A. S. *mīte,* a mite. **+** Low G. *mite,* Du.
mijt, O. H. G. *mīza,* a mite. Teut. type
*mītōn-, f. The word means 'cutter,' i. e.
biter; from Teut. base MEIT, to cut; cf.
Icel. *meita,* to cut. See **Emmet.**

mite (2), a very small portion. (Du.)
M. E. *mite.* – M. Du. *mijt, mite,* a very
small coin, mite, bit cut off. See above.

Mitigate. (L.) From pp. of L. *miti-
gāre,* to make gentle. – L. *mīt-is,* gentle;
-igāre, for *agere,* to make.

Mitre, a head-dress, esp. for a bishop.
(F. – L. – Gk.) O. F. *mitre.* – L. *mitra,* a

cap. **–** Gk. μίτρα, a belt, girdle, head-band, fillet, turban.

Mitten. (F. – G. *or* C. ?) M. E. *mitaine.* **–** F. *mitaine,* 'a mittain, winterglove,' Cot.; Gascon *mitano.* Origin disputed; · see Hatzfeld, Körting, Scheler.

Mix, to mingle. (E.) For *misk,* like *ax* for *ask.* A. S. *mixian* (C. Hall), *miscian,* to mix (not borrowed from Latin, but allied to it). **+** G. *mischen*; also W. *mysgu,* Gael. *measg,* O. Irish *mescaim,* I mix, Russ. *mieshate,* Lithuan. *maiszyti,* L. *miscēre,* Gk. μίσγειν (for *μίγ-σκειν), to mix. Cf. Skt. *miçra,* mixed. Extended from √MEIK; cf. Gk. μίγνυμι, I mix. Brugm. i. §§ 707, 760. **Der.** *mash,* q. v.

mixture. (L.) L. *mixtūra,* a mixture. **–** L. *mixtus,* pp. of *miscēre,* to mix (above).

Mixen, a dunghill. (E.) M. E. *mixen,* A. S. *mixen, meoxen,* the same. From A. S. *mix, meox,* dung. **–** A.S. *mig-,* weak grade of *migan,* to urine. Cf. G. *mist.*

Mizen, Mizzen, a sail in a ship. (F. – Ital. – L.) F. *misaine,* explained by Cotgrave as 'the foresaile of a ship.' – Ital. *mezzana,* 'a saile in a ship called the poope or misen-saile;' Florio. Cf. Ital. *mezzano,* 'a meane man, between great and little;' id. The orig. sense seems to have been 'of middling size,' without reference to its position. **–** Late L. *mediānus,* middle, also of middle size (whence also F. *moyen,* E. *mean*). **–** L. *medius,* middle. See **Medium.**

Mizzle, to rain in fine drops. (E.) Formerly *misle,* M. E. *miselen,* Cath. Angl. Cf. M. Du. *mieselen,* to drizzle, Hexham; Low G. *miseln* (Berghaus); E. Fries. *misig,* damp, gloomy. Cf. **Mist.**

Mnemonics, the science of aiding the memory. (Gk.) Gk. μνημονικά, mnemonics; neut. pl. of μνημονικός, belonging to memory. **–** Gk. μνημον-, stem of μνήμων, mindful. **–** Gk. μνάομαι, I remember. (From the weak grade of √MEN.)

Moan, sb. (E.) M. E. *mone,* a communication, also a complaint; corresponding to A. S. *mān-* (not found), supposed to be cognate with O. Fries. *mēne,* an opinion, O. H. G. *meina,* an opinion, thought. Hence was formed A. S. *mānan,* to mean, intend, relate, also to complain, moan, lament, M. E. *mēnen,* to lament, now obsolete, its place being supplied by the form of the sb., used as a vb. See further under **Mean** (1). ¶ Cf. *means*

(some edd. *moans*) in Shak. M. N. D. v. 330. **Der.** *bemoan,* vb., substituted for M. E. *bimenen,* A. S. *bi-mēnan,* to bemoan.

Moat. (F. – Teut.) M. E. *mote.* – O. F. *mote,* an embankment, dike; Norman dial. *motte,* a moat, foss. [As in the case of *dike,* the same word means either the trench cut out or the embankment thrown up, or both together; cf. Low L. *mota,* (1) a mound, (2) a mound and moat together; also spelt *motta.*] The same word as F. *motte,* 'a clod, lump, sodd, turfe, little hill, butt to shoot at;' Cotgrave. Cf. also Ital. *motta,* a heap of earth, also a hollow, trench (like E. *moat*), Span. *mota,* a mound; Romansch *muotta,* rounded hill. Of Teut. origin; from Bavarian *mott,* peat, heap of peat (Diez). Prob. allied to **Mud**; cf. Du. *modder,* mud.

Mob (1), a disorderly crowd. (L.) A contraction of *mōbile uulgus,* i. e. fickle crowd. Both *mob* and *mobile* were in use, in the same sense, A. D. 1692-5.– L. *mōbile,* neut. of *mōbilis,* moveable, fickle.– L. *mouēre,* to move. See **Move.**

Mob (2), a kind of cap. (Du.) From Du. *mopmuts,* a woman's nightcap (where *muts* means cap); M. Du. *mop,* a woman's coif (Sewel); Low G. *mopp,* a woman's cap (Danneil).

Mobile, easily moved. (F. – L.) F. *mobile.* – L. *mōbilis*; see **Mob** (1).

Moccasin, Mocasin, a shoe of deer-skin. (N. American Indian.) From the Algonquin *makisin* (Cuoq).

Mock, to deride. (F. – L.) M. E. *mokken.* **–** O. F. *mocquer,* later *moquer.* According to Körting, it is the Picard form of *moucher,* to wipe the nose; and Cotgrave has *moucher,* 'to snyte, or make cleane the nose; also, to frump, mocke, scoff, deride;' for which Corblet gives the Picard form *mouker.* Cf. Ital. *moccare,* 'to blow the nose, also to mocke;' Florio. **–** Late L. *muccāre,* to blow the nose.– L. *muccus, mūcus,* mucus. See **Mucus.**

Mode. (F. – L.) F. *mode.* – L. *modum,* acc. of *modus,* measure, manner, way. Allied to **Mete.** Brugm. i. § 412.

model. (F. – Ital. – L.) M. F. *modelle* (F. *modèle*). – Ital. *modello,* 'a modell, frame, mould;' Florio. From dimin. of L. *modulus,* a standard, measure, which is again a dimin. of *modus,* measure. **Der.** *re-model.*

moderate, temperate. (L.) From pp. of L. *moderārī,* to regulate. From a stem *moder* for *modes-*, extended from *mod-us*, a measure. See **modest**.

modern. (F. – L.) F. *moderne.* – L. *modernus*, belonging to the present mode ; extended from a stem *moder-* (above).

modest, moderate, chaste, decent. (F. – L.) F. *modeste.* – L. *modestus*, modest, lit. ' keeping within measure.' From a neuter stem *modes-*, with suffix *-tus* ; see **moderate** (above). Brugm. ii. § 132.

modicum, a small quantity. (L.) Neut. of L. *modicus*, moderate. – L. *modus*, measure.

modify. (F. – L.) F. *modifier.* – L. *modificāre.* – L. *modi-*, for *modus*, measure, moderation ; *-ficāre*, for *facere*, to make.

modulate, to regulate. (L.) From pp. of L. *modulārī*, to measure by a standard. – L. *modulus*, dimin. of *modus*, a measure ; see **model**.

Mogul, a Mongolian. (Pers.) Pers *Moghōl*, a Mogul ; another form of *Mongol*.

Mohair, cloth of fine hair. (Arab.) A changed spelling (by confusion with *hair*) of *mockaire* (Hakluyt, ii. 273) ; whence F. *mouaire* (1650), mod. F. *moire* ; also F. *moncayar.* – Arab. *mukhayyar*, a kind of coarse camlet or hair-cloth ; Rich. Dict., p. 1369.

Mohammedan. (Arab.) A follower of *Mohammed.* – Arab. *muhammad*, praiseworthy. – Arab. *hamada*, he praised.

Mohur, a gold coin. (Pers.) Pers. *muhr, muhar*, a gold coin worth 16 rupees (Wilson) ; *muhr, muhur*, Rich. Dict., p. 1534.

Moidore, a Portuguese gold coin. (Port. – L.) See Bailey's Dict. – Port. *moeda d'ouro*, a moidore, £1 7s. ; lit ' money of gold.' – L. *monēta*, money ; *dē*, of : *aurum*, gold. See **Money**.

Moiety, half. (F. – L.) F. *moitié*, a half. – L. *medietātem*, acc. of *medietās*, a middle course, a half. – L. *medius*, middle. See **Medium**.

Moil, to toil, drudge. (F. – L.) Formerly *moile*, to defile with dirt ; later *moil*, ' to dawbe with dirt, to drudge ;' Phillips. The older sense was to dirty, hence to drudge, from the dirt consequent on toil. Spenser has *moyle*, to sully, Hymn of Heav. Love, st. 32. Still earlier, we have M. E. *moillen*, to moisten, wet. – O.F. *moiller, moiler* (Littré), later *mouiller*, to wet, moisten : orig. sense, to soften, which (in the case of clay) is effected by wetting it.

This verb answers to a Late L. **molliāre*, to soften ; not found. – L. *molli-s*, soft. Thus the senses were, to soften, moisten, dirty, soil oneself, drudge.

Moire, watered silk. (F.) From F. *moire*, used in two senses. In the sense *mohair*, it is borrowed from E. *mohair* (Hatzfeld). In the sense of watered silk, it may represent L. *marmoreus*, shining like marble, from *marmor*, marble (Körting) ; but this may be only a transferred sense of the former.

Moist. (F. – L.) M. E. *moiste*, often with the sense ' fresh' ; Ch. C. T. 459, 12249. – O. F. *moiste*, later *moite*. Etym. disputed ; (1) from L. *musteus*, new, from L. *mustum*, must ; (2) from L. *mucci-dus, mūcidus*, mouldy, from L. *mūcus* (Körting) ; (3) from L. *muscidus*, mossy, from *muscus*, moss (Hatzfeld). Der. *moist-ure*, O. F. *moisteur*.

Molar, used for grinding. (L.) L. *molāris*, adj., from *mola*, a mill. Cf. *molere*, to grind. (√MEL.) Brugm. ii. § 690.

Molasses, syrup made from sugar. (Port. – L.) Formerly *melasses.* – Port. *melaço*, molasses ; cf. Span. *melaza* (same . – L. *mellāceus*, made with honey. – L. *mel*, honey.

Mole (1), a spot or mark on the body. (E.) M. E. *mole.* A. S. *māl*, a spot (whence *mole* by the usual change from *ā* to long *ō*). +O. H. G. *meil*, Goth. *mail*, a spot.

Mole (2), an animal. (E.) M. E. *molle.* + M. Du. and Du. *mol* ; Low G. *mull* (Berghaus). Prob. related to M. Du. *mul*, ' the dust or crumblings of turf,' Hexham ; M. E. *mul*, A. S. *myl*, dust ; which are further related to **Mould** (1). The sense may have been ' earth-grubber,' or ' crumbler,' from the weak grade of √MEL, to pound. Cf. E. Fries. *mullen*, to grub ; *mulle* a child that grubs in the ground ; *mulle, mul*, a mole ; Low G.*mull-worm*, a mole (Danneil). ¶ Another name was formerly *moldwarp* (1 Hen. IV. iii. 1. 149), lit. ' the animal that casts up mould.' M. E. *moldwerp* ; from *mold*, mould, *werpen*, to throw up. See **Warp**. Cf. Icel. *moldvarpa*, a mole, O. H. G. *mult-wurf*, G. *maulwurf*.

Mole (3), a breakwater. (F. – Ital. – L.) F. *môle.* – Ital. *molo, mole*, ' a great pile ;' Florio. – L. *mōlem*, acc. of *mōles*, a great heap.

molecule, an atom. (L.) Formerly *molecula* ; Bailey. Coined from L. *mōles*, a heap; the true form would have been *molicula*.

Molest, to annoy. (F. – L.) F. *molester*. – L. *molestāre*. – L. *molestus*, troublesome; formed with suffix *-tus*, from a stem *moles-*, extended from *mol-*, as seen in *mol-ere*, to grind. See **Molar**.

Mollify, to soften. (F. – L.) M. F. *mollifier*. – L. *mollificāre*. – L. *moll-is*, soft; *-ficāre*, for *facere*, to make. Cf. Skt. *mṛdu-*, soft. Allied to **Melt**; Brugm. ii. § 690.

mollusc. (F. – L.) F. *mollusque*. – L. *mollusca*, a soft-shelled nut; which some molluscs were supposed to resemble. – L. *moll-is*, soft.

Molten, old pp. of **Melt**, q. v.

Moly, a plant. (L. – Gk.) L. *mōly*. – Gk. μῶλυ; Homer, Od. x. 305.

Moment. (F. – L.) F. *moment*. – L. *mōmentum*, a movement; hence, an instant of time; short for **mouimentum*. – L. *mouēre*, to move. See **Move**. Doublets, *momentum*, *movement*.

Monad, a unit, &c. (L. – Gk.) L. *monad-*, stem of *monas*, a unit. – Gk. μονάς, a unit. – Gk. μόνος, alone.

monarch, a sole ruler. (F. – L. – Gk.) F. *monarque*. – L. *monarcha*. – Gk. μονάρχης, a sovereign, sole ruler. – Gk. μον- (for μόνος), alone; and ἄρχειν, to rule.

monastery. (L. – Gk.) L. *monastērium*. – Gk. μοναστήριον, a minster. – Gk. μοναστής, dwelling alone, a monk. – Gk. μονάζειν, to be alone. – Gk. μόνος, alone. Der. *monast-ic*, from Gk. μοναστικός, living in solitude.

Monday. (E.) M. E. *monenday*, later *moneday*, *monday*. A. S. *mōnan dæg*, day of the moon; where *mōnan* is the gen. of *mōna*, moon. See **Moon**. A translation of L. *diēs lunæ*.

Monetary, relating to money. (L.) L. *monētārius*, lit. belonging to a mint. – L. *monēta* (1) a mint, (2) money. See **Mint** (1).

money. (F. – L.) M.E. *moneie*. – O.F. *moneie* (F. *monnaie*). – L. *monēta*, (1) mint, (2) money; see **Mint** (1).

Monger, a dealer, trader. (L.) Hence *iron-monger, coster-monger*. M.E. *monger*; A. S. *mangere*, a dealer, merchant; A. S. *mangian*, to traffic. – L. *mango*, a dealer.

Mongoose; see **Mungoose**.

Mongrel, an animal of a mixed breed. (E.) Spelt *mungril* in Levins (1570). It stands for **mong-er-el*, i. e. a small animal of mixed breed; cf. *cock-er-el, pick-er-el* (small pike). – A. S. *mang*, a mixture. See **Mingle**.

Monition, a warning, notice. (F. – L.) F. *monition*. – L. acc. *monitiōnem*. – L. *monitus*, pp. of *monēre*, to advise, lit. to make to think. (√MEN.) Brugm. ii. § 794.

Monk. (L. – Gk.) M. E. *monk*. A. S. *munuc*. – L. *monachus*. – Gk. μοναχός, adj., solitary; sb., a monk. – Gk. μόν-os, alone.

Monkey, an ape. (Low G. – F. – Ital. – L.) Borrowed from M. Low G. *Moneke*, the name of the ape's son in Reinke de Vos (where *-ke* is for *-ken*, dimin. suffix; so that the F. version has *Monnekin*; Godefroy). Formed with Low G. dimin. suffix *-ken* = G. *-chen*, from M. F. *monne*, an ape. – M. Ital. *mona*, *monna*, 'an ape, a munkie, a munkie-face; also a nickname for women, as we say gammer, goodie;' Florio. *Monna* is a familiar corruption of *madonna*, i. e. my lady, mistress; Scott introduces *Monna Paula* in the Fortunes of Nigel. See **Madonna**. ¶ From the same source is M. Ital. *monicchio*, 'a pugge, a munkie, an ape;' Florio. This is the Ital. equivalent of the Low G. word.

Mono-, *prefix*, sole. (Gk.) Gk. μόνο-s, single.

monochord, a musical instrument having but *one* string; see **Chord**. So also *mono-cotyledon, mon ocular, mon-ode, mono-logue* (from Gk. λόγος, a speech), *mono-syllable, mono-tone*; see **Cotyledon, Ocular, Ode, Syllable, Tone**.

monopoly, exclusive sale. (L. – Gk.) L. *monopōlium*. – Gk. μονοπώλιον, right of monopoly; μονοπωλία, monopoly. – Gk. μόνο-s, sole; πωλεῖν, to sell, barter.

Monsoon, a periodical wind. (Ital. – Malay. – Arab.) Ital. *monsone*. – Malay *mūsim*, a season, monsoon, year. – Arab. *mawsim*, a time, season. – Arab. *wasm* (root *wasama*), marking.

Monster, a prodigy. (F. – L.) F. *monstre*. – L. *monstrum*, a divine omen, portent, warning. (For **mon-es-trum*.) – L. *mon-ēre*, to warn.

Month. (E.) M. E. *moneth*, later *month*. A. S. *mōnað*, a month; from *mōna*, moon. See **Moon**.+Du. *maand*; Icel. *mānuðr*, Dan. *maaned*, Swed. *månad*; G. *monat*, Goth. *mēnōths*, a month. Teut. stem **mǣnōth-*. Cf. also Lithuan. *mėnesis*, Russ. *miesiats'*, L. *mensis*, Irish and W.

mis, Gael. *mios,* Gk. μήν, Skt. *mās,* a month ; all connected with **Moon,** q.v.

Monument, a memorial. (F. – L.) F. *monument.* – L. *monumentum,* a memorial. – L. *monu-,* for *moni-,* as in *moni-tus,* pp. of *monēre,* to advise, remind; with suffix *-men-tum.*

Mood (1), disposition of mind. (E.) Prob. sometimes confused with *mood* (2), but properly distinct. M. E. *mood,* mind, also temper, anger, wrath. A.S. *mōd,* mind, courage, pride.+Du.*moed,* courage ; Icel. *mōðr,* wrath, moodiness ; Dan. Swed. *mod,* G. *muth,* courage; Goth. *mōds,* wrath. Teut. type **mō-do-* (where *-do* is a suffix). Cf. Gk. μαίομαι, I strive after. Brugm. i. § 196. **Der.** *mood-y,* A. S. *mōdig* ; Sweet, N. E. G. § 1608.

Mood (2), manner, grammatical form. (F. – L.) The same word as **Mode,** q.v.; but confused with *mood* (1).

Moon. (E.) M. E. *mone.* A.S. *mōna,* a masc. sb.+Du. *maan,* Icel. *māni,* Dan. *maane,* Swed. *måne,* Goth. *mēna,* G. *mond,* O. H. G. *māno.* Teut. type **mænon-,* masc. Cf. also Lithuan. *mėnů,* Gk. μήνη ; Skt. *mās,* moon, month. Perhaps it meant the 'measurer' of time. (√ME.) See Brugm. i. § 132, ii. § 132.

Moonshee, a secretary, interpreter. (Arab.) Arab. *munshī,* a secretary, a language-master or tutor.

Moor (1), a heath. (E.) M. E. *more.* A.S. *mōr.* + M. Du. *moer,* moor, mud ; *moerlandt,* peaty land ; Icel. *mōr,* Dan. *mor,* Low G. *moor*; O. H. G. *muor,* marsh, pool, sea. Teut. type **mōro-* ; perhaps related (by gradation) to Goth. *marei,* sea, lake ; or to Skt. *maru,* a desert, mountain. See **Mere.**

Moor (2), to fasten up a ship. (Du.) Du. *marren* (M. Du. *merren*), to tie, bind, moor a ship ; also to retard. Cognate with E. **Mar.**

Moor (3), a native of N. Africa. (F. – L. – Gk.) F. *More,* 'a Moor ;' Cot. – L. *Maurus.* – Gk. Μαῦρος, a Moor. **Der.** *black-a-moor,* corruption of *blackmoor* (Minsheu), i. e. *black Moor.*

Moose, the American elk. (W. Indian.) The native W. Indian name ; 'Knisteneaux *mouswah,* Algonquin *musu*;' cited in the Cent. Dict. Cuoq cites Algonquin *mons* (with *n*).

Moot, to discuss a point. (E.) Chiefly used in phr. 'a *moot* point.' Minsheu gives *moot* as a verb, to discuss. The proper sense of *moot* is 'meeting,' as in *moot-hall,* hall of assembly ; hence, to *moot* is to discuss at a meeting, and 'a *moot* point' is one reserved for public discussion. M. E. *motien,* to discuss. A.S. *mōtian,* to converse, address a meeting, discuss ; from A. S. *mōt,* a meeting, also *gemōt,* esp. in phr. *witena gemōt* = meeting of wise men, parliament.+Icel. *mōt,* M. H. G. *muoz,* a meeting. Teut. base **mōt-.* **Der.** *meet.*

Mop (1), an implement for washing floors. (F. – L.) In a late ed. of Florio's Ital. Dict., *pannatore* is explained by 'a maulkin, a *map* of clouts or rags to rub withal.' Halliwell gives *mop,* a napkin ; *Gloucestershire.* Prob. from O. F. *mappe,* a napkin (afterwards turned into *nappe*). – L. *mappa,* a napkin (of Punic origin). See **Map.** ¶ Cf. *strop, strap* ; *knop, knap.* The Celtic forms are from E.

Mop (2), a grimace ; to grimace. (E.) The same word as *mope* (below).

mope, to be dispirited. (E.) The same word as *mop,* to grimace; cf. 'in the *mops,*' i. e. sulky (Halliwell). + Du. *moppen,* to pout, be sulky ; M. Swed. *mopa,* to mock (Ihre); Westphal. *möpen,* to grimace; G. *muffig,* sullen, pouting (Flügel), Bavar. *muffen,* to growl, pout. And see *mow* (3).

Moraine, a line of stones at the edges of a glacier. (F. – Teut.) F. *moraine*; cf. Ital. *mora,* a pile of rocks. – Bavarian *mur,* sand and broken stones, fallen from rocks in a valley; the lit. sense being perhaps 'crumbled material.' Cf. G. *mürbe,* soft, O. H. G. *muruwi*; Icel. *merja,* to crush.

Moral. (F. – L.) F. *moral.* – L. *mōrālis,* relating to conduct. – L. *mōr-,* from nom. *mōs,* a manner, custom.

Morass, a bog. (Du. – F. – Low G.) Du. *moeras,* marsh, fen ; M. Du. *moerasch,* adj., belonging to a moor, as if from the sb. *moer,* moor, mire, but really an altered form of M. Du. *marasch, maerasch,* a marsh (Kilian). – O.F. *maresque, maresche,* adj., marshy ; also, as sb., a marsh ; Low L. *mariscus.* – Low G. *marsch,* a marsh. See **Marish, Marsh.** Cf. G. *morast* (for *morask), Swed. *moras,* Dan. *morads,* a morass ; all from Du. or Low G.

Morbid, sickly. (F. – L.) F. *morbide.* – L. *morbidus,* sickly. – L. *morbus,* disease. Allied to *mor-ī,* to die; Brugm. ii. § 701.

Mordacity, sarcasm. (F. – L.) Little used. – F. *mordacité.* – L. acc. *mordāci-*

tālem, from *mordācitās*, power to bite. – L.
mordāc-, stem of *mordax*, biting. – L.
mordēre, to bite. Cf. Skt. *mardaya*, to
rub, break in pieces, from *mṛd*, to rub.
Brugm. ii. § 794. (√MERD.)

More. (E.) This does duty for two
distinct M. E. words, viz. (1) *mo*, more in
number, (2) *more*, larger. α. The former
is from A. S. *mā*, more in number, orig.
an adv. form, like G. *mehr*, Goth. *mais*.
β. The latter is from the corresponding
adj. A. S. *māra*, greater; cognate with
Icel. *meiri*, Goth. *maiza*, greater. See
Most. ¶ The notion that *mo* is a positive form is quite wrong; the positive
forms are *much*, *mickle*, *many*. The *r*
in *more* represents an earlier -*z*-, which in
the adv. (being final) was regularly lost.
Brugm. i. § 200.

Morganatic. (Low L. – G.) Low L.
morganātica, in the phrase *matrimōnium
ad morganāticam*, a morganatic marriage.
Coined from G. *morgen*, here short for
morgengabe, lit. morning-gift, orig. a present made to a wife on the morning after
marriage, esp. if the wife were of inferior
rank. See **Morn.**

Morian, a Moor. (F. – L. – Gk.) In
Pss. lxviii. 31; lxxxvii, 4 (P. B. version). –
O.F. *Morien, Moriaine* (Godefroy). – Late
L. *Maurītānus, for L. *Maurītānicus*, a
Moor. – L. *Maurītānia*, the land of the
Moors. – L. *Maur-us*, a Moor. – Gk.
Μαῦρος. See **Moor** (3).

Morion, an open helmet. (F. – Span.)
F. *morion*. – Span. *morrion*; cf. Port.
morrião, Ital. *morione*, a morion. The
word is Spanish, if we may accept the
prob. derivation from Span. *morra*, the
crown of the head; a word of unknown
origin. Cf. Span. *morro*, anything round;
moron, a hillock.

Mormonite. The *Mormonites* are
the followers of Joseph Smith, who in
1827 said he had found the book of *Mor-
mon*. An invented name.

Morn. (E.) M. E. *morn*, a Northern
form. Short for M. E. *morwen*, Ancren
Riwle, p. 22. A. S. *morgen*, whence
morwen by the usual change of *rg* to *rw*.
O. Fries. *morn*.+Du. Dan. G. *morgen*;
Icel. *morginn*, Swed. *morgon*; Goth.
maurgins. Teut. type *murgenoz, m.
Cf. Lithuan. *merkti*, to blink. Orig. sense
prob. 'dawn.' **Doublet,** *morrow*, q. v.

morning. (E.) Short for *morwening*,
Ch. C. T., A 1062; formed from M. E.

morwen (above) by adding the substantival
(not participial) suffix -*ing* (= A. S. -*ung*).
So also *even-ing*, from *even*.

Morocco, a fine kind of leather. Named
from *Morocco*, in N. Africa; which was
named from the *Moors* dwelling there.

Morose. (L.) L. *mōrōsus*, self-willed;
(1) in a good sense, scrupulous; (2) in a
bad sense, peevish. – L. *mōr-*, nom. *mōs*,
(1) self-will, (2) custom, use. ¶ Confused
with L. *mŏra*, delay, in the 17th cent.

Morphia, Morphine, the narcotic
principle of opium. (Gk.) From Gk.
Μορφεύς, Morpheus, god of dreams (Ovid);
lit. 'shaper,' i. e. creator of dreams. – Gk.
μορφή, a shape, form. **Der.** *meta-morph-
osis, a-morph-ous*; from μορφή.

Morris, Morris-dance. (Span. –
L. – Gk.) The dance was also called a
morisco, i. e. a Moorish dance. – Span.
Morisco, Moorish. – Span. *Moro*, a Moor.
– L. *Maurus*, a Moor. See **Moor** (3 .

Morrow. (E.) M. E. *morwe*, from an
older form *morwen* (from A. S. *morgen*),
by loss of final *n*. See **Morn.** Thus
M. E. *morwen* gave rise (1) to *morrow*, by
loss of *n*; (2) to *morn*, by loss of *w*, and
contraction; cf. M. E. *moroun*, Gawain,
1208. [Or else *morne*, dat., is from A. S.
morgene, short form *morne*.] **Der.** *to-
morrow* = A. S. *tō morgene*, i. e. for the
morrow, where *tō* is a prep. (E. *to*), and
morgene is dat. case of *morgen*, morn.

Morse, a walrus. (F. – Finnish.) F.
morse. – Finnish *mursu*, a morse; whence
also Russ. *morj'*, a morse (with *j* sounded
as F. *j*). The true Russ. name is *morskaia
korova*, the sea-cow.

Morsel, a mouthful, small piece. (F.
– L.) M. E. *morsel*. – O. F. *morsel* (F.
morceau). Cf. Ital. *morsello*. Dimin. from
L. *morsum*, a bit. – L. *morsus*, pp. of
mordēre, to bite. See **Mordacity.**

Mortal, deadly. (F. – L.) F. *mortal*.
– L. *mortālis*, adj.; from *mort-*, stem of
mors, death. From L. *mor-ī*, to die; cf.
Skt. *mṛ*, to die, *mṛta*, dead; Russ. *mert-
vuii*, dead; Lithuan. *mirti*, to die; Pers.
murdan, to die; Gk. βροτός, mortal.
Allied to **Murder.** Brugm. i. § 500.

Mortar (1), **Morter,** a vessel in
which substances are pounded with a
pestle. (L.) M. E. *morter.* A.S. *mor-
tere.* – L. *mortārium*, a mortar.

mortar (2), cement. (F. – L.) M. E.
mortier. – F. *mortier*, 'mortar;' Cot. –
L. *mortārium*, mortar; lit. stuff pounded

together; a different use of the word above.

Mortgage, a kind of security for debt (F. – L.) O. F. *mortgage*, lit. a dead pledge; because, whatever profit it might yield, it did not thereby redeem itself, but became dead or lost to the mortgagee on breach of the condition. – F. *mort*, dead; *gage*, a pledge. – L. *mortuus*, dead, pp. of *morī*, to die; *gage*, a pledge; see **Mortal** and **Gage** (1). Der. *mortgag-ee*, where *-ee* answers to the F. *-é* of the pp.

mortify. (F. – L.) M.F. *mortifier*. – L. *mortificāre*, to cause death. – L. *morti-*, decl. stem of *mors*, death; *-ficāre*, for *facere*, to make.

Mortise, a hole in a piece of timber to receive the tenon. (F.) Spelt *mortesse* in Palsgrave. – F. *mortaise*, 'a mortaise in a piece of timber;' Cot. Cf. Span. *mortaja*, a mortise. Orig. unknown; Devic suggests Arab. *murtazz*, fixed in the mark (said of an arrow), very tenacious (said of a miser).

Mortmain. (F. – L.) Property transferred to the church was said to pass into *morte main*, lit. ' dead hand,' because it could not be alienated. – L. *mortuam*, acc. fem. of *mort-uus*, dead; *manum*, acc. of *manus*, hand. See **Mortal.**

mortuary, belonging to the burial of the dead. (L.) Chie.ly in the phr. ' a *mortuary* fee,' which was also called *mortuary* for short. – Late L. *mortuārium*, neut. of *mortuārius*, belonging to the dead. – L. *mortu-us*, dead; pp. of *morī*, to die.

Mosaic-work, ornamental work made with small pieces of marble, &c. (F. – Ital. – L. – Gk.) F. *mosaïque*, ' mosaicall work;' Cot. – Ital. *mosaico*, 'a kinde of curious stone worke of diuers colours;' Florio. – Late L. *mūsaicus*, adj., an extended form from L. *mūsæum* (*opus*), mosaic work. – Late Gk. μουσεῖον, mosaic work, lit. artistic, neut. of μουσεῖος, belonging to the muses, artistic. – Gk. μοῦσα, a muse. Cf. **Museum.**

Moslem, a Mussulman. (Arab.) Arab. *muslim*, 'a musulman, a true believer in the Mohammedan faith;' Richardson. Cf. Arab. *musallim*, one who acquiesces. A *mussulman* is one who professes *islām*, i. e. submission to the will of God and to the orthodox faith. – Arab. *salama*, to be resigned. ¶ The E. words *moslem*, *mussulman*, *islam*, and *salaam* are all from the same Arab. root *salama*.

Mosque, a Mohammedan temple. (F. – Span. – Arab. F. *mosquée*; Cot. – Span. *mezquita*, a mosque. – Arab. *masjad*, *masjid*, a temple, place of prayer. – Arab. root *sajada*, to adore, prostrate oneself.

Mosquito, a gnat. (Span. – L.) Span. *mosquito*, a little gnat; dimin. of *mosca*, a fly. – L. *musca*. a fly. Cf. Gk. μυῖα, Lithuan. *musè*, a fly.

Moss. (E.) M. E. *mos*; A. S. *mos*, a swamp. +Du. *mos*; Icel. *mosi*, moss, also a moss or moorland; Dan. *mos*, moss, *mose*, a bog, moor; Swed. *mossa*; G. *moos*, moss, a swamp, O. H. G. *mos*. Teut. base **mus-*; allied to M. H. G. *mies*, O. H. G. *mios*, A. S. *mēos*, moss (Teut. base **meus-*); and to **Mire.** Cognate with Russ. *mokh*', moss, L. *muscus*, moss. ¶ Note E. *moss* in sense of bog, moorland; hence *moss-trooper.* Brugm. i. § 105.

Most. (E.) M. E. *most*, *mēst*. – A. S. *mǣst*.+Du. *meest*, Icel. *mestr*, G. *meist*, Goth. *maists*; the superlative form corresponding to comp. *more*. See **More.** ¶ The *o* (for early M. E. *ē*) is due to the *o* in *more.*

Mote, a particle of dust, speck. (E.) M. E. *mot*. A. S. *mot*, a mote.+Du. *mot*, sawdust; E. Fries. *mut*, grit.

Motet, Motett, a short piece of sacred music. (F. – Ital. – L.) F. *motet*, ' a verse in musick;' Cot. – Ital. *mottetto*, ' a dittie, a wittie saying;' Florio. Dimin. of *motto*, a saying. – L. *muttum*, a murmur; see **Motto.**

Moth. (E.) M. E. *mothe*. A. S. *moððe*, *mohðe*. + Du. *mot*, Icel. *motti*, G. *motte*, a moth; Swed. *mått*, a mite. β. Perhaps related to A. S. *maða*, a maggot, Du. G. *made*, a maggot, Goth. *matha*, a worm. Kluge allies these forms to the verb *to mow*, i. e. to cut as if the sense were ' cutter.' Cf. E. *after-math.*

Mother (1), a female parent. (E.) M. E. *moder*. A. S. *mōder*, *mōdor*, a mother; the change from *d* to *th* is late, after A. D. 1400.+Du. *moeder*, Icel. *moðir*, Dan. Swed. *moder*, G. *mutter*; Irish and Gael. *mathair*; Russ. *mate*, Lithuan. *motė*, L. *māter*, Gk. μήτηρ, Pers. *mādar*, Skt. *mātā*, *mātr-*. Orig. sense uncertain.

mother (2), hysterical passion. (E.) In King Lear, ii. 4. 56. Spelt *moder* in Palsgrave; and the same word as the above.+Du. *moeder*, a mother, womb, hysterical passion; cf. G. *mutterbeschwerung* mother-fit, hysterical passion.

Mother (3), lees, mouldiness. (O. Low. G., Originally *mudder.* — M. Du. *modder*, mud or mire, also the lees, dregs, or 'the mother of wine or beere'; Hexham. +G. *moder*, mud, mould, mouldering decay (from Low G. *moder*); which is sometimes called *mutter* (as if 'mother'; from Low G. *mudder*, mud). Extended from **Mud**, q. v.

Motion. (F. — L.) F. *motion.* — L. *mōtiōnem*, acc. of *mōtio*, movement. — L. *mōtus*, pp. of *mouēre*, to move. See **Move.**

motive. (F. — L.) M. F. *motif*, 'a moving reason;' Cot. — Late L. *mōtivus*, moving. — L. *mōt-us*, pp. of *mouēre*, to move.

motor. (L.) L. *mōt-or*, a mover.

Motley, of different colours. (F.) M.E. *mottelee*, Ch. C. T. 271. Of uncertain origin. Perhaps from O. F. *mattelé*, 'clotted, curdled;' Cot. Cf. M. F. *mattonné*, as in *ciel mattonné*, 'a skie full of small curdled clouds;' id. [Thus the orig. sense of *motley* was merely 'spotted.'] — Bavarian *matte*, curds (Schmeller). 2. Or from O. F. *motel*, M. F. *motteau*, 'a clot of congealed moisture,' Cot.; app. a deriv. of M. F. *motte*, a clod, lump; see **Moat.** Der. *mottl-ed*, for O. F. *mattelé* above, by substituting the E. pp. suffix *-ed* for the F. pp. suffix *-é*.

Motto. (Ital. — L.) Ital. *motto*, a saying, a motto. — L. *muttum*, a murmur, muttered sound; cf. L. *muttīre, mūtīre,* to murmur. (√MU.) Allied to **Mutter.**

Mould (1), earth. (E.) M. E. *molde*. A. S. *molde*, dust, soil, earth. +Icel. *mold*, Dan. *muld*, Swed. *mull* (for *muld*), mould; Goth. *mulda*, dust; O. H. G. *molta*, mould. Allied to the shorter forms seen in Du. *mul*, G. *mull*, A. S. *myl*, dust; cf. O. H. G. *muljan*, Icel. *mylja*, to crush. The lit. sense is 'crumbled.' From Teut. *mul*, weak grade of √MEL, to grind. See **Meal, Mill.** Der. *mould-er*, to crumble; also *mould-y* (which seems to have been confused with **Mole** (1), q. v.).

Mould (2), a model, form. (F. — L.) M. E. *molde*, with excrescent *d*. — Norman dial. *molde*, O. F. *mole, molle* (F. *moule*), a mould; once spelt *modle* in the 12th cent. (Littré). — L. *modulum*, acc. of *modulus*, dimin. of *modus*, a measure. See **Mode.**

Mould (3), a spot. (E.) For *mole*; *mold* in Spenser, F. Q. vi. 12. 7. 'One yron

mole defaceth the whole peece of lawne,' Lyly, Euphues, p. 39. This is now called *iron-mould* (with added *d*). We also find M. E. *moled*, spotted; hence mod. E. *mouldy* (in some senses); by confusion with *mould* (1). See **Mole** (1).

Mouldy, musty. (Scand.) Orig. distinct from *mould*, ground; also from *mould* as used in *iron-mould*. Formed from the sb. *mould*, mustiness, in which the final *d* is excrescent. From the M. E. verb *moulen, mowlen*, to grow musty; formerly very common, and much used in the pp. *mouled*. Note also the M. E. *moul*, mould, mouldiness, answering to Dan. *mul*, Swed. dial. *mul, muel, mujel*, Swed. *mögel*. Cf. also Dan. *mullen*, mouldy, *mulne*, to become mouldy; Swed. dial. *mulas*, Swed. *möglas*, to grow mouldy; Icel. *mygla*, to grow musty. From *mug-*, as in Icel. *mugga*, mugginess. See **Muggy.** Thus *mould* is 'mugginess' in this use.

Moult, to cast fe.thers, as birds. (L.) The *l* is intrusive. M. E. *mouten.* A. S. *mūtian* (in comp. *bi-mūtian*). — L. *mūtāre*, to change. See **Mutable.**

Mound, an earthen defence, a hillock. (E.) M. E. *mound*, a protection. A. S. *mund*, protection, chiefly as a law-term; but also *mund-beorh*, a protecting hill, a mound. +O. Fries. *mund*, O. H. G. *munt*, a protector; cf. G. *vormund*, a guardian.

Mount (1), a hill. (F. — L.) M. E. *mount, mont.* — F. *mont.* — L. *mont-*, stem of *mons*, a hill. — √MEN, to jut out; see **Mound.** Cf. A. S. *munt* (borrowed from L.).

mount (2), to ascend. (F. — L.) F. *monter.* — F. *mont*, a hill. [The verb is due to O. F. *a mont*, up-hill.] — L. *montem*, acc. of *mons* (above).

mountain. (F. — L.) O. F. *montaine* (F. *montagne*). — Late L. *montānea*, by-form of *montāna*, a mountain. — L. *montāna*, neut. pl., mountainous regions; from *montānus*, adj. from *mons* (stem *mont-*), a mountain.

mountebank, a quack doctor. (Ital. — L. *and* G.) Lit. one who *mounts a bench*, to proclaim his nostrums. — Ital. *montambanco*, a mountebank; M. Ital. *monta in banco*, the same. — Ital. *montare*, to mount; *in*, on; *banco*, a bench. Here *montare* is the same word as F. *monter*, to mount; *in* = L. *in*, on; and *banco* is from O. H. G. *banc*, a bench; see **Bank** (2).

Mourn. (E.) M. E. *murnen.* A. S.

murnan, to grieve.+Icel. *morna*, Goth. *maurnan*, O. H. G. *mornēn*. Cf. A. S. *meornan*, to care, Gk. μέρ-ιμνα, sorrow. (√SMER.)

Mouse. (E.) M. E. *mous*. A. S. *mūs* (pl. *mȳs*). + Du. *muis*, Icel. *mūs*, Dan. *muus*, Swed. *mus*, G. *maus*, Russ. *muishe*, L. *mūs*, Gk. μῦς, Pers. *mūsh*, a mouse; Skt. *mūsha-*, a rat, a mouse. Perhaps from √MEUS, to steal; Skt. *mush*, to steal. See **Muscle** (1).

Moustache, Mustache. (F.–Ital. –Gk.) F. *moustache*. – Ital. *mostaccio*, 'a face, a snout, a mostacho;' Florio. – Gk. μύστακ-, stem of μύσταξ, the upper lip, a moustache, Doric form of μάσταξ, the mouth, upper lip. See **Mastic**.

Mouth. (E.) M. E. *mouth*. A. S. *mūð*.+Du. *mond*, Icel. *munnr*, Dan. *mund*, Swed. *mun*, G. *mund*, Goth. *munths*. Teut. type **munthoz*, masc.; Idg. type **mṇtos*; cf. L. *mentum*, the chin.

Move. (F.–L.) M. E. *mouen* (*u=v*). –O. F. *movoir* (F. *mouvoir*). – L. *mouēre*, to move, pp. *mōtus*. **Der.** *motion*.

Mow (1), to cut grass. (E.) M. E. *mowen*, pt. t. *mew*. A. S. *māwan*, to mow, strong vb. + Du. *maaijen*, Dan. *meie*, G. *māhen*, O. H. G. *māen*. Teut. base *mǣ-*. Allied to Gk. ἀ-μά-ω, I reap, L. *me-t-ere*, to reap. Brugm. ii. § 680.

Mow (2), a heap, pile of hay or corn. (E.) M. E. *mowe*, A. S. *mūga*, a mow. + Icel. *mūgr*, a swathe, also a crowd; Norw. *muga*, *mua*, a heap (of hay). Cf. **Muck.**

Mow (3), a grimace; *obsolete.* (F. – M. Du.) F. *moue*, 'a moe, or mouth;' Cot.; Norman dial. *moe*.–M. Du. *mouwe*, the protruded under-lip, in making a grimace (Oudemans). Cf. **Mop** (2).

Much. (E.) M. E. *moche*, *muche*, adj., later forms of M. E. *mochel*, *muchel*, *michel*. For the loss of final *l*, cf. E. *wench*, from A. S. *wencel*. The change of vowel (from *michel* to *muchel*) seems to have been due to association with M. E. *lutel*, little, from A. S. *lȳtel*. The orig. A. S. form was *micel* (cf. Low Sc. *mickle*), great. + Icel. *mikill*, great; O. H. G. *mihhil*; Goth. *mikils*. Cf. Gk. μεγάλ-η, fem. of μέγας, great.

Mucilage, a slimy substance, gum. (F.–L.) F. *mucilage*.–L. *mūcilāgo* (stem *mūcilāgin-*), mouldy moisture (4th cent.). –L. *mūcēre*, to be mouldy.

Muck, filth. (Scand.) M. E. *muck*.– Icel. *myki*, dung; *moka*, to shovel dung

out of a stable; Dan. *møg*, dung; Norw. *mok-dunge*, a muck-heap, allied to *mukka*, a heap. ¶ Not allied to A. S. *meox*, dung.

Muck, Amuck, a term applied to malicious rage. (Malay.) Only in phr. 'to run amuck,' where *amuck* is all one word; yet Dryden actually has 'runs *an Indian muck*,' Hind and Panther, iii. 1188. To *run amuck*=to run about in a rage.– Malay *āmuk*, 'rushing in a state of frenzy to the commission of indiscriminate murder;' Marsden.

Mucus, slimy fluid. (L.) L. *mūcus*, slime. + Gk. μύξα, mucus; μύκης, snuff of a wick. Cf. Skt. *much*, L. *mungere*, Gk. ἀπο-μύσσειν, to cast or wipe away.

Mud, wet soft earth, mire. (E.) M. E. *mud* (not common). Not found in A. S. Cf. E. Fries. *mudde*, Low G. *mudde*, mud; M. Swed. *modd*, mud (Ihre). + Bavarian *mott*, peat; whence E. *moat*, q. v. Hence *mother* (3), q. v.

muddle, to confuse. (E.) Lit. to dabble in mud; frequentative from *mud*. 'Muddle*, to rout with the bill, as geese and ducks do; also, to make tipsy and unfit for business;' Kersey.+Dan. *muddre*, to stir up mud, *mudder*, mud (from Du.); E. Fries. *muddelen*, to dirty; M. Du. *moddelen*, 'to mudd water,' Hexham; Pomeran. *muddeln*, to disorder.

Muezzin, a Mohammedan crier of the hour of prayer. (Arab.) Arab. *mu-azzin*, *mu-zin*, the public crier, who assembles people to prayers.–Arab. *azan*, the call to prayers (Palmer); *uzn*, the ear.

Muff (1), a warm, soft cover for the hands. (Walloon.–F.–Low L.) A late word. Formerly *muffe*; Minsheu. Prob. from Walloon *mouffe* (Sigart). Cf. Du. *mof*; Low G. *muff* (Berghaus); E. Fries. *muf*. The word *muffle* is found earlier, and is more widely spread; so that Wall. *mouffe* is merely a short form of F. *moufle*; see below.

muffle, to cover up warmly. (F.– Low L.) 'I *muffyll*;' Palsgrave. 'A *muffle*;' Levins (1570). – O. F. *mofle*, *moufle*, a kind of muff or mitten. – Low L. *muffula*, (occurring A. D. 817); also spelt *mulfola*. Cf. M. Du. *moffel*, a muff, mitten. ¶ The late appearance of Du. *mof*, and the Low L. form *mulfola*, remain unexplained. Cf. M. H. G. *mouwe*, a sleeve.

Muff (2), a simpleton. (E.) Lit. 'a mumbler,' or indistinct speaker; hence a stupid fellow. Cf. prov. E. *muff*, *muffle*, to mumble; also *moffle*, *maffle*. **+** Du. *muffen*, to dote; prov. G. *muffen*, to be sulky. Allied to **Mumble.**

Muffle; see **Muff** (1).

Mufti, a magistrate. (Arab.) Arab. *muftī*, a magistrate. Allied to Arab. *fatwā*, a judgment, doom, sentence. ¶ The phr. *in mufti* means in a civilian costume, not in military dress.

Mug. (Scand.) In Levins (1570). Cf. Irish *mugan*, a mug. – Norw. *mugga*, *mugge*, an open can; Swed. *mugg*, a mug. – E. Fries. *mukke*, a cylindrical earthen vessel; Groningen *mokke* (Molema, p. 543); whence also Norm. dial. *moque*, a cup, Guernsey *mogue*.

Muggy, damp and close. (Scand.) From Icel. *mugga*, soft drizzling mist; whence *mugguveðr*, muggy, misty weather. Cf. Norw. *mugg*, fine rain; *muggen*, moist, muggy; Dan. *muggen*, musty, mouldy, *mugne*, to grow musty.

Mugwort, a plant. (E.) M. E. *mogwort*. A.S. *mucgwort*. For the latter syllable, see **Wort** (1). The sense of A.S. *mucg* is unknown, unless it be a by-form of A.S. *mycg*, a midge; cf. Norw. *mugg*, O. Sax. *muggia*, Du. *mug*, a midge; O. H. G. *mucca*, a midge. [Like *flea-bane*.]

Mulatto, one of mixed breed. (Span. – Arab.) Span. *mulato*, a mulatto. Usually derived from Span. *mula*, a she-mule, as being one of a mixed breed. But the true forms for 'young mule' are *muleto*, m., *muleta*, f. Hence der. by De Sacy from Arab. *muwallad*, lit. 'begotten'; also used to mean 'one who has an Arabian father and a foreign mother'; allied to Arab. *walad*, a son. See Devic.

Mulberry. (L. *and* E.) M. E. *moolbery*. Here the *l* stands for an older *r*, by dissimilation; and M. E. *oo* answers to A. S. *ō*, as usual. Thus the M. E. *mool-* is the same as A. S. *mōr-*, in *mōr-bēam*, a mulberry-tree. Again, the A. S. *mōr* is borrowed from L. *mōrus*, a mulberry-tree. The word *berry* is E. ; see **Berry.** Cf. also Gk. μῶρον, μόρον, a mulberry, μορέα, a mulberry-tree. ¶ Similarly, G. *maulbeere*, a mulberry, is O. H. G. *mūrberi*, from L. *mōrus* and O. H. G. *beri*, G. *beere.*

Mulct, a fine. (L.) L. *mulcta*, a fine; also spelt *multa*. Perhaps orig. 'damage;' from L. *mulc-āre*, to injure. Brugm. i. § 756. **Der.** *mulct*, verb.

Mule. (F. – L.) F. *mule*. – L. *mūlus*, a mule (whence also A.S. *mūl*).

Mulled, applied to ale or wine. (E.) *Mulled ale* is a corruption of *muld-ale* or *mold-ale*, a funeral ale or feast. M. E. *molde-ale*, a 'mould-ale,' a funeral feast; from *molde*, the earth of the grave, and *ale*, a feast (as in *bride-ale*). The sense being lost, *mulled* was thought to be a pp., and a verb *to mull* was evolved from it.

Mullein, the verbascum. (E.) M. E. *moleyn*. A. S. *molegn*, mullein? The sense is doubtful; but see the Cent. Dict. and Cockayne, Leechd. iii. 339. (Cf. A. S. *holegn*, holly, whence prov. E. *hollin*, holly.)

Mullet (1), a fish. (F. – L.) M. E. *molet*, *mulet*. – F. *mulet*; Cot. Dimin. from L. *mullus*, the red mullet.

Mullet (2), a five-pointed star. (F. – L.) O. F. *molette*, a rowell, whence it came to mean the 'mullet' of heraldry; also M. F. *mollette*, 'a mullet, rowell of a spur;' Cot. Dimin. from L. *mola*, a mill, whence Ital. *mola*, a mill-stone, mill-wheel, *molla*, a clock-wheel with cogs. See **Mill.**

Mulligatawny, a hot soup. (Tamil.) Tamil *milagu-tannīr*, lit. 'pepper-water;' Yule. Cf. Malayālam *mulaka*, pepper.

Mullion, an upright division between lights of windows. (F.) A corruption of *munnion*, which occurs with the same sense. The lit. sense is 'stump,' because the *mullion* is, properly, the stump or lower part of the division below the tracery. – F. *moignon*, a stump. (Cf. E. *trunnion* = M.F. *troignon*, dimin. of F. *tronc* = Ital. *tronco*.) – O. F. *moing*, maimed (Suppl. to Diez). Cf. Bret. *mouñ*, *moñ*, maimed, also occurring in the forms *mañk*, *moñk*, *moñs*. Also Span. *muñon*, the stump of an arm or leg; Ital. *mugnone*, 'a carpenter's munion or trunion,' Torriano.

Multangular, &c. ; see **Multitude.**

Multitude. (F. – L.) F. *multitude*. – L. *multitūdinem*, acc. of *multitūdo*, a multitude. – L. *multi-*, for *multus*, many, much; with suffix *-tūdo*. From L. *multus* come also *mult-angular*, *multi-lateral*, &c.

multifarious. (L.) L. *multifāri-us*, manifold; with suffix *-ous*. The orig. sense seems to be 'many-speaking,' i.e. speaking on many subjects. – L. *multi-*, for *multus*, many; *fārī*, to speak; see **Fate.**

multiply. (F. – L.) F. *multiplier.*

– L. *multiplicāre.* **– L.** *multiplic-,* from *multiplex,* many-fold; cf. *plic-āre,* to fold. See Plait.

Mum, a kind of beer (Low G.). In Pope. Said to have been so named after Chr. *Mumm,* a brewer of Brunswick (ab. 1487). Cf. Du. *mom* in Franck; G. *mumme.*

Mum! silence! (E.) M. E. *mom, mum,* to express the least sound made with closed lips. Cf. L. *mu,* Gk. μῦ (the same).

mumble, to speak indistinctly. (E.) For *mumm-le.* M. E. *momelen, mamelen,* to speak indistinctly; frequent. form due to M. E. *mom,* mum (above). **+** E. Fries. *mummelen;* Du. *mommelen.*

mummer, a masker, buffoon. (F. – Du.) M. F. *mommeur,* 'a mummer, one that goes a-mumming;' Cot. **–** M. Du. *mommen,* to go a-mumming; cf. *momaensicht,* a mummer's mask; Low G. *mumme,* a mask. β. The word is imitative, from the sound *mum* or *mom,* used by nurses to frighten or amuse children, at the same time pretending to cover their faces. Cf. G. *mummel,* a bug-bear. **Der.** *mummer-y,* M. F. *mommerie* (F. *momerie.*

Mummy. (F. – Ital. – Arab. – Pers.) F. *momie* (*mumie* in Cotgrave). **–** Ital. *mummia, mumia* (Florio). **–** Arab. *mūmiyā,* a mummy; the substance with which mummies are preserved. (Cf. Pers. *mūmāyin,* a mummy.) **–** Pers. *mūm, mōm,* wax; much used in embalming.

Mump, to mumble, sulk, beg. (Du.) A *mumper* was a cant term for a beggar. **–** Du. *mompen,* to mump, cheat (Sewel); cf. *mommelen, mompelen,* to mumble (Hexham). Thus *mump* is merely an emphatic form of *mum,* M. Du. *mommen,* to say mum, also to mask. Cf. Norw. *mumpa,* to munch. See Mumble.

mumps. (Du.) 'To have the *mumps*' or 'to be in the *mumps*' was to be sulky or sullen; hence it was transferred to the disease which gave one a sullen appearance. From *mump* (above).

Munch, to chew. (E.) M. E. *monchen* (Chaucer). Doubtless an imitative word, like *mump.* Kilian has M. Du. *moncken, mompelen,* ' mussitare.' Cf. E. Fries. and Low G. *munkeln,* to mumble: and see Mump. ¶ It cannot be from F. *manger* (<L. *mandūcāre*).

Mundane, worldly. (F. – L.) M. E. *mondain.* **–** F. *mondain.* **–** L. *mundānus,* adj. from *mundus,* the world (lit. order). **–**

L. *mundus,* clean, adorned. **Der.** *supramundane;* from L. *suprā,* above; *mundus,* the world.

Mungoose, a kind of ichneumon. (Telugu.) Telugu *mangīsu;* ' Jerdon gives *mangūs,* however, as a Deccani and Mahratti word;' Yule.

Municipal. (F. – L.) F. *municipal.* **–** L. *mūnicipālis,* relating to a township. **–** L. *mūnicipium,* a township which had the rights of Roman citizenship, whilst retaining its own laws. **–** L. *mūnicip-,* stem of *mūniceps,* a free citizen, one who undertakes duties. **–** L. *mūni-,* for *munus,* obligation, duty; *capere,* to take. See Brugm. i. § 208.

munificence, liberality. (F. – L.) F. *munificence.* **–** L. *mūnificentia;* formed from *mūnificus,* bountiful. **–** L. *mūni-,* for *munus,* a duty, also a present; *-fic-,* for *facere,* to make.

Muniment, a defence, title-deed. (F. – L.) M.F. *muniment.* **–** L. *mūnimentum,* a defence. **–** L. *mūnīre,* to fortify; old form *moenire.* **–** L. *moenia,* neut. pl., walls, ramparts, defences. Brugm. i. § 208.

munition. (F. – L.) F. *munition.* **–** L. acc. *mūnītiōnem,* a defending. **–** L. *mūnītus,* pp. of *mūnīre* (above). **Der.** *ammunition.*

Munnion, old form of Mullion, q. v.

Mural. (F. – L.) F. *mural.* **–** L. *mūrālis,* belonging to a wall. **–** L. *mūrus,* a wall.

Murder, Murther, sb. (E.) M.E. *mordre, morthre.* A. F. *murdre,* sb. ; *murdrir,* vb. A.S. *morðor.* **+** Goth. *maurthr.* β. We also find A.S. *morð,* Du. *moord,* Icel. *morð,* G. *mord,* murder, death, cognate with L. *mors* (stem *mort-*); see Mortal. **Der.** *murder,* vb.

Muriatic, briny. (L.) L. *muriāticus,* lying in brine. **–** L. *muria,* brine, salt liquor.

Muricated, prickly. (L.) L. *mūricātus,* prickly. **–** L. *mūric-,* stem of *mūrex,* a prickly fish, a spike. **+** Gk. μύαξ (for *μύσαξ), a sea-muscle; from μῦς, a mouse, a sea-muscle. See Muscle (2).

Murky, Mirky. (Scand.) The *-y* is a modern addition. M. E. *mirke, merke.* **–** Icel. *myrkr* (for *mirkwoz,* Noreen), Dan. Swed. *mörk,* dark, mirky.**+**A.S. *mirce;* O. Sax. *mirki.* ¶ The A. S. form would have given *mirch.*

Murmur, sb. (F. – L.) F. *murmure.* **–** L. *murmur,* a murmur; *murmurāre,* to murmur.+Skt. *marmara-*, rustling sound of wind. A reduplicated form; cf. G. *murren*, Icel. *murra*, to murmur. Of imitative origin. Brugm. i. § 499.

Murrain, cattle-disease. (F. — L.) M. E. *moreine*, also *morin*. — O. F. *morine*, a carcase of a beast, also a murrain; Norm. dial. *murine*. Cf. Span. *morriña*, Port. *morrinha*, murrain. — O. F. *morir* (F. *mourir*), to die. — L. *morī*, to die. See **Mortal**.

Murrey, dark red; *heraldic*. (F. — L.) In Palsgrave. — M. F. *morée*, 'a kind of murrey, or dark red colour;' Cot. [Cf. Ital. *morato*, mulberry-coloured.] — L. *mōrum*, a mulberry. See **Mulberry**.

Murrion; see Morion.

Muscadel, Muscatel, Muscadine. (F. — Ital. — L. — Pers.) M.F. *muscadel*. — M. Ital. *moscadello, moscatello, moscatino*, names of wines, from their perfume. — M. Ital. *moscato*, scented with musk. — M. Ital. *musco*, musk. — L. *muscum*, acc. of *muscus*, musk; see further under **Musk**. And see **Nutmeg**.

Muscle (1), the fleshy part of the body. (F. — L.) F. *muscle*. — L. *musculum*, acc. of *musculus*, (1) a little mouse, (2) a muscle, from its creeping appearance when moved. Dimin. of L. *mūs*, a mouse; see **Mouse**. (Cf. F. *souris*, (1) mouse, (2) muscle.)

muscle (2), **mussel**, a shell-fish. (L.) In earlier use. M. E. *muscle*, A.S. *muxle*, *muscle* (Wright), a muscle (fish). — L. *musculus*, a sea-muscle, also a little mouse (as above).

.Muscoid, moss-like. (L. *with* Gk. *suffix*.) L. *musco-*, for *muscus*, moss; and Gk. suffix -ειδης, like, from εἶδος, form. See **Moss**.

Muse (1), to meditate. (F. — L.) M. E. *musen*. — F. *muser*, 'to muse, dreame;' Cot. — O. F. *muse*, the mouth, muzzle (Godefroy); see **Muzzle**. The image is that of a dog sniffing the air when in doubt as to the scent; cf. Ital. *musare*, to muse, also to gape about, 'to hould ones musle or snout in the aire,' Florio, from Ital. *muso*, snout.

Muse (2), a goddess of the arts. (F. — L. — Gk.) F. *muse*. — L. *mūsa*. — Gk. μοῦσα, a muse.

museum. (L. — Gk.) L. *mūsēum*. — Gk. μουσεῖον, temple of the muses, a study, a school. — Gk. μοῦσα, a muse.

Mushroom. (F. — O. H. G.) M. E.

muscheron. — M.F. *mouscheron, mousseron*, a mushroom; extended from F. *mousse*, moss (Hatzfeld). — O. H. G. *mos* (G. *moos*), moss; see **Moss**.

Music. (F. — L. — Gk.) M. E. *musik*. — F. *musique*. — L. *mūsica*. — Gk. μουσική, musical art, fem. of μουσικός, belonging to the muses. — Gk. μοῦσα, a muse.

Musit, a small gap in a hedge. (F. — C. ?) M. F. *mussette*, 'a little hole;' Cot. Dimin. of O. F. *musse*, a secret corner. — F. *musser*, to hide. Perhaps of Celt. origin; cf. O. Irish *mūch-aim*, I hide (Thurneysen, p. 108).

Musk, a perfume. (F. — L. — Gk. — Pers.) F. *musc*. — L. *muscum*. acc. of *muscus*. — Gk. μόσχος. — Pers. *musk, misk*. Cf. Skt. *mushka*, a testicle, because musk was obtained from a bag behind the musk-deer's navel; it also means 'little mouse,' from *mush*, to steal. See **Mouse**.

Musket. (F. — Ital. — L.) M. F. *mousquet*, a musket, orig. a kind of hawk; (another sort of gun was called a *falconet*, another a *saker*, a kind of hawk). — Ital. *mosquetto*, a musket, orig. a kind of hawk, so called from its small size. Deriv. of Ital. *mosca*, a fly. — L. *musca*, a fly. Doublet, *mosquito*.

Muslin. (F. — Ital. — Syriac.) F. *mousseline*; O. F. *mosolin*. — Ital. *mussolino*, dimin. of *mussolo*, muslin. — Syriac *Mosul*, a city in Kurdistan, whence it first came; Arab. *Mawsil* (the same).

Musquito; see Mosquito.

Mussel; see Muscle (2).

Mussulman, a true believer in the Mohammedan faith. (Pers. — Arab.) Pers. *musulmān*, an orthodox believer. — Arab. *moslim, muslim*, a moslem; see **Moslem**.

Must (1), part of a verb implying 'obligation.' (E.) Only the pt. t. remains, which is now only used as a present. M. E. *mot, moot*, preterito-pres. t., I am able, I am free to, I ought; pt. t. *moste, muste*, I was able, I ought. A. S. *ic mōt*, preterito-pres. t.; *ic mōste*, I must, new pt. t.; infin. **mōtan*. +O. Sax. **mōtan*, pr. t. *ik mōt*, pt. t. *ik mōsta*; Du. *moeten*, to be obliged; Swed. *måste*, I must (compare the E. use); G. *müssen*, pr. t. *ich muss*, pt. t. *ich musste*; Goth. pr. t. *ik ga-mot*, pt. t. *ik ga-mosta*, lit. 'I find room.'

Must (2), new wine. (L.) M. E. *must*. A. S. *must*. — L. *mustum*, new wine; neut. of *mustus*, fresh, new.

Mustachio; see **Moustache**.

Mustang, a wild horse of the prairies. (Span.–L.) Span. *mesteño* (with *ñ* as *ny*), formerly *mestengo* (Pineda), in the same sense as *mostrenco*, adj., stray, having no owner. The adj. *mesteño* also means belonging to a 'mesta.' – Span. *mesta*, a body of proprietors of cattle, a company of graziers. – L. *mixta*, fem. of pp. of *miscēre*, to mingle. Cf. Span. *mestura*, a mixture.

Mustard. (F.–L.; *with* Teut. *suffix.*) M. E. *mostard.* – O. F. *mostarde* (F. *moutarde*). Cf. Ital. *mostarda.* It took its name from being mixed with *must* or vinegar (Littré). – L. *mustum*, must; with suffix *-ard* (<G. *hart*).

Muster. (F.–L.) M. E. *moustre*, a muster of men, lit. display. – O. F. *mostre*, another form of *monstre*, 'a pattern, also a muster, view, shew;' Cot. The same word as F. *monstre*, a monster; see **Monster.** Cf. O. Norm. dial. *mustrer*, Gascon *mustra*, to shew.

Musty, mouldy, damp. (L.) A doublet of *moisty*, used by Chaucer in the sense of 'new,' but by Ascham in the sense of 'moist.' – L. *musteus*, like must, new. – L. *mustum*, must. See **Must** (2). Perhaps influenced by F. *moisi*, 'mouldy, musty, fusty,' Cot.; from which, however, it cannot possibly be derived.

Mutable. (L.) M. E. *mutable.* – L. *mūtābilis*, changeable. – L. *mūtāre*, to change. Prob. for *moitāre*; allied to *mūtuus*, mutual, and to Gk. μοῖτος, thanks, favour (Prellwitz).

Mutchkin, a pint. (Du.) From M. Du. *mudseken* (for *mutseken*), 'the halfe pint of Paris measure,' Hexham. Lit. 'small cap;' dimin. of M. Du. *mutse* (Du. *muts*), a cap. Cf. G. *mütze*, a cap. See **Amice** (2).

Mute (1), dumb. (L.) From L. *mūtus*, dumb. Cf. Skt. *mūka-*, dumb. ¶ The M. E. *muet, mewet*, mute, is from a Romanic form *mūtettus*, formed from L. *mūt-us* (O. F. *mu*) by adding *-ettus.*

Mute (2), to dung; used of birds. (F. M. Du.) M. F. *mutir*, 'to mute as a hawke;' Cot. Short for M. F. *esmeutir*, the same; oldest spelling *esmeltir.* – M. Du. *smelten, smilten*, to smelt, to liquefy; also to mute (Hexham). See **Smelt.**

Mutilate. (L.) From pp. of L. *mutilāre*, to maim. – L. *mutilus*, maimed. +Gk. μύτιλος, μίτυλος, curtailed, docked.

Mutiny. (F.–L.) Formed from the old verb to *mutine*; Haml. iii. 4. 83. – F. *mutiner*, 'to mutine;' Cot. – O. F. *mutin*, tumultuous. – O. F. *mute*, a sedition; (cf. Low L. *mōta*, a pack of hounds = mod. F. *meute*) – Folk-L. *movita*, (lit. moved, hence, a movement, bustle), fem. of *movitus*, new pp. of *mouēre*, to move. Cf. mod. F. *émeute.* See **Move.**

Mutter, to murmur. (E.) M. E. *muttren, moteren.* A frequentative verb, from a base *mut-*, to express inarticulate mumbling, as in E. Fries. *motjen*, to mutter; Swed. dial. *mutla, muttra*, Norw. *mutra.* So also L. *muttīre, mūtire*, to mutter, prov. G. *mustern*, to whisper.

Mutton. (F.–C.?) M. E. *motoun.* – O. F. *moton* (F. *mouton*), a sheep; Low L. *multo*, a sheep. Cf. Ital. *montone* (for *moltone*), a sheep. Prob. of Celtic origin, from Celt. type *moltos*, a sheep; whence Irish and Manx *molt*, Gael. *mult*, W. *mollt*, Corn. *mols*, Bret. *maout*, a wether sheep. ¶ Diez cites Prov. *mout*, Como *mot*, Grisons *mutt*, castrated, and derives all from L. *mutilus*, maimed; but this is not now accepted.

Mutual. (F. – L.) O. F. *mutuël.* Extended from L. *mūtu-us*, mutual, reciprocal, orig. 'exchanged.'– L. *mūtāre*, to change. See **Mutable.**

Muzzle, snout. (F.–L.) M. E. *mosel.* – O. F. *musel* (Burguy), *muzel* (A. D. 1521, Godefroy); later *museau*, 'muzzle,' Cot ; Norm. dial. *musel* (Du Bois). Diez shews that the orig. F. form was *morsel* (still preserved in Bret. *morzeel* or *muzel*, a muzzle, forms borrowed from O. F.). This O. F. *morsel* is a dimin. from Late L. *morsus*, a morsel, also a snout, beak. – L. *morsus*, a bite; from *morsus*, pp. of *mordēre*, to bite. See **Mordacity.** Cf. Ital. *muso*, snout, *morso*, a snaffle (Florio). ¶ Disputed.

My. (E.) M. E. *mi, my*; short for *min*, mine, by loss of final *n.* See **Mine.** Der. *my-self*, M. E. *mi-self*, formerly *me-self.*

Myriad. (Gk.) Gk. μυριάδ-, stem of μυριάς, the number of 10,000. – Gk. μυρίος, numberless.

Myrmidon. (L.–Gk.) Gen. in pl. *Myrmidons.* – L. *Myrmidones*, pl. – Gk. Μυρμιδόνες, pl., a warlike people of Thessaly, formerly in Ægina (Homer).

Myrrh. (F.–L.–Gk.–Arab.) M.E. *mirre.* – O. F. *mirre* (11th cent.); F. *myrrhe.* – L. *myrrha.* – Gk. μύρρα. – Arab.

murr, (1) bitter, (2) myrrh, named from its bitterness.+Heb. *mōr*, myrrh.

Myrtle. (F.–L.–Gk.–Pers.) O. F. *myrtil*, dimin. of *myrte*, *meurte*, the myrtle-tree. – L. *murtus*, *myrtus*. – Gk. *μύρτος*. – Pers. *mūrd*, the myrtle.

Mystery (1), a secret rite. (L.–Gk.) M. E. *mysterie.* – L. *mystĕrium.* – Gk. *μυστήριον* (Rom. xvi. 25).–Gk. *μύστης*, one who is initiated. – Gk. *μυεῖν*, to initiate.

Mystery (2), **Mistery**, a trade, handicraft; see **Mistery**.

Mystic, secret, allegorical. (F.–L.– Gk.) F. *mystique.*–L. *mysticus.*–Gk. *μυστικός*, mystic. – Gk.*μύστης*,fem.*μύστις*, one who is initiated; see **Mystery** (1).

mystify. (F.–Gk. *and* L.) F. *mystifier*, a modern and ill-coined word; coined from Gk. *μυστι-κός*, mystic, and F. *-fier*, from L. *-ficāre*, for *facere*, to make.

Myth, a fable. (Gk.) Gk. *μῦθος*, a fable.

mythology. (F.–L.–Gk.) F. *mythologie.* – L. *mȳthologia.* – Gk. *μυθολογία*, legendary lore. – Gk. *μῦθο-s*, a fable; *λόγ-ος*, a discourse, from *λέγειν*, to tell.

N.

Nab, to seize. (Scand.) Prov. E. *nap* (North). From Swed. and Norw. *nappa*, Dan. *nappe*, to catch, snatch at, nab. **Der.** *kidnap*.

Nabob, an Indian prince. (Hind.– Arab.) Hind. *nawāb* or *nawwāb*, orig. a pl. sb., but used in the sing. as a title of honour. Pl. of Arab. *nāib*, a vice-gerent, deputy, viceroy. Cf. Arab. *nawb*, supplying the place of another.

Nadir, the point of the sky opposite the zenith. (F.–Span.–Arab.) F. *nadir.* –Span. *nadir.*–Arab. *nazīr*, short for *naziru's 'samt*, the nadir; lit. ' corresponding to the zenith.' –Arab. *nazīr*, alike, corresponding to; *as'samt*, the azimuth, also the zenith. See **Azimuth, Zenith.** (The *z* is here the 17th letter of the Arab. alphabet.)

Nag (1), a horse. (M. Du.) M. E. *nagge.* – M. Du. *negghe*, *negge*, Du. *negge*, *neg*, a small horse; Du. dial. *knagge* (Molema). Cf. Low G. *nikkel*, a nag. Origin unknown.

Nag (2), to worry, tease. (Scand.) Norw. Swed. *nagga*, to nibble, peck; cf. Dan. *nage*, Icel. *gnaga*, to gnaw; Low G.

nagen, *naggen*, to gnaw, vex, nag; *gnaggen*, to nag (Berghaus). See **Gnaw.**

Naiad, a water-nymph. (L.–Gk.) L. *naiad-*, stem of *naias.* – Gk. *ναιάς*, a water - nymph. – Gk. *νάειν*, to flow. Cf. O. Irish *snáim*, I swim. (√SNĀ.)

Nail. (E.) M. E. *nayl.* A. S. *nægel.* +Du. *nagel*, Dan. *nagle*, Swed. *nagel*, G. *nagel*; Icel. *nagl*, the human nail, *nagli*, a nail or spike; and cf. Goth. *ganagljan*, to nail. β. The Teut. type is **nagloz*, masc. Allied to Lithuan. *nagas*, a claw, Russ. *nogote*, a nail, Pers. *nākhun*, Skt. *nakha-*, nail of the finger or toe; and further, to Gk. *ὄνυξ*, L. *unguis*, O. Irish *inga*, W. *ewin*, a nail, with a different gradation.

Naive, artless. (F.–L.) F. *naïve*, fem. of *naïf*, native, natural.–L. *nātiuus*, native.–L. *nātus*, born; see **Natal.**

Naked. (E.) A. S. *nacod.*+Du. *naakt*, G. *nackt*, Goth. *nakwaths*, Icel. *nökviðr*; cf. Dan. *nögen*, Swed. *naken*, mod. Icel. *nakinn*. All these are pp. forms; cf. *nake*, to strip, in Chaucer, tr. of Boethius, bk. iv. m. 7; which is a back-formation. Teut. type **nakwathoz*>**nakwadoz*; Idg. type **nog(w)otós.* Allied to Skt. *nagna-*, Russ. *nagoi*, L. *nūdus*, Irish *nochd*, W. *noeth*, stripped, bare. Brugm. i. § 165. See **Nude.**

Naker, a kettle-drum. (Arab.) In Chaucer. Arab. *naqqārah*, a kettle-drum; see Palmer's Pers. Dict.. col. 659.

Name. (E.) A. S. *nama.*+Du. *naam*; Icel.*nafn*, *namn*, Dan.*navn*,Swed. *namn*; Goth. *namo*, G. *name.* Further allied to L. *nōmen*, a name; Gk. *ὄνομα*, Pers. *nām*, Skt. *nāman*; and to Ir. *ainm*, W. *enw*, name. ¶ Not allied to **Know**; see Prellwitz. Brugm. i. §§ 399, 425.

Nankeen, Nankin, a kind of cotton cloth. (China.) So called from *Nankin*, in China. –Chin. *nan-king*, south court; cf. *pe-king*, north court (Yule).

Nap (1), a short sleep. (E.) M. E. *nappen*, verb, to doze. A. S. *hnæppian*, verb, to doze. Cf. O. H. G. *hnaffezen*, to nap.

Nap (2), the roughish surface of cloth. (M. Du.) M. E. *noppe*, nap (Prompt. Parv.). Prob. introduced by Du. cloth-workers. [A.S. **hnoppa* is unauthorised.] – M. Du. *noppe*, ' the haire or nap of wooll or cloath;' Hexham. Du. *nop.* Cf. M. Du. *noppen*,' to sheare of[f] the nap ;' Hexham.+Norw. *napp*, nap; *nappa*, to give a nap to; Dan. *noppe*, nap; *noppe*, to friz; Low G. *nobbe*, *nubbe*, nap. Allied to Norw. *nuppa*, to pluck off with the fingers; A.S. *hnoppian*, to pluck, Voc. 480. 23; Goth. *dis-hnupnan*, to be torn to pieces, *dis-hniupan*, to tear to pieces. Teut. root **hneup*.

Nape, the joint of the neck behind. (E.) M. E. *nape*; also *naupe* (Palsgrave). The same as O. Fries. *hals-knap*, nape of the neck; which links it with A. S. *cnæp*, the top of a hill; and with **Knop**.

Napery, linen for the table. (F. – L.) O. F. *naperie*. – Late L. *nāpāria*, *mappāria*, the office in a household for supplying table-linen. – Late L. *nāpa*, a cloth, for L. *mappa*, a cloth. See **Map**, **Napkin**.

Naphtha. (L. – Gk. – Arab.) L. *naphtha.* – Gk. ναφθα. – Arab. *naft*, *nift*, naphtha, bitumen.

Napkin, a small cloth. (F. – L.; *with* E. *suffix*.) M. E. *napekin*, also *napet*, both dimin. forms of O. F. *nape*, a cloth, from Late L. *nāpa*; see **Napery**.

Narcissus, a flower. (L. – Gk.) L. *narcissus.* – Gk. νάρκισσος; named from its *narcotic* properties. See below.

narcotic, producing stupor. (F. – Gk.) F. *narcotique.* – Gk. ναρκωτικός, benumbing. – Gk. ναρκόω, I benumb; ναρκάω, I grow numb. – Gk. νάρκη, numbness, orig. contraction; for **σνάρκη*, i. e. contraction. Allied to **Snare** (Prellwitz).

Nard, an unguent. (F. – L. – Gk. – Pers.) F. *nard.* – L. *nardus.* – Gk. νάρδος, Mk. xiv. 3. – Pers. *nard* (whence Skt. *nalada-*), spikenard.+Skt. *naḍa-*, a reed. Horn, § 1060. Der. *spike-nard*.

Nargileh, Nargili, Nargile, a pipe or smoking-apparatus in which the smoke is passed through water. (Pers.) – Pers. *nārgīl*, a coco-nut, because these pipes were originally made with a coco-nut, which held the water. Cf. Skt. *nārikera-*, *nārikela-*, a coco-nut. (Devic, Yule.)

Narration. (F. – L.) F. *narration.* – L. acc. *narrātiōnem*, a tale. – L. *narrātus*, pp. of *narrāre*, to relate, lit. to make known. – L. *nārus*, *gnārus*, knowing, acquainted with. – √GEN, to know; see **Know**. Brugm. i. § 457 (2).

Narrow. (E.) M. E. *narowe*, *narewe*, *narwe*. A. S. *nearu*, narrow, closely drawn.+O. Sax. *naro*; Du. *naar*, dismal, sad. Perhaps allied to **Nerve** (Franck).

Narwhal, sea-unicorn. (Scand.) Dan.

Swed. *narhval*; Icel. *nāhvalr*, a narwhal. The lit. sense is 'corpse-whale'; the fish being (often) of a pallid colour; perhaps a 'popular etymology.' – Icel. *nā-r*, corpse; *hvalr*, whale.

Nasal. (F. – L.) F. *nasal*. – Late L. *nāsālis*, belonging to the nose. – L. *nāsus*, nose. See **Nose**.

Nascent, springing up. (L.) L. *nascent-*, stem of pres. pt. of *nascī*, to be born, arise, spring up, inceptive verb from pp. *nātus*. See **Natal**.

Nasturtium, a flower. (L.) Lit. 'nose-wring;' from the sharp smell. – L. *nasturtium*, cress; better spelt *nasturcium*. – L. *nās-us*, nose; *torquēre*, to twist, torment; see **Torment**.

Nasty. (Scand.) Formerly also *nasky*; see *Mau-lavé* in Cot. Cf. Swed. dial. *naskug*, nasty, dirty, also spelt *snaskig*; Swed. *snuskig*, nasty. – Swed. dial. *snaska*, to eat like a pig, be slovenly; Dan. *snaske*, to eat like a pig.+Low G. *nask*, nasty; Norw. *nask*, greedy, *naska*, to champ; E. Fries. *nasken*, G. *naschen*, O. H. G. *nascōn*, to eat dainties.

Natal, belonging to one's birth. (F. – L.) F. *natal* (O. F. *noël*). – L. *nātālis*. – L. *nātus* (for *gnātus*), born (cf. Gk. κασίγνητος, a blood relation); pp. of *nascī*, to be born. – √GEN, to beget. See **genus**, **Kin**. Brugm. i. § 452.

Natation, swimming. (L.) From the acc. of L. *natātio*, a swimming. – L. *natātus*, pp. of *natāre*, to swim, frequent. of *nāre*, to swim. Cf. Gk. νήχειν, to swim, O. Irish *snā-im*, I swim. See **Naiad**.

Nation. (F. – L.) F. *nation*. – L. *nātiōnem*, acc. of *nātio*, a nation. – L. *nātus*, born. See **Natal**.

native. (F. – L.) F. *natif*, 'native;' Cot. – L. *nātīuus*, natural. – L. *nātus*, born. **Doublet**, *naive*.

nature. (F. – L.) F. *nature*. – L. *nātūra*, nature. – L. *nātus*, born.

Natron, native carbonate of soda. (F. – Span. – Arab. – Gk. – Heb.) A doublet of *nitre*; see **Nitre**.

Naught, Nought. (E.) M. E. *naught*. A.S. *nāwiht*, also *nāht*. – A.S. *nā*, not; *wiht*, a whit; see **No** and **Whit**. Der. *naught-y* (lit. naught-like, worthless). **Doublet**, *not*.

Nauseous. (L. – Gk.) L. *nauseōsus*, adj.; from *nausea*, sea-sickness. – Gk. ναυσία, sea-sickness. – Gk. ναῦς, a ship. See **Nave** (2).

Nautch, a kind of ballet-dance by women. (Hind. – Prakrit. – Skt.) Hind. (and Mahratti) *nāch,* a dance; Prakrit *nachcha.* – Skt. *nṛtya,* dancing, acting; orig. fut. pass. part. of *nṛt,* to dance, to act. Der. *nautch-girl,* a dancing-girl (Yule).

Nautical. (L. – Gk.) From L. *nautic-us,* nautical. – Gk. ναυτικός, pertaining to ships. – Gk. ναύτης, a sailor; from ναῦ-s, a ship. See **Nave** (2).

nautilus, a shell-fish. (L. – Gk.) L. *nautilus.* – Gk. ναυτίλος, a sea-man; also the nautilus (from its sailing). – Gk. ναύτης, a sailor; from ναῦ-s, a ship.

Naval. (F. – L.) F. *naval.* – L. *nāuālis,* belonging to ships. – L. *nāuis,* a ship. Cf. Gk. ναῦs. See **Nave** (2).

Nave (1), the hub of a wheel. (E.) M. E. *naue* (*u=v*). A. S. *nafu, nabu.* + Du. *naaf,* Icel. *nöf,* Dan. *nav,* Swed. *naf,* G. *nabe,* O. H. G. *naba.* Teut. type **nabā,* fem. Cf. Skt. *nābhi-,* the nave of a wheel, navel, centre, boss. See **Navel.** Der. *auger.*

Nave (2), the body of a church. (F. – L.) From O. F. *nave* (F. *nef*), a ship, also the body of a church; said to be named from its lengthy shape. – L. *nāuem,* acc. of *nāuis,* a ship. + Gk. ναῦs, a ship, O. Irish *nau,* Skt. *nau-.* Brugm. i. § 184.

Navel. (E.) M. E. *nauel* (*u=v*); A.S. *nafela, nabula,* navel. + Du. *navel,* Icel. *nafli,* Dan. *navle,* Swed. *nafle,* G. *nabel.* Teut. type **nabolon-;* from the form seen in Lettish *naba,* navel; see **Nave** (1). Cf. also Pers. *nāf,* navel; Skt. *nābhi-,* (1) nave, (2) navel; related (with a difference of gradation) to Gk. ὀμφαλός, navel, Lat. *umbilīcus,* O. Irish *imbliu.* Similarly, *nave* (1) is allied to L. *umbō,* boss (of a shield). Brugm. ii. § 76.

Navigable, that can be traversed by ships. (F. – L.) F. *navigable.* – L. *nāuigābilis.* – L. *nāuigāre,* to navigate. – L. *nāu-,* for *nāuis,* a ship; *-igāre,* for *agere,* to drive.

navigation. (F. – L.) F. *naviga-tion,* sailing. – L. acc. *nāuigātiōnem;* from pp. of L. *nāuigāre* (above).

navvy, a labourer employed on railways, &c. (L.) Short for *navigator,* formerly used to mean a labourer employed on canals for *navigation;* first used, according to Haydn, about 1830.

navy, a fleet. (F. – L.) M. E. *navie.* – O. F. *navie,* orig. a single ship. – L. *nāuia,* a vessel. – L. *nāui-s,* a ship.

Nay. (Scand.) M. E. *nay.* – Icel. *nei,* Dan. *nei,* Swed. *nej,* nay. Negative of Aye, q. v.

Nazarite, a Jew who made vows of abstinence, &c. (Heb.; *with* Gk. *suffix.*) Heb. *nāzar,* to separate oneself, vow, abstain; with suffix *-ite* (= L. *-īta,* Gk. *-ιτης*).

Neap, scanty, very low; said of a tide. (E.) M. E. *neep;* A. S. *nēp* (or *nep*).

Near, nigh. (E.) Now used as a positive, but orig. the comparative of *nigh.* [The form *nearer* is a double comparative.] M. E. *nerre,* adj., *ner,* adv., nigher; A. S. *nēar,* comparative adv. from *nēah,* nigh. + Icel. *nær,* adv., both positive and comparative; orig. the latter. See **Nigh.**

Neat (1), black cattle, an ox. (E.) M. E. *neet,* both sing. and pl. A. S. *nēat,* pl. *nēat,* cattle. + Icel. *naut,* pl. *naut,* cattle; Swed. *nöt;* Dan. *nöd;* M. H. G. *nōz,* cattle. Teut. type **nautom,* neut. β. Usually explained as 'domestic' or 'useful'; from the 2nd grade (*naut*) of Teut. **neut-an,* to employ; seen in A. S. *nēotan,* to use, employ, Icel. *njóta,* G. *geniessen,* Goth. *niutan,* to enjoy, get benefit from. Cf. Lithuan. *naudà,* usefulness. (√NEUD.) Brugm. i. § 221. Der. *neat-herd.*

Neat (2), tidy. (F. – L.) F. *net,* masc., *nette,* fem., neat, pure. – L. *nitidus,* shining, neat. – L. *nitēre,* to shine.

Neb, beak, nose. (E.) M. E. *neb,* face. A. S. *nebb,* face. + Du. *neb,* bill, nib, mouth; Icel. *nef,* nose; Dan. *næb;* Swed. *näbb.* β. Further allied to Du. *sneb,* bill, beak, *snavel,* bill; G. *schnabel,* bill, M. H. G. *snabel,* allied to M. H. G. *snaben,* to snap. And cf. Lith. *snapas,* bill.

Nebula, a misty patch of light. (L.) L. *nebula,* mist. + Gk. νεφέλη, cloud; Du. *nevel,* Icel. *nifl,* G. *nebel,* mist. Allied to Gk. νέφος, cloud, W. *nef,* O. Ir. *nem,* heaven, Russ. *nebo,* heaven; also Skt. *nabhas,* sky, æther. Brugm. i. § 554.

Necessary. (F. – L.) O. F. *neces-saire.* – L. *necessārius,* needful. – L. *necesse,* neut. adj., necessary.

Neck. (E.) M. E. *nekke.* A.S. *hnecca,* neck, orig. nape of the neck. + Du. *nek,* G. *genick;* Teut. type **hnekkon-.* Cf. also Icel. *hnakki,* Dan. *nakke,* Swed. *nacke,* G. *nacken,* O. H. G. *(h)nach,* nape of the neck, back of the head; from Teut. type **hnakkon-.* β. Orig. sense 'projection', further allied to Irish *cnoc,* hill.

Necromancy, divination by communion with the dead. (F.−L.−Gk.) M.E. *nigromancie* (since altered).−O. F. *nigromance,* 'nigromancy, conjuring, the black art;' Cot.−Late L. *nigromantia,* corrupt form of L. *necromantīa.* − Gk. νεκρομαντεία, necromancy. − Gk. νεκρό-s, a corpse; μαντεία, prophetic power. β. Gk. νεκρός, is allied to νέκυς, a corpse; cf. L. *necāre,* to kill. (√NEK.) Gk. μαντεία is from μάντις, a seer. ¶ *Necromancy* was called ' the black art' owing to a popular etymology from L. *niger,* black; cf. the Late L. *nigromantia.*

Nectar. (L.−Gk.) L. *nectar.* − Gk. νέκταρ, the drink of the gods.

Need. (E.) M. E. *need.* A.S. *nīed* (*nȳd*), also *nēad*; O. Merc. *nēd,* necessity. + Icel. *nauðr,* necessity, *nauð,* distress; Du. *nood,* Dan. Swed. *nöd,* G. *noth, not,* Goth. *nauths.* Teut. stem *naudi-.* In late A. S. texts this word is confused in form with *nēod, nīed* (*nȳd*), desire ; which is related to O. Sax. *niud,* O. H. G. *niot,* desire; Teut. base **neud-.* Brugm. i. § 427 b.

Needle. (E.) Also *neeld*; M.E. *nedle,* also *nelde.* A. S. *nǣdel*; earlier form *nǣðl.* + Du. *naald* (for **naadl*) ; Icel. *nál*; Dan. *naal* ; Swed. *nål*; G. *nadel*; Goth. *nēthla.* β. All from a Teut. type **nǣ-thlā,* from root **nē,* to sew, as in G. *nähen,* to sew, L. *nēre,* Gk. νήθειν, νέειν, to spin. Cf. √SNĒ, as in O. Irish *sním,* a spinning ; cf. Irish *snathad,* a needle, *snathaim,* I string together, *snaidhe,* thread. See Brugm. i. § 136, ii. § 62.

Neese, Neeze, to sneeze, puff. (E.) M. E. *nesen* ; not in A. S. + Du. *niezen,* G. *niesen,* O. H. G. *niusan,* Icel. *hnjōsa,* Swed. *nysa,* Dan. *nyse.* Teut. type **hneusan-.* See **Sneeze.**

Nefarious. (L.) L. *nefāri-us,* impious ; with suffix *-ous.* − L. *nefās,* that which is unlawful. − L. *ne-,* for *nē,* not ; *fās,* law, allied to *fāri,* to speak, declare. Cf. Skt. *bhāsh,* to speak.

Negation, denial. (F.−L.) M. F. *negation.* − L. acc. *negātiōnem,* denial. − L. *negātus,* pp. of *negāre,* to deny. Prob. from a particle (*neg-*) of negation ; cf. Lith. *negi,* also not. Brugm. ii. § 774.

Neglect. (L.) L. *neglectus,* pp. of *negligere,* to neglect.− L. *neg-,* not (see **Negation**) ; and *legere,* to gather, select.

negligence. (F.−L.) M. F. *negligence.* − L. *negligentia,* carelessness. − L.

negligent-, stem of pres. part. of *negligere,* to neglect (above).

Negotiate, to do business. (L.) From pp. of L. *negōtiāre,* to do business.− L. *negōtium,* business ; compounded of *neg-,* not (see **Negation**), and *ōtium,* leisure.

Negro. (Span.−L.) Span. *negro.* − L. *nigrum,* acc. of *niger,* black.

Negus. (E.) A beverage invented by Colonel *Negus* (one of a Norfolk family) in the time of Queen Anne.

Neif, Neaf, the fist. (Scand.) M. E. *neue* (*u=v*), dat. case. − Icel. *hnefi,* fist ; Swed. *näfve,* Dan. *næve.*

Neigh. (E.) M.E. *neȝen.* A.S. *hnǣgan,* to neigh. + Low G. *neigen* (Lübben), M. Du. *neyen,* to neigh. Cf. Icel. *gneggja,* *hneggja,* Swed. *gnägga,* Dan. *gnegge,* Norw. *kneggja.*

Neighbour. (E.) M. E. *neighebour*; A.S. *nēahgebūr* or *nēahbūr.* − A. S. *nēah,* nigh ; *būr,* or *gebūr,* a husbandman, the same word as Du. *boer,* a boor. See **Boor.** + G. *nachbar,* M.H.G. *nāchbūr*; from *nāch,* nigh, *būr,* a husbandman.

Neither. (E.) M. E. *neither*; for *ne* (negative particle), not, and *either.* See **Either.** With A.S. *ne,* not, cf. O. Sax. *ne, ni* ; Goth. and O. H. G. *ni,* not.

Nemesis. (L.−Gk.) L. *nemesis.* − Gk. νέμεσις, allotment, retribution, vengeance. − Gk. νέμειν, to distribute. (√NEM.)

Nenuphar, a kind of water-lily. (Pers.−Skt.) Pers. *nīnūfar,* for *nīlūfar, nīlūpar, nīlūpal,* a water-lily (Devic). − Skt. *nīlōtpala,* a blue lotus. − Skt. *nīla,* blue; *utpala,* a lotus.

Neology, the introduction of new phrases. (Gk.) Gk. *νέο-s,* new; *-λογία,* from λόγος, discourse, from λέγειν, to speak ; see **New.**

neophyte, a novice. (L.−Gk.) L. *neophytus.* − Gk. νεόφυτος, lit. new planted, hence, a novice. − Gk. *νέο-s,* new ; φυτ-όν, a plant, φυτ-ός, grown, from φύειν, to grow, cause to grow, allied to **Be.**

neoteric, novel. (L.−Gk.) L. *neōtericus.* − Gk. νεωτερικός, novel. − Gk. νεώτερος, comparative of νέος, new ; see **New.**

Nepenthe, Nepenthes, a drug which lulled sorrow. (Gk.) Gk. νηπενθές, an epithet of a soothing drug (in Homer) ; neut. of νηπενθής, free from sorrow. − Gk. νη-, neg. prefix; πένθος, grief, allied to πάθος. See **No** (1) and **Pathos.**

Nephew. (F. − L.) M. E. *neueu* (*= neveu* . − F. *neveu,* 'a nephew;' Cot. −

L. *nepōtem*, acc. of *nepōs*, a grandson, also a nephew.+Skt. *napāt*, a grandson ; Pers. *nawāda*, a grandson ; A. S. *nefa*, a nephew ; G. *neffe*, nephew ; Du. *neef*. Idg. type **nepōt*; whence orig. Teut. type **nefōd*, later **nefon-*. The fem. type is Idg. **neptī-* (Skt. *naptī*, L. *neptis*), Teut. **neftī->* **niftī-* (A. S. *nift*, Du. *nicht*). Der. *nepot-ism*, favouritism to relations, from L. *nepōt-*, stem of *nepōs*. Brugm. i. § 149.

Nereid, a sea-nymph. (L.–Gk.) L. *Nēreid-*, stem of *Nēreis*. ‒ Gk. Νηρείς, a daughter of *Nēreus* (Gk. Νηρεύς), an ancient sea-god. ‒ Gk. *νηρός*, wet ; cf. Gk. *νάειν*, to flow (Prellwitz). (√SNA.)

Nerve. (F.–L.) F. *nerf* ; Cot. ‒ L. *neruum*, acc. of *neruus*, a sinew. Perhaps allied to Gk. *νεῦρον*, a sinew, string ; Skt. *snāva-*, a tendon. See Prellwitz.

Nescient, ignorant. (L.) From L. *nescient-*, stem of *nesciens*, pres. pt. of *nescīre*, not to know. ‒ L. *ne-*, not ; *scīre*, to know. See **Science**, **Nice**.

Nesh, tender, soft. (E.) M. E. *nesh*. A. S. *hnesce*, soft.+Goth. *hnaskwus*, soft, tender.

Ness, a promontory. (E.) Seen in *Sheer-ness*, &c. A. S. *næss*, headland.+ Icel. *nes*, Dan. *næs*, · Swed. *näs*. Teut. types **nasoz* or **nassoz*, masc., **nasjom*, neut. Perhaps allied to **Nose**.

Nest. (E.) M. E. and A.S. *nest*. + Du. *nest*, O. H. G. and G. *nest* ; Bret. *neiz*, Irish and Gael. *nead*, O. Irish, *net* ; W. *nyth*, L. *nīdus* (for **nizdus*), Skt. *nīḍa-*, a nest, a den. β. Orig. 'a place to sit in.' Explained as short for **ni-sd-os*, a place in which to sit down ; cf. Skt. *ni-sad*, to sit down. Here *-sd-* is the weak grade of √SED, to sit. See **Sit**. Der. *nest-le*, from A.S. *nestlian*, to make a nest ; *nest-l-ing*. Brugm. i. § 81.

Net (1), an implement for catching fish. (E.) A. S. *net*, *nett*.+Du. *net*, Icel. Dan. *net*, Swed. *nät*, Goth. *nati*, G. *netz*. Teut. type **natjom*, neut. Cf. L. *nassa*, a wicker creel, Icel. *nōt*, a net.

Net (2), clear of all charges. (F.–L.) F. *net*, pure ; hence, free ; see **Neat** (2).

Nether, lower. (E.) M. E. *nethere*. A. S. *neoðera*, *nioðerra*, nether ; a comp. adj. due to *niðer*, adv., downward, also a compar. form. To be divided as *ni-ðer*, the suffix *-ðer* being comparative, as in *o-ther*, *nei-ther* (cf. Gk.-τερος, Skt. *-tara-*). We find Skt. *ni-tarām*, adv., excessively, continually, grammatically a comp. form

from *ni*, downward, into.+Icel. *neðri*, adj., *neðarr*, adv. ; Dan. *neder-* (in comp.), whence *ned*, downward ; Swed. *nedre*, G. *nieder*, nether ; Du. *neder*, adv., down. Cf. Russ. *nije* (*j* as in F.) adv., lower. Der. *nether-most*, corruption of A. S. *niðe-mest*, extended (by the usual superlative suffix *-est*) from an earlier **ni-ðem-a*, where *-ðe-m-* = Idg. *-to-mo* (as in L. *op-ti-mus*).

Nettle. (E.) M. E. *netle*. A.S. *netele*, *netle*.+Du. *netel*, Dan. *nelde* (for **nedle*), Swed. *nässla* (for **nätla*), G. *nessel*. Teut. type **natilōn-*, fem. An older form appears in O. H. G. *nazza*, fem., a nettle. Cf. O. Irish *nenaid*, nettles.

Neuralgia, pain in the nerves. (Gk.) From Gk. *νεῦρ-ον*, a nerve, and ἀλγ-ος, pain ; with suffix *-ια*. The Gk. *νεῦρον* may be allied to L. *neruus* ; see **Nerve**.

Neuter. (L.) L. *neuter*, neither ; hence, sex-less. ‒ L. *ne*, not ; *uter*, whether ; see **Whether**. Der. *neutr-al*, &c.

Never. (E.) M. E. *neuer* (*u* = *v*). A. S. *nǣfre*. ‒ A. S. *ne*, not ; *ǣfre*, ever ; see **Ever**.

New. (E.) M. E. *newe* ; A. S. *nīwe*, *nēowe*.+Du. *nieuw*, Icel. *nȳr*, Dan. Swed. *ny*, Goth. *niujis*, G. *neu*, L. *nouus*, W. *newydd*, Irish and Gael. *nuadh*, Lithuan. *naujas*, Russ. *novuii*, Gk. *νέος* (=νέϝος), Pers. *nau*, Skt. *nava(s)*, *navya(s)*, new. Idg. types **newios*, *newos* ; Brugm. i. §§ 120, 318 ; ii. § 63. Allied to Skt. *nu*, now ; hence new = 'that which is now,' recent. See **Now**.

newfangled, fond of novelty. (E.) The *d* has been added. M. E. *newefangel*, i. e. fond of what is new. Compounded of *newe*, new, and *fangel*, ready to catch, from the base *fang-*, as in A. S. *fangen*, pp. of *fōn*, to catch. The suffix *-el* is the same as in A. S. *sprec-ol*, fond of speaking, talkative, &c. See **Fang**.

news, tidings. (E.) Formerly *newes*, sb. pl., lit. new things ; see the Kingis Quair, st. 179. It is a translation of F. *nouvelles*, news, pl. of O. F. *novel*, new. Cf. Du. *nieuws* (Sewel).

Newel, the upright column round which a circular staircase winds. (F.–L.) Former-ly *nuell*. ‒ O. F. *nuel*, *noiel*, later *noyau*, 'the stone of a plumme, the nuell or spindle of a winding staire ;' Cot. ‒ L. *nucāle*, neut. of *nucālis*, lit. belonging to a nut ; hence a kernel or stone of a plum. ‒ L. *nuc-*, stem of *nux*, a nut. ¶ Named from its *central* position. Cf. F. *nueil*, a nut (dial. of La Meuse).

Newfangled, News; see **New.**

Newt, a kind of lizard. (E.) The initial *n* is unoriginal; *a newt* stands for *an ewt.* M. E. *newte*; also *ewte*, which is a shortened form of M. E. *evete.* — A. S. *efeta*, a lizard. See **Eft.**

Next, nighest. (E.) M. E. *next*; also *nehest*, superl. of *neh*, nigh; A. S. *nēhst*, superl. of *nēh*, *nēah*, nigh. See **Nigh.**

Nias, a young hawk, a ninny. (F.—L.) M. F. *niais*, 'a neastling, ninny;' Cot. — Late L. acc. type **nīdiācem* (Ital. *nidiace*). — L. *nīdus*, a nest. See **Nest.**

Nib, point of a pen. (E.) Another form of *neb*; see **Neb.** Cf. E. Fries. *nibbe*, *nib*, Low G. *nibbe*, a neb.

Nibble. (E.) Lit. 'to nip often;' the frequent. of *nip*, to pinch off the end of grass, &c.+Low G. *nibbeln*, *knibbeln*, to nibble, to gnaw slightly. (Cf. *dibble* from *dip*.) ¶ Or we may regard it as an attenuated form of Du. *knabbelen*, to nibble.

Nice, fastidious, delicious. (F.—L.) M. E. *nice*, foolish, simple, later fastidious, and lastly delicious. — O. F. *nice*, lazy, simple; orig. ignorant; Romanic **necium* (cf. Span. *necio*). — L. *nescium*, acc. of *nescius*, ignorant.—L. *ne*, not; *scī-re*, to know. See **No** (1) and **Science.**

Niche, a recess in a wall for a statue. (F.—Ital.—L.) F. *niche.*—Ital. *nicchia*, a niche, a shell-like recess in a wall.—Ital. *nicchio*, a shell, also a nitch (Florio).—L. *mītulum, mȳtilum,* acc. of *mītulus, mȳtilus*, a sea-muscle. 'Derived in the same way as Ital. *secchia* from *situla*, a bucket, and *vecchio* from *uetulus*, old; as to the change of initial, cf. Ital. *nespola* with L. *mespilum*, a medlar;' Diez. [The same change occurs in F. *natte*, a mat, and in *napkin*.] We also find L. *mūtulus*, a sea-muscle; cf. L. *musculus*, a sea-muscle; see **Muscle** (1). Cf. Gk. μυτίλος (Liddell).

Nick `(1), a small notch. (O. Low G.) *Nick* is an attenuated form of *nock*, a notch; see **Nock.** So also *tip* from *top*.

Nick (2), the devil. (F.—L.—Gk.) Short for *Nicolas*. [Not from A. S. *nicor*, a water-sprite, hobgoblin; Icel. *nykr*, Dan. *nök*, *nisse*, Swed. *näck*, G. *nix*, a water-goblin. See Kluge, s. v. *Nix*.]

Nickel, a grayish white metal. (G.— Swed.) G. *nickel*, nickel: *kupfernickel*, nickel of copper.—Swed. *nickel*. So named

by Cronstedt (a Swed. mineralogist) in 1754 (Cent. Dict.).

Nicknack; see **Knickknack.**

Nickname. (E.) M. E. *nekename*, also *ekename*; (*a nekename = an ekename*). See Prompt. Parv.; cf. Du. *toenaam*, G. *zuname.* From *eke* and *name.* + Icel. *auknefni*, Swed. *öknamn*, Dan. *ögenavn*, an eke-name, nickname.

Nicotian, belonging to tobacco. (F.) M. F. *Nicotiane*, 'Nicotian, tobacco, first sent into France by *Nicot* in 1560;' Cot. *Nicot* is a personal name.

Niece. (F.—L.) M. E. *nece*, *neyce.*— M. F. *niece* (F. *nièce*).—Late L. *neptia*, a niece.—L. *neptis*, a granddaughter, niece; used as fem. of L. *nepōs*, nephew. See **Nephew.**

Niggard, a miser. (Scand.) M. E. *nigard*; where the suffix *-ard* is of F. origin (=O. H. G. *hart*, hard). We also find M. E. *nigun*, a niggard, and *niggish*, adj., stingy; and even *nig.*—Icel. *hnöggr*, niggardly, Swed. *njugg*, niggardly, scanty; cf. Mid. Dan. *nygger*, Swed. dial. *nugger*, stingy.+A. S. *hnēaw*, niggardly (Noreen). Cf. M. Du. *nugger*, 'nimble, carefull, or diligent,' Hexham.

Nigh. (E.) M. E. *neh, neih, ney.* A. S. *nēah, nēh*, nigh; adv. and prep. + Du. *na*, adv., Icel. *ná-* (as in *ná-būi*, a neighbour); Goth. *nēhwa*, adv. and prep.; G. *nah, nahe*, adj., *nach*, prep., nigh. Teut. type **nêhwo-.* Root unknown.

Night. (E.) M. E. *night, niht.* A. S. *niht, neaht*; O. Merc. *næht.*+Du. G. *nacht*, Icel. *nátt, nótt*, Dan. *nat*, Swed. *natt*, Goth. *nahts.* Teut. type **naht-*; Idg. type **nokt-.* + W. *nos*, Irish *nochd*, Lithuan. *naktis*, Russ. *noche*, L. *nox* (stem *noct-*), Gk. νύξ (stem νυκτ-), Skt. *nakta-.* ¶ For the old system of reckoning by *nights*, cf. *sennight, fortnight.*

nightingale. (E.) M. E. *nightingale*, earlier *nightegale* (the *n* having been` inserted;) A. S. *nihtegale.* — A. S. *nihte-*, for *niht*, night; *gale*, a singer, from *galan*, to sing. Lit. 'singer by night.' A. S. *.gal-an* is from *gal-*, 2nd stem of *giellan*, to yell. See **Yell.** So also Du. *nachtegaal*, Dan. *nattergal*, Swed. *näktergal*, G. *nachtigall*, O. H. G. *nahtagala.*

nightmare, an incubus. (E.) M. E. *nightemare.* From A. S. *niht*, night; *mære*, a nightmare, incubus; allied to a Teut. verb **marjan-*, to crush, Icel. *merja* (pt. t. *marði*), to crush. [*Mara* is quite distinct from A. S. *mere*, a mare, but the two have been confused in Du. *nacht-merrie*, a nightmare.]+Icel. *mara*, Swed. *mara*, Dan. *mare*, Low G. *moor*, O. H. G. *mara*, *mar*; all with the sense of incubus or crushing weight on the breast. Cf. F. *cauche-mar*, nightmare; where *cauche* is from L. *calcāre*, to tread on, press upon. Also N. Fries. *naagtmäre*, G. *nachtmahr*, nightmare.

nightshade, a plant. (E.) A. S. *nihtscada*. Cf. Du. *nachtschade*, M. Du. *nachtschaede*, G. *nachtschatten*. Also Swed. dial. *natt-skate-gräs*, as if from *natt-skata*, a bat, and *gräs*, grass (Rietz).

Nigrescent, growing black. (L.) From stem of pres. pt. of *nigrescere*, to grow black, inceptive of *nigrēre*, to be black. ━ L. *nigr-*, for *niger*, black.

Nihilist, a member of a revolutionary secret society, esp. in Russia. (L.) Etymologically, one who denies real existence. ━ L. *nihil*, nothing.

Nilgau; see **Nylghau**.

Nimble, active. (E.) M. E. *nimel*; the *b* is excrescent. Lit. ' ready to catch;' from A. S. *nim-an*, to catch, take, seize; with suffix *-ol*, as in *sprec-ol*, talkative. We actually find A. S. *numol* or *numul*, taking, seizing, or able to receive; from the weak grade (*num-*) of the same verb. Cf. Icel. *nema*, Goth. *niman*, G. *nehmen*, to take. Perhaps related to Gk. νέμεσθαι, to occupy, νέμειν, to distribute. (√NEM.)

Nincompoop, a simpleton. (L.) Thought to be a corruption of L. *non compos* (*mentis*), not sound in mind.

Nine. (E.) M. E. *nine*, where the final *-e* is a pl. suffix, and *nin-* is for *niȝen*, nine (Layamon). A. S. *nigon*, *nigen*, nine. +Du. *negen*, Icel. *nīu*, Dan. *ni*, Sw. *nio*, G. *neun*, Goth. *niun*; cf. also W. *naw*, Ir. *naoi*, L. *nouem*, Gk. ἐννέα, Zend *nava*, Pers. *nuh*, Skt. *nava*, nine. Idg. type *newən. Brugm. ii. § 173.

Ninny, a simpleton. (Ital.) Ital. *ninno*, a child (Diez). Cf. Span. *niño*, a child, one of little experience. ━ Ital. *ninna*, a lullaby, nurse's song to lull children to sleep, also *nanna*. Of imitative origin.

Nip. (E.) M. E. *nippen*, for *knip-pen*; see G. Douglas, Prol. to Æn. xii. l. 94. Not in A. S. From the weak grade (*knip-*) of a Teut. verb **kneipan-*, to pinch, as seen in Du. *knijpen*, to pinch; Dan. *knibe*, Sw. *knipa*; G. *kneifen*, *kneipen*, to pinch (from Low G.). Allied

to Lith. *gnyb-ti*, to pinch; or to Lith. *knĕb-ti*, to pinch.

Nipple, a teat. (E.) Formerly *nible* (Nares); *neble* (Palsgrave); dimin. of *nib* or *neb*; see **Neb**. Cf. O. F. *nifle*, *niffle*, a nose, Ital. *niffolo*, *niffa*, a snout, from the Teutonic (Low G. *nibbe*, a beak). Der. *nipple-wort*.

Nit, egg of a louse; a louse. (E.) M. E. *nite*, a nit, also a louse; A.S. *hnitu*, a louse's egg. + Du. *neet*; Icel. *nitr*, pl., Dan. *gnid*, Swed. *gnet*; G. *niss*; Gk. κονίς (stem κονίδ-); W. *nedd*, pl., nits; cf. also Russ. *gnida*, a nit.

Nitre. (F.━L.━Gk.━Heb.) F. *nitre*. ━ L. *nitrum*. ━ Gk. νίτρον. ━ Heb. *nether*, nitre. ¶ *Nitre* and *natron* are doublets, but applied to different substances. *Natron* is from F. *natron*. ━ Span. *natron*. ━ Arab. *natrūn*, *nitrūn*. ━ Gk. νίτρον. ━ Heb. *nether*. Der. *nitro-gen*, that which produces nitre, from γεν-, base of γίγνειν, to produce.

Nizam, the title of a ruler in the Deccan, in Hindustan. (Hind. ━ Pers. ━ Arab.) From the Arab. *niẓhām*, government, which the Persians pronounce as *nizām*. Though the proper sense is ' government,' in the phrase *nizām-'l-mulk* it is used as a title, meaning ' governor of the empire '; first used by Asaf Jāh in 1713 (Yule.) ━ Arab. root *naẓhama*, he arranged or ordered. (Devic, Richardson.)

No (1), a word of refusal or denial. (E.) M. E. *no*; A. S. *nā*, *no*, adv., never, no. ━ A. S. *ne*, not; *ā*, ever (whence M. E. *oo*, *ō*, ever, now obsolete). See **Aye.** β. With A. S. *ne*, not, cf. Goth. *ni*, Russ. *ne*, Irish, Gael. W. *ni*, L. *ne* (in *non-ne*), Skt. *na*, not.

no (2), none. (E.) Short for *none*, q.v. Der. *no-body*, i.e. none body; it took the place of M. E. *no man*. So also *no-thing*.

Noble. (F. ━ L.) F. *noble*. ━ L. *nō-bilem*, acc. of *nōbilis*, well known. For O. L. *gnōbilis*. ━ L. *gnō-*, base of *nōscere* (i.e. *gnōscere*), to know; allied to E. **Know.** Der. *nobil-i-ty*, O. F. *nobilitet*, L. acc. *nōbilitātem*. Also *i-gnoble*.

Nobody; from *no* and *body*; see **No** (1).

Nock, an indentation, notch; *obs.* (M. Du.) M. E. *nokke*. ━ M. Du. *nocke* (Kilian), a notch in the head of an arrow; M. Swed. *nocka*, a notch; Swed. dial. *nokke*, *nokk*. The M. Swed. *nocka* also denotes the same as Icel. *hnokki*, i. e.

the small metal hooks holding the thread in a distaff. ¶ The M. Ital. *nocca*, a nock, is of Teut. origin. Distinct from *notch*.

Nocturn, a service of the church. (F.—L.) F. *nocturne*, a nocturn; orig. nocturnal. — Late L. *nocturna*, a nocturn; fem. of L. *nocturnus*, nocturnal. From *noct-*, stem of *nox*, night. See **Night**.

Nod. (E.) M. E. *nodden*. Not in A. S.; but the orig. form began with *hn*. The orig. sense was to push, beat, shake. Cf. Icel. *hnyðja*, a rammer for beating turf; O. H. G. *hnōtōn* (*hnotōn*?), to shake; Bavar. *notteln*, to move to and fro. Teut. base **hneud*.

Noddle, the head. (E.) M. E. *nodle*, *nodil*, the noddle, nape, back of the head. ' Occiput, a *nodyle* ;' Vocab. 673. Dimin. of **knod*, a word not found in M. E., but the same as M. Du. *knodde*, a knob (Hexham), Du. *knod*, a club; cf. G. *knoten*, a knot, knob. This is a mere variant of *knot* (Franck). Cf. Low G. *knuddel*, a ball of yarn, a hard swelling under the skin (Berghaus).

Node, a knot. (L.) L. *nōdus*, a knot.

Noggin, a wooden cup. (Scand.) Cf. Irish *noigin*, Gael. *noigean*, a noggin; Gael. *cnagan*, a little knob, a peg, an earthen pipkin, *cnagaire*, ' a knocker'; a gill, noggin; a quart measure;' all from E. (Macbain). Also Lowl. Sc. *noggin*, *noggie*; spelt *knoggin* by Swift. For **knogg-en*, with *-en* as in *wood-en*, from *knog*, variant of *knag*, a knob, peg, also a keg (Jamieson), *knaggie*, a keg (id.). Of Scand. origin; see **Knag**.

Noise. (F.—L.—Gk.) M. E. *noise*.— F. *noise*, O. F. *noise*, *nose*, a debate, quarrel, noise. Cf. Prov. *noisa*, *nausa*, *nueiza*. β. Diez holds that it can only be derived from L. *nausea*, sea-sickness, disgust, hence annoyance, &c.; the L. word being borrowed from Gk. See **Nausea**.

Noisome, annoying, troublesome. (F. — L.; *with* E. *suffix*.) Formed from M. E. *noy*, annoyance; with E. suffix *-some*. This M. E. *noy* is short for M. E. *anoy*, *anoi*. — O. F. *anoi*, vexation; see **Annoy**.

Nole, Noll, head; see **Noule**.

Nomad, wandering. (Gk.) Gk. νομαδ-, stem of νομάς, roaming in search of pasture. — Gk. νομός, a pasture, allotted abode. — Gk. νέμειν, to assign. (√NEM.)

Nomenclator, one who names things. (L.) L. *nōmenclātor*, lit. ' name-caller.'

—L. *nōmen*, name; *calāre*, to call; see **Calends**.

nominal. (F.—L.) F. *nominal*.—L. *nōminālis*, nominal; belonging to a name. — L.*nōmin-*, for *nōmen*, a name; see **Noun**.

nominate. (L.) From pp. of L. *nōmināre*, to name. — L. *nōmin-*, for *nōmen*; see **Noun**.

Non-, prefix, not. (L.) L. *nōn*, not.

nonage. (L. *and* F. — L.) I. e. *non-age*, minority. So also *non-conforming*, *non-descript*, *non-entity*, *non-juror*, *non-sense*, *non-suit*.

Nonce; see **One**.

Nonchalant, careless. (E.—L.) F. *nonchalant*, careless; pres. pt. of O. F. *nonchaloir*, to be careless about. — O. F. *non*, not; *chaloir*, to glow, hence to be hot over, take care for. — L. *non*, not; *calēre*, to glow.

None. (E.) M. E. *noon*, *non*. A.S. *nān*. — A. S. *ne*, not; *ān*, one; see **One**. Hence *no*, as in *no-thing*, *no-body*, by loss of final *n*.

Nones, the ninth day before the ides. (L.) From L. *nōna*, ninth (i. e. ninth day), fem. of *nōnus*, ninth; from *nouem*, nine. See **Nine**.

Nonpareil, matchless. (F.—L.) F. *non*, not; *pareil*, equal.—L. *nōn*, not; Late L. **pariculus*, equal, double dimin. from *par*, equal. Cf. **Apparel**.

Nonplus. (L.) ' To be at a *nonplus*,' to be in perplexity, not to be able to proceed.—L. *nōn*, not; *plūs*, more, further.

Nook. (E.) M. E. *nōk*, a corner. Lowl. Sc. *neuk*, whence (probably) Irish and Gael. *niuc*, a corner, nook; also Lowl. Sc. *nuik*, *nuk*, a headland. It answers to A. S. **nōc* (not found); cf. Norw. *nakke*, a corner cut off; Dan. dial. *nogg*, a bend in a river.

Noon, mid-day. (L.) Orig. the ninth hour or 3 P.M., but afterwards the time of the church-service called *nones* was shifted to mid-day. We find A. S. *nōn-tīd* (lit. noon-tide), the ninth hour, Mk. xv. 33.— L. *nōna*, i. e. ninth hour, fem. of *nōnus*, ninth. See **Nine**.

Noose, a slip-knot. (F. — L.) In Beaumont and Fletcher. The word was imported from Gascony by sailors. — Gascon *nus*; O. Prov. *notz*; Prov. *nous*, a noose or loop. [Cf. Prov. *nous courrént*, a running noose; pl. *nouses*; *nous de l'araire*, a noose for mooring ships; note Gasc. *nouset*, a knot, *nousera*, to tie a

knot.] − L. *nōdus*, nom., a knot. See
Knot.

Nor. (E.) M. E. *nor*, short for *nother*,
neither. − A. S. *nāwðer*, contracted form
of *nāhwæðer*, neither. − A. S. *nā*, not;
hwæðer, whether.

Normal, according to rule. (L.) L.
normālĭs, adj. − L. *norma*, a carpenter's
square, rule, pattern.

Norman, Norse; see North.

North. (E.) A. S. *norð*. + Du. *noord*,
Icel. *norðr*, Dan. Swed. G. *nord*. Root
unknown; some compare Umbrian *nertru*,
on the left hand (to one looking east-
wards); Gk. νέρτερος, lower.

norman. (F. − Scand.) O. F. *Normand*. − Dan. *Normand*; Icel. *Norðmaðr*,
pl. *Norðmenn*. Lit. 'North-man.'

norse. (Scand.) From Norw. and
Dan. *norsk*, Norse; Icel. *norskr*, Norse.
Short for *North-isk*, i. e. *North-ish*.

northern. (E.) A. S. *norðern*; cognate with Icel. *norræn*, O. H. G. *nordrōni*.
For the suffix, cf. L. *-āneus*. Der. *north-
er-ly*, put for *north-ern-ly*.

Nose. (E.) M. E. *nose*. A. S. *nosu*.
+ Du. *neus*. Related, apparently by
gradation, to A. S. *nasu*, nose, Icel. *nös*,
Dan. *næse*, Swed. *näsa*, G. *nase*, Russ.
nos', Lithuan. *nosis*, L. *nāsus*, *nāres*, pl.,
Skt. *nāsā*, dual. Allied to **Ness.** Der.
nose-gay; cf. prov. E. *gay*, a painted
picture in a book, from *gay*, adj.; *nos-tril*;
nozzle; *nuzzle*.

Nosology, science of disease. (Gk.)
Gk. νόσο-ς, disease; -λογία, from λόγος,
discourse, from λέγειν, to speak.

Nostril. (E.) *Nostril* = *nose-thrill* or
nose-thirl. M. E. *nosethirl*; A. S. *nosðyrl*.
− A. S. *nos-u*, nose; *ðyrel*, a perforation,
orifice; see **Thrill.**

Nostrum, a quack medicine. (L.) L.
nostrum, lit. 'our own,' i. e. a special drug
peculiar to the seller. Neut. of *noster*,
ours. − L. *nōs*, we. Cf. Skt. *nas*, us

Not (1), a word expressing denial. (E.)
M. E. *not*, short form of *nought*, *naught*;
see **Naught.**

Not (2), I know not. *or* he knows not.
(E.) *Obsolete.* M. E. *nōt*, *noot*. A. S. *nāt*.
− A. S. *ne*, not ; *wāt*, I know, *or* he knows;
see **Wit.**

Notable. (F. − L.) F. *notable*. − L.
notābilis, remarkable. − L. *notāre*, to mark.
− L. *nota*, a mark; see **Note.**

notary. (F. − L.) M. F. *notaire* − L.
acc. *notārium* (from *notārius*), one who

makes notes, a scrivener. − L. *nota*, a note ;
see **Note.**

Notch, an incision, a score; also, as
vb., to incise, nick. (F.) For *otch*, by
association with *nock*, which has a similar
meaning. M. E. *ochen*, to cut, cut into,
occurs in the Morte Arthure, 2565, 3676.
Notch was often particularly used with
reference to the scoring of tallies, and
cricket was once scored by counting *notches*.
− O. F. *oche* (F. *hoche*), 'a nick, nock, or
notch, the cut of a tally;' Cot. Also
ocher, 'to nick, nock, notch, to cut as a
tally;' id. The O. F. *oche*, Gascon *osco*,
is of unknown origin. ¶ There is a similar
difficulty as to initial *n* in the word *nouch*
or *ouch*; see **Ouch.**

Note, a mark. (F. − L.) F. *note*. − L.
nota, a mark, lit. that by which a thing is
known. Perhaps for *gnōta*, and allied to
nōtus, known, pp. of *noscere*; Bréal. (For
the short *o*, cf. L. *cognitus* = *cognōtus*.)
Der. *not-at-ion*, from L. *notātio*, from pp.
notātus; and see *not-able*, *not-ary* above.

Nothing. (E.) Short for *no thing*; see
None.

Notice. (F. − L.) F. *notice* − L. *nōtitia*,
a being known, knowledge − L. *nōtus*, pp.
of *noscere*, to know. See **Know.**

notify. (F. − L.) F. *notifier*. − L.
nōtificāre, to make known. − L. *nōti-*, for
nōtus, known ; *-ficāre* for *facere*, to
make.

notion. (F. − L.) F. *notion*. − L. acc.
nōtiōnem, an investigation, a notion. − L.
nōtus, pp. of *noscere*, to know. See
Know.

notorious. (L.) From L. *nōtōri-us*,
manifest ; with suffix *-ous*. − L. *nōtor*, a
voucher, witness. − L. pp. *nōtus*, known.
Der. *notori-e-ty*, M. F. *notorieté* (Cot.).

Not-pated, close shorn. (E.) See
1 Hen. IV. ii. 4. 78. From A. S. *hnot*,
close shorn ; and **Pate.**

Notwithstanding. (E.) M. E.
nought withstonding, Gower C. A. ii. 181.
From *naught* and *withstand*.

Nought, the same as **Naught.**

Noule, Nowl, Nole, Noll, head.
(E.) See Nares. Mid. Nt. Dr. iii. 2. 17.
M. E. *nol*. A. S. *hnoll*, the crown of the
head. + O. H. G. *hnol*, top.

Noun, a grammatical term. (F. − L.)
O. F. *noun*, *non*, *nun* (F. *nom*), a name. −
L. *nōmen* a name. See **Name.**

Nourish. (F. − L.) M. E. *norisen*. −
O. F. *nouris-*, *norris-*, stem of pres. pt. of

nourir (F. *nourrir*), to nourish. — L. *nūtrīre*, to nourish, suckle. Cf. **Nurse.**

Novel. (F. — L.) O.F. *novel* (F. *nouveau*). — L. *nouellus*, new, dimin. of *nouus*, new. See **New. Der.** *novel-ty*, from O. F. *noveliteit*, from L. acc. *nouellitātem*, newness.

novice, a beginner. (F. — L.) F. *novice*. — L. *nouicius*, *nouitius*, new, fresh, a novice. — L. *nouus*, new. **Der.** *noviti-ate*, from M.F. *novitiat*, ' the estate of a novice,' Cot., from Late L. *novitiātus*, sb.

November. (L.) L. *Nouember*, the ninth month of the Roman year. — L. *nouem*, nine. See **Nine.**

Now. (E.) M. E. *now, nou, nu*; A.S. *nū.+*Du. *nu*, Icel. *nū*, Dan. Swed. O.H.G. Goth. *nu*, Skt. *nu, nū*. Cf. Gk. *νῦ-ν*, L. *nu-nc*. **Der.** *new.* Brugm. i. § 1042.

Noway, Noways. (E.) The older form is *noways.* — A. S. *nānes weges*, by no way, the gen. case used adverbially. See **None** and **Way.**

nowhere. (E.) A.S. *nāhwǣr.* — A. S. *nā*, not; *hwǣr*, where. See **No** (1) and **Where.**

nowise. (E.) Short for *in no wise*, M. E. *on none wise*; where *none* is dat. of M. E. *noon*, none, and *wise* is dat. of *wise*, a way, from A. S. *wīse*, a way. See **None,** and **Wise,** sb.

Noxious. (L.) L. *noxius*, hurtful. — L. *noxa*, hurt. — L. *nocēre*, to hurt ; cf. *nex*, destruction. **+** Skt. *nāça(s)*, destruction. (√NEK.) Brugm. ii. § 794.

Nozzle, a snout. (E.) Formerly *nozle*; dimin. of *nose.*

Nucleus, core. (L.) L. *nucleus*, small nut, kernel. — L. *nuc-*, stem of *nux*, a nut.

Nude, naked. (L.) L. *nūdus*, bare ; for **nogwedos.* Allied to **Naked.**

Nudge, a slight push. (E.) Lowl. Sc. *nodge*, to push, strike, strike with the knuckles ; North. E. *nog*, to jog. Perhaps of imitative origin. Cf. Norw. *nugga*, to rub, push, allied to *nyggja* (pt. t. *nogg*), to push; Swed. dial. *nogga*, to move slightly.

Nugatory, trifling, vain. (L.) L. *nūgātōrius*, adj. from *nūgātor*, a trifler. — L. *nūgātus*, pp. of *nūgārī*, to trifle. — L. pl. *nūgæ*, trifles.

Nugget, a lump of metal. (E.) Formerly *niggot*; see Trench, Eng. Past and Present. Cf. prov. E. *nug*, a block of wood ; *nigg*, a small piece (Essex) ; *nog, knog*, a block of wood, knob, peg ; allied to **Knag.** See **Noggin.**

Nuisance. (F. — L.) F. *nuisance*, a hurt. — F. *nuisant*, hurtful ; pres. pt. of *nuire*, to hurt. — L. *nocēre*, to hurt.

Null, invalid. (F. — L.) F. *nul.* — L. *nullus*, none. — L. *ne*, not ; *ullus*, any, short for **ūnulus*, dimin. of *ūnus*, one.

Nullah, a water-course, bed of a torrent. (Hind.) Hind. *nāla*, a water-course (Yule).

Numb. (E.) M. E. *nome, nomen*, pp. seized, taken, caught with, overpowered, deprived of sensation. Pp. of M. E. *nimen* (A. S. *niman*), to take ; see **Nimble.+** Icel. *numinn*, bereft, pp. of *nema*, to take.

Number. (F. — L.) F. *nombre.* — L. *numerum*, acc. of *numerus*, a number. Cf. Gk. *νόμ-ος*, law, *νέμειν*, to distribute. (√NEM.) **Der.** *out-number.*

numeral. (L.) From L. *numerālis*, belonging to number. — L. *numerus* (above).

numeration. (F. — L.) F. *numeration.* — L. acc. *numerātiōnem*, a numbering. — L. *numerātus*, pp. of *numerāre*, to number. — L. *numerus*, a number.

numerous. (F. — L.) M.F. *numereux* (Cot.). — L. *numerōsus*, adj. ; from *numerus*, sb., a number.

Numismatic, relating to coins. (L. — Gk.) Coined from L. *numismat-*, stem of *numisma*, current coin. — Gk. *νόμισμα*, a custom, also current coin. — Gk. *νομίζειν*, to adopt, use as coin. — Gk. *νόμος*, usage. — Gk. *νέμειν*, to distribute. (√NEM.)

Nun. (L.) M. E. and A. S. *nunne.* — Late L. *nunna, nonna*, a nun ; orig. a title of respect ; oldest sense, ' mother.' It answers to L. *nonnus*, father, also a monk (Ducange). **+** Gk. *νάννη*, aunt ; Skt. *nanā*, mother, a familiar word used by children. Formed like *ma-ma, da-da* (*daddy*), and the like. **Der.** *nunn-er-y*, from O. F. *nonnerie*, which is from O. F. *nonne*, Late L. *nonna.*

Nuncheon, a luncheon. (Hybrid ; L. *and* E.) The ending is confused with that of *luncheon.* M. E. *nonechenche* (for *noneschenche*), Riley, Memorials of London, p. 265 ; lit. a 'noon-drink,' to accompany the *nonemete* or ' noon-meat.' — M. E. *none*, noon ; *schenche*, a pouring out of drink. — A. S. *nōn*, noon (of L. origin ; see **Noon**) ; *scencan*, to pour out drink. β. The A.S. *scencan* is lit. ' to pour out through a pipe ; ' derived from A. S. *scanc*, a shank, hollow bone, pipe ; see **Shank.**

Nuncio, a messenger. (Ital. — L.) Ital.

nuncio. – L. *nuntium,* acc. of *nuntius,* a bringer of tidings. Prob. for **nouentius,* a bringer of news, from *nouus,* new.

Nuncupative, declared by word of mouth. (F. – L.) F. *nuncupatif* (Cot.). – Late L. *nuncupātīvus,* nominal. – L. *nuncupātus,* pp. of *nuncupāre,* to call by name. For **nōmi-cupāre* ; from L. *nōmen,* name, *capere,* to take. Brugm. ii. § 34.

Nuphar, a kind of water-lily. (Pers. – Skt.) Pers. *nūfar,* short for *nīlūfar* ; see Nenuphar.

Nuptial. (F. – L.) F. *nuptial.* – L. *nuptiālis,* belonging to a marriage. – L. *nuptiæ,* s. pl., a wedding. – L. *nupta,* a bride ; fem. of pp. of *nūbere,* to marry, lit. 'to veil.' Cf. *nūbes,* a cloud.

Nurse. (F. – L.) Contracted from M. E. *norice, nurice.* – O. F. *norrice* (F. *nourrice*). – L. *nūtrīcia,* a nurse. – L. *nūtrīc-,* stem of *nūtrix,* a nurse. – L. *nūtrīre,* to nourish.

nurture. (F. – L.) M. E. *norture.* – O. F. *noriture* (F. *nourriture*). – L. *nūtrītūra,* nourishment ; from *nūtrītus,* pp. of *nūtrīre,* to nourish.

Nut. (E.) M. E. *note, nute* ; A. S. *hnutu.* + Du. *noot,* Icel. *hnot,* Swed. *nöt,* Dan. *nöd,* G. *nuss.* Cf. Irish *cnu,* Gael. *cno,* W. *cneuen,* a nut. Der. *nut-hatch,* i. e. nut-hacker ; see Hatch (3).

nutmeg, the musk-nut. (E. ; *and* F. – L. – Pers. – Skt.) M. E. *notemuge,* later *nutmegge.* Here *-muge* is from O. F. *mugue,* musk. – L. *muscum,* acc. of *muscus,* musk ; see Musk. Cf. O. F. *muguette,* a nutmeg ; also called *noix muscade,* Span. *nuez moscada,* Ital. *noce moscada,* Late L. *muscāta,* nutmeg.

Nutation, a nodding. (L.) From L. *nūtātio,* a nodding. – L. *nūtāre,* to nod, frequent. of *nuere,* to nod. + Gk. *νεύειν,* to nod. (√NEU.)

Nutriment, food. (L.) L. *nūtrīmentum,* food. – L. *nūtrīre,* to nourish, suckle, feed.

nutritious. (L.) L. *nūtrītī-us,* for *nūtrīcius,* adj., nourishing ; with suffix *-ous.* – L. *nūtrīc-,* stem of *nūtrix,* a nurse. – L. *nūtrīre* (above).

nutritive. (F. – L.) F. *nutritif.* Formed with F. suffix *-if* (L. *-īuus*), from *nūtrīt-us,* pp. of *nūtrīre* (above).

Nuzzle, to thrust the nose in. (E.) Formerly *nousle, nosyll* ; a frequent. verb ; from *nose,* sb. Cf. Swed. *nosa,* to smell ; also Bavar. *nuseln, nöseln,* to seek about for, also, to speak through the nose ;

E. Fries. *nüsseln,* Swed. dial. *nösla,* to nuzzle.

Nylghau, a kind of antelope. (Pers.) Pers. *nīlgāw,* a nylghau, lit. 'blue cow.' – Pers. *nīl,* blue (see Lilac) ; and *gāw,* a cow, allied to E. Cow.

Nymph. (F. – L. – Gk.) F. *nymphe.* – L. *nympha.* – Gk. *νύμφη,* a bride.

O.

O (1), **Oh,** interjection. (E.) M. E. *o* ; not in A. S. + Du. Dan. Swed. G. Goth. L. *ō* ; Gk. *ὦ, ὤ.* There was no distinction, formerly, between *o* and *oh.*

O (2), a circle. (E.) So called because the letter *o* is of a circular shape.

Oaf, a simpleton. (Scand.) Prov. E. *auf,* an elf. – Icel. *álfr,* an elf. Chaucer uses *elvish* in the sense of 'simple.' A variant of *elf* ; see Elf.

Oak. (E.) M. E. *ook* ; A. S. *āc.* + Du. Icel. *eik* ; Dan. *eeg, eg,* Swed. *ek,* G. *eiche* ; Teut. base **aik-.*

Oakum, tow from old ropes. (E.) A. S. *ācumba,* tow. (For the sound-change, cf. E. *oak* < A. S. *āc.*) Lit. 'that which is combed out.' – A. S. *ā-,* prefix ; *cemban,* to comb, from *camb,* a comb ; see A- (4) and Comb. Cf. O. H. G. *āchambi,* tow ; of like origin.

Oar. (E.) M. E. *ore* ; A. S. *ār.* + Icel. *ār,* Dan. *aare,* Swed. *åra.* Teut. type **airā,* fem. ; whence Finnish *airo* (Noreen, § 57). ¶ A connexion with Gk. *ἐρ-έτης,* oarsman, cannot be established.

Oasis. (L. – Gk. – Egypt.) L. *oăsis.* – Gk. *ὄασις, αὔασις,* a fertile islet in the Libyan desert. Of Egypt. origin ; cf. Coptic *ouahe,* an oasis, a dwelling-place, *ouih,* to dwell (Peyron).

Oast, Oast-house, a kiln for drying hops. (E.) M. E. *oost, ost.* A. S. *āst,* a kiln, drying-house. + Du. *eest,* M. Du. *ast* (the same). Allied to L. *æstus,* Gk. *αἶθος,* a burning heat. (√AIDH.) See Ether.

Oath. (E.) M. E. *ooth, oth.* A. S. *āð.* + Du. *eed,* Icel. *eiðr,* Dan. Swed. *ed,* Goth. *aiths,* G. *eid,* O. H. G. *eid.* Teut. type **aithoz* ; Idg. type **oitos,* as in O. Irish *oeth,* an oath.

Oats. (E.) M. E. *otes,* pl. A. S. *āte,* sing. ; pl. *ātan.* Perhaps allied to Icel. *eitill,* a nodule in stone, Norw. *eitel,* a gland, knot, nodule, Russ. *iadro,* a kernel, ball, Gk. οἶδος, a swelling. From the swollen shape. (√EID.)

Ob-, prefix. (L.) It changes to *oc-* before *c*, *of-* before *f*, *op-* before *p*. L. *ob*, with very variable senses; as, towards, at, before, upon, over, about, near. Cf. Oscan *op*, near, Gk. ἔπι, upon; Brugm. i. § 557.

Obdurate. (L.) L. *obdūrātus*, pp. of *obdūrāre*, to harden.—L. *ob*; and *dūrus*, hard. See **Dure.**

Obedient. (F.—L.) O. F. *obedient*. —L. *obēdient-*, stem of pres. pt. of *obēdīre* (O. L. *oboedīre*), to obey.—L. *ob-*, near; and *audīre*, to hear. See **Audience.** Brugm. i. § 250. Der. *dis-obedient*.

obeisance. (F.—L.) M. E. *obeisance*. — O. F. *obeissance*, later F. *obéissance*, service, a salute.—O. F. *obeissant*, pres. pt. of *obeir*, to obey.—L. *obēdīre* (above).

Obelisk. (F.—L.—Gk.) O. F. *obelis-que*.—L. *obeliscum*, acc. of *obeliscus*.—Gk. ὀβελίσκος, a pointed spit; hence a thin pointed pillar; dimin. of ὀβελός, a spit.

Obese, fat. (L.) L. *obēsus*, (1) eaten away, wasted; (2) fat, lit. 'that which has devoured.'—L. *obēsus*, pp. of *obedere*, to eat away.—L. *ob*, near; *edere*, to eat. See **Edible.** Der. *obes-i-ty*.

Obey. (F.—L.) M. E. *obeyen*.—O. F. *obeir*.—L. *obēdīre*, to obey; see **Obedient.** Der. *dis-obey*.

Obfuscate, to darken. (L.) From pp. of L. *ob-fuscāre*, to obscure.—L. *ob*, near; and *fuscus*, brown. See **Fuscous.**

Obit, a funeral rite. (F.—L.) O. F. *obit.*—L. acc. *obitum*, a going to or down, downfall, death. — L. *obitum*, supine of *ob-īre*, to go near. — L. *ob*, near; *īre*, to go.

Object, vb. (F.—L.) F. *objecter*.—L. *obiectāre*, to throw against, oppose; frequent. of *ob-icere* (*obiicere*), to cast towards. — L. *ob*, towards; *iacere*, to cast. See **Jet** (1).

Objurgation. (F.—L.) F. *objurgation.*—L. acc. *obiurgātiōnem*, a chiding.— L. *obiurgātus*, pp. of *obiurgāre*, to chide. —L. *ob*, against; *iurgāre*, to sue, chide, which stands for **iūrigare*; from *iūr-*, stem of *iūs*, law, and *-igāre*, for *agere*, to drive, pursue. Cf. **Navigate.**

Oblate, widened at the sides. (L.) L. *oblātus*, spread out (at the sides).—L. *ob*, towards; *lātus*, borne, carried out, pp. of *tollere*, to bear. See **Tolerate.**

oblation, an offering. (F.—L.) F.

oblation, an offering; Cot.—L. acc. *oblā-tiōnem*, acc. of *oblātio*, an offering.—L. *oblātus*, used as pp. of *offerre*, to offer (but from a different root); see **Tolerate.**

Oblige, to constrain. (F.—L.) F. *obliger.* — L. *obligāre*, to bind together, oblige.—L. *ob*, near; *ligāre*, to bind. See **Ligament.**

Oblique, slanting, perverse. (F.—L.) F. *oblique.*—L. *oblīquus*, *oblīcus*, slanting, sideways, awry.—L. *ob*; **līquus*, oblique (not in use).

Obliterate. (L.) From pp. of L. *oblitterare*, to efface.—L. *ob*, over; *littera*, a letter. See **Letter.** ¶ It seems to have been associated with L. *oblinere*, to smear over; though there is no etymological connexion.

Oblivion. (F.—L.) F. *oblivion.*—L. acc. *oblīuiōnem*, forgetfulness. — L. *oblī-uiscī*, to forget. Origin uncertain.

Oblong, long from side to side. (F.— L.) F. *oblong.*—L. *oblongus*, long across. —L. *ob*, over; *longus*, long; see **Long.**

Obloquy, calumny. (L.) L. *obloquium*, contradiction.—L. *obloquī*, to speak against. —L. *ob*, against; *loquī*, to speak. See **Loquacious.**

Obnoxious, offensive. (L.) Formerly in the sense of 'liable to.'—L. *obnoxi-us*, liable to; also, hurtful; with suffix *-ous*. — L. *ob*, against; *noxius*, hurtful. See **Noxious.**

Oboe. (Ital.—F.—L.) Ital. *oboe.* — F. *hautbois*; see **Hautbois.**

Obolus, a small Gk. coin. (L.—Gk.) L. *obolus.*—Gk. ὀβολός, a small coin, perhaps orig. in the shape of a spike or nail; allied to Gk. ὀβελός, a spit.

Obscene. (L.) L. *obscēnus*, *obscaenus*, *obscoenus*, repulsive, foul. Etym. unknown.

Obscure, dimin. (F.—L.) F. *obscur.* —L. *obscūrus*, dark, lit. 'covered over.'— L. *ob*; and *-scūrus*, i. e. covered; cf. Skt. *sku*, to cover. (√SKEU.) Brugm. i. § 109; ii. § 74. See **Sky.**

Obsequies. (F.—L.) M.F. *obseques*, 'obsequies;' Cot.—L. *obsequiās*, acc. of *obsequiæ*, funeral rites, lit. followings.—L. *obsequī*, to follow near, comply with.— L. *ob*, near; *sequī*, to follow. See **Sequence.**

obsequious. (F. — L.) M.F. *obse-quieux*; Cot.—L. *obsequiōsus*, full of compliance.—L. *obsequium*, compliance.—L. *obsequī*, to comply with (above.)

Observe. (F.—L.) O. F. *observer.*—

354

L. *obseruāre*, to take notice of, mark. – L. *ob*, near ; *seruāre*, to keep, heed.

Obsidian, a vitreous stone. (L.) From L. *Obsidiānus lapis* (false reading for *Obsiānus lapis*), a stone found by one *Obsidius* (false reading for *Obsius*) in Æthiopia (Pliny, lib. xxxvi. c. 26, lib. xxxvii. c. 10).

Obsolescent, going out of use. (L.) From pres. pt. of L. *obsolescere*, to grow old, inceptive form of *obsolēre*, to decay. Origin doubtful ; perhaps from L. *ob*, against ; *solēre*, to be wont.

obsolete. (L.) L. *obsolētus*, pp. of *obsolēre* (above).

Obstacle. (F. – L.) F. *obstacle.* – L. *obstāculum*, a hindrance. – L. *ob*, against ; *-stāculum*, double dimin. from *stā-re*, to stand.

obstetric, pertaining to midwifery. (L.) L. *obstetrīcius*, adj., from *obstetrīc-*, stem of *obstetrix*, a midwife ; lit. an assistant, stander near. – L. *obstāre*, to stand near ; with fem. suffix *-trix* (of the agent). – L. *ob*, near ; *stāre*, to stand. See **State.**

obstinate. (L.) L. *obstinātus*, resolute ; pp. of *obstināre*, to set about, be resolved on ; lit. ' to put oneself near.' – L. *ob*, near ; and **stanāre*, to place oneself ; cf. Russ. *stanovite*, to set ; from √STĀ. See **Destine.**

Obstreperous, clamorous. (L.) L. *obstreper-us*, clamorous ; with suffix *-ous.* – L. *ob*, against, near ; *strepere*, to rattle.

Obstriction, obligation. (L.) Coined from L. *obstrictus*, pp. of *obstringere*, to bind, fasten. – L. *ob*, over : *stringere*, to draw tight. See **Stringent.**

Obstruct. (L.) From L. *obstructus*, pp. of *obstruere*, to build in the way of anything, lit. build against. – L. *ob*, against ; *struere*, to build. See **Structure.**

Obtain. (F. – L.) F. *obtenir.* – L. *obtinēre*, to hold, obtain. – L. *ob*, near ; *tenēre*, to hold. See **Tenable.**

Obtrude. (L.) L. *obtrūdere*, to thrust against. – L. *ob*, against ; *trūdere*, to thrust. See **Thrust.**

Obtuse, blunt. (F. – L.) M. F. *obtus*, ' dull ; ' Cot. – L. *obtūsus*, blunted, pp. of *obtundere*, to beat against. – L. *ob*, against ; *tundere*, to beat.

Obverse, lit. turned *towards* one, used of the face of a coin. (L.) L. *obuersus*, pp. of *obuertere*, to turn towards. – L. *ob*, towards ; *uertere*, to turn. See **Verse.**

Obviate. (L.) From pp. of L. *obuiāre*,

to meet in the way, prevent – L. *ob*, against ; *uia*, way. See **Viaduct.**

obvious. (L.) L. *obui-us*, lying in the way, evident ; with suffix *-ous.* – L. *ob*, over against ; *uia*, the way.

Oca, the name of a certain edible root. (Peruvian.) Peruv. *occa*, the same.

Occasion. (F. – L.) F. *occasion.* – L. acc. *occāsiōnem.* – L. *oc-* (for *ob*), at ; and *cās-us*, pp. of *cadere*, to fall. See **Cadence.**

occident, west. (F. – L.) O. F. *occident*, west. – L. *occident-*, stem of pres. pt. of *occidere*, to fall, set (as the sun). – L. *oc-* (for *ob*), at ; *cadere*, to fall.

Occiput. (L.) L. *occiput*, back of the head. – L. *oc-* (for *ob*), over against ; *caput*, the head. See **Capital.**

Occult. (F. – L.) F. *occulte.* – L. *occultus*, pp. of *occulere*, to cover over, conceal. – L. *oc-* (for *ob*) ; and obs. L. **celere*, to hide, allied to *cēlāre*, to hide. Cf. O. Irish *cel-im*, I hide, A. S. *hel-an*, to hide.

Occupy. (F. – L.) M.E. *occupien.* – F. *occuper.* – L. *occupāre*, to lay hold of. – L. *oc-* (for *ob*), near ; *capere*, to seize. **Der.** *pre-occupy.*

Occur. (F. – L.) M. F. *occurrer.* – L. *occurrere*, to run to meet, occur. – L. *oc-* (for *ob*), against ; *currere*, to run. See **Current.**

Ocean. (F. – L. – Gk.) O. F. *ocean.* – L. *ōceanum*, acc. of *ōceanus.* – Gk. ὠκεανός, the great stream supposed to encompass the earth.

Ocelot, a quadruped. (Mexican.) Mexican *ocelotl*, a tiger ; applied by Buffon to the ocelot.

Ochre, a fine clay, commonly yellow. (F. – L. – Gk.) F. *ocre*, ' oker ; ' Cot. – L. *ōchra.* – Gk. ὤχρα, yellow ochre ; from its pale colour. – Gk. ὠχρός, pale, wan.

Octagon, a plane 8-sided figure. (Gk.) From Gk. ὀκτα-, for ὀκτώ, eight ; γων-ία, an angle, connected by gradation with γόνυ, knee ; see **Knee.**

octahedron, a solid 8-sided figure. (Gk.) From ὀκτα-, for ὀκτώ, eight ; ἕδρα, a base, from the base ἑδ-, to sit ; see **Sit.**

octangular, having eight angles. (L.) From L. *oct-ō*, eight ; *angulus*, angle.

octant, the aspect of two planets when distant by the eighth part of a circle. (L.) L. *octant-*, stem of *octans*, an instrument for measuring the eighth of a circle. – L. *oct-ō*, eight.

octave. (F. – L.) Lit. 'eighth;' hence, eight days after a festival, eight notes in music. – F. *octave*, an octave (Cot.). – L. *octāua*, fem. of *octāuus*, eighth. – L. *octō*, eight. +Gk. ὀκτώ, eight; cognate with E. **Eight.** Doublet, *utas*.

October. (L.) L. *Octōber*, the eighth month of the Roman year. – L. *octō*, eight.

octogenarian, one who is eighty years old. (L.) From L. *octōgēnārius*, belonging to eighty. – L. *octōgēnī*, eighty each, distributive form of *octōginta*, eighty. – L. *octō*, eight; *-ginta*, probably allied to *decem*, ten. Brugm. ii. § 164.

octoroon, the offspring of a white person and a quadroon. (L.) One who is, in an eighth part, a black. Coined from L. *octō*, eight; in imitation of *quadroon*.

octosyllabic. (L. – Gk.) L. *octōsyllabicus*, having eight syllables. – Gk. ὀκτώ, eight; συλλαβή, a syllable; see **Syllable.**

Octroi, a toll. (F. – L.) F. *octroi*, O. F. *otroi*, orig. a grant; verbal sb. from O. F. *otroier*, to authorise, grant. – Late L. *auctōritāre*, by-form of *auctōrizāre*, to authorise. – L. *auctor*; see **Author.**

Ocular. (L.) L. *oculāris*, belonging to the eye. – L. *oculus*, eye; cognate with Gk. ὄμμα, eye. See **Optic.**

Odalisque, a female slave in a Turkish harem. (F. – Turk.) F. *odalisque*; better *odalique* (Devic). – Turk. *odaliq*, a chambermaid. – Turk. *oda*, a chamber.

Odd, not even, strange. (Scand.) M. E. *odde*. – Icel. *oddi*, a triangle, a point of land; metaphorically (from the triangle), an odd number (orig. *three*); hence also the phr. *standask ī odda*, to stand (or be) at odds, to quarrel; *oddamaðr*, the odd man, third man who gives a casting vote, *oddatala*, an odd number. Allied to *oddr*, a point of a weapon (for **ozdr*). +A. S. *ord*, a point of a sword, point; Dan. *od*, a point, Swed. *udda*, odd, *udde*, a point; G. *ort*, a place, M. H. G. *ort*, extreme point. Teut. type **uzdoz*.

Ode, a song. (F. – L. – Gk.) F. *ode.* – L. *ōda*, *ōdē*. – Gk. ᾠδή, a song; for ἀοιδή, a song. – Gk. ἀείδειν, to sing. Allied to O. Irish *faed*, W. *gwaedd*, a cry, shout. (√WEID.) Der. *ep-ode*, *palin-ode*.

Odium, hatred. (L.) L. *odium*, sb. – L. *ōdī*, I hate; an old perfect tense. Cf. Armen. *at-eam*, I hate. Brugm. i. § 160.

Odour. (F. – L.) M. E. *odour.* – F. *odeur.* – L. *odōrem*, acc. of *odor*, scent.

Cf. Gk. ὄζειν (= **ὄδ-yειν*), to smell. (√OD.) Der. *odorous*, from L. *odōr-us*, with suffix *-ous*; the accent has been thrown back.

Of, from, &c. (E.) M. E. *of*; A. S. *of*. +Du. Icel. Swed. Dan. Goth. *af*; G. *ab*, O. H. G. *aba*; L. *ab*, Gk. ἀπό, Skt. *apa*, away. Brugm. i. § 560.

off, away from. (E.) An emphatic form of *of*. M. E. *of*; as in ' Smiteth *of* my hed' = smite *off* my head; Ch. C. T. 782 (Harleian MS.).

Offal, waste meat. (E.) M. E. *offal*, falling remnants, chips of wood, &c. From *off* and *fall.* +Du. *afval*, windfall, offal; Dan. *affald*, a fall off, offal; Swed. *affall*; G. *abfall*; all similarly compounded.

Offence. (F. – L.) O. F. *offence*, *offense*. – L. *offensa*, an offence; orig. fem. of pp. of *offendere*, to dash against (below).

offend. (F. – L.) M. E. *offenden.* – F. *offendre.* – L. *offendere*, to dash or strike against, injure. – L. *of-* (for *ob*), against; **fendere*, to strike. See **Defend.**

Offer. (L.) A. S. *offrian.* – L. *offerre*, to offer. – L. *of-* (for *ob*), near; *ferre* to bring, cognate with E. *bear*. Der. *offer-t-or-y*, from F. *offertoire*, L. *offertōrium*, a place to which offerings were brought.

Office, duty. (F. – L.) F. *office.* – L. *officium*, duty; lit. ' service.' Perhaps from *of-* (for *ob*), towards; and *facere*, to do (Bréal). Der. *offic-er*, F. *officier*, Late L. *officiārius*; *offit-i-ous*, F. *officieux*, L. *officiōsus*.

Officinal, pertaining to or used in a shop or laboratory. (F. – L.) F. *officinal.* – L. *officīna*, a workshop, office; contracted form of *opificīna* (Plautus). – L. *opi-*, for *opus*, work; *-fic-*, for *facere*, to do.

Offing, the part of the visible sea remote from the shore. (E.) Merely formed from *off*, with the noun-suffix *-ing*. See **off.**

Offscouring. (E.) From *off* and *scour*. So also *off-set*, *off-shoot*, *off-spring*.

Oft, Often, frequently. (E.) A. S. *oft*; whence M. E. *ofte*, with added *-e*, and lastly *ofte-n* with added *-n.* +Icel. *opt*, Dan. *ofte*, Swed. *ofta*, G. *oft*, Goth. *ufta*. Origin unknown.

Ogee, Ogive, a double curve. (F. – Span. – Arab.) ' An *ogiue* (*ogive*) or *ogee*, a wreath, circlet, or round band in architecture,' Minsheu. An *ogee* arch is a pointed arch, with doubly-curved sides. – M.F. *augive*, F. *ogive*, an ogive or ogee

(Cot.). – Span. *auge*, highest point, also meridian, apogee (cf. Port. *auge*, top); from the pointed top of Moorish arches, which have doubly-curved sides. – Arab. *āwj*, summit. ¶ Perhaps not a true Arab. word, but der. from Gk. ἀπόγαιον, the apogee (in which sense *āwj* is sometimes used). **Der.** *ogiv-al*, adj. (also written *ogee-fall !*).

Ogle, to glance at. (Du.) A frequent. form of Du. *oogen*, 'to cast sheepes eyes upon one;' Hexham. (Cf. Low G. *oegeln*, to ogle, from *oegen*, to look at.) – Du. *ooge*, eye; cognate with E. **Eye.**

Ogre, a monster. (F. – L.) F. *ogre.* Cf. Span. *ogro* (Diez; but not given in most Dict., and probably from F.). Of unknown origin. The deriv. from L. acc. *augurem*, soothsayer, hence, a wizard (Körting) is not convincing. **Der.** *ogr-ess*, F. *ogresse.*

Oh; see **O** (1).

Oil. (F. – L. – Gk.) M. E. *oile.* – A. F. *oile* (F. *huile*). – L. *oleum*; from *olea*, an olive-tree. – Gk. ἐλαία, an olive-tree. See **Olive.**

Ointment. (F. – L.) The former *t* is due to confusion with *anoint*; the M. E. form is *oinement.* – O. F. *oignement*, an anointing, also an unguent. – O. F. *oigne-r*, the same as *oindre*, to anoint; with suffix *-ment.* – L. *ungere*, to anoint. See **Unguent.**

Old. (E.) M. E. *old.* O. Merc. *ald*, later *āld*; (A. S. *eald*). + Du. *oud* (for **old*), G. *alt*; cf. Goth. *altheis.* Teut. type **aldóz*; Idg. type **al-tós*, formed with pp. suffix *-tós* from √AL, as seen in L. *al-ere*, Icel. *al-a*, to nourish, bring up; so that the sense was orig. 'brought up.' β. L. *altus*, high, is prob. the same word, with a newer sense.

Oleaginous. (L. – Gk.) L. *oleāgin-us*, oily, with suffix *-ous*; adj., from *olea*, an olive-tree. See **Oil.**

Oleander, the rose-bay-tree. (F. – Late L.) M. F. *oleandre*, rose-bay-tree (Cot.). The same as Ital. *oleandro*, Span. *eloendro* (Minsheu), Port. *eloendro*, *loendro*; all variously corrupted from Late L. *lōrandrum* (taken for *l'ōrandrum*). It seems to have been confused with *oleaster*. **2.** Isidore gives the name as '*arodandarum*, vulgo *lorandrum.*' This shews that the name was a corruption of *rhododendron*, due to confusion with L. *laurus*, laurel.

Oleaster, wild olive. (L. – Gk.) L.

oleaster, Rom. xi. 17; formed from *olea*, an olive-tree. – Gk. ἐλαία, an olive-tree.

Olfactory, relating to smell. (L.) L. *olfactōrius*, adj., from L. *olfactor*, one who smells, *olfactus*, a smelling. – L. *olfactus*, pp. of *olfacere*, *olefacere*, to scent. – L. *olĕ-re* (also *olēre*), to smell; *facere*, to make, cause. This L. *olere* stands for **odere*; cf. *od-or*, scent; and cf. L. *lacruma* for *dacruma.* Allied to Gk. ὀδ-μή, scent.

Oligarchy. (F. – L. – Gk.) F. *oligarchie.* – Late L. *oligarchia.* – Gk. ὀλιγαρχία, government by a few men. – Gk. ὀλιγ-, for ὀλίγος, few, little; and *-αρχια*, from ἄρχειν, to rule.

Olio, a mixture, medley. (Span. – L.) A mistaken form for *olia*, intended to represent Span. *olla* (pronounced *olya*), a round earthen pot, also an olio, esp. in phrase *olla podrida*, a hodge-podge. – L. *olla*, O. Lat. *aula*, a pot.

Olive. (F. – L. – Gk.) F. *olive.* – L. *olīua.* – Gk. ἐλαία (for **ἐλαίϝα*), an olive-tree. Brugm. i. § 121 (2).

Omadaun, Omadhawn, a simpleton. (C.) Anglo-Irish; from Irish *amadán*, a simpleton. – Irish *amad* (the same). – Irish *am-*, for *an-*, neg. prefix (cf. Gk. ἀν-); *-mad*, O. Irish *-met*, mind, cognate with L. *mens* and E. *mind.* Cf. L. *āmens*, mad.

Ombre, a game at cards. (Span. – L.) From Span. *juego del hombre*, lit. 'game of the man' (whence F. *hombre*). – L. *hominem*, acc. of *homo*, a man. See **Human.**

Omega, the end. (Gk.) Gk. ὠ, called ὠ μέγα, i. e. great *o*, long *o*; which is the last letter of the Gk. alphabet, as opposed to *alpha*, the *first* letter. Μέγα is neut. of μέγας, great, allied to E. **Mickle.**

Omelet, a pan-cake, chiefly of eggs. (F. – L.) F. *omelette*, *aumelette* (Cot.). These are from O. F. *amelette*, but this again was preceded by the form *alemette*, which is, through change of suffix, from *alemelle* (Scheler). The sense of *alemelle* was 'a thin plate,' still preserved in F. *alumelle*, sheathing of a ship. Godefroy gives O. F. *alemele*, blade of a knife; thus the *omelet* was named from its shape, that of a 'thin plate' of metal. **2.** Lastly *l'alemelle* is a corruption of *la lemelle*, the correct O. F. form. – L. *lāmella*, a thin plate, properly of metal; dimin. of *lāmina*, a thin plate; see **Lamina.** ¶ See this clearly traced by Scheler and Littré.

Omen, a sign of a future event. (L.)
L. *ōmen*; O. Lat. *osmen*. **Der.** *ominous*.

Omit, to neglect. (L.) L. *omittere*,
(pp. *omissus*), lit. 'to let go.' For **ommittere* < **ob-mittere*; from *ob*, by, *mittere*,
to send. See **Missile. Der.** *omiss-ion*,
from F. *omission*, 'an omission,' from L.
acc. *omissiōnem*; from the pp.

Omni-, prefix. (L.) L. *omnis*, all.
Der. *omni-potent*, all-powerful; *omnipresent*, everywhere present; *omni-scient*,
all-knowing; *omni-vorous*, all-devouring;
see **Potent, Present, Science, Voracious.**

omnibus, a public vehicle. (L.) So
called because intended for the use of all.
— L. *omnibus*, for all; dat. pl. of *omnis*.
¶ Commonly shortened to *bus.*

Omrah, a prince, lord. (Arab.) 'Aigrettes by *omrahs* worn;' Scott, Vis. of
Don. Roderick, st. 31. *Omrah* is properly
a plural, like **Nabob,** q. v. — Arab. *umarā*,
pl. of *amīr*, a prince, emir; see **Emir.**
Cf. the Arab. title *amīru'l-umarā*, prince
of princes (Yule).

On. (E.) M. E. *on*; A.S. *on.* **+** Du.
aan, Icel. *ā*, Swed. *å*, G. *an* (whence Dan.
an), Goth. *ana*, Gk. *ἀνά*, Russ. *na*. Idg.
type **ana.*

Once; see **One.**

Once, sometimes for **Ounce** (2).

One (1), single, sole. (E.) M. E. *oon.*
Already written *won* in M. E. See Guy
of Warwick, ed. Zupitza, note to l. 7927.
A. S. *ān*, one. **+** Du. *een*, Icel. *einn*, Dan.
een, Swed. *en*, G. *ein*, Goth. *ains*, W. *un*,
Irish and Gael. *aon*, L. *ūnus*, O. L. *oinos*,
Gk. **οἶνος*, one (fem. *οἴνη*, an ace on a die).
Teut. type **ainoz*; Idg. type **oinos*. Cf.
Lith. *vĕnas*; Brugm. ii. § 165. **Der.** *an*,
a, *on-ly*, *al-one*, *at-one.*

once. (E.) M. E. *ones*; A.S. *ānes*,
adv., once. Orig. gen. case (masc. and
neut.) of *ān*, one; the gen. case was used
adverbially, as in *need-s*, *twi-ce*, *thri-ce.*

one (2), a person, spoken of indefinitely.
(E.) In the phrase '*one* says,' *one* means
'a single person.' Merely a peculiar use
of the ordinary word *one.* ¶ Not F. *on.*

Onerous, burdensome. (F.—L.) M.F.
onereux. — L. *onerōsus*, adj. — L. *oner-*, for
*ones-, stem of *onus*, a burden.

Onion, a plant. (F.—L.) F. *oignon.* —
L. *ūniōnem*, acc. of *ūnio*, a large onion;
see **Union** (2).

Only. (E.) M. E. *oonli*, adj. and adv.;

A.S. *ānlīc*, adj., unique, lit. 'one-like.' —
A.S. *ān*, one; *līc*, like.

Onomatopœia, name-making, the
formation of a word with a resemblance
in sound to the thing signified. (Gk.) Gk.
ὀνοματοποιία, the making of a name. — Gk.
ὀνοματο-, combining form of *ὄνομα*, a name;
and *ποιεῖν*, to make; see **Name** and
Poem. Brugm. ii. § 117.

Onset, an assault. (E.) Due to the phr.
set on! i. e. attack! From *on* and *set.*

Onslaught, an attack. (E.) From *on*
and M. E. *slaht*, A. S. *sleaht*, a stroke,
blow, formed from *slēan*, to strike; see
Slay. And cf. *slaughter.*

Onward, Onwards. (E.) From *on*
and *-ward*, *-wards*; see **Toward.**

Onyx, a kind of agate. (L.—Gk.) L.
onyx. — Gk. *ὄνυξ*, a nail; a veined gem,
onyx, from its resemblance to the finger-
nail. See **Nail.**

Oolite, a kind of limestone. (F.—Gk.)
F. *oolithe* (with *th* sounded as *t*). — Gk.
ᾠό-ν, egg; *λίθ-ος*, stone. Lit. 'egg-stone.'
See **Oval.**

Ooze, moisture, soft mud. (E.) Formerly *wose*; M. E. *wose.* A. S. *wōs*,
moisture, juice. **+** Icel. *vās*, wetness. Perhaps confused with A.S. *wāse*, soft mud;
which is cognate with Icel. *veisa*, a stagnant pool. **Der.** *ooze*, vb.

Opacity; see **Opaque.**

Opal, a gem. (F.—L.) F. *opale.* — L.
opalus, an opal. Cf. Gk. *ὀπάλλιος*, an
opal; Skt. *upala-*, a stone, gem.

Opaque. (F.—L.) F. *opaque.* — L. *opācum*, acc. of *opācus*, dark, obscure. **Der.**
opac-i-ty, from F. *opacité*, L. acc. *opācitātem.*

Open, unclosed. (E.) The verb is from
the adj. *open*, which is sometimes shortened to *ope* (Coriol. i. 4. 43). A. S. *open*,
adj., open, with the form of an old pp.
+ Du. *open*, adj.; Icel. *opinn*; Swed.
öppen; G. *offen.* Teut. types **upenoz*,
*upanoz. Perhaps connected with the
idea of the lifting of a tent-door; cf. A. S.
ūp, up. See **Up. Der.** *open*, vb., A. S.
openian, to make open.

Opera. (Ital.—L.) Ital. *opera*, a work,
a musical play. — L. *opera*, work; see
below.

operate. (L.) From pp. of L. *operārī*,
to work. — L. *opera*, work; from *oper-* (for
*opes-), stem of L. *opus*, work, toil. **+**
Skt. *apas*, work.

Ophidian, relating to serpents. (Gk.)

Formed with suffix -an (L. -ānus), from Gk. ὀφίδιον, ὀφείδιον, dimin. of ὄφις, a serpent. Cf. the dimin. form ζῴ-διον (see Zodiac). + Skt. ahi-, L. anguis, a snake.

ophicleide, a musical instrument. (F.–Gk.) Lit. a 'key-serpent'; because made by adding keys to an old musical instrument called a serpent (from its twisted shape). – Gk. ὄφι-s, a serpent; κλειδ-, stem of κλείς, a key.

Ophthalmia, inflammation of the eye. (Gk.) Gk. ὀφθαλμία. – Gk. ὀφθαλμός, the eye, Boeotian ὄκταλλος, for *ὀκταν-λος (cf. Skt. akshan-, eye); Doric ὀπτίλος, the eye. From Idg. base *oq-, eye; cf. Russ. oko, eye, Skt. aksha-, akshi, Lith. akìs, L. oc-ul-us. See Prellwitz. And see Ocular.

Opinion. (F.–L.) F. opinion.–L. opīniōnem, acc. of opīnio, a supposition. – L. opīnārī, to suppose, opine.–L. opīnus, thinking, expecting; only in nec-opīnus, not expecting, unexpected, in-opīnus, unexpected. Der. opine, F. opiner, L. opīnārī (above).

Opium. (L.–Gk.) L. opium.–Gk. ὄπιον, poppy-juice.–Gk. ὀπός, sap.

Opossum, a quadruped. (W. Indian.) – W. Indian opassom; in the language of the Indians of Virginia; Capt. Smith, p. 59.

Oppidan. (L.) L. oppidānus, belonging to a town.–L. oppidum, a town; O. L. oppedum. Apparently from L. op- (ob), near; *pedum (Gk. πέδον), a field, plain; Brugm. i. § 65. (Explained as 'protecting the plain'; the derivation is clearer than the sense.)

Oppilation, a stopping up. (F.–L.) M. F. oppilation, 'an obstruction;' Cot. – L. acc. oppīlātiōnem. – L. oppīlātus, pp. of oppīlāre, to stop up. – L. op (for ob), against; pīlāre, to ram, from pīlum, a pestle. And L. pīlum is for *pins-lom, from pinsere, to pound.

Opponent. (L.) L. oppōnent-, stem of pres. part. of oppōnere, to oppose.–L. ob, against; pōnere, to place. See Position.

Opportune, timely. (F.–L.) F. opportun.–L. opportūnus, convenient, seasonable, lit. 'near the harbour,' or 'easy of access.'–L. op- (ob), near; portus, access, harbour. See Port (2).

Oppose. (F.–L. and Gk.) F. opposer, to withstand.–L. op- (for ob), against; F. poser, to place, from Late L. pausāre, used to translate L. pōnere, to place. See Pose.

Opposite. (F.–L.) F. opposite.–L

oppositus, pp. of oppōnere, to set against. – L. op- (ob), against; pōnere, to set. See Position.

Oppress. (F.–L.) F. oppresser.– Late L. oppressāre, frequent. of L. opprimere, to oppress.–L. op- (ob), near; premere (pp. pressus), to press. See Press.

Opprobrious. (L.) From L. opprobriōsus, full of reproach.–L. opprobrium, reproach.–L. op- (for ob), on, upon; probrum, disgrace.

Oppugn, to resist. (F.–L.) F. oppugner. – L. oppugnāre. – L. op- (ob), against; pugnāre, to fight, from pugnus, a fist. See Pugilism.

Optative, wishing. (F.–L.) Chiefly as the name of a mood.–F. optatif.–L. optātīuus, expressive of a wish.–L. optātus, pp. of optāre, to wish. Cf. Skt. āp, to attain.

Optic, relating to the sight. (F.–Gk.) F. optique. – Gk. ὀπτικός, belonging to the sight; cf. ὀπτήρ, a spy. From the base οπ- (for οκ-) seen in Ionic ὄπ-ωπ-α, I have seen, ὄψ-ομαι, I shall see; cf. L. oc-ulus, the eye. See Ocular.

Optimism, the doctrine that all is for the best. (L.) From L. optim-us, O. Lat. opitumus (Brugm. ii. § 73), best; with suffix -ism (Gk. -ισμος). L. op-ti-mus is a superl. form from a base op- (i.e. choice, select); cf. optāre, to wish.

option, choice. (F.–L.) F. option. – L. optiōnem, acc. of optio, choice. Allied to L. optāre, to wish; see Optative.

Opulent, wealthy. (F.–L.) F. opulent.–L. opulentus, wealthy.–L. op-, base of opes, wealth. Cf. Skt. apnas, wealth.

Or (1), conj., offering an alternative. (E.) Short for other, outher, auther, the M. E. forms, which answer to A. S. āhwæþer, āwþer. – A. S. ā, ever; hwæþer, whether. Cf. Either.

Or (2), ere. (E.) M. E. or, unemphatic form of ēr, ere. A. S. ǣr, ere; see Ere. (In the phrases or ere, or ever.)

Or (3), gold. (F.–L.) In heraldry. F. or.–L. aurum, gold.

Orach, a 'pot-herb. (F.–L.–Gk.) Also arrache. – F. arroche, 'orache, orage;' Cot. A Picard form corresponding to F. *arreuce (Hatzfeld). [Cf. Walloon arip, orach (Remacle); Ital. atrepice.] – L. atriplicem, acc. of atriplex, orach.–Gk. ἀτράφαξις, ἀτράφαξυς, orach.

Oracle. (F.–L.) F. oracle.–L. ōrāculum, a divine announcement; formed from *ōrā-re*, to pray, from *ōr-* (for *ōs*), the mouth (below).

oral, spoken. (L.) Coined from L. *ōr-* (for *ōs*), the mouth. **+** Skt. *āsya*, mouth ; Icel. *ōss*, mouth of a river.

Orang-outang, a large ape. (Malay.) Malay *ōrang-ūtan*, lit. 'wild man.' **—** Malay *ōrang*, a man ; *ūtan*, *hūtan*, woods, wilds of a country, wild.

Orange. (F. — Ital. — Arab. — Pers.) O. F. *orenge* (F. *orange*). For **narenge*, but the initial *n* was lost (in Italian), and then *arenge* became *orenge* by a popular etymology from *or*, gold. Cf. Span. *na-ranja*, an orange. **—** Ital. *arancia*, an orange; Low Lat. *arangia*. **—** Arab. *nāranj*, *nā-rinj*. **—** Pers. *nārang*, an orange. Allied to Pers. *nār*, a pomegranate.

Oration. (F. — L.) F. *oration*. **—** L. acc. *ōrātiōnem*. **—** L. *ōrātus*, pp. of *ōrāre*, to pray. **—** L. *ōr-* (for *ōs*), the mouth. See Oral. Doublet, *orison*.

orator. (F. — L.) Formerly *oratour*. **—** F. *orateur*. **—** L. *ōrātōrem*, acc. of *ōrātor*, a speaker. **—** L. *ōrātus*, pp. of *ōrāre*, to pray, to speak (above).

Orb. (F. — L.) F. *orbe*. **—** L. *orbem*, acc. of *orbis*, a circle, sphere.

orbit. (L.) L. *orbita*, a track, circuit ; formed with suffix *-ta* from *orbi-*, decl. stem of *orbis*, an orb, circle.

Orc, Ork, a large marine animal ; a narwhal, or grampus. (L.) See Nares. **—** L. *orca*, perhaps the narwhal (Pliny).

Orchard. (L. *and* E.) M. E. *orchard*. A. S. *orceard*, older form *ortgeard*. Cognate with Goth. *aurtigards*, a garden (Gk. κῆπος). The latter element, A. S. *geard*, is the mod. E. *yard*; see Yard. The former element is merely borrowed from L. *hortus*, a garden, both in E. and Gothic; see Horticulture. As the L. *hortus* is cognate with E. *yard*, the form *ort-geard* merely repeats the idea of 'yard.' ¶ So in Brugm. i. § 767 ; but some consider A. S. *ort-geard* as wholly Teutonic, and connect it with A. S. *wyrt-geard*, Dan. *urt-gaard*, Swed. *örte-gård*, a kitchen-garden, from A. S. *wyrt*, Dan. *urt*, Swed. *ört*, a wort. (See *Wort* in Franck.) See Wort.

Orchestra. (L. — Gk.) L. *orchēstra*. **—** Gk. ὀρχήστρα, an orchestra ; which, in the Attic theatre, was a space on which the chorus danced. **—** Gk. ὀρχέομαι, I dance.

Orchis, a plant. (L. — Gk.) L. *orchis*. **—** Gk. ὄρχις, a testicle, a plant with roots

of testicular shape. **Der.** *orchid*, where the suffix *-id* was suggested by the Gk. εἶδος, shape ; cf. *cyclo-id*, *cono-id*.

Ordain, to set in order. (F. — L.) M. E. *ordeinen*. **—** O. F. *ordener* (later *or-donner*). **—** L. *ordināre*, to set in order. **—** L. *ordin-*, declensional stem of *ordo*, order. **Der.** *pre-ordain*.

Ordeal, a severe test, judgment by fire. &c. (E.) M. E. *ordal*. A. S. *ordēl*, *ordāl*, a dealing out, judgment, decision. **·**O. Friesic *ordēl*. **—** A. S. *or-*, prefix, out ; *dēl*, *dāl*, a dealing; see Deal, Dole. The prefix *or-* = Du. *oor-*, G. *ur-*, Goth. *us-*, out (hence, thorough). **+** Du. *oordeel*, O. Sax. *urdēli*, G. *urtheil*, judgment; similarly compounded.

Order. (F. — L.) F. *ordre*, O. F. *or-dine*. **—** L. *ordinem*, acc. of *ordo*, order. Allied to L. *ordīrī*, to begin, *orīrī*, to arise. Brugm. ii. § 128. **Der.** *dis-order*.

ordinal, shewing the order. (L.) L. *ordinālis*, adj., in order. **—** L. *ordin-*, declensional stem of *ordo*, order.

ordinance. (F. — L.) O. F. *ordi-nance*. **—** Late L. *ordinantia*, a command. **—** L. *ordinant-*, pres. pt. of *ordināre*, to ordain. See Ordain.

ordinary. (F. — L.) F. *ordinaire*. **—** L. *ordinārius*, regular (as sb., an over-seer). **—** L. *ordin-*, decl. stem of *ordo*, order. **Der.** *ordinary*, sb.

ordination. (L.) From L. *ordinātio*, an ordinance, also ordination. **—** L. *ordin-ātus*, pp. of *ordināre*, to ordain. See Ordain.

ordnance, artillery. (F. — L.) Formerly, *ordinance*; it had reference to the *bore* or *size* of the cannon, and was thence transferred to the cannon itself (Cot. ; s. v. *ordonnance*) ; see ordinance.

Ordure, excrement. (F. — L.) F. *ordure*. **—** O. F. *ord* (fem. *orde*), filthy, foul, ugly, frightful. **—** L. *horridus*, rough, frightful. See Horrid. (So Körting.)

Ore. (E.) M. E. *or*, *oor*. A. S. *ōra*, ore of metal, allied to *ōre*, a mine. E. Fries. *ūr*, ore. **+** Du. *oer*, ore. ¶ Distinct from A. S. *ār*, brass, which is cognate with Goth. *ais*, L. *aes*, brass. But the words may have been confused.

Oread, a mountain-nymph. (Gk.) From Gk. ὀρειάδ-, stem of ὀρειάς, an oread. **—** Gk. ὄρος, a mountain.

Organ. (F. — L. — Gk.) F. *organe*. **—** L. *organum*, an implement. **—** Gk. ὄργανον, an implement; allied to ἔργον, work; see Work.

orgies, sacred rites, revelry. (F. – L. – Gk.) F. *orgies.* – L. *orgia*, sb. pl., a festival in honour of Bacchus, orgies. – Gk. ὄργια, sb. pl., orgies, rites, from sing. *ὄργιον, a sacred act; allied to ἔργον, work.

Orgulous, proud. (F. – O.H.G.) Also *orgillous*; M. E. *orgeilus*; Anglo-F. *or-guyllus.* – O. F. *orgoillos*, *orguillus*, later *orgueilleux*, proud. – O.F. *orgoil*, *orguil*, F. *orgueil*, pride. From an O. H. G. sb. *urguolī*, from O.H.G. *urguol*, remarkable, notable (Graff).

Oriel, a recess (with a window) in a room. (F. – L.) M. E. *oriol*, *oryall*, a small room, portico, esp. a room for a lady, boudoir. – O.F. *oriol*, a porch, gallery, corridor. – Late L. *oriolum*, a small room, recess, portico; prob. for *aureolum* (?), that which is ornamented with gold. – L. *aurum*, gold. ¶ See Pliny, lib. xxxiii. c. 3, for the custom of gilding apartments. Cf. Oriole.

Orient, eastern. (F. – L.) F. *orient.* – L. *orient-*, stem of *oriens*, rising, the east; orig. pres. pt. of *orīrī*, to rise, begin. + Skt. *r̥*, to rise.

Orifice. (F. – L.) F. *orifice*, a small opening. – L. *ōrificium*, an opening, lit. 'making of a mouth.' – L. *ōri-*, decl. stem of *ōs*, mouth; *facere*, to make.

Oriflamme, the old standard of France. (F. – L.) F. *oriflamme*, the sacred standard of France. – Late L. *auriflamma*, lit. 'golden flame,' because the banner was cut into flame-like strips at the outer edge, and carried on a gilt pole. – L. *auri-* (for *aurum*), gold; *flamma*, flame.

Origan, wild marjoram. (F. – L. – Gk.) F. *origan.* – L. *orīganum.* – Gk. ὀρίγανον, lit. 'mountain-pride.' – Gk. ὀρῑ = ὀρει-, related to ὄρος, a mountain; γάνος, beauty, ornament.

Origin. (F. – L.) F. *origine.* – Lat. *orīginem*, acc. of *orīgo*, a beginning. – L. *orīrī*, to rise.

Oriole, the golden thrush. (F. – L.) O.F. *oriol* (F. *loriot* = *l' oriot*). – L. *aureolus*, golden. – L. *aurum*, gold.

Orison, a prayer. (F. – L.) O. F. *orison*, *oreison* (F. *oraison*). – L. *ōrātiōnem*, acc. of *ōrātio*, a prayer; see Oration.

Orle, a kind of fillet, in heraldry, &c. (F. – L.) F. *orle*, m., M. F. *orle*, f., a hem, narrow border; cf. Late L. *orla*, a border, edge. – L. type *ōrula*, dimin.

of L. *ōra*, border, edge. Cf. L. *ōs*, mouth.

Orlop, a deck of a ship. (Du.) Formerly *orlope* (Phillips). Contracted from Du. *overloop*, a running over, a deck of a ship, an orlope (Sewel). So called because it traverses the ship. – Du. *over*, over; *loopen*, to run; see Elope, Leap.

Ormolu, a kind of brass. (F. – L.) F. *or moulu*, lit. 'pounded gold.' – F. *or*, from L. *aurum*, gold; and *moulu*, pp. of *moudre*, to grind, O. F. *moldre*, from L. *molere*, to grind.

Ornament. (F. – L.) M. E. *ornement.* – F. *ornement.* – L. *ornāmentum*, an adornment. – L. *ornāre*, to adorn.

ornate. (L.) From pp. of L. *ornāre*, to adorn.

Ornithology, the science of birds. (Gk.) Gk. ὀρνιθο-, for ὄρνις, a bird; -λογία, from λόγος, a discourse, λέγειν, to speak. Allied to A. S. *earn*, G. *aar*, W. *eryr*, an eagle, named from its soaring; cf. Gk. ὄρνυμι, I stir up, rouse.

ornithorhyncus, an Australian animal. (Gk.) Named from the resemblance of its snout to a duck's bill. – Gk. ὀρνιθο- (for ὄρνις), bird; ῥύγχος, a snout.

Orphan. (L. – Gk.) L. *orphanus.* – Gk. ὀρφανός, destitute; John xiv. 18. Allied to L. *orbus*, destitute.

Orpiment, yellow sulphuret of arsenic. (F. – L.) Lit. 'gold paint.' F. *orpiment.* – L. *auripigmentum*, gold paint. – L. *auri-* (for *aurum*), gold; and *pigmentum*, a pigment, paint, from *pingere*, to paint.

orpine, orpin, a kind of stone-crop. (F. – L.) Named from its colour. M. E. *orpin.* – F. *orpin*, 'orpin, or live-long'; also orpiment;' Cot. A docked form of *orpiment* above.

Orrery, an apparatus for illustrating the motion of the planets. (Ireland.) Constructed at the expense of Charles Boyle, earl of *Orrery*, about 1715. *Orrery* is a barony in co. Cork, Ireland.

Orris, a plant. (Ital. – L. – Gk.) Formerly *orice*, *oris*. These are E. corruptions of M. Ital. *irios* (Ital. *ireos*). – M. Ital. *irios*, 'oris-roote,' Florio; with reference to the *Iris florentina*. Modified from L. *iris*, a rainbow, an iris.

Ort; see Orts.

Orthodox, of the right faith. (L. – Gk.) Late L. *orthodoxus.* – Gk. ὀρθόδοξος, of the right opinion. – Gk. ὀρθό-s, upright,

right; δόξα, an opinion, from δοκεῖν, to seem. Cf. **Arduous**. Brugm. ii. § 143.

orthoepy, correct pronunciation. (Gk.) From Gk. ὀρθοέπεια, orthoepy. — Gk. ὀρθό-s, right; ἔπ-os, a word; see **Epic**.

orthography, correct writing. (F. – L. – Gk.) M. E. *ortographie*. – M. F. *ortographie*. – L. *orthographia*. – Gk. ὀρθο-γραφία. – Gk. ὀρθό-s, right; γράφειν, to write.

orthopterous, lit. straight winged. (Gk.) Gk. ὀρθό-s, straight; πτερόν, a wing.

Ortolan, a bird. (F. – Ital. – L.) O. F. *hortolan*. – M. Ital. *hortolano*, a gardener, also an *ortolan*, lit. ' haunter of gardens.' – L. *hortulānus*, a gardener. – L. *hortulus*, dimin. of *hortus*, a garden; allied to **Yard**.

Orts, remnants, leavings. (E.) M. E. *ortes*. From A. S. *or-*, out (what is left); *etan*, to eat. Prôved by M. Du. *orete*, *ooraete*, a piece left after eating, Swed. dial. *oräte*, *uräte*, refuse fodder. The same prefix *or-* occurs in *ordeal*. Cf. also Low G. *ort*, an ort; Dan. dial. *ored*, *orret*, an ort; N. Fries. *örte*, to leave remnants after eating.

Oscillate, to swing. (L.) From pp. of L. *oscillāre*, to swing. – L. *oscillum*, a swing.

Osculate, to kiss. (L.) From pp. of L. *osculārī*, to kiss. – L. *osculum*, a little mouth, pretty mouth; double dimin. of *ōs*, the mouth.

Osier. (F.) F. *osier*, ' the ozier, red withy, water-willow tree;' Cot. The proposed connexion with Gk. οἶσος, an osier, lacks evidence.

Osmium, a metal. (Gk.) The oxide has a disagreeable smell. – Gk. ὀσμή, ὀδμή, a smell. – Gk. ὄζειν (for *ὄδ-yειν), to smell; cf. ὀδμή, scent. See **Odour**.

Osprey, the fish-hawk. (L.) A corruption of *ossifrage*, the older name for the bird. – L. *ossifragus*, *ossifraga*, an osprey. – L. *ossifragus*, bone-breaking; (from its strength). – L. *ossi-*, decl. stem of *os*, bone; *frag*, base of *frangere*, to break.

osseous, bony. (L.) L. *osse-us*, bony; with suffix *-ous*. – L. *oss-*, stem of *os*, a bone. Cf. Gk. ὀστέον, Skt. *asthi*, a bone. Brugm. i. § 703.

ossifrage. (L.) In Levit. xi. 13; see **Osprey**.

ossify, to turn to bone. (F. – L.)

From L. *ossi-*, decl. stem of *os*, bone; F. *-fier*, for L. *-ficāre*, to make, from *facere*, to make. Der. *ossific-at-ion*.

Ostensible. (L.) Coined from *ostensi-* (for *ostensus*), pp. of *ostendere*, to shew; with suffix *-bilis*. See below.

ostentation. (F. – L.) F. *ostentation*. – L. *ostentātiōnem*, acc. of *ostentātio*, display. – L. *ostentātus*, pp. of *ostentāre*, intensive form of *ostendere*, to shew, lit. stretch before. – L. *os-* (for *ops-*, related to *ob*), near, before; *tendere*, to stretch. See **Tend** (1). For *ops-*, see Brugm. i. § 143.

Osteology, science of the bones. (Gk.) Gk. ὀστέο-ν, a bone; -λογία, from λόγος, a discourse, λέγειν, to speak. See **osseous**.

Ostler; see **Hostler**.

Ostracise, to banish by a vote written on a potsherd. (Gk.) Gk. ὀστρα-κίζειν, to ostracise. – Gk. ὄστρακον, a potsherd, tile, voting-tablet, orig. a shell; allied to Gk. ὄστρεον, an oyster, orig. a shell. See **Oyster**.

Ostrich, a bird. (F. – L. *and* Gk.) M. E. *ostrice*, *oystryche*. – O. F. *ostruce*; mod. F. *autruche*. [Cf. Span. *avestruz*, Port. *abestruz*, an ostrich.] – L. *auis strūthio*, lit. ostrich-bird. Here *strūthio* is from Gk. στρουθίων, an ostrich; extended from στρουθός, a bird.

Other, second, different. (E.) M. E. *other*; A. S. *ōðer*, other, second. + Du. *ander*, Icel. *annarr* (for *anthar-*), Dan. *anden*, Swed. *annan*, G. *ander*, Goth. *anthar*; Lithuan. *antras*, Skt. *antara-*, other. In Skt. *an-tara-*, the suffix is the same as the usual comparative suffix (as in Gk. σοφώ-τερος, wiser). Cf. Skt. *an-ya-*, other, different.

Otter. (E.) M. E. *oter*, A. S. *otor* + Du. *otter*, Icel. *otr*, Dan. *odder*, Swed *utter*, G. *otter*; Russ. *vuidra*, Lith. *údra*; also Gk. ὕδρα, a hydra, water-snake. Teut. type *otroz*, m.; Idg. types *udros*, m., *udrā*, f. Allied to *water*; compare Gk. ὕδρα, hydra, with ὕδωρ, water. The sense is ' dweller in the water.' Doublet, *hydra*, q. v.

Otto, the same as **Attar**.

Ottoman, a low stuffed seat. (F. – Turk.) F. *ottomane*, an ottoman, sofa. – F. *Ottoman*, Turkish. So named from *Othman* or *Osman*, founder of the Turkish empire.

Ouch, Nouch, the socket of a precious

stone, ornament. (F.—O. H. G.) Usually *ouch*; yet *nouch* is the true form. M. E. *nouche*. ‒ O. F. *nouche, nosche, nusche*, a buckle, clasp, bracelet (Burguy); Low L. *nusca*. ‒ M. H. G. *nuske*, O. H. G. *nusca*, a buckle, clasp, brooch. ¶ Perhaps of Celtic origin; cf. Irish *nasc*, a tie, chain, ring, *nasgaim*, I bind (Schade, Stokes).

Ought (1), pt. t. of Owe, q. v.

Ought (2), anything; see Aught.

Ounce (1), twelfth part of a pound. (F.—L.) M. E. *unce*. ‒ O. F. *unce* (F. *once*). ‒ L. *uncia*, (1) an ounce, (2) an inch. Allied to Gk. ὄγκος, mass, weight. See Inch.

Ounce (2), **Once,** a kind of lynx. (F.—L.—Gk.) F. *once*; M.F. *lonce*, Cot. Cf. Port., *onça*, Span. *onza*, Ital. *lonza*, an ounce; also Ital. *onza*, an ounce (Florio, 1598), obtained by treating *lonza* as if = *l'onza*. ‒ Late L. type **lyncea*, lynx-like, fem. ‒ L. *lync-*, stem of *lynx*, a lynx. ‒ Gk. λύγξ, a lynx; see Lynx. For F. *o* < Gk. *v*, cf. *grotto, tomb, torso*.

Ouphe, an elf, fairy. (Scand.) Mer. Wives, iv. 4. 49. A variant of *oaf = elf*. See Oaf and Elf.

Our. (E.) A. S. *ūre*, of us; gen. of *wē*, we. The possessive pronoun was also *ūre*, which was regularly declined. The form *ūre* stands for **ūs-er-*; cf. Goth. *unsara*, gen. pl. of Goth. *weis*, we.

Ourang-outang; see Orang-outang.

Ousel, a kind of thrush. (E.) M. E. *osel*. A. S. *ōsle*. For **omsal-*, which is for older **amsal-*. ✛ G. *amsel*, O. H. G. *amsala*, an ousel. The L. *merula* (whence E. *merle*) can stand for **mesula*, and may be connected with G. *amsel* by gradation. See Merle.

Oust, to eject. (F.—L.) A. F. *ouster* (Bozon), M. F. *oster*, 'to remove;' Cot. (F. *ôter*.) Of disputed origin; some derive it from *obstāre*, to thwart, which gives the right form, but does not suit the sense; Diez suggests L. **haustāre*, a derivative of *haurīre* (pp. *haustus*), to draw water. Cf. E. *ex-haust*; and L. *exhaurīre*, in the sense 'to remove.'

Out, without, abroad. (E.) M. E. *oute, ute*, adv., A. S. *ūte, ūtan*, adv., out, without; formed (with adv. suffix *-e* or *-an*) from A. S. *ūt*, adv., out, from. ✛ Du. *uit*, Icel. *ūt*, Dan. *ud*, Swed. *ut*, G. *aus*, Goth. *ūt* (= A. S. *ūt*), *ūta* (= A. S. *ūte*), *ūtana* (= A. S. *ūtan*); Skt. *ud*, up, out. ¶ Hence numerous compounds, such as

out-balance, out-bid, out-break, presenting no difficulty.

outer, comp. form; see Utter.

Outlaw. (Scand.) M. E. *outlawe*. ‒ Icel. *ūtlagi*, an outlaw, lit. out of (beyond) the law. ‒ Icel. *ūt*, out; *lög*, law; see Out and Law. Cf. L. *exlex*, lawless.

Outlet. (E.) M. E. *utlete*, lit. 'a letting out.' ‒ A. S. *ūt*, out; *lǣtan*, to let.

Outmost; see Utmost.

Outrage. (F.—L.) F. *outrage*, earlier form *oltrage*, excessive violence. (Cf. Ital. *oltraggio*.) ‒ O. F. *oltre*, F. *outre*, beyond; with suffix *-age* (< L. *-āticum*). ‒ L. *ultrā*, beyond. See Ultra-.

Outrigger. (E. and Scand.) A projecting spar for extending sails, a projecting rowlock for an oar, a boat with projecting rowlocks. From Out and Rig.

Outward. (E.) A. S. *ūteweard*, outward. ‒ A. S. *ūte*, out; *weard*, -ward; see Toward.

Oval, egg-shaped. (F.—L.) F. *oval*. Formed with suffix *-al* (< L. *-ālis*) from L. *ōuum*, an egg. ✛ Gk. ᾠόν, ᾤον, an egg. The Gk. ᾤον is for **ōwiom*, related by gradation to L. *auis*, a bird (like ᾤα, a sheep-skin, from ὄις, a sheep); see Aviary. Perhaps cognate with Egg. Der. *ov-ar-y*, Late L. *ōuāria*, the part of the body in which eggs are formed in birds; *ovi-form*, egg-shaped; *ovi-parous*, from L. *ōui-parus*, egg-producing (see Parent).

Ovation, a lesser Roman triumph. (F. —L.) F. *ovation*. ‒ L. acc. *ouātiōnem*, from *ouātio*, a shouting, exultation. ‒ L. *ouātus*, pp. of *ouāre*, to shout. ✛ Gk. εὐάζειν, to shout, from εὐαί, εὐοῖ, interjections of rejoicing, esp. in honour of Bacchus.

Oven. (E.) M. E. *ouen* (= *oven*). A. S. *ofen, ofn*. ✛ Du. *oven* Icel. *ofn, omn* (also *ogn*), Swed. *ugn*, G. *ofen*, Goth. *auhns*. Teut. types **uhno-, ufno-*; Idg. type **uqnos*. Allied to Skt. *ukhā*, a pot (cf. Gk. ἰπνός, an oven); this older sense is remarkably preserved in A. S. *ofnet*, a pot, vessel.

Over, above, across. (E.) M. E. *ouer* (= *over*). A. S. *ofer*. ✛ Du. *over*, Icel. *yfir, ofr*, Dan. *over*, Swed. *öfver*, G. *über*, Goth. *ufar*; Gk. ὑπέρ, L. *s-uper*; Skt. *upari*, above. The Idg. form is **uper-*, closely related to **uperos*, upper (Skt. *upara-*, L. *s-uperus*, A. S. *yfera*). This is a comparative form from Idg. **upo-* (Skt. *upa*, near, on, under; Gk. ὑπό, L. *s-ub*, Goth.

uf, under; cf. A. S. *ufan*, E. *-ove* in *ab-ove*) Closely allied to **Up**. ¶ Hence a large number of compounds beginning with *over*, which present no difficulty.

Overt, open, public. (F.—L.) O. F. *overt* (later *ouvert*), pp. of *ovrir* (later *ouvrir*), to open. The etymology is disputed. α. Diez suggests that *ovrir* is a shortened form of O. F. *a-ovrir*, *a-uvrir* (Livre des Rois), answering to Prov. *adubrir*, to open. The latter can be resolved into L. *ad*, *de*, *operīre*, where *ad* is a mere prefix, and *de-operīre* is to uncover. β. Littré considers *ovrir* to be for *avrir*, i.e. L. *aperīre*, to open; the change being due to association with *covrir* (F. *couvrir*), to cover. Cf. Port. *avrir*, to open.

overture, a proposal, beginning. (F. —L.) O. F. *overture*, latter *ouverture*, an opening, from O. F. *overt*, open (above).

Oviform, Oviparous; see Oval.

Owe, to possess; hence, to possess another's property, be in debt, be obliged. (E.) M. E. *aȝen*, *awen*, *owen*, orig. ' to possess.' A. S. *āgan*, to have, possess (whence long *o* from A. S. *ā*, and *w* for *g*). +Icel. *eiga*, to possess, have, be bound, own; Dan. *eie*, Swed. *äga*, O.H.G. *eigan*, Goth. *aigan*, to possess. Teut. type **aigan-*. Allied to Skt. *īç*, to possess.

ought. (E.) The pres. tense of A. S. *āgan* is *ic āh*, really an old perf. tense; hence was formed the new pt. t. *āhte*, M. E. *ahte*, *aughte*, *oughte*, mod. E. *ought*.

owing, in phr. *owing to* = due to, because of. (E.) Orig. pres. pt. of *owe*, vb.

Owl, a bird. (E.) M. E. *oule*. A. S. *ūle*.+Du. *uil*, Icel. *ugla*, Dan. *ugle*, Swed. *ugla*, G. *eule*, O. H. G. *ūwela*. Teut. types **ūwalōn-*, **uwwalōn-*, fem. Cf. also L. *ulula*, Skt. *ulūka-*, an owl. The sense is ' howler,' from an imitative root; cf. L. *ululāre*, to howl. See Howl.

Own (1), possessed by any one, peculiar to oneself. (E.) M. E. *aȝen*, *awen*, *owen*, contracted to *own* by loss of *e*. A. S. *āgen*, own, orig. pp. of *āgan*, to possess; see Owe.+Icel. *eiginn*, Dan. Swed. *egen*, G. *eigen*, Goth. *aigans*.

own (2), to possess. (E.) M. E. *aȝnien*, *ahnien*, *ahnen*, *ohnen*. A. S. *āgnian*, to appropriate, claim as one's own; denom. vb., from A. S. *āgen*, own (above).+Icel. *eigna*, to claim as one's own; from *eiginn*, one's own. **Der.** *own-er*.

own (3), to grant. (E.) A development from *own* (2), to appropriate, claim; hence, to acknowledge. See Johnson. ¶ Usually said to have been due to A. S. *unnan*, M. E. *unnen*, to grant, of which there is no clear trace.

Ox. (E.) M. E. *ox*, *oxe*, pl. *oxen*; A. S. *oxa*, pl. *oxan*.+Du. *os*, Icel. *uxi*, *oxi*, Dan. Swed. *oxe*, G. *ochse*, *ochs*, Goth. *auhsa*; also W. *ych*; Skt. *ukshan-*, an ox, bull. Teut. type**ohsan-*; Idg. type **oksen-*. The Skt. *ukshan-* is usually derived from Skt. *uksh*, to sprinkle, hence, to impregnate; Brugm. ii. § 114.

Oxalis, wood-sorrel. (L.—Gk.) L. *oxalis*.—Gk. ὀξαλίς, (1) sour wine, (2) sorrel; from its sourness.—Gk. ὀξύς, acid. See Oxygen.

oxide, a compound of oxygen with a non-acid base. (Gk.) Coined from *ox-* (for *oxy-*, as in *oxy-gen*) and *-ide*, Gk. -ειδής, like. See Oxygen.

Oxlip, a flower. (E.) A. S. *oxanslyppe*, orig. an ox-slop, piece of ox-dung (a coarse name, like some other plant-names).— A. S. *oxan*, gen. case of *oxa*, ox; *slyppe*, a slop; see Slop. (So also *cow-slip* = *cow-slop*.)

Oxygen, a gas often found in acid compounds. (Gk.) Lit. ' acid-generator.' — Gk. ὀξύ-ς, sharp, acid; γεν-, to produce, base of γίγνομαι, I am born.

oxymel, a mixture of honey and vinegar. (L.—Gk.) L. *oxymeli*. — Gk. ὀξύμελι. — Gk. ὀξύ-ς, sharp, acid; μέλι, honey; see Mellifluous.

oxytone, having an acute accent on the last syllable. (Gk.) Gk. ὀξύτονος, shrill-toned.—Gk. ὀξύ-ς, sharp; τόνος, a tone; see Tone.

Oyer, a term in law. (F.—L.) *Oyer and terminer* means, literally, ' to hear and determine.'—A. F. *oyer* (F. *ouïr*), to hear. —L. *audīre*, to hear.

oyez, oyes, hear ye! (F.—L.) Public criers begin by saying *oyes*, now corrupted into *o yes !*—A. F. *oyez*, 2 p. pl. imperative of *oyer*, to hear (above).

Oyster. (F.—L.—Gk.) M. E. *oistre*. —A. F. *oistre* (F. *huître*).—L. *ostrea*; also *ostreum*.—Gk. ὄστρεον, an oyster; named from its hard shell.—Gk. ὀστέον, a bone, shell; see Osseous, Ostracise.

Ozone, a substance perceived by its smell in the air after electric discharges. (Gk.) Gk. ὄζων, smelling; pres. pt. of ὄζειν, to smell. See Odour.

PA–PE.

Pabulum. (L.) L. *pābulum*, food; from the base *pā-*, as seen in *pā-ui*, pt. t. of *pascere*, to feed. See **Pastor**.

Pace, a step. (F.–L.) M. E. *pas.*–F. *pas.*–L. *passum*, acc. of *passus*, a step, pace, lit. a stretch, distance between the feet in walking.–L. *passus*, pp. of *pandere*, to stretch. See **Expand**.

Pacha; see **Pasha**.

Pachydermatous, thick-skinned. (Gk.) From Gk. παχύ-s, thick; and δερ-ματ-, stem of δέρμα, skin. Gk. παχύs is allied to L. *pinguis*, fat. And see **Derm**.

Pacify. (F.–L.) F.*pacifier.*–L.*pāci-ficāre*, to make peace.–L. *pāci-*, decl. stem of *pax*, peace; *-ficāre*, for *facere*, to make. See **Peace**.

Pack, a bundle. (Low G.–L.?) M. E. *pakke* (13th cent.).–M. Du. *pack* (Du. *pak*); cf. Icel. *pakki*, Dan. *pakke*, Swed. *packa*; G. *pack*. [Cf. also Irish *pac*, Gael. *pac*, from E.; Bret. *pak*, from Romanic; Ital. *pacco*, F. *paqu-et*; Late L. *paccus*.] Prob. of Late L. origin; from the L. base *pac-*, as in pp. *pactus*, from *pangere*, to fasten (Körting). See **Pact**. Der. *pack-age*, with F. suffix *-age* (cf. *bagg-age*); *pack-et*, from F. *paquet*, a packet, bundle, dimin. form from Low G. *pakk*, M. Du. *pack*.

Pact, a contract. (L.) L. *pactum*, an agreement.–L. *pactus*, pp. of *paciscī*, to agree, inceptive form of O. L. *pacere*, to agree (Bréal). Allied to *pangere* (pp. *pactus*), to fasten, fix; Skt. *paç*, to bind, Gk. πήγνυμι, I fasten. Brugm. i. § 200; ii. § 79.

Pad (1), a soft cushion. (Low G.?) Also in the sense of 'saddle' (Levins, 1570); also in the sense of ' bundle ' (Halliwell). Of obscure origin. In the sense of cushion beneath an animal's foot, it agrees with M. Du., Low G., and Pomeranian *pad*, sole of the foot; perhaps borrowed from Slavonic. Cf. Russ. *podoshva*, sole of the foot; *podushka*, a cushion, pad; also Lith. *padas*, (the same). Cf. **Pod**.

Pad (2), a thief on the high road. (Du.) We now say *foot-pad*. Formerly a *padder*, one who goes on the *pad*, i. e. foot-path.–Du. *pad*, a path; see **Path**. (Many cant words are Dutch.) Der. *pad*, a nag, orig. *pad-nag*, a road-nag; *pad*, vb., to tramp.

Paddle (1), to finger, dabble in water. (Low G.?) Formerly also to finger, handle;

Haml. iii. 4. 185; Oth. ii. 1. 259. It is a parallel formation to *pattle*, frequent. of *pat*; see **Pat** (1). Cf. Low G. *paddeln*, to tramp about (Danneil), frequent. of *pedden*, to tread, or *padjen*, to walk with short steps (Brem. Wört.); from *pad*, the sole of the foot. See **Pad** (1). Cf. also Low G. *pladdern*, to paddle in water.

Paddle (2), a little spade, esp. to clean a plough with. (E.) Formerly *spaddle*; dimin. of *spade*. See **Spade**.

Paddock (1), a toad. (Scand.) M. E. *paddok*, dimin. of M. E. *padde*, a toad.– Icel. *padda*, Swed. *padda*, Dan. *padde*, a toad, frog.+Du. *padde*, *pad*; E. Fries. *padde*.

Paddock (2), a small enclosure. (L.?) Not an old word; used by Evelyn; a corruption of M. E. *parrok*, spelt *parrocke* in Palsgrave. (So also *poddish* for *porridge*.) See **Park**.

Paddy, rice in the husk. (Malay.) Malay *pādī*, rice in the husk. It seems to have been confused with Hind. *bhāt*, cooked rice; from Skt. *bhakta*, (properly) boiled rice, food, orig. pp. of *bhaj*, to divide, possess, &c. (See Yule.)

Padlock, a loose-hanging lock. (E.) A lock for hampers, &c.; prob. coined by adding *lock* to prov. E. *pad*, a pannier (Norfolk). This word is also written *ped*; see **Pedlar**.

Pæan, a hymn to Apollo. (L.–Gk.) L. *pæan.*–Gk. Παιάν, Παιών, (1) Pæan, Pæon, physician of the gods, (2) Apollo, (3) a hymn to Apollo. **Der.** *peon-y*.

Pædobaptism, infant baptism. (Gk.) From Gk. παιδο-, representing παῖs, a child; and *baptism*. Cf. **Pedagogue**.

Pagan, a countryman; hence, a heathen. (L.) L. *pāgānus*, (1) a villager, (2) a pagan, because the rustic people remained longest unconverted.–L. *pāgānus*, adj., rustic.–L. *pāgus*, a village, district, canton. Some connect it with *pag-*, base of *pangere*, to fasten; as being marked out by fixed limits; see **Pact**.

Page (1), a boy attending a person of rank. (F.–Late L.–Gk.?) M. E. *page.*– F. *page.*–Late L. *pagium*, acc. of *pagius*, a servant. Cf. Span. *page*, Port. *pagem*, Ital. *paggio*, a page. Etym. disputed. Diez thinks that Ital. *paggio* was formed from Gk. παιδίον, a little child, dimin. of παῖs, a boy. (See Diez, Littré, Scheler.)

Page (2), one side of the leaf of a book. (F.–L.) F. *page.*–L. *pāgina*, a page, leaf. Orig. a leaf ; and named from the fastening together of strips of papyrus to form a leaf. — L. *pag-*, base of *pangere*, to fasten (pp. *pac-tus* < *pag-tus*).

pageant, an exhibition, spectacle. (Late L. — L.) Orig. the moveable scaffold on which the old ' mysteries' were acted. M. E. *pagent* (Prompt. Parv.), also *pagen, pagyn* ; formed, with excrescent *t* after *n*, from Late L. *pāgina*, a scaffold, stage for shows, made of wooden planks. — L. *pāgina*, a page of a book ; in Late L. a plank of wood. Named from being fastened together ; see **Page** (2). Der. *page-ant-r-y*.

Pagoda, an Indian idol's temple. (Port. — Pers.) From Port. *pagoda, pagode*, a pagoda. — Pers. *but-kadah*, an idol-temple. — Pers. *but*, idol, image ; *kadah*, habitation. (The initial Pers. sound is sometimes rendered by *p*, as in Devic's Supp. to Littré.) Perhaps confused with Skt. *bhagavatī*, f., venerable, as the name of a goddess (Yule).

Pail. (E.) M. E. *paile*. A. S. *pægel*, a pail (Bosworth-Toller). See Anglia, viii. 450. Cf. Dan. *pægel*, half-a-pint ; M. Du. *pegel*, the contents or capacity of a pot. The orig. *pail* was prob. a liquid-measure, with pegs to mark the depth. See **Peg**.

Pain. (F. — L. — Gk.) M. E. *peine*. — F. *peine*, a pain, a penalty. — L. *pœna*, punishment, penalty, pain. — Gk. ποινή, penalty. Idg. type *qoinā ; cf. O. Ir. *cin*, a fault (Ir. *cion*), Zend *kaēnā-*, punishment, Pers. *kīn*, revenge, Russ. *tsiena*, a price, Gk. τίνειν, to pay a price. Brugm. i. § 202. Cf. **Pine** (2).

Painim ; see Paynim.

Paint. (F. — L.) M. E. *peinten*, vb. — F. *peint*, pp. of *peindre*, to paint. — L. *pingere*, to paint. See **Picture**.

Painter, a rope for mooring a boat. (F. — L. — Gk.) Assimilated to *painter*, one who paints ; orig. M. E. *panter*, a noose, esp. for catching birds. — M. F. *pantiere*, a snare for birds, a large net for catching many at once ; Cot. — L. *panthēr*, a hunting-net for catching wild beasts. — Gk. πάνθηρος, adj., catching all sorts. — Gk. πᾶν, neut. of πᾶς, every ; θηρᾶν, to hunt, from θήρ, a wild beast. See **Pan-**. (And see *panther*.)

Pair, two equal or like things. (F. — L.) M. E. *peire*. — F. *paire*, ' a pair ;' Cot. — F. *pair*, ' like, equal ;' id. — L. *parem*, acc. of *pār*, equal. See **Par**.

Pajamas, Pyjamas, loose drawers. (Hind. — Pers.) Hind. *pāejāmā, pājāmā*, drawers, lit. ' leg-clothing.' — Hind. *pāe*, leg ; *jāma*, garment. — Pers. *pāi*, cognate with E. *foot* ; *jāmah*, a garment (Horn, § 412).

Palace. (F. — L.) M. E. *palais*. — F. *palais*. — L. *palātium*, orig. a building on the Palatine hill at Rome ; esp. a palace of Augustus on this hill. The *Palatine* hill is supposed to have been named from *Pales*, a pastoral divinity.

paladin. (F. — Ital. — L.) F. *paladin*, a knight of the round table. — Ital. *paladino*, a warrior ; orig. a knight of the *palace* or royal household. — L. *palātīnus* ; see Palatine.

Palæo- ; see Paleo-.

Palanquin, Palankeen, a light litter in which travellers are borne on men's shoulders. (Port. — Hind. — Skt.) Cf. F. *palanquin*. From Port. *palanquim*, a palankeen. All from Hindustani *palang*, a bed, bedstead (Forbes) ; otherwise *pālkī*, and (in the Carnatic) *pallakki* (Wilson) ; Pali *pallanko*, a palankeen (Yule). — Skt. *paryanka-* (Prakrit *pallanka-*), a couch-bed, bed. Apparently named from the support afforded to the body. — Skt. *pari* (= Gk. περί), round, about ; *anka-*, a hook, also the flank.

Palate. (F. — L.) O. F. *palat*. — L. *palātum*, the palate, roof of the mouth.

Palatine. (F. — L.) In phr. ' count palatine ;' the proper sense is ' pertaining to the palace or royal household.' — F. *palatin*. — L. *palātīnus*, (1) the name of a hill at Rome, (2) belonging to a palace ; see Palace.

Palaver. (Port. — L. — Gk.) A parley. — Port. *palavra*, a word, parole. — L. *parabola*. — Gk. παραβολή ; see Parable.

Pale (1), a stake, limit. (F. — L.) M. E. *paal*. — F. *pal*, ' a pale, stake ;' Cot. — L. *pālum*, acc. of *pālus*, a stake. For *pac-slus, from *pac-*, to fasten, as in *pac-iscī* to stipulate. Brugm. ii. § 76. ¶ The heraldic *pale* is the same word ; so is *pole* (1).

Pale (2), wan. (F. — L.) O. F. *pale*, later *pasle* (F. *pâle*). — L. *pallidum*, acc. of *pallidus*, pale. Allied to **Fallow**.

Paleography, the study of ancient modes of writing. (Gk.) — Gk. παλαιό-s, old, from πάλαι, adv., long ago ; γράφ-ειν, to write.

paleology, archæology. (Gk.) From

Gk. παλαιό-s, old ; -λογία, discourse, from λόγος, a word, λέγειν, to speak.

paleontology, the science of fossils, &c. (Gk.) From Gk.παλαί-os, old ; ὄντο-, decl. stem of ὤν, existing ; -λογία, discourse, from λόγος, a word, λέγειν, to speak.

Palestra, a wrestling-school. (L. – Gk.) L. *palæstra.* – Gk. παλαίστρα, a wrestling-school. – Gk. παλαίειν, to wrestle. – Gk. πάλη, wrestling.

Paletot, a loose garment. (F.) Mod. F. *paletot,* formerly spelt *palletot, palletoc,* a sort of coat ; whence M. E. *paletok,* used of a dress worn by soldiers, knights, and kings, and usually made of silk or velvet. Explained by Diez as *palle-toque,* a cloak with a hood ; from L. *palla,* a mantle, and W. *toc,* Bret. *tōk,* a cap. Littré derives O. F. *palletoc* from M. Du. *paltrok,* a mantle, but Franck says that this M. Du. word is taken (with alteration) from the O. F. word. Cf. Bret. *paltōk,* a peasant's robe ; from *pallen,* a covering (L. *palla*) ; and *tōk,* a cap. Whence also Span. *paletoque.*

Palette, a small slab on which painters mix colours. (F. – Ital. – L.) F. *palette,* orig. a flat blade, spatula, and lastly, a palette. – Ital. *paletta,* a flat blade, spatula; dimin. of *pala,* a spade. – L. *pāla,* a spade, shovel, flat-bladed ' peel ' for putting bread into an oven. See Peel (3).

Palfrey. (F. – Low L. – C.) M. E. *palefrai, palfrei.* – O. F. *palefrei* (F. *palefroi*). – Low L. *paraverēdus,* lit. ' an extra post-horse' (White). – Low L. *para-* (Gk. παρά), beside, hence, extra ; *uerēdus,* a post-horse, courier's horse. β. Here *uerēdus* stands for **vo-rēdus,* from a Celtic type **vo-reido-,* a carriage-horse. – Celtic **vo* (Ir. *fo-,* W. *go*), under, in ; and Celtic **reidā,* Gaulish L. *rēda, rhēda,* a carriage. The Celt. **vo-reido-* appears in W. *go-rwydd,* a horse. The Celt. **reidā* is from the verb seen in O. Irish *riad-aim,* I travel, ride, cognate with E. *ride* (Stokes). ¶ Cf. Du. *paard,* G. *pferd,* O. H. G. *pfer-frit,* a horse, also from *paraverēdus.*

Palimpsest, a MS. which has been twice written on, the first writing being partly erased. (Gk.) Gk. παλίμψηστον, a palimpsest, neut. of παλίμψηστος, scraped again (to renew the surface). – Gk. πάλιμ- (for πάλιν), again ; ψηστός, scraped, from ψάειν, to rub.

Palindrome, a word or sentence that

is the same whether read forwards or backwards. (Gk.) Such a word is *madam.* – Gk. παλίνδρομος, running back again. – Gk. πάλιν, again ; δρόμος, a running, from δραμεῖν, to run ; see Dromedary.

Palinode, a recantation, in song. (F. – L. – Gk.) F. *palinodie* (Cot.). – L. *palinōdia.* – Gk. παλινῳδία, a recantation, esp. of an ode. – Gk. πάλιν, back, again ; ῳδή, an ode. See Ode.

Palisade. (F. – L.) F. *palissade,* a row of pales. – F. *paliss-er,* to enclose with pales. – F. *palis,* a pale, extended from *pal,* a pale ; see Pale (1).

Pall (1), a cloak, mantle, shroud. (L.) A.S. *pæll.* – L. *pallium,* a coverlet, cloak ; Sievers, § 80.

Pall (2), to become vapid. (F. – L.) *Pall* is a shortened form of *appal,* formerly used in the same sense. Palsgrave has *palle* and *appalle,* both in the sense of losing colour by standing as drink does ; also ' I *palle,* I fade.' See Appal.

Palladium, a safeguard of liberty. (L. – Gk.) L. *Palladium* ; Virg. Æn. ii. 166, 183. – Gk. Παλλάδιον, the statue of Pallas on which the safety of Troy depended. – Gk. Παλλάς (stem Παλλαδ-), Pallas, an epithet of Athene.

Pallet (1), a kind of mattress, properly one of straw. (F. – L.) M. E. *paillet.* – F. *paillet,* a heap of straw, given by Littré as a provincial word. Cf. *paillat,* a palliasse, in pâtois of Lyons (Puitspelu). – F. *paille,* straw. – L. *palea,* straw, chaff. +Gk. πάλη, fine meal ; Skt. *palāla,* straw ; Russ. *polova,* chaff ; Lith. *pelai,* pl., chaff.

Pallet (2), an instrument used by potters, also by gilders ; also a palette. (F. – Ital. – L.) It is a flat-bladed instrument for spreading plasters, gilding, &c. ; and is a doublet of Palette.

Palliasse, a straw mattress. (F. – L.) F. *paillasse* (with *ll* mouillés), a straw-bed ; spelt *paillace* in Cotgrave. – F. *paille,* straw ; with suffix *-ace* (<L. *-āceus*). – L. *palea,* straw. See Pallet (1).

Palliate, to cloak, excuse. (L.) From L. *palliātus,* covered as with a cloak. – L. *pallium,* a coverlet, cloak. See Pall (1).

Pallid. (L.) L. *pallidus,* pale.

pallor. (L.) L. *pallor,* paleness. – L. *pallēre,* to be pale. See Pale (2).

Pall-mall; see Mall (2).

Palm (1), inner part of the hand. (F. – L.) M. E. *paume,* palm of the hand. – F. *paume.* – L. *palma,* the palm of the hand. +

Gk. παλάμη, the palm of the hand; A. S. *folm*, the same; O. Irish *lām*, W. *llaw*. Brugm. i. § 529 (2). Der. *palm-ist-r-y*.

Palm (2), a tree. (L.) A. S. *palm*.— L. *palma*, a palm-tree. Der. *palm-er*, M. E. *palmere*, one who bore a palm-branch in memory of having been to the Holy Land; hence a *palmer* or *palmer-worm*, a sort of caterpillar, supposed to be so named from its wandering about. Also *palm-ary*, deserving the palm (of victory).

Palpable, that can be felt. (F.—L.) F. *palpable* (Littré, Palsgrave).—L. *palpā-bilis*, that may be felt.—L. *palpāre, pal-pārī*, to feel, to handle.

Palpitate, to throb. (L.) From pp. of L. *palpitāre*, to throb.

Palsy. (F.—L.—Gk.) M. E. *palesy*, fuller form *parlesy*.—F. *paralysie*.—L. *paralysin*, acc. of *paralysis*.—Gk. παρά-λυσις; see Paralysis.

Palter, to dodge, shuffle, equivocate. (Scand.) Spelt *paulter* in Cotgrave, s. v. *harceler*. The orig. sense is to haggle, to haggle over such worthless stuff as is called *paltrie* in Lowland Scotch. More literally, it is 'to deal in rags, to trifle'; see further below.

paltry, worthless. (Scand.) Lowland Sc. *paltrie* is a sb., meaning trash; so also Norfolk *paltry*, 'rubbish, refuse,' Forby. But both sb. and adj. are from an old sb. *palter*, rags, which is still preserved in Danish and Swedish.—Swed. *paltor*, rags, pl. of *palta*, a rag, tatter; Dan. *pialter*, rags, pl. of *pialt*, a rag. β. We find the adj. itself in Low G. *paltrig*, ragged, from *palte*, a rag, piece torn off a cloth; and in prov. G. *palterig*, paltry, from *palter* (pl. *paltern*), a rag (Flügel). We find also M. Du. *palt*, a fragment, Friesic *palt*, a rag; E. Fries. *palterig*, *paltrig*, ragged. Possibly of Slavonic origin. Cf. Russ. *polotno, platno*, linen, *platite*, to patch.

Pampas, plains in S. America. (Peruvian.) The final *s* is the Span. pl. suffix.— Peruvian *pampa*, a plain.

Pamper, to glut. (O. Low G.) Frequent. from Low G. *pampen*, to cram.— Low G. *pampe*, broth, pap, nasalised form of *pappe*, pap. Cf. Low G. (Altmark) *pampen, pappen*, to cram oneself (Danneil). See Pap (1).

Pamphlet, a small book. (F.?—L.?— Gk.?) Spelt *pamflet*, Test. of Love, pt. iii. 9. 54. Etym. quite uncertain. We

find F. *pamphile*, the knave of clubs, from the Gk. name *Pamphilus*; similarly, I should suppose that there was a F. form **pamfilet*, or Late L. **pamphilētus*, coined from L. *Pamphila* (of Gk. origin), the name of a female historian of the first century, who wrote numerous *epitomes* of history. G. Paris suggests L. *Pamphilus*, the name of a medieval Lat. comedy. We find Low Lat. *panfletus* (A. D. 1344).

Pan. (E.?) M. E. *panne*. A.S. *panne*, a pan, broad shallow vessel; cf. Irish *panna*, W. *pan*, a pan.—Late L. *panna*, a pan (whence also Du. *pan*, G. *pfanne*, O. H. G. *pfanna*). If not of Teut. origin, it may be a corrupted form of L. *patina*, a shallow bowl, pan, bason. Der. *pan-cake; pannikin* (M. Du. *panneken*).

Pan-, prefix, all. (Gk.) Gk. πᾶν, neut. of πᾶς, all.

Panacea, a universal remedy. (L.— Gk.) L. *panacēa*.—Gk. πανάκεια, a universal remedy; allied to πανακής, all-healing.—Gk. πᾶν, all (above); ἀκέομαι, I heal, ἄκος, a remedy.

Pancreas, a fleshy gland, commonly called sweet-bread. (L.—Gk.) L. *pancreas*. —Gk. πάγκρεας, sweet-bread; lit. 'all flesh,' from its softness —Gk. πᾶν, all; κρέας, flesh, for **κρέϝας*; cf. Skt. *kravya-*, raw flesh, L. *crū-dus*, raw. See Pan- and Crude.

Pandect, a digest. (F. — L. — Gk.) Usually in pl. *pandects*.— M. F. *pandectes*, pl. (Cot.).—L. *pandectæ*, the title of a collection of laws made by order of Justinian; also (in sing.) *pandectēs*.—Gk. πανδέκται, pandects; from Gk. πανδέκτης, all-receiving, comprehensive.—Gk. πᾶν, all; δέχομαι, I receive. See Pan-.

Pandemonium. (Gk.) The home of all the demons.—Gk. πᾶν, all; δαίμονι-, for δαίμων, a demon; see Pan- and Demon.

Pander, Pandar, a pimp. (L.—Gk.) L. *Pandarus*.—Gk. Πάνδαρος, a personal name; the name of the man who procured for Troilus the favour of Chryseis. The *name* is from Homer (Il. ii. 827); but the *story* belongs to medieval romance.

Pane, a patch of cloth, plate of glass. (F.—L.) M. E. *pane*, a portion.—F. *pan*, 'a pane, piece, or pannell;' Cot.—L. *pannum*, acc. of *pannus*, a cloth, rag, patch. Allied to Vane.

Panegyric. (L.—Gk.) L. *panēgyri-cus*, a eulogy; from L. *panēgyricus*, adj.

—Gk. πανηγυρικός, fit for a full assembly, festive, solemn; hence applied to a festival oration. **—**Gk. πανήγυρις, a full assembly. **—**Gk. πᾶν, all; -ηγυρις, related to ἀγορά, a gathering, a crowd.

Panel, Pannel, a board with a surrounding frame, &c. (F.–L.) M. E. *panel,* (1) a piece of cloth, sort of saddle, (2) a schedule containing jurors' names; the general sense being 'little piece.'— O. F. *panel,* M. F. *paneau* (later *panneau*), 'a pannel of wainscot, of a saddle,' &c.; Cot.—Late L. *pannellum,* dimin. of *pannus,* a cloth; see **Pane. Der.** *em-panel, im-panel,* to put upon a panel, enroll jurors' names.

Pang, a sharp pain. (E.?) Spelt *'prange* of love'; Court of Love, l. 1150 (ed. 1561); M. E. *pronge,* a throe, a woman's pang (Prompt. Parv.). The sense is 'a sharp stab,' a prick; see **Prong.** For the loss of *r,* cf. *speak* for *spreak.*

Panic, extreme fright. (Gk.) Gk. τὸ πανικόν, Panic fear, supposed to be inspired by the god Pan. **—**Gk. πανικός, adj., from Πάν, Pan, the rural god of Arcadia.

Panicle, a form of inflorescence. (L.) L. *pānicula,* a tuft; double dimin. of *pānus,* the thread wound round the bobbin of a shuttle.**+**Gk. πῆνος, the same. Allied to L. *pannus,* cloth; see **Pane.**

Pannage, food of swine in woods. (F. –L.) Anglo-F. *panage*; M. F. *pasnage,* 'pawnage, mastage, monie for feeding of swine with mast;' Cotgrave.—Late L. *pasnāticum, pastiōnāticum,* pannage.— Late L. *pastiōnāre,* to feed on mast, as swine.—L. *pastiōn-,* stem of *pastio,* grazing, used in Late L. to mean right of pannage.—L. *past-us,* pp. of *pascere,* to feed.

Pannier, a bread-basket. (F.–L.) M. E. *panier.* **—**F. *panier.* **—**L. *pānārium,* a bread-basket.**—**L. *pānis,* bread. Cf. **Pantry** and **Company.**

Pannikin, a little pan. (L.; *with* E. *suffix.*) Dimin. of **Pan.** Cf. M. Du. *panneken,* Westphal. *pänneken,* the same.

Panoply, complete armour. (Gk.) Gk. πανοπλία, full armour. **—** Gk. πᾶν, all; ὅπλ-α, arms, armour, pl. of ὅπλον, an implement, from Gk. ἕπω, I am busy about. Brugm. ii. § 657. And see **Pan-.**

Panorama, a kind of large picture. (Gk.) Lit. 'a view all round.'**—**Gk. πᾶν, all; ὅραμα, a view, from ὁράω, I see. See **Pan-** and **Wary.**

Pansy, heart's-ease. (F. – L.) F. *pensée,* 'a thought; also, the flower paunsie;' Cot. (It is the flower of thought or remembrance.) Prop. fem. of pp. of F. *penser,* to think. **—**L. *pensāre,* to weigh, ponder, frequent. of *pendere,* to weigh. See **Pendant.** Cf. Chaucerian Pieces, xxi. 62 (note).

Pant, to breathe hard. (F.–L.?–Gk.?) M. E. *panten,* to pant (15th cent.). The O. F. *pantais* (Godefroy) meant 'shortness of breath, in hawks,' and was a term in hawking. So also F. *pantois,* short-winded, F. *panteler,* to pant; Gascon *pantacha,* to pant; A. F. *pantoiser.* The O. F. *pantais* is a verbal sb. from O.F. *pantaisier,* to breathe with difficulty; cf. Prov. *pantaisa,* to pant, dream. Prob. from Late L. **phantasiāre,* by-form of *phantasiārī,* to imagine, dream (Ducange). **—** Gk. φαντασία, a fancy; see **Fancy.** (G. Paris, in Romania, vi. 628.) ¶ Not from W. *pantu,* which does not mean to press (Diez), but to sink in, indent.

Pantaloon (1), a ridiculous character, buffoon. (F. – Ital. – Gk.) F. *pantalon.* **—** Ital. *pantalone,* a buffoon; from the personal name *Pantaleone,* common in Venice, St. *Pantaleone* being a well-known saint in Venice. Prob. from Gk. πανταλέων, lit. 'all-lion,' a Gk. personal name. **—** Gk. παντα-, all; λέων, lion.

pantaloons, a kind of trousers. (F.– Ital.–Gk.) F. *pantalon,* so called because worn by Venetians.–Ital. *pantalone,* a Venetian; see above.

Pantheism, the doctrine that the universe is God. (Gk.) From **Pan-** and **Theism**; see below.

pantheon. (L. – Gk.) L. *panthēon.* **—**Gk. πάνθειον, a temple consecrated to all the gods.**—**Gk. πᾶν, all; θεῖος, divine, from θεός, god.

Panther, a quadruped. (F.–L.– Gk.) M. E. *pantere.***—**O. F. *panthere.***—** L. *panthēra, panthēr.* **—** Gk. πάνθηρ, a panther; prob. of Skt. origin. ¶ A supposed derivation from πᾶν, all, θήρ, a beast, gave rise to numerous fables.

Pantomime, a dumb actor; later, a dumb show. (F.–L.–Gk.) F. *pantomime,* an actor of many parts in one play. **—**L. *pantomīmus.* **—** Gk. παντόμιμος, all-imitating, a pantomimic actor.**—**Gk. παντο-, for πᾶς, all; μῖμος, a mime, imitator; see **Pan-** and **Mimic.**

Pantry. (F.–L.) M. E. *pantrie.* **—**

O. F. *paneterie*. — Late L. *pānētāria, pāni-tāria*, a place where bread is made or kept. — Late L. *pānēta*, one who makes bread. — L. *pān-is*, bread, food; cf. *pascere*, to feed. (√PA.)

Pap (1), food for infants. (E.) ' *Papmete* for chylder;' Prompt. Parv. (A. D. 1440). Cf. M. E. *pappe*, only in the sense of ' breast.' Of infantine origin, due to the repetition of *pa, pa*, in calling for food; cf. L. *pāpa, pappa*, the word by which infants call for food. So also Du. *pap*, E. Fries. and G. *pappe*, pap; Dan. *pap*, Swed. *papp*, paste-board. Cf. **pap** (2), **Papa**.

pap (2), a teat, breast. (E.) M. E. *pappe*. Cf. M. Swed. *papp*, the breast; changed, in mod. Swedish, to *patt*. So also Swed. dial. *pappe*, N. Fries. *pap*, *pape*, Lithuan. *pápas*, the breast. Much the same as **Pap** (1); and due to the infant's call for food.

Papa, father. (F. — L.) Not found in old books; rather, borrowed from F. *papa*. — L. *pāpa*, a father, bishop, pope. Cf. L. *pappas*, a tutor, borrowed from Gk. πάππας, papa; Homer, Od. vi. 57. Due to the repetition of *pa, pa*; see **Pap** (1), **Pope**.

papal, belonging to the pope. (F. — L.) F. *papal*. — Late L. *pāpālis*, adj., from L. *pāpa*, a bishop, spiritual father. Cf. Gk. πάπας, πάππας, papa, father (above).

Papaw, a fruit. (Span. — W. Indian.) Span. *papaya* (Pineda). — Carib *ababaï*. See Yule.

Paper. (L. — Gk. — Egyptian?) A. S. *paper*; directly from L. *papyrus*; see **Papyrus**.

papier-maché, paper made into pulp, moulded, dried, and japanned. (F. — L.) F. *papier*, paper, from L. acc. *papȳrum*; F. *mâché*, lit. chewed, pp. of *mâcher*, L. *masticāre*, to chew. See **Masticate**.

Papilionaceous, having a winged corolla resembling a butterfly. (L.) Coined, with suffix -*āceus*, from L. *papiliōn-*, stem of *papilio*, a butterfly; see **Pavilion**.

Papillary, belonging to or resembling nipples or teats, warty. (L.) From L. *papilla*, a small pustule, nipple, teat; dimin. of *papula*, a pustule. + Lithuan. *pápas*, a teat, *pampti*, to swell out. See Prellwitz, s. v. πέμφιξ.

Papyrus. (L. — Gk. — Egyptian?) L.

papȳrus. — Gk. πάπυρος, an Egyptian rush or flag, of which a writing material was made. Prob. of Egyptian origin.

Par, equal value. (L.) L. *pār*, equal. Perhaps allied to **Pare**.

Para-, prefix. (Gk.) Gk. παρά, beside. Allied to Skt. *parā*, away, from, L. *per*, through, and to E. *for-* in *for-give*.

Parable. (F. — L. — Gk.) M. E. *parabole*. — O. F. *parabole*. — L. *parabola*, Mark iv. 2. — Gk. παραβολή, a comparison, a parable. — Gk. παραβάλλειν, to cast or put beside, to compare. — Gk. παρά, beside; βάλλειν, to cast. Brugm. ii. § 713.

parabola, a certain plane curve. (L. — Gk.) L. *parabola*. — Gk. παραβολή, the conic section made by a plane *parallel* to the surface of the cone; see **Parable**.

Parachute, an apparatus for breaking a fall from a balloon. (F. — L.) F. *parachute*, lit. that which parries or guards against a fall. — F. *para-*, as in *para-sol*; and *chute*, a fall. Here *para-* represents Port. or Ital. *parare*, to ward off; and *chute* is equivalent to Ital. *caduta*, a fall, orig. fem. of *caduto*, fallen, from L. *cadere*, to fall. See **Parasol**.

Paraclete, the Comforter. (L. — Gk.) L. *paraclētus*. — Gk. παράκλητος, called to one's aid, the Comforter (John xiv. 16). — Gk. παρακαλεῖν, to call to one's aid. — Gk. παρά, beside; καλεῖν, to call.

Parade, display. (F. — Span. — L.) F. *parade*, a show, also 'a stop on horseback,' Cot. The latter sense was the earlier in French. — Span. *parada*, a stop, halt, from *parar*, vb., to halt, also to get ready. — L. *parāre*, to get ready. See **Pare**. The sense 'display' was due to the F. verb *parer*, to deck, trim, from the same L. *parāre*.

Paradigm, an example, model. (F. — L. — Gk.) F. *paradigme*. — L. *paradigma*. — Gk. παράδειγμα, a pattern, model, example of declension. — Gk. παρά, beside; δείκνυμι, I point out, show. See **Diction**.

Paradise. (L. — Gk. — Pers.) L. *paradīsus*. — Gk. παράδεισος, a park, pleasureground; an oriental word of Pers. origin. — Zend *pairidaēza*, an enclosure, place walled in. — Zend *pairi* (= Gk. περί), around; *diz* (Skt. *dih*), to mould, form, shape (hence to form a wall of earth). √DHEIGH; see **Dough**.

Paradox. (F. — L. — Gk.) F. *paradoxe*. — L. *paradoxum*, neut. of *paradoxus*, adj. — Gk. παράδοξος, contrary to received opinion. — Gk. παρά, beside ; δόξα, opinion, from δοκεῖν, to seem ; see **Dogma.**

Paraffine. (F. — L.) Named from its having but small affinity with an alkali. — F. *paraffine.* — L. *par-um*, little ; *affinis*, having affinity ; see **Affinity.**

Paragoge, the addition of a letter at the end of a word. (L. — Gk.) [Thus, in *tyran-t*, the final letter is *paragogic*.] — L. *paragōgē.* — Gk. παραγωγή, a leading by or past, alteration. — Gk. παράγειν, to lead past. — Gk. παρ-ά, beyond ; ἄγειν, to lead ; see **Agent.**

Paragon. (F. — Span. — Gk.) M. F. *paragon.* — M. Span. *paragon*, a model of excellence. Cf. Ital. *paragone*, 'a paragon, a match, an equal;' Florio ; and Ital. *paragonare*, to compare. The latter answers to the Gk. παρακονάειν, to rub against a whetstone (hence, probably, to try by a touchstone, compare). — Gk. παρ-ά, beside ; ἀκόνη, a whetstone, allied to ἀκίς, a sharp point. (√AK.) See Tobler, in Zt. für roman. Philol. iv. 373.

Paragraph, a short passage of a book. (F. — L. — Gk.) Actually corrupted, in the 15th century, into *pargrafte*, *pylcrafte*, and *pilcrow* ! — F. *paragraphe.* — Late L. *paragraphum*, acc. of *paragraphus*. — Gk. παράγραφος, a line or stroke in the margin, a paragraph-mark ; hence the paragraph itself. — Gk. παρά, beside ; γράφειν, to write ; see **Graphic.** (N. B. The *pilcrow* or paragraph-mark is now printed ¶.)

Parallax, the difference between the real and apparent places of a star. (Gk.) Gk. παράλλαξις, alternation, change ; also parallax (in modern science). — Gk. παραλλάσσειν, to make things alternate. — Gk. παρά, beside ; ἀλλάσσειν, to change, alter, from ἄλλος, other ; see **Alien.**

Parallel, side by side, similar. (F. — L. — Gk.) M. F. *parallele*, Cot. — L. *parallēlus.* — Gk. παράλληλος, parallel, beside each other. — Gk. παρ-ά, beside ; *ἄλληλος, one another, only in the gen. dat. and acc. plural. β. The decl. stem ἀλληλο- stands for ἄλλο- ἄλλο-, a reduplicated form, lit. 'the other the other' or 'one another'; from Gk. ἄλλος, other ; see **Alien.**

parallelogram. (F. — L. — Gk.) M. F. *paralelograme*, Cot. — L. *parallēlogrammum.* — Gk. παραλληλόγραμμον, a figure contained by two pairs of parallel

lines. — Gk. παράλληλο-s, parallel (above); γράμμα, a line, from γράφειν, to write.

parallelopiped. (L. — Gk.) So written ; a mistake for *parallelepiped.* — L. *parallēlepipedum.* — Gk. παραλληλεπίπεδον, a body formed by parallel surfaces. — Gk. παράλληλ-ος, parallel ; ἐπίπεδον, a plane surface, neut. of ἐπίπεδος, on the ground, from ἐπί, upon, and πέδον, the ground.

Paralogism, a conclusion unwarranted by the premises. (F. — L. — Gk.) F. *paralogisme.* — L. *paralogismus.* — Gk. παραλογισμός, a false reckoning or conclusion. — Gk. παραλογίζομαι, I misreckon. — Gk. παρά, beside, amiss ; λογίζομαι, I reckon, from λόγος, reason ; see **Logic.**

Paralysis. (L. — Gk.) L. *paralysis.* — Gk. παράλυσις, a loosening aside, disabling of nerves, paralysis or palsy. — Gk. παραλύειν, to loosen aside. — Gk. παρά, beside ; λύειν, to loosen, allied to **Lose.** Der. *paralyse*, from F. *paralyser*, verb formed from F. sb. *paralysie*, paralysis. Also *paralytic*, from Gk. παραλυτικός, afflicted with palsy. Doublet, *palsy*.

Paramatta, a fabric like merino. (New S. Wales.) So named from *Paramatta*, a town near Sydney, New South Wales. Properly spelt *Parramatta* ; the lit. sense is ' place of eels '; where *parra* represents eels, and *matta*, place. *Parramatta* is also the name of the river ; *Cabramatta*, ten miles off, is not a river.

Paramount, of the highest importance. (F. — L.) O. F. *par amont*, at the top, above, lit. ' by that which is upwards.' — L. *per*, by ; *ad montem*, to the hill, upwards ; where *montem* is acc. of *mons*, a hill. See **Mount.**

Paramour. (F. — L.) M. E. *par amour*, with love ; orig. an adverb. phrase. — F. *par amour*, with love ; where *par <* L. *per*, and *amour* is from L. *amōrem*, acc. of *amor*, love. See **Amatory.**

Parapet, a rampart, breast-high. (F. — Ital. — L.) F. *parapet.* — Ital. *parapetto*, a wall breast-high ; lit. ' guarding the breast.' — Ital. *parare*, to adorn, also to guard, parry ; *petto*, breast. — L. *parāre*, to prepare, adorn ; *pectus*, the breast. See **Pare.**

Paraphernalia, ornaments. (L. — Gk.) Properly the property which a bride possesses beyond her dowry. Formed by adding L. neut. pl. suffix *-ālia* to Late L. *paraphern-a*, the property of a bride over and above her dower. — Gk. παράφερνα, that which a bride brings beyond her dower. — Gk. παρά, beside; φερνή, a dower, that which is brought, from φέρειν, to bring, allied to E. Bear (1).

Paraphrase. (F. – L. – Gk.) M. F. *paraphrase.* — L. *paraphrasin*, acc. of *paraphrasis.* — Gk. παράφρασις, a paraphrase, free translation. — Gk. παρά, beside; φράσις, a phrase, from φράζειν, to speak; see **Phrase.**

Paraquito, Parakeet, a little parrot. (Span.) Span. *periquito*, a little parrot, dimin. of *perico*, a parrot. Diez supposes *perico* to be a nickname, meaning 'little Peter,' dimin. of *Pedro*, Peter. See **Parrot.**

Parasang, a measure of distance. (Gk. — Pers.) Gk. παρασάγγης, of Pers. origin. Mod. Pers. *farsang*, *ferseng*, a league. (Horn, § 818.)

Parasite. (F. – L. – Gk.) F. *parasite.* — L. *parasītus.* — Gk. παράσιτος, eating beside another at his table, a flatterer, toad-eater. — Gk. παρά, beside; σῖτος, wheat, food. Orig. in a good sense; see Gk. Lex.

Parasol, a sun-shade. (F. — Port. – L.) F. *parasol*, 'an umbrello;' Cot. — Port. *parasol* (or Ital. *parasole*), an umbrella to keep off the sun's heat. — Port. *para-r* (or Ital. *parare*), to ward off; *sol* (Ital. *sole*), sun. — L. *parāre*, to prepare; *sōlem*, acc. of *sōl*, sun. See **Parry** and **Solar.**

Parboil. (F. – L.) It now means 'to boil insufficiently,' by confusion with *part.* The old sense is 'to boil thoroughly.' — O. F. *parboillir*, to cook thoroughly, also, to boil gently (Godefroy). — Late L. *parbullīre*, L. *perbullīre*, to boil thoroughly. — L. *per*, through; and *bullīre*, to boil; see **Boil** (1).

Parcel. (F. – L.) M. E. *parcel.* — F. *parcelle*, a small piece or part. — Late L. *particella*, only preserved in Ital. *particella*, a small part. Dimin. of L. *particula*; see **Particle.**

Parch, to scorch. (F. – L.) Very difficult. M. E. *parchen*, to parch. Prob. the same as M. E. *perchen*, to pierce, an occasional form of *percen*, to pierce. This is the most likely solution ; in fact, a careful examination of M. E. *perchen* fairly proves the point. It was at first used in the sense 'to pierce with cold,' and was afterwards transferred to express the effects

of heat. We still say '*piercing* cold.' See Milton, P. L. ii. 594. — Picard and Walloon *percher*, for F. *percer*, to pierce. See **Pierce.**

Parchment. (F. – L. – Gk.) M. E. *perchemin.* — O. F. *parchemin.* — L. *pergamīna*, *pergamēna*, parchment; fem. of L. *Pergamēnus*, belonging to Pergamos (where parchment was first invented). — Gk. περγαμηνή, parchment, from Πέργαμος, Πέργαμον, Pergamus, in Mysia of Asia Minor.

Pard, a panther, leopard. (L. – Gk.) L. *pardus.* — Gk. πάρδος. An Eastern word; cf. Pers. *pārs*, a pard ; Skt. *prdāku*, a leopard. **Der.** *leo-pard, camelo-pard.*

Pardon, forgiveness. (F. – L.) M. E. *pardoun.* — F. *pardon*, sb. — F. *pardonner*, to forgive. — Late L. *perdōnāre*, to remit a debt, pardon. — L. *per*, fully ; *dōnāre*, to give ; see **Donation.**

Pare, to shave off. (F. – L.) M. E. *paren.* — F. *parer*, to deck, trim, pare. — L. *parāre*; to get ready, prepare.

Paregoric, assuaging pain. (L. – Gk.) L. *parēgoricus*, assuaging. — Gk. παρηγορικός, addressing, encouraging, soothing. — Gk. παρηγορεῖν, to address. — Gk. παρά, beside ; ἀγορά, an assembly, whence also ἀγορεύειν, to address an assembly.

Parent. (F. – L.) F. *parent*, a kinsman. — L. *parent-*, stem of *parens*, a parent, lit. one who produces. — L. *parere*, to produce. Brugm. i. § 515.

Parenthesis. (Gk.) Gk. παρένθεσις, an insertion, a putting in beside. — Gk. παρ-ά, beside ; ἐν, in ; θέσις, a placing ; see **Thesis.**

Parget, to plaster a wall. (F. – L.) Nearly obsolete ; once common. M. E. *pargeten* ; as if from O. F. *pargeter*, to spread abroad, cast around, Late L. *perjactāre* (not in Ducange, but found in the 14th cent.). Cf. '*Perjacio*, Anglice, to perjette ;' Vocab. 602. 7. As if from L. *per*, fully ; *iactāre*, to cast, frequent. of *iacere*, to throw. See **Jet** (1). 2. But really substituted for O. F. *porgeter*, to rough-cast a wall (Godefroy). — L. *prōiectāre*, to cast forth ; from *prō* and *iactāre*. Cf. Walloon *porgeté*, to parget (Remacle). ¶ Also spelt *spargetten*, where the *s* of *spargetten* = O. F. *es-*, L. *ex* (intensive).

Parhelion, a mock sun. (L. Gk.) L. *parhēlion.* — Gk. παρήλιον, neut. of παρήλιος, beside the sun. — Gk. παρ-ά, beside ; ἥλιος, sun ; see **Heliacal.**

Pariah, an outcast. (Tamil.) Tamil *paṟaiyan*, corruptly *pariah*, Malayālim *parayan*, a man of low caste, performing the lowest menial services; one of his duties is to beat the village drum (called *paṟai* in Tamil), whence, probably, the appellation of the caste. (H. H. Wilson.)

Parian, belonging to Paros. (Gk.) *Paros* is an island in the Ægean sea.

Parietal, forming the walls, applied to two bones in the front of the skull. (L.) L. *parietālis*, belonging to a wall. − L. *pariet-*, stem of *pariēs*, a wall.

Parish. (F.−L.−Gk.) M. E. *parische.* − F. *paroisse.* − L. *parœcia.* − Gk. παροικία, a neighbourhood; hence an ecclesiastical district. − Gk. πάροικος, neighbouring. − Gk. παρ-ά, near; οἶκος, house, abode, allied to Vicinage. **Der.** *parishion-er*, formed by adding *-er* (needlessly) to M. E. *parisshen* < O. F. *paroissien*, a parishioner.

Paritory; see Pellitory.

Parity, equality. (F.−L.) F. *parité.* − L. *paritātem*, acc. of *paritās*, equality. − L. *pār*, equal.

Park, an enclosed ground. (E. ?) *Park* = O. F. *parc*, is a F. spelling. M. E. *parrok*, an enclosure, A. S. *pearruc*, *pearroc.* Cf. Irish and Gael. *pairc*, W. *park* and *parwg* (< E. *parrok*). The word is common in Teutonic tongues, as in Du. *perk*, Swed. Dan. *park*, G. *pferch*, and is prob. Teutonic; cf. M. E. *parren*, to enclose. Hence, probably, Late L. *parcus*, *parricus*, an enclosure; whence F. *parc*, Ital. *parco*, Span. *parque.*

Parley. (F.−L.−Gk.) F. *parler*, sb., speech, talk, a parley. − F. *parler*, vb., to speak. − Late L. *parabolāre*, to talk. − L. *parabola*; see Parable.

parliament. (F.−L.−Gk.; with F. suffix.) M. E. *parlement*. [We also find Late L. *parliāmentum*, corresponding to our spelling *parliament*.] − F. *parlement*, 'a speaking, parleying, a supreme court ;' Cot. − F. *parler*, to speak (as above) ; with F. suffix *-ment* (L. *-mentum*).

parlour. (F.−L.−Gk.) M. E. *parlour*, *parlur.* − O. F. *parloir*, a parlour, lit. a room for conversation. − F. *parl-er*, to speak ; with suffix *-oir* < L. *-ātōrium* ; so that *parlour* answers to a Late L. form **parabolātōrium*, a place to talk in. (Cf. F. *dortoir* < L. *dormitōrium*.) See above.

Parlous. (F.−L.) Short for *perilous*.

Parochial. (L.−Gk.) L. *parōchiālis.*

− L. *parōchia*, same as *parœcia*, a parish ; see Parish.

Parody. (F.−L.−Gk.) M. E. and F. *parodie.* − L. *parōdia.* − Gk. παρῳδία, also παρῳδή, a song sung beside (i. e. in imitation of) another. − Gk. παρ-ά, beside ; ᾠδή, an ode. See Ode.

Parole. (F.−L.−Gk.) F. *parole*, a word, esp. a promise ; the same word as Prov. *paraula*, Span. *palabra* (= **parabla*), Port. *palavra.* − Late L. *parabola*, a discourse ; L. *parabola*, a parable. See Parable, Palaver.

Paronymous, allied in origin ; alike in sound. (Gk.) Gk. παρώνυμος, formed from another word by a slight change. − Gk. παρά, beside ; ὄνυμα, a name. **Der.** *paronom-as-ia*, a slight change in a word's meaning, from Gk. παρωνομασία, better παρονομασία.

Paroxysm. (F.−L.−Gk.) F. *paroxysme.* − L. *paroxysmus.* − Gk. παροξυσμός, irritation, the fit of a disease. − Gk. παροξύνειν, to irritate. − Gk. παρ-ά, beside ; ὀξύνειν, to sharpen, from ὀξύς, sharp. See Oxygen.

Parquetry, a mosaic of wood-work for floors. (F. − Teut. ?) F. *parqueterie.* − F. *parqueter*, to inlay a wooden floor. − F. *parquet*, a wooden floor ; orig. a small enclosure ; dimin. of F. *parc*, a park. See Park.

Parricide, (1) the murderer of a father ; (2) murder of a father. (F. − L ; or L.) The former is the older E. sense, and answers to F. *parricide*, L. *parricīda*, for older *pāricīdas* (Brugm. ii. § 190), a murderer of a relative. − L. *parri-*, for *pāri-*, a relative (cf. Gk. πηός, a relative, Prellwitz, s. v. πάομαι) ; and *cædere*, to kill (whence *-cīda*, a slayer). 2. The second sense is directly from L. *parricīdium*, the murder of a relative, from the same sb. and vb.

Parrot. (F.−L.−Gk.) F. *Perrot*, of which the lit. sense is 'little Peter,' given to the bird as a nickname ; see Cotgrave. Also written *Pierrot*, both forms being from *Pierre*, Peter. − L. *Petrum*, acc. of *Petrus*, Peter. − Gk. πέτρος, a stone, rock ; also Peter. **Der.** F. *perroquet*, borrowed from Span. *perichito* or *periquito*, dimin. of *Perico*, Peter ; see Paraquito. ¶ The F. word is prob. imitated or translated from Span. or Portuguese.

Parry, to ward off. (F. − L.) Formerly *parree*, sb., a warding off. From F. *parée*, fem. pp.; used as equivalent to Ital. *parata*, a defence, guard. – F. *parer*, to prepare, also to guard, ward off. – L. *parāre*, to prepare. See Pare.

Parse, to tell the parts of speech. (L.) To *parse* is to tell ' quæ *pars* orationis,' i.e. what part of speech a word is. – L. *pars*, a part. See Part.

Parsee, an adherent of the old Persian religion, in India. (Pers.) Pers. *pārsī*, a Persian. – Pers. *Pārs*, Persia.

Parsimony, frugality. (F. – L.) M. F. *parsimonie*; Cot. – L. *parsimōnia*, better *parcimōnia*. – L. *parci*-, for *parcus*, sparing; with suffix -*mōnia* (Idg. -*mōnyā*). Allied to *parcere*, to spare.

Parsley. (F. – L. – Gk.) Formerly *persely.* – F. *persil*; older form *peresil*. – L. *petroselīnum.* – Gk. πετροσέλινον, rock parsley. – Gk. πέτρο-s, rock, stone; σέλινον, a kind of parsley; see Celery.

Parsnep, Parsnip. (F. – L.) Formerly *parsnep*, and still better *pasneppe*, as in Palsgrave; the *r* being intrusive. – O. F. *pastenaque*, a parsnip (by dropping *te*). – L. *pastināca*, a parsnep: perhaps orig. a root dug up. Perhaps from L. *pastināre*, to dig up. – L. *pastinum*, a two-pronged dibble. ¶ The ending -*nep* was assimilated to that of *turnep*.

Parson. (F. – L.) M. E. *persone*, which also means *person*; see Late L. *persōna*, a person of rank, a choir-master, curate, parson (Ducange). See Person. ¶ Blackstone gives the right etymology, but the wrong reason; the Late L. *persōna* was applied to ' rank ' or dignity, and had nothing to do with a fanciful embodiment of the church in the parson's person ! Der. *parson-age.*

Part. (F. – L.) F. *part*. – L. *partem*, acc. of *pars*, a part. Orig. ' a share,' that which is provided; from the same root as *portion*. Brugm. i. § 527. **Der.** *part*, vb.; *partake*, *partial*, &c.

partake. (F. – L ; *and* Scand.) For *part-take*, i. e. take part. Wyclif has *part-takynge*, 1 Cor. x. 16 (earlier version). See Part and Take.

Parterre. (F. – L.) F. *parterre*, an even piece of garden-ground. – F. *par terre*, along the ground. – L. *per terram*, along the ground. See Terrace.

Partial. (F. – L.) F. *partial*. – Late L. *partiālis*, referring to a part only. – L. *parti*-, decl. stem of *pars*, a part. See Part.

participate. (L.) From pp. of L. *participāre*, to take a part. – L. *particip*-, stem of *particeps*, sharing in. – L. *parti*-, decl. stem of *pars*, a part; *capere*, to take.

participle. (F. – L.) The *l* is an E. insertion, as in *syllable*. – F. *participe*. – L. *participium*, a participle; supposed to partake of the nature both of an adjectival sb. and a vb. – L. *particip*-, stem of *particip.*

particle. (F. – L.) F. *particule* (16th cent.). – L. *particula*, double dimin. from *parti*-, decl. stem of *pars*, a part.

partisan (1), an adherent of a party. (F. – Ital. – L.) F. *partisan*. – Ital. *partigiano*, a partner; answering to a Late L. form **partītiānus.* – L. *partītus*, pp. of *partīrī*, to part, divide. – L. *parti*-, decl. stem of *pars*, a part. Others (see Körting), give the Late L. form as *partensiānus, extended from *part*-, stem of *pars*, a part.

Partisan (2), **Partizan,** a halberd. (F. – Ital. – L. ?) M. F. *pertuisane*, ' a partisan, or leading-staffe,' Cot. ; O. F. *pourtisaine* (15th cent., Littré) ; *pertesane* (Godefroy, s. v. *pertuisanier*). – Ital. *partegiana*, ' a partesan, iauelin ;' Florio. [The M. F. *pertuisane* is an accommodated spelling, to make it look like M.F. *pertuiser*, to pierce through, due to L. *per-tundere*.] Cf. Late L. *partesāna*, *pertixāna*. β. Apparently connected with the word above, as if the weapon of a partisan (Diez).

Partition. (F. – L.) F. *partition*. – L. acc. *partītiōnem*, a sharing, partition. – L. *partītus*, pp. of *partīrī*, to divide. – L. *parti*-, decl. stem of *pars*, a part; see Part.

partner. (F. – L.) A curious corruption of M. E. *parcener*, frequently misread and misprinted as *partener*, by the common confusion between *c* and *t* in MSS., and through the influence of *part*. – O. F. *parcener*, M. F. *parsonnier*, ' a partener, or coparcener ;' Cot. – Late L. *partītiōnārius, of which the shorter form *partiōnārius* occurs. – L. *partītiōn-em*, acc. of *partītio*, a sharing, share ; see Partition.

Partridge, a bird. (F. – L. – Gk.) M. E. *pertriche.* – F. *perdrix*, where the second *r* is intrusive. – L. *perdīcem*, acc. of *perdix*. – Gk. πέρδιξ, a partridge.

Parturient, about to produce young. (L.) L. *parturient*-, stem of pres. pt. of *parturīre*, to be ready to produce young. From *part*-, as in *part-us*, pp. of *parĕre*, to produce. Brugm. ii. § 778. **Der.** *par-tur-it-ion*, F. *parturition.*

Party. (F.—L.) M. E. *partie*, usually 'a part.' — O. F. *partie*, a part, a party ; Cot. — L. *partīta*, fem. of *partītus*, pp. of *partīrī*, to divide. See **Partition.**

Parvenu, an upstart. (F.—L.) F. *parvenu*, lit. one who has arrived, hence, one who has thriven. Pp. of *parvenir*, to arrive, thrive. — L. *per-uenīre*, to arrive, come through. — L. *per*, through : *uenīre*, to come ; see **Venture.**

Parvis, a porch, room over a porch. (F.—L.—Gk.—Pers.) O. F. *parvis*, a porch, outer court before a house or church ; variant of *parevis, pareïs, paraïs*, paradise (Low L. *paravīsus*). — L. *paradī-sus*, a church-porch, outer court, paradise. See **Paradise.** The *v* was inserted in *pare-is*, to avoid hiatus.

Pasch, the Passover. (L.—Gk.—Heb.) A.S. *pascha*. — L. *pascha*. — Gk. πάσχα. — Heb. *pesakh*, a passing over ; the passover ; Exod. xii. 11. — Heb. *pāsakh*, he passed over.

Pash, to dash. (Scand.) Swed. dial. *paska*, to dabble in water, Norweg. *baska*, to dabble in water, tumble, work hard ; the same as Dan. *baske*, to slap, *baxes*, to box, Norw. *baksa*, to box ; Swed. dial. *baska, basta*, to beat ; from *bas-a*, to beat. Cp. prov. E. *bash*, of which it is a mere variant. And see **Plash, Baste** (1).

Pasha, Pacha. (Pers.) Also *bashaw*. Pers. *bāshā, bādshāh*, a governor of a province, great lord ; the same as *pādshāh*, a prince, great lord ; lit. 'protecting the king.' — Pers. *pād*, protecting ; *shāh*, king. See **Bezoar** and **Shah.**

Pasquin, Pasquinade, a lampoon. (F.—Ital.) (Formerly also *pasquil*; M. F. *pasquille*.) — F. *pasquin* (whence *pasquinade*), a pasquin, lampoon. — Ital. *Pasquino*, 'a statue in Rome on whom all libels are fathered ;' Florio. From the name of a cobbler at Rome, whose stall was frequented by gossips ; his name was transferred to a statue found near his stall at his death, on which the wits of the time secretly affixed lampoons ; see Haydn.

Pass, to move onward. (F.—L.) M. E. *passen*. — F. *passer*. — Late L. *pas-sāre*, to pass. — L. *passus*, a step ; see **Pace.** β. Diez takes Late L. *passāre* to be the frequent. form of *pandere*, to stretch ; it makes but little difference.

passage. (F.—L.) F *passage*. — Late

L. *passāticum*, a right of passage. — Late L. *passāre* ; see above. **Der.** *passenger*, for M. E. *passager.*

Passion. (F.—L.) F. *passion*. — L. *passiōnem*, acc. of *passio*, (properly) suffering. — L. *passus*, pp. of *patī*, to suffer. See **Patient.**

passive. (F.—L.) F. *passif*. — L. *passīuus*, suffering. — L. *passus* (above).

Passport. (F.—L.) F. *passeport*, written permission to pass through a gate, &c. — F. *passer*, to pass ; *porte*, gate, from L. *porta* ; see **Pass** and **Port** (3).

Paste. (F.—L.—Gk.) O. F. *paste*; F. *pâte*. — Late L. *pasta*, paste. — Gk. παστή, a mess of food ; orig. fem. of παστός, besprinkled, salted ; from πάσσειν, to sprinkle. The orig. sense was 'a salted mess of food.' **Der.** *past-y*, M. E. *pastee*, O. F. *pasté* (F. *pâté*), a pasty ; *past-r-y*, orig. a room in which pasties were kept (cf. *pantry, buttery*). And see **Patty.**

Pastel, a coloured crayon. (F.—Ital. —L.) An artist's term. — F. *pastel*, 'a pastel, crayon ;' Hamilton. — Ital. *pas-tello*, a pastel. — L. *pastillum*, acc. of *pas-tillus*, a little loaf or roll ; the pastel being named from being shaped like a roll. Dimin. of *pastus*, food. — L. *pastus*, pp. of *pascere*, to feed. ¶ *Not* allied to *paste* ; see **pastille** below.

pastern. (F.—L.) Formerly *pastron*; Palsgrave. — M. F. *pasturon*, 'the pastern of a horse ;' Cot. (F. *pâturon*.) So called because a horse at *pasture* was tethered by the *pastern* ; the tether itself was called *pasture* in O. French. — O. F. *pasture*, pasture. See **pasture.**

pastille, a small cone of aromatic substances, to be burnt in a room. (F.—L.) F. *pastille*, a little lump or loaf ; see Cotgrave. — L. *pastillum*, acc. of *pastillus*, a little loaf ; dimin. of *pastus*, food ; see **Pastel.**

Pastime. (F.—L. ; *and* E.) From *pass* and *time* ; imitating F. *passe-temps.*

Pastor, a shepherd. (F.—L.) Formerly *pastour*. — O. F. *pastour*. — L. *pas-tōrem*, acc. of *pastor*, a shepherd, lit. 'feeder.' — L. *pastus*, pp. of *pascere*, to feed, an inceptive verb ; pp. *pā-ui*. (√PA.) **Der.** *pastor-al*, F. *pastoral*, L. *pastorālis*, adj.

pasture. (F.—L.) O. F. *pasture*, a feeding. — L. *pastūra*, a feeding. — L. *pas-tus*, pp. of *pascere*, to feed.

Pat (1), to strike lightly. (E.) In

Bacon, Nat. Hist. § 63. Most likely from a by-form of A. S. *plættan*, M. E. *platten*, *pletten* (see Stratmann), to strike; for loss of *l* cf. *patch* (1). Cf. Swed. dial. *pjätta*, to pat, *plätta*, to tap (Rietz); Bavarian *patzen*, to pat; E. Fries. *patjen*, to splash; G. *patschen*, to tap, splash; G. *platzen*, to crack; M. Du. *pletten*, 'contundere,' Kilian. Of imitative origin; cf. **Tap, Dab, Paddle.**

Pat (2), a small lump of butter. (E.) Cf. Irish *pait*, a hump, lump, *paiteog*, a small lump of butter; Gael. *pait, paiteag* (the same); where the form *pait* is borrowed from E. Prob. from the verb *pat* (1) above, as being *patted* into shape; just as *dab*, a small lump, is from the verb *to dab*.

Pat (3), quite to the purpose. (E.) Due to a peculiar use of *pat*, to strike, tap; see **Pat** (1). 'It will fall [happen] *pat*;' Mid. N. Dr. v. 188. Cf. *dab*, sb., an adept, from the verb *to dab*.

Patch (1), a piece sewn on a garment, a plot of ground. (E.?) M. E. *pacche*. Apparently a by-form of *platch*. 'Platch, a large spot, a patch, a piece of cloth sewn on a garment to repair it;' Dial. of Banffshire, by W. Gregor. Cf. Low G. *plakke, plakk*, (1) a spot, (2) a patch, (3) a patch or plot of ground; also M. E. *plekke*, a plot (of land), Du. *plek*, a patch of ground.

patch (2), a paltry fellow. (E.?) Temp. iii. 2. 71. *Patch* meant a fool or jester, from the parti-coloured or patch-like dress; Wolsey had two fools so named (Nares). The same word as *patch* (1). Der. *patch-ock*, a clown, a dimin. form, Spenser, View of Ireland, Globe ed., p. 636, col. 2; spelt *pajock*, Hamlet, iii. 2. 295.

Patchouli, a scent. (F.—Dravidian.) F. *patchouli*; of obscure origin. Apparently from E. *patcha-leaf*, i. e. 'green leaf,' imitating the vernacular *pacha-pāt*, where *pāt* is Hind. for 'leaf.' Or from Dravidian words meaning 'green leaf.' Cf. Tamil *pachchai*, green, *ilai*, leaf (Knight); Malayālim *pachchila*, green leaf (Gundert); Canarese *pachcha*, green, *yele*, leaf (Reeve).

Pate, the head. (Unknown.) M. E. *pate*. Of unknown origin; perhaps suggested by Late L. *platta*, the clerical tonsure. Cf. M. Du. *platte*, 'vertex rasus,' Kilian; G. *platte* a plate, a bald pate, in

vulgar language, the head (Flügel); M. H. G. *plate*, a plate, shaven pate. All from Gk. πλατύς, flat, broad. Cf. M. F. *pate*, a plate; Cot.

Paten. (F.—L.—Gk.) M. F. *patene* (Cot.).—L. *patina, patena*, a flat dish.— Gk. πατάνη, a flat (open) dish. See **Pan** and **Patent.**

Patent, open, public; as sb., an official document conferring a privilege. (F.—L.) M. E. *patente*, a patent; so called because *open* to general inspection.—O. F. *patent* (fem. *patente*), patent, wide open. — L. *patent-*, stem of pr. pt. of *patēre*, to lie open. Cf. Gk. πετάννυμι, I spread out. (√PET.) Brugm. i. § 120 (note).

Paternal. (F. — L.) F. *paternel*.— Late L. *paternālis*, fatherly. — L. *paternus*, fatherly. — L. *pater*, father. Perhaps formed with suffix *-ter* of the agent from √PA, to feed, guard. See **Father.**

Path, a way, track. (E.) A. S. *pæð*, *pað*, a path.+Du. *pad*, G. *pfad*.

Pathos. (Gk.) Gk. πάθος, suffering, emotion.— Gk. παθεῖν, used as 2 aor. infin. of πάσχειν (for *παθ-σκειν), to suffer. Allied to πένθ-ος, grief. Der. *path-et-ic*, from O. F. *pathetique*, L. *pathēticus*, Gk. παθητικός; extended from παθητός, subject to suffering.

Patient. (F.—L.) O. F. *patient*.— L. *patient-*, stem of pres. pt. of *patī*, to suffer. Der. *patience*, F. *patience*, L. *patientia*.

Patois, a vulgar dialect of French. (F.—L.) F. *patois*, country talk; which stands for an older form *patrois*, given by Godefroy (Diez, Littré).—Late L. *patriensis*, a native; hence, belonging to the natives. — L. *patria*, native country. — L. *patri-*, for *pater*, a father.

patriarch. (F. — L. — Gk.) O. F. *patriarche*. — L. *patriarcha*. — Gk. πατρι-άρχης, chief of a race or tribe. — Gk. πατρι-ά, a race; ἄρχειν, to rule. See **Arch-** (prefix).

patrician, a Roman nobleman. (L.) Formed, with suffix *-an*, from L. *patrici-us*, noble; a descendant of the *patrēs*, i. e. senators or fathers of the state.

patrimony. (F.—L.) M. E. *patrimonie*.—F. *patrimoine*.—L. *patrimōnium*, an inheritance.—L. *patri-*, for *pater*, father; with suffix *-mōnium* (Idg. *-mōn-yom*).

patriot. (F.—Late L.—Gk.) O. F. *patriote*.—Late L. *patriōta*.—Gk. πατριώτης, properly, a fellow-countryman.—Gk.

πατριά, a race, from πατρι-, for πατήρ, a father. ¶ The mod. sense of *patriot* arose in *French*.

patristic, pertaining to the fathers of the church. (F.–L.) F. *patristique* (Littré). Coined from L. *patri-*, *pater*, a father; with the Gk. suffixes *-ist-* and *-ic*.

Patrol, a going of the rounds in a garrison. (F.) F. *patrouille*, 'a still nightwatch in warre;' Cot. Lit. a tramping about; from O. F. (Picard) *patrouiller*, to paddle in water, the same word (but with inserted *r*) as *patouiller*, to paddle or dabble in with the feet; also *patrolli*, in the pâtois of Lyons (Puitspelu). Formed from O. F. *pate* (F. *patte*), the paw or foot of a beast. Of uncertain origin; perhaps imitative. Cf. Late L. *pata*, the foot of a cup, base of a tower; also G. *patsche*, an instrument for striking the hand, *patsch-fuss*, web foot of a bird; *patschen*, to strike, dabble, walk awkwardly; Low G. *pattjen*, to paddle in water with the feet (Richey); Bavarian *patzen*, to pat; see **Pat** (1). ¶ Hence also Span. *pata*, paw, *patullar*, to run through mud, *patrullar*, to patrol; and Ital. *pattuglia*, a patrol (without the inserted *r*).

Patron. (F.–L.) F. *patron*.–L. *patrōnum*, acc. of *patrōnus*, a protector; extended from *patr-*, stem of *pater*, father.

patronymic. (F.–L.–Gk.) M. F. *patronymique*. – L. *patrōnymicus*. – Gk. πατρωνυμικός, belonging to the father's name. – Gk. πατρωνυμία, a name taken from the father. – Gk. πατρ-, for πατήρ, a father; ὄνομα, a name; see **Name.**

Patten, a clog. (F.) Formerly *paten*. – F. *patin*, a patten, ' also a foot-stall of a pillar;' Cot. – M. F. *pate* (F. *patte*), a paw or foot of a beast, 'also a foot-stall of a pillar;' Cot. See **Patrol.**

Patter, to strike frequently, as hail. (E.) A frequentative of *pat*; see **Pat** (1). Cf. prov. E. (Lonsdale) *pattle*, to pat gently.

Pattern, an example, model to work by. (F.–L.) M. E. *patron*; (the old spelling). – F. *patron*, 'a patron . . also a pattern, sample;' Cot. See **Patron.**

Patty, a little pie. (F.–L.–Gk.) Mod. F. *pâté*; O. F. *pasté*, a pasty. – Late L. *pastātum*, neut. of pp. of *pastāre*, to make paste. – Late L. *pasta*, paste; see **Paste.**

Paucity, fewness. (F.–L.) F. *paucité*.

–L. *paucitātem*, acc. of *paucitās*, fewness. –L. *paucus*, few; allied to **Few.**

Paunch. (F.–L.) O. F. *panche* (Picard); also *pance*; F. *panse*. –L. *panticem*, acc. of *pantex*, belly, paunch.

Pauper. (L.) L. *pauper*, poor. *Pau-* is allied to *paucus*, few; *-per*, (perhaps) to L. *parāre*, to provide. Lit. 'provided with little.'

Pause, a stop. (F. – L. – Gk.) F. *pause*.–Late L. *pausa*.–Gk. παῦσις, a pause, ceasing.–Gk. παύειν, to make to cease; παύεσθαι, to cease. **Doublet,** *pose*, q. v.

Pave. (F.–L.) M.E. *pauen=(paven)*. –F. *paver*, to pave.–Late L. *pavāre*, corrupt form of L. *pauīre*, to beat, strike, ram, tread down. Cf. Skt. *pavi-*, thunderbolt. **Der.** *pavement*, F. *pavement*, L. *pauīmentum*, a hard floor, from *pauīre*, to ram; also *pav-i-or* (cf. *law-y-er*), from F. *paveur*, 'a paver,' Cot.

Pavilion. (F.–L.) M.E. *pavilon.*– F. *pavillon*, a tent; so called because spread out like the wings of a butterfly.– L. *pāpiliōnem*, acc. of *pāpilio*, (1), a butterfly, (2) a tent.

Pavin, Pavan, a stately Spanish dance. (F.–Span. – L. – Pers. – Tamil.) F. *pavane*.–Span. *pavana*, a grave dance (see *Pavan* in Nares). Prob. from a Late L. **pāvānus*, peacock-like, from the row of stately dancers (Scheler); cf. Span. *pava*, a peahen, a turkey, *pavada*, a flock of turkeys, *pavo*, adj., like a peacock (whence *pavonear*, to walk with affected gravity).–Late L. *pāvus*, earlier L. *pāuo*, a peacock. See **Peacock.**

Pavise, a large shield. (F.) Also spelt *pavese*, *pavish*, *pauice*, *pauys*, *paues*. – F. *pavois*, 'a great shield;' Late L. *pavensis*. (Span. *paves*; Ital. *pavese*, *pavesce*, Florio.) Of uncertain origin; perhaps from the city of *Pavia*, in Italy. Godefroy has the adj. *pavinois*, *paviois*; *pavois*, *pavaiz*, adj. ' de Pavie;' as in the phr. *escus pavaiz*, shields of Pavia.

Paw. (F.) M.E. *pawe*, *powe*, a paw. – A.F. *powe*, O.F. *poe*, a paw; the same as Prov. *pauta*, Catalan *pota*, a paw. Cf. Low G. *pote*, Du. *poot* (whence G. *pfote*), a paw. Perhaps from an imitative root; cf. F. *patte*. Franck takes Du. *poot* to be of Teut. origin. Cf. E. Fries. *pote*, *pōt*, paw.

Pawl, a short bar, as a catch to a windlass. (F.–L.) O.F. *paul*, variant of *pal*, *pel*, a stake (whence Du. *pal*, Swed. *pall*, Norw. *pall*, a pawl; cf. W. *pawl*, a pole, stake, bar).—L. *pālum*, acc. of *pālus*, a stake. See Pale (1).

Pawn (1), a pledge. (F.—Teut.) F. *pan*, 'a pane, piece, panel, also a pawn, gage, skirt of a gown, pane of a hose,' &c.; Cot. In the sense of 'pane,' F. *pan* is of Latin origin; see Pane. In the sense of 'pawn,' F. *pan* is rather from Du. *pand*; cf. G. *pfand*, O. H. G. *phant*, a pledge. Der. *im-pawn*, to put in pledge, to pledge; *pawn*, vb.

Pawn (2), a piece at chess. (F.—L.) M. E. *paune, poune, poun.*—O. F. *paon*, a pawn (Roquefort), also *poon* (Littré); but the older form is *peon* (F. *pion*), agreeing with Span. *peon*, a foot-soldier, pawn, Ital. *pedone*, a foot-soldier, *pedona*, a pawn (Florio).—Late L. *pedōnem*, acc. of *pedo*, a foot-soldier.—L. *ped-*, stem of *pes*, foot. ¶ The O. F. *paon* is the same word; cf. F. *faon* (E. *fawn*), from Late L. *fētōnem*, shewing the same substitution of *a* for *e*; there is no need to connect it with F. *paon*, a peacock, as Littré does, ignoring the Ital. and Span. words.

Pawnee, drink. (Hind.—Skt.) Hind. *pānī*, water.—Skt. *pānīya*, allied to *pāna*, a beverage.—Skt. *pā*, to drink.

Paxwax, strong tendon in the neck of animals. (E.) M. E. *paxwax*, also *fexwax*, the latter being the right form (see Prompt. Parv.).—A. S. *feax, fex*, hair; *weaxan*, to grow. Thus the lit. sense is perhaps 'hair-sinew,' because it is where the hair ends; cf. G. *haarwachs*, a tendon.

Pay (1), to discharge a debt. (F.—L.) M. E. *paien.*—O. F. *paier, paer* (F. *payer*), to pay, to content.—L. *pācāre*, to pacify; in late Lat., to pay a debt.—L. *pāc-*, stem of *pax*, peace; see Peace.

Pay (2), to pitch the seams of a ship. (F.—L.) A. F. *peier* (O. F. *poier*, Godefroy), to pitch.—L. *picāre*, to pitch.—L. *pic-*, stem of *pix*, pitch; see Pitch. ¶ The M. E. word for 'pitch' is *peis*, from A. F. *peis* (O. F. *pois*), pitch; from L. acc. *picem*.

Paynim, Painim, a pagan. (F.—L.) 'The *paynim* bold;' F. Q. i. 4. 41. M. E. *paynim*, a pagan; but this sense is due to a singular mistake. A *paynim* is properly not a *man*, but a *country* or district, and is identical with *paganism*, formerly used to mean heathendom, or the country of pagans. Rightly used in

King Horn, 803, to mean 'heathen lands.' —O. F. *paienisme*, lit. paganism; Late L. *pāgānismus*. Formed with suffix *-ismus*, from L. *pāgān-us*, a pagan. See Pagan.

Pea, a vegetable. (L.) Formerly *pease*, *pese*; M. E. *pese*, pl. *pesen* or *peses*. A. S. *pisa*, pl. *pisan.*—L. *pīsum*, a pea.+Gk. πίσος, a pea. (√PIS.)

Peace. (F.—L.) M. E. *pais.*—O. F. *pais* (F. *paix*).—L. *pācem*, acc. of *pax*, peace, orig. a compact; cf. *pac-*, as in *pac-tum*, a bargain; see Pact.

Peach (1), a fruit. (F.—L.—Pers.) M. E. *peche.*—O. F. *pesche*, a peach.—L. *persicum*, a peach; so called from growing on the *Persica arbor*, Persian tree.—Pers. *Pārs*, Persia.

Peach (2), to inform against. (F.—L.) Short for M. E. *apechen*, to impeach, a variant of *impechen*, to impeach, by the substitution of prefix *a-* (L. *ad*) for *im-* (L. *in*). See Impeach.

Peacock. (L.—Pers.—Tamil; *and* E.) M. E. *pecok, pocok*; where *cok* = E. *cock*. We also find M. E. *po*; A. S. *pēa, pāwa*; all from L. *pāuo* (whence Du. *paauw*, G. *pfau*, F. *paon*). The same as Gk. ταῶς, for ταϝῶς, a peacock; the change from τ to *p* being due to the fact that the word was foreign both to L. and Gk.—Pers. *ṭāwus, ṭāus*, a peacock.—O. Tamil *tōkei, tōgei*, a peacock; see Max Müller, Lect. on Lang. i. 190 (ed. 1891). ¶ Also *pocock*, which is still a surname.

Pea-jacket, a coarse thick jacket. (Du. *and* F.) The prefix *pea-* is borrowed from Du. *pij, pije*, a coat of a coarse woollen stuff; Hexham has M. Du. *pije*, 'a pie-gowne, rough gowne, such as seamen weare.' The same as Low G. *pije*, N. Fries. *pie, pie-jäckert.*—M. Du. *pije*, or *pije-laken*, 'a rough or a hairy cloath;' Hexham. Prob. from F. *pie*, a mag-pie; cf. E. *pied*, spotted. See Pie (1). Also Low G. *pije, pigge, pyke* (Brem. W.), perhaps from L. *pīca*.

Peak. (F.—L.) M. E. *pec*. [Cf. Irish *peac*, a sharp-pointed thing; from E. *peak*.] A variant of *pike*, q. v. Cf. dial. of Normandy *pec*, a hob (or mark) in the game of quoits (Godefroy, s. v. *pec*); also Low G. *peek*, a pike, pointed weapon.

Peal, a loud sound, chime of bells, noise of a trumpet. (F.—L.) A shortened form of *appeal*, M. F. *apel, appel*; Cot. gives *appel*, pl. *appeaux*, 'chimes.' Note also

M. E. *apel*, an old term in hunting-music (Halliwell) ; this we now call a *peal*. The prefix *a-* was prob. mistaken for the E. indef. article. The O. F. *apel* is from O. F. *apeler*, vb. ; see **Appeal**.

Pean ; see **Pæan**.

Pear, a fruit. (L.) A. S. *peru, pere.* — L. *pirum*, a pear (whence also Ital. *pera*).

Pearl. (F. — L. ?) M.E. *perle.* — F. *perle*, 'a pearl, a berrie ;' Cot. Of unknown origin ; we find also Ital., Span., Prov. *perla*, Port. *perola, perla*. Cf. Low L. *perula*, the end of the nose (7th cent.). Perhaps for L. **pirula*, i. e. a little pear, from L. *pirum*, a pear ; cf. Span. *perilla*, (1) a little pear, (2) a pear-shaped ornament, M. Ital. *perolo*, a little button on a cap. Perhaps suggested by the various senses of L. *bacca*, (1) a berry, (2) olive-berry, (3) round fruit, (4) a pearl (Horace). See **Purl** (2).

Pearl-barley. (F. — L. ; *and* E.) F. *orge perlé*, pearl-barley (Hamilton) ; but this seems to be a corruption of *orge pelé*, 'pilled barley,' Cot. See **Peel** (1).

Peasant. (F. — L.) O. F. *paisant*, another form of O. F. *paisan*, a peasant ; (cf. Ital. *paesano*, Span. *paisano*, a compatriot). Formed with suffix *-an* (L. *-ānus*), from O. F. *pais* (F. *pays*), a country (cf. Ital. *paese*, Span. *pais*, Port. *pais*, a country). — Late L. *pāgense*, neut. of *pāgensis*, belonging to a village. — L. *pāgus*, a village, district. See **Pagan**.

Peat, a kind of turf for fuel. (L. ?) Latinised as *peta* (Ducange) ; whence *petāria*, a place for getting peat. Apparently from M. E. (Kentish) *pet*, O. Fries. *pet*, M. Du. *pet, pette*, a pit. See **Pit**.

Pebble. (E.) A. S. *papol-stān*, a pebble-stone.

Peccable, liable to sin. (L.) Coined as if from L. **peccābilis*, from *peccāre*, to sin. Brugm. i. § 585.

peccadillo. (Span. — L.) Span. *peccadillo, pecadillo*, a slight fault ; dimin. of *pecado*, a sin. — L. *peccātum*, a sin. — L. *peccātus*, pp. of *peccāre*, to sin.

peccant, sinning. (F. — L.) First used in phr. '*peccant* humours.' — F. *peccant*, sinning ; '*l'humeur peccante*, corrupt humour ;' Cot. — L. *peccant-*, stem of pres. pt. of *peccāre*, to sin.

Peccary, a quadruped. (F. — Caribbean.) F. *pécari*, a peccary (Buffon). — Carib. *pakira*, the name used in Guiana ; see N. and Q., 9 S. iv. 496. Cf. *pachira*,

the name given to the peccary in Oronoko (Clavigero, Hist. Mexico) ; Span. *pacquire* (Pineda).

Peck (1), to strike with the beak, to pick up. (L.) M. E. *pekken*, used as equivalent to *pikken*, to pick or peck up. A mere variant of *pick* ; see **Pick**.

Peck (2), a dry measure, 2 gallons. (F. — L. ?) M. E. *pekke*, a peck. A. F. and O. F. *pek*. From the verb *pekken*, to peck or snap up ; cf. E. *peck*, to pick up (as a bird) ; prov. E. *peck*, meat, victuals. [So also F. *picotin*, a peck (measure), *picoter*, to peck as a bird.] See **Peck** (1), **Pick**.

Pectinal, lit. comb-like. (L.) From L. *pectin-*, stem of *pecten*, a comb. — L. *pectere*, to comb. + Gk. πεκτεῖν, to comb, from πέκειν, to comb. (√PEK.)

Pectoral, belonging to the chest. (F. — L.) F. *pectoral.* — L. *pectorālis*, adj., from *pector-* (for **pectos*), stem of *pectus*, the breast. Der. *poitrel*.

Peculate, to pilfer. (L.) From pp. of L. *pecūlāri*, to appropriate to one's own use. Formed as if from **pecūlum*, for *pecūlium*, private property ; see below.

peculiar, one's own, particular. (F. — L.) M. F. *peculier.* — L. *pecūliāris*, one's own. — L. *pecūlium*, private property ; closely allied to *pecūnia*, money ; see below.

pecuniary. (F. — L.) M.F. *pecuniaire.* — L. *pecūniārius*, relating to money or property. — L. *pecūnia*, property. — O.L. *pecu*, cattle ; cf. *pecu-a*, neut. pl., cattle of all kinds, property ; *pecus*, cattle. Cf. Skt. *paçu*, cattle, cognate with Goth. *faihu*, property, A. S. *feoh*, G. *vieh*, cattle.

Pedagogue, a teacher. (F. — L. — Gk.) M.F. *pedagogue.* — L. *pædagōgus.* — Gk. παιδ-αγωγός, a slave who led a boy to school ; hence, a tutor. — Gk. παιδ-, stem of παῖς, a boy ; ἀγωγός, leading, from ἄγειν, to lead. The Gk. παῖς = παϝίς, allied to L. *puer*, a boy. See **Puerile, Puberty.**

Pedal, belonging to the foot. (L.) The *pedal* keys in an organ are acted on by the feet. — L. *pedālis*, belonging to the foot. — L. *ped-*, stem of *pēs*, foot. + A. S. *fōt*, foot. See **Foot.**

Pedant. (F. — Ital. — Gk. ?) M. F. *pedant.* — Ital. *pedante*, 'a pedante, or a schoolmaster, the same as *pedagogo* ;' Florio. The suffix *-ante* is a pres. participial form ; the stem *ped-* is prob. the same as in Ital. *pedagogo*, and therefore due to

Gk. παιδεύειν (whence a Lat. form *paedāre), to instruct; see **Pedagogue.**

Peddle, to deal in small wares. (E.?) Coined from the sb. *pedlar,* later form of *peddar*; see **Pedlar.**

Pedestal. (Span. — Ital. — L. *and* G.) Span. *pedestal,* 'the base of a pillar,' Minsheu; borrowed from Ital. *piedestallo,* 'a footstall or treshall [threshold] of a door;' Florio. Lit. 'foot-support.' Compounded as if from L. *pedem,* acc. of *pes,* a foot; and O. H. G. *stal* (G. *stall*), a stall; see **Stall.**

pedestrian. (L.) Properly an adj.; from L. *pedestri-,* decl. stem. of *pedester,* one who goes on foot. For **pedit-tr-*; from *pedit-,* stem of *pedes,* one who goes on foot; with suffix *-ter* (Idg. *-ter*). *Ped-it-* is from *ped-,* stem of *pes,* foot; and *it-um,* supine of *īre,* to go. Brugm. ii. § 123.

pedicel, pedicle, the foot-stalk of fruit. (F. — L.) *Pedicel* is from mod. F. *pédicelle*; but *pedicle* (older and better) from M. F. *pedicule,* a leaf-stalk; Cot. — L. *pediculus,* little foot, foot-stalk, pedicle; double dimin. of *ped-,* stem of *pēs,* foot.

pedigree. (F. — L.) Old spellings *pedegree* (1627); *pedigrew* (1570); *petygrewe* (1530). Also, in Prompt. Parv. (1440) *pedegru, petygru,* with slight variations, explained by ' lyne of kynrede and awncetrye, *Stemma, in scalis.*' Also *peedegrue,* Lydgate (1426; in Polit. Poems, ii. 138). A. F. *pee de grue,* foot of a crane; from a three-line mark (like the broad arrow) used in denoting succession in pedigrees. — L. *pedem,* acc. of *pēs,* foot; *dē,* of; *gruem,* acc. of *grus,* a crane, cognate with E. **Crane.**

pediment, an ornament finishing the front of a building. (Ital. — L.) Better *pedament.* From Ital. *pedamento,* a basis, foundation, ground-work; also, a prop for vines (Torriano). — L. *pedāmentum,* a stake or prop, with which vines are supported. The sense seems to be due to the allied word *pedātūra,* a prop, also (in Late L.) a space, site; since a pediment does, in fact, enclose a space which often supports sculpture on its base. History obscure. Form of the word from L. *pedāre,* to prop; from *ped-,* stem of *pes,* a foot.

Pedlar, Pedler, Peddler, a dealer in small wares. (E.?) The old word was usually *peddare, pedder,* a man who hawked about fish in baskets called *peds,* or occasionally *pads.* See *Pedde* in Prompt.

Parv.; Norfolk *ped* (Forby); Lowl. Sc. *peddir,* a pedlar (Jamieson). The orig. sense of *ped* was prob. 'bag,' and the word may be related to *pad.* See **Padlock.**

Pedobaptism, infant baptism. (Gk.) From Gk. παιδο-, for παῖς, a boy; and *baptism.* Cf. **Pedagogue.**

Peel (1), to strip off skin. (F. — L.) From F. *peler,* to 'unskin'; Cot. (Cf. M. Ital. *pellare,* 'to unskin;' Florio). — O. F. *pel,* skin. — L. *pellem,* acc. of *pellis,* a skin. See **Fell** (2). ¶ Confused with F. *piller*; see below.

Peel (2), to pillage. (F. — L.) In Milton, P. R. iv. 136. Distinct from *peel,* to strip; another spelling of *pill*; see **Pill** (2).

Peel (3), a fire-shovel. (F. — L.) Once a common word. — O. F. *pele* (Littré), F. *pelle,* a fire-shovel. — L. *pāla*; see **Palette.**

Peel (4), a small castle. (F. — L.) M. E. *pēl,* a small castle, orig. a stockade or wooden fortress. — O. F. *pel* (also *pal*), a stake. — L. *pālum,* acc. of *pālus,* a stake. See **Pale** (1).

Peep (1), to chirp, cry like a chicken. (F. — L.) M. E. *pipen.* — O. F. *piper,* to chirp as a bird. — L. *pipāre, pīpīre,* to chirp. See **Pipe** (1) and **Peep** (2).

Peep (2), to look through a narrow aperture. (F. — L.) Palsgrave has : ' I peke or prie, *Ie pipe hors;*' i. e. I peep out. Thus *peep* is directly from F. *piper,* lit. to pipe, but also used in the sense to peep. [It arose from the exclamation *pipe!* (Du. dial. *piep!,* Molema), made by a hider in the game of *peep-bo, bo-peep,* or hide-and-seek; cf. Du. dial. *piepen,* (1) to say *piep!* (2) to peep out.] Cot. gives F. *piper,* 'to whistle, chirp like a bird, cousen, deceive, cheat, beguile;' *pipée,* ' the peeping or chirping of small birds, counterfeited by a bird-catcher, also a counterfeit shew;' *pipe,* 'a bird-call.' The F. *piper* is from L. *pīpāre, pīpīre,* to chirp; see **Pipe.**

Peer (1), an equal. (F. — L.) The twelve *peers* of France were of *equal* rank. M. E. *pere, per.* — O. F. *per,* peer, later *pair,* a peer; or as adj., equal. — L. *parem,* acc. of *par,* equal. See **Par.** Der. *peer-less.*

Peer (2), to look narrowly, pry. (E.?) M. E. *piren,* E. Fries. *pīren,* Westphal. *pīren,* Low G. *piren,* to look closely. Cf. also *pliren,* to peer, orig. to draw the eyelids together, so as to look closely ; Swed. *plira*, Dan. *plire*, to blink.

Peer (3), to appear. (F.−L.) Short for *appear*, just as M. E. *peren* is short for *apperen* ; see **Appear**.

Peevish, fretful, whimpering. (E.) M. E. *peuisch*, *peyuesshe*; also *pevych*, *pevage*, uncouth, perverse (G. Douglas). The leading idea seems to be ' whining,' ' making a plaintive cry.' Cf. Dan. dial. *piæve*, to whine; Lowl. Sc. *peu*, to make a plaintive noise, E. *pew*- in *pewet*, a bird ; Low G. *pauen*, to whimper. See **Pewet**. Of imitative origin. For the suffix, cf. *thiev-ish*, *mop-ish*.

Peewit; see **Pewet**.

Peg, a wooden pin. (E.) M. E. *pegge*. Cf. Du. and Low G. *pegel*, a measure of liquid capacity, such as was marked by pegs in a ' peg-tankard.' Apparently allied to Dan. *pig*, Swed. *pigg*, a spike; W. *pig*, a peak, point; Corn. *peg*, a prick ; see **Peak**.

Peise, Peize, to weigh. (F.−L.) M. E. *peisen*; A. F. *peiser*, to weigh ; O.F. *poiser*; see **Poise**, which is a doublet.

Peitrel; see **Poitrel**.

Pelf, lucre, booty. (F.) M. E. *pelfyr*, *pelfrey*, ' spolium ;' Prompt. Parv.−O. F. *pelfre*, booty, spoil ; allied to *pelfrer*, to pilfer. See Körting, § 3221. Der. *pilfer*.

Pelican. (F.−L.−Gk.) F. *pelican*. −L. *pelicānus*, *pelecānus*.−Gk. πελεκάν, πελεκᾶς, wood-pecker, also a water-bird. Named from its large bill, as the wood-pecker was named from its pecking.−Gk. πελεκάω, I hew with an ax, peck.−Gk. πέλεκυς, an ax.+Skt. *paraçu*-, an ax.

Pelisse, a silk habit. (F.−L.) Formerly a furred robe.−F. *pelisse*, *pelice*, ' a skin of fur ;' Cot.−L. *pellicea*, fem. of *pelliceus*, made of skins.−L. *pellis*, a skin.

pell, a skin. (F.−L.) M. E. *pell*, *pel*.−O. F. *pel* (F. *peau*).−L. *pellem*, acc. of *pellis*, a skin. See **Fell** (2).

Pellet, a little ball. (F.−L.) M. E. *pelet*.−O. F. *pelote*, a tennis-ball. Dimin. from L. *pila*, a ball.

Pellicle, a thin film. (F.−L.) F. *pellicule*. − L. *pellicula*, a small skin ; dimin. of *pellis*, a skin. See **pell**.

Pellitory (1), **Paritory**, a wild flower that grows on walls. (F. − L.) *Pellitory* is for *paritory*. M. E. *paritorie*. −M. F. *paritoire*, ' pellitory ;' Cot. − L. *parietāria*, pellitory ; fem. of *parietārius*,

belonging to walls.−L. *pariet*-, stem of *pariēs*, a wall.

Pellitory (2), the plant pyrethrum. (Span.−L.−Gk.) Span. *pelitre* [Ital. *pilatro*].−L. *pȳrethrum*.−Gk. πύρεθρον, a hot spicy plant.−Gk. πῦρ, fire.

Pell-mell, confusedly. (F.−L.) O.F. *pesle-mesle*, ' pell-mell, confusedly ;' Cot. Spelt *pellemelle* in the XIIIth cent. (mod. F. *pêle-mêle*). [Apparently understood to mean ' stirred up with a fire-shovel.'−F. *pelle*, a fire-shovel ; O. F. *mesler*, to mix up ; see **Peel** (3) above, and **Medley**.] But orig. only a reduplicated form of *mesle*, as *mesle-mesle* and *melle-melle* also occur. See Körting, § 5336.

Pellucid. (F.−L.) F. *pellucide*.− L. *pellūcidus*, *perlūcidus*, transparent.−L. *per* ; and *lūcidus*, lucid. See **Lucid**.

Pelt (1), to throw, cast. (L.) M. E. *pelten*, also *pilten*, *pulten*, to thrust, cast. The forms *pilten*, *pulten*, answer to an A. S. form **pyltan*.−L. *pultāre*, to beat, strike, knock. *Pultāre* (like *pulsāre*) is a derivative of *pellere*, to drive. See **Pulsate**.

Pelt (2), a skin, esp. of a sheep. (F.− L.) M. E. *pelt*, a shortened form of *peltry*, skins, *peltry-ware*, dealing in skins.−O.F. *pelleterie*, the trade of a skinner. − O.F. *pelletier*, a skinner. Formed (like *bijou-tier*, with suffix -*tier* = L. -*tārius*) from O. F. *pel*, a skin.−L. *pellis*, a skin. See **Pell**. ¶ G. *pelz*, O. H. G. *pelliz*, answers to E. *pelisse*; see **Pelisse**.

Pelvis, the bony cavity in the lower part of the abdomen. (L.) L. *peluis*, a basin, hence the pelvis.

Pemmican, a preparation of dried meat. Of N. American Indian origin.

Pen (1), an instrument for writing. (F.−L.) O.F. *penne*.−L. *penna*, a feather ; O. L. *pesna* (for **petna* or **petsna*). Brugm. i. § 762 (2). From √PET, to fly. See **Feather**.

Pen (2), to shut up. (L.) M.E. *pennen*. A.S. *pennian*, only in the comp. *on-pennian*, to un-pen, unfasten. *Pennian* is properly to fasten with a *pin* or peg ; cf. Low G. *pennen*, to bolt a door, from *penn*, a pin or peg; see **Pin**. Note E. Fries. *penne*, *penn*, *pinne*, *pin*, a peg, a pin.

Penal. (F.−L.−Gk.) M.F. *penal*, ' penall ;' Cot.−L. *pœnālis*, belonging to punishment.−L. *pœna*, punishment.−Gk. ποινή, penalty. See **Pain**.

penance. (F. − L. − Gk.) O. F.

penance, older form *penëance.* – L. *pœni-tentia*, penitence. – L. *pœnitent-*, stem of pres. pt. of *pœnitēre*, to cause to repent. See **Penitent**.

Penchant, a strong inclination, bias (in favour of). (F. – L.) F. *penchant*, sb.; orig. pres. pt. of *pencher*, to lean, lean towards. – Late L. type *pendicāre; from L. *pendēre*, to hang.

Pencil. (F. – L.) The old sense was a small hair-brush for painting. – M. F. *pincel*, later *pinceau*, ‘a pensill, brush;’ Cot. – L. *pēnecillus*, a small tail, painter’s brush; dimin. of *pēniculus*, which is a double dimin. of *pēnis*, a tail. For *pes-nis; cf. Skt. *pasa(s)*, Gk. πέος; Brugm. i. § 877.

Pendant, anything hanging, a hanging ornament. (F. – L.) F. *pendant*, a pendant. – F. *pendant*, pres. pt. of *pendre*, to hang. – L. *pendēre*, to hang; allied to *pendere*, to weigh. Cf. Gk. σφενδόνη, a sling. (√SPHEND, SPHED.) Der. *pend-ent*, hanging, Latinised form of F. *pendant*; *pend-ing*, Anglicised form of F. *pendant*, during.

pendulous. (L.) For L. *pendulus*, hanging. – L. *pendēre*, to hang.

pendulum. (L.) L. *pendulum*, neut. of adj. *pendulus* (above).

Penetrate. (L.) From pp. of L. *penetrāre*, to pierce into. Compounded of *pene-*, base of *penes*, with, *peni-tus*, within, with which cf. *penus*, the inner part of a sanctuary; and *-trāre* (as in *in-trāre*) to pass over, allied to Skt. *tara-*, a crossing.

Penguin, Pinguin, a bird. (Unknown.) In a tract printed in 1588, we read that Sir F. Drake gave a certain island the name of *Penguin Island* in 1587, from the penguins found there. Selden (1613) derived it from W. *pen gwyn*, i.e. white head. In that case, it must first have been given to another bird, such as the auk (the puffin is common in Anglesey), since the penguin’s head is black.

Peninsula. (L.) L. *pēninsula*, a piece of land nearly an island. – L. *pēne*, *pæne*, almost; *insula*, an island. So also *pen-ultimate*, almost the last, last but one; *pen-umbra*, partial shadow.

Penitent. (F. – L. – Gk.) O. F. *peni-tent.* – L. *pœnitent-*, stem of pres. pt. of *pœnitēre*, to cause to repent, derivative of *pœnīre = pūnīre*, to punish. – L. *pœna*, penalty. – Gk. ποινή, penalty; see **Pain**.

Pennon, Pennant. (F. – L.) M. E. *penon, penoun.* – M. F. *pennon*, ‘a flag, streamer; also the feather of an arrow;’ Cot. – L. *penna*, wing, feather (hence a plume, standard). See **Pen** (1).

Penny. (E.) M. E. *peni*; pl. *penies*, contracted form *pens* (whence mod. E. *pence*). A. S. *pening, penning*, a penny; later *penig*, whence M. E. *peni*. By-form *pending* (Thorpe, Diplomatarium, p. 471); as if formed with E. suffix *-ing* from the base *pand. β. This base is usually identified with Du. *pand*, a pawn, pledge, G. *pfand*, O. H. G. *pfant*; see **Pawn** (1) above. In this case, the lit. sense may have been ‘ little pledge,’ i. e. a token, coin. + Du. *penning*, Icel. *penningr*, Dan. Swed. *penning*; G. *pfennig*, O. H. G. *phantinc*, *phentinc*, dimin. of *pfant*.

Penny-royal, a herb. (F. – L.) A popular form of the old name *pulial royal*. Cotgrave translates M. F. *pulege* by ‘ penny royall, puliall royall’; from Late L. *pūle-gium*. The above old name is due to L. *pūlēium rēgium*, a name given to the plant from its supposed efficacy against fleas (cf. E. *flea-bane*). From L. *pūlex*, a flea; *rēgius*, royal. See **Puce** and **Royal**.

Pensile, suspended. (F. – L.) M. F. *pensil*; Cot. – L. *pensilis*, pendent; from *pens-us, unused pp. of *pendēre*, to hang.

pension. (F. – L.) F. *pension.* – L. *pensiōnem*, acc. of *pensio*, a payment. – L. *pensus*, pp. of *pendere*, to weigh, weigh out money, pay.

pensive. (F. – L.) M. E. *pensif.* – F. *pensif*, thoughtful. – F. *penser*, to think. – L. *pensāre*, to weigh, ponder; frequent. of *pendere*, to weigh.

Pent, for *penned*, pp. of Pen (2), q. v.

Pentagon, a plane five-sided figure. (F. – L. – Gk.) F. *pentagone.* – L. *penta-gōnus*, adj., pentagonal. – Gk. πεντάγωνος, pentagonal; neut. πεντάγωνον, a pentagon. – Gk. πεντά-, for πεντέ, five; γωνία, an angle, from γόνυ, a knee; see **Knee**. And see **Five**.

pentameter, a verse of five metres. (L. – Gk.) L. *pentameter.* – Gk. πεντά-μετρος. – Gk. πεντά-, for πεντέ, five; μέ-τρον, a metre.

pentateuch, the five books of Moses. (L. – Gk.) L. *pentateuchus.* – Gk. πεντά-, five (above); τεῦχος, a tool, also a book.

pentecost, Whitsuntide; orig. a Jewish festival on the fiftieth day after the

Passover. (L. – Gk.) L. *pentēcostē.* –
Gk. πεντηκοστή, Pentecost, Acts ii. 1;
fem. of πεντηκοστός, fiftieth. – Gk. πεντή-
κοντα, fifty.

Penthouse, a shed projecting from
a building. (F. – L.) Formerly *pentice,*
whence it is corrupted. – M. F. *apentis,
appentis,* 'a penthouse;' Cot. – L. *ap-
pendicium,* an appendage, allied to *appendix* (the same). – L. *ap- (ad),* to ; *pendēre,*
to hang.

Pentroof, a roof with a slope on one
side only. (F. – L.; *and* E.) This has
affected the sense of *penthouse,* though
they mean quite different things. Here
pent is from F. *pente,* a slope, formed
from F. *pendre,* to hang. – L. *pendēre,* to
hang.

Penultimate, Penumbra; see
Peninsula.

Penury, want. (F. – L.) M. F. *penurie.*
– L. *pēnūria,* want, need. Cf. Gk. πεῖνα,
hunger.

Peony, Pæony, a flower. (F. – L. –
Gk.) Altered to suit the Lat. spelling.
M. E. *pione.* – O. F. *pione* (F. *pivoine).* –
L. *pæōnia,* medicinal, from its supposed
virtues ; fem. of *Pæōnius,* belonging to
Pæōn, its supposed discoverer. – Gk. παιω-
νία, pæony ; from Παίων, Pæon. See
Pæan.

People. (F. – L.) M. E. *people, poeple.*
– A. F. *people, pēple* ; O. F. *pueple* ; F.
peuple. – L. *populum,* acc. of *populus,*
people.

Pepper. (L. – Gk. – Skt.) A. S. *pipor.*
– L. *piper.* – Gk. πέπερι. – Skt. *pippalī,*
(1) fruit of the holy fig-tree, (2) long
pepper ; from *pippala-,* the holy fig-tree.

Pepsine, one of the constituents of
gastric juice. (F. – Gk.) Mod. F. *pepsine.*
– Gk. πέψις, digestion ; for *πεπτις<*πεq-
tis, related to πέπτειν, to cook. (√PEQ.)
See Cook.

Per-, prefix, through. (L. ; *or* F. – L.)
L. *per,* through ; whence F. *per-, par-,*
prefix. Allied to Gk. περί, around ; cf.
also παρά, beside ; Skt. *parā,* away, forth,
param, beyond ; E. *from.*

Perambulate, to walk about through.
(L.) L. *per,* through ; and *ambulātus,*
pp. of *ambulāre,* to walk about. See
Amble.

Perceive. (F. – L.) O. F. *percever.*
– L. *percipere,* to apprehend. – L. *per,*
thoroughly ; *capere,* to seize.

perception. (F. – L.) F. *perception.*

– L. acc. *perceptiōnem.* – L. *perceptus,* pp.
of *percipere* ; see above.

Perch (1), a rod for a bird to sit on ;
a measure. (F. – L.) F. *perche.* – L. *per-
tica,* a rod, bar.

Perch (2), a fish. (F. – L. – Gk.) F.
perche. – L. *perca.* – Gk. πέρκη, a perch ;
from the dark marks. – Gk. πέρκος, περκνός,
spotted, blackish ; cf. Skt. *pṛçni-,* spotted,
pied, *spṛç,* to sprinkle.

Percolate. (L.) From pp. of L. *per-
colāre,* to filter through. – L. *per,* through ;
colāre, to filter. See Colander.

Percussion. (L.) From L. *percussio,*
a striking. – L. *percussus,* pp. of *percutere,*
to strike. See Quash. Der. *re-percussion.*

Perdition. (F. – L.) F. *perdition.* –
L. acc. *perditiōnem,* utter loss. – L. *per-
ditus,* pp. of *perdere,* to lose. – L. *per,*
thoroughly ; *-dere,* to put, place, representing Idg. *dhə,* weak form of √DHĒ,
to place ; cf. Do.

Peregrination. (F. – L.) M. F. *peregrination.* – L. *peregrīnātiōnem,* acc. of
peregrīnātio, a wandering. – L. *peregrī-
nātus,* pp. of *peregrīnārī,* to travel. – L.
peregrīnus, foreign, adj. from *peregrī, pere-
grē,* adv., abroad ; cf. *pereger,* a traveller.
From L. *per-,* which is either = L. *per,*
through, or is related to A. S. *feor,* far ;
and *ager,* land, field. See Acre and
Pilgrim.

Peremptory, decisive. (F. – L.) M. F.
peremptoire. – L. *peremptōrius,* destructive,
decisive. – L. *peremptor,* a destroyer. – L.
peremptus, pp. of *per-imere,* to take away
entirely, destroy. – L. *per,* utterly ; *emere,*
to take. See Exempt.

Perennial. (L.) Coined from L. *per-
enni-s,* everlasting ; lit. lasting throughout
the year. – L. *per,* through ; *annus,* a year.
See Annual.

Perfect. (F. – L.) M. E. *perfit, parfit.*
– O. F. *parfit, parfeit* (F. *parfait).* – L.
perfectus, pp. of *perficere,* to complete. –
L. *per,* thoroughly ; *facere,* to make. See
Fact.

Perfidious. (L.) From L. *perfidiōsus,*
treacherous. – L. *perfidia,* treachery. – L.
perfidus, treacherous. – L. *per,* away (cf.
Skt. *parā,* from) ; *fidēs,* faith. See Faith.

Perfoliate. (L.) Coined from L. *per,*
through ; *folium,* a leaf. See Foil (2).

Perforate. (L.) From pp. of L. *per-
forāre,* to bore through ; where *forāre* is
cognate with E. Bore.

Perform, to achieve. (F. – O. H. G. ;

with L. *prefix*.) Corrupted from M. E. *parfournen*, later *parfourmen*. — O. F. *parfournir*, 'to perform;' Cot. — L. *per*, thoroughly; and O. F. *fournir*, to furnish, provide; see **Furnish**.

Perfume, vb. (F. — L.) F. *parfumer*, to perfume, lit. to smoke thoroughly. — L. *per*, thoroughly; *fūmāre*, to smoke, from *fūmus*, smoke; see **Fume**.

Perfunctory. (L.) L. *perfunctōrius*, carelessly done. — L. *perfunctus*, pp. of *perfungī*, to perform fully, get through with. — L. *per*, thoroughly; *fungī*, to perform; see **Function**.

Perhaps. (L. *and* Scand.) A clumsy hybrid compound. — L. *per*, by (as in *perchance*, where *per* is, strictly, F. *par*); *haps*, pl. of *hap*, chance.

Peri, a fairy. (Pers.) Pers. *parī*, a winged spirit. Lit. 'winged;' from Pers. *par*, a wing, feather, Zend *patara-*, a wing. See **Feather**. (√PET.) Brugm. ii. § 150.

Peri-, prefix, round. (Gk.) Gk. περί, around, about.+Skt. *pari*, round about. Allied to *per-*, prefix.

Pericardium, the sac surrounding the heart. (L. — Gk.) L. *pericardium*. — Gk. περικάρδιον. — Gk. περί, around; καρδία, the heart; see **Heart**.

Pericarp, a seed-vessel. (Gk.) Gk. περικάρπιον, shell of fruit. — Gk. περί, around; καρπός, fruit; see **Harvest**.

Pericranium, the membrane that surrounds the skull. (L. — Gk.) Late L. *pericrānium*. — Gk. περικράνιον, neut. of περικράνιος, surrounding the skull. — Gk. περί, round; κρανίον, skull.

Perigee, point of the moon's orbit nearest the earth. (Gk.) From Gk. περί, about, here 'near'; γῆ, earth. See **Geography**.

Perihelion, the point of a planet's orbit nearest the sun. (Gk.) Gk. περί, round, near; ἥλιος, the sun. See **Heliacal**.

Peril, danger. (F. — L.) M. F. *peril*. — L. *perīclum*, *perīculum*, danger, lit. 'a trial.' — L. *perīrī*, to try; an obsolete verb, of which the pp. *perītus* is common. Allied to Gk. πεῖρα, an attempt; and ultimately to E. *fare*; see **Fare**. Cf. E. *fear*; G. *gefahr*, peril. (√PER.) Der. *peril-ous*.

Perimeter, lit. 'the measure all round.' (L. — Gk.) L. *perimetros*. — Gk. περίμετρος. — Gk. περί, round; μέτρον, a measure. See **Metre**.

Period, time of a circuit, epoch, perfect

sentence. (F. — L. — Gk.) M. F. *periode*, a perfect sentence. — L. *periodus*. — Gk. περίοδος, a going round, circuit, complete sentence. — Gk. περί, round; ὁδός, a way; see **Exodus**. ¶ The sense of 'circuit' is *directly* from Gk.

Peripatetic, a walking about. (L. — Gk.) L. *peripatēticus*. — Gk. περιπατητικός, given to walking about, esp. while disputing; a name given to followers of Aristotle. — Gk. περιπατέω, I walk about. — Gk. περί, about; πατέω, I walk, from πάτος, a path.

Periphery, circumference. (L. — Gk.) L. *periferīa*, *peripheria*. — Gk. περιφέρεια, the circumference of a circle. — Gk. περί, around; φέρειν, to carry, cognate with E. **Bear**, vb.

Periphrasis. (L. — Gk.) L. *periphrasis*. — Gk. περίφρασις, circumlocution. Gk. περί, around; φράζειν, to declare, express. See **Phrase**.

Perish. (F. — L.) M. E. *perischen*. — O. F. *periss-*, stem of pres. pt. of *perir*, to perish. — L. *perīre*, to come to naught, perish. — L. *per-*, used with a destructive force (like E. *for-* in *for-do*); and *īre*, to go.

Periwig, a peruke. (F. — Ital. — L.) Formerly *perwigge*, *perwicke* (Minsheu). This is a corrupted form, used in place of *peruke*. — F. *perruque*; see **Perruque**.

Periwinkle (1), a plant. (L.) Formed, with suffixed *-le* and inserted *i*, from M. E. *pervenke*, a periwinkle; A.S. *peruince*. — L. *peruinca*, a periwinkle; also called *uinca peruinca*, a name doubtless orig. given to some twining plant. — L. *per*, through, thoroughly; *uincīre*, to bind, allied to **Withy**.

Periwinkle (2), a small univalve mollusc. (Gk. *and* E.) A corrupt form, due to confusion with the word above. The better name is simply *winkle*; see **Winkle**. Also found as *pennywinkle*; Halliwell.

Perjure. (F. — L.) F. *parjurer*. — L. *periurare*, to forswear. — L. *per*, in the sense of 'beyond, against'; *iūrāre*, to swear. See **Jury**.

Perk, to make smart or trim. (F. — L.) [Cf. W. *perc*, compact, trim; *percu*, to smarten, trim; *percus*, smart; all prob. from E.] M. E. *perken*, used of birds, to trim their feathers. Cf. prov. E. *perk up*, to recover from illness. All prob. from M. E. *perke*, a perch (on which a bird sits up). — North F. *perque*, *perke*, for F. *perche*; see **Perch** (1). Cf. Walloon *pierke*, a perch; and F. *être perché sur*, to be conceited of (like E. *perky*). Perhaps associated with **Pert.**

Permanent. (F. — L.) F. *permanent.* — L. *permanent-*, stem of pres. pt. of *permanēre*, to endure, lit. abide through. — L. *per*, through; *manēre*, to remain. See **Mansion.**

Permeate, to pervade, pass through small openings. (L.) From pp. of L. *permeāre*, to pass through. — L. *per*, through; *meāre*, to pass, go. See μοῖτος in Prellwitz.

Permit. (L.) L. *permittere* (pp. *permissus*), to let pass through, lit. send through. — L. *per*, through; *mittere*, to send. See **Missile.** Der. *permiss-ion.*

Permutation. (F. — L.) F. *permutation.* — L. acc. *permūtātiōnem*, a changing. — L. *permūtātus*, pp. of *permūtāre*, to change thoroughly. — L. *per*, thoroughly; *mūtāre*, to change. See **Mutable.**

Pernicious, hurtful. (F. — L.) F. *pernicieux.* — L. *perniciōsus*, destructive. — L. *perniciēs*, destruction. — L. *per*, thoroughly; *nici-*, for *neci-*, decl. stem of *nex*, slaughter; see **Internecine.**

Peroration. (F. — L.) M. F. *peroration.* — L. *perōrātiōnem*, acc. of *perōrātio*, the close of a speech. — L. *perōrātus*, pp. of *perōrāre*, to complete a speech. — L. *per*, through; *ōrāre*, to speak. See **Oration.**

Perpendicular. (F. — L.) F. *perpendiculaire.* — L. *perpendiculāris*, according to the plumb-line. — L. *perpendiculum*, a plummet, for careful measurement. — L. *perpendere*, to weigh or measure carefully. — L. *per*, thoroughly; *pendere*, to weigh.

Perpetrate. (L.) From pp. of L. *perpetrāre*, to perform thoroughly. — L. *per*, thoroughly; *patrāre*, to accomplish.

Perpetual. (F. — L.) M. E. *perpetuel.* — M. F. *perpetuel.* — L. *perpetuālis*, universal; in later use, permanent. — L. *perpetuus*, continuous, constant, perpetual. — L. *perpet-*, stem of *perpes*, lasting throughout, continuous. — L. *per*, through; *pet-*, as in *pet-ere*, to seek. See **Petition.**

Perplex. (F. — L.) *Perplexed*, pp., was first in use. — M. F. *perplex*, 'perplexed, intangled;' Cot. — L. *perplexus*, entangled, interwoven. — L. *per*, thoroughly; *plexus*, entangled, pp. of *plectere*, to weave; see **Plait.**

Perquisite, a small gain. (L.) Late

L. perquīsītum, an extra profit above the yearly rent, arising from fines, waifs, &c.; neut. of *perquīsītus*, pp. of *perquīrere*, to seek after thoroughly. — L. *per*, thoroughly; *quærere*, to seek. See **Query.**

Perruque. (F. — Ital. — L.) In use in the 16th cent. — F. *perruque.* — Ital. *perrucca*, M. Ital. *perucca*, 'a periwig,' Florio; also spelt *parucca*, id. The same as Port. *peruca*, Span. *peluca*, Sardinian *pilucca*, orig. a mass of hair, and allied to M. Ital. *piluccare*, 'to pick or pull out haires or feathers one by one;' Florio. From Ital. *pelo*, hair. — L. *pilum*, acc. of *pilus*, a hair.

Perry. (F. — L.) M. E. *pereye.* 'Piretum, *pereye*;' Vocab. 603. 11. From an A. F. form (mod. Norman *peiré*). Cf. F. *poiré*, 'perry, drink made of pears,' Cot.; which is formed with suffix *-é* (< L. *-ātus*, made of) from F. *poire*, a pear. — L. *pirum*, a pear. See **Pear.**

Persecute. (F. — L.) M. F. *persecuter*, vb. — L. *persecūtus*, pp. of *persequī*, to pursue. — L. *per*, thoroughly; *sequī*, to follow. See **Sequence.**

Persevere. (F. — L.) Formerly *persé-ver.* — O. F. *perseverer.* — L. *perseuērāre*, to persist in a thing. — L. *per*, thoroughly; *seuērus*, earnest. See **Severe.**

Persist. (F. — L.) M. F. *persister.* — L. *persistere*, to continue, persist. — L. *per*, through; *sistere*, to stand, orig. causal of *stāre*, to stand. See **State.**

Person. (F. — L.) M. E. *persone*, *persoune.* — O. F. *persone*, F. *personne.* — L. *persōna*, a mask used by an actor, a personage, character played by an actor, a person. — L. *personāre*, to sound through; the large-mouthed mask of the actor was named from the voice sounding through it. — L. *per*, through; *sonāre*, to sound, from *sonus*, sound. See **Sound** (3).

Perspective. (F. — L.) F. *perspective*, 'the optike art;' Cot. — L. *perspectīua*, the art of inspecting; orig. fem. of *perspectīuus*, looking through. — L. *perspectus*, pp. of *perspicere*, to look through. — L. *per*, through; *specere*, to look. See **Species.**

perspicacity, keenness of sight. (F. — L.) F. *perspicacité.* — L. acc. *perspicācitātem*, sharp-sightedness. — L. *perspicāci-*, decl. stem of *perspicax*, sharp-sighted. — L. *per-spicere*, to see through (above).

perspicuous, clear. (L.) L. *perspicu-us*, clear; with suffix *-ous.* — L. *perspicere*, to see through (above).

Perspiration, a sweating. (F. — L.)

F. *perspiration.* — Late L. acc. **perspīrā-tiōnem,* lit. a breathing through. — L. *per-spīrāre,* to breathe through. — L. *per,* through; *spīrāre,* to breathe. See Spirit.

Persuade. (F. — L.) F. *persuader.* — L. *persuādēre,* to advise thoroughly, succeed in advising. — L. *per,* thoroughly; *suādēre,* to persuade. See Suasion.

Pert, saucy. (F. — L.) M. E. *pert,* shortened form of *apert,* formerly used in the same sense. See Malapert.

Pertain. (F. — L.) M. E. *partenen.* — O. F. *partenir.* — L. *pertinēre,* to extend through to, belong. — L. *per,* thoroughly; *tenēre,* to hold, hold to. See Tenable.

pertinacity. (F. — L.) F. *pertinacité* (16th cent.). Coined, with suffix *-té* < L. *-tātem,* from L. *pertināci-,* decl. stem of *pertinax,* very tenacious. — L. *per,* thorough; *tenax,* tenacious, from *tenēre,* to hold.

pertinent. (F. — L.) F. *pertinent.* — L. *pertinent-,* stem of pres. pt. of *pertinēre,* to belong to, relate to; see Pertain.

Perturb. (F. — L.) M. F. *perturber;* Cot. — L. *perturbāre,* to disturb thoroughly. — L. *per,* thoroughly; *turbāre,* to disturb. See Turbid.

Peruke; see Perruque.

Peruse. (F. — L.) · The orig. sense was 'to use up,' to go through thoroughly; hence to examine thoroughly or all over, to survey; the only difficulty in the word is in its change of sense. From *per,* thoroughly; and *use,* q. v. Cf. O. F. *paruser sa vie,* to live out his life.

Pervade. (L.) L. *peruādere,* to go through. — L. *per,* through; *uādere,* to go. See Evade, Wade.

Pervert. (F. — L.) F. *pervertir.* — L. *peruertere,* to overturn, ruin, corrupt, pervert. — L. *per,* wholly; *uertere,* to turn. See Verse. Der. *perverse,* from pp. *peruersus.*

Pervicacious, wilful. (L.) Coined from L. *peruicāci-,* decl. stem of *peruicax,* wilful; allied to *peruicus,* stubborn. Perhaps from *per,* through; and *uic-,* weak grade of *uic-,* as in *uīc-ī,* pt. t. of *uincere,* to conquer. See Victor.

Pervious, penetrable. (L.) L. *perui-us,* passable; with suffix *-ous.* — L. *per,* through; *uia,* a way. See Viaduct.

Pessimist, one who complains that all is for the worst. (L.) Coined from L. *pessim-us,* worst; a superl. perhaps connected with *pēior,* worse. Brugm. ii. § 73.

Pest. (F. — L.) F. *peste.* — L. *pestem,* acc. of *pestis,* a plague.

Pester. (F. — L.) Formerly to encumber, clog; and short for *impester.* — M. F. *empestrer,* 'to pester, intangle, incumber;' Cot. (F. *empêtrer.*) Orig. 'to hobble a horse at pasture.' — Late L. *im-* (*in*), on, upon; *pastōrium,* a clog for a horse at pasture, from *pastus,* pp. of *pascere,* to feed. See Pastor.

Pestiferous. (L.) L. *pestifer-us,* or *pestifer,* plague-bringing; with suffix *-ous.* — L. *pesti-s,* plague; *ferre,* to bring. See Pest and Bear (1).

pestilent. (F. — L.) F. *pestilent.* — L. *pestilent-,* stem of *pestilens,* hurtul; formed as if from a verb **pestilēre,* from *pestilis,* pestilential. — L. *pesti-,* decl. stem of *pestis,* a plague (above).

Pestle. (F. — L.) M. E. *pestel.* — O.F. *pestel,* later *pesteil* (Cot.). — L. *pistillum,* a small pestle. See Pistil.

Pet (1), a tame animal, a child treated fondly. (Unknown.) Formerly *peat.* [Cf. Irish *peat,* sb., a pet; adj., petted; Gael. *peata,* a pet, a tame animal; borrowed from E.] The word is prob. of F. origin; but has not been traced. Perhaps from O. F. *peti,* short for *petit,* small; see Petty. And see *petiot,* dear little child, in Godefroy.

pet (2), a fit of peevishness. (Unknown.) We also find *pettish,* capricious, i. e. like a *pet* or spoilt child; see above. Hence the phr. 'to take *pet,*' or 'to take the *pet,*' i. e. to act like a spoilt child; and finally *pet,* sb., a fit of wilfulness.

Petal. (Gk.) Gk. πέταλον, a leaf (hence petal of a flower); neut. of πέταλος, spread out, flat; from the base πετ-, as in πετ-άννυμι, I spread. + L. *patulus,* spreading; from *patēre,* to spread. (√PET.)

Petard, an explosive war-engine. (F. — L.) M. F. *petard, petart,* 'a petard or petarre;' Cot. Lit. 'explosive.' Formed with suffix *-art* (= G. *hart,* hard, common as a suffix) from M. F. *peter,* to break wind. — F. *pet,* a breaking wind, slight explosion. — L. *pēditum,* neut. of *pēditus,* pp. of *pēdere* (for **pezdere*), to break wind. See Brugm. i. § 857.

Petiole, footstalk of a leaf. (F. — L.) F. *pétiole.* — L. *petiolum,* acc. of *petiolus,* little stalk.

Petition. (F. — L.) M. F. *petition;* Cot. — L. acc. *petītiōnem,* from *petītio,* a suit. — L. *petītus,* pp. of *petere,* to attack, to beseech, ask ; orig. to fall on. Allied to E. Feather. (√PET.) See Brugm. i. § 560.

Petrel, a bird. (F.–G.–L.–Gk.) Formerly *peterel*. – F. *pétrel, pétérel*; formed as a dimin. of *Pêtre*, i.e. Peter, and the allusion is to the action of the bird, which seems, like St. Peter, to walk on the sea. The F. form of Peter is *Pierre* ; *Pêtre* is for G. *Peter*, Peter ; cf. the G. name for the bird, viz. *Petersvogel* (= Peter's-fowl, Peter's-bird). – L. *Petrus*. – Gk. πέτρος, a stone, Peter (John i. 42).

petrify, to turn into stone. (F. – Gk. and L.) M. F. *petrifier*; as if from a L *petrificāre*, not used. – L. *petri-*, for *petra*, a rock ; *-ficāre*, for *facere*, to make. The L. *petra* is borrowed from Gk. πέτρα, a rock ; cf. πέτρος, a stone.

petroleum, rock-oil. (L. – Gk.) Coined from L. *petr-a*, rock ; *oleum*, oil. – Gk. πέτρα, rock ; ἔλαιον, oil ; see **Oil.**

Petronel, a horse-pistol. (F. – Span. – L.) M. F. *petrinal*, 'a petronell, or horse-man's piece;' Cot. Said to have been invented in the Pyrenees ; and almost certainly derived from Span. *petrina*, a belt, a girdle (so that *petrinal* would orig. mean what was attached to the belt). Allied to Span. *petral*, a poitrel ; and named from going round the breast. – L. *pector-* (for *pectos*), stem of *pectus*, the breast. See **Pectoral.**

Petty, small. (F. – C.?) M.E. *petit*. – F. *petit*, small. Cf. O. Ital. *pitetto*, small. Perhaps allied to *piece*, from a Gaulish base *pett-* (Celtic *qett-*) ; cf. Bret. *pez*, a piece ; W. *peth*, a part ; Irish *cuid*, O. Ir. *cuit*, a part, share. See Körting, § 6101 ; Stokes (s. v. *qetti*). Der. *petti-fogger*, where *fogger* is equivalent to M. Du. *focker*, 'a monopole or an engrosser of wares and commodities,' Hexham ; *focker* being prob. a corruption of the surname *Fugger*, Englished as *fogger* (N. E. D.).

Petulant. (L.) L. *petulant-*, stem of *petulans*, forward, pert, ready to attack. – L. *petere*, to attack. See **Petition.**

Pew. (F. – L. – Gk.) M. E. *pew, pue*. – A. F. *pui*, a platform (Liber Albus) ; O. F. *pui*, an elevated space ; *puie*, an open gallery with rails (hence applied to an enclosed space or to a raised desk to kneel at). – L. *podium*, a balcony, esp. near the arena, where distinguished persons sat. (So E. *pew* meant a place for distinguished persons in church.) – Gk. πόδιον, which came to mean a foot-stool, gallery to sit

in, &c. ; lit. 'little foot.' – Gk. ποδί-, for πούς, foot. See **Foot.** ¶ Cf. M. Du. *puye*, 'a pue,' Hexham ; borrowed from O. F. *puye, puie.*

Pewet, Peewit, the lapwing. (E.) Also *puet* (Phillips). Named from its plaintive cry ; cf. mod. Norman F. *pivit*, a pewet ; Lowl. Sc. *peu*, to make a plaintive noise ; Westphal. *pīwit, pīwik*, a pewet. Cf. E. *peevish.*

Pewter. (F. – Teut.?) M. E. *pewtir*. O. F. *peutre, peautre, piautre*, a kind of metal (Roquefort). Older form *peltre*, akin to Span. *peltre*, Ital. *peltro*, pewter. Diez remarks that the Ital. *peltro* is believed to be derived from English, which he rejects, but only on the ground that *pewter* could not become *peltro*. However, *peltro* is probably (like O. F. *peautre*), an adaptation of the form found in O. F. *espeltre (espeautre)*, E. *spelter* ; see **Spelter.**

<h2 align="center">PH.</h2>

Ph. Initial *ph* is distinct from *p*, and has the sound of *f* ; it represents the Gk. φ, almost every word beginning with *ph* being of Gk. origin. The only exceptions are *pheon* (also *feon*), *philibeg*, better *fillibeg*, which is Gaelic, and *Pharisee*, really of Hebrew origin, but coming to us through Greek.

Phaeton, a kind of carriage. (F. – L. – Gk.) F. *phaéton* ; occurring A.D. 1723. – L. *Phaethon.* – Gk. Φαέθων, son of Helios, and driver of the chariot of the sun ; lit. 'shining,' being pres. part. of φαέθειν, to shine. – Gk. ἀάειν, to shine. See **Phantom.** See Prellwitz, s. v. φάος. (√BHĀ.)

Phalanx. (L. – Gk.) L. *phalanx.* – Gk. φάλαγξ, a battalion. See **Plank.**

Phantasm; see below.

Phantom. (F. – L. – Gk.) M. E. *fantome*. – O. F. *fantosme.* – L. *phantasma* (whence E. *phantasm*). – Gk. φάντασμα, a vision, spectre, lit. apparition. – Gk. φαντάζειν, to display. – Gk. φαν-, as in φαίνειν (= φάν-γειν), to shew, lit. to cause to shine ; whence *φάντης, one who shews (as in ἱερο-φάντης. – Gk. φά-ειν, to shine. +Skt. *bhā*, to shine. (√BHĀ.)

Pharisee, one of a religious school among the Jews. (L. – Gk. – Heb.) L. *pharisæus, pharisæus.* – Gk. φαρισαῖος, Matt. ix. 11, lit. 'one who separates himself.' – Heb. *pārash*, to separate.

Pharmacy. (F. – L. – Gk.) M. E. *fermacy.* – O. F. *farmacie*, later *pharmacie.* – L. *pharmacia.* – Gk. φαρμακεία, knowledge of drugs. – Gk. φάρμακον, a drug.

Pharynx. (L. – Gk.) L. *pharynx.* – Gk. φάρυγξ, the joint opening of the gullet and wind-pipe, a cleft, a bore ; allied to φάραγξ, a chasm. From the root φαρ-, to bore ; see Bore (1). (√BHAR.)

Phase, Phasis, an appearance. (L. – Gk.) Late L. *phasis*, pl. *phases.* – Gk. φάσις, an appearance ; from base φα-, to shine ; cf. φά-ος, light. (√BHĀ.) β. The Gk. φάσις also means ' a saying, declaration,' in which sense it is connected with φημί, I speak, declare, from √BHĀ, to speak. Der. *em-phasis.*

Pheasant, a bird. (F. – L. – Gk.) Formed with excrescent *t* (after *n*) from M. E. *fesaun*, a pheasant. – O. F. *faisan.* – L. *phāsiāna*, a pheasant ; for *Phāsiāna auis*, Phasian bird. – Gk. φασιανός, a pheasant, lit. Phasian, i. e. coming from the river *Phāsis* in Colchis.

Pheeze ; see Feeze.

Phenix, Phœnix. (L. – Gk.) L. *phœnix.* – Gk. φοῖνιξ, a phœnix (Herod. ii. 73). Perhaps named from its bright colour, like that produced by the *Phœnician* dye ; see Pliny, bk. x. c. 2.

Phenomenon, a remarkable appearance. (L. – Gk.) L. *phænomenon.* – Gk. φαινόμενον (pl. φαινόμενα), an appearance, neut. of pass. part. of φαίνειν, to shew (pass. φαίνομαι, I appear). See Phantom, Hierophant, Sycophant.

Pheon, Feon, a barbed arrow-head. (F. – L.) M. E. *feon*, Bk. of St. Alban's. – O. F. *foene, fouane, foine, foisne* ; M. F. *fouine*, ' an eele-speare,' Cot. – L. *fuscina*, a trident. See Foin.

Phial, Vial. (F. – L. – Gk.) Formerly *fyole, vial, viol*, altered to *phial* in modern editions of Shakespeare. – M. F. *phiole*, ' a violl,' Cot. (Mod. F. *fiole*.) – L. *phiala.* – Gk. φιάλη, a broad, flat, shallow cup or bowl (applied in F. to a small bottle).

Philanthropy, love of mankind. (L. – Gk.) L. *philanthrōpia.* – Gk. φιλανθρωπία, benevolence. – Gk. φιλάνθρωπος, loving mankind. – Gk. φιλ-, for φίλος, friendly, kind ; ἄνθρωπος, a man.

philharmonic, loving music. (Gk.) From Gk. φίλ-ος, friendly, fond of ; and L. *harmoni-a* < Gk. ἁρμονία, harmony ; see Harmony.

philippic, a discourse full of invec-

tive. (L. – Gk.) L. *Philippicum*, pl. *Philippica*, used to denote the celebrated orations of Demosthenes against Philip. – Gk. Φίλιππος, Philip ; lit. ' a lover of horses.' – Gk. φίλ-ος, fond of ; ἵππος, a horse.

philology, study of languages. (L. – Gk.) L. *philologia.* – Gk. φιλολογία, love of discourse, love of literature and language. – Gk. φιλόλογος, fond of discourse ; also, a student of literature and language. – Gk. φίλο-ς, fond of ; λόγος, discourse, from λέγειν, to speak.

philosophy, love of wisdom. (F. – L. – Gk.) M. E. *philosophie.* – F. *philosophie.* – L. *philosophia.* – Gk. φιλοσοφία, love of wisdom. – Gk. φιλόσοφος, loving knowledge. – Gk. φίλο-ς, fond of ; σοφός, skilful, σοφία, skill ; see Sophist. Der. *philosoph-er*, for M. E. *philosophre*, which represents F. *philosophe*, L. *philosophus*, Gk. φιλόσοφος.

philtre, a love potion. (F. – L. – Gk.) F. *philtre.* – L. *philtrum.* – Gk. φίλτρον, a love charm, love potion, drink to make one love. – Gk. φίλ-ος, dear ; -τρον (cf. Idg. -*ter*-), denoting the instrument.

Philibeg, a kilt ; see Fillibeg.

Phlebotomy, blood-letting. (F. – L. – Gk.) M. F. *phlebotomie.* – L. *phlebotomia.* – Gk. φλεβοτομία, blood-letting, lit. cutting of a vein. – Gk. φλεβο-, for φλέψ, a vein, from φλέ-ειν, to gush ; τομός, cutting, from τέμνειν, to cut ; see Tome.

Phlegm, slimy matter in the throat, sluggishness. (F. – L. – Gk.) The use of the term was due to the supposed influence of the ' four humours' ; phlegm causing a sluggish or ' phlegmatic' temperament. – M. F. *phlegme.* – L. *phlegma.* – Gk. φλέγμα (base φλεγματ-), (1) a flame, (2) inflammation, (3) viscous humour, phlegm. – Gk. φλέγειν, to burn. + L. *flag-rāre*, to burn ; see Flame. Der. *phlegmat-ic*, from base φλεγματ-.

phlox, a flower. (Gk.) It means ' flame,' from its colour. – Gk. φλόξ, flame. – Gk. φλέγ-ειν, to burn (above).

Phocine, belonging to the family of seals. (L. – Gk.) From L. *phōca*, a seal. – Gk. φώκη, a seal. See Prellwitz.

Phœnix ; see Phenix.

Phonetic, representing sounds. (Gk.) From Gk. φωνητικός, belonging to speaking. – Gk. φωνέω, I produce a sound. – Gk. φωνή, a sound ; cf. φημί, I speak. (√BHĀ.) Der. *phono-graph*, -*logy*, &c.

Phosphorus. (L. – Gk.) L. *phosphorus.* – G. φωσφόρος, light-bringing, i. e. producing light. – Gk. φῶς, light (=φάος, light), from base φα-, to shine; -φορος, bringing, from φέρειν, to bring. (√BHĀ and √BHER.)

photography. (Gk.) From Gk. φωτο-, for φῶς, light (above); and γράφειν, to write.

Phrase. (F. – L. – Gk.) F. *phrase.* – L. *phrasem*, acc. of *phrasis.* – Gk. φράσις, a speaking, a speech, phrase. – Gk. φράζειν (=*φράδ-yειν), to speak; cf. φραδής, shrewd. Der. *anti-phrasis, meta-phrase, periphrasis, para-phrase*; with prefixes *anti-, meta-, peri-, para-.*

Phrenology, science of the functions of the mind. (Gk.) From Gk. φρενό-, for φρήν, mind; -λογία, from λόγος, a discourse, from λέγειν, to speak.

Phthisis, consumption of the lungs. (L. – Gk.) L. *phthisis.* – Gk. φθίσις, consumption, decay. – Gk. φθίνειν, to decay, wane. Cf. Skt. *kshi,* to destroy, *kshiti-,* decay. Der. *phthisic,* properly an adj., from L. *phthisicus,* adj., consumptive; but used as a sb. (=L. *phthisica passio*), with the same sense as *phthisis*; often called and spelt *tisic.*

Phylactery, an amulet, amongst the Jews. (F. – L. – Gk.) M. E. *filaterie,* Wyclif. – O. F. *filaterie* (Godefroy); Mod. F. *phylactère.* – L. *phylactērium.* – Gk. φυλακτήριον, a preservative; Matt. xxiii. 5. – Gk. φυλακτήρ, a guardian. – Gk. φυλάσσειν, to guard; φύλαξ, a guard.

Physic. (F. – L. – Gk.) Orig. the healing art; hence, medicine. – O. F. *phisique,* science of medicine; also, natural philosophy. – L. *physica,* natural science. – Gk. φυσική, fem. of φυσικός, natural, physical. – Gk. φύσι-s, nature, being. – Gk. φύ-ειν, to produce. + Skt. *bhū,* to be; L. *fu-i, fo-re*; E. *be.* (√BHEU.) Der. *physic-s*; *physic-i-an*; &c.

physiognomy, visage, expression of features. (F. – L. – Gk.) M. E. *fisnomie, visnomie.* – O. F. *phisonomie,* later *physiognomie,* a knowledge of a man's character by his features; hence features, expression. Formed as if from L. **physiognōmia,* but due to the longer form *physiognomonia.* – Gk. φυσιογνωμονία, the art of reading the features; sometimes φυσιογνωμία. – Gk. φυσιο-γνώμων, adj., judging character. – Gk. φυσιο-, for φύσις, nature; γνώμων, an interpreter; see **Gnomon.**

physiology, the science of nature. (F. – L. – Gk.) F. *physiologie*; Cot. – L. *physiologia.* – Gk. φυσιολογία, an enquiry into the nature of things. – Gk. φυσιο-, for φύσις, nature; -λογία, from λόγος, a discourse, from λέγειν, to speak.

PI – PY.

Piacular, expiatory. (L.) L. *piāculāris,* adj., from *piāculum,* an expiation. – L. *piāre,* to propitiate. – L. *pius,* devout. See **Pious.**

Pianoforte, Piano. (Ital. – L.) So called from producing *soft* and *loud* effects. – Ital. *piano,* soft; *forte,* strong, loud. – L. *plānus,* level (hence smooth, soft); *fortis,* strong; see **Plain** and **Force.**

Piastre. (F. – Ital. – L. – Gk.) F. *piastre.* – Ital. *piastra,* plate of metal, also a piastre or coin; allied to Ital. *piastro,* a plaster. – L. *emplastrum,* a plaster (with loss of *em-*). See **Plaster.**

Piazza. (Ital. – L. – Gk.) Ital. *piazza,* a market-place, chief street. – Folk-L. **plattia*; L. *platea, platēa*; see **Place.**

Pibroch, a martial tune. (Gael. – L.) Gael. *piobaireachd,* a pipe-tune, tune on the bagpipe. – Gael. *piobair,* a piper. – Gael. *piob,* a pipe. – E. *pipe.* See **Pipe.**

Pica; see **Pie** (1).

Picador, a horseman with a lance, in bull-fighting. (Span. – L.) Span. *picador,* lit. a pricker. – Span. *picar,* to prick. – Late L. *pīcāre*; see **Pick.**

Picaninny, a negro or mulatto infant. (Span.) From *peekaneenee,* a dimin. (in Surinam) of Span. *pequeño,* small, allied to Ital. *piccolo,* small. Of uncertain origin.

Piccadill; see **Pickadill.**

Pice, a small copper coin. (Marathi.) Hind. and Marathi *paisā,* a copper coin; sometimes rated at four to the anna, or sixty-four to the rupee (H. H. Wilson).

Pick, to peck, pierce, also to pluck, &c. (L.) M. E. *pikken, pekken,* used as equivalent words, Ch. C. T., Group B. 4157. [Cf. Irish *pioc,* Gael. *pioc,* to pick, nibble, pluck, peck; W. *pigo,* to pick, peck, prick, choose; Corn. *piga,* to prick.] Allied to A. S. *pīcan,* to peck, from Late L. *pīcāre,* to use a pickaxe, to peck; *pīca,* a pick, pickaxe. – L. *pīc-,* as in *pīc-us,* a woodpecker. Cf. Gk. πείκειν, to shear; πικρός, sharp, bitter. See **Pike.**

pickadill, piccadill, a piece set round the edge of a garment, a collar. (F.

—Span.—L.) Obsolete; but preserved in *Piccadilly*, a street in London, named from a certain house, which was 'a famous ordinary near St. James's'; see Blount and Nares.—M.F. *piccadille*; pl. *piccadilles*, 'the several pieces fastened together about the brimme of the collar of a doublet;' Cot. Formed, with Span. dimin. suffix -*illo*, from Span. *picado*, pp. of *picar*, to puncture; cf. Span. *picadura*, a puncture, an ornamental gusset in clothes.—Span. *picar*, to prick, from *pica*, a pike (hence a pricking instrument); a word of Latin origin; see Pike.

pickax. (F.—L.) Not an *ax* at all, but a corruption of M. E. *pikois, pikeis*, a mattock.—O. F. *picois*, later *picquois*, a mattock.—O. F. *piquer*, to pierce, thrust into.—F. *pic*, a 'pick' or kind of mattock. —Late L. *pīca*, a pickax. Cf. A. S. *pīc*, a pike; Bret. *pic*, a pick; W. *pig*, a point, pike, Irish *piocaid*, a mattock; see Pike.

picket, a peg for fastening horses, a small outpost. (F.—L.) F.*piquet, picquet*, a little pickax, a peg thrust in the ground. Dimin. of F. *pic* (above).

Pickle, a liquid in which substances are preserved. (L.?) M. E. *pikil, pykyl*; Prompt. Parv. Probably from *pickle*, frequent. of *pick*, in the sense to pick out or 'cleanse'; with reference to the gutting or cleansing of the fish with which the operation of pickling is begun. We find M. E. *pykelynge*, 'purgulacio,' derived from '*pykyn*, or clensyn, or cullyn owte the onclene, *purgo, purgulo, segrego*'; Prompt. Parv. See Pick. β. We also find Du. *pekel*, pickle; which some have derived from the name of the supposed inventor of pickling, whose name is variously given as *Beukeler, Böckel*, and *Pökel*; a story unsupported by evidence.

Picnic. (E.) Found in F. as early as 1740, and in Swedish before 1788; but borrowed in those languages from English. Origin obscure. *Pic* is prob. from *pick*, in the sense to nibble; cf. slang E. *peck*, food, *peckish*, hungry. *Nic* is for *knick*, a trifle; another name for a picnic was *nicknack* (Foote, Nabob, act 1).

Picture. (L.) L. *pictūra*, properly the art of painting.—L. *pictus*, pp. of *pingere*, to paint. Allied to Skt. *piñj*, to dye, colour; Gk. ποικίλος. Brugm. i. § 701.

Piddling, trifling. (Scand.?) From the verb *piddle*, to trifle (Ascham); other forms are *pittle* (Skinner), *pettle* (Halliwell).

—Swed. dial. *pittla*, to keep on picking at; frequent. of Swed. *peta*, to pick, poke.

Pie (1), a magpie; unsorted printer's type. (F.—L.) The unsorted type is called *pie*, i. e. a jumble; see pie (3); also *pi*, as if short for *pica*, from the common use of pica-type; see below. The magpie is M. E. *pie*.—F. *pie*.—L. *pīca*, a magpie. Cf. L. *pīcus*, woodpecker, Skt. *pika-*, Indian cuckoo.

pie (2), a book which ordered the manner of performing divine service. (F.—L.) Here *pie* is (as above) a F. form of L. *pīca*, which was an old name for the Ordinale; so called from the confused appearance of the black-letter type on white paper, resembling a magpie. Certain sizes of type are still called *pica*.

pie (3), a pasty. (F.—L.) M. E. *pie*; prob. the same word as *pie* (1); from the miscellaneous nature of its contents. E. *pies* seems to be Latinised as *pīcē*, Babees Book, pt. ii. 36. 51. Cf. **pie** (2). ¶ Gael. *pighe*, a pie, is from E.

piebald, of various colours, in patches. (F.—L.; *and* C.) Compounded of *pie*, a magpie, and *bald*; see Bald. The old sense of *bald*, or *ball'd*, is streaked, from W. *bal*, having a white streak on the forehead, said of a horse. Cf. *skew-bald*.

Piece. (F.—C.) M. E. *pece, piece*.— O. F. *piece*; F. *pièce*. Cf. Ital. *pezza*, Span. *pieza*, Prov. *pessa, pesa*, Port. *peça*, a piece.—Late L. *petia*, a piece; cf. Late L. *petium*, a piece of land (A. D. 757).— Celtic (Gaulish) **petti-*, a piece, portion, answering to O. Celtic **qetti-*, the same; evidenced by O. Irish *cuit* (Ir. *cuid*), a piece, share, W. *peth*, a piece, a thing, Corn. *peth*, Bret. *pez*, a piece (Thurneysen, Stokes, Körting). Esp. used of a piece of land.

piece-meal. (F.—C.; *and* E.) M. E. *pece-mele*, by pieces at a time. The M. E. suffix -*mele*, lit. 'by bits,' occurs in other compounds, and is also spelt -*melum*; from A. S. *mǣlum*, dat. pl. of *mǣl*, a portion; see Meal (2).

Piepowder court, a summary court of justice formerly held at fairs. (F.—L.) The E. *piepowder* represents O. F. *pied pouldre*, i. e. dusty foot. The court was called, in Latin, *Curia pedis pulverīsātī*, the court of the dusty foot, from the dusty feet of the suitors.—F. *pied*, foot, from L. *pedem*, acc. of *pēs*; O. F. *pouldre* (=*poul-*

dré), pp. of *pouldrer*, to cover with dust, from *pouldre*, dust; see **Powder**.

Pier, a mass of stone-work. (F. – L. – Gk.) M. E. *pere.* – O. F. *piere* (F. *pierre*), a stone. – L. *petra.* – Gk. πέτρα, a rock, stone.

Pierce. (F. – L. ?) M. E. *percen.* – F. *percer*; O. F. *percier* (Roland). Generally thought to be contracted from O. F. *per-tuisier*, to pierce, lit. to make a hole. – O. F. *pertuis*, a hole (Ital. *pertugio*). The O. F. *pertuis* (like Ital. *pertugio*), answers to a Late L. **pertūsium*, extended from L. *pertūsus*, pp. of *pertundere*, to thrust through, pierce. (Ennius has *latu' pertudit hasta* = the spear pierced his side; Lewis.) – L. *per*, through; *tundere*, to beat; see **Contuse**. ¶ Commonly accepted; some suggest Late L. **per-itiāre*, to go through; cf. L. *in-itiare*. See **Initiate** and **Commence**.

Piety. (F. – L.) M. F. *pieté.* – L. *pietā-tem*, acc. of *pietās*, devoutness. – L. *pius*, devout. See **Pious**. Doublet, *pity*.

Pig. (E.) M. E. *pigge*. Prov. E. *peg* (Berks.). Cf. A. S. *pecg* ; ' of swīnforda oð *pecges* ford ; ' Birch, Cart. Saxon. iii. 223. But the connexion is doubtful. ¶ Certain masses of molten metal are called *sows* and *pigs*; hence *pig-iron*.

Pigeon, a bird. (F. – L.) F. *pigeon*, a pigeon, a dove. – L. *pīpiōnem*, acc. of *pīpio*, lit. ' chirper.' – L. *pīpīre*, to chirp. See **Pipe**.

Piggin, a small wooden vessel. (E.) Cf. Gael. *pigean*, a pitcher, jar; dimin. of *pige*, *pigeadh*, an earthen jar; Irish *pigin*, small pail, *pighead*, earthen jar; W. *picyn*, a piggin; all borrowed from E. Prob. for **piggen*, adj., from *pig*, in the sense of ' earthen vessel,' as in G. Douglas, tr. of Vergil, bk. vii. See **Pig**.

Pight, old form of *pitched*; see **Pitch** (2).

Pigment. (L.) L. *pigmentum*, colouring matter. – L. *pig-*, base of *pingere*, to paint; with suffix *-mentum*. See **Paint**.

Pigmy; see **Pygmy**.

Pike, a sharp-pointed weapon, a fish. (L.) M. E. *pike*, a peaked staff, *pic*, a spike; also M. E. *pike*, a fish, named from its sharply pointed jaws. A. S. *pīc*, a point, a pike. (Hence Irish *pice*, a pike, fork, Gael. *pìc*, W. *pig*, Bret. *pīk*, pike, point, pickax.) Closely allied to *pick*, sb., a mattock. – L. *pīc-*, as in *pīc-us*, a woodpecker. See **Pick**. Der. *pik-er-el*,

a young pike (fish); *pike-staff*, also found as *piked-staff*, i.e. staff armed with a pike or spike.

Pilaster, a square pillar. (F. – Ital. – L.) F. *pilastre.* – Ital. *pilastro*, ' a pilaster, a piller ; ' Florio. – Ital. *pila*, ' a flatsided piller ; ' id. – L. *pīla*, a pillar. See **Pile** (2).

Pilch. (L.) Orig. a warm fur garment. M. E. *pilche*. A. S. *pilece*, *pylce.* – L. *pellicea* : see **Pelisse**.

Pilchard, a fish. (E. ?) Formerly *pilcher*; cf. Irish *pilseir*, a pilchard. Of unknown origin. Cf. Dan. dial. *pilke*, to fish (in a particular manner), Swed. dial. *pilka*; from Norw. *pilk*, an artificial bait.

Pilcrow, a curious corruption of **Paragraph**, q. v.

Pile (1), a tumour, lit. a ball. (L.) Only in the pl. *piles.* – L. *pila*, a ball.

Pile (2), a pillar, heap. (L.) M. E. *pile*; A. S. *pīl.* – L. *pīla*, a pillar, a pier of stone. ¶ In the phrase *cross and pile* (of a coin), answering to the modern ' head and tail,' the *pile* took its name from the *pile* or short pillar on which the coin rested when struck; see Cotgrave, s. v. *pile*.

Pile (3), a stake. (L.) A. S. *pīl*, a stake. – L. *pīlum*, a javelin; orig. a pestle. For **pins-lum.* – L. *pinsere*, to pound. + Skt. *pish*, *piñsh*, to pound. ¶ The heraldic *pile* (F. *pile*) is a sharp stake.

Pile (4), a hair, fibre of wool. (L.) L. *pilus*, a hair. Cf. Gk. πῖλος, felt. Brugm. ii. § 76. Der. *three-piled*, L. L. L. v. 2. 407.

Piles, small tumours. (L.) See **Pile** (1).

Pilfer. (F. – L. ?) O. F. *pelfrer*, to rob, pilfer. – O. F. *pelfre*, plunder; see **Pelf**.

Pilgrim. (Ital. – L.) Ital. *pellegrino*, a pilgrim. – L. *peregrīnus*, a foreigner, stranger; as adj. foreign. – L. *peregrī*, adv., away from home; see **Peregrination**. Cf. O. H. G. *piligrīm*, from Ital.

Pill (1), a little ball of medicine. (F. – L.) Short for *pilule*; cf. O. F. *pile*, a pill. – F. *pilule*, ' a pill ; ' Cot. – L. *pilula*, a little ball, globule; dimin. of *pila*, a ball. See **Pile** (1).

Pill (2), to plunder. (F. – L.) Also spelt *peel*; and, conversely, *peel*, to strip, is spelt *pill*; the words have been confused, but are really different; see **Peel** (2). M. E. *pillen*, to plunder. – F. *piller.* – L. *pīlāre*, to plunder, pillage, not common ;

but the deriv. *compīlāre* (whence E. *compile*) occurs often. **Der.** *pill-age*, F. *pillage*.
Pillage ; see above.
Pillar. (F. – L.) M. E. *piler.* – O. F. *piler*, later *pilier*. (Span. *pilar*.) – Late L. *pīlāre*, a pillar. – L. *pīla*, pillar, pier. See Pile (2).
Pillau, Pilaf, a dish of meat or fowl, boiled with rice and spices. (Pers.) Pers. *pilāv, pilav*, a dish made of rice and meat; Palmer.
Pillion. (F. – L.) Mod. Norman and Guernsey *pillon*; Span. *pellon*, a long robe made of skin, also a covering for a saddle (see Wedgwood). – L. acc. type **pellōnem*, augm. form from L. *pellis*, a skin. [Cf. Irish *pilliun, pillin*, a pack-saddle; Gael. *pillean, pillin*, a pack-saddle, cloth put under a rustic saddle; Irish *pill*, a covering, *peall*, a skin; Gael. *peall*, a skin, coverlet; all from E. or from L. *pellis*, a skin.] See **Pell**.
Pillory. (F.) F. *pilori*, 'a pillory;' Cot. Of unknown origin ; other remarkable variants occur, viz. O. F. *pilorin, pellorin*, Port. *pelourinho*, Prov. *espitlori*, Late L. *pilloriacum, spiliorium*. There seems to have been a loss of initial *s*.
Pillow. (L.) M. E. *pilwe* ; A.S. *pyle*; both from L. *puluīnus*, a cushion, pillow, bolster; whence also Du. *peuluw*, G. *pfühl*, Westphal. *pülf*.
Pilot, one who conducts ships in and out of harbour. (F. – Ital. – Gk.) M. F. *pilot*, Cot. (F. *pilote*); O. F. *pedot*; cf. M. F. *piloter*, to take soundings (Palsgrave). Prob. borrowed from Ital. *pilota*, also *pedota*, a pilot (Florio) ; cf. Late L. *pedotta*, a pilot. – Late Gk. **πηδώτης*, a steersman; formed from Gk. *πηδόν*, a rudder, blade of an oar.
Pimento, allspice. (Port. – L.) Also *pimenta.* – Port. *pimenta*, pimento. The same as O. F. *piment*, a spiced drink. – L. *pigmentum*, (1) a pigment, (2) the juice of plants; see **Pigment**.
Pimp, a pandar. (F. – L.) Prob. a smartly dressed fellow. – M. F. *pimper*, to dress up smartly. A nasalised form of F. *piper*, to pipe, also to beguile, cheat; cf. also Prov. *pimpar*, to render elegant, from *pimpa*, sb. (equivalent to F. *pipeau*) meaning (1) a pipe, (2) a bird-call, (3) a snare; besides which, F. *piper* meant to excel in a thing. Note also F. *pimpant*, smart, spruce ; and see Littré. – L. *pīpāre*, to chirp (hence to pipe). See **Pipe**.

Pimpernel, a flower. (F. – L.?) M.F. *pimpernelle* (F. *pimprenelle*). Cf. Span. *pimpinela*, Ital. *pimpinella*. Origin unknown. ¶ Diez considers these words to be borrowed from L. **bipinella,*bipennula*, a dimin. of *bipennis*, i. e. double-winged. The pimpernel was confused with burnet (Prior) ; and the latter (*Poterium sanguisorba*) has a feather-like arrangement of its leaves. Cf. *Rosa pimpinellifolia*. If this be right (which is highly doubtful), we refer the word to L. *bi-*, double ; *penna*, a wing.
Pimple. (F.?) [Cf. A. S. *pīplian*, to be pimply. The alleged A. S. *pinpel* is Lye's misprint for *winpel !*] Prob. not an E. word, but borrowed from some O. F. or Late L. form. Cf. F. *pompette*, 'a pumple or pimple on the nose or chin,' Cot. ; and Span. *pompa*, a bubble. Also Gk. *πέμφιξ*, *πομφός*, a bubble, blister, Lith. *pampti*, to swell ; L. *papula*, a pimple.
Pin, a peg, &c. (L.) M. E. *pinne*, a peg. A. S. *pinn*, a pen, style for writing (Toller). [We find also Irish *pion*, Gael. *pinne*, a pin, peg, spigot ; W. *pin*, pin, style, pen ; Du. *pin*, pin, peg, Swed. *pinne*, a peg, Dan. *pind*, a (pointed) stick, Icel. *pinni*, a pin, Low G. *penn*, a peg.] All from L. *pinna*, a wing, fin, pen ; cognate with E. Fin. See Brugm. ii. § 66 (note).
Pinch. (F. – L.) North F. *pincher*, F. *pincer*. A nasalised form of M. Ital. *pizzare, picciare*, to nip ; cf. Ital. *pinzo*, a sting, goad, *pinzette*, pincers. The orig. sense seems to have been a slight prick with a sharp-pointed instrument, from a Latin base *pic-*, whence E. *pike, pick* ; cf. L. *pīcus*, a woodpecker. Cf. also Du. *pinsen, pitsen*, to pinch (Hexham). **Der.** *pinchers* or *pinc-ers* ; cf. M. F. *pinces*, 'a pair of pincers ;' Cot.
Pinchbeck, a metal. (Personal name.) From the inventor, Mr. Chr. *Pinchbeck*, the elder, a London watchmaker (c. 1670-1732). From *Pinchbeck*, Lincolnshire.
Pindar, Pinner, an impounder. (E.) Formed with suffix *-er* of the agent from A. S. *pyndan*, to pen up. – A. S. *pund*, an enclosure. See **Pound** (2). ¶ Not allied to *pen* (2).
Pine (1), a tree. (L.) A.S. *pīn-trēo*, a pine-tree. – L. *pīnus*, a pine ; i. e. *pīnus.*+Gk. *πί-τυς*, a pine ; Skt. *pītu-dāru-*, lit. 'resin-tree ;' L. *pītuīta*, phlegm, also 'resin.' See **Pip** (1). **Der.** *pine-apple*, orig. 'a fir-cone.'

Pine (2), to long for; to suffer pain, waste away. (L.–Gk.) M. E. *pinen*, to suffer, more frequently, to torment; a verb formed from M. E. *pine*, torment.–A. S. *pīn*, pain; borrowed from L. *pœna*, pain; see **Pain**.

Pinfold, a pound. (E.) For *pind-fold*; (also spelt *pund-fold*, Birch, iii. 309). – A. S. *pyndan*, to pen up (from *pund*, an enclosure); and *fold*. See **Pindar**.

Pinion, joint of a wing. (F.–L.) F. *pignon*, a gable-end; Cot. O. F. *pignon*, a feather, a pennon on a lance. Cf. Span. *piñon*, a pinion. [Again, the mod. F. *pignon* has the sense of E. *pinion*, a small wheel working with teeth into another; in which case the derivation is from L. *pinna*, the float of a water-wheel.]–L. *pinna*, a wing; see **Pin**.

Pink (1), to pierce, prick. (L.?) M. E. *pinken*, to prick. Used as a nasalised form of *pick*. We may note E. *pink*, to cut round holes or eyes in silk cloth (Bailey), as equivalent to M. F. *piquer*, the same (Cotgrave). Cf. **Pinch**. ¶ Or from A. S. *pynca, pinca*, a point, which seems to have been borrowed from L. *punctum*; see **Puncture**.

Pink (2), half-shut, applied to the eyes. (Du.–L.) Obsolete; cf. '*pink eyne*,' Antony, ii. 7. 121.–M. Du. *pincken* (also *pinck-oogen*), to shut the eyes (Hexham). The notion is that of narrowing, bringing to a point; see **Pink** (1). Cf. Prov. E. *pink*, a very small fish, minnow.

Pink (3), the name of a flower, and of a colour. (L.) As in *violet, mauve*, the name of the colour is due to that of the flower. The flower is named from the delicately cut or *pinked* edges of the petals; see **Pink** (1). β. Similarly, M. F. *pince*, a pink, is from F. *pincer*, to pinch, nip; but F. *pince* and E. *pink* are not the same word; though they are related.

Pink (4), a kind of boat. (Du.) See **Nares**. Short for M. Du. *espincke*, also written *pincke*, 'a pinke, or a small fisher's boat,' Hexham; (whence also F. *pinque*, Span. *pingue*, a pink). The same word as Icel. *espingr*, Swed. *esping*, a long boat; named from Icel. *espi*, aspen-wood, M. Du. *espe*, an aspen-tree. See **Aspen**.

Pink-eyed, having small eyes; see **Pink** (2).

Pinnace. (F.–Ital.–L.) F. *pinace, pinasse*. 'the pitch-tree; also a pinnace;' Cot.–Ital. *pinaccia*, a pinnace (Florio).

So named because made of pine.–L. *pīnus*, a pine. See **Pine** (1).

Pinnacle. (F.–L.) F. *pinacle*, Cot. –L. *pinnāculum*, a pinnacle (Matt. iv. 5). Double dimin. of Late L. *pinna*, a pinnacle (Lu. iv. 9), L. *pinna*, a fin, &c. See **Pin**.

Pinnate, feather-like. (L.) L. *pinnātus*, substituted for *pennātus*, feathered. –L. *penna*, a feather. See **Pen**.

Pint, a measure for liquids. (F.–L.) F. *pinte*; cf. Span. *pinta*, a spot, mark, pint. Named from being a marked part of a larger vessel; cf. O. F. *pinter*, to measure wine.–Late L. *pincta*, a pint; for L. *picta*, fem. of *pictus*, painted, marked, pp. of *pingere*, to paint. So also Span. *pintura* = a picture.

Pioneer, a soldier who clears the way before an army. (F.–L.) Formerly *pioner*. F. *pionnier*, O. F. *peonier*, a pioneer: a mere extension of F. *pion*, O. F. *peon*, a foot-soldier, but esp. applied to sappers and miners. See further under **Pawn** (2).

Piony, the same as **Peony.**

Pious. (F.–L.) F. *pieux*.–Late L. *piōsus*, extended from L. *pius*, holy, devout. Brugm. ii. § 643.

Pip (1), a disease of fowls. (F.–L.) M. E. *pippe*.–M. F. *pepie*, 'pip;' Cot. (Mod. Norman *pipie*; Span. *pepita*, Port. *pevide*, Ital. *pipita*.)–L. *pītuīta*, phlegm, rheum, also the pip (whence **pītvīta, *pīpīta*, Late L. *pīpīdo*). Hence also Du. *pip*; Swed. *pipp*, &c. β. L. *pītuīta* is from a stem *pītu-*, for which see **Pine** (1).

Pip (2), the seed of fruit. (F.–L.–Gk.) Short for *pippin* or *pepin*, the old name.– M. F. *pepin*, a pip. Allied to Span. *pepita*, a pip [quite distinct from *pepita*, pip in fowls]; and prob. to Span. *pepino*, a cucumber. β. Some have supposed that *pepin* was first applied to the remarkable seeds of the cucumber and melon; and is derived from O. F. *pepon*, L. *pepō*, a melon, borrowed from Gk. πέπων, a melon. γ. This Gk. πέπων was orig. an adj., signifying 'ripened' or 'ripe'; (cf. πέπτειν, to cook, to ripen); allied to Skt. *pach*, L. *coquere*, to cook. See **Cook.**

Pip (3), a spot on cards. (F.–L.–Gk.) Apparently a peculiar use of **Pip** (2). β. We also find a form *pick*, formerly a spade at cards.–F. *pique*, a spade at cards; the same as **Pique.**

Pipe, a musical instrument formed of a long tube; a tube, cask. (L.) M. E. *pipe*;

A.S. *pipe.* An imitative word; but borrowed from Late L. *pipa,* pipe; from L. *pipāre,* to chirp. [So also Irish and Gael. *piob,* Irish *pib,* W. *pib;* Du. *pijp,* Icel. *pipa,* Swed. *pipa,* Dan. *pibe,* G. *pfeife.*] Cf. L. *pipīre,* Gk. πιπίζειν, to chirp. From the cry *pi-pi* of a young bird.

Pipkin, a small earthen pot. (L., *with* E. *suffix.*) A dimin. (with suffix -*kin*) of E. *pipe,* in the sense of cask. This particular sense of *pipe* may have been imported; it occurs both in F. and Du.; see *pipe* in Cotgrave, *pijpe* in Hexham.

Pippin, a kind of tart apple. (F. – L. – Gk.) Named from seed-pips; the old sense of *pippin* was a pip; see **Pip** (2). 'Perhaps an apple raised from the pip or seed;' Wedgwood. (So Arnold's Chron.) Cf. O. F. and Norm. dial. *pepin,* an apple raised from seed.

Pique, wounded pride. (F. – L.) M. F. *picque, pique,* 'a pike, pike-man; also a pike [pique], debate, quarrel;' Cot. The same word as *pike;* lit. 'a piercer,' that which pierces. See **Pike.** Der. *pique,* vb., *piqu-ant,* pres. part. of F. *piquer,* vb.

Piquet, a game at cards. (F. personal name?) Littré says *piquet* was named from its inventor; but see Hatzfeld.

Pirate. (F. – L. – Gk.) F. *pirate.* – L. *pirāta.* – Gk. πειρατής, one who attempts, one who attacks, a pirate. – Gk. πειράω, I attempt. – Gk. πεῖρα (for *πέρ-ια*), an attempt. See **Peril.**

Pirogue, a sort of canoe. (F. – W. Indian.) Defoe has *periagua.* – F. *pirogue* (Span. *piragua*). From the native W. Indian name; said to be Caribbean.

Pirouette, a whirling round, quick turn. (F.) F. *pirouette,* 'a whirling about, also a whirligig;' Cot. Dimin. of the Guernsey word *piroue,* a little wheel or whirligig (Métivier). The latter part of the word simulates F. *roue* (L. *rota*), a wheel. Allied to M. Ital. *pirolo,* a peg, a child's top. Origin unknown.

Pisces, the Fishes. (L.) L. *piscēs,* pl. of *piscis,* a fish; cognate with E. **Fish.**

Pish! (E.) Of imitative origin; beginning with expulsion of breath, and ending in a hiss.

Pismire, an ant. (F. *and* E.) The old name of the ant; from the strong urinous smell of an anthill. The first syllable is from F. *pisser* (below). β. The second is M. E. *mire,* an ant, prob. a native word. Cf. Du. *mier,* M. Du. *miere,*

E. Fries. *mire,* an ant. Teut. type **miron-.* β. We also find the similar (but unrelated?) forms: Swed. *myra,* Dan. *myre,* Icel. *maurr,* an ant. Also Irish *moirbh,* W. *mōr,* pl. *myr,* Russ. *muravei,* Gk. μύρμηξ, Pers. *mūr, mōr,* an ant; Corn. *murrian,* ants.

Piss. (F.) F. *pisser;* supposed to be a Romance word, and of imitative origin.

Pistachio, Pistacho, the nut of a certain tree. (Span. – L. – Gk. – Pers.) Span. *pistacho.* – L. *pistācium.* – Gk. πιστάκιον, a nut of the tree called πιστάκη. – Pers. *pistā,* the pistachio-nut.

Pistil, in a flower. (L.) Named from the resemblance in shape to the pestle of a mortar. – L. *pistillum,* a small pestle, dimin. of an obsolete form **pistrum,* a pestle. – L. *pistum,* supine of *pinsere,* to pound. + Gk. πτίσσειν, Skt. *pish,* to pound. (√PIS.) See **Pestle.**

Pistol, a small hand-gun. (F. – Ital.) F. *pistole.* – Ital. *pistola,* 'a dag or pistoll;' Florio. We also find M. Ital. *pistolese,* 'a great dagger,' in Florio; and it is agreed that the name was first applied to a dagger, and thence transferred to the pistol, which even in E. was at first called a *dag* (F. *dague,* a dagger). A pistol is to a gun what a dagger is to a sword. β. The Ital. *pistolese* (= Late L. *pistolensis*) means 'belonging to Pistola'; so also Ital. *pistola* is from *Pistola,* now called *Pistoja,* a town in Tuscany, near Florence. The Old Lat. name of the town was *Pistōrium.* See Scheler.

pistole, a gold coin of Spain. (F. – Ital.) The name, however, is not Spanish, but French, and the coins were at first called *pistolets.* The name is of jocular origin. – F. *pistolet,* a little pistol, also a pistolet; Cot. Diez explains that the crowns of Spain, being reduced to a smaller size than the French crowns, were called *pistolets,* and the smallest *pistolets* were called *bidets;* cf. F. *bidet,* 'a small pistoll;' Cot. – F. *pistole,* a pistol; see above.

Piston. (F. – Ital. – L.) F. *piston,* 'a pestell,' Cot.; also a piston. – Ital. *pistone,* a piston; *pestone,* a large pestle. – Ital. *pestare,* Late L. *pistāre,* to pound. – L. *pistus,* pp. of *pinsere,* to pound. See **Pistil.**

Pit. (L.) M. E. *pit, put;* A. S. *pyt.* – L. *puteus,* a well, pit (Luke xiv. 5). Perhaps a spring of pure water, from L. *putus*, pure, allied to *pūrus*; see **Pure.** Der. *pit*, vb., to set in competition, from the setting of cocks to fight in a *pit*.

Pitapat. (E.) A reduplication of *pat*, weakened to *pit* in the former instance.

Pitch (1), a black sticky substance. (L.) M. E. *pich*; older form *pik*; A. S. *pic.* ─ L. *pic-*, stem of *pix*, pitch.+Gk. πίσσα (for **πίκ-ya*). Cf. Pine (1).

Pitch (2), to throw, fall headlong, fix a camp. (L.) A palatalised form of *pick*, to throw, Cor. i. 1. 204, esp. to throw a *pike* or dart; also to plunge a sharp *peg* into the ground for fixing tents. M. E. *picchen*, pt. t. *pihte* (later *pight*). See Pike.

Pitcher. (F.─O. H. G.─L.) M. E. *picher.* ─ O. F. *picher*, also *pechir*; M. F. *pichier*, 'a pitcher; a Languedoc word;' Cot.─O. H. G. *pechāri* (G. *becher*). ─ Late L. **biccarium*, for L. *bīcārium*, a wine-vessel; prob. from Gk. βῖκος, (the same). See Beaker.

Pith. (E.) M. E. *pithe*. A. S. *piða*, pith.+Du. *pit*, M. Du. *pitte*, Low G. *peddik*.

Pittance, a dole. (F.) M. E. *pitaunce.* ─F. *pitance*, 'meat, food, victuall of all sorts, bread and drinke excepted;' Cot. Cf. Span. *pitanza*; Ital. *pietanza* (which is prob. corrupted by a supposed connexion with *pietà*, pity); also Span. *pitar*, to distribute or dole out allowances. β. Ducange explains Late L. *pictantia* as a pittance, orig. a dole of the value of a *picta*, which was a very small coin issued by the counts of Poitiers (Pictava). γ. But we also find Late L. *pittantia*, which Thurneysen connects with Ital. *pit-etto*, F. *pet-it*, small, allied to **Piece.**

Pity. (F.─L.) M. E. *pitee.* ─O. F. *pite*, *pitet* (12th cent.). ─ L. *pietātem*, acc. of *pietās*, devoutness. ─ L. *pius*, devout. **Doublet,** *piety.* Der. *pite-ous*, for M. E. *pitous*, from O. F. *piteus* < Late L. *pietōsus*, merciful.

Pivot, a pin on which a wheel, &c. turns. (F.─Ital.─L.?) F. *pivot*. Formed, with dimin. suffix *-ot*, from Ital. *piva*, a pipe. The Ital. *piva* meant (1) a pipe, (2) a tube with fine bore; cf. *pivolo*, a peg. ─ Late L. *pīpa*, a pipe; allied to L. *pīpāre*, to chirp; see Pipe. ¶ So Diez; much disputed.

Pixy, a fairy. (Scand.) Also *picksy*; Cornwall *pisky*. Of Scand. origin; cf. Swed. dial. *pyske*, a dwarf, goblin (Rietz).

Placable. (L.) L. *plācābilis*, easy to be appeased. ─L. *plācāre*, to appease.

Placard. (F. ─ Du.) F. *placard*, *plaquard*, 'a placard, inscription set up; also rough-cast on walls;' Cot. ─ F. *plaquer*, to rough-cast; also to stick or paste on; Cot. ─ Du. *plakken*, to glue or fasten up, formerly 'to plaister,' Hexham. Prob. of imitative origin (Franck).

Place. (F.─L.─Gk.) F. *place*. ─ Folk-L. **plattia*; L. *platea*, also *platĕa*, a broad way, a courtyard. ─ Gk. πλατεῖα, a broad way; fem. of πλατύς, broad. ¶ A *place* was orig. a courtyard or square, a piazza. Cf. Ital. *piazza* (=F. *place*). See Plaice, Plate.

Placenta, a substance in the womb. (L.) L. *placenta*, lit. a flat cake.+Gk. πλακοῦς, a flat cake; cf. πλάξ, a flat surface.

Placid. (F.─L.) F. *placide*, 'calm;' Cot. ─ L. *placidus*, pleasing, gentle. ─ L. *placēre*, to please. See Please.

Plack, a third of a (Scotch) penny. (Du.) From M. Du. *placke*, 'a French sous;' Hexham. Also, 'a spot.' ─ M. Du. *placken*, 'to plaister;' see Placard.

Plagiary. (F.─L.) F. *plagiaire*, one who kidnaps; also 'a book-theef'; Cot. ─L. *plagiārius*, a kidnapper. ─ L. *plagium*, kidnapping; *plagiāre*, to ensnare. ─ L. *plaga*, a net.

Plague. (F.─L.) M. E. *plage.* ─O. F. *plage*, *plague* (F. *plaie*). ─ L. *plāga*, a stroke, blow, injury, disaster.+Gk. πληγή, a blow, plague, Rev. xvi. 21, from πλήσσειν (=*πλήκ-γειν), to strike; cf. L. *plangere*, to strike. Brugm. i. § 569.

Plaice, a fish. (F.─L.) O. F. *plaïse*, *plaïs.* ─ L. *platessa*, a plaice; so called from its flatness. From the base *plat-*, as seen in Gk. πλατύς, flat, broad; cf. **Place.**

Plaid. (C.─L.) Gael. (and Irish) *plaide*, a blanket, plaid. Allied to *peal-laid*, a sheep-skin. ─ Gael. (and Irish) *peall*, a skin. ─ L. *pellis*, a skin. See Pell.

Plain, flat, evident. (F.─L.) F. *plain.* ─ L. *plānus*, flat.

Plaint, a lament. (F. ─ L.) M. E. *pleinte.* ─ O. F. *pleinte.* ─ Late L. *plancta*, for L. *planctus*, lamentation. ─ L. *planctus*, pp. of *plangere*, to bewail. See Plague.

plaintiff. (F.─L.) M.E. *plaintif.* ─ F. *plaintif*, 'a plaintiff;' Cot. Formed with suffix *-if* (L. *-īuus*), from *planctus*, pp. of *plangere* (above).

plaintive. (F. – L.) F. *plaintive*, fem. of F. *plaintif* (above).

Plait. (F. – L.) From M. E. *plait*, sb., a fold. – O. F. *pleit*, *ploit*, *plet*, a fold. – Late L. type **plectum*, for *plic'tum*, short form of *plicitum*, by-form of L. *plicātum*, neut. of *plicātus*, pp. of *plicāre*, to fold; see **Ply**. Cf. **Implicit**; and see **Pleach**.

Plan. (F. – L.) F. *plan*, 'the ground-plat of a building;' Cot. – F. *plan*, flat; learned form of F. *plain*. – L. *plānum*, acc. of *plānus*, flat. Properly, a drawing (for a building) on a flat surface.

plane (1), a level surface. (F. – L.) F. *plane*, fem. of *plan*, flat (above). – L. *plāna*, fem. of *plānus*, flat.

plane (2), a tool; also to render a surface level. (F. – L.) M. E. *plane*, a tool. – F. *plane*. – Late L. *plāna*, a tool for planing. 2. We find also M. E. *planen*, to plane. – F. *planer*. – L. *plānāre*, to plane. – L. *plānus*, flat.

Plane (3), a tree. (F. – L. – Gk.) M.E. *plane*. – F. *plane*. – L. *platanum*, acc. of *platanus*, a plane. – Gk. πλάτανος, a plane; named from its spreading leaves. – Gk. πλατύς, wide. Brugm. i. § 444.

Planet. (F. – L. – Gk.) M. E. *planete*. – O. F. *planete*. – L. *planēta*. – Gk. πλανή-της, a wanderer; also πλανής, a wanderer; the pl. πλάνητες means the wandering stars or planets. – Gk. πλανάομαι, I wander. – Gk. πλάνη, wandering.

Planisphere, a sphere projected on a plane. (L. *and* Gk.) From L. *plānus*, flat; and E. *sphere*, of Gk. origin; see **Sphere**.

Plank, a board. (F. – L.) M. E. *planke*. – N. F. (Picard) *planke*; Norman *planque*. – L. *planca*, a flat board. Nasalised from the base *plac-*, flat; see **Placenta**.

Plant. (L.) M. E. *plante*. A. S. *plante*. – L. *planta*, a plant; properly a spreading sucker or shoot; also, the sole of the foot. From the base *plat-*; see **Place**.

plantain. (F. – L.) F. *plantain*. – L. *plantāginem*, acc. of *plantāgo*, a plantain. Named from its spreading leaf; allied to **Plant** (above).

plantigrade, walking on the sole of the foot. (L.) From *planti-*, for *planta*, the sole or flat part of the foot; *grad-ī*, to walk. See **Plant, Place**.

Plash (1), a puddle, shallow pool. (E. ?) M. E. *plasche*. Cf. M. Du. *plasch*, a plash, pool; *plasschen in 't water*, to plash or plunge in the water; Hexham.

Cf. also G. *platschen*, Dan. *pladske* (for **platske*), Swed. *plaska* (for **platska*, to dabble; from the Teut. base **plat*, to strike, seen in A. S. *plættan*, to strike.

Plash (2), the same as **Pleach**.

Plaster. (L. – Gk.) M. E. *plastre*; A. S. *plaster*. [Also spelt *plaister* = O. F. *plaistre*.] – L. *emplastrum*, a plaster for wounds, the first syllable being dropped. – Gk. ἔμπλαστρον, a plaster, a form used by Galen instead of ἔμπλαστον, a plaster, neut. of ἔμπλαστος, daubed on or over. – Gk. ἐμπλάσσειν, to daub on. – Gk. ἐμ- (for ἐν), on; πλάσσειν, to mould, form in clay or wax. Here πλάσσειν = **πλατ-γειν*; allied to E. *fold*, vb.

plastic. (L. – Gk.) L. *plasticus*. – Gk. πλαστικός, fit for moulding. – Gk. πλάσσειν, to mould (above).

Plat (1), **Plot**, a patch of ground; see **Plot** (2).

Plat (2), to plait; see **Plait**.

Platane, a plane-tree. (L. – Gk.) L. *platanus*. – Gk. πλάτανος; see **Plane** (3).

Plate, a thin piece of metal, flat dish. (F. – L.) M. E. *plate*. – O. F. *plate*; properly the fem. of *plat*, flat. – Late L. *platta*, a lamina, plate of metal, fem. of Folk-L. *plattus*, flat. Cf. Span. *plata*, plate, silver; but the Span. word was borrowed from French; whence also Du. Dan. *plat*, G. Swed. *platt*, flat. + Lithuan. *platus*, G. πλατύς, broad; Skt. *prthus*, large. (√PLET.)

plateau, a flat space. (F. – L.) F. *plateau*, for O. F. *platel*, a small plate; dimin. of *plat*, a plate. – F. *plat*, flat (above).

platform, a flat surface, level scaffolding; formerly, a ground-plan, plan. (F. – L.) F. *plateforme*, 'a platform, modell;' Cot. – F. *plate*, fem. of *plat*, flat; *forme*, form. See above; and see **Form**.

platina, a metal. (Span. – F. – L.) Span. *platina*; named from its silvery appearance. – Span. *plata*, silver. – O.F. *plate*, hammered plate, also silver plate; see **Plate**.

platitude. (F. – L.) F. *platitude*, flatness, insipidity. Coined from F. *plat*, flat : see **Plate**.

Platoon, a company of men. (F. – L.) Earlier form *peloton* (Stanford). – F. *peloton*, a tennis-ball, also a group of men, a platoon. Dimin. of M. F. *pelote*, a tennis-ball; see **Pellet**.

Platter, a flat plate. (F. – L.) M.E. *plater*. – A. F. *plater* (Bozon). Formed (with suffix -*er*) from O. F. *plat*, a plate ; see Plateau.

Plaudit, applause. (L.) Formerly *plauditè* or *plaudity*. − L. *plaudite*, clap your hands; 2 pers. pl. imp. of *plaudere*, to applaud.

Play, a game. (E.) M. E. *play*. A. S. *plega*, a game, sport ; also (commonly), a fight, battle. Cf. A. S. *plegian*, to play, clap ; *plegian mid handum*, to clap hands. ¶ Not allied to *plight* (Franck).

Plea, an excuse. (F. − L.) M. E. *plee*, *play*. − A. F. *plee* (Bozon) ; O. F. *ple*, *plai*, occasional forms of O. F. *plait*, *plaid*, a plea. − Late L. *placitum*, a decree, sentence, &c. (with numerous meanings), orig. a decision, that which has seemed good. − L. *placitum*, neut. of *placitus*, pp. of *placēre*, to please. See Plead, Please.

Pleach, Plash, to intertwine boughs in a hedge. (F. − L.) M. E. *plechen*. − O. F. *plescier*, *plessier*, later *plesser*, ' to plash, plait young branches,' &c. ; Cot. − Late L. type *plectiāre*, later *plessāre*, to pleach. − Late L. type *plectia*, later *plessa*, a thicket of woven boughs. − L. *plectere*, to weave ; extended from base PLEK, to weave, whence also *plicāre*, to fold. See Ply.

Plead. (F. − L.) M. E. *pleden*. − O. F. *plaider*, to plead, argue. − O. F. *plaid*, a plea ; see Plea.

Please. (F. − L.) M. E. *plesen*. − O. F. *plesir*, *plaisir*, to please (F. *plaire*). − L. *placēre*, to please. Allied to *plācāre*, to appease. **Der.** *pleas-ant*, from O. F. *plesant*, pleasing, pres. pt. of *plesir* ; also *dis-please*.

pleasure. (F. − L.) An E. spelling of F. *plaisir*, pleasure (like E. *leisure* for A.F. *leisir*). This F. sb. is merely the infin. mood used substantively. − L. *placēre* ; see Please.

Pleat, another form of Plait.

Plebeian, vulgar. (F. − L.) O. F. *plcbeien* (F. *plébéien*) ; formed, with suffix -*en* (L. -*ānus*), from L. *plēbēius*, adj., from *plēbēs*, more commonly *plebs*, the people. Cf. Gk. πλῆθος, a multitude.

Pledge, a security, surety. (F. − O. Low G.) M. E. *plegge*, a hostage, security. − O. F. *plege*, a surety (F. *pleige*). [Allied to O. F. *plevir*, M. F. *pleuvir*, to warrant.] − O. Sax. *plegan*, to promise, pledge oneself ; cf. O. H. G. *pflegan*, to answer for (G. *pflegen*), A.S. *pléon*, to risk, *pleoh*, risk (Franck). See Plight (1).

Pleiocene, more recent; **Pleistocene,** most recent. (Gk.) From Gk. πλείω-ν, more, or πλεῖστο-s, most ; and καινός, recent, new. Πλείων, πλεῖστος are comp. and superl. of πολύς, much.

Plenary, full. (Late L. − L.) Late L. *plēnārius*, entire. − L. *plēnus*, full. +Gk. πληρής, πλέ-ως, full ; πίμ-πλη-μι, I fill. Allied to **Full**.

plenipotentiary, having full powers. (L.) Coined from L. *plēni*-, for *plēno*-, decl. stem of *plēnus*, full ; and *potenti*-, for *potens*, powerful ; with suffix -*ārius* ; see Potent.

plenitude, fullness. (F. − L.) O. F. *plenitude*. − L. *plēnitūdo*, fullness. − L. *plēni*-, for *plēnus*, full ; with suffix -*tūdo*.

plenty, abundance. (F. − L.) M. E. *plentee*. − O. F. *plente*, *plentet*. − L. *plēnitātem*, acc. of *plēnitās*, fullness. − L. *plēni*-, for *plēnus*, full. **Der.** *plenteous*, M. E. *plenteus*, often spelt *plentivous*, from O.F. *plentivos* ; from O. F. *plentif*, answering to Late L. form *plēnitīvus*.

Pleonasm. (L. − Gk.) L. *pleonasmus*. − Gk. πλεονασμός, abundance. − Gk. πλεονάζειν, to abound, lit. to be more. − Gk. πλέον, neut. of πλέων, πλείων, more, comparative of πολύς, much, allied to πλέως, full. See Plenary.

Plethora, excessive fullness, esp. of blood. (L. − Gk.) L. *plēthōra*. − Gk. πληθώρη, fullness. − Gk. πλῆθ-ος, a throng, crowd ; allied to πλήρης, full. See Plenary.

Pleurisy, inflammation of the *pleura*, or membrane which covers the lungs. (F. − L. − Gk.) F. *pleurésie*. − L. *pleurisis* ; also *pleurītis*. − Gk. πλευρῖτις, pleurisy. − Gk. πλευρά, a rib, side, pleura. **Der.** *pleurit-ic*, from πλευρῖτ-ις ; *pleuro-pneumonia*, inflammation of pleura and lungs, from πνεύμων, a lung; see Pneumatic.

Pliable, flexible. See Ply.

pliant. (F. − L.) F. *pliant*, pres. pt. of *plier*, to bend ; see Ply.

Plight (1), pledge; hence, as vb., to pledge. (E.) M. E. *pliht*, danger, also engagement, pledge. A. S. *pliht*, risk, danger. Formed, with suffix -*t* (Idg. -*ti*-), from the strong vb. *pléon*, (*pleh-an*), pt. t. *pleah*, to risk; cf. *pleoh*, danger.+ M. Du. *plicht*, duty, debt, use ; *plegen*, to be accustomed ; G. *pflicht*, duty, from O. H. G. *pflegan* (G. *pflegen*), to promise or engage to do. Teut. root, **pleh-*.

Der. *plight,* vb., A. S. *plihtan,* weak vb., from *pliht,* sb.

Plight (2), to fold; as sb., a fold, also state, condition. (F.–L.) Misspelt. In all these senses, the sb. was formerly M. E. *plite.* – O. F. *plite,* fem. (given as *plyte* in Godefroy, *pliste, plyte* in Roquefort), state, condition. – L. *plicita,* fem. of *plicitus,* pp. of *plicāre,* to fold. It is the fem. of *plait*; see **Plait** and **Ply.**

Plinth, the lowest part of the base of a column. (F. – L. – Gk. ; *or* L. – Gk.) F. *plinthe.* – L. *plinthus.* – Gk. πλίνθος, a brick, plinth. Perhaps allied to **Flint.**

Plod. (E.) Orig. to splash through water or mud; hence, to trudge on laboriously, toil onward. From M. E. *plod,* a puddle. Cf. Irish *plod, plodan,* a pool; *plodach,* a puddle, whence *plodanachd,* paddling in water; Gael. *plod, plodan,* a pool. Also E. Fries. *pludern,* to splash about in water; Dan. dial. *pludder,* Dan. *pladder,* mud. Of imitative origin; cf. **Plash** (1).

Plot (1), a conspiracy. (F.) Short for *complot*(?); for the loss of *com-,* cf. *fence* for *defence, sport* for *disport.* – F. *complot,* 'a complot, conspiracy;' Cot. Of unknown origin; Körting, § 2053. β. Or, more likely, short for *plotform,* variant of *platform,* a map or plan; see **platform.** For *plotform,* see Gascoigne, Art of Venerie, 40; and cf. *plat,* a map (Mirror for Magistrates).

Plot (2), a small piece of ground. (E.) M. E. *plotte.* [Cf. *plat,* 2 Kings ix. 26.] A. S. *plot,* a plot of ground; Cockayne's Leechdoms, iii. 286. Note Dan. *plet,* as in *græsplet,* a grass-plat.

Plough. (E.) M. E. *plouh, plow*; also A. S. *plōh,* in the sense 'plot of land.' E. Fries. *plōg.*+Du. *ploeg*; Icel. *plōgr,* a plough; Swed. *plog,* Dan. *plov*; also O. Fries. *ploch,* G. *pflug.* [Lithuan. *plugas,* Russ. *plug*' are borrowed from Teutonic.]

Plover, a bird. (F. – L.) M. E. *plover.* – O. F. *plovier,* later *pluvier.* Formed from L. **pluuārius,* equivalent to L. *pluuiālis,* rainy. – L. *pluuia,* rain; see **Pluvial.** These birds were said to be most seen and caught in a rainy season; whence also the G. name *regenpfeifer* (rain-piper).

Pluck, to snatch. (E.) M. E. *plukken.* A. S. *pluccian,* Matt. xii. 1.+Du. *plukken,* Icel. *plokka, plukka* (perhaps borrowed), Dan. *plukke,* Swed. *plocka,* G. *pflücken.* ¶ Some think it not a Teut. word; but

borrowed from Late L. *piluccāre,* whence Ital. *piluccare,* to pluck out hair; from L. *pilus,* a hair; see **Pile** (3). **Der.** *pluck,* sb., a butcher's term for the heart, liver, and lights of an animal, whence mod. E. *pluck,* courage, *plucky,* adj.

Plug. (Du.) M. Du. *plugge,* Du. *plug,* a peg, bung. Cf. Low G. *plugge,* Swed. *plugg,* G. *pflock,* a peg, plug.

Plum. (L. – Gk.) A. S. *plūme,* a plum ; formed (by change of *r* to *l*) from L. *prūnum,* a plum. See **Prune.**

Plumage. (F. – L.) F. *plumage,* 'feathers ;' Cot. – F. *plume.* – L. *plūma,* a feather ; see **Plume.**

Plumb, a lead on a string, as a plummet. (F. – L.) Formerly *plomb*; M. E. *plom.* – F. *plomb,* 'lead, a plummet ;' Cot. – L. *plumbum,* lead. Cf. Gk. μόλυβος, μόλυβδος, lead. **Der.** *plumb,* vb., to sound a depth ; *plumb-er,* sb., F. *plombier.*

plumbago, blacklead. (L.) L. *plumbāgo,* a kind of leaden ore. – L. *plumbum,* lead (above).

Plume. (F. – L.) F. *plume.* – L. *plūma,* a small feather, down. Allied to E. *fly,* vb. See **Fly.** Brugm. i. § 681.

Plummet. (F. – L.) M. E. *plommet.* – O. F. *plommet*; M. F. *plombet*; dimin. of *plomb,* lead; see **Plumb** (above).

Plump (1), full, round, fleshy. (E. *or* O. Low G.) M. E. *plomp,* rude, clownish; also *plump,* sb., a cluster or clump. The word seems to be E., especially if the prov. E. *plim,* to swell out, is an allied verb. Cf. *plump,* to swell (Nares).+M. Du. *plomp,* clownish, dull (a metaphorical use, from the notion of thickness); E. Fries. and Low G. *plump,* bulky, thick ; Swed. Dan. G. *plump,* clumsy, blunt, coarse. See **Plump** (3). **Der.** *plump-er,* a kind of vote (to *swell out* a candidate's chances against all the rest).

Plump (2), straight downward. (F. – L.) Formerly *plum, plumb*; Milton, P. L. ii. 933. – F. *à plomb,* downright (cf. Ital. *cadere a piombo,* to fall plump, lit. like lead). – F. *plomb,* lead. – L. *plumbum,* lead. See below, and see **Plunge.**

Plump (3), vb., to fall heavily down. (E. ?). Of imitative origin. Cf. E. Fries. *plumpen,* to fall heavily, *plempen,* to plunge into water; so also Du. *plompen,* G. *plumpen,* Swed. *plumpa,* to fall heavily. Under the influence of this word the form *plumb,* 'straight downward,' has become *plump.* See above.

Plunder, to pillage. (G.) G. *plündern*, to steal trash, to pillage; from *plunder*, sb., trumpery, trash, baggage, lumber; orig. of Low G. origin; cf. M. Du. *plunderen, plonderen*, to pillage, connected with Low G. *plunnen, plunden*, E. Fries. *plünde, plünne*, rags, worthless household stuff. Hence to *plunder* is to strip a house even of its least valuable contents.

Plunge. (F. – L.) F. *plonger*, 'to plunge, dive;' Cot. Formed from a Late L. **plumbicāre*, not found, but verified by Picard *plonquer*, to plunge; see Diez, s. v. *piombare*. A frequentative form from L. *plumbum*, lead; cf. Ital. *piombare*, to throw, hurl, fall heavily like lead, from *piombo*, lead. See Plump (2).

Pluperfect. (L.) Englished from L. *plusquamperfectum*, by giving to *plūs* the F. pronunciation, and dropping *quam*. The lit. sense is ' more than perfect,' applied to a tense. – L. *plūs*, more; *quam*, than; *perfectum*, perfect. See Perfect.

Plural. (F. – L.) M. E. *plural.* – O. F. *plurel* (F. *pluriel*). – L. *plūrālis*, plural, expressive of *more* than one. – L. *plūr-*, stem of *plūs*, more. Allied to Gk. πλείων, more, πλέως, full; and to **Plenary**. Brugm. ii. § 135.

Plurisy, superabundance. (L.; *mis-formed*.) Shak. uses *plurisy* to express plethora; so also Massinger and Ford. Formed from L. *plūri-*, from *plūs*, more, by an extraordinary (prob. a jocular) confusion with *pleurisy*.

Plush. (F. – L.) F. *peluche*, 'shag, plush;' Cot. (Cf. Span. *pelusa*, nap, Ital. *peluzzo*, soft down.) From the fem. of a Late L. form **pilūceus*, hairy, not found. – L. *pilus*, hair. See Perruque, Pile (3).

Pluvial, rainy. (F. – L.) F. *pluvial.* – L. *pluuiālis*, rainy. – L. *pluuia*, rain. – L. *plu-it*, it rains. Cf. Skt. *plu-*, to swim. From Idg. **plu*, weak grade of √PLEU, to swim; cf. Gk. πλέειν, to swim.

Ply. (F. – L.) M. E. *plien*, to bend, to mould as wax (hence, to toil at). – F. *plier*, 'to fould, plait, ply, bend;' Cot. – L. *plicāre*, to fold. +Gk. πλέκειν, Russ. *pleste*, G. *flechten*, to weave, plait. (√PLEK.) Der. *pli-ant*, bending, from F. *pliant*, pres. pt. of *plier*; *pli-ers* or *ply-ers*, pincers for bending wire; *pli-able* (F. *pliable*).

Pneumatic. (Gk.) Gk. πνευματικός, relating to wind or air. – Gk. πνεῦμα (stem πνευματ-), wind, air. – Gk. πνέειν (for πνέϝ-ειν), to blow. Allied to **Neese**.

Pneumonia. (Gk.) Gk. πνευμονία, disease of the lungs. – Gk. πνευμον-, stem of πνεύμων, for πλεύμων, a lung, by a false connexion with πνέειν, to breathe (above). The Gk. πλεύμων is allied to L. *pulmo*, a lung; Lith. *plauczei*, pl. the lungs.

Poach (1), to dress eggs. (F. – O. Low G.?) Formerly *poch.* – F. *pocher*; Cot. gives ' *œuf poché*, a potched (poached) egg.' The orig. sense was prob. ' a pouched' egg, i. e. an egg so dressed as to preserve it in the form of a pocket. – F. *poche*, a pocket; see **Pouch**. See Scheler's explanation.

Poach (2), to intrude into preserves. (F. – L.) M.F. *pocher*; Cot. explains *pocher le labeur d'autruy* by ' to poch into, or incroach upon, another man's imploiment, practise, or trade.' The old sense was ' to thrust or dig out with the fingers,' Cot. (if this be the same word) ; or rather, to put the thumb into. Cf. prov. E. *poach*, to tread into holes ; Picard *pocher*, ' tâter un fruit avec le pouce,' *peucher*, ' presser avec le *pouce* ;' Corblet. Perhaps from L. *pollicem*, acc. of *pollex*, the thumb; cf. O. F. *pochier, poucier*, the thumb (from the adj. *pollicāris*).

Pock (1), a pustule. (E.) *Small pox* = small *pocks*, where *pocks* is pl. of *pock*. M. E. *pokke*, a pock, pl. *pokkes*. A. S. *poc*, a pustule. + E. Fries. *pok, pokke* ; Du. *pok*, G. *pocke*, a pock. Cf. Gael. *pucaid*, a pimple, Irish *pucoid*, a pustule, *pucadh*, a swelling up, Gael. *poc*, to become like a bag (from E.).

Pocket, a small pouch. (F. – Scand.) M. E. *poket.* – Norman dial. **poquette*, dimin. of O. Norman *poque* (see Norman dial. *pouque*, Métivier), the same as F. *poche*, a pocket, pouch. – Icel. *poki*, a bag; cf. M. Du. *poke*, a bag (Hexham). See Poke (1).

Pod, a husk. (E.) Of doubtful origin. Cf. M. Du. *puden*, 'huskes,' Hexham ; Westphal. *puddek*, a lump, a pudding ; Low G. *puddig*, thick ; prov. E. *poddy*, fat and round ; *puddle*, short and fat. See Pudding and Pout.

Poem. (F. – L. – Gk.) M.F. *poëme*, Cot. – L. *poëma.* – Gk. ποίημα, a work, composition, poem. – Gk. ποιεῖν, to make.

poesy. (F. – L. – Gk.) M. E. *poesie.* – M. F. *poësie.* – L. *poësin*, acc. of *poësis*, poetry. – Gk. ποίησις, a composition. poem. – Gk. ποιεῖν, to make.

poet. (F. – L. – Gk.) O. F. *poëte.* – L.

poëta. — Gk. *ποιητής*, a maker. — Gk. *ποιεῖ-ν,* to make; with suffix *-της* of the agent.

Poignant. (F. — L.) F. *poignant,* stinging, pres. part. of *poindre,* to prick. — L. *pungere,* to prick.

point. (F. — L.) M. E. *point.* — O. F. *point, poinct,* a point, prick. — L. *punctum* ; orig. neut. of *punctus,* pp. of *pungere,* to prick.

Poise, Peise, to balance, weigh. (F. — L.) M. E. *poisen, peisen.* — O. F. *poiser,* later *peser,* to weigh ; A. F. *peiser.* — L. *pensāre,* to weigh. Allied to O. F. *pois,* A. F. *peis,* a weight (now misspelt *poids,* from a notion of its being derived from L. *pondus,* which is *not* the case). — Late L. *pensum, pensa,* a portion, weight ; L. *pensum,* a portion weighed out to spinners, a task. — L. *pensus,* pp. of *pendere,* to weigh. See **Pendant.**

Poison. (F. — L.) F. *poison,* poison. — L. *pōtiōnem,* acc. of *pōtio,* a draught, esp. a poisonous draught ; see **Potion.**

Poitrel, Peitrel, armour for a horse's breast. (F. — L.) M.F. *poitral,* Cot. ; A.F. *peitral.* — L. *pectorāle,* neut. of *pectorālis,* belonging to the breast. See **Pectoral.**

Poke (1), a bag, pouch. (Scand.) M. E. *poke.* [Cf. A. S. **poca, pocca, pohha, pohcha, poha,* a bag.] — Icel. *poki* ; M. Du. *poke,* a bag.

Poke (2), to thrust, push. (E.) M. E. *poken, pukken* (whence Irish *poc,* a blow, kick, Corn. *poc,* a shove, Gael. *puc,* to push). + Du. *poken* ; E. Fries. *pokern,* frequent., to keep on poking about ; Pomeran. *pök-en* ; G. *pochen.* From Teut. base **puk* ; of imitative origin. Der. *pok-er.*

Pole (1), a large stake. (L.) M. E. *pole,* formed (by usual change of *ā* to *ō*) from A. S. *pāl,* a pale, pole. — L. *pālus,* a stake ; see **Pale** (1).

Pole (2), a pivot, end of earth's axis. (F. — L. — Gk.) O. F. *pol.* — L. *polum,* acc. of *polus.* — Gk. *πόλος,* a pivot, hinge. — Gk. *πέλειν,* to be in motion ; allied to Russ. *koleso,* a wheel. (√QEL.) Brugm. i. § 632.

Pole-ax, a kind of ax. (L. and E.) From *pole* and *ax.* Cf. Westphal. *pål-exe,* from *pål,* a pole. The Low G. *pollexe,* as if from *polle,* the poll, is also spelt *bollexe,* and rather represents the obs. E. *bole-ax,* Icel. *bolöxi,* from the *bole* of a tree.

Polecat, a kind of weasel. (Hybrid.) M. E. *polcat,* where *cat* is the ordinary word ; also *pulkat.* From F. *poule,* a

hen, because the *pole-cat* slays capons ; see Chaucer, C. T. 12789. Cf. the pronunciation of *poul-try,* from A. F. *poletrie* ; and see **Catchpoll.**

Polemical, warlike. (Gk.) From Gk. *πολεμικός,* warlike. — Gk. *πόλεμος,* war.

Police. (F. — L. — Gk.) F. *police,* orig. civil government. — L. *polītīa.* — Gk. *πολιτεία,* polity, government. — Gk. *πολίτης,* a citizen. — Gk. *πόλις,* a state, city. Related to *πολύς,* much ; cf. Skt. *purī,* a town. Der. *polic-y,* O. F. *policie* < L. *polītīa* ; *polit-ic,* from Gk. *πολιτικός,* adj. Der. *acro-polis, metro-polis, cosmo-polite.*

Policy, a warrant for money in the funds, a contract of insurance. (F. — Late L. — Gk.) Confused with *policy,* from *police,* with which it has nothing to do. — F. *police* (Hamilton ; cf. M. Ital. *poliza,* a schedule, Florio). — Late L. *politicum, polecticum,* corruptions of *polyptychum,* a register (a common word ; Ducange). — Gk. *πολύπτυχον,* a piece of writing in many folds, hence a long register ; orig. neut. of *πολύπτυχος,* having many folds. — Gk. *πολύ-,* much ; *πτυχο-,* crude form of *πτύξ,* a fold, leaf, layer, connected with *πτύσσειν,* to fold up. (Supp. to Diez.) β. Better thus : the Port. form *apólice,* M. Span. *póliça,* M. Ital. *póliza, pólisa,* prob. represent Late L. *apódissa, apódixa,* 'cautio de sumpta pecunia ;' Duc. Cf. Port. *apodixe,* a plain proof. — Late Gk. *ἀπόδειξις,* a shewing forth, a proof. — Gk. *ἀποδείκνυμι,* I point out. — Gk. *ἀπό,* from, forth ; *δείκνυμι,* I shew. (Körting, § 6258.)

Polish, to make smooth. (F. — L.) F. *poliss-,* stem of pres. pt. of *polir.* — L. *polīre,* to make smooth.

polite. (L.) L. *polītus,* polished ; pp. of *polīre,* to make smooth (above).

Politic ; see **Police.**

Polka, a dance. (Polish.) Said to have been first danced by a Bohemian peasant-girl in 1831, and to have been named *polka* at Prague in 1835. — Pol. *Polka,* a Polish woman. Another dance is called the *Polonaise,* with the same literal sense ; another the *Cracovienne,* lit. a woman of Cracow ; another the *Mazurka,* q. v.

Poll, the head, esp. the back part (O. Low G.) Hence it means also a register of heads or persons, a voting-place, &c. M. E. *pol,* a poll ; *pol bi pol,* head by head, separately. — Low G. *polle* ; M. Du. *polle,* *pol, bol,* 'head or pate,' Hexham ; Swed. dial. *pull,* Dan. *puld* (for *pull*). Cf. E. Fries. *pol,* round, full, fleshy. **Der.** *poll,* to cut off the hair of the head. Also *poll-ard,* a tree that is *polled,* leaving a large knobby head ; also, formerly, a *clipped* coin.

Pollen. (L.) L. *pollen, pollis,* fine flour. Cf. Gk. πάλη, fine meal.

Pollock, Pollack, a fish. (E.) Prob. from E. *poll;* cf. E. *pollard,* which is a name of the chub. See *pollard,* under **Poll.** Hence Irish *pullog,* a pollock; Gael. *pollag,* a whiting. (Doubtful.)

Pollute. (L.) L. *pollūtus,* pp. of *polluere,* to defile. Orig. to wash over, as a flooded river. — L. *pol-,* allied to O. Lat. *por-,* towards ; *luere,* to wash ; see **Lave.**

Polo, a game. (Balti.) ' It comes from Baltí ; *polo* being properly, in the language of that region, the ball used in the game;' Yule. Balti is in the high valley of the Indus.

Polony, a Bologna sausage. (Ital.) Ital. *Bologna,* where they were made (Evelyn).

Poltroon, a dastard, lazy fellow. (F. — Ital. — L.) F. *poltron,* a sluggard ; Cot. — Ital. *poltrone,* a varlet, coward, sluggard; cf. *poltrare,* to lie in bed. — Ital. *poltro,* a bed, couch ; orig. ' a colt,' also ' a varlet,' Florio. Cf. F. *poutre,* a beam, M. F. *poutre,* ' a filly,' Cot. — Late L. *pullitrum,* acc. of *pullitrus,* a colt ; Duc. — L. *pullus,* a colt, foal. See **Foal.** For change of sense, cf. **Pulley, Chevron.**

Poly-, many. (L. — Gk.) L. *poly-.* — Gk. πολύ-, decl. stem of πολύς, much. + Skt. *puru-,* much. Allied to **Full.**

polyanthus, a flower. (L. — Gk.) L. *polyanthus.* — Gk. πολύανθος, many-flowered. — Gk. πολύ-, many ; ἄνθος, flower.

polygamy. (F. — L. — Gk.) F. *polygamie.* — L. *polygamia.* — Gk. πολυγαμία, a marrying of many wives. — Gk. πολύ-, much; -γαμία, from γάμος, marriage.

polyglot, speaking many languages. (Gk.) Attic Gk. πολύγλωττος. — Gk. πολύ-, much, many ; γλῶττα = γλῶσσα, tongue, language ; see **Gloss.**

polygon, a many-sided plane figure. (L. — Gk.) L. *polygōnum.* — Gk. πολύγωνον, neut. of πολύγωνος, having many angles. — Gk. πολύ-, many ; γωνία, an angle, from γόνυ, a knee.

polyhedron, a many-sided solid

figure. (Gk.) Gk. πολύ-, many ; -εδρον, for ἕδρα, a base, from the base ἑδ-, to sit ; see **Sit.**

polynomial. (Gk. *and* L.) Coined to go with *bi-nomial.* — Gk. πολύ-, many ; L. *nōmen,* a name, term.

Polypus, Polyp, an aquatic animal of the radiate type. (L. — Gk.) L. *polypus.* — Gk. πολύπους, many-footed. — Gk. πολύ s, many ; πούς, a foot. ¶ Cf. F. *polype,* Ital. and Span. *polipo,* L. *polypūs* (gen. *polypī*); all false forms, due to treating the Lat. ending *-pūs* as if it were *-p-ŭs.*

polysyllable. (Gk.) From *poly-* and *syllable.* Cf. Gk. πολυσύλλαβος, adj.

polytheism. (Gk.) From *poly-* and *theism.*

Pomade, Pommade. (F. — Ital. — L.) F. *pommade,* pomatum ; so called because orig. made with apples. — Ital. *pomada, pomata,* ' a pomado to supple one's lips, lip salve,' Florio. — Ital. *pomo,* an apple. — L. *pōmum,* an apple, fruit.

Pomander, a globe-shaped box for holding ointments or perfumes. (F. — L. *and* Arab.) Spelt *pomander* (1518); *pomaunder* (Skelton). Cf. M. F. *pomendier,* ' a pomaunder;' Palsgrave (prob. from E.) ; and note M. Span. *poma,* a pomander (Minsheu), which is a fem. form, from *pomo,* an apple. β. The suffix *-ander* is for *ambre,* amber. We find ' *pomum ambre* for the pestelence '; MS. Harl. 2378, p. 324, in Medical Works of the 14th cent., ed. Henslow, p. 122. Cf. O. F. *pomme d'ambre* (Rom. Rose, 21008). — L. *pōmum,* an apple ; and see **Amber.**

Pomegranate. (F. — L.) O. F. *pome grenate* (also turned into *pome de grenate* by confusion of the sense); the same as Ital. *pomo granato.* — L. *pōmum,* an apple ; *grānātum,* full of seeds, from *grānum,* a grain, seed ; see **Grain.**

pommel, a knob. (F. — L.) M. E. *pomel,* a boss. — O. F. *pomel* (later *pommeau*), a pommel ; lit. ' small apple.' Dimin. from L. *pōmum,* an apple.

Pomp. (F. — L. — Gk.) F. *pompe.* — L. *pompa.* — Gk. πομπή, a sending, escorting, solemn procession. — Gk. πέμπειν, to send.

Pond. (E.) M. E. *pond,* variant of *pound,* an enclosure ; it means a pool formed by damming up water ; see **Pound** (2). Cf. Irish *pont,* (1) a pound, (2) a pond.

Ponder, to weigh in the mind, consider. (L.) L. *ponderāre,* to weigh. — L.

ponder-, for **pondes-*, stem of *pondus*, a weight. **–** L. *pendere*, to weigh. See **Pendant.**

Ponent, western. (F. – L.) M.F. *ponent*, ' the west ; ' Cot. – L. *pōnent-*, stem of pres. pt. of *pōnere*, to lay, hence to set (as the sun). See **Position.**

Poniard. (F. – L. ; *with* G. *suffix*.) F. *poignard*, a dagger. **–** F. *poing* (O. F. *poign*), the fist ; with suffix *-ard* < G. *hart* (lit. hard). [So also Ital. *pugnale*, a poniard, from *pugno*, fist ; Span. *puñal*, a poniard, from *puño*, fist, handful, hilt.] **–** L. *pugnus*, fist. See **Pugnacious.**

Pontiff. (F. – L.) M. F. *pontif* ; F. *pontife*. **–** L. *pontifex*, a Roman high-priest ; lit. ' a path-maker ' or ' road-maker,' but the reason for the name is not known. **–** L. *ponti-*, representing *pons*, a path, a bridge ; *facere*, to make. Cf. Gk. πόντος, sea. Brugm. i. § 140.

Pontoon. (F. – L. – C.) F. *ponton*, a lighter, bridge of boats, ' a wherry,' Cot. **–** L. *pontōnem*, acc. of *ponto*, a boat, bridge of boats. The word is of Celt. origin ; see **Punt.**

Pony. (F. – L.) Cf. Gael. *ponaidh*, a little horse, a pony ; vulgar Irish *poni*, both borrowed from English. Lowl. Sc. *powney*. **–** O. F. *poulenet*, a little colt (Godefroy) ; dimin. of *poulain*, a colt, foal. **–** Late L. acc. *pullānum*, a young horse. **–** L. *pull-us*, a foal ; cognate with E. **Foal.**

Poodle, a dog. (G.) G. *pudel*, a poodle ; Low G. *pudel*, *pudel-hund*, allied to Low G. *pudeln*, to waddle, used of fat persons and short-legged animals. Cf. Low G. *pudel-dikk*, unsteady on the feet, *puddig*, thick. Allied to **Pudding.**

Pooh. (F.) M. F. *pouac*, ' faugh,' Cot. Cf. Icel. *pū*, pooh. Of imitative origin.

Pool (1), a small body of water. (E.) M. E. *pol*, *pool*. A. S. *pōl* ; [Irish *poll*, *pull*, a hole, pit ; Gael. *poll*, a hole, pit, bog, pool ; W. *pwll*, Corn. *pol*, Manx *poyl*, Bret. *poull*, a pool].**+**Du. *poel*, G. *pfuhl*, O. H. G. *pfuol*. Teut. type *pōloz ; cf. Lith. *balà*, a swamp. (The Celtic forms are borrowed.)

Pool (2), receptacle for the stakes at cards. (F. – L.) F. *poule*, (1) a hen, (2) a pool, at various games ; the stakes being the eggs to be got from the hen. **–** Late L. *pulla*, a hen ; fem. of L. *pullus*, a young animal ; see **Foal.**

Poop. (F. – L. ; *or* F. – Ital. – L.) *poupe*, *pouppe*. **–** L. *puppim*, acc. of *puppis*, hinder part of a ship. ¶ Or F. *poupe* is from Ital. *poppa*, poop ; Hatzfeld.

Poor. (F. – L.) From M. E. *poure* (= *povre*), poor. **–** O. F. *povre*, poor. **–** L. *pauperem*, acc. of *pauper* ; see **Pauper.**

Pop. (E.) ' To *poppe*, coniectare ; ' Levins. Of imitative origin ; allied to M. E. *poupen*, to blow a horn ; also to **Puff.**

Pope, the father of a church, bishop of Rome. (L. – Gk.) M. E. *pope* ; A. S. *pāpa*, pope, with the usual change from *ā* to *ō*. **–** L. *pāpa*, pope, father ; see **Papal.**

Popinjay, orig. a parrot. (F. – Bavarian *and* L. ; *with modified suffix*.) M. E. *popingay*, also spelt *papeiay* (= *papejay*). The *n* is inserted as in *passe-n-ger*, *messe-n-ger*. **–** F. *papegai*, ' a parrot or popinjay ; ' Cot. Cf. Span. *papagayo*, Port. *papagaio*, a parrot ; (whence Arab. *babaghā*, a parrot). β. But there is also O. F. *papegau*, a parrot (13th cent.), Ital. *papagallo*, a parrot, lit. ' a talking cock ; ' and this is the older form. [The change was due to the substitution of *jay* (F. *gai*, *geai*) for ' cock,' because the jay seemed to come nearer than a cock to the nature of a parrot.] Cf. Bavarian *pappel*, a parrot, from *pappeln*, to chatter (= E. *babble*). A similar name is Lowl. Sc. *bubblyjock* (i. e. babble-jack), a turkey-cock.

Poplar, a tree. (F. – L.) O. F. *poplier* ; F. *peuplier*. Formed with suffix *-ier* (= L. *-ārius*) from O. F. *pople, later *peuple*, a poplar. **–** L. *pōpulum*, acc. of *pōpulus*, a poplar.

Poplin. (F.) F. *popeline*, a fabric ; at first called *papeline*, A. D. 1667 (Littré). [Therefore not from *Poppeling* or *Popper-ingen*, near Ypres, in W. Flanders ; as in N. and Q. 6 S. vi. 305.]

Poppy. (L.) A. S. *popig*, also *popæg* ; from L. *papāuer*, a poppy (with change of suffix).

Populace. (F. – Ital. – L.) F. *populace*. **–** Ital. *popolazzo*, *popolaccio*, ' the grosse, vile, common people ; ' Florio. **–** Ital. *popolo*, people. **–** L. acc. *populum*. ¶ The suffix *-accio* is depreciatory.

popular. (F. – L.) F. *populaire*. **–** L. *populāris*, adj., from *populus*, the people.

Porcelain. (F. – Ital. – L.) Named from the resemblance of its polished surface to that of the univalve shell with the same name. **–** F. *porcelaine*, *pourcelaine*, ' the purple-fish, the Venus-shell ; ' Cot. **–** Ital. *porcellana*, ' the purple-fish, a kind of fine earth, whereof they make . . *porcellan* dishes;' Florio. β. The shell is named from the curved shape of its upper surface, like a pig's back. ‒ Ital. *porcella*, a pig, dimin. of *porco*, a hog, pig. ‒ L. *porcum*, acc. of *porcus*, a pig. See **Pork**.

Porch. (F.‒L.) F. *porche*.‒ L. *porticum*, acc. of *porticus*, a gallery, porch; formed, with suffix *-icus*, from L. *port-a*, a door; see **Port** (3).

Porcine, pig-like. (L.) L. *porc-īnus*, adj., from *porc-us*, a pig; see **Pork**.

Porcupine. (F.‒L.) M. E. *porkepyn* (3 syllables.‒ O. F. *porc espin*, Godefroy; (now called *porc-épic*). [So also Span. *puerco espin*, Ital. *porco spinoso*.] ‒ O. F. *porc*, a pig; *espin*, by-form of *espine*, a spine, prickle. ‒ L. *porc-um*, acc. of *porcus*; *spīna*, a thorn; see **Spine**. ¶ But mod. F. *porc-épic* was formerly *porc espi*, derived from *spīca*, spike, not *spīna*, a thorn. We also find E. *porpin*, short for *porkepin*; whence *porpint*, altered to *porpoint*, *pork-point*; whence *porpent-ine*; all these forms occur.

Pore (1), a minute hole in the skin. (F. ‒L.‒Gk.) F. *pore*.‒ L. *porum*, acc. of *porus*.‒ Gk. πόρος, a passage, pore. Allied to **Fare**. (√ PER.)

Pore (2), to look steadily, gaze long. (E.) M. E. *poren*. Cf. North Fries. *porre*, to stick, stir, provoke, E. Fries. *puren*, *purren*, to stick, thrust, bore, stir, vex; Low G. *purren*, to poke about, clean out a hole, Du. *porren*, to poke; Swed. dial. *pora*, *pura*, *påra*, to work slowly and gradually, to do anything slowly (Rietz); Norw. *pora*, to finger, poke, stir, thrust. The idea seems to be that of poking about slowly, hence to *pore over* a thing, be slow about it. We also find Gael. *purr*, to push, thrust, drive, urge, Irish *purraim*, I thrust, push; from M. E. *pouren*, *poren*; cf. Lowl. Sc. *porr*, to stab.

Pork. (F.‒L.) F. *porc*.‒ L. *porcum*, acc. of *porcus*, a pig.+Lithuan. *parszas*, Irish *orc* (with usual loss of *p*), A. S. *fearh*, a pig (whence E. *farrow*). Brugm. i. § 486.

Porphyry. (F.‒L.‒Gk.) M. E. *porphurie*, answering to an O. F. form *porphyrie*, which Cotgrave gives only in the form *porphyre*.‒ L. *porphyrītes*.‒ Gk. πορφυρίτης, porphyry, a hard rock named from its purple colour.‒ Gk. πορφύρα, the purple-fish. See **Purple**.

Porpoise, Porpess. (F.‒L.) M. E.

porpeys.‒ O. F. *porpeis*, a porpoise; now obsolete (except Guernsey *pourpeis*), and replaced by *marsouin*, borrowed from G. *meer-schwein* (mere-swine). For *porc-peis*.‒ L. *porc-um*, acc. of *porcus*, a pig; *piscem*, acc. of *piscis*, a fish. See **Pork** and **Fish**.

Porridge. (F.) Another form of *pottage*, which first became *poddige* (as preserved in Craven *poddish*) and afterwards *porridge*, just as the Southern E. *errish* is corrupted from *eddish* (A. S. *edisc*), stubble. Similarly, *pottanger* (Palsgrave) was an old form of *porringer*. Cotgrave has '*potage*, pottage, porridge.'

porringer. (F.) Formed from *porrige* (= *porridge*) by inserted *n*, as in *messenger* (F. *messager*); with E. suffix *-er*. It means a small dish for porridge (above).

Port (1), demeanour. (F.‒L.) M. E. *port*.‒ F. *port*, 'the carriage, or demeanor of a man;' Cot. A sb. due to the verb *porter*, to carry.‒ L. *portāre*, to carry. Allied to **Fare**. (√ PER.) **Der.** *port*, vb., as 'to *port* arms;' and (probably) 'to *port* the helm'; *port-ed*, P. L. iv. 980. Also *port-er*, a bearer of a burden, substituted for M. E. *portour*, from F. *porteur*. Hence *porter*, the name of a strong maltliquor, so called from being the favourite drink of London *porters* (1730); *port-folio*, a case large enough to carry *folio* paper in (cf. F. *porte-feuille*), *port-manteau*, F. *portemanteau*, see **Mantle**, **Mantua**; *port-ly*, *port-li-ness*.

Port (2), a harbour. (L.) M. E. *port*. A. S. *port*.‒ L. *portus*, a harbour; cognate with E. Ford. Closely allied to **Port** (3). Brugm. i. § 514.

port (3), a gate, entrance. (F.‒L.) F. *porte*.‒ L. *porta*, a gate. Allied to Gk. πόρος, a ford, way; see above. **Der.** *port-er*, F. *portier*, L. *portārius*; *port-al*, O. F. *portal*, Late L. *portāle*.

port (4), a dark wine. (Port.‒L.) Short for *Oporto wine*.‒ Port. *o porto*, i. e. the harbour; where *o* is the def. art. (= Span. *lo* = L. *illum*), and *porto* is from L. *portum*, acc. of *portus*, a harbour.

portal; see port (3) above.

portcullis. (F.‒L.) M. E. *portcolise*. ‒ O. F. *porte coleïce* (13th cent.), later *porte coulisse*, or *coulisse*, a portcullis, lit. sliding door.‒ L. *porta*, a door; Late L. *cōlātīcia* (sc. *porta*), from *cōlātus*, pp. of *cōlāre*, to flow, glide, slide; see **Colander** and **Cullis**. We find the Late L. forms *cōlā-*

dissus, cōlācius, porta cōlācia, port-cullis; from the same source.

porte, the Turkish government. (F. —L.) The *Sublime Porte* is a F. translation of *Babi Ali,* the chief office of the Ottoman government, lit. 'high gate;' (Arab. *bāb,* gate, *'alīy,* high). — F. *porte,* a gate. — L. *porta,* gate; see **port** (3) above.

Portend. (L.) L. *portendere,* to predict; lit. to stretch out towards, point out. — L. *por-* (O. Lat. *port-*), towards; *tendere,* to stretch. Der. *portent,* O. F. *portent,* L. *portentum,* neut. of pp. of *portendere.*

Porter (1), a carrier; see **Port** (1).

Porter (2), a gate-keeper; see **Port** (3).

Porter (3), a kind of beer; see **Port** (1).

Portesse, Portous, a breviary. (F. —L.) M. E. *portous, porthors.* — O. F. *portehors,* a translation of the Latin name *portiforium.* — F. *porter,* to carry; *hors,* forth (O. F. *fors*). — L. *portāre,* to carry; *foris,* abroad.

Portico. (Ital. — L.) Ital. *portico.* — L. *porticum,* acc. of *porticus* ; see **Porch.**

Portion. (F. — L.) F. *portion.* — L. acc. *portiōnem,* a share, from *portio*; closely allied to *part-,* stem of *pars,* a part. Brugm. i. § 527.

Portly; see **Port** (1).

Portrait. (F. — L.) M. F. *pourtraict,* 'a pourtrait;' Cot. — M. F. *pourtraict, pourtrait,* pp. of *pourtraire,* to portray (below).

portray, pourtray. (F. — L.) M. E. *pourtraien.* — O. F. *portraire, pourtraire,* to portray. — Late L. *prōtrahere,* to depict; L. *prōtrahere,* to draw forward, to reveal. — L. *prō,* forth; *trahere,* to draw. See **Trace** (1).

Pose (1), a position, attitude. (F. — L. —Gk.) Modern; but important. — F. *pose,* attitude. — F. *poser,* to place, set. — Late L. *pausāre,* to cease; also to cause to rest (substituted for L. *pōnere,* the sense of which it took up). — L. *pausa,* a pause. — Gk. παῦσις, a pause. — Gk. παύειν, to make to cease; παύεσθαι, to cease. ¶ One of the most remarkable facts in F. etymology is the extraordinary substitution whereby Late L. *pausāre,* coming to mean 'to cause to rest,' usurped the place of L. *pōnere,* to place, with which it has *no etymological connexion.* This it did so

effectually as to restrict F. *pondre* (=L. *pōnere*) to the sole sense 'to lay eggs,' whilst in all compounds it thrust it aside, so that *compausāre* (F. *composer*) usurped the place of L. *compōnere,* and so on throughout. But note that, on the other hand, the sb. *position* (with all derivatives) is veritably derived from the pp. of *pōnere* ; see **Position** ; and see **Repose.**

Pose (2), to puzzle by questions. (F.— L. *and* Gk.) M. E. *apposen,* to question; not really = F. *apposer,* but substituted for M. E. *opposen,* to oppose, hence, to cross-question ; see **Oppose.** ¶ Confused with *appose,* because of *apposite,* which see. See *Appose* in N. E. D.

Pose (3), a cold in the head. (C.) In Chaucer. A. S. *geposu,* a cough (where *ge-* is a mere prefix). Borrowed from W. *peswch* or *pâs,* a cough; allied to Irish *casachdas,* Russ. *kashele,* prov. E. *hoast,* a cough, Skt. *kās,* to cough. (√QAS.)

Position. (F. — L.) F. *position.* — L. *positiōnem,* acc. of *positio,* a placing. — L. *positus,* pp. of *pōnere,* to place. β. *Pōnere* is for *po-sinere,* where *po-* stands for an old prep., and *sinere* is to allow; see **Site.** ¶ Quite distinct from *pose* (1).

positive. (F. — L.) F. *positif.* — L. *positīuus,* settled. — L. *posit-us,* pp. of *pōnere,* to set, settle.

Posse. (L.) L. *posse,* infin. to be able; used as sb., meaning 'power.' See **Potent.**

Possess. (L.) L. *possessus,* pp. of *possidēre,* to possess. The orig. sense was 'to remain master.' — L. *pot-,* as in *pot-is,* able, having power; *sedēre,* to sit. Cf. **Potent.**

Posset, a warm curdled drink. (F.) M. E. *possyt.* — M. F. *possette,* 'a posset of ale and mylke,' Palsgrave. Origin unknown; cf. L. *posca,* sour wine and water. [Irish *pusoid,* a posset, W. *posel,* curdled milk, posset, are borrowed from E.]

Possible. (F. — L.) F. *possible.* — L. *possibilis,* that may be done. Cf. L. *posse,* to be able; see **Potent.**

Post (1), a stake set in the ground. (L.) M. E. *post* ; A. S. *post.* — L. *postis,* a post. Perhaps something firmly fixed. — L. *postus,* short for *positus,* pp. of *pōnere,* to set. See **Position.**

post (2), a military station, a public letter-carrier, stage on a road. (F. — Ital. —L.) Orig. a military post ; then a fixed place on a line of road, a station ; then a stage, also a traveller who used relays of horses, &c. — F. *poste*, masc., a carrier, messenger; fem., posting, a riding post. — Ital. *posta*. — Late L. *postus*, fem. *posta*, a post, station. — L. *positus*, pp. of *pōnere*, to place.

Post-, prefix. (L.) L. *post*, after, behind.

post-date; from *post* and *date*.

posterior, hinder. (L.) L. *posterior*, comp. of *posterus*, coming after. — L. *post*, after. Der. *posterior-s*, i. e. posterior parts.

posterity. (F. — L.) M. F. *posterité*. — L. *posteritātem*, acc. of *posteritās*, futurity, posterity. — L. *posteri-*, for *posterus*, coming after (above).

postern. (F. — L.) O. F. *posterle*, also spelt *posterne* (by change of suffix); later *poterne*, 'a back-door to a fort;' Cot. — L. *posterula*, a small back-door. — L. *posterus*, behind.

posthumous, postumous. (L.) L. *postumus*, the latest-born; hence, as sb., a posthumous child. Written *posthumus* owing to a popular etymology from *post humum*, forced into the impossible sense of 'after the father is in the ground or buried'; hence F. *posthume*, Port. *posthumo*; but Span. and Ital. *postumo* are right. β. L. *postumus* = *post-tu-mus*, a superl. form of *post*, behind; cf. *op-tu-mus*, best.

postil, an explanatory note or commentary on the Bible. (F. — L.) M. F. *postille*. — Late L. *postilla*, a marginal note in a Bible. Derived by Ducange from L. *post illa uerba*, i. e. after those words, because the glosses were added afterwards.

Postillion. (F. — Ital. — L.) F. *postillon*. — Ital. *postiglione*, a post-boy. — Ital. *posta*, a post; with suffix *-iglione* = L. *-iliōnem*. See post (2) above.

Post-meridian, Pomeridian, belonging to the afternoon. (L.) L. *pōmerīdiānus*, also *postmerīdiānus*, the same. — L. *post*, after; *meridiānus*, adj., from *merīdiēs*, noon; see **Meridian.**

post-mortem. (L.) L. *post*, after; *mortem*, acc. of *mors*, death.

post-obit. (L.) L. *post*, after; *obitum*, acc. of *obitus*, death.

postpone, to put off. (L.) L. *postpōnere*, to put after, delay. — L. *post*, after; *pōnere*, to put.

post-prandial, adj., after-dinner. (L.) From L. *post prandium*, i. e. after dinner. For L. *prandium*, see Brugm. ii. § 165.

postscript. (L.) L. *postscriptum*, that which is written after. — L. *post*, after; *scriptum*, neut. of pp. of *scrībere*, to write.

Postulate, a self-evident proposition. (L.) L. *postulātum*, a thing demanded (and granted); neut. of pp. of *postulāre*, to demand. Derived from *poscere*, to ask. Brugm. i. §§ 483(7), 502.

Posture. (F. — L.) F. *posture*. — L. *positūra*, arrangement. — L. *positus*, pp. of *pōnere*, to put. See Position.

Posy. (F. — L. — Gk.) In all its senses, it is short for *poesy*. It meant a short poem, esp. a short motto in verse on knives and rings, Hamlet, iii. 2. 162; hence it meant a nosegay, because the flowers chosen for it enigmatically represented a posy or motto. It even meant a collection of precious stones, forming a motto; Chambers, Book of Days, i. 221. See Poesy.

Pot. (E.) M. E. *pot*. A. S. *pott*. + E. Fries. Du. *pot*; Icel. *pottr*, Swed. *potta*, Dan. *potte*; Low G. *pott*. Also Irish *pota*, Gael. *poit*, W. *pot*, all from E. Also F. *pot*, Bret. *pôd*, Span. *pote*; from Low G. Teut. type *puttoz*. Hence Low L. *pottus*, also spelt *pōtus* (as if from L. *pōtāre*, to drink). Der. *to go to pot*, i. e. into the cooking-pot.

Potable, drinkable. (F. — L.) F. *potable*. — L. *pōtābilis*, drinkable. — L. *pōtāre*, to drink; *pōtus*, drunken. + Skt. *pā*, to drink. Allied to Gk. πόσις, drink, πῶμα, drink.

Potash. (E.) From *pot* and *ash*; ash obtained by boiling down burnt vegetable substances in a pot. Latinised as *potassa*; whence *potass-ium*.

Potation. (L.) From L. *pōtātio*, a drinking. — L. *pōtātus*, pp. of *pōtāre*, to drink. See Potable.

Potato. (Span. — Hayti.) Span. *patata*, a potato. — Hayti *batata*, a yam.

Potch, to thrust; see Poach (2).

Potent. (L.) L. *potent-*, stem of *potens*, powerful, pres. part. of *posse*, to be able, *possum*, I am able. *Possum* is short for *pot-sum* or *pote-sum*, from *potis*, powerful, orig. 'a lord;' allied to Skt. *pati-*, a master, lord, Lithuan. *-patis*, Russ. *-pode* in *gos-pode*, lord. Brugm. i. § 158. Der. *omnipotent*. And see Despot.

Pother, a bustle, confusion. (E.) Also *pudder*, the same; from *pudder*, vb., to stir, confuse, a variant of Potter.

Potion. (F. — L.) F. *potion*. — L.

pōtiōnem, acc. of *pōtio*, a draught. – L. *pōtus*, drunken; see **Potable, Poison.**

Pottage. (F. – Low G.) M. E. *potage.* – F. *potage*; formed with F. suffix *-age* (L. *-āticum*), from F. *pot*, a pot, of Teut. origin. See **Pot.**

Potter. (E.) To *potter* is to poke about, hence to stir, confuse, disorder, also to do a thing inefficiently; so also *pother*, to poke, disorder (Bailey, Halliwell). These are frequentative forms of *put*, to thrust; see **Put.** Cf. M. Du. *poteren*, ' to search one thoroughly,' Hexham; Du. *peuteren*, to fumble, poke about; Norw. *pota*, M. Swed. *potta*, to poke.

Pottle. (F. – Low G.) M. E. *potel.* – O. F. *potel*, a small pot, small measure; dimin. of F. *pot*, a pot. – Low G. *pott* ; see **Pot.**

potwalloper. (Hybrid.) Lit. ' one who boils a pot;' hence a voter who has a vote because he can boil a pot on his own fire. *Wallop*, to boil fast, is from M. E. *walopen*, to gallop. Golding has ' seething *a-wallop*,' boiling rapidly ; tr. of Ovid, f. 82. See **Gallop.**

Pouch. (F. – M. Du.) M. E. *pouche.* – O. F. *pouche*, variant of *poche*; see **Pocket.**

Poult, a chicken. (F. – L.) M. E. *pulte.* – F. *poulet*, a chicken; dimin. of *poule*, a hen. – Late L. *pulla*, a hen ; fem. of *pullus*, a young animal. See **Pool** (2). **Der.** *poult-er*, afterwards extended to *poult-er-er* ; *poult-r-y* (for *poult-er-y*), A.F. *poletrie.*

Poultice. (F. – L.) Gascoigne has the pl. *pultesses* (Steel Glas, 997). – M. F. **pult-ice*, formed from M. F. *pulte*, 'a poultice;' Cot. [Cf. M. Ital. *poltiglia*, ' a pultis,' Florio.] – Late L. *pulta*, a kind of pap; from *pult-*, as in L. *pult-is*, gen. of *puls*, a thick pap, or pap-like substance. + Gk. πόλτος, porridge.

Poultry; see **Poult.**

Pounce (1), to seize with the claws. (F. – L.) Orig. a term in hawking ; a hawk's claws were termed *pounces*; cf. O. F. *ponce*, a fist. A *pounce* is also a punch or stamp (Nares) ; a *pounson* was a dagger (Barbour). Cf. Gascon *pounchoun*) ; O.F. *poinc-on*, *punch-on* (Ital. *punz-one*, Span. *punz-on*), a punch, sharp point. Cf. Ital. *punzone*, ' a bodkin, a goldsmith's pouncer or pounce;' Florio. From the base seen in Ital. *punz-ellare*, to prick, goad, Span. *punz-ar*, to punch. The Span. *punzar*

answers to a Late L. **punctiāre*, not found, but regularly formed from L. *punctus*, pp. of *pungere*. See **Pungent.**

Pounce (2), fine powder. (F. – L.) F. *ponce*; ' *pierre ponce*, a pumis stone;' Cot. – L. *pumicem*, acc. of *pumex*, pumice; see **Pumice. Der.** *pouncet-box.*

Pound (1), a weight, a sovereign. (L.) Orig. a weight. M. E. *pund.* A. S. *pund*, pl. *pund.* – L. *pondō*, a weight, used as an indeclinable sb., though orig. meaning ' by weight ' ; allied to *pondus*, a weight. See **Ponder.**

Pound (2), an enclosure for strayed cattle. (E.) M. E. *pond.* A. S. *pund*, an enclosure. Hence *pindar*. **Doublet, pond.**

Pound (3), to bruise in a mortar. (E.) The *d* is excrescent. M. E. *pounen*; also *ponen*, as in comp. *to-ponen*, to pound thoroughly. – A. S. *punian*, to pound.

Pour. (F. – L.) M. E. *pouren, poren*, esp. used with *out*. The orig. sense was to purify, clarify, esp. by pressure or squeezing out. – O. F. *purer*, to clarify, also to pour out or drip ; so also *depurer*, to clarify, to be clarified, to drip or run out. – Late L. *pūrāre*, to purify. – L. *pūrus*, pure ; see **Pure.** So in Guernsey, ' J'o l'cidre qui *pure* dans l'auge,' I hear the cider pouring into the trough (Moisy).

Pourtray; see **Portray.**

Pout (1), to swell out, to sulk. (E.) See below. [W. *pwdu*, to pout, to be sullen, is from E.]

pout (2), a fish. (E.) A. S. *ǣle-pūtan*, pl., eel-pouts. The fish has the power of inflating a membrane above the eyes ; hence A. S. *-pūt-a − pout-er.* From a Teut. base **pūt-an-*, to swell out. Cf. Du. *puit*, a frog, from its rounded shape ; *puit-aal*, an eel-pout ; *puist*, a pimple (from a shorter base **pū-*) ; Swed. *puta*, a cushion (from its shape ; Swed. dial. *puta*, to be inflated). Cf. Prov. *pot, pout*, a full lip ; *fa de pots*, to pout (Mistral). Cf. **Pudding.**

Poverty. (F. – L.) M. E. *pouertee* (= *povertee*). – O. F. *poverte*, later *povreté*, poverty (F. *pauvreté*). – L. *paupertātem*, acc. of *paupertās*, poverty. – L. *pauper*, poor. See **Pauper.**

Powder. (F. – L.) M. E. *poudre.* – F. *poudre*, O. F. *poldre, puldre.* Formed with excrescent *d* from L. *puluerem*, acc. of *puluis*, dust. See **Pulverise.**

Power. (F. – L.) M. E. *pöer* ; later *po-w-er*, the *w* being inserted. – A. F. *poër*,

O. F. *pooir* (mod. F. *pouvoir*), to be able ;
hence, as sb., power. — Late L. *potēre*, to
be able ; for L. *posse*, to be able. See
Possible, Potent.

Pox ; see **Pock.**

Praam, Pram, a flat-bottomed boat.
(Du. — Slav.) Du. *praam* ; M. Du. *prame*.
— Pol. and Bohem. *pram.*

Practice. (F. — L. — Gk.) [Formerly
practise, from the verb *to practise.* — O. F.
practiser, pratiser. — Late L. *practicāre.*]
The M. E. form of the sb. was *praktike.* —
M. F. *practique*, practice. — L. *practica*, fem.
of *practicus.* — Gk. πρακτικός, fit for business ; whence ἡ πρακτική, practical science,
experience. — Gk. πράσσειν (= *πράκ-γειν),
to do, accomplish. **Der.** *practition-er*,
formed by needlessly adding *-er* to the
older term *practician*, from M. F. *practicien*,
' a practicer in law ;' Cot.

Prætor, Pretor, a Roman magistrate. (L.) L. *prætor*, lit. a goer before,
leader ; for *præ-itor.* — L. *præ*, before ;
*itor, a goer, from *ire*, to go.

Pragmatic. (F. — L. — Gk.) F. *prag-
matique*, belonging to business. — L. *prag-
maticus.* — Gk. πραγματικός, skilled in
business. — Gk. πραγματ-, stem of πρᾶγμα
(= *πρακ-μα), a deed, thing done. — Gk.
πράσσειν (= *πράκ-γειν), to do. See **Practice.**

Prairie, an extensive meadow. (F. —
L.) F. *prairie*, a meadow. — Late L.
prātāria, meadow-land. — L. *prātum*, a
meadow.

Praise, sb. (F. — L.) O. F. *preis*, price,
value, merit (hence, tribute to merit). — L.
pretium, price, value. **Der.** *dis-praise.*

Prance. (E.) M. E. *prancen, prauncen*,
used of a horse ; it means to make a show,
shew off ; apparently an A. F. adaptation
of M. E. *pranken*, to trim. Cf. Dan. dial.
prandse, pranse, to go proudly, as a
prancing horse ; *pransk*, proud ; Swed.
dial. *prånga*, to shew off. So also M. Du.
pronken, to make a show, to strut about ;
Low G. *prunken.* See below.

Prank (1), to deck, adorn. (E.) M.E.
pranken, to trim ; allied to obs. E. *prink*,
to trim (Nares). *Prink* is a nasalised
form of *prick* ; cf. Lowl. Sc. *preek*, to be
spruce, *prick-me-dainty*, finical, *prink*,
primp, to deck, to prick. *Prank* is an
allied form to these ; see further under
Prick. So also M. Du. *proncken*, to display one's dress, *pronckepinken, proncke-
prinken*, to glitter in a fine dress ; Low G.

Dan. Swed. *prunk*, show, parade ; M. Du.
pryken, to make a show. From a Teut.
type **prenkan-*, str. vb. (pt. t. **prank*, pp.
*prunkanoz).

prank (2), a trick. (E.) An act done
to shew off, a trick to make people stare ;
from **Prank** (1).

Prate. (E.) M. E. *praten.* Cf. M.
Swed. *prata*, Dan. *prate*, to prate, talk ;
Swed. Dan. *prat*, talk ; M. Du. and Low
G. *praten*, to prate ; Du. *praat*, talk. Of
imitative origin ; from a base **prat.* **Der.**
pratt-le, the frequentative form.

Prawn. (F. ? — L. ?) M. E. *prane*,
Prompt. Parv. Perhaps (through a lost
A. F. form) from L. *perna*, a sea-mussel ;
cf. M. Ital. *parnocchie*, ' a fish called
shrimps or praunes ;' Florio.

Pray. (F. — L.) M. E. *preyen.* — A. F.
and O. F. *preier* (F. *prier*). — L. *precārī*,
to pray. See **Precarious.** **Der.** *pray-er*,
M. E. *preiere*, O. F. *preiere*, from L. *pre-
cāria*, fem. of *precārius*, adj.

Pre-, beforehand. (L. ; *or* F. — L.) M. F.
pre-, L. *præ-*, from L. *præ*, prep., before.
For **prai*, a locative form. ¶ Hence
numerous compounds, many of which,
like *precaution*, are of obvious origin.

Preach. (F. — L.) M. E. *prechen.* —
O. F. *precher, prescher* (*prêcher*). — L. *prædicāre*, to declare. See **Predicate.**

Prebend. (F. — L.) O. F. *prebende*
(F. *prébende*). — L. *præbenda*, a payment,
stipend from a public source ; orig. fem.
of gerundive of *præbēre*, to afford, give.
— L. *præ*, before, *habēre*, to have ; whence
prahibēre, to hold forth, give, contracted
to *præbēre.* **Der.** *prebend-ar-y.*

Precarious. (L.) L. *precāri-us*, obtained by prayer or as a favour, doubtful,
precarious ; with suffix *-ous.* — L. *precārī*,
to pray. — L. *prec-*, stem of *prex*, a prayer.
+G. *fragen*, to ask ; Goth. *fraih-nan*,
A. S. *frignan*, to ask ; Lith. *praszyti* ;
Russ. *prosite* ; Pers. *pursīdan* ; Skt. *pracch*,
to ask. (√PREK.) Brugm. i. § 607.

Precaution. (F. — L.) From **Pre-**
and **Caution.**

Precede. (F. — L.) O. F. *preceder*
(F. *précéder*). — L. *præcēdere*, to go before.
— L. *præ*, before ; *cēdere*, to go. See
Cede. **Der.** *preced-ent* ; *pre-cess-ion*, from
the pp. *præcess-us.*

Precentor. (L.) L. *præcentor*, the
leader of a choir. — L. *præ*, before ; and
cantor, a singer, from *canere*, to sing ; see
Cant (1).

Precept. (F. – L.) O. F. *precept.* – L. *præceptum*, a prescribed rule. – L. *præceptus*, pp. of *præcipere*, to take beforehand, give rules. – L. *præ*, before ; *capere*, to take. Der. *precept-or*.

Precinct. (L.) Late L. *præcinctum*, a boundary. – L. *præcinctus*, pp. of *præcingere*, to gird about. – L. *præ*, in front ; *cingere*, to gird. See **Cincture**.

Precious. (F. – L.) O. F. *precieus* (F. *précieux*). – L. *pretiōsus*, valuable. – L. *pretium*, price, value. See **Price**.

Precipice. (F. – L.) F. *précipice.* – L. *præcipitium*, a falling headlong down ; a precipice. – L. *præcipit-*, decl. stem of *præceps*, headlong. – L. *præ*, before ; and *capit-*, decl. stem of *caput*, head. Der. *precipitate*, from L. *præcipitāre*, to cast headlong.

Precise. (F. – L.) O. F. *precis*, strict. – L. *præcīsus*, cut off, concise, strict ; pp. of *præcīdere*, to cut off. – L. *præ*, in front ; *cædere*, to cut. See **Cæsura**.

Preclude. (L.) L. *præclūdere*, to shut off, hinder access to. – L. *præ*, in front ; *claudere* (pp. *clūsus*), to shut. Der. *preclus-ion*, from the pp. *præclūsus*. Cf. **Conclude**.

Precocious. (L.) Coined (with suffix *-ous*) from L. *præcoci-*, decl. stem of *præcox*, prematurely ripe. – L. *præ*, before ; *coquere*, to cook, to ripen. See **Cook**.

Precursor. (L.) L. *præcursor*, a forerunner. – L. *præ*, before ; *cursor*, a runner, from *curs-us*, pp. of *currere*, to run. See **Current**.

Predatory, given to plundering. (L.) L. *prædātōrius*, plundering. – L. *prædātor*, a plunderer. – L. *prædārī*, to plunder. – L. *præda*, booty. β. *Præda* = **præhed-a*, that which is seized beforehand ; from *præ*, before, and *hed-*, base of *-hendere*, to seize, get, cognate with *get* ; see **Get**. (So also *prendere* = *pre-hendere*.) γ. Irish *spreidh*, cattle, W. *praidd*, flock, herd, booty, prey, are from L. *præda*.

Predecessor. (L.) L. *prædēcessor*. – L. *præ*, before ; *dēcessor*, one who retires from an office, from *dēcessus*, pp. of *dēcēdere*, to depart. – L. *dē*, from ; *cēdere*, to go. See **Cede**.

Predicate. (L.) From pp. of *prædicāre*, to publish, proclaim, declare. – L. *præ*, before ; *dicāre*, to tell, publish, allied to *dīcere*, to say. See **Diction**.

predicament. (L.) L. *prædicāmentum*, a term in logic, one of the most

general classes into which things can be divided. – L. *prædicāre*, to declare (above).

Predict. (L.) L. *prædictus*, pp. of *prædīcere*, to say beforehand, foretell. – L. *præ*, before ; *dīcere*, to say. See **Diction**.

Predilection, a choosing beforehand. (L.) From L. *præ*, before ; *dīlectio*, choice, from *dīligere*, to choose ; see **Diligent**.

Preface. (F. – L.) O. F. *preface.* – L. *præfātio*, a preface. – L. *præfātus*, spoken before, pp. of *præfārī*, to speak before. – L. *præ*, before, *fārī*, to speak. See **Fate**.

Prefect, a governor. (F. – L) M. E. *prefect.* – O. F. *prefect* (F. *préfet*). – L. *præfectus*, one set over others ; pp. of *præficere*, to set before. – L. *præ-*, before ; *facere*, to make, set. See **Fact**.

Prefer. (F. – L.) O. F. *preferer*. – L. *præferre*, to set in front, prefer. – L. *præ*, before ; *ferre*, to bear, set. See **Fertile**.

Prefigure. (F. – L.) From **Pre-** and **Figure**.

Pregnant, fruitful, with child. (F. – L.) M. F. *pregnant*, ' pregnant, pithy ; ' Cot. – L. *prægnantem*, acc. of *prægnans*, pregnant. *Prægnans* has the form of a pres. part. of an obs. verb **prægnāre* to be before a birth, to be about to bear. – L. *præ*, before ; **gnāre*, to bear, of which the pp. *gnātus* or *nātus* is used as the pp. of the inceptive infin. *nascī*, to be born. See **Natal**.

Prehensile, adapted for grasping. (L.) Coined with suffix *-ile* (L. *-ilis*) from L. *prehens-us*, pp. of *prehendere*, *prendere*, to lay hold of. – L. *præ*, before ; obsolete *-hendere*, to grasp, cognate with E. **Get**, q. v.

Prejudge. (F. – L.) O. F. *prejuger*. – L. *præiūdicāre*, to judge beforehand. – L. *præ*, before ; *iūdicāre*, to judge, from *iūdic-*, stem of *iūdex*, a judge. See **Judge**.

prejudice. (F. – L.) O. F. *prejudice*. – L. *præiūdicium*, a judicial examination, previous to a trial, also a prejudice. – L. *præ*, before ; *iūdicium*, judgment, from *iūdic-*, stem of *iūdex*, a judge.

Prelate, a church dignitary. (F. – L.) O. F. *prelat.* – L. *prælātus*, set above ; used as pp. of *præferre*, to prefer (but from a different root) – L. *præ*, before ; *lātus*, borne, set, pp. of *tollere*, to lift, bear. See **Tolerate**.

Preliminary, introductory. (F. – L.)

Coined from *pre-*, prefix, before ; and M.F. *liminaire*, ' set before the entry of, dedicatory,' Cot. From L. *præ*, before ; and *līmināris*, adj., coming at the beginning or threshold.—L. *līmin-*, stem of *līmen*, threshold. See **Limit.**

Prelude, an introduction. (F.—L.) M. F. *prelude*, 'a preludium, preface, preamble;' Cot.—Late L. **præludium*.—L. *præludere*, to play beforehand, give a prelude.—L. *præ*, before ; to *ludere*, to play. See **Ludicrous.**

Premature. (F.—L.) From Preand Mature.

Premier. (F.—L.) F. *premier*, first. —L. *prīmārium*, acc. of *prīmārius*, chief. —L. *prīmus*, first. See Prime (1).

Premiss, Premise. (F. — L.) Better *premiss* than *premise*.—O. F. *premisse* (F. *prémisse*), in use in the 14th century (Littré).—L. *præmissa* (*sententia* being understood), a premiss, lit. that which is sent before or stated beforehand. Fem. of *præmissus*, pp. of *præmittere*, to send before.—L. *præ*, before ; *mittere*, to send. See **Missile.** Der. *premis-es*, s. pl., the adjuncts of a building, first stated in full, in a lease, and afterwards referred to as the *premises* ; or otherwise, due to the custom of beginning leases with *premises* setting forth the names of the grantor and grantee of the deed. Also *premise*, vb., with accent on *i*.

Premium. (L.) L. *præmium*, profit; lit. 'a taking before;' for **præ-imium.* —L. *præ*, before ; *emere*, to take. Cf. **Exempt.**

Premonish, to warn beforehand. (F. —L.) Coined from *pre-*, before (for L. *præ*); and *monish*, a corrupted form of M. E. *monesten*, to warn, Wyclif, 2 Cor. vi. 1. See **Admonish.** Der. *premonitor-y*, from L. *præmonitor*, one who warns beforehand, from *præmonēre*, to warn beforehand.

Prentice, short for **Apprentice,** q. v.

Prepare. (F.—L.) M. F. *preparer*; Cot.—L. *præparāre*, to make ready beforehand.—L. *præ*, before ; *parāre*, to prepare. See **Pare.**

Prepense, premeditated. (F. — L.) 1. As if from M.F. *pre-*, beforehand; *penser*, to think.—L. *præ*, beforehand ; *pensāre*, to weigh, ponder, frequent. form of *pendere*, to weigh ; see **Pendant.** 2. But in the phr. *malice prepense*, it is an altered

form of A.F. *purpensé*, pp. of *purpenser*, to meditate on, with prefix *pur-* (F. *pour-*) from L. *prō*.

preponderate. (L.) From pp. of L. *præponderāre*, to outweigh.—L. *præ*, before ; *ponderāre*, to weigh ; see **Ponder.**

Preposition. (F.—L.) O. F. *preposition.*—L. acc. *præpositiōnem*, a setting before ; a preposition (in grammar).—L. *præpositus*, pp. of *præpōnere*, to set before. —L. *præ*, before ; *pōnere*, to place. See **Position.**

Preposterous. (L.) L. *præposter-us*, inverted, hind side before ; with suffix *-ous.* —L. *præ*, before ; *posterus*, later, coming after. See **Post-.**

Prerogative. (F.—L.) A. F. *prerogative*, a privilege.—L. *prærogātīua*, a previous choice, preference, privilege.— L. *præ*, before ; *rogāre*, to ask. See **Rogation.**

Presage. (F.—L.) O. F. *presage.*— L. *præsāgium*, a divining beforehand.—L. *præsāgīre*, to perceive beforehand.—L. *præ*, before ; *sāgīre*, to observe, perceive. See **Sagacious.**

Presbyter. (L.—Gk.) L. *presbyter.* —Gk. πρεσβύτερος, an elder ; orig. elder, comparative of πρέσβυς, old. Cf. L. *priscus*, ancient.

Prescience. (F. — L.) O.F. *prescience.* —L. *præscientia*, foreknowledge.—L. *præ*, before ; *scientia*, knowledge. See **Science.**

Prescribe. (L.) L. *præscrībere*, to write beforehand, prescribe ; pp. *præscriptus* (whence *prescription*).—L. *præ*, before ; *scrībere*, to write. See **Scribe.**

Present (1), near at hand. (F.—L.) O. F. *present.*—L. *præsent-*, stem of *præsens*, i. e. being in front or near.—L. *præ*, in front ; *-sens*, for **es-ens*, being, from √ES, to be. Cf. **Absent.** Der. *present-ly*; *presence*, sb., O. F. *presence*, L. *præsentia.*

present (2), to give. (F.—L.) O. F. *presenter.*—L. *præsentāre*, to place before, hold out, offer.—L. *præsent-*, stem of *præsens* (above). Der. *present*, sb., a gift.

Presentiment. (F.—L.) M. F. *presentiment*, 'a fore-feeling;' Cot.—L. *præsentī-re*, to feel beforehand.—L. *præ*, before ; *sentīre*, to feel. See **Sense.**

Preserve. (F.—L.) O. F. *preserver*, to preserve.—L. *præ*, beforehand ; *seruāre*, to keep. See **Serve.**

Preside. (F.—L.) O. F. *presider*, to

preside, govern.—L. *præsidēre*, to sit before, preside over.—L. *præ*, in front ; *sedēre*, to sit. See **Sedentary.**

Press (1), to squeeze. (F.—L.) M. E. *pressen.*—F. *presser.*—L. *pressāre*.frequent. of *premere* (pp. *pressus*), to press. Der. *press*, sb. : *press-ure.*

Press (2), to hire men for service, make men serve as sailors, &c. (F.—L.) *Press* is a corruption of the old word *prest*, ready ; whence *prest-money*, ready money advanced to a man hired for service, earnest money ; also *imprest*, a verb (now *impress*), to give a man earnest money. When it became common to use *compulsion* to *force* men into service, it was confused with the verb *to press*. *Prest money* was money lent.—O.F. *prester* (F. *prêter*), to lend, advance money.—L. *præstāre*, to stand forth, come forward, furnish, offer, give.—L. *præ*, in front ; *stāre*, to stand. See **State.** Der. *press-gang, im-press, im-press-ment.*

Prestige. (F.—L.) F. *prestige*, an illusion, fascination, influence due to fame. —L. *præstigium*, a deception, illusion, jugglery. For **præstrigium*, the 2nd *r* being lost (Brug. i. § 483).—L. *præstriugere*, to bind fast, to dull, dim, blind.—L. *præ*, before ; *stringere*, to bind. See **Stringent.**

Presume. (F.—L.) M. E. *presumen.* —O. F. *presumer.*—L. *præsūmere*, to take beforehand, presume, imagine.—L. *præ*, before ; *sūmere*, to take ; see **Assume.** Der. *presumpt-ion*, &c. (from the pp. *præsumpt-us*).

Pretend. (F.—L.) O. F. *pretendre.* —L. *prætendere*, to spread before, hold out as an excuse, allege, pretend.—L. *præ*, before ; *tendere*, to stretch. See **Tend** (1). Der. *pretence*, misspelt for *pretense* (O. F. *pretensse*, f., Godefroy), from the fem. of Late L. *prætensus*, used for L. *prætentus*, pp. of *prætendere.*

Preter-, prefix. (L.) L. *præter*, beyond ; comparative form of *præ*, before ; see **Pre-.**

Preterite. (F.—L.) M. E. *preterit.* —O. F. *preterit*, m., *preterite*, fem.—L. *præteritus*, pp. of *præterīre*, to pass by.— L. *præter*, beyond ; *īre*, to go.

Pretermit, to omit. (L.) L. *prætermittere*, to allow to go past.—L. *præter*, beyond ; *mittere*, to send. See **Missile.** Der. *pretermiss-ion*, from the pp.

Preternatural. (L.) From L. *præter*,

beyond ; and *natural*, adj., from *nature.* See **Nature.**

Pretext. (F.—L.) M. F. *pretexte*, a pretext.—L. *prætextum*, a pretext ; orig. neut. of *prætextus*, pp. of *prætexere*, lit. to weave in front.—L. *præ*, in front ; *texere*, to weave. See **Text.**

Pretty. (E.) M. E. *prati* ; A. S. *prætig, prættig, pætig*, orig. deceitful, tricky ; hence clever, cunning, the usual M. E. sense. Formed with suffix -*ig* from A. S. *præt*, deceit, trickery. Cf. Lowl. Sc. *pratty*, *pretty*, tricky, from *prat*, a trick (G. Douglas).✚Icel. *prettr*, a trick ; *pretta*, to cheat ; E. Fries. *pret*, a trick, *prettig*, jocose, droll, pleasant ; M. Du. *pratte, perte*, Du. *part*, a trick, deceit. Of uncertain origin.

Prevail. (F. - L.) O. F. *prevail*, 1 p. pr. of *prevaloir*, to prevail.—L. *præualēre*, to have great power.—L. *præ*, before, excessively ; *ualēre*, to be strong. See **Valid.** Der. *prevalent*, from L. *præualent-*, stem of pres. pt. of *præualēre*, to prevail.

Prevaricate. (L.) From pp. of L. *præuāricārī*, to straddle, hence to swerve, shuffle, shift, quibble.—L. *præ*, before, excessively ; *uāric-us*, straddling, from *uārus*, crooked. See **Varicose.**

Prevent. (L.) The old meaning was ' to go before' ; cf. M. F. *prevenir*, ' to prevent, anticipate, forestall ;' Cot.—L. *præuent-us*, pp. of *præuenīre*, to go before.— L. *præ*, before ; *uenīre*, to come. See **Venture.**

Previous. (L.) L. *præui-us*, on the way before, going before ; with suffix -*ous*. —L. *præ*, before ; *uia*, a way.

Prey, sb. (F.—L.) A. F. *preie* (F. *proie*).—L. *præda*, prey. See **Predatory.** Der. *prey*, vb.

Prial, three of a sort, at cards. (F.—L.) A contraction of *pair-royal* ; (see Nares).

Price. (F.—L.) M. E. *pris.*—O. F. *pris*, also spelt *preis*, price, value, merit.— L. *pretium*, price. See **Precious.**

Prick. (E.) M. E. *prikke, prike*, sb. A. S. *pricu, prica*, a point, prick, dot ; *prician*, to prick. ✚ M. Du. *prick*, Du. *prik*, a prickle ; Dan. *prik*, Swed. *prick*, a dot, mark ; E. Fries., Low G. *prik.* Also Du., E. Fries., Low G. *prikken*, to prick ; Dan. *prikke*, Swed. *pricka*, to dot. From a Teut. base **prik*, to prick, dot. Der. *prick*, vb. ; *prick-le*, sb., from A. S. *pricel.*

Pride. (F. - L.) M. E. *pride, prude.* A. S. *prȳte*, pride ; regularly formed (by

the usual change from *ŭ* to *y̆*) from A. S.
prūt, proud, of F. origin. See **Proud**.

Priest. (L. – Gk.) M. E. *preest*; A. S.
prēost. Contracted (like O. F. *prestre*, O.
Sax. *prēstar*, G. *priester*) from L. *presbyter.*
Cf. '*Prester John.*' See **Presbyter.**
¶ Abnormal; perhaps *presbyter* was ap-
prehended as **prebyster.*

Prig (1), to steal. (E.) Cant *prygge*, to
ride, ride off with a horse which a man has
to take care of; *prigger of prauncers*, a
horse-stealer; see Harman's Caveat, pp.
42, 43, and p. 84, col. 3. Modification of
prick, to spur, to ride; Spenser, F. Q. i.
1. 1. See **Prick.**

Prig (2), a pert, pragmatical fellow.
(E.) From the verb *to prick*, in the sense
to trim, adorn, dress up. Lowl. Sc. *prig-
me-dainty*, *prick-me-dainty*, a prig. See
above.

Prim, neat. (F. – L.) O.F. *prim*, masc.,
prime, fem., prime, forward, also *prime*,
masc. and fem., thin, slender, small, as *che-
veux primes*, 'smooth or delicate hair;'
Cot. The sense is first-grown, small, delicate. – L. *primus*, first (below). ¶ The
word was perhaps confused with *prink*, to
deck; see **Prank.**

prime (1), first, chief. (F. – L.) F.
prime, properly 'prime,' the first canonical
hour. – L. *prīma*, fem. of *prīmus*, first.
Prīmus is for **prismus*, and is related to
pris-cus, ancient, *pris-tinus*, primitive,
and to *prius*, adv., former. Brugm. ii.
§ 165. Cf. A. S. *for-ma*, first, from *fore*
(see **Former**); Gk. πρῶ-τος, first, from
πρό; Skt. *pra-ta-ma-*, first. **Der.** *primary*; *prim-ate*, O. F. *primat*, L. acc. *prīm-
ātem*, from *prīmās*, a chief man.

prime (2), to make a gun quite ready.
(F. – L.) Cf. *prime*, to trim trees; *prime*,
first position in fencing; and esp. the phr.
'to put into *prime* order.' A peculiar use
of *prime* (1).

primero, an old game at cards. (Span.
– L.) Span. *primero*, lit. 'first.' – L. *prīmārius*, chief; see **Premier.**

primeval. (L.) Coined from L. *prīmus*, first; *æu-um*, age; with suffix *-al*; cf.
L. *prīmæuus*, primeval.

primitive. (F. – L.) F. *primitif.* –
L. *prīmitīuus*, earliest of its kind. – L.
prīmit-us, adv., for the first time. – L.
prīmus, first.

primogeniture. (F. – L.) M. F. *primogeniture*, 'the being eldest;' Cot. – L..
prīmogenitus, first-born. – L. *prīmo-*, for

prīmus, first; *genitus*, pp. of *gignere* (base
gen-), to beget, produce; see **Genus.**

primordial, original. (F. – L.) F.
primordial. – L. *prīmordiālis*, original. –
L. *prīmordium*, origin. – L. *prīm-us*, first;
ordīrī, to begin, allied to *ordo*, order.

primrose. (F. – L.) As if from F.
prime rose, first rose; L. *prīma rosa.*
Such is the popular etymology; but, historically, *primrose* is a substitution for
M. E. *primerole*, a primrose. Dimin. of
Late L. *prīmula*, a primrose (still preserved
in Span. *primula*, the same). Again,
prīmula is a derivative of *prīmus*, first.
¶ Thus the word *rose* was only associated
with *primrose* by a popular blunder.

prince. (F. – L.) F. *prince.* – L. *prin-
cipem*, acc. of *princeps*, a chief, lit. 'taking
the first place.' – L. *prin-*, for *prim-us*,
first; *capere*, to take; see **Capital.**

principal. (F. – L.) F. *principal.* –
L. *principālis*, chief. – L. *princip-*, stem of
princeps, a chief (above).

principle. (F. – L.) The *l* is an E.
addition, as in *syllable.* – F. *principe*, a
principle, maxim; orig. beginning. – L.
principium, a beginning. – L. *princip-*,
stem of *princeps*, taking the first place;
see **prince** (above).

Print, sb. (F. – L.) M. E. *printe*,
prente, *preinte*; short for *empreinte*, borrowed from M. F. *empreinte*, 'a stamp,
print;' Cot. See **Imprint. Der.** *print*,
vb.; *re-print.*

Prior (1), former. (L.) L. *prior*,
former. Used as comparative of the superl. *prīmus*; see **Prime.**

prior (2), head of a priory. (F. – L.)
M. E. *priour.* – A. F. *priour*; F. *prieur.*
– L. *priōrem*, acc. of *prior*, former, hence,
a superior; see above.

Prise, Prize, a lever. (F. – L.) '*Prise*,
a lever;' Halliwell. Hence 'to *prise* open
a box,' or corruptly, 'to *pry* open.' – F.
prise, a grasp, tight hold (hence, leverage).
Orig. fem. of *pris*, pp. of *prendre*, to
grasp. – L. *prehendere*, to grasp. See
Prehensile.

Prism. (L. – Gk.) L. *prisma.* – Gk.
πρίσμα (stem πρισματ-), a prism; lit. a
piece sawn off. – Gk. πρίειν, for **πρίσειν*,
to saw. (Gk. √πρίς.) **Der.** *prismat-ic.*

Prison. (F. – L.) O. F. *prisun*, F.
prison; cf. Ital. *prigione*, a prison. – L.
acc. *prensiōnem*, acc. of *prensio*, a seizing,
seizure. – L. *prensus*, for *prehensus*, pp. of
prehendere, to seize. See **Prehensile.**

Pristine, ancient. (F. – L.) M. F. *pristine.* – L. *pristinus,* ancient; allied to L. *pris-cus,* former, and to prime (1).

Private. (L.) L. *prīuātus,* apart; pp. of *prīuāre,* to bereave. – L. *prīuus,* single; lit. put forward, sundered from the rest.

Privet, a shrub. (F. ? – L. ?) *Privet* seems to be a corruption of *primet,* which also means a primrose; confusion between the plants arose from the L. *ligustrum* being applied to both. We also find, for privet, the names *prim, primprint, primprivet;* where *print* is short for *primet* (*prim't*), and *primprint* stands for *prim-prim-et.* Prob. named from being formally cut and trimmed; cf. *prime,* to cut trees (Halliwell). See Prim and Prime (1). *Primet,* a primrose, is likewise from *prime.*

Privilege. (F. – L.) O. F. *privilege.* – L. *prīuilēgium,* (1) a bill against a person, (2) an ordinance in favour of one, a privilege. – L. *prīui-,* for *prīuus,* single; *lēg-,* stem of *lex,* law.

privy, private. (F. – L.) O. F. *prive* (F. *privé*), private. – L. *prīuātus,* private; see Private.

Prize (1), a thing captured from the enemy or won in a lottery. (F. – L.) F. *prise,* a seizure, also, a prize; see Prise.

Prize (2), to value highly. (F. – L.) M. E. *prisen.* – F. *priser,* to esteem. – O. F. *pris* (F. *prix*), a price, value. – L. *pretium,* value. See Price.

Prize (3), the same as Prise.

Pro-, prefix. (L. *or* Gk.; *or* F. – L.) L. *pro-,* prefix, before; cf. also *prō* (= *prōd*), an abl. form, used as a prep. Also Gk. προ-, prefix; πρό, prep., before; cf. Skt. *pra,* before, away. See *pre-,* prefix; *prior, pri-me, pri-vate, prow, pro-vost,* &c.

Proa, Proe, Prow, Prau, a small ship. (Malay.) Malay *prāhu, prāu,* a general term for small ships.

Probable. (F. – L.) F. *probable.* – L. *probābilis,* that may be proved. – L. *probāre,* to test, prove, orig. to try the goodness. – L. *probus,* good, excellent. See Prove.

probation. (F. – L.) F. *probation.* – L. acc. *probātiōnem,* a trial, proof. – L. *probātus,* pp. of *probāre,* to test.

probe. (L.) A coined word; cf. Late L. *proba,* a proof. – L. *probāre,* to test; see above.

probity. (F. – L.) F. *probité,* honesty. – L. *probitātem,* acc. of *probitās,* honesty. – L. *probus,* honest, excellent.

Problem. (F. – L. – Gk.) O. F. *probleme;* F. *problème.* – L. *problēma.* – Gk. πρόβλημα, a thing thrown forward, or put forward as a question for discussion. – Gk. πρό, forward; βλῆμα, a casting, from βάλλειν, to cast.

Proboscis. (L. – Gk.) L. *proboscis.* – Gk. προβοσκίς, an elephant's trunk or 'feeder.' – Gk. πρό, in front; βόσκειν, to feed; see Botany.

Proceed. (F. – L.) O. F. *proceder.* – L. *prōcēdere,* to go forward. – L. *prō,* before; *cēdere,* to go. See Cede. Der. *process* (mod. F. *procès*); *process-ion.*

Proclaim. (F. – L.) F. *proclamer,* 'to proclame;' Cot. – L. *proclāmāre,* to call out. – L. *prō,* forth; *clāmāre,* to cry out. See Claim.

Proclivity. (L.) From L. *prōclīuitās,* a downward slope, tendency. – L. *prōclīuus,* sloping forward. – L. *prō,* forward; *clīuus,* a slope. (√KLEI.) Cf. Acclivity.

Procrastinate, to postpone. (L.) From pp. of L. *prōcrastināre,* to delay, put off till the morrow. – L. *prō,* forward, off; *crastinus,* belonging to the morrow, from *crās,* morrow.

Procreate. (L.) L. *prōcreātus,* pp. of *prōcreāre,* to generate. – L. *prō,* before, forth; *creāre,* to produce. See Create.

Proctor. (L.) M. E. *proketour;* short form of *procuratour.* – O. F. *procurator.* – L. acc. *prōcūrātōrem;* see Procurator.

Procumbent, prostrate. (L.) L. *prōcumbent-,* stem of *prōcumbens,* pres. pt. of *prōcumbere,* to sink forwards. – L. *prō,* forwards; *cumbere,* to recline, allied to *cubāre,* to lie down. See Covey.

Procurator. (L.) L. *prōcūrātor,* a manager, deputy. – L. *prōcūrāre;* see below.

procure. (F. – L.) F. *procurer.* – L. *prōcūrāre,* to take care of, manage. – L. *prō,* before; *cūrāre,* to take care, from *cūra,* care. See Cure.

Prodigal. (F. – L.) O. F. *prodigal.* – Late Lat. *prōdigālis;* due to L. *prōdigus,* lavish; for **prōd-agus.* – L. *prōd-,* forth; and *agere,* to do, act. See Agent.

Prodigy. (F. – L.) Englished from F. *prodige,* a prodigy, wonder. – L. *prōdigium,* a token, portent, prophetic sign. β. Perhaps for **prōdagium,* i. e. a saying beforehand, from *prōd* (*prō*), before, and **agium,* a saying, as in *ad-agium;* see Adage. Brugm. i. § 759.

Produce, vb. (L.) L. *prōdūcere*, to bring forward. — L. *prō*, forward; *dūcere*, to lead. See **Duke.** Der. *product-ive*, *-ion* (from the pp. below).

product, sb. (L.) L. *prōductus*, produced; pp. of *prōdūcere* (above).

Proem. (F. — L. — Gk.) M. F. *proëme*, 'a proem, preface;' Cot. — L. *prooemium.* — Gk. *προοίμιον*, an introduction. — Gk. *πρό*, before; *οἶμος*, a way, path, from √EI, to go.

Profane, impious. (F. — L.) F. *profane.* — L. *profānus*, unholy; lit. before (i. e. outside of) the temple. — L. *prō*, before; *fānum*, a temple.

Profess. (F. — L.) We find M. E. *professed*, pp., Englished from O. F. *profes*, masc., *professe*, fem., professed. — L. *professus*, pp. of *profitērī*, to avow. — L. *prō*, forth; *fatērī*, to speak; see **Confess.**

Proffer. (F. — L.) M. F. *proferer*, to produce, adduce. — L. *prōferre*, to bring forward. — L. *prō*, forward; *ferre*, to bring, cognate with E. *bear*. See **Bear** (1).

Proficient. (L.) L. *prōficient-*, stem of pres. pt. of *prōficere*, to make progress, advance. — L. *prō*, forward; *facere*, to make. See **Fact.**

Profile. (Ital. — L.) Ital. *profilo*, a sketch of a picture, outline (Florio). — L. *prō*, before, in front; *fīlum*, a thread (Ital. *filo*, thread, line). ¶ The mod. F. *profil* is also from Ital. *profilo*.

Profit. (F. — L.) M.E. *profit.* — F. *profit.* — L. *prōfectum*, neut. of *prōfectus*, pp. of *prōficere*, to make progress, be profitable. See **Proficient.**

Profligate. (L.) L. *prōflīgātus*, cast down, abandoned, dissolute; pp. of *prōflīgāre*, to dash down. — L. *prō*, forward; *flīgere*, to strike, dash. See **Afflict.**

Profound, deep. (F. — L.) F. *profond.* — L. *profundum*, acc. of *profundus*, deep. — L. *prō*, forward, hence downward; *fundus*, bottom, allied to **Bottom.** Der. *profund-ity.* M. F. *profondité.*

Profuse, lavish. (L.) L. *profūsus*, pp. of *profundere*, to pour forth. — L. *prō*, forth; *fundere*, to pour. See **Fuse** (1).

Progenitor. (F. — L.) Formerly *progenitour.* — M. F. *progeniteur.* — L. *prōgenitōrem*, acc. of *prōgenitor*, an ancestor. — L. *prō*, before; *genitor*, a parent, from the base of *gignere*, to beget. (√GEN.) See **Genus.**

progeny. (F. — L.) O. F. *progenie.* — L. *prōgeniem*, acc. of *prōgeniēs*, lineage,

offspring. — L. *prō-*, forth; *genus*, kin. See **Genus.**

Prognostic, a presage. (F. — L. — Gk.) M. F. *prognostique*; Cot. — L. *prognōsticon.* — Gk. *προγνωστικόν*, a token of the future. — Gk. *πρό*, before; *γνωστικός*, good at knowing. See **Gnostic.**

Programme, Program. (F. — L. — Gk.) Now spelt as if from F. *programme*; formerly *programma* (1706), from L. *programma.* — Gk. *πρόγραμμα*, a public notice in writing. — Gk. *πρό*, beforehand; *γράμμα*, a writing, from *γράφειν*, to write.

Progress, advancement. (F. — L.) M. F. *progrez* (F. *progrès*). — L. *prōgressum*, acc. of *prōgressus*, an advance. — L. *prōgressus*, pp. of *prōgredī*, to go forward. — L. *prō*, forward; and *gradī*, to walk. See **Grade.**

Prohibit, to check. (L.) From L. *prohibitus*, pp. of *prohibēre*, to hold before one, put in one's way, prohibit. — L. *prō*, before; *habēre*, to have, keep. See **Habit.**

Project, sb., a plan. (F. — L.) M. F. *project* (F. *projet*), a project, purpose. — L. *prōiectum*, neut. of *prōiectus*, pp. of *prōicere* (*proiicere*), to fling forth; hence (in Late L.) to purpose, plan. — L. *prō*, forth; *iacere*, to cast. See **Jet** (1).

Prolate, extended in the direction of the polar axis. (L.) L. *prōlātus*, extended. — L. *prō*, forward; *lātus*, carried, pp. of *tollere*, to lift, bear. See **Tolerate.**

Prolepsis, anticipation. (L. — Gk.) L. *prolēpsis.* — Gk. *πρόληψις*, lit. a taking beforehand. — Gk. *πρό*, before; *λῆψις*, a seizing, from *λήψ-ομαι*, fut. of *λαμβάνειν*, to seize. See **Catalepsy.**

Proletarian, a citizen of the lowest class, useful only by producing children. (L.) From L. *prōlētārius*, one who served the state by help of his children only. — L. *prōles*, offspring (below).

prolific. (F. — L.) F. *prolifique*, fruitful. — L. *prōli-*, decl. stem of *prōles*, offspring; *-ficus*, from *facere*, to make. Perhaps L. *prōles* = *prō-oles*, from *prō*, before, and **olēre*, to grow, whence *ad-olescere*, to grow up; cf. *sub-oles*, *ind-oles*. See **Adult.**

Prolix. (F. — L.) F. *prolixe.* — L. *prōlixus*, extended. Lit. 'that which has flowed forth' or beyond bounds; from *prō*, forth, *liquēre*, *līquī*, to flow. Cf. *ē-lixus*, soaked. See **Liquid.**

Prolocutor, the chairman of a conference. (L.) L. *prōlocūtor*, an advocate. — L. *prōlocūtus*, pp. of *prōloquī*, to speak in public. — L. *prō*, publicly; *loquī*, to speak. See **Loquacious**.

Prologue, a preface. (F. — L. — Gk.) F. *prologue.* — L. *prōlogum*, acc. of *prōlogus*. — Gk. πρόλογος, a fore-speech. — Gk. πρό, before; λόγος, a speech. See **Logic**.

Prolong, to continue. (F. — L.) M. E. *prolongen.* — F. *prolonger.* — L. *prolongāre*, to prolong. — L. *prō-*, forward; *longus*, long. See **Long**. Doublet, *purloin*.

Promenade, a walk. (F. — L.) Formed with O. F. suffix *-ade* (< L. *-āta*) from O. F. *promener*, to walk. — Late L. *prōmināre*, to drive forwards. — L. *prō*, forwards; Late L. *mināre*, to drive, lead; from L. *minārī*, to threaten. See **Menace**.

Prominent, projecting, forward. (L.) L. *prōminent-*, stem of pres. pt. of *prōminēre*, to project forward. — L. *prō*, forward; *-minēre*, to project. See **Menace**.

Promiscuous, mixed, confused. (L.) For L. *prōmiscuus*, mixed. — L. *prō*, forward (here of slight force); *miscēre*, to mix. See **Miscellaneous**.

Promise, an agreement to do a thing. (F. — L.) Formerly *promes.* — F. *promesse*, 'a promise;' Cot. — L. *prōmissa*, fem. of *prōmissus*, pp. of *prōmittere*, to send or put forth, to promise. — L. *prō*, forward; *mittere*, to send. See **Missile**. Der. *promiss-o-ry*.

Promontory, a headland. (L.) L. *prōmonturium*, a ridge, headland. Prob. from *prōminēre*, to jut out; see **Prominent**, and cf. **Mount**.

Promote, to advance, further. (L.) From L. *prōmōt-us*, pp. of *prōmouēre*, to move forward. — L. *prō*, forward; *mouēre*, to move. See **Move**.

Prompt. (F. — L.) F. *prompt.* — L. *promptum*, acc. of *promptus*, *promtus*, brought to light, at hand, ready, pp. of *prōmere*, to bring forward; for **prōd-imere* — L. *prōd*, forward; *emere*, to take, bring. Cf. **Exempt**.

Promulgate. (L.) From pp. of L. *prōmulgāre* to publish. (Of unknown origin.)

Prone. (F. — L.) M. F. *prone.* — L. *prōnum*, acc. of *prōnus*, inclined towards. *Prōnus* is prob. allied to Gk. πρηνής, headlong; cf. Skt. *pravaṇa*, inclined to, prone.

Prong, spike of a fork. (E.) Spelt

prongue in Levins (1570). The M. E. *pronge*, a pang, sharp pain, is the same word. Cf. M. E. *prangelen*, to constrain (Havelok). Also Du. *prangen*, to pinch, oppress; M. Du. *prangen*, to oppress, shackle, constrain; *prange*, a muzzle, shackle, collar; Low G. *prangen*, to press, push hard; *prange*, a stake; G. *pranger*, a pillory; Goth. *ana-praggan* (= *-prangan*), to press. All from a Teut. base **prang*, to press, nip, push.

Pronoun. (F. — L) Coined from L. *prō*, for; and E. *noun*; suggested by F. *pronom*, L. *prōnōmen*, a pronoun. See **Noun**.

Pronounce. (F. — L.) F. *prononcer*. — L. *prōnuntiāre*, to pronounce, lit. tell forth. — L. *prō*, forth; *nuntiāre*, to tell. See **Nuncio**. Der. *pronunciat-ion*, from L. pp. *prōnuntiāt-us*, with suffix *-iōn-*.

Proof, a test, evidence. (F. — L.) Formerly *profe* (1551); altered from M. E. *preef*, *preove*. — F. *preuve*, a trial; Cot. — Late L. *proba*, a proof. — L. *probāre*, to test. See **Prove**, **Probable**.

Prop. (E.) M. E. *proppe*. [Also Irish *propa*, Gael. *prop*, a prop, support; borrowed from E.] Cf. Du. *prop*, a stopple; M. Du. *prop*, *proppe*, 'a prop, a stopple,' Hexham; *proppen*, 'to prop, stay, or bear up,' Hexham; Low G. *propp*, a plug, G. *pfropf*, a cork, also a graft. All from a Teut. base **prup*, to stop up, to support. ¶ In the sense of 'graft,' the G. *pfropf* is due to L. *propāgo*; see **Propagate**.

Propagate. (L.) From the pp. of L. *prōpāgāre* (or *pro-*), to peg down, propagate by layers; allied to *prōpāgēs*, *prōpāgo* (or *pro-*), a layer, and from the same source as *compāgēs*, a fastening together. — L. *prō*, forth; *pāg-*, base of *pangere*, to fasten, set (hence, to peg down). Der. *propagandist*, a coined word; from the name of the society entitled *Congregatio de propaganda fide*, constituted at Rome, A. D. 1622. And see **Prune** (1).

Propel, to urge forward. (L.)ʼ L. *prōpellere*, to drive forward. — L. *prō*, forward; *pellere*, to drive; see **Pulse** (1). Der. *propuls-ion*, from pp. *prōpulsus*.

Propensity, an inclination. (L.) Coined from L. *prōpensus*, hanging down, inclining towards; pp. of *prōpendēre*, to hang down or forward. — L. *prō*, forward; *pendēre*, to hang. See **Pendant**.

Proper, one's own, peculiar, suitable. (F. — L.) M. E. *propre.* — F. *propre.* — L.

proprium, acc. of *proprius,* one's own. Prob. akin to *prope,* near.

property. (F. – L.) M. E. *propertee.* – O. F. *properté,* property (Littré), also propriety, fitness. – L. *proprietātem,* acc. of *proprietās,* property, ownership; also propriety of terms. – L. *proprius,* one's own.

Prophecy. (F. – L. – Gk.) M. E. *prophecie,* sb. – O. F. *prophecie,* variant of *prophetie,* a prophecy. – L. *prophētīa.* – Gk. προφητεία, a prediction. – Gk. προφήτης, a prophet (below). Der. *prophesy,* vb.

prophet. (F. – L. – Gk.) O. F. *prophete.* – L. *prophēta.* – Gk. προφήτης, one who declares, an expounder, a prophet. – Gk. πρό, publicly, lit. before; φη-μί, I speak; with suffix -της of the agent. (√ BHĀ.) Allied to **Fame.**

Propinquity, nearness. (F. – L.) O. F. *propinquité.* – L. *propinquitātem,* acc. of *propinquitās,* nearness. – L. *propinquus,* near. – L. *prope,* adv., near.

Propitious, favourable. (L.) For L. *propitius,* favourable. Prob. a term in augury, with the sense ' flying forwards.' – L. *pro-,* forward; *petere,* to seek, orig. to fly. See **Petition.** Der. *propitiate,* from pp. of L. *propitiāre,* to render propitious.

Proportion. (F. – L.) F. *proportion.* – L. acc. *prōportiōnem,* from *prōportio,* comparative relation. – L. *prō,* before, in relation to; *portio,* a portion; see **Portion.**

Propose. (F. – L. *and* Gk.) F. *proposer,* lit. to place before. – L. *prō,* before; F. *poser,* to place, from Gk. See **Pose.**

Proposition. (F. – L.) F. *proposition.* – L. acc. *prōpositiōnem,* a statement. – L. *prōpositus,* pp. of *prōpōnere,* to put forth. – L. *prō,* forth; *pōnere,* to put.

propound. (L.) The *d* is excrescent; formerly *propoune, propone.* – L. *prōpōnere* (above).

Propriety. (F. – L.) M. F. *proprieté,* a property, also ' a comely assortment,' Cot. – L. acc. *proprietātem,* from *proprietās,* property; also, propriety. – L. *proprius,* one's own. Doublet, *property.*

Prorogue. (F. – L.) O. F. *proroguer.* – L. *prōrogāre,* to propose an extension of office, lit. to ask publicly; hence, to defer. – L. *prō,* publicly; *rogāre,* to ask. See **Rogation.**

Pros-, towards. (Gk.) Gk. πρός, towards; fuller form προτί, extended from πρό, before. + Skt. *prati,* towards, from *pra,* before. See **Pro-.**

Proscenium, the front part of a stage. (L. – Gk.) L. *proscēnium.* – Gk. προσκήνιον, the place before the stage (or scene). – Gk. πρό, before; σκηνή, a scene. See **Scene.**

Proscribe. (L.) L. *prōscrībere,* lit. to write publicly; pp. *prōscriptus* (whence *proscription*). – L. *prō,* publicly; *scrībere,* to write. See **Scribe.**

Prose. (F. – L.) F. *prose.* – L. *prōsa,* for *prorsa orātio,* direct speech; hence, unimbellished speech; fem. of *prorsus,* forward, short for *prōuersus,* lit. turned forward. – L. *prō,* forward; *uersus,* pp. of *uertere,* to turn. See **Verse.**

Prosecute. (L.) From L. *prōsecūtus,* pp. of *prōsequī,* to pursue. – L. *prō,* forward; *sequī,* to follow. See **Sequence.** Doublet, *pursue.*

Proselyte, a convert. (F. – L. – Gk.) O. F. *proselite.* – L. *prosēlytum,* acc. of *prosēlytus.* – Gk. προσήλυτος, one who has come to a place, a stranger, a convert to Judaism; Acts ii. 10. – Gk. προσέρχομαι, I approach, 2 aor. προσῆλθον (= προσήλυθον). – Gk. πρός, to; ἔρχομαι, I come. [Gk. ἔρχομαι and ἤλυθον are from different roots; the latter goes with ἐλεύσομαι, I will come; from √LEUDH.]

Prosody. (F. – L. – Gk.) F. *prosodie.* – L. *prosōdia.* – Gk. προσῳδία, a song sung to an instrument, a tone, accent, prosody, (or laws of verse). – Gk. πρός, to, accompanying; ᾠδή, an ode. See **Ode.**

Prosopopoeia, personification. (L. – Gk.) L. *prosōpopœia.* – Gk. προσωποποιία personification. – Gk. προσωποποιεῖν, to personify. – Gk. πρόσωπο-ν, a face, a person; ποιεῖν, to make. Πρόσωπον is from πρός, towards, and ὤπ-, stem of ὤψ, face, appearance. See **Pros-, Optic,** and **Poem.**

Prospect. (L.) L. *prospectus,* a view. – L. *prospectus,* pp. of *prospicere,* to look forward. – L. *prō,* forward; *specere,* to look. See **Species.** Der. *prospectus* = L. *prospectus,* a view.

Prosperous. (L.) L. *prosper,* adj., prosperous; with suffix *-ous.* Cf. L. *prosperus,* by-form of *prosper.* Lit. ' according to one's hope.' – L. *prō,* for, according to; *sper-,* weak grade of *spēr-* for *spēs,* hope. Der. *prosper,* vb.; O. F. *prosperer,* L. *prosperāre,* to prosper; from *prosper,* adj.

Prosthetic, prefixed. (Gk.) Modern; as if for Gk. *προσθετικός,* lit. disposed to add; due to Gk. πρόσθετ-ος, added, put to. – Gk. πρός, to; θε-τός, placed, put, verbal adj. from the base θε-, to place. See **Thesis.**

Prostitute. (L.) L. *prŏstitūta*, f. pp. of *prŏstituere*, to expose openly, prostitute. — L. *prō*, forth; *statuere*, to place, causal of *stāre*, to stand. See **State.**

Prostrate. (L.) L. *prŏstrātus*, pp. of *prŏsternere*, to throw forward on the ground. — L. *prō*, forward; *sternere*, to spread. See **Stratum.** Der. *prostrat-ion.*

Protean. (L. — Gk.) From L. *Prōteus* (misdivided as *Prōte-us*), a sea-god who often changed his form. — Gk. Πρωτεύς, a sea-god; cf. πρῶτος, first, chief.

Protect. (L.) From L. *prōtectus*, pp. of *prōtegere*, to protect; lit. cover in front. — L. *prō*, in front; *tegere*, to cover. See **Tegument.**

Protest. (F. — L.) F. *protester.* — L. *prōtestārī*, to protest, bear public witness. — L. *prō*, forth, in public; *testārī*, to witness, from *testis*, a witness. See **Testament.**

Prothalamium. (L. — Gk.) Late L. **prothalamium.* — Gk.*πρoθαλάμιον, a song written before a marriage; a coined word. — Gk. πρό, before; θάλαμος, a bedroom, bride-chamber. Coined to accompany *epithalamium*, q. v.

Protocol, the first draught of a document. (F. — L. — Gk.) M. F. *protocole*, 'the first draught or copy of a deed.' — Late L. *prōtocollum.* — Late Gk. πρωτόκολλον, explained by Scheler to mean orig. a first leaf, glued on to MSS., in order to register by whom the MS. was written, &c. By a decree of Justinian, certain MSS. were to be thus accompanied by a fly-leaf. It means 'first glued on,' i. e. fastened on at the beginning. — Gk. πρῶτο-s, first; κολλᾶν, to glue, from κόλλα, glue. Πρῶτος is a superl. form from πρό, before; see **Pro-.**

protomartyr. (F. — L. — Gk.) M. F. *protomartyre.* — Late L. *prōtomartyr.* — Gk. πρωτόμαρτυρ, lit. ' first martyr.' — Gk. πρῶτο-s, first (above); μάρτυρ, a martyr; see **Martyr.**

prototype. (F. — L. — Gk.) F. *prototype.* — L. acc. *prōtotypum.* — Gk. πρωτό-τυπον, a prototype, neut. of πρωτότυπος, according to the first form. — Gk. πρῶτο-s, first (above); τύπος, a type; see **Type.**

Protract. (L.) From L. *prōtractus*, pp. of *prōtrahere*, to draw forward, also to extend, prolong. — L. *prō*, forth; *trahere*, to draw. See **Trace** (1), **Portray.**

Protrude. (L.) L. *prōtrūdere*, to

thrust forth. — L. *prō*, forth; *trūdere* (pp. *trūsus*), to thrust. Der. *protrus-ion* (from the pp.). Cf. **Intrude.**

Protuberant. (L.) From stem of pres. pt. of *prōtūberāre*, to bulge out. — L. *prō*, forward; *tūber*, a swelling. See **Tuber.**

Proud. (F. — L.?) M. E. *prud*, later *proud*; older form *prut*. A. S. *prūt*, proud; whence the Icel. *prūðr*, proud, is supposed to have been borrowed; cf. Dan. *prud*, stately. β. A late word in A. S.; and prob. merely borrowed from O. French. — O. F. *prod*, *prud*, fem. *prode*, *prude*, valiant, notable (taken in a bad sense). See further under **Prowess.** Der. *pride.*

Prove, to test, demonstrate. (L.) The usual old sense is to test or try. — A. S. *prōfian.* [Cf. O. F. *prover*, later *prouver*, ' to prove, try, essay, verifie;' Cot.] — L. *probāre*, to test, try the goodness of. — L. *probus*, excellent. See **Probable.**

Provender. (F. — L.) The final *r* is an O. F. addition. — O. F. *provendre* (Godefroy), usually *provende*, ' provender, also, a prebendary;' Cot. — Late L. *præbenda*, an allowance of provisions, also a prebend; see **Prebend.**

Proverb. (F. — L.) F. *proverbe.* — L. *prōuerbium*, a common saying. — L. *prō*, publicly; *uerb-um*, a word, cognate with E. **Word.**

Provide. (L.) L. *prōuidēre* (pp. *prōuīsus*), to foresee, act with foresight. — L. *prō*, before; *uidēre*, to see. See **Vision.** Der. *provident*, *provis-ion.*

Province. (F. — L.) F. *province.* — L. *prōuincia*, a territory brought under Roman government. (Of doubtful origin.)

Provision. (F. — L.) F. *provision.* — L. acc. *prōuīsiōnem*, foresight, forethought, purveyance. — L. *prōuīs-us*, pp. of *prōuidēre*, to provide for. See **Provide.**

Provoke. (F. — L.) F. *provoquer*; Cot. — L. *prōuocāre*, to call forth. — L. *prō*, forth; *uocāre*, to call. See **Vocal.**

Provost, a prefect. (L.) A. F. *provost*; [cf. M. F. *prevost*, ' the provost or president of a college;' Cot.] A. S. *prāfost.* — L. *præpositus*, a prefect, one set over. — L. *præpōnere*, to set over. — L. *præ*, before; *pōnere*, to put. See **Position.**

Prow, front part of a ship. (F. — L. — Gk.) O. F. *prouë* (F. *proue*), prow. [Cf. Ital. *proda*.] — L. *prōra*, a prow; the 2nd *r* disappearing to avoid the double trill (as also in Prov. Span. Port. *proa*, Genoese *prua*). ─ Gk. πρῷρα, the prow. ─ Gk. πρό-, before, in front. See **Pro-**.

Prowess, bravery. (F.─L.) M. E. *prowes, pruesse.*─O. F. *prouesse,* prowess; formed with suffix *-esse* (<L. *-itia*) from O. F. *prou* (F. *preux*), valiant. β. Etym. disputed; we also find O. F. *prod, prud, proz, prous, pru*; Prov. *proz,* Ital. *prode,* valiant, notable (whence Ital. *prodezza,* prowess). Also O. F. *prou,* sb., advantage (whence M. E. *prow,* advantage). Although O. F. *prod* was used to translate L. *probus,* the spelling with *d* shows there is no connexion between these forms. γ. Scheler explains it from L. *prōd-,* as occurring in *prōd-esse,* to benefit; so that *prōd* was taken to mean 'for the benefit of'; and we even find F. *prou* used as an adverb, as in *prou,* 'much, greatly, enough;' Cot. *Prōd* is the old form of *prŏ,* before.

Prowl. (O. Low G.) M. E. *prollen,* to search after continually. 'I *prolle,* I go here and there to seke a thyng;' Palsgrave. '*Prollyn,* scrutor. *Prollynge,* or sekynge, perscrutacio;' Prompt. Parv. It also meant to rob, plunder. Like the word *plunder,* it prob. meant 'to filch trifles,' or 'to sneak after trifles'; from Low G. *prull, prulle,* a trifle, thing of small value (Bremen). Cf. Du. *prul,* 'a bawble' (Sewel), *prullen,* 'lumber, luggage, pelf, trumpery, toys' (id.); *prullen-kooper,* a ragman (Calisch); E. Fries. *prülle, prül,* a trifle. Root unknown.

Proximity. (F.─L.) F. *proximité.* ─L. *proximitātem,* acc. of *proximitās,* nearness. ─ L. *proximus,* very near; a superl. form from *prope,* near. See **Propinquity**.

Proxy. (Late L.─L.) Palsgrave has *prockesy*; short for *procuracy.*─Late L. *prōcūrātia,* used for L. *prōcūrātio,* management.─L. *prōcūrāre,* to manage, to procure. See **Procure**.

Prude, a woman of affected modesty. (F.─L.) F. *prude,* M. F. *preude,* orig. in a good sense, chaste; used (but not originally) as the fem. of F. *preux,* O. F. *preu,* excellent, which at first had but *one* form for the masc. and fem. (Godefroy). Perhaps the forms *preudomme, preude-femme* arose from misunderstanding the O. F. phrases *preu d'omme* and *preu de femme* (Tobler). O. F. *preu* is a variant of O. F. *prod, prou*; see **Prowess**.

Prudent. (F.─L.) F. *prudent.*─L. *prūdentem,* acc. of *prūdens,* contr. form of

prōuidens, foreseeing, pres. pt. of *prōuidēre,* to foresee.─L. *prō,* before; *uidēre,* to see. See **Vision**.

Prune (1), to trim trees. (F.?─L.?) Very difficult. M. E. *proinen, prunen,* to dress oneself up smartly, trim; Gascoigne has *proyne,* to prune off shoots. Prob. from a provincial form of F. *provigner* (also spelt *prougner, proignier,* Godefroy, *preugner, progner,* Littré), 'to plant or set a stocke, staulke, slip, or sucker,' Cot.; hence the sense, to clear off or to trim off suckers, stalks, &c. This verb is from F. *provin,* O. F. *provain,* a sucker.─L. *propāginem,* acc. of *propāgo,* a layer, a sucker. See **Propagate**.

Prune (2), a plum. (F.─L.─Gk.) F. *prune.* ─ L. *prūnum.* ─ Gk. προῦνον, shorter form of προῦμνον, a plum.

prunella, prunello, a strong woollen stuff, orig. of a *dark* colour. (F.─L.─Gk.) F. *prunelle,* a sloe (with ref. to the colour); whence *prünella* is a Latinised form. Dimin. of F. *prune* (above).

Prurient. (L.) L. *prūrient-,* stem of pres. pt. of *prūrīre,* to itch, orig. to burn. Allied to E. **Freeze.** Brugm. i. § 562.

Pry, to peer into, search inquisitively. (F.─L.) M. E. *prien.*─O. F. *prier, preër,* to pillage [to search for plunder].─ Late L. *prēdāre,* to plunder, also to investigate; Duc.─L. *præda,* prey; see **Prey**.

Psalm. (L.─Gk.) M. E. *psalm,* formerly *salm.* A. S. *sealm.*─L. *psalmus.*─ Gk. ψαλμός, a touching, twitching the strings of a harp; also a song, psalm.─ Gk. ψάλλειν, to touch, twitch, twang a harp. Der. *psalmod-y,* F. *psalmodie,* L. *psalmōdia,* Gk. ψαλμῳδία, a singing to the harp, from ᾠδή, a song; see **Ode**.

psaltery, a stringed instrument. (F. ─ L. ─ Gk.) O. F. *psalterie* (12th cent.).─L. *psaltērium.*─Gk. ψαλτήριον, a kind of harp.─Gk. ψαλτήρ, a harper.─ Gk. ψάλ-λειν, to twang a harp; with suffix -τηρ of the agent. Der. *psalter,* O. F. *psaltier,* a book of psalms, L. *psaltērium,* (1) a psaltery, (2) a psalter.

Pseudonym. (F.─Gk.) F. *pseudonyme* (1690). ─ Gk. ψευδώνυμος, adj., called by a false name.─Gk. ψεῦδ-ος, falsehood (ψευδής, false), from ψεύδειν, to lie; ὄνυμα, a name.

Pshaw, interjection. (E.) An imitative word; cf. *pish, pooh.*

Psychical, pertaining to the soul. (L.

—Gk.) From L. *psȳchicus.*—Gk. ψυχικόs, belonging to the soul or life.—Gk. ψυχή, soul, life, orig. breath.—Gk. ψύχειν, to blow.

psychology. (Gk.) Gk. ψυχο-, for ψυχή, soul, life; -λογία, from λόγοs, a discourse, from λέγειν, to speak.

Ptarmigan, a bird. (Gael.) Formerly *termigant.*—Gael. *tarmachan*; Irish *tarmochan.* ¶ The *p* was probably due to a notion of a Greek origin; but Gk. πταρμική means 'milfoil'!

Puberty. (F.—L.) F. *puberté,* youth. —L. *pūbertātem,* acc. of *pūbertās,* age of maturity.—L. *pūbēs,* the signs of manhood, hair. Allied to *pū-pus, pu-er,* a boy. Der. *pubescence,* sb. due to *pūbescent-,* stem of pres. pt. of *pūbescere,* to arrive at puberty.

Public. (F.—L.) F. *public,* masc., *publique,* fem.; Cot.—L. *publicus,* belonging to the people; also *poublicos, poplicos* (in inscriptions).—L. *populus,* the people.

publican. (L.) M. E. *publican.*—L. *publicānus,* a tax-gatherer, Luke iii. 12; orig. an adj., belonging to the public revenue.—L. *publicus* (above).

publication. (F.—L.) F. *publication.* —L. acc. *publicātiōnem.*—L. *publicātus,* pp. of *publicāre,* to make public.—L. *publicus,* public.

publish. (F.—L.) M. E. *publishen.* An analogical formation; founded on F. *publier,* to publish.—L. *publicāre* (above).

Puce, the name of a colour. (F.—L.) Lit. 'flea-colour.'—F. *puce,* a flea; *couleur puce,* puce; O. F. *pulce.*—L. *pūlicem,* acc. of *pūlex,* a flea. ¶ Said to be the same as *puke,* which was also the name of a dark-brown colour, but the form *puke* is difficult to explain. The Picard and Walloon form of *puce* was *puche.*

Puck. (E.) M. E. *pouke.* A. S. *pūca* (Napier); whence Irish *puca,* an elf, sprite; W. *pwca, pwci.*+Icel. *pūki,* an imp.

Pucker, to gather into folds. (Scand.) Particularly used of the folds in the top of a *poke* or bag, when gathered together by drawing the string tight. So also M. Ital. *saccolare,* to pucker, from *sacco,* a sack; and E. *purse,* as 'to *purse* up the brows.' Cf. Norman F. *pouque,* for F. *poche,* a pouch, bag. See **Poke** (1).

Pudding, an intestine filled with meat, a sausage; hence, a sort of light food, made of flour, eggs, &c. (E.) M. E. *pudding, poding.* Cf. Low G. *pudding,* a pudding; *pudde-wurst,* a black-pudding;

puddig, thick, stumpy; Westphal. *puddek,* a lump, a pudding. Apparently from a Teut. base **pud,* to swell out, similar to **put;* cf. A. S. *pud-uc,* a wen (Toller); and see **Poodle** and **Pout.** β. Cf. also Irish *putog,* a pudding, Gael. *putag;* W. *poten,* a paunch, a pudding; Corn. *pot,* a bag, pudding; also W. *pwtyn,* a short round body, Gael. *put,* a buoy, inflated skin; all borrowed words. See **Pout.**

Puddle (1), a small dirty pool. (E.) M. E. *podel.* Dimin., with E. suffix *-el,* of A. S. *pudd,* a ditch, a furrow (Toller).

puddle (2), to make thick or muddy. (E.) From the sb. above.

Puerile. (F.—L.) M. F. *pueril* (15th cent.).—L. *puerīlis,* boyish.—L. *puer,* a boy.

puerperal, relating to child-birth. (L.) From L. *puerpera,* fem. adj., bearing a child.—L. *puer,* a boy; and *parere,* to bear; see **Parent.**

Puff, to blow. (E.) M. E. *puffen;* of imitative origin.+G. *puffen,* to puff, pop, Dan. *puffe,* to pop, Swed. *puffa,* to crack, push; W. *pwff,* a puff (from E.).

puffin, a bird. (E.) From its *puffed out* appearance, or from its swelling beak.

Pug, a monkey, a kind of dog. (E.) Orig. an imp, or little demon (Ben Jonson); see Nares, s. v. *puck.* A later form of *puck.* Cf. Dan. dial. *puge,* a 'puck,' sprite; and (perhaps) Dan. dial. *pugge,* a toad. 'A *pug-dog* is a dog with a short monkey-like face;' Wedgwood.

Puggry, Puggery, a scarf round the hat. (Hind.) Hind. *pagrī,* a turban; Yule.

Pugilism. (L.) From L. *pugil,* a boxer. Allied to L. *pugnus,* Gk. πυγ-μή, the fist.

pugnacious. (L.) Coined from L. *pugnāci-,* decl. stem of *pugnax,* combative. —L. *pugnāre,* to fight.—L. *pugnus,* the fist.

Puisne, Puny. (F.—L.) *Puny* is for *puisne,* a law-term, implying inferior in rank. — A. F. and M. F. *puisné,* 'puny, younger, born after;' Cot.—L. *post nātus,* born after. See **Natal.**

Puissant, mighty. (F.—L.) F. *puissant,* powerful. Cf. Ital. *possente,* powerful. From **possient-* for **possent-,* stem of a barbarous L. **possens,* substituted for L. *potens,* powerful.

Puke, to vomit. (E.?) Prob. of imitative origin, partly suggested by *spew.* Cf.

G. *spucken*, to spit; O. F. *escoupir*, to spit, *sput*, *esput*, a spitting.

Pule, to chirp, to whimper. (F. – L.) F. *piauler*, 'to cheep as a young bird, to pule or howle;' Cot. In Gascon, *pioula*. Cf. Ital. *pigolare*, to chirp, moan. Imitative words; allied to L. *pīpilāre*, *pīpāre*, to chirp; see **Pipe**.

Pull. (E.) M. E. *pullen*; A. S. *pullian*, to pull, pluck.+Low G. *pulen*, to pick, pinch, pull, pluck, tear; Dan. dial. *pulle*. Cf. also Low G. *pullen*, to drink in gulps (cf. E. to take a *pull*).

Pullet. (F. – L.) M. E. *polete*. – O. F. *polete*, later *poulette*, fem. of F. *poulet*, a chicken, dimin. of F. *poule*, a hen. – Late L. *pulla*, fem. of *pullus*, a chicken. See **Pool** (2).

Pulley. (F. – L. – Gk.?) From F. *poulie*, 'a pulley;' Cot. Cf. Ital. *puleggia*; Late L. *poledia*, a crane; Duc. Perhaps from Late L. *pōlĭdia*, orig. pl. of *pōlĭdium*<Gk. *πωλίδιον*, a little colt, dimin. of *πῶλος*, a colt. Cf. O. F. *poulier*, a pulley, answering to Late Gk. *πωλάριον*, a little colt. β. The M. E. forms are *poliue* (= *polīvĕ*, riming with *drīvĕ*), Ch.; also *poleyne*, Prompt. Parv. The latter form is from F. *poulain*, 'a fole, a colt, also the rope wherewith wine is let down into a seller [cellar], a pulley-rope;' Cot. – Late L. *pullānus*, a colt. – L. *pullus*, a young animal; see **Pullet**. So also E. *pulley* answers to mod. F. *poulie*. γ. The transference of sense causes no difficulty; thus M.F. *poutre*, a filly, also means a beam, and F. *chèvre*, a goat, also means a kind of crane; the names of animals are applied to contrivances for exerting force. Cf. also Late L. *polānus*, a pulley or pulley-rope, also a kind of sledge. ¶ Diez derives E. *pulley* from F. *poulie*, and then, conversely, F. *poulie* from E. *pull*. This is very unlikely. G. Paris (*Romania*, July, '98, p. 486) suggests Gk. *πολίδιον*, dimin. of *πόλος*, a pivot, axis; see **Pole** (2).

Pulmonary, affecting the lungs. (L.) *pulmōnārius*, affecting the lungs. – L. *pulmōn-*, stem of *pulmo*, a lung.+Gk. *πλεύμων*, a lung. See **Pneumatic**.

Pulp. (F. – L.) F. *pulpe*. – L. *pulpa*, pulp of fruit, pith.

Pulpit. (F. – L.) O. F. *pulpite*. – L. *pulpitum*, a scaffold, stage for actors.

Pulsate, to throb. (L.) From pp. of L. *pulsāre*, to throb, beat; frequent. form of *pellere* (pp. *pulsus*), to drive. L. *pel-lo*

is for *pel-nō; cf. Gk. *πίλ-ναμαι*, 'I draw near quickly;' Brugm. ii. § 612.

pulse (1), a throb. (F. – L.) F. *pouls*, 'the pulse;' Cot. – L. *pulsum*, acc. of *pulsus*, the beating of the pulse. – L. *pulsus*, pp. of *pellere* (above).

Pulse (2), grain or seed of beans, peas, &c. (L.) M. E. *puls*. – L. *puls*, a thick pap or pottage made of meal, pulse, &c. (hence applied to the pulse itself).+Gk. *πόλτος*, porridge. **Der.** *poultice*, q. v.

Pulverise. (F. – L.) M.F. *pulverizer*; Cot. – Late L. *pulverīzāre*, to reduce to dust; L. *puluerāre*, the same. – L. *puluer-* (for **pulues-*), stem of *puluis*, dust. Allied to *pollis*, *pollen*, fine meal, *palea*, chaff; Gk. *πάλη*, meal, dust.

Puma, a quadruped. (Peruvian.) Peruv. *puma*.

Pumice. (F. – L.) [A.S. *pumic-stān*, pumice-stone.] M. E. *pomice*. – M. F. *pumice*. – L. *pūmic-*, stem of *pūmex*, pumice. From an Idg. base **poim-*, whence also A. S. *fām*, foam; from its foam-like appearance. See **Foam**.

Pummel, the same as **Pommel**.

Pump (1), a machine for raising water. (F. – Teut.) M. E. *pumpe*. – F. *pompe*. – G. *pumpe*, also *plumpe*, which is likewise an imitative form. Cf. prov. G. *plumpen*, to pump. β. The G. *plumpen* also means to plump, fall plump, move suddenly and violently, from the plunging action of the piston. It is therefore allied to E. **Plump** (2), of imitative origin. γ. We even find prov. E. *plump*, to pump, Corn. *plumpy*, to pump; also Du. *pomp*, Swed. *pump*, Dan. *pompe*, Russ. *pompa*, a pump, all borrowed words; and (the imitative forms) Span. and Port. *bomba*, a pump, a bomb.

Pump (2), a thin-soled shoe. (F. – L. – Gk.) So called because used for *pomp* or ornament; cf. F. *à pied de plomb et de pompe*, 'with a slow and stately gate,' i. e. gait; Cot. See **Pomp**.

Pumpion, Pumpkin, a kind of gourd. (F. – L. – Gk.) The old forms are *pumpion* and *pompon*. – M. F. *pompon*, 'a pumpion or melon;' Cot.; cf. Ital. *popone* (Florio); – L. *pepōnem*, acc. of *pepo*, a large melon. – Gk. *πέπων*, a kind of melon, eaten quite ripe. – Gk. *πέπων*, mellow, from *πέπτειν*, to ripen; see **Cook**.

Pun. (E.) Orig. to pound; hence to pound words, beat them into new senses, hammer at forced similes. Shak. has *pun*

=to pound, Troil. ii. 1. 42. – A. S. *punian*, to pound ; see Pound (3).

Punch (1), to perforate. (F. – L.) M. E. *punchen*, to prick ; which seems to have been coined from the sb. *punchion, punchon, punsoun*, a dagger, awl. See Puncheon (1).

Punch (2), to beat, bruise. (F. – L.) Short for *punish* ; M. E. *punchen* and *punischen* are equivalent (Prompt. Parv.). See Punish.

Punch (3), a beverage. (Hind. – Skt.) So called from consisting of *five* ingredients, spirit, water, lemon-juice, sugar, spice ; introduced from India, by way of Goa ; mentioned A.D. 1669. – Hind. *panch*, five. – Skt. *pañcha*, five. See **Five**. ¶ The Hind. short *a* is pronounced like E. *u* in *mud* ; it occurs again in *pundit, punkah*.

Punch (4), a short, hump-backed fellow in a puppet-show. (Ital. – L.) A contraction for *Punchinello*, which occurs A.D. 1666 (Nares). This is a corruption of Ital. *pulcinello* (by the change of *l* to *n*, the Ital. *ci* being sounded as E. *chi*). *Pulcinello* is the droll clown in Neapolitan comedy ; we also find Ital. *puncinella*, 'punch, buffoon,' Meadows. A dimin. form of Ital. *pulcino*, a young chicken ; cf. *pulcella*, a young girl ; from L. *pullus*, the young of any animal, allied to *puer*, a boy. See **Pullet**. The lit. sense of *pulcinello* is little chicken ; thence, a little boy, a puppet. ¶ Confused with prov. E. *punch*, short, fat, which is (perhaps) allied to **Bunch**. *Judy* is for *Judith*, once a common name.

Puncheon (1), a punch or awl. (F. – L.) M. E. *punchon, punsoun.* – Gascon *pounchoun*, M. F. *poinson* (F. *poinçon*), ' a bodkin, also a puncheon, a stamp,' &c. ; Cot. Cf. Span. *punzon*, a punch, Ital. *punzone*, a punch, bodkin, also a wine-barrel. – L. *punctiōnem*, acc. of *punctio*, a pricking, puncture. The gender of this word was changed from fem. to masc., whilst at the same time the sense was changed from 'pricking' to 'pricker.' – L. *punctus*, pp. of *pungere*, to prick ; see Pungent. See also Puncheon (2).

Puncheon (2), a cask. (F. – L.?) From Gascon *pounchoun*, a punch or awl ; M. F. *poinson* (F. *poinçon*), 'a bodkin, also a puncheon [steel tool], also a stamp, mark, print, or seale ; also, a wine-vessell ;' Cot. This is a difficult word ; but I conclude that the O. F. *poinson* (F. *poinçon*) remains the same word in all its senses, and that the cask was named from the ' mark,

print, or seale' upon it, which was made with a *puncheon* or stamp. See Puncheon (1). ¶ So also M. Ital. *punzone* means both puncheon or bodkin, and puncheon or wine-vessel.

Punchinello ; see Punch (4).

Punctate, dotted. (L.) Coined from L. *punct-um*, a point ; with suffix *-ate* (L. *-ātus*). – L. *punctus*, pp. of *pungere*, to prick ; see Pungent.

punctilio. (Span. – L.) Span. *puntillo*, a nice point of honour ; dimin. of *punto*, a point. – L. *punctum*, a point ; see Punctate, Point.

punctual. (F. – L.) M. F. *ponctuel*, ' punctuall ;' Cot. – Late L. *punctuālis.* – *punctu-m*, a point ; see Point.

punctuate. (L.) From pp. of Late L. *punctuāre*, to determine, define. – L. *punctu-m*, a point (above).

puncture. (L.) L. *punctūra*, a prick. – L. *punctus*, pp. of *pungere*, to prick.

Pundit, a learned man. (Skt.) Skt. *paṇḍita-* (with cerebral *ṇḍ*), adj., learned, sb., a wise man, scholar. – Skt. *paṇḍ*, to heap up or together. See note to Punch (3).

Pungent. (L.) L. *pungent-*, stem of pres. pt. of *pungere*, to prick, pt. t. *pupug-i*, pp. *punctus*. (Base PUG.)

Punish. (F. – L. – Gk.) M. E. *punischen.* – F. *puniss-*, stem of pres. pt. of *punir*, to punish. – L. *pūnīre*, to punish. – L. *poena*, penalty. – Gk. ποινή, penalty. See Pain.

Punkah, a large fan. (Hind. – Skt.) Hind. *pankhā*, a fan ; allied to *pankha*, a wing, feather, *paksha*, a wing. Allied to Skt. *paksha-*, a wing. Cf. Pers. *pankan*, a sieve, a fan. See note to Punch (3).

Punt (1), a flat-bottomed boat. (L. – C.) A.S. *punt.* – L. *ponto*, a punt (also a pontoon) ; a word of Gaulish origin. From Celtic type *qonto-* ; cf. L. *contus* < Gk. κοντός, a punting-pole, whence prov. E. *quont, quant*, a punting-pole.

Punt (2), to play at a game at cards called basset. (F. – Span. – L.) F. *ponte*, a punt, a punter, a red ace, *ponter*, to punt. – Span. *punto*, a point, also a pip at cards. – L. *punctum*, a point. See Point. ¶ Or immediately from Spanish.

Puny ; see Puisne.

Pupa, a chrysalis. (L.) L. *pūpa*, a girl, doll, puppet (hence, undeveloped insect). Fem. of *pūpus*, a boy ; allied to *putus, puer*, a boy. (√ PEU.)

pupil (1), a scholar, ward. (F. – L.) O. F. *pupile*, F. *pupille* (masc.). – L. *pūpillum*, acc. of *pūpillus*, an orphan-boy, ward; dimin. of *pūpus*, a boy (above).

pupil (2), the central spot of the eye. (F. – L.) F. *pupille* (fem.). – L. *pūpilla*, a little girl, also pupil (name due to the small images seen in the pupil). Fem. of *pūpillus* (above).

puppet. (F. – L.) M. E. *popet*. – M. F. *poupette*, 'a little baby, puppet;' Cot. Dimin. of L. *pūpa*; see **Pupa** (above).

puppy, (1) a whelp; (2) a dandy. (F. – L.) 1. F. *poupée*, 'a baby, a puppet;' Cot. Here 'baby' really means 'doll,' but it is clear that, in E., the term was applied to the young of an animal, esp. of a dog. The F. *poupée* (as if < L. **pūpāta*) is a derivative of L. *pūpa*; see **Pupa** (above). 2. In the sense of 'dandy,' *puppy* represents M. F. *poupin, popin*, spruce, trim (as if < L.**pūpīnus*); from the same source. Der. *pup*, short for *puppy*.

Pur-, prefix. (F. – L.) O. F. *pur-*, F. *pour-, pour*, (Span. *por*), for; a curious variation of L. *prō*, for. Thus *pur-* and *pro-* are equivalent; and *pur-vey, pro-vide* are doublets.

Purblind. (F. – L. *and* E.) Orig.*pure-blind*, i.e. wholly blind, M. E. *pur blind*, Rob. of Glouc. p. 376. See **Pure** and **Blind.** It afterwards came to mean partly blind, prob. through confusion with the verb *to pore*, as Sir T. Elyot writes *pore-blind*. (Similarly *parboil*, to boil thoroughly, came to mean to boil partially.) *Pure* = wholly, Tw. Nt., v. 86.

Purchase, vb. (F. – L.) M. E. *purchasen, purchacen.* – O. F. *purchacer*, to pursue eagerly, acquire, get. – O. F. *pur* (F. *pour*), from L. *prō*; and O. F. *chacer*; see **Chase** (1).

Pure. (F. – L.) F. *pur*, masc., *pure*, fem., pure. – L. *pūrus*, pure. Cf. Skt. *pū*, to purify. (√PEU).

purge. (F. – L.) F. *purger*. – L. *purgāre*, to purify. L. *purgare = *pūr-igāre* (Plautus has *expūrigātio*). – L. *pūr-us*, pure; *agere*, to make.

purify. (F. – L.) F. *purifier.* – L. *pūrificāre*, to make pure. – L. *pūri-*, for *pūrus*, pure; *facere*, to make. Der. *puri-fic-at-ion*.

Purim, an annual Jewish festival; the feast of lots. (Heb.) Heb. *pūrīm*, lots; pl. of *pūr*, a lot. See Esther ix. 26.

Puritan. (L.) A coined word, to designate one who aimed at great *purity* of life; see below.

purity. (F. – L.) M. E. *puretee*. – F. *pureté*, 'purity;' Cot. – L. acc. *pūritātem*, pureness. – L. *pūrus*, pure.

Purl (1), to flow with a murmuring sound. (E.) Cf. M. E. *prille, pirle*, a whirly-gig (toy). So also Swed. *porla*, to purl, bubble as a stream; a frequent. form from a base *pur-*, imitative of the sound. See **Purr**, **Purl** (4).

Purl (2), spiced beer. (F. – L.) In Phillips, ed. 1706. But it should be *pearl*. It was a term in cookery; thus *sucre perlé* is sugar boiled twice, *bouillon perlé*, jelly-broth. Cf. G. *perlen*, to pearl, rise in small bubbles like pearls. See **Pearl.**

Purl (3), to form an edging on lace, invert stitches in knitting. (F. – L.) Frequently misspelt *pearl*. Contraction of *purfle*. – M. F. *pourfiler*, to purfle, embroider on an edge. – F. *pour* (L. *prō*), confused (as often) with F. *par* (L. *per*), throughout; *fil*, a thread, from L. *filum*, a thread. See **File** (1), **Profile.**

Purl (4), to upset. (E.) Better *pirl*; from M. E. *pirle*, a whirligig, formed by the frequent. suffix *-l* from the imitative word *pirr*, to whirl. See **Purr**, **Pirouette.** So also Ital. *pirlare*, 'to twirle round;' Florio. See **Purl** (1).

Purlieu, the border of a forest, &c. (F. – L.) Formerly *pourallee*, altered to *purlieu* by confusion with F. *lieu*, a place; also spelt *purley*. The O. F. *pouralee, poralee* is a sort of translation of Late L. *perambulātio*, which meant 'all that ground near any forest, which, being made forest by Henry II., Rich. I., or king John, were (*sic*) by *perambulations* granted by Henry III., severed again from the same'; Manwood's Forest Laws. The etymology is from O. F. *pur* (F. *pour*) < L. *prō*, and O. F. *alee*, a going, for which see **Alley.**

Purloin, to steal. (F. – L.) O. F. *purloignier, porloignier*, to prolong, retard, delay (hence to keep back, detain, filch). – L. *prōlongāre*, to prolong. – L. *prō*, forward; *longus*, long. See **Long.** Doublet, *prolong.*

Purple. (F. – L. – Gk.) M. E. *purpre* (with *r*). – O. F. *porpre*, later *pourpre*, purple. – L. *purpura*, the purple-fish. – Gk. πορφύρα, the purple-fish; cf. Gk. πορφύρεος, purple, orig. an epithet of the surging sea. – Gk. πορφύρειν, reduplicated form of φύρειν, to mix up, stir violently, allied to Skt. root *bhur*, to be active.

Purport, to imply. (F.—L.) O. F. *purporter, pourporter*, to declare, inform (hence, imply); we also find *purport*, sb., tenor (Roquefort). — O. F. *pur*, F. *pour*, from L. *prō*, according to; *porter*, to carry, bring, from L. *portāre*. For the sense, cf. *import*. See Port (1).

Purpose (1), to intend. (F.—L. *and* Gk.) O. F. *purposer*, a variant of *proposer*, to propose, intend. — L. *prō*, before; and F. *poser*, to place; see Pose (1).

Purpose (2), intention. (F.—L.) M. E. *purpos.* — O. F. *pourpos*, a variant of *propos*, a purpose. — L. *prōpositum*, a thing proposed, neut. of pp. of *prōpōnere*, to propose. — L. *prō*, before; *pōnere*, to place. See Position.

Purr, Pur. (E.) An imitative word for various sounds, chiefly of the murmuring of a cat. Cf. Scotch *pirr*, a gentle wind; E. *buzz*; Irish *bururus*, a gurgling sound. See Purl (1), Purl (4), and Pirouette.

Purse. (L.—Gk.) M. E. *purs*; also *pors.* A.S. *purs*, Eng. Studien, xi. 65. [Also *burs.* — O. F. *borse*, later *bourse*, a purse.] — Late L. *bursa*, a purse. — Gk. βύρσα, a hide, skin; of which purses were made. **Der.** *purse*, vb., to wrinkle up, like a purse drawn together.

Purslain, Purslane, a herb. (F.—L.) M. E. *purslane, porseleyne.* — M. F. *porcelaine, pourcelaine*, purslane; Cot. Formed from L. *porcilāca*, purslain (Pliny); usually spelt *portulāca*.

Pursue. (F.—L.) O. F. *porsuir, pursuir, poursuir*; mod. Norman F. *porsuir*, mod. F. *poursuivre*, to pursue. — O. F. *por, pur* < L. *prō*; and *suir* < Late L. *sequere*, for L. *sequī*, to follow. **Der.** *pursu-ant*, from the pres. pt. of O. F. *pursuir*; *pursuiv-ant*, from the pres. pt. of *poursuivre*; *pursuit*, from F. *poursuite*, fem. sb. answering to L. *prōsecūta*, fem. of the pp. of L. *prōsequī*, to pursue.

Pursy, short-winded. (F.—L.) M. E. *purcy*, also *purcyf* (Palsgrave). — M. F. *pourcif* (Palsgrave), variant of *poulsif*, 'pursie, short-winded,' Cot. — M. F. *poulser*, F. *pousser*, to push, also to pant; see Push.

Purtenance. (F.—L.) Short for M. E. *apurtenance*; see Appurtenance.

Purulent. (F.—L.) F. *purulent.* — L. *pūrulentus*, full of matter. — L. *pūr-*, stem of *pūs*, matter; see Pus.

Purvey. (F.—L.) M. E. *purueien*,

porueien, (purveien, porveien), to provide. — A. F. *purveier, purveer* (O. F. *porvoir*, F. *pourvoir*), to provide. — L *prōuidēre*, to provide. See Provide.

purview, a proviso. (F.—L.) Now applied to the enacting part of a statute; so called because it orig. began with *purveu est*, it is provided. — O. F. *porveu*, pp. of O. F. *porvoir* (F. *pourvoir*), to provide. — L. *prōuidēre*, to provide (above).

Pus, white matter from a sore. (L.) L. *pūs* (gen. *pūris*), pus. + Gk. πύον, matter; Skt. *pūya-*, pus, from *pūy*, to stink. Allied to Foul. (√PEU.) Brugm. i. § 113.

Push. (F.—L.) M. E. *possen, pussen.* — O. F. *pousser, poulser*, to push, thrust. — L. *pulsāre*, to beat, thrust, frequent. of *pellere*, to drive. See Pulsate.

Pusillanimous. (L.) L. *pusillani-m-is*, mean-spirited; with suffix *-ous.* — L. *pusill-us*, mean, small; *animus*, courage. *Pusillus* is related to *pūsus*, small; cf. *putus*, a boy. (√PEU.)

Puss, a cat, hare. (E.) Prob. an imitative word, from the spitting of a cat. We find also Du. *poes*, Low G. *puus, puuskatte*, Swed. dial. *pus*, Norw. *puse, puus*; Irish and Gael. *pus* (from E.). And even S. Tamil *pusei*, a cat; *pusha* in the Cashgar dialect of Afghan.; Lith. *puž*, a word to call a cat.

Pustule. (F.—L.) F. *pustule.* — L. *pustula*, another form of *pūsula*, a blister, pimple. Perhaps allied to Gk. φυσαλίς, a bladder, φυσάω, I blow.

Put. (E.) M. E. *putten*; A.S. *potian*, to push, thrust; [whence also Gael. *put*, to push, thrust; W. *pwtio*, Corn. *poot*, to push, kick]. + Du. *poten*, to plant, set, *poot*, a twig, M. Du. *pote*, a scion, plant (see Franck); N. Fries. *putje*, Dan. *putte*, to put, place; Swed. dial. *putta*, to push.

Putative, reputed. (F.—L.) F. *putatif.* — L. *putātīuus*, presumptive. — L. *putātus*, pp. of *putāre*, to think, suppose. The orig. sense was to make clean, then to make clear, to come to a clear result. — L. *putus*, clean. (√PEU.)

Putrefy. (F.—L.) M. F. *putrefier*; as if from L. **putrificāre*; but the true L. forms are *putrefacere*, to make putrid, *putrefieri*, to become putrid. — L. *putri-s*, putrid (below); *facere*, to make.

putrid. (F.—L.) M. F. *putride.* — L. *putridus*, stinking. — L. *putri-*, decl. stem of *puter, putris*, rotten; cf. *putrēre*, to be rotten, *pūtēre*, to stink. See Pus.

Puttock, a kite, hawk. (E. ?) M. E. *pottok, puttok.* Of unknown origin. It seems to have been used in a contemptuous sense. A. S. *Puttoc* occurs as a name or nickname.

Putty. (F. – Low G.) M. F. *potée,* calcined tin, also putty; orig. a potful (of bits of broken metal); cf. M. F. *pottein,* bits of broken metal, *pottin,* solder. All from F. *pot,* a pot, of Germanic origin. See **Pot.**

Puzzle, a difficult question. (F. – L. and Gk.) Orig. a sb., and short for *opposal,* spelt both *opposayle* and *apposayle* in Lydgate, with the sense of question. These are from the verb *oppose,* like *deni-al* from *deny,* &c. See **Pose** (2).

Pygmy. (F. – L. – Gk.) M. F. *pygmé,* adj., dwarf-like; Cot. – L. *pygmæus,* adj., dwarf-like; from pl. *Pygmei,* the race of Pygmies. – Gk. Πυγμαῖοι, pygmies, fabulous dwarfs of the length of a πυγμή, i.e. about 13½ in. (from the elbow to the knuckles). – Gk. πυγμή, a fist; see **Pugilist.**

Pylorus. (L. – Gk.) L. *pylōrus.* – Gk. πυλωρός, the lower orifice of the stomach, entrance to the intestines; orig. a gatekeeper. – Gk. *πυλα-ϝορός* (Prellwitz); from πύλα = πύλ-η, a gate; ϝόρος (cf. οὖρος), a keeper, watcher, allied to **Wary.**

Pyramid. (L. – Gk.) Formerly *pyramis.* – L. *pyramis* (stem *pyramid-*). – Gk. πυραμίς (stem πυραμιδ-), a pyramid. Prob. of Egyptian origin.

Pyre. (L. – Gk.) L. *pyra.* – Gk. πύρα, a funeral pile. – Gk. πῦρ, fire; allied to E. **Fire.**

pyrites. (L. – Gk.) L. *pyrītes.* – Gk. πυρίτης, a flint, pyrites; orig. an adj., belonging to fire. – Gk. πῦρ, fire.

pyrotechnic, belonging to fireworks. (Gk.) Coined from Gk. πυρο-, for πῦρ, fire; τεχνικός, artistic, from τέχνη, an art; see **Technical.**

Python, a large snake. (L. – Gk.) L. *pythōn,* a serpent slain by Apollo near Delphi. – Gk. Πύθων (the same). – Gk. Πυθώ, a former name of Delphi.

Pyx. (L. – Gk.) Shortened from L. *pyxis,* a box. – Gk. πυξίς, a box. – Gk. πύξος, box-wood. Allied to **Box** (1), **Box** (2).

Q.

Quack (1), to make a noise as a duck. (E.) M. E. *queke,* as a duck's cry; an imitative word. +Du. *kwaken, kwakken,*

G. *quaken,* Icel. *kvaka,* Dan. *qvække,* to croak, quack. Cf. L. *coaxāre,* to croak, Gk. κόαξ, a croaking.

quack (2), to cry up a nostrum. (Du.) Due to the older word *quacksalver*; hence, to act as a *quack-salver* or a *quack.* – Du. *kwakzalver,* a quacksalver. – Du. *kwakzalven,* vb., to apply salves in a trifling way. Cf. Du. *kwakken,* to croak, which came to mean 'to trifle, linger' (Franck); and Du. *zalf,* a salve; see **Salve.**

Quadragesima, forty days of Lent. (L.) L. *quadrāgēsima,* lit. fortieth; fem. of *quadrāgēsimus*; older form *quadrāgensumus,* fortieth. – L. *quadrāgintā,* forty. – L. *quadrā-,* related to *quattuor,* four; *-gintā,* allied to Gk. -κοντα (for *δεκοντα), and to L. *decem,* ten. See **quadrate.**

quadrangle. (F. – L.) F. *quadrangle.* – L. *quadrangulum,* sb., neut. of *quadrangulus,* four-cornered. – L. *quadr-,* related to *quattuor,* four; *angulus,* angle. See **Angle** (1).

quadrant. (L.) M.E. *quadrant.* – L. *quadrant-,* stem of *quadrans,* sb., a fourth part. Extended from L. *quadr-* (above).

quadrate. (L.) L. *quadrātus,* pp. of *quadrāre,* to make square. – L. *quadr-,* allied to *quattuor,* four; see **Four.** Brugm. ii. § 168.

quadrennial. (L.) For *quadriennial,* adj. – L. *quadrienni-um,* a space of four years; with suffix *-al.* – L. *quadri-,* belonging to four; *annus,* a year; see **Annals.**

quadrilateral. (L.) L. *quadrilaterus,* four-sided; with suffix *-al.* – L. *quadri-* (above); *later-,* for *lates-,* stem of *latus,* a side. See **Lateral.**

quadrille. (F. – Span. – L.) Formerly a game at cards for four. – F. *quadrille,* (1) fem., a troop of horses; (2) masc., but orig. fem., a game at cards. The former answers to Ital. *quadriglia,* M. Ital. *squadriglia,* a troop; but the latter to Span. *cuadrilla,* a meeting of four persons. – Span. *cuadra,* a square. – Late L. *quadra,* fem. of *quadrus,* square.

quadrillion, a million raised to the fourth power. (L.) Coined by prefixing L. *quadr-* i.e. four, to *-illion,* which is *m-illion* without the *m.*

quadroon. (Span. – L.) For *quartroon.* – Span. *cuarteron,* the child of a creole and a Spaniard; one who is, in a fourth part, a black; also a fourth part. – Span.

cuarto, a fourth part. – L. *quartum*, acc. of *quartus*, fourth; see quartern.

quadruped. (L.) L. *quadrupedus*, four-footed; *quadruped-*, stem of *quadrupēs*, *quadripēs*, four-footed. – L. *quadru-*, four times; *pēs*, a foot; see quadrant.

quadruple. (F. – L.) F. *quadruple*. – L. *quadruplum*, acc. of *quadruplus*, four-fold. – L. *quadru-* (above); *-plus*, signifying 'fold'; see Double.

Quaff, to drink in large draughts. (C. – L. – Gk.) Here *ff* stands for guttural *ch*, as in *quach*, i. e. to drink out of a *quach* or cup, usually called *quaich*, *quech*, *queff* in Lowland Scotch, *quaff* in Humphrey Clinker (Supp. to Jam.). – Irish and Gael. *cuach*, a cup, bowl. – L. *caucus*, a cup. – Gk. καῦκα, a cup.

Quagga, a quadruped. (Kaffir.) A Xosa-Kaffir word. – Kaffir *iqwara* (W. J. Davis); where the *r* is guttural. See N. and Q. 9 S. v. 3.

Quagmire. (E.) Spelt *quake-mire* in Stanihurst; i. e. quaking bog.

Quaigh, Quaich, a cup. See under Quaff.

Quail (1), to cower. (E.) M. E. *quelen*, to die. A. S. *cwelan* (pt. t. *cwæl*), to die; whence *ācwelan*, to die utterly. + Du. *kwelen*, O. H. G. *quelan*, to pine. Teut. type **kwel-an-*. Cf. A. S. *cwalu*, destruction, Du. *kwaal*, Icel. *kvöl*, Dan. Swed. *qval*, G. *qual*, agony. Also allied to Lith. *gelti*, to pain; *gela*, pain. From Idg. root **g(w)el*. Brugm. i. § 656. ¶ Distinct from prov. E. *quail*, to coagulate, from O. F. *coailler* (F. *cailler*), from L. *coagulāre*. Der. *qualm*.

Quail (2), a bird. (F. – Low L. – Low G.) M. E. *quaille*. – O. F. *quaille*, F. *caille*. – Low L. *quaquila*, a quail. – M.Du. *quackel*, Du. *kwakkel*, a quail. – M. Du. *quacken*, Du. *kwaken*, to quack. From the noise which the bird makes. See Quack.

Quaint, neat, odd, whimsical. (F. – L.) M. E. *queint*, also *quoint*, *coint*, commonly with the sense of 'famous.' – O. F. and M. F. *coint*, 'quaint, compt, neat, fine;' Cot. – L. *cognitus*, well-known, pp. of *cognoscere*, to know; see Cognisance. Der. *ac-quaint*.

Quake. (E.) M. E. *quaken*, *cwakien*. A. S. *cwacian*, to quake; cf. *cweccan*, to wag; E. Fries. *kwakkelen*, to be unsteady. Der. *Quak-er* (A. D. 1650); see Haydn.

Quality. (F. – L.) M. E. *qualitee*. – F.

qualité. – L. *quālitātem*, acc. of *quālitās*, sort, kind. – L. *quāli-s*, of what sort. Allied to E. Which.

qualify. (F. – L.) F. *qualifier*. – Late L. *quālificāre*, to endue with a quality. – L. *quāli-s*, of what sort; *facere*, to make.

Qualm. (E.) M. E. *qualm*, usually 'a pestilence.' A. S. *cwealm*, pestilence. + O. Sax. *qualm*, destruction, death; O.H.G. *qualm*, destruction. [Perhaps not the same word as Du. *kwalm*, thick vapour.] Teut. type *kwalmoz, masc.; from *kwal, 2nd grade of **kwel-an-*, to die. See Quail (1).

Quandary, a perplexity. (L. – Gk.) Orig. a morbid state of mind; Knt. of Burning Pestle, i. 1. It probably arose from '*condarye*, for *hypo-condarye*, a morbid state of mind. 'I, seeing him so troubled, asked him what newes . . . had put him in so great a *hypo-condarye* ;' Blackhall, Brief Narration, ab. 1640 (Spalding Club), p. 175. See Hypochondria. (H. B.)

Quantity. (F. – L.) M. E. *quantitee*. – F. *quantité*. – L. *quantitātem*, acc. of *quantitās*, quantity. – L. *quanti-*, for *quantus*, how much. Related to *quam*; and to *quis*, who. Brugm. i. § 413.

Quarantine. (F. – L.) O. F. *quarantine* (Roquefort), usually *quarantaine*, a space of forty days. – F. *quarante*, forty. – L. *quadrāgintā*, forty; see Quadragesima.

Quarrel (1), a dispute. (F. – L.) M.E. *querele*. – O. F. *querele*, later *querelle*. – L. *querēla*, a complaint. – L. *querī*, to complain. See Querulous.

Quarrel (2), a square-headed cross-bow bolt. (F. – L.) M.E. *quarel*. – O.F. *quarrel*, M. F. *quarreau*, a diamond, square tile, cross-bow bolt. – Late L. *quadrellus*, a quarrel. – L. *quadrus*, square; see Quadrate.

quarry (1), a place where stones are dug. (F. – L.) Formerly *quarrer*; M. E. *quarrere*, a place where stones are squared. – O.F. *quarriere*, a quarry; F. *carrière*. – Late L. *quadrāria*, a quarry for *squared* stones. – L. *quadrāre*, to square. – L. *quadrus*, square. ¶ The sense was suggested by L. *quadrātārius*, a stone-squarer, also a stone-cutter (merely).

Quarry (2), a heap of slaughtered game. (F. – L.) M. E. *querrè*. – O. F. *curee*, *cuiree* (F. *curée*), intestines of a slain animal, the part given to hounds; so called because wrapped in the skin. – F.

cuir, a skin, hide. ─ L. *corium*, hide. See **Cuirass**.

Quart, the fourth of a gallon. (F. ─ L.) M. E. *quarte*. ─ F. *quarte*. ─ L. *quarta* (i. e. *pars*), a fourth part; fem. of *quartus*, fourth. Related to L. *quattuor*, four. Brugm. i. § 279.

 quartan. (F. ─ L.) F. *quartaine*, recurring on the fourth day (said of a fever). ─ L. *quartāna* (*febris*), a quartan fever; fem. of *quartānus*, belonging to the fourth. ─ L. *quartus*, fourth (above).

 quarter. (F. ─ L.) M. E. *quarter*. ─ O. F. *quarter*, *quartier*. ─ L. *quartārius*, fourth part. ─ L. *quartus*, fourth.

 quartern, fourth of a pint. (F. ─ L.) Short for *quarteron*. M. E. *quarteroun*. ─ O. F. *quarteron*, a quartern. ─ Late L. *quarterōnem*, acc. of *quartero*, a fourth part. ─ Late L. *quarterus*, from L. *quartus*, fourth.

 quartet, quartette. (Ital. ─ L.) Ital. *quartetto* (*quartette* is a F. spelling); dimin. of *quarto*, fourth. ─ L. *quartus*, fourth.

 quarto, having the sheet folded into four leaves. (L.) From L. phr. *in quartō*, in a fourth part; where *quartō* is abl. of *quartus*, fourth.

Quartz, a mineral. (G.) G. *quarz*, rock-crystal; M. H. G. *quarz*.

Quash. (F. ─ L.) M. E. *quaschen*. ─ O. F. *quasser*, later *casser*, to break, quash. ─ L. *quassāre*, to shatter; frequent. of *quatere* (supine *quassum*), to shake.

Quassia, a South-American tree. (Personal name.) Named by Linnæus (like *dahl-ia* from *Dahl*) from *Quassi*, a negro of Surinam, who pointed out the use of the bark as a tonic in 1730. *Quassi* is a common negro name.

Quaternary, consisting of fours. (F. ─ L.) F. *quaternaire*. ─ L. *quaternārius*. ─ L. *quaternī*, pl., four at a time. ─ L. *quattuor*, four.

 quaternion. (L.) L. *quaterniōn*-, stem of *quaternio*, a band of four men; Acts xii. 4. ─ L. *quaternī*, pl.; see above.

 quatrain. (F. ─ L.) F. *quatrain*, a stanza of four lines. ─ F. *quatre*, four. ─ L. *quattuor*, four.

Quaver, vb. (E.) Frequent. of *quave*, M. E. *quauen* (*u* = *v*), to quake. Allied to M. E. *quappen*, to throb, palpitate. Compare **Quake**. Der. *quaver*, sb., a note in music, orig. a trill, shake. And see *quiver* (1).

Quay, a wharf. (F. ─ C.) Formerly *kay*, *key*; M. E. *key*, *keye*. ─ M. F. *quay* (F. *quai*), 'the key of a haven;' Cot. ─ Bret. *kaé*, an enclosure, a quay; W. *cae*, an enclosure, hedge. Celt. type **kagi-*; allied to **Haw, Hedge**.

Quean, a woman; used slightingly. (E.) A. S. *cwene*. + O. H. G. *quena*, a wife; Goth. *kwinō*. Teut. type **kwenōn-*. Also Irish *ben*, W. *bun*, a woman; Russ. *jena*, wife; Idg. type **g(w)enā*. Cf. Gk. γυνή, Pers. *zan*. See **Queen**. Brugm. i. § 670.

Queasy. (Scand.) M.E. *quaysy*, *queysy*, causing or feeling nausea. ─ Norweg. *kveis*, sickness after a debauch; Icel. *iðra-kveisa*, colic. Cf. Icel. *kveisa*, a whitlow, boil; Low G. *quese*, a blister; *quesen-kopp*, a brain-disease in sheep; E. Fries. *kwäse*, a blister, boil, worm causing giddiness in sheep.

Queen. (E.) Differing in gradation from *quean*, which spelling is restricted to the use of the word in a lower sense. A. S. *cwēn*, a woman; O. Merc. *kwōen*. + Icel. *kvān*, wife; Goth. *kwēns*, woman. Teut. type **kwēniz*, fem.; Idg. type **g(w)ēni-*, cf. Skt. *-jāni-*, wife. Brugm. i. § 677. (√GwEN.)

Queer. (Low G.) A cant word. ─ Low G. *queer*, across; cf. *qŭere*, obliquity. In Awdelay's Fraternity of Vagabonds, p. 4, 'a *quire* fellow' is one who has just come out of prison; cf. Low G. *in der quere liggen*, to lie across, lie queerly. So also G. *quer*, transverse; *querkopf*, a queer fellow. G. *quer* answers to O. H. G. *twer*, transverse, Icel. *þverr* (whence E. *thwart*). See **Thwart**.

Quell, to subdue. (E.) M. E. *quellen*, to kill. A. S. *cwellan*, to kill; causal of *cwelan*, to die. + Du. *kwellen*, Icel. *kvelja*, Swed. *qvälja*, Dan. *qvæle*, to torment, choke; all causal forms. Teut. type **kwaljan-*; from **kwal*, 2nd stem of **kwel-an-*, to die. See **Quail** (1).

Quench. (E.) M. E. *quenchen*. A. S. *cwencan*, to extinguish; causal of A. S. *cwincan* (pt. t. *cwanc*), to go out, be extinguished. Cf. O. Fries. *kwinka*, to be extinguished.

Querimonious, fretful. (L.) From L. *querimōnia*, a complaint. ─ L. *querī*, to complain; with Idg. suffixes -*mōn-jā-*.

Quern, Kern, a handmill for grinding grain. (E.) M. E. *querne*. A. S. *cweorn*, *cwyrn*; orig. 'that which grinds.' + Du.

kweern, Icel. *kvern*, Dan. *qværn*, Swed. *qvarn*, Goth. *kwairnus*. Teut. type **kwernuz*. Cf. also Russ. *jernove*, a millstone; Lith. *girna*, stone in a hand-mill. Brugm. i. § 6;0.

Querulous, fretful. (L.) L. *querulus*, full of complaints. − L. *querī*, to complain. **+** Skt. *çvas*, to sigh. Brugm. i. § 355.

Query, an enquiry. (L.) For *quære*, i. e. enquire thou. − L. *quære*, imp. sing. 2 pers. of *quærere*, to seek; for **quæs-ere*, as in L. *quæso*, I beg. Brugm. ii. § 662.

quest, a search. (F. − L.) O. F. *queste*; F. *quête*. − L. *quæsīta* (*rēs*), a thing sought; fem. of pp. of *quærere*, to seek.

question. (F. − L.) F. *question*. − L. acc. *quæstiōnem*, an enquiry. − L. *quæs-*, base of *quærere*, to seek; with suffix *-tiōn-*.

Queue, a tail. (F. − L.) F. *queue*, a tail. − L. *cauda*, a tail; see **Caudal**.

Quibble. (L.) Dimin. of *quib*, a sarcasm (Ash); which is a weakened form of *quip*. See **Quip**.

Quick, living, lively. (E.) M. E. *quik*. A. S. *cwic*, *cwicu*.**+**Du. *kwik*, Icel. *kvikr*, Dan. *qvik*, Swed. *qvick*, O. H. G. *quec*. Teut. type **kwikuz* or **kwikwoz*, allied to the shorter Teut. type **kwiwoz*, as in Goth. *kwius*, living; cf. Irish *beo*, W. *byw*, L. *uīuus*, Lith. *gywas*, Russ. *jivoi*, alive; Gk. βίος, life; Skt. *jīv*, to live. Brugm. i. §§ 85, 318, 677. **Der.** *quick-silver*; A. S. *cwicseolfor*.

quicken. (E.) M. E. *quiknen*, orig. to become alive. − A. S. *cwic*, alive.

Quid, a mouthful of tobacco. (E.) Merely another form of *cud*; M. E. *quide*, cud. See **Cud**.

Quiddity, a nicety, cavil. (L.) Late L. *quidditās*, the nature of a thing. − L. *quid*, what; i. e. what is it? Neut. of *quis*, who; see **Who**.

Quiet, adj. (L.) L. *quiētus*, quiet; orig. pp. of **quiēre*, only used in the inceptive form *quiescere*, to be still. Cf. *quiēs*, rest. Allied to O. Pers. *shiyāti-*, a place of delight, home; Pers. *shād*, pleased; and to E. **While**. Brugm. i. §§ 130, 675; Horn, § 767. **Der.** *quiet*, sb. and vb.; *quietus*, sb.; *quiescent*, from stem of pres. pt. of *quiescere*.

Quill (1), a feather, pen. (E. ?) M. E. *quille*. 'Quylle, a stalk, Calamus;' Prompt. Parv. *Quill* also meant the faucet of a barrel, or a reed to wind yarn on. This is a difficult and doubtful word, not found at an early date. Apparently E.,

and of Teut. origin.**+**Low G. *kiil*, a goose-quill (Berghaus); Westphalian *kwiøle* (Woeste); G. *kiel*, M. H. G. *kil* or *kīl*.

Quill (2), to pleat a ruff. (F. − L.) From O. F. *cuillir* (F. *cueillir*), to gather, pluck; also used in the sense of to pleat; see Rom. Rose, 1219, and Chaucer's translation. − Folk-L. **colligīre*, for L. *colligere*, to cull, collect. See **Cull**. Allied to the Guernsey word *enquiller*, to pleat (Métivier).

Quillet, a sly trick in argument. (L.) Short for L. *quidlibet*, anything you choose. − L. *quid*, anything; *libet*, it pleases (you).

Quilt, a bed-cover, &c. (F. − L.) M.E. *quilte*. − A. F. and O. F. *cuilte*, a quilt (12th cent.). − L. *culcita*, a cushion, mattress, pillow, quilt.

Quinary, consisting of fives. (L.) L. *quinārius*, arranged by fives. − L. *quīnī*, five at a time. For **quinc-nī*, from *quinque*, five. Cf. *bīnī*, two at a time. See **Five**.

Quince. (F. − L. − Gk.) Formerly *quence*, *quyns*. (Cf. M. F. *coignasse*, 'the greatest kind of quince,' Cot.) Merely the pl. form of M. E. *quyne*, *coine*, or *coin*, a quince. − O. F. *coin*, F. *coing*, a quince. [The same as Prov. *codoing*; cf. Ital. *cotogna*, a quince.] − L. **cotōnium*, for **cydōnium*; (the Ital. *cotogna* being from L. *cydōnia*, a quince). − Gk. κυδώνιον μῆλον, a quince, lit. a Cydonian apple. − Gk. Κυδωνία, Κυδωνίς, Cydonia, one of the chief cities of Crete.

Quincunx, an arrangement by fives. (L.) Applied to trees arranged like the spots on the side of a die marked 5; L. *quincunx*. − L. *quinque*, five; *uncia*, an ounce, small mark, such as a spot on a die; see **Uncial**.

Quinine, extract of Peruvian bark. (F. − Peruv.) F. *quinine*, formed with suffix *-ine* (L. *-īna*), from F. *quina*, Peruvian bark. − Peruvian *kina*, or *kina-kina*, said to mean 'bark,' esp. that which we call Peruvian bark.

Quinquagesima. (L.) L. *quinquāgēsima* (*dies*), fiftieth (day); fem. of *quinquāgēsimus*, fiftieth. − L. *quinquā-*, for *quinque*, five, allied to E. **Five**; *-gēsimus*, for **-gensimus*, allied to *decem*, ten; see **Quadragesima**. ¶ So also *quinquangular*, having five angles; *quinqui-ennial*, lasting five years.

Quinsy. (F. − Gk.) Formerly also *squinancy*. − O. F. *quinancie* (Supp. to

Godefroy, s. v. *esquinance*); also *squinancie* (16th cent.) ; *squinance*, 'the squinancy or squinzie ;' Cot. Formed (sometimes with prefixed *s* = O. F. *es*-, L. *ex*, very) from Gk. κυνάγκη, lit. a dog-throttling, applied to a bad kind of sore throat. ━ Gk. κύν-, stem of κύων, a dog ; ἄγχ-ειν, to choke.

Quintain. (F. ─ L.) M. F. *quintaine*, a post with arms, for beginners to tilt at. The form of the word is such that it must be allied to L. *quintāna*, a street in the camp, which separated the *fifth* maniple from the sixth ; where was the market and business-place of the camp. Doubtless this public place was also the scene of martial exercises and trials of skill ; the Late L. *quintāna* means (1) a quintain, also (2) a part of a street (space) where carriages could pass. ━ L. *quintānus*, from *quintus*, fifth. For *quinc-tus, from *quinque*, five. See **Five**.

Quintal, a hundred-weight. (F. ─ Span. ─ Arab. ─ L.) F. *quintal* (Cot.). ─ Span. *quintal*. ─ Arab. *qintār*, a weight of 100 lbs. Not a true Arab. word ; but formed from L. *centum*, a hundred.

Quintessence, pure essence. (F. ─ L.) Lit. 'fifth essence.' ─ L. *quinta essentia*, fifth essence (in addition to the four elements). See below ; and **Essence**.

Quintuple, five-fold. (F. ─ L.) F. *quintuple*. ─ L. *quintuplus, a coined word. ─ L. *quintu-s*, fifth, for *quinctus ; from *quinque*, five ; *-plus*, i. e. -fold ; see **Double**.

Quip, a taunt, cavil. (L.) Formerly *quippy* ; Drant's Horace, bk. ii. sat. 1. ━ L. *quippe*, forsooth (ironical). For *quid-pe ; Brugm. i. § 585. Der. *quibble*.

Quire (1), a collection of sheets of paper. (F. ─ L.) Spelt *cwaer* in the Ancren Riwle. ━ O. F. *quaier* (13th cent.), later *quayer*, *cayer* ; mod. F. *cahier*. ━ Late L. *quaternum*, a collection of four leaves (we find Late L. *quaternus*, glossed by A. F. *quaer* in Wright's Voc. i. 116) ; whence also Ital. *quaderno*, a quire. Allied to L. *quattuor*, four. [The suffix *-num* is lost as in F. *enfer* from L. *infernum*.] ¶ Not from L. *quaternio*, which could not thus suffer loss of the acc. termination *-niōnem*.

Quire (2), a band of singers ; see **Choir**.

Quirk, a cavil. (M. Du. ─ F. ─ L.) M. Du. *kuerken*, 'a cunning trick,' Hexham. Dimin. of M. Du. *küre*, Du. *kuur*, a whim, also a cure. ━ F. *cure*, a cure. ━

L. *cūra* ; see **Cure**. Cf. E. Fries. *küre*, *kürke*, a whim.

Quit, freed, free. (F. ─ L.) Orig. an adj., as in '*quit* claim.' M. E. *quyt*, *quit*, also *quyte*, free ; adj. ━ O. F. *quite*, discharged, released, free. ━ Late L. *quītus*, *quittus*, altered forms of Late L. *quiētus*, at rest, hence, free. Cf. Late L. *quiēta clāmantia*, A. F. *quite claime*, E. *quit claim* ; *quiētum clāmāre*, *quītum clamāre*, to quit a claim ; *quiētāre*, *quitāre*, *quittāre*, to free from debt. See **Quiet**. Der. *quit*, vb., F. *quitter*, O. F. *quiter*, from the adj. ; hence *quitt-ance*, O. F. *quitance*, Late L. *quītantia*, *quiētantia* ; *acquit*. Cf. **Coy**.

quite. (F. ─ L.) M. E. *quite* ; an adverbial use of the M. E. adj. *quite*, free, now spelt *quit* ; see above.

Quiver (1), to shiver. (E.) Allied to obsolete adj. *quiver*, full of motion, brisk ; A. S. *cwifer*, in the comp. adv. *cwifer-līce*, eagerly. Cf. M. Du. *kuyven*, *kuyveren*, to quiver (Kilian) ; E. Fries. *kwifer*, lively, *kwifern*, to be lively.

Quiver (2), a case for arrows. (F. ─ O. H. G.) O. F. *cuivre*, *cuevre*, *coivre*, a quiver. ━ O. Sax. *cokar* ; cf. O. H. G. *kohhar* (G. *köcher*), a quiver ; A. S. *cocer*, a quiver. Teut. type **kukuro-*, whence Med. L. *cucurum*, a quiver.

Quixotic. (Span.) Named from *Don Quixote* or *Quijote*, a novel by Cervantes.

Quoif ; the same as **Coif**.

Quoin, a wedge. (F. ─ L.) The same as F. *coin* ; see **Coin**.

Quoit, Coit, a ring of iron for throwing at a mark. (F. ─ L. ?) M. E. *coite*, *coyte* ; cf. Lowl. Sc. *coit*, to push about, justle. Prob. from O. F. *coitier*, *quoitier*, to press, push, hasten, incite, urge on (which prob. also had the sense ' to hurl '). Of unknown origin. Cf. Prov. *coitar*, to hasten, urge.

Quorum. (L.) It was usual to nominate members of a committee, *of whom* (*quorum*) a certain number must be present to form a meeting. ─ L. *quōrum*, of whom ; gen. pl. of *quī*, who. Allied to **Who**.

Quota, a share. (Ital. ─ L.) Ital. *quota*, a share. ━ L. *quota* (*pars*), how great a part ; fem. of *quotus*, how great. ━ L. *quot*, how many ; allied to *quī*, who ; see **Who**.

quote. (F. ─ L.) Formerly also *cote*. ━ O. F. *quotĕr*, *coter*, to quote. ━ Late L. *quotāre*, to mark off into chapters and verses, for references ; hence, to give a reference.

–L. *quotus*, how many, how much, with allusion to chapters, &c. ; see above.

Quoth, he said. (E.) Properly a pt. t. M. E. *quoth, quod.* – A. S. *cwæð*, pt. t. of *cweðan*, to say.+Icel. *kvað*, pt. t. of *kveða*, to say ; Goth. *kwath*, pt. t. of *kwithan*, to say. Der. *quotha*, for *quoth he.*

Quotidian, daily. (F. – L.) F. *quotidien.* – L. *quotidiānus*, daily. – L. *quoti-*, for *quotus*, how many ; *diēs*, a day. Thus *quotidiānus* = on however many a day, on any day, daily.

quotient. (F. – L.; *or* L.) F. *quotient*, the part which falls to each man's share ; Cot. – L. **quotient-*, the imaginary stem of L. *quotiens*, how many times ; which is really indeclinable. – L. *quot*, how many. See **Quote.**

R.

Rabbet, to cut the edges of boards so that they overlap and can be joined. (F. – L. *and* G.) F. *raboter*, to plane, level, or lay even ; cf. *rabot*, a joiner's plane, a plasterer's beater. Of doubtful origin. Perhaps from F. *re-* (L. *re-*), again ; F. *a* (L. *ad*), to ; and M. F. *buter*, 'to joine unto by the ende,' Cot., from F. *but*, end. See. **Abut,** and **Butt** (1).

Rabbi, Rabbin, sir. (L. – Gk. – Heb.) L. *rabbī*, John i. 38. – Gk. *ῥαββί*. – Heb. *rabbī*, literally ' my master.' – Heb. *rab*, great ; as sb., master ; and *ī*, my. – Heb. root *rābab*, to be great. (The form *rabbin* is French.)

Rabbit. (O. Low G. ?) M. E. *rabet*. Dimin. of an older form only found in M. Du. *robbe*, dimin. *robbeken*, a rabbit (Kilian). ¶ The true E. name is *cony.*

Rabble. (M. Du.) From the noise made by a crowd. – M. Du. *rabbelen*, to chatter ; Low G. *rabbeln*, to chatter, babble. The suffix *-le* gives a frequentative force ; *rabble* = that which keeps on making a noise. Cf. **Rap** ; and see **Rapparee.**

Rabid, mad. (L.) L. *rabidus*, mad. – L. *rabere*, to rage, rave. Cf. **Rage.**

Raca. (Chaldee.) Matt. v. 22. Chaldee *rēkā*, worthless ; hence, foolish.

Raccoon, Racoon. (N. American Indian.) Spelt *rackoon* in Bailey (1735). The native W. Indian name. ' *Arathkone*, a beast like a fox ;' glossary of Indian Words subjoined to A Historie of Travaile into Virginia, by W. Strachey (pub. by the Hakluyt Soc. in 1849).

Race (1), a swift course. (Scand.) M. E. *ras* (North) ; [*rees* (South), from A. S. *ræs*]. – Icel. *rás*, a running, race. Teut. base **rēs-*. Hence it is not for **rans*, i. e. a running (as in Noreen).

Race (2), a family. (F. – Ital.) F. *race.* – Ital. *razza, raza*, also M. Ital. *raggia*, ' a race, broode,' Florio. Of doubtful origin ; but answering to L. type **radia*, allied to *radiāre*, to radiate. (Korting, § 6612.)

Race (3), a root. (F. – L.) ' A *race* of ginger ;' Wint. Ta. iv. 3. 50. – O. F. *rais*, *raiz*, a root. – L. *rādīcem*, acc. of *rādix*, a root. See **Radix, Radish.**

Raceme, a cluster. (F. – L.) F. *racème.* – L. *racēmum*, acc. of *racēmus*, a cluster.

Rack (1), a grating above a manger, an instrument of torture. (E.) In some senses the word is doubtless English ; cf. M. E. *rekke*, a rack for hay. In the particular sense ' to torture,' it may have been borrowed from M. Du. *racken*, to rack, to torture. The radical sense of *rack* is to extend, stretch out ; hence, as sb., *rack* is a straight bar (cf. G. *rack*, a rail, bar) ; hence, a frame-work, such as the bars in a grating above a manger, a frame-work used for torture, a bar with teeth in which a cog-wheel can work. *On the rack* = in great anxiety ; a *rack-rent* is a rent stretched to its full value, or nearly so. Allied words are Icel. *rakkr*, straight, *rekkja*, to strain, M. Du. *racken*, to stretch, reach out ; rack ; Swed. *rak*, straight, G. *rack*, a rack, rail, *recken*, to stretch ; esp. Low G. *rakk*, a shelf, as in E. *plate-rack*. Cf. Goth. *uf-rakjan*, to stretch out. ¶ *Rack* is used in many senses ; see *rack* (2), *rack* (3), &c.

Rack (2), light vapoury clouds, mist. (Scand.) See Hamlet, ii. 2. 506 ; Antony, iv. 14. 10. M. E. *rak*. – Icel. *rek*, drift, motion, a thing drifted ; cf. *skȳrek*, the rack or drifting clouds. – Icel. *reka*, to drive, thrust, toss ; cognate with A. S. *wrecan*, to drive. See **Wreak.** Cf. Swed. *skeppet vräker* = the ship drifts.

Rack (3), to pour off liquor, to clear it from dregs or lees. (F. – L. ?) Minsheu (1627) speaks of ' *rackt* wines.' – M. F. *raqué* ; whence *vin raqué*, ' small, or corse wine, squeezed from the dregs of the grapes, already drained of all their best moisture ;' Cot. Cf. Languedoc *raqua*, to glean grapes ; *raquo*, skin of grapes (D'Hombres) ; Span. *rascon*, sour ; *rascar*, to scrape. Prob. of L. origin ; see **Rascal.**

428

Rack (4), the same as *wrack*; in the phr. 'to go to *rack* and *ruin*'; see **Wrack**.

Rack (5); see **Arrack**.

Rack (6), a neck of mutton. (E.) A.S. *hracca*, the back of the head (*occiput*); see Somner, and Vocab. 463. 21. ¶ We also find *rack* (7), for *reck*, to care; *rack* (8), to relate, from A.S. *racu*, an account; *rack* (9), a pace of a horse, i.e. a *rocking* pace; see **Rock** (2). Also *rack* (10), a track, cart-rut, from A.S. *racu*, a track.

Racket (1), **Raquet**, a bat with a net-work blade. (F.–Span.–Arab.) M.E. *raket*; borrowed from O.F.; cf. M.F. *raquette*.–Span. *raqueta*, a racket, battle-dore.–Arab. *rāhat*, the palm of the hand (hence the game of fives, which preceded rackets). To this day, tennis is called in F. *paume*, i.e. palm of the hand, though now played with bats.

Racket (2), a noise. (E.) Of imitative origin; cf. *rattle*, *rap*. So also Gael. *racaid*, a noise; Irish *racan*, noise; Gael. *rac*, to make a noise like geese or ducks.

Racoon; see **Raccoon**.

Racy, of strong flavour, spirited. (F.–Ital.; *with* E. *suffix*.) *Rac-y* = indicative of its *race*, due to its breed. See **Race** (2).

Radiant. (L.) From stem of pres. pt. of L. *radiāre*, to shine.–L. *radius*, a ray.

Radical; see **Radix**.

Radish. (F.–Prov.–L.) F. *radis* (not a true F. word, but borrowed from Provençal).–Prov. *raditz*, a root.–L. *rādīcem*; see **Radix**. ¶ Or the F. *radis* is from Ital. *radice*.

Radius, a ray. (L.) L. *radius*, a ray. Doublet, *ray* (1).

Radix, a root. (L.) L. *rādix* (stem *rādīc-*), a root.+Gk. ῥάδιξ, a branch, rod; ῥάδαμνος, a twig. See **Root** and **Wort**. Der. *radic-al*, L. *rādīcalis*.

Raffle, a kind of lottery. (F. – G.) M.E. *rafle*, a game at dice.–M.F. *rafle*, *raffle*, a game at three dice; O.F. *rafle*, a gust of wind; F. *rafler*, to snatch up.–G. *raffeln*, to snatch up; frequent. of *raffen*, to snatch away, carry off hastily. See **Rap** (2).

Raft. (Scand.) M.E. *raft*, a spar, beam; orig. sense 'rafter.'–Icel. *raptr* (*raftr*), a rafter, beam (where the final *r* is merely the sign of the nom. case); Dan. *raft*, a rafter, a beam. Allied to Icel.

rāf, *ræfr*, a roof, cognate with O.H.G. *rāfo*, a spar, rafter. Allied to Gk. ὄροφος, a roof, ἐρέφειν, to cover. (√REPH.) ¶ Not allied to A.S. *hrōf*, a roof.

rafter, a beam to support a roof. (E.) A.S. *ræfter*. An extension of the word above.

Rag. (Scand.) M.E. *ragge*. We only find A.S. *raggie*, for **raggige*, rough, shaggy; as if formed from a sb. **ragg-*.– Norw. *ragg*, rough hair, whence *ragged*, shaggy (E. *ragged*); Swed. *ragg*, rough hair, whence *raggig*, shaggy; Icel. *rögg*, shagginess, *raggaðr*, shaggy. Orig. sense 'shagginess,' whence the notion of untidiness. ¶ The resemblance to Gk. ῥάκος, a shred of cloth, is accidental. Der. *rag-stone*, i.e. rugged stone; *rag-wort*, i.e. ragged plant.

Rage. (F.–L.) F. *rage*.–L. *rabiem*, acc. of *rabiēs*, rage.–L. *rabere*, to rage. And see **Rave**.

Ragout. (F.–L.) F. *ragoût*, a seasoned dish.–F. *ragoûter*, to coax a sick man's appetite.–F. *re-*, again; *a*, to; *goûter*, to taste.–L. *re-*; *ad*; *gustāre*, to taste. See **Gust** (2).

Raid. (North E.) A Northern form of E. *road*. Cf. Icel. *reið*, a riding, a road. See **Road**.

Rail (1), a bar. (F.–L.) M.E. *rail*. Not found in A.S.–O.F. *reille*, a rail, bar; Norman dial. *raile*.–L. *rēgula*, a bar. See **Rule**. Cf. Low G. *regel*, a rail, cross-bar; Swed. *regel*, a bar, bolt; G. *riegel*, O.H.G. *rigil*, a bar, bolt; all from L.

Rail (2), to brawl, scold. (F.) F. *railler*, to deride; O.F. *raille*, sb., mockery. Origin unknown. Der. *raill-er-y*, F. *raillerie*, banter.

Rail (3), a bird. (F.–Teut.) O.F. *raalle*; M.F. *rasle*, 'a rayle,' Cot.; F. *râle*. (From its cry.)

Rail (4), part of a woman's night-dress. (E.) See Halliwell and Palsgrave. M.E. *rejel*.–A.S. *hrægl*, *hregl*, a dress, robe, swaddling-clothes. +O. Fries. *hreil*, *reil*; O.H.G. *hregil*, a garment. Teut. type **hragilom*, neut.

Raiment. (F.–L. *and* Scand.; *with* F. *suffix*.) Short for *arrai-ment*; see **Array**.

Rain. (E.) M.E. *rein*. A.S. *regn*, also *rēn* (by contraction).+Du. *regen*, Icel. Dan. Swed. *regn*, G. *regen*, Goth. *rign*, rain. Cf. L. *rigāre*, to moisten.

Raindeer; see **Reindeer.**

Raise. (Scand.) M. E. *reisen.*—Icel. *reisa*, to make to rise, causal of *rīsa* (pt. t. *reis*), to rise; so also Dan. *reise*, Swed. *resa*, to raise. See **Rise, Rear** (1).

Raisin. (F.—L.) M. E. *reisin.*—O. F. *raisin*, a grape; also a bunch.—Folk-L. *racīmum*, for L. *racēmum*, acc. of *racēmus*, a cluster.

Rajah, prince. (Skt.) Skt. *rājā*, the nom. case from the stem *rājan*, a king. Cognate with L. *rex*; see **Regal.**

rajpoot, a prince. (Hind.—Skt.) Hind. *rajpūt*, a prince; lit. 'son of a rajah.'— Skt. *rāj-ā*, a king; *putra*, son.

Rake (1), an implement. (E.) A.S. *raca*, a rake.+Du. *rakel*, a rake, Dan. *rage*, a poker, Swed. *raka*, an oven-rake (with base *rak*-); also Icel. *reka*, a shovel, G. *rechen*, a rake (with base *rek*-). Allied to Goth. *rikan* (Teut. type **rek-an-*, pt. t. *rak*), to collect, heap up. Cf. Icel. *raka*, vb., to rake. **Der.** *rake*, vb.

Rake (2), a dissolute man. (Scand.) M. E. *rakel*, rash; oddly corrupted to *rake-hell* (Trench, Nares); finally shortened to *rake.*—Swed. dial. *rakkel*, a vagabond, from *raka*, to run hastily, M. Swed. *racka*, to run about. Cf. A.S. *racian*, to run.

Rake (3), the projection of the extremities of a ship beyond the keel, the inclination of a mast from the perpendicular. (Scand.) 'In sea-language, the *rake of a ship* is so much of her hull or main body, as hangs over both the ends of her keel;' Phillips (1706). Evidently from *rake*, vb., to reach, extend (Halliwell).—Swed. dial. *raka*, to reach, *raka fram*, to reach over, project; Dan. *rage frem*, to project, jut out. Cf. Icel. *rakr*, Swed. *rak*, straight. Allied to **Rack** (1).

Rakehell, a vagabond; see **Rake** (2).

Raki, arrack. (Turk.—Arab.) Turk. *rāqī*, arrack.—Arab. *'araq*, arrack; see **Arrack.**

Rally (1), to re-assemble. (F.—L.) F. *rallier.*—F. *re-*, again; *allier*, to ally; see **Ally.** Cf. prov. F. *raller*, to rally, grow convalescent; dial. de la Meuse (Labourasse).

Rally (2), to banter. (F.) We also find the sb. *rallery*, 'pleasant drolling,' Phillips, ed. 1706. This is, of course, another spelling of *raillery*; and *rally* is merely another form of *rail* (2), from F. *railler*, to deride. See **Rail** (2).

Ram. (E.) A.S. *ram.*+Du. *ram*, G.

ramm. Cf. Icel. *ramr*, strong. **Der.** *ram*, vb., to butt, push, thrust; *ram-rod.*

Ramadan, a great Mohammedan fast. (Arab.) So called because kept in the ninth month, named *Ramadan.*—Arab. *ramaḍān*, pronounced *ramazān* in Turkish and Persian. As it is in the ninth month of the lunar year, it may take place in any season; but it is supposed to have been originally held in the hot season. The word implies 'consuming fire'; from Arab. root *rameḍ*, it was hot. (Devic, Richardson.)

Ramble. (E.) Frequentative of M. E. *ramien* (?), prov. E. *rame*, to rove, to gad about (Yks.); cf. E. Fries. *ramen, rāmen*, to rove, ramble. The *b* is excrescent, and *ramble* is for prov. E. *rammle*, to ramble (Whitby Glossary).

Ramify. (F.—L.) F. *ramifier*, to put forth branches (hence, to branch off).—L. *rāmi-*, for *rāmus*, a branch, bough; *-ficāre*, for *facere*, to make. With L. *rāmus*, cf. Gk. ῥάδαμνος, a twig. Brugm. i. § 529.

Ramp, Romp, to bound, leap; properly to climb, scramble, rear; also to sport boisterously. (F.—Teut.) M. E. *rampen*, to rage; cf. *ramp-ant* (F. *rampant*), rearing, said of a lion.—F. *ramper*, 'to creep, run, crawle, climb;' Cot. Orig. sense 'to clamber'; cf. M. Ital. *rampare*, to clutch, *rampo*, a hook. According to Diez, the Ital. *rampare* (Prov. *rapar*) is a nasalised form from Low G. *rappen*, to snatch hastily, Dan. *rappe*, to hasten; cf. G. *raffen*, to snatch; see **Rape** (1). But Körting derives Ital. *rampa*, a grip, from Low G. *ramp* (Lübben), Bavar. *rampf*, a cramp, seizure; which is allied to *rampf*, 2nd grade of O. H. G. *rimpfan*, to cramp. Cf. **Ripple** (2).

Rampart. (F.—L.) Also spelt *rampire, rampier, rampar.*—M. F. *rempart*, rem1r., *rempar*, a rampart of a fort.—M. F. *remparer*, to put again into a state of defence. —L. *re-*, again; *im-* (*in*), in; *parāre*, to get ready. See **Pare.**

Ramsons, broad-leaved garlic. (E.) A double plural; for *rams-en-s.* Here *ramsen* = A. S. *hramsan*, ramsons; a pl. form, from a sing. *hramsa.*+Swed. *rams-lök* (*lök* = leek); Dan. *rams*; Lithuan. *kermusze*, wild garlic; Irish *creamh*, W. *craf*, garlic; Gk. κρόμυον, an onion (Stokes-Fick, p. 98).

Ranch, Rancho, a rude hut. (Span. —Teut.) Common in Mexico.—Span. *rancho*, a mess, set of persons who eat

and drink together; formerly, 'a ranke,'
Minsheu. Prob. borrowed from Prov.
renc, a rank; O. F. *reng*; see **Rank,
Range.**

Rancid. (L.) L. *rancidus,* rancid. Cf.
L. *rancens,* stinking, as if from an infin.
*rancēre, to stink.

rancour. (F.—L.) M. E. *rancour.* —
A.F. *rancour.* — L. *rancōrem,* acc. of *rancor,*
spite, orig. rancidness. See above.

Random, said or done at hazard. (F. —
Teut.) M. E. *randon*; esp. in phr. *in
randon,* in great haste. — O. F. *randon,* the
force and swiftness of a great stream;
whence phr. *à randon,* in great haste, with
impetuosity; from O. F. *randir,* to run
swiftly. So also Span. *de rendon, de rondon,*
rashly, impetuously. — G. *rand,* a brim,
edge, verge, margin; whence Ital. *a randa,*
with difficulty, exactly (lit. near the verge).
Cf. G. *bis am rande voll,* full to the brim.
The sense of O. F. *randir* has reference to
the course of a *full* or *brimming* river.✚
A. S. *rand,* Icel. *rönd,* Dan. *rand,* rim,
verge; Swed. *rand,* a stripe. See **Rind.**

Range. (F.—O.H.G.) The sense 'to
rove' arose from the trooping about of
ranks of armed men. — F. *ranger* (O. F.
renger), to range, rank, order, array, lit.
'to put into a rank.' — F. *rang* (O. F. *reng*),
a rank (below).

rank (1), a row, line of soldiers, class.
(F.—O.H.G.) M. E. *reng, renk.* — O. F.
reng (F. *rang*), a rank, row, list, range. —
O. H. G. *hrinc,* a ring, ring of men, hence
a row or rank of men. See **Ring.**

Rank (2), coarse in growth, very fertile;
also rancid. (E.) The sense 'rancid' is
due to confusion with O. F. *rance,* 'musty,'
Cot., which is from L. *rancidus.* But M.E.
rank means strong, forward; from A. S.
ranc, strong, proud, forward.✚Du. *rank,*
lank, slender (like things of quick growth);
Icel. *rakkr* (for **rankr*), straight, slender,
Swed. *rank,* long and thin, Dan. *rank,* erect.

Rankle, to fester. (F. — L. — Gk.)
A. F. *rankler,* to fester; O. F. *draoncler,
raoncler, rancler* (so that it once began
with *d*; see Godefroy). — O.F. *draoncle,
raoncle, rancle,* an eruption of the skin. —
Late L. *dracunculus, dranculus,* (1) a
little dragon; (2) a kind of ulcer (as
dragons were supposed to be venomous).
— Late L. *draco,* a dragon. See **Dragon.**
(Phil. Soc. Trans. 1891.)

Ransack. (Scand.) Icel. *rannsaka,* to
search a house, ransack; Swed. *ransaka,*

Dan. *rannsage.* — Icel. *rann,* a house, abode;
sak-, related to *sækja,* to seek. The Icel.
rann stands for **razn,* and is the same as
A. S. *ærn,* a cot, Goth. *razn,* a house; see
barn. Cf. A. S. *ræsn,* a plank, beam;
and see **Seek.** ¶ Cf. Norman dial. *ran-
saquer,* Gael. *rannsaich,* from Scand.

Ransom, redemption. (F.—L.) M. E.
ransoun (with final *n*). — O. F. *raënson,*
later *rançon,* a ransom. — L. *redemptiōnem,*
acc. of *redemptio,* a buying back. — L.
redemptus, pp. of *redimere,* to redeem; see
Redeem. Doublet, *redemption.*

Rant. (Du.) M. Du. *randten,* to dote,
be enraged; also spelt *randen*; see Kilian.
Cf. Westphal. *rantern,* to prate.

Rantipole, a romping child. (Low G.)
Cf. M. Du. *wrantigh,* E. Fries. *wranterig,*
Low G. *wrantig,* peevish, quarrelsome;
and **Poll.** See **Frampold.**

Ranunculus. (L.) L. *rānunculus,* a
little frog; also, a plant. Double dimin.
of *rāna,* a frog.

Rap (1), to strike smartly; a smart
stroke. (Scand.) Dan. *rap,* a rap, tap;
Swed. *rapp,* a blow; Swed. *rappa,* to beat;
cf. G. *rappeln,* to rattle. Of imitative
origin; allied to **Rattle, Racket** (2).

Rap (2), to snatch, seize hastily. (E.)
M. E. *rapen,* to hasten, act hastily. Cf.
M. Du. *rapen,* 'to rap up, gather,' Hexham; Du. *rap,* quick; Icel. *hrapa,* to
fall, tumble, hasten, hurry; Swed. *rappa,*
to seize, snatch, Dan. *rappe,* to make
haste; Swed. *rapp,* Dan. *rap,* quick,
brisk; G. *raffen,* to snatch. From Teut.
base **hrap-.* ¶ Chiefly in the phrase to
rap and rend. And see **Rapt, Rape** (1).

Rapacious. (L.) Coined from L.
rapāci-, for *rapax,* grasping. — L. *rapere,*
to grasp. Brugm. i. § 477.

Rape (1), a seizing by force. (F.—L.)
A. F. and Norm. dial. *rape, rap*; cf. Late
L. *rappus, rafus* (for L. *raptus*). O.F.
rapt. — L. *raptum,* acc. of *raptus,* a rape.
— L. *raptus,* pp. of *rapere,* to seize.
Cf. O. F. *raper,* Gascon *rapa,* to seize.
β. But, apparently, confused with M E.
rape, haste, hurry, a common word; see
Chaucer's lines to Adam Scrivener. — Icel.
hrap, ruin, falling down, *hrapaðr,* a hurry,
hrapa, to hasten; Swed. *rapp,* Dan. *rap,*
quick; see **Rap** (2). Der. *rape,* vb.

Rape (2), a plant. (L.) M. E. *rape.* —
L. *rāpa, rāpum,* a turnip, a rape.✚Gk.
ράπυς, a turnip, *ῥαφανίς,* a radish; Russ.
riepa, a turnip; G. *rübe.*

Rape (3), a division of a county, in Sussex. (Scand.) Icel. *hreppr*, a district; prob. orig. a share. — Icel. *hreppa*, to catch; cf. A. S. *hreppan*, to touch, lay hold of. Allied to **Rap** (2).

Rapid. (F. — L.) F. *rapide* — L. *rapidus*, quick, lit. snatching away. — L. *rapere*, to snatch. See **Rapacious**.

Rapier, a light narrow sword. (F. — Span. — O. H. G.) M. F. *rapiere, rappiere*, also *raspiere* (Littré); it was considered as Spanish. '*Rapiere*, Spanische sworde;' Palsgrave, p. 908. Perhaps *raspiere* was a name given in contempt, meaning 'a rasper' or poker; hence it was called 'a *proking-spit* of Spaine'; Nares.· Cf. Span. *raspadera*, a raker. — Span. *raspar*, to rasp, scratch. — O. H. G. *raspōn*, to rasp. See **Rasp.** ¶ So Diez; Littré rejects this probable solution.

Rapine. (F. — L.) F. *rapine*, ' ⅂apine, ravine;' Cot. — L. *rapīnia*, robbery, plunder. — L. *rapere*, to seize. See **Rapacious.**

Rapparee, an Irish robber. (Irish.) Irish *rapaire*, a noisy fellow, sloven, robber, thief; cf. *rapal*, noise, *rapach*, noisy. Cf. Gael. *rapair*, a noisy fellow. All perhaps from E. *rabble* (Macbain).

Rappee, a kind of snuff. (F. – O. H. G.) F. *râpé*, lit. rasped, reduced to powder; pp. of *râper*, to rasp; see **Rasp.**

Rapt, carried away. (L.) From L. *raptus*, pp. of *rapere*, to seize; see Milton, P. L. iii. 522. ¶ But in ' What thus *raps* you,' Cymb. i. 6. 51, the word may be E. See **Rap** (2).

raptorial. (L.) Used of birds of prey. — L. *raptōr-i-*, from *raptor*, one who seizes; with suffix *-al* — L. *rapere*, to seize.

rapture. (L.) Coined, as if from L. **raptūra*, from L. *raptus*, pp. of *rapere*.

Rare. (F. — L.) F. *rare*. — L. *rārum*, acc. of *rārus*, rare.

Rascal, a knave, villain. (F. — L.) M.E. *raskaille*, the common herd. [It was a term of the chase; certain animals, not worth hunting, were so called. The hart, till he was six years old, was accounted *rascayle*.] A. F. *raskayle*, a rabble; also **rascaille*, whence mod. F. *racaille*, 'the rascality or base or rascall sort, the scumme, dregs, offals, outcasts of any company,' Cot. Due to an O. F. word cognate with Prov. Span. Port. *rascar*, to scrape; the orig sense being ' scrapings'; cf. M. F. *rasque*, 'scurfe'; Cot. All from a Late L. **rāsicāre*, a frequent.

form from *rāsum*, supine of *rādere*, to scrape; see **Rase** (below); and **Rash** (2).

Rase, Raze, to scrape, efface. (F. — L.) M. E. *rasen*, to scrape. — F. *raser*. — Late L. *rāsāre*, to graze, to demolish. — L. *rāsum*, supine of *rādere*, to scrape. Allied to **Rodent.**

Rash (1), headstrong. (E.) M. E. *rash, rasch*, E. Fries. *rask*; cf. A. S. *ræscan* to flash.+Du. *rasch*, G. *rasch*; Dan. Swed. *rask*, quick, rash; Icel. *röskr*, vigorous; N. Fries. *radsk*, quick. ¶ Brugm. i. § 795, connects this word with O. H. G. *rad*, a wheel; see **Rotary.**

Rash (2), a slight eruption on the body. (F. — L.) O. F. *rasche, rasque, rache*. The same as Prov. *rasca*, the itch. So called from the wish to scratch it; cf. Prov. *rascar*, to scratch, equivalent to a Late L. **rāsicāre*. — L. *rāsum*, supine of *rādere*, to scrape. See **Rascal.**

Rash (3), to pull, tear violently. (F. — L.) ' *Rashing* off helmes;' F. Q. v. 3. 8. M.E. *aracen*, afterwards shortened to *racen*. — O. F. *esrachier* (F. *arracher*), to root up, pull away violently. — L. *exrādicāre*, to root out. — L. *ex*, out; *rādicāre*, to root, from *rādīc-*, stem of *rādix*, a root. See **Radix.**

Rash (4), a kind of serge. (F. — Ital.) M. F. *ras*, serge. — Ital. *rascia*, ' silk rash ;' Florio. From *Rascia*, a district in the S. of Bosnia.

Rasher, a thin slice of broiled bacon. (E.) ' *Rasher* on the coales, quasi *rashly* or hastily roasted,' Minsheu. This is right; cf. ' *Rashed*, burnt in cooking, by being too hastily dressed;' Halliwell. See **Rash** (1).

Rasorial. (L.) L. *rāsōr-i-*, from *rāsor*, one who scrapes; with suffix *-al.* — L. *rās-um*, supine of *rādere*, to scrape.

Rasp, vb. (F. — O. H. G.) M. E. *raspen* — O. F. *rasper* (F. *râper*). — O.H.G. *raspōn*, whence G. *raspeln* to rasp. Cf. O. H. G. *hrespan*, to pluck, to rake together. Cf. **Rap** (2).

rasp-berry, a kind of fruit. (F. — O.H.G.; and E.) Formerly called *raspis, raspes*, but this is merely a pl. form used as a singular. Named from its uneven surface. So also M. Ital. *raspo*, a rasp, also a raspberry.

Rat. (E.) M. E. *rat*. A. S. *ræt*.+M.Du. *ratte*, Du. *rat*, Dan. *rotte*, Swed. *råtta*, G. *ratte*, *ratz*; Low L. *ratus, rato* (whence F. *rat*); Irish and Gael. *radan*, Bret. *raz*.

Der. *rat*, vb., to desert one's party, as rats are said to leave a falling house. And see **Ratten.**

Ratafia, a liquor. (F.—Arab. *and* Malay.) F. *ratafia*; cf. *tafia*, rum-arrack. — Malay *araq tāfīa*, the spirit called *tafia*; where *araq* is borrowed from Arab. *'araq*, arrack.

Ratch, a rack or bar with teeth. (E.) A palatalised form of *rack* (1) above, in the sense of 'bar with teeth'; hence it came to mean a kind of a toothed wheel. **Der.** *ratch-et*, in watch-work, 'the small teeth at the bottom of the fusee or barrel that stop it in winding up;' Phillips.

Rate (1), a proportion, standard, tax. (F.—L.) A.F. *rate*, price, value. — L. *rata*, fem. of *ratus*, determined, fixed, settled, pp. of *reor*, I think, judge, deem. Brugm. i. § 200.

Rate (2), to scold, chide. (F.—L.) M. E. *raten*, Ch. C. T. 3463; *araten*, to reprove. Also spelt *retten*, *aretten*. — O.F. *reter*, *rateir*, *areter*, *aratter*, to accuse, to impute; Norman dial. *reter*, *retter*, to blame. — L. *ad*, to; and *reputāre*, to count. See **Repute.** ¶ Not from *rate* (1).

Rath, early; **Rather,** sooner. (E.) *Rather* is the compar. of *rath*, early, soon. A. S. *hraðe*, adv., quickly, *hræð*, adj., quick, swift; hence *hraðor*, sooner.+Icel. *hraðr*, swift; M. H. G. *rad*, *hrad*, quick; Du. *rad*, swift. Cf. O. Ir. *crothim*, I shake.

Ratify. (F.—L.) F. *ratifier*. — Late L. *ratificāre*, to confirm. — L. *rati-*, for *ratus*, settled; *-ficāre*, for *facere*, to make. See **Rate** (1).

ratio. (L.) L. *ratio*, calculation. — L. *ratus*, pp. of *reor*, I think, deem.

ration, rate or allowance of provisions. (F.—L.) F. *ration*. — L. *ratiōnem*, acc. of *ratio* (above). Doublet, *reason*.

Ratlines, Ratlins, Rattlings, the small transverse ropes crossing the shrouds of a ship. (E.; *and* F.—L.) Now turned into *rat-lines*, as if affording ladders for rats to get up by. But the old term was *raddelines*, or *raddelyng of the shrowdes*, Naval Accounts (1485–97), ed. Oppenheim, pp. 185, 207. Prob. the same as prov. E. *raddlings*, long pieces of underwood twisted between upright stakes (hence, *cross*-lines of the shrouds); cf. Du. *weeflijnen* (weave-lines), ratlines. Cf. prov. E. *raddle*, a hurdle; perhaps allied to *rod*. Palsgrave has '*radyll* of a carte.'

Rattan, a Malacca cane. (Malay.)

Also spelt *ratan* (Johnson). — Malay *rōtan*, the rattan-cane.

Ratten, to take away a workman's tools for offending the trades' union. (F.—Low L.—Teut.) *Ratten* is the Hallamshire (Sheffield) word for a rat; hence applied to working secret mischief, which is attributed to rats. 'I have been *rattened*; I had just put a new cat-gut band upon my lathe, and last night the *rats* have carried it off;' N. and Q. 3 S. xii. 192. M. E. *raton*, a rat. — F. *raton*, dimin. of F. *rat*; see **Rat.**

Rattle, to clatter. (E.) M. E. *ratelen.* A. S. **hrætelan*, only preserved in A. S. *hrætele*, *hrætelwyrt*, rattle-wort, a plant which derives its name from the rattling of the seeds in the capsules.+Du. *ratelen*, G. *rasseln*, to rattle; allied to Gk. κραδαίνειν, to shake. Cf. also Gk. κρόταλον, a rattle.

Raught, pt. t. of **Reach,** q. v.

Ravage, sb., plunder. (F.—L.) F. *ravage*, 'ravage;' Cot. — F. *ravir*, to bear away suddenly. — Folk-L *rapīre*, L. *rapere*, to seize. See **Rapid.** Der. *ravage*, vb., F. *ravager.*

Rave. (F.—L.) M. E. *raven.* — O. F. *raver*, cited by Diez, s. v. *rêver*, as a Lorraine word; hence the derivative *ravasser*, 'to rave, talk idly;' Cot. Godefroy has O. F. *resver*, *raver*, *rever*, to stroll about, also to rave; cf. F. *rêver*, dial. de la Meuse (Labourasse). Allied to Span. *rabiar*, to rave, a verb formed from the sb. *rabia*, rage, allied to L. *rabiēs*, rage. — L. *rabere*, to rage; see **Rabid.** ¶ This is the solution given by Diez; but see Körting, § 6598.

Ravel, to untwist, unweave, entangle. (M. Du.) The orig. sense has reference to the untwisting of a string or woven texture, the ends of threads of which become afterwards entangled. To *unravel* is to disentangle; to *ravel out* is to unweave. — M. Du. *ravelen*, to ravel; mod. Du. *rafelen*, E. Fries. *rafeln*, to fray out, unweave; Low G. *reffeln*, to fray out. Cf. Du. *rafel*, E. Fries. *rafel*, *räfel*, a frayed edge. Also Norman dial. *raviler*, to ravel; Pomeran. *rabbeln*, *uprabbeln*, to ravel out. Of unknown origin; but cf. A.S. *ārafian* (or *ārāfian*?), to unravel, Gregory's Pastoral Care, ed. Sweet, p. 245, l. 22. ¶ The M. Du. *ravelen*, to dote (from O. F. *rêver*, see **Rave**), is a different word. **Der.** *unravel.*

Ravelin, a detached work in fortification, with two embankments raised before the counterscarp. (F. – Ital.) F. *ravelin.* – M. Ital. *ravellino, revellino* (Ital. *rivellino*), a ravelin. Origin unknown; thought to be from L. *re-,* back, *uallum,* a rampart; which is unlikely.

Raven (1), a bird. (E.) M. E. *raven.* A. S. *hræfn, hrefn.*+Du. *raaf,* Icel. *hrafn,* Dan. *ravn,* G. *rabe.* Teut. type **hrabnoz,* m. Perhaps allied to Gk. κόραξ, a raven, L. *cor-uus.*

Raven (2), to plunder, to devour. (F. – L.) Better spelt *ravin.* From M. E. *ravine,* sb., plunder. – O. F. *ravine,* rapidity, impetuosity (oldest sense ' plunder,' as in L.). – L. *rapīna,* plunder; see **Rapine.**

ravine, a hollow gorge. (F. – L.) F. *ravine,* a hollow worn by floods, also a great flood; O. F. *ravine* (above).

ravish, to seize with violence. (F. – L.) M. E. *rauischen.* – F. *raviss-,* stem of pres. pt. of *ravir,* to ravish. – Folk-L. *rapīre,* for L. *rapere,* to seize.

Raw. (E.) M. E. *raw.* A. S. *hrēaw, hrǽw.*+Du. *raauw;* Icel. *hrár,* Dan. *raa,* Swed. *rå;* O. H. G. *rāo,* G. *roh.* Teut. types **hrawoz,* **hrǽwoz.* Allied to L. *crūdus,* raw, Skt. *krūra-,* sore, cruel, hard; also to Gk. κρέας (for **κρεϝας*), raw flesh, Skt. *kravya-,* raw flesh; Lat. *cruor,* blood; Russ. *krove,* Lith. *kraujas,* Irish *crū,* W. *crau,* blood. Brugm. i. § 492. (√KREU.)

Ray (1). (F. – L.) O. F. *raye* ; F. *raie.* – L. *radium,* acc. of *radius,* a ray. See **Radius.**

Ray (2), a fish. (F. – L.) O. F. *raye,* F. *raie.* – L. *rāia,* a ray.

Ray (3), a dance. (Du.) M. Du. *rey,* a dance; Du. *rei,* a chorus.

Rayah, a person, not a Mohammedan, who pays the capitation-tax, a word in use in Turkey. (Arab.) It may be explained as ' subject,' though the orig. sense is ' a flock,' or pastured cattle. – Arab. *ra'iyah, ra'iya(t),* a flock, subject, peasant; from *ra'y,* pasturing, tending flocks. Cf. **Ryot.**

Raze, the same as **Rase** (above).

razor. (F. – L.) F. *rasoir,* a razor, lit. a shaver. – F. *raser,* to shave; see **Rase.**

Razzia, a sudden raid. (F. – Algiers.) F. *razzia, razia;* borrowed from the Algerine *razia,* which is a peculiar pronunciation of Arab. *ghāzīa,* a raid, expedition against infidels (Devic). – Arab. *ghāzī,* a hero, a leader of an expedition.

Re-, Red-, *prefix,* again. (F. – L.; *or* L.) L. *re-, red-* ; commonly *re-,* except in *red-eem, red-olent, red-dition, red-ound, red-undant.* ¶ Hence a large number of compounds, such as *re-address, re-arrange,* which cause no difficulty.

Reach (1), to attain. (E.) M. E. *rechen,* pt. t. *raghte, raughte,* pp. *raught.* – A. S. *rǣcan, rǣcean,* pt. t. *rǣhte.*+Du. *reiken,* O. Friesic *reka;* G. *reichen.* The A. S. *rǣcan* is closely allied to the sb. *ge-rǣc,* opportunity; giving as the orig. sense ' to seize an opportunity.' Teut. type **raikjan-.* (Distinct from A. S. *reccan,* to stretch.) **Der.** *reach,* sb., which also means 'a stretch in a river.'

Reach (2), to try to vomit; see **Retch.**

Read. (E.) M. E. *reden.* A. S. *rǣdan* (strong verb), to counsel, consult, interpret, read; with the remarkable pt. t. *rēord.* [Also as a weak vb., pt. t. *rǣdde;* prob. by confusion with *rǣdan,* to dispose of, to govern.] Allied to Goth. *garēdan,* to provide, Icel. *rāða* (pt. t. *reð*), to advise, G. *rathen* (pt. t. *rieth*), to advise. Teut. type **rǣdan-.* Perhaps allied to L. *rē-rī,* to think. **Der.** *riddle* (1), q. v.

Ready. (E.) M. E. *rēdi;* with change of suffix from A. S. *rǣde,* ready; orig. ' equipped for riding,' or ' prepared for a raid' ; [*ready* = ' fully dressed,' is common in Tudor E.]; usual form *ge-rǣde.* – A. S. *rād,* and stem of *rīdan,* to ride. So also G. *be-reit,* ready, from *reit-en,* to ride; Goth. *garaids,* Icel. *g-reiðr,* ready; cf. Goth. *raidjan,* to order, appoint. And cf. G. *fertig,* ready, from *fahren,* to go. See **Ride.**

Real (1), actual. (F. – L.; *or* L.) Either from O. F. *reël* (F. *réel*), or directly from Late L. *rēālis,* belonging to the thing itself. – L. *rēs,* a thing. **Der.** *real-ist.*

Real (2), a small Spanish coin. (Span. – L.) Span. *real,* lit. a ' royal ' coin. – L. *rēgālis,* royal ; see **Regal.**

Realgar, red arsenic. (F. – Span. – Arab.) F. *réalgar.* – Span. *rejalgar,* red sulphuret of arsenic. – Arab. *rahj al-ghār,* powder of the mine, mineral powder. – Arab. *rahj,* powder; *al,* the; *ghār,* a cavern, mine.

Realm. (F. – L.) M. E. *roialme, realme.* – A. F. *realme* (F. *royaume*), a kingdom; answering to a Late L. **rēgālimen.* – L. *rēgālis,* royal; see **Regal.**

Ream. (F. – Span. – Arab.) M. E. *reeme.* – O. F. *raime* (F. *rame*), a ream or bundle of paper. **—** Span. *resma*, a ream. **—** Arab. *risma*(*t*), pl. *rizam*, a bundle.

Reap. (E.) M. E. *repen* (pt. t. *rep*, pp. *ropen*). O. Merc. *reopan*, A. S. *repan*, pt. t. *ræp*, pt. t. pl. *ræpon*. [But a commoner form is A. S. *rīpan* (pt. t. *rāp*, pp. *ripen*); whence A. S. *rīp*, E. *ripe*; see **Ripe**. The co-existence of these two strong verbs is remarkable.] The A. S. *repan* is from a Teut. base **rep-*, whence Du. *repel*, a flax-comb (see **Ripple** (1)), and Swed. *repa*, to rip up (see **Rip**). The A. S. *rīpan* is from a Teut. base **reip-*, whence **Ripe** and **Rope**.

Rear (1), to raise. (E.) M. E. *reren*. A. S. *rǣran*, to rear; the exact equivalent of Icel. *reisa*, to raise. Teut. type **raizján-* (cf. Goth. *ur-raisjan*, to raise up); whence A. S. *rǣran*, by Verner's law. See **Raise**. Causal form of *rīsan*, to rise (pt. t. *rās* = Goth. *rais*). Doublet, *raise*.

Rear (2), the back part. (F. **–** L.) M. E. *rere*, chiefly in adv. *arere*, *arrere*, in the rear. **—** O. F. *riere*, backward; whence *ariere* (F. *arrière*), behind, backward. **—** L. *retro*, backward; whence *ad retro* > F. *arrière*. See **Retro-**.

Rear (3), insufficiently cooked. (E.) M. E. *rere*. A. S. *hrēr*, half-cooked.

Rearmouse; see **Reremouse**.

Rearward, the rear-guard. (F. **–** L. *and* G.) The old spelling is *rereward*, M. E. *rerewarde*, i. e. guard in the rear. See **Rear** (2) and **Ward**.

Reason. (F. **–** L.) M. E. *resoun*, *reisun*. **–** A. F. and O. F. *reison* (F. *raison*). **–** L. *ratiōnem*, acc. of *ratio*, calculation, reason. See **Ratio**.

Reave, to rob. (E.) M. E. *reuen* (= *reven*); pt. t. *rafte*, *refte*, pp. *raft*, *reft*. A. S. *rēafian*, to despoil, lit. to strip; cf. A. S. *rēaf*, clothing, a robe, spoil, plunder. **—** A. S. *rēaf*, 2nd grade of strong verb *rēofan*, to break. **+** Icel. *raufa*, to reave, *rauf*, spoil, from *rauf*, 2nd grade of *rjūfa*, to break up, violate; G. *rauben*, to rob, *raub*, plunder. The strong verb is of the Teut. type **reuban-* (pt. t. **raub*). Cf. L. *rumpere*, to break. Brugm. i. § 701.

Rebate, to blunt a sword's edge. (F. **–** L.) O. F. *rebatre*, to beat back again. **—** F. *re-* (L. *re-*), back; O.F. *batre*, F. *battre*, to beat; see **Batter** (1).

Rebeck, a three-stringed fiddle. (F. **–** Arab.) O. F. *rebec*, also spelt *rebebe*; M. Ital. *ribecca*, also *ribebba*, a rebeck. **—** Arab. *rabāb*, *rabāba*(*t*), a rebeck (Devic).

Rebel. (F. **–** L.) The verb is from the sb., and the sb. was orig. an adj. M. E. *rebel*, adj., rebellious. **—** F. *rebelle*, rebellious. **–** L. *rebellem*, acc. of *rebellis*, renewing war. **–** L. *re-*, again; *bellum*, war = O. L. *duellum*, war; see **Duel**. Der. *rebel*, sb. and vb.; *rebell-ion*, *-ious*.

Rebound; see **Bound** (1).

Rebuff, a repulse. (Ital.) In Milton, P. L. ii. 936. **–** Ital. *rebuffo*, *ribuffo*, a check. **–** Ital. *ribuffare*, 'to check, chide;' Florio. **–** Ital. *ri-* (L. *re-*), back; *buffare*, a word of imitative origin, like E. *puff*; see **Puff**.

Rebuke, to reprove. (F. **–** L.) M. E. *rebuken*; A. F. *rebuker*. **–** O. F. (Picard) *rebouquer*, also *reboucher*, to blunt a weapon; metaphorically, to put aside a request; cf. Picard *se rebuker*, to revolt. **—** F. *re-*, back; *bouquer*, Picard form of *boucher*, to obstruct, shut up, also to hoodwink, nip with cold (hence to blunt); formed from *bouque*, Picard form of F. *bouche*, the mouth. **–** L. *re-*, back; *bucca*, the puffed cheek (later, the mouth). Thus *to rebuke* is to stop one's mouth, obstruct; cf. Gascon *rebouca*, 'refluer, en parlant d'eau.'

Rebus, a representation of a word by pictures. (L.) Thus *Bolton* was represented by pictures of a *bolt* and a *tun*. **–** L. *rēbus*, by things, i. e. by means of things; abl. pl. of *rēs*, a thing. See **Real** (1).

Rebut. (F. **–** L. *and* M.H.G.) O. F. *rebouter*, to repulse. **–** L. *re-*, again; M.H.G. *bōzen*, to beat; see **Beat**.

Recall. (L. *and* Scand.) From L. *re-*, back; and *call*, of Scand. origin.

Recant. (L.) L. *recantāre*, to sing back, echo; also, to recant, recall. **–** L. *re-*, back; *cantāre*, to sing. See **Cant** (1).

Recede. (L.) L. *recēdere*, to go back. **–** L. *re-*, back; *cēdere*, to go; see **Cede**.

Receive. (F. **–** L.) A. F. *receiv-*, a stem of *receivre*, O. F. *reçoivre*. **–** L. *recipere*, to take back. **–** L. *re-*, back; *capere*, to take. See **Capacious**.

Recent. (F. **–** L.) M. F. *recent* (F. *récent*). **–** L. *recent-*, stem of *recens*, fresh, new, orig. 'beginning anew.' **–** L. *re-*, again; *-cent-*, a stem allied to Russ. *po-chin-ate*, to begin, O. Irish *cét-*, first; and to Gk. καινός, new (Prellwitz).

Receptacle. (F. **–** L.) F. *réceptacle*. **–** L. *receptāculum*, a place to store away. **–** L. *recept-us*, pp. of *recipere*; see **Receive**.

reception. (F. – L.) F. *réception.* – L. acc. *receptiōnem*, a taking back. – L. *receptus* ; as above.

Recess. (L.) L. *recessus*, a retreat. – L. *recessus*, pp. of *re-cēdere*, to recede. See **Recede.**

Recheat, a signal of recall, in hunting. (F. – L.) From A.F. *rechet*, variant of O. F. *recet*, a place of refuge, a retreat (Godefroy). – L. *receptum*, acc. of *receptus*, a retreating, retreat. – L. *receptus*, pp. of *recipere*, to receive ; see **Receive.**

recipe. (L.) L. *recipe*, take thou ; imp. of *recipere*, to receive (above).

recipient. (L.) L. *recipient-*, stem of pres. pt. of *recipere*, to receive.

Reciprocal. (L.) From L. *reciprocus*, returning, alternating. Lit. ' directed backwards and forwards ; ' from L. **re-co-*, backwards (from *re-*, back) ; and **pro-co-*, forwards, whence *procul*, afar off. Brugm. ii. § 86.

Recite. (F. – L.) M. F. *reciter.* – L. *recitāre*, to recite. – L. *re-*, again ; *citāre*, to quote ; see **Cite.**

Reck, to regard. (E.) M. E. *rekken* ; often *recchen*. A.S. *reccan, reccean* (for *rak-jan) ; but the pt. t. in use is *rōh-te*, from an infin. *rēcan* (for *rōk-jan), from the strong grade **rōk-*. + Icel. *rækja* ; O. Sax. *rōkjan*, to reck, heed. Formed from a sb. with base *rac-*, strong grade *rōc-*, care, which exists in the cognate M. H. G. *ruoch*, O. H. G. *ruoh*, care, heed (whence the M. H. G. *ruochen*, O. H. G. *ruohhjan*, to reck). β. The Teut. stem **rōk-* is the strong grade of **rak-*, as seen in Icel. *rök*, a reason, A. S. *racu*, account, reckoning, O. Sax. *raka*, a business, affair, O. H. G. *rahha*. Der. *reck-less*, A.S. *rēce-lēas* ; cf. Du. *roekeloos*, G. *ruchlos*.

reckon. (E.) M. E. *rekenen*. A.S. *ge-recenian*, to explain ; allied to *ge-reccan, reccan*, to rule, order, direct, explain, ordain, tell. + Du. *rekenen* ; (whence Icel. *reikna*, to reckon, Dan. *regne*, Swed. *räkna*, are borrowed) ; G. *rechnen*, O.H. G. *rehhanōn*, to compute, reckon. β. All secondary verbs ; allied to the sb. seen in A. S. *racu*, an account, Icel. *rök*, neut. pl., a reason, ground, origin, O. H. G. *rahha*, a thing, subject. See **Reck.**

Reclaim ; from Re- and **Claim.**

Recline. (L.) L. *reclīnāre*, to lean back, lie down. – L. *re-*, back ; *clīnāre, to lean. See **Lean** (1) and **Incline.**

Recluse. (F. – L.) M. E. *recluse*, orig. fem. – O. F. *recluse*, fem. of *reclus*, pp. of *reclorre*, to shut up. – L. *reclūdere*, to unclose ; but in late Lat. to shut up. – L. *re-*, back ; *claudere*, to shut. See **Clause.**

Recognise. (F. – L.) Formed from the sb. *recognisance* (Chaucer, C. T. 13260). – O. F. *recognisance*, an acknowledgment. – O. F. *recognis-ant*, pres. part. of *recognoistre* (F. *reconnaître*). – L. *re-cognoscere*, to know again. See **Cognisance.** Der. *recognit-ion* (from L. pp. *recognit-us*).

Recoil, vb. (F. – L.) M. E. *recoilen.* – A. F. *recuiller* ; F. *reculer*, ' to recoyle, retire ; ' Cot. Lit. to go backwards. – F. *re-*, back ; *cul*, the hinder part. – L. *re-*, back ; *cūlum*, acc. of *cūlus*, the hinder part.

Recollect, to remember. (F. – L.) Lit. ' to gather again ; ' from *re-*, again, and *collect* ; see **Collect.**

Recommend, to commend to another. (F. – L.) From Re- and **Commend** ; imitated from F. *recommander*, ' to recommend ; ' Cot.

Recompense, to reward. (F. – L.) M. F. *recompenser*, ' to recompence ; ' Cot. – L. *re-*, again ; *compensāre*, to compensate ; see **Compensate.**

Reconcile. (F. – L.) O. F. *reconcilier.* – L. *re-*, again ; *conciliāre*, to conciliate ; see **Conciliate.**

Recondite, secret. (L.) L. *reconditus*, put away, hidden, secret ; pp. of *recondere*, to put back again. – L. *re-*, back ; *condere*, to put together. β. The L. *condere* (pt. t. *condidi*) is from *con-* (*cum*), with, and the weak grade of √DHĒ, to place, put. Brugm. i. § 573.

Reconnoitre, to survey. (F. – L.) O. F. *reconoistre*, M. F. *recognoistre*, 'to recognise, to take a precise view of ; ' Cot. – L. *re-cognoscere*, to know again. See **Recognise.**

Record. (F. – L.) M. E. *recorden.* – O. F. *recorder.* – L. *recordāre, recordārī*, to recall to mind. – L. *re-*, again ; *cord-*, stem of *cor*, heart. See **Heart.**

Recount. (F. – L.) F. *raconter*, to teil, relate. – F. *re-* (L. *re-*), again ; *aconter*, to account ; from *a* (L. *ad*), to, and *conter*, to count. See **Count** (2). *Recount = re-ac-count.*

Recoup, to diminish a loss. (F. – L. and Gk.) Lit. to secure a piece or shred. – F. *recoupe*, a shred. – F. *recouper*, to cut again. ‒ L. *re-*, again; and F. *couper*, to cut; see **Coppice.**

Recourse. (F.‒L.) F. *recours.* ‒ L. *recursum*, acc. of *recursus*, a running back; from pp. of *recurrere*, to run back. ‒ L. *re-*, back; *currere*, to run; see **Current.**

Recover. (F.‒L.) O. F. *recovrer*, *re-cuvrer* (F. *recouvrer*). ‒ L. *recuperāre*, to recover, also to recruit oneself. A difficult word; perhaps orig. 'to make good again,' from Sabine *cuprus*, good, of which the orig. sense may have been 'desirable,' from L. *cupere*, to desire. Brugm. ii. § 74.

Recreant. (F.‒L.) O. F. *recreant*, faint-hearted; pres. pt. of *recroire*, to believe again, also to give up, give back (hence, to give in). ‒ Late L. *recrēdere*, to believe again, recant, give in. ‒ L. *re-*, again; *crēdere*, to believe; see **Creed.**

Recreation. (F.‒L.) M. F. *recrea-tion.* ‒ L. *recreātiōnem*, acc. of *recreātio*, orig. recovery from illness (hence, amusement). ‒ L. *recreātus*, pp. of *recreāre*, to revive, refresh. ‒ L. *re-*, again; *creāre*, to make. See **Create.**

Recriminate. (L.) From L. *re-*, again; and *crīminātus*, pp. of *crīminārī*, to accuse of crime, from *crīmin-*, for *crīmen*, a crime. See **Crime.**

Recruit. (F.‒L.) F. *recruter*, to levy troops (Littré). An ill-formed word, from *recrute*, mistaken form of *recrue*, fem. of *recrû*, pp. of *recroître*, to grow again. F. *recrue*, sb., means 'a levy of troops,' lit. 'new-grown.' ‒ L. *recrescere*, to grow again. ‒ L. *re-*, again; *crescere*, to grow; see **Crescent.**

Rectangle, a four-sided right-angled figure. (F.‒L.) F. *rectangle*, adj., right angled (Cot.). ‒ L. *rectangulus*, having a right angle. ‒ L. *rect-us*, right; *angulus*, an angle. *Rectus* was orig. the pp. of *regere*, to rule. See **Regent** and **Angle** (1).

rectify. (F.‒L.) F. *rectifier.* ‒ Late L. *rectificāre*, to make right. ‒ L. *recti-*, for *rectus*, right (above); *-ficāre*, for *facere*, to make.

rectilinear. (L.) From L. *rectilīne-us*, formed by straight lines. ‒ L. *recti-*, for *rectus*, right, straight; *linea*, a line.

rectitude. (F.‒L.) F. *rectitude.* ‒ L. *rectitūdo*, uprightness. ‒ L. *recti-* (above); with suffix *-tūdo*.

Recumbent. (L.) L. *recumbent-*, stem of pres. pt. of *recumbere*, to recline; where *cumbere* is a nasalised form allied to *cubāre*, to lie down. See **Incumbent** and **Covey.**

Recuperative, tending to recover. (L.) L. *recuperātīuus*, (properly) recoverable. ‒ L. *recuperāre*, to recover. See **Recover.**

Recur. (L.) L. *recurrere*, to run back, recur. ‒ L. *re-*, back; *currere*, to run; see **Current.**

Recusant, opposing an opinion. (F.‒L.) F. *récusant*, 'rejecting,' Cot.; pres. pt. of *récuser.* ‒ L. *recūsāre*, to reject, oppose a cause or opinion. ‒ L. *re-*, back; *caussa*, a cause. See **Cause.**

Red. (E.) M. E. *reed* (with long vowel). A. S. *rēad.*+Du. *rood*, Icel. *rauðr*, Dan. Swed. *röd*, G. *roth*, Goth. *rauds.* Teut. type **raudoz.* Further allied to Gk. ἐρυθρός, Irish and Gael. *ruath*, W. *rhudd*, L. *ruber* (for **rudhro-*), red; cf. Russ. *ruda*, Skt. *rudhira-*, blood. Note also the Icel. strong verb *rjóða* (pt. t. *rauð*), to redden; A. S. *rēoðan*, to redden; Teut. type **reu-dan-*, pt. t. **raud.* (√REUDH.)

Reddition, a restoring. (F.‒L.) F. *reddition.* ‒ L. *redditiōnem*, acc. of *redditio*, a restoring. ‒ L. *reddere*, to give back. ‒ L. *red-*, back; *dare*, to give. See **Date** (1).

Redeem, to atone for. (L.) Formerly *redeme.* Coined from L. *red-*, back, and *emere*, to buy. [Cf. M. F. *redimer*, 'to redeem;' Cot. ‒ L. *redimere*, to buy back.] **Der.** *redempt-ion* (from the pp. *redemptus*).

Redgum, a disease of infants. (E.) M. E. *reed gounde*, lit. 'red matter' (of a sore); Prompt. Parv. From A.S. *rēad*, red; *gund*, matter of a sore.

Redintegration, renovation. (L.) From L. *redintegrātio*, restoration. ‒ L. *red-*, again; *integer*, whole, entire. See **Integer.**

Redolent, fragrant. (F.‒L.) M. F. *redolent.* ‒ L. *redolent-*, stem of pres. pt. of *redolēre*, to emit odour. ‒ L. *red-*, again; *olēre*, for **odēre*, to be odorous; see **Odour.**

Redoubt, an intrenched place of retreat. (F.‒Ital.‒L.) Ill spelt; through confusion with *redoubtable.* F. *redoute.* ‒ Ital. *ridotto*, a place of retreat. ‒ Ital. *ridotto*, *ridutto*, pp. of *ridurre*, to bring home. ‒ L. *redūcere*, to bring back. ‒ L. *re-*, back; *dūcere*, to lead. See **Duke.**

Redoubtable. (F.‒L.) M. F. *re-doubtable*, terrible. ‒ O. F. *redouter*, M. F. *redoubter*, to fear. See **Re-** and **Doubt.**

Redound. (F.‒L.) F. *redonder.* ‒ L. *redundāre*, to overflow. ‒ L. *red-*, again, back; *unda*, a wave. See **Undulate.**

Redress. (F.–L.) F. *redresser*, to put straight again. ‒ F. *re-*, again ; *dresser*, to erect, dress ; see **Dress**.

Redstart, a bird with a red tail. (E.) From **Red**; and *start*, a tail (A. S. *steort*).

Reduce. (L.) Orig. to bring back. ‒ L. *redūcere*, to bring back. ‒ L. *re-*, back ; *dūcere*, to lead. See **Duke**. **Der**. *reduction* (from the pp. *reduct-us*).

Redundant. (L.) From stem of pres. pt. of L. *redundāre*, to redound. See **Redound**.

Reechy, dirty. (E.) Lit. ‘ smoky ;’ palatalised form of *reeky* ; cf. Low. Sc. *reekie*, smoky. See **Reek**.

Reed. (E.) M. E. *reed*. A. S. *hrēod*, a reed.+Du. *riet*; G. *riet*, *ried*. Teut. type **hreudom*, neut.

Reef (1), a ridge of rocks. (Du.) Formerly *riff*. ‒ Du. *rif*, a reef. + Icel. *rif*, a reef, allied to *rifa*, a fissure, rift ; Dan. *rev*, a sand-bank (*revle*, a shoal, *revne*, to split); Swed. *refva*, *ref*, a sand-bank, a cleft, gap. Cf. L. *rīpa*, a bank ; Gk. ἐρίπνη, a broken cliff, scaur, ἐρείπειν, to tear down. The orig. sense seems to have been ‘ broken edge.’ Cf. **Rive**.

Reef (2), a portion of a sail. (Du.) M. E. *riff*. ‒ Du. *reef*, ‘ a riff in a sail,’ Sewel ; M. Du. *rif*, *rift*, a reef.+Icel. *rif*, a reef in a sail ; Dan. *reb*, Swed. *ref*, reef; Low G. *reff*, *riff*, a small sail ; Pomeran. *räff*, a little extra sail, bonnet.

Reek, vapour. (E.) M.E. *reke*. O.Merc. *rēc*, vapour ; O. Fries. *rēk*.+Icel. *reykr*; Swed. *rök*, Dan. *rög* ; Du. *rook*, G. *rauch* ; Teut. base **rauk-*. From **rauk*, 2nd grade of Teut. **reukan-*, to smoke ; as in A. S. *rēocan*, Icel. *rjūka*, O. H. G. *riohhan*, G. *riechen*. Brugm. i. § 217.

Reel (1), a small spindle for winding yarn. (E.) M. E. *rele* ; A.S. *hrēol*, a reel. +E. Fries. *rēl*; N. Fries. *reel*. Kluge derives A.S. *hrēol* from a form **hrōehil*, but this would give A.S. *hrēl* ; see Eng. Stud. xi. 512. **Der**. *reel*, vb., to wind, turn round, stagger.

Reel (2), a Highland dance. (Gael.) Gael. *righil*, *ruidhil*, *ruithil*, a reel.

Reest, the wood on which a plough-coulter is fixed. (E.) Also *wreest* (wrongly), *rest*. A. S. *rēost*.

Reeve (1), to pass a rope through a ring. (Du.) Du. *reven*, to reeve. ‒ Du. *reef*, a reef in a sail ; because a reeved rope is used for reefing ; see **Reef** (2).

Reeve (2), an officer, steward. (E.)

A. S. *gerēfa*, an officer ; orig. sense perhaps ‘ numberer,’ registrar (of soldiers); for **ge-rōfja*. From *-rōf*, a host (as in *secg-rōf*, a host of men) ; cf. O. H. G. *ruova*, a number. ¶ *Not* allied to G.*graf*. **Der**. *borough-reeve* ; *port-reeve* ; *sheriff*, q. v.

Refection, refreshment. (F. – L.) M. F. *refection*, a repast. ‒ L. acc. *refectiōnem*, lit. a remaking. ‒ L. *refectus*, pp. of *reficere*, to remake, restore. ‒ L. *re-*, again; *facere*, to make. See **Fact**.

Refel. (L.) L. *refellere*, to refute, shew to be false. ‒ L. *re-*, back ; *fallere*, to deceive ; see **Fallible**.

Refer, to assign. (F.–L.) O. F. *referer* (F. *référer*). ‒ L. *referre*, to bear back, relate, refer. ‒ L. *re-*, back ; *ferre*, to bear; see **Fertile**.

Refine. (F.–L.) Coined from *re-* and *fine* (1), but imitated from F. *raffiner*, to refine, comp. of L. *re-*, again, L. *af-=ad*, to, and F. *fin*, fine. **Der**. *refine-ment*; cf. F. *raffinement*.

Reflect. (L.) L. *reflectere*, lit. to bend back, hence to return rays, &c. ‒ L. *re-*, back ; *flectere*, to bend; see **Flexible**.

Reform. (F.–L.) F. *reformer*, to shape anew. ‒ L. *re-*, again ; *formāre*, to form; see **Form**.

Refract, to bend back rays of light. (L.) L. *refractus*, pp. of *refringere*, to bend back. ‒ L. *re-*, back ; *frangere*, to break; see **Fragile**. **Der**. *refract-or-y*, a mistaken form for *refractary*, from L. *refractārius*, stubborn, obstinate. Also *refrangible*, a mistaken form for *refringible*.

Refrain (1), to restrain, forbear. (F.– L.) M. E. *refreinen*. ‒ O. F. *refrener*, to repress ; Cot. ‒ L. *refrēnāre*, to bridle, hold in with a bit. ‒ L. *re-*, back ; *frēnum*, a bit, curb. The orig. sense of *frēnum* is ‘ holder ’ or ‘ keeper,’ from √DHER, to support, maintain ; cf. Skt. *dhṛ*, to support, *dhārana*, restraining. ¶ Prob. sometimes confused with M. F. *refraindre*, ‘ to bridle,’ Cot.; this is from L. *refringere*, to break back (below).

Refrain (2), the burden of a song. (F. – L.) F. *refrain* ; so also Prov. *refranhs*, a refrain, *refranher*, *refrenher*, to repeat. So called from frequent repetition ; the O. F. *refreindre*, to pull back, is the same word as Prov. *refrenher*, to repeat ; both are from L. *refringere*, to break back (refract, hence, to repeat). ‒ L. *re-*, back ; *frangere*, to break; see **Fragile**.

Refresh. (F.–L. *and* G.) M. E. *re-*

freschen. – O. F. *refreschir* ; Cot. – L. *re-*, again ; O. H. G. *frisc* (G. *frisch*), fresh. See **Fresh.**

Refrigerate. (L.) From pp. of L. *re-frīgerāre*, to make cool again. – L. *re-*, again ; *frīgerāre*, to cool, from *frīgus*, cold. See **Frigid.**

Reft, pp. of *reave* ; see **Reave.**

Refuge. (F. – L.) M. E. *refuge.* – F. *refuge.* – L. *refugium*, an escape. – L. *refugere*, to flee back. – L. *re-*, back ; *fugere*, to flee ; see **Fugitive.**

   refugee. (F. – L.) M. F. *refugié*, pp. of *se refugier*, to take refuge. – F. *refuge* (above).

Refulgent. (L.) From L. *refulgent-*, stem of pres. pt. of *refulgēre*, to flash back. – L. *re-*, back ; *fulgēre*, to shine. See **Fulgent.**

Refund, to repay. (L.) L. *refundere*, to pour back, also to restore, give back (see below).

   refuse, to deny a request. (F. – L.) M. E. *refusen.* – O. F. *refuser* (the same as Port. *refusar*, Ital. *refusare*, to reject). It answers to a Late L. type **refūsāre*, formed as a frequentative of *refundere*, to pour back, also to restore, give back (whence to reject). – L. *re-*, back ; *fundere*, to pour ; see **Fuse** (1). β. We may also note E. *refuse*, sb., O. F. *refus*, refuse ; cf. O. F. *mettre en refus, faire refus à*, to abandon, reject (Godefroy).

   refute, to oppose, disprove. (F. – L.) M. F. *refuter.* – L. *refūtāre*, to repel, rebut. The orig. sense was prob. ' to pour back ; ' see **Confute.**

Regain. (F. – L. *and* O. H. G.) F. *regagner.* – L. *re-*, back ; and F. *gagner*, to gain. See **Gain** (1).

Regal. (F. – L.) M. F. *regal*, royal; Cot. – L. *rēgālis*, adj., from *rēg-*, stem of *rex*, a king. Allied to L. *regere*, to rule. Cf. Skt. *rājan-*, a king ; O. Irish *rī.* Brugm. i. §§ 135, 549 c. Der. *regal-ia*, insignia of a king ; neut. pl. of *rēgālis.*

Regale, to entertain. (F. – Ital.?) M.F. *regaler*, to entertain. Not allied to *regal*, as Cotgrave suggests ; but the same as Span. *regalar*, to make much of, pamper ; orig. to melt (Diez). 1. Diez derives it from L. *regelāre*, to melt, thaw ; from L. *re-*, back, *gelāre*, to freeze (see **Gelid**). 2. Hatzfeld derives F. *régaler* (ultimately) from Ital. *regalare*, to give presents to ; from Ital. *gala*, mirth. See **Gala.**

Regard, vb. (F. – L. *and* O. H. G.)

F. *regarder*, to look, look at, view. – L. *re-*, back ; F. *garder*, to guard, observe ; of O. H. G. origin ; see **Guard.**

Regatta. (Ital.) Orig. a strife, contention, hence a race, rowing-match. – Ital. *regatta, rigatta*, ' a strife for the maistrie ; ' Florio. – M. Ital. *rigattare*, to contend for the mastery, to wrangle, to haggle as a huckster does. So also Span. *regatear*, to haggle, retail provisions, to rival in sailing. Of unknown origin.

Regenerate. (L.) From pp. of *re-generāre*, to produce anew. – L. *re-*, again ; *generāre*, to produce, from *gener-*, for **genes-*, stem of *genus*, kindred. See **Genus.**

Regent. (F. – L.) M. F. *regent*, a regent, vice-gerent. – L. *regent-*, stem of pres. pt. of *regere*, to rule. Allied to Gk. ὀρέγειν, to stretch, Goth. *uf-rakjan*, to stretch out, Skt. *ṛj*, to stretch, *rāj*, to govern. (√REG.) See **Right.** Brugm. i. § 474.

   regicide, slayer of a king ; slaying of a king. (F. – L.) M. F. *regicide* (Minsheu). – L. *rēgi-*, for *rex*, king, allied to *regere*, to rule ; *-cīda*, a slayer, from *cædere*, to slay. Also : from L. *rēgi-* (as before), *-cīdium*, a slaying, from *cædere.*

   regimen. (L.) L. *regimen*, guidance. – L. *regere*, to rule, direct.

   regiment. (F. – L.) M.F. *regiment*, ' a regiment of souldiers,' Cot. ; also, a government. – L. *regimentum*, rule, government. – L. *regere*, to rule.

   region. (F. – L.) M. F. *region.* – L. *regiōnem*, acc. of *regio*, territory. – L. *regere*, to rule, govern.

   Register. (F. – L.) M. F. *registre*, ' a record ; ' Cot. – Late L. *registrum*, more correctly *regestum*, a book in which things are recorded (L. *regeruntur*). – L. *regestum*, neut. of pp. of *regerere*, to bring back, record. – L. *re-*, back ; *gerere*, to carry. See **Gerund.** Cf. L. *regesta*, pl., a register.

   Regnant, reigning. (L.) L. *regnant-*, stem. of pres. pt. of *regnāre*, to reign. – L. *regnum*, kingdom. – L. *regere*, to rule. See **Regent.**

Regress, return. (L.) L. *regressus*, sb. – L. *regressus*, pp. of *regredī*, to go back. – L. *re-*, back ; *gradī*, to go. See **Grade.**

Regret, sorrow. (F. – L. *and* Scand.) F. *regret*, grief ; *regretter*, to lament (Cot.). The oldest form of the verb is *regrater.* Of disputed origin ; see Scheler. The most likely solution is that which derives O. F. *regrater* from L. *re-*, again, and the verb which appears in Icel. *grāta*, Swed. *grāta*, Dan. *græde*, A. S. *grǣtan*, Lowl. Sc. *greit*, to weep, bewail. See **Greet** (2). Cf. ' I mone as a chylde dothe for the wantyng of his nourse or mother, *je regrete*;' Palsgrave.

Regular. (L.) L. *rēgulāris*, according to rule. — L. *rēgula*, a rule ; *regere*,-to rule. See **Regent.**

Rehearse. (F. — L.) M. E. *rehersen*. — O. F. *reherser, rehercer*, to harrow over again ; hence, to go over the same ground. — L. *re-*, again ; O. F. *hercer*, to harrow, from *herce*, sb., a harrow. See **Hearse.**

Reign, sb. (F. — L.) M. E. *regne.* — M. F. *regne.* — L. *regnum*, kingdom. — L. *regere*, to rule. See **Regent.**

Reimburse, to refund. (F. — L. *and* Gk.) Adapted from F. *rembourser* by substituting L. *re-im-* for F. *rem-* (with the same force). — L. *re-*, again ; *im-* (for *in*), in ; F. *bourse*, a purse. See **Purse.**

Rein. (F. — L.) M. E. *reine.* — O. F. *reine*, rein of a bridle (The same as Ital. *redina*, Span. *rienda*, transposed form of *redina*.) — Late L. **retina*, not found, but a short form allied to L. *retināculum*, a rein. — L. *retinēre*, to hold back. — L. *re-*, back ; *tenēre*, to hold. See **Retain.**

Reindeer, Raindeer, a kind of deer. (Scand.) M. E. *raynedere*. Formed by adding *deer* (see **Deer**) to Icel. *hreinn*, a reindeer ; cf. also O. Swed. *ren*, a reindeer, A. S. *hrān*. [We also find Dan. *rensdyr*, Du. *rendier*, G. *rennthier*.] Teut. type **hrainoz* ; a true Teut. word, as the forms shew. β. Diez refers us to Lapp *raingo*, but this is merely a bad spelling of Swed. *renko*, i. e. rein-cow. The true Lapp word is *påtso*, a reindeer ; nor can the Icel. word have been suggested by Lapp *reino*, a pasturage for rein-deer ; Ihre, Lexicon Lapponicum, p. 374.

Reins, the lower part of the back. (F. — L.) O. F. *reins.* — L. *rēnēs*, pl., kidneys, reins.

Reject. (F. — L.) M. F. *rejecter* (16th cent.) ; F. *rejeter* ; oldest spelling *regeter*). — O. F. *re-*, back ; *geter, getter*, to throw, from L. *iactāre* ; see **Jet** (1).

Rejoice. (F. — L.) M. E. *reioisen.* — O. F. *resjoïs-*, stem of pres. pt. of *resjoir* mod. F. *réjouir*, to gladden, rejoice. — L. *re* again ; O. F. *esjoir*, to rejoice, from L.

ex, much, very, and *gaudēre*, to rejoice. See **Gaud.**

Rejoin. (F. — L.) Lit. to join again ; in legal language, to answer to a reply. — F. *rejoign-*, a stem of *rejoindre*, to rejoin. — L. *reiungere*, to join again. — L. *re-*, again ; *iungere*, to join. See **Join. Der.** *rejoinder*, which is the F. infin. mood used as a sb., as in the case of *attainder*.

Relapse, to slide back into a former state. (L.) From L. *relapsus*, pp. of *relābī*, to slide back. — L. *re-*, back ; *lābī*, to slide; see **Lapse.**

Relate, to describe, tell. (F. — L.) F. *relater*, 'to relate ;' Cot. — Late L. *relātāre*, to relate. — L. *relātus*, used as pp. of *referre*, to relate (but from a different root). — L. *re-*, again ; *lātus*, for *tlātus*, borne, pp. of *tollere*, to bear. See **Tolerate.**

Relax. (L.) L. *relaxāre*, to relax. — L. *re-*, again ; *laxāre*, to slacken ; see **Lax.** Doublet, *release*.

relay (1), a set of fresh dogs or horses, a fresh supply. (F. — L.) Orig. used of dogs and horses. — F. *relais*, a relay ; *chiens de relais, chevaux de relais*, dogs or horses kept in reserve ; Cot. The orig. sense is ' a rest,' and *chiens de relais* are dogs kept at rest ; cf. *à relais* ' at rest, that is not used,' Cot.; and see *relais* in Godefroy. — O. F. *relaissier*, to relinquish. — L. *relaxāre*, to loosen, let loose, allow to rest ; see **Lax.** Cf. Italian *cani di rilasso*, dogs kept in reserve (late edition of Florio by Torriano, 1688).

Relay (2), to lay again. (L. *and* E.) From *re-* and *lay*. See **Lay** (1).

Release. (F. — L.) M. E. *relessen, relesen.* — O. F. *relessier* (M. F. *relaisser*), to relax. — L. *relaxāre*, to relax; see **Relax.**

Relegate, to consign to exile. (L.) From pp. of L. *relēgāre*, to send away, remove. — L. *re-*, again, back ; *lēgāre*, to send, appoint ; see **Legate.**

Relent. (F. — L.) Altered from F. *ralentir*, to slacken, to relent (cf. L. *relentescere*, to slacken). — F. *ra-*, for *re-a-* (L. *re-ad*) ; L. *lentus*, slack, slow, allied to *lēnis*, gentle, and to E. *lithe*. See **Lenient** and **Lithe.**

Relevant. (F. — L.) The orig. sense is ' helpful ' ; hence, of use for the matter in hand. — F. *relevant*, pres. part. of *relever*, to raise up, assist, help. — L. *releuāre*, to raise again. — L. *re-*, again ; *leuāre*, to raise, from *leuis*, light. See **Levity.**

Relic, a memorial. (F. — L.) Chiefly

in the pl.; M. E. *relikes.*—F. *reliques*, s. pl., 'reliques;' Cot.—L. *reliquiās*, acc. of *reliquiæ*, pl., remains.—L. *relinquere*, to leave behind.—L. *re-*, back; *linquere*, to leave. See **Relinquish, Licence.**

relict, a widow. (L.) L. *relicta*, fem. of *relictus*, pp. of *relinquere*, to leave behind (above).

Relieve. (F.—L.) M. E. *releuen* (= *releven*).—F. *relever*, to raise up, relieve.—L. *releuāre*, to raise again; see **Relevant.** Der. *relief*, M. E. *relef*, O. F. *relief* (F. *relief*), a sb. due to the verb *relever*.

Religion. (F.—L.) F. *religion*; Cot.—L. acc. *religiōnem*, from *religio*, piety; allied to *religens*, fearing the gods, pious. *Re-ligens* is the opposite of *neg-ligens*, negligent; see **Neglect.** Allied also to *di-ligent*, and to Gk. ἀλέγειν, to reverence.

Relinquish. (F.—L.) O. F. *relenquis-*, pr. pt. stem of *relenquir*, to leave (Godefroy).—L. *relinquere*, to leave behind; see **Relic.**

reliquary, a casket for relics.(F.—L.) F. *reliquaire*, 'a casket wherein reliques be kept;' Cot.—Late L. *reliquiārium* (same sense).—L. *reliquiā-*, orig. stem of *reliquiæ*, relics; see **Relic** (above).

relique; the same as **Relic.**

Relish, orig. an after-taste. (F.—L.) M. E. *reles*, an after-taste, Sir Cleges, 208.—O. F. *reles, relais*, that which is left behind; also a relay; see **Relay** (1).

Reluctant. (L.) From stem of pres. pt. of *reluctāre, reluctārī*, to struggle against.—L. *re-*, back; *luctārī*, to struggle, from *lucta*, a wrestling. Allied to Gk. λυγ-ίζειν, to bend, writhe in wrestling; Lith. *lugnas*, flexible, Skt. *ruj*, to bend, break. (√LEUG.)

Rely, to repose on trustfully. (F.—L.) We find 'to *relye* their faithe upon'; where *relye* = fasten.—F. *relier*, to bind up, or together.—L. *religare*, to fasten. L. *re-*, back; *ligāre*, to bind; see **Ligament.** ¶ But much influenced by E. *lie*, vb., to repose, though this would have required a pp. *relain*. Der. *reli-ance.*

Remain. (F.—L.) O. F. pres. s. (*je*) *remain*; cf. M. F. impers. vb. *il remain-t*, it remains. [The infin. *remaindre* is preserved in E. *remainder*, used as a sb.]—L. *reman-eo*, I remain; *reman-et*, it remains; *remanēre*, to remain.—L. *re-*, behind; *manēre*, to stay. See **Mansion.**

Remand, to send back. (F.—L.) M.F. *remander.*—L. *remandāre*, to send back

word.—L. *re-*, back; *mandāre*, to send; see **Mandate.**

Remark, to take notice of. (F.—L. *and* Teut.) F. *remarquer*, to mark, note, heed.—L. *re-*, again; *marquer*, to mark, from *marque*, sb., a mark; see **Mark** (1).

Remedy. (F.—L.) M. E. *remedie.*—A. F. *remedie*, O. F. *remede*, mod. F. *remède.*—L. *remedium*, a remedy; that which heals again.—L. *re-*, again; *medērī*, to heal. See **Medicine.**

Remember. (F.—L.) O. F. *remembrer.*—L. *rememorārī*, to remember.—L. *re-*, again; *memorāre*, to make mention of, from *memor*, mindful. See **Memory.**

Remind, to bring to mind again. (L. *and* E.) From **Re-** and **Mind.**

Reminiscence. (F.—L.) M. F. *reminiscence.*—L. *reminiscentia*, remembrance.—L. *reminiscent-*, stem of pres. pt. of *reminiscī*, to remember.—L. *re-*, again; and base of *me-min-ī*, I remember. Allied to Gk. μέ-μον-α, I yearn, Skt. *man*, to think. (√MEN.)

Remit, to abate. (L.) L. *remittere* (pp. *remissus*), to send back, slacken, abate.—L. *re-*, back; *mittere*, to send; see **Missile.** Der. *remiss*, adj., from pp. *remissus*; *remiss-ion.*

Remnant. (F.—L.) M. E. *remanaunt.*—O. F. *remanant.*—L. *remanent-*, stem of pres. pt. of *remanēre*, to remain; see **Remain.**

Remonstrate. (L.) From pp. of Late L. *remonstrāre*, to expose, to produce arguments against.—L. *re-*, again; *monstrāre*, to show, from *monstrum*, a portent; see **Monster.**

Remorse. (F.—L.) M. F. *remors*; Cot.—Late L. *remorsus*, remorse.—L. *remorsus*, pp. of *remordēre*, to bite again, to vex.—L. *re-*, again; *mordēre*, to bite; see **Mordacity.**

Remote, distant. (L.) L. *remōtus*, pp. of *remouēre*, to remove; see **Remove.** Or from M. F. *remote*, f. 'remove, removed,' Cot.; from L. pp. f. *remōta.*

Remount, to mount again. (F.—L.) F. *remonter.*—F. *re-*, again; *monter*, to mount; see **Mount** (2).

Remove. (F.—L.) M.F. *remouvoir*, Cot. See **Re-** and **Move.**

Remunerate, to recompense. (L.) From pp. of *remūnerāre, remūnerarī*, to reward.—L. *re-*, again; *mūnerāre*, to bestow a gift, from *mūner-* (for **mūnes-*), stem of *mŭnus*, a gift, also, an office. See **Municipal**.

Renaissance, revival of learning. (F. – L.) M. F. *renaissance*, 'a new birth,' Cot. – L. *re*-, again ; *nascentia*, birth, from *nascent*-, stem of pres. pt. of *nascī*, to be born. See **Natal**.

Renal. (F. – L.) M. F. *renal*. – L. *rēnālis*, adj. ; from *rēnēs*, s. pl., reins. See **Reins**.

Renard; see **Reynard**.

Rencounter, Rencontre. (F. – L.) F. *rencontre*, a meeting. – F. *rencontrer*, to meet. – F. *re*-, again ; *encontrer*, to meet, encounter ; see **Encounter**.

Rend. (E.) M. E. *renden*. A. S. *rendan*, to cut or tear.+O. Fries. *renda*, to tear ; North Fr. *renne, ranne*, to tear apart. Der. *rent*, sb., from pp. *rent*.

Render. (F. – L.) M. E. *rendren*. – F. *rendre*. – L. *reddere*, to give back. – L. *red*-, back ; *dare*, to give ; see **Date** (1).

rendezvous. (F. – L.) F. *rendezvous*, 'a rendevous, place appointed for the assemblie of souldiers ;' Cot. – F. *rendez vous*<L. *reddite uōs*, render yourselves ; imperative pl. of *reddere* (above).

Renegade, Renegado. (Span. – L.) Span. *renegado*, an apostate, one who has denied the faith ; orig. pp. of *renegar*, to forsake the faith. – L. *re*-, again ; *negāre*, to deny. See **Negation**.

Renew. (L. *and* E.) From L. *re*-, again ; and E. *new*.

Rennet (1), the prepared inner membrane of a calf's stomach, used to make milk coagulate. (E.) M. E. *renet*; from M. E. *rennen*, to run ; prov. E. *run*, to congeal, coagulate. See **Run**. Hence *rennet* is also called *runnet* (Pegge's Kenticisms) ; also *erning* (Derbyshire), from A. S. *irnan*, to run. So also M. Du. *rinsel, runsel, renninge*, ' curds, or milk-runnet,' from *rinnen*, ' to presse, curdle ;' Hexham. Cf. G. *rinnen*, to run, curdle, coagulate.

Rennet (2), a sweet kind of apple. (F. – L.) Formerly spelt *renate*, from an odd notion that it was derived from L. *renātus*, born again! – F. *reinette, rainette*, a rennet ; the same as *rainette*, a little frog ; from the speckled skin. Dimin. of F. *raine*, a frog. – L. *rāna*, a frog. Cf. **Ranunculus**.

Renounce. (F. – L.) F. *renoncer*. – L. *renuntiāre*, to bring back a report, also to disclaim, renounce. – L. *re*-, back, again : *nuntiāre*, to tell, bring news, from *nuntius*, a messenger. See **Nuncio**.

Der. *renunciat-ion*, F. *renonciation*, from L. pp. *renuntiātus*.

Renovate. (L.) From L. *renouātus*, pp. of *renouāre*, to renew. – L. *re*-, again ; *nouāre*, to make new, from *nouus*, new. See **Novel**.

Renown, fame. (F. – L.) M. E. *renoun*. – A. F. *renoun, renun* ; O. F. *renon* (12th cent.). [Cf. Port. *renome*, Span. *renombre*, renown.] – O. F. *renomer*, to make famous. – L. *re*-, again ; *nōmināre*, to name, from *nōmen*, a name ; see **Noun**.

Rent (1), a tear ; see **Rend**.

Rent (2), annual payment. (F. – L.) M. E. *rente*. – F. *rente*. [Cf. Ital. *rendita*, rent.] – Late L. *rendita*, nasalised form of L. *reddita*, fem. of pp. of *reddere*, to render ; see **Render**.

Renunciation. (F. – L.) M. F. *renonciation*, ' renunciation ;' Cot. – L. acc. *renuntiātiōnem*, prop. an announcement. – L. *renuntiāt-us*, pp. of *renuntiāre*, orig. to announce ; see **Renounce**.

Repair (1), to restore, amend. (F. – L.) M. F. *reparer*. – L. *reparāre*, to recover, repair, make ready anew. – L. *re*-, again ; *parāre*, to get ready ; see **Pare**. Der. *repar-able*, M. F. *reparable*, L. *reparābilis*; *repar-at-ion*, M. F. *reparation*.

Repair (2), to resort to. (F. – L.) M.F. *repairer*, to haunt ; Cot. Older form *repairier* (Burguy). – L. *repatriāre*, to repair to one's own country. – L. *re*-, back ; *patria*, native country, from *patri*-, for *pater*, a father.

Repartee, a witty reply. (F. – L.) F. *repartie*, ' a reply ;' Cot. Orig. fem. of *reparti*, pp. of M. F. *repartir*, to re-divide, to answer thrust with thrust, to reply. – F. *re*-, again ; *partir*, to part, also to rush, dart off, burst out laughing. – L. *re*-, again ; *partīre*, to share, from *parti*-, for *pars*, a part. See **Part**.

Repast, a meal. (F. – L.) O.F. *repast*, later *repas*. – L. *re*-, again ; *pastum*, acc. of *pastus*, food, from *pascere*, to feed. See **Pastor**.

Repay. (F. – L.) O.F. *repaier*. – O. F. *re*- (L. *re*-), back ; *paier*, to pay ; see **Pay**.

Repeal. (F – L.) Altered from O. F. *rapeler*, F. *rappeler*, to repeal. – O. F. *re*- (L. *re*-) ; *apeler*, later *appeler*, to appeal. See **Appeal**. *Repeal = re-appeal*.

Repeat. (F. – L.) Formerly *repete*. – M. F. *repeter*, Cot. – L. *repetere*, to attack again, reseek, repeat. — L. *re-*, again; *petere*, to attack; see **Petition**. Der. *repet-it-ion*.

Repel. (L.) L. *repellere*, to drive back. — L. *re-*, back; *pellere*, to drive; see **Pulse**. Der. *repulse*, from pp. *repulsus*.

Repent, to rue. (F. — L.) F. *repentir*, to repent. — L. *re-*, again; *pœnitēre*, to cause to repent; see **Penitent**.

Repercussion. (L.) From **Re-** and **Percussion**.

Repertory, a treasury. (F. — L.) M. F. *repertoire*. — L. *repertōrium*, an inventory. — L. *repertor*, a finder, discoverer. — L. *reperīre*, to find out. — L. *re-*, again; *parīre* (Ennius), usually *parere*, to produce; see **Parent**.

Repine. (L.) Compounded of L. *re-*, again; and *pine*, to fret; see **Pine** (2).

Replace. (F. — L. *and* Gk.) From *re-* (F. *re-*, L. *re-*), again; and **Place**.

Replenish. (F. — L.) O. F. *repleniss-*, stem of pres. pt. of *replenir*, to fill up again; now obsolete. — L. *re-*, again; Late L. *plēnīre, to fill, from L. *plēnus*, full.

replete, full. (F. — L.) M. F. *replet*, masc.; *replete*, fem., full. — L. *replētus*, filled up; pp. of *re-plēre*, to fill again. — L. *re-*, again; *plēre*, to fill; see **Plenary**.

Replevy, to get back detained goods on a pledge to try the right in a suit. (F. — Teut.) F. *re-* (L. *re-*), again; O. F. *plevir*, to be surety. See **Pledge**.

Reply. (F. — L.) M. E. *replien*. — O. F. *replier*, the old form afterwards replaced by the 'learned' form *répliquer*, to reply. — L. *replicāre*, lit. to fold back; as a law term, to reply. — L. *re-*, back; *plicāre*, to fold. Der. *replica*, a repetition; from Ital. *replica*, a sb. due to L. *replicāre*, to repeat, reply.

Report. (F. — L.) M. E. *reporten*. — F. *reporter*, to carry back. — L. *reportāre*, to carry back. — L. *re-*, back; *portāre*, to carry; see **Port** (1). The E. sense 'to relate' is due to F. *rapporter*, O. F. *raporter*; with prefix *ra-* < L. *re-ad*.

Repose. (F. — L. *and* Gk.) F. *reposer*, to rest, pause; Late L. *repausāre*, to pause, rest. — L. *re-*, again; *pausāre*, to pause, from *pausa*, sb., due to Gk. παῦσις, a pause. ¶ Important; this is the verb which seems to have given rise to *poser* and its compounds. See **Pose**.

Repository, a storehouse. (F. — L.) M. F. *repositoire*, a storehouse. — L. *repositōrium* — L. *repositus*, pp. of *repōnere*, to

lay up, store. — L. *re-*, again; *pōnere*, to place; see **Position**.

Reprehend, to reprove. (L.) L. *reprehendere*, to hold back, check, blame. — L. *re-*, back; *prehendere*, to seize, to hold. See **Prehensile**.

Represent. (F. — L.) O. F. *representer*. — L. *repræsentāre*, to bring before again, exhibit. — L. *re-*, again; *præsentāre*, to present; see **Present** (2).

Repress. (F. — L.) From F. *re-*, again, and *presser*, to press; but used with sense of L. *reprimere* (pp. *repressus*) to press back, check. — L. *re-*, back; *premere*, to press; see **Press**.

Reprieve, vb. (F. — L.) [A doublet of *reprove*.] M. E. *repreven*, to reprove, reject, disallow; to *reprieve* a sentence is to disallow it. — O. F. *repreuve*, 3rd pres. sing. indic. of *reprover* (F. *réprouver*), to reprove; see **Reprove**. Cf. Schwan, § 348(4).

Reprimand. (F. — L.) F. *réprimande*, formerly *reprimende*, 'a reproof;' Cot. — L. *reprimenda*, a thing that ought to be repressed; hence, a check. Fem. of the gerundive of *reprimere*, to repress; see **Repress**.

Reprisal. (F. — Ital. — L.) M. F. *represaille*, a taking or seizing on, a reprisal. [The change of vowel is due to obs. verb *reprise*, to seize in return; from F. *repris*, pp. of *reprendre* < L. *reprehendere*, (here) to seize again.] — Ital. *ripresaglia*, booty. — M. Ital. *ripresa*, a taking again; fem. of *ripreso*, pp. of *riprendere*, to reprehend, also to retake. — L. *reprehendere*, to seize again, also, to reprehend; see **Reprehend**.

Reproach. (F. — L.) F. *reprocher*, to reproach. Cf. Span. *reprochar*, Prov. *repropchar*, to reproach; answering to Late L. *repropiāre, to bring near to, impute to, reproach. — L. *re-*, again; *propi-us*, nearer, comp. of *prope*, near. See **Propinquity**. ¶ A translation of L. *obicere* (*objicere*), to bring near or cast before one, to reproach.

Reprobate. (L.) L. *reprobātus*, reproved, rejected; pp. of *reprobāre*, to reject upon trial. — L. *re-*, back; *probāre*, to test. See **Probable**.

reprove. (F. — L.) M. E. *reproven*, also *repreven*. — O. F. *reprover* (F. *réprouver*), to reprove, condemn. — L. *reprobāre*, to reject, reprove (above).

Reptile, crawling; usually, as a sb. (F. — L.) F. *reptile*, 'crawling;' Cot. — L.

reptilem, acc. of *reptilis*, creeping. – L. *reptus*, pp. of *rēpere*, to creep. + Lithuan. *reploti*, to creep.

Republic. (F. – L.) M. F. *republique*, 'the commonwealth;' Cot. – L. *rēspublica*, a republic. – L. *rēs*, a matter, state ; *publica*, fem. of *publicus*, public. See **Real**.

Repudiate. (L.) From pp. of L. *repudiāre*, to reject. – L. *repudium*, a casting off, divorce. Perhaps from L. *re*-, away ; *pud*-, base of *pudēre*, to feel shame ; cf. *pudor*, shame, *prō-pudium*, a shameful action.

Repugnant. (F. – L.) M. F. *repugnant*, pres. pt. of *repugner*, 'to repugne, thwart;' Cot. – L. *re-pugnāre*, to fight against. – L. *re*-, back ; *pugnāre*, to fight ; see **Pugilism**.

Repulse. (L.) From L. *repulsa*, sb., a refusal ; or *repulsāre*, vb. – L. *repuls-us*, pp. of *repellere* ; see **Repel**. Cf. Norman dial. *repulser*, to repulse.

Repute. (F. – L.) M. F. *reputer*. – L. *reputāre*, to repute (lit. reconsider). – L. *re*-, again ; *putāre*, to think ; see **Putative**.

Request. (F. – L.) O. F. *requeste*. – L. *requīsīta*, a thing asked, fem. of pp. of *requirere*, to ask back. – L. *re*-, back ; and *quærere*, to seek. See **Quest**.

require. (F. – L.) M. E. *requeren*, but also *requiren*. – M. F. *requerir* ; O. F. *requerre*, with 1 pr. s. *requier*. – L. *requirere* (above). **Der.** *requis-ite*, from pp. *requīsītus*.

Requiem. (L.) The Mass for the Dead was called *requiem*, because it began 'Requiem æternam dona eis.' – L. *requiem*, acc. of *requiēs*, repose. – L. *re*- ; *quiēs*, rest. See **Quiet**.

Requite. (F. – L.) Also spelt *requit*, Temp. iii. 3. 71. From *re*- and *quit* ; see **Quit**.

Reredos, a screen at the back of a thing, esp. of an altar. (F. – L.) From M. E. *rere*, rear ; and F. *dos*, back, from L. *dorsum*, back. See **Rear** (2) and **Dorsal**.

Reremouse, Rearmouse, a bat. (E.) A. S. *hrēremūs*, a bat; from the flapping of its wings. – A. S. *hrēran*, to agitate, allied to *hrōr*, adj., stirring, quick ; *mūs*, a mouse. Cf. prov. E. *flitter-mouse*, a flutter-mouse or bat. And cf. **Uproar**. ¶ Perhaps a popular etymology ; cf. early A. S. *hreatha-mus*, a bat ; Epinal Gl. 978.

Rereward; see **Rearward**.

Rescind, to repeal. (F. – L.) F. *re-scinder*, to cancel ; Cot. – L. *rescindere*, to cut off, annul. – L. *re*-, back ; *scindere*, to cut. Allied to **Schism**. (✓SKHEID.)

Rescript. (F. – L.) M. F. *rescript*, a reply in writing. – L. *rescriptum*, neut. of pp. of *rescrībere*, to write back. – L. *re*-, back ; *scrībere*, to write ; see **Scribe**.

Rescue, vb. (F. – L.) M. E. *rescouen*. – O. F. *rescourre*, to rescue, save. [The same word as Ital. *riscuotere*.] – Late L. *rescutere* (A. D. 1308); for *re-excutere*, to drive away again. – L. *re*-, again ; *ex*, away ; *quatere*, to shake ; see **Quash**. ¶ The M. E. sb. was *rescous*, from O. F. *rescousse* < Late L. pp. fem. *rescussa*.

Research. (F. – L.) Compounded of **Re**-, again, and **Search**. Cf. Norman dial. *recerche*, research.

Resemble. (F. – L.) O. F. *resembler*. – O. F. *re*-, again ; *sembler*, to seem, be like. – L. *re*-, again ; *simulāre*, to make like ; see **Simulate**.

Resent. (F. – L.) M. F. *se resentir* (or *ressentir*), to have a deep sense of. – L. *re*-, again ; *sentīre*, to feel. See **Sense**. **Der.** *resentment*.

Reserve. (F. – L.) O. F. *reserver*. – L. *reseruāre*, to keep back. – L. *re*-, back ; *seruāre*, to keep ; see **Serve**.

reservoir. (F. – L.) F. *réservoir*. – Late L. *reseruātōrium*, a store-house, formed from *reseruāre*, to reserve. Cf. Late L. *seruatōrium*, a store-house (Lewis).

Reside. (F. – L.) M. F. *resider*, to reside, stay. – L. *residēre*, to sit or remain behind. – L. *re*-, back ; *sedēre*, to sit ; see **Sedentary**. **Der.** *resid-ence*.

residue. (F. – L.) O. F. *residu*. – L. *residuum*, a remainder, neut. of *residuus*, remaining. – L. *residēre* (above).

Resign, to yield up. (F. – L.) M. F. *resigner*. – L. *resignāre*, to unseal, annul. – L. *re*-, back ; *signāre*, to sign, from *signum*, a sign, mark. See **Sign**.

Resilient. (L.) L. *resilient*-, stem of pres. part. of *resilīre*, to leap back. – L. *re*-, back ; *salīre*, to leap. See **Salient**.

Resin, Rosin. (F. – L. – Gk.) M. E. *recyn, recine*. – M. F. *resine*, 'rosin;' Cot. Norman dial. *rosine*. – L. *rēsīna*, Jer. li. 8 (Vulgate). – Gk. ῥητίνη, resin, gum from trees. See Prellwitz.

Resist. (F. – L.) O. F. *resister*. – L. *resistere*, to stand back, withstand. – L. *re*-, back ; *sistere*, to stand, from *stāre*, to stand ; see **State**.

Resolute. (L.) L. *resolūtus*, pp. of *resoluere* (below).

resolve. (L.) L. *resoluere*, to loosen, melt; hence to separate into parts (also, to decide, resolve). — L. *re-*, back; *soluere*, to loosen; see **Solve.** Der. *resolut-ion* (from pp. *resolūtus*).

Resonant. (L.) From *resonant-*, stem of pres. pt. of L. *resonāre*, to sound back, echo, resound. — L. *re-*, back; *sonāre*, to sound, from *sonus*, sound. See **Sound** (3).

Resort, to betake oneself to. (F. — L.) M. F. *resortir, ressortir*, 'to issue, goe forth againe, resort;' Cot. Orig. a law term; to appeal. — Late L. *resortīre*, to resort to a tribunal; cf. *resortīrī*, to return to any one. — L. *re-*, again; *sortīrī*, to obtain; so that *re-sortīrī* is to re-obtain, gain by appeal. — L. *re-*, again; *sorti-*, for *sors*, a lot; see **Sort.**

Resound. (F. — L.) O. F. *resoner* (12th cent.). — L. *resonāre*; see **Resonant.**

Resource. (F. — L.) M. F. *resource*, later *ressource*, 'a new source;' Cot. — F. *re-*, again; *source*, source; see **Source.**

Respect, sb. (F. — L.) F. *respect*, 'respect, regard;' Cot. — L. *respectum*, acc. of *respectus*, a looking at. — L. *respectus*, pp. of *respicere*, to look at, look back upon. — L. *re-*, back; *specere*, to see; see **Species.** Der. *respect*, vb.; *respect-able*, *respect-ive*; also *dis-respect*.

respite, delay, reprieve. (F. — L.) O. F. *respit*, a respite. Orig. sense regard, respect had to a suit on the part of a judge. — L. acc. *respectum*, respect (above).

Respire, to breathe, take rest. (F. — L.) F. *respirer*. — L. *respīrāre*, to breathe again or back. — L. *re-*, back; *spīrāre*, to breathe; see **Spirit.**

Resplendent. (L.) From L. *resplendent-*, stem of pres. pt. of *resplendēre*, to glitter. — L. *re-*, again; *splendēre*, to shine; see **Splendour.**

Respond. (F. — L.) O. F. *respondre.* — L. *respondēre* (pp. *responsus*), to answer. — L. *re-*, back; *spondēre*, to promise; see **Sponsor.** Der. *response*, from O. F. *re-spons*, an answer, from L. *responsum*, neut. of pp. *responsus*.

Rest (1), repose. (E.) A. S. *rest, ræst*, rest. Cf. Du. *rust*, Dan. Swed. *rast*, Icel. *röst* (the distance between two resting-places), Goth. *rasta* (a stage), O. H. G. *rasta*, G. *rast*, rest. The A. S. *rest*, fem., answers to Teut. type **rast-jā*, orig. 'a

halting-place,' which (like O. H. G. *rasta*) is from Teut. root **ras*, to dwell, as seen in Goth. *raz-n*, a house. See **Ransack.** Brugm. i. § 903 c.

Rest (2), to remain, be left over. (F. — L.) F. *rester*, to remain. — L. *restāre*, to stop behind, remain. — L. *re-*, back; *stāre*, to stand; see **State.** ¶ Distinct from *rest* (1), repose.

Restaurant. (F. — L.) Mod. F. *restaurant*, lit. 'restoring;' pres. pt. of *restaurer*, to restore, refresh; see **Restore.**

Restharrow, a plant. (F. *and* E.) For *arrest-harrow*, because its tough roots stop the harrow. Cf. the F. name *arrête-bœuf*, lit. 'stop-ox.'

Restitution. (F. — L.) F. *restitution*. — L. *restitūtiōnem*, acc. of *restitūtio*, a restoring. — L. *restitūtus*, pp. of *restituere*, to restore. — L. *re-*, again; *statuere*, to set up, place, causal of *stāre*, to stand; see **State.**

Restive. (F. — L.) Confused with *restless*, but it really means stubborn, refusing to move. — M. F. *restif*, 'restie, stubborn, drawing backward;' Cot. — F. *rester*, to remain; see **Rest** (2). ¶ Hence E. *rusty* in the phr. *to turn rusty* = to be stubborn.

Restore. (F. — L.) O. F. *restorer*, also *restaurer*. — L. *restaurāre*, to restore. — L. *re-*, again; **staurare*, to set up; see **Store.** Brugm. i. § 198.

Restrain. (F. — L.) O. F. *restraign-*, as in *restraign-ant*, pres. pt. of *restraindre* (F. *restreindre*), to restrain. — L. *restringere*, to draw back tightly, bind back. — L. *re-*, back; *stringere*, to bind; see **Stringent.** Der. *restraint*, from O. F. *re-strainte*, fem. of pp. of *restraindre*.

restrict. (L.) From L. *restrictus*, pp. of *restringere*, to bind back (above).

Result, vb. (F. — L.) M. F. *resulter*, 'to rebound or leap back; also to rise of, come out of;' Cot. — L. *resultāre*, to rebound; frequent. of *resilīre*, to leap back; see **Resilient.** Der. *result-ant*.

Resume, to take up again. (F. — L.) M. F. *resumer*. — L. *resūmere*. — L. *re-*, again; *sūmere*, to take; see **Assume.** Der. *resumpt-ion* (from pp. *resumpt-us*).

Resurrection. (F. — L.) O. F. *resurrection*. — L. acc. *resurrectiōnem*. — L. *resurrectus*, pp. of *resurgere*, to rise again. — L. *re-*, again; *surgere*, to rise; see **Surge.**

Resuscitate, to revive. (L.) L. *resus-*

citātus, pp. of *resuscitāre*, to revive. — L. *re-*, again, *sus-*, up, and *citāre*, to rouse; see Cite.

Ret, to steep flax. (M. Du.) M. Du. *reten, reeten*, to steep flax; Du. *reten*. Cf. Pomeran. *röten*, Swed. *röta*, Norw. *röyta*, to ret; also Du. *rete, reute*, Low G. *rate*, E. Fries. *rötte*, a retting-pit. Lit. 'to make rotten;' formed by mutation from Teut. **raut*; for which see **Rotten**. Cf. Du. *rooten*, to ret.

Retail, sb. (F. — L.) To sell by retail is to sell by small pieces. — O. F. *retail*, a shred, paring, small piece. — O. F. *retailler*, to shred, cut small. — O. F. *re-* (= L. *re-*), again; *tailler*, to cut; see **Tailor**.

Retain. (F. — L.) F. *retenir*. — L. *re-tinēre*, to hold back; pp. *retentus*. — L. *re-*, back; *tenēre*, to hold; see **Tenable**. Der. *retent-ion* (from the pp.).

Retaliate, to repay. (L.) From pp. of L. *retāliāre*, to requite; allied to *tālio*, retaliation in kind, as in *lex tāliōnis*, the law of retaliation. — L. *tāli-*, decl. stem of *tālis*, such, of such a kind. Cf. Gk. τη-λίκος, of such an age. From the Idg. base *tā-*, allied to Gk. τό, E. *tha-t*. See **That**.

Retard, to delay. (F. — L.) F. *retarder*, to hinder. — L. *retardāre*, to delay. — L. *re-*, again; *tardāre*, to make slow, from *tardus*, slow. See **Tardy**.

Retch, Reach, to try to vomit. (E.) A. S. *hrǣcan*, to clear the throat, hawk, spit. — A. S. *hrāca*, spittle; cf. *hrǣcgebrǣc*, hoarseness. + Icel. *hrǣkja*, to spit; from *hrāki*, spittle. Prob. of imitative origin.

Retention. (F. — L.) M. F. *retention*, 'retention;' Cot. — L. acc. *retentiōnem*, a holding back. — L. *retent-us*, held back, pp. of *retinēre*; see **Retain**.

Reticent, silent. (L.) From stem of pres. pt. of L. *reticēre*, to be very silent. — L. *re-*, back, very; and *tacēre*, to be silent. See **Tacit**.

Reticule. (F. — L.) F. *réticule*, a net for the hair, a reticule. — L. *rēticulum*, a little net; double dimin. of *rēte*, a net. ¶ Formerly also *ridicule* (both in F. and E.), by confusion with **Ridicule** (Littré). Cf. prov. F. *rédicule*, a reticule, dial. of Verdun (Fertiault).

retina, the innermost coating of the eye. (L.) Neo-Lat. *rētina*; so called because resembling network. Coined from *rēti-*, for *rēte*, a net.

Retinue. (F. — L.) M. E. *retenue*. — O. F. *retenue*, a body of retainers; fem. of

retenu, pp. of *retenir*, to retain; see **Retain**.

Retire. (F. — Teut.) M. F. *retirer*, 'to retire, withdraw;' Cot. — F. *re-*, back; *tirer*, to pull; see **Tier, Tirade**.

Retort, a censure returned; tube for distilling. (F. — L.) M. F. *retort*, pp. 'twisted, violently returned,' *retorte*, 'a lymbeck,' Cot.; lit. a thing twisted back. — M. F. *retort*, pp. of *retordre*, to twist back. — L. *retorquēre*, to twist back. — L. *re-*, back; *torquēre*, to twist; see **Torture**.

Retract. (F. — L.) M. F. *retracter*, 'to revoke;' Cot. — L. *retractāre*, frequent. of *retrahere*, to draw back. — L. *re-*, back; *trahere*, to draw; see **Tract** (1).

retreat, sb. (F. — L.) M. E. *retrete*. — O. F. *retrete*, later *retraite*, a retreat, fem. of *retret*, pp. of *retraire*, to withdraw. — L. *retrahere*, to draw back (above).

Retrench. (F. — L.?) M. F. *retrencher*, 'to curtall, diminish;' Cot. — L. *re-*, back; and O. F. *trencher*, to cut; see **Trench**.

Retribution. (F. — L.) M. F. *retribution*. — L. acc. *retribūtiōnem*, requital. — L. *retribūtus*, pp. of *retribuere*, to pay back. — L. *re-*, back; *tribuere*, to pay; see **Tribute**.

Retrieve, to recover. (F. — L. and Gk.) Formerly *retreve*. — O. F. *retreuve*, 3rd pers. sing. indic. of *retrover*, later *retrouver*, to find again. — L. *re-*, again; O. F. *trover*, to find; see **Trover**.

Retro-, backwards. (L.) L. *retrō*, backwards; a case of a comparative form from *re-* or *red-*, back. The suffix *-trō* (*-trā*), in *ci-trō, ci-trā*, answers to Goth. *-þrō* in *þa-þrō*, thence; see Brugm. ii. § 75. See **Rear** (2).

Retrocession. (F. — L.) F. *rétrocession*. — Late L. *retrōcessiōnem*, acc. of *retrōcessio*, a going back. — L. *retrōcess-us*, pp. of *retrōcēdere*, to go further back. — L. *retrō*, backwards; *cēdere*, to go; see **Cede**.

Retrograde, going backward. (F. — L.) O. F. *retrograde*. — L. *retrōgradus*, retrograde (used of a planet). — L. *retrō-gradī*, to go backwards. — L. *retrō*, back-wards; *gradī*, to go; see **Grade**.

retrogression. (L.) Coined from pp. of L. *retrō-gradī* (above).

Retrospect. (L.) From L. *retrō-spectus*, (unused) pp. of *retrōspicĕ* look back. — L. *retrō*, back; *spece* look.

Return, vb. (F.−L.) F. *retourner* (Cot.). − F. *re-* (=L. *re-*), back; *tourner*, to turn; see **Turn**.

Reveal. (F.−L.) M. F. *reveler*, ' to reveale;' Cot. − L. *reuēlāre*, to draw back a veil. − L. *re-*, back; *uēlum*, veil; see **Veil**.

Reveille, an alarum at break of day. (F. − L.) [Cf. F. *réveil*, a reveille, M. F. *resveil*, 'a hunt's-up, or morning-song for a new married wife, the day after the marriage;' Cot.] The E. *reveillè* was a trisyllable, and represented F. *réveillez*, wake ye, imper. plural of *réveiller*, to awaken; O. F. *resveiller*. − O. F. *re-* (L. *re-*, again); and *esveiller*, to awaken, from L. *ex*, out, and *uigilāre*, to watch (from *uigil*, awake). See **Vigil**. ¶ The E. word is also spelt *reveillez*; Brand, Pop. Antiq., ed. Ellis, ii. 176. The F. *réveillez* is used as a sb. (in the E. sense) in the dialect of Forez, near Lyons (Graz).

Revel, a noisy feast. (F.−L.) M. E. *reuel* (*revel*), sb.−O. F. *revel*, pride, rebellion, sport, jest, disturbance, disorder (Roquefort). − O. F. *reveler*, to rebel, hence, to riot. − L. *rebellāre*, to rebel; see **Rebel**. Der. *revell-er*; whence *revel-r-y*.

Revenge. (F.−L.) O. F. *revengier*, also *revencher*, to avenge oneself (F. *re-vancher*). − F. *re-* (=L. *re-*), again; O. F. *vengier*, *venger*, from L. *uindicāre*, to vindicate; see **Vindicate**.

Revenue, income. (F.−L.) M. F. *re-venu*, m., and *revenuë*, f. ' revenue, rent;' Cot. From *revenu*, pp. of *revenir*, to come back. − F. *re-*, back; *venir*, to come. − L. *re-*, back; *uenīre*, to come; see **Venture**.

Reverberate. (L.) From pp. of L. *reuerberāre*, to beat back (hence, to re-echo). − L. *re-*, back; *uerberāre*, to beat, from *uerber*, a scourge.

Revere. (F.−L.) M. F. *reverer* (F. *révérer*), to reverence. − L. *reuerērī*, to revere, stand in awe of. − L. *re-*, again; *uerērī*, to fear, feel awe, allied to E. **Wary**. Der. *reverence*, O. F. *reverence*, L. *reuerentia*; also *rever-end*.

Reverie, Revery. (F. − L.) F. *rêverie*, a raving, a vain fancy, a revery. − F. *rêver*, formerly *resver*, *râver*, to rave. See **Rave**.

Reverse. (F. − L.) M. E. *reuers* (*revers*). − O. F. *revers*. − L. *reuersus*, lit. turned backwards; pp. of *reuertere*, to turn backward. − L. *re-*, back; *uertere*, to turn; see **Verse**.

revert. (F.−L.) M. F. *revertir*, ' to revert, returne;' Cot. − L. *reuertere* (above).

Review. (F.−L.) From **Re-** and **View**.

Revile. (F.−L.) M. E. *reuilen* (= *revilen*); A. F. *reviler* (Gower). − F. *re-*, again; and F. *vil* (L. *uīlis*), cheap; see **Vile**. Lit. ' to cheapen.'

Revise. (F.−L.) O. F. *reviser*. − L. *reuīsere*, to look back upon, revisit. − L. *re-*, again; *uīsere*, to survey, from *uīsus*, pp. of *uidēre*, to see; see **Vision**.

Revisit. (F. − L.) From **Re-** and **Visit**.

Revive. (F.−L.) F. *revivre*. − L. *re-uīuere*, to live again, revive. − L. *re-*, again; *uīuere*, to live; see **Vivid**.

Revoke. (F.−L.) O. F. *revocquer* (F. *révoquer*). − L. *reuocāre*, to recall. − L. *re-*, back; *uocāre*, to call; see **Vocal**.

Revolt, a rebellion. (F.−Ital.−L.) M. F. *revolte*, ' a revolt;' Cot. − M. Ital. *revolta* (Ital. *rivolta*), a revolt; fem. of *revolto*, turned, overthrown, pp. of *revolvere*, to turn, roll back, overturn. − L. *re-uoluere*, to roll back (below).

revolve. (L.) L. *reuoluere*, to turn again, revolve. − L. *re-*, again; *uoluere*, to turn; see **Voluble**. Der. *revolut-ion*, from pp. *reuolūtus*.

Revulsion. (F.−L.) M.F. *revulsion*, ' a plucking away; also the drawing of humours from one part of the body into another;' Cot.−L. *reuulsiōnem*, acc. of *reuulsio*, a plucking back.−L. *reuulsus*, pp. of *reuellere*, to pull back.−L. *re-*, back; *uellere*, to pull, pluck. Cf. **Convulse**.

Reward, vb. (F.−L. *and* O. H. G.) A. F. *rewarder*; O.F. *regarder*, to look back upon, regard (with favour); see **Regard**. Doublet, *regard*.

Reynard, Renard, a fox. (F.− Teut.) O.F. *renard*, *regnard* (F. *renard*). − Low G. (M. Flemish) *Reinaert*, the name given to the fox in the celebrated M. Flemish epic so called. Cognate with O. H. G. *Reginhart*, lit. ' strong in counsel;' from O. H. G. *regin-*, *ragin-*, answering to Goth. *ragin*, judgment, counsel, and *hart* (E. *hard*), strong.

Rhapsody. (F.−L.−Gk.) M.F.*rap-sodie*, Cot.−L. *rhapsōdia*.−Gk. ῥαψῳδία, the reciting of epic poetry, part of an epic poem, a rhapsody, tirade.−Gk. ῥαψῳδός, one who strings (lit. stitches) songs together, a reciter of epic poetry. — Gk. ῥαψ-, stem of fut. of ῥάπτειν, to stitch together, fasten together; ῷδή, an ode; see Ode.

Rhetoric. (F. – L. – Gk.) O. F. *rhetorique*; Cot. – L. *rhētorica*, i. e. *rhētorica ars*, the art of rhetoric; fem. of *rhētoricus*, adj. – Gk. ῥητορικός, rhetorical; adj. from ῥήτωρ, an orator, speaker. For Ϝρή-τωρ, related by gradation to εἴρειν, to speak (for *Ϝέρ-yειν). Allied to Verb.

Rheum. (F. – L. – Gk.) M.F. *rheume*, – L. *rheuma*. – Gk. ῥεῦμα (stem ῥευματ-), a flow, flux, rheum. – Gk. ῥεύ-σομαι, fut. of ῥέειν, to flow; (for *σρέϝ-ειν).+Skt. *sru*, to flow. Allied to **Stream.** (√SREU.) Der. *rheumat-ic*.

Rhinoceros. (L. – Gk.) L. *rhīnocerōs*. – Gk. ῥινόκερως, lit. ' nose-horned.' – Gk. ῥινο-, for ῥίς, nose; κέρας, a horn, allied to Horn.

Rhizome, a rootlike stem. (F. – Gk.) F. *rhizome*. – Gk. ῥίζωμα, root. – Gk. ῥιζοῦν, to cause to take root. – Gk. ῥίζα, root. See Root.

Rhododendron. (L. – Gk.) L. *rhododendron*. – Gk. ῥοδόδενδρον, the rose-bay, oleander. – Gk. ῥόδο-, for ῥόδον, rose; δένδρον, tree. Gk. ῥόδον is of Armenian origin; see Rose.

Rhodomontade; see Rodomontade.

Rhomb, Rhombus. (L. – Gk.) L. *rhombus* (F. *rhombe*). – Gk. ῥόμβος, a thing twirled round, whirling spindle, a thing in the shape of a whirling spindle, a four-sided figure with equal sides but unequal angles. – Gk. ῥέμβειν, to revolve. Allied to **Wrinkle** (Prellwitz). See also Rumb.

Rhubarb. (F. – Late L. – Gk.) O. F. *reubarbe*; F. *rhubarbe*. – Late L. *rheubarbarum* (= *rhēum barbarum*). – Gk. ῥῆον βάρβαρον, rhubarb; lit. ' Rhēum from the barbarian country.' Gk. ῥῆον is an adj. from ῥά, the rha-plant, rhubarb, which was also called *Rhā Pontīcum*. *Rhā* took its name from the river *Rha*, i. e. the Volga. And see Barbarous.

Rhumb; see Rumb.

Rhyme; see Rime (1).

Rhythm. (F. – L. – Gk.) M.F. *rithme*, Cot. – L. *rhythmus*. – Gk. ῥυθμός, measured motion, time, measure. – Gk. ῥέειν, to flow. See Rheum.

Rib. (E.) M. E. *ribbe*. A.S. *ribb*.+ Du. *rib*, Icel. *rif*, Swed. *ref-been* (rib-bone), Dan. *rib-been*; G. *rippe*; Russ. *rebro*,

Perhaps allied to G. *rebe*, a tendril ; from the idea of clasping (Kluge).

Ribald. (F. – Teut.) M. E. *ribald*, *ribaud*. – O. F. *ribald* (F. *ribaud*). – LowL. *ribaldus*, a ruffian ; cf. Low L. *ribalda*, a prostitute. Of Teut. origin. – O. H. G. *hrīpa*, M. H. G. *rībe*, a prostitute; cf. O. F. *riber*, to be wanton. The suffix *-ald* is due to O. H. G. *walt*, power. Cf. Körting, § 4019.

Riband, Ribbon. (F.) M. E. *riban*, *reban*. [Also Irish *ribin*, a ribbon; Gael. *ribean*, a ribbon, fillet; from E.] – O. F. *riban* (F. *ruban*), a ribbon (Littré); Gascon and Languedoc *riban*; Norman dial. *riban*. Low L. *rubānus* (A. D. 1367). Origin unknown; cf. Dan. *vride-baand*, a twisted band.

Rice. (F. – Ital. – L. – Gk. – O. Pers.) O. F. *ris*, rice ; F. *riz*. – Ital. *riso*. – L. *orȳza*. – Gk. ὄρυζα, ὄρυζον, rice, grain. From an O. Pers. form, preserved in the Pushto (Afghan) *wrijzey*, *wrijey*, rice ; *wrijza'h*, a grain of rice (Raverty). Hence also Arab. *uruzz*, *ruzz*, whence Span. *arroz*, rice. Allied forms are Pers. *birinj*, Armen. *brinj*, rice; Skt. *vrīhi-*, rice. (Horn, § 208; Yule.)

Rich. (E.) M. E. *riche*. – A. S. *rīce*, powerful, rich. [We also find O.F. *riche*, from O. Sax. *rīki*, allied to O. H. G. *rīhhi*, M. H. G. *rīche* (G. *reich*), powerful.]+ Du. *rijk*, Icel. *rīkr*, Swed. *rik*, Dan. *rig*, Goth. *reiks*. Teut. type *rīkiz*, powerful, from the base *rīk-* as seen in Goth. *reik-s*, a ruler; cognate with the Celtic base *rīg-*, as in Gaulish *rīx*, a king (cf. O. Irish *rī*, gen. *rīg*, a king, W. *rhi*, a chief); unless the Teut. base *rīk-* is merely borrowed from the Celtic *rīg-*. Cf. L. *rēx*, gen. *rēg-is*, a king. All from √REG, to rule (L. *reg-ere*). See Regent. Brugm. i. §§ 135, 549 c.

riches. (F. – O.H.G.) M. E. *richesse*, a sing. sb.; the pl. being *richesses*. – F. *richesse*, wealth. – O. H. G. *rīhhi*, M. H. G. *rīche* (G. *reich*), rich (above). The suffix is F. *-esse*, L. *-itia*.

Rick. (E.) *Rick* is from A. S. *hrycce*, as in *corn-hrycce*, corn-rick. We also find M. E. *reek*, A. S. *hrēac*, a heap, a rick.+ Icel. *hraukr*, a rick ; Du. *rook*. Cf. O. Irish *cruach*, a rick ; and see Ruck (2).

Rickets, a disease of children, accompanied by softness of the bones and great weakness. (E.) A prov. E. word first noticed about A. D. 1620 ; whence the medical term *rachītis* was coined about

448

1650, with allusion to Gk. ῥάχις, the spine. Cf. prov. E. *rickety*, i. e. tottery, weak, unstable. Formed from M. E. *wrikken*, to twist, wrest, still in use in the phrase 'to *wrick* one's ankle.' Allied to A. S. *wringan*, to twist; see **Wring** and **Wry**. Cf. Du. *wrikken*, Swed. *ricka*, to be rickety; Swed. *rickug*, rickety.

Ricochet, the rebound of a cannon-ball. (F.) F. *ricochet*, 'the sport of skimming a thinne stone on the water, called a Duck and a Drake;' Cot. Origin unknown.

Rid (1), to free. (E.) M. E. *ridden*, *redden*. A. S. *hreddan*, to snatch away, deliver.+O. Fries. *hredda*, Du. *redden*, Dan. *redde*, Swed. *rädde*; G. *retten*. Teut. type **hradjan-*. Cf. Skt. *çrath*, to untie.

Rid (2), to clear, esp. land. (Scand.) Prov. E. *rid*. M. E. *ruden* (pp. *rid*).— Icel. *ryðja* (orig. *hryðja*), to clear, clear out; Dan. *rydde*, to clear, grub up land. Teut. type **hrudjan-*, from **hrud-*, weak grade of **hreuthan-* (Icel. *hrjóða*), to strip. ¶ Confused with *rid* (1).

Riddle (1), an enigma. (E.) Properly *riddles*; and the pl. should be *riddles-es*. M. E. *redels.—* A. S. *rǽdels*, *rǽdelse*, a riddle, ambiguity, something requiring explanation.— A. S. *rǽdan*, to discern, explain; see **Read.**+Du. *raadsel*, for **raad-is-lo-*, the A. S. *-els* being for *-isl*; G. *räthsel*, a riddle. ¶ We still say *to read a riddle*, i. e. to explain it.

Riddle (2), a large sieve. (E.) M. E. *ridil*. A.S. *hridder*, a vessel for winnowing corn; older form *hrīder* (Sweet); the suffixed *-er* and *-il* (*-le*) being equivalent. +O. H. G. *rītera*; Irish *creathair*, Gael. *criathar*; L. *crībrum*. Lit. sense ' separater.' All from Idg. root **krei*, to separate; cf. Gk. κρί-νειν. See **Critic.**

Ride. (E.) M. E. *riden*, pt. t. *rood*, pp. *riden*. A. S. *rīdan*, pt. t. *rād*, pp. *riden*. +Du. *rijden*, Icel. *rīða*, Dan. *ride*, Swed. *rida*; G. *reiten*. Also O. Irish *riad-aim*, I drive, ride. (√REIDH.) Brugm. i. § 210. Der. *road*, *read-y*.

Ridge. (E.) M. E. *rigge*, *rugge*. A.S. *hrycg*, the back of a man or beast.+Du. *rug*, back, ridge, Dan. *ryg*, Swed. *rygg*, Icel. *hryggr*; G. *rücken*, O. H. G. *hrucki*. Cf. O. Irish *croccenn*, (1) hide, (2) the back.

Ridiculous. (L.) L. *rīdicul-us*, laughable; with suffix *-ous*. — L. *rīdēre*, to laugh.

Riding, one of the three divisions of the county of York. (Scand.) For *thriding*

(*North-riding = North-thriding*). — Icel. *þriðjungr*, the third part of a thing, third part of a shire. — Icel. *þriði*, third; cognate with A. S. *þridda*, third. See **Third**, **Three**. So also Norw. *tridjung*, a third part.

Rife. (Scand.) M. E. *rif*, late A. S. *rīf*. — Icel. *rīfr*, munificent, abundant; M. Swed. *rif*, rife; Norw. *riv.*+M. Du. *rijf*, abundant; Low G. *rive*, abundant, munificent, extravagant. Cf. Icel. *reifr*, glad; *reifa*, to bestow.

Riff-raff, refuse. (F. – Teut.) M. E. *rif and raf*, things of small value, hence every bit. — M. F. *rif et raf*, every bit; also *rifle et rafle*. 'Il ne luy lairra *rif ny raf*, he will strip him of all;' Cot. Here *rif* or *rifle* is a thing of small value, from *rifler*, to rifle, ransack; and *rafle* is from M. F. *raffler*, to rifle, ravage. Both are words of Teut. origin, drawn together by their sound, though of different origin. F. *rifler* is from Icel. *hrífa* (see **Rifle** (1)); M. F. *raffler* is from G. *raffen*, to seize.

Rifle (1), to spoil, plunder. (F. – Teut.) M. F. *rifler*, 'to rifle, spoile;' Cot. Norm. dial. *rifler* (Duméril). Formed, with frequentative *-l-*, from Icel. *hrífa*, *rífa*, to catch, grapple, grasp; allied to Icel. *hrifsa*, plunder.

Rifle (2), a kind of musket. (F. – Teut.) Short for *rifled gun*, from the verb *rifle*, to groove. – O. F. *rifler*, to scratch, graze (Godefroy). — Low G. *rifeln*, to furrow, chamfer; E. Fries. *riffeln* (the same), *riffel*, a groove; Dan. *rifle*, to rifle, groove, *rifle*, a groove; Swed. *reffla*, to rifle. So also G. *riefe*, a furrow; *riefen*, *riefeln*, to rifle (from Low G.). All allied to **Rivel**, and to **Rive**.

rift. (Scand.) Dan. and Norw. *rift*, rift, rent. — Norw. *riva*, Dan. *rive*, to tear. Cf. Icel. *ript*, a breach of contract. See **Rive.**

Rig (1), to fit up a ship. (Scand.) Spelt *rygge* in Palsgrave. — Norw. *rigga*, to bind up, wrap round, also to rig a ship; *rigg*, sb., rigging. Cf. Swed. dial. *rigga på*, to harness a horse. Also Westphal. *riggen*, Du. *rijgen*, G. *reihen*, to stitch together, orig. to put in a row; cf. E. Fries. *rige*, *rīge*, a row. See **Row** (1).

Rig (2), a frolic, prank. (E.?) We also find *rig*, to be wanton; *riggish*, wanton. For *wrig*, and allied to *wriggle*; see **Wriggle.** Cf. Norw. *rigga*, to rock; E. Fries. *wriggen*, to wriggle; Du. *wrikken*, to stir to and fro, *wriggelen*, to wriggle; and see **Rickets**.

Rig (3), a ridge. (E.) M. E. *rig*, Northern form of *rigge*, *rugge*, a ridge. See **Ridge**.

Right. (E.) M. E. *right*. A. S. *riht*, *ryht*; O. Merc. *reht*.+Du. *regt*, *recht*, Icel. *rēttr* (for *rēhtr), Dan. *ret*, Swed. *rät*, G. *recht*, O. H. G. *reht*, Goth. *raihts*. Teut. type *rehtoz; Idg. type *rektos, as in L. *rectus*. Cf. W. *rhaith*, sb., right, O. Ir. *recht*; Pers. *rāst*. See **Regent**. (✓REG.)

righteous. (E.) Corruption of M. E. *rightwis*; A. S. *rihtwīs*, i. e. wise as to what is right.—A. S. *riht*, right; *wīs*, wise.

Rigid. (L.) L. *rigidus*, stiff.—L. *rigēre*, to be stiff. Brugm. i. § 875.

Rigmarole. (Scand.; *and* F.—L.) Well known to be a corruption of *ragman-roll*, orig. a deed with many signatures, a long list of names; hence, a long stupid story. Lit. ʻcoward's roll.'—Icel. *ragmenni*, a coward, from *ragr*, a coward, and *maðr* (= *mannr*), a man; with the addition of *roll*, for which see **Roll**. The Icel. *ragr* seems to be allied to Icel. *argr*, a coward, A. S. *earg*.

Rigol, a circlet. (Ital.—O. H. G.) In Shak.—Ital. *rigolo*, a little wheel (Torriano); cf. *riga*, a line, a stripe.—O. H. G. *riga*, *rīga*, a line, the circumference of a circle (G. *reihe*). See **Row** (1).

Rile; see **Roil**.

Rill, a streamlet. (Low G.) Cf. Low G. *rille*, E. Friesic and Dan. dial. *rille*, a streamlet. Apparently for *rithele; cf. A. S. *rīðe*, a stream; Low G. *rīde*, a stream; G. -*reide* (in place-names). See Phil. Soc. Trans. 1888, p. 166. ¶ Norm. dial. *risle*, *rille*, the name of a river, written *Ridula*, *Risila*, *Risla* in old charters (Robin, p. 432).

Rim. (E.) M. E. *rim*. A. S. *rima*, a verge, edge; cf. W. *rhim*, *rhimp*, *rhimyn*, a rim, edge.+Icel. *rimi*, a strip of land. Perhaps allied to G. *rand*, a rim, and to **Rind** (Kluge). Brugm. i. § 421.

Rime (1), verse, poetry, &c. (F.—L.—Gk.) Usually spelt *rhyme*, by confusion with *rhythm*, but not before A. D. 1550. M. E. *rime*.—F. *rime*, ʻrime, or meeter;' Cot. Cf. M. F. *rithme*, ʻrime, or meeter;' id. Prob. from L. *rhythmus*, rhythm; of Gk. origin; see **Rhythm**. ¶ Hence also M. H. G. *rīm*, in the sense of ʻverse,'

which is a different word from M. H. G. *rīm*, O. H. G. *rīm* (A. S. *rīm*), in the sense of ʻnumber.' From F. *rime* came also Ital. Span. Port. *rima*; also Du. *rijm*, Icel. *rīma*, G. *reim*.

Rime (2), hoarfrost. (F.) For *hrime*. A. S. *hrīm*, hoarfrost. + Du. *rijm*, Icel. *hrim*, Dan. *riim*, Swed. *rim*. Allied to Du. *rijp*, G. *reif*, hoar-frost.

Rimer, a tool for enlarging holes in metal. (E.) From A. S. *rȳman*, to enlarge.—A. S. *rūm*, wide. See **Room**.

Rimple, to ripple, as the surface of water. (E.) To *rimple* is to shew wrinkles. — A. S. *hrympel*, a wrinkle. — A. S. *hrump-*, *rump-*, weak grade of *hrimpan* or *rimpan*, to wrinkle. + Du. *rimpel*, a wrinkle, *rimpelen*, to wrinkle; O. H. G. *hrimfan*, M. H. G. *rimpfen* (cf. G. *rümpfen*), to crook, bend, wrinkle. (See Franck.) See **Rumple**.

Rind. (E.) M. E. *rind*, *rinde*. A. S. *rinde*, bark of a tree, crust (of bread). + M. Du. and G. *rinde*, bark. Allied to **Rim**.

Ring (1), a circle. (E.) M. E. *ring*. A. S. *hring*.+Du. *ring*, Low G. *ring*, *rink*, Icel. *hringr*, Swed. Dan. G. *ring*, O. H. G. *hrinc*. Teut. type *hrengoz; Idg. type *krenghos; also *kronghos, as in O. Bulg. *kragŭ*, Russ. *krug(e)*, a circle. See **Rank** and **Harangue**.

Ring (2), to sound a bell. (E.) M. E. *ringen*. A. S. *hringan*, to clash, ring; a *weak* verb, as in Scand.; but English has pt. t. *rang*, by analogy with *sang* from *sing*. + Icel. *hringja*, Dan. *ringe*, Swed. *ringa*. Cf. Icel. *hrang*, a din; L. *clangere*, to clang.

Rink, a course for the game of curling, &c. (E.) A peculiar form of *ring*, in the sense of *prize-ring*, &c. Cf. Low G. *rink*, a ring.

Rinse. (F.) M. F. *rinser*, ʻto reinse linnen clothes;' Cot. F. *rincer*; from O. F. *raïncer* (Littré). Cf. O. F. *reincier*, to rinse (Godefroy). Of unknown origin.

Riot. (F.—O. H. G.?) O. F. *riote*, a brawling. The same as Prov. *riota*, Ital. *riotta*, dispute, strife. Of unknown origin; see Körting.

Rip. (Scand.; or F.—Scand.) M. E. *ripen*, to grope, search into; ʻ*rypen vp*, to seek out (cf. E. *rip up*). Cf. O. F. *riper*, to scratch (Godefroy). — Norweg. *ripa*, to scratch, Swed. dial. *ripa*, to scratch, pluck asunder (like E. *rip open*); Dan. *oprippe*, to rip up; Swed. *repa upp*, to rip up, *repa*, to scratch. Allied to Du. *repel*, G. *riffel*, a flax-comb; see **Ripple** (1). The Teut. base takes a double form; see **Reap**; cf. **Ripe** (below) and **Rope**.

Ripe. (E.) M. E. *ripe*. A. S. *rípe*, fit for reaping; cf. *ríp*, harvest. ‒ A. S. *rípan*, to reap. **+** Du. *rijp*, G. *reif*, ripe. See **Rip, Reap**.

Ripple (1), to pluck the seeds from flax-stalks. (E.) M. E. *ripplen, ripelen*, to ripple; from the sb. *ripple*, a flax-comb (Jamieson). Formed, with suffix -*le*, of the agent, from the weak grade, **rip-*, of A. S. *rípan*, to reap, cut; see **Reap**. Cf. Swed. *repa*, to ripple flax, orig. to scratch, rip; see **Rip** (above). **+** Du. *repelen*, to ripple, from *repel*, a ripple, from M. Du. *repen*, to beat flax; G. *riffeln*, to ripple, from *riffel*, a ripple.

Ripple (2), to cause or shew wrinkles on the surface, said of water. (Scand.) A late word; the same as **Ripple** (3) below. The older word was **Rimple**, q. v.

Ripple (3), to graze slightly. (Scand.) ' *Ripple*, rescindere ;' Levins (1570). Frequentative of **Rip** (above).

Rise. (E.) M. E. *risen*. A. S. *rísan*, pt. t. *rás*, pp. *risen*.**+**Du. *rijzen*, orig. to move, also in M. Du. to fall (contrary to the E. sense); Icel. *rísa* ; O. H. G. *rísan*, to move up or down, to rise, to fall ; Goth. *ur-reisan*, to arise. Teut. type **reis-an-*, to slip away. Der. *raise, rear*, vb.

Risible. (F.‒L.) F. *risible*.‒L. *rísibilis*, laughable.‒L. *rísus*, pp. of *rídére*, to laugh. See **Ridiculous**.

Risk. (F.‒Ital.‒L.) F. *risque*, peril ; Cot. Orig. a maritime word.‒Ital. *risco*, peril ; Florio ; the same word (probably) as Span. *risco*, a steep abrupt rock ; whence the sense of ' peril,' as shewn by Span. *arriesgar*, O. Span. *arriscar*, to venture into danger (lit. to go against a rock). The orig. sense of *risco* is cut off, sheer, like a sharp rock.‒L. *resecáre*, to cut back, cut off short (curiously verified by the use of the Como word *resega*, a saw, also risk ; Diez) ; and cf. Port. *risco*, (1) rock, (2) danger.‒L. *re-*, back ; *secáre*, to cut ; see **Section**. (See further in Diez and Körting.)

Rissole, a minced-meat fritter. (F.‒L.) F. *rissole* ; O. F. *roissole, roussole*.‒ Late L. type *russeola ; from L. *russeus*, reddish, or rather brownish ; from the colour.‒L. *russus*, red. See **Russet**.

Rite. (L.) L. *rítus*, a custom.**+**Skt. *ríti-*, a going, way, usage; from *rí*, to go, flow. Cf. Brugm. ii. § 498. **Der.** *ritu-al*, from L. *rítu-*, decl. stem of *rítus*.

Rival. (F.‒L.) F. *rival*.‒L. *ríuális*, sb., one who uses the same brook as another, a near neighbour, a rival.‒L. *ríuus*, a stream. Cf. Skt. *rí*, to go, flow.

Rive, to tear. (Scand.) M. E. *riuen* (*u=v*).‒Icel. *rífa*, pt. t. *reif*, pp. *rifinn* (>E. *riven*), to rive ; Dan. *rive*, Swed. *rifva*. Cf. Gk. ἐρείπειν, to dash down ; L. *rípa*, a bank (shore). See **Reef**.

Rivel, to wrinkle. (E.) M. E. *riuelen* (*u = v*). A. S. *rifeled*, wrinkled (Eng. Stud. xi. 66) ; cf. *ge-riflian*, to wrinkle ; a frequent. form from the weak grade of Teut. **reifan-*, as seen in Icel. *rífa*, to rive ; see **Rive** (above). Cf. A. S. *gerifod*, wrinkled ; Ælf. Hom. i. 614.

River. (F.‒L.) M. E. *riuer* (*u=v*). ‒ A. F. *rivere*, O. F. *riviere*. (F. *rivière*.) The same as Span. *ribera*, a shore, strand, sea-coast, Ital. *riviera*, shore, bank, also a river ; Late L. *ripária*, (1) shore, bank, (2) river.‒Late L. *ripárius*, belonging to a shore.‒L. *rípa*, shore, bank. Allied to **Rive**.

Rivet. (F. ‒ Scand.) F. *rivet*, ' the welt of a shoe,' Cot. ; also a rivet (Littré). ‒ F. *river*, to rivet, clench, fasten back. ‒ Icel. *rifa*, to tack, sew loosely together ; *rifa saman*, to stitch together. Cf. Shetland *riv*, to sew coarsely, Aberdeen *riv*, to rivet.

Rivulet. (L.) Dimin. from L. *ríuulus*, a small stream ; dimin. of *ríuus*, a stream ; lit. ' flowing.' Cf. Ital. *rivoletto* (Torriano). See **Rival**.

Rix-dollar, a coin. (Du.‒G.) Du. *rijks-daalder*, a rix-dollar.‒G. *reichsthaler*, a dollar of the empire.‒G. *reichs*, gen. case of *reich*, empire, allied to G. *reich*, rich ; and *thaler*, a dollar ; see **Rich** and **Dollar**.

Roach, a fish. (F.‒Teut.) M. E. *roche*. ‒ O. North. F. and Walloon *roche*, O. F. *roce* (*rosse* in Cot.).‒M. Du. *roch*, a skate ; cf. Dan. *rokke*, Swed. *rocka*, a ray ; Low G. *ruche*, whence G. *roche*, a roach, ray. Origin unknown. There is a remarkable confusion between roach, skate, ray, and thornback. Cf. A. S. *reohhe*, a fish.

Road. (E.) M. E. *rood, rode* (both for ships and horses).‒A. S. *rád*, a road, also a raid.‒A. S. *rád*, 2nd stem of *rídan*, to ride. See **Ride**. **Doublet**, *raid*.

Roam. (F. – L.) M. E. *romen.*
Coined from O. F. *romier,* a pilgrim to
Rome; cf. O. F. *romel,* a pilgrim, *romeree,*
a pilgrimage; Span. *romero,* a pilgrim;
M. E. *Rome-rennere,* a runner to Rome,
pilgrim; also Late L. *romeus,* Ital. *Romeo,*
one who goes to Rome, a pilgrim. All
from L. *Rōma,* Rome.

Roan. (F.) M.F. *rouën;* '*cheval rouën,*
a roane horse;' Cot. Mod. F. *rouan,*
Span. *roano,* Ital. *rovano, roano* (Florio).
Origin unknown. ¶ Sometimes derived
from the town of *Rouen,* with which
Ital. *rovano* can have nothing to do.

Roan-tree, Rowan-tree, the mountain ash. (Scand.) Spelt *roun-tree, roan-
tree, rowan-tree* in Jamieson. – Swed. *rönn,*
M. Swed. *runn, rönn,* roan-tree; Dan.
rön, Icel. *reynir.* The Icel. *reynir* is for
*reyŷnir < *rauŷnir, a derivative of *rauðr,*
red; from the colour of the berries (Noreen). See **Red.**

Roar. (E.) M.E. *roren.* A.S. *rārian,*
to bellow.+M. H. G. *rēren;* cf. Lith.
rēju, I scold, Brugm. ii. §§ 465, 741.
Perhaps of imitative origin.

Roast. (F. – G.?) M. E. *rosten.* – O. F.
rostir, 'to rost;' Cot. (F. *rôtir.*) – O.H.G.
rostĕn, to roast. – O. H. G. *rost,* a grate,
gridiron.+Du. *roosten,* to roast; *rooster,*
a gridiron. Cf. also Irish *rost,* roast meat,
Gael. *rost, roist,* W. *rhostio,* from E.;
Bret. *rosta,* from F.

Rob (1). (F. – O. H. G.) M. E. *robben.*
– O. F. *robber,* more commonly *rober,* to
disrobe, spoil, strip off clothing, plunder.
– F. *robe,* a robe; see **Robe.**

Rob (2), a conserve of fruit. (F. – Span.
– Arab.) F. *rob,* 'the juice of black
whortleberries preserved;' Cot. – Span.
rob, thickened juice of fruit with honey. –
Arab. *rubb,* 'a decoction of the juice of
citrons and other fruits, inspissated juice,
rob;' Richardson.

Robbins, Robins, ropes for fastening
sails. (E.) Lowl. Sc. *ra-band, rai-band.*
E. Fries. *rā-band;* where *rā* = yard of a
ship. Cf. Icel. *rā,* Dan. *raa,* Swed. *rå,* G.
rahe, yard; and Band.

Robe. (F. – O. H. G.) F. *robe,* formerly also *robbe.* – M. H. G. *roub,* O. H. G.
raup (G. *raub*), booty, spoil; hence, a
garment taken from the slain, clothing.+
A. S. *rēaf,* Icel. *rauf,* sb.; see under **Reave.**
Der. *dis-robe.*

Robin. (F. – O. H. G.) F. *Robin,*
proper name; pet name for *Robert.* –

O. H. G. *Ruodperht* (G. *Ruprecht,* i.e.
Rupert). Lit. 'fame-bright,' illustrious
in fame.– O. H. G. *ruod-,* allied to Icel.
hrōðr, fame; O. H. G. *perht* = E. *bright.*
See **Hobgoblin.**

Robust. (F. – L.) F. *robuste.* – L.
rōbustus, strong.– O. L. *rōbus* (L. *rōbur*),
strength; orig. a tough tree, oak.

Roc, a huge bird. (F. – Pers.) F. *rock*
(Littré). – Pers. *rukh,* the name of a huge
bird; also a hero.

Rochet, a fine white linen robe, like a
surplice, worn by bishops. (F. – M. H. G.)
F. *rochet,* 'a frock; a prelate's rochet;'
Cot. – M. H. G. *roc* (G. *rock*), a frock, coat.
+Du. *rok,* O. Fries. *rokk,* A. S. *rocc,* Icel.
rokkr, the same; Teut. type **rukkoz.*

Rock (1), a large mass of stone. (F.)
O. F. *roke* (13th cent.), also *roque, rocque;*
commonly *roche,* a rock. The same as
Walloon *roc,* Languedoc *roquo,* f., Prov.
roca, Span. *roca,* Port. *roca, rocha,* Ital.
rocca, roccia, a rock. Cf. Low L. *rocca*
(Ducange). We also find Ir. and Gael.
roc (prob. from E.), and Bret. *roch* (prob.
from F.). Also A. S. *stān-rocc* (11th c.).
Origin unknown.

Rock (2), to shake, totter. (E.) M. E.
rokken. A. S. *roccian* (C. Hall); N. Fries.
rocke. + Dan. *rokke,* to rock, shake,
Swed. dial. *rukka,* to wag. Allied to
Dan. *rykke,* to pull, *ryk,* a pull; Icel.
rykkr, a hasty pull; G. *ruck,* a pull, jolt;
Du. *ruk,* a jerk. Teut. types **rukkōjan-,*
*rukkjan-, to jolt, jerk (Franck). The
base **rukk-* may be related to **renkan-,*
to shake, as seen in Swed. dial. *rinka,* to
shake (pt. t. *rank,* supine *runkit*); Swed.
runka, to shake. See Rietz.

Rock (3), a distaff. (Scand.) Icel. *rokkr,*
Swed. *rock,* Dan. *rok,* a distaff.+G. *rocken;*
Du. *rok, rokken.*

rocket (1), a kind of fire-work. (Ital.
– G.) M.Ital. *rocchetto,* 'a bobbin to winde
silke upon; a squib of wilde fier;' Florio.
So named from its shape, resembling that
of a bobbin or a distaff. – M. H. G. *rocke,*
G. *rocken,* a distaff (above).

Rocket (2), a plant. (F. – Ital. – L.) F.
roquette. – Ital. *ruchetta,* dimin. of *ruca,*
garden-rocket. – L. *ērūca,* a sort of colewort; whence also G. *rauke,* rocket.

Rod, a wand. (E.) See **Rood.**

Rodent, gnawing. (L.) From *rō-
dent-,* stem of pres. part. of *rōdere,* to gnaw.
Allied to **Rase.**

Rodomontade, vain boasting. (F. –

Ital.) F. *rodomontade.* – Ital. *rodomontata*, a boast. Due to the boastful character of *Rodomonte*, in the Orlando Furioso of Ariosto, b. xiv.

Roe (1), a female deer. (E.) M. E. *ro.* A. S. *rā*, early form *rāha.*+Icel. *rā*, Dan. *raa*, Swed. *rå*, Du. *ree*, G. *reh.* **Der.** *roe-buck.*

Roe (2), spawn. (Scand.) For *roan*; the final *n* was dropped, being mistaken for the pl. suffix, as in *shoon* for shoes, *eyne* for eyes. M. E. *rowne.* – Icel. *hrogn*, Dan. *rogn*, Swed. *rom*, roe.+G. *rogen*, roe (whence F. *rogue*, roe).

Rogation. (F.–L.) F. *rogation.* – L. acc. *rogātiōnem*, a supplication. – L. *rogā-tus*, pp. of *rogāre*, to ask.

Rogue. (F.–C.) F. *rogue*, 'arrogant, proud, presumptuous, rude, surly;' Cot. Cf. E. *rogu-ish*, saucy. The orig. sense was a surly fellow; hence a vagabond. – Bret. *rok*, *rog*, arrogant, proud, haughty, brusque. Cf. Irish *rucas*, pride. (Doubtful; see Scheler.)

Roil, Rile, to vex. (F.?) The old word *roil* meant (1) to disturb, (2) to vex. See Davies, Supp. Gloss. Of doubtful origin; prob. French. Cf. O. F. *roeillier*, *roillier*, to roll, to give one a beating; M. F. *rouiller*, to pummel.

Roistering, turbulent. (F. – L.) From the sb. *roister*, a bully, turbulent fellow. – F. *rustre*, 'a ruffin, royster, sawcie fellow;' Cot. By-form of O. F. *ruste*, a rustic, the *r* being epenthetic; cf. O. F. *ruistre*, *ruiste*, *ruste*, adj., strong, vigorous, rude, violent (Godefroy). – L. *rusticum*, acc. of *rusticus*, rustic. See **Rustic.**

Roll, vb. (F. – L.) M. E. *rollen.* – O. F. *roler*, F. *rouler.* – Late L. *rotulāre*, to revolve, roll. – L. *rotula*, a little wheel; dimin. of *rota*, a wheel. See **Rotary. Der.** *roll*, sb., a scroll, O. F. *role*, L. *rotulus.*

Romance. (F. – L.) O. F. *romanz*, *romans*, a romance. The form is due to late L. adv. *rōmānicē*, as in the phr. *rō-mānicē loquī* = O. F. *parler romanz*, to speak Romance, i.e. the vulgar Latin dialect of every-day life, as distinguished from book-Latin. *Rōmānicē*, i.e. Roman-like, is from L. *Rōmānus*, Roman. – L. *Rōma*, Rome.

romaunt. (F. – L.) O. F. *romant*, oblique case of O. F. *romanz*, a romance; see above. **Der.** *romant-ic.*

Romp; see **Ramp.**

Rondeau. (F.–L.) F. *rondeau*, a kind of poem, O. F. *rondel*; see **Roundel.**

Rood, the cross; a measure of land. (E.) The same word as *rod*, which is shortened from M. E. *rood* (also *rod*), a rood, a rod. Both *rood* and *rod* are used as measures, though the former is restricted to square measure, and the latter to linear; both senses are due to the use of a rod for measurement. A. S. *rōd*, a gallows, cross, properly a rod or pole.+O. Fries. *rōde*, gallows; O. Sax. *rōda*, cross, gallows; Du. *roede*, rod, perch, wand; G. *ruthe*, a rod of land; O. H. G. *ruota*, a rod, pole. Teut. type **rōdā*, fem., a rod, pole. ¶ The short *o* in *rod* is due to the final *d*; cf. *red*, *head*, *dead.* M. E. *rod(de)* is not older than the 13th cent. Cf. **Ratlines.**

Roof. (E.) M. E. *rōf.* A. S. *hrōf.*+Du. *roef*, a cabin, Icel. *hrōf*, a shed. Cf. also Ir. *crō*, a hovel; W. *craw*, a pig-sty; Bret. *crou*, a stable. Teut. type **hrōfo-*; Idg. type **krāpo-.*

Rook (1), a kind of crow. (E.) M. E. *rook.* A. S. *hrōc.*+Icel. *hrōkr*, Dan. *raage*, Swed. *roka*, M. H. G. *ruoch*, O. H. G. *hruoh*, a jackdaw. Teut. type **hrōkoz*, masc.; cf. Gk. κρώζειν (for **κρώγ-γειν*), to caw. Of imitative origin; cf. Goth. *hrūkjan*, to crow.

Rook (2), a castle, at chess. (F. – Span. – Pers.) M. E. *rook.* – F. *roc.* – Span. *roque* (cf. Ital. *rocco*). – Pers. *rokh*, a rook. Said to have meant 'warrior' (Devic).

Room, space, a chamber. (E.) The old meaning is space, place. M. E. *roum.* A. S. *rūm*; 'næfdon *rūm*' = they had no room, Luke ii. 7. We also find adj. *rūm*, spacious. + Du. *ruim*, adj., spacious, *ruim*, sb., room; Icel. *rūmr*, spacious, *rūm*, space; Dan. and Swed. *rum*, adj. and sb.; Goth. *rūms*, adj. and sb., G. *raum*, sb. Teut. type **rūmoz*, adj., whence the sb. forms are derived. Allied to L. *rūs*, open country; see **Rural. Der.** *roomy*, adj., used for M. E. *roum*, adj.

Roost, sb. (E.) M. E. *roost*, a perch for fowls. A. S. *hrōst*, the same.+M. Du. *roest*, a hen-roost; O. Sax. *hrōst*, the woodwork of a roof. Cf. Lowl. Sc. *roost*, the inside of a roof; but the orig. *roost* was on the rafters inside a roof. **Der.** *roost*, vb.

Root (1), lowest part of a plant. (Scand.) M. E. *rote.* – Icel. *rōt*, Swed. *rot*, Dan. *rod*, a root. For **wrōt*, cognate with L. *rādix*, and allied to Goth. *waurts*, a root, A. S. *wyrt*, a wort, a root; the initial *w* being dropped, as is usual in Icelandic in the combination *wr* (later *vr*). See below. And see **Radix** and **Wort**.

Root (2), **Rout,** vb., to grub up, as a hog. (E.) A.S. *wrōtan,* to grub up (strong vb.); whence prov. E. *wrout,* the same. Cf. A. S. *wrōt,* sb., a swine's snout; G. *rüssel,* a snout.+M. Du. *wroeten,* the same; Icel. *rōta,* to grub up, Dan. *rode,* Low G. *wröten,* O. H. G. *ruozzan.*

Rope. (E.) M. E. *roop.* A.S. *rāp,* a cord, rope.+Du. *reep,* Icel. *reip,* Swed. *rep,* Dan. *reb*; Goth. *skauda-raip,* shoe-latchet; G. *reif,* circle, hoop, ring, sometimes a rope. All from Teut. base **raip-,* with the sense of 'strip,' hence 'string.' Perhaps from the 2nd grade of Teut. **reip-an-,* to cut; see **Reap** (Franck). And cf. **Ripe, Rip.** Der. *rop-y,* stringy, glutinous; *stir-rup.*

Roquelaure, a short cloak. (F.) Named after the duke of *Roquelaure* (ab. 1715).—Todd.

Rose. (L.—Gk.—Armenian.) A.S. *rose.* —L. *rosa*; borrowed from Gk. *ῥόδον,* a rose (whence a form ** ῥοδια > rosa*); Æolic *βρόδον* (for **Ϝρόδον*). — Armen. *ward,* a rose; whence also Pers. *gūl.* See **Julep.** Der. *rhododendron* (Gk. δένδρον, a tree).

Rosemary. (F.—L.) M.E. *rosmarin.* —O. F. *rosmarin* (Cot.). —L. *rōsmarīnus, rōsmarīnum,* rosemary, lit. sea-dew; called *rōs maris* in Ovid. —L. *rōs,* dew; *marīnus,* marine. Named from some fancied connexion with sea-spray; altered to *rosemary* (as if for *rose of Mary*).

Rosin; see **Resin.**

Roster, a military register. (Du.) From Du. *rooster,* a grate, gridiron; hence, a list in parallel lines; lit. ' roaster.' — Du. *roosten,* to roast; see **Roast.**

Rostrum. (L.) L. *rostrum,* a beak; pl. *rostra,* a pulpit for speakers in the forum, adorned with beaks of ships taken from the Antiates. For **rōd-trum.*—L. *rōdere,* to gnaw, to peck. See **Rodent.** (Cf. *claus-trum < *claud-trum.*)

Rot, vb. (E.) A weak verb; the proper pp. is *rotted,* but *rotten* is common, which is a Scand. form (see below). M. E. *roten,* pp. *roted.* A.S. *rotian,* pp. *rotod.*+Du. *rotten,* to rot; O. H. G. *rozēn* (also *rōzen*), to rot. See further under **Rotten.**

Rotary, turning like a wheel. (L.) Formed from L. *rota,* a wheel. + Gael.

and Irish *roth,* W. *rhod,* Lithuan. *ratas*; G. *rad,* a wheel. Also Skt. *ratha-,* a chariot, car. All from Idg. root RET, as in O. Irish *reth-im,* I run; Lith. *ritt-u,* I roll, turn round. Brugm. i. § 159. Der. *rotate,* from pp. of L. *rotāre,* to turn round.

Rote (1), routine, repetition. (F.—L.) M. E. *bi rote,* with repetition, by heart; lit. in a beaten track.—O.F. *rote* (F. *route*), a way, a beaten track. See **Route.**

Rote (2), an old musical instrument. (F. —G.—C.) O. F. *rote,* a kind of fiddle; answering to O. H. G. *hrota, rota,* a rote; Low L. *chrotta,* a violin; Of Celtic origin.—W. *crwth,* a violin; Gael. *cruit,* a harp; O. Irish *crot,* a harp. (Stokes-Fick, p. 99.) See **Crowd** (2).

Rother, an ox. (E.) M.E. *ruðer.* Late A.S. *hrūðeru,* pl.; orig. *hrȳðer, hrīðer*; and (in comp.) *hrīð-. Hrīð-< hrinð-,* cognate with G. *rind.* Cf. also Du. *rund.* See Kluge and Franck.

Rotten, putrid. (Scand.) M. E. *roten.* —Icel. *rotinn,* Swed. *rutten,* Dan. *raaden,* rotten. The Icel. *rotinn* is the pp. of a lost strong verb **rjóta,* to decay, orig. to soak, wet, allied to A. S. *rēotan,* O. H. G. *riuzan,* to weep, shed tears; cf. Lith. *raudóti,* Skt. *rud,* to weep. (√REUD.) See **Rot.** Brugm. i. § 594.

Rotundity. (F.—L.) F. *rotonditē.*— L. *rotunditātem,* acc. of *rotunditās,* roundness.—L. *rotundus,* round; see **Round.**

Rouble, Ruble, a Russian coin. (Russ.) Russ. *ruble,* a rouble, 100 copecks. Perhaps from Pers. *rūpīya,* a rupee (Miklosich). See **Rupee.**

Roué. (F.—L.) F. *roué,* lit. broken on the wheel; hence a profligate, supposed to merit that punishment. Pp. of *rouer,* to turn round (L. *rotāre*). —F. *roue,* a wheel. —L. *rota,* a wheel. See **Rotary.**

Rouge, red paint. (F.—L.) F. *rouge,* red. —L. acc. *rubeum,* red; (whence F. *rouge,* like F. *rage* from L. *rabiem*). Allied to L. *ruber,* red. See **Red.**

Rough. (E.) M.E. *rough, rugh, row, ruh,* &c. A.S. *rūh,* rough, hairy; also *rūg.*+Du. *ruig,* M. Du. *ru,* Dan. *ru,* Low G. *ruug,* O.H.G. *rūh,* G. *rauh.* Cf. Lithuan. *raukas,* a fold, *rùkti,* to wrinkle. ¶ Distinct from *raw.*

Rouleau. (F.—L.) F. *rouleau,* a roll of paper; hence, coins in a roll of paper. Dimin. of O. F. *role,* M. F. *roule,* a roll; see **Roll.**

roulette, a game of chance. (F.—L.)

F. *roulette*, a game in which a ball rolls on a turning table; dimin. of *rouelle*, a little wheel; see **Rowel**.

Roun, Round, to whisper. (E.) Shak. has *round*, with excrescent *d*. M. E. *rounen*. A. S. *rūnian*, to whisper. ─ A. S. *rūn*, a whisper. ✚ G. *raunen*, to whisper; from O. H. G. *rūn*, a secret; see **Rune**.

Round. (F. ─ L.) O. F. *roönd*, F. *rond*. ─ L. *rotundus*, round. ─ L. *rota*, a wheel. See **Rotary**.

roundel, a kind of ballad. (F. ─ L.) O. F. *rondel*, later *rondeau*, a poem containing a line which recurs or comes *round* again. ─ F. *rond*, round (above).

roundelay. (F. ─ L.) M. F. *rondelet*, dimin. of O. F. *rondel* above. ¶ Prob. confused, in spelling, with E. *lay*, a song.

Rouse (1), to excite, to wake up. (Scand.) '*Exciter*, to stir up, *rowse*;' Cot. ─ Swed. *rusa*, to rush, *rusa upp*, to start up; Dan. *ruse*, to rush. Cf. A. S. *hrēosan*, to rush, to fall down quickly; from Teut. base **hreus-*.

Rouse (2), a drinking-bout. (Scand.) In Shak. ─ Dan. *ruus*, intoxication; Dan. *sove rusen ud* = to sleep out a rouse, to sleep oneself sober; Swed. *rus*, drunkenness. ✚ Du. *roes*, drunkenness. Prob. allied to East Friesic *rūse*, noise, uproar, ' row;' *rūsen*, to make a noise. [G. *rausch*, a drunken fit, is borrowed from some other Teut. dialect.] ¶ Really a *Danish* word; such a bout being called 'the Danish *rowza*.' Cf. **Row** (3).

Rout (1) a defeat, (2) a troop or crowd. (F. ─ L.) F. *route*, ' a rowt, defeature; also a rowt, heard, flock, troope; also a rutt, way, path;' Cot. ─ L. *rupta*, pp. of *ruptus*, broken; from *rumpere*. This L. *rupta* came to mean (1) a defeat, flying mass of broken troops; (2) a fragment of an army, a troop; (3) a way broken or cut through a forest, a way, route.

route, a way, course. (F. ─ L.) F. *route*, a way, route; see the word above.

routine, a beaten track. (F. ─ L.) F. *routine*, usual course; lit. small path. Dimin. of F. *route* (above).

Rover, a pirate. (Du.) M. E. *rover*. ─ Du. *roover*, a robber, pirate, thief. ─ Du. *rooven*, to rob. ─ Du. *roof*, spoil. ✚ A. S. *rēaf*, Icel. *rauf*, G. *raub*, spoil; see **Reave**. Der. *rove*, vb., to wander; evolved from the sb.

Row (1), a line, rank. (E.) M. E. *rowe*. ─ A. S. *rāw*, *rǣw*, a row; *hegerāw*, a hedge-row. Teut. type **rai(g)wā*, fem., from a root-verb **reihwan*· (pt. t. **raihw*); whence also G. *reih-e*, a row, Du. *rij*, M. Du. *rij-e*, a row, O. H. G. *riga*, a line. Idg. root **reikh*, whence Skt. *rēkhā*, a line.

Row (2), to propel with oars. (E.) M. E. *rowen*. ─ A. S. *rōwan*, to row. ✚ Du. *roeijen*, Icel. *rōa*, Swed. *ro*, Dan. *roe*, M. H. G. *rüejen*. Allied to O. Ir. *rām*, L. *rēmus*, an oar, Skt. *aritra-*, a paddle, rudder, Lithuan. *irti*, to row; Gk. ἐρετμός, a paddle, oar. Der. *rudder*.

Row (3), an uproar. (Scand.) For *rouse*; for loss of final *s*, cf. *pea*, *cherry*, *sherry*, *shay* (*chaise*). See **Rouse** (2).

Rowan-tree; see **Roan-tree**.

Rowel. (F. ─ L.) M. F. *rouelle*, a little wheel (on a bit or a spur). ─ Late L. *rotella*, dimin. of *rota*, a wheel. See **Rotary**.

Rowlock, Rollock, Rullock, the place of support for an oar. (E.) Spelt *orlok* in the Liber Albus, pp. 235, 237. A corruption of *oar-lock*. ─ A. S. *ārloc*, a rowlock. ─ A. S. *ār*, oar; *loc*, cognate with G. *loch*, a hole. The orig. rowlocks were actual holes, and were called also *oar-holes*.

Royal. (F. ─ L.) M. E. *real*, *roial*. ─ O. F. *real*, *roial* (F. *royal*). ─ L. *rēgālis*, royal; see **Regal**. Doublet, *regal*.

Rub. (E.) M. E. *rubben*. Not in A. S. ✚ Dan. *rubbe*, Norw. *rubba*, E. Fries. *rubben*, to rub, scrub; Norw. *rubben*, rough, uneven; E. Fries. *rubberig*, rough; Du. *robbelig*, 'rugged,' Sewel; also (from E.) Gael. *rub*, to rub, Irish *rubadh*, a rubbing, W. *rhwbio*, to rub. Further allied to Icel. *rūfinn*, rough, Lith. *rupàs*, rough. ¶ Not allied to G. *reiben*; rather to L. *rumpere* and E. **Reave**.

Rubbish, broken stones, waste matter, refuse. (F. ─ O. H. G.) M. E. *robows*, *robeux*, Prompt. Parv.; pl. of an old form **robel*, clearly represented by mod. E. *rubble*; see below. ¶ *Rubbish* is, in fact, a corrupt form of the old plural of *rubble*.

rubble, broken stones, rubbish. (F. ─ O. H. G.) '*Rubble*, or *rubbish* of old houses;' Baret (1580). M. E. *robell*, Palladius, p. 13, l. 340. This answers exactly to an old form **robel*, O. F. **robel*, only found in the pl. *robeux*. 'A grete loode of *robeux*;' cited by Way in Prompt. Parv. A. F. *robous* (for **robeus*), rubbish, Liber Albus, p. 579. Obviously the dimin.

of F. *robe* in the sense of 'trash,' so well preserved in the cognate Ital. *roba*, 'a gowne, a robe, wealth, goods, geare, trash, pelfe,' Florio. Cf. Ital. *robaccia*, old goods, rubbish; *robiccia*, trifles, rubbish; from *roba*. See **Robe**.

Rubicund, ruddy. (F.—L.) F. *rubicond*. − L. *rubicundus*, very red. − L. *rubēre*, to be red. See **Red**.

rubric, a direction printed in red. (F. − L.) F. *rubrique*. − L. *rubrīca*, red earth; also a title written in red. − L. *ruber*, red (above).

ruby, a red gem. (F.−L.) O. F. *rubi*, *rubis*; F. *rubis* (where *s* is the old sign of the nom. case). Cf. Span. *rubi*, *rubin*, Port. *rubim*, Ital. *rubino*. − Late L. *rubīnus*, a ruby; from its colour. − L. *rubeus*, red; *rubēre*, to be red. Allied to **Red**.

Ruck (1), a fold, crease. (Scand.) Icel. *hrukka*, a wrinkle; cf. *hrokkin*, curled, pp. of *hrökkva*, to recoil, give way, curl; Norw. *rukka*, a wrinkle. Cf. Swed. *rynka*, Dan. *rynke*, a wrinkle. From Teut. base **hrenk-* (Noreen).

Ruck (2), a heap, small pile. (Scand.) Norw. and M. Swed. *ruka*, a heap; cf. Icel. *hraukr*, a rick, heap; see **Rick**.

Rudder. (E.) M. E. *roder*, *rother*. A. S. *rōðer*, a paddle. Here *rō-ðer* = rowing implement; from *rōw-an*, to row. (Paddles preceded rudders.) + Du. *roer* (for *roeder*), an oar, rudder; Swed. *roder*, *ror*; Dan. *ror*; G. *ruder*. See **Row** (2).

Ruddock, a red-breast. (E.) A. S. *rudduc*. Hence W. *rhuddog*, Corn. *ruddoc*, a red-breast. See below.

ruddy. (E.) M. E. *rody*, A. S. *rudig*, ruddy. From A. S. **rud-*, weak grade of *rēodan*, to redden, a strong verb, whence also A. S. *rēad*, red; see **Red**.

Rude. (F.−L.) F. *rude*.−L. *rudem*, acc. of *rudis*, rough, raw, rude.

rudiment. (F.−L.) F. *rudiment*.− L. *rudīmentum*, a thing in the first rough state, a first attempt.−L. *rudi-s*, rude.

Rue (1), to be sorry for. (E.) M. E. *rewen*. A. S. *hrēowan* (pt. t. *hrēaw*).+ O. Sax. *hrewan*, O. H. G. *hriuwan*, G. *reuen*. Cf. Icel. *hryggr*, grieved, *hrygð*, ruth. Teut. type **hrewwan-*, to pity.

Rue (2), a plant. (F.−L.−Gk.) F. *rue*.−L. *rūta*.−Gk. ῥυτή, rue; whence also G. *raute*. Cf. A. S. *rūde*, rue.

Ruff (1), a kind of frill. (E.) 'Ruffe of a shirt;' Levins (1570). So called from its uneven surface; apparently shortened from *ruffle*, verbal sb. from *ruffle*, vb., which was in early use. See **Ruffle** (1).

Ruff (2), the name of a bird. (E.?) Said to be named from the male having a *ruff* round its neck in the breeding season. But the female is called a *reeve*, which points to formation by vowel-change from some different source.

Ruff (3), a fish. (E.?) M. E. *ruffe*. Origin unknown.

Ruff (4), a game at cards. (F.) A modification of O. F. *roffle*, *roufle*, *ronfle*, M. F. *ronfle*, 'hand-ruffe, at cards,' Cotgrave; *jouer à la ronfle*, 'to play at handruffe, also to snort,' id. Cf. Ital. *ronfa*, ruff; *ronfare*, to snort, to trump at cards. From Tuscan *ronfiare* (F. *ronfler*), to snore, snort; supposed to be from L. *re-in-flāre*, to re-inflate (Körting). See **Inflate**. But it may be of imitative origin.

Ruffian, a bully. (F.—Ital.—Teut.) Walloon *rouffian*, M. F. *rufien*, *ruffien*, 'a bawd, pandar;' Cot.−Ital. *ruffiano*, *roffiano*, 'a pander, ruffian, swaggrer;' Florio. For **rufflānus*, formed with L. suffix *-ānus* from Low G. *ruffeln*, to act as pandar. See **Ruffle** (2).

Ruffle (1), to disorder a dress. (E.) M. E. *ruffelen*, to entangle, run into knots; also (apparently) to rumple, Cursor Mundi, 26391. Allied to **Ruff** (1) above.+M. Du. *ruyffelen*, to ruffle, wrinkle, *ruyffel*, a wrinkle, a crumple; E. Fries. *ruffelen*, *ruffeln*, to pleat. From **ruf*, weak grade of Teut. **reufan-*, to break, tear; see **Reave**. Cf. Lithuan. *ruple*, rough bark on old trees. Der. *ruffle*, sb.

Ruffle (2), to bluster, be turbulent. (M. Du.) Obsolete. *Rufflers* were cheating bullies, highwaymen, lawless or violent men (Nares).−M. Du. *roffelen*, *roffen*, to pandar (Oudemans); Low G. *ruffeln*, to pandar, *ruffeler*, a pimp, intriguant; Dan. *ruffer*, a pandar. A *ruffler* and a *ruffian* are much the same. See **Ruffian**.

Rug. (Scand.) Swed. *rugg*, rough entangled hair, cf. M. Swed. *ruggig*, rough, hairy; Icel. *rögg*, shagginess. Also Low G. *ruug*, rough, *rugen*, to be rough (like flocks of hair); E. Fries. *rūg*, rough, *ruge*, a roughness, a rough side of a skin; *ruger*, a rough-hided or furry animal (e. g. a cat). See **Rough**.

rugged. (Scand.) M. E. *rugged*; also *ruggy*, Ch. C. T., A 2883. The latter is from M. Swed. *ruggig*, rough, hairy.− Swed. *rugg*, rough entangled hair (above).

Rugose, full of wrinkles. (L.) L. *rūgōsus,* adj., from *rūga,* a wrinkle. Cf. Lith. *raŭkas,* a wrinkle, *runkù,* I grow wrinkled. Brugm. ii. § 628.

Ruin. (F. – L.) F. *ruine.* – L. *ruīna,* an overthrow. – L. *ruere,* to rush, fall down. Brugm. ii. § 529.

Rule, sb. (F. – L.) M. E. *reule, riwle.* – A. F. *reule,* O. F. *riule, reule* (F. *règle*). – L. *rēgula,* a rule. – L. *regere,* to rule. See **Regent.**

Rum (1), a spirituous liquor. (Prov. E.) Called *rumbo* in Smollett, Per. Pickle, c. ii and c. ix; this is short for the sailor's word *rumbowling,* grog. Orig. called *Rumbullion* in Barbadoes, A. D. 1651; from Devonsh. *rumbullion,* uproar, rumpus, which is prob. allied to **Rumble.**

Rum (2), strange, queer. (Hindi.) *'Rum,* gallant, a cant word;' Bailey (1737).· *Rum* really means ' Gypsy'; hence ' good' from a Gypsy point of view, but 'suspicious' from an outsider's point of view. Hence *rome bouze, rum booze,* good wine. *Rom* means 'a husband, a Gypsy'; *rŏmmani,* adj., Gypsy. This Gypsy word *rom* answers to Hindi *ḍom* (with initial cerebral *d,* resembling *r*), a man of low caste; Skt. *ḍomba-,* 'a man of low caste, who gains his livelihood by singing and dancing;' Benfey.

Rumb, Rhumb, a line for directing a ship's course on a chart; a point of the compass. (F. – Span. – L. – Gk.) See *Rumb* in Phillips. – F. *rumb,* 'a roomb, or point of the compasse, a line drawn directly from wind to wind in a compasse, traversboord, or sea-card;' Cot. – Span. (and Port.) *rumbo,* a ship's course (represented by spiral lines on a globe). – L. *rhombum,* acc. of *rhombus,* a magician's circle, a rhombus. – Gk. ῥόμβος, a top, a magic wheel, whirling motion; also a rhombus. See **Rhomb.** *Rhomb* meant revolution of the sphere, Milton, P. L. viii. 134; hence whirling or spiral lines, &c. ¶ No connexion with Du. *ruim,* which merely means room or space, or sometimes the hold of a ship, i. e. its room or capacity.

Rumble, to make a low, heavy sound. (E.) Prov. E. *rommle, rummle;* M. E. *romblen* (with excrescent *b*). Frequent. form, meaning 'to repeat the sound *rum*'; cf. L. *rūmor,* a rumour; Skt. *ru,* to hum. See **Rumour.** + Du. *rommelen,* Low G. and Pomeran. *rummeln,* Dan. *rumle,* to rumble, buzz.

Ruminate. (L.) From pp. of L. *rūmināre,* to chew the cud, ruminate. – L. *rūmin-,* for *rūmen,* the throat, gullet. Allied to L. *rū-gīre,* to roar, bray, Gk. ὠ-ρυ-γή, a roaring, ὠ-ρύ-ομαι, I roar; Skt. *ru,* to hum, bray, roar. (√REU.) See **Rumour.**

Rummage, to search thoroughly. (E.; *with* F. *suffix.*) Due to the sb. *roomage,* i. e. stowage; whence *roomage, romage,* vb., to find room for close packing of things in a ship, also *rummage,* vb., to clear a ship's hold, to search narrowly (Phillips).

Rummer, a sort of drinking-glass. (Du.) Used for Rhenish wine. ' Rhenish *rummers*;' Dryden. – Du. *roemer, romer,* a wine-glass; Low G. *römer,* a large wine-glass; hence G. *römer,* a rummer. Du. *roemer* is prob. from Du. *roem,* boasting, praise; as if 'a glass to drink in praise of a toast'; Franck. Cf. G. *ruhm,* praise; O. Sax. *hrōm;* also Icel. *hrōðr,* praise. ¶ Also M. Du. *roomer* (Hexham); which some explain as a ' Romish glass.'

Rumour. (F. – L.) M. E. *rumour.* – F. *rumeur.* – L. acc. *rūmōrem,* from *rū-mor,* a noise, murmur. Cf. L. *rūmitāre,* to spread reports. – √REU, to make a humming noise. See **Rumble, Ruminate.**

Rump. (E.) M. E. *rumpe.* + Icel. *rumpr,* Swed. *rumpa,* Dan. *rumpe;* M. Du. *rompe,* ' the bulke of a body or corps, or a bodie without a head,' Hexham; Du. *romp;* Low G. *rump,* trunk (of the body); G. *rumpf.*

Rumple. (E.) The M. E. form is *rimplen,* to rimple. *Rimple* and *rumple* are from the same verb, viz. A. S. *hrimpan* (pp. *gehrumpen*), to wrinkle; see **Rimple.** +M. Du. *rompelen, rompen,* to wrinkle; *rompel, rimpel,* a wrinkle; cf. G. *rümpfen,* to wrinkle; O. H. G. *hrimfan,* str. vb.

Run. (E.) M. E. *rinnen,* pt. t. *ran,* pp. *runnen, ronnen;* A. S. *rinnan,* pt. t. *rann,* pp. *gerunnen;* also found in the transposed form *irnan,* pt. t. *arn.* + Du. *rennen,* Icel. *renna,* Dan. *rinde,* Swed. *rinna,* Goth. *rinnan,* G. *rinnen.* See Brugm. i. § 67; ii. § 654.

Runagate, a vagabond. (F. – L.) A corruption of M. E. *renegat,* an apostate, villain; Ch. C. T. 5353. [The corruption was due to a popular etymology from *runne a gate,* run on the road, hence, to be a vagabond.] – O. F. *renegat,* ' a renegadoe;' Cot. — Late L. *renegātus*, pp. of *renegāre*, to deny again, forsake the faith. — L. *re.* again ; *negāre*, to deny ; see Negation.

Rundlet, Runlet, a small barrel. (F. – L.) Formerly *roundlet*; dimin. of O. F. *rondelle*, a little barrel, named from its roundness. — F. *rond*, round. — L. *rotundus*, round. — L. *rota*, a wheel ; see Round.

Rune, one of the old characters used for incised inscriptions. (E.) A learned term. A. S. *rūn*, a rune, mystery, secret conference, whisper. Orig. sense 'whisper' or murmur, hence a mystery, lastly an incised character, because writing was a secret known to few.+Goth. *rūna*, O. H. G. *rūna*, a secret, counsel ; O. Irish *rūn*, W. *rhin*, a secret. Idg. type **rūnā*, fem. Cf. Gk. ἐρευνάω, I search out, ἔρευνα, fem., an enquiry.

Rung, a round of a ladder. (E.) M. E. *ronge*, a stake. A. S. *hrung*, a stake of a cart, beam or spar.+M. Du. *ronge*, a beam of a plough ; G. *runge*, a pin, a bolt ; Goth. *hrugga* (= *hrunga*), a staff. Cf. also Icel. *röng*, rib in a ship. Perhaps allied to Ring. The sense seems to be 'rounded stick.'

Runnel, a stream. (E.) A. S. *rynel*; cf. *ryne*, a course, allied to *runn-*, weak grade of *rinnen*, to run ; see Run.

Runt, a bullock, heifer. (Du.) From Du. *rund* (Hexham). And see Rother.

Rupee, an Indian coin. (Hind. — Skt.) Hindūstānī *rūpiyah*, a rupee. — Skt. *rūpya-*, handsome, also (as sb.) wrought silver. — Skt. *rūpa-*, beauty.

Rupture. (F. – L.) F. *rupture*. — L. *ruptūra*, a breakage. — L. *rupt-us*, pp. of *rumpere*, to break (pt. t. *rūpī*). Allied to Reave. (√REUP.) Brugm. i. § 466.

Rural, belonging to the country. F. – L.) F. *rural*. — L. *rūrālis*, adj. — L. *rūr-*, stem of *rūs*, country. See Rustic.

Rusa, a kind of deer. (Malay.) Malay *rūsa*, a deer. See Babirusa.

Ruse, a trick. (F. – L.) F. *ruse*, a trick. — F. *ruser*, to beguile ; contr. from O. F. *reüser*, to refuse, recoil, escape, dodge. — L. *recūsāre*, to refuse, to oppose a cause. — L. *re-*, back ; *caussa*, a cause. See Recusant.

Rush (1), to move swiftly forward. (E.) M. E. *ruschen*. + M. H. G. *rūschen* (G. *rauschen*), to rush, rustle, roar (as water) ; Du. *ruischen*, to murmur (as

water), to rustle. Cf. M. Swed. *ruska*, to rush ; M. Swed. *rusa*, N. Fries. *ruse*, to rush. See Rouse (1).

Rush (2), a plant. (E. *or* L.) M. E. *rusche*, *rische*, *resche*. A. S. *risce*, *resce*, a rush ; oldest form *risc*. + Du. *rusch*, rush, reed ; E. Fries. *rüske* ; Low G. *rusk* ; N. Fries. *rusken*, pl., rushes. Perhaps borrowed from L. *ruscum*, butcher's broom ; the Teut. word was Goth. *raus* (cf. F. *ros-eau*), Du. *roer*, G. *rohr* (Teut. type **rauzom*, neut.) ; with which *ruscus* may have been confused. ¶ But this does not account for A. S. *risc*. **Der.** *bul-rush* (prob. for *bole-rush*, round-stemmed rush) ; cf. *bull-weed*, i. e. bole-weed, knapweed.

Rusk. (Span.) Span. *rosca de mar*, sea-rusks, a kind of biscuit ; *rosca*, a roll (twist) of bread, also a screw. Cf. Port. *rosca*, the winding of a snake. Origin unknown.

Russet. (F. – L.) M. E. *russet*. — M. F. *rousset*, 'russet, ruddy;' Cot. Dimin. of F. *roux* (fem. *rousse*), reddish. — L. *russus*, reddish. Allied to Gk. ἐ-ρυθ-ρός, red ; see Red. Cf. Brugm. i. § 759.

rust. (E.) Prov. E. *rowst*. A. S. *rūst*, rust ; orig. redness. Allied to A. S. *rudu*, ruddiness, and *rēad*, red. + Du. *roest*, Dan. *rust*, Swed. G. *rost*. Teut. type **rūsto-*, from Idg. **reudh-to-* ; see Ruddy. Cf. Lith. *rudis*, rust ; L. *rōbīgo*, *rūbīgo* ; Polish *rdza*, rust. Brugm. i. § 759.

Rustic. (F. – L.) F. *rustique.* — L. *rusticus*, belonging to the country. — L. *rūs*, the country. Cf. Russ. *raviina*, a plain, Zend *ravan*, O. Irish *roe*, a plain ; see Room.

Rustle. (E.) Cf. A. S. *ge-hruxl*, a noise, tumult. Frequent. of Rush (1), q. v. Cf. M. Du. *ruyselen*, 'to rustle,' Hexham ; Low G. and Pomer. *russeln* ; M. Swed. *ruska*, to shake, rush ; G. *rauschen*, *ruschen*, to rustle, to rush.

Rut (1), a track left by a wheel. (F. – L.) F. *route*, 'a rutt, way ;' Cot. See Rout. Doublets, *rout*, *route*.

Rut (2), to copulate, as deer. (F. – L.) M. E. *rutien*, to rut ; from *rut*, sb. — M. F. *rut*, *ruit*, 'the rut of deer or boars.' — L. *rūgītum*, acc. of *rūgītus*, the roaring of lions ; hence, the noise made by deer in rut-time. — L. *rūgīre*. to roar (whence M. F. *ruir*). See Rumour.

Ruth, pity. (E.) M.E. *reuthe*. Formed from A.S. *hrēow*, s. f., pity (cf. G. *reue*), by adding *-th* ; suggested by Icel. *hryggð*, *hrygð*, ruth, sorrow. From A. S. *hrēowan*, to rue; see Rue (1).

Rye. (E.) M. E. *reye*. A. S. *ryge*, rye. **+** Du. *rogge*, Icel. *rugr*, Dan. *rug*, Swed. *råg*, G. *roggen*; O. H. G. *rocco*. Cf. Russ. *roj(e)*, rye; Lithuan. *ruggei*, pl. sb., rye.

Ryot; the same as Rayah, q. v.

S.

Sabaoth, hosts. (Heb.) Heb. *tsevā'ŏth*, armies; pl. of *tsāvā'*, an army. — Heb. *tsāvā'*, to go forth as a soldier.

Sabbath. (L. — Gk. — Heb.) M. E. *sabat*. — L. *sabbatum*. — Gk. *σάββατον*. — Heb. *shabbāth*, rest, sabbath, sabbath-day. — Heb. *shābath*, to rest.

Sable, an animal. (F. — Slavonic.) O.F. *sable*. — Russ. *sobole*, the sable; also a fur-tippet; Polish *sobol*. ¶ As black sable was best liked, the word *sable* (in E. and F.) also means 'black.'

Sabre, Saber. (F. — G. — Gk. ?) F. *sabre*. — G. *säbel* (older form also *sabel*), a falchion. Said to be from Mid. Gk. *ζαβός*, crooked (Diez). We also find Russ. *sablia*, Pol. *szabla*, Hungar. *szablya*, Serv. *sablja*, Wallach. *sabie*; all supposed to be borrowed words.

Saccharine. (F. — L. — Gk. — Skt.) F. *saccharin*, adj.; from L. *saccharon*, sugar. — Gk. *σάκχαρον*. — Skt. *çarkarā*, gravel, candied sugar; see Sugar.

Sacerdotal. (F. — L.) F. *sacerdotal*. — L. *sacerdōtālis*, belonging to a priest. — L. *sacerdōt-*, stem of *sacerdōs*, a priest, lit. 'presenter of offerings or sacred gifts' (Corssen). — L. *sacer*, sacred; *dare*, to give. Cf. *dōs* (stem *dōt-*), a dowry, from *dare*.

Sack (1), a bag. (L. — Gk. — Heb. — Egyptian?) M. E. *sak*. A. S. *sacc*. — L. *saccus*. — Gk. *σάκκος*. — Heb. *saq*, sack-cloth, a sack of corn. Prob. of Egyptian origin; cf. Coptic *sok*, sack-cloth (Peyron). From L. *saccus* are borrowed Du. *zak*, G. *sack*, &c. Der. *sack-cloth*.

sack (2), to plunder. (F. — L., &c.) From the sb. *sack*, pillage. — F. *sac*, ruin, spoil. From the use of a *sack* in removing plunder; Cot. has *à sac, à sac*, 'the word whereby a commander authorizeth his souldiers to sack a place.' Cf. Late L. *saccāre*, to put into a bag; Late L. *saccus*, a garment, a purse, L. *saccus*, a sack; see above.

Sack (3), the name of an old Spanish

wine. (F. — L.) Formerly also *seck*, meaning a 'dry' wine. — F. *sec*, dry; *vin sec*, sack. Cf. Span. *seco*, dry. — L. *siccum*, acc. of *siccus*, dry. *Sherris sack* = Span. *seco de Xeres*; see Sherry.

Sackbut, a kind of wind-instrument. (F. — L. — Gk. — Chaldee.) F. *saquebute*, a sackbut. Substituted, by some perversion, for L. *sambūca*, Dan. iii. 5 (Vulg.), which was a kind of harp. — Gk. *σαμβύκη*. — Chald. *sabb(e)khā*,' a kind of harp. ¶ Cf. Span. *sacabuche*, a tube used as a pump; also, a sackbut, trombone. Explained, by popular etymology, as 'that which exhausts the chest,' from the exertion used; as if from Span. *sacar*, to draw out, exhaust, the same as M. F. *sacquer*, to draw out hastily, lit. to draw out of a sack, from Heb. *saq*, a sack; *buche*, maw, stomach, chest.

Sacrament. (L.) L. *sacrāmentum*, an engagement, military oath, vow; in late L.), a sacrament. — L. *sacrāre*, to render sacred. — L. *sacr-*, for *sacer*, sacred (below).

sacred. (F. — L.) *Sacred* is the pp. of M. E. *sacren*, to consecrate, render holy; a verb now obsolete. — F. *sacrer*, to consecrate. — L. *sacrāre*, to consecrate. — L. *sacr-*, for *sacer*, holy. From base *sac-* of L. *sancīre*, to make holy. Brugm. ii. § 744. (√SAK.)

sacrifice. (F. — L.) F. *sacrifice*. — L. *sacrificium*, lit. a rendering sacred; cf. *sacrificāre*, to sacrifice. — L. *sacri-*, for *sacer*, sacred; *-ficāre*, for *facere*, to make.

sacrilege. (F. — L.) M. F. *sacrilege*. — L. *sacrilegium*, the stealing of sacred things. — L. *sacri-*, for *sacer*, sacred; *legere*, to gather, steal; see Legend.

sacristan, sexton. (F. — L.) *Sacristan* is rare; it is commonly *sexton*, M. E. *sextein*, orig. a keeper of the sacred vestments, afterwards a grave-digger. — A. F. *secrestein*, M. F. *sacristain*, 'a sexton or vestry-keeper;' Cot. — Late L. *sacrist-a*, a sacristan; with suffix *-ānus*. — L. *sacr-*, for *sacer* (above); with suffix *-ista*.

Sad. (E.) The orig. sense was sated; hence tired, grieved. A.S. *sæd*, sated, satiated. **+** O. Sax. *sad*, Icel. *saðr*, Goth. *saths*, G. *satt*, sated, full. Teut. type **sa-doz*, sated; a pp. form. Allied to O. Ir. *sā-ith*, satiety, *sa-thech*, sated; L. *sa-tur*, full; Lith. *so-tùs*, full, *so-tas*, satiety; Gk. *ἄ-σαι*, *ἄ-μεναι*, to satiate. (√SĀ, SA.) Brugm. i. § 196. Allied to Sate, Satiate.

Saddle. (E.) M. E. *sadel*. A. S. *sadol*.
+Du. *zadel*, Icel. *söðull*, Swed. Dan.
sadel, G. *sattel*, O. H. G. *satul*. Teut.
type *saduloz; possibly borrowed from a
derivative of Idg. *sed, to sit, in some
other Idg. language. Cf. O. Slav. *sedlo*,
Russ. *siedlo*, L. *sella* (for *sedla, from *sedēre*,
to sit); but none of these exhibits the
grade *sad.

Sadducee. (L. – Gk. – Heb.) L. pl.
Sadducæi. – Gk. pl. Σαδδουκαῖοι. – Heb. pl.
tsedūqīm; pl. of *tsādōq*, just, righteous. –
Heb. *tsādaq*, to be just. Some derive it
from *Tsādōq* (*Zadok*), the founder of the
sect, whose name meant ' the just.'

Safe. (F. – L.) M. E. *sauf*. – F. *sauf*,
safe. – L. *saluum*, acc. of *saluus*, safe. See
Salvation. Cf. O. Norman dial. *saf*,
safe.

Saffron, a plant. (F. – Arab.) A. F.
saffran, F. *safran*. – Arab. *za'farān*,
saffron.

Sag, to droop. (E.) M. E. *saggen*.
Not in A. S. Low G. *sakken*, to settle (as
dregs); E. Fries. *sakken*, Du. *zakken*, to
sink; Swed. *sacka*, to settle, sink down;
cf. Dan. *sakke*, to have stern-way. Hardly
allied to *sink*.

Saga, a tale. (Scand.) Icel. *saga*, a
tale; cf. Icel. *segja*, to say. See Say (1),
Saw (2).

Sagacious. (L.) From L. *sagāci-*,
decl. stem. of *sagax*, of quick perception;
with suffix *-ous*. – L. *sāgīre*, to perceive by
the senses.+Goth. *sōk-jan*, A. S. *sēcan*, to
seek. See Seek. Brugm. i. § 187.

Sage (1), wise. (F. – L.) F. *sage*. –
Late L. *sabius, for L. *-sapius*, whence
nesapius, unwise (Petronius); see Schwan.
– L. *sapere*, to be wise. See Sapid.

Sage (2), a plant. (F. – L.) M. E.
sauge. – O. F. *sauge*. – L. *saluia*, sage;
from its supposed healing virtues. – L.
saluāre, to heal; *saluus*, safe, hale, sound.
See Salvation.

Sagittarius. (L.) L. *sagittārius*, an
archer. – L. *sagitta*, an arrow.

Sago, a starch. (Malay.) Malay *sāgu*,
sāgū, sago, pith of a tree named *rumbiya*.

Sahib, sir, master; a title. (Hind. --
Arab.) Hind. *sāhib*. – Arab. *sāhib*, lord,
master; orig. ' companion.' Rich. Dict.,
p. 924.

Sail, sb. (E.) M. E. *seil*. A. S. *segel*,
segl, a sail.+Du. *zeil*, Icel. *segl*, Dan. *seil*,
Swed. G. *segel*. Teut. type *seglom, neut.
Sense unknown; perhaps ' driver '; cf. Gk.

ἔχειν νῆας, to urge on ships, Od. ix. 279.
See Scheme.

Saint. (F. – L.) M. E. *seint*, *saint*. –
A. F. *seint*; F. *saint*. – L. *sanctum*, acc.
of *sanctus*, holy. – L. *sanctus*, pp. of *sancīre*,
to render sacred; see Sacred.

sainfoin. (F. – L.) F. *sainfoin*, M.F.
sainct-foin (Cot.); as if ' holy hay.' – L.
sanctum fænum, holy hay. ¶ But thought
to represent *sain foin*, i. e. ' wholesome
hay.' – L. *sānum fænum*; see Sane.

Sake. (E.) M. E. *sake*, purpose, cause.
A. S. *sacu*, strife, dispute, crime, law-suit;
orig. ' contention.' + Du. *zaak*, matter,
affair, business; Icel. *sök*, a charge, crime;
Dan. *sag*, Swed. *sak*, G. *sache*. Teut.
type *sakā, fem., strife. From Teut.
**sakan-*, to contend, as in Goth. *sakan*,
A. S. *sacan*, O. H. G. *sahhan*, str. vb. See
Soke.

Saker, a kind of falcon; a small piece
of artillery. (F. – Span. – Arab.) (The
gun was called after the falcon; cf. *musket*.)
– M. F. *sacre*, ' a saker; the hawk, and the
artillery so called; ' Cot. – Span. *sacre*, a
saker (in both senses). – Arab. *saqr*, a
hawk; Rich. Dict., p. 938. Engelmann
has shewn that the word is not of Lat.
origin, as said by Diez. (Devic; and
Körting, § 1642.)

Salaam, Salam. (Arab.) Arab.
salām, saluting, wishing peace; a salutation. – Arab. *salm*, saluting.+Heb. *shalōm*,
peace, from *shālam*, to be safe.

Salad. (F. – Ital. – L.) F. *salade*. –
M. Ital. *salata*, a salad of herbs; lit.
' salted; ' fem. of *salato*, salted, pickled,
pp. of *salare*, to salt. – Ital. *sale*, salt. –
L. *sāl*, salt. See Salt.

Salamander, a reptile. (F. – L. –
Gk.) F. *salamandre*. – L. *salamandra*.
– Gk. σαλαμάνδρα, a kind of lizard. Of
Eastern origin; cf. Pers. *samandar*, a
salamander.

Salary, stipend. (F. – L.) F. *salaire*.
– L. *salārium*, orig. salt-money, given to
soldiers to buy salt. – L. *sāl*, salt. See
Salt.

Sale. (E.) M. E. *sale*. A. S. *sala*.+
Icel. *sala*, fem., sal, neut., a sale, bargain;
Swed. *salu*; O. H. G. *sala*. Orig. sense
' delivery,' or ' a handing over '; as in
O. H. G. *sala*. Der. *sell*, *handsel*.

Salic, Salique. (F. – O. H. G.) F.
Salique, belonging to the Salic tribe. This
was a Frankish tribe, prob. named from
the river *Sala* (now Yssel).

Salient. (L.) From pres. pt. of L. *salīre*, to leap, spring forward.+Gk. ἄλλο-μαι, I leap. (√SAL.) Brugm. i. § 514 (3).

Saline. (F. – L.) F. *salin*, fem. *saline*, adj. – L. *salīnus*, as in *salīnæ*, salt-pits. – L. *sāl*, salt. See Salt.

Saliva. (L.) L. *salīua*, spittle; whence also O. Ir. *saile*, W. *haliw*, saliva. Der. *saliv-ate*.

Sallet, a kind of helmet. (F. – Ital. – L.) Also *salade*. – M. F. *salade*, a sallet, head-piece. – Ital. *celata* (or Span. *celada*), a helmet. – L. *cælāta* (*cassis*), an ornamented helmet. – L. *cælātus*, pp. of *cælāre*, to engrave, ornament (steel). – L. *cælum*, a chisel, graver. Allied to *cædere*, to cut. Brugm. i. § 944. See Cæsura.

Sallow (1), **Sally,** a kind of willow. (E.) M. E. *salwe*. – O. Merc. *salh* (A. S. *sealh*), a willow; pl. *salas*, later *salgas*, +Icel. *selja*, Swed. *sälg*, *sälj*, Dan. *selje*, G. *sahl-weide*, O. H. G. *salaha* (whence F. *saule*); also L. *salix*, Gael. *seileach*, Irish *sail*, *saileach*, W. *helyg* (pl.), Gk. ἑλίκη, a willow.

Sallow (2), pale, wan. (E.) M. E. *salow*. A. S. *salu*, sallow. + Du. *zaluw*, Icel. *sölr*, O. H. G. *salo*, tawny (whence F. *sale*, dirty). Teut. type *salwoz*. Brugm. i. 375 (9).

Sally. (F. – L.) M. E. *salien*. – F. *saillir*, to issue forth; also to leap. – L. *salīre*, to leap. See Salient. Der. *sally*, sb., from F. *saillie*, a sally, from the fem. of pp. *sailli*.

Salmagundi, a seasoned hodge-podge. (F. – Ital. – L.) F. *salmigondis*, spelt *salmagondin* in Cotgrave, who describes the dish. Orig. 'seasoned salt-meats.' – Ital. *salami*, pl. of *salame*, salt-meat, from L. *sāl*, salt; *conditi*, pl. of *condito*, seasoned, savoury, from L. *condītus*, pp. of *condīre*, to pickle, season.

Salmon. (F. – L.) M. E. *salmon*, *saumon*. – O. F. *saumon*; A. F. *salmon*. – L. *salmōnem*, acc. of *salmo*, a salmon. Perhaps 'a leaper.' – L. *salīre*, to leap.

Saloon. (F. – O. H. G.) F. *salon*, large room. – F. *salle*, room. – O. H. G. *sal* (G. *saal*), an abode, hall, room. + Du. *zaal*, Icel. *salr*, A. S. *sæl*, *sele*, *salor*, hall. Orig. 'an abode;' cf. Goth. *saljan*, to dwell.

Salt. (E.) M. E. *salt*. O. Merc. *salt*, A. S. *sealt*, both adj. and sb. So also O. Fries. *salt*, Icel. *saltr*, Dan. Swed. *salt*, Du. *zout*, all adjectives, from a Teut. type

saltoz; cf. W. *hallt*, adj. salt, and L. *salsus*, salted. The sb. forms appear in L. *sāl*, Gk. ἅλs, Russ. *sole*; also in Goth. *salt*, G. *salz*, Du. *zout*; also in O. Irish *salann*, W. *halen*, *halan*. (See Kluge and Prellwitz.) Brugm. i.

Saltation, dancing. (L.) Rare; from L. *saltātio*, a dancing. – L. *saltātus*, pp. of *saltāre*, to dance, frequent. of *salīre*, to leap. See Salient.

Salt-cellar. (E.; *and* F. – L.) For *salt-sellar* or *salt-selar*, where *selar* is an old word for 'salt-holder'; so that the prefix *salt* is superfluous. – A. F. *saler*; M. F. *saliere*, 'a salt-seller;' Cot. – L. *salārium*, salt-cellar (in late L.); from L. *salārius*, adj., belonging to salt. – L. *sāl*, salt. See Salient.

Saltire, in heraldry, a St. Andrew's cross. (F. – L.) A cross in this position (×). – O. F. *salteur*, a saltire (Godefroy); M. F. *saultoir*, St. Andrew's cross (Cot.). Also M. F. *sautoir*, orig. a stirrup of a triangular shape Δ, also, a saltire (the cross being named from the position of the stirrup's sides). – Late L. *saltātōrium*, a stirrup. – L. *saltātōrius*, belonging to leaping or springing; suitable for mounting a horse. – L. *saltātor*, a leaper. – L. *saltāre*, frequent. of *salīre*, to leap. See Salient.

Salt-petre, nitre. (E.; *and* F. – L. *and* Gk.) For M. F. *salpestre*, salt-petre (Cot.). – Late L. *salpetra*; L. *sal petræ*, salt of the rock. – L. *sāl*, salt; Gk. πέτρα, a rock; see Salt and Petrify.

Salubrious. (L.) From L. *salūbri-*, healthful. For *salūt-bris*, i. e. healthful. – L. *salūt-*, stem of *salūs*, health; *-bris*, adj. suffix (Brugm. ii. § 77). The L. *salūs* is allied to *saluus*, safe, whole; see Salvation.

salutary. (F. – L.) F. *salutaire*. – L. *salūtāris*, healthful. – L. *salūt-*, stem of *salūs*, health; allied to *saluus*, hale.

salute. (L.) L. *salūtāre*, to wish health to; to greet. – L. *salūt-* (above).

Salvage. (F. – L.) O. F. *salvage*, lit. 'a saving.' – O. F. *salver*, F. *sauver*, to save. – L. *saluāre*, to save. – L. *saluus* (below).

salvation. (F. – L.) O. F. *salvation*. – L. acc. *saluātiōnem*, acc. of *saluātio*, a saving. – L. *saluātus*, pp. of *saluāre*, to save. – L. *saluus*, safe. Brugm. i. § 860 c.

Salve, ointment. (E.) M. E. *salue* (= *salve*). A. S. *sealf*; O. Merc. *salb*, *salf*.+Du. *zalf*, G. *salbe*; cf. Goth. *salbōn*, vb., to anoint. Teut. type *salbā, fem. Allied to Gk. ἔλπos, oil, fat (Hesychius); Skt. *sarpis*, clarified butter. Brugm. i. § 562.

Salver, a plate on which anything is presented. (Span.–L.) In place of Span. *salva*, a salver, a plate on which anything is presented; it also means the previous tasting of viands before they are served up. – Span. *salvar*, to save, free from risk, to taste the food or drink of nobles to save them from poison. – L. *saluāre*, to save (below). ¶ A *salver* (*salva*) is properly a plate or tray on which drink was presented to the taster, and then to the drinker of a health; cf. Span. *hacer la salva*, to drink one's health, also, to make the essay.

Sambo, the offspring of a negro and mulatto. (Span.–L.–Gk.) Span. *zambo*, formerly *çambo* (Pineda), bandy-legged; also as sb., a sambo (in contempt). – Late L. *scambus*. – Gk. σκαμβός, crooked, said of the legs.

Same. (E.) M. E. *same*. A. S. *same*, only as adv., as in *swā same swā men*, the same as men, just like men. The adj. use is Scand.; from Icel. *samr*, Dan. Swed. *samme*, the same.+O. H. G. *sam*, adj., *sama*, adv.; Goth. *sama*, the same (cf. *samana*, together), Gk. ὁμός, Skt. *sama-*, same; cf. Russ. *samuii*, same. Allied to Skt. *sām*, with, Gk. ἅμα, together, L. *simul*, together, *similis*, like.

Samite, a rich silk stuff. (F.–L.–Gk.) O. F. *samit*. – Late L. *examitum*. – Late Gk. ἑξάμιτον, a stuff woven with six kinds of thread. – Gk. ἑξ, six; μίτος, a thread of the woof. See Dimity.

Samovar, a tea-urn. (Russ.) Russ. *samovar'*.

Sampan, a small boat. (Malay–Chin.) Malay *sampan*. – Chin. *sanpan* (Yule).

Samphire, a herb. (F.–L. *and* Gk.) Spelt *sampier* in Baret (1580). – F. *saint Pierre*, St. Peter; whence *herbe de saint Pierre*, samphire. – L. *sanctum*, acc. of *sanctus*, holy; *Petrum*, acc. of *Petrus*, Peter; see Petrel.

Sample. (F.–L.) M. E. *sample*. – O. F. *essample*, *exemple*. – L. *exemplum*, an example, sample; see Example.

   sampler. (F.–L.) O. F. *examplaire* (XIV cent.), the same as *exemplaire*, a pattern. – L. *exemplārium*, late form of *exemplar*, a copy. – L. *exemplāris*, serving as a copy. – L. *exemplum* (above).

Sanatory. (L.) From L. *sānātor*, a healer. – L. *sānāre*, to heal. – L. *sānus*, whole, sane; see Sane.

Sanctify. (F.–L.) F. *sanctifier*. – L. *santificāre*, to make holy. – L. *sancti-*, for *sanctus*, holy; *-ficāre*, for *facere*, to make. See Saint.

   sanctimony. (F.–L.) M.F. *sanctimonie*. – L. *sanctimōnia*, holiness. – L. *sanctus*, holy; see Saint.

   sanction. (F.–L.) F. *sanction*. – L. *sanctiōnem*, acc. of *sanctio*, a rendering sacred. – L. *sanctus*, pp. of *sancīre*, to render sacred. See Sacred.

   sanctity. (L.) From L. *sanctitās*, holiness; cf. F. *sainteté*. – L. *sanctus*, holy; see Saint.

   sanctuary. (F.–L.) M. E. *seintuarie*, a shrine. – O. F. *saintuarie* (F. *sanctuaire*). – L. *sanctuārium*, a shrine. – L. *sanctus*, holy (above).

Sand. (E.) A. S. *sand*. **+** Du. *zand*; Icel. *sandr*; Swed. Dan. G. *sand*; Bavarian *sam(b)d*. Teut. types *sam(a)doz*, m., *sam(a)dom*, n.; Idg. type *samadhos*. Cf. Gk. ἅμαθος, sand.

Sandal, shoe. (F. – L. – Gk. – Pers.) F. *sandale*, f. – L. *sandalia*, pl. of *sandalium*. – Gk. σανδάλιον, dimin. of σάνδαλον, a wooden sole bound on to the feet with straps. Of Pers. origin; cf. Pers. *sandal*, a sandal.

   Sandal-wood. (F. – L. – Gk. – Pers. – Skt.) F. *sandal*, *santal*. – Late L. *santalum*. – Gk. σάνταλον. – Pers. *sandal*, *chandal*, *chandan*. – Skt. *chandana-*, sandal, the tree.

Sandblind, half-blind. (E.) In Shakespeare; a corruption of *sam-blind*, half blind. The prefix ✕ A. S. *sām-*, half, cognate with L. *sēmi-*, Gk. ἡμι-; see Semi-, Hemi-.

Sandwich. (E.) Named from John Montague, 4th Earl of *Sandwich*, died 1792, who used to have *sandwiches* brought to him at the gaming-table. – A. S. *Sandwīc*, Sandwich, a town in Kent.

Sane. (L.) L. *sānus*, of sound mind, whole, safe. Prob. allied to Icel. *sōn*, G. *sühne*, atonement (Kluge).

Sanguine. (F. – L.) F. *sanguin*, bloody, of a sanguine complexion. – L. *sanguineus*, adj.; from *sanguin-* (for *sanguen-*), stem of *sanguis*, blood.

Sanhedrim. (Heb.–Gk.) Late Heb. *sanhedrīn*, borrowed from Gk. συνέδριον, a council; lit. a sitting together. – Gk.

σύν, together; ἕδρα, a seat, from ἕζομαι, I sit; see Sit.

Sans. (F.--L.) F. *sans*, without; O.F. *sens.*—L. *sine*, without.—L. *si ne*, if not, except.

Sanskrit. (Skt.) Skt. *saṁskṛta*, lit. 'symmetrically formed.'—Skt. *sam*, together; *kṛta*, made, from *kṛ*, to make; cf. L. *creāre*, to make. See **Create.**

Sap (1), juice of plants. (E.) A. S. *sæp.* + Du. *sap*; Low G. *sapp*; O. H. G. *saf*, cf. G. *saft*; Icel. *safi.* ¶ Not allied to Gk. ὀπός; but perhaps borrowed from L. *sapa.*

Sap (2), to undermine. (F.—Late L.) O.F. *sapper*, F. *saper.*—O. F. *sappe* (F. *sape*), a kind of hoe. (Cf. Span. *zapa*, Ital. *zappa*, mattock.)—Late L. *sappa, sapa*, a hoe. Origin unknown; Diez suggested Gk. σκαπάνη, a hoe; from σκάπτειν, to dig.

Sapid, savoury. (L.) Rare. L. *sapidus*, savoury.—L. *sapere*, to taste; also to be wise. Cf. O. H. G. *int-seffen*, to taste, mark. Brugm. ii. § 718. Der. *in-sipid.*

sapience. (F.—L.) F. *sapience.*—L. *sapientia*, wisdom.—L. *sapient-*, stem of pres. pt. of *sapere*, to be wise.

Saponaceous, soapy. (L. — Teut.) Coined, as if from L. **sāpōnāceus*, from L. *sāpōnem*, acc. of *sāpo*, soap (Pliny). See **Soap.**

Sapphic, a kind of metre. (L.—Gk.) L. *sapphicus*, belonging to Sappho. — Gk. Σαπφώ, Sappho of Lesbos, died about 592 B.C.

Sapphire. (F.—L.—Gk.—Heb.) F. *saphir.*—L. *sapphīrus.* — Gk. σάπφειρος, a sapphire. — Heb. *sappīr* (with initial *samech*), a sapphire. Cf. Pers. *saffīr*, sapphire.

Saraband. (F.—Span.—Pers.) F. *sarabande*, a Spanish dance.—Span. *zarabanda*, a dance of Moorish origin.—Pers. *sarband*, lit. 'a fillet for fastening a lady's head-dress.'—Pers. *sar*, head ; *band*, band.

Saracen. (L.—Gk.—Arab.) L. *saracēnus*, lit. one of the Eastern people.— Late Gk. Σαρακηνός.—Arab. *sharqīn*, pl. of *sharqīy*, eastern.—Arab. *sharq*, east, rising sun.—Arab. root *sharaqa*, it rose.

Sarcasm, a sneer. (F.—L.—Gk.) F. *sarcasme.*—L. *sarcasmus.*—Gk. σαρκασμός, a sneer. — Gk. σαρκάζειν, to tear flesh, to bite the lips in rage, to sneer. — Gk. σαρκ-, stem of σάρξ, flesh. **Der.** *sarcastic*, Gk. σαρκαστικός, sneering.

Sarcenet, Sarsnet, a thin silk. (F. —L. — Gk. — Arab.) O. F. *sarcenet*, a stuff made by the Saracens. — Low L. *saracēnicum*, sarcenet. — L. *Saracēnus*, Saracen; see **Saracen.**

Sarcophagus. (L.—Gk.) L. *sarcophagus*, a stone tomb ; made of a limestone which was supposed to consume the corpse (Pliny). — Gk. σαρκοφάγος, flesh-consuming; hence lime-stone. — Gk. σαρκο-, for σάρξ, flesh ; φαγεῖν, to eat. See **Sarcasm.**

Sardine (1), a small fish. (F.—L.— Gk.) F. *sardine.*—L. *sardīna, sarda.*— Gk. σαρδίνη, σάρδα, a kind of fish.

Sardine (2), a gem. (L.—Gk.) L. *sardīnus.*—Gk. σαρδίνος; Rev. iv. 3. Named from *Sardis*, in Asia Minor (Pliny).

sardius, a gem. (L.—Gk.) Rev. xxi. 20.—L. *sardius* (Vulgate).—Gk. σάρδιος, σάρδιον, a gem of Sardis (above).

Sardonic, used of grim laughter. (F. —L.—Gk.) F. *sardonique*, formerly *sardonien*, in phrase *ris sardonien*, 'a forced or carelesse mirth ;' Cot.—L. *Sardonicus*, usually *Sardonius.* — Gk. σαρδάνιος, also σαρδόνιος, said to be derived from σαρδόνιον, a plant of Sardinia (Σάρδω), said to screw up the face of the eater; see Vergil, Ecl. vii. 41.

Sardonyx, a gem. (L.—Gk.) L. *sardonyx.*—Gk. σαρδόνυξ, i. e. Sardian onyx. —Gk. σαρδ-, for Σάρδεις, Sardis, in Lydia; ὄνυξ, onyx. See **Onyx.**

Sarsaparilla. (Span.) Span. *zarzaparilla*, a plant. (Span.) *Zarza* means ' bramble,' perhaps from Basque *sartzia*, a bramble; *parilla* is generally referred to *Parillo*, the name of a physician who prescribed the use of sarsaparilla.

Sarsnet; see **Sarcenet.**

Sash (1), a case or frame for panes of glass. (F.—L.) Adapted from F. *châssis*, ' a frame of wood for a window,' Cot.; or from O. F. *chasse* (F. *châsse*), a case, shrine. —L. *capsa*, a case. See **Chase** (3) and **Case** (2).

Sash (2), a scarf, girdle. (Pers.) Formerly *shash.*—Pers. *shast*, of which one meaning is 'a girdle worn by the fire-worshippers'; also spelt *shest.*

Sassafras, a kind of laurel. (F.— Span.—L.) F. *sassafras.*—Span. *sasafras*, from O. Span. *sassafragia*, the herb saxifrage; sassafras was so named from being supposed to possess the like virtue.—L. *saxifraga*; see **Saxifrage.**

Satan. (Heb.) Heb. *sātān*, an enemy. — Heb. root *sātan*, to persecute.

Satchel, a small bag. (F. – L., &c.) O. F. *sachel*, a little bag. – L. *saccellum*, acc. of *saccellus*, dimin. of *saccus*, a sack; see **Sack.**

Sate, Satiate. (L.) *Sate* is from *sated*, used as a short form of *satiate* in sense of 'satisfied.' (Suggested by L. *sat* for *satis*; *satur*, full.) – L. *satiātus*, pp. of *satiāre*, to sate, fill full. – L. *sat*, *satis*, sufficient; *satur*, full. Allied to **Sad.** Brugm. i. § 196. Der. *satiety*, M. F. *satieté*, from L. acc. *satietātem*, fullness.

Satellite. (F. – L.) F. *satellite*, 'a sergeant, catchpole;' Cot. – L. *satellitem*, acc. of *satelles*, an attendant.

Satin. (F. – L.) F. *satin*. (Ital. *setino*, Port. *setim*.) – Late L. *sātīnus*, *sētīnus*, satin. – Late L. *sēta*, silk; L. *sēta*, *saeta*, a bristle, a hair. Brugm. i. § 209.

Satire. (F. – L.) F. *satire*. – L. *satira*, *satura*, a species of poetry; orig. 'a medley.' Derived from *satura lanx*, a full dish, dish full of mixed ingredients; where *satura* is fem. of *satur*, full. Cf. **Sate.**

satisfy. (F. – L.) O. F. *satisfier* (later *satisfaire*). Formed as if from Late L. **satisficāre*, substituted for L. *satisfacere*, lit. 'to make enough.' – L. *satis*, enough; *facere*, to make. Der. *satisfaction*, from pp. *satisfactus*.

Satrap, a Persian viceroy. (F. – L. – Gk. – Pers.) F. *satrape*. – L. *satrapam*, acc. of *satrapēs*. – Gk. σατράπης. – O. Pers. *khsatra-pāvā*, guardian of a province; from *khsatra*, province, and *pā*, to protect (Spiegel). Cf. Zend *shōithra-pān*, protector of a region (Fick, i. 305), from Zend *shōithra*, a region, *pān*, protector; Skt. *kshetra-*, a field, region, from *kshi*, to dwell, and *pā*, to protect.

Saturate. (L.) From pp. of L. *satur-āre*, to fill full. – L. *satur*, full. Cf. **Sate.**

Saturnine. (F. – L.) O. F. *saturnin* (usually *Saturnien*), under the influence of the malign planet Saturn; hence, melancholy. – L. *Sāturnus*, Saturn; said to mean 'the sower'; as if from *satum*, supine of *serere*, to sow (Festus); which is improbable.

saturday. (L. and E.) A. S. *Sæter-dæg*, also *Sætern-dæg*, *Sæternes dæg*, i. e. Saturn's day; a translation of L. *Sāturni diēs*; cf. Du. *Zaterdag*. – L. *Sāturnus*, Saturn; A. S. *dæg*, a day.

Satyr. (F. – L. – Gk.) F. *satyre*. – L. *satyrus*. – Gk. σάτυρος, a satyr, a sylvan god.

Sauce. (F. – L.) F. *sauce*. – L. *salsa*, a thing salted; fem. of *salsus*, salted. See **Salt.** Der. *sauc-er*, orig. a vessel for sauce; *sauc-y*, full of sauce, pungent.

Saunders, a corrupt form of **Sandal-wood.**

Saunter. (F. – L.) From A. F. *sauntrer*, to adventure oneself. I find mention of a man 'qe *sauntre* en ewe,' who ventures on the water, who goes to sea; Year-book of 11 Edw. III. p. 619. – A. F. *s-*, for *es-*, out (L. *ex*); and *auntrer*, for *aventurer*, to adventure or venture, from *aventure*, an adventure. See **Adventure.**

Saurian, one of the lizard tribe. (Gk.) From Gk. σαύρα, σαῦρος, a lizard.

Sausage. (F. – L.) Formerly *sausige* (for **sausice*); cf. Guernsey *sauciche*. F. *saucisse*. – Late L. *salsicia*, fem. of *salsicius*, adj. (Georges), made of salted or seasoned meat. – L. *salsus*, salted. – L. *sāl*, salt. See **Salt.**

Sauterne, a wine. (F.) From *Sauterne* in France, department of Gironde.

Savage. (F. – L.) M. E. *sauage*. – A. F. *savage*; O. F. *savaige*, *salvage* (F. *sauvage*). – L. *siluāticus*, belonging to a wood, wild. – L. *silua*, a wood. See **Silvan.**

Savanna, a meadow-plain. (Span. – L. – Gk.) Span. *sabana* (with *b* pron. as bi-labial *v*), a sheet for a bed, large cloth, large plain (from the appearance of a plain covered with snow). – L. *sabana*, pl. of *sabanum*, a linen cloth; used as a fem. sing. – Gk. σάβανον, a linen cloth, towel.

Save. (F. – L.) M. E. *sauuen* (= *sauven*). – A. F. *saver*, *sauver*; F. *sauver*. – L. *saluāre*, to save. – L. *saluus*, safe. See **Salvation.**

Saveloy, Cervelas, a kind of sausage. (F. – Ital. – L.) Formerly *cervelas* (Phillips). – F. *cervelas*, M.F. *cervelat*. – Ital. *cervellato* (Torriano), a saveloy; from its containing brains. – Ital. *cervello*, brain. – L. *cerebellum*, dimin. of *cerebrum*, brain. See **Cerebral.**

Savin, Savine, Sabine, a shrub. (L.) A. S. *safine*. – L. *sabina*; orig. *Sabīna herba*, a Sabine herb. The *Sabines* were a people of central Italy.

Savory, a plant. (F. – L.) M. F. *savorée*, a popular perversion of O. F.

sarrie (whence F. *sarriette*). – L. *saturēia*, savory.

Savour. (F. – L.) O. F. *savour*, later *saveur*. – L. *sapōrem*, acc. of *sapor*, taste. – L. *sapere*, to taste. See **Sapid.**

Savoy, a kind of cabbage. (F.) Brought from *Savoy.*

Saw (1), a cutting instrument. (E.) M. E. *sawe.* A. S. *sagu*, lit. a cutter; from 2nd grade of Teut. root SEG < √SEK, to cut.+Du. *zaag*, Icel. *sög*, Dan. *sav*, Swed. *såg*, G. *säge.* See **Secant.** Der. *see-saw*, a reduplicated form; cf. *scythe*, *sedge.*

Saw (2), a saying. (E.) M. E. *sawe.* A. S. *sagu*, a saying; cf. A. S. *secgan*, to say. Allied to Lith. *pa-saka*, a saying. Doublet, *saga.* See **Say.**

Saxhorn, a kind of horn. Named after the inventor, Adolphe *Sax*, a Frenchman; ab. 1840.

Saxifrage, a plant. (F. – L.) F. *saxifrage.* – L. *saxifraga*, spleen-wort; so named because it was supposed to break stones in the bladder. – L. *saxi-*, for *saxum*, a stone; *frag-*, base of *frangere*, to break. Cf. **Sassafras.**

Saxon, a Teut. race. (L. – Teut.) Late L. *Saxonēs*, pl., Saxons. – A. S. *Seaxan*, Saxons; because armed with a short sword. – A. S. *seax*, a knife, lit. ' cutter;' O. Fries. *sax*; cf. L. *saxum*, a stone implement. Brugm. i. § 549 c.

Say (1), to speak. (E.) M. E. *seggen*, pr. s. *sey-eth*, *sei-th.* A. S. *secgan*, North. pr. s. *seg-eð*, pt. t. *sægde*, pp. *gesægd.*+Du. *zeggen*, Icel. *segja*, Dan. *sige*, Swed. *säga*, G. *sagen*, O. H. G. *sagēn.* Cf. Lithuan. *sakýti*, to say; Gk. ἔννεπε (for *ἔν-σεπ-ε), O. L. *in-sec-e*, imp. s., tell, say. See Sweet, N. E. Gr. § 1293.

Say (2), a kind of serge. (F. – L. – Gk.) O. F. *saie*, say. (Cf. Span. *saya*, *sayo*, a tunic; *sayete*, a thin stuff.) So called because used for making a kind of coat called in Latin *saga*, *sagum*, or *sagus*; Late L. *sagum*, (1) a mantle, (2) a kind of cloth. – Gk. σάγος, a soldier's mantle; allied to σαγή, harness, σάγμα, a packsaddle; see **Sumpter.**

Say (3), to essay; short for *assay* or *essay*; see **Essay.**

Scab. (Scand.) Dan. Swed. *skab.*+G. *schabe*; A.S. *sceab*, *sceb*, scab, itch. Lit. 'something that is scratched;' cf. L. *scabere*, to scratch, *scabiēs*, itch. See **Shave** and **Shabby.**

Scabbard. (F. – Teut.) M. E. *scaubert*,

scauberk, scaberk, a scabbard; answering to O. F. *escauberc*, only found in the pl. *escaubers* (Godefroy). The F. word is made up of O. F. *escale*, a scale, husk, case; and *-berc*, a protection (as in O. F. *hauberc*, *hal-berc*, a hauberk). – O. H. G. *scala*, a scale, husk, case; *bergan*, to hide, protect. Thus *scabbard = scauberk = scaleberk*, with the reduplicated sense of 'cover-cover,' or protecting case. See **Scale** (1) and **Hauberk.**

Scabious. (F. – L.) M. F. *scabieuse*, f. – L. *scabiōsa* (*herba*), a plant supposed to be good for skin-eruptions. – L. *scabiēs*, an itch. See **Scab.**

Scaffold. (F. – L. and Gk.?) M. E. *scafold.* – O. F. *escafalt*, only found as *escafaut*, *eschafaut* (also *chafaut*), mod. F. *échafaud*, a scaffold. Short for *escadafalt* (Burguy), where *es-* represents L. *ex*, prep.; cf. Span. and Ital. *catafalco*, a funeral canopy, also a stage, scaffold (whence F. and E. *catafalque*). β. The former part of *catafalco* may be allied to Span. *catar*, in the sense 'to view.' The latter part is perhaps due to L. *fala*, a kind of scaffold. (Doubtful.)

Scald (1), to burn. (F. – L.) M. E. *scalden.* – O. F. *escalder*, later *eschauder*, to scald (F. *échauder*). – L. *excaldāre*, to wash in hot water. – L. *ex*, out, very; and *caldus = calidus*, hot. See **Caldron.**

Scald (2), scabby. (Scand.) For *scalled*, i. e. afflicted with the *scall*; see **Scall.**

Scald (3), a poet. (Scand.) Icel. *skald*, a poet, older form *skáld* (Noreen).

Scale (1), a shell, a flake. (F. – O. H. G.) M. E. *scale.* – O. F. *escale* (F. *écale*). – O. H. G. *scala* (G. *schale*). ✛ A.S. *scealu*, *scalu*, a shell, husk, scale; Dan. and Swed. *skal*, a shell, pod. From Teut. base *skal*, 2nd grade of str. vb. *skel-an-*, to cleave, divide; cf. Lith. *skel-ti*, to cleave; Gk. σκάλλειν, to stir up, to hoe. (√SKEL.) See **Shale, Shell**, and **Skill.**

scale (2), a bowl or dish of a balance. (F. – Teut.) [Formerly also *scole*; cf. Icel. *skál*, a scale of a balance.] M. E. *scale.* – O. F. *escale*, a cup (Godefroy). – Icel. *skál*, Dan. *skaal*, Swed. *skål*, bowl; Du. *schaal*, scale, bowl. Allied to **Scale** (1); being from Teut. base *skæl-*, 3rd grade of *skelan-.*

Scale (3), a ladder, gradation. (L.) L. *scāla*, a ladder. L. *scā-la* < *scan(t)-slā*, i. e. *scan(d)-slā*; from *scandere*, to climb. See **Scan.** Brugm. i. § 414.

Scalene. (L.–Gk.) L. *scalēnus*, adj. –Gk. σκαληνός, scalene, uneven.

Scall, scab on the skin. (Scand.) From Icel. *skalli*, a bald head; orig. a peeled head. Cf. Swed. *skallig*, bald, from *skala*, to peel. Allied to Swed. *skal*, a husk; see **Scale** (1). Der. *scald* (2)=*scalled*, afflicted with scall.

Scallion, a plant allied to garlic. (F. –L.–Gk.–Phoenician.) O. F. *escalogne*, a scallion; see further under **Shallot**.

Scallop, Scollop, a kind of shell-fish. (F.–Teut.) M. E. *skalop.*–O. F. *escalope*, a shell.–M. Du. *schelpe* (Du. *schelp*), a shell, especially a scallop-shell. Allied to **Scale** (1) and **Shell**. Der. *scallop*, vb., to cut an edge into scallop-like curves.

scalp. (Scand.) M.E. *scalp* (Northern). –Icel. *skálpr*, M. Swed. *skalp*, a sheath; Dan. dial. *skalp*, husk, shell of a pea; also M. Ital. *scalpo*, the scalp, a word borrowed from Teutonic. Cf. M. Du. *schelpe*, a shell (hence, skull). See **Scallop**.

Scalpel, a small sharp knife. (L.) L. *scalpellum*, dimin. of *scalprum*, a knife.– L. *scalpere*, to cut.

Scammony, a cathartic gum-resin. (F.–L.–Gk.) M.F. *scammonie*.–L. *scammōnia*.– G. σκαμμωνία, σκαμωνία, scammony, a kind of bind-weed.

Scamp. (F.–L.) Formerly a vagabond, or fugitive.–O. North F. *escamper*, *s'escamper*, to flee; O. F. *eschamper*, to decamp.–L. *ex*, out; and *campus*, battlefield. Der. *scamp-er*, to run or flee away.

Scan. (L.) Short for *scand*; the *d* was prob. mistaken for the pp. suffix *-ed.*–L. *scandere*, to climb; also, to scan a verse. +Skt. *skand*, to spring up. Brugm. i. § 635.

Scandal. (F.–L.–Gk.) F. *scandale*. –L. *scandalum.*–Gk. σκάνδαλον, a snare; also a scandal, offence, stumbling-block. Orig. the spring of a trap, the stick which sprang up when the trap was shut, and on which the bait was placed; usually called σκανδάληθρον.–√SKAND, to spring up. See **Scan**. Doublet, *slander*.

Scansion. (L.) From L. *scansio*, a scanning.–L. *scansus*, pp. of *scandere*, to scan; see **Scan**.

Scant, adj. (Scand.) M. E. *skant*, insufficient.–Icel. *skamt*, neut. of *skammr*, short, brief; whence *skamta*, to dole out (hence to scant or stint); Icel. *skamtr*, a dole. In Norwegian, *nt* appears for *mt*,

as in *skant*, a dole, *skanta*, to measure closely. Cf. O. H. G. *skam*, short. Der. *scant-y*.

Scantling, a cut piece of timber, a pattern. (F.–Teut.; *with* L. *prefix*.) From O. North F. *escantillon*, for O. F. *eschantillon*, 'a small cantle, scantling, sample;' Cot.–O. F. *es-*, prefix, from L. *ex*; *cantel*, a cantle; see **Cantle**.

Scapegoat. Here *scape* is short for *escape*; see **Escape**.

Scapular, belonging to the shoulder-blades. (L.) Late L. *scapulāris*, adj., from *scapulæ*, pl. shoulder-blades. Der. *scapular-y*, a kind of scarf (worn over the shoulders), F. *scapulaire*, Late L. *scapulāre*.

Scar (1), mark of a wound. (F.–L.– Gk.) M. F. *escare.*–L. *eschara*, a scar, esp. of a burn.–Gk. ἐσχάρα, a hearth, fireplace, scar of a burn.

Scar (2), **Scaur,** a rock. (Scand.) M.E. *scarre.*–Icel. *sker*, a skerry, isolated rock; Dan. *skiær*, Swed. *skär*. So called because cut off from the main land; see **Shear**.

Scaramouch, a buffoon. (F.–Ital.– O. H. G.) From *Scaramoche*, a famous Italian zany who acted in England in 1673 (Blount). Also called *Scaramouche*, which was the F. spelling; but his real name was *Scaramuccia*, of which the lit. sense is 'a skirmish,' being the same word as the O. F. *escarmouche*, a skirmish. See **Skirmish**.

Scarce. (F.–L.) M. E. *scars.*–O. F. *escars*, *eschars*, scarce, scanty, niggard (F. *échars*).–Late L. *scarpsus*, short form of *excarpsus*, used as a substitute for L. *excerptus*, pp. of *excerpere*, to select; see **Excerpt**. Thus the sense was 'picked out,' select, scarce.

Scare. (Scand.) M.E. *skerren*, to scare; from *skerre*, adj., timid, shy.–Icel. *skjarr*, timid, shy; allied to *skirrask*, to shun, lit. to sheer off; see **Sheer** (2).

Scarf (1), a light sash or band. (F.– O. Low G.) Confused, as to sound, with **Scarf** (2). The particular sense is due to O. North F. *escarpe*, O. F. and M. F. *escharpe*, a scarf; Cot. – M. Du. *scharpe*, a scrip (Oudemans); Low G. *schrap*. Cf. E. Fries. *scherpe*, a scarf, which, like G. *schärpe*, is prob. from F. See below.

Scarf (2), to join timber together. (Scand.) From Swed. *skarf*, a scarf, seam, joint.+Bavarian *scharben*, to cut a notch in timber, G. *scharben*, O. H. G. *scarbōn*, to cut small. From Teut. **skarb*, 2nd grade of *skerb-an-*, to cut, as in A. S. *sceorfan*, pt. t. *scearf*, to scrape.

Scarify. (F. – L. – Gk.) F. *scarifier*. – L. *scarificāre*, to scarify, scratch open; from *scarīfāre*, to scarify. – Gk. σκαριφάομαι, I scratch. – Gk. σκάριφος, a sharp pőinted instrument. Allied to L. *scrībere*, to write, and to E. Scribe.

Scarlet. (F. – Pers.) O. F. *escarlate*, scarlet. (Span. *escarlata*, Ital. *scarlatto*.) – Pers. *saqalāt*, *siqalāt*, *suqlāt*, scarlet cloth. Orig. the name of a stuff, which was often of a scarlet colour; cf. 'scarlet reed,' Ch. Prol. 456. ¶ Hence Pers. *saqlatūn*, scarlet cloth, whence M. E. *ciclatoun* (Chaucer). The Turkish *iskerlat*, scarlet, is merely borrowed from Ital. *scarlatto* (Zenker). See *Suclāt* in Yule.

scarlatina, scarlet fever. (Ital. – Pers.) Ital. *scarlattina*. – Ital. *scarlatto*, scarlet cloth (above).

Scarp. (F. – Ital. – Teut.) F. *escarpe*. – Ital. *scarpa*, 'a curtein of a wall;' so called because cut *sharp*, i. e. steep. – Du. *scherp*; M. H. G. *scharf*, *scharpf*, sharp; see Sharp.

Scathe, to harm. (Scand.) From Icel. *skaða*, Swed. *skada*, Dan. *skade*. **+** A. S. *sceaðan* (pt. t. *scōd*); G. Du. *schaden*; Goth. *ga-skathjan* (pt.t. *ga-skōth*). Cf.Gk. ἀ-σκηθής, unharmed. Der. *scathe*, sb., Icel. *skaði*.

Scatter. (E.) M. E. *scateren*. Northern form of Shatter, q. v. **+** Gk. σκεδάννυμι, I sprinkle, σκέδ-ασις, a scattering; Skt. *skhad*, to cut. Cf. Squander.

Scavenger. (F. – Teut.) Formerly *scavager*; the *n* is intrusive. The sense has much changed; a *scavager* was an officer who acted as inspector of goods for sale, and subsequently had to attend to cleansing of streets. *Scavage*, i. e. inspection, is an A. F. word, with F. suffix *-age* (< L. *-āticum*); from O. F. *escauw-er*, to examine, inspect. – O. Sax. *scawōn*, to behold; cognate with A. S. *sceāwian*, to look at. See Show.

Scene. (L. – Gk.) L. *scēna*, *scæna* (whence also F. *scène*). – Gk. σκηνή, a sheltered place, tent, stage, scene. Der. *pro-scenium*.

Scent, vb. (F. – L.) A false spelling for *sent*, as in Hamlet, i. 5. 58 (ed. 1623). – F. *sentir*, 'to feel, sent;' Cot. – L. *sentīre*, to feel, perceive. See Sense.

Sceptic. (F. – L. – Gk.) F. *sceptique*. – L. *scepticus*. – Gk. σκεπτικός, thoughtful,

inquiring; pl. σκεπτικοί, the Sceptics, followers of Pyrrho (3rd century, B. C.). – Gk. σκέπτομαι, I consider; see Species.

Sceptre. (F. – L. – Gk.) F. *sceptre*. – L. *sceptrum*. – Gk. σκῆπτρον, a staff to lean on, a sceptre. – Gk. σκήπτειν, to prop; also to hurl. Cf. L. *scāpus*, a shaft, stem.

Schedule. (F. – L. – Gk.) Formerly *cedule*. – M. F. *schedule*, *cedule*, 'a schedule, scrowle,' Cot.; F. *cédule*. – L. *schedula*, a small leaf of paper; dimin. of *scheda* (or *scida*), a strip of papyrus-bark. Late Gk. σχέδη, a tablet, is borrowed from L.; hence the L. word must be from the kindred Gk. σχίδη, a cleft piece of wood, from σχίζειν, to cleave. See Schism.

Scheme. (L. – Gk.) Formerly *schema*. – L. *schēma*. – Gk. σχῆμα, form, appearance, also used as a term in rhetoric. – Gk. σχη-, as in σχή-σω, fut. of ἔχ-ειν, to hold, have (base σεχ-). Cf. Skt. *sah*, to bear. (√SEGH.)

Schism. (F. – L. – Gk.) F. *schisme*. – L. *schisma*. – Gk. σχίσμα, a rent, split, schism. – Gk. σχίζειν (base σχιδ-), to cleave. **+** L. *scindere*, Skt. *chhid*, to cut. Brugm. i. §§ 586, 599.

schist, slate-rock. (Gk.) Gk. σχίστος, easily cleft. – Gk. σχίζειν (above).

School (1). (F. – L. – Gk.) M. E. *scole*. A. F. and O. F. *escole*, school. – L. *schola*. – Gk. σχολή, rest, leisure, employment of leisure time, also a school. Orig. 'a pause;' from σχο-, a grade of the base of ἔχειν, to hold; see Scheme. (√SEGH.) Der. *schol-ar*, A. F. *escoler*; *scholi-ast*, from Gk. σχολιαστής, a commentator.

School (2), a shoal of fish. (Du.) Du. *school visschen*, 'a shole of fishes,' Sewel. Doublet of *shoal*. See Shoal (1).

Schooner. (Scand.) Properly *scooner*, but spelt as if derived from Dutch, which is not the case, the Du. *schooner* being of E. origin. First called a *scooner* in 1713, when the first schooner was so named in Gloucester, Massachusetts, from the remark that 'she *scoons*,' i. e. glides swiftly. This verb is the Clydesdale *scon* or *scoon*, to glide swiftly, applied to stones with which one makes 'ducks and drakes' in the water. – Icel. *skunda*, to speed. See Shun.

Schorl, black tourmaline. (Swed.) Swed. *skörl* (with *sk* as E. *sh*). Perhaps suggested by Swed. *skör*, brittle.

Sciatic, pertaining to the hip-joint. (F. – L. – Gk.) F. *sciatique*, adj. – L. *sciaticus*, corruption of L. *ischiadicus*, subject to gout in the hips. — Gk. ἰσχιαδικός, subject to pains in the loins. — Gk. ἰσχιαδ-, stem of ἰσχιάς, pain in the loins. — Gk. ἰσχίον, the socket in which the thigh-bone turns. **Der.** *sciatic-a*, fem. of L. adj. *sciaticus*.

Science. (F. — L.) F. *science*. — L. *scientia*, knowledge. — L. *scient-*, stem of pres. pt. of *scire*, to know, orig. to discern. Allied to Skill. **Der.** *con-*, *pre-science*.

Scimetar, Cimetar. (F. *or* Ital. — Pers. ?) F. *cimeterre*, 'a scymitar;' Cot. Cf. Ital. *scimitarra*, 'a simitar,' Florio. Prob. from Pers. *shimshīr*, *shamshīr*, 'a cimeter,' Rich. Dict., p. 909. Lit. lion's claw. — Pers. *sham*, nail, claw; *shēr*, lion.

Scintillation. (F. — L.) F. *scintillation*. — L. acc. *scintillātiōnem*, a sparkling. — L. *scintillāre*, to sparkle. — L. *scintilla*, a spark.

Sciolist. (L.) Formed, with suffix *-ist*, from L. *sciol-us*, a smatterer. — L. *scius*, knowing. — L. *scī-re*, to know. See Science.

Scion. (F. — L.) M. E. *sioun*. — O. F. *cion*, M. F. *sion*, F. *scion*, 'a scion, shoot;' Cot. Orig. 'a cutting.' — O. F. *sier*, F. *scier*, to cut. — L. *secāre*, to cut. See Secant.

Scirrhous, pertaining to a hard swelling. (L. — Gk.) From Late L. *scirrhus*, sb., a form used for L. *scirros*, a hard swelling. — Gk. σκίρρος, σκίρος, σκίρρωμα, a hard swelling. — Gk. σκιρός, hard.

Scissors. (F. — L.) [Ill spelt, and not from L. *scindere*, to cut.] M. E. *sisoures*, *cisoures*. — O. F. *cisoires*, shears; used instead of *ciseaux*, 'sizars,' Cot. The latter is the pl. of O. F. *cisel*, chisel; see Chisel. Both words are due to L. *cædere*, to cut; see Cæsura. ¶ No doubt the word was confused with L. *scissor*, which properly means 'a cutter,' hence, a tailor; from L. *scindere*, to cut.

Scoff. (Scand.) M. E. *skof*. Swed. dial. *skoff-*, as in *skoffs-ord*, n. pl., words of abuse, *skoff-sera*, to abuse; O. Fries. *schof*, a scoff; Icel. *skaup*, *skop*, mockery. Cf. M. Du. *schoppen*, *schobben*, to scoff, Icel. *skopa*, to scoff; also Dan. *skuffe*, to deceive; see Scuffle. The orig. sense was prob. 'a rub' or 'a shove'; cf. Swed. *skuff*, a push, G. *schupfen*, to push; see Shove.

Scold. (Perhaps Frisian.) M. E. *scolden*; also *skalde*, *scolde*, sb., a scold. The sb. is formed from *skald*, 2nd grade

of Teut. *skeldan-*, to scold, blame, as seen in O. Fries. *skelda*, Du. *schelden* (pt. t. *schold*), G. *schelten* (pt. t. *schalt*), to scold; cf. Dan. *skielde*, wk. vb., to scold. If the orig. sense was 'to push,' it is allied to O. Sax. *skaldan*, to push off (a boat).

Scollop; see Scallop.

Sconce (1), a small fort, bulwark. (F. — L.) Also applied to a helmet, and even to the head. — O. F. *esconse*, a hiding-place, sconce; orig. fem. of pp. *escons*. — L. *absconsa*, fem. of *absconsus*, used (as well as *absconditus*) as pp. of *abscondere*, to hide; see Abscond.

sconce (2), a candle-stick. (F. — L.) M. E. *sconce*, *scons*, a covered light, lantern. — O. F. *esconse*, a dark lantern (Roquefort). — Late L. *absconsa*, a dark lantern; from L. *absconsus*, hidden.

Scoop. (F. — Scand.) M. E. *scope*, sb. — O. F. *escope* (F. *écope*), a scoop (Hatzfeld). — Swed. *skopa*, a scoop. ✛ M. Du. *schoepe*, M. H. G. *schuofe*, a scoop; cf. G. *schöpfen*, to draw water, to scoop. From Teut. *skōp*, 2nd grade of Teut. *skap-*, as in O. Sax. *skeppian* (for *skapjan*), Du. *scheppen*, O. H. G. *schepfan* (pt. t. *scuof*), to draw up water.

Scope. (Ital. — Gk.) Ital. *scopo*, a mark to shoot at, scope; Florio. — Gk. σκοπός, a mark, a watcher; allied to Gk. σκέπτομαι, I see, spy, which is cognate with L. *specere*; see Species.

Scorbutic, afflicted with scurvy. (Low L.) From Low L. *scorbūtus*, scurvy; said to be Latinised from M. Du. *scheur-en*, to break, tear, and *bot*, a bone (Weigand); which is doubtful. From L. *scorbūtus* were formed Low G. *scharbock*, *schärbuuk*, scurvy; M. Du. *scheurbuyck* (Du. *scheurbuik*), scurvy. These forms are due to popular etymology, as the lit. sense of M. Du. *scheurbuyck* is 'rupture of the belly,' from *scheuren*, to tear, and *buyck* (mod. Du. *buik*), the belly. See Scurvy.

Scorch. (F. — L.) Orig. to flay; Knt. de la Tour, p. 6. — O. F. *escorcher*, lit. to flay (Ital. *scorticare*). — L. *ex*, off; *cortic-*, stem of *cortex*, bark, rind, husk. Confused with M. E. *scorklen*, to burn, *scorknen*, to parch; cf. Norw. *skrokkna*, to shrivel, *skrokken*, shrunken; allied to Shrink.

Score. (Scand.) M. E. *score*, properly a cut; hence twenty, denoted by a long cut on a cut stick. — Icel. *skor*, a score, cut; also twenty; cf. Swed. *skåra*, Dan. *skaar*, score, cut. From Teut. *skor-*, Icel. *skor-*, weak grade of *sker-a*, to cut, shear; see **Shear.**

Scoria, slag. (L. – Gk.) L. *scŏria.* – Gk. σκωρία, dross, scum. – Gk. σκῶρ, dung, ordure. + A. S. *scearn*, dung.

Scorn. (F. – L.) M. E. *scorn.* – O. F. *escorne*, scorn; Cot. – O. F. *escorner*, to humiliate, mock at; orig. 'to deprive of horns;' from L. *ex*, out, *cornu*, a horn. ¶ But much influenced by M. E. *scarnen*, to scorn, from O. F. *escarnir*, *escharnir*, to deride; from O. H. G. *scernōn*, to deride, a vb. due to the sb. *scern*, derision.

Scorpion. (F. – L. – Gk.) F. *scorpion.* – L. *scorpiōnem*, acc. of *scorpio*, the same as *scorpius*. – Gk. σκορπίος, a scorpion, also a prickly sea-fish. (√SKERP.)

Scotch, to cut with narrow incisions. (Scand.) To *scotch* is to cut slightly ; short for *scor-ch*, an extension of score; see **Score.** 'With knyfe *scortche* not the Boorde;' Babees Book, p. 80. Confused with M. E. *scorchen*, to flay, which suggested its form.

Scot-free, free from payment. (F. – Teut.) A. F. and O. F. *escot* (F. *écot*), payment, esp. a contribution to a common fund, into which it is *shot*. – Icel. *skot*, a shot, a contribution. + Du. *schot*, G. *schoss*, a shot, a scot. From **skut-*, weak grade of Teut. **skeut-an-*, to shoot. See **Shoot.**

Scoundrel. (Scand.) Lit. 'a loathsome fellow.' Aberdeensh. *scoonrel* ; for **scunner-el*, where *-el* is an agential suffix. From Lowl. Scotch *scunner*, *sconner*, to loathe, also (formerly) to shrink through fear, act as a coward; so that a *scoonrel* is one who shrinks, a coward. See Barbour, Bruce, xvii. 651. The verb *scunner* is the frequentative of the North. form of A. S. *scun-ian*, to shun; see **Shun.** Cf. Swed. dial. *skunna sig*, Icel. *skunda*, to hasten.

Scour (1), to cleanse. (F. – L.) O. F. *escurer*, to scour. Cf. Span. *escurar*, M. Ital. *scurare*, to scour, rub up. – L. *excūrāre*, to take great care of. – L. *ex*, very; *cūrāre*, to take care, from *cūra*, care. (Körting.)

Scour (2), to run along. (F. – L.) 'Camilla *scours* the plain;' Pope. – O. F. *escorre*, *escourre*, to run out (as a spy). – L. *excurrere*. – L. *ex*, out; *currere*, to run.

Scourge. (F. – L.) A. F. *escorge*; cf. O. F. *escorgiee* (F. *écourgée*), a scourge. Cf. Ital. *scuriata*, M. Ital. *scoriata*, a scourge, *scoriare*, to whip. The M. Ital.

scoriata answers to L. *excoriāta*, lit. flayed off, hence a strip of leather for a whip, a thong; pp. of *excoriāre*, to flay off, in Late L., to whip; see **Excoriate.**

Scout (1), a spy. (F. – L.) M. E. *scoute.* – O. F. *escoute*, a spy. – O. F. *escouter*, to listen. – Folk-L. **ascoltāre*, for L. *auscultāre*, to listen; see **Auscultation.**

Scout (2), to ridicule an idea. (Scand.) Allied to Lowl. Scotch *scout*, to pour out a liquid forcibly, to *shoot* it out. – Icel. *skúta*, *skúti*, a taunt; cf. *skot-yrði*, scoffs. – Icel. *skút-*, a weak grade of the base of *skjóta*, to shoot. Cf. Swed. *skjuta* (1) to shoot, (2) to shove; *skjuta skulden på*, to cast the blame on; Dan. *skyde*, to shoot, cast (blame on), repel. See **Shoot.**

Scowl. (Scand.) M. E. *scoulen.* Not in A. S. – Dan. *skule*, to scowl, cast down the eyes; allied to E. Fries. and Low G. *schulen*, Du. *schuilen*, to hide oneself, prov. G. *schulen*, to hide the eyes, look slily, peep. From the sb. seen in E. Fries. *schûl*, Du. *schuil*, Dan. *skiul*, shelter, Icel. *skjól*, shelter, cover. See **Sheal.**

Scrabble, to scrawl. (Scand.) Lit. 'to scratch or scrape;' for prov. E. *scrapple*, frequent. of *scrape*. Cf. Du. *schrabben*, to scratch; E. Fries. *schrabben*, *schrappen*, *schrapen*, to scratch. See **Scrape.**

Scraggy, lean, rough. (Scand.) Allied to M. E. *scroggy*, covered with thin straggling bushes. From prov. E. *scrag*, a forked branch, lean person; cf. *scrog*, a stunted bush. – Swed. dial. *skragga*, a weak old man; cf. Icel. *skröggsligr*, scraggy; North Fries. *skrog*, a lean man; Dan. *skrog*, a carcase. See **Shrug, Shrink.**

Scramble. (Scand.) Nasalised form of prov. E. *scrabble*, to scramble, allied to *scraffle*, to scramble, *scrapple*, to grub about; frequentatives of *scrape*, prov. E. *scrap*, to scrape.

Scrannel, thin, weakly, wretched. (Scand.) In Milton, Lycidas, 124. Prov. E. *scranny*, thin, lean; *scrannel*, a lean person (Lincolnshire). – Swed. dial. *skran*, weak; Norweg. *skran*, thin, lean, dry; Dan. *skranten*, sickly, weakly. Cf. Swed. dial. and Norw. *skrinn*, thin, lean, weak, dry.

Scrap. (Scand.) Icel. *skrap*, scraps, trifles, lit. 'scrapings.' – Icel. *skrapa*, to scrape.

scrape. (Scand.) Orig. to scratch with something *sharp*. – Icel. *skrapa*, Swed.

skrapa, Dan. *skrabe*, to scrape. **+** Du. *schrapen*. From Teut. **skrap-*, 2nd grade of Teut. **skrepan-*, to scrape; as in A.S. *screp-an*, pt. t. *scræp*. Cf. Russ. *skrebok'*, a scraper.

Scratch. (Scand.) Due to the confusion of M. E. *skratten*, to scratch, with M. E. *cracchen*, to scratch. β. M. E. *skratten* stands for *s-kratten*, where the *s*- (due to F. *es-*, L. *ex-*) is intensive, and *kratten* is from Swed. *kratta* (below). γ. M. E. *cracchen* stands for **kratsen*. ─ Swed. *kratsa*, to scrape, *krats*, a scraper. ─ Swed. *kratta*, to rake, scrape; cf. Icel. *krota*, to engrave. From Teut. **kret-an-*, to cut (pt. t. **krat*, pp. **krot-anoz*). So also Du. *crassen* (for **kratsen*), G. *kratzen*, O.H.G. *shrazzōn*, to scratch. And see **Grate** (2).

Scrawl. (Scand.) A contraction of *scrabble*, to write carelessly. ¶ Confused with M.E. *scraulen*, to crawl, a form of *crawl* with prefix *s* (=O. F. *es-*< L. *ex*) used with an intensive force.

Scream. (Scand.) M. E. *scremen*. ─ Icel. *skræma*, Swed. *skräma*, Dan. *shræmme*, to scare; orig. to cry aloud. Cf. Swed. *skrän*, a scream; Dan. *skraale*, to roar.

Screech. (Scand.) Cf. M. E. *scriken*; Lowl. Sc. *scraik*. ─ Icel. *skrækja*, to shriek; cf. Swed. *skrika*, to shriek, Dan. *skrige*.**+** Gael. *sgreuch*, to shriek. Cf. **Shriek.**

Screen. (F. ─ Teut.) M. E. *scren*. ─ O. F. *escren* (Littré); *escran*, 'a skreen,' Cot. (Mod. F. *écran*.) Also found as as O.F. *escranne* (Godefroy). ─ G. *schranne*, a railing, grate. β. In the sense of 'coarse sieve,' it is the same word; so called because it *screens* (or wards off) the coarser particles, and prevents them from coming through.

Screw (1). (F. ─ Teut.) Formerly *scrue*. ─ M. F. *escroue*, 'a scrue;' Cot.; O. F. *escroe* (Godefroy). F. *écrou*. Perhaps from Low G. *schruve*; cf. M. Du. *schroeve*, Du. *schroef*, G. *schraube*, a screw. ¶ The Icel. *skrúfa*, Swed. *skruf*, Dan. *skrue*, are from Low G. ; and it is doubtful whether the Du. and G. words are really Teutonic.

Screw (2), a vicious horse. (E.) The North E. form of *shrew*, q. v.

Scribble. (L.; *with* E. *suffix*.) Formed from *scribe* with frequent. suffix *-le* ; the suffix giving it a verbal force.

scribe. (L.) L. *scriba*, a writer. ─ L. *scribere*, to write, orig. to scratch or cut slightly.

Scrimmage; see **Skirmish.**

Scrip (1), a small bag. (Scand.) A. F. *escrepe*, a scarf. ─ Icel. *skreppa*, Swed. *skräppa*, a scrip. Orig. sense 'scrap,' because made of a scrap of stuff; cf. N. Fries. *skrap*, a scrip.

Scrip (2), a piece of writing; the same word as *script* (below).

script. (F.─L.) M. F. *escript*, 'a writing.' ─ L. *scriptum*, neut. of pp. of *scribere*, to write.

scripture. (F.─L.) M. E. *scripture*, a writing. ─ M.F. *escripture*. ─ L. *scriptūra*, a writing. ─ L. *scriptus*, pp. of *scribere*, to write.

scrivener. (F. ─ L.) Formerly a *scriven*; the suffix *-er*, of the agent, is an E. addition. M. E. *scriuein* (=*scrivein*). ─ O. F. *escriuain*. ─ Late L. *scrībānum*, acc. of *scrībānus*, a notary. ─ L. *scrībere*, to write.

Scrofula. (L.) L. *scrōfula*, a little pig; whence the pl. *scrōfulæ*, used in the sense of scrofulous swellings; perhaps from the swollen appearance of the glands. Dimin. of *scrōfa*, a breeding sow, lit. a digger; from the habit of swine; cf. L. *scrobis*, a ditch.

Scroll, a roll of paper. (F.─Teut.) Dimin. (with suffix *-l*) of M. E. *scrowe*, a scroll. ─ M. F. *escroue*, 'a scrowle;' Cot. ─ M. Du. *schroode*, a shred, strip, slip of paper; O. H. G. *scrōt* (the same). Allied to **Shred.**

Scroyles, rascals. (F.─L.) In K. John, ii. 1. 373. ─ O. F. *escroelles*, later *escrouelles*, lit. 'the king's evil,' i.e. scrofula ; Cot. ─ Late L. **scrobellæ* (only found as *scroellæ*), scrofula, dimin. of **scrobula*, for *scrofula*; see **Scrofula.** Transferred, as a term of abuse, from the disease to the person said to be afflicted with it. (See Körting.)

Scrub (1), brush-wood. (Scand.) Dan. dial. *skrub*, brush-wood ; Norw. *skrubba*, the dwarf cornel-tree. See **Shrub.** Der. *scrubb-y*, mean, orig. shrubby, stunted.

Scrub (2), to rub hard. (Scand.) M. E. *scrobben*, to scrub. ─ Swed. *skrubba*, Dan. *skrubbe*, to scrub. **+** Low G. *schrubben*; Du. *schrobben* ; N. Fries. *skrobbe*, E. Fries. *schrubben*. According to Franck, it is allied by gradation to Du. and E. Fries. *schrabben*, to scratch; see **Scrabble**, **Scrape.** β. It is also, perhaps, related to *shrub*. Cf. E. *broom*, from the shrub so called; Lowl. Scotch *scrubber*, 'a handful of heath tied tightly together for cleaning culinary utensils;' Jamieson.

Scruff; see **Scuft.**

Scruple. (F.-L.) F. *scrupule*, 'a little sharp stone .. in a mans shooe,' Cot.; hence a hindrance, perplexity, doubt, also a small weight.-L. *scrūpulum*, acc. of *scrūpulus*, a sharp stone, dimin. of *scrūpus* (the same).

Scrutiny. (L.) L. *scrūtinium*, a careful enquiry.-L. *scrūtārī*, to search into carefully, as if among broken pieces.-L. *scrūta*, s. pl., broken pieces.

Scud, to run quickly. (Scand.) Cf. Dan. *skyde*, to shoot; *skyde over stevn*, lit. 'to shoot over the stem,' to scud along; *skudsteen*, a stone quoit, called in Scotch a *scudding-stane*. Cf. Swed. dial. *skudda*, to shoot the bolt of a door. See **Scuttle** (3), **Scout** (2), and **Shoot.**

Scuffle. (Scand.) The frequentative of Swed. *skuffa*, to push, shove, jog. Cf. M. Du. *schuffelen*, to drive on, also to run or shuffle off, from Du. *schuiven*, to shove. See **Shuffle, Shove.**

Scuft, Scuff, Scruff, the nape of the neck. (Scand.) O. Icel. *skopt* (pron. *skoft*), hair of the head, mod. Icel. *skott*, a fox's tail; N. Fries. *skuft*, the nape of a horse's neck.+G. *schopf*, a tuft of hair; O. H. G. *scuft*, hair; Goth. *skuft*, hair of the head. Allied to **Sheaf**; cf. Icel. *skauf*, a fox's brush.

Sculk, Skulk. (Scand.) M. E. *skulken.* — Dan. *skulke*, to sculk, slink; Swed. *skolka*, to play the truant. A derivative of Dan. *skule*, to scowl; see **Scowl.** Allied to Icel. *skolla*, to sculk, keep aloof.

Scull (1), **Skull,** the cranium. (Scand.) M. E. *skulle, scolle.* Named from its shell-like shape.—Swed. dial. *skulle*, variant of *skóllt*, scull; Norw. *skolt*, scull. From Teut. **skol*, weak grade of **skelan-* (pt. t. **skal*), to cleave, divide. From the form **skal* we have Swed. *hufvud-skalle*, the scull (also *hufvud-skål*), and Dan. *hjerne-skal*, scull; see **scale** (2).

Scull (2), a small light oar. (Scand.?) Perhaps named from the slightly hollowed blades. See **Scull** (1). Cf. M. Swed. *skolla, skålla*, a thin plate; Swed. *hufvud-skål*, scull (of the head); *våg-skål*, scale (of a balance); *skalig*, concave. Der. *scull*, vb., to use sculls.

Scull (3), a shoal of fish; see **School** (2).

Scullery, a place for swilling dishes,

&c. (F.-L.) The suffix -*y* (=F. -*ie*) is the same as in *butter-y, pantr-y*. The orig. sense was that of 'keeping the dishes.' — O. F. *escuelerie, esculerie*, the office of keeping the dishes (Godefroy).—O. F. *escuelle* (F. *écuelle*), a dish.—L. *scutella*, a dish; dimin. of *scutra*, a flat tray.

Scullion, a kitchen menial. (F.-L.) Not allied to *sculiery*. The true sense is a dish-clout, a name transferred to the maid who used it; just as *mawkin* meant both 'maid' and 'dish-clout.'—M. F. *escouillon*, 'a dish-clout, a maukin;' Cot. The same word as Span. *escobillon*, a sponge for cannon, formed from *escobilla*, dimin. of *escoba* (O. F. *escouve*), a brush, broom.—L. *scōpa*, a twig; pl. *scōpæ*, a broom or brush made of small twigs.

Sculpture. (F.-L.) F. *sculpture.*-L. *sculptūra*, sculpture, lit. a cutting.-L. *sculptus*, pp. of *sculpere*, to cut, carve; allied to *scalpere*, to cut.

Scum. (Scand.) Dan. *skum*, froth; Swed. *skum*, froth; E. Fries. *schüm.*+Du. *schuim*; G. *schaum* (as in *meer-schaum*). (√SKEU, to cover.) Der. *skim.*

Scupper. (E.) '*Scuppers*, the holes through which the water runs off the deck;' Coles (1684). Phillips has *scoper-holes.* For *scoop-er*, i. e. lader out of water; from *scoop*, vb., to lade out water. (The Du. name is *spiegat*, lit. 'spit-hole.') See **Scoop.**

Scurf. (Scand.) From Swed. *skorf*, Dan. *skurv*, scurf; Icel. *skurfur*, pl. + A. S. *scurf, scorf*; Du. *schurft*, G. *schorf.* From **skorf-*, weak grade of **skerfan-*, as in A. S. *sceorfan*, to scarify, gnaw. Der. *scurv-y.*

Scurrile, buffoon-like. (L.) L. *scur-rīlis*, adj., from *scurra*, a buffoon.

Scurvy, scabby, shabby. (Scand.) An adj. formed from *scurf* (above). Hence *scurvy disease*, the scurvy, much confused with F. *scorbut*, the scurvy (Littré).

Scutage, a tax on a knight's fee. (M. Lat.) From Med. L. *scūtāgium.*—L. *scūtum*, a knight's shield, orig. a shield. See **Esquire.**

Scutch, to beat flax. (F. – Scand.) From O. F. *escouche, escuche*, a scutch or swingle.—Norw. *skoka, skuku*, a scutch for beating flax.

Scutcheon; see **Escutcheon.**

Scutiform. (F. – L.) M.F. *scuti-forme*, shaped like a shield.—L. *scūti-*, for *scūtum*, shield; *forma*, form.

Scuttle (1), a shallow basket or vessel. (L.) A Northern form. Icel. *skutill*; A. S. *scutel*, a vessel.–L. *scutella*, allied to *scutula*, a small tray; cf. *scutra*, a tray. See **Scullery**.

Scuttle (2), an opening in a hatchway of a ship. (F. – Span. – Teut.) O. F. *escoutille*, scuttle.–Span. *escotilla*, the hole in the hatch of a ship.–Span. *escotar*, to cut, hollow out, or slope out a garment to fit the neck or bosom.–Span. *escote*, the sloping of a jacket, &c.–Du. *schoot*, lap, bosom; Low G. *schoot*; Icel. *skaut*; see **Sheet**. ¶ So Diez; but Span. *escotilla* is rather a dimin. from Low G. *schott*, a trap-door. Cf. E. **shutter**. Der. *scuttle*, vb., to sink a ship by making holes in it.

Scuttle (3), to hurry along. (Scand.) Cf. Swed. dial. *skutta*, to take a long jump; also prov. E. *scuddle* (Bailey), frequent. of *scud*; see **Scud** and **Shoot**.

Scythe. (E.) M. E. *sithe*. A. S. *sīðe*, old form *sigðe*. Lit. 'cutter;' from √SEK. + Icel. *sigðr*, Low G. *seged*, *segd*; cf. O. H. G. *segansa*, G. *sense*. See **Secant**.

Se-, away, apart. (L.) L. *sē-*, prefix; full form *sed*, without.

Sea. (E.) M. E. *see*. A. S. *sǣ*, sea, lake.+Du. *zee*; Icel. *sær*; Dan. *sö*; Swed. *sjö*; G. *see*; Goth. *saiws*. Teut. type *saiwiz*.

Seal (1), a stamp. (F.–L.) M. E. *seel*. –O. F. *seel*, a signet (F. *sceau*).–L. *sigillum*, a seal, mark; dimin. form allied to *signum*, a mark. See **Sign**. Der. *seal*, vb.

Seal (2), a sea-calf. (E.) M. E. *sele*. A. S. *seolh*.+Icel. *selr*; Dan. *sæl*; Swed. *själ*; O. H. G. *selah*.

Seam (1). (E.) A. S. *sēam*. + Icel. *saumr*; G. *saum*; Du. *zoom*; Dan. Swed. *söm*. Teut. type *saumoz*, m.; from root *seu-*, *siw*. (√SIW.) Cf. Skt. *sū-tra-*, a thread. See **Sew** (1).

Seam (2), a horse-load. (Late L.–Gk.) M. E. *seem*, A. S. *sēam*. Borrowed (like G. *saum*) from Late L. *sauma*, late form of *sagma*, a horse-load, pack.–Gk. σάγμα, a pack-saddle. See **Sumpter**.

Seamstress, Sempstress. (E.; with F. *suffix*.) A. S. *sēamestre*, a seamstress; with suffix *-ess* (< F. *-esse* < Gk. *-ισσα*).–A. S. *sēam*, a seam (see **Seam**); with suffix *-estre*; see **Spinster**.

Sear, Sere, withered. (E.) M. E. *sere*, A. S. *sēar*, dry; *sēarian*, to dry up. +M. Du. *sore*, Du. *zoor*, Low G. *soor*.

Allied to Russ. *suχoi*, dry; Lith. *sausas*, dry; Gk. αὖος (for *σαυσος), dry; cf. Skt. *çush*, for *sush*, to dry up. Idg. type *sausos*. See **Austere**. Brugm. i. § 214.

Search, to explore. (F.–L.) M. E. *serchen*, *cerchen*.–O. F. *cercher* (F. *chercher*); prov. F. *sercher*, dial. of Verdun (Fertiault).–L. *circāre*, to go round; hence, to explore.–L. *circus*, a ring; see **Circus**. Der. *re-search*; cf. *shark*.

Season. (F.–L.) M. E. *seson*.–O. F. *seson*, *seison*, *saison*. [Cf. Span. *sazon*, O. Prov. *sadons*, *sasos*, Bartsch.]–Late L. *satiōnem*, acc. of *satio*, sowing-time, i. e. spring, regarded as the chief season for preparing crops.–L. *satus*, pp. of *serere*, to sow. ¶ The Span. word is *estacion*, Ital. *stagione*; from acc. of L. *statio*, a station, hence a stage (period).

Seat, sb. (Scand.) Icel. *sæti*, a seat; Swed. *säte*; Dan. *sæde*.–Icel. *sāt-*, 3rd grade of *sitja*, to sit; see **Sit**. Der. *seat*, vb.

Secant, a line that cuts another, or that cuts a circle. (L.) From *secant-*, stem of pres. pt. of *secāre*, to cut.+Russ. *siech'*, to hew. Brugm. i. § 635. (√SEK.) See **Saw**, **Scythe**, **Sickle**.

Secede. (L.) L. *sēcēdere*, to go apart, withdraw.–L. *sē-*, *sed*, apart; *cēdere*, to go. See **Cede**. Der. *secess-ion* (from the pp. *sēcess-us*).

Seclude. (L.) L. *sēclūdere*, to shut off.–L. *sē* (for *sed*), apart; *claudere*, to shut. See **Se-** and **Clause**. Der. *seclus-ion*, from the pp. *sēclūs-us*.

Second. (F.–L.) O. F. *second*.–L. *secundus*, second, next following. – L. *sequī*, to follow. See **Sequence**.

Secret. (F.–L.) M. E. *secre*, *secree*. –O. F. *secret*, 'secret;' Cot.–L. *sēcrētus*, secret, set apart; pp. of *sēcernere*, to separate.–L. *sē*, apart; *cernere*, to separate. See **Se-** and **Concern**. Der. *secrete*, vb., from L. *sēcrētus*; *secret-ion*.

secretary. (F.–L.) O. F. *secretaire*. –Late L. *sēcrētārium*, acc. of *sēcrētārius*, a confidential officer.–L. *sēcrēt-us*, secret (above).

Sect. (F.–L.) F. *secte*, 'a sect or faction;' Cot.–Late L. *secta*, a set of people, a suit of clothes, a suit at law.–L. *sec-* (as in *sec-undus*), base of *sequi*, to follow, sue. ¶ Not from *secāre*, to cut.

Section. (F. – L.) F. *section*. – L. *sectiōnem*, acc. of *sectio*, a cutting. – L. *sect-us*, pp. of *secāre*, to cut. See **Secant**.

Secular. (F.–L.) M. E. *seculere*.–

M. F. *seculier*, ' secular, temporall ; ' Cot.
— L. *sēculāris*, secular, worldly. — L. *sēculum*, *sæculum*, a generation, an age, the world.

Secure. (L.) L. *sēcūrus*, free from anxiety. — L. *sē-*, apart from ; *cūra*, anxiety. Doublets, *sicker*, *sure*.

Sedan-chair. (F.) Named from *Sedan*, a town in France. Cf. F. *sedan*, cloth made at Sedan (Littré).

Sedate, quiet. (L.) L. *sēdātus*, pp. of *sēdāre*, to settle or make calm, causal of *sedēre*, to sit. See below.

sedentary. (F. — L.) F. *sédentaire*. — L. *sedentārius*, ever sitting. — L. *sedent-*, pres. pt. of *sedēre*, to sit. See Sit. (√SED.) Brugm. i. § 574.

Sedge. (E.) M. E. *segge*. — A. S. *secge*, g., d., and acc. of *secg*, f., sedge ; lit. ' cutter,' i. e. sword-grass ; from the shape ; cf. *secg*, m. a sword. The A. S. *secg*, f. = Teut. type *sag-jā* ; from *saχ-*, 2nd grade of Teut. root *seχ-*, to cut. + Low G. *segge*, coarse grass. Cf. Irish *seisg*, sedge. (√SEK, to cut.) See Secant.

Sediment. (F. — L.) M. F. *sediment*. — L. *sedimentum*, a settling (of dregs). — L. *sedēre*, to sit, settle. See Sit.

Sedition. (F. — L.) O. F. *sedition*. — L. acc. *seditiōnem*, a going apart, dissension, mutiny. — L. *sed-*, apart ; *it-um*, supine of *īre*, to go. (√EI.)

Seduce, to lead astray. (L.) L. *sēdūcere*, to lead aside. — L. *sē* (for *sed*), apart ; *dūcere*, to lead. See Se- and Duke. Der. *seduct-ion* (from the pp. *sēduct-us*).

Sedulous, diligent. (L.) L. *sēdulus*, diligent. Cf. *sēdulō*, adv. busily ; from *sē*, apart from, *dolō*, abl. of *dolus*, guile. Brugm. i. § 244.

See (1), to perceive by the eye. (E.) M. E. *seen*, *sen*. — A. S. *sēon* ; pt. t. *sēah*, pp. *gesewen*. + Du. *zien* ; Icel. *sjá* ; Dan. *see* ; Swed. *se* ; G. *sehen* ; Goth. *saihwan*, pt. t. *sahw*. Teut. type *sehwan-*. Brugm. i. § 665. Der. *seer*, i. e. see-er.

See (2), seat of a bishop. (F. — L.) M. E. *se*. — O. F. *sed*, *se*, seat. — L. *sēdem*, acc. of *sēdes*, a seat. — L. *sēd-*, as in *sēd-ī*, pt. t. of *sedēre*, to sit. See Sit.

Seed. (E.) A. S. *sǣd*, seed. From A. S. *sāwan*, to sow. + Du. *zaad*, Icel. *sǣði*, *sāð*, Dan. *sæd*, Swed. *säd*, G. *saat*. Cf. Goth. *mana-sēths*, the world, lit. ' man-seed ; ' Lat. *sē-men*, seed. The A. S. *sǣd* answers to Teut. type *sǣ-dom*, neut. See Sow. Brugm. i. § 132.

Seek. (E.) M. E. *seken*. A. S. *sēcan*, pt. t. *sōh-te*, to seek, strive after. + Du. *zoeken* ; Icel. *sœkja*, *sœkja* ; Dan. *söge* ; Swed. *söka* ; Goth. *sōkjan* ; G. *suchen*. Teut. type *sōk-jan-* ; from *sōk-* = Idg. *sāg-*, as in L. *sāgīre*, to perceive, Gk. ἡγέομαι, I consider ; cf. O. Ir. *sagim*, I seek for. Der. *be-seech*.

Seel, to close up the eyes. (F. — L.) M. F. *siller*, ' to seal up the eie-lids ; ' Cot. Also spelt *ciller*. — O. F. *cil*, eye-lid. — L. *cilium*, eye-lid ; which is probably allied to Gk. τὰ κύλα, the parts under the eyes. See Supercilious.

Seem. (E.) M. E. *semen*. A. S. *sēman*, to satisfy, conciliate (hence, to suit, a sense due to the adj. *seemly* ; see below). For *sōm-ian*, where *sōm-* is the strong grade of *sam-*, as in E. *same*. + Icel. *sœma*, to honour, bear with, conform to, allied to *sœmr*, fit, *sōma*, to befit, and to *samr*, same. See Same.

seemly, fit. (Scand.) M. E. *semlich*. — Icel. *sœmiligr*, seemly. — Icel. *sœmr*, fit ; with suffix -*ligr*, like (-ly) ; where *sœm*- is the mutated form of *sōm*- (as in Icel. *sōm-a*, to befit), strong grade of *sam*-, as in Icel. *sama*, to beseem, cognate with Goth. *samjan*, to please, lit. ' to be the same,' agree with. — Icel. *samr*, same ; see Same.

Seer ; see See.

Seesaw. (E.) A reduplicated form ; from the verb *to saw*. From the motion of a sawyer. See Saw (1).

Seethe, to boil. (E.) Pt. t. *sod* ; pp. *sodden*. M. E. *sethen*, pt. t. *seeth* (pl. *soden*), pp. *soden*. A. S. *sēoðan*, pt. t. *sēað*, pp. *soden*. + Icel. *sjóða*, pt. t. *sauð* ; Dan. *syde* ; Swed. *sjuda* ; G. *sieden*. Teut. type *seuthan-*, pt. t. *sauth*, pp. *sud-anoz*. Allied to Goth. *sauths*, a burnt-offering.

Segment. (L.) L. *segmentum*, a piece cut off ; for *sec-mentum*. — L. *secāre*, to cut. See Secant.

Segregate, to separate from others. (L.) From pp. of *sēgregāre*, to set apart from a flock. — L. *sē-*, apart ; *greg-*, stem of *grex*, a flock. See Se- and Gregarious.

Seignior. (F. — L.) O. F. *seignor*, *seigneur*, lord. — L. *seniōrem*, acc. of *senior*, oider, hence, greater ; see Senior.

Seine, a large fishing-net. (F. — L. — Gk.) F. *seine*. — L. *sagēna*. — Gk. σαγήνη, a large fishing-net.

Seize, to grasp. (F. — Late L.) M. E.

seysen, saisen, a law term, to put one in *seisin* or possession of a thing, also, to take possession ; hence, to seize, take. ‒ O. F. *saisir, seisir,* to put in possession of, to take possession. ‒ Late L. *sacīre,* to put, place. ¶ It is usual to refer this verb to O. H. G. **sazjan,* to set, put, place, but this is an impossible form (it was really *sezzen*) ; or else to Goth. *satjan,* to set, which would have given **sadir, *sair.* See **Set.** Der. *seis-in,* O. F. *seisine, saisine,* from the verb *saisir.*

Selah, a pause. (Heb.) Supposed to mean 'a pause.'

Seldom. (E.) A. S. *seldan, seldum, seldon,* seldom, lit. rarely ; cf. *seld-līc,* strange, *seld-sīene,* rarely seen, strange.+ Du. *zelden,* Icel. *sjaldan,* Dan. *sielden,* Swed. *sällan,* G. *selten,* adv., seldom. Allied to Goth. *sildaleiks,* wonderful.

Select, choice. (L.) L. *sēlectus,* pp. of *sēligere,* to choose. ‒ L. *sē-,* apart ; *legere,* to pick, choose. See **Se-** and **Legend.** Der. *select,* vb.

Self. (E.) A. S. *self,* also *seolf, silf,* self.+Du. *zelf;* Icel. *sjálfr;* Dan. *selv;* Swed. *sjelf;* Goth. *silba ;* G. *selb, selb-st.*

Sell (1), to deliver for money. (E.) A. S. *sellan, sillan, syllan,* to hand over, deliver; a secondary verb, from the sb. **Sale.**+Icel. *selja,* Dan. *sælge,* Swed. *sälja,* O. H. G. and Goth. *saljan,* to hand over, offer. Teut. type **saljan-.*

Sell (2), a saddle. (F. ‒ L.) O. F. *selle,* seat, saddle. ‒ L. *sella,* seat ; for **sed-la.* ‒ L. *sedēre,* to sit. Brugm. i. § 475. See **Saddle.**

Selvage. (Du.) Also *selvedge.* Lit. 'self-edge.' ‒ M. Du. *selfegge,* selvage. ‒ M. Du. *self,* self; *egge,* edge ; [mod. Du. *zelfkant,* selvage ; from *zelf,* self, *kant,* edge] ; Low G. *sulf-egge,* self-edge, selvage.

Semblance, appearance. (F. ‒ L.) *semblance,* appearance. ‒ F. *sembler,* to seem. ‒ L. *similāre, simulāre,* to make like. ‒ L. *similis,* like. See **Simulate.**

Semi-, half. (L.) L. *sēmi-,* half.+Gk. ἡμι-, half; A. S. *sām,* half; Skt. *sāmi,* half, prob. related to Skt. *sāmya-,* equality, from *sama,* even, same (Benfey). Allied to **Same.** Der. *semi-breve,* &c.

Seminal, relating to seed. (F. ‒ L.) M. F. *seminal.* ‒ L. *sēminālis,* relating to seed. ‒ L. *sēmin-,* for *sēmen,* seed. ‒ L. *sē-* as in *sē-uī,* pt. t. of *serere,* to sow; with suffix *-men.* See **Sow** (1).

seminary. (L.) L. *sēminārium,* a seed-garden, seed-plot (hence a place of education). ‒ L. *sēmin-* (above).

Semolina. (Ital. ‒ L.) Ital. *semolino,* m., small seed, paste for soups; dimin. of *semola,* bran. ‒ L. *simila,* fine wheaten flower. See **Simnel.**

Sempiternal, everlasting. (L.) F. *sempiternel.* ‒ L. *sempitern-us,* everlasting. ‒ L. *sempi-,* for *semper,* always; with suffix *-ter-nus.* β. L. *semper* was perhaps formerly **sem-perti,* where **sem-* probably meant 'one,' as in L. *sem-el,* once, *simplex,* one-fold. Brugm. i. § 1023 (12); ii. § 160 (1).

Sempster. (E.) Later forms **Seamstress, Sempstress;** *with F. suffix.* A. S. *sēamestre,* a sempster; with suffix *-ess* (= F. *-esse* < Gk. *-ισσα*). ‒ A. S. *sēam,* a seam (see **Seam**) ; with suffix *-estre*; see **Spinster.**

Senary, belonging to six. (L.) L. *sēnārius,* adj., from *sēnī,* six apiece; for **sex-nī.* ‒ L. *sex,* six; see **Six.**

Senate, a council of elders. (F. ‒ L.) O.F. *senat.* ‒ L. *senātum,* acc. of *senātus,* council of elders. ‒ L. *sen-,* as in *sen-ex,* old, *sen-ium,* old age. Cf. O. Gk. ἔνος, old, Goth. *sineigs,* O. Ir. *sen,* W. *hen,* O. Skt. *sana-,* old. Brugm. i. § 117.

Send. (E.) A. S. *sendan.*+Du. *zenden;* Icel. *senda;* Dan. *sende;* Swed. *sända;* Goth. *sandjan;* G. *senden.* Teut. type **sandjan-,* for **santhjan-,* by Verner's law, from **santh,* 2nd grade of **senthan-,* to go. Hence *send* is a causal verb, meaning 'to make to go.' The Teut. **senthan-* (pt. t. **santh*) is a lost strong verb, of which the prime grade appears in Goth. *sinth-s,* A. S. *sīð* (for **sinð*), a journey, way, Teut. type **senthoz,* m., Idg. type **sentos,* as seen in O. Irish *sēt* (for **sent*), W. *hynt,* Bret. *hent* (for **sent*), a way. Cf. G. *gesinde,* followers; Goth. *gasinthja,* a travelling companion.

Sendal, Cendal, a rich thin silken stuff. (F. ‒ Late L. ‒ Skt.) O. F. *sendal, cendal ;* Late L. *cendalum, cindādus, cindātus,* &c. So called because brought from India. ‒ Skt. *sindhu-,* the Indus, also Scinde. ‒ Skt. *syand,* to flow : see **Indigo.** Cf. Gk. σινδών, fine Indian linen.

Seneschal, a steward. (F. ‒ Teut.) O. F. *seneschal.* Orig. sense 'old servant.' ‒ Goth. *sin-,* old (only preserved in superl. *sin-ista,* eldest, and in *sin-eigs,* old); *skalks,* a servant. Cf. **Senate** and **Marshal.**

senile, old. (L.) L. *senīlis*, old; cf. *sen-ex*, old. See Senate.

senior. (L.) L. *senior*, older; comp. of *senex*, old.

Senna. (Ital. — Arab.) Ital. *sena* (Florio).—Arab. *sanā*, senna.

Sennet, a signal-call on a trumpet. (F. —L.) See Nares; and Wright's note to K. Lear, i. 1. 23. Also spelt *sinet*.—O. F. *sinet*, *senet*, *segnet*, presumably 'a signal'; dimin. of F. *signe*, a sign, mark, note.—L. *signum*, a signal; see Sign, Tocsin.

Sennight; short for *seven night*, a week.

Sense. (F. — L.) F. *sens*, 'sence;' Cot.—L. *sensum*, acc. of *sensus*, feeling. —L. *sensus*, pp. of *sentīre*, to feel, perceive.

sensual. (L.) Late L. *sensuālis*, endowed with feeling.—L. *sensu-s*, feeling.— L. *sensus*, pp. of *sentīre*, to feel.

sentence. (F.—L.) F. *sentence*.—L. *sententia*, a way of thinking; for **senti-entia*.—L. *sentient-*, stem of pres. pt. of *sentīre*, to feel, think.

sentiment. (F.—L.) M. E. *sentement*.—O. F. *sentement*; as if from a Late L. **sentīmentum*.—L. *sentīre* (above).

Sentinel. (F. — Ital.—L. ?) M. F. *sentinelle*.—Ital. *sentinella*, 'a watch, a sentinell;' Florio. Cf. M. F. *sentinelle*, a watch-tower (Godefroy). Etym. uncertain; apparently ultimately from L. *sentīre*, to perceive. See Körting, §§ 7365, 7377.

Sentry. (F.—Ital.—L. ?) Confused with *sentinel*, but apparently of different origin. Spelt *sentrie* in Minsheu (1627), *sentery* in Milton, P. L. ii. 412. Prob. from O. F. *senteret*, a path, track, with reference to the sentinel's beat; double dimin. of O. F. *sente*, a path.—L. *sēmita*, a path.

Sepal, a leaf or division of the calyx of a flower. (F. — L.) F. *sépale*, a sepal. Coined to pair off with F. *pétale*, a petal, by taking part of the Lat. adj. *sēp-ar*, separate, and adding the same suffix -*āle* (Littré). Thus *sep-al* is, as it were, short for *separ-al*, where *separ-* was regarded as being allied to L. *sēparāre*, to separate. See Separate.

Separate, to keep apart. (L.) L. *sēparātus*, pp. of *sēparāre*, to sever.—L. *sē*, apart; *parāre*, to get ready, set. Der. *separate*, adj., kept apart (not so old as the verb in E.). Doublet, *sever*.

Sepia, ink from the cuttlefish. (L.—

Gk.) L. *sēpia*.—Gk. σηπία, cuttle-fish, sepia.

Sepoy. (Pers.) Pers. *sipāhī* (pronounced nearly as *sepoy*), a horseman, soldier. — Pers. *sipāh*, *supāh*, an army (Horn, § 699).

Sept, a clan. (F.—L.) Used in the 16th cent. as synonymous with *sect*, of which it is an arbitrary variant. Ducange has Late L. *septa* for Ital. *setta* (< L. *secta*); and Wedgwood cites Prov. *cepte*, a sect. See Sect.

September. (L.) L. *September*, the seventh month of the Roman year.—L. *septem*, seven. See Seven.

septenary. (L.) L. *septēnārius*, consisting of seven.—L. *septēnī*, pl., seven apiece.—L. *septem*, seven.

septennial. (L.) From L. *septennium*, a period of seven years.—L. *septennis*, adj., of seven years.—L. *sept-em*, seven; *annus*, year.

septuagesima. (L.) Lit. 'seventieth' (day).—L. *septuāgēsima* (*diēs*) seventieth (day), fem. of *septuāgēsimus*, seventieth. — L. *septuāginta*, seventy. — L. *septem*, seven; -*ginta*, related to Gk. -κοντα, for **δέκοντα*, from δέκα, ten.

Sepulchre. (F.—L.) O. F. *sepulcre*. —L. *sepulcrum*, ill-spelt *sepulchrum*, a tomb.—L. *sepul-tus*, pp. of *sepelīre*, to bury. Der. *sepult-ure*, from the pp. *sepultus*.

Sequel. (F.—L.) M. F. *sequele*, 'a sequell;' Cot.—L. *sequēla*, a result.—L. *sequī*, to follow. See below.

sequence. (F.—L.) O. F. *sequençe*, a sequence.—L. *sequentia*, sb., a following; from *sequent-*, stem of *sequens*, pres. pt. of *sequī*, to follow.+Lith. *sekti*, to follow; Gk. ἕπομαι, Irish *seich-im*, I follow; Skt. *sach*, to follow. (√SEQ.) Brugm. i. § 118.

sequester. (F.—L.) M.F. *sequestrer*, to sequester or lay aside.—L. *sequestrāre*, to surrender, lay aside.—L. *sequester*, a mediator, trustee, agent. Prob. orig. 'a follower.'—L. *sequī*, to follow.

Sequin, a gold coin. (F.—Ital.—Arab.) F. *sequin*; Cot.—Ital. *zecchino*, a Venetian coin.—Ital. *zecca*, a mint; Florio.—Arab. *sikka*(*t*), pron. *sikkah*, a die for coins.

Seraglio. (Ital.—L.) Misused in E.; the true sense is merely 'enclosure'; but it was confused with Pers. *sarāy* or *serāī*, a palace, king's court, seraglio. Really from Ital. *serraglio*, an enclosure; formed with suffix -*aglio* (< L. -*āculum*) from Late L. *serāre*, to bar, to bolt, shut in. = L. *sera*, a bar, bolt. = L. *serere*, to join together ; see Series. And see below.

Serai, a palace. (Pers.) Pers. *serāī*, a palace (Horn, § 727).

Seraph. (Heb.) Coined from the pl. form *seraphim*. = Heb. *serāphīm*, s. pl., seraphs, lit. exalted ones (Gesenius).

Seraskier, a Turkish general. (F. — Turk. — Pers. *and* Arab.) F. *séraskier*, *sérasquier*. = Turk. *ser'asker*, chief of the army, with a light sound of *i* after the *k*. = Pers. *sar*, head (with initial *sin*) ; and Arab. *'askar*, an army (Devic). The Pers. *sar* is cognate with Skt. *çiras*, head ; cf. Gk. κάρα, head. And see Sirdar.

Sere ; see Sear.

Serecloth ; see Cerecloth.

Serene. (L.) L. *serēnus*, bright, clear. Brugm. i. § 920 (4).

serenade. (F. — Ital. — L.) M. F. *serenade*. = Ital. *serenata*, music beneath a lady's window ; orig. fem. of pp. of *serenare*, to make clear or to cheer, to be merry. = L. *serēnus*, bright.

Serf. (F. — L.) F. *serf*, a servant. = L. *seruum*, acc. of *seruus*, a slave. See Serve.

Serge. (F. — L. — Gk. — Chinese ?.) F. *serge*, a silken stuff. = L. *sērica*, fem. of *sēricus*, silken, the same as *Sēricus*, belonging to the *Sēres*. = Gk. Σῆρες, pl., Chinese ; cf. σήρ, a silkworm. The name *Sēres* is from the Chinese *se, sei*, silk.

Sergeant, Serjeant. (F. — L.) M.E. *sergeant, sergant*. = O. F. *sergant, serjant*, an officer. = Late L. *seruientem*, acc. of *seruiens*, an officer ; orig. pres. pt. of *seruīre*, to serve. See Serve.

Series, a row. (L.) L. *seriēs*, a row. = L. *serere*, to join or bind together (pp. *sertus*). + Gk. εἴρειν (for *σέργειν) ; cf. Lith. *sēris*, a thread ; Icel. *sörvi*, a necklace.

Serif, the short cross-line at the end of a stroke of a letter. (Du.) Adapted (with *ser-* for Du. *schr-*) from Du. *schreef*, M.Du. *schreve*, a dash, short line. Allied to O. H. G. *screvōn*, to scratch, incise.

Serious. (F. — L.) O. F. *serieux*. = Late L. *seriōsus*, serious. = L. *sērius*, grave, earnest. Cf. G. *schwer*, heavy ; Lith. *swarùs*, heavy. See Sore (2).

Sermon. (F. — L.) F. *sermon*. = L. *sermōnem*, acc. of *sermo*, a speech, discourse.

Serous ; see Serum.

Serpent. (F. — L.) F. *serpent*. = L. *serpentem*, acc. of *serpens*, a serpent ; orig. pres. pt. of *serpere*, to creep. + Gk. ἕρπειν, to creep ; Skt. *sṛp*, to creep, *sarpa-*, a snake. Brugm. i. § 477. (√SERP.)

Serrated, notched like a saw. (L.) L. *serrātus*, notched like a saw. = L. *serra*, a saw.

Serried, crowded together. (F. — L.) F. *serrer*, to compact, press close, lock. = Folk-L. *serrāre*, for L. *serāre*, to bolt. = L. *sera*, a bolt. = L. *serere*, to join. Cf. Seraglio.

Serum, whey. (L.) L. *serum*, whey, serum. + Gk. ὀρός, whey ; Skt. *sara(s)*, adj., flowing, sb., whey. (√SER, to flow.) But cf. Brugm. i. § 466. Der. *ser-ous*, adj.

Serve. (F. — L.) F. *servir*. = L. *seruīre*, to serve. = L. *seruus*, a slave ; cf. *seruāre*, to keep, protect. Der. *serv-ant*, from pres. pt. of F. *servir* ; *serv-ice*, F. *service*, L. *seruitium* ; *serv-ile*, L. *seruīlis* ; *servitude*, F. *servitude*, L. acc. *seruitūdinem* ; also *serf, sergeant*.

Service-tree, a kind of wild pear-tree. (L. *and* E.) *Service* is a corruption of *serv-ës* (dissyllabic), the M. E. plural of *serf* or *serve*, the name of the fruit. A.S. *syrf-*, the fruit of the service-tree ; *syrftrēow*, a service-tree (correctly, sirf-tree). = L. *sorbus*, the tree ; *sorbum*, its fruit.

Session. (F. — L.) F. *session*. = L. *sessiōnem*, acc. of *sessio*, a sitting. = L. *sessus*, pp. of *sedēre*, to sit. See Sit.

Set (1). (E.) A. S. *settan*, to set, make to sit ; causal of *sittan*, to sit (derived from the 2nd grade *sat*). + Icel. *setja* ; Dan. *sætte* ; Swed. *sätta* ; G. *setzen* ; Du. *zetten* ; Goth. *satjan* ; all causal forms. Teut. type *satjan-*. See Sit.

Set (2). When we speak of a *set* of things, this is a variant of *sect*. The Late Latin word is *secta*, common in old wills ; for which we also find *setta*.

Seton, an artificial irritation under the skin. (F. — L.) F. *séton*, in use in the 16th century ; the orig. sense is 'a thread.' Formed (as if from Late L. *sēto*) from L. *sēta*, a bristle, stiff hair. See Satin.

Settee, a seat with a long back ; apparently an arbitrary variation of *settle*, sb., which see below.

settle (1), a long bench with a high back. (E.) A.S. *setl*, a seat. + Goth. *sitls* ; G. *sessel* ; L. *sella* (for *sed-la*). See Sell (2), Sit.

settle (2), to fix, adjust. (E.) M. E. *setlen.* A. S. *setlan*, to fix; also, to take a seat, settle down as in a seat, from A. S. *setl*, a seat; see above. ¶ Perhaps it may have been affected by M. E. *sahtlen*, to reconcile, A. S. *sahtlian*, *sæhtlian*, to reconcile. − A. S. *seht*, *sæht*, reconciliation; borrowed from Icel. *sātt*, *sætt*, reconciliation, peace; which Noreen (§ 73) connects with L. *sanctus*, holy.

Seven. (E.) A.S. *seofon*, *sibun*.+Du. *zeven*; Icel. *sjau*, *sjö*; Dan. *syv*; Swed. *sju*; G. *sieben*; Goth. *sibun*; L. *septem*; Gk. ἑπτά; W. *saith*; Irish *seacht*; Russ. *seme*; Lith. *septyni*; Skt. *sapta*. Idg. type **septom.* **Der.** *seven-teen*, A. S. *seofontyne*; *seven-ty*, A. S. *hund-seofontig* (*hund* being dropped); *seven-th.*

Sever, to separate. (F. − L.) O. F. *sevrer.* − L. *sēparāre*, to separate. See Separate. **Der.** *dissever.*

several, adj. (F.−L.) O. F. *several.* − Late L. *sēparāle*, a thing set apart. − L. *sēparāre*, to separate (above).

Severe. (F.−L.) O. F. *severe.*−L. *seuērus*, severe, serious, grave. **Der.** *sever-ity*, M. F. *severité.*

Sew (1), to fasten with thread. (E.) M. E. *sowen*, *sewen.* A. S. *siwian*, to sew. +Icel. *sȳja*; Dan. *sye*; Swed. *sy*; O.H.G. *siuwan*; Goth. *siujan*; L. *suere*; Lith. *suti*; Russ. *shite*; Skt. *siv*, to sew. Cf. Gk. κασσύειν, to sew together; and see Hymen. (✓SIW.)

Sew (2), to follow; the same as Sue; see Sequence.

Sewer (1), a large drain. (F.−L.) Frequently spelt *shore*. From O. F. *sewiere*, *seuwiere*, a sluice, channel for draining a pond. − Late L. type **exaquāria*, short for Late L. *exaquātōrium*, a channel for draining.−L. *ex*, out ; *aqua*, water. (The derivation of E. *ewer* from L. *aquāria* is parallel.)

Sewer (2), the officer who formerly set and tasted dishes, &c. (E.) ' *Seware, at mete,* Depositor, dapifer, sepulator ;' Prompt. Parv. [Hence M. E. *sewen*, to set meat, bring in dishes, &c.] The M. E. *seware*, *sewere* is short for *assewer*, *asseour* (N. E. D.).−O. F. *asseour*, one who sets the table.−O. F. *asseoir*, to set, place; orig. to sit beside.−L. *assidēre*, to sit by. −L. *as-*, for *ad*, near ; *sedēre*, to sit. See Sit and Assess. ¶ Perhaps confused with M. E. *sew*, pottage, from A. S. *sēaw*, juice.

Sex. (F.−L.) F. *sexe.*−L. *sexum*, acc.

of *sexus*, sex; also *secus*, n. Was it orig. ' division ;' from *sec-āre*, to cut ? See Segment, Secant. **Der.** *sex-u-al*, L. *sexuālis.*

Sexagenary. (L.) L. *sexāgēnārius*, belonging to sixty. − L. *sexāgēnī*, sixty each; distribute form of *sexāginta*, sixty. − L. *sex*, six; and *-ginta*, related to Gk. -κοντα, for **δέκοντα, from δέκα, ten. See Six and Ten.

sexagesima. (L.) L. *sexāgēsima* (*diēs*), i. e. sixtieth (day); fem. of *sexāgēsimus*, sixtieth, ordinal form of *sexāginta*, sixty.

sexennial. (L.) From L. *sexennium*, a period of six years.−L. *sex*, six; *annus*, a year.

sextant, the sixth part of a circle. (L.) L. *sextant-*, stem of *sextans*, a sixth part. − L. *sext-us*, sixth, from *sex*, six; with suffix *-ans*, like that of a pres. pt. of a verb in *-āre.*

Sexton; see Sacristan.

Sextuple, sixfold. (L.) Coined from *sextu-s*, sixth ; with suffix *-ple* (as in *quadru-ple*), answering to L. *-plic-*, stem of *-plex*, as seen in *du-plex*, *com-plex.*

SH.

Shabby, mean. (E.) Also *shabbed*; *shabby* and *shabbed* are the native E. equivalents of the Scand. *scabby* and *scabbed.* See Scab. For the sense, cf. *scurvy* (= *scurfy*); E. Fries. *schabbig*, scabby, also miserable, mean.

Shackle. (E.) A.S. *sceacul*, bond, fetter; orig. a loose bond; from its *shaking* about.+Icel. *skökull*, pole of a carriage, from *skaka*, to shake; Swed. *skakel*, loose shaft of a carriage; Dan. *skagle*, the same. Cf. Swed. dial. *skak*, a chain. See Shake.

Shad, a fish. (E.) A.S. *sceadd*.+Prov. G. *schade*, a shad; cf. Irish *sgadan*, O. Irish *scatán*, a herring; W. *ysgadan*, pl., herrings.

Shaddock, a large species of orange. (E.) Named from Captain *Shaddock*, who first introduced it into the West Indies from China, early in the eighteenth century.

Shade, Shadow. (E.) M. E. *shade*, *shadwe.* A. S. *sceadu*, shadow, fem. sb. The M. E. *shade* is from the A. S. nom. *sceadu*; the M. E. *shadwe* (mod. E. *shadow*) is from the dat. case *sceadwe.* + Du. *schaduw*, Goth. *skadus*, shadow;

G. *schatten*, O. Irish *scáth*, Corn. *scod*, shade; Gk. σκότος, σκοτία, gloom.

Shaft. (E.) A. S. *sceaft*, shaft of a spear.+Icel. *skapt*, *skaft*, Dan. Sw. *skaft*; G. *schaft*, Du. *schacht* (for *schaft*). Further allied to L. *scāpus*, a shaft, stem, stalk; Gk. σκῆπτρον, Doric σκᾶπτον, a staff, sceptre. All apparently from Idg. root *skap*, to support. 2. Or else *shaf-t* = that which is *shaven* or cut smooth; from Shave, q. v.

Shag, rough hair. (E.) A. S. *sceacga*, hair. + Icel. *skegg*, Swed. *skägg*, a beard, Dan. *skiæg*, beard, awn, wattle; cf. Icel. *skaga*, to jut out. The orig. sense is 'roughness.' See Shaw. Der. *shagg-y*, adj. *Shag* tobacco is rough tobacco.

Shagreen, a rough-grained leather. (F. – Turkish.) F. *chagrin*. It was orig. made of the skin of the *back* of the horse or mule. – Turk. *sāghrī*, *saghrī*, back of a horse, shagreen.

Shah, king of Persia. (Pers.) Pers. *shāh*, a king. O. Pers. *khshāyathiya*, a king; allied to Skt. *kshatra(m)*, dominion, from *kshi*, to rule; cf. Gk. κτάομαι, I possess. Lit. sense 'ruler'; Horn, § 772; Brugm. i. § 920. See Check. Der. *pa-sha*.

Shake. (E.) A. S. *sceacan*, *scacan*, pt. t. *scŏc*, pp. *scacen*.+Icel. *skaka*, Sw. *skaka*, Dan. *skage*. Teut. type *skakan-*.

Shako, a military cap. (F. – Hung.) F. *shako*. – Hungarian *csako*, a cap, shako; spelt *tsākō* in Dankovsky's Magyar Lexicon, p. 900.

Shale, a slaty rock. (G.) G. *schale*, a shell, peel, scale; whence *schal-gebirge*, a mountain formed of thin strata. Hence also O. F. *escale* and E. *scale* (1). See Scale (1).

Shall. (E.) A. S. *sceal*, I shall, I must; pt. t. *sceolde*, I should, ought. The orig. sense was 'to owe,' to be liable for; cf. Lith. *skilti*, to owe, be liable.+Icel. *skal*, pt. t. *skyldi*; Sw. *skall*; Dan. *skal*; Du. *zal*; G. *soll*; Goth. *skal*, infin. *skulan*. Cf. G. *schuld*, debt, guilt; Lith. *skelēti*, to be liable. Brugm. i. § 795.

Shalloon, a light woollen stuff. (F.) From *Chalons*, in France, E. of Paris.

Shallop, a light boat. (F. – Du.) F. *chaloupe* [whence Span. *chalupa*, 'a flat-bottomed boat,' Minsheu (1623); Port. *chalupa*]. – Du. *sloep*, a sloop. See Sloop.

Shallot, Shalot, a kind of onion. (F. – L. – Gk. – Heb.) O. F. *eschalote*, variant of *escalogne*, a shallot. – L. *ascalōnia*, a

shallot; fem. of *Ascalōnius*, belonging to Ascalon. – Gk. Ἀσκάλων, Ascalon; a chief city of the Philistines. – Heb. *Ashqelōn*.

Shallow. (E.) M. E. *schalowe*; cf. also *schold*, *schald*, Barbour, Bruce, ix. 354; for which see Shoal. An E. word; but of doubtful origin. However, M.E. *schalowe* is allied to M. E. *schal-d*, shallow, as they have a common base *schal-*. And perhaps allied to Low G. *schaal*, *schalig*, G. *schal*, insipid, stale (as liquids when little is left in the vessel); cf. Du. *verschalen*, to grow stale or flat.

Shalm; see Shawm.

Sham. (E.) A London slang term, due to Northern E. *sham*, a shame, disgrace (hence, trick). 'Whea's *sham* is it' = whose fault is it? Whitby Glossary. See Shame.

Shamble, to walk awkwardly. (E.) Lowl. Sc. *shammel*, *shamble*, to rack the limbs with long strides; also, to distort; *shammel shanks*, crooked legs. Cf. E. Fries. *schamel*, shamefaced, modest, also poor, miserable; O. Fries. *skamel*, poor; Du. *schamel*. If this connexion be right, the adj. is formed from the sb. *shame*; see Shame.

Shambles. (L.) Orig. stalls on which butchers expose meat for sale; pl. of *shamble*, a bench, butcher's bench or stall. A.S. *scamel*, a stool. – L. *scamellum*, a stool, little bench; allied to *scamnum*, step, bench, *scabellum*, foot-stool. L. *scamnum* is for **scab-num*, **scap-num*, allied to *scāpus*, a stem. Brugm. i. § 241.

Shame. (E.) A.S. *sceamu*, *scamu*.+ Icel. *skömm*; Dan. Sw. *skam*; G. *scham*. Allied to Goth. *skanda*, shame, G. *schande*.

shamefaced, modest. (E.) Corruption of M. E. *shamefast*, modest. – A.S. *scamfæst*, lit. firm in shame, i. e. in modesty. – A.S. *scamu*, shame, modesty; *fæst*, fast, firm; see Fast.

Shammy, Shamoy, a kind of leather. (F. – G.) Orig. *chamois* leather; see Blount and Phillips. See Chamois.

Shampoo. (Hind.) Hindustani *chāmpnā*, to join, to stuff, press, thrust in, shampoo; from the kneading or pressure used in the operation. Perhaps directly from the imperative *chāmpo* of the same verb; Yule.

Shamrock. (C.) Irish *seamrog*, trefoil, dimin. of *seamar*, trefoil; Gael. *seamrag*.

Shank, lower part of the leg. (E.) A.S. *sceanca*, *scanca*, bone of the leg.

+Du. *schonk*, Dan. *skank*, Swed. *skank*. Further related to G. *schenkel*, shank; G. *schinken*, ham. **Der.** *skink*.

Shanty, a hut. (Irish.) Said to be from Irish *sean*, old; *tigh*, a house.

Shape, vb. (E.) M. E. *schapen*; a new formation from the sb. *schap*, A. S. *ge-sceap*; or from the pp., on the analogy of *sceacan*, pp. *sceacen*. The A. S. vb. is *sceppan*, *scieppan*, with a weak infin.; pt. t. *scōp*, pp. *scapen*. **+** Icel. *skapa*, Swed. *skapa*, Dan. *skabe*, Goth. *ga-skapjan*, G. *schaffen*; Du. *scheppen* (weak). All from Teut. type **skapan-*, **skapjan-*, pt. t. **skōp*. Cf. Lith. *skabèti*, to cut, hew. Brugm. i. § 701.

Shard, Sherd, fragment. (E.) A. S. *sceard*, a fragment; lit. ' cut thing.' From **skar*, 2nd grade of **sker-an-*, to shear. See **Shear.** Cf. Icel. *skarð*, a notch. **Der.** *pot-sherd*.

share (1), a portion. (E.) A. S. *scearu*, a share, part. From **skar* (above).

share (2), a plough-share. (E.) A. S. *scear*, plough-share. From the same.

Shark, a voracious fish. (F.−L.) The name of the fish is from the Tudor verb *to shark*, to prowl; *to shark* for a dinner, to try to get one; *to shark* for a living; see Cent. Dict. Prob. from North F. (Picard) *cherquier*, equivalent to O. F. *cercher* (E. *search*), to hunt after. F. *chercher*. Cf. *cercher le broust*, 'to hunt after feasts;' Cot. Godefroy has two examples of the spelling *cherquier*. Cf. Ital. *cercare del pane*, ' to shift for how to live;' Torriano.−L. *circāre*, to go round. −L. *circus*, a ring. See **Search.** If this be right, *to shark* is a variant of *to search*, but was much used (formerly) in the sense of to prowl about for a living. Hence *shark*, sb. (1), a greedy fellow (Johnson); (2) a greedy fish.

Sharp. (E.) A. S. *scearp*.**+**Du. *scherp*, Icel. *skarpr*, Swed. Dan. *skarp*, G. *scharf*. Teut. type **skarpoz*. Prob. allied to **Scrape. Der.** *scarp, escarpment*.

Shatter. (E.) M. E. *schateren*, to scatter, to dash as a falling stream; hence to break in pieces. A. S. *scaterian*, to scatter, A. S. Chron. 1137. Cf. E. Fries. *schattern*, Du. *schateren*, to resound; M. Du. *schetteren*, to rattle. See **Scatter,** which is a doublet; cf. Milton, Lyc. 5.

Shave. (E.) A. S. *sceafan*, *scafan*, pt. t. *scōf*, pp. *scafen*.**+**Du. *schaven*; Icel. *skafa*; Swed. *skafva*, Dan. *skave*, Goth.

skaban, G. *schaben*; Lith. *skapoti*, to shave, cut, Russ. *skopite*, to castrate, Gk. σκάπτειν, to dig. Cf. also L. *scabere*, to scrape. (√SQAB, SQAP.) Brugm. i. §§ 569, 701.

Shaw, thicket. (E.) A. S. *scaga*.**+**Icel. *skōgr*, a shaw, wood; Swed. *skog*, Dan. *skov*, North Fries. *skōg*. Allied to Icel. *skagi*, a ness (Noreen); N. Fries. *skage*, a nook of land; cf. Icel. *skaga*, to jut out. Allied to **Shag.**

Shawl. (Pers.) Pers. *shāl* (pron. *shawl*), a shawl, mantle.

Shawm, Shalm, a musical instrument. (F.−L.−Gk.) O. F. *chalemie*, a reed pipe; allied to *chaume*, a straw; cf. M. H. G. *schalmīē*.−L. *calamus*, a reed. −Gk. κάλαμος, a reed. See **Haulm.**

She. (E.) M. E. *sche*, *scho*; also *scæ*, A. S. Chron. 1140. In the Northumbrian dialect, we find *scho* used as a dem. pronoun, though the A. S. *sēo* is the fem. of the def. article. The A. S. *sēo* would have become *see*, but this form never occurs; rather, it became *seō* (Lind. *sio*, John iv. 23); whence (perhaps influenced by the Icel. m. and f. demonstr. pron *sjā*, that), came Northumb. *scho* or *sho*; and this seems to have suggested the Midland *sche*, *she*, *s*ᵹ*e*; the true South. form being *heo*, *he* (which caused confusion with the masc. *he*). ⌊We also find such forms as *hyo*, *hio*, *ho*, ᵹ*ho*, ᵹ*o*, mod. Lanc. *hoo*, all from *heō*.⌋ The A. S. *sēo* is the fem. of *se*, orig. 'that;' cognate with Goth. *sa*, that.**+**Du. *zij*, G. *sie*; Icel. *sū*, fem. of *sā*, that; Goth. *sō*, fem. of *sa*, that; Gk. ἡ, fem. of ὁ; Skt. *sā*, she, fem. of *sa*, *sas*, he. For Icel. *sjā* see Noreen, § 399. See Sweet, E. Gr. § 1068.

Sheaf. (E.) M. E. *scheef*. A. S. *scēaf*, a sheaf, pile of corn shoved together.− A. S. *scēaf*, 2nd grade of *scūfan*, to shove. **+** Du. *schoof*, Icel. *skauf*, Bavar. *schaub*, sheaf; from Teut. **skaub*, 2nd grade of **skūban-*, to shove; see **Shove.**

Sheal, a temporary summer hut. (Scand.) Also spelt *shiel*, *shieliṅ*, *sheelin*.−Icel. *skjōl*, a shelter, cover, Dan. Swed. *skjul*, a shed; Icel. *skȳli*, a shed. Cf. Skt. *sku*, to cover.

Shear. (E.) A. S. *sceran*, pt. t. *scær*, pp. *scoren*.**+**Du. *scheren*, Icel. *skera*, Swed. *skära*, Dan. *skære*, G. *scheren*, to shear. Teut. type **skeran-*, pt. t. **skar*, pp. **skoranoz*. Allied to O. Ir. *scar-aim*, I separate, Gael. *sgar*, to sever; W. *ysgar*, to part;

Gk. κείρειν (for *(σ)κέργειν), to cut; Lith. *kirwis*, an axe. (√SQER.) Brugm. i. §§ 515, 631.

Sheath. (E.) A. S. *sceáð, scǽð*, a sheath, orig. that which separates, hence a husk, shell, pod. + Du. *scheede*, Dan. *skede*, Swed. *skida*, G. *scheide*, a sheath; Icel. *skeiðir*, fem. pl., a sheath (lit. things that separate or open). All from the Teut. base *skaith*; for which see **Shed** (1). Der. *sheathe*, vb.

Shebeen, a liquor-shop. (Irish—E.) Apparently a dimin. (with suffix -*in*) of Irish *seapa*, a shop. — E. *shop*; see **Shop**.

Shed (1), to part, pour, spill. (E.) Orig. 'to separate.' A. S. *sceádan, scádan*, pt. t. *scéad, scéd*, pp. *sceáden*, to shed; whence M. E. *schēden*, weak verb (with long *e*, but the *e* has been shortened, the pt. t. being *shadde* or *shedde*). + Goth. *skaidan*, G. *scheiden*, to part; O. Sax. *skéðan*, O. Fries. *skéða, skéda*. From Teut. base *skeith*, varying to *skeid*, to split (see **Shide**); or from the 2nd grade *skaith, skaid*. The Idg. root would, regularly, be *skheit*, but we only find √SKHEID; cf. Gk. σχίζειν, for *σχίδγειν, to cleave; L. *scindere*, to cut; Lith. *skēdziu*, I separate. All from an older √SKHEI. Brugm. i. §§ 201, 599.

Shed (2), a slight shelter, hut. (E.) O. Kentish *shed* (written *ssed*), shade; a dialectal form; Ayenbite of Inwyt. See **Shade**.

Sheen, fairness, splendour. (E.) M. E. *schene*, adj., fair. A. S. *scéne, sciene, scýne*, fair, 'showy;' allied to *scéawian*, to show, see. + O. Sax. *scóni*, adj.; Du. *schoon*, adj.; G. *schön*, adj.; cf. Goth. *ibna-skauns*, of like appearance. Teut. type *skau-niz*, 'showy;' see **Show**. ¶ Not allied to *shine*.

Sheep. (E.) A. S. *sceáp, scép*; pl. unchanged. + O. Sax. *skáp*; Du. *schaap*; G. *schaf*. Teut. type *skǽpom*, neut.

Sheer (1), bright, pure, perpendicular. (Scand.) A *sheer* descent is a clear (unbroken) one. M. E. *shere*, bright. — Icel. *skœrr*, Dan. *skær*, sheer, bright; Teut. type *skairiz*. Cf. Icel. *skírr*, A. S. *scír*, bright; G. *schier*, Goth. *skeirs* (Teut.type *skeiroz*); from the base (*skei*-) of the verb *to shine*; see **Shine** (Noreen). ¶ The *sh* (for *sk*) is due to A. S. *scír*. Der. *Sheer-Thursday*, the day before Good Friday; cf. Icel. *skíra*, to cleanse, baptize.

Sheer (2), to deviate from one's course. (Du.) Du. *scheren*, to shear, cut, with-

draw, go away; *scheerje van hier*, sheer off! (Sewel). Cf. Low G. *schere hen*, get out! See **Shear**.

Sheet. (E.) M. E. *schete*. Anglian *scéte*, A. S. *sciete, scýte*, a sheet; also (without mutation) *scéat, scéata*, a corner, nook, fold of a garment, corner of a sail, hence a *sheet* or rope fastened to a corner of a sail, called in A. S. *scéat-líne* (sheet-line). Cf. A. S. *scéat*, 2nd grade of *scéotan*, to shoot, hence to jut out. The orig. sense of *sheet* was 'projection,' hence 'corner,' &c.+Icel. *skaut*, corner, sheet of a sail; Swed. *sköte*, the lap; Du. *schoot*, shoot, sprig, sheet; Goth. *skauts*, hem of a garment; G. *schooss*, flap of a coat, lap, bosom. All from Teut. *skaut*, 2nd grade of *skeutan*-, to shoot; see **Shoot**.

Sheet-anchor, an anchor to be 'shot' out in emergency. (E.) From prov. E. *sheet*, M.E. *schēten*, A.S. *scéotan*, to shoot. See **Shoot**.

Sheik, a chief. (Arab.) Arab. *sheikh*, an elder, chief; orig. sense 'old.'

Shekel, a Jewish weight and coin. (Heb.) Heb. *sheqel*, a shekel (weight). — Heb. *shāqal*, to weigh.

Shekinah. (Heb.) It signifies the visible presence of God; lit. 'dwelling.' — Heb. *shekanāh*, dwelling. — Heb. *shākan*, to dwell.

Sheldrake. (E.) For *sheld-drake*, i.e. variegated or spotted drake. Cf. Orkney *sheld-fowl*, a sheldrake (Cent. Dict.). '*Sheld*, flecked, party-coloured;' Coles (1684). M. E. *sheld* is a shield; and the allusion is to the patch round the breast. Cf. A. S. *scild*, a shield, used also of part of a bird's plumage (Grein). So also Icel. *skjöldungr*, a sheldrake, *skjöldóttr*, dappled, from *skjöldr*, a shield. See **Shield**.

Shelf. (E.) M. E. *schelfe, shelfe*. A. S. *scilfe*, story (of a building), shelf. Orig. a thin piece, flake; allied to *shell* and *skill*.+Low G. *schelf*, a board, shelf; cf. *schelfern*, to flake off; also E. Fries. *schalfer, schilfer*, a chip, splinter; Du. *schilfer*, a scale. Extended forms, from the root of **Skill** and **Scale**.

Shell. (E.) M. E. *shelle*, sb. A. S. *scell, scyll*. + Du. *schel*; Icel. *skel*; Goth. *skalja*, a tile. Teut. type *skaljā*, fem. The sense is 'thin flake'; cf. Swed. *skala*, to peel. See **Scale, Skill**. Der. *shell*, verb.

Shelter. (E.) A curious development of M. E. *sheldtrume*, a body of guards or troops, a squadron; frequently spelt *sheltron*, *sheltrun*; it came to mean a guard or protection of any kind (P. Plowm., Halliwell). **–** A. S. *scildtruma*, lit. 'shield-troop,' a guard. **–** A. S. *scild*, shield; *truma*, a band of men, allied to *trum*, firm. See **Shield** and **Trim**.

Shelve, to slope down. (E.) A derivative of *shelf*, but the connexion is not clear. A *shelf* came to mean a slab of stratified rocks, also a sand-bank; and the sense of 'slope' prob. refers to the sloping edges of the latter. Torriano translates M. Ital. *stralare* by 'to shelve or go aside, aslope, awry'; a sense perhaps suggested by M. Du. *scheel*, awry, G. *schel*, *scheel*.

Shepherd. (E.) A.S. *scēaphyrde*, a keeper of sheep; see **Herd** (2). **Der.** *shepherd-ess*.

Sherbet, a drink. (Arab.) Arab. *sharbat*, a drink, draught, sherbet, syrup. **–** Arab. root *shariba*, he drank. **Der.** *shrub* (2), *syrup*.

Sherd; see **Shard**.

Shere-Thursday; see **Sheer** (1).

Sheriff. (E.) For *shire-reeve*. A. S. *scīr-gerēfa*, a shire-reeve; see **Shire** and **Reeve**. **Der.** *sheriff-al-ty*, usually spelt *shrievalty*.

Sherry. (Span.–L.) Formerly *sherris*; *sh* being an old pron. of Span. *x*. **–** Span. *Xeres*, a town in Spain, near Cadiz. **–** L. *Cæsaris*, gen. case of *Cæsar*, proper name (Dozy).

Shew; see **Show**.

Shibboleth, a test-word of pronunciation. (Heb.) Heb. *shibbōleth*, an ear of corn, also a river; see Judges xii. 6.

Shide, a thin piece of board. (E.) A.S. *scīd*, a billet of wood; from the base (**skeid*) of the verb *to shed*.**+**Icel. *skīð*, G. *scheit*, a billet; O. Irish *scīath*, a shield. See **Shed**, **Sheath**.

Shield. (E.) A. S. *scild*, *sceld*.**+**Du. *schild*, Icel. *skjöldr*, Dan. *skiöld*, Swed. *sköld*, Goth. *skildus*, G. *schild*. Teut. type **skelduz*, m. Perhaps 'thin board'; cf. Lith. *skel-ti*, to split.

Shieling; see **Sheal**.

Shift. (E.) M. E. *schiften*, to divide, change, shift, remove; orig. 'to divide.' A.S. *sciftan*, to divide. **+** Icel. *skipta* (for *skifta*), to divide, part, shift, change; Swed. *skifta*, Dan. *skifte*, the same. Allied to Icel. *skīfa*, to cut into slices, *skīfa*, a slice, prov. E. *shive*, a slice, *sheave*, a

wheel of a pulley, Du. *schijf*, G. *scheibe*, a slice, disc. See **Shiver** (2).

Shillelagh, an oaken stick used as a cudgel. (Irish.) Named from *Shillelagh*, a barony in Wicklow famous for oaks. It means 'descendants of Elach'; from Irish *siol*, seed, descendants.

Shilling. (E.) A.S. *scilling*. **+** Du. *schelling*; Icel. *skillingr*; Dan. Swed. *skilling*; Goth. *skilliggs* (for **skillings*); G. *schilling*. β. The suffix -*ing* is a diminutive which occurs also in E. *farthing*, and in A.S. *pen-ing*, a penny. The base is either **skel-*, to resound, ring; or **skil-*, to divide; see **Skill**. Reason for the name uncertain; but cf. Swed. *skiljemynt*, Dan. *skillemynt*, small change, small money.

Shillyshally. (E.) Formerly *shill I*, *shall I*; a reduplicated form of *shall I*.

Shimmer, to glimmer. (E.) A.S. *scimrian*, frequent. form of *scīman*, *scimian*, to shine, allied to *scīnan*, to shine; see **Shine**.**+**Du. *schemeren*; Swed. *skimra*; G. *schimmern*. Cf. O. H. G. *scīmo*, a bright light, Icel. *skīmi*, a gleam, Irish *sgeimh*, *sgiamh*, beauty.

Shin. (E.) A. S. *scinu*; also *scinbān*, shin-bone. **+** Du. *scheen*; G. *schiene*, also a splint; Swed. *sken-ben*, Dan. *skinnebeen*, shin-bone. Orig. sense perhaps 'thinly covered bone,' and allied to **Skin** (Franck; doubtful). Cf. A.S. *scīa*, shin.

Shine. (E.) A. S. *scīnan*, pt. t. *scān*, pp. *scinen*. **+** Du. *schijnen*, Icel. *skīna*; Dan. *skinne*; Swed. *skina*; Goth. *skeinan*; G. *scheinen*. (Base SKEI.) Cf. **Sheer** (1), **Shimmer**.

Shingle (1), a wooden tile. (L.) M.E. *shingle*, corruption of *shindle* (Minsheu), as shewn by the corresponding G. *schindel*, a shingle, splint, thin piece of wood. **–** L. *scindula*, a shingle, as if from L. *scindere*, to cleave; but really for *scandula*, a shingle.

Shingle (2), coarse round gravel on the sea-shore. (Scand.) Corruption of Norweg. *singl* or *singling*, coarse gravel, shingle, named from the crunching or ringing noise made by walking on it. **–** Norweg. *singla*, to ring, tinkle, Swed. dial. *singla* (the same); frequent. form of Swed. dial. *singa*, the same word as E. *sing*; see **Sing**. Cf. Lowl. Sc. *chingle*, shingle, allied to *chink*.

Shingles. (F. – L.) A variant of *sengles*, pl. of the old word *sengle*, a girth; the disease encircling the body like a belt.

— O. North. F. *chengle,* O. F. *cengle, sangle,* 'a girth, a sengle;' Cot. **—** L. *cingula,* a belt. **—** L. *cingere,* to surround; see Cincture.

Ship. (E.) A. S. *scip.* **+** Du. *schip,* Icel. *skip,* Dan. *skib,* Swed. *skepp,* Goth. *skip,* G. *schiff.* Teut. type **skipom,* neut. Hence *skiff, skipper, equip.*

Shire. (E.) A. S. *scīr,* a shire, province; orig.' employment, government.' Cf. A. S. *scirian,* to appoint, allot; O. H. G. *scira,* business. ¶ Not allied to **Shear.**

Shirk. (F. **—** L. ?) The verb *to shirk* seems to be a variant of *sherk* or *shark,* to prowl about; hence, to act in a paltry way, to keep out of danger. See **Shark.**

Shirt. (E.) M. E. *shirte, shurte.* A. S. *scyrte.* **—** A. S. *scort,* short; see **Short.+** Icel. *skyrta,* a shirt, kind of kirtle; Swed. *skjorta,* Dan. *skiorte.* So called because *short.* Doublet, *skirt.*

Shittah-tree, Shittim-wood. (Heb.) *Shittim* is a pl. form. **—** Heb. *shittāh,* pl. *shittim,* a kind of acacia (the *t* is *teth*). Of Egypt. origin (Gesenius).

Shive, Sheave; see **Shiver** (2).

Shiver (1), to tremble. (E.) Formerly *shever,* in Baret (1580); M. E. *chiueren, cheueren* (*chiveren, cheveren*), where *ch* stands for earlier *c(k),* as if from an A. S. **cifer,* which I suppose to be a variant of *cwifer.* See **Quiver** (1). ¶ The spelling with *sh* was due to confusion with the word below.

Shiver (2), a splinter, small piece of wood. (E.) A *shiver* is a small piece; hence *to shiver,* to break in pieces. Again, *shiver* is the dimin. of *shive,* a thin slice, the same as prov. E. *sheave,* a thin disc of wood, wheel of a pulley. E. Fries. *schife, schive, schif',* N. Fries. *skiv, skeev.* **+** Du. *schijf;* Icel. *skīfa,* Dan. *skive,* Swed. *skifva;* G. *scheibe,* a slice. Teut. base **skeib,* Idg. root **skeip;* whence Gk. σκοῖπος, a potter's disc (Hesychius). See **Shift.**

Shoal (1), a multitude of fishes, a troop, crowd. (E.) Spelt *shole* in Spenser; M. E. *scole,* a troop, throng, crowd. A. S. *scolu,* a troop.+O. Sax. *skola,* a troop, band; Du. *school,* a shoal. Teut. type **skulā,* fem.; from **skul-,* weak grade of **skel-,* to separate, set apart. See **Skill.** ¶ The sailor's phrase ' a *school* of fish ' exhibits the Du. form of the same word; it also appears as *scull,* Troil. v. 5. 22.

Shoal (2), a shallow, a sandbank. (E.)

Orig. an adj., meaning ' shallow,' formerly *shole;* M. E. *shold* or *shald;* see **Shallow.** A. S. *sceald,* shallow; found in place-names. Cf. Pomeran. *scholl,* shallow water; and note E. *old,* prov. E. *ole,* from O. Merc. *ald,* A. S. *eald.*

Shoar, a prop; see **Shore** (2).

Shock (1), a violent jolt. (E.) M. E. *schokken,* to shock, jolt. E. Fries. *schok-ken.+*Du. *schok,* sb., *schokken,* vb. ; Low G. *schokken, schukken,* vb. ; O. H. G. *scoc,* sb. (whence F. *choc,* sb., *choquer,* vb.). Cf. G. *schaukel,* a swing. See **Shog.**

Shock (2), a pile of sheaves of corn. (E.) M. E. *schokke.+*M. Du. *schocke,* a shock, cock, heap; so called from being tossed together; from M. Du. *schocken,* to jolt, shock, cock, heap up; see **Shock** (1) above. Cf. Swed. *skock,* a heap, flock; Dan. dial. *skok,* N. Fries. *skock,* a heap of six sheaves.

Shock (3), a rough-coated dog. (E.) *Shock-headed* is rough-headed, with shaggy hair. Perhaps from **Shock** (2), a heap.

Shoddy, a material obtained from tearing into fibres old woollen goods. (E.) Etym. uncertain ; but cf. Devon *shod,* shed, spilt, M.E. *schoden, scheden,* to separate; see **Shed.**

Shoe. (E.) M. E. *scho.* A. S. *sceō, scōh;* pl. *sceōs, scōs.+*Du. *schoen;* Icel. *skōr;* Swed. and Dan. *sko;* Goth. *skōhs;* G. *schuh.* Teut. type **skōhoz,* masc.

Shog, to jog on. (E.) M.E. *schoggen,* to jog; variant of *schokken,* to jolt. See **Shock** (1); and cf. **Jog.**

Shoot. (E.) A. S. *sceōtan,* later form of *scēotan,* str. vb. [with *eō* for *ēo* as in *choose*] ; pt. t. *scēat,* pp. *scoten,* of which only the pp. *shotten* is preserved (in the phrase *shotten herring* = a herring that has lost its roe).+Du. *schieten;* Icel. *skjōta;* Dan. *skyde;* Sw. *skjuta;* G. *schiessen.* Teut. type **skeutan-,* pt. t. **skaut,* pp. **skutanoz.* Brugm. i. § 623.

Shop. (E.) A. S. *sceoppa,* a stall, booth. Allied to *scypen,* a pen for cattle. **+** Low G. *schupp,* a shed; G. *schoppen,* a shed, covert (whence O. F. *eschoppe,* a shop).

Shore (1), strand of a lake or sea. (E.) M. E. *schore.* A. S. *score* (Somner); cf. A. S. *scoren clif,* a shorn cliff, precipice. Cf. A. S. *scor-,* weak grade of *sceran,* to shear. See **Shear.**

Shore (2), **Shoar,** a prop. (E.) M. E. *schore.* Not in A. S. E. Fries. *schōr, schore* (also *schār, schare*), a prop. Cf.

A. S. *sceorian*, to project, jut out. **+** Du. *schoor*, a prop; M. Du. *schooren*, to under-prop; Norweg. *skora*, prop. Cf. also Icel. *skorða*, a prop, stay, esp. under a boat; *skorða*, vb., to under-prop, shore up.

Shore (3), a sewer; see **Sewer**.

Short. (E.) A. S. *sceort*, short. Cf. Du. *schorten*, to lack (fall short), Icel. *skortr*, shortness, O. H. G. *scurz*, short. The Teut. base would appear to be **skert-*, to cut; as if extended from **sker-*, to cut; see **Shear**. Cf. also Icel. *skarðr*, diminished, cut down. ¶ But as the G. *kurz* is from L. *curtus*, short, it is usual to explain all these words as borrowed from a L. type **ex-curtus*; which is improbable.

Shot. (E.) M. E. *schot*. A. S. *scot*, a shot, *ge-sceot*, implements for shooting; cf. A. S. *scot-*, weak grade of *scēotan*, to shoot. **+**Icel. *skot*, Du. *schot*, a shot, shooting; G. *schuss*, a shot. See **Shoot**.

Shoulder. (E.) A. S. *sculder*, *sculdor*. **+**Du. *schouder*, Swed. *skuldra*, Dan. *skulder*, G. *schulter*. Perhaps allied to O. H. G. *skerti*, the shoulder; cf. also O. H. G. *harti*, the shoulder-blade.

Shout. (E.) M. E. *shouten*; Chaucer, Troil. ii. 614. Cf. Icel. *skūta*, *skūti*, a taunt; see **Scout** (2).

Shove. (E.) M. E. *shouven*. A. S. *scūfan*, pt. t. *sceaf*, pp. *scofen*, to shove.**+** Icel. *skūfa*; Du. *schuiven*, G. *schieben* (pt. t. *schob*); Goth. *skiuban*. Teut. type **skeuban-* or **skūban-*, pt. t. **skaub*, pp. **skubanoz*. Cf. Lith. *skubùs*, quick, hasty, industrious; Skt. *ksubh*, to become agitated, *kshobha-*, agitation. Brugm. i. § 992.

shovel. (E.) A. S. *scofl*, a shovel, for lifting and shoving; cf. A.S. *scof-*, weaker grade of *scūfan* (above).**+**Du. *schoffel*; G. *schaufel*, O. H. G. *skūvala* ; a form which makes a connexion with *shove* doubtful. Der. *shovel-er*, a kind of duck.

Show, Shew. (E.) M. E. *schewen*, vb. A. S. *scēawian*, to see, behold ; later, to make to see, point out, show.**+**Du. *schou-wen*, Dan. *skue*, G. *schauen*, to behold. Cf. Goth. *us-skaws*, cautious, wakeful. Teut. base **skaw*, Idg. root **skau* ; cf. Gk. θνο-σκόος, an inspector of an offering ; also L. *cau-ēre*, to heed, *cau-tus*, watchful ; Gk. κοέω, I observe; Skt. *kav-i-*, wise. From the same root we have *cautious*. Brugm. i. §§ 163, 639. **Der.** *sheen*, *scavenger*.

Shower. (E.) M. E. *schour*. A. S. *scūr*. **+** Du. *schoer*; Icel. *skūr*; Swed.

skur; Goth. *skūra*, a storm ; G. *schauer*, O. H. G. *scūr*. Brugm. i. § 627.

Shred. (E.) M. E. *shrēde*, sb. A. S. *scrēade*.**+**M.Du. *schroode*, a shred (Kilian); Pomeran. *schrood*. From Teut. **skraud*, 2nd grade of **skreud-* ; for which see **Shroud**.

Shrew, a scold. (E.) M. E. *shrewe*, adj., applied to both sexes, wicked, bad. A. S. *scrēawa*, a shrew-mouse, fabled to have a very venomous bite. **Der.** *shrew*, to curse, talk like a shrew ; *be-shrew*.

shrewd, malicious, cunning. (E.) The old sense is 'malicious.' M. E. *schrewed*, accursed, depraved, hence malicious ; pp. of *schrewen*, to curse, from the adj. *schrewe*, malicious, bad (above).

shrew-mouse, an animal like a mouse. (E.) A. S. *scrēawa*; see **Shrew** (above).

Shriek. (E.) A native form of *screech*; from M. E. *schriken*, to shriek. See **Screech**. Imitative ; see **Shrike**.

Shrievalty; see **Sheriff**.

Shrift, confession. (L.) A. S. *scrift*, confession, prescribed penance. Cf. A. S. *scrif-*, weak grade of *scrif-an*, to shrive, to impose a penance ; ult. of L. origin ; see **Shrive**.**+**Icel. *skript*, Swed. *skrift*, Dan. *skrifte*; Du. and G. *schrift*, writing. See **Shrive**.

Shrike, the butcher-bird. (E.) Cf. Westphalian *schrīk*, a shrike; Icel. *skrīkja*, a shrike, lit. 'shrieker,' from Icel. *skrīkja*, to titter, orig. to shriek, and allied to Icel. *skrækja*, to screech. See **Shriek** and **Screech**.

Shrill. (E.) M. E. *shril*; cf. Lowl. Scotch *skirl*, a shrill cry, *skirl*, to cry aloud. Cf. E. Fries. *schrel*, Low G. *schrell*, G. *schrill*, shrill ; A. S. *scralletan*, to cry aloud ; Norweg. *skryla*, *skræla*, to cry shrilly. From Teut. root **skrel* (2nd grade **skral*), to cry aloud.

Shrimp. (E.) M. E. *shrimp*; cf. Lowl. Scotch *scrimp*, to straiten, *scrimpit*, dwarf-ish. A parallel form to *shrink*; cf. A. S. *scrimman*, to shrink ; Dan. dial. *skrimpe*, a lean cow. See the traces of O. Swed. *skrimpa*, strong verb, to contract, in mod. Swed. dialects (Rietz) ; and cf. M. H. G. *schrimpfen*, to shrink, G. *schrumpfen*, Dan. *skrumpen*, shrivelled ; Du. *schrompe*, a wrinkle. See **Shrink**.

Shrine. (L.) A. S. *scrīn*, a box. **–** L. *scrīnium*, chest, box.

Shrink. (E.) A. S. *scrincan*, pt. t.

scranc, pp. *scruncen*. to contract, shrivel up.**+**M. Du. *schrinken*, to shrink, grow smaller; Swed. *skrynka*, a wrinkle. Allied to **Shrimp, Shrug.**

Shrive; see **Shrove-tide.**

Shrivel. (E.) In Shak. An E. word. **+**Swed. dial. *skryvla*, to shrivel up, to wrinkle; *skryvla*, a wrinkle. Perhaps allied to Swed. *skroflig*, rough, and to G. *schroff*, rugged.

Shroud. (E.) A. S. *scrūd*, garment, clothing.**+**Icel. *skrūð*, ornament, shrouds of a ship; Dan. and Swed. *skrud*, dress, attire. Orig. a ' shred ' of stuff, a piece cut or torn off; cf. A. S. *scrēade* (= mod. E. *shred*). The Teut. base is **skreud*, to cut; the 2nd grade **skraud* appears in **Shred,** q. v. Cf. L. *scrūta*, broken bits? **Der.** *scroll.*

Shrove-tide, Shrove-Tuesday. (L. *and* E.) The time for *shrift* or confession. The sb. *shrove* is formed from *shrove*, 2nd grade of *shrive* (M. E. *schriuen*, pt. t. *schroof*).—A.S. *scrifan*, to shrive, impose a penance, pt. t. *scrāf*, pp. *scrif-en* (whence *scrif-t*, shrift).**+**O Fries. *skrīva* (pt. t. *skrēf*); O. Sax. *skrīban*, to write; Du. *schrijven* (pt. t. *schreef*); Dan. *skrive* (pt. t. *skrev*); Swed. *skrifva* (pt. t. *skref*); G. *schreiben* (pt. t. *schrieb*). Teut. type **skreiban-*, pt. t. **skraib*, pp. **skribanoz.* Conjugated as a genuine Teut. verb, but probably an early borrowing from Lat. *scrībere*, to write. See **Scribe.**

Shrub (1), a low dwarf tree. (E.) M. E. *schrob.* A.S. **scrob*, a shrub; whence *scrybb*, underwood. Cf. prov. E. *shruff*, light rubbish wood, *scroff*, refuse of wood; Norw. *skrubba*, the dwarf cornel; E. dial. *scrub*, underwood; Dan. dial. *skrub*, brushwood.

Shrub (2), a drink, chiefly made with rum. (Arab.) Arab. *shirb, shurb*, a drink. **—** Arab. root *shariba*, he drank. See **Sherbet.**

Shrug. (E.) M. E. *shruggen*, to shiver. The old sense was to shrink, shrink up. Cf. Dan. *skrugge, skrukke*, to stoop; Swed. dial. *skrukka, skrugga*, to huddle oneself together, allied to *skrinka*, to shrink, Norw. *skrukken*, shrunken. See **Shrink.**

Shudder. (E.) M. E. *schoderen, schudderen.* Low G. *schuddern*; Dan. dial. *skuddre*, to shudder. A frequentative verb. Cf. E. Fries. *schüdden*, to shake; O. Sax. *skuddian*, to shake; M. Du. *schudden*, to shake, tremble. Also G.

schütteln, to shake, frequent. of O. H. G. *skuttan.*

Shuffle. (E.) Frequentative of *shove.* E. Fries. *schuffeln*, to shuffle along, from *schufen*, to shove, push. Cf. *scuffle*, which is the frequentative of Swed. *skuffa*, to push, shove. See **Scuffle.**

Shun. (E.) M. E. *shunien, shonien.* A. S. *scunian*, to shun, avoid; orig. sense (perhaps) to hurry away, hasten. Cf. Icel. *skunda, skynda*, Swed. *skynda sig*, Dan. *skynde*, to hasten, hurry, speed. **Der.** *scoundrel, schooner.*

Shunt. (E.) Prov. E. *shunt*, to turn aside; M. E. *shunten*, to start aside, avoid. Perhaps allied to **Shun** (above).

Shut. (E.) M. E. *shutten, shitten.* A. S. *scyttan*, to shut; to fasten a door with a bolt (called a *shuttle*). We still say ' to *shoot* a bolt.' The A. S. *scyttan* is a weak verb; cf. *scut-*, weak grade of *scēotan*, to shoot.**+**Du. *schutten*, G. *schützen* (from the same grade). See **Shoot.**

shuttle. (E.) So called from being *shot* across the threads in weaving. M. E. *schitel*, also a bolt of a door; A. S. *scyttel*, a bolt. Formed, with suffix *-el* of the agent, from Teut. **skut*=A. S. *scut-*, weak grade of *scēotan*, to shoot.**+**Dan. *skytte, skyttel*, a shuttle; cf. Du. *schiet-spoel*, a shuttle, lit. ' shoot-spool.' **Der.** *shuttle-cock*; from its being *shot* backwards and forwards like a *shuttle*, and because furnished with feathers. ¶ Not for *shuttle-cork.*

Shuttle-cock; see above.

Shy. (E.) M. E. *shey, scheouh*, said of a shy horse.**—** A. S. *scēoh*, timid; cf. E. Fries. *schöi.*+Dan. *sky*, shy; Swed. *skygg*, skittish, shy, coy; Du. *schuw*, shy; G. *scheu*, timid, shy, M. H. G. *schiech.* Teut. type **skeuhoz.* See **Eschew.**

Si–Sy.

Siamang, a large ape. (Malay.) Malay *siāmang.*

Sib, related. (E.) A. S. *sibb*, akin to; see **Gossip.** Cf. M. Swed. *sif*, akin to.

Sibilant, hissing. (L.) L. *sībilant-*, stem of pres. part. of *sībilāre*, to hiss. **—** L. *sībilus*, hissing. Imitative.

Sibyl. (L.—Gk.) L. *Sibylla.* **—** Gk. Σίβυλλα, a Sibyl or prophetess.

Sicca, in phr. *sicca rupee*, newly coined rupee. (Hind. — Pers. — Arab.) Hind. *sikka*, a die for coining. **—** Pers. *sikka(h)*, the

same. – Arab. *sikka(h)*, *sakk*, the same. Rich. Dict., pp. 839, 837. Cf. **Sequin.**

Sick. (E.) M. E. *sik*, *sēk*. A. S. *sēoc*. +Du. *ziek*; Icel. *sjūkr*; Dan. *syg*; Swed. *sjuk*; G. *siech*; Goth. *siuks*, which is related to Goth. *siukan*, to be ill (pt. t. *sauk*). Teut. type **seukoz*.

Sicker, Siker, certain, secure. (L.) M. E. *siker*. Borrowed from Late L. *sécurus*, for L. *sēcūrus*, secure; whence also O. Fries. *siker*, *sikur*, Du. *zeker*, G. *sicher*, O. H. G. *sichur*, Swed. *säker*, Dan. *sikker*, W. *sicr*. See **Secure.**

Sickle. (L.) A. S. *sicol.* – L. *secula*, a sickle, cutter. – L. *sec-āre*, to cut. See **Secant.** Cf. **Scythe, Saw (1).**

Side. (E.) M. E. *side*. A. S. *sīde*, side; allied to A. S. *sīd*, long, wide.+Du. *zijde*; Icel. *sīða* (allied to Icel. *sīðr*, long, hanging down); Dan. *side*; Swed. *sida*; G. *seite*.

Sidereal, starry. (L.) For *sideral*, from L. *sīderālis*, relating to the stars. – L. *sīder-*, for **sīdes-*, stem of *sīdus*, a star. Cf. *con-sider.*

Sidesmen. (E.) Officers chosen to assist a churchwarden; also called *side-men*, i.e. men at one's side. Cf. L. *assessor*, one who sits beside another.

Siege. (F. – L.) The orig. sense was 'seat,' or 'a sitting down,' esp. in order to besiege a town. – O. F. *siege*, a seat, throne; F. *siège*. Not immediately from L. type **sedicāre*; cf. Late L. *assedium*, a siege, for L. *obsidium*, a siege; both words being due to L. *sedēre*, to sit; see **Sedentary.** Der. *be-siege*, with E. prefix.

Sienna, a pigment. (Ital.) Made from earth of *Sienna*, a place in Tuscany.

Sierra, a chain of hills. (Span. – L.) Span. *sierra*, a saw, an outline of hills. – L. *serra*, a saw.

Siesta, orig. a noon-day nap. (Span. – L.) Span. *siesta*, the hottest part of the day, the time for a nap, gen. from one to three o'clock. But orig. the sixth hour, or noon. – L. *sexta (hōra)*, sixth hour, noon; fem. of *sextus*, sixth. – L. *sex*, six.

Sieve. (E.) M. E. *sive*. A.S. *sife*; oldest spelling *sibi* (8th cent.).+Du. *zeef*; G. *sieb*. Teut. types **sibiz*, **siboz*, neut.; cf. Lith. *sijote*, to sift.

sift. (E.) A. S. *siftan*, to sift; allied to A.S. *sife*, a sieve.+Du. *ziften*, to sift, *zift*, a sieve; *zeef*, a sieve.

Sigh, vb. (E.) M. E. *sighen*, also *syken*.

A. S. *sīcan*, to sigh, pt. t. *sāc* (in *on-sāc*), pp. *sicen*. Cf. Swed. *sucka*, Dan. *sukke*, to sigh, groan. Of imitative origin.

Sight. (E.) M. E. *sight*. A. S. -*siht*, *gesiht*, commonly *gesihð*. Verbal sb. allied to A. S. *sēon*, to see. + Du. *gezigt*; Dan. *sigte*; Swed. *sigt*; G. *sicht*. See **See.**

Sign. (F. – L.) O.F. *signe.* – L. *signum*, a mark. Der. *sign*, vb.; *sign-at-ure*, from the pp. of the L. verb *signāre*, to sign. Brugm. i. § 762 (3). Der. *sennet.*

signal. (F. – L.) F. *signal.* – Late L. *signāle*, sb., neut. of L. *signālis*, belonging to a sign. – L. *signum*, a sign.

signet. (F. – L.) F. *signet*; dimin. of F. *signe*; see **Sign** (above).

signify. (F. – L.) F. *signifier*, to betoken. – L. *significāre*, to shew by signs. – L. *signi-*, for *signum*, a sign; *-ficāre*, for *facere*, to make.

Signor. (Ital. – L.) Ital. *signore*, sir. – L. acc. *seniōrem*; see **Seignior.**

Silence. (F. – L.) F. *silence.* – L. *silentium*, silence. – L. *silent-*, stem of pres. pt. of *silēre*, to be silent. Cf. Goth. *ana-silan*, to be silent. Der. *silent*, from L. *silent-*, stem of *silens*, pres. pt. of *silēre*.

Silex, flint. (L.) L. *silex* (stem *silic-*), flint. Der. *silic-a.* Brugm. i. § 980.

Silhouette. (F.) This meagre form of portrait, made by tracing the outline of a shadow, was named (in derision) after Étienne de *Silhouette*, French minister of finance in 1759.

Silk. (Chinese?) A.S. *seolc*, *seoluc* (cf. *milk*, A. S. *meolc*); Icel. *silki*; Ch. Slav. *shelkū* (Russ. *shelk′*). Perhaps from Chinese *se*, *sei*, silk; cf. L. *Sēricum*, silk, neut. of *Sēricus*, adj., belonging to the *Sēres*; from Gk. Σῆρες, pl., Chinese. See **Serge.**

Sill, base of a door. (E.) A.S. *syll*, a base, support.+Icel. *syll*, *svill*, a sill; Swed. *syll*, Swed. dial. *svill*; Dan. *syld*; G. *schwelle*, sill, threshold. Cf. Goth. *ga-suljan*, to lay a foundation. The Teut. base appears to be **swel*, to found, to form as a base; 2nd grade **swal*, whence G. *schwelle*; the weak grade **swul*, **sul* gives Goth. *ga-suljan* and A. S. *syll*, f. (Teut. type **sul-jā*). Der. *ground-sill*, spelt *grunsel* in Milton, P. L. i. 460.

Sillabub, a mixture of wine with milk, &c. (E.) Formerly *sillibouk*, or *merribouk*. '*Laict aigre*, a sillibub or merribowke;' Cot. Apparently from E. *silly* (merry) and M. E. *bouk*, A. S. *būc*, the belly. A jocose name.

Silly. (E.) Orig. 'timely;' then happy, lucky, blessed, innocent; lastly, simple, foolish. M. E. *seli, sili*; thus *syly man* in Seven Sages, ed. Wright, 1361 = *seli man* in Seven Sages, ed. Weber, 1473. A.S. *sǽlig, gesǽlig*, timely; from *sǽl*, time, season, happiness.+Du. *zalig*, G. *selig*, blest, happy; cf. also Icel. *sǽll*, Swed. *säll*, Goth. *sēls*, good.

Silo, a pit for storing grain or fodder. (Span.—L.—Gk.) Span. *silo.*—L. *sīrum*, acc. of *sīrus.*—Gk. σῑρός. **Der.** *en-sil-age.*

Silt. (Scand.) 1. Either formed, with participial suffix -*t*, from *sile* (M. E. *silen*), to drain. — Swed. *sila*, to drain, strain, filter; *sil*, a filter. 2. Or from M. Swed. *sylta*, mud; allied to A.S. *syl-u*, a miry place. See **Sully.**

Silvan, Sylvan. (L.) The spelling with *y* is bad.—L. *siluānus*, belonging to a wood.—L. *silua*, a wood. Cf. Gk. ὕλη, a wood (connexion with *silua* doubtful; Brugm. i. § 102).

Silver. (E.) O. Merc. *sylfur* (Matt. x. 9); A.S. *seolfor*; earlier *siolofr.*+Du. *zilver*; Icel. *silfr*; Dan. *sölv*; Swed. *silfver*; G. *silber*; Goth. *silubr*; Russ. *serebro*; Lith. *sidábras.*

Similar. (F.—L.) F. *similaire*; as if from L. *similāris, extended from *similis*, like. Cf. O. Ir. *samail*, Ir. *samhail*, W. *hafal*, like. Allied to *simul*, together, and to E. **Same.** Brugm. i. §§ 438, 442.

simile. (L.) L. *simile*, a comparison, a like thing; neut. of *similis*, like.

similitude. (F.—L.) F. *similitude.*— L. acc. *similitūdinem*, likeness. — L. *similis*, like.

Simious, monkey-like. (L.) From L. *sīmia*, an ape.—L. *sīmus* (Gk. σιμός), flat-nosed.

Simmer. (E.) A frequentative form, from the base *sim*, to express the sound of gentle boiling. Cf. Dan. *summe*, G. *summen*, Swed. dial. *summa*, to hum, buzz.

Simnel, a kind of rich cake. (F.—L.) O. F. *simenel*; Late L. *simenellus, siminellus*, bread of fine flour; also called *sim-ella* in Late L. — L. *simila*, wheat-flour of the finest quality; whence *siminellus*, for *similellus. Allied to Gk. σεμίδαλις, fine flour. Cf. **Semolina.**

Simony, traffic in ecclesiastical preferment. (F.—L.—Gk.—Heb.) F. *simonie*; Late L. *simōnia*. Named from *Simon Magus* (Acts viii. 18).—Gk. Σίμων, Simon.

—Heb. *Shim'ōn*, Simeon; lit. 'hearkening.' —Heb. root *shāma'*, to hear.

Simoom. (Arab.) Arab. *samūm*, a sultry pestilential wind; from its poisonous nature.—Arab. root *samma*, he poisoned (Devic).

Simper, to smirk. (Scand.) From Scand.; cf. Norw. *semper*, fine, smart; Dan. dial. *semper, simper*, affected, coy, prudish; M. Swed. *semper*, one who affectedly refrains from eating; cf. Bavar. *zimpern*, to be affectedly coy (from Low G.). Formed from M. Swed. *sipp, simp*, an affected woman, Swed. *sipp*, adj., finical, prim. All from the notion of *sipping*, or taking only a little at a time; hence, prudish, affected, coy, &c. Cf. Low G. *sipp*, prim, *den Mund* sipp *trekken*, to make a small mouth; and M. Du. *sippen*, to sip. See note to **Sip.**

Simple. (F.—L.) F. *simple.*—L. *simplicem*, acc. of *simplex*, lit. 'one-fold.'— L. *sim-* (appearing also in *sin-guli*, one by one, *sem-el*, once, *sin-ul*, together); and *plic-*, from *plicāre*, to fold; see **Simulate** and **Ply. Der.** *simplicity*, F. *simplicité*, from L. acc. *simplicitātem*; *simpli-fy*, to make simple.

simpleton. (F.—L.) I.e. *simple-t-on*, with double suffix; formed with F. suffix -*on* from Picard and M. F. *simplet*, a simple person, fem. *simplette*, 'a simple wench;' Cot.—F. *simple*, simple; with suffixed -*t*. (So also *musk-et-oon*.) Cf. Span. *simplon*, a simpleton.

Simulate. (L.) From pp. of L. *simulāre*, also *similāre*, to make like.—L. *similis*, like; *simul*, together, lit. 'at once.' From Idg. **sem-*, one; cf. Goth. *sim-lē*, once; Gk. ἕν, neut., one, μία, f. (for *σμ-ία); Skt. *sa-kṛt*, once; Gk. ἅ-παξ, once; Brugm. ii. § 165.

simultaneous. (L.) Late L. *simultāneus*; coined from L. *simult-im*, at the same time.—L. *simul*, together.

Sin. (E.) A.S. *synn* (*sinn, senn*).+Du. *zonde*; Icel. *synd, synð*; Dan. Swed. *synd*; G. *sünde*, O. H. G. *suntea*. Thus the A.S. *synn* represents a Teut. type *sundjā, fem., or rather an Idg. type *sṇtjā; where *sṇt is the weak grade of *sent*: *sont*. Allied to L. *sons* (stem *sont-*), guilty, sinful, orig. 'real.' [' Language regards the *guilty* man as the man *who it was*;' Curtius.] Cf. Ion. Gk. ἐ-οντ-, stem of ἐών (for *ἐσ-ων), being, pres. pt. of εἰμί, I am. See **Sooth. Der.** *sin*, vb.

Since. (E.) Written for *sins*, which is short for M. E. *sithens*, since. This is formed, with adverbial suffix -*s*, from M. E. *sithen*, since, a modification of A. S. *siððan*, for *sið ðan*, after that. β. The A. S. *sið* was orig. an adj., meaning 'late,' but here represents the compar. adv., later, after; cf. Goth. *seithus*, late, *seithu*, adv., late, -*seiths*, adv., later. The A. S. *ðan* is the instrumental of the definite article or demonst. pronoun. The G. *seitdem*, since, is similarly formed. See Sievers, §§ 323, 337.

Sincere. (F. – L.) O. F. *sincere*. – L. *sincērus*, pure, sincere. **Der.** *sincerity*, from M. F. *sinceritĕ*, from L. acc. *sincēritātem*.

Sinciput. (L.) The fore part of the head; lit. 'half head.' – L. *sinciput*, half the head. – L. *sēmi-*, half; and *caput*; see Semi- and Capital. Brugm. i. § 121.

Sinder, the true spelling of **Cinder,** q. v.

Sine. (L.) From L. *sinus*, a bosom, a fold, a curve; peculiarly used. See Sinus.

Sinecure. (L.) For *sine curā*, without cure of souls; hence, an office without work.

Sinew. (E.) M. E. *sinewe*. A. S. *sinu* (dat. *sinwe*), *seonu*. + Du. *zenuw*; Dan. *sene*; Swed. *sena*; G. *sehne*; also Icel. *sin*. Perhaps allied to Skt. *snāva(s)*, a tendon.

Sing. (E.) A. S. *singan*, orig. to sing, resound; pt. t. *sang*, pp. *sungen*. See Song; and see singe. + Du. *zingen*; Icel. *syngja*; Dan. *synge*; Swed. *sjunga*; Goth. *siggwan* (for **singwan*); G. *singen*.

singe, to scorch. (E.) For *senge*; M. E. *sengen*. A. S. *sengan*, to singe; lit. ' to make to sing,' from the hissing of a burning log, &c. Causal of *singan*, to sing (above). + Du. *zengen*, G. *sengen*, causal verbs, similarly formed.

Single. (L.) L. *singulus*, single, separate, in Plautus and in late Latin; in classical Latin, we have only *singulī*, pl., one by one. Allied to Simple, q. v. Brugm. i. § 441. ¶ M.E. and O. F. *sengle*.

singular. (F. – L.) M.E. *singuler*. – F. *singulier*. – L. *singulāris*, single. – L. *singulī*, pl., one by one (above).

Sinister. (L.) L. *sinister*, on the left hand, inauspicious.

Sink. (E.) Properly intransitive [the transitive form should rather end in -*ch*; cf. *drench* from *drink*]. – A. S. *sincan*,

intrans., pt. t. *sanc*, pp. *suncen*. + Du. *zinken*; Icel. *sökkva* (for *sinkva*); Dan. *synke*; Swed. *sjunka*; G. *sinken*; Goth. *sigkwan* (for **singkwan*). β. For the trans. form, cf. A. S. *sencan*, to cause to sink, G. *senken*. Der. *sink*, orig. a place into which filth *sank* or was collected; Cor. i. 1. 126. Brugm. i. §§ 421(3), 679.

Sinople, green. (F. – L. – Gk.) F. *sinople*, ' green; ' Cot. – Late L. *sinōpis*, greenish, also reddish; L. *sinōpis*, red ochre. – Gk. σινωπίς, σινωπική, a red earth found in Cappadocia, and imported -from *Sinope*, on the Black Sea.

Sinus, a bend, fold, &c. (L.) L. *sinus*, a bosom, bend, bay, fold. Now only used in anatomy, and, in the form *sine*, in mathematics. **Der.** *sinuous*, L. *sinuōsus*, full of curves.

Sip, vb. (E.) M. E. *sippen*. It answers to A. S. *sypian*, to absorb moisture, a causal form allied to A. S. *sūpan*, to sup. See Sup. ¶ In the E. Fries. *sippen*, to sip, M. Du. *sippen*, to sip, Norw. *sipla*, to sip, the *i* suggests a connexion with Low G. *sipen*, to drip; but cf. E. Fries. *süpken*, to sip, Swed. dial. *syppa*, to drink. **Der.** *sip*, sb.

Siphon. (F. – L. – Gk.) F. *siphon*. – L. *sīphōnem*, acc. of *sīphō*, a siphon, bent pipe for drawing off liquids. – Gk. σίφων, a small pipe or reed.

Sippet, a little sop. (E.) Dimin. of *sop*, with vowel-change (from Teut. *u* to *y* > *i*). See Sop.

Sir, Sire. (F. – L.) *Sir* is short for *sire*. – F. *sire*, sir. – L. *senior*, older, elder; (the word *seignior* being from the acc. *seniōrem*). *Sire* is a variant of O. F. *senre* < L. *senior* (see Schwan).

Sirdar, a commander. (Pers.) Pers. *sardār*, a chief. – Pers. *sar*, head (cf. Gk. κάρα), possessing, holding.

Siren. (L. – Gk.) L. *sīrēn*. – Gk. σειρήν, a nymph who enticed seamen to destruction by her magic song.

Sirloin, Surloin. (F. – L.) M.E. *surloyn*; XV cent. – O. F. *surlonge* (14th cent.), the surloin. – F. *sur*, upon, above (from L. *super*); *longe*, loin; see Loin. ¶ The story about turning the *loin* into *sir-loin* by knighting it is mere trash.

Sirname, for **Surname,** q. v.

Sirocco, a hot wind. (Ital. – Arab.) Ital. *sirocco*, south-east wind. – Arab. *sharq*, east (Devic). See Saracen.

Sirrah. (F. – L.) *Sirra* (Minsheu);

serrha (Levins). A contemptuous extension of *sire*, perhaps by addition of *ah!* or
ha! (so Minsheu). ─ O. F. *sire*, Prov. *sira*,
sir. ─ L. *senior*; see **Sir.**

Sir-reverence. (L.) Short for *save-
reverence*, a translation of L. *saluā reuerentiā*, i. e. reverence to you being preserved,
or, by your leave. ─ L. *saluā*, abl. fem.
of *saluus*, safe; and *reuerentiā*, abl. of
reuerentia.

Sirup; see **Syrup.**

Siskin, a song-bird. (Low G. ─ Slavonic.) Low G. *zieske, ziseke*, a siskin;
Du. *sijsje*, where the dimin. suffix *-je*
answers to an older suffix *-ken*, so that
sijsje implies an older form **sijsken*. Cf.
Dan. *sisgen*, a siskin; Swed. *siska*. Of
Slavonic origin. ─ Polish *czyżik*, dimin.
form of *czyż*, a siskin; Sloven. *chizhek*;
Russ. *chij'*. See Miklosich, p. 36.

Sister. (E.) A. S. *sweostor, swuster*;
M. E. *suster*; affected by Icel. *systir*.+Du.
zuster; Icel. *systir*, Swed. *syster*, Dan.
söster, Goth. *swistar*; G. *schwester*. Further
allied to L. *soror* (for **swesor*); O. Ir. *suir*,
W. *chwaer*, Lith. *sesů*; Skt. *svasar-*.
Brugm. ii. § 122. Der. *cousin*, q. v.

Sit. (E.) A. S. *sittan*, pt. t. *sæt*, pp.
seten.+Du. *zitten*; Icel. *sitja*; Dan. *sidde*;
Swed. *sitta*; G. *sitzen*. Teut. type **setjan-*,
pt. t. **sat*, pp. **setanoz*. Further allied to
Goth. *sitan*; W. *seddu*; L. *sedēre*; Gk.
ἕζομαι, I sit; Skt. *sad*. See **Sedentary.**
(√SED.) Der. *set*.

Site. (F. ─ L.) F. *site*; M. F. *sit*. ─ L.
situm, acc. of *situs*, a site, place. ─ L. *situs*,
pp. of *sinere*, to let, suffer, permit; the orig.
sense seems to have been to place.
Position, q. v. But see Brugm. i. § 920.

Sith, since. (E.) Short for M. E. *sithen*;
see **Since.**

Situate. (L.) Late L. *situātus*, pp. of
situāre, to place. ─ L. *situ-*, for *situs*, a
place. See **Site.**

Six. (E.) A. S. *six*.+Icel., Dan., and
Swed. *sex*; G. *sechs*; Goth. *saihs*; Russ.
sheste; W. *chwech*; Gael. and Irish *se*;
L. *sex*; Gk. ἕξ; Lith. *szeszi*; Pers. *shash*;
Skt. *shash*. See Brugm. ii. § 170. Der.
six-th, M. E. *sixte*, A. S. *six-ta*; *six-ty*,
A. S. *sixtig*. See **Sexagenarian.**

Sizar, a student admitted at lower fees,
at Cambridge, than a pensioner. (F. ─ L.)
Named from *size*, formerly a farthing's-
worth of bread or drink (Blount). *Size* is
short for *assize*, an allowance of provisions;
see **Assize** (1). See below.

Size (1), an allowance of food; also
magnitude. (F. ─ L.) Short for *assize*;
see **Assize** (1).

Size (2), weak glue. (Ital.─L.) Ital.
sisa, 'syse or glew;' Florio. Short for
assisa, size. So called from making colours
lie flat. ─ M. Ital. *assisare*, 'to sute [suit]
well;' Florio. ─ Ital. *assiso*, pp. of *assidere*,
to sit; also, to situate. ─ L. *assidēre*, lit.
to sit near. ─ L. *as-* (for *ad*), near; *sedēre*,
to sit. See **Sit.**

Skain, Skene, Skean, Skein, a
dagger, knife. (Irish.) Irish and Gael.
sgian, a knife; O. Irish *scían*; W. *ysgien*,
a cutting instrument. Cf. W. *ysgi*, a
cutting off; Gk. σχάειν, to slit.

Skate (1), a large flat fish. (Scand.)
M. E. *scate*. ─ Icel. *skata*; Norw. *skata*.
Cf. L. *squātus*, a skate (Pliny); also Irish
sgat, a skate (from E.)

Skate (2), **Scate,** a frame with a
steel blade, for sliding on ice. (Du. ─ F. ─
Low G.) Properly *skates*; the *s* being
dropped because *skates* looked like a pl.
form. [Cf. *scatches* (another form of
skateses, pl., but usually meaning 'stilts').]
─ Du. *schaatsen*, skates, a pl. form, from a
sing. *schaats*, whence *schaatsryder*, a skate-
rider, skater (Sewel); M. Du. *skaetsen*, pl.
─ O. North. F. *escache*, Picard form of O.F.
eschace, a stilt (12th cent.); whence F.
échasse. [So also M. Du. *kaetsen*, lit. 'to
catch;' from Picard *cacher*, for O. F.
chacer.] ─ Low G. *schake*, a shank, leg.
Thus *scatches* or *skaies* are 'shanks,' contrivances for lengthening the stride; cf. F.
échasse, a stilt, as above.

Skein, Skain, a knot (or quantity) of
thread or silk. (F. ─ C.?) M. E. *skeyne*,
a quantity of yarn. ─ M. F. *escaigne*, 'a
skain;' Cot.; F. *écagne*. Perhaps of Celtic
origin; cf. Gael. *sgeinnidh*, flax, thread
(unless this is from E.). Der. (probably)
skainsmates, companions (Shak.), as if associated in winding yarn; but cf. **Skain.**

Skeleton. (Gk.) Gk. σκελετόν, a
dried body; neut. of σκελετός, dried. ─ Gk.
σκέλλειν, to dry, parch.

Skellum, a cheat. (Du.) See Nares.
Du. *schelm*, a rogue, villain; the Du. *sch*
being rendered (as in *landscape*) by *sk* = *sc*.
+G. *schelm*; O. H. G. *scelmo*, a pestilence,
carrion, worthless rogue.

Skeptic; see **Sceptic.**

Skerry, a rock surrounded by sea.
(Scand.) From Icel. *sker*, a skerry; see
Scar (2).

Sketch. (Du. – Ital. – L. – Gk.) Du. *schets*, a draught, sketch. – Ital. *schizzo*, a first rough draught. – L. *schedium*, a thing made hastily; from *schedius*, adj., hastily made. – Gk. σχέδιος, sudden; allied to σχεδόν, near; from the base σχε-, to hold. Allied to **Scheme.**

Skew. (O. Low G.) M. E. *skewen*, verb, to turn aside. – M. Du. *schuwen*, *schouwen*, to avoid, shun; Low G. *schuwen*, *schouen*, to avoid. + O. H. G. *sciuhen*, G. *scheuen*, to avoid; from *scheu*, adj., shy. Thus *to skew* is to turn aside, like a shying horse, and is derived from the adj. appearing in E. *shy*. See **Shy.** Der. *askew*, i. e. *on the skew*.

Skewbald, piebald. (O. Low G. *and* C.) Marked in a *skew* or irregular manner; see **Bald.** Cf. *pie-bald*. ¶ We find, however, M. E. *skewed*, pie-bald; perhaps from M. E. *skewes* (blotches?), used as the pl. of *sky*, a cloud. If so, there is no connexion with **Skew** (above).

Skewer. (Doubtful.) Formerly *skuer* (A. D. 1411). Etym. unknown. ¶ Prov. E. *shiver*, a skewer, is the Scand. form answering to E. *shiver*, a small piece; cf. Dan. dial. *skivrt*, small sticks for fuel. See **Shiver** (2).

Skid. (Scand.) Orig. a thin slip of wood, to put under a wheel. – Norw. *skida*, a thin plank; cf. Icel. *skíð*, a billet of wood; see **Shide.**

Skiff. (F. – M. H. G.) M. F. *esquif*, 'a skiffe, little boat;' Cot. – M. H. G. *skif*, G. *schiff*, a ship; see **Ship.**

Skill, discernment, tact. (Scand.) M.E. *skil*, often in the sense of 'reason.' – Icel. *skil*, a distinction; cf. *skilja*, to part, separate, distinguish; Dan. *skiel*, Swed. *skäl*, reason; Dan. *skille*, Swed. *skilja*, to separate. Allied to Lith. *skelti*, to cleave; Swed. *skala*, to peel. From Teut. root *skel*; see **Scale** (1). Der. *skill*, vb., as in phr. 'it *skills* not,' i. e. makes no difference; from Icel. *skilja*, often used impersonally, with the sense 'it differs.'

Skillet, a small pot. (F. – L.) Formerly *skellet*. – O. F. *escuellette*, 'a little dish;' Cot. Dimin. of O. F. *escuelle*, a dish. – L. *scutella*, a dish; dimin. of *scutra*, a tray. See **Scuttle.**

Skim, to take off scum. (Scand.) Dan. *skumme*, Swed. *skumma*, to skim; from *skum*, scum. The E. verb preserves an old vowel-change from *u* to *y*, later *i*; cf. *fill* from *full*. And cf. Dan. dial. *skimmel*,

a thin film on milk; E. Fries. *schümen*, to skim.

Skin. (Scand.) Icel. *skinn*, Swed. *skinn*, Dan. *skind*, skin. Cf. G. *schinden*, to skin, flay; also W. *cen*, skin, *ysgen*, dandriff.

Skink, to serve out wine. (Scand.) M. E. *skenken*; [also *schenken*, from A. S. *scencan*, to pour out; orig. to draw off through a pipe; from A.S. *scanc*, a shank, shank-bone, hollow bone (hence, a pipe)]. – Icel. *skenkja*, Dan. *skienke*. + Du. *schenken*, G. *schenken*, to skink. Teut. type *skankjan-*; from *skank-*, a shank, pipe of bone. See **Nunchion.**

Skip. (Scand.) M. E. *skippen*; also *skeppen* (Cursor Mundi). Cf. Swed. dial. *skopa*, to skip, leap (as animals), to dance; M. Swed. *skuppa*, *skoppa*, Rietz; Icel. *skoppa*, to spin like a top. And cf. M. H. G. *sciuften*, to gallop. (The E. *i* is for *y*, mutation of *u*.) Cf. Dan. dial. *skippe sig*, to move aside.

Skipper. (Du.) Du. *schipper*, a mariner. – Du. *schip*, a ship; cognate with E. *ship*; see **Ship.**

Skirmish. (F. – O. H. G.) Also spelt *scrimmage*. M. E. *scarmishe*, sb., from *scarmishen*, vb. – O. F. *eskermiss-*, a stem of *eskermir*, to fence, fight. [Cf. M. F. *escarmouche*, 'a skirmish, bickering;' Cot.] – O. H. G. *skerman*, to defend, fight, also *scirman*. – O. H. G. *scirm* (G. *schirm*), a shield, screen, shelter, guard, defence. To *skirmish* is, properly, to fight behind cover, hence to advance, under shelter, to fight. β. Note also O. F. *eskermisor*, *escremisseor*, a fencer; *escremissement*, fencing.

Skirr, Scur, to scour a country. (F. – L.) Variants of **Scour** (2). Cf. M. E. *scurrour*, a scout.

Skirret, the water-parsnip. (Scand.) M. E. *skirwit*; older form *skirwhit*. As if 'sheer white,' from the colour of the root; from Icel. *skírr*, sheer, bright; *hvítr*, white. Prob. a popular form, and perverted from O. F. *eschervis* (M. F. *chervi*), a skirret. – Span. *chirivia*. – Arab. *karawīā*, *karwīā*; whence also **Carraway.**

Skirt. (Scand.) M. E. *skyrt*. – Icel. *skyrta*, a shirt, kind of kirtle; see **Shirt.** A doublet of *shirt*, but restricted to the lower part of a garment.

Skittish. (Scand.) From Lowl. Scotch *skit*, to flounce, caper about. This is a secondary verb, of Scand. origin, from the verb *to shoot*. – Swed. dial. *skutta*, *skötta*, to leap about; cf. *skut*, weak grade of Swed. *skjuta*, to shoot. 2. Note Swed. *skytt*, Icel. *skyti*, a marksman; whence the verb *to skit* in the sense to aim at or reflect upon a person, and the sb. *skit*, an oblique taunt. See Shoot.

skittles, a game. (Scand.) Formerly *skittle-pins*; so called because *shot* at by a *skittle* or projectile. — Dan. *skyttel*, a shuttle; Icel. *skutill*, a projectile, harpoon, bolt of a door. Cf. Icel. *skut-*, weak grade of *skjōta*, to shoot; see Shoot.

Skua, a gull, bird. (Scand.) Icel. *skūfr*, *skūmr*, the skua, or brown gull. Prob. from the colour. Cf. Icel. *skūmi*, dusk; Swed. and Norweg. *skum*, dusky, dull (of the weather), dusky (in colour); cf. Sky.

Skulk; see Sculk.

Skull; see Scull.

Skunk, a quadruped. (N. American Indian.) Said to be from the Abenaki *seganku*, a skunk; this is a dialect of Algonquin (Lower Canada).

Sky, (Scand.) M. E. *skye*, a cloud. — Icel. *skȳ*, a cloud; Dan. Swed. *sky*, a cloud. Allied to A. S. *scēo*, O. Sax. *scio*, a cloud; A. S. *scūa*, shade; Skt. *sku*, to cover. (✓SKEU.)

Slab (1), a thin slip of timber or stone. (F. — Teut.) M. E. *slab*, *slabbe*. Apparently a weakened form of prov. E. *slap*, a slab (Halliwell). — O. F. *esclape*, 'éclat; de menues *esclapes* de bois,' i. e. thin slabs of wood; Godefroy. Prob. of Teut. origin. (Wedgwood cites ' Languedoc *esclapa*, to split wood, *bos esclapa*, split logs, *esclapo*, a slab of wood or stone.') Cf. Ital. *schiappare*, to split. Perhaps from the prefix *es-* (L. *ex*), and Low G. *klappen*, to clap, make an explosive sound. (Körting, § 5453.)

Slab (2), slimy. . (E.) The same as prov. E. *slabby*, sloppy, dirty; from prov. E. *slab*, a puddle; cf. Norw. *slabb*, filth; Irish *slab*, *slaib*, Gael. *slaib*, mire, mud. Also M. E. *slabben*, to wallow; E. Fries. *slabben*, Du. *slabben*, to lap up; Swed. dial. *slabba*, to splash, to soil. And see Slabber below.

Slabber, to slaver. (E.) M. E. *slaberen*, frequent. of M. E. *slabben*, to wallow (above).+E. Fries. *slabbern*, to lap, sup, or lick up; Low G. *slabbern*, *slubbern*, to slabber, lap, sip, frequent. of *slabben*, to lap; G. *schlabbern*, *schlabben*, to lap, to slabber. Cf. prov. E. *slap*, to lick up food, eat quickly; Dan. dial. *slabbe*, *slappe*, to

lap up. Of imitative origin; cf. *slobber*, *slubber*. See Slaver.

Slack. (E.) M. E. *slak*. A. S. *slæc*, *sleac*, slack, slow.+Icel. *slakr*; Swed. Dan. *slak*; prov. G. *schlak*, slack, loose. Teut. type **slakoz*. Orig. sense 'fluid'; see below. Allied to Lax; Brugm. i. § 193.

slag, dross, scoria. (Swed.) Swed. *slagg*, dross of metal; so called from flowing over when fused; Norw. *slagga*, to flow over. Cf. Icel. *slagna*, to flow over, *slag*, *slagi*, wet, damp, water penetrating walls. It is a variant of *slack*, as seen by G. *schlacke*, 'dross, slacks, sediment,' Flügel; *schlackern*, to trickle, *schlack*, slack, drossy, sloppy; Low G. *slakke*, slag.

slake, to slacken, quench, wet. (E.) A. S. *slacian*, to grow slack; cf. prov. E. *sleck*, to quench, A. S. *sleccan*, to grow slack (hence, to make slack, slacken). — A. S. *sleac*, slack; see Slack.+Icel. *slökva* (pp. *slokinn*), to slake; Swed. *släcka*, to quench, allay, slake, from *slak*, adj.

Slade, a valley. (E.) M. E. *slad(e)*. A. S. *slæd*. + Westphal. *slade*, a ravine; Dan. dial. *slade*, a flat piece of land.

Slag, Slake; see Slack.

Slam. (Scand.) Norweg. *slemba*, *slemma*, to smack, bang, slam a door; Swed. dial. *slämma*, to push hastily; Icel. *slamra*, to slam. Cf. Swed. *slammer*, a noise. Allied to Slap. Of imitative origin.

Slander, scandal. (F. — L. — Gk.) M. E. *sclandre*, *sclaundre*. — O. F. *esclandre*, scandal. The oldest O. F. form was *escandle*, whence *escandre*, and finally *esclandre*, with inserted *l*. It is merely another form of Scandal, q. v.

Slang, vulgar language. (Scand.) Norweg. *sleng*, a slinging, a device, a burthen of a song, *slengja*, to sling, *slengja kjeften*, to slang, abuse (lit. 'to sling the jaw'), *slengjenamn*, a slang-name, *slengjeord*, a slang word, insulting word. All from *slengja*, to sling, causal form from the 2nd grade of the Icel. *slyngva*, to sling. See Sling.

Slant, to slope. (Scand.) M. E. *slenten*, to slope, glide. — Swed. dial. *slenta*, *slänta*, causal of *slinta* (pt. t. *slant*), to slide, slip with the foot; Swed. *slinta*, to slip, glance aside. The E. adj. *slant*, sloping, answers to Swed. dial. *slant*, slippery. Der. *a-slant*, i. e. *on the slant*.

Slap. (E.) M. E. *slappe*, a smart blow; an imitative word; allied to Slam.+Low

G. *slapp*, sound of a blow, a slap; G. *schlapp*, interj., slap! *schlappe*, sb., a slap, *schlappen*, to slap. **Der.** *slap-bang*, violently; *slap-dash*, off hand.

Slash. (F. – Teut.) [Lowl. Sc. *slash*, to work in wet, is from Swed. *slaska*, Dan. *slaske*, to dabble in water.] The sense 'to cut' appears in '*slish* and *slash*,' i. e. much cutting; Tam. Shrew, iv. 3. 90. – O. F. *esclachier*, to break in pieces. – O. F. *es-* (L. *ex*), very; and Teut. type **klakjan*, M. H. G. *klecken*, to break with a *clack*; cf. F. *claque*, a clack, M. H. G. *klac*. (Körting, § 4541.)

Slat, a thin bar of wood. (F. – O. H. G.) M. E. *slat*, a slate; see below. ¶ Hardly from Gael. and Irish *slat*, a rod, twig; though these are related to *lath*.

Slate (1), a flake of stone. (F. – O.H.G.) M. E. *slat*, *sclat*. – O. F. *esclat*, a splinter, slice of wood, &c. (hence, a thin slice of slate). – O. F. *esclater*, to split, burst, shiver. This answers to a Late L. type **exclapitāre*, to break with a clap; from L. *ex*, and Low G. *klapp*, a clap, loud noise. (Körting, § 4543.) ¶ The *a* in *slate* was orig. short.

Slate (2), to bait, ridicule, criticise sharply, abuse. (E.) M. E. *slēten*; A.S. *slǣtan*, to bait, set dogs on (an animal); causal vb. from *slītan*, to slit, tear, rend; see **Slit**.

Slattern, an untidy woman. (Scand.) From prov. E. *slatter*, to waste, to be untidy, to throw about; frequent. of *slat*, to dash or throw about. – Icel. *sletta*, to slap, dab, dash liquids about; Norweg. *sletta*, to fling about, jerk; Icel. *sletta*, sb., a dab, spot of ink. Allied to which are Dan. *slat*, a slop; *slat*, *slatten*, *slattet*, loose, flabby; *slattes*, to become slack; *slatte*, a slattern; Low G. *slatje*, a slattern. ¶ *Slut* is quite distinct.

Slaughter, sb. (Scand.) M. E. *slaghter*. – Icel. *slátr*, slaughter, whence *slátra*, to slaughter cattle; cf. Noreen, § 224. The A. S. word is -*sleaht*, whence M. E. *slaught*. +Du. Swed. *slagt*, G. *schlacht* (Teut. type **slah-tā*). All from **slah*, the base of **Slay**, q. v.

Slave. (F. – L – Gk. – Slavonic.) F. *esclave*. – Late L. *sclavus*, a Slavonian captive, a slave. – Late Gk. Ἐσκλαβηνός, the same. The origin of *Slavon-ian* is unknown; Miklosich, p. 308.

Slaver, to slabber. (Scand.) Icel. *slafra*, to slaver; cognate with Low G.

slabbern, to slabber. See **Slabber. Der.** *slaver*, sb., from Icel. *slafr*, *slefa*, slaver.

Slay (1), to kill. (E.) The form *slay* is due to the pp. *slai-n*; else, the infin. would have been *slee*. Orig. to smite. M. E. *sleen*. – A. S. *slēan* (contracted form of **slahan*), to smite, pt. t. *slōh*, pp. *slegen* (whence M. E. *slein*, E. *slain*).+Du. *slaan*; Icel. *slá*; Dan. *slaae*; Swed. *slå*; Goth. *slahan*; G. *schlagen*. Teut. type **slah-an*-; cf. O. Irish *slig-im*, I strike.

slay (2), **sley**, a weaver's reed. (E.) A.S. *slahæ*; see *sleahe* in A.S. Dict.; orig. form **slæge*, gen. **slagan*; Camb. Phil. Trans. 1899, p. 139 (231). So called from *striking* the web together. – A. S. *slēan* (<**slahan*), to strike; see **Slay** (1).

Sleave, Sleave-silk, soft floss silk. (Scand. ?) 'Ravelled *sleave*,' i. e. tangled loose silk. Cf. Dan. dial. *slöve*, a knot, twist, tangle (in thread). Perhaps the orig. sense was 'loose'; cf. Icel. *slæfa*, to slacken.

Sled, a sledge. (Du.) M. E. *slede*. – M. Du. *sledde* (Du. *slede*). + Icel. *sleði*, Dan. *slæde*, Swed. *slede*, a sledge; G. *schlitten*, a sledge. From the weak grade of the verb *to slide*; see **Slide**.

sledge. (Du.) This is a corrupt form; apparently due to *sleds*, pl. of *sled*.

Sledge-hammer. (E.) A reduplicated form; a *sledge* means 'a hammer.' – A.S. *slecg*, dat. *slecge*, a heavy hammer, smiter. For Teut. type **slag-jā*, fem.; from **slag*, for **slah*, base of A. S. *slēan*, to smite.+Du. *slegge*, *slei*, Swed. *slägga*, Icel. *sleggja*, a sledge or heavy hammer. See **Slay** (1).

Sleek, Slick, smooth, glossy. (E.) M. E. *slike*. + Icel. *slíkr*, sleek, smooth. Allied to Du. *slijk*, North Fries. *slick*, E. Fries. *slîk*, slime; G. *schlick*, grease; cf. the Low G. strong verb *sliken* (pt. t. *sleek*, pp. *sleken*)= G. *schleichen* (pt. t. *schlich*), to slink, crawl, move as if through mire; see **Slink**. The Teut. type of the verb is **sleikan-*, pt. t. **slaik*, pp. **slikanoz*. Orig. sense 'greasy,' like soft mud.

Sleep, vb. (E.) A.S. *slǣpan*, *slēpan*, pt. t. *slēp*.+Du. *slapen*; Goth. *slēpan*; G. *schlafen*, to sleep. The sb. is A.S. *slǣp*, Du. *slaap*, Goth. *slēps*, G. *schlaf*, O. H. G. *slāf*, orig. 'drowsiness;' allied to Low G. *slapp*, G. *schlaff*, lax, loose, flabby, unbent, relaxed (as in sleep). Teut. type **slǣpan-*, redupl. vb. Allied to L. *lābī*, to glide;

Russ. *slabuii*, weak, slack. Cf. E. *sleepy*, i. e. inactive.

sleeper, a block of wood under rails; from the vb. above. (E.) Cf. F. *dormant*, a sleeper; from *dormir*, to sleep.

Sleet. (E.) M. E. *sleet*. From O. Merc. **slēte*, A. S. **slȳte*, not found. Cf. E. Fries. *slaite*, hail; Low G. *sloten*, pl. hailstones (Lübben); G. *schlosse*, hailstone. From Teut. type **slauti-*; orig. sense unknown. Cf. also Dan. *slud*, sleet. ¶ Norw. *sletta*, sleet, seems to be unrelated.

Sleeve. (E.) O. Merc. *slēf*, a sleeve; A. S. *slȳf*.✛M. Du. *sleve*, a sleeve; N. Fries. *slief*; cf. M. Du. *sloove*, a veil, cover; Du. *sloof*, an apron; Low G. *sluwe*, a husk, shell. From Teut. root **sleub*; variant form of **sleup*, whence M. H. G. *sloufe*, a cover, allied to M. H. G. *sloufen*, to let slip, cover. Cf. Goth. *sliupan* (pt. t. *slaup*, pp. *slupans*), to slip, creep into. It is thus allied to *slip*, from the *slipping* of the sleeve on and off, in dressing and undressing. See **Slip**, and **Slop** (2).

Sleigh. (Du.) An ill-spelt word; there is no final guttural. — Du. *slee*, short for *slede*, a sledge; cf. Du. *sleekoets*, for *sledekoets*, lit. 'a sledge-coach.' Cf. Norw. *slee*, for *slede*, a sledge; see **Sled**.

Sleight, dexterity. (Scand.) For *sleighth*; M. E. *sleighthe*. — Icel. *slægð*, slyness, cunning. — Icel. *slægr*, sly. So also Swed. *slöjd*, dexterity, from *slög*, dexterous. See **Sly, Sloid.**

Slender, thin, feeble. (F. — O. Low G.) M. E. *sclendre*, *slendre*. — O. F. *esclendre*, 'sklendre;' Palsgrave, p. 323. — M. Du. *slinder*, slender, thin; as sb., a watersnake, named from its gliding or trailing. — M. Du. *slinderen*, also *slidderen*, to drag, train along, trail; Low G. *slindern*, to slide on the ice (whence Low G. *slender*, a trailing gown). Nasalised forms from the verb *to slide*. Cf. O. H. G. *slintan* in Schade.

Sleuth - hound, a slot-hound; see **Slot** (2).

Slice, sb. (F. — O. H. G.) M. E. *slice*, *sclice*. — O. F. *esclice*, a splinter, shiver, piece of split wood. — O. F. *esclicir*, to slit (whence E. *slice*, vb.). — O. H. G. **slitjan*, *slizzen*, related to *sclīzan*, *slīzan*, to slit, shiver (whence O. F. *esclier*, to shiver); cognate with E. *slit*; see **Slit**.

Slick; see **Sleek**.

Slide, vb. (E.) A. S. *slīdan*, pt. t. *slād*, pp. *sliden*. Cf. also A. S. *slidor*, slippery;

O. H. G. *slītan*, to slide, G. *schlitten*, a sledge. Also Lith. *slidus*, slippery.

Slight, adj. (O. Low G.) M. E. *slight*, orig. sense even or flat; then plain, smooth, simple, trivial, &c. — M. Du. *slicht*, even, plain, *slecht*, slight, simple, vile; cf. *slichten*, 'to slight, to make even or plaine,' Hexham; O. Low G. *slight*, even, simple, bad.✛Icel. *slēttr*, flat, smooth, trivial; Dan. *slet*, level, bad; Swed. *slät*, smooth, worthless, slight; Goth. *slaihts*, smooth; G. *schlecht*, bad, *schlicht*, smooth, plain, homely; O. H. G. *sleht*, smooth. Teut. type **slehtoz*, smooth. Root unknown.

Slim. (Du.) Orig. sense 'oblique'; thence weak, poor, thin, bad, slight; prov. E. *slim*, crafty. — M. Du. *slim*, awry, crafty. ✛ G. *schlimm*, bad, cunning; M. H. G. *slimp*, oblique, slanting, awry; Dan. Swed. *slem*, worthless; Icel. *slæmr*, vile.

Slime. (E.) A. S. *slīm*.✛Du. *slijm*; Icel. *slīm*; Swed. *slem*; Dan. *sliim*; G. *schleim*. Cf. L. *līmus*, mud.

Sling, vb. (Scand.) From Icel. *slyngva*, *slöngva*, to sling, throw, pp. *slunginn*; Swed. *slinga*, to twist; cf. O. H. G. *schlingan*, to wind, twist, sling, Du. *slingeren*, to toss, sling. Teut. type **slengwan-*; pt. t. **slang*. ¶ A. S. *slingan* (rare), to creep, seems to be a variant of *slincan*. See below. **Der.** *sling*, sb.; *slang*, q. v.

Slink. (E.) A. S. *slincan*, to creep; nasalised form of A. S. **slīcan* (not found), which is cognate with Low G. *slīken*, to creep (pt. t. *sleek*, pp. *sleken*) and G. *schleichen*, to creep (pt. t. *schlich*).✛Swed. dial. *slinka* (pt.t. *slank*); cf. Lith. *slinkti*, to creep. Allied to **Sleek**; also to **Sling**.

Slip. (E.) A weak verb; due to the weak grade of A. S. **slūpan*; cf. A. S. *slipor*, *slipig*, slippery. ✛ Du. *slippen*, Swed. *slippa*, O. H. G. *slipfan*, to slip, weak verbs; allied to Du. *slijpen*, G. *schleifen*, to grind smooth, whet, polish. We also find A. S. *slūpan*, pt. t. *slēap*, pp. *slopen*; cf. Goth. *sliupan*, pt. t. *slaup*, pp. *slupans*, to slip or creep into. Teut. types **sleipan*- and **sleupan-*. The latter is allied to L. *lūbricus*, slippery; see **Lubricate**. Cf. Brugm. i. §§ 553, 563. **Der.** *slipp-er*, a loose shoe easily slipped on; *slipper-y*, from A. S. *slipor*, slippery, with added *-y*. And see *sleeve*, *sloop*.

Slit. (E.) M. E. *slitten*, weak verb; from the weak grade of *slīten*, strong verb. — A. S. *slītan*, to slit, rend; pt. t. *slāt*, pp. *sliten*.✛Icel. *slīta*, Swed. *slita*, Dan. *slide*, to rend; Du. *slijten*, to wear out; O.H.G. *slīzan*, G. *schleissen*, to slit, whence *schlitzen*, to slice. Teut. type *sleitan-, pt. t. *slait. **Der.** *slice*.

Sliver, a splinter, twig. (E.) M.E. *sliver*, dimin. of prov. E. *slive*, a slice, chip; from M.E. *sliuen* (*sliven*), to cleave. — A.S. *-slīfan*, to cleave, pt. t. *-slāf*; in *to-slīfan*. A parallel form to A.S. *slītan*, pt. t. *slāt*; see **Slit**.

Slobber, Slubber, to do carelessly, to sully. (Scand.) Dan. *slubbre*, to slabber; Swed. dial. *slubbra*, to slubber, slobber, be disorderly, frequent. of Swed. dial. *slubba*, to mix liquids carelessly, to be careless. Cf. also Du. *slobberen*, to sup up; Low G. *slubbern*, to lap, sip. Allied to **Slabber**.

Sloe. (E.) M.E. *slo.* A.S. *slā*, *slāh*, pl. *slān.* — Du. *slee*, M.Du. *sleeu*; Dan. *slaaen*; Swed. *slån*; G. *schlehe*, pl. *schlehen*; O.H.G. *slēha*.

Slogan, war-cry. (Gael.) Gael. *sluagh-ghairm*, the signal for battle, lit. 'cry of the host.' — Gael. (and Irish) *sluagh*, host, army (W. *llu*); *gairm*, outcry, *gairm*, to cry out; cf. Irish *gairm*, W. *garm*, outcry, O. Irish *gāir*, W. *gawr*, outcry, L. *garrīre*, to prate. Cf. **Slughorn**.

Sloid, manual dexterity. (Swed.) Englished from Swed. *slöjd*; see **Sleight**.

Sloop, a ship. (Du. — Low G.) Du. *sloep*, M.Du. *sloepe*, a sloop. — Low G. *sluup*, *slupe*, a sloop; whence (apparently) the O.F. *chaloupe*, a shallop; see **Shallop**. Perhaps from Low G. *slupen*, to glide, orig. to slip. See **Slip**.

Slop (1), a puddle. (E.) M.E. *sloppe*, a pool. — A.S. *-sloppe*, *-slyppe*, the sloppy droppings of a cow, as in *cū-sloppe* (cowslip); also A.S. *slyppe*, a viscid substance. Orig. sense 'something slippery'; cf. Icel. *slöp*, slimy offal of fish. See further below.

slop (2), a loose garment. (E.) M.E. *sloppe*. A.S. *-slop*, *-slype*, in comp. *ofer-slop*, *ofer-slype*, an upper garment. From A.S. *slop-* (Teut. *slup-), weaker grade of *slūpan*, to slip; because the outer garment is easily slipped on. So also Du. *slop*, a gap in a hedge to slip through; prov. E. *sloppy*, loose.+Icel. *sloppr*, a slop, long loose gown. Compare **Sleeve**.

slope, an incline. (E.) M.E. *slope*; *a-slope*, on the slope, ready to slip. From the weak grade (*slop*-) of A.S. *slūpan*, to slip. See above.

Slot (1), a bolt of a door, bar. (Du.)

O. Fries. and Du. *slot*, a lock, fastening. — Du. *slot-* (Teut. *slut-), weak grade of *sluiten*, to shut; so also Low G. *slot*, a bar, from *sluten*, to shut; G. *schloss*, a lock, a castle. We find also Swed. *sluta*, G. *schliessen*, O.H.G. *sliozan*, to shut; allied to O. Fries. *slūta*, also *sklūta*, to shut; and hence to L. *claudere*, to shut; see **Clause**. (√SKLEUD.) ¶ *Slot*, a narrow depression or aperture, is prob. the same word; it is shaped like a bar.

Slot (2), track of a deer. (O.F. — Scand.) O.F. *esclot*, track, trace. — Icel. *slōð*, a track, trail (whence, immediately, M.E. *sloth*, *sleuth*, a track, E. *sleuth-hound*); Swed. dial. *slo*, a track.

Sloth. (E.) Lit. 'slowness.' For *slow-th, directly from the adj. *slow*. See **Slow**. ¶ The M.E. word was *slewth*, from A.S. *slǣwð*, sloth; Teut. type *slaiwiþā. **Der.** *sloth*, an animal (translating Span. *perezoso*, slothful, a sloth); *slothful*.

Slouch, to have a clownish look or gait. (F.) Cf. *slouch*, sb., a great lubberly fellow (Phillips). — O.F. *esloucher*, *eslochier*, to be loose in the joint, to waver. — O.F. *es-* (L. *ex*), out, away; *lochier* (F. *locher*), to shake, to be loose, prob. from M.H.G. *lucke*, G. *locker*, loose. Perhaps affected by Norw. *sloka*, to go slowly and heavily, Swed. *sloka*, to droop.

Slough (1), a muddy pool, mire. (E.) M.E. *slogh*, *slough*. A.S. *slōh* (stem *slōg*-), a slough. Hardly allied to Irish *slugpholl*, a whirlpool; *slugaim*, I swallow up; Gael. *slugan*, a gulf, from *sluig*, to swallow up. Rather, to E. *slag*.

Slough (2), the cast skin of a snake, &c.; the dead part which separates from a sore. (E.) Pronounced *sluf*. M.E. *slouh*, *slughe*, *slouʒe*, skin of a snake. The corresponding word appears in Swed. dialects as *slug* (Rietz), which is prob. allied to G. *schlauch*, M.H.G. *slūch*, a skin, bag.

Sloven. (Du.) M.E. *sloveyn*. — M.Du. *slof*, *sloef*, a sloven; with M.E. suffix *-ein* (= F. *-ain*, L. *-ānus*). Cf. Du. *slof*, careless; *slof*, sb., neglect, an old slipper; *sloffen*, to neglect, to go slipshod. So also Low G. *sluf*, slovenly; *sluffen*, to be careless; E. Fries. *sluf*, *sluffe*, a sloven; *sluffen*, to be careless.

Slow. (E.) A.S. *slāw*, slow.+Du. *sleeuw*, Icel. *slær*, *sljōr*; Dan. *slöv*, Swed. *slö*, blunt, dull; O. Sax. *slēu*; O.H.G. *slēo*.

Teut. type *slaiwoz*; allied to L. *laeuus*, Russ. *lievuii*, Gk. λαιός, left (of the hand).

Slow-worm. (E.) In popular etymology, it is 'a slow worm,' but the true sense is 'slay-worm,' the snake that strikes. A. S. *slā-wyrm*; where *slā* seems to be borrowed from Icel. *slā*, to strike. This is clearer from Swed. *slå* or *ormslå*, a slow-worm, where *orm* = E. *worm*, and *slå* is 'striker,' from *slå*, to strike; so also Norw. *ormslo*, a slow-worm, also called *slo*, from *slaa*, to strike.

Slubber; see **Slobber**.

Sludge, soft, greasy mud. (E.) M. E. *sluche, sliche*. North Fries. *slick*, E. Fries. *slīk*, slime.+Du. *slijk*, prov. G. *schlick*, grease; see **Sleek**. ¶ The *u* is due to confusion with E. dial. *slud*, wet mud; cf. Du. *slodder*, a sloven.

Slug, to be inactive. (Scand.) M. E. *sluggen*, vb., *slugge*, a sluggard. — Dan. *slug*, weakened form of *sluk*, appearing in *slugoret, slukoret*, having drooping ears; Swed. dial. *slogga*, to be sluggish; cf. Norw. *sloka*, to slouch, Swed. *sloka*, to droop. Note also Low G. *slukkern, slakkern*, to be loose, *slukk*, melancholy, downcast; Du. *sluik*, slender, thin. **Der.** *slugg-ard*, with F. suffix -*ard* (= O. H. G. -*hart*, cognate with E. *hard*).

Slug-horn, a battle-cry. (C.) Ignorantly used by Chatterton and Browning to mean a sort of *horn*; but really Mid. Sc. *slogorne*, a corruption of *slogan*, a war-cry. See **Slogan**.

Sluice, a flood-gate. (F. — L.) O. F. *escluse*, 'a sluce, floudgate;' Cot. — Late L. *exclūsa*, a flood-gate; lit. shut off (water); pp. of *ex-clūdere*, to shut out. — L. *ex*, out; *claudere*, to shut.

Slum, pl. *slums*, dirty back streets. (E.) Cf. prov. E. *slump*, wet mire; Low G. *slam*, mire (Lübben); Dan. and Swed. *slam*, G. *schlamm*, mire.

Slumber, verb. (E.) The *b* is excrescent. M. E. *slumeren*, frequent. of M. E. *slūmen*; to slumber; from *slume* (also *sloumbe*), sb., slumber, A. S. *slūma*, sb., slumber. + Du. *sluimeren*; Dan. *slumre*, frequent. of *slumme*, to slumber; Swed. *slumra*, vb.; G. *schlummern*, vb. The sb. *slūma* is from Teut. root *sleu*-, to be silent; 2nd grade *slau*, whence Goth. *slawan*, to be silent (Kluge).

Slump, a sudden fall or failure. (E.) Prov. E.. Cf. Swed. Dan. *slump*, a chance, accident; Low G. *slump* (Danneil); G.

schlump. Of imitative origin; cf. Norw. and Lowl. Sc. *slump*, the noise made by an object falling into water. Cf. *plump*, *dump*.

Slur, to contaminate, pass over lightly with slight notice. (M. Du.) The orig. sense is to trail in mud, draggle; hence, to pass over slightingly. — M. Du. *sleuren, slooren*, to drag, trail; cf. *sloorigh*, 'filthie,' Hexham, and M. E. *slor*, mud; Du. *sleuren*, to trail. Also Low G. *slüren, slören*, to draggle, Swed. dial. *slöra*, to be negligent; Norw. *slöra*, to be negligent, sully, *slöda*, *slöa*, to draggle, *slöda*, *slöe*, a trail; E. Fries. *sluren, slüren*, to go about carelessly and noisily.

Slut. (Scand.) M. E. *slutte*. Cf. Icel. *slöttr*, a heavy, loglike fellow; Swed. dial. *slåta*, a slut, *slåter*, an idler; Dan. dial. *slöter*, a slovenly person; Norw. *slott*, an idler. Also Icel. *slota*, to droop, Norw. *sluta*, to droop; allied to Dan. *slat, slatten*, loose, flabby. Cf. *slot*-, weak grade of Norw. *sletta* (strong verb), to dangle, drift, idle about (Aasen). β. From the 2nd grade *slat(t)* we have Dan. *slatte*, a slut, and *slat*, loose; see **Slattern**. Note also Bavarian *schlotzen, schlutzen*, a slut; *schlotzen*, to be careless.

Sly, cunning. (Scand.) M. E. *sligh, sleih, slēh*. — Icel. *slægr*, sly, cunning; Swed. *slög*, handy, dexterous; prob. allied to **Slay**. ¶ Distinct from **sleight**; Dan. *slug, slu*; Du. *sluw*; G. *schlau*. Der. *sleight*.

Smack (1), taste. (E.) M. E. *smak*, *smach*. A. S. *smæc*, taste, flavour; cf. *smæccan*, to taste. + M. Du. *smaeck*, Du. *smaak*; Dan. *smag*, Swed. *smak*; G. *geschmack*, taste. **Der.** *smack*, vb., to taste.

Smack (2), a sounding blow. (Scand.) Confused with the word above, but perhaps distinct; prob. of imitative origin. — Swed. *smacka*, to smack, Swed. dial. *smakka*, to throw down noisily; *smäkka*, to hit smartly; Dan. *smække*, to rap; E. Fries. *smakken*, to smack the lips. Cf. Dan. *smæk*, a smack, rap; Du. *smak*, a loud noise.

Smack (3), a fishing-boat. (Du.) M. Du. *smacke*, Du. *smak*, a smack, hoy; whence also Dan. *smakke*. Generally thought to stand for *snack*; cf. A. S. *snacc*, a small vessel; Icel. *snekkja*, a swift vessel, Dan. *snekke*, Swed. *snäcka*.

Small. (E.) A. S. *smæl*.+Du. Dan.

Swed. *smal*, narrow, thin; Goth. *smals*, small; G. *schmal*, narrow.   Allied to Icel. *smali*, small cattle, sheep; Gk. μῆλον, a sheep; Russ. *maluii*, small. ¶ Icel. *smār*, Dan. *smaa*, Swed. *små*, small, are allied to O. H. G. *smāhi*, small.

smallage, celery. (E. ; *and* F.—L.) For *small ache*; from F. *ache*, parsley < L. *apium*, parsley.

Smalt, blue enamel. (Ital.—O. H. G.) Ital. *smalto*, enamel.   From the 2nd grade of O. H. G. *smelzan*, str. vb.. to become liquid, whence also O. H. G. *smelzen*, G. *schmelzen*, weak vb., to smelt; from the method of preparation; see **Smelt** (1). See also **Enamel**.

Smaragdus. (L.—Gk.) L. *smaragdus*. —Gk. σμάραγδος, an emerald.   Cf. Skt. *marakata*(*m*), *marakta*(*m*), an emerald. See **Emerald**.

Smart, to feel pain. (E.)   M. E. *smerten*.   A. S. *smeortan*.+Du. *smarten*, Dan. *smerte*, Swed. *smärta*, G. *schmerzen*. Also allied to L. *mordēre*, to bite; Skt. *mṛd*, to rub, grind, crush; Gk. σμερδαλέος, terrible. (√SMERD.)   Der. *smart*, sb. ; *smart*, adj., painful, also pungent, brisk, lively, A. S. *smeart*.

Smash. (E.)   A late word. Apparently formed from E. *mash*, to mix up, by prefixing *s*- (from O. F. *es*-, L. *ex*), an intensive prefix.

Smattering, sb. (E.)   M.E. *smateren*, to make a noise; hence, to prate, talk ignorantly.   Cf. Swed. *smattra*, to clatter; G. *schmettern*, to smash, to resound. From a repetition of *smat*, an imitative sound; see **Smack** (2).   Cf. M. H. G. *smetzen*, to prattle.   [Parallel to *prat-tle*, *chat-ter*; cf. Swed. *snattra*, to chatter.]

Smear. (E.)   A. S. *smirian*, to smear. —A. S. *smeru*, *smeoru*, fat, grease.   So also Icel. *smyrja*, Dan. *smöre*, Swed. *smörja*, G. *schmieren*, to smear ; and Du. *smeer*, Dan. Swed. *smör*, G. *schmeer*, fat, grease, O. H. G. *smero* ; Goth. *smairthr*, fatness.   Cf. O. Irish *smir*, marrow; W. *mēr*, marrow; Lith. *smarsas*, fat; Gk. μύρον, unguent.   Der. *smir-ch*.

Smell, odour. (E.)   M. E. *smel*, *smul*. Allied to Du. *smeulen*, Low G. *smelen*, E. Fries. *smälen*, to smoulder.   Cf. **Smoulder**.   Der. *smell*, vb.

Smelt (1), to fuse ore. (Scand.)   Dan. *smelte*, to smelt ; Swed. *smälta*, to smelt. (Properly a Swed. word.)+M. Du. *smilten*, *smelten*, G. *schmelzen*, to smelt.   These

are causal forms; cf. Westphal. *smelten*, O. H. G. *smelzan*, str. vb., to melt.   From the Teut. verb **smeltan*-, to melt, pt. t. **smalt* (whence E. *smalt*), pp. **smultanoz*. And cf. Gk. μέλδειν, to melt, render fluid. Brugm. i. § 475.

Smelt (2), a fish. (E.)   A.S. *smelt*, *smylt*. +Dan. *smelt*, Norw. *smelta*.   The prov. E. *smolt* means a young salmon, when it first assumes its silvery scales; and prov. E. *smolt* means 'smooth and shining.'

Smew, a small diving-bird. (E.)   Also called *smee*, *smeeth*.   Cognate with E. Fries. *smēnt*, Du. *smient*, smew.   The Du. *smient* is explained as 'small duck'; from O. Du. **smēhi anud*, small duck; where **smēhi* is cognate with O. H. G. *smāhi*, Icel. *smā-r*, Swed. *små*, small; and **anud* (**anid*) is Du. *eend*, A.S. *ened*, G. *ente*, duck.   Cf. G. *schmal-ente*, small wild duck.

Smile, vb. (Scand.)   Swed. *smila*, to smile, smirk ; Dan. *smile*.   Allied to L. *mīrārī*, to wonder at; Russ. *smiekh'*, a laugh; Gk. μειδάω, I smile; Skt. *smi*, to smile. (√SMEI.)

Smirch, to besmear. (E.)   Extended from M. E. *smer-en*, to smear ; see **Smear**.

Smirk. (E.)   A.S. *smercian*, *smearcian*, to smile.   Cf. O. Northumb. *smerdon*, 'deridebant,' Mat. ix. 24.

Smite. (E.)   A.S. *smītan*, pt. t. *smāt*, pp. *smiten*.+Du. *smijten*; Dan. *smide*, to fling; G. *schmeissen*, to smite, fling, cast; O. H. G. *smīzan*, to throw, stroke, smear. Cf. Goth. *bismeitan*, to besmear.   β. The orig. sense was to 'smear' or rub over, as in Gothic; cf. M. Swed. *smita*, to smite, *smeta*, to smear.   'To rub over' seems to have been a sarcastic expression for 'to beat'; we find *well anoynted* = well beaten, Romance of Partenay, l. 5653.

Smith. (E.)   A. S. *smið*, a worker with the hammer.+Du. *smid*; Icel.*smiðr*; Dan. Swed. *smed*; G. *schmied*; Goth. *-smitha*.   Cf. Icel. *smíð*, smith's work; Du. *smijdig*, G. *geschmeidig*, malleable (with *ī*).   The forms **smith*, **smiþ*, point to a lost strong verb **smeith-an-*, to forge, pt. t. **smaith*, pp. **smithanoz*, to forge, actually preserved in Swed. dial. *smida*, to forge, pt. t. *smed*, pp. *smiden* (Rietz).   Hence, as weak verbs, Dan. *smede*, Swed. *smida*, to forge.   Cf. O.H.G. *smīda*, metal, Gk. σμί-λη, a graver's tool. Brugm. i. § 849.   **Der.** *smith-y*, A. S. *smiððe* (Icel. *smiðja*).

Smock, a woman's shirt. (E.) M. E. *smok.* A. S. *smoc.* For *smocc*; Teut. type **smugnoz,* Idg. type *smuqnos; Brugm. i. § 899. The Teut. **smug-* is represented by A. S. *smog-,* weaker grade of *smūgan,* to creep into. So called because 'crept into,' or put over the head. Cf. Shetland *smook,* to draw on a glove or stocking. + Icel. *smokkr,* a smock; from *smog-,* weak grade of *smjūga,* to creep through a hole, to put on a garment over the head. Cf. M. Swed. *smog,* a round hole for the head.

Smoke, sb. (E.) A. S. *smoca.* Cf. A. S. *smoc-,* weak grade of the strong verb *smēocan* (pt. t. *smēac*), to smoke, reek.+ Du. *smook,* sb.; G. *schmauch,* sb. Perhaps Irish *múch,* smoke, W. *mwg,* smoke, are from E. Cf. Lith. *smaug-iu,* I choke; Gk. σμύχειν (2 aor. ἐσμύγην), to smoulder. Der. *smoke,* vb., from A. S. *smocian,* weak verb. Brugm. i. § 849.

Smooth, adj. (E.) M. E. *smoothe*; also *smēthe.* A. S. *smēðe,* Northumb. *smoeðe*; sometimes *smōð,* smooth. The form *smēðe* represents *smōth-joz (with mutation of *ō* to *ē*); and further, the base **smōth-* represents a Teut. base **smanth-,* so that *smōthjoz is for **smanth-joz,* ' creamy.' The base appears in Bohem. *smant,* cream (Russ. *smetana*); whence the G. *schmant,* cream, is borrowed. Cf. Bavar. *schmand,* cream. Der. *smoothe,* vb.

Smother, sb. (E.) Formerly *smorther*; M. E. *smorther,* a suffocating smoke, lit. ' that which stifles ;' formed (with suffix *-ther* of the agent) from A. S. *smor-ian,* to stifle, smother.+Du. and E. Fries. *smoren,* to stifle, smother.

Smoulder, vb. (E.) M.E. *smolderen,* vb.; from M. E. *smolder,* sb., a stifling smoke. *Smol-der* < **smol-ther.* Cf. Low G. *smelen, smölen,* to smoulder ; *smöln,* to give out fumes (Danneil); Du. *smeulen.* Allied to **Smell.**

Smudge. (Scand.) M. E. *smogen* (Hall.); weakened form of *smutch.* ─ Dan. *smuds,* smut, dirt; *smudse,* to soil. Cf. M. E. *smod,* dirt; E. Fries. and Low G. *smudden,* to soil; Du. *smoddig,* dirty. See **Smut.**

Smug, neat, spruce. (Scand.─G.) Formerly *smoog, smug*; weakened form of **smuk.* ─ Dan. *smuk,* pretty, fine, fair; (South Dan. *smugg,* N. Fries. *smock, schmuck,* Outzen); M. Swed. *smuck,* elegant, fair.─Low G. *smuk,* neat, trim ;

G. *schmuck,* trim, spruce; cf. *schmücken,* to adorn, M. H. G. *smucken,* to clothe, adorn, derived from the weak grade of the M. H. G. strong verb *smiegen,* to creep into, cognate with A. S. *smūgan,* to creep. β. Thus *smug* meant ' dressed ' or ' trim ' ; allied to *smock,* attire. See **Smock.**

smuggle, to import or export secretly. (Scand.) Dan. *smugle,* to smuggle; cf. *i smug,* secretly, *smughandel,* contraband trade ; Swed. *smuga,* a lurking-hole, Icel. *smuga,* a hole to creep through. ─ Icel. *smug-,* weak grade of *smjūga,* to creep, creep through a hole, cognate with A. S. *smūgan,* to creep ; see **Smock.**

Smut, a spot of dirt or soot. (E.) For the base *smut-,* cf. M. E. *smotten, bi-smoteren,* to smut; G. *schmutz,* dirt. β. We also find *smutch,* for *smuts ; from Swed. *smuts,* smut, dirt; whence Swed. *smutsa,* to soil ; see **Smudge.**

Snack; see **Snatch.**

Snaffle. (Du.) For *snaffle-piece,* i.e. nose-piece.─Du. *snavel,* a horse's muzzle; M. Du. *snavel, snabel,* bill, snout ; cf. O. Fries. *snavel,* mouth ; G. *schnabel,* bill. Dimin. of M. Du. *snabbe, snebbe,* Du. *sneb,* bill, lit. 'snapper;' from **snabben,* parallel form to M. Du. *snappen,* to snap up; see **Snap.** Cf. Du. *snebbig,* snappish; Lith. *snapas,* bill.

Snag, a short branch, knot on a stick, abrupt projection. (Scand.) Prob. of Scand. origin; cf. Norw. *snage,* a projecting tongue of land ; Icel. *snagi,* a clothespeg. Hence, perhaps, prov. E. *snag,* to trim, cut small branches from a tree ; Gael. *snaigh,* to hew, cut down, trim trees ; Irish *snaigh,* a hewing, cutting.

Snail. (E.) M.E. *snayle.* A.S. *snægl, snegel,* a snail.+Icel. *snigill,* Dan. *snegl*; Swed. *snigel,* a slug. Teut. types **snagiloz,* **snegiloz,* masc. Allied to A.S. *snaca,* a snake (Noreen, § 252). See below ; and cf. Low G. *snigge,* G. *schnecke,* a snail.

snake. (E.) A.S. *snaca,* a snake +Icel. *snakr, snokr*; Dan. *snog*; Swed. *snok.* From Teut. verb **snak-an-,* to creep, pt. t. **snōk,* as seen in O. H. G. *snahhan,* pt. t. *snuoh.*

Snap, vb. (Du.) Du. *snappen,* to snap, snatch. + Dan. *snappe,* Swed. *snappa,* G. *schnappen* ; M. H. G. *snaben.* Base **snap,* similar to **snak.* See **Snaffle,** **Snatch.**

Snare, a noose. (E.) A.S. *sneare,* cord,

string, noose.**+**Du. *snaar*, a string; Icel. *snara*; Dan. *snare*; Swed. *snara*; O.H.G. *snarahha*, a noose. β. The O. H. G. *snarahha* shews an orig. final guttural; the sb. is from a strong verb, seen in O. H. G. *snerhan*, to twist tightly; from a base SNERH = Idg. √SNERK, whence Gk. νάρκη, cramp; see **Narcissus**. Cf. √SNER, to twist, wind; see **Nerve**. γ. All from √SNĒ, to wind, spin; whence L. *nēre*, to spin, G. *schnur*, a string.

Snarl, vb. (E.) Frequentative form of *snar*, to shew one's teeth like a dog, spelt *snarre* in Palsgrave. Not found in A. S.; but cf. M. Du. *snarren*, 'to brawl, to scould, or to snarle,' Hexham. **+** G. *schnarren*, to growl, snarl; M. H. G. *snar*, a growling. And see **Sneer, Snort**.

Snatch. (E.) M. E. *snacchen*, as if from **snak-*; cf. Lowland Sc. *snak*, a snap of the jaws.**+**Du. *snakken*, to gasp. Base **snak*, parallel to **snap*. See **Snap**. Der. *snack*, sb., a portion, lit. ' a bit snatched up,' a hasty meal, a share; *to go snacks* = to go shares. Also prov. E. *sneck*, snap or latch of a door.

Sneak. (E.) Variant of M. E. *snīken*, A.S. *snícan*, to creep, Teut. type **sneikan-*; pt. t. **snaik*, pp. **snikanoz*. The A.S. pt. t. *snác* would give a deriv. **snǣcan*, representing E. *sneak*. Cf. Guernsey *snēquer*, to rob slily.**+**Icel. *snik-inn*, hankering after, from a lost strong verb; Swed. dial. *snika* (pt. t. *snek*), to hanker after; Dan. *sniga sig*, to sneak, slink; Gael. and Irish *snaig, snaigh*, to creep (from E.).

Sneap, to pinch, check; see **Snub**.

Sneer, to scoff. (E.) M. E. *sneren*. Cf. E. Fries. *sniren*, to frizzle, to cause a hissing noise, to sneer at; Dan. *snærre*, to grin like a dog, shew one's teeth at a person; allied to **Snarl**.

Sneeze, vb. (E.) M.E. *snesen*; Chaucer has *fnesen* (Cant. Tales, H. 62), of which *snesen*, occurring in the Camb. MS., is a modification. A. S. *fnēosan*, to sneeze. **+**Du. *fniezen*; Swed. *fnysa*; Dan. *fnyse*. Cf. Gk. πνέω, I breathe; see **Pneumatic**. Base **fneus-*, parallel form to **hneus-*; see **Neese**.

Sniff, to scent. (Scand.) M. E. *sneuien* (*snevien*). **–** Icel. **snefja*, to sniff, a lost verb, whence *snafðr*, sharp-scented, *snefill*, a slight scent; Dan. *snive*, to sniff. Similar to Icel. *snippa*, to sniff; and cf. *snoppa*, a snout.

Snip, vb. (Du.) Du. *snippen*, to snip,

clip; allied to *snappen*, to snap, intercept; see **Snap**.**+**E. Fries. *snippen*; Low G. *snippeln*, to cut small; G. *schnippen*, to snap, allied to *schnappen*. Cf. E. Fries. *snip*, sharp; *snip*, *snippe*, a small piece of land. ¶ Prob. confused with **Nip**. Der. *snip*, sb.; *snipp-et*, a small piece.

Snipe, a bird. (Scand.) M. E. *snype*. **–** Icel. *snipa*, a snipe; Dan. *sneppe*, a snipe; Swed. *snäppa*, a sand-piper.**+**Du. *snip*, *snep*, M. Du. *snippe, sneppe*; G. *schnepfe*. It refers to the long bill; lit. 'snipper.' See **Snip, Snap**.

Snite (1), to wipe the nose. (E.) A. S. **snȳtan*, whence *snȳting*, sb., a sneezing; E. Fries. *snüten*, to snite.**+**Du. *snuiten*, from *snuit*, snout, nose; Icel. *snȳta*, Swed. *snyta*, Dan. *snyde*, to snite; from Swed. *snut*, Dan. *snude*, snout; see **Snout**.

Snite (2), a snipe. (E.) M. E. *snite*. A. S. *snīte*, a snite or snipe. Cf. **Snipe**.

Snivel, to snuffle, to whimper. (E.) M. E. *snuvelen, sneuelen (snevelen)*; as if from A. S. **snyflian*. From A. S. *snofl*, mucus. Cf. Swed. *snöfla*, Dan. *snövle*, to snuffle; Low G. *snüff, snuff*, a nose, snout. See **Snuff**.

Snob. (Scand.) Prov. E. *snob*, a vulgar person, also, a journeyman shoemaker, *snap*, a lad, servant, usually in a ludicrous sense; Lowl. Sc. *snab*, a cobbler's boy. **–** Dan. dial. *snopp, snupp*, bashful, silly; Icel. *snápr*, a dolt, with the notion of impostor, a boaster, used as a by-word; Swed. dial. *snöpp*, a boy, anything stumpy; cf. Swed. dial. *snöppa*, to cut off, make stumpy; and see **Snub**. Cf. Swed. *snopen*, ashamed.

Snood, a fillet, ribbon. (E.) A. S. *snōd*, a fillet; orig. 'a twist,' wreath. Cf. Icel. *snúðr*, a twist; Swed. *snodd*, a string; also W. *ysnoden*, a fillet; Irish *snáthe*, a thread. All from Idg. root **snē, *snā*, to spin, to twist; whence G. *schnū-r*, a string; cf. Icel. *snúa*, Dan. *snoe*, Swed. *sno*, to twist, twine.

Snore, vb. (E.) M. E. *snoren*; for **fnoren*; cf. A. S. *fnora*, sb., a snoring, snore. From A. S. *fnor-* (< *fnus-*), weak grade of *fnēosan*, to sneeze; see **Sneeze**. Influenced by **Snort**.

Snort, vb. (E.) M. E. *snorten*, to snore. Low G. *snurten, snarten*, to make an explosive noise. From **snur-*; as in Low G. *snurren*, to hum, M. Du. *snorren*, to murmur. Variant forms are Dan. *snorke*, to snort; Swed. *snorka*, to threaten (orig. to fume, be angry); Du. *snorken*; G. *schnar-chen*. And see **Snarl**.

Snot, mucus from the nose. (E.) M. E. *snotte*. A. S. *ge-snot*; O. Fries. *snotte*; Du. Dan. *snot*. Allied to **Snite** (1) and **snout**.

snout. (E.) M. E. *snoute*, E. Fries. *snute*. + Du. *snuit*; Swed. *snut*, snout, muzzle; Dan. *snude*; G. *schnauze*. Cf. Dan. *snue*, to sniff, Low G. *snau*, prov. G. *schnau*, snout, beak. From a base **sneu*; whence Teut. vb. **snūtan-*, pt. t. **snaut*, pp. **snutanoz*. From the 1st grade we have Swed. *snūt*, Du. *snuit*, E. *snout*; from the 2nd, G. *schnauze*; and from the 3rd, E. *snot*.

Snow. (E.) A. S. *snāw*. + Du. *sneeuw*, Icel. *snær*, Dan. *snee*, Swed. *snö*, Goth. *snaiws*, G. *schnee*; also Lith. *snëgas*, Russ. *snieg'*, L. *nix* (gen. *niuis*), Gk. acc. νίφα, Irish *sneachd*, W. *nyf*. (√SNEIGH.) Cf. Lith. *snigti*, to snow, L. *ningit*, Gk. νείφει, it snows. Brugm. i. § 394.

Snub, to check, reprimand. (Scand.) Also *sneb*, *snib*. M. E. *snibben*. – Dan. *snibbe*, to reprimand; Swed. *snubba*, Icel. *snubba*, N. Fries. *snubbe*, to snub, chide. Orig. to 'snip off' the end of a thing; cf. Icel. *snubbōtr*, snubbed, nipped, with the tip cut off; Swed. dial. *snubba*, to snip or clip off; E. Fries. *snubbeln*, to snap or snatch away. β. Allied to obs. E. *sneap*, to pinch, nip, answering to Icel. *sneypa*, to castrate, also to disgrace, snub; Swed. *snöpa*, to castrate. Cf. also Dan. dial. *sneve*, to dock, to snub, to nip. **Der.** *snub-nosed*, i. e. with a short or stumpy nose, as if with the end cut off.

snub-nosed; see above.

Snuff (1), to sniff, smell. (Du.) From M. Du. *snuffen*; cf. *snuyven* (Du. *snuiven*), 'to snuffe out the filth out of ones nose,' Hexham; Du. *snuf*, smelling, scent; E. Fries. *snufen*, *snuven*, to snuff up. + Swed. *snufva*, a catarrh, *snufven*, a sniff, scent; cf. G. *schnauben*, *schnaufen*, *schnieben*, to snuff, snort (from a Teut. base **sneub*); G. *schnupfen*, a catarrh, *schnupfen*, to take snuff. **Der.** *snuff*, powdered tobacco; also *snuff-le*, prov. G. *schnuffeln*, *schnüffeln*.

Snuff (2), to snip off the top of a candle-wick. (E.) M. E. *snuffen*, to snuff out a candle; cf. *snoffe*, sb., the snuff of a candle. Parallel to **snuppen*; cf. prov. E. *snop*, to eat off, as cattle do young shoots; Swed. dial. *snōppa*, to snip off, snuff a

candle; Dan. *snubbe*, to nip off. See **Snub**. **Der.** *snuff*, sb.

Snug. (Scand.) Cf. prov. E. *snug*, tidy, trimmed up; *snog*, the same. – Icel. *snöggr*, smooth, said of wool or hair; M. Swed. *snygg*, short-haired, trimmed, Swed. *snygg*, cleanly, neat, genteel; Dan. dial. *snög*, neat, smart. Cf. E. Fries. *snügge*, *snigge*, smooth, neat. Orig. 'trimmed;' hence neat, smart, tidy, comfortable. Cf. **Snag**.

So. (E.) M. E. *so*. A. S. *swā*. + Du. *zoo*, Icel. *svā*, *svo*, *so*; Dan. *saa*, Swed. *så*, G. *so*, Goth. *swa*; Teut. types **swē*, **swō*, **swa*. Cf. Gk. ὡς. β. From a case of Idg. **swos*, one's own; cf. L. *suus*, Skt. *sva*, one's own. Lit. 'in one's own way.' See Prellwitz; Brugm. i. § 362.

Soak. (E.) It also means to suck up, imbibe. M. E. *soken* (1) to suck, (2) to soak. A. S. *socian*, to soak; from A. S. *soc-* (Teut. *suk-*), weak grade of *sūcan*, to suck. See **Suck**. Cf. W. *swga*, soaked, *sugno*, to suck.

Soap. (E.) M. E. *sope*. A. S. *sāpe*. + Du. *zeep*; [cf. Icel. *sāpa*, Swed. *såpa*, from A. S.]; G. *seife*. Teut. type **saipōn*, fem.; from **saip*, 2nd grade of **seipan-*, to trickle (M. H. G. *sīfen*); hence also A. S. *sāp*, resin, pomade, allied to *sāpe*. ¶ L. *sāpo* (whence F. *savon*, &c.) was borrowed from Teutonic; the true L. (cognate) word seems to be *sēbum*, tallow, grease.

Soar. (F. – L.) M. E. *soren*. – F. *essorer*, to expose to air; in M. F., 'to sore up,' Cot. – Late L. **exaurāre*, to expose to air. – L. *ex*, out; *aura*, breeze, air. Perhaps L. *aura* was borrowed from Gk. αὔρα, a breeze; formed, apparently, with suffix -*ra* from √AW, variant of WE, to blow. See **Air**.

Sob, vb. (E.) M. E. *sobben*, related to A. S. *sēofian*, to lament. + G. *seufzen*, to sigh, O. H. G. *sūftōn*, to sob, O. H. G. *sūft*, a sigh, sob; all from O. H. G. *sūfan*, to sup, sup up. Allied to **Sup**. **Der.** *sob*, sb.

Sober. (F. – L.) M. E. *sobre*. – F. *sobre*. L. *sōbrium*, acc. of *sōbrius*, sober. – L. *sō-* = *sē-*, apart, hence, not; -*brius*, drunk, as in *ē-brius*. See **Ebriety**. (Doubtful.) **Der.** *sobriety*, M. F. *sobrieté*, L. acc. *sōbrietātem*.

Sobriquet, Soubriquet, a nickname. (F.) F. *sobriquet*, 'surname, nickname, a jeast broken on a man;' Cot. He also spells it *sotbriquet*, *soubriquet*.

From O. F. *soubzbriquet*, a chuck under the chin (14th cent.); hence, a quip, an affront, a nickname. Here O. F. *soubz*, F. *sous*, is from L. *subtus*, below; *briquet* has been conjectured to stand for *bequet*, dimin. of *bec*, beak, mouth; cf. Ital. *sotto-becco*, a chuck under the chin. 'Percussit super mentonem faciendo dictum *le soubriquet*;' A. D. 1335. See Körting, and Littré.

Soc, Socage; see S oke.

Sociable. (F. – L.) F. *sociable*. – L. *sociābilis*, companionable. – L. *sociā-re*, to accompany. – L. *socius*, companion, follower; allied to L. *sequī*, to follow. See Sequence. Der. *as-sociate*, *dis-sociate*.

social. (L.) L. *sociālis*, adj., from *socius* (above).

society. (F. – L.) M. F. *societé*. – L. acc. *societātem*, from nom. *societās*, fellowship. – L. *socius*, a companion; see Sociable.

Sock. (L.) A. S. *socc*. – L. *soccus*, a light shoe, slipper, sock, buskin of a comedian.

Socket. (F. – L.?) Cf. F. dial. *soquette*, a stump of dead wood, patois de la Meuse (Labourasse); Walloon *sokett*, a stump. Godefroy has *socquet*, (apparently) a cupboard. Prob. an A. F. dimin. of O. F. *soc*, a wooden clog (A. D. 1473). Cotg. has '*socque*, a sock or sole of durt, cleaving to the foot in a cloggy way.' Cf. Port. *socco*, wooden shoe or clog, mod. F. *socque*, a clog. β. All from L. *soccus*, sock, shoe, hence, a wooden shoe or clog. I conclude that *socket* is a dimin. of *sock*, notwithstanding the change in sense; cf. E. *shoe*, a kind of socket, as a term in machinery (Webster). ¶ O. F. *soket*, a small ploughshare, is from a Celtic source, being allied to O. Irish *socc*, a ploughshare.

Sod. (E.) So called from the use of turf as fuel (?); or from its frequent wetness (?). The connexion with the verb *to seethe* appears clearly in Du. *zode*, sod, green turf, M. Du. *zode*, seething, also sod; G. *sode*, sod, *sod*, bubbling up of boiling water; Low G. *sood*. a well, *sode*, a turf, sod; E. Fries. *sōd*, a well; *sode*, a cut turf, also, boiling, cooking; Dan. dial. *sodd*, *saadd*, a sod. (See Franck.) Cf. also A. S. *sēað*, a well, pit, *sēað*, pt. t. of *sēoðan*, to seethe; O. Fries. *sātha*, sod, *sāth*, a well; A. S. *ge-sod*, a cooking. See Seethe.

Soda. (Ital. – L.) Ital. *soda*, 'a kind of fearne ashes whereof they make glasses;' Florio. Fem. of Ital. *sodo*, 'solide, tough;'

ibid. (Similarly O. F. *soulde*, glasswort, answers to L. *solida*; prob. from the hardness of the products obtained from glasswort.) – L. *solidus*, solid, hard. See Solid. Der. *sod-ium*, a coined word.

Sodden; see Seethe.

Soder, Solder, a firm cement from fusible metals. (F. – L.) Formerly *soder*, *sowder*, sometimes *soulder*; now pronounced (sod·ər). – F. *soudure*, M. F. *souldure*, 'a souldering, and particularly the knot of soulder which fastens the led [lead] of a glasse window;' Cot. – O. F. *souder*, *soulder*, to consolidate, make firm. – L. *solidāre*, to make firm. – L. *solidus*, firm. See Solid.

Sodomy. (F. – L. – Gk. – Heb.) F. *sodomie*, a sin imputed to the inhabitants of Sodom. – F. *Sodome*, Sodom. – L. *Sodoma*. – Gk. Σόδομα. – Heb. *Sedōm*.

Sofa. (Arab.) Arab. *suffat*, *suffah*, 'a sopha;' Rich. Dict. p. 936. – Arab. root *saffa*, to draw up in line, to put a seat to a saddle; ibid.

Soft. (E.) A. S. *sōfte*, adv.; *sōft*, also *sēfte* adj. (with *i*-mutation). + O. Sax. *sāfto*, adv., softly; G. *sanft*, soft; O.H.G. *samfto*, adv., gently; Du. *zacht*, for *zaft* (whence G. *sacht*). Der. *soft-en*.

Soil (1), ground, country. (F. – L.) M. E. *soile*. – A. F. *soil*; (cf. F. *seuil*, threshold of a door < L. *solium*). – Late L. *solea*, soil, ground. Allied to L. *solum*, ground; whence F. *sol*, soil, ground (from which, however, the E. word cannot be directly derived). Cf. Gk. ἔδ-αφος, foundation, ground. See Sole (1).

Soil (2), to defile. (F. – L.) M. E. *soilen*. [Not allied to M. E. *sulen*, E. *sully*.] – O. F. *soillier*, F. *souiller*, to soil; *se souiller*, to wallow as a sow. – O. F. *soil*, *souil*, 'the soile of a wild boar, the mire wherein he hath wallowed;' Cot. – Late L. *suillus*, a pig; L. *suillus*, adj., belonging to swine. – L. *sūs*, a sow. See Sow. Der. *soil*, sb., a stain; quite distinct from *soil*, ground.

Soil (3), to feed cattle with green grass, to fatten with feeding. (F. – L.) O. F. *soeler*, *saoler*, M. F. *saouler*, to glut, satiate (F. *soûler*); cf. O. F. *soelement*, satiety (Godefroy). – O.F. *saol*, full, cloyed. – L. acc. *satullum*, filled with food. – L. *satur*, full. See Satiate.

Soirée, an evening party. (F. – L.) F. *soirée*, evening; hence, an evening party. Cf. Ital. *serata*, evening. – L. *sēr·us*, late in the day (whence Ital. *sera*, F. *soir*, evening) ; with suffix -*āta* (>F. -*ée*).

Sojourn, to dwell. (F.–L.) O.F. *sojorner, sojourner*.–L. *sub*, under; *diurnāre*, to stay, from *diurnus*, daily ; which is from *diēs*, a day. See **Diary**.

Soke, Soc, a franchise, land held by socage. (E.) The A.S. *sacu* meant 'a contention,' a 'law-suit'; whence the Law term *sac*, the power of hearing suits and administering justice within a certain precinct. The A.S. *sōcn* meant 'investigation,' or 'a seeking into'; whence the Law term *soke*, the right of hearing disputes and enquiring into complaints, also, the precinct within which such right was exercised ; see Blount, Spelman, Ellis, Thorpe, Schmid. β. Etymologically, *sac* (A.S. *sacu*) is the same word as **Sake**, q. v. *Soke* (A.S. *sōc*-) is the exercise of judicial power; and *soken* (A.S. *sōcn*, *sōcen*) is an enquiry; both allied to E. *seek*, and derived from A.S. *sōc*, strong grade of *sacan*, to contend; see **Seek**. Der. *soc-age*, a barbarous law term made by adding F. -*age* (L. -*āticum*) to A.S. *sōc*-. (The *o* is long.)

Solace, a relief. (F.–L.) M.E. *solas*. –O.F. *solaz* (where *z* = *ts*).–L. *sōlātium*, a comfort.–L. *sōlātus*, pp. of *sōlārī*, to console. Allied to L. *sollus*, Gk. ὅλος, whole (Prellwitz). Der. *solace*, vb.

Solan-goose, a bird. (Scand. *and* E.) The E. *goose* is an addition.–Icel. *sūlan*, lit. ' the gannet,' where -*n* stands for the definite article ; def. form of Icel. -*sūla*, in *haf-sūla*, i. e. sea-gannet, solan goose ; Norweg. *sula*, the same.

Solar, belonging to the sun. (L.) L. *sōlāris*, solar. – L. *sōl*, sun. + Icel. *sōl*, Goth. *sauil*, Lith. *sáule*, Irish *sūl*, Gk. ἥλιος (see Prellwitz); Skt. *sūra*-, sun, splendour. Brugm. i. § 481.

Solder; see **Soder**.

Soldier. (F.–L.) M.E. *sodiour, soudiour, souldier*.–O.F. *soldier, soudoier, souldoyer*, one who fights for pay; Late L. *soldārius*.–Late L. *soldum*, pay.–Late L. *solidus*, a piece of money (whence O.F. *sol*, F. *sou*); orig. 'a solid piece.'–L. *solidus*, solid; cf. E. 'hard cash.' See **Solid**.

Sole (1), under side of foot or shoe. (L.) A.S. *sole*.–Late L. *sola*, for L. *solea*, sole of the foot, or of a shoe.–L. *solum*, the ground. See **Soil**.

Sole (2), a fish. (F.–L.) M.E. *sole*.– F. *sole* ; Cot.–L. *solea*, the sole-fish.

Sole (3), alone. (F.–L.) O.F. *sol* (F. *seul*).–L. *sōlum*, acc. of *sōlus*, alone.

Solecism, impropriety in speaking or writing. (F.–L.–Gk.) M.F. *soloecisme* ; Cot.–L. *solœcismus*.–Gk. σολοικισμός, a solecism.–Gk. σολοικίζειν, to speak incorrectly.–Gk. σόλοικος, speaking incorrectly, like an inhabitant of Σόλοι (*Soloi*) in Cilicia, where the Gk. dialect was corruptly spoken. Der. *solecist*, sb.

Solemn. (F.–L.) M.E. *solempne*.– O.F. *solempne*. – L. *sōlemnem*, acc. of *sōlemnis*, older forms *sōlennis, sollennis*, annual, occurring yearly like a religious rite, religious, solemn.–L. *sollus*, entire, complete; *annus*, a year. Hence *solemn* = returning at the end of a complete year. The O. Lat. *sollus* is cognate with W. *holl*, whole, entire. Brugm. i. § 417. Der. *solemn-ity, -ise*.

Sol-fa, to sing the notes of the gamut. (L.) It means to sing the notes by the names *si, la, sol, fa, mi, re, ut* (where, for *ut, do* is now used). These names are of L. origin; see **Gamut**. Der. *solfeggio*, from Ital. *solfeggio*, the singing of the gamut; cf. *sol-mi-sation*, coined from *sol* and *mi*.

Solicit. (F.–L.) M.F. *soliciter*.–L. *sollicitāre*, to agitate, arouse, urge, solicit. –L. *sollicitus*, lit. wholly agitated.–L. *solli*-, for *sollus*, whole ; *citus*, aroused, pp. of *ciēre*, to shake, excite. See **Solemn** and **Cite**. Der. *solicitous*, for L. *sollicitus*; *solicit-ude*, M.F. *solicitude*, from L. *sollicitūdo*, anxiety.

Solid. (F.–L.) F. *solide*.–L. *solidum*, acc. of *solidus*, firm. Der. *solidar-i-ty*, ' a word which we owe to the F. communists, and which signifies a fellowship in gain and loss, a being, so to speak, all in the same bottom;' Trench. Also *solid-i-fy*, from F. *solidifier*, to render solid.

Soliloquy. (L.) Late L. *sōliloquium*, a speaking to oneself (Augustine).–L. *sōli*-, for *sōlus*, alone; *loquī*, to speak. See **Loquacious**.

Soliped, an animal with uncloven hoof. (L.) Short for *solidiped*. – L. *solidiped*-, stem of *solidipēs*, solid-hoofed (Pliny).–L. *solidi*-, for *solidus*, solid ; *pēs*, a foot ; see **Foot**.

Solitary. (F.–L.) M.E. *solitarie*.– A.F. *solitarie* ; cf. F. *solitaire*.–L. *sōlitārius*, solitary. Short for **sōlitātārius*, from *sōlitāt*-, stem of *sōlitās*, loneliness.– L. *sōlus*, alone.

solitude. (F.—L.) F. *solitude.*—L. *sŏlitūdo.*—L. *sŏli-*, for *sŏlus*, alone; and suffix *-tūdo*.

solo. (Ital.—L.) From Ital. *solo*, alone.—L. *sŏlus*, alone.

Solmisation: see **Sol-fa**.

Solstice. (F.—L.) F. *solstice.*—L. *solstitium*, the solstice; lit. a point (in the ecliptic) at which the sun seems to stand still.—L. *sŏl*, the sun; *-stit-um*, for *statum*, supine of *sistere*, to make to stand still, from *stāre*, to stand. See **State**.

Soluble. (F.—L.) F. *soluble.*—L. *solūbilis*, dissolvable.—L. *solū-*, base of *solū-tus*, pp. of *soluere*, to loosen; with suffix *-bilis*. See **solve**.

solution. (F.—L.) F. *solution.*—L. *solūtiōnem*, acc. of *solūtio*, a loosing.—L. *solūt-us*, pp. of *soluere*, to loosen, solve.

solve. (L.) Late L. *solvere*; L. *soluere*, to loosen, relax, explain; pp. *solūtus.*—L. *so-* (for *sē-*), apart; *luere*, to loosen, allied to Gk. λύ-ειν, to set free, and to E. **Lose**. Brugm. i. § 121. **Der.** *solvent*, from the stem of the pres. pt.; and see above.

Sombre, gloomy. (F.—L.) F. *sombre*, gloomy. Cf. Port. and Span. *sombrio*, gloomy, from Port. and Span. *sombra*, shade. Diez refers these to L. *umbra*, shade, with prefix *sub*; cf. Prov. *sotz-ombrar*, to shade. (See Körting.) Littré refers them to L. *umbra*, shade, with prefix *ex* (intensive). Either solution seems possible; the latter is the simpler. See **Umbrage**.

sombrero, a broad-brimmed hat. (Span.—L.) Span. *sombrero.* — Span. *sombra* (above).

Some. (E.) A. S. *sum*, some one, a certain one, one; pl. *sume*, some.+Icel. *sumr*, Goth. *sums*, O. H. G. *sum*, some one; Dan. *somme*, pl.; cf. Swed. *somlige*, pl., some. Allied to **Same**. **Der.** *some-body*, *-thing*, *-time*, *-times* (where *-s* is an adverbial suffix).

-some, suffix. (E.) A. S. *-sum*, as in *wyn-sum* = E. *win-some*. Cf. G. *lang-sam*, slow. From the weak grade of Teut. *samo-*, same; see **Same**.

Somersault, Somerset. (F.—Ital.—L.) M.F. *soubresault*, 'a sobresault or summersault, an active trick in tumbling;' Cot.—Ital. *soprasalto.*—Ital. *sopra*, above, over; *salto*, a leap.—L. *suprā*, above, over; *saltum*, acc. of *saltus*, a leap, from pp. of L. *salīre*, to leap; see **Salient**.

Somnambulist, one who walks in his sleep. (L.) Coined (with suffix *-ist* = L. *-ista* = Gk. -ιστης, as in *bapt-ist*) from L. *somn-us*, sleep, and *ambul-āre*, to walk. See below, and see **Amble**.

somniferous, causing sleep. (L.) L. *somnifer*, sleep-bringing; with suffix *-ous*. —L. *somni-*, for *somnus*, sleep; *-fer*, bringing, from *ferre*, to bring. β. The L. *somnus* is for **swepnos*, allied to Skt. *svapna-*, Irish *súan*, W. *hun*, sleep. (√SWEP.) See **Soporiferous**.

somnolence. (F.—L.) F. *somnolence.* —L. *somnolentia*, sleepiness.—L. *somnolentus*, sleepy.—L. *somno-* (for *somnus*), sleep (above); with suffix *-lentus*.

Son. (E.) M.E. *sone*. A.S. *sunu.*+ Du. *zoon*; Icel. *sunr*, Dan. *sön*, Swed. *son*, G. *sohn*, Goth. *sunus*. Teut. type **sunuz*. Cf. Lith. *sūnus*, Russ. *suin'*; Skt. *sūnu-*, from Skt. *su*, *sū*, to beget; Gk. νἰός, νἱύς (for **σνγύς*); O. Irish *suth*, birth. (√SŪ.) Brugm. i. §§ 104, 292.

Sonata. (Ital.—L.) Ital. *sonata*, a sounding, a sonata. From the fem. of pp. of Ital. *sonare*, to sound.—L. *sonāre*, to sound, from *sonus*, sound. See **Sound** (3).

Song. (E.) M.E. *song*. A.S. *sang.*— A.S. *sang*, 2nd grade of *singan*, to sing + Du. *zang*; Icel. *söngr*; Swed. *sång*; Dan. and G. *sang*; Goth. *saggws* (for *sangws*); cf. Gk. ὀμφή, voice. See **Sing**.

songster. (E.) A.S. *sangystre*, *sang-estre*, a singer.—A.S. *sang*, 2nd grade of *singan*, to sing; with double suffix *-es-tre* of the agent. **Der.** *songstr-ess*, with F. suffix, from Gk. -ισσα.

Sonnet. (F.—Ital.—L.) F. *sonnet.*— Ital. *sonetto*, a sonnet, canzonet; dimin. of *sono*, a sound, tune.—L. *sonum*, acc. of *sonus*, a sound. **Der.** *sonnet-eer*, Ital. *sonettiere*, a sonnet-writer. See **Sound** (3).

sonorous. (L.) For L. *sonōrus*, loud-sounding. —L. *sonōr-*, stem of *sonor*, sound, noise.—L. *sonāre*, to sound.—L. *sonus*, sound.

Soon. (E.) M.E. *sone*. A.S. *sōna.*+ O. Sax. *sāna*, *sāno*; O. Fries., O. Sax, M. H. G. *sān*; cf. Goth. *suns-aiw*, *suns*, immediately.

Soot. (E.) A.S. *sōt.*+Icel. *sōt*, Swed. *sot*, Dan. *sod*; cf. Lith. *sódis*, soot. Perhaps from the *ō-* grade of Idg. root SED (Teut. SET), to sit, rest upon. See **Sit**. (Noreen, § 146; Streitberg, § 95.) Cf. also Gael. *sùith*, soot.

Sooth, true. (E.) A.S. *sōð*, true;

whence *sōð*, neut. sb., the truth. [The A.S. *sōð* stands for *south-, Teut. *santh-; the loss of *n* following the lengthening of *o*.] +Icel. *sannr* (for *santhr), Swed. *sann*, Dan. *sand*; from Teut. base *santhoz, Idg. *sontos, short for *es-ont-, lit. being, that which is, from √ES, to be. Allied to L. -*sens*, being, as in *ab-sens* (stem *ab-sent-*), *præ-sens* (stem *præ-sent-*); Skt. *sat-ya-*, true. See **Suttee** and **Essence.** Der. *for-sooth*, i. e. for a truth; *sooth-say*, to say truth.

soothe. (E.) The orig. sense was to assent to as being true, hence to say yes to, humour, flatter, approve of. 'Is't good to *soothe* him in these contraries?' Com. Errors, iv. 4. 82. M. E. *sōðien*, to confirm, verify. A. S. *ge-sōðian*, to confirm, prove to be true.—A. S. *sōð*, true; see **Sooth.**

soothsay. (E.) To *say sooth*, i. e. tell truth, predict.

Sop, sb. (E.) M. E. *soppe*. It answers to an A.S. *soppe, a sop (whence *soppian*, to sop up); regularly formed from *sop-* (Teut. *sup-) weaker grade of *sūpan*, to sup. Cf. Icel. *soppa*, a sop, from the weaker grade of *sūpa*, to sup; also Du. *sop*, M. Du. *zoppe*, M. Swed. *soppa*, Low G. *soppe*, G. *suppe*. See **Sup.**

Sophist, a captious reasoner. (F.—L. —Gk.) Usually *sophister* in old authors, but the final *r* is unoriginal.—O. F. *sophiste.*—Late L. *sophista.*—Gk. σοφιστής, a skilful man, also a Sophist, teacher of arts for money (see Liddell).—Gk. σοφίζειν, to instruct.—Gk. σοφός, wise. Der. *sophist-r-y*, *sophist-ic* (Gk. σοφιστικός); *sophis-m* (Gk. σόφισμα, a device).

Sophy, a shah of Persia, A. D. 1505–1736. (Pers.—Arab.) In Shak. Merch. Ven. ii. 1. 26. Pers. *Safi*, a title.—Arab. *safīy*, pure. ¶ Distinct from *Sufi*, a Moslem mystic; from Arab. *sūfīy*, intelligent.

Soporiferous, inducing sleep. (L.) From L. *sopōrifer*, sleep-bringing; by adding -*ous*.—L. *sopōri-*, from *sopōr-*, stem of *sopor*, sleep; -*fer*, bringing, from *ferre*, to bring. The L. *sopor* is allied to Skt. *svapna-*, sleep (from *svap*, to sleep), Gk. ὕπνος, sleep, A.S. *swefen*, a dream. (√SWEP.) Brugm. i. § 551. See **Somniferous.**

soporific, causing sleep. (L.) L. *sopōri-* (above); and -*fic-*, for *facere*, to make, cause.

Soprano. (Ital.—L.) Ital. *soprano*,

supreme; highest voice in music.—Late L. *superānus*, chief; see **Sovereign.**

Sorcery. (F.—L.) O. F. *sorcerie*, casting of lots, magic.—O. F. *sorcier*, a sorcerer.—Late L. *sortiārius*, a teller of fortunes by lots, sorcerer.—L. *sorti-*, from *sort-*, stem of *sors*, a lot.

Sordid, dirty, vile. (F.—L.) F. *sordide.*—L. *sordidus*, dirty.—L. *sordi-*, for *sordēs*, dirt. Cf. Russ. *sor'*, filth. Brugm. i. p. 1092.

Sore, adj. (E.) M. E. *sor*. A. S. *sār*, painful. + Du. *zeer*, Icel. *sārr*, Swed. *sår*, O. H. G. *sēr*, wounded, painful; cf. G. *sehr*, sorely, very, *versehren*, to wound. Teut. type *sairoz, adj. Cf. O. Irish *sáeth*, *sóeth*, tribulation; but hardly L. *sæuus*, dire. Der. *sore*, sb., A.S. *sār* (Goth. *sair*); and *sore*, adv., very; see **Sorry.**

Sorrel (1), a plant. (F.—M. H. G.) O. F. *sorel* (F. *surelle*).—M. H. G. *sūr* (G. *sauer*), sour; from its taste. So also A. S. *sūre*, sorrel, from *sūr*, sour. See **Sour.**

Sorrel (2), of a reddish-brown colour. (F.—Teut.) O. F. *sorel*; dimin. from O.F. *sor*, F. *saur*, sorrel of colour.—Low G. *soor*, sear, dried up, withered; cognate with E. *sear*. See **Sear.**

Sorrow, grief. (E.) M. E. *sorwe*, *sorȝe*. A. S. *sorge*, gen. dat. and acc. of *sorh*, *sorg*, sorrow, anxiety. + Du. *zorg*, Dan. Swed. *sorg*, G. *sorge*, Goth. *saurga*, care, grief. Teut. type *sorgā, f. Cf. O. Irish *serg*, sickness, Lith. *sirgti*, to be ill, suffer. ¶ Not allied to *sore* or *sorry*, though the present sense of *sorry* shews confusion with it. See below.

Sorry, sore in mind, aggrieved. (E.) M. E. *sory*. A. S. *sārig*, adj., sorry, sad, sore in mind; from *sār*, sore.+Du. *zeerig*, Swed. *sårig*, sore, full of scres, words which preserve the orig. sense. ¶ Spelt with two *r*'s owing to the shortening of M. E. *ō* in *sory*, due to the addition of the suffix -*y* (A. S. -*ig*); but not orig. allied to *sorrow*.

Sort, a kind. (F.—L.) F. *sorte*, fem., sort, kind; O. F. *sorte*, fem., a company; allied to F. *sort*, masc., luck, fate.—L. *sortem*, acc. of *sors*, lot. Perhaps allied to **Series.** Brugm. i. § 516 (1).

Sortie. (F.—L.) F. *sortie*, a going forth; fem. of *sorti*, pp. of *sortir*, to sally forth. Cf. Span. *surtida*, a sortie, from O. Span. *surtir*, to rise. β. F. *sortir*, Span. *surtir*, answer to a Folk-L. form *sortīre, to rise up, from *sortum, for L.

surrectum, supine of *surgere,* to rise up; see **Surge.** The contraction of *surrectum* to *sortum* is proved to be correct by Ital. *sorto,* occurring as pp. of *sorgere,* to rise; and by Span. *surto,* pp. of *surgir.*

Sot, a stupid fellow, drunkard. (Late L.) M. E. *sot* (Ancren Riwle). A. S. *sot,* *sott.* Late L. *sottus* (Ducange); ab. A.D. 800. Prob. of Teut. origin; cf. M. Du. *zot;* M. H. G. *sote,* a sot. ¶ Distinct from Span. *zote,* a blockhead; Ital: *zotico* (Florio has *zottico*). The Ital. *zotico* has been referred to L. *idiōticus,* idiotic, in which case Span. *zote* may represent L. *idiōtes,* of Gk. origin; see **Idiot.** Ducange has *jotticus,* a foolish game; cf. M. E. *jottes,* unlearned people.

Sou. (F. — L.) F. *sou,* O. F. *sol,* a coin. — Late L. *solidus,* solid, also a coin; cf. *l. s. d.,* i. e. *libræ, solidi, denarii.* See **Solid.**

Soubriquet; see **Sobriquet.**

Souchong, a kind of tea. (Chinese.) Cantonese *siu-chung,* for *siao-chung,* 'little sort;' Yule, p. 691.

Sough, a sighing sound. (E.) M. E. *swogh, swough,* from A. S. *swōgan,* to resound. Cf. Icel. *arn-sūgr,* the rushing sound of an eagle's wings; and see **Surf.**

Soul. (E.) A. S. *sāwel, sāwl.* + Du. *ziel,* Icel. *sāla, sāl,* Dan. *siæl,* Swed. *själ,* G. *seele,* Goth. *saiwala.* Brugm. i. § 200.

Sound (1), adj., healthy. (E.) M. E. *sound.* A. S. *sund.* + Du. *gezond;* Swed. Dan. *sund;* G. *gesund.* Perhaps allied to *sane.*

Sound (2), strait of the sea. (E.) M. E. *sound.* A. S. *sund,* (1) a swimming, (2) power to swim, (3) a strait of the sea, that could be swum across. + Icel. *sund.* Swed. G. *sund.* Probably derived from **swum* (A. S. *swum-*), weak grade of *swimman,* to swim; with suffix *-doz* for Idg. pp. suffix *-tós.* Brugm. i. § 377 (2). See **Swim.** Der. *sound,* swimming-bladder of a fish, another use of the same word; Shetland *soond,* Icel. *sund-magi.*

Sound (3), a noise. (F. — L.) The final *d* is added. M. E. *soun.* — F. *son.* — L. *sonum,* acc. of *sonus* (for **swenos*), a sound. + Skt. *svana-,* sound; A. S. *swin,* melody. (√SWEN.) Brugm. ii. § 519.

Sound (4), to measure depth of water. (F. — L.) In Palsgrave. — F. *sonder,* to sound the depth of. Cf. Span. Port. *sondar,* to sound; Span. Port. *sonda,* F. *sonde,* a

sounding-lead. Diez derives F. *sonder* from a supposed L. **sub-undare,* to go under the water; from L. *sub,* under, and *unda,* a wave; cf. *ab-ound, red-ound,* and *sombre.* ¶ Yet we find A. S. *sund-gyrd,* a sounding-rod; *sund-līne, sund-rāp,* a sounding-line or rope; which point to a derivation from **Sound** (2).

Soup. (F. — Teut.) F. *soupe.* — F. *souper,* to sup. — Low G. *supen,* to drink, quaff. See **Sup,** and **Sop.**

Sour. (E.) A. S. *sūr.* + Du. *zuur,* Icel. *sūrr,* Dan. *suur,* Swed. *sur,* G. *sauer;* W. *sur,* sour, Lith. *surus,* salt; Russ. *surovuii,* raw, coarse, harsh, rough. Brugm. i. § 114.

Source. (F. — L.) M. E. *sours.* — O. F. *sorse, surse* (F. *source*), a source. Here *sorse* is fem. of *sors,* old pp. of O. F. *sordre* (F. *sourdre*), to rise. — L. *surgere,* to rise; see **Surge.**

Souse (1), pickle. (F. — L.) Merely another spelling of **Sauce;** cf. M. E. *sowser,* a saucer; Vocab. 661. 17. Hence *souse,* vb., to soak in brine.

Souse (2). **Sowse,** to swoop down upon. (F. — L.) From M. E. *sours,* the upward spring or the swoop of a bird of prey; Ch. — O. F. *sorse,* a rise, also a source; see **Source.** Phil. Soc. Trans. 1888, p. 18.

South. (E.) A. S. *sūð.* + Du. *zuid;* Icel. *sūðr,* also *sunnr,* south (cf. *suðreyjar,* lit. southern islands, Sodor, the Hebrides); Dan. Swed. *syd,* Swed. *sunnan,* the south; O. H. G. *sund,* G. *süd.* β. The Teut. base is **sunth-,* south; perhaps allied to **Sun,** q. v. Connexion with Gk. *νότος,* south wind (Brugmann), is doubtful; see Prellwitz. **Der.** *south-ern;* cf. O. H. G. *sundrōni,* southern, Icel. *suðrœnn.*

Souvenir. (F. — L.) F. *souvenir,* sb., a remembrance; merely the verb *souvenir,* to remember, used as a sb. — L. *subuenīre,* to occur to one's mind. — L. *sub,* under, near; *uenīre,* to come. See **Venture.**

Sovereign. (F. — L.) M. E. *souerain* (*soverain*). — A. F. *soverein;* O. F. *souverain.* — Late L. *superānus,* chief. — L. *super,* above. See **Super-.**

Sow (1), to scatter seed. (E.) A. S. *sāwan,* pt. t. *sēow,* pp. *sāwen.* + Du. *zaaijen,* Icel. *sā,* Dan. *saae,* Swed. *sā,* O. H. G. *sāwen,* G. *säen,* Goth. *saian.* Also W. *hau,* Lith. *sēti,* Russ. *sieiate,* L. *serere* (pt. t. *sē-ui,* pp. *sa-tum*), to sow; Gk. *ἵημι* (for **σί-ση-μι*), I send, throw. (√SE, to cast.) Brugm. i. §§ 132, 310. **Der.** *seed*; cf. *season*.

Sow (2), a female pig. (E.) Also applied to oblong pieces of melted metal, whence smaller pieces branch out, called *pigs*. M. E. *sowe*. A. S. *sugu*, also *sū*.+ Du. *zog*, Icel. *sȳr*, Dan. *so*, Swed. *so, sugga*, G. *sau*; W. *hwch*, Irish *suig*, L. *sūs*, Gk. *ΰs*, a sow; Zend *hu*, a boar. Perhaps ' producer,' from the prolific nature of the sow. (√SŪ, to produce.) **Der.** *swine*.

Soy, a sauce. (Japanese.) Also *sooja*, ' which has been corrupted into *soy*;' Eng. Cycl. Japanese *shōyu*, soy, sauce ; though the name is now given to the bean (*Do-lichos soja*) whence *soy* is made. But the Jap. name for the bean is *daidzu*.

Spa, a place where is a spring of mineral water. (Belgium.) Named after *Spa*, S.W. of Liège, in Belgium.

Space. (F.—L.) F. *espace*.—L. *spatium*, a space. Allied to **Span**. Brugm. i. § 193. **Der.** *spac-i-ous*.

Spade (1). (E.) A. S. *spædu, spada*, a spade.+Du. *spade*, Icel. *spaði*, Dan. Swed. *spade*, G. *spaten* ; Gk. σπάθη, broad blade, sword-blade, spathe of a flower (whence L. *spatha*, F. *épée*). From its flat surface. (√SPA, to draw out.) **Der.** *spaddle*, a paddle.

spade (2), at cards. (Span.—L.—Gk.) A substitution for the Span. *espada*, meaning (1) a sword, (2) a spade at cards. **Der.** *spad-ille*, ace of spades, F. *spadille*, Span. *espadilla*, small sword, ace of spades, dimin. of Span. *spada*, a spade (< L. *spatha* < Gk. σπάθη). See **Spade** (1).

Spalpeen, a mean fellow. (Irish.) Irish *spailpin*, a common labourer, a mean fellow, Gael. *spailpean*. From Ir. *spailp*, a beau; orig. pride.

Span, to measure, grasp. (E.) M. E. *spannen*. A. S. *spannan*, to bind, pt. t. *spěnn* ; *gespannan*, to bind, connect.+ O. H. G. *spannan*, to extend, connect; Du. *spannen*, to span, stretch, put horses to, Dan. *spænde*, Swed. *spänna*, to stretch, span, buckle; Icel. *spenna*, to clasp. Allied to **Space** and **Spin**. (√SPA.) **Der.** *span*, sb., stretch of the hand, 9 inches in space.

Spancel. (North E.) ' A rope to tye a cows hinder legs ;' Ray. From *span*, to tie, and Icel. *seil* (A. S. *sāl*), a rope. +Du. *spanzeel* ; G. *spannseil*.

Spandrel. (F.—L.) The space be-

tween the outer mouldings of an arch and a horizontal line above it. As if from O. F. **espanderel*, from O. F. *espandeur*, that which spreads.—O. F. *espandre*, to spread, expand. See **Expand, Spawn**.

Spangle. (E.) M. E. *spangel*, dimin. of *spang*, a metal fastening (hence, small shining ornament). A. S. *spange*, a metal clasp.+E. Fries. and M. Du. *spange*, a thin plate of metal; Icel. *spöng* ; G. *spange*, brooch, clasp, buckle.

Spaniel. (F. — Span. — L.) M. E. *spaniel, spaneȝeole*. — O. F. *espagneul*, a spaniel, Spanish dog. — Span. *Español*, Spanish.—Span. *España*, Spain.—L. *His-pania*, Spain.

Spank, to slap, move quickly. (E.) We also have *spanker*, a large active man or animal ; *spanking*, large, lusty. An E. word.+Low G. *spakkern, spenkern*, to run and spring about quickly ; E. Fries. *spenkelen, spenkern*, to burst, fly about; Dan. *spanke*, to strut about. From a base **spak*, significant of quick action ; cf. E. Fries. *spaken*, to split, burst with heat. **Der.** *spank-er*, an after-sail in a barque.

Span-new, quite new. (Scand.) The *a* has been shortened by the stress upon it. M. E. *span-newe*. — Icel. *spánnȳr, spānȳr*, span-new, lit. ' new as a chip.' — Icel. *spánn*, a chip, shaving, spoon ; *nȳr*, new. See **Spoon**.

Spar (1), a beam, bar. (E.) M. E. *sparre*. The A. S. sb. is vouched for by the derived verb *sparrian*, to fasten a door with a bar.+Du. *spar*, Icel. *sparri*, Dan. Swed. *sparre* ; O. H. G. *sparro*, G. *sparren*, spar, bar. [Irish and Gael. *sparr*, beam, are from E.] **Der.** *spar*, vb., to fasten a door.

Spar (2), a mineral. (E.) A. S. *spær-stān*, a spar-stone. Cf. G. *sparkalk*, plaster. ¶ Distinct from G. *spat, spath*, spar.

Spar (3), to box, wrangle. (F. — Teut.) Used of fighting-cocks.— M. F. *esparer*, ' to fling or yerk out with the heels ;' Cot.— Low G. *sparre*, sb., a struggling, striving ; G. *sich sperren*, to struggle against, resist, oppose. Allied to Skt. *sphur*, to throb, struggle ; Gk. σπαίρειν, άσπαίρειν, to strug-gle convulsively ; Russ. *sporite*, to quarrel, wrangle. (√SPER.) And see **Spur, Spurn.** Brugm. i. § 509 (3).

Sparable, a small nail used for boots. (E.) Formerly *sparrow-bill* ; from the shape.

Spare, frugal, lean. (E.) A. S. *spær,* spare; whence *sparian,* vb., to spare.+ Icel. *sparr,* Dan. *spar-som,* Swed. *spar-sam,* G. *spar-sam, spär-lich,* thrifty. Der. *sparing, spare-rib*; *spare,* vb., from A. S. *sparian* (above); so also Du. and G. *sparen,* Icel. and Swed. *spara,* Dan. *spare.*

Spark (1), a small particle of fire. (E.) O. Merc. *spærca* (Sweet); A.S. *spearca.*+ M. Du. *sparcke*; Low G. *sparke.* Perhaps so called from the crackling of a fire-brand, which throws out sparks; cf. Icel. *spraka,* to crackle, Lith. *spragéti,* to crackle like burning fire-wood, Gk. σφάραγος, a crackling. Brug. i. § 531.

Spark (2), a gay young fellow. (Scand.) The same as Wiltsh. *sprack,* lively. — Icel. *sparkr,* sprightly, also *sprækr*; Swed. dial. *spräker, spräk, spräg,* talkative. Cf. **Spark** (1). Der. *sprag,* i. e. *sprack,* used by Sir Hugh, Merry Wives, iv. 1. 84.

Sparkle, vb., to throw out sparks, to glitter. (E.) Cf. Du. *sparkelen,* to sparkle. The form *spark-le* is frequentative. See **Spark** (1).

Sparrow. (E.) A. S. *spearwa.*+Icel. *spörr,* Dan. *spurv,* Swed. *sparf,* Goth. *sparwa*; O. H. G. *sparo,* G. *sper-ling.* Lit. 'flutterer;' from √SPER, to quiver. See **Spar** (3). Der. *sparrow-hawk*; and see *sparable, spavin.*

Sparse, thinly scattered. (L.) L. *sparsus,* pp. of *spargere,* to scatter, sprinkle. Allied to Gk. σπείρειν; see **Sperm.**

Spasm. (F. — L. — Gk.) F. *spasme,* the cramp. — L. *spasmum,* acc. of *spasmus.* — Gk. σπασμός, a spasm. — Gk. σπᾶν, σπάειν, to draw, pluck. (√SPA.) Der. *spasm-od-ic,* from Gk. σπασμώδης, convulsive.

Spat (1), a blow, a slap. (E.) Of imitative origin; cf. *slap, slam, pat.*

Spat (2), young of shell-fish. (E.) From *spat-,* to eject, the base of *spatter.* Cf. Du. *spat,* a speckle, spot; and see **Spatter.**

Spate, a river-flood. (F. — Teut.) Cf. Irish *speid,* a great river-flood; borrowed from E. *spate.* The same as North E. *spait,* a torrent of rain; also spelt *speat.* G. Douglas has *spait,* a torrent; cf. Verg. Aen. ii. 496. — A. F. **espeit* = O. F. *espoit,* a spouting out (Godefroy). — E. Fries. *speiten, speuten, spoiten,* W. Flem. *speeten,* Du. *spuiten,* to spout; see **Spout.**

Spats, gaiters. (E.) Short for *spatterdashes.*

Spatter, to besprinkle. (E.) A fre-

quentative of *spat-,* with the sense to throw, to splash. E. Fries. *spatten,* to burst, fly out, spirt.+Du. *spatten,* to throw, spatter, splash. Der. *spatterdashes,* gaiters, to protect against *spatterings* and *dashes.* See **Spats.**

Spatula, a broad-bladed knife for spreading plaisters. (L. — Gk.) L. *spatula,* dimin. of *spatha.* — Gk. σπάθη, a broad blade. See **Spade** (1).

Spavin, a swelling near the joints of horses, producing lameness. (F. — Teut.) M. E. *spaveyne.* — O. F. *esparvin* (13th c., in Hatzfeld); M. F. *esparvain,* 'a spavin in the leg of a horse;' Cot. The same as Span. *esparavan,* (1) a sparrow-hawk, (2) spavin; answering to a Low L. adj. **sparvānus,* belonging to a sparrow, parallel to Late L. *sparvārius,* a sparrow-hawk, lit. belonging to sparrows; cf. G. *sperber,* a sparrow-hawk. Perhaps the lit. sense is 'sparrow-like,' from the hopping or sparrow-like motion of a horse afflicted with spavin. Derived from O. H. G. *sparwe,* a sparrow, cognate with E. **Sparrow,** q. v. ¶ Generally explained as 'sparrow-hawk-like,' contrary to grammar and sense. However, the result is, in any case, doubtful.

Spaw, the same as **Spa,** q. v.

Spawn, the eggs of fish or frogs. (F. — L.) From M. E. *spawnen, spanen,* to spawn, as fishes; Prompt. Parv. For *spaund,* with loss of *d.* See Wright's Voc. i. 164; N. & Q. 6 S. v. 465. — M. F. *espandre,* 'to shed, spill, pour out, scatter abroad in great abundance;' Cot. — L. *expandere,* to spread out, shed abroad; see **Expand.**

Speak. (E.) M. E. *speken,* also (before A. D. 1200) *spreken*; the word has lost an *r.* Late A. S. *specan,* A. S. *sprecan,* pt. t. *spræc,* pp. *sprecen.* + Du. *spreken*; G. *sprechen,* pt. t. *sprach.* All perhaps from Teut. base SPREK, to make a noise; cf. Icel. *spraka,* to crackle; see **Spark** (1), and Prellwitz, s. v. σφάραγος.

Spear. (E.) M. E. and A. S. *spere.*+ Du. *speer,* Icel. *spjör,* Dan. *spær,* G. *speer*; cf. L. *sparus,* a small missile-weapon, dart. Perhaps allied to *spar,* a beam, bar (hence, a pole).

Special. (F. — L.) Short for *especial*; see **Especial.**

Specie, money in gold or silver. (L.) Evolved as a sb. from the old word *species,* 'money paid by tale,' Phillips; prob. by confusion with L. abl. *speciē,* as if *paid in specie* = paid in visible coin.

species, a kind. (L.) L. *speciēs*, look, appearance, kind, sort. ‒ L. *specere*, to look, see. +O. H. G. *spehōn*, G. *spähen*, to spy; Skt. *paç*, *spaç*, to spy. (√SPEK, to see.) Brugm. i. § 551.

specify. (F. ‒ L.) O. F. *specifier*, to particularise. ‒ L. *specificāre*. ‒ L. *specificus*, specific, particular. ‒ L. *speci-ēs*, kind; *-fic-*, for *facere*, to make.

specimen. (L.) L. *specimen*, an example, something shown. ‒ L. *speci-*, for *specere*, to see; with suffix *-men*.

specious, showy. (F. ‒ L.) M. F. *specieux*, fair. ‒ L. *speciōsus*, fair to see. ‒ L. *speci-ēs*, appearance; with suffix *-ōsus*.

Speck, a small spot. (E.) A. S. *specca*, a spot, mark. Allied to Low G. *spakig*, spotted with wet, *spaken*, to spot with wet; M. Du. *spickelen*, to speckle, frequentative of M. Du. *spicken*, to spit; Du. *spikkel*, a speckle, spot. Der. *speck-le*, a little speck; *speck-le*, vb.

Spectacle. (F. ‒ L.) F. *spectacle*, a sight. ‒ L. *spectāculum*, a show. ‒ L. *spectāre*, to behold, frequentative of *specere*, to see.

spectator. (L.) L. *spectātor*, a beholder. ‒ L. *spectā-re*, to see; with suffix *-tor*. ‒ L. *spect-um*, supine of *specere*, to see.

spectre. (F. ‒ L.) F. *spectre*, 'an image, ghost;' Cot. ‒ L. *spectrum*, a vision. ‒ L. *spec-ere*, to see.

specular. (L.) L. *speculāris*, belonging to a mirror. ‒ L. *speculum*, a mirror. ‒ L. *spec-ere*, to see. ¶ But Milton uses it with reference to L. *specula*, a watch-tower; also from *spec-ere*; see below.

speculate. (L.) From pp. of L. *speculārī*, to behold. ‒ L. *specula*, a watch-tower. ‒ L. *spec-ere*, to see. Der. *speculation*, *-ive*.

Speech. (E.) M. E. *speche*. Late A. S. *spǣce*, dat. of *spǣc*, earlier form *sprǣc*, speech. ‒ A. S. *sprǣc*, 3rd grade of *sprecan*, to speak. +Du. *spraak*, G. *sprache*, speech. See Speak.

Speed, success, velocity. (E.) A. S. *spēd*, haste, success. For *spōdiz*, with the usual change from *ō* to *ē*. ‒ A. S. *spōw-an*, to succeed; with suffix *-diz* (Idg. *-tis*). + Du. *spoed*, speed; O. H. G. *spuot*, *spōt*, success, from *spuon*, to succeed. Allied to Skt. *sphīti-*, increase, prosperity, from *sphāy*, to enlarge. Brugm. i. § 156. Der. *speed*, vb., A. S. *spēdan*; from *spēd*, sb.

Speir, to ask. (E.) Northern E. A. S. *spyrian*, to ask, track out. ‒ A. S. *spor*, a foot-track; allied to *spora*, a spur; see **Spur.** + Du. *speuren*,. Icel. *spyrja*, G. *spüren*; Low G. *späören*, to track, from *spaor*, a spoor, trail (Danneil).

Spelicans, thin slips of wood. (Du.) M. Du. *spelleken*, a small pin; dimin. of M. Du. *spelle* (Du. *speld*), a splinter. See **Spell** (4). ¶ Distinct from Du. *spalk*, A. S. *spele*, a splint.

Spell (1), an incantation. (E.) M. E. *spel*. A. S. *spel*, *spell*, a saying, story, narrative; hence a form of words, spell. +Icel. *spjall*, a saying; O. H. G. *spel*, narrative; Goth. *spill*, fable. Der. *go-spel*.

spell (2), to tell the names of letters in a word. (F. ‒ Teut.) M. E. *spellen*, of spell; also, to tell. ‒ O. F. *espeler*, 'to spell;' Cot. ‒ Du. *spellen*, to spell; or from O. H. G. *spellōn*, to tell, relate. + A. S. *spellian*, to tell, recount, from A. S. *spell*, a story (above); Goth. *spillon*, to narrate. ¶ M. E. *spellen*, in the sense 'to relate,' is from A. S. *spellian*. We also find *speldren*, to spell, in the Ormulum, from *spelder*, a splinter; see **Spell** (4); but this is a different word.

Spell (3), a turn of work. (E.) Cf. A. S. *spelian*, to supply another's room, to act or be proxy for; allied to Du. *spelen*, Icel. *spila*, G. *spielen*, to act a part, play a game; from the sb. appearing as Du. Swed. *spel*, Icel. Dan. *spil*, G. *spiel*, a game.

Spell (4), **Spill,** a thin slip of wood, slip of paper. (E.) Formerly *speld*. M. E. *speld*, a splinter. A. S. *speld*, a torch, spill to light a candle. Orig. a splinter; from Teut. **spaldan-* (G. *spalten*), to cleave; a reduplicating verb, like O. H. G. *spaltan*. +Du. *speld*, a pin, splinter; Icel. *speld*, a square tablet, orig. thin piece of board, *spilda*, a slice; Goth. *spilda*, a tablet; M. H. G. *spelte*, a splinter. Cf. Shetland *speld*, to split.

Spelt, a kind of corn. (L.) A. S. *spelt*, corn. Cf. Du. *spelt*, G. *spelz*. Apparently borrowed from Late L. *spelta*, spelt; whence also Ital. *spelta*, *spelda*, F. *épeautre*, spelt.

Spelter, pewter, zinc. (Low G.) In Blount (1674). Perhaps from Low G. *spialter*, pewter; cf. Du. *spiauter*, M. Du. *speauter*, O. F. *espeautre*. ¶ This seems to be the original of **Pewter,** q. v. The history of these words is very obscure.

Spencer, a short over-jacket. (F. ‒ L.) Named after Earl *Spencer*, died 1845. The

name is from M.E. *spenser*, also *despenser*.
— O.F. *despencier*, a spender, a caterer,
clerk of a kitchen; Cot. — O.F. *despenser*,
to spend; frequent. of *despendre*. — L. *dis-pendere*, to weigh out, pay. — L. *dis-*, apart;
pendere, to weigh. See **Pendant**.

spend. (L.) A.S. *spendan*, to spend.
Shortened from L. *dispendere*, to spend,
waste, consume. We find Late L. *spendium*
for *dispendium*, *spensa* for *dispensa*; also
spendibilis moneta, money for expenses
(A.D. 922). So also Ital. *spendere*, to
spend, *spendio* (< L. *dispendium*), expense. — L. *dis-*, away, part; *pendere*, to
weigh out, pay. ¶ Or (as usually said)
from L. *expendere*, which does not suit
the F. forms; see above. It makes no
great difference.

Sperm, spawn, spermaceti. (F. — L. —
Gk.) M. E. *sperme*. — F. *sperme*, ' sperm,
seed;' Cot. — L. *sperma*. — Gk. σπέρμα. —
Gk. σπείρειν (for *σπερ-γειν), to sow;
orig. to scatter with a jerk of the hand.
(√SPER.) Der. *sperm-at-ic* (Gk. σπερματι-κός); *spermaceti*, L. *sperma-cēti*, i. e. sperm
of the whale; see **Cetaceous**.

Spew, Spue. (E.) A.S. *spīwan*,
pt. t. *spāw*, pp. *spiwen*, to vomit.+Du.
spuuwen, Icel. *spȳja*, Dan. *spye*, Swed. *spy*,
G. *speien*, Goth. *speiwan*; L. *spuere*, Lith.
spjauti; Gk. πτύειν (for *σπιύειν), to spit.
(√SPIW.) Allied to *puke* (1), *spit* (2).
Brugm. i. § 567.

Sphere, a globe, ball. (F. — L. — Gk.)
M. E. *spere*. — O. F. *espere*, M. F. *sphere*. —
L. *sphæra*. ⁓ Gk. σφαῖρα, a ball.

Sphinx. (L. — Gk.) L. *sphinx*. — Gk.
σφίγξ (gen. σφιγγός), lit. ' the strangler,'
because the Sphinx strangled travellers
who could not solve her riddles. — Gk.
σφίγγειν, to throttle. ¶ The story suggests
that this is a ' popular' etymology; and
that the word is foreign to Greek.

Spice. (F. — L.) M. E. *spice*, formerly
used also in the sense of *species* or kind. —
O. F. *espice*, spice. — L. *speciem*, acc. of
speciēs, a kind, which in Late L. meant
also a spice, drug. See **Species**.

Spick and Span-new, wholly new.
(Scand.) Lit. ' spike and spoon-new,'
where *spike* is a nail, and *spoon* is a
splinter. See **Spike** and **Spoon**. Cf.
Swed. dial. *spik spangande ny* in Rietz
(with many variants), and Icel. *spān-nȳr*,
lit. spoon-new, splinter-new.

Spider. (E.) M. E. *spither*, *spiðre*.
A. S. *spīder* or **spīðer* (for **spinðer*),

Leechdoms, iii. 42. Formed from the verb
to spin; cf. prov. E. *spinner*, a spider. +
Du. *spin*, Dan. *spinder*, Swed. *spindel*, G.
spinne, spider or spinner. And cf. **Spindle**.

Spigot. (F. — L.) M.E. *spigot*, *spikket*,
a peg for a cask. Cf. Irish and Gael.
spiocaid, a spigot (from E.). — O. F. **espigot*,
(not found); but cf. O. F. *espigeot*, a
bad ear of corn, a dimin. from L. *spīca*, an
ear of corn (Godefroy); Walloon *spigot*,
the peak of a shoe. Also Port. *espicho*,
a spigot, from L. *spīculum*. — L. *spīca*, a
point; see below.

Spike (1), a sharp point, a nail.
(Scand.) From Icel. *spīk*, Swed. *spik*;
cf. Dan. *spiger*, Du. *spijker*, a nail. Apparently distinct from L. *spīca*; and allied
by gradation to **Spoke**.

Spike (2), an ear of corn. (L.) L.
spīca, an ear of corn, a point.

spikenard. (F. — L. *and* Gk. — Pers.
— Skt.) O. F. *spiquenard*. — L. *spīca
nardī*, spike of nard; also *nardus spīcātus*,
i. e. nard furnished with spikes, in allusion
to the mode of growth. And see **Nard**.

Spill (1), a slip of paper for lighting
candles; see **Spell** (4).

Spill (2), to destroy, shed. (Scand.)
(Not allied to *spoil*.) M. E. *spillen*, to
destroy, mar; also, to perish. — Icel. *spilla*,
to destroy; Swed. *spilla*, Dan. *spilde*, to
spill. + A. S. *spildan*, to destroy; O. Sax.
spildian. Teut. type **spelth-jan-*; allied
to G. *spalten*, to split.

Spin, to draw out threads. (E.) A. S.
spinnan, pt. t. *spann*, pp. *spunnen*.+Du.
spinnen, Icel. Swed. *spinna*, Dan. *spinde*,
G. *spinnen*, Goth. *spinnan*. Allied to
Lith. *pin-ti*, to weave. See **Span**.

Spinach, Spinage, a vegetable.
(F. — Span. — Arab. — Pers.) *Spinage* is a
' voiced' form of *spinach*. O. F. *espinache*,
espinage, *espinace*. — Span. *espinaca*. —
Arab. *aspanākh*, *isfānāj*; of Pers. origin
(Devic.). ¶ The Ital. *spinace* and Span.
espinaca are referred, by popular etymology, to L. *spīna*, a thorn; some say the
fruit is prickly, some say the leaves are so.
See **Spine**.

Spindle. (E.) The *d* is excrescent
after *n*. M. E. *spinel*, also *spindele*. A.S.
spinl, i.e. ' spinner,' from *spinnan*, to spin.
+ M. Du. *spille* (for **spinle*); G. *spindel*,
O. H. G. *spinnila*. Der. *spindl-y*, thin
like a spindle; *spindle-tree* (Euonymus)
formerly used for spindles and skewers.

Spine, a prickle. (F. — L.) O. F. *espine*,

a thorn.— L. *spīna*, a thorn, prickle; also the back-bone. ¶ Observe that in the sense of 'back-bone' the word is Latin only, not F.

spinet, a kind of musical instrument. (F. — Ital.— L.) So called because struck by a *spine* or pointed quill. O.F. *espinette*. — Ital. *spinetta*, a spinet, also a prickle; dimin. of *spina*, a thorn.— L. *spīna*.

Spink, a finch. (Scand.) M. E. *spink*. — Swed. dial. *spink*, a sparrow; *gull-spink*, a gold-finch; Norw. *spikke* (for **spinke*), Dan. dial. *spinke*, small bird. **+** Gk. σπίγγος, a finch, i. e. 'chirper;' from σπί-ζειν, to chirp. Cf. σπίζα, a finch, σπίνος, a small bird. **Doublet,** *finch*.

Spinny, a thicket. (F. — L.) O. F. *espinei*; M. F. *espinoye*, 'a thicket, grove, a thorny plot,' Cot.; F. *épinaie*. — L. *spīnētum*, a thicket of thorns.— L. *spīna*, a thorn. See **Spine.**

Spinster, orig. a woman who spins. (E.) M. E. *spinnestere*. From A. S. *spinnan*, to spin; with A. S. suffix *-estre* (E. *-ster*). **β.** This suffix is a compound one (*-es-tre*). It was used in A. S. (as in Du.) solely with reference to the feminine gender, but this restricted usage was soon set aside in a great many M. E. words. Cf. Du. *spinster*, a spinster, *zangster*, a female singer; also E. *seamstress* (i. e. *seam-ster-ess*), *songstress* (i. e. *song-ster-ess*), where the F. fem. suffix *-ess* is superadded.

Spiracle. (F.—L.) F. *spiracle*, 'a breathing-hole;' Cot. — L. *spīrāculum*, air-hole. — L. *spīrāre*, to breathe.

Spire (1), a tapering stem, sprout, steeple. (E.) A. S. *spīr*, spike, stalk.**+** Icel. *spīra*, spar, stilt, Dan. *spire*, germ, sprout, Swed. *spira*, a pistil, G. *spiere*, a spar. ¶ Distinct from **Spire** (2).

Spire (2), a coil, wreath. (F.—L.—Gk.) F. *spire*. — L. *spīra*, a coil, twist, wreath. —Gk. σπεῖρα (for **σπερ-ya*), a coil; allied to σπάρτον, a rope, σπυρίς, a basket. (√SPER.) **Der.** *spir-al*, F. *spiral*, L. *spīrālis*.

Spirit. (F.—L.) M. E. *spirit*.— A. F. *espirit*; F. *esprit*.— L. acc. *spīritum*, from *spīritus*, breath.— L. *spīrāre*, to breathe. **Doublet,** *sprite*.

Spirt; see **Spurt.**

Spit (1), a skewer, iron prong for roasting meat. (E.) M. E. *spite*. A. S. *spitu*, a spit.**+**Du. *spit*, Dan. *spid*, Swed. *spett*; M. H. G. *spiz*, G. *spiess*, a spit; cf. *spitze*, a point, top.

Spit (2), to eject from the mouth. (E.) M. E. *spitten*, A. S. *spittan*; cf. *spǣtan*, pt. t. *spǣtte*, to spit. But we also find Dan. *spytte*, Swed. *spotta*, prov. G. *spützen* (cf. G. *spucken*); from Teut. **sput-*; see **Spout.** Perhaps **spit-*, **sput-* are both from **spēw-*, the root of **Spew.** Cf. Brugm. i. §§ 279 (1), 567. **Der.** *spittle*, formerly also *spettle*, *spatil*, *spotil*, A. S. *spǣtl*, *spātl*.

Spite. (F. — L.) M. E. *spyt*, *spite*. Merely short for *despite*, by loss of the first syllable (as in *fence* for *de-fence*). See **Despite.** **Der.** *spite-ful*.

Spittle (1), saliva; see **Spit** (2).

Spittle (2), a hospital. (F.—L.) M. E. *spitel*.— O. F. *ospital*, *hospital*; see **Hospital.**

Splash, to dash water about. (E.) Coined, by prefixing *s-* (= O. F. *es-*, L. *ex*) used for emphasis, *to plash*, used in the same sense (White Kennett). See **Plash** (1); and cf. Du. *plassen*, to plash; E. Fries. *plassen*, *plasken*, *platsken*, Dan. *pladske*, to splash, dabble.

Splay, to slope, in architecture; to dislocate a bone. (F.—L.) In both senses it can be proved to be a contraction for **Display.** **Der.** *splay-footed*.

Spleen. (L. — Gk.) M. E. *splen.* — L. *splēn.*—Gk. σπλήν, the spleen. Cf. Skt. *plihan-*; L. *liēn*. Brugm. i. § 549 (c). **Der.** *splen-etic*.

Splendour. (F.—L.) F. *splendeur.* — L. *splendōrem*, acc. of *splendor*, brightness. — L. *splendēre*, to shine. **Der.** *re-splendent*.

Spleuchan, a tobacco-pouch. (Gael.) Gael. *spliuchan*, Irish *spliuchan*, a pouch.

Splice. (Du.) M. Du. *splissen*, to interweave rope-ends; so named from *splitting* the rope-ends beforehand; ·from Du. *splitsen*, to splice (really an older form). Formed from *split-*, weak grade of Du. *splijten*, to split. **+** Dan. *splidse*, to splice (for **splitse*), allied to *splitte*, to split; Swed. *splissa*; G. *splissen*, to splice. See **Split.** **Der.** *splice*, sb.

splint, splent, a thin piece of split wood. (Scand.) Formerly *splent*; from O. F. *esplente*, a thin steel plate. — Swed. *splint*, a kind of spike, a forelock (flat iron peg); Dan. *splint*, a splinter; cf. Low G. *splinte*, an iron pin; E. Fries. *splinte*, *splint*, the same. Cf. Swed. *splinta*, to splinter, ultimately allied to Dan. *splitte*, Swed. dial. *splitta*, to split; see **Split.** **Der.** *splinter*; cf. Du. and E. Fries. *splinter*.

Split. (Du.?) Apparently borrowed from M. Du. *splitten*, to split; cf. Dan. *splitte*, to split, Swed. dial. *splitta*, to disentangle or separate yarn. From the weak grade *split-* of the Teut. strong verb **spleitan-*, as seen in O. Fries. *splīta*, Du. *splijten*, E. Fries. *spliten*, Low G. *spliten*, G. *spleissen*, to split, cleave. Hence also Dan. *split*, Du. *spleet*, a split, rent, G. *spleisse*, a splinter.

Splutter, to speak hastily and confusedly. (E.) Of imitative origin; a variant of *sputter*, which is a frequentative of *spout*; see Spout, Spurt. It means 'to keep on *spouting* out'; *spout* being formerly used (as now) in the sense 'to talk.' 'Pray, *spout* some French;' Beaum. and Fletcher, Coxcomb, iv. 4. Cf. Low G. *sprutten*, to spout, spurt.

Spoil, to plunder. (F.–L.) M. E. *spoilen*. – O. F. *espoillier*; F. *spolier*, 'to spoile;' Cot. – L. *spoliāre*, to strip off spoil. – L. *spolium*, spoil, booty; orig. skin stripped off, dress of a slain warrior. Der. *spoil*, sb.; *spoliation*, from L. pp. *spoliātus*.

Spoke, a bar of a wheel. (E.) A.S. *spāca*, a spoke.+Du. *speek*, a spoke, G. *speiche*, prov. G. *spache*, a spoke. Teut. types **spaikon-*, **spaikōn-*. Allied by gradation to Spike (1).

Spokesman. (E.) In Shak. Two Gent. ii. 1. 151. Formed from *spoke*, pt. t. of *speak*, instead of from the infin. *speak*; for the *s*, cf. *hunt-s-man*, *sport-s-man*.

Spoliation; see Spoil.

Spondee. (L.–Gk.) The metrical foot marked (– –). – L. *spondēus*. – Gk. σπονδεῖος, a spondee, used for solemn melodies at treaties or truces. – Gk. σπονδαί, a solemn treaty, truce; pl. of σπονδή, a drink-offering, libation to the gods. – Gk. σπένδειν, to pour out. Prob. allied to Sponsor. Brugm. i. § 143, ii. § 802. Der. *sponda-ic*.

Sponge. (F.–L.–Gk.) O. F. *esponge* (F. *éponge*). – L. *spongia*. – Gk. σπογγιά, a sponge; also σπόγγος (Attic σφόγγος . +L. *fungus*, a fungus (from its spongy nature).

Sponsor. (L.) L. *sponsor*, a surety. – L. *sponsus*, pp. of *spondēre*, to promise. Prob. allied to Gk. σπονδαί, a truce, and to Spondee. Brugm. i. § 143.

Spontaneous. (L.) L. *spontāne-us*, willing; with suffix *-ous*. – L. *spont-*, as seen in abl. *sponte*, of one's own accord, from a lost nom. **spons*.

Spook, a ghost. (Du.) Du. *spook*; Low G. *spook*, Swed. *spöke*, a ghost; cf. Du. *spoken*, Low G. *spöken*, Swed. *spöka*, to haunt.

Spool, a reel for winding yarn on. (M. Du.) M. E. *spole*. – M. Du. *spoele*, Du. *spoel*, a spool, quill; Low G. *spöle*.+Swed. *spole*, Dan. *spole*, G. *spule*, spool, bobbin. Cf. Icel. *spölr* (base *spal-*), a bar.

Spoom, to run before the wind. (L.) Lit. 'to throw up *spume* or foam.'–L. *spūma*, foam.

Spoon, an instrument for supping liquids. (E.) M. E. *spon*. A.S. *spōn*, a chip, splinter of wood (which was the orig. spoon).+Du. *spaan*, Icel. *spānn*, *spōnn*, Dan. *spaan*, Swed. *spån*, G. *spahn*, a chip.

Spoor, a trail. (Du.) Du. *spoor*; see Spur. Cf. A.S. *spor*, a foot-track; see Speir.

Sporadic, scattered here and there. (Gk.) Gk. σποραδικός, scattered. – Gk. σποραδ-, stem of σποράς, scattered. – Gk. σπείρειν (for **σπερ-γειν*), to scatter.

spore. (Gk.) Gk. σπόρος, seed-time; also a seed. – Gk. σπείρειν, to sow.

Sporran. (Gael.–L.–Gk.) Gael. *sporan*, a purse, pouch worn with the kilt; Irish *sparan*, *sburan*, the same. For **s-burran*<**s-burs-an*. – L. *bursa*, a purse. – Gk. βύρσα, a hide. See Purse.

Sport, mirth. (F.–L.) Short for *dis-port*, *desport*; (so also *splay* for *display*). The verb is M. E. *disporten*, to amuse; see Disport.

Spot, a blot, mark made by wet, piece of ground. (E.) M. E. *spot*. Cf. Norw. *spott*, m., a spot, a small piece of ground (distinct from *spott*, f., mockery); Icel. *spotti*, *spottr*, a small piece; E. Fries. *spot*, a spot; cf. M. Du. *spotten*, to spot, stain. From Teut. **sput-*, weaker grade of **spūtan-*; see Spout.

Spouse. (F.–L.) From O. F. *espouse*, a spouse. – L. *sponsa*, a betrothed woman; fem. pp. of *spondēre*, to promise; see Sponsor.

Spout, to squirt out, rush out as a liquid out of a pipe. (E.) M. E. *spouten*. Cf. Swed. *sputa*, occasionally used for *spruta*, to squirt, spout, spurt, spatter; Du. *spuiten*, to spout, *spuit*, a squirt; Dan. *spyte*, to spit, sputter. From Teut. **spūtan-*, to spit out, with weaker grade **sput-* (Franck).

Sprack, Sprag; see Spark (2).

Sprain, vb. (F.–L.) Formed from O. F. *espreign-*, a stem of O. F. *espreindre*, 'to press, wring,' Cot.; (cf. *strain* from O. F. *estreindre*). Mod. F. *épreindre*. — L. *exprimere*, to press out (whence *esprein-dre*, by analogy with F. forms from verbs in *-ingere*). — L. *ex*, out; *premere*, to press. See **Press**. Der. *sprain*, sb.

Sprat, a small fish. (E.) M. E. *sprot*. A. S. *sprott*. Cf. A. S. *sprot*, a sprout.+ Du. *sprot*, a sprat; also (in M. Du.) a sprout of a tree. '*Sprat*, a small fish, considered as the fry of the herring;' Wedgwood. From A. S. *sprot*- (Teut. **sprut-*), weaker grade of *sprūtan-*, to sprout; with the sense of 'fry,' or young one. See **Sprout**.

Sprawl, to toss about the limbs. (E.) M. E. *spraulen*. A. S. *spreawlian*, to move convulsively, to sprawl. + Norw. *sprala*, Dan. *sprælla*, *sprælde*, Swed. dial. *sprala*, *spralla*, N. Fries. *sprawle*.

Spray (1), foam tossed with the wind. (Low G.) A late word, given in Bailey's Dict. (1735). From Low G. *sprei*, a slight drizzle (Schambach); in Coburg, *sprœ*; cf. Bavar. *sprœen*, to drizzle (Schmeller); G. *sprühen*; M. H. G. *sprœjen*, *sprœwen*; Du. *sproeien* (see Franck).

Spray (2), sprig of a tree. (E.) M. E. *spray*; answering to A. S. **sprœg*, allied to A. S. *sprœc*, a shoot, spray; cf. Dan. *sprag*, a spray (Molbech), Swed. dial. *spragge*, a green branch, Icel. *sprek*, a stick. Cf. also Lith. *sproga*, a spray of a tree; also a rift, from *sprog-ti*, to crackle, split, sprout, bud. (Difficult and doubtful.)

Spread. (E.) A. S. *sprǣdan*, to extend. +Du. *spreiden*, Low G. *spreden*, G. *sprei-ten*; cf. Swed. *sprida*, Dan. *sprede*, to spread. Teut. type **spraidjan-*; from a Teut. root **spreid*.

Spree, a frolic. (Scand.?) Cf. Irish *spre*, a spark, flash, animation, spirit; Lowl. Sc. *spree*, a frolic, also spelt *spray* (Scott); cf. Swed. dial. *sprag*, lively conversation. Perhaps allied to **Spry**.

Sprig. (E.) M. E. *sprigge*. Allied to A. S. *sprǣc*, a twig.+Icel. *sprek*, a stick; Low G. *sprikk*, E. Fries. *sprikke*, *sprik*, stick, twig. Allied to **Spray** (2).

Sprightly, Spritely. (F. — L; *with* E. *suffix*.) *Sprightly* is a false spelling; *spritely* is from **Sprite**, q. v.

Spring, vb. (E.) A. S. *springan*, pt. t. *sprang*, pp. *sprungen*. + Du. G. *springen*, Swed. *springa*, Dan. *springe*; Icel. *springa*, to burst, split. β. Orig. sense to 'split or crack,' as when we say

that a cricket-bat is *sprung*; or to *spring* (i. e. burst) a mine. Teut. type **sprengan-*. Perhaps allied to Gk. σπέρχειν, to drive on (Prellwitz); but this is doubtful. Der. *spring*, sb., a leap, also a bursting out of water, also the budding time of year, also a crack in a mast; *springe*, a snare made with a flexible (springing) rod, like O.H.G. *springa*.

Sprinkle. (Du.?) Formerly *sprenkle*; perhaps borrowed from Du. *sprenkelen*, to sprinkle. Cf. G. *sprenkeln*, to sprinkle, from M. H. G. *sprenkel*, a spot, allied to Icel. *sprekla*, Swed. *spräkla*, a little spot. See Kluge (s. v. *sprenkel*).

Sprint; see **Spurt** (2).

Sprit, a spar extending a fore-and-aft sail. (E.) M. E. *spret*, a pole. A. S. *sprēot*, a pole; orig. a sprout, shoot, branch of a tree. Allied to A. S. *sprūtan*, to sprout; see **Sprout**.+E. Fries. *sprēt*; Du. *spriet*; M. Swed. *spröte*.

Sprite, a spirit. (F. — L.) The false spelling *spright* is common, and is retained in the adj. *sprightly*. M. E. *sprit*, *sprite*. — F. *esprit*, the spirit; hence, a spirit. — L. *spīritum*, acc. of *spīritus*; see **Spirit**.

Sprout, to germinate. (E.) M. E. *spruten*. A. S. **sprūtan* (found in the pp. *ā-sproten*); O. Fries. *sprūta*, strong verb, pp. *spruten*, to sprout.+Low G. *spruten*, to sprout; Du. *spruiten*, G. *spriessen* (pt.t. *spross*); Swed. *spruta*, Dan. *sprude*, to squirt, spurt, spout. Teut. type **sprūtan-*, pt. t. **spraut*, pp. **sprutanoz*. Compare **Spout**.

Spruce, fine, smart. (F. — G.) Hall's Chronicle tells us that a particular kind of fashionable dress was that in which men 'were appareyled after the manner of *Prussia* or *Spruce*'; see Richardson's Dict. M. E. *spruce*, Prussia, P. Plowman, C. vii. 279, B. xiii. 393; also written (more usually) *pruce*. — O. F. *Pruce* (F. *Prusse*), Prussia. — G. *Preussen*, Prussia. See **Spruce-beer**.

Spruce-beer, a kind of beer. (G.; confused with F. *and* E.) The E. name for German *sprossen-bier*, i. e. 'sprouts-beer,' obtained from the young sprouts of the black spruce fir. — G. *sprossen*, pl. of *spross*, a sprout (from *spriessen*, to sprout); and *bier*, cognate with E. *beer*; see **Sprout** and **Beer**. β. Englished as *Spruce-beer*, i. e. Prussian beer, where *Spruce* meant *Prussia*; see **Spruce** above. So also *spruce fir* (substituted for *sprossen-fichte*) meant Prussian fir; and *spruce leather* meant Prussian leather.

Spry, active. (E.?) Cf. Swed. dial. *sprygg,* very active, skittish; allied to Swed. dial. *spräg, spräk,* spirited, mettlesome. See **Spark** (2).

Spue; see **Spew.**

Spume, foam. (L.) L. *spūma,* foam; for **spoima;* Brugm. i. § 791. Cf. Skt. *phena-,* A.S. *fām,* foam.

Spunk, tinder; a match, spark, spirit, mettle. (C. – L. – Gk.) Orig. 'tinder.'– Gael. *spong,* Irish *sponc,* sponge, spongy wood, tinder. – L. *spongia,* a sponge; see **Sponge.** Cf. W. *ysbwng,* a sponge, from Latin.

Spur. (E.) M. E. *spure.* A. S. *spura, spora,* a spur.+Du. *spoor,* a spur (allied to *spoor,* a track); Icel. *spori,* Dan. *spore,* Swed. *sporre,* O. H. G. *sporo,* spur. From the weak grade of Teut. **sper-an-,* to kick. Brugm. i. § 793 (2). (√SPER.) See **Spar** (3). The orig. sense is 'kicker'; from its use on the heel; cf. Lith. *spir-ti,* to kick. **Der.** *spur,* vb. See **Spoor, Spurn.**

Spurge, a plant. (F. – L.) Named from its corroding (and so cleansing away) warts. – O. F. *spurge, espurge.* – O. F. *espurger,* to purge away. – L. *expurgāre,* to cleanse away. – L. *ex,* away; *purgāre,* to cleanse. See **Purge.**

Spurious. (L.) L. *spuri-us,* false; with suffix *-ous.*

Spurn. (E.) M. E. *spurnen,* to kick against, hence to reject. A. S. *spurnan,* to kick against (pt. t. *spearn,* pp. *spornen*). Allied to **Spur.** + Icel. *sperna* (pt. t. *sparn*); Swed. *spjärna;* L. *spernere,* to despise, a cognate form. (Base **spern;* √SPER.) See **Spar** (3). Brugm. i. § 565.

Spurry, a plant. (F. – G. – Late L.) M. F. *spurrie,* 'spurry or frank, a Dutch [German] herb;' Cot. Of Teut. origin; cf. G. *spörgel, spergel, spark,* spurry.– Late L. *spergula,* A. D. 1482 (Weigand).

Spurt (1), **Spirt,** to spout out. (E.) The older sense is to germinate. *Spurt* stands for *sprut;* M. E. *sprutten,* to sprout or shoot. A. S. *spryttan,* to produce as a sprout or shoot; causal form from A. S. *sprūtan,* to sprout. See **Sprout.**

Spurt (2), a violent exertion. (Scand.) Formerly *spirt.* – Icel. *sprettr,* a spurt, spring, bound, run. – Icel. *spretta* (pt. t. *spratt*), to start, spring; also to sprout, to

spout. Icel. *spretta* is for **sprenta, *sprinta* (Noreen). See **Sprint.**

Sputter. (E.) The frequentative of *spout.* It means 'to keep on spouting out'; hence to speak rapidly and indistinctly. Cf. Du. dial. (Groningen) *spöttern,* to sputter; Low G. *sputtern,* Norw. *sputra,* to spout. ¶ Distinct from but allied to *spatter* and *spot.*

Spy, to see. (F. – O. H. G.) Short for *espy;* see **Espy. Der.** *spy, sb.*

Squab, (1) to fall plump; (2) a sofa, a young bird. (Scand.) See *squab, squob* in Halliwell. And see *squab,* to fall plump, *squab,* with a sudden fall, in Johnson. 1. From Swed. dial. *skvapp,* a word imitative of a splash; cf. G. *schwapp,* a slap, E. *swap,* to strike. 2. From Swed. dial. *skvabb,* loose or fat flesh, *skvabba,* a fat woman, *skvabbig,* flabby; allied to Norw. *skvapa,* to tremble, shake, and cf. M. E. *quappen,* to throb, and E. *quaver;* see **Quaver.** Cf. Icel. *kvap,* jelly, jelly-like things.

squabble, to wrangle. (Scand.) Swed. dial. *skvabbel,* a dispute. – Swed. dial. *skvappa,* to chide, lit. make a splashing, from the sb. *skvapp, sqvapp,* a splash. Cf. Prov. E. *swabble,* to squabble, allied to *swab,* to splash over, *swap,* to strike.

Squad, a small troop. (F. – Ital. – L.) M. F. *esquadre, escadre.* – Ital. *squadra,* a squadron; see **Square.**

squadron. (F. – Ital. – L.) M. F. *esquadron.* – Ital. *squadrone;* augmentative of *squadra* (above).

Squalid. (L.) L. *squālidus,* rough, dirty. – L. *squālēre,* to be rough, parched, dirty. **Der.** *squal-or, sb.*

Squall, to cry out. (Scand.) Swed. *sqvala,* to gush out violently, *sqval,* a rush of water, *sqval-regn,* a violent shower of rain (E. *squall,* sb., a burst of rain); Dan. *sqvaldre,* to clamour, *sqvalder,* clamour, noisy talk; Swed. dial. *skvala,* to gush out, cry out, chatter. + Gael. *sgal,* a loud cry, sound of high wind; allied to G. *schallen,* Icel. *skjalla* (pt. t. *skall*), to resound, and W. *chwalu,* to babble.

Squander, to dissipate. (E.) Orig. to disperse, scatter abroad; Dryden, Annus Mirabilis, st. 67. Nasalised form allied to Lowl. Sc. *squatter,* to splash about, scatter, squander, prov. E. *swatter,* to throw water about; Swed. dial. *skvättra,* to squander. These are frequentatives from Dan. *sqvatte,* to splash, spurt, also to squander; Swed.

sqvätta, to squirt, Icel. *skvetta* (for
*skwenta, perhaps allied to G. σπένδειν, to
pour out; see Noreen), to squirt out water.
The *d* appears in M. Du. *swadderen*, to
dabble in water; Swed. dial. *skvadra*, to
gush out of a hole (as water). Cf. *scatter*
and *squirt*.

Square. (F. − L.) M. E. *square*. −
O. F. *esquarré*, squared; *esquarre*, a square,
squareness. Cf. Ital. *squadrare*, to square;
squadra, a square, also a squadron of men
(orig. a square). All from Late L. **ex-
quadrāre*, intensive (with prefix *ex*) of L.
quadrāre, to square. − L. *quadrus*, four-
cornered; see **Quadrate**.

Squash, to crush. (F. − L.) **a.** The
mod. E. *squash* appears to be due to *quash*,
with the prefix *s*- = O. F. *es*- < L. *ex*-,
used as an intensive. − O. F. *esquasser*,
to break in pieces, from O. F. *es*-, and
quasser, casser, to break; see **Quash.**
β. But it commonly keeps the sense of
M. E. *squachen*, to crush. − O. F. *esqua-
chier*, to crush, also spelt *escacher*, 'to
squash;' Cot. (Mod. F. *écacher*). The
F. *cacher* answers to a Late L. type **coac-
ticāre*, due to L. *co-actāre*, to constrain,
force, press. The prefix *es*- = L. *ex*, extremely; L. *coactāre* is formed from *coact-us*,
pp. of *cōgere* (= *coigere*), to drive together.
See **Ex**- and **Cogent**; also **Con**- and
Agent. Der. *squash*, sb., an unripe
peascod (nearly flat).

squat, to cower. (F. − L.) Lit. to lie
flat, as if pressed down; the old sense is to
press down, squash. M. E. *squatten*, to
crush flat. − O. F. *esquatir*, to flatten,
crush. − O. F. *es*- (= L. *ex*), extremely;
quatir, to beat down. Diez shows that
O. F. *quatir* (Late L. type *coactīre) is
a derivative of L. *coactus*, pp. of *cōgere*,
to press, compel; see above. Cf. M. Ital.
quattare, 'to squat, lie close.'

Squaw, a female. (W. Indian.) Massachusetts *squa,eshqua*, Narragansett *squāws*,
a female (Webster); Cree *iskwew*.

Squeak, to cry out shrilly. (Scand.)
M. Swed. *skwæka*, to squeak; Swed.
sqväka, to croak; Norw. *skvaka*, to cackle;
Icel. *skvakka*, to sound like water shaken
in a bottle. Allied to **Quack.**

Squeal. (Scand.) M. Swed. *sqwæla*,
Swed. dial. *sqväla*, Norw. *skvella*,to squeal.
Used as a frequentative of *squeak*, and ap-
plied to a continuous cry. See **Squall.**

Squeamish, over-nice. (F. − Teut. ?)
Squamish, Baret (1580). M. E. *skeymous*,

sweymous, Prompt. Parv.; also *squaimous,
skoymus*, disdainful. − A. F. *escoymous*,
delicate, nice as to food (Bozon). Perhaps
suggested by M. H. G. *schemig*, ashamed,
from O. H. G. *scam*, shame; cf. Swed.
skämma, to disgrace. If so, it is related
to **Shame.**

Squeeze, to crush, press tightly. (E.)
The prefixed *s* is due to O. F. *es*- (= L. *-ex*),
very; *queeze* = late M. E. *queisen*, to
squeeze. This M. E. *queisen* probably
represents O. Merc. *cwēsan, answering to
A. S. *cwīesan, cwȳsan*, to crush, chiefly in
the comp. *tō-cwīesan*.

Squib, (1) a paper tube, with combustibles; (2) a lampoon. (Scand.) **1.**
Squibs were sometimes fastened slightly to
a rope, so as to run along it like a rocket;
whence the name. From M. E. *squippen,
swippen*, to move swiftly, fly, sweep, dash.
− Icel. *svipa*, to flash, dart, *svipr*, a swift
movement; Norw. *svipa*, to run swiftly.
2. A *squib* also means a political lampoon,
but was formerly applied, not to the *lampoon itself*, but to the *writer* of it; see
Tatler, no. 88, Nov. 1, 1709. A *squib*
thus meant a firework, a flashy fellow,
making a noise, but doing no harm. *Squib*
also means child's squirt, from its shooting
out water instead of fire. Cf. G. *schweif-
stern*, a comet.

Squill. (F. − L. − Gk.) M. F. *squille*,
'squill, sea-onion;' Cot. − L. *squilla,
scilla*. − Gk. σκίλλα, a squill.

Squinancy, old spelling of *quinsy*.

Squint, to look askew. (E.) The same
as prov. E. (Suffolk) *squink*, to wink. Of
obscure origin. Cf. M. Du. *schuyn*, 'cross,
oblique, byas-wise,' Hexham; E. Fries.
schün, oblique, awry; Du. *schuin*, oblique;
schuinen, to slant; *schuinte*, a slope, obliquity.

Squire (1), the same as **Esquire.**

Squire (2), a square, carpenter's rule.
(F. − L.) M. E. *squire*. − O. F. *esquire,
esquierre*; mod. F. *équerre*. A variant
of O. F. *esquarre*; see **Square.**

Squirrel. (F. − L. − Gk.) M.E. *squirel,
scurel*. − O. F. *escurel* (F. *écureuil*). −
Late L. *scūrellus*, a squirrel; for **sciūrel-
lus*, dimin. of *sciūrus*, a squirrel. − Gk.
σκίουρος, a squirrel; lit. 'a shadow-tail,'
from his bushy tail. − Gk. σκι-ά, shadow;
οὐρά, tail. ¶ The explanation of the Gk.
word may be due to popular etymology.

Squirt, vb. (E.) Prov. E. *swirt*. Cf.
Low G. *swirtjen*, to squirt; from *swiren*,

orig. to whir, like G. *schwirren* ; see **Swirl.** So also E. Fries. *kwirtjen*, to squirt out, to dart about, from *kwirt*, turning quickly about.

Stab, vb. (Scand.) Cf. Irish *stob-aim*, I stab ; Gael. *stob*, to fix a stake in the ground, from *stob*, a stake, pointed iron or stick, stub. Apparently from Swed. dial. *stabbe*, a thick stick or stump; Icel. *stabbi*, a stub, stump, allied to *stafr*, a staff ; Dan. dial. *stabb*, a short peg. Allied to **Stub, Staff,** q. v. Der. *stab*, sb.

Stable (1), a stall for horses. (F. – L.) O. F. *estable*, a stable. – L. *stabulum*, a stall. – L. *stāre*, to stand still. Brugm. ii. §§ 62, 77. See **Stall.**

stable (2), firm. (F. – L.) O.F. *estable*. – L. *stabilis*, firm. – L. *stāre* (above).

stablish. (F. – L.) Short for **Es-tablish.**

Stack, a large pile of wood, &c. (Scand.) M. E. *stak*. – Icel. *stakkr*, a stack of hay ; *stakka*, a stump (as in our chimney-stack); Swed. *stack*, a rick, heap, stack; Dan. *stak*. Teut. type **staknoz* (Noreen). The sense is 'a pile.' Cf. Russ. *stog'*, a heap, hay-rick. Allied to **Stake.**

Staff. (E.) A. S. *stæf*; pl. *stafas*, staves. + Du. *staf*, Icel. *stafr*, Dan. *stab, stav*, Swed. *staf*, Goth. *stafs* or *stabs*, G. *stab*. Allied to O. H. G. *staben*, to be stiff, E. Fries. *staf*, unmoved ; cf. Skt. *stambh*, to make firm.

Stag, a male deer. (Scand.) Also applied (in dialects) to a male animal generally. Late A. S. *stagga* (from Norse). – Icel. *steggr, steggi*, a he-bird, drake, tom-cat ; Norw. *stegg*, a cock. Icel. *steggr* is said to be for **stig-joz*, lit. ' mounter ;' from *stig-*, weak grade of *stīga*, to mount ; see **Stair.** (Noreen, § 140; but doubtful.)

Stage. (F. – L.) A. F. and M. F. *estage*, ' a story, stage, loft, also a dwelling - house ;' Cot. [Hence it meant a stopping-place on a journey, or the distance between stopping-places.] Cf. Prov. *estatge*, a dwelling-place ; answering to Late L. form **staticum*, a dwelling-place. – L. *stat-um*, supine of *stāre*, to stand.

Stagger, to reel, vacillate. (Scand.) A weakened (voiced) form of *stacker*, M. E. *stakeren*. – Icel. *stakra*, to push, to stagger ; frequentative of *staka*, to punt, push, also to stagger ; Norw. *stakra*, *staka*, to stagger; Swed. dial. *stagra*; Dan. dial. *stagge, stagle*. Allied to Icel. *stjaki*, a punt-pole ; and to **Stake.**

Stagnate, to cease to flow. (L.) From L. *stagnātus*, pp. of *stagnāre*, to be still, cease to flow. – L. *stagnum*, a still pool, a stank ; see **Stank.** Der. *stagnant*, from stem of pres. pt. of *stagnāre*.

Staid, grave. (F. – M. Du.) Formerly *stay'd*, pp. of *stay*, vb., to support, make steady. See **Stay** (1).

Stain, vb. (F. – L.) Short for **Distain.** ' I *stayne* a thynge, *Je destayns* ;' Pals-grave. The orig. sense was to dim the colour of a thing. Der. *stain*, sb.

Stair, a step up. (E.) M. E. *steir, steyer*. A. S. *stǣger*, a stair, step; lit. a step to climb by. Formed (with mutation to *ǣ*) from *stág*, 2nd grade of *stīgan*, to climb. +Du. *steiger*, a stair ; cf. Icel. *stegi*, step, Swed. *stege*, ladder, Dan. *stige*, ladder, G. *steg*, a path ; respectively from Du. *stijgen*, Icel. *stíga*, Swed. *stiga*, Dan. *stige*, G. *steigen*, to mount, climb ; Teut. verb **steigan-*, pt. t. **staig*, pp. **stiganoz*. Allied to Skt. *stigh*, to ascend, Gr. στεί-χειν. (√STEIGH.)

Staithe, a landing-place. (E.) A. S. *stæð*, bank, shore. + Icel. *stöð*, harbour, roadstead ; M.Du. *stade*, 'a haven.' Allied to **Stead.**

Stake, a post, strong stick. (E.) M. E. *stake*. A. S. *staca*, a stake. + Du. *staak*, Swed. *stake*, Dan. *stage*. From the Teut. base **stak*, 2nd grade of **stek-an-*, to pierce, appearing in G. *stach*, pt. t. of *stechen*, to stick, pierce; see **Stick** (1).

Stalactite, a kind of crystal hanging from the roof of some caverns. (Gk.) Formed, with suffix *-ite* (Gk. *-ιτης*), from σταλακτ-ός, trickling. – Gk. σταλάζειν (= σταλάγ-γειν), to drip; allied to στα-λᾶν, to drip.

stalagmite, a cone of carbonate of lime on the floor of some caverns. (Gk.) Gk. στάλαγμ-α, a drop; with suffix *-ite* (Gk. *-ιτης*). – Gk. σταλάζειν (above).

Stale (1), too long kept, vapid, trite. (E. ; *or* F. – Teut.) 1. *Stale*, as a sb., means urine of cattle or horses. Cf. E. Fries. and Low G. *stallen*, Swed. *stalla*, to put into a stall, also to stale (as cattle); Dan. *stalde*, to stall-feed, *stalle*, to stale (as horses). From *stall*, sb. 2. *Stale*, adj., is that which stands too long, from M. F. *estaler*, to display wares on a stall, from *estal*, a stall. Cf. M. Du. *stel*, stale, Du. *stel*, a stall, place ; G. *stelle*, a place, *stellen*, to place, from G. *stall*, a stall. See **Stall.**

Stale (2), a decoy, bait; Shak. (F. — Teut.) — A. F. *estale*, a decoy-bird (Bozon). Perhaps adapted from A. S. *stæl-*, as in *stæl-hrān*, a decoy reindeer, allied to M. E. *stale*, theft, A. S. *stalu*, theft; allied to **Steal**.

Stale (3), **Steal,** the handle of anything. (E.) M. E. *stale, stele.* The latter answers to A. S. *stela, steola,* a stalk, stem. + Du. *steel,* stalk, stem, handle; G. *stiel,* stalk, handle. Cf. Gk. στελεόν, a handle. Allied to *still* and *stall;* the *stale* being that by which the tool is held firm and unmoved. And see **Stalk** (1).

Stalk (1), a stem. (E.) M. E. *stalke,* of which one sense is the side-piece (stem) of a ladder. A dimin. form, with suffix -*k*, from M. E. *stale,* variant of *stele*; see **Stale** (3) above.+Icel. *stilkr,* Swed. *stjelk,* Dan. *stilk,* stalk; cf. Gk. στέλεχος, stem of a tree, allied to στελεόν, a handle.

Stalk (2), to stride. (E.) M. E. *stalken.* A. S. *stealcian,* to walk warily; allied to *stealc,* steep. + Dan. *stalke,* to stalk. The notion is that of walking cautiously. Cf. perhaps A. S. *stellan, styllan,* to leap. Der. *stalk-ing-horse,* a horse for stalking game; see Halliwell.

Stall, a standing-place for cattle, &c. (E.) M. E. *stal.* A. S. *steall,* station, stall.+Du. *stal,* Icel. *stallr,* Dan. *stald,* Swed. *stall,* G. *stall.* Teut. type **stalloz,* perhaps for **stadloz*; cf. A. S. *standan,* to stand, E. *stead*; Gk. σταθ-μός, a stall; L. *stab - ulum* (for **stadh - lom*). Allied to **Stead.** Brugm. i. 593 (4). Der. *stalled ox,* a fatted ox; cf. Swed. dial. *stalla,* to fatten, *stalloxe,* fatted ox (Möller).

stallion, an entire horse. (F. — O. H. G.) M. E. *stalon.* — O. F. *estalon* (F. *étalon*), a stallion; so called because kept in a *stall* and not made to work. — O. H. G. *stal* (G. *stall*), a stall, stable; see **Stall.**

Stalwart, sturdy. (E.) For *stalworth.* M. E. *stalworth, stelewurðe, stealewurðe, stalewurðe*; A. S. *stælwyrðe,* pl., serviceable (said of ships); A. S. Chron. an. 896. β. We find A. S. *gestælan* used as short for *gestaðelan.* Hence Sievers explains the form *stæl-* or *stēl-* as being contracted from *staðol,* a foundation [or from a parallel form **stæþl*]. Thus *stæl-wyrðe* is for **staðol - wyrðe,* lit. ' foundation-worthy,' i. e. firmly fixed, firm, constant; cf. A. S. *staðol-fæst,* steadfast. The A. S *staðel, staðol* is allied to **Stead.** Cf. **stead-fast.**

Stamen, male organ of a flower. (L.) Lit. ' a thread.' — L. *stāmen,* a thread, the warp standing up in an upright loom. — L. *stāre,* to stand. Der. *stamina,* orig. pl. of *stāmen,* lit. threads in a warp, a firm texture.

stamin, a kind of stuff. (F. — L.) M. E. *stamin.* — M. F. *estamine,* ' the stuffe tamine;' Cot. — L. *stāmineus,* consisting of threads. — L. *stāmin-,* stem of *stāmen,* a thread (above). Also spelt *stammel,* *tamine, tammy.*

Stammer, to stutter. (E.) M. E. *stameren,* vb.; A. S. *stomrian* (Shrine, p. 42); from A. S. *stamer, stamor,* adj., stammering; where the suffix *-er, -or* is adjectival. From a base **stam,* extended from √STA, to stand, remain fixed; cf. prov. E. *stam,* to amaze, confound; related by gradation to G. *stumm,* dumb. + Du. *stameren, stamelen,* G. *stammern, stammeln*; Icel. *stamma,* Dan. *stamme,* Swed. *stamma,* to stammer; Icel. *stamr,* O. H. G. *stam,* Goth. *stamms,* adj., stammering. See **Stem** (1).

Stamp, to tread heavily, to pound. (E.) M. E. *stampen.* A. S. *stempan* (for **stampian*).+Du. *stampen,* Icel. *stappa,* Swed. *stampa,* Dan. *stampe,* G. *stampfen*; also Gk. στέμβειν, to stamp.

stampede, a panic. (Span. — Teut.) *Stampede* is a sudden panic, causing cattle to take to flight and run for many miles; any sudden flight due to panic. — Span. (and Port.) *estampido,* a crash, sudden sound of anything bursting or falling. Formed as if from a verb **estampir,* akin to *estampar,* to stamp. The reference appears to be to the noise made by the blows of a pestle upon a mortar. Of Teut. origin; see **Stamp** above.

Stanch, Staunch, to stop a flow of blood. (F. — L.) O. F. *estancher,* to stanch; Walloon *stanchi* (Remacle). Late L. *stancāre,* to stanch, a variant of Late L. type **stagnicāre,* to cause to stagnate, from L. *stagnāre,* to cease to flow; see **Stagnate.** ¶ It is probable that the sense was influenced by G. *stange,* a pole, a bar (Körting, § 7733). Der. *stanch,* adj., firm, sound, not leaky; cf. F. *étanche,* water-tight.

Stanchion, a support, beam, bar. (F. — L.) O. North F. *estanchon,* Norm. dial. *étanchon*; M. F. *estançon, estanson,* ' a prop, stay;' Cot. Not derived from the O. F. *estancher,* to prop (allied to E. *stanch*), but a diminutive of O.F. *estance,* a situation,

condition, also a stanchion (Scheler). —
Late L. *stantia*, a chamber, a house, lit.
'that which stands firm.' — L. *stant*-, stem
of pres. pt. of *stāre*, to stand. See **State.**
¶ But the word may have been confused
with O. F. *estancher*, to prop (as above),
which is the same word as *estancher*, to
staunch; for which see **Stanch.** The
ultimate root is the same either way.
(√STĀ.)

Stand. (E.) A. S. *standan*, pt. t. *stōd*,
pp. *standen*.+Icel. *standa*, Goth. *standan*;
cf. Du. *staan* (pt. t. *stond*); Swed. *stå*
(pt. t. *stod*); G. *stehen* (pt. t. *stand*).
Teut. type *standan-*, pt. t. *stōth*; base
stath, *stad*, the *n* being orig. characteristic
of the pres. tense. Allied to L. *stāre*, Gk.
ἱστην, I stood, Russ. *stoiate*, Skt. *sthā*, to
stand. (√STĀ.) See **State. Der.** *stand*,
sb.; *standish*, short for *stand-dish*, a standing dish for pen and ink.

Standard. (F. — L.) A. F. *estandard*,
a standard or ensign, O. F. *estendard*, a
standard measure. The flag was a large
one, on a fixed (standing) pole; and hence
was modified by the influence of the verb
to stand. The O. F. *estendard*, Ital. *sten-
dardo*, are unmodified forms; from L.
extend-ere, to extend; with suffix *-ard*
(= O. H. G. *-hart*, suffix, orig. the same
as *hart*, hard). See **Extend.**

Stang, a pole, stake. (Scand.) M. E.
stange. — Icel. *stöng* (gen. *stangar*), a pole,
stake; Dan. *stang*, Swed. *stång*, Du. *stang*,
G. *stange*; A. S. *steng.* From the 2nd
grade of the verb *to sting.* Cf. **Stake.**

Staniel, a kind of hawk. (E.) A. S.
stāngella; lit. 'rock-yeller.' — A. S. *stān*,
rock (see **Stone**); and *gellan*, to yell (see
Yell).

Stank, a pool, tank. (F. — L.) An old
word; once common. — Walloon *stank*,
O. F. *estang*, a pond. (The same as Prov.
estanc, Span. *estanque*, Port. *tanque*, a
pond, pool.) — L. *stagnum*, a pool of stagnant or standing water. See **Stagnate,
Stanch, Tank.**

Stannary, relating to tin-mines. (L.)
Late L. *stannāria*, a tin-mine. — L. *stannum*, tin.

Stanza. (Ital. — L.) Ital. *stanza*, M.
Ital. *stantia*, 'a lodging, chamber, dwelling, also *stance* or *staffe* of verses;' Florio.
So called from the stop or pause at the
end of it. — Late L. *stantia*, an abode. —
L. *stant*-, stem of pres. pt. of *stāre*, to
stand · see **Stanchion, State.**

Staple (1), a loop of iron. (E.) A. S.
stapol, a post, pillar; also, a step. Orig.
sense a prop, something that holds firm.
— A. S. *stap-*, base of *stæppan*, strong
verb, to step, tread firmly; cf. *stamp.* +
Du. *stapel*, staple, stocks, a pile; Dan.
stabel, Swed. *stapel*; G. *staffel*, a step,
stapel, a staple (below).

staple (2), a chief commodity of a
place. (F. — Low G.) The sense has
changed; it formerly meant a chief market,
with reference to the place where things
were most sold. — O. F. *estaple*, M. F.
estape, 'a staple, a mart or general market,
a publique storehouse;' Cot. (F. *étape*.) —
Low G. *stapel*, a heap; hence a heap laid
in order, store, store-house; the same
word as **Staple** (1). The Du. *stapel* means
(1) a staple, (2) the stocks, (3) a pile or
heap. All from the notion of fixity or
firmness.

Star. (E.) M. E. *sterre.* A. S. *steorra.*
+Du. *ster*; O. H. G. *sterro.* Cf. Icel.
stjarna, Dan. *stierne*, Swed. *stjerna*, Goth.
stairnō, G. *stern*; also L. *stella* (for *ster-
la*), Gk. ἀστήρ, Corn. *steren*, Bret. *sterenn*,
W. *seren*, Skt. *tārā.* Orig. sense uncertain.
Cf. Brugm. i. § 473 (2).

Star-board, the right side of a ship.
(E.) M. E. *sterebourde.* A. S. *stēorbord*,
i. e. steer-board, the side on which the
steersman stood; in the first instance, he
used a paddle, not a helm. Cf. Icel.
ā stjōrn, at the helm, or on the starboard
side. — A. S. *stēor*, a rudder or paddle to
steer with; *bord*, board, border, edge or
side; see **Steer** (2) and **Board.** The
O. H. G. *stiura* (G. *steuer*) means a prop,
staff, paddle, rudder, allied to Icel. *staurr*,
a post, stake, Gk. σταυρός, an upright pole
or stake. (√STEU, allied to √STĀ.)
+Du. *stuurboord*, Icel. *stjörnborði*, Dan.
Swed. *styrbord*; all similarly compounded.

Starch. (E.) *Starch* is stuff that
stiffens; from the adj. **Stark**, stiff, strong.
Cf. G. *stärke*, (1) strength, (2) starch;
from *stark*, adj., strong.

Stare (1), to gaze fixedly. (E.) A. S.
starian; from a Teut. adj. *staroz*, fixed,
appearing in G. *starr*, fixed; cf. Skt. *sthira-*,
fixed, allied to *sthā*, to stand; and Gk.
στερεός, firm. (√STĀ.) +Du. *staren*;
Icel. *stara*, *stira*, to stare; Swed. *stirra*,
Dan. *stirre*, to stare; O.H.G. *starēn.*
¶ Hence 'staring hair' is 'stiff-standing
hair.' Brugm. i. § 200.

stare (2), to glitter. (E.) M. E.

staren; whence *staring colours* = bright colours. The same word as *stare* (1); from the glittering of staring eyes.

Stark, stiff, rigid, entire. (E.) A. S. *stearc*, stiff, strong.+Du. *sterk*, Icel. *sterkr*, Dan. *stærk*, Swed. *stark*. From Teut. verb **sterkan-*, to stiffen; of which the weak grade appears in Goth. *ga-staurk-nan*, to become dry, Icel. *storkinn*, pp. coagulated. Further allied to Lith. *strĕgti*, to become rigid, Pers. *suturg*, big, strong. Root STERG, extension of √STER; see Stare (1). Der. *stark*, adv., as in *stark mad*.

Stark-naked, quite naked. (E.) A substitution for M. E. *start-naked*, lit. 'tail-naked,' i. e. with the hinder parts exposed, but used in the sense of wholly naked. From A. S. *steort*, a tail; as in *red-start*, i. e. red-tail, a bird.+Du. *staart*, Icel. *stertr*, Dan. *stiert*, Swed. *stjert*, G. *sterz*, a tail; cf. Gk. στόρθη, a spike.

Starling. (E.) M. E. *sterling*, double dimin. of \M. E. *stare*, a starling.–A. S. *stær*, a starling. + Icel. *starri*, *stari*, Dan. *stær*, Swed. *stare*, G. *staar*, L. *sturnus*. Cf. A. S. *stearn*, a tern.

Start, to move suddenly. (E.) M. E. *sterten*; pt. t. *stirte* (Havelok, 873), *sturte*, *storte* (Layamon, 23951). Allied to Du. *storten*, to precipitate, fall, rush, G. *stürzen*. Also, perhaps, to M. Du. *steerten*, to flee, run away. Some even connect it with A.S. *steort*, a tail. See Stark-naked. Der. *start-le*; A.S. *steartlian*, to stumble.

Starve. (E.) M. E. *steruen* (*sterven*), to die (without reference to the means of death). A. S. *steorfan*, pt. t. *stearf*, pp. *storfen*, to die; whence *-stierfan*, to kill (weak verb).+Du. *sterven*, G. *sterben*. Teut. type **sterban-*, pt. t. **starb*. Der. *starve-l-ing*, double dimin., expressive of contempt; *starv-ation*, a hybrid word, introduced from the North about 1775.

State, a standing, position, condition, &c. (F.–L.) O. F. *estat*.–L. *statum*, acc. of *status*, condition. – L. *statum*, supine of *stāre*, to stand.+Gk. ἔστην, I stood; Skt. *sthā*, to stand; cognate with E. *stand*. (√STĀ.)

Statics, the science treating of bodies at rest. (Gk.) From Gk. στατικός, at a standstill; ἡ στατική, statics.–Gk. στατ-ός, placed, standing; verbal adj. from στα-, allied to -στη- in ἵστημι, I place, stand. (√STĀ.)

Station. (F.–L.) F. *station* – L.

statiōnem, acc. of *statio*, a standing still. – L. *statum*, supine of *stāre*. Der. *station-er*, orig. a bookseller who had a *station* or stall in a market-place; hence *station-er-y*, things sold by a *stationer*. Also *station-ary*, adj. See State.

statist, a statesman, politician. (F.– L.; *with* Gk. *suffix*.) Coined from *state* by adding *-ist* (L. *-ista*, Gk. *-ιστης*).

statue. (F.–L.) O. F. *statuĕ* (trisyllabic).–L. *statua*, a standing image. – L. *statu-*, for *status*, a position, standing. – L. *statum*, supine of *stāre*, to stand.

stature, height. (F.–L.) F. *stature*. – L. *statūra*, an upright posture, height. – L. *statum*, supine of *stāre* to stand.

status, condition. (L.) L. *status*; see State.

statute. (F.–L.) F. *statut*.–L. *statūtum*, a statute; neut. of *statūtus*, pp. of *statuere*, to place, set, causal of *stāre*, to stand.

Staunch; see Stanch.

Stave, piece of a cask, part of a piece of music. (E.) Merely another form of *staff*, due to M. E. dat. sing. *staue* (*stave*) and pl. *staues* (*staves*). Cf. Icel. *stafr*, a staff, a stave; Dan. *stav*, staff, *stave*, stave. See Staff.

Stavesacre, the seeds of a larkspur; *Delphinium staphisagria*. (L.–Gk.) Lat. form of Gk. σταφὶς ἄγρια; where ἄγρια, wild, is from ἀγρός, a field (E. *acre*).

Stay (1), to prop, delay, remain. (F.– M. Du.) M. F. *estayer*, 'to prop, stay;' Cot.–M. F. *estaye*, sb. fem. 'a prop, stay;' id.–M. Du. *stade*, also *staeye*, 'a prop, stay,' Hexham; O. Flem. *staey*, a prop; allied to E. Stead. [The loss of *d* between two vowels is usual in Dutch, as in *broer*, brother, *teer* (for *teder*), tender.] See Stay (2).

Stay (2), a rope supporting a mast. (E.) A. S. *stæg*, a stay (whence F. *étai*, a ship's stay; Hatzfeld). + Du. *stag*, Icel. Dan. Swed. G. *stag*. Der. *stay-sail*. ¶ It is difficult to decide whether E. *stay* (2) is a survival of A. S. *stæg*, 'a rope for a mast,' or is from O. F. *estaye*, a prop, for which see Stay (1).

Stays, a bodice. (F.–M. Du.) Merely a pl. of *stay*, a support. (So also *bodice* = *bodies*). See Stay (1).

Stead. (E.) M. E. *stede*. A. S. *stede*, a place.+Du. *stede*, *stee*, a place; cf. Du. *stad*, a town, Icel. *staðr*, *staða*, a place;

Dan. Swed. *stad*, town, Dan. *sted*, place; G. *stadt*, *statt*, town, place, Goth. *staths* (gen. *stadis*), a place. Allied to L. *statio*, a station; Gk. στάσις, Skt. *sthiti-*, a standing. (√STĀ.) **Der.** *home - stead*, *bed-stead*.

steadfast. (E.) A. S. *stedefæst*, firm in its place.—A. S. *stede*, place; *fæst*, firm; see **Fast.** + M. Du. *stedevast*, Icel. *staðfastr*, Dan. *stadfast*.

steady, firm. (E.) Spelt *stedye* in Palsgrave. (The sole example of *stedi* in Stratmann has another form and sense.) A new formation from *stead*, sb., with suffix *-y*; suggested by *steadfast*.

Steak, a slice of meat for cooking. (Scand.) M. E. *steike*. — Icel. *steik*, a steak; so called from being stuck on a wooden peg, and roasted before the fire; cf. Icel. *steikja*, to roast on a spit or peg. Allied to Icel. *stika*, a stick; and to **Stick** (1). + Swed. *stek*, roast meat, *steka*, to roast; allied to *stick*, a prick, *sticka*, to stick, stab; Dan. *steg*, a roast, *at vende steg*, to turn the spit. Cf. G. *anstecken*, to put on a spit, *anstechen*, to pierce.

Steal. (E.) A. S. *stelan*, pt. t. *stæl*, pp. *stolen.*+Du. *stelen*, Icel. *stela*, Dan. *stiæle*, Swed. *stjäla*, G. *stehlen*, Goth. *stilan*. Teut. type **stelan-*, pt. t. **stal*, pp. **stulanoz*.

Steam, sb. (E.) M. E. *steem*. A. S. *stēam*, vapour, smell, smoke.+Du. *stoom*. **Der.** *steam*, vb.

Stearine, one of the proximate principles of animal fat. (F.–Gk.) F. *stéarine*; formed, with suffix *-ine*, from Gk. στέαρ, tallow, hardened fat. Allied to Gk. στῆναι, to stand; Brugm. ii. § 82. See **Statics.**

steatite, a soft magnesian rock with a soapy feel. (F.–Gk.) Formed with suffix *-ite*, from Gk. στέατ- as in στέατ-ος, gen. of στέαρ, tallow, fat. See above.

Steed. (E.) M. E. *stede*. A. S. *stēda*, a stud-horse, stallion, war-horse; Teut. type **stōd-jon-.* — A. S. *stōd*, a stud (with the usual change from *ō* to *ē*). Cf. G. *stute*, a stud-mare; Icel. *stōðhestr*, stud-horse, *stōðmerr*, stud-mare. See **Stud** (1).

Steel. (E.) M. E. *steel*. O. Merc. *stēli*; A. S. *style*, which is a late Wessex spelling.+Du. *staal*, Icel. *stāl*, Dan. *staal*, Swed. *stål*, G. *stahl*, O. H. G. *stahal*. The O. H. G. *stahal* answers to O. Pruss. *stakla-*, as in *panu-stakla*, steel for kindling fire; cf. also Skt. *stak*, to resist, Zend *staχra-*, strong. Named from its firm re-

sistance. Brugm. ii. § 76. **Der.** *steel*, vb., A. S. *stȳlan* (Icel. *stæla*).

Steelyard (1). (Low G.) Said to be the *yard* in London where *steel* was sold by German merchants (Stow); but really for Low G. *staal-hof*, 'sample-yard,' from *staal*, a sample of goods; see Bremen Wört. Low G. *staal* is from O. F. *estale*, a sample.—O. F. *estaler*; see **Stale** (1).

Steelyard (2), a kind of balance, with unequal arms. (F.–L.?) Now generally misunderstood as meaning a yard or bar of steel; but spelt *stelleere* by Cotgrave, s. v. *Crochet*. Perhaps from O. F. *astelier*, a spit-cratch, in which spits lay horizontally (Roquefort); cf. Span. *astillero*, the same, and *astil*, the beam of a balance. From L. *hasta*, a lance.

Steenbok, a S. African antelope. (Du.) Du. *steenbok*, lit. 'rock-goat.'—Du. *steen*, stone, rock; *bok*, he-goat; see **Buck** (1).

Steep (1), precipitous. (E.) M. E. *steep*. A. S. *stēap*, steep, high. + Icel. *steypðr*, steep, lofty. Allied to *stoop*, whence the notion of sloping down, or tilted up; cf. Swed. *stupande*, sloping; Norweg. *stupa*, to fall, *stup*, a steep cliff. See **Stoop.**

steep (2), to soak in a liquid. (Scand.) M. E. *stepen*, Icel. *steypa*, to make to stoop, overturn, pour out liquids, cast metals (hence to pour water over grain or steep it); causal of *stūpa*, to stoop; see **Stoop.** So also Swed. *stöpa*, to cast metals, steep corn; Dan. *stöbe*, the same.

steeple. (E.) O. Merc. *stēpel*, A. S. *stȳpel*, a lofty tower; so called from its height. — A. S. *stēap*, steep, high (with regular change from *ēa* to *ȳ*). + Icel. *stöpull*; Low G. *stipel*.

Steer (1), a young ox. (E.) A. S. *stēor.* +Du. and G. *stier*, a bull, Icel. *stjörr*, Goth. *stiur*; Teut. type **steuroz*, m. [Also **theuroz*, for Idg. **teuros*; as in Icel. *þjörr*, Swed. *tjur*, Dan. *tyr*, a steer. Cf. also L. *taurus*, Gk. ταῦρος, Russ. *tur'*.] β. The sense is 'full-grown' or 'large,' as in Skt. *sthūla-* (for *sthūra-*), great, large, powerful, *sthūra-*, a man, *sthūrī*, a pack-horse; cf. Zend *staora-*, Pers. *sutūr*, a beast of burden. **Der.** *stir-k*, a bullock, A. S. *stȳr-ic* (with vowel-change from *ēo* to *ȳ*); Low G. *stärk*.

Steer (2), to guide. (E.) M. E. *steren*. A. S. *stēoran*, *stȳran*, to steer.+Du. *sturen*, Icel. *stȳra*, Dan. *styre*, Swed. *styra*, G.

steuern, to steer; Goth. *stiurjan*, to confirm. **β**. Weak verb; from the sb. appearing in M. E. *stere*, Du. *stuur*, Icel. *stȳri*, G. *steuer*, a rudder, still retained in *star-board*; see **Star-board**. The O. H. G. *stiura* meant (1) a prop, staff, support, (2) a rudder; and is allied to Icel. *staurr*, a stake. Noreen, § 143; Brugm. i. § 198.

Stellar. (L.) L. *stellāris*, starry.—L. *stella*, star; for **ster-la*, a dimin. form allied to E. **Star**. Brugm. i. § 473.

Stem (1), trunk of a tree. (E.) M. E. *stem*. A. S. *stefn*, *stemn*, (1) stem of a tree; (2) stem, prow of a vessel, for which *stefna* (*stæfna*) is also used. Apparently allied to **Staff**; but the primitive forms are uncertain. **+** Du. *stam*, trunk, *steven*, prow; Icel. *stafn*, *stamn*, stem of a vessel, *stofn*, trunk; Dan. *stamme*, trunk, *stævn*, prow; Swed. *stam*, trunk, *stäf*, prow, *framstam*, fore-stem, *bak-stam*, back-stem, stern; G. *stamm*, trunk, *vorder steven*, prow-post, stem, *hinter steven*, stern-post. Some compare O. Irish *tamon* (Ir. *tamhan*), the stem of a tree.

stem (2), prow of a vessel. (E.) See above.

Stem (3), to check, stop. (E.) E. Fries. *stemmen*, to check, stop, hinder. So Icel. *stemma*. Dan. *stemme*, to dam up; G. *stemmen*, to dam up water, check, resist. From Teut. **stam*, to stop; see **Stammer**.

Stench, sb. (E.) A. S. *stenc*, a strong smell, often in the sense of fragrance.— A. S. *stanc*, 2nd grade of *stincan*, to stink, also to smell sweetly.**+**G. *ge-stank*. See **Stink**.

Stencil, to paint in figures by help of a pierced plate. (F.—L.) From O. F. *estenceler*, to sparkle, also to cover with stars, to adorn with bright colours (Godefroy).—O. F. *estencele*, a spark.—L. type **stincilla*, mistaken form of L. *scintilla*, a spark. See **Scintillation**.

Stenography, shorthand writing. (Gk.) From Gk. στενό-s, narrow, close; γράφ-ειν, to write.

Stentorian, extremely loud. (Gk.) From Gk. Στέντωρ, Stentor, a Greek at Troy, with a loud voice (Homer).—Gk. στέν-ειν, to groan; with suffix -τωρ. (✓ STEN.) See **Stun**.

Step, a pace, degree, foot-print. (E.) M. E. *steppe*. From A. S. *steppan*, *stæppan* (for **stapjan*), a str. verb with a weak present; pt. t. *stōp*, pp. *stapen*. Cf. Du.

stap, G. *stapfe*, a footstep; Russ. *stopa*, a step. Allied to **Stamp**.

Stepchild. (E.) A. S. *stēopcild*; where *cild* = E. *child*; see **Child**. We also find A. S. *stēopbearn*, step-bairn, stepchild. *stēopfæder*, stepfather, *stēopmōdor*, stepmother, &c. **β**. The sense of *stēop* is ' orphaned,' and *stēopcild* is the oldest compound; we find A. S. *āstēapte*, pl., made orphans, also O. H. G. *stiufan*, to deprive of parents.**+**Du. *stiefkind*, stepchild; Icel. *stjúpbarn*, step-bairn; Swed. *styfbarn*; G. *stiefkind*.

Steppe, a large plain. (Russ.) Russ. *stepe*, a waste, heath, steppe.

Stereoscope, an optical instrument for giving an appearance of solidity. (Gk.) From Gk. στερεό-s, solid, stiff; σκοπ-εῖν, to behold.

stereotype, a solid plate for printing. (Gk.) Gk. στερεό-s, hard, solid; and *type*, q. v.

Sterile. (F.—L.) O. F. *sterile*.—L. *sterilem*, acc. of *sterilis*, barren. Cf. Gk. στεῖρα (for **στέρ-ya*), a barren cow; Goth. *stairō*, a barren woman. Brugm. i. § 838.

Sterling. (E.) M. E. *sterling*, a sterling coin; A. F. *esterling*. Said to be named from the *Esterlings* (i. e. easterlings, men of the east); this was a name for the Hanse merchants in London, temp. Henry III.—M. E. *est*, east. See **East**; and see *Easterling* in N. E. D.

Stern (1), severe, austere. (E.) M. E. *sterne*, *sturne*. A. S. *styrne*, stern. Allied to G. *störrig*, morose, stubborn; Goth. *and-staurran*, to murmur against.

Stern (2), hind part of a vessel. (Scand.) Icel. *stjörn*, a steering, steerage, helm; hence a name for the hind part of a vessel. Cf. Icel. *stjōr-i*, a steerer, allied to E. *steer* (2).

Sternutation, sneezing. (L.) L. *sternūtātio*, a sneezing.—L. *sternūtātus*, pp. of *sternūtāre*, to sneeze, frequentative of *sternuere*, to sneeze. Allied to Gk. πτάρνυσθαι, to sneeze.

Stertorous, snoring. (L.) Coined from L. *stertere*, to snore.

Stethoscope, the tube used in auscultation, as applied to the chest. (Gk.) Lit. ' chest-examiner.'—Gk. στῆθο-s, chest; σκοπ-εῖν, to consider.

Stevedore, one who stows a cargo. (Span. — L.) Span. *estivador*, a woolpacker; hence a *stower* of wool for exportation, and generally, one who stows a cargo. ━ Span. *estivar*, to compress wool, to stow a cargo. ━ L. *stīpāre*, to press together. Allied to **Stiff**. Cf. Span. *estiva*, O. F. *estive*, stowage; Ital. *stiva*, ballast.

Stew, to boil slowly. (F. ─ Teut.) M. E. *stuwen*, orig. to bathe; formed from the old sb. *stew* in the sense of bath or hot-house (as it was called); the pl. *stews* generally meant brothels. An Anglicised form of O. F. *estuve*, a stew, stove, hot-house (F. *étuve*). ─ O. H. G. *stupa*, a hot room for a bath (mod. G. *stube*, a chamber). Allied to **Stove**, q. v. ¶ The history of O. F. *estuve* and of O. H. G. *stupa* is much disputed.

Steward. (E.) A.S. *stīweard*, *stīward*, a steward. Lit. 'a sty-ward;' from A. S. *stigu*, a farmyard, *weard*, a ward. The orig. sense was one who looked after the domestic animals, and gave them their food; hence, one who provides for his master's table, or who superintends household affairs. We also find *stīwita*, *stigwita*, a steward, where the former element is the same. See **Sty** (1) and **Ward**.

Stick (1), to stab, pierce, thrust in, adhere. (E.) The orig. sense was to sting, pierce, stab, fasten into a thing; hence, to be thrust into a thing, to adhere. Two verbs are confused in mod. E., viz. (1) *stick*, to pierce; (2) *stick*, to be fixed in. **a.** We find (1) M. E. *steken*, strong verb, to pierce, pt. t. *stak*, pp. *steken*, *stiken*; answering to an A. S. *stecan, pt. t. *stæc, pp. *stecen (not found); cognate with O. Fries. *steka*, O. Sax. *stekan* (pt. t. *stak*), E. Fries. *steken*, Low G. *steken* (pt. t. *stak*, pp. *steken*); G. *stechen* (pt. t. *stach*, pp. *gestochen*). Teut. type *stekan- (pt. t. *stak); transferred to the *e*-series from an older type *steikan- (weak grade *stik*); cf. Goth. *staks*, a mark, *stiks*, a point. Further allied to Gk. στίζειν (= στίγ-γειν), to prick, L. *instīgāre*, to prick, Skt. *tij*, to be sharp; and to E. **Sting**. (√STEIG.) **β.** We also find (2) A.S. *stician*, pt. t. *sticode*, weak verb; allied to Icel. *stika*, to drive piles, Swed. *sticka*, Dan. *stikke*, to stab, sting, *stecken*, to stick, set, also to stick fast, remain.

stick (2), a small branch of a tree. (E.) M. E. *stikke*. A. S. *sticca*, a stick, peg, nail. So called from its piercing or sticking into anything; the orig. sense being 'peg,' also a small bit of a tree. Allied to **Stick** (1) above. ╋ Icel. *stika*,

a stick, E. Fries. *stikke*, *stik*; Du. *stek*; G. *stecken*.

stickleback, a small fish. (E.) So called from the *stickles* or small prickles on its back. *Stick-le* is a dimin. of *stick* (2); cf. E. Fries. *stikel*, a thorn.

Stickler, one who parts combatants, or settles disputes between two who are fighting. (E.) Now only used of one who insists on etiquette or persists in an opinion. Corruption of a sb. formed from M. E. *stightlen*, *stightlien*, to dispose, order, arrange, govern, subdue; commonly used of a steward who arranged matters, acting as a master of ceremonies. See Will. of Palerne, 1199, 2899, 3281, 3841, 5379; Destruction of Troy, 117, 1997, 2193, 13282, &c. This M. E. *stightlen* is a frequentative of A. S. *stihtan*, *stihtian*, to control. Cognate with M. Du. *stichten*, to build, impose a law; Dan. *stifte*, to institute, Swed. *stifta*, *stikta*, G. *stiften*, to found, institute. Cf. also Icel. *stētt* (for **stīhti-*), a foundation, base.

Stiff. (E.) M. E. *stif*. A. S. *stīf*, stiff. ╋ Low G. *stif* (Danneil); Du. *stijf*, Dan. *stiv*, Swed. *styf*. Allied to Lith. *stiprus*, strong, *stip-ti*, to be stiff, L. *stīpes*, a stem, *stīpāre*, to pack tight, *stipulus*, firm.

stifle. (Scand.) XVI. cent. From Icel. *stīfla*, to dam up, choke ; Norweg. *stīvla*, to stop, hem in, lit. to stiffen; *stivra*, to stiffen; frequentatives of Norw. *stiva*, Dan. *stive*, to stiffen. All from adj. above. ¶ The prov. E. *stive*, to stuff, from O. F. *estiver*, to pack tight, is ult. from the same root; see **Stevedore**.

Stigmatise. (F. ─ Gk.) F. *stigmatiser*, to brand with a hot iron, defame. ━ Gk. στιγματίζειν, to mark, brand. ━ Gk. στιγ-ματ-, base of στίγμα, a prick, mark, brand. ━ Gk. στίζειν (= *στίγ-γειν), to prick. Allied to **Stick** (1). (√STEIG.)

Stile (1), a set of steps for climbing over. (E.) M. E. *stile*. A. S. *stigel*, a stile. ━ A. S. *stig*-, weak grade of *stigan*, to climb; with suffix -*el*. See **Stair**. ╋ M. Du. and O.H.G. *stichel*.

Stile (2), the correct spelling of **Style** (1), q. v.

stiletto, a small dagger. (Ital. ─ L.) Ital. *stiletto*, a dagger; dimin. of M. Ital. *stilo*, a dagger. ━ L. *stilum*, acc. of *stilus*, an iron pin; see **Style** (1).

Still (1), motionless. (E.) M. E. *stille*. A. S. *stille*, still; cf. *stillan*, vb., to remain in a place or stall. For *steljoz;

allied to A. S. *stellan*, to place, from A. S. *stæl*, a place; cf. *steall*; see **Stall.** + Du. *stil*, still, *stillen*, to be still, *stellen*, to place, from *stal*, a stall; Dan. *stille*, Swed. *stilla*, G. *still*, still; Dan. *stille*, to still, also to place, Swed. *stilla*, to quiet; G. *stillen*, to still, *stellen*, to place; Dan. *stald*, Swed. G. *stall*, a stall. Der. *still*, adv., A. S. *stille*, continually, ever.

Still (2), to distil, trickle down. (L.; or F.–L.) In some cases, it represents L. *stillāre*, to fall in drops; more often, it is short for **Distil**, q. v.

still (3), sb., an apparatus for distilling. (L.) Short for M. E. *stillatorie*, a still, from *stillāt-us*, pp. of *stillāre* (above).

Stilt. (Scand.) M. E. *stilte.* – Swed. *stylta*, Dan. *stylte*, a stilt; Dan. *stylte*, to walk on stilts.+Du. *stelt*; G. *stelze*, a stilt; O. H. G. *stelza*, prop, crutch. Perhaps allied to **Stalk** (1); cf. E. Fries. *stilte*, a stem, stalk.

Stimulate. (L.) From pp. of L. *stimulāre*, to prick forward. – L. *stimulus*, a goad.

Sting. (E.) A. S. *stingan*, pt. t. *stang*, pp. *stungen.*+Icel. *stinga*, Swed. *stinga*, Dan. *stinge.* Teut. type *stengan-.* Der. *stang.*

stingy, mean. (E.) The same as Norfolk *stingy*, pronounced (stin-ji), nipping, unkindly, ill-humoured. Merely the adj. from *sting*, sb., which is pronounced (stinj) in Wiltshire. So also Swed. *sticken*, pettish, fretful, from *sticka*, to sting.

Stink. (E.) A. S. *stincan*, pt. t. *stanc*, pp. *stuncen.* + Du. *stinken*, Dan. *stinke*, Swed. *stinka*, G. *stinken.* Cf. Gk. ταγγός, rancid.

Stint, to limit, restrain, cut short. (E.) Orig. 'to shorten.' M. E. *stinten* (also *stentan*). A. S. *styntan*, in *for-styntan*, properly 'to make dull'; formed from A. S. *stunt*, stupid, by vowel-change from *u* to *y*. The peculiar sense is Scand.+ Icel. *stytta* (for *stynta*), to shorten, from *stuttr*, short, stunted; Swed. dial. *stynta*, to take short steps, from *stunt*, short; Dan. dial. *stynte*, to crop. See **Stunted.**

Stipend, salary. (L.) L. *stīpendium*, a tax, tribute; for *stip-pendium*, a payment in money. – L. *stip-*, stem of *stips*, small coin; *pendere*, to weigh out, pay; see **Pendant.** β. *Stips* is supposed to mean 'pile of money'; cf. *stīpāre*, to heap together.

Stipple, to engrave by means of small dots. (Du.) Du. *stippelen*, to speckle, dot over. – Du. *stippel*, a speckle; dimin. of *stip*, a point. Allied to Low G. *stippelen*, to drip as raindrops (Danneil), *stippen*, to speckle; G. *steppen*, to stitch, *stif 't*, a tack, peg, pin.

Stipulation, a contract. (F.–L.) F. *stipulation.* – L. acc. *stipulātiōnem*, a covenant. – L. *stipulātus*, pp. of *stipulārī*, to settle an agreement. – O. Lat. *stipulus*, firm, fast; allied to *stīpes*, a post. ¶ Not from *stipula*, a straw, though this is an allied word.

Stir. (E.) M. E. *stiren, sturen.* A. S. *styrian*, to move, stir. Allied to Icel. *styrr*, a stir; Du. *storen*, Swed. *störa*, G. *stören*, to disturb, O. H. G. *stören*, to scatter, destroy, disturb. Teut. types *sturjan-,*staurjan-* (Franck). Prob. allied to **Storm.**

Stirk; see **Steer** (1).

Stirrup. (E.) For *sty-rope*, i. e. a rope to mount by; the orig. stirrup was a looped rope for mounting into the saddle. M. E. *stirop.* A. S. *stī-rāp*, *stig-rāp.* – A. S. *stig-*, weak grade of *stīgan*, to mount; *rāp*, a rope; see **Stair** and **Rope.**+Icel. *stig-reip*, Du. *steg-reep*, G. *steg-reif.*

Stitch, a pain in the side, a passing through stuff of a needle and thread. (E.) M. E. *stiche.* A. S. *stice*, a pricking sensation. – A. S. *stician*, to prick, pierce. See **Stick** (1).

Stith, an anvil. (Scand.) M. E. *stith.* – Icel. *steði*, an anvil; allied to *staðr*, a fixed place; named from its firmness; see **Stead.** + Swed. *städ*, an anvil; M. Du. *stiet.* Der. *stith-y*, properly a smithy, but also an anvil, like M. E. *stethi.*

Stiver, a Dutch penny. (Du.) Du. *stuiver*, a small coin. Perhaps orig. 'bit' or small piece. Franck connects it with Low G. *stuuf*, stumpy, Icel. *stūfr*, a stump, Icel. *stȳfa*, to cut off.

Stoat, an animal. (Scand.) A late word; *stote*, Phillips, 1706; Levins, 1570. M. E. *stot*, a stoat, also a bull, stallion. See **Stot.**

Stoccado, Stoccata, a thrust in fencing. (Ital. – Teut.) *Stoccado* is an accommodated form, as if it were Spanish. – Ital. *stoccata*, 'a foyne, thrust,' Florio. – Ital. *stocco*, 'a short sword, a tuck,' Florio; with pp. suffix *-ata.* – G. *stock*, a stick, staff, trunk, stump; cognate with E. stock.

stock, a post, &c. (E.) The old sense

was a stump; hence a post, trunk, stem, a fixed store, fund, capital, cattle, stalk, butt-end of a gun, &c. A. S. *stocc*, stock, stump. + G. *stock*, O. H. G. *stoch*; Du. *stok*, Icel. *stokkr*, Dan. *stok*, Swed. *stock*. Allied to A. S. *stykke*, G. *stück*, a bit, fragment.

Stockade, a breastwork formed of stakes. (Span. – Teut.) Coined as if from E. *stock* (above); but adapted from Span. *estacada*, a palisade, fence. – Span. *estaca*, a stake, pale. – M. Du. *stake*, Du. *staak*, a stake; see **Stake.**

Stocking. (E.) *Stocking* is a dimin. form of *stock*, used as short for *nether-stock*. 'Un bas des chausses, *a stocking, or nether-stock*;' Cot. The clothing of the lower part of the body consisted of a single garment, called *hose*, in F. *chausses*. It was afterwards cut in two at the knees, and divided into *upper-stocks*, and *nether-stocks* or *stockings*. In this case, *stock* means a piece or stump, a piece cut off; see **Stock.**

Stoic. (L. – Gk.) L. *Stoicus*. – Gk. Στωϊκός, a Stoic; lit. 'belonging to a colonnade,' because Zeno taught under a colonnade at Athens. – Gk. στοά, στοιά (for *στοϝ-γά*), a colonnade, row of pillars; cf. στῦ-λος, a pillar. (√STEU.)

Stoker, one who tends a fire. (Du.) Orig. used to mean one who looked after a fire in a brew-house (Phillips). – Du. *stoker*, 'a kindler, or setter on fire,' Hexham. – Du. *stoken*, to kindle a fire, stir a fire. Allied to Du. *stok*, a stock, stick (hence, a poker for a fire); cognate with **Stock.** Cf. Westphal. *stoken*, to poke a fire.

Stole, long robe, scarf. (L. – Gk.) L. *stola*. – Gk. στολή, equipment, robe, stole. – Gk. στέλλειν, to equip.

Stolid, stupid. (L.) L. *stolidus*, firm, stock-like, stupid.

Stomach. (F. – L. – Gk.) M.E. *stomak*. – O. F. *estomac*. – L. acc. *stomachum*. – Gk. στόμαχος, mouth, gullet, stomach; dimin. of στόμα, mouth. Brugm. i. § 421.

Stone. (E.) M. E. *stoon*. A. S. *stán*. + Du. *steen*, Icel. *steinn*, Dan. Swed. *sten*, G. *stein*, Goth. *stains*. Cf. Gk. στία, a stone; O. Bulgarian *stěna*, Russ. *stiena*, a wall. **Der.** *stan-iel*.

Stook, a shock of corn. (E.) It answers to A. S. **stóc*, from **stók-*, strong grade of **stak-*, as in E. **Stack.**+Low G. *stuke*, a stook; Swed. dial. *stuke*.

Stool. (E.) M. E. *stool*. A. S. *stól*, seat.+Du. *stoel*, Icel. *stóll*, Dan. Swed.

stol, Goth. *stols*, seat, chair; G. *stuhl*, chair, pillar. Lit. 'that which stands firm.' (√STĀ.) Brugm. i. § 191.

Stoop (1), to lean forward. (E.) Prov. E. *stowp*; M. E. *stoupen*. A. S. *stūpian*. +M. Du. *stuypen*, O. Icel. *stūpa*, to stoop; Swed. *stupa*, to tilt, fall. Allied to **Steep** (1).

Stoop (2), a beaker; see **Stoup.**

Stop. (L.) Of L. origin. M. E. *stoppen*, A. S. *-stoppian*, to stop up; so also Du. *stoppen*, to stop, stuff, cram, Swed. *stoppa*, Dan. *stoppe*, G. *stopfen*; Ital. *stoppare*, to stop up with tow, Late L. *stuppāre*, to stop up with tow, cram, stop. All from L. *stupa*, *stuppa*, coarse part of flax, hards, oakum, tow. Cf. Gk. στύπη, στύππη, the same. **Der.** *stopp-le*, i. e. *stopper*; also *estop*, A. F. *estoper*, from Late L. *stuppāre*.

Storax, a resinous gum. (L. – Gk.) L. *storax*, *styrax*. – Gk. στύραξ.

Store, sb. (F. – L.) M. E. *stor*, *stoor*, provisions. – O. F. *estor*, store, provisions (Godefroy); Late L. *staurum*, the same as *instaurum*, store. – L. *instaurāre*, to construct, build, restore; Late L. *instaurāre*, to provide necessaries. – L. *in*, in; **staurāre*, to set up, place, also found in *re-staurāre*, to restore. From an adj. **staurus* = Skt. *sthāvara-*, fixed; cf. Gk. σταυρός, an upright pole. (√STĀ.) **Der.** *store*, vb., O. F. *estorer*, from Late L. *staurāre = instaurāre*.

Stork, bird. (E.) A. S. *storc*.+Du. *stork*, Icel. *storkr*, Dan. and Swed. *stork*; G. *storch*. Cf. Gk. τόργος, a large bird (vulture, swan). Prob. allied to **Stark.**

Storm. (E.) A. S. *storm*, storm.+Icel. *stormr*, Du. Swed. Dan. *storm*, G. *sturm*. Teut. type **stur-moz*. From the same root as E. **Stir.**

Story (1). (F. – L. – Gk.) M. E. *storie*. – A. F. *storie* (Bartsch), O. F. *estoire*, a history, tale. – L. *historia*. – Gk. ἱστορία, information; see **History.**

Story (2), set of rooms on a level or flat. (F. – L.) Orig. merely 'a building' or 'thing built.' – O. F. *estorée*, a thing built; fem. of pp. of *estorer*, to build. – Late L. *staurāre*, for L. *instaurāre*, to construct, build, &c. See **Store.** **Der.** *clere-story*, i. e. *clear-story*, story lighted with windows, as distinct from *blind-story*.

Stot, stallion, bullock. (E.) M. E. *stot*. Cf. Icel. *stútr*, a bull, Swed. *stut*, Dan. *stud*, a bull; allied to Swed. *stöta*, to push, G. *stossen*.

Stoup, Stoop, flagon. (M. Du.) M. E.
stope. – M. Du. *stoop,* a large cup (Kilian);
Du. *stoop,* a gallon; cf. Icel. *staup,* a
knobby lump, also a stoup; Low G. *stoop,*
a stoup (whence Swed. *stop,* three pints;
Dan. dial. *stob,* a stoup). + A. S. *stēap,*
a cup; G. *stauf,* a cup. Allied to A. S.
stēap, steep; perhaps as being high and
upright; see **Steep** (1), and **Stoop.**

Stout. (F. – O. Low G.) M. E. *stout.* –
O. F. *estout,* stout, bold. – M. Du. *stolt,*
stout, stout, bold; Low G. *stolt,* A. S. *stolt,*
the same. + G. *stolz,* proud. Perhaps all
from L. *stultus,* foolish, foolhardy. **Der.**
stout, sb., a strong beer.

Stove. (E.) A. S. *stofa.* +M. Du. *stove,*
'a stewe, hot-house, or a baine,' Hexham; Low G. *stove;* cf. Icel. *stofa, stufa,*
a bath-room with a stove; G. *stube,*
O.H.G. *stupa,* a room (whence Ital. *stufa,*
F. *étuve*). See **Stew.**

Stover, food for cattle. (F. – L.?) In
Shak.; M. E. *stouer* (*stover*), necessaries.
– O. F. *estover, estovoir,* necessaries; orig.
the infin. mood of a verb which was used
impersonally with the sense 'it is necessary.'
Perhaps from L. *est opus* (Tobler).

Stow, to pack away. (E.) M. E. *stowen,*
lit. to put in a place. – A. S. *stōwigan*
(Sweet); from *stōw,* a place. +Icel. *eld-stō,*
fire-place. Also Lith. *stowa,* place where
a thing stands, from *stōti,* to stand.
(√STA.)

Straddle. (E.) Formerly *striddle*
(Levins); frequentative of **Stride.**

Straggle. (E.) Formerly *stragle.*
For *strackle;* cf. prov. E. *strackle-brained,*
thoughtless. Apparently the frequentative
of M. E. *strāken,* to roam, wander; P.
Plowman's Crede, 82; with *ā* shortened
before *k-l.* Allied to **Strike.** Perhaps
Swed. dial. *strakla,* to stagger, totter, is
related.

Straight. (E.) M. E. *streiȝt,* orig. pp.
of M. E. *strecchen,* to stretch; A. S. *streht,*
pp. of *streccan,* to stretch; see **Stretch.**
Der. *straight,* adv., M. E. *streiȝt; straight-
way; straight-en.*

Strain (1), vb. (F. – L.) From *estraign-,*
a stem of M. F. *estraindre,* 'to wring hard;'
Cot. – L. *stringere,* to draw tight. See
Stringent.

Strain (2), descent, lineage, birth. (E.)
Strain in Shak.; *strene* in Spenser. M. E.
streen, Chaucer, C.T., Cl. Tale, 157. A.S.
strēon, gain, product, lineage, progeny;
whence *strȳnan,* to beget.

Strait, adj. (F. – L.) M. E. *streit.* –
A. F. *estreit* (F. *étroit*), narrow, strict. –
L. *strictum,* acc. of *strictus;* see **Strict.**

Strand (1), shore. (E.) A. S. *strand.* +
Icel. *strönd* (gen. *strandar*), margin, edge;
Dan. Swed. G. *strand.*

Strand (2), thread of a rope. (Du.)
The final *d* is added. – Du. *streen,* a skein,
hank of thread. + G. *strähne,* a skein,
hank, O. H. G. *streno.* Cf. Du. *striem,*
a stripe.

Strange, foreign, odd. (F. – L.) O. F.
estrange. – L. *extrāneum,* acc. of *extrāneus,* foreign, on the outside. – L. *extrā,*
without. See **Extra** and **Estrange.**

Strangle, to choke. (F. – L. – Gk.)
O. F. *estrangler.* – L. *strangulāre.* – Gk.
στραγγαλόειν, στραγγαλίζειν, to strangle.
– Gk. στραγγάλη, a halter. – Gk. στραγγός,
twisted. Allied to **String** and **Strict.**

strangury. (L. – Gk.) L. *strangūria.*
– Gk. στραγγουρία, retention of urine, when
it falls by drops. – Gk. στραγγ-, base of
στράγξ, a drop, that which oozes out (allied
to στραγγός, twisted); οὖρ-ον, urine.

Strap. (L.) Prov. E. *strop;* A. S.
stropp. – L. *struppus* (also *stroppus*), a
strap, thong, fillet. (Hence F. *étrope.*)

Strappado. (Ital. – Teut.) A modified
form of *strappata* (just as *stoccado* was used
for *stoccata*). – Ital. *strappata,* a pulling, a
wringing the strappado. – Ital. *strappare,*
to pull, wring. – H. G. (Swiss) *strapfen,*
to pull tight, allied to G. *straff,* tight,
borrowed from Low G. or Du. – Du. *straf-
fen,* to punish, from *straf,* severe; cf. E.
Fries. *strabben,* to be stiff.

Stratagem. (F. – L. – Gk.) M.F.
stratageme. – L. *stratēgēma.* – Gk. στρατή-
γημα, the device of a general. – Gk. στρατηγός, general, leader. – Gk. στρατ-ός, army,
camp; ἄγ-ειν, to lead. The Gk. στρατός
is allied to στόρνυμι, I spread. See
Stratum.

strategy. (F. – L. – Gk.) F. *stratégie.*
– L. *stratēgia.* – Gk. στρατηγία, general-
ship. – Gk. στρατηγός (above).

Strath, a flat valley. (C.) Gael. *srath,*
a valley with a river, low-lying country beside a river; Irish *srath, sratha,* the bottom
of a valley, fields beside a river; W. *ystrad,*
a flat vale. Allied to **Stratum** (below).

Stratum. (L.) L. *strātum,* a layer,
that which is spread flat; neut. of *strātus,*
pp. of *sternerè,* to spread. + Gk. στόρνυμι,
I spread out. (√STER.)

Straw, sb. (E.) A. S. *streaw* (*streow*).

+Du. *stroo*, Icel. *strā*, Dan. *straa*, Swed. *strå*, G. *stroh*. Teut. type **strawom*, n. Allied to L. *strāmen*, straw, *sternere*, to strew; see **Strew, Stratum.**

straw-berry. (E.) A.S. *streawberige*, straw-berry; perhaps from its propagation by runners; cf. *strew.*

Stray, to wander. (F. − L.) O.F. *estraier*, to wander; orig. to rove about the streets or ways. Cf. Prov. *estradier*, a wanderer in the streets, one who strays, from Prov. *estrada* (= O.F. *estree*), a street; M. Ital. *stradiotto*, a wanderer, from *strada*, street. − L. *strāta*, a street; see **Street.** **Der.** *stray*, *estray*, sb.

Streak, a line or long mark. (E.) M. E. *streke*, more commonly *strike*. A.S. *strica*, from **stric-*, weak grade of *strīcan*, to stroke, rub. Cf. E. Fries. *streke*, *sträke*, a stroke, streak; Du. *streek*; Swed. *streck*, a dash, streak, line; Dan. *streg*, the same. Also Goth. *striks*, a stroke with the pen; G. *strich*, from Teut. **strik*, weak grade of **streikan-*; see **Strike.** Cf. also L. *striga*, a swath, furrow.

Stream. (E.) A.S. *strēam*. **+** Du. *stroom*, Icel. *straumr*, Swed. Dan. *ström*, G. *strom*. Teut. type **straumoz*, m. Allied to Russ. *struia*, Irish *sruaim*, a stream. All from √SREU, to flow, which in Teut. and Russ. became STREU; cf. Skt. *sru*, Gk. ῥέειν (for **σρέϝ-ειν*), to flow. Cf. **Rheum.**

Street. (L.) A.S. *strêt*; O. Merc. *strēt* ; a very early loan-word; cf. Du. *straat*, G. *strasse*. − L. *strāta*, i. e. *strāta uia*, a paved way ; *strāta* being fem. of pp. of *sternere*, to strew, pave.

Strength. (E.) A.S. *strengðu*; (for **strang-i-thu*). − A.S. *strang*, strong. See **Strong.**

Strenuous. (L.) L. *strēnu-us*, vigorous, active; with suffix *-ous*. **+** Gk. στρηνής, strong, allied to στερεός, firm.

Stress, strain. (F. − L.) Sometimes short for *distress*; see **Distress.** Otherwise, from O. F. *estrecier*, *estressier*, to straiten, pinch, contract. This answers to a Folk-L. type **strectiāre*, regularly formed from L. *strictus*, tightened ; see **Strict.**

Stretch. (E.) M. E. *strecchen*. − A.S. *streccan*, pt. t. *strehte*, pp. *streht*. Formed as a causal verb from A. S. *stræc*, hard, rigid, violent, strong. Thus *stretch* = to make stiff or hard, as in straining a cord. **+**Du. *strekken*, to stretch, from *strak*, stretched, tight, rigid; Dan. *strække*, Swed.

sträcka ; G. *strecken*, from *strack*, adj., tight. Perhaps allied to **Strong.**

Strew, Straw, vb. (E.) M. E. *strewen*. A. S. *streowian*, to strew, scatter. Closely allied to A. S. *streaw*, straw. **+**Du. *strooijen*, to strew, allied to *stroo*, straw ; G. *streuen*, to strew, allied to *stroh*, straw ; Goth. *straujan* (pt. t. *strawida*), to strew. From a derivative of the root STER, as in L. *ster-nere* (pt. t. *sträui*), to strew ; cf. Gk. στόρνυμι, I spread ; Skt. *str̥*, to spread. See **Stratum.** Brugm. i. § 570. **Der.** *be-strew.*

Stricken ; see **Strike.**

Strict. (L.) L. *strictus*, pp. of *stringere*, to tighten, draw together, &c. See **Stringent. Doublet,** *strait.*

Stride, vb. (E.) M. E. *striden*, pt. t. *strad*, *strood*. A. S. *strīdan*, to stride, pt. t. *strād* (rare ; but cf. *bestrād*, Ælf. Hom. ii. 136). So also Low G. *striden* (pt. t. *streed*), to strive, to stride ; Du. *strijden*, G. *streiten*, Dan. *stride*, strong verbs, to strive, contend ; Icel. *strīða*, Swed. *strida*, weak verbs, to strive. β. Teut. type **streidan-*, pt. t. **straid*, pp. **stridanoz* ; whence also Icel. *strīð*, woe, strife ; *strīðr*, hard, stubborn. Cf. Skt. *sridh*, to assail ; also, an enemy. The orig. sense was ' to contend,' hence to take long steps (as if in contention with another). **Der.** *bestride, strid, straddle, strife, strive.*

strife. (F. − Scand.) O.F. *estrif*, strife. Apparently modified from Icel. *strīð*, strife, contention. Cf. O. Sax. and O. Fries. *strīd*, strife ; Du. *strijd*; G. *streit*. From the verb **Stride** (above). ¶ The connexion with G. *streben*, Du. *streven*, is obscure. **Der.** *strive*, vb., q. v.

Strike, to hit. (E.) M. E. *striken*, orig. to proceed, advance, or flow ; hence used of smooth swift motion, to strike with a rod or sword. The verb is strong ; pt. t. *strak*, pp. *striken* ; the phrase ' *stricken* in years' meant ' *advanced* in years.' A.S. *strīcan*, to go, proceed, advance swiftly and smoothly ; pt. t. *strāc*, pp. *stricen*. **+**Du. *strijken*, to smooth, rub, stroke, spread, strike ; G. *streichen*, the same. [Cf. Icel. *strjūka*, to stroke, rub, wipe, strike ; Swed. *stryka*, Dan. *stryge*, the same.] Allied to L. *stringere*, to graze, touch lightly with a swift motion ; *striga*, a row of mown hay. **Der.** *strike*, sb., the name of a measure, orig. an instrument with a straight edge for levelling (striking off) a measure of grain. Also *streak, stroke.*

String. (E.) A.S. *strenge*, cord; from its being tightly twisted. − A.S. *strang*, strong, violent. Cf. Gk. στραγγάλη, a halter; from στραγγός, tightly twisted. + Du. *streng*, string, allied to *streng*, severe; so also Icel. *strengr*, Dan. *stræng*, Swed. *sträng*, G. *strang*, cord, string. See **Strong.**

Stringent. (L.) L. *stringent*-, stem of pres. pt. of *stringere*, to draw tight, compress, urge, also to graze, stroke; pp. *strictus*. Perhaps allied to **Strike.**

Strip. (E.) M.E. *stripen.* A.S. *striepan*, *strýpan*, to plunder, strip; in comp. *be-strýpan.* + Du. *stroopen*, to plunder; E. Fries. *stropen*, *strōpen*; G. *streifen*, from M.H.G. *stroufen.* Teut. type *straupjan-*; from the 2nd grade of the strong verb *streupan*, for which cf. Norw. *strūpa*, to grip, to throttle, pt. t. *straup.* **Der.** *strip*, sb., a piece stripped off; see below.

Stripe. (Du.) Orig. a streak; M.E. *stripe*; not an old word; prob. a weaver's term. − M. Du. *strijpe*, a stripe in cloth, variant of *strepe* (Kilian); Du. *streep*; Low G. *stripe*, a stripe. + Norw. *stripa*, Dan. *stribe*, a stripe, streak; G. *streifen*, M.H.G. *streif.* From a Teut. base *streip*, allied to *streik*; see **Strike.** Cf. O. Irish *sríab*, a stripe. ¶ Low G. *stripe*, a stripe, also means a strip of cloth; although *strip* belongs strictly to the verb above.

Stripling. (E.) A double dimin. from *strip*, variant of *stripe*; hence a lad as thin as a *strip*, a growing lad not yet filled out.

Strive. (F. − Scand.) M.E. *striuen* (*striven*), properly a weak verb. − O.F. *estriver*, to strive; Walloon *striver.* − O.F. *estrif*, strife; see **Strife.**

Stroke (1), a blow. (E.) M.E. *strook.* From *strāc*, 2nd grade of A.S. *strīcan*, to strike. Cf. G. *streich*, a stroke.

stroke (2), to rub gently. (E.) M.E. *stroken.* A.S. *strācian*, to stroke; a causal verb; from *strāc*, 2nd grade of *strīcan*, to strike. Cf. G. *streicheln*, to stroke, from *streichen*, to stroke; see **Strike.**

Stroll, to wander. (F. − Teut.) Formerly *stroule*, *stroyle.* Formed by prefixing *s*- (O.F. *es*-, L. *ex*) to *troll*, used (in P. Pl.) with the sense 'to range'; see **Troll.** Cf. Guernsey *étreûlaï* [= *estreulé*], adj., idle, vagabond (Métivier; who notes that, at Valognes, dep. Manche, the equivalent term is *treulier*, i.e. 'troller'); cf. Norm. dial. *treuler*, to rove (Moisy), dial. of Verdun *trôler*, *trauler.*

Strong. (E.) A.S. *strang*, *strong.* + Du. *streng*, Icel. *strangr*, Dan. *streng*, Swed. *sträng*; G. *streng*, strict. Cf. Gk. στραγγός, tightly twisted.

Strop, a piece of leather, for sharpening razors. (L.) A.S. *stropp*, a strap, from L.; see **Strap.** Cf. Westphal. *strop.*

Strophe, part of a poem or dance. (Gk.) Gk. στροφή, a turning; the turning of the chorus, dancing to one side of the orchestra, or the strain sung during this evolution; the *strophe*, to which the *antistrophe* answers. − Gk. στρέφειν, to turn.

Strow; see **Strew.**

Structure. (F. − L.) F. *structure.* − L. *structūra*, a structure. − L. *structus*, pp. of *struere*, to build, orig. to heap together.

Struggle, vb. (F. − M. Du. ?) M.E. *strogelen*, *strugelen*; apparently from A.F. *es-* (L. *ex*) prefixed to M. Du. *truggelen* (Du. *troggelen*), Low G. *truggeln*, to beg persistently, which prob. also had the same sense as E. Fries. *trüggeln*, to struggle against, as when a horse jibs or refuses to move forward, also to beg persistently. All from Teut. base *thrüg-*, as in Icel. *þrúga*, Dan. *true*, to press, ultimately related to A.S. *þryccan*, G. *drücken*, to press. (Doubtful.)

Strum, to thrum on a piano. (E.) An imitative word. Made by prefixing an intensive *s*- (= O.F. *es*- = L. *ex*) very, to the imitative word *trum* (also *thrum*), as seen in Low G. *trummen*, Du. *trommen*, to drum; see **Drum** and **Thrum.**

Strumpet. (F. − Teut. ?) M.E. *strompet.* The form answers to O.F. *estrompette* (not found), as if from M. Du. *strompe*, a stocking. Or (if the *m* be an insertion) it is from O.F. *strupe*, Late L. *strupum*, dishonour, violation; from L. *stuprum.* (Unexplained.)

Strut (1), to walk about pompously. (Scand.) M.E. *strouten*, to spread or swell out. − Swed. dial. *strutta*, to walk with a jolting step; Dan. *strutte*, *strude*, to strut; cf. Norw. *strut*, a spout that sticks out, a nozzle. The orig. sense seems to be 'to stick out stiffly'; cf. Icel. *strūtr*, a hood sticking out like a horn; Low G. *strutt*, rigid. + G. *strotzen*, to strut, be puffed up; cf. *strauss*, a tuft, bunch.

strut (2), a support for a rafter. (Scand.) Orig. a stiff piece of wood; from *strut*, to stick out or up. Cf. Icel. *strūtr*, Low G. *strutt* (above).

Strychnine. (Gk.) From Gk. στρύχ-

vos, nightshade, poison; with F. suffix *-ine*.

Stub, stump of a tree. (E.) A. S. *stybb*, a stub; E. Fries. *stubbe*.+Du. *stobbe*, Icel. *stubbi*, Dan. *stub*, Swed. *stubbe*. Allied to Icel. *stūfr*, a stump (Noreen); and see Stab. Also to Gk. στύπος, a stump, Skt. *stūpa-*, a heap. Allied to **Stump**.

Stubble. (F. — Late L.) M. E. *stobil*, *stoble*. — A. F. *estuble*, O. F. *estouble*. — Late L. *stupula*, *stupla*, stubble; a variant of L. *stipula*, stubble, due to the influence of Low G. *stoppel*, stubble (Lübben), Du. and E. Fries. *stoppel*, cognate with M. H. G. *stupfel*, O. H. G. *stupfila*, stubble.

Stubborn. (E.) M. E. *stoburn*, *stiborn*; also *stibornesse*, *stybornesse*, stubbornness, for which Palsgrave has *stubblenesse*. The final *n* is prob. due to misunderstanding *stibornesse* as *stiborn-nesse*; in any case, it has been added; cf. *bitter-n*, *slatter-n*. *Stubor*, *stibor* represent an A. S. form *styb-or*; *-or* being a common adj. suffix, as in *bit-or*, bitter. From A. S. *stybb*, a stub. Thus *stubborn* = stock-like, not easily moved, like an old stub or stump. See **Stub**.

Stucco. (Ital. — O. H. G.) Ital. *stucco*, hardened, encrusted; stucco. — O. H. G. *stucchi*, a crust; G. *stück*, a piece, patch; cognate with A. S. *stycce*, a piece, bit. Allied to **Stock**.

Stud (1), a collection of breeding-horses and mares. (E.) M. E. *stood*. A. S. *stōd*, a stud; orig. an establishment or herd in a stall.+Icel. *stōð*, Dan. *stod*, M. H. G. *stuot* (whence G. *gestüt*). Cf. Russ. *stado*, a herd or drove, Lith. *stodas*, a drove of horses. (√STĀ.) Der. *stud-horse*, steed.

Stud (2), a rivet, large-headed nail, &c. (E.) Also a stout post, prop; hence a projection, boss, support. — A. S. *studu*, *stuþu*, a post.+Icel. *stoð*, Swed. *stöd*, a post; Dan. *stöd*, stub, stump; G. *stütze*, a prop. Cf. Gk. στῦ-λος, a pillar. (√STEU, allied to √STĀ.)

Student. (L.) From L. *student-*, stem of pres. pt. of *studēre*, to be busy about, to study.

study, sb. (F. — L.) M. E. *studie*. — A. F. *estudie* (F. *étude*). — L. *studium*, zeal, study. Der. *studio*, Ital. *studio*, a school, from L. *studium*.

Stuff, materials. (F. — L.) O. F. *estoffe*, 'stuffe;' Cot.; Walloon *stoff* (Remacle). — L. *stupa*, *stuppa*, the coarse part of flax, hards, tow; the pronunciation of this L.

word being Germanised before it passed into French (Diez). Cf. G. *stoff*, stuff, materials. β. The sense of the L. word is better preserved in the verb *to stuff*, i. e. to cram, to stop up, M. F. *estouffer*, to stifle (Cot.), G. *stopfen*, to fill, stuff, quilt, from Late L. *stuppāre*, to stop up; whence also E. **Stop**, q. v.

stuffy, close, stifling. (F. — L.) From O. F. *estouffer*, to choke (F. *étouffer*); the same as O. F. *estoffer*, to stuff or cram up. Cf. Walloon *stofé*, stifled (Remacle). — O. F. *estoffe*, stuff (above). ¶ So Scheler, disputing the suggestion of Diez, who needlessly goes to the Gk. τῦφος, smoke, mist, in order to explain *estoffe*.

Stultify. (L.) Coined, with suffix *-fy* (F. *-fier*, L. *-ficāre*), from L. *stulti-*, for *stultus*, foolish.

Stumble, vb. (E.) The *b* is excrescent. M. E. *stomblen*, *stomelen*, *stumlen*; also *stomeren*. E. Fries. *stummeln*, to go stumbling along; cf. Dan. dial. *stumle*, to stumble; Icel. *stumra*, Norw. *stumra*, to stumble; Swed. dial. *stambla*, *stomla*, *stammra*, to stumble, falter. From the base *stum*. Practically a doublet of *stammer*, with reference to hesitation of the step instead of the speech; see **Stammer**. Cf. O. Sax. and O. H. G. *stum*, mute.

Stump. (E.) M. E. *stumpe*; E. Fries. *stump*.+Icel. *stumpr*, Swed. Dan. *stump*, stump, end, bit; Du. *stomp*; G. *stumpf*, Allied to G. *stumpf*, blunt, stumpy; Du. *stomp*, blunt. Also to Lith. *stambras*, stalk of grass, &c. Brugm. i. § 424.

Stun, to make a loud din, to amaze, esp. with a blow. (E.) M. E. *stonien*. A. S. *stunian*, to make a din; *ge-stun*, a din. Cf. Icel. *stynja*, to groan, *stynr*, a groan; Du. *stenen*, G. *stöhnen*, to groan, Russ. *sten-ate*, Lith. *sten-èti*, Gk. στέι-ειν, to groan; Skt. *stan*, to sound, to thunder. (√STEN.) Brugm. i. § 818 (2). And see **Thunder**.

Stunted, hindered in growth. (E.) From A. S. *stunt*, adj., dull, obtuse, stupid, orig. 'short;' hence, metaphorically, short of wit; also not well grown; but the peculiar sense is Scand. + Icel. *stuttr* (for *stuntr*), short, stunted (Noreen); M.Swed. *stunt*, cut short. Cf. **Stint**.

Stupefy. (F. — L.) F. *stupéfier*; due to L. *stupefacere*, to stupefy; cf. F. *stupéfait*, pp., directly from L. *stupefactus*, made stupid. — L. *stupē-re*, to be stupid; *facere*, to make.

stupendous. (L.) For L. *stupend-us*, amazing, to be wondered at, gerundive of *stupēre*, to be amazed; with suffix *-ous*.

stupid. (F. – L.) F. *stupide.* – L. *stupidus*, senseless. – L. *stupēre*, to be amazed.

Sturdy. (F.) It formerly meant rash or reckless; hence, brave, bold. M. E. *sturdi*, *stordy*, rash. – O. F. *estourdi*, amazed, also rash, heedless; pp. of *estourdir*, 'to amaze;' Cot. (Mod. F. *étourdir*, Ital. *stordire*, to stun, amaze.) Of unknown origin; see Körting.

Sturgeon, a fish. (F. – O. H. G.) O. F. *estourgeon*, *esturgeon*; Late L. acc. *sturiōnem*, from nom. *sturio.* – O. H. G. *sturjo*, *sturo*, a sturgeon. Sometimes explained as 'a stirrer,' because it stirs up mud by floundering at the bottom of the water; cf. O. H. G. *stören*, to spread, stir (G. *stören*); see **Stir.** + A. S. *styria*, *styriga*, a sturgeon, as if from *styrian*, to stir; Swed. Dan. *stör*, sturgeon, as if from Swed. *störa*, to stir; Icel. *styrja*; Du. *steur* (see Franck). Origin doubtful.

Stutter. (E.) Frequentative of *stut*, once common in the same sense. 'I *stutte*, I can nat speake my wordes redyly;' Palsgrave. M. E. *stoten*. Cf. E. Fries. *stuttern*, to stutter; Du. *stotteren* (whence G. *stottern*). From M. E. *stot-* (Teut. **stut*) weak grade of Teut. root **steut*, for which cf. Du. *stuiten*, to stop; 2nd grade **staut*, as in Icel. *stauta*, to beat, strike, also to stutter, Swed. *stöta*, Dan. *stöde*, to strike against, G. *stossen*, Goth. *stautan*, to strike. Orig. 'to strike against,' to trip. (√STEUD; from the weak grade come Skt. *tud*, L. *tundere*, to strike.)

Sty (1), enclosure for swine. (E.) M.E. *stie.* A. S. *stigu*, a sty, a pen for cattle. + Icel. *stía*, *stí*, sty, kennel, Swed. *stia*, pig-sty, pen for geese, Swed. dial. *sti*, *steg*, pen for swine, goats, or sheep, G. *steige*, pen, chicken-coop, O. H. G. *stīa*.

Sty (2), small tumour on the eyelid. (E.) The A. S. name was *stīgend*, lit. 'rising;' as if from the pres. pt. of *stīgan*, to ascend, climb, rise; but this is doubtful. M. E. *styanye*, as if it meant 'sty on eye.' + Low G. *stieg*, *stige*, sty on the eye, as if from *stigen*, to rise; E. Fries. *stiger*; Norw. *stig*, *stigje*, also *stigköyna* (from *köyna*, a pustule).

Style (1), a pointed tool for writing, a mode of writing. (F. – L.) It should be

stile, as it is not Gk. M. E. *stile.* – M. F. *stile*, *style*, 'a stile, manner of indicting;' Cot. – L. *stilus*, an iron pin for writing; a way of writing. Der. *stiletto*.

Style (2), the middle part of the pistil of a flower; gnomon of a dial. (Gk.) Gk. στῦλος, a pillar, long upright body like a pillar. Cf. Skt. *sthūṇā*, a pillar, post. (√STEU, by-form of √STĀ.)

Styptic, astringent. (F. – L. – Gk.) F. *styptique.* – L. *stypticus.* – Gk. στυπτικός, astringent. – Gk. στύφειν, to contract, draw together, to be astringent; orig. to make firm; allied to στύπος, a stump, stem, block.

Suasion, advice. (F. – L.) M. F. *suasion.* – L. acc. *suāsiōnem*; from *suāsio*, persuasion. – L. *suāsus*, pp. of *suādēre*, to persuade, lit. 'to make sweet.' Allied to *suāuis* (= **suaduis*), sweet. See **Sweet.** Brugm. i. § 187.

suave, pleasant. (F. – L.) F. *suave*; Cot. – L. *suāuis*, sweet (above).

Sub-, prefix. (L., *or* F. – L.) L. (and F.) *sub-*, prefix. Orig. form **sup*; whence the comparative form *sup-er*, above, allied to Skt. *upari*, above. The prefix *s-* prob. answers to Gk. ἐξ; cf. *s-uper* with ἐξύπερθε, 'from above.' *Sub* seems to have meant 'up to'; hence it also came to mean just under or below; it is allied to E. **Up**, q. v., and to Gk. ὑπό; see **Hypo-.** ¶ *Sub* becomes *suc-* before *c*, *suf-* before *f*, *sug-* before *g*, *sum-* before *m*, *sup-* before *p*, *sur-* before *r*; and see **Sus-** (below).

Subaltern, inferior to another. (F. – L.) F. *subalterne*; Cot. – L. *subalternus*, subordinate. – L. *sub*, under; *alter*, another.

Subaqueous, under water. (L.) L. *sub*, under; *aqua*, water. See **Aqueous.**

Subdivide. (L.) L. *sub*, under; and *dīuidere*, to divide. See **Divide.** Der. *subdivision* (from the pp.).

Subdue. (F. – L.) M. E. *soduen* (afterwards 'learnedly' altered to *subdue*). First used in the pp. *sodued*, *sodewed.* – A. F. **subdut*, as in *subduz* (for *subduts*), pp. pl., subdued. – Late L. **subdutus*, for L. *subditus*, subdued. – L. *subdere*, to subdue. – L. *sub*, under; *-dere*, to put, weak grade of √DHĒ, to put. ¶ Not from L. *subdūcere*, with an alien sense.

Subjacent. (L.) From stem of pres. pt. of L. *sub-iacēre*, to lie under. – L. *sub*, under; *iacēre*, to lie. See **Jet** (1).

subject. (F. – L.) M.E. *suget*, *subjet.* – O. F. *suiet*, *suiect* (later *subiect*), mod. F. *sujet*, a subject. – L. *subiectus*, pp. of *sub-*

icere, to put under, subject. — L. *sub*, under ; *iacere*, to cast, to put.

Subjoin. (F.–L.) M. F. *subjoign-*, a stem of *subjoindre*.—L. *subiungere*, to join beneath, annex, subjoin.—L. *sub*, beneath ; *iungere*, to join. See Join.

subjugate, to bring under the yoke. (L.) From pp. of L. *subiugāre*, vb. — L. *sub iugō*, under the yoke; where *iugō* is abl. of *iugum*, a yoke. See Yoke.

subjunctive. (L.) L. *subiunctīuus*, lit. joining on dependently, from the use of the subjunctive mood in dependent clauses. —L. *subiunctus*, pp. of *subiungere*, to subjoin; see Subjoin (above).

Sublime. (F.–L.) F. *sublime*. — L. *sublīmis*, lofty, raised on high. Perhaps from L. *sub*, and *līmen*, lintel ; ' up to the lintel ;' Brugm. ii. § 12.

Sublunar, under the moon, earthly. (L.) Coined from L. *sub*, under ; and E. *lunar*, belonging to the moon, from L. *lūna*, moon ; see Lunar.

Submerge, to plunge under water. (F. —L.) F. *submerger*. — L. *submergere*. — L. *sub*, under ; *mergere*, to dip ; see Merge.

Submit. (L.) L. *submittere*, to let down, submit, bow to (pp. *submissus*).— L. *sub*, under ; *mittere*, to send. See Missile. Der. *submiss-ion, -ive*.

Subordinate, of lower rank. (L.) From the pp. of Late L. *subordināre*, to place in a lower rank.—L. *sub*, below ; *ordināre*, to rank, from *ordin-*, stem of *ordo*, order. See Order.

Suborn, to procure secretly, bribe. (F. —L.) F. *suborner*. — L. *subornāre*. — L. *sub*, secretly ; *ornāre*, to furnish, properly, to adorn. See Ornament.

Subpœna, a writ, commanding attendance under a penalty. (L.) L. *sub*, under ; *pœnā*, abl. of *pœna*, a penalty. See Pain.

Subscribe. (L.) L. *subscrībere*, to write (one's name) under ; pp. *subscriptus* (whence *subscription*). — L. *sub*, under ; *scrībere*, to write. See Scribe.

Subsequent. (L.) From stem of pres. pt. of *subsequī*, to follow close after. — L. *sub*, under, near ; *sequī*, to follow. See Sequence.

Subserve. (L.) L. *subseruīre*, to serve under another. — L. *sub*, under ; *seruīre*, to serve. See Serve.

Subside. (L.) L. *subsīdere*, to settle down. — L. *sub*, under, down ; *sīdere*, to

settle, allied to *sedēre*, to sit. See Sedentary. Brugm. i. § 882.

subsidy. (F. — L.) A. F. *subsidie* (Godefroy) ; F. *subside*. — L. *subsidium*, a body of troops in reserve, assistance ; lit. that which sits in reserve. — L. *sub*, under, in reserve ; *sedēre*, to sit. Der. *subsidi-ary*, from L. adj. *subsidiārius*.

Subsist, to live, continue. (F.–L.) F. *subsister*, 'to subsist ;' Cot. — L. *subsistere*, to stay, abide. — L *sub*, near to ; *sistere*, to stand, also to place, from *stāre*, to stand. See State.

substance. (F.–L.) F. *substance*.— L. *substantia*, substance, essence.—L. *substant-*, stem of pres. pt. of *substāre*, to exist, lit. ' to stand near or beneath.'—L. *sub*, near ; *stāre*, to stand. Der. *substanti-al* ; also *substant-ive*, F. *substantif*, L. *substantīuus*, self-existent, used of the verb *esse*, and afterwards applied, as a grammatical term, to nouns substantive.

substitute, sb. (F.–L.) F. *substitut*, a substitute.—L. *substitūtus*, pp. of *substituere*, to put in stead of.—L. *sub*, near, instead of ; *statuere*, to put, place, causal of *stāre*, to stand.

Subtend. (L.) L. *subtendere*, to stretch or extend beneath.—L. *sub*, beneath ; *tendere*, to stretch. See Tend (1).

Subterfuge. (F.–L.) F. *subterfuge*, ' a shift ;' Cot.—Late L. *subterfugium*.— L. *subterfugere*, to escape by stealth.—L. *subter*, stealthily (from *sub*, under, with compar. suffix); *fugere*, to flee. See Fugitive.

Subterranean, Subterraneous. (L.) From L. *subterrāne-us*, underground. —L. *sub*, under ; *terra*, ground. See Terrace.

Subtle. (F.–L.) Formerly *sotil, sotel* ; the *b* was a pedantic insertion, and is never sounded.—O. F. *sotil, soutil*, later *subtil*. —L. *subtīlem*, acc. of *subtīlis*, fine, thin, accurate, subtle. The orig. sense of *subtīlis* was 'finely woven'; from L. *sub*, under, closely, and *tēla*, a web, for which see Toil (2). Der. *subtle-ty*, M. E. *soteltee*, from O. F. *sotilleté*, subtlety, from L. acc. *subtīlitātem*. Brugm. i. § 134.

Subtract. (L.) From L. *subtractus*, pp. of *subtrahere*, to draw away underneath, to subtract.—L. *sub*, beneath ; *trahere*, to draw. See Trace (1).

Suburb. (F.–L.) A. F. *suburbe* (A. D. 1285). — L. *suburbium*, suburb. —L. *sub*, near ; *urbi-* decl. stem of

urbs, a town. **Der.** *suburb-an*. See
Urbane.

Subvert. (F.–L.) F. *subvertir*; Cot.
–L. *subuertere*, to turn upside down,
overthrow. –L. *sub*, beneath; *uertere*, to
turn. See **Verse**. **Der.** *subvers-ion*, from
the pp. *subuers-us*.

Succeed. (F.–L.) F. *succéder*; Cot.
–L. *succēdere* (pp. *successus*), to follow
after. –L. *suc-* (*sub*), next; *cēdere*, to go,
come. **Der.** *success*, O. F. *succes*, L. *successus*, result, from pp. *successus*.

Succinct, concise. (L.) L. *succinctus*,
pp. of *succingere*, to gird up, tuck up short.
–L. *suc-* (*sub*), up; *cingere*, to gird. See
Cincture.

Succory; see **Chicory.**

Succour. (F.–L.) M. E. *socouren.–*
O. F. *sucurre* (Burguy). Mod. F. *secourir.*
–L. *succurrere*, to run near or to, run
to help, aid. –L. *suc-* (for *sub*), near;
currere, to run. See **Current.**

Succulent, juicy. (F.–L.) F. *succulent.–* L. *sūculentus*, *succulentus*, full of
juice. –L. *sūcu-s*, *succu-s*, juice; with suffix
-lentus. See **Suck.**

Succumb. (L.) L. *succumbere*, to lie
under, to sink down.–L. *suc-* (for *sub*),
under; **cumbere*, to recline, allied to
cubāre, to lie down. See **Covey.**

Such, of a like kind. (E.) M. E. *swulc,
swilc, swich, such.* A. S. *swylc.*+O. Sax.
sulik, Du. *zulk*, Icel. *slíkr*, Dan. *slig*, Swed.
slik, G. *solch*, Goth. *swaleiks*. β. The Goth.
swaleiks is from *swa*, so, and *leiks*, like;
hence *such = so-like*; see **So** and **Like.**

Suck. (E.) M. E. *souken.* A. S. *sūcan,*
pt. t. *sēac*, pp. *socen*. [There is an A. S.
by-form *sūgan*; cognate with Icel. *sjūga,
sūga*, Dan. *suge*, Swed. *suga*, G. *saugen,*
Du. *zuigen*.] β. The A. S. *sūcan* is cognate with L. *sūgere*, W. *sugno*, to suck,
O. Irish *sūg-im*, I suck; cf. O. Ir. and W.
sug, Gael. *sugh*, L. *sūcus*, juice; see **Succulent**. Brugm. i. § 112.

suction. (F.– L.) M. F. *suction.*
Formed (as if from L. **suctio*) from L.
suct-us, pp. of *sūgere*, to suck.

Sudatory, a sweating-bath. (L.) L.
sūdātōrium, a sweating-bath; neut. of
sūdātōrius, serving for sweating. – L.
sūdātōr-, stem of *sūdātor*, a sweater.–
L. *sūdā-re*, to sweat; with suffix *-tor* (of
the agent). Cognate with E. **Sweat.**

Sudden. (F.–L.) M.E. *sodain.–*O.F.
sodain, sudain (F. *soudain*). [Cf. Ital.
subitaneo, subitano, sudden.] – Late L.

*subitānus, for L. *subitāneus*, sudden,
extended from *subitus*, sudden, lit. that
which has come stealthily, orig. pp. of
subīre, to come or go stealthily.–L. *sub*,
under, stealthily; *īre*, to go.

Sudorific. (F.–L.) F. *sudorifique*,
causing sweat; as if from L. **sūdōrificus.*
–L. *sūdōri-*, for *sūd-or*, sweat, allied to
sūdāre, to sweat; *-ficus*, making, from
facere, to make. See **Sudatory.**

Suds. (E.) The proper sense is 'things
sodden'; pl. of *sud*, which is derived from
A. S. *sud-*, weak grade of *sēoðan*, to seethe.
Cf. prov. E. *sudded*, flooded; M. Du. *zode*,
a seething, boiling; Low G. *sod*, cooked
broth, *sōde*, a boiling. Cf. **Sod.**

Sue. (F.–L.) M. E. *suen, sewen.–*
A. F. *suer*; O. F. *sevre, suir* (F. *suivre*),
to follow.–Late L. *sequere*, to follow, used
for L. *sequī*, to follow. See **Sequence.**
Der. *en-sue, pur-sue, suit, suite.*

Suet. (F.–L.) M. E. *suet*. Formed,
with dimin. suffix *-et*, from O.F. *seu, suis*
(Norman *sieu*, Walloon *sew*, Littré; F.
suif), suet, fat.–L. *sēbum*, tallow, suet,
grease.

Suffer. (F.–L.) M. E. *soffren, suffren.*
–O. F. *soffrir* (F. *souffrir*). – Folk-L.
sufferīre, for L. *sufferre*, to undergo.–L.
suf- (*sub*), under; *ferre*, to bear. See
Fertile.

Suffice. (F.–L.) From F. *suffis-*, base
of *suffis-ant*, pres. pt. of *suffire*, to suffice.
–L. *sufficere*, to supply.– L. *suf-*, for *sub*,
under; *facere*, to make, put. See **Fact.**

Suffix. (L.) From L. *suffix-us*, pp. of
suffigere, to fix beneath, fix on.–L. *suf-*
(for *sub*), beneath; *figere*, to fix. See
Fix.

Suffocate. (L.) From pp. of L.
suffōcāre, to choke; lit. to squeeze the
throat.–L. *suf-* (for *sub*), under; *fauc-*,
stem of *fauc-ēs*, sb. pl., gullet, throat.

Suffrage, a vote. (F.–L.) F. *suffrage.*
–L. *suffrāgium*, a vote, suffrage.

Suffusion. (F.–L.) F. *suffusion.–*L.
suffūsiōnem, acc. of *suffūsio*, a pouring
over.–L. *suffūsus*, pp. of *suffundere*, to
pour over.–L. *suf-* (for *sub*), under, also
over; *fundere*, to pour. See **Fuse** (1).

Sugar. (F. – Span. – Arab. –Pers. –
Skt.) F. *sucre*. ▬ Span. *azucar.*–Arab.
assokkar; for *al*, the, *sokkar*, *sakkar*, sugar.
▬Pers. *shakar*.– Skt. *çarkarā*, gravel, also
candied sugar. Prob. allied to Skt. *kar-
kara-*, hard.

Suggestion. (F.–L.) F. *suggestion.*

- L. acc. *suggestiōnem.* **-** L. *suggestus,* pp. of *suggerere,* to bring under, supply, suggest. **-** L. *sug-* (for *sub*), under; *gerere,* to bring. See Gerund.

Suicide, self-murder; one who dies by his own hand. (F. **-** L.) A word coined *in England* (before A. D. 1750), but on a F. model; yet the F. *suicide* was borrowed from us. Like *homicide,* the word has a double meaning, (1) answering to L. **suīcīdium,* from L. *suī,* of himself, and *-cīdium,* a slaying, from *cædere,* to slay; (2)=L. **suīcīda,* from L. *suī,* of himself, and *-cīda,* a slayer. See Cæsura.

Suit. (F. **-** L.) F. *suite,* a pursuit, suit at law, also a suite or 'following.' **-** Late L. **sequita,* variant of *secta* (L. *secūta*), a following, a sect, a suite, a suit at law, suit of clothes, set, &c.; see Sect.

suite. (F. **-** L.) F. *suite;* see above.

Sulcated, furrowed. (L.) L. *sulcātus,* pp. of *sulcāre,* to furrow. **-** L. *sulcus,* a furrow. **+** Gk. ὁλκός, a furrow; from ἕλκειν, to draw along; cf. A. S. *sulh,* a plough.

Sulky, obstinate, silently sullen. (E.) Not an old form, but deduced from the sb. *sulkiness,* by dropping *-ness.* However, *sulkiness* is itself a corrupt form for *sulkenness,* formed by adding *-ness* to the adj. *sulken.* This appears as A. S. *solcen,* slothful, remiss; chiefly in the comp. *ā-sŏlcen,* also *be-solcen,* with a like sense. The sb. *āsolcennes,* sloth, disgust, sulkiness, is quite a common word. β. Further, *ā-solcen* was the pp. of a strong verb **ā-seolcan,* to be slothful or languid. Cf. Skt. *sṛj,* to let flow, let loose.

Sullen, morose. (F. **-** L.) Orig. solitary, hating company. M. E. *solain, sulain,* solitary; also, a mess of food for *one* person. **-** O. F. *solain,* lonely; given as ' a pittance for one monk ' in Roquefort, and in Ducange, s. v. *solatium* (5). **-** Late L. **sōlānus;* equivalent in sense to O. F. *soltain,* solitary, Late L. *sōlitāneus,* rare. **-** L. *sōlus,* alone; see Sole (3).

Sully, to tarnish, spot. (E.) M. E. *sulien.* A. S. *sylian,* to sully, defile, lit. to bemire. Formed (with the usual change from Teut. *u* (**>** A. S. *o*) to *y*) from A. S. *sol,* mud, mire. **+** Swed. *söla,* to bemire, Dan. *söle,* Goth. *bisauljan,* G. *sühlen;* from the sb. appearing as Dan. *söl,* G. *suhle,* O. H. G. *sol,* mire. ¶ Not allied to the verb *to soil,* with which it was doubtless often confused.

Sulphur. (L.) L. *sulphur.* Cf. also Skt. * çulvāri-,* sulphur.

Sultan. (F. **-** Arab.) F. *sultan.* **-** Arab. *sultān,* victorious, also a ruler, prince; orig. ' dominion.' Cf. Chaldee *sholtān,* dominion. Der. *sultan-a,* from Ital. *sultana,* fem. of *sultano,* sultan, from Arab. *sultān.*

Sultry, Sweltry, very hot and oppressive. (E.) *Sweltry* is the older form, and is short for *swelter-y,* from the verb to *swelter* (M. E. *swelteren, swalteren*). Again, *swelter* is a frequentative form from M. E. *swelten,* to swoon, faint, die. **-** A. S. *sweltan,* to die. **+** O. Sax. *sweltan;* Icel. *svelta* (pt. t. *svalt*), Dan. *sulte,* Swed. *svälta;* Goth. *swiltan,* to die. Cf. Icel. *sultr,* Dan. *sult,* hunger, famine; from the weak grade **swult* **>** **sult.* Also O.H.G. *schwelzan,* to burn, to be consumed by fire or love. The Teut. root **swelt-* seems to be an extension of **swel-,* to burn, as in A. S. *swelan,* to burn, perish with heat, Lith. *swilti,* to shine, burn, Skt. *svar,* splendour, M. Du. *zoel,* ' sultrie,' Hexham.

Sum, amount, total. (F. **-** L.) M. E. *summe.* **-** F. *somme.* **-** L. *summa,* sum, chief part, amount; orig. fem. of *summus* (**sup-mus*), highest, superl. form from *sub* (**<** **sup*), above. Brugm. i. § 762. Der. *summ-ar-y,* sb., from F. *sommaire,* ' a summary,' Cot., from L. *summārium,* a summary.

Sumach, a tree. (F. **-** Span. **-** Arab.) F. *sumac,* M. F. *sumach.* **-** Span. *zumaque.* **-** Arab. *summāq,* a species of shrub, sumach.

Summer (1), hot season. (E.) M. E. *somer, sumer.* A. S. *sumer, sumor.* **+** Du. *zomer,* Icel. *sumar,* Dan. *sommer,* Swed. *sommar,* G. *sommer,* O. H. G. *sumar.* Further allied to O. Irish *sam, samrad,* O. Welsh *ham,* W. *haf,* Zend *hama,* summer; Skt. *samā,* a year. Brugm. i. § 436.

Summer (2), a beam; see Sumpter.

Summerset; see Somersault.

Summit, top. (F. **-** L.) F. *sommet,* top. Dimin. of O. F. *som,* top of a hill. **-** L. *summum,* highest point, neut. of *summus,* highest; see Sum.

Summon. (F. **-** L.) A. F. *sommoner* (Godefroy); O. F. *somoner* (Roquefort), early altered to *semoner* and *semondre* (F. *semondre*), to summon. **-** L. *summonēre;* to remind privily. **-** L. *sum-* (for *sub*), under, privily; *monēre,* to remind.

summons, sb. (F. **-** L.) M. E. *som-*

529

ouns. — A. F. *somons,* earlier *somonse,* fem.; M. F. *semonce,* 'a warning, summons,' Cot.; orig. the fem. of the pp. of the verb *somoner, semondre* (above). ¶ Thus the final *s* of *summons* is not due to L. *summoneās,* as some have suggested.

Sumpter, a pack-horse. (F. — Low L. – Gk.) *Sumpter* is a derivative from M. E. *somer,* a pack-horse, which must be first considered. β. M. E. *somer* is from O. F. *somier, sommier,* a pack-horse, the same as Late L. *sagmārius,* corruptly *salmārius,* a pack-horse. — Gk. σάγμα, a pack-saddle. — Gk. σάττειν (base σακ-), to pack, fasten on a load, orig. to fasten. γ. Hence E. *sumpter,* which orig. meant (not a pack-horse, but) a pack-horse-driver, baggage-carrier. — O. F. *sommetier,* a pack-horse-driver; answering to a Late L. **sagmatarius,* for which Ducange has *summatārius, saumatērius.* — Gk. σαγματ-, stem of σάγμα (above). δ. The old word *summer,* a beam, was so called from its bearing a great weight, and is the same as M. E. *somer* (above); cf. F. *sommier,* 'a summer,' Cot. Hence E. *bressomer,* familiar form of *breast-summer,* a beam placed breastwise, to support a superincumbent wall. ¶ I explain *sumpter* in K. Lear, ii. 4. 219, as meaning 'pack-horse-driver'; a man, not a horse.

Sumptuary, relating to expenses. (L.) L. *sumptuārius,* adj. from *sumptu-s,* expense. See below.

sumptuous, costly. (F. — L.) F. *somptueux* (Cot.) — L. *sumptuōsus,* costly. — L. *sumptus,* expense. — L. *sumptus,* pp. of *sūmere,* to take, use, spend; a derivative from *emere,* to take. Brugm. i. § 240.

Sun. (E.) M. E. *sonne.* A. S. *sunne,* fem. sb.+Du. *zon,* G. *sonne,* Goth. *sunnō,* all feminine; Teut. type **sunnōn-,* fem. ¶ Cf. Icel. *sól,* Swed. Dan. *sol,* L. *sōl,* Goth. *sauil,* Lith. *saulė,* W. *haul,* Gk. ἠέλιος (ἥλιος), Skt. *sūra-, sūrya-,* the sun. Der. *Sun-day,* A. S. *sunnan-dæg.*

Sunder, to divide. (E.) A. S. *syndrian, -sundrian,* to put asunder. — A. S. *sundor,* adv., asunder, apart. + Icel. *sundra,* Dan. *söndre,* Swed. *söndra,* G. *sondern,* to sunder; from Icel. *sundr,* Dan. Swed. *sönder,* adv., apart, G. *sonder,* adj., separate. Cf. Gk. ἄτερ (for **sənter*), without; allied to Gk. ἄνευ, L. *sine,* without. Brugm. i. § 500.

Sup, to imbibe, lap up. (E.) M. E. *soupen.* A. S. *sūpan* (pt. t. *sēap,* pp. *sopen*),

to sup, drink in. + Du. *zuipen,* Icel. *sūpa,* Swed. *supa,* G. *saufen,* O. H. G. *sūfan.*

Super-, prefix. (L.) L. *super,* above; cf. L. *superus,* upper. For *s-uperus:* where *s-* corresponds to Gk. ἑξ-; see **Sub-.** Cf. Gk. ὑπέρ, above; ὑπό, from under; Skt. *upari,* above, allied to *upara-,* upper, comparative of *upa,* near, close to.

Superannuate. (L.) Formerly (and better) *superannate.* — Late L. *superannātus,* orig. that has lived beyond a year. — L. *super,* beyond; *annus,* a year. See **Annals.**

Superb. (F. – L.) F. *superbe.* — L. *superbus,* proud; one who thinks himself above others. For **super-fu-os,* one who is above (cf. L. *fu-ī,* I was); Brugm. ii. § 4. — L. *super,* above. See **Super-.**

Supercargo. (L.; *and* Span. – C.) From L. *super,* above; and Span. *cargo,* a freight. Suggested by Span. *sobrecargo,* a supercargo; where *sobre* < L. *super.* See **Cargo.**

Supercilious, disdainful. (L.) From L. *supercili-um,* (1) an eyebrow, (2) haughtiness, as expressed by raising the eyebrows. — L. *super,* above; *cil-ium,* eyelid, allied to Gk. τὰ κύλα, the parts under the eyes (Prellwitz).

Supererogation. (L.) From acc. of Late L. *supererogātio,* that which is done beyond what is due. — L. *supererogāre,* to pay out in excess. — L. *super,* beyond; *ē,* out; *rogāre,* to ask. (L. *ērogāre*=to lay out, expend.) See **Rogation.**

Superficies. (L.) L. *superficiēs,* surface, outer face. — L. *super,* above; *faciēs,* face.

Superfine. (F. – L.) From L. *super,* above; and *fine* (1).

Superfluous, excessive. (L.) L. *superfluus,* overflowing; with suffix *-ous.* — L. *super,* over; *fluere,* to flow; see **Fluent.** Der. *superflui-ty,* F. *superfluité,* from L. acc. *superfluitātem.*

Superinduce. (L.) L. *super,* beyond; and *in-dūcere,* to induce. See **Induce.**

Superintendent, an overseer. (F. – L.) M.F. *superintendant;* Cot. — L. *superintendent-,* stem of pres. pt. of *superintendere,* to superintend. — L. *super,* above; *intendere,* to apply the mind to; see **Intend.**

Superior. (F. – L.) Formerly *superiour.* — M. F. *superieur.* — L. *superiōrem,* acc. of *superior,* higher; comparative from *superus*, high, which is itself an old comparative form. See **Super-**.

Superlative. (F.−L.) F. *superlatif*, Cot. − L. *superlātīuus*, as a grammatical term.−L. *superlātus*, excessive, lit. ' borne beyond.' − L. *super*, beyond ; *lātus*, pp. of *tollere*, to bear. (√TEL.) See **Tolerate**.

Supernal. (F.−L.) M. F. *supernel*, ' supernall ; ' Cot. Answering to a Late L. *supernālis*, from L. *supern-us*, upper ; from *super*, above ; see **Super-**.

Supernatural. (L.) From L. *super*, beyond ; and *natural*, adj., from *nature*.

Supernumerary. (F.−L.) M. F. *supernumeraire* (Cot.).−L. *supernumerārius*, excessive in number. − L. *super*, beyond ; *numerus*, number.

Superscription. (F.−L.) M. F. *superscription* ; Cot.−L. acc. *superscriptiōnem*.−L. *superscriptus*, pp. of *superscrībere*, to write above or over. − L. *super*, above ; *scrībere*, to write ; see **Scribe**.

Supersede. (F.−L.) O.F. *superseder*, to leave off, desist (hence to suspend or defer a matter). − L. *supersedēre*, to sit upon, to preside over, refrain, desist from. − L. *super*, upon ; *sedēre*, to sit. See **Sedentary**. Der. *supersess-ion* (from pp. *supersess-us*); cf. *surcease*.

Superstition. (F.−L.) F. *superstition*.−L. acc. *superstitiōnem*, a standing near a thing, amazement, dread, religious awe, scruple. − L. *superstit-*, stem of *superstes*, one who stands near, a witness. − L. *super*, above, near ; *statum*, supine of *stāre*, to stand.

Superstructure. (L.) From L. *super*, above ; and **Structure**.

Supervene. (L.) L. *superuenīre*, to come upon or over, to follow, occur. − L. *super*, beyond ; *uenīre*, to come. See **Venture**.

Supervise; see **Vision**.

Supine, on one's back, lazy. (L.) L. *supīnus*, lying on one's back. − L. **sup*, orig. form of *sub*, up ; with suffix *-īnus*.

Supper. (F.−Teut.) M. E. *soper*. − O. F. *soper* (F. *souper*), a supper. It is the infin. mood used as a sb. − O. F. *soper*, to sup (F. *souper*).−Low G. *supen*, Icel. *sūpa*, Swed. *supa*, to sup. See **Sup**.

Supplant. (F.−L.) F. *supplanter*.− L. *supplantāre*, to put something under the sole of the foot, trip up, overthrow.− L. *sup-* (> *sub*), under ; *planta*, sole ; see **Plant**.

Supple. (F.−L.) M. E. *souple*. − F.

souple, supple, pliant.−L. *supplicem*, acc. of *supplex*, with the old sense of ' bending under.' − L. *sup-* (> *sub*), under ; *plic-*, as seen in *plicāre*, to fold. See **Ply**.

Supplement. (F. − L.) F. *supplément* ; Cot. − L. *supplēmentum*, a filling up.−L. *supplēre*, to fill up.−L. *sup-* (*sub*), up ; *plēre*, to fill. See **Plenary**.

Suppliant. (F. − L.) F. *suppliant*, pres. pt. of *supplier*, to pray humbly.−L. *supplicāre* ; see below.

supplicate. (L.) From pp. of L. *supplicāre*, to beseech. − L. *supplic-*, stem of *supplex*, bending under or down, beseeching ; see **Supple**.

Supply. (F. − L.) Formerly *supploy* (Levins).−O. F. *supploier*, F. *suppléer*, to supply ; Cot.−L. *supplēre*, to fill up ; see **Supplement**.

Support. (F.−L.) M. E. *supporten*. −F. *supporter*.−L. *supportāre*, to carry to a place ; in Late L., to endure.−L. *sup-* (*sub*), near ; *portāre*, to carry. See **Port** (1).

Suppose. (F.−L. *and* Gk.) F. *supposer*, to imagine. − L. *sup-* (*sub*), under, near ; F. *poser*, to place, put. See **Pose**.

Supposition. (F.−L.) F. *supposition*. − L. acc. *suppositiōnem*. − L. *suppositus*, pp. of *suppōnere*, to suppose. − L. *sup-* (*sub*), near ; *pōnere*, to place. See **Position**.

Suppress. (L.) From L. *suppressus*, pp. of *supprimere*, to suppress. − L. *sup-* (*sub*), under ; *premere*, to press. See **Press**.

Suppurate. (L.) From pp. of L. *suppurāre*, to gather pus underneath.− L. *sup-* (*sub*), under ; *pūr-*, for *pūs*, matter. See **Pus**.

Supra-, prefix. (L.) L. *suprā*, above, adv. and prep.; allied to *superus*, upper ; see **Super-**. Der. *supra-mundane*; see **Mundane**.

Supreme. (F.−L.) F. *suprême*.−L. *suprēmus*, highest. *Suprē-mus* is from **suprē*, an adverb, with suffix *-mus* ; Brug. ii. § 75. This **suprē* is allied to L. *super*, above.

Sur- (1), prefix. (L.) For *sub* before *r*; only in *sur-reptitious*, *sur-rogate*.

Sur- (2), prefix. (F.−L.) F. *sur*, above. −L. *super*, above. See **Super-**.

Surcease, to cease, cause to cease. (F.−L.) Not allied to *cease* (except in popular etymology). A corruption of O. F. *sursis*, masc., *sursise*, fem., ' surceased, intermitted ;' Cot. This word was also used as a sb., to signify ' delay ' ; hence *surcease*, vb., to delay. *Sursis* is the pp. of O. F. *surseoir*, ' to surcease, delay,' Cot. – L. *supersedēre*, to desist from, hence to delay proceedings ; see **Supersede**.

Surcharge, sb. (F. – L. *and* C.) F. *surcharge*, an over-charge. – F. *sur* (< L. *super*), above ; and **Charge**.

Surd, having no rational root (in mathematics). (L.) L. *surdus*, deaf ; hence, deaf to reason, irrational. *Surdus* also means dim ; and connexion with *sordid* is possible. Brugm. i. § 362.

Sure. (F. – L.) O. F. *seür* (F. *sûr*), earliest form *segur*. – L. *sēcūrus*; see **Secure**. Doublet, *secure*.

Surf, the foam of the waves on the shore. (E.) The *r* is intrusive; spelt *suffe*, with the sense of ' rush,' in Hakluyt's Voyages, ed. 1598, vol. ii. pt. i. 227 : ' The *suffe* of the sea [sweep or rush of the inflowing wave] setteth her [a raft's] lading dry on land.' I suppose *suffe* to be the same as ' *sough* of the sea,' also spelt *souf*, *souch* in Jamieson. M. E. *swough*, from *swoughen*, *swowen*, to make a rushing noise. Cf. ' the *swogh* of the see,' Morte Arth. 759. – A. S. *swōgan*, to make a rushing noise ; see **Sough**.

Surface. (F. – L.) F. *surface*, upper face. – F. *sur*, above; *face*, face. – L. *super*, above; *faciēs*, face. See **Face**.

Surfeit, sb. (F. – L.) O. F. *surfait*, *sorfait*, excess; orig. pp. of *sorfaire*, to augment, exaggerate. – L. *super*, above; *facere*, to make. See **Fact**.

Surge, the swell of waves. (F. – L.) ' *Surge* of the see, *uague*;' Palsgrave. Coined from O. F. stem *sourge-*, as in *sourge-ant*, pres. pt. of *sourdre*, to rise. – L. *surgere* (= *sur-rigere*, i.e. *sub-regere), to rise. – L. *sub*, up ; *regere*, to direct. See **Regent**.

Surgeon, contracted form of *chirurgeon*; see **Chirurgeon**. So also Gascon *surgen*, a surgeon; O. F. *surgien* (Godefroy). **Der.** *surgical*, short for *chirurgical*; *surgery*, corruption of M. E. *surgenry*, i.e. *surgeon-ry*, or of O.F. *cirurgerie*.

Surloin; see **Sirloin**.

Surly, proud, churlish. (E.) Spelt *serly* (Levins) ; *syrly*, Spenser, Shep. Kal. July, 203. Prob. from A.S. *sūr-līc, lit. ' sour-like.' We find *sowre*, meaning ' morose ' (Baret) ; see **Sour**. Cf. G. *sauer*, sour, surly ; Swed. Dan. *syrlig*, sourish. Also M. E. *surdagh*, ' sour dough ;' Wrt. Vocab. 663. 22.

Surmise, an imagination, guess. (F. – L.) O. F. *surmise*, an accusation, charge; orig. fem. of *surmis*, pp. of *surmettre*, to put upon, lay to one's charge. – F. *sur*, above; *mettre*, to put. – L. *super*, above; *mittere*, to send, put. See **Missile**.

Surmount. (F. – L.) F. *surmonter*. – F. *sur* (L. *super*), above; *monter*, to mount; see **Mount** (2).

Surname. (F. – L.; *and* E.) From F. *sur* (L. *super*), above, over; and E. **Name**.

Surpass. (F. – L.) F. *surpasser*, to excel. – F. *sur* (L. *super*), beyond ; *passer*, to pass ; see **Pass**.

Surplice. (F. – L.) M. E. *surplis*. – F. *surplis*; Cot. – Late L. *superpelliceum*, a surplice. – L. *super*, over; *pelliceus*, made of skins, from *pellis*, a skin; see **Pelisse**.

Surplus. (F. – L.) F. *surplus*, ' an over-plus ;' Cot. – Late L. *superplūs*, a residuum. – L. *super*, above; *plūs*, more. See **Plural**.

Surprise, sb. (F. – L.) O. F. *sorprise*, *surprise*, a taking unawares. Fem. of *sorpris*, pp. of *sorprendre*, *surprendre*, to surprise. – L. *super*, upon ; *prehendere*, to seize, from *præ*, before, and *-hendere*, to seize. See **Prehensile**.

Surrebutter. (F. – L. *and* O. H. G.) A legal term, meaning an answer or reply to a *rebut*. From F. *sur* (L. *super*), upon, in reply to ; and M.F. *rebouter*, to rebut, the infin. mood being used as a sb. See **Rebut**. And see **Surrejoinder**.

Surrejoinder. (F. – L.) A *rejoinder* in reply. ' The plaintiff may answer him by a *rejoinder*; upon which the defendant may *rebut*; and the plaintiff may answer him by a *surrebutter*;' Blackstone, Comment. b. iii. c. 20. From F. *sur*, upon, in reply to; and F. *rejoindre*, to rejoin, used as a sb. See **Rejoin**.

Surrender. (F. – L.) O. F. *surrendre*, to give up. – F. *sur* (L. *super*), above; *rendre*, to render, from L. *reddere*, to restore. See **Render**.

Surreptitious. (L.) L. *surreptīti-us*, better *surreptīcius*, done stealthily ; with suffix *-ous*. – L. *surreptum*, supine of *surripere*, to pilfer, purloin. – L. *sur-* (*sub*), under, secretly ; *rapere*, to seize. See **Rapid**.

Surrogate, a substitute. (L.) L. *surrogātus*, pp. of *surrogāre*, to elect in place of another. – L. *sur-* (for *sub*), in place of; *rogāre*, to ask, elect. See **Rogation**.

Surround. (F. – L.) Confused with *round*. Orig. *suround*, i.e. ' to overflow ; ' as in Caxton's Statutes of Hen. VII, leaf c 7. – O. F. *suronder.* – L. *superundāre*, to overflow (Lewis). – L. *super*, over, above ; *undāre*, to flow, from *unda*, a wave. Cf. *ab-ound*, *red-ound*.

Surtout. (F. – L.) From F. *sur tout*, lit. ' over all.' – L. *super*, over ; *tōtum*, acc. of *tōtus*, all. See **Total**.

Surveillance, inspection. (F. – L.) F. *surveillance*, superintendence. – F. *surveiller*, to superintend. – L. *super*, over ; *uigilāre*, to watch, from *uigil*, adj., awake. See **Vigil**.

Survey. (F. – L.) A. F. *surveier*, *surveër* (O. F. *sourveoir*), to survey. – Late L. *superuidēre*, to supervise. – L. *super*, over ; *uidēre*, to see. See **Vision**. Doublet, *supervise*.

Survive. (F. – L.) F. *survivre*, to outlive. – L. *superuiuere*, to live beyond, outlive. – L. *super*, beyond ; *uiuere*, to live. See **Victuals**.

Sus-, prefix. (L.) L. *sus-*, prefix ; for **sups*, extended form of **sup*, *sub*, under.

Susceptible. (F. – L.) F. *susceptible*. – L. *susceptibilis*, ready to receive. – L. *sus-*, for **sup-s*, under ; and *capt-um*, supine of *capere*, to take. See **Capacious**.

Suspect. (F. – L.) M. E. *suspect*, orig. a pp. with the sense suspected or suspicious. – F. *suspect*, suspected. – L. *suspectus*, pp. of *suspicere*, to suspect, lit. ' to look under,' mistrust. – L. *su-* (for *sus-*, *sups-*), under ; *specere*, to look. See **Species**.

Suspend. (F. – L.) F. *suspendre.* – L. *suspendere* (pp. *suspensus*), to hang up. – L. *sus-* (for *sups-*), extension of *sub*, under ; *pendēre*, to hang. See **Pendant**. Der. *suspense*, *suspension*.

Suspicion. (F. – L.) M. E. *suspecion*. – A. F. *suspeciun* ; O. F. *suspeccion*, suspicion ; later *souspeçon*, Cot. (mod. F. *soupçon*). – L. *suspiciōnem*, acc. of *suspicio*, suspicion. – L. *suspicere*, to suspect ; see **Suspect**.

Sustain. (F. – L.) M. E. *susteinen.* – A. F. *sustein-*, a stem of O. F. *sustenir*, *sostenir* (F. *soutenir*). – L. *sustinēre*, to uphold. – L. *sus-* (for *sups-*), up : *tenēre*, to hold. See **Tenable**. Der. *sustenance*, O. F. *sustenance*, L. *sustinentia*, sb. ; *sustentation*, from L. *sustentātio*, maintenance, from *sustentāre*, frequentative of *sustinēre*.

Sutler, one who sells provisions in a camp. (Du.) Du. *soetelaar* (Sewel) ; usually *zoetelaar* ; M. Du. *zoetelaer*, ' a scullion, a sutler, or a victualler,' Hexham. Orig. a scullion, drudge, menial who does dirty work ; formed with suffix *-aar* (= E. *-er*) from *zoetel-en*, ' to sullie,' Hexham. Cognate with Low G. *suddeln*, Dan. *sudle*, G. *sudeln*, to sully, daub. All these are frequentative forms, with suffix *el-* or *-l-* ; from Teut. **sud-*, as in Swed. *sudda*, to daub, stain, soil. Allied to Icel. *suddi*, steam from cooking, drizzling rain, *suddaligr*, wet and dank, *soð*, broth in which meat has been sodden ; all from the weak grade of Teut. **seuthan-*, Icel. *sjóða*, to seethe. Further allied to E. *suds*, and to the verb **Seethe**, q. v.

Suttee. (Skt.) Skt. *satī*, a true or virtuous wife, a term applied to a widow who immolates herself on the funeral pile of her husband ; hence (incorrectly) the burning of a widow. – Skt. *satī* is the fem. of *sant*, being, existing, true, right, virtuous ; pres. pt. of *as*, to be. (✔ES.) See **Sooth**.

Suture, a seam. (F. – L.) F. *suture.* – L. *sūtūra.* – L. *sūtus*, pp. of *suere*, to sew ; see **Sew**.

Suzerain, a feudal lord. (F. – L.) F. *suzerain*, ' sovereign, yet subaltern ; ' Cot. A coined word, made from F. *sus* < L. *sūsum* or *sursum*, above ; so that F. *suzerain* answers to a Late L. **sūserānus* or **surserānus*. β. The L. *sursum* = **suuorsum*, lit. turned upwards ; from *su-*, for *sub*, up, and *uorsum* = *uersum*, neut. of pp. of *uertere*, to turn. See **Verse**. ¶ Prob. imitated from O. F. *soverain* (from **superānus*), which accounts for the *-er-*.

Swabber. (Du.) Older than *swab*, vb. – Du. *zwabber*, ' a swabber, the drudge of a ship ; ' Sewel. Cf. Du. *zwabberen*, to drudge ; Swed. *svabb*, a fire-brush, *svabla*, to swab ; Dan. *svabre*, to swab ; G. *schwabber*, a swabber. Cf. also Norw. *svabba*, Pomeran. *swabbeln*, to splash about ; E. Fries. *swabbeln*, G. *schwabbeln*, Low G. *swappen* (Danneil), to shake about (said of liquids). Of imitative origin. Compare M. E. *quappen*, to palpitate ; and E. *swap*, *swash*.

Swaddle, to swathe an infant. (E.) Formerly *swadle*, *swadell* ; for *swathel*. M. E. *swathlen*. It means to wrap in a swaddling-band, which was called a *swathel* or *swethel.* – A.S. *sweðel* (once *swæðil*), a swaddling-band; lit. 'that which swathes;' cf. O. H. G. *swedil*, a bandage; see **Swathe**.

Swagger. (Scand.) Frequentative of *swag*, to sway from side to side. ' I *swagge*, as a fatte persons belly *swaggeth* as he goth;' Palsgrave. — Norw. *svagga*, to swag; cf. Icel. *sveggja*, to cause to sway. *Swag* is allied to *sway*; see **Sway**.

Swain. (Scand.) Icel. *sveinn*, a boy, lad, servant; Swed. *sven*, Dan. *svend*, a swain, servant.+Low G. *sween*; O. H. G. *swein*, a swine-herd; A. S. *swān*, a swine-herd. Teut. type *swainoz*; allied (by gradation) to *sweinom*, A. S. *swīn*, a swine, pig. Thus 'swine-herd' was the orig. sense.

Swallow (1), a bird. (E.) A. S. *swealwe*.+Du. *zwaluw*, Icel. *svala*, Dan. *svale*, Swed. *svala*, G. *schwalbe*. Teut. type *swalwōn*, f. Cf. E. Fries. *swālke*, Low G. *swaalke*, a swallow.

Swallow (2), to absorb. (E.) M. E. *swelȝen*, *swelwen*, *swolȝhen*, *swolwen*; A.S. *swelgan*, to swallow, strong verb, pt. t. *swealh*, pp. *swolgen*. + Du. *zwelgen*, Icel. *svelgja*, Dan. *svælge*, Swed. *svälja*, G. *schwelgen*. (The weak and strong forms are confused.) Der. *groundsel*, q. v.

Swamp. (Scand.) Not an old word in E. — Dan. Swed. *svamp*, a sponge, fungus; (hence applied to swampy ground, which is the usual E. use); Icel. *svöppr*, a sponge. Cf. G. *sumpf*, a swamp (whence Du. *somp*); allied to M. H. G. *swam*, *swamp*, G. *schwamm*, a sponge, fungus; Goth. *swamms*, sponge; Low G. *swamm*, *swamp*, fungus; Du. *zwam*, A. S. *swamm*, fungus. We find also prov. E. *swank*, *swang*, a swamp; Swed. dial. *svank*.

Swan. (E.) A. S. *swan*.+Du. *zwaan*, Icel. *svanr*, Dan. *svane*, Swed. *svan*, G. *schwan*. The form resembles that of Skt. *svan*, to resound, sound, sing (L. *sonāre*).

swan-hopping, taking up swans to mark them. (E.) The usual explanation, that it stands for *swan-upping*, is right. See old tract on *upping* in Hone, Every-day Book, ii. 958. From the prep. *up*.

Swap, to strike. (E.) M. E. *swappen*, to strike; also, to go swiftly. E. Fries. *swappen*, to strike with a noise, from *swap*, a slap, noise of a blow; cf. Low G. *swaps*, interj. crack!, said of a slap. Imitative; cf. *slap*, *whap*; prov. E. *swack*, a blow.

Sward. (E.) It orig. meant skin, rind. or covering. A.S. *sweard*, the skin of

bacon, rind. *Green-sward* is the grassy covering of the land, green turf (of Scand. origin).+Du. *zwoord*, rind of bacon; Icel. *svörðr*, skin, sward, *grassvörðr*, green-sward; Dan. *fleskesvær*, flesh-sward, *grönsværd*, green-sward; G. *schwarte*, rind, bark, skin.

Swarm. (E.) A. S. *swearm*; lit. 'that which hums;' from √SWER, to hum, buzz, as in Skt. *svṛ*, to sound, *svara-*, voice, L. *susurrus*, a hum; G. *schwirren*, to buzz. +Du. *zwerm*, Icel. *svarmr*, Dan. *sværm*, Swed. *svärm*, G. *schwarm*. Cf. Lith. *surma*, a pipe. Brugm. i. § 375 (8).

Swart, Swarthy. (E.) The proper form was *swart*, afterwards *swarth*, whence *swarth-y*. M. E. *swart*. A. S. *sweart*.+ Du. *zwart*, Icel. *svartr*, Dan. *sort*, Swed. *svart*, G. *schwartz*, Goth. *swarts*. Cf. A. S. *sweorcan*, to grow dark.

Swarth, a quantity of grass cut down at one stroke of the scythe. (E.) In Tw. Nt. ii. 3. 162. An error for *swath*, as in Troil. v. 5. 25. See **Swath**.

Swash, to strike forcibly. (E.) Of imitative origin. Cf. Swed. dial. *svasska*, to make a swashing noise, as when one walks with water in the shoes. It stands for *svak-sa*; cf. Norweg. *svakka*, to make a noise like water under the feet; prov. E. *swack*, a blow, fall, *swacking*, crushing, huge. Der. *swash-buckler*, one who strikes or flourishes his shield.

Swath, a row of mown grass. (E.) A. S. *swæð*, a track; *swaðu*, a track, foot-track, trace. E. Fries. *swad*, a swath.+Du. *zwad*, *zwade*, a swath (Sewel); G. *schwad*. The sense of ' mown grass' is original; cf. Low G. *swad*, a swath, *swade*, a scythe. The earliest meaning may have been ' shred' or ' slice'; cf. Norweg. *svada*, vb., act. and neut., to shred or slice off, to flake off. Franck suggests that *swath* answers to an Idg. pp. form *swa-to-*, from the root of the verb *to sway*; with reference to the sweep of a scythe.

Swathe, to enwrap, bandage. (E.) M. E. *swathen*; also *swethen*. From a base *swath-*; whence A.S. *sweðel* (*swæðil*), a swaddling-band; *be-sweðian*, to enwrap. Cf. O. H. G. *swedil*, *swithel*, a bandage; M. H. G. *swede*, a plaster.

Sway, to swing, incline, rule over. (E.) M. E. *sweyen*. E. Fries. *swäien*, *swäjen*, to sway about, to swing. Cf. Swed. *svaja*, to jerk, Dan. *svaie*, Du. *zwaaijen*, to sway, swing. Allied to **Swagger**.

Swear. (E.) M. E. *sweren*. A. S. *swerian*, pt. t. *swōr*, pp. *sworen*, to swear.+Du. *zweren*, Icel. *sverja*, Dan. *sværge*, Swed. *svärja*, G. *schwören*. Allied to Goth. *swaran*, Icel. *svara*, to answer. Orig. 'to speak loudly;' cf. Skt. *svara-*, sound, voice. See Swarm. (√SWER.) **Der.** *an-swer*.

Sweat, sb. and vb. (E.) M. E. *swoot*, sweat, sb.; whence *sweten*, to sweat. A. S. *swāt*, sb.; whence *swǣtan*, vb. The A. S. *swǣtan* became M. E. *swēten*, and should be mod. E. *swet*, the vowel having been shortened; similarly A. S. *lǣtan* > M. E. *lēten* > mod. E. *let*. The spelling *sweat* is now unsuitable. The A. S. sb. *swāt* would now be *swote*, but has been superseded by the verb. + Du. *zweet*, sb.; Icel. *sveiti*, Dan. *sved*, Swed. *svett*, G. *schweiss*. Teut. stem **swaito-*. Allied to L. *sūdor*, sweat; G. *ίδίω*, I sweat, *ίδρώς*, sweat; W. *chwys*, sweat; Skt. *svēda-*, sweat, from *svid*, to sweat. (√SWEID.) See **Sudatory**. Brugm. i. § 331 c.

Sweep, vb. (E.) M. E. *swēpen*. A weak verb, formed from the base *swǣp-*, as in *swēpð*, 3 p. s. pres. t. of A.S. *swāpan*, to sweep. Cf. also O. Fries. *swēpa*, to sweep; E. Fries. *swēpen* (pt. t. *swēpde*), to swing, sway, vibrate. Cf. Icel. *sōpa*, to sweep, M. Swed. *swepa*, Swed. *sopa*. From Teut. base **swaip-*; seen also in O. H. G. *sweifan* (pt. t. *swief*), whence G. *schweifen*, to rove, stray, sweep along; Icel. *sveipa*, to sweep along, a weak verb, from an old verb *svípa* (pt. t. *sveip*, pp. **svipinn*). Teut. root **sweip*. See **Swoop**, **Swipe**. Brugm. i. § 701.

Sweet. (E.) M. E. *swete*, with by-forms *swote*, *sote*. A.S. *swēte*, sweet (for **swōti-*); *swōte*, adv. sweetly. + O. Sax. *swōti*, Du. *zoet*, Icel. *sœtr*, Dan. *söd*, Swed. *söt*, G. *süss*, O. H. G. *suozi*; Goth. *sūts*. β. From the Idg. √SWAD, to please; whence Skt. *svad*, *svād*, to taste, eat, please, *svādu-*, sweet, Gk. *ήδύς*, L. *suāuis*. See **Suave**.

sweetheart. (E.) M. E. *swete herte*, lit. sweet heart, i.e. dear love; see Chaucer, Troil. iii. 1181, 1210, and last line.

Swell. (E.) M. E. *swellen*, pt. t. *swal*. A. S. *swellan*, pt. t. *sweall*, pp. *swollen*.+Du. *zwellen*, Icel. *svella*, Swed. *svälla*, G. *schwellen*. Teut. type **swellan-*, pt. t. **swall*, pp. **swullanoz*. Cf. Goth. *uf-swalleins*, a swelling up. Brugm. i. § 903.

Swelter; see **Sultry**.

Swerve, to turn aside. (E.) M. E. *sweruen swerven*). A. S. *sweorfan*, pt. t.

swearf, pp. *sworfen*, to rub, file, polish (hence to move swiftly to and fro, to turn aside in moving).+Du. *zwerven*, to swerve, wander, riot, rove; O. Sax. *swerban*, to wipe; O. Fries. *swerva*, to rove; Icel. *sverfa* (pt. t. *svarf*), to file; O. H. G. *swerban*, to run round, whirl round; Goth. *biswairban*, to wipe. Teut. type **swerban-*, pt. t. **swarb*, pp. **swurbanoz*. Cf. E. Fries. *swarven*, to wander, Swed. *svarfva*, to turn.

Swift. (E.) A. S. *swift*. From *swif-*, weak grade of A. S. *swīfan*, to move quickly; with suffix *-t* (Idg. *-tos*). Cf. Icel. *svifa*, to rove, turn, sweep; O. H. G. *sweibōn*, to move or turn quickly. Teut. base **sweib*.

Swill, to wash dishes, drink greedily. (E.) M. E. *swilien*. A. S. *swilian*, to wash. **Der.** *swill*, sb.. hog's-wash; whence *swill*, vb., to drink like a pig, Rich. III, v. 2. 9.

Swim (1), to move about in water. (E.) A. S. *swimman*, pt. t. *swamm*.+Du. *zwemmen*, Icel. *svimma*, Dan. *svömme*; Swed. *simma*; G. *schwimmen*. Teut. type **swemman-*, pt. t. **swamm*, pp. **swummanoz*.

Swim (2), to be dizzy. (E.) From M. E. *swime*, a dizziness. A. S. *swīma*, a swoon, swimming in the head. + Du. *zwijm*, a swoon; E. Fries. *swīm*; cf. Icel. *svimi*, dizziness, Dan. *svimle*, to be giddy, *besvime*, to swoon; Swed. *svimma*, to be dizzy, *swimning*, swoon; Pomeran. *swimen*, to swoon; Low G. *swimeln*, to reel (Danneil). β. A. S. *swīma* = *swī-ma*; the real base is **swī* (**swei*) whence also O. H. G. *swīnan*, to decrease, disappear, allied to Swed. *svindel*, G. *schwindel*, dizziness; Swed. *försvinna*, to disappear, Icel. *svina*, to subside (as a swelling). The orig. notion is that of failure, giving way, subsidence, &c.; see **swindler**.

swindler, a cheat. (G.) XVIII cent. — G. *schwindler*, an extravagant projector, a swindler. — G. *schwindeln*, to be dizzy, act thoughtlessly. — G. *schwinden*, to decay, sink, vanish, fail. + A. S. *swindan*, pt. t. *swand*, to languish; allied to O. H. G. *swīnan*, to fail. See above.

Swine, a sow, pig, pigs. (E.) M. E. *swin*, both sing. and pl. A. S. *swīn*, a pig; pl. *swīn*, swine. + Du. *zwijn*, a swine, hog; Icel. *svín*, pl. *svín*; Dan. *sviin*, pl. *sviin*; Swed. *svin*, G. *schwein*, O. H. G. *swīn*; Goth. *swein*, neut. sb.

sing.; Teut. type *swīnom*, neut. So also Russ. *svineya*, a swine, *svinka*, a pig, *svinoi*, swinish. All diminutive or adjectival forms, like L. *suīnus* (Varro), related to swine, from *sus*, a sow. See Sow. Brugm. i. § 95.

Swing. (E.) M. E. *swingen*, pt. t. *swang*, pp. *swungen*. A. S. *swingan*, pt. t. *swang*, pp. *swungen*, to scourge, also to fly, flutter, flap with the wings. + Swed. *svinga*, Dan. *svinge*, to swing, whirl; G. *schwingen*; cf. also Goth. *af-swaggwjan*, to cause to doubt or despair. Teut. type *swengwan-*, pt. t. *swangw*, pp. *swungwanoz*.

swinge, to beat, whip. (E.) M. E. *swengen*. A. S. *swengan*, to dash, strike (cf. *sweng*, a blow); the causal form of Swing. As if 'to flourish a whip.'

swingle, a staff for dressing flax. (M. Du.) M. E. *swinglen*, to beat flax; *swingle*, a swingle. From M. Du. *swingelen*, or *swingen*, 'to beate flax,' Hexham; see Swing. Cf. A. S. *swingele*, a scourging; E. Fries. *swengel*, G. *schwengel*, a pump-handle.

swingle-tree, the bar that swings at the heels of harnessed horses. (E.) M. E. *swingle-tre*. = M. E. *swingle*, a beater, but lit. 'a swinger,' or that which swings ; *tre*, a piece of wood; see Tree. Cf. Du. *zwengel*, a swing; Low G. *swengel* (Danneil), G. *schwengel*, a swingle-tree.

Swink, to toil. (E.) Obsolete; once very common. A.S. *swincan*, pt. t. *swanc*, pp. *swuncen*, to labour, work hard. From the violent action; allied to Swing. Cf. Du. *zwenk*, a swing, a turn; G. *schwenken*, to swing, whirl about.

Swipe, to strike with a sweeping stroke. (E.) Allied to M. E. *swippen*; A.S. *swipian, swippan*, to scourge, beat, from *swip-*, weak grade of Teut. *sweipan-*; cf. Icel. *sveipa*, to sweep, swoop. Cf. A. S. *swipe*, a whip; Icel. *svipa*, to whip, *svipa*, a whip. In form, mod. E. *swipe* answers to O. Icel. *svipa*, to sweep, swoop. See Sweep.

Swirl, to whirl in an eddy. (Scand.) Norweg. *svirla*, to whirl round; frequent. of *sverra* (= Dan. *svirre*), to whirl, orig. to hum. Note also Norw. *svervel*, a whirlpool, *svervla*, to swirl. Cf. Swed. *svirra*, to murmur; G. *schwirren*, to whir; Skt. *svr*, to sound. See Swarm.

Switch, a pliant rod. (M. Du.) For *swich*, palatalised form of *swick*. = M.

Du. *swick*, ' a swich, or a whip;' Hexham; cf. Low G. *zwukse* (Hanov. *swutsche*), a long thin rod. We also find Norw. *svige*, *sveig*, a switch, Icel. *svigi, sveigr*, a switch; Swed. *sveg*, a green twig; all allied to Icel. *sveigja*, to bend; cf. Sway.

Swivel, a link turning on a pin or neck. (E.) Spelt *swiuell* in Minsheu (1627); formed, with suffix *-el*, from *swif-*, weak grade of A. S. *swīfan*, to move quickly (revolve). Allied to Swift. Lit. sense 'that which readily revolves.' Cf. Icel. *sveifla*, to spin round; from *svifa*, to turn. Brugm. i. § 818 (2).

Swoon, to faint. (E.) M. E. *swounen, swoghenen, swowenen*, to swoon. Formed (with formative *n*, usually with a passive sense, as in Goth. verbs in *-nan*) from M. E. *swowen, swoghen*, to swoon, to sigh deeply, also to sough, sigh. This is a strong verb, from A. S. *swōgan*, to move or sweep along noisily, to sough, to sigh as the wind, a strong verb, of which the pp. *geswōgen* occurs with the actual sense of 'in a swoon.' 'Se læg *geswōgen*' = he lay in a swoon, Ælfric's Hom. ii. 336. So also A. S. *geswōwung*, a swooning, A. S. Leechdoms, ii. 176, l. 13. Cf. Low G. *swōgen*, to sigh, *swugten*, to swoon; Lith. *swageti*, to resound. Allied to Sough, q. v.

Swoop, vb. (E.) M. E. *swōpen*, usually in the sense to sweep. [The *ō*, orig. open (<A. S. *ā*) became close owing to the preceding *w*.] A. S. *swāpan*, to sweep along, rush, swoop; also, to sweep (pt. t. *swēop*, pp. *swāpen*). + Icel. *sveipa*, to sweep, swoop; *sōpa*, to sweep; G. *schweifen*, to rove. Base *swaip*, allied to *swaip*, 2nd grade of Teut. *sweipan-*, as in O. Icel. *svīpa*, to move quickly. See Sweep.

Sword. (E.) M.E. *swerd*. A.S. *sweord*. + Du. *swaard*, Icel. *sverð*, Dan. *sværd*, Swed. *svärd*, G. *schwert*. Teut. type *swerdom*, neut.

Sybarite, an effeminate person. (L. – Gk.) L. *Sybarīta*. = Gk. Συβαρίτης, an inhabitant of *Sybaris*, a town named from the river *Sybaris*, on which it was situated; in Lucania, Lower Italy.

Sycamine, a tree. (L. – Gk. – Heb. ?) L. *sȳcamīnus*. = Gk. συκάμινος; Luke xvii. 6. Prob. a Gk. adaptation of Heb. *shiqmīm*, pl. of *shiqmāh*, a sycamore; that it has been confused with *sycamore* is obvious.

Sycamore, a tree. (L. – Gk. – Heb. ?)

Better *sycomore.* ▬ L. *s̄ycomorus.* ▬ Gk. *συκόμορος,* as if it meant 'fig-mulberry'; [Gk. *σῦκο-ν,* fig; *μόρον,* a mulberry]; but prob. a Gk. adaptation of Heb. *shiqmāh,* a sycamore; see above.

Sycophant. (L.–Gk.) L. *s̄ycophanta,* an informer, parasite. ▬ Gk. *συκοφάντης,* lit. 'fig-shewer,' also an informer, a false adviser. [Etymology certain, but the reason for the peculiar use is unknown. The usual explanation, 'informer against those who exported sacred figs from Attica,' is unauthorised.] ▬ Gk. *σῦκο-ν,* a fig; *-φαντης,* lit. 'shewer,' from *φαίνειν,* to shew. See Hierophant.

Syllable. (F.–L.–Gk.) The third *l* is intrusive. M. E. *sillable.*–O. F. *sillabe,* also *sillable.*–L. *syllaba.*–Gk. *συλλαβή,* a syllable, lit. 'holding together,' so much of a word as makes a single sound or element.▬Gk. *συλ-,* for *σύν,* together; *λαβ-,* base of *λαμβάνειν,* to take, seize.

Syllogism, a reasoning from premises. (F.–L.–Gk.) F. *syllogisme.*–L. *syllogismus.*–Gk. *συλλογισμός,* a reasoning.▬ Gk. *συλλογίζομαι,* I reckon together, reason. ▬Gk. *συλ-* (=*σύν*), together; *λογίζομαι,* I reckon, from *λόγος,* discourse, reasoning.

Sylph, an imaginary being inhabiting the air. (F.–Gk.) F. *sylphe.*▬Gk. *σίλφη,* a kind of worm or grub (Aristotle). On this word it would seem that Paracelsus formed the name *sylphe*; he also used the names *gnome, salamander,* and *nymph* (all of Greek origin), to signify, respectively, a genius of earth, fire, and water. Hence the form *sylph-id,* a false form, but only explicable on the hypothesis of a Greek origin; as if from a nom. *σιλφις (base *σιλφιδ-*). ¶ Littré's explanation, that *sylph* is of Gaulish origin, seems to me futile; Paracelsus could hardly have known Gaulish.

Sylvan, misspelling of Silvan.

Symbol, a sign. (F.–L.–Gk.) F. *symbole.*–L. *symbolum.*–Gk. *σύμβολον,* a token, pledge, a sign by which one infers a thing.▬Gk. *συμβάλλειν,* to throw together, compare, infer. ▬ Gk. *συμ-* (*σύν*), together; *βάλλειν,* to throw, put.

Symmetry. (F.–L.–Gk.) M. F. *symmetrie*; Cot. ▬ L. *symmetria.*▬Gk.*συμμετρία,* due proportion. ▬ Gk. *σύμμετρος,* of like measure with. ▬Gk. *συμ-* (= *σύν*), with; *μέτρον,* a measure. See Metre.

Sympathy. (Gk.) From Gk. *συμ-*

πάθεια, fellow-feeling.▬Gk. *συμ-,* for *σύν,* with; *παθεῖν,* to suffer. See Pathos.

Symphony. (F.–L.–Gk.) F. *symphonie,* Cot. ▬ L. *symphōnia.* ▬ Gk. *συμφωνία,*music(Lukexv. 25).▬Gk. *σύμφωνος,* harmonious.▬Gk. *συμ-,*for *σύν,* together; *φωνή,* sound. See Phonetic.

Symposium, a merry feast. (L.–Gk.) L.*symposium.* ▬ Gk. *συμπόσιον,* a drinking-party, banquet. ▬ Gk. *συμ-* (for *σύν*), together; *πο-,* base of *πέ-πω-κα,* I have drunk, *πόσις,* a drink. See Potable.

Symptom, an indication of disease. (F.–L.–Gk.) Properly a medical term. M. F. *symptome*; Cot. ▬ L. *symptōma.* ▬ Gk. *σύμπτωμα,* a casualty, anything that befals one. ▬ Gk. *συμπίπτειν,* to fall in with.▬Gk. *συμ-* (*σύν*), together; *πίπτειν,* to fall. (✓PET.)

Syn-, prefix. (L.–Gk.; *or* F.–L.– Gk.) A Latinised spelling of Gk. *σύν-,* together. It becomes *syl-* before *l; sym-* before *b, m, p, ph*; and *sy-* before *s* or *z.*

Synæresis, the coalescence of two vowels into a diphthong. (L.–Gk.) L. *synæresis.* ▬ Gk. *συναίρεσις,* a taking together. ▬ Gk. *σύν,* together; *αἵρεσις,* a taking, from *αἱρεῖν,* to take. See Heresy.

Synagogue. (F.–L.–Gk.) F. *syna-gogue.* ▬ L. *synagōga.* ▬ Gk. *συναγωγή,* a bringing together; congregation.▬Gk.*σύν,* together; *ἀγωγή,* a bringing, from *ἄγειν,* to bring, drive. (✓AG.)

Synalœpha, a coalescence of two syllables into one. (L.–Gk.) L. *synalœpha.* ▬Gk. *συναλοιφή,* lit. a smearing together. ▬ Gk. *σύν,* together; *ἀλείφειν,* to anoint, allied to *λίπος,* grease. Cf. Skt. *lip,* to besmear, anoint.

Synchronism, concurrence in time. (Gk.) Gk. *συγχρονισμός.*▬Gk. *σύγχρονος,* contemporaneous.▬Gk. *συγ-,* for *σύν,* together; *χρόνος,* time. See Chronicle.

Syncopate, to shorten a word by dropping a syllable. (L. ▬ Gk.) From pp. of L. *syncopāre,* of which the usual sense is 'to swoon.'–L. *syncopē, syncopa,* a swoon; also, syncope. ▬ Gk. *συγκοπή,* a cutting short, syncope, loss of strength. ▬Gk. *συγ-* (written for *σύν,* together, before *κ*); *κοπ-,* base of *κόπτειν,* to cut. See Apocope.

Syndic. (F.–L.–Gk.) F. *syndic,* 'a syndick, censor, controller of manners;' Cot. ▬ L. *syndicus.* ▬ Gk. *σύνδικος,* adj., helping in a court of justice; as a sb., a syndic. — Gk. σύν, together ; δίκη, justice. Allied to Diction. (√DEIK.)

Synecdoche, a figure of speech whereby a part is put for the whole. (L. — Gk.) L. *synecdochē.* — Gk. συνεκδοχή, lit. a receiving together. — Gk. σύν, together ; ἐκδέχομαι, I receive, from ἐκ, out, and δέχομαι (Ion. δέκομαι), I receive. (√DEK.)

Synod. (F. — L. — Gk.) F. *synode.* — L. *synodum,* acc. of *synodus.* — Gk. σύνοδος, a coming together, a meeting. — Gk. σύν, together ; ὁδός, a way, a coming. See Method. (√SED.)

Synonym. (F. — L. — Gk.) F. *synonyme.* — L. (pl.) *synōnyma,* lit. synonyms ; from the adj. *synōnymus,* synonymous, having the same sense as another word. — Gk. συνώνυμος, of like meaning. — Gk. σύν, together ; ὄνομα, a name. **Der.** *synonymous,* from L. *synōnymus ;* *synonymy,* from L. *synōnymia,* Gk. συνωνυμία, likeness of name. See Onomatopœia.

Synopsis, a general view. (L. — Gk.) L. *synopsis.* — Gk. σύνοψις, a seeing all together. — Gk. σύν, together ; ὄψις, sight. **Der.** *synoptic-al,* from Gk. adj. συνοπτικός. See Optic.

Syntax. (F. — L. — Gk.) F. *syntaxe.* — L. *syntaxis.* — Gk. σύνταξις, arrangement ; hence, arrangement of words. — Gk. σύν, together ; τάξις, order, from τάσσειν, to arrange. See Tactics.

Synthesis. (L. — Gk.) L. *synthesis.* — Gk. σύνθεσις, a putting together. — Gk. σύν, together ; θέσις, a putting, from τιθέναι, to set, place. See Thesis. **Der.** *synthetic-al,* from Gk. συνθετικός, skilled in putting together.

Syphon, Syren ; see Siphon, Siren.

Syringe. (F. — L. — Gk.) M. F. *syringue,* 'a siringe, squirt ;' Cot. — L. *syringem,* acc. of *syrinx,* a reed, pipe, tube. — Gk. σύριγξ, a reed, pipe, shepherd's pipe, whistle. **Der.** *syring-a,* a flowering shrub, so named because the stems were used for making Turkish pipes.

Syrup, Sirup. (F. — Span. — Arab.) M. F. *syrop ;* F. *sirop.* — M. Span. *xarope,* a drink ; Span. *jarope.* — Arab. *sharāb, shurāb,* wine, beverage, syrup. — Arab. root *shariba,* he drank. See Sherbet.

System, method. (L. — Gk.) XVII cent. — L. *systēma.* — Gk. σύστημα, a complex whole put together, a system. — Gk. σύ-ν, together ; στῆ-ναι, to stand, pres. t. ἵστημι, I stand. See Statics.

Systole, contraction of the heart,

shortening of a syllable. (Gk.) Gk. συστολή, a drawing together. — Gk. συστέλλειν, to draw together. — Gk. σύ-ν, together ; στέλλειν, to place, put. See Diastole, Stole.

Syzygy, conjunction. (Gk.) Gk. συζυγία, conjunction. — Gk. σύζυγος, conjoined. — Gk. σύ-ν, together ; ζυγ-, weak grade of ζεύγνυμι, I join ; see Yoke, Conjugal. (√YEUG.)

T.

Tabard, a herald's coat. (F.) M. E. *tabard.* — O. F. *tabart, tabard,* also *tribart* (Ducange), a kind of coat. Etym. unknown. Cf. M. Ital. and L. *trabea,* a robe of state.

Tabby, a kind of waved silk. (F. — Span. — Arab.) A *tabby* cat is one marked like the silk. — F. *tabis* (15th cent.) ; also *atabis* (Godefroy). — Span. *tabi,* a silken stuff ; Low L. *attabi.* — Arab. *'utābī,* a rich watered silk. It was the name of a quarter in Bagdad where the silk was made ; named after prince *Attab,* great-grandson of Omeyya. (See Dozy and Devic.) **Der.** *tabi-n-et,* a variety of tabby ; from Ital. *tabin-o,* 'tabine, tabby ;' Torriano.

Tabernacle. (F. — L.) F. *tabernacle.* — L. *tabernāculum,* a tent ; double dimin. of *taberna,* a booth. See Tavern.

Tabid. (L.) L. *tabidus,* wasting away. — L. *tabēre,* to waste away, languish.

Table. (F. — L.) F. *table.* — L. *tabula,* a plank, flat board, table. **Der.** *tabul-ate, tabul-ar,* from L. *tabula ;* *tabl-eau,* from F. *tableau,* dimin. of F. *table.* Also *en-tablature, tafferel.*

Taboo, Tabu, to forbid the use of. (Polynesian) The verb is formed from the sb. *taboo,* which is the E. pronunciation of New Zealand *tapu,* a prohibition or interdict ; pronounced *tambu* in the Solomon Islands. Kotzebue mentions the 'Tabu, or interdict,' in his New Voyage Round the World, London, 1830, ii. 178. ¶ Not in any way connected with the custom of *te pi,* as erroneously said in some former editions.

Tabour, Tabor, a small drum. (F. — Span. — Arab.) M. F. *tabour* (mod. F. *tambour*). — Span. *tambor,* M. Span. *atambor* (where *a = al,* the Arab. def. article). — Arab. *tambūr,* 'a kind of lute or guitar with a long neck, and six brass strings, also a drum.' Prob. of imitative origin ;

cf. Arab. *tabl*, a drum, *tabbāl*, a drummer. Der. *tabour-et* or *tabret*, a dimin. form ; also *tambour*.

Tabular, Tabulate ; see Table.

Tache (1), a fastening. (F. – Low G.) 'A *tache*, a buckle, a claspe ;' Baret (1580), s. v. *Claspe*. – O. F. *tache*, a nail, fastening (Godefroy). – E. Fries. *take*, a point, prick, thorn ; allied to *tak, takke*, a pointed thing, a twig ; Low G. *takk*, a point, pointed thing. See Tack. Cf. *at-tach, de-tach.*

Tache (2), a blemish. (F.) M. E. *tache*, also *tecche*, a bad habit, blemish, vice, caprice, behaviour. – F. *tache*, 'a spot, staine, reproach ;' Cot. Also formerly spelt *taiche, teche, teque, teke*, a natural quality, esp. a vice, ill habit ; mod. F. *tache*, a stain ; Picard *take*. Cf. Ital. *tacca, taccia*, defect, stain ; Port. and Span. *tacha*, defect, flaw, crack. Root unknown ; it is difficult to connect it with Tache (1) ; yet this may be right. Ital. *tacca* also means 'notch' or 'dent' ; cf. E. Fries. *takke*, a notch, *takje*, a small notch, small twig, *take* (Du. *tak*), a twig.

Tacit, silent. (L.) L. *tacitus*, silent. – L. *tacēre*, to be silent. + Goth. *thahan*, Icel. *þegja*, Swed. *tiga*, O. H. G. *dagēn*, to be silent. Der. *tacit-urn*, F. *taciturne*, L. *taciturnus*, silent ; *tacit-urnity*, F. *taciturnité*, L. acc. *taciturnitātem*, silence ; also *re-ticent*.

Tack, a small nail, a fastening ; also to fasten. (E.) M. E. *takke, tak*, a fastening ; *takken*, to fasten together. Of E. or Low G. origin ; cf. E. Fries. Dan. *takke*, a tine, pointed thing ; Low G. *takk* (the same) ; G. *zacke*, a tooth, tine, prong, twig. Allied to E. Fries. *tak*, 'a twig, bough ;' the same as Du. *tak*, a twig. [The Irish *taca*, pin, peg, nail, fastening, Gael. *tacaid*, tack, peg, are from E.] Cf. Norman dial. *taque*, a nail. β. Hence a *tack* or rope fastening a sail ; also the verb *tack*, to sew slightly, attach. γ. Perhaps a *tack*, in sailing, refers to branching out in a given direction ; from Du. *takken*, to branch.

Tackle, equipment, gear, tools. (Scand.) M. E. *takel*. – Swed. and M. Swed. *tackel*, tackle of a ship ; Dan. *takkel*, tackle, whence *takle*, to rig. Cf. Du. *takel*, a pulley, *takelen*, to rig. The suffix *-el* denotes the agent ; *tack-le* is that which *takes* or holds firmly ; cf. M. Du. *taeckel*, 'a rope to drawe a boate.' – Icel. *taka*, to grasp, seize, &c., also to take ; cf. E. Fries.

taken, to grip. ¶ The W. *tacl*, a tool, is borrowed from M. E. *takel*.

Tact. (L.) L. *tactus*, touch ; hence, delicacy. – L. *tactus*, pp. of *tangere*, to touch. See Tangent.

Tactics, the art of manœuvring forces. (Gk.) Gk. τακτικά, neut. pl., tactics. – Gk. τακτικός, adj., fit for arranging. – Gk. τακτός, arranged, ordered ; verbal adj. of τάσσειν (for *τάκ-yειν), to arrange, order. Der. *tactic-ian.*

Tadpole. (E.) Lit. a *toad* which is nearly all *poll* or head ; from its shape ; see Poll. Formerly called a *bullhead*, which was also the name of a small fish with a large head.

Tafferel, Taffrail, upper part of the stern of a ship. (Du.) Du. *tafereel*, a panel, a picture, a tablet or board. For *tafel-eel, dimin. of Du. *tafel*, a table ; cf. G. *täfelei*, boarded work, from G. *tafel*, a table. – L. *tabula*, a table, plank, board. Doublet, *tableau*. ¶ The spelling *taffrail* points to confusion with *rail*.

Taffeta, Taffety, a thin silk stuff. (F. – Ital. – Pers.) F. *taffetas*, 'taffata ;' Cot. – Ital. *taffetà*, 'taffeta ;' Florio. – Pers. *tāftah*, twisted, woven, taffeta. – Pers. *tāftan*, to twist, spin, curl (Horn, § 372).

Tag, a point of metal at the end of a lace, &c. (Scand.) 'An aglet or *tag* of a poynt ;' Baret (1580). – Swed. *tagg*, a prickle, point, tooth ; Norw. *tagge*, a tooth, cog. + Pomeran. *tagg*, a point, tack ; Low G. *takk*, point, tooth. See Tack. Der. *tag-rag*, for *tag* and *rag* = every appendage and shred.

Tail (1), hairy appendage, appendage. (E.) M. E. *tayl*. A. S. *tægel, tægl*, a tail. + Icel. *tagl*, Swed. *tagel*, hair of mane or tail ; Goth. *tagl*, hair ; O. H. G. *zagel*, a tail. Cf. Irish *dual*, a plait, lock of hair, Skt. *daçā*, a skirt. Brugm. i. § 783.

Tail (2), the term applied to an estate which is limited to certain heirs. (F. – L.) Better spelt *taille* ; see Todd's Johnson. – F. *taille*, a cutting, shred ; the same word as Tally (below). And see Entail.

tailor. (F. – L.) Properly 'a cutter,' or cutter out. M. E. *taylor*. – O. F. *tail-leor*, later *tailleur*, 'a cutter ;' Cot. – F. *tailler*, to cut ; cf. F. *taille*, a slitting, an incision. – Late L. *tāliāre*, to cut ; cf. L. *tālea*, a thin rod, stick, slip ; an agricultural term for a slip or layer.

Taint, sb. (F. – L.) F. *teint*, 'a stain ;'

Cot. — F. *teint*, pp. of *teindre*, to tinge. — L. *tingere*, to dye. See **Tinge**.

Take. (Scand.) M. E. *taken*, pt. t. *tok*, pp. *taken*. — Icel. *taka*, pt. t. *tōk*, pp. *tekinn*, to lay hold of, seize, grasp, take; Swed. *taga*, O. Swed. *taka*, Dan. *tage*. + Goth. *tēkan*, to touch.

Talc, a mineral. (F. — Span. — Arab.) F. *talc*. — Span. *talco*. — Arab. *talq*, talc, mica.

Tale, a number, a narrative. (E.) M. E. *tale*. A. S. *tæl*, a number, *talu*, a narrative. + Du. *taal*, speech; Icel. *tal*, speech, *tala*, number; Dan. *tale*, speech, Swed. *tal*, number, speech, G. *zahl*, number. Der. *tal-k*, *tell*.

Talent. (F. — L. — Gk.) The sense of 'ability' is from the parable; Matt. xxv. F. *talent*, 'a talent in money; also will, desire;' Cot. — L. *talentum*. — Gk. τάλαν-τον, a balance, weight, sum of money, talent. Named from being lifted and weighed; cf. Skt. *tul*, L. *tollere*, to lift, Gk. τάλ-ας, sustaining. (√TEL.) Allied to Tolerate. Der. *talent-ed*, in use before A. D. 1640.

Talisman, a spell. (Span. — Arab. — Gk.) Span. *talisman*, a magical character. — Arab. *tilsamān*, pl. of *tilsam*, *tilism*, a talisman, magical image. — Late Gk. τέλεσμα, mystery, initiation; Gk. τέλεσμα, a payment; τελεσμός, an accomplishment. — Gk. τελέειν, to accomplish, end. — Gk. τέλος, end; also initiation into a mystery.

Talk. (E.) E. Fries. *talken*, to talk; cf. *talke*, a short tale. The Low G. *taalke* means (1) a jackdaw, (2) a talkative woman. Extended (like *wal-k*, q. v.) from A. S. *tal-*, as in *talu*, a tale, *talian*, to account, with suffix *-k-*, which seems to give a frequentative force. Cf. Icel. Swed. *tala*, Dan. *tale*, to talk. See **Tale** and **Tell**.

Tall, high in stature, lofty. (C. ?) [We find M. E. *tal*, which meant seemly, also obedient, obsequious, valiant; allied to A. S. *tæl*, appearing in *lēof-tæl*, friendly. So also Goth. *un-tals*, indocile, uninstructed, from which we infer *tals*, docile. Note also A. S. *ge-tal*, quick, prompt; O. H. G. *gi-zal*, quick.] But mod. E. *tall* seems to be quite distinct, and of Celtic origin. Cf. W. *tal*, high, Corn. *tal*, high; Corn. *tal carn*, the high rock; W. *taldra*, tallness, loftiness.

Tallow. (E.) M. E. *talgh*. E. Fries. *talg*, *tallig*. + M. Du. *talgh*, *talch*, tallow; Du. *talk*, Low G. *talg*; Dan. Swed. *talg*; Icel. *tōlgr*. So also G. *talg*, tallow (bor-

rowed from Low G.); cf. O. Merc. *tælg*, a dye.

Tally, a stick notched so as to match another stick; an exact match. (F. — L.) M. E. *taille*, a tally; for keeping accounts. — F. *taille*, a notch, cut, incision, cutting; also a tally, or score kept on a piece of stick by notches. — F. *tailler*, to cut. — Late L. *tāliāre*, to cut; cf. L. *tālea*, a slip of wood. ¶ The final *-y* in *tall-y* is due to the frequent use of F. *taillé*, pp., to signify 'notched'; cf. *lev-y*, *jur-y*, *pun-y*, where *-y* = F. *-é*.

Talmud, the body of Hebrew laws, with comments. (Chaldee.) Chaldee *talmūd*, instruction, doctrine; cf. Heb. *talmīd*, a scholar, from *lāmad*, to learn, *limmad*, to teach.

Talon. (F. — L.) Particularly used of a hawk's hind claw and toe. — F. *talon*, a heel. — Late L. *tālōnem*, acc. of *tālo*, heel. — L. *tālus*, heel.

Tamandua, an ant-eater. (Brazil.) From Guarani *tamānduá*, an ant-eater (where *à* is nasal); see Granada, Vocab. Rioplatense.

Tamarind. (F. — Span. — Arab. *and* Pers.) M.F. *tamarind*. — Span. *tamarindo*. — Arab. *tamr*, a ripe date; *Hind*, India. Lit. 'Indian date.' β. The Arab. *tamr* is allied to Heb. *tāmār*, a palm-tree. *Hind* is borrowed from Pers. (which turns *s* into *h*), and is derived from Skt. *sindhu-*, the river Indus. See **Indigo**.

Tamarisk, a tree. (L.) L. *tamariscus*, also *tamarix*, *tamarīcē*; of foreign origin. Cf. Gk. μυρίκη, a tamarisk.

Tambour, a small drum-like frame, for embroidering. (F. — Span. — Arab.) F. *tambour*, a tambour, also a drum; see **Tabour**.

tambourine. (F. — Span. — Arab.) F. *tambourin*, a tabour, dimin. of F. *tambour*, a tabour or drum: see **Tabour**.

Tame, adj. (E.) M. E. *tame*. A. S. *tam*, tame; whence *temian*, to tame. + Du. *tam*, Icel. *tamr*, Swed. Dan. *tam*, G. *zahm*. Allied to L. *domāre*, Skt. *dam*, Gk. δαμάειν, W. *dofi*, to tame. (√DAM.) See **Daunt**.

Tammy, Tamine; the same as **Stamin**.

Tamper, to meddle, interfere with. (F. — L.) The same word as *temper*, used actively, but in a bad sense; 'to influence in a bad way.' Godefroy gives *tramper* as another form of *temprer*; and *tempreure*, *tampreure*, moderation, manner of operating, temper of a weapon. See **Temper**.

Tampion, a kind of plug. (F. – Teut.) F. *tampon*, bung, stopple; nasalised form of F. *tapon*, the same, augment. of O. F. *tampe, tape*, a bung. Cf. F. *taper, tapper*, to stop with a bung (a Picard word). – Du. *tap*, a bung, tap; Low G. *tappe*, the same. See **Tap** (2).

Tan. (F. – G.) From F. *tan*, 'the bark of a young oak, wherewith leather is tanned;' Cot. (Bret. *tann*, an oak, also tan.) – G. *tanne*, fir-tree. + Du. *den*, a fir-tree; M. Du. *dan*, as in '*abies*, eyn dan,' Mone, Quellen, p. 302. Der. *tan*, vb., &c.; *tan-ling*, Cymb. iv. 4. 29.

Tandem. (L.) L. *tandem*, at length; applied to two horses harnessed *at length*. A University joke.

Tang (1), a strong taste. (Du.) Cf. M. Du. *tanger*, sharp, biting to the taste; lit. pinching. – Du. *tang*, a pair of pincers; see **Tongs**. Cf. O. H. G. *zangar*, sharp to the taste; A. S. *ge-tingan*, to press hard upon (pt. t. *getang*).

Tang (2), to make a shrill sound. (E.) To *tang* is to ring out; an imitative word; allied to *tinker, tingle, twang*.

Tang (3), tongue of a buckle, the part of a knife which goes into the haft. (Scand.) Icel. *tangi*, tang of a knife, which is *nipped* by the handle; Norw. *tange*, tang of a knife, tongue of land; allied to *töng*, tongs; see **Tang** (1), **Tongs**.

Tang (4), seaweed; see **Tangle**.

Tangent. (L.) From L. *tangent-*, touching, stem of pres. pt. of *tangere* (base *tag*), to touch; pp. *tactus*. + Gk. base ταγ-, as in τεταγών, taking.

tangible. (F. – L.) F. *tangible*. – L. *tangibilis*, touchable. – L. *tangere*, to touch.

Tangle, to knot confusedly. (Scand.) Spelt *tangell* in Palsgrave. To *tangle* is 'to keep twisting together like seaweed'; a frequentative verb from North E. *tang*, sea-weed. – Dan. *tang*, Swed. *tång*, Icel. *þang*, kelp or bladder-wrack, a sea-weed (whence the idea of confused heap); cf. Icel. *þöngull*, sea-weed, Norw. *tongul*, a tangle-stalk. So also prov. E. *tangle*, sea-weed; Norman F. *tangon*, a kind of sea-weed (*Fucus flagelliformis*, Métivier). Der. *en-tangle*, with F. prefix *en-* (< L. *in*).

Tanist, a presumptive heir to a prince. (Irish.) Irish *tanaiste*, apparent heir. – Irish *tanaise*, second in rank (Rhŷs).

Tank, a pool. (Port. – L.) Port. *tanque*, cognate with Span. *estanque*, O. F. *estang*, a stank, pool. – L. *stagnum*, a pool. See **Stank.** ¶ Anglo-Indian; see Yule.

Tankard. (F.) O. F. *tanquard*, a tankard (Rabelais); M. Du. *tanckaert*, 'a wodden [wooden] tankard,' Hexham (from F.). Prob. from Swed. *stånka*, a wooden tankard; with F. augment. suffix -*ard*. Swed. *stånka* is a dimin. of *stånna, stånda*, a vat (Rietz); note the *aa* in Norw. *taankar*, a tankard. Cf. Tudor E. *standard*, a tankard, standing-bowl (Greene).

Tansy, a plant. (F. – Low L. – Gk.) M. E. *tansaye, tansey*. – O. F. *tanasie, tanaisie*; earlier form *athanasie, atanasie*. (Cf. M. Ital. *atanasia*, Port. *atanasia*, tansy.) – Late L. **athanasia*, merely the Latinised form of Gk. ἀθανασία, immortality. Cf. M. Ital. *atanato* (lit. immortal), the rose-campion; Florio. Prob. from its supposed virtue, and its use in medicine. – Gk. ἀθάνατος, immortal. – Gk. ἀ-, not; θαν-εῖν, 2 aor. of θνῄσκειν, to die.

Tantalise. (Gk.) Formed with F. suffix -*iser* (< L. -*īzāre* < Gk. -ιζειν), from Gk. Τάνταλ-ος, Tantalus, in allusion to his story. The fable was that he was placed up to his chin in water, which fled from his lips whenever he desired to drink. Allied to τανταλίζειν, τανταλεύειν, to oscillate, sway like a balance; intensive form from ταλ-, as in τάλαντον, a balance. See **Talent.**

Tantamount. (F. – L.) First used as a verb, with the sense 'to amount to as much.' – F. *tant*, so much, as much, from L. *tantum*, neut. of *tantus*, so great; and E. *amount* (of F. origin); see **Amount.**

Tap (1), to knock gently. (F. – Teut.) F. *taper*, M. F. *tapper*, 'to tap, hit;' Cot. – Low G. *tappen*, to grope, fumble, *tappe*, a paw; E. Fries. *tappen*, to grope, *tap*, a light blow; Icel. *tapsa*, to tap. Prob. of imitative origin; cf. Russ. *topate*, to stamp with the foot, Arab. *tabl*, a drum; E. *dub-a-dub*. ¶ Perhaps a native word; M. E. *tappen* occurs rather early.

Tap (2), a short pipe to draw liquor from a cask, a plug. (E.) M. E. *tappe*. A. S. *tæppa*, (Toller); we also find A. S. *tappere*, one who taps casks. + Du. *tap*, Icel. *tappi*, Dan. *tap*, a tap; Swed. *tapp*, a tap, handful, wisp, G. *zapfen*, a tap. β. The orig. idea was prob. a tuft or wisp of something, to stop a hole with; cf. Swed. *tapp* (above), *halm-tapp*, a wisp of straw. **Der.**

tap-root, tap-ster, A. S. *tæppestre,* a fem. form of *tæppere* (above); *tampion,* q. v.

Tape. (L. – Gk.) M. E. *tape,* also *tappe.* A. S. *tæppe,* a tape, a fillet; closely allied to A. S. *tæppet, tæpped,* a tippet, a carpet. The A. S. pl. *tæppan* probably meant strips of stuff or cloth. Borrowed from L. *tapēte,* cloth; see **Tapestry.**

Taper (1), a small wax candle. (E.) M. E. *taper.* A. S. *tapor, taper.* Cf. Irish *tapar,* a taper, W. *tampr,* a taper, torch.

taper (2), long and slender. (E.) *Taper* means *taper-like,* shaped like the tapers used in churches, which were sometimes thinner at the top. Holland has: ' *taper-wise,* sharp-pointed in the top;' tr. of Pliny, xvi. 16. See above. ¶ The A.S. *taper-ax,* a kind of ax, is unallied; cf. Russ. *topor',* Pers. *tabar,* an ax.

Tapestry. (F. – L. – Gk.) A corruption of the old form *tapisserie.* – F. *tapisserie,* tapestry. – F. *tapisser,* to furnish with tapestry. – F. *tapis,* tapestry, hangings; Late L. *tapēcius.* – L. *tapēte,* cloth, hangings. – Gk. ταπητ-, stem of τάπης, a carpet, woollen rug. Cf. Pers. *tabastah,* a fringed carpet; *tābīdan,* to spin, *tāftah,* taffeta; see **Taffeta.**

Tapioca. (Brazilian.) Brazilian *tapioka,* the poisonous juice which issues from the root of the cassava when pressed (Littré); hence tapioca, which is also prepared from the root of the cassava. The Tupi or Brazilian *tipi-ōca* means 'dregs squeezed out'; from *tipi,* residue, dregs, and the verbal root *og, ōk,* to take by force, pull, pluck off, hence to squeeze (Cavalcanti).

Tapir, a quadruped. (Brazilian.) Tupi or Brazilian *tapyra, tapīra,* a tapir.

Tar. (E.) M. E. *terre.* A.S. *teoru, teru,* tar; cf. also *tyrwa.* + Du. *teer,* Icel. *tjara,* Dan. *tiære,* Swed. *tjära.* β. Cf. Icel. *tyri, tyrvi,* resinous wood; allied to Lithuan. *darwa, derwa,* resinous wood, particularly the parts of the fir-tree that readily burn; also to Russ. *drevo,* a tree, *derevo,* wood, timber, W. *derw,* an oak-tree, and E. *tree.* Orig. sense ' wood,' esp. resinous wood for fuel; hence resin from such wood. Allied to **Tree.**

Tar (2), a sailor; see **Tarpauling.**

Tarantella. (Ital.) A dance so called (also a tarantula); so named from Ital. *Taranto,* Tarento, a town in S. Italy.

Taraxacum, the dandelion. (Arab.) From Arab. *tarasacon,* explained as a kind of succory, Pers. *tarkhashqūn,* wild endive; Latinised as *taraxacon,* in Avicenna. (Devic; supp. to Littré.)

Tardy. (F. – L.) F. *tardif,* tardy. (Cf. Ital. *tardivo,* tardy.) From L. *tard-us,* slow; with suffix *-īuus.*

Tare (1), a plant. (E.) M. E. *tare,* darnel (Matt. xiii. 25). Not in A. S.; but the sense is peculiar to English, as the mod. E. *tare* is short for *tare-vetch,* i. e. darnel-vetch. + M. Du. *terwe,* Du. *tarwe,* Low G. *tarve,* wheat; Lith. *dirwa,* corn-field; Skt. *dūrvā,* a kind of grass.

Tare (2), an allowance. (F. – Span. – Arab.) F. *tare,* loss, waste in merchandise. – Span. *tara,* tare, allowance in weight. Lit. ' what is thrown away.' – Arab. *tarha,* what is thrown away, detriment (Devic); *tirh, turrah,* thrown away. – Arab. root *taraha,* he threw prostrate, threw down.

Target, a small shield, &c. (F. – Scand.; *with* F. *suffix.*) Formerly also *tergat;* the *-et* is the F. dimin. suffix. – O. F. *targuete* (Godefroy), a small shield; dimin. of O. F. *targue* (as in Cot.), F. *targe.* – Icel. *targa,* a target, small shield; A.S. *targe;* O. H. G. *zarga,* a frame, side of a vessel, wall, G. *zarge,* frame, case, edge, border. ¶ Distinct from Arab. *darkat, darakat,* a shield, whence Port. and Span. *adarga,* a small square target.

Targum, a Chaldee paraphrase of the Old Testament. (Chaldee.) Chaldee *targūm,* an interpretation. – Chal. *targēm,* to interpret. Cf. Arab. *tarjumān,* an interpreter; see **Dragoman.**

Tariff. (F. – Span. – Arab.) F. *tarif.* M. F. *tariffe,* a casting of accounts. – Span. *tarifa,* a list of prices, book of rates. – Arab. *ta'rīf,* giving information, notification (because a tariff gives notice). – Arab. *'irf,* knowing, knowledge. – Arab. root *'arafa,* he knew.

Tarn, a pool. (Scand.) M. E. *terne.* – Icel. *tjörn* (gen. *tjarnar*), a tarn, a pool; Swed. dial. *tjärn, tärn,* Norw. *tjörn,* a pool without an outlet.

Tarnish. (F. – O. H. G.) F. *terniss-,* stem of pres. pt. of *se ternir,* to become dim, lose lustre (Cot.). – M. H. G. *ternen,* O. H. G. *tarnen,* to obscure, darken; from O. H. G. *tarni,* secret (whence F. *terne,* dim). + A. S. *dernan, dyrnan,* to hide, from *derne, dyrne,* adj., secret; cf. O. Sax. *derni,* hidden, secret.

Tarpauling, a cover of tarred canvas. (E. *and* L.) It means *tarred pauling* or *tarred palling;* a *palling* is a covering, from the verb *pall*, to cover. This verb is from *pall*, sb., a cover; see **Pall**. Der. *tarpaulin*, an old name for a sailor (Smollett), now abbreviated to *tar*.

Tarragon, a plant. (Span.—Arab.— Gk.) Span. *taragona* (Diez); usually *taragontia* (cf. M. F. *targon*, *tragon*).—Arab. *tarkhūn*, dragon-wort. — Gk. δράκων, a dragon. See Devic, s. v. *estragon*; and see **Dragon**.

Tarre, to incite, set on. (E.) In Shak. Hamlet, ii. 2. 370. M. E. *terren, terien, tarien*, to irritate, provoke.—A. S. *tergan* (rare), *tirgan*, to vex, provoke ; N. Fries. *tarre, terre*, to set on a dog. See **tarry**.

tarry. (E.) The present form is due to M. E. *tarien, terien*, to irritate, provoke, worry, vex; hence to hinder, delay. [This is the true source of the word, though its meaning may have been affected and fixed by the O. F. *targer*, to delay, from Late L. *tardicāre, to delay, from L. *tardus*, slow; see **Tardy**.]—A.S. *tergan*, usually *tirgan*, to vex, provoke. **+** Du. *tergen*, Low G. *targen, tarren*, to provoke ; prov. G. *zergen*, to provoke.

Tart (1), acrid, sharp, severe. (E.) A. S. *teart*, tart, severe. Perhaps lit. tearing, i. e. bitter. — A. S. *tar (*tær*), 2nd grade of *teran*, to tear. See **Tear** (1).

Tart (2), a small pie. (F.—L.) M. E. *tarte.* — O. F. *tarte*, ‘a tart;’ Cot. It seems to be a perverted form of O. F. *torte*, F. *tourte*, a tart, Ital. *tartera, torta*, a pie or tart, Span. *torta*, a round cake. — L. *torta*, fem. of *tortus*, pp. of *torquēre*, to twist. Perhaps confused with L. *tracta*, a long piece of dough.

Tartan, a woollen stuff. (F.—Span.) F. *tiretaine*, ‘linsie-wolsie, or a kind therof, worn ordinarily by the French peasants;’ Cot. — Span. *tiritaña*, a thin woollen stuff; so named from its flimsiness; cf. Port. *tiritana*, a light silk. — Span. and Port. *tiritar*, to shiver, shake with cold. Perhaps of imitative origin.

Tartar (1), an acid salt in casks, a concretion on the teeth. (F.—Late L.— Arab.) A term due to the alchemists ; called *sal tartre*, or *tartre*, in Chaucer. — F. *tartre*, ‘tartar,’ Cot. ; Late L. *tartarum* (by confusion with *Tartarus*). — Arab. *durd*, dregs, sediment, tartar of wine; *durdīy*, dregs. Cf. Arab. *darad*, a shedding of teeth; which Devic connects with tartar on the teeth.

Tartar (2), a native of Tartary. (Tatar.)

A perverse spelling of *Tatar*, owing to a popular etymology which regarded Tatars as let loose out of *Tartarus* or hell (see below). From *Tātar*, a Tatar or inhabitant of Tatary (as it should be spelt).

Tartar (3), Tartarus, hell. (L.—Gk.) ‘ The gates of *Tartar* ;’ Tw. Nt. ii. 5. 225. —L. *Tartarus.*—Gk. Τάρταρος, Tartarus, the infernal regions; conceived to be a place of extreme cold; cf. Gk. ταρταρίζειν, to shiver with cold.

Task, sb. (F.—L.) Lit. a tax. M.E. *taske.* — O. North F. *tasque*, Norm. dial. *tasque*, a tax, O. F. *tasche*, a task (mod. F. *tâche*).—Late L. *tasca*, a tax, another form of Late L. *taxa*, a tax.—L. *taxāre*, to tax. See **Tax**.

Tassel (1), a bunch of silk, &c., as an ornament. (F.—L.) M. E. *tassel.*—O. F. *tassel*, an ornament, fringe; also a piece of square stuff (cf. Ital. *tassello*, a square, a collar of a cloak).—L. *taxillum*, acc. of *taxillus*, a small die; dimin. of *tālus*, a knuckle-bone, a die made of knuckle-bone. *Tālus* = *tax-lus, as shewn by the dimin. *taxillus*, and means a bone cut or squared; cf. Skt. *taksh*, to hew, prepare, make. **¶** The application to a tassel is curious; a woodcut at p. 272 of Guillim’s Display of Heraldry (1660) shews a tassel ornamented with strings and dots; these strings divide it into squares, each of which (having a dot in the middle) resembles *an ace on a die*. It was confused with L. *tessella* (see **Tesselated**) ; cf. ‘ *Tessera*, tasol ;’ O. E. Texts.

Tassel (2) ; the same as Tercel.

Taste. (F.—L.) Orig. to handle, feel, the usual sense of M. E. *tasten.* — O. F. *taster*, to handle, feel, taste. Cf. Late L. *taxta*, O. F. *taste*, a probe for wounds; so that O. F. *taster* answers to a Late L. *taxitāre, iterative form of *taxāre*, to feel, handle (Gellius). Again *taxāre* (<*tagsāre) is an intensive form of L. *tangere*, to touch. See **Tangent**.

Tat, to make trimming. (Scand.) North E. *tat*, to entangle.—M. Swed. *tatte*, Dan. dial. *tat*, Norw. *taatt*, a thread, strand of a rope, whence Norw. *tætta*, to interweave. Cf. Icel. *þáttr*, Swed. *tåt*, a strand, filament ; Dan. *tot*; G. *docht*, a wick.

Tatter, a shred. (Scand.) Also spelt *totter.* — Icel. *töturr*; pl. *tötrar, töttrar*, rags, tatters ; Norw. *totror, tottrar*, also *taltrar*, pl., rags, tatters.**+**Low G. *taltern*, rags, *taltrig*, ragged ; E. Fries. *talte*, a rag, *taltrig*, ragged. Thus *tatter* stands for *talter*, with loss of *l*; cf. Low G. *talt'r*, *tadler*, a rag (Danneil); perhaps also A. S. *tættec*, a rag. I suppose the orig. sense was 'that which flaps or flutters about,' and that it is closely allied to *totter*, q. v.

Tattle, vb. (E.) M. E. *tatelen*, *totelen*, *tateren*, to tattle, prattle. We also find M. E. *titeren*, to tattle, whence mod. E. *tittle*, in the phrase *tittle-tattle*. *Tattle* and *tittle* are frequentative forms, from a base TAT or TIT, expressive of the iteration of the syllables *ta*, *ta*, *ta*, or *ti*, *ti*, *ti*, to indicate constant prattling. So also Du. *tateren*, to stammer, E. *taratantara*, the sound of a trumpet, Low G. *tateln*, to tattle, *titetateln*, to tittle-tattle, *taat-goos*, a gabbling goose, a chatterer; Ital. *tatta-mella*, chat, prattle. Der. *tittle*, weakened form of *tattle*, as above; whence *tittletattle*.

Tattoo (1), the beat of a drum recalling soldiers to their quarters. (Du. *or* Low G.) Formerly *taptoo* (Phillips); used as early as A.D. 1663. — Du. *taptoe*, tattoo. — Du. *tap*, a tap; *toe*, to, i.e. shut, closed. Due to the phrase appearing in Low G. *tappen to slaan*, lit. 'to strike a tap to,' a proverbial phrase (like E. *shut up*) signifying to close, conclude; esp. used of closing the taps of the public-houses, at the sound of the drum. So also G. *zapfenstreich*, the tattoo, is lit. 'tap-stroke;' and Low G. *tappenslag*, the tattoo, is its equivalent. β. The Du. *tap* is cognate with E. *tap*; and Du. *toe* with E. *to*, prep. See **Tap** and **To**.

Tattoo (2), to mark the skin with figures, by pricking in colouring matter. (Tahitian.) See Cook's First Voyage, b. i. c. 17, b. iii. c. 9. — Tahitian *tatau*, tattoo-marks; derived from *ta*, a mark (Littré). The Maori *ta* means to tattoo, to mark.

Taunt, vb. (F. — L.) Hardly from O.F. *tanter* (see Littré), occasional form of *tenter*, 'to tempt, prove, essay, suggest, provoke, or move unto evill;' Cot. — L. *tentāre*, to try, prove, attack, assail, &c.; see **Tempt**. β. Rather from the M.F. phrase *tant pour tant*, 'one for another,' Cot.; cf. *tit for tat*. — O. F. *taunt*, *tant*, so much. — L. *tantum*, neut., so much.

Taurus. (L.) L. *taurus*, a bull. ╋Gk. ταῦρος. Allied to **Steer** (1).

Taut, tight, firm. (E.) M. E. *togt*, *toght*. Lit. 'pulled tight;' pp. of M. E. *togen*, to tow, pull. See **Tow**.

Tautology. (F. — Gk.) L. *tautologia*. — Gk. ταυτολογία, a repetition of what has been said already. — Gk. ταυτολόγος, repeating what has been said. — Gk. ταυτό, short for τὸ αὐτό or τὸ αὐτόν, the same thing; -λογος, speaking, from λέγειν, to speak.

Tavern. (F. — L.) F. *taverne*. — L. *taberna*, a hut, orig. a hut of boards; a tavern. Perhaps allied to L. *tabula*, a plank, board; see **Table**.

Taw, a game at marbles. (Gk.) Orig. the mark from which the marbles were shot, and marked (originally) with a T, to denote an exact spot. From Gk. ταῦ, among schoolboys; a letter-name of Semitic origin. Cf. **Tee**.

Taw, Tew, to prepare skins, curry; also to toil. (E.) M. E. *tawen*, *tewan*. A. S. *tawian*, to prepare, dress, get ready; also, to scourge. Cf. A.S. *getawa*, implements. ╋Du. *touwen*, to curry leather; O. H. G. *zouwen*, to make, prepare; Goth. *taujan*, to do, cause. See **Tool**.

Tawdry, showy, gaudy. (E.) Formerly used in the phrase *tawdry lace*, which meant lace bought at *St. Awdry's* fair, held in the Isle of Ely (and elsewhere) on St. Awdry's day, Oct. 17. *Tawdry* is a familiar contraction of *St. Awdry*. β. Again, *Awdry* is a popular form of *Etheldrida*, the Latinised form of the A. S. female name *Æþelþrȳð*. It means 'noble strength'; from A.S. *æðel* or *æþel*, noble, and *þrȳð* or *þrȳðu*, strength. Cf. Icel. *prūðr*, the name of a goddess; and the suffix in *Ger-trude*, a name of O. H. G. origin.

Tawny. (F. — G.) For *tanny*; spelt *tenny* in heraldry. '*Tanny* colowre, or *tawny*;' Prompt. Parv. — F. *tanné*, tawny; lit. tanned; pp. of *tanner*, to tan. — F. *tan*, sb., tan. — G. *tanne*, a fir-tree. See **Tan**.

Tax, sb. (F. — L.) M. E. *taxe*. — F. *taxe*. — F. *taxer*, to tax. — L. *taxāre*, to handle, value, appraise, tax. For **tag-sāre*; from *tag-*, base of *tangere*, to touch. **Doublet**, *task*.

Taxidermy, the art of stuffing the skins of animals. (Gk.) From Gk. τάξι-s, order (see **Tactics**); δέρμ-α, a skin, from δέρ-ειν, to flay, cognate with **Tear** (1).

Tea. (Chinese.) Spelt *tee* in Pepys' Diary, Sept. 28, 1660; *cha* in Blount (1674). From the Amoy pronunciation (*tē*) of the Chinese name for the plant, which is (in other parts of the empire) called *ch'a* or *ts'a*; Williams, Chin. Dict.

p. 5; Douglas, Chin. Dict. of the Amoy vernacular, p. 481. Hence Ital. *cià*, tea; F. *thé*, G. *thee*, Malay *tēh*, tea.

Teach. (E.) M. E. *techen*. A. S. *tǣcan*, to shew how to do, shew, pt. t. *tǣhte*, pp. *tǣht*. Formed (with change of *ā* to *ǣ* before *j*, as in Teut. **taikjan-*), from *tāc-* (Teut. **taik-*), base of *tāc-en*, a token. Allied to Gk. δείκ-νυμι, I shew. See **Token**.

Teak, a tree. (Malayālam.) Malayālam *tēkka*, the teak-tree; Tamil *tēkku*, the same (H. H. Wilson).

Teal, a bird. (E.) M. E. *tele* (13th cent.); not in A. S. **+** Du. *taling*, older form *taeling* (Sewel), M. Du. *teelingh*, a teal (Kilian). The A.S. form would be **tǣle*.

Team, a family, set, animals harnessed in a row. (E.) M. E. *tēm*, *teem*. A. S. *tēam*, a family, offspring. **+** Du. *toom*, a rein (from the notion of drawing or guiding); Low G. *toom*, offspring, also a rein; Icel. *taumr*, a rein; Dan. *tömme*, Swed. *töm*, a rein; G. *zaum*, a bridle. Teut. type **tau-moz*, for **taug-moz* (Noreen), from *tauh*, 2nd grade of **teuh-an-*, to draw. See Tow (1). (√DEUK.) Der. *teem*.

Tear (1), to rend. (E.) M. E. *teren*. A. S. *teran*, pt. t. *tær*, pp. *toren*. **+**Goth. *ga-tairan*, to break, destroy; Lith. *dir-ti*, to flay, Gk. δέρ-ειν, to flay; Russ. *dra-te*, to tear; Pers. *darīdan*, to tear; cf. W. *darn*, a fragment; Zend *dar*, to cut; Skt. *dāraya*, to tear. Teut. type **teran-*, pt. t. **tar*; pp. **turanoz*. (√DER.) Cf. also G. *zehren* (weak verb). Brugm. i. § 594.

Tear (2), a drop of fluid from the eye. (E.) M. E. *tere*. A. S. *tēar*, *tǣr*, also *teagor*; O. Northumb. *tæher*. **+** Icel. *tār*, Dan. *taar*, *taare*, Swed. *tår*, Goth. *tagr*, O. H. G. *zahar* (pl. *zaheri*, whence mod. G. *zähre*). Cf. O. Lat. *dacruma*, L. *lacrima*, Gk. δάκρυ, δάκρυμα, W. *dagr*, a tear, O. Irish *dēr*. Brugm. i. § 178. Der. *train-oil*.

Tease, to card wool, to vex, plague. (E.) M. E. *tēsen*. A. S. *tǣsan*, to pluck, pull. **+**M. Du. *teesen*, to pluck wool; Swed. dial. *tesa*, Dan. *tæse*, Bavarian *zaisen* (Schmeller), O. H. G. *zeisan*. All from Teut. base **teis*.

teasel, a plant. (E.) M. E. *tēsel*. A. S. *tǣsl*, *tǣsel*, lit 'teaser,' from its use in teasing wool.**—** A. S. *tǣsan*, to tease. **+** O. H. G. *zeisala*, teasel; from *zeisan*, to tease.

Teat, nipple of the female breast. (F.

—Low G.) M. E. *tete*, *tette*. **—** O. F. *tete*, *tette*; F. *tette*.**—**Low G. *titte*, M. Du. *titte*.**+**A. S. *tit* (pl. *tittas*), whence E. *tit*, a teat; G. *zitze*. Cf. also W. *didi*, *did*, a teat. (As if from an Idg. base DI.) ¶ Distinct from Gk. τίτθη, τιτθός, a teat, which appears to be allied to Skt. *dhē*, to suck, Goth. *daddjan*, to suckle.

Teazle, i. e. teasel; see **teasel**.

Technical. (Gk.) Formed with suffix *-al* (=L. *-ālis*) from Gk. τεχνικός, belonging to the arts.**—**Gk. τέχνη, art, allied to τέκτων, a carpenter. Cf. Skt. *takshan*, a carpenter, from *taksh*, to cut wood. Allied to **Text**.

Techy, fretful; see **Tetchy**.

Ted, to spread mown grass. (Scand.) Icel. *teðja*, to spread manure, from *tað*, manure; cf. *taða*, hay grown in a well-manured field, *töðu-verk*, hay-making, lit. 'ted-work.' So also Norw. *tedja*, Swed. dial. *täda*, to spread manure; from *tad*, manure.**+**Bavarian *zetten*, O. H. G. *zettan*, to strew; cf. G. *ver-zetteln*, to scatter.

Tedious. (L.) L. *tædiōsus*, irksome. **—**L. *tædium*, irksomeness.**—**L. *tædet*, it irks one. (We also use *tedium*, sb.)

Tee, a mark. (E.) From the use of a T to denote an exact spot. Cf. *tee-totum*; and see **Taw**.

Teem (1), to be prolific. (E.) M. E. *tēmen*, to teem; *tēm*, sb., progeny, offspring; whence mod. E. *team*. See **Team**. The M. E. *tēmen* answers to A. S. *tēman*, *tȳman*, older *tīeman*, to teem. Teut. type **taumjan-*, from **taumoz*, a team.

Teem (2), to empty. (Scand.) Icel. *tæma*, Dan. *tömme*, Swed. *tömma*, vb.; from the adj. *toom*; see **Toom**.

Teen, vexation, grief. (E.) M. E. *tene*. A. S. *tēona*, accusation, vexation.**—**A. S. *tēon*, contracted form of **tīhan*, to accuse. **+**Goth. *gateihan*, to tell, make known; G. *zeihen*, to accuse; cf. L. *dicāre*, to make known. Allied to **Diction**. (√DEIK.) ¶ *Teen* means a making known, public accusation, reproach, injury, vexation, grief, harm.

Teetotaller, a total abstainer. (F. — L.; *with E. prefix and suffix*.) *Tee-total* is an emphasised form of **Total**, q.v. The word originated with R. Turner, of Preston, who, at a temperance meeting about 1833, asserted that nothing but *te-te-total* will do; see the Staunch Teetotaller, ed. by J. Livesey, of Preston, Jan. 1867. (Haydn.) See below.

Teetotum, Totum, a spinning toy. (L.) Formerly *totum* (Ash, 1775, Phillips, 1706). So called from the side formerly marked *T*, which signified *totum*, i. e. all the stake, from L. *tōtum*, neut. of *tōtus*, the whole; see **Total.** Hence the name *totum*, or *T-totum*; which may have suggested *T-total*.

Tegument, a covering. (L.) L. *tegumentum*, a covering. – L. *tegere*, to cover. +Gk. στέγειν, Skt. *sthag*, to cover. Cf. O. Irish *tech*, W. *tŷ*, a house. Allied to Thatch. (√STEG.) Brugm. i. § 632.

Teil-tree, a linden tree. (F. – L.; *and* E.) O. F. *teil*, a lime-tree; also, the inner bark of a lime-tree (mod. F. *tille*). – L. *tilia*, a lime-tree; also, the inner bark of a lime-tree.+Irish *teile*.

Telegraph. (Gk.) Modern. From Gk. τῆλε, afar; γράφειν, to write. **Der.** *telegram*, coined to express 'telegraphic message'; from γράμμα, a written character.

telescope. (Gk.) From Gk. τῆλε, afar; σκοπ-εῖν, to behold. See **Scope.**

Tell, to count, narrate. (E.) A. S. *tellan*, pt. t. *tealde*, pp. *teald*; a weak verb (for **tal-jan*). – A. S. *talu*, number, narrative; see **Tale.**+Du. *tellen*, Icel. *telja*, Dan. *tælle*, Swed. *tälja*, G. *zählen*; all from sbs. Teut. type **taljan-.*

Telluric, belonging to earth. (L.) From L. *tellūr-*, stem of *tellūs*, earth. **Der.** *telluri-um*, a rare metal.

Temerity. (F. – L.) M.F. *temerité.* – L. acc. *temeritātem*, rashness. – L. adv. *temere*, rashly. The orig. sense of *temere* was 'in the dark'; cf. Skt. *tamas*, gloom.

Temper, vb. (L.) M. E. *tempren.* A. S. *temprian*, to temper. – L. *temperāre*, to apportion, regulate, qualify. Allied to *temperī, temporī*, adv., seasonably, and to *tempus*, time; see **Temporal** (1). Brugm. ii. § 132.

tempest. (F. – L.) O. F. *tempeste* (F. *tempête*), a storm; answering to a Late L. *tempesta*, fem. of Late L. *tempestus*, adj., used instead of L. *tempestās*, season, fit time, weather, also bad weather, storm. From L. *tempus*, time (above). Brugm. ii. §§ 102, 132.

Temple (1), a fane. (L.) A. S. *templ, tempel.* – L. *templum*, a temple. + Gk. τέμενος, a sacred enclosure, piece of ground cut off; allied to τέμνειν, to cut. (√TEM.) Brugm. ii. § 76. **Der.** *tempi-ar*, Late L. *templārius.*

Temple (2), flat portion of the side of the head above the cheek-bone. (F. – L.) M. E. *templis*, pl. – O. F. *temples*, pl., temples (mod. F. *tempes*, Norm. dial. *temples*). – L. *tempora*, pl., the temples. **Der.** *tempor-al*, adj., belonging to the temples.

Temporal (1), worldly, secular. (F. – L.) M. E. *temporal.* – O. F. *temporal, temporel*, adj. – L. *temporālis*, temporal. – L. *tempor-*, for **tempos-*, stem of *tempus*, time.

Temporal (2), belonging to the temples; see **Temple** (2).

Tempt. (F. – L.) O.F. *tempter*, later *tenter*, to tempt, prove. – L. *temptāre, tentāre*, to handle, try the strength of, assail, tempt; frequentative of *tendere* (pp. *tentus*), to stretch (Bréal). See **Tend** (1).

Ten. (E.) A. S. *tŷn, tīen*, with mutation; O. Merc. *tēn.* The long vowel appears in *-teen.* + Du. *tien*; Icel. *tíu*, Dan. *ti*, Swed. *tio*; Goth. *taihun*; G. *zehn*; L. *decem*, Gk. δέκα, Lith. *deszimtis*, Russ. *desiate*, W. *deg*, Irish and Gael. *deich*, Pers. *dah*, Skt. *daça.* Teut. type **tehon*; Idg. type **dekam.* Brugm. ii. § 174. **Der.** *ten-th*; see **Tithe.**

Tenable, that can be held. (F. – L.) F. *tenable*, 'holdable,' Cot. – F. *tenir*, to hold. – L. *tenēre*, to hold, keep; orig. to extend.+Skt. *tan*, to extend, stretch; Gk. τείνειν (for **τένγειν*), to stretch. Allied to **Thin.**

tenacious. (L.) Coined from L. *tenāc-i-*, decl. stem of *tenax*, holding fast; with suffix *-ous.* – L. *tenēre* (above).

tenacity. (F. – L.) M.F. *tenacité.* – L. *tenācitātem*, acc. of *tenācitās*, a holding firm. – L. *tenāci-* (above).

tenant. (F. – L.) F. *tenant*, holding, pres. pt. of *tenir.* – L. *tenēre*, to hold. **Der.** *lieu-tenant*, q. v.

Tench, a fish. (F. – L.) O. F. *tenche* (F. *tanche*). – L. *tinca*, a tench.

Tend (1), to aim at, move towards, incline, bend to. (F. – L.) F. *tendre.* – L. *tendere*, to stretch, extend, direct, tender. Allied to *tenēre*, to hold; see **Tenable.** (√TEN.) Brugm. ii. § 696 (3). **Der.** *tend-enc-y*, formed by adding *-y* to the obs. sb. *tendence*, coined from the stem of *tendere.*

Tend (2), to take care of. (F. – L.) A docked form of **Attend.**

Tender (1), soft, delicate. (F. – L.) F. *tendre.* – L. *tenerum*, acc. of *tener*, tender, orig. thin; allied to *tenuis*, thin. (✓ TEN.) See **Thin**. Der. *tender*, vb., to regard fondly, a word more or less confused with *tender* (2); whence *tender*, sb., regard, care, K. Lear, i. 4. 230.

Tender (2), to proffer, offer, shew. (F. —L.) F. *tendre*, 'to tend, .. also to tender or offer unto;' Cot. —L. *tendere*, to stretch out. See **Tend** (1).

tender (3), a small vessel that attends a larger, a coal-carriage attached to a locomotive engine. (F. — L.; *with* E. *suffix*.) Short for *attender*, i. e. attendant on; see **Tend** (2) and **Attend**.

tendon. (F.—L.) F. *tendon*, 'a tendon, or taile of a muscle;' Cot. From a Late L. form **tendo*, gen. *tendōnis* and *tendinis*; cf. Span. *tendon*, Ital. *tendine*, a tendon; Port. *tendāo*. Lit. 'stretcher.' —L. *tendere*, to stretch.

Tendril. (F.—L.) From O. F. *tendrillons*, pl. 'tendrells;' Cot.; or from an O. F. **tendrille*, not recorded. We also find O. F. *tendron*, 'a tender fellow, also a tendrell;' Cot.—F. *tendre*, tender; see **Tender** (1).

Tenebrous, Tenebrious, gloomy. (F.—L.) M. F. *tenebreux*.—L. *tenebrōsus*, gloomy.—L. *tenebræ*, pl., darkness. Allied to Skt. *tamisra-*, darkness, *tamas*, gloom. Brugm. i. § 413. (✓TEM.) See **Dim**.

Tenement, a holding. (F.—L.) M.F. *tenement*.—Late L. *tenēmentum*, a fief.— L. *tenēre*, to hold.

tenet. (L.) L.*tenet*, he holds; 3rd pers. sing. pres. of *tenēre*. (Cf. *habitat*, *exit*.)

Tennis. (F.—L.) M.E. *tenétz* (accented on latter *e*); Gower, Balade to Henry IV, l. 295, also *tenise*, *teneis*, *teneys*; whence Late L. *tenisia*, *teniludium*.—A. F. *tenetz*, F. *tenez* (< L. *tenēte*), imp. pl. of *tenēre*, to hold; perhaps used to mean 'take this,' and ejaculated by the player in serving.

Tenny, a colour in heraldry. (F.—G.) The same as *tawny* or *tanny*; see **Tawny**.

Tenon. (F.—L.) F. *tenon*, 'a tenon, the end of a rafter put into a morteise;' Cot. So called because it *holds fast*.—F. *tenir*, to hold fast.—L. *tenēre*, to hold.

tenor. (F. — L.) Formerly (better) *tenour*. M. E. *tenour*, import.—F. *teneur*, import, content of a matter.—L. *tenōrem*, acc. of *tenor*, a holding on; a course, tenor of a law.—L. *tenēre* to hold. ¶ The sense of *tenor* in music (Ital. *tenore*) is due to the notion of holding or continuing the dominant note (Scheler).

Tense (1), part of a verb, indicating time of action. (F.—L.) M. E. *temps*, Chaucer, C. T. 16343. — F. *temps*, time (also O. F. *tens*). — L. *tempus*, time, also a tense.

Tense (2), tightly strained. (L.) L. *tensus*, pp. of *tendere*, to stretch; see **Tend** (1). Der. *tense-ness*, with E. suffix.

tension, the act of straining, a strain. (F.—L.) F. *tension*, used in 16th cent. —L. *tensiōnem*, acc. of *tensio*, a stretching. —L. *tens-um*, supine of *tendere* (above). So also *tens-or*, a coined word.

tent (1), a pavilion. (F.—L.) F. *tente*. —Late L. *tenta*, a tent; fem. of L. *tentus*, pp. of *tendere*, to stretch, spread out.

Tent (2), a roll of lint used to dilate a wound. (F.—L.) M. E. *tente*.—F. *tente*; Cot. A verbal sb. from F. *tenter* < L. *tentāre*, to try, prove, probe. Cf. Span. *tienta*, a probe. See **Tempt**.

Tent (3), a wine. (Span.—L.) From Span. *vino tinto*, a deep-coloured (lit. tinted) wine.—L. *tinctus*, pp. of *tingere*, to dye. See **Tinge**.

Tent (4), heed, attention. (F.—L.) In Lowl. Sc. *tak tent*. Short for *attent*, i. e. *attention*.

Tentacle, feeler of an insect. (L.) Coined from L. *tentā-re*, to feel; with suffix *-cu-lum*; see **Tempt**.

tentative. (L.) L. *tentātīuus*, adj., trying, tentative.—L. *tentāre*, to try; see **Tempt**.

Tenter, a frame for stretching cloth. (F.—L.) Properly *tenture*; but a vb. *tent* was coined, and from it a sb. *tenter*, which supplanted M.E. *tenture*. — M.F. *tenture*, a stretching.—L. *tentūra*, a stretching.— L. *tentus*, pp. of *tendere*, to stretch. See **Tend** (1). Der. *tenter-hook*.

Tenth. (E.) M. E. *tenþe*, coined (by analogy with *seven-th*, *nin-th*) from *ten*; the true E. word is *tithe*.

Tenuity, thinness. (F. — L.) M. F. *tenuité*. — L. *tenuitātem*, acc. of *tenuitās*, thinness.—L. *tenui-s*, thin; lit. 'stretched out.' Cognate with **Thin**. (✓TEN.)

Tenure. (F.—L.) F. *tenure*.—Late L. *tenūra*, a holding (of land).—L. *tenēre*, to hold. See **Tenable**.

Teocalli, a temple. (Mexican.) From *teotl*, a god; and *calli*, a house.

Tepid. (L.) L. *tepidus*, warm. — L. *tepēre*, to be warm. **+** Skt. *tap*, to be warm; Russ. *topite*, to heat; Irish *tē*, hot. (✓TEP.)

Teraphim, idols, household gods. (Heb.) Heb. *teráphīm,* s. pl., images connected with magical rites.

Terce, the same as Tierce.

Tercel, Tassel, the male of any hawk. (F.—L.) M. E. *tercel*; dimin. *tercel-et.* —O. F. *tercel, tiercel*; whence the dimin. *tiercelet,* 'the tassell, or male of any kind of hawke; so tearmed because he is, commonly, a third part lesse then the female;' Cot. [Another alleged reason is, that every third bird hatched was, in popular opinion, sure to be a male. So also Ital. *terzolo,* 'a tassel gentle of a hauke;' Florio.]—O. F. *tiers, tierce,* third.—L. *tertius,* third; see Tierce.

Terebinth, turpentine-tree. (L.—Gk.) L. *terebinthus.*—Gk. τερέβινθος, the turpentine-tree; earlier form τέρμινθος.

Tergiversation, a subterfuge, fickleness. (F.—L.) F. *tergiversation.*—L. *tergiuersātiōnem,* acc. of *tergiuersātio,* a subterfuge.—L. *tergiuersātus,* pp. of *tergiuersāri,* to turn one's back, turn right round, shuffle.—L. *tergi-,* for *tergum,* the back; *uersāri,* to turn about, pass. of *uersāre,* frequent. of *uertere,* to turn; see Verse.

Term. (F.—L.) M. E. *terme.* —F. *terme.*—L. *terminum,* acc. of *terminus,* boundary, limit. **+** Gk. τέρμα, limit; Skt. *tāraya,* to cause to pass over. (√TER.)

Termagant. (F.—Ital.—L.) M. E. *Termagant, Teruagant,* a (supposed) Saracen idol, hence a ranting character in old moralities [plays], and finally a scolding woman.—O. F. *Tervagant, Tervagan,* a (supposed) Saracen idol (Chanson de Roland). **—** Ital. *Trivigante,* the same (Ariosto, xii. 59). Explained as *Trivagante,* the moon, wandering under the three names of *Selene* (or *Luna*) in heaven, *Artemis* (*Diana*) in earth, *Persephone* (*Proserpina*) in the lower world.—L. *ter,* thrice; *uagant-,* stem of pres. pt. of *uagāri,* to wander. But perhaps Eastern.

Termination. (F.—L.) M.F. *termination.*—L. acc. *terminātiōnem,* a bounding, ending.—L. *terminātus,* pp. of *termināre,* to bound, end.—L. *terminus,* boundary. See Term.

terminus, end. (L.) L. *terminus* (above).

Tern, a bird. (Scand.) Dan. *terne, tærne,* Swed. *tärna,* Icel. *þerna,* a tern. Cf. A. S. *stearn,* a tern; and Starling.

Ternary. (L.) L. *ternārius,* consisting

of three.—L. *ternī,* pl., by threes.—L. *ter,* three times; *trēs,* three; see Three.

Terra cotta, a kind of hard pottery. (Ital.—L.) Ital. *terra cotta,* baked earth. — L. *terra,* earth (below); *cocta,* fem. of *coctus,* pp. of *coquere,* to cook; see Cook.

terrace. (F.—Ital.—L.) M.F. *terrace, terrasse,* a terrace, platform, plat.—M. Ital. *terraccia, terrazza,* a terrace, long mound of earth.—Ital. *terra,* earth.—L. *terra,* earth. β. *Terra=*tersa,* i. e. dry ground; allied to O. Irish *tīr,* W. *tir,* earth; also to Gk. τέρσεσθαι, to dry up. (√TERS.) See Torrid, Thirst. Brugm. i. § 706 (b).

terreen, tureen, a large bowl for soup. (F.—L.) Both spellings are bad; *terrine* would be better.—F. *terrine,* an earthen pan.—L. *terr-a,* earth; with suffix *-īna,* fem. of *-īnus.*

terrene, earthly. (L.) L. *terrēnus,* earthly.—L. *terra,* earth.

terrestrial. (L.) From L. *terrestri-s,* earthly; with suffix *-ālis.* **—** L. *terra,* earth; with suffix *-st-tr-.*

Terrible. (F.—L.) F. *terrible.*—L. *terribilis,* causing terror.—L. *terrēre,* to frighten. See Terror.

Terrier (1), a kind of dog. (F.—L.) M. E. *terrere,* a 'burrow-dog,' one who pursues rabbits, &c. at their holes.—F. *terrier,* as in *chien terrier,* 'a terrier;' Cot. Cf. *terrier,* 'the hole, berry, or earth of a conny [rabbit] or fox; also, a little hillock;' Cot.—Late L. *terrārius,* belonging to earth. **—** L. *terra,* earth. See Terrace.

terrier (2), a register of landed property. (F.—L.) M.F. *papier terrier,* a roll of tenants' names, &c.—Late L. *terrārius,* as in *terrārius liber,* a book wherein landed property is described.—L. *terra,* land.

Terrific. (L.) L. *terrificus,* causing terror.—L. *terri-,* for *terrēre,* to frighten; *-ficus,* causing, from *facere,* to make.

Terrine; see terreen.

Territory, domain. (F.—L.) F. *territoire,* a territory.—L. *territōrium,* a domain, land round a town.—L. *terra,* land. Formed as if from a sb. with decl. stem *territōri-,* i. e. possessor of land.

Terror, dread. (F.—L.) Formerly also *terrour.* **—** F. *terreur.*—L. *terrōrem,* acc. of *terror,* dread.—L. *terrēre,* to scare, make afraid, orig. to tremble. Cf. Gk. τρέειν (for *τρέσειν), to tremble; Skt. *tras,* to tremble, be afraid; Lith. *triszéti,* to tremble, Russ. *triasti,* to shiver. Allied to **Tremble.** Brugm. ii. § 657.

Terse, concise, neat. (L.) L. *tersus,* wiped off, clean, neat, pure, nice, terse; pp. of *tergere,* to wipe, wipe dry, polish a stone.+Gk. τρίβειν, to rub.

Tertian, recurring every third day. (F. —L.) M.F. *tertiane,* a tertian ague.—L. *tertiāna,* fem. of *tertiānus,* tertian.—L. *tertius,* third.—L. *ter,* thrice, *trēs,* three. See Tri-.

tertiary. (L.) L. *tertiārius,* containing a third part; used to mean belonging to the third.—L. *tertius,* third (above).

Tesselated. (L.) L. *tessellātus,* checkered, furnished with small square stones (as a pavement).—L. *tessella,* a small square piece of stone, little cube; dimin. of *tessera,* a die (to play with), small cube.

Test, a pot in which metals are tried, a trial, proof. (F.—L.) M.E. *test,* a pot or vessel used in alchemy.—O.F. *test* (F. *têt*), a test, in chemistry.—L. *testum,* an earthen vessel. Closely allied to O.F. *teste* (F. *tête*), a pot-sherd, a skull, answering to Late L. *testa,* a vessel used in alchemy. So also Ital. *testo,* a test, melting-pot, from L. *testum*; *testa,* an earthen pot, potsherd, skull, head, burnt tile or brick, from L. *testa,* a piece of baked earthenware, potsherd, shell, skull. Perhaps *testa* = *testa,* i.e. dried, baked, allied to *terra* (=*tersa*), dry ground; from √TERS, to dry. See Terrace.

testaceous, having a hard shell. (L.) L. *testāce-us,* having a shell; with suffix *-ous.*—L. *testa,* tile, shell, &c.

Testament. (F.—L.) F. *testament,* a will.—L. *testāmentum,* a will.—L. *testā-rī,* to be a witness.—L. *testis,* a witness. Der. *in-testate,* i.e. without a will; *testa-tor,* one who makes a will, fem. *testa-trix.*

Tester, a sixpence; flat canopy over a bed or pulpit. (F.—L.) Mod. E. (slang) *tizzie,* a sixpence; the *tester, testern,* or *testoon* was named from a French coin with a head upon it (of Louis XII of France); in England *all* coins bore the head, so that our use of the term was borrowed.—O.F. *testre,* the head-piece of a bed; M.F. *teston,* 'a testoon, piece of silver worth xviijd. sterling;' Cot.—O.F. *teste,* a head. —L. *testa,* tile, skull. ¶ A *tester* for a bed also appears as M.F. *testiere,* 'a head-piece,' Cot.; from O.F. *teste* (as before).

Testicle. (F.—L.) F. *testicule.*—L.

testiculum, acc. of *testiculus,* dimin. of *testis,* a testicle.

Testify. (F.—L.) M.F. *testifier.*—L. *testificārī,* to bear witness.—L. *testi-s,* a witness; *-ficārī,* for *facere,* to make.

testimony. (L.) L. *testimōnium,* evidence.—L. *testi-s,* a witness; with Idg. suffixes *-mōn-io-.*

Testy, fretful. (F.—L.) M.E. *testif,* Ch.—O.F. *testif* (not found); M.F. *testu,* 'heady;' Cot.—O.F. *teste,* the head; see Tester.

Tetchy, Techy, fretful, peevish, touchy. (F.—Low G.) The sense is full of freaks, whims, or caprices; from *tetch,* M.E. *teche, tecche, tache,* a bad habit, whim; see Tache (2). ¶ This is the word which is now altered to *touchy,* as if sensitive to the *touch.*

Tether, a rope for fastening up. (E.) Formerly written *tedder.* M.E. *tedir.*— A.S. *tēoder* (not found) = O. Fries. *tiader, tieder.*+Icel. *tjōðr,* a tether, Swed. *tjuder,* Dan. *töir,* Norw. *tjōr, tjoder*; Low G. *tider,* O.H.G. *zeotar, zieter.* Teut. type *teu-dro-,* of uncertain origin; sometimes referred to Teut. root *teuh-*; see Team. ¶ Gael. *teadhair* is from E. Cf. Bahder, p. 147; Brugm. ii. § 62.

Tetragon, a figure with four angles. (F.—L.—Gk.) M.F. *tetragone,* adj., four-cornered.—L. *tetragōnus,* adj.—Gk. τετράγωνος, four-cornered. — Gk. τετρα-, allied to τέσσαρες, four, cognate with E. **Four**; and γωνία, an angle, from γόνυ, a knee, cognate with E. **Knee.**

tetrahedron, a solid figure contained by four equilateral triangles. (Gk.) Gk. τέτρα- (as above); -έδρον, from ἕδρα, a base, which is from ἕδ-ειν, to sit; see Sit.

tetrarch. (L.—Gk.) L. *tetrarcha.* — Gk. τετράρχης, one of four chiefs; Luke, iii. 1.—Gk. τετρ-, allied to τέσσαρες, four; and ἄρχειν, to rule. See Four and Arch-, prefix.

tetrasyllable, a word of four syllables. (F.—L.—Gk.) Coined from Gk. τέτρα-, four (as above); and συλλαβή, a syllable. Cf. M.F. *tetrasyllabe,* L. *tetra-syllabus,* Gk. τετρασύλλαβος, of four syllables. See Syllable.

Tetter, a cutaneous disease. (E.) M.E. *teter.* A.S. *teter,* a kind of itch. Cf. G. *zittermal,* a tetter; Bavar. *zittaroch,* O.H.G. *zitaroch.* Allied to L. *derbiōsus,* scabby; Skt. *dadru-,* a tetter.

Teutonic. (L.—Gothic.) L. *Teuto-*

nicus, adj., from *Teutones*, sb. pl., the Teutons, a people of Germany; lit. 'men of the nation,' or 'the people.' — Goth. *thiuda*, a people, nation (or from a dialectal variant of this word). See Dutch.

Text. (F. — L.) M. E. *texte*. — F. *texte*, a text, subject of a book. — L. *textum*, a thing woven, fabric, style of an author, text of a book. — L. *textus*, woven, pp. of *texere*, to weave. + Skt. *taksh*, to cut wood, to prepare; cf. Russ. *tesiate*, to hew. Further allied to **Technical.** (√TEK.) Brugm. i. § 594. **Der.** *textu-al*, from M. F. *textu-el*.

textile. (L.) L. *textīlis*, woven. — L. *textus*, pp. of *texere*, to weave.

texture. (F. — L.) F. *texture*, 'a texture, web;' Cot. — L. *textūra*, a web. — L. *textus*, pp. of *texere*, to weave.

TH.

Th. This is distinct from *t*, and should have a distinct symbol. Formerly, the A. S. *þ* and *ð* were used (but indiscriminately) to denote *both* the sounds now denoted by *th*. When *þ* degenerated into a symbol closely resembling *y*, *y* was at last substituted for it; hence we find *y^e* and *y^t* used, by early printers, for *the*, *that*; it is needless (I hope) to remark that *y^e* *man* was never *pronounced* as *ye man* in the Middle Ages, as it often is *now*.

I here use *ð* for A.S. words, and *ð* or *th* for M. E. words, beginning with the sound of *th* in *that*; and *þ* for A. S. and M. E. words, beginning with the sound of *th* in *thin*. Observe these facts. (1) Initial *th* is always pronounced as in *thin* except (*a*) in words allied to *that*; and (*b*) in words allied to *thou*. (2) At the end of a word, it is pronounced as *th* in *thin*, except when a written *e* follows; compare *breath* with *breathe*; exceptions are *with*, *smooth*. (3) No word beginning with *th* (except *thurible*, formed on a *Greek* base) is of *Latin* origin; some (easily known) are *Greek*; *thummim* is *Hebrew*; all the rest are *English* or *Scandian*.

Than, conj. (E.) Frequently written *then*, and orig. the same word as *then*. M. E. *thanne*, *thonne*. A. S. *ðonne*, than. Closely allied to the def. art.; see **That**, § β. + Du. *dan*; G. *dann*, *denn*. Cf. L. *tum*.

Thane, a dignitary among the English. (E.) M. E. *þein*. A. S. *þegen*, *þegn*, *þēn*, a thane. Lit. 'child' or 'begotten.' +

Icel. *þegn*; G. *degen*, a warrior, O. H. G. *degan*. Teut. type **thegnóz*, m. Allied to Gk. *τέκνον*, a child; from *τεκ-*, as in *τεκ-εῖν*, 2 aor. inf. of *τίκτειν*, to beget. (√TEK.) Brugm. ii. § 66.

Thank, Thanks. (E.) M. E. *þank*, a thought, kindly remembrance, goodwill; hence *thanks*, pl., expressions of goodwill. A. S. *þanc*, *þonc*, sb., thought, favour, content, thank. + Du. *dank*, Icel. *þökk*, Dan. *tak*, Swed. *tack*, Goth. *thagks*, i.e. **thanks*, remembrance, thank. Teut. type **thankoz*, m.; from **thank*, 2nd grade of **thenkan-*, to think. See **Think.** (√TENG.) **Der.** *thank*, vb., A. S. *þancian*.

That. (E.) M. E. *that*. A. S. *ðæt*, orig. neuter of a demonstrative pronoun, which came to be used as the definite article. The masc. and fem. forms in use were *sē* (*se*), *sēo*, which in late A. S. were replaced by *ðe*, *ðēo*, by analogy with the neuter and other cases. The neut. *ðæt* is from the Teut. pronominal base THA = Idg. TO, meaning 'he' or 'that.' The suffix *-t* is merely the sign of the neut. gender, like Lat. *-d* in *i-d*, *illu-d*, *istu-d*, *qui-d*. β. The declension was as follows. SING. NOM. *sē*, *sēo*, *ðæt* [replaced in late A. S. by *ðe*, *ðēo*, *ðæt*]; GEN. *ðæs*, *ðære*, *ðæs*; DAT. *ðæm*, *ðăm*, *ðære*, *ðæm*, *ðăm*; ACC. *ðone*, *ðā*, *ðæt*; INSTRUMENTAL (*ðȳ*, *ðon*): PLURAL; NOM. AND ACC. *ðā*; GEN. *ðæra*, *ðăra*; DAT. *ðăm*. + Du. *de*, the, *dat*, that; Icel. neut. *þat*, the; Dan. *den*, neut. *det*, the; Swed. *den*, neut. *det*, this; G. *der*, *die*, *das*, the, *dass*, that; Goth. *thata*, neut. of def. article. Cf. Lith. *tas*, *ta*, that; Russ. *tot'*, *ta*, *to*, that; Gk. *τό*, neut. of def. art.; Skt. *tat*, it, that; L. *-te*, *-ta*, *-tud* (in *is-te*, *is-ta*, *is-tud*).

Thatch, sb. (E.) M.E. *þak*. A. S. *þæc*, thatch; whence *þeccan*, to thatch. + Du. *dak*, sb., whence *dekken*, vb. (whence E. *deck* is borrowed); Icel. *þak*, sb., Dan. *tag*, Swed. *tak*, G. *dach*. Teut. type **thak-om*, n. From **thak*, 2nd grade of Teut. root **thek-*, to cover, cognate with L. *teg-*, as in *teg-ere*, to cover. + Gk. *τέγος*, *στέγος*, a roof; Irish *teagh*, Gael. *teach*, *tigh*, O. Irish *tech*, W. *tŷ*, a house; Lith. *stogas*, a thatch, *stègti*, to thatch; Skt. *sthag*, to cover. (√STEG, TEG.) Allied to **Tegument.**

Thaw, vb. (E.) M. E. *thōwen*; prov. E. *thow* (*ow* as in *snow*); A.S. *þawian*, to melt. + Du. *dooijen*, to thaw, from *dooi*, thaw; Icel. *þeyja*, from *þá*, sb.; Dan. *töe*, Swed. *töa*. Cf. G. *verdauen*, to digest, concoct; *thauen*, O. H. G. *douwen*, to thaw. Perhaps allied to Gk. τήκειν, to melt; W. *toddi*, to melt. ¶ *Not* allied to *dew*.

The (1), def. art. (E.) M.E. *the*. A. S. *ðe*, used as nom. masc. of def. art. in late MSS., but early common as an indeclinable relative; see **That**, § β.

the (2), in what (or that) degree. (E.) Only in such phrases as '*the* more, *the* merrier.' This is the *instrumental case* of the def. art. M. E. *the*; A.S. *ðȳ*; see **That**, § β. + Goth. *thē*, Icel. *þvī*, *þī*, inst. case of art. or dem. pronoun.

Theatre. (F.−L.−Gk.) M.F. *theatre*; Cot.−L. *theātrum*.−Gk. θέατρον, a place for seeing shows. − Gk. θεάομαι, I see. Cf. θέα, a sight; see Prellwitz.

Thee (1). (E.) A. S. *ðē*, dat. and acc. of *ðū*, thou; see **Thou**.

Thee (2), to prosper, thrive. (E.) Obsolete. M. E. *theen*.−A. S. *þeon*, *þīon* (for **þīhan*), pt. t. *þāh*, *þēah*, pp. *þigen*, *þogen*, also *geþungen*, to thrive. + Goth. *theihan*, to thrive, increase; G. *gedeihen*; Du. *gedijen*. The A. S. pp. *ge-þungen* shews that the A. S. **þīhan* is for **þinhan* (cf. O. Sax. *ge-þengian*, to fulfil). Teut. root **þinχ*, **þenχ*, Idg. root **tenk*, as in Lith. *tenku*, it suffices, O.Irish *tocad*, prosperity; W. *tynged*, luck; cf. Lith. *tekti*, to suffice. Brugm. i. § 421 (3).

Theft. (E.) In place of *thefth*. M. E. *þefte*; for A.S. *þīefþ*, *þēofþ*, theft.−A. S. *þēof*, a thief. + Icel. *þȳfð*, O. Fries. *thiufthe*. See **Thief**.

Their, belonging to them. (Scand.) M. E. *thair*. − Icel. *þeirra*, of them, used as gen. pl. of *hann*, he, but really the gen. pl. of a dem. pronoun, as shewn by A. S. *þāra*; see **They**, and **That**, § β.

Theism, belief in a God. (Gk.) Coined, with suffix *-ism* (Gk. *-ισμος*), from Gk. θε-ός, a god. Perhaps for an older form **θεσος*; cf. O. Ir. *dess*, God (Stokes-Fick, p. 151), Gk. θέσ-φατος, spoken by God (Prellwitz).

Them, objective case of *they*. (Scand.) Really an old dat. case. − Icel. *þeim*, dat. of *þeir*, they; see **They**. + A. S. *þām*, dat. pl. of def. art.; see **That**, § β.

Theme. (F.−L.−Gk.) M.E. *teme*.− O.F. *teme*, M.F. *theme*, 'a theam;' Cot.− L. *thema*.−Gk. θέμα, that which is laid down, a theme for argument.−Gk. base θε-, to place; τί-θη-μι, I place. + Skt. *dhā*, to put; see **Do** (1). (✓DHĒ.)

Then. (E.) Frequently written *than* in old books, and originally identical with it; see **Than**.

thence. (E.) M. E. *thennes* (dissyllabic); whence *thens*, by contraction, later written *thence*. The *s* is an adverbial suffix; earlier forms were *thenne*, *thanne*, in which a final *n* has been lost. − A. S. *ðanan*; formed from base *ða-*, with the suffix *-na-n-*, or *-na-na*. The base *ða-* = Teut. base THA; see **That**. + G. *dannen*, O. H. G. *dannana*, thence; from base *da-*.

Theocracy. (Gk.) Lit. 'government by God.' From θεο-, for θεός, God; -κρα-τία, government, from κρατεῖν, to govern, which is from κρατύς, strong. Cf. *aristo - cracy*, *auto - cracy*, *demo - cracy*. See **Theism**.

Theodolite, an instrument used in surveying. (F.−Gk.?) Generally said to be Greek. Formerly *theodelitus*, meaning 'a circle with a graduated border'; used A. D. 1571. Also *theodolet*, *theodelet*. Apparently imitated (it is not known why) from O. F. *theodelet*, *theodolet*, the name of a treatise, lit. 'a work by *Theodulus*.'−Gk. Θεοδοῦλος, Theodulus; lit. 'servant of God.' 'Ung *theodelet* coute viij. s.;' Godefroy.

Theogony. (L.−Gk.) L. *theogonia*. − Gk. θεογονία, the origin of the gods. − Gk. θεό-s, a god; -γονία, origin, from γεν-, base of γίγνομαι, I become; see **Genus**.

theology. (F.−L.−Gk.) M. E. *theologie* −M.F. *theologie*; Cot.−L. *theologia*. −Gk. θεολογία, a speaking about God.− Gk. θεολόγος, adj., speaking about God. −Gk. θεό-s, a god; λέγειν, to speak.

Theorbo, a large lute. (Ital.) Formerly *theorba*.−Ital. *tiorba*; the *th* being due to the occasional F. spelling *théor·be* for *téorbe*. (*Said* to have been named after the inventor.)

Theorem. (L.−Gk.) L *theōrēma*.− Gk. θεώρημα, a spectacle: a subject for contemplation, theorem.−Gk. θεωρεῖν, to behold.−Gk. θεωρός, a spectator.−Gk. θεάομαι, I see. See **Theatre**.

theory. (F.−L.−Gk.) M. F. *theorie*, 'theory;' Cot.−L. *theōria*.−Gk. θεωρία, a beholding, contemplation, speculation. − Gk. θεωρός, a spectator (above).

Therapeutic, pertaining to the healing art. (F.−L.−Gk.) M. F. *therapeutique*, healing; Cot. −L. *therapeutica* (*ars*), the healing art; fem. of *therapeuticus*.−Gk. θεραπευτικός, tending.−Gk. θεραπευτής, an attendant. ━ Gk. θεραπεύειν, to wait on. ━ Gk. θεραπ-, stem of θέραψ, an assistant; cf. θεράπ-ων, a servant. From √DHER, to maintain, support; cf. Skt. *dhṛ*, to maintain, bear, *dharitrī*, a supporter.

There, in that place. (E.) M. E. *ther*, *thar*. A. S. ðǣr. The suffix -*r* seems to be due to a locatival formation like that in Skt. *upa-ri*, Gk. ὑπέ-ρ. The base is Teut. base THA; see **That**.+Du. *daar*, Icel. *þar*, Dan. Swed. *der*, Goth. *thar*, G. *da*. Compare **Here**, **Where**. Hence *there*-, in *there-by*, *there-in*, *there-of*, &c. Cf. G. *dar*- in *dar-in*, *dar-an*.

Thermometer, an instrument for measuring the temperature. (Gk.) From Gk. θερμό-s, warm (allied to L. *formus*, warm, Skt. *gharma*- heat); and μέτρον, a measurer; see **Metre**.

Thesaurus. (L. ─ Gk.) See **Treasure.**

These. (E.) M. E. *thise*, *these*, *theos*; a new pl. of *this*. The old pl. (A. S. *þās*) is the mod. E. *those*. See **Those**.

Thesis. (L.─Gk.) L. *thesis*.─Gk. θέσις, a thing laid down, a proposition. ━ Gk. base θε-; cf. τίθημι, I place. **Der.** *apo-thesis*, *para-thesis*, *pros-thesis*, *pro-thesis*, all rare words, with prefixes ἀπό, παρά, πρός, πρό respectively; also *anti-thesis*, *hypo-thesis*, *meta-thesis*, *par-en-the-sis*, *syn-thesis*, which see.

Theurgy, supernatural agency. (L. ─ Gk.) L. *theurgia*. ━ Gk. θεουργία, divine work, magic. ━ Gk. θεό-s, a god; ἔργ-ον, a work, cognate with E. **Work.**

Thews, pl. sb., sinews; (formerly) manners. (E.) *Thews* in Shak. means sinews or strength; but M. E. *thewes* almost always means habits or manners. A. S. *þēawas*, pl. of *þēaw*, habit, custom, demeanour (orig. sense 'strength').+O. Sax. *thau*, custom; O. H. G. *dau*, *thau*, discipline. Cf. Skt. *tavas*, strong.

They. (Scand.) M. E. *thai* (gen. *thair*, dat. and acc. *thaim*, *tham*); chiefly in the Northern dialect. This usage is Scand., not E., as the A. S. corresponding forms were used as pl. of def. art. ━ Icel. *þeir*, nom. pl., they; *þeirra*, gen. pl., their; *þeim*, dat. pl., them. So also Dan. Swed. *de*, they, *dem*, them; Dan. *deres*, Swed. *deras*, their, theirs.+A. S. *þā*, nom. pl. of def. art.; gen. *þāra*; dat. *þām*; see **That**, § β.

Thick. (E.) M. E. *þikke*. A. S. *þicce*, thick.+O. Sax. *thikki*, Du. *dik*, Icel. *þykkr*, Dan. *tyk*, Swed. *tjok*, *tjock*; G. *dick*.

Allied to Gael. and Irish *tiugh*, fat, thick; W. *tew*, plump, from Celtic base **tegu*-; also to **Tight**. ¶ Not Scand.; see below.

thicket. (E.) A. S. *þiccet*, i. e. a thick set of bushes, &c.+Dan. dial. *tykke*.

Thief. (E.) Pl. *thieves*. M. E. *þeef*, pl. *þeues*. A. S. *þēof*, pl. *þēofas*. + Du. *dief*, Icel. *þjófr*, Dan. *tyv*, Swed. *tjuf*, G. *dieb*, Goth. *thiubs*. Teut. type **theuboz*, for **theufoz*. Perhaps allied to Lith. *tupéti*, to squat down (hence, to hide oneself).

Thigh. (E.) M. E. *þih*, *þeh*. O. Merc. *þēh*, A. S. *þēoh*, thigh.+Du. *dij*, Icel. *þjó*, thigh, rump, O. H. G. *dioh*. Teut. type **theuhom*, n. The orig. sense is 'thick or plump part'; allied to Lith. *tùk-ti*, to become fat, Russ. *tuch-nite*, to fatten; Russ. *tuk*', Pol. *tuk*, sb., fat; Lith. *taukas*, sb., fat (of animals).

Thill, shaft of a cart. (E.) Also spelt *fill*; whence *fill-horse*. M. E. *þille*. A. S. *þille*, slip of wood, thin board, plank, flooring; allied to *þel*, n., a plank, as in *benc-þel*, a bench-board.+Icel. *þilja*, plank, Swed. *tilje*, a plank, floor; G. *diele*, plank, board; Du. *deel*, a plank. Teut. types **theljōn*, f., **thelom*, n. Cf. Lith. *tille*, a little plank in the floor of a boat. Cf. Skt. *tala*-, bottom, floor. (See Franck.) Doublet, *deal*, a thin board.

Thimble. (E.) M. E. *þimbil*; formed (with excrescent *b*) from A. S. *þýmel*, a thumb-stall.━A. S. *þūma*, thumb (with the usual change from *ū* to *ȳ*). Cf. G. *däumling*, a thumb-stall; from *daum*, thumb.

Thin. (E.) M. E. *þinne*. A. S. *þynne*.+Du. *dun*, Icel. *þunnr*, Dan. *tynd* (for **tynn*), Swed. *tunn*, G. *dünn*, O. H. G *dunni*. Cf. W. *teneu*, Gael. Irish *tana*, Russ. *tonkii*, L. *tenuis*, Gk. ταναός, Skt. *tanu*-, thin; Pers. *tunuk*, slender. Lit. 'stretched out.' (√TEN.) See **Tend** (1).

Thine, Thy. (E.) M. E. *thīn*, shortened to *thy* before a following consonant. A. S. ðīn, thy, possessive pronoun, declined as an adj.; allied to A. S. ðū, thou.+Icel. *þínn*, Dan. Swed. *din*, G. *dein*, Goth. *theins*. **Der.** *thy-self* (=*thine self*).

Thing. (E.) A. S. *þing*, *þinc*, *þincg*, a thing, cause, orig. a discussion; cf. *þingian*, to discuss, *þingere*, a pleader.+Du. G. *ding*; Icel. *þing*, a thing, also an assembling, meeting, council (so also Dan. Swed. *ting*). Kluge compares it with Goth. *theihs*, season, time; and even with

L. *tempus*; but see *tempus* in Brugm. i.
§ 412, ii. § 132. **Der.** *hus-tings*, q. v.

Think. (E.) M. E. *þenken*, to think ;
orig. distinct from the impers. vb. *þunchen*,
to seem, for which see **Methinks**. [But
confusion between the two was easy and
common. The pt. t. of M. E. *þenken*
should have been *thoghte*, and of M. E.
þunchen should have been *thughte*; both
were merged in the form *thoughte*, mod. E.
thought.] – A. S. *þencan*, to think, pt. t.
þōhte. A weak verb; allied to A. S. *þanc*,
a thought, also a thank. + Icel. *þekkja*,
Dan. *tænke*, Swed. *tänka*, G. *denken* (pt. t.
dachte); Goth. *thagkjan*, i. e. **thankjan*
(pt. t. *thāhta*). Teut. type **thankjan-*;
from **thank*, 2nd grade of root **thenk*,
Idg. **tenk*; cf. O. L. *tongēre*, to think. See
Thank. Der. *be-think*, with prefix *be-* = *by*.

Third. (E.) Formerly *thrid*. M. E.
þridde, *þride*. A. S. *þridda*, third. – A. S.
þri-, for *þrēo*, three. + Du. *derde*, Icel. *þriði*,
Dan. *tredie*, Swed. *tredje*, G. *dritte*, Goth.
thridja, W. *trydydd*, Russ. *tretii*, Gk. τρίτος,
Skt. *tṛtīya-*.

Thirl, to pierce; see **Thrill.**

Thirst, sb. (E.) Lit. 'dryness.' M. E.
þurst. A. S. *þurst*, *þyrst*, thirst; whence
þyrstan, vb., to thirst. + Du. *dorst*, Icel.
þorsti, Dan. *törst*, Swed. *törst*, G. *durst*,
Goth. *thaurstei*. β. Goth. *thaurstei* is
from the Goth. weak stem *thaurs-*, as in
-thaurs-ans, pp. of *-thairsan* (pt. t. *-thars*),
to be dry; with suffix *-tei*. The Goth.
-thairsan (Teut. **þersan-*) is cognate with
Gk. τέρσεσθαι, to become dry. Cf. Skt.
tṛsh, to thirst; *tarsha-*, thirst. (√TERS.)
Allied to **Terrace** and **Torrid.**

Thirteen. (E.) M. E. *þrettene*. A. S.
þrēotȳne. – A. S. *þrēo*, three; *tȳn*, ten; with
pl. suffix *-e*. + Du. *dertien*, Icel. *þrettān*,
Dan. *tretten*, Swed. *tretton*, G. *dreizehn*.

thirty. (E.) M. E. *þritti*. A. S. *þrītig*,
þrittig. – A. S. *þrī*, also *þrēo*, three; *-tig*,
suffix denoting 'ten'; see **Ten**. + Du. *der-
tig*, Icel. *þrīr tigir*, Dan. *tredive*, Swed.
trettio, G. *dreissig*.

This. (E.) M. E. *this*, *thes*; pl. *these*,
thuse, *thos*, &c., the forms *these* and *those*
being both used as plurals of *this*; the
plural of *that* being *tho*. Gradually *these*
became the settled pl. of *this*, whilst *those*
supplanted *tho* as pl. of *that*. – A. S. *ðes*,
ðēos, *ðis*, this; pl. *ðās*. [M. E. *tho* answers
to A. S. *ðā*, pl. of def. art.; see **That**, § β.]
β. *This* (A. S. *ðe-s*) is an emphatic form,
due to suffixing an emphatic particle to

the Teut. pronom. base THA. + Du. *deze*,
Icel. *þessi*, G. *dieser*.

Thistle. (E.) M. E. *þistil*. A. S. *þistel*.
+ Du. *distel*, Icel. *þistill*, Dan. *tidsel*, Swed.
tistel, G. *distel*. The *i* was once long, as
in some E. and G. dialects; cf. Somersets.
daash-l, a thistle; E. Fries. *dīssel*. Teut.
types **þīstiloz*, m., **þīstilā*, f.

Thither. (E.) M. E. *thider*. A. S.
ðider. Cf. Icel. *þaðra*, thére; Goth.
thathrō, thence; also Skt. *tatra*, there,
thither. Formed from Teut. base THA
(Idg. TO) with a suffix which is to be
compared with L. *-tro* in *ul-tro*.

Thole (1), **Thowl**, a peg to steady an
oar. (E.) M. E. *thol*. A. S. *þol* (8th cent.).
+ Du. *dol*; Icel. *þollr*, young tree, wooden
peg, thole; Dan. *tol*; Swed. *tall*, pine-tree;
Norw. *tall*, *toll*, fir-tree, *toll*, a thole. Orig.
sense 'young tree'; hence a bit of fir-wood
for a peg. Cf. Icel. *þella*, a young pine,
þöll (gen. *þallar*), a young fir.

Thole (2), to endure. M. E. *þolien*.
A. S. *þolian*, to suffer, endure. + Icel. *þola*,
Dan. *taale*, Swed. *tåla*, O. H. G. *dolēn*
(whence O. H. G. *geduld*, patience), Goth. *thulan*.
Cf. L. *tollere*, *tolerare*; Gk. τλῆναι, to
suffer; Skt. *tul*, to lift. See **Tolerate**.

Thong, a strip of leather. (E.) For
thwong. M. E. *thwong*, a thong; A. S.
þwang, a thong, string, cord; also a bit.
+ Icel. *þwengr*, a thong. From **þwang*,
2nd grade of Teut. **þwengan-*, to constrain
(O. Fries. *thwinga*). See **Twinge**. Cf.
O. Fries. *thwong*, *thwang*, compulsion;
Du. *dwang*, Dan. *tvang*, Swed. *tvång*, G.
zwang, constraint.

Thorax. (L. – Gk.) L. *thorax*. – Gk.
θώραξ, a breast-plate; also the breast, chest.
Lit. 'defender;' cf. Skt. *dhāraka-*, a trunk
to protect clothes, from *dhṛ*, to carry,
maintain, keep. (√DHER.)

Thorn. (E.) A. S. *þorn*. + Du. *doorn*,
Icel. *þorn*, Dan. *tiörn*, Swed. *torn*, G.
dorn, Goth. *thaurnus*. Teut. type **þur-
nuz*, m. + Russ. *tern'*, the black-thorn;
Polish *tarn*, a thorn; cf. Skt. *tṛna-*, a grass-
blade. Perhaps 'piercer;' cf. L. *terere*,
to pierce.

Thorough. (E.) Merely a by-form
of the prep. *through*, spelt *þoru* in Havelok, and *þuruh* in the Ancren Riwle. It
became an adverb, whence *thoroughly*,
adv., with added suffix. And hence, finally,
thorough, adj.

Thorp, Thorpe, a village. (E.)
A. S. *þorp*, a village. + Du. *dorp*, Icel. *þorp*,

Dan. Swed. *torp*, G. *dorf*; Goth. *þaurp*, a field. Teut. type **thurpo-*. Cf. Lith. *troba*, a building, house. Also Irish *treabh*, village, W. *tref*, hamlet; Idg. type **trebo-*. Brugm. i. § 553.

Those. (E.) A. S. *ðās*, originally the pl. of A. S. *ðes*, this. See **This.**

Thou. (E.) A. S. *ðū*, thou.+Icel. *þu*, Goth. *thu*, Dan. Swed. G. *du*; Irish and Gael. *tu*; W. *ti*; L. *tu*, Russ. *tui*; Gk. *σύ*, *τύ*; Pers. *tū*; Skt. *tvam*.

Though. (Scand.) M. E. *thogh*; [also *theigh*, A. S. *ðēah*, *ðēh*.] — Icel. *þō* (for **þauh*); cf. Dan. *dog*, Swed. *dock*.+O. Sax. *thōh*, Du. *doch*, yet, but; G. *doch*, Goth. *thauh*. Teut. type **thau-h*, in which *-h* seems to be an enclitic; cf. L. *que*, 'and.' *Thau-* is prob. from the same base as **That.** ¶ In the Du. and G. *doch*, &c., the short *o* is due to loss of emphasis.

Thought, sb. (E.) Better *thoght*. M. E. *þoght*. A. S. *þōht*, *ge-þōht*, a thought, lit. thing thought of. — A. S. *þōht*, pp. of *þencan*, to think; see **Think.**+Icel. *þōtti*, *þōttr*; cf. G. *gedacht*, adj., thought of, orig. pp. of *denken*, to think.

Thousand. (E.) M. E. *þousand*. A. S. *þūsend*.+Du. *duizend*, Icel. *þūsund*, *þūs-hund*, *þūshundrað*; Dan. *tusind*, Swed. *tusen*, G. *tausend*, Goth. *thusundi*. Cf. also Lith. *tukstantis*, Russ. *tuisiacha*, a thousand. ¶ Not yet explained; in Icel. *þūs-hund*, the syllable *hund* = A. S. *hund*, a hundred, and is due to popular etymology, which may (however) be correct.

Thowl; see Thole (1).

Thrall, a slave. (Scand.) O. Northumb. *ðrǣl*, borrowed from Norse, Mk. x. 44; the *ǣ* was perhaps shortened in M. E. *þraldom*, from Icel. *þrældōmr*. — Icel. *þrǣll*, a thrall, serf; Dan. *træl*, Swed. *träl*. The Icel. *þrǣll* stands for **þrāhiloz*, m., and is cognate with O. H. G. *dregil*, *drigil*, a thrall, serf; lit. 'a runner,' i. e. one who runs on messages. From base of Goth. *thragjan*, A. S. *þrægan*, to run; allied to Gk. *τρέχειν*, to run. See **Trochee**, **Feuterer.** Der. *thral-dom*, Icel. *þrældōmr*. Brugm. i. § 784.

Thrash, Thresh. (E.) *Thresh* is older; M. E. *þreshen*, for *þershen*. — A. S. *þerscan*, to thrash (strong verb). + Du. *dorschen*, Icel. *þreskja*, Dan. *tærske*, Swed. *tröska*, G. *dreschen*, Goth. *thriskan* (pt. t. *thrask*). Orig. to rattle, make a din or rattling noise; cf. Russ. *tresk-ate*, to crackle, burst, *tresk'*, a crash, O. Slav. *troska*, stroke

of lightning; Lith. *treszkéti*, *traszkéti*, to rattle, crack. Teut. base **thresk*; Idg. root **tresk*. Prob. first used of thunder, then of the noise of the flail. Der. *thresh-old*.

Thrasonical, vain-glorious. (L. — Gk.) Coined from *Thrasōn-*, stem of *Thraso*, the name of a bragging soldier in Terence's Eunuchus. Evidently from Gk. *θρασ-ύς*, bold, spirited; allied to **Dare** (1). (√DHERS.)

Thrave, a number of sheaves of wheat. (Scand.) M. E. *þraue*, *þreue* (*thrave*, *threve*). — Icel. *þrefi*, a thrave; Dan. *trave*, a score of sheaves; Swed. *trafve*, a pile of wood; Swed. dial. *trafve*, 24 or 30 sheaves set up in shocks (F. Möller). Cf. Icel. *þref*, a loft for corn.

Thread. (E.) M. E. *þreed*, *þrēd*. A. S. *þrǣd* (< **þrǣ-diz*), thread; lit. 'that which is twisted.' — A. S. *þrāwan*, to twist.+Du. *draad*, Icel. *þrāðr*, Dan. *traad*, Swed. *trād*, thread; G. *draht*, O. H. G. *drāt*, wire. Teut. type **þrǣ-diz*. See **Throw.**

Threat, sb. (E.) M. E. *þret*. A. S. *þrēat*, a crowd, crush of people, also great pressure, calamity, trouble, threat. — A. S. *þrēat*, 2nd grade of str. vb. *þrēotan*, to afflict, vex, urge. + Goth. *us-thriutan*, to vex greatly, G. *verdriessen*, to vex; Russ. *trudite*, to make one work, urge, vex; L. *trūdere*, to push, crowd, urge. (Base TREUD.) Der. *threat-en*, vb.

Three. (E.) M.E. *þre*. A. S. *þrī* (*þrȳ*), *þrīo* (*þrēo*), three.+Du. *drie*, Icel. *þrīr*, Dan. *tre*, Swed. *tre*, Goth. *threis*, G. *drei*. Cf. Irish, Gael. and W. *tri*, Russ. *tri*, L. *tres* (neut. *tri-a*), Gk. *τρεῖς* (neut. *τρί-a*), Lith. *trys*, Skt. masc. nom. pl. *trayas*; Idg. masc. nom. pl. **treyes*.

Threnody, a lament. (Gk.) Gk. *θρην-ῳδία*, a lamenting. — Gk. *θρῆν-ος*, a wailing, from *θρέ-ομαι*, I cry aloud; *ῳδή*, ode; see **Drone** (1) and **Ode.**

Thresh; see Thrash.

Threshold, a piece of wood or stone under an entrance-door. (E.) *Thresh-old* was usually written *thresh-wold*, as if it were the piece of wood threshed or beaten by the tread of the foot; but this was due to a popular etymology (suggested by *wald*, perhaps = floor). A. S. *þerscwald*, late form of A. S. *þerscold*. — A. S. *þersc-an*, to thresh; with *-old*, suffix. + Icel. *þreskölder*, threshold; from *þresk-ja*, to thresh. β. The A. S. *þerscold* is from a form **þersc-o-ðl(o)-*; cf. O. H. G. *drisc-u-*

fti. And *-ðlo-* represents Idg. *-tro-*; see Princ. of E. Etym. i. § 228 (*h*).

Thrice. (E.) For *thrīs*, contr. form of M. E. *priës*, *pryës* (dissyllabic), where the suffix *-s* is adverbial (orig. a mark of gen. case). Earlier form *prië.* ‒ A. S. *príwa*, thrice. ‒ A. S. *prí*, three. See **Three.**

Thrid, a thread. (E.) Another form of *thread* (Dryden, Hind and Panther, iii. 278).

Thrift, frugality. (Scand.) M. E. *prift.* ‒ Icel. *prift*, thrift; also *prif*, the same. ‒ Icel. weak grade *prif-*, as in *prif-inn*, pp. of *prífa* to thrive. Cf. Dan. *trivelse*, prosperity. See **Thrive.**

Thrill, Thirl, to pierce. (E.) The old sense of *thrill* was to pierce; also spelt *thirl*, which is an older spelling. M. E. *pirlen*, *prillen*. A. S. *pyrlian*, to pierce; shorter form of *pyrelian*, the same; lit. ‘to make a hole.’ ‒ A. S. *pyrel*, *pyrel*, a hole, orig. an adj. with the sense ‘pierced,’ for **pyrh-il*, as shewn by the cognate M. H. G. *durchel*, pierced. Derived from A. S. *purh*, through (with change of *u* to *y*), just as M. H. G. *durchel* is from G. *durch*, through. See **Through.**

Thrive. (Scand.) M. E. *priuen* (*thriven*), pt. t. *praf*, *prof*, pp. *priuen.* ‒ Icel. *prífa* (pt. t. *preif*, pp. *prifinn*), to clutch, grasp, grip, seize; hence *prifask* (with suffixed *-sk = -sik*, self), lit. to seize for oneself, to thrive. + Dan. *trives*, Swed. *trifvas*, reflex. verb, to thrive; cf. Norw. *triva*, to seize. Der. *thrift-t*, q. v.

Throat, the gullet. (E.) M. E. *prote*. A. S. *protu*, also *-prote*, throat.+O. H. G. *drozza*, whence G. *drossel*, throat, throttle. Prob. allied to Du. *strot*, M. Du. *stroot*, *stroote*, the throat, gullet; Ital. *strozza*, the gullet (a word of Teut. origin). We also find Swed. *strupe*, Dan. *strube*, the throat. Der. *throttle*, q. v.

Throb, to beat forcibly, as the heart. (E.) M. E. *probben*, to throb. Allied to Russ. *trepete*, palpitation, throbbing; L. *trepidus*, trembling. See **Trepidation.**

Throe, a pang. (Scand. ?) M. E. *prowe*, *thrawe*. [Cf. O. Merc. *thrauu*, ‘argutiæ,’ O. E. Texts; A. S. *prēa*, a rebuke, affliction, threat, evil; which seem to have been confused with it.] Prob. from Icel. *prá*, a throe. Cf. A. S. *prōwian*, to suffer; O. H. G. *drōa*, burden, suffering, *druoēn*, *drōēn*, to suffer.

Throne. (F. ‒ L. ‒ Gk.) Formerly *trone* (Wyclif). ‒ O. F. *trone* (F. *trône*). ‒

L. *thronum*, acc. of *thronus*. ‒ Gk. θρόνος, a seat; lit. a support. (√DHER.)

Throng, a great crowd of people. (E.) M. E. *prong.* A. S. *ge-prang*, a throng. ‒ A. S. *prang*, 2nd grade of *pringan*, to crowd, press. + Du. *drang*, Icel. *pröng*, G. *drang*, a throng; cf. Dan. *trang*, Swed. *trång*, adj., narrow, close. Allied to Goth. *threihan*, to throng, Lith. *trenk-ti*, to jolt, push. Der. *throng*, vb.

Thropple, Thrapple, wind-pipe. (E.) *Thropple* is prob. a reduction of A. S. *prot-bolla*, the wind-pipe; from *prot-u*, throat, and *bolla*, prominence. See **Throttle, Throat,** and **Bowl** (2).

Throstle, the song-thrush. (E.) M. E. *prostel.* A. S. *prostle*, a throstle.+M.H.G. *trostel.* Teut. type **prustlā*, fem.; Idg. type **tərzdlā*; cf. L. *turdus*, a thrush, and Icel. *pröst* (gen. *prastar*), Swed. and Norw. *trast*, a thrush (from the 2nd grade, **prast*, of a Teut. base **prest*). Also, with initial *s*, Lith. *strazdas*, m., *strazda*, f., a thrush. See further under **Thrush** (1). *Throstle* has a variant *throshel* (M. E. *thrusshil*, Prompt. Parv.). Brugm. i. §§ 818 (2), 882.

Throttle, the wind-pipe. (E.) Dimin. of *throat*; cf. G. *drossel*, throat. Der. *throttle*, vb., to press on the wind-pipe; M. E. *throtlen.*

Through, prep. (E.) M. E. *purh.* A. S. *purh*, O. Northumb. *perh.*+Du. *door*, G. *durch*, O. H. G. *duruh* ; Teut. type **purh* ; allied to Goth. *thairh*, through (Teut. type **perh*). β. The Goth. *thairh*, through, is allied to *thairkō*, a hole ; from Teut. base **perk* = Idg. base **terg*, an extension of √TER, as in L. *ter-ere*, to bore. Cf. Gk. τρώγλη, a hole. Brugm. i. § 527. **Der.** *thrill.*

Throw, to cast, hurl. (E.) M. E. *prowen*, pt. t. *prew*, pp. *prowen.* A. S. *prāwan*, to twist, hurl, whirl ; pt. t. *prēow*, pp. *prāwen.* [The orig. sense, to twist, is preserved in *thread.*] Allied to Du. *draaijen*, to twist, whirl ; O. H. G. *drāen*, G. *drehen*, to turn ; all from Teut. base **prē* = Idg. base **trē*, as in Gk. τρητός, bored through, τρῆμα, a hole. The grade **ter* appears in L. *terere*, to bore, Gk. τείρειν (for **τέρyειν*), to bore. (√TER.)

Thrum (1), the tufted end of a weaver's thread. (E.) M. E. *prum*, not found in A. S. + Icel. *prömr* (gen. *pramar*), the edge, verge, brim of a thing (hence the edge of a web) ; Norw. *tröm*, *tram*, *trumm*, edge, brim ; Swed. dial. *trumm*, *trömm*, a stump, the end of a log; M. Du. *drom*, thread on a weaver's shuttle; G. *trumm*, end of threads, thrum. Teut. base *þru, weak grade of *þer = Idg. *ter. Hence it is allied to Gk. τέρμα, end, L. *terminus*; see **Term.**

Thrum (2), to play noisily. (Scand.) Icel. *þruma*, to rattle, thunder; Swed. *trumma*, to beat, drum; cf. Dan. *tromme*, a drum. See **Drum, Strum.**

Thrush (1), a bird. (E.) M. E. *þrusch.* A. S. *þrysce*, a thrush; Teut. type *thruskjōn,f. Cf. O.H.G. *drosca* or *drōsca*, a thrush; whence G. *drossel.* Allied to **Throstle**, q. v.

Thrush (2), a disease marked by small ulcerations in the mouth. (E.) In Phillips (1706). Orig. 'a dryness;' or lit. 'dry-ishness.' Formed by adding the A. S. suffix *-isc* (=*-ish*) to A. S. *þyrr-e*, cognate with Icel. *þurr*, dry, as proved by Dan. *tröske*, Swed. *torsk*, Swed. dial. *trösk*, the thrush; forms which are to be compared with Dan. *törke*, Swed. *torka*, Icel. *þurka*, drought, and with M. E. *thurst*, thirst. Closely allied to **Thirst**, q. v.

Thrust, vb. (Scand.) M. E. *þrusten*, *þristen.* ‒ Icel. *þrýsta*, to thrust, press, compel. Allied to **Threaten**, and to L. *trūdere*, to thrust.

Thud, a dull sound of a blow. (E.) Used by G. Douglas and Burns. A. S. *þyddan*, to strike. Cf. L. *tundere.*

Thug, an assassin. (Hindustani.) Hind. *thag*, *thug* (with cerebral *th*), a cheat, knave, a robber who strangles travellers; Marāthī *thak*, *thag*, a thug (H. H. Wilson).

Thumb. (E.) M. E. *þombe*; with ex-crescent *b.* A. S. *þūma*, the thumb. **+** Du. *duim*, Swed. *tumme*, G. *daumen*; also Icel. *þumall*, the thumb of a glove, Dan. *tommel-finger*, thumb. Lit. 'the *thick* finger;' from √TEU, to grow large. See **Tumid. Der.** *thimble.*

Thummim, perfection. (Heb.) *Urim and thummim* = light and perfection ; though the forms are, strictly, plural. ‒ Heb. *tummīm*, pl. of *tōm*, perfection, truth. ‒ Heb. root *tāmam*, to be perfect.

Thump, vb. (E.) Allied to Icel.*dumpa*, to thump, Swed. dial. *dompa*, to thump, *dumpa*, to make a noise.

Thunder, sb. (E.) For *thuner*; the *d* is excrescent. M. E. *þoner.* A. S. *þunor.* ‒ A. S. *þunian*, to rattle, thunder; cf. *ge-þun*, a loud noise.**+**Du. *donder*; Icel.*þôrr* (for *þonr*), Thor, god of thunder; G.

donner; L. *tonāre*, to thunder, Skt. *tan*, to sound. **β.** We further find A.S. *tonian*, to thunder, prob. from L.; but compare Skt. *stan*, to sound, thunder, sigh, *stanita-*, thunder, and E.*stun.* (√STEN.) See **Stun.**

Thurible, a censer. (L.‒Gk.) English from L. *thūribulum*, *tūribulum*, a vessel for holding incense. ‒ L. *thūri-*, *tūri-*, decl. stem of *thūs*, *tūs*, frankincense; with suffix *-bulum* (as in *fundi-bulum*, from *fundere*). L. *thūs* is borrowed from Gk. θύος, incense. ‒ Gk. θύ-ειν, to burn a sacrifice. Allied to **Fume.** (√DHEU.) See **Thyme.**

Thursday. (Scand.) M. E. *þurs-day*, *þors-day.* A. S. *þūres dæg*, Thursday. ‒ A. S. *þūres*, gen. of *þūr*, Thor; *dæg*, day. Borrowed from Icel. *þôrsdagr*, Thursday; from *þôrs*, gen. of *þôrr*, Thor, and *dagr*, a day; cf. Swed. Dan. *Torsdag.* So also A. S. *þunresdæg* (the native word); Du. *Donderdag*, G..*Donnerstag.* All translations of L. *diēs Iouis.* (See Sweet, Hist. E. Sounds, § 578.)

Thus. (E.) M. E. *thus.* A. S. *ðus.* **+** O. Fries. and O. Sax. *thus* ; Du. *dus.* Allied to **That** ; and perhaps to **This.**

Thwack, Whack, to beat. (E.) Prob. imitative. Compare Icel. *þjökka*, to thwack, thump; also *þjaka*, the same; prov. G. *wackeln*, to cudgel.

Thwaite, a clearing. (Scand.) Common in place-names. Icel. *þveit*, a pad-dock, orig. a clearing in woods, a cutting. ‒ Icel. *þveit, 2nd grade of *þvīta, not found, but = A. S. *þwītan*, to cut. See **Thwite.** Cf. Norw. *tveit*, a cutting, also a clearing; Dan. dial. *tved.*

Thwart, transversely, transverse. (Scand.) Properly an adv.; afterwards an adj.; lastly, a verb. M. E. *thwert*, *thwart*, across. ‒ Icel. *þvert*, neut. of *þverr*, adj., perverse, adverse. Used adverbially in phrases such as *um þvert*, across, *athwart*, *taka þvert*, to take athwart, to deny flatly. **β.** The Icel. *þverr*, adj., is cognate with A.S.*þweorh*, perverse, transverse, Dan. *tvær*, transverse (whence *tvært*, adv., across), Swed. *tvär*, across (whence *tvärt*, adv., rudely), Du. *dwar(s)*; Goth. *thwairhs*, angry; G. *zwerch*, adv., across, awry. From Teut. base *þwerh, Idg. root *twerk ; cf. L. *torquēre*, to twist ; Skt. *tarku-*, a spindle. Brugm. i. § 593 (3). Allied to **Twirl.**

Thwite, to cut. (E.) Obsolete. A.S. *þwītan*, pt. t. *þwāt*, pp. *þwiten*, to cut. Der. *thwaite*, *whittle*, q. v.

Thy; see Thine.

Thyme, a plant. (F. – L. – Gk.) The *th* is pronounced as *t*, because borrowed from French. M. E. *tyme.* – M. F. *thym,* 'the herb time;' Cot. – L. *thymum,* acc. of *thymus.* – Gk. θύμος, θύμον, thyme, from its sweet smell. Cf. Gk. θύος, incense; see Thurible. (√DHEU.)

TI-TY.

Tiara, a wreathed ornament for the head. (L. – Gk. – Pers.) L. *tiāra.* – Gk. τιάρα, τιάρας, a Persian head-dress. Doubtless of Pers. origin.

Tibert, a cat. (F. – Teut.) See Nares. O. F. *Thibaut,* Theobald. – O. Sax. *Thiodbald;* O. H. G. *Dietbald.* – O. Sax. *thiod,* O. H. G. *diet, diot,* people (see **Dutch**); *bald,* bold.

Tibia, the large bone of the leg. (L.) L. *tibia,* shin-bone.

Tic, a twitching of the muscles. (F. – Teut.) F. *tic,* a twitching; *tic douloureux,* painful twitching, a nervous disease. Formerly F. *ticq, tiquet,* a disease suddenly seizing a horse (Cot.). Cf. Ital. *ticchio,* a vicious habit, caprice. Most likely allied to Low G. *tukken,* to twitch; G. *zucken* (M. H. G. *zucken, zücken*), to twitch, shrug; with which cf. *zug,* a draught, *ziehen,* to draw (Scheler). See **Touch.**

Tick (1), a small insect infesting dogs, sheep, &c. (E.) M. E. *tyke, teke;* cf. A.S. *ticia* (Sweet, O. E. T.). [The F. *tique* is borrowed from Teutonic.] **+** M. Du. *teke,* Du. *teek,* Low G. *teke, täke,* G. *zecke* (whence Ital. *zecca*). Cf. Lith. *dygus,* sharp, *dégti,* to sting (Franck).

Tick (2), cover of a feather bed. (L. – Gk.) M. E. *teke,* 14th cent. – L. *tēca, thēca,* a case (whence F. *taie*). – Gk. θήκη, a case to put a thing in. – Gk. θη-, base of τίθημι, I put, put away.

Tick (3), to beat as a watch. (E.) An imitative word, like *click;* perhaps suggested by **Tick** (4). Cf. G. *ticktack,* pit-a-pat; E. Fries. *tik-tak,* the ticking of a clock.

Tick (4), to touch lightly. (E.) M. E. *teck,* a light touch; whence the game called *tick* or *tig,* in which children try to touch each other. Not in A.S. E. Fries. *tikken,* to touch lightly. **+** Du. *tik,* a touch, pat, tick, *tikken,* to tick, pat; Low G. *tikk,* a light touch; Norw. *tikka,* to touch lightly.

Tick (5), credit. (F. – G.) Short for

ticket; Nares shews that to take things on credit was 'to take on *ticket.*' See below.

Ticket, a bill stuck up, a label. (F. – G.) M. F. *etiquet,* 'a little bill, note, or ticket, esp. such as is *stuck up* on the gate of a court;' Cot. O. F. *estiquet, estiquete* (Godefroy). – G. *stecken,* to stick, stick up, fix; see **Stick.** And see **Etiquette.**

Tickle. (E.) M. E. *ticklen;* frequentative form from the base *tik-,* to touch lightly; see **Tick** (4). It means 'to keep on touching lightly.' Hence also M. E. *tikel,* unstable, ticklish, easily moved by a touch; mod. E. *ticklish,* unstable. ¶ Not necessarily a variant of Icel. *kitla,* to tickle; but a parallel formation.

Tide. (E.) M. E. *tide.* A. S. *tīd,* time, hour, season. **+** Du. *tijd,* Icel. *tíð,* Dan. Swed. *tid,* G. *zeit.* Teut. type **tī-di-.* Allied to **Time.** Der. *tide-waiter,* an officer who *waits* for arrival of vessels with the *tide,* to secure payment of duties.

tidings. (Scand.) M. E. *tidinde,* also *tidinge;* afterwards *tidings.* Orig. 'things that happen;' cf. A. S. *tīdung,* tidings; *tīdan,* to happen. But rather from Icel. *tīðindi,* neut. pl., tidings, news, Dan. *tīdende,* tidings; cf. Du. *tijding,* G. *zeitung.* All from the sb. above.

tidy, seasonable, neat. (E.) M. E. *tidy,* seasonable, from M. E. *tid* or *tide,* time; see **Tide. +** Du. *tijdig,* Dan. Swed. *tidig,* G. *zeitig,* timely.

Tie, vb. (E.) M. E. *tien, tiȝen, teyen,* to tie; A. S. *tīegan, ge-tīgan;* an unoriginal verb, from A. S. *tēag,* a bond, chain, rope. – A. S. *tēah,* Teut. type **tauh,* 2nd grade of **teuhan-,* to pull, draw; see **Tow, Tug.** Cf. Icel. *taug,* a tie, *tygill,* a string.

Tier, a rank, row. (F. – Late L.) Formerly *tire,* a better spelling; Florio explains Ital. *tiro* by 'a *tyre* of ordinance.' – F. *tire,* 'a draught, pull, . . also a *tire;* a stroke, hit, reach, gate, course, or continuance of course;' Cot. [Cf. Span. *tiro,* a set of mules; Ital. *tiro,* 'a shoot, shot, tire, reach, . . a stones caste, a *tyre* of ordinance;' Florio (1598).] – F. *tirer,* to draw, drag, pull, &c. – Late L. *tirāre,* to draw, pull, extend, hurl; whence also Ital. *tirare,* Span. Port. Prov. *tirar.* Of unknown origin. ¶ The A. S. *tīer,* occurring but once, is an obscure and doubtful word, and has nothing to do with it.

Tierce, Terce. (F. – L.) It meant a third hour, a third of a pipe or cask, a third card, a third thrust (in fencing). –

O. F. *tierz, tierce*, third. – L. *tertius*, third. – L. *ter*, thrice; *trēs*, three. See **Tri-**, **Three**.

Tiff (1), to deck, dress out. (F. – O. Low G.) M. E. *tiffen*. – M. F. *tiffer, tifer* (more commonly *attiffer*), 'to deck, trim, adorn;' Cotg. – Du. *tippen*, to cut, clip, cut off the *tip* of the hair; Low G. *tippen*, to touch lightly. See **Tip** (1).

Tiff (2), a pet, fit of ill-humour; also liquor, drink. (Scand.) Orig. 'a sniff;' hence (1) a pet, (2) a sip or draught of beer. – Norweg. *tev*, a drawing in of the breath, sniff, *teva*, to sniff; Swed. dial. *täv*, smell, taste; Icel. *þefa*, to sniff.

Tiffin, luncheon. (Scand.) Anglo-Indian; orig. Northern English *tiffin*, i. e. *tiffing*, sipping, eating and drinking out of due season. From *tiff*, a draught of beer. See above.

Tiger. (F. – L. – Gk. – Pers.) M. E. *tigre*. – F. *tigre*. – L. *tigrem*, acc. of *tigris*, a tiger. – Gk. τίγρις. – Zend *tighri-*, an arrow (hence perhaps a tiger, from its swiftness, also the river *Tigris*, from its swiftness); mod. Pers. *tīr*, an arrow, the river Tigris. – Zend *tighra*, sharp; allied to Skt. *tigma-*, sharp, from *tij*, to be sharp. Perhaps allied to **Stigma**.

Tight. (Scand.) For **thight*; but, as both Dan. and Norw. have *t* for *th*, it easily became *tight*. Orkney *thight*, water-tight; prov. E. *thite*, tight, close, compact; M. E. *tiȝt*, also *þiȝt, thyht*. – Icel. *þéttr*, tight, esp. water-tight; Norw. *tjett, tett*, close, water-tight; Swed. dial. *tjett, titt*; Swed. *tät*, close, tight, solid, compact; Dan. *tæt*, tight, close, compact, water-tight. M. E. *tiȝt* shews the old guttural; the Icel. *þéttr* is for **þíhtr*, as shewn by Du. *dicht*, *digt*, G. *dicht*, tight, M. H. G. (*ge*)*dîhte*, adv., continually. Teut. type **þíhtoz*, for **þenχtoz*. Allied to Lith. *tenku*, I have enough, *tankus*, close, tight.

Tike, a dog, low fellow. (Scand.) M. E. *tike*. – Icel. Norw. *tík*, Swed. *tik*, a bitch; Dan. dial. *tiig*, a male dog.

Tile. (L.) M. E. *tile*, contracted form of A. S. *tigele*, a tile. – L. *tēgula*, a tile. – L. *tegere*, to cover. See **Tegument**.

Till (1), to cultivate. (E.) M. E. *tilien*. A. S. *tilian*, to labour, endeavour, strive after, to till land. + Du. *telen*, to breed, cultivate, till; G. *zielen*, to aim at, O. H. G. *zilōn*, to strive after, Bavar. *zelgen*, to till. From A. S. *til*, adj., beneficial, excellent; cf. O. H. G. *zil*, a goal, mark; Goth.

ga-tils, fit, convenient; A. S. *til*, sb., use. **Der.** *til-th*, A. S. *tilð*, a crop, cultivation; cf. Du. *teelt*, crop.

Till (2), to the time when. (Scand.) M. E. *til*; chiefly in the Northern dialect; O. Northumb. *til*, Matt. xxvi. 31. – Icel. *til*, Dan. *til*, Swed. *till*, prep., to. Also O. Fries. *til*, prep. Apparently allied to Icel. *tili, tíli*, aim, bent, cognate with O. H. G. *zil*, aim, mark; see **Till** (1).

Till (3), a drawer for money. (E.) The proper sense is 'drawer,' something that can be pulled out. Dryden has *tiller* in this sense, tr. of Juvenal, vi. 384. From M. E. *tillen*, to draw, draw out, also to allure; also spelt *tullen*. A. S. *tyllan*, only in the comp. *for-tyllan*, to draw aside, lead astray. Cf. **Toll** (2).

tiller, the handle of a rudder. (E.) Prov. E. *tiller*, a handle, lit. 'puller.' From M. E. *tillen*, to draw, pull (above).

Tilt (1), the covering of a cart. (E.) M. E. *teld*, later *telt*, the same. A. S. *teld*, a tent. The final *t* was due to the cognate E. Fries., Low G., and Dan. *telt*, Swed. *tält*, a tent. + M. Du. *telde*, Icel. *tjald*, G. *zelt*.

Tilt (2), to cause to heel over, to joust in a tourney. (E.) Orig. sense 'to totter'; hence to cause to totter, to upset, tilt over, upset an enemy in a tourney. M. E. *tilten*, *tulten*, to totter, be unsteady; answering to an A. S. **tyltan* (not found), regularly formed (by change from *ea* to *ie, y*) from A. S. *tealt*, adj., unsteady, unstable. + Icel. *tölta*, to amble; Norw. *tylta*, to walk on tiptoe; Swed. *tulta*, to waddle; G. *zelt*, an ambling pace. Cf. **Totter**. **Der.** *tilt*, sb.

Tilth; see **Till** (1).

Timber, wood for building. (E.) A. S. *timber*, material to build with; for **timro-* (the *b* being excrescent). + Icel. *timbr*, Dan. *tömmer*, Swed. *timmer*; G. *zimmer*. Cf. Goth. *timrjan*, to build. From Teut. base **tem-*, to build; cf. Gk. δέμ-ειν, to build; L. *dom-us*, a house. See **Dome**. Brugm. i. § 421 (8). (√DEM.)

Timbrel, a kind of tambourine. (F. – L. – Gk.) Dimin. of M. E. *timbre*, a small tambourine. – O. F. *timbre*, a timbrel. – L. *tympanum*, a drum. – Gk. τύμπανον, a drum. See **Tympanum**.

Time. (E.) A. S. *tíma*. + Icel. *tími*; Dan. *time*; Swed. *timme*. Teut. type **tī-man-*. Allied to **Tide**.

Timid, fearful. (F. – L.) F. *timide*. – L. *timidus*. – L. *timēre*, to fear.

timorous. (L.) Coined, with suffix *-ous*, from L. *timor*, fear. — L. *timēre*, to fear.

Tin. (E.) A. S. *tin*. + Du. *tin*, Icel. *tin*, Dan. *tin*, Swed. *tenn*, G. *zinn*. ¶ Distinct from L. *stannum* (F. *étain*).

Tincture. (L.) L. *tinctūra*, a dyeing. — L. *tinctus*, pp. of *tingere*, to dye. See Tinge.

Tind, to light or kindle. (E.) Also spelt *tine*; nearly obsolete. M.E. *tenden*. A. S. *-tendan*, to kindle. + Dan. *tænde*, Swed. *tända*, Goth. *tandjan*. Teut. type **tandjan-*, from the 2nd grade of a lost strong verb **tendan-*, making pt. t. **tand*, pp. **tundanoz*. See below.

tinder. (E.) M. E. *tinder*, more commonly *tunder*, *tondre*. A. S. *tyndre*, f., anything for kindling fires from a spark. Cf. O. H. G. *zuntira*, tinder. Teut. type **tund-ir-ōn*; from **tund*, weak grade of lost verb **tendan*, to kindle; see above. + Icel. *tundr* (cf. *tandri*, fire); Dan. *tönder*, Swed. *tunder*; Du. *tonder*; G. *zunder*, tinder.

Tine (1), the tooth or spike of a fork or harrow. (E.) Formerly *tind*. M. E. *tind*. A. S. *tind*. + Icel. *tindr*, Swed. *tinne*, Dan. dial. *tind*, tooth of a rake; M. H. G. *zint*. Teut. type **tendoz*, m. ; allied to L. *dens* (gen. *dent-is*), a tooth ; cf. also Skt. *danta-*, a tooth. Noreen, § 144. See Tooth.

Tine (2), to kindle; see Tind.

Tine (3), to lose. (Scand.) Icel. *tȳna*, to lose. — Icel. *tjōn*, loss, damage; allied to A. S. *tēona*, harm; see Teen.

Tinge, to dye. (L.) L. *tingere*, pp. *tinctus*, to dye (see Tint). + Gk. τέγγειν, to wet, dye; O. H. G. *thunkōn*, G. *tunken*, to dip, steep (from the weak grade). (√TENG.)

Tingle. (E.) M. E. *tinglen*, a by-form of *tinklen*, to tinkle, which, again, is a frequentative form of M. E. *tinken*, to tink (see tinker), of which a weaker form is *ting*. 'To *ting*, tinnire; *tingil*, tinnire;' Levins (1570). Cf. E. Fries. *tingeln*. The orig. sense was to ring, then to vibrate, thrill, to feel a sense of vibration as when a bell is rung.

tinker. (E.) M. E. *tinkere*. So called because he makes a *tinking* sound, in the mending of metal pots, &c. From M. E. *tinken*, to ring or tinkle; Wyclif, 1 Cor. xiii. 1. Of imitative origin; cf. M. Du. *tinge-tangen*, to tingle, *tintelen*, to tinkle; E. Fries. *tinken*, *tingen*, *tengen*, to make

a bell ring; L. *tinnīre*, to tinkle, ring, *tintinnum*, a tinkling. Cf. Tudor E. *tinkler*, a tinker (Levins).

tinkle, to jingle. (E.) Frequentative of M. E. *tinken*, to ring; see tinker.

Tinsel, gaudy ornament. (F. — L.) From M. F. *estincele*, a spark, a star-like ornament; for **escintele*. — L. *scintilla*, a spark. See Scintillation, Stencil.

Tint, a tinge of colour. (L.) Formerly *tinct*. Spenser has *tinct* = dyed. — L. *tinctus*, pp. of *tingere*, to dye; see Tinge. Or from Ital. *tinta*, a dye. — L. *tincta*, fem. of *tinctus*.

Tiny, very small. (F. — L.) Preceded, in Shakespeare, by the word *little*; as, 'a *little tiny* boy,' 'my *little tiny* thief,' 'pretty *little tiny* kickshaws;' spelt *tine* or *tyne* in ed. 1623. Lydgate has *a little tyne*, a little bit. Perhaps from O. F. *tinee*, a tubful (hence, quantity, bit); from O. F. *tine*, a tub. (Athen., July 21, 1900.)

Tip (1). (E.) Often associated with *top*, but not etymologically connected with it. M. E. *tip*. + Du. Swed. Dan. *tip*, Low G. *tipp*; cf. G. *zipfel*, a small tip. Allied to Du. and E. Fries. *tepel*, a nipple, teat, and to E. Tap (2). Cf. M. Du. *tipken*, a teat. Der. *tip*, vb., chiefly in pp. *tipped*, i. e. furnished with a silver top or iron spike; whence *tipped-staff*, later *tipstaff*, an officer with a tipped staff; cf. *tipple*.

Tip (2), to tilt. (E.) Generally in the phrase *tip up*, or *tip over*; a secondary form of *tap*. Cf. *tip and run*, i. e. tap and run (a game); *tip for tap*, blow for blow (Bullinger's Works, i. 283), now *tit for tat*. E. Fries. *tippen*, to tap lightly. + Low G. *tippen*; Swed. *tippa*, to tap, tip, strike gently, touch lightly. Cf. Icel. *tapsa*, to tap. See Tap (1).

Tippet. (L. — Gk.) M. E. *tipet*, *tepet*. A. S. *tæppet*, a carpet, tippet. — L. *tapēte*, cloth, hangings; see Tapestry.

Tipple, to drink habitually. (Scand.) Norweg. *tipla*, to tipple, frequentative of *tippa*, to drip from a point or tip; Swed. dial. *tippa*, to drip, from *tipp*, a tip; cf. Du. *tepel*, a nipple, teat; see Tip (1).

Tipsy. (E.) Lit. 'unsteady.' Formed from *tip* (2) with suffix *-sy*, as in *trick-sy*, &c.; see Tip (2) above.

Tirade, a strain of reproof. (F. — Ital. — Late L.) F. *tirade*, lit. 'a lengthening out.' — Ital. *tirata*, a drawing, a pulling. — Ital. *tirare*, to pull, draw, pluck; the same as F. *tirer*; see Tier.

Tire (1), to exhaust. (E.) M. E. *tirien*, *teorien*. A. S. *teorian*, (1) to be tired, (2) to tire; weak verb; see *Atire* in New E. Dict. '*Fatigatus*, atered;' Voc. 170. 30.

Tire (2), to deck. (F.) Both as sb. and vb. M. E. *tir*, *tyr*, sb.; which is merely M. E. *atir* with the initial *a* dropped. Thus *tire* is short for *attire*, like *peal* (of bells) for *appeal*. See **Attire**.

Tire (3), a hoop of iron that binds the fellies of wheels. (F.) '*Tire*, the ornament of womens heads, the iron band of a cart-wheel,' Phillips, ed. 1706. Prob. identical with *tire*, a woman's head-dress. *Tire* meant to deck, also to arrange, being short for *attire*. Palsgrave has: 'I *tyer* an egge, *Je accoustre*; I *tyer* with garmentes,' &c. See **Tire** (2).

Tire (4), to tear a prey, as is done by predatory birds. (F. – Late L.) M. E. *tiren*, to tear a prey.– F. *tirer*, to pull, drag. See **Tirade**.

Tire (5), a train. (F. – Late L.) Only in Spenser, F. Q. i. 4. 35. From F. *tirer*, to draw; see **Tirade** and **Tier**.

Tiro, Tyro, a novice. (L.) L. *tīro*, a novice, recruit. ¶ The frequent spelling with *y* is absurd.

Tisic; see **Phthisis**.

Tissue. (F. – L.) F. *tissu*, 'a ribbon, fillet, or headband of woven stuffe;' Cot. Also *tissu*, masc., *tissue*, fem., woven; old pp. of *tistre* (mod. F. *tisser*), to weave.– L. *texere*, to weave. See **Text**.

Tit (1), a small horse or child. (Scand.) Icel. *tittr*, a tit, bird; Norw. *tita*, a little bird, small trout. Cf. prov. E. *titty*, small.

Tit (2), a teat. (E.) A. S. *tit*, *titt*, a teat; see **Teat**.

Titan, a giant. (L. – Gk.) L. *Tītān*; cf. *titio*, a firebrand. – Gk. Τιτάν, a giant; perhaps allied to τιτώ, day (Prellwitz).+ Skt. *titha-*, fire. (√TEITH, to burn.) **Der.** *titan-ic*.

Tit for tat, blow for blow. (Scand.) A corruption of *tip for tap*, where *tip* is a slight tap (Bullinger, Works, i. 283).

Tithe, a tenth part. (E.) M. E. *tithe*, also *tethe*. A. S. *tēoða*, tenth; O. Merc. *-tegða*; fuller form *teogoða*, corresponding to Gk. δέκατος, tenth. See **Ten**.

Titillation, a tickling. (F. – L.) F. *titillation*.– L. acc. *tītillātiōnem*, a tickling.– L. *tītillātus*, pp. of *tītillāre*, to tickle.

Titlark. (Scand. *and* E.) Lit. 'small lark;' from **Tit** (1) and **Lark**.

Title. (F. – L.) M. E. *title*.–O. F. *title* (F. *titre*).–L. *titulum*, acc. of *titulus*, a superscription on a tomb or altar. **Der.** *titul-ar*, from F. *titulaire*, titular.

Titmouse, a kind of small bird. (Scand. and E.) Not connected with *mouse*; the true pl. should be *titmouses*, but *titmice* is used, by confusion with *mice*. M. E. *titmose*. Compounded of *tit*, small (see **Tit** (1)); and A. S. *māse*, a name for several small birds, e. g. A.-S. *fræc-māse*, *col-māse*, *spic-māse*, all names of birds. + Du. *mees*, G. *meise*, a titmouse, small bird; Icel. *meisingr* (F. *mésange*). Teut. type*maisōn-*, f.; the sense of which was 'twittering'; cf. L. *maerēre* (for *maesēre*, cf. *maes-tus*), to lament, mourn (Franck).

Titter, to giggle. (E.) The same as M. E. *titeren*, to prattle; from a repetition of the syllable *ti*, which was also used to indicate laughter, as in the word *te-hee* (in Chaucer). See also *twitter* and *twaddle*. And see **Tattle**.

Tittle, a jot. (F. – L.) M. E. *titel*.– O. F. *title*, a title; M. F. *titre*, *tiltre*, 'a tittle, a small line drawn over an abridged word, also a title;' Cot. – L. *titulum*, acc. of *titulus*, a title. β. In late Latin *titulus* must have meant a mark over a word, as shewn by O. F. *title* (above). Wyclif has *titel* for the Vulgate *titulus* (Matt. v. 18).

Tittle-tattle, prattle; see **Tattle**.

To. (E.) M. E. *to*. A. S. *tō*. + Du. *toe*, G. *zu*; O. Irish *do*, Russ. *do*, to, up to. Cf. Gk. -δε, towards.

to- (2), prefix, to. (E.) Only in *to-day*, *to-gether*, *to-morrow*, *to-night*, *to-ward*; and in the obsolete M. E. *to-name*, nickname, and a few other words; see **To-day**.

To- (1), prefix, in twain, asunder, to pieces. (E.) Only retained in the phrase *all to-brake* = utterly broke asunder, Judges ix. 53. The M. E. phrase *al to-brake* meant wholly brake-asunder, the *al* being adverbial, and *to-brake* the pt. t. of *tobreken*, to break asunder. But about A. D. 1500, it was mistakenly written *all-to brake*, as if *all-to* meant 'altogether,' and *brake* was separate from *to*; and later writers much confused the matter, which is still often wrongly explained. The A. S. *tō-*, prefix, was very common, as in *tōbrecan*, to break asunder, *tōblāwan*, to blow asunder; cognate with O. Friesic *to-*, *te-*; and allied to O. H. G. *zar-*, G. *zer-*, signifying 'asunder.'

To- (2), prefix; see **To**.

Toad. (E.) M. E. *tode*. A. S. *tádige*, *tádie*, a toad. Der. *tad-pole*.

toad-eater. (E.) Formerly a companion or assistant to a mountebank, who pretended to eat toads, swallow fire, &c.; now represented by *toady*.

Toast (1), scorched bread. (F.–L.) O. F. *tostée*, a toast of bread; orig. pp. fem. –L. *tosta* (for *tors-ta), pp. fem. of *torrēre*, to parch; see **Torrid**.

toast (2), a person whose health is drunk. (F.–L.) The reference is to the *toast* usually put in stirrup-cups, &c., in drinking healths; see the story in the Tatler, no. 24, June 4, 1709 (Todd).

Tobacco. (Span.–Hayti.) Span. *tabaco*. A word taken from the language of Hayti (Clavigero, Hist. of Mexico). Las Casas says that *tabaco* was the name of the pipe in which the Caribs smoked the plant.

Toboggan, a kind of snow-sledge. (Amer. Indian.) A Canadian perversion of an Amer. Indian *odabagan*, a sledge.

Tocher, a dowry. (Gael.) Gael. and Irish *tochar*, a dowry, assigned portion.– O. Irish *tochur*, a putting; *tochurim*, I put.– O. Irish *to-*, *do-*, to; *cuir-im*, I put, assign.

Tocsin, sound of an alarm-bell. (F.– Teut. *and* L.) M. F. *toquesing* (F. *tocsin*), an alarm-bell, or its sound; see Cot. Lit. 'striking of the signal-bell.'– O. F. *toqu-er*, to strike, touch (Picard *toker*, Norm. dial. *toquer*, to strike); O. F. *sing* (Norm. dial. *sin*), a bell, from Late L. *signum*, a bell, L. *signum*, a sign; see **Touch** and **Sign**.

Tod, a bush, a measure of wool, a fox. (Scand.) Icel. *toddi*, a tod of wool, bit, piece (the fox being named *tod* from his bushy tail).+E. Fries. *todde*, a bundle; Du. *todde*, a rag; G. *zotte*, *zote*, a tuft of hair, anything shaggy.

To-day, this day. (E.) Compounded of *to*, prep., and *day*; *to* being formerly used in the sense of 'for.' Thus A. S. *tō dæge* = for the day, to-day; *dæge* being the dat. of *dæg*, day. So also *to-night*, *to-morrow*.

Toddle, to walk unsteadily. (E.) The same as Lowl. Sc. *tottle*, to walk with short steps, and equivalent to E. *totter*; see **Totter**. Cf. *tottlish*, tottery, unsteady (Cent. Dict.); Bavarian *zotteln*, *zotten*, to toddle, walk feebly.

Toddy. (Hindustani – Pers.) Hind. *tāṛī*, *tāḍī*, 'vulgarly toddy, juice or sap of the palmyra-tree,' &c.; H. H. Wilson.– Hind. *tār*, a palm-tree, palmyra-tree.–

Pers. *tār*, a palm-tree yielding toddy; Skt. *tāla-*. ¶ The Hind. *ṛ* has a peculiar [cerebral] sound, which has come to be represented by *d* in English.

Toe. (E.) A. S. *tā*, pl. *tān*. A contracted form; O. Merc. *tāhae*. **+** Du. *teen*, Icel. *tā*, Dan. *taa*, Swed. *tå*, G. *zehe*; O. H. G. *zēha*, a toe. Teut. type *taihōn. (Further connexions unknown.)

Toft, a green knoll, open ground, homestead. (Scand.) M. E. *toft*, a knoll.– Icel. *topt* (pron. *toft*), also *tupt* (pron. *tuft*), *toft*, *tomt* (the oldest spelling), a place to build on. Perhaps for **tumft-*<**tump-* (Noreen, §§ 83, 238), as if 'suitable place'; from **tum-*, weak grade of **tem-an-*, O. Sax. *teman*, to suit. Cf. G. *zunft*, a guild, O. H. G. *zumft*; and Goth. *ga-timan*, to suit.

Toga. (L.) L. *toga*, a mantle, lit. covering.– L. *tegere*, to cover. See **Tegument**.

Together. (E.) M. E. *togedere*.– A. S. *tō-gædere*, *tō-gædere*.– A. S. *tō*, to, *gador-*, *geador*, together; see **Gather**.

Toil (1), labour; to labour. (F. – L.) M. E. *toil*, disturbance, tumult; *toilen*, to pull about (the sense having somewhat altered). – O. F. *toillier*, M. F. *touiller*, to entangle, shuffle together, mix confusedly, trouble, &c.; see Cotgrave. Godefroy also gives the sb. *tooil*, *toeil*, *toil*, *toel*, a massacre, trouble, confusion, disorder. – L. *tudiculāre*, to stir up (Hatzfeld). – L. *tudicula*, a machine for bruising olives, d.min. of *tudes*, a mallet. – L. *tud-*, as in *tu-tud-ī*, pt. t. of *tundere*, to beat. ¶ *Toil* is often derived from M. Du. *tuylen*, to till or manure land, but it is impossible to explain it from this source; the M. E. usage is completely at variance with this view.

Toil (2), a net, snare. (F.–L.) F. *toile*, cloth; pl. *toiles*, toils, snares for wild beasts.– L. *tēla*, a web, thing woven; for *tex-la, from *texere*, to weave. See **Text**.

toilet, toilette. (F.–L.) F. *toilette*, 'a toylet, the stuff which drapers lap about their cloths, a bag to put nightcloths in;' Cot. – F. *toile*, a cloth (above).

Toise, a measure, 6 ft. 4½ in. (F.–L.) F. *toise*, 'a fadome;' Cot. – L. *tensa*, sc. *brāchia*, neut. pl. of *tensus*, pp. of *tendere*, to stretch (reach). See **Tend**.

Tokay, a wine. (Hungary.) From *Tokay*, a town in Hungary, E. N. E. from Pesth.

Token. (E.) M. E. *token*. A. S. *tácen*, *tácn*. **+** Du. *teeken*, Icel. *teikn*, Dan.

tegn, Swed. *tecken*, G. *zeichen*, Goth. *taikns*. Teut. types **taiknom*, n., *taikniz*, f. ; allied to **Teach**. Usually referred to an Idg. base **deig-*, by-form of **deik-*, as in Gk. δείκ-νυμι, I shew, cognate with Goth. *ga-teihan*, to point out; which is not wholly satisfactory.

Tolerate. (L.) From pp. of L. *toler-āre*, to put up with; allied to *tollere*, to lift, bear, take.+Skt. *tul*, to lift, Gk. τλῆναι, to suffer, A. S. *þolian*, to endure. (√TEL.) β. From L. *tlātum*, supine of *tollere*, usually written *lātum*, are formed numerous derivatives, such as *ab-lat-ive*, *collat-ion*, *di-late*, *e-late*, *ob-late*, &c.·

Toll (1), a tax. (E.; *or* L.–Gk.) M.E. *tol*. A.S. *toll*, tribute.+Du. *tol*, Icel. *tollr*, Dan. *told* (for **toll*), Swed. *tull*, G. *zoll*. Teut. type **tulloz*, m. ; which might be explained as < **tulnoz*, from the weak grade **tul* (with suffix *-noz*) of **tel*, the root of **Tale**; with the sense 'that which is counted out or paid.' But the existence of by-forms, as A.S. *toln* (whence *tolnere*, a toller), O. Sax. *tolna*, O. Fries. *tolne*, toll, O. H. G. *zollan-tuom*, as well as O. H. G. *zolonari*, M. Du. *tol-lenaer*, a toller, suggest that the forms are borrowed from Late L. *tolōnium*, for L. *telōnium*, which is from Gk. τελώνιον, a toll-house (Matt. ix. 9); from Gk. τέλος, an end, a toll. Cf. F. *tonlieu*, a toll; from Late L. *tonleium*, *tolneum*, for L. *telōnium*.

Toll (2), to pull a bell, sound as a bell. (E.) The old use was 'to *toll* a bell,' i. e. to pull it; from M. E. *tollen*, to stir, draw, pull, allied to *tullen*, to entice, allure, and prob. to A. S. *fortyllan*, to allure; see **Till** (3).

Tolu, a kind of resin. (S. America.) Said to be named from *Tolu*, a place on the N. W. coast of New Granada, now Colombia, in S. America.

Tom, pet name for Thomas. (L.–Gk.–Heb.) M. E. *Thomme*. – L. *Thōmās*. – Gk. Θωμᾶς, Thomas; 'a twin.' Cf. Heb. *tōmīm*, pl., twins.

Tomahawk, a light war-hatchet. (W. Indian.) Algonkin *tomehagen*, Mohegan *tumnahegan*, Delaware *tamoihecan*, a war-hatchet. 'Explained by Lacombe from the Cree dialect: *otomahuk*, knock him down; *otāmahwaw*, he is knocked down;' Cent. Dict.

Tomato, a love-apple. (Span.–Mexican.) Span. (and Port.) *tomate*. – Mexican *tomatl*, a tomato.

Tomb. (F. – L. – Gk.) F. *tombe*.–L. *tumba*. – Gk. τύμβα, a late form of τύμβος, a tomb. Allied to **Tumulus**.

Tomboy, a rude girl. (L. – Gk. – Heb.; *and* E.) From **Tom** and **Boy**.

Tome, a volume. (F. – L. – Gk.) F. *tome*.–L. acc. *tomum*. – Gk. τόμος, a section, a volume. – Gk. τομ-, 2nd grade of τεμ-, as in τέμ-νειν, to cut. Allied to **Tonsure.** (√TEM.)

To-morrow; see **To-day**.

Tomtit, a small bird. (L. – Gk. – Heb.; *and* Scand.) From **Tom** and **Tit**.

Tomtom, a kind of drum. (Bengāli.) Bengāli *tantan*, vulgarly *tomtom*, a small drum. Prob. named from the sound.

Ton, Tun, a large barrel, great weight. (L.) M. E. *tonne*, a large barrel, hence a great weight. A.S. *tunne*, a barrel. So also Du. *ton*, Icel.Swed. *tunna*, Dan. *tönde*, tun, cask; G. *tonne*, cask, weight; Gael. and Irish *tunna*, W. *tynell*, tun, barrel. All from Late L. *tunna*, a cask (9th cent.). If the orig. sense was ' wine-skin,' perhaps from O. Irish *tonn*, skin.

Tone. (F. – L. – Gk.) F. *ton.*–L. acc. *tonum.*–Gk. τόνος, a thing stretched, a string, note, tone. – Gk. τον-, 2nd grade of τεν-, as in **τενγειν* > τείνειν, to stretch. +Skt. *tan*, to stretch. (√TEN.)

Tongs, sb. pl. (E.) M.E. *tonge, tange*, sing. sb.; the pl. is due to the *two* arms of the instrument. A.S. *tange*, a pair of tongs, pincers; also *tang*.+Du. *tang*, Icel. *töng* (pl. *tangir*), Dan. *tang*, Swed. *tång*, G. *zange*. Orig. sense 'a biter' or 'nipper'; from a nasalised form of √DAK, to bite, as in Gk. δάκνειν. Brugm. i. § 420.

Tongue. (E.) M.E. *tunge, tonge*. A.S. *tunge*. +Icel. Swed. *tunga*, Dan. *tunge*, Du. *tong*, G. *zunge*, Goth. *tuggō* (=*tungō*). Teut. type **tungōn*, f. + O. Lat. *dingua* (L. *lingua*), a tongue. Root uncertain. Allied to **Lingual**. Brugm. i. § 441.

Tonic. (Gk.) Lit. 'giving tone.'–Late Gk. τονικός, adj., from τόνος; see **Tone**.

To-night; see **To-day**.

Tonsil. (F. – L.) M. F. *tonsille* ; Cot. – L. *tonsilla*, formed from the pl. *tonsillæ*, the tonsils. 'There is one [Latin] sb. in *-li*, Lat. *tōlēs*, pl. m. "wen on the neck," for **tons-li-*, from *tens-* "stretch" (Goth. *at-thinsan*, to draw towards one, Lith. *tęs-ti*, to stretch by pulling); *tonsillæ*, "tonsils," points to an older form **tons-lo-* or **tons-lā*;' Brugm. ii. § 98.

Tonsure. (F. – L.) F. *tonsure*. – L.

tonsūra, a clipping. − L. *tonsus*, pp. of *tondere*, to shear, clip. Cf. Gk. τένδειν, to gnaw; see **Tome**.

Tontine, a kind of lottery. (F.−Ital.) F. *tontine*. Named from Laurence *Tonti*, a Neapolitan (about A. D. 1653).

Too. (E.) The emphatic form of *to*, prep.; used adverbially.

Tool. (E.) M. E. *tol*, *tool*. A. S. *tōl*, a tool. ╇ Icel. *tōl*, neut. pl., tools. Lit. an implement for working with; Teut. type **tōlom*, n., for **tōu-lom* ; where **tōu-* is related to **tau*, as in A. S. *tawian*, to prepare, dress, get ready. See **Taw**. Streitberg, § 85.

Toom, empty. (Scand.) M. E. *tom*, *toom*. − Icel. *tōmr*, Swed. Dan. *tom*, empty.

Toot (1), to peep, spy; see **Tout**.

Toot (2), to blow a horn. (O. Low G.) Spelt *tute* in Levins (1570). − M. Du. *tuyten*, 'to sound a cornet,' Hexham; cf. Du. *toethoren*, a toot-horn, bugle. Cf. Swed. *tjuta*, Dan. *tude*, to howl, to toot; Icel. *þjóta* (pt. t. *þaut*), to resound, blow a horn; E. Fries. and Low G. *tuten*, to toot; A. S. *þeotan*, to howl; cf. Goth. *thuthaurn*, a trumpet. Of imitative origin; but the M. Du. form may have been borrowed from Scandinavian.

Tooth. (E.) A. S. *tōð*, pl. *teð* and *tōðas*. Lengthened *o* produced loss of *n* (*tōð* < *tonth*).╇Du. *tand*, Icel. *tönn*, Dan. *tand*, Swed. *tand*, G. *zahn*, O. H. G. *zand*, *zan*. Teut. stem **tanth-* ; or (in Goth. *tunthus*) **tənth-*.╇L. *dens* (stem *dent-*), Lith. *dantis*, W. *dant*, Skt. *danta-*, Gk. ὀδούς (stem ὀδόντ-). All participial forms; Idg. stem **(e)dónt-*; orig. sense ' eating '; from √ ED, to eat; see **Eat**.

Top (1), summit. (E.) M.E. *top*. A. S. *top*.╇Du. *top*; Icel. *toppr*, tuft, top; Dan. *top*, tuft, crest, top ; Swed. *topp*, summit ; G. *zopf*, tuft, top. **Der**. *topp-le*, to be top-heavy, tumble over.

Top (2), a child's toy. (F.−G.) M. E. *top*. − A. F. **top*, only found in the dimin. form *topet*. ' Trocus, *topet* ;' Glasgow MS. (Godefroy); cf. O. F. *topier*, to turn as a top ; also *tupin*, a pipkin (Cot.). − M. H. G. *topf*, a top, pot, scull (apparently with reference to the large hollow humming-top).╇Low G. *dop*, a shell ; M. Du. *dop*, *doppe*, a top (also *top*, from H. G.), *dop*, a shell, *doppe*, a little pot ; E. Fries. *dop*, *doppe*, a shell. Prob. allied to M. E. *doppen*, to dive, dip (a water-pot) ; and to E. **Dip**, **Deep**. Cf. M. Du. *toppen*, ' to

whipe a top ; ' Hexham. ¶ Or from M. Du. *top*, borrowed from M. H. G. *topf*.

Topaz, a gem. (F.−L.−Gk.) M. F. *topase*. − L. *topazus*, *topazion*. − Gk. τόπαζος, τοπάζιον, a topaz. ¶ Pliny derives it from an island called *Topazas*, in the Red Sea, the position of which is ' conjectural '; from Gk. τοπάζειν, to conjecture. This is ' conjectural ' indeed.

Toper, a great drinker. (F. *or* Ital.− Teut.) Certainly allied to F. *tôper*, to cover a stake, a term in dice-playing ; whence *tôpe*, interjection (short for *je tôpe*, I accept your offer) in the sense ' agreed ! ' Also used as a term in drinking; cf. M. Ital. *topa*, in dicing, agreed ! throw ! also (in drinking), I pledge you ! Cf. Span. *topar*, to butt, strike, accept a bet. Of Teut. origin; from the *striking* of hands or of glasses together, as in Picard *toper*, to strike hands in bargaining, Ital. *in-toppare*, to strike against an obstacle. Originally from the placing together of the tops of the thumbs, at the same time crying *topp!* See Ihre, Outzen, Brem. Wörterbuch.

Topiary. (L.−Gk.) *Topiary* work is a term applied to clipped trees and shrubs. L. *topiārius*, belonging to landscape gardening. − L. *topia*, fancy gardening. − Gk. τόπος, a place, district.

topic. (F.−L.−Gk.) M.F. *topiques*, ' topicks, books or places of logical invention.' − L. *topica*, sb. pl., title of a work by Aristotle. − Gk. τοπικά (the same), neut. pl. of τοπικός, local, relating to τόποι or common-places. − Gk. τόπος, a place.

topography. (F.−L.−Gk.) F. *topographie*. − L. *topographia*. − Gk. τοπο-γραφία, description of a place. − Gk. τόπο-s, a place ; γράφ-ειν, to describe.

Topple ; see under **Top** (1).

Topsyturvy. (E.) Formerly *top-turvy*, *topsydturvy*, *topsy-tervy* (1528). [Not for *top-side-turvy*, where *top-side* = upper side; for *topsytervy* is the older form.] Just as *upside down* was formerly *upsodown*, so *topsytervy* prob. = *top so tervy*. *Tervy* is from M. E. *terven*, to roll, roll back (hence, overthrow) ; see my Gloss. to Chaucer ; cf. M. E. *over-tyrven*, to upset ; A. S. *tearflian*, to turn, roll over ; Low G. *tarven*, to roll or turn up a cuff. ¶ Explained *topside t'other way* by late writers, where *t'other way* is a false gloss.

Torch. (F. − L.) M. E. *torche*.−F.

torche, a torch, also a wreath, wreathed wisp or piece of tow (Low L. *tortia*, a torch), twist. **–** Late L. *tortica*, a torch; (cf. *porche* from *porticum*). **–** L. *tortus*, pp. of *torquēre*, to twist. See Torture.

torment. (F.**–**L.) O. F. *torment* (F. *tourment*). **–** L. *tormentum*, an engine for throwing stones, or for inflicting torture. Formed with suffix *-mentum* from *tor-*, for *torc-*, base of *torquēre*, to twist, hurl.

tormentil, a herb. (F.**–**L.) F. *tormentille* (Cot.); Late L. *tormentilla*, Voc. 713. 6. Said to be so called from its relieving tooth-ache. **–** O. F. *torment*, torment, pain (above).

Tornado, a hurricane. (Span. **–** L.) Dampier speaks of ' *tornadoes* or thundershowers.' For **tronada*. **–** Span. *tronada*, a thunder-storm. **–** Span. *tronar*, to thunder. **–** L. *tonāre*, to thunder.

Torpedo. (L.) L. *torpēdo*, numbness; also a cramp-fish (which electrifies or numbs). **–** L. *torpēre*, to be numb (below).

torpid, sluggish. (L.) L. *torpidus*, benumbed. **–** L. *torpēre*, to be numb or stiff. Cf. Lith. *tirpti*, to grow stiff; Russ. *terpnute*, to grow numb. Brugm. i. § 521.

Torque, a collar of twisted gold. (F. **–** L.) F. *torque*, in Littré. **–** L. *torquem*, acc. of *torques*, a twisted collar, a torque. **–** L. *torquēre*, to twist. See Torture. Cf. W. *torch*, a wreath, O. Irish *torc*.

Torrent. (F. **–** L.) F. *torrent*. **–** L. acc. *torrentem*, a raging stream; from *torrens*, raging, impetuous, boiling, hot; orig. pres. pt. of *torrēre*, to heat (below).

torrid. (F.**–**L.) F. *torride*. **–** L. *torridus*, scorched. **–** L. *torrēre*, to scorch. **+** Gk. τέρσεσθαι, to become dry. See Terrace, Thirst. (√TERS.)

Torsion. (F. **–** L.) F. *torsion*, ' a wresting;' Cot. **–** L. acc. *torsiōnem*, a wringing. **–** L. *tors-*, as in *tors-ī*, pt. t. of *torquēre*, to twist.

Torso, trunk of a statue. (Ital.**–**L.**–** Gk.) Ital. *torso*, stump, trunk, stalk. **–** L. *thyrsus*, stalk, stem. **–** Gk. θύρσος, a stalk, rod, thyrsus.

Tort, a wrong. (F. **–** L.) F. *tort*, a wrong, harm; pp. of *tordre*, to twist. **–** L. *tortus*, pp. of *torquēre*, to twist.

tortoise. (F. **–** L.) M. E. *tortuce*, *tortu*; later, *tortoise*, with changed suffix; cf. Prov. *tortesa*, a tortoise. The M. E. *tortu* answers to F. *tortue*, a tortoise; Late L. *tortūca*. So named from the twisted

feet; cf. O. F. *tortis*, crooked. All due to L. *tort-us*, pp. of *torquēre*, to twist.

tortuous. (F.**–**L.) M. E. *tortuos*. **–** F. *tortueux*. **–** L. *tortuōsus*, crooked. **–** L. *tortus*, pp. of *torquēre*, to twist (below).

torture. (F.**–**L.) F. *torture*. **–** L. *tortūra*, torture, wringing pain. **–** L. *tortus*, pp. of *torquēre*, to twist, wring, whirl. (√TERQ.)

Tory. (Irish.) First used about 1680 in the political sense. The Irish State Papers, Jan. 24, 1656, mention ' *tories* and other lawless persons.'**–** Irish *toiridhe*, *toruighe*, lit. a (hostile) pursuer, also a searcher (hence, a plunderer); cf. *toireacht*, pursuit, search, &c. **–** Irish *toirighim*, I fancy, I pursue, search closely. Cf. Gael. *toir*, pursuit, search; O. Irish *toracht* (for **do-fo-racht*), pursuit; where *do* (to) and *fo* (under) are prefixes, and *racht* is from √REG, as in L. *reg-ere*, to direct, Irish *rig-im*, I stretch out.

Toss, to jerk. (Scand. ?) Cf. W. *tosio*, to jerk, toss; *tos*, a quick jerk, toss; borrowed from E. Perhaps from Norw. *tossa*, to scatter, spread out; cf. ' to *toss* hay ;' Dan. dial. *tusse*, to stir, move, shake. Allied to Touse.

Total. (F.**–**L.) F. *total*. **–** Late L. *tōtālis*, adj.; extended from L. *tōtus*, entire.

Totter, to be unsteady. (E.) Prov. E. *tolter*, a form occurring in Clare's Village Minstrel; cf. Lowl. Sc. *tolter*, adj. and adv., unsteady (not a *verb*, as Jamieson says). *Tolter*, as a vb., is related to M. E. *tulten*, to tilt, be unsteady (see Tilt (2)); and is allied to A. S. *tealtrian*, to totter, from the adj. *tealt*, unsteady. **+** M. Du. *touteren* (<**tolteren*), to tremble, shake. Cf. prov. E. *totter*, a swing; Bavar. *zeltern*, to hobble along.

Toucan, a bird. (F.**–**Brazil.) F. *toucan*; a Brazilian word (Littré). **–** Guarani *tucà*; whence Port. *tucano*. Granada gives Guarani *tùcà* (*ù* and *à* both nasal).

Touch. (F.**–**Teut.) F. *toucher*. [Also O. F. *toquer*, Walloon *toquer*, to knock or strike against; Ital. *toccare*, to touch, strike, smite.] **–** Teut. **tukkōn*, represented by Low G. *tukken* = O. H. G. *zucchen*, G. *zucken*, to twitch, draw with a quick motion; cf. M. Du. *tucken*, *tocken*, ' to knock head to head; to touch;' Hexham. A secondary verb, due to the weak grade (**tuh*) of Teut. **teuhan-*, as in Goth. *tiuhan*, A. S. *tēon* (<**teohan*), to pull, draw, O. H. G. *ziohan* (G. *ziehen*), cognate with

L. dūcere, to draw, lead. (√DEUK.) See **Tuck** (1), **Tow** (1). **Der.** *toc-sin, tuck-et.*

Touchy, corruption of Tetchy, q. v.

Tough. (E.) M. E. *tough.* A. S. *tōh,* tough.+Du. *taai,* flexible, pliant, viscous, tough; G. *zäh,* O. H. G. *zāhi,* tough, tenacious. Teut. type **tanχuz* (>**tāhuz*); allied to A. S. *ge-teng-e,* close to, oppressive, O. Sax. *bi-teng-i,* oppressive. The orig. sense is 'holding close together' or 'tenacious'; cf. Tongs.

Tour, a circuit. (F.—L.) Lit. 'a turn.' — F. *tour,* lit. a turn; also 'a turner's wheel,' Cot. — L. *tornum,* acc. of *tornus.* —Gk. τόρνος, a lathe. See **Turn.**

Tourmaline, the name of a mineral. (F.—Cingalese.) F. *tourmaline.* Formed from the native name in Ceylon, where it was called *tōramalli.* Explained (vaguely) as 'a general name for the cornelian'; Clough, Singhalese Dict. (1830), ii. 246.

Tournament. (F.—L.—Gk.) M. E. *turnement.* — A. F. *tournement,* O. F. *tornoiement,* a tournament. — A. F. *tourneier,* O. F. *tornoier,* to joust; cf. A. F. *turney, torney,* O. F. *tornoi,* a tourney, joust, lit. a turning about. — O. F. *torner,* to turn; see **Turn.**

tourney. (F.—L.—Gk.) A. F. *turney,* O. F. *tornoi* (above).

tourniquet. (F.—L.—Gk.) F. *tourniquet,* lit. 'that which turns about;' a name given to a stick turned round to tighten a bandage, to stop a flow of blood. — F. *tourner,* to turn (above). Cf. Picard *torniker,* to turn round.

Touse, to pull about, tear. (E.) M. E. *tūsen,* in comp. *tō-tūsen,* to pull about. [Cf. mod. E. *Towser,* a dog's name, lit. 'tearer.'] This answers to E. Fries. *tūsen,* to tear, pull, rend. + G. *zausen,* O. H. G. *(er)zūsan, (zir)zūsōn,* to tug, pull, drag about. **Der.** *tussle;* cf. *toss.*

Tout, to solicit custom. (E.) A dialectal form of *toot.* M. E. *toten,* orig. to peep; hence to be on the look-out for custom. A. S. *tōtian,* to project, stick out (hence, peep out); whence *Toothill, Tothill,* a look-out hill (W. *Twthill* at Carnarvon).

Tow (1), to tug along. (E.) M. E. *towen, toƷen.* O. Fries. *toga,* to pull, tow; cf. A. S. *toh-line,* a tow-line, towing-rope. —A. S. *tog-,* as in *tog-en,* pp. of *tēohan, tēon,* to pull, draw.+E. Fries. *tagen,* Icel. *toga,* to pull; O. H. G. *zogōn;* all similarly formed from Teut. **tuh* (>**tug*),

weak grade of **teuhan-,* to draw, cognate with L. *dūcere,* to draw, lead. (√DEUK.)

Tow (2), coarse part of hemp. (E.) M. E. *tow.* A. S. *tow-,* occurring in *tow-līc weorc,* material for spinning, lit. 'tow-like stuff,' and in *tow-hūs,* a tow-house, house for spinning. Orig. the *operation,* not the *material;* cf. A. S. *getawa,* implements. Allied to A. S. *tawian,* to prepare, work; see **Taw** and **Tool.** + M. Du. *touw,* tow, *touwen,* to tan leather, *touwe,* a weaver's implement; Icel. *tō,* a tuft of wool for spinning.

Toward, Towards. (E.) M. E. *towardes,* formed by adding *-es* (genitive suffix used adverbially) to M. E. *toward.* The A. S. *tōweard* is usually an adj., with the sense 'future, about to come;' *tōweardes* was a prep., usually put after its case. — A. S. *tō,* to; *-weard,* in the direction of, cognate with Icel. *-verðr,* M. H. G. *-wert,* Goth. *-wairths,* and allied to L. *uersus,* towards. β. All these suffixes are derivatives of the verb appearing in E. as *worth,* to become; see **Worth** (2). The same suffix appears in *after-ward, in-ward,* &c.; the lit. sense is 'that which has become' or 'that which is made to be,' or 'that which is turned'; hence *in-ward* = turned in, *to-ward,* turned to, &c.

Towel. (F.—O. H. G.) M. E. *towaille.* — F. *touaille,* 'a towel;' Cot. O. F. *toaille* (Low L. *toacula,* Span. *toalla,* Ital. *tovaglia*). —O. H. G. *twahila, dwahila* (G. *zwehle*), a towel. —O. H. G. *twahan,* to wash.+A. S. *þwēan* (<**þwahan*), O. Sax. *thwahan,* Icel. *þvā,* Swed. *tvā,* Dan. *toe,* Goth. *thwahan,* to wash. Cf. A. S. *þwēle,* a towel (Sweet, O. E. T.); *þwēal,* a bath; from *þwēan.*

Tower. (F.—L.—Gk.) O. F. *tur, tour.* —L. *turrem,* acc. of *turris,* a tower. —Gk. τύρσις, τύρρις, a tower, bastion; cf. Gael. *torr,* conical hill, tower, castle. ¶ A. S. *torr* is from L. *turris;* and late A. S. *tur* from O. F. *tur.*

Town. (E.) M. E. *toun,* an enclosure, town. A. S. *tūn,* a fence, farm, town.+Du. *tuin,* fence, Icel. *tūn,* enclosure, homestead, O. H. G. *zūn,* hedge; Irish and Gael. *dūn,* a fortress, W. *dīn,* a hill-fort. Lit. 'fastness;' cf. Gk. δύ-ναμις, strength, Irish *dūn,* L. *dūrus,* firm. Brugm. i. § 112, ii. § 66.

Toxicology, the science which investigates poisons. (Gk.) From Gk. τοξικό-ν, poison for arrows (from τόξον, a bow);

-λογία, from λέγειν, to discourse. β. Τόξον may be from √TEKS, to hew, shape; see **Technical.** But cf. L. *taxus*, yew-tree.

Toy, sb. (Du.) Du. *tuig*, tools, utensils, implements, stuff, refuse, trash; whence *speel-tuig*, playthings, toys, lit. ' stuff to play with.' M. Du. *tuyg*, ' silver chains with a knife, cizzars, pincushion, &c. as women wear,' Sewel. **+** Icel. *tygi*, gear, Dan. *töi*, gear, *legi-töi*, a plaything, toy, Swed. *tyg*, gear, trash, G. *zeug*, stuff, trash, G. *spielzeug*, playthings. β. The orig. sense was stuff, material, gear ; and G. *zeug* is connected with G. *zeugen*, to beget, to produce, and even to witness. So also Du. *tuig* is connected with Du. *tuigen*, to equip, to witness, E. Fries. *tügen*, to produce, prepare, equip, O. Fries. *tiuga, tioga*, to witness, M. H. G. *ziugen*, to produce, equip, witness; all weak verbs, due to the strong Teut. verb **teuhan-* (Goth. *tiuhan*, A. S. *téon*, O. H. G. *ziohan*, G. *ziehen*), cognate with L. *dūcere*, to lead. (√ DEUK.) ¶ As to the sound, cf. *hoy* = Flemish *hui*. See **Tow** (1), **Team.**

Trace (1), a track, foot-print. (F.—L.) F. *trace*, ' trace, path, tract ;' Cot. A verbal sb. from M. F. *tracer*, to trace, follow, also spelt *trasser*, to trace out, delineate. The same as Ital. *tracciare*, Span. *trazar*, to trace out, plan, sketch. These answer to a Late L. **tractiāre*, formed from *tractus*, pp. of *trahere*, to draw, drag.

trace (2), one of the straps by which a vehicle is drawn. (F.—L.) M. E. *traice*, *trace*, which Palsgrave explains by O. F. *trays* ; this is a plural form = mod. F. *traits*, pl. of *trait*. — O. F. *trays*, later *traits, traicts*, pl. of *traict*, explained by Cotgrave as ' a teame-trace or trait.' Thus *trace* = *traits*, pl. of *trait* ; see **Trait.**

Trachea, wind-pipe. (L.—Gk.) L. *trāchēa.* — Gk. τραχεῖα, lit. ' the rough,' from the rings of gristle round it ; fem. of τραχύς, rough. Allied to τέ-τρηχ-α, pt. t. of θράσσειν, ταράσσειν, to disturb.

Track, a course. (F.—Teut.) From F. *trac*, ' a track, beaten way ;' Cot. Norm. dial. *trac.*—Du. *trek*, a draught ; *trekken*, to draw, pull, tow, travel, march, &c. Allied to Low G. and E. Fries. *trekken*, O. Fries. *trekka*, and O. H. G. strong verb *trehhan*, to scrape, shove, draw ; see Franck. Scheler regards F. *trac* as due to F. *tracer*, to trace; see **Trace** (1); but N. Fries. has *tracke* for Du. *trekken.*

Tract (1), a continued duration, a

region. (L.) L. *tractus*, a drawing out, course, region. —L. *tractus*, pp. of *trahere*, to draw.

tract (2), a short treatise. (L.) Short for *tractate*, now little used. —L. *tractātus*, a tractate, treatise, tract. **—** L. *tractātus*, pp. of *tractāre*, to handle ; see **Treat.**

tractable. (L.) L. *tractābilis*, manageable. —L. *tractāre*, to handle, frequent. of *trahere* (pp. *tractus*), to draw.

traction, a drawing along. (F.—L.) M. F. *traction.* —Late L. acc. **tractiōnem*, acc. of **tractio.* **—** L. *tractus*, pp. of *trahere* (above).

Trade. (E.) The old sense was ' path '; hence a beaten track, regular business. Cf. M. E. *trede*, a tread, a step; from A. S. *tredan*, to tread ; see **Tread.** Cf. A. S. *trod*, a track, from the weak grade of *tredan*. But the right form occurs in Low G. *trade*, Swed. dial. *trad*, a beaten path, track ; from the 2nd grade of the verb. Der. *trade-wind*, a wind that keeps a beaten track, or blows always in the same direction.

Tradition. (L.) From acc. of L. *trāditio*, a surrender, a tradition (Col. ii. 8). —L. *trāditus*, pp. of *trādere*, to deliver. —L. *trā-*, for *trans*, across; *-dere*, for *dare*, to give. See **Trans-, Date.**

Traduce, to defame. (L.) L. *trādūcere*, to lead over, transport, also, to defame. Here *trā-* = *trans*, across; and *dūcere* is ' to lead.' See **Trans-** and **Duke.**

Traffic, vb. (F.—Ital.) F. *trafiquer*, ' to traffick ;' Cot. **—** Ital. *trafficare* ; cf. Span. *trafagar*, Port. *traficar, trafeguear*, to traffic. β. Origin unknown. It is proposed to derive the Ital. word from *traffik*, a late Hebrew form of Gk. τροπαϊκός, Gk. rendering of L. *uictōriātus*, a silver coin bearing the image of Victory (Athen., Apr. 7, 1900).

Tragedy. (F. — L. — Gk.) O. F. *tragedie*. — L. *tragœdia*. — Gk. τραγῳδία, a tragedy ; lit. ' a goat-song ;' prob. because the actors were clad in goat-skins to resemble satyrs. **—** Gk. τραγῳδός, a tragic singer ; lit. ' goat-singer.' — Gk. τράγ-ος, a he-goat; ῳδός, a singer, contracted from ἀοιδός; see **Ode.** Der. *trag-ic*, F. *tragique*, L. *tragicus*, Gk. τραγικός, lit. ' goatish.'

Trail, vb. (F.—L.) M. E. *trailen*, to draw along, answering to A. F. *trailer*, to trail, occurring in *trailebaston* (below).

─O. F. *trailler*, to tow a boat; allied to
F. *traille*, a ferry-boat with a cord. **─ L.**
trāgula, a drag-net, sledge, *traha*, a sledge;
from *trahere*, to draw. Cf. Gascon *trailho*,
a track; Port. *tralha*, a net; Span. *tralla*,
a cord. ¶ M. Du. *treylen*, to draw along,
is merely borrowed from F. *trailler*, ' to
traile a deer, or hunt him upon a cold
sent, to reel, or wind yarn,' Cot.; or else
from E. *trail* (see Franck). [The A. S.
trǣglian is a very scarce word, in a gloss,
and means ' to pluck.']

trailbaston, a law term. (F.─L.)
Anglo-F. *traylebastoun*, a term applied to
certain lawless men. It meant ' trail-stick'
or ' stick-carryer.' Fully explained in
Wright's Polit. Songs, p. 383; but constantly misinterpreted. The *justices of
traylbaston* were appointed by Edw. I to
try them. From *trail*, vb. (above); and
O. F. *baston*, a stick. See **Baton.**

train, sb. and vb. (F.─L.) M. E.
train, sb., *trainen*, vb.─M.F. *train*, a great
man's retinue; *traine*, a sledge; *trainer*,
to trail along (Cot.).─Late L. *tragināre*,
to drag along (Schwan). ─ L. *trahere*, to
draw. Der. *train-band*, corruption of
train'd-band.

Train-oil. (Du.; *and* F.─L.─Gk.)
For *oil*, see Oil. Formerly *trane-oyle* or
trane. ─ M. Du. *traen*, ' trayne-oyle made
of the fat of whales; also a tear, liquor
pressed out by the fire;' Hexham. The
orig. sense is ' tear'; then drops forced out
in boiling blubber, &c. Mod. Du. *traan*, a
tear; cf. G. *thräne.* The G. *thräne* is really
a pl. form = M. H. G. *trehene*, pl. of *trahen*,
O. H. G. *trahan*, a tear; cf. O. Sax. *trahni*,
pl., tears; E. Fries. *trän*, tear-drops. We
also find M. H. G. *treher*, pl., tears, which
may be connected with O. Northumb.
tæher, a tear, and A. S. *tēar*, a tear.
Similarly, Du. *traan* may be allied to
Dan. *taar*, a tear, and to E. *tear.*

Trait, a feature. (F.─L.) F. *trait*, a
line, stroke; Cot.─F. *trait*, pp. of *traire*,
to draw.─L. *trahere*, to draw.

Traitor, one who betrays. (F.─L.)
O. F. *traitor*, oblique case from nom.
traitre. ─ L. *trāditōrem*, acc. of *trāditor*,
one who betrays. ─ L. *trādere*, to betray;
see **Tradition.**

Trajectory, the curve which a projectile describes. (F.─L.) Suggested by
M.F. *trajectoire*, ' casting;' Cot. Formed
as if from L. **trāiectōrius*, belonging to
projection. ─ L. *trāiectus*, pp. of *trāicere*

(= **trā-jicere*), to throw across, fling. ─
L. *trā-*, for *trans*, across; *iacere*, to cast.
Der. *traject* (M. F. *traject*, a ferry), the
right reading for *tranect*, Merch. Ven. iii.
4. 53.

Tram, a coal-waggon, car on rails.
(Scand.) The words *dram-road* and *tram-
road* occur as early as A.D. 1794; we even
find *tram* in a will dated 1555 (Surtees
Soc. Public. xxxviii. 37). The same as
Lowl. Sc. *tram*, shaft of a cart, beam, bar,
prov. E. *tram*, a milk-bench (orig. a log of
wood). The *tram-road* was prob. at first
a log-road, then a rail-road on sleepers.─
Norw. *tram*, door-step (of wood); *traam*,
a frame; cf. Swed. dial. *tromm*, log, stock
of a tree, also a summer-sledge; M. Swed.
tråm, *trum*, piece of a cut tree. Orig.
sense a beam, shaft, bar, log; then a shaft
of a cart, a sledge; cf. E. Fries. *trame*,
trime, step of a ladder, handle of a barrow;
Low G. *traam*, a beam, handle of a wheel-
barrow; O. H. G. *dräm*, *träm*, M. Du.
drom, a beam, O. Icel. *þram* (in *þram-
valr*). ¶ The 'derivation' from *Outram*
(about 1800) is ridiculous; it ignores the
accent, and contradicts the history.

Trammel. (F.─L.) M. E. *tramaile.*
─ M. F. *tramail*, ' a tramell, or a net
for partridges;' Cot. (Mod. F. *trémail*,
Littré; Gascon *tramail*; Ital. *tramaglio*.)
Late L. *tremac(u)lum*, a kind of net (Lex
Salica). Prob. from L. *tri-*, threefold, and
macula, a mesh, net (Diez). ¶ The Span.
form *trasmallo* is corrupt.

Tramontane, foreign to Italy. (F.─
Ital.─L.) M. F. *tramontain.* ─ Ital. *tra-
montano*, living beyond the mountains.─L.
trā-, for *trans*, beyond; *mont-*, stem of
mons, mountain.

Tramp, vb. (E.) M. E. *trampen*; not
in A. S.; E. Fries. *trampen.*+Low G. and
G. *trampen*, Dan. *trampe*, Swed. *trampa*,
to tramp, tread; cf. Goth. *ana-trimpan*
(pt. t. *ana-tramp*), to tread on. Nasalised
form of base TRAP; see **Trap** (1).

trample. (E.) M. E. *trampelen*, frequent. of M. E. *trampen* (above); E. Fries.
trampeln.+G. *trampeln.*

Tram-way; see **Tram.**

Trance. (F.─L.) F. *transe*, ' a trance,
or swoon;' Cot. Lit. a passing away
(from consciousness). ─ O. F. *transir*, to
depart, die. ─ L. *transīre*, to pass away;
see **Transit.**

Tranquil. (F. ─ L.) F. *tranquille*,
calm.─L. *tranquillus*, at rest.

Trans-, prefix. (L.) L. *trans,* beyond, across, over. Orig. pres. pt. of a verb **trāre* (whence *in-trāre*), to pass over; cf. Skt. *tara-,* a crossing over. ¶ It occurs as *trans-, tran-,* and *trā-.* Brugm. ii. § 579.

Transact, to perform. (L.) From L. *transactus,* pp. of *transigere,* to complete. − L. *trans,* beyond, fully; *agere,* to do. See **Agent.**

Transalpine. (L.) From L. *transalpīnus,* beyond the Alps; see **Alp.**

Transcend. (L.) L. *transcendere,* to climb over, to surpass. − L. *tran-,* for *trans,* beyond; *scandere,* to climb.

Transcribe. (L.) L. *transcrībere,* to copy out from one book into another. − L. *tran-,* for *trans,* across, over; *scrībere,* to write. Der. *transcript,* from neut. of pp. *tran-scriptus ;* also *transcript-ion.*

Transept. (L.) Lit. cross-enclosure. − L. *tran-,* for *trans,* across; *septum,* enclosure, orig. neut. of pp. of *sēpīre, sæpīre,* to enclose, from *sæpēs,* a hedge.

Transfer. (F.−L.) F. *transférer.* − L. *trans-ferre,* to convey across. − L. *trans,* across; *ferre,* to bear; see **Bear** (1).

Transfigure. (F. − L.) F. *transfigurer.* − L. *transfigūrāre,* to change the figure or appearance. − L. *trans,* across (implying change); *figūra,* figure.

Transfix. (L.) From L. *transfix-us,* pp. of *transfīgere,* to transfix. − L. *trans,* through; *fīgere,* to fix; see **Fix.**

Transform. (F.−L.) F. *transformer.* − L. *transformāre,* to change the shape of. − L. *trans,* across (implying change); *formāre,* to form, from *forma,* shape; see **Form.**

Transfuse. (L.) From L. *transfūsus,* pp. of *transfundere,* to pour out of one vessel into another. − L. *trans,* across; *fundere,* to pour; see **Fuse** (1).

Transgression. (F.−L.) F. *transgression.* − L. acc. *transgressiōnem,* a passage across, in late Lat. a transgression. − L. *transgressus,* pp. of *transgredī,* to go across. − L. *trans,* beyond; *gradī,* to step, go; see **Grade.**

Transient. (L.) From *transient-,* supposed stem of L. *transiens,* passing away, though the real stem is *transeunt-;* pres. pt. of *transīre,* to pass across or away. − L. *trans,* beyond; *īre,* to go.

transit. (L.) L. *transitus,* lit. a passing across. − L. *transitum,* supine of *transīre,* to pass across (above).

Translate. (F.−L.) F. *translater,* Cot. − Late L. *translātāre,* to translate (12th cent.). − L. *translātus,* transferred; used as pp. of *transferre* (but from a different root). − L. *trans,* across, beyond; *lātus,* borne, used as pp. of *ferre,* to bear. See **Tolerate.**

Translucent, allowing light to pass through. (L.) L. *translūcent-,* st m of pres. pt. of *translūcēre,* to shine through. − L. *trans,* beyond; *lūcēre,* to shine; see **Lucid.**

Transmigration. (F.−L.) F. *transmigration.* − L. acc. *·transmigrātiōnem,* orig. a removing from one country to another. − L. *transmigrāre,* to migrate across. − L. *trans,* across; *migrāre,* to go; see **Migrate.**

Transmit. (L.) L. *transmittere.* − L. *trans,* across; *mittere,* to send; see **Missile.** Der. *transmiss-ion* (from pp. *transmissus*).

Transmutation. (F.−L.) F. *transmutation.* − L. acc. *transmūtātiōnem.* − L. *transmūtātus,* pp. of *transmūtāre,* to change over, shift, transmute. − L. *trans,* across; *mūtāre,* to change; see **Mutable.**

Transom, a thwart-piece across a double window, lintel, cross-beam. (L.) Shortened from *transtrom* (see Florio, under *Transtri* and *Trasti*). − L. *transtrum,* a transom (Vitruvius). − L. *trans,* going across; *-trum,* suffix (as in *arātrum,* that which ploughs, a plough).

Transparent. (F. − L.) F. *transparent,* ' clear-shining ;' Cot. − L. *trans,* through; *pārent-,* stem of pres. pt. of *pārēre,* to appear; see **Appear.**

Transpicuous, transparent. (L.) Coined, as if from L. **transpicuus,* from *transpicere,* to see through. − L. *tran-,* for *trans,* beyond; *specere,* to look. Compare *perspicuous.*

Transpire, to ooze out. (L.) From L. *tran-,* for *trans,* through; *spīrāre,* to breathe; see **Spirit.**

Transplant. (F.−L.) F. *transplanter.* − L. *transplantāre,* to plant in a new place. − L. *trans,* across; *plantāre,* to plant, from *planta,* a plant; see **Plant.**

Transport. (F.−L.) F. *transporter,* ' to carry or convey over ;' Cot. − L. *transportāre,* to carry across. − L. *trans,* across; *portāre,* to carry; see **Port** (1).

Transpose. (F. − L. *and* Gk.) L. *transposer,* to transpose, remove. − L. *trans,* across; F. *poser,* to put; see **Pose** (1).

Transposition. (F.−L.) F. *transposition.* − L. acc. *transpositiōnem.* − L. *transpositus,* pp. of *transpōnere,* to transpose. − L. *trans,* across; *pōnere,* to put; see Position.

Transubstantiation, the doctrine that the bread and wine in the Eucharist are changed into Christ's body and blood. (F. − L.) F. *transsubstantiation.* − Late L. acc. *transubstantiātiōnem* ; see Hildebert of Tours (died 1134), sermon 93. − Late L. *transubstantiātus,* pp. of *transubstantiāre* ; coined from *trans,* across (implying change) and *substantia,* substance ; see Substance.

Transverse. (F.−L.) O. F. *transvers,* placed across. − L. *transuersus,* turned across, laid across ; pp. of *transuertere,* to turn across. − L. *trans,* across ; *uertere,* to turn ; see Verse.

Trap (1), a snare, gin. (E.) M. E. *trappe.* A.S. *treppe,* a trap, for **træppe,* whence *be-træppan,* vb., to entrap (cf. F. *trappe,* of Teut. origin) ; E. Fries. *trappe, trap* (1) a step, (2) a trap.+M. Du. *trappe,* mouse-trap ; O. H. G. *trappa.* Orig. sense 'step' ; a *trap* is that on which an animal steps, or puts its foot. Cf. Westphal. *trappe,* a step ; Du. *trap,* a stair, step, kick, Swed. *trappa,* a stair. Allied to Du. *trappen,* to tread on, Norw. *trappa,* E. Fries. and Low G. *trappen,* to tread on, trample. Allied to Tramp. Cf. Span. *trampa,* a trap. **Der.** *trap,* vb.; *trap-door, trap-bat.*

Trap (2), to adorn, deck. (F.−Teut.) M. E. *trapped,* decked ; from M.E. *trappe,* trappings of a horse, &c. Coined, with unusual change from *dr* to *tr,* by sound-association with *trap* (1), from F. *drap,* cloth, as proved by Chaucer's use of *trappure,* trappings of a horse, from O. F. *drapure,* with the same sense (Godefroy). Cf. also Late L. *trapus,* cloth (usually *drappus*), *trappatura,* a horse's trappings, Span. and Port. *trapo,* cloth. See Drape. **Der.** *trapp-ings,* sb. pl.

Trap (3), a kind of igneous rock. (Swed.) Swed. *trappa,* a stair ; whence *trapp,* trap-rock ; cf. Dan. *trappe,* stair. So called from its appearance ; its tabular masses seem to rise in steps. Cf. Trap (1).

trapan, trepan (2), to ensnare. (F. −O. H. G.) Formerly *trapan.* − O. F. *trappan, trapant,* a snare, trap - door (Roquefort) ; a plank (Godefroy). − Late L. *trapentum,* a plank for a trap-door. −

F. *trappe,* a trap. − O. H. G. *trappa,* a trap ; see Trap (1).

Trapezium, an irregular four - sided figure. (L. − Gk.) L. *trapezium.* − Gk. τραπέζιον, a small table, also a trapezium. Dimin. of τράπεζα, a table, of which the orig. sense was a four-footed bench. − Gk τρα-, a reduced form of the Idg. word for 'four' ; πέζα, foot, allied to πούς (stem ποδ-), a foot ; see Foot. See Brugm. ii. § 168. **Der.** *trapeze,* F. *trapèze,* a swing in the shape of a trapezium, as thus : △. From L. *trapezium* (above).

Trappings ; see Trap (2).

Trash, refuse. (Scand.) The orig. sense was bits of broken sticks found under trees ; ' trash and short sticks,' Evelyn. Cf. Icel. *tros,* rubbish, twigs used for fuel ; Norweg. *tros,* fallen twigs, half-rotten branches easily broken ; Swed. *trasa,* a rag, tatter, Swed. dial. *trås,* a heap of sticks. Derived from the Swed. dial. phrase *slå i tras,* to break in pieces, the same as Swed. *slå in kras,* to break in pieces ; so that *tr* stands for *kr,* just as Icel. *trani* means a crane (see Crane). − Swed. *krasa,* Dan. *krase,* to crash, break ; see Crash. *Trash* means ' crashings,' i. e. bits readily *cracked* off, dry twigs that break with a *crash* or snap.

Travail, toil. (F. − L.) F. *travail,* toil, labour. The same as Ital. *travaglio,* Span. *trabajo,* Port. *trabalho,* toil, labour. According to P. Meyer (Rom. xvii. 421) it answers to Late L. *trepālium,* a kind of rack for torturing martyrs (Ducange) ; perhaps made of three beams (*trēs pālī*). Others make it answer to Late L. **trabāculum,* formed from L. *trab-em,* acc. of *trabs, trabes,* a beam. Cf. Late L. *trabāle,* an axle-tree. And see below.

Trave, a shackle. (F.−L.) A *trave* was a frame of rails for confining unruly horses. − O. F. *traf,* a beam (Supp. to Roquefort), usual form *tref* (Cot.). Cf. F. *en-traver,* to shackle, *en-traves,* shackles ; (Cot.) ; Span. *trabar,* to clog, *traba,* a shackle. − L. *trabem,* acc. of *trabs,* a beam. **Der.** *archi-trave,* q. v.

Travel, to journey. (F.−L.) The same word as *travail* ; from the toil of travelling in olden times.

Traverse, laid across. (F.−L.) M. F. *travers,* maso., *traverse,* fem. ' crosse-wise ;' Cot. − L. *transuersus,* transverse. − L. *trans,* across ; *uersus,* pp. of *uertere,* to turn ; see Verse. **Der.** *traverse,* vb., F.

traverser, 'to thwart or go overthwart,' Cot.

Travertine, a kind of white limestone. (Ital.–L.) From Ital. *travertino*, formerly *tivertino* (Florio). – L. *Tīburtīnus*, adj., belonging to *Tibur*, the modern Tivoli.

Travesty. (F.–Ital.–L.) Orig. a pp., borrowed from F. *travesti*, disguised, pp. of *se travestir*, to change one's apparel. – M. Ital. *travestire*, to disguise, mask. – L. *trā-* (for *trans*), implying ' change '; *uestīre*, to clothe, which is from *uestis*, a garment ; see **Vest**.

Trawl, to fish with a drag-net. (F.– Teut.) Walloon *trauler*, O. F. *trauler*, to go hither and thither (Roquefort) ; also spelt *troller*, mod. F. *trôler* ; see **Troll**.

Tray, a shallow vessel. (E.) M. E. *trey*. A. S. *tryg*, written *trig* (A. S. Leechdoms, ii. 340). – A. S. *trog*, a trough. + Low G. *trügge* (Stratmann) ; deriv. of *trog*. See **Trough**. (Doubtful ; the alleged A. S. *treg* is an error for *trog*.)

Treachery. (F.–L.) M. E. *trecherie*, *tricherie*. – O. F. *trecherie*, treachery. – O. F. *trechier*, *trichier*, to trick ; cf. Ital. *treccare*, to cheat. – Late L. **triccāre*, for L. *trīcare*, to dally (Ecclus. xxxii. 15), *trīcārī*, to make difficulties. – L. *trīcae*, pl. difficulties, wiles ; see **Intricate**.

Treacle. (F.–L.–Gk.) Formerly a medicament ; the mod. *treacle* is named from resembling it in appearance. M. E. *triacle*, a sovereign remedy. – O. F. *triacle*, also spelt *theriaque* (the *l* being unoriginal, as in *syllable*). – L. *thēriaca*, an antidote against poisons, esp. venomous bites. – Gk. θηριακὰ φάρμακα, sb. pl., antidotes against the bites of wild beasts. – Gk. θηριακός, belonging to a wild beast. – Gk. θηρίον, a wild animal. – Gk. θήρ, a wild beast.

Tread, vb. (E.) M. E. *treden*. A. S. *tredan*, pt. t. *træd*, pp. *treden*. + Du. *treden*, G. *treten*. We also find Icel. *troða*, pt. t. *tra*), pp. *troðinn* (cf. E. *trodden*) ; Dan. *træde*, Swed. *tråda*, Goth. *trudan* (pt. t. *trath*). Der. *tread-le*, a thing to tread on (in a lathe) ; also *trade*.

Treason. (F.–L.) M. E. *traison*. – O. F. *traïson*. – L. acc. *trāditiōnem*. – L. *trāditus*, pp. of *trādere*, to deliver over, betray. Doublet, *tradition*.

Treasure. (F.–L.–Gk.) The former *r* is intrusive. M. E. *tresor*. – O. F. *tresor* (F. *trésor*) ; the same as Ital. *tesoro*, Span. *tesoro*. – L. *thēsaurum*, acc. of *thēsaurus*,

a treasure. – Gk. θησαυρός, a treasure, store, hoard. – Gk. base θη-, θησ-, as in τί-θη-μι, I place, store up, fut. θήσ-ω ; (the suffixes are not clear). Der. *treasur-y*, O. F. *tresorie*.

Treat, vb. (F.–L.) F. *traiter*. – L. *tractāre*, to handle ; frequentative of *trahere* (pp. *tractus*), to draw.

treatise. (F.–L.) M. E. *tretis*. – O. F. *tretis*, *traitis*, a thing well handled or nicely made ; answering to a Late L. form *tractitius*. – F. *traiter*, to treat (above).

treaty. (F.–L.) M. E. *tretee*. – O. F. *traite* [i.e. *traité*], a treaty, pp. of *traiter*, to treat (above) ; Late L. *tractātus*.

Treble, threefold. (F.–L.) O. F. *treble*. – L. *triplum*, acc. of *triplus*, threefold ; see **Triple**.

Treddle, for **Treadle** ; see **Tread**.

Tree. (E.) M. E. *tree*, *tre* (which also means dead wood, timber). A. S. *trēo* or *trēow*, a tree, timber. + Icel. *trē*, Dan. *træ* ; Swed. *trä*, timber, also *träd*, a tree (for *trä-et*, lit. the wood, with post-positive article) ; Goth. *triu*. Teut. type **trewom*, n. Cf. Russ. *drevo*, a tree, W. *derw*, an oak, Irish *darag*, Gk. δρῦς, oak, Skt. *dru*, wood ; cf. Skt. *dāru*, a kind of pine ; Gk. δόρυ, a spear-shaft. Der. *tar* (1), *trough*.

Trefoil. (F.–L.) O. F. *trefoil*. – L. *trifolium*, lit. ' three-leaf.' – L. *tri-*, allied to *trēs*, three ; *folium*, a leaf. See **Foliage**.

Trellis, lattice-work. (F.–L.) M. E. *trelis*. – F. *treillis*, 'a trellis ;' Cot. Ultimately from F. *treille*, a latticed frame. – Late L. *trichila*, *tricla*, an arbour. But the suffix *-is* is due to O. F. *treilis*, *treslis* (mod. F. *treillis*, sack-cloth), adj., applied to armour covered with a sort of lattice-work, Late L. *trislicium*, a covering of sack-cloth. – L. *trēs*, three, *licium*, a thread ; cf. L. *tri-lix*.

Tremble. (F.–L.) F. *trembler*. – Late L. *tremulāre*. – L. *tremulus*, adj., trembling. – L. *tremere*, to tremble. + Lith. *trim-ti*, Gk. τρέμ-ειν, to tremble. (√ TREM.) Brugm. i. § 474. Der. *trem-or*, L. *tremor*, a trembling ; *tremulous*, from L. *tremulus* (above) ; *tremendous*, from L. *tremendus*, lit. to be feared, gerundive of *tremere*, to fear.

Trench, vb. (F.–L.?) M. E. *trenche*. – A. F. and O. F. *trencher*, vb., ' to cut, carve, slice, hew,' Cot. Now spelt *trancher*. β. Etym. much disputed. Cf. Prov. *trencar*, *trinquar*, Span. and Port.

trinchar, Ital. *trinciare*. Apparently from Late L. *trencāre*, to cut, substituted for L. *truncāre*, to lop, from *truncus*, the trunk of a tree. **Der.** *trench-ant*, cutting, from the pres. part. of *trencher*; also *trench-er*, a wooden plate, to cut things on, O. F. *trencheor*.

Trend, to bend away, said of direction. (E.) M. E. *trenden*, to roll, turn round. Allied to A. S. *trendel*, a circle round the sun, a ring; *ā-trendlian*, to roll; A. S. *tryndel*, a ring; Du. *om-trent*, about; Dan. Swed. *trind*, round; M. H. G. *trendel*, O. H. G. *trennila*, a ball; O. H. G. *trennilōn*, to revolve. See **Trundle**.

Trental, a set of thirty masses for the dead. (F. — L.) O. F. *trentel*, *trental* (Roquefort). — F. *trente*, thirty. — L. *trīgintā*, thirty. — L. *trī-*, thrice; *-ginta*, allied to Gk. -κοντα, short for *δεκοντα, a decad, from δέκα, ten.

Trepan (1), a small saw for removing a piece of a broken skull. (F. — L. — Gk.) M. F. *trepan*. — Late L. *trepanum*. — Gk. τρύπανον, an auger, borer; also a trepan. — Gk. τρυπᾶν, to bore. — Gk. τρῦπα, τρύπη, a hole. From √TER, to pierce, as in L. *ter-ere*, Gk. τείρειν (= *τέργειν).

Trepan (2); to ensnare. See **Trapan**.

Trepang; see **Tripang**.

Trepidation. (F. — L.) M. F. *trepidation*. — L. acc. *trepidātiōnem*, a trembling. — L. *trepidātus*, pp. of *trepidāre*, to tremble. — L. *trepidus*, trembling, agitated. Cf. Brugm. ii. § 797 (note).

Trespass. (F. — L.) O. F. *trespasser*, to exceed, pass beyond (hence, in E., to sin). — O. F. *tres-*, from L. *trans*, beyond; *passer*, to pass; see **Pass**.

Tress, a plait of hair, ringlet. (F. — Gk.) M. E. *tresse*. — F. *tresse*, a tress; *tresser*, to braid hair. [The same as Ital. *treccia*, a braid, plait, Span. *trenza*.] — Late L. *tricia*, variant of *trica*, a plait. — Gk. τρίχα, in three parts, threefold; from a common way of plaiting hair (Diez, Scheler). — Gk. τρι-, thrice, allied to τρεῖς, three; see **Three**. (Doubtful.)

tressure, an heraldic border. (F. — Gk.) Formed, with F. suffix *-ure*, from F. *tresser*, to plait. — F. *tresse*, a plait (above).

Trestle, Tressel, a support for a table. (F. — L.) O. F. *trestel*, later *tresteau*, 'a tresle for a table,' Cot. (Mod. F. *tréteau*.) — Late L. *transtellum*, the same as L. *transtillum*, dimin. of *transtrum*,

a cross-beam. See **Transom**. ¶ For O. F. *tres-* < L. *trans*, cf. *tres-pass*.

Tret. (F. — L.) *Tret*, 'an allowance made for the waste, which is always 4 in every 104 pounds;' Phillips. It prob. meant an allowance for waste in transport. — F. *traite*, 'a draught, . . also a transportation, shipping over, and an imposition upon commodities;' Cot. — L. *tracta*, fem. of *tractus*, pp. of *trahere*, to draw; see **Trace** (1). Cf. M. Ital. *tratta*, 'leaue to transport merchandise;' Florio.

Trey, three. (F. — L.) A. F. *treis*. — L. *trēs*, three.

Tri-, relating to three. (L.) L. *tri-*, three times; allied to *trēs* (neut. *tri-a*) three. So also Gk. τρι-, prefix; from τρεῖς (neut. τρί-a), three. See **Three**.

triad, the union of three. (F. — L. — Gk.) F. *triade*; Cot. — L. *triad-*, stem of *trias*, a triad. — Gk. τριάς, triad. — Gk. τρι-, thrice (above).

Trial; see **Try**.

Triangle. (F. — L.) F. *triangle*. — L. *triangulum*, sb.; neut. of *triangulus*, three-angled. — L. *tri-*, thrice; *angulus*, an angle; see **Tri-** and **Angle** (1).

Tribe, a race. (F. — L.) F. *tribu*, 'a tribe;' Cot. — L. *tribu-*, decl. stem of *tribus*, a tribe; cf. Umbrian *trifo*. Said to have been one of the *three* original families in Rome; as if from L. *tri-*, three. But see Brugm. ii. § 104.

Tribrach, a metrical foot containing 3 short syllables. (L. — Gk.) L. *tribrachys*. — Gk. τρίβραχυς. — Gk. τρι-, three; βραχύς, short.

Tribulation. (F. — L.) F. *tribulation*. — L. acc. *tribulātiōnem*, affliction. — L. *trībulātus*, pp. of *trībulāre*, to rub out corn; hence, to afflict. — L. *trībulum*, a sledge for rubbing out corn, consisting of a wooden frame with iron spikes beneath it. — L. *trī-*, as in *trī-tus*, pp. of *terere*, to rub; with suffix *-bulum*, denoting the agent. See **Trite**.

Tribune. (F. — L.) M. E. *tribun*. — F. *tribun*. — L. *tribūnum*, acc. of *tribūnus*, lit. the chief officer of a tribe. — L. *tribus*, a tribe; see **Tribe**.

Tribute, sb. (F. — L.) M. E. *tribut*. — F. *tribut*, tribute. — L. *tribūtum*, tribute, lit. a thing paid; neut. of pp. of *tribuere*, to assign, pay. Perhaps from L. *tribu-s*, a tribe (Bréal).

Trice (1), a short space of time. (Scand.) M. E. *at a tryse*, at a (single) pull;

Ipomydon, 392. From **Trice** (2), below β. Later, in the phr. *in a trice*, as if imitated from Span. *en un tris*, in a trice, in an instant ; from *tris*, the noise made by the cracking of glass, a crack, an instant. So also Port. *triz*, cracking of glass, a crash, crack, instant ; *en hum triz*, in a trice. Prob. of imitative origin ; cf. Span. *tris tras*, a noise ; *trisca*, a cracking, crashing ; *triscar*, 'to make such a noise as of treading on glass, nut-shells, or the like ; ' Pineda.

Trice (2), **Trise**, to haul up, hoist. (Scand.) M. E. *trisen*, to hoist sail (orig. with a pulley). — Swed. *trissa*, a pulley, *triss*, spritsail-brace ; Norw. *triss*, also *trissel*, a pulley ; Dan. *tridse*, a pulley, *tridse*, vb., to trice. Cf. also Low G. *trisel*, anything that revolves, a dizziness, a top. The Brem. Wört. also cites Hamburg *drysen*, to trice ; *dryse-blok*, a pulley. ¶ Orig. initial = þ.

Tricentenary. (L.) Coined from L. *tri-* and **Centenary**, q. v.

Trick (1), a stratagem. (Du. — F. — L.) XVI cent. — M. Du. *treke*, a trick ; Du. *treek*. Prob. distinct from Du. *trek*, a pull, draught ; and borrowed from O. F. *triquer*, Norman form of O. F. *tricher*, to trick. In fact, E. *trickery* is from O. F. *triquerie*, dial. form of *tricherie*, whence E. *treachery* ; see **Treachery** ; and *trick* may have been borrowed directly from Norm. dial. *trique*, a trick. ¶ But doubtless influenced by Du. *trek*, a pull, stroke, touch ; from *trekken*, to pull ; see below.

Trick (2), to deck out. (Du.) From the vb. *trick* below ; the sb. also meant a neat contrivance, a toy, trifle, &c.

trick (3), to delineate a coat of arms. (Du.) Du. *trekken*, to draw, also (in M. Du.) to delineate, trick, or sketch out.+ O. H. G. *trehhan*, str. vbs., to push.

Trickle, vb. (E.) M. E. *triklen*, short for *striklen*, *strikelen*, to trickle, frequentative of M. E. *striken*, to flow (Spec. of English, ed. Morris and Skeat, p. 48, l. 21). — A. S. *strīcan*, to flow, a particular use of *strīcan*, to strike ; see **Strike**. Cf. *streak*, and G. *streichen*. ¶ The loss of *s* arose in the phr. *teres striklen* = tears trickle ; see Ch. C. T., B. 1864, &c.

Tricolor. (F. — L.) F. *tricolore*, for *drapeau tricolore*, three-coloured flag ; cf. F. *tricolor*, the three-coloured amaranth. — L. *tri-*, three ; *color-*, stem of *color*, colour.

trident. (F. — L.) F. *trident*. — L. *tridentem*, acc. of *tridens*, a three-pronged spear. — L. *tri-*, three ; *dens*, tooth, prong.

triennial. (L.) Coined from L. *triennium*, a period of three years. — L. *tri-*, three ; *annus*, year.

Trifle. (F. — L.) M. E. *trufle*, *trefle*, rarely *trifle*. — O. F. *trufle*, mockery, raillery, a little jest, dimin. of *truffe*, a gibe, jest (Cot.). Properly a truffle, a thing of small worth ; the O. F. *truffe* also means a truffle (Cot.) ; cf. Prov. *trufo*, a truffle, mockery. See *truffe* in Scheler. See **Truffle**.

Trifoliate, three-leaved. (L.) From L. *tri-*, three ; *foli-um*, leaf.

triforium, a gallery above the arches of the nave and choir of a church. (L.) From L. *tri-*, for *trēs*, three ; *fori-s*, a door, opening. ¶ Now usually with but *two* arches (within a third) ; some early examples had *three* such.

triform, having a triple form. (L.) L.*triformis*. — L. *tri-*, three ; *form-a*,form.

Trigger. (Du.) Formerly *tricker*. — Du. *trekker*, a trigger ; lit. 'that which draws or pulls.' — Du. *trekken*, to pull. See **Track**.

Triglyph, a three-grooved tablet. (L. — Gk.) L. *triglyphus*. — Gk. τρίγλυφος, a triglyph ; lit. 'thrice-cloven.' — Gk. τρι-, thrice ; γλύφειν, to carve, groove.

trigonometry. (Gk.) 'Measurement of triangles.' — Gk. τρίγωνο-ν, a triangle ; -μετρια, measurement, from μέτρον, a measure. Gk. τρίγωνον is from τρι-, three ; γων-ία, angle, allied to γόνυ, knee.

trilateral, trilingual, triliteral. (L.) From L. *tri-*, three ; and *lateral*, &c.

Trill (1), to shake, quaver. (Ital.) In music. — Ital. *trillare*, to trill, shake ; *trillo*, sb., a shake. An imitative word, like Span. *trinar*, to trill.

Trill (2), to turn round and round. (Scand.) Perhaps obsolete. M. E. *trillen*, Chaucer, C. T. 10630. — Swed. *trilla*, Dan. *trille*, to roll, turn round ; the same as Du. *drillen* ; see **Drill** (1).

trill (3), to trickle, roll. (Scand.) Merely a particular use of the word above. Perhaps confused with *trickle*.

Trillion. (F. — L.) A coined word ; to express *tri-million* ; see **Billion**.

Trilobite, a kind of fossil. (Gk.) It has three lobes. — Gk. τρι-, for τρεῖς, three ; λοβ-ός, a lobe ; -ιτ-ης, suffix.

Trim, vb. (E.) M. E. *trimen, trumen.*
A. S. *trymman*, to set firm, to strengthen,
set in order, prepare, array. Formed
(by usual change of *u* to *y*) from A. S.
trum, adj., firm, strong. **Der.** *trim*, sb. ;
be-trim.

Trinity. (F. – L.) M. E. *trinitee.*–
O. F. *trinite.* – L. acc. *trīnitātem*, a triad.
– L. *trīnus*, pl. *trīnī*, by threes ; for **tris-
nus*, allied to *trēs*, three. Brugm. ii.
§ 66.

Trinket (1), a small ornament. (F.)
M. E. *trenket*, a shoemaker's knife ; also
spelt *trynket* (Palsgrave). Tusser speaks
of ' *trinkets* and tooles.' Hence it seems
to have meant a toy-knife, such as ladies
wore on chains ; and, generally, a small
ornament. Prob. from O. North F. *tren-
quer*, to cut, by-form of *trencher*, to cut ;
cf. Span. *trinchar*, Ital. *trinciare*, to cut,
carve ; Span. *trinchete*, a cook's mincing-
knife, a shoemaker's knife (Minsheu). See
Trench.

Trinket (2), **Trinquet**, the highest
sail of a ship. (F. – Span. – L.) M. F. *trinquet*, the highest sail ; Cot. – Span. *trin-
quete*, a trinket. Cf. Ital. *trinchetto*, a
trinket ; Port. *traquete*, a foresail. Prob.
from L. *triquetrus*, triangular (from the
shape). – L. *tri-*, allied to *trēs*, three ; see
Tri- ; *-quetrus*, of doubtful origin. The
n may be due to Span. *trinca*, a rope.

Trio. (Ital. – L.) Ital. *trio*, music in
three parts. – L. *tri-*, three ; see **Tri-**.

Trip, vb. (E.) M. E. *trippen*, to step
lightly. A lighter form of the base
TRAP, to tread ; see **Trap** (1) and **Tramp.**
+ Du. *trippen*, to skip, whence *trippelen*,
to trip, dance ; Swed. *trippa*, Dan. *trippe*,
to trip, tread lightly.

Tripang, an edible sea-slug. (Malay.)
Malay *trīpang.*

Tripe. (F.) M. E. *tripe.* – F. *tripe* ;
cf. Span. and Port. *tripa*, Ital. *trippa*, tripe.
Also Irish *triopas*, sb. pl., entrails, tripes ;
W. *tripa*, intestines ; Bret. *stripen*, tripe,
pl. *stripou*, intestines. Of unknown origin.
Perhaps from Low G. *stripe*, a stripe, also
a strip.

Triple, three-fold. (F. – L.) F. *triple.*
– L. *triplum*, acc. of *triplus*, threefold. –
L. *tri-*, three ; *-plus*, allied to *plēnus*, full.
See **Tri-** and **Double.**

triplicate, threefold. (L.) From
pp. of L. *triplicāre*, to treble. – L. *tri-*,
three ; *plicāre*, to weave, fold ; see **Ply.**

tripod. (L. – Gk.) L. *tripod-*, stem

of *tripūs.* – Gk. τρίπους (stem τρίποδ-), a
tripod, three-footed brass kettle, three-
legged table. – Gk. τρι-, three ; πούς, foot ;
see **Foot.**

tripos, an honour examination at Cambridge. (L. – Gk.) Better spelt *tripus*, as
in An Eng. Garner, vii. 267 (1670). It was
orig. applied to a certain M.A. chosen at
a commencement to make an ingenious
satirical speech ; hence the later *tripos-
verses*, i. e. facetious Latin verses on the
reverse side of which the *tripos-lists* were
printed. Thus the orig. reference was
(not to the *three* classes, but) to the three-
legged stool used by the *Tripus*, who was
also called a *Prævaricator*, or (at Oxford)
a *Terræ filius* ; and the lists were named
from the verses which took the place of
the speech delivered by the M.A. who sat
on the *tripus*. From L. *tripūs* (above).

trireme, galley with three banks of
oars. (L.) L. *trirēmis*, having three banks
of oars. – L. *tri-*, three ; *rēmus*, oar.

trisect. (L.) Coined from L. *tri-*, in
three parts ; and *sect-um*, supine of *secāre*,
to cut.

Trist ; see **Tryst.**

Trite. (L.) L. *trītus*, worn, pp. of
terere, to rub, wear away.+Russ. *terete*,
Lith. *triti*, to rub ; Gk. τείρειν (< **τέργειν*), to rub. (√TER.)

Triton, a sea-god. (L. – Gk.) L. *trītōn.*
– Gk. Τρίτων, a Triton. Cf. Irish *triath*,
the sea ; Skt. *trita-*, the name of a deity.

Triturate. (L.) From pp. of L. *trī-
tūrāre*, to rub down, thrash, grind. – L.
trītūra, a rubbing. – L. *trītus*, pp. of
terere, to rub. See **Trite.**

Triumph. (F. – L.) O. F. *triumphe*,
later *triomphe.* – L. *triumphum*, acc. of
triumphus, a public rejoicing for a victory.
+Gk. θρίαμβος, a hymn to Bacchus.

Triumvir. (L.) One of three men
associated in an office. L. pl. *triumuirī*,
three men, evolved from the gen. pl. *trium
uirōrum*, belonging to three men. – L.
trium, gen. pl. of *trēs*, three ; *uirōrum*,
gen. pl. of *uir*, a man ; see **Virile.**

Trivet, Trevet, a three-footed support. (L.) Spelt *trevid* (1493). A. S.
trefet, Cart. Sax. iii. 367. – L. *tripedem*,
acc. of *tripēs*, having three feet. – L. *tri-*,
three ; *pēs*, a foot. Cf. **tripod.**

trivial, common. (F. – L.) F. *trivial.*
– L. *triuiālis*, belonging to three cross-
roads ; that which may be picked up any-
where, common. – L. *triuia*, a place where

three roads meet. – L. *tri-*, three; *uia*, a way; see **Viaduct**.

Trochee. (L. – Gk.) L. *trochæus.* – Gk. τροχαῖος, running; also the tripping foot which consists of a long syllable followed by a short one. – Gk. τρέχειν, to run. Allied to **Thrall**.

Troglodyte, a dweller in a cave. (F. – L. – Gk.) F. *troglodyte.* – L. *trōglodyta.* – Gk. τρωγλοδύτης, one who creeps into holes, a cave-dweller. – Gk. τρωγλο-, for τρώγλη, a hole, cave; δύειν, to enter. β. Τρώγλη is from τρώγειν, to gnaw, bite, gnaw a hole. Cf. **Trout**.

Troll, to roll, sing a catch, fish for pike. (F. – Teut.) M. E. *trollen*, to roll; *to troll a catch* is to sing it irregularly (see below); *to troll a bowl* is to circulate it; *to troll* is also to draw hither and thither. – M. F. *troller*, which Cotgrave explains by 'hounds to *trowle*, raunge, or hunt out of order'; O. F. *trauler*, to run or draw hither and thither; mod. F. *trôler*. – G. *trollen*, to roll, troll.+M. Du. *drollen*, 'to troole,' Hexham; Low G. *drulen*, to roll, troll. Prob. allied to E. Fries. *drallen*, to turn, roll; and to **Drill** (1). ¶ Distinct from *trail*.

Trombone. (Ital. – G. – Slav.) Ital. *trombone*, a trombone, augmentative form of Ital. *tromba*, a trumpet; see **Trump** (1).

Tron, a weighing-machine. (F. – L.) O. F. *trone*, a weighing-machine; Low L. *trona* (Ducange). – L. *trutina*, a pair of scales. Cf. Gk. τρυτάνη, tongue of a balance, pair of scales. **Der.** *tron-age*.

Troop, a crew. (F.) F. *troupe*; M. F. *trope*. Also Span. *tropa*, M. Ital. *troppa*. Origin unknown. Cf. M. Du. *trop*, Late L. *troppus*, a troop. Perhaps from Norw. *torp*, a flock, crowd, Icel. *þorp*; cf. Icel. *þyrpast*, to throng.

Trope, a figure of speech. (L. – Gk.) L. *tropus.* – Gk. τρόπος, a turn, a trope. – Gk. τρέπειν, to turn. + O. Lat. *trepere*, to turn.

trophy. (F. – L. – Gk.) F. *trophée*, 'a trophee;' Cot. – L. *tropæum*, a sign of victory. – Gk. τροπαῖον, a trophy, monument of an enemy's *defeat*. Neut. of τροπαῖος, belonging to a defeat. – Gk. τροπή, a return, putting to flight of an enemy. – Gk. τρέπειν, to turn (above).

tropic. (F. – L. – Gk.) M. E. *tropik.* – F. *tropique*, 'a tropick;' Cot. – L. *tropicum*, acc. of *tropicus*, tropical. – Gk. τροπικός, belonging to a turn; the *tropic* is

the point where the sun appears to turn from N. to S., or from S. to N. in the zodiac. – Gk. τρόπος, a turn; see **Trope**. And see **Trepan** (1), **Trover**.

Trot, vb. (F. – L.) F. *trotter*; O. F. *troter*. We also find O. F. *trotier*, Low L. *trotārius*, a trotter, messenger, supposed to be from L. *tolūtārius*, going at a trot. – L. *tolūtim*, adv., at a trot; lit. 'liftingly,' i.e. lifting the feet. – L. *tollere*, to lift; see **Tolerate**. (So Diez, Scheler, and Littré.) But cf. M. H. G. *trotten*, to run, perhaps allied to *treten*, to tread; M. Du. *tratten*, ' to goe, to pace, or to trot.'

Troth. (E.) Merely a variant of *truth*. M. E. *trowþe*, Ormulum; see **Trow**.

Troubadour. (Prov. – L. – Gk.) A F. modification of Prov. *trobador*, also *trobaire*, a troubadour, inventor of songs or verses. Here *trobador* answers to a Late L. acc. **tropātōrem* (= Ital. *trovatore*, Span. *trovador*); whilst F. *trouvère* answers to a Late L. nom. **tropātor*. Both from the verb **tropāre* (as seen in Ital. *trovare*, Span. *trovar*, Prov. *trobar*, F. *trouver*), to find. See **Trover**.

Trouble, vb. (F. – L.) F. *troubler*; O. F. *trubler*. It answers to a Late L. **turbulāre*, a verb made from L. *turbula*, a disorderly group, dimin. of L. *turba*, a crowd. In fact, we find O. F. *torbleur*, *tourbleur*, one who troubles. Cf. Gk. τύρβη, disorder, throng; Skt. *tvar*, *tur*, to hasten. See **Turbid**.

Trough. (E.) M. E. *trogh*. A.S. *troh*, *trog*, a hollow vessel, trough. + Du. Icel. G. *trog*, Dan. *trug*, Swed. *tråg*. Teut. type **trugóz*, Idg. type **dru-kóz*; from **dru-*, as in Skt. *dru*, a tree, with adj. suffix. Thus the sense is ' wood-en'; see **Tree**.

Trounce, to beat. (F. – L.) To beat with a truncheon. – O. F. *trons*, a truncheon, m.; *tronce*, f., variant of *tronche*, a great piece of timber, allied to *tronc*, a trunk; see **Truncheon**.

Trousers, Trowsers. (F.) The latter *r* is modern; from the old word *trowses*, or *trouses*, breeches; older forms *trowze*, *trooze*; also *trews*; esp. used of the Irish *trews* or breeches; (whence Irish *trius*, *triubhas*, trousers; M. Irish *tribus*; Gael. *triubhas*). – F. *trousses*, trunk-hose, breeches (Littré), pl. of *trousse*, O. F. *tourse*, a bundle, package, case; from O. F. *tourser*, *trousser*, to pack; see **Truss**.

trousseau, a package; bride's outfit.

(F.) F. *trousseau*, a little bundle; dimin. of *trousse*, a bundle, a pack; from O. F. *trousser*, to pack. Of doubtful origin. See **Truss.**

Trout. (L. – Gk.) A. S. *trúht.* – L. *trúcta.* – Gk. τρώκτης, a nibbler, also a fish with sharp teeth. – Gk. τρώγειν, to bite, gnaw. Lit. 'nibbler.' Cf. **Troglodyte.**

Trover, an action at law arising out of the finding of goods. (F. – L. – Gk.) O. F. *trover* (F. *trouver*), to find; orig. to devise, invent, make up poetry. The same as Prov. *trobar*, Port. Span. *trovar*, Ital. *trovare*, to versify. β. Since Ital. *v* and Prov. *b* arise from L. *p*, the corresponding Late L. form is **tropāre*, to versify. – L. *tropus*, a trope; Late L. *tropus*, a song, manner of singing. – Gk. τρόπος, a trope, also a mode in music. See **Troubadour, Trope.**

Trow, to believe, suppose. (E.) M. E. *trowen.* O. Fries. *trouwa*, E. Fries. *trōen*, to believe. A. S. *trúwian*, to trow, trust, from Teut. base **trū-* ; also *treowian*, to believe, which is allied to the sb. *treow*, faith, trust, and to the adj. *treowe*, true, from Teut. base **trew(w)-*. Cf. Icel. *trúa*, to trow, *trúr*, true; Dan. *troe*, to trow, *tro*, true; Swed. *tro*, to trow; Low G. *trouen*, to trow, *trou*, true; Du. *trouwen*, to marry, *trouw*, true; G. *trauen*, O. H. G. *trūwēn*, to trust, Goth. *trauan*, to believe. See **True.**

Trowel. (F. – L.) M. E. *truel.* – F. *truelle*, O. F. *truele*; Late L. *truella*, a trowel. Dimin. of L. *trua*, a stirring-spoon, skimmer, ladle (hence a trowel, from the shape); cf. L. *trulla*.

Trowsers; see **Trousers.**

Troy-weight. (F. *and* E.) Orig. a weight used at the fair of *Troyes*, a town in France, S. E. of Paris. See Arnold's Chronicle, ed. 1811, pp. 108, 191; Haydn, Dict. of Dates, &c.

Truant, an idler. (F. – C.) F. *truand*, a beggar; *truand*, adj., beggarly; Cot. [The same as Span. *truhan*, Port. *truhão*, a buffoon, jester.] – W. *truan*, wretched, a wretch; Bret. *truek*, a beggar; Gael. and Irish *truaghan*, a wretch, miserable creature. Cf. W. *tru*, wretched, Corn. *troc*, wretched, Gael. *truagh*, Irish *trogha*, miserable, O. Irish *trúag*; Celt. type **trougos*, wretched (Stokes, 138). The Late L. *trútānus*, a wandering beggar, is from the same source.

Truce. (E.) It should rather be *trews*, i. e. pledges; it is the pl. of *trew*, a pledge of truth. (This is proved by the M. E. forms.) – A. S. *trēow*, a compact, promise, pledge, faith; cf. A. S. *trēowe*, true; see **True.**

Truck (1), to barter, exchange. (F.) M. E. *trukken.* – F. *troquer*, 'to truck, barter;' Cot. So also Span. *trocar*, to barter; whence some have thought that the F. form was borrowed. Cf. Ital. *truccare*, 'to truck, barter, to skud away;' Florio (1598). Origin disputed; the sense 'skud away' is clearly due to Gk. τρόχος, a course, from τρέχειν, to run; see **Truck** (2). β. But the Vocab. du haut Maine has *tric pour troc*, a simple exchange; and we find Norm. dial. *faire la troque*, to barter, from W. Flemish *trok*, used with respect to the (good or bad) 'sale' of goods; cf. *in trok zijn*, to be in vogue; and W. Flem. *trok* = Du. *trek*. The form *trok* is from Du. *trok-*, weak grade of *trekken*, to pull, for which W. Flemish employs *trokken*.

Truck (2), a small wheel, low-wheeled vehicle. (L. – Gk.) Modified from L. *trochus*, a wheel. – Gk. τροχός, a runner, wheel, disc. – Gk. τρέχειν, to run. **Der.** *truckle-bed*, a bed on little wheels, where *truckle* = L. *trochlea*, a pulley; Baret has: '*Pullie*, trochlea; a *truckle*, or pullie.' Cf. Span. *trocla*, a pulley.

truckle, to submit servilely to another. (L. – Gk.) From the phrase *to truckle under*, due to the old custom of putting a *truckle-bed* under a larger one; the truckle-bed being occupied by a servant, pupil, or inferior. It prob. originated in University slang, from L. *trochlea* (as above).

Truculent, barbarous. (F. – L.) F. *truculent.* – L. acc. *truculentum*, cruel. – L. *truc-*, stem of *trux*, fierce, wild.

Trudge, to march heavily. (F. – Teut.?) Perhaps to slouch along, or go about as an idle beggar. – F. *trucher*, to beg idly; obsol. (Littré). Of Teut. origin; cf. Low G. *truggelen*, to beg fawningly, to wheedle; Du. *troggelen*, to beg, wheedle; M. Du. *truggelen*, 'to trugge up and downe a Begging,' Hexham; W. Flem. *troggelen*, to walk with difficulty; Dan. *trygle*, to importune; E. Fries. *trüggeln*, to press, push backward, also to be importunate. Allied to G. *drücken*, to press, A. S. *þryccan*, to press, afflict, prov. E. *thrutch*, to press.

True, firm, certain. (E.) M. E. *trewe.* A. S. *trēowe, trȳwe,* true. Orig. 'believed;' allied to O. Prussian *druwit,* to believe (Fick); Lith. *drútas,* firm. **+** Du. *trouw,* Icel. *tryggr,* Swed. *trogen,* G. *treu,* Goth. *triggws,* true. Cf. also Icel. *trūr,* true, Goth. *trauan,* to believe,trust, be persuaded. See **Trow.**

Truffle. (F. – L.) M. F. *trufle,* F. *truffe,* a round edible fungus, found underground. Span. *trufa,* a truffle. It is thought that the F. *truffe,* Span. *trufa,* answer to L. pl. *tūbera,* truffles, whence was formed a F. fem. sb. **tufre,* easily altered to *truffe.* We also find Ital. *tartufo,* a truffle < L. *terræ tūber,* i. e. truffle of the earth; whence G. *kartoffel,* earlier form *tartuffel,* a potato. See **Trifle.**

Trull, a worthless woman. (G.) G. *trulle, trolle* (whence Picard *troulle*), a trull. Cognate with M. Du. *drol,* a jester, Icel. *troll,* a merry elf; see **Droll** and **Troll.**

Trump (1), a trumpet. (F. – G. – Slav.) M. E. *trumpe, trompe.* – F. *trompe,* 'a trump;' Cot. Cf. Span. *trompa,* Ital. *tromba,* a trump. – O. H. G. *trumpa, trumba,* a trumpet. – O.Slav.type **tromba,* as in O. Slav. and Pol. *traba* (with former *a* nasal), Slovenian *tromba, trôba,* a trumpet, Russ. *truba,* a pipe, tube, trumpet.

Trump (2), one of a leading suit of cards. (F. – L.) Well known to be a corruption of *triumph;* see Latimer's Sermons, and Nares. – F. *triomphe,* 'the card-game called ruffe, or trump; also the ruffe or trump at it;' Cot.: *triompher,* 'to triumph, to trump at cards;' Cot. – L. *triumphus,* triumph; see **Triumph.**

Trumpery, nonsense. (F. – G. – Slav.) F. *tromperie,* 'a wile, fraud;' Cot. **–** F. *tromper,* to deceive; orig. to sound a horn; whence the phrase *se tromper de quelqu'un,* to play with any one, amuse oneself at their expense. See **Trump** (1).

trumpet. (F. – G. – Slav.) F. *trompette,* dimin. of *trompe,* a horn; see **Trump** (1).

Truncate, to cut off short. (L.) From pp. of L. *truncāre,* to cut off. – L. *truncus,* a stump. See **Trunk** (1).

truncheon. (F. – L.) M. E. *tronchoun.* – O. North F. *tronchon* (Norm. dial.); O. F. *tronson,* a thick stick; formed from *tronc,* a trunk; see **Trunk.** Mod. F. *tronçon.*

Trundle, to roll. (F. – Low G.) Cf.

trundle-bed, a bed running on wheels; *trundle-tail,* a curly tail of a dog; A. S. *tryndyled,* rounded; Voc. 152. 5. – M. F. (Picard) *trondeler,* 'to trundle;' Cot.; Walloon *trondeler,* to roll (Sigart). Of Low G. origin; cf. Low G. *tröndeln,* Pomeran. *tründeln,* to trundle a hoop; O. Fries. *trund,* round; N. Fries. *trind,* round. From Teut. **trund-,* weak grade of a lost verb **trendan-,* to roll (pt. t. **trand*); whence also A. S. *sin-tryndel,* a large round shield. The *i* appears in Dan. Swed. *trind,* round; the *a,* modified to *e,* appears in M. E. *trenden,* to turn, roll, secondary verb from **trand,* 2nd grade of **trendan-.* See **Trend.**

Trunk (1), stem of a tree, &c. (F. – L.) F. *tronc,* trunk. – L. *truncum,* acc. of *truncus,* trunk, stem, bit cut off. – L. *truncus,* adj., cut off, maimed. Brugm. i. § 144. **Der.** *trunk-hose,* i. e. *trunk'd-hose,* knee-breeches, breeches cut short.

Trunk (2), of an elephant. (F. – G. – Slav.) Formerly *trump,* signifying (1) trumpet, (2) tube. – F. *trompe,* 'a trump, or trumpet, the snowt of an elephant;' Cot. Cf. O. F. *tromper,* to blow a trumpet; see **Trump** (1).

Trunnion, one of the projecting stumps on each side of a cannon, on which it rests in the carriage. (F. – L.) F. *trognon,* a stump; from *tronc,* a trunk; cf. M. F. *tron,* a stump; see **Trunk** (1).

Truss, to pack, fasten up. (F.) O. F. *trousser, tourser,* to pack up; whence the sb. *trousse, tourse,* a bundle; and the dimin. *troussel, toursel,* later *trousseau;* see **Trousseau.** Cf. Port. *trouxa,* a pack, Span. *troja,* a soldier's knapsack. Origin doubtful; perhaps from O. F. *tros, trous,* a small piece; from Late L. *tursus,* L. *thyrsus,* a stalk. – Gk. θύρσος; see **Thyrsus.** So Körting.

Trust. (Scand.) M. E. *trŭst.* – Icel. *traust,* trust, protection, firmness; Dan. Swed. *tröst,* consolation. **+** G. *trost,* consolation, Goth. *trausti,* a covenant. Related to **Trow, True.**

truth. (E.) M. E. *trewthe, trouthe;* A. S. *trēowð,* truth. – A. S. *trēowe,* true; see **True.** **+** Icel. *tryggð,* truth. And see **Troth.**

Try, to select, test, examine, &c. (F. – L.) M. E. *trien,* to select, pick out, choose. – F. *trier,* 'to cull out;' Cot. The same as Prov. *triar,* to separate corn from the straw, also to choose. – Late L.

trītāre, to pound small ; cf. Ital. *tritare*, to pound, mince, also to ponder, consider, scan.—L. *trītus*, pp. of *terere*, to rub. It meant to thresh, pulverise, separate, purify, cull, pick. (Disputed.) **Der.** *tri-al.*

Tryst, Trist, an appointment to meet. (F.—Teut.?) See Jamieson ; orig. a set station, place of meeting. M. E. *triste, tristre*, a station (in hunting), place to watch. — O. F. *triste, tristre*, station to watch (in hunting), ambush ; Low L. *trista.* Of doubtful origin ; but perhaps related to Frankish L. *trustis*, one in a place of trust (see Ducange). Allied to O. H. G. *trōst*, help, M. H. G. vb. *troesten*, to assist ; see **Trust.**

Tub, a small cask. (O. Low G.) M. E. *tubbe.*—M. Du. *tobbe*, a tub ; Low G. and E. Fries. *tubbe*, a tub.

Tube. (F.—L.) F. *tube.*—L. *tubum*, acc. of *tubus*, a tube, pipe ; akin to *tuba*, a trumpet. **Der.** *tub-ul-ar*, from L. *tubulus*, dimin. of *tubus.*

Tuber, a rounded root. (L.) L. *tūber*, a bump, tumour, also a truffle. Lit. 'swelling ;' allied to **Tumid.** Brugm. i. § 413 (8). **Der.** *tubercle*, a little swelling.

Tuck (1), to gather in a dress. (O. Low G.) M. E. *tukken.* — Low G. *tukken*, to pull up, draw up, tuck up, also to entice (= M. Du. *tocken*, to entice). + G. *zucken*, to twitch up ; O. H. G. *zucchen.* Teut. base **tukk* ; intensive form from the weak grade (**tuh*) of Teut. **teuhan-*, to pull ; see Tow (1), Tug, Touch.

Tuck (2), a rapier. (F. — Ital. — G.) Short for F. *étoc*, occasional form of *estoc*, 'the stock of a tree, a rapier, a tuck ;' Cot. — Ital. *stocco*, a truncheon, rapier, tuck ; Florio. — G. *stock*, a stock, stump, &c. ; see **Stock, Stoccado.**

Tuck (3), beat of drum. (F. — Teut.) From Picard or Walloon *toquer, toker*, to touch, strike ; variant of F. *toucher*, to touch ; see **Touch, Tocsin.**

tucker, a fuller. (F.—Teut.) M. E. *touker*, lit. 'beater ;' though the cloth was worked up with the feet. — O. North F. *touker, toquer*, to beat ; variant of F. *toucher*, to touch. See **Tocsin.**

tucket, a flourish on a trumpet. (F. — Teut.) North F. *touquet*, for O. F. *touchet*, a stroke ; equivalent to Ital. *toccata*, a prelude, tolling of a bell, a tucket, a striking ; from *toccare*, to strike, touch ; see **Touch.** ¶ Or from Italian.

Tuesday. (E.) A. S. *Tīwes dæg*, the day of *Tīw*, the god of war. + Icel. *Tȳs-dagr*, the day of *Tȳr* ; Dan. *Tirsdag*, Swed. *Tisdag* ; O. H. G. *Zies tac*, the day of *Ziu*, god of war. β. The A. S. *Tīw*, Icel. *Tȳr*, O. H. G. *Ziu* are the same as Skt. *dēva-s*, god, and allied to L. *deus*, god, and even to L. *Iu-* in *Iu-piter*, Gk. *Zeús*, Skt. *Dyaus.* ¶ A translation of L. *dies Martis.*

Tufa, a soft stone. (Ital.—L.) For *tufo.* — Ital. *tufo.* — L. *tōfus, tōphus.* Cf. Gk. τόφος. Origin unknown.

Tuft (1), a crest, knot. (F. — Teut.) M. E. *tuft*, but the final *t* is excrescent' ; prov. E. *tuff*, a tuft.—F. *touffe*, a tuft or lock of hair.—Swed. dial. *tuppa*, a tuft, fringe ; Icel. *toppr*, a top, tuft, or lock of hair ; M. Du. *top*, a tuft ; G. *zopf.* ¶ W. *twff* is borrowed from E., and preserves the correct form.

Tuft (2), a plantation, a green knoll. (Scand.) See **Toft.**

Tug, vb. (Scand.) M. E. *toggen.* From Icel. *tog*, M. Swed. *tog*, a rope to pull by ; allied to E. Fries. *tokken*, to pull ; Low G. *tukken*, to pull up, draw up ; cf. Low G. *togg*, a pull (Danneil). From the weak grade (*tuh-*) of Teut. **teuh-an-*, to pull ; see Tow (1), **Tuck** (1).

Tuition. (F.—L.) F. *tuition.*—L. acc. *tuitiōnem*, protection.—L. *tuit-us*, pp. of *tuērī*, to guard, protect.

Tulip, a flower. (F. — Ital. — Turk. — Pers.) M. F. *tulippe*, also *tulipan*, a tulip ; so called from its likeness to a turban. — Ital. *tulipa, tulipano*, a tulip. — Turk. *tulbend*, a turban ; also *dulbend.*—Pers. *dulband*, a turban ; see **Turban.**

Tulle, a kind of silk open-work or lace. (F.) Named from *Tulle*, the chief town in the department of Corrèze (France), where it was first made (Littré).

Tumble, vb. (E.) M. E. *tumblen* ; frequent. of *tomben, tumben*, to tumble.— A. S. *tumbian*, to turn heels over head, dance. + Du. *tuimelen* ; cf. G. *tummeln*, from O. H. G. *tūmōn*, to turn over and over (whence F. *tomber*) ; Dan. *tumle.* **Der.** *tumbler*, sb., (1) an acrobat, (2) a glass without a foot, which could only be set down when empty ; *tumb-r-el*, a cart that falls over, O. F. *tomberel*, from F. *tomber*, to tumble, fall over, a word of Teut. origin.

Tumefy, to cause to swell. (F. — L.) M. F. *tuméfier* ; Cot. — Late L. **tumeficāre*, for L. *tumefacere*, to make to swell. ▬ L. *tumē-re*, to swell; *facere*, to make.

tumid. (L.) L. *tumidus*, swollen. ▬ L. *tumēre*, to swell. Cf. Gk. τύλη, a swelling; Skt. *tu*, to increase. Brugm. i. § 413 (8). (√TEU.) Der. *tum-our*, F. *tumeur*, from L. acc. *tumōrem*, a swelling.

Tump, a hillock. (C.) W. *twmp*, a tump, is perhaps from E. But the word seems to be Celtic; from W. *tom*, Gael. and Irish *tom*, a hillock; cf. Gk. τύμβος, L. *tumulus*, a mound. See Tomb.

Tumult. (F.–L.) F. *tumulte*. ▬ L. acc. *tumultum*, an uproar.▬L. *tumēre*, to swell, surge up.

tumulus. (L.) L. *tumulus*, a mound. ▬L. *tumēre*, to swell. And see Tomb.

Tun; see Ton.

Tune, tone, melody. (F.–L.–Gk.) M. E. *tune*. ▬ A. F. *tun*, F. *ton*, 'a tune, or sound;' Cot. ▬ L. acc. *tonum*. ▬ Gk. τόνος, a tone. See Tone.

Tungsten, a heavy metal. (Swed.) Swed. *tungsten*, lit. 'heavy stone.'▬Swed. *tung*, heavy; *sten*, stone. Swed. *tung* = Icel. *þungr*, heavy; *sten* is cognate with E. *stone*.

Tunic. (F.–L.) O.F. *tunique*.▬L. *tunica*, an under-garment; whence A.S. *tunicæ*. Der. *tunic-le*, *tunic-at-ed*.

Tunnel. (F.–L.) O.F. *tonnel* (later *tonneau*), a tun, great vessel; hence a tunnel (or trap) for partridges, which was an arched tunnel of wire, strengthened by *hoops* at intervals (whence the name; it was also called *tonnelle* in F.). It came to mean any kind of tunnel or shaft, e.g. the shaft or pipe of a chimney, &c. Dimin. from Late L. *tunna*, a ton; see Ton.

Tunny, a fish. (F.–L.–Gk.) F. *thon*; Cot. ▬ L. *thunnum*, acc. of *thunnus*. ▬ Gk. θύννος, θῦνος, a tunny. Lit. 'the darter.' ▬ Gk. θύνειν, allied to θύειν, to rush along. (√DHEU.)

Tup, a ram. (Scand.) Prob. a transferred name; cf. Swed. and Norw. *tupp*, a cock, allied to Dan. *top*, a cock's crest, and to Icel. *toppr*, a top, a crest. See Top.

Turban. (F. – Ital. – Turk. – Pers.) Formerly *turbant*, *turribant*, *turband*; also *tolipant*, *tulipant*, *tulibant*. ▬ M. F. *turbant*, *turban*, a turban; Cot. ▬ Ital. *turbante*, 'a turbant;' Florio. ▬ Turk. *tulbend*, vulgar form of *dulbend*, a turban.▬ Pers. *dulband*, a turban. Cf. Tulip.

Turbary, a right of digging turf, or a

place for digging it. (F.–O. H. G.) O. F. *torberie*; Low L. *turbāria*, the same. ▬ O. H. G. *turba, older form of *zurba*, turf. +A. S. *turf*. See Turf.

Turbid. (L.) L. *turbidus*, disturbed. ▬ L. *turbāre*, to disturb. ▬ L. *turba*, a crowd, confused mass of people. See Trouble.

Turbot. (F.–L.) F. *turbot*, a fish.▬ Late L. *turbo*, a turbot; L. *turbo*, a spindle, reel; from its rhomboidal shape. So also L. *rhombus*, a spindle, rhombus, turbot.

Turbulent. (F.–L.) F. *turbulent*.▬ L. *turbulentus*, full of commotion. ▬ L. *turbāre*, to disturb; see Turbid.

Tureen, the same as Terreen, q. v.

Turf. (E.) M. E. *turf*, pl. *turues* (*turves*). A. S. *turf*.+Du. *turf*, Icel. *torf*, sod, peat; Dan. *törv*, Swed. *torf*, O. H. G. *zurba*. Cf. Skt. *darbha-*, a matted grass, from *dṛbh*, to bind.

Turgid. (L.) L. *turgidus*, swollen.▬ L. *turgēre*, to swell out.

Turkey. (F.–Tatar.) Called a *Turkey* cock, or a cock of *India*, from the notion that it came from Turkey or from India; so also G. *Calecutischer hahn*, a turkey-cock, is lit. a cock of Calicut. (It really came from the New World.) From F. *Turquie*, Turkey. ▬ F. *Turc*, a Turk. ▬ Tatar *Turk*, a Turk; orig. an adj. meaning 'brave.' ¶ The usual Turkish word for 'Turk' is '*Osmānlī*.

Turmeric. (Arabic?) New L. *turmerica* (Minsheu). Cf. F. *terre-mérite*, turmeric (Littré ; s. v. *Curcuma*); as if L. *terra merita*, apparently 'excellent earth'; but cf. *terræ meritum*, 'the produce of the earth,' in Ducange. ¶ But *terra merita*, like *turmeric*, is prob. a corruption of an Eastern word. Span. Port. *curcuma*, turmeric, are from Arab. *kurkum*, saffron; whence also L. *crocus*.

Turmoil, sb. (F.?–L.?) Formerly *turmoyl*; probably a corrupt form, the latter part of the word being assimilated to *moil*, q.v.; and the former part to *turn*. Prob. from M. F. *tremouille*, 'the hopper of a mill,' also called *trameul* (Cotgrave); O. F. *trameure*. β. So named from being in continual motion. ▬ L. *tre-mere*, to tremble, shake. Cf. O. F. *tram-oier*, to tremble.

Turn, vb. (L.–Gk.) M. E. *turnen*, *tournen*; A.S. *tyrnan*, *turnian*. [Cf. O. H. G. *turnen*, to turn.] ▬ L. *tornāre*, to turn in a lathe. ▬ L. *tornus*, a lathe.▬

Gk. τόρνος, a tool to draw circles with; allied to τορός, piercing, L. *terere*, to rub, bore. (√TER.) **Der.** *turn*, sb.

Turnip, Turnep, a plant. (F. – L.; *and* L.) The latter part of the word is in M. E. *nepe*, a turnip, A. S. *nǽp*, borrowed from L. *nāpus*, a kind of turnip; cf. Irish and Gael. *neip*, a turnip. β. The origin of the former part is unknown; the suggestion *terræ nāpus* does not agree with the spelling, which rather resembles the F. *tour* in the sense of 'wheel,' as signifying its round shape; it looks as if it had been turned. A turner's wheel was formerly called a *turn* in English, and *tour* in French. Cf. Irish *turnapa*, a turnep, *turnoir*, a turner (from E.).

Turnpike. Formerly a name given to the old-fashioned turn-stile, which revolved on the top of a post, and resembled a frame with pikes, used for defence. From Turn and Pike.

Turpentine, exudation from the terebinth. (F. – L. – Gk.) M. F. *turbentine*; Cot.; Norman dial. *turbentine*. – L. *terebinthus*. – Gk. τερέβινθος, the terebinth-tree. See Terebinth.

Turpitude. (F. – L.) F. *turpitude*. – L. *turpitūdo*, baseness. – L. *turpis*, base.

Turquoise, Turkis, a gem. (F. – Ital. – Tatar.) F. *turquoise*; orig. fem. of *Turquois*, Turkish. – M. Ital. *Turchesa*, a turquoise, or Turkish stone. – Tatar *Turk*, a Turk.

Turret. (F. – L.) M. F. *tourette*; Cot. Dimin. of O. F. *tur*, F. *tour*, a tower. – L. acc. *turrem*. See Tower.

Turtle (1), a turtle-dove. (L.) A. S. *turtle*; formed, by change also of *r* to *l*, from L. *turtur*, a turtle (whence also G. *turtel*, Ital. *tortora, tortola*). An imitative word; due to a repetition of *tur*, used to express the coo of a pigeon.

Turtle (2), the sea-tortoise. (L.) English sailors, ill understanding the Port. *tartaruga*, Span. *tortuga*, a tortoise or sea-turtle, turned these words into *turtle*; see above. The Span. and Port. words are allied to Tortoise.

Tush, an exclamation of impatience. (E.) Formerly *twish*, an expression of disgust. Cf. *pish* and *tut*; and cf. Low G. *tuss*, silence! Also Dan. *tysse*, to silence.

Tusk. (E.) South E. *tush* (as in Shak.). A. S. *tusc*, usually spelt *tux*; prob. originally **tūsc*. Cf. O. Fries. *tusch, tusk*; E.

Fries. *tūsk*; Icel. *toskr*. Perhaps related to Tooth. Brugm. i. § 795.

Tussle, to scuffle. (E.) The same as *tousle*, to disorder; frequent. of *touse*, to pull about. See Touse. Cf. Westphal. *tusseln*, to pull about, and E. *toss*.

Tut, an exclamation of impatience. (E.) Cf. M. F. *trut* (the same); and cf. *tush*.

Tutelage, guardianship. (L.; *with* F. suffix.) From L. *tūtēl-a*, protection; with F. suffix *-age* (< L. *-āticum*). – L. *tūt-us*, short for *tuitus*, pp. of *tuērī*, to guard, protect; see Tuition.

tutelar. (L.) L. *tūtēlāris*, protecting. – L. *tūt-us*, short for *tuitus* (above).

tutor. (L.) L. *tūtor*, a guardian, tutor. – L. *tūt-us* (above).

Tutty, a collyrium. (F. – Pers.) F. *tutie*; M. F. *tuthie*, 'tutie,' Cot. – Pers. *tūtiyā*, green vitriol. Cf. Skt. *tuttha-*, blue vitriol.

Twaddle, to tattle. (E.) Formerly *twattle*, a collateral form of *tattle*.

Twain; see Two.

Twang, to sound with a sharp noise. (E.) A collateral form of *tang*; see Tang (2). Cf. Tingle.

Tweak, to twitch, pinch. (E.) M. E. *twikken*; A. S. *twiccian*, pt. t. *twicc-ode*, (spelt *twiccede*, Shrine, 41); cf. A.S. *twicce*, as in A. S. *angel-twicce*, a hook-twitcher, the name of a worm used as a bait. + Low G. *twikken*, E. Fries. *twikken*, G. *zwicken*, to pinch. See Twitch.

Tweezers, nippers. (F. – Teut.; *with* E. suffix.) A surgeon's box of instruments was formerly called a *tweese*, whence small surgical instruments were called *tweezes*, a form afterwards turned into *tweezers*, and used of small nippers in particular. β. Again, the word *tweese* was really at first *twees*, the plural of *twee* or *etwee*, a surgical case; *etwee* being merely an Englished form of M. F. *estuy*, F. *étui*. – M. F. *estuy*, 'a sheath, case, a case of little instruments, now commonly termed an *ettwee*;' Cot. γ. The M. F. *estuy* is cognate with Span. *estuche*, Port. *estojo*, M. Ital. *stuccio, stucchio*, 'a little pocket-case with cisors, pen-knives, and such trifles in them' (*sic*); Florio. – M.H.G. *stūche* (prov. G. *stauche*), a short and narrow muff (hence a case). + Icel. *stūka*, a sleeve. ¶ Etymology quite clear; *estuy* became *etwee, twee*, then *twees*, then *tweeses*, and lastly *tweezers*, which might be explained as 'instruments belonging to a *tweese* or *twee*.'

Twelve. (E.) M. E. *twelf*, whence *twelf-e*, a pl. form, also written *twelue* (=*twelve*). A. S. *twelf*, *twelfe*.+O. Fries. *twilif*, Du. *twaalf*, Icel. *tōlf*, Dan. *tolv*, Swed. *tolf*, G. *zwölf*, O.H.G. *zwelif*, Goth. *twalif*. β. The Goth. *twa-lif* is composed of *twa*, two; and *-lif*, the equivalent of the Lithuan. *-lika*, occurring in *dwy-lika*, twelve. Again, the suffix *-lika* is allied to Lithuan. *lėkas*, remaining, left over, from *lik-ti*, to remain. Hence *twa-lif* = two over ten, i. e. twelve. Brugm. ii. § 175. Der. *twelf-th*, for *twelft* = A. S. *twelfta*, twelfth; *twelvemonth* = M.E. *twelfmonthe*.

twenty. (E.) A. S. *twentig*. ─ A. S. *twen* = *twēn*, short for *twegen*, twain; and *-tig*, suffix allied to Goth. *-tigjus* and E. *ten*. +Goth. *twaitigjus*, Du. *twintig*, Icel. *tut-tugu*, G. *zwanzig*; all similarly formed.

twibill, twybill, a two-edged bill. (E.) M. E. *twibil*. A. S. *twibill*. ─ A. S. *twi-*, double; *bill*, a bill; see **twice** (below).

twice. (E.) M.E. *twiës* (dissyllabic). A. S. *twiges*, a late form, for the older *twiwa*, twice. ─ A. S. *twi-*, double; like L. *bi-*, Gk. δι-, Skt. *dvi-*; allied to *twā*, two. See **Two.**

twig (1), a shoot of a tree. (E.) A. S. *twig* (pl. *twigu*), a twig; Northumb. *tuigge* (pl. *tuiggo*), Jo. xv. 5, 6; orig. the fork of a branch, and named from being double, the small shoot branching off from the larger one. ─ A. S. *twi-*, double; see above.+Du. *twijg*, Low G. *twig* (Danneil), Westphal. *twich*, *twick*, G. *zweig*. Cognate with Skt. *dvi-ka-*, ' consisting of two,' Gk. δισσός, double, twofold. Brugm. ii. § 166.

Twig (2), to comprehend. (C.) Irish *tuig-im*, O. Irish *tucc-im*, I understand; Gael. *tuig*, to understand.

Twilight. (E.) M. E. *twilight*. The prefix *twi-* (A.S. *twi-*) is lit. 'double' (see **twice** above); but is here used rather in the sense of doubtful or between; cf. L. *dubius*, doubtful, from *duo*, two. + G. *zwielicht*, M. Du. *tweelicht*; similarly compounded.

twill, to weave, shewing ribs. (Low G.) The word has reference to a peculiar method of doubling the warp-threads, or taking two of them together; this gives an appearance of diagonal lines, in textile fabrics. From Low G. *twillen*. [One Low G. *twillen*, to bifurcate, is allied to O. H. G. *zwinel*, twin, and to E. **Twin.**]

But *twillen* is here a Low G. spelling of M. H. G. *zwilhen*, to double; from M. H. G. *zwilch*, O. H. G. *zwilīh*, adj., two-threaded, a word suggested by L. *bilix*, two-threaded (from L. *bi-*, double, *līcium*, thread). Cf. G. *zwillich*, ticking.

twin. (E.) A. S. *ge-twinnas*, twins.+ Icel. *tvinnr*, in pairs; Lithuan. *dwyni*, twins; cf. L. *bīnī*, two at a time. From the A. S. *twi-*, double; the *-n* gives a distributive force, as in L. *bī-n-i*, two at a time. Cf. Goth. *tweihnai*, two apiece; Bavar. *zwin-ling*, G. *zwil-ling*, a twin.

twine, vb. (E.) M. E. *twinen*, to twist together. From A. S. *twin*, sb., a twisted or doubled thread.+Du. *twijn*, sb., a twist, twine, Icel. *tvinni*, twine; Swed. *tvinntråd*, twine-thread; also Du. *tweern*, G. *zwirn*. β. All from Teut. type *twis-no->*twiz-no-*, double; the *iz* becomes *ī* in A. S. *twīn*, Du. *twijn*; the *zn* becomes *nn* in Icel. and Swed.; and the *z* becomes *r* in Du. and G. The base *twis-* occurs in E. *twis-t*, Goth. *twis-*, prefix; cf. L. *bis* (for **dwis*), Gk. δίς, Skt. *dvis*, twice. Brugm. i. § 903 (c, note 2).

Twinge, to nip. (E.) M. E. *twengen*, weak vb. (*g=j*). Causal of *twingen*, str. vb., O. Fries. *twinga*, *thwinga* (pt. t. *twang*), to constrain, O. Sax. *bi-thwingan*, Icel. *þvinga*, Du. *dwingen*, G. *zwingen*, O.H.G. *dwingan*; Teut. type **thwengan-*, pt. t. *thwang*. Cf. also Lith. *twenkti*, to be hot, to smart; *twankas*, sultry. (√TWENK.) Der. *thong*.

Twinkle. (E.) A. S. *twinclian*, to twinkle; a frequentative form of *twink*, appearing in M. E. *twinken*, to blink, wink. Again, this is a nasalised form of M. E. *twikken*, to twitch (hence to quiver); see **Tweak.**+Bavarian *zwinkern*, frequent. of *zwinken*, to blink.

twinkling. (E.) M.E. *twinkeling*, the twitching of an eye.─M.E. *twinkelen*, to wink; the same word as E. *twinkle.*

Twinter, a beast two years old. (E.) A.S. *twi-wintre*, adj., of two years. ─ A.S. *twi-*, double (see **twice**), and *winter*, a winter, a year.

Twire, to peep out. (E.) In Shak. Son. 28. Only recorded in the cognate Bavarian *zwiren*, *zwieren*, to peep (Schmeller), M. H. G. *zwieren*, to peep out (Schade). ¶ Nares is wrong in citing *twire* = *twitter* from Chaucer; the true reading is *twitreth*.

Twirl, to turn rapidly round. (E.) It stands for *thwirl* (like *twinge* for *thwinge*).

Frequentative of A. S. *-þweran*, to turn, whence *þwiril*, the handle of a churn. Cognate with G. *querlen, quirlen,* to twirl, *querl,* a twirling-stick ; from O. H. G. *tweran, dweran,* to whirl round. β. The frequent.form appears also in Du.*dwarlen,* to twirl, *dwarlwind,* a whirlwind ; cf. Low G. *dweerwind,* a whirlwind. We also find Icel. *þvara,* a stirring-stick ; from *thwar,* 2nd grade of Teut. **thweran-,* as seen in A. S. *-þweran.* Also E. Fries. *dwīreln, dwirlen,* to twirl, *dwarrel,* a whirl, from *dweren,* to turn ; cf. Gk. τορύνη, a stirrer. (√TWER.)

Twist, vb. (E.) M. E. *twisten,* vb. formed from A. S. *twist,* sb., a rope or twisted cord. — A. S. **twis-,* double (see **Twine**) ; with suffix *-t* (Idg. suffix *-to-*). The Du. *twist,* Dan. Swed. *tvist,* G. *zwist,* mean ' discord,' which is another sense of the same word ; so also M. E. *twist,* a twig or fork of a branch ; Icel. *tvistr,* the deuce, in card-playing.

Twit, to remind of a fault. (E.) Shortened from M.E. *atwiten,* to reproach. — A. S. *ætwītan,* to twit, reproach. — A. S. *æt,* at, upon ; *witan,* to blame, orig. to observe, hence to observe what is amiss. β. This A. S. *wītan* answers to Goth. *-weitan* in comp. *fra-weitan,* to avenge ; cf. *weitjan,* to observe ; allied to Goth. *witan,* to know ; see **Wit** (1). Cf. Du. *wijten,* to reproach, G. *ver-weisen,* from Teut. base **weit.* (√WEID.)

Twitch, to pluck. (E.) M.E. *twicchen,* palatalised form of M. E. *twikken,* A.S. *twiccian,* to tweak. See **Tweak.** For the form, cf. A. S. *angel-twicce,* prov. E. *angletwitch,* an earthworm (N. E. D.).

Twitter, vb. (E.) Frequentative from a base *twit* ; cf. *titter, tattle,* and *twaddle* ; all of imitative origin.+G. *zwitschern,* to twitter, Bavar. *zwitzern* ; Du. *kwetteren,* Dan. *qviddre,* Swed. *qvittra.*

Two, Twain. (E.) The A. S. forms shew that the difference between *two* and *twain* was orig. one of gender only. A.S. *twegen,* masc., two (M. E. *tweien, twein,* E. *twain*) ; *twā,* fem., two ; neut. *twā* or *tū,* two. + Du. *twee,* Icel. *tveir,* Dan. *to,* Swed. *två, tu,* Goth. *twai,* G. *zwei* (also *zween,* masc.) ; Irish *da,* Gael. *da, do,* W. *dau,* Russ. *dva,* Lith. *dwi,* L. *duo* (whence F. *deux,* E. *deuce*), Gk. δύο, Skt. *dvāu, dvā.* Cf. also L. *bi-, bis,* twice ; and the prefixes *di-, dia-, dis-.* **Der.** *a-two,* i. e. *on two* = in two.

Tybalt, the ' prince of cats.' (Low G.) In Shak. A. F. *Tebald, Tebaud.* — O. Sax. *Thiod-bald,* Theobald. Cf. *Tybert,* the cat ; in ' Reynard the Fox.'

Tympanum, the hollow part of the ear, &c. (L. — Gk.) L. *tympanum,* a drum, tympanum. — Gk. τύμπανον, a drum, roller ; the same as τύπανον, a drum. — Gk. τυπ-, base of τύπτειν, to strike. **Der.** *tympany,* Gk. τυμπανίας, a dropsy in which the belly is tightly stretched, as a drum.

type. (F. — L. — Gk.) F. *type* (Sherwood). — L. *typum,* acc. of *typus.* — Gk. τύπος, a blow, mark of a blow, stamp, impress, mark, mould, type, &c. — Gk. τυπ-, base of τύπτειν, to strike. Cf. Skt. *tup, tump,* to hurt ; allied to Gk. στυφελίζειν, to strike. (√STEU.) **Der.** *typ-ic,* Gk. τυπικός ; whence *typic-al,* &c.

Typhoon, a violent whirlwind. (Arab. — Gk.) [Sometimes claimed as a Chinese word meaning ' a great wind.' — Chinese *ta,* great ; *fāng* (in Canton *fung*), wind, whence *ta fung,* a gale, a typhoon (Williams).] But this seems to be a late mystification. In old authors the forms are *tuffon, tuffoon, tiphon,* &c. — Arab. *ṭūfān,* a hurricane, storm. — Gk. τυφῶν, better τυφώς, a whirlwind. The close accidental coincidence of these words in sense and form is very remarkable, as Whitney notes. See below.

Typhus, a kind of fever. (L. — Gk.) L. *typhus.* — Gk. τῦφος, smoke, mist ; also stupor, esp. if arising from fever ; *typhus fever* = stupor-fever. — Gk. τύφειν, to smoke. (√DHEU.) **Der.** *typho-id,* i. e. typhus-like, from εἶδος, resemblance.

Tyrant. (F. — L. — Gk.) The final *t* is added. O. F. *tiran,* also *tyrant.* — L. *tyrannum,* acc. of *tyrannus,* a tyrant. — Gk. τύραννος, a lord, sovereign, master ; orig. in a good sense (see Prellwitz). **Der.** *tyrann-y,* F. *tyrannie,* Late L. *tyrannia,* Gk. τυραννία, sovereignty.

Tyro, misspelling of **Tiro,** q. v.

U.

Ubiquity, omnipresence. (F. — L.) F. *ubiquité,* ' an ubiquity ; ' Cot. As if from L. acc. **ubiquitātem,* a being everywhere ; a coined word. — L. *ubīque,* everywhere. — L. *ubī,* where ; with suffix *-que,* allied to L. *quis,* who. **Der.** *ubiquit-ous.*

Udder. (E.) A. S. *ūder,* an udder. + M. Du. *uder,* Du. *uijer,* Icel. *jūgr* (for *jūdr), Swed. jufver, jur, Dan. yver; G. euter, O. H. G. ūter; also L. über, Gk. οὖθαρ, Skt. ūdhar, ūdhan, an udder. Brugm. i. § 113.

Ugly, frightful. (Scand.) M. E. ugly, uglike. – Icel. uggligr, fearful, dreadful. – Icel. ugg-r, fear; -ligr = A. S. -līc, like. Allied to Icel. ugga, to fear. Der. ugliness.

Uhlan, Ulan, a lancer. (G. – Polish. – Turkish.) G. uhlan, a lancer. – Pol. ulan, a lancer. Borrowed from Turk. oglān, also ōlan, a youth, lad. Of Tatar origin.

Ukase, an edict. (F. – Russ.) F. ukase. – Russ. ukaz', an edict; cf. ukazate, to indicate, shew, order, prescribe. – Russ. u-, prefix, allied to Skt. ava, away, off; kazate, to shew, Ch. Slav. kazati. Brugm. i. §§ 163 (note), 616.

Ulcer, a dangerous sore. (F. – L.) F. ulcère. – L. ulcer-, for *ulces-, stem of ulcus, a sore. + Gk. ἕλκος, a wound, sore; Skt. arças, hemorrhoids.

Ullage, the unfilled part of a cask. (Prov. – L.) 'Ullage of a cask, that which it wants of being full;' Phillips. – Mod. Prov. ulhage; O. F. ouillage, eullage, a filling up. – Mod. Prov. ulha; O. F. ouillier, eullier, to fill a cask up to the bung. Cotgrave spells it oeiller, and the sb. as oeillage. The Late L. type of the vb. is *oculāre, i. e. to fill up to the oculus, eye, orifice. We also find O. F. aouillier, as if for *adoculāre.

Ulterior, further. (L.) L. ulterior, further; comp. of O. L. ulter, adj.

ultimate, furthest. (L.) L. ultimātus, pp. of ultimāre, to be at the last. – L. ultimus, last; ul-ti-mus being a double superl. form from the base ul-; see ultra-.

ultra-, beyond. (L.) L. ultrā, beyond, adv. and prep. Allied to O. Lat. ul-s, beyond, ollus, that one.

ultramarine, beyond sea; as sb. sky-blue. (Span. – L.) Span. ultramarino, beyond sea; also a blue colour. – L. ultrā, beyond; mar-e, sea; and suffix -īnus; see Marine.

ultramontane, beyond the Alps. (F. – Ital. – L.) F. ultramontain. – Ital. oltramontano. – L. ultrā, beyond; mont-em, acc., a mountain; with suffix -ānus; see Tramontane and Mountain.

ultramundane, beyond the world. (L.) L. ultrā, beyond; mundānus, worldly, from mundus, world; see Mundane.

Umbel, an umbrella-like inflorescence. (L.) L. umbella, a parasol; dimin. of umbra, a shade; see Umbrage.

umber. (F. – Ital. – Lat.) F. ombre, short for terre d'ombre, lit. 'earth of shadow,' a brown earth used for shadowing in paintings. – Ital. terra d'ombra, lit. earth of shadow (Torriano). – L. terra, earth; dē, of; umbra, shadow.

Umbilical, pertaining to the navel. (F. – L.) M. F. umbilical, adj., from umbilic, navel (Cot.). – L. umbilīcum, acc. of umbilīcus, navel, middle, centre. + Gk. ὀμφαλός, navel; cf. Skt. nābhi-, navel; see Nave (1). Brugm. i. § 467.

Umbrage, shade of trees; offence. (F. – L.) Properly 'shadow'; hence, shadow or suspicion of injury. – M. F. ombrage, umbrage, shade, also suspicion. – F. ombre, shadow (with suffix -age < L. -āticum). – L. umbra, shadow.

umbrella. (Ital. – L.) Ital. umbrella, ombrella, a parasol; dimin. of Ital. ombra, a shade. – L. umbra, a shade.

Umpire. (F. – L.) For numpire, 'the old form of the word; M. E. nompere, noumpere, also nounpere, nounpier, P. Plowman, B. v. 337. – O. F. nomper, later nompair, peerless, odd (Cot.); earliest form nonper (Roquefort). – L. non, not; parem, acc. of pār, equal. Used, like L. impar, in the sense of arbitrator; the lit. sense is unequal, odd, hence a third man called in to arbitrate, a 'non-peer.' See Non- and Peer.

Un- (1), neg. prefix. (E.) Prefixed to sbs., adjs., and advs. (Distinct from un- (2) below.) A. S. un-, neg. prefix. + Du. on-, Icel. ō-, ū-, Dan. u-, Swed. o-, Goth. un-, G. un-, W. an-, L. in-, Gk. ἀν-, ἀ-, Zend. an-, a-, Skt. an-, a-. Readily prefixed to a large number of words; a few of these, such as un-couth, of which the simple form is not used, will be found below.

Un- (2), verbal prefix, expressing the reversal of an action. (E.) Quite distinct from un- (1) above; only used with verbs. Thus to un-lock = to reverse locking, to open that which was closed by locking. A. S. un-. + Du. ont-, G. ent-, O. H. G. ant-, Goth. and- (as in and-bindan, to unbind). Precisely the same as E. an- in an-swer, A.S. and-, Gk. ἀντι-; see Anti-. ¶ In the case of past participles, the prefix is ambiguous; thus un-bound may either mean 'not bound,' with prefix un- (1), or may mean 'undone' or released, with prefix *un-* (2).

Un- (3), prefix. (E.) Only in *un-to*, *un-til*, which see.

Unaneled, without having received extreme unction. (E.; *and* L.—Gk.) In Hamlet, i. 5. 77. Lit. 'un-on-oiled.'—A.S. *un-*, not; M. E. *an-eled*, from *an* (for A.S. *on*) and *eled*, pp. of M. E. *elien*, to oil, vb., from *ele*, sb., oil. The A.S. *ele*, oil, is borrowed from L. *oleum*, Gk. ἔλαιον, oil; see **Oil**.

Unanimous, of one mind. (L.) L. *ūnanim-us*, of one mind; with suffix *-ous*. — L. *ūn-us*, one (see **One**); *animus*, mind.

Uncial, large, applied to letters. (L.) L. *unciālis*, adj. from *uncia*, inch; see **Inch**. (From the large size of the letters.)

Uncle. (F.—L.) M. E. *uncle*.—A. F. *uncle*; F. *oncle*.—L. *auunculum*, acc. of *auunculus*, a mother's brother, lit. 'little grandfather;' dimin. of *auus*, a grandfather.

Uncouth. (E.) A.S. *uncūð*, orig. unknown; hence, strange, odd.—A. S. *un-*, not; and *cūð*, known, pp. of *cunnan*, to know. See **Can**.

Unction. (F.—L.) F. *onction*.—L. *unctiōnem*, acc. of *unctio*, an anointing.—L. *unct-us*, pp. of *ungere*, to anoint. **Der.** *unctu-ous*, Late L. *unctu-ōsus*. Brugm. i. § 398. See **Unguent**.

Under, beneath. (E.) A.S. *under*.+ Du. *onder*, Icel. *undir*, Dan. Swed. *under*, Goth. *undar*, G. *unter*, under. Common as a prefix. Brugm. i. § 446, ii. § 75.

Undern, a certain period of the day. (E.) The time denoted differed at different periods. The A. S. *undern* meant the third hour, about 9 a. m.; later, it meant about noon; and, still later, the afternoon, in which sense it survives in prov. E. *aunder*, *aandorn*, *orndorns*, *doundrins*, &c.+Icel. *undorn*, O.H.G. *untorn*, Goth. *undaurni-*; the lit. sense being 'intervening or middle period.' Perhaps from A.S. *under*, with the sense 'among' or 'between,' like G. *unter*. Cf. L. *internus*, inward; from L. *inter*. ¶ Kluge explains it as equivalent to A. S. *un-dyrne*, 'not dark,' hence 'dawn.' (But *dyrne* usually means 'not manifest.') See Eng. Stud. xx. 334.

Understand. (E.) A.S. *understandan*, lit. to stand under or among, hence, to comprehend (like L. *intel-ligere*).—A.S. *under*, under; *standan*, to stand.

Undertake, to take upon oneself, attempt. (E. *and* Scand.) M. E. *undertaken*, compounded of *under* and M. E. *taken*, to take. **Der.** *undertak-er*, lit. one who takes a business in hand; Oth. iv. 1. 224.

Undulate, to wave. (L.) From pp. of L. *undulāre*, to fluctuate.—L. **undula*, dimin. of *unda*, a wave. Allied to **Water**; cf. Skt. *udan*, water, *und*, to wet, Lith. *wandŭ*, water, Russ. *voda*, water. Brugm. i. §§ 102, 594.

Uneath, scarcely, with difficulty. (E.) Obsolete. M. E. *uneþe*. A.S. *unēaðe*, adv., from adj. *unēaðe*, difficult.—A.S. *un-*, not; *ēaðe*, *ēað*, easy; the orig. sense being waste, empty, hence easy to occupy. Cf. O. Sax. *ōði*, easy; G. *öde*, waste, deserted, Icel. *auðr*, empty, Goth. *auths*, *authis*, desert, waste. ¶ But some dissociate A. S. *ēaðe*, O. Sax. *ōði*, from the rest.

Ungainly, awkward. (Scand.; *with* E. *prefix and suffix*.) Formed by adding *-ly* to M. E. *ungein*, inconvenient.—A. S. *un-*, not; Icel. *gegn*, ready, serviceable, convenient, allied to *gegna*, to meet, suit, *gegn*, against, and to E. **Again**. Cf. Icel. *ō-gegn*, ungainly.

Unguent, ointment. (L.) L. *unguentum*, ointment. — L. *unguent-*, stem of pres. pt. of *ungere*, to anoint. + Skt. *añj*, to smear. Brugm. i. § 398.

Unicorn. (F.—L.) M. F. *unicorne*, a fabulous one-horned animal. — L. *ūnicornem*, acc. of *unicornis*, one-horned. — L. *ūni-*, for *ūnus*, one (see **One**); *corn-ū*, a horn. See **Horn**.

uniform, adj. (F.—L.) F. *uniforme*. —L. *ūniformem*, acc. of *ūniformis*, having one form.—L. *ūni-*, for *ūnus*, one; *form-a*, form; see **Form**.

union (1), concord. (F.—L.) F. *union*. —L. acc. *ūniōnem*, oneness.—L. *ūni-*, for *ūnus*, one.

union (2), a large pearl. (F.—L.) The same word as the above; the L. *ūnio* means oneness, also a single pearl of a large size, also a kind of onion.

unique. (F.—L.) F. *unique*, single. — L. *ūnicum*, acc. of *ūnicus*, single. — L. *ūni-*, for *ūnus*, one.

unison, concord. (F.—L.) F. *unisson*. —L. *ūnisonum*, acc. of *ūnisonus*, having a like sound.—L. *ūni-*, for *ūnus*, one; *sonus*, sound; see **Sound** (3).

unit. (F.—L.) Formed by dropping the final *-y* of *unity*. '*Unit, Unite*, or

Unity, in arithmetic, the first significant figure, or number 1,' &c., Phillips; see **Unity**.

unite. (L.) L. *ūnītus*, pp. of *ūnīre*, to unite.—L. *ūnus*, one.

unity, oneness. (F.—L.) M. E. *unitee*. —M. F. *unite* (*unité*).—L. *ūnitātem*, acc. of *ūnitās*, unity.—L. *ūni-*, for *ūnus*, one, cognate with **One**.

universal. (F.—L.) F. *universel* (Latinised).—L. *ūniuersālis*, belonging to the whole.—L. *ūniuersus*, turned into one, combined into a whole.—L. *ūni-*, for *ūnus*, one; *uersus*, pp. of *uertere*, to turn; see **Verse**. Der. *univers-ity*, F. *université*, from L. acc. *ūniuersitātem*.

univocal, having but one meaning. (L.) From L. *ūniuoc-us*, univocal; with suffix *-ālis*.—L. *ūni-*, for *ūnus*, one; *uoc-*, allied to *uox*, voice, sense; see **Voice**.

Unkempt, i. e. uncombed; for *un-kemb'd*. From A. S. *cemban*, to comb; formed (by vowel-change of *a* to *e*) from *camb*, a comb. See **Comb**.

Unless, if not, except. (E.) Formerly *on les*, *on lesse*, in the phrase *on lesse that*, i. e. in less than, on a less supposition than. Thus *un-* here stands for *on*. See **On** and **Less**.

Unruly, disregarding restraint. (E.; and F.—L.) From *un-*, prefix, and *rule*; with suffix *-y*; a coined word. See **Rule**. Fabyan has *unruled*.

Until. (E.) The same word as below, with the substitution of North E. (and Scand.) *til*, to, for E. *to*. See **Till**.

unto, even to. (E.) M. E. *unto* (not in A. S.). For *und-to*; where *to* is the usual E. prep., and *und* is the O. Fries. *und*, *ont*, Goth. *und*, O. Sax. *und*, unto, whence O. Sax. *un-tō*, unto. A related form *oð* (<* *anth*) is common in A. S.; cf. also A. S. *and-*, prefix, for which see **Un-** (2).

Up. (E.) M. E. *vp*, *up*; A. S. *ūp*, *upp*, adv. + Du. *op*, Icel. *upp*, Dan. *op*, Swed. *upp*, Goth. *iup*, G. *auf*, O. H. G. *ūf*. Allied to **Over**; cf. *ab-ove*.

Upas, the poison-tree of Java. (Malay.) Malay *ūpas*, a poisonous juice; *pūhun ūpas*, poison-tree (*pūhun*=tree).

Upbraid, to reproach. (E.) M. E. *vp-breiden*, to reproach.—A. S. *up*, up, upon, on; *bregdan*, to braid, weave, also to lay hold of, seize. The orig. sense seems to have been to lay hold of, hence to attack, accuse, &c. The A. S. *bregdan*, also = E. *braid*, to weave; so that *-braid* in *up-braid* is the usual verb *braid*, used in a special sense. So also Dan. *be-breide* (lit. be-braid), to upbraid.

Upholsterer. (E.) Lengthened from *upholster*, for *uphold-ster*, another form of *upholder*, which was formerly used of a dealer in furniture; lit. one who *holds up* for sale.

Upon. (E.) A. S. *uppon*, upon.—A. S. *upp*, *up*, up; *on*, on, on. + Icel. *upp ā*, upon; Swed. *på*, Dan. *paa* (reduced forms).

Uproar, tumult. (Du.) The spelling shews confusion with E. *roar*.—Du. *oproer*, 'uprore, tumult;' Hexham.—Du. *op*, up; *roeren*, to excite, stir, move; so that *oproer* = a stirring up, commotion.+Low G. *upp-rōr* (Danneil); Swed. *uppror*, Dan. *uprör*, G. *aufruhr*. β. The verb is Du. *roeren*, Swed. *röra*, Dan. *röre*, G. *rühren*, A. S. *hrēran*, to stir; see **Reremouse**. The A. S. *hrēran* is from *hrōr*, adj., active, busy.

Upsidedown. (E.) From *up*, side, and *down*. But the M. E. form was *up-so-doun*, i. e. 'up as it were down.'

Upstart, sb. (E.) From *upstart*, vb., to start up; Spenser, F. Q. i. 1. 16; Chaucer, C. T., A. 1080. See **Start**.

Upwards; see **Up** and *-ward*, suffix.

Urbane, courteous. (L.) L. *urbānus*, belonging to a city. — L. *urb-s*, a city. Der. *urban*, doublet of *urbane*; *urban-i-ty*, F. *urbanité*, from L. acc. *urbānitātem*, courteousness.

Urchin, a hedgehog, goblin, imp, small child. (F.—L.) Orig. hedgehog; hence, goblin, imp, small child (Tempest, i. 2. 326); it being supposed that some imps took a hedgehog's shape. — Walloon *urechon*, *irchon* (Sigart); Norm. dial. *hérichon*; O. North. F. *herichon*; O.F. *ireçon*, *eriçon*, *herisson*, a hedgehog; formed with suffix *-on* (= L. *-ōnem*) from L. *ēricius*, a hedgehog, lengthened form of *ēr* (gen. *ēri-s*), a hedgehog.+Gk. χήρ, hedgehog; cf. χαράσσειν, to scratch.

Ure, practise, use. (F.—L.) Obsolete, except in *in-ure*, *man-ure*. (Distinct from *use*.)—O. F. *eure*, *uevre*, *ovre*, work, action. —L. *opera*, work; see **Operate**.

Urge. (L.) L. *urgēre*, to urge, drive. Allied to **Wreak**. (√WERG.) Der. *urg-ent*, from stem of pres. part.

Urim. (Heb.) Heb. *ūrīm*, lights; pl. of *ūr*, light. See **Thummim**.

Urine. (F.—L.) F. *urine*.—L. *ūrīna*. +Gk. οὖρον, urine; Skt. *vāri*, *vār*, water;

Icel. *úr*, drizzling rain; Icel. *ver*, A. S. *wær*, sea. Orig. 'water.'

Urn. (F.–L.) M. E. *urne*.–F. *urne*. –L. *urna*, urn. For **urc-na*; cf. *urc-eus*, a pitcher. Brugm. i. § 756.

Us. (E.) A. S. *ūs*, dat. pl. of *wē*, we; *ūs*, *ūsic*, acc. pl. of *wē*.+Du. *ons*, Icel. *oss*, Swed. *oss*, Dan. *os*, G. *uns*; Goth. *uns*, *unsis*, dat. and acc. pl. Teut. base **uns-*. Cf. L. *nōs*, Skt. *nas*; also Gk. ἡμᾶς, Skt. *asmān*, us. Brugm. i. § 437 (2); ii. § 436.

Use (1), sb. (F.–L.) M.E. *use, v* – O.F. *us*, use, usage. –L. *ūsum*, acc. of *ūsus*, use.–L. *ūsus*, pp. of *ūtī*, to use. Der. *use*, vb., F. *user*, Late L. *ūsāre*, frequent. of L. *ūtī*, to use; *us-age*, F. *usage*; *usu-al*, L. *ūsuālis*, adj., from *ūsu-*, stem of *ūsus*, use; &c.

Use (2), profit, benefit. (F.–L.) When *use* is employed, legally, in the sense of ' benefit,' it is a modernised spelling of the Anglo-F. form of the Lat. *opus*, employment, need. We find the Anglo-F. spellings *oes, oeps, uoes*; O. F. *oes, eus, ues*.

Usher, a door-keeper. (F.–L.) M. E. *uschere, ussher*.–A. F. *usser*; O. F. *ussier, uissier*, later *huissier*, ' an usher, or doorkeeper;' Cot.–L. *ostiārium*, acc. of *ostiārius*, a door-keeper.–L. *ostium*, a door. Extended from L. *ōs*, mouth; see **Oral**.

Usquebaugh. (Irish.) Irish *uisge beatha*, usquebaugh, whisky.–Irish *uisge*, water (see **Whisky**); *beatha*, life, O. Ir. *bethu*, allied to Gk. βίος, life. Brugm. i. §§ 85, 368.

Usurp, to seize to one's own use. (F.– L.) F. *usurper*.–L. *ūsurpāre*, to employ, acquire; also, to usurp. β. Clearly derived from *ūs-us*, use, but the rest of the word is obscure; Brugmann (ii. § 4) suggests *ūsu-* and *rapere*, to seize to one's own use.

usury. (F.–L.) M. E. *usurye, usure*. –F. *usure*, usury, the occupation of a thing.–L. *ūsūra*, use, enjoyment, interest, usury.–L. *ūs-us*, pp. of *ūtī*, to use.

Ut, the first note of the musical scale. (L.) L. *ut*. See **Gamut**.

Utas, the octave of a feast. (F.–L.) *Utas* is for *utaves*, an A. F. word corresponding to O. F. *oitauves*, pl. of *oitauve*, octave, eighth day.–L. *octāua* (*diēs*), eighth day; fem. of *octāuus*, eighth.–L. *octō*, eight. See **Octave**.

Utensil. (F.–L.) M. F. *utensile*, sb. –L. *ūtensīlis*, adj., fit for use; whence *ūtensīlia*, neut. pl., utensils. For **ūtent-*

tīlis, from the stem of pres. pt. of *ūtī*, to use. Cf. **Use** (1).

Uterine, born of the same mother by a different father. (F.–L.) M. F. *uterin*, ' of the womb, borne of one mother;' Cot.–L. *uterīnus*, born of one mother.–L. *uterus*, womb. Cf. Gk. ὑστέρα, womb. Brugm. i. § 706.

Utilise. (F.–L.) F. *utiliser*, a modern word; coined from *util-e*, useful, with suffix *-iser* (Gk. -ιζειν).–L. *ūtilis*, useful.–L. *ūtī*, to use. Cf. **Use** (1).

utility. (F.–L.) F. *utilité*.–L. acc. *ūtilitātem*, from nom. *ūtilitās*, usefulness. –L. *ūtili-s*, useful.–L. *ūtī*, to use.

Utis, festival merriment; see **Utas**.

Utmost. (E.) M. E. *outemest*. A. S. *ūte-m-est*, double superl. form, from *ūt*, out. Doublet of *outmost*. See **Out**.

Utopian. (Gk.) An adj. due to Sir T. More's description of *Utopia*, an imaginary island, situate *nowhere*. – Gk. οὐ, not; τόπος, a place; see **Topic**.

Utter, outer. (E.) M. E. *utter*. A. S. *uttera*, which occurs as well as *ūtera*; both are comparative forms of *ūt*, out; see **Out**. Der. *utter*, vb.; cf. G. *äussern*, vb., from *äusser*, outer; also A. S. *ūt-ian*, to put out, from *ūt*, out.

utterance (1), an uttering. (E.; *with* F. *suffix*.) From the verb *to utter*, M. E. *outren*; formed from M. E. *outer*, *utter*, compar. of A. S. *ūt*, out. See **Out**.

Utterance (2), extremity. In Shak. (F.–L.) F. *outrance*, extremity. – F. *outre*, beyond.–L. *ultrā*, beyond; see **Ultra-**.

Uvula. (L.) Late L. *ūvula*, dimin. of L. *ūua*, a grape, a cluster, also the uvula. +Lith. *ūga*, a berry. Brugm. i. § 223 (2).

Uxorious, excessively fond of a wife. (L.) L. *uxōri-us*, fond of a wife; with suffix *-ous*.–L. *uxōr-*, stem of *uxor*, a wife.

V.

V. In Middle-English, *v* is commonly written as *u* in the MSS.; conversely, *v* is put for *u* in a few words, chiefly *vp, vnder, vnto, vs, vse*, and the prefix *vn-*.

Vacation. (F.–L.) F. *vacation*.–L. acc. *uacātiōnem*, leisure.–L. *uacātus*, pp. of *uacāre*, to be empty or at leisure. Cf. L. *uacuus*, W. *gwag*, empty.

Vaccinate. (L.) Coined as if from pp. of **vaccināre*, to inoculate.–L. *uaccīnus*, belonging to cows.–L. *uacca*, a cow. **+** Skt. *vaçā*, a cow. ¶ First used about 1798.

Vacillation. (F. – L.) F. *vacillation*, 'a reeling, staggering;' Cot. – L. *uacillā-tiōnem*, acc. of *uacillātio*, a reeling, wavering. – L. *uacillātus*, pp. of *uacillāre*, to reel. Cf. Skt. *vank*, to go tortuously, *vakra-*, bent.

Vacuum. (L.) L. *uacuum*, an empty space; neut. of *uacuus*, empty. – L. *uacāre*, to be empty; see **Vacation**.

Vade, to fade. (Du. – F. – L.) M. Du. *vadden*, 'to fade.' Hexham. – O. F. *fader*, to fade; see **Fade**.

Vagabond. (F. – L.) F. *vagabond*, 'a vagabond;' Cot. – L. *uagābundus*, adj., strolling about. – L. *uagā-rī*, to wander; with suffix *-bundus*.

vagary. (L.) Also *vagare* (trisyllabic; Stanyhurst); orig. used as a verb; [cf. F. *vaguer*, 'to wander, vagary;' Cot.] – L. *uagārī*, to wander; see **Vague**.

Vagrant. (F. – G.) A. F. *wakerant*, a vagrant; O. F. *walcrant*, wandering, pres. pt. of *walcrer*, to wander. – M. G. *welkern*, M. H. G. *walgern*, to walk about; allied to E. **Walk**. ¶ Confused with L. *uagārī*, to wander, but *not* derived from it. See Phil. Soc. Trans., 1885, 1888, 1889.

Vague, unsettled. (F. – L.) F. *vague*, wandering; *vaguer*, to wander. – L. *uagus*, wandering; whence *uagārī*, to wander.

Vail (1), the same as **Veil**.

Vail (2), to lower. (F. – L.) From O. F. *avaler*, to let fall down. – F. *aval*, downward. – L. *ad uallem*, to the valley.

Vail (3), a gift to a servant. (F. – L.) A headless form of *avail*, sb., in the sense of profit, help (Palsgrave). From **Avail**, vb.

Vain. (F. – L.) F. *vain*. – L. *uānum*, acc. of *uānus*, empty, vain. Brugm. i. § 414 (3).

Vair, a kind of fur. (F. – L.) F. *vair*, 'a rich fur;' Cot. – L. *uarius*, variegated. Der. *vair-y* (in heraldry), from M. F. *vairé*, 'diversified with argent and azure;' Cot. Hence *meni-ver* (= F. *menu vair*), 'little vair.'

Valance, a fringe of drapery, now applied to a part of the bed-hangings. (F. – L.) Chaucer has 'a litel kerchief of *valence*'; Assembly of Foules, 272. Prob. named from *Valence* in France, near Lyons (still famous for silks). – L. *Valentia*, a name given to several towns, evidently from the name *Valens*, lit. 'strong.' – L. *ualent-*, stem of pres. pt. of *ualēre*, to be

strong; see **Valid**. ¶ Johnson derives it from *Valentia* in Spain, which is also famous for silks.

Vale, a valley. (F. – L.) M. E. *val*. – F. *val*. – L. *uallem*, acc. of *uallis*, valley.

Valediction, a farewell. (L.) Formed from L. *ualēdictus*, pp. of *ualēdīcere*, to say farewell. – L. *ualē*, farewell; *dīcere*, to say. β. L. *ualē*, lit. 'be strong.' is the 2 p. s. imp. of *ualēre*, to be strong.

Valentine. (F. – L.) Named from *St. Valentine's* day, Feb. 14. – F. *Valentin*. – L. *Valentīnus*. – L. *ualent-*, stem of pres. pt. of *ualēre*, to be strong.

valerian. (F. – L.) M. F. *valeriane*, valerian; a flower. – Late L. *ualeriāna*, valerian. Fem. of *Valeriānus*, prob. a personal name; from L. *ualēre*, to be strong.

Valet. (F. – C.) F. *valet*, 'a groom;' Cot. The same word as **Varlet**, q. v.

Valetudinary. (F. – L.) M.F. *valetu-dinaire*, sickly. – L. *ualētūdinārius*, sickly. – L. *ualētūdin-*, stem of *ualētūdo*, health (good or bad). – L. *ualē-re*, to be strong.

Valhalla, the hall of the slain. (Scand.) Icel. *valhöll* (gen. *valhallar*), lit. the hall of the slain. – Icel. *valr*, the slain, slaughter; *höll*, *hall*, a hall; see **Hall**.

Valiant, brave. (F. – L.) F. *vaillant*, valiant; O. F. *vailant*, pres. pt. of F. *valoir*, to profit. – L. *ualēre*, to be strong.

valid, having force. (F. – L.) F. *valide*. – L. *ualidus*, strong. – L. *ualēre*, to be strong.

Valise, a travelling-bag. (F. – Ital.) F. *valise*, 'a male [mail], wallet;' Cot. – Ital. *valigia*; corrupted in German to *felleisen*. β. Etym. unknown; Diez supposes it to be founded on L. *uidulus*, a leathern travelling-trunk. Devic suggests Pers. *walīchah*, a large sack, or Arab. *walihat*, a corn-sack.

Valkyrie, Valkyria, one of the handmaidens of Odin. (Scand.) Icel. *Valkyria*, a goddess; lit. 'chooser of the slain.' – Icel. *val*, acc. of *valr*, the slain (A.S. *wæl*); *-kyrja*, f., a chooser, from *kur-* (<*kus-*), weak grade of *kjōsa*, to choose, cognate with E. *choose*.

Valley. (F. – L.) M. E. *vale*, *valeie*. – O. F. *valee* (F. *vallée*), a valley; parallel to Ital. *vallata*, a valley, which appears to mean, literally, 'formed like a valley.' Formed with suffix *-ee* (< L. *-āta*), from F. *val*, a vale, representing L. *uallem*, acc. of *uallis*, a vale.

Valour. (F.—L.) O. F. *valor, valur, valeur,* value, worthiness. — L. *ualōrem,* acc. of *ualor,* worth. — L. *ualēre,* to be strong, to be worth.

value. (F.—L.) M. F. *valuĕ,* fem. 'value;' Cot. Fem. of *valu,* pp. of *valoir,* to be worth.—L. *ualēre,* to be worth.

Valve. (F.—L.) F. *valve,* 'a foulding, or two-leafed door, or window;' Cot.— L. *ualua,* sing. of *ualuæ,* the leaves of a folding-door. Allied to L. *uoluere,* to revolve; see **Voluble.**

Vambrace, Vantbrace, armour for the fore-arm. (F.—L.) The word simply means 'fore-arm.' It is short for *avantbrace.*—M. F. *avant-bras,* 'a vambrace, armour for an arm; also, the part of the arm which extends from the elbow to the wrist;' Cotgrave. (The latter is the orig. sense.) — F. *avant,* before; *bras,* the arm. —L. *ab ante,* from before, in front; *brāchium,* arm (the pl. of which gave O. F. *brace,* arm; see Scheler). See **Van** (1) and **Vamp.** ¶ Similarly, armour for the upper part of the arm was called a *rerebrace,* i. e. rear-brace.

Vamp, the fore-part of a shoe. (F.—L.) Short for M. E. *vampay,* also *vaumpè,* a vamp.—M. F. *avant-pied,* 'the part of the foot that's next to the toes.'—F. *avant,* before; *pied* (A. F. *pee*), foot, from L. *pedem,* acc. of *pēs,* foot.

Vampire. (F.—G.—Servian.) F. *vampire.* — G. *vampyr.* — Servian *vampir,* a blood-sucker, a supposed ghost that sucked men's blood. Prob. of Turkish origin; cf. N. Turk. *uber,* a witch (Miklosich).

Vamplate, an iron plate protecting a lance. (F.—L.) From F. *avant,* in front, fore; and *plate.* See **Vambrace.**

Van (1), the front of an army. (F.—L.) Short for *van-guard,* which stands for M. E. *vantwarde.* — O. F. *avant-warde,* later *avant-garde,* 'the vanguard of an army;' Cot. — F. *avant,* before; O. F. *warde,* a guard; see **Advance** and **Guard** or **Ward.**

Van (2), a fan. (F.—L.) F. *van,* a fan. —L. *uannum,* acc. of *uannus,* a fan. Doublet, *fan.*

Van (3), a covered waggon for goods. (F.—Pers.) Short for *caravan,* like *bus* for *omnibus.* See **Caravan.**

Vandal, a barbarian. (L.—Teut.) One of the tribe of *Vandalī* (Pliny); answering to A.S. *Wendlas,* pl. (from *Wendil-*). Cf. Icel. *Vendill* (also *Vandill*), a proper name.

Vane, a weather-cock. (E.) A Southern form; formerly also *fane.* A. S. *fana,* a small flag.+Du. *vaan,* Icel. *fāni,* Dan. *fane,* Swed. Goth. *fana,* G. *fahne.* Teut. type **fanon-,* m. Orig. a bit of cloth; allied to L. *pannus,* a cloth; see **Pane.**

Vanguard; see **Van** (1).

Vanilla, a plant. (Span.—L.) Span. *vainilla,* a small pod, or capsule (which is the orig. sense). Dimin. of Span. *vaina,* a scabbard, a pod.—L. *uagīna,* scabbard, sheath, pod.

Vanish. (F. — L.) M. E. *vanissen, vanisshen;* also *evanisshen.* Derived from an O. F. vb. **vanir,* with pres. pt. **vanissant.* The verb is only recorded as A. F. *evanir,* O. F. *esvanir, esvanuir;* but we find O. F. *esvanuir* and *vanuir.* Cf. Ital. *svanire,* to vanish (where *s* = L. *ex*); Late L. type **exvanīre,* for L. *ēuānescere.* — L. *ē,* out, away; *uānescere,* to vanish, lit. to become empty, from L. *uānus,* empty. See **Vain.**

vanity. (F. — L.) F. *vanité.* — L. *uānitātem,* acc. of *uānitās,* emptiness.— L. *uānus,* vain, empty.

Vanquish. (F.—L.) M. E. *venkisen, venquishen.* — A. F. *venquis-,* O. F. *veinquiss-,* stem of pres. pt. of A. F. *venquir, veinquir,* occurring as a collateral form of *veincre,* to conquer (F. *vaincre*). — L. *uincere,* to conquer. Brugm. i. § 367.

Vantage. (F.—L.) Short for M. E. *avantage;* see **Advantage.**

Vapid, insipid. (L.) L. *uapidus,* stale, flat, said of wine; cf. L. *uappa,* vapid or palled wine; wine that has emitted its vapour or strength. Allied to *uapor* (below).

vapour, mist. (F.—L.) F. *vapeur.*— L. *uapōrem,* acc. of *uapor,* vapour. + Gk. καπνός, smoke. Brugm. i. § 193.

Varicose, permanently dilated, as a vein. (L.) L. *uārīcōsus.*—L. *uārīc-,* stem of *uārix,* a dilated vein; named from its crooked appearance.—L. *uārus,* crooked.

Variegate. (L.) From pp. of L. *uariegāre,* to make of various colours. — L. *uario-,*for *uarius,* of divers colours; *igāre,* due to *agere,* to drive, to make.

various. (L.) L. *uari-us,* variegated, diverse, manifold; with suffix *-ous.* Der. *varie-ty,* M. F. *varieté,* from L. acc. *uariĕtātem,* variety.

Varlet. (F. — C.) M. F. *varlet,* 'a groom, stripling, youth;' Cot. An older spelling was *vaslet,* dimin. of O. F. *vasal, vassal,* a vassal; see **Vassal.** The successive spellings were *vaslet, varlet, vallet, valet.*

Varnish. (F.) F. *vernis,* 'varnish;' Cot. Cognate with Ital. *vernice,* Port. *verniz,* Span. *berniz,* varnish; Late L. *vernicium, vernix, bernix.* Origin unknown. Perhaps from M. Gk. βερνίκη; see Schade, p. 1439.

Vary. (F.–L.) F. *varier.*–L. *uariāre,* to vary.–L. *uarius,* various.

Vascular. (L.) From L. *uasculum,* a small vessel; double dimin. of *uās* (below).

vase. (F.–L.) F. *vase,* a vessel.–L. *uāsum,* allied to *uās,* a vessel. Allied to Skt. *vāsana-,* a receptacle, cover.

Vassal, a dependant. (F.–C.) M. E. *vassal.*– F. *vassal,* 'a vassall, subject, tenant;' Cot. The Celtic sense is 'servant'; Low L. *uassallus;* extended from Low L. *uassus, uasus,* a servant. – O. Bret. *uuas,* Bret. *gwaz,* a servant, vassal; W., Corn. *gwas,* youth, servant; O. Irish *foss.* Celtic type **wassos.*

Vast. (F.–L.) F. *vaste.*–L. *uāstus,* vast, great, of large extent. See **Waste.**

Vat, a large vessel for liquors. (E.) M. E. *vat* (Southern); also *fat* (Northern). A. S. *fæt,* a vessel, cask. + Du. *vat,* Icel. *fat,* Dan. *fad,* Swed. *fat,* G. *fass.* Teut. type **fatom,* n. Lit. 'that which contains;' cf. E. Fries. *faten,* O. Fries. *fatia,* Du. *vatten,* to catch, contain, G. *fassen,* to seize, contain.

Vaticinate, to foretell. (L.) From L. *uāticinātus,* pp. of *uāticinārī,* to prophesy.–L. *uāticin-us,* prophetic.–L. *uāti-,* for *uātes,* a prophet, allied to Wood (2); *-cin-,* from *can-ere,* to sing, proclaim (Bréal).

Vaudeville. (F.) F. *vaudeville,* orig. a country ballad; ' so tearmed of *Vaudevire,* a Norman town, wherein Olivier Bassel [or Basselin], the first inventer of them, lived;' Cot. Basselin was a Norman poet (died ab. 1418), whose songs were named after his native valley, the *Val de Vire;* *Vire* is in Normandy, S. of Bayeux.

Vault (1), an arched roof, cellar. (F.–L.) For *vaut;* the *l* was pedantically inserted. M.E. *voute, vowte, vawte, vaute.*– M.F. *voute* (also *voulte,* with inserted *l*), ' a vault, arch, a vaulted roof;' Cot. O.F. *volte,* a vault (whence the later form *voute,* mod. F. *voûte*); this is the fem. of O. F. *volt,* vaulted, lit. bent, bowed, the same as Ital. *volta.*–Late L. **voltus,* substituted

for *uolūtus,* pp. of *uoluere,* to roll, turn round. Thus a *vault* meant a ' bowed ' roof, hence a chamber with bowed roof, a·cellar which has an arched roof.

vault (2), to bound, leap. (F.–Ital.– L.) M. F. *volter,* ' to vault ;' Cot.–M. F. *volte,* a round, turn, tumbler's gambol.– Ital. *volta,* a sudden turn ; the same word as *volta,* a vault (above). See **Volute.**

Vaunt. (F. – L.) F. *se vanter,* to boast.– Late L. *vānitāre,* to speak vanity, flatter; (F. *se vanter* = to flatter oneself). A frequentative form from *uānus,* vain ; see **Vain.**

Vavasour, a vassal of the second rank. (F.–C.) A. F. *vavasour.*–Low L. *vassus vassōrum,* vassal of vassals ; see **Vassal.**

Vaward, another spelling of *vanward* or *vanguard;* see **Van** (1).

Veal. (F.–L.) O. F. *veël,* a calf.–L. *uitellum,* acc. of *uitellus,* dimin. of *uitulus,* a calf.+Gk. ἰταλός, a calf ; cf. Skt. *vatsa-,* a calf, properly 'a yearling,' from Skt. *vatsa-,* Gk. ἔτος, a year. Allied to **Wether** and **Veteran.**

Veda, knowledge ; one of the ancient sacred Skt. books. (Skt.) Skt. *veda-,* lit. knowledge. – Skt. *vid,* to know ; allied to **Wit.**

Vedette, Vidette, a cavalry sentinel. (F.–Ital.–L.) M.F. *vedette,* a sentinel.– Ital. *vedetta,* a horse-sentry ; formerly a watch-tower.– Ital. *vedere,* to see.–L. *uidēre,* to see ; see **Vision.**

Veer. (F.–L.?) F. *virer,* to turn, veer. Said to be derived from L. *gȳrāre,* to turn round (see **Gyrate**), but influenced by L. *uiriola,* dimin. of *uiria* (only in pl. *uiriæ*), an armlet, large ring. Allied to **Environ.** Cf. also M. F. *virolet,* 'a boy's wind-mill;' Cot. (Doubtful.)

Vegetable. (F.–L.) M. F. *vegetable,* adj., ' vegetable, fit or able to live;' Cot. This is the old sense.–L. *uegetābilis,* full of life, animating.–L. *uegetāre,* to quicken, enliven.–L. *uegetus,* lively.–L. *uegēre,* to quicken, arouse. Allied to **Vigour.** Der. *vegetat-ion,* M. F. *vegetation* (Cot.).

Vehement, passionate. (F.–L.) M.F. *vehement* (Cot.). – L. *uehement-,* stem of *uehemens,* passionate ; lit. ' out of one's mind.' β. *Uehe-* has been explained as equivalent to *uē-,* ' apart from,' as in *uē-cors,* senseless ; cf. Skt. *vahis,* apart. For *mens,* mind, see **Mental.**

Vehicle. (L.) L. *uehiculum,* a carriage. – L. *uehere,* to carry, convey.+Skt.

vah, to carry. Allied to **Weigh** and **Wain**. (✓WEGH.) Brugm. i. § 128.

Veil, sb. (F – L.) O. F. *veile*, later *voile*. – L. *uēlum*, a sail; also a cloth. For *uexlum = *uecslum ; cf. *uexillum*, a standard. Lit. 'propeller' of a ship; from *uehere*, to carry along. Brugm. i. § 883.

Vein. (F.–L.) F. *veine*.–L. *uēna*, a vein. For *uecsna. Lit. 'conveyer' of the blood.–L. *uehere*, to carry. Brugm. ii. § 66.

Vellum. (F.–L.) M. E. *velim*.–O.F. *velin* (F. *vélin*); cf. Late L. *vitulīnium*, or *pellis vitulīna*, vellum, calf's skin.–L. *uitulīnus*, adj., from *uitulus*, a calf. See **Veal**.

Velocity. (F.–L.) M.F.*velocité*, swiftness. – L. acc. *uēlōcitātem*. – L. *uēlōci-*, decl. stem of *uēlōx*, swift. Allied to **Volatile**. Der. *veloci-pede*, lit. 'swift-foot,' coined from L. *uēlōci-* (above), and L. *ped-*, stem of *pēs*, a foot.

Velvet. (Ital.–L.) M. E. *velouette*, *velouet*; Spenser has *vellet*. A. F. *velwet*, *veluet*; Low L. *velluētum*; answering to a Romanic type *villūlettum. Cf. M. Ital. *veluto* (Ital. *velluto*), velvet; answering to a Late L. *uillūtus, shaggy, by-form of L. *uillōsus*, shaggy. All from L. *uillus*, shaggy hair; allied to *uellus*, fleece, and to E. **Wool**.

Venal. (F.–L.) M. F. *venal*, saleable. –L. *uēnālis*, saleable.–L. *uēnus*, *uēnum*, sale. Allied to Gk. ὦνος, a price, ὠνή, a buying; Brugm. i. § 329. Der. *venal-ity*.

vend, to sell. (F.–L.) F. *vendre*.– L. *uendere*, to sell; short for *uēnundāre*, lit. to give or offer for sale, also written *uēnum dare*. – L. *uēnum*, sale; *dare*, to give, offer.

Veneer, to overlay with a thin slice of wood. (G.–F.–O. H. G.) Formerly *fineer*. – G. *furniren*, to furnish or provide small pieces of wood, to veneer.–F. *fournir*, to furnish; a word of G. origin; see **Furnish**.

Venerable. (F.–L.) M. F. *venerable*. –L. *uenerābilis*, to be reverenced.–L. *uenerā-rī*, to reverence. – L. *uener-*, for *uenes, stem of *uenus*, love. Der. *venerat-ion*, from pp. of *uenerārī*.

venereal. (L.) Coined from L. *uenere-us*, *ueneri-us*, pertaining to Venus or love. – L. *ueneri-*, decl. stem of *uenus*, love. Allied to Skt. *van*, to love, honour.

Venery, hunting. (F. – L.) M. F.

venerie, 'hunting;' Cot. – O. F. *vener*, to hunt. – L. *uēnārī*, to hunt; see **Venison**.

Venesection, blood-letting. (L.) L. *uēnæ*, of a vein, gen. of *uēna*; and *section*. See **Vein** and **Section**.

Venew, Venue, Veney, (1) a turn or bout or thrust in fencing; (2) a locality. (F.–L.) M. F. *venuë*, 'a coming, a *venny* in fencing, turn, trick;' Cot. Lit. a coming, home-thrust; fem. of *venu*, pp. of *venir*, to come. – L. *uenīre*, to come; see **Venture**. 2. As a law-term, *venue* is the same word, and signifies a place of arrival, locality. ¶ Apparently confused by Blackstone with O. F. *visné*, vicinity (a derivative of L. *uīcīnus*, near).

Vengeance. (F.–L.) F. *vengeance*, 'vengeance;' Cot. – F. *venger*, to avenge. –L. *uindicāre*; see **Vindicate**.

Venial. (F. – L.) O. F. *venial*.–L. *ueniālis*, pardonable. – L. *uenia*, pardon; also grace, favour. Allied to **venereal**.

Venison. (F.–L.) M. E. *veneison*.– A. F. *veneisun*, M. F. *venaison*, 'venison, flesh of beasts of chase;' Cot. – L. *uēnā-tiōnem*, acc. of *uēnātio*, the chase, also game.–L. *uēnātus*, pp. of *uēnārī*, to hunt. Cf. **Gain**, vb. And see **Venery**.

Venom. (F.–L.) M.E. *venim*.–A. F. *venim* (F. *venin*).–L. *uenēnum*, poison.

Venous, belonging to a vein. (L.) For L. *uēnōsus*, adj.; from *uēna*, a vein. See **Vein**.

Vent (1), an air-hole, flue. (F.–L.) 'A *vent*, meatus, porus ; *To vent*, aperire, euacuare;' Levins. Doubtless influenced by a popular etymology from F. *vent*, wind, as if 'air-hole'; but the true sense was 'fissure.' Formerly *fent*. '*Fent* of a gowne, *fente*;' Palsgrave. – M. F. *fente*, 'a cleft, rift;' Cot. – F. *fendre*, to cleave. – L. *findere*, to cleave. See **Fissure**. Der. *vent*, vb., Temp. ii. 2. 111 ; certainly confused with F. *vent*, wind ; see **Vent** (3).

Vent (2), sale, utterance. (F. – L.) Formerly common. – F. *vente*, sale, selling. – F. *vendre*. – L. *uendere*, to sell; see **Vend**.

Vent (3), to snuff up air, breathe, expose to air. (F.–L.) See Spenser, Shep. Kal. Feb. 75 ; F. Q. iii. 1. 42. The word was prob. due to a misuse of *vent* (1); but the popular etymology is obvious. – F. *vent*, wind. – L. *uentum*, acc. of *uentus*, wind; cognate with **Wind** (1). Der. *vent-age*, air-hole, Hamlet, iii. 2. 373.

ventail, lower half of the moveable

part of a helmet. (F.−L.) M.E. *auentaile*
(with prefix *a* = F. *a* < L. *ad*).−M.F. *ven-
taille*, 'breathing-part of a helmet;' Cot.
−F. *vent-er*, to puff; with suffix -*aille* (<
L. -*ācula*).−F. *vent*, wind (above).

ventilate. (L.) From pp. of L. *uen-
tilāre*, to blow, winnow.−L. *uentulus*, a
light wind.−L. *uentus*, wind.

Ventral, belonging to the belly. (L.)
L. *uentrālis*, adj.; from *uenter*, the belly.

ventricle. (F.−L.) F. *ventricule*,
'the ventricle, the place wherein the meat
sent from the stomach is digested;' Cot.
−L. *uentriculum*, acc. of *uentriculus*,
stomach, ventricle; double dimin. of *uenter*,
the belly.

ventriloquist. (L.) Coined from
L. *uentriloqu-us*, lit. speaking from (or
in) the belly. −L. *uentri-*, decl. stem of
uenter (above); *loquī*, to speak. See
Loquacious.

Venture, sb. (F. − L.) A headless
form of M.E. *auenture* (*aventure*), an
adventure, chance. − F. *aventure*, a chance,
occurrence. − L. *aduentūra*, fem. of *aduentūrus*, about to happen.−L. *ad*, to; *uen-
tūrus*, fut. of *uenīre*, to come. Cognate
with E. **Come.** (√GwEM.) **Doublet,**
adventure. **Der.** *venture,* vb.

Venue; see Venew.

Veracious, truthful. (L.) From L.
uērāci-, decl. stem of *uērāx*, true; with
suffix -*ous*.−L. *uērus*, true. See Very.

Veranda, Verandah, a covered
balcony. (Port. − Span. − L.) Port. *varanda.*−O. Span. *varanda*, a stair-railing;
in Pedro de Alcala (1505). If of native
Span. origin, it may be from Span. *vara*,
a rod, rail.−L. *uāra*, a forked pole. Cf.
L. *uārus*, crooked. ¶ Hence also was
borrowed Skt. *varaṇḍa*, a portico, which
is quite a modern word; see *veranda* in
Yule.

Verb, the word; the chief word in a sentence. (F.−L.) F. *verbe.*−L. *uerbum*, a
word. For **uerdhum*, cognate with E.
Word. **Der.** *verb-iage,* F. *verbiage,* from
O. F. **verbier, verboier,* to talk.

Verbena. (L.) L. *uerbēna*, orig. a
sacred bough; afterwards, vervain. Allied to *uerber*, a rod. See Vervain.

Verdant, flourishing. (F.−L.) A false
form ; as if from F. **verdant,* substituted
for *verdissant,* pres. pt. of *verdir,* to flourish.
−O. F. *verd*, green.−L. *uiridis*, green.
See Vert. Cf. also *verdure,* F. *verdure,*
lit. greenness.

Verdict. (F.−L.) M.E. *verdit* (the
correct form). − A. F. and O. F. *verdit,
veirdit.* − L. *uērē dictum*, truly said;
whence Late L. *uērēdictum*, true saying,
verdict.−L. *uērē*, adv., from *uērus*, true;
dictum, neut. of *dictus*, pp. of *dicere*, to
say. ¶ Mod. F. *verdict* is from E.

Verdigris, rust of copper. (F.−L.)
M. F. *verd de gris*, 'verdigrease, Spanish
green;' Cot. Spelt *verte grez* in the 13th
cent., and *verd de grice* in the 14th (Littré).
A better form is the M.E. *verdegrece,* i.e.
verd de Grece, lit. 'green of Greece;' so
also A.F. *vert de Grece*, Vie de S. Gile,
853. Cf. '*uiride grecum*, Ang. verdegrece;'
Wülker, Voc. 619. 35. M.F. *verd* (*verd,
vert*) is from *uiridem*, acc. of *uiridis*,
green. (See Acad. 1118, Oct. 1893.)

verditer, a green pigment. (F.−L.)
M.F. *verd de terre*, a green mineral; Cot.
−L. acc. *uiridem*, green (above); *dē*, of;
terra, earth.

Verge (1), a wand of office, edge, brink.
(F.−L.) Distinct from *verge* (2) below.
M.E. *verge*, a wand, rod, yard (in measure).
− F. *verge*, 'a rod, wand, yard, hoope, ring,
rood of land;' Cot. From the sense of
rod it came to mean hoop, ring (hence,
edge); the sense of edge also easily followed from the Law-term *verge,* i.e. limit
of jurisdiction.−L. *uirga*, a rod, pliant
twig. **Der.** *verg-er,* a rod-bearer, mace-
bearer, F. *verger*, L. *uirgārius.*

Verge (2), to tend towards. (L.) L.
uergere, to bend, tend, incline towards, incline. ¶ The phrase 'to be on the *verge*
of' is quite distinct, and belongs to **Verge**
(1).

Verify. (F.−L.) M.F. *verifier*; Cot.
−Late L. *vērificāre*, to make true.−L.
uēri-, for *uērus*, true; -*ficāre*, for *facere*,
to make.

verisimilitude, likelihood. (F.−
L.) M.F. *verisimilitude.*−L. *uērisimili-
tūdo.*− L. *uērī similis*, like the truth.−L.
uērī, gen. of *uērum*, the truth, orig. neuter
of *uērus*, true; *similis*, like.

verity, truth. (F.−L.) M.F. *verité.*
−L. *uēritātem*, acc. of *uēritās*, truth.−L.
uēri-, for *uērus*, true. See Very.

Verjuice. (F. − L.) F. *verjus*, verjuice; lit. 'green juice,' i.e. juice of green
grapes.−O. F. *verd*, green, from L. *uiridem*, acc. of *uiridis*; *jus*, juice, from L.
iūs; see Juice.

Vermicelli. (Ital.−L.) Ital. *vermicelli*, lit. 'little worms;' from the shape.

Pl. of *vermicello*, dimin. of *verme*, a worm. **–** L. *uermem*, acc. of *uermis*, a worm. See **Worm**.

vermicular, pertaining to a worm. (L.) From L. *uermicul-us*, a little worm; dimin. of *uermis*, a worm.

vermilion. (F. **–** L.) F. *vermillon*, 'a little worm, vermillion;' Cot. **–** F. *vermeil*, vermilion. **–** L. acc. *uermiculum*, dimin. of *uermis* (above). ¶ So named from the cochineal insect (see **Crimson**); but *vermilion* is now generally made from red lead.

vermin. (F. **–** L.) F. *vermine*, vermin; applied to obnoxious insects, &c. As if from a Lat. adj. **uermīnus*, formed from *uermi-*, decl. stem of *uermis*, a worm, cognate with E. **Worm**.

Vernacular, native. (L.) From L. *uernācul-us*, adj., native; lit. belonging to a home-born slave. **–** L. *uerna*, a home-born slave. Lit. 'dweller;' cf. Skt. *vas*, to dwell. (√WES.) Brugm. ii. § 66.

Vernal. (L.) L. *uernālis*, extended from *uernus*, belonging to spring. **–** L. *uēr*, spring. **+** Gk. ἔαρ (for **Ϝέσαρ*), Russ. *vesna*, Icel. *vár*, Dan. *vaar;* Swed. *vår*, spring; the time of increasing brightness. Cf. Lith. *wasara*, summer; Skt. *vasanta-*, spring, *ush*, to burn, glow; also O. Irish *áir*, W. *gwawr*, dawn.

Vernier, a kind of scale, for fine measurement. (F.) Invented by *P. Vernier*, b. 1580, died Sept. 14, 1637.

Verse. (L.) M. E. *vers, fers* (Ormulum); A. S. *fers* (perhaps from O. Irish *fers*, also from L.). **–** Late L. *versus*, L. *uersus*, a turning, course, row, line of poetry. **–** L. *uersus*, pp. of *uertere*, to turn. Allied to **Worth** (1). (√WERT.) **Der.** *vers-ed*, imitated from L. *uersātus*, pp. of *uersārī*, pass. of frequent. of *uertere*; *vers-at-ile*, quickly turning, M. F. *versatil* (Cot.), L. *uersātilis*, versatile; likewise from L. pp. *uersātus*.

versify. (F. **–** L.) F. *versifier*. **–** L. *uersificāre*, to make verses. **–** L. *uersi-*, for *uersus*, a verse; *-ficāre*, for *facere*, to make. **Der.** *versificat-ion*, from pp. *uersificātus*.

version. (F. **–** L.) F. *version*. **–** Late L. *uersiōnem*, acc. of *uersio*, a version, translation. **–** L. *uersus*, pp. of *uertere*, to turn.

verst, a Russian measure of length. (Russ.) Russ. *versta*, 3500 English feet;

also, *age*. For **vert-tā*; from √WERT (Russ. *vertiete*), to turn.

Vert, green. (F. **–** L.) F. *vert*, O. F. *verd*. **–** L. *uiridem*, acc. of *uiridis*, green. Cf. L. *uirēre*, to be green. **+** W. *gwyrdd*, green; Corn. *guirt*. Or (if these Celtic words are borrowed) allied to *vivid*; cf. Skt. *ji-ra-*, active, *jī-va*, living. Brugm. ii. § 74.

Vertebra. (L.) L. *uertebra*, a joint, vertebra. **–** L. *uertere*, to turn.

vertex, top. (L.) L. *uertex*, top, pole of the sky (which is the turning-point of the stars), but afterwards the zenith. **–** L. *uertere*, to turn. **Der.** *vertic-al*, L. *vertical*, from L. *uerticālis*, vertical, which is from *uertic-*, for *uertec-*, stem of *uertex*, top.

vertigo, giddiness. (L.) L. *uertīgo*, giddiness. **–** L. *uertere*, to turn round.

Vervain. (F. **–** L.) F. *verveine*, 'vervaine;' Cot. **–** L. *uerbēna*, a sacred bough; afterwards, vervain. See **Verbena**.

Very, true. (F. **–** L.) M. E. *verrai*. **–** O. F. *verai* (F. *vrai*), true. Cf. Prov. *verai*, true. It answers to a Late L. type **vērācus*, allied to L. *uērāx*, true. **–** L. *uērus*, true, credible (whence O. F. *voir*). **+** W. *gwir*, O. Irish *fīr*, true; G. *wahr*, A. S. *wǣr*, true. Cf. Russ. *viera*, faith. Brugm. i. § 367.

Vesicle, a small tumour or cell. (L.) L. *uēsicula*, dimin. of *uēsīca*, a bladder.

Vesper. (L.) M. E. *vesper*, the evening-star (Gower). **–** L. *uesper*, evening-star, evening; cf. *uespera*, even-tide. Hence O. F. *vespre* (F. *vêpre*), evening, and *vespres* (F. *vêpres*), vespers, even-song. **+** Gk. ἕσπερος, adj. and sb., evening; O. Irish *fescor*, W. *ucher*, evening. Brugm. i. § 329.

Vessel. (F. **–** L.) M. E. *vessel*. **–** A. F. *vessel;* O. F. *vaissel*, a vessel, ship, later *vaisseau*, a vessel (of any kind). **–** L. *uascellum*, a small vase or urn; dimin. of *uās*, a vase. See **Vase**.

Vest, a garment. (L.) L. *uestis*, a garment, clothing. **+** Goth. *wasti*, clothing; cf. Gk. ἕν-νυμι (= Ϝέσ-νυμι), I clothe, ἔσθής, clothing, Skt. *vas*, to put on clothes. (√WES.) See **Wear**.

Vestal. (F. **–** L.) F. *Vestale*, a Vestal virgin. **–** L. *Vestālis*, belonging to a Vestal, also a priestess of Vesta. **–** L. *Vesta*, goddess of the flocks and household. **+** Gk. ἑστία, goddess of the domestic hearth.

Vestibule. (L.) L. *uestibulum*, a fore-court; lit. 'separated from the abode.' **–**

L. *uĕ-*, separate from, *stabulum*, an abode; see Stable (Vaniček).

Vestige. (F. – L.) F. *vestige*, a step, foot-track. – L. *uestīgium*, foot-track.

Vestment. (F. – L.) M. E. *vestiment.* – O. F. *vestement* (F. *vêtement*). – L. *uestīmentum*, clothing. – L. *uestīre*, to clothe; from *uestis*, clothing. See Vest.

vestry. (F. – L.) M. E. *vestrie*; shortened from O. F. *vestiarie*; cf. M. F. *vestiaire*, 'vestry;' Cot. – L. *uestiārium*, a wardrobe; neut. of *uestiārius*, adj., from *uestis*, a robe.

vesture. (F. – L.) O. F. *vesture*, *vestéure.* – Late L. *vestītūra*, clothing. – L. *uestīre*, to clothe. – L. *uestis*, a robe.

Vetch, a plant. (F. – L.) Also *fitch.* M. E. *feche* (of which the Southern form was *veche*). – O. F. *veche, vece,* M. F. *vesce,* vetch (where *veche* is a Walloon and North F. form). – L. *uicia*, a vetch; whence also G. *wicke*, Du. *wikke.*

Veteran. (L.) L. *ueterānus*, experienced; as sb., a veteran. – L. *ueter-*, for **uetes*, stem of *uetus*, old, lit. 'advanced in years.' Cf. Gk. ἔτος, Skt. *vatsa-*, a year. See Veal.

veterinary. (L.) L *ueterīnārius*, of or belonging to beasts of burden; as sb., a cattle-doctor. – L. *ueterīnus*, belonging to beasts of burden. The L. *ueterīna* meant an animal at least a year old, one that had passed its first year; from the base **uet-*, year (above). See Wether.

Veto, a prohibition. (L.) L. *ueto*, I forbid; O. L. *uoto.*

Vex, to harass. (F. – L.) F. *vexer.* – L. *uexāre*, to vex; orig. intensive form of *uehere* (pt. t. *uex-i*). See Vehicle.

Viaduct. (L.) L. *uia ducta*, a road conducted across (a river, &c.). – L. *uia*, a way, road; *ducta*, fem. of pp. of *dūcere*, to carry, conduct. β. L. *uia*, formerly *uea* = Skt. *vaha-*, a road; from L. *uehere* = Skt. *vah*, to carry; see Vehicle, Way.

Vial, Phial, a small bottle. (F. – L. – Gk.) M. E. *viole, fiole.* – O. F. and F. *fiole.* – L. *phiala.* – Gk. φιάλη, a shallow cup or bowl.

Viands, food. (F. – L.) Pl. of *viand.* – F. *viande*, food. – L. *uīuenda*, neut. pl., provisions, food; from the gerundive of *uīuere*, to live. See Victuals.

Vibrate. (L.) From pp. of L. *uibrāre*, to swing, shake. Cf. Skt. *vep*, to tremble. (√WEIP.) Brugm. i. § 701.

Vicar. (F. – L.) F. *vicaire*, a deputy.

– L. *uicārius*, a deputy, orig. an adj., deputed, put in place of. – L. *uic-*, base of *uicis*, gen. case, a turn, change, succession. (√WEIQ.) Brugm. i. § 701,

Vice (1), a fault. (F. – L.) F. *vice.* – L. *uitium*, blemish, fault. Der. *vic-i-ous*, F. *vicieux*, L. *uitiōsus*, faulty; *viti-ate*, from pp. of L. *uitiāre*, to injure. And see Vituperation.

Vice (2), an instrument for holding things firmly. (F. – L.) M. E. *vice*, orig. 'a screw,' because tightened by a screw. – F. *vis*, 'vice, a winding-staire;' Cot. O. F. *viz.* – L. *uītis*, a vine, bryony, lit. 'that which winds or twines.' (√WEI.) See Withy.

Vice-gerent. (F. – L.) M. F. *vicegerent*, a deputy; Cot. – L. *uice*, in place of; *gerent-*, stem of pres. pt. of *gerere*, to carry on, rule; see Gesture. ¶ So also *vice-admiral; vice-roy* (from F. *roi*, L. acc. *rēgem*, king), *vice-regal.*

Vicinage, neighbourhood. (F. – L.) Altered from F. *voisinage*, neighbourhood. – F. *voisin*, near. – L. *uīcīnus*, near, lit. 'belonging to the same street.' – L. *uīcus*, a village, street; see Wick (2).

vicinity, neighbourhood. (F. – L.) M. F. *vicinité.* – L. acc. *uīcīnitātem*, neighbourhood. – L. *uīcīnus*, near (above).

Vicissitude. (L.) L. *uicissitūdo*, change. Allied to *uicissim*, by turns. – L. *uic-is* (genitive), a change; see Vicar.

Victim. (F. – L.) F. *victime.* – L. *uictima*, a victim. Cf. Goth. *weihan*, to consecrate. Brugm. i. § 606.

Victor. (L.) L. *uictor*, a conqueror. – L. *uic-*, base of *uincere*, to conquer (pt. t. *uīc-i*); with suffix *-tor.* + Goth. *weihan*, to fight; cf. A. S. *wig*, war. (√WEIQ.) Brugm. i. § 367. Der. *victor-y*, A. F. *victorie*, L. *uictōria.*

Victuals. (F. – L.) Pl. of *victual*, a pedantic spelling of M. E. *vitaille*, provisions. – O. F. *vitaille*, usually in pl. *vitailles*, provisions. – L. neut. pl. *uictuālia*, provisions; from *uictuālis*, adj., belonging to nourishment. – L. *uictu-*, stem of *uictus*, food. – L. *uictus*, pp. of *uīuere*, to live; allied to *uīuus*, living, and to E. Quick. (√GwEI.) Brugm. ii. § 488.

Vicuna, a quadruped of the camel tribe. (Span. – Peruv.) Span. *vicuña*; of Peruvian origin (Acosta, iv. 40).

Videlicet, viz., namely. (L.) In old MSS. and books, the abbreviation for *et* resembled *z*; hence *viet* (short for *vide-*

licet) was misread as *viz.* — L. *uidēlicet*, short for *uidēre licet*, it is possible to see, it is evident, hence, to wit, namely. — L. *uidēre*, to see ; *licet*, it is allowable ; see Vision and Licence.

Vidette ; see Vedette.

Vie, to contend for superiority. (F. — L.) M. E. *vien*, a contracted form of *en-vien*, to vie, contend for superiority. (Cf. *fence* for *defence*, *story* for *history*, &c.) — O. F. *envier* (*au ieu*), 'to vie ;' Cot. The lit. sense of O. F. *envier* was to invite [quite distinct from *envier*, to envy], esp. used in gaming in the sense ' to open a game by staking a certain sum ' ; precisely as Span. *envidar*, Ital. *invitare*, to invite, to vie, or propose a stake. — L. *inuītāre*, to invite (of which *vie* is thus seen to be a doublet). See Invite. ¶ The sense was to stake a sum to draw on or invite a game, then to wager, bet against, contend, strive for the upper hand.

View, sb. (F. — L.) A. F. *view, vewe, vue* ; M. F. *veuë*, 'a view, sight ;' Cot. Fem. of *veu*, pp. of O. F. *veoir* (F. *voir*), to see. — L. *uidēre*, to see. See Vision.

Vigil. (F. — L.) Lit. 'a watching.' F. *vigile*, 'a vigile, eve of a holy day ;' Cot. — L. *uigilia*, a watch. — L. *uigil*, awake. — L. *uigēre*, to be lively ; cf. *uegēre*, to arouse ; allied to Wake. See Vigour. Der. *vigil-ant*, F. *vigilant*, from stem of pres. pt. of L. *uigilāre*, to watch.

Vignette, a small engraving with ornamented border. (F. — L.) First applied to borders in which vine-leaves and tendrils were introduced ; XVIIth cent. — F. *vignette*, a little vine ; pl. *vignettes*, ' branch-like flourishes ;' Cot. Dimin. of F. *vigne*, a vine ; see Vine.

Vigour, energy. (F. — L.) O. F. *vigor* ; F. *vigueur*. — L. *uigōrem*, acc. of *uigor*, liveliness. — L. *uigēre*, to be lively ; see Vigil. Der. *vigor-ous*.

Viking, a Northern pirate. (Scand.) Icel. *vīkingr*, a pirate, free-booter, rover. Lit. 'a warrior ;' for *vīgningr (*ign* > *īk*) ; allied to *vīg*, war, Goth. *weihan*, to fight, L. *uincere*, to conquer. See Victor. (So Noreen, § 252 ; cf. Sweet, Hist. E. Sounds, § 319.) + A. S. *wīcing*. ¶ Usually explained as ' creek-dweller ' ; from Icel. *vīk*, a creek.

Vile. (F. — L.) F. *vil*, fem. *vile*, base. — L. *uīlis*, base, mean. + W. *gwael*, vile.

Villa. (L.) L. *uilla*, a farm-house ; O. L. *uella*. Perhaps for *ues-la, i. e. a

dwelling, from √WES, to dwell ; see Was.

village. (F. — L.) F. *village*. — L. *uillāticus*, adj., belonging to a farm-house. — L. *uilla* (above).

villain. (F. — L.) M. E. *vilein*. — A. F. *vilein*, servile ; as sb., a bondman, slave, villain. — Late L. *villānus*, orig. a farm-servant, hence a slave, serf, villain. — L. *uilla*, a farm-house. Der. *villain-y*, A. F. *vilanie*, servitude, baseness.

Vinculum, a link. (L.) L. *uinculum*, a bond, fetter. — L. *uincīre*, to bind.

Vindicate. (L.) From pp. of L. *uindicāre*, to arrogate, lay claim to ; cf. *uindic-*, stem of *uindex*, a claimant.

vindictive. (F. — L.) Shortened from F. *vindicatif*, ' revenging ;' Cot. From L. *uindicāt-us*, pp. of *uindicāre*, to avenge ; with suffix *-īuus*, F. *-if*.

Vine. (F. — L.) F. *vigne*. — L. *uīnea*, a vineyard ; in Late L. (apparently) a vine. Fem. of L. *uīneus*, adj., from *uīnum*, wine ; see Wine. Der. *vine-yard*, substituted for A. S. *wīn-geard*, a vineyard, lit. ' wine-yard.' See Yard (1).

vinegar. (F. — L.) M. E. *vinegre*. — O. F. *vin egre* (F. *vinaigre*). — L. *uīnum*, wine ; *ācrem*, acc. of *ācer*, sharp. See Wine and Eager.

Vinewed, mouldy. (E.) A Southern form. Also *finewed, fenowed* (Nares). From M. E. *fenow*, mouldiness ; with suffix *-ed* ; cf. A. S. *fynegian*, to become mouldy. — A. S. *fynig*, mouldy (Joshua, ix. 5). — A. S. *fyne*, mould, moistness. Allied to Du. *vuns*, rank ; M. Du. *vunstigh*, ' mustie (as hay) ;' Hexham.

Vintage. (F. — L.) An alteration of M. E. *vindage, vendage* ; by influence of *vint-ner*. — F. *vendange*, M. F. *vendenge*, vintage. — L. *uindēmia*, vintage. — L. *uīn-um*, wine, grapes ; *-dēmia*, a taking away, from *dēmere*, to take away. *Dēmere* = *dē-imere, from *emere*, to take.

vintner. (F. — L.) M. E. *vintener*, altered form of earlier *vineter, viniter*. — M. F. *vinetier*, ' a vintner ;' Cot. — Late L. *uīnētārius*, a wine-seller. — L. *uīnētum*, a vineyard. — L. *uīnum*, grapes, wine.

Viol. (F. — Prov. — Late L.) M. F. *viole, violle*, ' a violin ;' Cot. — Prov. *viula*. — Late L. *vīdula, vītula*, a viol ; whence also O. H. G. *fidula*, A. S. *fiþele*, a fiddle. See Fiddle.

Violate. (L.) From pp. of L. *uiolāre*, to treat with force, violate. Formed as if from an adj. *uiolus, due to uī-s, force. Brugm. i. § 655.

Violent. (F. − L.) F. violent. − L. uiolentus, full of might. Formed as if from an adj. *uiolus; see Violate.

Violet, a flower. (F.−L.) M. F. violet, m., violette, f. (Cot.). Dimin. of M. F. viole, ' a gilliflower;' Cot. − L. uiola, a violet. + Gk. ἴον, a violet. Der. violet, adj.

Violin. (Ital.−Late L.) Ital. violino, dimin. of Ital. viola, a viol; see Viol.

violoncello. (Ital.−Late L.) Ital. violoncello, dimin. of violone, a bass-viol, an augmentative form of viola, a viol.

Viper. (F.−L.) F. vipère.−L. uīpera, a viper. Usually explained as ' that produces living young'; short for uīuipara, fem. of uīuiparus, producing living young; see viviparous.

Virago. (L.) L. uirāgo, a manlike woman.−L. uir, a man; see Virile.

Virgate, a measure of land. (L.) From Late L. terra uirgāta, land measured with a rod.−L. uirga, a rod; see Verge (1).

Virgin. (F.−L.) O. F. virgine.−L. uirginem, acc. of uirgo, a maid. Der. virgin-als, the name of a musical instrument, played upon by virgins.

Viridity, greenness. (L.) L. uiriditās, greenness.−L. uiridis, green. See Vert.

Virile, manly. (F. − L.) F. viril, ' manly;' Cot.−L. uirīlis, adj., from uir, a man.+A. S. wer; O. H. G. wer; Goth. wair; Icel. verr; O. Irish fer, W. gwr, a man; cf. Skt. vīra-, a hero.

virtue. (F.−L.) M. E. vertu.−F. vertu.−L. uirtūtem, acc. of uirtūs, manly excellence.−L. uir, a man.

virtuoso. (Ital.−L.) Ital. virtuoso, one skilled in the fine arts, orig.' virtuous.' −Ital. virtù, shortened form of virtute, virtue, also, a love of the fine arts.−L. uirtūtem (above).

Virulent. (F.−L.) F. virulent.−L. uīrulentus, full of poison. − L. uīrus, poison.+Gk. ἰός, Skt. visha-, poison. Cf. Wizen.

Visage, look, face. (F.−L.) F. visage, face, look. − M. F. vis, visage; with suffix -age (<L. -āticum). − L. uīsum, acc. of uīsus, sight, afterwards look; face. − L. uīsus, pp. of uidēre, to see.

visard, the same as visor.

Viscera, entrails. (L.) L. uiscera, neut. pl., entrails. Der. e-viscer-ate, to remove the entrails.

Viscid, sticky, clammy. (L.) L. uis-

cidus, sticky, clammy. − L. uiscum, mistletoe, birdlime.+Gk. ἰξός, mistletoe.

Viscount. (F. − L.) Also spelt vicounte (and the inserted s is not pronounced). A. F. visconte, viconte; F. vicomte, ' a vicount, at first the deputy of an earl,' Cot.; O. F. viscomte (12th cent.). −L. uice, in place of; comitem, acc. of comes, a count; see Count (1).

Visible. (F. − L.) F. visible. − L. uisibilis, that can be seen.−L. uīs-us, pp. of uidēre, to see.+Gk. ἰδεῖν, to see; Skt. vid, to know. Allied to Wit. (√WEID.)

vision. (F.−L.) F. vision.−L. uīsiōnem, acc. of uīsio, sight. − L. uīsus, pp. of uidēre, to see.

visit. (F.−L.) F. visiter.−L. uīsitāre, to visit, go to see, frequent. of uīsere, to behold; from uīsus, pp. of uidēre, to see.

visor, visard, vizor. (F. − L.) The d is added. M. E. visere. − M. F. visiere, ' the viser, or sight of a helmet;' Cot. Formed from M. F. vis, the face; see Visage. A visor also meant a mask, from its covering the face; Cotgrave has ' faux visage, a maske, or visard.'

vista. (Ital.−L.) Ital. vista, lit. a view.−Ital. vista, fem. of visto, seen, from vedere, to see. − L. uidēre, to see.

visual. (F.−L.) M. F. visual.−L. uīsuālis, belonging to the sight.−L. uīsu-, decl. stem of uīsus, sight.−L. uīsus, pp. of uidēre, to see.

Visier; see Vizier.

Vital. (F.−L.) F. vital.−L. uītālis, belonging to life.−L. uīta, life; allied to uīuere, to live. See Victuals.

Vitiate; see Vice (1).

Vitreous. (L.) L. uitre-us, glassy; with suffix -ous.−L. uitri-, for uitrum, glass. The i in uitrum is common; some connect the word with uidēre, to see. ¶ L. uitrum, ' woad,' is cognate with E. Woad.

vitriol. (F.−L.) F. vitriol,' vitrioll;' Cot. Said to be so called from its glassy look.−L. uitreolus, glassy.−L. uitreus, glassy.−L. uitrum, glass (above).

Vituperation, blame. (F.−L.) M.F. vituperation.−L. acc. uituperātiōnem.− L. uituperātus, pp. of uituperāre, to blame, lit. ' to prepare (or find) a blemish.'−L. uitu-, for uiti-, base of uitium, a vice, fault; parāre, to prepare, provide.

Vivacity. (F.−L.) F. vivacité, liveliness.−L. uīuācitātem, acc. of uiuācitās, liveliness.−L. uīuāci-, decl. stem of uīuāx, tenacious of life. − L. *uīuere*, to live. See **Victuals**.

vivid. (L.) L. *uīuidus*, lively. − L. *uīuere*, to live.

vivify. (F. − L.) F. *vivifier*, to quicken. − L. *uīuificāre*, to quicken. − L. *uīui*-, for *uiuus*, living; *-ficāre*, for *facere*, to make.

viviparous. (L.) From L. *uīui-parus*, producing living young. − L. *uīui*-, for *uīuus*, living; *parere*, to produce.

vivisection. (L.) Coined from L. *uīui*- (above); and *section*.

Vixen. (E.) M. E. *vixen, fixen*, a she-fox; answering to A. S. *fyx-en*, made from *fox* by vowel-change of Teut. *u* (A. S. *o*) to *y*, with fem. suffix *-en* (for *-īn-jŏ-*); precisely as A. S. *gyden*, a goddess, from *god*, a god. See **Fox**. Cf. G. *füchsin*, f. of *fuchs*, fox. The *v* for *f* is Southern.

Viz.; see Videlicet.

Vizard; see Visor.

Vizier, Visier, a councillor of state. (F. − Arab.) F. *vizir*. − Arab. *wazīr*, a councillor of state; orig. a porter, one who bears the burden of state affairs. − Arab. root *wazara*, to bear a burden, sustain.

Vocable, a term, word. (F. − L.) F. *vocable*. − L. *uocābulum*, an appellation, name. − L. *uocāre*, to call. − L. *uoc-*, related to *uōc-*, stem of *uōx*, voice, name (below). Der. *vocabulary*, from Late L. *uocābulārium*, a list of words.

vocal, uttering sound. (F. − L.) F. *vocal*. − L. *uōcālis*, adj., from *uōc-*, stem of *uōx*, voice, sound. ✚ Gk. ἔπος, a word; Skt. *vacha-s*, speech, from *vach*, to speak. (√WEQ.) Brugm. i. § 678.

vocation. (F. − L.) F. *vocation*. − L. acc. *uocātiōnem*, a calling, invitation. − L. *uocātus*, pp. of *uocāre*, to call.

vociferation. (F. − L.) M.F. *vociferation*. − L. acc. *uōciferātiōnem*, an outcry. − L. *uōciferātus*, pp. of *uōciferārī*, to lift up the voice, cry aloud. − L. *uōci*-, decl. stem of *uōx*, voice; *fer-re*, to bear, carry, cognate with E. *bear*.

Vogue, mode, fashion. (F. − Ital. − Teut.) Formerly *vogue* meant sway, authority, power. − F. *vogue*, 'vogue, sway, power; a cleere passage, as of a ship in a broad sea;' Cot. Orig. 'sway of a ship,' verbal sb. of F. *voguer*, 'to saile forth;' id. − Ital. *voga*, sb., stroke of an oar, *vogare*, to row in a galley. − M. H. G. *wāgen*, G. *wogen*, to fluctuate, be in motion on the sea. − M. H. G. *wāg*, G. *woge*,

a wave; O. H. G. *wāc*. ✚ A. S. *wǣg*, Goth. *wēgs*, a wave; Teut. type **wǣgoz*, m.; from **wǣg-*, 3rd stem of Teut. **wegan-*, to move; see **Weigh**.

Voice. (F. − L.) M. E. *vois*. O. F. *vois* (F. *voix*). − L. *uōcem*, acc. of *uōx*, voice, sound. See **vocal**.

Void, empty. (F.) O. F. *vuide, voide* (F. *vide*); a fem. form of which the masc. is *vuit*. Origin unknown.

Volant, flying. (F. − L.) F. *volant*, pres. pt. of *voler*, to fly. − L. *uolāre*, to fly. Cf. Gk. βολή, a throw; Brugm. i. § 663.

volatile. (F. − L.) F. *volatil*, 'flying;' Cot. − L. *uolātilis*, flying. − L. *uolātus*, flight. − L. *uolāre*, to fly.

Volcano, a burning mountain. (Ital. − L.) Ital. *volcano*, a volcano. − L. *Volcānum*, acc. of *Volcānus, Vulcānus*, Vulcan, god of fire, fire. Cf. Skt. *varcha-s*, lustre.

Vole, a field-mouse. (Scand.) Also called *vole-mouse, field-mouse, meadow-mouse, campagnol*; L. *arvicola*. A modern word; abbreviated from North E. *vole-mouse*, i. e. field-mouse. From Norw. *voll*, field; cognate with E. **Wold**. Der. *water-vole*, i. e. water field-mouse.

Volition. (F. − L.) F. *volition*. − Late L. **volitiōnem*, acc. of **volitio*, volition (prob. a term of the schools). − L. *uolo*, I wish. See **Voluntary**.

Volley. (F. − L.) F. *volée*, 'a flight;' Cot. Hence, a flight of shot. − L. *uolāta*, fem. of pp. of *uolāre*, to fly.

Volt, another spelling of **Vault** (2).

Voltaic, originated by Volta. (Ital.) From *A. Volta*, of Como, died March 5, 1826.

Voluble, fluent. (F. − L.) M.F. *voluble*, 'voluble, easily rolled, glib;' Cot. − L. *uolūbilis*, easily turned about. − L. *uolū-*, as in *uolū-tus*, pp. of *uoluere*, to roll; with suffix *-bilis*. ✚ Goth. *walwjan*, to roll, Gk. εἰλύειν, to enfold; allied to Russ. *valite*, to roll. (√WEL.) See **Helix**.

volume, a roll, a book. (F. − L.) F. *volume*. − L. *uolūmen*, a roll, scroll; hence, a book on a parchment roll. − L. *uolū-*, as in *uolū-tus*, pp. of *uoluere*, to roll.

Voluntary. (F. − L.) M.F. *voluntaire, volontaire*. − L. *uoluntārius*, willing. − L. *uoluntās*, free will. − L. **uolunt-*, related to *uolent-*, stem of *uolens*, willing, from *uelle*, to wish, *uolo*, I wish. ✚ Skt. *vṛ*, to choose, select. Allied to **Will** (1). (√WEL.) Brugm. ii. §§ 102, 493.

voluptuous. (F. – L.) F. *voluptuëux*, Cot. – L. *uoluptuōsus*, addicted to, or full of pleasure. – L. *uolupt-ās*, pleasure. – L. *uolup, uolupe*, adv., agreeably. – L. *uol-o*, I wish. Cf. Gk. ἐλπίς, hope.

Volute, a spiral scroll on a capital. (F. – L.) F. *volute* (Cot.). – L. *uolūta*, a volute; fem. of *uolūtus*, pp. of *uoluere*, to roll; see **Voluble.**

Vomit, sb. (L.) L. *uomitus*, a vomiting; whence *uomitāre*, to vomit. – L. *uomitus*, pp. of *uomere*, to vomit. +Gk. ἐμεῖν, Lith. *wemti*, Skt. *vam*, to vomit. (√WEM.)

Voracity. (F. – L.) F. *voracité*. – L. *uorācitātem*, acc. of *uorācitās*, hungriness. – L. *uorāci-*, for *uorax*, voracious, greedy to devour. – L. *uorāre*, to devour. – L. *-uorus*, devouring, as in *carni-uorus*, flesh-eating. Allied to Skt. *-gara-*, as in *aja-gara-*, goat-devouring; Gk. βορός, gluttonous. (√GwER.) Brugm. i. § 653.

Vortex, a whirlpool. (L.) L. *uortex*, also *uertex*, whirlpool. – L. *uertere*, to turn; see **Verse.**

Vote, sb. (L.) L. *uōtum*, a wish; orig. a vow. – L. *uōtum*, neut. of *uōtus*, pp. of *uouēre*, to vow. Der. *vot-ive*, L. *uōtīuus*, promised by a vow; *vot-ary*, a coined word, like *votaress*, *votress*.

Vouch, to warrant. (F. – L.) M. F. *voucher*, 'to vouch, cite, pray in aid in a suit;' Cot. O. F. *vochier*. – L. *uocāre*, to call, call upon, summon. See **Vocable.**

vouchsafe. (F. – L.) Formerly *vouch safe*, i. e. warrant as safe; from *vouch* and *safe*.

Vow, sb. (F. – L.) M. E. *vow, vou*. – O. F. *veu, vou* (F. *vœu*), a vow. – L. *uōtum*, a vow; see **Vote.** ¶ Hence the M. E. *avow*, sb., common in the sense of 'vow,' Chaucer, C. T. 2237, 2414; and hence the verb *avow*, to vow. Another *avow* answers to F. *avouer*, L. *aduocāre*, and is a doublet of *avouch*.

Vowel. (F. – L.) O. F. *vouel, voiel*; F. *voyelle*, 'a vowell;' Cot. – L. *uocālem*, acc. of *uocālis* (*littera*), a vowel, vocal letter; see **Vocal.**

Voyage. (F. – L.) M. E. *viage, veage*. – O. F. *veiage*, later *voyage*. – L. *uiāticum*, properly provisions for a journey. – L. *uiāticus*, belonging to a journey. – L. *uia*, a way. See **Viaduct.**

Vulcanise, to combine caoutchouc with sulphur by heat. (L.) Coined, with suffix -*ise*, from *Vulcan*, god of fire,

fire. See **Volcano.** Der. *vulcan-ite*, vulcanised caoutchouc.

Vulgar. (F. – L.) F. *vulgaire*. – L. *uulgāris*, belonging to the common people. – L. *uulgus, uolgus*, the common people; a throng, crowd. Der. *vulgar-ity*; also *vulgate*, the E. name for the L. version of the Bible known as the *ēditio vulgāta*, where *vulgāta* is a later form of the fem. of the pp. of *uulgāre*, to publish.

Vulnerable. (F. – L.) M. F. *vulnerable*. – L. *uulnerābilis*, liable to injury. – L. *uulnerare*, to wound. – L. *uulner-*, for **uulnes-*, stem of *uulnus*, a wound; O. L. *uolnus*. Allied to *uellere*, to pluck, tear. Cf. Skt. *vraṇa-*, a wound, fracture; Gk. οὐλή, W. *gweli*, a wound. (√WEL.)

Vulpine, fox-like. (F. – L.) M. F. *vulpin*; Cot. – L. *uulpīnus*, fox-like. – L. *uulp-*, base of *uulpes*, a fox. Allied to **Wolf** (Darbishire, Reliquiæ Philologicæ, p. 92).

Vulture. (L.) L. *uultur*, a vulture; O. L. *uolturus*; lit. 'tearer.' – L. *uul-* (*uol-*), as in *uul-si*, pt. t. of *uellere*, to pluck, tear. Allied to **Vulnerable.**

W.

Wabble, Wobble, to reel, move unsteadily. (E.) Frequentative of *wap*, *whap*, to flutter (Halliwell); see **Wave**, **Whap.** Cf. E. Fries. *wabbeln*, to wabble; Löw G. *wabbeln*, *quabbeln*, to palpitate, to wabble; Swed. dial. *vabbla*, to move food to and fro in the mouth.

Wacke, a rock derived from basalt. (G.) G. *wacke*, wacke; M.H.G. *wacke*, O.H.G. *waggo*, a kind of flint.

Wad, a small bundle of stuff, little mass of tow. (Scand.) Swed. *vadd*, wadding, M. Swed. *wad*, clothing, stuff; cf. Icel. *vaðmál*, wadmal, a plain woollen stuff. + G. *watte*, wadding, wad (whence F. *ouate*). Der. *wadd-ing*, *wad-mal*. Cf. **Weed** (2).

Waddle, to walk clumsily. (E.) Frequentative of *wade* (below).

Wade, to walk slowly, esp. through water. (E.) A. S. *wadan*, pt. t. *wōd*, to wade, go. + Du. *waden*; Icel. *vaða*, pt. t. *óð*, to wade; (cf. Icel. *vað*, a ford); Dan. *vade*, Swed. *vada*, G. *waten*, O. H. G. *watan*, to wade, go. Further allied to L. *uadum* (for **uadhom*), a ford, *uādere*, to go.

Wadi, a water-course, river. (Arab.) Arab. *wādī*.

Wafer. (F.—Teut.) M. E. *wafre.*—
A. F. *wafre*, O. F. *waufre* (F. *gaufre*),
a wafer. — M. Du. *waefel*, a wafer (Du.
wafel); Low G. *wafel*, whence G. *waffel*,
wafer. β. F. *gaufre* also means 'honey-
comb'; hence Low G. *wafel* may be allied
to G. *wabe*, a honey-comb, Icel. *vaf*, a weft;
from Teut. *waf, 2nd grade of **weƀan-*, to
weave; see **Weave**.

Waft. (E.) For *waff*, like *graft* for
graff. Again, *waff* is the same as *wave*,
in the sense 'to beckon by waving something'; see *waft*, pt. t. of *waff*, in Merch.
Ven. v. i. 11. See **Wave** (1).

Wag (1). (Scand.) M. E. *waggen.*—M.
Swed. *wagga*, Swed. *vagga*, to wag, sway,
rock. Cognate with A. S. *wagian* (>M. E.
wawen), to wag, which is a secondary verb
derived from the 2nd grade of A. S. *wegan*,
to carry, move. Similarly, the Swed. *wagga*
is a secondary verb, from O. Swed. *wega,
Icel. *vega*, to weigh; see **Weigh**. So also
Goth. *wagjan*, to shake. **Der.** *wag-tail*;
waggle, q. v.

wag (2), a merry knave. (E.) Short
for *wag-halter*, one who deserves hanging
(jocosely).

Wage, a gage, pledge; pl. **Wages,** pay
for service. (F.—Teut.) M. E. *wage*, pl.
wages.—O. F. *wage*, later *gage*, a gage,
pledge; hence a stipulated payment; whence
O. F. *wager*, to pledge, Low L. *wadiāre.*
—Low L. *wadium*; formed from Goth.
wadi, a pledge; see **Wed**. **Der.** *wage*,
vb., as in *to wage war*, orig. to declare (or
pledge oneself to) war; cf. Walloon *wager*,
to pledge.

wager, a bet. (F.—Teut.) M. E.
wager, *waiour.* — O. F. *wageure*, later
gageure, 'a wager;' Cot.—Low L. *wa-
diātūra*, from *wadiāre*, to pledge (above).
Der. *wager*, vb. See also **Gage** (1).

Waggle, to wag frequently. (Scand.)
Frequent. form of **Wag** (above); cf. Swed.
dial. *vagla*, Swed. *vackla*, to totter; also G.
wackeln, Pomeran. *waggeln*, to waggle;
Low G. *wigelwageln*, to wiggle-waggle.

wagon, waggon. (Du.) XIVth cent.
Borrowed from Du. *wagen*, a wagon; which
is cognate with **Wain**.

wagtail; from **Wag** and **Tail**.

Waif, sb., a thing abandoned, a thing
found astray. (F.—Scand.) M. E. *waif*,
weif; pl. *wayues, weyues,* (*wayves, weyves*).
—A.F. and O.F. *waif*, later *gaif*, pl.
waives, gaives; *choses gayves*, 'weifes,
things forsaken, or lost;' Cot. —O. Icel.

*weif, Icel. *veif*, anything moving or
flapping about (applied, e. g. to the fin
of a seal); allied to *veifa*, to vibrate, move
about; see **Waive**.

Wail, to lament. (Scand.) M. E. *weilen.*
—O. Icel. *wæla, Icel. *væla*, to wail;
also *vāla.* Lit. 'to cry wo;' from *væ*,
vei, interj., wo! See **Wo**. Cf. Swed.
dial. *väla*, to wail; Dan. dial. *vælle*, to
wail, *væl*, a wail; Norw. *væla*, to bleat.

Wain, a waggon. (E.) M. E. *wain*,
wayn; formed (by the usual change of *æg*
to *ay*) from A. S. *wægn*, a wain; we also
find A. S. *wǣn*, a contracted form. From
the 2nd grade (*wag) of *wegan*, to carry;
see **Weigh**. ♣ Du. *wagen* (whence E.
wagon), Icel. *vagn*, Dan. *vogn*, Swed.
vagn, G. *wagen.* Allied to L. *ueh-iculum*,
Gk. ὄχ-ος, O. Irish *fēn*, a car. (√WEGH.)

Wainscot, panelled boards on walls of
rooms. (Du.) XIVth cent.—Du. *wagenschot*,
'wainscot,' Hexham; cf. Low G. *wagenschot*,
the best kind of oak-wood. As if from
Du. *wagen*, a wain; but really an alteration of M. Du. *waeghe-schot*, which Kilian
explains as 'oak-wood with a waving
grain'; from M. Du. *waeghe* (G. *woge*,
M. H. G. *wāg*), a wave, and *schot*, 'a wainscot, partition,' &c., Sewel, or 'a closure of
boards,' Hexham. The Du. *schot* is cognate with E. *scot* and *shot.* ¶ Not from
M. Du. *weegh*, a wall.

Waist. (E.) M. E. *wast*, waist; lit.
'the growth' of a man, or the part of the
body where size and strength are developed.
The same word as M. E. *wacst*, strength,
answering to an A. S. form *wæxt, not
found, but nearly allied to A. S. *wæstm*,
growth. — A. S. *weaxan*, to grow; see
Wax (1). ♣ Goth. *wahstus*, growth, increase, stature; Icel. *vöxtr*, stature, shape;
Swed. *växt*, Dan. *væxt*, growth. Brugm.
i. § 795 (2). **Der.** *waist-coat.*

Wait, sb. (F.—O. H. G.) Orig. a
watchman, sentinel, afterwards one who is
awake at night, a night-musician.—O. F.
waite, a guard, watchman; cf. F. *guet.*—
O. H. G. *wahta*, a watchman, orig. a
watch, a guard, a being awake. From the
Teut. base **wak-*, as in Goth. *wak-an*, to
be awake; see **Wake** (1); with Teut. suffix
-ton-. ¶ Also used in the phr. *to lie in
wait*; cf. Walloon *weitier*, to spy.

wait, vb. (F.—O. H. G.) O. F. *waiter*,
waitier, *gaiter*, later *guetter*, to watch,
wait.—O. F. *waite*, a watchman, a watching (above).

Waive, to relinquish a claim. (F.—Scand.) M. E. *waiuen, weiuen (waiven, weiven)*, to set aside, shun, push aside, remove.—A. F. *weiver*, M. F. *guesver*, 'to waive, refuse, abandon, give over, surrender, resigne;' Cot. (Low L. *waviāre*, to waive.)—O. Icel. **weifa*, Icel. *veifa*, to vibrate, flap, flutter, whence *veifi-skati*, a spendthrift. Cf. Norw. *veiva*, to turn (a grindstone), *veiv*, a crank, Swed. *vefva*, to wind. Allied to O. H. G. *weibōn*, to hover, move about; M. Du. *weyfelen*, to be inconstant; E. Fries. *wif*, restless. And to **Vibrate.** (√WEIP.) Cf. **Waif.** ¶ Distinct from *wave.*

Wake (1), to be brisk, cease from sleep. (E.) M. E. *waken*, pt. t. *wook*: properly intransitive; whence the weak verb *wakien*, pt. t. *waked*, to cause to wake, rouse. A. S. *wacan*, to arise, come to life, be born, pt. t. *wōc*, pp. *wacen*; whence *wacian*, weak verb, to make, watch, pt. t. *wacode.* + Goth. *wakan* (pt. t. *wōk*), *wakjan* (pt. t. *wakida*); Du. *waken*, Icel. *vaka*, Dan. *vaage*, Swed. *vaka*, G. *wachen* (whence Du. *wekken*, Icel. *vekka*, Dan. *vække*, Swed. *vācka*, G. *wecken*). Ultimately allied to **Vigil**; see Brugm. ii. § 804. **Der.** *wake*, sb., a vigil, A. S. *-wacu.*

Wake (2), the track of a ship. (Scand.) In Norfolk, a *wake* means a space of unfrozen water in a frozen tarn or ' broad.' The proper sense is an opening in ice, passage through ice, hence a track of a ship through a frozen sea, or a track generally. — O. Icel. **wak-*, Icel. *vak-*, stem of *vök*, a hole, opening in ice; Swed. *vak*, Norweg. *vok* (the same). Hence Norweg. *vekkja*, Dan. *vække*, to cut a passage for ships through ice. The orig. sense was ' a wet place.' — Icel. *vökr*, wet (Lowl. Scotch *wak*); cf. Du. *wak*, moist, Gk. *ὑγ-ρός*, wet.

Waken, to awake. (E.) Now usually transitive, but orig. *intransitive only*, in the sense ' to become awake.' M. E. *waknen, wakenen.* A. S. *wæcnan*, to be aroused, be born; intrans. form from *wacan*, to wake; see **Wake.** ¶ The verbal suffix *-en* has now usually a *transitive* force; the M. E. suffix *-n-en* is properly *intransitive*, as in Gothic. Cf. Goth. *gawaknan*, Swed. *vakna*, Dan. *vaagne*, to become awake. **Der.** *a-waken*, where the prefix *a* = A. S. *ā-*; see **A-** (4).

Wale, Weal, the mark of a blow. (E.) M. E. *wale.* A. S. *walu*, a weal; also

wyrt-walu, the root of a tree (with the idea of ridge). + E. Fries. *wale*, a weal; O. Fries. *walu*, rod, wand, Icel. *völr*, a round stick, Goth. *walus*, a staff. Cf. E. Fries. *walen*, to turn round, roll; Russ. *val'*, a cylinder, *valiate*, to roll. β. The sense of rod or beam is preserved in *gun-wale*, the plank along the edge of a ship protecting the guns.

Walk, vb. (E.) M. E. *walken*, pt. t. *welk*, pp. *walken.* A. S. *wealcan*, pt. t. *wēolc*, pp. *wealcen*, to roll, toss oneself about, rove about; hence, generally, to ramble, walk. Cf. M. Du. *walcken*, to press, full cloth, Swed. *valka*, to roll, full, work, Dan. *valke* (same), G. *walken*, to full. Allied to Skt. *valg*, to go by leaps. ¶ M. E. *walker*, a fuller, is from M. Du.

Wall. (L.) A. S. *weall*, borrowed from L. *uallum*, a rampart, orig. a row of stakes; Cf. L. *uallus*, a stake, palisade, lit. protection. Allied to O. Irish *fāl*, a hedge.

Wallah, lit. an agent. (Hind.) H. H. Wilson explains Hind. *wālā* as one who is charged with doing any duty; Yule says it is practically an adj. suffix, like the L. *-ārius* (or E. *-er*); orig. an agent, doer, &c. See *Competition-wallah* in Yule; we may explain this as *competition-er* = *competitor.*

Wallet, a bag, budget. (E.? or F.—O. H. G.?) M. E. *walet*, apparently equivalent to M. E. *watel*, a wattle, also a bag. In P. Plowman, C. xi. 269, where some MSS. express ' bag-full ' by *watel-ful*, others have *walet-ful*. Again, Shakespeare has *wallets* for bags of flesh upon the neck (Temp. iii. 3. 46), which is the same as *wattles.* ¶ Very doubtful; the form suggests an A. F. **walet*, possibly from O. H. G. *wallōn*, to go on pilgrimage. Cf. O. F. *gauler*, to wander (Ducange).

Wall-eyed, with diseased eyes. (Scand.) ' *Glauciolus*, an horse with a *waule eye*;' Cooper (1565). — Icel. *vald-eygðr*, corruption of *vagleygr*, wall-eyed, said of a horse. — Icel. *vagl*, a beam, also a beam in the eye, disease of the eye; *eygðr, eygr*, eyed, from *auga*, eye, cognate with E. *eye.* The Icel. *vagl* is the same as Swed. *vagel*, a perch, roost, sty in the eye, Norw. *vagl*, a hen-roost. Cf. Wars of Alexander, 608, 1706.

Wallop; see **Potwalloper.**

Wallow. (E.) M. E. *walwen.* A. S. *wealwian*, to roll round. Cf. Goth. *walwjan*, L. *uoluere*, to roll; see **Voluble.**

Walnut. (E.) Lit. ' foreign (Gaulish)

nut.' O. Merc. *walh-hnutu*, from O. Merc. *walh*, A. S. *wealh*, foreign; *hnutu*, a nut. +Du. *walnoot*, Icel. *valhnot*, Dan. *valnöd*, Swed. *valnöt*, G. *wallnuss*. β. The A. S. *wealh* makes the pl. *wealas*, O. Merc. *walas*, which is the mod. E. *Wales* (now applied to the country itself); cognate with O. H. G. *walah*, a foreigner, whence G. *Wälsch*, Italian. ¶ The explanation 'foreign' is inexact; the A. S. *wealh* meant a Celt, either of Wales or Gaul. In form it answers to ' one of the tribe of *Volcæ*,' who occupied Southern Gaul.

Walrus, a large seal. (Du.—Scand.) Du. *walrus*. − Swed. *vallross*, Dan. *hvalros*, a morse; lit. a 'whale-horse'; the same as A. S. *hors-hwæl*, a morse, horse-whale. − Swed. *vall*, Dan. *hval*, a whale; Icel. *hross*, a horse. Said to be named from the neighing sound made by the animal. See **Whale** and **Horse**.

Waltz, a dance. (G.) Short for G. *walzer*, a waltz (with *z* sounded as *ts*).− G. *walzen*, to roll, revolve; see **Welter**.

Wampum, small beads, used as money. (N. American Indian.) Amer. Indian *wampum*; from the Massachusetts *wômpi*, Delaware *wápi*, white (Mahn). Cf. Algonkin *wab*, white (Cuoq).

Wan, colourless. (E.) M. E. *wan*. A. S. *wann*, *wonn*, dark, black, colourless; now applied to *pale* objects deficient in colour.

Wand, a slender rod. (Scand.) M. E. *wand*. − Icel. *vöndr* (gen. *vand-ar*), a switch; M. Swed. *wand*; Dan. *vaand*. + Goth. *wandus*, a rod, orig. a pliant stick; prob. from *wand*, 2nd grade of *windan*, to wind, bind. From the use of *wands* in wicker-work.

Wander, to ramble. (E.) A. S. *wandrian*, to wander; used as frequentative of *wend*, to go, but formed from *wand*, 2nd grade of *windan*, to wind; see **Wend**. +E. Fries. *wandern*, *wandeln*; Du. *wandelen*, G. *wandeln*; Swed. *vandra*, Dan. *vandre*.

Wane, to decrease (as the moon), to fail. (E.) A. S. *wanian*, to wane, decrease. − A. S. *wan*, *won*, deficient. + Icel. *vana*, vb., from *vanr*, deficient. Cf. Goth. *wans*, lacking, Gk. ἐῦνις, bereft of, Skt. *ūna-*, wanting. Brugm. ii. § 67.

wanion. (E.) In the phr. *with a wanion*, i. e. with ill-luck. I believe *wanion*=North E. *waniand*, waning, pres. pt. of M. E. *wanien*, to wane; see **Wane** (above). Sir T. Moore (Works, p. 306)

writes *in the waniand*, which I explain to mean ' in the waning of the moon,' i. e. with ill-luck; see Brand, Popular Antiq. on *The Moon*. (So also Wedgwood.)

want, lack. (Scand.) M. E. *want*, first used as an adj., signifying ' deficient.'− Icel. *vant*, neut. of *vanr*, adj., lacking, which was formerly used with a gen. case following; as, *var þeim vettugis vant*, there was lacking to them of nothing, i. e. they wanted nothing. The Icel. *vanr* = A. S. *wan*; see **Wane** (above). Der. *want*, vb., Icel. *vanta*, from the neut. adj. *vant*.

wanton, unrestrained. (E.) M. E. *wantoun*, unrestrained, not educated; full form *wantowen*. − M. E. *wan-*, prefix, lacking, a neg. prefix (from A. S. *wan*, lacking); *towen* < A. S. *togen*, pp. of *teon*, to draw, to educate. See **Wane** and **Tow** (1).

Wap, to strike; see **Whap**.

Wapentake, a district. (Scand.) M. E. *wapentake*. A. S. *wæpengetæc*, not an E. word, but borrowed from Icel. *vápnatak*, lit. a weapon-touching, hence, a vote of consent so expressed; and, finally, the district governed by a man whose authority was confirmed by the touching of weapons. See Thorpe, Ancient Laws, i. 455. − Icel. *vápna*, gen. pl. of *vápn*, a weapon; and *tak*, a touching, grasping; see **Weapon** and **Take**.

Wapiti, the N. Amer. elk. (Amer. Indian.) Cree *wapitik*, ' white deer;' cf. Delaware *wápi*, white (see **Wampum**).

War. (F.—Teut.) M. E. *werre*; A. S. Chron. an. 1119. Also *war-*; we find: ' armorum oneribus, quod Angli *war-scot* dicunt,' Laws of Cnut, De Foresta, § 9. [Not common, the usual A. S. words being *wig*, *hild*, *winn*, *guð*.]−O. F. *werre*, later *guerre* (see Low L. *werra*, *guerra*), war. − M. Du. *werre*, war, cf. *warren*, to embroil; O. H. G. *werra*, broil, confusion, strife.−O. Sax. and O. H. G. *werran*, str. vb., to confuse. Base *werr-*, for *werz-*; allied to **Worse**. Cf. G. *verwirren*, to embroil. Der. *war-fare*, i. e. war-expedition; from A. S. *faran*, to go.

Warble, to sing as a bird. (F.−O. H. G.) M. E. *werbeln*, *werbelen*. − O. F. *werbler* (Burguy). − M. H. G. **werbelen*, old form of G. *wirbeln*, to whirl, run round, warble; see **Whirl**.

Ward, a guard, watch, &c. (E.) M. E. *ward*. A. S. *weard*, masc., a guard, watchman, defender; also *weard*, fem., a guarding, protection, defence. Allied to **Wary**.

(Base *war.) **+** Icel. *vörðr*, (1) a watch-man, (2) a watching; G. *wart*, Goth. *-wards* in *daura-wards*, a door-keeper. Cf. also A. F. *warde*, sb.; see **Guard**. Der. *ward*, vb., *ward-er*, sb.; also *bear-ward*, *ste-ward*, &c.

warden, a guardian. (F. − Teut.) M. E. *wardein*. **−** A. F. *wardein*, old spelling of O. F. *gardein*, *gardain*, Low L. *gardiānus*, a guardian. **−** O. F. *warder*, later *garder*, to guard; with L. suffix *-iānus*. **−** O. Sax. *wardōn*, to watch; see **Guard**. **Doublet**, *guardian*.

wardrobe. (F.−G.) M. E. *warde-robe*. **−** O. F. *warderobe*, later *garderobe*, a guardrobe, i. e. place for keeping robes. See **Guard** and **Robe**.

Ware (1), merchandise. (E.) M. E. *ware*. A. S. *waru* (L. *merx*; Wright). The orig. sense was prob. ' valuables,' and the word may be allied to A. S. *waru*, pro-tection, guard, custody. **+** Icel. *vara*, Dan. *vare*, Swed. *vara*, Du. *waar*, G. *waare*, a commodity; prob. allied to Dan. *vare*, Swed. *vara*, care; see **Wary** and **Worth** (1).

Ware (2), aware. (E.) See Acts xiv. 6. M. E. *war*; A. S. *wær*, cautious. (The true form, whence *wary* was made by adding *-y*.) See **Wary**.

Wariness; see **Wary**.

Warison, Warisoun, protection, reward. (F.−O. H. G.) M. E. *warisoun*, protection (the true sense); more com-mon in the sense of reward or help; it also meant recovery from illness or healing. **−** O. F. *warison*, *garison*, surety, safety, provision, healing. **−** O. F. *warir*, to pro-tect, heal. **−** O. H. G. *warjan*, *werjan*, to protect; see **Weir**.

Warlock, a wizard. (E.) M. E. *war-loghe*, a wicked one, the devil; *warlawe*, a deceiver. **−** A. S. *wǣrloga*, a traitor, per-fidious man, liar, truce-breaker; (hence, a witch, wizard). Lit. ' liar against the truth.' **−** A. S. *wǣr*, truth (cognate with L. *uērum*, truth) ; *loga*, a liar, from *log-* (Teut. **lug-*), weak grade of *lēogan*, to lie. See **Very** and **Lie** (2).

Warm. (E.) A. S. *wearm*. **+** Du. G. *warm*, Icel. *varmr*, Dan. Swed. *varm*. Teut. type **warmoz*. Cf. Lith. *wirti*, to cook, Russ. *varite*, to boil, scorch. Brugm. i. § 680. (Doubtful; some com-pare *warm* with L. *formus*, Gk. θερμός, warm, Skt. *gharma-s*, heat; with labio-velar *gh*.)

Warn. (E.) A. S. *wearnian*, *ware-nian*, (1) to take heed, which is the usual sense, (2) to warn. Cf. the sb. *wearn*, refusal, denial, orig. an obstacle ; whence *wiernan*, to refuse. Prob. allied to **Weir**. **+** Icel. *varna*, to warn off, from *vörn*, a defence ; Swed. *varna*, G. *warnen*. **Der.** *fore-warn*, *pre-warn*.

Warp, sb. (E.) M. E. *warp*. A. S. *wearp*, a warp, in weaving. **−** A. S. *wearp*, for **warp*, 2nd grade of *weorpan* (strong verb), to cast, throw, hence, to throw the shuttle. **+** Icel. *varp*, a throwing, from *varp*, 2nd grade of *verpa*, to throw ; Swed. *varp*, a warp ; O. H. G. *warf* (G. *werft*), from *werfen*, to throw ; cf. Goth. *wairpan*, to throw. From Teut. str. vb. **werpan-* (pt. t. **warp*, pp. **wurpanoz*). Allied to Russ. *vergate*, to throw. **Der.** *warp*, vb., from Icel. *varpa*, to throw, cast (hence, to twist out of shape) ; this mod. E. *warp* is a secondary (weak) verb, not the same as A. S. *weorpan*. So also Swed. *varpa*, Dan. *varpe*, to warp a ship, from Swed. *varp*, the draught of a net.

Warrant, sb. (F.−O. H. G.) M. E. *warant*. **−** O. F. *warant*, *guarant*, later *garant*, ' a warrant ;' Cot. The form *war-ant* is that of the pres. pt., with the sense ' warranting.' **−** O. H. G. *werĕnt-*, stem of pres. pt. of *werĕn* (G. *gewähren*), to cer-tify, to warrant. Of obscure origin. **Der.** *warrant*, vb. ; *warrant-y*, O. F. *warantie*, fem. sb. formed from *warantir*, to war-rant ; see **Guarantee**.

Warren, sb. (F. − O. H. G.) M. E. *wareine*. **−** O. F. *warenne*, *varenne*, later *garenne*, ' a warren of conies,' Cot. ; Low L. *warenna*, a preserve for hares, &c. **−** O. H. G. *warjan*, to protect, preserve ; see **Warison**.

Warrior. (F.−O. H. G.) M. E. *wer-riour*. **−** A. F. *werreiur*, old spelling of A. F. *guerreiur*, a warrior. **−** A. F. *wer-reier*, *guerreier*, to make war (whence E. *warray* in Spenser, F. Q. i. 5. 48, ii. 10. 21). **−** O. F. *werre*, *guerre*, war. **−** O. H. G. *werra*, strife ; see **War**.

Wart. (E.) M. E. *werte*, A. S. *wearte*, a wart. **+** Du. *wrat*, Icel. *varta*, Dan. *vorte*, Swed. *vårta*, G. *warze*. Perhaps ' growth ' as from a root ; and allied to **Wort** (1). Some connect it with L. *uerrūca*, wart ; A. S. *wearr*, a callosity.

Wary, Ware, cautious. (E.) M. E. *war* ; *war-y* is a rather late form, with added *-y* (as in *murk-y*). A. S. *wær*, cau-

tious.**+**Icel. *varr*, Dan. Swed. *var*, Goth.
wars. Cf. G. *gewahr*, aware. Allied to
Gk. ὁρ-άω, I perceive, L. *uer-ēri*, to regard, dread. (√WER.) **Der.** *wari-ness*.

Was, pt. t. of the verb *to be*. (E.) M. E.
was, pl. *weren*. A.S. *wæs*, I was, he was;
wêre, thou wast; pl. *wêron*, were; subjunctive sing. *wêre*, pl. *wâren*. Mod. E.
substitutes *wast* for the A. S. *wêre* in the
indicative, and *wert* for the same in the
subjunctive; both are late forms. β. The
infin. is A. S. *wesan*, to be; cognate with
Du. *wezen*, O. Icel. *vesa*, Dan. *være*, Swed.
vara, Goth. *wisan*, to be, dwell, remain;
Skt. *vas*, to dwell. (√WES, to dwell.)
γ. The form *was* answers to O. Icel. *vas*, Du.
was, Dan. Swed. *var*, G. *war*, Goth. *was*;
and the pl. *were* to Icel. *vârum*, *vârut*,
vâru, Du. G. *waren*, Swed. *voro*, Goth.
wesum, wesuth, wesun.

Wash, vb. (E.) M. E. *waschen*, pt. t.
wessh. A. S. *wæscan*, *waxan*, pt. t. *wôx*,
pp. *wæscen*.**+**Du. *wasschen*, Icel. Swed.
vaska, Dan. *vaske*, G. *waschen* (pt. t. *wusch*).
Allied to **Water.** Brugm. i. § 942.

Wasp. (E.) Prov. E. *waps*, *wops*; A.S.
wæps, *wæfs*. **+** G. *wespe*, L. *uespa*; Lith.
wapsà, a gad-fly; Russ. *osa*, a wasp.
Allied to **Weave.** Brugm. i. § 918.

Wassail. (E.) M. E. *wasseyl*, *wassayl*,
orig. a drinking of a health, from the
Northern E. *wes heil*, answering to A.S.
wes hâl, lit. 'be whole,' a form of wishing
good health. Here *wes* is imperative sing.
of *wesan*, to be; and *heil* is cognate with
mod. E. *whole*. The dialectal *heil* is the
Scand. form; Icel. *heill*, whole. See
Hail (2) and **Whole.**

Waste, desert, unused. (F.–O.H.G.
–L.) M. E. *wast*. **–** O. F. *wast*, in the
phrase *faire wast*, to lay waste (Roquefort); whence mod. F. *gâter* (<*gaster*
<*waster*).–M. H. G. *waste*, sb., a waste,
wasten, to lay waste. Borrowed from L.
uastus, waste, desolate, also vast, *uastâre*,
to lay waste. β. We also find A.S. *wêste*,
O. H. G. *wuosti*, waste; these forms are
not *borrowed* from Latin, but are *cognate*.
So also O. Irish *fâs*, empty. Idg. types
*wâstos, *wâstios. Brugm. i. § 317.

Watch, sb. (E.) M. E. *wacche*; A.S.
wæcce, a watch, guard. **–** A.S. *wacan*, to
wake; see **Wake** (1). **Der.** *watch*, vb.,
M. E. *wacchen*, A.S. *wæccan*, weak verb.

Water, sb. (E.) A.S. *wæter*. **+** Du.
water, G. *wasser*. Allied to Icel. *vatn*,
Dan. *vand*, Swed. *vatten*, Goth. *wato*;

Russ. *voda*, Gk. ὕδωρ, L. *unda*, Lith.
wandù, Skt. *udan-*, water. Brugm. i. § 594.
Der. *water*, vb.; *otter*.

Wattle, a flexible rod, hurdle; fleshy
part under the throat of a cock or turkey.
(E.) The orig. sense was something twined
or woven together; hence a hurdle, woven
stuff, a fleshy flap on a cock's neck. M.E.
watel, a bag; A.S. *watel*, *watul*, a hurdle.
Cf. **Weed** (2).

Wave (1), to fluctuate. (E.) M. E.
wauen. A. S. *wafian*, to wave with the
hand; also, wonder at or waver in mind;
cf. the adj. *wæfre*, wavering, restless. Cf.
Icel. *vafra*, *vafla*, to waver; *vafl*, hesitation; Bavar. *wabern*, to sway to and fro
(Schmeller). **Der.** *wave*, sb., from the
verb above (not the same word as M. E.
wawe, a wave, which is allied to *wag*).

waver, vb. (E.) M. E. *waueren*
(*waveren*), to wander about.–A.S. *wæfre*,
restless, wandering.**+**Icel. *vafra*, to waver;
cf. O. H. G. *wabar-*, adj., wavering; see
above.

Wax (1), to grow. (E.) M. E. *waxen*,
pt. t. *wox*, *wex*, pp. *woxen*, *waxen*. A.S.
weaxan, pt. t. *wēox*, pp. *geweaxen*. **+** Du.
wassen, Icel. *vaxa*, Dan. *voxe*, Swed. *växa*,
G. *wachsen*, Goth. *wahsjan*, pt. t. *wōhs*.
Further allied to Gk. αὐξάνειν, Skt. *vaksh*,
to wax, grow. Brugm. ii. § 657.

Wax (2), a substance made by bees.
(E.) M. E. *wax*; A.S. *weax*. **+** Du. *was*,
Icel. Swed. *vax*, Dan. *vox*, G. *wachs*, Russ.
vosk', Lith. *waszkas*.

Way. (E.) M. E. *wey*, *way*. A.S. *weg*.
+Du. *weg*, Icel. *vegr*, Dan. *vei*, Swed. *väg*,
G. *weg*, Goth. *wigs*. Also Lith. *weža*, the
track of a cart; L. *uia*; Skt. *vaha-*, a
way, from *vah*, to carry. See **Weigh.**
(√WEGH.) **Der.** *al-way*, *al-ways*, see **All**;
way-faring, i. e. faring on the way, A. S.
weg-farende, where *farende* is the pres. pt.
of *faran*, to travel; *way-lay*, *way-worn*.

wayward, perverse. (E.) M. E. *wei-
ward*, headless form of M.E. *aweiward*,
adv., in a direction away from a thing;
from M. E. *awei*, away, and *-ward*, suffix.
See **Away.**

We, pl. of the 1st pers. pronoun. (E.)
M.E. *we*. A.S. *wē*.**+**Du. *wij*; Icel. *vēr*;
Dan. Swed. *vi*; G. *wir*; Goth. *weis*; Skt.
vay-am.

Weak. (E.) [The verbal form has
ousted the M. E. *wook*, A.S. *wâc*, adj.,
weak.] A back-formation from the verb
signifying to weaken; from M. E. *wēken*

(Ch.), to make weak, A. S. *wācan*; the M. E *k* being due to association with the adj. *wook*. This verb is for **wāc-ian*, from A. S. *wāc*, weak. **+** Icel. *veikr*, adj., weak, Swed. *vek*, Dan. *veg*, pliant, Du. *week*, G. *weich*, O. H. G. *weih*. All from Teut. **waik*, 2nd grade of **wīkan-*, as in A. S. and O. Sax. *wīcan*, G. *weichen*, to yield.

Weal (1), sb. (E.) M. E. *wele*; A. S. *wela*, weal, prosperity; allied to A. S. *wel*, adv., well; see **Well** (1). **+** Dan. *vel*, Swed. *väl*, G. *wohl*, welfare.

Weal (2); see **Wale**.

Weald, a wooded region, an open country. (E.) The M. E. *wald* became *wold*; but Layamon has a by-form *wæld*; l. 21339. Caxton speaks of ' the *weeld*' of Kent, which is apparently connected with this M. E. *wæld*, but seems also to have been more or less confused with **Wild**. Shakespeare and Lyly speak of ' the *wilde*' of Kent; see **Wild** and **Wold**.

Wealth, riches. (E.) M. E. *welthe*; not in A. S. Extended from M. E. *wele*, weal; see **Weal** (1).**+**Du. *weelde*, luxury; O. H. G. *welida*, riches.

Wean, to accustom a child to bread and meat, to reconcile to a new custom. (E.) We also use the word, less properly, in the sense, ' to disaccustom,' because a child that is *weaned to* meat is also being *weaned from* the breast. M. E. *wenen*; A. S. *wenian*, to accustom; *āwenian*, to wean away or disaccustom. From an adj. base **wano-*, accustomed, found in the cognate Icel. *vanr* (Swed. *van*), accustomed (cf. *vani*, custom); from **wan*, 2nd grade of Teut. **wenan-*, to crave; see **Ween**. The weak grade appears in A. S. *gewuna*, accustomed, *wunian*, to dwell.**+**Du. *wennen*, to accustom, *afwennen*, to wean from; Icel. *venja*, Dan. *vænne*, Swed. *vänja*, G. *gewöhnen*, to accustom; Dan. *vænne fra*, Swed. *vänja af*, G. *entwöhnen*, to wean from.

Weapon. (E.) M. E. *wepen*. A. S. *wǣpen*, a weapon. **+** Du. *wapen*, Icel. *vāpn*, Dan. *vaaben*, Swed. *vapen*, G. *waffe*; Goth. *wēpna*, neut. pl., weapons. Cf. A. S. *wǣpnmann*, *wǣpmann*, a full-grown man, a male.

Wear (1), to wear clothes, to consume by use. (E.) M. E. *weren*, pt. t. *wered*. A. S. *werian* (pt. t. *werode*). **+** Icel. *verja*, O. H. G. *werian*, to wear; Goth. *wasjan*, to clothe. Allied to **Vest**. (√WES, to clothe.) See **Vest**. ¶ All the senses of

wear come from the sense of carrying clothes on the body; hence it means to consume or use up by wear, to destroy, efface. The pt. t. *wore* is modern. Not allied to A. S. *werian*, to defend, which is a different word.

Wear (2) a weir; see **Weir**.

Wear (3), to veer a ship; the same as **Veer**, q. v.

Weary, exhausted, tired. (E.) M. E. *weri*. A. S. *wērig*, tired; cf. A. S. *wōrian*, to tramp about, wander, travel.—A. S. *wōr-*, a moor, swampy place (tedious to tramp over) in the comp. *wōr-hana*, moorcock; O. E. Texts, p. 465.**+**O. Sax. *wōrig*, weary. (The change from *ō* to *ē* is regular.) ¶ Not allied to *wear* (1).

Weasand, Wesand, the wind-pipe. (E.) A. S. *wāsend*, the gullet; but the mod. E. *wesand* answers rather to a by-form **wāsend*. **+** O. Fries. *wāsende*, wind-pipe; Bavar. *waisel*, the gullet.

Weasel. (E.) M. E. *wesel*, *wesele*. A. S. *wesle*, *wesulæ*, a weasel.**+**Du. *wezel*, Icel. *-vīsla*, Dan. *væsel*, Swed. *vesla*, G. *wiesel*.

Weather. (E.) M. E. *weder*; A. S. *weder*. (The *-ther* for *-der* seems to have arisen in prov. (Northern) E.; cf. *father*.) **+**Du. *weder*, Icel. *veðr*, Dan. *veir*; Swed. *väder*, wind, weather; G. *wetter*. Allied to G. *gewitter*, a storm, Icel. *land-viðri*, a land-wind; Russ. *vietr'*, wind, breeze, Lith. *wĕtra*, storm. Allied to **Wind** (1); cf. Goth. *waian*, to blow, O. Irish *feth*, air.

weather-beaten, weather-bitten. (E.) Both forms seem to be correct. The former means ' beaten by the weather,' from *beat*. The latter means ' bitten by the weather,' from *bite*, and occurs in Wint. Tale, v. 2. 60; derived from Norw. *vederbiten*, Swed. *väder-biten*, lit. bitten by the weather.

Weave. (E.) M. E. *weuen* (*weven*). A. S. *wefan*, pt. t. *wæf*, pp. *wefen*. **+** Du. *weven*, Icel. *vefa*, Dan. *væve*, Swed. *vefva*, G. *weben*. Also Gk. ὑφ-αίνειν, to weave. Teut. type **weban-*. (√WEBH.) Brugm. i. § 562.

web. (E.) A. S. *webb*, a web; Teut. type **wabjom*, n.; from **wab*, 2nd grade of **weban-* (above).**+**Du. *web*, Icel. *vefr*, Dan. *væv*, Swed. *väf*, G. *gewebe*.

Wed, vb. (E.) M. E. *wedden*. A. S. *weddian*, lit. to pledge, engage; hence to betroth. — A. S. *wedd*, a pledge; Teut. type **wadjom*, n. **+** M. Du. *wedde*, Icel.

veð, Swed. *vad*, G. *wette*, Goth. *wadi*, a pledge, wager. Allied to L. *uas* (gen. *uad-is*), a pledge, Gk. ἄ-εθλον (= ἄ-Ϝεθ-λον), the prize of a contest; Lith. *wadoti*, to redeem a pledge. (√WEDH.)

Wedge. (E.) M. E. *wegge*. A. S. *wecg*. **+** Du. *wig*, Icel. *veggr*, Dan. *vægge*, Swed. *vigg*, O. H. G. *wecki*, a wedge; G. *weck*, *wecke*, a kind of wedge-shaped loaf; cf. prov. E. *wig*, a kind of cake. Also Lith. *wágis*, a wedge, wooden peg. Teut. type *wagjoz*, m. Lit. 'a mover,' from its effect in splitting trees; allied to **Wag**. (√WEGH.)

Wedlock, marriage. (E.) A. S. *wedlác*, lit. a pledge, pledging. – A. S. *wed*, *wedd*, a pledge; or *lác*, a sport, also, a gift, often a mere suffix. See **Wed**.

Wednesday. (E.) M. E. *wednesday*. A. S. *wódnesdæg*, Woden's day; O. Fries. *wernisdei* (for *wédnisdei*), where *é* is the mutation of *ó*; N. Fries. *weensdi*, Outzen, p. 38. **+** Du. *woensdag*, Icel. *óðinsdagr*, Swed. Dan. *onsdag*; all meaning 'Woden's (or Odin's) day.' β. The name *Wóden* signifies 'furious,' from A. S. *wód*, mad, furious (= Icel. *óðr*, Goth. *wods*); or else 'filled with divine frenzy.' See **Wood** (2). ¶ A translation of L. *diēs Mercurii*; *Woden* was identified with L. *Mercurius*. Brugm. i. § 190.

Wee, tiny. (E.) M. E. *we*, *wei*, only as sb., in the phrase 'a litel *we*' = a little bit, a short time. I have little hesitation in assuming the O. Northern E. *we*, or *wey* (Barbour), or *wei* (Cursor Mundi), a way, space, to be the same as M. E. *wei*, a way, also a distance, mod. E. **Way**, q. v. Cf. North. E. *way-bit*, also *wee-bit*, a small space. ¶ Certainly not allied to G. *wenig*, little.

Weed (1), a noxious plant. (E.) M. E. *weed*; A. S. *wéod*, *wiod*, a weed. **+** O. Saxon *wiod*; whence Du. *wieden*, vb., to weed. Root unknown.

Weed (2), a garment. (E.) M. E. *wede*. A. S. *wæde*, neuter, *wæd*, fem., a garment. **+** O. Fries. *wéde*, O. Sax. *wádi*; Icel. *vāð*, *vóð*, a piece of stuff, cloth; O. H. G. *wāt*, *wōt*, clothing, armour. Lit. 'something woven;' from the Idg. root WE, Skt. *vā*, to weave.

Week. (E.) M. E. *weke*, *wike*; A. S. *wice*, *wicu*, a week. (There was a later A. S. *wucu*, a week, which became M. E. *wouke*, a week, and is obsolete.) **+** Du. *week*, Iccl. *vika*, Swed. *vecka*, O. H. G.

wecha, *wehha* (mod. G. *woche*). We also once find Goth. *wiko* in the sense of order or succession (Luke i. 8), answering to L. *ordine* (not to *uicis*) in the Vulgate version. The orig. sense seems to have been 'succession,' series; cf. Icel. *víkja*, to turn, return; from *wik-*, weak grade of *wīkan-*, to give way; see **Weak**. And cf. G. *wechsel*, a change.

Ween, to suppose, think. (E.) M. E. *wenen*, A. S. *wénan*, to imagine. – A. S. *wén*, sb., expectation; orig. 'a striving after.' Teut. type *wâniz*, f. (Sievers, § 269); from *wân*, 3rd grade of a supposed Teut. str. vb. *wenan-*, to crave, desire. Cf. A. S. *wine*, friend, Skt. *van*, to crave; L. *uenus*, desire. **+** Du. *wanen*, Icel. *vāna*, G. *wähnen*, Goth. *wénjan*, to expect, fancy; from Du. *waan*, Icel. *vān*, G. *wahn*, Goth. *wéns*, expectation, conjecture, orig. 'a wish.' See **Wish**.

Weep. (E.) M. E. *wepen*, pt. t. *weep*, *wep*. A. S. *wépan*, pt. t. *wéop*, to cry aloud, raise an outcry; cf. A. S. *wóp*, a clamour, outcry (note the change from *ó* to *é*). **+** O. Sax. *wôpian*, to cry out, *wôp*, outcry; Icel. *æpa*, to shout, *óp*, outcry; Goth. *wôpjan*, wk. vb., to cry out. ¶ Not allied to *whoop*.

Weet, to know. (E.) Another spelling of **Wit** (1); in Spenser, F. Q., i. 3. 6; &c.

Weevil, a small beetle. (E.) M. E. *weuel*, *wiuel* (*wevel*, *wivel*); A. S. *wifel*, *wibil*.**+**Icel. *-yfill*, M. Du. *wevel*, O. H. G. *wibil*; cf. E. Fries. *wefer*, (1) a weaver, (2) a beetle. A dimin. form; cf. A. S. *wibba*, a beetle. Apparently allied to **Weave**. Cf. Lith. *wábalas*, a chafer, winged insect.

Weft. (E.) A. S. *weft*, *wefta*, the threads woven across the warp; from *wefan*, to weave. **+** Icel. *veftr*. See **Weave**.

Weigh. (E.) M. E. *weghen*. A. S. *wegan*, pt. t. *wæg*, to carry, bear; also, to move; also to raise, lift (cf. to *weigh* anchor); to weigh. **+** Du. *wegen*; Icel. *vega*, to move, lift; Dan. *veie*, Swed. *väga*; G. *bewegen*, to move, *wiegen*, to rock; and cf. *wägen*, to weigh. Allied to L. *uehere*, Skt. *vah*, to carry. (√WEGH.)

weight. (E.) M. E. *weght*, *wight*. A. S. *wiht*, *gewiht*, weight; for *wehti-*< *weg-ti-*; from *wegan* (above).**+**Du. *gewigt*, Icel. *vætt*, Dan. *vægt*, Swed. *vigt*, G. *gewicht*.

Weir, Wear, a dam. (E.) M. E. *wer*; A. S. *wer*; allied to *werian*, to defend, protect, also dam up. **+** Low G. *ware*, a weir; M. Du. *weer*, a rampart; Icel. *vörr*, a fenced-in landing-place, *verja*, to defend; G. *wehr*, a defence, *mühlwehr*, a milldam; Goth. *warjan*, to defend. Allied to Skt. *vr*, to cover, *vāraya*, to stop, hinder, keep off.

Weird, fate, destiny. (E.) Properly a sb.; but used as adj. M. E. *wyrde, wirde*. A. S. *wyrd*, fate; Teut. type **wurd-iz*, f.; from **wurd* (for **wurð<*wurþ*, by Verner's law), weak grade of Teut. **werthan-*, to become, take place, happen; see **Worth** (1). **+** O. Sax. *wurð*, Icel. *urðr*, fate.

Welcome. (Scand.) For *well come*. **−** Icel. *velkominn*, welcome, lit. well come. **−** Icel. *vel*, well; *kominn*, pp. of *koma*, to come. So also Dan. *velkommen*, Swed. *välkommen*, welcome. Hence A. F. *welcomer*, to welcome (Godefroy). ¶ Distinct from A. S. *wilcuma*, one who comes at another's pleasure; where *cuma* is 'a comer,' from *cuman*, to come.

Weld (1), to beat metal together. (Swed.) Late M. E. *well* (G. Douglas). The final *d* is modern; the word is Swedish, from the iron-works there. **−** Swed. *välla*, orig. to well, whence *välla up*, to well up, *välle ihop*, to weld (iron); cf. Dan. *vælde*, to well up (with excrescent *d*, as in English). Cognate with E. *well*, vb.; from **Well** (2).

Weld (2), dyer's weed. (E.) M. E. *welde, wolde*; Lowl. Sc. *wald*. **+** Du. *wouw*; Low G. *wolde* (Lübben); G. *wau* (from Du.). Teut. base **wald-*, as shewn by Span. *gualdo*, F. *gaude*, weld. Prob. 'belonging to the wood;' cf. A. S. *weald*, a wood; see **Wold.** ¶ Quite distinct from *woad*.

Welfare. (E.) M. E. *welfare*. **−** M. E. *wel*, well; *fare* = A. S. *faru*, a faring, lit. a journey, from A. S. *faran*, to fare; see **Fare.**

Welkin, sky, clouds. (E.) M. E. *welkne, welkene*; also *wolkne, wolkene*, A. S. *wolcnu*, clouds, pl. of *wolcen*, a cloud. **+** O. Sax. *wolkan*, Du. *wolk*, Low G. *wulke*; G. *wolke*, O. H. G. *wolka*, f., *wolcan*, n., a cloud. All from the base **wulk-*, weak grade of **walkan-*, to roll (see **Walk**); or else allied to O. H. G. *welc*, moist.

Well (1), excellently. (E.) M. E. *wel*;

A. S. *wel*, orig. 'agreeably to a wish;' allied to *will*, sb. and vb. **+** Du. *wel*, Icel. *vel*, Dan. *vel*, Swed. *väl*, Goth. *waila*; G. *wohl*, O. H. G. *wela, wola*. Cf. W. *gwell*, better; also Skt. *vara-*, better, *vara-*, a wish; *prati varam*, according to a wish. See **Will** (1) and **Weal.**

Well (2), a spring, fount, (E.) M. E. *welle*; A. S. *wylla, wella*, a spring; with two other by-forms. Teut. type **walljon-*, m.; cf. A. S. *weallan* (pt. t. *wēoll*), to well up, boil; [but the mod. E. *well*, vb., is derived from the sb.]. **+** Icel. *vell*, ebullition, from *vella*, to boil (pt. t. *vall*); Du. *wel*, a spring; Dan. *væld*; G. *welle*, a wave, surge; cf. *wallen*, to boil. Further allied to Skt. *val*, to move to and fro, Russ. *val'*, a wave, *valiate*, to roll. See **Walk, Helix.** (√WEL.) Der. *well*, vb., as above.

Wellaway, an exclamation of sorrow. (E.) M. E. *weilawey*; also *wa la wa*. It stands for *wei la wei* or *wa la wa*. A.S. *wā lā wā*, lit. wo! lo! wo! **−** A. S. *wā*, wo; *lā*, lo; *wā*, wo; cf. Icel. *vei*, wo. ¶ Early misunderstood, and turned into *wellaway*, and even into *welladay*, Merry Wives, iii. 3. 106. See **Wo.**

Welsh, pertaining to Wales. (E.) M.E. *walsh*, foreign. A.S. *wælisc, welisc, wylisc*, Celtic. Formed, with suffix *-isc* (E. *-ish*) and vowel-change, from A. S. *wealh*, a Celt; whence *Wealas*, pl., mod. E. *Wales*. **+** G. *wälsch*, Italian. See **Walnut.**

Welt. (E.) The old sense seems to be border, hem, fringe. M. E. *walt, welte*; cf. Lowl. Sc. *waut*, a welt, prov. E. *welt*, to turn down the upper leather of a shoe. Perhaps from A. S. *wyltan, wæltan*, to roll; cf. Icel. *velta*, to roll over; see **Welter.+**W. *gwald*, a hem, welt, *gwaltes*, the welt of a shoe; *gwaldu*, to welt, hem.

Welter, to wallow, roll about. (E.) Formerly also *walter*. *Walter, welter*, are frequentatives from M. E. *walten*, to roll over, tumble, turn over. **−** A. S. *wæltan* to roll (cf. *gewælten*, strong pp., Matt. xvii. 14, Lind.). Cf. Icel. *velta* (pt. t. *valt*), to roll, Dan. *vælte*, to overturn; Swed. *vältra*, to welter, frequent. of *välta*, to roll; G. *wälzen*, to roll, welter, from *walzen*, to roll. Cf. Goth. *us-waltjan*, to subvert; L. *uoluere*, to roll. (√WEL.)

Wen, a tumour. (E.) A.S. *wenn*.**+** Du. *wen*; Low G. *ween*; Dan. dial. *van*. A. S. *wenn<*Teut. type **wanjoz*, m. Prob. from *wann*, 2nd grade of A.S. *winnan*, to toil, to win, to suffer from illness (whence E. *win*). See **Win, Wound**.

Wench. (E.) M. E. *wenche*, earlier form *wenchel*, a child (male or female).— A. S. *wenclo, winclo*, sb. pl., children (of either sex). Allied to A. S. *wancol*, tottery (hence weak, infantine). From the base **wank*, seen in G. *wanken*, to totter, M. H. G. *wenken*, to render unsteady. Allied to **Wink**.

Wend, to go. (E.) Little used except in the pt. t. *went* (used as pt. t. of *to go*). M. E. *wenden*; A. S. *wendan*, to turn, also to turn oneself, proceed, go. The pt. t. *wende* became *wente*, and finally *went*. Causal of A. S. *windan*, to wind; see **Wind** (2). **+** Du. *wenden*, Icel. *venda*, Dan. *vende*, Swed. *vända*, Goth. *wandjan*, G. *wenden*, to turn; all causal forms.

went. (E.) See above.

Were, pl. of **Was**, q. v.

Werwolf, a man-wolf. (E.) A.S. *werewulf*, a werwolf, the devil. — A.S. *wer*, a man; *wulf*, a wolf. **+** G. *währwolf*, M. H. G. *werwolf*, a man-wolf; from M. H. G. *wer*, a man, and *wolf*. (Hence O. F. *garoul*, F. *garou*, now *loupgarou*, i.e. wolf-werwolf.) See **Virile**. ¶ It was supposed that fierce men could turn into wolves; cf. Gk. λυκάνθρωπος, i. e. wolf-man.

West. (E.) A. S. *west*, adv., westward; *west-dǣl*, west part or quarter.**+**Du. *west*, Icel. *vestr*, Dan. Swed. *vest*, G. *west*. Perhaps allied to **Vesper**.

Wet, moist. (E.) M. E. *wet, weet*; A. S. *wǣt*, wet. **+** Icel. *vātr*, Dan. *vaad*, Swed. *vȧt*, wet. Teut. type **wǣtoz*. Allied (by gradation) to **Water**. Der. *wet*, vb., A. S. *wǣtan*.

Wether, a castrated ram. (E.) A.S. *weðr*.**+**O. Sax. *wethar, withar*, Icel. *veðr*, Dan. *væder*, Swed. *vädur*, G. *widder*, Goth. *withrus*, a lamb. Lit. 'a yearling;' allied to **Veal**. Brugm. i. § 118.

Wey, a heavy weight; from two to three cwt. (E.) M. E. *wege*. A. S. *wǣge, wǣg*, a weight.— A.S. *wǣg-*, 3rd grade of *wegan*, to weigh.**+**Icel. *vāg*, O. H. G. *wāga*. See **Weigh**.

WH.

Wh. This is distinct from *w*. The mod. E. *wh* answers to A. S. *hw*, Icel. *hv*, L. *qu*, Gk. π, τ, κ, Idg. *kw*.

Whack, to beat; see **Thwack**. But

cf. E. Fries. and Westphal. *wackeln*, to beat, to cudgel.

Whale. (E.) M.E. *whal, qual*. A. S. *hwæl*.**+**Du. *walvisch* (whale-fish), G. *walfisch*, Icel. *hvalr*, Dan. Swed. *hval*. It also meant a porpoise, grampus, &c. Cf. Gk. πέλωρ, a monster. **Der.** *wal-rus*.

Whap, to beat, flutter. (E.) Also *whop, wap, wop*. M. E. *quappen*, to palpitate, throb. E. Fries. *kwabben, kwappen*, to strike violently. From a base **kwap*, to throb; see **Quaver**. Cf. also W. *chwap*, a sudden stroke, *chwapio*, to strike, slap.

Wharf (1), a place for landing goods. (E.) A.S. *hwerf*, a dam or bank to keep out water (Thorpe, Diplomatarium, pp. 341,361); *mere-hwearf*, sea-shore (Grein). — Teut. **hwarb*, A. S. *hwearf*, 2nd grade of *hweorfan*, to turn, turn about. β. This difficult word, with a great range of senses, meant a turning, reversion, turning-place, space, dam, shore, dockyard, as proved by the cognate words, viz. Du. *werf*, Icel. *hvarf*, Dan. *værft*, Swed. *varf*, M. Swed. *hwarf*, &c. The A. S. *hweorfan* answers to Goth. *hwairban*, to turn oneself about, walk, and to Icel. *hverfa*, to turn. (Base HWERB.) ¶ *Not* allied to G. *werfen*, to throw; but rather to Gk. καρπός, the wrist. **Der.** *wharf-inger*, for *wharfager*; with inserted *n* as in *messenger, passenger*.

wharf (2), bank of a river. (E.) In Shak. Hamlet, i. 5. 33. Cf. A. S. *mere-hwearf*, sea-shore (Grein); it is the same word as **Wharf** (1).

What. (E.) A.S. *hwæt*, neut. of *hwā*; see **Who**.

Wheal (1), a pimple. (E.) Distinct from *weal, wale*, a mark of a blow. Perhaps from A. S. *hwele*, a wheal (Somner); A. S. *hwelian*, to form pus; *ge-hweled*, inflamed. Cf. also W. *chwiler*, a maggot, wheal, pimple.

Wheal (2), a mine. (C.) A Cornish word.—Corn. *hwēl*, a work, a mine. Cf. W. *chwel, chwyl*, a course, a turn.

Wheat. (E.) M. E. *whete*. A.S. *hwǣte*, wheat; Teut. type **hwaitjo-*, m.; from **hwait*, 2nd grade of **hweit-*; named from the whiteness of the meal; see **White**. **+** Du. *weite, weit*, Icel. *hveiti*, Dan. *hvede*, Swed. *hvete*, Goth. *hwaiteis*, G. *weizen*. **Der.** *wheat-en*, adj., A. S. *hwǣten*.

Wheedle. (E.?) Spelt *wheadle* in Blount, ed. 1674; who connects it (quite unsatisfactorily) with W. *chwedla*, to gossip, *chwedl*, a fable, tale. But perhaps from A. S. *wǣdlian*, to beg, orig. to be poor ; from *wǣdl*, poverty.

Wheel. (E.) A. S. *hwēol*, shorter form of *hweowol*, *hweogul*, a wheel ; also spelt *hweohl*.+Icel. *hjōl*, Dan. *hiul*, Swed. *hjul*, O. Swed. *hiughl* (Ihre). Teut. type *hweg-wlōm, n., for *hwehwlōm, Idg. **qeqló-*, as in Skt. *chakrá-*, a wheel, Gk. κύκλος, a wheel. Idg. **qe-qlo-* is a reduplicated form, from √QEL, to drive ; whence Gk. πόλος, an axis, Russ. *koleso*, Icel. *hvel*, a wheel. See **Cycle** and **Pole** (2). Brugm. i. § 658.

Wheeze. (E.) A. S. *hwēsan* (pt. t. *hwēos*), to wheeze. Allied to A. S. *hwōs-ta*, prov. E. *hoast*, a cough, Du. *hoest*, G. *husten*. From Teut. **hwōs-*, Idg. *qās, as in Skt. *kās*, to cough ; from √QAS, as in Irish *cas-achdach*, W. *pas*, a cough ; cf. Lith. *kosti*, to cough. See **Pose** (3).

Whelk (1), a mollusc with a spiral shell. (E.) Ill spelt ; it should be *welk* or *wilk*. M. E. *wilk* ; A. S. *wiloc*, also *weoluc*, *weluc*.+Du. *wulk*, also spelt *welk*, *wilk*, *willok*, *wullok*. Prob. named from its convoluted shell ; cf. Gk. ἕλιξ (ϝέλ-ιξ), a volute ; see **Helix**. Der. *whelk'd*, i. e. convoluted, K. Lear, iv. 6. 71 ; spelt *wealk'd* in the first folio.

Whelk (2), a small pimple. (E.) M. E. *whelke*, Chaucer, C. T., A. 632. Dimin. of **Wheal** (1).

Whelm, to overturn, cover over by something that is turned over, to overwhelm, submerge. (Scand.) M.E.*whelmen*, to turn a hollow vessel upside down (Palsgrave), to turn over ; Lowl. Sc. *quhemle*, *whommle*, *whamle*, to turn upside down. Closely related to M. E. *wheluen* (*whelven*) and *ouerwheluen* (*overwhelven*), used in the same sense. β. The only difficulty is to explain the final *-m* ; this is due to the fact that *whelm*, vb., is really formed from a sb. *whelm*, standing for *hwelf-m*, the *f* being dropped because unpronounceable. This appears from M. Swed. *hwalma*, to cock hay, derived from the sb. *hwalm*, a hay-cock ; where *hwalm* is for *hwalfm, being derived from M.Swed.*hwalf*,an arch, vault ; cf. *hwälfwa*, to arch over (make into a rounded shape). Thus the suffix *-m* is substantival (as in *doo-m*, *bloo-m*, &c.), and the Teut. base is HWELB, to become convex (M. H. G. *welben*, pt. t. *walb*), the derivatives of which appear in A. S. *hwealf*, adj., convex, sb., a vault, Icel. *hválf*, *hólf*,

a vault, *hvālfa*, *hólfa*, to ' whelve ' or turn upside down, G. *wölben*, to arch over. γ. We thus trace the following forms, viz. base HWELB, to swell out, become convex, Icel. *hvelfa*, to vault, turn a round vessel upside down ; hence *whelm*, sb., a thing made convex, *whelm*, vb., to make convex, turn a round vessel over, capsize. Forby remarks that *whelm*, in the E. Anglian dialect, signifies ' to turn a tub or other vessel upside down, whether to cover anything with it or not.' From √QELP ; whence also Gk. κόλπος, bosom, a hollow. Der. *over-whelm*.

Whelp, a puppy. (E.) A. S. *hwelp*, sb. + Du. *welp*, Icel. *hvelpr*, Dan. *hvalp*, Swed. *valp*, M. H. G. *welf*. Root unknown.

When. (E.) M. E. *whan* ; A. S. *hwænne*, *hwonne*, when. + M. Du. *wan*, G. *wann*, Goth. *hwan* ; W. *pan*. Allied to Goth. *hwas*, A. S. *hwā*, who. Cf. L. *quan-do*, Gk. πό-τε, when.

whence. (E.) M. E. *whennes*, older form *whanene*.–A. S. *hwanon*, whence ; closely allied to **When** (above).

where. (E.) M. E. *wher* ; A.S. *hwǣr*, where ; allied to *hwā*, who.+Du. *waar*, Icel. *hvar*, Dan. *hvor*, Swed. *hvar*, G. *war* (in *war-um*), Goth. *hwar* ; Lith. *kur*.

Wherry, a shallow, light boat. (E.) Spelt *whirry* by Latimer. Perhaps allied to Whir ; cf. Sc. *whirry*, to whir, to hurry. Origin unknown.

Whet. (E.) M. E. *whetten*. A. S. *hwettan*, to sharpen (<*hwat-jan.)–A. S. *hwæt*, keen, bold, brave.+Du. *wetten*, Icel. *hvetja*, Swed. *vätja*, G. *wetzen*, to sharpen, encourage ; from O. Sax. *hvat*, Icel. *hvatr*, bold, O. H. G. *hwaz*, sharp. Der. *whetstone*, A. S. *hwetstān*.

Whether, which of two. (E.) See Matt. xxvii. 21. A. S. *hwæðer*, which of two ; formed with comparative suffix *-ðer* (Idg. *-tero-*) from the base of *who*.+ Icel. *hvārr*, Goth. *hwathar* ; cf. Lith. *ka-tras*, Gk. κότερος, πότερος, Skt. *katara-*.

Whey. (E.) M. E. *whey*. A. S. *hwǣg*, whey.+M. Du. *wey* ; Du. *hui*, *wei*. Cf. W. *chwig*, whey fermented with sour herbs.

Which. (E.) M. E. *which* ; *quhilk* (Barbour). A. S. *hwilc*, *hwelc*, which ; short for *hwi-līc*, lit. ' of what form.' – A. S. *hwi-*, allied to *hwā*, who ; *līc*, like ; see **Who** and **Like**. + O. Sax. *hwilik*, O. Fries. *hwelik*, Du. *welk*, Goth. *hwileiks*, *hwēleiks*, Icel. *hvīlīkr*, Dan. Swed. *hvilken*, G. *welcher*, O.H.G. *hwelih*. Cf. L. *quālis*, Gk. πηλίκος. Brugm. ii. § 88.

Whiff, sb., a puff. (E.) M. E. *weffe*, vapour. An imitative word, like *puff*, *fife*. +W. *chwiff*, a puff, *chwaff*, a gust; Dan. *vift*, a puff, gust. Cf. A.S. *hwiða*, Icel. *hvíða*, a breeze.

whiffle, to blow in gusts, veer as the wind. (E.) Frequentative of *whiff*, to puff. **Der.** *whiffl-er*, a piper, fifer, hence one who goes first in a procession.

Whig. (E.?) See Todd's Johnson and Nares. *Whig* is a shortened form of *whiggamor*, applied to certain Scotchmen who came from the west to buy corn at Leith; from the word *whiggam*, employed by these men in driving their horses. A march to Edinburgh made by Argyle (in 1648) was called 'the *whiggamor's* inroad;' and afterwards those who were opposed to the court came (in 1680) to be called *whigs*. (Burnet, Own Times, b. i.) But the term had previously been applied (in 1667) to the Scotch Covenanters (Lingard). The Glossary to Sir W. Scott's novels has: '*whigamore*, a great whig; *whigging*, jogging rudely, urging forward.' To *whig awa'* is to jog on briskly. Perhaps for *wig*; cf. E. Fries. *wiggen*, Norw. *vigga*, to rock; Icel. *vigg*, a horse; E. *wiggle* and *wag*.

While, a time. (E.) A.S. *hwīl*, sb., a pause, a time. +Icel. *hvíla*, a place of rest; Dan. *hvile*, rest; Swed. *hvila*, rest; G. *weile*, Goth. *hweila*, a time. Prob. allied to L. *qui-es*, rest. (√QEI.) Brugm. i. § 675. **Der.** *while*, adv.; *whiles*, M. E. *whiles*, adv. (with gen. suffix *-es*); whence *whils-t*, with added *t* (as in *amongs-t*, *amids-t*); also *whil-om*, formerly, from A.S. *hwīlum*, dat. pl. of *hwīl*, a time. Also *mean-while*, see **Mean** (3); also *whiling-time*, the waiting a little time before dinner (Spectator, no. 448), whence the phrase *to while away time*, probably with some thought of confusion with *wile*.

Whim, a freak. (Scand.) Skelton has *whim-wham*. – Icel. *hvima*, to wander with the eyes, as a silly person; Norw. *kvima*, to whisk about, trifle. Cf. Swed. dial. *hvimmerkantig*, giddy in the head; Norw. *kvim*, foolery (Ross). **Der.** *whimsey*, a whim, from the allied Norw. *kvimsa*, Swed. dial. *hvimsa*, Dan. *vimse*, to be giddy, skip or whisk about.

Whimper, to whine. (E.) The same

as Lowland Sc. *whimmer*, to whimper, frequentative of *whim*, another form of *whine*; see **Whine**. '[They] wil *whympe* and *whine*;' Latimer, Seven Sermons, ed. Arber, p. 77.+G. *wimmern*.

Whin, gorse. (C.) M. E. *whynne*, *quyn*. – W. *chwyn*, weeds; cf. Bret. *chouenna* (with guttural *ch*), to weed.

Whine, vb. (E.) A.S. *hwīnan*, to whine.+Icel. *hvína*, Swed. *hvina*, Dan. *hvine*, to whir, whiz, whine. [Cf. Icel. *kveina*, to wail, Goth. *kwainōn*, to mourn.] **Der.** *whimp-er*, q. v.

Whinyard, a kind of sword. (Scand.) Lit. *whine-yard*, where *yard* (probably) is a mere suffix (*-i-ard*). – Icel. *hvin-a*, to whiz, whistle through the air like a weapon; the same word as E. *whine*, but used in a different way. Cf. also E. *whinny*; and Lowl. Sc. *whing-er*, a whin-yard, from the verb *whinge*, an extension of *whine*.

Whip, to move quickly, to flog. (E.) M.E. *whippen*, to overlay a cord by rapidly binding the twine round it, *whippe*, a scourge. From the sense of rapid movement; M. E. *wippen*, to jump up and down suddenly, to jig.+Du. *wippen*, to skip, formerly to shake; Low G. *wippen*, to bob up and down; Dan. *vippe*, to see-saw, bob; Swed. *vippa*, to wag, jerk; G. *wippen*, to move up and down, see-saw, jerk. (I find no very early authority for the *h*.) Cf. L. *uibrāre*; see **Vibrate**. **Der.** *whip*, sb., M. Du. *wippe* (Hexham).

whipple-tree, a swing-bar for traces. (E.) The sense is 'piece of swinging-wood,' composed of *tree* (as in *axle-tree*) and the verb *whipple*, frequent. of *whip*, to move about quickly, to see-saw (above).

Whir, to buzz. (Scand.) An imitative word, like *whiz*. – Dan. *hvirre*, to whirl, twirl; Swed. dial. *hvirra*, to whirl. Allied to **Whirl**.

Whirl. (Scand.) M. E. *whirlen*; a contraction for **whirf-len*, frequent. of M. E. *wherfen*, to turn. – Icel. *hvirfla*, to whirl; frequent. of *hverfa* (pt. t. *hvarf*), to turn round; Dan. *hvirvle*, Swed. *hvirfla*, to whirl; M. Du. *wervelen*, to whirl; G. *wirbeln*, to whirl, to warble. (Base HWERB.) Allied to **Wharf**. Cf. Goth. *hwairban*, to go about; Gk. καρπός, the wrist. Brugm. i. § 675. **Der.** *whirl-wind*, from Icel. *hvirfilvindr*, Dan. *hvirvelvind*, Swed. *hvirfvelvind*, a whirlwind; also *whirl-pool*; *whirl-i-gig* (see **Gig**).

Whisk, to move or sweep quickly. (Scand.) The *h* is intrusive. It is properly *wisk*, orig. to wipe, brush, sweep, esp. with a quick motion, as when using a light brush; the *h* was due to confusion with *whiz, whir, whirl,* &c.— Dan. *viske,* to wipe, rub, sponge, from *visk,* a wisp, rubber; Swed. *viska,* to wipe, also to wag (or whisk) the tail, from *viska,* 'whisk (*sic*), a small broom,' Widegren; Icel. *visk,* a wisp of hay, something to wipe with, a rubber.+G. *wischen,* 'to wipe, wisk, rub,' Flügel; from the sb. *wisch,* 'whisk (*sic*), clout,' id. Cf. A.S. *weoxian* (for **wiscian*), to wipe. β. The sb. which thus appears as Icel. *visk,* Swed. *viska,* G. *wisch,* meant orig. 'a wisp.' Der. *whisker,* from the likeness to a small brush. 'Nestor *brush'd* her with his *whiskers*;' Dryden, Troilus, iv. 2. Also *whisk-y,* a light gig, easily *whisked* along.

Whisky, Whiskey, a spirit. (Gaelic.) Gaelic *uisge-beatha,* water of life, whisky; the latter element being dropped; see **Usquebaugh.**

Whisper, vb. (E.) M. E. *whisperen.* O. Northumb. *hwisprian,* to murmur, Luke xix. 7, John vii. 12.+M. Du. *wisperen, wispelen,* G. *wispeln.* Cf. also Icel. *hvīskra,* Swed. *hviska,* Dan. *hviske,* to whisper. (Imitative base HWIS.) Allied to **Whiz** and **Whistle.**

Whist, a game requiring silence. (E.) Orig. called *whisk,* from the sweeping up of the tricks (see **Whisk**); renamed as *whist,* from the use of the word *whist* to enjoin silence; cf. *hist* and *hush.* Chaucer has both *hush* and *whist* in the sense of 'silenced' or 'quiet'; tr. of Boethius, b. ii. met. 5, l. 1341.

Whistle, vb. (E.) A.S. *hwistlian,* to hiss; *hwistlere,* a whistler, piper. + Icel. *hvīsla,* to whisper; Dan. *hvisle,* to hiss, whistle; Swed. *hvissla,* to whistle. (Base HWIS.) See **Whisper.**

Whit, a thing, particle. (E.) The *h* is misplaced; *whit* is for *wiht,* the same as *wight,* a person, also a thing, bit, whit.— A.S. *wiht,* a wight, a thing, bit; see **Wight** (1). Der. *aught* = A.S. *āwiht,* one whit; whence *n-aught, n-ot.*

White. (E.) M. E. *whit.* A.S. *hwīt.* +Du. *wit,* Icel. *hvītr,* Dan. *hvid,* Swed. *hvit,* Goth. *hweits,* G. *weiss.* Allied to Skt. *çvēta-,* white, from *çvit,* to shine, to be white; also to Russ. *svietite,* to shine; Lith. *szwaitinti,* to illuminate. Brugm. i.

§ 319. (✔KWEI.) Der. *whit-ing,* a fish with delicate white flesh, also ground chalk; also *whit-ster,* a whitener, bleacher; *whittle* (2), *wheat,* **Whit-sunday,** q. v.

Whither. (E.) M. E. *whider.* A.S. *hwider, hwæder,* whither.+Goth. *hwadrē.* Cf. *hither, thither.* Allied to **Who.**

Whitlow, a painful swelling on the fingers. (Scand.) Corruption of *whick-flaw,* a whitlow (Halliwell); where *whick* is the Northern pronunciation of *quick,* i.e. the sensitive part of the finger round the nail; Icel. *kvika. Flaw* is the Swed. *flaga,* a flaw, crack, breach, flake. See **Quick** and **Flaw.** The sense is 'crack near the quick,' hence a painful sore, afterwards a painful swelling. It was corrupted first to *whitflaw* (Holland), or *whitflowe* (Palsgrave), and afterwards to *whitlow*; by confusion with *white* and *low* (4). '*Paronychia,* a *whitflaw*;' Wiseman, Surgery, b. i. c. 11.

Whit-sunday. (E.) Lit. *white Sunday,* as is perfectly certain from the A.S. name *hwīta sunnan-dæg,* Icel. *hvītasunnudagr,* Norwegian *kvitsunndag*; these are *facts,* though constantly denied by the lovers of paradoxical and far-fetched etymologies. The difficulty lies *only* in the reason for the name. 'The great festivals, Yule, Easter, and Pentecost, but esp. the two latter, were the great seasons for christening; in the Roman Catholic church especially Easter, whence in Roman usage the Sunday after Easter was called *Dominica in Albis*; but in the Northern churches, perhaps owing to the cold weather at Easter-time, Pentecost .. seems to have been esp. appointed for christening and for ordination; hence the following week was called the Holy Week, *Helga Vika*;' Icel. Dict. The case is parallel to that of *noon,* which at first meant 9th hour, or 3 P.M., but was afterwards *shifted.* So also in other cases. Cf. W. *sulgwyn,* Whitsunday; from *sul,* sun, *gwyn,* white. Der. *Whitsun-week,* short for *Whitsunday's week* (Icel. *hvīta-sunnudags-vika*); *Whitsun-tide,* short for *Whitsunday-tide*; cf. *Palmson* for *Palm-sunday, Lowson* for *Lowsunday.*

Whittle (1), to pare or cut with a knife. From the obsolete sb. *whittle,* a knife, the same as M. E. *þwitel,* a knife, lit. 'a cutter.'—A.S. *þwit-,* weak grade of *þwītan,* to cut. See **Thwite.**

Whittle (2), to sharpen. (E.) Used as

a slang term; 'well-*whittled*'=thoroughly drunk. Lit. sharpened like a *whittle* or knife; see **Whittle** (1) above. Doubtless confused with *whet*, to sharpen.

Whittle (3), a blanket. (E.) M. E. *whitel*; A. S. *hwītel*. Named from its white colour. **–** A. S. *hwīt*, white.

Whiz, to hiss. (E.) 'The woods do *whizz*;' Surrey, tr. of Æneid, b. ii. 536. An imitative word; allied to **Hiss, Whisper, Whistle.** **+** Icel. *hvissa*, to hiss.

Who, pronoun. (E.) Formerly *who*, *what*, *which*, were interrogative pronouns. *What*, *whose*, *whom*, occur as *relatives* as early as the end of the 12th century, but *who*, nom., as a *relative*, is not found before the 14th century. (Morris.) A. S. *hwā*, who; neuter, *hwæt*, what; gen. *hwæs*, whose; dat. *hwǣm*, *hwām*; acc. masc. and fem. *hwone*, whom [obsolete], neut. *hwæt*, what; instrumental *hwī*, in what way, how, why. **+** Du. *wie*, Icel. *hverr*, Dan. *hvo*, Swed. *hvem*, G. *wer*, Goth. *hwas*, Irish. *co*, L. *quis*, Lith. *kas*, Skt. *kas*. (Base QO = Teut. HWA.) Brugm. ii. § 411.

Whole. (E.) M. E. *hole* (without *w*). A. S. *hāl*, whole. **+** Du. *heel*, Icel. *heill*, Dan. *heel*, Sw. *hel*, Goth. *hails*, G. *heil*. Teut. type **hailoz*. Cf. W. *coel*, an omen. Doublet, *hale*. Der. *hol-y*; *heal-th*.

Whoop, to shout. (F. – Teut.) The initial *w* is modern; formerly *hoop*. M. E. *houpen*. **–** F. *houper*, 'to hoop unto;' Cot. From F. *houp!* an exclamatory interjection. Of Teut. origin; cf. E. Fries. *hup!* up! G. *hopsa*, 'heyday!' Flügel. Cf. **Hoot.** Der. *whooping-cough* or *hooping-cough*.

Whore, sb. (Scand.) The *w* is unoriginal. M. E. *hore*. **–** Icel. *hōra*, an adulteress, fem. of *hōrr*, an adulterer; Dan. *hore*, Swed. *hora*. **+** Du. *hoer*, G. *hure*, O. H. G. *huora*; Goth. *hōrs*, masc., an adulterer. Allied to Polish *kurwa*, Church-Slavonic *kuruva*, an adulteress; L. *cārus*, loving; W. *caru*, to love; O. Irish *caraim*, I love. (√KAR.) ¶ Certainly not allied to *hire*! Brugm. i. § 637.

Whorl. (E.) The same as *wharl*, a piece of bone placed on a spindle to twist it by. The likeness between a *wharl* on a spindle and a *whorl* of leaves is sufficiently close. M. E. *wharl*, *wherl*, *whorl*, Cath. Angl. Contraction of M. E. *whorvil*, for **whervil*; from A. S. *hweorfa*, a wharl. **–** A. S. *hweorfan*, to turn; see **Wharf.**

Whirl. **+** M. Du. *worvel*, a whårl, *worvelen*, to twist or twine; Du. *wervel*, G. *wirbel*, a thing that turns round.

Whortle-berry, the bilberry. (E.) Formerly *hurtle - berry*, and later (in America) *huckle-berry*; also *hurt*, by confusion with M. F. *heurte*, a small azure ball (in heraldry). But the true name is (Dorset) *hart-berry*, A. S. *heorot-berige*. From **Hart** and **Berry.**

Why. (E.) M. E. *whi*; *for whi* = on what account (common). A. S. *hwī*, in what way, instrumental case of *hwā*, who; see **Who.**

WI–WY.

Wick (1), a twist of threads for a lamp. (E.) M. E. *wicke*, *weyke*, *wēke*. A. S. *weoce*, a wick. **+** M. Du. *wiecke*; Low G. *weke*, lint; Dan. *væge*, Swed. *veke*, a wick; Norw. *veik*; M. H. G. *wieche*, a wick; O. H. G. *wioh* (lucubrum). Origin doubtful. Perhaps 'a twist'; cf. O. Irish *figim*, I weave.

Wick (2), a town. (L.) A. S. *wīc*; borrowed from L. *uīcus*, a village. See **Vicinity.**

Wick (3), **Wich**, a creek, bay, salt-pit. (Scand.) O. Icel. **wīk*, Icel. *vīk*, a small creek, inlet, bay. From *vīk-ja*, to recede; see **Weak, Wicker.**

Wicked. (E.) Orig. a pp. form with the sense 'rendered evil,' from the obsolete adj. *wikke*, evil, also weak; evidently allied to **Weak**, q. v. From the weak grade *wic-* of A. S. *wic-an*, Icel. *vīk-ja*, to give way. Cf. also A. S. *wicca*, a wizard; see **Witch.**

Wicker, made of twigs. (Scand.) M. E. *wiker*, a pliant twig, properly a sb.; cf. A. S. *wic-*, weak grade of *wīcan*, to give way, bend, ply; see **Weak.** It corresponds to Swed. dial. *vekare*, *vikker*, willow, from Swed. *vika*, to bend, ply; Dan. dial. *vegre*, a pliant rod, allied to Dan. *veg*, pliant, weak. See **Witch-elm.**

Wicket, a small gate. (F. – Teut.) M. E. *wiket*. **–** A. F. *wiket*, also written *wisket*; O. F. *guischet* (Supp. to Godefroy); Prov. *guisquet* (Diez); mod. F. *guichet*; Walloon *wichet*. Origin doubtful; apparently formed with F. dimin. suffix *-et*, from Teut. base **wisk-*, to whisk or move quickly, from its lightness. Cf. E. Fries. *wisken*, (1) to wipe, (2) to move quickly; Norw. *viska* (the same); Swed.

dial. *viska*, to throw, swing; G. *wischen*, to rub, to slip aside. See **Whisk**. Used of a small door, easily opened, made within a large gate; cf. Norw. *viskjen*, light and quick (Ross). (Körting, § 8714.) Der. *wicket* (at cricket), which was at first 'a small gate,' being made 2 feet wide by 1 foot high (A.D. 1700).

Wide. (E.) A. S. *wīd*. + Du. *wijd*, Icel. *viðr*, Swed. Dan. *vid*, G. *weit*. Teut. type **wīdoz*. Der. *wid-th*, XVI cent.; in place of the old word *wide-ness*.

Widgeon, a bird. (F. – L.?) Spelt *wigion* in Levins (1570). – A. F. **wigeon*, for O. F. *vigeon*, a whistling duck (Littré). Prob. from L. *uīpiōnem*, acc. of *uīpio*, a kind of small crane (Pliny, x. 49).

Widow. (E.) M. E. *widewe*; A. S. *widwe*, *widuwe*.+Du. *weduwe*, G. *wittwe*, Goth. *widuwo*. Further allied to L. *uidua*, fem. of *uiduus*, bereft of, deprived of; Irish *feadhb*, W. *gweddw*; Russ. *vdova*, Skt. *vidhavā*, a widow. Brugm. ii. § 64. √WIDH, as in Skt. *vidh*, to lack (St. Petersburg Dict. vi. 1070). Der. *widow-er*, M. E. *widewer*, coined from *widow* by adding *-er*; so also G. *witwer*.

Wield. (E.) M. E. *welden*, to govern, possess, manage. A. S. *gewyldan*, to have power over. This is a weak verb, due to A. S. *wealdan* (pt. t. *wēold*), to have power over, govern, rule, possess. + Icel. *valda*, G. *walten*, Goth. *waldan*, to govern; allied to Lith. *waldyti*, Russ. *vladiete*, to rule, possess. Cf. W. *gwlad*, a region.

Wife. (E.) A. S. *wīf*, a woman, neut. sb. with pl. *wīf* (unchanged). + Du. *wijf*, Icel. *vīf*, Dan. *viv*, G. *weib*, O. H. G. *wīp*, a woman. Teut. type **wībom*, n. Root obscure; certainly not allied to *weave* (A. S. *wefan*), as the fable runs. Der. *woman*.

Wig. (Du.– F.– Ital.– L.) Short for *periwig*, which see.

Wight (1), a person, creature. (E.) M. E. *wight*, *wiȝt*. A.S. *wiht*, a creature, animal, person, thing (very common). + Du. *wicht*, a child; Icel. *vættr*; Dan. *vætte*, an elf; G. *wicht*, Goth. *waihts*, fem. a wight, *waiht*, neut. a whit. Teut. type **wehtiz*, f. Perhaps it meant 'something moving,' from A. S. *wegan*, to move; see **Weigh, Whit**.

Wight (2), nimble, strong. (Scand.) In Spenser, Shep. Kal., March, 91. M. E. *wight*, valiant. – Icel. *vīgr*, fit for war, neut. *vīgt*, serviceable (accounting for the final *t*), Swed. *vig*, nimble, *vigt*, adv., nimbly. From Icel. *víg* (= A. S. *wíg*), war; cf. Icel. *vega*, to fight, smite; Goth. *weihan* (pt. t. *waih*), to fight, strive; L. *uincere*, to conquer. Cf. Lith. *vĕkl*, strength.

Wigwam, an Indian hut. (N. Amer. Indian.) Massachusetts *wēk*, his house; this word, with possessive and locative affixes, becomes *wēkou-om-ut*, in his house; whence E. *weekwam* or *wigwam* (Webster). Cuoq gives Algonquin *mikiwam*, also *wikiwam*, a house (pp. 221, 438).

Wild. (E.) M. E. *wilde*; A.S. *wilde*, wild, untamed. + Du. *wild*; Icel. *villr*, wild, also astray, bewildered, confused (whence Lowl. Sc. *will*, astray); Dan. Swed. *vild*, G. *wild*, Goth. *wiltheis*. Teut. type **welthjoz*. Cf. W. *gwyllt*, wild. Root uncertain.

wilderness, a waste place. (E.) M. E. *wildernesse*, Layamon, 30335. From A. S. *wilder*, a wild animal; also *wildor*; Teut. type **wilthos*, n., a derivative of *wilde*, wild. Sievers, § 289.+M. Du. *wildernisse*. And see **Bewilder**.

Wile, a trick. (E.) M. E. *wile*; A.S. *wīl*, a wile. Cf. Lithuan. *wilti*, to deceive. And see **Guile**. ¶ The A. S. *wīl* is a late word; and a derivation from A. S. *wiglian*, to practise sorcery, is possible; cf. '*wilung*, divinatio,' Kentish Glosses, 554; also *His* [the devil's] *wiȝeles*, Ancr. Riwle, 300; A. S. *wígl*, divination (Napier).

Wilful. (E.) M. E. *wilful*; formed with suffix *-ful* from M. E. *wil-le*, will; see Will (2) below.

Will (1), to desire, be willing. (E.) M. E. *willen*, pt. t. *wolde*; A.S. *willan*, *wyllan*, to wish, be willing; pres. *wille*, *wile* (2 p. *wilt*), pt. t. *wolde*.+Du. *willen*, Icel. *vilja*, Dan. *ville*, Swed. *vilja*, Goth. *wiljan* (pt.t. *wilda*), G. *wollen* (pres. *will*, pt. t. *wollte*), Lithuan. *weliti*, L. *uelle* (pres. *uolo*); Skt. *vṛ*, to choose. (√WEL.) Der. *will-ing*, orig. a pres. part. Also *willy-nilly*, answering both to *will I, nill I*, and to *will he, nill he*; from A. S. *nillan*, short for *ne willan*, not to wish (= L. *nolle*, not to wish).

will (2), sb., desire. (E.) M. E. *wille*, A.S. *willa*, sb. – A. S. *willan*, to will; see Will (1) above.+Du. *wil*, Icel. *vili*, Dan. *ville*, Swed. *vilja*, G. *wille*, Russ. *volia*.

Willow. (E.) M. E. *wilow*, *wilwe*; A.S. *welig*.+Du. *wilg*, Low G. *wilge*.

Wimberry, Winberry. (L. and E.)

A. S. *wīnberie, wīnberige*, a grape, lit. a wine-berry. — A. S. *wīn*, from L. *uīnum*, wine ; *berige*, a berry ; see **Berry.**

Wimble (1), a gimlet. (E.) M. E. *wimbil*. Cf. Dan. *vimmel*, a boring-tool ; Low G. *wemel, wemmel*, a wimble (Lüb- ben) ; M. Du. *weme*, ' a pearcer, or a wimble,' Hexham ; M. Du. *wemelen*, ' to pearce or bore with a wimble,' Hexham. Apparently from a Teut. base **wem*, to turn ; see below. Cf. Shropsh. *wim-wam*, a turnstile. **Der.** *gimlet.*

Wimble (2), active. (Scand.) In Spenser, Shep. Kal., March, 91. — Swed. dial. *vimmla*, to be giddy or skittish, fre- quent. of Swed. dial. *vima*, to be giddy, allied to Icel. *vim*, giddiness. Compare **Wimble** (1) and **Whim.**

Wimple, a covering for the neck. (E.) M. E. *wimpel* ; A. S. *winpel*, a wimple. + Du. *wimpel*, a streamer, pendant ; Icel. *vimpill*, Dan. Swed. *vimpel*, G. *wimpel*, a pennon, O. H. G. *wimpal*, a summer robe. **β.** The A. S. *winpel* suggests **wind-pel* ; from *wind*, the wind, and (perhaps) A. S. *pæll, pell* (L. *pallium*), a covering ; cf. O. H. G. *wim-pal*. See **Wind** (1) and **Pall** (1). ¶ This would also account for the sense of ' streamer,' if *pel* can mean a strip of bright-coloured stuff. (A guess.)

Win, to gain by labour, earn. (E.) M. E. *winnen*, pt. t. *wan, won*, pp. *wonnen*. A. S. *winnan*, to fight, struggle, try to get, labour, suffer ; pt. t. *wann*, pp. *wunnen*. + Du. *winnen*, Icel. *vinna*, Dan. *vinde*, Swed. *vinna* ; G. *gewinnen*, O. H. G. *win- nan*, to fight, strive, earn ; *Goth. winnan*, to suffer. Allied to Skt. *van*, to beg, ask for, honour ; L. *uenerāri*, to honour, *uenus*, desire ; W. *gwên*, a smile. (√WEN.)

Winberry ; see **Wimberry.**

Wince. (F. — Teut.) M. E. *wincen*. — A. F. **wencir*, necessarily the old form of A. F. *guencir* (Toynbee), for O. F. *guen- chir*, later *guincher*, to wriggle, writhe aside (Cot.). — O. Sax. *wenkian* ; M. H. G. *wenken*, to wince, start aside ; for Teut. **wankjan-*. — M. H. G. *wank*, 2nd grade of *winken*, to move aside, nod, beckon ; see **Wink.**

winch, the crank of an axle. (E.) M. E. *winche* ; prov. E. *wink* ; A. S. *wince*, a winch, orig. a bent handle. Cf. A. S. *wincel*, a corner, lit. bend ; from the strong verb **wincan* ; see **Wink.** Note also Lithuan. *winge*, a bend or turn of a river or road.

Wind (1), air in motion. (E.) M. E. *wind* ; A. S. *wind.* + Du. *wind*, Icel. *vindr*, Dan. Swed. *vind*, G. *wind*, Goth. *winds*. Teut. type **wendoz.* Further cognate with W. *gwynt*, Bret. *gwent*, L. *uentus*, wind. Orig. a pres. part., with the sense of ' blowing.' From √WE, to blow ; whence also Skt. *vā*, to blow, *vātas*, wind, Goth. *waian*, to blow, Russ. *vieiate*, to blow, *vieter'*, wind, Lithuan. *wèjas*, wind. From the same root is E. *weather*, q.v. **Der.** *wind*, to blow a horn, pt. t. and pp. *winded*, Much Ado, i. 1. 243, often oddly corrupted to *wound*! Cf. Sweet, Gr. 1367. Also *wind-fall*, *wind- mill*, &c.

Wind (2), to turn round, twist. (E.) M. E. *winden*, pt. t. *wand*, *wond*, pp. *wunden*. A. S. *windan*, pt. t. *wand*, pp. *wunden*. + Du. *winden*, Icel. *vinda*, Dan. *vinde*, Swed. *vinda* (to squint), G. *winden*, Goth. *-windan* (in *bi-windan*). Teut. type **wendan-*, pt. t. **wand*, pp. **wund- anoz.*

windlass (1), a machine with a turn- ing axis. (Scand.) M. E. *windelas* ; from Icel. *vindil-āss* (still in use), a compound of Icel. *vindill*, a winder, and *āss* (ex- plained below). Here Icel. *vindil* = M.E. *windel*, Swed. dial. *vindel*, a winder ; from the verb *to wind*. **β.** We also find M. E. *windas*, a windlass ; Chaucer, C. T. 10498, &c. — Icel. *vindāss*, a windlass. — Icel. *vind-a*, to wind ; *āss*, a pole, rounded beam, + Du. *windas*, M. Du. *windaes*, a windlass. **γ.** Here M. Du. *aes*, Icel. *āss*, is cognate with Goth. *ans*, a beam (distinct from Du. *as*, M. Du. *asse*, an axis, for which see **Axis**).

windlass (2), a circuit. (Scand.) Formerly *windlasse* ; Hamlet, ii. 1. 65 ; &c. A peculiar use of **Windlass** (1), perhaps misunderstood as if used for *wind- lace*, a winding course ; from *wind*, vb., and *lace*, a snare, twist, mod. E. *lace.*

Window. (Scand.) Orig. sense ' wind- eye,' an eye or hole for the admission of air and light. M. E. *windowe, windohe, windoge*. — Icel. *vindauga* (for **windauga*), a window ; lit. ' wind-eye ;' Dan. *vindue*. — Icel. *vindr*, wind ; *auga*, eye ; see **Eye.** ¶ Butler has *windore*, a corrupted form, as if for *wind-door.*

Wine. (L.) A. S. *wīn*, wine ; borrowed from L. *uīnum*, wine (whence also G. *wein*, &c.). + Gk. οἶνος, wine ; οἴνη, a vine. The Gk. οἴνη is from √WEI, to wind, twist, twine (see **Withy**); from the twining growth of the vine. Brugm. ii. § 66.

Wing. (Scand.) M. E. *winge, wenge.* — Icel. *vængr* (for **wængr*), a wing; Dan. Swed. *vinge*; N. Fries. *winge.*

Wink, to move the eyelids quickly. (E.) 1. M. E. *winken*, pt. t. *winkede.* — A. S. *wincian*, to wink. 2. But we also find *winken*, strong verb, pt. t. *wank, wonk*, shewing that there was also a strong A. S. verb **wincan*, (pt. t. **wanc*, pp. **gewuncen*), whence A. S. *wanc-ol*, wavering, and other forms. ✛ M. Du. *wincken, wencken*, to wink; *wanck*, sb., a twinkling of an eye, an instant; Icel. *vanka*, to wink; Dan. *vinke*, Swed. *vinka*, to beckon; G. *winken*, to nod; O. H. G. *winkan*, str. vb., to move aside, stir, waver (see Schade). Cf. Lith. *wingis*, a bend of a river, *wangus*, idle, *wengti*, to shirk work, to flinch.

winkle, a kind of shell-fish. (E.) A. S. *-wincla* (in *wine-wincla*), a winkle. Named from the convoluted shell; cf. Dan. dial. *vinkel*, a snail-shell; allied to *wince*, a winch (orig. a bend, turn?). See also **Wench.**

Winnow. (E.) M. E. *windewen, winewen*, to winnow. A. S. *windwian*, to winnow, expose to wind. — A. S. *wind*, wind. So also O. H. G. *wintôn*, from *wint*; L. *uentilare*, from *uentus.*

Winsome, pleasant. (E.) A. S. *wynsum*, delightful; formed with suffix *-sum* from *wynn*, joy. A. S. *wynn* < Teut. **wunjā*, f., is formed (by vowel-change of *u* to *y*) from *wun-*, as in Goth. *unwun-ands*, unrejoicing, weak grade of Idg. **wen*, to desire. See **Wont.** Cf. G. *wonne*, joy, O. Sax. *wunnia.*

Winter. (E.) A. S. *winter*, a winter, also a year. ✛ Du. *winter*, Icel. *vetr*, Dan. Swed. *vinter*, G. *winter*, Goth. *wintrus.* Teut. type **wintruz.* Root unknown.

Wipe. (E.) A. S. *wîpian*, to wipe; orig. to rub with a wisp of straw. From a sb. preserved in E. Fries. *wîp*, Low G. *wiep*, a twist or wisp of straw. Allied to Goth. *waips*, a wreath; from the str. vb. *weipan*, to crown (twine).

Wire. (E.) A. S. *wîr*, a wire. ✛ Icel. *vîrr*, wire; cf. Swed. *vira*, to twist; O. H. G. *wiara*, an ornament of (twisted) gold; L. *uiriæ*, armlets. Some compare Irish *fiar*, crooked (bent); from ✓WEI, to twine.

Wis; see **Ywis.**

Wise (1), discreet, learned. (E.) A. S.

wîs, wise. ✛ Du. *wijs*, Icel. *vîss*, Dan. *viis*, Swed. *vis*, G. *weise*, wise. Teut. type **wîsoz*, for **wit-toz*, from Idg. ✓WEID, to know. See **Wit** (1). Thus *wise* = 'knowing'; cf. *cunning.* Brugm. i. §§ 759, 794. Der. *wis-dom*, A. S. *wîs-dôm.*

wise (2), manner, way. (E.) M. E. *wise*; A. S. *wîse*, way. Orig. sense 'wiseness' or skill; from *wîs*, adj., wise (above). ✛ Du. *wijs*, Dan. *viis*, Swed. *vis*, G. *weise*, sb. Der. *like-wise* (i. e. in like wise); *other-wise.* Doublet, *guise.*

wiseacre. (Du. — G.) Borrowed from M. Du. *wijssegger*, supposed to mean a wise sayer, sooth-sayer. — G. *weissager*, supposed to mean 'wise sayer.' β. But the G. word is itself a corruption of O. H. G. *wîzago*, a prophet, seer; from O. H. G. *wîzan*, to see. The cognate A. S. word is *wîtega*, a prophet, seer; from A. S. *wîtan*, to observe. β. The verbs *wîzan, wîtan*, are cognate with L. *uidêre* (pt. t. *uîd-i*), to see; and closely allied to A. S. *witan*, to know; see **Wit** (1).

Wish, vb. (E.) M. E. *wischen.* A. S. *wýscan*, to wish; for Teut. **wunskjan-*, formed from Teut. **wunsko-*, sb., a wish. Compare A. S. *wûsc-* (in comp.), which is cognate with M. Du. *wunsch*, Icel. *ôsk*, G. *wunsch*, O. H. G. *wunsc*, a wish [the derived verbs being Icel. *æskja*, G. *wünschen*, to wish]. Allied to Skt. *vâñch*, to desire, wish, formed (with verbal suffix *-sko-*) from *van*, to ask. Similarly the E. word is a derivative from ✓WEN, to desire, whence E. *win*; see **Win.** Brugm. ii. § 90. Der. *wishful*; and see *wistful.*

Wisp, a small bundle of straw or hay. (E.) M. E. *wisp*, also *wips.* The form *wips* may be connected with the verb *to wipe.* Allied to Low G. *wiep*, Norweg. *vippa*, a wisp, Swed. dial. *vipp*, a little sheaf or bundle, Goth. *waips*, a crown (orig. a twisted wreath). Cf. Dan. *vippe*, to see-saw, go to and fro, Swed. *vippa*, G. *wippen*, to go up and down, see-saw. Perhaps from the vibratory motion in rubbing; see **Whip, Vibrate.**

Wist, knew; see **Wit** (1).

Wistful, eager. (E.) The history of the word shews it to be a substitution for *wishful*, 3 Hen. VI, iii. 1. 14; which is from *wish*, sb., with suffix *-ful.* β. But it seems to have been confused with *wistly*, a word used by Shakespeare in place of M. E. *wisly*, certainly, verily, exactly, formerly a common word; see Chaucer, C. T. 1865, 3992, &c. This M. E. *wisly* is from Icel. *viss*, certain (distinct from, yet allied to, *vīss*, wise), orig. pp. of Icel. *vita*, to know (Noreen); see **Wit** (1).

Wit (1), to know. (E.) The parts of this verb are often ill understood and wrongly given. M. E. infin. *witen*; pres. t. *I wot*, with 3 p. *he wot* (later *wotteth*), and 2 p. *thou wost* (later *wottest*), pl. *witen*; pt. t. *wiste*, pp. *wist*. A. S. *witan*; pres. t. *ic wāt*, *þū wāst*, *he wāt*, pl. *witon*, pt. t. *wiste*, also *wisse*, pl. *wiston*; pp. *witen*; gerund *tō witanne* (mod. E. *to wit*).+Du. *weten*, Icel. *vita*, Dan. *vide*, Swed. *veta*, G. *wissen*, Goth. *witan*, to know. Further allied to L. *uidēre*, to see, Gk. ἰδεῖν, to see (perf. t. οἶδα = I *wot*, I know), Skt. *vid*, to see, *vēda*, I know. (√WEID.)

wit (2), sb., knowledge, &c. (E.) M. E. *wit*; A. S. *witt*, knowledge; Teut. type **wit-jom*, neut. — A. S. *witan*, to know; see **Wit** (1). + Icel. *vit*, Dan. *vid*, Swed. *vett*, G. *witz*, wit.

wit (3), a wise man. (E.) M.E. *wite*; A. S. *wita*, lit. ' one who knows.' — A. S. *witan*, to know. Der. A. S. *witena gemōt*, a meeting of ' wits,' a parliament.

Witch. (E.) M. E. *wicche*, both masc. and fem., a wizard, a witch; A. S. *wicce*, fem.; also *wicca*,m. Allied to A.S. *wiccian*, to practise witchcraft; E. Fries. *wikken*. +M. Du. *wicker*,' a soothsayer,' Hexham; Low G. *wikken*, to predict. Cf. Norw. *vikja*, (1) to turn aside, (2) to conjure away. This links it with Icel. *vīkja* (pp. *vik-inn*), to move, turn, push aside; and with E. **Weak**. Thus *witch* perhaps = ' averter.' Der. *bewitch*, vb. (above).

Witch-elm, Wych-elm. (E.) M.E. *wiche*. A. S. *wice*. The sense is ' bending,' or drooping; from the pendulous branches. — A. S. *wic-en*, pp. of *wīcan*, to bend; see **Wicker**.

With. (E.) A.S. *wið*, by, near, among; it also means ' against,' as in mod.E. *withstand*, *with-say*. + Icel. *við*, against, by, at; Dan. *ved*, Swed. *vid*, near, by, at. Allied to A. S. *wiðer*, against; see **Withers**. Der. *with-al*, from M.E. *with*, with, *alle*, dat. case of *al*, all; *with-in*, A. S. *wiðinnan*; *with-out*, A.S. *wiðūtan*. Hence also *with-draw*, *with-hold*, *with-say*, *with-stand*.

Withdraw. (E.) From *with*, i. e. back, towards oneself; and *draw*. Hence

with-draw-ing-room, a retiring-room, now oddly contracted to *drawing room*.

Withe; see **Withy**.

Wither. (E.) Orig. trans.; M. E. *widren*, *wederen*, to expose to weather. From M. E. *weder*, weather; see **Weather.** Cf. G. *verwittern*, to wither; from *wetter*, weather.

Withers, the ridge between the shoulder-blades of a horse. (E.) So called because it is the part which a horse *opposes* to his load, or on which the stress of the collar comes in drawing. — A. S. *wiðer*, against; as sb., resistance; cf. also A.S. *wið*, against (above). Cf. G. *wider-rist*, withers of a horse; from *wider*, by-form of *wieder*, against, and *rist*, an elevated part. A. S. *wiðer* is further related to Icel. *viðr*, against, O. H. G. *widar*, Goth. *withra*, against (for *wi-thra*, a compar. form). Cf. Skt. *vi*, apart, *vi-taram*, further. Brugm. i. § 86.

Withhold. (E.) From *with*, i.e. back, towards oneself; and *hold*.

Within, Without; see **With**.

Withsay, to contradict. (E.) From *with*, in the sense ' against '; and *say*.

Withstand, to resist. (E.) From *with*, in the sense ' against '; and *stand*.

Withy, Withe, a flexible twig. (E.) M.E. *wiði*; A.S. *wiðig*, a willow. Named from its flexibility; from √WEI, to twine, plait, as in L. *ui-ēre*, Russ. *vite*, to twine. +M. Du. *weede*, hop-plant (twiner); Icel. *viðja*, a withy, *við*, a withe, *viðir*, a willow; Dan. *vidie*, Swed. *vide*, willow; G. *weide*, willow. Also Lith. *wytis*, a withe, *žil-wittis*, a willow (cf. *žill-as*, gray); L. *uītis*, a vine; Gk. ἰτέα, a willow; W. *gwden*, a withe. Cf. L. *uī-men*, a twig. Brugm. ii. §§ 685, 789.

Witness, testimony. (E.) Properly an abstract sb. A. S. *witnes*, testimony. — A. S. *wit-an*, to know, with suffix *-nes*; thus the orig. sense was ' knowledge ' or ' consciousness.' Cf. Icel. *vitna*, Dan. *vidne*, to testify; Goth. *weit-wōds*, a witness. Der. *witness*, vb.

Wittol, a cuckold. (Low G.) Formerly supposed to mean ' wit-all '; also thought to represent A. S. *witol*, knowing, wise, from *witan*, to know. There is no foundation for this, as the word is not used in the M. E. period. Bp. Hall writes *witwal*; i.e. *wittol* is the same as *witwall*, or *woodwale*, the name of a bird. Florio (ed. 1598) explains Ital. *godano* by ' the bird called a *witwal* or *woodwall*'; and in a later edition, 'a *wittal* or *woodwale.*' If this be so, we may be sure that allusions were made to the *witwall* similar to those endless allusions to the *cuckoo* which produced the word *cuckold*. *Witwall* represents the M. Du. or Low G. form of E. *woodwale*; and, while *woodwale* usually means the wood-pecker, *witwall* seems to have been applied to the oriole. See **Woodwale.**

Wivern; see **Wyvern.**

Wizard, Wisard. (F. – Teut.) M. E. *wisard.* – A. F. *wischard*, necessarily the orig. form of O. F. *guischard, guiscart,* sagacious. – Icel. *vizk-r*, clever, sagacious, knowing (where *-r* is merely the suffix of the nom. case); with F. suffix *-ard* = G. *hart*, hard, strong, confirmed in (as in numerous other words). **β.** The Icel. *vizkr = vitskr*, with *z* for *ts*; from *vit-a,* to know, with suffix *-sk-* (=E. *-ish*). Hence *wiz-ard = wit-ish-ard.*

Wizen, to shrivel or dry up. (E.) M. E. *wisenen,* to become shrivelled ; O. North-umb. *wisnian,* to become dry, John xv. 6 ; we find also A. S. *for-wisnian,* to dry up. **+** Icel. *visna,* to wither, allied to the old pp. *visinn,* wizened, occurring also as Dan. and Swed. *vissen.* This is a pp. of a lost strong verb, from a base WEIS, to dry up. Cf. O. H. G. *wesanēn,* to dry up. And cf. **Virulent.**

Wo, Woe. (E.) M. E. *wo* ; A. S. *wā*, interj. and adv. ; *wēa*, wo, sb. **+** Du. *vee,* interj. and sb. ; Icel. *vei,* Dan. *vee,* Swed. *ve,* G. *weh,* Goth. *wai,* interj. ; also Dan. *vee,* G. *weh,* sb. Allied to W. *gwae,* woe, L. *uæ,* wo ! Orig. an exclamation ; hence a cry of pain, &c. **Der.** *wo-begone,* i. e. wo-surrounded, from M. E. *begōn,* pp. of *begōn* = A. S. *begān,* to surround, lit. to go round about ; from A. S. *be-* (= E. *by*), and *gān,* to go. Also *wo worth,* i. e. wo be to ; see **Worth.**

Woad, a plant, used for dyeing. (E.) M. E. *wod, wood,* woad. A. S. *wād,* woad. **+** Du. *weede,* Dan. *vaid, veid,* Swed. *veide,* G. *waid,* M. H. G. *weit* (whence O. F. *waide,* mod. F. *guède*). Allied to L. *uitrum,* woad. **¶** Distinct from *weld* (2).

Wold, a down, plain, open country. (E.) M. E. *wold, wald.* A. S. *weald, wald,* a wood, forest (hence waste ground, and even open country, as in Icelandic). **+** Du. *woud,* O. Sax. and O. Fries. *wald,* a wood ; G. *wald* ; O. H. G. *walt,* a

wood ; Icel. *völlr,* gen. *vallar,* a field, plain. Teut. type **walthuz.* Cf. **Weald.**

Wolf. (E.) M. E. *wolf,* pl. *wolues* (= *wolves*). A. S. *wulf,* pl. *wulfas.***+**Du. G. *wolf,* Icel. *ūlfr,* Dan. *ulv,* Swed. *ulf,* Goth. *wulfs.* Further allied either to L. *uulpēs* (see **Vulpine**) ; or else (together with Icel. *ylgr,* a she-wolf) to Lith. *wilkas,* Russ. *volk',* Gk. λύκος, Skt. *vṛka-,* a wolf. Teut. type **wulfoz,* Idg. type **wᵊlqos* ; from **welq,* to tear ; cf. Skt. *vraçch,* to tear, Lith. *wilkti,* to pull. Brugm. ii. § 60. **Der.** *wolv-er-ene,* a coined word ; *wulverin* in Hakluyt, i. 277.

Woman. (E.) A phonetic alteration of A.S. *wīfman,* lit. wife-man, the word *man* being formerly applied to both sexes. This word became *wimman,* pl. *wimmen,* in the 10th century, and this pl. is still in use in *spoken* English. In the 12th century, it became *wumman* (just as, in A. S., *widu* became *wudu,* see **Wood**), whence E. *woman* and prov. E. *wumman* [wum·un]. **¶** Cf. *leman* from A.S. *lēofman, Lammas* from A. S. *hlāfmæsse* ; see **Leman, Lammas.**

Womb. (E.) Lowl. Sc. *wame,* the belly. M.E. *wombe, wambe.* A.S. *wamb, womb,* the belly.**+**Du. *wam,* belly of a fish; Icel. *vömb,* Dan. *vom,* Swed. *våmb, våmm,* G. *wampe, wamme,* Goth. *wamba,* the belly.

Wombat, a marsupial mammal. (Australian.) A corruption of *womback,* the native Australian name. (Collins, New South Wales, 1802 ; Bewick, Quadrupeds ; E. E. Morris, Austral English.)

Won, to dwell, remain. (E.) M. E. *wonen,* A. S. *wunian,* to dwell ; see **Wont.**

Wonder, sb. (E.) A. S. *wundor,* a portent, wonder.**+**Du. *wonder,* Icel. *undr,* G. *wunder,* O. H. G. *wuntar* ; Teut. type **wundrom,* n. Origin unknown.

wondrous, wonderful. (E.) A corruption of the old word *wonders,* won-drous, orig. an adv., but also an adj. ' *Wonders* dere' = wondrously dear ; '*wonders* men ' = wonderful men. *Wonders* was formed by adding the adv. suffix *-s* (orig. a gen. case) to the M. E. *wonder,* adj., wonderful, Chaucer, C. T. 455. This adj. is short for *wonderly,* adj. = A. S. *wunderlic,* wonderful, *-ly* being dropped because it seemed like an adverbial ending.

Wont, used, accustomed. (E.) M. E. *woned,* pp. of *wonien,* to dwell, remain, be used to; it came to be used as a sb.; and, its origin being forgotten, the pp. suffix -*ed* was again added, producing a form *wont-ed* = *won-ed-ed*! Chaucer has *woned*, i. e. *wont*, as a pp.; C. T. 8215; Troilus, i. 511. A.S. *wunod*, pp. of A.S. *wunian*, to dwell, be used to. **–** A.S. *ge-wuna*, sb., custom, use, 'wont.' **–** A.S. *wun-*, weak grade of √WEN, to desire, strive after; see **Win, Wish.** *Wont* is a habit due to acquiescence in what seems pleasant. Cf. Icel. *vanr*, adj., accustomed, *vani*, a usage, allied to *vinr*, a friend; G. *gewohnt*, wont, pp. of *wohnen*, to dwell. **Der.** *wont*, sb., for M. E. *wone*, usage (by confusion); hence *wont*, vb., *wont-ed*, accustomed.

Woo, to court. (E.) M. E. *wo3en*, *wowen*. A. S. *wōgian*, to woo; of obscure origin.

Wood (1), timber, forest. (E.) M. E. *wode*. A.S. *wudu*, of which the orig. form was *widu*, wood. **+** Icel. *viðr*, a tree, wood; Dan. Swed. *ved*; O. H. G. *witu*. Cf. Irish *fiodh*, a wood, tree; O. Irish *fid*, a tree; W. *gwŷdd*, trees. Teut. type *widuz*. **Der.** *wood-en*, *-y*, *-ed*; *wood-bine*, A.S. *wudu-binde*; *-ruff*, *-wale*.

Wood (2), mad, furious. (E.) In Mids. Nt. Dr. ii. 1. 192. M. E. *wod*. A. S. *wōd*, mad, raging. **+** Icel. *ōðr*, Goth. *wōds*, frantic. Cf. G. *wuth*, madness. Perhaps allied to L. *uātes*, a prophet, one filled with divine frenzy; O. Irish *fáith*, a prophet. Hence the name *Wōden*; see **Wednesday.**

Woodruff, a plant. (E.) M. E. *wod-ruffe*, *woderoove*. A.S. *wuderōfe*, *wudurōfe*, woodruff. Perhaps allied to A. S. *rōf*, meaning 'strong' or 'famous.' Cf. G. *waldmeister*, woodruff; L. *hastula regia*.

woodwale, a bird. (E.) Also called *witwall*, *wittal*. M. E. *wodewale*, perhaps a woodpecker. From A.S. *wudu*, a wood; the form *witwall* being due to the Low G. and M. Du. forms. The sense of *-wale* is not known. **+** M. Du. *weduwael*, a kind of yellow bird; Low G. *widewaal*; M.H.G. *witewal*, an oriole. (Cf. **Wittol.**)

Woof, the weft. (E.) This curious word is a corruption of M. E. *oof*, the *w* being prefixed owing to a popular etymology from *weave* (which is true, but not in the way which popular etymologists would understand). The M. E. *oof* is a contraction of A.S. *ōwef*, the woof. **–** A.S. *ō-*, variant of *ā-* (as in *ā-wefan*), *wef*, a sb. due to *wefan*, to weave. Cf. prov. E.

abb, A. S. *āweb*, woof; from *ā-wefan*, to weave together.

Wool. (E.) M. E. *wolle.* A.S. *wull*, *wul*. **+** Du. *wol*, Icel. *ull*, Dan. *uld*, Swed. *ull*, G. *wolle*, Goth. *wulla*, wool. Allied to Lith. *wilna*, Russ. *volna*, Skt. *ūrṇā*, wool; L. *uellus* (for **velnus*), fleece. Also to Gk. λῆνος (for **Fλῆνος*), L. *lāna*, Irish *olann*, W. *gwlan.*

woolward, clothed in wool only, for penance. (E.) See L. L. L. v. 2. 717. M. E. *wolleward*, lit. with the skin towards (against) the wool. From *wool* and *-ward*, suffix. See **Toward.**

Woon, a governor, officer. (Burmese.) Burm. *wun*, a governor or officer of administration; lit. 'a burden,' hence presumably 'the bearer of the burden'; Yule, p. 867. See **Vizier** for the sense.

Word. (E.) A. S. *word*. **+** Du. *woord*, Icel. *orð*, Dan. Swed. *ord*, G. *wort*, Goth. *waurd*. Teut. type **wurdom*, n.; Idg. type **wordho-*. Cf. Lith. *wardas*, a name; L. *uerbum*, a word. Lit. 'a thing spoken;' from √WER, to speak; cf. Gk. εἴρειν, to speak. **Doublet**, *verb.*

Work, sb. (E.) M. E. *werk.* A. S. *weorc*, *werc*. **+** Du. *werk*, Icel. *verk*, Dan. *værk*, Swed. *verk*, G. *werk.* Teut. type **werkom*, n. Further allied to Gk. ἔργον, work, ἔοργα, I have wrought, Zend. *vareza*, a working, Pers. *warz*, gain. (√WERG.) Allied to **Organ**. **Der.** *work*, vb., *wright.*

World. (E.) M. E. *werld*. A. S. *weoruld*, *weorold*. **+** Du. *wereld*, Icel. *veröld*, Dan. *verden* (where *-en* is the article), Swed. *verld*, G. *welt*, M. H. G. *werlt*, O. H. G. *weralt*. β. The lit. sense is 'age of man' or 'course of man's life,' hence a life-time, course of life, experience of life, &c. The component parts are A. S. *wer* (Icel. *verr*, O. H. G. *wer*, Goth. *wair*), a man; and A. S. *eld*, an age (Icel. *öld*, Goth. *alds*, an age); see **Virile** and **Eld.**

Worm. (E.) M. E. *worm*. A.S. *wyrm*, a worm, snake. **+** Du. *worm*, Icel. *ormr*, Dan. Swed. *orm*, G. *wurm*, Goth. *waurms*; also L. *uermis*, a worm. Teut. type **wurmiz*, Idg. type **wrmiz*. Brugm. i. § 371; ii. § 97. Prob. allied to Gk. ῥόμος (for **Fρόμος*), a wood-worm.

Wormwood, a bitter plant. (E.) A corrupted form, the word having no reference either to *worm* or to *wood*. M. E. *wermode*, later *wormwod*. A.S. *wermōd*. **+** G. *wermuth*, O. H. G. *werimuota*. Origin unknown.

Worry, to harass. (E.) M. E. *wirien, worowen,* orig. to strangle, and used of the worrying of sheep by dogs or wolves. A. S. *wyrgan,* to strangle, harm; see O. E. Texts, p. 99. **+** Du. *worgen,* O. Fries. *wergia, wirgia,* G. *würgen,* to strangle, suffocate. β. G. *würgen* is the causal form of the M. H. G. strong verb -*wergan,* only in comp. *ir-wergan,* to strangle. Teut. base *werg,* Idg. √WERGH; as in Lith. *wersz-ti,* to strangle, oppress. Brugm. i. § 624.

Worse, comparative adj. and adv., more bad. (E.) M. E. *wurs, wers,* adv., *wurse, werse,* adj.; A. S. *wyrs;* adv., *wyrsa,* adj., worse. **+** O. Sax. *wirs,* adv., *wirsa,* adj.; Icel. *verr,* adv., *verri,* adj.; Dan. *værre,* Swed. *värre,* adj.; M. H. G. *wirs,* adv., *wirser,* adj.; Goth. *wairs,* adv., *wairsiza,* adj. β. The common Teut. type is *wersizon-,* adj., where -*izon-* is the comparative suffix, and the base is *wers,* to twist, entangle, confuse; cf. O. H. G. *werran,* G. *wirren,* to twist, entangle; see **War.** Der. *wors-en,* vb. See **Worst.**

Worship, sb. (E.) Short for *worth-ship.* A. S. *weorðscipe, wyrðscipe,* honour. **–** A. S. *weorð, wyrð,* adj., honourable; with suffix -*scipe* (E. -*ship*), allied to E. *shape.* See **Worth.** Der. *worship,* vb.

Worst, superlative. (E.) A. S. *wyrst,* adv., *wyrsta,* contracted form of *wyrsesta,* adj., which also occurs as *wyrresta,* Matt. xii. 45.**+**O. Sax. *wirsista,* adj.; Icel. *verst,* adv., *verstr,* adj.; Dan. *værst,* Swed. *värst,* O. H. G. *wirsisto.* Teut. type *wers-ist-oz,* adj.; see **Worse.**

Worsted, twisted yarn. (E.) M. E. *worsted,* Chaucer, C. T. 264. Named from the town of *Worsted,* in Norfolk. *Worsted* stands for *Worth-stead;* from *Worth,* an estate, and *stead,* a place.

Wort (1), a plant. (E.) M. E. *wort.* A. S. *wyrt,* a wort, plant, herb. **+** O. Sax. *wurt,* G. *wurz,* Goth. *waurts;* cf. Dan. *urt,* Swed. *ört.* Teut. type *wurtiz,* f.; Idg. type *wṛdis.* Allied to Icel. *rót,* L. *rādix,* Gk. ῥίζα, a root; ῥάδ-αμνος, a young shoot; W. *gwreiddyn,* O. Irish *frem,* a root. See **Radix, Root.** Brugm. i. §§ 350, 529.

Wort (2), an infusion of malt, new beer. (E.) M. E. *wort* or *worte.* A. S. -*wyrt,* in the compound *māx-wyrt,* lit. mash-wort, an infusion of worts.**+**Icel. *virtr,* Norw. *vyrt, vört;* Swed. *vört,* G. *bier-würze,* beer-

wort; M. H. G. *wirz.* β. The Icel. *virtr,* M. H. G. *wirz* are from a Teut. base *werti-;* which differs in gradation from **Wort** (1), but is closely allied to it.

Worth (1), adj., deserving of; sb., desert, value. (E.) M. E. *wurth, worth.* A. S. *wyrðe,* adj., mutated by-form of *weorþ,* adj. valuable; *wyrþ, weorþ,* sb., value. **+** Du. *waard,* adj., *waarde,* sb.; Icel. *verðr,* adj., *verð,* sb.; Dan. *værd,* adj. and sb.; Swed. *värd,* adj., *värde,* sb; G. *werth,* adj. and sb.; Goth. *wairths,* adj. and sb. β. Teut. type *werðoz,* adj., valuable; cognate with Lith. *wertas,* worthy; cf. W. *gwerth,* value; L. *uer-ērī,* to respect. Prob. from √WER, to guard, keep. Allied to **Ware** (1) and **Wary.** Der. *worth-y,* adj., suggested by Icel. *verðugr,* worthy; *worth-less.*

Worth (2), to become, to be, to befall. (E.) In phr. *wo worth the day* = wo be to the day. M. E. *worthen,* to become. A. S. *weorðan,* to become, pt. t. *wearð,* pl. *wurdon.* **+** Du. *worden,* pt. t. *werd;* Icel. *verða,* pt. t. *varð;* Dan. *vorde;* Swed. *varda;* G. *werden;* Goth. *wairthan,* to become, pt. t. *warth.* β. All from Teut. base WERTH, to become = √WERT, to turn; cf. L. *uertere,* to turn, *uertī,* to turn to, become. See **Verse.**

Wot, I know, or he knows; see **Wit** (1).

Would; see **Will** (1).

Wound, a hurt. (E.) A. S. *wund.* **+** Du. *wond, wonde,* Icel. *und,* Dan. *vunde,* G. *wunde,* sb. We also find an older type in A. S. *wund,* G. *wund,* Goth. *wunds,* wounded, harmed; Teut. type *wun-dōz;* Idg. type *wṇ-tos.* Origin doubtful. Cf. Wen, Win.

Wourali, Ourali, Oorali, Ourari, Curari, a resinous substance, used for poisoning arrows. (Guiana.) From 'ourali, written also *wourali, urali, urari, curare,* &c., according to the pronunciation of the various tribes'; W. H. Brett, Indian Tribes of Guiana, 1868, p. 140.

Wrack, a kind of sea-weed; shipwreck, ruin. (E.) Lit. 'that which is cast ashore;' well shewn by mod. F. *varech,* (1) sea-weed cast ashore, (2) pieces of a wrecked ship cast ashore; this F. word being borrowed from English. M.E. *wrak,* a wreck; a peculiar use of A. S. *wræc,* 'what is driven' (Lat. *actuārius*), O. E. Texts, 37. 62. **–** A. S. *wræc,* for *wrac,* 2nd grade of *wrecan,* to drive, urge, wreak; see **Wreak.** **+** Du. *wrak,* sb., a wreck, adj., broken; Icel. *rek*, anything drifted ashore; Dan. *vrag*, Swed. *vrak*, wreck, trash. Cf. Du. *wraken*, Dan. *vrage*, to reject.

Wraith, an apparition. (Scand.) Lowl. Sc. *wraith*, G. Douglas, tr. of Virgil, Æn. x. 641. The only similar word is Icel.*reiðr*, formerly *vreiðr*, angry, offended, equiv. to E. *wroth*; but the sense does not suit. ¶ Jamieson gives also an Ayrshire *warth*, with the sense of 'apparition.' Cf. Icel. *varða*, *varði*, a beacon, a pile of stones to warn a way-farer, Norw. *varde*, a beacon, *vardyvle* (= ward-evil?), a guardian or attendant spirit seen to follow or precede one, *vord*, an attendant spirit, Dan. dial. *vardyr*, *varedyr*, a ghostly creature resembling a man, who attends and preserves him. (Doubtful.)

Wrangle, vb. (E.) M. E. *wranglen*, to wrestle, also to dispute. Frequentative of *wring*, formed from the A. S. *wrang*, 2nd grade of *wring-an*; see **Wring.** Thus the sense was to keep on twisting or urging; hence to wrestle or argue vehemently. Cf. Dan. *vringle*, to twist, entangle. Der. *wrangle*, sb.; *wrangl-er*, a disputant in the schools (at Cambridge), now applied to a first-class man in the mathematical tripos.

Wrap, to enfold. (E.) M. E. *wrappen*; also *wlappen*, whence **Lap** (3). Cf. N. Fries. *wrappe*, to stop up. **Doublet,** *lap* (3). Cf. *en-velop*, *de-velop*.

Wrath, anger. (E.) M. E. *wraththe*, *wreththe*, A. S. *wrǣþþu*, wrath; Teut. type*wraithithā*. ─ A. S.*wrāð*, adj., wroth; Teut. type *waithoz*; see **Wroth**. **+** Icel. *reiði*, Dan. Swed. *vrede*, sb., wrath; from Icel. *reiðr*, Dan. Swed. *vred*, adj., wroth. See **Wroth.**

Wreak, to revenge. (E.) M. E. *wreken*. A.S. *wrecan*, pt. t. *wræc*, pp. *wrecen*, to wreak, revenge, punish, orig. to drive, urge, impel.**+**Du. *wreken*; Icel. *reka*, pt. t. *rak*, to drive, thrust, repel, wreak; G. *rächen*, to avenge; Goth. *wrikan*, to persecute. β. Allied to Lith. *wargti*, to suffer affliction; Gk. εἴργειν (for *ἐϝέργειν), to shut in; and to **Urge**. (✓WERG.)

Wreath, a garland. (E.) M. E. *wrethe*. A. S. *wrǣð*, a twisted band, bandage, fillet. Formed (with vowel-change of *ā* to *ǣ*) from *wrāð*, 2nd grade of *wriðan*, to writhe, twist. See **Writhe.** Der. *wreathe*, vb.

Wreck, ruin, remains of what is wrecked. (E.) Formerly *wrack*; the same as **Wrack.**

Wren, a small bird. (E.) M. E. *wrenne*. A. S. *wrenna*, *wrænna*, a wren. Cf. Icel. *rindill*, a wren.

Wrench, a twist, sprain. (E.) M. E. *wrenche*, only in the metaphorical sense of perversion, deceit. A. S. *wrenc* (dat. *wrence*), guile, fraud, orig. crookedness or perversion, lit. 'a twist.' **+** G. *rank* (pl. *ränke*), a trick. Teut. type *wrankiz*, m. From *wrank-*; perhaps allied to A. S. *wringan*, to wring, twist; see **Wrinkle.** Der. *wrench*, vb.

Wrest, to distort. (E.) M. E. *wresten*. A. S. *wrǣstan*, to twist forcibly. From *wrǣst*, adj., firm, strong (orig. tightly strung or twisted); formed with the suffix *-t* and vowel-change of *ā* to *ǣ*, from *wrāð*, 2nd grade of *wriðan*, to twist. (For the form, see Sievers, § 232; cf. A. S. *lāst*, foot-track, from *lið-an* (pt. t. *lāð*), to travel.) Cf. Icel. *reista*, to wrest, Dan. *vriste*, to wrest.

wrestle. (E.) M. E. *wrestlen*. A. S. *wrǣstlian*, to wrestle; frequentative of *wrǣstan*, to wrest, twist about; see above. **+**M. Du. *wrastelen*, *worstelen*, to struggle, wrestle; E. Fries. *worsteln*; N. Fries. *wrassele*.

Wretch, a miserable creature. (E.) Lit. 'outcast.' M. E. *wrecche*. A. S. *wrecca*, *wrǣcca*, an outcast, an exile. **+** O. Sax. *wrekkio*, O. H. G. *racheo*, G. *recke*, a warrior (adventurer). Teut. type *wrakjon-*, m. ─ Teut. *wrak*, 2nd grade of *wrekan-*, to drive, urge, hence to exile; see **Wreak.** Cf. Lithuan. *wargas*, misery. Der. *wretch-ed*, i. e. made like a wretch.

Wretchlessness, the same as *recklessness*; see **Reck.**

Wriggle, vb. (E.) Frequentative of *wrig*, to move about, Skelton, Elinour Rumming, 176; which is a weakened form of M. E. *wrikken*, to twist; [we actually find A. S. *wrigian*, but this passed into the form *wry*.] O. Fries. *wrigia*, E. Fries. *wriggen*, Norw. *rigga* (whence *rigla*), to move about, rock. By-form of E. Fries. *wrikken*, to turn hither and thither. **+** Du. *wriggelen*, to wriggle, frequent. of *wrikken*, to move or stir to and fro; Low G. *wrickeln* (Richey); Dan. *vrikke*, to wriggle, Swed. *vricka*, to turn to and fro. See **Rickets** and **Wry.**

Wright, a workman. (E.) M. E. *wrighte*. A. S. *wyrhta*, a worker.─ A. S. *wyrht*, a deed, work; formed with suffix *-t* from *wyrc-an*, to work. [Teut. type

wurhtiz; related to *werkjan-*, to work.]
— A. S. *weorc*, work, sb. See **Work**. +
O. Sax. *wurhtio*, O. H. G. *wurhto*, a wright.
Der. *cart-wright, ship-wright, wheel-wright*.

Wring, to twist. (E.) M. E. *wringen*,
A. S. *wringan*, pt. t. *wrang*, pp. *wrungen*,
to press, compress, strain, wring. + Du.
wringen; G. *ringen* (pt. t. *rang*), to
wrestle, to twist, turn. Allied to **Wry**,
and perhaps to **Worry**. Der. *wrong*.

Wrinkle (1), a small ridge or unevenness on a surface. (E.) M. E. *wrinkel*.
Perhaps allied to **Wrench**, and to A. S.
wringan, to twist. The lit. sense is 'a
little twist,' causing unevenness. + M. Du.
wrinckel, a wrinkle, allied to *wringen*, to
twist. ¶ Dan. *rynke*, Swed. *rynka*, Icel.
hrukka (for **hrunka*), a wrinkle, forms
due to the pp. of an old strong vb.
*hrenkan, are related to **Ruck** (1). Der.
wrinkle, vb.

Wrinkle (2), a hint. (E.) Lit. 'a
small trick;' dimin. of A. S. *wrenc*, a
trick; see **Wrench**.

Wrist. (E.) M. E. *wrist, wirst*. A.S.
wrist, also called *handwrist*, i. e. that
which turns the hand about. Formed
(like *wrest*, q. v.) with suffix *-t* from
wrið-, weak grade of *wriðan*, to writhe,
twist about. + Low G. *wrist*; Icel. *rist*,
instep, from *rið-*, weak grade of *rīða*, to
twist; Dan. Swed. *vrist*, instep, from *vride*
or *vrida*, to twist; G. *rist*, instep, wrist.

Write. (E.) The orig. sense was 'to
score,' i. e. to scratch the surface of wood
with a knife. M. E. *writen*, pt. t. *wroot*,
pp. *writen* (with short *i*). A. S. *wrītan*,
pt. t. *wrāt*, pp. *writen*. + O. Sax. *wrītan*,
to cut, write; Du. *rijten*, to tear; Icel.
rīta, to scratch, write; Swed. *rita*, to
draw; G. *reissen*, to cut, tear. Teut.
type **wreitan-*, pt. t. **wrait*, pp. **writanoz*.
Der. *writ*, sb., A. S. *gewrit*, from the weak
grade *writ-*.

Writhe. (E.) M. E. *writhen*, pt. t.
wroth, pp. *writhen* (with short *i*). A.S.
wrīðan, pt. t. *wrāð*, pp. *wriðen*, to twist
about.+Icel. *rīða*, Dan. *vride*, Swed. *vrida*,
to wring, twist, turn; O. H. G. *rīdan*.
Teut. type **wreithan-*. Der. *wroth, wrath,
wreath, wrest, wrist*.

Wrong, perverted, bad. (Scand.) M. E.
wrong. Late A. S. *wrang*, a wrong, sb.;
orig. an adj. — Icel. *rangr*, O. Icel.
*wrangr > *vrangr*, awry, wrong; Dan.
vrang, Swed. *vrång*, perverse. From

vrang, 2nd grade of *vringa*, to wring
(only preserved in the pt. t. 3 p. pl.
vrungu); cognate with E. **Wring**.+Du.
wrang, acid, sour (because acids *wring*
the mouth).

Wroth, angry. (E.) A.S. *wrāð*; from
wrāð, 2nd grade of *wrīðan*, to writhe. +
Du. *wreed*, cruel; Icel. *reiðr*, Swed. Dan.
vred; O. H. G. *reid, reidi*, twisted, curly.
See **Writhe**.

Wry, twisted, turned aside. (E.) From
the M. E. *wrien*, vb., to twist, bend aside;
A. S. *wrigian*, to turn, incline towards.
See **Wriggle**. Der. *a-wry*, for *on wry*,
Barbour, Bruce, 4. 705.

Wych-elm; see **Witch-elm**.

Wyvern, Wivern, a two-legged
dragon, in heraldry. (F. – L.) The final
n is added, as in *bitter-n*. M. E. *wiuere*
(*wivere*), a serpent. – A. F. *wyvre*, O. F.
wivre (F. *givre*), a viper. – L. *uīpera*, a
viper; see **Viper**. ¶ The *w* is due to G.
influence; as if from O. H. G. **wīpera*,
borrowed from L.

X.

Xebec, a small three-masted vessel.
(Span. – Turk.) Span. *xabeque*. – Turk.
sumbakī, a kind of ship. Cf. Pers. *sum-
buk*, Arab. *sumbūk*, a small boat, a pinnace. (Devic; Rich., p. 852.)

Y.

Y-, prefix. (E.) In *y-clept, y-wis*. M.E.
y-, i-; A. S. *ge-*, a common prefix. This
prefix appears as *e-* in *e-nough*, and as *a-*
in *a-ware*.+Du. G. *ge-*, prefix; Goth. *ga-*,
prefix.

Yacht. (Du.) Du. *jagt*, M. Du. *jacht*,
a swift boat, a hunting.—Du. *jagen*, to
hunt, chase. + G. *jagen*, to hunt. See
Yaw.

Yak, a wild ox. (Thibet.) Thibetan
ɣyag, a male yak, where the symbol ɣ is
used to denote a peculiar Thibetan sound;
H. A. Jäschke, Dict. p. 668.

Yam, a large esculent tuber. (Port. –
W. African.) Port. *inhame*, a yam
(Littré). Formerly called *inamia* in
Benin; Hakluyt, ii. 2. 129.

Yankee, a citizen of New England, or
of the United States. (North. E.) In use
in Boston, 1765. Dr. Wm. Gordon, in his
Hist. of the American War, ed. 1789, vol. i.
pp. 324, 325, says it was a favourite cant

word in Cambridge, Mass., as early as 1713, and that it meant 'excellent,' as 'a yankee good horse.' The word may have spread from the students through New England, and have thence obtained a wider currency. It appears to be the same as Lowl. Sc. *yankie*, a sharp, clever, forward woman; cf. Lowl. Sc. *yanker*, an agile girl, an incessant talker, a smart stroke, *yank*, a jerk, smart blow, *yanking*, active (Jamieson). We also find *yank*, to jerk, noted by Buckland (Log of a Naturalist, 1876, p. 130) as an American word. β. Thus *yank-y* is quick, spry, from *yank*, to jerk. ¶ Dampier (Voyages, 1699, i. 38) mentions a Captain *Yanky* several times.

Yap, to yelp. (E.) Of imitative origin; cf. E. Fries. and Low G. *jappen*, to gasp; F. *japper*, to yap. Note also Lowl. Sc. *yaup*, to yelp, from Icel. *gjálpa*. See **Yelp.**

Yard (1), an enclosed space. (E.) M.E. *yerd.* A.S. *geard*, an enclosure, court. + Icel. *garðr* (whence E. *garth*), Dan. Du. *gaard*, Swed. *gård*; Goth. *gards*, a house; O.H.G. *gart*, a circle; allied to O.H.G. *garto*, a garden, Goth. *garda*, a fold. Teut. type **gardoz*, m.; Idg. type **ghortos*, as in O. Irish *gort*, a field, *lub-gort*, a garden; L. *hortus*, a garden; Gk. χόρτος, a courtyard. But the connexion with Gk. χόρτος is not certain. **Doublets,** *garden, garth.* Der. *court-yard, orchard.*

Yard (2), a rod, 36 inches, cross-bar on a mast. (E.) M.E. *yerde, yerde*, a stick, rod. A.S. *gyrd, gerd*, a rod.+Du. *garde*, a twig, rod, G. *gerte*, a switch; O.H.G. *gerta*; Teut. type *gardjā*, f. Allied to O. Bulg. *žrŭdĭ* (Russ. *jerde*), a rod. But not to Icel. *gaddr*, Goth. *gazds*, a goad. Streitberg, § 125 (4).

Yare, ready. (E.) M.E. *ʒare, yare*, ready. A.S. *gearu, gearo*, ready, quick, prompt. + Du. *gaar*, done, dressed (as meat); Icel. *görr*, ready; O.H.G. *garo*, ready; cf. G. *gar*, adv., wholly. Teut. type **garwoz*. Allied to **Gear.**

Yarn. (E.) M.E. *yarn.* A.S. *gearn*, thread. + Du. *garen*, Icel. Dan. Swed. G. *garn.* Allied to Gk. χορδή, a cord, orig. a string of gut; cf. Lith. *žarnos*, Icel. *garnir*, guts. See **Cord, Chord.**

Yarrow, the plant milfoil. (E.) M.E. *yarowe, yarwe.* A.S. *gæruwe, gearuwe, gearwe*, yarrow. + Du. *gerw*, G. *garbe*, O.H.G. *garawa.* If allied to **Yare**, perhaps it meant 'that which dresses,' or puts

in order; from the old belief in its curative properties as a healer of wounds.

Yataghan, Ataghan, a dagger-like sabre, with doubly curved blade. (Turk.) Turk. *yātāghān*, the same; Zenker's Dict. pp. 947, 958.

Yaw, to go unsteadily, as a ship. (Scand.—Du.) Icel. *jaga*, to move to and fro; also, to hunt.—Du. *jagen*, to hunt. See **Yacht.**

Yawl (1), a small boat. (Du.) Du. *jol*, a yawl, a Jutland boat; M. Du. *jolleken*, 'a small barke.'+Dan. *jolle*, Swed. *julle*, a yawl; E. Fries. *jül, jülle*; Low G. *jolle* (Lübben). Root unknown.

Yawl (2), to howl. (E.) Also *yole, yowl* (Halliwell). M. E. *ʒaulen.* Also M. E. *goulen.* Cf. E. Fries. *jaueln*, Low G. *jaueln*, to yawl. + Icel. *gaula*, Norw. *gaula*, to low, bellow, roar; cf. Du. *jolen*, to groan. Imitative. Cf. **Yell.**

Yawn, to gape. (E.) M.E. *geonien, yonien*; whence E. *yawn*, by lengthening of ǒ to open long *o*; cf. E. *frost, broth.*—A.S. *geonian*, to yawn. Also *ginian*; from *gin-*, weak grade of *-gīnan*, strong verb, to gape widely.+O.H.G. *ginēn*, to yawn; cf. Icel. *gīna*, to gape, pt. t. *gein.* Allied to L. *hiare*, to gape; see **Hiatus.** (√GHEI.)

Ye. (E.) M.E. *ye, ʒe*, nom.; *your, ʒour*, gen.; *you, ʒou, yow*, dat. and acc. pl. A.S. *gē*, nom. ye; *ēower*, gen. of you; *ēow*, to you, you, dat. and acc. + Du. *gij*, ye, *u*, you; Icel. *ēr, ier*, ye, *yðar*, your, *yðr*, you; Dan. Swed. *i*, ye, you; G. *ihr*; Goth. *jūs*, ye, *izwara*, your, *izwis*, you. β. The common Idg. base is YU; whence Lith. *jus*, ye; Gk. ὑ-μεῖς, ye, Skt. *yū-yam*, ye. Brugm. ii. § 436.

Yea, verily. (E.) This is the simple affirmative; *yes* is a strengthened form, often accompanied by an oath in our early writers. M.E. *ye.* A.S. *gēa, geá*, yea.+ Du. Dan. Swed. G. *ja*, Icel. *jā*, Goth. *ja, jai*; W. *ie*; Gk. ἤ, truly. Der. *yes.*

Yean, Ean, to bring forth young. (E.) Here the prefixed *y-* answers to the A.S. prefix *ge-.* A.S. *ēanian*, to ean; *ge-ēanian* to yean. We find *ge-ēane eowa* = the ewes great with young, Gen. xxxiii. 13; cf. Swed. dial. *öna*, to yean, *vara i ön*, to be with lamb (Rietz, p. 114). Teut. type **aunōjan*, to yean. From Teut. type **auno-* (for **agwno-*), corresponding to L. *agnus*, a lamb (Kluge). Cf. Irish *ūan*, W. *oen*, Corn. *oin*, Bret. *oan*, Manx *eayn*, a lamb. Hence Manx *eayney*, to yean. ¶ Sievers derives *ean* from A. S. *eowu*, a ewe; see **Ewe.** Brugm. i. § 671. Der. *yean-ling*, a new-born lamb.

Year. (E.) M. E. *ȝeer, yeer*, often unaltered in the plural (hence 'a *two-year* old colt'). A. S *gēar, gĕr*, a year; pl. same.+Du. *jaar*, Icel. *ār*, Dan. *aar*, Swed. *år*, G. *jahr*, Goth. *jĕr.* Teut. type *yêrom*, n. Cf. Zend *yār(e)*, a year. Perhaps allied to Gk. ὥρος, a season, year, ὥρα, season, hour; Skt. *yātu-*, time. Lit. 'that which passes.' (√YE, to pass; from √EI, to go.) Brugm. i. § 308, ii. § 587.

Yearn (1), to long for. (E.) M. E. *yernen.* A. S. *giernan*, to yearn, be desirous. – A. S. *georn*, adj., desirous. + Icel. *girna*, to desire, from *gjarn*, eager; Goth. *gairnjan*, to long for, from *-gairns*, desirous (Teut. type *gernoz*). β. Again, the adj. is from the verb appearing in O. H. G. *gerōn*, G. *be-gehren*, to long for; allied to Gk. χαίρειν, to rejoice, χαρά, joy, Skt. *hary*, to desire. (√GHER.)

Yearn (2), to grieve. (E.) Also spelt *earn, ern*; Hen. V. ii. 3. 3, ii. 3. 6; Jul. Cæs. ii. 2. 129; Merry Wives, iii. 5. 45; Rich. II. v. 5. 76; Hen. V. iv. 3. 26; the prefixed *y-* being due to A. S. prefix *ge-*, as in the case of *yean*. From A. S. *eorn-*; as in *eorn-igende*, murmuring; *eorn-ful*, anxious; *eorn-lic*, diligent; perhaps allied to **Earnest.**

Yeast. (E.) M. E. *yeest, yest.* A. S. *gist*, yeast. + Du. *gest, gist*, N. Fries. *jêst*, Icel. *jast, jastr*, Swed. *jäst*, Dan. *giær*, G. *gäscht, gischt.* Teut. base *yest-*. All from √YES, to ferment, appearing in O. H. G. *jesan*, G. *gähren*, to ferment, Gk. ζέειν, to boil, ζεστός, fervent. See **Zeal.** Der. *yeast-y* or *yest-y*, frothy, Hamlet, v. 2. 199.

Yede, went. (E.) M. E. *yede, ȝede*; also *eode.* A. S. *ge-ēode*, also *ēode*, went, only in the pt. t. Cf. A. S. *ēodon*, pt. t. pl., with Goth. *iddjēdun*, pt. t. pl. Perhaps A. S. *ēo- = *ī-o*, from √EI, to go. Cf. Skt. *ayāt, iyāt*, he went. Brugm. i. § 309 (2); ii. § 478.

Yelk; see **Yolk.**

Yell. (E.) M. E. *yellen.* A. S. *gellan, giellan*, to cry out, resound. + Du. *gillen*. Icel. *gella*, also *gjalla* (pt. t. *gall*), Dan. *giælle*, gialde, Swed. *gälla*, G. *gellen*, to sound loud and shrill. Teut. type *gellan-*, pt. t. *gall.* Allied to Icel. *gala*, pt. t. *gōl*, to sing, O. H. G. *galan*; A. S. *galan*,

pt. t. *gōl*, whence E. *nightin-gale*. Der. *stan-iel.*

Yellow. (E.) M. E. *yelwe, yelu.* A.S. *geolo, geolu*, yellow. + Du. *geel*, G. *gelb.* Teut. type *gelwoz*, Idg. type *ghelwos.* Allied to L. *heluus*, light yellow, Gk. χλόη, young verdure of trees, Russ. *zelenŭi*, green, Skt. *hari*, green, yellow. Further allied to **Gall** (1). Der. *yolk.*

yellow - hammer, yellow - ammer, a song-bird. (E.) The *h* is an ignorant insertion; *ammer* answers to A. S. *amore*, a small bird.+M. Du. *emmerick*, a yellow-ammer, G. *gelbammer, goldammer*, yellow-ammer or gold-ammer, *emmerling*, the same; O. H. G. *amero.*

Yelp, to bark shrilly. (E.) M. E. *yelpen*, also to boast. A. S. *gielpan*, pt. t. *gealp*, pp. *golpen*, to boast, exult, talk noisily. + Icel. *gjālpa*, to yelp; M. H. G. *gelfen.* Allied to **Yell.** Cf. **Yap.**

Yeoman. (E.) M. E. *yoman*, also *yeman.* It appears to answer to an A. S. *gēaman* (not found), which might become *gēaman*; these would give *yeman, yoman* in M. E. The word is cleared up by the existence of O. Fries. *gāman*, a villager, from *gā*, also *gō*, a village, and *man*, a man; so also M. Du. *goymannen*, arbitrators appointed to decide disputes, from M. Du. *gouwe*, a hamlet (Hexham). Cf. also G. *gau*, a province, Goth. *gawi*, a district; O. H. G. *gawi* (without mutation), and O. H. G. *gewi* (with mutation), like Bavarian *gäu*, whence *gäumann*, 'landmann.' Observe *yore*, as compared with *year.* Many solutions have been proposed of this difficult word.

Yerk, the same as **Jerk.**

Yes. (E.) A strengthened form of *yea.* M. E. *yis, yus.* A. S. *gise, gese*, yes. Prob. short for *gēa swā*, i. e. yea, so; see **Yea.**

Yesterday. (E.) M. E. *yisterdai*; from A. S. *geostra, giestra* (yester-), and *dæg*, a day.+Du. *gisteren, dag van gister*, G. *gestern*; Goth. *gistradagis*, tomorrow. β. Cf. Lat. *hester-* in *hes-ter-nus*, adj., belonging to yesterday; where again the syllable *hes-* is cognate with Icel. *gær*, Dan. *gaar*, Swed. *går*, Lat. *her-i*, Gk. χθές, Skt. *hyas*, yesterday. The suffix *-ter* is of a comparative form, as in *in-ter-ior*, &c. Brugm. i. §§ 624, 923.

Yet. (E.) M. E. *yet, yit.* A. S. *git, get, giet*, moreover. + O. Fries. *ieta, ita*, M. H. G. *iezuo, ieze*, yet; cf. G. *jetz-t*, now. Origin obscure.

Yew, a tree. (E.) M. E. *ew.* A. S. *īw.* + Icel. *ȳr,* G. *eibe,* O. H. G. *īwa,* yew. We also find Irish *eo,* W. *yw, ywen,* Corn. *hivin,* Bret. *ivin,* a yew. ¶ *Not* allied to *ivy.*

Yex, to hiccough. (E.) M. E. *yexen, yesken.* A. S. *giscian,* to sob, sigh. Prob. allied to L. *hiscere,* to yawn, *hiāre,* to yawn; see **Yawn.** (√GHEI.)

Yield. (E.) M. E. *gelden, yelden,* pt. t. *yald,* pp. *yolden,* to pay; hence, to yield up. A. S. *gieldan, gildan,* pt. t. *geald,* pp. *golden,* to pay, give up. + Du. *gelden,* Icel. *gjalda,* Dan. *gielde,* to pay; Swed. *gälla,* to be worth; G. *gelten,* pt. t. *galt,* to be worth; Goth. *fra-gildan,* to pay back. (Teut. base GELD.) **Der.** *guild.*

Yoke, sb. (E.) M. E. *yok.* A. S. *geoc, gioc, ioc,* a yoke for oxen. + Du. *juk,* Icel. *ok,* Dan. *aag,* Swed. *ok,* Goth. *juk,* G. *joch.* Teut. type **yukom,* n.; Idg. type **jugom;* cf. W. *iau,* L. *iugum,* Russ. *igo,* Lith. *jungas,* Gk. *ζυγόν,* Skt. *yuga-,* a yoke, a couple. Lit. 'that which joins;' all from the weak grade of √YEUG, to join. See **Join. Der.** *yoke,* vb.

Yolk, Yelk, yellow part of an egg. (E.) M. E. *yolke, yelke.* A. S. *geoleca, geolca,* the yolk, lit. 'yellow part.' – A. S. *geolu,* yellow; see **Yellow.**

Yon, adj., at a distance. (E.) M. E. *yon, ȝon.* A. S. *geon, yon;* Ælfred, tr. of Gregory's Past. Care, ed. Sweet, p. 443. + Icel. *enn,* the, orig. that, confused with *hinn;* Goth. *jains,* G. *jener,* yon, that. β. Allied to Skt. *ya-s,* who, orig. that; Gk. *ὅς* (for *yós*). From the same base are *ye-a, ye-s, ye-t.* **Der.** *yond-er,* M. E. *yonder,* adv.; cf. Goth. *jaindre,* adv., yonder, thither.

Yore, formerly. (E.) M. E. *yore.* A. S. *geāra,* adv., formerly; lit. ' of years, during years,' orig. gen. pl. of *geār;* see **Year.**

You. (E.) Properly the dat. and acc. of *ye;* see **Ye.**

your. (E.) M. E. *your.* A. S. *eōwer,* your; orig. gen. pl. of *gē,* ye; see **Ye.** **Der.** *your-s,* M. E. *youres,* from A. S. *eowres,* gen. sing. masc. and neut. of *eower,* your, possessive pronoun.

Young. (E.) M. E. *yong, yung.* A. S. *geong, giung, iung,* young. + Du. *jong,* Icel. *ungr,* Dan. Swed. *ung,* G. *jung,* Goth. *juggs* (for **jungs*). Teut. **yun-goz,* short for **yuwungoz.* β. These forms answer to Lat. *iuuencus,* a young animal, heifer; cf. Skt. *yuvaça-,* W. *ieuanc,*

young. Other forms (without the final guttural) are L. *iuuenis,* Lith. *jaunas,* Skt. *yuvan,* Russ. *iunuii,* young; from Idg. base **yuwen-.* **Der.** *young-ling, young-ster;* also *youn-ker,* borrowed from Du. *jonker, jonkheer,* i. e. young sir, compounded of *jong,* young, and *heer,* sir, a lord.

youth. (E.) M. E. *youthe;* earlier *ȝuweðe, ȝuȝeðe,* youth. A. S. *geogoð, geoguð, iuguð.* [The middle *g* became *w,* and then disappeared.] + O.Sax. *juguð,* Du. *jeugd,* G. *jugend,* O. H. G. *jugund;* Teut. type **yugunthiz,* f. (where *-unth-* > A. S. *-ūð* > *-uð*); from Idg. base **yuwnt-,* which is from **yuwen-* (above). Cf. L. *iuuenta;* also L. *iuuentās,* Skt. *yuvatā,* youth.

Yowl; see **Yawl** (2).

Yucca, a genus of American liliaceous plants. (Span. – Caribbean.) Span. *yuca,* said to be a word of Caribbean origin.

Yule, Christmas. (E.) M. E. *ȝole, yole.* A. S. *gēol, geohol,* the feast; also *iula, gēola,* the name of a month. December was called *se ǣrra geōla,* the former yule; and January *se æftera geōla,* the latter yule. We also find Icel. *jōl,* a feast in December, *ȳlir,* December, and Goth. *jiuleis,* November. Of disputed origin. ¶ The attempt to connect this word with *wheel* is futile.

Ywis, certainly. (E.) M. E. *ywis, iwis;* often written *Iwis, I-wis,* in MSS., whence, by a singular error, the fictitious verb *wis,* to know, has been evolved by lexicographers, though unknown to our old MSS. A. S. *gewis,* adj., certain, which came to be used as an adverb. β. Here the *ge-* is a mere prefix; see **Y-** (above); the adj., *wis,* certain, answers to Teut. type **wissoz,* Idg. type **wid-tos,* an old pp. signifying ' known,' hence ' sure '; from √WEID, to know. (*dt* > *ss.*) See **Wit,** vb. + Du. *gewis,* adj. and adv., certain, certainly; G. *gewiss,* certainly; Icel. *viss,* certain, Dan. *vis,* Swed. *viss,* certain; Dan. *vist,* Swed. *visst,* certainly.

Z.

Zamindar, Zemindar, a landholder. (Hind. – Pers.) Hind. *zamīndār,* a land-holder. – Pers. *zamīn,* earth, land (allied to L. *humus*); *dār,* holding, possessing.

Zanana, Zenana, the female apartments. (Hind. – Pers.) Hind. *zanāna,* the women's apartments. — Pers. *zanān*, women; pl. of *zan*, a woman, which is cognate with E. **Quean.**

Zany, a buffoon. (Ital. — Gk. — Heb.) O. Ital. *Zane*, Ital. *Zanni*, a familiar form of *Giovanni*, John; used to mean 'a sillie John, a gull, a noddie, clowne, foole, simple fellowe in a plaie,' Florio. — Gk. Ἰωάννης, John. — Heb. *Yōkhānān*, i. e. the Lord graciously gave. — Heb. *Yō*, the Lord; *khānan*, to shew mercy.

Zariba, Zareeba, an enclosure, slight defence. (Arab.) Used in newspapers with reference to the war in the Soudan. — Arab. *zarībat*, 'a fold, a pen, an enclosure for cattle; den or haunt of wild beasts; lurking-place of a hunter;' Rich. Dict. p. 775.

Zeal. (F. — L. — Gk.) Formerly *zele*. — M. F. *zele*, 'zeale;' Cot. (Mod. F. *zèle*.) — L. *zēlum*, acc. of *zēlus*, zeal. — Gk. ζῆλος, ardour. Doric ζᾶλος, Idg. type *yā-los*; perhaps from *yā*, to drive; as in Skt. *yātṛ*, a driver (Prellwitz). Der. *zeal-ot*, M. F. *zelote*, 'zealous,' Cot.; from L. *zēlōtes*, Gk. ζηλωτής, a zealot.

Zebra. (Port. — W. African.) Port. *zebra* (Span. *cebra*, *zebra*). According to Littré, the word is of Ethiopian origin, but this is due to some mistake, as the name originated in Congo. (N. and Q., 9 S. v. 480.)

Zedoary, an E. Indian root resembling ginger. (F. — Low L. — Pers.) M. F. *zedoaire*, Cot. — Low L. *zedoāria*. — Pers. *zadwār*, *zidwār*, zedoary; also spelt *jadwār*. ¶ The O. F. forms were *citouart*, *citoual*, *citoal*; whence M. E. *cetewale*, Chaucer, C. T. 13691.

Zend, an ancient Persian dialect. (Zend.) Properly the translation into the Pehlevi language of the *Avesta*, or Zoro-astrian scriptures; but commonly used to denote the language, an ancient Persian dialect, in which the *Avesta* is written. It is supposed that *Avesta* means the 'text,' and *Zend* the 'commentary' or 'explanation.' The word *zend* is mod. Persian (Palmer); also written *zand* (Richardson); and corresponds to Zend *zaiñti*, knowledge, information, appearing in the compounds *ā-zaiñti*, *paiti-zaiñti*, knowledge, and answering to an Idg. form *ganti*, from the Idg. root GEN, to know (Fick, i. 67, 321). See **Can** (1). β. *Avesta* has been explained as meaning 'the settled' text (Skt. *ava-*

sthita, from *ava-sthā*, to be firm: root STĀ); or, otherwise, as meaning 'that which is proclaimed or made known' (cf. Skt. *ā-vid*, to report: root WEID). See Max Müller, Lectures, 8th ed. i. 237.

Zenith. (F. — Span. — Arab.) M. E. *senyth*. — O. F. *cenith*; F. *zénith*. — Span. *zenit*, O. Span. *zenith*. — Arab. *samt*, a way, road, path, tract, quarter; whence *samt-ur-ras*, the zenith, vertical point of the heavens; also *as-samt*, an azimuth. β. *Samt* was pronounced *semt*, of which Span. *zenit* is a corruption; again, *samt* is here short for *samt-ur-ras* or *semt-er-ras* (as above), lit. the way overhead, from *ras*, the head. See **Azimuth.**

Zephyr. (F. — L. — Gk.) M. F. *zephyre*, the west wind. — L. *zephyrum*, acc. of *zephyrus*, the west wind. — Gk. ζέφυρος, the west wind.

Zero. (Ital. — Low L. — Arab.) Ital. *zero*, short for *zefiro*. — Low L. *zephyrum* (Devic). — Arab. *sifr*, a cipher; see **Cipher.**

Zest. (F. — L. — Gk.) Formerly a chip of orange or lemon-peel, used for flavouring drinks; hence, something that gives a relish, or simply a relish. — M. F. *zest*, 'the thick skin whereby the kernell of a wallnut is divided,' Cot.; hence, a slice of lemon-peel. — L. *schistus*, *schistos*, lit. cleft, divided. — Gk. σχιστός, divided. — Gk. σχίζειν, to cleave; see **Schist.**

Zigzag, having sharp, quick turns. (F. — G.) F. *zigzag*. — G. *zickzack*, a zigzag; [whence *zickzack segeln*, to tack, in sailing.] Reduplicated from *zacke*, a tooth; with reference to *zacken-werk*, notched work; hence *zickzack* is 'in an indented manner.' Cf. E. Fries. *takken*, to notch (whence E. *tack*, in sailing). See **Tack.**

Zinc, a metal. (F. — G.) F. *zinc*. — G. *zink*, zinc; of uncertain origin. Perhaps allied to *zinn*, tin; and meaning 'tin-like.' But see Schade.

Zodiac, an imaginary belt in the heavens, containing the twelve *signs*. (F. — L. — Gk.) F. *zodiaque*. — L. *zōdiacus*. — Gk. ζωδιακός, sb., the zodiacal circle; so called from containing the twelve con-stellations chiefly represented by animals. — Gk. ζωδιακός, adj., belonging to animals. — Gk. ζῴδιον, a small animal; dimin. of ζῷον, a living creature. See **Zoology.**

Zone. (F. — L. — Gk.) F. *zone*. — L. *zōna*. — Gk. ζώνη, a girdle; for *ζώσ-νη. — Gk. ζώννυμι (= *ζώσ-νυμι), I gird.

Cf. Lith. *jōsta*, a girdle, from *jōsti*, to gird. (√YŌS.)

Zoology. (Gk.) From Gk. ζῶο-ν, a living creature, animal; and -λογία, allied to λόγος, discourse, from λέγειν, to speak. β. Gk. ζῶον is neut. of ζῶος, living; allied to ζωή, life, ζάειν, ζῆν, to live. Allied to Zend *ji*, to live; see **Vivid.** (√GwEI.) Brugm. ii. § 488.

zoophyte. (F. — Gk.) F. *zoophyte.* — Gk. ζωόφυτον, a living being; an animal-plant. — Gk. ζωό-s, living; φυτόν, a plant, that which has grown, from φύειν, to produce, grow, from √BHEU, to exist. See **Be.**

Zouave, one of a body of soldiers in the French service, orig. Arabs. (F. — N. African.) F. *Zouave.* — N. African *Zouaoua*, a tribe of Kabyles living among the Jurjura mountains in Algeria.

Zymotic, a term applied to diseases, in which a poison works through the body like a ferment. (Gk.) Gk. ζυμωτικός, causing to ferment. — Gk. ζυμόω, I cause to ferment. — Gk. ζύμη, leaven. Allied to L. *iūs*, broth; see **Juice.**

APPENDIX

I. LIST OF PREFIXES

THE following is a list of the principal prefixes in English, shewing their origin. It is, perhaps, not quite exhaustive, but contains nearly all of any consequence. For further information, see the etymologies of the words *a-down*, &c., in the Dictionary.

A- (1), in a-down. (E.) See **Of-** (below).

A- (2), in a-foot. (E.) See **On-** (below).

A- (3), in a-long. (E.) See **An-** (5).

A- (4), in a-rise. (E.) A.S. *ā-*, intensive prefix to verbs.✠Goth. *us-*, *ur-*; G. *er-*.

A- (5), in a-chieve. (F.—L.) See **Ad-**.

A- (6), in a-vert. (L.) See **Ab-**.

A- (7), in a-mend. (F.—L.) See **Ex-** (1).

A- (8), in a-las. (F.—L.) O.F. *a-*; from L. *ah!* interj.

A- (9), in a-byss. (Gk.) See **An-** (2).

A- (10), in a-do. (E.) For *at do*.

A- (11), in a-ware. (E.) M. E. *i-*; *y-*; A. S. *ge-*, prefix. See **Y-**.

A- (12), in a-pace. (E.) For *a pace*; *a* for *an*, indef. art.

A- (13), in a-vast. (Du.) Du. *hou vast*, hold fast. (Doubtful.)

A- (14), in a-pricot. (Arab.) Arab. *al*, def. art. See **Al-** (4).

Ab- (1); ab-dicate, ab-undance. (L.; *or* F.—L.) L. *ab*, from. Lengthened to *abs-* in *abs-cond*; cf. Gk. *ἄψ*. ✠ E. *of*; Gk. *ἀπό*; Skt. *apa*, away from. See **Apo-**, **Of-**. This prefix also appears as *a-*, *adv-*, *av-*, *v-*; ex. a-vert, adv-ance, av-aunt, v-anguard.

Ab- (2); ab-breviate. (L.) Used for L. *ad*; see **Ad-**.

Abs-; abs-cond, abs-ent, abs-tain, abs-tract. (L.; *or* F.—L.) L. *abs-*, extended form of *ab*; see **Ab-** (1).

Ac-; see **Ad-**. Also for **A-** (4) in ac-cursed; and for **A-** (2) in ac-knowledge.

Ad-; ad-apt, ad-dress. (L.; *or* F.—L.) L. *ad*, to, at, for. A.S. *æt*, E. *at*. This prefix appears as *a-*, *ab-*, *ac-*, *ad-*, *af-*, *ag-*, *al-*, *an-*, *ap-*, *ar-*, *as-*, *at-*; ex.: a-chieve, ab-breviate, ac-cede, ad-mire, af-

fix, ag-gress, al-lude, an-nex, ap-pend, ar-rogate, as-sign, at-tract.

Adv-; see **Ab-** (1).

Af-; see **Ad-**. Also for **A-** (11) in af-ford; for **A-** (4) in af-fright; and for **Ex-** (1) in af-fray.

After-. (E.) E. *after*, prep.; A.S. *æfter*.

Ag-; see **Ad-**.

Al- (1), all; al-most. See **All**, p. 12.

Al- (2); see **Ad-**.

Al- (3); al-ligator. (Span.—L.) Span. *el*, def. art.—L. *ille*, he.

Al- (4); al-cohol. (Arab.) Arab. *al*, def. art. This also appears as *a-*, *ar-*, *as-*, *el-*, *l-*. Ex.: a-pricot, ar-tichoke, as-sagai, el-ixir, l-ute. See **L-** (2).

Am- (1); am-bush. (F.—L.) F. *em-*.— L. *im-*, for *in*, prep.; see **In-** (2).

Am- (2); am-brosia. (Gk.) See **An-** (2).

Am- (3); am-bassador; see **Ambi-**.

Am- (4); am-putate. (L.) Short for *amb-*, *ambi-*; see below.

Ambi-, **Amb-**; ambi-dextrous; amb-ition. (L.; *or* F.—L.; *or* C.) L. *ambi-*, on both sides, around.✠Gk. *ἀμφί*; O. Irish *imm-*; see **Ambassador**, p. 14. See below.

Amphi-. (Gk.) Gk. *ἀμφί*, on both sides, around.✠L. *ambi-*; see **Ambi-**.

An- (1); see **Ad-**.

An- (2), **A-** (9), negative prefix. (Gk.) Gk. *ἀν-*, *ἀ-*, neg. prefix. Hence *am-* in am-brosia; *a-* in a-byss.✠L. *in-*, E. *un-*; see **In-** (3), **Un-** (1).

An- (3); see **Ana-**.

An- (4); an-oint. (F.—L.) For F. *en-*. —L. *in*, prep.; see **In-** (2).

An- (5); an-swer. (E.) A.S. *and-*, in reply to, opposite to. **+** Goth. *and-*; Du. *ent-*; G. *ent-*; Gk. ἀντί. Shortened to *a-* in a-long; and allied to *un-* in verbs. See Anti- (1), Un- (2).

An- (6); an-cestor. (F−L.) See Ante-.

Ana-, An- (3); ana-gram, an-eurism. (Gk.) Gk. ἀνά, upon, on, up. **+** A.S. *on*, Goth. *ana*. See On-.

Anci-; anci-ent. (F.−L.) See Ante-.

Ann-; ann-eal. (E.) See Anneal in the Dictionary, p. 18.

Ant-; ant-agonist. (Gk.) See Anti-.

Ante-. (L.) L. *ante*, before. Also *anti-, anci-, ant-, an-*; as in anti-cipate, anci-ent, ant-ique, an-cestor.

Anth-; anth-em. (Gk.) See below.

Anti- (1), **Ant-**. (Gk.) Gk. ἀντί, against, opposite to. Also *ant-, anth-*, as in ant-agonist, anth-em. See An- (5), Un- (2).

Anti- (2); see Ante-.

Ap-; ap-pend; see Ad-.

Aph-; aph-æresis; see below.

Apo-. (Gk.) Hence *aph-* in aph-æresis. Gk. ἀπό, from, off. **+** L. *ab*; A.S. *of*; see Ab- (1), Of-.

Ar- (1); see Ad-.

Ar- (2); ar-tichoke; see Al- (4).

Arch-, Archi-, Arche-; arch-bishop, arch-angel, archi-tect, arche-type. (Gk.) Gk. ἀρχί-, chief.−Gk. ἄρχειν, to be first.

As- (1); as-sign; see Ad-.

As- (2); as-tonish; see Ex- (1).

As- (3); as-sagai; see Al- (4).

At-; see Ad-.

Auto-, Auth-, self. (Gk.) Gk. αὐτό-s, self. Hence *auth-* in auth-entic; *eff-* in eff-endi.

Av-; av-aunt. (F.−L.) F. *av-*; from L. *ab*; see Ab- (1).

Ba-; ba-lance; see Bi-.

Be-. (E.) A.S. *be-, bi-*, the same as *bi*, by, prep.; E. *by*.

Bi-, double. (L.) L. *bi-*, double, from an earlier form *dui-*, related to *duo*, two. **+**Gk. δι-, double, allied to δύω, two; Skt. *dvi-*, allied to *dva*, two; E. *twi-* in twi-bill. Hence F. *bi-* in bi-gamy, F. *ba-* in ba-lance; and see below.

Bin-; bin-ocular. (L.) L. *bīn-ī*, distributive form allied to *bi-* (above).

Bis-; bis-cuit. (F.−L.) F. *bis*, L. *bis*, twice; extended from *bi-* (above). Cf. E. *twice*; see Dis-.

By-; by-path. A.S. *bī*; see By, p. 70.

Cat-; cat-echism; see Cata-.

Cata-, down. (Gk.) Gk. κατά, down, downwards. Hence *cat-, cath-*, in cat-echism, cath-olic.

Cath-; cath-olic; see below.

Circum-, round. (L.) L. *circum*, around, prep. Hence *circu-* in circu-it.

Co-, Coi-; see Com-.

Col-; see Com-.

Com-. (L. *or* F.−L.) L. *com-*, together, used in composition for *cum*, prep. together. **+** Gk. σύν, together; see Syn-. It appears as *co-, col-, com-, con-, cor-, coun-*; ex.: co-agulate, col-lect, com-mute, con-nect, cor-rode, coun-cil. Also as *coi-* in coi-l; *cou-* in cou-ch, cou-sin; *co-* in co-stive, co-st; *cu-* in cu-ll, cu-stom; *cur-* in cur-ry (1). ¶ *Combustion* is perhaps for comb-ustion.

Con-; con-nect; see Com-.

Contra-, against. (L.) L. *contrā*, against. Allied to *contrō-* in contro-vert, contro-versy; loses final *a* in Ital. contr-alto. Hence F. *contre*, against, as in contr-ol; but the F. form is usually written *counter-* in English. Hence also *country-*.

Cor-; cor-rode; see Com-.

Cou-; cou-ch, cou-sin; see Com-.

Coun-; coun-cil; see Com-.

Counter-. (F.−L.) See Contra-.

Cu-; cu-ll, cu-stom; see Com-.

Cur-; cur-ry (1); see Com-.

D-; d-affodil; see De- (1).

De- (1); de-scend, de-bate. (L.; *or* F.− L.) L. *dē*, down, downward. Used with an oppositive sense in de-form; with an intensive sense in de-clare, &c. Changed to *di-* in di-stil. Distinct from the prefix below.

De- (2); de-face, de-fame, de-feat, de-fray. (F.−L.) F. *dé-*, O.F. *des-*, from L. *dis-*, apart; see Dis-. Distinct from the prefix above.

De- (3); de-vil; see Dia-.

Dea-; dea-con; see Dia-.

Demi-, half. (F.−L.) F. *demi.−* L. *dī-midius*, half; see Demi- in Dict., p. 135.

Des-; des-cant; see Dis-.

Di- (1), double. (Gk.) Gk. δι-, double, allied to δίs, twice, and δύο, two; see Bi-. Ex. di-lemma, di-syllable (*often written* dissyllable).

Di- (2), apart, away. (L.) See Dis-.

Di- (3); di-stil; see De- (1).

Dia-. (Gk.) Gk. διά, through, between.

I. LIST OF PREFIXES

apart; allied to **Di-** (1). Shortened to *di-* in di-æresis; appearing as *de-, dea-*, in de-vil, dea-con.

Dif-; see **Dis-**.

Dis-, apart, away. (L.; *or* F.—L.) *dis-*, apart, in two, another form of *bis-*, double; *dis-* and *bis-* are variants from an older form *duis-*, double, also used in the sense in two, apart; see **Bis-**. *Dis-* becomes *des-* in O. French, also *dé-* in later F.; but the O. F. *des-* is sometimes altered to *dis-*, as in dis-cover. The various forms are *di-, dif-, dis-, des-, de-*, and even *s-*; as in di-verge, dif-fuse, dis-pel, descant, de-feat, de-luge, s-pend.

Dou-; dou-ble; see **Duo-**.

Duo-, Du-, two, double. (L.) L. *duo*, two; cognate with E. *two*. Only in duodecimo, duo-denum; shortened to *du-* in du-al, du-plicate, &c. Appearing as *dou-* in dou-ble, dou-bt; as *do-* in do-zen.

Dys-, badly. (Gk.) Gk. δύς, badly, with difficulty. Some connect it with **To-** (2).

E- (1); e-normous; see **Ex-** (1).

E- (2); e-nough; see **Y-**.

E- (3); e-lope. A. F. *a-*, perhaps for O. F. *es-*, L. *ex*; see **Ex-** (1).

E- (4); e-squire. (F.) This *e-* is a F. addition, of purely phonetic value, due to the difficulty which was experienced in pronouncing initial *sq-, sc-, st-, sp-*. So also in e-scutcheon, e-state, e-special; to which add e-schew.

Ec-; ec-logue. (Gk.) Gk. ἐκ, also ἐξ, out. + L. *ex*, Lithuan. *isz*, Russ. *iz'*, out; see **Ex-** (1). Also *el-, ex-*, as in el-lipse, ex-odus.

Ef-; see **Ex-** (1).

Eff-; eff-endi; see **Auto-**.

El- (1); el-lipse; see **Ec-**.

El- (2); el-ixir; see **Al-** (4).

Em- (1); em-brace. (F.—L.) F. *em-*; L. *im-*, for *in*; see **In-** (2).

Em- (2); em-piric; see **En-** (2).

Em- (3); em-bassy; see **Am-** (3).

En- (1); en-close. (F.—L.) F. *en-*; L. *in-*; see **In-** (2).

En- (2); en-ergy. (Gk.) Gk. ἐν, in. + L. *in*; A.S. *in*. Becomes *em-* before *p*, in em-piric. See **Em-** (2), **In-** (1), **In-** (2).

En- (3); en-emy. (F.—L.) Negative prefix; see **In-** (3).

Endo-, within. (Gk.) Gk. ἔνδο-ν, within; extended from ἐν, in; see **En-** (2), and **Indi-**.

Enter-; enter-tain. (F.—L.) F. *entre*.

—L. *inter*, among; see **Inter-**. Shortened to *entr-* in entr-ails.

Ep-, Eph-; see below.

Epi-, upon. (Gk.) Gk. ἐπί, upon. + Skt. *api*; allied to L. *ob-*. See **Ob-**. It appears as *ep-, eph-*, in ep-och, eph-emeral.

Es-; es-cape; see **Ex-** (1).

Eso-, within. (Gk.) Gk. ἔσω, within; from ἐς, εἰς, into.

Eu-, well. (Gk.) Gk. εὖ, well; neut. of ἐύς, good. + Skt. *vasu-s*, good; cf. Goth. *ius-iza*, better. Hence *ev-* in ev-angelist.

Ev-; ev-angelist; see above.

Ex- (1), out of, very. (L.; *or* F.—L.) L. *ex*, also *ē*, out of; also used intensively. + Gk. ἐξ, ἐκ, out. See **Ec-**, and see below. It appears as *a-, as-, e-, ef-, es-, ex-, iss-, s-*, in a-mend, as-tonish, e-normous, ef-fect, es-cape, ex-tend, iss-ue, s-ample; also as *af-, a-*, in af-fray, a-fraid.

Ex- (2), out of, away. (Gk.) Gk. ἐξ, out; as in ex-odus. See above.

Exo-, without. (Gk.) Gk. ἔξω, outside, without; adv. from ἐξ, out (above).

Extra-, beyond. (L.) A comparative abl. form, from L. *ex*, out; see **Ex-** (1). Cf. *exter-* in exter-ior, exter-nal. It appears also as *stra-* in stra-nge; *cf.* estra-nge.

For- (1), in place of. (E.) E. *for*, prep.; in *for-as-much, for-ever*, which might just as well be written as separate words instead of compounds. Allied to **Per-, Pro-**.

For- (2); for-give. (E.) A.S. *for-*, intensive prefix. + Icel. *for-*, Dan. *for-*, Swed. *för-*, Du. G. *ver-*, Goth. *fra-*, Skt. *parā-*.

For- (3); for-feit. (F.—L.) F. *for-*, prefix. — L. *forīs*, outside, out of doors. Also in *for-close*, sometimes spelt *foreclose*; and in *for-judge*.

For- (4); for-ward; see **Forth-**.

Fore- (1), before. (E.) A.S. *fore*, for; before, prep.; *fore*, adv. Allied to **For-** (1). See **Fore**, p. 194.

Fore- (2); fore-go. (E.) A bad spelling of *for-go*; see **For-** (2).

Forth-. (E.) In *forth-coming, forth-with*. A.S. *forð*, forth; see p. 195.

Fro-; fro-ward. (Scand.) Icel. *frá*; see **Fro**, p. 200.

Gain-, against. (Scand.) Icel. *gegn*, against. Ex. gain-say.

Hemi-, half. (Gk.) Gk. ἡμι-, half. + L. *sēmi-*, half; see **Semi-**. Shortened to *me-* in me-grim.

Hetero-, other. (Gk.) Gk. ἕτερο-s, other.

Holo-, entire. (Gk.) Gk. ὅλο-s, entire.

Homo-, same. (Gk.) Gk. ὁμό-s, same; cognate with E. *same.* Lengthened to *homœo-,* like, in homœo-pathy.

Hyper-, above, beyond. (Gk.) Gk. ὑπέρ, above; see **Over-.**

Hypo-, Hyph-, Hyp-. (Gk.) Gk. ὑπό, under. + L. *sub,* under; see **Sub-.** Hence *hyph-* in hyph-en; *hyp-* in hyp-allage.

I- (1); i-gnoble; see **In-** (3).

I- (2); i-wis; A. S. *ge-*; see **Y-.**

Il- (1); il-lude; see **In-** (2).

Il- (2); il-legal; see **In-** (3).

Im- (1); im-bed; see **In-** (1).

Im- (2); im-mure, im-merge; see **In-** (2).

Im- (3); im-mortal; see **In-** (3).

In- (1); in-born. (E.) A. S. *in,* prep. It also becomes *im-* before *b* and *p*; as in im-bed, im-park. See below.

In- (2); in-clude. (L.; *or* F.—L.) L. *in,* in. + Gk. ἐν, in; A. S. *in.* See **In-** (1), **En-** (2). It appears as *am-, an-, em-, en-, il-, im-, in-, ir-,* in am-bush, an-oint, em-brace, en-close, il-lude, im-mure, in-clude, ir-ritate.

In- (3); negative prefix. (L.) L. *in-,* neg. prefix. + Gk. ἀν-, ἀ-, neg. prefix; E. *un-,* before nouns. See **An-** (2), **A-** (9), **Un-** (1). It appears as *en-, i-, il-, im-, in-, ir-,* in en-emy, i-gnoble, il-legal, im-mortal, in-firm, ir-regular.

Indi-, Ind-; indi-genous, ind-igent. (L.) O. Lat. *indu,* within. + Gk. ἔνδον, within; see **Endo-.**

Intel-; see below.

Inter-, between. (L.) L. *inter,* between. A comparative form, allied to L. *inter-ior,* within; cf. L. *inter-nus,* internal. It appears as *intel-* in intel-lect, *enter-* in enter-tain; and cf. entr-ails; see **Enter-.** Closely allied are L. *intrō-,* within, *intrā-,* within.

Intra-, within; see **Inter-.**

Intro-, within; see **Inter-.**

Ir- (1); ir-ritate; see **In-** (2).

Ir- (2); ir-regular; see **In-** (3).

Iss-; iss-ue. (F.—L.) F. *iss-,* from L. *ex*; see **Ex-** (1).

Juxta-, near. (L.) L. *iuxtā,* near.

L- (1); l-one. (E.) Short for *all*; l-one = al-one. See **Al-** (1).

L- (2); l-ute. (Arab.) Short for Arab. *al,* the, def. art. See **Al-** (4).

Male-, Mal-, Mau-, badly. (L.; *or* F.—L.) L. *male,* badly, ill; whence F. *mal,* which becomes *mau-* in mau-gre.

Me-; me-grim; see **Hemi-.**

Meta-, Meth-, Met-, among, with, after; also used to imply change. (Gk.) Gk. μετά, among, with, after. + A. S. *mid,* G. *mit,* Goth. *mith,* with. It appears also as *meth-* in meth-od, *met-* in met-eor.

Min-; min-ster; see **Mono-.**

Mis- (1); mis-deed; mis-take. (E. *and* Scand.) A. S. *mis-,* wrongly, amiss. + Icel. Dan. Du. *mis-*; Swed. *miss-*; Goth. *missa-,* wrongly. Allied to *miss,* vb.

Mis- (2), badly, ill. (F.—L.) O. F. *mes-,* from L. *minus,* less; used in a depreciatory sense. Appearing in mis-ad-venture, mis-alliance, mis-chance, mis-chief, mis-count, mis-creant, mis-nomer, mis-prise, mis-prision. Quite distinct from **Mis-** (1).

Mono-, Mon-, single. (Gk.) Gk. μόνο-s, single, sole, alone. Hence *mon-k, min-ster.*

Multi-, Mult-, many. (L.; *or* F.—L.) From L. *multus,* much, many.

N- (1); n-ewt, n-ickname, n-uncle. (E.) *A newt* = *an ewt,* where the prefixed *n* is due to the indef. article. *N-ickname* = *an eke-name. My nuncle* = *mine uncle,* where the *n* is due to the possessive pronoun. In *n-once,* the prefixed *n* is due to the dat. case of the def. article, as seen in M. E. *for then anes,* lit. ' for the once.'

N- (2), negative prefix. (E. *or* L.) In *n-one,* the prefixed *n* is due to A. S. *ne,* not. In *n-ull,* it is due to the cognate L. *ne,* not. See **Ne-.**

Ne-, Neg-. (L.) L. *ne,* not; *nec* (whence *neg-* in *neg-ligere*), not, short for *ne-que,* nor, not. In ne-farious, neg-ation, neg-lect, neg-otiate, ne-uter. See **N-** (2).

Non-, not. (L.; *or* F.—L.) L. *nōn,* not; O. Lat. *noenum,* for **ne oinom,* i. e. *ne ūnum,* not one; see above. It appears as *um-* in um-pire, for *numpire.*

O-; o-mit; see **Ob-.**

Ob-. (L.; *or* F.—L.) L. *ob,* near; allied to Gk. ἐπί, upon, near; Skt. *api,* moreover, Lith. *apë,* near. See **Epi-.** The force of *ob-* is very variable; it appears as *o-*, *ob-*, *oc-*, *of-*, *op-*, also as extended to *os-* (for *ops*?) in o-mit, ob-long, oc-cur, of-fer, op-press, os-tensible.

Oc-; oc-cur; see **Ob-**.

Of- (1); of-fal. (E.) A. S. *of*, of, off, away. This word is invariably written *off* in composition, except in the case of *offal*, where its use would have brought three *f*'s together.+L. *ab*, Gk. ἀπό; see **Ab-** (1), **Apo-**. It appears as *a-* in *a-down*.

Of- (2); of-fer; see **Ob-**.

Off-; see **Of-** (1).

On-, on, upon. (E.) A. S. *on*, on.+Gk. ἀνά. See **Ana-** (above). It often appears as *a-*, as in a-foot, a-sleep, &c.

Op-; op-press; see **Ob-**.

Or- (1); or-deal, or-ts. (E.) A. S. *or-*; cognate with Du. *oor-*, O. Sax. and G. *ur-*, Goth. *us*, away, out of.

Or- (2); or-lop. (Du.) Short for Du. *over*, cognate with E. *over*; see **Over-**.

Os-; os-tensible; see **Ob-**.

Out-. (E.) A. S. *ūt*, adv., E. *out*.+ Goth. *ut*, G. *aus*, Skt. *ud*, out. Shortened to *utt-* in utt-er; and to *ut-* in ut-most.

Outr-; outr-age. (F. — L.) F. *outre.* — L. *ultrā*, beyond; see **Ultra-**.

Over-. (E.) A. S. *ofer*, E. *over*, prep.+ Goth. *ufar*, L. *s-uper*, Gk. ὑπέρ, Skt. *upari*, above. A comparative form allied to **Up**, q. v. See **Hyper-**, **Super-**, **Or-** (2).

Pa-; pa-lsy; see **Para-**.

Palin-, Palim-, again. (Gk.) Gk. πάλιν, back, again. It becomes *palim-* in palim-psest.

Pan-, Panto-, all. (Gk.) Gk. πᾶν, neut. of πᾶς, all; παντο-, decl. form of the same, occurring in panto-mime.

Par- (1); par-son; see **Per-**.

Par- (2); par-ody; see **Para-** (1)

Para- (1), beside. (Gk.) Gk. παρά, be-side. Allied to E. *for*, L. *per*, also to Gk. περί. See **Per-, Peri-**, and **For-** (1). It becomes *pa-* in pa-lsy, *par-* in par-ody. ¶ Quite distinct from *para-* in para-chute, para-pet, para-sol, from L. *parāre*.

Para- (2); para-dise. Zend *pairi* = Gk. περί; see **Peri-**.

Pel-; pel-lucid; see **Per-**.

Pen-; pen-insula. (L.) L. *pæn-e*, almost.

Per-, through. (L.; *or* F. — L.) L. *per*, through. Allied to **Para-** and **For-** (1). It appears also as *par-* in par-son, par-don; as *pel-* in pel-lucid; and as *pil-* in pil-grim.

Peri-, around. (Gk.) Gk. περί, around. +Skt. *pari*, Zend *pairi*, round about. Allied to **Para-**, &c.

Pil-; pil-grim; see **Per-**.

Po-; po-sition; see **Por-** (1).

Pol-; pol-lute; see **Por-** (1).

Poly-, many. (Gk.) Written for Gk. πολύ-, decl. form of πολύ-s, much, many. Allied to E. *full*.

Por- (1); por-tend. (L.) L. *por-*, to be compared with Gk. παρά, beside (Brugmann, ii. § 35). See **Para-** (1). It appears as *pol-*, *por-*, in pol-lute, portend; and is allied to *po-* in po-sition.

Por- (2); por-trait; see **Pro-** (1).

Post-, after. (L.) L. *post*, after, behind. Hence F. *puis*, appearing as *pu-* in pu-ny.

Pour-; pour-tray; see **Pro-**.

Pr- (1); pr-ison; see **Pre-**.

Pr- (2); pr-udent; see **Pro-** (1).

Pre-, Præ-, before. (L.) L. *pre-*, for *præ*, prep., before; for older, * *prai*. Allied to **Pro-**. This prefix occurs also in pr-ison; and is curiously changed to *pro-* in pro-vost; and appears as *prea-* in prea-ch.

Preter-, beyond. (L.) L. *præter*, beyond; comparative form of *præ*, before.

Pro- (1), before, instead of. (L.; *or* F. — L.) L. *prŏ-*, before, in front, used as a prefix; also *prō*, short for *prod*, abl. case used as a preposition, which appears in *prod-igal*. Allied to Gk. πρό, before, Skt. *pra*, before, away; also to E. *for*. See below; and see **For-** (1). It appears also as *prof-*, *pour-*, *por-*, *pur-*, *pr-*, in prof-fer, pour-tray, por-trait, pur-vey, pr-udent; where *pour-*, *por-*, *pur-* are due to the F. form *pour*.

Pro- (2), before. (Gk.) Gk. πρό, before; cognate with **Pro-** (1). In pro-logue, pro-phet, pro-scenium, pro-thalamium.

Pro- (3); pro-vost; see **Pre-**.

Prod-; prod-igal; see **Pro-** (1).

Prof-; prof-fer; see **Pro-** (1).

Pros-, in addition, towards. (Gk.) Gk. πρός, towards. Allied to **Forth-** and **Por-** (1).

Proto-, Prot-, first. (Gk.) From Gk. πρῶτο-s, first; superl. form of πρό, before; see **Pro-** (2). Shortened to *prot-* in prot-oxide.

Pu-; pu-ny; see **Post-**.

Pur-; pur-vey. (F. — L.) See **Pro-** (1).

R-; r-ally; see **Re-**.

Ra-; ra-bbet; see **Re-**.

I. LIST OF PREFIXES

Re-, Red-, again. (L.) L. *re-, red-* (only in composition), again, back. *Red-* occurs in red-eem, red-integration, red-olent, red-ound, red-undant, red-dition; and is changed to *ren-* in ren-der, ren-t. In re-ly, re-mind, re-new, it is prefixed to purely E. words; and in re-call, re-cast, to words of Scand. origin. It appears as *r-* in r-ally (1), r-ansom; and as *ru-* in ru-nagate. **2.** *Re-* is frequently prefixed to other prefixes, which sometimes coalesce with it, so that such words require care. For example, rabbet = re-a-but; ragout = re-a-gout; rampart = re-em-part; cf. also re-ad-apt, re-col-lect, re-con-cile, re-sur-rection, &c.

Rear-; see Retro-.
Red-, Ren-; see Re- (above).
Rere-; rere-ward; see Retro-.
Retro-, backwards, behind. (L.) L. *retrō-,* backwards, back again; a comparative form from *re-,* back; see Re-. The prefixes *rear-, rere-,* in rear-guard, rere-ward, are due to L. *retrō,* and are of F. origin.

S- (1); s-ober, s-ure; see Se-.
S- (2); s-pend; see Dis-.
S- (3); s-ample; see Ex- (1).
S- (4); s-ombre; see p. 501.
Sans-, without. (F.—L.) F. *sans,* without.—L. *sine,* without; see Sine-.
Se-, Sed-, away, apart. (L.) L. *sē-,* apart; O. Lat. *sed-,* apart, which is probably retained in sed-ition. The orig. sense was probably 'by oneself.' It appears as *s-* in s-ure; *cf.* sober.
Semi-, half. (L.) L. *sēmi,* half.+Gk. ἡμί-, half; see Hemi-. It appears as *sin-* in sin-ciput./
Sine-, without. (L.) L. *sine,* without; lit. if not.—L. *si,* if; *ne,* not. Hence F. *sans,* without.
So-; so-journ; see Sub-.
Sover-, Sopr-; see Super-.
Stra-; stra-nge; see Extra-.
Su-; su-spect; see Sub-.
Sub-, under. (L.) L. *sub,* under, (sometimes) up. Allied to Gk. ὑπό, under; Skt. *upa,* near, under; also to E. *up* and *of.* See Hypo-, Of-, Up-. *Sub* also appears as *s-, so-, su-, suc-, suf-, sug-, sum-, sup-, sur-,* in s-ombre (?), so-journ, su-spect, suc-ceed, suf-fuse, sug-gest, sum-mon, sup-press, sur-rogate. It is also extended to *sus-* (for *sups-*); as in sus-pend.
Subter-, beneath. (L.) L. *subter,*

beneath; comparative form from *sub,* under; see Sub-.
Suc-, Suf-, Sug-, Sum-, Sup-; see Sub-.
Super-, above, over. (L.) L. *super,* above. + Gk. ὑπέρ, over, beyond; A.S. *ofer,* E. *over.* See Hyper-, Over-; also Sub-. Hence *supra-,* beyond, L. *suprā.* Also *sover-* in sover-eign, which is a F. form; and *sopr-* in sopr-ano, which is an Ital. form. Also F. *sur-* = L. *super.*
Supra-, beyond; see above.
Sur- (1); sur-rogate; see Sub-.
Sur- (2); sur-face; see Super-.
Sus-; sus-pend; see Sub-.
Sy-, Syl-, Sym-; see Syn-.
Syn-, with, together with. (Gk.) Gk. σύν, with. It appears as *sy-, syl-, sym-,* and *syn-,* in sy-stem, syl-logism, symmetry, syn-tax.

T- (1); t-wit. (E.) *Twit* is from A.S. *æt-wītan,* to twit, reproach; thus *t-* is here used for E. *at.*
T- (2); t-awdry. (F.—L.) *Tawdry* is for *Saint Awdry;* thus *t-* is here the final letter of *saint.*
T- (3); t-autology. (Gk.) Here *t-* represents Gk. τό, neuter of def. article.
Thorough-, through. (E.) Merely another form of E. *through.*
To- (1), to-day. (E.) A.S. *tō,* to.
To- (2), intensive prefix. (E.) Obsolete, except in *to-brake.* A.S. *tō-,* apart, asunder; prob. cognate with L. *dis-,* apart. See Dis-. ¶ Some connect it with Gk. δύς-; see Dys-.
Tra-, Tran-; see below.
Trans-, beyond. (L.) L. *trans,* beyond. Shortened to *tran-* in tran-scend; and to *tra-* in tra-duce, tra-verse, &c. Hence F. *tres-,* occurring in tres-pass; and *tre-* in tre-ason.
Tre- (1), **Tres-.** (F.—L.) See above.
Tre- (2); tre-ble. (F.—L.) See below.
Tri- (1), thrice. (L.) L. *tri-,* thrice; allied to *trēs,* three. Hence tri-ple, tre-ble, &c.; and *tra-* in tra-mmel.
Tri- (2), thrice. (Gk.) Gk. τρι-, thrice; allied to τρία, neut. of τρεῖς, three. Hence tri-gonometry, &c.
Twi-, double, doubtful. (E.) A.S. *twī-,* double; allied to *twā,* two. Hence twi-bill, twi-light.

Ultra-, beyond. (L.) L. *ultrā,* beyond; allied to O. Lat. *ulter,* adj., appearing in *ulter-ior*, which see in Dict. Hence F. *outre*, beyond, appearing in outr-age; also in E utter-ance (2), corruption of F. *outr-ance*.

Um- ; um-pire; see **Non-**.

Un- (1), negative prefix to nouns, &c. (E.) A.S. *un-*, not; cognate with L. *in-*, not, Gk. ἀν-, not. See **An-** (2), **In-** (3).

Un- (2), verbal prefix, signifying the reversal of an action. (E.) A. S. *un-*, verbal prefix; cognate with Du. *ont-*, *ent-*, G. *ent-*, O.H.G. *ant-*, Goth. *and-*. The same as E. *an-* in *an-swer*; see **An-** (5), **Anti-**.

Un- (3); un-til, un-to. (O. Low G.) See *un-to* in Dict., p. 584.

Un- (4), **Uni-**, one. (L.) L. *ūn-us*, one; whence uni-vocal, with one voice; un-animous, of one mind; &c. Cognate with E. *one*.

Under-. (E.) A. S. *under*, E. *under*, prep.

Up-. (E.) A.S. *up*, E. *up*, prep. Allied to **Of**, **Sub-**, **Hypo-**.

Ut-, Utt-. (E.) See **Out**.

Utter-. (F. – L.) Only in *utter-ance* (2). F. *outre*, L. *ultrā*; see **Ultra-**.

V- ; v-an (1). (F. – L.) See **Ab-** (1).

Ve-, apart from. (L.) L. *uē-*, apart from. Only in ve-stibule, and (possibly) in ve-stige.

Vice-, Vis-, in place of. (L.; *or* F. – L.) L. *uice*, in place of, whence O. F. *vis*, the same. The latter appears only in vis-count.

Wan-, negative prefix; see **Wanton** in its due place; p. 599.

With-, against. (E.) A.S. *wið*, against; the sense is preserved in with-stand. In with-hold, with-draw, it signifies 'back.'

Y- ; y-wis, y-clept. (E.) A.S. *ge-* prefix; M. E. *i-*, *y-*. This prefix appears as *a-* in a-ware, as *i-* in i-wis (*for* y-wis) and as *e-* in e-nough. See **A-** (11), **E-** (2).

II. SUFFIXES

THE number of suffixes in modern English is so great, and the forms of several, especially in words derived through the French from Latin, are so variable, that an attempt to exhibit them all would tend to confusion. The best account of their origin is to be found in Brugmann, Grundriss der Vergleichenden Grammatik der Indogermanischen Sprachen. An account of Anglo-Saxon suffixes is given at p. 119 of March, Comparative Grammar of the Anglo-Saxon Language. Lists of Anglo-Saxon words, arranged according to their suffixes, are given in Loth, Etymologische angelsæchsisch-englische Grammatik, Elberfeld, 1870. Simple accounts of English suffixes in general are given in Morris, Historical Outlines of English Accidence, pp. 212–221, 229–242, in Nesfield, Historical English and Derivation, pp. 185–252, and in the two Series of my Principles of English Etymology, to which the reader is referred. See also Koch, Historische Grammatik der Englischen Sprache, vol. iii. pt. 1, pp. 29–76. It is clearly established that the Indo-germanic languages abound in suffixes, each of which was originally intended slightly to modify the meaning of the root to which it was added, so as to express the radical idea in a new relation. The force of many of these must, even at an early period, have been slight, and in many instances it is difficult to trace it ; but in some instances it is still clear, and the form of the suffix is then of great service. The difference between *lov-er*, *lov-ed*, and *lov-ing* is well marked, and readily understood. One of the most remarkable points is that most Indo-germanic languages delighted in adding suffix to suffix, so that words are not uncommon in which two or more suffixes occur, each repeating, it may be, the sense of that which preceded it. Double diminutives such as *parti-c-le*, i. e. a little little part, are sufficiently common. The Lat. superl. suffix -*is-si-mus* is a simple example of the use of a treble suffix, which really expresses no more than is expressed by -*mus* alone in the word *prī-mus*. The principal Indo-germanic suffixes, as given by Brugmann, are these: -*o*, -*i*, -*u*, -*yo*, -*wo*, -*mo*, -*mi*, -*men* (-*mon*), -*meno* (-*menā*), -*no*, -*tno*, -*ni*, -*nu*, -*en* (-*on*), -*ent* (-*ont*), -*lo*, -*li*, -*ro*, -*ri*, -*ru*, -*er* (-*or*), -*es* (-*os*), -*to*, -*mento*, -*ti*, -*ti-on*, -*tā-ti*, -*tu*, -*tū-ti*, -*ter* (-*tor*, -*tr*), -*tūro*, -*id*, -*d*, -*d-en*, -*d-on*, -*tū-den*, -*do*, -*go*, -*ko*, -*k*, -*sqo*, -*sqā*, -*bho*. But these can be readily compounded, so as to form new suffixes; so that from -*men-to* was formed -*mento* (as in E. *argu-ment*).

One common error with regard to suffixes should be guarded against, namely, that of mis-dividing a word so as to give the suffix a false shape. This is extremely common in such words as *logi-c*, *civi-c*, *belli-c-ose*, where the suffix is commonly spoken of as being -*ic* or -*ic-ose*. This error occurs, for instance, in the elaborate book on English Affixes by S. S. Haldemann, published at Philadelphia in 1865; a work which is of considerable use as containing a very full account, with numerous examples, of suffixes and prefixes. The truth is that *civi-c* (Lat. *cīuicus*) is derived from Lat. *cīui-*, declensional stem of *cīui-s*, a citizen, with the suffix -*cus* (Idg. -*ko*); and *logi-c* is from Gk. λογι-κός, from λογι-, for λόγο-, declensional stem of λόγος, a discourse, with the suffix -*κος*, as before. Compare Lat. *cīui-tās*, Gk. λογο-μαχία. Of course, words in -*i-c* are so numerous that -*ic* has come to be regarded as a suffix at the present day, so that we do not hesitate to form *Volta-ic* as an adjective of *Volta*; but this is English misuse, not Latin etymology. Moreover, since both -*i-* and -*ko* are Idg. suffixes, such a suffix as -*i-κos*, -*i-cus*, is possible both in Greek and Latin; but in the particular words above cited it is clearer to consider the -*i-* as due to the original stem.

One more word of warning may perhaps suffice. If we wish to understand a suffix, we must employ comparative philology, and not consider English as an absolutely isolated language, with laws different from those of other languages of the Aryan family. Thus the -*th* in *tru-th* is the -ð of A. S. *trēow-ð*, gen. case *trēow-ðe*, fem. sb. This suffix answers to that seen in Goth. *gabaur-ths*, birth, gen. case *gabaur-thais*, fem. sb., belonging to the -*i*-stem declension of Gothic strong substantives. The true suffix is therefore to be expressed as Teut. -*thi*, cognate with Idg. -*ti*, so extremely common in Latin; cf. *dō-ti-*, dowry, *men-ti-*, mind, *mor-ti-*, death, *mes-si-* (<*met-ti-*), harvest, that which is mown. Hence, when Horne Tooke gave his famous etymology of *truth* as being 'that which a man *troweth*,' he did in reality suggest that the -*ti-* in Lat. *mor-ti-* is identical with the -*t* in *mori-t-ur* or in *ama-t*; in other words, it was a mere whim.

III. SELECT LIST OF LATIN AND GREEK WORDS

IN the former edition of this work a list of Indo-germanic roots was given, as determined, for the most part, by Fick. The later researches of Brugmann and others have much modified the former results, chiefly because the vowel-sounds have been more exactly appreciated. As a list of roots is not usually much required in practice, it has been here replaced by a useful and practical list of some of the more important words in Latin and Greek which are, mostly, of rather frequent occurrence in English compounds and derivatives. In some cases, the form of the root is given, chiefly when the derivatives from it are rather numerous. Both of these lists might be largely increased, but it has not been deemed worth while to include such words as present no difficulty. For example, the Greek word κόσμος, order, is purposely omitted, because its derivatives (viz. *cosm-ic*, *cosm-etic*, and words beginning with *cosmo-*) can readily be found at p. 114. On the other hand, the Greek ἄλλος is inserted, for the sake of such derivatives as *par-all-ax*, *par-all-el*.

SELECT LIST OF LATIN WORDS

THE following list contains the principal Latin words which are (mostly) productive of rather numerous derivatives in English, and readily admit prefixes. Words that have produced but few derivatives, or that are of no especial interest, are excluded.

ac-, as in *āc-er*, *ac-idus*, *ac-ūtus*, sharp — acerbity, acid, acrid, acrimony, acumen, acute, aglet, ague, eager, eglantine, exacerbate. (✓AK, to be sharp.)

ǣdē-s, a temple — edify, edile; *cf.* estuary, ether, oasthouse. (✓AIDH, to burn.)

ǣqu-us, equal — adequate, equal, equanimity, equation, equilibrium, equinóx, equipollent, equity, equivalent, equivocal, iniquity.

ag-ere, to drive — act, agent, agile, agitate, agriculture, ambiguous, coagulate, cogent, cogitate, counteract, enact, essay, exact, examine, exigent, peregrination, pilgrim, prodigal, transact. Cf. Gk. ἄγειν; p. 644. (✓AG to drive.)

alb-us, white — alb, album, albumen, auburn.

al-ere, to nourish, grow up — adolescent, adult, aliment, alimony, altar, altitude, alto, coalesce, contralto, exalt, haughty, hautboy, proletarian. (✓AL, to nourish.)

al-ius, other — alias, alien, alibi, aliquot, alter, altercation, alternate, subaltern. Cf. Gk. ἄλλος; p. 645.

am-āre, to love — amatory, amenity, amiable, amicable, amity, amorous, amour, enamour, enemy, enmity, inimical, paramour.

ambul-āre, to walk — amble, ambulance, ambulation, circumambulate, perambulate.

ang-ere, to choke — angina, anguish, anxious; *cf.* ail, anger, awe, ugly. (✓AGH, to choke.)

anim-a, breath, *anim-us*, mind — animal, animadvert, animate, animosity; equanimity, magnanimous, pusillanimous, unanimous. (✓AN, to breathe.)

ann-us, a year — annals, anniversary, annual, biennial, triennial, &c.; perennial, superannuate.

apt-us, fit — adapt, adept, apt, aptitude, attitude, inept. (✓AP, to bind.)

aqu-a, water — aqua-fortis, aquatic, aquarium, aquarius, aqueduct, aqueous, ewer, sewer (1), subaqueous; *cf.* ait, eyot, island.

arm-a, arms — alarm, alarum, ambry (aumbry), arm (2), arms, armada, armadillo, armament, armistice, armour, army.

art-em, acc., skill — art, artifice, artillery, artisan, inert.

asper, rough — asperity, exasperate.

audī-re, to hear — audible, audience, audit, obedient, obeisance, obey, oyer, oyez.

aug-ēre, to increase — auction, augment, august, author, auxiliary; *cf.* eke (1). (✓AUG, to increase.)

aur-is, the ear — auricula, auricular, auscultation, scout (1); *cf.* ear (1).

aur-um, gold — aureate, dory, loriot, or (3), oriel, oriflamme, oriole, ormulu, orpiment, orpine.

aui-s, a bird — auspice, aviary, bustard, ostrich.

barb-a, beard — barb (1), barbel, barber; *cf.* beard.

barr-a (Late L.) — bar, barracks, barrel, barricade, barrier, barrister, debar, embargo, embarrass.

bass-us, low — abase, base (2), basement, bass (1), bass-relief, bassoon, debase.

bat-ere (popular L.), to beat — abate, battalion, batter (1), batter (2), battery, battle, battledoor, combat, debate, rebate.

bell-us, beautiful — beau, beauty, beldam, belladonna, belle, embellish.

bib-ere, to drink — beaver (3), beverage, bevy, bib, imbibe, imbrue (embrew).

bon-us, good — bonny, boon, *adj.*, bounty.

brāchi-a, arms — brace, bracelet, brassart, embrace, vambrace.

breu-is, short — abbreviate, abridge, breve, brevet, breviary, brevity, brief (1), brief (2).

brocc-a (Late L.), a pointed stick — broach, brocade, broccoli, brochure, brocket, broker, brooch.

bucc-a, mouth — debouch, disembogue, embouchure.

bull-a, a bubble, boss — bill (3), billet (1), boil (1), budge (1), bull (2), bullet, bulletin, bullion, ebullition, parboil.

busc-us (popular L.), a bush — ambuscade, ambush, bush (1), bouquet, emboss (2).

bux-us, a box-tree — box (1), box (2), bush (2); *cf.* bushel, pyx.

caball-us (popular L.), a horse – cavalier, cavalcade, cavalry, chevalier, chivalry.

cad-ere, to fall – accident, cadaverous, cadence, caducous, cascade, case (1), casual, chance, cheat, coincide, decadence, decay, deciduous, escheat, incident, occasion, occident.

cæd-ere, to cut – cæsura, circumcise, concise, decide, excision, incise, precise; *also* homi-cide, sui-cide, &c.; *also* chisel, scissors.

cæl-um, heaven – ceil, ceiling, celestial.

cal-āre, to summon – calends, calendar, conciliate, council, intercalate, reconcile; cf. *clāmāre* (below).

calc-āre, to tread – caulk, causeway, cockatrice.

calc-em, acc., lime – calcareous, calcine, calculate, calx, chalk.

cal-ēre, to be hot – caldron, calenture, caloric, calorific, caudle, chafe, chaldron, nonchalant, scald (1).

camer-a, a chamber – camera, chamber, chamberlain, comrade. (√KAM, to bend, cover, vault over.)

camp-us, a plain – camp, campaign, campestral, champagne, champaign, champion, decamp, encamp, scamp.

canāl-is, a canal – canal, channel, kennel (2).

cancrī, lattice-work – cancel, chancel, chancellor, chancery.

cand-ēre, to shine – candelabrum, candid, candidate, candle, candour, cannel-coal, censer, chandelier, chandler, incandescent, incendiary, incense (1), incense (2), kindle (2). (√QEND, to shine.)

can-is, a dog – canine, kennel (1); cf. cynic, hound.

cant-āre, to sing – accent, canorous, cant (1), canticle, canto, canzonet, chant, descant, enchant, incantation, incentive, precentor, recant; cf. hen.

cāp-a (popular L.), a cape – cap, caparison, cape (1), capuchin, chapel, chaperon, chaplet, cope (1), escape, scape.

cap-er, a goat – cab, cabriolet, caper, capricorn, capriole, cheveril, chevron.

cap-ere, to seize, lay hold of, contain – accept, anticipate, cable, caitiff, capable, capacious, capsule, captious, captive, captor, capture, case (2), casement, cash, casket, catch, cater, chase (1), chase (2), chase (3), conceit, conceive, conception, deceive, deception, encase, enchase, except, imperceptible, inceptive, incipient, intercept, occupy, perceive, perception, precept,

purchase, receive, receptacle, reception, recipe, recipient, sash (1), susceptible; cf. haft, heave, heft. (√QAP, to seize, take hold of.)

cap-ut, the head – achieve, cabbage (1), cad, cadet, cape (2), capital (1), capital (2), capital (3), capitation, capitol, capitular, capitulate, captain, cattle, chapiter, chapter, chattels, chief, chieftain, corporal (1), decapitate, hatchment, occiput, precipice, sinciput.

carn-, stem of *caro*, flesh – carnage, carnal, carnation, carnival, carnivorous, carrion (from *caro*), charnel, incarnadine, incarnation.

carp-ere, to cull – excerpt, scarce; cf. harvest. (√QERP, to cut.)

cār-us, dear – caress, charity, cherish; cf. whore.

cas-a, a cottage – casino, cassock (?), chasuble.

cast-us, chaste – caste, castigate, chaste chasten, chastise, incest.

catēn-a, a chain – catenary, chain, chignon, concatenation.

caud-a, the tail – caudal, coward, cue, queue.

causs-a, a cause – accuse, because, cause, excuse, recusant, ruse.

cau-us, hollow – cage, cajole, cave, concave, excavation, gabion, gaol, jail.

cēd-ere, to come, yield – abscess, accede, access, ancestor, antecedent, cease, cede, cess, cessation, cession, cess-pool, concede, decease, exceed, excess, incessant, intercede, precede, predecessor, proceed, recede, recess, retrocession, secede, succeed.

cēl-āre, to hide – cell, cellar, conceal, occult; cf. hall, hell, hole. (√QEL, to hide.)

cent-um, a hundred – cent, centenary, centennial, centesimal, centigrade, centipede, centuple, centurion, century, quintal.

cēr-a, wax – cerecloth, cerement, ceruse.

cerebr-um, brain – cerebral, cervelas (saveloy).

cern-ere, to separate – concern, decree, decretal, discern, discreet, discriminate, excrement, excretion, secret, secretary. *See* Gk. κρίνειν; p. 645.

cert-us, sure – ascertain, certain, certify.

cing-ere, to gird – cincture, enceinte, precinct, shingles, succinct.

circ-us, a ring – circle, circus, research, search, shark.

cist-a, a chest – chest, cist, cistern, cistvaen.

cit-āre, to incite – cite, excite, incite, recite, resuscitate, solicit.

cīu-is, a citizen – cit, citadel, citizen, city, civil.

clām-āre, to call out – acclaim, acclamation, claim, clamour, declaim, declamation, exclaim, exclamation, proclaim, proclamation, reclaim, reclamation.

clār-us, clear – claret, clarify, clarion, clear, declare, glair.

claud-ere, to shut – clause, cloister, close (1), close (2), closet, conclude, exclude, include, preclude, recluse, seclusion, sluice ; *cf.* slot (1). (√SKLEUD, to shut.)

clāu-is, a key – clavicle, clef, conclave.

clī-uus, a slope – acclivity, declivity, proclivity ; *cf.* decline, encline, incline, recline ; *also* lean (1), low (3). Cf. Gk. κλίνειν ; p. 645. (√KLEI, to lean.)

cohort-em, acc., an enclosure – cohort, cortege, court (1), court (2), courteous, courtesan, courtesy, courtier, curtain, curtsey; *cf.* garden, garth, yard (1). (√GHER, to contain.)

col-āre, to trickle – colander, culvert (?), cullis, percolate, portcullis.

col-ere, to till – colony, cultivate, culture ; agriculture; *cf.* bucolic. (√QEL, to turn round, to till.)

coll-um, the neck – collar, collet, colporteur, decollation.

cond-ere, to hide – abscond, sconce (1), sconce (2).

contrā, against – counter, encounter, rencontre, rencounter.

coöper-īre, to cover – cover, coverlet, covert, curfew, discover, kerchief.

cōpula, a bond – copulate, couple.

coqu-ere, to cook – biscuit, concoct, cook, decoct, kitchen, precocious ; *also* apricot, terra-cotta. (√PEQ, to cook.)

cord-, from *cor*, the heart – accord, concord, cordial, courage, discord, quarry (2), record ; *cf.* heart.

cor-ium, leather – cuirass, excoriate, scourge.

corn-u, a horn – core (?), corn (2), cornea, cornel, cornelian, corner, cornet, cornucopia, unicorn ; *cf.* horn, hart.

corōn-a, a wreath – corolla, corollary, coronal, coronation, coroner, coronet, crown.

corp-us, body – corporal (2), corps, corpse, corpulent, corpuscle, corse, corset, corslet, incorporate.

cost-a, a rib – accost, coast, costal, cutlet.

crass-us, thick, dense – crass, cresset, grease.

crāt-es, a hurdle – crate, creel, grate (1), griddle, gridiron, grill ; *cf.* hurdle.

creāre, to create, make – create, creole, procreate, recreation.

crēd-ere, to believe – credible, credit, credulous, creed, grant, miscreant, recreant.

crep-āre, to crackle, burst – crevice, decrepit, discrepant.

cresc-ere, to grow – accretion, accrue, concrete, crescent, crew, decrease, decrement, excrescence, increase, increment, recruit.

crēt-a, chalk – cretaceous, crayon.

crocc-us (popular L.), a hook – crochet, crosier, crotchet, crouch.

cruc-em, acc., a cross – cross, crucial, crucify, cruise, crusade, excruciate.

cub-āre, to lie down – concubine, covey, incubate, incubus ; *cf.* incumbent, procumbent, recumbent, succumb.

culp-a, blame – culpable, culprit, exculpate, inculpate.

culter, a coulter – coulter, curtleaxe, cutlass, cutler.

cumul-us, a heap – accumulate, cumulate.

cune-us, a wedge – coign, coin, cuneate, quoin.

cūp-a, a vat – coop, cowl (2), cupola, goblet ; *cf.* cup.

cup-ere, to desire – concupiscence, covet, cupid, cupidity.

cūr-a, care – accurate, assure, curate, cure, curious, ensure, proctor, procurator, procure, proxy, scour, secure, sicker, sinecure, sure.

curr-ere (*curs-*), to run – coarse, concourse, concur, corridor, corsair, courier, course, current, curricle, cursive, cursory, discourse, discursive, excursion, incur, incursion, intercourse, occur, precursor, recourse, recur, succour. *Also* hussar, kraal ; *cf.* horse.

curu-us, bent – curb, curve, curvet, incurvate, kerbstone.

damn-um, loss – condemn, damage, damn, indemnify, indemnity.

da-re, to give – condone, dado, date (1), die (2), donation, dowager, dower, pardon, reddition, render, rendezvous, rent (2), surrender, tradition, traitor, treason. (√DO, to give.)

decem, ten – dean, decanal, decemvir, decennial, decimal, decimate, decussate, denary, dime ; *cf.* decade, ten, tithe.

dec-ēre, to become – decent, decorate, decorum.

dent-em, acc., tooth — dandelion, dental, denticle, dentifrice, dentist, dentition, indent, indenture; *cf.* tine, tooth.

deus, god — adieu, deify, deity, deist; *cf.* jovial; and see *diēs* (below).

dīc-ere, to say, *dic-āre*, to tell — abdicate, addict, condition, contradict, dedicate, dictate, diction, dictionary, dight, ditto, ditty, edict, index, indicate, indict, interdict, preach, predicament, predicate, predict; *cf.* avenge, benediction, benison, judge (adjudge, adjudicate, judicature, judicial, judicious, prejudge, prejudice), malediction, malison, valediction, verdict, vindicate. (√DEIK, to show.)

diē-s, a day — adjourn, dial, diary, dismal, diurnal, journal, journey, sojourn.

dign-us, worthy — condign, dainty, deign, dignify, dignity, disdain.

dol-ēre, to grieve — condole, doleful, dolour, indolence.

dom-āre, to tame — daunt, indomitable; *cf.* tame. (√DAM, to tame.)

domin-us, a lord — dam (2), dame, damsel, danger, demesne, domain, dominate, domineer, dominical, dominion, domino, don (2), donna, dungeon; *cf.* monkey.

dūc-ere, to lead — abduction, adduce, conduce, conduct, conduit, deduce, deduct, doge, douche, ducal, ducat, duchess, duchy, duct, ductile, duke, educe, induce, induct, introduce, produce, product, redoubt, reduce, seduce, superinduce, traduce; *cf.* educate. (√DEUK, to lead.)

duo, two — belligerent, deuce (1), deuce (2), double, doublet, doubloon, doubt, dozen, dual, dubious, duel, duet, duodecimal, duodenum, duplicate, duplicity, indubitable, rebel, redoubtable; *cf.* two.

dūr-us, hard — durance, duration, dure, duress, endure, indurate, obdurate.

ed-ere, to eat — edible, esculent, obese; *cf.* eat. (√ED, to eat.)

em-ere, to take — assume, consume, ensample, example, exemplar, exemplify, exempt, impromptu, peremptory, premium, presume, prompt, ransom, redeem, resume, sample, sampler, sumptuary, sumptuous.

err-āre, to stray — aberration, err, erratum, erroneous, error.

es-se, to exist, be — absent, entity, essence, present, quintessence. Cf. are, sin, sooth; *also* suttee. (√ES, to dwell, exist.)

exter-, as in *exter-ior*, outer — estrange, exterior, external, extra, extraneous, extreme, extrinsic, strange.

fac-ere (pt. t. *fē-ci*), to do — affair, affect,

comfit, confect, counterfeit, defeasance, defeat, defect, deficient, difficulty, discomfit, effect, efficacy, efficient, facile, facsimile, fact, faction, factitious, factotum, faculty, fashion, feasible, fetish, feat, feature, fiat, forfeit, hacienda, infect, mallecho, perfect, prefect, proficient, profit, refection, suffice, sufficient, surfeit. (√DHĒ, to put, place.)

faci-ēs, face — deface, efface, façade, face, superficies, surface.

fall-ere, to deceive — default, fail, fallacy, fallible, false, faucet, fault, refel.

fā-rī, to speak — affable, confabulate, confess, defame, fable, fairy, fay, ineffable, infamy, infant, infantry, nefarious, preface, profess; *cf.* ban. ·(√BHA, BHĀ, to speak.)

·*fend-ere*, to strike — defend, fence, fend, offend.

fer-re, to bear — circumference, confer, defer (1), defer (2), differ, fertile, infer, offer, prefer, proffer, refer, suffer, transfer; *cf.* bear (1), barrow (2), bier. (√BHER, to bear.)

feru-ēre, to boil — effervesce, fervent, fervid, ferment.

fest-um, a feast — feast, festal, festival, festive, fête.

fid-em, acc., faith — affiance, affidavit, confide, defy, diffident, faith, fealty, fidelity, fiducial, infidel, perfidious; *cf.* bide. (√BHEIDH, to trust.)

fig-ere (*fix-*), to fix — affix, fix, prefix, suffix, transfix.

fīl-um, a thread — defile (2), enfilade, filament, file (1), filigree, fillet, profile, purl (3).

fing-ere (*fig-*), to fashion — configuration, effigy, faint, feign, fiction, figment, figure, transfigure; *cf.* dairy, dike, ditch, dough. (√DHEIGH, to knead, mould.)

fin-is, end — affinity, confine, define, final, finance, fine (1), fine (2), finial, finical, finish, finite, refine, superfine; *cf.* paraffine.

firm-us, firm — affirm, confirm, farm, firm, firmament, infirm. (√DHER, to support.)

flāgrā-re, to burn — conflagration, flagrant; *cf.* flambeau, flame, flamen (?), flamingo. (√BHLEG, to burn.)

flect-ere, to bend — circumflex, deflect, flection, flexible, inflect, reflect.

flīg-ere (*flict-*), to strike — afflict, conflict, inflict, profligate.

flōr-em, acc., a flower — deflower, efflorescence, ferret (2), fleur-de-lis, floral, florid, florin, floscule, flour, flourish, flower, inflorescence; *cf.* blow (2), bloom, blossom.

III. SELECT LIST OF LATIN WORDS

flu-ere, to flow — affluence, confluence, defluction, effluence, floss, fluctuate, fluent, fluid, fluor-spar, flux, influence, influenza, influx, superfluous.

foc-us, a hearth — focus, fuel, fusil (1).

fōd-ere (*foss-*), to dig — foss, fossil.

foli-um, leaf — exfoliate, foil (2), foliage, folio, perfoliate, trefoil.

form-a, form — conform, deform, form, formula, inform, reform, transform. (√DHER, to support.)

fort-em, acc., strong — comfort, deforce, effort, force (1), fort, forte, fortify, fortitude, fortress ; *cf.* borough. (√BHERGH, to protect.)

frang-ere (*frag-*), to break — fraction, fracture, fragile, fragment, frail, frangible, infraction, infringe, irrefragable, refract, refrain (2) ; *cf.* break. (√BHREG, to break.)

fric-āre, to rub — fray (3), friction.

front-em, acc., forehead — affront, confront, effrontery, front, frontal, frontier, frontispiece, frontlet ; *cf.* flounce (2).

fru-ī (*fruct-*), to enjoy — fructify, fruit, fruition, frumenty ; *cf.* frugal, brook (1). (√BHREUG, to enjoy.)

fug-ere, to flee — fugitive, fugue, refuge, refugee, subterfuge ; *cf.* bow (1). (√BHEUG, to bend.)

fund-ere (*fūs-*), to pour — confound, confuse, confute, diffuse, effuse, foison, fuse (1), fusil (3), futile, infuse, profuse, refund, refuse, refute, suffuse, transfuse ; *cf.* gut, chyle, chemist. (√GHEU, to pour.)

fund-us, bottom — found (1), founder, fund, fundament, profound ; *cf.* bottom.

fung-ī (*funct-*), to perform — defunct, function, perfunctory.

gaudi-um, joy — enjoy, gaud, joy, rejoice.

gel-u, frost — congeal, gelatine, gelid, jelly ; *cf.* chill, cool.

gen-us, kin — congenial, congenital, degenerate, engender, engine, gender (1), gender (2), general, generate, generic, generous, genial, genital, genitive, genius, genteel, gentile, gentle, gentry, genuine, genus, gin (2), indigenous, ingenious, ingenuous, progenitor, progeny, regenerate ; *cf.* kin. (√GEN, to produce.)

ger-ere (*gest-*), to bear — congeries, congestion, digest, exaggerate, gerund, gestation, gesticulate, gesture, jest, register, suggestion.

glūtin-, for *glūten*, glue — agglutinate, conglutinate, glue, glutinous.

grad-ī (*gress-*), to step — aggress, congress, degrade, degree, digress, egress, grade, gradient, gradual, graduate, grail (1), grallatory, grise, ingredient, ingress, progress, regress, retrograde, retrogression, transgression. (√GHREDH, to go.)

grand-is, great — aggrandise, gaffer, gammer, gramercy, grand, grandee, grandeur, grandiloquent ; *cf.* grampus.

grān-um, grain — engrain, garner, garnet, grain, granary, grange, granite, granule, grenade, pomegranate ; *cf.* corn. (√GER, to grind.)

grāt-us, pleasing — agree, congratulate, grace, grateful, gratify, gratis, gratitude, gratuitous, gratuity, gratulate, ingratiate, ingrate.

grau-is, heavy — aggravate, aggrieve, grave (2), grief, grieve.

greg-em, acc., a flock — aggregate, congregate, egregious, gregarious, segregate.

gross-us, thick — engross, grocer, grog, grogram, gross.

gust-us, a tasting — disgust, gust (2), ragout ; *cf.* choose, choice. (√GEUS, to taste.)

hab-ēre, to have — able, avoirdupois, binnacle, cohabit, debenture, debt, deshabille, devoir, due, duty, endeavour, exhibit, habiliment, habit, habitable, habitant, habitat, habitation, habitude, inhabit, inhibit, prebend, prohibit, provender.

hær-ēre (*hæs-*), to stick — adhere, cohere, hesitate, inherent.

hēr-ēs, an heir — heir, hereditary, heritage, inherit.

hom-o, a man — homage, homicide, human, humane, ombre.

horr-ēre, to bristle — abhor, horrible, horrid, horrify, horror, ordure ; *cf.* hirsute.

hum-us, the ground — exhume, humble, humiliate, humility.

int-us, within — denizen, intestine ; *cf.* entrails, interior, internal.

ī-re, to go — adit, ambient, ambition, arrant, circuit, commence, concomitant, constable, count (1), county, exit, eyre, initial, initiate, issue, itinerant, obit, perish, prætor, preterite, sedition, sudden, trance, transient, transit ; *cf.* isthmus. (√EI, to go.)

(i=y.) iac-ere, to throw — abject, adjacent, adjective, agistment, amice (1), circumjacent, conjecture, deject, ejaculate, eject, gist, inject, interjacent, interjection, jesses, jet (1), jetsam, jetty, joist, jut, jutty, object, project, reject, subjacent, subject, trajectory.

636

ioc-us, a jest—jeopardy, jewel, jocose, jocular, joke, juggler.

iūdex, a judge ; see *dīcere* ; p. 635.

iung-ere (*iug-*), to join—adjoin, conjoin, conjugal, conjugate, enjoin, injunction, join, joint, jugular, junction, juncture, junta, junto, rejoin, subjoin, subjugate, subjunctive ; *cf.* yoke, syzygy. (✓YEUG, to join.)

iūr-āre (*iūs-*), to swear—abjure, adjure, conjure, injure, juridical, jurisdiction, jurist, juror, jury, just (1), justice, justify, objurgation, perjure.

iuu-āre, to help—adjutant, aid, coadjutor.

lāb-ī (*laps-*), to glide, slip — collapse, elapse, illapse, lapse, relapse ; *cf.* sleep.

labōr-em, acc., labour—belabour, elaborate, laboratory, laborious, labour.

lac-ere, to entice — delectable, delicate, delicious, delight, dilettante, elicit.

læd-ere (*læs-*), to hurt—collide, collision, elide, elision, illision, lesion.

lau-āre, *lu-ere*, to wash—ablution, alluvial, antediluvian, deluge, dilute, laundress, lava, lave, lavender, lotion ; *cf.* lather, lye. (✓LOU, to wash.)

lax-us, slack—lax, laxative, lease (1), leash, lessee, relax, relay (1), release, relish ; *cf.* slack.

lēg-āre, to appoint — allege, colleague, college, delegate, legacy, legate, legatee, relegate ; cf. *legere* (below).

lĕg-ere, to collect, read—coil (1), collect, cull, diligent, elect, elegant, eligible, intellect, intelligence, intelligible, lection, lecture, legend, legible, legion, lesson, neglect, negligence, predilection, recollect, select ; *cf.* leal, legal, legislator, legitimate, loyal ; also *lēg-āre* (above). (✓LEG, to collect.)

leu-is, light—alleviate, elevate, leaven, legerdemain, leger-line, levant, levee, lever, levity, levy, relevant, relieve.

līber, free — deliver, liberal, liberate, libertine, liberty, livery.

lībra, a balance — deliberate, level, librate.

lic-ēre, to be allowable—illicit, leisure, licence, licentiate, licentious.

lig-āre, to bind—alligation, alloy, ally, league (1), liable, lictor, lien, lime-hound, ligament, ligature, oblige, rally (1).

līmen, a threshold — eliminate, lintel, preliminary.

linqu-ere, to leave — delinquent, dereliction, relic, relict, relinquish, reliquary ; *cf.* eclipse, ellipse. (✓LEIQ, to leave.)

līn-um, flax, *līn-ea*, a line—align (aline), delineate, line, lineage, lineal, lineament, linear, linen, lint ; *cf.* lining, linnet, linseed, linsey-woolsey.

liqu-ēre, to be fluid—deliquesce, liquefy, liquescent, liquid, liquidate, liquor.

lītera, a letter—alliteration, letter, literal, literature, obliterate.

loc-us, a place—allocate, allow (1), collocate, couch, dislocate, lieu, lieutenant, local, locate, locomotion, locus.

long-us, long—eloign, elongate, longevity, longitude, lunge, oblong, prolong, purloin ; *cf.* long.

loqu-ī, to speak—allocution, circumlocution, colloquy, elocution, eloquent, loquacious, obloquy, prolocutor, soliloquy, ventriloquist.

lūc-ēre, to shine — elucidate, illuminate, illustrate, limn, lucid, lucubration, luminary, luminous, lunar, lunatic, lustre (?), pellucid, sublunar, translucent ; *cf.* light (1). (✓LEUQ, to shine.)

lūd-ere, to play—allude, collude, delude, elude, illude, illusion, ludicrous, prelude.

mag-n-us, great — magistrate, magnanimous, magnate, magnificent, magnify, magniloquence, magnitude, main (2), majesty, major, master, maxim, maximum, mayor, merino, miss (2), mister, mistress.

mal-us, bad—malady, malapert, malaria, malediction, malice, malign, malinger, malison, maltreat, malversation, maugre.

mand-āre (*cf. manus*), to put into the hands of, enjoin — command, commend, commodore, countermand, demand, mandate, maundy Thursday, recommend, remand. See *manus*.

man-ēre, to remain — manor, manse, mansion, mastiff (?), menagerie, menial, messuage, permanent, remain, remnant. (✓MEN, to remain.)

man-us, hand — amanuensis, maintain, manacle, manage, manciple, manege, manifest, maniple, manipulate, manner, manœuvre, manual, manufacture, manumit, manure, manuscript.

mās (*māri-*), a male—emasculate, male, mallard, marital, marry, masculine.

meā-re, to go—congé, permeate.

med-ērī, to be a remedy — medicine, remedy.

medi-us, middle — demi-, immediate, mean (3), mediate, medieval, mediocre, mediterranean, medium, meridian, mezzotinto, mizen, moiety.

mel, honey — marmalade, melilot, melli-fluous, molasses ; *cf.* mildew.

memor, remembering — commemorate, memoir, memory, remember. (✓SMER, to remember.)

mend-um, a fault — amend, amends, emendation, mend.

ment-em, acc., mind, *mon-ēre,* to advise — comment, demented, memento, mental, mention ; admonish, demonstrate, mint (1), moidore, monetary, money, monition, monster, monument, muster, premonish, remonstrate, summon, summons ; *cf.* mind, mean (1) ; *also* amnesty, automaton, mnemonics. (✓MEN, to think.)

mer-ēre, to earn — demerit, meretricious, merit.

merx (merc-), traffic — amerce, commerce, market, mart, mercantile, mercenary, mercer, merchandise, merchant, mercury, mercy.

mēt-īrī (mens-), to measure — commensu-rate, dimension, immense, measure, mensuration.

migrā-re, to wander — emigrate, immi-grate, migrate, transmigrate.

min-ārī, to threaten — amenable, com-mination, demean (1), demeanour, menace, promenade.

min-ēre, to project — eminent, imminent, prominent. (✓MEN, to project.)

minu-ere, to diminish, *min-or,* less — ad-minister, comminute, diminish, diminution, minim, minish, minister, minor, minstrel, minuet, minus, minute, mistery.

mīr-us, wonderful — admire, marvel, mi-racle, mirage, mirror ; *cf.* smile. (✓SMEI, to wonder at.)

misc-ēre, to mix — meddle, medley, mis-cellaneous, promiscuous ; *cf.* mix.

mitt-ere (miss-), to send — admit, com-missary, commit, compromise, demise, dimissory, dismiss, emit, immit, intermit, mass (2), mess (1), message, missal, missile, mission, missive, omit, permit, premiss, premises, pretermit, promise, remit, sub-mit, surmise, transmit.

mod-us, manner — accommodate, com-modious, incommode, mode, model, moderate, modern, modest, modicum, modify, modulate, mood (2), mould (2) ; *cf.* meditate, mete. (✓MED, to measure.)

mol-ere, to grind — mill, molar, mullet (2) ; *cf.* molest ; *also* meal (1). (✓MEL, to grind.)

mōl-es, a heap — demolish, emolument, mole (3), molecule.

moll-is, soft — emollient, moil, mollify, mollusc ; *cf.* melt, smelt (1). (✓MELD, Teut. SMELT, to melt.)

mon-ēre ; see *ment-em.*

mont-em, acc., a hill — amount, mount (1), mount (2), mountain, mountebank, paramount, remount, surmount, tanta-mount, tramontane ; *cf.* mound. See *minēre.* (✓MEN, to project.)

mord-ēre (mors-), to bite — mordacity, morsel, remorse ; *cf.* muse (1), muzzle. (✓MERD, to rub, bite.)

mor-ī, to die — morbid, mortal, mortgage, mortify, mortmain, mortuary, murrain ; *cf.* murder ; *also* amaranth, ambrosia. (✓MER, to die.)

mou-ēre (mōt-), to move — commotion, emotion, mob (1), mobile, moment, motion, motive, motor, move, mutiny, promote, remote, remove.

mūn-us, a duty — municipal, munificence, remunerate.

mūt-āre, to change — commute, mew (3), moult, mutable, mutual, permutation, transmutation.

nascī, to be born, *nāt-us (gnāt-us),* born — agnate, cognate, impregnate, innate, naive, nascent, natal, nation, native, nature, pregnant, preternatural, supernatural. (✓GEN, to beget.)

nect-ere (nex-), to bind — annex, connect, connexion.

negā-re, to deny — abnegate, deny, nega-tion, renegade, runagate.

noc-ēre, to hurt — innocent, innocuous, noxious, nuisance, obnoxious. (✓NEK, to destroy.)

nōmen, a name — cognomen, denominate, ignominy, nomenclator, nominal, nomi-nate, noun, pronoun, renown ; *cf.* nun-cupative ; *also* name, onomatopœia, syn-onym, &c.

noscere (gnoscere, *gnōt-), to get to know — acquaint, cognisance, cognition, connoisseur, ignoble, ignore, incognito, noble, notice, notify, notion, notorious, quaint, recognise, reconnoitre. Cf. Gk. γνῶναι ; E. kin, &c. (✓GEN, GNŌ, to know, get to know.)

not-a, a mark — annotate, denote, notable, notary, note.

nou-us, new — innovate, novel, novice, renovate ; *cf.* neology, neophyte, neoteric ; *also* new.

nūb-ere (nupt-), to marry — connubial, nuptial.

numer-us, a number — enumerate, number,

numeral, numeration, numerous, super-numerary. (√NEM, to apportion.)

nunti-us, a messenger — announce, annunciation, denounce, enunciate, nuncio, pronounce, renounce.

nūtrī-re, to nourish — nourish, nurse, nurture, nutriment, nutritious, nutritive.

ocul-us, eye — binocular, inoculate, inveigle, monocular, ocular; *cf.* ophthalmia, optics, canopy; eye. (√OQ, to see.) See Gk. ὀπτικός; p. 646.

odi-um, hatred — annoy, ennui, noisome, odium.

od-or, scent — olfactory, odour, redolent; *cf.* osmium, ozone. (√OD, to smell.)

opt-āre, to wish — adopt, optative, optimism, option; *cf.* copious, copy, office, opulent.

opus (*oper-*), work — co-operate, inure, opera, operate, ure, use*(2).

orb-is, a circle — exorbitant, orb, orbit.

ord-o (*ordin-*), order — co-ordinate, extraordinary, inordinate, ordain, order, ordinal, ordinance, ordinary, ordination, ordnance, primordial, subordinate.

orī-rī, to rise — aborigines, abortion, orient, origin.

orn-āre, to adorn — adorn, ornament, ornate, suborn.

ōs (*ōr-*), the mouth — adore, inexorable, oracle, oral, oration, orator, orifice, orison, osculate, peroration.

pac-ere, pac-iscī (*pact-*), to agree; *pangere* (*pact-*), to fasten — appease, compact (1), compact (2), dispatch, impact, impinge, pacify, page (2), pageant, pale (1), palette, palisade, pallet (2), pay (1), peace, peel (3), pole (1), propagate, repay. (√PĀG, PĀK, to fasten.)

pann-us, a cloth — counterpane, pane, panel, pannel, panicle.

pār, equal — apparel, compeer, disparage, disparity, pair, par, parity, peer (1), prial, umpire.

par-āre, to prepare — apparatus, compare, emperor, empire, imperative, imperial, parachute, parade, parapet, parasol, pare, parry, prepare, rampart, repair (1), separate, sever, several; *cf.* sepal.

par-ere, to produce, *pār ēre*, to come to sight — apparitor, appear, parent, parturient, repertory, transparent.

part-em, acc., part — apart, apartment, apportion, compartment, depart, impart, parcel, parse, part, partake, participate, participle, particle, partisan (1), partition,

partner, party, portion, proportion, repartee.

pasc-ere (*pā-, past-*), to feed — pabulum, pannage, pastel, pastern, pastille, pastor, pasture, pester, repast; *cf.* feed, fodder, food, foster. (√PĀ, to feed.)

pater (*patr-i-*), father — expatriate, paternal, patois, patrician, patrimony, patristic, patron, pattern, repair (2); *cf.* patriarch, patriot, patronymic (*from* Gk.); *also* father.

pat-ēre, to lie open, *pand-ere*, to spread — compass, expand, pace, pass, passage, passport, pastime, patent, surpass, trespass; *cf.* paten. (√PET, to spread out.)

pat-ī (*pass-*), to suffer — compassion, compatible, passion, passive, patient.

pauper, poor — impoverish, pauper, poor, poverty; *cf.* few.

pectus (*pector-*), the breast — expectorate, pectoral, peitrel (poitrel).

ped-em, acc., foot — biped, expedite, impede, pawn (2), pedal, pedestal, pedestrian, pedicel, pedigree, pediment, piepowder, pioneer, quadruped; *cf.* impeach; *also* tripod, tripos (Gk.); *also* foot, fetter.

pell-ere (*puls-*), to drive — appeal, appellant, compel, dispel, expel, impel, interpellation, peal, pelt (1), propel, pulsate, pulse (1), pursy, push, repeal, repel.

pell-is, skin — peel (1), pelisse, pell, pellicle, pelt (2), pilch, pillion (?), plaid (?), surplice; *cf.* fell (2).

pend-ere (*pens-*), to weigh, *pend-ēre*, to hang — append, compendious, compensate, counterpoise, depend, dispense, expend, impend, pansy, pendant, pending, pendulous, pendulum, pensile, pension, pensive, penthouse, pentroof, perpendicular, poise, ponder, pound (1), prepense, preponderate, propensity, recompence, spencer, spend, suspend.

-perī-rī, to try — experience, expert, parlous, peril; *cf.* pirate, pore (1); *also* fare, ford. (√PER, to fare.)

pet-ere, to fly, attack — appetite, competent, competitor, impetus, petition, petulant, repeat; *also* pen, pennon; *cf.* feather. (√PET, to fly.)

pil-a, a ball — pellet, pile (1), piles, pill (1), platoon; *cf.* bullace (in Supplement, p. 662).

pil-us, a hair — depilatory, periwig, perruque, peruke, pile (3), plush, wig.

ping-ere (*pict-*), to paint — depict, paint, picture, pigment, pimento, pint.

pi-us, holy — expiate, piacular, piety, pious, pity.

plac-ēre, to please — complacent, complaisant, placable, placid, plea, plead, please, pleasure.

plang-ere, to lament — complain, plaint, plaintiff, plaintive.

plant-a, a plant — plant, plantain, plantigrade, supplant, transplant.

plān-us, flat — esplanade, explain, pianoforte, plain, plan, plane (1), plane (2), planisphere; *cf.* placenta, plank.

plaud-ere, to applaud — applaud, explode, plaudit, plausible.

plē-nus, full, *(com)plē-re*, to fill — accomplish, complement, complete, compliance, compliment, compline, comply, depletion, expletive, implement, plenary, plenitude, plenty, replenish, replete, supplement, supply; *cf.* polygon; full. (✓PLĒ, to fill.)

plic-āre, to fold, *plect-ere* (*plex-*), to plait — accomplice, apply, complex, complexion, complicate, complicity, deploy, display, employ, .explicate, explicit, exploit, implicate, imply, perplex, plait, pleach (plash), pleat, pliant, plight, ply, reply, splay, supple, suppliant, supplicate; *hence also* -ple *in* sim-ple, tri-ple, quadruple, -ble *in* dou-ble; *cf.* simplicity, duplicate, treble, triplicity, &c.

plōr-āre, to weep — deplore, explore, implore.

pōn-ere (*posit-*), to place — apposite, component, composite, composition, compost, compound, deponent, deposit, deposition, disposition, depot, exponent, exposition, expound, imposition, impost, impostor, interposition, juxtaposition, opponent, opposite, ponent, positive, post (1), post (2), postillion, postpone, posture, preposition, proposition, propound, provost, purpose (2), repository, supposition, transposition.

popul-us, people — depopulate, populace, popular, public, publican, publication, publish.

port-āre, to carry — comport, deport, disport, export, import, importable, port (1), porter (1), porter (3), portesse (portous), portfolio, portly, portmanteau, purport, report, sport, support, transport.

port-us, a harbour, *port-a*, a gate — importune, opportune, porch, port (2), port (3), port (4), portcullis, porte, porter (2), portico.

pos-se (*pot-ent-*) — posse, possible, potent, power, puissant. (✓ES, to exist.)

pōtā-re, to drink — poison, potable, potation; *cf.* potion.

prec-ārī, to pray — deprecate, imprecate, precarious, pray. (✓PREK, to ask.)

præd-a, prey — depredation, predatory, prey (see below).

prehend-ere, to seize — apprehend, apprentice, apprise, comprehend, comprise, emprise, enterprise, impregnable, imprese, imprison, prehensile, prentice, prise (prize), prison, prize (1), prize (3), reprehend, reprisal, surprise; *cf.* get. (✓GHwED, to seize.)

prem-ere (*press-*), to press — compress, depress, express, impress, imprint, oppress, print, repress, reprimand, sprain, suppress.

preti-um, price — appraise, appreciate, depreciate, praise, precious, price, prize (2).

prīm-us, first — premier, prim, prime (1), prime (2), primero, primeval, primitive, primogeniture, primrose, prince, principal, principle; *cf.* prior (1), prior (2), pristine; *also* first, fore, former.

prīu-us, single — deprive, private, privilege, privy.

prob-us, good — approbation, approve, disprove, improve, probable, probation, probe, probity, proof, prove, reprieve, reprobate, reprove.

prop-e, near — approach, approximate, propinquity, proximity, reproach.

propri-us, one's own — appropriate, impropriate, proper, property, propriety.

pugn-us, fist — impugn, oppugn, poniard, pugnacious, repugnant; *cf.* pugilism; pygmy (Gk.).

pull-a (late L.), a hen — pool (2), poult, poultry, pullet; *cf.* foal, filly.

pung-ere (*punct-*), to prick — appoint, compunction, counterpoint, expunge, poignant, point, pounce (1), punch (1), puncheon, punctate, punctilio, punctual, punctuate, puncture, pungent, punt (2); *cf.* embonpoint.

pūr-us, pure — expurgate, pour, pure, purge, purify, puritan, purity, spurge. (✓PEU, to purify.) See *put-us*.

pūs (*pūr-*), matter — purulent, pus, suppurate; *cf.* putrid; foul. (✓PŪ, to stink.)

put-us, clear — account, amputate, compute, count (2), depute, discount, dispute, impute, putative, recount, repute.

quær-ere (*quæst-*), to seek — acquire, conquer, conquest, disquisition, enquire, exquisite, inquest, inquire, inquisition, perquisite, query, quest, question, request, require.

quat-ere (*quass-*), to shake — concussion, discuss, percussion, quash, rescue; *cf.* squash.

quattuor (whence *quadr-us*), four — quadrangle, quadrant, quadrate, quadriennial, quadrilateral, quadrille, quadrillion, quadroon, quadruped, quadruple, quarantine, quarrel (2), quarry (1), quart, quartan, quarter, quartern, quartet, quarto, quaternary, quatrain, quire (1), squad, squadron, square, squire (2); *cf.* four.

quer-ī, to lament — quarrel (1), querimonious, querulous.

quiēt-em, acc., rest — acquiesce, aquit, coy, quiet, quit, quittance, quite, requiem, requite; *cf.* while.

rab-ere, to rave — rabid, rage.

rād-ere, to scrape — abrade, erase, rascal, rase, rash (2), rasorial, razor.

rādīc-em, acc., a root — eradicate, race (3), radish, radix, rash (3); *cf.* root, wort.

radi-us, a ray — irradiate, radiant, radius, ray.

rap-ere, to seize — rapacious, rapid, rapine, raptorial, rapture, ravage, raven (2), ravine, ravish; *cf.* rape (1).

reg-ere, to rule — address, adroit, alert, correct, direct, dirge, dress, erect, escort, insurgent, insurrection, interregnum, real (2), realm, rectangle, rectify, rectilineal, rectitude, regal, regent, regicide, regimen, regiment, region, regnant, regular, reign, resource, resurrection, royal, rule, sortie, source, surge, unruly; *cf.* rajah, rich, right. (✓REG, to rule.)

rē-rī (*rat-*), to suppose — arraign, rate (1), ratify, ratio, ration, reason.

rīd-ēre, to laugh — deride, ridiculous, risible.

rōd-ere, to gnaw — corrode, erode, rodent, rostrum; *cf.* rat (?).

rog-āre, to ask — abrogate, derogate, interrogate, prerogative, prorogue, rogation, supererogation, surrogate.

rot-a, a wheel — comptroller, control, controller, roll, rondeau, rotary, rotundity, roué, rouleau, roulette, round, roundel, roundelay, rowel, rundlet (runlet).

rub-er, red — erubescent, rouge, rubicund, rubric, ruby; *cf.* russet; *also* red, ruddy, rust. (✓REUDH, to be red.)

rump-ere (*rupt-*), to break — abrupt, corrupt, disruption, cruption, interruption, irruption, rote (1), rout (1), route, routine,

rupture, rut (1); *cf.* loot, reave, rove, rob. (✓REUP, to tear, seize.)

sac-er (*sacr-*), holy — consecrate, desecrate, execrate, sacerdotal, sacrament, sacrifice, sacrilege, sacristan, sexton; *cf.* saint, sanctify, &c.

sal, salt — salad, salary, saline, salmagundi, salt-cellar, sauce, sausage, souse (1).

sal-īre, to leap, spring forward — assail, assault, desultory, exult, insult, resilient, result, salient, sally, saltire, saltation.

salu-us, safe — safe, sage (2), salubrious, salutary, salute, salvage, salvation, salver, save.

sap-ere, to savour of, be wise — insipid, sage (1), sapid, sapience, savour.

sat-is, enough, *satur*, full — assets, sate, satiate, satire, satisfy, saturate, soil (3).

scand-ere, to climb — ascend, condescend, descend, escalade, scale (3), scan, scansion, transcend; *cf.* scandal, slander.

scī-re, to know — ascititious, conscience, conscious, prescience, science, sciolist.

scrīb-ere, to write — ascribe, circumscribe, conscript, describe, descry, inscribe, postscript, prescribe, proscribe, rescript, scribble, scrip (2), script, scripture, scrivener, subscribe, superscription, transcribe.

scūt-um, a shield — escuage, escutcheon, esquire, scutage, scutcheon, scutiform.

sec-āre, to cut — bisect, dissect, insect, intersect, scion, secant, section, segment, sickle, trisect; *cf.* saw (1), scythe, sedge. (✓SEK, to cut.)

sed-ēre, to sit — assess, assiduous, assize (1), assize (2), dissident, hostage, insidious, possess, preside, reside, residue, sedate, sedentary, sediment, see (2), sell (2), session, sizar, size (1), size (2), subside, subsidy, supersede, surcease; *cf.* seat, set, settle (1), settle (2); *also* cathedral, chair, chaise, polyhedron. (✓SED, to sit.)

sēmen, seed — disseminate, seminal, seminary.

sent-īre (*sens-*), to feel — assent, consent, dissent, presentiment, resent, scent, sense, sensual, sentence, sentiment.

sequ-ī (*secūt-*), to follow (*soci-us*) — associate, consecutive, consequent, dissociate, ensue, execute, exequies, intrinsic, obsequies, obsequious, persecute, prosecute, pursue, second, sect, sept, sequel, sequence, sequester, sociable, social, society, subsequent, sue, suit, suite. (✓SEQ, to follow.)

ser-ere, to join — assert, concert, desert (1), dissertation, exert, insert, series, serried; *cf.* seraglio.

III. SELECT LIST OF LATIN WORDS

seru-us, a slave — conserve, desert (2), deserve, dessert, disservice, observe, preserve, reserve, reservoir, serf, sergeant, servant, serve, service, servile, servitude, subserve.

seuēr-us, serious — asseverate, persevere, severe.

sign-um, a sign — ancient (2), assign, consign, countersign, design, ensign, insignia, resign, seal (1), sennet, sign, signal, signet, signify.

simil-is, like, *simul*, together — assemble, assimilate, dissemble, dissimilar, dissimulate, resemble, semblance, similar, simile, similitude, simulate, simultaneous; *cf.* same.

solid-us, solid — consolidate, soda, soder (solder), soldier, solid, soliped, sou.

solu-ere, to loosen — absolute, absolve, assoil, dissolute, dissolve, resolute, resolve, soluble, solution, solve.

sōl-us, alone — desolate, sole (3), soliloquy, solitary, solitude, solo, sullen.

son-us, sound — assonant, consonant, dissonant, parson, person, resonant, resound, sonata, sonnet, sonorous, sound, unison. (√SWEN, to sound.)

sort-em, acc., lot — assort, consort, resort, sorcery, sort.

sparg-ere (*spars-*), to scatter — asperse, disperse, intersperse, sparse.

spec-ere (*spect-*), to look — aspect, circumspect, conspicuous, despise, despite, especial, espy, expect, inspect, introspection, perspective, perspicacity, perspicuous, prospect, respect, respite, retrospect, special, species, specify, specimen, specious, spectacle, spectator, spectre, specular, speculate, spice, spite, spy, suspect, suspicion, transpicuous; *cf.* auspice, frontispiece.

spēr-, from *spēs*, hope — despair, desperado, desperate, prosper.

spīr-āre, to breathe — aspire, conspire, expire, inspire, perspiration, respire, spiracle, spirit, sprightly, sprite, transpire.

spond-ēre (*spons-*), to promise — correspond, despond, espouse, respond, sponsor, spouse.

stagn-um, a pool — stagnate, stanch, stank, tank.

stā-re (*stat-*, *sist-*), to stand — arrest, assist, circumstance, consist, constant, constitute, contrast, cost, desist, destitute, distant, establish, estate, exist, extant, insist, instance, institute, interstice, obstacle, obstetric, persist, press (2), prostitute, resist, rest (2), restitution, restive, stable (1),

stable (2), stablish, stage, stamen, stamin, stanza, state, station, statist, statue, stature, status, statute, subsist, substance, substitute, superstition, transubstantiation; *cf.* statics, &c.; see Gk. ἵστημι; p. 645. (√STĀ, to stand.)

-staur-āre, to set up — restaurant, restore, store, story (2).

stern-ere (*strāt-*), to strew — consternation, prostrate, stratum, stray, street; *cf.* strath, straw, strew. (√STER, to strew.)

still-a, a drop — distil, instil, still (2), still (3).

-stingu-ere (*-stinct-*), to prick — distinct, distinguish, extinguish, instinct.

stīp-āre, to press together — constipate, costive, stevedore; *cf.* stipend, stipulation.

string-ere (*strict-*), to draw tight — astriction, astringent, constrain, distrain, distress, district, obstriction, restrain, strain, strait, stress, stringent, strict; *cf.* strike.

stru-ere (*struct-*), to build up — construct, construe, destroy, instruct, instrument, obstruct, structure, superstructure.

suād-ēre (*suās-*), to persuade — assuage, dissuade, persuade, suasion, suave; *cf.* sweet.

sup-, as in *sup-er*, above — consummate, soprano, sovereign, sum, summit, super-, superior, supernal, supine, supra-, supreme, sur- (2), sus-, suzerain.

tabula, a plank — entablature, table, tableau, tabular, tabulate, tafferel.

tac-ēre, to be silent — reticent, tacit.

talea (popular L.), a thin rod — detail, entail, retail, tail (2), tailor, tally; *cf.* intaglio.

tang-ere (*tag-*, *tact-*), to touch — attain, attainder, attaint, contact, contagion, contaminate, contiguous, contingent, entire, integer, redintegration, tact, tangent, tangible, task, taste, tax. (√TAG, to touch.)

teg-ere (*tect-*), to cover — detect, integument, protect, tegument, tile, toga; *cf.* thatch, deck, tight. (√STEG, to cover.)

temper-āre, to regulate — attemper, distemper (1), distemper (2), tamper, temper.

temp-us (*temp-or-*), time — contemporaneous, contemporary, extempore, tempest, temporal, tense (1).

tend-ere, to extend — attend, contend, distend, extend, intend, intense, intent, ostensible, ostentation, portend, pretend, subtend, superintendent, tend (1), tend (2), tender (2), tender (3), tendon, tense (2), tension, tent (1), tent (4), tenter, toise. (√TEN, to stretch.)

ten-ēre, to hold — abstain, appertain, appurtenance, attempt, contain, content, continent, continue, continuous, countenance, countertenor, detain, entertain, impertinent, obtain, pertain, pertinacity, pertinent, purtenance, rein, retain, retinue, sustain, tempt, tenable, tenacious, tenacity, tenant, tenement, tenet, tenon, tenor, tent (2), tentacle, tentative, tenure; *cf.* tend, lieutenant, maintain.

tenu-is, thin — attenuate, extenuate, tenuity; *cf.* thin. (✓TEN, to stretch.)

ter-ere (*trīt-*), to rub — attrition, contrite, detriment, tribulation, trite, triturate; *cf.* try. (✓TER, to bore.)

termin-us, end — determine, exterminate, term, termination, terminus.

terr-a, earth — inter, parterre, subterranean, terrace, terreen (tureen), terrene, terrestrial, terrier (1), terrier (2), territory; *cf.* torrid, thirst. See *torr-ēre*.

terr-ēre, to scare — deter, terrible, terrific, terror.

test-is, a witness — attest, contest, detest, intestate, protest, testament, testify, testimony.

tex-ere, to weave — context, pretext, subtle, text, textile, texture, tissue, toil (2), toilet. (✓TEK-S, from TEK, to cut out.)

tim-ēre, to fear — intimidate, timid, timorous.

ting-ere (*tinct-*), to dye — distain, stain, taint, tent (3), tincture, tinge, tint.

toll-ere (*lāt-*), to lift — ablative, collation, correlate, delay, dilate, elate, extol, oblate, oblation, prelate, prolate, relate, superlative, translate; *cf.* emblements, legislator, tolerate; *also* atlas, talent, tantalise; thole. (✓TEL, to endure.)

torn-us, a lathe — attorney, contour, detour, return, tour, tournament, tourney, tourniquet, turn, turnpike. (*Borrowed from* Gk. τόρνος; *from* ✓TER, to bore.)

torqu-ēre (*tort-*), to twist — contort, distort, extort, retort, torch, torment, tormentil, torque, torsion, tortoise, tortuous, torture; *cf.* tart (2).

torr-ēre (*tost-*), to dry up — toast, torrent, torrid; *cf.* thirst. (✓TERS, to be dry.)

trah-ere (*tract-*), to draw — abstract, attract, contract, detract, distract, entreat, estreat, extract, portrait, pourtray, protract, retract, retreat, subtract, trace, tract, tractable, trail (?), train, trait, treat, treatise, treaty.

trēs (*tri-*, *ter-*), three — tercel, ternary,

tertian, tierce, treble, trental, trey, triangle, tricentenary, tricolor, &c., trillion, trinity, trio, triple, triplicate, trireme, triumvir, trivet, trivial; *cf.* triad, tribrach, triglyph, trigonometry, trihedron, tripod, tripos (Gk.); *perhaps* tress, tressure; *cf.* three.

tribu-s, a tribe — attribute, contribute, distribute, retribution, tribe, tribune, tribute.

trūd-ere, to thrust — abstruse, detrude, extrude, intrude, obtrude, protrude; *cf.* thrust. (✓TREUD, to thrust.)

tu-ērī (*tuit-*, *tūt-*), to protect — intuition, tuition, tutelage, tutelar, tutor.

tum-ēre, to swell — intumescence, tumefy, tumid, tumult, tumulus; *cf.* tuber, thumb. (✓TEU, to swell.)

tund-ere (*tūs-*), to beat — contuse, obtuse, pierce (?). (✓TEUD, Teut. STEUT, to beat.)

turb-a, a crowd — disturb, perturb, turbid, turbulent.

ultrā, beyond — antepenultima, outrage, penultima, ulterior, ultimate, ultramarine, ultramontane, ultramundane, utterance (2).

umbr-a, shade — adumbrate, umbel, umber, umbrage, umbrella.

und-a, a wave — abound, abundance, inundation, redound, redundance, superabound, surround, undulate; *cf.* hydrogen, hydra; water, wet, otter. (✓WED, to be wet.)

ung-ere (*unct-*), to anoint — anoint, ointment, unction, unctuous, unguent.

ūn-us, one — annul, null, onion, unanimous, unicorn, uniform, union (1), union (2), unique, unison, unit, unite, unity, universal, univocal.

ūt-ī (*ūs-*), to use — abuse, peruse, use, usurp, usury, utensil, utilise, utility.

(*u* = *w*.) *uād-ere* (*uās-*), to go — evade, evasion, invade, pervade; *cf.* wade. (✓WADH, to go.)

uag-ārī, to wander — extravagant, vagabond, vagary, vague.

ual-ēre, to be strong — avail, convalesce, countervail, prevail, vail (3), valediction, valentine, valerian, valetudinary, valiant, valid, valour, value.

uall-is, a valley — avalanche, vail (2), vale, valley.

uān us, vain — evanescent, vain, vanish, vanity, vaunt.

uap-or, vapour — evaporate, vapour: *cf.* vapid.

uari-us, various — meniver, vair, variegate, variety, various, vary.

uār-us, crooked (whence *uāric-*) – divaricate, prevaricate, varicose.

uās, a vessel – extravasate, vascular, vase, vessel.

ueh-ere (*uect-*), to carry – convex, inveigh, vehement, vehicle, vex; *cf.* reveal, veil, vein, venesection; *also* wag, waggon, wain, way, weigh, wey. (√WEGH, to carry.)

uell-ere (*uuls-*), to pluck – convulse, revulsion.

uend-ere, to sell – vend, vent (2); *cf.* venal. (√DO, to give.)

uen-īre (*uent-*), to come – advent, adventure, avenue, contravene, convene, convenient, convent, convention, covenant, covin, event, intervene, invent, parvenu, prevent, revenue, saunter, souvenir, supervene, venture, venew; *cf.* come; *see* Gk. βαίνειν; p. 645. (√GwEM, to go, come.)

uerb-um, a word – adverb, proverb, verb, verbal, verbiage; *cf.* word.

uerg-ere, to incline – converge, diverge, verge.

uert-ere (*uers-*), to turn – adverse, advert, advertise, avert, controversy, converse, convert, divers, diverse, divert, divorce, inverse, invert, obverse, pervert, prose, reverse, revert, subvert, transverse, traverse, verse, versify, version, vertebra, vertex, vertigo, vortex; *cf.* verst, worth (2), weird. (√WERT, to become.)

uēr-us, true – aver, veracious, verdict, verify, verisimilitude, verity, very.

uest-is, clothing – divest, invest, travesty, vest, vestment, vestry, vesture; *cf.* wear (1). (√WES, to clothe.)

uet-us (*ueter-*), old – inveterate, veteran, veterinary; *cf.* wether.

uia, a way – convey, convoy, deviate, devious, envoy, impervious, invoice, obviate, obvious, pervious, previous, viaduct, voyage. See *uehere*. (√WEGH, to carry.)

uid-ēre (*uīs-*), to see – advice, advise, envy, evident, improvise, invidious, provide, proviso, prudent, purvey, purview, review, revise, revisit, supervise, survey, videlicet, view, visage, visard, visible, vision, visit, visor, vista, visual; *cf.* wise, wiseacre, wit (2), wot; *and* Gk. ἰδεῖν; p. 645. (√WEID, to see.)

uig-il, wakeful (*uig-or*), – invigorate, reveille, surveillance, vigil, vigour; *cf.* wake. (√WEG, to wake.)

uinc-ere (*uict-*), to conquer – convince, evict, evince, invincible, vanquish, victor.

uirid-is, green – farthingale, verdant, verdigris, verjuice, vert, viridity.

uīu-ere (*uict-*), to live – convivial, revive, survive, viands, victuals, vital, vivacity, vivid, vivify, viviparous, vivisection; *cf.* viper, wyvern; *also* quick, biology. (√GwIW, to live.)

uol-o, I wish, *uel-le*, to will – volition, voluntary, voluptuous.

uolu-ere (*uolūt-*), to roll – circumvolve, convolve, devolve, evolve, involve, revolt, revolve, vault (1), vault (2), voluble, volume, volute; *cf.* helix. (√WEL, to wind, turn, roll.)

uou-ēre (*uōt-*), to vow – devote, devout, vote, vow.

uox (*uōc-*), voice, *uoc-āre*, to call – advocate, advowson, avocation, avouch, convoke, evoke, invocation, invoke, provoke, revoke, vocable, vocal, vocation, vociferation, voice, vouch, vouchsafe, vowel; *cf.* epic. (√WEQ, to speak.)

SELECT LIST OF GREEK WORDS

The following list contains the principal Greek words that appear in compounds or in several derivatives. Such as have produced but few derivatives, or are of but little interest, are excluded.

ἄγ-ειν, to drive – agony, antagonist, axiom; epact, paragoge, stratagem, strategy; dem-, ped-, syn-agogue. Cf. L. *agere*; p. 632. (√AG, to drive.)

αἱρ-εῖν, to take – aphæresis, diæresis, heresy, heretic, synæresis.

αἰσθάν-ομαι, I perceive – æsthetic, anæsthetic.

ακ-, as in ἀκ-μή, a point, ἄκ-ρος, pointed – acacia, acme, aconite, acrobat, acropolis, acrostic. *See* L. *ac-*; p. 632. (√AK, to pierce.)

ἀλλ-ος, other — allopathy, parallax, parallel, parallelogram. Cf. L. *alius*; p. 632.

ἀρχ-ή, a beginning — anarchy, arch-, arch, archæology, archaic, archetype, archipelago, architect, architrave, archives, heptarchy, hierarchy, monarch, oligarchy, patriarch, tetrarch.

ἀστήρ, a star — aster, asterisk, asteroid, astrology, astronomy; *cf.* disaster.

βαίν-ειν (βα-), to go, come — base (2), basis, diabetes. Cf. L. *uenīre*, E. *come.* (✓GwEM, to come.)

βάλλ-ειν, to cast (βελ-, βολ-) — belemnite, devil, diabolic, emblem, embolism, hyperbole, palaver, parable, parabola, parley, parliament, parlour, parole, problem, symbol.

βίο-s, life — amphibious, biography, biology. (✓GwĪW, to live.)

βόμβ-os, a humming — bomb, bombard, bound (1), bumper; *cf.* boom (1).

βύρσ-η, a hide — bursar, disburse, purse, reimburse; *cf.* sporran.

γάμ-os, marriage — bigamy, cryptogamia, monogamy, polygamy.

γέν-, as in γέν-os, race — endogen, exogen, genealogy, genesis; *cf.* cosmogony. (✓GEN, to beget.)

γῆ, earth — apogee, geography, geometry, georgic, perigee; *cf.* ogee.

γλῶσσ-α (γλωττ-), the tongue — epiglottis, gloss (2), glossary, glossographer, glottis, gloze; *also* bugloss, polyglot.

γνῶ-ναι, to know — diagnosis, gnome, gnomon, gnostic, prognostic. Cf. L. *noscere*; p. 638. (✓GEN, GNŌ, to know.)

γράφ-ειν, to write, γράμ-μα, a letter — autograph, digraph, lithograph, paragraph, photograph; -graphy (*as in* biography, &c.); graphic, graft; anagram, diagram, epigram, glamour, gramarye, grammar, grammatical, programme, telegram. Cf. E. *carve.* (✓GREBH, to carve.)

δέρμ-α, skin — derm, epidermis, pachydermatous. Cf. E. *tear* (1). (✓DER, to flay.)

δο-, cf. δί-δω-μι, I give — anecdote, antidote, dose. Cf. L. *do*, I give. (✓DO, to give.)

ἕδρα, a seat — cathedral, chair, chaise; octahedron, polyhedron, tetrahedron. Cf. L. *sedēre*, E. *sit.* (✓SED, to sit.)

ἔργ-ον (ὀργ-), work — energy, exergue, organ, orgies; lit-, metall-, the-urgy; *cf.* work. (✓WERG, to work.)

ἔχ-ειν (ὀχ-, σχη-), to hold — epoch, hectic, Hector, scheme. (✓SEGH, to endure, hold in.)

ἥλι-os, sun — aphelion, heliacal, heliotrope, parhelion, perihelion.

θεάο-μαι, I see — amphitheatre, theatre, theorem, theory.

θέ-μα, a theme, θέσ-ις, a thesis, τί-θη-μι, I place — anathema, antithesis, apothecary, epithet, hypothec, hypothesis, metathesis, parenthesis, synthesis, theme, thesaurus, thesis, treasure. Cf. E. *do.* (✓DHĒ, to put, place.)

θε-όs, a god — apotheosis, atheism, enthusiasm, pantheon, polytheism, theism, theocracy, theogony, theology, theurgy.

ἰδ-εῖν (εἰδ-), to see — idea, idol, idyll; *cf.* wit. (✓WEID, to see.)

ἴδιο-s, own — idiom, idiosyncrasy, idiot.

ἴστη-μι (στα-), I stand — apostasy, apostate, ecstasy, hypostasis, imposthume, statics, system; *cf.* stand. (✓STĀ, to stand.)

καί-ειν (καύ-σω), to burn — caustic, cauterise, encaustic, holocaust, ink.

κάλυξ, a cup — calyx. See L. *cēlāre*; p. 633.

κεῖμαι, I lie down — cemetery, coma. (✓KEI, to lie.)

κέλλειν, to drive — bucolic, pole (2), cylinder; *cf.* accelerate, celerity. (✓QEL, to drive.)

κέντρ-ον, a spike, goad — centre, centrifugal, centripetal, concentric, eccentric.

κλί-νειν, to lean, slope — anticlimax, climacter, climate, climax, clime, clinical, enclitic; *cf.* lean (1), low (3). See L. *clīuus*; p. 634. (✓KLEI, to lean.)

κόλαφος, a blow — cope (2), coppice, copse, coupon, recoup.

κρατ-ύς, strong — aristo-cracy, auto-, demo-, theo-cracy; *cf.* hard.

κρί-νειν, to judge — crisis, criterion, critic, diacritic, hypocrisy. See L. *cernere*; p. 633.

κρύπτ-ειν, to hide — apocrypha, crypt, cryptogamia, cryptogram, grot, grotesque, grotto.

λαμβάν-ειν (λαβ-, ληψ-), to seize — catalepsy, epilepsy, syllable; dilemma, lemma.

λόγ-os, a saying, λέγ-ειν, to speak — analogy, apologue, apology, catalogue, decalogue, dialect, dialogue, eclectic, eclogue, epilogue, eulogy, lexicon, logarithm, logic, monologue, prologue, syllogism; *also* -logy, *as in* astro-logy, &c. (✓LEG, to collect.) See L. *legere*; p. 637.

μέτρ-ον, a measure — diameter, metre, perimeter, symmetry; *cf.* baro-meter, chrono-meter, &c. (✓MĒ, ME, to measure.)

μόν-os, single — minster, monad, monarch, monastery, monk, monochord, monopoly, mono-.

νέμ-ειν, to assign — nemesis, nomad, numismatic; astro-nomy, eco-nomy, &c. (✓NEM, to apportion, take.)

ὁδ-ός, a way — episode, method, period, synod.

ὄζ-ειν (ὀδ-), to smell — osmium, ozone; cf. odour. (✓OD, to smell.)

ὄνομα, a name — anonymous, homonymous, metonymy, onomatopœia, paronymous, patronymic, pseudonym, synonym; cf. noun, name. See L. nōmen; p. 638.

ὀξ-ύ-s, sharp — oxalis, oxide, oxygen, oxymel, oxytone, paroxysm.

ὀπτικ-ός, visual — catoptric, dioptric, optic; cf. autopsy, ophthalmia, synopsis; also ocular. See L. oculus; p. 639. (✓OQ, to see.)

πάθ-os, suffering — antipathy, apathy, pathos, sympathy; allo-, homœo-pathy.

παῦσ-ις, a pause — pause, pose (1); whence appose, compose, decompose, depose, dispose, expose, impose, interpose, oppose, pose (2), propose, purpose (1), repose, suppose, transpose; also puzzle.

πέτρ-os, stone, πέτρ-α, rock — petrel, petrify, petroleum, pier, samphire.

ποιν-ή, a penalty — impunity, pain, penal, penance, penitent, pine (2), punch (2), punish, repent, repine, subpœna. (✓QEI, to appraise, fine, pay.)

πυξίς, a box — pyx, bush (2), bushel. See L. buxus; p. 632.

πῦρ, fire — bolt (2), bureau, empyrean, pelleter, pellitory (2), pyre, pyrites, pyrotechnic; cf. fire.

ῥέ-ειν (ῥευ-), to flow — catarrh, diarrhœa, rheum, rheumatism, rhythm, rime (1) or rhyme; cf. stream. (✓SREU, to flow; Teut. root STREU.)

σκέπτο-μαι (σκοπ-), I consider — bishop, episcopal, sceptic, scope, stereoscope, telescope, &c.

σπείρ-ειν (σπερ-, σπορ-), to sow — sperm, spore, sporadic. (✓SPER, to scatter.)

στέλλ-ειν (στολ-), to send — apostle, diastole, epistle, stole, systole.

στρέφ-ειν (στροφ-), to turn — antistrophe, apostrophe, catastrophe, strophe.

τάσσ-ειν (τακτ-, ταξ-), to arrange — syntax, tactics, taxidermy.

τλῆ-ναι, to suffer, endure — atlas, tantalise, talent; cf. L. tollere; p. 643. (✓TEL, TLĒ, to endure.)

τόμ-os, a section — anatomy, atom, entomology, epitome, tome; cf. litho-tomy, phlebo-tomy; also contemplate, temple. (✓TEM, to cut.)

τόν-os, a tone — attune, barytone, diatonic, intone, monotonous, oxytone, tone, tonic, tune; cf. hypo-tenuse. (✓TEN, to stretch.) See L. tendere; p. 643.

τόρν-os, a tool to draw circles with; see tornus in the list of Latin primitives; p. 643. (✓TER, to bore.)

τρόπ-os, a turn — trope, trophy, tropic; also contrive, retrieve, troubadour, trover.

τύπ-os, a blow — antitype, archetype, stereotype, timbrel, tympanum, type.

ὕδ-ωρ, water — dropsy, hydra, hydrangea, hydraulic, hydro-, hydropsy; cf. water, otter. (✓WED, to wet.)

φαίν-ειν (φαν-), to shew — diaphanous, epiphany, fancy, fantastic, fantasy, phantom, phenomenon; cf. hiero-phant, sycophant.

φέρ-ειν (φορ-), to bear — diaphoretic, metaphor, periphery, phosphorus. (✓BHER, to bear.)

φλέγ-ειν, to burn — phlegm, phlox; cf. flagrant. (✓BHLEG, to burn.)

φύ-ειν, to produce — physic, physiology, physiognomy; neo-phyte, zoo-phyte; imp. (✓BHEU, to become.)

φων-ή, sound — anthem, antiphon, euphony, phonetic, symphony, telephone; cf. blame, blaspheme, euphemism, prophet. (✓BHĀ, to speak.) Cf. L. fārī; p. 635.

χάρτ-η, a leaf of paper — card, carte, cartel, cartoon, cartouche, cartridge, cartulary, chart, charter, écarté.

χέ-ειν, to pour — chyle, chyme; cf. alchemy. (✓GHEU, to pour) Cf. L. fundere; p. 636.

χρόν-os, time — anachronism, chronicle, chronology, chronometer, isochronous, synchronism.

ᾠδ-ή, a song — epode, monody, ode, palinode, parody, prosody. (✓WEID, to cry out.)

IV. DISTRIBUTION OF WORDS ACCORDING TO THE LANGUAGES FROM WHICH THEY ARE DERIVED

THE Dictionary shews from what language each word is derived, as far as its etymology is at present ascertained. The largest classes of words are the following.

1. Words of purely ENGLISH origin, most of which are found in Anglo-Saxon, or in Old Friesian, or are words of imitative origin.

2. Words of SCANDINAVIAN or OLD DANISH origin, due to the frequent incursions of the Danes, many of whom permanently settled in England. Their speech was closely allied to the oldest English as represented by Anglo-Saxon.

3. Words of CELTIC origin, few of which can be due to the ancient Britons. Most of the words in this class have been borrowed from Welsh, Gaelic, or Irish in comparatively modern times.

4. Words of LATIN origin; borrowed (1) from Latin directly; (2) through the medium of French. Both these classes of words are very large. Here also may be included words of Late Latin origin, chiefly borrowed from the debased or rustic Latin, which employed words not to be found in the best classical authors.

5. Words of GREEK origin; borrowed (1) from Greek directly; (2) through the medium of Latin; (3) through the medium of Latin, and afterwards of French; (4) through the medium of French (the word not being used in Latin).

6. HYBRID WORDS, made up from two different languages. Such a word is *bankrupt, bank* being of Teutonic, but *-rupt* of Latin origin. Words of this character are rather numerous, but their component parts are, in most cases, easily accounted for.

Words *strictly* belonging to the above classes are numerous, and will not be further noticed here. But there are also other smaller classes of words which are here brought particularly under the reader's notice.

Before proceeding to enumerate these at p. 655, a few remarks upon some of the classes already mentioned may be useful.

1. ENGLISH. Among these we must include :

Place-names : canter, carronade, dunce, galloway, jersey, kersey. *Personal names* : kit-cat, negus, pinchbeck, shaddock, shrapnel.

Also a word that seems to have been originally English, and to have been reborrowed.

Portuguese from English : dodo (?).

2. Among SCANDINAVIAN WORDS we must also include the following :

Icelandic : geysir.
Swedish : dahlia, gantlet (gantlope), slag. sloid, trap (3), tungsten, weld (1).
German from Swedish : nickel.
Danish : floe, jib (1), jib (2).
Norwegian : lemming (leming).
French from Scandinavian : abet, baggage, barbed, bet, bondage, brandish, brasier (brazier), breeze (3), equip, flounder (2), gable, gallop, gauntlet, gawky, jib (3), jolly, locket, Norman, pocket, rivet, slot (2), strife, strive, waif, waive, wicket.
Dutch from Scandinavian : doit, furlough, walrus.
Russian from Swedish : knout.

3. Among CELTIC WORDS we may also include the following :

Welsh : bragget, coracle, cromlech, crowd (2), eisteddfod, flannel, flummery, maggot, metheglin (*of* L. *origin* ; p. 663).
Gaelic : airt, capercailzie, cateran, clachan, clan, claymore, coronach, corrie, duniwassal, fillibeg (philibeg), gillie, inch

(2), loch, mackintosh, ptarmigan, reel (2), slogan, spleuchan, whisky.

Irish: colleen, culdee, gallow-glass, kern (1) *or* kerne, lough, mavourneen, orrery, rapparee, skain (skene), shanty, shillelagh, spalpeen, tanist, Tory, usquebaugh.

Cornish : wheal (2).

Breton: dowlas.

Latin from Celtic : punt (1).

French from Celtic (or Breton) : beak, bijou, bilge, bound (2), bourn (1), bracket, brail, bray (2), budget, bulge, car, cark, career, carpenter, carry, carriage, charge, chariot, cloak (cloke), dolmen, garter,

gobbet, gobble (*with* E. *suffix*), gravel, javelin, lay (2), lockram, mavis, mien, mine (2), mutton, petty, piece, quay, truant, valet, varlet, vassal.

Spanish from Celtic : cargo, galliard, garrote (garrotte).

Italian from Celtic: caricature.

French from Italian from Celtic: caroche.

French from Latin from Celtic : ambassador, barge, bark (1), embassy, feuterer, league (2), marl, palfrey, pontoon.

French from German from Celtic: rote (2).

4. Among LATIN WORDS we may also include the following:

Late Latin from French from Latin : crenellate.

Italian from French from Latin : oboe.

Spanish from French from Latin : platina.

Dutch from French from Latin : buoy, cashier, commodore, domineer, excise, foy, quirk.

Provençal from Latin : battledoor.

French from Provençal from Latin : badinage, fad, fig, radish. *Also, from Southern French* : cabin, cabinet, funnel, noose, puncheon (1), puncheon (2), tulle.

Spanish from Provençal from Latin : flamingo.

Italian from Latin : accordion, allegro, alto, antic, askance, attitude, belladonna, breve, broccoli, canto, canzonet, caper (1), casino, catacomb, cicerone, comply, contralto, cupola, curvet, dado, dilettante, ditto, doge, donna, duel, duet, ferret (2), forte, granite, gurgle, incognito, influenza, infuriate, intaglio, isolate, lagoon (lagune), lava, league (1), levant, macaroni (maccaroni), madonna, manifesto, maraschino, Martello tower, mezzotinto, miniature, motto, nuncio, opera, pediment, pianoforte, piano, pilgrim, portico, profile, punch (4), punchinello, quartet (quartette), quota, semolina, seraglio, signor (signior), size (2), soda, solo, sonata, soprano, stanza, stiletto, travertine, trio, tufa, umbrella, velvet, vermicelli, virtuoso, vista, volcano.

French from Italian from Latin : accolade, alarm (alarum), alert, apartment, arcade, artisan, battalion, bulletin, burlesque, cab (1), cabbage (2), cabriolet, cadence, camp, campaign, cape (2), caprice,

capriole, caress, carnival, cascade, cavalcade, cavalier, cavalry, citadel, colonel, colonnade, compartment, compliment, concert, contour, corridor, corsair, cortege, costume, countertenor, courier, courtesan, cuirass, custard, disgrace, dome, douche, ducat, escort, esplanade, façade, faggot (?), falchion, favourite, festoon, filigree, florin, fracas, fugue, gabion, galligaskins, gambit, gambol, gelatine, imprese, improvise, incarnadine, infantry, junket, lavender, lutestring, macaroon, manage, manege, marmot, mizen (mizzen), model, mole (3), motet, musket, niche, ortolan, paladin, palette, pallet (2), parapet, partisan (1), pastel, peruke, pilaster, pinnace, piston, pivot, poltroon, pomade (pommade), populace, porcelain, post (2), postillion, redoubt, reprisal, revolt, rocket (2), salad, sallet, salmagundi, saveloy (cervelas), sentinel ?, sentry ?, serenade, somersault (somerset), sonnet, spinet, squad, squadron, termagant, terrace, tramontane, ultramontane, umber, vault (2), vedette (vidette).

Dutch or Low German from French from Italian from Latin : monkey.

German from Italian from Latin : barouche.

Spanish from Latin : alligator, ambuscade, armada, armadillo, booby, brocade, capsize, carbonado, cask, casket, chinchilla, cork, corral, corregidor, cortes, desperado, disembogue, dispatch, don (2), duenna, firm (2), funambulist, grandee, hacienda, hidalgo, junta, junto, lasso, llano, mallecho, matador, merino, mosquito (musquito), mustang, negro, olio, ombre, peccadillo, picador, primero, punctilio, quadroon, real (2), renegade (renegado), salver, sherry, sierra, siesta, sombrero, stevedore, tent (3), tornado, vanilla.

Portuguese from Spanish from Latin: verandah.

French from Spanish from Latin: calenture, capstan, casque, comrade, creole, doubloon, dulcimer, escalade, farthingale (fardingale), grenade, jade (2), jonquil, manchineel, parade, petronel, punt (2), quadrille, risk, sassafras, spaniel.

Portuguese from Latin: auto-da-fe, ayah, binnacle, caste, cobra, joss, junk (2), lingo, madeira, moidore, molasses, pimento, port (4), tank.

French from Portuguese from Latin: corvette, fetich (fetish), parasol.

Dutch from Portuguese from Latin: kraal.

Dutch from Latin: anker, bung, cant (2), cornel, cruise, easel, pink (2), tafferel (taffrail).

Scandinavian from English from Latin: kindle.

German from Latin: drilling.

French from High German from Latin: baldric, coif, fife, pitcher, spurrey, waste.

Scandinavian from Latin: bush (1).

Russian from Teutonic from Latin: czar.

French from Portuguese from Arabic from Greek from Latin: apricot.

French from Spanish from Arabic from Latin: quintal.

Late Latin: baboon, barrister, campanula, cap, capital (3), cope (1), edible, elongate, elucidate, fine (2), flask, grate (1), hoax, hocus-pocus, implement, indent (1), intimidate, pageant, plenary, proxy; *and perhaps others.*

French from Late Latin: ambush, ballet, bar, barbican, bargain, base (1), bassoon, bittern, burden (2), burl, cape (1), dominion, felon ?, ferret (1), festival, flagon, flavour, frock, funeral, gauge (gage), gouge, hutch, oleander.

French from Provençal from Late Latin: ballad.

French from Italian from Late Latin: basement, canton, capuchin.

French from Spanish from Late Latin: caparison.

German from Hungarian from Servian from Late Greek from Latin: hussar.

---

5. Among GREEK WORDS we must also include the following :

Latin from Greek: abyss, acacia, allegory, alms, amaranth, amethyst, &c., &c.

Late Latin from Greek: bursar, cartulary, catapult, chamomile (camomile), hulk, imp, intoxicate, magnesia, pericranium, &c.

Italian from Latin from Greek: biretta, grotto, madrigal, orris, piazza, torso.

French from Italian from Latin from Greek: agate, air (2), baluster, balustrade, cannon, canopy, espalier, grotesque, medal, mosaic, piastre.

Dutch from Italian from Latin from Greek: sketch.

Spanish from Latin from Greek: melocotone, morris, pellitory (2), sambo, savanna (savannah), silo, spade (2).

French from Spanish from Latin from Greek: castanets, cochineal, rumb (rhumb).

Portuguese from Latin from Greek: buffalo, palaver.

French from Portuguese from Latin from Greek: marmalade.

Provençal from Latin from Greek: troubadour.

Scandinavian from Latin from Greek: beaker.

Dutch from Latin from Greek: bush (2).

French from German from Latin from Greek: chamberlain, petrel (peterel).

Celtic from Latin from Greek: sporran, spunk.

French from Late Latin from Greek: acolyte, anchoret (anchorite), apoplexy, apostasy, apothecary, bombast, bottle (1), butler, buttery, bushel, calender (1), calm, card (1), carte, cauterise, celandine, chronicle, clergy, climacter, *climate, clinical, dredge (2), embrocation, fleam, galoche, gash, germander, liturgy, lobe, mangonel, patriot, policy.

Dutch from Late Latin from Greek: mangle (2).

Italian from Greek: archipelago, banjo, barytone, gondola, scope.

French from Italian from Greek: cartel, cartridge (cartouche), emery, gulf, mandolin, manganese, moustache (mustache), pantaloon (1), pantaloons, pedant?, pilot.

French from Spanish from Greek: paragon.

French from Greek: acrobat, catalogue, mandrel (?), ophicleide, stearine, steatite, stigmatise.

French from German from Greek: sabre?

Scandinavian from English from Greek: kirk.

Arabic from Greek: elixir, typhoon.

Spanish from Arabic from Greek : talisman, tarragon.

Portuguese from Spanish from Arabic from Greek: albatross.

French from Spanish from Arabic from Greek: alembic, limbeck.

French from Arabic from Greek: alchemy.

French from Italian from Arabic from Greek: carat.

Hebrew from Greek: sanhedrim.

Turkish from Greek: effendi.

6. Words of HYBRID origin cannot very well be classed, from the nature of the case. To the above six classes we may add these following.

7. Words of LOW GERMAN origin. The following words I call ' Old Low German ' for want of a better name. Many of them may be truly English, but are not to be found in Anglo-Saxon. Some may be Friesic. Others may yet be found in Anglo-Saxon. Others were probably borrowed from the Netherlands at an early period, but it is difficult to assign the date. The list will require future revision, when the history of some at least may be more definitely settled.

askew, bought, bout, brake (1), bully, cranberry, cringle, fib, fob, frampold, fraught, hawk (2), hawker, huckaback, huckster, kit (1), knurr (knur), lazy, loon (1) (lown), mate (1), minx, mum, nick (1), nock, pamper, plump ?, poll, prowl, queer, rabbit, rabble, rantipole, rill, skew, slight, toot (2), tuck (1), twill.

French from Old Low German: border, butty, chuck (1), dace, dare (2), dart, filter, fur, garment, garnish, garrison, goffer, growl, gruel, guard, guile, hackbut,

hamlet, heinous, lampoon, loop-hole ?, massacre ?, mute (2), pledge, poach (1)?, pottage, pottle, putty, staple (2), stout, supper, wafer. *Perhaps* paw.

Late Latin from Old Low German: allodial.

Dutch from Low German: groat (2), sloop.

French from Low Latin from Low German : quail (2).

Dutch from French from Low German: morass, skate (2).

8. Words borrowed from DUTCH.

aloof, avast, beleaguer, bluff, boom (2), boor, bouse (boose), brackish, brandy, bruin, bulk (2), bumpkin, burgher, buskin, caboose, cam, catkin, cave in, clamp, clank, clinker, dapper, deal (3), delf, derrick, dirk ?, dock (3), drawl, drill (1), duck (4), duffel, foist, freebooter, frolic, fumble, gas, geck, golf, groove, gruff, guelder-rose, guilder, heyday (1), hold (2), holland, hop (2), hope (2), hottentot, hoy (1), hoy (2), hull (2), hustle, isinglass, jerkin, kails, kilderkin, knap, knapsack, knickerbockers, landgrave, landscape, lay (4), leaguer, lighter, link (2), linstock (lintstock), litmus, loiter, margrave, marline, mob (2), moor (2), mump, mumps, mutchkin, ogle, orlop, pad (2), pink (4), plack, plug, quacksalver, rant, ray (3), reef (1), reef (2), reeve (1), roster, rover, ruffle, rummer, runt, school (2), selvage (selvedge), serif, sheer (2), skellum, skipper, sled (sledge, sleigh),

slim, sloven, slot (1), slur, smack (3), snaffle, snap, snip, snuff (1), spelicans, splice, spook, spoor, steenbok, stipple, stiver, stoker, strand (2), stripe, sutler, swab, switch, tang (1), tattoo (1), toy, trick (2), trick (3), trigger, uproar, wagon (waggon), wainscot, yacht.

Middle Dutch: deck, doxy, firkin, hoiden (hoyden), hoist, lollard, lop, mite (2), mother (2), nag (1), nap (2), ravel, ret, split, spool, stoup, swingle, tub.

Named from towns in Flanders or Belgium: cambric, dornick, spa.

French from Dutch (or Middle Dutch): arquebus, brick, clinquant, clique, cracknel, dig, droll, fitchet, frieze (1), friz (frizz), gleek (1), gleek (2), hackbut, hoarding, hotch-pot (hodge-podge), manikin (manakin), mow (3), mummer, mute (2), placard, pouch, shallop, staid, stay (1), stays.

Spanish from Dutch: filibuster.

9. Words borrowed from GERMAN. The number of words borrowed *directly* from German is very small; but many came in indirectly through the medium of French. See 10 below.

bantling, bismuth, cobalt, Dutch, elk, feldspar, fuchsia, fugleman, gneiss, hock (2), huzzah, landau, mangelwurzel, maulstick, meerschaum, mesmerise (*with* F. *suffix*), plunder, poodle, quartz, shale, spruce-beer, swindler, trull, wacke, waltz, zinc.

German (Moravian) personal name: camellia.
Dutch from German: crants, dollar, etch, holster, luck, rix-dollar, wiseacre.
Polish from German: hetman.

10. Other words of TEUTONIC origin. *Teutonic* is here used as a general term, to shew that the following words (derived through French, Spanish, &c.) certainly or probably belonged originally to the Teutonic family, though they cannot in all cases be referred to a definite Teutonic language.

French from Teutonic: abandon, agraffe, allegiance, allure, attach, attire, bacon, ball (1), bale (3), balloon, band (2), bandy, banish, bank (2), banner, banneret, baste (3), bawd, bawdy, beadle, belfry, bend (2), bistre, bivouac, blanch (1), blank, blanket, blister, block, blue, board (2), booty, border, boss, botch (2), bottle (2), brach, brawl (2), brawn, bray (1), bream, brewis, browse, brunette, brush, burgeon, burgess, burin, burnet, burnish, butcher, butt (1), button, buttress, carcanet, carousal (1), carouse, chamois, chine, choice, chuck (1), coat, coif, coterie, cotillon, cramp, cratch, crayfish, cricket (1), croup (2), cruet, crupper, crush, dally, dance, éclat, egret, enamel, equerry, ermine, eschew, escrow, espy, etiquette, fauteuil, fee (fief), feuter, filbert, flange, flank, flatter, flawn, flinch, flunky, forage, foray, franc, franchise, frank, franklin, freight, frisk, frown, furbish, furnish, gaff, gage (1), gaiety, gain (2), gaiter, gallant, galloon, garb (1), garb (2), garden, garland, garret, gay, gimlet, gimp, giron, goblin, gonfanon (gonfalon), grape, grapnel, grapple, grate (2), grimace, grisette, grizzled, grizzly, guarantee, guipure, guise, grumble, habergeon, haggard (1), haggard (2), halbert (halberd), hale (haul), halyard, halt (2), hamlet, hamper (2), hanseatic, harangue, harbinger, hardy, hash, haste, hatch (3), hatchet, hauberk, haunch, haversack, herald, heron, hob (2), hobby, hoe, hoop (2), housings, hovel, hubbub, hue (2), huge, Huguenot, hut, jay, jig, jog, lampoon, lansquenet, lattice, lecher, liege, list (2), lodge, lumber (1), lure, mail (2), main, malkin, marque (letters of), marquee, marquetry, marquis, marshal, marten, mason (?), mazer, moat, moraine, motley, mushroom, orgulous, ouch (nouch), pawn (1), perform (*with* L. *prefix*), pewter, pump (1), quiver (2), quoif, raffle, rail (3), ramp, random, range, rank (1), rappee, rasp, raspberry (*partly* E.), ratten, rebut (*with* L. *prefix*), retire (*with* L. *prefix*), reynard (renard), ribald, riffraff, rifle (1), riches, roast, rob, robe, robin, rochet, romp, rubbish, rubble, Salic (Salique), saloon, scabbard, scale (1), scale (2), scallop (scollop), scarf (1), scavenger, scot(free), screen, screw (1), scroll, seneschal, shammy (shamoy), skiff, skirmish, slab (1), slash, slat, slate (1), slender, slice, sorrel (1), sorrel (2), soup, spar (3), spate, spavin, spell (2), spruce, spy, stale (1), stallion, stew, stroll, strumpet?, sturgeon, supper, tache (1), tampion, tan, tap (1), tarnish, tawny, teat, tenny, tetchy, Tibert, tic, tick (5), ticket, tiff (1), top (2), touch, towel, track, trap (2), trapan, trawl, trepan (2), trist, troll, trudge, tuck (3), tucker, tuft (1), tweezers, vagrant, wafer, wage, wager, wait, war, warble, warden, wardrobe, warison, warrant, warren, warrior, whoop, wince, wizard, zigzag.
German from French from Old High German: veneer.
Low Latin from French from Teutonic: feud (2), feudal.
Low Latin from Teutonic: allodial, bedell, bison, corrody, faldstool, marchioness, morganatic, Vandal.
Italian from Teutonic: balcony, ballot, bandit, bunion, fresco, lobby, loto (lotto), rocket (1), smalt, stoccado (stoccata), strappado, stucco, tucket.
French from Italian from Teutonic:

attack, bagatelle, banquet, escarpment, gala, group, guide, guy, ruffian, scaramouch, scarp, tuck (2), vogue.

Spanish from Teutonic: demarcation,

flotilla, gabardine, guerilla (guerrilla), marquess, ranch, stampede, stockade.

French from Spanish from Teutonic: amice (2), rapier, scuttle (2).

11. Words of indeterminate ROMANCE origin. The *Romance* languages, which include French, Italian, Spanish, and Portuguese, are, strictly speaking, unoriginal, but we cannot always trace them. A large number of terms belonging to these languages are derived from *Latin, Greek, Celtic*, &c. Those in this section are words of which the origin is local, obscure, or unknown.

French: abash, agog, antler, arras, artesian, average, awning, baboon, barnacles, barren, barter, basket, bastard, bastile, baton (batoon), batten (2), battlement, bauble, bavin, bayonet, beaver (2), beg, beggar, beguine, bevel, bezonian, bice, biggen, bigot, billet (2), billiards, blazon (2), blemish, blond, blouse, bobbin, boisterous, bonnet, boot (2), boudoir, bourd, bran, brattice, breeze (2), brisket, broider, broil (1), broil (2), budge (2), buff (2), buffer (1), buffer (2), buffet (1), buffet (2), buffoon, bugle (3), burbot, burganet (burgonet), busk (2), cabbage (2), caddis, cajole, caliber (calibre), calipers, caliver, carp (1), caul, chablis, chagrin, champagne, chaudron, cheval-de-frise, chiffonier, cockade, crare, curlew, dagger, debonair, disease, drab (2), drape, dupe, ease, embattle, emblazon, embrasure, embroider, embroil, flout, flute, fricassee, frieze (2), frill, frippery, furbelow, gallery, galley, galliot, gallon, garboil, gasconade, gavotte, gewgaw, gibbet, gibbon, giblets, gill (3), glean, gobelin, gormandize, gourmand, greaves, (2), grebe, grouse, grudge, guillotine, gusset, guzzle, haberdasher, hackney, haha, halloo, harass, haricot, harlot, harridan, haunt, havoc, hod, holla, lawn (2), lees, lias, lists, loach, loo, lozenge, lurch (2), magnolia, maraud, maroon (1), merelles, mignonette, minion, mortise, musit, Nicotian, notch, paletot,

pamphlet ?, patrol, patten, pavise, paw, pillory, pirouette, piss, pittance, poplin, rail (2), ricochet, rinse, riot, roan, roquelaure, sauterne, savoy, sedan (chair), shalloon, silhouette, sobriquet, sturdy, tabard, tire (2), tire (3), tripe, troop, trousers, trousseau, truck (1), truss, tulle, valise, varnish, vaudeville, vernier, void.

French from Provençal: charade, flageolet.

Italian: andante, bergamot (1), bravo, cameo, caviare, fiasco, galvanism, imbroglio, mantua, milliner, ninny, polony, rebuff, regatta, sienna, trill, voltaic.

French from Italian: bastion, brigade, brigand, brigantine, brig, brisk, brusque, buckram, bust, canteen, canton, carcase, carousal (2), casemate, cassock, catafalque, charlatan, cornice, frigate, gallias, gazette, jane, pasquin, pasquinade, pistol, pistole, rash (4), ravelin, rodomontade, theorbo, tontine.

Spanish: anchovy, banana, bastinado, bilbo, bilboes, bravado, cachucha, cigar, cinchona (chinchona), cockroach, embargo, fandango, galleon, launch (2), paraquito, quixotic, rusk, sarsaparilla ; *cf.* trice (1).

French from Spanish: barricade, bizarre, cannon (2), caracole, chopine, cordwainer, embarrass, fanfare, maroon (2), morion (murrion), tartan.

Portuguese: cocoa (1), dodo, emu.

Dalmatian: argosy, dalmatic.

12. Words of SLAVONIC origin. This is a general term, including Russian, Polish, Bohemian, Servian, &c.

French from Slavonic: cravat, sable.

French from German from Slavonic: calash, trump (1), trumpery, trumpet.

Italian from German from Slavonic: trombone.

Low German from Slavonic: siskin.

Dutch from Slavonic: praam.

Polish: mazurka, polka.

German from Bohemian: howitzer.

French from German from Servian: vampire.

French from Latin from Greek from Slavonic: slave.

Russian: copeck, drosky, rouble (ruble), samovar, steppe, verst.

French from Russian: ukase.

13. A word of LITHUANIAN origin.

Dutch from German from Lithuanian: eland.

14. Words of PERSIAN origin.

Persian: bakshish, bashaw, bazaar, bulbul, caravansary, carboy, dervis (dervish), divan, durbar, firman, giaour, houri, Lascar, mogul, mohur, nargileh, nylghau, Parsee, pasha (pacha, pashaw, bashaw), peri, roc, sash (2), sepoy, serai, shah, shawl, sirdar.

Hindustani from Persian: pajamas, toddy, zamindar, zanana.

Greek from Persian: parasang.

Latin from Greek from Persian: asparagus, cinnabar, laudanum, Magi, paradise, tiara?.

French from Latin from Greek from Persian: jujube, magic, musk, myrtle, nard, parvis, sandal, satrap, tiger.

French from Italian from Latin from Greek from Persian: rice.

Spanish from Latin from Greek from Persian: pistachio (pistacho).

Italian from Greek from Persian: gondola.

Dutch from Slavonic from Low Latin from Greek from Persian: gherkin.

French from Latin (or Late Latin) from Persian: peach (1), zedoary.

French from Italian from Latin from Persian: muscadel (muscatel), muscadine.

Italian from Persian: scimetar (cimeter)?.

French from Italian from Persian: jargonelle, taffeta (taffety).

French from Spanish from Persian: julep, marcasite, rook (2), saraband.

Portuguese from Persian: pagoda.

French from Persian: bezique, calender (2), caravan, check, checker (chequer), checkers (chequers), chess, chicanery, exchequer, gueber, khedive, lemon, lime (3), scarlet, tutty, van (3).

Latin from Greek from Arabic from Persian: arsenic.

Low Latin from Arabic from Persian: borax.

French from Latin from Arabic from Persian: balas (ruby).

French from Arabic from Persian: azure, jasmine.

French from Italian from Arabic from Persian: mummy, orange.

Spanish from Arabic from Persian: lilac.

French from Spanish from Arabic from Persian: bezoar, calabash, galingale, spinach.

Turkish from Persian: jackal, kiosk.

French from Italian from Turkish from Persian: tulip, turban.

15. Words of SANSKRIT origin.

Sanskrit: avatar, brahmin (brahman), champak, juggernaut, pundit, rajah, Sanskrit, suttee, Veda.

Latin from Greek from Sanskrit: pepper.

French from Latin from Greek from Sanskrit: beryl, brilliant, ginger, mace (2), saccharine.

French from Low Latin from Sanskrit: sendal (cendal).

Persian from Sanskrit: bang (2), lac (1), nenuphar, nuphar.

French from Latin from Greek from Persian from Sanskrit: sandal(wood).

French from Spanish from Latin from Greek from Persian from Sanskrit: indigo.

French from Portuguese from Persian from Sanskrit: lacquer (lacker).

French from Persian from Sanskrit: lake (2).

French from Spanish from Arabic from Persian from Sanskrit: aniline, sugar.

Arabic from Sanskrit: kermes.

Spanish from Arabic from Sanskrit: carmine.

French from Arabic from Sanskrit: crimson.

French from Italian from Arabic from Sanskrit: candy.

Hebrew from Sanskrit: algum.

Hindustani from Sanskrit: cheetah, chintz, ghee, gunny, jungle, lac (2), loot, maharajah, nautch, pawnee, punch (3), punkah, rajpoot, rupee.

Portuguese from Hindustani from Sanskrit: palanquin.

Canarese from Sanskrit: jaggery.

Portuguese from Malay from Sanskrit: mandarin.

Portuguese from Sanskrit: banyan.

16. Words of MAGYAR or HUNGARIAN, or of FINNISH origin. (These languages do not belong to the Indo-germanic family.)

Hungarian: tokay.

French from Hungarian: coach, shako.

French from Finnish: morse.

IV. DISTRIBUTION OF WORDS, ETC.

17. Words of TURKISH origin. (This language does not belong to the Indo-germanic family.)

Turkish: agha (aga), bey, caftan, chibouk, chouse, horde, turkey.
Persian from Turkish: begum.
French from Turkish: caïque, dey, odalisque, ottoman, shagreen.
French from Italian from Turkish: bergamot (2), janizary, turquoise.
Spanish from Turkish: xebec.
German from Polish from Turkish: uhlan.
French from German from Hungarian from Turkish: dolman.

18. Words of SEMITIC origin. The principal Semitic languages are Hebrew, Arabic, Chaldee, Syriac, &c.; the borrowed words in English being somewhat numerous.

Hebrew: alleluia (allelujah), bedlam, cab (2), cherub, corban, ephod, gopher, hallelujah, hin, homer, Jehovah, jug, log (3), Messiah, mishna, Nazarite (*with* Gk. *suffix*), purim, Sabaoth, Satan, Selah, seraph, shekel, Shekinah (Shechinah), shibboleth, shittah (tree), shittim (wood), teraphim, thummim, urim. *Cf.* davit.
Greek from Hebrew: hosannah; *from Phoenician*: alphabet, delta, iota.
Latin from Greek from Hebrew: amen, bdellium, cassia, cinnamon, cumin (cummin), Jacobite, Jesus, jesuit, jot, Levite, manna, Pasch, Pharisee, rabbi (rabbin), sabbath, Sadducee, sycamine?, sycamore?, Tom. *Also* balsam?, jordan?.
French from Latin from Greek from Hebrew: cade, camel, cider, earnest (2), ebony, elephant, Hebrew, hyssop, jack (1), Jacobin, Jew, jockey, lazar, maudlin, nitre, sapphire, shallot, simony, sodomy.
French from Spanish from Arabic from Greek from Hebrew: natron.
Italian from Greek from Hebrew: zany.
Latin from Hebrew: damson, leviathan.
French from Latin from Hebrew: jubilee.
French from Hebrew: cabal.
French from a place in Palestine: gauze.
Syriac: Maranatha.
Latin from Greek from Syriac: abbot, damask, mammon.
French from Latin from Greek from Syriac: abbess, abbey.
French from Italian from Syriac: muslin.
Chaldee: raca, talmud, targum.
French from Latin from Greek from Chaldee: sackbut.
Arabic: alkali, alkoran, arrack, attar (of roses), azimuth, cadi, drub (2), emir, fellah, hadji, hakim, harem, hashish,

hegira, henna, hookah (hooka), imam, islam, jerboa, jinn, koran, mahdi, Mahometan (Mohammedan), mohair, moonshee, moslem, muezzin, mufti, omrah, otto, rack (5), ramadan, rayah, ryot, salaam (salam), sheik, sherbet, shrub (2), simoom, sofa, taraxacum.
Latin from Greek from Arabic: gypsum, naphtha, saracen, sarsnet.
French from Greek from Arabic: civet.
French from Latin from Greek from Arabic: jasper, myrrh.
Low Latin from Arabic: alcohol, algebra.
French from Low Latin from Arabic: tartar (1).
Italian from Arabic: artichoke, botargo, felucca, senna, sirocco, zero.
French from Italian from Arabic: arabesque, baldachin, benzoin, magazine, sequin.
Spanish from Arabic: alguazil, arsenal, atabal, bonito, caraway (carraway), cid, dragoman, maravedi, minaret, mulatto.
French from Spanish from Arabic: alcove, amber, basil (2), borage, carafe, cipher, cotton (1), cubeb, garble, gazelle, genet, giraffe, hazard?, jennet (gennet), lackey (lacquey), martingale, mask (masque), masquerade, mosque, nadir, ogee (ogive), racket (1) (raquet), realgar, ream, rob (2), saker, sumach, syrup (sirup), tabby, talc, tabor, tambour, tambourine, tare (2), tariff, zenith.
French from Portuguese from Spanish from Arabic: marabout.
Portuguese from Arabic: albacore, assagai (*Moorish*).
French from Arabic: admiral, assassin, bedouin, burnouse, calif (caliph), camlet, carob, fardel?, faquir, furl?, jar (2), lute (1), Mamaluke (Mameluke), mate (2), mattress, moire, rebeck, saffron, sultan, vizier.

French from Algerine: razzia.
Persian from Arabic: ghoul, houri, mussulman, sophy.
Hindustani from Arabic: houdah, nabob, sahib.

Hindustani from Persian from Arabic: nizam, sicca.
Turkish from Arabic: coffee, raki.
Italian from Malay from Arabic: monsoon.

19. Words of ASIATIC origin, but NEITHER ARYAN NOR SEMITIC.

Hindustani: anna, bandanna, bangle, bungalow, chutny, cowry, dacoit, ghaut, mahout, nullah, shampoo, thug, wallah.
French from Hindustani: gavial.
E. Indian place-names: calico, cashmere (kerseymere).
Hindi: dawk, rum (2).
Bengali: dingy, jute, tomtom.
Balti: polo.
Marathi: pice.
Portuguese from Canarese: areca.
Malay from Canarese: bamboo.
Malayalim: teak.
Portuguese from Malayalim: betel.
Tamil: catamaran, cheroot, coolie, mulligatawny, pariah; *cf.* pavin (pavan), peacock.
Portuguese from Malay from Tamil: mango.
Telugu: bandicoot, mungoose.
French from Dravidian: patchouli.
Cingalese: anaconda (?).
French from Cingalese: tourmaline.
Malay: babirusa, bamboo [from *Canarese*], caddy, cajuput (cajeput), cassowary, cockatoo, crease (2) *or* creese, dugong, durian, gecko, gong, gutta-percha, junk, ketchup, lory (lury), mangosteen, muck (amuck), orang-outang, paddy, proa, rattan, rusa, sago, siamang, tripang, upas.
French from Malay: gingham, ratafia.
French from Arabic from Malay: camphor.
Chinese: bohea, china, Chinese, congou, hyson, nankeen, souchong, tea; *cf.* silk.
Malay from Chinese: sampan.
French from Latin from Greek from Chinese: serge.
Japanese: harakiri, japan, soy.
Portuguese from Japanese: bonze.
Java: bantam.
Annamese: gamboge.
Tatar: tartar (2).
Russian from Tatar: cossack, mammoth.
Persian from Tatar: khan.
French from Turkish from Tatar: horde.
French from Italian from Tatar: turquoise.
French from Tatar: turkey.
Mongolian (*through Persian*): mogul.
Thibetan: lama (1).
Australian: boomerang, dingo, kangaroo, parramatta, wombat.
Tahitian: tattoo (2).
Polynesian: taboo.
Maldive: atoll.

20. Words derived from various AFRICAN languages.

Hebrew from Egyptian: behemoth, ephah.
Latin from Greek from Hebrew from Egyptian: sack (1).
French from Latin from Greek from Hebrew from Egyptian: sack (2), satchel.
Latin from Greek from Egyptian: ammonia, ibis, leo, oasis, paper?, papyrus?.
French from Latin from Greek from Egyptian: gum (2), gypsy, labyrinth?, lion.

French from Italian from Low Latin from Egyptian: fustian.
French from Barbary: barb (2).
Morocco: fez, morocco.
West African: baobab, canary, chimpanzee, guinea; *also* gorilla (Old African), yam. *From a negro name*: quassia.
Congo: zebra; *cf.* banana.
Kaffir: gnu, quagga.
French from Malagasy: aye-aye.

21. Words derived from various AMERICAN languages.

North-American Indian: caucus?, hickory, hominy, manito, moccasin (mocassin), moose, opossum, pemmican, racoon (racoon), skunk, squaw, toboggan, tomahawk, wampum, wigwam.
Mexican: coyote, jalap, ocelot.

IV. DISTRIBUTION OF WORDS, ETC.

Spanish from Mexican: cacao, chocolate, copal, tomato?.

Cuba: maguey.

Hayti: mahogany.

Spanish from Hayti: cassava, guaiacum, maize, manatee, potato, tobacco.

Caribbean (or other West Indian languages): cayman, hammock, macaw.

Spanish from West Indian: cacique, cannibal, canoe, guava, hurricane, iguana, papaw.

French from West Indian: buccaneer, caoutchouc, peccary, pirogue.

Peruvian: inca, jerked (beef), llama, oca, pampas, puma.

Spanish from Peruvian: alpaca, coca, condor, guanaco, guano.

French from Peruvian: quinine.

Brazilian: ai, manioc, tapioca, tapir.

Portuguese from Brazilian: ipecacuanha.

Spanish from Brazilian: ananas.

French from Spanish from Brazilian: agouti.

French from Brazilian: cashew-nut, jaguar, toucan.

South American (Colombia): tolu.